The Kaiser in 1891

# WILHELM II

## THE KAISER'S PERSONAL MONARCHY, 1888–1900

JOHN C. G. RÖHL

TRANSLATED BY

SHEILA DE BELLAIGUE

CAMBRIDGE
UNIVERSITY PRESS

PUBLISHED BY THE PRESS SYNDICATE OF THE UNIVERSITY OF CAMBRIDGE
The Pitt Building, Trumpington Street, Cambridge, United Kingdom

CAMBRIDGE UNIVERSITY PRESS
The Edinburgh Building, Cambridge, CB2 2RU, UK
40 West 20th Street, New York, NY 10011–4211, USA
477 Williamstown Road, Port Melbourne, VIC 3207, Australia
Ruiz de Alarcón 13, 28014 Madrid, Spain
Dock House, The Waterfront, Cape Town 8001, South Africa

http://www.cambridge.org

Originally published in German as *Wilhelm II: Der Aufbau der
Persönlichen Monarchie* by C. H. Beck 2001 and © John C. G. Röhl 2001
First published in English as *Wilhelm II: The Kaiser's Personal Monarchy,
1888–1900* by Cambridge University Press, 2004
English translation © John C. G. Röhl 2004

Printed in the United Kingdom at the University Press, Cambridge

*Typeface* Walbaum 12/14 pt.     *System* LaTeX 2$_\varepsilon$     [TB]

*A catalogue record for this book is available from the British Library*

*Library of Congress Cataloguing in Publication data*
Röhl, John C. G.
[Wilhelm II. English]
Wilhelm II: the Kaiser's personal monarchy, 1888–1900 / John C. G. Röhl; translated by Sheila de Bellaigue.
p.   cm.
Includes bibliographical references and index.
ISBN 0 521 81920 2
1. William, II, German Emperor, 1859–1941.   2. Germany – Kings and rulers – Biography.
I. Title.
DD229.R6412813    2004
943.08′4′092 – dc22    2003065264
[B]

ISBN 0 521 81920 2 hardback

For
ROSEMARIE

# Contents

# Illustrations

# Preface to the English edition

After many decades of neglect, Kaiser Wilhelm II is at last coming to be recognised internationally as the powerful and pernicious ruler that he actually was,[1] a
kind of missing link, as it were, between Bismarck and Hitler, thereby helping to
render not only the vagaries of his own long reign but also Germany's twisted road
to the Third Reich historically a little more understandable. Biographies, mono-
graphs and dissertations about him are now appearing thick and fast, including
the first-ever study of his life to be written in French,[2] some penned by the
very historians who have hitherto downplayed his significance by emphasising
the supreme influence of anonymous structures and social forces. Wolfgang
J. Mommsen, one of the leading German authorities on the history of the
Wilhelmine era, who only recently proclaimed that those historians who placed
Wilhelm 'into the centre of things' were simply 'bad historians',[3] has himself now
published a biography highlighting the Kaiser's central importance, beginning
with a quotation from a letter of 1906 from Max Weber to Friedrich Naumann
which could well serve as the leitmotiv for the present volume: 'The degree of
contempt heaped upon us as a nation abroad (in Italy, America, everywhere!) –
and quite *rightly* so! That is the decisive thing – *because* we are willing to put
up with *this* regime of *this* man, has now become a factor of first-rate "world
political" significance for us.'[4]

True, Mommsen presents his study as a mild corrective to my own interpretation of Wilhelm's role, arguing that the 'Prusso-German power elites' were
sometimes able to manipulate the Kaiser and should therefore be saddled with
greater blame than I have allowed, but the observant reader will soon establish that the disagreement between us, at least for the period here at issue, is
more apparent than real. For one thing, it is a gross exaggeration to suggest, as
Mommsen's title *War der Kaiser an allem schuld?* seems to do, that I hold the

xiii

Kaiser 'alone' responsible for all of imperial Germany's ills. The build-up of his personal power was gradual, and then after a few years of – always dysfunctional – dominance it disintegrated into polycratic confusion. For another, as the following pages will demonstrate, I heap sharp criticism on the 'Prusso-German power elites', though for rather different reasons from Mommsen. Whereas he sees them as at times successfully controlling the monarch in their own interest, I both emphasise the blindness of those at court who assisted the young monarch in his bid for personal power and bewail the political and moral weakness of those in the Wilhelmstrasse and elsewhere who tried and failed to stop him. Mommsen appears to me to overestimate the cohesion of the 'Prusso-German power elites', who were in fact, politically speaking, at each other's throats and allowed themselves all too readily to be controlled by the Kaiser and his court through what Norbert Elias has termed the 'kingship mechanism' – the monarch's ability to choose which of several rival cliques and conflicting courses he preferred at any given moment. The evidence for this interpretation is overwhelming. It is clearly set out in this volume and will, I am confident, prove persuasive in the end. But even now such differences are trivial when compared with the times, not so long ago, when I stood virtually alone and most historians, Wolfgang Mommsen included, banished Kaiser Wilhelm II to the shadows as a political irrelevancy and an embarrassing buffoon.

Gratifying as the international acceptance of the important if catastrophic role played by Wilhelm II in the history of Germany and the wider world may be, it was by no means axiomatic that a work as voluminous as this should be translated into English. Making my research accessible to English-speaking readers became possible only as a result of the generous financial support I received from the Arts and Humanities Research Board and the Stiftungsfonds Deutsche Bank, together with the award in 1994 of the Wolfson Prize and in 2002 of the Gissings Prize, and I should like to thank Dr Ulrich Cartellieri of the Deutsche Bank and Mr Sean Breslin of Gissings in particular for their extraordinary generosity.

The almost superhuman task of faithfully translating the many hundreds of pages that follow, replete as they are with at times rather idiosyncratic extracts from the letters and diaries of Europe's royalty, aristocracy and political and military leadership of more than a century ago, was undertaken by Sheila de Bellaigue, formerly Registrar of the Royal Archives at Windsor Castle and hence well acquainted with the personalities and issues of that vanished world. Not only did she fulfil the daunting task of translating my German text with characteristic professionalism and selfless commitment, however; she also checked and re-checked many of the quotations from the extensive correspondence held in the Royal Archives to ensure their accuracy. Puzzling archaic phrases, obscure aristocratic titles and arcane terms of courtly ritual were discussed at length between us in the hope of arriving at the closest equivalent in current English usage. I cannot praise or thank Sheila de Bellaigue enough for her uncomplaining dedication during what must at times have seemed a Sisyphean sentence. The footnotes were expertly transformed into English by Anna Menge. The entire text has been copy-edited with admirable virtuosity, sensitivity and devotion to the English language by Karen Anderson Howes. The responsibility for any errors that may remain naturally rests entirely with me.

I have seized the opportunity presented by this happy collaboration on the English edition to review the entire text, to shorten the account where it appeared overloaded with detail and to streamline the argument wherever it seemed unnecessarily serpentine, without, I hope, losing the immediacy and authenticity which it has been my aim throughout to achieve. If nothing else, the plentiful and often previously unknown archival evidence gathered together in this volume should stand as the solid foundation upon which future informed debate on this question of world historical significance, which has, for whatever reason, been obscured for far too long, will be able to build.

*John Röhl*
Sussex, June 2003

# Preface to the German edition

I began the first volume of this biography of Wilhelm II, which dealt with the future Kaiser's childhood and youth up to his accession, with Heraclitus's saying that the soul of another person is a distant continent that cannot be visited or explored.[1] In this second volume on the first half of his long and much-debated reign I am returning to a country I first visited more than forty years ago, some of whose inhabitants seem more familiar to me than my own contemporaries. Both for my first book, *Germany without Bismarck*[2] and during the many years I spent compiling the three-volume edition of the correspondence of Philipp Eulenburg,[3] Wilhelm II's best friend, I studied the events and personalities of the transitional epoch between Bismarck and Bülow and examined the almost incalculable wealth of letters, diaries and notes written by the Kaiser, the imperial family and the statesmen and diplomats of the time, both in Germany and beyond, which has survived in public and private archives.

During my archival research for these early studies it became incontrovertibly clear to me, contrary to the opinion of professional German historians, that Wilhelm II was a key figure in modern German history as it followed its fatal course from Bismarck to Hitler. His narcissistic coldness, his dynastic arrogance, the aggressive attitude he adopted towards the federal constitution of the Reich, parliamentarism, political Catholicism, social democracy, the Jewish minority and the democratic aspirations which were beginning to emerge everywhere, even among the Conservatives, led him from the very outset to use the most wounding terms of abuse against the majority of his own people, thereby very rapidly undermining the stability of the Hohenzollern throne. His thirst for glory, his overweening nationalism, his pronounced militaristic tendencies and his passion for the navy provided the impetus for a breathtakingly ambitious, long-term goal: the transformation of imperial Germany into the foremost great power – *the* European world power – on earth, an endeavour which represented so mortal a threat to the established and hitherto far from harmonious world powers, Russia, France and Great Britain, that it caused them to unite against the common danger.

Although these perceptions gained acceptance in the wake of the great controversies over the work of Fritz Fischer in the 1960s and 1970s as far as Wilhelmine Germany in general was concerned, the decisive role which Wilhelm II played in introducing this illusory and self-destructive *Weltmachtpolitik* and naval policy was not recognised, and was even – despite the overwhelming weight of documentary evidence – vehemently denied. The last Kaiser, so the argument ran, had been no more than a *Schattenkaiser* – a shadow Kaiser – too impulsive to be able to intervene effectively in politics, too ridiculous to be taken seriously by historians.[4] The practical result of this neglect, however, was a virtual exoneration of the Kaiser, for in the absence of critical research the ample documentary evidence which could have thrown light on his true character and his disastrous political activity remained undiscovered. Diametrically opposed judgements on Wilhelm II were left abruptly juxtaposed in a limbo of unexplained contradiction – always a sign that the research essential to the furtherance of consensus has not been carried out.[5] For many years I was almost alone in my views on the true nature of the monarchical constitution which Bismarck had created – even at the moment of his dismissal in 1890 the founder of the Reich proudly described the system of Personal Monarchy, in which the King and Kaiser actually ruled, as one of his greatest achievements – and on the overriding decision-making power of Wilhelm II.[6] It is true that, especially in the English-speaking world, several other studies based on empirical archival research had reached similar conclusions.[7] But the general revision of the historical picture of this era that should have followed on from these findings was still lacking.[8]

In this volume I therefore return to the land I know so well, the Prusso-German Kaiserreich of the 1890s. With the benefit of richer sources than were available to me on my first expedition, and from a higher vantage-point – that of the imperial court rather than of the bureaucracy in the Wilhelmstrasse – I have set out to describe in detail the way in which Kaiser Wilhelm II's personal power grew within the monarchical and militaristic structures provided by the Bismarckian constitution and to point to the consequences of such a regime. Clearly, what is in question here is much more than the history of personalities; indeed we are dealing with some of the most fundamental issues of history in general. For there is no doubt that German policy would have taken a different course if the power struggle between the Kaiser and the leading German statesmen, which forms the main theme of this biography, had turned out differently. This book is therefore concerned not only with Kaiser Wilhelm II but also with the question of who controlled the powerful machinery of government in the German Empire at the heart of Europe, and how the guidelines of domestic and foreign policy were decided upon. It is concerned with the conditions necessary for the survival of the monarchical form of government in the twentieth century. And it is concerned with the question of the continuity, or inevitability, of German history in the course it followed from the foundation of the Second Reich by Bismarck to the Third Reich of Adolf Hitler.

For the gradual assumption of power by Wilhelm II in the period from 1889 to 1896, as this volume very clearly demonstrates, was anything but inevitable or predestined. Rather, it was the result of innumerable crises and machinations at the Hohenzollern court, in the officer corps and in the administrative offices of the Wilhelmstrasse, and it had to be more or less forcibly carried through against the growing democratic spirit of the time. From the earliest days urgent warnings came not only from members of parliament and journalists but also from the Reich chancellors, Prussian ministers, Reich secretaries of state, privy councillors, diplomats, generals, federal princes, foreign monarchs and ambassadors and even members of the Kaiser's own family. They all cautioned against the reintroduction, a hundred years after the French Revolution, of a semi-absolute Personal Monarchy in the federalist Reich, in an age of industrialised and urbanised mass society with unrestrained freedom of thought and expression. Everywhere, and with increasing alarm, comparisons were made with the fall of the Stuarts in England in the seventeenth century and of the Bourbons in France in the eighteenth century. The end of the Hohenzollern monarchy, the encirclement of the Reich and a war that would destroy everything were widely predicted. Not long after Wilhelm's accession there was already widespread speculation as to whether an All-Highest Sovereign who made such anachronistic and megalomaniac claims to power could still be in his right mind, and a few years later, as the last chapter shows, serious consideration was being given to the idea of a forced abdication. But in vain. In the end all his opponents, numerous, prominent and influential though they were, proved helpless against the elemental will to power of their young ruler with his faithful military retinue (the Flügeladjutanten), cunning court officials and blindly devoted favourites. From mid-1896 the dramatic power struggle behind the scenes was as good as over, with only the two Berlin parliaments, the Reichstag and the Prussian Landtag, still providing some constraint on Wilhelm II's decision-making power, but only in domestic and armaments policy. In accordance with the Bismarckian system of Personal Monarchy their opinion was not even sought where foreign and military policy were concerned. It was not long before the anticipated consequences began to show themselves.

In view of the unresolved state of research and of the controversy still surrounding the fundamental questions involved, I have again opted for a narrative

style in which the very expressive letters and diary entries of the main protagonists are quoted extensively. In this way the reader can get to know the archival
sources which have led me to my own view of the growing power and the pernicious influence of Wilhelm II. From these it should become plain that the
interpretation offered here of the dramatic developments behind the glittering
scenes of imperial Germany is not mine alone, but was also very much that of
the people directly involved. Through the documents on which this biography
draws heavily, long-forgotten expressions of opinion by Wilhelm II's contemporaries, kept secret at the time for good reason, are brought back to life, enabling
us a hundred years later to enter into the thought patterns, convictions, passions, intrigues and human weaknesses of that generation. They should help
to deepen our understanding of the vanished civilisation of the last days of the
Hohenzollern throne, with a Kaiser who either could not or would not understand what was required of monarchy if it were to survive in a modern pluralist
society.

A further reason for adopting a closely source-based narrative form is that
several printed editions of letters and diaries which were published after the
trauma of 1918 – Article 227 of the Treaty of Versailles stipulated that Wilhelm,
who had taken refuge in Holland, was to be handed over to an international
tribunal and tried as a war criminal – can be shown to have been corrupted by
omissions from and distortions of the authentic text calculated to gloss over the
truth. As a result of this falsification a highly inaccurate historical picture, above
all of Kaiser Wilhelm II and the manner in which he ruled, has been perpetuated
until this day. It can be corrected only by returning to the original sources. This
is particularly true of the diaries of the ambitious, arch-conservative and always
well-informed General Count Alfred von Waldersee, which were published in
1922–3 in a scandalously expurgated version.[9] The original text of the diaries,
with his scathing comments on Wilhelm II, has been fully utilised for the first
time in this biography; the disparities with the printed version are indicated in
the notes.

A further important source, but one to which little attention has been paid in
Germany, provides striking evidence of the extent of Kaiser Wilhelm II's power,
and that is the correspondence of his British relations which is preserved in the
Royal Archives at Windsor Castle. In drawing on these papers and in giving them
their due place in the narrative I hope to have been able to throw more light on
the personality of the last German Emperor, and above all to have contributed to
our understanding of the international implications of his restless and scheming
political activity. I thank Her Majesty Queen Elizabeth II for again allowing me
to make use of the Royal Archives for this part of my biography.

As I stated in the preface to the first volume, I began the archival research for
this book more than twenty years ago, after I had finished editing Eulenburg's

correspondence. The work has required many visits to a variety of archives, and in this I have been greatly helped by generous grants from the British Academy, the Robert Bosch Foundation and the Robert Bosch Jubilee Foundation 1986 in the Stifterverband für die Deutsche Wissenschaft. Once again I thank the archivists of the then Central State Archives of the German Democratic Republic in Merseburg and Potsdam (both now in Berlin) for their help, above all in assisting me to consult the holdings in the Brandenburg–Prussian House Archive and the records of the Kaiser's Civil Cabinet. The Bundesarchiv in Koblenz, the Bundesarchiv-Militärarchiv in Freiburg and the Politisches Archiv of the German Foreign Office, then in Bonn and now also back in Berlin, also hold important collections – papers of major statesmen and military figures, diplomatic reports and the secret reserve collection with the Kaiser's outrageous marginal comments, which had to be locked away on the orders of successive Reich chancellors and foreign secretaries – all of which I was able to consult for this biography, for which I wish to express my thanks. I am most particularly grateful to HRH Landgrave Moritz of Hesse and Prince Rainer of Hesse for permission to work for several months in the Hesse Family Archives in Schloss Fasanerie near Fulda and to make unrestricted use of the extensive papers of Wilhelm II's remarkably progressive mother Victoria, the Empress Frederick, for this volume as for the previous one. My thanks are also due to HH Prince Ferdinand von Bismarck and the Director of the Otto von Bismarck Foundation, Dr Michael Epkenhans, for making available the secret file at Friedrichsruh on the purchase of Wilhelm II's embarrassing letters to Miss Love. And last but not least, the archivists of the Royal Archives, particularly Sheila de Bellaigue, have earned my thanks for their enduring support for my work, both in making material available to me and through their expert knowledge and wise advice, and have saved me from many an error.

In addition, many private individuals have given me access to papers in their possession relevant to this biography. In this connection my particular thanks go to the Earl of Lonsdale, at Lowther, Cumbria; Ramona Countess von Oeynhausen-Sierstorpff and Peter Count von Wedel, at Bad Driburg; Gustav Count von Wedel, at Frankfurt am Main; Hermann Count Stolberg-Wernigerode, at Frankfurt am Main; Karl-Wilhelm Freiherr von Plettenberg, at Essen; Herr and Frau Joachim von Natzmer at Munich; Frau Margot Leo-Hoffmann at Freiburg; Frau Ruth von Santen at Wennigsen, Lower Saxony; Adrian Freiherr von Holzing-Berstett, at Bollschweil, Breisgau; and Freifrau von Seyfried-Marschall at Oberkirch, Baden. My thanks for information and material of great value to this book are also due to Professor Dr Margarete Jarchow, Dr Anastasia Hackett, Dr Ragnhild Fiebig-von Hase, Hagen Count Lambsdorff, Dr Thomas Otte, Dr Roderick McLean, Dr Annika Mombauer, Dr Matthew

Seligmann, Dr Matthew Stibbe, Dr Christopher Duggan, Dr Jost Rebentisch, Miss Frances Dimond, Mr Arthur Addington, Frau Liesbeth Ruitenberg, Frau Dr Friedhild den Toom-Jacobi and Drs Th. L. J. Verroen.

I was able to begin writing this second volume of the biography in ideal conditions in January 1994 at the Institute for Advanced Study in Princeton, and to continue during the academic year of 1997–8 at the National Humanities Center in North Carolina. Stays at the Moses Mendelssohn Centre for European Jewish Studies in Potsdam and at the Bellagio Study and Conference Center of the Rockefeller Foundation on Lake Como contributed considerably to my progress on the manuscript. My own university, the University of Sussex, also generously helped further the work by allowing me leave of absence from teaching and administrative duties on several occasions. During the last stage of the preparation of the book, thanks to a generous research grant from the Arts and Humanities Research Board, I had the good fortune to be able to obtain scholarly assistance, without which this study would have taken a great deal longer to complete. The help which I received from Annika Mombauer and above all Pauline von Hellermann, both in carrying out research on particular aspects of the biography and in the stylistic revision of my drafts, was outstanding. Dr Holger Afflerbach, who visited the University of Sussex in the spring of 2001 as the holder of a Feodor Lynen scholarship, assisted me in the concluding phases of the work with his valuable advice and specialist knowledge. My pupils, and above all my old friends Wilhelm Deist, Hartmut Pogge von Strandmann, Bernd and Britta Sösemann and Manfred Count von Roon encouraged me at moments when the work seemed too much to cope with. I thank my editors at the C. H. Beck Verlag in Munich, Dr Stefan von der Lahr and Peter Schünemann, as well as Frau Dr Jäger, for their accurate and sensitive work in editing the final manuscript. But above all I reserve my warmest thanks for my children Stephanie, Nicky and Christoph and my wife Rosemarie von Berg Röhl, to whom this volume is dedicated, for their patient interest in this lifelong project.

*John Röhl*
Sussex, June 2001

# CHAPTER ONE

# The accession

## IN PLACE OF A CORONATION

IN any other monarchy the death of two Emperors within three months would no doubt have been followed by the coronation of their successor in a solemn and magnificent ceremony designed to demonstrate the stability of the throne. In the complicated German Reich constructed by Bismarck, with its delicately counterbalanced forces, such a ceremony would have been impossible. The coronation of Wilhelm II as Kaiser was ruled out by the federal structure of the Reich, with its four kingdoms (Prussia, Bavaria, Saxony and Württemberg), six grand duchies (Baden, Hesse-Darmstadt, Mecklenburg-Schwerin, Mecklenburg-Strelitz, Oldenburg and Saxe-Weimar-Eisenach), five duchies (Anhalt, Brunswick, Saxe-Altenburg, Saxe-Coburg-Gotha and Saxe-Meiningen), seven principalities (Lippe, Schaumburg-Lippe, Reuss of the senior and junior lines, Schwarzburg-Rudolstadt, Schwarzburg-Sonderhausen and Waldeck), three free Hanseatic cities (Hamburg, Bremen and Lübeck) and the imperial provinces of Alsace-Lorraine. Nor would it have struck the right note in the new Reich for Wilhelm to follow the example of his grandfather Wilhelm I in October 1861, by crowning himself king of Prussia far away in Königsberg, and this idea was not seriously considered by anyone. Instead, following the disruption which this 'year of the three Kaisers' had brought with it, other methods were sought to stabilise the Hohenzollern throne and to legitimise the rule of the 29-year-old former Crown Prince as German kaiser and king of Prussia.

As early as 15 June 1888, immediately after the death of his father, Wilhelm II issued two proclamations which attracted universal attention as indications of what the new regime might bring. In an 'Army Order' of the day, his 'first word'

1

to 'His Army', Wilhelm emphasised the special relationship which his 'glorious ancestors' had always had with the military. 'In the army', its new supreme commander declared, 'the firm, inviolable bond with the commander-in-chief is the inheritance which passes from father to son, from generation to generation, and for that reason I point to my grandfather, who stands before you all in your mind's eye, the picture of the glorious, revered Commander, and no finer or more stirring picture can be imagined – and to my dear Father, who already as crown prince won himself a place of honour in the annals of the army – and to a long series of renowned ancestors, whose names shine brightly in history and whose hearts beat warmly for the army. And so we belong together, I and the army; we were born for one another and it will be our endeavour to hold together in an indissoluble union, through calm or storm, according to God's will.' The army, he continued, would now take the oath of loyalty and obedience to him, and he on his side would pledge 'always to be mindful that the eyes of my forefathers look down upon me from the next world and that I shall one day have to answer to them for the glory and the honour of the army!'[1]

At the same time Wilhelm – this time in his capacity as German Kaiser – issued a proclamation entitled 'To the Navy!' in which he spoke in similar tones of his particularly close relationship to the fleet. Only the previous year his grandfather had expressed 'in the warmest terms his lively satisfaction and appreciation with regard to the development of the navy under his glorious rule', and his beloved father had also taken 'such great pleasure and such a lively interest in the growth and progress of the navy'. He wished the navy to know that he too, the new Kaiser, had been held by bonds of 'lively and warm interest in the navy, since my earliest youth, in complete accord with my dear brother, Prince Heinrich of Prussia'. Thus he could 'declare with full confidence that we shall stand firm and fast together in good and in bad times, in storm as in sunshine, always mindful of the German Fatherland and always ready to give our life's blood for the honour of the German flag'.[2] This was the first time that a Prussian monarch had addressed the navy as well as the army on his accession, and the warm words of the young Kaiser filled his naval officers, as Admiral Gustav Freiherr von Senden-Bibran later recalled in his memoirs, 'with great joy and raised our hopes for the future'. Even in these circles, however, no one could have suspected – as Senden added – 'that Wilhelm II would see it as his task to raise up not only the army but also the navy, with all the means at his command, with his thorough knowledge of it, his great devotion to it, and his whole personality, and to set it beside the army on as near as possible an equal footing'.[3]

It was not until three days later that Wilhelm, reverting this time to his capacity as king of Prussia, issued a proclamation to the Prussian people. In it he invoked dynastic tradition and Christianity in order to weave a special bond between ruler and subjects. 'Called to the throne of my Fathers,' he announced, 'I enter upon my reign with my eyes raised to the King of all Kings, and I have made a pledge to God, following the example of my Fathers, to be a just and merciful ruler of my people, to foster piety and the fear of God, to defend peace, to further the welfare of this country, to be a helper to the poor and oppressed and a true guardian of justice. In asking God for strength to fulfil these Royal duties which His will lays upon me, I rely upon the trust in the Prussian people which I derive from looking back on our history. In good and evil times the people of Prussia have remained ever loyal to their King; upon this loyalty, which has proved an indissoluble bond to My Fathers in all times of difficulty and danger, I also depend, in the knowledge that I return it with all my heart, as the loyal Prince of a loyal People, both equally strong in their devotion to their common Fatherland. This knowledge of the mutual love which binds Myself and My People gives me confidence that God will grant me strength and wisdom to discharge the duties of my Royal office for the good of the Fatherland.'[4]

All three proclamations were received with much sympathy, although the conspicuous singling-out of the army drew criticism from the left-wing liberals and in Western foreign countries.[5] The 'Army Order' was greeted with enthusiasm in the Prussian officer corps above all. Helmuth von Moltke, the future Chief of the General Staff, who was serving as personal adjutant to his uncle the old Field Marshal at this time, wrote delightedly to his Swedish wife: 'You will have read in the newspapers the young Kaiser's splendid Proclamation to the army. — There is a decidedly new wind blowing in everything. The young Kaiser is in constant activity, he has spent the whole day conferring, issuing orders and signing documents. We received the first Cabinet Order with the signature Imperator Rex the night before last [15 June]' in the General Staff. The younger Moltke was convinced that Wilhelm had composed all three proclamations himself; there was 'no other hand involved', he claimed; the 'young Master' had 'rejected all suggestions and seen to the matter himself'.[6] It is more probable, however, that Wilhelm had sought Count von Waldersee's advice on the composition of all three proclamations,[7] and that Prince Bismarck and his son had also seen and approved the texts in advance; had it not been so, it would certainly have been remarked upon later in the numerous embittered writings of the Bismarcks about their dismissal. At any rate Waldersee, the elder Moltke's deputy, who in a few weeks would himself be promoted to chief of the General Staff, was more than satisfied when he wrote in his diary on 19 June: 'The . . . proclamations of the Kaiser "To the Army and Navy" and "To My People" have made an excellent impression; in the army there is general jubilation over the new sovereign. There is a widespread feeling that we have successfully overcome a serious illness and are now moving forward to good times. The uncertainty, the mistrust, the dissatisfaction were having a dreadfully oppressive effect on everyone's minds. The gentlemen of the Progressive Party and their Jewish hangers-on have certainly been dealt a hard blow.'[8]

On 24 June 1888 the new Kaiser and Kaiserin moved out of the small Marmorpalais in Potsdam into the Stadtschloss in Berlin. As their carriage drove through the Brandenburg Gate, accompanied by two outriders and with detachments of the aristocratic Gardes-du-Corps regiment preceding and following the carriage, Unter den Linden was as crammed with onlookers as it had been three months earlier for the funeral of the old Kaiser.[9] The next day the grandiose ceremony of the opening of the Reichstag took place; it was even more effective than the proclamations of 15 and 18 June as a spectacular prelude to the new era. The impetus for it came from a suggestion made by Grand Duke Friedrich I of Baden, who, because of the double change of sovereign, wished to rally the German federal princes demonstratively around the young Kaiser.[10] As there was no precedent for a ritual of this kind the ceremony had to be improvised behind the scenes, which also necessitated – not surprisingly, with such a large number of exalted participants – making allowances for numerous special requests and soothing a series of wounded vanities. The first difficulty arose from the fact that the Kingdom of Bavaria, which as the biggest of the federated states could claim the first place after Prussia in the ceremony, was formally under the rule of the hopelessly deranged King Otto; but the Prince Regent, Prince Luitpold, was of inferior rank to King Albert of Saxony. The problem was resolved by the King of Saxony yielding to Prince Regent Luitpold 'the precedence to which he was unquestionably entitled' for the duration of the ceremony.[11] A comparable problem arose with Württemberg, whose highly eccentric King Karl I had been for some years completely under the influence of two American favourites named Woodcock and Jackson and had not the least inclination to travel to Berlin. He appointed as his representative his nephew, the heir presumptive, Prince Wilhelm of Württemberg, to whom the Grand Duke of Baden – Württemberg being a kingdom – yielded precedence.[12] Thus, with the single exception of Grand Duke Friedrich Wilhelm of Mecklenburg-Strelitz, all of the federal princes (or their representatives) were present at the magnificent ceremony of the opening of the Reichstag in the White Hall of the imperial palace – a fact that made a strong impression on all observers. The Austro-Hungarian ambassador Count Imre Széchényi reported to Vienna: 'This great act of homage paid by Germany's princes to the youthful Kaiser Wilhelm II acquires increased significance because no invitations of any kind had been sent out for this purpose; the homage arose from a completely spontaneous decision by the German princes, a fact that understandably gave the greatest pleasure in influential circles here.'[13]

Until the last moment, however, organisational blunders threatened to upset the ceremony. When the two Moltkes, the Field Marshal and his nephew, returned to Berlin from Ratzeburg on the evening of 24 June, they discovered that the old Chief of the General Staff, victor of three wars of unification, was not mentioned anywhere in the programme for the opening ceremony. The 88-year-old was, as his nephew remarked, 'deeply hurt and declared at first that he wished to leave at once' and to hand in his resignation. The following morning he sent a letter to the Flügeladjutant (aide-de-camp) on duty, in which he announced that 'since he, as the most senior Field Marshal, Chancellor of the Order of the Black Eagle etc. might well have expected to find a place in His Majesty's suite, namely directly behind the Reich Chancellor, but is not in fact mentioned at all in the programme, and finds it incompatible with his military dignity to appear as a member of parliament, he would request that His Majesty be informed that he found himself obliged to absent himself from the ceremony'. The younger Moltke attributed the blame for this omission entirely to court toadies who, he suspected, wished to be done with the old man and attach themselves to the new stars. But the Kaiser, beside himself with anger, sent a Flügeladjutant to Bismarck immediately before the ceremony to ask whether it would be permissible to have the old Field Marshal appear together with the federal princes, to which Bismarck assented. Moltke, however, who was still in the palace, declared 'no, he did not belong there', and chose for himself the place behind the crown insignia, directly in front of the Kaiser.[14]

The impressive festivities of 25 June 1888 in the White Hall of the Stadtschloss in Berlin reminded many of the proclamation of the Kaiser in the hall of mirrors at Versailles nineteen years earlier, which had been immortalised – as this ceremony was to be – in a celebrated group portrait by Anton von Werner.[15] The ceremony began at 12 noon with a service in the chapel of the imperial palace. The text of the court chaplain's sermon was 'By God's grace I am what I am' and had been selected by Wilhelm himself.[16] After the service the members of the Reichstag, almost four hundred in number – only the eleven Social Democrats had refused to take part in the ceremony – the members of the government of the Reich and of the Prussian state government, and finally the court, assembled in the White Hall, which had been decorated under the direction of Anton von Werner. 'The throne richly draped with yellow velvet, the red velvet dais for the Kaiserin, the seats right and left of the throne for the princes' – everything made a magnificent impression, Moltke recorded.[17]

Particularly impressive was the entrance of a company of the Palace Guard, marching with shouldered arms, the officers with drawn swords. Bismarck, clad in his cuirassier's uniform, led in the members of the Bundesrat 'like a flock of lambs'. When they were all assembled he announced to the Kaiser that the members of the court could now enter. 'First pages in black breeches with mourning ribbons at the knee, then the insignia of the Reich', followed by Field Marshal Count von Moltke with his marshal's baton supported on his hip, then the Kaiser with the Prince Regent of Bavaria on his left and the King of Saxony on his right, followed by the remaining German princes, twenty in number, all in the great red velvet mantles of the Supreme Order of the Black Eagle, the highest Prussian honour.[18] Behind the Kaiser the new, six-year-old Crown Prince took his place with the young Kaiserin, pregnant with Prince Oskar; next to them sat the Hereditary Princess Charlotte of Saxe-Meiningen, the Kaiser's eldest sister, and a handful of other ladies, all still dressed in black. Facing the Kaiser were ranged the highest court officials, the Reich Chancellor, his son Herbert and the other secretaries of state of the Reich, together with the Prussian ministers of state and the remaining members of the Bundesrat. The people's representatives, the elected members of the German Reichstag, the opening of which was the ostensible reason for the ceremony, stood in the background and melted into the obscurity of insignificance. The speech from the throne, which the young Kaiser was thus to address both to all the federal princes and to the elected members of parliament, and which was seen as a kind of programme for the coming reign, was received 'with breathless attention'.[19]

On his entrance into the White Hall the Kaiser struck the younger Moltke as 'extraordinarily dignified and deeply serious'. The manner in which Wilhelm 'walked with a firm step up to the throne dais and greeted the assembly with a solemn inclination of the head' had been 'truly majestic'. Once complete silence was established, the Reich Chancellor handed him the text of the speech from the throne. Wilhelm grasped the manuscript, set the helmet on his head 'with a resolute gesture' and threw his mantle back, 'his head held high, allowing his glance to roam over the silently waiting assembly'. Although his hand did not shake – Moltke watched closely for this – his voice was at first 'muffled and unclear. The sentences came out jerkily and with difficulty, and in spite of the dead silence he could hardly be understood. But gradually the voice rose, the delivery became fluent, and when he came to the words: I am resolved to maintain peace with everyone, insofar as this depends on me, he emphasised the word *me* so loudly and clearly that it flashed through all his audience like an electric spark, it was so charged with meaning, the full consciousness of the ruler's power, while at the same time there resounded in it the warning: but woe to him who dares to tread too close to me; an extraordinary strength and confidence lay in that one word, so that everyone broke out spontaneously into loud and enthusiastic applause. He spoke the last sentences of the speech in a fine, penetrating voice, every trace of self-consciousness had vanished, and he stood there, strong and proud, the powerful, self-confident ruler of a mighty empire.'[20]

1. The young Kaiser surrounded by the German princes, Bismarck and the ministers at the opening of the Reichstag on 25 June 1888

After a few introductory sentences expressing his grief at the loss of his grandfather and father Kaiser Wilhelm II's speech declared: 'I have called you together, gentlemen, to announce to the German people, in your presence, that as kaiser and king I am resolved to follow the same path by which my late, revered grandfather won the trust of his allies, the love of the German people and the goodwill of other nations. Whether I too shall succeed in this lies with the Almighty; I will strive towards it with earnest endeavour. The greatest tasks of the German kaiser lie in safeguarding the military and political position of the Reich with regard to foreign relations, and, in internal matters, in watching over the execution of the laws of the Reich. The chief of these laws is the constitution of the Reich; to guard and defend it, in all the rights which it vouchsafes to both legislative bodies of the nation and to every German citizen, but also in those vouchsafed to the kaiser and to each of the federated states and their rulers, is among the foremost rights and duties of the kaiser. In the legislation of the Reich, according to the constitution, it is my duty to act more in my capacity as king of Prussia than as German Kaiser; but in both roles it will be my endeavour to continue the work of the legislation of the Reich in the same way as my late, revered grandfather began it. In particular I adopt in its entirety the declaration issued by him on 17 November 1881 [concerning social policy], and I shall continue to work in the spirit of this declaration, to ensure that the legislation of the Reich strives further to give the working population the protection that it is able, in accordance with the principles of Christian morality, to provide for the weak and the oppressed in the struggle for existence. I hope that in this way we shall succeed in bringing closer the elimination of unhealthy social differences, and I am confident that in my care for the internal well-being of the nation I shall receive the unanimous support of all true adherents of the Reich and of the federated governments, support undivided by party differences. At the same time I consider it imperative to maintain our national and social development on the path of the law, and to take firm action against all aspirations which have the aim and effect of undermining national order. With regard to foreign policy I am resolved to maintain peace with everyone, insofar as this depends on me. My love for the German army and my relationship with it will never lead me into the temptation of depriving my country of the benefits of peace unless war becomes a necessity forced upon us by an attack on the Reich or on its federated states. Our army shall safeguard peace, and if in spite of it our peace is breached, it shall be ready to fight for it with honour. This it will be able to do with God's help, thanks to the strength which it has been given by the recent legislation on national defence, passed unanimously by you. To use this strength in wars of aggression is far from my intent. Germany needs neither new military glory nor any conquests, having finally won itself the right to exist as a single and independent nation. Our alliance with Austria-Hungary is publicly known; I hold fast to it with German loyalty, not only because it has been entered into, but because I see in this defensive bond one of the basic elements of the balance of power in Europe, as well as a legacy of German history, the sense of which is shared today by public opinion throughout the German people, and which accords with traditional European international law as it stood, undisputed, until 1866. Similar historical links and similar national needs of the present bind us to Italy. Both countries desire to hold fast to the blessings of peace . . . Our existing agreements with Austria-Hungary and Italy allow me, to my satisfaction, to nurture my personal friendship with the Tsar of Russia and the peaceful relations which have existed for a hundred years with the Russian Empire, as is consistent both with my own feelings and with the interests of Germany. Both in the conscientious preservation of peace and in caring for our army I place myself willingly in the service of the Fatherland, and I rejoice in the traditional relations with foreign powers through which my endeavours towards the former goal will be furthered. Trusting in God and in the valour of our people I am confident that it will be granted to us for the foreseeable future to preserve and to consolidate what was won in battle under the leadership of my two predecessors on the throne, who now rest in God.'[21]

The speech, the beginning of which was received with complete silence, was interrupted several times by cheers from all sides. When it was over the Kaiser handed the text back to Bismarck and held out his hand to him. The Chancellor, deeply moved, kissed the hand of his Kaiser and King. Bavarian Minister-President Freiherr von Lutz called for three cheers for the Kaiser, with which the assembled company joined in; then the monarch and the remaining ruling princes left the hall in the same order as that in which they had entered.[22]

The ceremony with the carefully considered speech from the throne made an excellent impression in all circles in Germany and almost everywhere abroad.[23] Wilhelm himself could look back on this favourable beginning to his reign with satisfaction. 'The first days left nothing to be desired in the way of impressive moments', he wrote delightedly to his grandmother Augusta, 'and the gift of God which was bestowed on me in the gathering of the German princes by common consent must surely be the most magnificent gift that He has given to a young sovereign! May he continue to stand as graciously by my side! Uncle Fritz [of Baden] and Uncle Albert [of Saxony] above all showed themselves quite outstandingly excellent and kind in their longstanding loyalty and friendship; may Heaven reward them both for it. They can both count on me.'[24] With similar enthusiasm Hildegard von Spitzemberg wrote: 'The most magnificent thing of all was the opening of the Reichstag with the German princes!' It was an act 'which must fill every German heart with joy and pride and which vis-à-vis

foreign countries is the equivalent of winning a war . . . It filled the eyes of all
with tears, who saw the young ruler standing in his place of great responsibility,
surrounded by all the German princes, Moltke behind him, the Iron Chancellor
before him, bending over his hand, the young Kaiserin with child, beside her
the little Crown Prince!'[25]

Only in the Progressive camp, in London and in the British royal family were
critical voices heard. The Empress-Mother Victoria − she now took the title
Kaiserin Friedrich or the Empress Frederick − pronounced the whole 'pageant
and pomp' of the opening of the Reichstag 'very silly and absurd and out of place'.
She was indignant that her daughter Charlotte had attended the ceremony in
spite of being in deep mourning. In the eyes of the widowed Kaiserin the true
meaning of the opening ceremony lay in Bismarck's wish to demonstrate to the
world his pleasure at the beginning of a new era which was incomparably more
congenial to him than the short reign of Friedrich III. She was bitter in her
condemnation of the initiative taken by the Grand Duke of Baden, who had
taken a fancy to the role of protector of the Reich and could not see how much
he was playing into the hands of Bismarck.[26] 'The opening of the Reichstag
with this completely unnecessary pomp hurts me *deeply*!', she wrote in her
diary. 'Calling together of all German Princes − a *demonstration* in favour of
the present system! . . . It was Prince Bismarck who wanted this farce! And
Fritz v. Baden whose idea it was for the Princes to come here. All this will go to
Wilhelm's head even more! Anton v. Werner has been brought here to decorate
the White Hall as if for a *celebration*! How *cruel* and unfeeling, with the grave
only just sealed! What absence of dignity and decency! − if the German Reich
needs such an artificial *mise-en-scène* and hocus-pocus to prove to the world
that it is not breaking up, then I am *sorry* for it! Quiet, solemn silence, and
*mourning* . . . would have been more dignified and fitting than this childish
haste to create a spectacle.'[27]

Two days later the ritual was virtually repeated in the same place, only this
time without the participation of the federal princes, when Wilhelm opened
the Prussian parliament in his capacity as king of Prussia, with a speech from
the throne in which he took the oath on the Prussian constitution. In this
speech, which had been communicated to the Prussian ministers and approved
by them that morning at the first Crown Council at which Wilhelm presided,
he again emphasised his wish to carry on quietly pursuing the same policies as
his grandfather. 'I have no intention', he declared, 'of shaking the confidence
of our people in the permanence of our legislative system by attempting to
broaden the rights of the Crown. The legal position as regards my rights, so
long as it is not called into question, is quite sufficient to secure the measure
of monarchical intervention which Prussia requires in accordance with her

historical development, her present structure, her position in the Reich and the feelings and usages of her own people.' Wilhelm closed his speech by taking to heart Frederick the Great's principle that the king is the first servant of the state.[28] On his return to Wilhelmstrasse from the ceremony Bismarck threw his cap on to the table and, beaming with pleasure, exclaimed: 'Im Sattel hew ick en jetzt!' ('I've got him in the saddle now!')[29] He did not ask himself whither the proud rider would now ride on his high horse.

### THE FATEFUL ALLURE OF CHARISMATIC KAISERDOM

The newfangled ceremony of the opening of the Reichstag by the Kaiser, with the court, the federal princes and the elected members of the Reichstag all playing their part, illustrated more clearly than any other ritual could have done the complicated constitutional structure of Bismarck's Reich. The competing forces of authoritarian and popular, centralist and federalist elements were held together in a state of unsteady equilibrium by a delicately balanced mechanism. Any shift of power towards one side or the other – whether towards the Prussian hegemonic state, the centralised Reich authorities, the intermediate states led by the Kingdoms of Bavaria, Saxony and Wurttemberg or the democratically elected Reichstag – would have imperilled the whole edifice of the Reich. Nevertheless such shifts were inevitably happening as a result of population growth, internal migration, industrialisation and urbanisation. With every year of unification the German people grew closer together, in spite of all confessional and particularistic differences, in such a way that the initially feared separatist aspirations in Bavaria, Saxony and Württemberg gradually lost ground. Nonetheless the fear of the disintegration of the Reich (possibly in the course of a civil war with foreign intervention) continued to haunt the highest authorities in Berlin right up to the turn of the century, as we shall see. On the other hand these same powerful social and intellectual fluctuations were strengthening democratic tendencies throughout the land.

To create a bulwark against the dangerous growth of parliamentary and democratic power in the Reich Bismarck was obliged to bring the so-called state-supporting monarchical principle increasingly to the fore, even though this involved an uncomfortable paradox for him: for reasons of *state* he needed to propound the romantic fiction of a genuinely ruling monarch. As his son Herbert expressed it on 5 October 1888, the 'state-supporting Prussian principle' of the *genuinely* ruling monarch must be defended by all possible means; everything depended on preventing 'the modern parliamentary system without a personally ruling monarch' from establishing itself in the Kaiserreich – on ensuring that the Prussian–German monarch did not degenerate into an 'automatic signing-machine', as for example in England or Belgium.[30] The German Kaiser and King of Prussia must continue to wear 'the most powerful crown on the entire planet'.[31] This 'monarchical principle' was elaborated into a political ideology through which Prussia–Germany increasingly detached itself from the parliamentary monarchies and republics in the north, west and south of Europe. In the autumn of his chancellorship Bismarck let loose upon the world a dubious form of monarchical myth which would cast a widespread and lasting spell and would ultimately undermine his own position.

How this 'state-supporting Prussian principle' of 'personal monarchy' was projected on to the young Kaiser Wilhelm II in 1888 can be seen from the speech which the Free Conservative member of the Reichstag, Count Hugo Sholto von Douglas, made in the small provincial town of Aschersleben on 4 October. As the full text of this sensational speech was printed three days later in the official *Norddeutsche Allgemeine Zeitung* and then published as a semi-official pamphlet entitled 'What we can expect from our Kaiser', it is hardly surprising to discover that Douglas was not its author, but that it had been drafted in the Wilhelmstrasse by Franz von Rottenburg, the head of Bismarck's Reich Chancellery. The speech was originally to have been made by District Magistrate Dietz, as the Empress Frederick discovered, and it was only when he refused to act as Bismarck's mouthpiece that the speech was passed on to Douglas, 'who was servile enough to make it. *C'est ainsi que l'on fait l'Histoire!*' was the Dowager Empress's biting comment on this episode.[32] Douglas's action may seem more comprehensible, however, in the light of the fact that he had been created a count by Wilhelm not long beforehand, on 20 August 1888.[33]

The speech declared the dual aims of the Kaiser to be the strengthening of the power of the German Reich vis-à-vis the outside world and the establishment of a strong, genuinely ruling monarchy within the country. 'In the memorable speeches from the throne with which he opened the Reichstag and the Landtag in June, Kaiser Wilhelm proclaimed his loyalty to the legacy of his great predecessors', Douglas declared. 'And this legacy consists in the strengthening and consolidation of the German Reich on the one hand and the strengthening and consolidation of the monarchical principle on the other . . . What Kaiser Wilhelm I won for Germany with his victorious sword Kaiser Wilhelm II will and shall hold fast for Germany. No less will he and shall he hold fast to all that Kaiser Wilhelm did to instil the idea and the consciousness of a strong monarchy into the hearts of his people. There was a time, not long ago, when people mocked the influence of the sovereign and sought to consign him to the role of a purely representative figurehead, as is still the aim today of the democratic and democratically inclined parties. The achievements of Kaiser Wilhelm I showed the whole world what great things a powerful ruler can accomplish, and if there were ever any doubt about it, everyone who loves his Fatherland today has the deep conviction that Prussia has not only become great through the Hohenzollerns, but that the whole future of Germany and Prussia, indeed of the peace of the world, is inseparably bound up with the House of Hohenzollern. That is the great legacy that has come down to our illustrious Kaiser from his predecessors, and he would be no Hohenzollern if he did not see it as his foremost task to build further upon the foundations laid by his fathers, to Germany's, to Prussia's, honour and blessing.'[34]

Undeniably, the personal characteristics of the Kaiser were a problematic aspect of this daring monarchical concept, for in a hereditary monarchy the continuity of suitably statesmanlike talent from generation to generation cannot be guaranteed. But on the very grounds of this inner logic, in drafting the speech Rottenburg was obliged to emphasise how outstandingly well qualified Kaiser Wilhelm II was for the mighty Prussian–German throne. That in so doing he had to set the truth on its head in every single particular, against his better judgement, was quite a different matter.

It was therefore no accident that the speech began with a heroic description of the quite exceptional preparation Wilhelm had undergone for the heavy responsibilities of office.[35] Never before had a Prussian prince 'seen so much of everyday life with his own eyes', Douglas declared. With 'perceptive wisdom' Kaiser Friedrich III had broken through the 'traditional boundaries of royal education' by sending his son to school in Kassel, and had thus brought him 'into contact with circles of everyday life'. 'It was a bold experiment to set the heir to the Prussian throne on the school bench at the gymnasium in Kassel and to give him the task of learning what his fellow pupils had to learn'; yet thanks to the 'tenacious will-power' of the prince the experiment had been a 'brilliant' success, 'so that the practical impressions gained during his time at the gymnasium' could 'continue to be felt and to develop further in his academic life in Bonn'. Still today, according to Douglas's idealised account, Wilhelm's fellow students at Bonn spoke enthusiastically of 'his lively, truly comradely character and of his unrivalled talents as a forceful swordsman'. 'Our young Kaiser has had the benefit of a thorough, scientific education; he has learnt to work with persistence and perseverance, and he has succeeded most happily in uniting the impressions of practical life with the conclusions drawn from his scientific studies.' This successful education in combination with his 'exceptional natural gifts' was 'undoubtedly responsible for the excellent judgement and the quick, felicitous perception which distinguish our present Kaiser, to the astonishment of all those to whom it falls to have dealings with him'. After Kassel and Bonn, as was well known, a 'strict military training' had ensued. 'With the purposeful energy characteristic of him, and with the warm interest in the army innate in the House of Hohenzollern . . . Prince Wilhelm became a smart and enthusiastic soldier' who 'learnt to obey . . . in order to be able to command in days to come'. In spite of all his passion for the military life, however, the Kaiser never allowed his interest in the civil affairs of the nation to recede. 'Already as prince, while he was receiving instruction from the highest officials of our national administration about the work of the civil authorities, of the general provincial administration, of the church and educational authorities, about the economic and social functions of the state, about the fiscal, financial and budgetary principles on which the prosperity of the Prussian state so heavily depends, he surprised everyone with his quick understanding, his healthy, practical intelligence, his lively interest in all these things, characterised by a desire to get to the root of the matter on every subject. So it has remained after his accession', Count Douglas assured his audience.

This 'all-embracing education' of the Prince had brought out a straightforward and yet regal disposition in Wilhelm. Thanks to it the young sovereign had developed 'a restless instinct for activity and a genuine love of work', together with the conviction 'that the duties of a sovereign were also service, a service which must be carried out faithfully and without respite, and to which all personal considerations had to be subordinated'. The magic of the Hohenzollerns, which was so characteristic of all three German Kaisers, showed itself also in Wilhelm II 'in the most natural simplicity and geniality, heart-conquering benevolence, combined with the highest degree of majesty'. Kaiser Wilhelm II knew 'no inactivity, no respite. No hour is too early for him, no discomfort or exertion too great, if it is a matter of fulfilling his duties as ruler. Good health, steeled by energetic physical exercise and temperance, and an admirable steadiness, achieved by iron self-discipline, in all his conduct and habits of life, enable him to bring an efficacy and dedication to his royal calling which, recalling so much our great King Friedrich II [Frederick the Great] and continuing the ideal example of his illustrious grandfather, must indeed stand as a model for all classes of our people.' In all his indefatigable work for land and people the Kaiser always maintained an 'imperturbable calm', Douglas claimed. 'Never does he become impatient, never hasty or agitated.' Moreover, by 'generous planning of his day', in spite of heavy military commitments the Kaiser 'always found enough time to settle government business conscientiously in every sphere, with the same love, the same interest and the same lively intelligence'. It should also be noticed that the Kaiser 'allowed no one to speak to him, or listened to what he had to say, about matters which that person's office did not entitle him to raise with the Kaiser', and it was precisely this which provided 'the guarantee which could not be valued too highly, that the Kaiser is the determined enemy of all coteries and camarillas, and that he never listens to whisperings from unauthorised sources . . . He is likewise characterised by absolute imperviousness to personal flattery and sycophancy and a sure eye for the true evaluation of those who approach him, a resolute rejection of all importunate ambition, as well as, on the other hand, a rare receptiveness to an open, honest and true word, which the Kaiser knows how to appreciate even if it does not correspond to his personal views. These are qualities of the young Kaiser which not only do his character the greatest honour, but are also of incalculable worth for the country.' Furthermore he showed a 'truly royal gratitude' and a 'reverent appreciation' of the services of his leading advisers.

With regard to internal politics the Kaiser stood on the lofty ground of the 'monarchical principle', above all parties. He wanted no 'party government'; his vision was 'far too broad and impartial' for that. Of his government he demanded 'objective action . . . and he has repeatedly declared that his life belongs to the whole people regardless of religious belief, ethnic origin or party political affiliation. The Kaiser knows only one yardstick in this connection: real love for the Fatherland and the throne. This is the only yardstick which fits the monarchical principle. He alone remains and will remain when the ephemeral catch-phrases of the party political activity of the day have long since faded away.' Certainly Wilhelm had a strong 'interest in all humanitarian and welfare work', asserted the speaker. 'Wherever it is a question of alleviating want and creating institutions that are designed to improve the lot of our oppressed fellow creatures, there is no more willing and ready hand than his.' At the same time Wilhelm II had the ability to look calmly and dispassionately at the practical consequences of a new idea. 'That unfortunate romantic impulse which, particularly in the highest echelons of human society, can so easily become a reef on which practical judgement and creative power are shipwrecked, is quite foreign to our Kaiser and finds no place in the conduct of his life.'

The deeper source of all these magnificent qualities, according to the speech, is 'to be found in the quiet assurance which is the fruit of a genuine trust in God grounded in personal experience'. This 'high moral seriousness of the Kaiser, resting on a deep inner religious conviction', nevertheless did not prevent him from 'joyfully looking real life straight in the eye, with a healthy, clear vision, and nothing is more foreign to our young Kaiser than a gloomy, morbid view of life. Anyone who has ever had the opportunity of meeting him will have gained the impression that in him he has a healthy, manly, cheerful nature that places all its strength at the service of land and people with joyous energy, but is absolutely inaccessible to any gloomy, sluggish and melancholy quietism.' 'All these traits are united in an overall picture of such fresh, promising colours, that our people are indeed justified in looking up with the fullest confidence to him who wears the crown.' No sovereign understood his times as Wilhelm did, no king would turn this understanding into deeds better than he, and the people would 'thank him with ever-increasing loyalty'. Thus the monarchy, which under Kaiser Wilhelm I had already attained hitherto unknown glory, and which in the last twenty years had 'sunk its roots deeper than ever into the heart of our people', would in future be still more firmly anchored. All Germans, regardless of which party orientation they favoured, felt assured that the monarchy was 'the guardian of our freedom, our culture, our national welfare'. And 'our present young Kaiser' was the man 'not only to uphold the blessings of a strong and free monarchy for our Fatherland, but to develop them to an even richer and finer degree'.[36]

Even if Bismarck thought of the 'monarchical principle' as a politically necessary fiction which would safeguard his own leadership as 'first counsellor of the crown' under the new Kaiser as before, it was nevertheless clear that other forces were also at work seeking to turn the myth of Personal Monarchy into reality. The first among these was of course Kaiser Wilhelm II himself, who was impatient to bring about the actual beginning of his personal rule, as we shall see. But other influential people also spoke up for a strengthening of monarchical power on constitutional and conservative socio-political grounds. They too argued in favour of building up the 'monarchical principle' under the dynamic young Kaiser as the 'guardian of the concept of the Reich' and as a bastion against the ever-rising democratic tide. Thus for instance the Saarland industrialist Carl Freiherr von Stumm-Halberg expressed the conviction that, in view of the growing democratic threat, 'it was absolutely out of the question for our kings to avoid any longer intervening personally in the fight against the disintegrating tendencies'.[37] Nonetheless even the most ardent royalist could see that there were also great dangers in endowing the Hohenzollern monarchy with such charisma. Bernhard von Bülow, the future Reich Chancellor, spoke of 'Untergehen [downfall]' if the experiment failed,[38] and Philipp Eulenburg, the Kaiser's best friend, captured the desperate 'all-or-nothing' quality of this crisis strategy in the words: 'No, under such circumstances the only outcome can be to give one's support *to the Kaiser sans phrase*. If we do not work to consider *Him* the personification of Germany − even if his character makes it hard work for us! − we shall lose *everything*.'[39]

### THE MATERIAL COST OF PERSONAL MONARCHY

The renewed emphasis on the monarchical principle found its first audible echo when shortly after the accession of Wilhelm II a lively disagreement broke out both in government circles and among the public over the financial circumstances of the imperial court. Everyone accepted that the relatively modest means which had been at the disposal of the Prussian–German crown under Wilhelm I would not be sufficient under the dynamic new sovereign. Everyone also knew that while Wilhelm I, whose old-style Prussian frugality was proverbial, thought of himself primarily as king of Prussia and considered the office of kaiser almost as a tiresome honorary position, his grandson had completely different ideas of his tasks as German kaiser – ideas that were shared by many Germans of all classes.

There was no reluctance to talk about the sums involved. According to conversations with 'one of the highest court officials here' (it was probably Count Stolberg), the Austrian chargé d'affaires Arthur von und zu Eissenstein-Lhotta was able to report to Vienna on 28 October 1888, the old Kaiser Wilhelm I had left a private fortune of 24 million marks in securities in addition to landed property to the value of 3 million marks. Out of the securities his widow the Kaiserin Augusta had received 3 million marks at his death, and his daughter Luise, Grand Duchess of Baden, had received 1.7 million marks, while the landed properties went to Prince Heinrich, the brother of the present Kaiser. The remainder of the estate of Wilhelm I had been turned over to the Prussian crown entail fund (Kronfideikommiss). With the knowledge and approval of Wilhelm II, Kaiser Friedrich III had taken the sum of 9 million marks from Wilhelm I's estate; of that, at Friedrich's death, his widow Victoria had inherited 1 million marks and each of her four daughters had received 2 million. Both Dowager Empresses – Augusta and Victoria – also received a widow's pension of 600,000 marks a year, in addition to which the costs of Kaiserin Augusta's household were defrayed from Wilhelm II's privy purse, but not those of the Kaiser's mother. She, however, could draw on 200,000 marks a year from her private means. Kaiser Wilhelm II himself, as the chargé d'affaires was informed, had at his disposal 'an annual income of 20 million marks, of which 13 ½ million was civil list and the remainder was revenue from the Prussian Kronfideikommiss'.[40] These latter sums, however, were far from adequate for the manner in which Wilhelm intended to conduct his reign. The grandiose, rather heavy and overladen interior redecoration of the rooms of the Berlin Schloss had alone cost twice as much as the renovation of Charlottenburg which Friedrich and Victoria had undertaken.[41] A new imperial yacht was ordered for four and a half million marks.[42] The reorganisation and 'expansion of the household in general' – soon to be swelled by 'two men accustomed to the sea, a royal cook and a valet', as well as two brushers, five porters, one cellarman and two court quartermasters[43] – which arose from the restless lifestyle of the young Kaiser, led to demands soon after his accession for an increase both of the Prussian Crown Endowment (or civil list) and of the 'Allerhöchster Dispositionsfonds', the sum allocated to the monarch for the fulfilment of his duties in his capacity as German Kaiser.

Oberhofmarschall Eduard von Liebenau, the Senior Marshal of the Court, persuaded the Kaiser to ask the Prussian parliament for an additional 6 million marks a year – he also pressed for a royal train to be built – while House Minister von Wedell favoured an increase of the civil list of 3 million marks and was of the opinion that such a request would 'go through without a hitch' in the Prussian parliament.[44]

At first these proposed increases came up against determined resistance from Bismarck, who feared that a parliamentary debate on the cost of the monarchy might endanger the monarchy itself. He warned that even in the Prussian parliament, where thanks to the three-class franchise at least there were no Social Democrats, the deliberations should last for no more than five minutes and no debate should be allowed, for 'any discussion harms the prestige of the crown'; if the increase were rejected the ministry would even have to resign. Only the Conservatives could be relied upon to support an increased civil list, and even among them there were several who would agree only 'with trembling hearts', the Chancellor opined. Among the Free Conservatives there were many who were 'already uncertain', and support for the measure from the National Liberals was probably quite out of the question. That the Kaiser 'had heavy expenses because of the 2 dowager empresses, who each received 900,000 [sic] marks a year and because of his 5 children, was quite clear', he admitted; an exceptional request based on this fact would therefore be only fair. 'But a permanent increase, when all the world knew that Kaiser Wilhelm I had made savings of 27 million in 25 years, would cause much bad blood.' So it was on this very question, which foreshadowed the coming power struggle between crown and government, that the first direct confrontation between Kaiser and Chancellor threatened to arise. On 2 December 1888 General Count Alfred von Waldersee, the successor to the old Field Marshal Count von Moltke as chief of the General Staff, recorded: 'the affair is causing . . . the Chancellor serious anxiety; he must . . . soon come to a decision . . . He will be in a difficult position.'[45] In the end a compromise solution was reached, after Wilhelm II had held personal discussions with National Liberal and Free Conservative Party leaders (in the first instance with Bennigsen and Douglas).[46]

When the proposal came up for discussion in the Prussian parliament the Free Conservative Party leader Christoph von Tiedemann spoke in favour of unanimous acceptance. 'You may depend upon it that the whole German people is behind you on this question', he declared to the house in ringing tones. He pointed out that since the creation of the Reich the representational duties of the Prussian crown, particularly with regard to the South German and the non-German states, had increased enormously. Addressing the question of whether the Reich as a whole was not 'under an obligation to provide an endowment for the imperial crown', he argued 'that the duty to provide the crown with an endowment must be regarded as a point of honour for Prussia'. The only opposition came from the ranks of the Progressive Party: Rudolf von Virchow abstained from voting, and Eugen Richter spoke out against a permanent increase of the annuity from the Kronfideikommiss by 3.5 million marks as an unjustified measure, although he recognised the necessity of a one-off extra payment. Both in committee and in plenary session Richter pointed out that the old Kaiser had been able to save up millions, and maintained that the additional duties of the Kaiser's role had already been provided for by the increase of the crown endowment in 1868. In the end, however, the proposal was accepted with a large majority. The Prussian parliament approved an increase of the civil list by 3.5 million marks a year, raising it from 12.2 million to 15.7 million per annum.[47]

Not only this parliamentary success but also other indications suggest that Bismarck's fear of a general debate on the purpose of the monarchy may have been exaggerated.[48] Since the creation of the Reich seventeen years earlier the imperial role of the Hohenzollerns had taken root even in the south and west of the Reich and even in sections of the working class.[49] The leading role which the dynamic young monarch intended to play as German Kaiser was in perfect accord with a widespread desire for it in the people and in the Reichstag.[50] After the sense of stagnation produced by an old Kaiser followed by a sick one, a powerful new impetus was in the air. Thus, for example, in Frankfurt am Main the construction of a new Reich Post Office was approved by an All-Highest Cabinet Order of 26 January 1889 with the proviso that 'lodgings for His Majesty's occasional use' must be incorporated into it; the new apartments cost no less than 2 million marks.[51] At the same time the Reichstag took the decision that a palace should be built for the Kaiser in Strassburg. The popularity of the imperial concept was so great that some saw in it a threat to the federal character of the Reich: the Prince Regent of Bavaria expressed the fear that if Wilhelm II received an additional civil list as *Kaiser*, the civil lists of the other German monarchs − at least at their existing levels − might be called into question. The Bavarian envoy and member of the Bundesrat in Berlin, Hugo Count von Lerchenfeld-Köfering, acknowledged that the Kaiser had onerous public duties, that these would increase greatly under the energetic new monarch and that therefore some remuneration from the Reich's resources was indeed required. He nevertheless argued for the retention of the ersatz solution represented by the 'Allerhöchster Dispositionsfonds', and rejected a 'civil list as such' for the Reich.[52] Bismarck also took a decisive stance against an imperial civil list at first. In August 1888 he declared that he had 'never yet heard the present Kaiser make any mention of it, nor did he expect him to. He had opposed or diverted similar suggestions in the time of Kaiser Wilhelm I *a limine*, and he would continue to do this if they should be made to him.'[53]

In spite of these federalist misgivings the pressure for an imperial civil list continued to grow. As the Austrian chargé d'affaires Eissenstein was able to report in November 1888, among the members of the Reichstag there was a firm determination to introduce soon 'a motion for the creation of a civil list for the German Kaiser'; it was to be set at a level of 5 million marks per annum. The semi-official newspapers had also been suggesting for some time 'that the German Kaiser, to whom in this capacity a great deal of heavy expenditure had accrued, could not make do with the income of a king of Prussia, which was in any case modest. The German Reich therefore had the obligation to do away with this unsatisfactory state of affairs, and must place at the disposal of the Kaiser a certain sum every year to cover the many expenses which have to be incurred in the interest of the nation.' As the government-supporting newspapers had emphasised, the old Kaiser Wilhelm had been 'reluctant, out of delicacy, to accept that the Reich should vote a civil list to him, since His Imperial Majesty, as first German kaiser, chose to see the bestowal of the imperial crown, for Himself, as no more than an honorary position, to which no pecuniary advantages of any kind were attached'. The old Kaiser had always insisted, however, that his successors could not be expected to defray the expenses which accrued to the king of Prussia in his role as German Kaiser out of their Prussian income alone. There was therefore no doubt, Eissenstein reported, 'the Reichstag would accept with acclaim a resolution to this effect to which it had itself given birth'.[54]

In early 1889 the Reichstag voted in favour of a large increase in the funds made available annually to the Kaiser, even though the Prussian crown endowment had already taken the duties of the imperial crown expressly into account. In deference to the character of the Reich as a monarchical alliance the name 'imperial civil list' was avoided, but the so-called Allerhöchster Dispositionsfonds, introduced for this purpose in 1874, was increased tenfold, that is to say from 300,000 to 3 million marks. Thus the total amount of money approved by the two parliaments which Wilhelm II received rose immediately after his accession, as Liebenau had demanded, by 6.2 million marks, from 12,500,000 to 18,700,000 marks per annum.[55]

### THE 'WILHELMINE ERA' BEGINS

A new era – the 'Wilhelmine epoch', as it was to be named – had undoubtedly dawned. For anyone who had had the opportunity to observe the Kaiser's proclamations, the opening ceremonies of the Reichstag and of the Prussian parliament in the White Hall of the Berlin Schloss, the officially published

flattering speeches and loyal addresses,[56] the public debates on the increase of
the crown endowments in Prussia and in the Reich, the countless inaugural visits
to German and foreign courts or the newly devised celebration of the Kaiser's
birthday, it was obvious that the accession of the 29-year-old Kaiser was an event
of no ordinary significance, but a crucial turning-point in what was as yet the
short history of Bismarck's Reich.[57] The combination of the inherited power of
the Hohenzollern crown with the youthful energy and strength of will which
Kaiser Wilhelm II radiated represented, both in the direct political realm and
in the social and cultural spheres beyond, an almost invincible – if as yet still
latent – new force.[58]

Shortly after his accession, pamphlets and newspaper articles about the Kaiser
appeared in numerous cities of the Reich, echoing – partly from ignorance, partly
from calculation – the whitewashing and wishful thinking that characterised
Count von Douglas's speech. In September 1888 the *Schwäbische Merkur* was
already applauding the fact that the German people had now acquired 'what we
need at the helm of the Reich: a *man of character*'. The certainty that Wilhelm II's
regime 'would not lag behind that of his grandfather in honour and constancy
quickly won all hearts for him', the Stuttgart newspaper commented. On all
sides there was 'a firm confidence that Germany's destiny [was] on the right
path'.[59] In the summer of 1889 the anonymous publication *Wallende Nebel und
Sonnenschein*, which even in the opinion of the Wilhelmstrasse amounted to a
'glorification of the reigning Kaiser', caused a great stir throughout the country.[60]
The *Badische Presse*, a Karlsuhe newspaper, rejoiced that the 'youthful Reich
now [has] the good fortune to acquire a Kaiser who is capable of being his own
chancellor'. Hitherto, since Kaiser Wilhelm I had been 'already too advanced in
years' and 'his noble son Kaiser Friedrich already too ill', the 'beneficial influence'
of an 'active, strong monarchy' had not reached its full potential. 'But Kaiser
Wilhelm II in his youthfulness and energy is, for the next phase of the development of the Reich, ... the right man in the right place.'[61] Even abroad there was
great admiration for him at first. In the summer of 1889 a commentary on the
German sovereign which was astonishingly favourable for a French publication
appeared under the title of *L'Empereur Guillaume II et la première année de
son règne*.[62] The writer of this work, Edouard Simon, was admittedly German
by birth and had taken French nationality, but the renowned French historian
Ernest Lavisse, writing on the German Kaiser in the *Figaro*, remarked no less
admiringly: 'To reign [régner] is not sufficient for Wilhelm II: he wishes to rule
[gouverner] like his forefathers, who put Prussia together piece by piece with
their own royal hands.'[63] An Italian newspaper spoke of the great 'love ... which
[is] shown by the German people towards the Hohenzollern family and in particular towards the illustrious head of this dynasty'.[64] The American friend of the

Kaiser's youth, Poultney Bigelow, unburdened himself of a flattering character sketch of the Kaiser in a Polish newspaper.[65] The Englishman Harold Frederic compiled a 'glorification' of the early life of Wilhelm II, which was well received everywhere except in Bad Homburg and Windsor.[66] But behind the scenes of the apparatus of power, even in these very early days of the Wilhelmine era, grave anxieties about the new state of affairs and the new ruler were perceptible and would indeed never again disappear.

Although the 73-year-old founder of the Reich was still firmly in the saddle, when Wilhelm II came to the throne on 15 June 1888 the balance of power between Chancellor and Kaiser had shifted noticeably and with lasting effect. Scarcely three weeks later the British ambassador Sir Edward Malet summed up the fundamental transformation which had taken place with Wilhelm II's accession, even though there had been no formal constitutional change, and gave a perceptive warning of the fragility of Bismarck's position: 'The scene has changed: a young Prince has come to the throne. The power of Prince Bismarck is dependent upon the will of the Kaiser & . . . whereas in all the latter years of the Emperor William's reign we had only to consider the intentions of Prince Bismarck, we should now in a considerable measure turn our attention to the Emperor, who has just succeeded . . . If we were dealing with a country in which the foreign policy was guided by the Government & not by the Sovereign this would be a matter of small moment, but that is not the case . . . It is therefore of special importance that the Emperor should be on our side. His sentiments will count as a strong factor in the policy which may be adopted towards us. The Chancellor's position is no longer as strong as it was during the reign of the Emperor William, & he will have to humour the young Sovereign in order to maintain his own power.'[67]

The solemn proclamations and theatrical ceremonies of the first days contrasted sharply with the hectic, unconventional style which Wilhelm rapidly brought to his conduct of affairs. There was little sign of grieving for his dead father; on the contrary, observers spoke of a state of intoxication which lasted the whole summer.[68] Wilhelm's mother expressed the opinion to Queen Victoria and also to Kaiserin Augusta that nothing could have been more destructive for the Kaiser's character than his early accession. 'I cannot imagine anything *worse* for his disposition than becoming Kaiser!, or than rising to this position so utterly unripe and so ignorant of the world, of *other* countries & other *sets* than the one he has unfortunately lived & moved in & identified himself with against our will! His good qualities have *not* been developed & the bad ones have been *forced* as in a hot bed', she warned in April 1889.[69] Not only Wilhelm and his Kaiserin but also the entire court and the whole new style of life were 'so far from what I think dignified, "tactvoll" − & refined!'[70]

Most observers were inclined to attribute the 'furious' pace which Wilhelm had kept up in Berlin since mid-June 1888 to a personality which had not yet found its equilibrium, and they found some consolation in the fact that Bismarck was still in office to stave off the dangers of such an intemperate style of conducting business. Only three weeks after the succession the astute Austro-Hungarian ambassador Széchényi reported apprehensively to Vienna: 'When Kaiser Friedrich III came to the throne and, although his reign had hardly begun, made one change and innovation after another in rapid succession with a morbid urge, one could understand this, taking into account the weaknesses of human nature, in a ruler who had to live with the premonition, if not the certainty, that his time for action might be of short duration and passing rapidly by; but if a strong young monarch who probably has a long life ahead of him, at a time when the mortal remains of his father and predecessor are scarcely cold in the grave, begins organising, dismissing, pensioning off with almost greater haste and speed, this is of a nature to arouse serious misgivings.' In such circumstances it was anything but surprising that people in Berlin were 'anxious . . . , looked towards the future not without concern, and that many in the higher posts in the government and in the army are beginning to feel unsafe in their skins'.[71] Similarly Baroness Spitzemberg recorded in her diary in mid-August: 'Yes, the young Kaiser is having a fine time chasing his people around, especially the soldiers, and the wind that is blowing in Berlin at present might seem more dangerous than a military campaign to many! The senile pace of the old Kaiser is followed directly by that of a boisterous young man thirsting for action – it gives one a certain pleasure, and the army needed sorting out. But if our Chancellor, as the last of the heroes of the great days, were not standing behind the young daredevil, one might occasionally become alarmed by the excessive zeal that rushes in all too keenly.'[72] Even Waldersee, who remained one of Wilhelm II's closest advisers after his accession and who was one of those who profited most from the favour of the young ruler, was worried about the Kaiser's restlessness.[73] On 26 August 1888 he recorded in his diary: 'the Kaiser is incredibly, not to say even immoderately, active, and indeed rather too much so in the military sphere. There is hardly any time left for audiences and so it is very difficult to approach the Kaiser.'[74]

Széchényi interpreted as a characteristic 'signature of the new era' the new-style celebration of the Kaiser's birthday which was introduced in January 1889. He reported thus to Vienna on it: 'Whereas under Kaiser Wilhelm I the congratulations were received only in the private apartments of the Palace, and of the foreign diplomats only the ambassadors took part, this time there is to be a great *church ceremony*, which the congratulating parties have to attend and to which the entire male Diplomatic Corps is invited.'[75] The old ambassador also found it strange that the new Kaiser expressed his 'All-Highest thanks' for the numerous congratulations offered to him on the occasion of his birthday in an order addressed to the Reich Chancellor, which he commanded to be published.[76] 'To the astonishment of all' Prince Bismarck had appeared at the birthday ceremony in the Schloss chapel, and when Széchényi remarked to him that this was the first time that he had seen him at a ceremony at court the Reich Chancellor replied that this was 'the first birthday of the present Kaiser and if I did not come my young master might think that I meant to leave him in the lurch'. The ambassador considered this significant episode as 'proof' that Bismarck 'is avoiding everything which might displease the young Kaiser'.[77]

Another novelty introduced by Wilhelm was the New Year meeting of the commanding generals at the Berlin Schloss – an institution which was to last until January 1914. Quite new – and in itself refreshing and modern – was also the tendency of the new ruler to venture into wider, informal social circles and thereby to throw the traditional court etiquette into confusion. Széchényi reported with surprise and mild irony in March 1889 on a 'hitherto non-existent circumstance that causes much talk here, and not without mockery' – a 'beer party' in the house of the Bavarian envoy Lerchenfeld, who like the Kaiser and Herbert Bismarck was a member of the Bonn student fraternity Borussia, at which the Kaiser was able to meet about twenty-eight gentlemen, principally 'Bonn Borussians' and 'a selection of the Bavarians who are living here while in the service of the Reich', in an informal gathering, and at which 'by way of reinforcement for the inner man . . . sausages with sauerkraut, augmented with cold meats and the host's own beer, ordered from his home, [was] served'. The Kaiser, the ambassador was able to report, had left this all-male party towards midnight, but the remaining 'more or less aged youths . . . continued to amuse themselves until around three in the morning carousing, making speeches and conversing together in the spirit of student brethren'. No one had drawn the Kaiser's attention to the precedent he was setting by his participation in this 'beer party', Széchényi commented with disapproval. 'Kaiser Wilhelm I accepted invitations from the diplomatic corps only if they came from ambassadors', he asserted, 'but if this happened to one of them, naturally all the others competed for the same honour.' After the evening entertainment at Lerchenfeld's house it was therefore to be feared 'that the other accredited envoys, particularly those who are also members of the Bundesrat, would conclude from the above-mentioned "beer party" that they were justified in claiming a similar favour'. So the Chief Marshal of the Kaiser's household had had to make it known through the press that the Kaiser 'is accustomed to visit only those private houses to which He Himself announces His intention of going. If however His Majesty wishes to continue as he has done before in this respect, certain contradictions or inconsistencies might nevertheless be impossible to avoid altogether', Széchényi feared. For instance the Kaiser had recently accepted an invitation to dine with his Flügeladjutant Gustav von Kessel and had attended the baptism of the newborn child of his old regimental comrade Oskar von Chelius in Potsdam. The ambassador warned: 'Although one sees a noble and pleasing trait of character in the fact that Kaiser Wilhelm, now that he has come to the throne, has not ceased to maintain the youthful friendships he struck up when he was still Prince Wilhelm, yet one fears that if this is not handled with more moderate and systematic restraint the Imperial Master could be placed in the undesirable position either of seeing the devaluation of the great favour bestowed by his personal support, or of neglecting or offending people who might have a longer-standing and better claim to it.'[78]

The 'beer party' at Lerchenfeld's house indeed proved no exception. Only a few days later a 'parliamentary dinner at Prince Bismarck's house caused a great stir', as Count August zu Eulenburg remarked, and immediately after that the Kaiser attended a large party at the British Embassy.[79] The dinner at Bismarck's house was, according to Malet's report to London, the first time that a Prussian sovereign had honoured members of parliament with his presence, and the impression of a new relationship between the monarch and the parliamentarians had been further strengthened by the Kaiser's declaration that it was his intention to get to know the representatives of the people better than had been customary hitherto for a head of state.[80] Széchényi also pointed out the unprecedented nature of this event in his report to Vienna: the attention attracted by Wilhelm's presence had been all the greater 'as it was the *first time* that the ruling Kaiser [had taken part] in a parliamentary banquet'. 'His Majesty had all the members of parliament present, who included some Poles, presented to him, and after the dinner he circulated among all the Reich Chancellor's guests in the friendliest manner.'[81]

In a strikingly perceptive confidential report, which was transmitted to all ambassadors of the Habsburg monarchy, the Austrian ambassador summed up his views of the political, social and mass psychological significance of the new reign in these words: 'If the youthful Kaiser Wilhelm II holds His head somewhat higher than He should considering His age and the natural absence of a successful past, this is in truth not to be wondered at, if one considers how and in what circumstances He came to the throne, and what the personal satisfactions were that have already fallen to His lot in such a short time. The young ruler ascends the throne almost without a transition, when scarcely half a year earlier, by all human reckoning, this was only a very distant prospect. He wishes that all the sovereigns of the German Empire should gather around him for this ceremony; it is done, and takes place before one's very eyes like a formal act of homage. He wishes that all commanders of the German army corps should take part in the New Year congratulations, something which was never demanded by Kaiser Wilhelm I; they appear in full strength, and among them two royal princes: Prince Georg of Saxony and Prince Leopold of Bavaria. If the Kaiser drives out, in the courtyard of the Schloss around the waiting royal carriages the crowds are scarcely smaller than those which gathered in honour of the "venerable Kaiser-Hero" in front of the Imperial Palace and the so-called historic window; and what is more, in the streets during his drive the All-Highest is often applauded, which even with his grandfather generally happened only on special occasions.' Furthermore, the entourage of the young ruler 'not only owes its present existence to the favour of its Imperial Master but also counts on Him for its future', with the consequence that it 'always guards against expressing a view contrary to His Majesty's intentions . . . so that in many cases the youthful and hasty initiative of the sovereign does not find the counterweight that would be desirable'. Although those closest to the monarch could still exercise some influence over him, they could not necessarily be relied upon to put this to good effect. 'So it is possible that, just as Kaiser Wilhelm I was sometimes taken advantage of during the last years of his reign in consequence of his old age, and Kaiser Friedrich was taken advantage of in consequence of his incurable physical illness, so Kaiser Wilhelm II might be taken advantage of because of his youth', the ambassador warned. The Kaiser's new manner of conducting his reign had met with very differing reactions among the population, observed Széchényi in his remarkable *tour d'horizon*. 'The most dissatisfied are probably all the middle-aged people in both civilian and military life who had pinned all their hopes on the reign of Kaiser Friedrich, and who now, as things have turned out, see themselves to a certain extent passed over, as well as all free-thinking and Progressive Party groups which hoped to see their political ideals realised by the deceased Kaiser. Dissatisfaction is also felt by all those who had a role to play during the era of Kaiser Wilhelm I and who now find themselves relegated to complete obscurity, although their day lasted quite unusually long, beyond any human reckoning. Those who are really content are only the young people in military, civil or court service, who consider not only the future, but already also the present, as belonging to them. And yet it cannot be denied that in spite of everything Kaiser Wilhelm II is much more popular, especially among the public at large and in the broader social classes, than one would think judging by the given circumstances and the way people talk. Yes, youth is indeed that powerful talisman which is capable of finding a softer side in even the most embittered character.'[82]

# CHAPTER TWO

# The first state visits

IMMEDIATELY after his accession to the throne, Wilhelm was keen to show himself off in the great capitals of Europe, but there were strict limits to where he could go. Paris was quite out of the question, not only because of the fresh memory of the defeat of 1870–1 and the still festering wound of Alsace and Lorraine, but also because the young sovereign epitomised 'Christian–German' racial ideals, Prussian militarism and authoritarian monarchy which were anathema on the Seine. But even Brussels, which was briefly considered for a state visit in 1888, was speedily ruled out as a no-go area for a German Kaiser. As Wilhelm recalled many years later, the German embassy in the Belgian capital warned when the idea of a royal visit was mooted that Brussels must be regarded as a suburb of Paris: it was strongly French ethnically and in sentiment, and one would in addition have to reckon with the influx of whole trainloads of Parisians of all sorts from the south. 'The Brussels mob is the just about the worst in the whole of Europe', Wilhelm wrote in 1904, remembering the warnings of the embassy. 'Miners and other workers would stream in in their thousands from the surrounding countryside and from Paris etc., in short such a huge rabble would gather there that the very poor police force and the weak, wholly inadequate army would be unable to master it. On top of that, all the anarchists of London, Paris and Brussels itself would be present in great numbers, so that the Belgian government could not guarantee the safety of my person. Moreover, one could never be sure that several thousand bribed Camelots [du Roi] – whether Parisians or from within the country itself – would not at any moment provoke demonstrations with shrieks, whistles etc., leading to the most unpleasant situations and the most painful consequences.' Both Prince Bismarck and the Belgian government concurred with this advice, the Kaiser recalled, and hence the proposed visit was cancelled. The ugly scenes that he had had to contend with when embarking some months later at Ostend were quite bad enough and proved that a visit to Belgium should be considered only in return for 'quite massive concessions by the King [such as] an alliance or agreement with us'.[1] In eastern Europe the situation was of course utterly different.

### THE JOURNEY TO PETERHOF

As he had announced in his speech from the throne on 25 June 1888, it was Wilhelm's intention to build up a particularly close relationship between Germany and its ally Austria-Hungary and at the same time to maintain the personal friendship between the German and Russian imperial houses. The idea, which Wilhelm had vigorously championed on his two visits to Russia in 1884 and 1886, of the three Emperors uniting to form a bastion against democracy and socialism came distinctly to the fore again now. The day before the speech Széchényi had been able to ascertain that the Kaiser's address would 'make a show of the greatest devotion to peace and that Kaiser Wilhelm would refer to the Austro-German alliance in the warmest terms'.[2] Shortly before the ceremony there had been an exchange of letters between Kaiser Franz Joseph and the young German Kaiser which would have long-term repercussions on the foreign policy of the Reich. One gains the impression from this correspondence that the Habsburg monarch, with whom Wilhelm had hunted so often and with such enjoyment in his youth, had now inherited the position which for Wilhelm had hitherto been held by his grandfather: that of the revered older emperor as role-model. In an initial telegram after the death of Friedrich III, Franz Joseph had assured the young Wilhelm that he could count on his loyal friendship in all circumstances,[3] and in a letter written in Budapest on 17 June 1888 and brought to Berlin by his brother Paul, the Habsburg monarch emphasised 'how sincerely I feel for you in everything which Providence has meted out to you before and at your accession to the throne'. Franz Joseph expressed his firm conviction 'that you – true to your conservative principles and to the tradition inherited from your unforgettable grandfather – will do your utmost to lead your people into happiness and well-being with a firm and calm hand, and to maintain the blessings of peace for them. It is, first and foremost, in the immutability of our friendship, in the strength of the ties which bind our empires together, that the pledge of Europe's peaceful future lies. May both our endeavours be directed above all to achieve and maintain this goal: you may be as sure that you will always find me at your side on this path as I am sure of my trust in your inviolable friendship.'[4]

In response to this letter Wilhelm II sent the Austrian Emperor on 23 June the text of his forthcoming speech from the throne and added, using a draft prepared by Herbert Bismarck: 'My dear, valued Friend. Your affectionate, kind letter in which you express your sympathy for me in such a warm and friendly manner has moved me most deeply; and I thank you most sincerely for your kind words, and particularly for the fact that you have such complete and justifiable confidence in my firm attachment to the traditions inherited from my dear Grandfather. I take possession unreservedly of this inheritance, in domestic as in foreign policy, and notably as regards the immutability of our friendship and the strength of the ties which bind our empires. With joyful gratitude I receive your assurance of this and return it with all my heart. As I have the good fortune of having been known to you from my earliest youth, there is no longer any need for me to assure you of these feelings of mine, to which, as you will see from my enclosed speech for the opening of the Reichstag, I am giving public utterance. The more strongly my late Grandfather was convinced of the necessity of warding off Russian attacks in partnership with you, the more earnestly he strove to prevent them from taking place. I follow him in the endeavour to do everything to bring the blessings of peace to our empires and to preserve them there, and to this end to nurture our relations with Emperor Alexander. The friendship that binds me to you stands so firm that it needs no outward action. But I believe I shall be acting in the interest of our mutual aims if I openly refute all the calumnies concerning our love of peace circulating in Russia as in France, by paying a visit to the Emperor of Russia in the near future. I intend to combine an inspection of my fleet with a recreational sea voyage at the end of July, which I shall conclude by calling on the Tsar at Peterhof. I have no doubt that you and I will be satisfied with the result of this visit. I hope that you will allow me to pay you a visit in the course of the autumn or in the late summer. For I should be very happy if you would agree that we should uphold the tradition of my grandfather also with regard to meeting each other in person where possible every year, even if perhaps not always at Gastein itself, in order to keep up our old friendship by exchanging ideas in person . . . In constant loyalty and devotion I remain your true Friend and Brother Wilhelm.'[5] This hand-written letter was brought to Franz Joseph by Waldersee, who had been commissioned by Wilhelm to convey the formal notification of his accession to the throne to the Austrian Emperor.[6]

In a letter to his grandmother Kaiserin Augusta, Wilhelm likewise emphasised the importance of a German–Russian understanding for the future of Austria as well as for European peace. 'With the Chancellor's full agreement and approval I shall have a meeting with the Tsar near Kronstadt, in order to make the peace of Europe even more secure', Wilhelm informed her. 'But I am making the journey principally for the sake of our dear ally the Emperor of Austria. I am hopeful that if we are able to exchange ideas I may succeed in persuading the Tsar to adopt a calm and sensible attitude towards the various ups and downs and problems with Austria. So that there might then be a calmer time in which diplomatic ways could be found of settling justified claims on both sides. Of course much depends on the extent to which the Emperor [Alexander] still holds the real power in his hands.'[7] Just before his departure for Kiel Wilhelm also informed his 'friend', Crown Prince Rudolf of Austria, 'in all frankness' of the 'threefold aim' of his coming journey to visit the Tsar. In a letter of 12 July he explained that he wanted to set the economic and financial relations between Germany and Russia in order, to settle the dispute between Austria and Russia over Bulgaria and to put an end to the dangerous situation on the Russian–Austrian frontier.[8]

It was in a distinctly cooler, indeed almost frosty, atmosphere that the news of his travelling plans reached his English grandmother. If Queen Victoria and Lord Salisbury had already been taken aback by the absence of mention of Britain in the speech from the throne, and by the indications of a rapprochement between Germany and Russia,[9] the Queen made no secret of her annoyance when Wilhelm's travelling plans were reported in the press. 'There are many rumours of your going & paying visits to Sovereigns', she wrote to her grandson on 3 July. 'I hope at least you will let some months pass before anything of this kind takes place, as it is not 3 weeks yet since your dear beloved Papa was taken & we are all still in such deep mourning for him.'[10] In his reply Wilhelm emphatically rejected the Queen's intervention and in so doing clearly revealed the foreign and domestic policy aspects of his 'Kaiser-ideology': he laid strong emphasis on the importance of his personal relations with Franz Joseph and the Tsar in the battle against parliamentarism, democracy and socialism. 'At the end of this month I shall inspect the fleet & take a trip in the Baltic; where I hope to meet the Emperor of Russia', he wrote, 'which will be of good effect for the peace of Europe & for the rest & quiet of my allies. I would have gone later if possible; but state interest goes before personal feelings, & the fate which sometimes hangs over nations does not wait till the etiquette of court mournings has been fulfilled. And as I am quite d'accord with Prince Bismarck, I hope & trust that much good will come of the proposed meeting; as I deem it necessary that monarchs should meet often & confer together to look out for dangers which threaten the monarchical principle from democratical & republican parties in all parts of the world. It is far better that we Emperors keep firm together with Italy, than that two of them should go pitching into one another without any earthly reason except for a few miserable villages more or less; which would only be arranging & preparing the way for anarchists at home & abroad.' The curious signature, 'Willy I. R.', on this first letter as Kaiser to his English grandmother betrayed how closely personal and family ties were here entangled with high politics, a state of affairs which, as we shall see, was to lead to countless conflicts.[11]

In his unpublished memoirs Herbert von Bismarck claims that the idea of a visit to the Tsar's court had been deliberately conceived as an act of revenge against the British royal family, and that it had been in Wilhelm's mind even before the death of Friedrich III, when Queen Victoria was visiting Berlin.[12] 'The anti-English urge, once again strongly prevalent, the wish to "astonish" at the very start of his reign, had allowed the plan of the Baltic journey to ripen as early as May — shortly after the departure of the Queen, and after Grand Duke Vladimir had come to Berlin at the end of April: after the funeral [of Kaiser Friedrich III on 18 June] it was divulged to Grand Duke Vladimir and was accepted with alacrity on the Russian side.'[13] Herbert Bismarck's claim is given some credence by the letter from Wilhelm to Crown Prince Rudolf of 12 July mentioned earlier, in which he speaks of the necessity of putting an end, in St Petersburg, to the machinations of France and above all of Britain against him. He would have to 'destroy, in St Petersburg, the last manifestations of French intrigues, which have been augmented since my accession by the intrigues of England . . . The latter, which under certain circumstances could increase the strength and effectiveness of the former, I even consider as the more dangerous', the Kaiser declared.[14]

Wilhelm II did not in fact wait until the end of the month but left Berlin as early as the evening of 13 July, to sail in the *Hohenzollern* from Kiel via Stettin and Danzig to Kronstadt. Only a week after the death of his father he had issued an All-Highest Order cancelling the planned fleet manoeuvres and commanding the navy to hold itself in readiness for his further orders.[15] His mother wrote in her diary on 13 July: '*How* unseemly this journey seems to me, when not even 4 weeks have gone by, I really cannot say! It hurts me unspeakably — and *must* cause *painful surprise* abroad! — As if one could not wait to show oneself, to amuse oneself, to go out, to be fêted, to enjoy the outward honours of the new position It disgusts me! Of course he is also pushed into it so as to turn his head completely!'[16] In this opinion the Dowager Empress was not alone. The Austrian ambassador reported to Vienna that everyone was wondering 'not without misgivings whether it was really necessary to announce this visit as early as the first days of the reign, and also to carry it out so soon, after scarcely a month had passed??'[17]

Certainly the Kaiser's first visit to his Baltic neighbours did not show much evidence of mourning. On his arrival in Kiel the admirals and commanders on parade at the station were delighted to see him descending from the train dressed in the new rear-admiral's uniform which he had himself designed: 'Nothing like this has ever happened before!', exclaimed of one of the commanders in high delight.[18] In the harbour the fleet was dressed overall. A salute of 330 guns was fired for the Kaiser. A naval review followed, to the accompaniment of music and cheering.[19] On the eighteen-day tour to St Petersburg, Stockholm and Copenhagen the imperial yacht, under the command of Prince Heinrich, was escorted by a squadron of ten larger warships – four iron-clads, four training ships and two corvettes – and over a dozen torpedo boats.[20] With the Kaiser and his brother travelled Secretary of State Count von Bismarck, the serving Adjutant-General Adolf von Wittich and the Kaiser's aide-de-camp, Flügeladjutant Gustav von Kessel, House Minister Maximilian Freiherr von Lyncker, physician-in-ordinary Dr Rudolf Leuthold, the diplomat Alfred von Kiderlen-Wächter as representative of the Foreign Office and Privy Court Councillor Willisch as head of the cipher office, together with Prince Heinrich's adjutant, Albert Freiherr von Seckendorff. The convoy sailed at a deliberately leisurely pace so as not to arrive at St Petersburg before the afternoon of 19 July. The atmosphere on board the *Hohenzollern* was exuberant and unconstrained. 'H.M. is in high spirits', reported Herbert Bismarck to his father on 14 July, 'and we are all inhaling the invigorating sea air with delight. The review this morning was a magnificent spectacle, the 10 big ships of our squadron sailed by in perfect order, and the two torpedo divisions (14 little ships) sped by twice at top speed in a shower of spray, overtaking us.'[21] Even when Wilhelm and a few of the other passengers became seasick he remained in the best of moods and declared his intention of undertaking a similar sea-voyage every year.[22]

Despite all the high spirits the diplomats and court officials knew only too well what risks lay hidden in a meeting between two imperial courts. In an audience with the Kaiser the Foreign Secretary urged him 'not to *initiate* any discussion on politics with the Tsar and to pay special attention to his comfort while riding etc.'[23] The first misunderstanding was nevertheless not long in coming. The German naval attaché in St Petersburg, Freiherr von Plessen, came on board at 4 a.m. with the Russian pilots and brought the programme of festivities for the coming days, together with the news that the Tsar would leave Peterhof at half past one in the afternoon. That was interpreted to mean that the Tsar, in his steamer *Alexandrie*, would sail to meet the *Hohenzollern*. At the same time the German squadron was informed of the order in which the ten ships should sail in and drop anchor before Kronstadt: the training ships should moor in front of the iron-clads. Wilhelm II, as Kiderlen-Wächter reported, was 'very angry' at this, as he wanted 'to show off his battleships first'. Seckendorff finally succeeded in calming him with the argument 'that by coming along behind the battleships he would make a far greater impression!!! Next he wanted absolutely to sail past the Tsar as admiral at the head of his squadron, could also not be induced to put on Russian uniform, but continued to wear his own newly designed naval uniform! Despite all the peeping through the telescope, no Tsar came into sight and we hove to and anchored.' Not for another two hours, when the Tsarevich

Nicholas came on board, was it discovered that the Russian court – the Tsar in his yacht, the Tsarina Maria Feodorovna on the landing stage – had been waiting for the *Hohenzollern* in the harbour since half past one. The Kaiser, who had meanwhile hurriedly donned a Russian uniform, was therefore two and a half hours late in setting foot on the Tsar's yacht, which was filled 'with grand dukes of every age and every kind, ministers, and some of the highest officers of the court'. Alexander III's greeting was warm; the 'remaining public had become definitely nervous on account of the wait! We were asked by everyone about our delay', Kiderlen reported to Berlin. 'The two Emperors sat by themselves for a long time. Ours spoke every now and then; one could see how the other was searching for a subject.'[24] Among the German naval officers it was widely felt that the 'cold' reception was intended as a deliberate snub to the German monarch. It was 'very noticeable', wrote one of them, 'that the Tsar did not sail to meet our Kaiser, that only the son, and not the father too, had come on board the Hohenzollern to greet him'.[25]

In spite of this faltering start the six-day programme passed off fairly well, at least outwardly. The political discussions centred on the private audience which Herbert Bismarck had with Tsar Alexander on 22 July, when the German Foreign Secretary, with staggering frankness, talked at length about the most intimate relationships in the German imperial family. As Herbert recorded, the Tsar had the strange idea that the position of German Kaiser was not automatically linked to the crown of Prussia, so that at the death of Kaiser Friedrich III it would have been possible for another German monarch to put forward a claim to the imperial crown. Herbert was able to convince the Tsar not only that the German kaisership was tied hereditarily to the Prussian royal house under the constitution of the Reich, but also that, of the four kings in Germany, only the Prussian monarch was a king by virtue of indigenous sovereignty, as the Kings of Bavaria, Saxony and Württemberg had only received their crowns from Napoleon in the disastrous year of 1806. But in any case, the Secretary of State continued, the princes of the German Reich had long since recognised that 'the firm cohesion of the different parts of the Reich' provided 'the only sure bastion against radical levelling tendencies and threats to the rights of the monarchical crown'. For that very reason the princes had decided on the 'magnificent demonstration that they made by their unanimous appearance at the opening of the Reichstag', as a result of which 'the edifice of the Reich stands more firmly held together now than ever'.

Alexander III then turned his attention to the relationship between Wilhelm II and his mother, whereupon the Foreign Secretary replied with the greatest frankness that the estrangement between mother and son continued beneath the surface, and that the widowed Kaiserin was alone to blame for it, for she had 'never shown . . . what is [understood] in normal life as motherly feelings' towards the present Kaiser. The Dowager Empress thought of herself 'entirely as an Englishwoman' and until the death of her husband she had seen her life's goal in 'ruling the Germany she disliked for as long as possible, as an Englishwoman'. Not satisfied with that, the Chancellor's son then gave a cynical description of the conduct of the various members of the imperial family in the Battenberg affair; he spoke of the interference of the British royal family in it and 'of the systematic efforts of Kaiserin Victoria to prejudice Kaiser Friedrich against our present Master. This went back for many a year and unfortunately had not always been unsuccessful', he added. Many years before, Herbert continued, Wilhelm II himself had once said to him, when he 'was speaking of his fruitless efforts with his exalted Mother: "I see that everything I can do will be in vain: we stand on different ground, my mother will always remain an Englishwoman and I am a Prussian; so how can we ever be in harmony with one another?"'

As if even that were not enough, the younger Bismarck then spoke 'about the role of the English doctors, about the nursing, about the reasons behind the glossing over of the facts, about the conduct of business, as well as about the behaviour of the English–Progressive camarilla' during the last Kaiser's death throes. He further informed the Tsar that 'the Prince of Wales [had] pestered our Kaiser with tiresome advice' and had 'expressed all kinds of wishes regarding Cumberland through his wife and in person'. 'In the English family and its closest offshoots' there was 'a kind of cult of the family principle', Herbert Bismarck explained to the Tsar, 'and Queen Victoria is considered as a kind of absolute head of all members of the Coburg tribe and its offshoots'. Moreover it was Britain's political aim to 'create discord and conflict on the continent and to goad the other great powers for England's benefit'. For precisely this reason the Prince of Wales had 'blackened' the name of the present Kaiser to him, the Tsar, the previous autumn, 'in order to create mutual distrust, and the Queen had written to Kaiser Wilhelm 3 days before our departure to advise him strongly against the journey here. His Majesty, however, has had enough of this uninvited tutelage and has sent the Queen such a plain answer that it is scarcely likely that it will happen again.'[26] Even if one were to take the view that the disclosure of such intimate family relationships to a foreign monarch is acceptable in the national interest, the lack of restraint with which Herbert Bismarck spoke of the Tsar's brother-in-law in this conversation is still astounding – for the Tsarina Maria Feodorovna was of course the sister of Alexandra Princess of Wales.

Otherwise the visit to Russia consisted of ceremonies, banquets and reviews. Wilhelm and Heinrich laid wreaths on the grave of the assassinated Tsar Alexander II.[27] The bachelors Herbert Bismarck and Kiderlen-Wächter, who spun out their nights with visits to bars or to ladies, sometimes did not get to bed until 6 or

7 a.m.[28] On the second day the entire party drove out to Krasnoe Selo, the Tsar's summer residence a few kilometres south-west of St Petersburg, where they all spent the night. Everywhere there were troops lining the roads and cheering, not three times as in the West, but continuously for as long as any member of the suite was still in sight. 'One became quite dizzy from all this Asiatic howling', complained Kiderlen. After a lengthy ride the whole party gathered round a tent where 'a great tattoo, prayers, firing of cannon, etc.' ensued. On the next morning there was a parade which, as Kiderlen reported, was 'led by the Russian Tsar mounted on a small, horribly fat, horse. Our Kaiser mounted on his big elegant chestnut subsequently led his regiment in parade, to the universal admiration of the Russians.' The parade, at which 'in the Russian fashion there were all sorts of extra turns', went off in fine style. 'The white Tsar was obviously in a good humour that reached its height when our sovereign at lunch in the marquee replied in Russian to the toast given by the Tsar in French. This made a really tremendous impression on all the Russians, all the more so because it was quite unexpected. Our sovereign said his little piece quite smartly and without stumbling', Kiderlen reported.[29]

According to the original programme, after the Russian mass, the luncheon and a state banquet, the German party was to re-embark on the evening of Sunday 22 July and sail that night for Stockholm. But by Wilhelm's wish the visit was prolonged for two days, as he wanted to take part in a large cavalry exercise – the horses, specially broken in for the Kaiser, had been transported from Berlin – and above all to show off one of his iron-clads to the Tsar. The cavalry exercise was proposed to the Kaiser by Grand Duke Vladimir and the Tsarevich Nicholas and was at first accepted with delight; but then Wilhelm began to have doubts, as he wondered whether the good impression created by the visit might not be endangered by too long a stay. In addition he was concerned that the invitation had not come from the Tsar himself, who was known to be no lover of riding. These problems were initially solved by the Tsar extending the invitation in person, and at the same time announcing that in any case he did not wish to accompany Wilhelm and Vladimir to the camp. 'On Sunday the Tsar, whose mood was improving all the time, suddenly said that he would go too. Since, however, the Tsar does not like to get up as early as would have been necessary if they were to leave for the camp in the early morning, everybody left that evening for Krasnoe, where they stayed the night.' Kaiser Wilhelm, as Kiderlen reported, was far from pleased with this change of plan. 'He had particularly hoped to have a really good gallop round on his horse and to take the jumps etc., as he did in Potsdam when he last inspected the Hussars.' He had been irritated by the appointment of the 'very ancient' General Glinka to be in honorary attendance on him – this eighty-year-old had been chosen

simply because he was the only holder of the ribbon of the Order of the Red
Eagle! – and had been looking forward 'enormously' to 'chasing the old man
*à la* Albedyll over the jumps'. It was probably quite fortunate that this did not
happen, the diplomat considered, and that instead 'our sovereign had to watch
the manoeuvres in a neat and proper way from a marquee in the Tsar's company',
for 'it would hardly have made a good impression if an old Russian general had
broken his neck'.[30]

On the last evening there was a family dinner for Wilhelm and his brother
with their Russian relations. The imperial occasion reached its high point with a
battle with wet towels between the Tsar and his son on one side and Wilhelm and
Heinrich on the other, which in Kiderlen's opinion 'certainly struck the typical
domestic tone of the Peterhof court of the Autocrat of all the Russias'. On the
Tuesday morning before the departure both Emperors, each with his retinue,
visited the smartly turned-out German flagship *Baden*.[31] Among the Russian
visitors were the Grand Duke Vladimir with his wife Marie of Mecklenburg-
Schwerin, together with Grand Duke Sergei and his Hessian wife Ella, sister-
in-law of Prince Heinrich and Wilhelm's first love.[32] 'Nothing was spared us',
commented Kiderlen after the visit was over. 'Upstairs and downstairs – everything had to be seen, engine-room, galley, men's quarters etc. Then gunnery
drill, marines' drill with blank cartridges etc.'[33] Finally there was lunch on
board the *Hohenzollern*, in bright sunshine on a glassy sea. 'We took our leave
with the greatest cordiality', accompanied by 'a continuous thunder of cannon-
fire', Herbert Bismarck wrote to his brother-in-law Kuno Count Rantzau. 'There
was no further talk of politics at all, our master has kept quite quiet, and this
is probably what has put the Tsar so much at ease.'[34] The mood of the German
Kaiser was no less gratified. 'Whether it was the feeling as we steamed away of
being free from ceremonial obligations, whether it was a good lunch combined
with pleasure that the visit had gone off so well that induced a peculiarly festive
mood', reflected Kiderlen in his report to Holstein, 'H.M. was in the most boisterous spirits and . . . gave us one in the tummy, only this time quite literally.' On
the journey from Kronstadt to Stockholm on 25 July Kiderlen summed up his
general impression of the St Petersburg visit with the comment that the Russians
had never been 'so conciliatory, so humble, so compliant, and in everything one
could clearly see their efforts and desires to get peace and quiet, and to be freed
from the nightmare caused by a worsening in their relations with us; hence also
the fearful avoidance of all "ticklish" questions'.[35]

If Kaiser Wilhelm II's first official visit to St Petersburg can count as a success
at all, it is only in the sense that it did not turn out to be a disaster, as many had
feared.[36] Both sides registered with relief that during the entire visit political
conversations had been successfully avoided. The First Secretary at the German
Embassy in St Petersburg, Count Friedrich von Pourtalès, regarded it as a success

'that we have shown that we did not *want* anything from this visit, but at the
same time that we are not disposed to comply with certain demands that they
would like to make of us'. His one hope was that the two monarchs had gained
a favourable impression of one another, Pourtalès wrote to Holstein. 'I believe
that our young Kaiser with his frank guileless character found favour in Tsar
Alexander's eyes and by his mere presence dispelled much of the artificially
created mistrust of him.'[37] Pourtalès and also the ambassador, General Lothar
von Schweinitz, were seriously mistaken, however, if they thought that Wilhelm
had won back the Tsar's earlier confidence in him.[38] In the imperial family and in
the Russian upper class in general there was great indignation at Wilhelm's lack
of piety and Herbert Bismarck's spiteful enmity towards the late Kaiser Friedrich
and his widow. After the visit the Tsar commented to the future Foreign Minister
Count Vladimir Lamsdorff that the young Kaiser was a 'rascally young fop, who
throws his weight around, thinks too much of himself and fancies that others
worship him'.[39] As the British ambassador in St Petersburg, Sir Robert Morier,
ascertained, the family of Alexander III, whose life was a totally domestic one,
were '*outrés* by this hideous persecution under the sanction of the son of the
memory of the father'. He reported to London on the 'profound effect of disgust
produced by the order to put off mourning during the Emperor's stay here
and the giving the signal for every sort of feasting & jollity'. The behaviour
of Herbert Bismarck had been particularly offensive: 'as usual beastly drunk',
in a loud voice which could be heard from the other side of the street, he had
welcomed Friedrich's early death as a deliverance. His theme was 'all that wd.
have befallen Germany, & how the flood gates of democracy & Jews & God knows
what more besides wd. have been opened if the reign of the Emperor Frederick
& the Empress Victoria had been prolonged. But, he added, *un bon petit cancer
nous a sauvé!*' This story was 'quite authentic, quite in character and has left
behind the profoundest sense of loathing', Morier wrote.[40]

The Kaiser's physician also considered that the outcome of the Russian visit,
in spite of all the professed friendliness, had been unsatisfactory, and that the
young Kaiser was aware of this. In a conversation with a diplomat at the Austro-
Hungarian embassy Leuthold acknowledged that 'the reception accorded to
Kaiser Wilhelm in St Petersburg had certainly been very warm outwardly, and
in particular the personal relations between the All-Highest Persons had left
nothing to be desired; nevertheless the German gentlemen had received the
impression that all these manifestations lacked spontaneity and that "it had
been more a matter of acting than of feeling". The free, unaffected tone which
Wilhelm had adopted in everything seemed to please the Russians, yet it never
came to the point of real inner warmth of feeling, everyone was extremely
polite, but remained fundamentally cold and distant.' When the German ships
finally sailed away, Leuthold continued, 'the Russian gentlemen were as pleased

that everything had gone off in the best possible way in accordance with the programme, as that the visit had come to an end'. The doctor had been able to establish that the Kaiser had come away with the same impression.[41]

When Gustav Freiherr von Senden-Bibran, who had taken part in the voyage as commander of the *Bayern*, looked back over the visit it was, likewise, the 'frosty' reserve of the Russians that struck him most. At both higher and lower levels he had the distinct feeling of a 'cold reception'. During the entire visit it had been clear 'that the Russian naval officers were not anxious to make any closer contact with our officer corps'. The ships' commanders were invited to meet them, certainly, but even these meetings had had a 'stiff quality', and none of the other German officers was invited, which was 'quite unusual' on a foreign visit. He had noticed on numerous occasions, Senden wrote, that the Russian officers 'did not *want* to speak German', but 'always began the conversation in French'. In the Russian officers' cabins there had been many pictures of Napoleon hanging next to portraits of the Tsar. He had not seen a single German flag flying. All in all he had the impression 'that the cold reception was instigated from on high'. There had also been much talk in St Petersburg of a party sympathetic to France which was gaining influence under Alexander III.[42]

Of the ambitious objectives which Wilhelm had announced in his letters to the Emperor Franz Joseph, Crown Prince Rudolf, Kaiserin Augusta and Queen Victoria, not one was realised. Before the journey Waldersee had taken the view that the antagonism between Russia and Austria was much too strong to be resolved by anything short of a European war. In a letter to the future Minister of War General von Verdy du Vernois, a friend of his, the acting Chief of the General Staff predicted: 'There are indications that the Kaiser's journey to Russia will change nothing in the political sphere; the difference between Austria's and Russia's interests is so great, and on both sides the inclination to yield in any way at all is so slight, that a clash is inevitable; all that we shall achieve is to delay it a little, which is Bismarck's aim; you will probably agree with me that it would be better for us to bring it on. For the moment the Russians still seem to be short of money, but they will find it after we have helped to raise the exchange.'[43] When the visit to the Tsar was over Waldersee drove the point home with his laconic verdict: however favourable an impression Kaiser Wilhelm might have made in St Petersburg, 'that does not alter the situation as a whole'.[44]

## THE STATE VISIT TO THE SCANDINAVIAN COURTS

The four-day visit to Sweden was an undoubted success, which – not least because the visit to Peterhof had proved disappointing – left a lasting impression on Wilhelm II. He named his fifth son, who was born at this time, after King

Oscar II of Sweden and Norway.[45] On their arrival in Stockholm on 26 July the beauty of the city and the warmth of their reception delighted the Kaiser and his suite.[46] The King sailed out to meet the Kaiser's yacht, and on the way into the harbour 'the people were standing in large crowds on the shore; they greeted our Kaiser in the heartiest fashion, both from the land and from steamers . . . Wherever one looked there were . . . waving handkerchiefs and friendly faces', Senden commented. 'It was quite a different matter from Russia.' As the Queen of Sweden was in Norway, the Kaiser led in the Swedish Crown Princess Viktoria, his cousin from Baden, to dinner.[47] Looking back on the visit Herbert Bismarck recorded with relish: 'After the dinner in the enchantingly situated Drottningholm Castle, from which the return journey on Lake Mälaren, gilded by the sinking sun, was fabulously beautiful, we continued with a *souper* on the Hohenzollern, with cannon-fire and fireworks, and this after the harbour had already rocked on its foundations with the din of salutes from our big iron-clads at midday, in confirmation of the birth of the 5th Prince. The Swedes were extremely warm-hearted; the monarch was so moved that huge tears rolled down his cheeks; and he was immediately asked to be godfather. Stockholm is magnificently positioned: probably the only royal city in which the iron-clads can tie up directly at the quay of the imposing castle.'[48]

At the end of August, when Wilhelm II looked back on his Baltic cruise, it was the visit to Stockholm which brought back the happiest memories. He wrote to his friend Philipp Eulenburg, the author of the 'Skalden Songs' evoking the Viking past, with rapturous enthusiasm for the Nordic world: 'What an eventful summer it has been! But what marvellous moments it brought me! What would I have given if you could have been in Stockholm when we sailed in! How proud I felt when we sailed in round Sandhammer and then passed through the magical girdle of the skerry reefs with our mighty squadron. Impressive as my "dragons" looked as they sailed on the open sea, now in the serpentine narrows through which they made their way, they seemed truly gigantic. And then came the moment when we rounded the last point, the splendid city lay before us and the first German squadron sent its brazen greeting to the palace of the Nordic King, as it steamed in before the eyes of hundreds of thousands of people. Yes, that was indeed a moment to remember! I felt as if I could see our old Norse friends in the clouds, watching the procession of "dragons" with smiles of pleasure, and rejoicing that a race worthy of them was coming to its ancient ancestral land with warriors a thousand in number! – The whole of Stockholm seemed to me like a dream, for I was transported to the days of Erik, Hokan and Fritjof and hence almost forgot about living people, and yet not quite, for I have never in all my life seen such a quantity of beautiful girls and women together as in Stockholm. And how fresh and rosy, gay and friendly they all looked. I thought to myself that if they were Valkyries, it would be a real delight to be a hero in Valhalla. I picked up flowers thrown by the most beautiful of them, to the gratification of the King, and put them in my buttonhole; the King pointed this out to each lovely benefactor with a wave, which gave great pleasure. When we mounted the stairs of the telephone exchange – unfortunately the only thing we mounted in it – the most beautiful telephonists were standing on the landings and scattering flowers. The lower floor was dressed in tulle montant, the upper floor in very low-cut satin, and furthermore a lovely redhead with a dazzling complexion! Which I particularly admire! What more could one ask? Answer: darkness and a bed! – That was beloved Sweden . . . The King of Sweden made me à la suite of his Navy, just as he wears the uniform of ours, so now I am partly Swedish too, and I am getting closer to the ancient land of the Jarls and Vikings.'[49] King Oscar knew well how to exploit the Germanic racial cult to secure for his country the goodwill of the new ruler of the powerful neighbouring empire.[50] At the state banquet in Stockholm he proposed a cordial toast in German to the 'brother peoples of Germanic origin, both to those who live in Germany and to those who are settled in the North'.[51] Unfortunately in his words of thanks the Kaiser spoke 'very fast', so that his speech failed to make 'as much of an impression as the King's, with his dignified way of speaking'.[52]

The danger that lay in this blend of Nordic romanticism with the Kaiser's naval passion was not something to which German diplomats were as yet particularly alive. Kiderlen merely scoffed at the Kaiser's disappointment that 'the two heaviest armoured ships had . . . to be left behind at Oskar-Friederiksborg because their draught was too great to allow them to enter the harbour. And oh! the pity of it!', he exclaimed sarcastically, 'at Copenhagen we will have to leave *three* behind!' The diplomat was irritated that in Stockholm the Kaiser insisted on going through the 'whole programme' again on the iron-clad *Baden*. He mocked Wilhelm's obvious delight in the joint salute fired by the German and Swedish ships for the birth of his fifth son, making 'an infernal noise' which echoed round the cliffs surrounding the harbour. The bibulous Swabian *bon vivant* was more inclined to appreciate the warm hospitality of the Swedish court, whose 'sole endeavour was to amuse us to the utmost from morning till night'.[53]

After four days the journey continued to Copenhagen, where the imperial squadron arrived on 30 July, although for a stay of only twelve hours, which in view of the shortage of accommodation in the Tivoli and of the strongly anti-German mood of the Danish people seemed only advisable.[54] Senden-Bibran recalled: 'The decoration of the city was minimal and the crowds also very small. We saw no German flags on private buildings. We heard not a single cheer' as the two monarchs drove through the streets.[55] After the journey was over Wilhelm's physician commented that the reception in Copenhagen had been 'very cool and reserved . . . In the streets of Copenhagen the Prussian national anthem and the *Wacht am Rhein* were, it is true, sung as the Kaiser drove by, but this was done by the numerous Germans who are there at the moment, and the Danes were not at all happy at these demonstrations.'[56]

The longstanding distrust which existed between the Danish and the Prussian courts, and which was further inflamed by letters from Queen Victoria,[57] had become acute again as a result of the Danish royal family's championship of the rights of Ernst August, Duke of Cumberland, whose father had been forced to surrender the Kingdom of Hanover to Prussia in 1866. Thyra — the youngest sister of the Tsarina Maria Feodorovna, of Alexandra Princess of Wales and of the King of Greece — was married to the Guelph pretender. Just as the Prince and Princess of Wales had spoken up for the cause of their Hanoverian brother-in-law in Berlin, and the Tsarina likewise in St Petersburg, the mother of the three influential Danish princesses, Queen Luise, born a princess of Hesse-Cassel in 1817, now took up the cudgels in Copenhagen for the interests of the House of Cumberland. As the Kaiser wrote to his grandmother Augusta on his return to Potsdam: 'The Empress [of Russia] was more charming than ever, but as we were leaving she regaled me with a few Cumberland complaints and wishes, of which I naturally could do no more than take note . . . The Queen [of Denmark], whose intelligent and incredibly youthful features betray an inclination for mischief-making, regaled me with the whole Cumberlandiana again, in the most charming way while we were at dinner, which I handled as coolly as in Russia. Later she approached Count H. Bismarck as well; he gave her a fairly plain answer in mine and the Chancellor's names.'[58]

On the evening of 31 July 1888 the *Hohenzollern* arrived back at Kiel, and the party travelled on that night by special train to Friedrichsruh, the elderly Reich Chancellor's residence east of Hamburg. Out of consideration for the Chancellor, Wilhelm II had originally wished to spend another night on the yacht and to travel to Friedrichsruh on 1 August, but Herbert Bismarck explained to him that his father would sleep less well in the expectation of the Kaiser's arrival than if he knew him to be safely under his roof. To this Wilhelm replied: 'Very well, my only concern is to disturb your father as little as possible; so please telegraph to him my express order that he should go to bed at the customary time and should not receive or wait up for me.' When Herbert smilingly answered 'As Your Majesty commands', the Kaiser 'raised his finger threateningly and said "You don't think that your Father will act directly against my imperial command?" — But joking aside, H.M. simply wants to go from the station straight to bed', the Foreign Secretary added reassuringly.[59]

With this Kaiser Wilhelm II's first official visits to the neighbouring courts to the east and north came to an end. In a letter to his grandmother Augusta of 9 August 1888 he commented on how the journey had gone and expressed decided optimism about its foreseeable consequences. 'I did not discuss politics with the Emperor of Russia, as he did not speak to me about them and I had nothing in particular to say', he declared. 'That had been agreed with the Reich Chancellor. On the other hand Count H. v. Bismarck had a long audience with the Tsar in which the latter was extremely open and friendly towards the Count and spoke to him for a long time. For the first time not a word about Austria or Bulgaria passed his lips, which may be considered as a good sign . . . The visible success in Russia is that, according to news just received, a Russian division destined for the Austrian frontier has received the order to return to its quarters. In Stockholm we were shown the highest degree of warmth and friendliness and we felt quite at home. The King was also extremely anxious to accentuate as sharply as possible their firm dependence on Germany; and the French influence which was formerly dominant has almost completely disappeared. Copenhagen did not lag behind the other countries in any way. The family was as friendly as the others and the King was particularly charming . . . So I can confidently declare, as the general result of the journey, that the French influence, formerly predominant everywhere in the North, has suffered a palpable and perhaps fatal blow, everywhere where it previously held sway.'[60]

### THE VISIT TO THE SOUTH GERMAN COURTS, VIENNA AND ROME

Scarcely had Wilhelm returned from his Baltic cruise when preparations had to be made for his first official visits to Saxony, Baden, Württemberg, Bavaria, Vienna and Rome, which he had announced immediately after his accession. The Chancellor was decidedly in favour of the visits, and when Wilhelm hinted in mid-August that he might prefer to leave out the South German courts, Bismarck let him know how important he considered the Kaiser's visits to the capitals in question to be. As Kuno Rantzau informed Under-Secretary of State Count Maximilian von Berchem on 16 August, the Kaiser had 'told [the Chancellor] during the All-Highest stay at Friedrichsruh that His Majesty had the intention of going to see the King of Saxony from Berlin, and of visiting the King of Württemberg and the Prince Regent of Bavaria in Friedrichshafen and Munich, from Baden-Baden, where the Kaiser wished to go for the birthday of Kaiserin Augusta, on his way to Vienna. From your letter the Reich Chancellor perceived that these intended visits to the German courts had become uncertain again. He would ask you to put it to His Majesty, when the occasion arises, that he would regret it if the visits did not take place, seeing that the German princes had come to Berlin for the opening of the Reichstag and, by their presence, had rendered considerable service to the Kaiser in reinforcing his position. The character of these gentlemen being what it is, the good relations brought about by their co-operation could be preserved only through careful nurture of personal links with them, which in certain circumstances are more valuable than political links. After His Majesty had visited the monarchs of Russia, Sweden and Denmark it would be all the more remarked upon if the All-Highest did not visit the German princes, who had not only been the first to visit the Kaiser, but had also thereby rendered His Majesty an important political service.'[61]

On 25 September 1888 the Kaiser left Berlin again, to go hunting at Detmold. At the end of September he travelled from there via Frankfurt (where Herbert Bismarck joined him) and Stuttgart to Mainau Island on Lake Constance, to celebrate Kaiserin Augusta's birthday. On 1 October he arrived in Munich for a two-day stay, travelling on to Vienna where he arrived on the morning of 3 October.[62] From Mürzsteg, where he hoped to hunt with the Emperor Franz Joseph as in the old days, he wrote to his grandmother Augusta with the news that the weather was appalling and the hunting had therefore been cancelled, but that otherwise the journey was going extremely well, as 'the friendly feelings of the people and of the ruling houses had tried to outdo each other in the warmth of the reception' that they gave him.[63] Seasoned diplomats in the Kaiser's suite judged the Viennese reception more soberly. Ludwig von Raschdau reported that in comparison with Stuttgart and Munich the welcome in Vienna had been 'a *succès d'estime*, to put it mildly'. There had been 'more curiosity than jubilation', and 'nor were there many decorations. The people in the Hofburg, on the other hand were very friendly, and relations with the imperial family seemed to me affectionate.' Franz Joseph, however, had been put out by the deliberate refusal of Wilhelm II to confer a decoration on Minister-President Taaffe — the Bismarcks and the Kaiser considered Taaffe the 'ruination of his country', guilty of undermining the Habsburg monarchy by his pro-Czech policy in Bohemia.[64] As in St Petersburg, Herbert Bismarck made himself unpleasantly conspicuous by his tactless behaviour.[65] Differences between Wilhelm II and Crown Prince Rudolf, which will be discussed later, together with the ceaseless rain which spoiled the days in the mountains, contributed further to turning the German Emperor's first visit to Austria into a failure. 'What pleases me least about the result of the Kaiser's journey', wrote Waldersee, 'is the fact that our relations with Austria have become not better, but worse. On both sides mistrust is taking root again . . . I am afraid that Herbert Bismarck, who cannot bear the Austrians and always stirs the Kaiser up against Austria, is partly to blame here.'[66]

The public reception in Rome on 11 October was decidedly more grandiose and demonstrative.[67] The young Italian state took every imaginable trouble to impress its illustrious guest from the powerful empire to which it was allied – Wilhelm II was the first reigning monarch to pay a state visit to the united Italy – and his huge retinue. Workmen spent weeks removing unsightly buildings from the neighbourhood of the Palazzo Quirinale; the route from the station was adorned with the banners of all the Italian cities, and the entrance to the Via Nazionale with a gigantic arch of papier mâché painted with brightly coloured knights and horses. Before the Quirinal itself stood a triumphal arch of wood and cardboard. The crowds shouted 'Viva la Germania' and other such greetings. In order to demonstrate Italy's martial strength to its mighty ally, on 13 October a colossal military review was held, at which 32,500 infantry and 4,650 cavalry troops with 108 pieces of field artillery marched past the Kaiser. (To bring this mass of humanity to Rome the Italians 'borrowed' 1,000 railway carriages from Austria-Hungary, which they afterwards somehow forgot to return.) A state banquet on the Capitol, with 3,000 guests, ended with a toast by King Umberto, to which the Kaiser replied in Italian. Three days later in Naples Wilhelm witnessed the launch of the latest Italian iron-clad and an impressive naval review with no fewer than forty-seven warships.[68]

There is no doubt that outwardly the Kaiser's visit was a great success. The German Cardinal Prince Gustav zu Hohenlohe-Schillingsfürst wrote delightedly that the 'great Kaiser days' had filled 'the whole population with incredible enthusiasm and myself likewise. It was altogether wonderful, and I thanked God heartily for allowing me to live long enough to witness this magnificent historic moment, through which the two nations will become ever more closely united, which for both of them and for the whole world is a great blessing.'[69] As Raschdau reported to Berlin, the scene beneath the balcony of the royal palace in Rome on 11 October was 'le comble de l'enthousiasme'. 'On such ceremonial occasions', he commented to Holstein, 'the Kaiser looks very serious, almost hard, and in my opinion this suits the occasion. The soldiers are especially impressed by this imperial attitude. But in general this manner is effective in those countries where the monarchy adopts a frivolous attitude. In society, however, the Kaiser displays his winning charm of manner.'[70] Herbert Bismarck likewise remarked that 'our Master, who is as charming as he could conceivably be, is playing his part quite superbly'.[71] With satisfaction he reported back to Wilhelmstrasse that 'everything goes splendidly, H.M. makes a first-rate impression everywhere, and for his part is thoroughly content'.[72]

Behind the scenes, however, Wilhelm II and his retinue showed another side of themselves. As in Russia and Austria, in Italy also many people were repelled by the malicious way in which the young Kaiser spoke of his parents and of Queen Victoria.[73] His 'somewhat imperious and brusque' manner displeased the Italians, with the exception of the military. He made no attempt to conceal his contempt for parliaments and civilians and scarcely spoke to the Lord Mayor of Rome or the presidents of the Senate and the Chamber of Deputies.[74] He made

2. Kaiser Wilhelm II and Prince Heinrich of Prussia with the Italian royal family in
Rome, October 1888

a disagreeable impression by his tactlessness, above all towards the diminutive
Italian Crown Prince. The British chargé d'affaires in Rome, Kennedy, sent a
secret dispatch to Lord Salisbury which the latter immediately forwarded to
the Queen, remarking that it showed 'that the Emperor William's rude ways
are beginning to attract notice'.[75] The Kaiser's military suite took the liberty
of inspecting all barracks, munitions stores, port installations and ministries.
Herbert Bismarck, who according to Holstein 'gave way once or twice to his habitual outbursts of rage',[76] spoke openly to the Italian Prime Minister Francesco
Crispi about the coming war to be waged by both countries against France, and
Wilhelm himself told the King that they would soon meet again in Paris after
the victory over France. 'After that you will return to Italy with your three hundred thousand victorious men and then you will be able to kick the Chambers
out of the door', the Kaiser assured the shocked Umberto.[77]

If, in spite of all this, his first visit to the leaders of the Italian state can be considered a success on the whole, Wilhelm's audience with Pope Leo XIII on 12 October was a complete disaster, for which, however, the chief blame lay less with the Kaiser himself than with Herbert Bismarck. The embittered relationship between the pope, who in 1870 had lost all territorial power and was a virtual prisoner in the Vatican, and the anti-clerical Italian state demanded the highest degree of diplomatic sensitivity, and that was exactly what the German visitors lacked.[78] According to Holstein, whose account was based on a note dictated by Wilhelm, in his private conversation with the Kaiser the Pope had called for the 'restoration of temporal power' and to this end demanded that Germany should conclude an alliance with Russia, Austria and Spain against Italy and France. If Germany did this the Vatican would ensure that the 15 million Catholics in Germany would remain loyal to the Kaiser and the Reich; if not he would be forced to regard the German Empire as a hostile power. To this the Kaiser had made the 'spirited reply' that if Rome were no longer the capital of Italy the Italian monarchy would not be able to survive. But the radical republic which would then follow would throw the Pope and all the cardinals out of the Vatican. As to the loyalty of the German or at least of the Prussian Catholics, he, Wilhelm, could see to that himself.[79] The private audience was to have lasted half an hour, by previous agreement between the Cardinal Secretary of State Rampolla, the prelate Johannes de Montel and the Prussian envoy Kurd von Schlözer, but it was forcibly interrupted by Herbert Bismarck, who sent Prince Heinrich into the audience chamber prematurely, with the brusque declaration that 'a Prussian prince does not wait around in an antechamber; either immediately or not at all'.[80] The Pope was a 'hypocritical Lenten preacher' who had 'very greatly bored us', Herbert Bismarck commented afterwards. Wilhelm was 'very disappointed with him', the Chancellor's son added.[81]

What had really happened in the Vatican Waldersee discovered later from conversations with several of the men who had taken part in the trip to Rome. 'The programme had been arranged', he recounted, 'so that the Kaiser should lunch with Schlözer [in the Palazzo Capranica, the residence of the Prussian envoy] and should go from there, that is from German soil, to the Vatican, and not in Italian royal carriages but in his own.' The carriage and horses had been brought from Berlin expressly for this purpose. 'After the visit had gone on for a precise length of time Prince Heinrich was then to appear and to be taken in to see the Pope too. Now at Schlözer's house there was a great deal of drinking – the Kaiser is always very moderate – and Herbert as well as Prince Heinrich had drunk more than was good for them, and had also used the time after the Kaiser's departure for further drinking. They arrived in the Vatican in a very obstreperous mood, were politely received and asked to wait in an antechamber as the Kaiser was still in conversation with the Pope. This did not please Herbert; in the most uncouth manner possible he declared that a Prussian prince could not wait, and had then held forth very rudely in German – which naturally various people in the papal household understood very well – about the behaviour of courtiers, guards etc. Finally he had transgressed so far as to use violence to gain entry: he simply pushed aside a senior court official in front of the door. Thereupon Prince Heinrich entered and unfortunately arrived at a moment when the conversation between the Kaiser and the Pope had just begun to get warm. The Pope broke off completely at this, and we have probably done ourselves a great deal of harm. The Kaiser deeply deplored the incident. The unbelievably tactless Herbert bragged that evening at the royal court about the way he had behaved, and made lamentable jokes about popish mummery.' In the Vatican people had been 'violently angry' at this incident, Waldersee noted, and had 'decided in the first flush of rage to take up the Kulturkampf again with full force'. After negotiations with Herbert Bismarck they had then 'withdrawn the declaration of war', but he, Waldersee, was convinced 'that the war will still break out again now. The people in the Vatican are too conceited to forgive us this day, they will set everything in motion to do us harm. We shall soon see from our Centre Party how things stand. That the Pope virtually used France as a threat is also very characteristic.'[82] In the following days Waldersee heard from various sides and on good authority that the Kaiser's visit to the Pope, 'but particularly the forceful irruption into the papal apartments by Prince Heinrich, will have a disastrous influence on the mood of the Catholic world'. In such circles people were 'beside themselves' at the 'violent entrance by Prince Heinrich into the Pope's apartments' and were determined to have a question asked in the Reichstag about the incident. Leo XIII had 'complained bitterly about Prince Heinrich's forcing his way in' while he had been in the process of 'discussing with the Kaiser a subject which would have been agreeable to him: the fight against social democracy'. At any rate with this 'uncivil treatment . . . of the Holy Father' the Catholics had been handed 'an excellent means of stirring up agitation', the Chief of the General Staff commented disapprovingly.[83] Months after the incident the Vatican was still 'indignant' and had the lowest opinion of Germany's leadership. Bismarck was old, 'Herbert drinks too much, and the Kaiser is too busy and has too many demands on him' was the verdict of one cardinal.[84]

## WILHELM II'S 'PASSION FOR TRAVEL'

Soon the Kaiser's 'passion for travel'[85] became a problem of general political concern. Queen Victoria observed at the beginning of November 'that the young Emp's unfeeling & indecent conduct in rushing abt so early uninvited to other Courts, his marked slights & rudeness to England & his relatives is much remarked upon'.[86] On 6 November she wrote to her daughter: 'It is beginning to be much talked of here; & every where abroad, W's indecently early & hurried Journies have shocked people & while of course one wishes not to quarrel *if possible* with the German Govt. there is a *limit* to that.'[87] The Grand Duke of Hesse expressed anxiety that Wilhelm's 'glorious triumphal progress' could go to his head, as he was inclined to take the ovations he received as demonstrations of admiration for his own person.[88] Only with difficulty and with Liebenau's help could the Bismarcks prevent Wilhelm from returning to Vienna on his way back to Germany from Italy.[89] When suggestions were advanced for a visit to Spain and a cruise to Athens and Constantinople while they were still in Mürzsteg, Herbert Bismarck tried in vain to convince the Kaiser that he would weaken the impact of the visits he had already made by adding more visits. He wrote to his father: 'I would regard those journeys as politically impractical and ill-advised for the simple reason that they would inevitably reduce the impression made by the great state visits of this year. Multiplication weakens. Furthermore there is nothing for us to gain in the Orient; the grandeur of an imperial visit is too much to fritter away on those shabby regions. The sense of the mighty weight of an imperial progress is not yet sufficiently developed [in the Kaiser], the inclination towards recreational cruises with Henry the Navigator [Prince Heinrich, the Kaiser's brother] prevails too much as yet.'[90] The Kaiser's journeys to Athens and Constantinople took place nevertheless, as we shall see.

The new Emperor's excessive love of travelling had thus proved to be a double-edged sword within the first few months of his reign. His first official visits to St Petersburg, Stockholm, Copenhagen, Vienna and Rome may indeed have served to show the world that, following the aged Kaiser Wilhelm I and the sick Kaiser Friedrich III, the empire in the centre of Europe was now ruled by a dynamic young monarch with whom everyone would have to reckon; but not every court or government found such a demonstration of strength particularly edifying. There was no question of a visit to republican Paris – that was perfectly comprehensible; but the fact that in the first round of visits his closest relatives in London had been passed over attracted lively comment and was widely interpreted as a deliberate snub to the mighty British nation. Not only in the British royal family, but also in German liberal circles, Wilhelm's restless drive to travel so soon after his father's death was seen as a gross impiety which cast a harsh light on his adulation-seeking character and his political ambitions. Although reasons of foreign policy were advanced to justify the journeys, it was nevertheless clear to everyone that the real reasons were of a personal, emotionally motivated nature: that Wilhelm wanted to show himself, to be paid court to, to 'astonish' – and also that he lacked inner repose.[91] In the capital cities he visited, highly complex political circumstances prevailed, of which he understood very little, and for which the alcoholic Herbert Bismarck and the insomniac old Prince-Chancellor could prepare him only very inadequately. The intrusive German attempt to strengthen monarchical forces and to undermine the position of those dynasties and statesmen who championed constitutional forms of government by ostentatiously cold-shouldering them made an offensive impression and was often counterproductive. Thus these first visits, with the exception of that to Stockholm, on balance brought more damage than profit. The damage was, however, small in comparison to the truly incredible conflict with the British royal family which Wilhelm stirred up soon after his accession. The background to it lay in the disastrous relationship between him and his mother.

# CHAPTER THREE

# The Kaiser and his mother

## THE EMPRESS FREDERICK AND KAISER WILHELM II

THE mental and physical state of the Dowager Empress after the death of her husband was pitiful. Furthermore, the new circumstances in which she found herself were very hard to bear. For the first weeks she wept and lamented incessantly;[1] she had frequent attacks of 'rheumatism' and 'neuralgia';[2] she shut herself away completely with her three younger daughters and Frau von Stockmar, and as far as possible avoided any contact with the world around her.[3] There were moments when she harboured thoughts of suicide.[4] For three months she had stood at the centre of events as German empress (and sometimes even beforehand, as crown princess); now she was avoided, isolated, attacked in the pro-government press. On 4 July the ministers of state – '*not* the Reich Chancellor, of course' – and the aides-de-camp came to offer their condolences and take their leave from her formally. 'Apart from Friedberg, I think the only ones who spoke from the heart or had even a glimmer of sympathy for me were – at the most – Bronsart or Lucius!', the Empress commented.[5] The isolation which she had at first sought soon weighed heavily on her. 'I have to get accustomed to be a person who is *not* considered or remembered by the present Régime, & I find it rather hard!', she complained in September.[6] She saw her eldest son only rarely. He visited his grandmother every day at Babelsberg, but to her, his mother, he came as good as never. '*This* House does *not exist!* William never comes; & I am taken no notice of!'[7] As ever, she had no illusions about her son's loveless, cold, self-centred character. '*Affection* people cannot give – who do not know the feeling & have it not in their heart!', she wrote to her mother on 21 August. 'He will get through the world a great deal easier than his beloved Papa or I, but he will never attach people to him or have half the love that Fritz had, & I really do not think he wants it, or would care for it or understand it!'[8] Comparing Wilhelm with his brother, she commented that both had equally repugnant political opinions, but Heinrich had 'certainly more feeling, & is less spoilt, & is less selfish & rücksichtslos [inconsiderate]!'[9] Wilhelm's coldness made itself felt in both minor and major matters.[10] She was hurt that Wilhelm did not name his fifth son after her but after the King of Sweden, since the fourth son, August Wilhelm, had been named in honour of Kaiserin Augusta.[11] Even the sixth son, Joachim, did not receive the name Victor at baptism, as both the Dowager Empress and her mother had hoped. 'I think they *might* have called *one* of the 6 boys *Victor* after me! Particularly as they know how much I wished it', the younger Victoria wrote to *her* daughter Victoria. It was not until the birth of Wilhelm's daughter Viktoria Luise that her wish was fulfilled.[12]

Victoria was now completely excluded from political affairs, never asked for her opinion, avoided by officialdom, and thus no longer had the slightest influence on politics.[13] At the court too she was relegated to an inferior position which she found very hard to bear. Of the three Empresses she now held the lowest place, third after Kaiserin Augusta and Kaiserin Auguste Viktoria ('Dona'), as she commented in August 1888. 'You know how *very* indifferent rank and etiquette, honours etc. are to me', she wrote to the Queen. 'But yet I am often shocked at the want of courtesy and considerate behaviour I meet with. I am *quite* ready to give way to the Empress Augusta on account of her age and her being my mother-in-law, but to have to knock under to my own daughter in law besides, makes it rather trying & almost ludicrous sometimes.'[14] As her 'widow's pension' amounted to only 600,000 marks, from which she had to pay all salaries and allowances, she reduced her household to a minimum: she retained only one marshal of the court (Hofmarschall Hugo Freiherr von Reischach), one chief master of the court (Oberhofmeister Götz Graf von Seckendorff), one senior lady in waiting (Palastdame Hedwig Countess von Brühl) and two other ladies in waiting (Hofdamen). She was forced to limit her expenditure to a third of what it had been while she was Crown Princess. Kaiserin Augusta was much richer and had a very much larger household.[15] Sorrowfully Victoria compared her widowhood with earlier, happier years. 'Our House here is really like a convent, nothing but Ladies, & only 2 gentlemen, sometimes only *one*, and at other times (though rarely!) *none*! Formerly it used to be principally gentlemen, and so many coming and going – people wanting to speak to one every minute, carriages driving up & away etc . . . Now *all* is *silent*. I am only *too* thankful to be quiet at this moment . . . But the contrast is terrible. The Bees seem to have deserted this hive and flown to the next one, & one is left in the empty one alone!'[16] For his part, Wilhelm complained bitterly about his mother and was still claiming at the end of 1890 that 'he had given her a generous allowance and various castles and had put her generally in the position of being able to do or not do whatever she wanted. But there was no question of thanks. Recently she had even threatened him and prophesied that his autocratic conduct must lead to disaster.'[17]

The contrast with the new lifestyle of her son could hardly have been more flagrant. Wilhelm's grandiose ceremonies, the innumerable court festivities and parades so soon after his father's death, his visits to St Petersburg, Stockholm and Copenhagen, his journeys to Vienna and Rome and the unmistakable cold-shouldering of London[18] – all this the widowed Empress took as a personal insult. 'Since our terrible Loss', she wrote in September 1888, '*not 2* days have been devoted to mourning or to quiet! . . . It has been *one whirl*, of visits, receptions, *dinners*, journeys, parades, manoeuvres, shooting & entertaining. Of course it *jars* on my feelings.'[19] She looked back on the early days of her son's reign with nothing but scorn for his achievements. 'What has William done in those 3 months. Certainly nothing lasting or useful! He has rushed & torn about all over the place fr. morning till night; visited half the courts in Europe, made 2 or 3 most illadvised speeches, allowed that abominable Pamphlet to be published about his Father's illness . . . Some new excitement must be provided for every day!!! Receptions, Dinners, Parades etc . . . To me it seems utterly childish, when I think of how his beloved Father read, & wrote & worked, & tried to help on each good & useful thing.'[20] Two years later the Dowager Empress was still complaining of his astonishing behaviour: Wilhelm was doing 'the very oddest things, the element of show off, – noise, and "sensation", dramatic effects etc. is very preponderant and in these serious times seems to me *very* youthful.'[21]

### THE 'CRUSADE' AGAINST THE CROWN PRINCE'S PARTY

In addition to the deplorable personal relations between mother and son, in the first months after Wilhelm's accession the public attacks on the Empress Frederick and the late Kaiser's political intimates took on an increasingly brutal form. The Empress wrote in disgust to her mother that the Bismarcks and their 'pupil' Wilhelm were now trying 'to *crush* & annihilate *all* that is in any way *liberal*, or *independent* or cosmopolitan' in Germany.[22] She found the attacks on her in the pro-government press particularly despicable – she cited above all the semi-official *Norddeutsche Allgemeine*, the right-wing conservative *Kreuzzeitung* and the Free Conservative *Post* – but she was completely powerless to defend herself against them.[23] 'The language of the semi-official press is insolent and disgraceful', she commented in her diary only a few days after the death of her husband. 'I am no longer astonished at *any lies* or impertinence. The most impudent gang in the world, without principles or conscience, is now in power!'[24] 'I feel *utterly without any protection* whatsoever!', she wrote to her mother at the end of July. '*Any*body fr. Pce. Bismark [sic] to a Dr. or Professor can accuse, blacken or calumniate me, excite the public against me! William or Henry would *never* stop it or interfere & it would be the easiest thing in the world to make them believe the *greatest falsehoods* & say such attacks were patriotic, necessary for German interests, the authority of the Crown or some such rubbish!!'[25]

Almost anything that her son ordered, did or said was repugnant to her.[26] She was 'half dead with despair' and '*mad* with sorrow, anger and agitation' when she heard that 'at William's wish and command' an autopsy had been carried out on the body of her husband.[27] When she heard of the 'abominable' decision of Bergmann, Gerhardt and other German doctors to publish an official pamphlet about the illness of Kaiser Friedrich III, she implored Wilhelm 'verbally, in writing and by telegram, most earnestly not to allow this', as it would be unbearably painful for her, but 'all in vain, – he had already given his consent . . . He has no tact or delicacy.'[28] She was naturally horrified, too, when in August 1888 Wilhelm sent a telegram to Heinrich von Treitschke expressing his praise and thanks for a pamphlet in which the historian derided Friedrich III and his principles, and portrayed his reign as one of the most regrettable episodes in German history.[29]

A series of draconian measures were taken in the early stages of his reign by Wilhelm and the Bismarcks against members of the so-called Crown Prince's party. The Hamburg diplomat and constitutional lawyer Heinrich Geffcken was arrested for high treason because he published extracts from the Franco-Prussian war diaries of the then Crown Prince Friedrich Wilhelm in the *Deutsche Rundschau*. When the authorities had no alternative but to discharge him, as a broken man, after ninety-nine days of imprisonment, the Jewish Minister of Justice Heinrich von Friedberg – the 'only remaining friend and prop' of the Empress Frederick in government circles – was made a scapegoat and dismissed, while the lawyer who had drawn up the indictment against Geffcken, Ober-Reichsanwalt Tessendorff, was awarded the cross of a commander of the Hohenzollern royal family order by Wilhelm II in his birthday honours.[30] Shortly after Geffcken's arrest the German translation of Sir Morell Mackenzie's book refuting the Bergmann pamphlet was confiscated (the government prosecutor released it again soon afterwards as unobjectionable), while Mackenzie's arch-enemy Sir Felix Semon was honoured by Wilhelm with the Order of the Red Eagle.[31]

Then the *Kieler Zeitung* was confiscated on the personal orders of Wilhelm II because it had published extracts (which had long since been public knowledge) from the Crown Prince's diary – this time from the 1866 campaign. As if that were not enough, Franz von Roggenbach's house was searched in his absence by the secret police — at Geffcken's arrest letters and writings by Roggenbach had been found, which were said to have contained 'crude outbursts' against the young Kaiser,[32] the widowed Bogumilla von Stockmar was cross-questioned in her home by an examining magistrate of the supreme court of the Reich, and the British ambassador in St Petersburg, Sir Robert Morier, was accused in the semi-official *Kölnische Zeitung* of having passed on German military secrets to the French in the Franco-Prussian war.[33] There was no respite: as the Empress commented in one of her stream of letters of lament, when the left-wing liberal *Volkszeitung* was also confiscated in March 1889, 'The crusade goes on against all & everything that we approved of & stood by!'[34]

'These things are allowed & sanctioned by William against his Father's most trusted & oldest friends!!!', Victoria wrote bitterly to her mother.[35] She was afraid that the Reich was well on the way to becoming 'a sort of military Paraguay'.[36] Many people were already talking of a 'reign of terror' or of 'despotism' which might perhaps be customary in Russia, but which could in no way be permitted in Germany in the nineteenth century. 'Russian conditions hold sway here, the police-state flourishes, it makes me feel faint!!', the dead Kaiser's widow recorded in her diary. 'Such nightmares are possible now. There is no longer any right, decency, respect, piety or justice', she lamented; and the Grand Duke of Hesse and his daughter Princess Irène of Prussia took a very similar view.[37] But Wilhelm, according to his mother, considered it all 'very grand'.[38] He regarded any public mention of his father or his mother as 'an offence to *him*!'[39] He behaved 'unspeakably', 'abominably', 'heartlessly', 'harshly and slightingly' and acted with 'brutal ruthlessness' like a 'tyrant', complained his despairing mother.[40] 'Fritz saw it all, & it *broke* his *heart*, and I am sure the mental worry and distress predisposed him to this disease.'[41]

Writing in November 1888 the Empress Frederick poured scorn on what she considered the reactionary German system of government, and particularly on the role which her son played in it. She told the Queen that Wilhelm was '*so green* and *so suspicious* and prejudiced!!' He read 'only the papers prepared for him, does not understand or care for all the difficult and intricate questions of internal government, & is *utterly ignorant* of *social*, industrial, agricultural, commercial, financial questions etc . . . *only* occupied with military things, with a little smattering of foreign affairs, & *constantly* being *fétéd* [sic], — travelling about having dinners, receptions &c. . . . It is *sad* indeed for me as a mother, but it is *not* surprising. The Clique supported by the Emp: William and the Empss Augusta (who both meant no harm & thought they were right) have brought this about and we *could not* prevented [sic].'[42] In a last letter from Germany before she left for England in mid-November 1888 with her three unmarried daughters, the Empress gave vent to her feelings about her son's superficial character and reactionary views. He was 'considered the right & real representant of his Grandfather's views – & Pce Bismark's [sic] policy, – & is *much* elated at this, – *much flattery* is poured upon him, so he never doubts that all he does & thinks is perfect, and there is no counterbalance or moderating influence in his wife that I can see! She quite approves the present system, gives it her full support & is very happy.' Wilhelm would never replace 'the antediluvian & autocratic ideas of most of the Hohenzollerns' with a 'wider, more *humane*, liberal, tolerant & moderate spirit', she foretold. He was too obstinate, and the people who could influence him in the right way were unknown to him and had no opportunity of approaching him. 'His *whole* mode of thought is so completely different that he would never *read* or understand or study anything which *could* open his eyes. He has never travelled and he has *not one* eminent man as a friend.' His entourage consisted of men like Gustav von Kessel and Maximilian von Lyncker, the former false and dangerous, the latter narrow-minded, violent and always advocating the strongest measures, and their influence on him was pernicious. The young Kaiser was like 'a child that pulls off a flies [sic] legs or wings & does not think the fly minds it, or that it matters'. Even Prince Bismarck had recently expressed surprise at Wilhelm's unstable personality, the Empress Frederick informed her mother. It appeared that the Chancellor had remarked to the ambassador Count Münster that 'the Emperor is like a balloon, if one did not hold him fast on a string, he would go no one knows whither'.[43]

As for the question of who was the driving force behind the new regime – the Bismarcks or the young Kaiser – and in particular who was responsible for the terrorisation of her free-thinking supporters, the Dowager Empress was in no doubt as to the answer. Writing bitterly to her mother and her brother Albert Edward ('Bertie'), her constant refrain was that Wilhelm was now wholly in the hands of 'Bismarck and his gang', and that he was being exploited by them as a tool.[44] Her son was surrounded by those whom she and her husband had fought against for thirty years.[45] Bismarck's wish was for 'his head to be thoroughly turned, his vanity & pride to be still greater than they are already, and *then* he will of course dash into *anything* they may propose'.[46] Her three eldest children, Wilhelm, Charlotte and Heinrich, were almost completely unaware of how they were being used. 'By nature they *do not understand* politics, nor do they *care* about them, they only join the general cry of the circles in which they move, & support William with all the roughness & violence of his disposition.'[47] 'I close my *eyes* & *ears* to the official world and find it the only way not to feel the profoundest irritation with W.', she wrote. 'I am only too ready to make *all* allowances for him, when I think of the deplorable friends he has had, & of all the nonsense with wh. his head has been *so* systematically stuffed!!'[48] There was no point in getting irritated with this or that action of Wilhelm's, she commented stoically, for once one began one would never know when to stop.[49] 'I try never to think of William, so as not to make myself ill with bitterness, indignation and anger', she noted in her diary at Christmas 1888. Nevertheless her bitterness repeatedly broke through, as at the end of December 1888, when she wrote of the Bismarcks and Wilhelm: 'What else can one expect from such a rough, vile person [as Herbert Bismarck] and from such an *infamous* system as that of our Government – with an inexperienced, rather rough and heartless young man at its helm, who is *completely* in the hands of these people – blind and deaf to *all truth*, stuffed with prejudices, indoctrinated with wrong opinions, full of *himself* and his dignity – and of the new power which has gone to his head.'[50]

The Empress Frederick believed that she had detected the political goal behind the hate campaign against her and her political friends orchestrated by the Bismarcks. 'It is now a struggle for Prince Bismarck's power to shake off all obligations and fetters which might be a *gêne* – to those belong Fritz's memory and my person! I must be run down and annihilated, as I am a relic of that fabric of hopes and plans he wishes to destroy once and for all! He fears that William might some day fall under my influence and therefore this must be prevented in time by making me out a danger to the state and an enemy to the Government.' In this struggle for power Bismarck '*could* not have a better tool than William. He has carefully had him prepared by his *own* son Herbert for two years. *All* other voices and views are excluded.'[51] So she was sharing 'the fate of *all* our friends, all the *best*, most experienced & enlightened patriots who wd. have been our support & help. War to the knife is waged against them *all*, with the most unheard-of & unjustifiable means!', she wrote at the beginning of November.[52] At a time when Queen Victoria was having a statue of Friedrich III placed at Windsor and a bust of him at Balmoral, where she had seen him for the last time,[53] his widow in Potsdam was coming to the conclusion that the Bismarcks' goal was the systematic obliteration of all memory of the liberal hopes of the short reign of Friedrich III, so as to create the impression among the people that Wilhelm II had followed directly on from Wilhelm I.[54] She had already observed in early July 1888 that it was the aim of the gentlemen now in power in Berlin 'to wipe out all trace of Fritz's reign, as of an *interlude* without importance . . . William the IInd succeeds William the 1st – in a *perfect* continuity of system, aims and tradition! Frederick III *would* have had to be *submitted* to, but was happily removed by Providence before he had time to set *his* mark and *his* stamp on the German Empire; the sooner *he* is forgotten the better, therefore the sooner his widow disappears the better *also*.'[55] In government circles it was considered a blessing that Friedrich III had not lived longer, for as they saw it he would have destroyed the Reich with his liberal principles. 'These are the *sentiments* & this is the *Language* which has been held during 30 years, but especially during the *2 last*, in *Government*, *Court*, Society & *Berlin* military circles, with which our 3 eldest children have been embued.'[56]

If the Bismarcks used the glorification of Kaiser Wilhelm I chiefly as a calculated tactic in the battle against left-wing liberalism, for Wilhelm II a feeling of almost mystical reverence for his grandfather still played a part, the Empress Frederick observed. The young Wilhelm had tried all his life 'either consciously or unconsciously to place his Grandfather on a pinnacle, in *contrast* to his father. That it should pain, annoy & irritate *me*, you cannot wonder. Certainly I am the last to wish that the Emperor William [I] should [not] have his due. But neither in *character*, intelligence nor education was he to be *compared* to his son! He was a thorough Tyrant & autocrat, & could never understand his task as a sovereign from the same elevated & modern point of view as beloved Fritz did; William has not learnt to appreciate or understand his Father as he should, nor to feel that *he*, W., cannot do better than try to reign in *his* spirit! He considers himself the representative of his *Grandfather's* ideas; & this is very unfortunate indeed! He is of course encouraged in this by everyone around him. Either he will find out his mistake too late or not at all.'[57] It is not difficult to guess the effect of such reports from Germany on the royal family in Britain.

### FROM POTSDAM TO KRONBERG

In the first weeks after Wilhelm's accession the relationship between mother and son was put under further strain by the question of accommodation for the widowed Empress, and almost inevitably the discussions over this led to conflict between the new Kaiser and the British royal family. For the grief-stricken widow it was hard to leave Friedrichskron – as the Neues Palais in Potsdam was now called – where her husband had been born and had died, and where she had spent thirty happy years with him.[58] Her eldest brother, the future King Edward VII, who had come to Potsdam with his Danish wife Alexandra to attend the funeral of their late brother-in-law in the Friedenskirche on 18 June 1888, persuaded her that Wilhelm would let her keep the palace if she would only ask him for it directly.[59] 'If you put it to him personally he could not refuse his own Mother & widow of his beloved Father!', he assured her.[60] When this hope was disappointed, the Prince of Wales urged that his sister should at least be given the nearby palace of Sans Souci as her residence, not least because he hoped that if Victoria could continue to live at Potsdam she might in time gain some influence over her son. 'That you have bitter feelings about people & things is indeed not to be wondered at after what you have told me & all I have heard', he wrote to her at the end of June after his return to Windsor. 'But I would beg you dearest Sister to endeavour to dispel those feelings as much as you possibly can . . . Above all things endeavour to have influence over W. This is I know no easy task, but do not despair, do not give up the hope eventually that the example & views of his ever to be regretted Father may yet be an example to him in the difficult task which he has to fulfil. Let no estrangement exist between you both, & remember he is his father's eldest son & your first born.'[61] The Prince entreated her never to quarrel with Wilhelm, whatever happened.[62] 'There will I know be endless difficulties with W.', he wrote to her, 'but you must not be disheartened, dearest Vicky, & try to surmount them. Above all if possible try & have some influence with him — so that he may not be entirely at the mercy of those in whose political opinions you cannot share.'[63] The Empress Frederick was well aware of how illusory such hopes were,[64] but on the other hand she was 'also very keen' to be given Sans Souci as her residence; she thought 'it would make it easier for me to leave Friedrichskron, and it would be so close to the Friedenskirche', where not only her husband but also her two favourite sons, Sigismund and Waldemar, were buried.[65] But this wish was likewise rejected by Wilhelm, and so too was her request to be allocated at least a few rooms in Charlottenburg. She noted bitterly in her diary for 28 June: 'I would have liked Sans Souci — it was curtly and rudely refused! Fritz had wished that I should be given rooms in Charlottenburg — this is also *refused* to me. I am to leave Friedrichskron and only the Villa Liegnitz is to be reserved for me.'[66] This small house, built by Friedrich Wilhelm III for his second wife Auguste Countess Harrach, in which first Vicky's daughter Charlotte and then Prince Heinrich had lived, would at least serve as an overnight lodging for her on her visits to the Friedenskirche and to the school in Bornstedt, she reported to Windsor.[67]

Although she received the Crown Prince's Palace Unter den Linden as her Berlin residence, a stay of any length in Potsdam was made impossible for her by these decisions. Again the Empress Frederick felt she knew what calculations lay behind them. 'They would like me to go right away, for fear I might gain some influence over William, remind the public of Fritz, keep the love for him — the longing for him — alive, and possibly retain some connections with the Liberal Party and give them support', she conjectured.[68] 'The Court wants me away from here, the whole of Wilhelm's entourage would like to be rid of me! They find me tiresome and uncomfortable! I have been asked whether I would not like to go to Italy for the winter?'[69]

Given such circumstances, why did she remain in Germany? She gave a partial answer to this question in a letter to her mother of August 1890: 'It is out of love — to my own darling's memory & to his country — to my girls — & so many charitable institutions that need me, — & kind friends that would be miserable if I went, — that I remain in Germany *at all* — after the treatment I have received!', she explained. It would be 'foolish and wrong — & undignified — to allow oneself to be frightened away or bullied out of the country – for wh. one has toiled as best one could for 30 years; – still it is gall and wormwood to me to have to remain at Berlin under the present circumstances.'[70] Whether in addition to this other considerations of a personal or material kind influenced her decision need not detain us here.[71]

Even before her husband's death, in fact, Victoria had been planning to buy a property well away from Berlin, although for financial reasons it was nevertheless to be in Germany, and if possible in Prussia. Towards the end of June two houses were offered to her through the agency of Roggenbach and Stosch, one of which, in the Rhine-Main area which she had always favoured, seemed particularly attractive.[72] After turning down houses near Gotha and Dresden, as well as Schloss Weikersheim in the Hohenlohe domains, she finally chose the Villa Reiss in Kronberg, which she enlarged to create Schloss Friedrichshof.[73] The prospect of building herself a home of her own in the Taunus, where she could live independently of the Berlin court, consoled her to a certain degree for having to give up Friedrichskron.[74] When she subsequently received a legacy of 5 million French francs from the Duchesse de Galliéra at the beginning of 1889 the building of the new castle, which she directed from Bad Homburg, became a source of happiness for her.[75] Nevertheless she found it unbearably difficult to leave the old rooms in Potsdam. 'Now everything, everything is over!', she wrote in her diary on 1 October 1888. 'Never again will I set foot in this dear house! . . . The rooms, the walls will *not* be able to speak to those who move in here after us!' She could not take this in, she recorded, but only write it down in floods of tears. Now she had no home any more, for the new one in the Taunus would not be ready for two years.[76]

## KAISER FRIEDRICH III'S PAPERS

The tense relationship between the young Kaiser and his mother was put under still further pressure by the question of the papers left by Kaiser Friedrich III which had been sent to Windsor in several boxes before 15 June 1888, as described in the first volume of this biography.[77] The volume ends with an account of Wilhelm's action immediately after the death of his father: he had the Neues Palais surrounded by Hussars to prevent documents from being smuggled out. On his instructions General von Winterfeldt and Gustav von Kessel rifled through every desk in the palace in search of secret papers. They were looking in particular for the book containing the secret ciphers of the Foreign Office which every reigning monarch and every crown prince carried about with him, and when this could not be found Wilhelm told his mother that he was convinced that Dr Morell Mackenzie had stolen the cipher-book on orders from a foreign power – that is, from Britain. All the servants were interrogated in the House Ministry and depositions taken down. Then it was said that the Empress herself had removed the cipher-book; hints to that effect even appeared in the press. She was said to have sent abroad not only the cipher-book – which was discovered in late October, sealed, in the Crown Prince's Palace! – but also the secret state papers of the deceased Kaiser. Even in the semi-official press 'W[illiam], Bism[arck] and accomplices' (as the Empress Frederick called them in her diary) spread the word that she, Victoria, had 'purloined the papers of Kaiser Friedrich and sent them abroad to *publish* them there'.[78] The papers which had been deposited in Windsor by Friedrich himself or by his express wish were without exception private papers, she assured her mother. 'He wished *my private* correspondence & *his* to be safe fr. the ruthless hands of people who were traitors to him & to me! – Never never give them up *please*, even if they *try* to make you!' The Queen could deny having any papers of her late son-in-law, her daughter urged, for no one could know what Friedrich had sent to Windsor, if anything, or indeed where he had secreted his papers at all. In any case he had torn up and burned heaps of his papers in Charlottenburg, in Potsdam, in Baveno and San Remo, and even before their last journey to England.[79]

Not long afterwards, however, Friedberg and the new House Minister Wilhelm von Wedell succeeded in gradually allaying the Empress Frederick's mistrust. Wedell visited her on 10 July and persuaded her, in a 'kind and polite' manner, to hand over to him the keys to her husband's desk, tables and cupboard in the Crown Prince's Palace, which had hitherto been sealed, having promised to show her all the papers before they were deposited in the family archives.[80] On 18 July she went to Berlin for the first time since the death of her husband. In the presence of Friedberg, Wedell and Count von Unruh from the House Ministry the writing tables and the iron safe cupboard were unsealed and the papers examined. The Empress handed over to the House Ministry all documents which were not of a private character: she was allowed to keep every paper she wished to have. It was a 'very painful' task for her, but one that also helped restore her confidence.[81]

Four days previously Friedberg had come to her with the urgent advice that she should have all the boxes which the late Kaiser had deposited in Windsor sent back to Berlin, as Wilhelm II, Bismarck and the ministers of state were expressing the view that it was she who had removed Friedrich III's papers, and that they were German state property. Friedberg promised to examine the papers with Wedell in her presence, so that she would be in a position to prove that they did in fact consist purely of private papers. Once she had convinced Friedberg and Wedell of this, they would be able to speak authoritatively in her support to Bismarck and the other ministers. On the strength of this advice the

Empress Frederick wrote confidentially to her mother on 12 July 1888 asking her after all to return all the boxes stored at Windsor to Potsdam. The boxes should be sent as unobtrusively as possible with the luggage of her sister Helena ('Lenchen'), who was coming to Potsdam soon.[82]

The boxes, guarded by a footman named Schobert, arrived safely at Friedrichs-kron as early as 19 July, with Lenchen.[83] Friedberg went out to Potsdam the very next day and satisfied himself that the papers were indeed the private property of the Empress Frederick and that the House Ministry could not stake any claim to them.[84] On the following day Friedberg returned with Wedell, and the House Minister now ascertained for himself, as the widowed Empress recorded, 'that in *every* box a note in beloved Fritz's hand lay on top – "*All the papers in this box are the property of the Crown Princess my wife*" . . . These were all his *private papers* & now are *mine*; but nevertheless I made a selection with the gentlemen & had a quantity sent to the Family Archives to be deposited there.' As they were her private property these documents could be examined only with her express permission, she insisted.[85] After this 'obliging' co-operation from the Empress Frederick Friedberg and Wedell were in fact able to fend off Herbert Bismarck's demand that the Foreign Office should also participate in the sorting of the papers.[86] To her mother Victoria justified her decision to hand over some of the records with the explanation that 'Whatever there is wh. I think Fritz would not mind their having, or wh. would be of *use*, I will give up to them, retaining all else for ever more! I shall then put them *in a safe place where no one* can get at them!' Depositing the papers in Windsor had however been their salvation, she wrote gratefully to the Queen, for at the time immediately after the death of her husband the palace was searched by 'foolish & false people' who had been ready 'like Harpies to seize everything and anything they could lay hands on'. Now she was alone with Lenchen and could arrange the papers undisturbed.[87] But in this task she missed both her faithful old adviser Stockmar and her former Marshal of the Court Karl von Normann, who had wanted to help her sort the papers but had suddenly died on the way to join her.[88]

The two sisters arranged the papers left by Kaiser Friedrich III in three groups. The first consisted of letters which were to be returned to their authors. Thus the letters of Friedrich's Weimar grandparents were returned to Weimar, and similarly Kaiserin Augusta, Grand Duchess Luise of Baden, King Leopold of the Belgians, Friedrich's tutor Pasteur Godet, General Albrecht von Stosch, General Albert von Mischke, Eduard von Liebenau, Albert Freiherr von Seckendorff, Dr Georg Hinzpeter, Dr Heinrich Geffcken and Pastor Persius received their letters. The documents which were to be kept securely, including Queen Victoria's and Prince Albert's letters to their daughter and son-in-law, were put back into the cases, which were sent back to Windsor temporarily via the British embassy on 26 July, until the Empress could build a safe hiding place for them in her new castle in the Taunus.[89] The third group was destroyed. 'Arranged the remaining correspondence with Lenchen', Victoria noted in her diary for 22 July 1888. 'All from my brothers and sisters − *30* years' worth − *burnt*, with a heavy heart − likewise those from many friends and acquaintances.'[90] At the same time she made arrangements for her own letters to other people to be destroyed, including, for instance, her entire correspondence with Stockmar.[91]

KAISER FRIEDRICH'S WAR DIARY

It was in fact Victoria's intention, as her enemies feared, to write a biography of her husband. In September 1888 she asked her mother to have extracts made from the letters she had written to her, which would provide source material for such a work, since she, unlike her husband, had kept no diary. 'Some day the world *shall* have a true picture of him and all he suffered', she vowed in a letter of 14 September, 'but *now* it is *much* too soon.'[92] A week later she, like everyone else, was startled by the publication of extracts from the war diary of her husband in the *Deutsche Rundschau*. She at once feared that the public might think her responsible for the publication.[93] Shortly thereafter she recorded that 'great excitement' had been caused both on the left and on the right by the article in the *Rundschau*: 'Delight among all well-meaning & non-partisan people, great anger in the Marmor Palais, at Court etc. The publication contains fine and true material, but also incautious remarks, and it is altogether a great and inexplicable indiscretion! How it happened I do not know! . . . The Secret [diary] I have never seen − it is in the Archives! But I am abused again as always and at every opportunity.'[94] Many people thought that *she* had arranged the publication to get her revenge on Bismarck. 'Of course, this is all a mischievous lie! in order to excite his Party, William, &c . . . against me.'[95] In the following days it turned out that the Empress had mistakenly handed over her husband's Franco-Prussian war diary, which he himself had sent on a roundabout journey from San Remo first to the British embassy in Berlin and from there to Windsor,[96] to the House Ministry on 21 July when she had allowed the 'non-private' papers of her husband to be deposited in the House Archives by Friedberg and Wedell; she had taken the sealed diaries for a collection of military writings.[97]

No one was more infuriated by the publication of the war diary than Wilhelm II.[98] As his mother reported to Windsor on 24 September, 'The Marmor Palais & Berlin are in a state of fury & excitement about the publication of Fritz's "Tagebuch". It does *not suit* the "powers that be" at all of course. William was in a rage & called it "high treason" and theft of State papers! Of course this is non-sense!' The only explanation she could think of, she wrote, was that her husband had several lithographic copies of the diary made, which he had given to his more intimate friends.[99] Although it was thoroughly well meant, she commented, the publication of the diaries had only poisoned the atmosphere in Berlin still more, deepened the gulf between her and Wilhelm and inflamed 'evil passions' in the government and in Bismarck's party; 'their violence is untold!' she wrote on 26 September. 'This publication utterly infuriates them. *Where* it was got from, *what it is*, I do not know! I possess nothing of the kind in my papers, and yet every word is true, and the facts are correct, — the writing seems to me Fritz's own, they are his words and opinions, but I never saw them put together in this form! An *outburst* of delight in the public has been followed by an outburst of fury by William, who bitterly criticized his Papa to me, & said "*how could* he write such imprudent things down . . ." I only thought to myself — how deeply is William to be pitied for so little understanding his Father.'[100] Bismarck's anger over the publication was easy to understand, commented Victoria, for did not the diary entries make clear the important role which the Crown Prince had played in the foundation of the German Reich, which was a revelation to the German public, schooled as it was to believe that Wilhelm I and Bismarck alone had founded the Reich? The liberal ideas that her husband had confided to his diary were those which Bismarck and his people had fought against and tried to discredit for decades. 'You can imagine *how indignant* I feel at the tone in which the Government and Bismarck papers *dare* to speak of Fritz & of his Diary. It *is not* "überarbeitet" [reworked], there is *not* a word that is not his *very own* and in his own dear writing. *Of course* it ought *not* to have been published without my permission and *not now*. It was done in a good intention, & the public are delighted! The facts *long known* to me, and which now *leak out*, are of course *odious* to the Govt. and Bismark [sic] Party, — & the *opinions* wh. Fritz *so modestly* & simply puts forth are of course "gall and wormwood" to them, as they are the very principles they have been treading & trampling down, & holding up to opprobrium for *20* years, *calumniating* and persecuting each individual who dared to uphold them! *Now* this Party B. try to cast doubt, contempt & ridicule on Fritz's word & on his character, wh. makes me feel quite *savage*! . . . I *want* the Tagebuch *back*! I am so afraid William and Bismark [sic] will order it to be burnt, & it is such a *valuable* and precious *record* of the *real* truth of things, that *if* they do *that*, I do *not* see *how* I can *ever* be on a footing of peace with them again! . . . I have *not* published this Diary, nor had anything to do with it! I fear it was Dr Geffcken who did it.' She predicted that he and all her friends would now be persecuted 'à la "Arnim"'.[101]

Even as Victoria wrote these lines the hunt was already on for Heinrich Geffcken, who (as we have already seen) was indeed responsible for the publication of the diary extracts. When the police discovered that he was staying on the island of Heligoland (at that time still British) Wilhelm II ordered police searches of all passenger steamers from Heligoland. At his command a gunboat was ordered to Heligoland in case Geffcken should try to reach the German coast by sailing boat.[102] The next day Geffcken was arrested in Hamburg. 'What an everlasting *disgrace*!', the Empress Frederick commented in her diary. 'Bism. is behaving *unspeakably*!'[103] She wrote to her mother: 'The way Bism. has behaved, and *how* the matter has been treated, is simply *disgraceful*, *much*, *much* worse than the indiscretion and the want of tact in publishing the diary! . . . These arbitrary acts of high handed despotism seem to go down with the people of Berlin in the most extraordinary way! The "Party" are of course exultant & triumphant. "Brutality" in every shape and form is what they admire, practise and preach!'[104]

### THE RUPTURE OF RELATIONS BETWEEN MOTHER AND SON

The official discrediting of the dead liberal Kaiser which accompanied the Geff-cken affair – the government went so far as to publish a report to the crown by Bismarck which contained insulting passages concerning Friedrich III – brought the widowed Empress's feelings towards Bismarck and her own son to new heights of bitterness in the autumn of 1888. In her letters to England she deplored the 'terrorisation' by the Bismarcks and Wilhelm of the now leaderless free-thinking forces in Germany, in language of mounting vehemence. '*All* must be done to raise William on a Pinnacle, because he is Bismark's [sic] *Pedestal*, wh. Fritz would never have stooped to be! So Fritz must be diminished in the eyes of the nation, and *I* must be calumniated, accused, vilified . . . Independent people are *silent*, cowed into holding their tongues! The whole machinery of the press is in Bismark's hands – in Berlin alone, the Government employés, "Beamten", are 33,000 people; all of these have *no* other opinion than what *he* orders them to have! *Caprice*, *tyranny* and despotism are *rampant*. It is very sad indeed . . . William allows his Father and me to be insulted & attacked, and *sanctions* it! . . . *Fritz* of Baden, Louise & the Empress Augusta are on Bism: side. Fritz of Baden especially has completely changed in politics & sails with William. It is his *interest* to do so . . . Seeing my sons side with our enemies makes me guess what Caesar felt when Brutus stabbed him.'[105] '*What am* I to think and feel', she asked despairingly on 12 October 1888, 'when I see my *own* son approve of and *encourage* the *insults* to his father's memory & his mother's reputation! He is either too lazy & careless, or he *does not* understand, or he intends to break the 5th Commandment [to honour one's parents], or he is so blunt of perception & so blind – in his prejudices – that he does *not* understand *how* disgraceful is the part he *has played*, is playing, or is *made* to play!! He has had a long and careful training & preparation in the Bism: atmosphere – so that his sense of right and wrong, of *gratitude*, *chivalry*, respect, affection for his Parents, – and *pity* for those who are so stricken has been thoroughly destroyed! It well nigh broke Fritz's heart, it may have been the cause of his illness – when he saw how his sons were having their minds wharped [sic] and their judgement & opinions perverted. They were young, easily caught – and their Grand Parents contributed *largely* to this result!'[106]

Victoria's position became so intolerable that she began to suspect that it was the Bismarcks' intention to force her to leave Germany. She would not do that, she assured her mother, although she was completely defenceless against attacks and calumnies. To appeal to Wilhelm in her hour of need would be useless. 'William does not read letters – if they are unpleasant to him he tosses them on one side! He does not *see* or *feel* what is an insult or injury to his Parents, – & does not think it worth his while to trouble about it; – to get on easily and undisturbed with the Chancellor, to do exactly what he pleases – with as little bother as possible is all he cares about . . . His Mama is a consideration he never dreams of remembering! As Pce B. & Herb: know this very well, – they become more and more daring, as they know & feel that against my darling Fritz, against *me* and *mine*, they may say, write, print, do – *what* they like with *complete* impunity! I have *no* one here to defend or advise me!!'[107]

As we have seen, in October she discovered that on Bismarck's orders the police had drawn up a list of all those who had been friendly with the late Kaiser and herself, and that he intended to have the houses of all these friends searched. As a few letters from Roggenbach containing critical remarks about the Bismarcks and Wilhelm II had been found among Geffcken's papers, Roggenbach's house in Schopfheim was searched, his writing table broken open and his papers ransacked. 'These things are allowed and sanctioned by William against his Father's most trusted and oldest friends!!!', the Empress commented indignantly to her mother.[108] Nevertheless Geffcken – meanwhile reduced to physical and mental breakdown – had to be released and the proceedings against him dropped. The cup was now full to overflowing. Shortly before she left Friedrichskron the Empress Frederick wrote her son a letter expressing her profound concern over his attitude towards the memory of his dead father. She could not have made her meaning plainer. 'If you had not enough feeling of filial affection and reverence towards your beloved Father to make you prevent the publication of that passage (in the "Immediat-Bericht" of Prince Bismark [sic] to yourself relative to your Father's Diary) – I am sorry for *you*. It was a passage as unnecessary as it was unjustifiable and a *direct* insult to your Father's memory – and a *distortion*

of the bright historical Picture he left behind him. I repeat, that I regret it
for yourself, as it has injured you in the eyes of all impartial and rightminded
people, destroying the respect which should be felt towards a ruler. But *one* thing
I would beg you to remember, – that even though you do not feel any obligation
of respect towards *us your Parents*, it is still binding on you as Emperor & King to
*uphold* & cultivate *such* in your People. *Truth* & Justice, and a reverence for that
which should inspire loyalty – are the surest foundation for the state, which your
own hands should be the last to destroy. It is *not* for our sakes, but for your *own*,
that I bid you remember this; & remain with deepest concern Your sorrowing
Mother Victoria.'[109]

Even before the Empress could send this letter to Wilhelm, violent arguments broke out between mother and son which led to the formal breaking-
off of relations between them. On 5 November, on the strength of a piece of
tittle-tattle, Wilhelm accused his mother of having arranged to meet Prince
Alexander of Battenberg at the railway station in Frankfurt. At Bornstedt the
next day her daughter Viktoria ('Moretta') approached her imperial brother
with the wish to be allowed at long last to marry Battenberg. Her request was
brusquely rejected by Wilhelm, who gave no reasons. 'W. behaved like a tyrant',
the Empress recorded despondently in her diary. His 'unheard of tyranny', his
'brutal lack of consideration', his 'want of piety' had 'deeply wounded' her.[110]
On 7 November she wrote him a second, bitterly angry letter, in which she
broke off all relations with him. 'You have, with perfectly heartless disregard for
your sister's feelings, in direct opposition to the will of your Parents, & for no
urgent reason of State policy or expediency, *refused* to allow her marriage with
Pce. Alexander (Prince of Battenberg), a Prince whose bravery compelled the
admiration, & whose illtreatment enlisted the sympathies of the greater part of
Europe, because you choose to say that such a marriage would be a mesalliance.
You have *repeatedly* proved beyond doubt, that your Father's dying wishes have
absolutely no weight with you. To *me*, they are *sacred*. You have shown that
the happiness of your sister is a matter of perfect indifference to you. – It is
the only thing I have left in the world to care for, & watch over, for my son
who *should* be my natural support and protector seems to find his chief delight
in doing all he can think of to insult & to wound me. – It is *best* therefore
we should understand each other. I cannot prevent my son from insulting his
Father's memory if it is his good pleasure to do so, but such conduct coming
from a son must necessarily inspire me with the deepest indignation and horror.
I therefore intend for the future to hold no communication with you, beyond
what is absolutely necessary. – One word of warning. – You are now young, well
and prosperous, and arrogant & overbearing in the pride of your newly acquired
power, you have not experience enough to know that a selfish disregard of

the wishes & feelings of others *always* brings sooner or later a heavy punishment on the selfish person himself, & want of filial piety is never left unavenged. Yr. sorrowing Mother V.' In a postscript the Empress added: 'It is needless to say that it gives me great pain to have to write all this to my own dear child. I *had hoped* that it could have been possible to live in *Harmony*, but so long as your ear is given to those who make it their business to sow discord between us, I fear there is *no* hope of it. Later in Life you will perhaps learn to understand me better, and realize that I *had your interest* at heart *after all.* – I expect no answer to either of my letters.'[111]

## THE INTERVENTION OF QUEEN VICTORIA

The Empress Frederick saw clearly the dangers for Anglo German relations to which her ever-worsening relations with her son were giving rise, but it did not occur to her to moderate the tone of her letters on that account. 'Of course – it must be our endeavour, that the relations of England and Germany should *not* suffer in spite of Pce Bismark's [sic] wickedness and William's folly', she wrote to Queen Victoria on 2 November 1888. 'You & dear Bertie & I – & your Ministers will do all that is possible – to keep everything on the best footing, but still I hope that this state of things is *not* ignored in England, & that the sorrows and sufferings of your daughter are known, as well as their sources and reasons.'[112] Her own despairing letters, together with the verbal accounts of the Prince and Princess of Wales of their experiences in Germany, ensured that the British royal family and above all Queen Victoria herself received a distinctly unfavourable impression of developments in Berlin, and especially of Wilhelm's behaviour. This effect was reinforced by numerous other letters from family members.[113] As early as 27 June 1888 the Queen had a long conversation with Lord Salisbury about 'this all engrossing misfortune of poor darling Fritz's death, which is such an untold tragedy, – of the symptoms in William's Opening Speech, of a leaning towards Russia, & there having been no mention of England, – of Pce Bismarck's violent language, when talking to Bertie, which showed how untrue & heartless he is, after all he seemed to promise me, & after poor Fritz had placed Vicky's hand in his, as if to recommend her to him! It is incredible & disgraceful.'[114] In the first days of July she wrote bitterly to one of her granddaughters: 'It is too dreadful to us all to think of Willy & Bismarck & Dona being the supreme head of all now! Two so unfit & one so wicked. He [Bismarck] spoke so shamefully about dear Aunt V[icky] to Uncle Bertie & A[unti]e Alix!'[115] And in a letter to Princess Maria Anna of Prussia on 30 July 1888 the Queen wrote: 'The loss of our dear Fritz is quite irreplaceable and a great misfortune for Germany and Europe, and it is fearful for my poor child, . . . whose whole existence is quite ruined! William seems to be enjoying himself a great deal – and it is only 6 weeks since the death of his beloved father!!'[116]

The Queen was particularly incensed, as was seen in the previous chapter, by Wilhelm's decision to visit the courts of St Petersburg, Stockholm, Copenhagen, Vienna and Rome immediately after the death of his father. The remonstrances she addressed to her grandson on 3 July merely gave offence and aroused further defiance, and the cold attempt at justification, cited earlier, which Wilhelm wrote to her on 6 July did nothing to lessen the Queen's annoyance.[117] In her letters to relatives near and far she roundly and repeatedly condemned the impious, pleasure-seeking conduct of her grandson. On 17 July, while Wilhelm was steaming towards St Petersburg, she complained in a letter to her eldest son: 'William has started his Journey far too soon – & it is certainly rather significant that he shd. pay his 1st visit to any Sovereign to the Russian Tsar – being so far more nearly related to us.'[118] A week later she wrote again: 'How sickening it is to see Willy not 2 months after his beloved & noble Father's death going to Banquets & Reviews. It is very indecent & very unfeeling! Why does he have to go to Copenhagen? It is so unnecessary & I am sure (& hope) your Parents in Law will not receive him with open arms tho' they must be civil.'[119] On 25 July she assured her eldest daughter that she entered into her feelings: 'If I do not express my more than regret & surprise at Willy's Visit to St. Petersburg & at the Reviews & Parades & at the visits to Stockholm & Copenhagen – all so foolish & unnecessary, not to speak of the gt. impropriety of doing so so soon, it is because I do not wish to pain you still more by alluding to it – or to add fuel to the irrita[tio]n & deep pain it must cause you. All I can say is – that he is v[er]y young & foolish, – has certainly not the right sort of feeling & is not well surrounded. It is much remarked on here.'[120]

Urged by the Prince of Wales to intervene in the argument over a residence at Potsdam for her daughter, on 3 July Queen Victoria wrote to Wilhelm: 'I am naturally very much occupied with poor dear Mama's future home. She feels probably a certain awkwardness amounting to pain to ask for anything, where so lately all was her own, but as Uncle Bertie told me you were only too anxious to do what she wished in that respect. Would you not (if you are not going to live there yourself) offer her to stay – at any rate for the present let her have Friedrichskron – or else Sans Souci? Uncle Bertie told me you had mentioned the Villa Liegnitz but that is far too small & would not do I think for *your* mother who is the first after you – & who is the 1st Princess after Aunt Alix in Great Britain. An Empress could not well live in a little Villa where Charlotte & afterwards Henry lived. Mama does *not* know I am writing to you on this subject nor has she ever mentioned it to me; but after talking it over with Uncle Bertie he advised me to write direct to you.'[121]

3. The Empress Frederick and Queen Victoria in mourning for Kaiser
Friedrich III, 1889

Given all that we know of the personality of Wilhelm II, and notably of his
fear of being treated like a child by his mother's family, it is no surprise that his
reaction to his grandmother's letter – in which she also reproved him for not
replying to her last letter – was one of offended vanity. In the reply he wrote in
his own hand on 6 July 1888 he was certainly at pains to stress his co-operative
attitude towards his mother, but he remained unbending on the matter in hand.
'In regard to what you say about Mama I am doing my uttermost to fullfill her
desires. Today I had a long talk with her relating to her wishes concerning her
future home – somewhere on the Rhine – & when I found out that the capital

she wanted was not free because it is meant as a legacy for us children after her death, I at once renounced for my part once for all, & promised to bring my sisters to do the same! With respect to her living at Friedrichskron or Villa Liegnitz Uncle Bertie seems not to have been informed in detail. I have proposed to Mama to stay at "Friedrichskron" for this year, & to help her find a house of her own. On the other hand, *Mama herself* named the Villa, as one of the houses to be left to her by Papa when her "Witthum" [the arrangements for her widowhood] was beeing [sic] drawn up, besides the Schloss at Homburg, at Wiesbaden & the Palace at Berlin were also named by her as houses she most preferred to live in; so they were entered in the will accordingly. Sans-Souci is the only castle left to me in case of strangers coming to us, as all the other palaces, − except the small Stadtschloss at Potsdam, town −, are in the hands of Grandmama. She told me − Mama − that she only wanted a "pied à terre" here and that was why she wished to have the Villa which she adores.'[122] But the conflict was only seemingly resolved by this exchange of letters. Wilhelm was infuriated by what he regarded as the unacceptable interference of his grandmother and uncle, a state of affairs that Herbert Bismarck skilfully exploited,[123] and on both sides of the North Sea anger and mistrust took on increasingly serious forms.

Another and more far-reaching effect of the conflict between mother and son became apparent at the very outset of the new reign. Just as Waldersee was sent to Vienna and Schlieffen to Bucharest and Sofia to convey the formal announcement of the accession of Wilhelm II, the Kaiser sent Adjutant-General Hugo von Winterfeldt together with his aide-de-camp Albano von Jacobi to London as his emissaries. Unlike Waldersee, who had been received in the Hofburg with particular warmth,[124] Winterfeldt, who was regarded by the Queen, on the strength of her daughter's letters,[125] as Bismarck's spy and an odious enemy of her deceased son-in-law, was deliberately badly treated at Windsor.[126] After his return to Berlin Winterfeldt reported to Herbert Bismarck on his frosty reception: 'Her Majesty addressed a few words of condolence to me on the decease of His Late Majesty Kaiser Friedrich, greeted Lieutenant von Jacobi whom Her Majesty knew from former days, announced Her intention of having a letter for His Majesty the Kaiser delivered to me and took leave of my companion and myself . . . Later I learned from a letter from Sir Henry Ponsonby that Her Majesty had changed Her mind and would not be giving me a letter. Consequently my companion and I left London the following morning.'[127] When Herbert laid this report before him Wilhelm wrote a furious marginal note on it, which Bismarck had to have placed under restriction: 'The reception seems to confirm the bad manners and discourtesy shown several times to German officers at the English Court. Our treatment of the British in the future ought to be modified accordingly.'[128] On 4 July the young Kaiser spoke to the British military attaché Colonel Leopold Swaine, with whom he had been on friendly terms for several years, and who wrote the same day in great alarm to the Queen's Private Secretary: 'The Emperor is much hurt. I gather from my interview with him after the parade today that he feels he is treated as a grandson and not as German Emperor. I don't think he will resent it this time, but I am very anxious even on that head, for there are many advisers here who, feeling as he does, are ready to recommend it. No man is striving harder than Malet [the British ambassador] to bring about and foster a good understanding between the two countries, and it is literally cutting away the ground from under his feet if all he does is undermined by our court. I know you are doing all you know to throw oil on the troubled waters, and you will see . . . how necessary it is to continue to do so at every opportunity. I am quite upset by this unfortunate turn matters have taken and am longing to get away from here.'[129]

Queen Victoria, however, was not at all inclined to regret her treatment of Winterfeldt. When Ponsonby sent her Swaine's letter her response was emphatic: 'The Queen is *extremely* glad to hear that Gl. Winterfeldt says he was recd. coldly tho' civilly for such was her *intention*. He was a traitor to his beloved Master & never mentioned *his* name even, or a word of regret, & spoke of the *pleasure* wh. he experienced at being chosen to announce *his* new Master's accession!! *Could* the Queen, devoted as she is to the dear memory of the beloved & noble Emperor Frederic to whom & to her daughter Gl. Winterfeldt has behaved so treacherously receive him otherwise – & she *hopes* & *asks* Sir Henry to *tell Col. Swaine* what she has just *said*. – Ld. Salisbury *does not* think Col. S. at all a wise man. – He certainly does not see *thru' people*.'[130]

Despairingly the British ambassador in Berlin, Sir Edward Malet, drew attention to the dangers posed by this feud in the Anglo-German royal family for the relations between the two empires, particularly since from the accession of Wilhelm II the monarchical element in the German Reich had gained so much in importance vis-à-vis the power of the state as embodied by Bismarck. As things now stood the most personal feelings of the Kaiser would inevitably play a part in shaping German policy towards Britain. As Swaine had done, so too Malet warned that Britain must therefore avoid everything which might antagonize the immature and oversensitive young Kaiser. 'Nothing is more calculated to change his feelings with regard to England than the suspicion that all his efforts to show friendliness towards us in the reception which he has given to English officers, & other minor matters . . . have been unavailing to correct the false impression which has got abroad regarding his [anti-English] views. He

administration in Alsace-Lorraine in a conversation with Herbert Bismarck and
had also expressed the hope that the Kingdom of Hanover, annexed by Prussia
in 1866, would one day be returned to Ernst August, Duke of Cumberland.
Count Bismarck passed this on to Wilhelm, which the Empress considered 'very
nasty' of him, whereupon Wilhelm publicly attacked his uncle in his speech
at Frankfurt.[3] In the pro-government press she herself was described as being
responsible for the Prince of Wales's remarks, which she vehemently denied. As
she complained to her mother, the Bismarcks wanted to create the impression
that '*I* instigated Bertie & Alix, wh. is most absurd, as I really hardly know what
they *did* say!' It was 'rather unfortunate that anything *was* said, as the Bismarks
[sic] use it as a weapon against *me*, not only have they represented it so to William
and caused him to make that foolish speech at Frankfort a.d.O., but they also
spread it through the Norddeutsche and Cölnische Zeitung to injure me, and it
is then largely believed. I am utterly innocent of all this . . . It is rather silly, to
talk of my intriguing for "Danish aspirations", as Fritz & I always did what we
could for Schleswig Holstein aspirations and *not* Danish ones . . . One is really
ashamed of such rubbish, but it *all profits* the Bismarks & William in the eyes
of a widespread class in Germany. Their superior "Patriotism" is aired again on
this occasion, and *distrust* sown against me, and doubt cast on Fritz's intentions.
It is an abominable game, & apparently always succeeds with a certain set!'[4] The
Prince of Wales gave a rather different account of his conversation in Berlin.
He had in fact believed, he said, that Friedrich III had considered handing back
Alsace-Lorraine in order to put an end to the hostility between France and
Germany. In his conversation with Herbert Bismarck in June 1888, however, he
had only asked whether this was true. When Herbert replied that it was nothing
but a rumour without substance, he had let the matter drop. As to the return of
northern Schleswig to Denmark and the restitution to the Duke of Cumberland
of the King of Hanover's private property, confiscated in 1866, the Prince of Wales
maintained in a letter of April 1889 to his brother-in-law Prince Christian of
Schleswig-Holstein that he had mentioned these matters only in passing. He
presumed that Herbert Bismarck, in repeating this conversation to his father
and to Wilhelm II, had turned this *question* into a concrete *suggestion*, which the
Chancellor had then shamelessly used against his sister, the widowed Empress.
Herbert had further misused this incident to prejudice Wilhelm against Britain
and in favour of Russia. In view of this distortion of events by the Bismarcks it
was not surprising that the young Kaiser had been so enraged.[5]

   For his part, the Reich Chancellor was anxious to put the best complexion on
the Frankfurt speech with regard to Russia. He instructed the Wilhelmstrasse
to make clear, in confidential conversations with the Russian Foreign Minister
and the Russian grand dukes, that in his speech the Kaiser 'had intended to

repudiate the continual insinuations of his uncle, the Prince of Wales, and that one would be on quite the wrong track to see a threat against France in it. One would find His Majesty's remarks quite understandable if one knew that the Prince and, notably, the Princess of Wales, had made all kinds of demands for concessions to the Guelphs, and that in the days of Kaiser Friedrich, partly with and partly without Battenberg interference, the hope had been aroused and nourished that Germany might somehow be inclined to hand back the hard-won national bulwark of Alsace to the French as an offensive base for them. His Majesty's irritation at these demands and insinuations was certainly understandable and had given rise to the vehemence of his language, but if this outburst of displeasure had had any particular target, it was an English one, and more especially the Anglo-French one to which the Prince of Wales had belonged.'[6]

In Herbert Bismarck's retrospective account, written in 1891, the conversation with the Prince and Princess of Wales is shown in yet another light, and the responsibility for Wilhelm's overreaction is ascribed to tale-bearing by Princess Charlotte and intrigues on the part of the Russian Grand Duke Vladimir. During the funeral of his father, the Kaiser had been treated by his uncle 'not enough as . . . Kaiser, but too much as . . . nephew, and still as a green "bad boy"', according to this account. The Prince of Wales's claim that 'the Emperor Frederick would have handed back the Reich's territory etc.' was reported to the Kaiser 'with malicious pleasure' by his sister Charlotte of Saxe-Meiningen and 'with skilful political calculation' by Grand Duke Vladimir, writes Herbert, with the result that Wilhelm's 'anti-English urge' was again brought strongly to the fore. The direct incentive for Wilhelm's speech against the Prince of Wales in Frankfurt probably came from 'reminiscences of Peterhof and renewed provocation from the Meiningen Princess', the Chancellor's son concluded. In any case he himself had certainly not played the role later ascribed to him as the 'scapegoat' in this affair. The Prince of Wales's remarks in June had not occurred in conversation with him, Herbert, but when the Prince and Princess had met the Reich Chancellor. 'At that time they both received the Chancellor and embarrassed him with various indiscreet questions & demands concerning Cumberland, Brunswick, Guelphic funds, so that H[is] H[ighness] was much put out when he returned from the audience. The next morning Malet sent me a memorandum of several pages drawn up by the Pr[ince] of W[ales] about the previous day's audience, with the request that I lay it before H.H., so that he could ratify and if necessary correct it. I sent for Malet at once, and asked him to take the document back brevi manu [there and then] and in confidence', the Foreign Secretary recalled. 'It could not be regarded as an official document, as Malet had received no instructions from Salisbury, and I should be rightly criticised by the Chancellor and would have been put in the most awkward position vis-à-vis H.M. as well as H.H. if by officially accepting it from the ambassador I had obliged my Government to explain itself and bind itself in writing quite unilaterally and on important internal matters to the Pr. of W., who had no official standing. Malet became red-faced and embarrassed, agreed that I was quite right, excused himself by saying that the Prince was staying with him and would not leave him in peace, so he had given in, although he had foreseen my reaction. He concluded: "I wish the Royalties had not come at all, they have now been staying for a week with me but I feel sure that their presence has only done harm." Later [Lord] Rosebery told me that the Prince of W. had been so "hurt", because that memorandum was the first "State Paper" he had written, and he had been very proud of it. But Rosebery also agreed that I had been perfectly right.'[7]

It cannot be denied that Herbert Bismarck's detailed description of the incident has a more plausible ring to it than the vague version given by the Prince of Wales. Herbert's account is supported by the information which he gave Tsar Alexander in St Petersburg on 22 July 1888 (more than three weeks before the Frankfurt speech), and which he set down in writing a few days later. At his audience Herbert told the Tsar 'that the Prince of Wales had importuned our Kaiser with tiresome suggestions which were refused'. This, as Herbert had learned from the British ambassador, had annoyed the Prince. The younger Bismarck went on to tell the Tsar 'that the Prince of Wales had expressed all kinds of wishes with regard to the Cumberlands, both through his wife and direct. For reasons of state he had to be answered with a *fin de non recevoir* [rejection], which had evidently awakened in the Prince the painful feeling that he had gone too far.' Then it had been discovered in Berlin that the Prince of Wales had tried to 'blacken' Prince Wilhelm in the eyes of Alexander III in the autumn of 1887, which had naturally strained relations between Kaiser Wilhelm II and his English uncle. Finally the Kaiser had been greatly angered by a letter from his grandmother in which she had strongly advised him not to go to Russia – advice which he considered gratuitous and patronising.[8] The records of the German Foreign Office confirm Herbert Bismarck's claim that Grand Duke Vladimir, the Tsar's brother, who was married to Duchess Marie of Mecklenburg-Schwerin, had contributed to Wilhelm's ill-feeling towards his English uncle. In a conversation with a member of the German embassy in St Petersburg in September 1888 Vladimir stated that in Berlin the Prince of Wales had spoken to him 'in all seriousness of the possibility of a surrender of Alsace-Lorraine by Germany'.[9]

But regardless of whether the Prince of Wales made suggestions or merely asked questions in a meeting with Bismarck, whether Kaiser Wilhelm considered his grandmother's letter as patronising, or whether Grand Duke Vladimir and Charlotte Meiningen increased Wilhelm's ill-feeling by their tale-bearing, there was no doubt that public abuse of the heir to the British throne in a speech by the Kaiser eight weeks later amounted to an insult which was bound to have lasting repercussions. It would be tempting to describe the Frankfurt speech by the young Kaiser as an absolute low point in his relationship with his British family, if the next confrontation, which followed hard on its heels, had not cast an even more singular light on Wilhelm's feelings for them. This arose from his decision, to which historians have paid very little attention hitherto and which a psychologist would be hard put to explain, to ban his Uncle Bertie from Vienna throughout the several days of his own first official visit to the Austrian capital in October 1888.

### THE VIENNA INCIDENT

At the beginning of September 1888 a group of British officers, including Count 'Eddie' Gleichen, son of Prince Victor of Hohenlohe-Langenburg and Laura Seymour, visited Potsdam and Berlin to attend army manoeuvres. Wilhelm received the officers with great friendliness. He laid stress on the importance of such meetings between officers in helping to maintain good relations between the two countries. He treated Count Gleichen as a prince, spoke German to him and used the familiar 'du' form of address, thus emphasising the fact that they were related.[10] There were other signs, too, of Wilhelm's wish to restore good relations with Great Britain. For a brief period he visited his mother several times to discuss the wish of the young Crown Prince of Greece, Constantine, to marry Princess Sophie of Prussia, Wilhelm's sister; Constantine's father was the brother of the Princess of Wales, the Tsarina and the Duchess of Cumberland.[11] Also around this time Wilhelm expressed the wish to have a railway carriage like that of the Prince of Wales, and sent an official from the Marshal of the Court's office to Gmunden to inspect the Prince's carriage.[12] For one deceptive moment the mutual mistrust and annoyance of the summer seemed to have fled and the relations between mother, uncle and son appeared at last to be improving.

On 2 September the Prince of Wales, who was staying at Bad Homburg on his way to Austria, wrote the Kaiser a warm letter thanking him for his friendly reception of the British officers and ending with the hope that he would be seeing Wilhelm in Vienna shortly. He never received a reply. When he arrived in Vienna on 10 September and discussed the programme for his stay in Austria-Hungary with Kaiser Franz Joseph and Crown Prince Rudolf, the Prince of Wales learnt that Wilhelm would be arriving in Vienna on 3 October. Although he was scheduled to be in Hungary at that time, the Prince felt that he should return to Vienna, as his absence from the Austrian capital during his nephew's visit might be misinterpreted. He even decided to send a messenger to Berlin to

4. The Prince of Wales in Marienbad around 1890

fetch the uniform of his Prussian Hussar regiment to wear at his meeting with
Wilhelm. On 11 September, however, he discovered that the German ambassador in Vienna, Prince Heinrich VII Reuss, had informed the Austro-Hungarian
Foreign Minister Count Kálnoky, the Obersthofmeister (principal Grand Master
of the Court) Prince Constantine zu Hohenlohe-Schillingsfürst and the British
ambassador in Vienna, Sir Augustus Paget, 'that it would not be agreeable to the
Emperor William to meet his uncle at Vienna – in fact that it might mar the
success of his visit were they to be there simultaneously'. This official communication through the German ambassador, of which the Prince of Wales learnt

with the 'utmost surprise' and with 'great pain', was soon common knowledge throughout Vienna and led to serious consequences. The Prince's equerry, General Arthur Ellis, commented: 'I have never seen the P. of W. so upset about anything and he is racking his brains in vain to discover the cause.' The Prince found it particularly regrettable that the Kaiser should not have written to him directly, if he had some personal grudge against him, his uncle, instead of choosing the official route through the ambassador. In order to avoid placing Emperor Franz Joseph in an even more difficult position, Ellis wrote, the Prince of Wales would go to Romania during Wilhelm II's stay in Vienna, but Colonel Swaine should find out as soon as possible what was the reason behind this quite extraordinary insult. The Prince could only imagine 'that this unfortunate mal attendu [sic] must be based on some unaccountable misunderstanding to clear up which no time must be lost'.[13]

Although he was otherwise on such friendly terms with the Kaiser, the British military attaché was unable to obtain any clear explanation of Wilhelm's motives. His request for a personal audience was refused by Wilhelm with the comment that Swaine could speak to him before the military review. But when the colonel tried to approach him there he found the Kaiser surrounded by generals, so that it was impossible for him to bring up the delicate subject of what had happened in Vienna. He decided instead to write to the Kaiser about it, enclosing General Ellis's letter. On 19 September the Kaiser had several opportunities of exchanging a word with Swaine, but he acted as if he had not seen him and, although Swaine was standing very close to the Kaiser, he was not even given the chance of greeting him. On 20 September the Kaiser left Berlin for Munich, Vienna and Rome without having addressed a single word to Swaine. The colonel, who had placed so much confidence in Wilhelm, felt that to remain in Berlin in such circumstances would be intolerable. 'With all the kindness and almost attachment I feel for the young Emperor I cannot allow or countenance any such treatment of Your Royal Highness', he told the Prince of Wales, 'and my position here would certainly lead to a complete estrangement between The Emperor and myself, which would not be to the advantage of the service and would destroy the object I have had in view and to which I have devoted these last six years.'[14] At the end of September Colonel Swaine handed in his resignation.[15]

Swaine's letter, together with General Ellis's, were sent to Queen Victoria and copied to the Prime Minister Lord Salisbury.[16] The Queen wrote indignantly to her son Arthur, Duke of Connaught, who was married to Princess Louise Margaret of Prussia, about 'the most *outrageous* behaviour of Willie the Gt. (& I fear "the bad hearted") towards Bertie'. Wilhelm, she said, had actually informed his uncle officially through Reuss, Kálnoky and Paget that it would not be agreeable to him to meet him in Vienna, 'Bertie having graciously written

3 weeks before, how much pleasure it wd. give him to meet him there!!! Bertie
was naturally shaken & pained beyond measure. However to give Wm. every
opportunity of getting out of it, Bertie had Col: Swaine written to to ask to see
Wm. & taken him Bertie's or rather Genl. Ellis's letter (dictated by B[ertie], &
an excellent letter) to Wm. asking what this meant & what was the cause of
this. Wm. while saying he *wd.* see him on Parade avoided Col: Swaine in every
way & then went away! Bertie is, as you will easily imagine, *furious*, as well as
*deeply pained* & says if he does not receive an apology he "will never speak to
him again". Col: Swaine is so shocked that he says if W. does not answer B. he
will resign & leave Berlin where he cannot remain after such an insult. To treat
the Pce of W. – the oldest son of one of the gtst Sovereigns in the World [sic], &
his own kind Uncle in such a manner is one of the greatest insults ever comitted!
B. has had to change his arrangements & doubtless this shameful affair will soon
come out. People will be furious here & everywhere & I am sure Louischen will
be horrified.'[17]

The disastrous affair continued to spread. Soon the story reached the gutter
press.[18] Crown Prince Rudolf, who had invited the Prince of Wales to hunt
with him in Siebenbürgen and wrote to his wife Stephanie that he would 'only
invite Wilhelm along . . . so as to hasten him out of this world through an
elegant hunting adventure', stoked up the fire in Vienna by making indiscreet
remarks.[19] In this dangerous situation the British ambassador in Vienna, Paget,
took the unusual step of warning the Prince of Wales not to say anything about
Wilhelm II, for in Vienna, as everywhere, there were malicious gossips at both
high and low levels who would only too gladly misrepresent and pass on *every*
remark of the Prince about his nephew. He knew for a certainty that this affair
itself arose from just such tittle-tattle – people had passed on to Kaiser Wilhelm
remarks that the Prince of Wales was said to have made.[20]

The question arose of how the ambassador was to behave on meeting the
Kaiser. Lord Salisbury telegraphed from Nice, where he was holidaying, instructing Paget to absent himself, if he could, from any ceremony at which Wilhelm II
would be present, and to avoid him as far as possible without causing a scandal.[21]
That, however, was a contradiction in terms, as Paget pointed out in his reply,
for if he wished to avoid a scandal he would have to behave like every other
ambassador; any departure from the norm would be noticed and unfavourably
commented upon.[22] The Prince of Wales and Ellis asked the ambassador, in his
audience with the Kaiser, to signal to Wilhelm that his uncle was eager for a
reconciliation, and to ask him directly whether he had any message to convey to
the Prince. Unlike Paget, who feared that this would merely invite a rejection
from the Kaiser and thus aggravate the situation still further, they were confident that it would bring about a clarification of the whole mysterious affair.[23]

But in a second telegram from Salisbury Paget received instructions not to raise the matter on any account unless the Kaiser himself spoke of it. Although in the event the audience lasted for more than ten minutes, the ambassador had no opportunity to carry out the Prince of Wales's request, as the Kaiser spoke only of indifferent matters.[24] Wilhelm did not even enquire after the Queen's health! Later Queen Victoria and the Prince of Wales heard through Crown Prince Rudolf that Wilhelm had even intended, originally, to turn his back on the ambassador, and had only been dissuaded from doing so by Franz Joseph and Rudolf. When Rudolf – at the request of the Prince of Wales – asked Wilhelm whether he had any message for his uncle, whom Rudolf would be seeing shortly in Siebenbürgen, Wilhelm answered in the negative and merely said that if his uncle wrote him a very kind letter he, Wilhelm, '*might perhaps answer it!!*'[25]

The crisis became more acute still when on 26 September 1888 the German Foreign Secretary informed Sir Edward Malet in Berlin that the following year – possibly in May – Kaiser Wilhelm II wished to pay a visit to Britain![26] Not only the British royal family but the British government too found it unthinkable that such an invitation should be issued until the Kaiser had made a full apology for his behaviour to the Prince of Wales. At this point at the latest the feelings of both royal families stood in direct opposition to the political interests of the two nations.

It soon transpired that Count Paul von Hatzfeldt, the German ambassador in London, was not only in the dark about the Vienna incident but was positively terrified of bringing up the subject with the Bismarcks. On 13 October Hatzfeldt read Salisbury a lengthy memorandum from the Reich Chancellor in which Bismarck attempted to justify the enforced absence of the Prince of Wales during the Kaiser's visit to Vienna on foreign policy grounds: the Tsar, he claimed, would have been annoyed by a meeting between the heir to the British throne and the German and Austrian Emperors, and this would have been dangerous for Germany, as Britain was not yet prepared, by way of compensation for the mistrust the meeting would arouse in Russia, to conclude a genuine alliance with Germany. Bismarck's memorandum did then touch on the personal aspects of the Vienna incident, if only tentatively and indirectly. Kaiser Wilhelm II, Salisbury gathered from the Chancellor's statement, had three things with which to reproach the Prince of Wales. First, Albert Edward had told a Russian grand duke, who had repeated it to the Kaiser, that if Emperor Friedrich III had lived longer he would have offered concessions on the Alsace and North Schleswig questions and recognised the claims of the Duke of Cumberland; second, the Prince of Wales and his wife, in a conversation with Bismarck, had put forward Cumberland's interests and thereby abused the respect the Chancellor had to show to the Princess, and had subsequently tried to force a written record of this

conversation on Prince Bismarck; and, third, the Prince of Wales had treated
Wilhelm as his nephew and not as an emperor, even though the latter, although
still young, had been of age for some time. Bismarck's memorandum, according
to Salisbury, had said nothing about 'the request that the Prince would leave
Vienna on personal grounds; or of the Emperor William's announcement that
he would not go to Vienna while the Prince of Wales was there; or of the failure to
notice Col: Swaine's letter; or of the omission to ask after the Queen in speaking
to Sir A. Paget'. This was clearly the first time Hatzfeldt had heard about these
matters. Salisbury warned him strongly against encouraging a visit to Britain
by the Kaiser in these circumstances, for any such suggestion would be quite
unacceptable in the present situation. The Prime Minister nevertheless insisted
that the personal conflict between Kaiser Wilhelm and the Prince of Wales must
not be allowed to affect the general policy of the two nations towards each other.
This view, Hatzfeldt assured Salisbury, was entirely shared by Prince Bismarck.[27]

On the following evening Salisbury and Hatzfeldt met again. The Prime
Minister was disturbed to discover, as he reported to the Queen, that the ambassador had not communicated with Berlin at all on the matter of the Vienna
incidents, out of fear of Bismarck, and in particular he had failed to warn his
government 'that so long as those incidents were unexplained it was impossible for Your Majesty to receive the Emperor. He was simply afraid to do so.'
Salisbury again urged the ambassador to send some kind of warning to Berlin,
since if the Kaiser proposed himself and the Queen were obliged to turn him
away, the gulf between the two nations would only become deeper. Salisbury
spoke of the 'terror of the Ambassador' and concluded from his behaviour that
Hatzfeldt's post was at risk. The situation made him very uneasy, for 'if nobody
dares tell Prince Bismarck the truth, there is no knowing what he might do'.[28]

These conversations, together with further information about Wilhelm's
behaviour which she received through the Princess of Wales, convinced Queen
Victoria that her grandson was no longer quite responsible for his actions. Anxious as she was to maintain good relations between Britain and Germany, she
nonetheless doubted that this would be possible as long as Wilhelm was on the
throne and the Reich was in the hands of the two Bismarcks. She found the
reasons given by the Chancellor for the Kaiser's impossible behaviour 'simply
absurd'. How could Bismarck claim that the Tsar would have been annoyed
by a meeting between Wilhelm and his uncle, when the Prince of Wales was
the Tsar's brother-in-law, she asked in astonishment. It was not yet clear what
Albert Edward had said about Alsace-Lorraine. He was certainly on very intimate terms with all the Russian grand dukes, so that it was not unthinkable that
he had made a remark about Friedrich III's willingness to make concessions.
What he had said in his conversations with both Bismarcks about Brunswick

and Cumberland was well known to the Prime Minister, the Queen declared. She continued indignantly: 'As regarding the Prince's not treating his nephew as Emperor this is really too *vulgar* and too absurd as well as untrue almost *to be believed*. We have always been very intimate with our grandson and nephew, and to pretend that he is to be treated *in private* as well as in public as "His Imperial Majesty" is *perfect madness*! He has been treated just as we should have treated his beloved Father & even Grandfather, and as the Queen *herself* was always treated by her dear uncle King Leopold. *If* he has *such* notions he better *never* come *here*. The Queen will not swallow this affront.' As for what Crown Prince Rudolf had told the Prince of Wales, namely that Wilhelm had intended to turn his back on the British ambassador and had been deterred from doing so only at the urgent instances of Rudolf and Franz Joseph, and that Wilhelm had told Rudolf that he would 'perhaps' be willing to answer a letter from his uncle, but only if it were a particularly friendly letter, Queen Victoria's verdict was that 'all this shows a very unhealthy and unnatural state of mind & he *must* be made to feel that his Grandmother and Uncle will not stand such insolence. The Prince of Wales must *not* submit to such treatment. As regards the political relations of the 2 Governments, the Queen quite agrees that that should not be affected (if possible) by these miserable personal quarrels, but the Queen much *fears* that, with such a hot headed, conceited and wrongheaded young man, devoid of all feeling, this may at *any* moment become *impossible*.'[29]

In spite of all efforts to keep the political repercussions of the affair within bounds, the crisis continued to deepen. Since Bismarck had cited as one of the reasons for Wilhelm's behaviour the lack of proper respect with which Queen Victoria had corresponded with her grandson, copies of her letter to Wilhelm of 3 July and of his answer of 6 July were made and sent to Vienna. All who read the correspondence – Sir Augustus Paget, Count Kálnoky, Kaiser Franz Joseph – were struck by the inexplicable discrepancy between the irreproachable wording of both letters and the way in which they were represented subsequently.[30] On 14 November Queen Victoria wrote to Kaiserin Augusta to complain 'about our grandson Wilhelm', who 'has behaved in such an unkind, inconsiderate and peculiar way towards his Uncle Bertie, who has always been so very kind, and in general scarcely treats his British relations as relations at all'. It would be a very good thing, she advised, if Augusta would draw the young monarch's attention to the consequences of such conduct, which could lead to a cooling of relations between the two countries. Wilhelm evidently did not know how to behave, did not keep good company and did not listen to good advice.[31] The ninety-year-old Kaiserin retorted that she could intervene only if Wilhelm asked for her advice. But he was 'altogether less amenable to advice' than the Queen supposed. Augusta expressed the opinion that Wilhelm's ill feeling towards Britain went back for more than a year, for he had felt 'hurt' when he returned to Germany after the Queen's Jubilee. Moreover the Battenberg marriage project had played a very damaging role.[32]

The Prince of Wales, like his mother, could see no other explanation for Wilhelm's 'outrageous' behaviour than that it was a sign of insanity.[33] He even commented that this explanation was more advantageous for Wilhelm than the only other possible one – that he knew what he was doing! After his return from Austria he wrote to his sister: 'Nothing that your son William does surprises me – my only doubts are whether he is sane! Perhaps it is more charitable to think that he is insane.' Be that as it may, 'till he makes some apology for the gross insults he has heaped upon me in a foreign country I must naturally cease having any further acquaintance with him'.[34]

Although a political crisis was avoided for the time being, Wilhelm II's behaviour had undoubtedly done great long-term harm. On 17 October 1888, four months after Wilhelm's accession, the Princess of Wales wrote to her son, the future King George V, of the atonement that would one day have to be sought for this insult. Wilhelm was an 'ass' whose behaviour, particularly to his mother, was getting worse every day. Now he had also been 'personally most *frightfully rude & impertinent* towards Papa' and had 'actually refused to meet him at Vienna!! He is perfectly infuriated against *England* that beast . . . Oh he is mad & a conceited ass – who also says that Papa & Grandmama don't treat him with proper respect as the *Emperor* of *all & mighty Germany*! But my hope is that *pride* will have a *fall* some day!! – Won't we rejoice then.'[35]

### THE ROLE PLAYED BY THE BISMARCKS AND
### KAISER FRANZ JOSEPH

The only other explanation which suggested itself in London for Wilhelm II's extraordinary behaviour was that the young Kaiser had been manipulated by the Bismarcks. For the Prince of Wales there was no question that Wilhelm had been 'aided & abetted by that scoundrel Herbert Bismarck, whose ingratitude for all the kindness I have shown him for so many years knows no bounds'.[36] Queen Victoria's third son, the Duke of Connaught, also thought that Wilhelm's 'most extraordinary & unbecoming' behaviour must be the result of an anti-British and anti-constitutional intrigue by the Bismarcks. 'My own impression is that *someone* has intentionally made mischief between William & Bertie with a view to prevent their meeting. I should not be surprised if the Bismarks [sic] had something to say to it as they appear to be so afraid of *any* English influence being brought to bear on William. They are clearly afraid of any constitutional ideas being put into Willie's head & they think that any of his family might interfere with the dictatorial gov't they wish him to exercise & that Bertie in particular may wish to give William good advice.'[37]

What was the role of the two Bismarcks in this puzzling incident? The account written by Herbert Bismarck after his dismissal is once again of particular interest. As we have seen, he denied all responsibility and claimed that the cause of the incident was to be found at the Austrian court. He thought it quite possible that Wilhelm II had not even read the closing passage of the Prince of Wales's letter, in which the latter expressed his pleasure at their forthcoming meeting in Vienna. Furthermore, 'with the growing number of hurried journeys and because of the manoeuvres . . . many things [had been] neglected, many official papers not even opened for weeks. At any rate the Pr. of Wales received no answer, and this, combined with the gossip about the genesis of H.M.'s Frankfurt speech, certainly put him into a bad temper. When the Archduke Carl Ludwig came to Potsdam at the end of August or the beginning of September H.M. spoke very disparagingly to him about the Pr. of Wales, so that the Archduke was left with the impression that a meeting between the two of them in Vienna would be very undesirable, indeed painful, for the Kaiser: this impression was all the more justified because H.M. had made no mention of the Prince of Wales's letter nor of his publicly announced presence in Austria, so that Kaiser Franz Joseph also thought he was acting in accordance with H.M.'s wishes if he sent the Pr. of W. away. He took the initiative and had the British ambassador informed through Kalnoky that he regretted that because of the large German suite he had no room in the Burg, and wished to offer the Prince hunting in Hungary for the period in question. The Pr. of W. did not take this hint, or did not want to take it, and sent a message to say that he would go to a hotel during the Kaiser's visit, but would wish to be invited to all festivities. Kaiser Franz Joseph, with his back to the wall, now made himself quite clear and told the ambassador that it would not be possible for the Pr. of W. to participate in the meeting of the Kaisers. Whether Franz Joseph also gave as a reason for this the fact that the presence of his uncle would not suit H.M. I have not been able to discover, but I think it not unlikely. The result was that the Pr. of W. was deeply offended, departed in great anger and immediately wrote furious letters to the Queen and the Empress Frederick to the effect that "his imperial nephew had had him thrown out of Vienna". The Queen wrote indignantly to various people (the Duchess of Edinburgh among others) "that Willie has grossly insulted Uncle Bertie", using all possible epithets about her grandson. As those on the British side did not want to push the whole responsibility for these "insults" onto H.M. I was chosen as scapegoat, and his "unheard-of behaviour" was credited to me.' But he, Herbert Bismarck, had been on holiday in Ostend when the incident occurred in Vienna on 11 September. 'Nor was there anything in our records about it, and it was not until several weeks later that I was in a position to reconstruct the episode. In the subsequent discussions we were at first faced with the difficulty that we did not want to expose Kaiser Franz Joseph and therefore always had to refer to Paget.'[38]

Herbert Bismarck was indeed away from Berlin at the critical moment. On 31 August he travelled to Ostend and he did not return to Friedrichsruh until 15 September. On the following day, as he noted in his diary, he attended a 'dinner at the Schloss with Archduke Albrecht, Grand Duke Nicholas etc.', after which he had time only for a 'hurried audience with H.M.'.[39] On 17 September Herbert left Berlin again for five days' hunting on the Livonian estates of the Russian ambassador Count Paul Shuvalov. He did not return to Berlin until 24 September and the next morning he and his father had an audience at the Marmorpalais before the Kaiser left for Detmold to go shooting. On 26 September Herbert Bismarck travelled to Frankfurt am Main, as has already been described, from where he journeyed on, 'united with H.M.', to Stuttgart, Munich and Vienna.[40]

Despite Herbert's claim that the records of the Auswärtiges Amt contained nothing about the incident, documents preserved there do in fact show precisely how the Prince of Wales came to be given this insulting brush-off. After the departure of the Foreign Secretary for Ostend on 31 August a report arrived from the military attaché in Vienna, Adolf von Deines, stating that the heir to the British throne would be arriving there on 10 September and would accompany the Austrian Emperor to the manoeuvres in Croatia the following day.[41] To this Kaiser Wilhelm II responded with an acerbic note written on the envelope containing the report: 'It would be advisable to draw the Kaiser [Franz Joseph]'s attention to the Prince's taste for intrigue. Inform him confidentially of the claim about Papa surrendering Reich territory and warn him against telling the Prince militarily important things about troop deployment or frontier defence. As such things could easily become known in Russia via Copenhagen, through the sisters-in-law.'[42]

When this note reached Friedrichsruh Prince Bismarck, through his son-in-law Count Kuno Rantzau, gave orders for the Kaiser's suspicions about the Prince of Wales to be communicated immediately to Vienna. The Chancellor was anxious to keep the relationship between Germany and Great Britain on a distant footing, and saw an opportunity to sow discord between Wilhelm and his British relations by exaggerating the importance of the Kaiser's scribbled comment. The Wilhelmstrasse was instructed to inform the German ambassador in Vienna, Reuss, and the military attaché, Deines, that the Kaiser had 'expressly commanded that attention should be drawn in Vienna to the advisability of observing caution towards the Prince of Wales with regard to military matters, as he is unreliable by nature, and to judge by his general attitude and inclination he would not be deterred even by goodwill for us and Austria from misusing secret information. His Majesty had grounds for being ill-disposed towards his uncle because he had spread all kinds of untrue claims about Kaiser Friedrich being disposed to make concessions to France. His Highness [Prince Bismarck] did not himself know the details of these matters, but he knew from elsewhere that our French, Danish and Guelphic conquests had been regarded with disfavour at the English court . . . His Majesty had expressly ordered that the Kaiser of Austria should be asked in some discreet way not to consider the Prince of Wales as a safe recipient of secret information, since information given to him would immediately go to Petersburg and Copenhagen.'[43] On 6 September 1888 the Under-Secretary of State at the Foreign Office, Count Maximilian von Berchem, accordingly drew up instructions for Prince Reuss, emphasising the 'express wish' of Kaiser Wilhelm that he should draw Kaiser Franz Joseph's attention to the unreliability of the Prince of Wales, particularly with regard to secret military matters. By way of explanation for this unusual step, Reuss was informed that Kaiser Wilhelm was annoyed with his uncle 'on the one hand because of the continued insinuations made by the Prince and his wife, aimed at concessions in favour of the Guelphs, and also because of the fact that in the days of Kaiser Friedrich, partly through the agency of the Prince of Wales, hopes had been raised and nourished suggesting that there was an inclination on the part of the late Emperor to hand back the national bulwark of Alsace and German Lorraine, won with heavy sacrifices, to the French as an offensive bastion for them'. These matters had also given rise to the well-known speech by Wilhelm II in Frankfurt an der Oder, which had been directed not against France, but rather against 'that English, and indeed *French*–English party to which the Prince of Wales belongs and which regards our political power in Europe with jealousy and mistrust'.[44]

It is not surprising that when Wilhelm II's 'express wish' was officially communicated to him, Franz Joseph gained the impression that the German Kaiser bore his British uncle a deep grudge and did not wish to meet him during his visit to Vienna. The Austrian Emperor decided to accompany the Prince of Wales as far as Gödöllö after the manoeuvres in Croatia, and to take his leave of him there, because – as Reuss reported to Berlin on 13 September – 'it did not please him to have the Prince remaining here as his guest during the visit of our All-Gracious Master'. But the Prince of Wales, who 'always likes to be present wherever exceptional events are taking place', embarrassed his host by stating that he wanted to come to Vienna after all, to 'shake the hand' of his nephew. When the Grand Master of the Court of Vienna, Prince Constantin zu Hohenlohe-Schillingsfürst, discussed the ticklish situation that had now arisen

with the German ambassador, Reuss strongly supported Hohenlohe 'in his intention . . . to prevent the Prince from reappearing at court here', since he assumed
'that His Majesty our All-Gracious Master would likewise prefer not to meet
other princely personages here, and that this assumption would be particularly
applicable with regard to His Royal Highness the Prince of Wales'. Significantly
for the subsequent course of events, Reuss also spoke directly to the British ambassador, Sir Augustus Paget, and urged him too to dissuade the Prince of Wales
from returning to Vienna. According to his own report the German ambassador
gave two reasons for this plea: first, the Prince of Wales would 'only embarrass
the court *here*' by such a visit, and second 'His Majesty [Wilhelm II] would
probably not' expect 'to find the Prince here'. Paget's first attempt to keep the
Prince of Wales away from Vienna was unsuccessful, however, as Albert Edward
refused to understand these objections. He declared that he would stay at a
hotel so as not to be a burden to the Viennese court; he considered it 'useful for
the public impression and for the relations between the two families "because
of all the stories of the last few months" to have a friendly meeting with our
Kaiser here'. The Prince's deliberate unwillingness to understand the situation
only increased the embarrassment of Kaiser Franz Joseph. Reuss reported that
as the Habsburg monarch 'was aware, through the secret communication that
I was instructed to make to Count Kálnoky about the Prince of Wales, that the
confidence which our All-Gracious Master places in His Uncle is not exactly
of the highest order, the Kaiser [Franz Joseph] seized the opportunity to talk
to Sir A. Paget after the court dinner the day before yesterday, and to ask him
to tell the Prince that He would prefer it if His Royal Highness did not come
here on the occasion of the Kaiser's visit in October, because He had reason to
believe that our All-Gracious Master would prefer not to meet any other foreign
Princes here'. This 'imperial message', which he received through the British
ambassador, 'greatly surprised' the Prince of Wales, as Reuss reported. 'He has
sensed that the court here [in Vienna] is of the opinion that his presence would
not please our All-Gracious Master, and it seems that this realisation, which has
at last dawned upon him, has upset him very much.' The ambassador would very
much have welcomed it, he wrote, 'if the Prince's staying away could have been
achieved without employing the harsh method used by Kaiser Franz Joseph'.
But Kálnoky had assured him that the problem could not be solved in any other
way, after the Prince 'absolutely refused to take the hints given him in the beginning'. For the Austrian Emperor, Kálnoky had explained, it had been chiefly a
question of ensuring that Kaiser Wilhelm 'did not have any meetings here which
could have been unwelcome to Him, and He therefore had no alternative but
to speak as he had done to the British Ambassador'.[45] This report makes it clear
beyond doubt that the root cause of the Vienna incident lay in Wilhelm II's

grudge against his uncle; that Franz Joseph found himself obliged to act purely on account of the secret information conveyed to him officially several times; and that the explanation of the incident which attributed the initiative for putting off the Prince of Wales entirely to Franz Joseph was not in accordance with the facts.[46] It is quite plain that in his conversations with the British ambassador, the Austrian Foreign Minister and Obersthofmeister Prince Hohenlohe, Prince Reuss strongly and repeatedly stressed that a meeting between Wilhelm II and his uncle in Vienna would be unwelcome. In so doing Reuss was acting on the express official instructions of Prince Bismarck, who was evidently keen to bar the way to the 'French–British' influence of the Prince of Wales on the young Kaiser. Although Wilhelm II had never directly expressed the wish not to see the Prince in Vienna, the origin of the Vienna incident is nevertheless to be seen in his 'grudge' against his uncle, which had been noticeable not only in his Frankfurt speech and in his remarks to the Archduke Carl Ludwig, but also and above all in an angry marginal note whose contents had been conveyed officially, on the personal orders of the Reich Chancellor, through the German ambassador and the Austrian Foreign Minister to Kaiser Franz Joseph. Franz Joseph did *not* act 'entirely on his own initiative', but because he believed that he had to take account of the deep antipathy of Wilhelm II towards the Prince of Wales, to which his attention had been drawn repeatedly. As early as 16 September 1888 Herbert Bismarck wrote gleefully to his father, after his 'hurried' audience, that 'H.M. was wild with delight at Kaiser Franz Joseph turning away the Prince of Wales, who wanted to join in on the Vienna visit. *He bears him a grudge.*'[47] The Habsburg Emperor saw far more clearly than the Bismarcks the damaging political risks which lay in the unprecedented slight to the Prince of Wales. After an audience of an hour and a half with Franz Joseph on 4 October 1888, Herbert Bismarck commented laconically in his diary on the elderly monarch's attitude: 'Prince of Wales, unnecessary worry about repercussion on England'.[48]

The Vienna episode was especially damaging because Germany's international position was anything but secure. As the Empress Frederick commented in a letter to Windsor on 20 April 1889, 'all *serious*, *important* and well informed people' were concerned about the internal and external situation of the Reich. In his European policy, Bismarck had made the 'fatal mistake' of weakening Austria so much that it had become almost useless as an ally. As soon as the Russian regiments stationed in Poland were ready, Russia would 'attack Austria to *a certainty*', even if the Tsar were against it. The French were not quite ready yet either, it was true, but their new infantry rifle would be introduced in the course of the next twelve months, while '*ours* in Germany will *not*. If the Russians attack Austria and we are forced to help them, the French will *not* be

brought to him from the Kaiser by Swaine that he should first write a letter
to Wilhelm, to which the latter promised to send a conciliatory reply. Similarly
the Prince refused to accept Hatzfeldt's suggestion that he should simply let
the unpleasant episode rest until both men had the opportunity to express their
mutual regret over the misunderstanding when they met. For his part, the heir
to the throne asked his brother-in-law Prince Christian of Schleswig-Holstein
to mediate for him during his forthcoming visit to Berlin. Christian, however,
was not known for his skill as a negotiator,[57] and the Prince of Wales's Private
Secretary, Sir Francis Knollys, took the view that no one was in a better position
to settle the family quarrel than Queen Victoria herself.[58]

With the agreement of the Chancellor and Wilhelm and much to the surprise of the British government and the German ambassador, Herbert Bismarck
turned up in London at the end of March. His intention was to bring about an
improvement in Anglo-German relations, in view of the danger of a military
confrontation on the continent, or of a French invasion of Italy, and also of the
growing American influence in the Pacific. According to Waldersee it was the
German Foreign Secretary's aim to achieve 'a firm union between us and England
against Russia'. Herbert had explicit instructions from Wilhelm II to 'emphasise
his pleasure at the kind invitation' while he was in London.[59] In two conversations with Salisbury he stressed that it was important 'that England & Germany
should appear friendly before the world' and pointed to the significance of the
Kaiser's forthcoming visit in this regard. He went so far as to draw the Prime
Minister's attention to the danger to the British monarchy of openly opposing
public opinion as embodied in Parliament.[60] The Kaiser, he informed Salisbury,
wished to come 'quite quietly' to Osborne for two or three days at the end of
July. He proposed to spend two or three more days visiting dockyards, weapons
arsenals and other military installations in the south of England. The Foreign
Secretary spoke in a markedly friendly manner of the Kaiser's 'great affection
& veneration' for the Queen and described the death of Kaiser Friedrich III as
'an appalling calamity'.[61] Even so, the Vienna incident continued to cast a dark
shadow over Anglo-German relations.

In a letter to Prince Christian of Schleswig-Holstein of 3 April 1889 the
Prince of Wales gave a detailed account of the incident and asked him to use his
influence with Kaiser Wilhelm during his forthcoming visit to Berlin to try to
induce the latter to express his regret over the affair in some form or other. 'If he
does not, I shall be obliged to absent myself during his visit which it is needless
to say would have a most deplorable effect. I have always been on the terms of
the greatest friendship & intimacy with every member of his family, & with
many of them before he was born!, but the close relationship between him & me
would render an estrangement between us a matter of serious importance!'[62]

Prince Christian had an initial conversation with Wilhelm II on 8 April 1889. Earlier the same morning the Kaiser had conferred with Herbert Bismarck about 'Christian & Wales'.[63] Although Wilhelm claimed several times that he had never expressed the wish not to see his uncle in Vienna, Christian nevertheless detected 'a certain indisposition towards the Prince of Wales'. Above all, the Kaiser remained unbending on the crucial matter of a written explanation. He declared with some vehemence, which Christian nevertheless did not quite understand, that he could not write to the Prince of Wales 'as this was not a simple affair between uncle and nephew, but between Emperor and Prince of Wales'.[64] On the following day Christian asked the British ambassador Malet to telegraph the Prince of Wales to say that the Kaiser certainly wished to settle the quarrel but was not willing to take the first step in writing. Instead he had suggested that the Austrian Foreign Minister Kálnoky should be asked, through Reuss, how he had gained the – ostensibly false – impression that the Kaiser had not wanted to see the Prince.[65] Malet suspected that this suggestion would only cause more trouble, and therefore asked the Prince of Wales to send a cipher telegram expressing his satisfaction with the Kaiser's explanation that Kálnoky must have been given the wrong impression. This would enable the unedifying quarrel to be finally laid to rest, relieving Anglo-German relations of the strain it had caused.[66] The Prince again expressed astonishment at his nephew's behaviour and commented that if the whole affair had been a misunderstanding the Kaiser could surely write a few lines signalling his regret.[67] Salisbury also believed that the means of putting an end to the whole tiresome story now lay within reach: if the Kaiser would write a letter to Prince Christian repeating his declaration that he had never expressed the wish not to see the Prince of Wales, there would be no further reason for the quarrel, and Wilhelm and Albert Edward would be able to meet in the Isle of Wight.[68] In a letter to the Prince of Wales, the Prime Minster went even further and said that such a declaration would purge the personal injury to His Royal Highness even if it were *not* in accordance with reality. The truthfulness of the Kaiser's declaration was not a matter for the British government; it could happily be left to Reuss and his imperial master to sort out between them.[69]

On 11 April Christian saw the Kaiser for the second time and again received a verbal assurance from him that neither he nor the Foreign Office had ever said that he did not wish to meet the Prince of Wales in Vienna. But again the Kaiser 'most explicitly' declared that he could not write to the Prince to this effect. The reason for this, he said, was that he did not know whether Prince Bismarck would agree to his doing so. At any rate Wilhelm was prepared this time to *dictate* to Prince Christian a telegram to be sent to the Prince of Wales, giving the assurance that 'the Emperor has not ever expressed any such wish;

consequently the affair was a misunderstanding'. On his own initiative Christian added that Wilhelm undoubtedly wanted to see the Prince of Wales and had expressed the hope that he would not absent himself during the Kaiser's visit to England.[70] But this attempt at reconciliation also failed because of the Kaiser's refusal, incomprehensible to all on the British side, to set down in writing the verbal declaration he had made to Christian.[71] The Prince of Wales, for his part, refused to be satisfied either by his nephew's oral declaration or by a dictated telegram, and demanded that his letter of 3 April 1889 to Christian should now be shown to the Kaiser. 'If he really wishes to be friends with me again the request I ask of him is very easy to grant', the Prince insisted.[72] 'I *must* have an expression of regret on paper; no verbal message will suffice.'[73] But the Kaiser maintained his stand: he could go no further.[74] A disaster with momentous consequences seemed inevitable.

Unwilling to aggravate what was already an extremely critical situation, Christian refused to show the Prince of Wales's letter to the Kaiser. He pointed out that 'the Emperor is still too young in his position to feel quite sure of himself and always to do the right thing. He is constantly apprehensive of doing something incompatible with his dignity, and he is especially haunted by the thought that his older relatives might treat him as "nephew" and not as "Emperor". Under these circumstances I am firmly convinced that, even if I had given the letter to the Emperor, he would not have complied with the wish of the Prince of Wales. Possibly the situation might have become still more acute and an irreparable rupture would have been caused.' Christian also warned against any attempt to unearth the real reasons for the Vienna incident. 'To do this', he cautioned anxiously, 'some diplomatic steps would have to be taken the consequences of which are beyond my calculations and which might be attended by the most serious dangers.'[75]

Malet tried despairingly to avert a public scandal, which would have been damaging not only to Anglo-German relations but also to the image of the crown in both countries. There were two theories in circulation, he reported, about the Kaiser's refusal to set down his declaration in writing. The first claimed that 'the Kaiser' had indeed expressed the wish not to see the Prince of Wales in Vienna, but that the Kaiser in question had been Franz Joseph, not Wilhelm II. According to this theory Wilhelm did not want to embarrass the Austrian Kaiser, whom he greatly respected, by making a written declaration. The second theory retailed by Malet was that a high-ranking German official (in all probability the ambassador Prince Reuss), in a zealous attempt to prevent a meeting between Wilhelm and Albert Edward in Vienna at all costs, had spoken out on behalf of the Kaiser, but without authorisation. Although Wilhelm was very anxious to be on friendly terms with his uncle again, he was held back from making a written declaration by the feeling, in itself honourable, that he could not disavow this high-ranking official. Both theories allowed the Kaiser's desire for reconciliation with his uncle to appear genuine; the reasons for his refusal to apologise in writing, according to these interpretations, lay elsewhere.[76] Queen Victoria's Private Secretary, General Sir Henry Ponsonby, after reading the numerous reports from Berlin, came to the conclusion that a mysterious game was being played out. Like Queen Victoria he suspected that the Bismarcks were behind the Vienna incident. 'They probably originated the whole difficulty at Vienna and when they found matters had gone too far and that it was necessary to have a reconciliation before the Emperor came to England, Count Herbert was sent.'[77]

But even this perceptive guesswork did not help resolve the problem. The Prince of Wales wrote bluntly to the Prime Minister: 'In asking the Emperor to write me a few lines instead of sending me a vague, verbal message, I do not think that my demand is excessive but should the Emperor refuse to do so, I shall look upon it as a clear proof that the Emperor does not wish to make it up with me, and I shall ask the Queen's permission to absent myself when the Emperor comes over to England.'[78] To his brother-in-law he stated flatly that he had a duty to protect his own dignity. If Wilhelm did not write a letter, he would stay away during the visit of the 'German Emperor and his Fleet' and would also take care 'that every one knows the reason'.[79] He sent Christian a note for the latter to show to the Kaiser, saying: 'Please let William *clearly* understand that unless I do receive a few lines from him as I have asked for in my previous letters to you, I shall be unable to meet him when he comes to England this summer.'[80] Queen Victoria fully shared her son's view that he must insist on receiving 'a few kind words' in writing from Wilhelm.[81]

The Prince of Wales's eldest sister, Wilhelm's mother, was of the same opinion. She considered it absolutely essential that the Kaiser apologise in writing for the Vienna incident. Vicky saw Wilhelm's behaviour as an expression not of malevolence but of embarrassment. 'It is *only laziness* & indifference a little awkward shyness wh. makes William reluctant to write, as he *must* feel that he has behaved very ill, has made a great *bévue* & been very rude! He now does not like to own it, and as he is singularly "*gauche*" & "*ungeschickt*" – does not know how to get out of it.' She nevertheless found it incomprehensible that Wilhelm had not long since written a few simple lines to his uncle.[82]

Prince Christian's attempts at mediation had thus succeeded in worsening, rather than improving, relations between Wilhelm and his British family.[83] Queen Victoria wondered whether Christian had been the most suitable go-between, in view of his close family relationship to Kaiserin Auguste Viktoria, and suggested another German son-in-law, Grand Duke Ludwig of Hesse, instead.[84] But as Christian explained to the Prince of Wales, the Kaiser had been most reluctant to enter into any kind of discussion of the affair with him. 'He was always in a hurry. My interview the other day only lasted a few moments, and when we left the room together we stumbled on Herbert B., the last person I wished to see. W. told him to speak to me on the subject, which I much disliked . . . I showed him [Wilhelm] your memo upon which he again said he could not write.' Christian nevertheless had the impression that 'if he were left to himself his better nature would prevail'.[85] He blamed Wilhelm's attitude on the harmful influence of Herbert Bismarck, who had behaved so 'boorishly and roughly' that Christian 'nearly lost all patience' with him.[86]

This unpleasant affair was still completely unresolved in mid-May 1889. The Prince of Wales, in a solemn memorandum on the subject, spoke of the Kaiser's 'ominous silence' and stated that he, the heir to the British throne, could only interpret Wilhelm's conduct 'as an admission that the affront was intended and that the Emperor William declines any offer of reconciliation'.[87] Relations between Berlin and London were so tense that the Kaiser's visit seemed in jeopardy and Hatzfeldt's position again looked insecure. Prince Ernst zu Hohenlohe-Langenburg, who had recently taken up a post at the German embassy in London, and who as a close relative of the British royal family had an insider's view of the entangled situation, wrote to his father on 11 May to say that 'disagreements' had 'yet again' arisen over the planned visit by the Kaiser. 'The way in which the Kaiser and H. Bismarck have made a point of ignoring the Prince of Wales, whom they have treated, from what I gather, with the utmost lack of consideration, will not improve matters, as relations between the Queen and the Prince are very good. Hatzfeldt is said to have behaved very skilfully in the affair and to have shown great tact in overcoming all the difficulties which Berlin's rudeness and suspicion caused him. If the visit should now be thwarted by new thunderbolts from the Berlin sky, he would have no alternative but to take his leave.'[88]

On the same day Salisbury — acting on Herbert Bismarck's hint — wrote to the Queen warning her again of the serious political consequences, above all for the standing of the crown, which must inevitably result from an estrangement between Britain and Germany caused by personal disagreements in the two royal families. He expressed the anxious hope 'that no decision may be arrived at, which will, in effect or in appearance, give ground to the world to think that a rupture or estrangement with so powerful & important a nation as Germany has arisen out of discussions of a personal or family character. Such an impression would produce a formidable effect on public opinion: which would be regrettable at a time when so many politicians seem ready to rush into extreme opinions. Lord Salisbury dreads the *internal* effect of a rupture with Germany arising out of non-political differences, much more than the general effect upon European politics — though that of course would be prejudicial.'[89] Other ministers and advisers of the Queen likewise recognised the danger for the monarchy that would arise if republican agitators seized upon the royal family quarrel to further their cause among the lower classes.[90]

At this dangerous juncture Sir Francis Knollys and Sir Henry Ponsonby, private secretaries to the Prince of Wales and the Queen respectively, reverted to the suggestion that only Queen Victoria had the sureness of touch and the authority required to bring about a reconciliation. 'I have *long* thought that the only person to take it in hand was the Queen, and no one else . . . She would do it much better than all the Christians, Hatzfeldts & Malets in the world', wrote Knollys. 'I don't say she would succeed, but the best chance of success would be for her to write a carefully composed letter to the Emperor, and for her to suggest at the end of it that he should consult Prince Bismarck on the subject. This however I doubt Her being able to make up Her mind to propose.'[91] On 13 May Ponsonby advised the Queen that she should write a friendly letter to Kaiser Wilhelm II expressing her regret at the conflict between him and the Prince of Wales; Wilhelm would then have no alternative but to reply expressing his own regret at the misunderstandings.[92]

Ponsonby submitted to the Queen a draft letter to the Kaiser drawn up by Lord Salisbury. She made several corrections to it in her own hand, on the grounds that the wording proposed by the Prime Minister simply accepted the Kaiser's denial 'and makes us swallow all the lies'. She also crossed out a passage which could have given the impression that Wilhelm's visit was awaited with pleasure in Britain. To Salisbury's horror she insisted on adding a passage expressing the hope that the Kaiser would order an official investigation into the Vienna incident.[93] After much heart-searching the Prince of Wales, who still felt deeply injured, agreed to the draft as altered by the Queen. He let it be known that he would refuse to dine with the Prime Minister on the Queen's birthday if Salisbury raised any objections to his mother's amendments.[94] Evidently the royal family had reached the limits of its willingness to compromise. But at least its advisers at court were convinced that the Queen's letter would have the desired result and put an end to the quarrel. As Ponsonby remarked on 23 May: 'If the Germans don't like the letter they may put in their pipes & smoke it. Then the fault wd. be theirs. But of course they will answer and I believe all will come right. Very possibly they won't "enquire" — because an enquiry wd. lead to awkward revelations. But we can't make them enquire.'[95]

After the customary exchange of affectionate telegrams on the Queen's birthday on 24 May 1889,[96] the moment arrived to launch the much-discussed correspondence. The final version of the crucial passage in the Queen's letter read: 'My dear Willie, . . . I was very glad to hear from Uncle Christian that you entirely deny the assertion of your having expressed to the Emperor of Austria a wish not to meet Uncle Bertie at Vienna. Lord Salisbury reports to me that you have also instructed Count Hatzfeldt to repeat to him that you never expressed any such wish and I will tell this to your Uncle who will be much pleased to hear it. I cannot understand how the mistake could have arisen which might really have led to very serious consequences, & I hope you will enquire into the circumstances.'[97] The Prince of Wales sent a copy of the letter to his sister in the Taunus, commenting that he thought it too mild and that he feared Wilhelm might consider that it put an end to the matter. 'We must hope', he wrote, 'that in turn he will see how unjust he has been to an Uncle who has always been a kind friend & affect[ionat]e relation to him. I will however do him the justice to say that I think if he *had* been left alone without the pernicious advice of the B[ismarck]s he would have sent me a line, telegram or conciliatory message before now.'[98]

The hopes of the British court and government for a prompt end to this smouldering conflict proved premature, for the Kaiser's rude reply − probably composed with the collaboration of Herbert Bismarck, and at any rate approved by him on 28 May and sent to London by dispatch rider[99] − only made matters worse.[100] 'With respect to the Vienna mistake I have had the matter enquired into immediately when I heard of it from Uncle Christian. I even had Count Kalnoky asked. The result of the enquiry is that the whole affair is absolutely invented, there not having been an atom of a cause to be found. The whole thing is purely a fixed idea which originated either in Uncle Bertie's own imagination or in somebody else's, who put it into his head. I am very glad to hear that this affair has at last come to an end. If you wish for any detailed information Count Hatzfeldt is in possession of all the documents which have reference to the case & can explain the facts to you at any time.'[101]

The Queen sent Wilhelm's letter to her son with the remark that the Kaiser's answer 'will and *must* annoy you very much. It is incredible!!' 'The affair is becoming more and more disagreeable', she commented despairingly. It would now be necessary to recall Sir Augustus Paget from Vienna and carefully compare both versions of the incident. It was clear that several people had told 'great *untruths*'. 'I will believe, at least I *hope* so, that William did not give the message − & that that horrid Herbert & Prince Reuss did it. I shall of course have to answer William . . .'[102] At Marlborough House, the Prince of Wales's residence, the Emperor's answer to the carefully formulated attempt at reconciliation was greeted with incredulity. The Kaiser was trying to dismiss the entire affair as nonsense, Knollys wrote indignantly. 'He simply pooh poohs the whole matter.' This confirmed Knollys's belief that it would have been better not to have been so 'milk and watery' with the Kaiser. It was of course possible that Wilhelm had really had nothing to do with the Vienna episode, and that either the Bismarcks or Crown Prince Rudolf were behind it. But the Kaiser's assertion that the Prince of Wales had simply dreamt up the whole affair was 'a most extraordinary and offensive one and increases the affront which has already been put upon the Prince of Wales'. As the latter had now decided not to forgo his visit to Cowes after all, a meeting with the Kaiser in the Isle of Wight was inevitable, but in the existing circumstances any contact between them must be limited to the purely outward, ceremonial minimum. Naturally the Queen would have to receive her grandson, Knollys opined, 'as otherwise from the Platform and in the Press a howl of abuse will emanate from all the Radical and Socialistic elements in the country', but 'if the Prince were to *receive* the Emperor it would look as if he were *welcoming* him', and he could not be expected to do that.[103] The anger felt at Windsor against Wilhelm was scarcely assuaged by news from the Empress Frederick that her son had been boasting that he could 'do what he liked with his Grandmama'.[104]

Opinion at the German embassy in London was no less critical than at the British court. As the Hereditary Prince of Hohenlohe reported to his father on 9 June, the planned visit by the Kaiser was still 'a precarious matter'. The Prince of Wales, he said, was 'piqued, chiefly because last year he was pushed aside on account of the Kaiser's visit to Vienna, and now this is stubbornly denied, and it is made to appear as if it were an *idée fixe* of his, although in fact there are official documents which show that the greatest zeal was used to make sure that he was out of the way on that occasion. I have read the relevant correspondence and must say that judging from it the Prince has every right to be piqued. It is possible that Reuss will be disavowed so as to bring about a reconciliation. Hatzfeldt is doing the best he can and making use of every possible diplomatic ruse. In the end politics are nothing but a vile game of intrigue, and as we are not having much success at the moment with our brutality, which is given the fine names of sincerity and frankness, and are telling clumsy lies, our position is not exactly a happy one.'[105]

In London there were feverish attempts to formulate yet another letter to the Kaiser which would persuade him to offer some explanation for his insulting behaviour in a manner acceptable to the Prince of Wales. In a first draft of a reply from the Queen to Wilhelm, Salisbury suggested that she should declare herself 'very satisfied' with her grandson's letter, with the single exception of one sentence. 'I wish you had not suggested that the story about your not having wished to see your Uncle at Vienna might possibly be "a fixed idea originating in his own imagination". The proofs that the idea did not originate in *his* imagination are in writing, for my Ambassador Sir Augustus Paget sent home reports at the time showing that this story was communicated to him by people who should have been better informed and was communicated by him to the Prince of Wales. I do not refer to this for the purpose of reviving a matter which has now been happily set at rest but to remove the notion in your mind that the Prince of Wales had any prejudice or any unkind thought towards you.'[106]

For the second time Queen Victoria replaced the title 'Prince of Wales' with 'your Uncle'; but above all she insisted that the German ambassador, Prince Reuss, should be named as the man who had conveyed the Kaiser's wish to Paget, not least so as to avoid creating the impression that she wished to lay the blame for the 'misunderstanding' on Kaiser Franz Joseph or (the now deceased) Crown Prince Rudolf.[107] The draft composed at Marlborough House by the Prince of Wales with the help of Prince Christian of Schleswig-Holstein and Sir Francis Knollys was more direct. The heir to the throne and his advisers put forward a text strongly emphasising the offence caused to him and thus decidedly less conciliatory than the Prime Minister's draft.[108]

On 7 June, however, Salisbury wrote to Ponsonby expressing his 'most distinct disapproval' both of the alteration of his own draft and of the Prince of Wales's proposed wording. Any express mention of Prince Reuss by Queen Victoria would cause 'endless trouble', he warned. He pointed out that it would provoke two possible reactions, both of which would be harmful to British interests. The most probable result would be a flat, insulting denial by the Kaiser which would make further contact with him impossible; alternatively, a large-scale inquiry into the affair, including German complaints against the British side, might actually be launched in Berlin, which would leave the two Kaisers, Wilhelm and Franz Joseph, with a 'rancorous feeling' at a critical moment when a good understanding between the three empires was of the greatest importance. The Prime Minister objected categorically to the naming of Reuss, since that would immediately give the correspondence, which had hitherto been 'personal', a 'political' nature. He strongly advised against replying to the Kaiser's letter at all; but if an answer must be sent, it should be his original draft. What the Queen might later say privately to her grandson was her own affair.[109]

Salisbury's resolute opposition, on grounds of national interest, put an end to the matter, since the Queen could not carry out any action for which her Prime Minister was not prepared to take responsibility,[110] but his attitude was deeply resented in the royal family and generally at court. Prince Christian spoke of it as a 'deplorable end', and Knollys described it as the 'miserable termination' of an affair which had put his master in a 'very awkward' situation. The general verdict of the court was that in adopting a conciliatory stance Salisbury had sacrificed the Prince of Wales on the altar of political expediency.[111] But it was precisely this willingness to allow reasons of state, put forward by a constitutional government, to prevail over personal wishes in matters of politics, that marked the essential difference between the British parliamentary monarchy on the one hand and the 'personal monarchy' of Prussia–Germany on the other. No one was to feel this difference more keenly in the coming months than the Bismarcks themselves.

## THE ADMIRAL'S UNIFORM

Meanwhile Salisbury not only maintained his conciliatory stance – under pressure from Hatzfeldt it was decided not to send any reply to the Kaiser's letter[112] – but also pulled off a coup which, at a stroke, transformed Wilhelm's attitude to Britain – at least temporarily – into rapturous gratitude. During Herbert Bismarck's visit to London in March he had raised with Leopold Swaine, the recently recalled military attaché in Berlin, the question of whether the Kaiser might be made colonel of a British regiment, since – as the German Foreign Secretary put it – 'if he receives any English uniform he will be beside himself with joy . . . He sets far more store by new uniforms than even his Uncle Wales.'[113] Now, in June, Salisbury informed the Kaiser confidentially through the British ambassador in Berlin that Queen Victoria intended to create him a British admiral before his forthcoming visit to the Isle of Wight. The Queen would be glad to be given a German regiment in return; the First Dragoon Regiment was selected, as the only cavalry regiment in which Kaiser Friedrich III had served.[114] Finally, to flatter the vanity of the increasingly touchy Prince Bismarck, the British Prime Minister sent word that the Queen had consented to confer her portrait on the Chancellor in honour of the Kaiser's visit.[115]

Wilhelm II was indeed beside himself with delight at being created a British admiral, and all anglophobia seemed forgotten. On 14 June 1889, the eve of the first anniversary of his accession, he wrote to Sir Edward Malet: 'You can not imagine with what joy I read the welcome news, which you so kindly sent me this evening. I shall immediately set to work in order to select a Regiment fit for the great honour of having Her Majesty as Honorary Colonel. But the last sentence of your letter fairly overwhelmed me! What a surprise and an agreeable one too! I am indeed deeply grateful for the intention of Her Majesty to make me a British Admiral! Fancy wearing the same uniform as St. Vincent and Nelson; it is enough to make one quite giddy. I feel something like Macbeth must have felt, when he was suddenly received by the witches with the cry "All Hail who art Thane of Glamis and of Cawdor too!" I shall of course gladly accept the kindness Her Majesty so graciously has preferred with all my heart. Of course I shall not breathe a word to anybody.' Wilhelm added jokingly that in quoting Macbeth he naturally did not mean to liken the ambassador to a witch; on the contrary he regarded him as a good fairy.[116]

5. Oil portrait by Rudolf Wimmer of Kaiser Wilhelm II in the uniform of a
British admiral of the fleet on the terrace of Osborne House, 1889

The bestowal of this new uniform, according to Herbert Bismarck, had the
effect of intensifying 'to the utmost' the 'enslavement to England' which he had
already observed in Wilhelm in March.[117] The Kaiser was 'like a child' in his
delight at being created a British admiral, Philipp Eulenburg commented during
the Scandinavian cruise.[118] From India the Duke of Connaught wrote that the
Kaiser was overjoyed at his appointment and that the political effect in Germany

would certainly be excellent.[119] The full significance of the admiral's uniform for Wilhelm himself was apparent from his words to Herbert Bismarck when the latter joined him at Wilhelmshaven after his summer cruise. He declared that 'his appointment as an English admiral was a great event; apart from the flattering honour for him (through which field marshal's rank in the British armed forces had been conferred on him, a distinction that he did not even hold at home) he would now have the right, as admiral of the fleet, to have a say in English naval affairs and to give the Queen his expert advice. I looked up in surprise, but H.M. was perfectly serious in what he said . . . During the visit to England General Wittich repeated several times the remark he had made the previous year, "things are going the same way as with [King] Ludwig II [of Bavaria]"', the German Foreign Secretary recalled.[120]

With this skilful move Salisbury had swept away the last hindrance to Wilhelm II's visit to England. As early as 15 June the First Secretary at the German embassy in London, Count Casimir von Leyden, sent the Queen's Private Secretary the list which Wilhelm had personally drawn up of his suite for the journey.[121] Through the London embassy the Queen asked the Kaiser to come to the Isle of Wight on 2 August, as delegates from the British Parliament had decided to attend the naval review planned for that day. Again Wilhelm was delighted. 'I am very much gratified by this mark of kindness shown to us by the Representatives of the whole British nation; which shows the world, that the Country fully concur & sympathise with their illustrious Sovereign in tightening of the bonds of friendship between our two families & countries', he wrote to the Queen on 23 June 1889. He referred to the unpleasant Vienna episode only in a single, unobjectionable sentence: 'At the same time I am happy to see that you regard the Vienna affair as concluded in which I heartily concur & I shall be happy to meet the [sic] Uncle Bertie in Osborne.'[122]

## THE KAISER'S VISIT TO ENGLAND

When Kaiser Wilhelm, his brother Heinrich and his suite arrived in the *Hohenzollern* off the Isle of Wight on the evening of 2 August 1889, the Prince of Wales, accompanied by his two sons Albert Victor ('Eddy') and George (the future King George V), together with his brothers-in-law Prince Christian of Schleswig-Holstein and Prince Henry of Battenberg, sailed out to meet the imperial yacht and brought the German guests back to Osborne House, where they were received by Queen Victoria with her daughters Helena, Louise and Beatrice and her daughter-in-law Alexandra, the ladies and gentlemen of the royal household and Lord Salisbury. The Kaiser, who his grandmother thought had grown 'very large & puffed in the face',[123] was wearing, with evident delight, his new admiral's uniform. Here in Osborne, as Herbert Bismarck contemptuously remarked, he became 'the complete anglomaniac'.[124] He greeted the Queen warmly and kissed her 'very affectionately' on both cheeks. He led the Queen in to the formal dinner for forty guests, held in a marquee in the garden – all the gentlemen were in uniform, with the band of the marines playing softly in the background – and, as on every evening, the Queen sat between Wilhelm and her other Prussian grandson, Heinrich.[125] Among the political guests there were, on the German side, Count Herbert von Bismarck, Count Paul von Hatzfeldt, Generalleutnant Wilhelm von Hahnke, Geheimrat Hermann von Lucanus, Oberhofmarschall Eduard von Liebenau, Generalleutnant Adolf von Wittich and Kapitän zur See Gustav Freiherr von Senden-Bibran.[126] The Queen did her best to conceal her disgust at 'that horrid Herbert B. . . . & that traitor [Flügeladjutant Gustav von] Kessell [sic]'.[127] Outwardly, there was no sign of the ill-feeling of the past weeks and months.

Over the following days, too, the full programme for the Kaiser's visit proceeded perfectly satisfactorily both for him and for his British hosts. Wilhelm described the result of his conversations with Lord Salisbury as 'eminently reassuring' and commented that a 'thorough consonance of views' had prevailed.[128] Accompanied by General von Hahnke and the full complement of princes and princesses, the Kaiser watched the British naval review on 5 August, while Queen Victoria reviewed the German ships, which played *God Save the Queen* one after the other as she sailed past. In the evening, before dinner, Wilhelm introduced to his grandmother, with a 'very pretty speech', a delegation of 'her' First Dragoon Regiment of which she had become colonel-in-chief.[129] On the morning of 7 August Wilhelm travelled to Aldershot with his Uncle Bertie and his brother Heinrich to attend a Field Day.[130] On his return he commented happily to Herbert Bismarck: 'Things are going better and better, tomorrow The Queen has even invited me to her breakfast in the tent, that is a rare honour.' The Foreign Secretary retorted that it was in fact an honour for the Queen 'that Your Majesty should give yourself the trouble to do so', but the Kaiser answered 'irritably': 'You do not understand, . . . you do not know what a secluded life my Grandmother always lives and how much she dislikes receiving in the morning.' For Herbert this remark was one more proof 'that in his English family relationships H.M. had not yet grown up; he was still completely under the influence of his earlier visits to the Isle of Wight when he was treated as a child and as a youngster as his mother thought fit'.[131]

On 8 August, the last day of the visit, while the two monarchs breakfasted in the tent, all the German sailors and marines came ashore to be inspected by the Queen. Wilhelm led the march-past in person. The Queen commented in her journal on how fine the men looked and how well they marched, although 'in that peculiar Prussian way, throwing up their legs'. She conferred the Order of the Garter on Prince Heinrich, which greatly delighted both him and his imperial brother. For his part, the Kaiser bestowed the Order of the Black Eagle on Prince George, and presented the Queen with a bust of himself by Reinhold Begas.[132] Herbert Bismarck and the German officers present saw this demonstration of family affection rather differently. As Herbert commented in his memoirs: 'The worst part was the march-past, led by H.M. himself, of 1200 sailors who had come ashore, on the lawn in front of the tent in which the Queen sat in her armchair waving. H.M. gave the commands and lined them up like a lieutenant in a barracks square, and led the detachment, with drawn sword, at goosestep past the tent. Our generals turned away angrily, and murmured the words "undignified farce".'[133]

On the British side, and for Wilhelm II too, there was relief that the visit had passed off so successfully.[134] 'William came up to see me, & we talked generally of things', wrote the Queen of her grandson's departure. 'He was all the time very amiable, & seemed delighted with his visit.'[135] Salisbury congratulated the Queen on the great success of the visit and above all 'upon the admirable effect produced upon the mind of the Emperor and those who were with him by your Majesty's cordial and most gracious welcome'. He hoped that with time the Empress Frederick would also have reason to be thankful that her son's visit to England had led to happier and more peaceful family relationships.[136]

On his arrival back at Wilhelmshaven the Kaiser sent the Queen an affectionate telegram of thanks: 'I reiterate from the depth of my heart the thanks for your unbounded love and kindness to me, Henry, and all of us, which will never be forgotten, especially for the commission as Admiral of the Fleet.'[137] A few days later in Berlin the Kaiser, the Prince Regent of Brunswick and a number of gentlemen from the British embassy attended a banquet in honour of Queen Victoria's appointment as colonel-in-chief of the First Dragoon Regiment, at which all the speakers proposed toasts to the long and successful co-operation of the German and British armed forces and to the friendship of the two nations.[138] On 17 August, in a letter from Bayreuth, Wilhelm expressed his confidence that, with British maritime power making common cause with the German army and navy, world peace would be safeguarded, or if it should come to war, that both countries would fight shoulder to shoulder. 'May I be allowed to reiterate my most fervent thanks for all the kindness which you lavished on Henry & me, and which I scarcely know how to repay?', he wrote. 'We have felt so comfortable & quite at home at Osborne through all the pains you gave your self to arrange everything for me . . . But personally I beg to be allowed once more to express my warmest thanks for the quite unexampled honour, which you conferred on me with the commission as "Admiral of the Fleet". It really gave me such an immense pleasure, that I now am able to feel & take interest in your fleet as if it were my own; & with keenest sympathy shall I watch every phase of its further development.' Here too he proclaimed it as his most earnest wish that in a future war the German fleet might fight alongside the English, and the 'Pomeranian Grenadier' shoulder to shoulder with the 'Red Coat'.[139] When the Channel Squadron of the British navy sailed in to Kiel at the beginning of October Wilhelm not only went there to attend a large naval dinner, but also made arrangements – as he proudly announced to the Queen – for Admiral Baird and his officers to attend a reception held by the Empress Frederick in Berlin.[140]

The astonishing, almost alarming effect on the Kaiser of the admiral's commission became most clearly apparent in October 1889 during his cruise to Athens. For days on end Wilhelm hoped that the British Mediterranean squadron would come to meet him, 'but no one came'; early each morning he went on deck and surveyed the horizon, telling the ship's commander to hold the Union Jack ready for hoisting if British warships came in sight; at midday he did not eat with the officers but had his meal brought up to him – increasingly tense with expectation – in the chartroom on deck. Eventually, when the British ships hove into view in the Bay of Phaleron he had the Union Jack – which is the badge of rank of the British admiral of the fleet when flown at topmast – hoisted beside the imperial standard. When the Kaiser sailed into the harbour of Piraeus in the *Hohenzollern* the imperial standard was lowered on the great German warship, 'but the English admiral of the fleet's badge was left flying on the order of the Kaiser. A German warship with an English admiral's flag!', exclaimed the ship's commander. The passing ships of all nations were compelled to salute the admiral of the fleet's flag with nineteen guns.[141] The Kaiser, dressed in his admiral of the fleet's uniform, spent several hours inspecting the ships of the British Mediterranean fleet off Athens, and reported to the Queen by telegraph on the excellent state of both equipment and crews.[142] In a 'brilliant' speech in honour of the Queen and the Royal Navy he pointed out that he had felt a bond with the British fleet since his earliest childhood. 'From the time when he was a "little urchin" he accompanied his parents to Osborne and was taken over to see the Royal Dockyard at Portsmouth. It was then, said His Imperial Majesty, that his uncle the Duke of Edinburgh took him by the hand, and gave him his first instruction in nautical matters. Since then his naval education had, he hoped, steadily progressed, till it culminated in the much valued honour which the Queen had recently bestowed upon him. The Emperor said further [so the British envoy in Athens reported] that the German Navy was beholden to that of England for instruction and example, and that the best officers derived the best part of the knowledge from their association with and experience of English ships.'[143]

A remarkable change had come about thanks to an invitation, a uniform and a few friendly gestures. As Lord Salisbury — who had no doubt reflected more than once in the previous months on John Erichsen's warning that Wilhelm would never be a normal person and would be subject to periodic fits of rage[144] — was able to assure the Queen in the autumn of 1889, the attitude of the Kaiser to his grandmother and to Britain was now very satisfactory. 'He is a changed man, from what he was twelve months ago.'[145] 'His present mood is all that could be desired & shows a great improvement in tone & mental grasp.'[146] At the German embassy in London too there was jubilation at the predominantly German-friendly tone of the British press, which since the Kaiser's visit had praised 'Germany, the Kaiser and the Reich Chancellor to the skies'.[147]

The transformation of the Kaiser's personal stance towards Britain had immediately discernible consequences for the international political scene in Europe. Following a visit to Berlin by Kaiser Franz Joseph, the Austrian Foreign Minister, in mid-August 1889, expressed his pleasure at the Anglo-German understanding, which would also enable the Danube monarchy to act more confidently in eastern and southern Europe. If a war should break out, he would now be able to reckon on British participation on the side of Austria and Germany. During his stay in Berlin, Kálnoky reported, he had furthermore been able to establish that the close relationship which had prevailed between the St Petersburg and Berlin courts in the days of Wilhelm I no longer existed, so that the ambivalence which had formerly characterised German policy towards Russia and Turkey would henceforth be replaced by a more clear-cut attitude.[148] The Shah of Persia, in Budapest at the end of his great European tour, also spoke to the British diplomat Sir Arthur Nicolson of his pleasure at the successful visit of Kaiser Wilhelm II to England: it was necessary for all the great powers to hold together, he declared, in order to keep Russia under control.[149]

Less obvious, but nevertheless perceptible under the surface, was the effect of the Anglo-German royal family reconciliation on the position of the Bismarcks, not only because their leanings were towards friendship with Russia and scepticism towards Austria, but above all because in recent months they had taken their attacks on Wilhelm's mother and uncle to new heights. Herbert Bismarck had already sensed the danger on 30 July 1889 in Wilhelmshaven before the departure of the imperial party for England; but with characteristic cynicism he tried to make light of the Kaiser's changing mood, writing to his brother-in-law Rantzau: 'For the time being joy at the British admiral's uniform has the upper hand; but if the Tsar in his turn produces a similar token the scales will tilt back to the other side again.'[150] All too soon his eyes were to be opened to the seriousness of the new situation. Officially he expressed his satisfaction that the visit to England had brought an end to the 'ill-natured stories' that 'evil-disposed persons' had spread about to create 'bad feelings between the families',[151] but he feared that in private conversations the Queen might have stirred up her grandson 'against the name of Bismarck' and also against Russia, for he was in no doubt that 'H.M. had become decidedly more distant after the journey.'[152]

Wilhelm's mother could not but greet the improvement in Anglo-German relations resulting from the Kaiser's visit to Osborne as a natural and necessary development that she herself had long sought. It had after all been the chief goal of her husband, in the interests of world peace and progress within Germany, to bring about the closest possible relationship between the two countries. Nonetheless, 'the part wh. only appears so *ironically* sad to me is that the *very persons* should suddenly profess this creed *now*, that did *all* in their power to *thwart* this, who denounced *me* as a traitor to Germany & *abused* Fritz in the most unjust & ungrateful way for remaining true to his Principles. These same people now make all these demonstrations of friendship!! I see *no* more urgent reason for it now, than *last year*, or than *always*, but this fitful capricious policy has long shocked me!'[153]

# CHAPTER FIVE

# The young Kaiser: a sketch drawn from life

I N the months after his accession several attempts to throw light on the mercurial personality and as yet unfathomable mindset of the dynamic new ruler were published. At the same time as Count Douglas made the glowing eulogy of 4 October 1888 discussed in chapter 1,[1] the Kaiser's former tutor Hinzpeter, now living in retirement in Bielefeld, published a pamphlet entitled *Kaiser Wilhelm II. A Sketch Drawn from Life*, which was rapidly reprinted in dozens of editions, and which began, with the brazenness characteristic of its author: 'In all Germany the question is now being asked, with nervous anxiety, warm interest or at least with lively curiosity: What is the young Kaiser like?'[2] In astonishingly frank terms, Hinzpeter described the difficulties he had faced with Wilhelm's education. Quoting almost word for word from his anxious correspondence with the Prince's parents in the 1870s, he spoke of the 'curiously strongly developed individuality' of his pupil, the 'curiously crystalline composition' of his nature, the 'curious capacity of this mind, so unwavering in its course, to seize what pleases it everywhere', and the striking resistance which the 'very girlish boy, whose delicacy was increased to the point of weakness by a very troublesome clumsiness of the left arm', had shown towards any attempt to force his inner nature 'into a particular form'. The 'Doctor' described Wilhelm's 'muddle-headedness in thinking and condescending attitude in feeling', his 'dangerously low powers of concentration' which he, Hinzpeter, had tried to combat with 'the utmost rigour', but without any lasting success, for 'the inner being of the growing Prince always eluded . . . even this pressure, sometimes immense . . . ; it developed steadily according to his own nature, touched, modified, directed by outward influences, but never fundamentally changed or displaced'. Hinzpeter openly admitted his 'bitter feelings of disappointment' when it became clear that in spite of his efforts '[Wilhelm's] essential being remained unchanged.' He recorded with satisfaction, however, the strong, always easily aroused German national feeling and the 'eminently Prussian' nature of the Kaiser, and in a breathtaking (but thoroughly characteristic) sideswipe at his pupil's English mother he wrote of the 'discomfort of the hen who hatches a duck's egg': the 'pair of eagles', the Crown Prince and Princess, had had no right, Hinzpeter opined, to 'blame the egret who chooses his own trajectory'. If the 'young Prince bubbling over with words and show' had now become a 'steady, reserved, digni-fied ruler', this 'almost tropically fast ripening' could only be attributed to the profound emotional shocks which Wilhelm had suffered during the last months before his accession, his tutor claimed.[3]

The previous chapters have already shown the disturbing extent to which the political pronouncements and actions of the new Kaiser were determined by uncontrolled emotions. It is now time to take a closer look behind the façade of the Berlin Schloss and to echo Hinzpeter's question: what sort of a person was the young Kaiser? The aim will be to use his own writings, together with contemporary sources from his closest entourage, to investigate the pattern of the Kaiser's working day, the picture he had of his rights and duties as emperor and king, how he viewed the other reigning princes of Europe and how he stood in relation to the various parties and social classes in the German Reich in this initial phase of his reign. The next chapter will seek to throw light on the thinking of the Kaiser with regard to foreign affairs.

### THE KAISER AND AFFAIRS OF STATE

In his first letters after coming to the throne Wilhelm self-righteously stressed the great burden of work which had fallen upon him as a result of the double crisis of the previous months, during which countless matters of state had not been attended to. In a letter to the Kaiserin Augusta on 11 July 1888 he claimed that he had been 'not at all prepared for the avalanche of work which engulfed me'. 'I would not have thought it possible for there to be such a stagnation in affairs of state as there was! In the last month under poor dear Papa things had come *de facto* to a complete standstill. All that had to be worked through now! Documents requiring signature piled up like sand on the seashore, and these now have to be gradually dealt with. For instance at Albedyll's audiences, which almost always last for 2 hours, I always have to sign 200 or more documents. Principally patents which date from last summer in Gastein! . . . Today I put in a good day's work with 250 signatures, and am really longing for a moment of rest.'[4] A week earlier he had used similar arguments to justify to Queen Victoria his failure to answer letters. 'The complete stagnation which had set in during the second half of Papa's time, left such an enormous amount of work to be done, especially unnumbered heaps of unsigned orders, Papers, Patents etc., so that for the first 3 weeks I had to work nearly night & day to get rid of all these things', he wrote to her.[5]

On the other hand the experiences of statesmen, diplomats, court officials and military officers in dealing with him immediately after the accession bear unmistakable witness to the very opposite of a regular, dutiful, 'dignified' way of life and work. During his first state visit to Russia and Sweden in July 1888 none of his travelling companions succeeded in persuading him to do any work. 'Nobody here has any luck with "reports", which H.M. avoids as far as possible', Kiderlen-Wächter observed; Wilhelm 'only wants to amuse himself'.[6] Kiderlen, the Foreign Office representative in the imperial suite, then reported to Holstein how Herbert Bismarck had tried in vain for days 'to get hold of H.M. to report to him' until he had at last succeeded, half an hour before lunch on 18 July, in reading out and handing over to Wilhelm the Reich Chancellor's instructions for his meeting with the Tsar. But the Kaiser, Kiderlen continued acidly, 'seems to regard all this as very insignificant compared with the question of how he will bring in his fleet'.[7] In his own memoirs Herbert Bismarck recorded that his father, at the request of the Kaiser, had drawn up a memorandum on the attitude which Wilhelm should adopt at the Russian court during his visit, and had given it to Herbert. 'General Wittich, to whom I gave it to read on the journey, was full of admiration for it, said H.M. should read it twice every day, instead of carrying out tedious naval manoeuvres, and was quite stupefied when I remarked that H.M. had not even looked at it yet. Eventually, just before Kronstadt, H.M. read it through quickly on the fore-deck.'[8] During the visit to Russia, Kiderlen went on to report, the Kaiser had only once taken an interest in political affairs. As a 'small point characteristic of our new sovereign', he told Holstein, Wilhelm 'could hardly be persuaded to attend to business' until he spent the night in Krasnoe Selo for the second time. But then he had suddenly had the military plenipotentiary von Villaume hauled out of bed at half past midnight 'and questioned him for a whole hour about all sorts of things!!!'[9]

On the journey from St Petersburg to Stockholm, Kiderlen again expressed surprise at the attitude of 'our new sovereign' to his official duties. The diplomat repeatedly complained of the difficulty everyone had in persuading the Kaiser to sign papers or grant audiences. 'To conduct business with W. II is, however, in many respects not easy', he wrote to Holstein. 'It is so difficult to get hold of him for that purpose. Wittich has carried around with him during the entire voyage the new drill regulations, which are to be submitted in draft form to a commission if approved by H.M. But H.M. could not be got hold of to approve them. Moreover Wittich reckons that there will be much more travelling, for apart from Vienna and Rome . . . H.M. will probably accept a number of hunting invitations; Wi[ttich] says he still lacks the ability to discriminate as to which should be accepted. People are already asking what will happen when he gets home, where a whole pile of things await him. Everything is being staked on the energy of Herr von Lucanus.'[10]

During the Baltic cruise the diplomats and military officers accompanying the new Kaiser had the opportunity of observing other personality traits which were scarcely in accord with the public image that was being propagated of him. Thus for instance Kiderlen-Wächter reported disapprovingly in a letter to Holstein on the argument which took place between the Kaiser and his brother Heinrich when the latter was given a regiment by the Tsar. When Wilhelm heard of the award he remonstrated with his brother, saying that this was 'quite out of the ordinary and could not be done, one could only be a colonel-in-chief when one was a colonel, but he, Prince H., was only a lieutenant-commander, that is to say major. Prince H. has now established that there were no majors or lieut.-colonels in the Russian Guards, and therefore the next highest rank after captain was colonel. He had this next highest rank and therefore was a Russian colonel; *quod erat demonstrandum!!!*'[11]

As to the 'high moral seriousness of the Kaiser' over which the Douglas speech and countless other publications enthused, the imperial travelling companions on board the *Hohenzollern* had another tale to tell. As early as the third day of the cruise Kiderlen wrote to Holstein: 'We always take our meals at H.M.'s table; up to now the chief subjects of conversation have been shitting, vomiting, pissing, fucking; pardon me for hurting your ear with these harsh words, but I cannot choose any others if I am to give you a true picture.'[12] The Kaiser's personal physician likewise had ample opportunity to reflect on the immaturity of his exalted patient. He blamed Wilhelm's excessively long service in Potsdam for the uncouth demeanour of the imperial entourage, which he considered positively dangerous. 'He [Wilhelm] knows too little of the world and still judges everything from the standpoint of the former colonel in the Hussars', Leuthold commented in a conversation with the Austrian embassy counsellor Eissenstein. 'I am very much afraid', the physician continued, 'that my gracious master will have many a disappointment and many a sad experience to face before his judgement becomes mature and unprejudiced. In his own circle the Kaiser has not yet become accustomed to his new position', he said. 'So for instance on board ship, particularly in the evening, there were wild goings-on, and it was very difficult to strike the right note again the next day. Many of the gentlemen had already been spoilt by the atmosphere of intimacy which so often takes over, and consequently they allow themselves various liberties, which then displeases the Kaiser. All this will no doubt change with time, but for now these incidents hold dangerous germs of unseemly conduct which could easily lead to storms and crises.'[13] Waldersee, who learned of it through Holstein, was likewise disturbed by the 'sort of table-talk that is going on' on the imperial yacht. He had hoped, he remarked, that accession to the throne would have brought about a change in this respect, and blamed Herbert Bismarck's influence for the unimperial tone on board.[14] After conversations with many of those who travelled in the yacht he noted in his diary at the end of August 1888: 'Unfortunately the tone did not improve on the cruise, chiefly of course because of the presence of [Herbert] Bismarck. The Kaiser is certainly inclined to adopt a rather light tone, but nevertheless he sees quite clearly that it is tactless for B. to permit himself to take the same tone towards him which was already scarcely acceptable when Wilhelm was still a Prince.'[15]

In court and government circles people wondered nervously whether such lapses of conduct on the part of the Kaiser were only temporary problems of adjustment, or whether they would prove to be a lasting characteristic. Only a few days after Count Douglas's speech in October 1888, Waldersee, who at this time was still cautiously optimistic, remarked that the Kaiser's entourage continued to be concerned about his restless and unfocused lifestyle. 'The people who have to work with him have been complaining for some time now that it is difficult to get him to grant audiences – he likes finding excuses and puts things off until the last moment', the General noted. 'If one considers what he has taken on and how occupied his time is as a result, it is certainly understandable that there is little time left for audiences; but on the other hand the work must be done and the other activities ought therefore to be limited. I hope that when the [foreign] journeys are over the Kaiser's whole way of life will become more calm and regular, for dealing with affairs in a rush is to be avoided at all costs. The inevitable and deplorable result will be that the Kaiser puts himself too much into the hands of the people to whom he gives audience.' Waldersee urged the introduction of an agreed schedule to bring more regularity and stability into the exercise of imperial authority. 'If the Kaiser wishes to conduct business like his grandfather – and that is what he would like – first the week and then the day must be precisely planned; without a firm plan it certainly cannot be done. There are some people who have misgivings in this regard; I am not among them. The Kaiser is indeed unusually lively, interests himself in countless matters which in the end always take up some of his time, and also aims not to give up his own pleasures entirely. But on the other hand the core of his nature is so good that he will certainly find the right way. The first period of his reign, with so many journeys, is not at all a good basis on which to form a clear judgement. Nor should it be forgotten that the Kaiser can work extraordinarily fast. He has a quick understanding, an excellent memory and makes swift decisions. That makes up for lost time.'[16] In spite of his readiness to enumerate Wilhelm's good

qualities and to blame the Kaiser's initial failures on the particular circumstances
of his accession, Waldersee saw clearly the danger that his new position and the
intoxication of success might go to Wilhelm's head. It was to be feared, he warned
on 13 October 1888, 'that the great successes which the young lord has achieved
in his short reign, and the fact that he is cheered wherever he goes, and that
all destructive elements already fear him . . . could give him false impressions
of his own worth. The danger definitely exists that he considers himself more
important than he is and that he is becoming less open to good advice. But the
successes will not continue in the same way and there will inevitably be setbacks.
He is rising too quickly.'[17]

Months after the accession there were still complaints on all sides that
Wilhelm took plenty of interest in military matters but none in domestic affairs.
'It is said that Kaiser Wilhelm II practically never reads a political report', Count
Széchényi reported to Vienna in January 1889, 'while he always examines the
military ones closely himself. Thus as regards the former he will only listen to
what he is told in audience, so that naturally a great deal depends on the way
the matter is explained to him.'[18] In the imperial family it was even said that
letters that were unpleasant to Wilhelm were thrown unread into a corner.[19] On
the other hand he read the newspaper articles which were laid before him with
passionate interest. As early as October 1888 Prince Bismarck had to reject, as
both hopeless and dubious, a demand from Wilhelm for an amendment of the
law which would restrict press freedom: Wilhelm would simply have to develop
'the necessary thick skin towards the press' and not allow himself to be so upset
by newspaper criticism. The Chancellor likewise rejected his son's suggestion
that the Under-Secretary of State in the Prussian State Ministry, rather than the
Literary Bureau as hitherto, should be responsible for selecting the newspaper
extracts to be laid before the Kaiser. Prince Bismarck thought this unworkable
because no official would be able, in making the selection, to find 'the middle
way between the dull and the dubious'. The extracts for the Kaiser needed to be
'piquant', and that would always be dangerous as long as the monarch allowed
himself to be influenced and upset by newspaper articles.[20]

In the summer of 1889, a year after the accession, Herbert Bismarck summarised for his father the chief characteristics of the Kaiser's method of working.
In a letter to his brother-in-law Rantzau he described it thus: 'In his politics H.M.
acts hurriedly and in fits and starts, and that is because up to now he lacks a
solid grounding based on study and reflection. H.M. does not like reading long
documents (Wittich told me that whenever they run to more than 4 pages he
regularly writes "oral report" on them without reading them); at least, whenever there are arguments and differences of opinion: he prefers narrative reports,
and best of all newspaper articles. Ph. Eulenburg has also repeatedly observed

that whenever papers are sent in to him he likes reading the newspaper extracts first, and usually puts written documents on one side to begin with. Thus it is that H.M. forms his views on the basis of *oral* information and discussions, occasionally influenced by press opinions. I have repeatedly spoken to Papa of my experience that one gets much further with H.M., and can do business with him more easily, by speaking rather than writing to him. So I often request an audience even if I only have things to read out to him, for I am sure that H.M. always raises one question or another on which it is then easy to reach agreement *in conversation. Written* reports, as I said, are read only in passing, and if they do not square with H.M.'s preconceived opinion they provoke contradiction and obstinacy and have rude marginal comments added. In conversation H.M. is always very polite and obliging. His grandfather was exactly the same, in fact.'[21] It was all very well for Herbert to speak, for he had almost unlimited access to the sovereign; apart from military officers and naval commanders, the other ministers and secretaries of state did not get near him. Even Holstein, who at this time still admitted to having 'a certain liking for him', recorded in November 1889 the 'complaints from everyone that H.M. dodges political reports'. Meanwhile Wilhelm would read thirty to forty newspaper clippings at one sitting, making marginal comments on them. He was 'a curious personality'.[22]

The complaints about the Kaiser's lack of order, both outward and inward, grew ever louder. At the time of the Douglas speech, which praised his 'imperturbable calm', and of the publication of Hinzpeter's pamphlet, which drew attention to Wilhelm's 'steady, reserved, dignified' character, in government circles there was widespread criticism of his 'passion for travel'.[23] In Potsdam, because of his constant absences, he was nicknamed 'Wilhelm the External'.[24] After his first Scandinavian cruise in the summer of 1889 Philipp Eulenburg deplored the Kaiser's hyperactivity, commenting: 'The health of the Kaiser was excellent – his restlessness immeasurable. His changeable appearance unfortunately indicates a certain nervousness of disposition which worries Leuthold, but then Leuthold is a pessimist of the worst kind.'[25]

From 21 October until 12 November 1889 a middle-class outsider, the commander of the battleship *Kaiser*, Vice-Admiral Paul Hoffmann, had the opportunity of observing Wilhelm II closely during the Mediterranean cruise from Genoa to Athens and Constantinople. He too was struck by the obvious reluctance of the monarch to grant audiences. On numerous occasions the Kaiser had said to the Chief of the Military Cabinet, who was accompanying him, 'at sea no audiences are held'.[26] During the entire voyage Wilhelm only once granted audiences, and that was in Athens; 'otherwise he refuses everything', Hoffmann commented in amazement. When the Flügeladjutant Freiherr von Senden-Bibran, on their arrival in Athens, asked permission to make a report on behalf of the Foreign Office, the Kaiser turned to Hoffmann and said: 'I surely cannot be expected to listen to reports when I have my first opportunity to see Greece.'[27]

If the Kaiser refused to hold audiences at sea, he nevertheless spent several hours every day in childish games. Hoffmann commented with bewilderment on the 'great tenacity' with which Wilhelm II played the quoits game 'Bleiglatt' on deck. 'This game is played to the point of exhaustion and I have absolutely no taste for it. All the other participants became heartily tired of it eventually, but the Kaiser is indefatigable.'[28] For light reading Wilhelm had brought with him the recently published lectures of his former German teacher Carl Werder on Schiller's *Wallenstein*,[29] but there was no question of serious work, the Vice-Admiral concluded, having observed the Kaiser for more than two weeks. This is how he described the course of a typical day on board: 'In the afternoon "Bleiglatt" was played again on the aft deck until dark. After luncheon the Kaiser sat down to play piquet. On extremely rare occasions the Kaiser occupies himself for an hour, when he reads for pleasure, e.g. lectures on Schiller's Wallenstein. But I have never yet known him to "work" on his own, that is, see to official business by himself. As a rule he demands social entertainment, distraction of some kind, and whatever kind it is he joins in with great vigour, more persistently than all other participants.'[30]

In November 1889 Waldersee noted in his diary for the first time a decline in the popularity of the Kaiser. Suddenly, he reported, there were complaints on all sides that Bismarck was being too lenient with the Kaiser. Only the Reich Chancellor had the authority to raise objections to two of Wilhelm's extravagant projects – the new *Hohenzollern* for four and a half million marks and the imperial residence in Frankfurt for two million. The initial popularity of the Kaiser, which rested on the fact that apart from the extreme left every party wanted to win his support, had already passed its climax and would soon 'go backwards', in Waldersee's view. 'It soared to the heights far too quickly and a fall is therefore natural and not at all harmful; the Kaiser must go through hard times in order to reach the heights to which he is entitled by virtue of his talents and his many excellent qualities. Very gradually a certain disappointment is setting in; the many journeys, the restless activity, the innumerable and varied interests naturally lead to a lack of thoroughness.'[31]

For the first time, now that he had gained a deeper insight, the Chief of the General Staff criticised Wilhelm's personality and the manner in which he exercised his rule, although he interpreted the latter as a consequence of the Bismarckian system. 'The Cabinet chiefs complain that they have difficulty in obtaining audiences and when they do, they are too short and hurried. The ministers have the feeling that the Kaiser ought to have thorough discussions of their departmental affairs with each of them from time to time, but he almost never does so. The Minister of War has regular audiences, and I myself have an adequate number, but Count Bismarck has far too many.'[32] Waldersee urged strongly that more 'regularity in the Kaiser's conduct of business' must be introduced. 'It is frequently asserted that he goes away too much and that this inevitably detracts from the thoroughness with which business is conducted. Unfortunately there is some truth in this', he admitted, 'although one must not forget that the Kaiser has a very quick understanding, and therefore works more quickly than many other people. Nevertheless I too wish that he would concentrate a little more. He shows plenty of interest in the matters which I bring before him, and no doubt likewise in military affairs in general, most particularly naval affairs. But his audiences on civil business cannot be very thorough; although he hears more from the Foreign Office, he hears very little indeed from the other ministries. I think, however, that all this will sort itself out. This year [1890] will bring many a serious internal problem in the country, and consequently the necessity of paying more attention to these matters; I hope that 1890 will prove a serious but excellent school for the Kaiser.'[33]

Waldersee failed to see that his own intimate relationship with Wilhelm was inconsistent with the well-regulated, responsible conduct of affairs of state. As with Wilhelm's friendship with Philipp Eulenburg, Waldersee's close contact with the Kaiser was the living contradiction of the claim made in Count Douglas's speech and elsewhere that the Kaiser was inaccessible to personal flattery and sycophancy and hostile to all types of coterie and camarilla. Like Bismarck, Waldersee — and later Eulenburg — was to experience in person how matters really stood with Wilhelm's willingness to receive an 'open, honest and true word' and with the 'truly royal gratitude' of the Kaiser.

## THE KAISER AND THE 'MONARCHICAL PRINCIPLE'

It was certainly one of the foremost aims of Wilhelm II, as Douglas pointed out in his speech, to secure the 'monarchical principle' in Prussia and Germany, but his conception of this task differed in several essential respects from that of Bismarck. Whereas for the founder of the Reich the constitutional principle of Personal Monarchy was a legal fiction with which the authoritarian state could defend itself against the floodtide of parliamentarism and democracy, Wilhelm took the theory literally and saw it as the legitimisation of his personal power, indeed more than that, as the obligation laid upon him by heaven to defend monarchy by Divine Right. Nothing enraged him more than the suspicion that the Reich or state government, the Reichstag, the political parties or the press might be trying to interfere with his prerogatives as Kaiser, king of Prussia and supreme

war lord. 'I am accustomed to being obeyed, . . . I do not enter into discussions . . . The word of a Kaiser should not be twisted or quibbled with', he
insisted, even before Bismarck's dismissal.[34] In his eyes the rights of the Prussian crown inherited from absolutist times were now augmented by the dignity
and immense power of the new kaiserdom, which he saw — and here his concept of the constitution differed sharply from Bismarck's interpretation — as the
continuation of the medieval emperorship with its claims to universal domination. This was perhaps most clearly expressed in his memorable comment to his
mother shortly after Bismarck's death: 'For ever & for ever, there is only *one real
Emperor* in the world, & that is the *German*, regardless of his Person & qualities,
but by *right* of a *thousand years tradition.* And his Chancellor has to *obey*!'[35]

From the beginning of his reign until the end of his life Wilhelm II regarded
the battle for the defence of the monarchical principle against democracy as an
international conflict between good and evil, the conduct of which devolved first
and foremost on him as German Kaiser. In 1893 he declared to Pope Leo XIII:
'We monarchs represent Divine Right and conservative politics. Republicanism,
and with it radicalism, on the other hand, is based on regicide, the abolition of
God, and aims to overthrow all existing order . . . The people [of France] cannot
find calm and stability because they have beheaded their King whom God set
over them, dishonoured the Church and mocked the deity.'[36] Even in the First
World War, when millions had died, he declared to the incredulous American
envoy that only emperors and kings like himself, that is the Tsar and George
V, had the right to decide over peace and war; mere republics like the United
States and France could not have a say in such questions.[37]

With every year — with every electoral victory of social democracy, with every
new sign of the democratisation in the Catholic Centre Party, with the success of
the United States of America in achieving world power status — the Kaiser should
have recognised that he was fighting a losing battle in defending his monarchical
ideology. Moreover, the principle of Personal Monarchy which he upheld was
increasingly called into question, not only from below and in the Western world
abroad, but also from within — by his weaker and less autocratically inclined
kingly 'colleagues', and Wilhelm reacted to these tendencies with a violence
probably unprecedented in the history of the ruling houses of Europe. In the
summer of 1895 he wrote to Crown Prince Gustav of Sweden and Norway, urging
that his father Oscar II pull himself together and act with greater severity if he
did not want to go down in world history as a traitor to the monarchical principle.
'The monarchical principle itself would suffer most seriously', he warned, if King
Oscar did not take decisive action against the freedom movement in Norway. The
monarchical principle had 'already fallen into disrepute through the Kings of
Portugal, Serbia and Greece. May your father be preserved from being counted

among such colleagues. His duty as monarch and king is to set his personal feelings aside and to do his duty, which requires of him that he impose respect and obedience to the royal authority in his lands.'[38]

The most remarkable source from which insight can be gained into the idiosyncratic thinking of Kaiser Wilhelm consists of his marginal notes on diplomatic reports. Countless such annotations, in the early days often written on small mourning envelopes, have remained unknown until today, as the Bismarcks had them secreted in a metal trunk in the Foreign Office: they were too explosive even for internal circulation within the Wilhelmstrasse offices.[39] Even while Wilhelm was Crown Prince, deputising for his father, the Reich Chancellor had to have documents bearing his marginalia locked away.[40] In the first months of the new reign Bismarck gave orders for several dozen foreign dispatches to be confiscated because of excessively crude marginal comments by Wilhelm. Even the founder of the Reich, it seems, did not have the courage to advise the young Kaiser to abstain from this disastrous habit. Instead a clerk was given the task of copying out the dispatches without the marginalia, as the original text was needed for the work of the Foreign Office.[41] Bismarck's successor General von Caprivi at first continued Bismarck's practice, but in the latter half of his time in office he allowed more and more documents to be circulated with Wilhelm's marginal comments. Under Reich Chancellor Prince Hohenlohe, and even more under Bernhard von Bülow, no one thought it possible or necessary any more to conceal Wilhelm's marginalia. This creeping moral decline in public life exactly corresponds to the rise of the Kaiser's power vis-à-vis the state and Reich administration in the first twelve years of Wilhelm II's reign. But it later led to a kind of optical illusion, when the records of the Foreign Office were published in more than forty volumes in the 1920s. Unaware of the confiscated marginalia the observant reader could not help gaining the impression from the published records that Wilhelm had only gradually acquired the taste for decking out the official reports of his diplomats with scathing annotations. In actual fact, as we have seen, the mischief had begun even before his accession. The early marginalia, which today are preserved in a reserve collection in the archive of the Foreign Office, throw a harsh light not only on Wilhelm II's strange ideology but also on his contemptuous opinion of other monarchs at the very beginning of his reign.

Wilhelm's dizzying, quasi-absolutist conception of his role as Kaiser expressed itself (as in a mirror image that shows one's own face in reverse, but nevertheless truthfully) in his derisive contempt for other rulers who sought or were obliged to maintain constitutional forms. He especially despised his Coburg relation Dom Pedro, who had abdicated as emperor of Brazil. Since then the country had been in a dreadful state, he thundered, and all 'because the cowardly monarch abandoned the post which God had entrusted to him!'[42] Contempt was mixed with indignation when he heard that Wilhelm, Hereditary Grand Duke of Luxemburg, who as a member of the Nassau family was descended from William of Orange, was to be received into the Catholic Church. The Kaiser described this conversion as 'disgraceful' and 'frightful!' 'The epigones are utterly unworthy of the great Prince of Orange', he pronounced, and declared that 'now the duty [to be the bulwark of Protestantism] passes to my House as next in line'.[43]

With disgust Wilhelm observed developments in Romania, which were strikingly portrayed in the colourful reports, carefully tailored for him, written by the German envoy Bernhard von Bülow, the future Foreign Secretary and Reich Chancellor. The Kaiser reproached King Carol, who was descended from the related (Catholic) House of Hohenzollern-Sigmaringen, with working 'valiantly' towards the overthrow of monarchical order in his country through his constitutional style of government. This 'short-sighted' monarch did not even notice that people were trying to get rid of him; he did not listen to Berlin, which had already tried 'who knows for how long' to open his eyes to the danger of a pro-parliamentary policy. Thanks to the 'limpness' and blindness of the King, Romania was going the best way to become a second Poland, which would be simply 'gobbled up' by Russia. 'Polish conditions' already ruled in Romania, Wilhelm claimed in February 1889, and he annotated a report with a quotation from *Wallenstein*: 'You are blind with your seeing eyes!' As we have seen, he had just been reading Carl Werder's lectures on Schiller. The Romanian monarchy would 'be destroyed by its muddle-headed idealism!!', prophesied the young German ruler. 'Incredible!' was his verdict on the appointment, reported by Bülow, of a liberal government under Lascar Catargis in February 1889: the new Prime Minister, he declared, was a 'cur!', he and his foreign minister were 'milksops!', the Cabinet was a 'fine rabble!' that resembled 'a Richter-Windthorst-Rickert-Virchow ministry'. The 'blessing of parliamentarism combined with constitutional kingship' would be anarchy, Wilhelm predicted in November 1889. Carol's willingness to make concessions – Wilhelm mockingly named him 'Carol the Great'[44] – he could only understand as a wrong-headed calculation that he should give the 'billy-goat . . . a few cabbages so that he does not devour the whole garden'. 'Landgrave, Landgrave, be firm', on the other hand, would have been the only wise motto for the King. When Bülow reported the comment of a Romanian politician that the King ought to cut himself out of politics, Wilhelm was shocked and remarked, 'The public prosecutor ought to be called in here!'[45]

Of the Romanian Queen Elisabeth, born a Princess of Wied, who wrote poems under the pen-name of Carmen Sylva, Wilhelm had as disparaging an opinion as of the King himself. 'Obstinacy and vanity on the part of the monarch and poetic, humanistic fantasising and attacks verging on nymphomania on the part of his consort are hard to combat, but give one little confidence in a level-headed reign and future', he commented in an annotation of March 1889.[46] The Queen's constitutional ideas — she was said to have expressed the wish to be queen of a republic — the Kaiser considered 'high treason and treason to the country'; in his view Elisabeth belonged in a 'padded cell!'[47] The King really ought to put her away 'in a hydrotherapic institution', he remarked; she was after all nothing but 'a crazy bluestocking!'[48] In any case she ought to keep her fingers out of politics, for 'petticoats don't belong in politics, especially when they have blue stockings'.[49] 'Wherever there is mischief: chercher la femme!', he scribbled in the margin of one report from Bucharest.[50] In view of the progressive parliamentarisation of Romania, Wilhelm was only too glad not to have any closer connection with this country. Commenting on a complaint by a Romanian nationalist that Romania, because of its German ruling house, had sunk to the level of a German province, the Kaiser retorted: 'Thank God no, what would I want with such brutes?! You are all frog-arses in Germany's eyes!'[51] It would do nothing but good if the Russian influence in Romania became ever stronger. 'In any case the ruble goes on doing its work at every level.'[52]

Wilhelm also poured scorn and mockery on Bulgaria, where his cousin Ferdinand of Saxe-Coburg and Gotha had been elected king in July 1887 by the national assembly. On the back of a mourning envelope, which Bismarck locked away at Friedrichsruh, the young Kaiser wrote: 'Petit Ferdinand holds out only because the powers cannot agree on anyone else, and only so long as mama [born a princess of Bourbon-Orléans] throws money around. A few clauses of the old Treaty of Berl[in] are energetically defended because they seem to be appropriate at the moment; and they are apparently to be considered sacred and unassailable.'[53]

Wilhelm II took an equally avid interest in the dramatic events in Serbia, where King Milan, the friend of his youth, divorced his wife in October 1888 and then renounced the throne on 6 March 1889. At first the Kaiser did not believe Milan's intentions were serious. 'If someone runs about with a pistol in his pocket and assures everyone he is going to kill himself', he observed in November, 'then one can wager 100 to 1 that he certainly will not do it! And likewise in this case!'[54] But as the rumours of the forthcoming abdication grew stronger Wilhelm responded by suggesting ways of persuading Milan to stay, in order to maintain Austrian influence in the Balkan state. In December 1888, when Prince Reuss reported from Vienna that the Russians might offer the Serbian king, whom they hated, a pension to help him decide to give up the throne, Wilhelm declared: 'As far as I know King Milan's character and personality, the idea of the "Russ. Pension" seems perfectly probable and credible. Could he not be helped with an Austrian pension? Austria's influence in Serbia must not be lost, and must be upheld there by all means. Otherwise the Austrians will later have a threat to their flank!' Patiently, Bismarck had to point out the absurdity of this idea with the comment: 'But if Milan *has* abdicated then nothing more can be gained by a subvention. Austr. would have to bribe him to stay!'[55] A few days later Wilhelm suggested that as he was 'very close to the King and intimate' with him, he could himself write a 'persuasive and encouraging letter'.[56] This suggestion was accepted by the Chancellor, who drafted a letter from the Kaiser to the Serbian King designed to persuade the latter to give up the idea of abdication. When Reuss thereupon sent word to Berlin that Milan was insisting that he had no alternative but to abdicate, 'because he feared that he would certainly go mad if he remained in his present situation', a distinct change took place in Wilhelm's attitude. Several times in his marginal comments he recommended the dispatch of his friend to the cold-water treatment institute in Bad Godesberg, and wrote: 'Cold water on the head and Friedrichshall [hot salt] waters everywhere else will at least help!' At the beginning of March, when the news of Milan's imminent abdication reached the German capital, Wilhelm commented spitefully: 'Better a nasty end than prolonging the agony!'[57] And in response to a further report, on the oriental journey on which Milan embarked after his abdication, the Kaiser observed that the ex-King seemed 'to have been very busy f . . . ing [sic]'.[58]

The fascination with the sexual life of other monarchs and members of their families apparent in such comments was a characteristic of Wilhelm's marginalia in general, from which interesting conclusions may be drawn about his own psychosexual constitution. He once joked that he would 'very gladly' visit the Sultan again, 'if I could go into the harem'.[59] Of Crown Prince Ferdinand of Romania, who for a time contemplated marrying Wilhelm's youngest sister, the Kaiser wrote on an official diplomatic report: 'He can't do anything but f . . . [sic], and he already takes care of that here anyway.'[60] When news arrived to the effect that King Carol was concerned about Ferdinand's delicate health, His Majesty noted in the margin: 'He survived very well in Potsdam and the way he bedded the girls was a delight!'[61] The marriage of the former ruling Prince of Bulgaria, Prince Alexander of Battenberg, to the actress Johanna Loisinger in February 1889, as might be expected, drew equally disgraceful comments from the Kaiser. He described the Prince as a 'cur!' and accused the bride of imprudent behaviour 'of a horizontal nature'. On Prince Alexander's changing his name to Count Hartenau after his marriage, the Kaiser commented contemptuously, 'Once a Polack always a Polack.'[62] He perhaps sank lowest with his jibes in July 1889 when Schweinitz reported from St Petersburg that the Russian Princes Ivan and Gabriel Constantinovich would have to look for Orthodox brides in the Balkans one day. Kaiser Wilhelm II saw fit to record, on the ambassador's official report, his opinion that the Princes would 'probably look after themselves elsewhere meanwhile!'[63] At this time the Grand Duke Constantine's sons were respectively three and two years old.

Such comments were not at all exceptional. When Schweinitz reported that the Tsarevich Nicholas had 'gained a broader knowledge of the fair sex' on his educational tours in Egypt, India and Japan, the Kaiser observed: 'That would be a blessing, for up to now he has refused to go near any woman.'[64] Commenting on a dispatch from Count Casimir Leyden in Cairo according to which the Russian heir and the Greek Crown Prince George had given diamond brooches to the little girls who offered them flowers on their Nile cruise, the All-Highest wrote: 'As these girls are usually naked, it might be interesting to know where they put the brooches?'[65] Learning from a further report from St Petersburg of a feud between the 'bigoted' Grand Duke Sergei and an archimandrite of the Russian Orthodox Church, Wilhelm II gave his explanation of the incident: 'That is because the worthy old man discovered that Sergei was buggering his handsome young domestic chaplain. He transferred the latter at once. This enraged the pious prince so much that he contrived to have the old man transferred!! I have spoken out before now of my fear that Grand Duke Sergei would bring about the downfall and destruction of his family. It almost looks as if that were so.'[66] He accused the (originally middle-class) wife of the aristocratic ambassador of the French Republic in St Petersburg, Count Gustave Lannes de Montebello, of being 'also available for adjutant generals and grand dukes', and moreover of having 'travelled successfully on the Isle of Lesbos'.[67] When the German embassy reported on the great social success of Countess Montebello especially in grand-ducal circles of St Petersburg, the Kaiser observed: 'So it is as I said before, they will all have had their turn.'[68]

Other ruling princes served simply as targets for imperial mockery. Thus for instance Wilhelm noted on a report from Athens, in which attention was drawn to the organisational talents of the King of Greece, a scion of the House of Denmark, that the King was perhaps better fitted to be a court marshal 'than to be Rex'.[69] On a British newspaper article praising the constitutional methods of the Greek King, Wilhelm wrote angrily 'balderdash!', 'rubbish!' and 'utter nonsense!'[70] When it was reported to him that French diplomats feared that the engagement of his (Wilhelm's) sister to the heir to the Greek throne could turn Greece away from France and towards Germany, Wilhelm saw it as merely a sign of incipient madness on the part of the French and wrote one of his favourite sayings, 'Quos deus perdere vult! etc.' in the margin of the report. Nevertheless he hoped that this French attitude would bring about a beneficial effect on the Danish royal house. 'I trust this conduct will deal a hearty blow to the Francophile inclinations probably still latent in Copenhagen', he commented.[71]

When the Empress Frederick told her mother of the primitive conditions in which her daughter Sophie had brought her first child into the world in Athens, she begged her not to repeat any of it to Wilhelm, for 'He always abuses the King & the Greeks − & it *comes round* to them again, & makes things difficult & uncomfortable, he is *so* rash imprudent injudicious & thoughtless.'[72] After Sophie's conversion to the Greek Orthodox Church[73] the relationship of the German Kaiser to the Greek royal house, which had long been tense, became increasingly hostile. The King of Greece had 'perhaps been coached by his Mama in Copenhagen', Wilhelm wrote scornfully on a report from Athens.[74] 'These petticoats should just keep their fingers out of things', he commented angrily on receiving a report in 1897 on the influence of Danish, Russian and British relations in Athens.[75] Echoing a comment by the King of Saxony, Wilhelm wrote that the King of Greece 'is and remains the "Greek gamin" as King Albert always calls him. And rules over a band of robbers.'[76] 'How can one expect courtesy from such a worthless and ill-mannered man as the "Greek gamin"!!', he asked.[77] The King's sons were 'louts without any education'.[78] In further marginal comments the Kaiser characterised the Greeks as 'miserable scoundrels' and the Athenians as 'unreliable blackguards'.[79] On a report from the German envoy in Athens in which it was stated that neither the Greek court nor the Greek people had taken much notice of the Kaiser's birthday, Wilhelm commented that the coolness of the Greek King and Queen was 'very indicative', for 'we do not love each other'. The Greeks were 'piqued', he considered, 'because I have not arranged for them to have Constantinople'.[80] When a report arrived from Lisbon announcing that on 27 January the Portuguese King Carlos had not sent anyone to the German embassy to bring his congratulations, Wilhelm II denounced this 'colleague' too, as a 'bad-mannered boor like the Hellene'.[81]

The gathering of monarchs in Athens on the occasion of the marriage of his sister Sophie on 27 October 1889 confirmed the predominantly negative opinions of the Kaiser about his fellow rulers. When the Kaiser arrived in Piraeus in the *Hohenzollern* there was no welcoming party of Greek ships, the reception was disorganised, nothing had been prepared and neither the King nor the Queen of Greece was present. Wilhelm would not even have credited the King with the ability of a court marshal now, as he gave vent publicly to 'his displeasure at the prevailing confusion'.[82] From now on the Greeks were nothing but a 'wretched, pretentious people' in his eyes.[83] The commander of the battleship *Kaiser*, who attended the banquet at Athens, gave a vivid description of the royalties assembled for the wedding: the bride's mother, the Empress Frederick, looked much younger again dressed in a pale grey gown; her brother the Prince of Wales was as usual the picture of health; his Danish wife Alexandra looked 'almost as young as her two daughters, the son Eddy [Albert Victor] rather foppish with his swan-neck, the second [George] very sensible'. The Tsarevich Nicholas, on the other hand, gave the impression of a 'juvenile Muscovite youth' and was 'as brash as could be in his manner'; the King and Queen of Denmark seemed more like a 'fusty bourgeois councillor and his wife'. At the ceremony known as the 'baisemain' next day, at which Princess Sophie appeared in modern Greek costume, the American and French envoys – 'no doubt as republicans!' – refused to kiss the bride's hand.[84]

On 31 October the German squadron, consisting of the *Kaiser, Hohenzollern, Deutschland, Preussen, Friedrich der Grosse, Irene, Pfeil, Wacht*, the Lloyd's steamer *Danzig* which had been hired for the very large suite and the flagship of Admiral Deinhard, the *Leipzig*, sailed onwards to Constantinople, where three large steamers packed with Germans came out to meet them, greeting them 'with continuous cheering, singing of patriotic songs and waving of handkerchiefs'.[85] For the reception by Sultan Abdul Hamid II, Kaiser Wilhelm II put on his red Hussar uniform, 'doubtless', Vice-Admiral Hoffmann assumed, 'because the green sash of the order looks very Turkish against it'.[86] Here, for German eyes, an exotic, almost sinfully opulent monarchical world revealed itself. The pavilion in which the Emperor and Empress were accommodated in Yildiz was 'excessively rich' and furnished with every possible luxury.[87] 'The dinner was very elaborate, the table was a magnificently arranged, we ate off nothing but gold. The centre-pieces on the table were all of gold and bronze, likewise spoons, knives and forks . . . The extravagance which is shown off in the Sultan's palace disgusts one because one knows how wretched things are in the country. The Sultan is in his middle forties', Hoffmann observed; 'he is thin, has very sharp, Jewish features and gives the impression of having some nervous disorder.'[88] As a present for the Sultan the Kaiser had brought a large rococo clock decorated with figures costing 1,800 marks and two nine-branched candelabra worth 1,100 marks,[89] but these costly gifts were far outdone by the Sultan's presents to his guest. On the Kaiser's departure Abdul Hamid presented him with 'an extraordinarily costly sabre' and the Kaiserin with gifts including a piece of jewellery which alone was valued at £10,000.[90] In general the members of the imperial entourage were repelled by the 'senseless luxury', the 'court flim-flam, the humbug about orders, the miserable business of etiquette' in Constantinople.[91] When they embarked on 6 November Hoffmann observed that even 'our exalted master and mistress' were glad to be back on board, particularly as the Kaiserin claimed to have found bed-bugs in her rooms.[92] In political terms Wilhelm II's visit to Constantinople, which was viewed with suspicion in Russia, brought few advantages. On taking leave of the Sultan the Kaiser expressed the hope that he would look on 'his (the Kaiser's) policies from now on no longer with mistrust', to which Abdul Hamid replied that people were 'unfortunately attempting to arouse his suspicion of

German policies and that this had even been attempted again in the course of his exalted guest's visit'.[93]

Thus the impressions that Kaiser Wilhelm II formed of his royal 'colleagues' in Athens and Constantinople were not of a kind to reinforce his belief in the power of the monarchical system to withstand the struggle against the democratic current of the times. Nor was it exactly strengthened by the secret information about the death of King Luiz of Portugal which arrived during the wedding festivities in Athens: when the doctors began the autopsy on the 'corpse', they heard the apparently dead king begging them not to hurt him so much![94] The Kaiser's meeting with Shah Nassr ed-Din of Persia, the 'King of Kings', in Berlin in June 1889 was equally ill calculated to sweep away any lingering inner doubts. On his Mediterranean cruise in November the Kaiser was still telling 'all kinds of tales' about the Shah, and said to Hoffmann: 'He was a queer customer. When my wife showed him our children he said "Sont tous de vous Madame?"'[95] A certain surprise speaks out of the letter in which Wilhelm reported to the Reich Chancellor on his conversations with the Persian ruler. 'The Shah *wants*, without a doubt, to be amiable. He makes what is for him a very considerable effort to show his admiration and satisfaction.' Nevertheless he was clearly upset by the treatment he had received in Russia, and above all by having been bundled off to Warsaw, where he had been forced to spend thirteen days. 'Varsovie pas belle ville', the Shah had complained to the Kaiser. At dinner on 11 June he had questioned Wilhelm closely about the state of the Italian army and navy and had wanted to know, when the 'March for the Entry into Paris' was played to him, 'whether we would march in there again, to which I replied yes, if we have to'. Thereupon the Shah had whispered softly to him 'Français méchants, très méchants', and when the Kaiser admitted 'that it was not very easy to live with them', the Shah responded: 'Ce sont des Saltimbanques.'[96] Wilhelm subsequently told the British ambassador that the Tsar had threatened the Shah with an invading force of 100,000 men if he made concessions to the British; the Persian monarch had twice asked him, the German Kaiser, for help in such an event.[97]

The Kaiser could scarcely contain his contempt for his British — and admittedly very odd — cousin Albert Victor, the elder son of the Prince of Wales and presumptive future king of England, when he was granted the title of Duke of Clarence in 1890. In a lengthy marginal note, in which he went so far as to allude to current rumours about the homosexuality of the newly created Duke, the Kaiser wrote: 'Well! I must say! He can't speak German, nor French; he didn't know whether Munich was a river or a town and had no idea who Fred. the Great was! And furthermore he was under serious suspicion last autumn. And that is called being superbly prepared [for his calling as a monarch]!!! In the end it is of no consequence in England as he is not expected to have anything to say anyway, nor will he.'[98] When the news of the sudden death of the Duke reached him in January 1892 the Kaiser did not even break off his shooting expedition in Bückeburg, which was taken very much amiss by the family.[99] Colonel Leopold Swaine, who returned to Berlin as military attaché in early 1892 after an absence of three years, was shocked by Wilhelm's coldness and especially by his refusal to attend the service held in Berlin in honour of his dead cousin. 'The extraordinary behaviour — almost heartlessness — of the Emperor on the occasion of the death of the Duke of Clarence caused surprise and regret even amongst the immediate surroundings of the Court, but none of them had the courage openly to express their opinion', the military attaché wrote in disgust.[100]

As for the German federal princes, Kaiser Wilhelm II expected them to maintain a 'national' demeanour, an expectation in which he found himself not infrequently disappointed. This was particularly true with the Catholic Bavarian royal house, which demonstrated a strongly particularist attitude. When the Württemberg envoy in Munich, Soden, found himself being attacked in Bavaria because of military agreements which had been reached between Württemberg and Prussia, Wilhelm II wrote on the report from Munich: 'Then Soden should do his duty and tell the stuck-up Wittelsbachs that what the King of Württemberg does is nobody else's business!'[101] The Kaiser regarded the close relationship between Grand Duke Ludwig IV of Hesse-Darmstadt and the British and Russian royal families with suspicion. Ludwig had been married to Princess Alice of Great Britain, the Empress Frederick's sister, who had died in 1878, and his daughter Ella was married to the younger brother of Tsar Alexander III. When Schweinitz reported early in 1889 that the Grand Duke was to prolong his stay in St Petersburg until after the Tsar's birthday, Wilhelm wrote scornfully on the report: 'I'll be damned a million times! He'll be given the title of a Russian grand duke next!'[102] To the amazement of many, Wilhelm II's behaviour was quite different in the case of another German prince with British connections. When his great-uncle Duke Ernst II of Saxe-Coburg and Gotha died in August 1893, the Kaiser was said to have 'knelt, or as some say lain, before the coffin, bathed in tears', as Waldersee reported, although he was unable to take the imperial grief seriously, as Duke Ernst had 'never been really close to the Kaiser', and it could 'not have escaped the latter's attention how little esteem the Duke had enjoyed in the world'. In Waldersee's eyes there could indeed be 'scarcely anyone who does a throne so little honour as this Coburger'. The late Duke, he maintained, had been 'a man of a very low moral calibre', who was 'a thoroughly bad character, false, lying, a braggart and an intriguer'. The successor to the dukedom was Alfred, Duke of Edinburgh, Queen Victoria's second son, which was at first considered undesirable, as a British prince and admiral seemed unlikely to make a satisfactory German ruling prince. But the mood changed when the new Duke 'chased away' some of his predecessor's favourites and mistresses.[103]

The Kaiser was particularly enraged by King Karl of Württemberg's habit of spending the winter enjoying the delights of life on the French Riviera with his homosexual American favourites. On a report from Stuttgart he recommended that 'the person in question be advised that it is not fitting for ruling princes of the Reich to amuse themselves in Cannes in international company, while German citizens have no rights or protection in France'. Wilhelm had to admit, however, that 'unfortunately' other German princely personages were just as disinclined to allow the tense political situation to deter them from spending every winter in Cannes or Nice.[104] After King Karl's death in October 1891 Waldersee warned the Kaiser against the particularist inclinations of his successor, Wilhelm II of Württemberg, whose anti-Prussian attitude was reinforced by the influence of his Hofmarschall Plato, 'a very nasty fellow', and of his scheming wife. 'The Kaiser, however, considered that he had such a hold over the Prince [Wilhelm] that he would not be able to step out of line.'[105] In the end there were only two federal princes for whom Wilhelm II retained a certain respect: King Albert of Saxony and Grand Duke Friedrich of Baden, but even their influence on the young Kaiser was limited and temporary, as we shall see.

There was, however, one instance in which the Kaiser's closest confidants thought they could still detect an uncharacteristic youthful diffidence on his part, which indicated that he 'still did not [have] a sufficiently strong sense of being sovereign and kaiser in dealing with his older relatives'. 'Time must change that', Herbert Bismarck observed.[106] This remark related to the uneasy impression which the Kaiser made in his conversations with Philipp Eulenburg on 2 January 1889 about the 'strange Guelphic ambitions' of Prince Albrecht of Prussia, an uncle of the Kaiser, who had been acting as regent in Brunswick since 1885. Albrecht was married to Princess Marie of Saxe-Altenburg, whose aunt was the mother of Duke Ernst August of Cumberland, the pretender to the throne of Hanover, Brunswick and Lüneburg, hence Wilhelm's suspicions. Yet the Kaiser, so Eulenburg reported to Herbert Bismarck, was unusually restrained in his condemnation of his uncle's 'Guelphic ambitions'. 'I have so much admiration for him – he has so much admiration for me', Wilhelm had declared. Eulenburg gained the impression from this conversation 'that it is painful for His Majesty to play preceptor to his uncle'.[107] Later Wilhelm confided to his best friend that he was deeply concerned for Prince Albrecht's 'character and frame of mind in general'. 'The various cures which my uncle undertakes in Dresden are officially intended to strengthen his nerves. In fact matters are much more serious: by taking colossal quantities of snuff he has overstrained the nerves in his head and nose so much that the effects of the overstrain are already spreading dangerously towards the brain. In short, nicotine poisoning of the brain through snuff is looming in the background; this could lead to a cold-water treatment institution or a lunatic asylum.'[108]

Nothing demonstrated more clearly the human and political fragility of the traditional monarchical world which Kaiser Wilhelm II represented and was determined to uphold against the tide of changing times than the death of his contemporary and erstwhile friend, Crown Prince Rudolf of Austria, in Mayerling on 29 January 1889. With good reason Herbert Bismarck reported to Friedrichsruh that the Kaiser was 'very shocked' by this event and could 'even now scarcely believe that it was suicide'.[109] The Austrian ambassador in Berlin reported that after hearing the news of the death the Kaiser had spent a considerable time with him, 'and I can assure you that he did not put on any conventional demonstration of sorrow, but showed a profound sense of shock and a sincere, heartfelt sympathy. The Kaiser could not keep still, moving about constantly, sometimes standing, sometimes sitting, and everything he said revealed his inner agitation.' Wilhelm expressed the wish, 'only natural' for him although it remained unfulfilled, of going to Vienna in person for the funeral, Széchényi reported. Again, after the memorial service in Berlin, Wilhelm and the Kaiserin lingered for some time at the Austrian embassy and demonstrated 'the heartfelt sympathy and deep distress with which Their Majesties were both filled'. The Kaiserin had been exceedingly upset by the news, Széchényi reported, and had broken down in tears.[110] Through Rudolf's friend Prince Philipp of Coburg, however, Wilhelm heard, as he wrote to Queen Victoria, 'that lunacy was looming in the background & that the monomania of suicide had done its silent but sure work on the overexcitable brain'.[111] When Wilhelm was about to visit the grave of 'the unfortunate Rudolf' for the first time in September 1890 Auguste Viktoria wrote feelingly: 'A friend of your youth in the same position in life, and *how* different, thank God, the course of your lives! One can easily see there what a difference it makes whether someone has built on the right ground or not!!'[112]

In the judgement of many contemporaries, above all those who knew nothing about the torments of his childhood, Kaiser Wilhelm II's blatant arrogance was a consequence of the apparently carefree life he had led hitherto. Thus for instance Vice-Admiral Hoffmann commented in 1889 while on board ship with the Kaiser: 'Great self-esteem is an essential characteristic of the Kaiser ... With a young, very gifted person, who suddenly becomes Kaiser, who has never had any unpleasant experiences, for whom everything is made palatable, it can hardly turn out otherwise. The great eloquence which he possesses to a rare degree is also part of it. Yesterday he told us that neither the Kaiser of Austria nor the King of Italy was able to say a single word of their own accord; they read every after-dinner speech etc. from a paper.'[113] Whatever the truth of that may be, it is quite clear that his strange imperial ideology and his extraordinary self-satisfaction led him to despise weaker and less imperious fellow monarchs to an extent which is probably unequalled in the history of the royal houses of Europe.

Surveying the ruling dynasties at the time of Kaiser Wilhelm II's accession, however, one is forced to admit that his sense of superiority, viewed objectively, was not altogether unfounded. With the possible exception of the British royal family, among monarchs and their heirs there was no prince who came anywhere near Wilhelm in eloquence, energy or breadth of interests, no charismatic power-figure to match him. Wherever he looked he saw suicide, abdication, imminent (or actual) madness, marital breakdown, sexual excess, conceited narrow-mindedness, petty bourgeois obtuseness, sheer incapacity and poisonous scheming. In comparison with his 'colleagues' Wilhelm could indeed be seen, in spite of all his failings, as 'the most important man in Europe', as a British peer was later to describe him,[114] and likewise in 1910, after the death of King Edward VII, a South German baron was able to say of Wilhelm II: 'Now that his Uncle-King is dead, he is more than ever the decisive voice in the world. He and Roosevelt will be the masters of history from now on.'[115] At any rate his experiences with his fellow monarchs can only have reinforced his conviction that Prussia–Germany under the Hohenzollerns had been chosen by God and world history to be the bulwark of the 'monarchical principle'. Doubts as to whether his dizzyingly ambitious monarchical programme was at all practicable under such circumstances clearly did not enter his mind in these early years.

### THE KAISER AND GERMAN SOCIETY

Internally the Kaiser's monarchical ideology expressed itself on the one hand in his glorification of the armed services, the Protestant Church and the aristocracy as the natural pillars of the throne, and on the other in his contempt for civilians and above all for Left Liberal and Social Democratic parliamentarians, Catholics and Jews. In August 1888 he took over the patronage of the Protestant Order of St John of Jerusalem and gave a speech in Sonnenburg in which he alluded to the 'great tasks' which lay before him 'in the sphere of the inner development of my people'. Elaborating on this theme, he declared: 'In order to raise up the people, to strengthen and develop their moral and religious feeling, I need the support of the noblest of them, of my noblemen . . . I hope with all my heart that I may succeed . . . in bringing about the elevation of the spirit of religion and Christian discipline and morality in the people, and thus in achieving the high aims which I have set myself as ideals.'[116] Not only Wilhelm's mother and her left liberal Progressive Party friends were incensed at this speech; even aristocratic diplomats found that 'to address that band of frauds the Order of St John of Jerusalem as "the noblest of the nobility" . . . was going a little too far'.[117]

Civilians, above all democratically minded ones, were third-class citizens for Wilhelm. Not long after his accession he declared to the Italian ambassador Count Launay: 'After the French, the people I hate most are diplomats and deputies.'[118] He made it abundantly clear what sort of behaviour he expected of his diplomats and officials in a crude comment in the margin of a submission in which Prince Hohenlohe had argued for the title of governor to be conferred on the most senior officials in all German colonies. 'As far as I am concerned the gentlemen can stick a blue button in their navels and a peacock feather up their arses too! So long as they pay increased attention to their duty to match their increased rank.'[119] Some of his remarks about civil servants were simply insulting. He described Burghard Freiherr von Cramm, the veteran delegate to the Bundesrat from Brunswick, as 'this evil little toad!'[120] Referring to one of his diplomats, who presumably had a conspicuously large nose, Wilhelm wrote on a report submitted to him by the Reich Chancellor: 'With this gentleman's facial characteristics he only needs to put on a fez and anyone would take him for a Cretan fellow at the very least, if not indeed for an Armenian!'[121] He spoke of members of parliament and other elected politicians with deep contempt. When he visited the King of Italy in Rome in October 1888 he remarked: 'At home [in Germany] if one sees a black coat and asks "Who is that?", if the answer is a deputy, one turns one's back on him.'[122] When he was informed from Madrid that the American President Cleveland did not wish to call on the King of Spain for 'democratic' reasons, Wilhelm II wrote: 'Once a bumpkin always a bumpkin!'[123] On a diplomatic report from St Petersburg about the French ambassador there, Count Gustave Lannes de Montebello, the Kaiser wrote that one could not expect decent behaviour 'from a republican'.[124] When Wilhelm and his entourage were compared by a French newspaper to Friedrich Wilhelm I and his tobacco club, the Kaiser noted in the margin: '*He* would not have sat down with civilians.'[125] But on reading another report from France, according to which the French army command was financially independent of parliament and had raised army units without budgetary authorisation, Wilhelm commented: 'That is exactly right . . . I shall do the same if the Reichstag does not consent.' He gave orders for the 'excellent' article to be 'thoroughly aired and discussed in the press'.[126]

The Progressive movement, which advocated the parliamentarisation of the Prusso-German military monarchy on British lines, and which had been particularly closely associated with his father and mother, was singled out for Kaiser Wilhelm II's special contempt. On 18 October 1888, Friedrich III's birthday, an article in memory of the late Kaiser appeared in the *Berliner Zeitung*, which

Wilhelm II passed on to Bismarck as, in his words, 'proof of the attitude border-ing on lèse-majesté of the democratic Press'.[127] A few days later, in a speech to a deputation from the city of Berlin, which had come to greet him on his return from Rome and to present him with the deed of gift of the fountain designed for the Schloss by Reinhold Begas, the Kaiser declared that he had encountered warm sympathy for the German Reich among the foreign rulers and people he had visited, but that he had also brought back a 'most painful' memory from his journey. 'While I have invested all My health and strength in creating bonds of friendship in order to ensure the peace and welfare of our Fatherland, and thus also of its capital city, the daily newspapers of My capital city and My residence have dragged the affairs of My family before the public and discussed them in a way which a private citizen would never have accepted. This does not only painfully affect Me, but it has also aroused My anger. Above all I must insist that the continual invoking of My Father against My person should finally cease. It offends Me very deeply as a son and is unfitting in the highest degree. It is My expectation that, if I choose Berlin as My principal residence – and as a Berliner I am always drawn back here – others will abstain from making the intimate relationships of My family a subject for discussion in the press.'[128] Thereupon the Kaiser dismissed the deputation without shaking hands with the Chief Burgomaster Max von Forckenbeck, who was a Progressive, and without allowing the members of the deputation to be presented to him.

There was general astonishment and bewilderment at this speech.[129] The Austrian chargé d'affaires reported to Vienna: 'Various gentleman of the court, high-ranking officers and government officials expressed to me the fear that the incident in question would make a highly unfavourable impression on the broad mass of the population, and would be, so to speak, grist to the mill of the Progressive Party. It is considered that the occasion was ill chosen for the Kaiser to express his otherwise well-justified indignation against the activities of a certain party, just at the moment when the city is preparing to offer a lasting tribute to the Kaiser in grateful remembrance of His Majesty's journey, and it is thought that the imperial words were misdirected, as one cannot hold the Chief Burgomaster of Berlin responsible for the behaviour of a section of the national press.'[130] The British chargé d'affaires, Beauclerk, was likewise of the opinion that Wilhelm's speech would cost the government camp many votes in the forthcoming elections. No one really knew, he commented, which newspaper reports the Kaiser meant to condemn – whether it was the article about the Battenberg marriage project, Sir Morell Mackenzie's published defence of himself or Friedrich III's war diary that had aroused the Kaiser's fury. Everyone thought that to castigate the Berlin deputation for newspaper articles which they had neither inspired nor could control had been extremely inappropriate and unwise. 'In fact the speech can only be regarded as one more of the regrettable incidents which seem to be becoming of almost daily occurrence in this city . . . The speech forms the one subject of conversation in all circles here. It is remarked that His Majesty showed scant courtesy to the Members of the Town Council who, though nearly all prominent Liberals, have little or nothing to do with the Control of the Press; and the words addressed to them are generally deplored and condemned.'[131]

Friedrich von Holstein was also concerned about the effect of the speech, and thought that its timing was 'extraordinary', just when the City of Berlin had spent several thousand marks on the fountain to please the Kaiser. He could only imagine that the Kaiser's 'remarkable address' had been a consequence of Herbert Bismarck's campaign against the Progressive newspapers, 'in which Kaiser Friedrich III's reign and personality are always contrasted favourably with the present'.[132] Holstein was undoubtedly right in this assumption. When the malicious rumour was spread in the Left Liberal and Catholic press that the Kaiser's anger had been directed not at the Progressive press, but at the pro-government Kartell parties and especially at Count Douglas's speech, the Bismarcks felt compelled to persuade the Kaiser to issue a categorical statement. 'It seems to me', Herbert Bismarck wrote to his father, 'that after this systematic, deliberate, uniform pack of lies has been circulated by the radical press of the whole world we should make . . , an authoritative declaration that: "H.M. meant the Progressive press, and in particular the exploitation of the diary [of Friedrich III]." Shall I put this to H.M. in audience? I am afraid that otherwise the false rumour will take root.'[133] With the Chancellor's approval Herbert 'extracted' an appropriate declaration against the left-liberal newspapers from the Kaiser in an audience on 3 November.[134]

Almost as strong as Wilhelm II's hatred for the Progressives was his antipathy at this time towards the Catholic Centre Party led by Ludwig Windthorst. On a report from Dresden according to which the death of both Counts Platen had removed the principal supporters in Saxony of the Guelphic dynasty, the Kaiser wrote in January 1889: 'Good . . . May Windhorst [sic] follow soon!'[135] Another Centre Party leader he dubbed a 'blockhead' who had 'ridiculous ideas' and talked 'rubbish'.[136] He called the participants in the German Catholic assembly in Munich 'insolent hounds' against whom one must 'at all costs give cover' to the pro-Prussian Bavarian government of Freiherr von Lutz. 'Give Lutz strong support against the blacks [i.e. the clericals] and assure him from here of my warmest approval and interest', he ordered. On the Kaiser's personal instructions the Bavarian Minister-President was given the Order of the Black Eagle in the summer of 1889.[137] In countless sarcastic marginal notes the Kaiser also mocked the Pope and Vatican policy. Very soon after acceding to the throne he called Pope Leo XIII a 'sheep!' and an 'old idiot!', and exclaimed: 'The old man must have gone mad!'[138] Ten years later the imperial tone showed no sign of mellowing. The Pope was an 'old donkey' and 'an incorrigible old bletherer', who was probably 'cracked', Wilhelm wrote on the reports of his envoys to the Holy See.[139] Of the papal hopes for a restoration of temporal power with Germany's help Wilhelm wrote: 'Might it already have got very hot in Rome? In that case an icy blast would be a good thing . . . We'll be damned if we do any such thing!'[140]

As far as the Kaiser's attitude to his half-million Jewish subjects is concerned, the evidence shows that in the period immediately following his accession Wilhelm's anti-Semitism remained as vehement as before. Waldersee's diary bears witness to the fact that during his visits to the Marmorpalais and then to the Berlin Schloss 'the Jewish question' was often the subject of 'lively conversation'.[141] In September 1888 the Chief of the General Staff recorded that the Kaiser 'in truth [could] not bear Jews', and that the monarch had also 'often stated' this.[142] The following month Waldersee noted indignantly in a lengthy diary entry that people were now trying 'to depict the Kaiser as the Jews' friend, or at least as no enemy of the Jews'; that alone was enough to show how influential the Jews had become. When Wilhelm II came to the throne, Waldersee continued, the Jews had been very worried about their future because they did not know how the new Kaiser would act towards them; but now, as no measures had been taken against them, they were full of confidence and had 'gone on the offensive; they know that they have many friends among the National Liberals and Free Conservatives and they are trying to ally themselves with them so as to attack the Conservatives, in whom they see their only enemies'. Waldersee was convinced, however, that Kaiser Wilhelm II's basic anti-Semitic attitude had not changed in the slightest. 'In my view the Kaiser's antipathy towards Jewry, at least towards the arrogance it shows so plainly, towards the sucking-dry of Christians' as well as towards the excessive influence which the Jews exercised, 'is so deeply rooted that not even Bismarck can do anything about it'. Of course, Waldersee reflected, 'whether the Kaiser is strong enough to keep up a perpetual front against the Jews is another question; no doubt we have already sunk too far into this affliction to be able to find a legal [sic!] way out of it again'.[143] Towards the end of 1891, when the anti-Semitic movement was growing alarmingly and spreading into ever broader circles, Waldersee, who must have known precisely what the situation was, again noted: 'The Kaiser is a decided enemy of the Jews and has often said so, right up until very recently, and has called Bleichröder a dog and a scoundrel often enough, but he is not in a position to see through what is going on because he has many dealings with people who are of Jewish origin or who are completely dependent on Jews.'[144]

The marginal comments made by Wilhelm II and locked away in the Foreign Office safe by Bismarck leave the accuracy of Waldersee's assessment of Wilhelm in no doubt. When in the spring of 1889 the Kaiser read a report in a British newspaper of a conspiracy against the Tsar, in which Jews were said to have been implicated, he annotated the report with 'Those dogs, of course!!'[145] A few weeks later he read of the appointment of Nathaniel Mayer Rothschild, on whom Queen Victoria had already conferred a peerage in 1885, as lord lieutenant of Buckinghamshire. He wrote derisively in the margin: 'I'll be damned!! Incredible! Perhaps we should consider appointing Bleichröder governor of Pomerania now!?'[146] In November 1889, when Schlözer reported to Berlin that the papal nuncio in Vienna, Cardinal Luigi Galimberti, 'had been staying, in the company of a beautiful woman of Semitic origin, with whom he seemed to have a very close relationship', at the Adriatic resort of Abbazia, Wilhelm commented: 'The lucky fellow! It is better that he sees the Semitic beauty only in the evening!'[147] The contrast with the attitude of his uncle, the Prince of Wales, was stark. Prince Ernst zu Hohenlohe-Langenburg, who was attached to the German embassy in London, wrote in the summer of 1889 that the heir to the British throne often took him with him to visit Jewish families, 'who give very good dinners in magnificent houses. They play an important part in society here. It is at their houses that one sees the most elegant people and the most beautiful women and enjoys oneself the most. As the Prince is very much in favour of them, I have no reason to be fastidious.'[148] When Wilhelm II read a newspaper account in June 1889 of the Prince of Wales's visit to Auteuil, during which his uncle had accepted an invitation from Baron Gustave de Rothschild to go out for a drive in his carriage, he wrote on the report: 'Good Heavens! My son sitting next to Bleichröder's coachman would be a very odd sight in the Thiergarten.'[149] If a diplomat criticised a foreign envoy in an official dispatch, the Kaiser might well note in the margin: 'He was a Jew too!'[150] When Schweinitz reported in 1891 that a Mr White had arrived in St Petersburg to negotiate with Pobedonostzew on behalf of Baron Hirsch over the emigration of Russian Jews to Argentina, Wilhelm II commented 'Fancy that!', adding that Hirsch was after all 'the friend of "Ich Dien"' — that is, of the Prince of Wales. But he added regretfully: 'If only we could send ours [i.e. Germany's Jews] there too.'[151]

Kaiser Wilhelm II's animosity towards Jews, recorded in such marginalia and also in Waldersee's diary, was anything but peripheral: rather, it formed a key element of his thinking, even if for tactical reasons it had to be hidden from public view. His anti-Semitic attitude lay at the root of many of his actions and utterances and it explains much that contemporary and later observers found baffling. We have seen how for most people the Kaiser's hostile speech to the Berlin city deputation at the presentation of the Schloss fountain on 27 October 1888 seemed utterly incomprehensible. Waldersee and his ultra-conservative party friends knew, however, exactly what was going on in Wilhelm's mind: the deputation had consisted principally of 'Progressive Jewish gentlemen', whose intention it had been 'to get themselves on a good footing with the Kaiser in the eyes of the world, and if possible to reclaim him for their own'. Wilhelm's first concern had been to defend himself against this by taking harsh action.[152] We shall examine the demonic role that his hatred of Jews was to play in the Bismarck crisis in more detail later.

The Kaiser's anti-Semitic attitude almost inevitably brought him close to the Wagnerian circle out of which, even in these early days, a dangerous counterforce to the pragmatic statecraft embodied by Bismarck was growing. Immediately after his accession Wilhelm II wrote a letter to Cosima Wagner which led her to hope that the Kaiser might agree to become the patron of the Bayreuth festival. She sent a fulsome reply on 23 August: 'Your Majesty's graciousness towards me is too great to allow me to feel any apprehension that I aroused Your Majesty's displeasure with my request. Nevertheless I beg Your Majesty most humbly to forgive me that I . . . took the liberty of laying this supplication at Your Majesty's feet . . . Your Majesty's most gracious words to me filled my soul like a divine summons, and with hot tears, in the solitude in which my feeling for myself and for the work is most profound, I praised and thanked God that the protection which we need is coming to us from the most exalted height. Now I could understand why I had suffered, and far more powerful than any suffering was the feeling of hope which penetrated my heart with Your Majesty's words . . . Whatever decision Your Majesty reaches, . . . all will be sacred to me, and with feelings that I could never put into words and which turn to God as my most fervent prayer, I beg the All-Highest Lord for grace to be allowed to subscribe myself Your Majesty's most thankful, humblest servant Cosima Wagner.'[153]

This letter, which recalls Philipp Eulenburg's style, initially did not fail to achieve its aim. As Head of the Civil Cabinet Hermann von Lucanus informed the Reich Chancellor on 18 September, 'His Majesty . . . [was] not disinclined to grant this request, particularly as the All-Highest has reason to believe that His Royal Highness the Regent of Bavaria does not take a very close interest in the festival.'[154] The Kaiser's inclination to accept the patronage was encouraged by Philipp Eulenburg, who had been responsible for establishing the connection between Wilhelm and Bayreuth through their visit to see *Parsifal* together in the summer of 1886.[155] In the press too there was support for the Kaiser's taking over the patronage of Bayreuth 'in the interests of national art': his predilection for the works of Wagner was described as characteristic of 'the Kaiser's disposition and taste', and the imperial patronage was presented as a fait accompli.[156] Bismarck, however, was firmly opposed to the idea, expressing grave doubts about it in a submission to the Kaiser on 20 September. For one thing, he wrote, he feared that the monarch would find himself being called upon increasingly for financial support for the festival. Moreover he believed that 'closer personal contacts between Your [Majesty] and the festival would give new nourishment to the mistrust of the Bavarians, which we have with difficulty but successfully overcome, with regard to the maintenance of their position vis-à-vis the kaiserdom, and would furnish the Ultramontane and Jesuit party with plausible excuses for stirring up feeling against us in Bavaria. Precisely because Bayreuth belongs to the Old Brandenburg lands, and because no one in Bavaria has forgotten that it was only after lengthy and difficult negotiations that Kaiser Wilhelm I granted the cession of Bayreuth, and because the similarity of religious denomination in itself already inclines the Franconian provinces to look northwards, precisely for these reasons Bayreuth is a sensitive point for Bavarian rivalries and fears.' He was therefore convinced 'that the fulfilment of the wish of Frau Cosima Wagner would be a favour which would not fail to be financially exploited at the expense of Your Majesty, and that a patronage held by Your [Majesty] in Bayreuth would harm the internal political situation of the German Reich in no small degree'. As in the case of the Stoecker meeting in the autumn of 1887, Bismarck again warned the Kaiser 'in the All-Highest interest to decline connections with private associations, whether in the form of patronage or in any other form, as it is very difficult for the sovereign to defend himself from the financial and even political exploitation which inevitably arises from such connections'.[157] This submission was laid before the Kaiser on his return from Italy by Herbert Bismarck, but for lack of time the Kaiser could look at it 'only fleetingly', and he therefore took no immediate decision.[158] On 31 October 1888, the Reich Chancellor was able to have a personal audience with the monarch to discuss this awkward affair. As Herbert informed the Head of the Civil Cabinet afterwards, Wilhelm had decided 'to decline the patronage'.[159] Prince Regent Luitpold of Bavaria took over the patronage a few months later.

Harmony between Kaiser and Chancellor was more easily achieved when it came to freemasonry, since Wilhelm showed he fully understood the necessity of maintaining the connection between the monarchy and the freemasons, even though – unlike his father and grandfather – he refused to join the movement himself. As Wilhelm's brother Heinrich had no wish to become a member either, the Kaiser suggested that Prince Friedrich Leopold of Prussia – who was to marry the Kaiserin's younger sister in June 1889 – should be appointed honorary patron of the three Old Prussian lodges, for it was 'an old tradition' that 'a royal prince' should be a freemason.[160] Bismarck was 'in complete agreement with H.M.'s intention to nominate Prince Leopold to the freemasons . . .; he said that freemasonry, like Judaism, was an element that had considerable influence and should therefore not be alienated from the monarchy'.[161] The arch-conservative Waldersee naturally had less understanding for this statesmanlike gesture, and when a few years later Wilhelm 'created' a special order for Prince Leopold in his role as a high dignitary of the freemasons and even allowed his brother-in-law to wear this order 'at non-masonic occasions', the General poured scorn on this symbolic concession to the Liberals and remarked that he was prepared to believe that the Kaiser 'is even beginning to flirt with the idea of becoming a freemason himself'.[162]

In the domain of foreign politics, which both sides – the thirty-year-old monarch and the 74-year old Chancellor – regarded as their sphere of activity par excellence, it was far harder for them to agree. Since the 'Supreme War Lord' also saw himself as an 'officer' and looked on military questions as a field in which he alone, by virtue of his powers of command and without any civilian 'interference', should give the orders, the risk of conflict breaking out over foreign policy or military matters was particularly high. What were Wilhelm's views in this sphere, and how far did they coincide or conflict with the policies pursued by the Bismarcks?

# CHAPTER SIX

# First steps in foreign affairs

WILHELM II had shown a lively interest in foreign affairs even before his accession. From the very beginning of his reign he took to annotating diplomatic and military reports with angry, contemptuous and often crude comments describing statesmen and diplomats of foreign powers as 'scoundrels', 'blackguards', 'villains', 'swine', 'hounds', 'filthy hounds', 'insolent dogs', 'curs', 'apes', 'dolts', 'asses', 'toads', 'milksops' and other such epithets.[1] Whatever other conclusions may be drawn from marginalia of this kind, they are clear evidence of the passionate intensity with which the Kaiser followed the course of international affairs. But can one detect in these spontaneous and sporadic utterances any coherent elements which might indicate, if not a systematic foreign policy, at least a pattern of thought where foreign affairs were concerned? To answer this question we shall need to take a closer look at Wilhelm's attitude towards the major European powers during the period immediately following his accession.

## THE 'APPROACHING BATTLE WITH FRANCE AND RUSSIA'

The Kaiser's initial hopes of reviving the eastern Three Kaiser Alliance against France, Great Britain and the parliamentary systems prevalent in western Europe were dashed within a matter of weeks. The reason for this was the cool, if not positively frosty conduct of the Russian imperial family, together with the continuing Russian and French rearmament which seemed to indicate that a general war was in the offing. The aspirations of friendship with which Wilhelm had set out on his state visit to St Petersburg were replaced by feelings of frustration and offence. He did not set much store by the influence of Alexander III, whom he considered to be under the thumb of his Danish wife and his francophile advisers: the Tsar, he commented, clearly had 'not the faintest idea' about the belligerent intentions of the Russian military establishment.[2] The Kaiser's relations with Nicholas, the heir to the Russian throne, remained cool and distant. When the latter planned to stop for an hour and a half in Berlin early in the morning of 13 November 1888 on his way to Darmstadt he asked to be left alone and to be received by the Kaiser only on his return journey.[3] The subsequent visit of the 'strikingly small, . . . very ill-at-ease and gauche' Tsarevich to Berlin on 21–2 November was not a success. 'People were very polite to him here', Waldersee noted, and the Kaiser even went so far as to be 'very warm', but Nicholas 'seemed to me to remain extraordinarily cold', and his entourage likewise avoided anything 'which could in any way be connected with politics'.[4] The Kaiser's disillusionment was so profound that at the official reception for his thirtieth birthday on 27 January 1889 he shook hands demonstratively with the Austrian, Italian and British ambassadors but not with the Russian ambassador Count Shuvalov. 'I am convinced that it was on purpose', the anti-Russian Chief of the General Staff noted with satisfaction, 'for the Kaiser is very displeased with the conduct of the Russian imperial family.'[5] In March 1889 Waldersee concluded that as far as Russia was concerned the Kaiser was 'without any illusions and quite certain that we have no friends there any more'.[6]

Wilhelm II now kept a very close eye on the Russian troop movements and the mobilisation of the Russian Empire by land and sea. Before his accession he had noted on a military attaché's report on Russian operational plans that it was clear 'that a very precise system is being followed in order to ensure at all events – while taking advantage of our loyally standing by and consenting – an initial victory, and to disrupt their opponent's deployment of his forces . . . So there is twice as much hurry for our artillery!!'[7] After his failed attempt to ingratiate himself at Peterhof in July 1888 he returned to this earlier attitude. In early August 1888 a dispatch from Count Yorck von Wartenburg reached Berlin from St Petersburg, reporting that Russian non-commissioned officers who were prepared to remain at the front until July 1890 were to receive a bonus of 150 rubles. This information prompted an excited marginal note by the Kaiser: 'It would be of interest to check to see whether within the period of time specified here (until 1890) the big ships in the Black Sea are fitted out and made ready to sail. For if that were the case, an advance on Stamboul possibly through Bulgaria would not be unthinkable.'[8] In the ensuing months Wilhelm wrote note after note on diplomatic dispatches from St Petersburg and Paris. 'Yet another proof of the calm and uninterrupted progress of what are obviously systematic preparations for a war! All this persistence would be worthy of a better cause!'[9] Or, similarly: 'The view I have often expressed, that the French war preparations are tacitly but indisputably linked to those of Russia, is further borne out by this report! Avis au lecteur! So we must get to work strengthening

our army at home, especially the artillery!'[10] When in late 1888 he heard of
Russian troop movements towards the west he concluded that they marked the
last stage of a programme that had begun several years earlier and declared: 'So
now the deployment is completed and – – –. What comes next we shall no doubt
find out!'[11] In November 1888 when news arrived from Warsaw of the transfer
of the 19th Russian Division from the Caucasus to the Austro-Hungarian border,
Wilhelm again inferred that a Russian attack was in the offing and wrote: 'If it
has already come to the point when Ural Cossacks, Kirghizes etc. are brought
over from the steppes, that is deployment in preparation for a later attack in the
fullest sense of the word!'[12]

Confronted with such russophobic marginalia, the Reich Chancellor felt
obliged to reveal the secrets of his foreign policy in a memorandum for Wilhelm
dated 19 August 1888. Bismarck asked the monarch to burn his letter 'after due
perusal', as it referred to matters and questions which as a rule he did not think it
expedient to commit to paper. In particular, the Chancellor's letter mentioned the
secret Reinsurance Treaty concluded between Germany and Russia in 1887 for
a period of three years, although he conceded that this agreement clashed 'with
our Austro-Italian obligations'. Alluding to the marginalia in which Wilhelm
warned of an approaching attack by Russia on Turkey, the Chancellor argued
that in view of confidential remarks made repeatedly by high-ranking Russian
statesmen during the treaty negotiations, he was of the opinion that, although
both the Russian army and the Russian Black Sea fleet would indeed be 'ready'
by 1890, this fact 'was important only as an indication of preparedness, not of
intended action'. On the other hand he did not doubt Russia's intention 'to make
a play for Constantinople and once the Black Sea fleet is ready, that is to say
in the early 1890s, choose the moment for action according to the dictates of
the situation in Europe. In my most humble estimation', the Chancellor continued, revealing the guiding principle of his foreign policy, 'it is not part of
our policy to hinder Russia in the fulfilment of her plans for Constantinople,
but to leave this entirely to other powers, if they think it in their interest; our
interest in the Bosphorus question is not worth the major war on two fronts that
a clash with Russia would entail; on the contrary, if Russia becomes involved
there, she will become less dangerous for us because she will withdraw from our
frontier and because there will be a provocative tension in her relations with
the Mediterranean powers, particularly with England and in the long run also
with France.' If Russia eventually secured 'control over the opening and closing
of the Bosphorus by occupying a fortified position, she will be able to use her
expansionist power against Persia and India. That will make it impossible for
England to maintain her present fiction that she is an indifferent spectator, and
we can wait and see how the constellation of the remaining powers develops,

since a Russian attack on Constantinople does not in itself constitute a casus foederis between Austria and ourselves.'[13]

This machiavellian, indeed almost diabolical peace strategy was beyond the comprehension of both Kaiser Wilhelm II and his mentor, the newly appointed Chief of the General Staff Count von Waldersee. Both dismissed Bismarck's hope for a Russian war against Turkey in which Germany would not intervene as a 'delusion'.[14] Instead, they considered that a war in the near future, between Germany, Austria-Hungary and Italy on the one hand and Russia and France on the other, was not only inevitable but also – at the right moment – thoroughly desirable. For Wilhelm and Waldersee, both Russia and France were irreconcilable enemies of the German Reich and had to be defeated in good time before they had the chance to destroy Germany. As his notorious speech of 16 August 1888 at Frankfurt an der Oder had already made plain,[15] in addition to his mounting russophobia a constant factor in Wilhelm II's view of the world was his pronounced hatred for republican France.[16] When for example in November 1888 the French General de Miribel made a speech expressing confidence that the sons would win through where their fathers had won through before them, Wilhelm wrote, just as he had done as Prince, that 'Lutetia' – Paris – would have to be 'destroyed'. 'Just as the fathers came over our border as prisoners, the sons will have to do so too! Nomen omen! Caeterum [sic] censeo Lutetiam etc.'[17] The following month, when Schweinitz, the German ambassador in St Petersburg, reported to Berlin that the Russian army had ordered 1.5 million rifles, but that it would take at least five more years for them to be made, Wilhelm noted on the report that this news at any rate gave Germany the 'opportunity to smash the Gauls'.[18]

In this bellicose attitude the young Kaiser was powerfully seconded by Waldersee. The Chief of the General Staff convinced the monarch that the Russians, in systematic collusion with the French, were preparing to attack Germany and Austria-Hungary soon. Russia was aiming to be 'ready by the end of the year', even if it did not make an immediate strike then, Waldersee claimed in September 1888.[19] During an audience in March 1889 the two discussed in detail German prospects in a war with France, and Waldersee stated his view that in war it was 'absolutely immaterial who had been right or wrong at the outset. In the long run only the victor was right.' When the Kaiser expressed the opinion that 'we must also be prepared to fight the great battle alone', the Chief of the General Staff added that in fact 'all alliances suffer from great weaknesses, and I hoped that we would be victorious even if we were alone; Germany was still in the ascendant, and I had the greatest faith in her future. The Kaiser agreed with me and spoke with complete confidence.'[20] Waldersee admitted in April 1889, however, that in fact the German army still needed 'a year and a half of peace . . . in order to be ready', as 'the French [were] still a year to eighteen months ahead'. 'So we must not act too boldly', he warned.[21] Nevertheless the great war could not be put off for too long, in his view, since Austria would be 'encircled' as a result of Russian efforts to undermine the countries in the Russian sphere of influence south and east of the Danube monarchy, and would thus become increasingly incapable of taking action. This development was putting Austria 'into a worse and worse situation . . . and unfortunately the same is true for us'.[22] Reading these documents one might easily believe they were reports from the years immediately preceding the First World War.

The latent opposition between Kaiser and Chancellor in their assessments of the international political and military situation created a potential time bomb of which the Chief of the General Staff was fully aware. In the autumn of 1888 he noted in his diary: 'The Chancellor does not entirely trust the Kaiser as regards either internal or external political affairs and lives in a very salutary state of anxiety that the Kaiser may occasionally come out with his own ideas; meanwhile I myself am always regarded with a certain disquiet.'[23] Nevertheless Waldersee availed himself of every opportunity to 'contest the Chancellor's view that our opponents are gradually becoming weaker and weaker'.[24] When reports on improvements in the French army reached Berlin in October 1888, Waldersee saw them as renewed proof of his 'long-held view that we have missed our moment. In the Foreign Office the light is slowly dawning about this. They are very much afraid there that I could become troublesome for the Chancellor by explaining the true state of affairs. I now intend', the General observed, 'to remain quite quiet until the end of the year; but then I shall conscientiously report what I believe to the Kaiser.'[25] For Waldersee, as he recorded as early as 1 November, it was 'an incontrovertible fact that the Chancellor has run aground with his policy; all his art has not helped him to prevent the Franco-Russian alliance or to get the Russians engaged in the Orient. For years things have been patched up and put off and opportune moments have been missed. Our adversaries are not getting worse as the Chancellor claims, but better. Only a particularly lucky chance, like discord in France or Russia, can preserve us from a war which we shall have to undertake under not very favourable circumstances.'[26]

The first direct clash between Wilhelm and Waldersee on the one hand and the two Bismarcks on the other came in November 1888. After he had submitted a report to the monarch on French rearmament measures and had been received for a two-hour audience on the progress of Russian rearmament, the Chief of the General Staff commented on 3 November that the Kaiser was now convinced that the general situation 'indicated a war in the course of the next year. In the face of the immense power of Russia and France the assistance of Austria and Italy should not be overestimated. We agreed', Waldersee noted after the audience, that 'the Russian measures had reached a degree which [was] no longer tolerable.' 'Unfortunately it turns out that I was right in my predictions and also that I was not wrong when I claimed that Bismarck had run himself thoroughly aground with his policy.' Waldersee rejected the Kaiser's hope for Turkish participation in a war against Russia on the grounds that the Sultan would take part in a war only if he were compelled by force to do so, and that Russia had more opportunity to use force in that regard than Germany or any other power. In the course of the discussion, Waldersee recorded, he had floated his favourite idea 'that given the seriousness of the situation we had no alternative but to bring the Poles on to our side by working towards the restoration of Poland'. The Kaiser and his Chief of the General Staff were in complete agreement as to the necessity of increasing the number of troops on Germany's eastern borders and strengthening the artillery.[27] It is no surprise that after this audience the Chancellor accused the Chief of the General Staff of stirring the Kaiser up against Russia. Waldersee, however, protested: '*I* did not excite the Kaiser's feelings at all, but found him already in this state; indeed he became even more excited after Herbert's audience which followed mine, and after which the Kaiser said to me: Schweinitz is at last beginning to think that the situation is serious.'[28]

In the following days and weeks Wilhelm II was seriously preoccupied with the thought of an approaching European war. While hunting at Königswusterhausen on 10 November he called Waldersee to see him several times 'to talk about our political situation and, in relation to that, about our armaments question'. The same theme then became the subject of a discussion lasting several hours that evening at the Berlin Schloss, in which the Foreign Secretary also took part. Waldersee described this memorable conversation as follows: 'The Kaiser was very grave and is beginning to be alarmed; he thinks that Russia and France have [agreed] to go to war soon, and he is now confirmed in this belief by the outline I gave him recently of the progress of the Russian arms preparations and by the news that the Russians are intending to take out a loan of a billion marks, while in France a similar sum is being sought for army purposes. He wishes to increase our peacetime artillery establishment substantially, and to expedite the production of the new infantry rifle.' The three men then discussed the likely attitude of Great Britain towards a European war, upon which Herbert Bismarck put forward the view that the British would be 'very foolish if they did not side with us in the great war because, if we are defeated, they would be hopelessly overpowered by France and Russia. The Kaiser quite rightly remarked', Waldersee commented, that the English were too 'short-sighted' for that. 'They wanted above all to make money and a war on the continent was the best means of doing so. What might follow was too far off for them; moreover they were scarcely in a position at the moment to achieve anything significant with their navy or army, nor did they show any inclination to prepare themselves for anything more. In addition there is Ireland, which is causing them a great deal of trouble.' The Chief of the General Staff expressed the opinion that in all probability the war would not begin on both fronts simultaneously; so it would be 'the business of the diplomats . . . to tell us how much time [we] had before we needed to reckon with the other adversary as well', for that would determine 'the deployment of our resources'. Finally the General gave 'further information on the probable intentions of the Russians' in the coming war. Summing up, he commented: 'the whole conversation was very lively and I cannot deny that [Herbert] Bismarck was very quick-witted in his remarks. The Kaiser mostly listened, but from time to time he cut in with forceful and clear opinions. The conclusion was that I reckoned our requirement with regard to increasing the peacetime artillery establishment at approximately 100 batteries; the Kaiser accepted this and ordered [Herbert] Bismarck [to inform] his father' of this decision.[29] Not surprisingly, as we learn from Waldersee's diary, the Reich Chancellor was 'very put out'[30] by the Kaiser's demand for an increase in the artillery, and no doubt still more by the manner in which this order had come about, although his subsequent invitation to the Chief of the General Staff to a confidential discussion at Friedrichsruh, in order to talk over matters which he was 'unwilling to commit to paper', was politeness itself.[31]

The attitude which Wilhelm II and Waldersee took towards a European war was, however, far less confident at this time than it had been six months earlier, for they did not rate the actual state of preparedness of the German and Austrian armies very highly in comparison to that of the French and Russian forces. At the end of November 1888 the Chief of the General Staff frankly stated his fatalistic views. Among the people in the know in Berlin, there was no one who believed that peace could be maintained until the earliest possible moment for the termination of the treaty of alliance with Austria in 1891, he said. It was therefore important 'that we should be on a good footing with Austria'. Above all Germany should 'not make Kaiser Franz Joseph, who is utterly loyal by nature, suspicious'. At the same time it was necessary for Germany 'to continue to work diligently at rearming our infantry, and if possible the artillery too, so that we shall be in good shape in early 1890. But if the circumstances are such that we must be prepared for a war next summer [1889], I suggest that it would be better to start the war at once; for at this moment it suits neither the French nor the Russians.'[32]

Towards the end of 1888, Waldersee recorded after speaking to the Kaiser that Wilhelm regarded 'the general political situation . . . as extremely grave'.[33] The General summarised his own view, which undoubtedly coincided with that of the Kaiser, in pessimistic terms: 'France and Russia are preparing to go to war together against us. We have watched this coming for years, we have seen how the clouds have gathered increasingly, but we have found no way of dispersing them, nor do we dare take the great decision to forestall them. On the other hand we do nothing to bind our friends more closely to us, and have even [made] our trustiest friend, Austria, suspicious by various measures we have taken. The Chancellor is assured from time to time that we can never win the Russians back, but he does not believe it and persists in the illusion that they might make an attack on Turkey. Unfortunately his agents scarcely dare to tell him the plain truth. I cannot deny that I do not at all like the general situation. As things are now, I have strongly urged that war should be avoided; a year ago, or best of all early this year, we would have had good prospects if we had taken action; now it is too late. The Russians have carried out considerable troop redeployments towards the west; they have also strengthened their field artillery; France has introduced a new rifle and has definitely overtaken us in this field. We must not have a war in 89 in any circumstances; we may even have to avoid it in 90. But I have not yet given up hope that our rifles will be ready by [1 April 1890]. Whether we shall succeed in postponing war for so long, however, seems to me questionable, as our weaknesses are very well known abroad.'[34]

At the beginning of 1889, Waldersee repeated that he was doing all he could to speed up the arming of the infantry so as to be 'ready to strike' in 1890, but the Reich Chancellor was opposed to this intensified rearmament 'because he is suspicious and thinks that the Kaiser could strike out whenever he considers the army ready'.[35] Philipp Eulenburg also concluded, after a visit to the Foreign Office, that Bismarck was afraid that the Kaiser might 'strike out' as soon as the army was 'prepared', and that he was therefore '*in favour of* proceeding slowly in the formation of the artillery etc.'. Eulenburg found that this view was not shared by Holstein and other officials in the Foreign Office, however; instead, they harboured 'a strong desire for very rapid preparation of the army', for 'only with *immediate* preparation would we be ready to face the situation of the moment'.[36] To his satisfaction Holstein had been able to establish from the Kaiser's marginal comments 'that the mistrust of Kaiser Wilhelm towards Russia is growing steadily'.[37] Eulenburg's interlocutors in the Wilhelmstrasse also considered 'any suspicion of Austria on His Majesty's part' very dangerous; they thought the alliance with the Danube monarchy '*absolutely essential for us*'. This was an allusion to Herbert Bismarck's anti-Austrian influence, and they deplored the fact that the 'bad treatment Herbert once received from a pair of Viennese countesses' still rankled with him.[38]

### KAISER WILHELM II AND AUSTRIA-HUNGARY

If the Kaiser and Waldersee shared the same view of the French and Russian threat, they did not at first see eye to eye over Germany's ally Austria-Hungary.

Waldersee deplored the Kaiser's mistrust of the Danube monarchy, which he attributed to Herbert Bismarck's influence and to the 'immoral' policy of the Reich Chancellor in favouring Russia at the expense of Austria.[39] He set out to open Wilhelm's eyes and to bring home to him the military necessity of strengthening the bond between Germany and Austria. 'I hope the Kaiser will take firm action once he understands the situation', Waldersee remarked in January 1889.[40] Although Wilhelm veered between the Bismarcks and Waldersee over this question it is clear that here too there was increasing potential for a future explosion.

Waldersee's attempts to support Austria and undermine the Bismarcks' pro-Russian policy can be clearly traced in his diary. On 1 November he noted: 'My impression that the Kaiser has been prejudiced against Austria has been confirmed. I am convinced that this is chiefly the work of Count [Herbert] Bismarck . . . It is a misfortune that the Bismarcks, father and son, have such an attachment to Russia and however badly things go they always come back to it. I am now quite determined to speak up resolutely for our alliance with Austria; we certainly cannot stand alone or we should undoubtedly be defeated; we need allies, as France and Russia are collaborating against us, and I do not know on whom we can count if not on Austria; certainly not on Italy. I would understand their policy if it were possible to believe that we could gain any advantage by the collapse of Austria; but this is not the case and it must be in our interest not only to uphold but also to strengthen her.'[41] Not long afterwards the Chief of the General Staff sent Bismarck a report in which he tried 'to give a better impression of the Austrian army', and drew attention to Austria's military measures in Galicia, which revealed the 'clearly discernible intention' of the Austrians to take an offensive stance in the forthcoming war.[42] But even Waldersee was indignant at the conciliatory policy followed by the government in Vienna towards the Czechs: in that way Austria would become 'first a federal state and then fall apart completely'. Bismarck's unequivocal warning to Austria that a federal state 'is considerably less acceptable to us as an ally' met with Waldersee's approval.[43]

Waldersee's subversive influence in favour of Austria and against Bismarck's policy is reflected almost verbatim in the Kaiser's marginalia. Wilhelm greeted as 'very pleasing' the news sent by Adolf von Deines, the military attaché in Vienna, that Austria wished to be as strong an ally of the German army as possible.[44] When reports arrived of the 'excellent morale' in the Austrian army, the Kaiser again welcomed this as a sign that the 'idea of *offensive* action, which is otherwise so foreign to the Austrian character', was now spreading to all parts of the army. 'If that is the case', he commented, 'there are very strong grounds indeed to hope that the Austrian army will have some healthy surprises in store for the Russians in any clash with them!'[45] Like Waldersee, the Kaiser believed that the 'logical consequence' of the Vienna government's pro-Czech policy would be 'a coronation in Prague!'[46] A report by the German Consul-General in Budapest, Count Anton Monts, which contrasted the pleasure-seeking indolence of the German-Austrian aristocracy with the industriousness of the 'small, but energetic and politically talented race' of the Hungarians, who formed a bulwark against the 'Slavic deluge', earned a delighted comment by Wilhelm II: 'A quite outstandingly well-written report! So the "transfer of the centre of gravity" to Budapest will still go ahead thanks to the greater insight and cleverness of the Hungarians!'[47] The Kaiser also spoke out strongly for the maintenance of Austrian influence in Serbia.[48] After the abdication of King Milan, which led to a marked increase of Russian influence in Serbia at Austria's expense, the Kaiser remarked while sailing between Corfu and the Albanian coast: 'One gets a real craving for annexation here; it is just as well that we shall soon be cooling off again in our cold North.'[49]

In the spring of 1889 Waldersee observed with disquiet that Wilhelm II seemed once more to have come under the pro-Russian, anti-Austrian influence of the Bismarcks. During a long walk he took with the Chief of the General Staff, the Kaiser remarked critically that Austria had refused to agree to a partition of Turkey: this 'foolishness' on the part of the Austrians, he believed, arose from their 'expansionist ideas', which were aimed at creating a huge Danubian empire stretching down to the Black Sea and across to Bessarabia and Odessa. Waldersee thought he recognised an 'old idea' of Bismarck's in these remarks. The Chancellor wished for the 'gradual downfall' of Austria, because he still believed he could come to an agreement with Russia. Waldersee, however, considered this idea 'quite wrong' and 'very sad'. 'I have nothing against helping to break up Austria, if it is necessary in our interest, but I must first be convinced that we should really gain some advantage and benefit from it; as things are at the moment Russia would be happy to join us if it were against Austria; but it would not last long and we would find ourselves alone, without allies, and would be overpowered by Russia and France.' Waldersee was astonished to learn from Wilhelm that he had never discussed Austria's supposed 'plans for the future' directly with Kaiser Franz Joseph himself.[50]

## BRITAIN, THE UNITED STATES AND COLONIAL POLICY

Since a great war on two fronts on the continent was expected shortly, a firm understanding with Britain, which must at least remain neutral in the conflict, was urgently needed. In order to ensure this neutrality there could be no question of Germany pursuing an expansionist colonial policy for the time being. On this point Wilhelm II and Waldersee were at first in complete agreement with the Bismarcks. The Chief of the General Staff considered the 'whole colonial policy' to be 'nonsense' and sharply condemned the colonial enthusiasts, who wanted to 'take energetic action and impress people by a show of strength' overseas.[51] His influence on the Kaiser is unmistakable here too. 'I told the Kaiser plainly that I considered that our African colonies could never amount to anything, and that I was even convinced that in 30 years all Europeans would be driven off African soil', he declared perceptively in January 1889, adding that 'this might be a slight exaggeration; I should have said: "wherever the Mohammedans rule". But this is still my view and it can be seen that their power is constantly spreading. In the South, however, it may take longer for the native population to become aware of its strength. The days of colonies are altogether over. My only wish now is that we should avoid becoming more deeply embroiled.'[52] In early 1889 Waldersee recorded anxiously that German policy in East Africa had ventured further than was wise.[53] He was afraid, in particular, that Germany might easily 'get into a squabble . . . with England' in East Africa.[54]

Still more dangerous, in the eyes of the Chief of the General Staff, was the deployment of German troops in Samoa, for this Pacific adventure could even lead to differences with the United States. 'An entanglement with America is just what we need!', Waldersee exclaimed despairingly.[55] In March 1889 he recorded that light had at last dawned in the Foreign Office, which had recognised 'that our colonial policy has been extremely foolish'.[56] He strongly criticised those naval officers and diplomats who favoured 'energetic action even to the point of fighting America', for Germany could not conduct a war with the United States; it would be 'the greatest misfortune . . . which could happen to us'. He implored the Kaiser to avoid any aggressive measures over Samoa because the consequences were unforeseeable and 'we should have nothing on our minds now except preparing ourselves for the forthcoming struggle with France and Russia'. 'I found the Kaiser calm, and he had evidently given much thought to the question; he promised me that serious complications would be avoided, and also thought that the Chancellor was taking a calmer view of the question.'[57]

The colonial question had become acute because the situation on the island of Zanzibar, where both Germany and Britain had substantial interests, had been threatening to spiral out of control since the autumn of 1888. A British officer reported that the German East Africa Company, supported by a German squadron, had already executed several natives and an uprising against the Sultan of Zanzibar was imminent. 'Zanzibar itself is very unpleasant, full of Germans who drink all day, rail at the Sultan & scowl at the English', he informed London.[58] This critical view was fully borne out by German reports. In September 1889 Prince Ernst zu Hohenlohe wrote to his father, the President of the

German Colonial Society, from the German embassy in London: 'I have recently heard (from a German) that our representatives in Africa are behaving quite incredibly and are ruining our standing both with the natives and with the Europeans by their behaviour. [Carl] Peters is said to have acted like a madman on his arrival in Africa, [Hermann von] Wissmann is said to have been completely drunk when he arrived in Cairo . . . and to have scandalised everyone by his behaviour there. The officers and officials in Africa are reported to be making the natives everywhere rebellious by their immoral and brutal conduct. All this and more was told me, as I said, not by an Englishman but by a German, who is close to the Foreign Office and is very much concerned with colonial policy.'[59]

In this tense situation Kaiser Wilhelm at first showed an uncharacteristic level-headedness, to the relief of the Bismarcks and Waldersee. After an audience on 16 September 1888 Herbert Bismarck was able to report to his father: 'With regard to East Africa H.M. was as cool and sensible as could be, agreeing entirely with your opinion and needing no persuasion. H.M. said of his own accord that in East Africa we ought to do everything *through* the Sultan, to make use of his Mohammedan authority as a wire-puller without appearing on the scene ourselves, and on no account to allow ourselves to become involved in enterprises in the interior – and even on the coast only on condition that the Sultan's standing is not compromised. [The Kaiser spoke] of the East Africa Company with contemptuous disparagement and called Peters a misguided fantasist. So when Berchem delivers your P[ro] M[emoria] . . . to H.M. the day after tomorrow it will receive the fullest All-Highest approval.'[60] Even when the Kaiser manifested 'a little colonial chauvinism' in the summer of 1889, attributed by Herbert Bismarck to the influence of the 'transoceanically minded' Bennigsen, the Foreign Secretary did not take it seriously, since the Kaiser was in complete agreement with his principle of 'harmony with England on matters of colonial policy'.[61] The younger Bismarck believed he had all the more reason to feel reassured since even senior naval officers were speaking to the Kaiser in support of his dispassionate view of German interests in Zanzibar.[62]

It seems not entirely unlikely that the restraint which the Kaiser showed in his attitude to colonial politics in the first eighteen months of his reign was partly rooted in his half-English identity. It is certainly difficult, given the constant oscillation between hatred and love in his attitude towards his mother's country, to detect any consistent line. But Wilhelm's extensive comments on the activities of British military forces in northern East Africa during this period bear witness to a personal interest in their fate which is absent from his marginal comments on other international events. When, for instance, Ambassador Count Hatzfeldt reported in November 1888 on a government statement in the House of Commons announcing that an expeditionary force of ten officers and three hundred men, drawn from Egyptian and Scottish regiments, under the command of General Francis Grenfell, had left Cairo and was marching through the desert to the Sudan in order to suppress the Mahdi's Islamic rebellion, the Kaiser criticised both the size and the composition of the force as inadequate. 'They are always making the same mistake! A totally inadequate detachment is sent off with great show – with at least 1 General. It is supposed to act purely defensively but nevertheless it later finds itself forced to undertake offensive action, for which it is of no use. The combination with black regiments seems risky to me. To judge from their performance up to now they are not worth a great deal. And add to that a march through the desert!'[63] Similarly, two weeks later, it is clear from the Kaiser's detailed comments on Lord Salisbury's optimistic assurances that the 5,000 British soldiers assembled in Suakin on the Red Sea would be perfectly adequate to defend the port against 2,000 rebels how anxious he was for a British victory. 'M[eo] V[oto] the detachment in Suakin is *not* sufficient', he observed. 'Even a simple defence of the most defensive nature requires occasional offensive action. They have only a very imprecise idea of the strength of the enemy. The reconnaissances have failed because the mounted detachments were driven back by the besieging forces; according to private reports they even ran away. The enemy is well armed and has artillery which has been dug into trenches for weeks, and which is said to fire with great precision. If one reckons on 2000 men to cover occupation and guard duties, sick, wounded &c, that leaves a figure of 2,500–2,000 [sic] infantry and about 500–700 cavalry for the sortie. This would suffice only to drive the enemy out of, or destroy, the trenches. And then, if successful, to go back, and to have to do the same thing again 14 days later. But in the face of an enemy such as the one besieging Suakin the only thing that is of any use is an energetic offensive. Suakin can be protected only by capturing Sinkrat and Tokar and by occupying and fortifying them. For that at least one division of 12000 infantry; 1 cavalry regiment of 1000 horse and 2 batteries of mounted cannon and 4 of rapid fire cannon are required. If the news of Emin's fall is true, the Mahdi or Osman Digna has sufficient reserves of victorious troops to hand to make the Englishmen's task very difficult.'[64] Even though Wilhelm did not send these words of advice to Queen Victoria, in many respects they anticipate the two highly controversial imperial memoranda which he sent to London at the turn of the century, to help the British to victory in their war against the Boers.[65] In the event the Anglo-Egyptian army under Grenfell defeated the rebels in August 1889 even without the benefit of the Kaiser's advice.

As has already been shown, the anglophile side of the Kaiser came to the fore suddenly and much more strongly than ever before after his visit to Osborne and his appointment as a British admiral. After his dismissal, Herbert Bismarck recalled that the British government, having agreed with Germany on a joint approach to the forthcoming Samoa Conference, had proposed the exchange of Heligoland for parts of German South-West Africa. 'My letter about this was submitted by H.H. [the Chancellor] to the Kaiser, who was absolutely delighted, and wanted to accept *immediately*. We had difficulty', wrote Herbert, 'in making it clear to H.M. that it was not yet time for this.' Instead, if the Kaiser set such store by Heligoland it would be better not to show any enthusiasm, but to wait for a situation to arise 'in which England needed us, and this would happen soon enough'. The Kaiser yielded to 'these rational arguments, even if very reluctantly'. At the request of the Foreign Secretary, who feared that the acquisition of Heligoland might be 'made known through the confidential conversations which the Kaiser liked to have with naval officers . . . and as a result only made more expensive for us', the Kaiser ordered the exchange plan to be locked away. But as soon as Herbert had left for his summer holiday in June 1889 the Kaiser asked Under-Secretary of State Count Berchem to take the matter up, so that he could sign the treaty while he was at Osborne. It was only with great difficulty that Herbert succeeded in making it clear to the Kaiser that if *Germany* suggested the cession of Heligoland at this moment, Britain would either put forward an unacceptable counterclaim or reject the whole arrangement, 'because Salisbury would not want to expose himself to opposition accusations of giving up English territory for the sake of a family visit to *Osborne*'. The idea of signing the pact at Osborne was a particularly unfortunate one, in Herbert's eyes, and moreover it would be impossible to achieve an acceptable basis for negotiations so quickly. The Kaiser gave way with bad grace.[66]

At the end of 1889, however, the first indications of imperial enthusiasm for colonialism began to appear. In December Wilhelm ordered the Foreign Secretary to inform Hermann von Wissmann by telegraph 'that in recognition of his achievements hitherto, and for the accomplishment of his duties, I am giving him a battery of 6 naval guns with ammunition (including landing carriages)'.[67] If Herbert Bismarck was disturbed by this evidence of the influence of the navy on the Kaiser, he was horrified to discover, a few weeks later, that Wilhelm was suddenly 'fiercely against England in the colonial question, especially Zanzibar, which He wishes to take'. He was 'embittered against England because of East Africa', and 'inclined to violent action'.[68] Once again it was the Empress Frederick who recognised the mechanisms that were at work here. Prince Bismarck, she wrote, had 'never seriously thought' of acquiring colonies or fighting for them, but he had stoked up enthusiasm for colonies because he thought he could 'use it for electioneering purposes, & that flourishing the patriotic flag, & blowing the national trumpet' would enable him to put pressure on the Reichstag. But he had been caught in his own trap, for meanwhile 'not only the Chauvinist

Party but William have taken it *quite* "au sérieu" [sic], − & wish it followed up. The Chancellor does not *dare* to say that it would be wiser to drop all such undertakings for the present, & while the state of European Peace is so uncertain, but I have no doubt he *thinks* it.'[69]

## THE KAISER'S 'PASSION FOR THE NAVY'

Still more significant for the future than the Kaiser's growing enthusiasm for colonies was, of course, his enthusiasm for the navy, which even in these early days struck all observers as strange. In political circles in Berlin it was either mocked as a personal fad or criticised as a dangerous threat to the necessary supremacy of the army. Herbert Bismarck described it contemptuously as 'hydrophilia',[70] and the young Alfred von Kiderlen-Wächter, reporting on the Baltic cruise in July 1888, commented mockingly that Wilhelm was manifesting 'a colossal interest in naval matters'. He was constantly reading naval signals with a telescope. A naval battle had been arranged 'to the accompaniment of much thunder from the guns', followed by a great sailing exercise on another day. Then 'we one and all shot with a revolver-cannon at a barrel thrown overboard as a target, which H.M. to his great joy also hit'.[71] Even senior naval officers considered some aspects of the imperial passion for the navy questionable. Thus for instance the future Chief of the Naval Cabinet, Gustav Freiherr von Senden-Bibran, criticised the fact that throughout his state visit to Russia, apart from the uniform of his Russian regiment, the Kaiser had worn only the new admiral's uniform which he himself had designed; this would cause bad feelings in the army, he predicted.[72] A year later Vice-Admiral Paul Hoffmann commented that on their voyage from Genoa to Athens the Kaiser aspired 'to act completely as an admiral, to give direct orders, to receive direct reports as commanding officer of the squadron, and in addition to dress and behave as a seaman'. His enthusiasm for the navy made itself felt everywhere.[73] 'His interest in these things takes precedence over everything else',[74] the Vice-Admiral recorded; and the Kaiser even found it embarrassing to be seasick.[75] However gratified Hoffmann was by the Kaiser's naval interests, he clearly recognised the dangers that lay in the superficiality of his knowledge, combined with his articulacy and with the inhibitions that his exalted status called forth in others. On several occasions the monarch had started lively discussions on naval matters and marine tactics, and it was pleasing to note 'how clearly and calmly the Kaiser thinks, and how superbly gifted he is intellectually. The fault lies only in his dilettantism; he thinks he can give an opinion on anything, even if his knowledge is only superficial. If an opposing, clear and well-founded view is expressed to him, he disputes it, but then agrees with the opposing view and recognises its force. The only difficulty is being able to defend one's opinion straight away and skilfully to the Kaiser. If his opponent is not practised in this, which of course unfortunately often happens, then the Kaiser is even more convinced of his own opinion and very self-satisfied at having confounded the experts.'[76] Waldersee, as Chief of the General Staff, was shortly to have very similar experiences during the army manoeuvres.

Wilhelm was deeply imbued with the idea that his grandfather had, in a sense, entrusted him with the task of building up the navy to be 'a sister-force to the army, of equal value'. Many years later, in exile in Holland, the Kaiser could still vividly remember the 'solemn moment' during the laying of the foundation stone of the Kaiser Wilhelm Canal at Kiel in June 1887, when the old Kaiser surprised him with the words: 'Heinrich has just told me that your interest in and understanding of the navy is so great that the navy wishes that the bond which already links you with it should be outwardly visible as well. After the splendid impressions left by today I am especially glad to fulfil this wish, which you yourself no doubt also cherish in your heart. Therefore I now place you à la suite of the I. Marine Battalion.'[77] 'I was completely overcome with joy and surprise, and speechless', the exiled Kaiser recalled. 'It was the fulfilment of a fervent wish! Heinrich embraced me at once and pressed me to him so tightly that I could scarcely breathe. The senior naval officers who were present for our departure . . . shook my hand warmly after I had kissed the Kaiser's hand in respectful thanks.' On the train journey from Kiel to Potsdam, however, conflict arose with the Prussian Minister of War as representative of the interests of the army. Admittedly Chief of the Military Cabinet Emil von Albedyll and most of the other generals who were in the compartment congratulated the young Prince 'most warmly' on the new honour and Albedyll went so far as to say, 'You deserved it, for I have already heard from naval circles how surprisingly at home you are in maritime affairs.' But Prussian Minister of War General Paul Bronsart von Schellendorf went on reading a document 'without taking any notice of the event. When I announced the news to him, full of happy excitement [the Kaiser continued] he looked at me over his pince-nez and said with cold condescension: "I see! – Well, you certainly should take an interest in such things", and resumed his reading. Burning with anger I answered him: "I beg your pardon, Excellency. The navy is the equal sister-force of the army! It represents the honour of the German flag abroad, and it is high time and quite proper that the army should also take an interest in such things. In the regiments to which I have the honour to belong I have already awakened this interest", and abruptly left the compartment. When we arrived at Potsdam His Excellency von Albedyll came up to me and while strongly disapproving the conduct of His Exc. von Bronsart . . . he expressed the latter's regret over the affair, upon which I thanked the General and added: "When it is for me to speak, things will be different."' As the Kaiser explained, Bronsart, like Caprivi, belonged 'to the group of older Prussian generals, who lacked any understanding of questions of naval prestige and of a correspondingly strong navy. They looked on it as an appendage to the army, and considered money spent on the navy as wrongfully taken away from the army.'[78] Shortly after Wilhelm II's accession, both Bronsart as Prussian minister of war and Caprivi as chief of the Admiralty were obliged to hand in their resignations.

In his aim of building up the navy into 'the equal sister-force of the army' Kaiser Wilhelm received warm support from his brother Heinrich, who was at this time in command of the torpedo boat division, and was soon to be promoted to admiral and fleet commander.[79] After the bill on naval organisation ordered by Wilhelm had been passed by the Reichstag early in 1889, giving the navy a similar administrative structure to the army (more will be said about this in the next chapter), Heinrich sent an enthusiastic reply to a telegram from his brother: 'I shall never forget your words and shall inform my new officer corps of them tomorrow, as on a day on which I shall hoist our proud flag to your and the Fatherland's glory. Only in such a spirit shall we be able to be named in the same breath as your glorious army.'[80]

In the army, on the other hand, the Kaiser's obsession with the navy aroused grave misgivings. Only a few weeks after the accession Waldersee, who on this point at least was in complete agreement with his rival War Minister Paul von Bronsart, was strongly criticising the 'passion' of the new Kaiser for the sea. The navy must realise, Waldersee warned, that it 'is only one part of our armed forces, and by no means the most important, though certainly the most costly'. He castigated the naval officers and others in the imperial entourage who fuelled this dangerous passion in Wilhelm.[81] At the naval exercises in September 1888 Waldersee was shocked by the evident strength of 'the Kaiser's passion for the navy'. Wilhelm was 'incredibly enthusiastic' and spent the whole day on deck, except for meals. This 'very pronounced' obsession of the Kaiser with the navy was 'stronger than is good for us' and was being exploited improperly by the naval authorities. 'The Kaiser is now determined to make considerable demands for money for the navy so as to build bigger ships again, which Caprivi did not think right', Waldersee complained on 9 October 1888.[82] Only a month later the Chief of the General Staff expressed the hope that the Kaiser would give up his plans for a large naval building programme for the sake of urgently needed reinforcement of the army. 'My wish', he confessed, 'is for the Kaiser to drop his huge demand for the navy – I think it is 100 million; he will be very reluctant to do so, but I hope that he will agree nevertheless, if he acknowledges that we shall have a war soon. Iron-clads take three years to build, but the war will not be kept waiting that long.'[83]

The ample evidence of Wilhelm II's enthusiasm for naval affairs at this initial stage of his reign should not, of course, mislead us into thinking that we are already dealing with plans to build a battlefleet against Britain. The idea that the new German Reich with its minimal naval strength might aspire within a few years to dispute the maritime supremacy of Great Britain seemed so fantastic, so far removed from reality, to both the supporters and the opponents of the Kaiser's naval passion that it was not even thought of as a remote possibility. Indeed, Wilhelm clearly regarded his love for the navy as an expression of his English heritage and declared to one of his Flügeladjutanten in Doorn: '[M]y very particular passion for the navy . . . arose not least from the English blood I inherited from my mother.'[84] And Bülow, as Reich chancellor, once had to point out to him that it would not do, as he proposed, to describe the expensive and highly risky German battleship building programme in public as the expression of his personal predilection and of his youthful experiences in Portsmouth and Plymouth![85]

In these first years Wilhelm II's naval plans were, on the contrary, rooted in the wishful notion that the Royal Navy, the German fleet and the Prusso-German army would together safeguard world peace and that if a war should nevertheless prove inevitable they would carry off the victory jointly. In this expectation the Kaiser positively urged an expansion of the British navy and deplored the fact that the British were 'hardly in a position at the moment to achieve anything significant with either navy or army', nor did they seem to show any desire 'to prepare themselves for more'.[86] When the Westminster Parliament approved the funding of seventy new warships in early 1889 Wilhelm expressed his delight.[87] After his appointment as admiral of the fleet and his successful visit to England in the summer of 1889 Wilhelm's wish for Anglo-German military co-operation by land and by sea seemed to be on the verge of fulfilment. In August that year he wrote to Queen Victoria saying that he knew that 'the British ironclads coupled with mine & my army are the strongest guarantees of peace; which Heaven may help us preserve! Should however the Will of Providence lay the heavy burden on us of fighting for our homes & destinies, then may the British fleet be seen forging ahead side by side with the German, and the "Red Coat" marching to Victory with the "Pommeranian Grenadier"!'[88] In the same spirit he annotated an English newspaper report in which much was made of the independence of the British navy and of the fact that it did not exist to serve the interests of either Germany or other countries, with the comment: 'Short-sighted! History will teach them to know better.'[89] This Anglo-German dream reached its peak in a memorable Christmas letter to Queen Victoria of 22 December 1889, in which the Kaiser strongly urged doubling the strength of the British Mediterranean fleet. 'My journey to Athens and Constantinople was immensely interesting', he wrote.

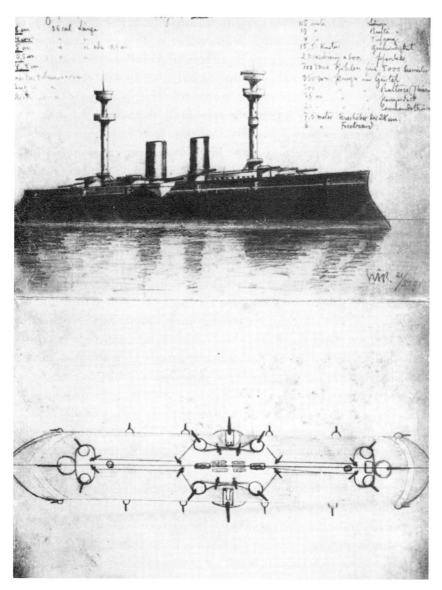

6. A ship of the line designed by Kaiser Wilhelm II in May 1891

'I was very much pleased & interested in seeing the ships of the Mediterranean Squadron. It is in most able & excellent hands; except Adm. Hornby I hardly ever met [?] a more distinguished gentleman, finer seaman, & better political head than S[ir] Anth. Hoskins; he is what the sailors say a "splendid fellow". I only wish – this as Adm. of the Fleet – that I saw a *dozen* 1 class battleships under his command instead of 5! Admiral Hoskins' Squadron is to[o] small to fullfill [sic] all the duties incumbent upon it, especially in case of war, I among many other points only take the liberty of submitting one to you. France has now in commission *9 first class* battleships at Toulon; according to their last full speed trial this fleet took one day to reach Toulon from Villefranche. Now, should the French, – this boite à surprise for Europe – suddenly run wild & fall foul of Italy, for instance, their Mediterranean fleet would be able to pounce upon any Italian town or division of their fleet in 1 or 2 days. Well, if, as Lord Salisbury told me at Osborne, England never would allow France to hurt Italy without good cause, Adm. Hoskins would have to do something or other to help them. But what? What can he do with 5 ships against *9*? These 9, which will be followed in 24 hours by the whole of the first reserve of Toulon? Adm. Hoskins must be reinforced, as soon as is deemed expedient; a man in whose hands the responsibility for the British prestige in the Mediterranean is placed must be able to muster such a commanding number of battleships, that neither the simplest gamin in Paris, Rome or Constantinople can be in doubt for one second who will be the victor when it comes to fighting. I can assure you, dearest Grandmama, this question has weighed heavily on me ever since my return! I have culled information from all sources in the South & East & have regularly found the same answer: "the French look down upon the British Mediterranean Squadron with disdain, & are sure of doing away with it in short time after the opening of hostilities!" Fancy! What would Lord Nelson say! I sent a scheme I drew up some time ago through L[ord] Ch. Beresford to Ld. Salisbury, a copy of a scheme as it is worked out for my Navy. It shows the British Navy & French Navy told off in Squadrons for war; I believe it would interest you to see it. – But I must be[g] your pardon for taking up your precious time; when this "Admiral of the Fleet" gets hold of me, then I am for a while unable to shake him off.'[90] One wonders how Queen Victoria reacted to this advice from her Prusso-German grandson!

Only years later, when Wilhelm II began to carry out his 'boundless' naval plans, did critics recognise the explosive force, in terms of international politics, which lay in the imperial 'passion for the navy'. At the beginning of his reign only the Grand Duchess Augusta Caroline of Mecklenburg, born in England in 1822, sent out a warning after a visit by the restless young Kaiser to Strelitz, that Wilhelm was 'a passionate *Sailor*, more even than his brother Henry is, his aim being to out-do *all* other *Fleets*'. The old Grand Duchess underlined the word 'all' three times.[91]

# CHAPTER SEVEN

# The pillars of imperial power

As soon as he came to the throne Wilhelm embarked upon a thorough and – in the view of many observers – overhasty reorganisation of his court. The appointments he made were his own strictly personal choices, and they ranged from officials of the household and court, adjutant-generals and Flügeladjutanten (aides-de-camp), the Secret Cabinets for Civil, Military and Naval Affairs, to the highest posts in the army and in the civil administration of the state. They included appointments of men who were little suited to their posts; they led to conflicts, both among the new court officials themselves and between them and the military suite – conflicts which were exacerbated by the power struggles between the Bismarcks and their adversaries in the army and within ultra-conservative circles. Nevertheless, through this reorganisation of the court Wilhelm II created for himself a compliant instrument of power which enabled him to carry out a successful campaign against Bismarck and then, over the course of the next ten years, gradually undermine and finally control the power of the state. As early as 1896 the influential Privy Councillor Friedrich von Holstein described the imperial entourage as one of the three factors – the others being the Kaiser himself and the government – which had to be reckoned with in political decision-making.[1] In contrast to the chancellors and ministers, a surprisingly large number of these men appointed at the beginning of the reign retained their posts for decades, some until death and others until the fall of the monarchy in November 1918. The court, which consisted of over 2,000 officials and military officers, thus served literally as the Kaiser's own power base.[2]

### THE MINISTRY OF THE ROYAL HOUSEHOLD

The Household Ministry was situated at 73 Wilhelmstrasse, close to the Reich chancellor's palace and the Foreign Office, and it administered the business affairs, estates and Royal Archive of the Hohenzollern family and all its branches. It also included the Office of Heralds, which dealt with matters of noble rank and privilege, and consequently played an important role in the upper echelons of German society. It nevertheless stood outside the constitution, in the personal domain of the reigning monarch. The minister of the Royal Household was thus the only minister in Prussia who was not a member of the Ministry of State.

The House Minister at the time of the double succession in 1888, Otto Count zu Stolberg-Wernigerode, was not only a member of one of the most illustrious aristocratic families in Europe, but had also made a brilliant career in government service, having been Oberpräsident of Hanover, a member of the Reichstag, ambassador at Vienna, vice-chancellor and vice-president of the Ministry of State under Bismarck; since 1884 he had served as principal chamberlain, and from 1885 also as minister of the Royal Household (as successor to Count von Schleinitz).[3] At the grand opening ceremony of the Reichstag on 25 June 1888, Stolberg stood very near the Kaiser, just beside the imperial crown. It therefore came as a painful shock to court society when Stolberg was dismissed as house minister shortly after the accession. Wilhelm II had simply invited him to hand in his resignation. Stolberg, as the Kaiser announced to the Prussian ministers in his first Crown Council, had missed the opportunity to buy up for 30,000 marks the entire edition of the controversial memoirs of the Hofrat Louis Schneider, who had spent many years as reader and private librarian to Friedrich Wilhelm IV and Wilhelm I, and had thus damaged the reputation of the old Kaiser.[4] It was true that Stolberg had in any case intended, as was generally known, to ask to be relieved of his post in the course of the next few months. 'But the fact that although he wanted to go, he has been pushed out now, gave him the greatest offence', Count Imre Széchényi reported. The change at the Ministry of the Royal Household caused all the more head-shaking because the successor named by Wilhelm II, the ultra-conservative former President of the Reichstag, Wilhelm von Wedell-Piesdorf, could, as Széchényi commented acidly, 'offer no special qualifications for the post except that he is a friend of Count Waldersee and likewise belongs to the party of the Protestant zealots'. No one would ever have thought, 'even as the remotest possibility', of Wedell as a candidate for this post, Széchényi maintained.[5] He could hardly have suspected that the new House Minister would remain in office until 1907. Even Waldersee criticised the unnecessary haste with which Wilhelm had made the change. Stolberg – who much against his will remained in his post as principal chamberlain until

1893 — was 'undoubtedly the most respected man in our society and the most distinguished member of the Protestant aristocracy', the General commented. 'With his position, fortune and family connections he is a personality the Kaiser must reckon with.'[6] Wilhelm, however, treated the matter lightly; he wrote to his grandmother Augusta concealing the true facts of the case and saying that Stolberg had 'asked, in a most firm and decided manner, to be relieved of his post, as he could no longer manage it because he had to look after his own domains'. The Kaiser added that he had known Wedell well for a long time, and he was 'in every respect perfectly fitted for the position'.[7] When Prince Stolberg died in November 1896, Waldersee paid tribute to his popularity, distinction and tact, but added: 'He no longer liked the way things were in Berlin, and in this he was not alone . . . His relations with the Kaiser have always remained good outwardly, but at heart they were cool.'[8]

Stolberg's dismissal attracted all the more attention because numerous other court officials were retained and even promoted at the accession. Physician-General Dr Rudolf Leuthold, who had been on terms 'almost of friendship' with Wilhelm for years, was appointed his personal physician.[9] Others were taken over from his father's household and court establishment, as for instance were Hugo Count Radolinski, who (now as Prince Radolin) was appointed Lord High Steward, Maximilian Freiherr von Lyncker, the Hausmarschall (Marshal of the Household), and Count August zu Eulenburg, the Senior Master of Ceremonies. They were later to exercise an unparalleled influence at the court in Berlin. Countess Therese von Brockdorff was granted the title 'Excellency' and became Oberhofmeisterin (Senior Mistress of the Court) to Kaiserin Auguste Viktoria. The Kaiser's mother wrote of her that she was certainly 'devoted to her mistress, but not my idea of a Lady!', adding that she was very narrow-minded, spoke 'such common German', and altogether had 'the manners and ideas of a "Bourgeoise"'. In general, she claimed, the people now at the new court were 'very second rate'.[10] The two ladies in waiting, Mathilde Countess von Keller and Claire von Gersdorff likewise remained in the Kaiserin's close entourage. Her erstwhile Chamberlain, the zealously Protestant Ernst Freiherr von Mirbach, was promoted to be her Senior Master of the Court and Chief of her Cabinet.[11]

### THE 'MILITARY RETINUE'

With equally unseemly haste (and cunning dissimulation of his feelings, as in Stolberg's case) Wilhelm brought about the dismissal of the elderly generals who had set the tone for decades at his grandfather's court, and who had remained in office for the time being because of the difficult circumstances of his father's accession.[12] Adjutant-Generals Karl Friedrich Count von der Goltz, Heinrich

August Count von Lehndorff and Anton Prince Radziwill, who belonged to 'the closest entourage of Kaiser Wilhelm I, and for whom the old monarch had feelings of genuine friendship', as Széchényi recorded in his report of 4 July 1888, found themselves 'pensioned off without warning, and numerous other measures of a similar kind may well be forthcoming soon for the senior generals'. The ambassador's comment on this brusque new style was telling: 'If all this had happened, not in the very first days of the new reign, but only quietly and gradually after several months, no one would have been surprised, given the advanced age of those affected; but as it was, the impression made on the circles to whom the latter belong was a very painful one.'[13]

   The elderly gentlemen were replaced by younger career officers whom Wilhelm had got to know during his service at Potsdam. The 'dashing' General Max von Versen, who had been in command of the Hussar Guards regiment when Wilhelm was colonel, was appointed adjutant-general, while General Adolf von Wittich, who had been giving him lectures on military history since the beginning of 1888, was promoted to adjutant-general in waiting. The period during which the Kaiser had two adjutant-generals in his suite did not last long, however, for in March 1889 Versen was appointed general in command of the III Army Corps in Metz and was hence discharged from his appointment at court.[14] Even Versen's friend and defender Waldersee had to admit with hindsight that the Adjutant-General had exercised a considerable, but in his eyes 'questionable' influence on the young monarch: he was 'not the man to give the Prince the right advice, after the problems began', Waldersee considered. It was true that Versen had 'made a bold horseman' of Prince Wilhelm, and had 'really taken a great deal of trouble' in so doing. But Waldersee considered that this extraordinarily energetic, hard-working and physically tough, but only moderately intelligent and increasingly vain man had been partly responsible for the rough tone of the court. In addition it was he who was chiefly to blame for the arming of the cavalry with lances, and in general for the military deployment of the cavalry, 'about which the Kaiser [had] the unhealthiest ideas'. Above all Waldersee reproached the Adjutant-General with having whipped up Wilhelm 'against the entire entourage of his grandfather and especially against Albedyll'. At the time when his father's cancer became known, Wilhelm had thought 'very highly' of Versen and had discussed numerous 'future plans' with him, in the course of which 'much confused nonsense' had been talked. In the first months of his reign Wilhelm had 'singled him out a great deal' and 'showered him with favours', but soon his star began to wane. Versen had become 'an uncomfortable presence' for the Kaiser 'by constantly putting himself forward'; the Kaiser had suddenly withdrawn his confidence from the General and since then had avoided being alone with him. Although Versen's influence decreased sharply as a result, and although it became increasingly apparent that he was suffering from a brain disorder, he continued to be regarded as an important factor even after his transfer to Metz, and was thus numbered among the most hated people in the Kaiser's circle.[15] The Empress Frederick considered him one of her worst enemies and thought him 'half mad', but others too had nothing but contempt for him and mocked Versen with the punning nickname of 'das Versehen' (the mistake).[16] The British military attaché Swaine, who spoke of Versen's 'domination', later recognised what inner court circles had long known, that the General was 'nothing but a vulgar flatterer'.[17] Both Versen and Waldersee were convinced that the transfer of the Adjutant-General to Metz was the result of an intrigue, blaming in particular the 'ambitious' Flügeladjutant Adolf von Bülow for his downfall.[18] The second Adjutant-General, Adolf von Wittich, remained in office until the summer of 1892, in spite of countless disagreements with his imperial master.[19]

Wilhelm's personal adjutants, Moritz Ferdinand Freiherr von Bissing and Major Kurt Wolf von Pfuel, were both promoted to the position of Flügeladjutant.[20] According to Colonel Swaine, Bissing was the only man in the entire imperial entourage who had the courage to talk openly and frankly to Wilhelm.[21] Friedrich von Holstein likewise considered him the only reliable military officer in the Kaiser's entourage and later, after Bissing had been transferred elsewhere, tried to bring him back to court as Wilhelm's 'bodyguard', although Philipp Eulenburg was of the opinion that Bissing's *excessive irascibility* made him seem, 'even to His Majesty, not quite suited for the position'.[22] Among Wilhelm II's Flügeladjutanten in waiting in these early days were also Lieutenant-Colonel von Lippe, Colonel Carl Count von Wedel and Majors Gustav von Kessel, Adolf von Bülow (his former military tutor), Cölestin von Zitzewitz and Friedrich von Scholl. Bissing, Bülow, Wedel and Kessel were repeatedly demonised by the Empress Frederick as 'dreadful', 'selfish', 'ambitious', *dangerous* and 'very pernicious', while Zitzewitz (who was married to an Englishwoman) and Scholl she considered merely as 'second rate, inferior, common & vulgar'. The tone and manners of these men were 'far from what they should be at Court & about W.', she maintained; and their inclination towards 'abject flattery' was sheer poison for him.[23] Kessel in particular was an unscrupulous opportunist in her eyes, who had purchased his position with Wilhelm by treachery towards his dying sovereign. 'Of course W. is beholden to him & looks upon his conduct as a proof of K's devotion to his person; *we* were *sacrificed*...My blood boils with indignation the same as it did *then* when I think of it all', she declared in the summer of 1891.[24] When Kessel was promoted to colonel a few months later but not put in command of a regiment, the widowed Empress rightly assumed that this meant that he 'is going to be kept *on* in the Household and then become "General Adjutant" wh. is a post of influence & confidence!

Considering the *past* this fact speaks *volumes* to *me*, and they are *not* consolatory or encouraging.'[25]

Some of these officers remained Wilhelm II's closest companions and advisers until the end of the monarchy. All officers on the new Kaiser's staff, including Waldersee, belonged from December 1888 onwards to the 'Military Retinue of Kaiser Wilhelm II', while those who had served with his grandfather and father were designated as belonging to the retinue of Kaiser Wilhelm I or of Kaiser Friedrich III. The old name of 'Maison Militaire' was abandoned.[26] In its place came the 'Headquarters of His Majesty the Kaiser and King', established on 7 July 1888, and comprising all the adjutant-generals, generals à la suite and Flügeladjutanten. As commandant of the 'Kaiser's Headquarters', Adolf von Wittich was responsible for the division of duties of the 'Military Retinue'.[27]

The adjutant-generals and Flügeladjutanten gave the Wilhelmine court its particular character, and hence the atmosphere in which Wilhelm II took his decisions. Even under the old Kaiser, a Master of Ceremonies had declared proudly that nothing showed the predominantly military character of the Prusso-German court more clearly than the fact that 'in Prussia, more than at many other courts, the King's Flügel-Adjutanten are at the same time his gentlemen in waiting, and the ceremonial of the Prussian court in many ways reveals the military organisation beneath it'. It was, he maintained, 'the Prussian national character which is also clearly reflected in the life of the court'.[28]

The reverse of the medal, as far as this military accent was concerned, was the roughness of tone and the fondness for obscene stories which it often encouraged. The Chief of the Military Cabinet later admitted that he had suggested to the Kaiser early in 1889 that he should appoint Carl Wedel to his entourage, because 'its tone left much to be desired at that time. The Kaiser', Hahnke recalled, 'accepted this suggestion with enthusiasm, because he himself had been keenly aware that not everything was quite as it should be.'[29] However, observers continued to be struck by 'the bad tone' of the Kaiser's entourage. 'Scholl distinguished himself particularly in that respect', Waldersee commented some years later.[30]

One of Wilhelm II's Flügeladjutanten has left behind a precise account of the daily routine at the Schloss which shows how omnipresent the Military Retinue was. There were always two Flügeladjutanten in attendance on the Kaiser. They drove or rode out with him, they advised him on the questions on which he had to take decisions, they answered enquiries addressed to him from the outside world, they announced the people who were granted audience or whom the Kaiser had summoned, they assisted him in arranging his daily programme and they kept the 'All-Highest diary'. Normally an adjutant was on duty for two days, followed by two free days, so that each of them spent about fourteen days a month with the monarch. While on duty they lived at the Schloss, where they had a spacious study and two bedrooms beneath the Sternensaal at their disposal. In Berlin the two Flügeladjutanten usually began their work at about 8.30 a.m. when they accompanied the Kaiser and Kaiserin for an hour's ride in the Tiergarten. After returning to the Schloss the Kaiser gave audience to hear reports (Immediatvorträge) until just before 'second breakfast' (luncheon). At one o'clock (and then again at 8 p.m.) the Flügeladjutanten sat with the Kaiserin's ladies in waiting and the Hofmarschall at the imperial table, at which the Kaiser led the conversation, while the Kaiserin made no effort to disguise her preference for taking meals without a retinue, so as to have 'more of her beloved husband' to herself. About twice a week guests were also invited to luncheon. After the meal the Kaiser smoked a cigar with his two Flügeladjutanten in his study or in the adjutants' room. If the Kaiser and Kaiserin were driving out together in the afternoon, the Flügeladjutanten remained behind in the Schloss, but otherwise one of them drove out with the Kaiser. From 5 p.m. until dinner the Kaiser generally withdrew to his own apartments. After dinner Their Majesties both went into the library with their retinue, 'and one often remained sitting there for a very long time, sometimes without the Kaiser entering into any interesting conversation at all', the Adjutant recalled.[31]

The Flügeladjutanten may have had little independent influence on the Kaiser in the very early part of his reign. They were too new to court service, Wilhelm's personality was too strong and his self-assurance too great. Waldersee, who knew all the members of the military suite personally and kept a close eye on them, commented in August 1888: 'It is quite clear that he [Wilhelm] is ruled by no one in his entourages . . . The Flügeladjutanten have no influence.'[32] Little had changed by the summer of 1891, when Wilhelm's sister Viktoria (Moretta) observed that his entourage was too afraid of him to give him any advice.[33] Waldersee was dismayed to discover, shortly after his dismissal as chief of the General Staff, that of all the high-ranking army officers whose duty it was to advise the Kaiser − Chief of the General Staff Count Schlieffen, Minister of War von Kaltenborn-Stachau, Adjutant-General von Wittich and Chief of the Military Cabinet von Hahnke − 'not a single one' had 'exchanged a word with the Kaiser' during the autumn manoeuvres of 1891.[34] But within a few years it was widely recognised that the Military Retinue had become a powerful factor in German politics; in parliamentary and journalistic circles 'adjutant politics' and 'adjutant intrigues' became catch-phrases, and Bismarck, in discussing with a Bavarian newspaper editor the question of whether the Kaiser could be deposed, went so far as to sound the warning that ousting Wilhelm II 'from the midst of his generals' would 'not be as easy as the removal of King Ludwig II of Bavaria'.[35] Some of the adjutant-generals and Flügeladjutanten even developed a mystical, Knights-of-the-Holy-Grail relationship to their monarch, and for that reason alone would not have dreamt of contradicting, let alone ousting him. When in 1893 the Kaiser appointed as Flügeladjutanten not only Colonel Hans von Arnim, the son of a Potsdam architect, but also the musical and effete Kuno Count von Moltke, the latter's close friend Philipp Count zu Eulenburg wrote ecstatically: 'Your Majesty will become increasingly aware of what a pearl Your Majesty has acquired in this Adjutant – and I am filled with a pleasant, comforting feeling to know that *he* of all people is with my dearly beloved Kaiser.'[36] The world-famous equestrian Max Freiherr von Holzing-Berstett, who was appointed Flügeladjutant to the Kaiser around the turn of the century, openly admitted to his mother: 'I love him',[37] adding later, 'I rave about him like a silly girl, or rather, like a man who appreciates power and importance.'[38] When another officer, Heinrich Prince von Schönburg-Waldenburg, was addressed by the Kaiser during manoeuvres on 14 August 1900 with the question: 'Will you be my Flügeladjutant?', he was too stunned to reply, but expressed his gratitude 'wordlessly' by bowing 'to kiss the hand that is always so good to me'.[39] Gustav von Neumann-Cosel, as Flügeladjutant in attendance, kissed the Kaiser's hand at every possible opportunity. But even he found service at court so stressful that on returning to his bachelor apartments he 'first swore three times very loudly and crudely across the room and then retired to bed for 24 hours'.[40]

### LIEBENAU AND THE MARSHALS OF THE COURT

If the Flügeladjutanten had no noticeable influence on the Kaiser in the early days, the same could not be said of his Oberhof- und Hausmarschall (Senior Marshal of the Court and the Household), Eduard von Liebenau and his assistants, the Hofmarschälle. In his short time as Crown Prince Wilhelm had expressed the intention of 'breaking the power of the marshals of the court'; to this end he had planned with Waldersee to appoint a strong-willed general as commandant of his Imperial Headquarters.[41] In reality, however, during the first months of the reign of Wilhelm II the influence of the marshals grew markedly – and indeed chiefly because in August 1888 the Kaiser appointed Liebenau, hitherto his Hofmarschall, to the post of senior marshal of the court and the household, conferring on him the title of 'Excellency'. Liebenau was assisted by the Senior Cupbearer Karl Count von Pückler, who had served as lieutenant in the elite Gardes-du-Corps regiment and was a nephew of the Senior Master of Ceremonies under Wilhelm I. The immaculately dressed Pückler, whom Wilhelm II nicknamed 'Suleiman the Magnificent', was described by a middle-class naval officer as 'every inch the courtier, an elegant air, obliging cordiality mingled with slight condescension'.[42] Under Liebenau and Pückler the 'power of the marshals' grew steadily. In October 1888 Waldersee grumbled that their 'influence [has] grown greater than ever'.[43] 'It is quite extraordinary how this Kaiser allows the influence of these gentlemen to increase, and everywhere one hears complaints of their arrogance.'[44]

In Waldersee's eyes, Liebenau's appointment was incomprehensible except as an expression of gratitude for past services for, apart from the two Bismarcks and Carl Wedel, the Oberhofmarschall had no friends at court and, although he was economical and efficient as an administrator, in every other respect he was thoroughly unsuited to his post. He was 'so vain and puffed-up, so uncouth and at the same time so domineering, that he will give great offence and will perhaps come to grief one day', Waldersee observed in August 1888.[45] A few months later the Chief of the General Staff remarked that Liebenau's influence had grown greater still. 'It is really very much to be deplored that the Kaiser has made Herr von Liebenau Oberhofmarschall', he wrote in his diary. 'There is nothing distinguished about him; even his outward appearance is far from agreeable; and now he suffers from a kind of megalomania which brings him into conflict with everyone. At the court there is not *one* gentleman who does not complain about him; his subordinates are unhappy because of his rough tone and his lack of consideration. Everywhere he tries to exceed the authority of his office . . . He has been on a bad footing with the Kaiserin and the ladies for a long time; this alone speaks against him, for the Kaiserin is an excellent woman, of a most noble and distinguished nature, a model for all women.'[46] It was clear to the Chief of the General Staff that the Reich Chancellor and his son were promoting Liebenau's position in order to put a stop to the pious-orthodox influence of the Kaiserin and her close entourage.[47] Not long afterwards Waldersee began to suspect that Liebenau was even aiming '*to bring about discord or coolness between the Kaiser and the Kaiserin* by every means at his disposal'. At any rate Liebenau was trying 'to be the sole influence' on the Kaiser, and was 'jealous of anyone else who approaches the Kaiser; so it is particularly unpleasant for him when Their Majesties are together, because he feels that the Kaiserin's excellent influence is making itself felt'.[48] Liebenau had long since become the sworn enemy of Freiherr von Mirbach, who as the Kaiserin's Hofmarschall acted as the hub of the strict religious faction at court.[49]

The Oberhofmarschall was indeed making more and more enemies with his tactless behaviour.[50] In November 1888, when arranging a visit to Breslau for the Kaiser, he managed to exclude both the new Chief of the Military Cabinet, General Wilhelm von Hahnke, and the new Chief of the Civil Cabinet, Hermann von Lucanus, and failed to invite the Commanding General in Silesia, Oktavio von Boehn, either to shoot or to dine with the Kaiser. 'That is a crass violation of all traditions, which would have been absolutely impossible under Kaiser Wilhelm

I', was Waldersee's verdict on the incident. Liebenau was 'on the way to losing the Kaiser the support of the army. Boehn wants to hand in his resignation as a result and he is quite right; the act does him credit. Hahnke remonstrated, but the damage had already been done.'[51]

It was not long before Liebenau's nerves and those of other senior court officials gave way. They had overtaxed themselves 'in a quite ridiculous way' in their office work, Senior Master of Ceremonies August Count zu Eulenburg wrote in March 1889. Liebenau had had to go to Wiesbaden for a fortnight 'for his nerves to recuperate' — 'oh if only he would never come back!', sighed Waldersee — and Pückler had 'completely collapsed for months'.[52] The newspapers speculated about Liebenau's retirement and his replacement by August Eulenburg, but Waldersee knew better. It was certainly almost everyone's wish that Liebenau should retire, and one could not deny that he was 'a very regrettable element in the Kaiser's entourage', but he, Waldersee, knew 'for certain that the Kaiser will continue to hold on to him for the time being'.[53] And that was indeed the decisive factor. In spite of many a fiasco and much hostility Liebenau managed to cling on until May 1890, which was after all two months longer than the Reich Chancellor and his son the Foreign Secretary.

THE NEW CABINET CHIEFS

In the political sphere the changes in the two Cabinet posts were probably even more significant than the new appointments to the court and household and to the Kaiser's Military Retinue. A change at the top of the Secret Civil Cabinet, which was responsible for liaison with the non-military authorities of the Reich and Prussia, was certainly overdue. The 71-year-old Karl Freiherr von Wilmowski had been chief of the Civil Cabinet since 1861; his political role had been further enhanced in recent years because in addition to his customary work he had the responsibility of reporting to the monarch on matters concerning the Prussian Ministry of State. Lately, however, he had several times asked to be relieved of his post because of a serious eye disorder. It was therefore perfectly understandable on humanitarian grounds that permission was given for Wilmowski's retirement on 1 July 1888.[54] As Wilhelm informed his grandmother on 11 July, 'poor Wilmowski . . . had become so completely blind that he had to be operated on and he looked so incredibly pleased when I reluctantly gave my consent to his resignation, which had been refused several times, that he must really have wanted it very badly'. His successor was to be the former Under-Secretary in the Prussian Ministry of Ecclesiastical Affairs, Dr Hermann von Lucanus, who, as Wilhelm added, is 'qualified in every respect to fill the post'.[55] As the son of an apothecary, Lucanus had risen in the administration purely on

7. Hermann von Lucanus, Head of the Kaiser's Secret Civil Cabinet 1888–1908

his own merits. He had been ennobled only weeks earlier, in the last days of the reign of Friedrich III, and thus became a very isolated example at court of the tradition of the intelligent, profoundly loyal and dedicated middle-class Prussian government official. That of course did not please everyone in court society. Count Waldersee complained that Lucanus had no 'independent opinions', and danced 'entirely to Bismarck's tune'.[56] Years later, when he was awarded the Order of the Black Eagle, he was still being mocked in aristocratic circles as 'the apothecary'. When Privy Councillor von Holstein heard that Count Philipp zu Eulenburg used the phrase 'most obedient' in his letters to Lucanus, he declared that he was shocked: it was 'enough to turn the heads of all the apothecaries in the Prussian monarchy'.[57] Aristocratic court officials and army officers complained that the 'characterless' Lucanus 'complied with the Kaiser's wishes in everything', in order to remain in his well-paid post.[58] Nonetheless Lucanus led the Secret Civil Cabinet until his death in the summer of 1908, and became in time a key figure in Wilhelm II's reign.[59] Simultaneously with the replacement of Wilmowski by Lucanus, at the Kaiser's request Privy Councillor Miessner took over the running of the imperial private chancellery as secret correspondence secretary. Some time later he was also entrusted with the administration of Wilhelm II's Privy Purse.[60] The Correspondence Secretary, as we have already seen in the first volume, found himself immediately faced with a number of highly delicate matters to settle.[61] Like Lucanus he too remained in office until his death in 1909.

8. General Wilhelm von Hahnke, Head of the Kaiser's Military Cabinet 1888–1901

The Secret Military Cabinet, which was responsible for all matters of army personnel, also received a new chief directly after Wilhelm II's accession. General Emil von Albedyll imagined himself quite secure in the Kaiser's favour, although privately Wilhelm had decided to have no more to do with him since their conflict over the Union Club.[62] It was therefore to the General's considerable surprise that he found himself dismissed in the first few days of the new reign and replaced by General Wilhelm von Hahnke, who was appointed adjutant-general at the same time.[63] Like Versen and Wittich, the monarch had known Hahnke, a man of gigantic height, from his soldiering days in Potsdam: he had been Wilhelm's brigade commander when the young Prince was serving in the First Regiment of Foot Guards, and he was related by marriage to Wilhelm's erstwhile military tutor and current Flügeladjutant Adolf von Bülow.[64] He made an excellent impression on Queen Victoria, who met him in August 1889 during Wilhelm's visit to the Isle of Wight: she pronounced him 'a very pleasing man, with a straightforward manner', who was 'the principal person about William'.[65] Waldersee's verdict on Hahnke, on the other hand, was critical in the extreme: he described him as 'a man below the level of mediocrity' and 'a notoriously narrow-minded person' who was not capable of fulfilling the duties of his post properly.[66] When Waldersee asked a Commanding General who had come to Berlin in the autumn of 1890 whether he intended to call on the Chief of the Military Cabinet, the General replied: 'Why? He knows nothing about anything.'[67] And in

1891, shortly before his own downfall, the Chief of the General Staff said of the 'small-minded' Hahnke that he had not given up hope 'that the Kaiser will come to realise what kind of an adviser he has; the feeling against the man is very much on the increase'.[68] Only once, in the spring of 1891, did Hahnke proffer his resignation; 'the Kaiser, who will certainly not find a more compliant man again, naturally declined it', noted his rival Waldersee in his diary.[69] Hahnke served until 1901 as an influential chief of the Military Cabinet. His son married the daughter of Waldersee's successor as chief of the General Staff, Count Schlieffen.

## THE NEW NAVAL CABINET

Shortly after coming to the throne Wilhelm II proposed fundamental changes to the organisation of the imperial navy. Instead of a single body, the Admiralty, which had hitherto held sole responsibility for all naval affairs, the highest level of naval administration was to be divided into three authorities, analogous to the command structure of the army. The Reich Navy Office would be responsible for ship-building, and would thus have the duty of making the case for the naval establishment in the Reichstag, as the Prussian minister of war did for the army budget. The High Command would be responsible for naval operations and the strategic planning, echoing the General Staff's role for the army. Finally, a newly established Naval Cabinet, like the Military Cabinet, would have charge of personnel matters.[70] The Kaiser's aim was obvious: he was not prepared 'to tolerate an intermediate authority with powers such as the Chief of the Admiralty had possessed between himself and his favourite creation'.[71] A major administrative department of the Reich, which was directly answerable to the Reich chancellor, was broken up so that the Kaiser could intervene more easily in naval affairs.[72] The highly respected Chief of the Admiralty, General Leo von Caprivi, warned that although the army was 'so firmly grounded . . . that the interference of the Kaiser [could] not cause any serious damage', matters were 'quite different' in the navy.[73] The fact that on 5 July 1888 the young Kaiser was already ordering extensive changes to naval uniform only confirmed Caprivi in his conviction that he could not continue in office under the new sovereign.[74] To the delight of the naval officer corps it was Vice-Admiral Count Alexander XVI von Monts de Mazin, rather than yet another general, who was placed in charge of the Admiralty, at least until the reorganisation of the administrative structure of the navy could come into effect.[75]

In November 1888 Kaiser Wilhelm appointed a naval officer as Flügeladjutant, for only the second time in the history of the Prussian court. The first had been Albert Freiherr von Seckendorff, who had meanwhile been promoted to the post of Hofmarschall to Prince Heinrich.[76] Wilhelm had got to know the then

9. Admiral Gustav Freiherr von Senden-Bibran, Head of the
Kaiser's Naval Cabinet 1889–1906

41-year-old Captain Gustav Freiherr von Senden-Bibran during his state visits
to St Petersburg, Stockholm and Copenhagen and also at the naval exercises in
September 1888, when Senden had been commandant of the iron-clad *Bayern*; he
was also warmly recommended to the Kaiser by Prince Heinrich and Seckendorff.
When Senden received the imperial order appointing him Flügeladjutant on
13 November he became 'fearfully agitated', for 'the post as Flügeladjutant [and]
the life of a courtier which went with it' seemed to him 'an absolutely horrifying
idea'. 'It did not suit me at all', he reminisced in his memoirs, 'to move in exalted
circles, be cautious in expressing opinions . . . or make stimulating drawing-
room conversation.' Nevertheless he travelled to Potsdam the next day in his
new Flügeladjutant's uniform to present himself to the Kaiser. In his agitation
he was somewhat reassured to find, in the small office in the Marmorpalais
allocated to the Flügeladjutanten, officers of aristocratic birth such as Moritz
Freiherr von Bissing, whom he and his brothers had known since childhood.
The Kaiser received Senden in Hussar's uniform and said that he was glad 'that
he would now always have a naval officer about him'.[77] Commandant of the
Imperial Headquarters General von Wittich instructed him in the duties of the
Flügeladjutanten. Over the next few days he called personally on all the princes
of the royal house, and wrote to all adjutant-generals, generals à la suite and
Flügeladjutanten, to introduce himself as Flügeladjutant in attendance. 'This

is an old custom which is intended to demonstrate the solidarity between the officers attached to the person of the Kaiser', he explained. He was received cordially everywhere, even by the most senior naval authorities in Berlin, as the man who 'was to become the mouthpiece of the Kaiser'.[78]

Although the reorganisation of the naval authorities desired by the Kaiser was still being debated, it was already settled that Senden would in future administer naval personnel questions in addition to his personal service with the Kaiser. The acting Chief of the Admiralty, Count Monts, who like Caprivi was an opponent of the reorganisation, resigned himself to the new order, not least because Senden had been put in charge of personnel matters.[79] Prior to the establishment of a Naval Cabinet Senden-Bibran was detailed to serve in the Military Cabinet under Hahnke, in order to learn from the latter and from the two departmental heads, General à la suite von Brauchitsch and Colonel von Oidtman, how army personnel questions and disciplinary matters were dealt with.[80] Then, before the year was out, a Naval Cabinet analogous to the Military Cabinet was set up with Senden as chief, with responsibility for all naval personnel questions.

With the appointment of Gustav Freiherr von Senden-Bibran as Flügeladjutant and head of the Naval Cabinet the imperial court acquired a figure who ruthlessly stoked up Wilhelm II's passion for the navy and who, after Bismarck's dismissal, looked down with the greatest contempt on the statesmen who bore the responsibility for the policies of the Reich.[81] German diplomats regarded him as 'a monstrosity', who gave them 'terrible . . . headaches'.[82] Count Münster, the elderly German ambassador in Paris, commented after a meeting with Senden that it was 'a positive disgrace' to have to listen to so much nonsense and megalomania.[83] Yet all attempts to get rid of Senden from the court misfired. Until his retirement in 1906, as Privy Councillor von Holstein was forced to acknowledge through gritted teeth, he remained one of the most influential men in the Kaiser's entourage.[84]

## THE GENERAL STAFF AND THE MINISTRY OF WAR

In August 1888 the old Field Marshal Count von Moltke stepped down from his post as chief of the Great General Staff and was succeeded by Wilhelm's fatherly friend Count Alfred von Waldersee, whose influence now became so apparent that he was regarded everywhere – even abroad – as the future Reich chancellor.[85] Immediately after Wilhelm II's accession Waldersee noted in his diary that he had reason to be 'almost too proud', for he was 'definitely greatly in favour with the Kaiser, which the whole world knows, and plenty of people run after me in consequence. The Kaiser thinks a great deal of me, likes

to hear my opinion on many things and in fact has friendly feelings towards
me.'[86] After his appointment as chief of the General Staff Waldersee reflected
with some self-satisfaction: 'I am well aware that the Kaiser has placed great
confidence in me and that a tremendous responsibility may fall on my shoulders.
If war breaks out, my position is the most important not only in our army, but
also in the country, even in the whole world. On the achievements of our army
depend the future of Germany and thereby of the whole European states system . . . How wonderful are God's ways! I have one of the most brilliant careers
behind me and the whole world looks to me, for as things are the chief of the
General Staff of the German Army is in fact the most respected of all military
officers.'[87]

Since Wilhelm II listened to Waldersee's advice on all military decisions and
frequently disregarded the established division of responsibilities, the power of
the General Staff within the army increased so fast and to such an extent that
Minister of War General Paul Bronsart von Schellendorf felt obliged to hand in
his resignation at the end of 1888. The Kaiser positively welcomed this battle
between Waldersee and Bronsart, particularly as the latter had aroused his anger
earlier that year with his contemptuous attitude towards the navy.[88] In December
Wilhelm declared that he was glad 'to have direct fights with the Minister of War
and others, which enabled Him to sharpen His teeth; yesterday He had already
had Bronsart in tears!'[89] As Waldersee confided to his friend General Julius von
Verdy du Vernois, who was to be appointed Bronsart's successor as minister of
war at Waldersee's suggestion, Bronsart had lost his 'balance' since the death of
Wilhelm I; he had become nervy and allowed 'trifles' to annoy him. 'From the
very beginning he did not know how to get on with the present Kaiser, and there
is an uncomfortable feeling on both sides. Now Bronsart has got it into his head
that the Kaiser has more confidence in me than in him, which he thinks is an
intolerable situation, and of course in this he is just seeing things. The position is
that the young Kaiser is very independent, does not always observe divisions of
responsibility strictly enough and sometimes expresses His will to the Minister
of War in a very decided manner. So the position of a minister is naturally
different from before, and all the more so because the Kaiser wishes to give the
chief of the General Staff more powers.' If, as Waldersee had recommended, the
Kaiser should appoint Verdy minister of war, it would be conditional on Verdy
declaring himself in favour of a 'further demarcation of powers between the
Ministry and the General Staff', Waldersee wrote. He added with machiavellian
disingenuousness: 'I hope that you will not make any difficulties, and I am sure
that we shall agree. I feel that this is a great moment and in this way you can
begin to render great service to the army and the Fatherland.'[90] At this Verdy
himself suggested that on his appointment 'a few of the powers of the minister

of war' could be taken away from him.[91] A few days later Waldersee had to inform Verdy that Bronsart had withdrawn his resignation for the time being, at Bismarck's urgent request, and that the Minister of War had received strong support from the officers in his ministry in his battle against the increase in the power of the General Staff. Nevertheless the Kaiser would triumph, Waldersee assured him. 'I believe that the Kaiser has the intention of making you the successor', he wrote to Verdy on 2 December 1888. 'He brought the matter up himself today. It could be that he encounters opposition from the Chancellor; but as things stand at the moment it will not be strong. The Chancellor is no longer what he used to be; he knows the strength of his sovereign's will and just now he has other plans for which he badly needs to win concessions, so he will be careful not to play too high a card here.'[92] The observation was accurate: after Verdy's appointment as minister of war in April 1889 Waldersee was able to note with satisfaction: 'Another sign that the Chancellor is very ready to give in to the Kaiser is that he raised absolutely no objection to Verdy's appointment.' Indeed, Bismarck had even put a brave face on it and told 'all the world that he was very pleased that the Kaiser [had] chosen Verdy'.[93] Only after his dismissal did Bismarck show his resentment at the appointment of a long-standing personal opponent to be his colleague as a minister, when he wrote: 'Verdy treated me as an enemy from 1870 in France (demi-gods) and because he falsely blamed me for his transfer to Königsberg; also because he is of a progressive–liberal turn of mind.'[94]

Since the Kaiser exercised unlimited 'power of command' in the military sphere as supreme war lord, and moreover (after hearing the advice of the Chief of the Military Cabinet) took decisions on all matters of army personnel entirely on his own, the Reich chancellor and Prussian minister-president had absolutely no say in the choice of the minister of war. And yet, because the minister of war was a member of the Prussian Ministry of State, and also because of the anomaly that he had to present the army budget in the Reichstag since there could be no Reich minister of war in the federated German Reich, he had to work closely with the chancellor. The new distribution of functions between the Ministry of War and the General Staff therefore represented – like the introduction of a Naval Cabinet and a Naval High Command – both a reduction of the authority of the state that was more than symbolic, and an increase in the powers of the crown. But even after the concessions made by Verdy to the General Staff in the spring of 1889 the 'all-highest, all-gracious Ministry of War' was still too powerful in the eyes of Wilhelm II. As the Kaiser's brother-in-law, himself a commanding general, commented ten years after Verdy's appointment, Wilhelm was convinced that 'the omnipotence of the Ministry of War must be broken; there is only one way of doing this: greater decentralisation'.[95]

The Kaiser, of course, made full use of his right of appointment to select the commanding generals and to fill the remaining high-ranking posts in the army with his personal choices. As late as 1904 we find an officer, commenting on the appointment of one of the Flügeladjutanten as 'commander of the most illustrious brigade in the army,' writing: 'It is quite clear that the Kaiser's wish is absolutely decisive in such nominations.'[96] What such appointments meant for the social life of a province is vividly illustrated by a letter from the Commanding General in Breslau, Bernhard, Hereditary Prince of Saxe-Meiningen. 'In accordance with the longstanding tradition everyone looks to the commanding general, how he conducts himself here and there, how he receives people and where he goes, and where he does not. The nobility and society instinctively take the lead from the commanding general, which is at present even more the case than hitherto.'[97] At the beginning of each year and in times of crisis the Kaiser summoned the commanding generals to Berlin — this too was an innovation brought in by him. They were expected to act as a body, like an Areopagus hovering over the state, to reinforce his authority and legitimise his decisions. Thus it was that they were summoned to Berlin on 18 March 1890, when Bismarck was forced to hand in his resignation.[98]

## 'THE ENTOURAGE OF THE YOUNG SOVEREIGN'

The radical reorganisation of the structure and personnel of the court and of the high command of the country's defence forces which took place immediately after the accession of Wilhelm II was undoubtedly the Kaiser's own work. Waldersee was quite right in recording on 23 June 1888 that the Kaiser had 'selected the personalities and the adjutants himself'.[99] Consistent with this was his observation four months later that Wilhelm was 'undoubtedly the master . . . where his entourages are concerned',[100] for the power of appointment and dismissal is the key to power itself. All too soon the Hohenzollern court acquired an atmosphere of mawkish sycophancy which repelled many observers. 'God knows', one of the Flügeladjutanten exclaimed in disgust at the sight of the 'swarm of courtiers', 'one cannot help laughing, but one often feels sick at this wretched craning upwards of eyes and ears!'[101] The military suite, however, showed no more character than the civilian courtiers. As the British military attaché Leopold Swaine remarked in 1892 on being reappointed to Berlin after an absence of three years: 'What we suffer under here is a hornets nest of fulsome flatterers whose sole interest is to remain in favour in order to draw their salleries [sic] and obtain decorations from all arriving Royalties . . . The Emperor is either no judge of character or else he prefers having silly people about him who can't, or dare not, give him contrary advice to his own inclinations.' Swaine preferred the latter explanation.[102]

The men whom Wilhelm had gathered around himself were mostly young and inexperienced. Many of them were professional soldiers from minor aristocratic families, while a few, like Lucanus and Müller, were of middle-class stock. Apart from the holders of the senior honorary posts at court, the higher aristocracy and great landowners were not represented in the new imperial entourage. The court lacked the kind of older, more experienced and prudent person who could have dissuaded the young, immature, impulsive monarch from his notorious 'suddennesses'. The Hungarian *grand seigneur* Count Széchényi reported from Berlin on 29 December 1888 that 'the entourage of the young sovereign' was 'a subject of serious concern to most right-thinking and well-disposed people' and certainly left much to be desired 'in that the Kaiser has no one about him with sufficient experience of the world and knowledge of what is customary, traditional and seemly to make up for what His Majesty himself, being so young, naturally lacks in that regard'. The Kaiser's court consisted of 'nothing but insignificant young people', he wrote, 'who have been so to speak catapulted out of the limited circumstances of the small princely court at the Stadtschloss in Potsdam on to the broad, high plateau of the Imperial Court'. Even General von Wittich, the senior Adjutant General, and General von Hahnke, the Chief of the Military Cabinet, were 'undoubtedly two outstanding experts in their field and in that respect a very fortunate choice; but since they have hitherto lived only within and for their profession' they were 'lacking in any knowledge or experience of the world'. The only person who had had the opportunity to acquire such knowledge, namely Count Herbert Bismarck, either did not possess 'the necessary tact' to make appropriate use of his experience, or lacked influence, perhaps 'because he does not yet feel safe enough in the saddle to use [his influence] without endangering it'. The Reich Chancellor, who could have played the most effective role in this respect, was staying 'well out of the line of fire' at Friedrichsruh, following his ploy of not intervening in insignificant questions in order to preserve the full weight of his influence for matters of great political import. 'The state of affairs here' in the new Reich, the ambassador reflected, 'is in general so very unsettled and still only at the formative stage, especially as it has not evolved step by step and gradually, but has arisen suddenly and developed by leaps and bounds. It is a state which can well be compared with that of fermenting, bubbling young wine. The finer the juice of the vine, the more it works and the better and stronger the wine will then become, when all impure and foreign elements have at last settled. – May it be so!'[103]

At the beginning of 1889 the perspicacious Széchényi returned to this central theme and emphasised how much Wilhelm II dominated his entourage. 'When one . . . considers', he wrote, 'that the entourage of the young sovereign is of the kind that I tried to describe in my . . . secret report . . . of the 29th of last month, and that it not only owes its present existence to the favour of its Imperial Master but also counts on Him for its future, it is perfectly comprehensible that it always guards against expressing a view contrary to His Majesty's intentions, and only ventures such a view when He expressly asks for it, so that in many cases the youthful and hasty initiative of the sovereign does not find the counterweight that would be desirable. At the same time this close entourage nonetheless retains, at least in those cases where it is consulted, sufficient room for manoeuvre to be able to exercise a not inconsiderable influence, although it can by no means be taken for granted that the best use is always made of this.'[104] In the Bismarck crisis that began to emerge soon after the accession, the court that Wilhelm had built around himself formed a bastion of imperial power against which the Reich Chancellor, even with the support of Liebenau, could not in the end prevail.

# CHAPTER EIGHT

# The domination of the Bismarcks

## THE KAISER AND THE BISMARCKS

I N the first months of his reign Wilhelm II's relationship with the Bismarcks was nothing if not harmonious. In October 1888, when it was suggested to him that he ought to develop 'his own ideas as Kaiser', he exclaimed: 'It is too stupid that people simply refuse to understand that the young and the old generations can work excellently together. There is no such thing as the Kaiser and the Chancellor having separate ideas; the troublemakers always forget that I worked in the Foreign Office for $2^1/_2$ years.'[1] Also forgotten, apparently, were the Bismarcks' grim premonitions of the previous year[2] and even the conflicts of the previous few weeks, for while Friedrich III was still on the throne Herbert Bismarck had had to seek a vote of confidence from the then Crown Prince Wilhelm, so badly had the latter treated him.[3] Now, however, after the accession, the Foreign Secretary reported with gratification to Friedrichsruh that the young Kaiser was 'very affable, just as always'.[4] 'Our new sovereign is very attentive, and at the same time calm and objective; he is excellent to work with.'[5] 'Our Kaiser does his job extremely well', the Chancellor's son wrote to Holstein on 15 October 1888 from Rome. 'He pleases and impresses everywhere he goes.'[6] Two days later, in a further letter to the influential Privy Councillor, he commented: 'It is very easy to get along with H.M., at all events easier than with any other sovereign with whom I have hitherto been acquainted.' Herbert added that Wilhelm had been 'quite exceptionally nice' to him on the journey to Austria and Italy; he had 'often come into my room in the evening with his brother to recover from the day's exertions with the help of beer, cigars, and jokes. Everything goes splendidly, H.M. makes a first-rate impression everywhere, and for his part is thoroughly content.'[7]

No doubt some of this optimism was only for show, for the Bismarcks were of course fully aware of the instability of their position, dependent as it was entirely on the 'confidence' of the dynamic, impatient and unpredictable young monarch. That is evident from their carefully calculated conduct. In August 1888 the old Reich Chancellor refused to travel to Hamburg with Wilhelm, 'because he feared becoming a burden to the Kaiser, and putting H.M. in the shade through the ovations that he receives'. In order to 'get out of everyone's way' Prince Bismarck, who had been living at Friedrichsruh since 12 July 1888, took the decision to withdraw even further to his Pomeranian property of Varzin. His daughter Marie and her husband Kuno Count von Rantzau tried to talk him out of this idea 'because of the cold and the great distance from Berlin', but the Chancellor remained at first 'quite firm, and said that he had things to do at Varzin, which to my knowledge is not true, and that Mama wanted to go there'. Rantzau decided to co-opt Bismarck's doctor Schweninger as an ally against the move to Pomerania, for quite apart from the danger that it would scarcely be possible for government business to be carried on during parliamentary sessions if he were at Varzin, to stay so far away from Berlin would be inadvisable on health grounds as well.[8] Although Bismarck did remain at Friedrichsruh for the time being – Herbert also considered a move to Varzin would be 'disastrous' and set out to 'frustrate' his parents' decision[9] – the Chancellor's arguments nevertheless show how precarious he considered his position to be as far as the Kaiser was concerned. This is also demonstrated by the overcautious, courtier-like attitude which the Chancellor adopted towards the young Kaiser during his absence from Berlin. 'Don't forget at the next audience to thank His Majesty for his greetings and for allowing me to remain here longer for my health in spite of the Reichstag', he telegraphed in cipher from Friedrichsruh to his son in Berlin on 7 December 1888.[10]

Wilhelm for his part found Bismarck's absence extremely agreeable. At the end of December 1888, when Herbert Bismarck handed him a letter from the Chancellor, the Kaiser read it with a smile and remarked that it was a very good thing that the Chancellor had 'remained in the country until now', both because it suited Prince Bismarck better and because it obliged him, the Kaiser, to deal directly with the ministers.[11] In June 1889, when the Chancellor carried out his original plan of going to Varzin,[12] Wilhelm expressed pleasure at this decision. The Kaiser was 'in the happiest of moods', Herbert reported to his father, and had said 'it was a real blessing that Schweninger had at last succeeded in persuading you to go to Varzin, and he hoped that you would have a complete rest there'.[13] Apart from a few short trips to Berlin to greet visiting foreign monarchs, Bismarck was not to return to the capital until 24 January 1890.

Given the international significance of this development, it is not surprising to find that the latent threat to the power of the Bismarck family under the new Kaiser was a central theme in the reports written by German and foreign diplomats at the time. As early as October 1888 Count Hatzfeldt, the German ambassador in London, intimated to the British Prime Minister 'that the young Emperor was very difficult to manage, that Prince Bismarck was in great perplexity, and his temper had consequently become more than usually unbearable'.[14] The Austro-Hungarian ambassador recorded in February 1889 that the old Prince was avoiding 'everything which might displease the young Kaiser.' As evidence of this Széchényi cited the fact that Bismarck, 'to the astonishment of all', had attended the service in the Schloss chapel to celebrate the Kaiser's birthday on 27 January 1889. When Széchényi expressed his surprise at this, the Prince replied that if he had not come, his 'young sovereign' might have thought that he was failing to show due respect. As the ambassador aptly observed, it was widely felt in Berlin 'that Prince Bismarck is no longer the only driving-wheel of the state, and that as such he often chooses to keep still, accommodating himself to the new circumstances, whether in order to avoid wearing himself out unnecessarily, or to pave the way for his son'. The undeniable result of this restraint, however, was that other political figures in Berlin 'generally have the tendency to follow whichever paths they think will lead to good, secure positions in the new era'.[15]

Only a few days later Széchényi was commenting on the numerous 'very significant' assertions in the official and pro-government press to the effect that 'the relationship between the Reich Chancellor and Kaiser Wilhelm II continued to be an untroubled one'. As mouthpiece for this announcement Bismarck had chosen the *Hannover'sche Courier*, but the article which appeared in that newspaper entitled 'Kaiser and Chancellor' had been reprinted in the *Norddeutsche Allgemeine Zeitung*, and again in the *Post*, with the additional assurance that the article had received 'full approval in the highest and most authoritative political circles'. The conclusion which one must draw from these 'resounding and persistent trumpet blasts', Széchényi opined, was 'that Prince Bismarck still possessed the confidence of his sovereign, and that his position was therefore in no way compromised or indeed weakened, but that he had ceased to be all things in all respects, partly from the prudent, self-imposed moderation of his influence, partly because of the drive towards independent action which is natural both to the age and to the character of the young sovereign'.[16] Others were less diplomatic in their language. The Empress Frederick, disgusted at the old Chancellor's behaviour, wrote on 20 April 1889 that he 'toadies William as he never did his grandfather or his father'.[17]

10. Count Herbert von Bismarck, German Foreign Secretary 1886–1890

For months on end the Reich Chancellor deliberately remained away from the capital, returning only for a few short visits, and these during the time when Herbert Bismarck was abroad.[18] The actual conduct of government business therefore rested on the shoulders of his son Herbert, who however kept in close touch with his father through his brother-in-law Kuno Rantzau and the Chief of the Reich Chancellery, Franz von Rottenburg. A vivid description of the outward appearance of this little-known key figure in German politics has reached us from the pen of Heinrich von Eckardt, a Baltic baron. The Chancellor's son, he wrote, was 'tall, broad-shouldered and heavily built'; he had 'a rather reddened face with a very determined expression, large eyes with a steady, rather overpowering gaze' and wore his hair 'not smooth but curly', so that he looked as if he had run his hand through his hair. He spoke very fast, 'without pronouncing the words very clearly'. In all, the Foreign Secretary gave the impression of a 'very determined, rather rough, perhaps even brutal personality', but he did not allow himself to be governed by emotions, but demanded 'manly German conduct' from his colleagues. With him one had to be 'able to work very hard; also to be lively and able to drink beer, smoke and talk frankly'.[19]

In the interval between Wilhelm's accession on 15 June 1888 and the beginning of the fateful year of 1890, Herbert Bismarck had 112 private audiences or other opportunities to discuss political questions face to face with the Kaiser; *in addition* to this he spent no fewer than seventy-four days travelling with the

Kaiser. Over the same period the Reich Chancellor saw the monarch – apart from at a few banquets for foreign sovereigns – only about ten times altogether, and Herbert was also present at four of his private audiences during these eighteen months.[20] Undoubtedly, therefore, Herbert Bismarck's relationship with the young Kaiser formed the cornerstone of the whole system of government. As Széchényi reported to Vienna in January 1889, it was 'the people in daily, close contact who gain most influence on His Majesty, and these are Count Herbert von Bismarck and Herr von Liebenau'.[21] For every appointment, every dismissal, every measure of domestic, foreign or colonial policy, Herbert had to 'extract' the consent of the Kaiser, but he succeeded in doing so. As the Empress Frederick observed in April 1889: 'Herb: Bismarks [sic] influence is supreme.'[22]

That the Foreign Secretary was doing his utmost to foster his relationship with Wilhelm can be seen in the – cynically calculating – obsequious tone of his letters, which dripped with expressions like 'most condescending', 'respectfully', 'all-gracious' and 'all-humblest'.[23] He advised Rantzau to remember the Kaiser's penchant for gossip when he wrote his reports from Munich.[24] Waldersee's verdict on this system and on Herbert Bismarck's servile attitude was contemptuous: 'This pathetic adviser throws himself at the Kaiser in an almost laughable way; people rightly see it as proof of the Bismarck system's weakness; it thinks itself very shaky if it cannot constantly work on the Kaiser. Young people are already laughing at Count Bismarck when they see him in society or at dinners etc. laying siege to the Kaiser and watching everyone who speaks to him. The Kaiser takes a very firm attitude towards everyone . . . and easily overcomes any opposition.' Under no circumstances, maintained Waldersee, could one say that the Kaiser had any respect for Herbert Bismarck.[25]

The fact that in a system like this decisions were sometimes based more on a desire to maintain an individual's position of power than on objective considerations led to criticism from many sides. Széchényi, for instance, found it incomprehensible that the Berlin government openly launched a strong attack on the British ambassador in St Petersburg, although 'they need England's support for their policy both on peace and on colonial affairs'. He likewise commented incredulously on the arrest of Geffcken for the publication of extracts from the war diary of the late Kaiser Friedrich, for this affair was undeniably 'a dangerous gamble with the prestige of the throne and the reputation of the courts'.[26] According to Széchényi, in well-informed circles in Berlin erroneous decisions such as these were attributed not to the Reich Chancellor, but to the relationship between Herbert Bismarck and the Kaiser. 'If one asks who was the driving force behind these matters, the answer is usually Count Herbert Bismarck, or even His Majesty the Kaiser, but as for the Reich Chancellor himself having played any part in them, that is denied outright.'[27]

The 39-year-old Herbert Bismarck was vulnerable not only because of the huge burden of work which he had to carry and his fear of rivals in the imperial favour, but also because of his unconventional lifestyle. He was still unmarried at this time: his father, by threatening suicide, had forced him to abandon his marriage in 1881 to the divorced Princess Elisabeth Carolath, née Hatzfeldt-Trachenberg, who was related to the Loë and Schleinitz families.[28] Herbert's diary shows that he regularly went out drinking into the early hours of the morning at large receptions or in smaller groups; occasionally he would have to dress hurriedly after only three or four hours' sleep because the Kaiser was at his door early in the morning with one of his Flügeladjutanten.[29] As secretary of state at the Foreign Office he frequently had to hold receptions for well over 100 guests, but other evenings were of a less formal order. The prudish Protestant Waldersee recorded indignantly in February 1889 that in Berlin 'much scandal is caused by Count Bismarck's parties. He invites ladies now too, the tone is very vulgar from the start and becomes worse by the hour as the drink takes its effect; by the end — yesterday morning the end was between 7 and 8 o'clock — the whole thing was said to have resembled a party in a brothel.' After this particular 'dance' the Kaiser called at Herbert's residence at 9.45 a.m. with Major von Pfuel.[30] Waldersee identified the female members of Herbert Bismarck's circle as the Dutch-born Frau Alide von Schrader, Countess Sibylle von Bismarck (née Arnim-Kröchlendorff, wife of his brother Bill Bismarck), Princess Maria Radziwill (née Countess Branicki in Paris in 1863, daughter-in-law of Prince Anton Radziwill) and Hereditary Princess Dorothee von Fürstenberg (née Talleyrand-Périgord in 1862, daughter of the Duc de Sagan). As foreign diplomats were also present at the parties, the whole world knew about these scandalous proceedings, the Chief of the General Staff commented, adding a note of warning: 'It cannot go on much longer like this.'[31] At the beginning of June 1889 Prince Heinrich and Waldersee were at one in agreeing that 'Count Bismarck is a real misfortune for the Kaiser.' On all his journeys, whether to St Petersburg, Stockholm, Copenhagen, Stuttgart, Munich, Vienna or Rome, Herbert Bismarck had drawn attention to himself by his 'uncouth, brutal and tactless nature'.[32] 'Wherever he has been abroad, and unfortunately he has been to many places, . . . people are horrified by his manners, by the rough tone of his conversation and by innumerable tactless remarks. It is deeply to be deplored that he has accompanied the Kaiser so often; the Kaiser has done everything well abroad, while Count Bismarck has undone much of the good he had done.'[33]

The Foreign Secretary was criticised not only for his marked weakness for drink[34] and his uninhibited bachelor life. His general manner and his misanthropic contempt for his colleagues and for subordinate officials made him positively hated. 'That he is really loathed by his subordinates for his inconsiderate, brutal behaviour is certainly not a good sign', Waldersee noted in autumn 1889. 'The diplomatic profession has unfortunately declined so much that there are no men of character to be found in it any more; some of them unwillingly resign themselves and keep quiet; others try to survive by toadying and flattery. This is true of those abroad as well as of the officials here at home. Abroad as well as among the diplomats here he [Herbert Bismarck] is really detested . . . He has inherited his father's worst characteristics, but unfortunately none of the good ones.'[35]

Whether Waldersee's harsh criticism of his arch-rival was justified or not, it is undeniable that for the time being the Bismarck family maintained tight control on the power of the state through this system. In February 1889 Waldersee complained that the position of the Chancellor was 'more powerful than ever'; no minister, no head of a Reich Office, no diplomat dared to express an independent opinion or make an independent judgement. 'The ministers are completely his creatures, he is in command of the Ministry of State and tolerates no opposition; all diplomatic agents report only what they think he likes to hear. Everyone pays court to him, and not only to him but to his family as well. It is truly disgusting to see how lamentably servile people are to his sons.' Although the Chancellor sensed that he had come up against 'a self-willed Kaiser', his handling of the monarch was 'masterful'. 'He flatters him to an unbelievable degree, sometimes gives in to him in lesser things, acting as if he were making a great sacrifice; he shows himself ostentatiously before the world as the humble servant of his sovereign, whom he nevertheless *de facto* controls. He makes his son go to see the Kaiser as often as he possibly can, and the latter's strength lies in all kinds of stories and jokes with which he keeps the Kaiser amused. Unfortunately the Kaiser has no idea that he is being led, and is equally unaware that he is constantly lied to in the most shameless manner.'[36]

Yet in the course of 1889 the situation gradually changed in two respects. First, not least because of the ever-growing and ever more conspicuous independence of the Kaiser, criticism of the Bismarckian style of government became increasingly vocal in political circles in Berlin. Second, the old Chancellor's powers were visibly on the wane. Both developments were closely watched and recorded by Waldersee. Until the summer of 1889, he wrote, the admirers of the Reich Chancellor were 'still very numerous'. They remained convinced that it was best 'to let the old, experienced Chancellor do as he thought fit; he would be sure to see that everything turned out well'. The entire diplomatic corps, Waldersee complained, was in any case well schooled in the habit of 'blindly obeying the orders they received without expecting any explanations'.[37] But since the autumn of 1889 a different mood had begun to prevail. In government circles there was an increasing recognition of the 'web of lies' spun by Bismarck, from

11. Before the storm – Kaiser Wilhelm II with Bismarck at Friedrichsruh
in autumn 1888

which ministers and close colleagues had greatly suffered.[38] There was much
ill-feeling among them: they all complained that they 'do not know what the
Chancellor wants and that he changes his mind every instant'.[39]

As to the health of the Reich Chancellor, in April 1889, immediately after
Bismarck's seventy-fourth birthday, Waldersee commented on how much the
Chancellor had aged recently. 'He is far less decisive, less efficient and much
feebler.'[40] Six months later, after visiting Friedrichsruh on 16 October, Waldersee
noted that, although Bismarck had been complaining about his state of health
for years, this time he had emphasised that 'his powers were visibly failing, his
walks were becoming shorter and shorter, his capacity and zest for work were
greatly diminished'.[41] A year after Wilhelm II's accession Herbert noted in his
diary: 'Papa overtired, depressed', and added that he had put on weight again and
weighed 200 pounds.[42] At the beginning of 1890 other visitors to Friedrichsruh
reported that the Chancellor had become very old and weak and sometimes

broke down in tears. As Waldersee wrote: 'He is witnessing the collapse of what he has built up and he no longer has the strength for bold action. His great days were over with the death of Kaiser Wilhelm I. Since then . . . , i.e. in the time of the present Kaiser, his power [has] gradually declined and he says quite openly that the Kaiser is a self-willed sovereign with whom it is difficult to work; he sees that he will escape from his control and will not take his son as his successor; at the same time his powers are failing, he has lost his resolve and has become discouraged. But it could not be otherwise; such a web of lies as he and his creatures have spun round the Kaiser cannot last forever. I still believe strongly', Waldersee affirmed, 'that divine providence will in the long run cause good to triumph and evil to be defeated, and I am therefore firmly convinced that Bismarck will come to an inglorious end and that his son will depart, unlamented by anyone.'[43]

At the beginning of the decisive year of 1890 Waldersee's diary provides a revealing analysis of the Bismarckian system of government in its last throes. 'The Chancellor wishes to control everything', the General commented, 'but no longer has the strength to do so. He is Foreign Minister and interferes in each of the Reich departments without considering the views of their heads; he is the Prussian Minister-President and Minister of Trade and treats the individual ministers as mere subordinates; he feels free to interfere in the most brazen fashion in their areas of responsibility. What is more, he sits at Friedrichsruh and is therefore difficult to get hold of. Not a single minister nor a single head of a Reich department dares to contradict him. They all complain about the lack of instructions or about uncertainties in the decisions taken, and especially about the Chancellor's lies, and in times like the present, when the Reichstag and the Landtag are assembled, they are often placed in the most difficult position.'[44] Waldersee was by no means alone in thinking that this state of affairs was intolerable and degrading for the Kaiser.

## PHILIPP EULENBURG, 'THE KAISER'S BEST FRIEND'

One of the first signs that the Bismarckian ascendancy was under threat from the determination of the passionate and strong-willed young Kaiser to go his own way appeared very early, and not by coincidence, in the form of a dispute over an appointment. Wilhelm's deep-rooted friendship with Philipp Count zu Eulenburg, who had been Prussian secretary of legation in Munich since 1881, had begun in May 1886 and had been reinforced by the enthralling reports Eulenburg had written on the dramatic death of King Ludwig II of Bavaria. Wilhelm had taken a cure lasting several weeks at Bad Reichenhall in the summer of that year, when he and Eulenburg had travelled together to the Bavarian

12. Count (later Prince) Philipp zu Eulenburg-Hertefeld, the Kaiser's best friend

royal castles and to Bayreuth; they had also gone on rowing expeditions together
(with the young fisherman Jakob Ernst) on the Starnberg lake, all of which
had served to strengthen the bond between Wilhelm and the diplomat, poet,
novelist, singer and composer, who was some twelve years his senior. Their common interest in spiritualist seances with mediums and secret writing provided
further stimulus to the friendship between the two men.[45] Soon it became clear
to all those in the know that Kaiser Wilhelm II 'loves Philipp Eulenburg more
than any other living person'.[46] And Eulenburg loved the Kaiser no less. In the
reign of Wilhelm II he was destined to play the powerful but dangerous role of
the imperial protégé, the favourite. It was a relationship which threatened the
Bismarcks' monopoly of influence at its weakest point.

In the first few weeks after the accession Eulenburg was still uncertain of
how the Kaiser's feelings for him would be affected by the new circumstances.
His letters to the monarch continued to be warm, almost affectionate. 'I need
not say how painful it is to me that our journey to Bayreuth now also has to be

given up', he wrote on 5 July 1888, scarcely three weeks after his 'dearly beloved' friend had succeeded to the 'most powerful crown on this earth'. 'Your Majesty will understand how deeply it affects me to have to remain so far away, after everything Your Majesty has gone through . . . How proud it made me to picture the princes gathered around Your Majesty – around my King!' Eulenburg did not miss the opportunity of adding a detailed description of the strange goings-on at the court of King Karl I of Württemberg, knowing that it would appeal to the Kaiser's taste for such tales.[47]

At the end of July Eulenburg received a sign that Wilhelm's friendship for him had not changed. In an allusion to one of the Nordic 'Skaldic Songs' composed by Eulenburg with the biographical title 'How they became friends', the Kaiser telegraphed to him from Sweden to say that he was writing 'from the land of Skaldic Songs, of beautiful women and of the Sea King. From the land of the Nordic Urwala, from the skerries, my greeting rings out to my friend the Skald.' As the Kaiser signed the telegram with the name 'Hokan', identifying himself with the powerful hero-figure in Eulenburg's Skaldic Song, Eulenburg replied with a new poem, 'King Hokan' which included the telling lines:

> *Auf loderndem Drachen, im rauschenden Meer*
> *Versank König Helge mit Schild und Speer . . .*
> *'Jetzt gilt unser Ruf einem neuen Mann!*
> *Herr Hokan, der junge, in strahlender Wehr,*
> *Der führt uns wohl sieghaft weit über das Meer!'*

> [On his flame-spewing dragon, in the stormy sea drear
> Sank downwards King Helge with shield and with spear . . .
> 'Now sounds out our summons to a new man!
> Lord Hokan, the youthful, in bright armour arrayed
> Will lead us victorious o'er seas far and wide!'][48]

After his return from Scandinavia Wilhelm wrote again stressing how glad he would have been to have Eulenburg with him in Stockholm. He gave a rapturous description of the great parade which he had held on 1 September in Berlin in the presence of the King of Sweden, exclaiming: 'What a feeling it is to call these troops *mine!*' Finally he expressed his pleasure that he and Eulenburg were soon to meet in Munich, where they would be able to talk 'undisturbed'.[49] This letter threw Eulenburg into a 'frenzy of joy'. He had 'the greatest difficulty' in controlling himself, 'so as not to write four pages of thanks!' The Kaiser would know well, he declared, 'what feelings stirred me at the sight of this beloved handwriting!' He was 'delighted with the soaring spirit of imagination which dwells in Your Majesty's breast'. 'That is the element which provides the counterweight to the energetic realism which Your Majesty's high calling demands.' If the Kaiser were able to come to Eulenburg's home in Munich, he would sing him a new ballad over a glass of Swedish punch from a Viking recipe.[50]

The Kaiser's meeting with Eulenburg in Munich in early October brought another unmistakable demonstration of friendship. As Eulenburg reported afterwards to his mother, he had '*never* doubted the Kaiser's sentiments towards me – but I was surprised by the *demonstrative* manner in which he favoured and honoured me'. Wilhelm had obviously wished 'to show others that he is fond of me – and how touching that is! A young man who does not flinch at the mightiest crown on the earth, who holds to his convictions with simplicity and truth, cannot but have a fine, distinguished nature. The mediocre man loses his head – not he!' When he saw Eulenburg again on 1 October at the train station in Munich, Wilhelm told him that he needed to speak to him again that evening. Eulenburg therefore waited until the royal family dinner at the Residenz was over and visited the Kaiser in his room at 11.30 p.m. 'He kept me with him until 1 o'clock, tête à tête – quite his old self – talking about everything which concerns us.'[51] The next morning at 10 o'clock, when Eulenburg arrived at the Residenz, the Kaiser had already sent for him. He gave him '*personally*', as Herbert Bismarck immediately reported to his father, 'the Hohenzollern Order . . . , although he had received the Order of the Red Eagle Class IV only in April'.[52] The other men at the legation received no decorations at all. The Kaiser also singled out Eulenburg's Swedish wife 'very conspicuously' and invited her and all her six children to Potsdam. 'Finally the Kaiser gave the Bavarians the following demonstration of his esteem for me', Eulenburg told his parents. 'On his departure, while he was standing at the carriage window, with the whole Bavarian royal family, all the ministers etc. assembled in front of him after he had taken leave of them, he beckoned me to the carriage last. I had to climb on to the footboard and he spoke to me quietly for a few minutes – again expressing the wish to come and hunt at Liebenberg in the autumn. This demonstration was intended to show Munich that he values me – and that this should be noted for the future.'[53]

It was not until 15 October that Eulenburg felt able to thank the Kaiser for these marks of friendship, for 'if I had tried earlier, I should have become sentimental, and that is as repugnant to Your Majesty as to myself! But now I write these lines with a cool head, although with a burning heart – my thanks for the expression of true friendship which every word and every look proved to me! The most powerful crown on this earth has no power over Your Majesty's heart and true mind – and he who wears such a crown unwaveringly is a noble man indeed! If it were possible, my love for my Kaiser would be many thousand times stronger now!' The impression made in Munich by Wilhelm's visit had been 'very striking and beneficial', Eulenburg reported; it had produced 'an overflow of German national enthusiasm' which would provoke 'the particularist gentlemen' into 'hoisting the blue and white colours of Bavaria again for some time to come'. He, Eulenburg, could see through these aspirations better than anyone else, he claimed. 'My experiences in Bavaria lead me to this conclusion: enthusiasm for the Kaiser must be instilled into the Germans *even more*, for only *a few months ago* there was still a possibility that the whole of southern Germany might be thrown off balance by Battenberg nonsense!'[54] With ardent assurances of friendship and political hints such as these, targeted at the Kaiser's innermost wishes, Eulenburg struck home with deadly accuracy. The longer-term significance of this friendship can scarcely be overestimated; but it also concealed an immediate danger. During the reign of Friedrich III, Bismarck had appointed his son in law, Count Rantzau, Prussian envoy in Munich, thus making him Eulenburg's superior, although Wilhelm − Crown Prince at the time − had strongly urged the appointment of Eulenburg to this influential post. With the new reign it was inevitable that this issue should again raise its head. During the great ceremony of the opening of the Reichstag at the Berlin Schloss on 25 June 1888 Wilhelm spoke to Bavarian Minister-President Freiherr von Lutz of his intention of appointing Eulenburg envoy in Munich, adding: 'Unfortunately one cannot always do as one wishes − but what has not happened can still be made to happen!' Both Lutz and Bavarian Foreign Minister Christoph Freiherr von Crailsheim had the impression, as Eulenburg sensed, 'that the Kaiser means business'. Herbert Bismarck, on the other hand, was intent on sending Eulenburg as far away as possible, to a distant post abroad as secretary at an embassy.[55]

A serious argument broke out between Wilhelm II and the Foreign Secretary at the end of September 1888 on Mainau Island. The Kaiser declared that 'he would like to make Philipp Eulenburg an envoy as soon as possible, preferably in Munich'. Herbert Bismarck at once recognised the danger concealed in this arrangement and wrote to his father: 'From the seriousness with which H.M. spoke of Eulenburg's promotion I conclude that he is absolutely set on it and will be angry if he is opposed. Liebenau merely confirms what I have known for a long time, that H.M. loves Ph. Eulenburg more than any other living person. We shall therefore have to reckon with him, and I am in favour of making this concession to the Kaiser, who is otherwise so tractable, sensible and easy to win over. When I told H.M. that Eulenburg ought first to go to an embassy in order get away from the one-sided view from Munich, he argued that this was not necessary, as he knew him well and he was an intelligent person. H.M. brushed aside the question of seniority . . . and said that Eulenburg was more senior in years (which is true) and had lost time, which should not be allowed to count against him. When I objected that there was no available vacancy [for Rantzau] he retorted that one could easily be made – he seemed quite inclined to get rid of [Alfred von] Bülow-Bern or Wesdehlen [the Prussian envoy in Stuttgart] immediately. I then said that Rantzau had only just been appointed; to which H.M. replied that that was exactly why he did not know the form in Munich as well as Eulenburg and would be better off in another post, as soon as there was a vacancy.'[56]

In the course of their conversation in the Munich Residenz on the night of 1 October the Kaiser told Eulenburg bluntly that he intended to appoint him envoy in Munich, but that *'for the moment* there were a few problems to be overcome'. Eulenburg pointed out 'that the sudden and forcible removal of Rantzau would *inevitably* put [him, Eulenburg] in a very difficult position in relation to Bismarck and Herbert'; it would therefore be preferable to find a 'peaceful way' of achieving the goal. When Eulenburg met Herbert Bismarck the next morning the latter was 'tight-lipped and would not talk freely'. He then offered Eulenburg the position of counsellor at the Constantinople embassy, which Eulenburg turned down on financial grounds: he would have been glad to go to Constantinople had he been a bachelor, but with a wife and six children he could barely afford to live even in Munich. Eulenburg then frankly declared that he would not misuse the influence which he had over the Kaiser to cause trouble to the Chancellor and his family. 'I shall not *force* Rantzau out of Munich – but I cannot set myself against the specific wish of my Kaiser.' Herbert should show him the way 'out of this dilemma'. At these words, Eulenburg reported to his parents, the Foreign Secretary 'almost fell on my neck', and said: 'I am impressed by the Kaiser's brazenness, talking to me so calmly of getting rid of Rantzau and my sister. That is how a King should be!' On the other hand the Kaiser's wish put him in an awkward position where his brother-in-law was concerned. 'Of course I *have to* bear this business in mind and I shall do so', Herbert promised. 'Perhaps there will be a rearrangement soon and the Kaiser will put you into another post for a short time, from which you can then move to Munich. Oldenburg is free at the moment, but it is so frightful that you cannot go there. You are also much more valuable in Munich, which is what the Kaiser wishes. If only Wesdehlen would clear off!'[57]

Writing to his father from Vienna, the Foreign Secretary explained the whole dilemma and strongly supported the appointment of Eulenburg as an envoy – but not in Munich for the present. If only to secure Rantzau's post in Munich for a few years, he thought it advisable to lose no time in finding a posting elsewhere for Eulenburg. The Prussian legation to the minor states of Oldenburg, Brunswick and Lippe was vacant and could perhaps provide a temporary solution. What was more important, however, was to avoid provoking Wilhelm II by opposing his wishes in this matter. 'As he has such a particular liking for Ph. Eulenburg,

I believe there is little that would give him more pleasure than making him an envoy. Oldenburg would do very well, and no doubt Stuttgart too. I have my doubts about Bern because of all the tricky Socialist and legal questions.' Herbert therefore advocated Eulenburg's promotion as envoy and asked his father to decide whether this would be better achieved by the enforced retirement of Count Wesdehlen from Stuttgart or by appointing Eulenburg to the vacant post in Oldenburg, Brunswick and Lippe.[58]

The reaction of the Reich Chancellor to this suggestion speaks volumes, and throws into sharp focus the difference between the old statecraft which he represented and what was now becoming the personal style of rule practised by Wilhelm II. Prince Bismarck commented that if important government appointments were filled according to the wishes of the Kaiser, and government ministers did not dare take a stand against the monarch's candidates because they did not want to provoke him, the ministers would be reduced to the status of royal cabinet counsellors. Furthermore, as secretary of state it was well beyond Herbert Bismarck's lawful competence to negotiate with the Kaiser on these matters, for according to the Deputisation Law of March 1878 only the Reich Chancellor was authorised to submit proposals to the Kaiser on appointments in the foreign service. 'They cannot be lawfully settled without my *personal* participation, therefore not until *after* His Majesty has returned home.' This was a question of absolutely fundamental significance, and he, Bismarck, could not 'fly in the face of the experience in these matters which I have accumulated over forty years'. He declared that he could not 'abandon, in the last act of my drama, the clear conscience which I have insisted on maintaining towards the *country* in hard battles fought with my old master, despite all the love I bore him'.[59]

As far as Eulenburg's character and abilities were concerned, the Reich Chancellor thought him wholly unsuited for the difficult post of envoy in Munich. He was certainly 'amiable, but hitherto lacking in political judgement'. He allowed himself to be influenced by 'carping gossip', had 'no political insight, makes no distinction between what is important and what is not, listens to gossip and slander and can thereby cause much damage'. He could have the insignificant post in Oldenburg with pleasure, the Chancellor wrote, but Munich was out of the question: he could not 'pull it off'. To transfer Rantzau or to sack Wesdehlen or another envoy merely to create a vacancy for Eulenburg would be dishonourable and would also be very harmful to the diplomatic service, for such 'acts of violence', through which the better and more reliable elements in the foreign service were deliberately 'sacrificed for *untried* and undeserving favourites', created insecurity and acted as a deterrent. If the Kaiser really loved Philipp Eulenburg more than any other human being he should be at court, not in a legation. In circumlocutory but unmistakable terms the Chancellor hinted that he knew things about Eulenburg which he could not commit to paper but would keep until he could speak privately to Herbert.[60]

Eulenburg was at first relieved that he had been able to ward off the looming conflict with the Bismarck family by his frank conversation with Herbert Bismarck in Munich. He was aware, however, that the Kaiser had not given up his wish but only postponed it, and sounded a note of warning to the Foreign Secretary: 'You know the power of his will, as I do!'[61] Writing to the Kaiser on 15 October to report his conversation with Herbert, Eulenburg conveyed the impression that Rantzau's transfer to another legation in order to free Munich for him was almost a settled arrangement, although one which could not take effect for some months. 'Knowing Your Majesty's will with regard to the post of envoy, he [Herbert] wriggled like an eel and spoke of future rearrangements. For Rantzau, Brussels, The Hague or the Vatican would be as good as Munich', Eulenburg maintained. At the Vatican there was little work in summer, so that Rantzau's service at Friedrichsruh would scarcely be affected. 'I took leave of Herbert on good terms – but it was not easy! I had to be devilishly careful what I said.'[62]

On 31 October Wilhelm II surprised his friend with the news that he had appointed him envoy to Oldenburg, Brunswick and the two Lippe states.[63] Although he may have been disappointed by this development, Eulenburg must also have been relieved, both because of the financial advantages of the promotion and because, for the time being, it removed the danger of conflict with the Bismarcks. He knew, moreover, that his transfer to the lowlands of north-western Germany would not last long. So his reply to the Kaiser was effusive in its thanks: 'I am so overjoyed and grateful – but also so completely overcome at receiving such an unexpected honour from Your Majesty, that I scarcely know what to say. Your Majesty is indescribably good to me and has shown a truly fatherly concern for me. For through this appointment I shall be spared any conflict with my superiors – everything will take its natural course. I cannot get over the surprise! . . . I have never known such a day in my life – and I owe it to the Kaiser, my truest friend.'[64] Since he had expected to be left at Munich Eulenburg could only imagine that the Oldenburg appointment was attributable to the Bismarcks, and he wrote also to Herbert, expressing his 'boundless' thanks.[65] Bismarck's son-in-law Rantzau, who was thus able to remain in his post as envoy in Munich for the present, was relieved at Eulenburg's transfer both for this and for other reasons. 'I wish Eulenburg well', he wrote to Herbert, 'but I am heartily glad that he can now practise his spiritualist mumbo-jumbo in a different setting.'[66] In reality, however, the Kaiser had by no means abandoned his intention of appointing his friend in Rantzau's place. He detested Rantzau and said to Eulenburg: 'If he [Rantzau] had not made the arrangement during my father's reign, you would be in Munich now! But I have declared *definitely* that I wish to have you there!'[67] So the first storm clouds were brewing on the horizon.

It has to be said that Eulenburg continued skilfully to exploit both his advantages and Wilhelm's interests and weaknesses to court favour with the young Kaiser. On 16 December 1888, before his departure for Oldenburg, he had a lengthy private audience with the Kaiser during which the two friends discussed not only the political situation in Munich and the question of imperial patronage for the Bayreuth festival, but also various spiritualist experiences.[68] Eulenburg believed strongly in the continued existence of the 'individuality' of human beings, 'in a purified, continually self-purifying form' after death. 'Related feelings, earthly relationships of many kinds between humans, live on in wonderfully transfigured form; for what is highest, purest and best on this earth is not the ideal, but the actual seed-corn for the form of our existence in the hereafter.'[69] He wrote ballads and Viking fables for the Kaiser and sang or read them to him. 'How wonderful was the last evening which I was permitted to spend with Your Majesty', he wrote in his first letter to the Kaiser from Oldenburg. 'My thoughts are still filled with it and with Your Majesty's understanding for my old-fashioned feelings. How could I ever have dreamed that my Kaiser would be the *only* one who really and truly understands these feelings!!'[70] Though he warned the Kaiser against spiritualists who would try to force themselves on his attention, and urged him to rely only on *his* mediation in these 'delicate and exciting matters', Eulenburg at the same time kept the Kaiser's interest in the spirit world alive and zealously collected secret writings and reports of seances with the intention of reading them to the monarch when they next met.[71] 'H.M. spoils me terribly', he wrote in February 1889, adding that it was difficult to 'keep lurking envy within bounds!'[72]

In the autumn of 1888 Eulenburg invited Wilhelm to hunt on his parents' estate of Liebenberg in the Uckermark, less than an hour's journey north of Berlin. While the Kaiser was still in Italy Eulenburg wrote to him: 'If only Your Majesty were here with us in the old Mark again. One sleeps better beneath fir trees than pines, and since Signora Lucretia Borgia left the Vatican, nothing much happens there any more. Her lovely eyes would have opened wide at the sight of the German Kaiser with his black Trakhener stallion! I know such marvellous stories about Lucretia – what a pity that I cannot tell them! It gives me the greatest pleasure to think that I shall be able to sing a few ballads to Your Majesty again, and the prospect of a day's hunting in Liebenberg makes me quite *overjoyed*!!'[73] On 19 November 1888 news arrived at Liebenberg from the Flügeladjutant Gustav von Kessel – a cousin of Eulenburg – that the Kaiser wished to hunt there from 25 to 27 November. 'I am quite beside myself with joy and happiness and do not know how to express my gratitude!', Eulenburg assured his imperial friend. 'What a great occasion! What an honour for my beloved old home!' He promised the Kaiser to arrange 'a sort of singing contest' with his musical friends Kuno Count von Moltke and Oskar von Chelius. If his cousin Eberhard Count Dohna could also come, he would make 'a tolerable Lady Venus'. In addition, he wanted to invite Herbert Bismarck, Gustav von Kessel, Richard Count Dohna, August Count zu Eulenburg and two more cousins – Heinrich von Keszycki and Walther Freiherr von Eseberck – to the imperial hunt at Liebenberg. 'The thought of having my beloved Kaiser staying comfortably here makes me quite mad with joy! . . . How good Your Majesty always is to me – but *how* I love my Kaiser too!!'[74] Because of the visit of the Duke of Aosta and other obligations, the imperial hunt at Liebenberg had to be postponed until the beginning of January 1889. But in the following years Wilhelm paid regular visits there in October or November.[75]

Immediately after Wilhelm's first visit to Schloss Liebenberg, the observant Austro-Hungarian ambassador reported to Vienna: 'This is probably the moment to tell Your Excellency of a man who, although not part of the Kaiser's official entourage, nevertheless plays a significant role about the person of the monarch, which could become even more significant with time. This is a certain Count Philipp Eulenburg, who is already quite often described as "the Kaiser's best friend". He . . . is neither a contemporary of the ruling Kaiser, for he is already in his forty-second year, nor is he a member of the military profession. His Majesty first became closely acquainted with him when, as Prince Wilhelm, he went to Reichenhall to take a cure of several months because of his ear complaint. The Count in question, who is very pleasant company, artistically talented, writes prose and poetry and makes music most delightfully, was then Secretary of Legation in Munich and had been instructed to go to Reichenhall from time to time to put himself at the disposal of the young Prince. He succeeded in winning the latter's approval and affection to such an extent that from that time onwards he remained in constant and growing favour with the future heir to the throne. When Kaiser Wilhelm II came to the throne one of his first acts was to appoint the said Secretary of Legation to be envoy in Oldenburg, over the heads of all the counsellors. However, the new Head of Mission is to be found far less at his post than in Berlin, where he spends almost all his time in the royal palace, attending Their Majesties' meals and generally spending the evening in the bosom of the Imperial Family. Only a short time ago Kaiser Wilhelm returned from a hunting trip of several days, for which he had betaken himself to Liebenberg, which is half an hour by train from here, . . . less on account of the hunting than for the undisturbed company, which he enjoys so much, of the son of the house. At present the threads by which the Kaiser feels himself bound to Count Philipp Eulenburg seem to be rather of an aesthetic nature, spun from literature and music; but whether they are destined to grow into serious political bonds only the future will reveal. However that may be, the said Count is certainly a personality on whom one should keep a close eye.'[76]

A few days after the first imperial hunt at Liebenberg, Wilhelm and Eulenburg met again in Bückeburg, for Eulenburg was also accredited to both Lippe courts. There the Kaiser introduced him to his tutor Hinzpeter, who had come over from Bielefeld, with the words: 'My bosom friend Philipp Eulenburg – and the only one I have.' Presciently, Eulenburg commented: 'Such remarks please me and make me happy – but if repeated they will make *many* people envious of me.'[77] He soon had an opportunity, however, to make himself useful to the monarch in yet another sphere. Wilhelm entrusted him with a secret mission to investigate the private circumstances of Prince Adolf of Schaumburg-Lippe, the youngest son of the ruling Prince, born the same year as Wilhelm himself. After the final failure of the Battenberg marriage project Wilhelm was looking for a suitable husband for his sister Moretta, not least in order to pre-empt his mother's active efforts in this direction.[78] When Eulenburg's favourable secret report on Prince Adolf's financial position and private life arrived at the Berlin Schloss at the end of February, Wilhelm thanked his friend 'with all [his] heart' for his communication, which he burned at once, and told him that it was 'exactly what I need, and invaluable. I am delighted to see that in you I have found the right person for such services, and that you take the right view of your position as my friend; please continue in this way.'[79] Eulenburg's joy at these words of thanks knew no bounds. 'It is a glorious feeling', he wrote, 'to receive words of appreciation from the one to whom one owes everything. It makes me indescribably happy to feel how Your Majesty has taken the spirit of my friendship. Until my last breath I shall always be the same!'[80] Eulenburg was virtually predestined to play a central role, with Waldersee, in the Bismarck crisis which began in the spring of 1889.

### MISS LOVE – THE END OF THE AFFAIR

There was, apart from his closest friend's promotion, a second personal matter in the life of the young Kaiser which urgently needed to be dealt with but which was no less fraught with danger for the Bismarck family. Whereas ambassador Prince Reuss in Vienna was able, with Waldersee's help, to buy the silence of Ella Sommssich and of Anna Homolatsch, who had borne Wilhelm a daughter,[81] and whereas Geheimrat Miessner, the monarch's Privy Correspondence Secretary, took on the messy case of the emotionally disturbed Countess Elisabeth von Wedel,[82] it was left to Herbert Bismarck to confront the Kaiser with the embarrassing news that another of his mistresses, Emilie Klopp, or Miss Love as she called herself, had approached him with a demand for money in return for the six letters and a signed photograph she claimed to have received from Wilhelm. Readers of the first volume of this biography will recall how the Prince had first met this Parisienne cocotte while on manoeuvres in Alsace and had then, in 1887, summoned her to Potsdam, where she lived for many months in a furnished apartment in the Russian quarter, though without ever receiving payment for her – evidently rather exotic – services.[83]

Upon his accession to the throne, Wilhelm turned his back on the fiercely proud Miss Love. Dangerously disaffected, she left Potsdam in October 1888 to return to her home outside Strassburg, determined to exact what she felt was her due, which she valued at around 20,000 marks. In November 1888 Emilie contacted another former lover of hers, Bismarck's younger son Bill, and then, when that approach appeared to be leading nowhere, in April 1889 she wrote to Waldersee. As was shown in the first volume, Herbert and Bill Bismarck were more acutely aware than either the Reich Chancellor or the Chief of the General Staff of the dangers inherent in this situation, both in regard to the damaging international scandal that could ensue if Emilie Love's demands were not met, and also with respect to the hypersensitive young monarch's continued confidence in anyone who caused him to lose face through familiarity with his peculiar sexual proclivities as revealed by the letters. Despite his sons' forebodings, however, Prince Bismarck insisted that Herbert must confront the Kaiser with the problem and act only with his express consent.

The Foreign Secretary's dilemma deepened immeasurably when, in an audience on 28 November 1888, the Kaiser, while eventually admitting to intercourse with Emilie during the manoeuvres in Alsace, flatly denied all further contact with her, just as he was to do when Waldersee offered to mediate in the affair some months later. There were no letters or photographs, Wilhelm insisted, the entire Potsdam story was pure fabrication, and therefore no measures of any kind were to be undertaken. Miss Love's threats to publish the Kaiser's acutely embarrassing letters in the French press could not, on the other hand, be ignored. It was without Wilhelm's prior knowledge, therefore, that Bill Bismarck met Emilie Love in a hotel in Frankfurt on 1 May 1889 and handed over an envelope containing 25,000 marks sent to him by his brother, in exchange for four – not six – handwritten letters and the signed photograph.

How the Foreign Secretary resolved the tricky question of submitting the letters – he kept the photograph – to the Kaiser is not clear from the evidence. His younger brother's suggestion that Herbert should send them in a sealed package and claim that he had acquired the documents without reading them testifies by virtue of its implausibility to the delicacy of the task. Herbert Bismarck's diary for 9 May 1889 records cryptically only that on that day he discussed the issue of the 'burned letter' with Wilhelm.[84] But are we mistaken in sensing that this was the moment the Kaiser came to feel the dominant power of the Bismarcks, which he would have to confront in the event of any disagreement? Did he now feel himself compromised in their eyes and begin to turn against them? Many years later, in conversation with Philipp Eulenburg, Wilhelm II identified this early period of his reign as the point at which he had broken with Herbert Bismarck. The issue which would divide the Kaiser from Herbert 'for all time to come', Eulenburg informed Geheimrat Friedrich von Holstein in 1894 after his conversation with Wilhelm, was the younger Bismarck's attempts to '*separate* the imperial couple inwardly — and outwardly from one another and work towards a regime of mistresses'[85] — presumably a reference, however distorted by self-righteousness and moral indignation, to the Miss Love imbroglio. What is clear is that from May 1889 onwards the Foreign Secretary was received less frequently in audience, even if we take into account that from mid-June to mid-November the monarch was almost constantly on his travels.[86] What is also clear is that, from now on, a new tone is noticeable in the Kaiser's dealings with the Bismarck family, not just in personal matters, but in all issues of home and foreign policy. The great crisis which was to culminate in the Iron Chancellor's dismissal ten months later was about to begin.

---

# CHAPTER NINE

# The Bismarck crisis begins

## WALDERSEE AS THE KAISER'S CONFIDANT

WHILE the domination of the Bismarcks was increasingly viewed as oppressive by both their opponents and their underlings in the Wilhelmstrasse, at the same time the not exactly underdeveloped self-confidence of 'our courageous and energetic Kaiser' – as Waldersee put it on 3 June 1889 – was growing stronger by the day.[1] The enthusiastic ovations that greeted the young monarch wherever he went – even in Bayreuth, Alsace, the Catholic Rhineland and Guelphic Hanover – visibly increased his self-assurance.[2] Even in South-West Germany the press welcomed the more prominent role he had adopted and enthusiastically demanded that the young Kaiser take personal control of governmental power.[3] After a ceremonial presentation of colours in Potsdam in May 1889 the Chief of the General Staff praised Wilhelm's 'outstanding' oratorical gifts and commented: 'He has developed very quickly in this respect and is already a confident speaker. All his speeches have a fresh, soldierly and highly patriotic note, always combined with pious respect for his predecessors.'[4] Nine months after his accession there were increasing signs everywhere that for the Kaiser the time of waiting was now over. In his dealings with the Reich Chancellor and his son there was an unmistakable new tone which showed clearly that in future he was determined to decide for himself the essential guidelines of both foreign and domestic policy. Not only in questions of high politics but also in difficult personal and family matters[5] Wilhelm II relied on the advice of his father-figure, Waldersee, whom he had appointed Chief of the General Staff in November 1888. On 26 January 1889 Széchényi reported that it was widely remarked 'that the young Kaiser is beginning to like Count Waldersee better than Prince Bismarck'.[6] Ten months later Waldersee was able to note with satisfaction that 'a better relationship' with the Kaiser was 'scarcely imaginable'. 'But I am very cautious, I do not run after him or bother him unnecessarily, and I am convinced that he respects me, which is definitely not the case e.g. with Herbert Bismarck.'[7] Although he was not an uncritical admirer of the young monarch,[8] nor did the latter by any means always follow his advice,[9] there is no doubt that during the first two years of the Wilhelmine era Waldersee exercised a greater and more constant influence on Wilhelm II than any other person in his entourage, and that this influence extended into every area of politics. Despite the harsh criticism that he meted out to others who overstepped the boundaries of their authority, at no time did Waldersee apply the same criterion to himself. On the contrary, he prided himself on being the only person in the imperial entourage, with the exception of the Kaiserin, who could speak openly and frankly to the monarch on any subject. In February 1889 he noted in his diary: 'Lucanus is nothing but a creature of Bismarck, Liebenau has given himself over to them entirely, neither of the two adjutant-generals has been able to create any kind of position for himself; of the Flügeladjutanten, Bissing was the only one who could still put in a word, and unfortunately he has now gone, so the Kaiserin and I are the only ones left who can get anywhere with the Kaiser.' Waldersee confidently predicted that as far as the Bismarckians at court were concerned, 'the Kaiser's eyes will one day be opened and then this band of villains and wretches will be thrown out'.[10]

The General had frequent opportunities to speak to the Kaiser in private, for in addition to the official audiences granted to him as chief of the General Staff, Wilhelm regularly called at his house to take him off for walks and rides[11] and invited him to numerous court events.[12] If he fell ill the Kaiser sent his personal physician to make sure that he had the best possible medical care. Waldersee often accompanied Wilhelm on his regular morning rides as if he were a Flügeladjutant.[13] Even on Bismarck's birthday on 1 April 1889, when the Kaiser appeared at the Reich Chancellor's palace to offer his congratulations, he made a point of taking his Chief of General Staff with him.[14]

At the beginning of March 1889 Waldersee took advantage of a formal audience, when he was alone with Wilhelm and could therefore talk 'completely openly and freely', to spur the Kaiser on towards greater independence. He proposed that, since diplomats simply echoed everything Bismarck said, the Kaiser should grant the military attachés, who were 'independent characters' and 'spoke their minds fearlessly', the right to report directly to the General Staff and thereby to the Kaiser. In general it would be a good thing for the monarch to hear a variety of opinions, Waldersee asserted, for, 'if everyone he listened to was in agreement, that would be a kind of conspiracy against which he would be powerless. He would be able to rule with more security if he kept his advisers

13. General Count Alfred von Waldersee

separate. The *divide et impera* principle would work here too', Waldersee urged, in effect advocating the future system of 'personal rule'. The Kaiser 'laughed heartily and nodded his head meaningfully', the Chief of the General Staff noted in his diary.[15] It may have been this conversation to which Herbert Bismarck was alluding when he recorded that Waldersee had told the Kaiser that Frederick the Great would never have become 'the Great' if he had been confronted with such a powerful chancellor at his accession and had kept him on.[16]

From the spring of 1889 Waldersee's criticism of the personal power of the Bismarck family became increasingly harsh; at the same time he denounced what he saw as their dishonest practices and corruption. He complained incessantly that lying had now become a 'routine practice' for the Bismarcks.[17] In April 1889, when Bismarck had the Prussian parliament dissolved prematurely despite the opposition of the ministers, the Chief of the General Staff saw this as nothing but a corrupt action by which the Chancellor sought to prevent the passing of the new income tax law announced by the Kaiser in his speech from the throne. Prince Bismarck, the General alleged, suspected that he would have to 'pay much more under the new system of assessment than before, and at the same time to allow an inspection of his fortune, which is probably colossal. Both would be very unwelcome to him, as since he has become rich, he has also become greedy.' It was thus purely for personal advantage that Bismarck had had the assembly closed, Waldersee claimed.[18]

But in spite of all his criticisms it would be quite wrong to categorise Waldersee as an advocate of Bismarck's dismissal at this early stage, for he was far too keenly aware of the catastrophic consequences which a premature *belle sortie* by the founder of the Reich would entail for the future position of the Kaiser. Indeed, the Chief of the General Staff occasionally went so far as to toy with the idea of harnessing the Reich Chancellor's unrivalled prestige to the furtherance of two great projects: abroad, the preparation of a war against Russia and France; at home, to anti-democratic revision of the Reich constitution. The shrewd General recognised that the Reich Chancellor's international reputation would work to his advantage in his preparations for what was, in his eyes, an inevitable war. On 15 April 1889, alluding to the now 74-year-old Bismarck, he declared: 'We must use his great skill and his great position throughout the world . . . to maintain peace for a time, but we must also recognise that as soon as we have finished arming it will be our duty to bring about the battle, of which our opponents are hoping to determine the timing, ourselves. Until then we need the Chancellor, but not when matters become serious, and if necessary we must even go against him; but I am convinced that he will then be glad to withdraw voluntarily, since he would scarcely be equal to such great stress.'[19] Waldersee then pressed for an internal *coup d'état* with the aim of abolishing universal manhood suffrage, while the right-leaning 'Kartell' majority still existed in the Reichstag. Bismarck's declared intention of getting rid of run-off elections[20] was not radical enough, in the General's eyes. 'I am of the opinion that if we want to do something, we must do it thoroughly. The universal suffrage that we have is proving to be increasingly dangerous; since we now have a good Reichstag, [we must] make the attempt to get another electoral law passed. It can be done now, but later only with great difficulty, perhaps only by force.'[21] In general, he commented in the spring of 1889, 'the whole party system' was in a shambles, 'and no one can foresee how it will develop'.[22] Only the recognition that pursuing such a policy of force would greatly strengthen the position of the Bismarcks held the reactionary Chief of the General Staff back.

## THE FIRST CONFLICTS

Bismarck may have succeeded in temporarily circumventing Wilhelm II's stubborn insistence on Philipp Eulenburg's appointment as envoy in Munich by adopting the compromise solution of the Oldenburg-Brunswick-Lippe post in October 1888,[23] and he had put a good face on the choice, made entirely without reference to him, of General von Verdy as minister of war.[24] But although these potential conflicts were avoided, in the spring of 1889 a long tug-of-war began between the Chancellor on the one hand and the Kaiser and Kaiserin with Waldersee on the other, over the position of the 'Christian–Social' (in other words anti-Semitic) agitator Adolf Stoecker as court preacher. This was the first warning signal marking the beginning of a long-drawn-out crisis.

In response to the official press attacks on Stoecker instigated by Bismarck – Waldersee described them as a 'witch-hunt by the Wilhelmstrasse' – the deeply anti-Semitic Chief of the General Staff asserted, as he had in previous years, that Stoecker was fighting 'for the Christian faith against the Jews and their countless Christian camp-followers', who he was convinced reached 'into the highest circles'; ultimately, he argued, Stoecker was in fact fighting 'for the crown, against which heavy storm clouds are gathering'. Waldersee succeeded in persuading the Kaiser, who had at first agreed to disciplinary proceedings against Stoecker,[25] that the latter's fall would signify a 'triumph for the Jews and Progressives' and that the 'evil man' Bismarck wanted 'at all costs to deliver up a sacrifice to the Jews and to inflict a heavy blow on the Conservative Party'.[26] This anti-Jewish influence directed against Bismarck by Waldersee was not without effect, for the Kaiser decided to leave Stoecker in his post as court preacher, on condition that he abstained from political agitation. Waldersee commented jubilantly: 'The Chancellor has once again failed to enforce his will.' Bismarck's defeat in this question, he said, was 'yet another proof that the Chancellor is losing his touch'. Moreover it would not last long, the Chief of the General Staff predicted confidently, and 'Stöcker will be asked to take up his political activity again.'[27] In the course of the next chapters we shall have further occasion to observe the hitherto-unsuspected role played by anti-Semitism in the crisis which began in the spring of 1889 and ended a year later with the dismissal of both Bismarcks.

At the beginning of April 1889 Waldersee's diary recorded a further instance in which the Kaiser acted 'completely in accordance with his own feelings and not at the behest of the Chancellor'. He had 'simply but very decisively refused' the Chancellor's wish for an order to be conferred on the Russian Consul-General in Hamburg, Count Artur Pavlovich Cassini.[28] The lengthy marginal comment in which the monarch rejected the Reich Chancellor's suggestion survives in the confidential records of the Foreign Office. 'In the staff records of the Hussar Guards Regiment', Wilhelm recalled, 'from the time when I was in command of the Regiment, there are various *reports from Kusserow* [the Prussian envoy in Hamburg] about Cassini. He is described as a *very nasty piece of work*, who enjoys the worst possible reputation in Hamburg and is seen in society only on sufferance, because he is the Russian Consul. He has a mad passion for gambling and took a lot of money off an officer of my Regiment. What is more he lives in sin with a lady of rank, and that in itself causes such anger in Hamburg that decent people will have nothing to do with him. I know him personally, and I have rarely seen anyone looking more like a consummate rogue and crook. I consider the whole panegyric on Cassini in the report [from Bismarck] to be either a gross exaggeration or a piece of collusion with the Russian Embassy.'[29] (Several months later Wilhelm II called Cassini a 'swine of the first order!' in a note on an official report.[30]) The Chancellor was 'furious' at this rebuff, but would have to resign himself to it, Waldersee recorded with glee.[31] Cassini, the 'very nasty piece of work', was eventually promoted to Russian ambassador in Washington and was to represent his country at the Algeciras Conference in 1906, at which Germany was made painfully aware of its international isolation.

In mid-May 1889 the General took the opportunity of a train journey to Potsdam to warn the Kaiser about 'the Chancellor's Russian leanings', to which Wilhelm II responded: 'I have recently told the Chancellor exactly what I think about that.' The Kaiser had spoken out 'very bluntly against Russia' on this occasion.[32] Both Bismarcks again repudiated the accusation so often directed at them of being 'russophile', and adopted a much more hard-headed, realistic attitude, which the Foreign Secretary, after a long morning walk with his father on 22 July 1889, summed up tersely with the comment that one must 'forge links with Russia as long as there is still the smallest connecting link', since the Triple Alliance with the disintegrating Austria-Hungary and the increasingly republican Italy did not offer any reliable security.[33] Waldersee took no heed, but continued his anti-Russian and anti-Bismarck 'mischief-making', as Herbert Bismarck called it.[34]

In May Otto von Bismarck invited the Chief of the General Staff to visit him and urged him to write to Colmar Freiherr von der Goltz, the Prussian colonel

Conflicts arose over lesser matters too, now that the wills of the two men at the summit of power were pitted against each other. On the occasion of the Kaiser's visit to Oldenburg in the spring of 1889 Eulenburg, the newly appointed Prussian envoy there, had applied for an unusually large number of high-ranking orders to be distributed among the small population of the Grand Duchy (a quarter of a million). Eulenburg was formally reprimanded for this by the Chancellor, and a copy of the Chancellor's order containing the reprimand was laid before the Kaiser. Not long afterwards, while Wilhelm was visiting Brunswick and summoned Eulenburg – who was also accredited there – to an audience to discuss the distribution of orders, the latter replied that he should no doubt restrict himself to the most essential ones, since the Chancellor was of the opinion that too many orders had been conferred the previous month in Oldenburg. At once the 'All-Highest displeasure' made itself felt. 'Very angrily' the Kaiser asked how Eulenburg knew of Bismarck's opinion, and was 'furious when I told Him that it had been conveyed to me through an order'.[47] Eulenburg could not have guessed that the Reich Chancellor's order had been copied to the Kaiser only *after* it had been dispatched, and that the latter had covered the copy with irate marginal comments.[48] The Kaiser, Eulenburg recounted, had 'struck the table with his fist and shouted furiously, who rules now, I or Bismarck!'[49] Not long afterwards Eulenburg returned from the imperial deer hunt in East Prussia and reported – as Herbert Bismarck recalled after his dismissal – that 'H.M. was irritated by a submission [from the Chancellor] advising him against repeating his visit to Rome this year. H.M. said sharply that He did not wish to be treated like a child all the time, only He knew what He should do etc.'[50]

As if that were not more than enough, in the same month differences arose between Germany and Switzerland which led to further serious arguments between Bismarck and Wilhelm II. The Chancellor's aim – such at least was Waldersee's suspicion – was nothing less than to bring Germany and Russia together in a joint invasion of Switzerland. According to Waldersee, Bismarck clearly wished to use the arrest and 'brutal' treatment of the German police agent Wohlgemuth in Switzerland to bring about a 'great coup', in which he hoped 'to win Russia over to a move against Switzerland, and the moment is favourable in so far as the anarchists in Zürich' had been caught 'in the process of making bombs' which were destined for Russia. Bismarck was even contemplating 'war against Switzerland and a partition of the country', claimed the Chief of the General Staff, who was vehemently opposed to the Chancellor on this matter too. He expressed concern at 'the atmosphere of hostility' towards Germany that had arisen in Switzerland as a result of Bismarck's policy. The Chief of the General Staff even feared that in the event of Germany going to war against

France the sympathies of the Swiss would be so much on the side of the French that their neutrality would be called into question.[51] He drew up a memorandum on Swiss neutrality which he hoped would prevent 'overhasty steps', and urged this view on the Kaiser.[52]

Wilhelm II had at first given his approval to the action against Switzerland, but without fully realising its implications.[53] Waldersee claimed that he had been 'badly served', especially by Herbert Bismarck, who 'showed great lack of skill in the matter'. 'The father knew very well how poor the support offered by the son had been, but did not want to disavow him and therefore probably became more deeply involved in the matter than he wanted.' Bismarck's policy gave rise to increasing protests, especially in South Germany and in Progressive circles, whereupon the Grand Duke of Baden – the German ruling princes had assembled in Stuttgart on 25 and 26 June 1889 for the twenty-fifth anniversary of the accession of King Karl of Württemberg – felt obliged to intervene with the Kaiser. At Holstein's instigation, Waldersee also had a discussion with the Kaiser in which he drew his attention to 'the utterly foolish idea of a war with Switzerland'.[54]

The result of this pressure on the Kaiser was soon apparent. Even before he left for Stuttgart he had instructed Under Secretary of State Berchem to write to the Reich Chancellor 'that he hoped we would not get too heated about it and would succeed in avoiding a conflict'. After his return from Stuttgart the Kaiser had 'expressed the same idea in more detail and more definitely through Berchem to H.H. [the Reich Chancellor] and positively *refused* to sign the Cabinet Order for the control of passports'.[55] Bismarck complained bitterly that he had 'already noticed that contrary influences are at work on His Majesty the Kaiser along the lines of the policies advocated by His Royal Highness the Grand Duke' and for the first time since Wilhelm's accession he threatened to resign.[56] He was 'very annoyed' when conciliatory remarks made by the Kaiser to a Swiss general appeared in the newspapers and were greeted with approval throughout Germany.[57] For the Kaiser the effect of the ill-thought-out and highly unpopular policy of the Bismarcks in the Wohlgemuth affair was to undermine still further his confidence in them. Waldersee summed it up with the words: 'The whole affair did nothing . . . to enhance Bismarck's reputation; it was a completely failed enterprise on his part, and it began to shake the Kaiser's confidence in the superiority of his statecraft.'[58] And that was not all: the Wohlgemuth case had also produced the anti-Bismarck coalition between Waldersee, Holstein, the Grand Duke of Baden and his representative in Berlin, Adolf Freiherr Marschall von Bieberstein. Together with Philipp Eulenburg, these were to be the Kaiser's most influential advisers in the crisis leading to the Bismarcks' dismissal.[59]

## THE 'DECISIVE TURNING-POINT'

When he looked back in later years on the Bismarck crisis, Waldersee picked out the fierce conflict which broke out in mid-June 1889 over the question of the Russian conversion as the 'decisive turning-point' in Wilhelm II's relations with the two Bismarcks; from that point, he claimed, the Kaiser had 'broken with the Bismarcks, father and son, in his heart'.[60] What had happened? What was so important that it led to an irreparable breach in the critical relationship between the Kaiser and the Chancellor?

Within only a few days of making his absurd anti-Semitic accusations against Bismarck — that the Chancellor wanted 'at all costs to deliver up a sacrifice to the Jews'[61] — in the Stoecker affair at the beginning of 1889, Waldersee repeated the same sentiments with regard to Bismarck's financial policy towards Russia. At this time the Chief of the General Staff was watching, with growing anxiety, the increasing strength of Russian finances, which had resulted in German capital flowing to Russia again. For Waldersee there was never any question of who was responsible for what he considered an extremely undesirable development. On 25 March he wrote: 'The House of Rothschild seems to have helped considerably, and so Bleichröder and his gang were of course also involved.'[62] Gerson Bleichröder, the Reich Chancellor's banker, was accused by Waldersee not only of strengthening Russian military power but also of simultaneously attempting to undermine the financial stability of Austria-Hungary. 'Lately that rogue Bleichröder, who is helping the Russians to convert their loans, has been working with all his might to damage Austrian credit, and has been sending bleak reports of the situation there', he claimed. Reuss, the German ambassador in Vienna, was 'convinced that the Jew is exaggerating greatly, and this is also my opinion'.[63]

In June 1889 this question, on which, as Waldersee stressed, he took 'exactly the same point of view as the Kaiser', came to the fore once more. During a shooting display for the Shah of Persia at Tegel on 11 June 1889 the Kaiser called the Chief of the General Staff over and said: 'There is fine news from Russia again. According to Yorck's latest report it now seems that a conversion of 250 million rubles is to be arranged in Berlin. This is going too far; I will not stand for it. What is your opinion?' When Waldersee asked for time to reflect, the Kaiser called out to him: 'Here comes the Minister of War, talk to him and then you can both give me your advice together.' After the display Waldersee and Verdy rode up to Wilhelm and advised him to have the conversion stopped by Bismarck. The Kaiser had wanted to give orders for a press campaign through Rudolf Lindau, the press officer of the Foreign Office, but the two generals doubted that this would be effective; the Chancellor himself must intervene with all his authority, they urged. 'If the Jews know that he is strongly against it they will keep their hands off, but not otherwise', they declared.[64] Upon returning from Tegel the Kaiser sent his Flügeladjutant Carl Wedel to the Foreign Office to summon the Foreign Secretary to the Schloss immediately. Herbert Bismarck found the Kaiser 'in a very excitable state', he recalled later, as those about him had been whipping up his feelings against the Chancellor's alleged 'russophilia'. He had already sent for Lindau. 'I drove into the Schloss where Lindau was standing in the ante-room; I was received, and H.M. at once gave orders that the new Russian loan must be condemned in the press, He did not wish any more German money to go to Russia in exchange for Russian paper, as Russia would only use it to pay for its war preparations. "One of my senior army officers has drawn my attention to this danger today, and something must be done absolutely at once."' The Foreign Secretary tried to explain to the Kaiser that 'that was not how matters lay, it was merely a question of a conversion of earlier Russian loans, and thus the best opportunity for German stockholders to take cash and to get *rid* of Russian papers . . . The French would take the Russian papers which were got rid of here. The business would be done in *Paris*. H.M. seemed not to understand', Herbert recorded in some perplexity, 'for He insisted that articles must be written in our press against this Russian financial operation, and He had summoned Lindau to give him instructions accordingly.' The Foreign Secretary insisted: 'If I have not succeeded in making the situation clear to Your Majesty, I beg Your Majesty to request a report from the Finance Ministry. Official articles cannot be written to that effect without reference to H.H. [the Reich Chancellor], because they would influence overall policy substantially; and in any case I consider them pointless in the present case.' At this the Kaiser directed Herbert to write to his father and urge the importance of the press campaign on him. He also spoke 'sharply' to Lindau, who was 'quite dumbfounded at his arrogant tone'. Not content with that, the Kaiser ordered the Reich Secretary for the Interior, Heinrich von Boetticher, to write to the Reich Chancellor; he also gave instructions to his Flügeladjutant, Kurt Wolf von Pfuel, to write to Lucanus. He sent another adjutant, Friedrich von Scholl, to the Prussian Finance Minister's deputy, Meinecke, with orders that the latter should instruct the Supervisory Board of the Stock Exchange, by imperial order, to 'put a stop to the Russian loan issue'. Meinecke, taken by surprise during a meal, replied that it was not the Finance Ministry but the Prussian Ministry of Trade that was responsible for the matter, and then sought Herbert Bismarck's help, 'in a state of consternation'.[65]

The Kaiser's frenetic activity reached its peak when he himself wrote a letter to the Reich Chancellor on 12 June 1889, demanding, in stridently imperious terms, the prohibition of the Russian conversion. 'Yesterday in the course of the day I heard by chance that Bleichröder and his associates intend in the very near future to bring a very large quantity (250 Million) of Russian rubles back here and to accommodate them in Germany. I am most strongly against this. That the Russians arm themselves and mobilise has become a matter of indifference to us; that they insult and scorn us, likewise; but I cannot allow German money to flow into Russian hands so that they can all the more surely attack [and] destroy us. I therefore request Your Highness . . . to give orders for a vigorous campaign to be waged against the Russian securities.'[66]

Waldersee, who was kept informed by Wilhelm himself of the progress of this extraordinary interlude, also made detailed notes on it which provide an interesting supplement to Herbert Bismarck's recollections. 'After [Herbert] Bismarck had admitted that the news of the conversions was correct, there were fierce arguments', he wrote. 'The Kaiser was especially vehement in attacking Bleichröder, of whom he said, among other things, that he frequented the Chancellor's house. With great determination he expressed his intention of preventing the conversion. Lindau was given a direct order to influence the newspapers in this sense. Of course [Herbert] Bismarck took this direct attack very much amiss.'[67] This was how Waldersee recorded the episode in his diary. Later, in a retrospective note on the 'very fierce' discussion between Herbert and Wilhelm, the General added that the monarch had railed against Bleichröder 'in strong language', to which the Foreign Secretary had 'angrily' retorted that he had absolutely no connection with the banker and the Kaiser had countered: 'I know that, but it makes no difference at all to me, for he is a constant visitor at your father's house.' Herbert also reacted very badly to the fact that the Kaiser gave Lindau direct orders to have articles against the conversion published in the press. Even in the eyes of the Chief of the General Staff this was an unwarranted interference by the Kaiser in the domain of the Foreign Secretary and therefore also in that of the Reich Chancellor himself.[68]

The Bismarcks, furthermore, found the role played by the Flügeladjutanten in the quarrel deeply insulting. They considered that such 'orders by adjutant' issued by the Kaiser were 'quite inadmissible' and could not be accepted by a minister or civil servant. For the Reich Chancellor this point of political principle was even more important than the conversion itself, and he told his son through Rantzau that 'in political matters it was not permissible to act upon an order conveyed through the Flügeladjutant on duty, for then the position of the Foreign Minister would become quite untenable, and one ought not to let the sovereign get away with that'.[69] Herbert pointed out that the Kaiser would have to be told this in person, otherwise he would not notice the 'stab' aimed at him.[70]

The younger Bismarck had no doubt that 'the affair had been exploited to stir up trouble', but he could not at first find out 'who had informed H.M. about it'.[71] Later he discovered that, among others, the King of Saxony had told the Kaiser that it was a scandal that Berlin bankers were supplying the Russians with cheap money which would only be used for military purposes against Germany. Others, Herbert reported to Varzin, had expressed the view that 'one had to be rough with the Russians'; then they always 'knuckled under'. With arguments such as these, 'troublemakers' had persuaded the Kaiser that 'Papa's policy was too pro-Russian'.[72] Among the Flügeladjutanten too the general opinion was that 'the pernicious Bleichröder–Rottenburg coalition must be broken up *à tout prix*'.[73] But not surprisingly, and justifiably, Herbert Bismarck's suspicions rested above all on Waldersee and Verdy. At the state banquet for the Shah he asked Verdy point blank: 'What gave you the idea of stirring up H.M. to involve himself in things which are none of your business? You are interfering with foreign policy.' He warned Verdy 'in future to refrain from making comments that have nothing to do with the responsibilities of the minister of war'. But he was well aware that the generals would persist in their subversive work.[74] And indeed the counter-measures which Waldersee advised the Kaiser to take to thwart 'all the Chancellor's clever ruses' are symptomatic of the course of the long crisis which was to end nine months later with the dismissal of both Bismarcks. The General recommended him to discuss the Russian conversion directly with Prussian Finance Minister Adolf von Scholz. This 'greatly displeased the Chancellor', who arranged for Scholz to go on leave before the monarch could speak to him. On 30 June 1889, at the beginning of the first Scandinavian cruise, Waldersee allied himself with Philipp Eulenburg – both believed that 'a major conflict was possibly in the offing' – and together they urged the Kaiser to have a daily report on the state of the Russian loan on the Berlin stock exchange telegraphed to him.[75]

In the last days of June and in early July 1889 this question actually threatened to bring about the resignation of the Reich Chancellor and with him the entire Prussian Ministry of State. Bismarck's colleagues – Rottenburg, Boetticher, Berchem, Magdeburg – had, as Holstein warned Eulenburg in a letter of 3 July, acted only on the instructions of the Chancellor; 'so that if His Majesty is rude to one of them and he is forced to resign', Bismarck would resign too. 'But I think', Holstein continued, 'that the Ministry [of State] will also ally itself to the Chancellor. Maybach is happy to take the opportunity to do so whenever he has the Chancellor nearby, and moreover the other ministers are very annoyed that the Kaiser only deals with them through Lucanus, like Friedrich Wilhelm III in the days of Cabinet politics. In short, there would be a fearful scene.' The forthcoming Reichstag elections, which in any case threatened to go very badly, would be catastrophic and the Kaiser would 'be obliged to tackle an internal conflict without Bismarck . . . with France and Russia looking on'. The Kaiser must realise 'that it really is dangerous for there to be an *open* breach between him and the Chancellor now, just because He wants to prevent a Russian financial operation. In that way war could actually break out sooner than we would like.' If Wilhelm did not want to bring about a break with Bismarck, he ought not to 'go too far in his rudeness, so as not to give anyone . . . an excuse to hand in his resignation'.[76] Writing to Herbert Bismarck, Holstein expressed the hope that the Kaiser would give in. The Chancellor's reply to the Kaiser's letter of 12 June had certainly looked 'rather like a resigning matter', but Wilhelm would want to avoid a chancellor crisis 'if for no other reason than that he would have to give up his travelling plans in the event of a change of ministry. Hopefully we shall be spared the mournful sight of Prince Bismarck disappearing from the scene on account of Bleichröder.'[77]

While Holstein warned against further 'rudeness' on the part of the Kaiser, Herbert Bismarck put pressure on his father to make some concession to the monarch over the Russian loans question. 'H.M. has got his teeth very firmly into this affair, and He is not entirely wrong in saying that the Russians would not have been able to pull it off and thereby save themselves about 20 millions in annual interest unless the big Berlin bankers had agreed to go along with it', he wrote to Rantzau on 27 June.[78] On 4 July 1889 he wrote again urging that his father should 'make some allowance' for the Kaiser's *present* disposition', 'while at the same time guiding him into better ways'. He warned of the efforts of those who were trying to stir up antagonism at court towards the Chancellor, 'first and foremost Waldersee and the orthodox cathedral preachers with their hangers-on', who wished to bring about a rupture between Bismarck and the Kaiser. Their tactic with the Chancellor was 'to make him lose his patience and annoy him into leaving'; they expected that Bismarck would eventually be driven into saying: 'If H.M. treats me like this and interferes so much, I would rather go, I am too old and too tired to allow myself to be tormented.' Herbert Bismarck, however, was determined not to let the 'unprincipled troublemakers, whom H.M. does not see through', win the day, and therefore argued strongly in favour of making concessions to the Kaiser. 'I would consider a great war a lesser misfortune than if Papa resigned', he wrote to Rantzau, 'for *if he does*, war will come *at once*, and with unskilled, new diplomatic leadership we shall have to be prepared for the worst: that would be to court disaster. H.M. holds very strongly to Papa, when all is said and done. But if Papa allows himself to be annoyed and wants to leave on his own account, the Fatherland will be ruined.'[79] Herbert went on to criticise Gerson Bleichröder bitterly, complaining that he had 'long wished for Papa to get rid of this dangerous Jew as a banker, he is too unscrupulous a liar, and Papa has had more annoyance and trouble because of him than he realises: so long as this money-grubbing Semite can earn a few millions he does not care what becomes of Papa and our Fatherland'.[80] Only recently the Kaiser had been told (as was unfortunately true, Herbert commented) that 'Bleichröder was spreading the lie around that the Reich Chancellor was not against the conversion [Prince Bismarck wrote in the margin beside this: 'That is quite right'], and through years of unscrupulous lying at Papa's expense Bleichröder had built himself up such a position at the stock exchange that the other members all now believed that his transactions had the blessing of the government, *otherwise he would certainly not make them.*'[81]

At the beginning of July 1889 the Reich Chancellor was indeed on the point of giving up. He wrote despondently to the Prussian envoy in Karlsruhe, Karl von Eisendecher, 'I can only conduct policy as I understand it, and in any case I am heartily tired of it all    My strength is not sufficient to cope with contrary influences in counselling His Majesty.'[82] Through Rantzau, he replied to his son with the comment that 'if the sovereign believes he can conduct political affairs more skilfully on his own, then let him do so'; it was his, Prince Bismarck's, duty to avoid arousing ill-feeling on the part of Russia 'so long as we are not prepared', 'if only because we have no way of knowing what might erupt in France . . . If the sovereign did not wish to carry on with him, there was nothing to be done about it; as to that, he was far more inclined than you not to give a damn about it.'[83] Herbert's answer to this letter speaks volumes. He wrote to Rantzau on 8 July: 'The reason why I do give a damn about Papa's relationship with H.M. is that we would face great danger and perhaps go to the devil if H.M., with his present immaturity and lack of experience, set out to reign without Papa with *homines novi.* With our old sovereign it was quite different: he had a strong sense of duty, no desire to seek his own pleasure, long experience and, last but not least, he had not only gone through heavy misfortunes in his childhood and in 1848, but had ruled himself into such an impasse in 1862 that he wanted to abdicate. He *knew* what he had in Papa, and would never have let him go, even in the most serious disagreement. But our present sovereign is not like that, he has only known the sunny side of life *et il ne doute de rien.* I was therefore thinking only of *the country* when I wrote recently that one ought to accommodate oneself a little to H.M.'s disposition from time to time.'[84]

If this highly explosive difference of opinion was eventually overcome without the major crisis anticipated by some, it was purely thanks to the Reich Chancellor's unusual willingness to make concessions. On 4 July Bismarck sent telegraphic instructions to the Foreign Office to advise the German public — as the Kaiser had demanded — through a notice in the *Norddeutsche Allgemeine Zeitung,* to cash in the old Russian securities, and not to take up the converted stock.[85] When the news of the Chancellor's intervention reached the *Hohenzollern,* it was greeted with 'the greatest delight'; Kiderlen-Wächter was instructed by the Kaiser to express 'the All-Highest thanks for the highly satisfactory news' to the Chancellor.[86] Eulenburg reported on 17 July to Berlin that the Russian conversion had certainly been 'of lively concern' to the Kaiser in the first days of the Scandinavian cruise, but since the affair had been 'brought to a happy conclusion, there is no more dancing to political tunes'. The Kaiser's travelling companions were 'all taking care not to disturb the restful atmosphere', and for his part the Kaiser was so absorbed by the impressions made on him by the journey itself that he had more or less lost interest in the conversion.[87] But we should not be misled by this outcome into underestimating the significance of the incident itself. As Waldersee pointed out retrospectively, even if the Kaiser had little desire 'to spoil the cruise for himself by getting angry with the Bismarck family', he had nevertheless 'by no means forgotten the whole affair'.[88] Quite the contrary: from this point onwards he had in fact 'done no more than to put on an act with the Chancellor'.[89]

## THE CONFLICT BETWEEN BISMARCK AND WALDERSEE

In the summer of 1889 the Reich Chancellor decided to make a frontal attack on Waldersee, whom he considered increasingly as a threat, by means of a press campaign against the 'military undercurrents' which were pushing the Kaiser towards war with Russia.[90] The General, who proudly admitted to having repeatedly put forward his anti-Russian views to the Kaiser 'in person and in writing', commented defiantly: 'As these views are not those of the Chancellor, and as the great man discovered that I was in correspondence with the Kaiser, war had to be waged against me once again, and this time it was with great force.'[91] He asserted, however, that 'for everyone capable of reading it was unmistakable that the thrust of the attacks was directed at the Kaiser, and one could see with total clarity the outrageous effrontery of the Chancellor'. He, Waldersee, had held back 'in order not to cause any difficulties for the Kaiser, who was still obliged to keep the Chancellor for a little longer'; but he had also had the reassuring feeling of knowing that the Kaiser was 'absolutely on my side'.[92] The solidarity between Wilhelm and Waldersee was again demonstrated when on 20 June 1889 the Kaiser wrote on a copy of an article inspired by Bismarck in the *Berliner Tageblatt*, against 'military interference in politics', a furious marginal note: 'Please find out where this shameless concoction comes from and who the author is. And give the paper a thorough dressing-down at the same time. I think it comes from Bleichröder's financial circles?? and his associates?? I shall want an answer on 28th or 29th.'[93]

During the Scandinavian cruise of 1889 – when the Kaiser and his Chief of General Staff spent almost four weeks at close quarters in the cramped cabins of the old *Hohenzollern*, while the Bismarcks were far away in Varzin or Berlin – the public feud between Bismarck and Waldersee took on increasingly dangerous forms. From the *Hohenzollern* Wilhelm issued a rebuke to the editor of the semi-official *Norddeutsche Allgemeine Zeitung* for an article which was patently aimed against Waldersee. With his 'cunning bordering on genius' (as Philipp Eulenburg put it), Waldersee took advantage of the imperial rebuke to send an almost simultaneous telegram of protest to the *Hamburger Nachrichten*, which had published similar attacks on him.[94] The telegram did not fail to attract attention. Writing of the explosive atmosphere on board at this time, Eulenburg recorded that Waldersee was intending to exploit the situation still further by writing an open letter, and could not be dissuaded by either Eulenburg or Kiderlen. It was plain to Eulenburg that 'the rupture between the Chancellor and Waldersee would inevitably become an open one as a result', and he tried another tack. 'In desperation I dropped hints to the Kaiser, and on the last morning in the "Hohenzollern" Waldersee told me that the Kaiser had spoken to him so kindly and reassuringly about his relations with the Chancellor that he would now give up the idea of the letter.' Eulenburg nevertheless had a gloomy feeling that such peaceful outcomes were only of a transitory nature. 'This unfortunate antagonism will go on and on doing damage both in the Fatherland and abroad.' Moreover the differences of opinion between Herbert Bismarck and Waldersee, 'in spite of their shared opposition to the power of the stock exchange', were even more intense than those between Waldersee and the Chancellor. 'The antagonism lies in the insuperable antipathy of their whole beings towards each other', Eulenburg observed with alarm. The Kaiser was certainly '*convinced* of the necessity' of keeping the Chancellor; but he would never drop Waldersee, with whom he had a very deep and close relationship.[95]

This incident led to a definitive break between the influential anti-Semitic Chief of the General Staff and the Bismarcks. In his hatred for the Reich Chancellor, the General strayed into the realms of hallucination – one can scarcely call it otherwise – in persuading himself that Prince Bismarck and his closest colleagues were completely 'Jew-ridden' and that therefore every aspect of the foreign and domestic policy of the German Reich was controlled by Jews. For the Chief of the General Staff there was no longer any question that the Reich Chancellor and his closest counsellors were in league with the Jewish bankers. 'It is quite clear that filthy money-interests now play an important role, and quite probably the only role', he claimed. Bismarck had got himself 'so involved with Bleichröder', Waldersee alleged, that it was obvious that 'he was doing a lot of financial business with him'. The Chancellor knew that his banker would lose 12 million marks if the Russian conversion did not go through; that was the only way in which 'the Chancellor's fury' at the Kaiser's intervention could be interpreted. The head of the Reich Chancellery, Franz von Rottenburg, was very

intimate with the banker Schwabach, and the 'otherwise so honest and hitherto completely upright' Boetticher had also got caught 'in the Bleichröder net':
Bleichröder had saved Boetticher's father-in-law Berg from bankruptcy, and 'the
cur does not let anyone go so easily, once he has him in his clutches'.[96] 'Wherever
one looks', Waldersee wrote in December 1889, 'one finds Bleichröder's traces.
When people said to me a year ago: "The Chancellor is completely Jew-ridden",
I laughed or said that it was an enormous exaggeration. After what I have been
through since then – e.g. Russian conversions – I have been converted. It is truly
terrible: the Jew Bleichröder has a great influence on our foreign and domestic policies.'[97] In the eyes of the Chief of the General Staff the 'pro-Russian'
policy adopted by Bismarck could be explained only by this Jewish influence.
On 7 December 1889 he noted in his diary: 'The more I am able to look into
the situation, the more firmly I am convinced and the more anxious I am that
we are gradually becoming more and more Jew-ridden. The Chancellor has
thrown himself completely into the arms of Herr Bleichröder; we are dabbling
in friendly relations with Russia so as to raise Russian funds and to make their
conversions easier for them. It is frightful but unfortunately true.'[98]

### RELATIONS WITH RUSSIA AND THE VISIT OF TSAR ALEXANDER

It was not only the Kaiser's anti-Semitic prejudices which Waldersee managed to
exploit so skilfully against Bismarck, but also Wilhelm's antipathy towards the
Russian imperial family. Since early in 1889 Wilhelm had become increasingly
annoyed with the 'boorishness' of the Tsar, who had still given no indication of
when he intended to make a return visit to Berlin.[99] 'The other great sovereigns
had announced their arrival months beforehand and the Tsar could at least have
sent word of whether he intended to come at all, even if he wanted to keep the
date a secret', he complained.[100] In June Waldersee welcomed the news that
the Tsar had again 'given considerable offence' to the Kaiser by toasting the
Prince of Montenegro as Russia's 'only true and honest friend'.[101] In October he
noted with satisfaction, when Alexander III at last announced that he would visit
Berlin, that 'both Kaiser and Kaiserin strongly resent his discourtesy in delaying
so long over the return visit. The Kaiser is quite convinced that nothing more
can be done with Russia through friendly means; he says: I have made up my
mind, I shall not speak to the Chancellor about it any more, for he has his own
views and we shall never agree.'[102]

   The sudden improvement in relations between Wilhelm and the British
court which had resulted from his August visit to Osborne and his appointment as admiral of the fleet also brought about a noticeable cooling of relations
between the Kaiser and Bismarck.[103] Although on the one hand warmer relations

between Germany and Britain were very much in accordance with the Reich Chancellor's thinking – 'the mere prospect of England's co-operating with us in the Mediterranean in case of war' contributed materially 'to the reinforcement of peace', according to Ernst Hohenlohe[104] – on the other hand the Kaiser's growing mistrust of Russia presented a growing danger to the Bismarcks' pro-Russian policy. Herbert Bismarck believed that there was a hidden connection between these two developments, for he attributed Wilhelm's suspicion of Russia to 'gossip against the Tsar at Osborne'. He presumed that it was above all 'highly spiced versions of remarks that the Tsar had made about H.M. and which had become known through the Princess of Wales' which had influenced the Kaiser in turning against Russia. There was no other explanation, he asserted, for 'the animosity . . . which H.M. felt towards the Tsar at the beginning of the autumn of 1889', for there were no tangible political reasons for it.[105] In this the Foreign Secretary was seriously underestimating the effects on the Kaiser of the anti-Russian sentiment fomented by the Chief of the General Staff.

Waldersee watched the Russian war preparations and troop movements with an eagle eye, although at this time he did not believe that there was any imme-diate intention on the part of the Russians to go to war. In his judgement Russia's armaments programme would not be completed until the spring of 1891, and even then Russia would not necessarily have any desire 'to start a war; but she wishes to be in a position to be able to call the tune in case of any complication that might arise, or to be able to intervene at a moment that suited her in any war between us and France. That would be the most inconvenient situation in which we could possibly find ourselves.'[106] Waldersee nevertheless continued to regard Russia with the deepest suspicion. The Russians 'are arming in great haste and on a huge scale and are gradually adopting a position that is scarcely tolerable for us', he observed.[107] In direct contrast to the pro-Russian policy of the Chancellor the Chief of the General Staff warned the Kaiser 'that the war for which we are preparing ourselves will be the mightiest that has ever been waged and that everything is at stake'. During a joint audience with Minister of War von Verdy in October 1889 Waldersee did his best 'to leave the Kaiser in no doubt as to the seriousness of the situation. He is after all the principal person concerned.'[108]

Whether it was English gossip or Waldersee's promptings, the Kaiser at first refused to receive the Tsar in Berlin for a full state visit. As Herbert Bismarck later recalled: 'Although King Umberto had been received in May and Kaiser Franz Joseph in August with maximum military honours, the whole garrison lining the route, mounted escorts, gun salutes etc., H.M. could not be persuaded to do the same for the Tsar in October; I had to call in Wittich and Hahnke to help, so that from the point of view of personal safety there would at least be a full military cordon from the station for the Tsar; at my request Hahnke then went a little beyond the imperial authorisation, because he realised that any difference in the reception from what was done for the other great sovereigns would be politically undesirable and there was nothing to justify it.'[109]

The next obstacle that the Reich Chancellor and the Foreign Secretary had to tackle with regard to the Tsar's visit was the Kaiser's selfish attitude to hunting. They had difficulty in making the young monarch understand that on this occasion he must be 'simply a refined and charming host', who must make allowances for his illustrious Russian guest's 'slow and hesitant' shooting and take care 'that the Tsar shot more than he did'. The Kaiser must not fail to invite the three high-ranking members of the Tsar's suite, Voronzov, Richter and Cherevin; it would be far better to give up the idea of the hunt altogether than to limit the Tsar to fruitless deer-stalking trips and not to invite his three companions. The Kaiser himself could, after the Tsar had left, 'shoot away to his heart's content. *This* is a *political* act, to make a pleasant impression on the Russian guests by helping them get a good bag', the responsible statesmen urged.[110]

The omens were therefore not particularly good for Alexander III's visit to Berlin from 11 to 13 October 1889. The reception of the Russian guests by the population was 'icy'.[111] No fewer than six times the Tsar complained of Waldersee's 'warlike' influence on the Kaiser.[112] He also expressed anxiety about Wilhelm II's forthcoming visit to Constantinople: he could not help taking it amiss, as it looked 'as if we wanted to turn the Turks against him'.[113] But Wilhelm suddenly swung round 'to the opposite extreme', Herbert Bismarck recalled. At a luncheon for the Alexander Regiment 'H.M. proposed a rousing toast to the old brotherhood in arms, with particular emphasis on Borodino and Sebastopol, in the anti-French sense, and ordered it to be published in full in the press, in spite of all arguments against this, which were based on the fact that casting aspersions on France was rash with regard to the Tsar at present, and as a guest he ought to be treated with consideration.'[114] If the Kaiser greatly overstepped the mark with this speech, even in Herbert's eyes, it was the russophobe Waldersee who found the most to regret in the imperial faux-pas. 'Things have gone somewhat wrong with our Kaiser', he lamented; 'he drank to the memory of the heroes of Borodino, Arcis sur Aube, Sebastopol and Plevna and to the Russian army. I do not think that this will please the Russians, the Turks, the French or the Austrians.'[115] In general, the Kaiser had positively besieged the Tsar with his attentions, so that someone in Alexander's retinue had commented that in Berlin 'everyone grovelled before us'.[116] In the Russian imperial family it was firmly believed that on this occasion Wilhelm had suggested to the Tsar the division of 'the whole of Europe' between Germany and Russia, whereupon Alexander − who could not help wondering about the Kaiser's mental state – immediately retorted: 'Stop whirling about like a dervish, Willy, just look at yourself in the mirror!'[117] After taking leave of the Tsar in his saloon carriage at the Lehrter station Wilhelm hurried up to Herbert Bismarck with the words: 'Everything has gone famously, the Tsar has invited me to Krasnoe and we have given each other our cipher codebooks.'[118] The Kaiser took this as a guarantee that Germany could count on peace at least for the coming year; it was 'a fine success', he said, which he attributed entirely to his own charm.[119] Later Waldersee learned that during a lively conversation with the Tsar in the saloon carriage Wilhelm had 'announced his intention of visiting Russia next year'; but 'no invitation from Tsar Alexander was forthcoming'. When Wilhelm informed the Reich Chancellor of this, in the belief that he had carried off a skilful coup, Bismarck was 'very embarrassed and dissatisfied', as Waldersee observed, for he too was of the opinion that one ought 'not to run after the Russians in any circumstances'.[120] Soon there were reports of 'bad-tempered remarks' by the Tsar about the Kaiser's proposed visit, which had been 'forced on him'.[121] As for the exchange of personal cipher codebooks, Herbert Bismarck commented: 'The A. cipher codebook for H.M. was soon ready and he carried it about everywhere, even in shooting costume. When Villaume received the W. cipher codebook to give to the Tsar, he reported that the latter expressed his thanks and put it in his desk.' In the eyes of the Tsar, such cipher codebooks were for adjutants to carry; 'a sovereign [could] not outwardly brand himself the adjutant of another'.[122]

The failed attempt to court the friendship of the House of Romanov reached its culmination in a painful epilogue. 'Certain incidents' which took place while the heir to the Russian throne, the Tsarevich Nicholas, was taking part in the imperial hunt at Springe am Deister in December 1889 embarrassed the Chief of the General Staff so much that he did not have the courage to mention the affair in his diary until several years later, and then only in veiled terms. The mysterious events in Springe, 'which I hesitate to set down on paper', Waldersee wrote after Nicholas's accession in December 1894, had undoubtedly 'made a lasting impression on the then heir to the throne'.[123]

In the weeks following the Tsar's visit Wilhelm's feelings towards Russia remained 'changeable, but still tolerable'. Although Herbert Bismarck recorded that he made many spiteful, mistrustful comments about Russia and the Tsar, 'full of the antipathy he still felt', he continued to have great faith in 'his own irresistible charm, . . . to the influence of which . . . the Tsar would again yield. To give this charm as much scope as possible to do its work, H.M. was even thinking of extending his announced visit, and inviting himself for 14 days' autumn shooting at the little hunting lodge at Spala, for then – by H.M.'s reckoning – the Tsar would be completely and lastingly under his spell.'[124] The relationship between the Kaiser and the Tsar was seen in quite another light by Bismarck's arch-rival Waldersee and yet confirmed in its essential elements. Waldersee complained that the Reich Chancellor, using a different tactic, had begun to flatter the Kaiser and not without success. Bismarck had assured Wilhelm 'that it is entirely to his, that is the Kaiser's, credit if Tsar Alexander now has quite different views about us, and then he tells the Kaiser quite shamelessly that he has considerable diplomatic talents. Unfortunately the Kaiser swallows this only too easily. Today the *Norddeutsche* sings the Kaiser's praises in a positively disgusting way as a great and wise sovereign, on the occasion of his visit to Constantinople. The Chancellor is unfortunately the cleverer and more cunning of the two.'[125]

In spite of the repeated requests of the Tsar, it did not occur to Wilhelm to give up his journey to Athens and Constantinople. He and the Kaiserin travelled to Italy, visiting the King and Queen in Monza on 19 October 1889 and, as we have already seen, continued their journey by sea from Genoa to Athens, where the Kaiser's sister Sophie was married to Crown Prince Constantine on 27 October. While at Monza on 20 October he wrote a lengthy report to Kaiser Franz Joseph on his meeting with Alexander III, which shows how he himself assessed the Tsar's visit.[126] He claimed that 'the Berlin public behaved very well, and to my astonishment greeted the Tsar much more warmly than I expected and than was described. As to the visit itself, it was more or less as follows: (Prince Bismarck and I compared our impressions afterwards and talked them over). The Tsar came to Berlin with a heart full of heavy forebodings and anxious cares. He had again been hard pressed last year, and the 2 months in Fredensborg had not been left unexploited by the illustrious members of the fair sex assembled there. For instance, from the questions which his tormented heart prompted him to ask the Chancellor, whom he had summoned to an audience, it became clear that he had been fooled into believing that I had allied myself with you, Umberto and the Queen of England – and now the Sultan was to be brought in too – in order to make a united and unexpected attack on the Tsar in the near future, to destroy his empire and to annihilate him and his family!! The Prince, in his calm, clear and conciliatory way, managed to contradict every bit of this nonsense so masterfully, and also to give an oversight of European politics in general, that afterwards the Tsar said to me in high delight: "Ah je suis tout a fait soulagé maintenant, et la conversation du Prince de Bismarck m'a dissipé toute[s] mes craintes, ce qui me laisse entierement satisfait." He had also personally been told many lies about me personally to make him as *soupçonneux* as possible, but all that was swept away with a magic wand. He was cheerful, contented, felt at home and was so loyal at the luncheon with the Alexander Regiment that he gave the toast in German and drank toasts with almost all his lieutenants.

Woronzoff told me that that was the first time for 25 years that he had heard the Tsar speak German in public. He set off on his journey home in the best of spirits and invited me to Krasnoe Selo for his big manoeuvres next year, an outcome which came as a complete but very pleasant surprise to the Chancellor. At any rate for the time being we are sure of peace for another year, and I hope for longer, if it is God's will. This was how things went, which I venture to tell you about. With many sincere greetings to the Kaiserin, I remain ever Your sincere Friend and Cousin Wilhelm.'[127]

In order to neutralise what he saw as the dangerous pro-Russian effect of the Tsar's visit, Waldersee held discussions with the Austrian military attaché von Steininger and the chargé d'affaires von Eissenstein and proposed a meeting between Wilhelm II and Kaiser Franz Josoph.[128] The latter made use of his letter of thanks for Wilhelm's long report to express the hope that on the return journey from Constantinople, 'somewhere on the way through Austria', he would have an opportunity to embrace the German Kaiser.[129] The Chief of the General Staff was nervous, however, that this might not be as warm an encounter as he hoped, since under Bismarck's influence the Kaiser was again speaking of Austria 'in a dismissive manner'.[130] The meeting took place on 14 November in Innsbruck and passed off fairly well, not least because the German military attaché, Major Adolf von Deines, went to meet the Kaiser at Bozen and had the opportunity to talk Wilhelm II out of Herbert Bismarck's disparaging views on Austria. The atmosphere was further 'improved' – in the anti-Russian, pro-Austrian sense – by a secret report which Waldersee sent to the Kaiser in Venice and which Wilhelm burned[131] during his second visit to Monza, where he had insisted on going in spite of strong opposition from Herbert Bismarck.[132] After the Kaiser's return to Berlin on 15 November Waldersee was relieved to discover that Wilhelm had not spent much time with Herbert during the journey to the eastern Mediterranean. 'While they were at sea – that is for more than 14 days – they were apart; in Athens and Constant[inople] the days were so fully occupied that the Kaiser could speak to him only infrequently and briefly. Of course the worthy Count again drew attention to himself by his rough and tactless behaviour', the General remarked.[133] Nonetheless Waldersee was still apprehensive, even after the meeting between Wilhelm and Franz Joseph, 'that we are once again faced with a cooling-off of relations with Austria. What we have so often seen before is happening again: the Chancellor is retreating into his old love of Russia, but Russia and France are continuing to rearm with all their might, and we are getting into a worse and worse situation, all the more so because things do not look good in Italy and Austria and each is full of sensitivities towards the other.'[134] After a conversation with Ambassador Count Münster on 8 December 1889 the General expressed the fear 'that we are going the best way about falling out with Austria without making sure of Russia's friendship'.[135]

Bismarck's lack of concern over Russian and French rearmament remained quite incomprehensible to Waldersee. When the Reichstag reassembled at the end of October during the Kaiser's absence, Bismarck sent instructions through Rottenburg to Minister of War von Verdy to postpone the planned creation of the new army corps until the following autumn, because France would take such redeployments amiss, and 'the most serious complications' could arise. Waldersee was furious at the Reich Chancellor's interference in military affairs and wrote: 'It is outrageous that he should express such wishes at this moment, and Verdy has sent him word that it is too late, that all the preparations are fully under way, the Kaiser having approved of the deployment &c. I am extremely anxious to know what will come of this; the Kaiser's being so far away may be a problem. But it is clear how afraid of war the Chancellor is. If our redeployments do not please the French, let them have it out with us, we are ready.'[136] Bismarck's attitude was all the more puzzling to Waldersee since everyone was aware that 'the new Reichstag which is to be elected . . . will be bad'; it would therefore have been 'much better to put forward even greater demands, while they can still be obtained'.[137] After making enquiries into the reasons for Bismarck's attitude and being able to find no convincing explanation, Waldersee once again suspected the influence of Jewish profiteers. 'It can only be Bleichröder who is behind it again' – as a 'well-informed person' had confirmed to him.[138]

At the beginning of December 1889 Waldersee noted with concern that 'thanks to the skill of the Chancellor' Kaiser Wilhelm II had 'without doubt gone over to the Russian camp altogether'.[139] As Waldersee saw it, Bismarck's foreign policy consisted in trying 'to get on a good footing with Russia through flattery and solicitousness'; but this policy destabilised the whole Triple Alliance, for it was making the army and leading circles in Austria feel unsafe and suspicious; the old differences between Austria and Italy were coming to the fore again, and France was making great efforts towards reconciliation with Italy. But the Chancellor could only continue with his policy by practising a massive confidence trick on the Kaiser. It was 'really infuriating' to see, Waldersee commented, 'how the Kaiser is deceived by the Chancellor; he only gives him reports which are written in accordance with his policy'. In any case Bismarck's diplomats reported nothing but what Bismarck ordered, and no newspaper articles which revealed the true atmosphere in Russia were allowed to be laid before the Kaiser. 'Yet in spite of all these despicable measures the Chancellor is not at all sure of the Kaiser', and was therefore feeling 'extremely uncomfortable', Waldersee observed at the beginning of 1890.[140]

The Chief of the General Staff was still confident, however, that 'from one day to the next' the Kaiser would 'begin to see clearly, in spite of all Bismarck's attempts to deceive him'.[141] On 23 December 1889 he recorded, after a conversation with the Kaiser in the Neues Palais, that Wilhelm had again become more sceptical about Russia. 'I am very glad to see that the Kaiser realises that the Russians are unsteady people, and that he is much less drawn along in their wake than he was 6 weeks ago. It was inevitable that this would happen.'[142] The Chief of the General Staff was also delighted to note, during a journey with Wilhelm to Dessau, that the Kaiser had 'recognised the restoration of Poland as a necessity'.[143]

## WALDERSEE'S FALL FROM GRACE

It is plain from all these conflicts that throughout the critical year of 1889 Waldersee was the Kaiser's closest confidant not only in the military sphere but also in foreign and domestic policy and political appointments. Indeed his role was almost that of a rival chancellor. But in December came the first signs – the reasons for it are not clear – of a certain disillusionment, which already indicated that the Chief of the General Staff would not after all become Bismarck's successor, as most observers expected, but would himself fall from grace soon after Bismarck's downfall. As the course of German and European history would certainly have been different if Waldersee had become Reich Chancellor in 1890, the slight ill-feeling which can be seen to have arisen between Kaiser and General from the end of 1889 – in early December Wilhelm called him, half-jokingly, a 'poisoner'[144] – is of no small significance.

The cooling of relations between Wilhelm and Waldersee became noticeable above all in the rejection of the renewed attempt by the Chief of the General Staff and the Minister of War to set up a kind of 'military railway dictatorship', as Herbert Bismarck described it.[145] The Chancellor wrote no fewer than three papers setting out his objections to an increased military influence over the Reich Railway Office, and stressing the necessity of securing the strategic interest of the army through the *Prussian* railway administration.[146] As Bismarck was more concerned with the constitutional aspects of this disagreement, while the Minister of War's preoccupation was with practical matters, an agreement was reached in a discussion between Herbert Bismarck and Verdy on 10 December.[147] It was indicative that relations between the Kaiser and Waldersee were no longer so close that – as Herbert observed – Verdy was not unwilling to distance himself from his 'rather sinister protector Waldersee', against whom he was 'desperately seeking a counterweight'.[148] Nevertheless there was still deep suspicion on both sides: from the Reich Chancellor's memoranda Verdy gained the impression 'that he intends to make me responsible for the result of the elections if these amount to a vote of no confidence in his domestic policies',[149] while for their part the Bismarcks suspected that the minister in charge of the army wanted to be able to say, if there were a war with France and Germany were defeated, 'Il vivrait, s'il m'avait suivi!' ('He would still be alive if he had followed me!') They were afraid that Verdy's aim was to collect written evidence of Bismarck's refusal, so that he would be able to claim later that it was not he but the Chancellor who had rejected the army's proposals, who was responsible for the defeat.[150] However that may be, the decisive factor was that in this intense conflict of political and military interests the Kaiser finally came down against the army's plans. On 10 December the Chief of the General Staff was still writing hopefully in his diary: 'I am anxious to know what attitude the Kaiser will adopt in the matter.'[151] Herbert Bismarck heard from one of the Flügeladjutanten on duty that Waldersee had been stirring up feeling against the Chancellor at luncheon in the Neues Palais, whereupon the Kaiser had complained 'in strong terms' about Prince Bismarck, who was always causing him problems.[152] But the next day the monarch had already adopted a different tone, and Waldersee was disappointed to realise that Wilhelm was inclined to agree with Bismarck on the railway question. 'I am very worried about his giving way like this', the General lamented for the first time since Wilhelm II's accession.[153] Finally, during a lengthy audience on the journey to Springe, Herbert Bismarck succeeded in winning over the Kaiser to the Chancellor's point of view, and in convincing him of the Minister of War's 'incredible ignorance of the constitution &c'.[154] The monarch had complained of the 'obstinacy and the purely civilian attitude' of Railways Minister Maybach, which would have seriously harmed the country's defence capabilities, but he had quickly seen the force of the constitutional objections put forward by the Reich Chancellor to the 'Waldersee–Verdy plan' and had expressed his pleasure that Bismarck was not opposed to the reform itself. Finally he said to Herbert: 'Good, then let us give up the Reich for the moment, and take up the matter in Prussia first. All I want is to improve our railway network quickly.' The Kaiser had been 'very calm and in an excellent mood', the Foreign Secretary reported to Friedrichsruh. 'I sat alone with him for an hour and three-quarters and discussed all kinds of important things that would take too long to write down and are partly too confidential as well.'[155]

The cooling of relations with Waldersee corresponded with an improvement – albeit only temporary – in Wilhelm II's relationship with the Bismarcks. When Herbert Bismarck called on the monarch on New Year's Eve he was 'very warmly' received. Wilhelm wanted 'detailed news about every member of the family' and added that the Reich Chancellor should 'of course stay at Friedrichsruh' and not put himself at the mercy of the Reichstag again before its dissolution. 'You were too precious for that', Herbert reported to his father, and went on: 'H.M. was simply as nice and considerate as he could be and sent warm greetings to you and Mama.'[156] A few days later, when Kaiserin Augusta died of influenza, the Kaiser sent the Reich Chancellor '*his command* not to come on any account'; he ought not to leave his wife alone and could catch something in Berlin.[157] Meanwhile, during a conversation with the Chief of the General Staff, Holstein observed that Waldersee was 'very nervous of the Kaiser'. Suddenly the General seemed to Holstein 'not a clear thinker after all, nor a consistent, logical character, more a blabbermouth than a worker. I would not be surprised', he commented in a letter to Eulenburg, 'if our sharp-witted Kaiser soon had no more use for him.'[158] Eulenburg thought he knew his 'most beloved Kaiser'[159] better, and cautioned Holstein: 'Do not lose patience with Waldersee! You are one of the few who have a conciliatory influence when there are differences between him and the Chancellor. If he becomes a burden to you the balance will shift and we shall be closer to a collision, the consequences of which *must* be *very* harmful to the relationship between the Kaiser and the Chancellor. For Waldersee is still in high favour. He will remain so for longer than you perhaps suppose. The Kaiser loves certain people *with* their weaknesses. Why should not Waldersee be one of these?'[160] Nevertheless, in the final phase of the Bismarck crisis which began in the autumn of 1889, the arch-conservative Chief of the General Staff no longer stood in the limelight. At this decisive stage the leading roles were played by Eulenburg and Holstein, seconded by the Kaiser's tutor Dr Hinzpeter, who suddenly re-emerged from obscurity at Bielefeld, Grand Duke Friedrich I of Baden and the Badenese envoy in Berlin, Adolf Marschall Freiherr von Bieberstein. All five were far more firm in supporting the Kartell of 'middle parties'. It was they, and not Waldersee, who were to join with Wilhelm in determining the policies of the post-Bismarckian era.

# CHAPTER TEN

# The Kaiser, the Chancellor and the Kartell

MANY observers, remembering Wilhelm's participation in the Stoecker meeting at Waldersee's house in November 1887, assumed that after his accession, and spurred on by the Kaiserin, Mirbach and Waldersee, he would maintain his alliance with the zealously Lutheran, reactionary wing of the German Conservative Party around the dismissed Interior Minister von Puttkamer, the editor of the *Kreuzzeitung* Freiherr von Hammerstein, the right-wing leader of the Conservatives Rauchhaupt and Adolf Stoecker himself, against the party's moderate wing and the liberal 'middle parties', that is to say the Free Conservatives and the National Liberals. And indeed in the autumn of 1889 a young diplomat at the British embassy was still bewailing the fact that 'poor' Friedrich III had omitted to sack Puttkamer, Stoecker and Waldersee the very day he came to the throne, for since then the 'political bigotry' of this right-wing 'rival government' at court had been gaining more and more influence over the Kaiser. This was fatal, for 'the men that are *very fast* destroying him [Bismarck] are our 10 times worse foes, the representatives of that tendency which ruined Fred[erick] W[illia]m II and VI'.[1] This contemporary interpretation of Bismarck's dismissal as the result of an extreme-right conspiracy has maintained its hold on historical research until the present day. It has much to be said for it, for Wilhelm's spiritual affinity with these ultra-conservative and anti-Semitic circles in the early days is beyond doubt. But it is equally clear that in his public utterances at the beginning of his reign the Kaiser supported the 'Kartell' of the 'middle parties' against the ultra-conservatives and it was this very fact that brought him into sharp conflict with Bismarck in the winter of 1889–90. Let us try to unravel this paradox, which from mid-1889 onwards forms the kernel of the confrontation between the Kaiser and the Chancellor over domestic policy.

## THE 'KARTELL KAISER'

In the initial phase of his reign Wilhelm II had no quarrel with Bismarck from a party-political point of view, at least outwardly. On several occasions he spoke out openly in support of the Kartell coalition which Bismarck had brought together in 1887 between the German Conservatives, the Free Conservative Reich party and the National Liberals. In so doing he was in effect showing preference for the latter party and administering a rebuff to the extreme orthodox, anti-Semitic right wing of the Conservative Party, which would rather have allied itself with the Catholic Centre Party than with the anti-clerical Liberals. Within weeks of Wilhelm's accession, when the leader of the Conservative group in the Prussian parliament, Wilhelm von Rauchhaupt, called for a campaign against the National Liberals in the forthcoming Prussian elections, the Kaiser did not conceal his displeasure. Herbert Bismarck reported to the ministers on 4 August 1888 that 'H.M. wished to call Rauchhaupt to order directly' and had personally suggested that, as a counter-demonstration against the right wing of the Conservatives, the National Liberal Party leader Rudolf von Bennigsen should be appointed Oberpräsident of the province of Hanover.[2] The next day the Kaiser informed Herbert that 'he had seen to it that Rauchhaupt was given a sharp dressing-down, so that he would probably keep quiet now'.[3] When Bennigsen accepted the post in Hanover – Bismarck had sent him word that this was the Kaiser's personal wish – Herbert commented that the move would 'make an excellent impression everywhere'.[4]

It was thus perfectly logical that in Count Douglas's election speech of October 1888, which as we have seen was written by Rottenburg on Bismarck's orders,[5] the Kaiser's pro-Kartell attitude should be strongly emphasised. In a striking passage in the speech the Free Conservative deputy declared that the young Kaiser could quite rightly be called the 'Kartell Kaiser', and not in the narrow, party political meaning of the word, but in the broadest, most patriotic sense. Since the Kartell parties were those which 'associate themselves with the Kaiser's endeavours, since they gladly and joyfully declare their support for kaiserdom and the monarchy, without any ulterior motives or subsidiary aims, they can also say with good reason of themselves: "We stand on the ground on which our Kaiser stands."' The appointment of Bennigsen, he continued, which was 'in accordance with the *personal wish of our Kaiser* . . . is above all a proof that in his reign the Kaiser is determined to call on the support of all those who are at one with him on the fundamental questions, regardless of their particular party allegiances'. As long as the Catholic Centre and the left-liberal Progressive Party refused to adopt the same position on the fundamental questions affecting the life of the nation, but persisted in 'carping, constantly negative opposition on principle',[6] the Kartell parties would remain the only ones on which the Kaiser's government could and must rely for support.

It was also completely in line with the Bismarck's thinking that Douglas should emphatically reject the idea that the Kaiser supported Adolf Stoecker's views on religious policy or indeed his anti-Semitism.[7] 'As you know', he pointed out in his speech, 'a meeting which was held at the house of the present Chief of the General Staff, Count Waldersee, and at which the then Prince Wilhelm was present, was exploited to bring the Prince under suspicion in the public mind and to identify him with the party political aspirations of strict church circles, in particular with those of Court Preacher Stoecker.' All such interpretations of the Kaiser's position, however, were based on 'sheer distortion of the truth', Douglas asserted. He must emphasise that, on the contrary, 'the links which Kaiser Wilhelm had with Court Preacher Stoecker were only very temporary, and were limited purely to genuinely Christian and hence genuinely humane endeavours with regard to giving practical assistance to the lower classes in their need . . . Apart from this there has been no connection with Court Preacher Stoecker, and least of all does our Kaiser subscribe to the extreme political and confessional party opinions which are customarily linked with the name of this deputy. On this matter the position is absolutely, unambiguously clear. And if attempts have been made even to link the Kaiser with the anti-Semitic movement, this is yet more effrontery, which I can refute with the greatest certainty.'[8]

The appointment of Bennigsen as Oberpräsident, the Douglas speech, Wilhelm's visit to Friedrichsruh on 29 October 1888, which was intended as 'a demonstration of opposition to all extremes',[9] and finally Stoecker's endangered position as court preacher, which from March 1889 he seemed increasingly likely to lose,[10] gradually led to a change in the public perception of Wilhelm II's party political inclinations. As the Austrian chargé d'affaires, Eissenstein, noted in a perceptive report to Vienna, at Wilhelm's accession it was still widely thought that he subscribed to 'extreme-conservative Christian views'; the Stoecker party had not failed to exploit this belief, which undeniably had some basis in utterances made by Wilhelm as prince, in their own interest. The 'reactionary tendencies ascribed to the young Kaiser, however, have not been confirmed subsequently', Eissenstein commented, and as a result 'the hopes of the Stoecker party [have been] greatly reduced'. The best evidence that Wilhelm had no intention of 'throwing himself into the arms of the ultra-conservatives' was – according to Eissenstein – Bennigsen's appointment.[11]

Outwardly, therefore, in party political terms the elderly founder of the Reich and the youthful Hohenzollern Kaiser were in perfect harmony, supported by the moderate Conservative–National Liberal Kartell coalition. But was it all an empty pretence? In spite of public assurances and demonstrations, many in the inner circles of the ruling elite still had their doubts as to whether the ideas officially described by the Wilhelmstrasse as representing the Kaiser's thinking really corresponded to his innermost convictions. Thus for instance no less a person than the Kaiserin herself wrote to her husband after reading the Douglas speech: 'I think much of it is good but some of what he [writes] about your political and religious opinions is a pity, because it is not quite right.'[12] Similarly, the ultra-conservative Waldersee was of the opinion that, even if Wilhelm were obliged to give public support to the Kartell for tactical reasons, in his heart he continued to sympathise with the 'strict religious' tendency in the Conservative Party around Stoecker and Hammerstein, and had only reluctantly accepted the alliance with the progressively inclined National Liberals. In September 1888 he recorded in his diary: 'The Chancellor is still afraid that the Kaiser is actually on the side of the *Kreuzzeitung* in his heart of hearts . . . The Kaiser is [however] much too clever to identify himself with one party, even if he feels otherwise.'[13] Waldersee was able to note with satisfaction in November of that year that the 'Kaiser's ideas' were still 'as sound as a bell'.[14]

Precisely because there was always a risk that the Kaiser could switch sides and join his right-wing conservative enemies, Bismarck could not but regard the latter as his most dangerous rivals. On 23 October Waldersee wrote that the Chancellor, whose secret aim was to ensure the succession for his son Herbert, needed to fight 'the Conservatives above all'. 'The only rivals he fears are people from the Conservative Party, especially on account of the Kaiser's opinions, and he is now trying to discredit both the party and the individuals whom he considers worthy of notice.'[15] To eliminate the danger that arose from Wilhelm's inner inclination towards the ultra-conservatives, the Bismarcks – according to Waldersee – were intent on splitting the Conservative Party and drawing political and moral odium on to its right wing. With the help of their agents at court – Waldersee picked out Liebenau and Lucanus above all – the Bismarcks were even trying to neutralise the influence of the pious Kaiserin on the Kaiser. In October 1888 he recorded in his diary: 'The Chancellor wants to break up the Conservative Party; he is now using all his press . . . to attack the *Kreuzzeitung* and cast suspicion on it in a most despicable way. They have no scruples in accusing it of hostility to the Reich and would like to make the public at large think that it is in league with the real enemies of the Reich, that is to say Ultramontanes, Progressives and Socialists . . . The Kaiser is being drawn into this and claims that he is not a firm supporter of any extreme party, and thus not of the strict church party either . . . And now Bismarck is flirting with the National Liberals', Waldersee continued in disgust. 'But he is in danger of being seriously misled and then he will find out that many among the National Liberals are of a strong left-wing

tendency, and that . . . the result will be to strengthen the Progressives. Naturally
every possible means is being tried to influence the Kaiser and persuade him that
the Conservatives . . . have no support in the country; the person most involved
in this is of course Herbert Bismarck, and then Liebenau, these two being the
people who see him most here; then Lucanus, who has no independent opinions
but dances entirely to Bismarck's tune. But I do not think that they will have
complete success. The Kaiser rightly takes the view – and I have often encouraged
him in it – that he must base himself on the Kartell parties, and consequently
that the machinery of government must work towards keeping these parties
together, and not try to split off the right wing, as Bismarck is now doing.'[16]

The political agitation stirred up by the ultra-conservatives, so dangerous for
Bismarck, reached a peak in January 1889 when Hammerstein published an
article in the *Kreuzzeitung* condemning government policy – and in particular
the publication of the charges against Geffcken – as un-Prussian and harmful
to the monarchy. In tones that were quite obviously aimed at winning over
the Kaiser, the newspaper editor wrote: 'The monarchical sentiments of Old
Prussian patriots cannot but have been deeply wounded by recent events. Highly
distressing as it then was to observe, after the Waldersee meeting, that nearly
all German newspapers – with the single exception of those of the conservative
right – had no compunction in conspiring with the entire foreign Jewish–liberal
press to give the world the sad example of shameful criticism of, and malicious
allegations against, members of the Imperial Family, without even a word from
the official organs to call them to order; . . . deeply as all men of a truly monarchical
way of thinking have deplored the tactless attempt by Count Douglas, Konstantin
Rössler and others to draw the person of our present Imperial Master into the
election campaign and party conflicts; and finally, profoundly displeased as every
patriot has been by the shameless utterances of the Progressive press concerning
the persons of the Kaisers Friedrich and Wilhelm II in connection with the
publication of the Crown Prince's diary – the Prussians, whose motto is "With
God for King and Fatherland!", are now confronted with the publication of the
indictment [against Geffcken], with all its accompanying circumstances, and are
filled with sadness and anxiety . . . The principle of authority not majority, the
basis of the Christian state, is beginning to falter. But this is the soil in which
Prussia's greatness is rooted, the Prussia in which His Majesty is King by the
Grace of God.'[17] For the first time since the Manteuffel era the *Kreuzzeitung* was
impounded on account of this article, and its editor, Hammerstein, was arrested.[18]
The Kartell block, the parliamentary base of the government in Prussia and in
the Reich, was already beginning to develop rifts. 'The Kartell is now a year old,
but still has no firm framework; on the contrary, it seems to be coming apart',
Waldersee noted in March 1889.[19]

## THE CHANCELLOR AND CATHOLIC GERMANY

If the situation in Berlin was already complicated enough, the party-political confusion was greatly increased by the federal structure of the Reich. Bavaria, the second-largest federal state, was governed, to a certain extent against the will of its Catholic majority and also against the personal convictions of Prince Regent Luitpold, by a National Liberal ministry led by Freiherr Johann von Lutz. His government was regarded as a guarantor of the Reich principle and of Prussian hegemony, against Bavarian particularist aspirations. In political circles everyone knew that Lutz was safe in his position as long as he was openly supported by Berlin; but if a more Centre-friendly policy, or a wish to form a 'black–blue' clerical–conservative coalition in the Reichstag, were signalled from the capital, the Prince Regent would be only too glad to replace the Protestant Lutz by some aristocratic Catholic Centre leader such as Georg Arbogast Freiherr von Franckenstein. Many in Berlin feared, however, that such a development in Bavaria might lead to a break-up of the Reich, for, as they argued, if a Bavarian Catholic and particularist came to power in Munich, the leaders in Austria and the Vatican (and perhaps even in France and Russia) would be tempted to sabotage Bismarck's Reich and seek to return the central European states system to its pre-1866 status quo. The result might easily be – and this was the nightmare which haunted many statesmen in Berlin – a civil war with foreign intervention.

Even the orthodox Protestant Waldersee was convinced of the necessity of strengthening the position of the Liberal Prime Minister of Bavaria. 'The Catholic Church is busier than ever', he wrote in his diary. 'It has got itself on to a good footing with the French government and is now trying to do the same with Russia. In Bavaria it is making great efforts to overthrow Lutz's ministry. It seems that the Holy Father is joining the Franco-Russian alliance and I grieve to see our situation worsening all the time.'[20] In the summer of 1889 the Chief of the General Staff called on Minister-President Lutz in Munich to convey greetings to him from Wilhelm II, and to assure him of the latter's support in his struggle against his numerous enemies in South German aristocratic circles and in the Centre Party. He persuaded the Kaiser to confer the Order of the Black Eagle, the highest Prussian order, on Lutz. 'The first time he was unwilling', the Chief of the General Staff recalled; 'but the second time he was more accommodating. I was very glad that Lutz received the Order a few days after my visit.'[21]

Since mid-1889 Lutz's government had been under threat as a result of an insignificant question of religious policy which was to acquire a disproportionately important place in the conflict between the Kaiser and the Chancellor: the recall of the Redemptorists, a small religious order which, together with the Jesuits, had been banned from the whole of Germany during the *Kulturkampf*. When the question of allowing the return of the Redemptorists became acute in June 1889, Herbert Bismarck reminded his father that he had rejected this eighteen months earlier after the Bundesrat had established that the Redemptorists were still affiliated to the Jesuits. The Foreign Secretary went on to warn that it would be senseless to use this measure to gain the co-operation of the ultramontane Catholics: they would immediately demand that the Jesuits be allowed to return next. 'We shall never win over the intransigents in any case', he advised his father. 'They would only be satisfied if *all* Germans became Catholics and the Reich were split up into a mass of small powerless states with a constitution *à la* Paraguay.'[22] Accordingly the Reich Chancellor wrote to Lutz on 6 August 1889 refusing permission for the return of the order.[23]

The Kaiser's two friends, Waldersee and Eulenburg, were also decidedly of the opinion that the Redemptorists should on no account be allowed to return, for this would at once be seen as signalling support for the Centre, it would cause the fall of Lutz's pro-Reich government in Bavaria, and the moderate Conservative–National Liberal Kartell in the Reichstag would be broken up. Indeed, in their eyes even the existence of the Triple Alliance would be threatened, as such a change in German domestic policy would alienate anti-clerical Italy. Remarkably enough, these two influential advisers of Wilhelm II suspected that the Bismarcks, of all people, intended to adopt a pro-Centre course with the aim of provoking both internal and external unrest, which they hoped would increase the strength of their own position. The Kaiser must at all costs be warned of this devilish plot. 'The Kaiser, thank God, is very steady now', Waldersee wrote in July 1889 during the Scandinavian cruise, 'and here on the "Hohenzollern" he shall not be influenced in the other direction.' But he added presciently: 'I hope different influences will not be brought to bear later, for there will certainly be attempts.'[24] Just as a little stream can split a cliff when it freezes, this question, insignificant in itself, developed enormous explosive potential and threatened to break up the powerful German Reich and its alliance system.

### IMPERIAL SUPPORT FOR THE KARTELL

In autumn 1889 the crisis came to a dramatic head. On his return from a walking holiday Friedrich von Holstein, the so-called Grey Eminence in the Foreign Office, heard that Bismarck's son-in-law Rantzau, as Prussian envoy in Munich, had sent a report directly to the Reich Chancellor at Friedrichsruh, in which he stated that Bishop of Fulda Georg Kopp had claimed in a letter to Lutz that the recall of the Redemptorists was now wished for 'in Berlin'.

The Chancellor had forwarded the report to Holstein, who was directed to lay it before the Kaiser, after consultation with Prussian Minister for Ecclesiastical Affairs Gustav von Gossler. The Kaiser, Holstein informed Eulenburg with relief on 28 September, had declared himself 'categorically' opposed to the recall of the order.[25] Encouraged by this imperial declaration of confidence in Lutz and in the Kartell combination in the Reichstag, Holstein devised a tactical coup through which the Kaiser could achieve three important aims: by making a public declaration in favour of the Kartell, Wilhelm would secure a majority for his government in the next Reichstag; he would unite moderate Conservative, nationalist and liberal public opinion behind him; and he would thereby deprive Bismarck of the chance of using a serious internal crisis to set himself up as a saviour in the hour of need, to the detriment of the monarch. Holstein's exposition of his plan to Eulenburg was shrewd and subtle. 'The elections will be bad, i.e. the moderate parties will suffer heavy losses, if the Kaiser himself does not in some way express his sympathy for the moderate groups. He would be doing himself a great service, for if his *first* Reichstag elections are won by the opposition, that is a vote of no confidence by the people in *him*, or at least it will be seen as such. The Chancellor does not need to worry about that. I have even come across some supporters of the Chancellor who think that bad elections are good for the Chancellor, although otherwise they take a pessimistic view of the regime. So the Kaiser is doing *himself* a good turn if he does something for the elections. It is nonsense when thoughtless people tell him that it does not matter for him whether there is a majority or a minority.' If the Reichstag elections due at the beginning of 1890 did indeed go badly, Bismarck would try 'to govern with the Centre and the Conservatives', Holstein predicted. But this would mean the appointment of a Centre Party deputy like Karl Freiherr von Huene as minister in Berlin, and the replacement of Lutz by someone like Franckenstein in Munich. 'That will dislocate the whole structure of the Reich, because Bavaria will assume the role destined for it by the curia ... as the *Catholic* hegemonial power in Germany. If that happens, whenever we want to obtain a war loan from parliament we shall first have to negotiate with the Pope, and buy his agreement.' Holstein asked Eulenburg whether he agreed in principle on the usefulness of a declaration in favour of the Kartell by the Kaiser; they could discuss the *modus operandi* later.[26]

Holstein himself was surprised by the lightning speed with which his suggestion took effect. Two days after Holstein's letter to Eulenburg, Herbert Bismarck returned to the Foreign Office from an audience with the Kaiser with instructions to publish a solemn imperial declaration in favour of the Kartell in the *Reichsanzeiger*, the official government gazette. The Kaiser, as Holstein informed Eulenburg, had stipulated the contents of the declaration with the words: 'His

Majesty is indignant at the misuse made of his name, in that several newspapers dared to claim that he was against the Kartell. On the contrary, &c . . .' Holstein presumed that Eulenburg had been responsible for the imperial order. 'Did *you* have something to do with it, you little rogue?', he asked. 'That would be a commendable achievement.' Holstein was curious to know how the Reich Chancellor, to whom the declaration would have to be shown before publication, would react. But in taking this action the Kaiser had undoubtedly shown 'a high degree of political *sangfroid* . . . such as many much older people do not possess'.[27]

So on 2 October 1889 the *Reichsanzeiger* published the following sensational declaration: 'His Majesty the Kaiser and King has taken notice of the contents of the *Kreuzzeitung* of the 26th of the month and strongly disapproves of the political opinions expressed therein and of the attacks on other political groups. His Majesty does not allow any party to claim the distinction of possessing the imperial ear. But the Kaiser sees the understanding and mutual restraint shown to each other by the parties supporting the state as a genuinely useful benefit to our parliamentary life, and has unambiguously expressed All-Highest disapproval of the attacks and insinuations directed against it by the *Kreuzzeitung*. His Majesty sees in the Kartell a political formation which corresponds to the principles of His government, and cannot see how the manner in which the *Kreuzzeitung* attacks it can be reconciled with the respect due to the All-Highest Person and to our constitutional institutions.'[28] The Kaiser was 'delighted with the effect of his anti-Kreuzzeitung declaration' and 'wished to see as many supportive articles as possible', Herbert Bismarck subsequently reported to Friedrichsruh. In complete accordance with the line taken by Waldersee, Holstein and Eulenburg, the monarch declared to his astonished Foreign Secretary that 'the Kartell is as essential for peace at home as the Triple Alliance is for peace abroad'.[29]

Eulenburg spent 8 October 1889 in Berlin, where for several hours he held a 'serious discussion' with Holstein and the German ambassador at the Quirinal, Eberhard Count zu Solms-Sonnenwalde, on the importance of the survival of the Kartell for domestic policy and of the Triple Alliance for foreign policy. That same evening Holstein recorded the main points of agreement in an aide-mémoire. 'No concessions (e.g. Redemptorists) through which Lutz could be brought down. An ultramontane ministry in Bavaria *must* be avoided. *No manifestation of any kind* through which advances might be made to the Catholics at the expense of our relations with the *Italian government*. The latter must on no account be made mistrustful or allowed to think that our relations with the Pope are more important to us than those with Italy. Even if the Pope, instead of being Franckenstein's ally, were imbued with the best possible intentions towards us and decided to give expression to these intentions, his *power* would not be nearly significant enough to replace the loss of strength which we should suffer if Italy ceased to trust us and turned away from us. There are plenty of enticements for her to do so. – The Centre will never become a *German* party. It remains a foreign element even if it *sometimes* deigns to support the government; this support remains dependent on the will of the Pope, behind whom hide Ledochowski [the Polish cardinal], Windthorst and the Jesuits. For the imperial government it will be easier, in the case of real need, to come to an agreement with *any German* party *at all*, than with the two international parties: the Centre and Social Democracy.'[30]

As a reaction against the apparently pro-Centre shift in Bismarck's policy, in the autumn of 1889 the strict church, ultra-conservative Waldersee surprisingly also went over to the Kartell camp. He was just as intent as before on using religion, as Stoecker urged, as a weapon against the dangers of democracy and socialism, which he regarded as the 'most important of all questions', but he was deeply suspicious of the Catholic Church and therefore resolutely opposed to any rapprochement between Bismarck and the Centre.[31] On 4 November he noted in his diary: 'There is general uncertainty as to what the clever Chancellor is planning; there is a feeling that an evolution is in the offing, but no one knows in what direction. I still fear that he wants to get involved with the ultramontanes. The Redemptorist question is being pursued very hard in Bavaria and people hope it will bring down Lutz; if the Chancellor decided to give in over this I should consider it highly deplorable.'[32] In reaction to Bismarck's swing towards the Centre, Waldersee not only made contact publicly with the Free Conservatives, who embodied the principle of the Kartell, but even 'became slightly more friendly' towards the National Liberals, as he said on 21 October 1889. The Chief of the General Staff knew very well that this change of direction on his part would be a 'considerable blow' for Bismarck.[33] Waldersee's action strengthened his ties with Holstein, who had repeatedly urged him since July 1889 to speak out 'for the Kartell, the sooner the better'.[34] From then on the two men, whose personalities and views could not have been more contradictory, met regularly for lengthy discussions.[35] The circle of Bismarck's opponents was beginning to close around him.

At the beginning of October 1889 the Kaiser's secret clique of advisers thought they had received confirmation of their worst fears: that the Chancellor was engineering a 'black–blue' clerical–conservative party block behind Wilhelm's back. During the Kaiser's three-week absence in Italy, Greece and Turkey, Eulenburg (who, it should be remembered, was now no longer accredited to Munich but to Oldenburg, Brunswick and Lippe) heard that the categorical 'expression of his will' opposing the recall of the Redemptorists made by the Kaiser at the end of September had not 'reached the ears of the Bavarian ministry' but had been 'held up at the Prussian legation'. On 5 October Eulenburg informed Wilhelm that instead of conveying his, the Kaiser's, clear decision to the Bavarian government, Bismarck's son-in-law Rantzau had hinted 'that the *Chancellor* was *in favour* of the recall', whereupon the Bavarian government had decided to allow the Redemptorists to return to Bavaria. This triumph for the ultramontane party was a serious blow to Lutz's position, Eulenburg told the Kaiser. But he also warned him of the next, inevitable step: soon Bavaria would propose a motion in the Bundesrat for the suspension of the relevant Bundesrat resolution, thereby enabling the return of the Redemptorists throughout Germany. 'And now that the Chancellor, in response to Rantzau's direct reports, has actually taken the step of moving closer to the Centre by agreeing to the recall, the more malleable elements in the Bundesrat could easily reach a decision which would greatly surprise Your Majesty. The timing of this action in Munich was cleverly planned to coincide with Your Majesty's absence. Everything therefore depends on a declaration of Your Majesty's will, to enlighten the Bundesrat on Your Majesty's views about the recall of the Redemptorists into the Reich.' Eulenburg strongly urged the Kaiser 'to destroy this letter at once – in strange hands it would look like an intrigue!' The Kaiser should not mention the letter to Herbert Bismarck – otherwise Eulenburg would be blacklisted – but he must refer to newspaper reports as his source. This was a matter of the greatest possible importance. 'I have often written to Your Majesty about Bavaria as "the Catholic hegemonial power in the Reich"; this is now a distinct possibility. If we support these tendencies we are doing ourselves damage, and *the day that we make concessions to Roman policy, Italy will cease to trust us.*' Eulenburg had already written to Lutz to inform him of the Kaiser's true opinion and to seek further information about other 'Catholic questions': the Kaiser had, after all, ordered him 'to keep in touch with matters in Bavaria'![36]

A few days later Eulenburg wrote a second letter to the Kaiser, who by now was on the way from Athens to Constantinople. In it he recounted that on a recent visit to Berlin he had found 'a state of immense alarm in the hallowed halls of the Wilhelmstrasse'. Holstein, Kiderlen-Wächter, Ludwig Raschdau, Dr Paul Kayser and the other counsellors in the Foreign Office were all 'at their wits' end' at the success of the 'coalition' between Rantzau in Munich and the 'ultramontane' Bavarian envoy in Berlin, Hugo Count von Lerchenfeld-Köfering. The Foreign Office men were 'of course powerless against the word put about by Friedrichsruh – and yet filled with the inner urge to bring Your Majesty's will to the fore in this important question'. All were of the opinion that it 'would be *of great importance* for the good of Your Majesty that, unless Your Majesty preferred to have the matter out with the Prince himself, or even *via Herbert*, Your Majesty should have the view which Your Majesty takes with regard to the recall of the Redemptorists clearly stated *before the representatives of the federal states, through Boetticher'*. The Reich Chancellor, Eulenburg asserted, would 'certainly not make this a resignation issue', for he could not face Germany with a threat to resign *'on account of the ultramontanes'*. Furthermore, 'the whole Ministry shares Your Majesty's point of view out of conviction'. Vice-President of the Ministry of State Heinrich von Boetticher and Minister for Ecclesiastical Affairs Gossler were particularly 'infuriated' by Bismarck's change of heart towards the Centre.[37] In support of his action Eulenburg also called on the Grand Duke of Baden to help by obtaining a 'formal declaration of the will of His Majesty The Kaiser to the federal governments (via Boetticher)', in order to put a stop to the 'intrigue' in which the Chancellor, Rantzau and Lerchenfeld were involved.[38] A head-on collision between the Kaiser and the Chancellor now seemed inevitable, for while there were increasing indications that Bismarck intended 'to go along with the ultramontanes', Holstein was able to observe from the Kaiser's marginal notes received at the Foreign Office on 4 November that the latter was 'still absolutely firm at the moment' on the church question.[39] He was nevertheless worried that as the Kaiser was 'unfortunately very impressionable', the Reich Chancellor might make him change his mind on his return. 'In a word', he warned Eulenburg on 5 November 1889, 'the Kaiser is not yet rated as a political factor. If he gives way this time too, his rating will sink down to near zero.'[40]

The very next day, as a direct result of Eulenburg's two letters, which the Kaiser had not received until after he had left Constantinople on 6 November,[41] two telegraphic ultimata arrived from Pera which put paid all to Holstein's doubts. The first telegram, addressed to Bismarck, was dictated by the Kaiser directly to the telegraph clerk. He did not mince his words. 'I see from articles in the *Kölnische* and the *National-Zeitung* that the recall of the Redemptorists has been proposed, not without prospects of success. I request you to declare that never in any circumstances can I or will I give my consent to this measure. Envoy in Munich notified direct, for information of government there.'[42] At the same time Boetticher received a telegram from Lucanus, just as Eulenburg had suggested, which read: 'His Majesty has telegraphed direct to the Reich Chancellor today concerning the Redemptorists. His Majesty asks Your Excellency to act in accordance with this telegram in the Bundesrat.'[43]

Holstein noted that, although the Kaiser's declaration had come too late to alter Lutz's position, which the latter had already made public under the impression that the Chancellor favoured the recall of the Redemptorists, it had nevertheless been in time to have a decisive influence on the Bundesrat and the federal governments, and was 'particularly well timed to influence our own ministers'. He hoped for a still more active participation by the Kaiser in the conduct of policy in the future, which would oblige the monarch to work more closely with individual ministers. 'Our All-Gracious Sovereign will *perhaps* learn from these events that he really must take some interest in work . . . It is not as if he will need to bury his imperial nose in papers for very long; it will be quite enough if he reads newspapers and asks *departmental ministers* to report to him from time to time.'[44] Eulenburg was confident that the Kaiser would not have his mind changed again on the Redemptorist question. 'The Redemptorists will *not* be forgotten by His Majesty – in any respect. I am certain of that', he assured Holstein. 'His Majesty has been warned and can no longer be easily trapped.'[45]

At the beginning of December 1889 Holstein recorded with satisfaction that the Kaiser, now back in Berlin, had spoken 'firmly' to the leader of the moderate, pro-Kartell wing of the Conservatives, Otto von Helldorff-Bedra, against the extreme right-wing tendency in the party, and had authorised him to make his views known.[46] He was even more pleased when Wilhelm praised the services of the Oberbürgermeister of Frankfurt am Main, the National Liberal Party leader Dr Johannes Miquel, in a speech on 9 December, for his toast was at once interpreted as a further demonstration of support for the Kartell. Jubilantly Holstein commented: 'It was the best speech that the Kaiser has made for a long time – the people can see from it that the sovereign is taking his work seriously.'[47]

Bismarck, who was 'rather taken aback' by the 'bluntness' of the imperial telegram,[48] tried to neutralise its effect as far as possible. He answered the Kaiser soothingly that he would act in accordance with his command as soon as the question came up in the Bundesrat or in the Reichstag; meanwhile he did not believe that the Bavarian government was likely to make a proposal respecting this matter in the Bundesrat.[49] He sent word to Lerchenfeld that he must forbid any declaration by the Bavarian government which would reveal the opposition of the other federal states to the return of the Redemptorists, for the confidentiality of the sittings of the Bundesrat must be preserved.[50] He published the imperial telegram to him, not least, Holstein suspected, in order to draw attention to the '*youthfulness*' of the Kaiser.[51]

Is it really true that Bismarck, shortly before his fall, pursued this plan to break up the Kartell coalition which suited the government so well, and replace it by a black–blue block in the Reichstag, as his secret enemies suspected? This thesis goes so much against the grain of orthodox research on Bismarck that it seems implausible even to Bismarck's great American biographer Otto Pflanze.[52] And yet there is no doubt of the authenticity of the sources cited above. The documents indisputably testify that men of such differing characters and political standpoints as Eulenburg and Holstein, Waldersee and Boetticher, Paul Kayser and the Grand Duke of Baden were convinced that this was Bismarck's aim, and were prepared to provoke direct conflict between the Kaiser and the Chancellor over it. Even if we accept that for a few of them – Holstein and Waldersee, for example – manipulative calculation may have played a part, and even if it cannot be denied that all the documentary evidence of Bismarck's sudden turning against the Kartell comes from the writings of the Kaiser's advisers, and none from the Bismarckians themselves, it is nevertheless scarcely conceivable that so many well-informed diplomats, civil servants, military officers and journalists should have fallen victim to a mere illusion. The likeliest explanation of the riddle seems to be that from the autumn of 1889 onwards Bismarck became increasingly aware of how much his position was threatened by the growing impatience of the young Hohenzollern ruler, and that, scenting danger, he began contemplating ways of frustrating the impending take-over of power by the Kaiser. The creation of a new majority in the Reichstag on a clerical–conservative basis was only one of the available solutions, and in itself not the most attractive. But the founder of the Reich must have foreseen – just as his secret opponents did – the internal and external tensions and crises that would be unleashed by such a change of coalition; and he would have calculated that the resultant chaos would make it impossible for the inexperienced monarch to dispense with his now almost 75-year-old Reich Chancellor. In the anxiety-ridden, paranoid world in which the conspirators supporting the Kaiser found themselves, these calculations on the part of Bismarck will certainly have been predicted and thought through to the end, even if Bismarck himself had not formulated them so fully. Hence also their subjective feeling – although objectively speaking they were the vanguard of a new regime under the personal leadership of the Kaiser – that they were mounting a heroic defence against the overly powerful Chancellor-Dictator Bismarck.

What is unmistakable is that within a short period there had been a massive shift of power. Six months earlier the Reich Chancellor had still held the monopoly of decision-making power in civil affairs; now, at the end of 1889, he could not even push through a minor religious measure, through which he might have hoped to engineer a new constellation of parties in the Reichstag, against the will of the Kaiser. From the autumn of 1889, instead of the dictatorship of the Chancellor which had existed hitherto, there was a dualism of power which could not last long. Nor was there much doubt as to which was the stronger element. 'Very few people suspect how weak the Chancellor is in relation to the Kaiser', Waldersee commented on 13 November. 'This is the clearest sign of his weakness. He is extremely worried about a conflict with the Kaiser because he fears that the Kaiser might dismiss him. The Kaiser knows this very well, and he uses it very skilfully to work on the Chancellor. He follows him in many things, but in others he remains absolutely independent.'[55] In so doing he received the advice of a heterogeneously assembled clique of whose existence the apparently all-powerful Reich Chancellor was completely ignorant.

### THE CONSPIRATORS AGAINST BISMARCK

As we have seen, the numerous collisions between Kaiser and Chancellor from early in 1889, especially the violent disagreements over the coal miners' strike and the Russian conversion in the summer and over the Kartell in the autumn, had led to the formation of an influential group of advisers around the Kaiser, in addition to the civilian and military officials of his court. It remained an informal group: its members corresponded with each other but rarely met, and then almost always only in secret; and they had little in common either socially or ideologically. Their motives were varied and yet closely entwined. They combined personal ambition and objective conviction with a strong desire to increase the power of the Kaiser, of whom the members of the group had formed a totally idealised image, and to reduce the domination of the Bismarcks, which they saw increasingly as dictatorial. Although Waldersee and Eulenburg continued to be key figures in this group, the circle of Wilhelm II's advisers cannot in any way be described as orthodox-evangelical or reactionary-conservative, for even Waldersee recognised the tactical necessity of publicly aligning the Kaiser with the Kartell. Other members of the group of advisers, like the Grand Duke of Baden and his representative in Berlin, Adolf Freiherr Marschall von Bieberstein, were South-West German liberal–conservative in their thinking, while men such as the influential Friedrich von Holstein in the Foreign Office and the journalist Franz Fischer of the National Liberal *Kölnische Zeitung* represented an almost progressive tendency, or at any rate a constitutional, anti-clerical rationalist one. Indeed the group even included idealists such as Dr Georg Hinzpeter, the Kaiser's former tutor, and Dr Paul Kayser, the (Jewish) Colonial Director in the Foreign Office, who showed astonishing radicalism in putting forward a programme of state social reform for the benefit of the working classes. This heterogeneous group, and not the *Kreuzzeitung* faction, were the Kaiser's supporters in his historic conflict with the Bismarcks.[54]

After his return to Bielefeld Hinzpeter had not lost touch with Wilhelm, but continued to correspond with him and visit him occasionally in Berlin and Potsdam. At the beginning of 1889 Eulenburg, who since his posting to the North German courts often came into contact with the former tutor, warned Herbert Bismarck of the 'liberal' influence exercised by Hinzpeter, who had pushed himself forward 'in his discourteous and thick-skinned way' to speak to the Kaiser during a train journey from Bückeburg to Hanover. Commenting on the relationship between the 'Doctor' and his pupil, Eulenburg wrote: 'You know that he writes a great deal to the Kaiser, and that the Kaiser is sincerely attached to his old teacher . . . The one thing that strikes me as strange about all this is that we owe our glorious Kaiser to the education given him by this man!'[55]

In November 1889, however, it was precisely Hinzpeter's liberal views which Eulenburg and Holstein began to see as a useful weapon in the battle to defeat the Bismarcks and preserve the Kartell. Holstein urged Eulenburg to arrange for Hinzpeter to be in Berlin on the day the Kaiser returned from his oriental journey, 'because of the church question'.[56] Suddenly the tutor had become 'intelligent and sensible' in their eyes, 'an exceptionally clever man', if 'slightly inclined to strike a pose as an original'. On 9 November 1889 Eulenburg visited Hinzpeter in Bielefeld and subsequently reported to Holstein that the pedagogue shared 'our point of view and will put forward these opinions in Berlin'.[57] Not the least of their hopes was that Hinzpeter's influence would result in a less 'youthful' style in the Kaiser's telegrams.[58] In fact he had exactly the opposite effect.

Early in the new year a letter from Hinzpeter produced a violent reaction from the Kaiser in connection with the critical question of the Kartell. He wrote on 4 January 1890 from Bielefeld, commenting that the candidature there of Hammerstein, the editor of the *Kreuzzeitung*, in the forthcoming Reichstag elections was of serious concern, because 'it shows particularly clearly how the extreme Conservative Party is trying to destroy the Kartell's majority at all costs and in any way it can, and to force the Kaiser and his Chancellor to change the domestic policies it hates'. The Bielefeld Conservatives, he reported, had not only got in touch with the Centre Party leader, Ludwig Windthorst, to ensure his support for them, as half the voters in the constituency were Catholics; they were repeating 'with redoubled energy and clarity the insinuation . . . that the declaration in the *Reichsanzeiger* [of 2 October 1889] had been issued only under pressure from Prince Bismarck; the Kaiser was in complete agreement with the Kreuzzeitung party at heart; it would be rendering him a service to vote for the party'. Hinzpeter ensured that this information would make an even greater impact on the Kaiser by adding: 'That this insinuation constitutes gross *lèse-majesté*, for it makes the Kaiser look like a cowardly weakling who does not have the courage to think for himself, matters less to them in their passion for their party than a possible triumph of the party over their opponents.' It had even been claimed at an election meeting that 'the Kaiser read the *Kreuzzeitung* as he always did; it was even the only political newspaper that he read; the Kaiser was a Hammerstein man through and through!'[59]

Hinzpeter should have known what rage such language would unleash in his pupil. Wilhelm covered the letter with exclamation marks and comments. For days he continued to fume with anger. He telegraphed to Hinzpeter immediately, *en clair*, instructing him to 'let it be most distinctly understood' how 'outraged' he had been at the behaviour of the Conservative–clerical faction in Bielefeld.[60] He forwarded Hinzpeter's letter to the Reich Chancellor with orders 'to take the most appropriate and severe steps in my name to counteract immediately and vigorously the activities of Hammerstein which Hinzpeter has described so excellently'.[61] On 6 January he called on Herbert Bismarck and spoke 'very indignantly' about the 'outrageous public fraternisation between Windthorst and Hammerstein', of which he had heard through Hinzpeter. As Herbert reported to Friedrichsruh, the Kaiser expressed 'furious resentment over the †Zeitung and that creature of the Guelphs, Hammerstein, whom he described as a "traitor"'; he expected the Chancellor to put forward suggestions as to how to 'publicly brand this shameful alliance between the hypocritical †Zeitung and Windthorst, the enemy of the Reich, which is aimed purely against the Kartell, and to turn it to account for the elections'. As he put it: 'After all, I have repeatedly declared in public, and had it declared on my behalf, that I regard the †Zeitung gang as enemies, that I stand by the Kartell absolutely; and yet people still have the temerity to claim that I read the †Zeitung and do not take any other paper: it really is a scandal that I should be defenceless against such lies!'[62] The Chancellor tried to dissuade the Kaiser from issuing another declaration against the *Kreuzzeitung* party with the argument that it would not be feasible to take the initiative publicly since 'the grounds for it are not apparent in the form of a public statement of the untruths which are to be denied'.[63] But Wilhelm was not satisfied with this answer. On 8 January he again called on Herbert Bismarck, and in his presence dictated 'an order to the Flügeladjutant that the Kreuzzeitung should no longer be subscribed to or found in any palace or adjutant's room; the Adjutant was also to write to Her Majesty's Cabinet Counsellor to say that H.M. must get rid of the Kreuzzeitung. Finally he had it noted for Hahnke's benefit that subscribing to the Kreuzzeitung was to be forbidden for all officers.'[64] Not satisfied with that, the next day the Kaiser once more called on the Foreign Secretary and instructed him to telegraph to the Reich Chancellor to say that with the imperial ban on the *Kreuzzeitung* 'the starting-point described as necessary' in his submission had now been provided.[65] This left Bismarck with no alternative but to order a second imperial declaration in the press in support of the Kartell and against the *Kreuzzeitung* party. Unlike Herbert, who wanted to have the notice published in the semi-official *Norddeutsche Allgemeine Zeitung*, the Chancellor preferred the 'less official' *Berliner Politische Nachrichten*, and the declaration appeared there on 10 January.[66] Marshall von Bieberstein, who was spending the day with Holstein, noted in his diary: 'Imperial declaration about *Kreuzzeitung* imminent. Count Bismarck wanted it in *Nord. Allg.* Reich Chancellor ordered "*Pol. Nachrichten*". Incredible.'[67]

Only a few days later Hinzpeter sent a second letter to Wilhelm, in which he warned him against receiving a deputation of Conservative voters from Biele-feld, as such a distinction would only be seen as support for Hammerstein's candidature.[68] When Bismarck, to whom Hinzpeter had sent a copy of his letter, likewise advised against receiving the deputation, Wilhelm wired to him on 17 January: 'Quite agree with your opinion. Had already telegraphed to Hinzpeter refusing.' He added a menacingly autocratic declaration of principle: 'I am accustomed to being obeyed, but I will not enter into discussions with such people. A kaiser's word should not be twisted or quibbled with.'[69]

If the Bismarcks were less affected by the imperial anger with the *Kreuzzeitung* party than many people had expected, the reason was that Wilhelm's telegrams and orders were met with 'shouts of triumph over the defeat of Waldersee'.[70] Clearly Wilhelm's anger at the right-wing Conservatives had strengthened his resolve, apparent since December, not to appoint Waldersee as chancellor after all. Only a short time later, on 1 February 1890, the Kaiser summoned General von Caprivi from Hanover and ordered him to be prepared if necessary to become Bismarck's successor.[71] Understandably therefore the Chief of the General Staff was not exactly delighted by the 'quite useless and ill-considered interference' by Hinzpeter in a matter which was none of his business. On 11 January he commented that Wilhelm had wildly overreacted to Hinzpeter's report that the right-wing Conservatives in Bielefeld had claimed that 'the Kaiser was still on the side of the Kreuzzeitung and against the Chancellor in his heart', by wielding 'another blow, and again very overhastily, against the Kreuzzeitung'. The embargo on the *Kreuzzeitung* at court would 'create a colossal uproar' and was 'undoubtedly a mistaken measure'. It was altogether wrong of the Kaiser to have intervened in the election campaign. 'If he had used his influence to get rid of Hammerstein, I should have had no objection; but to take this action against the newspaper will do great damage.'[72] Not long afterwards Waldersee noted that Bismarck was trying 'to exploit the punishment of the Kreuzzeitung by the Kaiser for his own ends'.[73]

With the recruitment of the liberal commoner Hinzpeter to the ranks of the secret group of imperial advisers, tensions had inevitably arisen among them which could be masked only temporarily by tactical considerations. Waldersee in particular, intent as he was on combating socialism through a religious revival, disapproved of Hinzpeter's pro-worker and anti-clerical influence on the Kaiser.[74] Even so the two men, tutor and General, found they had much in common in their assessment of the situation when they met on 11 January 1890 after the funeral of Kaiserin Augusta. Like Waldersee, Hinzpeter thought that the relationship between the Kaiser and the Chancellor was becoming 'worse by degrees'. Waldersee was gratified to hear from Hinzpeter 'that the Kaiser has at last realised that much is kept from him, that the Chancellor therefore acts behind his back; he [Wilhelm II] also knows of the rumours that the Chancellor is involved in financial dealings in grand style – in short, light is beginning to dawn'. Hinzpeter and Waldersee were also at one in their criticism of Herbert

Bismarck. The General was delighted to hear from Hinzpeter 'that the Kaiser speaks of him [Herbert Bismarck] with little respect and actually values him only for his jokes'. Hinzpeter dropped meaningful hints to the Chief of the General Staff, that he should not waste his energy on little things, but should 'keep himself fresh and intact for great ones'.[75] For his part, Waldersee commented in his diary on the great influence which Hinzpeter exercised over the Kaiser. The tutor was now 'very much in the foreground', he noted in mid-February 1890, four weeks before Bismarck's fall; and Hinzpeter had 'probably been principally responsible for persuading the Kaiser to take action on the worker question and also corresponded on many other matters with the Kaiser'.[76]

Remarkably, in this meeting between the schoolmaster and the Chief of the General Staff, anxieties about Wilhelm II's mental state also came to the fore, based in both cases on many years of experience. Immediately on arriving Hinzpeter remarked: 'What do you think of the Kaiser's nervous state? He is increasingly overhasty. It is true I wrote and told him that his name was being misused in Bielefeld, and asked him whether he still stood by the declaration in the Reichsanzeiger – which by the way I never approved of and thought greatly exaggerated – and he telegraphed to me at once in the most vehement terms; as it was an open telegram of course it soon became known, and now he has taken the step of banning the newspaper at court.' After this explanation Waldersee was in no doubt that Hinzpeter had 'set the thing in train and therefore bears a considerable part of the blame'.[77] 'Herr Hinzpeter, the actual originator of the whole wretched affair, no doubt greatly regrets his action', he noted.[78]

No less important for the development of the Bismarck crisis was the contact established on 3 January 1890 between Waldersee and the Grand Duke of Baden. 'We had a very frank conversation and I spoke my mind freely, because I know that the Grand Duke truly means well by the Kaiser and because he is discreet', the General recorded after their first meeting.[79] When Kaiserin Augusta died Waldersee was at first afraid that this might weaken the bond between Wilhelm II and the Grand Duke and Grand Duchess Luise, who was Augusta's daughter. 'In both the Kaiser has true and devoted friends, who wish only the best for him', he wrote.[80] In the event Grand Duke Friedrich, who had already played a significant part in the Wohlgemuth affair, in the conflict over the Russian conversion and in bringing about the Kaiser's pro-Kartell declaration, now took centre stage in the role of fatherly adviser to Wilhelm at the start of the most critical phase of the crisis. Through the monarchical and militaristic instincts which set him against what was perceived as the dangerous 'omnipotence' of the Bismarcks, he gave a semblance of legitimacy to Wilhelm II's rapidly growing hunger for power.

14. Grand Duke Friedrich I of Baden

The significance of his alliance with Waldersee became clear when the Grand Duke showed the Kaiser an article in the official *Norddeutsche Allgemeine Zeitung* in which Waldersee was again attacked as anti-Russian. On 12 January 1890 the Grand Duke was able to assure the latter that 'the attack against you has been beaten off. I showed the Kaiser the article, which had of course been withheld from him, and he soon saw that it is a product of the House of Bismarck and is in actual fact directed against him. He has now given very strict orders that the newspaper retract it.'[81] And indeed Herbert Bismarck found himself obliged to publish an apologetic explanation on 12 January stating that Prince Bismarck's peace policy was naturally 'the Kaiser's policy' and that there was no question of contrary views in the political or military sphere within the All-Highest entourage.[82]

In a second meeting on 12 January, Waldersee and the Grand Duke exchanged frank views on the relationship between Bismarck and the Kaiser. Waldersee said he had the impression that 'the Kaiser is now beginning to see clearly how Bismarck is deceiving him, and I believe that Your Royal Highness has greatly contributed to this'. The Grand Duke replied that he had certainly talked things over 'thoroughly' with the Kaiser, and had observed that Wilhelm was 'absolutely

determined to keep the Chancellor, even *against the latter's will*, but he wants
to look more closely into affairs so as to remain in control of them'.[83] A week
later the Grand Duke received Waldersee for another lengthy discussion during
which he assured the General 'that the Kaiser now sees things more clearly and
wants to free himself from the Chancellor's absolute power'.[84]

The Grand Duke had a permanent representative in Berlin in the person of
Adolf Freiherr Marschall von Bieberstein, Baden's envoy and delegate to the
Bundesrat, who soon developed an excellent rapport with the Grey Eminence
of the Foreign Office, Friedrich von Holstein – and who was to become Herbert
Bismarck's successor as foreign secretary. On 18 March 1890, the day on which
the founder of the Reich was forced to tender his resignation, Herbert Bismarck
confronted Marschall with the words: 'Your Grand Duke is the involuntary
gravedigger of the Reich Chancellor.' The Chancellor's son later recalled that
this remark threw Marschall into a state of 'very evident dismay' and he protested
'stammeringly' that 'his Grand Duke had always been a warm supporter of His
Highness. I interrupted him with the words "I did say *involuntary*; if you prefer
it, *unwitting*; the Grand Duke did not realise what he was bringing about and how
he was made use of during the 3 quiet weeks after the death of Kaiserin Augusta.
But I know exactly what happened, so you can spare yourself the trouble of an
apology."' As Herbert did not learn of Marschall's own 'undermining work in
league with Bötticher and the wives of both' until later, he was at first surprised
by the Baden envoy's overreaction. It was only when Lerchenfeld remarked
that he had hit the target more precisely than he realised, for it was Marschall
himself who 'has influenced and led his Grand Duke all along', that Herbert saw
why the envoy had been so strangely affected. And to understand Marschall's
efforts to stir up trouble, Herbert believed, one needed to know about his wife's
ambition.[85] Neither Herbert Bismarck nor his father, however, ever discovered
how much Marschall came under the intellectual domination of Holstein during
the crisis.

King Albert of Saxony, who had already come forward as a critic of Bismarck
during the Russian conversion crisis, became another member of the group of
imperial advisers in January 1890. In mid-January he had a long and 'very
anxious' conversation with General von Verdy, the Minister of War, and he saw
'as clearly as the Grand Duke of Baden how things stand'.[86] The Kaiser's secret
advisers recognised the significance – but also the danger – of this monarchical
alliance against the Chancellor. On 17 January Eulenburg wrote to Waldersee:
'I hope that in the present very difficult situation the Kaiser will form a closer
link with the King of Saxony and the Grand Duke of Baden, and that with
Boetticher's support he will find in them a kind of substitute for the lack of
support he is receiving from his Cabinet chiefs.'[87] 'The Kaiser's determination

15. King Albert of Saxony

to ally himself more closely with the princes is of such inestimable value', he
commented in a letter to Holstein, 'that I shudder to think what would happen
if he met with a setback and was thereby distracted from the path he has just
begun to follow. I know the Kaiser and I am well aware how much the lively
and joyful pursuit of an idea he has had captivates him and "makes him happy".
Everything now depends on persuading the King of Saxony and the Grand Duke
of Baden to make *written guarantees*, in order to consolidate the new alliance
round the Kaiser against possible encroachments by the Chancellor.'[88] Before
long, however, Eulenburg was dismayed to realise that the monarchical alliance
which he had encouraged had led to a kind of 'Anti-Chancellor League'. 'Princes
of the blood are prone to join forces and take extreme steps against major domos',
he warned in some alarm.[89]

### THE WITCH-HUNT AGAINST THE BISMARCKIANS AT COURT

The aim of the clique assembled by Holstein, Eulenburg and Waldersee in
support of Wilhelm II was not, in fact, Bismarck's dismissal – the secret advisers
were far too conscious of the consequences which a spectacular resignation by
the founder of the Reich would entail – but the gradual build-up of the Kaiser's

power behind the façade of Bismarck's chancellorship, which they hoped would
continue for the time being. To give the Kaiser more freedom in making decisions
there were two prerequisites: first, the Bismarckians among the court officials
and Flügeladjutanten must be removed from the Kaiser's entourage; and, second,
the Bismarcks' monopoly on information must be broken. As the Chancellor had
an extraordinarily strong desire for power or, as he himself would put it, a highly
developed sense of his responsibility, in addition to a deep conviction that his
complicated constitutional creation must in no way be tampered with, these
aims were of course far from easy to achieve.

Among the mainstays of Bismarck's power at court were General Wilhelm
von Hahnke, the Chief of the Military Cabinet, Hermann von Lucanus, the
Chief of the Civil Cabinet, and three of the Flügeladjutanten, Carl Count von
Wedel, Gustav von Kessel and Adolf von Bülow. But the key figure was Eduard
von Liebenau, the Oberhof- und Hausmarschall.[90] For Waldersee there was no
doubt that Liebenau had 'sworn complete allegiance' and 'sold' himself 'to the
House of Bismarck'.[91] He had 'curried favour with Count [Herbert] Bismarck
from the beginning, he receives gross flattery from that quarter and naturally he
always stands up for Count Bismarck with the Kaiser'.[92] For the Bismarck family
it was of course 'very pleasant' to have a Hofmarschall who represented 'their
interests to the Kaiser'.[93] Vice-Senior Master of Ceremonies August Count zu
Eulenburg, a cousin of Philipp, likewise complained at the beginning of 1890 that
Liebenau was behaving 'more and more as the agent of Casa Bismarck'.[94] From
the autumn of 1889 onwards all possible means were tried to remove Liebenau
from the vicinity of the Kaiser. The witch-hunt against this Bismarckian at
the Wilhelmine court provides a perfect example of the conspiratorial methods
which became common from now on under the new Kaiser's rule.

The lengthy campaign carried out against Liebenau seemed to have achieved
its goal in November 1889. During his journey to Athens and Constantinople
the Kaiser treated Liebenau badly and on one occasion even 'gave him such
a dressing-down that the stupid man' — as Waldersee heard — 'went to the
Kaiserin to ask for her protection! To the Kaiserin, towards whom he has behaved
uncouthly, whom he has often offended and who loathes him. One can see what a
truly wretched fellow he is.'[95] Finding the Kaiser in a 'very irritable mood' against
Liebenau on 17 November 1889, Waldersee seized the opportunity of expressing
his opinion that the Senior Marshal was 'quite unsuited' to his post. He told the
Kaiser frankly: 'He makes trouble with everyone apart from Count [Carl von]
Wedel who thinks it to his advantage to stand by Liebenau; there is not *one* person
in the entire court who would not have complaints, and justifiable complaints,
about him. In society there are protests from the highest to the lowest about
his inconsiderate behaviour and his coarse manners. In the end Your Majesty is

inevitably harmed by this, because the world believes the inconsiderate conduct in fact stems from Your Majesty. He suffers from delusions of grandeur and thinks he has to be the first person at court and in society. He has no political tact at all . . . I think Y.M. would spare yourself much annoyance if You made a change. The directorship of the Gardens would be quite a good way of getting rid of him.' The Kaiser said nothing in Liebenau's defence, but confirmed some of Waldersee's comments, leaving the latter with the impression 'that a change is not far off, but it might turn into a real rumpus, which I would be happy to see, in the Kaiser's interest. Liebenau does the Kaiser real harm; the sovereign is rather inclined to inconsiderate behaviour himself and he must at all costs have people around him who try to have a softening influence. What is more he [Liebenau] is nothing but a creature of Bismarck and is guilty of the greatest disloyalty towards his real master.'[96]

A week later the Kaiser discussed the matter with August Eulenburg, using Waldersee's arguments almost word for word. Eulenburg immediately hurried to report to Waldersee, who repeated his advice that Liebenau should be relieved of his post as Oberhof- und Hausmarschall and appointed director-general of the Royal Gardens; the 'best successor' to Liebenau would be August Eulenburg himself. 'I asked him just to speak to his cousin Philipp, whom the Kaiser is visiting at the moment and has doubtless told about this business.'[97]

The days of the hapless Oberhofmarschall now seemed to be numbered. 'The Kaiser was . . . very worked up yesterday and the day before about blunders made by Liebenau and is now in a mood in which the latter cannot do anything right in his eyes', Waldersee recorded at the end of November. Wilhelm discussed the situation with Philipp Eulenburg, who had the 'happy idea' of saying to the Kaiser: 'Do you know that Liebenau is in very good odour with the Bismarck family?', which provoked the defiant reply from Wilhelm: 'I care nothing about that, I choose my own Hofmarschall.'[98] Yet although the two Eulenburgs and Waldersee continued to take systematic action against Liebenau, and although Wilhelm repeatedly expressed himself highly dissatisfied with him, Liebenau's fall did not materialise.[99] When Waldersee arrived at the Schloss for lunch on 11 December the Kaiser summoned him in front of the other guests and immediately began discussing Liebenau, who he said had behaved very discourteously towards the ambassador in Paris, Count Münster. 'I reprimanded him severely for his impoliteness only a week ago and gave him a good dressing-down, but it does not seem to help', Wilhelm said. But there was still no sign of any firm intention to get rid of Liebenau.[100]

Over the Christmas period Philipp Eulenburg, on the prompting of his cousin August,[101] brought the Grand Duke and Hinzpeter into the cabal to give it further support. He told them of the Kaiser's complaints that Liebenau 'found a thousand excuses to keep away from him, systematically, all the people whom he, the Kaiser, would like to see at luncheon or dinner!' Yet as it was '*a matter of life and death* for us all that His Majesty should be in frequent contact with men of politics, high officials &c'. 'What a splendid effect contact with an influence of this kind would have on the development of our most beloved Kaiser's great intelligence and quick understanding, his great qualities of leadership!', sighed Wilhelm's bosom friend. Liebenau had to be removed at all costs, Eulenburg insisted. He begged the Grand Duke to provide the Kaiser with further material 'to document the impossibility of keeping Liebenau'; the Kaiser would be grateful to him for this, for he himself was trying to break free from this connection. Hinzpeter too had deplored the '*the bantering manners of an adjutant*' which were the hallmark of Liebenau's exercise of his office. Eulenburg warned the Grand Duke, however, that the Kaiser should not be allowed to detect any 'collaboration' between them.[102]

Even with this additional support, and in spite of several more clashes, Wilhelm still hesitated to dismiss his Oberhofmarschall. When Philipp Eulenburg brought up this vexatious subject again early in 1890 the Kaiser replied: 'The pot is gradually coming to the boil, and I shall find the right moment to get rid of him.'[103] A few days later the Kaiser, in conversation with August Eulenburg, gave vent to 'another very violent outburst against Liebenau'. This time the cause was truly ridiculous: the Kaiser had given Kamilla von Mirbach, the Belgian wife of the Kaiserin's Oberhofmeister, permission to spend the night in her husband's quarters in the Schloss after court parties. Liebenau had protested against this, but under pressure from the Kaiserin the Kaiser had upheld his 'command'. On 18 January the Kaiser received, as August Eulenburg recorded, 'a 20-page report from Liebenau in which he explained the impossibility of carrying out the All-Highest command, emphasising the wrongful use of bed-linen, crockery – His Majesty thought even chamber-pots had been mentioned'. The Kaiser covered Liebenau's memorandum 'with very strong comments' such as 'rubbish, nonsense, ridiculous', so that the Flügeladjutant on duty, Kessel, hesitated to send the original back to Liebenau. He drew up a reply which was dispatched to the Oberhofmarschall with the All-Highest signature. 'The report itself is to remain in the Schloss, in the keeping of the adjutants, for the amusement of its occupants', August Eulenburg mockingly recorded. 'The Kaiser described all this in the most forceful terms, using the strongest expressions, . . . in short he held forth . . . in a way that would have made anyone seeing such a scene for the first time swear that the final break was bound to happen that very day.' But the result had been as disappointing as on all the previous occasions, the Vice-Senior Marshal of Ceremonies complained, 'except that the impossibility of the situation and the damage to the dignity of the court is becoming more and more widely known and is talked about on the street, where people say that Liebenau must have some dangerous knowledge, on account of which His Majesty does not dare put an end to the business'.[104]

The longer the Liebenau crisis lasted, the more people racked their brains to find 'the mysterious reasons . . . which prevented action being taken against Liebenau'.[105] And from the evidence of the Kaiser's ambiguous attitude to him – violent animosity on one side, and indecisiveness and hesitancy on the other – it is indeed not easy to form a clear picture of what was going on. Did feelings of loyalty, gratitude, complacency or fear of awkward secrets coming to light outweigh the pressure from his advisers to sack Liebenau? Did Wilhelm want to maintain his independence from them too? The sources reveal nothing of his inner motives. What is beyond doubt, however, is that Liebenau's influence on Wilhelm in the critical weeks before Bismarck's dismissal was greatly weakened by the numerous attacks on him from all sides.[106] Only after the Chancellor's dismissal was Liebenau willing to recognise how untenable his position at court had become. But even then the Kaiser put off Liebenau's dismissal until May 1890.[107]

Almost as venomous, but in this case completely unsuccessful, was Waldersee's campaign against Cabinet Chiefs von Hahnke and von Lucanus, which also began in the autumn of 1889. The importance of the intermediary role played in the crisis by the Chief of the Military Cabinet is revealed by Herbert Bismarck's remark in December 1889 that Hahnke was 'the most reliable of all the generals', who saw the Kaiser most frequently and to whom he, Herbert, could speak daily.[108] This of course was the very reason why Waldersee's plans required him to be removed from the Kaiser's entourage. On 24 September Herbert Bismarck warned his father: 'As Liebenau told me in the strictest confidence, Waldersee is mounting an assault on Hahnke, who is to be given a Corps, to get him out of the Military Cabinet. Liebenau wants to appeal direct to H.M. not to go along with this.'[109] Six weeks later Waldersee did indeed try to convince the Kaiser that Hahnke was 'not a good chief of Cabinet', had no 'understanding of the significance of his position' and was doing the army 'much damage'. But Wilhelm was determined to keep him and remarked that 'he could not easily do without Hahnke, having just got used to working with him'.[110] Wilhelm's answer by no means satisfied the Chief of the General Staff, who continued his intrigues, convinced that the monarch had not yet seen through Hahnke's weaknesses. The Kaiser was 'definitely not well advised' by Hahnke, who was 'a very mediocre Cabinet Chief', Waldersee wrote. 'Unfortunately the Kaiser still does not see this at all and I am afraid that much damage will be done.'[111]

In mid-January 1890 Waldersee set out to win the support of the Grand Duke of Baden and Philipp Eulenburg in his campaign against Hahnke and Lucanus, as he had done in Liebenau's case. But although the Grand Duke professed himself convinced that 'Lucanus must go because he is the Chancellor's right-hand man, not the Kaiser's',[112] he refused to take any concrete steps against the Chief of the Civil Cabinet. In a letter to Eulenburg of 13 January Waldersee bemoaned the fact that the two officials who were supposed to be the Kaiser's 'right-hand men', namely the chiefs of the Military and Civil Cabinets, were failing to fulfil their duties adequately. Hahnke was certainly a 'thoroughly decent, honourable man', but he was incompetent. He did not have a good command of his responsibilities, '*he does not even fully comprehend them* and, what is now so important, he has no judgement and understanding of important questions and is quite unqualified to give His Majesty advice on serious matters'. Lucanus, on the other hand, was 'an unprincipled man and completely the Chancellor's creature at the moment'. Waldersee pressed for Eulenburg's help in this matter, with a view to enabling the Kaiser to become 'more independent of the Chancellor'.[113] Eulenburg agreed with Waldersee's views in principle but could see no prospect of bringing the two Cabinet Chiefs down, given the good relationship both enjoyed with Wilhelm.[114] He did not add that in these two cases, unlike that of Liebenau, there was no family advantage to be gained for him.

The second important prerequisite for enabling the Kaiser to play a more active role was the breaking of the monopoly on information exercised by the Chancellor. Wilhelm did not even read a daily newspaper, but only extracts which were selected for him in the Foreign Office under Herbert Bismarck's supervision, Holstein complained in December 1889; nor did he read his ambassadors' reports, but heard about their contents, with the appropriate anti-Austrian, anti-Italian and pro-Russian gloss, only through Herbert's oral reports. As a chancellor crisis must at all costs be avoided, one must proceed by small steps, the wily diplomat cautioned, suggesting that 'instead of newspaper extracts, or in addition to these, the Kaiser must *read a whole newspaper*'. Philipp Eulenburg or Hinzpeter would have to persuade him to subscribe either to the Free Conservative *Post* or – better still, because it was less subject to Bismarck's influence – the National Liberal *Kölnische Zeitung*. The *Nationalzeitung* was out of the question, because it was an organ of Bleichröder, Bismarck's banker. If it were too much to expect the Kaiser to read a daily newspaper, he must order the weekly edition of the *Kölnische*, in which at least the most important articles were reprinted. 'But this is the minimum that the sovereign can do. He *must* read *one* newspaper in order to make himself independent of the trends and tendencies which influence the choice of the extracts. This is *urgent*!', Holstein emphasised. It was a matter 'of the *most immense* importance for the Kaiser and for the Reich'.[115] The Grey Eminence of the Wilhelmstrasse failed to reveal that he had close links to the Berlin representative of the *Kölnische Zeitung*, Dr Franz Fischer.

In his subtle, manipulative way, Eulenburg used his New Year letter to the Kaiser to put forward a plea that in order to free himself from the possibility of being influenced by the selection of the newspaper extracts submitted to him, the monarch might perhaps '*read through* one of the more important newspapers each day'. Following Holstein's lead, he advised against the 'narrow-minded Kreuzzeitung', as also the *Post* and the *Nationalzeitung*, and suggested the *Kölnische Zeitung* as the best solution; if this were too long for the Kaiser, however, he could 'at least regularly read the whole weekly edition'.[116] After the Grand Duke of Baden had also hinted to the Kaiser that 'much was being withheld from him', Wilhelm did indeed order the weekly review of the National Liberal *Kölnische Zeitung* on 13 January 1890.[117]

Simultaneously Waldersee too took steps to break through the system by which Bismarck manipulated the Kaiser. In a furious diary entry of 14 January 1890 he recorded: 'A deception of the most flagrant kind is practised by the Chancellor in submitting newspaper extracts to the Kaiser. One would think that the Kaiser had such extracts laid before him because he did not have time to read whole newspapers but nevertheless wished to have an overall picture of the opinions expressed in the press. One would also think that the authorities responsible would have the moral and sacred duty to act with the greatest conscientiousness. But that is a mistake. The Chancellor demands that only those newspaper reports that meet his approval should be laid before the Kaiser. He quite deliberately carries out a shameless deception.' The extracts were selected, Waldersee continued, by Rudolf Lindau in the Foreign Office, 'a completely spineless fellow' (Waldersee's choice of words indicates that Lindau was of Jewish extraction), and by Konstantin Rössler in the Prussian Ministry of State, 'an elderly civil servant and a good man' who in spite of inner struggles was in the end obliged to submit to the Bismarcks.[118]

On 18 January 1890 Waldersee made use of his scheduled audience as chief of the General Staff to show the Kaiser a large number of extracts from Russian newspapers and to tell him that he was 'in a good position to do this more often', even if it aroused the Chancellor's hostility towards him. Wilhelm replied: 'Let that be my concern; from now on I wish you to bring me Russian newspaper extracts every week.' It was apparent from the tone of the whole conversation, the General reported, 'that there is great ill-feeling towards the Chancellor'.[119] At the end of January the Kaiser openly told Adjutant-General Max von Versen that he was having Russian newspapers submitted to him through the General Staff, since he received 'nothing or only mangled reports' from the Foreign Office.[120]

Bismarck's attempts to control the information on foreign affairs which reached Wilhelm II were under threat not only from Waldersee's extracts

from Russian newspapers. The confidential reports sent by military attachés
to the General Staff or directly to the Kaiser led to violent arguments with
the Chancellor and the Foreign Secretary, especially as Waldersee was aiming
to build up this military correspondence into a kind of rival diplomacy, and
Wilhelm had no scruples in expressly allowing some military attachés to write
to him personally. At the end of 1889 both Waldersee and Verdy predicted that
Bismarck would soon try to undermine the position of the military attaché in
Paris, Freiherr von Huene, who had been conducting a secret military-political
correspondence with the Kaiser for the past year. As Waldersee explained, 'Count
[Carl] Wedel found out that Huene has written to me . . . a few times and that I
gave the letters to the Kaiser to read, and unfortunately he told the Chancellor; it
is really a scandal and a betrayal of his master, whom he should serve exclusively.
He [Wedel] even knows that the Kaiser has invited Huene to write confidentially to him directly. Whether he approves of this or not he ought not to tell
anyone about it. In his suspicious way the Chancellor has now built himself up a
great framework of fantasies; he thinks I run a regular political bureau in which
correspondence with all the military attachés plays a central role.'[121]

However serious a threat Waldersee and his military attachés posed, however,
it was not they but the clique led by Eulenburg, Holstein, Hinzpeter, Marschall
von Bieberstein and the Grand Duke of Baden who represented the greatest
danger for the Bismarcks in the final phase of the dismissal crisis, in which the
principal point at issue was not foreign policy but the future course of domestic
politics.

# CHAPTER ELEVEN

# Constitutional conflicts

## BISMARCK'S PLANS FOR A *COUP D'ETAT*

I N May 1889, at the time of the serious disturbances among the Rhineland coal
miners, the Kaiser had whispered to Philipp Eulenburg during his first official
visit to Brunswick: 'I am having fearful difficulties with the Prince; constitutional change and other things.'[1] Subsequently, however, this problem, important
though it was, had receded into the background again. During the winter months
Wilhelm had made frequent and belligerent comments about the socialist threat,
so that until December 1889 there was very little perceptible difference between
his views on 'the social question' and those of the Chancellor. Towards the end
of November Waldersee noted that on all sides the opinion was current 'that
social democracy is making great strides and that, as massive strikes were to
be expected next year, there might easily be bloodshed'.[2] On 24 November he
recorded that Wilhelm II was 'not yet at all anxious' about the internal political
crises which were clearly in the offing. He had recently remarked: 'My grandfather reigned for several years while there was constitutional conflict, and I shall
be able to manage it too.' The General pointed out that circumstances had become
infinitely more complicated since the Prussian conflict of the 1860s. 'A conflict in
Prussia would not greatly alarm me either', he commented. 'But in the Reich it is
highly dangerous.'[3] He admitted, however, that 'serious people' were 'very worried about the way we are developing and saying: "It cannot go on like this."'[4]

Only the recognition that a massive political clash would greatly strengthen
Bismarck's position deterred Wilhelm, Waldersee and a few of the Kaiser's other
advisers from pursuing the idea of a *coup d'état*, which otherwise seemed to them
highly desirable. In the turmoil of a constitutional conflict or even a bloody *coup
d'état* it would be impossible to manage without the founder of the Reich,

who would then be able to impose harsh conditions on the Kaiser.[5] Waldersee suspected Bismarck of making secret plans along these very lines as early as mid-December 1889, when the Kaiser told him of the Chancellor's intention of strengthening the Berlin garrison 'in case of socialist uprisings'. The Chief of the General Staff thought this idea 'utterly foolish' and expressed the view to the Kaiser that 'we really have not come to that yet; there can be absolutely no question of uprisings yet; conditions would have to be very different for that to happen'. On the contrary, it was in fact the main aim of the Socialists 'to remain absolutely quiet'. In any case, Waldersee pointed out, there was no room for an increased military presence in the barracks of Berlin. He could see, however, that Bismarck's idea had 'made an impression' on the Kaiser.[6] On 26 December he remarked that in making such suggestions Bismarck was obviously trying 'to frighten the Kaiser and make him mistrust the workers, because in his view the Kaiser took the workers' side too much over the strike. At any rate the big industrialists, and in particular Herr Bleichröder, have been working on the Chancellor not to give way to the workers any more', the General claimed.[7] At the beginning of 1890 he noted that 'there is a difference of opinion just now between the Kaiser and the Chancellor over the handling of the strikes, and of the social question in general. The Kaiser favours the workers too much for the Chancellor. I have heard it said that the Chancellor would like the strikes to reach the point where the troops will intervene and shoot, so as to bring the Kaiser round. It is quite clear that he is trying to frighten him with socialist disturbances.'[8]

These differences of opinion had already become apparent in the previous weeks. In the negotiations with the Kartell parties over the renewal of the Anti-Socialist Bill, which Bismarck had made still more severe by adding an expulsion clause, the Chancellor gave vent to his deep displeasure with the National Liberals, who were prepared to support the extension only of a watered-down version of the bill beyond 1890. As the Conservatives, by contrast, welcomed the strengthening of the bill, the Kartell, with which the Kaiser had repeatedly and publicly identified himself, threatened to split apart over this question.[9] When Otto von Helldorff, the leader of the moderate Conservatives, went to Friedrichsruh for discussions at the end of November 1889, he found Bismarck 'in an angry mood over the attitude of the National Liberals to the Anti-Socialist Bill question'. Helldorff urged the Chancellor 'very strongly' 'to show forbearance to the National Liberals so as not to destroy the Kartell'.[10] Only when the three participating parties made a joint declaration, deferring the question of the renewal of the Anti-Socialist Bill until after the Reichstag elections, did the Kartell crisis seem to have been overcome.[11] But the conflicts within the coalition soon broke out again, fanned by the power struggle between the Kaiser and the Chancellor.

On 13 January 1890 the Kaiser took Philipp Eulenburg for a two-hour walk through the Tiergarten in the rain, and poured out his heart to him. 'I have scarcely ever discussed such important and far-reaching matters with the Kaiser before', Eulenburg commented afterwards. 'To have such wholehearted trust placed in me made me happy – but how painful it is to have to see him in difficulties that would dishearten the most experienced of men.' The Kaiser complained that 'the Chancellor wanted a *strong Anti-Socialist Bill*, which in itself was not a bad thing, but its severity would certainly lead to a conflict, which would – yes, is perhaps *intended to* – bring a constitutional change in its wake. He, the Kaiser, was in a really dreadful position, for he thought it dangerous to begin his reign with a sort of revolution, shooting and other measures of force.' For Eulenburg, who had conferred at length with Holstein, Hinzpeter and August Eulenburg in the preceding days, Bismarck's 'secret' purpose was no mystery. The Chancellor wanted to 'keep the reins of government and *the young Kaiser in his hand*', and had calculated 'that through a constitutional change with all the attendant furore, the consequences, the continual feuds – in a word: that through the *helplessness* to which this would reduce the Kaiser, the latter would certainly very soon find himself actually dependent on the Chancellor'. Eulenburg therefore advised the Kaiser that 'how he wanted to deal with the Social Democrats *eventually* was his affair; but I considered it extremely unwise for his *first* significant act of government to be a constitutional change – that is, in this case, a *coup d'état* – in the Reich. That would be to inflict upon the expectant German people a severe disappointment whose effects would be lasting, and to intensify the *opposition* which has always existed between Prussia and the whole of West and South Germany – to become a complete foreigner as Kaiser there.' The Kaiser, Eulenburg recalled, replied by saying that he wished 'to show the people, and especially the workmen, my good will, and to help them, but I have no intention of shooting at them!'[12] A year after Bismarck's dismissal Wilhelm II recalled the dilemma of those crisis-filled weeks in a marginal note. 'When the Prince demanded that I dissolve the Reichstag, let the masses go on strike and rise up in revolt, and then fire on them, I declared that there was time enough for that, but that some of their demands were justified, and these would have to be satisfied first. Then I should have "a clear conscience", and give the orders to shoot if necessary.'[13]

## WILHELM'S SOCIAL WELFARE PLANS

These differences, at first sight more tactical than fundamental, over the handling of the social democratic threat became potentially explosive differences of principle from the beginning of 1890, when Kaiser Wilhelm II, under the

influence of Hinzpeter, threw himself enthusiastically behind a comprehensive programme for social welfare. Greeted with universal astonishment, the
programme promised – as was no doubt Wilhelm's main aim – to make him
immensely popular with the people. But to combine this with the kind of *coup
d'état* policy demanded by the Reich Chancellor would not only torpedo the
programme but also expose the young Kaiser to universal public ridicule. In the
wake of the crucial struggle for power which now began between Kaiser and
Chancellor, Wilhelm's initially hesitant and unfocused ideas on social reform
acquired a radicalism that went far beyond his original intentions.[14]

The former tutor's pro-labour influence on the Kaiser in this difficult area was
deplored by almost everyone else in the group of advisers around Wilhelm, and
criticised as one-sided and doctrinaire. Holstein, who had recruited Hinzpeter
as an ally in the battle to save the Kartell, now described him as 'an undirected
force of nature', 'a pike in the fishpond, nothing more, for he has no political
judgement'. He reproached Hinzpeter with wanting 'to achieve fame at the
Kaiser's side through the social question'.[15] The Empress Frederick took much
the same view, lamenting that she had to stand silently by while her own son
plunged rashly into things that he did not understand. 'He listens to Hintzpeter
[sic] on these subjects, who is a very passionate "Christian Socialist". His ideas
are very good to listen to, but alas too doctrinaire & theoretical to be the *only* ones
to go by! After all Hintzpeter is *not* a political man by profession; he is kind &
charitable to the poor, but he has a *one* sided view of the question.'[16] The tutor
had won Wilhelm over to his social reform programme, she believed, with the
argument that 'he would find it "a mine of popularity for himself", & it would
make him a gt. man etc.'[17] Queen Victoria forwarded these comments to Lord
Salisbury, whose reaction was similar: 'If the Empress is right in thinking that
he [Wilhelm] has fallen under the guidance of two or three fanciful favourites,
there are dangerous times in front of him. He is meddling with very sharp
edge tools indeed.'[18] To his own surprise Waldersee, like the Empress Frederick,
found himself on Bismarck's side in this question. The latter, as the General
recorded on 20 January, was 'furious' that Hinzpeter 'is advising the Kaiser on
the labour question. The Chancellor's view is that there should not be too great
concessions to the workers, and I think he is right.'[19] On 8 February Waldersee
had to admit that 'this time, to my sincere regret, I am more on the side of the
Chancellor'.[20] Many years later he recalled the ambiguity of the Kaiser's attitude
at this critical stage, recording that he had told Wilhelm at the beginning of
1890 that 'he would not have any success with his ideas of social reform, for in
their greed people would ask for more and more and would never be satisfied; he
replied that I might well be right, but he considered it his duty to try everything;

if people were still not satisfied, then – and he launched into threats of what he would do to punish them'.[21]

At the Kaiser's request Hinzpeter had a long conversation with the Chancellor at the end of January 1890 on Wilhelm's ideas for workers' welfare, in the course of which Bismarck contemptuously remarked, revealing his annoyance at the extent of Hinzpeter's influence, 'I shall propose you as Reich Chancellor.'[22] Hinzpeter certainly considered the social welfare question of vital importance to the whole nation,[23] but he justified his role in spurring the Kaiser on, as his adviser on the subject, with a strange mixture of pedagogical ambition and blindly monarchist zeal. As Eulenburg admitted to Holstein, the tutor was combining what was in itself the very laudable idea of 'making the Kaiser *work*' with the social welfare question.[24] Hinzpeter and he, Eulenburg, were striving to foster and develop the 'self-reliance' of the 'most beloved' Kaiser, and that could be achieved to some extent by his playing his part confidently in the social welfare question.[25] In his own letters Hinzpeter openly admitted that his first concern was for the 'spiritual salvation' of the Kaiser; the welfare question itself was of secondary importance to him.[26] After the first clash between Wilhelm and Bismarck over the social welfare question, Hinzpeter wrote to Eulenburg saying that he had 'pitied and at the same time admired the object of our mutual concern' – meaning of course the Kaiser. 'Bitter feelings were aroused in the principal person [Wilhelm II], not excluding that of humiliation, and the half victory for which he fought was dearly bought. But on the whole I believe that he has come out of this first severe contest stronger, more confident and also wiser. As this last was especially desirable, he has at least achieved some personal progress . . . Besides everything else it was also a spiritual crisis', the tutor claimed.[27] In his correspondence with Eulenburg, Hinzpeter referred to the Kaiser as the 'master' and to the Chancellor as the 'servant'.[28] The Chancellor's attitude, Hinzpeter discovered during his conversation with Bismarck, was that 'the master had no right to order important measures to be taken without consulting his servant and without having secured his consent: a surprise attack with the help of other authorities was inadmissible'.[29]

Prompted by Hinzpeter and with Eulenburg's support, Wilhelm II had persuaded the King of Saxony, who had come to Berlin for the funeral of Kaiserin Augusta, to put forward a proposal to the Bundesrat for a Social Welfare Bill. At the same time he ordered Boetticher to cast the Prussian vote in the Bundesrat for the Saxon proposal.[30] With that, open conflict with the Reich Chancellor was a foregone conclusion, since the Chancellor bore sole responsibility for Reich policy, while in his capacity as Prussian minister of foreign affairs he alone had the right to direct the Prussian vote in the Bundesrat. 'What do you think of my position?', Boetticher complained in despair. 'The Chancellor tells me to refuse, the Kaiser tells me to agree.'[31] The pro-Bismarck Bavarian envoy, Count Lerchenfeld, reported scathingly to Munich: 'It is not yet known how the Chancellor has reacted to the fact that his sovereign has ordered a draft bill which runs counter to his, the Chancellor's, convictions, from another federal prince.'[32] Eulenburg, however, worked himself up into a fever over the 'newly formed monarchical alliance' of the Kaiser with the King of Saxony and the Grand Duke of Baden, which he hoped would strengthen the Kaiser's power significantly.[33] In order to bring Bavaria into the new alliance as well, Eulenburg wrote on 14 January to the influential Bavarian Adjutant-General, Freiherr von Freyschlag, the confidant of Prince Regent Luitpold, assuring him that the Kaiser was as committed as ever to the Kartell and would therefore be 'painfully affected' if Bavaria were to agree in the Bundesrat to the strengthening of the Anti-Socialist Bill as desired by Bismarck, which the National Liberals could not accept. Both in this letter and in another to Minister-President Lutz he urged the Bavarian state government 'in terms which could not be misunderstood' to support the measures planned by the Kaiser in the sphere of social welfare legislation, including the forthcoming Saxon proposal.[34] 'The federal governments are aware of Your Majesty's views on the labour question', Eulenburg assured the Kaiser on 20 January.[35]

### CONFLICT IN THE CROWN COUNCIL

As the Reichstag had to be dissolved on 25 January 1890 to enable the elections to take place, the crisis over the way forward – *coup d'état* or reform programme – came to a head rapidly. Only if the Chancellor stayed away until after the dissolution of the Reichstag, and only if the Anti-Socialist Bill were modified or postponed until after the elections, in the view of the Kaiser's advisers, could conflict between the Kaiser and the Chancellor be held off.[36] After a conversation with Holstein on 19 January Marschall noted in his diary: 'The Kaiser must not give way.' Discussing the situation with the Grand Duke of Baden he expressed the fear 'that the Reich Chancellor . . . wants to crush the Kaiser. The Kaiser must win the battle now.' The Grand Duke also became convinced, as a result of a meeting with Herbert Bismarck on 21 January, that the Reich Chancellor was planning 'to use force against the workers'. The Kaiser, however, was standing firm; it was his 'unalterable will' either to postpone the Anti-Socialist Bill until after the Reichstag elections, or to amend it in such a way as to make it acceptable to all three Kartell parties.[37] A collision between Kaiser and Chancellor, who were pursuing diametrically opposed programmes, seemed inevitable and indeed imminent, particularly as Bismarck was planning to return to Berlin after an absence of eight months.

On 22 January the Kaiser took Waldersee for a walk in the Tiergarten and again discussed the Anti-Socialist Bill with him. Wilhelm repeated his view that the bill should be brought before the next Reichstag, not the present one. The two men called on Herbert Bismarck and raised the question with him, only to receive the response: 'My father is coming tomorrow and he will deal with the Anti-Socialist Bill.' The Kaiser replied: 'I have heard nothing about that, and would consider it most deplorable; I thought that it was to be left to the new Reichstag when it is elected. Just now it can only cause harm and we shall ruin our chances in the elections.' Herbert hinted that his father was prepared to make this a resignation issue and said: 'My father is very experienced in these things and I think it will be as well to follow his advice.' As Waldersee noted, however, 'the Kaiser was of course not to be won over, and the majority of the Reichstag is probably on his side'.[38] Late on the morning of 23 January, a Thursday, Boetticher, as Vice-President of the Prussian State Ministry, was informed by one of the Flügeladjutanten that the Kaiser had ordered a council of ministers at which he would preside – in other words, a Crown Council – for the following evening at 6 o'clock in the royal palace. The agenda for the meeting was not divulged.[39] Herbert Bismarck and the other ministers could only suppose that the Kaiser wished to discuss social policy issues at this Crown Council.[40] Herbert telegraphed his father asking whether he would wish to request an audience with the Kaiser before the Crown Council, to which the Chancellor answered in the affirmative and prepared to leave for Berlin at once.[41] The Foreign Secretary thereupon decided to go to the Kaiser himself in order to clarify matters for his father, and to ask 'what the Council was to consider' and whether the Chancellor's presence was desired. The Kaiser replied, 'I have summoned the Council in order to put my ideas about the handling of the labour question to the ministers; if your father wishes to take part, I shall be very pleased.' Herbert then asked whether the Prince might be granted an audience a quarter of an hour before the Crown Council, to which the Kaiser agreed 'most readily'. In his telegram to Friedrichsruh recommending immediate departure for Berlin, Herbert expressed the optimistic belief that it would be 'not at all difficult' for the Chancellor to come to an agreement privately with the Kaiser on the social welfare question; moreover it was surely important that he should 'hear for himself what H.M. has to say to the ministers, and *how*'. If, on the other hand, he was not concerned with how the session went, the Chancellor could put off coming to Berlin until Saturday. But Herbert warned his father that, if experience were anything to go by, in the Kaiser's presence the other ministers would all 'remain silent, or agree with reservations to a greater or lesser degree'.[42]

Bismarck's arrival in Berlin on 24 January marked the beginning of the last phase of the crisis which was to end seven weeks later with the angry resignation of both Bismarcks. Everyone sensed the gathering storm. On the eve of his father's arrival Herbert Bismarck spent two hours in a state of great agitation at Holstein's bedside, the latter being ill with influenza at the time.[43] Eulenburg, smitten with the same illness in North Germany, commented that the thought of the crisis in Berlin gave him 'the oppressive feeling of an approaching thunderstorm'.[44] The very first act of the elderly Prince on reaching Berlin demonstrated that he was in no mood to shirk the struggle for power with the Kaiser. Before his audience he called the Ministry of State together for a 'confidential' consultation and made the ministers promise to support him against the monarch in the Crown Council. Waldersee recorded later that Bismarck had been 'very unfriendly towards his colleagues' during the meeting,[45] but from other sources we know that 'almost all the ministers' were deeply discontented with the Kaiser's treatment of them, and some of them were in any case thinking of resigning. Minister for Ecclesiastical Affairs Gossler had complained at length to Herbert Bismarck about the Kaiser a few days earlier, and had declared only at the last minute that he had decided to withdraw his threat to resign. Public Works Minister von Maybach also continued to feel 'piqued with H.M.', and in constant anxiety that he might 'receive a rude note' from the Kaiser. Both ministers supported Bismarck and thought that the Kaiser's attitude to the Ministry of State would in any case make it impossible for them to stay on much longer.[46] Nevertheless the ministers found themselves facing an acute dilemma. Although they were not at all accustomed to defying the all-powerful founder of the Reich, as non-political government officials they were deeply imbued with the monarchical principle, and to reject the express wish of the King of Prussia seemed to them simply inconceivable. How were they to vote in the forthcoming Crown Council?

Immediately before the Council met at 6 p.m. Bismarck had his audience with the Kaiser. The Prussian ministers – except Maybach, who did not attend – then assembled and Wilhelm II took the chair. He opened the session with a lengthy exposition contrasting the rapid industrialisation of Germany with the slower economic development of Britain. The rapid industrialisation of Germany had led to the exploitation and proletarianisation of the workforce in the major cities, which in turn had made them receptive to the doctrines of social democracy. Since almost all revolutions arose from the failure to make timely reforms, he wished to issue a proclamation to the Ministry of State demonstrating his 'heartfelt interest in the welfare of the workers' and announcing improvements in the sphere of Sunday and night work and of women's and children's work. He wished to introduce workers' committees in conjunction with government-run factory inspections, to set up arbitration bureaus for strike situations, and to build savings banks, churches, schools and hospitals for workers. He suggested that an international agreement on these questions should be sought and proposed that a congress be convened in Berlin with representatives from all industrialised countries. Finally he asked Boetticher to read out a programme written in his own hand, setting out all the points he had mentioned.[47]

How had Wilhelm II suddenly got hold of this astonishingly modern, indeed ground-breaking programme, that was criticised even by his liberal mother as 'state socialism'?[48] Immediately after Bismarck's dismissal the Kaiser called on the British ambassador, Malet, and claimed that he had written the document himself. He had certainly had 'the advantage of the advice of able and disinterested men', but the social policy programme was his own work. 'One night I sat up for two hours by myself and wrote down my views as to what ought to be done.' The Kaiser emphatically denied the widely believed rumour 'that Dr Hinzpeter was the author of that document'; Hinzpeter had seen the programme for the first time when Bismarck showed it to him at the end of January.[49] In the Crown Council itself, in addition to Hinzpeter Wilhelm named his advisers on this question as Hans Hermann Freiherr von Berlepsch, Oberpräsident of the Rhine Province, Count Hugo von Douglas and the painter and former director of mines August von Heyden, and these four names quickly found their way into the contemporary press and into Bismarck's memoirs, and thence into countless works of history until the present day.[50] In fact, however, no indications have been found that these alleged advisers influenced the Kaiser on social policy questions, with the sole exception of Hinzpeter. In all likelihood Wilhelm mentioned these names only to distract attention from those who were actually responsible. For the same reason he copied out in his own hand the memorandum which he brought to the Crown Council and had read out there. In reality the author of the famous imperial social welfare programme was not the Kaiser but a man named Kayser.

Dr Paul Kayser, one of the very few (baptised) Jews who had achieved acceptance in the highest ranks of the Reich administration, had been tutor in the 1870s to Philipp Eulenburg and Axel Varnbüler and also to Bismarck's two sons. Since then he had risen to become Director of the Colonial Department, at that time still a subdivision of the Foreign Office.[51] It was there that Eulenburg sought him out on 13 January, immediately after his memorable walk in the Tiergarten with the Kaiser, and asked him to draft 'an exposé' on the social question for the Kaiser, 'as quickly as possible'.[52] When Holstein heard of this he approached the journalist Dr Franz Fischer of the *Kölnische Zeitung* with the request that he too draw up a social policy programme and send it secretly to Eulenburg.[53]

Two days later both Kayser and Fischer had completed their reform plans. Both sent their work to Eulenburg on 15 January, asking not to be named as authors, and Eulenburg forwarded Kayser's exposé to Wilhelm II on 20 January.[54] (It is not clear whether he also sent Fischer's project.) It is an incontestable fact that the Kaiser copied out Kayser's exposé in full, for the Colonial Director's social programme is identical, word for word, with the 'Proposal by H.M. the Kaiser on the labour question' of 22 January which Wilhelm brought to the Crown Council with two other memoranda and had read out by Boetticher. The Bismarcks never found out that the programme had been worked out under their noses in the Foreign Office by one of their closest colleagues. It was not until the 1970s, when Eulenburg's correspondence was published, that the true identity of the author came to light.[55]

After the ministers had resolved (as arranged in their prior meeting with Bismarck) to examine the various social policy proposals in the memorandum and to draft the text of an imperial proclamation, the Kaiser moved on to the second part of the agenda, the Anti-Socialist Bill. 'In a thorough and well-reasoned manner', he expounded his view that the government ought to make a formal declaration that the Anti-Socialist Bill was acceptable to it even without the controversial expulsion clause, for only through such a declaration could the consent of the German Conservative Party be obtained and the Kartell prevented from disintegrating. Without the declaration not only would the Anti-Socialist Bill be lost, but the Kartell would be in complete disarray in the forthcoming elections. When the Kaiser had finished speaking, Bismarck rose to his feet and declared bluntly, without entering into the monarch's arguments, that in these circumstances he had no alternative but to ask to be relieved of all his offices, as he could not agree with the Kaiser's views. Boetticher later recalled that the Chancellor had spoken 'particularly vehemently', and had become increasingly heated in his exchanges with the Kaiser, finally remarking with great bitterness: 'I see more and more that this is no longer the place for me!' The Kaiser 'remained calm and measured', and asked each of the ministers in turn for his opinion. All supported the Reich Chancellor's view. The Kaiser was forced to give in, with the result that on the following day the Anti-Socialist Bill was rejected by 167 votes to 98; the German Conservatives voted with the Centre Party and the Social Democrats against the bill, and the Kartell entered the election campaign in a badly damaged state.[56] The Kaiser complained bitterly afterwards that 'the ministers are not my ministers, they are Prince Bismarck's ministers'.[57]

As Wilhelm insisted, against Bismarck's express wish, on dissolving the Reichstag with a speech from the throne in the White Hall of the Schloss, expressing his warm personal interest in the workers,[58] the conflict between Chancellor and Kaiser was plain for all to see. The mere fact that Bismarck stayed away from the ceremony was enough to demonstrate the rift.[59] 'Great excitement', Marschall noted in his diary that day. 'No one understands the

Reich Chancellor.'[60] Waldersee observed that 'the antagonism between Kaiser and Chancellor is growing. It is caused . . . by the fact that the Kaiser wishes to go on trying to calm the workers by making concessions and showing his interest in them, while the Chancellor thinks there should be no more giving way; instead, the workers must be shown the greatest severity, including firing on them.'[61] The Kaiser was indignant, Waldersee recorded, that Bismarck 'has no qualms about misusing the army to fire on the workers, and he thinks that in this matter too the Chancellor wants to rob him of the glory of having settled this very important question himself'.[62] With this remark the Chief of the General Staff had shrewdly hit upon the core of the conflict between the Kaiser and the Chancellor. Neither was concerned about the issue itself. It had long since become a pawn in their contest for decisive power in the Reich.

## TOWARDS A NEW SYSTEM

Although the Chancellor's behaviour on 24 and 25 January caused passions to run high – for days Wilhelm 'repeatedly let fly with furious complaints about it'[63] – none of the Kaiser's advisers was in favour of dismissing Bismarck at this juncture. They were all still agreed that a grand exit by the founder of the Reich would cause great harm to the monarchy; they also realised that, although the personal prestige of the young Kaiser was growing, it had not yet reached the point at which personal rule by the monarch would be politically acceptable. Holstein summed up his views in a letter to Eulenburg on 27 January: 'The Kaiser has shown magnificent self-control. He was right not to let the Chancellor go yet. His Majesty must first create a personal position for himself; this is by no means identical with the inherited position of sovereign.'[64] The Kaiser had rightly perceived that time was on his side, not the Chancellor's; he would soon – in months, not years – have everything for himself.[65] The relationship between Wilhelm and Bismarck was therefore, according to Holstein, 'a question of *time*'. On 4 February he stressed the point again: 'There will always be opportunities for a break. *Today* it is too early. Today the Kaiser is not yet well enough known among the people. But he is rapidly gaining in stature and the Chancellor is losing.' Wilhelm had realised that 'it is not enough to be Kaiser in order to rule; one must also be a man of character . . . In the present difficult situation the Kaiser is learning more and more each day. He has already achieved considerable self-control in the past ten days.'[66]

All the Kaiser's advisers shared Holstein's opinion. The Baden envoy, Marschall, recognised the vital importance of avoiding a break with Bismarck before the Reichstag elections.[67] Holstein came to the conclusion – wrongly, as it turned out – that Hinzpeter had advised the Kaiser to break with Bismarck before the elections so as to be able to win a triumphant victory by making a proclamation to the people, and was lost for words to describe the apparent stupidity of this 'schoolmaster who has gone mad'.[68] Hinzpeter, however, was also firmly convinced of the necessity of creating 'the possibility of further co-operation on a basis of trust, through mutual concessions' between Bismarck and the Kaiser.[69] As Eulenburg was able to assure Holstein, he was 'profoundly convinced that the Kaiser [was] *not capable of surviving without* the Chancellor'. 'He did not commit the *folly* of advising the Kaiser to dismiss the Chancellor before the elections', Eulenburg continued. 'Such thoughts may arise in the *unpolitical* minds of those who hate the Chancellor, military or princely minds.' Eulenburg himself was also working 'with all my strength to keep the two "great men" together', not least because he had realised that Bismarck's dismissal – for whatever reasons – would 'still be regarded by the people as a terrible thing to happen'.[70]

Even Paul Kayser, the author of the social welfare programme, could see that keeping Bismarck in office was more important than the Kaiser's social policy initiative. 'If the Chancellor goes before the elections the Kartell cannot be saved; its individual components will be sent spinning around like atoms in space. It would not matter in the least . . . for what reason he left; the fact itself would be enough to unsettle the whole population of the Reich.' It was significant, the Colonial Director warned, that 'even quite outspoken political opponents of the Chancellor' were now afraid 'that he might go very soon'.[71] He no doubt had Waldersee in mind, and it was indeed true that, although the Chief of the General Staff considered the dismissal of Bismarck inevitable in the long run, he did not think the moment yet ripe. On 12 January 1890, when for the first time in his diary he posed the question of how the dismissal of the Chancellor should be handled tactically, he commented: 'It is essential to give the Kaiser the right advice, so that he is not outmanoeuvred; however much he may have declined, the Chancellor is still a clever and very cunning man. His strength always was in his ability to find a way out of difficult situations. The break must at all costs be handled in such a way that it does not look to the world as if the Kaiser had wanted to get rid of the Chancellor.'[72] In a letter of 13 January the General commented that, if Bismarck noticed that 'a new era is about to begin, he will try to get out altogether', but he would try to ensure the succession for his son, 'and this, I think, will give His Majesty the chance to play for time . . . For as long as it can be managed the Chancellor must be kept in office; if he should in fact want to break away . . . he will choose the moment in such a way as to keep public opinion on his side. This must not be allowed; the goal must be to achieve the opposite effect.'[73] Now, after the clash of 24 January, the General expressed his admiration for the Kaiser in resisting the temptation to turn the Reich Chancellor out on the spot. 'In fact it is almost incredible', he observed, 'that he should be willing to continue working with a man who he believes is capable of bringing about bloodbaths simply to safeguard his own reputation! . . . I do not think that this will go on for much longer, but I am in favour of it and I am trying . . . to make sure that the Kaiser does not allow the Chancellor to go or send him away, but waits for the elections to take place first!'[74]

In adopting this attitude the Kaiser's secret advisers were nevertheless assuming that Wilhelm would be able to determine many matters of policy even with Bismarck as chancellor. They privately hoped that Bismarck would withdraw into the domain of foreign affairs, which would at least give the Kaiser room to manoeuvre in questions of domestic policy.[75] Eulenburg accurately summarised their principal aim in stating that Bismarck must be kept on for the time being, but that *at the same time* [we must] make the Kaiser *independent . . .* because we *need* him to be independent for what lies before us when the old Chancellor is living out his dotage'.[76] In this concept of a reduced degree of power for the Reich Chancellor the characteristics of the later Wilhelmine regime were already beginning to appear in the last stage of the Bismarck era. As we shall see, it was precisely Bismarck's refusal to accept such a system that finally provoked the Kaiser into dismissing him.

In their optimistic assessment of the situation Wilhelm's advisers were encouraged by the thought that the young monarch had after all managed to achieve a considerable amount, despite the opposition of the Iron Chancellor. He had closed the Reichstag with a speech expressing support for the workers and had set in train ministerial consultations on his social welfare programme. At a session of the Ministry of State on 26 January Bismarck gave orders for an imperial proclamation to be drawn up in accordance with the Kaiser's proposals, and he himself took on the responsibility of convening an international congress.[77] Though Wilhelm's wish to appoint Johannes von Miquel as Prussian minister of trade was thwarted, he did succeed in obtaining the appointment for Oberpräsident Hans Hermann Freiherr von Berlepsch, whom Bismarck had bitterly criticised for his pro-labour attitude in the crisis caused by the strikes of the previous year. The promotion of Berlepsch was the first ministerial appointment in the civilian domain that was entirely due to Wilhelm II's initiative; it was Berlepsch's express responsibility to put the Kaiser's social welfare programme into action. The Kaiser's success was all the more striking in that the Ministry of Trade had to this point been administered by Bismarck himself. What was more, the new minister's responsibilities were extended by the transfer of the Departments of Mining, Metallurgy and Saltworks from Maybach's Ministry of Public Works to the Ministry of Trade and Commerce.[78]

To develop this new system further the Kaiser now decided to receive the departmental ministers and other officials individually once a week or once a fortnight to hear their reports.[79] Like Holstein, Eulenburg thought this decision 'all the more admirable' because at the Crown Council on 24 January the ministers had presented 'a wretched display of lack of independence'; but he acknowledged that as a result 'the question of Chancellor or Kaiser' had become much more acute.[80] On 31 January Wilhelm arrived unannounced at a meeting of the Ministry of State and enquired about the progress of the consultations on his social welfare programme; he expressed satisfaction at Bismarck's response that the ministers had just resolved to draft two proclamations – one to the Reich Chancellor on the international congress to be convened, the other to the ministers of public works and of trade and commerce.[81] The 'little Kayser' too was able to note with satisfaction that through this resolution the proposals that he had submitted to the monarch in his secret memorandum would now be carried out. He wrote delightedly to Eulenburg, 'I think the success of the Kaiser's initiative is remarkable; in my opinion it has achieved the right thing in objective terms, and if the Proclamations prove to be noble in form as well as content, I am convinced that we shall soon see hymns of praise to the Kaiser in all the newspapers both here and abroad . . . I see the forthcoming proclamations of Kaiser Wilhelm II as the new leitmotiv which we need.'[82] The author of the second memorandum written for Wilhelm on the social welfare question, Franz Fischer, took a similar view: 'Our youthful Kaiser has indeed taken a great, bold step by his courageous, wise intervention in these questions, and he will surely succeed.'[83] When the two imperial proclamations were published – significantly without Bismarck's countersignature – on 4 February, Kayser's jubilation over the 'phenomenal success' of the young monarch knew no bounds, especially as he recognised in the proclamation to the Prussian ministers all the ideas he had included in his own programme. Bismarck would be forced to acknowledge, he thought, 'that *he* was blind and the Kaiser could see. All the successes and all the recognition which he could at least have shared with his sovereign will now come to the latter alone. Things will get better still. The press has not yet entered into it in enough detail. It is still gazing with amazement at the mere fact, like some traveller high in the Alps when the mist clears and he is blinded by the shining landscape in the valley below.'[84] Eulenburg was no less enthusiastic. He wrote to Paul Kayser: 'How wonderfully have we been guided into a way which leads to the noblest of goals: to the salvation of the poor and the wretched! The spark which *at best* glows in our hearts has become a burning flame in the heart of the beloved Kaiser – we should thank God for it from the depths of our souls.'[85] He sent fervent congratulations to Wilhelm II: 'This magnificent success will richly repay Your Majesty for much that has been difficult in recent days – but

Your Majesty's personal success has been so great that it gives me some concern to imagine the mood of the Chancellor and to ponder the consequences.' He sent the Kaiser extracts from the 'little' Kayser's letters and suggested that Kayser be appointed under-secretary of the Prussian Council of State which was to be convened to consider social welfare legislation, as announced in the proclamations. Kayser, he argued, was not only 'the best-qualified and most knowledgeable' man in this sphere, but was also 'congenial and useful' and above all 'not independent by nature', so he would 'simply implement Your Majesty's thoughts'.[86]

A few days later Bismarck and the Kaiser met to decide on the composition of the Council of State. Wilhelm agreed that Dr Robert Bosse, the under-secretary of state in the Reich Office of the Interior, who had been suggested by Bismarck and the ministers, should be appointed secretary of state of the Council of State. He insisted, however, on the appointment of Dr Kayser as acting secretary of state. In addition he demanded that the Prince of Pless, the industrial magnates Ritter, Krupp, Jencke and Stumm-Halberg, the conservative Centre Party member Freiherr von Huene and his own tutor Hinzpeter should be invited to join the Council, which Bismarck was obliged to concede.[87] Thus in the first half of February it actually looked as if Bismarck had reconciled himself to the new power structure, in which it was no longer he but Wilhelm II who would lay down the guidelines of domestic policy and take the most important decisions on government appointments. How was it that a crisis nevertheless arose and ended in Bismarck's abrupt dismissal on 18 March?

# CHAPTER TWELVE

# Bismarck's fall from power

## THE REICH CHANCELLOR'S TACTICS

SINCE his violent clashes with the Kaiser on 24 January 1890 the Reich Chancellor's position had changed radically. On that day Wilhelm had taken over the chairmanship of the Prussian Ministry of State, laid a precisely worked-out programme of social welfare reform before the ministers and succeeded in appointing a new minister of trade with responsibility for implementing the programme. At the dissolution of the Reichstag he had made a speech favourable to workers' causes and had insisted on announcing his programme of social reform in the two imperial proclamations of 4 February. At his instigation an international conference to regulate social welfare legislation in all industrialised nations had been arranged, and the Prussian Council of State had been convened under his personal chairmanship. In addition, Wilhelm had decided to receive individual ministers as well as lesser officials on a regular basis, with the intention of circumventing Bismarck's control over them and of making them *his* ministers and *his* tools. But how would the 75-year-old founder of the Reich react to such a fundamental undermining of his power?

Several possible courses of action were open to Bismarck, who reflected on each in turn without ever quite making up his mind. First, he could simply have accepted the new power structure, withdrawn to Friedrichsruh or Varzin and lent his name to the Kaiser's initiatives, regardless of whether he thought them right or wrong. Second, he considered reducing the formal powers of the Reich chancellor, so as to retain the responsibility for making decisions without the monarch's interference at least in those areas still under his control – for instance in foreign policy. A third option consisted in resigning all his offices – Reich chancellor, Prussian minister-president and Prussian foreign minister – thus drawing a line under his political activity after twenty-eight eventful years at the top. Finally, however, it was also open to him to take up the fight for power with the young Kaiser. The fact that by following this course he might bring about the destruction of his life's work, the mighty Hohenzollern empire with its personal monarchy virtually independent of parliament, and might even provoke a civil war with foreign intervention, was plain for all to see.

For a short time after the Crown Council of 24 January Bismarck seemed to have reconciled himself to the new situation. At the next ministerial meeting he remarked resignedly that 'the moods of a monarch are like fair and foul weather, one cannot escape them, one takes an umbrella and still gets wet. I think we must make the best of it!'[1] When the Chancellor accompanied the other ministers to congratulate the Kaiser on his birthday on 27 January his behaviour was so friendly that everyone had the impression that the differences of opinion that had arisen at the Crown Council would not have any further repercussions. The Kaiser seemed to have come to an understanding with the Chancellor and even announced his intention of attending a parliamentary dinner to be given by Bismarck on 4 February.[2] The members of the Kaiser's entourage were well aware, however, that the truce was only outward and certainly would not last.[3]

The idea, widely aired at this time, that the excessively powerful position enjoyed by Bismarck as chancellor ought to be dismantled in formal terms, originated in the Kaiser's camp, where thoughts were already turning towards getting rid of the post of Reich chancellor altogether.[4] As the crisis became more acute, Wilhelm II expressed the wish, on 27 January, that Bismarck should restrict himself to the Foreign Office and hand over control of internal policy in the Reich and in Prussia to someone else.[5] Significantly, however, similar ideas were also being considered by the Bismarcks and their circle. On 30 January 1890 the Chancellor informed the Saxon envoy, Count Hohenthal, that he intended 'to "crumble away" his post bit by bit', and to limit himself to the 'retirement zone', by which he meant foreign affairs and his work in the Bundesrat.[6] He went even further in a conversation with the Bavarian envoy, Count Lerchenfeld, to whom he said that he needed to put the 'excessively puffed-up Reich chancellor' on a slimming diet, give up his offices gradually and retain only the 'rump', the control of foreign affairs. Once he had quitted his Prussian posts − including that of Prussian foreign minister − the Prussian vote in the Bundesrat could even be cast against his views, if the occasion arose.[7] On 8 February Bismarck told the Kaiser in the course of a 'violent argument' that he wished to withdraw from Prussia completely and to remain in office only as Reich chancellor. He suggested that General von Caprivi, of all people − whom the monarch had himself received a few days earlier − be appointed minister-president, and his son Herbert Prussian foreign minister.[8] 'The Chancellor put on a very good act and even wept', Waldersee commented in his diary. 'He was particularly eager to find out who the Kaiser might have in mind as his successor. The Kaiser was wise enough not to name anyone to him; the Chancellor would have set out at once to ruin the reputation of whoever it was . . . The Kaiser is in a very agitated state and complains bitterly about the Chancellor, whose lies he has now experienced for himself; he is also very annoyed with Lerchenfeld, who – undoubtedly at the Chancellor's instigation – has written to Munich about a chancellor crisis, as a result of which the importance of keeping the Chancellor is being emphasised there. Can this state of affairs last long without causing great damage?', the Chief of the General Staff asked himself.[9] The next day Bismarck declared in the Ministry of State that his departure from the two Prussian posts had become unavoidable, as the Kaiser had plans with regard to domestic policy which he, Bismarck, could not agree to implement. He had already agreed on this 'irrevocable' decision with the Kaiser; his withdrawal to the 'retirement zone of the Foreign Office' must be publicly announced on 20 February, the day of the forthcoming Reichstag elections. Thereafter he would have no more contact with the Prussian ministers than with the Bavarians. The ministers did not protest, because they too saw this withdrawal as the only way to 'prevent a total break'.[10] Waldersee claimed to have heard after this meeting, however, that 'the Chancellor criticised the ministers without sparing a single one of them, and told them that none of them could be his successor'.[11]

On 8 February Lerchenfeld heard further details of the Chancellor's intentions from Herbert Bismarck. It should not be forgotten, said Herbert, 'that the present Reich Chancellor would not live for ever, and since it was unlikely that a successor of his calibre would ever be available again, it was perhaps a good thing that the transition should be made during his lifetime'.[12] It was generally assumed that Boetticher would be appointed Prussian minister-president, but meanwhile nothing further could be done than 'to duly await the decision of His Majesty the King'.[13] On 10 February Prince Bismarck himself remarked to the British ambassador, Sir Edward Malet, 'I cannot approve or agree in what the Emperor is doing and it has come to this that I have made up my mind to resign all the offices I hold except those of Chancellor of the Empire and Minister for Foreign Affairs of the Empire . . . My position will be a difficult one.' He added, presciently, 'Herr von Boetticher as Prussian Prime Minister will be over me in the Bundesrath while as Chancellor I direct the policy of the Empire. I doubt its working and it will probably end in my complete retirement.'[14]

That very evening, however, Bismarck had a discussion with Lerchenfeld as a result of which he was to abandon all these considerations. The Chancellor began by stating that he was intending to give up both his Prussian offices 'so as to have nothing more to do with the instruction of the Prussian vote' in the

Bundesrat. He wanted to build up a new bastion of authority for himself, based on the Bundesrat and the Reich offices. But the conversation constantly came back to the central difficulty in this combination, namely 'what would happen if the Prussian vote [in the Bundesrat] were instructed against his opinion'. The non-Prussian states would certainly not be in favour of such a solution, Lerchenfeld declared, for 'the confidence of the states in the central executive rested on their knowledge that what Prussia wanted, the Chancellor wanted too, and what the Chancellor wanted, Prussia wanted too. This was the cement which held the German states together'. The Bavarian envoy subsequently reported to Munich 'that the Reich Chancellor is not yet clear in his own mind about his future position. But he is well aware of the difficulties the new arrangement would create everywhere'.[15] That same evening Bismarck gave up his plans. He summoned Boetticher and told him that he had no intention of allowing himself to be 'buried alive'; he could not accept a situation in which Boetticher would sit beside him as Prussian minster-president and tell him how to vote in the Bundesrat.[16] The next day he informed a visibly displeased Kaiser that on no account would he retire from his Prussian offices. When August Eulenburg heard that the planned separation of offices had been abandoned, he deplored Bismarck's decision, arguing that it was '*he* of all people [who] should have tried to draw the dividing line [between the Reich chancellorship and the Prussian Ministry] which will surely be needed in the future, and in the short term this has the evil effect that from now on with every storm that breaks we shall have to be prepared for a full-blown chancellor crisis'.[17]

In parallel with these complicated deliberations on reducing his sphere of authority, Bismarck was also seriously considering the possibility of simply retiring altogether. He had already threatened to retire from all his offices at the Crown Council of 24 January. He fired a second warning shot on 30 January, telling Hohenthal that the day on which the Saxon government brought the proposal on social welfare instigated by the Kaiser before the Bundesrat would be his last day in office.[18] Shortly afterwards, when he was due to meet the Kaiser on 3 February to discuss the two social welfare proclamations, he warned that his desire to hand in his resignation was growing 'as fast as a hothouse plant'.[19] When the differences between the Kaiser and the Chancellor on social policy became public knowledge many people wondered why Bismarck remained in office in such circumstances, and why the Kaiser did not simply dismiss him. The British ambassador, for instance, assumed that the Kaiser must have overriding reasons for wishing to keep Bismarck. 'He is the creator of the Empire: and it is everywhere felt he is a guarantee of peace. On the other hand it is thought even in Germany that if the Emperor's ambition does not find vent peacefully it will take a more dangerous form, and he himself knows that public confidence would be shaken if Prince Bismarck were to leave his side. The Chancellor probably feels it would be unchivalrous & also unsafe to do so.'[20] But these were only guesses. Two days later, on 10 February 1890, Malet was to hear from Bismarck himself how he really felt.

In his conversation with the ambassador that day the Reich Chancellor made no secret of his thoughts. With astonishing frankness, he condemned the system of personal rule which the Kaiser had introduced. As Malet stated in a confidential letter to Lord Salisbury, the gist of Bismarck's comments was that 'the Emperor deemed himself quite able to stand alone and to direct the internal and external affairs of the Empire without any anxiety as to his own capacity'. The Chancellor gave repeated indications that he considered his days were over, even if he remained in office for form's sake. He was in a nervous and exhausted state because of the untenable position in which he found himself. His decision to retire from his Prussian offices had been made inevitable by the Kaiser's desire to govern himself; but the division of offices could not be permanent. It was only out of consideration for the monarch's wishes and because of the forthcoming Reichstag elections that he remained in office at all. As he put it to Malet, 'I would retire altogether, but the Emperor wishes me to remain and I cannot refuse – for if I were to go now on the eve of the elections it might have an effect upon them which I desire as little now as before the present situation arose. I have had no hand in making it. The young Emperor has been launched in the path which he has taken by outsiders. Those chiefly responsible', Bismarck claimed, 'are Hinzpeter, his old tutor, Freiherr von Douglas, whom he has created Graf, the Grand Duke of Baden and the King of Saxony.' In their personal relations the Kaiser was extremely friendly, 'but he wishes to govern himself. He has not realised the utility of having a screen between himself and his subjects on which the blows of unpopularity may fall without injuring him', the Chancellor explained. 'He has no doubts. He thinks he can do all things and he wishes to have the entire credit all to himself. He was not in the least annoyed when I declined to countersign the rescript . . . He does not foresee any reaction in popularity when his scheme fails.' Even in foreign affairs the Kaiser believed he could overcome any problem himself. 'He is elated with what he considers to be the success of his visit to Russia and other countries. He only wants me to remain in order that I may make speeches in the Reichstag and induce it to vote money', Bismarck observed bitterly. He was glad, he said, 'that seventy five years are behind me and not before me – my work is done – but it is sad to see the edifice which I have raised brick by brick in danger of crumbling'. The new system would also cause difficulties in Anglo-German relations which Bismarck himself would no longer be able to prevent.[21]

Six days later Herbert confirmed in a letter to his brother Bill that their father had abandoned the idea of separating his offices as impracticable and was now thinking of 'complete retirement on 1 April', his seventy-fifth birthday. 'I do not know what will happen in the end, but more animosity is being stirred up than ever, and as this of course destroys confidence, the constant living together becomes more and more difficult.'[22] The Reich Chancellor's attitude was much the same when he and his wife visited the Empress Frederick a few days later. He spoke to her at length about Wilhelm's social policy 'coup' and about his own forthcoming retirement, and said 'he could not keep pace with innovations so suddenly resolved on and carried out in such a hurry and on the advice of people he thought in no way competent to give it'. The Dowager Empress found him 'looking remarkably strong & well & inclined to take things very philosophically. He is exceedingly fond of W. . . . but I fancy he is *uneasy* at the *very* great self-confidence and the naiveté with wh. he exercises his will & takes responsibilities, and also at the curious people who have access to him & are listened to.' She believed that Bismarck's intention to retire was entirely honest, but doubted whether the Kaiser would accept his resignation.[23]

## THE DECISION APPROACHES

As we have seen, in the first weeks of 1890 Wilhelm II's advisers remained convinced of the necessity of keeping Bismarck in office. For all their criticism of his style of government and his policies, they were too afraid of the repercussions of a spectacular departure by the founder of the Reich to be willing to risk a violent break with him. So Bismarck might well have remained in office for a few months longer[24] had not the idea taken root in the Kaiser's camp during the month of February that the Chancellor was pursuing tactics which would make it acutely dangerous for the monarchy for him to stay on. Whether Bismarck had in fact decided to go on the offensive against Wilhelm and the crown, as the monarch's secret advisers feared, or whether their anxieties were mere fantasy, is still a matter of debate among historians today.[25] What seems quite clear from the wealth of sources available, however, is that Wilhelm's close advisers — *all* of them — were *sincerely* convinced of their interpretation of Bismarck's intentions, not least because after years of working with him they knew his mentality and methods, and could only too easily put themselves in his place.[26] This fact in itself is enough to explain the fatal process which led Kaiser Wilhelm II to decide, as early as mid-February, that Bismarck had to be dismissed in the near future.

Immediately after the Crown Council of 24 January and the subsequent fiasco in the Reichstag, when the Kartell broke apart over the strengthened

anti-socialist law, Holstein became convinced that he had seen through
Bismarck's tactics, which were highly dangerous for the Kaiser. He wrote to
Eulenburg in some agitation: 'What just happened has the purpose of making
the Centre into a government party. As a result of the disgrace which the Chancellor has brought on the Kartell parties in the socialist question, the elections
cannot but turn out badly, i.e. the Kartell will lose its majority. The Chancellor
will then say to the Kaiser: "We must move closer to the Centre, therefore it is
necessary for Your Majesty to appoint a member of the Centre – for instance
Huene – to the Ministry." The moment that the Centre becomes a government
party in *Prussia*, it also becomes a government party in Bavaria. Then Lutz will
be out within a few months . . . I do not think the consequences of that could
ever be reversed. A good Reichstag can always follow on a bad one. But if the
ultramontanes are once at the helm in Bavaria and are given the chance to alter
the constituency boundaries to suit themselves, we shall never get them out –
not without violence, anyway.' Holstein pointed to the similarity between the
domestic and foreign policies of the Chancellor: 'In both cases he holds sway
over a group of three. But he despises and mistreats them in order to run after
a fourth which has its back turned to *him*. The fourth is the Centre in the one
instance and Russia in the other.'[27]

With the publication of the two imperial proclamations on 4 February 1890 the
ever-suspicious Holstein scented new dangers. Not only had Bismarck refused
to countersign the rescripts, he had strengthened their wording in such a way as
to cause disquiet among German industrialists and foreign governments. 'The
longer of the two imperial proclamations has had the effect of alarming the propertied classes because of the general way in which it is expressed, which does not
come from the Kaiser *but from the corrections made by the Chancellor*', Holstein
warned on 7 February. 'It has led people to believe that a general redistribution
of property is in the offing. It will not be a good thing for this uncertainty to
continue for long, since the Kaiser needs the support of the propertied classes.
The Kaiser, who is certainly an intelligent man, will know how to counteract
these anxieties', he added. In this letter, parts of which Eulenburg forwarded
to the Kaiser, Holstein commented that Bismarck had not made the corrections
with the deliberate aim of putting the Kaiser in a difficult position, and added
that 'much of what looks like deceitfulness in the Chancellor is simply the consequence of mental weakness, which is rapidly increasing'.[28] After discussions with
Adolf Marschall von Bieberstein, Paul Kayser and Franz Fischer, however, he
became convinced that Bismarck was consciously deceiving the Kaiser. 'The fact
that the Chancellor undoubtedly feels deeply hurt by the Kaiser's independent
conduct makes the situation very dangerous', Holstein warned on 10 February.
'He will certainly not rest until he has succeeded in making the Kaiser see it as a

mistake to have acted alone and not followed his Chancellor. Even in the proclamations of the 4th of this month he made various additions which will make it
more difficult for them to be carried out, so as to wreck the Kaiser's ideas, leaving
the latter – as is the plan – entirely in the hands of the Chancellor.'[29] The Baden
envoy, Marschall, was also of the opinion that Bismarck was trying to portray
the Kaiser as 'a heaven-storming idealist', while he himself was 'the protector
of the propertied classes'. The Chancellor was proclaiming his 'innocence of the
Kaiser's action on all sides'.[30] Marschall indignantly recorded on 12 February
that Bismarck had put the question of the eight-hour day on the agenda of the
international social welfare conference, although he was very well aware that
this point was anathema, particularly for the British government.[31]

The secret advisers were afraid, on the one hand, that Bismarck would exag-
gerate the Kaiser's ideas on social reform to the point of absurdity, while on the
other hand they suspected him of intending to sabotage the work of both the
Prussian Council of State and the international conference in Berlin, in order to
wreck Wilhelm's initiative. 'There is no need to point out how dangerous it would
be for the reputation of the Kaiser and of the monarchy if the proclamations were
to remain nothing more than fine words', Holstein, Kayser and Fischer warned
in a joint memorandum of 10 February. 'There is no doubt that the Kaiser is now
in a very serious position . . . As things are now, a fiasco is very much to be feared.
The Council of State could become a noose for the Kaiser.'[32] The longer this
atmosphere of mistrust persisted, the more unbearable it became to both sides.
In mid-February 1890 Wilhelm II and his group of advisers gradually came
round to the idea that Bismarck would have to be dismissed in the interest of the
monarchy. On 30 January Waldersee had noted contemptuously in his diary that
the Chancellor no longer knew what he wanted: 'he wavers, tells lies and makes
everyone who works with him ill-tempered'; but most significantly, 'he will not
resign on any account and so . . . the great man will end his days as a small man'.[33]
Ten days later the Chief of the General Staff was already pondering the question
of when and under what circumstances Bismarck should be dismissed. Although
on 9 February he still took the view that the inevitable 'great clash' should be
delayed 'until the Reichstag has met and the Chancellor has reached a deadlock
with it',[34] the following day he expressed the opinion that the present moment
would be advantageous for the Kaiser. His thinking was almost schizophrenic
at this point, for he sided entirely with Bismarck on the questions actually at
issue, as he repeatedly admitted.[35] The social reform initiative had caused great
disquiet among the middle parties, precisely the people whose support the Kaiser
needed. 'Yesterday's stock exchange gave the Kaiser the answer to his proclamation by panicking over industrial securities!', Waldersee observed in alarm. It was
a case of 'the big capitalists, including the Jews, against the Kaiser's ideas. The

Kaiser will realise that there are some very unreliable people among the National Liberals and Free Conservatives, to whom he recently gave much support. They love the Kaiser as long as he helps them do good business, and [he] is in for many disappointments.'[36] Like Holstein, Waldersee became convinced that Bismarck would exploit the agitated mood among the propertied classes for his own benefit, and would 'not hesitate to attack the Kaiser' in the process. This perception marked a decisive moment for the Chief of the General Staff.[37] On 10 February he wrote for the first time: 'I do not doubt for a moment that the Chancellor must fall, and the present moment is really not a bad one for the Kaiser.'[38] It was two days later that he first told others of his view that the Kaiser must dismiss Bismarck immediately after the opening of the new Reichstag. 'Believe me', he wrote to Philipp Eulenburg on 12 February, 'it cannot go on like *this* for long.' It was obvious to everyone that the Chancellor was opposed to Wilhelm II's social reform policy. 'How can our beloved sovereign possibly continue the great work which is engaging the whole world's attention now, if the Chancellor does not commit himself to supporting it with all the power and influence he has?', he asked. 'It cannot help but give rise to a completely untenable situation, and therefore in my opinion we are now facing a really serious chancellor crisis.' Bismarck, he had heard, was outwardly calm, but inwardly very agitated. 'I think that the Chancellor must at all costs remain until the Reichstag has assembled and he has shown his face; but I *doubt* that it would be in the Kaiser's interest for him to remain any longer than that.'[39] In a conversation with Hinzpeter on 15 February the Chief of the General Staff stated frankly that he thought Bismarck must be got rid of soon, for if he remained in office for long the Kaiser would not be able to carry out many of his ideas and would therefore suffer a defeat at the hands of the Chancellor. At this point Waldersee did not consider that there was much danger of a pro-Bismarck movement against the Kaiser after the dismissal. 'Once the Chancellor has gone', he observed contemptuously, 'he will collapse under the weight of his 75 years and his present friends will desert him; they will have no interest in seeing him return to power, and in any case the Kaiser would never lend his hand to that.'[40] Johannes von Miquel, to whom Waldersee spoke at length, also considered Bismarck's days to be numbered. In contrast to the Chief of the General Staff, however, he preferred 'a slow fading away'.[41]

On 18 February 1890, two days before the first round of the Reichstag elections, the Kaiser had in fact already made up his mind. 'The chancellor crisis is in full swing', Waldersee recorded in his diary. 'The Chancellor is wavering – another indication of how he has become an old man – at one moment he wants to go, the next he wants to stay. But he is indignant because he is convinced that the Kaiser would like to be rid of him.' The latter was certainly 'quite prepared in his mind' for the dismissal, Waldersee wrote, 'and my experience tells me that he will not go back on it now'.[42] 'The Kaiser has definitely had done with the Chancellor now', he recorded after further discussions with Wilhelm on 19 and 20 February.[43] Not only had the manner in which Bismarck 'ran down' his ministerial colleagues left the Kaiser 'outraged'; but 'the dishonesty of the Chancellor has at last become too much for the Kaiser, and he is beginning to realise that he has frequently been deceived by the great man'.[44]

On the day of the elections Wilhelm called on the Chief of the General Staff during his morning walk and discussed with him the issues which were still unresolved. Waldersee's account of this conversation shows once again how much he was in fact on his arch-enemy Bismarck's side on the social welfare question. His diary states: 'In the labour question he [the Kaiser] believes that the Council of State will put forward good proposals and that much can be achieved. This is quite true: some things will be achieved, such as workers' committees, limitation of Sunday working hours and women's working hours. Unfortunately, however, this will nowhere near satisfy the workers. He has stimulated their greed and brought unrest throughout the world of labour. The outcome can only be great disappointment for him. He has unleashed a current which will be hard to stem. If all workers were noble or even merely sensible people, all would be very well But they are not, unfortunately, and, what is more, socialists will now stir them up into further madness. It will not be long before the Kaiser greatly regrets what he has done.'[45] In spite of this fatalistic prediction, which could have come from Bismarck himself, Waldersee continued to press for the Chancellor to be dismissed soon.

On 22 February the Kaiser again took Waldersee for a walk and almost immediately began to speak of the chancellor crisis, this time with 'a considerable degree of bitterness'. Wilhelm was 'completely convinced', according to the General, 'that the Chancellor is working against him with the greatest possible audacity in the labour question; it sounds incredible, but it is unfortunately true'. Bismarck, in the Kaiser's words, had 'wanted to go and then withdrawn his request the next day. I will not tolerate such games; from now on I shall decide on the date when he shall go and he must first wait a while. His misfortune is his immeasurable desire to rule. So he has gradually got everyone under his thumb and he is spoilt. But with me, for once, he is tackling the wrong person.'[46]

## 'COMPLETE VICTORY FOR THE KAISER'S CAUSE'

On 14 February 1890 Philipp Eulenburg arrived in Berlin, at almost the same moment as Hinzpeter. 'It is my impression that he [Eulenburg] is the only really close friend and I am sure that he gives wise advice', Waldersee commented.[47]

In the course of the following days and nights Eulenburg had numerous long conversations with Hinzpeter and Waldersee, Paul Kayser, Holstein, Marschall von Bieberstein, Rudolf Lindau, his two cousins August Eulenburg and Gustav Kessel, his intimate friends Axel Varnbüler and Kuno Moltke, and many of Wilhelm II's other advisers. Eulenburg also had several 'endless dialogues' with his old friend Herbert Bismarck, which 'unfortunately were not calculated to reassure me about the present state of affairs'.[48] Above all, however, he had daily 'discussions of all kinds of important matters' with Kaiser Wilhelm. They talked of the 'complicated state of social affairs', of the 'important questions of social welfare legislation and of foreign policy which are causing such a stir at the moment', as well as of colonial policy. Whereas Herbert gave the impression of being 'tense' and 'out of sorts', Wilhelm was in the best of spirits. 'The Kaiser was very merry and cheerful about several welcome developments in domestic politics', his friend recorded in his diary on 22 February 1890.[49]

The smouldering crisis now moved swiftly towards its climax. On the night of 22–3 February Eulenburg reported to the Kaiser: 'Today the whole Ministry was ransacked for an old regulation according to which ministers are supposed to have the right to speak to the King only in the presence of the minister-president. But all that was found was a ruling that in the case of a dispute between two ministers they were to appear before the king with the president.'[50] Bismarck was in fact looking for a Cabinet Order of 1 September 1852, and sent Counsellor Dr Erich von Schwarzkoppen to the Ministry of State's secretariat and then to the Finance Ministry to search for it. It was found the next day, 23 February. Barely three weeks later it became the direct cause of the final break between the Kaiser and the Chancellor.[51] Eulenburg's letter to the Kaiser also contained the news that Bismarck would ask for an audience in the next few days. He wanted to discuss the Reichstag elections, the programme for the international conference and 'general matters' with the Kaiser. Eulenburg urged the Kaiser to take care that the Chancellor did not introduce any discussion of the regulation of working hours into the conference programme, as it would alienate foreign powers. Following this warning, Wilhelm at once wrote to Queen Victoria deriding the 'nonsense' about fixing standard working hours as 'unadulterated blarney from beginning to end', which went some way towards reassuring the British government.[52] Eulenburg also reported to the Kaiser that Bismarck was aiming to cut down the social welfare bill and to delay it until after the international conference.[53]

Thus when a submission by Bismarck containing just such proposals arrived at the Schloss on 26 February the Kaiser had been amply forewarned.[54] He wrote furious marginal notes on the memorandum objecting to the postponement of the bill. He sent for Paul Kayser and complained that Bismarck was trying to put 'a spoke in his wheel', which he would not allow.[55] At Waldersee's audience on 1 March the Kaiser told him that Bismarck had suggested 'waiting until after the international conference had finished its work before bringing bills for the protection of labour before the Reichstag; the Kaiser at once realised that his intention was to put the whole thing off, and wrote to him to say that the bills should be put before the Reichstag as quickly as possible'.[56] The Kaiser's firm stand led some to hope that Bismarck would now give way. 'There is a growing hope that with Your Majesty using such tactics the Chancellor will be more circumspect in his wishes, and an understanding with him will be possible', Eulenburg assured the Kaiser.[57]

At the same time, however, there were increasing indications that Bismarck was aiming at a policy of force which would completely overshadow the Kaiser's initiative on social welfare, and with it his political power and independence. Waldersee was enraged when he heard on 16 February that Bismarck had attempted to convince the Kaiser that a revolution was imminent. The Chancellor, he noted, was constantly trying to frighten Wilhelm by predicting 'danger for the Kaiser himself and revolution in the spring or at the latest in the summer'. But this was 'all sheer trickery. The Socialists consider that the Kaiser is working in their interest and want to keep him alive at all costs. We shall have strikes, perhaps even bloody conflicts, but anyone who foresees a revolution now is either too inclined to see ghosts or is a swindler. A great deal more would have to happen before we reached that point.'[58] When Marschall met Eulenburg on 20 February both agreed that, although Bismarck was willing to concede the social reform proclaimed by the Kaiser, he was simultaneously aiming at a 'change of system': in other words, a reactionary constitutional change imposed forcibly from above.[59] Otto Prince von Stolberg-Wernigerode likewise expressed the view that, while the Kaiser was in favour of making a last attempt at satisfying public opinion before 'extreme measures' were employed, Bismarck on the other hand was convinced 'that we have already more or less reached the extreme point'.[60] On 26 February Waldersee and Minister of War General von Verdy du Vernois, after reporting to the Kaiser at a joint audience, heard from him what had happened at Bismarck's audience the previous day. Bismarck had declared that he was 'filled with anxiety that if there were serious disturbances and perhaps even riots the Kaiser would not take vigorous action and would not allow any shooting. When the Kaiser responded that he might set his mind at rest, for if it were necessary he would not shrink even from the most extreme measures, the Chancellor was gratified and said that he was now free of the nightmare which had oppressed him night after night.' Waldersee commented acidly: 'Both Verdy and I laughed and said that this was nothing but another piece of play-acting, in other words humbug, and I believe the Kaiser is of the same opinion.' Wilhelm went on to relate that Bismarck had spoken about the election result which had destroyed the Kartell[61] and had expressed the opinion that the National Liberals had lost votes because 'many of them were dissatisfied with the imperial proclamations and had voted with the Left-Liberals. This is an outrageous lie!' In the end, Wilhelm reported, Bismarck had said that as far as the social welfare question was concerned, from now on he was prepared 'to go along with the Kaiser, although he doubted that anything would be achieved. So the Chancellor gave way to the Kaiser, and the latter was very pleased', Waldersee commented.[62] Marschall reported to Karlsruhe on similar lines, stating that at his audience on 25 February the Chancellor had promised his support for the social welfare bill on condition that the Kaiser declared himself ready, 'in the event that the disastrous consequences feared by the Prince should materialise, to use force and to allow shooting'.[63]

During the last days of February Kaiser Wilhelm II demonstrated his powers of leadership to a broad and knowledgeable forum by presiding daily at the Prussian Council of State which he had convened, a task which he carried out 'with great confidence throughout'.[64] Even Waldersee, whose attitude to the Kaiser's initiative was sceptical in the extreme, saw great benefit in the fact 'that the Kaiser has the feeling of having promoted a good cause, and that many people who scarcely knew him before have come to know and appreciate him'.[65] Paul Kayser, the actual originator of the social welfare programme, described the result of the consultations as 'complete victory for the Kaiser's cause'. 'All the points in His Majesty's programme' had been accepted in principle by the Council of State, he commented enthusiastically. 'But the victory of the Kaiser's cause is a *personal* victory for His Majesty, and what Wilhelm I said of the organisation of the army, Wilhelm II will say of the social welfare legislation: "It is my own work."' Writing to Eulenburg, the 'little Kayser' observed that the previous few days must have been 'a time of severe trial' for the Kaiser, but it was also 'a time of apprenticeship culminating in mastery'. Eulenburg lost no time in forwarding this flattering letter to the monarch. During the sessions of the Council Wilhelm had 'shown qualities which it would truly be a sin to keep confined to the relatively small circle [of the Council of State]. The Kaiser maintained such a lively interest for seven hours each day that at the end of the day he seemed as fresh as he had been in the morning. He was always dignified, even in jest; he kept to the subject all the time with skill and flexibility, like any grey-haired parliamentary chairman, well-informed, and cutting short all unnecessary speeches. Finally, without any preparation . . . he set out his views on the latest major strike in a speech as perfect in form as in content, showing such profound awareness of his responsibility as head of state, such a warm, patriotic heart, such calm and objectivity, that the whole Council of State was spellbound. It would really be a very good thing if this were reported in the press . . . The nation has a right, after all, to know what kind of a ruler it has.'[66] After the last session of the Council of State *'the great Kaiser'* singled out *'the little Kayser'* for special attention; he *'was even permitted to kiss the Kaiserin's hand, and she thanked him for his support!'*, Holstein reported to Eulenburg with amusement. This was an early and conspicuous example of the corrupting effect of the 'kingship mechanism' on Prussian–German officialdom. 'You should hear the little fellow now!', Holstein commented mockingly. He was 'more imperial than the Emperor'.[67]

Wilhelm's success in the Council of State was generally considered to have strengthened his position vis-à-vis Bismarck to a significant degree.[68] After the Council's sessions Waldersee observed that the Chancellor was 'unbearable' and 'in the blackest of moods'. While he continued to behave with the utmost affability towards outsiders, he treated his closest colleagues abominably, Waldersee reported on 1 March.[69] On the same day Paul Kayser commented that Bismarck must have realised that his days of glory were over; but he could not get over 'the defeat he had suffered at the hands of his Imperial Master' and was still laying mines 'to bring down the work which has begun and lead the Kaiser into absurd extremes'.[70] By way of a defensive strategy, Kayser and Holstein suggested that the Kaiser should refuse to sign any bills until the Council of State had discussed the measures in full. In this way Wilhelm could win in the Council of State the support which the Ministry of State ought to give him, but which, under Bismarck's domination, it 'cannot provide at present'.[71] Waldersee too was confident that with his success in the Council of State Wilhelm had outmanoeuvred Bismarck. 'I no longer feel anxious that he might be able to cause the Kaiser great problems in the labour question, now that I have seen how the Kaiser has remained master of the situation and has overpowered the Chancellor. The Kaiser's great success is also plain for all to see. No one now speaks of the Chancellor's social policy, but only of the Kaiser's. People can see who is master; this is vital, and an outstanding achievement for the Kaiser.' In well-informed circles it was now the universal opinion that Bismarck's days were numbered, for it was obvious that the rift between him and the Kaiser was too deep and the bitterness on both sides too great ever to be healed. Wilhelm had clearly emerged as the victor in the struggle over social welfare legislation. Confident that the end was not far off, Waldersee expressed the opinion that 'a clash in the near future should be avoided, and the Chancellor should be left to

bring about his own ruin little by little'. Bismarck would have to appear before
the newly elected Reichstag first, however, for 'its unsatisfactory composition is
after all chiefly his fault', Waldersee opined.[72]


## NEW PLANS FOR A *COUP D'ETAT*

In parallel with the Kaiser's victorious initiative on social policy, however, another
development took place which convinced a growing number of the governing
elite that Bismarck was right to advocate a reactionary revision of the constitution of the Reich. The Kaiser's policy was overshadowed by the results of the
Reichstag elections, which were disastrous for the Prussian–German monarchy.
The results came out shortly before the Council of State began its sittings, and
were confirmed by the second round at the beginning of March. Of the 7,261,600
votes cast in all, the former opposition parties won no less than 4,658,900. The
Kartell parties' mandate was reduced from 220 to 135 seats. The losses of the
National Liberals and Free Conservatives, for whom the Kaiser had repeatedly
demonstrated his support, were particularly painful. The left-liberal Progressive
Party, however, climbed from 32 to 66 seats, while the Catholic Centre reached
its peak in the history of the Reich with 106 seats. Without its support, or that
of the Progressive Party, there could no longer be a government majority in
the Reichstag. If that was not alarming enough, the electoral success of the
Social Democrats was seen as little short of a catastrophe. With 1,427,000 votes
(19.7 per cent) this republican and Marxist popular movement had become the
strongest party in the German Reich in terms of numbers of votes.[73] All told,
enormous numbers of people had turned against the Hohenzollern monarchy
and called the existing political and social order into question.[74] How could the
new situation be brought under control? Was this really the ideal moment to
dismiss the founder of the Reich and to put the power of the state into the hands
of an untried and impulsive young Kaiser?

When the results of the first round of the elections were announced on
23 February, Waldersee's furious reaction showed clearly, once again, that regardless of all personal rivalry he fully shared the fatalistic views of the old Reich
Chancellor. After a meeting with the Kaiser at Potsdam on that day he noted:
'The election result turns out to be even worse than anyone thought. The Kartell
has disintegrated, as there is no question of it having a majority any more. The
true picture will not emerge until after the second-round elections, of which
there will be more than a hundred, but it is certain that the Social Democrats
have gained enormously. The Kaiser has not yet realised the full significance of
all this; we are facing an important turning-point. This Reichstag will certainly
not approve the demands of the military; its dissolution can hardly improve

matters.'[75] After the results of the second round were declared the Chief of the General Staff summed up the new internal political situation thus: 'The elections . . . have resulted in the complete defeat of the National Liberals and probably of the Free Conservatives too, and thus in the annihilation of the Kartell's position: it is very far off having a majority now. The Conservatives have lost a few seats, but they still form a very strong group. The Progressives have increased greatly, likewise the Social Democrats. More alarming than the number of socialists in the Reichstag, however, is the number of socialist votes in the country. Never has an election aroused so much passion as this one, and it has shown very clearly the disturbing aspects of universal suffrage.' The way in which the Social Democratic movement was spreading into rural constituencies was particularly dangerous, in Waldersee's eyes. The reawakening of republican aspirations in South Germany was also alarming. 'It is a question that must be treated with the utmost seriousness and remedies must be considered', Waldersee commented anxiously.[76]

Waldersee laid the blame for the electoral catastrophe partly on Bismarck, who 'as the responsible, almost supreme, ruling Reich Chancellor' had suffered 'a terrible defeat', He also blamed the Kaiser, who had 'given powerful stimulation to the greed of the working population' through his proclamations on social reform.[77] The political effect of the imperial proclamations would be very slow in materialising, if it happened at all. 'I am afraid that they do not help at all – and the Kaiser himself already shares this view.' Waldersee had 'not the slightest doubt that the general dissatisfaction will increase, and I see no reason to believe that future elections will turn out much better; the only thing that would help would be if the socialists rushed ahead too quickly and it came to bloodshed; then it is possible that property-owners and people living from the state would make common cause'.[78] For the Chief of the General Staff there could be no doubt about the conclusions which must be drawn from 'the bad elections'. As early as 23 February he commented in his diary: 'There is no alternative but to abolish universal suffrage. I shall be glad to help with that.'[79] A week later he went further: 'In the event that the Kaiser should wish to suspend universal suffrage and cannot do this through the Chancellor', he himself was ready to take Bismarck's place and would 'gladly risk my life for it'.[80] The leader of the Free Conservative Party, Wilhelm von Kardorff, was likewise 'very anxious about the future' and believed that 'the abolition of universal suffrage [was] necessary'; but in his opinion Bismarck's presence was 'absolutely essential' if a *coup d'état* of that nature were to be carried out.[81]

The dilemma that the election results represented for the Kaiser was stark: should he continue with the pro-worker policy of social reform which he had already proclaimed *urbi et orbi*? Could he risk Bismarck's resignation in the changed political situation? If he gave way − if he switched course towards a policy of force − would he not then be admitting his mistake and capitulating to the Chancellor? Wilhelm seems at first not to have understood the position of constraint in which he found himself. At the closure of the Council of State he announced emphatically: 'As far as the battle against social democracy is concerned, that is *my* own affair.' This he said in such a tone, according to Waldersee, 'that everyone felt that he was determined to take strong measures'.[82] The election results prompted thoughts of a *coup d'état* even in the otherwise soft-hearted Eulenburg, who did not at first give much thought to the political disadvantages of such a course for the Kaiser. In a letter to Holstein of 28 February he summed up the basic parliamentary dilemma for all future governments with the observation that the new Reichstag would not accept either a new Anti-Socialist Bill or an Army Bill unless, as a quid pro quo for the latter, the two-year military service demanded by the Progressive Party were granted, or political concessions were made to the Catholic Church. But '*the Chancellor is too old, the Kaiser too young and the Social Democrats too strong* for us to govern with a minority. To govern with the Centre means the *permanent* presence of Rome in the Bundesrat and the end of the Italian alliance . . . How about a demand by all the federal princes for a revision of the electoral law under the Chancellor's leadership? I admit that this would amount to a *coup d'état* and that shooting could hardly be avoided. But I almost think the Prince [Bismarck] could be persuaded to accept such a course, for *at bottom he is dissatisfied with his electoral law*. If the [German] princes supported it, he would become their standard-bearer "in the crisis of the Fatherland".'[83]

This was precisely what Bismarck proposed at the sitting of the Prussian Ministry of State on 2 March 1890. He told the ministers that he intended to bring into the new Reichstag an Anti-Socialist Bill which would be even more stringent than the one rejected by the Kartell-dominated Reichstag five weeks earlier. Social Democrat agitators would be disqualified from voting or standing for election and could be exiled. Bismarck's aim was plainly to dissolve the Reichstag several times in succession after it had rejected the bill, as it could be relied upon to do, and then finally to proclaim a new electoral law. He put forward the theory that the German Reich was founded on an alliance of *princes*, not of *states*. Therefore 'the princes . . . could decide, if need be, to withdraw from the joint treaty'. According to the minutes of the meeting he went on to say: 'In this way it would be possible to free oneself from the Reichstag if the results of the elections continued to be bad.'[84]

It was Holstein, Kayser and Marschall who drew attention to the dangerous consequences of such a policy for the Kaiser. 'We must save the Kaiser from that fate', Marschall noted in his diary on 2 March after a visit from Holstein.[85] The introduction of a more severe Anti-Socialist Bill would be 'a dark blot on the imperial chronicle, which has looked very good hitherto'. The Social Welfare Bill, on which the Council of State had just finished deliberating, would become 'an object of derision' if a more severe Anti-Socialist Bill including expulsion provisions were introduced at the same time.[86] For Paul Kayser, Bismarck's plan to persuade the Kaiser to introduce a more stringent Anti-Socialist Bill was 'the most masterful move in the whole game of chess; it means checkmate for the King', he warned. Writing to Eulenburg, he commented: 'It is unthinkable that the next Reichstag would accept a more severe Socialist Bill . . . Its reintroduction would therefore be a useless demonstration which would destroy the last remnant of the Kartell and throw down the apple of discord again. After the rejection of such a bill there would be no point in a dissolution. On the contrary, that would unleash the worst possible elements. For it would be death to the Kaiser's proclamations . . . The whole social welfare legislative programme would collapse and the blessing hoped for and rightly expected from it would become a curse.' A more severe Anti-Socialist Bill at this moment would be like a slap in the face for the Kaiser, and it was precisely that, and not the defeat of social democracy, which was quite obviously the Reich Chancellor's real aim. The next consequence of the introduction of such a bill would be the resignation of newly appointed Minister of Trade von Berlepsch, which would be closely followed by that of Heinrich von Boetticher. 'The Chancellor's haste is understandable', Kayser maintained. 'He is 75 years old and no longer has much to lose. But the Kaiser is the *future* of the country; a blow against *him strikes home!*' Since the ministers were still in awe of Bismarck, the Kaiser would have to convene the Council of State again. That would be the only way to prevent surprise attacks from the Chancellor. Then His Majesty would be on the crest of the hill at last. 'Post nubila Phoebus!'[87] Eulenburg sent extracts from this letter to the Kaiser on 4 March. He too warned that a more severe Anti-Socialist Bill would weaken 'the great impact of Your Majesty's proclamations' at home and abroad. The Chancellor's policy was aimed at 'destroying the existing state of affairs, and the sooner the better'.[88] The Kaiser's advisers were incensed to discover that Bismarck had told the ministers at the sitting of the Ministry of State on 2 March that the new, drastic Anti-Socialist Bill was 'particularly wished by the Kaiser'.[89] The crisis came rapidly to a head. In a conversation with Wilhelm II on 3 March, Marschall gained the impression that, although the monarch was thoroughly convinced of the dangers of Bismarck's policy, he was afraid to dismiss the Chancellor. Marschall therefore went with Holstein to visit the leader of the moderate wing of the Conservatives, Helldorff, and persuaded him to talk to the Kaiser the next day. After Helldorff's audience Marschall was able to note with satisfaction that the Kaiser was 'firm and ready for a break'. On 4 March he telegraphed to the Grand Duke of Baden:

'Helldorff saw the Kaiser today, pleaded with him not to concede the bill: this was a totally unnecessary provocation of the people, a policy aimed at creating scandal whereas calm was essential, and would destroy everything the Kaiser was trying to do. Helldorff has the impression that the Kaiser is firm.'[90]

His resolve stiffened by Eulenburg's and Kayser's letters and by Helldorff's visit, Wilhelm II took an uncompromising stand in his confrontation with Bismarck on 4 March. Immediately after the audience Marschall telegraphed to the Grand Duke of Baden reporting that the Kaiser had been determined 'not to give way, and to telegraph to Caprivi if the Chancellor threatened to resign'.[91] On 5 March Wilhelm wired to Eulenburg to say that Bismarck had 'finally given up the Anti-Socialist Bill yesterday upon my urging him to do so'.[92] 'So it would seem that we are over the worst', Eulenburg commented with relief to Holstein, praising the Kaiser's 'steadfastness'.[93] In the next few days, indeed, relations between the Kaiser and the Chancellor seemed to improve. Through Eulenburg's influence Paul Kayser was appointed secretary and personal observer for the Kaiser at the international social welfare conference.[94] At the same time Wilhelm showed that he recognised the difficult position in which the Prussian ministers found themselves by conferring the Order of the Black Eagle on Vice-President and Vice-Chancellor Heinrich von Boetticher, on the anniversary of the death of Kaiser Wilhelm I.[95] There was renewed hope that a *modus vivendi* might be reached, on the basis of mutual willingness to compromise and recognition of the Kaiser's need 'to rule according to his conscience'.[96] In conversation on 10 March 1890 with his banker, Gerson Bleichröder, as the latter reported to the Rothschilds in London, the Reich Chancellor indicated that he would not resign for the time being. 'Whether this will still be the case in a few months' time will depend on circumstances which cannot be foreseen today.'[97] Eulenburg's mood was optimistic, not least because he had just received news of his appointment as Prussian envoy at Stuttgart – a further sign of the Kaiser's increasing power and of the gradual decline of Bismarck's influence.[98]

## THE LAST DAYS OF BISMARCK'S RULE

Soon, however, news of a very different order reached Eulenburg from Berlin, and it became only too clear that the Reich Chancellor was determined to go on fighting against the Kaiser. Bismarck was still refusing to introduce the Social Welfare Bill in the Reichstag before the end of the international conference; he had informed the participating nations that they could send an unlimited number of delegates; he had at first invited the larger German federal states, but had then withdrawn the invitations to certain states, including the highly industrialised kingdom of Saxony; he had invited countries such as Spain and Portugal which had no export industry and no labour problems; and he had deliberately selected nonentities to serve on the Prussian delegation and had left out the best candidates, for example Theodor Lohmann and Robert Bosse. It was perfectly clear that Bismarck was out to wreck the international conference, which was 'His Majesty's own work'. The group around Holstein became convinced 'that everything is coming to a head and *the Prince is pushing for conflict*'.[99] As one of them aptly remarked, it was 'as if there were two governments, and whatever the Kaiser does, others undo'.[100]

Suddenly a new controversy arose to add to their troubles: a 'massive Army Bill' drafted by Verdy, the War Minister, under which the Reichstag was expected to approve expenditure of 280 million marks with a yearly increase of 70 million marks. It was plain that the Reichstag would refuse unless major concessions were made in return.[101] Verdy, who was in any case reputed to sympathise with the democratic Progressive Party, seemed ready to concede two-year in place of three-year military service, but in this he was fiercely opposed by Holstein and Marschall, who again appealed for Eulenburg's help. The concession of two-year military service would permanently increase the power of the Reichstag and would certainly add to the social democratic threat within the army, they argued. But to introduce such a major Army Bill without being prepared to make concessions of this kind would be to invite conflict with the Reichstag. 'Today, at the age of 75, Bismarck would no longer fight to get it through; *on the contrary*, the Kaiser would have to fight for Bismarck's policy and in the process he would lose the trust that he has gradually earned through his calm and moderate conduct hitherto, and which must underpin the personal position of every true ruler.' The Kaiser's advisers in the Foreign Office warned strongly of 'the Chancellor's current liking for extreme situations in which he wishes to involve not only himself but the Kaiser'.[102] Just as they had brought first the federal princes and then the Council of State into the campaign against the centralised power of the state controlled by Bismarck, they now advised the Kaiser to summon the commanding generals to a council over which Wilhelm himself should preside. 'This would have a dual advantage', Holstein urged. 'First the Kaiser would hear the wisest views, for the quota of intelligence to be found among our commanders . . . does not exist in *any* other group of people in Germany. . . . Second, for their part the generals would have the chance to get to know their Kaiser. If His Majesty presides as he did in the Council of State he will make an impression on the leaders of his army which they are unlikely ever to forget . . . It is important the the army should acquire such an impression of its Supreme Commander, perhaps soon, for who knows what fate has in store for us!'[103] As was his wont, Eulenburg immediately forwarded this letter to the Kaiser, and when the Grand Duke of Baden returned to Berlin on

8 March Marshall succeeded in convincing him too that 'the Kaiser ought to listen to the commanding generals'. As we shall see, they were summoned to Berlin for 18 March 1890.[104]

The arrival of the Grand Duke in Berlin after an absence of two months led to a marked intensification of the long-drawn-out crisis in which the German government had found itself since the autumn of 1889. Waldersee noted in his diary that the Grand Duke was 'very concerned about the state of affairs' which he had found in the capital, and was pressing for decisive action. 'He sees the full extent of the rift between Kaiser and Chancellor; the former has also talked quite openly about it and said that the Chancellor is continuing to intrigue against him; but nevertheless he wants to keep him for the time being and behave outwardly as if he were on good terms with him. The Grand Duke now thinks, quite rightly, that this state of affairs ought not to go on for too long, and that it is not a good thing for it to become gradually obvious to the whole world that the Kaiser is play-acting. The Grand Duke is very worried about the elections; he says that in South Germany a very marked hostility to the Reich has emerged', partly due to 'antagonism against the Chancellor'.[105] Grand Duke Friedrich was also anxious, however, about the planned Army Bill. On 11 March he had a discussion with Waldersee and the War Minister which shocked him deeply and which was to trigger the last phase of the chancellor crisis. He discovered that these two very senior military figures, and other generals too, were by no means unwilling to make far-reaching concessions to the Reichstag in order to obtain the expansion of the army which they sought. 'What kind of men are these?', exclaimed Marschall with horror on hearing this from the Grand Duke. 'Two-year military service, the strength of the army establishment to be fixed annually — they are prepared to trade it all off!'[106] The Baden envoy hurried to the Foreign Office to convey his master's urgent plea to Holstein that he should get Eulenburg to leave Oldenburg for Berlin at once. The Grand Duke had 'learned from highly placed people that there is an immediate danger of a conflict either at home or abroad'. Marschall and Holstein, 'seriously perturbed and worried', joined in the plea to Eulenburg to come quickly; they were convinced that 'every hour is of value for the Kaiser'. Eulenburg should pretend that his sudden departure was a matter of private business; he should telegraph from Hanover, not from Oldenburg, to let them know the time of his arrival in Berlin, and even then he should not sign his name. Paul Kayser was to know nothing of the visit. Holstein gave no hint of the reason for this panic-stricken appeal; he merely told Eulenburg that the summons had nothing to do with the international social welfare conference. 'Much may go against our wishes at the conference, but the Kaiser's future does not depend upon it.'[107]

Eulenburg hesitated. He complained of nervous ailments in the head and stomach, said that he was expecting a visit from his mother and maintained that he could in any case do no more than mediate, which the Grand Duke of Baden, as the Kaiser's uncle, could do just as well. On the other hand, he cautioned, the Grand Duke was inclined 'to look on the dark side', and the 'feverish atmosphere' which pervaded Berlin had evidently affected and alarmed him, so that he was convinced that a great crisis was inevitable. But of course if the Kaiser had decided to dismiss Bismarck, Eulenburg observed, his own mediation would not be needed.[108]

Even before he had time to find out more about the concessions Verdy and Waldersee were willing to make on the Army Bill, news reached Eulenburg of another sensational development in Berlin. On 12 March 1890 Bismarck had a meeting with the leader of the Catholic Centre, Ludwig Windthorst, to discuss co-operation with the latter's party in the Reichstag. During the interview Bismarck made no secret of the fact that he needed the support of the Centre 'in order to hold his own'. It would be impossible for him to remain in office unless 'the Centre supported his policy in the Reichstag and in the [Prussian] Chamber of Deputies', he admitted. 'Would Windthorst be inclined to do this?' The two erstwhile arch-enemies then discussed the terms of a possible collaboration and seemed to agree in principle. Subsequently Bismarck brought up the demands of the Centre with regard to schools and the possible readmission of the Redemptorist order to Germany for discussion in the Prussian Ministry of State. After Bismarck's dismissal Windthorst remarked to a colleague that 'from our point of view B[ismarck] certainly left office too soon'; only he would have had the necessary authority to dismantle the *Kulturkampf* legislation.[109]

The news of this meeting, which Bismarck made no effort to keep secret, aroused 'anxious misgivings' in the 'patriotic souls' of the Holstein circle. 'Saving the Reich with the aid of the Jesuitical Guelphs is really the limit!', exclaimed Paul Kayser indignantly. The worst thing, however, was that Bismarck had set his 'machinations' in train *without the Kaiser having any idea of it*. The Chancellor was exploiting the fact that the Kaiser was in favour of the Army Bill in order to lure him on to thin ice. The Progressive Party was prepared to accept the Army Bill in return for the concession of two-year military service and annual army budgets; Windthorst would accept triennial budgets, but only in return for concessions in the sphere of ecclesiastical policy. 'At home he will perhaps be content with the Redemptorists and the fall of Lutz's government [in Bavaria] – the Jesuits will be next, and the schools will become the victims of Catholicism. Abroad some concession will have to be made to the Papacy … That will jeopardise the alliance with Italy, and the way overtures are being made to

Russia shows that in any case it is considered unimportant if the Triple Alliance is destroyed.' The common denominator in all these intrigues was Bismarck's desire to deprive the Kaiser of his power. 'Every possible trick is being tried in the art of complicating matters', Kayser warned. 'It is a time-honoured practice, and it left Wilhelm I helpless, so that he had to give his Minister complete freedom of action. Will Wilhelm II be the same? A great turning-point seems to have been reached. For the Kaiser, the crossing of the Rubicon would in this case be a pilgrimage to Canossa.'[110]

In Marschall's view it was now beyond doubt that 'Prince Bismarck is continuing to use all possible methods not only to prevent a positive success for His Majesty in the field of social welfare, but to oppose His Majesty's intentions in everything, leading domestic policy not on to the path of reform but into the ways of scandal, provocation and confusion. As soon as his plan for a more severe Anti-Socialist Bill had failed, the Reich Chancellor threw himself with his characteristic energy into promoting the Army Bill . . . I am no army officer . . . but in *political* terms I am absolutely convinced that if this bomb is thrown into the new Reichstag, not only will His Majesty's initiative in social welfare policy be pushed completely into the background, but we shall be heading for chaos at home.' The concessions which were required in order to obtain a majority for the bill could not be made. But if an *Army* Bill were rejected, the Reichstag would have to be dissolved, Marschall observed. 'One does not need much political foresight to imagine the consequences which a dissolution of the Reichstag, say in June this year, would entail. To hold a new election which the opposition could turn into a plebiscite on the length of military service would in my view be no less than to destroy the already weakened government parties and to create a Reichstag which it would be impossible to live with.' The introduction of the huge Army Bill would amount to a direct negation of the calm, measured, reforming policy which the Kaiser had rightly initiated, Marschall argued. 'That the Reich Chancellor is now rushing ahead with the bill although until recently he opposed it, is symptomatic of the situation. The Social Welfare Bill is to be destroyed, and the Reichstag blown sky-high – then the time could come when the propertied classes regard the Reich Chancellor as the only saviour in their hour of need.'[111] A Prussian minister with whom Marschall discussed the situation agreed with him in thinking that Bismarck was trying to use the Army Bill, as he had done with the Anti-Socialist Bill earlier, to destroy the Kaiser's power. His 'transparent' aim was 'to blow up the Reichstag so as to wreck the Kaiser's social welfare programme and to create the measure of confusion in Germany which Bismarck needs in order to make himself indispensable'.[112] Eulenburg's decision to forward this letter from Marschall to the Kaiser on 14 March also contributed to the final break between Wilhelm and Bismarck, particularly as

even Waldersee wrote to the Kaiser to say that in his opinion Bismarck's plans
to dissolve the Reichstag again were 'an absolute disaster'.[113] So the moment of
truth was now imminent.


## 'THE GREAT CLASH'

After a meeting with Wilhelm II on 9 March 1890 Waldersee recorded that
the Kaiser, who had good sources of information, had heard that Bismarck had
complained about him to the French ambassador. Wilhelm had nevertheless
declared: 'I think it expedient to keep him on for the time being, and I am
therefore acting as if I had not noticed how badly he is behaving towards me;
and I shall dine with him again very soon so that people think that we are on
good terms.'[114] Four days later the Chief of the General Staff was still able to
observe that only a very small inner circle was aware of the 'breach between the
Kaiser and the Chancellor'. Even in the Foreign Office there was 'a certain sense
of oppression, without anyone believing that a catastrophe was in the offing'.
True, a few people were expecting that the Chancellor would 'quit the helm'; but
others believed that 'the Chancellor could still recover the upper hand'. On the
same day, however, Waldersee noted that Windthorst's visit to the Chancellor
had had a decisive effect 'in all right-thinking circles'.[115]

The news of Bismarck's interview with the leader of the Centre Party was
like a red rag to a bull in its effect on Wilhelm II. But his anger grew beyond all
bounds when he learned that the meeting had come about through the mediation of the Jewish banker Bleichröder. In the eyes of Wilhelm and Waldersee
the Bismarck-Bleichröder-Windthorst combination confirmed their own lurid
vision of Bismarck's rule as a thoroughly corrupt system under Jewish domination. At the end of January 1890, after the first bitter argument with the Chancellor, Waldersee had already noted that there were 'other reasons for ill-feeling'
between Wilhelm II and Bismarck, and that these were 'the most important
thing'. 'It has become clear to the Kaiser that the Chancellor has considerable
dealings with the stock exchange, especially with Bleichröder, and furthermore
he thinks it quite likely – as indeed everyone claims – that the reason why the
Chancellor constantly postpones the long-promised tax reform is merely that
he has discovered that he will have to pay far more, and in particular he will
have to declare the extent of his fortune, which is probably colossal.'[116] A few
observers who knew Bismarck well went further still, the Chief of the General
Staff recorded in February. 'People are even wicked enough to believe that he
makes Bleichröder work in his interest. Herr Schwabach has also been received
by the Chancellor.'[117] In view of such suspicions one can hardly be surprised
at the Kaiser's remark on 15 March 1890 to Generals Waldersee, Hahnke and

Wittich that he was convinced that Bleichröder's mediation between Bismarck and Windthorst meant that there was 'collusion between the Jesuits and the rich Jews'.[118]

The anti-Semitic Chief of the General Staff, as we know, had long harboured a deep personal antipathy towards Bismarck. Now, in the last phase of the chancellor crisis, he exercised a malign influence over Wilhelm through a constant and poisonous whispering campaign against his enemy. At the beginning of March 1890 he wrote contemptuously of Bismarck: 'I have not the least desire ever to have any dealings with him again; he has acted despicably towards me too often and I want no more to do with him; the only question, now that he is in decline, is whether I should forgive him everything or call him to account for it.'[119] Waldersee found it 'incomprehensible' that Bismarck had not resigned long ago. The only reason he could think of for the Chancellor's remaining, he said, was 'that he cannot leave because he is afraid of his successor and of the anger which will be unleashed in many whom he has oppressed, lied to and deceived. One already hears it said that he has a very bad character; he has not hesitated to disclaim his friends and those who have helped him most; lying has become a habit with him; he has made use of his official position to enrich himself on a colossal scale and has had his sons promoted with unbelievable ruthlessness although no one thinks them competent!' In spite of Bismarck's outstanding achievements at times of conflict and in the wars of unification, which would ensure him 'an exalted place in history for all times', the Chancellor's 'great errors of judgement' had begun immediately after the establishment of the Reich. Since 1871 his government had been 'permeated with too much evil passion, which detracts greatly from its fine appearance'. In the end, history would judge Bismarck harshly, Waldersee predicted.[120] When the Berlin stock exchange suffered a sharp fall at the beginning of March in the wake of the Bismarck crisis, Waldersee saw that too as 'a trumped-up show by the big capitalists, above all Bleichröder', behind whom stood Bismarck. One could be sure, he claimed, that the Jews would use Bismarck's fall to bring about 'a massive slump', for 'no harm can come to these people as a result; on the contrary, fluctuations always bring them profit; the people who pay the bill are the small speculators and people of limited means, who are naturally very anxious'.[121] The Jews were 'mostly fellows with no homeland, who have no interest in anything but making money, and who − wonder of wonders − mostly support the Progressives, and often even vote for Socialists at elections'.[122] On this point too the Kaiser was of the same mind as Waldersee and saw 'the downward trend of the stock exchange ... as a trumped-up show', although he was content to 'let it take its course'.[123]

It was yet another issue which proved to be the last straw. This was the Cabinet Order of 1852, mentioned earlier in this chapter, under which the minister-president had to be informed whenever another minister wished to make a report to the monarch. After many days of searching the order was eventually found, and Bismarck read it out to the Prussian ministers – with the exception of the minister for war, who had direct access to the Kaiser as supreme war lord – and asked them to act accordingly.[124] At the same time he pointed out that 'in the German Reich . . . according to the constitution, the Reich Chancellor is the only minister', which meant that direct contact between the secretaries of state of the Reich offices and the Kaiser was not permissible.[125] It was the Chancellor's last attempt to recover his monopoly of power over the central apparatus of government.[126]

On 15 March 1890 Waldersee recorded in his diary: 'The great clash has come!'[127] Bismarck's own description of the dramatic collision between him and the Kaiser in his son's official residence that morning is among the most striking and best-known passages in his memoirs. At 9 a.m. he had been awoken with the news that the Kaiser expected to receive him in audience at the Foreign Office in half an hour's time. The 75-year-old Chancellor did not believe Wilhelm's excuse that he had given the order the previous afternoon. Bismarck began the audience by stating that Windthorst had come to see him, whereupon the Kaiser exclaimed: 'Well, of course you had him thrown out?' The Reich Chancellor tried to explain that he had not only had the right, but the official duty, to find out the intentions of the leader of what was now the strongest party in the Reichstag. When the Kaiser insisted that the Chancellor ought to have 'asked him about it first', Bismarck that he could not allow 'my personal freedom of movement in my own house' to be subject to control. The Kaiser's characteristic retort was 'Not even when your sovereign commands it?' Wilhelm went on to complain that Windthorst's visit had been arranged through Bleichröder – 'Jews and Jesuits', he declared, always acted hand in glove. The Chancellor pointed out that it was not he but the Centre Party leader who had asked Bleichröder to mediate. The Kaiser then suddenly changed the subject to the Cabinet Order of 1852, which he described as 'a dusty old order . . . which had been long forgotten'. Bismarck stood his ground with the young monarch, maintaining that the order 'had been in force as long as our constitution had existed' and that a minister-president could not carry the entire responsibility for government policy without such a regulation. 'His Majesty's three predecessors' had all governed the country under this order. Wilhelm II, however, maintained that it restricted his royal prerogative and peremptorily demanded its withdrawal. Finally Bismarck seized the offensive: taking up a handful of secret reports on Tsar Alexander's current attitude, he strongly advised the Kaiser to cancel the visit to Russia which he had announced. Wilhelm took the papers from Bismarck's hand and was 'quite rightly hurt' and 'undoubtedly deeply insulted' by the reports they contained of remarks made by Alexander III about him and his last visit to St Petersburg. The whole audience, according to Bismarck's account, gave him the impression 'that the Kaiser wanted to be rid of me, that he had altered his intention of going through the initial negotiations with the new Reichstag with me, and of waiting until early summer, when it would be clear whether the dissolution of the new Reichstag would be necessary or not, before deciding on the question of parting with me'. Nevertheless the Chancellor refused to allow himself to be provoked into resigning by the 'ungracious behaviour' of his King. He was still of the opinion, he wrote, 'that it is not for me to take the initiative and thereby assume the responsibility for my own departure'.[128]

So much for Bismarck's own, highly compelling account of the clash on 15 March 1890, from which Wilhelm II emerges with little credit. But how did Wilhelm himself see this decisive quarrel? Only a few days after what had probably been one of the most powerful scenes ever played out in the Wilhelmstrasse, the Kaiser gave the British ambassador an emotional account of how Bismarck had become 'so violent . . . that I did not know whether he would not throw the inkstand at my head'.[129] Years later the Kaiser still recalled that the Chancellor had lost his self-control to such an extent that he might almost have struck him, his King, dead. 'The "Old Man" was raging with anger that day – whipped up beforehand by those villains Herbert and Lerchenfeld – so much so that I could not get a word in, and he seized the inkstand and threatened me with it, quite senseless with fury and forgetting himself completely. That was the first "outward" cause of his dismissal', he wrote in his own hand in the winter of 1903.[130]

Immediately after the violent set-to between Wilhelm and the Reich Chancellor, Waldersee arrived at the Schloss with Hahnke, the Chief of the Military Cabinet, and Adjutant-General von Wittich to report to the Kaiser. The Chief of the General Staff wrote a lengthy and hitherto largely unknown account of what had happened at the Wilhelmstrasse. According to this account, Wilhelm began the meeting with his top generals by announcing 'I have just come from seeing the Chancellor.' He went on: 'We had a serious dispute which will probably bring things to an end, and it is my wish that you should be aware of the whole episode. I told the Chancellor that it was not acceptable for him to enter into negotiations with Herr Windhorst [sic] at the present moment without telling me about it beforehand. He responded at once with great vehemence that as responsible minister-president he could receive whomever he wished; moreover he was cleverer than Windhorst and had no one else who could negotiate with him. On my replying that I must insist on my right to be informed in advance, and that at this moment negotiations with the Centre would make the worst possible impression in the country, and that I had heard only last night from Herr v.

Helldorff that the Conservatives would dissociate themselves from government policy at once, and that it gave me great cause for concern that Bleichröder had been the intermediary, he became absolutely enraged and talked nonsense, for instance saying that he was surrounded by spies, forgetting that his meeting with Windhorst had been reported in all the newspapers; sometimes he became subdued and even wept.' 'I am convinced', the Kaiser continued, 'that there is collusion between the Jesuits and the rich Jews. A second cause of conflict was his order to the ministers – on the basis of a Cabinet Order of 1852 – not to make any direct reports to me. After a violent argument I ordered him to submit a new order to me, suspending that of 1852.' Following this peroration from the Kaiser, Waldersee ventured the opinion that 'in spite of all this the Chancellor would not hand in his resignation, for he clung to office too much; he could not go because he would be leaving too much dirty linen behind, his son would not be his successor after all, and finally because by holding on he still hoped to regain the upper hand, and unfortunately also because he was too closely allied with the Jews and could not escape from them. But as the present situation was quite untenable it would be best, if he did not seek his own discharge, to *give* it to him, and as soon as possible.' 'Both Wittich and Hahnke agreed with that', Waldersee recorded. 'But the Kaiser replied that he would prefer the Chancellor to tender his own resignation, as it would look better in the eyes of the world.' At this, Waldersee made his final pitch against Bismarck by giving the Kaiser 'for the first time, a frank account of my views on the Chancellor, without sparing him anything. Hahnke and Wittich were astonished, but the Kaiser not at all; he was very well aware of the various accusations I had to make. Among other things I said: he has been very skilful in maintaining his reputation as a past master in handling foreign affairs, and as irreplaceable in that respect. But it seems to me that the situation in which we find ourselves is a not a good one; with all his skill he has not succeeded in preventing both France and Russia becoming our enemies, and growing stronger and bolder year by year. This is really a very serious state of affairs! Your Majesty has taken over the Reich at a very difficult time.' To this the Kaiser replied: 'It is strange, Herr v. Helldorff put exactly the same argument to me yesterday evening and thought it absolutely justified. Things are indeed going very badly with Russia at the moment; strong opposition is being whipped up against me and Tsar Alexander speaks of me in the most derogatory way; among other things he says I am mad. The ill-feeling towards us is constantly growing, and I shall not go to Krasnoe under any circumstances. As for our domestic affairs, everyone can see that things look very bad. What is the great Chancellor doing about that? What services has he rendered?' Waldersee derived some satisfaction from these remarks, since 'this was how I had seen the situation for years, but I was rarely believed'. He went on to record how the conversation ended. 'After much discussion of the Chancellor's outrageous behaviour in making derogatory remarks about the Kaiser to foreign diplomats I said finally: "As things stand, it is impossible for Your Majesty to do business with the Chancellor any longer. The present situation is intolerable for You and harmful for the Fatherland. I suggest that Your Majesty should come to a firm decision on the persons to appoint, and then act." In conclusion I added: "God grant that Your Majesty may hold Your head up high and direct Your choice to the right people." He then gave me his hand and said, "I think all will be well", adding "Good hunting!" in his usual lively manner. I replied in kind, "Good hunting."'[131]

Since Bismarck refused to resign of his own accord and Wilhelm was reluctant to take on himself the odium of dismissing the Chancellor, the next two days saw both attempting to seize the tactical advantage. On 16 March the Kaiser sent the Chief of his Military Cabinet to Bismarck with instructions to demand 'the order . . . or his resignation!'[132] Bismarck repeated his contention of the previous day that the minister-president could not function without the rights assured him by the Cabinet Order; if the Kaiser abolished the order, 'the title "president of the Ministry of State" would have to be abolished too'. Hahnke returned to the Schloss convinced that he would nevertheless succeed in accomplishing his mission. But when he called on Bismarck again the following morning, this time with the specific order – as the Chancellor recalled – 'that I was to hand in my resignation; I was to come to the Schloss in the afternoon to be released from my duties', Bismarck claimed to be too unwell to do so and said he would write instead.[133] Early that afternoon the Kaiser was able to inform the Chief of the General Staff that 'everything is in order. Hahnke has been to see the Chancellor; he is not sending an order, but his resignation.'[134] When the resignation letter failed to arrive Wilhelm sent Chief of the Civil Cabinet Hermann von Lucanus to the Reich Chancellor's palace to enquire 'why the letter of resignation demanded in the morning has not yet been delivered'. Bismarck responded that the Kaiser could dismiss him at any time without the need for him to tender his resignation. But he was intending, he said, to draw up the letter in such a way that he could publish it. 'I would not presume', he said, 'to take the responsibility for my resignation on myself, but would leave it to His Majesty.' Although Lucanus disputed Bismarck's justification for 'public explanation of the genesis' of his resignation, the Chancellor reiterated that he was tendering his resignation only on the orders of the Kaiser.[135]

One reason for Wilhelm's impatience to secure Bismarck's resignation was that a number of consular reports from Kiev, some of them long out of date, happened to be submitted to him at precisely this tense moment. Not only did these lead him to believe that a Russian attack on Austria was imminent; he was also convinced that Bismarck had tried to conceal the reports from him. On the morning of 17 March he told Waldersee that he had 'discovered that the Chancellor had held back many reports from Russia from him, and that things looked much worse there than he could have known; only recently the Chancellor had had an important report from Odessa about armaments filed away without submitting it to him first'. Instead of trying to calm the Kaiser down Waldersee fanned the flames of his anger, no doubt still hoping that his own appointment as Reich chancellor was not far off. 'A great deal of wrong has been done in this way and that is one of the reasons why the Chancellor cannot leave his post. He has too much dirty linen to hide', he told the Kaiser.[136] Bismarck was incredulous at these new accusations from the Kaiser, especially as they concerned his conduct of foreign policy, which he had always regarded as his forte. 'So, because a consul had reported on a few military events within his purview, some of them three months old . . . Austria was to be put on the alert, Russia threatened, preparations for war put in hand, and the visit which His Majesty himself had announced on his own initiative, cancelled; and because the consul's reports had arrived late, I was implicitly accused of high treason', he wrote in his memoirs. He went on to point to the 'caprices of fate' by which, the very day on which he was accused of suppressing the news of an imminent Russian attack, the Russian ambassador had called on him to announce that he had been authorised to negotiate with him the renewal of the Reinsurance Treaty, which was due to run out in June 1890![137] At the special sitting of the Ministry of State which Bismarck convened in his official residence on 17 March, the Reich Chancellor was thus able to make it appear that the fact 'that he could no longer support His Majesty's foreign policy' was the principal reason for his resignation.[138] He did it again with a vengeance in his celebrated resignation letter of 18 March 1890.[139]

That evening all the commanding generals and inspector generals of the army assembled in the Schloss. In an address lasting some twenty minutes, spoken according to Waldersee 'with great composure', the Kaiser set out his differences with the Reich Chancellor, and explained 'that in order to remain master of the situation he had had to issue an ultimatum to him insisting that he submit. The Chancellor had promised to tender his resignation; he would accept it and appoint Gen[eral] Caprivi Chancellor. Then the Kaiser spoke of our relations with Russia, which were bad, but about which the Chancellor had tried to deceive him.' He would never permit the Russians to invade Bulgaria, he added, for he had 'sworn to keep faith with the Emperor of Austria the previous year, and would hold to it'.[140] None of those present contradicted the Supreme War Lord. Only as they left was the old Field Marshal General von Moltke overheard to remark: 'Our young master will give us a lot to think about.'[141]

### THE BISMARCK CRISIS: A POWER STRUGGLE BETWEEN
### KAISER AND CHANCELLOR

The confused story of Bismarck's dismissal is often, and quite rightly, presented as the end of a long and successful epoch, the story of the 'decline and fall from power' of the founder of the Reich.[142] But at the same time it was also a beginning, the story of a young ruler's assumption of power, the birth of a new, completely different system of government with new values and a new style. Indeed Bismarck's dismissal can only be understood at all as the conflict between two powerful men and the two systems of government which they embodied. For some of those involved – second-ranking figures like Paul Kayser, for instance – the conflict may have been about a particular cause; but for the main actors in the drama almost all differences of opinion on objective issues were secondary, as we have repeatedly seen. Throughout the months over which the dismissal crisis was played out the real issue was the struggle for power. On both sides the attitude taken to the ostensible cause of conflict usually depended on the advantage that could be derived from it and the damage that could be inflicted on the other camp. The true cause of the bitter feud can be detected in numerous remarks by those involved. At the end of January 1890, for instance, when the crisis had just entered its most acute phase, Wilhelm II's closest confidant, Waldersee, noted: 'The Kaiser is hurt that the Chancellor always makes his newspapers refer to "the Chancellor's policy"; he wants to be regarded as having the overall direction of policy himself.'[143] Prince Heinrich, the Kaiser's brother, rightly observed that Bismarck's resignation was 'the natural outcome of the growing independence of the Kaiser'.[144] Wilhelm himself confirmed this view of the crisis when he spoke in April 1890 of Bismarck's 'open disobedience and perfidy', and exclaimed: 'The Hohenzollern dynasty is surely worth enough not to have to give way to Bismarck.'[145] The Kaiser's tutor Hinzpeter was convinced that the only historically correct interpretation of Bismarck's dismissal was that it was 'an act of self-defence of the monarchy against the looming danger of strangulation by a bureaucracy which had become too powerful in the person of the Chancellor'.[146] Hinzpeter went further still. Perhaps the person who knew his pupil's character better than anyone else, he commented later that, for Wilhelm II, Bismarck's dismissal had been 'a natural desire to save his own personality'. This desire was 'particularly strong' in him, 'even stronger than all other tendencies and intentions, as was indeed seen in 1890'.[147] Similar psychological interpretations of Bismarck's attitude were also current. Paul Kayser, for instance, expressed the opinion in early March 1890, when the Chancellor's dismissal had already been decided upon and was only a matter of time, that his resistance to the social welfare programme could really only be explained as the 'psychological process in the soul of a powerful man ... who after years of absolute monarchy [sic] feels threatened in his *monopoly* of power'.[148]

There were, admittedly, a few exceptional instances on both sides when inner conviction or personal passion played a greater role than tactical manoeuvring for political advantage. Wilhelm II's suspicions about the intentions of the Russian army or his constantly recurring feelings of hatred for 'Jesuits and Jews' are examples of this. It is more difficult to find instances when Bismarck was driven by conviction. His insistence, during the final clash with Wilhelm, on his right to receive any member of parliament whenever he wished in his own house, and on his right as minister-president to be informed of the intentions of any of his ministerial colleagues before they reported personally to the Kaiser, may seem to have been a matter of immutable conviction. Yet in both cases it was a question of repudiating imperial demands which would have strengthened the power of the monarch enormously while reducing that of the chancellor beyond recognition, had Bismarck given way. Moreover, in this final conflict between the Kaiser and the Chancellor on 15 March 1890 it was already so evident that Wilhelm intended to dismiss Bismarck that the latter would certainly have been on the look-out for tactically advantageous reasons for his retirement. The claim which was put about from Friedrichsruh very soon after the dismissal, and which proved so damaging to the Hohenzollern monarchy, namely that Bismarck had been anxious about Wilhelm's sanity and had wanted to stay in office only in order to rescue his life's work, was only the logical continuation of this struggle for power by other means.

But apart from these very few exceptions, was there a single difference of opinion between the young monarch and his 75-year-old opponent which was not determined principally by tactical considerations, in the long crisis which lasted from the summer of 1889 until March 1890? Ever since Wilhelm attended the Stoecker meeting of November 1887, his and his wife's intellectual affinity with the orthodox right wing of the German Conservative Party had been common knowledge. That he continued to hold these views inwardly is very clearly confirmed by Waldersee's diary. Yet at the instigation of Holstein, Eulenburg and Hinzpeter, who suspected that Bismarck might change tack and form a blue–black coalition dangerous to the monarchy, the Kaiser repeatedly and demonstratively spoke up for the Kartell parties, thus securing himself the support of the moderate Conservative and National Liberal bourgeoisie in the coming conflict with the Chancellor. Wilhelm II's initiative on social welfare policy may well have had its roots in earlier Christian charitable impulses implanted by Hinzpeter, but the actual motive behind it in January 1890 was his quest for popularity among the masses and his determination to take personal control of policy in this field at least. Wilhelm himself revealed how small a part inner conviction played in this dramatic intervention in social policy when he declared to Waldersee on 7 February 1890: 'I want to do all I can and I would not wish to be accused later of having failed to do anything. We shall soon see; if it does not work, at least I have done my duty.'[149] And yet from the moment he took action – from the Crown Council on 24 January and the issue of the uncounter-signed imperial proclamations on 4 February 1890 – there was no going back for Wilhelm II. From then on Bismarck's every action was judged not for its intrinsic worth but only for its capacity to endanger, or even merely to over-shadow, the Kaiser's social reform initiative and hence his reputation and future position. We have seen how several members of the Kaiser's coterie of advisers, Waldersee and Eulenburg in particular, were convinced of the need for a *coup d'état* to revise the constitution and do away with universal suffrage, especially after the catastrophic Reichstag election results of 20 and 27 February. But all agreed that this solution was impracticable *for the time being*, since a policy of force would simply have restored Bismarck's power and made the Kaiser's social reform initiative look like a ludicrous blunder. In the Kaiser's camp there was a strong feeling that a major Army Bill was needed – indeed, barely a year later the Kaiser was to give orders to the new Chancellor Caprivi to introduce just such a bill[150] – yet when on 12 March 1890 Bismarck put out feelers towards the Centre Party, whose support in the Reichstag was now indispensable for all legislation, his action was regarded by all the Kaiser's advisers as an attempt to destabilise the situation and permanently undermine the Kaiser's authority. As Marschall von Bieberstein put it: the Chancellor's goal was 'to blow the Reichs-tag sky-high, so as to frustrate the Kaiser's social reform plans and cause the degree of confusion in Germany which Prince Bismarck needs in order to prove himself indispensable'.[151]

Clearly, in this struggle for power the Kaiser had seized the initiative while the Chancellor had been forced on to the defensive from the start. Wilhelm's starting-point had been his inherited power, above all as king of Prussia and supreme war lord, and his extensive military and aristocratic court. Since mid-1889, however, an influential clique of advisers had formed around Friedrich von Holstein and Count Philipp zu Eulenburg, which had been joined by the envoy from Baden, Adolf Freiherr Marschall von Bieberstein, the Director of the Colonial Department Dr Paul Kayser and the journalist Dr Franz Fischer, and which also maintained close contact with Waldersee as Chief of the General Staff, Wilhelm II's former tutor Hinzpeter, and Grand Duke Friedrich of Baden. This secret and completely informal group was almost always extremely well informed about Bismarck's views and intentions – it was not for nothing that he complained of being surrounded by spies – while he had scarcely an inkling of the existence of the clique and its machinations. He blamed people who had no part whatever in the crisis, such as Count Douglas and the painter Heyden, and regarded his unfortunate deputy, Heinrich von Boetticher, as the worst of traitors. Even when writing his memoirs in exile at Friedrichsruh he had to admit that he had still not discovered, 'with any reliable certainty, the true reason for the break'.[152]

In the battle for power Bismarck's strength – apart, of course, from his incomparable political skill and his enormous prestige after twenty-eight years in power – lay in his rigorous control of the central apparatus of the state. We have seen how the Kaiser tried to circumvent this stronghold in the first weeks of the conflict by appealing for the support of the federal princes, in particular the Grand Duke of Baden and the King of Saxony. He pursued the same aim later by convening the Prussian Council of State and the international conference on social welfare, and finally by holding the meeting of commanding generals. But inevitably the real core of the conflict was the struggle for control of the power of the state. All Bismarck's attempts to reduce his own power to a degree acceptable to Wilhelm by giving up his Prussian offices were frustrated, both by the indissolubility of the symbiotic relationship between Prussia and the Reich and by the personal 'constitutional responsibility' which he held.[153] The stronghold of state power could not be bypassed. It was thus entirely within the logic of the situation that the final clash between Kaiser and Chancellor on 15 March was not a question of material differences of opinion, but of which of them had the right to negotiate with the Prussian ministers and the party leaders in the Reichstag.

With Bismarck's removal the way now lay open for Kaiser Wilhelm II to take over personal control of German policy. The dangers which this entailed for the monarchy were clearly recognised by none other than his tutor Hinzpeter. Writing to the future Minister for Ecclesiastical Affairs, Konrad Studt, five years after the event, he said of Bismarck's dismissal: 'That catastrophe was nothing other than an attempt by the monarchy to free itself from the suffocating hold of the bureaucracy. It seems that by an extraordinary effort of strength the attempt succeeded. The responsibility which the monarchy thereby took upon itself is very great. If it does not prove itself equal to this responsibility, it has incurred a danger which may bring about its destruction.'[154]

# CHAPTER THIRTEEN

# The haphazard transition: from the Bismarcks to the New Course

## 'WHAT A DAGGER IN MY HEART!'

IMMEDIATELY after the fall of Bismarck the battle to win the approval of governments abroad and of public opinion at home, which had been fundamental to the dismissal crisis from the outset, was resumed by both sides by other means. The founder of the Reich appeared in public more often in the eight days following his resignation than had been his custom in a whole year.[1] Deeply offended and angry, he took care to spread his own version of his downfall, according to which he had been 'thrown out' by a Kaiser who was perhaps not entirely of sound mind.[2] Herbert Bismarck had resigned with his father, and he and his mother talked of the Kaiser 'in the most disrespectful terms'.[3] Even before he left Berlin Prince Bismarck made it clear that he intended to create a 'Fronde' against the Kaiser. He had a 'stormy' interview with the Grand Duke of Baden during which he accused the Kaiser's uncle of interfering in matters which concerned only the Reich Chancellor. Tempers ran so high that the Grand Duke stormed out of the room.[4] After months of attempts by Bismarck and Wilhelm to take advantage of each other, Wilhelm suddenly could not do enough to soften the disastrous impression that the dismissal of the founder of the Reich was bound to make. He heaped Bismarck with titles and honours, offered him the Reich Chancellor's palace as his permanent home[5] and sent telegrams and lengthy self-justifying letters to Emperor Franz Joseph, Queen Victoria and others, in which he portrayed the resignation as an act of mercy which had become necessary for the sake of a highly meritorious but now regrettably dangerously unwell old servant. He went so far that even his Flügeladjutanten occasionally had the impression that he would have preferred to call Bismarck back.[6]

The Kaiser's tactic of killing his opponent with kindness was already apparent at the moment of Bismarck's dismissal. On 20 March 1890 Cabinet Chiefs von Hahnke and von Lucanus appeared at the Reich Chancellor's palace with two formal letters in which the Kaiser, while accepting the Prince's resignation 'with a heavy heart', conferred on him the Dukedom of Lauenburg (which Bismarck declined with the caustic remark that, at most, he would use the title if ever he wanted to travel incognito)[7] and announced that he had been appointed colonel-general with the rank of field marshal.[8] On 22 March (his grandfather's birthday) he sent Hinzpeter a hypocritical telegram undoubtedly intended for publication in which he lamented: 'My heart is as heavy as if I had lost my grandfather again! But it was destined by God, and so I must bear it, even if it should destroy me. The position of Officer of the Watch on the Ship of State has fallen to me. We must continue to steer the old course: and so full steam ahead!'[9]

If the reaction to Bismarck's fall was at first astonishingly calm in most parts of Germany, in the capitals of Europe there was considerable anxiety at the idea that the powerful German Reich was now to be governed by an 'immature youth' of thirty-one. The mood in Russia was carefully analysed by a young diplomat in St Petersburg who was destined to have the task, as ambassador in 1914, of transmitting the German declaration of war to Russia. In a private letter to Friedrich von Holstein of 20–1 March 1890, the First Secretary at the German embassy, Count Friedrich von Pourtalès, stated that there was great consternation in the Russian capital at events in Berlin, not only because Bismarck had pursued a distinctly pro-Russian policy and had served as the guarantor of peaceful existence between the two empires – the Reich Chancellor even told the Russian ambassador that he had been dismissed because of his pro-Russian policy[10] – but also because the relationship between Alexander III and Wilhelm II, which was in any case tense, had been further strained by Wilhelm's pro-labour initiative. There was 'the utmost astonishment' in St Petersburg, Pourtalès reported, 'that the Kaiser can have brought himself to accept his [Bismarck's] resignation'. The decision had given the Russian government all the more cause for concern because 'the Kaiser's recent activities in the field of social welfare' had seemed 'highly suspect to the Tsar' and had alienated him even more from the German monarch. Pourtalès also described the recent rapid change in Russian opinion of 'our young ruler'. 'Only a few months ago all that was known of him was that he liked travelling about and spreading alarm, and would occasionally deliver a fiery speech.' But since Bismarck was in charge, this behaviour had been regarded 'with a certain rather malicious pleasure'. 'Things are now substantially changed. Various events have taught the Russians that Kaiser Wilhelm II represents a force to be reckoned with. But his most recent conduct has at the same time provoked a change in anti-German circles here.' Among the Russian middle classes, in which 'democratic ideas are widely disseminated', the traditional hatred for Germany had given way to a more positive mood as a result of Willhelm II's initiative on social welfare. 'On the other hand recent events in Germany have caused some shaking of heads in conservative circles . . . where monarchical considerations still caused many people to desire co-operation with Germany; these events . . . have destroyed any remaining spark . . . of desire to be on good terms with us. These circles see our young Kaiser's behaviour as the action of a frivolous young man who is thereby undermining his own throne and the monarchical principle in general. In these circles I heard it said repeatedly yesterday that Prince Bismarck's resignation makes war seem more likely.'[11]

Another future ambassador, Count Anton Monts, who was at this time serving at the German embassy in Vienna, sent an equally pessimistic report on 24 March on the reaction in the Austrian capital to Bismarck's dismissal. Writing privately to the imperial Flügeladjutant Carl Count von Wedel, he commented that events in Berlin had made Kaiser Franz Joseph 'very worried; he is afraid of war and of unpleasant surprises, particularly if our sovereign's social policy should fail and he decided to try his hand at foreign politics'. According to Monts the Austrian people had at first been very much inclined to take Bismarck's side against Wilhelm II, but had since been reassured by the calm atmosphere in Berlin and the striking indifference towards the fall of Bismarck in South Germany. While there was much talk in the Danube monarchy of the ingratitude of the young Kaiser, 'the masses' were visibly impressed by the 'courage and independence of His Majesty'. Statesmen and politicians in Vienna, on the other hand, were 'all very discouraged', Monts continued. 'Uncertainty lay ahead, one was at the mercy of an immature youth who had shown the most unbelievable ingratitude towards his father and towards the benefactor of his dynasty.' The end result, Monts observed, was that 'the deplorable circumstances of the departure, the Fronde which it is unfortunately all too clear the Chancellor has already begun, the immaturity of the decisions taken, in short the last 8 days have used up the entire capital of authority which the great and good Kaiser Wilhelm I and his still greater Chancellor had built up over decades, the interest on which would have sustained the successors of both, and the organs dependent on it, for many years.' It was 'quite impossible to predict' what further consequences there might be, Monts warned, in view of Italy's doubtful fidelity as an ally. 'It is also an immense loss to Salisbury.' 'It is high time', his jeremiad concluded, 'that the sun shone on Germany once more. Since the passing of Kaiser Wilhelm we have had little to rejoice about.'[12] No less concerned than Monts was his superior, the ambassador Prince Heinrich VII von Reuss, who in a letter of 2 April deplored the 'alarming impression' created by Bismarck's dismissal 'in South Germany and abroad', and commented: 'It is impossible not to be anxious about it still, and it has been very severely criticised.'[13]

The Habsburg Emperor was still further unsettled by his correspondence with Bismarck, which left no room for doubt as to the true reasons for the Chancellor's dismissal. In a particularly friendly letter of 22 March Kaiser Franz Joseph (who, it must be remembered, knew nothing of the Russo-German Reinsurance Treaty) thanked Bismarck for his 'consistent and loyal co-operation' and expressed the hope that the 'firm bonds of friendship between Austria and Germany' which Bismarck had forged would be maintained 'in the difficult times in which we live . . . as a sure defence not only for the Allies, but also for the peace of Europe'.[14] The ex-Reich Chancellor's reply made no bones about revealing not only that he had been dismissed against his will, but also that he viewed the future with the greatest possible anxiety. He declared himself convinced that the continuation of the Austro-German alliance would be 'unaffected by any change of ministry' because it was based on 'the unalterable needs of both empires and of their peoples'; but he regretted being unable to carry on working to further 'strengthen and develop these relations and those of the Reich and its princes'. That, however, had not been 'the wish of my all-gracious sovereign', he wrote. 'I have always striven', Bismarck proudly proclaimed, 'to win for our personal monarchy, *qui règne et qui gouverne*, its constitutional right, which has been wrongly obscured, and when I think back to the day in September 1862 when I found my late lamented sovereign in front of the deed of abdication he had himself drawn up, and became his minister, I can claim that since then the authority of the monarchy in Prussia and in the rest of Germany has regained its strength. To strengthen it still further I would gladly have continued to serve my all-gracious sovereign, and my health is still good enough to do so. His Majesty did not allow it, and now I can support our great sovereign only with my prayers.' After which the ex-Chancellor stated, with unequivocal emphasis, 'that I am too dutiful an officer and vassal of my sovereign to desert my post *of my own free will*, in view of the crises which we seem to be facing in the internal affairs of our country'.[15]

It was now Wilhelm II's turn to justify his conduct to the Habsburg monarch.[16] On 3 April he sat down to compose a twenty-page letter, 'written in his own hand and composed absolutely without assistance',[17] which took him two days to finish. This letter, which was delivered to the Austrian Emperor by Carl Wedel, is not only the most complete account of the Bismarck crisis from the young Kaiser's point of view, but also the longest document he wrote during these critical years, and it provides several interesting insights into his mentality at the time. As Prince Bülow was to remark in his memoirs, the document contains numerous 'exaggerations and fantastic notions, not to speak of some palpable untruths'.[18]

Wilhelm began with the affirmation that he considered it his duty, 'given the deep and warm bonds of friendship which unite our countries and above all ourselves', to give his 'dear friend' Franz Joseph 'frankly and clearly a confidential survey of what lay behind, and eventually led to, the resignation of Prince Bismarck'. Contrary to the 'spate of suppositions and deductions in the press' and the 'official and semi-official hints' he wanted to give his imperial ally 'no more than a simple description of the course of events . . . without polemics or criticism'. He wished to observe at the outset, Wilhelm wrote, 'that it was not a matter of foreign policy which gave rise to differences of opinion between the Prince and myself, but purely internal and mostly tactical points of view'. Then he went back in time, tracing the beginning of the crisis to the spring of 1889. 'When the coal strike broke out in May last year and quickly grew to dimensions which threatened the whole nation in every aspect of its working life, once the normal security measures had been taken through troop deployments etc., the causes of the strike were investigated, as is natural. There were consultations in the Ministry of State, with which I did not concern myself at first; meanwhile, however, through my friends – particularly through my tutor, Privy Councillor Hinzpeter, who is Westphalian and lived on the spot – I instigated surveys and investigations concerning the relationship between employers and workmen, the state of the industry etc. . . . Soon, however, the ministers asked me to attend their consultations, as the Prince was quite intractable and the negotiations were not making the slightest progress', Wilhelm claimed, continuing: 'I appeared and assisted. It became clear at once that the Prince took a diametrically opposite view from myself and the ministers. He wanted to let the strike "rage and burn itself out completely" throughout the country. He rejected all notions of the state exercising its authority to intervene and expressed the opinion that that was the industry's own business; it must be allowed to fight out its private feuds. I, on the other hand, was of the opinion that this movement had already gone beyond the bounds of a private industrial dispute, and I found myself in agreement with the entire Ministry of State that if the King did not speedily take this matter in hand, no end of damage and mischief would be done to the country. Accordingly the old officials, who had lost their heads and had only made the confusion worse, were dismissed and replaced by excellent, qualified staff. As soon as that had happened I received deputations from the workers and the proprietors of the mines, which, as is well known, was successful. The Prince disapproved of this action too, for it was clear that he was increasingly inclined to take the side of the big industrialists, and regarded the workers' movement as partly revolutionary and totally unjustified, and thought that it should be curbed and cured with "Blood and Iron" alone, that is to say with grape-shot and repeating rifles.'

Once this crisis was over, Wilhelm continued, 'the Prince withdrew to the country, where he remained for 8–9 months until 25 [sic] January of this year'; what was more, 'during this time he had as good as cut himself off from the rest of the country, and the only person with whom he was in contact regarding the social welfare initiative was the old Commercial Councillor Baare – one of our biggest employers – who was the sworn enemy of this idea'. Wilhelm himself, however, had used this time 'to collect information on social welfare legislation; I sought guidance from all sides on the situation of the workers and on their possible and impossible wishes; I made contact with the Reichstag through its leaders etc. In the autumn I reached the clear conclusion and conviction that time was precious and that it was imperative to tackle the law on social welfare quickly, so that the Social Democrats could not steal a march on us and take up the same cause, which I had clear information that they intended to do. Therefore in the course of the autumn and continuing into January, on three different occasions, I first asked the Prince, then begged him, and finally informed him that it was my wish, that he should start work on amending social welfare legislation and submit an order to me on the subject for publication. He refused this three times very abruptly, saying that he did not wish it, that he was fundamentally opposed to it, and that was the end of the matter. Thereupon I sat down [the Kaiser continued] and worked through 2 nights on a memorandum giving a historical description of industrial relations in our country and indicating a series of principal points which in everyone's view constituted the worst evils, which must be tackled immediately through legislation. As soon as I had finished the memorandum I convened a Council of Ministers and summoned the Prince from Friedrichsruh. During this time the debates on the Anti-Socialist Bill were taking place in the Reichstag. They were very unpleasant, and in the course of them the Kartell parties went over to the opposition, driven to it by the Chancellor's inflexible self-will. They had undertaken to get the bill through for him if he would only declare that the expulsion clause would be formulated as "for consideration" – not dropped. On 25 [sic] January I held the Council of Ministers of State and explained my views on the basis of my memorandum, and concluded with the request that the Ministry should discuss the points in it under the chairmanship of the Prince, and also that an international conference should be convened, and that they should submit two proclamations to me on the subject, for publication. This was followed by a discussion during which the Prince at once repeated, with emphasis, the hostile viewpoint he had taken in the spring [of 1889], and condemned the whole affair as impracticable. The ministers were so afraid of him that none dared venture an opinion on the matter. Finally I came to the expulsion clause in the Anti-Socialist Bill, which was to be accepted or rejected the next day, and I earnestly implored the Prince to help the government parties and save the affair from ending on a note of discord in the Reichstag in such a lamentable way, by holding out the prospect, at the final vote, that the clause would be treated as "to be considered". At the same time I mentioned that I had received the most earnest entreaties on the subject directly from men who were loyal to the King and to the government. By way of answer he flung his resignation at my feet – it hurts me to use the expression – most disrespectfully and curtly. The ministers remained silent and gave me no support. I of course did not accept his resignation, the Prince got his way, the bill was rejected and the Reichstag broke up in an atmosphere of universal rage and displeasure, about which I was regaled with a variety of comments about feebleness etc., so this was the mood that was spread around the country by way of preparation for the new elections. The direct results of this are now absolutely plain for us to see.'

With that, the Kaiser recalled, the Bismarck crisis had entered into an acute phase. 'You will surely be able to imagine the deep pain I felt from that moment on, when I was forced to recognise that the Prince *did not want* to work together with me', the Kaiser's letter to Franz Joseph continues. 'Now began a terrible time for me. While the proclamations were being discussed, he tried to bring in all kinds of other things, and constantly angered the ministers. When he finally brought me the 2 proclamations to sign he declared that he was absolutely opposed to them; they would bring ruin and disaster on to the Fatherland and he advised against them. If I nevertheless signed them, he would co-operate with this policy only *as long as* he found it compatible with his own views. If that were no longer the case he would go. The proclamations were published and the enormous success they had showed the Prince, who was utterly taken aback, that he had been altogether on the wrong track, that his opposition had been useless and that I had been right. Now began the preparations for the invitations to the conference, the convening of the Council of State under my chairmanship. He immediately started a little war against me, behind the scenes, not always by the most honourable means. It pained me most bitterly, but I accepted it calmly. On the one hand I was too proud to allow myself to be drawn into it; on the other I was still too fond of the man whom I worshipped! Soon, however, the conflicts multiplied on all sides. He suddenly prevented the ministers from reporting directly to me by digging out an unknown order which had been buried for 30 years. He took away all the work of the Reich secretaries of state and wanted to do everything and countersign everything himself. Meanwhile his health worsened from week to week, he could no longer sleep, his nerves gave way. He had weeping fits in the night and sometimes also during audiences. His doctor declared that if this state of affairs continued for 3 weeks longer the Prince would die of apoplexy! Eventually towards the end of February the Prince announced to me during an audience that he could not continue with his nerves and health in the state they were in, and asked to be released from some of his duties. I asked him to suggest to me what should be done, entirely in accordance with his own will and wishes, as I wished to avoid giving even the slightest impression that I was sending him away, or looking forward to his departure.

After lengthy negotiations he came to an agreement with the Chief of my Civil Cabinet, whom he had been to see for this purpose, that he would give up the presidency of the Ministry of State and wished only to retain the chancellorship and foreign affairs. After a few weeks he wanted to give that up too and retire completely on about 20 February or at the beginning of March. I agreed to his proposals with a heavy heart', declared Wilhelm, 'and accordingly an order was drawn up in accordance with his instructions and completed, except for the date, which he reserved the right to determine. He himself told me that he was quite satisfied with this solution and declared that he would now inform the Council of Ministers of what he had done. 2 days later he came to report to me and to my immense astonishment he abruptly informed me that he had absolutely no intention of going; he was staying! When I asked him the reason, in bewilderment, he said it was because when he had informed them of his departure the ministers of state had not immediately begged him to stay at all costs, and that the gentlemen's expressions had been "too pleased" about it. From this he had concluded that they wished to get rid of him, and that had aroused the old spirit of resistance in him, and he would now certainly stay on "just to annoy the ministers"! That was all he said. I could only reply that I was very glad to know that he would remain at my side, but hoped that the increasing burden of work and worry would not harm his health.'

That, according to the Kaiser's account, was the beginning of the last stage of the crisis. 'From that day onward war broke out', he wrote. 'In every report the Prince sought to discredit the Ministry; the gentlemen whom he had himself chosen 12 years ago and trained, he now vilified in the most abominable way, and tried to force me to dismiss them *en masse*, to which I did not agree. The time of the conference was approaching and he used all the resources of diplomacy to try to prevent it from happening. Then, when the sittings of the Council of State went so splendidly, and the results were such striking proof that I was on the right track with the above-mentioned memorandum and its proposals, the Prince was overcome with jealousy of his poor young Kaiser and he resolved to ruin his success! At first, behind my back, he tried to induce various diplomats to send reports home opposing the conference, and finally he tried to persuade the Swiss minister to ask the Bern government not to give up their conference for my sake, so that my conference would fall through. The Swiss minister, a good, honest fellow – whom I happen to know well – was incensed at such deceitful, unpatriotic conduct towards the German Kaiser, and telegraphed at once to the government in Bern to say that if the official cancellation of the Swiss conference was not in his hands within 12 hours he would hand in his resignation, but he would also say why. The next morning the requested announcement arrived and my conference was saved! When this plan failed the Prince tried another.

The new Reichstag had been elected; he was furious at the election results and
wanted to break it up as soon as possible. The Anti-Socialist Bill would have to
serve the purpose again. He told me he proposed to bring in a new, harsher bill.
The Reichstag would reject it and he would dissolve the Reichstag. The people,
he said, were already unsettled, the socialists would vent their anger by causing
a putsch, there would be the beginnings of a revolution and then it would be up
to me to let rifles and cannon-fire do their worst. In the process – and this was
his secret intention – the conference and the Social Welfare Bill would of course
be lost, and ruled out for a long time as an election manoeuvre or a Utopian idea.
I refused to accept this but declared roundly that it was impossible to advise a
young king at the beginning of his reign – who was suspected of all kinds of
things – to answer the requests and wishes of his working-class subjects with
rapid fire and grape-shot. At this he became very angry. He declared that it
would have to come to shooting in the end, and so the sooner the better, and if I
were unwilling, he would resign at once. So once again I was faced with a crisis!',
bewailed the Kaiser. 'I summoned the leaders of the Kartell parties to see me and
asked them whether or not I should introduce an Anti-Socialist Bill and break up
the Reichstag. With one voice they declared themselves against this. They said
that the proclamations and the Council of State were already having a calming
effect, and the conference would do the same. There was no question of putsches
or revolutionary movements and the social welfare legislation would pass the
Reichstag with ease; if the bills put before it were not too severe it would behave
quite reasonably. They authorised me to convey this to the Prince as the opinion
of their voters, and to warn him against any attempt to force Anti-Socialist Bills
upon them, as he would not receive a single vote for them. The Prince then
came, and with some anxiety as to the outcome of the interview I explained to
him that I could not consent to his bringing in the bill. Thereupon he declared
that the whole affair did not matter to him in the least! and if I did not wish to
introduce the bill, there was no more to be said! The stand which he had taken
towards me only a few days earlier had completely vanished from his memory!
And as for the business over which he had managed to keep the ministers, me
and the government parties in a state of the greatest agitation for over 4 weeks,
and for which he had been willing to bring down ministers and stir up conflicts,
he dropped it as if it were a mere trifle! But as a result of all these machinations and intrigues, disagreements and quarrels on every possible subject, and
also of the failure of his little "ambuscades" the Prince had got into the most
extraordinary state of agitation. The ministers had to endure outbursts of fury
and the rudest possible behaviour, until they refused to go on with their work.
Business ground to a halt and piled up, nothing was settled; no project, however
urgent, could be submitted to me since the ministers were forbidden – N.B.

behind my back – to report directly to me. Everything had to be submitted to him first, and what he did not want he simply rejected and did not allow it to reach me. There was general dissatisfaction among the civil servants, which also spread to parliamentary circles. In addition I was informed by my personal physician that the Prince's doctor was greatly concerned by his state of health, and that he was in danger of a total collapse which would end in nervous fever and apoplexy! All my attempts to bring the Prince some relief by taking a greater part in business, he took as attempts to push him out. Any gentlemen and councillors whom I summoned to discuss matters with him, he treated with disfavour and suspected them of intriguing with *me* against him! Eventually matters came to a climax and all the pent-up electricity discharged itself on to my "guilty head"! The Prince, eager for battle and inspired by the motives I mentioned above, to the horror of those in the know and in spite of my orders to the contrary, began secretly preparing a campaign against the new Reichstag. Everyone was to be roused to anger and given a beating. First the Kartell parties were to be over-trumped and then the Socialists provoked, until the whole Reichstag was blown sky-high and H.M. would after all be forced, willy-nilly, to shoot! Then came the interview with Windhorst [sic], engineered by the Jew Bleichröder, which let loose a storm of indignation in the country, and was officially shrouded in mystery, which gave rise to all kinds of speculations. Furthermore an attempt was made to give the impression that I had known about it and approved it. Whereas I heard of it only 3 days later from the newspapers and from shocked enquiries which I received from all sides. When I saw the Prince on the third day after this affair, which had ever-increasing repercussions and began to take on a very unpleasant aspect for him, he brought up the subject of Windhorst's visit and described it in such a way as to make it appear that the latter had appeared almost unannounced in his antechamber and taken him by surprise. I had however heard for certain that Bleichröeder [sic] had arranged this inter-view with his consent. When I told the Prince this and asked him to give me notice of such important matters at least by sending me a note or a verbal mes-sage through his secretary, the storm broke! Without the slightest courtesy or consideration he told me that he would not be kept in leading reins by me; he refused once and for all to accept such treatment from me; I understood nothing of parliamentary life; it was most certainly not for me to give him any orders in such matters etc. etc. When he eventually stopped raging at me, I tried to explain to him that it was not a question of orders, but that what mattered to me was that when he took such important steps, which could result in decisions that might be binding on me, and which I could not evade, I should hear about it from him, and not discover it from the press after the event, so that I should know what was going on. But that did not help at all. When I put it to him how

much confusion and disturbance this visit had caused among the people, who
were still in an excitable state because of the elections, and said that this surely
cannot have been his intention, he let slip the fateful remark: "On the contrary,
that is exactly my intention! There must be such utter confusion and chaos in
the country that no one can tell what the aim of the Kaiser's policy is!!" When I
declared that this was not at all my intention, but that my policy must be open
and as clear as daylight to my subjects, he announced that he had nothing more
to say, and angrily threw his resignation at my feet. I did not react to this *third*
scene in the course of 6 weeks. Instead I changed the subject and spoke of the
Council of Ministers, and the Cabinet Order through which he had prevented
them from reporting directly to me. He declared that he did not trust "his"
ministers; they went behind his back to bring things to me which "he" could
not approve, and he had therefore cautioned them against this. When I pointed
out that this was a grave insult to me, his sovereign, who was so loyally and
sincerely devoted to him, and whom he was accusing of secret intrigues behind
his back, he refused to admit it. But he said that if I demanded it, he would send
me the order at once, in the course of the day, so that it could be revoked, for it
did not really matter. When I again asked him − purely with the intention of
relieving a man who was plainly very ill and under excessive nervous strain from
some of his work and anxieties − to let me take a greater part in business, to take
me into his confidence and consult me when there were important decisions to
be made, he refused categorically, with the comment that it was necessary for
him to take decisions in advance, before he came to me! I now realised, with
great pain and a sore heart, that lust for power had taken a demonic hold on this
noble, great man, and that he was using every opportunity, no matter what it
was, to pursue his battle against the Kaiser. He wanted to do everything alone
and rule alone and the Kaiser was not even to be allowed to work with him. In
that moment it was clear to me that we must separate, or everything would be
morally ruined and destroyed. God is my witness that for many a night in my
prayers I strove and pleaded to be able to reach the heart of this man, and to be
spared the fearful prospect of sending him away. But it was not to be! When the
order that was to be revoked still had not arrived from the Prince 2 days later, I
sent a message to him enquiring whether he would send it. He replied that he
had no intention of doing so; he needed to use it against "his" ministers! At that
I lost my patience and the old family pride of the Hohenzollerns was aroused in
me. The stubborn old man now had to be forced to obey or else it must come to a
parting of the ways, for now it was a question of who should prevail, the Kaiser
or the Chancellor. I asked him once more to send the revocation of the order
and to comply with the wishes and requests I had earlier expressed to him. He
refused point-blank. With that the drama was over.'

Finally, in tones of deep self-pity, Wilhelm stressed how hard the decision had been for him. 'The man whom I had idolised all my life, for whom I had endured the torments of hell through moral persecution in my parents' home; the man for whom I *alone* had thrown myself into the breach to keep him on after my grandfather's death, which earned me my dying father's anger and my mother's ineradicable hatred: this man thought nothing of all that and pushed me out of his way because I would not do his bidding! What a dagger in my heart! The boundless contempt for humankind with which he regarded everyone, even those who would have gone to their deaths for him, did him an evil turn in making him despise even his sovereign, whom he wished to reduce to the role of his minion. When he announced to me that he was leaving and accused me of driving him away I remained silent and said nothing, but after he had gone I broke down − I am ashamed to say − and wept.'[19]

On the basis of this description of 'the barely credible events' which had taken place, Franz Joseph conceded that Wilhelm could not have acted otherwise than to dismiss Bismarck. After reading the long letter he could indeed imagine, he wrote, 'how difficult it must have been for you to take this decision and what painful times you have had to go through since the beginning of the crisis. Although I share your deep regret that it had to come to this, no less do I deplore the fact that such a great man, who has served Prussia, Germany and peace with such merit, could allow himself to be so carried away as to act towards his Kaiser and sovereign in a manner for which the ultimate reasons could be more easily explained than excused.' That Wilhelm, 'guided by wise impartiality and clear judgement', had chosen Caprivi as Bismarck's successor Franz Joseph saw as a particular guarantee that judicious policies would prevail, 'although on an earlier occasion you did have a difference of opinion with him'. With Caprivi's support Wilhelm would certainly 'keep a firm hand on the helm in both domestic and foreign affairs, and face the present immensely difficult period with quiet prudence and deliberation'.[20] In his reply on 14 April Wilhelm II, alluding to the secret Reinsurance Treaty with Russia, the decision not to renew which was being taken at precisely this time, commented that for him the struggle with Bismarck had been 'immensely difficult and bitter', 'but it is better thus; and better also for our relationship to one another, for the Prince acted with such independence and at the same time with such secrecy that unfortunately I would not have been able to discover for certain what steps he was taking in foreign policy without my knowledge, and how these could be justified to my allies'.[21]

In parallel with his attempts to justify himself in the eyes of the Habsburg monarch, Kaiser Wilhelm II also sought to put the best construction on the historic events which had led to Bismarck's dismissal for the benefit of his grandmother and the British government. With the obvious intention of representing the Chancellor's resignation as a regrettable necessity rendered inevitable by failing health and old age, Wilhelm telegraphed to Queen Victoria as early as 19 March 1890: 'I deeply regret to have to announce to you that Prince Bismarck has placed his resignation in my hands. His nerves and strength having given out and beginning to fail in the hope of preserving and refreshing his broken health I have accepted his resignation hoping to be able to consult him in any difficult question when he is better and to have him as Councillor as long as he lives. My policy will undergo no change whatever. Gen. v. Caprivi has been named Chancellor. William I. R.'[22] Three days later he called on the British ambassador, Sir Edward Malet, and gave him a lengthy explanation of the reasons for his decision. Malet's confidential report to the Queen – he sent a copy privately to Lord Salisbury at the same time – is eighteen pages long and quotes the Kaiser in direct speech throughout. According to the report, Wilhelm expounded the long history of his differences with the Reich Chancellor on the social welfare question and the Anti-Socialist Bill. He reproached Bismarck with deliberately seeking to drive the class conflict to the limit so as to be able to 'sweep the streets with grape shot'. His grandfather would have had sufficient respect in the country to be able to approve such a policy if necessary, Wilhelm declared; 'but for me, a young Monarch, just come to the throne, to have allowed my people to be shot down in the streets, without making an effort first of all to examine their grievances, would have been disastrous to me and my whole House. It would have been said that my only idea of governing was by bayonets.' But instead of listening to him Bismarck had tried to undermine his social reform initiative behind his back and treated him 'like a schoolboy'. 'The moment came when I was obliged to think of my own dignity.' As he had told Franz Joseph, the Kaiser repeated to Malet: 'I was assured by the doctors that his state of mental excitement was such that it might end in a crisis at any moment . . . I finally decided that, if I wished his life to be preserved, I must relieve him of his duties. He and all his family are at present intensely incensed against me, but I hope that in a few months they will see that they have reason to thank me.' He went on: 'I cannot tell you the pain and anxiety I have gone through this winter on his account. I have always had the greatest admiration for him, and when I was Prince I went through bitter moments from taking his side. I used to say to myself: "Ah! if, when I am Emperor, I could have such a Minister!" – for of course I never thought that I should come to the throne before I was sixty. When I became Emperor, I was overjoyed at having him as my Minister, and I looked forward to keeping [him] at my side until old age should force him to retire and now my real aim is to keep him alive for the sake of Germany and of Europe. I look upon him as a Capital of which Europe enjoys the interest. The universal confidence felt in him is so great, that a word from him in difficult moments of European Conflicts can arrest a crisis, and I still hope to make use of the enormous power which he thus wields for our benefit. One thing which has really cut me to the quick is that in all these painful moments he has never seemed to have the slightest personal regard for me or gratitude for the little efforts which I made to help him when I was Prince. He unfortunately regards everybody as a machine; sentiment in dealing with people is not in his character.'[23] The ambassador was rightly suspicious of Wilhelm's claim that he had parted with Bismarck in the latter's own interest and only on the grounds of urgent medical advice. In his covering letter to Queen Victoria he remarked sceptically: 'The point which remains at issue is whether the health of the Chancellor was really in so precarious a state as the Doctors asserted     Probably the vehemence of Prince Bismarck's manner to the Emperor led His Majesty to believe that a crisis was imminent when it was not. For the Prince has carried his point over and over again, especially with the late Emperor William, by violence of manner and he very likely, in his discussions with the young Emperor, assumed this manner in the hopes that it would have like effect.'[24] The ambassador did not venture to suggest to the Queen that the whole story of the doctors' urgent warning was purely an attempt by his imperial visitor to justify himself.

A few days after his conversation with Malet the Kaiser repeated his version of events in a personal letter to his grandmother. He claimed hypocritically that he had parted from the founder of the Reich in tears after a 'warm embrace'. In this letter Bismarck's apparently shattered health – his life had been in danger – stood as the only reason for the 'very difficult' decision which Wilhelm had had to take. 'I hope & trust that the woods of Friedrichsruh will do him good & help to recruit his forces, & strengthen his nerves; for he was very much shaken. I spoke to his doctor 2 days ago [sic], who assured me, that if the Chancellor had kept on a few weeks longer, he would infallibly have died of apoplexy. The nights he could not sleep, & in day time, as well as in bed, even sometimes when he worked with me, he suddenly would break down, with crying fits. After this had gone on for a month I became afraid of the consequences & after much discussion & with deep regret, I resolved to part from him, in order to keep him alive.' Here the Kaiser repeated the metaphor he had used to Malet: 'I look upon the Prince as an international European capital, which I must try to keep going as long as possible, & not use him up in guerilla warfare with the Reichstag. It was a very hard trial, but the Lord's will be done. I have been educated politically by the Prince, & now I must show what I can do.'[25] When the Queen sent Salisbury the Kaiser's letter he commented with perfect accuracy, as Holstein had done two years earlier: 'It is a curious Nemesis on Bismarck. The very qualities which he fostered in the Emperor in order to strengthen himself when the Emperor

Frederick should come to the throne, have been the qualities by which he has been overthrown.'[26]

Several years later, during his Scandinavian cruise in July 1896, while reminiscing with his best friend Philipp Eulenburg on Bismarck's dismissal, Wilhelm II still spoke with self-pity of the shattering events of March 1890. 'How I loved Prince Bismarck!', he exclaimed. 'What sacrifices I made for him! I sacrificed *my parental home* to him. For his sake I was *maltreated* for years of my life, and I endured it because I regarded him as the living expression of our Prussian Fatherland. And he repaid me for all that with *hatred*! *That* I cannot forget!' It was only during the preparations for the international conference on social welfare that he had recognised the necessity of dismissing Bismarck, he claimed. 'I had considered it the highest of my duties to take care of the welfare of the workers and of old people. The conference was convened in Berlin. There I discovered that the Prince had been to see the French, English and Italian ambassadors to persuade them to ensure that their countries *refused to attend* the conference to which I had invited them . . . This behaviour of the Prince towards me was *open rebellion, which was paraded before the whole of Europe*. I *owed* it to the crown to part with the man! As to the manner in which the Prince's resignation took place, I sent accounts in my own hand to my grandmother in England and to Kaiser Franz Joseph. They will be published under my will, for then I wish to be shown as *justified*. As long as live I shall bear the burden – I have no wish to spoil the German people's ideal for them.'[27]

### THE NEW REICH CHANCELLOR

The appointment of the Commanding General of the X Army Corps in Hanover, Georg Leo von Caprivi, to be Bismarck's successor as Reich chancellor, Prussian minister-president and Prussian minister of foreign affairs, was one of the most genuinely personal decisions that Wilhelm II ever took in his thirty-year reign. Not even his brother knew of his intention. Indeed, when Prince Heinrich, who was with his ship *Irene* in the Mediterranean, read an announcement in a local Spanish newspaper that Caprivi had been appointed Reich chancellor and that Waldersee was to remain Chief of the General Staff, he exclaimed in astonishment to his officers: 'But how ridiculous – that is what it says . . . and yet we all know that it is the other way round!'[28] This anecdote, recorded by Baroness Spitzemberg in 1908, is borne out by the diary of one of the naval officers present. Vice-Admiral Paul Hoffmann noted several times that Prince Heinrich had commented that Caprivi was 'the last person my brother would take'. When the news of Caprivi's appointment was subsequently confirmed, there had been 'great surprise on the part of the Prince' and, 'at any rate, not a pleasant surprise'.[29]

When and why did the young Kaiser come to the surprising decision to appoint Caprivi, of all people, whom he thought 'stiff and rigid', and who had resigned as head of the Admiralty in 1888 in protest at Wilhelm's interference in naval affairs, to be Bismarck's successor? The question of the timing of the decision is more easily answered than that of the reasons behind it. In late January 1890 — that is, shortly after the relationship between Wilhelm and Waldersee had grown several degrees cooler[30] — the Baden envoy and intimate of Holstein, Baron Adolf Marschall von Bieberstein, was able to record in his diary: 'Today I tell the Grand Duke that Caprivi will be chancellor.'[31] It is known that Caprivi had been summoned to Berlin by the Kaiser at the beginning of February and had discussed the question of Bismarck's successor with him for an hour.[32] On 18 February 1890 Wilhelm called on Waldersee to take him for a walk and, although he made no direct reference to the question, the Chief of the General Staff already suspected at this time that the Kaiser's choice had fallen on Caprivi. Waldersee, who claimed not to wish to be Bismarck's immediate successor, seemed at first to welcome this decision: Caprivi was perhaps not particularly talented, but he was nevertheless a 'thoroughly honourable man of steadfast character' who was greatly respected in the Reichstag. The only question was 'whether he will be able to work well with the Kaiser', for Caprivi had 'a very strong will' and was the kind of person who could not take any opposition. Furthermore, 'he left the Admiralty as soon as the Kaiser, whose inclinations towards the navy he knew very well, came to the throne'.[33] It will surely have been no coincidence that Philipp Eulenburg called on the stubborn General in Hanover on 6 March on his way back to Oldenburg from Berlin. The Kaiser's friend was impressed by Caprivi's 'cleverness' and his 'calm, dignified, objective attitude', but could find no 'exceptionally intelligent insights in the political sphere'; above all, however, Eulenburg was astonished by Caprivi's radical views — he revealed himself as a firm opponent of the Anti-Socialist Bill and a proponent of the reduction of military service, at least for the infantry, from three to two years.[34] Eulenburg later remarked that he would have been in favour of the appointment of the ambassador Lothar von Schweinitz or of the Statthalter of Alsace-Lorraine Prince Chlodwig zu Hohenlohe-Schillingsfürst as Reich chancellor, but he would 'never have thought' of Caprivi.[35]

Very little is recorded about Wilhelm's motives for this surprising choice. Eulenburg discovered that the Kaiser 'had retained a great admiration for Caprivi from the time when he was still in charge of the navy', although for this admiration to have survived Caprivi's angry resignation as head of the Admiralty is something of a rarity in the history of Wilhelm II's reign.[36] Another factor which should not be underestimated is the high regard in which Kaiserin Auguste Viktoria and her entire entourage held Caprivi, who — without means of his own and unmarried — had reached the rank of commanding general purely

on the strength of his ability and his upright character.[37] And indifferent as
Wilhelm was to his mother's opinion, she too thought well of Caprivi, although
she considered him better fitted for the post of minister of war than for that
of Reich chancellor. 'He is an honest straightforward respectable man, of *great*
energy – a *very* stubborn and determined will – not given to any compromises –
and rather violent. I should not think he understood *politics* in the least, but he is
incapable of saying what he does not mean, or of an intrigue of any kind!'[38] Three
days later, after the newly appointed Chancellor had called to introduce himself
to her, the Empress Frederick wrote to Queen Victoria saying that Caprivi was
'extremely sensible', but she doubted whether he would get on with Wilhelm,
for he was 'a *very consciencious* [sic] man, and thoroughly in earnest, – & if
W. means (as he says sometimes) merely to have people who "obey him" and
"carry out his orders" – I fear he will find it very difficult – almost impossible –
to fulfill [sic] all the duties of his office'.[39] Such views of Caprivi's honesty and
integrity were widely held.[40] But no one was more aware than Caprivi himself
of how little these admirable qualities would help him to master the domestic
and international political situation in which the German Reich found itself
after Bismarck's departure. He described politics as a mysterious dark-room and
said of Bismarck's sophisticated alliance system that he, unlike his predecessor,
would never be able to juggle with several balls at once.[41] In December 1891
the Hereditary Prince of Saxe-Meiningen, the Kaiser's brother-in-law, although
still acknowledging the Reich Chancellor to be 'a thoroughly distinguished,
upright and noble-minded man', had to admit that there was a widespread view
among high-ranking officers in the army that Caprivi did not possess the necessary abilities 'to direct the policy of a great power of the first rank'.[42] It is
small wonder that some observers of the old school regarded the appointment
of the unsophisticated General to the most responsible position in the entire
Reich as a disastrous mistake. Kurd von Schlözer, the Prussian envoy to the Holy
See, was quick to pass disparaging judgement on the new Chancellor, whom he
described as a man 'of almost crass ignorance in non-military questions' who
did not understand political affairs 'because he has practically never been out
of Berlin circles and has no knowledge of human nature. One might just as
well make any battalion commander chancellor. All that so-called uprightness
of character is as good as useless!'[43] That Bismarck in his bitterness should also
belittle his successor as 'a man with a small horizon' who had failed even as a
soldier is no surprise.[44]

   In the end the choice of the honest General can probably only be explained as a
provisional solution which Wilhelm had intended as such from the outset. For the
difficult transition period in the immediate aftermath of Bismarck's resignation
he needed as Reich chancellor a strong-willed military man who in this case

16. General Georg Leo von Caprivi, Reich Chancellor 1890–1894

had the added benefit of a bald head and a white moustache which made him look not unlike his predecessor. Thereafter the excessive power of the chancellor would be gradually dismantled, perhaps even stripped away entirely; or a 'man of straw' – as Caprivi's successor Prince Hohenlohe was to call himself – would be installed. The Kaiser did not conceal from Caprivi that these were his intentions. As the newly appointed Chancellor confided to the Chief of the General Staff on 20 March 1890, the Kaiser had 'a new organisation in mind': he had appointed Caprivi only 'to put this into effect, and had told him . . . that he was not to remain for long'.[45] At any rate there is no doubt that Wilhelm now intended to rule himself, and to determine personally the guidelines of domestic and foreign policy.

The very fact that even today we know so little about the background to the appointment of Caprivi as chancellor is evidence that in taking this significant political step Wilhelm II was carrying out a totally personal decision. Even if Waldersee and other men around Holstein got wind of Caprivi's forthcoming appointment in late January or early February, it was only ever in the form of rumours about the Kaiser's intentions, and did not indicate that they had played any active part in the choice. Nearly everyone – whether for or against the appointment – was taken aback by the choice. Almost as if he were afraid that the influence of others would limit his freedom of action, Wilhelm kept his decision to offer the appointment to Caprivi to himself until the last minute.

Only his wife, Waldersee and his intimate – and in this case somewhat sceptical – friend Philipp Eulenburg seem to have been let in on the secret. Thus this most important of all decisions in the field of public appointments was made without consultation and without the agreement of anyone else. Nor was it, of course, ratified after the event by any committee or parliamentary body. In acting in this way, however, the Kaiser had infringed neither the Prussian constitution nor that of the Reich. Bismarck himself had after all seen to it that the 'Personal Monarchy' in Germany did not exist merely on paper but was the real and present form of government.

### THE NEW SECRETARY OF STATE FOR FOREIGN AFFAIRS

During his walk with Waldersee on 18 February 1890 the Kaiser hinted that he intended not only to appoint Caprivi as Reich chancellor, but also, at least in the short term and for tactical reasons, to retain Herbert Bismarck as secretary of state at the Foreign Office. The Chief of the General Staff welcomed this decision and acknowledged that the retirement of the founder of the Reich would 'look better in the eyes of the world if the son does not follow until some time later'. That Herbert would also have to be dismissed sooner or later, however, Waldersee did not doubt, for 'every chancellor has to keep control of foreign policy and he will soon rid himself of this boorish, most unpleasant man who is so dangerous for our international position'. Waldersee even took a certain malicious pleasure in anticipating conflict between Caprivi and Herbert Bismarck. 'I should be happy to see Caprivi becoming his [Herbert's] Chancellor', he wrote. 'He knows him very well and considers him far from competent . . . – and he utterly detests his behaviour and activities.'[46]

Simultaneously with his ultimatum to Prince Bismarck demanding his letter of resignation, on 18 March, Wilhelm II therefore took action to keep Herbert in office. He offered him, in addition to the Foreign Office, the post of Prussian minister of foreign affairs, which brought with it responsibility for casting the Prussian vote in the Bundesrat.[47] He sent Philipp Eulenburg to Herbert several times to try to persuade him to remain, but in vain. 'He is in an alarming mood', Eulenburg observed in his diary.[48] There were long consultations in the Foreign Office itself, but nothing would deflect Herbert from his firm resolve to resign at the same time as his father. Holstein went so far as to call on Bleichröder in the hope that he would be able to persuade the departing Chancellor to put pressure on his son to remain. But the elder Bismarck told his banker that he could not advise Herbert to do so. In direct discussions with Herbert Bismarck himself, Holstein pointed out that as secretary of state he could play an important intermediary role between his father and the Kaiser, and that he would thereby enjoy 'considerable status with the latter'. Herbert continued to hold out, and gave as a reason for his departure, in addition to his health and the state of affairs in the Reichstag, 'His Majesty's methods of work'. On 21 March 1890 he handed in his resignation.[49]

The Kaiser had nevertheless not abandoned all hope of persuading the younger Bismarck to resume his office after a few months' leave. Paul Hatzfeldt could stand in for him in the meantime, Wilhelm told Waldersee on the evening of 22 March.[50] Again on 28 March, although Freiherr Marschall von Bieberstein's appointment as foreign secretary had already been confirmed, the Kaiser remarked that Herbert must 'come back as soon as he has recovered, and take up the place he held before! . . . He valued Herbert's efficiency, could work with him and they were friends.' As one of the Flügeladjutanten observed, 'our young sovereign' showed by such comments that he was not satisfied with the choice of Marschall and was already thinking of replacing him.[51] Wilhelm also informed the British ambassador on 28 March that Marschall's appointment was only 'for the present & that he hoped to have Count [Herbert] Bismarck back again in 6 or 8 months'.[52]

In contrast with his conduct over the choice of the new Reich chancellor, therefore, Wilhelm II had evidently given no thought to the possibility   likely as it had always been – that the younger Bismarck would also resign, and that it would therefore be necessary to appoint a new foreign secretary. Although the Bismarck crisis had lasted for several months and had been at an acute stage since at least 24 January, a successor to Herbert Bismarck had to be found in great haste. The choice of a new foreign secretary was all the more crucial because the new Chancellor had absolutely no experience in the realm of foreign policy. Of the seven German ambassadors, however, none seemed to fit the post. In the course of a detailed discussion on 17 March of 'what advice to give the Kaiser' Eulenburg and Waldersee came to the conclusion 'that here too we lack able people'. Count Hatzfeldt, in London, was impossible because of his personal circumstances. Count Münster, in Paris, was too old and 'his mental powers are declining'. Prince Reuss, in Vienna, had 'not the slightest desire' for the post; and Lothar von Schweinitz in St Petersburg was 'disliked by the Kaiser'.[53] Joseph Maria von Radowitz, the ambassador in Constantinople, was a very gifted man but because of his Russian wife he was 'impossible, since Austria, England and Italy consider him a Russian spy', Eulenburg informed the Kaiser.[54] Count Eberhard zu Solms-Sonnenwalde, the ambassador in Rome, was in Waldersee's and Eulenburg's eyes 'too insignificant' for this important appointment. Holstein pointed out that, although Solms might have had the right qualities, he was sixty-five years old and would not be willing to give up his comfortable post.[55]

Holstein too was forced to admit, in his own telling phrase, that 'new growth has not flourished beneath Bismarck's oak, and there is nobody one could recommend'.[56] Like many others, he thought at first of Count Friedrich Johann von Alvensleben, the German envoy in Brussels. But when Caprivi summoned him to Berlin Alvensleben proved to be 'in a state of nervous tension and generally so "broken down" in health . . . that there could be no question of appointing him'.[57] Alvensleben himself told Count Otto von Stolberg-Wernigerode that he had refused the post because he had been away from the world of high politics for too long to take over such a responsibility, 'which is even heavier now, since Caprivi himself is not yet familiar with the work'.[58]

Alvensleben having definitely turned down the appointment, numerous other candidates were considered. The Under-Secretary of State at the Foreign Office, the Bavarian Count Maximilian von Berchem, was turned down by Caprivi as 'too Catholic'.[59] Bernhard von Bülow 'or even Eulenburg (Ph.)' were suggested as possible secretaries of state.[60] However, both Berchem and Holstein spoke out strongly against the choice of Bülow. '*Bülow* is unacceptable to the Kaiserin because of his [divorced] wife, let alone his social qualities, that is to say, failings', Holstein asserted.[61] Prince Bismarck himself had described Bülow to Caprivi as a 'not very reliable [he had first written "completely unreliable"] man'.[62] Bismarck's recommendation that the position should be offered to the Conservative member of the Prussian Landtag, Count Friedrich Wilhelm zu Limburg-Stirum, who had been the temporary head of the Foreign Office briefly in 1880, Holstein considered 'pure mockery', which merely showed 'which way Bismarck would like to push things', and Eulenburg likewise found the suggestion unacceptable, as Limburg-Stirum was 'of Jewish extraction' on his mother's side, 'which permeates his being'. Indeed, Eulenburg went so far as to consider Bismarck's recommendation of Limburg as positively 'perfidious'.[63]

The fact that the choice eventually fell on Baden's envoy and representative in the Bundesrat, Adolf Freiherr Marschall von Bieberstein, completely inexperienced in foreign affairs as he was, was chiefly due to the widespread desire in diplomatic circles to find someone who would work successfully with Friedrich von Holstein. Why Holstein himself did not wish to become secretary of state remains one of the unsolved riddles of Germany history. Philipp Eulenburg, who must have known what he was talking about, wrote of this solitary bachelor that there were such 'marked peculiarities' about his private life that it would be impossible for him to accept the top office, and that the Kaiser also knew this.[64] After Bismarck's departure, however, Holstein's knowledge and ability were considered indispensable. As Count Monts wrote on 24 March 1890 from Vienna, 'Here we are afraid that it may not be possible to come to an arrangement which would allow Holstein to stay on as right-hand man to the chief, or perhaps that H. may not feel able to continue to serve after the events of recent days. And in my opinion this man is now the only one capable of keeping the diplomacy of the Reich on course.'[65] Others, however, viewed the idea of entrusting the Foreign Office to Marschall, as a South German and a non-diplomat, with consternation. Herbert Bismarck exclaimed in horror that it would now be necessary 'to hand over all secret papers to a fellow from Baden!' And Carl Wedel, equally appalled, commented: 'My God, I really do not like the arrangement at the Foreign Office! Marschall is a completely unknown quantity and not even of the Bismarckian school. He has no standing at all in Europe.'[66] Everyone predicted that under Marschall the Foreign Office would be completely under the influence of Holstein, which was indeed the aim of many of those involved.

Despite all misgivings, Marschall's candidature gained ground day by day. As early as 17 March 1890 Philipp Eulenburg had described the Baron as 'very capable, fresh and well-disposed' and had pondered his suitability to take charge of the Foreign Office. Subsequently Waldersee had recommended Marschall to the new Chancellor. Count Berchem also spoke up for Marschall's appointment. Two days later Eulenburg informed Marschall that the Kaiser wished to appoint him secretary of state if Herbert Bismarck did in fact step down. Marschall pointed out that Caprivi could not expect much support from him in foreign policy initially and also that the older officials at the Foreign Office might resent the appointment of 'a young non-Prussian'. But he did not refuse the post in principle.[67] Caprivi told the Chief of the General Staff on 22 March that he liked Marschall very much, but that in his view it was 'questionable whether it was wise to begin with a novice'.[68] A further difficulty was that the Grand Duke of Baden expressed decided opposition to Marschall's appointment. Holstein, on the other hand, made no bones about his preference for the Baden envoy. He dismissed the criticism made of Marschall that he did not know 'the courts', for 'to be well-informed, one does not need to have been on the spot oneself'. Marschall would 'soon, very soon, work his way into the great questions of foreign policy: he already knows their general outlines', Holstein stated confidently in a letter to Eulenburg.[69] As so often in the long crisis which had begun in the early summer of 1889, the influence of Eulenburg, who passed on Holstein's thoughts to the Kaiser, proved decisive. In a letter to Wilhelm of 26 March he ruled out both Radowitz and Limburg-Stirum; he praised Bernhard von Bülow's talents, but warned that Holstein, who was indispensable, would resign if Bülow were appointed. Alvensleben, he said, was universally respected and might perhaps overcome his doubts if the Kaiser expressed it as his personal wish. The best man for the job, however, would undoubtedly be the 'excellent' Marschall, who as a South German would make an attractive partnership with the Old Prussian Caprivi. He was a good speaker and practised in dealing with the Reichstag;

he had a very sound knowledge of German internal affairs and would also 'very soon master the great questions of foreign policy'. Eulenburg closed his letter by repeating his warning that it was particularly important in the Kaiser's own interest 'that Holstein, who is familiar with all the secret paths of Bismarckian policy, should stay. Odd creature that he is, he would certainly pack his bags if for instance Bülow, Radowitz or Stirum were appointed.'[70] The next morning Caprivi – 'after he had received the Kaiser's consent'   offered Marschall the Foreign Office, arguing that the great powers would see his appointment as proof 'that the Kaiser is not pursuing any warlike policy'.[71]

At the last moment an embarrassing incident occurred which was symptomatic of the confusion inherent in the new distribution of power between the Kaiser and the Chancellor. On 27 March, after Marschall had accepted the post offered to him by Caprivi on the Kaiser's instructions, Wilhelm II, with strong support from his Flügeladjutant Carl Wedel, began to negotiate with Alvensleben again, pressing him to accept the post 'at least on trial'. Alvensleben would not be persuaded, and even threatened to resign from the diplomatic service altogether 'when the Kaiser began to apply a kind of coercion'. But what would have happened if Alvensleben had given in? When Caprivi heard of the renewed negotiations with Alvensleben, he told Herbert Bismarck, General von Hahnke and Lothar von Schweinitz, who were all waiting to be received in audience in the Schloss, that if Alvensleben accepted he himself would have to resign, for he was now comitted to Marschall.[72] 'What a strange sign of the way things are done now, and what chaos this must lead to!', Wedel remarked.[73]

The decision to appoint a Badenese lawyer without any experience of foreign affairs as secretary of state at the Foreign Office may indeed have reassured the other powers, as Caprivi hoped, that the Kaiser harboured no warlike intentions. It undoubtedly had the effect not only of safeguarding Friedrich von Holstein's influence on the formulation of German foreign policy in the years that followed, but even of greatly increasing it, particularly as the new Chancellor likewise had no experience in this field. Stolberg showed a perspicacious grasp of the situation in a letter of 28 March 1890 to the German ambassador in Vienna, remarking that Marschall was 'a very intelligent, efficient, reliable and respectable man, and to have gained him for the service is in itself to be welcomed; but with the best will in the world he cannot yet know anything about the actual work'. In the Bundesrat and in the Reichstag he was greatly respected, but not in the Foreign Service. 'By and large everything will depend on Holstein at first; but how far he can be relied on remains to be seen.'[74] After only a few weeks the dominance of Holstein and his South German confidants Marschall and Kiderlen-Wächter (who was from Württemberg) in the Foreign Office was so great that the Under-Secretary of State Count Berchem resigned in protest.[75] One

17. Adolf Freiherr Marschall von Bieberstein, German Foreign Secretary 1890–1897

of the Flügeladjutanten made the far-sighted observation that 'with Berchem one of the strongest corner-stones has been torn out of the building, and we are moving more and more towards a downhill road! Servility and self-seeking are more and more in evidence! One cannot help wondering whether this is purely the product of our new circumstances or whether it is also partly a pernicious result of the Bismarckian system which suppressed all independence.'[76] The paucity of experience and political skill at this time, in comparison to the period of the Bismarck family's ascendancy, was certainly immense, and all the talent and secret knowledge of the cranky Privy Councillor Friedrich von Holstein, who shrank from the glare of publicity, could not make up for it. As a South German Prince wrote from Berlin to his father in April 1890: 'It is a pity that the two most important posts are now occupied by people who are not yet at all familiar with the responsibilities of the offices which they hold.'[77] Nature abhors a vacuum. The void which now opened up in the field of foreign policy acted on the eager young Kaiser like a lure.

### THE NEW MINISTERS AND SECRETARIES OF STATE

A fundamental difference between the constitutional practice of Personal Monarchy as established by Bismarck in Prussia–Germany and the parliamentary system prevailing in northern, western and southern Europe was the absence in the German Reich of the principle of collective responsibility of ministers of the Crown. The Prussian Ministry of State, as Holstein complacently observed in February 1890, was 'a Ministry of Civil Servants and as such more comfortable . . . for the monarch than a parliamentary Cabinet'.[78] When Bismarck was dismissed none of the Prussian ministers or the secretaries of state of the Reich offices – apart from Herbert – declared their solidarity with him. Heinrich von Boetticher above all, Vice President of the Ministry of State and Secretary of State at the Reich Office of the Interior, earned himself Bismarck's irreconcilable hatred by showing himself ready to fulfil Wilhelm's wishes, for which he was rewarded with the Order of the Black Eagle. In the Bismarck family Boetticher's wife was maliciously accused of having designs on the post of minister-president for her husband, as she would then have field marshal's rank and would enjoy the highest precedence at court.[79]

When Bismarck convened the Prussian Ministry of State for the last time on 17 March 1890 three of the ministers spoke out – albeit without great conviction – in favour of resignation *en bloc*. Finance Minister Adolf von Scholz stated his opinion that in view of the forthcoming dismissal of Prince Bismarck the Ministry of State should consider 'whether it ought not to join in this step' and even ventured to suggest that a collective resignation might yet avert the 'fateful event'. Scholz was seconded by Minister of Public Works Albert von Maybach (who was in any case tired of his job), who put forward the view that all the ministers should 'put their offices at His Majesty's disposal and he, at least, was determined to do so'. Minister of Agriculture Robert Freiherr Lucius von Ballhausen also declared that he would resign if Bismarck wished.[80] If it had come to collective resignation by these ministers, Minister of Ecclesiastical Affairs Gustav von Gossler would probably have joined them. But when the Prussian ministers assembled again that evening at Boetticher's house, this time without the two Bismarcks, none of them spoke out in favour of resigning *en bloc*. In a declaration characteristic of the non-political, civil-service mentality of the ministers, Boetticher stated 'that it was not in the Prussian tradition for ministers to put their portfolios at the king's disposal *in corpore*. In the present situation there was in any case no reason to do so, since the All-Highest wishes concerning the choice of the new minister-president were still quite unknown. There was no reason to believe that His Majesty wished to pursue policies at home which were opposed in principle to those pursued under Prince Bismarck. Besides, so far as one could see His Majesty would not accept the resignations of the ministers of state. The entire step would thus have a merely formal character which would not be in keeping with the position and prestige of the Ministry of State. If His Majesty desired changes in other offices, one could expect him to take the initiative himself.'[81] Nothing shows more clearly than the passive arguments and deferential turn of phrase adopted by Boetticher how much the Prussian ministers of state took it for granted that the young Kaiser would determine policy guidelines and appointments to the principal positions in Prussia and the Reich from now on. With the exception of Herbert Bismarck, therefore, all the Prussian ministers and the secretaries of state of the Reich offices at first remained at their posts in March 1890. (Five of them − Scholz, Lucius, Maybach, Gossler and Minister of War von Verdy − were to resign in the course of the next few months.) The unpolitical attitude demonstrated by the ministers, which Holstein at this time still welcomed but was later bitterly to regret, was an essential prerequisite to the growing personal power of the Kaiser.

Wilhelm's mother also recognised the lack of a strong, politically self-confident collective ministry both as the chief weakness of the Bismarckian system and as the basis of the increasingly 'despotic' power of Wilhelm II's position. On 22 March 1890 she wrote to Queen Victoria saying that Bismarck's resignation would have been no great misfortune if only his regime had been replaced by a collective ministry with Prince Chlodwig zu Hohenlohe as Reich chancellor, Count Paul von Hatzfeldt as foreign minister, Caprivi as minister of war and a liberal statesman as minister of the interior. Had that happened, 'wise and experienced & conciliatory men would have had the confidence of Germany & *of Europe*, & in time *I am sure* would have had the best influence on W.'. With a collective government of that kind an era of peace and stability would have begun, just as would have happened under her husband. But as things actually stood she could see 'nothing but confusion − sudden resolution not sufficiently considered − suddenly carried out, with truly Bismarkian [sic] contempt for people's feelings − but without the "coup d'oeil de maitre" wh. B. often had!'[82]

### LIEBENAU'S DOWNFALL

If on the one hand the Prusso-German system of government lacked a responsible Reich Cabinet, on the other the men at court − the Oberhofmarschall, the military entourage and the three cabinets − played a political role which would not have been tolerated in a parliamentary system. Given that relations between the Wilhelmstrasse and the court were therefore closely intertwined, the departure of the two Bismarcks could not but affect the composition of the Kaiser's entourage. Above all, the long-heralded fall of the Oberhofmarschall, Eduard von Liebenau, became inevitable the moment that the protection of the Bismarck family vanished.

At the height of the Bismarck crisis Liebenau informed the Kaiser that the state of his nerves was so poor that he wished to ask for other employment. In response Wilhelm, following the advice of Liebenau's adversaries, Waldersee and

18. Count August zu Eulenburg, Senior Marshal of the Court and
Household 1890–1918

Eulenburg, offered him the post of intendant of the Royal Gardens. Liebenau,
however, requested an ambassadorial appointment; he had already come to an
agreement with Herbert Bismarck over this, he said. 'The Kaiser laughed out
loud' and asked what qualifications he had for such a post. Liebenau declined
the Intendancy of the Royal Gardens, stating that he could not demean himself
to take it. 'The Kaiser rubbed his hands and was glad that the initiative to leave
had come from L. himself.'[83]

Aside from the witch-hunt conducted by his enemies, Liebenau's notorious
incompetence also contributed to his downfall. He provided further proof of it
when at the end of March 1890, to the Kaiser's utter bafflement, he failed to
invite the new Reich Chancellor to a state banquet for the Prince of Wales, on
the grounds that Caprivi had not yet officially informed him – Liebenau – of
his return from a visit to Hanover.[84] Finally, on 23 May 1890, Wilhelm II took
the decision to sack his longstanding companion.[85] He cited a series of other
gaffes – Liebenau had for instance failed to inform him that during a night
journey through Elbing a large group of shipyard workers were waiting to greet
him as the train passed through the station[86] – as the reason for dismissing the
Oberhofmarschall and appointing August Eulenburg in his place. Waldersee
commented that there was 'unanimous' satisfaction at Liebenau's departure. He
had congratulated the Kaiserin upon it, for she above all had 'had to suffer a great

deal from the wretched man'.[87] A deeply embittered Liebenau left Potsdam the instant the question of his retirement pay had been settled.[88]

Liebenau's dismissal was regretted not only by the Bismarcks at Friedrichsruh but also by some at the Hohenzollern court. The Flügeladjutant Carl von Wedel commented bitterly on the Oberhofmarschall's fall: 'So that is what the Kaiser thinks of a man like Liebenau, who has stood by him loyally for fourteen years . . .! He drives him out of the house like a lackey, throws him away like a worn-out glove! – My God, the English blood has brought nothing good to the Hohenzollern dynasty, for our young sovereign has inherited this heartlessness from his mother! It will show itself in much worse outbreaks in the course of time!'[89] In actual fact, the Kaiser's English mother herself deeply deplored the change. She acknowledged that Liebenau was difficult and had offended many people; but he had kept the staff under control and had supervised court functions efficiently, which could not be expected from his successor.[90]

That Liebenau should be replaced as Oberhofmarschall by her old enemy August Eulenburg, who combined three other court posts (he became senior house marshal and senior master of ceremonies at the same time, and later also minister of the royal house), the Empress Frederick found extremely disturbing. Eulenburg was not to be trusted. 'He is very grasping & ambitious but he can make himself very agreeable & has the manners of the world . . . I do not think matters *can* go smoothly as long as many elements are still about William who have done such endless mischief!'[91] Waldersee, of course, saw the role of the new Oberhofmarschall in another light. August Eulenburg, he wrote, was extremely cautious and understood perfectly how to judge the Kaiser's mood and to act accordingly. Not until later did the General remark with some surprise that the Oberhofmarschall was trying to exert an independent influence on the monarch.[92] Though he bore no constitutional responsibility, he was soon to become one of the most influential of the figures at the Hohenzollern court, someone whose advice Wilhelm often chose to follow.

# CHAPTER FOURTEEN

# In Bismarck's footsteps: the conduct of foreign policy under the New Course

## THE NON-RENEWAL OF THE RUSSIAN REINSURANCE TREATY

WILHELM'S repeated assurances, in the letters that he wrote to his fellow sovereigns justifying his conduct, that Bismarck's dismissal had been the result of differences of opinion of an exclusively domestic nature were not, as we have seen, the whole truth. At the very outset of the chancellor crisis a violent confrontation between Bismarck and the Kaiser over the Russian loan conversion had come about as a result of constant warnings from Waldersee, and indirectly also from Holstein, that the Bismarcks were relying to a dangerous degree on Russia while neglecting the two powers to which Germany was bound by the Triple Alliance, Austria-Hungary and Italy. And in the final phase of the crisis, in mid-March 1890, Waldersee succeeded in convincing the Kaiser, on the basis of the delayed consular reports from Kiev, that Bismarck had deliberately withheld important information from him about Russian military preparations for an attack on the Triple Alliance. In addition, Wilhelm's personal relationship with the Russian imperial family had continued to deteriorate during these crucial months. This put the relations between Kaiser and Chancellor under renewed strain, notably during the weeks before Alexander III's visit to Berlin in October 1889, and again in December that year during the hunt at Springe with the Tsarevich Nicholas. In the last violent quarrel with Wilhelm on 15 March Bismarck took his revenge by showing him the Tsar's deeply insulting remarks about him, from which the young Kaiser was forced to conclude that Alexander III thought him 'insane'. As luck would have it, it was precisely at this time, in the highly unsettled days immediately after Bismarck's fall and before the diplomatically inexperienced new men Caprivi and Marschall had had the chance to take stock of their responsibilities, that one of the most momentous decisions in the history of German foreign policy was made: the non-renewal of the secret Reinsurance Treaty with Russia. What part did Kaiser Wilhelm II play in this fateful step, which historians have almost unanimously seen as one of stupidity verging on the suicidal?[1] Although the records reveal that ultimately the young monarch followed the advice of the responsible statesmen of the Wilhelmstrasse, they also convey an alarming picture of the confusion and superficiality that prevailed behind the glittering façade of the German Reich during this transitional period.

The Reinsurance Treaty with Russia, entered into by Bismarck on 18 June 1887 for a three-year period, was intended to replace the Three Emperors' League between Germany, Russia and Austria-Hungary which was shortly to expire.[2] The treaty bound Germany to remain neutral in the event of an Austrian attack on Russia and Russia to do the same if France attacked Germany. On the instigation of the Russian ambassador, Count Shuvalov, Bismarck had also agreed to a 'very secret' additional clause in the treaty which was irreconcilable with the Dual Alliance between Germany and Austria-Hungary. According to this clause the German Reich was to provide diplomatic and moral support to Russia in the event that it took possession of the Straits or protected its interests by a military invasion of Bulgaria.[3] As the date for the renewal of the treaty drew near, at the end of 1889, neither the Tsar nor his Foreign Minister Giers had any doubt that the extension of so advantageous an agreement would be in Russia's interest.[4] Early the next year, on 10 February 1890, Shuvalov approached Bismarck about the renewal.[5]

As was recorded in an earlier chapter, Prince Bismarck had let Wilhelm II in on the secrets of his Russian policy very soon after his accession, and in so doing had informed him of the existence of the treaty.[6] Now – in mid-February 1890 – according to Herbert Bismarck the Kaiser gave his consent to the renewal of the treaty, whereupon Shuvalov left for St Petersburg in order to set the appropriate negotiations in train. When he returned to Berlin on 17 March with the official authorisation of the Tsar and was immediately invited to hold conversations with Bismarck, he was met with the disturbing news that the Reich Chancellor – not least because of differences with the Kaiser over policy towards Russia – was about to be dismissed. Bismarck evidently wished to exploit to his own tactical advantage the irate handwritten note about troop movements in Kiev which the Kaiser had sent to him on the morning of 17 March, by painting a graphic picture of the momentous international consequences of his fall for the benefit of the Russian ambassador. Shuvalov was duly appalled, and telegraphed the news immediately to St Petersburg.[7]

On 19 March the ambassador also expressed his anxiety to Herbert Bismarck, who was still in office as secretary of state, 'over a glass of beer'. Russia's disquiet was recognised by Herbert as an opportunity, if not of preventing his father's dismissal, then at least of showing it in an advantageous light. In a letter to Wilhelm he went so far as to claim that Tsar Alexander was keen to reach agreement on the renewal of the treaty with new conditions that would be extremely favourable to Germany, but that he would do so only with Prince Bismarck. The letter, dating from 20 March and steeped in cynical self-interest, stated: 'This is to inform Your Majesty, with my most humble duty, that the Russian ambassador told me last night in confidence that he had been authorised by the Tsar to extend for six years the secret treaty between Russia and Germany which guarantees us Russia's neutrality in the event of a French attack, and which expires in June of this year; indeed the intention is that the agreement should be regarded as permanent. Count Shuvalov therefore called on the Reich Chancellor immediately on his return from St Petersburg, on the 17th of the month, to give him the above-mentioned information. He then learned that Your Majesty had sent word to the Reich Chancellor that same morning to say that You were expecting the Reich Chancellor's letter of resignation. Count Shuvalov thereupon withdrew his proposals; when he heard last night that Your Majesty would not hesitate to proceed with the dismissal of Prince Bismarck, he said Tsar Alexander would give up the renewal of the secret treaty, as such a secret matter could not be negotiated with a new Reich chancellor.'[8] This was of course pure fabrication.

We know of the Kaiser's furious mood during these crucial days from the notes kept by his Flügeladjutant Carl von Wedel. He saw Wilhelm on the evening of 17 March and recorded that he had been greeted with the words 'that it was all over with the Prince!' The Kaiser had then told him that Bismarck had 'started up an intrigue with Shuvalov', the aim of which was 'to make Russia invade Bulgaria, thereby causing Austria to launch an attack, and then for us to dispute the *casus foederis*. Such an intrigue carried on behind his back "was the absolute limit". Austria would have fallen into a terrible trap, and poor Kaiser Franz Joseph, to whom he had pledged his word and intended to keep it, would have had to pay the price. Of course it would never have come to that, for on the day that Russia made as if to do anything of the sort, he would have given the order for mobilisation, together with Austria. He now understood why the Chancellor had for several days been waiting "so longingly" for Shuvalov's return. Luckily he had been informed about this whole intrigue − for Shuvalov had brought back approval for Bismarck's plan from St Petersburg − in good time: he had been warned this morning and the whole plan had been revealed to him.' Wedel assumed that this warning had been conveyed to the Kaiser by the Grand Duke of Baden, who had received the news from Holstein.[9]

When he received Herbert Bismarck's letter three days later, however, Wilhelm seems to have forgotten the devilish conspiracy between Bismarck and Shuvalov to start an Austro-Russian war, for he wrote at the top of the letter: 'I agree to the renewal of the treaty and authorise you to inform Shuvalov 20.III.90.' He did not understand, however, why the renewal could be negotiated only with the old Reich Chancellor, as his 'Why?' at the end of the letter indicates. He sent the letter back to the Foreign Secretary with these marginal notes. As the Kaiser clearly had not grasped the real purpose of his letter, Herbert wrote him a second one, in which he again drew attention, mendaciously, to Shuvalov's insistence that Prince Bismarck was indispensable to the renewal of the treaty. 'From Your Majesty's All-Highest marginal note on my respectfully submitted report of this morning, which I return herewith, I observe that it was not sufficiently clearly expressed, and I therefore take the liberty of submitting the following explanation to Your Majesty, with my humble duty. Already before Count Shuvalov's departure for St Petersburg Your Majesty had authorised Prince Bismarck to say to the Russian ambassador, as then confidentially suggested by him, that it was the All-Highest inclination to renew the secret treaty which was due to expire in three months, and this was conveyed to Count Shuvalov at that time. The latter had intended to enter into negotiations with Prince Bismarck at the present time, as the Tsar had authorised him to do. In the meantime, however, Prince Bismarck has been relieved of his offices by Your Majesty, and Count Shuvalov, as I respectfully stated in the last sentence of the enclosed report, has now informed me that on the Russian side the extension of the treaty would be given up. After this notification from Count Shuvalov I therefore cannot return to this matter, since he is aware that Your Majesty had previously authorised negotiations for the renewal of the secret agreement, and yet in spite of this he spoke to me last night in the negative sense which I respectfully reported to Your Majesty in the enclosed report.'[10]

The Kaiser probably did not receive this second letter from Herbert until late in the evening. For a second time, perhaps deliberately, he failed to see that this was a ploy by the son to force him to reinstate the father, and he still refused to understand why the negotiations could not be continued without Bismarck. Dramatically asserting his own claim to be in charge, he had Shuvalov woken that same night with a message 'summoning the Count to see the Kaiser the next morning at a quarter to nine in frock coat'.[11] During their early morning discussion Wilhelm assured Shuvalov, as the future Russian Foreign Minister Count Vladimir Nikolaievich Lamsdorff recorded in his diary, 'that apart from a few differences of opinion on domestic policy, which I ascribe to the very agitated state of mind of the Chancellor, nothing, really absolutely nothing at all, has changed with regard to our foreign policy, which I have directed until now and shall continue to direct . . . Herbert Bismarck told me that you have had a discussion with his father about the renewal of the secret treaty and that your Emperor, like myself, is favourably inclined towards the renewal of our agreement; Herbert added that you no longer wished, in view of recent events, to continue the discussions. I should deeply regret that and I ask you to tell your Emperor that I, for my part, stand by our obligations. I am ready to renew them in complete agreement with the wishes of His Majesty. Our policy was after all not his, that is to say Bismarck's, policy. It was the policy of my grandfather and it has remained mine.'[12]

An hour later the Kaiser saw Herbert Bismarck at the station, where he had gone to meet the Prince of Wales, and told him that he had just spoken to Shuvalov. Herbert had misunderstood Shuvalov, Wilhelm said. He would call in the afternoon and 'set the matter straight'.[13] Herbert, however, refused to take any further part in these proceedings, as he intended to hand in his own resignation. The Kaiser was at first unwilling to take any notice of this. When the resignation letter arrived the same afternoon, however, Wilhelm instructed the new Chancellor, General von Caprivi, to arrange the renewal of the treaty. He did not of course inform Caprivi that he had already given Shuvalov his express approval.

In the turmoil of the next few days Kaiser Wilhelm seems temporarily to have put the affair out of his mind. When he found himself again confronted with the question of the renewal, several days later, the tide had turned completely. Caprivi had gone immediately to the Political Department of the Foreign Office on 22 March, to consult the relevant documents on the secret treaty and to seek advice. Holstein, who was the only person present on that day, a Saturday,[14] recorded that 'on the day of the investiture Caprivi asked to see a secret document which the Kaiser wished to discuss with him immediately afterwards. I let him have the document, to Herbert's unbounded fury.'[15] From Caprivi Holstein learned for the first time of the Kaiser's intention of renewing the treaty. He immediately took steps to prevent this, convincing the new Chancellor that he should not reach any decision until he had heard the views of the experts in the Foreign Office, and arranged a consultative meeting for the next day. He wrote at once to Philipp Eulenburg: 'Tomorrow at 10 Berchem, Raschdau and I will have a joint interview with Caprivi, at my suggestion. Then we shall have to see what Caprivi can do.'[16]

On the Sunday the consultation went according to Holstein's plan. The Privy Councillor convinced not only Caprivi, who immediately took a dislike to the double-dealing represented by the Reinsurance Treaty, but also Ludwig Raschdau, who at first argued for a more cautious approach, and the Under-Secretary Count Berchem, who was initially unsure of his opinion.[17] The latter drew up a joint report on the results of the consultation, in which he cited reasons for non-renewal which certainly could not be rejected out of hand. The treaty had 'the aim of provoking warlike incidents which it is highly unlikely to be possible to localise'. It was 'in direct contradiction, if not of the letter, then at least of the spirit of the Triple Alliance'. Moreover, it did not guarantee any 'reciprocity'; all the advantage was on the Russian side. The report gives a detailed picture of the diplomatic chaos which would ensue if Russia actually launched the 'oriental war' which was 'the object of the treaty'. From now on a 'calm, clear and loyal policy' must be pursued, for the 'lively enthusiasm' of the people, which was so important in modern times, would be entirely lacking for such a war. Therefore, the report concluded, Germany must withdraw 'in an amicable way' from the agreement with Russia.[18] It did not mention what was probably the most important reason why the leading advisers in the Foreign Office were convinced that the renewal of the secret treaty would be too risky. Simply by threatening to reveal its existence the vindictive former Chancellor would be able to blackmail the Kaiser and the new leadership of the Reich, perhaps even to bring about his own return to power. Worse still: by betraying the dark secret Bismarck would be able to wreck the Triple Alliance between Germany, Austria and Italy and thus prolong, after his dismissal, the very policy of chaos with which he had almost succeeded in checkmating the Kaiser.

Before the Kaiser and Caprivi were able to discuss the matter, Wilhelm II met Herbert Bismarck by chance on the evening of Monday 24 March. Herbert, who was enraged by Holstein's involvement in the affair,[19] submitted a new proposal to the monarch which was designed to cancel out the influence of Holstein and the other advisers: namely that the question of extending the Reinsurance Treaty could best be settled in St Petersburg between the Russian Foreign Minister, Giers, and the German ambassador, General Lothar von Schweinitz. The Kaiser also approved this suggestion, as Shuvalov telegraphed to Giers on 26 March. The ambassador went on to inform the astonished Russian Foreign Minister that Herbert Bismarck had persuaded the Kaiser to accept his new proposal with the argument that 'in view of the complete ignorance of this question on the part of those who would have to conduct the negotiations after him, it would be better to put the negotiations in the hands of persons who have already participated in them on both sides, and who know the situation well'.[20]

Schweinitz was in Germany at this time, but was soon to return to St Petersburg. As he was to take a message from Wilhelm to the Tsar, he was invited to tea with the Kaiser; but when the latter showed no signs of wishing to talk about the treaty, the ambassador was forced to bring up the subject himself. As he recalled: 'I was invited to take tea with Their Majesties at 8 o'clock in the evening with General Caprivi and the Statthalter Prince Hohenlohe. When we took our leave the Kaiser said goodbye to me, but I said that I must beg for a reply to the message which I had brought him at the request of Tsar Alexander.

At this he commanded the Chancellor and myself to come to see him the next day at a quarter to one.' So the Kaiser was prepared to lavish as much as a quarter of an hour (before lunch at 1 p.m.) on this vital matter![21]

Not until he called on Caprivi at 10.30 the next day did Schweinitz learn of the latter's view that the renewal should be rejected. The ambassador listened in alarm to the new Chancellor, whom he described as 'unassuming, honest and serious', explaining 'that the greatest problem facing him now was the question of the renewal of the Russian treaty, for unlike Prince Bismarck, in Kaiser Wilhelm I's famous metaphor, he could not be a juggler playing with five glass balls, he could only hold two glass balls at one and the same time'. Schweinitz, who knew from Shuvalov that the Kaiser had already given his consent to the renewal, was now confronted with a difficult decision. In the end the elderly ambassador – 'the model of Old Prussian loyalty and statesmanship'[22] – decided to stand by the Reich Chancellor. Indeed, he even allowed himself to be convinced, for the time being at least, by Caprivi's arguments. Describing this decisive moment, he wrote: 'He showed me the secret treaty with Romania, of whose existence I was aware without knowing anything of its contents. I could not but be convinced that it was impossible to reconcile the obligations which we had undertaken towards King Karl [of Romania] with the provisions of the Russian treaty. I fully recognised that under the changed circumstances it was dangerous to continue with such an ambiguous policy as Prince Bismarck had pursued in order to "dig out" Russia's mines on every side.' He went on: 'If Bismarck had remained at the helm, I would have been in favour of renewing the treaty without the [additional] clause. After a short and earnest discussion, in which Count Berchem was later also invited to take part, I declared to the Reich Chancellor that I should not wish to raise any objection if he put it to the Kaiser that the treaty should not be renewed.'[23]

Afterwards, when Caprivi and Schweinitz arrived for their joint audience with the Kaiser, the Chancellor delivered himself of a 'short, cogent report in which he maintained that he could not reconcile the various secret agreements with each other and therefore proposed that the Russian treaty should not be renewed, especially in order to avoid the danger to which we should be exposed if it became known; if it were brought to the knowledge of the Cabinet in Vienna, whether deliberately or by chance, it would alienate them from us. The Kaiser listened in silence and then asked: "Well now, what does the ambassador say to this?" I replied [Schweinitz wrote] that I accepted the arguments of the Chancellor . . . With this the matter was settled.'[24]

Wilhelm took the volte-face in his stride, commenting 'Well, then it won't do, although I am sorry about it.'[25] For his own part he explained his decision to Shuvalov a few years later by saying that Caprivi had threatened to resign if the treaty were renewed. He himself had 'only just come to the throne and had appointed a new Chancellor. The latter had confronted him with an ultimatum. There had been no question of provoking yet another ministerial crisis within 24 hours. He had given in to the stubborn obstinacy of Count [sic] Caprivi. Caprivi had been an honest, but at the same time stubborn person and he lacked insight.'[26] Leaving aside the misrepresentation and exaggeration in this piece of retrospective self-justification, it is certainly remarkable how quickly and uncomplainingly the Kaiser gave in to the Chancellor. That Wilhelm – who spent the afternoon drawing a design for a flower arrangement for Bismarck's retirement ceremony[27] – had not even begun to understand the consequences of this abrupt change of mind became clear when the question of the renewal of the treaty came up again in May 1890.

After his discussion with the Kaiser and Caprivi, Schweinitz had to muster all his diplomatic skill to explain the sudden about-turn in Germany's position, first to Shuvalov in Berlin and then to Giers and Lamsdorff in St Petersburg, who were understandably confused and annoyed, and to placate them. In so doing he laid particular stress on the fact that in all the confusion caused by the Bismarck crisis the new government was not yet in a position to take such major decisions, but that nothing had changed as far as relations between Germany and Russia as a whole were concerned. In May 1890 Giers therefore made a second attempt to obtain the renewal of the Reinsurance Treaty from the German government. On 16 May Schweinitz – who in the meantime had come to see the non-renewal as a serious error – sent a dispatch-rider to Berlin to take Caprivi an official report, the text of Shuvalov's telegram in French of 21 March, reproduced from memory by Schweinitz himself, and a private letter in his own hand, all pointing out valid arguments for renewal.[28]

The reaction from Berlin, however, was even now brusque and unfriendly. Holstein, Marschall von Bieberstein, Kiderlen-Wächter and Raschdau prepared formal opinions on 20 May, in which they set out their arguments of March even more forcibly, in support of Caprivi's decision to turn down the offer a second time.[29] Caprivi wrote a summary on 23 May explaining his decision as follows: 'In the reply to General von Schweinitz his attention should be drawn to the impossibility, with regard to public opinion in this country, of maintaining a complicated system of alliances after the departure of Prince Bismarck. To conclude secret alliances is all the more out of the question now because the conduct of the former Reich Chancellor in any case makes the danger of indiscretions more likely and fosters uncertainties and misunderstandings. But our policy can only be, and should be, a simple one.' The Kaiser, to whom Caprivi submitted the document, commented 'in a most resolute manner' that he 'would not commit himself to any verbal or written statement to the Tsar which did

not conform with the sense of the summary'.[30] Wilhelm II therefore gave orders
on 23 May 1890 that the Russian request for renewal of the treaty should again
be refused. Like Caprivi, he considered that this could be done 'in a polite and
friendly way', 'so that no ill-feeling remains on the Russian side'.[31]

In spite of the courteous tone of the refusal and the validity of some of
the objections expressed by Holstein and Caprivi — above all the irreconcilabil-
ity of the secret treaty with the Dual Alliance and the danger of betrayal by
the resentful Bismarck — the non-renewal of the Reinsurance Treaty is still
today considered by most historians to have been one of the most fatal decisions of the 'New Course'.[32] It is true that there is less inclination now than in
the Bismarckian orthodoxy of earlier years to see in this abandonment of the
'direct line to Russia' the beginning of the catastrophic events leading up to
the First World War. Nevertheless the 'enormous consequences', in the longer
term, of the non-renewal of the treaty in the spring of 1890 are unmistakable, as Thomas Nipperdey has rightly perceived. 'It cleared the way to the
anti-German alliance of 1893/4 with France for the Russian radical nationalists; . . . but even for the moderates the isolation of Russia vis-à-vis Germany and
England was not acceptable. The decision put the Reich on a new footing with
Austria, its only ally and a weak one at that: it made the Reich more suscepti-
ble to Austrian decisions and Austrian pressure because there was no Russian
"counterweight", something which Bismarck had wanted to avoid at all costs.
Finally, it gave European politics a stronger impetus towards the creation of
power blocs and confrontation; it was more offensive than Bismarck's defensive
tactics. There were good reasons for the decision . . . Nevertheless it was still a
calamity.'[33]

Not only the decision itself, but also the rushed and clumsy way in which
it was taken could not but cause offence to Russia. The solution repeatedly
put forward by Raschdau, of entering into serious negotiations in the hope of
achieving a different, less risky agreement with Russia, would undoubtedly
have been more tactful, even if it had failed in the end. Whatever one thinks of
the cynical conduct of the Bismarcks, the astute and pessimistic arguments of
Holstein and the straightforward, unpolitical standpoint of the newly appointed
Chancellor-General, the role of Kaiser Wilhelm II in the process which brought
about a decision of such importance in international history is shocking in its
superficiality and inconsistency. He stated his claim – not only verbally but also,
and above all, by his dismissal of Bismarck – to decide policy guidelines himself,
and yet lost track of this matter for days on end. He gave his consent several
times for the renewal, apparently without having grasped the full significance of
the secret alliance, and then changed his mind equally hastily, partly following
the advice of his official advisers, but partly driven by feelings of wounded

*amour propre* and especially by his desire to prove his personal authority. This combination of authoritarian conduct and outrageous frivolity did not bode well for the new era without Bismarck.

## THE KAISER AND THE FOREIGN POLICY OF THE NEW COURSE

When he dismissed Bismarck, did the Kaiser have foreign policy goals or even firm plans which he could now pursue unhindered? His very first actions stood in such marked contrast to his attitude during the dismissal crisis that they aroused the suspicion that his differences with Bismarck had been mere pretexts in a tactical struggle for power. Wilhelm's acceptance of Tsar Alexander's invitation to take part in the Russian army manoeuvres only days after he had declared that he would not go to Russia under any circumstances; the appeal to the despised Bleichröder to act as intermediary in the attempt to give financial assistance to Germany's ally Italy; his order to the commanding generals in the Ruhr 'to let the repeating rifles do their work at the first opportunity' after his frequent solemn declarations that he could not besmirch the first years of his reign with the blood of his subjects – all this and more led to the conviction that the young Kaiser was vacillating and lacking in a sense of purpose.[34]

The Chief of the General Staff, Count Waldersee, above all, was struck by Wilhelm II's apparent aimlessness. 'Many people thought that the Kaiser would have ascended the throne with firm and great plans for the future', he wrote less than six months after Bismarck's dismissal. 'It is quite plain to me that this is not the case. His thoughts were certainly lofty, he hoped to win great esteem for the German Reich and no doubt also to do great deeds himself. But he had no firm plan as to how to achieve this.'[35] As early as April 1890 he commented after a discussion with Philipp Eulenburg: 'What makes me most anxious is to observe that the Kaiser still has no firm opinions. He wavers back and forth . . . How often I have seen him wavering between Austria and Russia! How many different opinions I have heard him express about certain people! A man can be excellent today but in a few days' time he will be quite worthless, and vice versa! . . . He is still too impressionable.'[36] A few months later the General again noted in his diary: 'The Kaiser still has no firm opinions on any subject and does not know what he is aiming at. Anyone reasonably clever can easily influence him and he makes the most surprising leaps in all directions.'[37] By the autumn of 1891 the tenor of Waldersee's comments on the Kaiser had not greatly changed: 'And he is supposed to be an energetic man who knows exactly what he wants! Unfortunately he is like a reed before the wind who is still unsure of where he wants to be, in whatever sphere.'[38] 'When I think of how the Kaiser assured me 2–3 years ago that he would never stray from the path he had chosen, after I had begged him to be consistent, as nothing was more harmful than constant changes of system!'[39]

Other observers in the immediate circle around the Kaiser, it must be said, took a much more favourable view of his activities in the field of foreign affairs at this time. His Flügeladjutant Count von Wedel, for instance, following a conversation with Wilhelm II not long after Bismarck's dismissal, commented: 'My God, what outstanding qualities of mind our young sovereign has! What great and original ideas he has, and yet how irritated one can be sometimes by the strange course he adopts! May Heaven grant its blessing!'[40] On several occasions Wedel praised the 'clear, calm and cool judgement of the Kaiser . . . in questions of foreign policy', and even after two and a half years' service in close attendance on the Kaiser, in May 1891, he still felt able to comment that 'our young sovereign . . . pursues his plans with rare thoughtfulness and consistency'.[41] Similarly, the Kaiser's friend Philipp Eulenburg, as Waldersee concluded after a meeting with him, was an 'idealist' who firmly believed 'that Providence has great things in store for the Kaiser'; he was 'full of hope and confidence'.[42] The clearest testimony to the Kaiser's strongly developed will-power was given by those who suffered most directly from it. Reich Chancellor von Caprivi, for one, complained on 6 June 1890 of 'the constant torrent of new plans from the Kaiser and the millions needed, but not available, to carry them out'.[43]

If the disappointed Waldersee complained of the Kaiser's lack of a clear foreign policy plan, he too had no illusions about Wilhelm's immense power, his steely determination to shine in the eyes of the world, to rule in person and especially to decide on the foreign policy pursued by the German Reich. His own diary bears witness to the energetic and self-confident political activity of the young monarch. As he commented not long after Bismarck's fall, '*One* thought runs through . . . all his actions – concern for his personal position. He wants to be popular!'[44] Even if Wilhelm II's aims were still vague and unclear, one thing is certain: the Chief of the General Staff was to have direct experience of the Kaiser's power from at least the autumn of 1890, when his own position began to be threatened. A year after Bismarck's departure Waldersee observed that the Reich Chancellor was having 'a dreadfully difficult time with the Kaiser' because 'the good man cannot resist governing alongside the government; he would like to control everything and above all to make the world believe that he is the man who has everything under his control. So he goes gaily on, negotiating directly with this person or that, on his own initiative; this must lead to confusion and I cannot conceive how much Caprivi has to put up with.'[45] Six months later the General noted anxiously that an increasing number of observers were coming to think that, however many mistakes Caprivi had made, the principal blame for policy failures lay not with the Chancellor but with the Kaiser himself. 'With a Kaiser of such limited experience, so few clear opinions, such a changeable nature and at the same time such a strong inclination do everything himself and such a firm conviction that he knows everything better – no chancellor can govern. None could help but fail.'[46] Above all, Wilhelm had a deplorable habit of corresponding with the military attachés at various German embassies abroad, and of using them to make contact with foreign monarchs while bypassing the Reich Chancellor and the Foreign Office. Even in the eyes of Waldersee, who as chief of the General Staff had tried to build up just such an information network via the military attachés, this could not but create further chaos. In January 1892 he recorded indignantly that the Chancellor, 'in a towering rage', had made a vain attempt to prevent the Kaiser from corresponding with King Umberto of Italy through the military attaché Engelbrecht.[47] Not long afterwards the Kaiser revealed to Waldersee that he had bypassed the Foreign Office and the ambassador in St Petersburg by asking the military attaché there, Villaume, to assure Tsar Alexander on his behalf that he had no thoughts of war. Waldersee was horrified when, after a discussion of the military repercussions of the Russian famine, the Kaiser remarked to him: 'Hinzpeter takes a similar view.' 'So this wretched, scheming schoolmaster discusses such matters too', the General commented in disgust.[48] Caprivi was only indirectly to blame for the unhappy mood and serious state of the country, Waldersee considered, for 'the Kaiser wants to rule in person and to put everything to rights by himself. In that case he must also bear the responsibility, and indeed he can be shown to have been the cause of all the discontent.' The Chancellor was responsible for the bungled state of affairs only insofar as 'he does not provide a strong counterweight'.[49]

Waldersee saw more clearly than anyone that the Kaiser's opportunities for making his mark in the field of foreign policy were greater, more direct and considerably more dangerous than in the internal affairs of Prussia and the Reich. Shortly before his dismissal from the post of chief of the General Staff in January 1891 Waldersee held discussions with the ambassadors Reuss (Vienna), Radowitz (Constantinople) and Münster (Paris) during which all four acquiesced in the view that Bismarck's retirement had left a vulnerable gap in foreign policy which Caprivi had been unable to fill. Previously, the ambassadors agreed, all foreign governments, whenever a crisis arose, had asked what Bismarck's view was. But that was no longer so, for no one asked the opinion of the new German Chancellor. In general the representatives of the Reich abroad had come to think that Caprivi himself 'does not know in which direction he should steer'. While the Chancellor held back too much, the Kaiser, for his part, showed 'a strong inclination to dabble in politics himself', the diplomats commented. Although he pointed out that Wilhelm was by no means pursuing 'a completely new aim', Waldersee conceded that the Kaiser loved 'sudden jumps' and acted 'quickly, often too quickly, on momentary impulses'. 'If such a thing is dangerous anywhere, it is in the field of high politics', he warned. The ambassadors' comments also gave Waldersee the distinct impression that the views expressed by the Kaiser often did not coincide with those of the Chancellor and his advisers in the Wilhelmstrasse.[50]

Nothing demonstrates more clearly the growing anxiety of the Chief of the General Staff over the Kaiser's intervention in foreign policy than his comments on relations with Russia. Waldersee himself, of course, deeply distrusted Russia, and the relationship between the two countries had grown increasingly tense since Bismarck's fall and the non-renewal of the Reinsurance Treaty. The General recognised, however, that on the German side a policy of steadiness, caution and courtesy was required if the gigantic Russian Empire was not to be driven entirely into the arms of France. Instead, Wilhelm allowed his own vanity and thoughtlessness to mislead him into making such critical comments about Russia both in private conversation and in public speeches that his advisers were often horrified and sometimes even doubted his sanity. Only a few days after Bismarck's dismissal Waldersee noted with disapproval that in his attitude towards Russia Wilhelm was indulging in 'frequent and rapid scene-changes'. He was referring to Wilhelm's wish to go to Russia after all, to attend the manoeuvres in the summer. '8 days ago the Kaiser was absolutely determined not to go to Russia . . . under any circumstances, although shortly before that the contrary was the case.' But then Schweinitz had come to Berlin with the Tsar's personal invitation, and the Kaiser instantly decided 'that Russia is not so bad after all and now he does want to go there!'[51] In spite of the fact that he was about to visit Russia, in May 1890 Wilhelm was provoked by interviews which Bismarck had given to Russian and French journalists into exclaiming that Austria could not be grateful enough to him for having 'turned out Bismarck', as the latter had been planning the 'destruction' of the Danube monarchy in collusion with Russia. As even the loyal Carl Wedel remarked: 'With such stories I often wonder how far it is the Kaiser's imagination which is playing tricks on him, or how far it is libellous busybodies who are secretly telling him untrue or distorted, exaggerated things, for such tales surely cannot be really true!!'[52]

Still in this overexcited state of mind, Wilhelm II made a speech during a visit to the province of East Prussia which gave cause for alarm in Russian government and army circles. He would do his best to safeguard peace, he declared in Königsberg; 'but if it should be God's will that I be required to defend myself and to protect my country's borders, East Prussia's sword will show no less keen an edge in fighting the enemy than it did in 1870'. Those who dared to overturn peace would not be spared a lesson 'which they will not forget in a hundred years', he added threateningly, and promised: 'I shall not let the province be touched, but if any one should attempt it, my sovereignty will stand against it like a rocher de bronce.'[53] These bombastic words, clearly destined for Russian ears, were received with anger and alarm. Waldersee noted on 21 May that people in Russia were 'highly incensed by the Kaiser's speech'. But then again the Kaiser had taken the Russian reaction 'very badly', so that the 'much-discussed journey' to Russia was once more hanging in the balance.[54]

Wilhelm was particularly enraged by the russification of Finland, which began with the Tsar's manifesto on the Finnish postal system in the summer of 1890. He considered this to be a 'constitutional violation'. In a marginal note on a report from St Petersburg he commented that he fully shared the pessimistic view that the Russian government's aim was to turn Finland gradually into a province of the Russian Empire. One could not blame the Finnish people, let alone the Swedes, for resenting the Russian measures.[55] Neither the German nor the Russian side, therefore, pinned any great hopes on the Kaiser's visit to the Russian capital in August 1890. After Wilhelm's return to Potsdam on 27 August Prince Ernst zu Hohenlohe-Langenburg, who was working in the Foreign Office, commented that 'everything went off satisfactorily in Russia and at least the personal relations between the two Emperors became warmer'. But there had been no political benefits worth recording.[56] In fact, however, what had once been a good relationship between the two Emperors could not be restored, and gave way to an ill-natured indifference on both sides.[57]

In the course of a conversation during which the Kaiser explained to the Tsar why Germany had not been able to renew the secret Reinsurance Treaty, the two had a curious argument about France, triggered by the Tsar's remark that in their common struggle against nihilism and socialism the central and eastern European monarchies would be greatly assisted if the monarchy could be restored in France; at any rate, he said, he would never ally himself with France as long as it remained a republic.[58] The acting Chief of the French General Staff, General Boisdeffre, who was in Russia at the time, also came out with the assertion that the senior officers in his country were planning to restore the monarchy.[59] When the Flügeladjutant Carl Wedel, in discussing the question with the Kaiser, adopted Bismarck's well-known view that the French Republic would always have more difficulty than a French monarchy in finding allies among the other great powers, and went on to express the opinion that a restored French monarchy would try to legitimise itself through a war against Germany to recover Alsace and Lorraine, Wilhelm strongly contradicted this view. 'Strange to say, the Kaiser did not share this opinion', Wedel recorded with surprise. 'He thinks that we can enter into peaceful discussions more easily with the French monarchy, and that the latter will see its primary aim as the inner rebirth of the nation, rather than risking an adventure abroad.'[60] To Waldersee too the Kaiser expressed his conviction 'that Boisdeffre is right and would be supported by the Russians'. The Chief of the German General Staff commented: 'I cannot share in this beautiful dream, although unrest and civil war in France would certainly be the best thing that could happen for us.'[61] In the next few months Wilhelm II continued his attempts 'to hook the French'. He treated Jules Simon, President Carnot, the French ambassador Herbette and General Gallifet with particular courtesy and corresponded openly with Boisdeffre and with the widow of the painter Jean-Louis-Ernest Meissonier, who died at the beginning of 1891.[62]

In February 1891 Count Münster, the German ambassador in Paris, put forward a proposal that a number of French artists should be persuaded to exhibit their pictures in Berlin. Wilhelm and Caprivi took up the suggestion and had the idea of sending the Empress Frederick incognito – she took the name Countess Lingen on such occasions – to Paris for this purpose. She should make contact with the French artists and select appropriate pictures.[63] Waldersee, who suspected that the influence of Hinzpeter's French wife was behind this swing towards France, had nothing but scorn for this 'childish idea' which the Kaiser and Caprivi were pursuing 'to conciliate the French! We are making ourselves a laughing-stock for the whole world!', he wrote in his diary. In fact the attempted reconciliation proved all too soon to be 'a fiasco on a grand scale'.[64] Above all, the idea that the presence of the Empress Frederick and her daughter Margarethe could be kept a secret in Paris was a complete illusion. In a letter to her son written on 21 February from her apartments in the German embassy in Paris, Vicky commented: 'The newspaper reporters are a perfect pest, they follow us about everywhere like our shadows but we succeed in dogging [sic] them now & then, & it is rather amusing to read in the newspapers of the places we have visited (many of which we have never gone near).'[65] They were less amused, however, when chauvinistic articles appeared in the press calling for mass demonstrations against the 'German' Empress, who was forced to leave hastily for England. The German ambassador expressed the opinion that the Empress's visit would have been very useful if it had lasted four days, as planned, instead of ten, and 'if the royal lady had brought a more tactful escort than Seckendorff'.[66] 'I only hope in Germany they will not attach too much importance to it, and this ridiculous excitement will in the end not prevent the French artists from sending their things to the Berlin Exhibition!', the Empress Frederick wrote to her daughter Moretta.[67] But the right-wing Berlin newspapers brought out a stream of articles, apparently originating in diplomatic circles, stirring up feeling against the liberal Empress. Among other things, she was falsely accused of refusing to receive the Russian ambassador Mohrenheim and his wife, of going to see mainly Jewish art collections in Paris, of buying nothing in the shops, and of failing to give a single *sou* to the poor of Paris although she had inherited millions from the Duchesse de Galliera.[68] In Conservative circles the joke went around that after this debacle the Empress Frederick would not call herself Countess Lingen any more, but only Miss Lingen – a pun on the German word for failure.[69]

In spite of being on such bad terms with his mother, the Kaiser threatened serious repercussions if there were any 'unseemly behaviour towards the All-Highest person of the Kaiserin' in Paris. In response to the demonstrations against her in Paris, he ordered the rule requiring passports to be carried in Alsace-Lorraine to be enforced with the utmost severity, which the *'very distressed'* Empress Frederick condemned as 'so unnecessary and as *wrong-headed* as could be'.[70] After the Paris incident Wilhelm resumed his hostile attitude towards France. He took a malicious delight in the news that the 'French luminaries' who wanted to exhibit their pictures in Moscow had been forced to flee from Russia.[71] He spoke contemptuously of the French republicans – calling them 'infamous curs!' – and completely failed to recognise the looming threat of an alliance between France and the Russian Empire. 'The saying "Do not come near your Prince unless you are called!" is also valid for the Frenchmen in Moscow', he wrote on a diplomatic report of May 1891. When the Austrian Foreign Minister, Count Kálnoky, pointed out that Russia was convinced that even without a treaty of alliance France would take the Russian side in a war between Russia and Germany, the Kaiser remarked scornfully: 'Like a whore, without having to marry her.'[72]

Wilhelm's relationship with Denmark, which would play a strategically important role in a European war, remained tense and full of mistrust. A 'diffident' request directed by King Christian IX to the Kaiser, asking for the return of a few towns and villages in North Schleswig, was politely but firmly turned down by Wilhelm after consultation with Caprivi.[73] Discussing the matter with Waldersee in November 1890, however, the Kaiser spoke 'quite sharply about the Queen of Denmark and Prince Waldemar and about the intrigues of all the female relations, that is to say the Empress of Russia, the Princess of Wales and the Duchess of Cumberland. I had gathered from earlier remarks', Waldersee wrote, 'that the mood was gradually improving in that regard, but certainly only on condition that the King completely accepted the present situation. As this does not now seem to be the case, we shall after all be well advised to reckon with Denmark in the next war. The Kaiser thinks it best to send a fleet to Copenhagen straight away with an ultimatum. If we have time, this is of course an appropriate action to take, but only if war should break out surprisingly just at a time when we had a suitable fleet to hand! The fact that the Norwegians have not been on very friendly terms with the Danes lately seemed to please the Kaiser particularly. But unfortunately it is of very little significance.'[74]

On 18 April 1891, at a large military banquet in the White Hall of the Berlin Schloss, Kaiser Wilhelm II made a speech which according to Wedel sounded 'very warlike'. In an allusion to Bismarck's famous saying that the German Reich had been established not by parliamentary majorities and resolutions but by blood and iron, Wilhelm proclaimed that 'the German Reich was forged not by parliamentary majorities and resolutions but by the soldier and the army. My trust lies in the army. We live in solemn times, and there may be bad times before us in the next few years . . . Whatever the future brings, we shall hold aloft our flags and our traditions, mindful of the words and deeds of [the Margrave of Brandenburg] Albrecht Achilles, who said: "I know of no nobler place to die than in the midst of one's enemies." This is also my own heartfelt belief, and on it rests my unshakeable faith in the loyalty, courage and dedication of My army, particularly of all the comrades who are posted at our borders.'[75] Although government and court officials tried to pass on a watered-down version of the speech to the press, the actual text reached the German newspapers via the *Pester Lloyd* and the Viennese *Fremdenblatt*. Both the Reich Chancellor and the Flügeladjutanten Wedel and Zitzewitz wondered what had caused the 'warlike mood of the Kaiser'. Wedel thought that it was just another insignificant gaffe, and that Wilhelm's 'inclination to make speeches in general and his lack of preparation' were alone to blame. But he was forced to retract this opinion when he discovered that Wilhelm had recently given orders for a mobile headquarters to be built and a mobilisation plan to be worked out for the royal stables.[76]

Waldersee also expressed scathing opinions about the Kaiser's weakness for handing out new colours and standards 'which are mostly far-fetched', and for accompanying these with fulminating speeches. Commenting on the belligerent speech of 18 April 1891 he said that the strong emphasis on Luther had offended the Catholics, and that Wilhelm had 'once again needlessly roused' enemies within. Such remarks, together with the Kaiser's pessimistic utterances about a future war, Waldersee noted, made 'all discerning listeners . . . go hot and cold'. 'But the Kaiser himself believes he made an outstanding speech and the next morning he was indignant not to find it reported word for word in the newspaper.'[77] Meanwhile the Russians were quietly continuing to pursue their goals without a care for anyone, the General observed. 'They are trying to suppress completely and neutralise all nationalities which are not pure Russian, and at the same time to increase their military power and to be prepared for a rapid transition to war. The Kaiser, who is of course very easily influenced, at one moment thinks that everything looks perfectly peaceful, and at the next − when he receives news such as the redeployment of a division or something of the sort − that war is imminent.' Caprivi wavered back and forth with the Kaiser and had neither the intelligence nor the energy to pursue a consistent policy, Waldersee complained. For him it was clear that there were only two courses open to Germany, and one must be chosen. 'Either we say to ourselves that war must certainly come, and in that case we must go on arming ourselves with all our might; it would be best for us to fix our eyes firmly on a date when we can bring about the decisive moment ourselves. Or we believe that there is a way round, and in that case we must take it, i.e. try to turn our policy in a different direction: get out of the Triple Alliance and have a rapprochement with Russia, with or without Austria. But what do we do? Militarily, nothing; politically, we ride around on the broken-backed Triple Alliance and flirt in the clumsiest possible way with the Poles. Meanwhile we are most certainly rushing towards our doom.'[78] In May 1891 the General confided to his diary that the Kaiser was 'in an anxious state of mind and he believes there will be war before this year is out . . . He is naturally not at all pleased that the French are sending a fleet to Kronstadt in the summer. He sees clearly that Russia is quite openly making a show of her friendship with France for our benefit.'[79]

## FIRST STEPS IN COLONIAL AND NAVAL POLICY

Caprivi's foreign policy was directed principally towards ensuring the security of the German Reich on the continent of Europe.[80] To this end he wished first of all to strengthen the Triple Alliance between Germany, Austria-Hungary and Italy, prerequisites for which were the abandonment of the secret agreements with Russia and the establishment of relations of trust with Great Britain. This last, in turn, depended on a policy of restraint in German colonial affairs and particularly in naval armament. The advocates of this straightforward and moderate continental policy with its main focus on central Europe included not only Friedrich von Holstein, Adolf Marschall von Bieberstein and Alfred von Kiderlen-Wächter at the Foreign Office, but also – at first – the General Staff under Waldersee. The latter had a long conversation on 1 May 1890 with Caprivi about foreign policy, in the course of which he set out for the Chancellor the strategy and tactics to be adopted in any future war.[81] Caprivi expressed himself entirely satisfied with the Chief of the General Staff's analysis, and for his part Waldersee was glad to observe that Caprivi wanted 'to stick firmly to Austria'. 'I am sure that we shall get along well', noted Waldersee, who for the time being was still optimistic about his relationship with his fellow General at the Reich chancellor's palace.[82] The newly appointed Chancellor also told General Carl von Wedel that he wished to create both a 'Central European Customs Union' between Germany, Austria-Hungary and Italy and a maritime alliance with Denmark and the Netherlands, for 'if we can win over both [the latter] countries with their large sea-faring populations we shall be in a position to build up and maintain a large, powerful battlefleet, for which Germany does not have sufficient manpower on her own'.[83] As far as overseas policy was concerned, Caprivi professed himself an 'opponent' of colonies in principle, although he could not deny that to give up the colonies acquired so far by Germany would not be compatible with the national honour.[84] Like Caprivi, Waldersee rejected not only German colonialism, but also the 'whole colonial policy' of the European powers, and predicted, far-sightedly, that their imperialism would not last long. 'Africa belongs to the Africans! That is my view; and I consider it shameful on the part of the European powers simply to cut up the continent between them', he declared in the summer of 1890. 'The Mohammedans are working slowly but surely to convert the inhabitants to their creed and are far superior to us in their methods. I believe that Africa will belong to them and that after a few decades all Europeans will be driven out!'[85] In spite of the restraint in German colonial policy, however, Waldersee was concerned to note as early as June 1890 that the mood in Britain was becoming increasingly hostile towards Germany.[86]

The calm and restrained attitude required by Caprivi's cautious continental policy did not accord well either with Kaiser Wilhelm II's temperament or with his long-held, overweening ambitions. In the immediate aftermath of Bismarck's dismissal there was widespread 'fear of surprises, and unexpected escapades by our Kaiser', who was thought perfectly capable of 'going off at a tangent in the field of foreign policy'. In particular it was feared that Wilhelm might, 'if his social welfare policy were to run aground, perhaps start experimenting with diplomacy'.[87] It seemed at first that Wilhelm would favour an expansive colonial policy in Africa and thereby come into conflict with the Chancellor and the Foreign Office. In early April 1890 Caprivi confided to the Flügeladjutant Wedel that, as far as colonial policy was concerned, the Kaiser was pursuing 'far-reaching goals, with which he did not agree'.[88] From Waldersee's diaries we know that the Kaiser was 'determined' at this time 'not to give ground' to Britain in East Africa, but to extend and establish German influence 'as far as the lakes, to annex Zanzibar or at least to acquire a protectorate over it'. He had often expressed such sentiments recently, Waldersee recorded, as a result of which he had roused great hopes in colonial circles.[89] The Chief of the General Staff immediately recognised that this was an area 'in which differences of opinion between the Kaiser and the Chancellor' might arise.[90] When at the end of April 1890 Eulenburg drew the Kaiser's attention to the danger of an agreement between France and Britain which would cause 'great difficulties in Africa' for Germany, the impression made upon Wilhelm by this remark was unmistakable.[91]

In May 1890 Major Eduard von Liebert, the future governor of German East Africa, returned to Berlin from Africa in high spirits, after German troops had come to the aid of the German East Africa Company to put down the Bushiri rebellion in 1889. Liebert spoke so enthusiastically about the potential for development of this German protectorate (the present Tanzania) that the Foreign Office was seriously concerned that 'he might make the Kaiser even more enthusiastic and thereby cause us problems with England'.[92] The African explorer Hermann Wissmann also came to Berlin in the summer of 1890 – he received his patent of nobility at the Neues Palais on 24 June – and spoke 'very despondently of the bureaucratic attitude of the Chancellor and his people in dealing with African affairs'.[93] Seen from the point of view of the Wilhelmstrasse it was also alarming that Waldersee, who hitherto had argued for restraint in colonial policy, was now taking a vigorously defiant attitude towards Great Britain, whose expansionist aims in Africa certainly strike us as excessive today.[94] 'I do not wish to pass judgement on our relations with England', he wrote in his diary on 4 May 1890; 'I only know that we have been unbelievably submissive and timid hitherto, and also that the English have persisted in behaving in the most shameless and ruthless way in East Africa.'[95] In the conflict which was thus beginning to develop between the military and the Wilhelmstrasse it was of course the Kaiser's attitude which tipped the balance. Waldersee wrote on 24 May: 'In our East African policy we are coming up against many difficulties with England and would certainly give way if the Kaiser did not vigorously oppose it. All the officers who come here from Africa are full of hopes for the successful development of the colony so long as matters are handled with resolution here in Berlin.'[96] After Wilhelm had had a long conversation with Liebert during a military review at Spandau, Waldersee was able to note that the Kaiser had 'not the slightest inclination to give in to the excessive demands of the English, and there will be a difficult passage with Caprivi'.[97] The international repercussions of the Kaiser's attitude soon made themselves felt: on 23 May Lord Salisbury had to inform Queen Victoria that his negotiations with the German ambassador Count Hatzfeldt had failed, as the Kaiser wanted to cut Britain off from the great inland lake, 'which we cannot admit'.[98] In August 1890, after a conversation with the Prime Minister, the Queen complained of the great difficulties which her government was having with Germany over Africa.[99]

Wilhelm's confidence in Wissmann and Liebert was so great that he was also quite prepared to defend these officers against the colonial enthusiasts who advocated still more ambitious aims. An example of this occurred in December 1890 when Wissmann felt compelled to urge restraint on the celebrated African explorer and adventurer Eduard Schnitzer, who called himself Emin Pasha and who was leading a German expedition to Lake Nyanza in central Africa, now Lake Victoria.[100] The president of the German Colonial Society was none other that the Kaiserin's uncle, Prince Hermann zu Hohenlohe-Langenburg, who sent an urgent petition to the Kaiser on 25 December following newspaper reports of the recall of Emin Pasha. In it Hohenlohe gave a prophetic warning that the news of Emin's recall would spread like wildfire in central Africa and would put the man himself in grave danger. The chiefs of the warrior tribes and the Arabs who had entered into treaties with him as the Kaiser's representative and had ceded territory to Germany would 'look upon the disgraced Pasha as a deceiver and a traitor' and his authority would be severely damaged. 'If Emin should fall victim to the greed and vengeance of the natives . . . the imperial government would be accused of responsibility for the downfall of the man whom Europe admired for the selflessness with which he has devoted his life to winning Africa for the cause of civilisation.' In any case, Hohenlohe argued, the possibility should be borne in mind that on receiving the news of his recall Emin 'will feel compelled to throw himself into the arms of the English, which [would have] the worst possible consequences for the entire future development of the East African territories'. 'The high reputation and powerful position of the German Reich would be seriously impaired in the eyes of the natives' and grave problems would inevitably ensue. 'Everything which has been gained in East Africa over the past year, with so much effort and such heavy sacrifices, could hang in the balance. Filled with a passionate desire to see Germany's colonial possession achieving rapid and prosperous development', Hohenlohe appealed 'most humbly' to the Kaiser to cancel Emin Pasha's recall.[101]

Kaiser Wilhelm II replied to this petition with characteristic firmness on 27 December 1890: 'My dearest Uncle, I have received your letter concerning Emin Pasha and I hasten to answer it. First of all I must clear up a misunderstanding which is affecting you as well as many of our colonial friends. Emin *is not at all in disgrace* and has therefore not been recalled. Following orders from here Emin has by agreement placed himself under the Reich Commissar [Wissmann] and has pledged himself to obey his instructions. That he is in the service of the Reich at all is my own work for I instructed the former Reich Chancellor to take him on. Orders were given to Emin to advance to Nyanza equipped with a certain sum of money, gifts and bearers, to set up one or more bases – at any rate one fully equipped one – there, and then to return home. He was also ordered not to get involved in any fighting and only to enter into treaties, so as to have as reassuring an effect as possible. Only attacks on the caravan itself, of course, should be vigorously resisted. That is why the detachment which is accompanying him is so small, sufficient to protect the bearers but not for purposes of war. Emin has been at Nyanza for a long time now and has had plenty of time to look around, set up bases, explore the land around them and make it secure as agreed. As he was not making any preparations to come home, despite his orders, he received a second, repeated order to return after the completion of his task. Where is the disgrace or recall in that?! Reports and more detailed information cannot be expected for some time yet, to show what Emin has achieved. But if differences have arisen as a result of disobedience by Emin, giving the Reich Commissar cause to remind Emin of his orders again, that is simply Wissmann's duty. He bears the whole responsibility for military protection and for the measures that are required. The whole of Wissmann's past life provides a guarantee that he thoroughly understands what he is doing in Africa. But if there is to be any hope for the prosperous development of the colony, then the first requirement is that there should be discipline among those involved there. Without discipline no national institution can flourish and develop. So if anyone is sent out with instructions from the Commissar and then does not follow his instructions, he must learn to knuckle under, whether his name is Emin, Schulze or Lehmann. For if we cannot do without obedience in Europe, how much more necessary is it in Africa, where everything still has a half-military, warlike aspect, and the smallest mistake may be disastrous and could cost the lives of many. For the government here to interfere with Wissmann's orders, at a distance, ex officio, without more detailed reports, is absolutely out of the question. I have the fullest confidence in Wissmann and in his judgement. Emin must also learn that "Bravery even a Mameluke displays; obedience earns the Christian praise", which is quite good in relation to the Arabs. Your devoted nephew Wilhelm I. R. Happy New Year.'[102] Prince Hohenlohe declared himself reassured that all the rumours that Wilhelm was dissatisfied with Wissmann had been proved baseless by this confidential explanation from his 'All-Gracious Kaiser and Sovereign'.[103] As is well known, the ill-starred expedition led by Emin Pasha, who refused to acknowledge Wissmann's orders to return, ended with his murder by Arab slave-traders on 23 October 1892, just as Hohenlohe had predicted.[104]

If Wilhelm II had one aim that he pursued with even more enthusiasm than the expansion of the German colonial empire in Africa, it was to build up a large naval force. That this was his first priority became apparent in June 1890 when the astonishing agreement with Britain, under which Germany received the strategically important North Sea island of Heligoland in exchange for Zanzibar, became known.[105] The colonial enthusiasts and representatives of the export trade, who were chiefly to be found in the ranks of the Free Conservatives and National Liberals, were suddenly bitterly resentful of the Kaiser, by whom they felt they had been first 'urged on and then disowned and deserted'. A certain malicious hostility towards Caprivi also began to spread, and eventually led to the foundation of the Pan-German League.[106] The Kaiser, however, was enthusiastically in favour of the Heligoland–Zanzibar Treaty. At the beginning of his Scandinavian cruise in late June 1890, he discoursed on the strategic value of Heligoland in the presence of the newly appointed Secretary of State of the Reich Navy Office, Admiral Friedrich von Hollmann. He emphasised that if necessary he would have given up 'even more' than Zanzibar to obtain this little North Sea island, for he valued Heligoland 'very highly and he intends to set up cannon or howitzers on it. The English had no idea of Heligoland's strategic importance, and in order that they should remain in the dark he had also instructed that the German press should not mention it until the treaty had been ratified. Once that had been done he would soon show them how valuable the island was for us.'[107]

The Heligoland–Zanzibar Treaty and the Kaiser's brief visit to the South of England at the beginning of August 1890 led to a noticeable improvement in Anglo-German relations that summer. 'The English and the Belgians seem to be quite delighted with him [Wilhelm II]', as Ernst Hohenlohe at the Foreign Office reported to his father on 13 August 1890. 'The English newspapers are vying with each other in their panegyrics and assurances of friendship for Germany. The "Standard", the organ of the government, even says that England belongs in effect, if not formally, to the Triple Alliance and will stand shoulder to shoulder with it. The reception given to the Kaiser is said to have been very warm, as [August] Eulenburg told me. The notorious [Heligoland–Zanzibar] Treaty has had one good effect after all, in that the present mood towards us in England, even on the part of Gladstone and the opposition, has changed entirely for the better; and that makes up for a great deal. I thought the pompous handing-over of Heligoland [on 10 August 1890] rather ridiculous, and the comparison between this act and the Battle of Wörth in the imperial speech not very appropriate.'[108] This last remark referred to the Kaiser's address to his 'Comrades in the Navy!', in which he declaimed 'Four days have passed since we celebrated the memorable day of the Battle of Wörth, when under My late, revered grandfather the first hammer-blow in the construction of the new German Reich was struck by My father. Today, twenty years later, I reincorporate this island, as the last piece of German soil, into the German Fatherland, with neither battle nor blood. The island's destiny is to become a bulwark on the sea, a refuge for German fishermen, a base for my warships, a stronghold and a shield for Germany's seas against any enemy who should venture into them.'[109]

The ambivalence of Wilhelm II's attitude towards Great Britain, and the wishful thinking with which it was permeated, is exemplified by the fact that he chose the moment of taking possession of Heligoland to propose a toast in which he described Britain as a 'kindred land' and his grandmother as the 'noble lady whom we have to thank for the fact that the island is German once more. The Queen reigns over her country with far-seeing vision and lofty wisdom, and she attaches great importance to living in friendship with Me and My people. She values German officers, German melodies. Long live the Queen of England!'[110]

It was entirely in keeping with this attitude that the German Kaiser made use of the — supposed — permission which he had from the Queen to hand out advice to her on naval matters. As he wrote to her in February 1891, he had 'very grave doubts in the soundness & efficiency of the heaviest guns' in the battleships of the Royal Navy. The root of the evil lay in the English supply system, under which the fleet was obliged to accept the guns manufactured by Sir William Armstrong in Elswick. His advice was that the navy should manufacture its own guns in the Woolwich Arsenal, or at least have the right to inform the manufacturers of its requirements. In Germany the naval experts would say to Krupps: 'Such & such a gun is wanted in the fleet; it must have a certain number of qualities, which are named; then when the gun is made it is tested at the works. First by Krupp, then by a committee of officers, & if that is not enough it is sent to the Government Range.' He recommended that the German procurement system should be introduced in the Royal Navy.[111] Ten days later he sent his grandmother a warmly worded telegram of congratulations on the launch of two new Royal Navy ships, again emphasising the affinity between the two fleets. 'May the two fine new ships built by British hands prove a powerful addition to the Royal Navy and may they always . . . uphold the honour of the British flag. The whole of my Navy feels with me the honour done to our comrades in arms and begs to lay the most respectful congratulations at Your Majesty's feet.' He signed the telegram 'William German Emperor, King of Prussia, Admiral of the Fleet'.[112] Lord Salisbury suggested to the Queen that she confer a high-ranking British order on Admiral von der Goltz, who attended the launch as the Kaiser's representative, 'merely as a matter of policy'. It had the desired effect on Wilhelm.[113]

No observer could fail to see how much at home the Kaiser felt in the company of senior German naval officers. When he arrived at Wilhelmshaven on 22 April 1890 in the *Lahn* he was to have disembarked, according to the agreed pro-gramme. But instead he went on board the *Deutschland*, which had just returned from the Mediterranean. 'There were hearty greetings', Vice-Admiral Paul Hoff-mann recorded in his diary. The Kaiser inspected the crew and 'then betook himself to the cabin, where he felt so much at home that he said to his suite: "Come in to my cabin, gentlemen."' There he presented Admiral Friedrich von Hollmann with his patent of appointment as secretary of state at the Reich Navy Office and talked to him at length about Bismarck's dismissal. The monarch's conspicuous camaraderie with Hollmann was demonstrated again that evening when the latter was on his way to the Casino club with Hoffmann. Just as the two admirals were about to enter the building the Kaiser's carriage drew up at

the door. Hoffmann recorded: 'We hid behind a sentry box, but when we followed the Kaiser in he noticed us and was very pleased. Because of the rain the
Admiral [Hollmann] was wearing large rubber galoshes, with his trousers rolled
up, and a grey cloth draped round his neck over his raincoat. The Kaiser gave
him no time to take off his coat. "I shall take my guest in", he said, taking the
Admiral by the arm, and led him up the stairs into the brightly lit corridor where
many officers were standing, and then said: "Hollmann, old fellow, take your
overshoes off now, I will hold you steady", so that the Admiral was overcome
with embarrassment at the way he was dressed.'[114]

This friendly relationship was bound to have its consequences. Naval officers,
above all Chief of the Naval Cabinet Freiherr von Senden-Bibran and Navy Secretary von Hollmann, who was in the habit of lying in wait for the Kaiser during
his morning walks in the Tiergarten, did their best to encourage Wilhelm's personal commitment to the enlargement of the fleet. Prince Heinrich, stationed in
Kiel and enthusiastically dedicated to his career as a naval officer, also exercised
an anti-British influence on his brother. When his mother praised British rule
in Egypt in his presence in early 1891 Heinrich became 'quite savage'. 'He is
alas *so* jealous of England as a nation & as a power!', she commented.[115] During
the Scandinavian cruise in the summer of 1890 Alfred von Kiderlen-Wächter,
the Foreign Office representative in attendance, became aware of the disproportionate influence of the navy on the Kaiser. He deplored the fact that Wilhelm
was accommodated not in the *Hohenzollern* but in the bigger and more comfortable *Kaiser*, where he was completely under the thumb of the navy and was
rarely available to receive Kiderlen-Wächter's reports on foreign affairs. Even
Chief of the Military Cabinet General von Hahnke, who was travelling in the
*Kaiser*, 'being of course a mere general' was 'treated badly by the sailors!'[116]
Kiderlen urged the Reich Chancellor to come to Wilhelmshaven, where the
Kaiser intended to spend four or five days after the Scandinavian cruise, in order
to prevent Wilhelm from 'falling entirely into the navy's clutches'.[117] After the
combined military and naval manoeuvres in Schleswig-Holstein in the late summer of 1890 Kiderlen reported that 'of course praise was again lavished on the
navy' by the Kaiser, to the extent that 'even Hollmann felt quite embarrassed'.[118]
In March 1891 Caprivi complained that it was 'altogether very difficult to get
anywhere with the navy people, as he knew from his own experience how
obsessed they were and how they suffered from delusions of grandeur'.[119] Only
weeks later there were 'very serious arguments between the Kaiser and the senior
naval officers' in Kiel, triggered by the officers' avowal 'that our navy is in fact
incapable of anything and is by no means equal to its task if it came to the test'.
The naval officers even hinted to the Kaiser 'that his endless travelling around
with the fleet was seriously prejudicing the training of commanders, officers and

crew', which made him 'furiously angry'. Carl Wedel, who described this clash in his diary, commented far-sightedly: 'This will not bring about any change, for unfortunately the navy is and will remain a malady of our All-Highest Master which can be cured only by a war and the insignificance of the navy which would no doubt be revealed in the course of it.'[120] Waldersee, who was also at the naval review in Kiel, described the same episode in equally critical terms: 'It is quite extraordinary how the Kaiser has developed a stronger passion for naval affairs than for anything else, and here one can see very clearly that he is much more interested in the navy than in the army. Unfortunately there are many people in the navy who exploit this and drive the Kaiser even further; I would not exclude Prince Heinrich from their number. But most of the older officers are sensible and are very well aware of how the Kaiser exaggerates and overestimates the importance of the navy. Admiral Hollmann, the new Secretary of State, is already seriously worried; the Kaiser has far-reaching ideas which naturally cost a great deal, while the Reichstag is not at all inclined to spend large sums of money on the navy.'[121]

Wilhelm II's enthusiasm for the navy represented a constant if as yet latent threat to the cautious continental policy which Caprivi was trying to pursue. Directly after the appointment of the new Chancellor Waldersee predicted 'an immediate explosion caused by differing opinions on the development of our navy', for 'Caprivi will probably not yield and the Kaiser will do so only with the utmost reluctance.'[122] And indeed in the autumn of 1890 he learned that Wilhelm II was pressing for an enlargement of the fleet at the expense of the army, noting almost disbelievingly in his diary that the Kaiser was making 'very substantially increased demands for the navy', and was inclined to give these naval requirements 'very decided priority' if approval could not be obtained in the Reichstag at the same time for army expenditure. He continued anxiously: 'Heligoland of course needs to be fortified and this will not be cheap. And now the Kaiser comes up with the bizarre idea of turning Memel [now Klaipeda, Lithuania] into a naval base, which he justifies on the grounds that Russia is building a naval base at Libau [now Liepaja, Latvia]. If he brings it up before the National Defence Committee he will find scarcely anyone willing to vote for it. Another outrageous plan is to give up Wilhelmshaven and to make Cuxhaven a naval base!!! I hope he does not put that forward seriously.'[123]

Wilhelm's idea of fortifying Memel as a naval base was by no means allowed to lapse, as Waldersee had hoped. While the Chief of the General Staff was making his report to the Kaiser on 20 December 1890 the latter remarked almost casually that he had given orders for Memel to be fortified and had instructed the Finance Minister, Miquel, to find the money for it. Waldersee – who once again assumed that naval officers had won the Kaiser over to the idea – still considered the plan senseless, for fortification would require a significant amount of artillery and a large garrison, and would thereby 'swallow up considerable millions'. And for all that it would be 'scarcely a cannon-shot' away from the Russian frontier. 'How are we to get a garrison there if the Russians do not want to let us do it?', he asked in despair. Despite his misgivings, however, the Chief of the General Staff decided to act as if he had not rightly understood the Kaiser – 'which was not difficult, as the Kaiser himself immediately embarked on another subject' – since he had already expressed contradictory views on several other questions.[124] On that winter morning at least, Waldersee is unlikely to have thought the young Kaiser 'too impressionable' or lacking opinions of his own. Only a few days later Wilhelm dismissed him as chief of the General Staff.

### THE VISIT TO ENGLAND IN JULY 1891

At the end of June 1891 the Kaiser visited Heligoland. During the journey he jubilantly announced to Waldersee that the Triple Alliance had recently been renewed for six years.[125] The General did not share the monarch's satisfaction at this, for he had radically different ideas. 'I should consider it a much greater political success if we had freed ourselves from the Triple Alliance and had come to an understanding with Russia and Austria instead', he wrote. 'Shared conservative interests and solidarity against the republicanism threatening us from the Romance nations, probably combined with the partition of Turkey, could well provide the basis for it, in my view.' He was well aware, he commented, that the Kaiser would try to persuade the United Kingdom to join the Alliance during his forthcoming visit. But this was 'a vain effort', for 'England will never bind herself, and why should she? If she is attacked in Asia, she will be very glad to have the Triple Alliance as her ally; but until then she will keep a free hand, for which no one can blame her. She can still take sides at the last minute.'[126] In the General's view the British were businessmen who considered their options dispassionately, and 'they are very unlikely to do what the Kaiser wants – to join the Triple Alliance'.[127] Waldersee's sceptical opinion was to prove only too accurate, for Wilhelm's excitable and unpredictable attempts to press for an Anglo-German alliance aroused suspicion in London and, even in these early days, led the British government to wonder whether they might not do better to form an alliance with France and Russia.

At the beginning of July 1891 the Kaiser travelled via Holland, where the size of his entourage caused some astonishment, to Britain.[128] For the crossing from Flushing he wore his British admiral's uniform with the blue riband and collar of the Order of the Garter. He was accompanied not only by Kaiserin Auguste Viktoria but also by the latter's brother Duke Ernst Günther of Schleswig-Holstein.

The imperial suite included Secretary of State Adolf Marschall von Bieber-stein, the three Chiefs of the Military, Naval and Civil Cabinets, General von Hahnke, Gustav Freiherr von Senden-Bibran and Dr Hermann von Lucanus, the Kaiser's physician Dr Rudolf Leuthold, the new Oberhofmarschall Count August zu Eulenburg, Adjutant-General Adolf von Wittich, the Flügeladjutanten von Kessel, von Scholl, von Brandis and von Hülsen. The Kaiserin's suite consisted as usual of Baron Mirbach, Bodo von dem Knesebeck, Countess Brockdorff and Fräulein von Gersdorff. When the *Hohenzollern* arrived at Sheerness (then called Port Victoria) on 4 July 1891, the German guests were met by the Prince of Wales, his elder son the Duke of Clarence, known as Eddy, and his brother Prince Arthur, Duke of Connaught. All three wore Prussian Hussar uniform with the yellow sash of the Order of the Black Eagle.[129] Also present at Sheer-ness were Count Hatzfeldt, Count Wolff-Metternich and Prince Pless, from the German embassy in London. The party travelled together by train to Windsor, where the ladies and members of the wider royal family were waiting at the station. In the course of the next few days the Kaiser received the diplomatic corps and a delegation from the extensive German colony in London.[130]

On 10 July Kaiser Wilhelm II and the Kaiserin were the guests of the Lord Mayor and the financial world of the City of London, and on the way from Buckingham Palace to the Guildhall and back, driving through streets decked with flags and lined with troops in colourful uniforms, they were cheered for the first time by considerable numbers of the ordinary people of London. Wilhelm wore the white uniform of the Cuirassier Guards, a golden helmet adorned with a silver eagle, and the blue Garter riband. He saluted repeatedly in response to the enthusiastic cheers of the crowd, which drowned out the protests of a few German socialists gathered at Ludgate Circus. He was accorded the respect due to 'the most powerful of Continental monarchs' and it was proudly reported that no foreign ruler – not even Napoleon III on his visit after the victorious war in the Crimea in 1855 – had ever been greeted with anything approaching the warmth shown to Kaiser Wilhelm II.[131]

During the visit crowds assembled daily in front of Buckingham Palace. Wher-ever the young Kaiser with the gleaming eagle helmet went – a military review in Wimbledon, a visit to the Crystal Palace, dinner with Lord Salisbury at Hatfield House – the yellow and black imperial standard with the device 'Gott mit uns, 1870' was hoisted, transparencies and triumphal arches of branches and flowers were set up, bearing slogans (of which many were in German) such as 'England and Germany; the peace of Europe', and everywhere the national anthem – the tune was of course the same in both countries – was enthusiastically sung and played.[132] The visit also gave rise to lengthy disquisitions in the London press on the successful co-operation between Germany and Great Britain, particularly in the Seven Years War and in the campaign against Napoleon, to maintain peace and stability in Europe.[133] This was precisely the theme of the important speech which Wilhelm made, looking 'pale and rather exhausted' as one observer commented, to the ruling elite of Britain assembled in the Guild-hall. 'I have always felt at home in this lovely country, being the grandson of a Queen whose name will ever be remembered as the most noble character, and a lady great in the wisdom of her counsels, and whose reign has conferred lasting blessings on England', he declared. 'Moreover, the same blood runs in English and German veins. Following the examples of my grandfather and of my ever-lamented father, I shall always, as far as it is in my power, maintain the historical friendship between these two our nations, which . . . have so often been seen side by side in defence of liberty and justice . . . My aim is above all the maintenance of peace − (cheers) − for peace alone can give the confidence which is necessary to the healthy development of science, art and trade . . . You may rest assured, therefore, that I shall continue to do my best to maintain and constantly to increase the good relations between Germany and the other nations, and that I shall always be found ready to unite with you and them in a common labour for peaceful progress, friendly intercourse, and the advancement of civilisation. (Loud applause).'[134] The Berlin newspapers of every political hue judged the Kaiser's speech very favourably, and its conciliatory tone impressed even the Russian and French press, even if a few Moscow journalists voiced the suspicion that an Anglo-German agreement would only make more German troops available to attack Russia.[135]

As a souvenir of his state visit the Kaiser presented the Lord Mayor with a lifesize portrait of himself as British admiral of the fleet, with the Order of the Garter, painted by Rudolf Wimmer. He had given the Queen a similar portrait by the same painter a few weeks earlier.[136] On the night of 13−14 July he travelled by night train to Edinburgh, where he joined the *Hohenzollern* and departed for his annual Scandinavian cruise. Meanwhile the Kaiserin, who unlike Wilhelm had created 'a very disagreeable impression by her stiffness, rudeness and arrogance towards the royal family and even towards the Queen',[137] went to Felixstowe on the east coast of England, where the *Hohenzollern* had taken her five eldest sons for a seaside holiday on the 'German Ocean', as the North Sea was still called in Britain at that time.

Wilhelm's visit was undoubtedly a great success, and in his telegram of thanks to his grandmother from Scotland he had good reason to express the hope that he had helped 'to bring our two Nations a step nearer to each other'.[138] He followed this with a letter from Norwegian waters on 20 July. 'The stay in England was to me a great treat, & I am deeply touched by the friendly & warm reception I met at the hands of Your loyal subjects', he told the Queen. 'The old & strong feeling for their Dynasty & monarchical principles showed itself in all its vigour in the bearing of the people wherever one met them. It showed the loyal & devoted love the British cherish for their beloved Sovereign, as well as the wish to make me feel quite at home among them, beeing [sic], as I am a good deal of an Englishman myself. But what also accrued the feeling of contentment in me, was the open approval by the thinking people of the unswerving & honest labour I am given to, for the maintenance of peace & the development of good will amongst all nations – nota bene – as far as it is possible. This approval is a great recompense, & makes one forget all the trouble & disagreeable moments one has had to pull through. I hope & feel sure that my visit has been for the good of our subjects, & that it has tended to bring our two nations into nearer & warmer relations, which will be a benefit to them & the world at large. With Your benevolent encouragement & kindly interest . . . I hope to be able to persue [sic] my way, which Providence has marked down, & continue to strive for the fullfilment [sic] of those great problems which were so ably begun by dear Grandpapa Albert. With much love & respect I kiss Your hands & remain Ever Your most dutiful & aff^{ate} grandson Willy.'[139] When the completion of the first direct cable link between Britain and Germany was announced to him on his return to Kiel he sent a telegram to his grandmother expressing 'the confident hope that this successful result of the diligence and hard work of our officials and subjects on both sides may form a new link in the chain of friendly and sincere relations between our two realms'.[140] In another letter he described her as 'the "Nestor" or the "Sybilla" of Europe's sovereigns, venered [sic] & revered by all; feared only by the bad'.[141]

The burgeoning Anglo-German friendship gave rise to some embarrassment on the British side when it emerged that Prince Heinrich and his wife would be staying with Queen Victoria at Osborne at the time when a French naval squadron was due to pay an official visit to Cowes. It was therefore with some relief that an offer by the Kaiser's brother to go on an excursion in the Prince of Wales's yacht *Aline* from 19 to 21 August was accepted.[142] During his 'diplomatic' absence, however, Heinrich decided to take the opportunity of inspecting the 'arch-enemy squadron' from the outside, as he reported to his 'dear big brother'.[143] A few days later he was able to send the result of his spying activities, during which Princess Irène had 'diligently' photographed the French warships, to Berlin. 'The ships make no claim to any beauty, but are certainly well prepared for war. They are armour-plated throughout, and well equipped with large numbers of guns. The "Marceau" looks like a town shimmering with lights from a distance – and offers an excellent target with its high superstructure. Fore and aft and on both sides there are *long* heavy-calibre cannon (about 28 cm) in extended supports, but they are quite unprotected. In the battery there are 16 quick-loading cannon, apparently 15cm or 17cm, that is to say 8 on each side. Wherever else there is any space the ship is dotted with small quick-firing cannon, as are the other ships too, although there is a great variety of models and calibres. The "Furieux" has certain similarities with our "Siegfried" class . . . Neither "Requin" nor "Furieux" seems to have anti-torpedo cladding, or at least I have not been able to detect any! The torpedo boats are very inferior craft and have a certain similarity with the English ones.'[144] Wilhelm immediately passed on this secret information to his Naval Cabinet.

The press reports of the Kaiser's enthusiastic reception in Britain reminded Waldersee of past times when Wilhelm's thoughts about his second home had been of quite another order. 'If I think back to many a time in Prince Wilhelm's life, but also since he became Kaiser, when the English were treated as the most good-for-nothing people, as our enemies, as miserable shopkeepers, when English affairs were discussed in the most contemptuous way and the army was described as completely worthless, I have to keep reminding myself never to be surprised by anything.'[145] At the end of the visit the General was sceptical about its likely effect on British policy. As Konrad Canis has recently pointed out, the very fact that following the break with Russia Germany seemed to be more dependent on London than before convinced Lord Salisbury that Britain's independent stance towards the Triple Alliance could be maintained without compromise.[146] Waldersee was well aware, however, that the display of wealth and pomp which he had seen on his visit would impress the Kaiser, 'and his own love of pomp will have increased even more'. It was also to be feared, he thought, that the Kaiser's visit to Great Britain would arouse 'suspicion in France and Russia' which could be exploited against Germany.[147]

## WILHELM AND THE FRANCO-RUSSIAN RAPPROCHEMENT

For all his personal success in London, however, on the international political scene Wilhelm II's assurances of friendship for Great Britain, together with the Heligoland–Zanzibar accord and the ostentatious renewal of the Triple Alliance, contributed to the emergence of a closer relationship between Russia and France.[148] It was no coincidence that the conspicuous public fraternisation between the absolutist empire of the tsars and the west European republic – during the visit of the French navy to Kronstadt the Tsar stood bare-headed while the revolutionary Marseillaise was played – took place immediately after the Kaiser's visit to London, which had seemed to herald a closer bond between Britain and the Triple Alliance. The Empress Frederick saw a clear causal link between these two historic events. 'William's reception in England certainly brought about the Cronstadt demonstration', she commented, and expressed horror at what she saw as the danger of a European war latent in this development. 'The more one thinks of a European war the more *terrible* & awful the thought is. – *No* one has anything to *gain*, & the destruction of our civilisation would be very near.'[149] The reaction of the Kaiserin Auguste Viktoria was quite different. In a confused letter to her husband from Felixstowe she asked: 'What do you say to the French Russian friendship, they are really making such a fuss, the Tsar stood up for the Marseillaise.'[150] After the Kronstadt demonstrations, which he likewise interpreted as a response to Wilhelm II's visit to Britain, Waldersee was in no further doubt as to Germany's endangered position. 'What a lot of nonsense has been babbled about the Triple Alliance', he exclaimed on 27 August 1891. 'How certain everyone was only a few weeks ago that the Kaiser's visit to England would be enough to make the Triple Alliance a Quadruple Alliance! . . . All reports indicate that the Franco-Russian friendship must be taken very seriously this time and that it would take only a trifle to make the French decide to go to war . . . The shamelessness of the Russians and their presumption are quite outrageous.'[151] The first years of Wilhelm II's reign had led to a foreign policy fiasco, Waldersee complained, 'for what we needed to avoid, what we have been trying to prevent for 15 years, namely a Franco-Russian alliance, has happened.'[152] In September 1891 he received a report from Paris that leading figures there were anxious 'at all costs to avoid war now', as time was clearly working in France's favour. 'The Kaiser is gradually taking the German Reich further and further backwards.'[153]

The Kaiser himself reacted to these signs of a Franco-Russian alliance nervously and with increased aggressiveness. During a long conversation with Waldersee on board the *Hohenzollern* on 12 August 1891 he declared that 'the Kronstadt celebrations had opened people's eyes, and it was not impossible, especially as the French are in a highly excited state, that a war could quickly develop out of some incident or another'.[154] Not long afterwards, during the autumn manoeuvres, Waldersee observed that the Kaiser was still 'extremely irritated with the Russians and the French'.[155] When Bernhard von Bülow reported from Romania in August 1891 on a conversation with a French observer who had said that after securing initial successes in a European war the French would come to an arrangement with Germany in order to avoid Russian hegemony, Wilhelm wrote scornfully on the report: 'Now hold on, old boy, I shall certainly come to an arrangement with you people! But I wonder if it will really suit you too!?' It was clear from the report, the Kaiser commented, 'how sure the two nations are of their position with regard to us. And how dangerous the resultant arrogance and presumption are.' They were behaving as if Germany were already 'beaten and divided up'.[156] In other marginal notes he reviled the French and the Russians, whom he referred to from now on as 'Gauls and Slavs!', calling them 'insolent dogs'.[157]

Wilhelm's anger also made itself felt in the aggressive anti-French toast which he proposed on 14 September 1891 in Erfurt at the gala dinner of the IV Army Corps. He proclaimed: 'In this place the Corsican *parvenu* utterly humiliated us and dishonoured us abominably, but it was from this place too that the beam of avenging light shone out in 1813 and struck him to the ground.'[158] The German ambassador in Paris reported that the entire French press was 'very indignant' and even the usually moderate *Temps* considered 'the language belligerent and the revival of memories on which the irreconcilable rancour of German chauvinism feeds, very dangerous . . . The yellow press, particularly the Bonapartist papers, use it as a pretext for outrageously violent attacks on the Kaiser, who dared to gravely abuse France.' When Caprivi forwarded this report to Wilhelm II in cipher and without comment, the latter wrote on the telegram: 'Thank God. How annoyed they must have been!' He followed this with a defiant telegram *en clair* to the Reich Chancellor: 'Many thanks for telegram . . . which gave me and all present boundless pleasure. Wilhelm.'[159] The Kaiser's mother was scandalised and wrote to Queen Victoria: 'W. has made one of his most unfortunate speeches at Erfurt in wh. he calls Napoleon the "Corsican parvenu". The Ministers thought this would not do, & had it changed into "Corsican conqueror" – but rather late as everyone knew the first! Erfurt of all places was the last to say such a thing because it was the place where almost all the German sovereigns cringed & grovelled in the dust before Napoleon. – Besides the year 1870 & 1871 settled accounts – with Napoleon's descendants & army, so it is not necessary or good taste or becoming especially in an Emperor to allude to him in these terms.'[160]

## THE KAISER'S AIM: 'A SORT OF NAPOLEONIC SUPREMACY' IN EUROPE?

Is it possible to detect, in Wilhelm II's numerous and often seemingly contradictory utterances and actions in the field of foreign, colonial and armament policy during these first years after Bismarck's fall, any common denominators which might point to a fundamental idea behind them? Waldersee's comments, quoted earlier, to the effect that for all his inconsistency Wilhelm held fast to two goals – he wanted 'to win great esteem for the German Reich'[161] and to reinforce and win popular suppport for 'his personal position'[162] – contain the germ of two dominant ideas which we can perhaps consider as something of a key to his activity in foreign affairs. The two themes reappear as a leitmotiv in a number of Wilhelm's statements dating from the early part of his reign.

During a two-hour walk with Philipp Eulenburg near Tromsø in northern Norway in July 1892 Wilhelm II revealed the 'underlying thought' behind his policy, namely the establishment of German domination in Europe, although unlike Napoleon he intended to achieve this goal by peaceful means. 'I hope', he said according to Eulenburg's account, 'that Europe will gradually see the underlying purpose of my policy: leadership in the peaceful sense – a sort of Napoleonic supremacy – a policy which expressed its ideas by force of arms – in the peaceful sense.'[163] Six months later Kaiser Wilhelm felt moved to define the outlines of his foreign policy again, this time in several conversations with the heir to the Russian throne, the Tsarevich Nicholas, who had come to Berlin in January 1893 for the wedding of Wilhelm's youngest sister. In a letter to his 'dear friend' Kaiser Franz Joseph, Wilhelm set out the main points of his interviews with the future Tsar, which he hoped would help bring about a shift in Russian policy against France and in favour of the Triple Alliance. He had discussed the aims of the Alliance in several very detailed conversations with 'the young heir to the throne'. Germany, Austria-Hungary and Italy had been motivated only by their desire for self-preservation, he said. 'In concluding the alliance the powers had borne in mind the serious dangers which threatened the monarchies from the Republic of France, through the spread of republican propaganda. It was after all chiefly from Paris that all revolutionary teaching was spread, the aim of which was to undermine monarchical traditions in all states in a wide variety of [missing word]. These shared dangers were thus to be seen in the first place as the basis of the Alliance, and any power which wished to defend the interests of peace and of monarchy in the same way could join this Alliance at any time. Political matters were not, however, in any way the only area in which the three Allied powers shared common interests', the Kaiser continued. 'On the contrary, the Triple Alliance also wanted to bring the European powers closer to each other in the economic field as well, through trade agreements. In this way the Alliance wished both to reduce the causes of friction between European states and also, above all, to confront the dangers which threatened the entire trade of Europe through the fact that the Republic of North America was showing ever more inclination to seize all trade, including that of South America, for itself.'[164] In thus setting out his main lines of thought Kaiser Wilhelm revealed that his goal was to unite the European continent under German leadership against French republicanism and the growing economic power of the United States. Franz Joseph likewise expressed the hope 'that Russia will also feel at one with the other monarchical powers. May the necessity for this be realised in good time', he wrote in answer to Wilhelm's letter.[165]

In April 1893 the Kaiser went to Rome for the silver wedding celebrations of the King and Queen of Italy and took the opportunity of having a lengthy discussion with Pope Leo XIII, in the course of which he repeatedly stressed his ideology of monarchical leadership in Europe and his determined rejection of the democratic tendencies prevalent in France, in the Catholic Church and the Centre Party. Philipp Eulenburg had encouraged him to take up this theme, pointing out that 'the idea of the great monarchical bastion against revolution' had come from him, the Kaiser, and that he had 'voiced it many times' in their discussions.[166] In his interview with Leo XIII, Wilhelm emphasised 'that all the monarchies of Europe found themselves compelled by the advance of radical ideas to make a stand, in monarchical solidarity, against these ideas wherever they came from. Radicalism was the enemy of a well-ordered monarchy, and at the same time also the sworn enemy of the Church. Radicalism did not stand on its own, however, but was rooted in republicanism, for republican tendencies were its real basis. It was therefore equally dangerous to all monarchies, whether they were worldly or spiritual.' He, the Kaiser, therefore could not understand why the Pope supported the republican form of government in France. This attitude could not but seem strange to him, as to any observer. The policy of the Holy See towards France, Wilhelm told the Pope, had 'caused much anxiety to a great number of my fellow monarchs, as well as myself personally, since he was giving support to a republic, even if only in appearance. We monarchs represented the divine right of kings and conservative policy. The republic and radicalism, on the other hand, were based on regicide and the abolition of God and their purpose was to overturn the existing order . . . The [French] people could not find peace and stability because they had cut off the head of the King whom God had set over them, dishonoured the Church and scorned the Deity. The curse of the Lord lay on their land, and these afflictions were his punishment.' Moreover, by his attitude the Pope had 'caused uncertainty among a not insignificant proportion of my Catholic subjects, who saw him supporting an anti-monarchical type of state in another country', the Kaiser complained. Recently democratic leaders of the Centre Party like Lieber, Daller, Fusangel and Orterer had been elected to the Reichstag, he said, and they were causing problems to the government. 'They had used language towards My government which was scandalous and surely not in accordance with the spirit of the Pope, for they incited the masses to direct disobedience against the government.'[167]

In February 1894, while presiding over a meeting of the Prussian Ministry of State at which the commercial treaty with Russia was on the agenda, the Kaiser declared: 'Our supremacy must be demonstrated to Europe not only by our army, but also through commercial policy.' The policy pursued by the United States of America of cutting off Germany from its 'principal market, South America' must be counteracted by establishing a unified European tariff policy under German leadership. The Reich's aspirations towards supremacy must, however, be kept strictly secret from the Russians, for otherwise Russia's objections to the recent expansion of the German army would only be increased. Canis has rightly drawn attention to the similarity between these sentiments and the 'Napoleonic' ideas of domination which the Kaiser had expressed on his Scandinavian voyage in July 1892.[168]

The idea of an international monarchical order in Europe in which he as German kaiser would play the leading role was evidently a central aim of Wilhelm II. But this ambitious goal could not be achieved by peaceful means alone, any more than the Napoleonic system of a hundred years earlier. It was much more likely, as Wilhelm himself no doubt suspected, that military means would have to be used to create the new European order under German leadership. The military implication of his grand idea emerges in the final quotation from the Kaiser which we shall examine here. In the summer of 1895, by which time he had adopted a racist vocabulary and regularly referred to the Germans as Teutons, the Russians as Slavs and the French as Gauls or Romance peoples, the Kaiser defined the supreme aim of his foreign policy as the leadership of the entire Germanic population of Europe, including Scandinavia, against the Slav threat emanating from Russia. In a letter of 25 July 1895 he confided to the Crown Prince of Sweden: 'All my ideas and endeavours and all my policies are directed towards bringing the Germanic peoples in the world, especially in Europe, closer together and forging a stronger relationship between them, so as to guard ourselves more securely against the Slavic–Czech invasion which threatens us all to a most dangerous degree. Sweden–Norway is one of the principal factors in this league of Germanic peoples. What will become of us if this great northern union of states suddenly falls away and is perhaps absorbed by the Slavs (Russians)? In this respect the whole Germanic North of Europe constitutes the left flank of Germany, or rather of Europe, and is therefore of great importance for our security. Its disappearance would leave our flank exposed and would represent a grave danger for us all.'[169]

Given his notoriously erratic temperament, it would certainly be going too far to see such utterances as evidence that Wilhelm II had developed a coherent foreign policy strategy which he was now attempting to put into action. Nevertheless these declarations, scattered as they were over a number of years, reveal a recurring pattern of thought which suggests that his extremely active and strong-willed intervention in the field of diplomacy and arms policy was motivated by more than the vainglorious wish to be seen to be in control of Germany's foreign policy. The very fact that his remarks were tactically geared to suit each of his interlocutors gives particular significance to the consistency with which two basic elements – *German* supremacy in a *monarchically* structured Europe – come into play in each of the Kaiser's utterances. Wilhelm II's emotionally charged, fragmented thinking in the earliest phase of his reign, exemplified in the coarse marginal notes confiscated by Bismarck, had now resolved itself, after Bismarck's departure, if not by any means into a clear programme, then at least into an instinctive perception of his future role as German kaiser and king of Prussia. In later chapters we shall trace the way in which Wilhelmine policy on international affairs and naval armament evolved out of this initial stage. But first we shall examine the role which Kaiser Wilhelm II played in domestic politics during the first years of the New Course.

# CHAPTER FIFTEEN

# The dualism of power

## THE KAISER AND THE 'RESPONSIBLE GOVERNMENT'

THE dominant role Wilhelm II was already able to play in foreign and military policy soon after Bismarck's fall should not, of course, mislead us into seeing him as a dictator or a tyrant. He was certainly determined to make full use of the enormous inherited power of the Prusso-German military monarchy, and he was imbued with strange anachronistic ideas of his divine right, which he proclaimed increasingly loudly and often, to the consternation of his advisers. But he was and remained a legitimate king and Kaiser, who was obliged to co-operate in matters of domestic policy with the government authorities and parliaments prescribed by the constitutions of Prussia and the Reich. As a result, with the monarch on the one hand and the 'responsible government' (that is to say the Reich chancellor, the Prussian departmental ministers and the secretaries of state of the Reich offices) on the other, a dualism of power emerged, which was inevitably characterised by conflicts, crises and growing frustration on both sides. In tracing the development of this phenomenon we shall see how the balance of power within the leadership of the country gradually shifted in favour of the Kaiser and his court. We shall begin by taking a closer look at the tensions between Wilhelm II and his 'responsible' advisers in the period immediately following Bismarck's fall.

In this post-Bismarck system of parallel power centres, the newly appointed Reich Chancellor and Minister-President, General von Caprivi, was at first at an advantage in that Wilhelm could not immediately dismiss him. As Waldersee observed in May 1890, Caprivi's strength lay in the fact the Kaiser could not afford 'to change chancellors rapidly' and was therefore obliged 'to treat him with great care' and even 'to give way to him sometimes'.[1] Indeed the controversial Cabinet order of 1852, which Bismarck had invoked in order to strengthen his authority over his ministerial colleagues vis-à-vis the crown and which had provided the final impetus for his fall, was replaced by a new decree giving the minister-president much the same rights.[2] And at first Wilhelm and the Kaiserin were in fact, as they frequently declared, 'quite delighted' with the 'new regime', which they compared favourably with the latter days of Bismarck's government.[3] In December 1890 the Kaiser wrote effusively to Queen Victoria about the new Reich Chancellor: 'Here we are getting on very well with Caprivi who is already adored by friends & revered by his opposition. I think he is one of the finest charakters [sic] Germany ever produced, & am sure You would immensely like him as soon as You saw him.'[4] Privy Councillor von Holstein also recorded with satisfaction at this time that Caprivi enjoyed the confidence of the Kaiser,[5] while even Waldersee was forced to admit that the Kaiser was 'still very pleased' with the Chancellor, even if this had been possible only because Caprivi had so far 'skilfully made concessions and given way'.[6]

This relationship was not destined to last long, however, for the further the Bismarck crisis receded into the past, the more self-confident the Kaiser became. Furthermore, despite his conciliatory attitude the new Chancellor was certainly not a man to 'cling' to his thankless task whatever the circumstances. Thus Waldersee predicted as early as 20 April 1890 that after the 'initial' harmony between the Kaiser and the Chancellor it was inevitable that they would come into serious conflict, for Caprivi was 'an earnest, conscientious man who holds fast to his opinion once he has decided that it is right, and who is not cut out for intrigues. It really will not be easy for him to get along with the Kaiser, who is lively, likes to be cheerful and is sometimes even childishly high-spirited, taking pleasure in all kinds of tomfoolery, but also inclined to obstinacy. Anyone who knows the Kaiser well realises that one can achieve much by temporarily giving in to him and waiting a little, and occasionally by a joke; but that is not Caprivi's style.'[7] Furthermore the new Chancellor's state of health gave cause for concern. 'He seemed to me to have aged, and in particular he had grown very thin', Waldersee noted soon after Caprivi's appointment, adding that he had heard confidentially that the Chancellor 'is said to be suffering from quite a severe case of diabetes. The doctor at Carlsbad is said to have stated that he could not last long unless he spared himself and avoided straining his nervous system too much; otherwise he would not survive beyond this autumn.'[8] From the outset Caprivi recognised that the greatest difficulty facing him in carrying out the functions of his office lay in the Kaiser's character and behaviour.[9] In June 1890 he was already complaining about the expensive, ceaseless 'torrent of new plans from the Kaiser'.[10] It was entirely characteristic of this conscientious and honourable man, however, that he shouldered all troublesome questions himself in order to relieve his colleagues. As Arthur von Brauer, Baden's new representative in the Bundesrat, perceptively reported to Karlsruhe in December 1890, Caprivi's position 'in relation to the All-Highest is so strong, and he feels so secure in it, that it has become positively the custom among the ministers to pass on any delicate matters, or anything that might displease His Majesty, to the Minister-President so that he can report on it, a task which he willingly takes upon himself. The General uses H.M.'s regard for him to protect his ministerial colleagues – conduct which certainly does great credit to the Chancellor's character, but which also carries the risk that he will wear himself out over trifles and sometimes arouse the imperial ire over things which, in terms of their importance and of the existing division of ministerial responsibilities, are not the concern of the minister-president or the chancellor.'[11] All too soon the honeymoon period with the Kaiser came to an end and gave way to the day-to-day realities of life.

The problems which Caprivi and the ministers and secretaries of state faced with the Kaiser in the initial period of the New Course were not merely a matter of ill-considered speeches and actions on his part, much as they deplored these. Wilhelm intervened increasingly in the conduct of affairs of state, or created difficulties by his refusal to accept compromises with political parties which the 'responsible' statesmen considered necessary. One of the first clashes with the Chancellor occurred in June 1890 over the Army Bill introduced by Minister of War General von Verdy du Vernois. Caprivi asked for the Kaiser's authority to offer concessions to the Catholic Centre Party or the two Left Liberal Progressive parties if this proved necessary (in spite of the reduction of the proposed increase from 30,000 to 10,000 men), in order to get the bill through the Reichstag.[12] In particular, Caprivi asked for the abolition of the septennate (under which the Reichstag was entitled to debate the army establishment only at seven-year intervals) and for the introduction of two-year (instead of three-year) military service for certain army units. The Chancellor was reported to have returned from Potsdam 'in a very depressed frame of mind', as the Kaiser had 'rejected everything out of hand and expressed himself very strongly', Waldersee learned. He commented that Caprivi 'is now very pessimistic; he is probably put out by his first difference of opinion with the Kaiser and does not know what to do next ... I share Verdy's opinion that the Reichstag will give in if one shows that one is really in earnest and threatens it with dissolution; none of the parties wants new elections, and arrangements will be made so that the bills are adopted with very small majorities. Caprivi does not agree and wants to avoid a dissolution in all circumstances. If the Kaiser wants one, he will resign. I can already see that his nerves will not hold out, and the situation is therefore really serious. How the Bismarck family will rejoice to hear it.'[13]

It was not only the relations between Wilhelm II and his new Chancellor which were under strain. The first victim of the monarch's growing claims to power was the Minister of War. The conflict over the Army Bill in the Reichstag in the summer of 1890 led to the dismissal of Verdy, in which the Kaiser and Chief of the Military Cabinet von Hahnke were instrumental. Verdy had long since made himself unpopular with the Kaiserin by his tactlessness, and Bismarck's insinuations that the General had democratic inclinations had not failed to have the desired effect on the Kaiser. Only four weeks after Bismarck's fall Waldersee recognised the first signs that Wilhelm had taken against Verdy, which he attributed to Hahnke's influence. Verdy had not succeeded in 'curbing Hahnke's influence', he wrote. 'On the contrary, Hahnke has entrenched himself very firmly with the Kaiser.'[14] Then in June 1890, during the parliamentary negotiations over the Army Bill, the Minister of War was accused of 'the grossest errors and blunders'. It was said in government circles that by revealing his future plans, which would require even greater increases in the strength of the army, he had 'jeopardised the whole development' and 'welded the disintegrating Progressive Party together again'. In the Reichstag too the War Minister did not command 'the least respect', and when Caprivi disavowed him by declaring that he, the Chancellor, knew nothing of any further plans to enlarge the army, the General's fate was sealed.[15]

A violent disagreement between the Kaiser and the Minister of War as to whether heavy artillery guns should be cast in steel or bronze – Wilhelm considered himself qualified to pass judgement even on this – brought matters to a head. The Kaiser sided with the Essen firm of Krupp in favour of steel, while Verdy considered bronze to have an overwhelming advantage because it would not crack. When three bronze guns nevertheless did crack, it was generally held to be 'a great triumph for His Majesty' and a fiasco for Verdy.[16] After his return from Essen Wilhelm took action against Verdy 'with the greatest severity': on his instructions the Minister of War was given three months' leave with the proviso that he was then to return to his post *pro forma* for eight days, and resign on 1 October 1890, in order to avoid creating the undesirable impression that a Prussian minister of war had given way to the Reichstag.[17] The Chief of the General Staff acknowledged that his protégé had made mistakes and had often given offence, but he insisted that Verdy was a highly competent minister of war and that the army owed him a great deal. He had received no thanks for this. 'In fact the Kaiser has been extremely unfriendly and ungrateful towards him', he wrote, adding that Verdy might have done better to give way less and from the first to stand up to the Kaiser more.[18] Waldersee deplored the fall of his friend for several reasons, not least because his own position had been weakened by it.[19] He advised the outgoing Minister of War not to attend the autumn manoeuvres or the military review at Pasewalk, as he would only invite 'unfriendly attention from the Kaiser', which was indeed precisely what happened.[20] Waldersee predicted, however, that Wilhelm would have occasion to regret Verdy's departure, as he would never find 'a more compliant minister of war'.[21] When Verdy duly handed in his resignation on 1 October Waldersee commented that he was 'extremely embittered, with every right to be so', and saw trouble ahead. 'I am afraid that in his private capacity he will be unable to resist making skilful use of his pen. In him the Kaiser has made himself an enemy who should not be underestimated.'[22]

The Chief of the General Staff was hurt to realise that the Kaiser was avoiding discussing the subject of Verdy's successor with him. It was not until September that he finally heard from Caprivi what had been decided. He discovered that the Chancellor had first suggested the Kaiser's Adjutant-General, Adolf von Wittich, for the post and that the Kaiser had indeed offered it to Wittich, although 'by no means pressing him to accept',[23] But when the Flügeladjutant Count Wedel also proposed Wittich for the War Ministry, Wilhelm told him that this was an impossible choice because Wilhelm himself and Wittich were 'both such strong characters that before three days had gone by they would be disagreeing violently with each other'.[24] He suggested to Wittich that he remain at court until the autumn, when he would appoint him commanding general of the Corps of Guards.[25] The Ministry of War was then offered to General Hans von Kaltenborn-Stachau, who held the post until 1893. Waldersee at first considered him 'a very competent and experienced general and a clever and high-minded man' who was too good for the post. But he too would soon be at loggerheads with the Kaiser, Waldersee predicted, for 'no minister of war who has any self-esteem can work with him for long'.[26] In the Chief of the General Staff's view the whole affair proved once again that the Kaiser had 'far too low an opinion of the importance of the Ministry of War'. What Wilhelm really wanted, Waldersee considered, was to run the army exactly as he wished; the war minister's role was simply to 'obey' and 'carry out everything' ordered by the monarch. The Kaiser had Hahnke's backing in taking this line, and Verdy had not had the energy to combat it.[27] Moreover Wilhelm had not had 'the slightest anxiety' over the change of minister, for it mattered very little to him who was minister of war. He had told Caprivi that 'the new minister will probably not last longer than nine months anyway!' 'Is this not appalling?', exclaimed Waldersee. 'Where are we heading? The whole world will lose all respect for us if the most important appointments change hands so often. Every such change harms the Kaiser.'[28] Shortly after taking over the Ministry of War Kaltenborn – just like Caprivi and Waldersee – came to recognise that 'the problems lie mainly with the Kaiser'.[29]

The extent to which the Kaiser took it for granted that the choice of civilian ministers was also the prerogative of the crown was demonstrated repeatedly in these first months after the fall of Bismarck. When Prussian Minister of Finance Adolf von Scholz handed in his resignation on 14 June 1890, Wilhelm II

took advantage of his visit to Essen on 20 June to offer this key appointment
to the director-general of the Krupp works, Johann Friedrich Jencke, without
consulting Caprivi in advance. Jencke had earned his respect during the meetings of the Prussian Council of State, even though he had vigorously opposed
Wilhelm's social welfare plans. The Prussian ministers, especially Boetticher,
were incensed. They considered Jencke to be a tool of heavy industrial interests
who would try to undermine the government's policies on social welfare and
railways. Only one of them – it was of all people the reform-minded Minister
of Trade Freiherr von Berlepsch – was confident that Jencke would 'completely
dissolve his ties with Krupp and industry'. Caprivi also had serious reservations
about the choice of Jencke, but he was convinced that the Kaiser would not
rescind his decision and argued that it would therefore be wiser for the Ministry
to accept it.[30] It was not on account of any ministerial protest, however, but
rather because Jencke turned down the finance portfolio – he declared that he
would prefer the Ministry of Public Works, which was responsible for Prussian
railways – that the Kaiser gave up the idea of this appointment, thus avoiding a
serious clash with the Chancellor. The issue was one of principle for, apart from
objecting to Jencke's political views, Caprivi claimed the right at least 'to be consulted [and] if possible to make suggestions himself' where appointments of his
close colleagues were concerned.[31] Instead of Jencke, Wilhelm offered the post to
the National Liberal mayor of Frankfurt am Main, Johannes von Miquel, whom
he had also met in the Council of State and who had asked the Flügeladjutant,
Wedel, to present him to the Kaiser during a musical soirée at the Neues Palais
on 12 June – just before Scholz's resignation.[32] Miquel's appointment was unanimously welcomed by the Prussian ministers on 22 June, and even Caprivi found
it acceptable at first, until Miquel proved to be something of a cuckoo in the
nest. The new Finance Minister, who was to become one of the most powerful
figures in German politics in the next few years, rapidly embraced right-wing
policies and made himself highly uncongenial to the Chancellor by becoming
the champion of agrarian, heavy industrial and Bismarckian interests within the
Ministry of State. This ministerial appointment thus did nothing to reinforce the
cohesion of the government.[33] It was not long before the Kaiser had also changed
his mind about Miquel. In December 1890 he complained that Miquel was 'a
real know-all Hanoverian', prompting a comment by Waldersee that this was
'rather quick, considering the delight with which the Kaiser spoke [of him] only
a few months ago, but a real sign of the times'.[34] Two and a half years later the
General recorded that the Kaiser had 'alternated between praising [Miquel] to
the skies and criticising him, trusting and then mistrusting him'.[35] Nonetheless
many people predicted as early as 1891 that Miquel would soon take Caprivi's
place as chancellor.[36]

Wilhelm II's influence was predominant in two further ministerial appointments in the winter of 1890. In November the Prussian Minister of Agriculture, Robert Freiherr Lucius von Ballhausen, proffered his resignation on the grounds that he could not accept 'the retreat of agricultural interests behind those of industry' and left office with Caprivi's agreement and, according to Lucanus, 'extremely amicably'.[37] But his successor Wilhelm von Heyden-Cadow, a major landowner and hitherto Oberpräsident in Frankfurt an der Oder, owed his appointment above all to the fact that he was 'a particular favourite of the Kaiser'.[38]

The departure of the Minister of Public Works, Albert von Maybach, at first took a similarly smooth course. Maybach handed in his resignation at the beginning of 1891 as a result of the growing criticism which his railway policy was attracting from the General Staff, industrialists and the general public.[39] The Kaiser immediately demanded that he be replaced by Jencke, who had staked his claim to this post in the summer, as we have seen. Since the Kaiser's undertaking to Jencke at that time, Caprivi had certainly always reckoned with the latter's eventual appointment,[40] but this time he had more opportunity to ensure that his own views were taken into account. He convened a secret meeting of the Ministry of State and with the help of his colleagues framed a list of conditions which Jencke would have to fulfil if he wished to become minister of public works. He would have to explain his views on social welfare, particularly in relation to railway workers, clarify his position vis-à-vis Prussia and the Reich (Jencke was a Saxon) and above all guarantee that he would not 'protect industry unfairly at the expense of agriculture'. Caprivi took this list to the Kaiser and asked him to keep Maybach in office until Jencke had given his answer on the points at issue.[41] In the end the director of the Krupp works was not appointed to the post; it is not clear why. Both Holstein and Eulenburg, who were anxious to 'rally the propertied classes, big business etc. as much as possible' and to 'reassure the big industrialists' through Jencke's appointment, were disappointed.[42] All that is known is that the Kaiser, the Chancellor and the ministers eventually agreed on the choice of a worthy but non-political railway official, Karl Thielen (*von* Thielen from 1900), who remained in office until 1902 but who very soon fell completely under the influence of Miquel.

Another 'very serious' conflict, again between the Kaiser and the entire Prussian Ministry, arose in September 1890 when the monarch refused to ratify the re-election of the Mayor of Berlin, the Radical Max von Forckenbeck. 'I'll never confirm that fellow in office', he told Conservatives in Breslau, and when the Chief of his Civil Cabinet submitted the matter to the Kaiser during manoeuvres at Rohnstock in Silesia he was met with a point-blank refusal.[43] Caprivi and the other ministers were unanimously in favour of ratification, since otherwise any bills laid before the Prussian Landtag, and in particular the new local government bill, would be jeopardised.[44] In Silesia the Reich Chancellor spelt out to the Kaiser the consequences of non-ratification: the people of Berlin would re-elect Forckenbeck or vote for someone 'even worse', in which case the only thing to do would be to govern the capital by special commission; this would lead to the resignation of the majority of the honorary city councillors and the situation would become completely untenable. Still the Kaiser refused to budge.[45] As Waldersee tersely commented, if Wilhelm persisted in his attitude, 'there will be a ministerial crisis, perhaps even a chancellor crisis'.[46] Caprivi spoke threateningly of a resignation of the whole Ministry, since it clearly no longer enjoyed the confidence of the monarch. With the support of Lucanus, who argued that Forckenbeck was not worth such a crisis, an arrangement was reached by which the question would be submitted once more to the decision of the Ministry of State, and the Chancellor became 'quite cheerful again', commenting to Kiderlen-Wächter: 'The Kaiser will give in this time.'[47] On 10 October Waldersee recorded in his diary: 'Today is an important day. Caprivi has gone to Potsdam to ask the Kaiser to ratify Forckenbeck's appointment. If he refuses the whole Ministry will resign.'[48] The next day he registered the first 'victory' of the Reich Chancellor over the monarch, commenting: 'Caprivi obtained Forckenbeck's ratification yesterday. I do not know whether it was a hard struggle. At any rate it is a great victory for the Chancellor. The only question is whether the Kaiser will take it very badly and whether it will mean that there is ill-feeling from now on.'[49]

The Chancellor's 'victory' in this case was the exception that proves the rule. A year later another incident showed all too clearly who even at this early stage was calling the tune as far as appointments were concerned. Deputy Reich Chancellor and Secretary of State of the Reich Office of the Interior Heinrich von Boetticher and Foreign Secretary Baron Marschall von Bieberstein sent a cipher telegram to the Flügeladjutant on duty, asking almost timidly for the 'All-Highest decision' on how the Prussian ministers of state should respond to an invitation to a banquet in honour of the Mayor of Berlin, Forckenbeck, and of the world-renowned physician and Progressive Party parliamentarian, Rudolf Virchow. In reply the Kaiser wired imperiously from his hunting box at Hubertusstock: 'Participation in banquet for Forckenbeck *and* Virchow *not appropriate*. I agree to personal *congratulations* to Forckenbeck. Virchow is to be ignored. He has completely forgotten and failed in his duty as a civil servant. W.'[50] Not until November 1891 did relations between the Kaiser and the Mayor of Berlin improve for a time. At the inauguration of the fountain designed by Begas, Wilhelm singled Forckenbeck out for particularly courteous treatment, a volte-face which prompted Waldersee to observe that 'two years ago he maltreated this same man when he offered the fountain as a gift from the city, and even described him on several occasions as one of the most wicked democrats. O quae mutatio rerum!'[51]

The position of the government in the Reichstag, where the Centre Party held a key position between right and left thanks to its strong mandate in the elections of February 1890, was even more critical than in the Prussian parliament. On 14 June 1890 Wilhelm told one of his Flügeladjutanten that he had 'had his first battle with the new Reich Chancellor today'. Caprivi had asked him to invite the leader of the Centre Party, Ludwig Windthorst, to the forthcoming soirée for members of parliament on the Pfaueninsel, the lake island in the Wannsee. He had 'emphatically refused, for Windthorst was a most dangerous man of hostile intentions, who had already done fearful harm to his [Wilhelm's] family'. Caprivi recorded later that he had had 'fought hard' with the Kaiser until Wilhelm had put an end to the argument by declaring that it was 'against his honour to invite Windthorst'. When Carl Wedel went to the Reichstag on 20 June he heard regrets expressed on all sides that 'the Kaiser allowed himself to be carried away by personal antipathies into politically unwise rebuffs'. Miquel, above all, pointed out that Wilhelm would have to reckon with the Centre Party 'if he wanted to avoid a *coup d'état*'.[52]

In the autumn of 1890 Caprivi made a renewed attempt to bring the Kaiser and Windthorst together at a parliamentary dinner, this time successfully, although, as Waldersee recorded, 'the Kaiser hesitated for a long time before he made up his mind to meet Windthorst at Caprivi's house'. In spite of his reservations, he talked at some length with the leader of the Centre on this occasion. The Chief of the General Staff was convinced, however, that Windthorst and his party would not co-operate with the government in the Reichstag unless they received a quid pro quo such as the recall of the Jesuits or the implementation of clerical school reform in Prussia, neither of which the government could concede.[53] Nevertheless his meeting with Windthorst led to a change in the Kaiser's tactical attitude to the Centre. When the party leader fell down stairs and injured himself in January 1891 the Kaiser wondered whether it would be overdoing it to send a Flügeladjutant to enquire after his health. And not long afterwards, while checking the invitation list for the next court ball, he asked, 'Why is Windthorst not on the list?'[54] Once again Waldersee was amazed by this rapid change of mind and complained that Germany was now 'dancing entirely to the Catholic tune' and would 'certainly come off worst' in the process.[55] At the other end of the political spectrum the Empress Frederick was no less struck by the change. When Windthorst died in March 1891 she wrote in astonishment to Frau von Stockmar that 'Flowers were sent to him from the Court etc . . . That would no doubt *not* happen if one of our German-Progressives fell ill, or for our very deserving Mayor etc . . . In spite of all his opposition, all his Guelph sympathies and Ultramontanism, the conservative Windhorst [sic] is nevertheless closer to those in power now than a free, independent, clear-thinking liberal man.'[56]

The tactical rapprochement of the Kaiser and the government in general with both the Centre and the Left Liberal Parties in the Reichstag, which will be discussed in more detail below, undermined the position of the Prussian Minister for Ecclesiastical Affairs, Education and Medicine, Gustav von Gossler, who had worked with the Conservative–National Liberal Kartell under Bismarck. In the summer of 1890 members of the Centre Party were already complaining vociferously and 'furiously' about the minister and demanding that he be replaced by an ultra-conservative more sympathetic to them, such as the Silesian Count Robert von Zedlitz-Trützschler.[57] It was not the wishes of the parliamentary parties, however, but those of the monarch and of his irresponsible advisers behind the scenes which determined the composition of the closely intertwined governments of Prussia and the Reich. Thus while on a train journey to Kiel with the Kaiser, Waldersee was able to bring the conversation round to the social question and to demand the dismissal of both Gossler and Minister of the Interior Ernst Ludwig Herrfurth. The evil of socialism must be rooted out, he urged the Kaiser, and to that end church and school must co-operate instead of fighting one another. Wilhelm listened calmly, but complained that he could not 'make the slightest progress on school reform', as Gossler wanted 'preliminary consultations with countless people, i.e. to put off the whole matter indefinitely'.[58]

The dominant role played by Wilhelm II in December 1890 in the school reform question is an example of the way in which, with the help of his unofficial advisers, he was able quite simply to bypass the state bureaucracy in matters which interested him personally.[59] It was he, and not the minister responsible, Gossler, who invited forty-five delegates to Berlin for a conference on education lasting several days. Instead of seeking Gossler's advice he listened to his former tutor Dr Hinzpeter, who – as the generals and the Prussian and Reich bureaucrats discovered to their consternation – was suddenly spending all his time at court.[60] What was more, for weeks on end Wilhelm granted regular audiences to Professor Konrad Schottmüller, who drafted the 'powerful' speech which the Kaiser made at the opening of the school conference on 4 December 1890 and which still attracts both guarded admiration and passionate criticism today.[61] In this startling speech Wilhelm inveighed against 'excessive education', with express reference to his own experience at Kassel, and coined the influential watchword: 'We ought to educate young Germans, not young Greeks and Romans.' The task of the secondary schools was to take up 'the fight against social democracy' and against the 'centrifugal tendencies' in the Reich, he declared.[62]

It is not difficult to imagine the enormous sensation which this speech caused. Arthur von Brauer reported that it was 'almost the only subject of conversation in corridors and salons, and one cannot be surprised that a speech from such an exalted source, which goes into so much detail and contains a quite specific, rather radical programme, will give rise to the most diverse opinions, and that in private and more restricted circles criticism will not always be kept within the bounds that should be observed at all costs when the speaker is so illustrious a personage. Firstly, many people think it highly undesirable that the monarch should have entered so much into details and that he should have publicly expressed such a firmly rooted preconceived opinion, so that in the course of further discussion, any frank expression of opinion which leads to different conclusions will seem almost like a deliberate rebellion against the All-Highest will ... In two diametrically opposed camps there is much dissatisfaction with the speech even on purely formal grounds: among the strict Conservatives, because they fear that by descending into the arena where burning issues of the day are fought out the sovereign will damage the reputation of the monarchy; and among the strict constitutionalists, because as a matter of principle they reject personal intervention by the monarch, on doctrinaire grounds . . . No German who has any thought and feeling for the upbringing of children and for schools can fail to be powerfully affected by the Kaiser's words. He will not have changed the minds of any of the fanatical supporters of one side or another with his speech. On the other hand, among the wider public his positive suggestions have in fact met with enthusiastic support. It is well known that His Majesty prides himself on understanding the mood and wishes of the younger generation better than his ministers and advisers, and the success of his latest utterances seems to confirm this claim. At any rate I have frequently heard the opinion expressed, particularly among younger people, that the Kaiser has hit the nail on the head again this time, and they expect the abolition of the Realgymnasien [secondary schools for Latin, modern languages and sciences] and the elimination of Latin composition in the Gymnasien [grammar schools] to bring about a miraculously rapid end to all the shortcomings of our schools ... On the other hand the resounding patriotic tone of the speech has awakened a joyous echo on many sides. The idea that in the interest of the schools' national duty, the German language and especially German composition and the history of the Fatherland should be moved to a dominant position at the heart of the curriculum, has really taken hold . . . It is natural and only to be expected that His Majesty's remarks about journalists, whom he described as "starving paupers" and "old Gymnasium boys down on their luck", should be unfavourably commented on in the press of all shades of opinion ... What is incomprehensible is that apparently neither the Ministry of Ecclesiastical Affairs and Education nor the Civil Cabinet thought it prudent to examine H.M.'s speech before it was sent to be printed. At least I assume they did not, or it would be even more incomprehensible that the passage about the press and much else besides could be allowed to remain . . . Nothing is known for certain about the authorship of the imperial speech. What is clear is that no *official* adviser knew anything about it beforehand. Hinzpeter had nothing to do with it either. He spoke to me directly after it and commented on the content in terms that were anything but laudatory. Professor Schottmüller is said by many to have been the author . . . I have the impression that in essence the speech was the product of His Majesty's own direct inspiration, for his words clearly expressed the resentment which took root in him at the Gymnasium in Kassel against excessive classical formalism imposed by unskilful and pedantic teachers. In general one can say of the Kaiser's speech, as is true of many of the things his sense of power and his youthful enthusiasm have inspired him to say and do hitherto, that H.M. has earned more criticism and head-shaking than approval in official, cautious-minded circles, but that among the broad mass of the people his words have been greeted with jubilation and enthusiasm.'[63]

Waldersee was one of the many people who regretted that the Kaiser had put forward his own views so prominently, and thought he would have done better not to try to influence the deliberations of the conference.[64] 'The Kaiser's conduct at the opening of the school conference has displeased many people', he wrote. 'They think that he put himself and his own views forward altogether too much, and this is quite true.'[65] In the course of the conference the Kaiser said to Gossler, after a dinner at the Schloss, 'In the next few days I shall go back once more and take the chair; I am told on all sides that the gentlemen are very pleased when I speak.' Waldersee commented acidly: 'It is a mixed blessing for them, to say the least, and once again one can see how sycophantic individuals have managed to get at the Kaiser.'[66] In the speech which he made to the closing session of the school conference on 17 December 1890 Wilhelm spoke complacently of his 'full appreciation' of the fact that the learned delegates, after their free exchange of ideas, had finally 'arrived at the conclusions to which I pointed the way'.[67]

In these circumstances it is scarcely surprising that the Minister of Ecclesiastical Affairs and Education lost the desire to remain in office. During the school conference all the participants were 'absolutely horrified . . . by the wretched performance of the Minister, Gossler'.[68] When in January 1891 a bill rescinding discriminatory measures against Catholics, through which the government hoped to purchase the support of the Centre for the trade treaty with Austria, was introduced, Gossler again played 'a most wretched' role. 'It is my belief that he cannot possibly stay on as minister', Waldersee commented.[69] Wilhelm stood by his Minister at first. He sent him his portrait and publicly declared that he was the best minister of ecclesiastical affairs that Prussia had ever had. But then he suddenly dropped him when it was reported to him that Gossler's wife had strongly criticised the inscription 'sic volo sic jubeo' ('my will is my command') which the Kaiser had written on the portrait.[70] Finally, when Gossler was heavily defeated on his anti-clerical School Bill in the Prussian Landtag in March 1891 Wilhelm approved his dismissal. The Kaiser promised to appoint him Oberpräsident of the province of East Prussia by way of compensation, but dropped this idea too after members of the East Prussian aristocracy carried out a 'putsch' against Gossler, who was 'not grand enough' for them, while the Kaiser was hunting at Prökelwitz.[71] On 10 March Caprivi received the Kaiser's authority to offer the Prussian Ministry of Ecclesiastical Affairs to Count Robert von Zedlitz-Trützschler, who accepted.[72]

Looking back over all the decisions on appointments made during the first twelve months after Bismarck's fall, two characteristic features are immediately apparent: vacillation and uncertainty within the 'responsible' government, and overwhelming strength of will on the part of the young sovereign. When the Grand Duke of Baden came to Berlin in October 1890 for the ninetieth birthday of Field Marshal Count von Moltke he stressed the importance of 'more stability in high places', for 'the rapid changes and the persistent rumours of further changes' were having a highly unsettling effect.[73] Wilhelm von Rauchhaupt, the leader of the Conservatives, also thought 'the worst thing is the constant unease, the frequent changes and the resultant insecurity in many areas'.[74] No one doubted that the Kaiser was to blame for the unease. In June 1890 a member of the Reichstag observed that it was incredible 'how much the Kaiser is feared in the Reichstag',[75] and the same was even more true in the Reich and Prussian governments. With a self-assurance bordering on frivolity the monarch took it upon himself to offer the highest offices in the land to men whom he had happened to meet somewhere and who had won his personal favour. It is no wonder that the leadership of the country quickly lost any kind of unity through this behaviour and became increasingly psychologically dependent on the monarch. It was only very hesitantly – and usually only when there was a stalemate because the Kaiser's preferred candidate (Herbert Bismarck, Alvensleben, Jencke) turned down the post offered to him – that Caprivi, in conjunction with the Ministry of State, sometimes took the opportunity to come forward with counter-proposals. But without the right to decide on appointments and dismissals within the Prusso-German government, the authority of the Reich chancellor and minister-president inevitably lost ground in comparison with that of the kaiser and king.

### THE FIRST CHANCELLOR CRISIS OF THE NEW COURSE

From early 1891 onwards, as if one year after the fall of Bismarck he now felt that he had held himself back long enough, Wilhelm II's high-handed behaviour and utterances increased alarmingly. He made a succession of speeches which left little room for doubt of his autocratic intentions and which displayed notions of ancestor-worship and divine right so out of tune with the times that they caused universal shock and dismay. The absolutist motto 'sic volo sic jubeo' which the Kaiser had written on the portrait he gave to Gustav von Gossler proved to be no momentary aberration but an authentic reflection of the young Hohenzollern ruler's innermost convictions. On 20 February 1891, in a speech to the provincial diet of Brandenburg, he railed against 'the spirit of disobedience' which was rife throughout the land and invoked the spirit of the Great Elector, calling on his audience to follow him on the path 'which I tread, and which I have marked out for myself, to lead you and all of us towards My goal and towards the salvation of the whole nation . . . You know that I regard My position and My task as one which Heaven has laid upon me and that I am called to serve a Higher One, by whom one day I shall be called to account', he declaimed.[76] A similar peroration followed in May 1891, on the occasion of a festival performance of *Barbarossa* in the concert hall at Düsseldorf. 'I for My part must not flinch from the paths marked out for me, for which I alone must answer to My conscience and to My God', he proclaimed, finishing with the declaration that there was only one ruler in the Reich and that was himself; he would tolerate no other.[77] On 24 February 1892 these absolutist pronouncements reached new heights in a speech (again at a banquet held by the provincial diet of Brandenburg) which aroused universal indignation and disapproval, especially as it was published in the official *Reichsanzeiger*. 'Unfortunately', the Kaiser declaimed, 'it has of late become customary to find fault with everything that the government does. On the slightest pretext the tranquillity of the people is disturbed and their pleasure in the existence, vigour, and prosperity of our great Fatherland is embittered. All this carping and fault-finding finally gives rise in the minds of many people to the idea that our country is the most unfortunate and the worst-governed in the world, and indeed that it is torture to live in it. That this is not the case we, of course, know perfectly well, but would it not be better if these dissatisfied grumblers shook the dust of Germany from their feet and withdrew as quickly as possible from these miserable and distressful surroundings? They would thus be put out of their misery, and they would at the same time do us a great favour. We live in a state of transition! Germany is gradually growing out of her childhood and will soon be entering upon her period of youth. It is, therefore, high time that we should throw off our childish ailments. We are passing through difficult and exciting times, in which, unfortunately, the judgement of the great majority of people is wanting in objectivity. They will be followed by more tranquil days if only our people will earnestly concentrate their energies, realise their duties, and, refusing to be led away by outside influences, will place their trust in God and in the unsparing diligence and paternal care of their hereditary

Ruler . . . Brandenburgers, a great future is still reserved for us, and I am still leading you on to a glorious destiny. Only do not let a gloom be cast on your outlook into the future, or the pleasure you take in united effort be lessened by mere carping criticism and discontented partisan talk. Catchwords alone are powerless to effect anything, and to the incessant, captious criticisms of the new course of our policy and those who are responsible for it I quietly but firmly reply, "My course is the right one, and in it I shall continue to steer."'[78]

Brauer was so dismayed by these utterances that he felt compelled to offer some sort of psychological explanation of them to his Grand Duke. 'It is not easy to detect the direct motivation behind decisions which are so much His Majesty's own', he commented. 'But perhaps it would not be too far off the mark to see the immediate reason not so much in a current political objective as in H.M.'s habit of surprising the world with an extraordinary oratorical performance at every banquet of the provincial diet of Brandenburg . . . The speech . . . was made on the initiative of the Kaiser himself, who said to a gentleman in his entourage the day before yesterday: "I shall make a thundering good speech today." The speech was sent from the Schloss to the *Reichsanzeiger* printers in the morning, before it had been delivered. This was fortunate, for if it had been transcribed after the event, even more extraordinary remarks would have come to public notice. For instance, His Majesty allowed himself to be carried away into saying "Everything that is finest and best in Germany we owe to the House of Hohenzollern which brought it all about, and so it shall be in my reign too"! . . . What concerns me more than anything else, for the future of our political life, is the fact that nothing will dissuade H.M. from believing that these speeches of his have the most excellent effect possible. When honest people have drawn his attention, or tried to do so, to the dangers of the Kaiser making such remarks, his response has been to say triumphantly: "My speech has hit home; they are making a fearful fuss about it in the newspapers." In fact His Majesty particularly enjoys reading the opposition newspapers after such speeches. When he was shown the perfidious article in the *Berliner Tageblatt*, which reproduced H.M.'s speech without any criticism, simply printing Article 27 of the Prussian Constitution (the right of every Prussian to free expression of opinion) in full beneath it, H.M. laughed and said: "They ought to have added that the *King* also has the right to express his opinion freely"! . . . The respectable newspapers, on the whole, show admirable restraint. But reading between the lines one can see deep resentment or a strong sense of discouragement, according to temperament or political standpoint. In particular one can detect the underlying thought that the days of enlightened despotism are over and that it is no longer possible for any prince nowadays to determine what course the state and the national cultural life should follow purely on the basis of his own ideas. In government circles and among the parliamentarians of the moderate tendency with whom I have occasion to be in contact, I have not found a single person prepared to defend the Kaiser's words on principle. But in these circles people are naturally careful about what they say. Unpleasant incidents have shown that even confidential private remarks are not immune from being repeated maliciously to the Kaiser, and everyone knows that while H.M. is indifferent to press comments, however disparaging, he is very sensitive indeed to the slightest criticism from his officials or other people in the higher ranks of society. Hence the great reserve, which of course contrasts strongly with the disrespectful remarks which are said to be doing the rounds in other circles.'[79]

The increasingly overbearing behaviour of the young monarch made itself felt even more strongly behind the scenes, in his handling of civilian statesmen. In March 1891 Friedrich von Holstein deplored the fact that 'the relations between Kaiser and Chancellor . . . have suddenly changed for the worse'. For example, he commented, 'His Majesty is now suddenly dissatisfied about Gossler's departure – for which the Reich Chancellor was not responsible – and today he said to the latter, in reference to Boetticher, "as if we had not had enough changes already", and then commanded the Reich Chancellor in so many words "to restore the Kartell".'[80] By treating the Chancellor in this way the Kaiser was only encouraging the rumours that Caprivi's position was 'shaky'; Philipp Eulenburg warned him that 'nothing is more dangerous than that for Your Majesty at the moment'.[81] 'The worst thing about the whole business', Holstein warned in his turn, 'is that in parliamentary circles the Kaiser is increasingly thought to be not in his right mind. An elderly member of parliament, Hobrecht, said to me "It is the Kaiser himself who is the cause of all the uncertainty." If His Majesty takes on another new chancellor now the mood in the country will be unbelievably bad. That may mean that His Majesty finds very strange things happening.'[82]

Alfred von Kiderlen-Wächter, who accompanied the Kaiser on his Scandinavian cruise in the summer of 1891 as representative of the Foreign Office,[83] reported anxiously to Berlin that 'since last year H.M.'s autocratic tendencies have decidedly increased. The *sic volo sic jubeo* makes itself felt in matters both great and small.' Kiderlen thought it a telling sign of the All-Highest attitude that the Kaiser had grown a full beard (as he had done two years earlier), and had remarked that 'with a beard like this you could thump on the table so hard that your ministers would fall down with fright and lie flat on their faces'. The worst aspect of this autocratic attitude was that it was 'not accompanied by any serious scrutiny or weighing of the facts; he just talks himself into an opinion. Anyone in favour of it is then quoted as an authority; anyone who differs from it "is being fooled"', Kiderlen complained.[84] Wilhelm's idea of the appropriate relationship between a Reich chancellor and his kaiser was further illustrated by a marginal note of September 1891 in which he criticised Bismarck for having been 'guilty of disobedience towards his sovereign'.[85] It was again apparent in the wording of a letter he wrote to the King of Saxony in February 1892: 'I have already fulfilled your wish regarding the lottery and have given the ministers instructions.'[86] Equally typical of Wilhelm II's attitude, in the eyes of his contemporaries, was the 'very stern' telegram which he sent from Rominten, his East Prussian hunting lodge, to the Minister of Justice, Hermann von Schelling, and the sensational imperial proclamation on prostitution issued in the autumn of 1891, which he had composed with the help of Lucanus, the Chief of his Civil Cabinet, and with which he set himself up as 'supreme guardian of the law'.[87]

In the military sphere, where as supreme war lord he could exercise unlimited, extra-constitutional authority, Wilhelm II's increasingly autocratic behaviour was particularly noticeable. In July 1891 it was the main topic of conversation between Waldersee and the former Adjutant-General, Max von Versen. Waldersee, by now also dismissed from his post as chief of the General Staff, was informed by Versen that at a sitting of the Commission on Home Defence chaired by the Kaiser himself Wilhelm had insisted on transferring the chairmanship of this important body to Prince Albrecht of Prussia in spite of the fact that the latter had firmly refused to accept the appointment, 'being quite rightly convinced that he was in no way equal to the post'. Wilhelm had dismissed his uncle's objections and declared that he thought it particularly important to have a member of his family as chairman. When the fortification of Heligoland subsequently came up for discussion by the committee Wilhelm allowed neither discussion nor a vote, but simply declared the draft proposal which he had earlier agreed with an admiral and a general to be the final decision. Moreover, Wilhelm decided, against the advice of the General Staff, to abandon the fortress at Dirschau (now Tczew) on the Vistula, on which work had already begun, and to fortify Marienburg instead, as it would not be right to expose 'the beautiful Schloss Marienburg to destruction by the Cossacks'. Versen assumed that while the Kaiser was hunting at Prökelwitz, 'where many a matter has been settled before', East Prussian influences had been brought to bear against the military arguments of the General Staff. 'Sic volo, sic jubeo!' Waldersee angrily exclaimed on hearing of the manner in which these decisions were taken.[88]

The General was rendered almost speechless by a remark made by the Kaiser in the autumn of 1891 to the leader of the Conservatives, Rauchhaupt. When the latter tried to thank him for an order conferred on him, Wilhelm replied 'My dear Rauchhaupt, voluntas regis suprema lex', and turned away from him, remarking to another member of parliament, 'I really let the old greybeard have it.' 'What sort of behaviour is that, and how should Conservatives, who thank God are all still loyal monarchists here, react?', Waldersee asked. 'It really will dishearten some people, but also push many others into the anti-monarchist camp.'[89] When it was discovered that Wilhelm had already written the same absolutist maxim in the Golden Book of the City of Munich (see illus. 25), Waldersee was appalled and commented that the inscription would 'naturally cause a great scandal and do *nothing* but harm. It is quite a good thing, although extremely sad, that for some time now the Kaiser's utterances have no longer been taken seriously.'[90] The blame for the utter confusion of both domestic and foreign policy lay 'with the Kaiser *alone*, for he thinks that he can reign alone, that he understands *everything* and knows *everything* better than anyone else, while in fact he has no clear idea about *any* goal, nor does he thoroughly understand *anything*. The fact that the Chancellor and the ministers remain in their posts only proves that they are all characterless people. Perhaps the good Lord has better things in mind for us than we deserve, and the "voluntas regis suprema lex" will help to clear the air. All parties seem to be agreed in condemning this pronouncement, and indeed it could not be otherwise. But can a Ministry exist if it condones such a remark? I think not; it cannot but fall victim to contempt.'[91]

Simultaneously with the growth of Wilhelm II's appetite for autocracy, the conviction was spreading that Caprivi was a spent force, despite his considerable success in parliament, and would soon resign. The dismissed Minister of War, General von Verdy du Vernois, wrote to Waldersee in May 1891: 'More and more people are beginning to see the light about Caprivi: in the commercial world people think that the sooner he goes the better it will be; the groups who are still most attached to him acknowledge his hard work, his eloquence etc., but claim that he has an irremediable fault: he has become dull.' The Chancellor's diabetes, although officially denied, was evident in his increasing irritability, Verdy reported. He was 'under extreme nervous strain because of pressure of work' and was evidently close to 'forgetting himself completely', which was noticeable in his catastrophic relationship with the War Office. 'Having recently treated the Ministry of War in the most ruthless way', Verdy wrote in May 1891, Caprivi had 'added insult to injury' by making a written statement on the Pension Bill which 'was more merciless and insulting than the most extreme of Bismarck's pronouncements. And this statement was not only sent to Kaltenborn, but circulated to all the other ministers too. As a result the Minister of War is said to be extraordinarily . . . upset and those in the know in the Ministry expect that he will ask to be relieved of his office.' 'It certainly would be madness for him to stay!', commented Kaltenborn's predecessor.[92]

It was no coincidence that the Reich Chancellor's first threat to resign was over a question of military policy, especially as Wilhelm II's identification of himself with his 'grandpapa', the 'powerful' Emperor-Hero Wilhelm I, made itself felt most strongly in military matters.[93] On 15 June 1891, the third anniversary of his accession, the Kaiser ordered the introduction of a huge new Army Bill, which was destined to be at the centre of political conflict for the next two years. The Kaiser's orders were contained in two lengthy memoranda, written in his own hand and addressed to the Minister of War and the Reich Chancellor respectively, which cast a highly revealing light on his way of thinking as a military monarch.[94] In the memorandum to Kaltenborn the Kaiser began with the question which had long been a matter of lively debate among the generals, in the Reich government and in the parties in the Reichstag: whether the enlargement of the army should be linked to a reduction in military service from three to two years, as demanded by the parties of the left and above all by the Centre Party. Modelling himself on the unyielding attitude of his grandfather in the Prussian constitutional conflict three decades earlier, the young Wilhelm held out resolutely for the retention of three-year service. His memorandum acknowledged that there were 'undoubtedly tempting advantages' in two-year service. 'But there is no denying that the reliability, efficiency and especially the discipline of the army will be put at considerable risk by this measure (two years instead of three) and may indeed actually be damaged. I have thought it over again, conscientiously examining the reasons for and against, and I have again come to the conclusion that all the arguments of my grandfather of most blessed memory are still absolutely valid today. Moreover, success in three victorious campaigns is a momentous and weighty argument in favour of the three-year service, to which it bears shining testimony. But there are also other significant factors, in my view', the Kaiser continued. 'The question of two-year service is no longer purely a matter of military expediency . . . No; from the time of the conflict onwards parliament has turned it into a trial of strength, to which it constantly reverts at any given moment in order to force the King eventually to accept it. But I, as my grandfather's grandson, as war lord of the Prussian Army, who strives to defend his prerogative as supreme commander of the army and to give what orders he sees fit — within the bounds of *tradition* — to promote the welfare of his army, I cannot act differently from Grandpapa. You will surely understand and share my feelings, my dear Kaltenborn. And I tell you frankly, on the very anniversary of the death of the victor of Wörth and Sedan [i.e. Kaiser Friedrich III], that I will never accept two-year military service; come what may, whatever the consequences, I cannot and will not do it.' After this solemn, emotional and very determined declaration Wilhelm got to the point. His aim, he explained, was on the one hand to increase the infantry establishment and on the other to train officers for reserve units. After giving a precise list of orders the Kaiser concluded: 'These, my dear General, are the guidelines which you are to follow. As soon as you have acquainted yourself with them and worked through them I shall expect your report . . . There will certainly be a fight with those rogues in parliament. But that will not do any harm; in 1860–6 it was just the same and Grandpapa found his Bismarck and Roon and won, and was then magnificently justified by success in war. In the same way I expect to gain my victory with the help of Caprivi and Kaltenborn, and then – with God's help – to prove the rightness of my principles in the next battle for Germany's existence, which will surely come. Knowing the man that you are, I have no doubt that you will stand fast by me and fight hard for our cause. I remain, my dear Kaltenborn, your affectionate King Wilhelm R.'[95]

On the same anniversary Wilhelm II also wrote a long letter to the Reich Chancellor, the immediate outcome of which was a letter of resignation from the latter. The imperial missive began with an expression of his 'most sincere royal thanks' for the passage of the three great reform bills in the latest round of legislation, namely the Social Welfare Bill, the Prussian Finance Bill and the Rural District Bill. Wilhelm wrote: 'You were as intrepid as you were politically skilful in supporting your colleagues when it was needed, and the selfless cool-headedness which you have shown in the face of great adversity and difficulties of all kinds and from all sides is mainly responsible for the fact that in one session three such important laws, the like of which no government of any state has succeeded in launching before, were successfully passed. You have made yourself an undying name for all time in the annals of our country's history, and may the grateful thanks of your King give you some consolation and satisfaction after all the unpleasantness which unfortunately you were often obliged to endure.' After these three bills it was necessary to have a pause in domestic legislation for the time being, the Kaiser decreed. 'Therefore my concern is now once again for the army, and I wish to return to the questions of reorganisation which I postponed last year at your particular request until you had fought out your winter campaign.' In similar terms to those of his letter to Kaltenborn, and again alluding to his late grandfather, Wilhelm explained that he was firmly opposed to 'the experiment with two-year military service'. 'Even if the army gained in numbers it would lose in inner worth and discipline. Moreover, as a result of the conflict of 1860–6 the question of two-year service has since then been turned into a trial of strength in which parliament – particularly the radical Democrats – is constantly trying to force its will upon the King and compel him to accept it. My grandfather was criticised and blamed for the conflict by these very same people, and they still consider that it has not been fought to the finish. I, as the grandson of this great man, who grew up in his traditions and under his teaching, cannot act in any other way than exactly as he did. I should be sinning against His Name, His Memory, if I were not to follow in his footsteps completely, and continue to build where he left off.' The Kaiser expressed his utmost determination 'never to accept two-year service'. He had 'personally worked out a reorganisation which – with the knowledge of no one else – I have sent to the War Minister today, with a letter in which I laid down my principles, according to which he is to proceed henceforth. I have instructed him to be in touch with you in order to prepare a bill for the autumn and next winter, postponing all other army bills except for Heligoland ... The whole thing, with the greatest possible economy of means, amounts to a sum of 40 million. The War Minister will show you the scheme and my letter. We have reached the same point as in the year [18]60, when my grandfather was forced by the high age of the recruits to the reserve units and the territorial army to abolish both of these, so setting the ball rolling. I do not for one moment doubt that we shall have to fight for this bill as much as Grandpapa fought for his. But that does not matter. This is a good opportunity; a firm stand will clear the air both in parliament and among the people, like a thunderstorm. In his day Grandpapa found Bismarck, who helped him to fight and win. Today I have Caprivi, and I trust him absolutely to fight and win with me now. In addition we have the advantage of being able to point to the rightness of Grandpapa's principles as shown by the glorious wars. And if Bismarck really wishes for a rapprochement with the King, or to show that he sometimes takes the King's side, he may perhaps use his remaining strength to fight with us too. After all, he joined in the fight for the three-year service. It would have been different the other way round. So I look with confidence to you as my active collaborator in the absolutely essential and vital work to whose success you will contribute. Your truly devoted King Wilhelm R.'[96]

One can imagine Caprivi's feelings on receiving this directive, particularly when he learned that the Kaiser had worked out his plan with one of his Flügeladjutanten; according to information given to Waldersee by Adolf von Bülow the culprit was the 'stupid' Freiherr Gustav von Seckendorff, brother of Prince Heinrich's Hofmarschall.[97] The Chancellor was not only faced with the most crass example he had yet experienced of 'personal rule', with the monarch coolly handing down orders to the constitutionally 'responsible' Reich Chancellor and Minister of War instructing them to introduce and push through the Reichstag a legislative measure which he had worked out in detail and whose consequences were incalculable. Worse still, in direct emulation of the 'sacred' decisions of his grandfather in the Prussian constitutional conflict, Wilhelm II had ordered a fight with the Reichstag, which – as Caprivi was well aware – could easily lead to a *coup d'état* and even civil war, with the risk of foreign intervention. Holstein threw up his hands in despair when he heard of Wilhelm's peremptory demand. It was proof, he wrote to Eulenburg, 'that His Majesty has no idea of the difference between the Prussian constitution and the covenant between the German ruling princes on which the constitution of the Reich is based. Do *you*

believe that Saxony, Bavaria and Württemberg would side *with* the Kaiser if he
demanded an increase in the army when the Reichstag had voted *against* it? And
if they do not, we shall have civil war with Russia and France looking on; the
latter would certainly seize the opportunity of recapturing the Reich territories
[Alsace and Lorraine].'[98]

Caprivi's immediate response was to submit his resignation, the first time he
had taken this step since his appointment in March 1890. 'In the light of Your
Majesty's firm resolve it is not for me to put forward the different opinion I have
of the advisability of the measure', he wrote on 16 June 1891. 'On the other hand
I have had to ask myself whether and to what extent the All-Highest intention
could be carried out and whether it was in my power to do so. In my humble
opinion there would be difficulties which I consider insuperable. In the course
of last year's negotiations in the Reichstag I became convinced that to burden
the Reich with considerable additional expenditure for military purposes would
be very difficult in any event, and with the present Reichstag it is only possible
if two-year military service for the infantry etc. is conceded. I have already
taken the liberty, on a former occasion, of respectfully stating that I consider
two-year service, with certain compensations, better than the present state of
affairs with half-pay leave and reserves.' Even if the Reichstag were dissolved
and new elections held, this would not change the fundamental situation, the
Reich Chancellor asserted, for in order to get the Army Bill through the new
Reichstag two-year military service would still have to be conceded. 'In pursuing
Your chosen path Your Majesty would then be faced with the question of whether
and how, by some means akin to a *coup d'état* – perhaps by altering the electoral
law – it might be possible to achieve the aim in view. It would be irresponsible
on my part to conceal from Your Majesty my conviction that such a *coup d'état* in
the loosely knit German Reich and under the present circumstances would bring
that Reich close to disintegration. The political situation is quite different from
that which obtained in Prussia in the 1860s. I doubt that the federal governments
would agree to all the increased expenditure planned by Your Majesty, but I have
no doubt at all that they would not favour a *coup d'état*, whatever form it took,
at present. Therefore not only am I unable to foresee a successful outcome to
Your Majesty's planned course of action, but I am even more sure that it is well
beyond my powers to carry out the All-Highest intentions. Taking a risk of this
order can only succeed when the person who carries the official responsibility for
the matter believes it can succeed. But I lack this belief, as well as other qualities
essential to the fulfilment of so difficult a task. Nor can I conceal the fact that
because it has pleased Your Majesty to take crucial decisions in a question of
such great political importance without seeking my views beforehand, I have
become convinced that I do not possess the All-Highest confidence to the degree

without which I should be hindered at every step by the fear of making a false move.' Caprivi therefore asked to be relieved of all his offices.[99] Holstein, to whom the Chancellor showed both letters, urged Eulenburg to come to Berlin under whatever private pretext he could find, in order to avert a crisis which in his view could easily result in Waldersee's appointment as Reich chancellor and that of Herbert Bismarck as foreign secretary.[100]

The Kaiser sent a conciliatory reply to Caprivi's letter. 'When you accepted the position you now hold, you said "Whether one lays down one's life as a soldier in the face of the enemy or by exhausting one's strength in the interest of the Reich; both are of equal value in the end." At that time these words gave me the assurance that you would devote all your strength, trusting in God and your King, to the execution of the office which I entrusted to you. We should not and must not be separated by a misunderstanding — for such it undoubtedly is — of what I committed to paper yesterday in a solemn and hallowed moment. There can be no question of lack of confidence. You received yesterday, my dear Caprivi, certain indications of the way in which my army must be expanded in the future, which I consider essential in order to defend Prussia and the Reich as may be necessary in grave and critical situations. On the basis of these directives I expect a detailed report from the man whom I have chosen as my adviser, once he has studied the question thoroughly. I rely fully on you — as you must rely on me — and with God's help we cannot fail. The serious political objections which you have raised may, if necessary, result in the postponement of the decisions I have made after careful consideration, but never in their abandonment. I therefore expect you, my dear Caprivi, at 9.15 tomorrow morning to make your report. I gladly repeat today what I have already said, that you will always have my full confidence and my deepest admiration for the services you have rendered me as Reich Chancellor.'[101] In his audience of 17 June the Kaiser accused Caprivi of sending him 'a nasty letter' and complained: 'You made yesterday very unpleasant for me', to which the Chancellor showed both courage and dignity in replying: 'I shall always write to Your Majesty like that when I see that You wish to do something which will harm the Reich or Your Majesty Yourself.' After the Kaiser had declared himself ready to put off the large army increase until the following year — though still insisting on retaining three-year military service — Caprivi withdrew his resignation.[102] But this compromise did little to resolve the crisis.

When the Kaiser landed in Kiel on 10 August 1891 after his Scandinavian cruise, Caprivi was waiting for him in order to discuss the Army Bill. After the audience Kiderlen wrote to Holstein in some relief that he was now 'much easier in my mind', for 'with H.M.'s incessant talking himself into the need for an Army Bill, which he discussed constantly with his "restricted retinue" for no other reason than to win authoritative approval', the situation had seemed 'really serious'.[103] On 12 August Wilhelm received Waldersee on board the *Hohenzollern*. The General impressed upon him his strong objections to the abolition of three-year military service, maintaining that in view of the grave political situation Germany had no time 'for experimenting, but that the aim ought to be to strengthen the army if any means could be found of doing so'. Waldersee adroitly reminded the Kaiser of the Prussian constitutional conflict of the 1860s when his grandfather 'held fast to the three-year service and carried through the increase of the army against a hostile Landtag, against the advice of countless supposedly well-meaning people, against the opposition of the Crown Prince and against the opinion of many generals'. Retention of the three-year service and immediate enlargement of the army were indispensable, he insisted, since 'we are probably . . . facing a struggle for our existence'. If Germany lost this war the Reich would break apart, the monarchy would be jeopardised and Prussia would be destroyed, which would result in the most appalling state of affairs within the country. For him, the Kaiser, there was no better battlefield than the expansion of the army, for any party which persisted in voting against it would be digging its own grave. The Kaiser acknowledged the gravity of the international situation and promised Waldersee that 'under *no* circumstances would there be any question' of giving up three-year service.[104]

At the end of August 1891 the Reich Chancellor handed the Minister of War a long memorandum setting out his view of how Germany's military strength should be developed, a view diametrically opposed to that of the Kaiser. He agreed that since war was inevitable 'in the long or the short run' the German armed forces should be increased 'to the greatest extent permissible'. In order to achieve this increase, however, 'the support of the nation' must be won, and this could be achieved only through the timely concession of two-year service. Without this concession, conflict with the Reichstag leading to a *coup d'état* would be inevitable, but this must 'at all costs be avoided'. Caprivi argued that 'before one takes the first step towards a conflict one must be clear whether one is able and willing to take the eventual consequences of it'. One could argue about the advisability of a *coup d'état* for other reasons, for instance in order to achieve a change in electoral law after street battles. 'But if it were for the sake of three-year service it could lead to the disintegration of the German Reich and might be more catastrophic than losing a military campaign.' Like Friedrich von Holstein, Caprivi was convinced that the 'loosely knit Reich' would not tolerate extreme measures, and that 'any serious dispute between the federal governments or between them and the people . . . would be of benefit only to hostile foreign countries. To our enemies abroad a conflict at the present moment would look like a sign of weakness, an invitation to make war.' The Chancellor brusquely rejected Wilhelm's emotional evocation of his grandfather's steadfastness in the Prussian constitutional conflict with the comment: 'Just because this question became a trial of strength 30 years ago in Prussia in completely different circumstances it does not follow that it must do the same today.' This view of the importance of avoiding conflict with the Reichstag was, however, of fundamental significance for the proposed Army Bill, Caprivi continued, since 'from the answer to the question, whether one can or cannot risk a *coup d'état*, one must work backwards, for everything thereafter depends on it. If the answer is no, everything else is reduced to the question of whether to keep the *status quo* in military matters or to accept two-year service.' The question at issue was quite simple, Caprivi remarked. 'Is a significant increase of our military strength attainable without conceding two-year service?' This question too had to be answered with a firm negative, he said. By his reckoning, given the present composition of the Reichstag scarcely anyone other than the seventy-one Conservatives – and some of them only very unwillingly – would vote with the government if two-year military service were not conceded. Caprivi stressed, however, that he favoured the reduction of military service to two years for important reasons of military policy and not purely on grounds of parliamentary tactics. 'The closer one believes one is to war', he argued, the more vital it was 'to make the population feel that what is required of them is unavoidable'. The increase in the army must therefore take place in a way that was 'understood and approved at least by the majority of the people'. The implementation of compulsory military service for all was just such a 'popular, more general idea' and two-year service was a step on the way to the Scharnhorstian principle of the nation in arms. The Chancellor-General went even further and wondered whether the government should not also give up the septennate when it brought in the great Army Bill. He pointed out that in practice it was rare for seven years to go by without the government being obliged to break the septennate of its own accord. He thought it worth considering 'whether a peacetime military establishment calculated as a percentage of the population' could be achieved. Finally, Caprivi expressed his objections to the description of the Army Bill as a 'reorganisation'. That word, used by the Kaiser in an allusion to the reconstruction of the Prussian army in 1861, would create the dangerous impression abroad that Germany had been on the wrong track before and was therefore weak now, which was not the case. But even if these views of his were approved, the Chancellor concluded, 'very serious parliamentary battles' could still ensue. Even if the path of compromise were followed, the dissolution of the Reichstag might still be inevitable. 'But the prospects for new elections will be quite different if a longstanding wish of broad sections of the population is granted by the concession of two-year service. I have no doubt that this wish can be granted without military disadvantages. The fiction that the present so-called three-year service is better than a well-implemented two-year service cannot be maintained . . . But however that may be, it is my opinion that the decision lies in the answer to the question: Can we afford to risk conflict among the legislative bodies of the German Reich at this time for the sake of three-year military service? And I believe this question must be resolutely answered in the negative.'[105] As we shall see hereafter, the struggle over the form of the Army Bill, and especially the thorny question of the length of military service, would cast a dark shadow over the relationship between Wilhelm II and the Reich Chancellor until the summer of 1893.[106]

From the summer of 1891 the responsible government lived with the constant possibility of receiving some order from above which would put its entire legislative strategy at risk. Holstein, who had 'lost all sense of security', decided that one of the Flügeladjutanten – he thought first of Gustav von Kessel – would have to be recruited to tell the Kaiser unwelcome truths and draw his attention to the consequences of his orders. 'As the Kaiser generally lives only with his military entourage it is very important that there should be one among them who can occasionally teach him something', he argued.[107] When in December 1891 the Trade Treaties were passed by the Reichstag with a majority of 195 votes, to the delight of the Liberals and of the general population,[108] the Kaiser raised Caprivi to an earldom.[109] He conferred on Privy Councillor von Holstein – on his own birthday, in order to make the honour 'still more precious' – the cross of a commander of the Royal Order of the House of Hohenzollern which, as Caprivi explained, 'will by His Majesty's wish henceforth rank above the other orders'.[110] Philipp Eulenburg wrote to Holstein to congratulate him, emphasising that this distinction was 'a *quite exceptional* mark of His Majesty's confidence . . . If you but knew *what value* he attaches to his Order of the Household! It almost borders on eccentricity – and how the class of the decoration enhances the value!'[111] In spite of such outward signs of the Kaiser's confidence, however, there was still a general feeling of insecurity and dissatisfaction.[112] Not without reason Waldersee observed, after shooting with the Kaiser at Springe in November 1891, that the chancellor crisis had already begun, for Wilhelm had several times spoken of the choice of a successor and in the process had expressed the opinion, not exactly flattering to Caprivi, that anyone who had not yet become a 'nasty brute' in the post of chancellor would certainly become one in time.[113]

### THE KAISER AND DOMESTIC POLICY

Is it possible to detect, in the Kaiser's numerous speeches, marginal comments, letters and actions during the months following Bismarck's dismissal, anything approaching a consistent line on domestic policy which would throw light on his fundamental ideological stance? As in foreign policy, here too there were endless contradictions, which led many an observer to see Wilhelm as vacillating helplessly over internal policy and having no clearly defined goals, except perhaps that of making himself popular. Waldersee, for one, commented irritably on the Kaiser shortly after Bismarck's fall: 'With regard to his attitude to the political parties I have already seen him showing ultra-Conservative, Free Conservative and National Liberal leanings; many people claim he is now working in favour of the Progressive Party, while others of course say that he is going to sacrifice all to the interests of the workers. It has almost reached the point that no party knows where it stands with him. If there were a definite plan behind this it would be an excellent thing, for he must not belong to any party and can deal with them all best if each believes he favours it. *But no such plan exists!* . . . His desire to make himself popular, which is becoming increasingly obvious, is most regrettable.'[114] In the ensuing months the Chief of the General Staff was to revise this early verdict on Wilhelm II's political inconsistency, as we shall see, but on one important point – the Kaiser's attitude towards the worker question – he was essentially right.

Once Bismarck was out of the way, little more was heard of the Kaiser's great social reform initiative. On the contrary, fear of a socialist revolution made him increasingly inclined to favour a *coup d'état*, which he had angrily rejected when Bismarck had suggested it. Within a few days of the latter's dismissal the first signs of a volte-face became apparent. When an article appeared in the *Hamburger Nachrichten* on 26 March 1890 calling for 'firm and resolute use of the power of the state in all its rigour' to counter the 'increasingly arrogant conduct' of the workers' movement, Wilhelm, furious at the non-renewal of the anti-socialist law which Bismarck had deliberately engineered, scribbled bitterly in the margin of the article: 'You rejected the Anti-Socialist Bill! Now you can draw your conclusions!'[115] The next day he told one of his Flügeladjutanten that another strike had begun at Gelsenkirchen, and that he had instructed the commanding generals 'to let loose with repeating rifles at the first opportunity!' The Flügeladjutant commented in astonishment: 'How strangely the Kaiser changes . . . What has happened to his high-sounding vow "that he would not besmirch the first years of his reign with the blood of his subjects"?'[116] Wilhelm's willingness to crush the Social Democratic workers' movement with military force was also apparent in his Proclamation to the Army of April 1890, in which in principle he granted the patriotic bourgeoisie the same opportunities as the aristocracy to take up the career of an officer. As he explained to his Flügeladjutant Carl Wedel, his intention was 'to win over the bourgeoisie, which is now more than ever looking to the crown for help, out of fear of social democracy, and to bind it to him. It was important to bring together as many elements as possible in the struggle against social democracy.' Wedel ridiculed the Kaiser's remark, commenting that 'the bourgeois elements . . . in the army are in any case far and away the majority' and that 'there has never been a glaring difference between aristocracy and bourgeoisie in the army anyway'. Nevertheless he was deeply impressed by the decisiveness which the young monarch displayed in this question.[117]

The change which was beginning to emerge in Wilhelm's attitude towards the workers was welcomed by Waldersee, who commented after his meeting with Philipp Eulenburg on 24 April 1890 that it had now 'gradually become plain to everyone that the Kaiser has not achieved his planned goal. I myself have been of this opinion from the beginning and have therefore been on Bismarck's side in this matter; on the other hand I have no objection to the Kaiser trying to solve the problem, but he has gone about it in the wrong way. There are bound to be many disappointments, for the workers can never be satisfied and have now evidently lost all sense of reality.'[118] Waldersee continued to be a determined advocate of the view that the social democratic threat could be combated only with military force, for which riots and violence in the streets would afford a welcome pretext. When the Socialists declared 1 May 1890 an international holiday the Chief of the General Staff commented revealingly: 'I am afraid that it will all go off peacefully, except perhaps for some brawling; at least here in Germany.'[119] The day having passed without any disturbance anywhere, he admitted: 'I do not like this; it shows . . . that the leaders of the movement are in control.'[120] The General lost no opportunity of trying to convince the young Kaiser of the soundness of his views on class conflict.

At the end of April 1890, while on a journey to Bremen, Wilhelmshaven and Oldenburg together, Wilhelm II and his Chief of General Staff discussed 'the possibility of disturbances'. The Kaiser expressed 'very determined views' on the subject. 'I pointed out', Waldersee wrote, 'that it was very difficult to recognise the right moment to intervene in earnest, so that as a rule it was missed; I also mentioned that people have scruples about giving orders to fire, for fear that there might be many innocent people, women and children, in the line of fire, and that experience showed that difficulties arose from this.'[121] At Potsdam in May 1890 Waldersee observed that Wilhelm was 'more serious than usual', apparently because 'many things are not going as smoothly as he thought. The worker question is causing him much anxiety; he sees that people are quite shameless and always want more.'[122] During the manoeuvres that autumn the Social Democrats were a frequent topic of conversation with the Kaiser, and Waldersee was gratified to note that Wilhelm was beginning 'to realise that these people are superbly organised and increasingly dangerous'.[123] As the National Liberal Johannes von Miquel also noticed shortly after his appointment as Prussian minister of finance in the summer of 1890, the Kaiser was 'really afraid only of the Social Democrats'.[124] Members of the Kaiser's closer entourage, Waldersee learned, were convinced that the monarch's recently adopted hard line against the workers arose particularly from 'concern for his personal safety'.[125]

In the late summer of 1890 the Kaiser repeatedly expressed the opinion that it was dangerous to remove troops from Berlin and other major cities, as always happened for the manoeuvres, and suggested that at such times reserve battalions should be sent to the cities.[126] When he returned to Berlin from the manoeuvres in East Prussia at the end of August, Lucanus told him of the violence which had broken out recently following a Social Democratic rally in the suburb of Friedrichshagen, but which had been easily brought under control by the local police. In disbelief Waldersee recorded. 'The Kaiser, without consulting anyone, immediately sent the Flügeladjutant to the 3rd Army Corps with orders to send a brigade to Berlin; even Hahnke was passed over, and Verdy and Caprivi by the same token; the Governor [of Berlin] was not even asked whether he needed troops!' Waldersee condemned Wilhelm's action as 'a very overhasty act' which would create a general sensation and would be derided by the Social Democrats. If a revolution had really been in the offing, he commented, the guard detachment of about 700 men who had remained behind after the Corps of Guards had left for the manoeuvres would in any case have been insufficient to control the situation, even with the assistance of the 3,000-strong Berlin police force. But there was no question of that, for the leaders of the Social Democrats had not the slightest intention of attempting to overthrow the government. So the Kaiser's order had been completely superfluous. 'It seems as if something has made the Kaiser nervous', Waldersee wrote.[127]

On 20 November 1890 Kaiser Wilhelm made one of the most notorious speeches of his long reign at the swearing-in of recruits to the Corps of Guards in Berlin. He told the young recruits that they were called to fight not only against foreign enemies, but also against enemies within. 'The spirit of opposition, rebellion and insurrection was stalking the land', he declared, and he warned the young men against 'listening to the deceivers and agitators. They belonged to him now and must be prepared perhaps even to fire on their fathers and brothers, if he commanded it.' Wedel, who heard the speech, commented: 'As almost always, our sovereign's speech was lively and gripping, and yet I think it a great pity that in such speeches he lowers himself too much from his exalted position, and puts himself too much on the level of a mere superior officer. On the other hand remarks like these are psychologically interesting because they show how concerned the Kaiser is about the destructive tendencies of the Social Democrats and how concerned he is personally to put a stop to their agitation.'[128] Even in military circles the Kaiser's conduct was 'very strongly condemned'. Nevertheless he repeated his admonitions the next day when he swore in more recruits at Potsdam.[129]

It is thus indisputable that a radical change took place in Wilhelm's attitude towards the workers' movement as soon as he had dismissed Bismarck. But this fact should not lead to a generalised assumption that he pursued no aims at all in domestic policy. His closest friend, Philipp Eulenburg, had the impression at the beginning of 1892 that 'His Majesty's ideal' was to form two major parties in the Landtag and the Reichstag. Eulenburg welcomed this, although he had to admit that 'in Germany more than in any other country such desires are quite illusory!'[130] At about the same time Waldersee recorded in his diary that the Kaiser had recently declared to the gentlemen of his suite that 'differences between parties did not matter to him at all; he saw only two differences: those who were loyal to the King or monarchically inclined, and those who were not!'[131] On the second anniversary of Bismarck's dismissal Waldersee, who in 1890 had described the young Kaiser as completely aimless and as 'a shapeless piece of elastic that could be stretched in any direction',[132] was forced to acknowledge that a succession of measures of considerable importance could now be attributed to Wilhelm II's personal initiative. He listed these as: 'eradication of social democracy through improvement in the welfare of the working classes, international action on the same lines, school reform, raising of moral standards, strengthening of the position of the German emperor, reconciliation with Russia, firm friendship with England, friendly relations with Denmark, improvement of the army'.[133]

What is surprising is that the internal policy measures cited by Waldersee were carried out not so much with the support of the right-wing parties as with that of the Catholic Centre and of the two Left–Liberal Progressive parties. In February 1891 the Badenese envoy reported in astonishment that public life in Berlin now presented 'one of the most curious phenomena that has perhaps ever been seen since we have lived under a constitution. We have a Government which faces a parliament elected under another Government by a very large oppositional vote. And yet the present Government . . . meets with curiously little difficulty in this oppositional parliament. Its budget is passed almost without cuts; its bills are accepted – but in the strangest manner.' The government 'naturally raises no objections to this assistance from the Left and the Centre', Brauer reported to Karlsruhe, even if accepting the 'assistance of the entire German democratic movement' seemed 'a dangerous policy in the eyes of many a friend of the Fatherland'.[134] The moderate policy of the New Course is undoubtedly to be attributed mostly to the constellation of parties in the Reichstag, for without the support of the Left Liberals and/or of the Catholic Centre no legislative measure could have been passed. It is nevertheless astonishing that not only General von

Caprivi but also Kaiser Wilhelm II was evidently much in favour of co-operation with these erstwhile opposition parties.

We have seen how the Kaiser overcame what were at first very strong prejudices against the Centre Party leader, Ludwig Windthorst, in the summer of 1890. As we have also seen, Wilhelm even agreed – although very reluctantly – to the re-election of the Left Liberal Max Forckenbeck as Mayor of Berlin. When Caprivi set to work on the renewal of the Trade Treaties in the late autumn of 1890 and in so doing moved increasingly towards the pro-free trade position of industry and away from the protectionism favoured by agriculture, the question inevitably arose of how the Kaiser would react to this change of direction. On 16 November, when it became known that the Prussian Minister of Agriculture, Robert Lucius von Ballhausen, had resigned in protest against precisely this development, Waldersee recorded in his diary: 'Unfortunately there are already people who believe that the Kaiser, who has expressed warm support for the agricultural interest in several speeches, for instance in Königsberg and Münster, might nevertheless become a free-trader, at least with regard to corn duties.'[135] Barely two weeks later one of the Flügeladjutanten remarked that the public had the impression that the Kaiser's relations with his mother had greatly improved and that her liberal influence over him was growing.[136]

The most striking evidence of a rapprochement between Wilhelm II and the Liberals, however, was his dismissal of the anti-Semitic Court Preacher Adolf Stoecker in November 1890, carried out despite the opposition of Kaiserin Auguste Viktoria and during the absence of her Oberhofmeister Baron Mirbach. In October the ultra-conservative Protestant Waldersee had learned that Stoecker had 'again spoken out vigorously' at the conference of provincial synods, but in so doing he had 'aroused the anger of the Kaiser, whipped up by Hinzpeter'.[137] Moreover Stoecker had made a number of speeches in South Germany which, according to Waldersee, had received 'enormous acclaim', but for which he had been officially reprimanded in Berlin.[138] After an audience on 1 November 1890 Waldersee and Wilhelm discussed Stoecker, whom the Kaiser criticised 'severely'. 'So there must have been another campaign against him recently', the Chief of the General Staff concluded in alarm, quick to realise the implications for his own position.[139] To cap it all, Wilhelm had nominated the preacher Ernst von Dryander to deputise for the ailing Kögel at the forthcoming marriage of his sister Viktoria (Moretta) with Prince Adolf of Schaumburg-Lippe, which Stoecker, who as court preacher had the right to conduct all services in the Court Chapel, took as an affront to himself. He and two other court preachers asked to be relieved of their offices, on the assumption that Wilhelm would turn down their request.[140] The Kaiser, however, told Wedel during a hunt on 4 November that Stoecker had promised to refrain from political agitation, but that he had not kept this promise and must now go. Everyone was aware that he, the Kaiser, did not approve of Stoecker's behaviour, but the Court Preacher 'clung to the Kaiserin and to Mirbach's coat-tails, and a stop must be put to that'.[141]

The anti-Semitic Court Preacher's spectacular fall from grace was widely greeted as a liberation, and not least by many people at the court. 'Bravo, bravo!', Wedel exclaimed in delight, a sentiment echoed by Adjutant-General von Wittich. 'It is a pleasure to see our young sovereign showing such deep, clear and thoughtful insight!'[142] The Empress Frederick reported joyfully to her mother: 'The pleasure in the town & the public is great at his [Stoecker's] dismissal fr. Court.' She thought it a 'pleasing accident' that it was the marriage of her daughter which had provided the occasion for the dreaded Court Preacher's dismissal. On hearing of Kögel's illness she had declared 'I would *not* go to Church if that evil man "Stöcker" officiated – & Vicky [Moretta] said she refused to be married by him. – However, our opinion was not needed, as the matter was already decided.' For fifty years the court preachers in Berlin had been 'a wretched set & clique' and had created much mischief under Friedrich Wilhelm IV and Wilhelm I, she claimed. 'They are a strong Party as all that is orthodox and reactionary, the whole of the "Kreuzzeitung" & aristocracy belong to them; *Dona* & her court especially.'[143]

Those in the know suspected that this sensational decision by the Kaiser was principally due to a revival of the influence of his former tutor Georg Ernst Hinzpeter. Wittich claimed to have 'fairly precise information' that Hinzpeter 'was behind this affair and had been the prime mover in it'.[144] Waldersee also gathered through the Oberhofmarschall, Count August zu Eulenburg, and other court officials 'that Hinzpeter had campaigned strongly' against Stoecker.[145] In addition to Hinzpeter the Chief of the Civil Cabinet, Hermann von Lucanus, was thought to have played a part in prompting the dismissal. Waldersee, who could see 'nothing but a victory for Jewry' in Stoecker's fall, laid 'most of the blame on that unprincipled fellow Lucanus'. The duty of the Chief of the Civil Cabinet ought to have been 'to give the Kaiser accurate information, but he gave way to pressure from Mirbach's enemies and even egged the Kaiser on . . . The Kaiser will take note of the wholehearted applause of the Jews, Social Democrats and Liberals of all shades which he will receive for this! Will it agree with him?'[146] 'The Kaiser's action is not at all laudable and cannot lead to anything good', the General angrily complained on 7 November. 'Unfortunately Minister Gossler is a very weak man and offered no resistance at all; on the contrary, he is said to be very glad to be rid of Stoecker. But the fault lies mainly with the wretched Lucanus, who I now know is utterly false.'[147] On 23 November Waldersee was still lamenting the episode. 'The saddest thing about it, as ever, is that the Kaiser allows himself to be so easily influenced; in this case – naturally without suspecting it – he gave in to Jewish pressure; he is in the process of undermining the foundations on which he stands, by paralysing one of his best resources at a time when as he himself has often said the forces of insurrection are at work. If Stöcker were not such a dangerous enemy of revolution he would certainly not be attracting so much hostility.'[148]

In the immediate aftermath of the fall of the Court Preacher it became positively dangerous for members of the imperial entourage to be seen at Stoecker's church services. Both Wilhelm von Wedell, the House Minister, and the Hofmarschall Maximilian Freiherr von Lyncker thought themselves lucky not to have been noticed in the cathedral when Stoecker preached a sermon condemned by the Kaiser as 'quite outrageous' in January 1891. Waldersee's presence, on the other hand, was at once relayed to the Kaiser. The latter sought him out directly after a dinner for the commanding generals and remarked that the sermon had been 'of such a kind that a few gentlemen would have liked to walk out'. 'It is really scandalous what a disgraceful campaign has been whipped up again here!', the Chief of the General Staff wrote indignantly afterwards. 'These worthless cowards who do not dare to come forward openly but worm their way to the Kaiser by flattery! Oh if I could but once catch someone *in flagrante*!'[149]

In the course of a deeply pessimistic survey of the eventful year of 1890 Waldersee observed, shortly before his own dismissal as chief of the General Staff, that the Kaiser was still in the process of 'learning the lesson that one can get nowhere with the Liberals; . . . I have no doubt that he will eventually return to the Conservatives, as many another king has done before him.'[150] But this prophecy was not to come true for a long time yet. In fact in the spring of 1891 violent disagreements arose between the Kaiser and the German Conservative Party. The Conservative leader, Rauchhaupt, commented despairingly that 'in the party and in the country there is real sadness about much that is happening, nor can it be denied that Germany is in truth divided into two camps, and that the Kaiser has many opponents, particularly among the great industrialists in the West and in South Germany'.[151] The immediate cause of the conflict with the monarch was the refusal of the Conservatives to approve the 22 million marks required for the construction of 'his long-cherished favourite wish', the cathedral in Berlin.[152] There were, however, several more profound issues over which the Kaiser took a surprisingly modern view, bringing him into conflict with the East Elbian landed nobility.

At the end of 1890 the Conservatives began a campaign designed to replace the Prussian Minister of the Interior, Ernst Ludwig Herrfurth, a middle-class career bureaucrat with liberal leanings, with one of their own. They accused him of appointing too many liberal commoners to the influential post of Landrat in the Prussian provincial administration. Waldersee complained that Herrfurth was 'a clumsy bureaucrat' who did not know 'the country and its needs' and was trying 'to bring his creatures into the administration', while persecuting Conservative officials.[153] Wilhelm not only rejected these accusations out of hand; he also criticised the Conservative provincial officials for their opposition to the rural district reform plans being championed by Herrfurth. During a hunt in the Grunewald in January 1891 the Kaiser expressed support for Caprivi's decision to take disciplinary measures against the rebellious Landräte led by Count Kanitz. In Waldersee's opinion 'Minister Herrfurth's utter worthlessness' was demonstrated by the fact that he had shown the Kaiser an article published by Kanitz in the *Kreuzzeitung*.[154] A week later he recorded that the Conservatives were being 'constantly insulted' by Wilhelm. 'He is happy to hob-nob with *feeble Liberals*, who pay court to him shamelessly.'[155] In June 1891 Wilhelm II again had cause to complain about the 'supercilious and brusque behaviour' of the Conservatives towards the bourgeois Minister of the Interior, who was 'a thorn in their side, just because he is plain Herr Herrfurth and not a count', as Carl Wedel observed. The Conservative leaders charged that Herrfurth was 'acting in the Liberal interest in his appointment of provincial officials, for he is an avowed enemy of the aristocracy. The Kaiser rejected this', the Flügeladjutant recorded, 'by saying that the appointment of provincial officials was carried out through him; their suitability was examined by the Civil Cabinet, and Lucanus made sure that Conservative principles were taken into account.' Under no circumstances would he be prepared to drop Herrfurth. Wedel could not help wondering, in his account of this episode, whether the Kaiser was unaware 'that Herrfurth and Lucanus are close friends and that the latter also has strong Liberal leanings?'[156]

Waldersee saw yet another sign of the Kaiser's inclination to act against the Conservative Party 'in the most passionate way' when he went to Berlin in June 1891 to attend a session of the Upper House of the Prussian Landtag. Shortly before the Landtag closed Wilhelm invited a large number of members of both houses to the Pfaueninsel on the Wannsee. He received them personally at the lakeside, where two steamers awaited them, and accompanied them back there afterwards. Throughout the excursion he treated them with the utmost affability, with the intention of obtaining a majority both for the Game Damage Bill and Herrfurth's Rural District Bill. He went from one parliamentarian to another stressing that he set great store by the passage of these bills, with the result that both were indeed passed. 'Without his intervention the opposite would have happened', Waldersee observed, although in his view neither law was important enough to justify the sovereign's use of 'the full weight of his personal influence' in support of them, for had he failed he would have caused immeasurable damage. 'If there is serious trouble over a matter of great moment I have no objection to the King intervening personally', he wrote; but such action was 'dangerous in any circumstances'.[157] In the months that followed Waldersee complained repeatedly of the Kaiser's tendency to rule with the liberal 'middle parties' against the Conservatives. 'It is quite plain to me that we are steering strongly towards the left, and under Caprivi's deliberate leadership', he noted angrily in November 1891.[158]

## HINZPETER *REDIVIVUS*

If General Count Alfred von Waldersee blamed Wilhelm II's surprising and to him highly unwelcome swing towards the liberal middle parties on the Kaiser's need to co-operate with a Reich administration that in its turn had to answer to a Reichstag in which the balance of parties had shifted fundamentally since early 1890, in his eyes this was not the principal cause of the problem. Much more to blame for the monarch's left-wing tendencies, as Waldersee saw it, was the influence of two men who had already played a decisive role in the Bismarck crisis, namely Wilhelm's former tutor Dr Georg Ernst Hinzpeter and his ally Dr Paul Kayser, the (Jewish) Director of the Colonial Department at the Foreign Office. This astonishing conclusion cannot be seen merely as a delusion which had arisen in the mind of a Chief of General Staff whose position at court was becoming more and more insecure, for Waldersee was by no means alone in this opinion. In June 1890 the Flügeladjutant Count Carl von Wedel warned the Chancellor of the intrigues which Hinzpeter and Kayser were devising. Both men, he said, were 'unscrupulous intriguers' who enabled 'secret sources' to reach the Kaiser. Wedel pointed particularly to Hinzpeter as 'the mediator, who abuses the Kaiser's trust'.[159] On a train journey to Kiel an incensed Hermann von Lucanus told the Flügeladjutant that the Kaiser's recent speech at Essen had been corrected and sent back to Wilhelm by Hinzpeter. Lucanus, Wedel recorded, was 'furious and asked whether it was Hinzpeter or he, Lucanus, who was responsible to the Kaiser and the Ministry for his speeches . . . Since then Hinzpeter had of course been doubly hostile towards him and was seeking to overthrow him at the earliest opportunity.'[160] The commanding generals, who came to Berlin for Moltke's ninetieth birthday, likewise had the former tutor in mind when they expressed the unanimous opinion that 'the depressed and uncertain mood' in the country had come about 'principally . . . because of the Kaiser's inclination to consult private and unofficial individuals'.[161]

Hinzpeter's influence on Wilhelm, and through him on matters of domestic policy and public appointments, became apparent (as we have seen) when the Kaiser dismissed Court Preacher Adolf Stoecker.[162] It reached its zenith a few weeks later when the Kaiser intervened dramatically in the Prussian school reform question. Waldersee was horrified to find Hinzpeter back in Berlin in

19. Dr Georg Ernst Hinzpeter, the Kaiser's tutor from 1866 to 1877

the winter of 1890–1 and now described the schoolmaster from Bielefeld as the most dangerous of Wilhelm II's irresponsible advisers 'because he has contrived to keep himself in a strong position'.[163] 'The driving force is said to be the wife', he noted in his diary. 'She is ambitious and wants to get whatever she can for her husband. She is French, and although she has lived in Germany for 20 years she can still hardly speak German.'[164] The General predicted bitterly 'that people around the Kaiser will soon notice that this evil fellow has been here; in fact many people now see him for what he is. I am intrigued to see how Caprivi will get on with him.'[165] At present it was Minister of Ecclesiastical Affairs Gustav von Gossler who was suffering most from the misdeeds of this irresponsible adviser, Waldersee observed, for the 'Hinzpeter influence' was proving 'uncomfortably strong with regard to the question of school reform'.[166]

With Hinzpeter's arrival in Berlin at the beginning of December 1890 to attend the conference on school reform, his 'great influence on the Kaiser' became apparent to everyone.[167] Holstein and Eulenburg seriously wondered whether it would not be wise to appoint Hinzpeter to an under-secretaryship of state or a ministerial directorship in the Prussian Ministry of Ecclesiastical Affairs and Education. 'His relations with H.M. are the same – whether from Berlin or Bielefeld', they reasoned. 'The advantage of a man who has been using his influence anonymously having to answer for it publicly is obvious . . . Much gossip would be silenced . . . Anyone who disliked Hinzpeter would have the satisfaction of knowing that as under-secretary of state he will at least be given enough rope to hang himself.'[168]

However unmistakable the influence exercised by the former tutor, suddenly re-emerging from his Westphalian retreat into the limelight, on his now powerful pupil, the nature of the relationship between Hinzpeter and the Kaiser baffled contemporaries and is still hard to fathom today. Did Wilhelm II see the stern preceptor as a substitute for his dead father, and perhaps even for his deeply venerated grandfather, whose praise and encouragement he now needed more than ever? Had 'the Doctor' learned how to manipulate Wilhelm and direct his mood at will, during his long years in attendance on the young Prince?[169] Whether they liked or loathed the influence of this middle-class pedagogue over their high-handed monarch, contemporary observers agreed in sensing a strange mixture of domination and subjection on both sides of the relationship. Thus Waldersee remarked in December 1890: 'Hinzpeter's influence is undoubtedly in the ascendant; the Kaiser sees a great deal of this obsequious hypocrite. Several times when he has been with their Majesties he has not been deterred even by the presence of the entourage from his malicious intrigues. In this instance, too, the Kaiser is incredibly unaware of what is going on and, just as with Herbert Bismarck, he does not notice how much he allows Hinzpeter to influence and push him. The Kaiserin is wiser, as always, and hates the villain.'[170] When, at a dinner with the Chancellor and several ministers, the Chief of the General Staff deplored the tutor's hold over the Kaiser, Gossler and Boetticher, of all people, sprang to Hinzpeter's defence with the argument that 'anyone who disparages the Kaiser as strongly and criticises him as openly as Hinzpeter does can hardly have much influence' over him. Waldersee refused to be convinced, however, and retorted: 'This shows just how false Hinzpeter is; he is in fact very often with the Kaiser, who pays much attention to his views, and then immediately afterwards he criticises his former pupil!'[171] When in January 1891 Professor Schottmüller lamented the fact that the Kaiser began many things but never finished anything, Hinzpeter replied self-importantly: '*That does not matter in the least; the main thing is that I always keep him in suspense*; unless there is always something new he becomes apathetic.' Waldersee, who recorded this remark in his diary, commented: 'So the scoundrel gives himself credit for controlling the Kaiser completely, and does not care in the least what becomes of the Fatherland.'[172] Not long afterwards he wrote angrily, 'Wherever one goes one comes across people who think Hinzpeter dangerous; I have just been assured by eyewitnesses that on several occasions this wretched fellow has kissed the Kaiser's hand in front of many witnesses! It just shows what unscrupulous wretches these liberal gentlemen are. On the one hand outrageously presumptuous, [on the other] crawling to the Kaiser and prostrating themselves before him.'[173] In 1893 Poultney Bigelow, the American friend of the Kaiser's youth, also expressed his surprise at the tutor's attitude to his pupil after meeting Hinzpeter at the American Legation. 'I think he has gone mad', he reported to the Kaiser. 'He accused me of having compared you with *Alexander* and of attacking you in a periodical called Die Zukunft! . . . I think the dear old gentleman has "a screw loose" – he was so serious and critical!'[174]

Observers of all shades of opinion saw Hinzpeter's influence over appointments as particularly dangerous, especially as he openly boasted that the Kaiser even discussed changes in ministerial appointments with him. In January 1891, for instance, he told Kropatschek, the editor of the *Kreuzzeitung*, with whom he was working on the Commission for School Reform, that he had 'talked to the Kaiser about replacing Ministers Gossler and Herrfurth', and that the Kaiser had exclaimed: 'Finding replacements for ministers is difficult; when I get rid of generals I can find as many new ones as I want.'[175] Although Waldersee had nothing but contempt for Lucanus, whom he considered 'thoroughly unprincipled' and a 'very poor Chief of Cabinet' who gave the Kaiser bad advice,[176] he was outraged when it appeared that as a result of one of Hinzpeter's intrigues Lucanus might be replaced by Dr Paul Kayser. The three Generals, Caprivi, Waldersee and Wedel, otherwise at daggers drawn, agreed that this must be prevented at all costs. The Chancellor contrived to get 'the notorious Dr Kayser' appointed director of the Colonial Department at the Foreign Office, not least in the hope of 'pinning him down and rendering him harmless', as Carl Wedel put it. Wedel doubted, however, that this tactic would succeed, for 'the secret channels leading to the Kaiser via Hinzpeter will still be open to Kayser, and both have such a thirst for illicit intrigues and interference that they will certainly keep these channels accessible'.[177] The anti-Semitic Waldersee, above all, was adamant that Paul Kayser should not be given the influential Civil Cabinet post. 'He is an extraordinarily clever man but I would deeply deplore his appointment', he wrote, citing as his reason that Kayser was 'of Jewish extraction and has a Jewish wife'.[178] In October 1890 he commented: 'If Herr Hinzpeter protects such wretched fellows [as Kayser] he proves that he is himself good for nothing. For a time Herr Kayser's relationship with His Majesty went to his head and I think it quite credible that he planned – with Hinzpeter's support, of course – to get himself appointed Chief of the Civil Cabinet. I have reached the point where I think everything is possible, so what is to prevent a Jew obtaining even this position.'[179]

After the school conference Hinzpeter's influence seems to have receded a little. At the beginning of 1891 the 'Doctor' expressed the intention of staying on in Berlin for a while in order to bring about a reconciliation between the Kaiser and his mother, although Waldersee saw this as mere self-glorification, for Hinzpeter knew as well as he did that this was a hopeless task.[180] In the autumn of 1894, however, Waldersee heard from Count Botho zu Eulenburg, at that time Prussian Minister-President and Minister of the Interior, that Hinzpeter was 'unfortunately' still keeping in touch with the Kaiser 'in the same way as before', and in later years Philipp Eulenburg was likewise constantly discovering to his surprise that Wilhelm was maintaining close contact with his waspish tutor.[181] In the winter of 1890–1, at any rate, Hinzpeter was undoubtedly in great favour with the Kaiser, and under his influence Wilhelm II was able to nerve himself to take the momentous decision to part company with his longstanding, arch-conservative mentor Waldersee. As Flügeladjutant Carl von Wedel remarked shortly after Waldersee's dismissal, the fact that Hinzpeter had been involved in bringing about the fall of the Chief of the General Staff was 'beyond all doubt, just as I suspect that he has a hand in *all* these things'.[182]

# CHAPTER SIXTEEN

# The fall of the court generals

T HE fundamental cause of the break with the two Bismarcks and the dismissal of Liebenau as Oberhofmarschall was Wilhelm II's ambition to take the most important decisions for himself. This conclusion is reinforced by the fact that only a year later Wilhelm consolidated the independence of his position by dismissing Waldersee and moving the two generals in his suite, Count Carl von Wedel and Adolf von Wittich, to other posts. All three officers had stood by him loyally in his conflict first with his parents and then with the Bismarcks. The first two, moreover, had handled delicate negotiations on his behalf in the murky affairs involving Anna Homolatsch and Elisabeth Countess Wedel, the sister-in-law of the Flügeladjutant. The knowledge they shared of very private political and personal events made the removal of the three generals from the court a highly dangerous manoeuvre, and Wilhelm felt compelled to avoid the slightest semblance of a clash in carrying it out. It was important that these influential officers should continue to feel beholden to him even when they were no longer in court service. That he nevertheless insisted on their removal from his immediate entourage is symptomatic of the growing self-confidence of the young Kaiser, who would not tolerate any strong-willed adviser at his side and was already bragging that he intended to be his own chief of General Staff. The story of Waldersee's dismissal, above all, demonstrates some of the least admirable aspects of Wilhelm II's personality: his inability to accept criticism, his craving for admiration and his sense of injured vanity at any unfavourable comment about him.

## WALDERSEE'S 'DOWNFALL'

The dismissal of Count Alfred von Waldersee as chief of the General Staff was undoubtedly one of the most significant decisions taken by Kaiser Wilhelm II in the early part of his reign. The first volume of this biography described in detail the role of surrogate father played by Waldersee in the 1880s, when Wilhelm stood in venomous opposition to his liberal parents.[1] At the height of this conflict in 1887–8 Wilhelm entrusted certain private and secret papers to Waldersee for safekeeping. Precisely when and why the young Kaiser began to feel hampered by his close relationship with the powerful General cannot be clearly established, but it is not impossible that the first rift occurred when Waldersee tried to mediate in the blackmail episode involving Miss Love in April 1889. It will be remembered that Wilhelm had at first denied any intimate relationship with this woman but was later caught out when the Bismarcks felt compelled to buy back his letters to her.[2] At any rate, the first sign of trouble in the relationship between Wilhelm and Waldersee appeared in the spring of 1889. In March 1890 when Prince Heinrich heard what seemed to him the surprising news that Waldersee had not been appointed Reich chancellor, he remarked in front of his fellow naval officers that he had in fact heard of differences between his brother and Waldersee 'as much as a year ago'.[3] As the Flügeladjutant Colonel von Lippe also reported, the Kaiser complained several times in the course of 1889 about Waldersee 'interfering in everything' and 'stirring up trouble' everywhere.[4]

As we have already seen, the relationship came under further strain when the Bismarck crisis became acute towards the end of 1889 and Wilhelm was forced to consider whom he would appoint as Bismarck's successor.[5] After his dismissal as chief of the General Staff, Waldersee, looking back over the past year, noted in his diary that since January 1890 he had been 'pushed aside' by the Kaiser, which he attributed principally to the influence of Chief of the Military Cabinet General Wilhelm von Hahnke.[6] But the decisive break came – certainly not by coincidence – in mid-March 1890, at the height of the Bismarck crisis.

Sharp-eyed observers noticed that Waldersee's star was on the wane soon after Bismarck's dismissal. They dated the change in the Kaiser's mood from an incident in spring 1890 when the Kaiser criticised Waldersee in front of all his subordinates at the General Staff headquarters. Immediately beforehand Wilhelm had taken the Chief of the General Staff with him as usual for his morning walk, during which Waldersee must have made political comments which displeased the Kaiser, for on the way back Wilhelm remarked angrily to one of his adjutants: 'I don't understand W.; he's my Chief of General Staff, and ought not to worry his head about things which don't concern him.' After his harsh criticism of Waldersee at the General Staff headquarters, the Kaiser told the Chief of the Military Cabinet that he had wanted to show Waldersee that he could live without him.[7] The Flügeladjutant Wedel's view of this incident was that in accepting this insult from the Kaiser without protest, Waldersee had shown weakness, and that it had 'lowered him irretrievably in the eyes of the Kaiser'.[8] During his Scandinavian cruise in 1890 Wilhelm told his close friend Eulenburg that Waldersee was 'an intriguer pure and simple and wishes to become chancellor, although I have told him *I* shall *never* appoint him'. Politics were no business of the Chief of the General Staff; they were a matter for the Kaiser himself. Waldersee should 'kindly refrain from meddling in such matters'. Commenting on the Kaiser's changed attitude to Waldersee, Eulenburg observed: 'What H.M. resents is the way he [Waldersee] has exploited his close relationship with H.M. for his own purposes. H.M. holds the very correct view that people should work for *him* and not for themselves.'[9] Wilhelm also held Waldersee responsible for recommending Minister of War von Verdy, whom he had 'recognised too late' for what he was, and whom he had wanted to dismiss since the summer of 1890, as we have seen.[10] An increasing number of generals, including the Chancellor himself, expressed the opinion that Waldersee's 'worst crime' had been to advise the Kaiser to appoint Verdy minister of war.[11]

Waldersee naturally felt Wilhelm's growing coolness towards him in their almost daily meetings. After making his report to the Kaiser on 8 June 1890, in the course of which he obtained imperial approval for the deployment of troops against France and also for 'a few personal matters', Waldersee reflected that as far as the Kaiser was concerned he had never had any 'problems on official [!] business until now [!]'. The double qualification of this remark makes it clear that he had sensed a deterioration in his relationship with Wilhelm. He noted in his diary that 'in spite of his great amiability I thought I detected an underlying mood of gravity'.[12] The more coolly the Kaiser behaved towards him, the more critical became the General's opinion of the Kaiser. Thus at the manoeuvres at Memel Waldersee gained 'a very distressing impression' of Wilhelm's 'relationship with his entourages' and of the 'hasty and harsh judgements' which he passed on others in the presence of his Hofmarschall, his personal physician and the servants. Such frivolous conduct would never have been possible with the old Kaiser Wilhelm.[13] After the autumn manoeuvres in Silesia, which were particularly difficult to carry out because of floods, the Kaiser upbraided the participating generals 'very sharply' in the presence of young officers and foreign guests, which Waldersee condemned, since neither 'lack of judgement nor laziness' was to blame. 'Everyone has the best intentions, everyone is completely dedicated and does the best he can; people work for months at full stretch only to be rewarded with a harsh, overhasty verdict', he wrote, complaining that 'the Kaiser does not take the trouble to look at the circumstances . . . Those who are treated so mercilessly go away full of bitterness and lose all pleasure in their service. The subordinates lose all respect for their superiors, and so authority is undermined.'[14] Waldersee took it as a bad sign that commanding generals who visited the capital no longer reported to the Kaiser on arrival. 'Would it have been conceivable two years ago', he wondered in dismay, 'for a commanding general to come to Berlin and not to wish above all else to see the Kaiser?'[15]

Waldersee — and he was not alone — was appalled by Wilhelm II's practice of making sure that the side which he himself led in the manoeuvres was always victorious. When Philipp Eulenburg broached this sensitive subject with Wilhelm during the Scandinavian cruise of 1890 the Kaiser became '*very heated* and proved to me by an exposition of the military situation that he had won "according to the rules"'. Eulenburg argued that the army would always try to let the Kaiser win if he were participating, but Wilhelm refused to accept this, and claimed that it was 'a grave affront to all my commanding generals, who likewise regard me simply as a commanding general . . . Moreover if any commanding general opposing me in battle were to act dishonestly towards me, I should *dismiss him from the service at once.*' Eulenburg's suggestion that the Kaiser should in future abstain from active participation in the manoeuvres fell on deaf ears. Wilhelm considered it his right to 'undergo military training' and remarked 'that he hoped the army was satisfied he was *capable* of victory'. The Kaiser, Eulenburg reported, 'was so heated that my secretary . . . asked me whether H.M. had been reading me some document — the Kaiser's voice had sounded so consistently loud'. Wilhelm's friend was also amazed 'that no soldier has yet had the courage to discuss this question with H.M. The fact is they all go in holy terror of H.M.'[16] The Kaiser's personal intervention in manoeuvres, which was to cause trouble until the eve of the First World War, played an important part in Waldersee's dismissal, as we are about to see.

## TRANSFER TO STUTTGART AS 'VICEROY OF SOUTH GERMANY'?

When Waldersee returned to Berlin on 9 August 1890 after a period of leave, it was at once clear to him that a battle with the Reich Chancellor and the Foreign Office was looming, for Caprivi, 'spurred on' by that 'scoundrel' Friedrich von Holstein, as the General maintained, had issued an order that military attachés would henceforth be answerable to their heads of mission and that they should not allude to political questions in their reports. As Waldersee had been trying for years to raise the status of the attachés and to make them independent of the ambassadors, the order signified a direct challenge to him as chief of the General Staff.[17] The attitude of the Kaiser, who had previously been 'in complete agreement with me', as Waldersee remarked, was naturally of crucial importance in this question. 'I must handle the whole military attaché affair with the greatest care, and first try to find out what the Kaiser's view is', he wrote.[18] 'I shall probably see the Kaiser in the next few days and then I shall be able to tell if there is any specific reason behind this business.'[19] He now became increasingly convinced that he would do well to distance himself from Wilhelm II and the current regime. He noted resignedly in his diary on 11 September 1890: 'To my way of thinking everything is going so badly and I see such a decline that it has long been my wish not to be regarded as one of the chief advisers, sharing the responsibility for it. I am also convinced that things will go further and further downhill; why should I allow myself to be buried by the avalanche which I cannot halt?'[20]

It was after the joint manoeuvres of the XIII Army Corps and the navy in Schleswig-Holstein at the beginning of September 1890 that the Kaiser mentioned for the first time the possibility that Waldersee might take over the command of the Württemberg Army Corps at Stuttgart. The Swabian diplomat, Alfred von Kiderlen-Wächter, who as always was accompanying the Kaiser as the Foreign Office's representative, was surprised to find himself suddenly being asked by the Kaiser, on the train, whether he should send Waldersee to Stuttgart as corps commander. 'As you can imagine I was completely dumbfounded', he told Friedrich von Holstein. Kiderlen had the impression that Wilhelm did not relish the idea of informing Waldersee of his transfer to Stuttgart. He was obviously afraid that the General would hand in his resignation and had hit upon the idea of offering Waldersee the inspectorship of the two Bavarian Army Corps at the same time, 'to soften the blow'. Wilhelm even asked Kiderlen to sound out Waldersee about this solution, which the young diplomat declined to do. Instead he reported the Kaiser's intention to the Chancellor. Through an oversight Caprivi's answer to Kiderlen, written in his own hand and addressed to the latter in person, fell into the Kaiser's hands. Wilhelm opened the Chancellor's letter with the words: 'Let's commit a breach of confidence for once!' Luckily Caprivi had declared himself in favour of Waldersee's transfer to Stuttgart. But Kiderlen wondered whether 'the secret urge to have a peep behind the scenes for a change' had played a part in the imperial 'breach of confidence'.[21]

On his arrival in Breslau for the Silesian manoeuvres, the Kaiser had an initial, hesitant discussion with Waldersee on 17 September 1890 as to whether the General might move to Stuttgart, where he would to a certain extent be 'viceroy of South Germany'.[22] According to Kiderlen 'the crafty W. at once pretended he was very glad to go but pointed out to H.M. that Prince Leopold of Bavaria was senior to him in the service and could therefore not be subordinated to him'. After this Wilhelm left the difficult task of resolving the matter to the Reich Chancellor, only remarking that he did not want to 'force' Waldersee to go.[23] In an hour-long interview with the Chief of the General Staff, Caprivi made it clear that he wished Waldersee to take on the Stuttgart post. He was the right man and the only man for the job, and his wife too was 'ideally suited to help him'. The Chancellor declared that the Kaiser also wished for this transfer, although only on condition that Waldersee was happy to go to Stuttgart, and that he should not 'in any circumstances' gain the impression, as Waldersee noted in his diary, that the Kaiser 'wanted to part company with me'. He 'was to receive the Order of the Black Eagle immediately, and the Kaiser would also agree to my other wishes'.[24] Kiderlen discovered that Caprivi had told the Chief of the General Staff 'pretty bluntly' that 'there was simply no room for him' in Berlin.[25]

Waldersee spent a restless night weighing up these proposals. Next morning the Kaiser burst into his bedroom, whereupon the Chief of the General Staff told him he could not accept the Stuttgart post. The people of Württemberg, he explained, hated the arrangement by which a Prussian general always held the command of the Württemberg Army Corps. The South German particularist movement, which had in any case grown stronger of late, would be given further momentum by Waldersee's appointment, for the entire liberal and Catholic press would denounce him as a 'Stoeckerite, a bigot and a *Kreuzzeitung* man'. As a result he would have to take severe military measures from the start, which would only create more dissatisfaction. Furthermore he had absolutely no desire to mix with the Württemberg court, which was 'contemptible in some respects'; in particular he could not tolerate the 'way of life' of the (homosexual) King Karl. Waldersee therefore suggested to the Kaiser that he should break with former practice and entrust a reliable Württemberger general with the Stuttgart command. The Kaiser reacted favourably to this proposal, but said that he also wished to discuss with the Chancellor a suggestion made by the King of Saxony that Prince Wilhelm, the heir to the throne of Württemberg, should take over the command.[26] Following this conversation Waldersee wrote to the Chancellor stating that he would not be able to bring the necessary enthusiasm to the post in Stuttgart. Both Caprivi and the Chief of the Military Cabinet thought Waldersee's decision a mistake, since he would not be able to hold out for much longer in Berlin, and 'H.M. would not make him such an offer a second time.'[27]

All in all Waldersee had the impression that Caprivi would not be displeased if he left Berlin. 'I do not believe that the Kaiser wanted to get rid of me', he reflected, 'but at the same time I realise that I cannot stay with him permanently. He is beginning to feel sure of himself in military matters, and does not want to appear dependent on me. In the same way that he thinks his own judgement is sound on every imaginable subject and has already caused much head-shaking, he fails to recognise that he is nothing but a dilettante in the military sphere. If he should take it into his head that he could command major troop formations himself it would really be very dangerous, even disastrous!'[28]

## THE FATEFUL IMPERIAL MANOEUVRES ON THE NEISSE

Waldersee's bedroom conversation with the Kaiser about the Stuttgart command took place on 18 September 1890 at Rohnstock in Silesia. The next day a conflict arose between him and Wilhelm that was to seal the end of the General's career as chief of the Great General Staff and favourite of the monarch. The imperial manoeuvres, in Waldersee's disparaging words, had always gone well 'as long as the Kaiser was not in command . . . As soon as he entered the fray, however, everything became very artificial; indeed one would not hesitate to call it a childish game. Last year it was far better; but now he has gained confidence and really believes he knows something about commanding troops. In my opinion he has a certain grasp of parade-ground exercises, but not of the actual command of troops; of course he has no war experience at all and he refuses to believe that the cavalry has only limited usefulness in battle. He is extraordinarily restless and rushes about; he is usually right up at the front, interfering in the generals' command, issuing innumerable, often contradictory orders and paying scant attention to his advisers. Added to this he is extremely vain: he always wants to win and takes it very badly whenever the judges' decision goes against him.'[29] Waldersee particularly derided Wilhelm II's practice of sending his Flügeladjutanten 'quite brazenly over to the enemy' before the manoeuvre began. They then galloped back with secret reports to convey to the Kaiser, 'who later boasts in all seriousness of having been supplied with excellent information'.[30]

As ill luck would have it, on 19 September the Kaiser insisted on commanding the VI Army Corps, quite unaware that according to the plan for the manoeuvre drawn up by Waldersee this very corps would in all probability be thoroughly defeated. This was indeed what happened, particularly as the Kaiser's troop dispositions were 'extremely bad': he finished up with the river Neisse separating the two divisions he commanded.[31] The Chancellor-General also acknowledged that the Kaiser had made the unfavourable position of his side in the exercise even worse by 'one or two gross errors'.[32] The Chief of the General Staff's private verdict on Wilhelm's competence in command was terse. 'Extremely inadequate leadership, immature ideas, inexperience combined with a very self-confident manner. Playing to the gallery, in other words – a mere game, and no seriousness!'[33] Many of those taking part, among them the King of Saxony and the Hereditary Prince of Saxe-Meiningen (the Kaiser's brother-in-law), Waldersee recorded, had greeted the defeat of the monarch in the manoeuvres as a 'great stroke of luck' which might make him more circumspect in future.[34]

At the end of the exercise the hapless Waldersee was obliged to give a critical assessment of the manoeuvre in the presence of the Emperor of Austria, King

Albert and Prince Georg of Saxony, Prince Ludwig of Bavaria, the Austrian General Beck, Adjutant-General von Wittich and countless other officers and Flügeladjutanten. He did his best to mention all mistakes without giving offence. 'The Kaiser, whom people were of course watching closely, is said to have looked rather surprised and then very serious', Waldersee wrote. 'When I had finished he took over. He said first that he agreed with all I had said, but then began trying to make excuses for himself. Unfortunately his explanations were very weak, indeed lame. In the evening I could see that he was rather out of sorts and I also heard that he had been very angry and was in the mood to put the blame for his poor command on me.'[35] All those present noticed that Wilhelm did not shake hands with Waldersee as usual. A clumsy attempt by General von Versen to redeem the situation by flattery failed completely. Kiderlen reported that 'a high-ranking person' summed up the scene with the words: 'Versen was trying to lick H.M.'s boots but he wasn't having any!'[36] Wedel thought his rival Waldersee's assessment of the manoeuvre a masterpiece, as it 'dressed up strong criticism of the Kaiser in such a tactful form', but he suspected that the monarch had been deeply wounded by it nonetheless. 'If only Waldersee had spoken out as clearly and distinctly from the very beginning', the Flügeladjutant sighed, 'what a good effect he might then have had upon the Kaiser's military development! As it is, two years have gone by during which the Kaiser has constantly had his praises sung for his "talent as a military commander", while his most blatant mistakes have been passed over instead of being pointed out to him. Is it any wonder, particularly with his character and with the great gifts that he undoubtedly possesses, that he has gone astray and has finally come to believe in his own much-praised "talent"! Is it any wonder, and is not the psychological explanation only too easy to see, if he finds today's criticism disagreeable if not insulting, however tactfully expressed.' That evening Wedel heard that 'the Kaiser spoke very disparagingly of Waldersee's assessment'. Waldersee had 'risen somewhat' in the estimation of Wedel himself, 'although his star may have waned in the All-Highest circle because of his criticism'.[37]

When Wilhelm II returned to Berlin from Austria on 9 October he had reached 'a critical point', in the view of many observers, which Waldersee defined as follows: 'If he bears me a grudge because of his poor command of troops he shows that he lacks greatness of spirit and deserves to be treated as a little man. But if he has allowed himself to reflect calmly and to examine himself a little, he cannot but be grateful to me and tell himself that I acted without fear and did my duty. Then one could say: there is nobility in him after all.'[38] Although the newspapers were full of rumours of Waldersee's dismissal after this incident, Wilhelm II showed great friendliness at their next few meetings. The Chief of the General Staff nevertheless suspected that the Kaiser planned to move him to another post in the spring of 1891. 'Perhaps the Kaiser . . . will want to get rid of me then', he wrote, for Wilhelm was after all 'clever enough to think that it is not yet the right moment to make the break'.[39] Carl Wedel also realised that 'Waldersee's star is really sinking now.' 'Knowing the Kaiser's determined will, I am convinced that he has made up his mind to send him [Waldersee] away and that he will carry out this intention fairly soon, in one way or another. Who would have thought that the catastrophe would come so soon!?'[40]

## WALDERSEE'S DISMISSAL

As several weeks passed without any change in the Kaiser's behaviour towards him, Waldersee's anxieties were gradually stilled. But in mid-December 1890, when Wilhelm gave his approval to Caprivi's directive that military attachés should abstain from political reporting, the Chief of the General Staff's feeling that he no longer possessed the Kaiser's confidence was reawakened.[41] Bitterly he complained: 'As usual Hahnke has not understood what is happening and has failed to warn the Kaiser of the consequences, so that the Kaiser has now decided to do exactly the opposite of what he considered to be right in the spring.' Waldersee was also disappointed with the attitude of Minister of War von Kaltenborn, who was likewise annoyed about the directive but claimed that, 'since the Kaiser has decided', he could do nothing.[42] On 16 December Waldersee had 'a conversation that at times became somewhat heated' with the Kaiser on the subject. Hahnke was also brought in on the discussion. The monarch, with Hahnke's backing, claimed that those attachés who were also Flügeladjutanten — that is to say the most important of them, in St Petersburg, Vienna, Paris and Rome — still had the right, and indeed the duty, to report directly to him, and he intended to 'impress this on them thoroughly now, as he would be seeing them again for the New Year'. Waldersee was perplexed by this and noted in his diary that it showed 'that the Kaiser does not know exactly what is in the directive, and that Hahnke has not understood it at all either', for it was precisely Caprivi's aim to cut off direct and indirect contact between the military attachés and the Kaiser. On Hahnke he commented: 'And this is supposed to be a Cabinet chief and adviser? It is truly pitiful!'[43] After this argument with Waldersee the Kaiser loudly declared: 'I've just repulsed an attack on Caprivi. There is no hope whatever of driving a wedge between C. and myself. I know perfectly well why Waldersee always tries to do so: he'd very much like to become chancellor himself.'[44]

Waldersee felt he understood the inner conflict which was now troubling Wilhelm. Writing at the beginning of 1891 he remarked: 'I can often tell that the Kaiser is struggling with himself inwardly. Partly he is his old self, and tells himself that I am too; partly his vanity makes him feel uncomfortable with me; partly he still feels stung by the business of the imperial manoeuvres.'[45] Others occasionally noticed 'an irritable mood' towards Waldersee on the Kaiser's part, for instance when he discovered from a newspaper that the General had been present at Stoecker's farewell sermon.[46] In mid-January 1891 Waldersee detected a further sign that the final crisis was near: he was no longer invited to dinners given by other people for the Kaiser. As the guest lists were always submitted to the monarch and Wilhelm made ample use of the opportunity to strike out the names of those he did not wish to see, the Chief of the General Staff had the distinct feeling that the Kaiser was behind his exclusion from these occasions.[47]

The precise moment at which the Kaiser decided to dismiss Waldersee as chief of the General Staff was recorded by the Flügeladjutant Carl von Wedel, to whom Wilhelm recounted in some agitation a conversation he had had with the Chancellor and the moderate leader of the Conservatives, Otto von Helldorff. The latter had complained that he no longer had any influence in the party, since he had been 'completely pushed out' by Count Waldersee. Asked by the Kaiser for his views, Caprivi then said that he 'considered it absolutely essential to send Waldersee away from Berlin at least for a time, because he would not stop his scheming'. The Kaiser had thereupon decided to move Waldersee to another post.[48] He nevertheless maintained a markedly friendly tone in his personal contacts with his Chief of Staff, so that the end came as an unpleasant shock for the latter.

During Waldersee's regular audience on 24 January 1891 the conversation came round to the imperial manoeuvres planned for the following autumn. They were to take place in Bavaria following the manoeuvres in Austria. It emerged that the Kaiser, without asking anyone, had fixed on 9, 10 and 11 September for the Bavarian manoeuvres, on the assumption that the Austrian manoeuvres would take place from 2 to 8 September, immediately *before* the German ones. In fact, however, the Austrian manoeuvres had been planned for 11 to 15 September. The Chief of the General Staff's attempts to bring forward the Bavarian manoeuvres were thwarted by the Bavarian Minister of War's urgent request that the appointed dates should not be changed. Prince Regent Luitpold, he explained, for whom it was 'not at all convenient that the Kaiser was coming', refused to hear 'so much as another word about the manoeuvres'. At his audience Waldersee therefore asked Wilhelm II to accept the Austrian invitation with a day's postponement. The Kaiser, however, stood firm and ordered Waldersee to write to the military attaché Adolf von Deines in Vienna saying that Wilhelm could come to Austria only from 2 to 8 September, and that he therefore requested that the manoeuvres there be brought forward. The reason for the Kaiser's uncompromising attitude was, as Waldersee despairingly recorded in his diary, that he wanted '*come what may* to go hunting on the Rominter Heide on 23 September!' The General was 'thoroughly depressed' as he left the audience. 'Stags, in other words pleasure, take first place!', he sighed. 'And such great interests are harmed by this desire to pursue pleasure!'[49]

That same evening the Kaiser asked Waldersee to 'return to him certain private papers concerning him which he had given me for safekeeping in 1888, and said the reason was that he had now obtained an iron safe. He seems to have had a dark suspicion that it might be awkward for him if these papers remained in my possession after our separation', Waldersee noted in a later account of his dismissal.[50] In spite of this omen the Chief of the General Staff was taken completely by surprise when the Kaiser, after conferring on him the Cross of Grand Commander of the Order of Hohenzollern on 27 January 1891, Wilhelm's thirty-second birthday, announced that he wanted to make Waldersee happy, and that he therefore intended to give him command of an army corps. During a meal with his officers – among them Count Alfred von Schlieffen and the future Minister of War, Heinrich von Gossler – Waldersee made up his mind to ask the Kaiser to be allowed to retire from the army. He was determined 'to make my view of the situation very plain . . . I believe I shall be doing a service to the army and to the Kaiser himself if I act firmly and show him that there are still people who do not simply submit to his will without further ado', he wrote.[51]

The Kaiser told Wedel during a drive in the Grunewald that in dismissing Waldersee he wished to show 'that the Chief of the General Staff was only his agent and as such was certainly not in command of the commanding generals'. In Wedel's view, however, Wilhelm was merely deceiving himself about his real motives in bringing out this argument. On the other hand he agreed with the opinion expressed by the Kaiser that Waldersee no longer enjoyed the confidence of the army as a whole. He also recorded that all the military officers in the inner circle at court had the impression that 'since the criticism [by the Kaiser] of the work of the General Staff in the previous spring [1890] relations [between Wilhelm and Waldersee] had changed, and also that there was a general feeling that the coldness between them had grown since Waldersee's criticism of last autumn'. Wedel gave no credence to Wilhelm's claim that he had not taken Waldersee's criticism amiss. 'So now Waldersee has also met his downfall', he reflected; 'and another star of the new era, which shone so brightly at first, has set!'[52]

In the course of a violent argument which took place on 28 January 1891 in the Berlin Schloss Wilhelm refused point-blank to accept Waldersee's resignation from the army. The Chief of the General Staff listened in astonishment as the Kaiser sought to justify his transfer to the army corps at Altona on the grounds that both Bismarck and the 'socialist conspirators' who had their headquarters in

Hamburg must be kept under surveillance, and that developments at the North German courts were beginning to take a 'very alarming' turn; moreover Waldersee's wife (the widow of Prince Friedrich of Schleswig-Holstein-Sonderburg-Augustenburg, Prince of Noer) would surely be glad to return to her old homeland. And finally, the Kaiser explained, it was his wish to lower the status of the chief of the General Staff in relation to the Prussian minister of war and the commanding generals. As he put it, 'the chief of the General Staff is to be no more than a kind of amanuensis for me, and for that reason I need a younger man'. Waldersee was undeterred, and told the Kaiser bluntly that he was convinced he would be doing him and the army a greater service by resigning than by staying on. 'Whether he grasped the meaning of these words I do not know, but in time he will understand.' After the audience Waldersee met his predecessor, Field Marshal Count von Moltke. He too found the proposed transfer of Waldersee to Altona 'quite incomprehensible, and expressed great concern about the Kaiser'. Waldersee reflected with distress that 'the saddest thing' about his dismissal as chief of the General Staff was the fact 'that everyone agrees with me – even the stupid Hahnke – that the Kaiser's misfortune at the manoeuvre is the real reason why he wants to get rid of me and that Caprivi has made skilful use of this. The whole world will see it as we do. It will be so damaging for the Kaiser!' He saw the future as 'very black'. 'The Kaiser wants to be his own chief of General Staff! God protect the Fatherland!'[53]

Waldersee's removal was regarded by many, not only in the army and in the Conservative Party, as a mistake of considerable political significance, although others naturally greeted it as a great relief. The old Field Marshal Count von Moltke, the King of Saxony and Kaiser Franz Joseph all expressed deep regret at his departure. For the first time for three years Waldersee was received kindly by the Empress Frederick. Wedel, however, saw the dismissal as a positive step, for Waldersee had always been 'a corrosive element' who interfered in everything 'using all kinds of underhand methods' and who was filled with 'immeasurable ambition'. Chief of the Military Cabinet General von Hahnke told Wedel that 'Waldersee had been in league with Verdy to bring down not only Bismarck but also him [Hahnke].'[54]

When he received Waldersee's resignation letter on 31 January 1891 the Kaiser became 'extremely agitated' and hurried to Caprivi, who gained the impression that Wilhelm was toying with the idea of keeping Waldersee on as chief of the General Staff after all. 'Caprivi sees it as a sign of the Kaiser's tender heart', Wedel wrote after a conversation with the Chancellor. Both generals – Caprivi and Wedel – nevertheless agreed that the Kaiser must stand firm. 'If Waldersee stayed in his present post', Wedel commented, 'it would be . . . no more than papering over the cracks. Before long the Kaiser would certainly feel that it was a humiliation to have given in, and in a few months an abrupt break would be more than likely – the Bismarck episode is a very instructive precedent for this.'[55]

On the same day Waldersee had a 'fierce battle' with Wilhelm II, which in many ways resembled the violent argument between the latter and Bismarck on 15 March 1890. Waldersee was summoned to make his report, and when this was over he asked for Hahnke and Wittich to be sent away as he wished to speak to the monarch alone. Face to face with the Kaiser, he told him that an independent chief of the General Staff was a source of strength for the king, for on the one hand both the minister of war and the Reich chancellor were dependent on parliamentary majorities and could therefore easily be brought down; but, on the other, both were also in a position to play off these majorities against the monarch. He declared bluntly that 'hardly anyone ever dares give a frank opinion to Your Majesty; I therefore think it my duty to do so now', whether or not it was hurtful to the Kaiser. First, to his regret, he had to say that since the accession the army had deteriorated. 'The ideal relationship between the war lord and the officer corps which he had inherited no longer existed; there was a prevailing sense of uncertainty, ill-feeling and lack of zest for service in the upper echelons, and this mood had spread quite a long way downwards, while at the bottom a youthful element was growing up which was anything but well-disposed', for respect for authority was disappearing because of the rapid changes in senior appointments. Yet the principle of authority was the foundation on which the army was built, and he, the Kaiser and King, 'depended entirely on the support of the army'. Wilhelm replied: 'No one has ever said anything like that to me', whereupon Waldersee retorted: 'General von Hahnke ought to have done so long ago and I blame the former Minister of War [Verdy] for this too. Neither of them had the courage to do it.' The Kaiser again tried to persuade Waldersee to accept the Altona command: he would show the world, he said, 'what it meant to be a friend of the German Emperor. Anyone who dared say a word against me would be destroyed; he would send the press packing and so on and so forth, in a way that would scarcely have impressed a lieutenant. Eventually he even begged me to agree, with the tenderest of gestures: he took my hand and said: "You will accept, won't you? Your Kaiser begs you." But I remained adamant and I thank God that he gave me the strength to do so', Waldersee boasted. The General went on to tell the Kaiser that the whole crisis had been instigated by the Reich Chancellor, who not only wanted him away from Berlin but was also trying to bring the General Staff under the control of the War Ministry. 'His aim was also to reduce the minister of war to a secretary of state', Waldersee continued, 'in the same way as he was trying to reduce the power of the High Command of the Navy in favour of the secretary of state, so as to have a free hand in the army and the navy.' The Kaiser strongly disputed this assertion, but Waldersee maintained that he was right, and named not only Caprivi but also Holstein, Kiderlen, Lindau and Raschdau 'and all the rest of them' as his enemies, who had been working for his downfall for weeks. At the close of the interview the Kaiser became 'elegiac' and said 'It is too sad to think of what I have already had to go through. My best friends are deserting me!' Waldersee returned home 'very depressed' by the interview, and consoled himself with the thought that it was the carnival season, so that it was no wonder 'if madness were in the air, for the whole business is crazy and senseless. I am to leave the job which I do well, so as to make way for someone more insignificant.'[56]

Waldersee's frankness had its effect — at least temporarily — on Wilhelm. When August Eulenburg called on the departing Chief of Staff on 1 February he too was 'very depressed about the Kaiser' and told Waldersee that after his audience the monarch 'had been in a more serious mood than he had ever seen him in before; he had cancelled all other audiences and had given everyone in his entourage the impression of being in a highly emotional state'.[57] Although Waldersee was increasingly inclined to blame his downfall on the hostile machinations of Caprivi, who had 'made skilful use of the Kaiser's sensitivity over his misfortune at the manoeuvres' in order to get rid of Waldersee, in his eyes the intrigue cast a harsh light on the character of the Kaiser himself, who was 'so gullible' as to have been convinced that he must send Waldersee away from Berlin 'in the interest of his reputation'.[58] The Kaiser had shown himself weak and indecisive. 'He could not summon up the courage to speak openly to me, so that we could part as good friends and in a way that would have done him no harm. The fact that in the end he did not even have the courage to tell me the real reason, and what I am supposed to have done — that is unbelievably cowardly; he was obviously too ashamed to make any accusation, because he knew how groundless it would have been. But it is profoundly sad to see what a weak man he is; he has allowed himself to be systematically manipulated against me without even noticing, much less having any sense of how unworthy this is.'[59]

Waldersee then accepted the post of commanding general of the IX Army Corps in Altona after all, which led Wilhelm to remark scornfully: 'I should jolly well think so, too — the man thinks himself as grand as a grand mogul.' When Wedel resumed his duties after a few days' absence and took a drive with the Kaiser, the latter gave him his version of the 'fierce battle' with Waldersee, exclaiming as he climbed into the carriage: 'Well, since I last saw you terrible things have happened!' The Kaiser talked for an hour about the events of the past few days. It was worst on 31 January, he said, when Waldersee had lectured him for an hour and a half. 'That was when he revealed himself in his true colours and showed what a great man he thinks he is', the Kaiser mocked. Waldersee had claimed that he could not accept the army corps 'because it meant a reduction in rank for him, for the chief of the General Staff has much greater weight than a commanding general', which he said Field Marshal von Moltke had confirmed. When Wilhelm retorted that this was not the case, and that the exceptionally high standing of the chief of the General Staff was entirely due to the personal prestige of Moltke, Waldersee replied 'that he had been the person who had reorganised the General Staff'; the high regard which the General Staff now enjoyed and its good relationship with the Ministry of War were entirely his own work. 'If he now took command of a corps the whole world would shout about it and he would be depicted as "fallen" and "removed", for he had held "a position in the world".' To this, as Wedel recorded, the Kaiser had replied 'that he had dismissed Bismarck without fear of the press' and that he gave Waldersee 'his word of honour that he would protect him as his friend against any attack, from the press or elsewhere'. Wilhelm categorically rejected Waldersee's 'vicious attack' on Caprivi, who Waldersee claimed had always hated him and had now brought about his downfall; he declared that 'the Chancellor, who was so calm and high-minded in both thought and action, and whom he, the Kaiser, had chosen for himself', had 'never said so much as a word against him, Waldersee'. He had objected equally vigorously to Waldersee's claim that there had been a conspiracy against him among the officials in the Foreign Office, who were now congratulating themselves on his fall. When Waldersee, 'having been evasive, was eventually pressed by the Kaiser into naming Holstein, Kiderlen and Lindau', Wilhelm declared that his suspicion was 'absolutely unfounded'. In the course of the conversation Waldersee had become 'more and more critical and impertinent towards him', the Kaiser complained. As a result Wilhelm had finally told him that the only reason why he had not been transferred to the Stuttgart command the previous autumn had been that the King of Württemberg had declared that 'they could send him any general so long as it was not Waldersee'. Although Waldersee had obviously been deeply hurt by this remark, he had become increasingly harsh in his criticisms and had finally accused the Kaiser of causing a feeling of 'extreme insecurity' in the army. 'At this the Kaiser indignantly interrupted the Count and asked him how he, who claimed to be his friend and who enjoyed his full confidence, could have concealed such a fact from him for so long, if it were true.' And when Waldersee had gone on to claim that the whole army would be 'very deeply affected' by his retirement, Wilhelm had replied that he was deceiving himself, for he knew from his 'very wide range of sources' that Waldersee did not enjoy the confidence of the army. The Kaiser had again listed the reasons why it was desirable for Waldersee to go to Altona: the particular honour of being in command of the Kaiserin's home corps; the need to keep the social democratic movement in Hamburg under surveillance; the fact that various contingents from small North German princely states belonged to this army corps; and finally the necessity of keeping an eye on Bismarck, 'the hermit of Friedrichsruh'. Waldersee had rejected all these arguments, again alluding to his 'position in the world', and on taking his leave had said: 'I am sure that Your Majesty will think the matter over again.'

Not long after this heated argument, as the Kaiser went on to relate, he had received from Waldersee a letter 'whose impertinence exceeded all bounds, the like of which had probably never before been written by a Prussian general to his king'. The letter ended with a request to retire from the army. Immediately afterwards Hahnke came to see the Kaiser with the news that he had just received a visit from an intermediary sent by Waldersee to make the necessary arrangements for him to take over the army corps in Altona. The Kaiser showed Hahnke Waldersee's letter, whereupon the 'thunderstruck' Chief of the Military Cabinet brought his fist down on the table and exclaimed: 'Your Majesty must dismiss him at once; he really is going too far!'[60]

The Kaiser, 'as his friend', nevertheless stood by his decision to send Waldersee to Altona. But he gave vent to 'violent outbursts' over press reports containing details of their private conversation, which he believed could only have come from Waldersee. The latter's farewell audience on 4 February lasted barely two minutes, and afterwards the monarch merely remarked: 'Well, he seems to have calmed down.' After a conversation with his old rival Wedel wrote: 'Every word betrayed how swollen with venom Waldersee was. He had probably felt too secure ever to dream of such a downfall.'[61] If the fall of his adversary gave the Flügeladjutant any malicious pleasure, for which he could hardly be blamed, the pleasure was short-lived, for only a few weeks later he too was forced to leave his post at court.

## COUNT VON WEDEL'S TRANSFER TO THE FOREIGN OFFICE

As we have already seen, Count Carl von Wedel played an exceptional role among the Flügeladjutanten in the first years of Kaiser Wilhelm II's reign, possibly because he knew certain secrets of the Kaiser's private life from his time as military attaché in Vienna.[62] Philipp Eulenburg was quick to recognise Wedel's important position in the imperial entourage but was relieved to establish that Wilhelm had no 'inward interest' in the General.[63] His other rival, Waldersee, condemned Wedel as a 'blatant egoist' who had been 'foolish' enough to 'give himself great airs and push himself forward when he became a serving Flügeladjutant; he thought he could supplant General Wittich at that time'.[64] The mere fact that Wedel loyally supported Bismarck, then Caprivi and finally the Oberhofmarschall Liebenau too, was sufficient to arouse Waldersee's anger. Immediately after Bismarck's fall the Chief of the General Staff remarked maliciously that Wedel had 'become quite a changed man since he saw the Chancellor fall; he gives the impression of being completely defeated. The Kaiser has at last recognised his falseness and wants to be rid of him; unfortunately for him the crisis happened too quickly, so that he could not distance himself from the Chancellor; otherwise he would no doubt have disavowed him.'[65] Waldersee's gloating prophecy turned out at first to be a grave mistake. Wedel not only held out until the summer of 1891, but he had daily discussions with the Kaiser on vital questions of foreign and domestic policy and public appointments, was sent on confidential missions to Friedrichsruh, Vienna, Copenhagen and Stockholm, and accompanied the Kaiser on his trip to Russia in August 1890. All in all, he played a significant role in the first years of Caprivi's chancellorship, and not least in Waldersee's dismissal.[66] His position at the Hohenzollern court was even strengthened temporarily by the appointment of his cousin Ernst as Oberstallmeister (senior master of the stables) to the Kaiser in the autumn of 1890.[67] But then he too found his time in the imperial entourage running out. Wedel was reluctantly obliged to leave court service for the diplomatic service because he too had spoken his mind too often and too freely.

The strange story of how the transfer of a Hanoverian general and Flügeladjutant to a diplomatic career came about, and what role the personal wishes of the Kaiser played in it, emerges from Friedrich von Holstein's correspondence with Philipp Eulenburg and from a retrospective memorandum written by Wedel himself in the summer of 1894. According to Holstein, on 10 May 1891 the Chancellor received a telegram several pages long from the Kaiser, who was in Darmstadt. In it he claimed that the former military attaché in Paris, Ernst Freiherr von Hoiningen-Huene, with whom he had had a discussion in Karlsruhe about French intentions to begin a war, was better informed about France 'than the entire present embassy put together'. He therefore demanded that the ambassador Count Münster, whom he had long since condemned for 'hollow phrase-mongering with no serious background' and 'naivety and childish trust', be immediately replaced by his Flügeladjutant Carl von Wedel.[68] The Chancellor's first response was to ask for an audience, but he was determined to resign if the Kaiser insisted on sending a general to Paris, which in the eyes of the world would look like a threat of war. Holstein warned that throughout Germany people would say: 'Prince Bismarck is right when he says that His Majesty is mad.'[69] At his audience Caprivi succeeded in persuading the Kaiser to postpone Münster's recall until the autumn – in fact he remained ambassador in Paris until 1900 – but Wilhelm insisted that Wedel be appointed to the foreign service anyway. The Reich Chancellor sent for the Flügeladjutant and told him that for a long time the Kaiser had been considering appointing him to an embassy. Wilhelm's wish was also partly prompted, the Chancellor revealed, 'by his intention . . . to place another, younger general in command of His headquarters', and Wedel was an obstacle to this plan. There was, however, a problem with the choice of the embassy to be allocated to the General. Recently the Kaiser had been so strongly influenced against Münster in Paris that he had wanted to sack him and put Wedel in his place. But the Chancellor had political scruples about sending a general as ambassador to Paris, 'because an ulterior motive could easily be seen in it'. Caprivi had therefore advised the Kaiser to send Wedel to St Petersburg instead of Paris, for the recall of the ambassador there, Lothar von Schweinitz, would fall due soon. But the Kaiser had wanted to stick to his original plan, 'and so he, Caprivi, did not wish to raise any further difficulties; as far as he was concerned the French could think what they wanted'. Nevertheless the Chancellor had suggested to the Kaiser that Wedel should be seconded to the Foreign Office as a kind of transition, because this would somewhat reduce the sensitivity of his appointment as ambassador in Paris later. The Kaiser had eagerly seized on this suggestion and had ordered Wedel's secondment on 15 June 1891, the third anniversary of his accession, the Chancellor stated.

The unhappy Flügeladjutant then admitted that he too had sensed for some time that the Kaiser was 'not comfortable' with him. But he did not feel in any sense qualified to be ambassador in Paris and wanted to discuss his future with the monarch himself. That same evening Wedel went to the Neues Palais to take his turn in waiting as Flügeladjutant. The Kaiser 'soon appeared in our office, dictated a few telegrams to me and then asked me, as Major von Scholl was present, whether I could spare some time (!) as He would like to discuss something with me. We went into the next room, the one in which Kaiser Friedrich died, and He began the conversation by saying straight out that it was His aim to make use of me in *higher* diplomacy, for which not only He, but also others, thought me particularly suited. When I protested at this He remarked that I could not deny that I had a better understanding in this domain than the others, which was why He had often discussed politics with me. In the course of the conversation H.M. told me He had decided to recall Münster, and then He declared that he intended to send me to Paris in place of Münster, while reserving the right to send me to Petersburg later, when Schweinitz left, as He must be represented by an adjutant-general there.' After Wedel had asked for time to think it over, Wilhelm ended the interview with the remark that in the event of his acceptance he would second Wedel to the Foreign Office initially. Three days later, while driving with Wilhelm from the Neues Palais to the carnival of flowers in Westend, Wedel told the Kaiser that he did not feel equal to the post of ambassador in Paris. The Kaiser did not raise any objections, Wedel recalled, but asked him 'what I would think of St Petersburg, although he was not yet

planning to recall Schweinitz from there', whereupon the General replied that
he would 'at least venture an attempt' there, although he had doubts about his
suitability. He was quite prepared to be seconded to the Foreign Office by way
of transition – a step which, as he admitted in his memorandum of June 1894,
he had since 'seen only too clearly as a grave mistake, and regretted'.[70] During a
dinner to mark his departure from court service on 19 June 1891, at which the
Kaiser appeared, the latter referred to Wedel several times as ambassador and
remarked: 'Who knows, maybe he will be the ambassador who will spark a war
for us one day.'[71]

Following the autumn manoeuvres in Austria in September 1891, Caprivi
asked Wedel whether he would consider taking on a post as an envoy for a short
time. To his 'utter astonishment' the Chancellor then told him on 18 October that
'H.M. has commanded that I should go to Belgrade as envoy.' The next morning
Wedel turned down this 'second-class' post and asked the 'visibly embarrassed'
Reich Chancellor 'in very definite terms' to be allowed to return to the army.[72]
When he told the Kaiser that evening after a dinner at the Neues Palais that
he had refused the Belgrade posting, Wilhelm replied: 'My dear friend, do not
imagine that it was my idea. In your place I should also have refused, and there is
an end to the matter.' Nevertheless the Kaiser rejected Wedel's urgent plea to be
allowed to return to the army with the remark that something would certainly
be found for him.

Wedel's transfer to the the diplomatic corps was not exactly welcomed at the
Foreign Office. The influential Privy Councillor Holstein complained that 'he
did not know how he was going to get rid of him [Wedel], and spoke very disparagingly about the generals who were being given diplomatic appointments on
All-Highest orders, and were thereby ruining the service and putting off decent
people from going into diplomacy'.[73] Wedel's secondment caused even more
alarm among diplomats themselves, when Eulenburg discovered that he even
had 'a sort of promise from H.M. of an embassy'.[74] Yet although Wedel's position
in the Foreign Office became 'increasingly difficult and almost laughable', Chief
of the Military Cabinet von Hahnke persisted in blocking his return to the army
on the grounds that the Kaiser wished to obtain a suitable diplomatic post for
him. It was not until 19 June 1892 that Wedel managed to get himself invited
to luncheon at the Neues Palais through the good offices of his friend Friedrich
von Scholl, who was on duty as Flügeladjutant at the time. While he was in the
ante-room removing his sword, Wilhelm came in and asked 'Well, what is the
matter?', to which the General replied that his position at the Foreign Office had
become impossible and that he must therefore beg to be put in command of a
division. By way of an answer the Kaiser asked whether Wedel would be prepared
to accept the post of envoy at Stockholm as '*a short transition* to an embassy',

adding that 'I would be doing him a favour if I accepted the offer, as he had very few capable people in the foreign service and I showed a particular gift for diplomacy.'[75] Much against his will Wedel agreed to take on the Stockholm post, and then only after the Kaiser had 'firmly and solemnly' repeated his promise that this post would be 'only a short transition' to an embassy. 'H.M. immediately afterwards spoke to the Secretary of State [Marschall von Bieberstein], who was also at the luncheon.'[76]

The next day, while riding in the Tiergarten, Wedel informed Caprivi of his agreement with the Kaiser. An uncomfortable conversation ensued. Caprivi made it plain that he still considered Wedel's refusal of the Belgrade post the previous year a mistake; since then he had abstained from any intervention, nor could he give Wedel any advice now. Wedel pointed out that his own hands were tied by the Kaiser's solemn promise, 'as I certainly could not have told him that I did not believe his promises'. The Chancellor agreed but observed that no embassy would be available for the foreseeable future. 'Vienna, where he would have preferred to send me and where I should be *persona gratissima*, was not free and one could not turn out an old and meritorious public servant like [Prince Heinrich VII] Reuss.' On 24 June 1892 Caprivi summoned the General and informed him that the Kaiser had appointed him envoy at Stockholm and had also directed that he 'should go to Vienna later in place of Reuss'. When and how Reuss would leave his post was still undecided, but the Prince might perhaps be offered the St Petersburg embassy. Wedel pointed out that this solution was impossible as Reuss was married to Princess Maria (Sitta) of Saxe-Weimar-Eisenach, whose grandmother was a Russian Grand Duchess. And it was unlikely that he, Wedel, could any longer be considered a candidate for St Petersburg either, as he had heard that in the previous year the Tsarina of Russia, whose sister was married to the Duke of Cumberland, had 'made extremely derogatory remarks about the Kaiser and had described it as a callous act on his part to entrust me, a Hanoverian, with a mission to the Danish court. In view of the influence the Tsarina had over her husband, her attitude needed to be taken very seriously, for in consequence I could hardly be considered persona grata in St Petersburg', Wedel declared.[77]

Wedel took up his post in Stockholm with bad grace and consoled himself with the thought of the 'Vienna post officially promised' to him.[78] According to Eulenburg, who was '*incensed* by such ingratitude towards the Kaiser', Wedel complained to a friend that 'the Kaiser mistreats me, the Foreign Office likewise. I have *never* aspired to anything but a division. (!!) I am thrown out and given a *paltry* legation like Stockholm.' Eulenburg's Swedish wife also heard that Wedel had tactlessly told people in Stockholm that he would be staying there only for a very short time.[79] He was so sure of his imminent nomination as

ambassador in Vienna that he ordered a magnificent dinner service adorned
with his monogram and a count's coronet from a porcelain shop in the Austrian
capital. 'That is for Count Wedel, who is to be German ambassador here!', the
shop's proprietor told the astonished Princess Reuss when she enquired after the
owner of the service.[80]

Wedel was deeply dismayed when he heard soon afterwards of the appointment of the Hofmarschall Hugo Prince Radolin as ambassador at Constantinople. He rightly attributed this – to him – surprising development to Radolin's
'particular friendship [with] the camarilla in the Wilhelmstrasse', of which
Holstein was the ringleader. Wedel was again passed over when Schweinitz was
replaced at St Petersburg in January 1893 by General von Werder. When he
spoke to the Kaiser in April that year in Berlin, Wilhelm was at pains to point
out that it had not been his fault, remarking: 'Well yes, in fact I did want to
send you there, but I had to accept the direct request of the Tsar [for Werder].
But in any case it is perhaps quite a good thing, for as a Hanoverian you would
not have been persona grata to the Tsarina.' Neither the Kaiser nor the General
suspected that the 'direct request' of Tsar Alexander for General von Werder had
been engineered by the 'camarilla in the Wilhelmstrasse'.[81] But Wedel's greatest disappointment, of course, came when the Vienna post which he so ardently
desired was allotted not to him but to Count Philipp zu Eulenburg, the Kaiser's
best friend and at that time still in very close collaboration with Holstein.

Rumours began to reach Stockholm as early as the autumn of 1893 that
Eulenburg was behaving quite openly as future ambassador in Vienna. His close
acquaintances maintained that he had set his sights on this post because Vienna
was the only place where he could have his children educated. When Wedel came
to Berlin in November 1893 he called on the Reich Chancellor to challenge him
on these rumours. Caprivi, visibly embarrassed by Wedel's complaints, responded
that he knew nothing of the matter, although he had recently heard a remark
by the Kaiser to the effect that Eulenburg would be 'very well received in
Vienna'. Four weeks later, when he took leave of the Chancellor on his return
to Stockholm, Caprivi offered words of reassurance to the disconsolate envoy:
'*I give you my word* that you will become an ambassador. You are now first in
line, as Count Berchem has refused the post in Washington, but there is nothing
available and Vienna is out of the question for you.' With great bitterness Wedel
reminded the Chancellor of his promise regarding the Vienna embassy when he
had accepted the Stockholm legation in the summer of 1892. 'I had not doubted
that the Kaiser would forget about it; his [Caprivi's] words, however, had given
me a guarantee.' The Reich Chancellor was visibly discomposed at this, Wedel
later recalled, and replied with a shrug of the shoulders 'that he was powerless
where Count Eulenburg was concerned, and I must content myself with another

embassy'. Rome was a possibility in the near future, for Count Solms had 'lost favour' — he had aroused the Kaiser's anger during the latter's visit to Rome by failing to tell him of a garden party given by an English nobleman[82] — and was likely to be recalled soon. No sooner had he returned to Stockholm in December 1893, however, than Wedel was astounded to hear that Solms had been replaced by the former envoy in Bucharest, Bernhard von Bülow. This new blow was the final proof for Wedel 'that the highest official in the Reich has no influence . . . at all' and that his promises were therefore worthless. Wedel bitterly told the Chief of the Military Cabinet that he had decided to resign the following summer. Hahnke broached the subject with the Kaiser, pointing out that Wedel had reason to be surprised that preference had been given to Bülow, who was several years younger, whereupon Wilhelm replied: 'Count Wedel will not be forgotten, but I have to be free to appoint ambassadors as the need dictates; moreover as a diplomat W. is younger than Bülow.'[83] As it turned out, the former Flügeladjutant remained in his post in Stockholm but eventually achieved promotion to the higher echelons of the diplomatic service in 1897, when he succeeded Bülow as ambassador in Rome. Thereafter he was appointed to Vienna in 1902 in succession to Philipp Eulenburg, finally becoming governor of Alsace-Lorraine in 1907. A few weeks before the outbreak of war in 1914 Kaiser Wilhelm II created Count Wedel a Prince (Fürst) with the title 'Highness'.

When Wedel looked back over the two and a half years he had spent as Flügeladjutant, in the course of a conversation with Hahnke in May 1891, he agreed with the latter that 'at the beginning everything had gone splendidly, until I opposed the Kaiser in the Bismarck and Liebenau affairs . . . which convinced him that I did not approve of everything he did. There is certainly something very peculiar about the favour of our All-Highest Master.'[84] Wedel affirmed that he had long felt 'that I was an embarrassment to the Kaiser and I fully accepted that he, as sovereign, had the absolute and exclusive right to choose his entourage entirely according to his own preference.' Hahnke disclosed to him that various people, especially Waldersee, had been intriguing against him. In his record of the conversation Wedel added that he had felt for a long time that even Hahnke no longer took his side. He went on to comment: 'I am glad that I am out of it all, for my character does not suit the Kaiser! He demands creatures for whom he has no respect but with whom he is at ease. At least I am leaving with a clear conscience in the knowledge that even if it was not always permissible or possible for me to say what I thought, I never consciously said anything that I did not think, nor ever agreed to any opinion or action that I did not approve. Furthermore in the 2 $\frac{1}{2}$ years of my service it was my constant and to a certain degree successful endeavour, regardless of whom I had to deal with, to curb the uncouth tone and the indecent stories circulating in the Kaiser's entourage . . . My intentions were honest and true, but honourable people do not suit the young court.'[85]

## THE DEPARTURE OF ADJUTANT-GENERAL ADOLF VON WITTICH

Shortly after Waldersee's dismissal as chief of the General Staff and the transfer of the reluctant Wedel to the diplomatic service, Kaiser Wilhelm II dismissed the second Adjutant-General whom he had appointed at his accession – the first, Max von Versen, having already been transferred to Metz in March 1890.[86] Unlike Wedel, Adolf von Wittich was sent back to active service as commander of the XI Army Corps in Kassel. In the first years of the Wilhelmine era both he and Versen had exercised a controversial influence both on the decisions of the Kaiser and on the prevailing tone of his immediate entourage. Wittich, it is true, had from the beginning found it difficult to adapt himself to life at court, and soon after the accession of the young Kaiser Carl Wedel had confided to the Austrian ambassador that the Adjutant-General had been quite unable to 'reconcile himself to the official duties of his present post'. Wittich constantly complained of the 'great, pointless waste of time that the numerous court festivities caused him' and consequently suffered from 'nervous irritability which became increasingly apparent every day'. It could not be denied, Wedel maintained, that 'General von Wittich is cut out for a purely military sphere of activity, and the sooner he gets it the better.' Not only Wittich himself and the Flügeladjutanten around him, but also Kaiser Wilhelm, felt that his 'personal qualities are not those which the duties of his present post require'.[87] Waldersee likewise recorded as early as August 1888 that Wittich was not happy at court. 'He is under immense strain, so that he will scarcely be able to endure it for long, and has little taste for court life', he wrote.[88] The root of the problem lay in Wittich's personal relationship with the Kaiser. As Waldersee remarked, the Adjutant-General was 'of a critical disposition, and is therefore inclined to raise objections; the Kaiser knows this very well and contradicts him frequently and apparently deliberately'. At any rate Wittich could not claim to 'lead [the Kaiser] in any way'.[89] 'That Wittich has no position at all, or rather has one which is unworthy of a man of any competence, is now clear to everyone', Waldersee noted in November 1888. 'Now he is to resume his lectures on military history for the Kaiser and he will do this very well, but to keep someone on as a serving adjutant-general just for this purpose really is an extraordinary luxury.'[90] The surprising thing about this state of affairs was that Wittich was kept on in his post at the imperial court until mid-1892. His own frustration showed itself meanwhile in a growing cynicism which had a very unfavourable effect on the character of the Kaiser and on the

20. General Adolf von Wittich, Adjutant-General and Commander of
the All-Highest Headquarters 1888–1892

general tone of the court. In the summer of 1890 Waldersee commented that
Wittich was responsible for many of the Kaiser's boorish remarks. It was 'really
infuriating', he complained, how instead of moderating the Kaiser's disparaging
utterances the Adjutant-General gave them 'even greater harshness'.[91] Wittich
enjoyed 'biting criticism', Waldersee commented disapprovingly. 'He has not a
good word to say for anyone and has a deplorable weakness for openly criticising
and finding fault in the presence of younger officers . . . He has already done great
harm by his way of behaving . . . for the Kaiser is very ready to accept criticisms
of people and is himself very critical. Wittich is very largely responsible for the
fact that the Kaiser has lost all respect for age and experience; he has greatly
sinned!'[92] The Adjutant-General even committed the outrage, Waldersee wrote,
of 'speaking in the most disparaging way about the Kaiser, and not in private
among trustworthy people, but quite openly!'[93]

Rumours thus arose soon after his appointment as adjutant-general that
Wittich would shortly be sent back to active service, whether as minister of
war, chief of the General Staff or commander of an infantry division. When the
fall of Minister of War von Verdy was in the offing in summer 1890 it looked for
a time as if the Kaiser would indeed appoint his difficult Adjutant-General to the
post. Waldersee reported that 'Wittich had prepared to make a lengthy speech as
to why he did not wish to accept the post; as soon as he had begun, and the Kaiser

realised what he was getting at, he said "I am truly glad that you do not want to leave me", clapped him on the shoulder and left him standing there with his speech.' Waldersee rightly suspected that Wilhelm was afraid of coming into conflict with Wittich as minister of war, and that he was relieved to be able to tell the Chancellor that the Adjutant-General had refused the post.[94] In May 1891 Wittich called on Verdy to discuss his future with him. As he had got wind of the conflict between Kaltenborn and Caprivi and had also noticed that the new Chief of the General Staff, Alfred von Schlieffen, 'is already beginning to bore the Kaiser',[95] Wittich had declared that he would never accept the post of chief of the General Staff, but that he would perhaps agree to take on that of minister of war, 'although only under certain conditions, such as private audiences with His Majesty, etc.!!' The experienced Verdy's comment on this was: 'I should be sorry if he were to take over this post; within a few weeks he would be in the most terrible conflict with the Kaiser and Caprivi!'[96]

In spite of these soundings Wittich's dismissal and transfer to Kassel in the summer of 1892 took everyone by surprise. Waldersee knew only that the Kaiser, who had suddenly lost his temper with the Adjutant-General, had declared: 'I have given that poltroon an A[rmy] Corps.'[97] The Empress Frederick regretted Wittich's departure from the court, for he was 'an honest, straightforward, trust-worthy man – not afraid to speak his mind', although she doubted that he was particularly enlightened in his views or had much influence on Wilhelm.[98] The loss of Wittich also affected Chancellor von Caprivi, for whom he had been a source of strong support close to the Kaiser.

Wittich was replaced as adjutant-general by the elegant Hans von Plessen, who had served as Flügeladjutant to the old Kaiser Wilhelm from 1879 to 1888, and who was to remain 'a good comrade and a dear friend' to Wilhelm II from 1892 until the end of the Hohenzollern monarchy.[99] Even he, however, did not succeed in improving the general tone in the Kaiser's entourage. 'The Kaiser treats him with little consideration and has already attacked him rudely on several occasions', Waldersee noted in autumn 1894.[100] Plessen joined in the 'customary brash tone' at court and was 'not the man to influence the Kaiser in any direction'.[101]

The general opinion on the removal of Generals Versen, Waldersee, Wedel and Wittich from the entourage was that it must now be feared that, even more than hitherto, Wilhelm would decide what course to follow in all political and military matters on his own authority and without the advice of experienced older men. Immediately after Waldersee's fall the British military attaché, Colonel Russell, commented perceptively in a report to London that the Kaiser evidently wanted to be 'his own Chancellor, Chief of the Staff & his own Min[iste]r in every department – a task beyond any human Powers'. As far as public opinion

21. General Hans von Plessen, Adjutant-General and Commander of
the All-Highest Headquarters 1892–1918

was concerned, people often expressed more regret over the downfall of the
Chief of the General Staff than over that of Prince Bismarck eleven months earlier, Russell reported. The new man, Count von Schlieffen, certainly came from
the same school as Waldersee, so that a change in military policy need not be
expected, but Schlieffen was extremely reserved, did not have a strong personality and would therefore not acquire any great influence over Wilhelm II.[102] A
few years after his fall Waldersee himself was distressed to have to record, after
close observation of the imperial entourage, that all its members were afraid
of the Kaiser and 'do not dare make the slightest protest or objection'. Wilhelm
liked talking a great deal, and 'all agree with him in the most servile fashion'.[103]
What was certainly true was that he had no experienced and courageous general at his side when in the spring of 1892 he was confronted with the biggest
political crisis of the New Course. It was to lead to the separation of the office
of Reich chancellor from that of Prussian minister-president and thereby to an
aggravation of the crisis of government which had begun soon after Wilhelm II's
accession.

# CHAPTER SEVENTEEN

# The School Bill crisis and the fragmentation of power

## THE SCHOOL BILL CRISIS IN PRUSSIA

IT is not without irony that soon after Waldersee's departure from Berlin the otherwise liberal-minded Reich Chancellor veered towards a conservative–clerical course which most of his contemporaries found difficult to comprehend and which went much too far even for the fallen Chief of General Staff. This shift occurred exactly two years after Bismarck's dismissal and caused the most serious crisis of Caprivi's chancellorship. Two factors seem to have persuaded the Chancellor-General, who made no secret of his growing frustration, to make this dramatic change of course: the need to secure a majority in the Reichstag for the huge Army Bill ordered by the Kaiser in July 1891, and a defiant sense of solidarity with the newly appointed Conservative Prussian Minister of Ecclesiastical Affairs, Count Robert von Zedlitz-Trützschler, whom he had recommended to the Kaiser in the spring of 1891 as Gossler's successor. In shifting towards the right and against the liberal middle parties the Chancellor was unwittingly touching on one of the most sensitive points in the whole structure of the 'kleindeutsch' Prusso-German Reich, which had played an extraordinary role in the Kulturkampf and (as we have observed) also in the Bismarck crisis in 1889–90. This was the deep-rooted perception within the ruling elite, and not least at court, that both the Reich and the Triple Alliance could disintegrate if the Berlin government were to move closer to the Catholic Centre Party. In May 1891 Caprivi was reported to have stated to the 'very unpleasantly surprised' Kaiser that 'the only party from which we can seek support was the Centre, for it formed the only cohesive body!' Immediately Waldersee condemned this suggestion as 'a really hair-raising idea', for according to him the Centre consisted 'for the most part of notorious enemies of the Reich', on whom one could not possibly rely for support.[1] Caprivi's suggestion, the General wrote to his friend Verdy, 'certainly annoyed our royal master very much, but as you know that will not rule out his ordering a pact to be made with these people at a moment's notice'.[2]

As soon as he took over the Prussian Ministry of Ecclesiastical Affairs, Education and Medicine, Zedlitz-Trützschler personally set about devising a new Primary School Bill. It caused a furore when it was laid before the Prussian House of Representatives because it was of a strongly clerical nature and could have been passed only with the support of the German Conservatives and of the Catholic Centre Party against the liberals of all shades of opinion. It declared religion to be the highest goal of education and placed schools under the authority of the two main Christian churches, stipulating that the children of dissenters be compelled to attend religious education classes; the churches were given direct control over religious education in state schools and were also permitted to set up their own confessional schools.[3] The draft bill, which was seen as deeply reactionary, aroused unprecedented protests throughout Germany and above all among the nationalistically minded middle classes, who together with the East Elbian landed aristocracy formed the mainstay of the Reich. In liberal circles both right and left the bill was condemned as a 'disastrous mistake'.[4] Rudolf von Bennigsen made a sensational speech in the Reichstag on 22 January 1892 in which he urged all the liberal parties to unite against the new policy.[5] From Munich, where the Kaiser had recently appointed him Prussian envoy, Philipp Eulenburg expressed grave concern about the School Bill, which could become 'of decisive significance for the existence of the government'.[6] Ernst Prince zu Hohenlohe-Langenburg commented angrily that 'the concessions which have been made to ultramontanism and Polish interests for the sake of temporary advantages are surely very ill-advised, for history shows where such weakness towards the greatest enemies of our national existence has led and must lead, especially at a time when we should all be joining forces within the country in order to counter the dangers from abroad'.[7] Even Waldersee, who admired the ultra-conservative Zedlitz and was generally in favour of strengthening the Christian element in education, considered the bill a serious mistake which would lead to a dangerous increase in the influence of the Catholic Church and perhaps even to the return of the Jesuits to Germany. After all, he claimed, the Catholic Church was 'the fiercest opponent of the German Reich' and 'its destruction would be her greatest triumph'.[8] On the other hand there were misguided hotheads around the Kaiser who were hoping that the Zedlitz initiative would bring about a 'violent and brutal . . . war . . . on all fronts' between the government which was 'spoiling for a fight' and the entire German liberal movement, leading to a 'very healthy' solution to the 'mental apathy' of the 'stagnating masses'.[9]

So once again at the beginning of 1892 all eyes were on the Kaiser, to see whether he would withstand the 'liberal clamour' against the School Bill or disavow the Minister of Ecclesiastical Affairs and the Reich Chancellor who supported him. Philipp Eulenburg was convinced, just as he had been two and a half years earlier when Bismarck began to move closer to the Centre, that a deal between the Berlin government and the Catholic Church would bring about the fall of the liberal minority government in Munich, and with it the disintegration of the 'kleindeutsch' Reich.[10] He wrote urgently to the Kaiser on 21 January 1892 warning him of the dangers that would ensue for Crailsheim's government and the liberal parties in Bavaria, who provided 'the only support for the unity of the Reich' there, if the Centre were raised to the status of a government party in Berlin. He doubted whether Zedlitz had properly weighed up these dangers and advised Wilhelm to discuss the matter confidentially with him, so as to make clear to him that he, the Kaiser, took the moderate view on this question.[11] On 24 January Holstein was able to report to Munich that on 22 January in the afternoon, before he had received Eulenburg's letter, the Kaiser had gone straight from the station to see the Chancellor to find out what was happening, presumably because he had heard 'all kinds of strange things about the situation' from certain quarters. 'Then yesterday [23 January – that is, after receiving Eulenburg's letter] Zedlitz was suddenly summoned to luncheon. His Majesty told him that He would come and have a glass of beer with him that evening, and asked him to invite Helldorff, Manteuffel, Miquel, Benda, Tiedemann-Bomst and Douglas. Whether others were mentioned I do not know. In the evening the conversation was of almost nothing but the School Bill. His Majesty declared that "He would never accept a School Bill which was brought to him only by the Conservatives and the Centre. He demanded that the Free Conservatives and the majority of the National Liberals should also agree to it. If he made himself dependent on the Centre the next thing would be that the Redemptorists and then the Jesuits would come back. Moreover, in South Germany every minister who was not an ultramontane would fall, etc." His Majesty told Marschall all this at his audience this morning. Marschall replied that as a member of the Reichstag he had fought against the National Liberals, but that he could not deny that outside Prussia it was the National Liberals who were the supporters of the Reich idea. Marschall expressed to me his anxiety about the influence that Zedlitz – who *had been in complete agreement* with the Kaiser yesterday evening – would now exercise over Caprivi. Z[edlitz] went to see C[aprivi] this morning; then Marschall went over and found the R[eich] C[hancellor] in an agitated state and convinced that it was his duty as a decent man to stand by Zedlitz.'[12] Three days later Holstein's fears were confirmed. During a conversation with the Chancellor on 27 January, the Kaiser's birthday, the diplomat was 'very sad' to note that Caprivi 'wants to go along with the Centre; he thinks he will find stronger support there than with the National Liberals. The Conservatives are already firmly engaged as well . . . He, the R[eich] C[hancellor], therefore thinks that the committee will approve the bill without amendment. As I gather from [Franz] Fischer, in that case not only Miquel but also Bennigsen will go, and then the *reductio ad absurdum* of the conservative–clerical principle will come into play: that is to say, the Centre will bring forward its claims. How long do you think the German people will tolerate that, and how do you think the next elections will turn out?'[13]

A massive tug-of-war now began both within the government and in the public at large over Wilhelm II's decision. As Waldersee wrote at the end of January: 'On both sides people are trying to influence the Kaiser, and he has not yet reached a decision on which way to go.' 'As he . . . has no intention of giving up his unfortunate inclination to direct everything himself . . . he creates great uncertainty and unrest. He has expressed the most widely differing views to many people, and then when they compare notes it turns out that he has said very different things, which were mostly what those concerned wanted to hear!' It was a strange state of affairs and the outcome was not at all clear. 'The Liberals, who praised Caprivi to the skies only a few weeks ago, are now bitterly attacking him', Waldersee noted. 'In the Ministry there seem to be people who are ready to give way, and the Kaiser's favourite advisers like Hinzpeter and Helldorf[f] would have to deny their whole past if they were not trying to fish in murky waters again here.' In Waldersee's eyes, of course, the most desirable outcome of the School Bill crisis would have been the dismissal of Caprivi, with whom more and more people were becoming disillusioned. 'Lucanus called him two-faced not long ago; Boetticher has more or less fallen out with him; Miquel hates him' and was working to bring him down.[14] A 'wretched game of intrigue' was afoot, he noted on 21 February, 'with Caprivi, Boetticher, Miquel, Zedlitz and Lucanus each trying to go his own way; they do not trust each other and no one knows exactly what the Kaiser wants.' Clearly the latter had had no idea of how much unrest the bill would cause and now wanted to find a solution that would be acceptable to all parties.[15] 'Probably the only thing that is certain is that the Kaiser does not know which way to steer; he is beginning to be completely incapable of making a decision', Waldersee commented.[16]

Wilhelm's attitude towards religion in general and towards the Protestant zealots such as Zedlitz in particular kept everyone guessing. Early assumptions that he, like the Kaiserin, as a proponent of the Stoeckerite tendency, had been shaken by the dismissal of the anti-Semitic Court Preacher and the fall of Waldersee. But then came his solemn declaration, in his closing speech to the conference on school reform in December 1890: 'It goes without saying that I will, as king of Prussia, as well as *summus episcopus* of my Church, make it my most sacred duty to take every care that the religious sentiments and the Christian spirit are fostered and increased in the schools. May the school respect and revere the Church, and may the Church in its turn assist the school and facilitate the further accomplishment of its tasks. Then we shall be able to educate our young people up to the requirements of our modern national life.'[17] The speculation as to which side the monarch would take in the national crisis that had arisen over Zedlitz's bill began to take an even more serious form when 'the question of the Kaiser's madness', as Eulenburg noted anxiously in Munich, began to 'haunt us . . . again' in the winter of 1891–2.[18]

For those hoping for a clear lead from the monarch, the first signs were anything but reassuring. At a dinner given by Caprivi on 3 February, and again ten days later at another given by Boetticher, the Kaiser spoke out as he had originally done over the glass of beer at Zedlitz's house: he would approve the School Bill only if it received the support of the liberal middle parties. But then, angered by the attitude of the National Liberals and the two Progressive parties on military matters, he had spoken so disparagingly about them that his remarks were interpreted as support for Zedlitz's clerical School Bill.[19] The confusion reached its climax with Wilhelm II's alarming speech to the provincial diet of Brandenburg on 24 February 1892 in which he challenged 'the dissatisfied grumblers' to shake the dust of Germany off their feet and leave the country as soon as possible, which was generally taken to refer to the anti-clerical opponents of the School Bill.[20]

Simultaneously with the growing pressure on the Kaiser, who had the final power of decision in this momentous question – all were at least agreed on that – a small group close to the Chancellor was secretly exercising its influence to thwart the far-reaching concessions to political Catholicism Caprivi was planning to make, just as had happened two and a half years earlier in response to the Bismarcks' attempts at a rapprochement with the Centre Party.[21] This group, led like the earlier one by Holstein, was all the more dangerous to the Chancellor because it had direct access to Wilhelm II through Eulenburg. Writing to the latter on 27 January, Holstein admitted that he could see only two ways out of the present danger: 'First, for the Kaiser to ask the Reich Chancellor, as a favour to him, not to oppose an amendment of the bill at the committee stage but to leave the whole thing to Zedlitz . . . 2.: for His Majesty to get hold of a few Conservatives, members of the committee, and try to influence them quietly. His Majesty asked for members only of the Reichstag and of the Upper House [of the Prussian Landtag] (apart from Benda) to be invited for a glass of beer at Zedlitz's house, so members of [Prussian] House of Representatives were offended, on top of everything else. Helldorff and Manteuffel are both in the Upper House. As a last resort the Upper House could of course amend the bill to make it more moderate and conciliatory, in accordance with the Kaiser's wish, and then send the amended version back to the House of Representatives. The Upper House would gain a great deal of prestige in the country by doing so . . . I am afraid that the Reich Chancellor will speak [in the House of Representatives] tomorrow and commit himself completely. If he does not, it may perhaps still be possible to make a few suggestions to His Majesty.'[22]

With his long experience in Bavaria Eulenburg did not need to be told by Holstein of the dangers of a swing towards the Centre. In his view, such a shift could be justified only 'if the government is firmly resolved, directly they have attained their ends [in parliament], to begin a war and to alter the electoral system [i.e. undertake a *coup d'état*] etc., etc.' If this were not the intention, the reaction of the enraged liberal middle parties and of the social democratic workers' movement against black–blue clericalism would inevitably lead to parliamentary government and 'other embarrassments for the monarch'. 'The struggle of the united Liberals will be the more violent', Eulenburg shrewdly warned at the end of January 1892, 'in that their banner will read *suprema lex salus republicae* as against *suprema lex regis voluntas*. His Majesty's vigorous emphasis on the personality of the monarch will stamp the imprint of absolutism on the brow of any Conservative–Centre government' and thereby lead to the loss of the moderate parties 'which in my view form the natural basis nowadays for monarchical government'. The danger for Germany, which had been 'rocked to her foundation since the death of the old Kaiser', was plain for all to see, he warned. 'In Bavaria and Württemberg the Reich idea is enshrined only in Liberal hearts.' If the government in Berlin supported Zedlitz's School Bill it would 'lose the whole of Württemberg, the greater part of Bavaria and probably the greater part of the other federal states too'; they would all go over to the Bismarck camp 'with drums beating'. If the National Liberal Finance Minister Johannes von Miquel should resign in protest against the new policy he would 'enjoy *enormous prestige* throughout the Reich', which Bismarck could exploit for his purposes. 'We shall have some appalling experiences in the elections.' All these dangers were so great that the tactical gain would bear no relation to the loss. 'There are all kinds of surprises in store for Caprivi!'[23]

The dilemma for Holstein and Eulenburg in this rapidly developing crisis lay in the fact that any attempt to influence the Kaiser against the Zedlitz School Bill could easily provoke Caprivi's resignation. Although he considered the situation almost 'hopeless',[24] under pressure from Holstein Eulenburg agreed in principle to write a second letter to the Kaiser. He pointed out, however, that 'the more

H.M.'s attention is drawn to the dangerous consequences of the School Bill, the
more easily may annoyance with Caprivi gain a hold. But that simply must be
avoided. You know H.M. is inclined to criticise Caprivi – and I assume he is
already silently reproaching him over this school question.' As a solution to the
dilemma Eulenburg suggested the removal of the Prussian Interior Minister,
Herrfurth; Zedlitz could then take his place and the School Bill could be withdrawn under the pretext of the appointment of a new minister of ecclesiastical
affairs. 'I cannot imagine the Chancellor would stand by Herrfurth', Eulenburg
argued, 'if H.M. urged this solution on him.'[25] But after a conversation with the
Chief of the Reich Chancellery Karl Goering, Holstein, who was better able to
gauge the prevailing mood in the Wilhelmstrasse, warned that Caprivi would
certainly resign if the School Bill were not passed or if the Kaiser refused to
approve it. The only way out, in his eyes, was therefore to make sure that the bill
became 'bogged down' at the committee stage in the Landtag.[26] In his second letter of warning to the Kaiser on 10 March, therefore, Eulenburg expressed himself
with the greatest possible caution, pointing out that the dilemma confronting
Wilhelm was acute, for on the one hand Caprivi's resignation was *impossible* as
far as the Reich was concerned, but on the other hand a School Bill which was
accepted only by the Centre Party and the Conservatives was *equally impossible*',
for it would 'provoke conflict in the Reich with consequences which would be
disastrous for Your Majesty's position'. Therefore the bill must at all costs be
'buried' in committee, if no compromise could be found, 'although boundless
discretion will be required if we are not to cause Caprivi's fall!'[27] Although
Eulenburg later expressed his alarm at the 'bomb-like' effect which his letter
seemed to have, it was actually the intervention of another 'irresponsible adviser'
which was to be the immediate cause of the furore that followed.

As in the Bismarck crisis two years earlier – and just as Waldersee had
predicted – the influence of the moderate leader of the Conservatives, Otto
von Helldorff-Bedra, on the Kaiser now made itself felt. Helldorff was still convinced that the right wing of his own party, led by Hammerstein, was working
with the Catholic Centre to transform the German Reich into a clerical state.
Determined to resist, he declared, 'I am fighting with all my strength for this
one fundamental idea, that the Reich can only be governed and kept in existence
if it is supported by the forces through which the Hohenzollerns have attained
their position – the Protestant North – and if we keep the real and irreconcilable
enemy, the policy of Rome, in our sights.'[28] On 7 March 1892 he wrote urgently
to Eulenburg: 'How can we save the situation? We must keep Caprivi – and correct the Kaiser's position.' To achieve these goals a compromise acceptable both
to the National Liberals and to the Centre must first be sought. 'That is Kartell
policy on a grand scale – doing justice to the needs of the Catholics and allowing

them to remain in the national arena. – That is in fact also the fundamental idea of the bill, which Caprivi supports, but which has been dangerously distorted by Zedlitz and his *Kreuzzeitung* advisers.' If no such consensus could be achieved there was only one other way out of the wilderness, and this was the 'adjournment' of the bill, in other words 'a decent burial'. 'This also corresponds to the Kaiser's original view. – But it is a question of how to bring it about, and I think that direct intervention by His Majesty is necessary. – I think he should speak out, not publicly – not in a speech (he must be strongly warned against that) – but to carefully selected individuals. He must make his real aims clear and contradict the misrepresentation of his [Brandenburg] speech. He does not need to tell everyone everything, only what each needs to know.' Helldorff insisted that it was 'absolutely imperative that I should explain the situation to His Majesty as I see it, for at moments like this there is no shortage of people around him who are very skilful at exploiting likes and dislikes or temporary bouts of rage, against Bennigsen for instance. I shall therefore ask for an audience today.'[29] Because of a mysterious illness from which the Kaiser had been suffering for weeks it was not until the evening of 16 March 1892 that Helldorff managed to speak to the monarch. But then his intervention did indeed work 'like a bomb'.

What was the matter with the Kaiser in this, the most serious domestic crisis since Bismarck's fall? Not least as a result of his disastrous Brandenburg speech on 24 February, in which he promised to lead his people towards 'a glorious destiny' and challenged his critics to leave Germany,[30] the warning uttered by Eulenburg in January about 'the question of the Kaiser's madness' seemed to be proving accurate at the very moment when the School Bill crisis was approaching its climax. For some time now observers had noticed a strange indisposition in the Kaiser which seemed to undermine his ability to take decisions. The official explanation given was that he had a cold. However, the Empress Frederick reported to London that the illness was not serious; Wilhelm looked well and had gone away to Hubertusstock, where he would be able to spend the whole day in the fresh air. 'His ear is in no way affected, he has not had an "Ohren Catarrh" for some time now', she wrote, although it was true that Wilhelm had been very upset at the dreadful press comments on his latest Brandenburg speech.[31] Many people suspected some kind of nervous breakdown.[32] The Oberhofmarschall, Count August zu Eulenburg, confided to his cousin Philipp that the heated arguments about his speech combined with the 'high degree of agitation' over the School Bill had affected the Kaiser 'so badly that His latest indisposition [had been] far more psychological than physical'.[33] Wilhelm's personal physician, Rudolf Leuthold, spoke of a 'marked inclination to fall asleep' combined with physical fatigue and 'slight feverishness with a mild cold'. He considered this to be 'simply the result of a certain nervous fatigue, which was to be expected given the many demands on our All-Highest Master . . . and his present psychic state, which is probably not quite balanced'. He forbade his imperial patient to go out or do any work and prescribed 'several days of absence from Berlin and the whole business of government', preferably at Hubertusstock. There was no cause for alarm over his condition and there was no question of his ear being involved, Leuthold confirmed.[34] The British ambassador reported to London that the illness was feverish and that the Kaiser was 'quite unnerved by worry',[35] while Wilhelm himself sent a telegram to his grandmother admitting that 'I was too much overworked and the doctor wishes some rest for me.'[36]

Whatever the cause of the Kaiser's indisposition, the 'long and detailed conversation' that Wilhelm had with Helldorff after dinner on 16 March unleashed a serious crisis the next day. The moderate leader of the Conservative Party, who was to lose his position not long afterwards, said of the evening's interview with the Kaiser that he had found him 'still looking rather unwell – and in a very depressed mood'. 'The state of affairs, the malicious criticism of his speech etc. . . . had deeply upset him – he is said not to have slept for several nights.' Helldorff 'explained his view of the situation and told His Majesty . . . that in my opinion the only sensible way of resolving this difficult situation was for an appropriate group of Conservatives in the House of Representatives to amend the excessively pro-Catholic points [in the bill], which would pave the way either for an understanding on a broader basis or for a decent burial. As others were working with all their might to use the Centre and the Conservatives to force the bill through if possible without amendment, and to obscure the Kaiser's true intentions, I considered it important that His Majesty should inform Miquel that he wished the bill to be handled in this way and ask him to bring the National Liberals round to an agreement or a conciliatory attitude – and then to speak confidentially to a few Conservatives, principally . . . His Majesty agreed to this . . . – I had no idea that there would be a Crown Council the next morning.'[37]

Although the School Bill was not on the agenda and the Kaiser had not intended to state his personal views on it until after the first reading in committee, he nevertheless brought up the subject of the situation created by the bill at the end of the Crown Council on 17 March. The manner in which he did so not only went down badly with the Minister of Ecclesiastical Affairs but also offended Caprivi as minister-president.[38] Wilhelm's remarks, which (as Helldorff was at pains to stress) 'came purely from his own initiative', and in which he repeated that he would approve the School Bill only if it were accepted in the Prussian House of Representatives with the support of the liberal middle parties, had worked 'like a bomb', for they had 'blown Zedlitz and his whole policy sky-high' – and 'unfortunately almost did the same to Caprivi'.[39] As Zedlitz asked for time to consider his position after the Crown Council, members of the Kaiser's entourage were at first confident that the minister would stay in office and that the threat of a chancellor crisis could therefore also be discounted.[40] These hopes were however dashed by the indiscretion of other ministers, who regaled their fellow guests at a dinner given by the Württemberg envoy with accounts of the Kaiser's dramatic intervention, as a result of which 'the whole affair was spread about town'. That evening Zedlitz handed in his resignation, and on the morning of 18 March 1892 (two years to the day after the dismissal of Bismarck) Caprivi handed in his own resignation as Reich chancellor, Prussian minister-president and Prussian minister of foreign affairs. The Kaiser tried in vain to persuade Zedlitz to stay by writing him 'an explanatory letter . . . about the meaning of the All-Highest remarks at the Crown Council'. Zedlitz asked for two days to think it over, but Countess Zedlitz declared openly that 'they were leaving in any case'. The crucial question now was whether Caprivi could be persuaded to stay. 'A chancellor crisis at this moment would really be more than disastrous', August Eulenburg commented.[41] On 19 March the Kaiser wrote on Caprivi's letter of resignation: 'No. I wouldn't dream of it. It is not nice to drive the cart into the mud and leave the Kaiser sitting in it. Caprivi has made a mistake; that can happen to anyone. His departure now would be a national disaster and is out of the question.'[42]

In Munich Philipp Eulenburg received the news of the dramatic developments in Berlin through a cipher telegram from Holstein on 18 March. 'At yesterday's Crown Council the Kaiser again expressed the wish that moderate elements should join in working on the School Bill, and that Kartell policy should be followed as before. The rest of the session passed uneventfully. But afterwards Zedlitz came to the Reich Chancellor and declared that he could not cut himself off from the Centre and had therefore sent in his resignation. Von Caprivi then did the same, with a long, not uncivil explanation. He told me "that he could not let Zedlitz drown at his side" . . . The Kaiser left for Hubertusstock this afternoon for eight days, having turned down Zedlitz's resignation in writing and that of the Reich Chancellor verbally through Lucanus. But neither has yet relented, and there is no one available who would be in a position to mediate. Best arrangement would be to make Count Zedlitz minister of the interior or postpone whole thing until after first reading. If Zedlitz stays the Chancellor will stay too.'[43] Eulenburg immediately forwarded these comments to the Kaiser and pointed out another argument against a change of chancellor. There was a real danger that at any moment a publication in Zürich would reveal the fact that Bismarck had purchased the agreement of King Ludwig II of Bavaria to the foundation of the Reich in 1870 with millions from the secret Guelph Fund. If this 'Ludwig II–Bismarck dirty trick', which could shake Bavarian national consciousness to its core and lead to very dangerous debates about the events surrounding the creation of the Reich, were to become public knowledge at a time when the Kaiser was about to dismiss the Chancellor, there would be 'a great upheaval in South Germany' which could put both Kaiser and Reich in grave danger. 'To allow *two such disturbing events to coincide is simply impossible*', the Kaiser's friend warned.[44] At the same time Eulenburg wrote to Caprivi drawing his attention to the inadvisability of a chancellor crisis at a moment when the Guelph Fund revelations were looming.[45] Others also tried to placate Caprivi, among them Prince Heinrich and the respected President of the Prussian House of Representatives, Georg von Köller, but without success.[46] All attempts to mediate were thwarted by the embittered resolve of the departing Minister of Ecclesiastical Affairs, who cast 'all the blame on the Kaiser'.[47] 'Majesty must have left Z[edlitz] badly in the lurch', Verdy wrote to Waldersee, adding with bitter irony: 'We know all about that, through thick and thin!'[48]

Holstein, whose principal fear was that his *bête noire* Waldersee might be appointed Reich chancellor, found it 'quite horrifying that at this terribly important moment His Majesty is sitting at Hubertusstock with a couple of adjutants. There is a real similarity with Louis XVI. And who knows what decisions are being made there, without a single sensible person to consult.' The military suite, with which the Kaiser once again found himself sitting 'for 8 days . . . alone in the forest', would think it quite natural if their master appointed another general as Reich chancellor, while all politicians considered such a decision 'impossible', the diplomat observed. Furthermore, to his alarm, the Kaiserin also expressed herself in favour of Waldersee. The only person who could break through the 'magic circle' surrounding Wilhelm was Philipp Eulenburg.[49]

Caprivi's solidarity with the former Minister of Ecclesiastical Affairs was admired by some as the 'upright conduct' and 'comradely kindness' of a 'man of unswerving honour'. At the same time it was criticised as evidence of his lack of political instinct. The Chancellor seemed to Holstein, Marschall, Helldorff and many others to have been 'hypnotised' and to have behaved 'as if shackled to Zedlitz'. The Chief of the Reich Chancellery, Goering, said of him that 'since the beginning of this year a complete change has taken place in him'.[50] Others discerned an element of calculation in the Chancellor's attitude: he was convinced that 'in a few weeks or at most months he would come to blows with the Kaiser over military demands and the two-year service which might be linked to them', and he thought he could make a better exit now.[51]

When Caprivi went to visit the Kaiser at Hubertusstock on 20 March he had already made up his mind that, if he were stay in office at all, he would remain only as Reich chancellor and give up both his Prussian offices, the minister-presidency and the position of Prussian foreign minister. Wilhelm seems to have accepted this suggestion, for after Caprivi's return from Hubertusstock Marschall

von Bieberstein was obliged to point out to him that he would have to retain
at least the post of Prussian foreign minister, since the latter was responsible
for instructing the Prussian vote in the Bundesrat.[52] As Caprivi would therefore continue to be a member of the Prussian Ministry of State, and as the
minister-president did not enjoy any special constitutional privileges in Prussia,
his supporters hoped to have found a modus vivendi, especially if in addition
Marschall could be appointed to the Prussian Ministry of State as minister
without portfolio. But everything would depend on who was appointed as the
new minister-president.[53] Upon Caprivi's return from Hubertusstock August
Eulenburg reported to his cousin: 'C. suggested several names to the Kaiser
today, none of which aroused particular enthusiasm at first. Boetticher is *on no
account* to become minister-president, *nor* Miquel or any other National Liberal,
but a Conservative who could pursue a Kartell policy.' Caprivi finally settled on
Count Botho zu Eulenburg, the Oberhofmarschall's brother, and asked the latter *'without the Kaiser's consent'*, to invite Botho to Berlin as unobtrusively as
possible.[54] The latter accepted the minister-presidency after Caprivi had paid
a second visit to Hubertusstock on 23 March, during which he succeeded in
'fulfilling Botho's chief condition', namely the appointment of the Secretary of
State in the Reich Justice Office, Dr Robert Bosse, as the new Prussian minister of ecclesiastical affairs. Both Caprivi and Bosse himself expressed scruples
about this change of office, 'but the Kaiser decided on him at once', August
Eulenburg reported to Munich.[55] Bosse pointed out that he was a civil servant, not
a politician, and that he could not speak in parliament without embarrassment.
The Kaiser, however, declared bluntly 'Bosse and no other'. And with that and
Caprivi's admonition that 'as a decent man' he must obey the Kaiser's command,
Bosse had little alternative but to accept the thorny office proffered to him.[56]

On 24 March the envoys of Baden and Saxony, Brauer and Hohenthal, received
orders to go to Hubertusstock next day. Wilhelm explained to them his position
on the School Bill crisis, with a view to their informing the Grand Duke and
the King respectively. Brauer wrote to his master: 'It was a great relief to me
to discover, contrary to the many foolish rumours, how well H.M. looked and
obviously felt. H.M. was extremely cheerful and his conversation at table was
very lively and spiced with jokes . . . "I have sent for you", H.M. soon began in
his unaffected, jovial way, "so that you can report to my uncles on the course
of the crisis, and what *really* happened, and on my view of the situation. From
the beginning I have consistently held the opinion that the draft of the School
Bill was certainly a suitable basis on which to work out a successful result with
the co-operation of all moderate parties. But I have never left anyone in any
doubt that I would not ratify any bill which was acceptable only to the Centre
and the extreme Conservatives. I often asked Zedlitz whether he was sure of

*all* Conservatives, and he always assured me that he had them safely under control . . . I had no reason, after the Crown Council, to suppose that my words would lead to a crisis. I was very surprised when I received Zedlitz's letter of resignation that very evening and another from Caprivi next day. Particularly in the latter case there was no reason for it. Caprivi is a touchy, pigheaded fellow. He has often threatened to leave me in the lurch and tried to resign before now. I have given in countless times in order to keep him. I had warned him, indeed I had *ordered* him, not to commit himself to the School Bill. What was the use, he did it anyway! This time too I have implored him to stay. But I still could not prevent him giving up the presidency of the Ministry of State, out of utterly needless sensitivity. – It was just the same last autumn, when I asked the Reich Chancellor to demand the resignation of Herrfurth, who is now so unpopular with the Conservatives, from his Ministry after the Rural District Bill had been approved. The Chancellor absolutely refused to do it. But I was right! I am not as stupid as I look! Now we cannot get rid of him for the time being, because the liberal newspapers would immediately make a fuss" . . . The first task of the new minister-president, H.M. stated, would be "to break in the Conservative nags again: those fellows have become nothing but a bunch of snipers; he must turn them back into a regular battalion". Finally H.M. remarked: "Tell your gracious masters how difficult it is to manage with Caprivi. It could do no harm if your King or your Grand Duke gave him a good talking-to from time to time. I am too young to impress him"!'[57]

Wilhelm was also anxious to prove to the British government that he had not, as was universally claimed, 'behaved like a tyrant'. Summoning Sir Edward Malet, he gave him his version of the events leading up to the crisis. He began by complaining that Caprivi had not informed him of the new School Bill until the previous autumn; in his view he should have been consulted much earlier. He stated that he would have refused his consent to the bill there and then, had not Lucanus persuaded him to give in, since otherwise the Reich Chancellor and several of the ministers would have resigned. Public disquiet during the winter had only confirmed him in his view, Wilhelm told the British ambassador, that it would be a mistake to force the Zedlitz bill through in the Landtag. On 27 January, his birthday, he had gone personally to the Ministry of Ecclesiastical Affairs and had made it clear to Zedlitz that he did not wish the School Bill to be a party-political measure and that a compromise with the liberal parties must be found. Three days later he had begged Caprivi not to identify himself with the bill. His surprise and annoyance had therefore been all the greater, the Kaiser declared, when Caprivi had thrown down the gauntlet in favour of the bill in his speech in the House of Representatives. 'The feeling had now spread beyond Prussia. The National Liberal party in Germany, the backbone of the Empire outside Prussia, espoused the cause of the National Liberals in Prussia. General Caprivi & Count Zedlitz were throwing themselves blindly into the arms of the right fractions of Conservative and Clerical parties.' He, Wilhelm, had therefore called for reports from all parts of Germany, which proved to be unanimously against the bill. When Sir Edward Malet intervened to ask the Kaiser whether he had not in fact supported the School Bill in his Brandenburg speech, the latter replied that his intention had been exactly the opposite. He had meant that he would fight to the bitter end to prevent his ministers pushing through the School Bill in this form. According to Malet's report, the Kaiser described the end of the crisis as follows: 'Then came the famous Crown Council: at which the Emperor asked Count Zedlitz if he could not adopt some compromise. The latter looked annoyed and said nothing. The Emperor asked Count Caprivi his opinion, who said he believed the Bill met with the approval of the Majority of the House [of Representatives]: *only* the Minister of Finance thought it should be modified. The next day to his intense surprise the Emperor received the resignation first of Count Zedlitz, then of Count Caprivi.' Meanwhile the Kaiser had learned that Zedlitz drafted the bill himself; the officials in his ministry had refused to assist. 'If Count Zedlitz had had his way', the Kaiser told Malet, 'the Culturkampf would have been renewed in its most aggressive form & the National Liberal party alienated.' Malet's report concluded: 'The Emperor attributed Count Caprivi's action to lack of Parliamentary Education and to chivalry to his colleague. It was a fine sentiment but had led him into a mire from which attention to his Sovereign would have saved him.' Although the Kaiser told Malet he hoped that Caprivi would resume the Prussian minister-presidency in the autumn, in the ambassador's view it was obvious that the relationship of trust between Wilhelm II and his second chancellor, which was in any case fragile, had been irreparably damaged.[58] Philipp Eulenburg thought likewise. 'I am afraid that Caprivi's prestige has suffered greatly in the Kaiser's eyes', he wrote on 26 March 1892.[59]

As with Bismarck's dismissal, Wilhelm felt the need to show his own role in this chancellor crisis in the best possible light for the benefit of his grandmother. On 12 April he wrote to the Queen, who was staying in the South of France, saying: 'I had rather a bad winter this year caused by the trouble given me in the school law . . . The whole thing was very badly managed by the Ministry as a whole & by Count Zedlitz in person. He did the direct contrary to what I from the beginning told him to do; snubbed the liberals, instigated the Centre & Ultra-Conservatives († Zeitung) & finally behind my back & against my expressed wish entangled the Chancellor in the whole affair, a week after the latter had promised me not to make a speech alluding to the law or to take any active part in the debate. When I warned C[ount] Zedlitz for the last time before the dangers he was incurring he made no answer but simply resigned ab irato & without any positive reasons; pulling the Chancellor after him; who in, what the French call un exces de vertu, thought he was bound to keep the other Minister company & resigned too. It was rather hard lines upon me, considering that I was opposed to the law from the first moment I had cognizance of it; & considering that I had done my utmost to keep the Count from making a mess of it! The most extraordinary thing in this whole affair was, that the Ministry never even agreed when they sanctioned the law last autumn by signing it; & that now they were all dead against it excepting the Chancellor & Zedlitz who seem to have overruled their colleagues to such a degree, that they did not dare open their mouths or send word to me that my Ministry was hopelessly split, which they ought to have done at once.'[60]

## THE SEPARATION OF OFFICES

With the ill-considered, almost panic-stricken resolution of the School Bill fiasco by means of the separation of the Reich chancellorship from the Prussian minister-presidency in March 1892, the Kaiser's ability to intervene in government business was greatly increased. Instead of having to contend with a head of government who periodically, with a soldierly integrity sometimes verging on misguided obstinacy, refused to obey 'commands' of his monarch which he considered disastrous, Wilhelm II was now faced with a state apparatus with two leaders, one of whom had only reluctantly remained in office.[61] The other, meanwhile, closely linked to the Kaiser, the court and the Conservative Party and initially free of the burdens of running a ministry, naturally hoped the two posts would eventually be reunited in his hands. 'I am *very* sorry that Ct. Botho Eulenburg (the Brother of the Hofmarschall) is to be Vice Chancellor [sic] & I am sure it will not be long before he takes Caprivi's place too', the Empress Frederick predicted on 24 March 1892.[62]

Five months after his appointment as Prussian minister-president, Botho Eulenburg's position was considerably strengthened when he was given the additional appointment of minister of the interior. Once again the Kaiser was responsible for this appointment: as Marschall recorded in his diary on 12 April, Wilhelm had spoken out 'very strongly against Herrfurth, whom he wishes to replace with B. Eulenburg'. The next day he noted: 'H.M. very angry with R[eich] C[hancellor], who has already twice threatened to resign. Has had a letter sent to B. Eulenburg about Herrfurth.' Caprivi, who had protected the liberal Minister of the Interior from the Kaiser the previous year, eventually abandoned his opposition to Herrfurth's dismissal and the appointment of Botho Eulenburg to this influential Prussian post, whereupon the Kaiser triumphantly announced to the Chief of the Civil Cabinet: 'My dear Lucanus! I went to see the Chancellor yesterday and sounded him out carefully in the course of the conversation about our further progress in ministerial appointments. I am happy to say he was quite resigned and prepared for Herrfurth's departure, for which he no longer wished to set a date; and when I indicated that Eulenburg would be the best successor to H. he at once gave his agreement and expressed the hope that he would accept the post. So all our anxieties on this score are settled and you may inform Eulenburg of it immediately. W. I. R.' The Kaiser agreed, however, to postpone the change of minister until after the closure of the Landtag.[63] The Empress Frederick thought the departure of Herrfurth from the government regrettable from every point of view and saw Botho Eulenburg's promotion as a further weakening of the Chancellor, for Eulenburg was 'a very oily slippery ambitious sly man'.[64]

Caprivi's position after the separation of offices was widely seen as untenable in the long run, a view he himself shared. In April 1892 Marschall noted in his diary that the Reich Chancellor was 'very depressed' and had 'nothing to do'.[65] In May Verdy reported to Waldersee from Berlin that the Chancellor was seen 'as a dead man, not only in the eyes of the many but also by the privileged few in the know. Lucanus, for instance, told me 14 days ago when I was dining privately with him and a few ministers at Douglas's house, that he gave him another 6 weeks and then things would get hot again.'[66] Waldersee himself at first thought that Caprivi would soon retire and be replaced as chancellor too, by Botho Eulenburg. 'As soon as the Kaiser has reason to be pleased with Eulenburg . . . he will dismiss Caprivi on the most trivial grounds; with the Kaiser the new has the advantage over the old', besides which the malleable Botho Eulenburg could count on 'very valuable support from his brother August, his cousin Philipp and the whole East Prussian clique'.[67] It was only after a visit to Berlin, when he found the Kaiser in a more serious mood than usual, that the General realised that in appointing Botho Eulenburg the Kaiser's intention had not in fact been to make him Reich chancellor later. He was still looking for a suitable candidate in the event of Caprivi's resignation and had entered into negotiations with the Governor of Alsace-Lorraine, Prince Chlodwig zu Hohenlohe-Schillingsfürst. In Waldersee's opinion Hohenlohe was already a 'worn-out man with no energy' at this time, although the fact that he had turned down the post of chancellor at least proved 'that he still [possesses] some self-knowledge'. (Two and a half years later Hohenlohe was to succeed Caprivi and Botho Eulenburg as Reich chancellor and Prussian minister-president respectively.) Wilhelm had also discussed the chancellorship with the ambassador at Vienna, Heinrich VII Prince Reuss. 'The worst thing, as always, is that the Kaiser has no definite system at all in mind when he makes new appointments', Waldersee very justifiably complained. Nor had he 'any understanding at all of the fact that a Ministry needs to be unified and harmonious. The School Bill catastrophe has made him completely unsure of himself; he does not know where he is going or with whom he should ally himself. The ship is adrift! He really is not the right captain to steer it through such tricky waters!'[68] He, Waldersee, who was often approached about it, had no intention of seeking the post of Reich chancellor. That would only be possible 'if the Kaiser recognised that his way of ruling will not work, and decided not to lend his ear to secret advisers and to pursue policies without the Chancellor and the ministers knowing anything about them'.[69]

Caprivi's position was further weakened by the fact that the two most influential military officers at court, Adjutant-General von Wittich and Chief of the Military Cabinet von Hahnke, who had hitherto admired and supported him, were 'finished' with him, as Waldersee recorded after a train journey with his two fellow generals in April 1892.[70] Wittich, who took a 'very pessimistic' view, reported that Caprivi was bitter and rarely appeared in public, while Marschall was no longer taken seriously anywhere, 'not even by the Kaiser'. The Foreign Office was ruled by Holstein, who had allied himself with Kiderlen-Wächter 'because of his relationship with the Kaiser'.[71] 'I found Hahnke also in the mood to make critical judgements', Waldersee observed.[72] Among the Flügeladjutanten, who had long since ceased to admire Caprivi, a positively hostile attitude towards the Chancellor was spreading. Helmuth von Moltke, the future Chief of the General Staff, confided to Waldersee: 'The more I get to know Caprivi, the more convinced I am that he is a man of very questionable character.' In support of this judgement Moltke 'indignantly' recounted that Caprivi had prejudiced the Kaiser against Zedlitz and had thrown all the blame for the crisis on him, with the result that the Kaiser now spoke of Zedlitz, whom he had recently regarded as the man of the future, 'in the most dismissive manner'. 'Really not nice, either of the Kaiser or of Caprivi!', Waldersee commented. 'It seems to me that it must gradually dawn on everyone who has ever had anything to do with the Kaiser how fickle he is. In fact I do not know anyone with whom he has been on intimate terms about whom he has not spoken disparagingly; Philipp Eulenburg is perhaps the exception; but there are some who deny even that.'[73]

Similar views on the confused state of affairs were now to be heard from all parts of the political spectrum. On a visit to Berlin in May 1892 Waldersee was shocked by how critically the Free Conservatives and the National Liberals in particular spoke of Caprivi and Marschall, who were generally considered 'completely finished'. The Finance Minister, Miquel, complained that there were ministers but no ministry; everything was going in different directions. Waldersee recorded that there was open talk of a possible reconciliation between the Kaiser and Bismarck, which would inevitably lead to Caprivi's resignation and

Botho Eulenburg's appointment as chancellor. It was presumed that Marschall's successor at the Foreign Office would be the ambassador in Madrid, Ferdinand Freiherr von Stumm.[74] In the ensuing months new names were constantly mentioned for both key posts; Waldersee was repeatedly named, as was the Catholic General Walther Freiherr von Loë.[75] Significantly, no one expected leadership qualities from the civil service types who headed the Prussian ministries. There was a total lack of 'independent, self-assured men' in the Ministry of State, Waldersee lamented in October 1892, for 'Thielen, Bosse, Schelling, Berlepsch, Kaltenborn, Heiden are all only second-rate people.'[76]

For the first few months after the separation of the top offices in the Reich and Prussia the Kaiser behaved with restraint, recognising that another chancellor crisis would seriously harm the prestige of the monarchy. He did his best to avoid conflicts and sent the new Minister-President instructions via Philipp Eulenburg 'to maintain the closest contact with Caprivi'.[77] Added to this was the fact that, as Wittich and Hahnke confided to Waldersee on their train journey in April, the Kaiser had to a certain extent lost his nerve as a result of the crisis. Wittich, Waldersee noted, judged the Kaiser 'increasingly severely, and says he is quite incapable of making decisions; his main aim at present is to be spared any serious business, nor does he want to be reminded of serious consequences, he does his best to divert himself with all kinds of distractions'.[78] Information of this kind from the immediate entourage of the Kaiser led Waldersee to the conclusion that there would after all be no change of chancellor for the time being. The Kaiser wanted 'to keep moving for several months', he wrote, and all the disruption associated with a change of chancellor was 'too troublesome' for him, besides which he would find it 'very difficult' to make any major decision.[79]

At this time of latent crisis and nervous indecision Kaiserin Auguste Viktoria proved herself a loyal ally to Caprivi. During Wilhelm's absence on his Scandinavian cruise in 1892 she invited the increasingly isolated Chancellor to dinner and discussed the Bismarck Fronde and the domestic and foreign situation with him in detail. 'I liked him so much for his decent and unselfish attitude to everything', she wrote to her husband.[80] Briefly, during that summer, the Kaiserin became an intermediary for letters and messages between the Kaiser and the Chancellor, particularly in the quarrel over whether an international exhibition should be staged in Berlin. Caprivi's dealings with industrialists had convinced him of the benefits of such an exhibition and he had already written both to the German federal governments and to the French government. The Kaiser, on the other hand, made his antagonism to the idea plain in a succession of 'very sharp remarks' and marginal comments. On the basis of a newspaper report Wilhelm had formed the opinion that an exhibition of this kind would result in great economic disadvantages for Germany. He was also afraid of the effect of 'workmen crowding to Berlin'. In July 1892 he said to Alfred von Kiderlen-Wächter, who was again serving as representative of the Foreign Office, 'Six months ago when there was first talk of an international exposition I urgently requested the Chancellor to put a stop to it. He then wanted to wait and see. I have however repeatedly told him that I was opposed to it; but he has always shut up like an oyster and now we have a pretty kettle of fish; if it is now stated that I do not want it, then people will again say I do not know what I want and had changed my mind; and yet from the outset I left no doubt that I was against it.' The Kaiser was 'more depressed than angry' as he spoke, the diplomat reported. In Kiderlen's opinion it would have been better for the Chancellor to give way and avoid a conflict, since he was well aware of the Kaiser's views and must have known he would not yield.[81] Immediately after this conversation on board the *Hohenzollern* Wilhelm wrote to his wife, who hastened to reply: 'I *wrote at once* to Caprivi with your message about the exhibition in Berlin as I do not know when he will have time to come here again, and it was urgent . . . I enclose Caprivi's answer . . . but he tells me that he had already written to you saying the same thing. If only things would calm down again; this agitation from all sides is unbearable!'[82]

The Kaiser replied to his Chancellor's letter on 20 July 1892 in tones of defiant, autocratic self-satisfaction which marked the end of the close season as far as relations between them were concerned. He abruptly dismissed the Chancellor's arguments in favour of an international exhibition. He was 'absolutely opposed to it'. Two and a half years earlier Bismarck had turned down a similar proposal after an audience with him, the Kaiser, and 'all outcry in favour of an exposition thereupon ceased'. Caprivi should have responded to the renewed demands for an exhibition with a 'decisive No. In this connection a reference to the decision taken by Prince [Bismarck] after an audience with the Kaiser would not have failed to be of effect, and would probably have nipped every movement in the bud.' One must not give in to the avarice of the Berlin *demi-monde* and underworld, Wilhelm declared. 'The fame of the Parisians gives the Berliners no peace', he commented mockingly. 'Berlin is a great city, cosmopolitan (perhaps?), therefore it must also have an exposition! It is easy to see that this line of thought is very understandable and acceptable for *Berlin* hotels, theatres, music-halls, etc. They will be the only ones to profit from it! Hence the propaganda. But the *proton pseudes* is to be found in the conclusion that it was the tourist traffic alone that brought Paris such good returns. This is completely false. The hundreds of real millionaires who settled there to *live*, and to amuse themselves for months, and who attract new acquaintances from all countries – it is all this that has fattened the calf. Paris is after all – what I hope Berlin will never be – the greatest whore-house in the world, hence another attraction quite apart from the exposition. There is nothing in Berlin to hold the foreigner with the exception of a few museums, palaces and the soldiers. He has seen everything with the red book in his hand in six days . . . The Berliner does not understand this and would be thoroughly offended if one told him so.' Almost sarcastically Wilhelm then turned to Caprivi's attempts to restore the Kaiser's popularity by encouraging nationalist feeling. 'I am deeply moved', he wrote, 'to see from your proposal – to place me at the head – how you are trying, in these times that are so difficult for us both, to find a good opportunity to increase my subjects' affection for me, and I warmly thank you. But my will is firm as a rock, and I will hold fast to what I hold right, and no devil – not even Prince Bismarck – can dissuade me. I will not have an exposition because it can injure my Fatherland and my capital! Moreover we Hohenzollerns are accustomed only to advance slowly and painfully amidst trouble, conflicts, party divisions, and lack of appreciation. How often have my ancestors, most recently my grandfather who rests with God, had to battle for measures in direct opposition to the will of the uncomprehending populace which first opposed, then criticised, but finally blessed them. *What do I care about popularity!* For as the guiding principles of my actions, I have only the dictates of my duty and the responsibility of my clear conscience towards God. Dear Caprivi, think of it, I was prepared for bullets and dynamite when I ascended the throne and I am still alive! Yes – even the Socialists say that one can talk to me; well! More cannot be expected in two years after Prince [Bismarck] and the disappearance of the Socialist law. Our time will come as for everyone. Let us be patient and persevering, let us do our duty whether people are annoyed or not, it is all the same. Respect will come, it is already "on the march" owing to your distinction and my trust in God. Only *trust in my leadership* and fight bravely where I point the way, and we will have no trouble in managing the *canaille* either in this affair or later on in *rebus militariis!* . . . Hence don't worry! As my Berliners say, Ausstellung is nich [exposition? No way!]. Farewell, best greetings to your colleagues and counsellors, as well as to Holstein. Your very affectionate King Wilhelm I. R.'[83] Philipp Eulenburg and Kiderlen-Wächter were well aware that the 'sometimes crude, sometimes arrogant' tone of this letter would be insulting to the Reich Chancellor and maintained that it was 'at all events *intended* to be friendly' and not intended to be 'ironical'. Even Wilhelm was at pains to avoid the dreaded possibility of the Chancellor handing in his resignation, and he explained that he had 'put this in writing because in that way I can more emphatically emphasise my position as king and father of his country; it might easily seem provocative if I as a young man were to say anything like this orally to someone much older'. Nonetheless Kiderlen thought it advisable to conceal from the Chancellor that he and Eulenburg had read the letter and that Holstein had also received a copy on the Kaiser's instructions.[84] The international exhibition did not take place.

When Robert Zelle of the Progressive Party was elected to succeed the late Forckenbeck as mayor of Berlin in September 1892 it was generally expected that the Kaiser, having only very reluctantly agreed to ratify Forckenbeck's election under pressure from the Ministry of State, would hold out against this appointment likewise. Instead, he ratified Zelle's election at once and even sent him a congratulatory telegram.[85] This surprising change of heart can be attributed to the influence of Eulenburg and Holstein, who had impressed on the Kaiser that to delay ratification would 'cause *very* bad blood and would be *thoroughly* exploited against His Majesty'. Holstein had written despairingly to Eulenburg: 'My God, if only our sovereign would use the gifts which nature has so richly bestowed on him to increase his power by winning popularity! It is not a question of vanity but of *power*! By flattering Zelle in showing how willing he is to ratify the appointment, H.M. will make him more or less *his* candidate.'[86] Waldersee was thunderstruck when the Kaiser's telegram appeared in the press. 'Once again one can only say that we should be prepared for anything at any time and that nothing should surprise us', he commented. 'How often and in what terms I myself have heard the Kaiser abusing the Progressive Party and its people! But he can be blown in any direction, from one day to the next; he who is in disgrace today can be praised to the skies tomorrow, and vice versa.'[87] The impression that the Kaiser was anxious to make a good showing with the Progressives was strengthened by his friendly reception of Rudolf Virchow when the latter was appointed rector of the University of Berlin. 'That would not have been possible a year ago', Waldersee exclaimed.[88] The reason for this 'flirtation' with the Progressive Party was, however, clear to all — it was intended to win their support for the Army Bill.[89]

## THE GREAT ARMY BILL

The demand for a huge increase in the army put forward by the Kaiser in July 1891 continued to overshadow domestic politics in Germany more than any other question during these years.[90] As we have just seen, Caprivi's swing towards conservative–clerical school reform in Prussia had been prompted largely by his desire to win the votes of the Catholic Centre party for the Army Bill in the Reichstag. With the withdrawal of Zedlitz's School Bill in March 1892 the Chancellor was again confronted with the question of how to achieve a majority for the Army Bill. Caprivi himself was from the outset in favour of reducing the statutory period of military service from three to two years, at least for the infantry. He took this view not only for reasons of parliamentary tactics, although he certainly recognised that the Reichstag would never approve an increase in the army if three-year service, which was deeply unpopular in the country, were retained. The Chancellor-General also favoured the reduction of military service to two years on military grounds, seeing it as a welcome step on the path towards universal conscription and as a means of rejuvenating the infantry.[91] Other senior military figures – not least the former Minister of War General von Verdy and the future Field Marshal Colmar Freiherr von der Goltz – were equally keen on the idea of a nation in arms and therefore supported the introduction of two-year service as a long overdue measure to modernise and popularise the army.[92] The Kaiser, however, had shown almost religious zeal in categorically rejecting the concession of two year service in his letters to Kaltenborn and Caprivi in July 1891,[93] and now agreed only with great reluctance to a compromise put forward by the Chancellor, under which two-year service would indeed be introduced but only for certain units. Everyone was aware of how unconvincing a solution this was, and of the precarious situation it had brought about. As the compromise by no means satisfied the Left Liberals – the parties of the left held the view that the increase in the army constituted an unacceptable burden for the population as a whole[94] – it was evident that the Chancellor would in any case be forced to make further concessions, either to the two Progressive parties or to the Catholic Centre, in order to achieve a majority.

Waldersee, naturally enough, was one of the most determined opponents of Caprivi's reform plans. From the beginning the influential former Chief of General Staff recorded in his diary that to his 'horror' Caprivi had declared himself in favour of two-year service and had won round Minister of War Hans von Kaltenborn to his point of view.[95] The Chancellor would now start 'working on the Kaiser in this sense', he predicted. 'Until recently the Kaiser very strongly supported 3-year military service; but regrettably I no longer have any confidence in his reliability and I do not think that there is any subject on which a change of heart can be ruled out.'[96] In early 1892 Waldersee welcomed a report that the Kaiser had 'recently spoken out decisively against two-year service', but he added: 'If only I could be more confident that he would keep to it!'[97] Caprivi's willingness to exploit his contacts with the press on this question reminded Waldersee of the last phase of Bismarck's domination and seemed to him 'one of the most brazen and vile acts' imaginable; if 'the Chancellor and General' had indeed 'started a press campaign against his Kaiser and War Lord', both civil and court martial proceedings ought to be instituted against him.[98] A new chancellor crisis seemed inevitable, despite the fact that the Kaiser told General von Versen at the end of 1891 that he really could not 'let [Caprivi] go now'.[99]

In the Kaiser's entourage Caprivi could at first count on the support of Adjutant-General von Wittich (although after the School Bill crisis even he turned his back on the Chancellor),[100] but otherwise his plans were regarded with hostility both at court and in army circles, and certain of the ruling federal princes also urged the Kaiser to retain three-year service for the entire army. They argued that one could not train young recruits to be reliable soldiers loyal to the monarchy in under three years. Some even predicted the downfall of the Prusso-German military monarchy and the advent of parliamentary government if the concessions proposed by Caprivi went through. Prince Bernhard of Saxe-Meiningen, who was at this time working in the General Staff under Schlieffen, expressed the opinion that the average German was 'a refractory type who [could] be turned into a competent soldier only by strict discipline maintained for a considerable time', hence the need to retain three-year service.[101] In early 1892 Prince Bernhard felt able to reassure Waldersee that the Kaiser had spoken to him 'in such strong terms' against two-year service that he was convinced that 'he would not let himself be won round by the Caprivi-Kaltenborn-Wittich triad'. He, Bernhard, respected all three Generals greatly, but he would 'never' understand how they could champion such an idea, for 'a measure so damaging to the efficiency of the army . . . could bring about the downfall of Germany's sovereign independence and might perhaps even cost the Kaiser his crown'.[102] In the months that followed, Wilhelm's brother-in-law repeatedly expressed his 'patriotic anxieties and apprehensions . . . with regard to the great Army Reorganisation Bill'.[103] The Grand Duke of Baden and the new King of Württemberg also proved to be determined opponents of two-year military service and had 'a violent argument with Caprivi' about it.[104] Both South German monarchs took it upon themselves in the summer of 1892 to implore the Kaiser never to give up three-year military service.[105] Waldersee told the Grand Duke that he found it 'incomprehensible that Caprivi could persist in working against the views of his Kaiser, although he was perfectly well aware of them'.[106] Foreign Secretary Marschall feared that it might come to 'a second edition of the School Bill', with the Chancellor and the Kaiser pursuing irreconcilable policies, 'for on the main issue, two-year service, H.M. is intransigent'.[107] After a conversation with the Chancellor on 16 September the Foreign Secretary noted in his diary: 'The Army Bill has been forced on us by H.M., as I expected. I am worried about the coming winter and fear there will be a Reich chancellor crisis.'[108]

The difficulty for Wilhelm lay in the fact that he could not risk Caprivi's resignation, for after the debacle over the School Bill a chancellor crisis over the Army Bill would have been nothing less than a catastrophe amounting to 'bankruptcy for the Kaiser'.[109] Waldersee summed up the monarch's dilemma thus: 'If it is true that the Kaiser will not hear of concessions, a row can scarcely be avoided; if he makes significant concessions – and without them nothing is likely to be achieved – the army will suffer damage and his own reputation will be diminished.'[110] All eyes were therefore on the Kaiser when on 18 August 1892 he made a passionate speech declaring his preference for three-year military service and going so far as to say that he would prefer a small, efficient army with three-year service to 'a great horde with two years'.[111] Although Waldersee was among the most prominent champions of three-year service, he roundly condemned this remark as 'totally useless'. As he pointed out, the Kaiser had 'declared himself – as he has already done at least a dozen times in the course of the last few years – against two-year service, while at the same time the Ministry of War, with his consent, has planned the reorganisation of the army on the basis of two-year service', and this plan was shortly to be laid before the Reichstag. 'Now he suddenly bursts in with his speech, so that no one knows what is actually happening.' After the speech, Caprivi had at first thought that he would have to resign, but then he had 'soon calmed down', Waldersee reported, adding contemptuously, 'treacherous scoundrel that he is!'[112]

In the following weeks, to the disgust of the opponents of army reform, Wilhelm again allowed Caprivi to talk him into a compromise solution by which two-year service would be introduced for infantry regiments but not for the cavalry.[113] As Prince Bernhard wrote indignantly to Waldersee: 'As recently as 18 August His Majesty made his aversion to the introduction of two-year service absolutely clear in his speech; very soon afterwards those who rule the roost at the moment must have succeeded in allaying our All-Highest sovereign's fears and converting him to the opposite view . . . I am astonished . . . at their boldness in wanting to introduce something completely untried all at once, while giving in to misguided public opinion, clearly to the disadvantage of the real efficiency of the principal arm of our defence forces, and all for the sake of achieving other gains. This yielding to the pressure of public opinion I find alarming, for there is nothing one should be more careful to avoid than giving in to this treacherous power when it is motivated not by the desire for improvement, but by the selfish wish to rid itself of a burden. The most popular solution would of course be zero-year military service or at any rate a militia system on the Swiss model. There is no doubt where that would lead us.' In the opinion of the Kaiser's brother-in-law Germany was approaching an exceptionally critical moment in its military history. It was even possible that 'the incomparable work of Kaiser Wilhelm I will be irreparably ruined and the country will be spending billions on an army which is incapable of success on the battlefield'.[114]

The credibility of the government now depended on its maintaining a consistent line and adhering to the compromise which had been achieved with such difficulty, even at the risk of conflict with the Reichstag. The Kaiser, however, continued to manoeuvre indecisively between the different camps. After a discussion at Rominten, his East Prussian hunting lodge, with Philipp Eulenburg in September 1892, he gave orders for the political parties to be informed that he would not hesitate to dissolve the Reichstag if the Army Bill were rejected.[115] Barely three weeks later he indicated that he was determined to stick to Caprivi 'through thick and thin', and that he had accepted the necessity of two-year service for the infantry. Waldersee noted incredulously in his diary: 'The Kaiser has given up the struggle completely and has suddenly become a decided supporter of two-year service! As he is a master of the art of deceiving himself and freeing himself from blame, he now says that he had never before known that our infantry served for only $2\frac{1}{4}$ years, not 3!!! . . . Did anyone ever pride himself more than he did on knowing everything about the army, he who of course knows everything better than experienced men? And now he confesses to complete ignorance on one of the most important questions in the army, on which he has for years, on countless occasions, stated his opinion! . . . What are we to expect next from a man of such a character!'[116]

The Kaiser's support for Caprivi's bill proved decisive, at least within the military and civilian elite. Many observers were troubled by the spineless attitude towards the monarch shown even by the highest-ranking army officers over this issue. The leading members of the army establishment now knew what was wanted 'on high' and adjusted their reports accordingly, Arthur von Brauer complained. 'On whom can the Kaiser still depend, if such highly placed officers simply echo his words?', this Bismarckian statesman commented. 'The number of men who still have the courage of their own convictions grow fewer and fewer.'[117] However, the parliamentary fate of the bill remained extremely uncertain even after the decision to concede two-year service for some army units. The Centre Party, on whom the adoption or rejection of the bill ultimately depended, concealed its hand in order to extract as many concessions as it could for itself and the Catholic Church in Germany. On the other hand no one except the Social Democrats and the Progressives wanted to face new elections. The leaders of the Centre Party hoped to do further business with Caprivi and recognised that rejection of the Army Bill would lead to his dismissal; the Conservatives and Free Conservatives were unwilling to come into conflict with the Kaiser over a military question; and the National Liberals feared that they would lose votes to the anti-militaristic Left Liberals if the Reichstag were dissolved.[118] Following a visit to the capital in October 1892 Waldersee recorded: 'The Kaiser of course takes the matter very lightly and goes on living without a care in his head.'[119]

When the much-debated Army Bill was brought before the Reichstag at the end of November 1892 few trusted the Kaiser's resolve.[120] Doubtless for that very reason Wilhelm at first identified himself fully with the bill as being 'his own work' and let it be known that he would regard any opposition to it 'with great displeasure'.[121] In a letter to Franz Joseph he expressed confidence that the 'opposition' to 'our bill' was in decline everywhere, while the people's appreciation of it and 'hence its chances of success' were growing daily.[122] This staunch support, however, also attracted bitter criticism, and there was renewed talk of the downfall of the monarchy and even of the German Reich. Waldersee condemned the Kaiser's 'unfortunate passion for making all such causes his own; instead of putting the ministers in the forefront he allows them to push him forwards, and indeed probably pushes himself forwards. If the bill is rejected', he warned, 'it will now be a defeat for him!' The Kaiser had no inkling 'of what a grave situation he is facing; it is by far the biggest step that he has taken since he came to the throne and a complete failure . . . would mean the beginning of the break-up of the Reich', he predicted. The Kaiser was reported to have said that if the bill did not go through the first time it would perhaps do so at the fourth or fifth attempt. 'What immature, childish ideas', Waldersee complained.[123]

    There were thus conflicting reactions to the Kaiser's New Year address to the commanding generals in January 1893, which Eulenburg, urged on by Holstein and Kiderlen, had advised him to make.[124] Holstein thought the effect of Eulenburg's letter had been 'almost too powerful', for the Kaiser had gone so far as to speak of 'sweeping away the Reichstag',[125] which had made an undesirable impression particularly on the non-Prussian generals present − Prince Georg of Saxony, Prince Arnulf of Bavaria, the Bavarian General von Parsefal and General Wilhelm von Wölckern from Württemberg. Waldersee, who also heard the address, recorded in his diary that the Kaiser had claimed that the Army Bill had been 'carefully considered; all the princes had agreed to it; it was essential and he would see it through. He stated that it had come to his attention that in the army it was being adversely criticised by some individuals; he could not allow this; when he put forward a bill it was the duty of every officer not to find fault with it under any circumstances; he laid on us the duty of ensuring that the officers desisted from any criticism. Then he became livelier and turned his attention to the Reichstag, saying in effect: I shall get the bill through whatever it takes; what does this bunch of civilians know about military matters. I shall not lose a single man or a single mark, and I shall *send this half-crazy Reichstag to the devil if it opposes me!*' Commenting on the apprehensive mood among senior army officers after the speech Waldersee noted: 'When the Kaiser had gone groups immediately formed and the universal impression seems to have been that under *no circumstances* should a single word of the speech become public knowledge . . . But both the princes, and Generals Parceval and Wölckern too, are in duty bound to report the speech to their sovereigns; they in turn will speak to their ministers, and thus it will inevitably become public knowledge in the end. What might happen if the remarks about the Reichstag should become known! It would be an incalculable disaster!'[126] It was deplorable that the Kaiser had again committed himself so personally to the bill, for 'after what he has said it is impossible for him to retreat . . . unless, that is, he has fully realised the consequences of a dissolution of the Reichstag and has decided to fight the thing out. But he lacks the energy to do so.'[127] In fact the Kaiser's derogatory remarks did not remain a secret. The Hereditary Prince zu Hohenlohe-Langenburg, for example, wrote to his father about them, commenting: 'That the Kaiser expressed his firm determination not to give way over the army question pleases me very much. A surrender would damage his prestige at home and abroad. I think we need strong action by the government above all, even at the risk of a conflict. A repetition of the retreat over the School Bill would only help the opposition and would badly damage the standing of the Reich.'[128]

At the end of April 1893, after negotiations with Karl Freiherr von Hoyningen-Huene, the leader of the right wing of the Centre Party, Caprivi had hopes that a compromise would be reached, especially as the Kaiser declared himself willing to give up his visit to the Görtz family in Schlitz and shorten his stay in Karlsruhe in order to return to Berlin for the critical vote in the Reichstag. 'That will make a good impression', the Chancellor believed. 'God grant that we shall see Kaiser and Reich emerge unscathed from this difficult situation.'[129] Eulenburg urged the Kaiser 'to come roaring back to Berlin like Jupiter *tonans* from Karlsruhe or wherever else *within* Germany' he might be for the vote. Kiderlen likewise argued that '*for the sake of the Kaiser's prestige*' the dissolution of the Reichstag must not take place during his absence in Italy. 'If H.M. is in Karlsruhe it does not matter – on the contrary, it would make a colossal impression if he came storming back unexpectedly from there at the crucial moment.'[130] Wilhelm returned to Berlin on 3 May in time for the decisive parliamentary vote.

On 6 May 1893 the Army Bill was rejected by 210 votes to 162 and the Reichstag was dissolved. Germany now faced one of the most severe political crises since the fall of Bismarck.[131] The situation was drifting 'perilously close to a *coup d'état*', Waldersee commented.[132] Eulenburg, who had come from Munich to Berlin for the vote, noted in his diary that the Kaiser was 'very serious and violently attacked the Centre and the Bavarian wing, declaring that the Centre had burnt its bridges for at least 10 years. He intended to deliver to the Bavarian government, in the person of Crailsheim, who is to dine at the Neues Palais tomorrow with the other prime ministers who have come to Berlin for the dissolution, a stern reminder of its national obligations. I begged him to speak only in "Olympian" generalities, as kaiser, and to leave the details to me, which he agreed to do. I tried to calm the Kaiser by reminding him that the dissolution had taken place in much more favourable circumstances than could have been expected even eight days ago.'[133] When the ministers and envoys of the federal states arrived at the Neues Palais for a reception on 7 May the Kaiser made his views plain. To the Minister-President of Baden he said: 'When I returned to Germany [from Italy] the situation was clear. Acceptance of Huene's proposal or dissolution! I had already told the Grand Duke this when I was in Karlsruhe; in Berlin it was even plainer to me than from afar that this was inevitable . . . With a shortfall of 48 votes there was no alternative to dissolution.' To the Württemberg envoy Wilhelm remarked that 'these gentleman now had to be shown that we were in earnest. It would be no bad thing if a large number of Social Democrats were to get into the Reichstag, for it would give the philistines a fright and in the end they would themselves beg the government to free them from the impossible electoral system.' The Kaiser was in a good mood, Brauer reported to the Grand Duke of Baden, and had expressed 'his particular satisfaction that the situation was now "clear-cut" and the haggling was over'.[134]

Two days later Wilhelm made an angry speech to his generals on the Tempelhof Field which had the effect of intensifying the crisis to a dangerous degree. Referring to the Army Bill, he said: 'I could not have anticipated its rejection, and had hoped that it would have been passed unconditionally by the patriotic spirit of the Reichstag. I was, unfortunately, deceived in that expectation. A minority of patriotically minded men was unable to do anything against the majority. In the debates passionate words were spoken which are not heard with pleasure among educated men. I had to proceed to a dissolution, and I hope to obtain from a new Reichstag the approval of the Army Bill. Should, however, I be disappointed in this hope too, I am determined to do all I can to attain my object, for I am too strongly convinced that these proposals are necessary in order that I may be able to preserve the general peace. There has been some talk of inciting the masses. I do not believe that the German people will allow themselves to be stirred up by outsiders. On the contrary, I know that in these army proposals I am at one with the federal princes, with the people and with the army.'[135]

This speech, like most of Wilhelm's previous outbursts, did not escape Waldersee's censure. 'If only he could stop speaking without thinking! Such a speech cannot help in the slightest, but it can do great harm.'[136] Wilhelm's mother was outraged by this new proof of his anti-constitutional attitude and wrote: 'I was grieved and horrified to hear of the frightful speech! − I still *cannot* understand how a child of mine − a grandson of my father's − so utterly fails to understand the *importance*, the meaning and the value of a constitution, − and how there is such a world of difference between *all* his opinions and mine!'[137]

With the dissolution of the Reichstag in May 1893 the question arose of what would happen if the newly elected parliament again rejected the Army Bill. Caprivi threatened to seek another dissolution. The Prussian Minister of Finance,

Johannes von Miquel, who was becoming increasingly hostile to Caprivi,[138] warned that a constitutional conflict of this kind would only strengthen Caprivi's faltering relations with Wilhelm II. Herbert Bismarck, who had been elected to the Reichstag, was able to report to his father on a secret conversation between Miquel and the Free Conservative Party leader, Wilhelm von Kardorff, in which Miquel had declared 'that Caprivi's position with the Kaiser would only be strengthened if the bill were rejected and there were another dissolution; that was in the Kaiser's character. But if the bill were accepted by a few votes, H.M., who had already had enough of Caprivi, would grow so tired of him that Caprivi would be defeated in the regular autumn session by the determined onslaught which the Agrarians were planning to make on him then, and thus the country would be rid of the incompetent Caprivi within 5 months. The Kaiser had recently said [according to Miquel] that "he was beginning to realise that the commercial treaties recommended by Caprivi had been a stupid mistake". H.M. was beginning to doubt Caprivi's competence; this process would be interrupted if H.M.'s anger were aroused and he granted Caprivi a second dissolution. Miquel added [Herbert wrote] that he wanted to get rid of Caprivi because his narrow-mindedness was doing us harm both inside and outside the country; and he believed that this could most safely be achieved by leaving him in peace now, letting the Army Bill through by under 10 votes, and deferring the attack until the autumn.' Miquel claimed 'to know H.M. better now than anyone else', Herbert Bismarck added.[139]

The new elections resulted in heavy losses for the two Conservative parties (19 per cent down) but also for both Left Liberal parties (21 per cent down), while the Centre and the National Liberals maintained their share of the vote and the Social Democrats increased theirs by a further 18 per cent to 1.79 million (23.3 per cent of all votes). A worrying development was the increase in the number of Agrarians in the German Conservative Party and the election of sixteen overt anti-Semites to the Reichstag.[140] In spite of this polarisation the right wing of the Centre Party voted with the Conservatives, the anti-Semites and the Poles in favour of the Army Bill on 14 July 1893 to produce a small majority. The passage of the bill temporarily strengthened Caprivi's relations with the Kaiser.[141] The latter telegraphed his delight to his grandmother in Windsor: 'Army Bill passed easily. Great victory for my Government. Are all very happy.'[142] Philipp Eulenburg wrote enthusiastically from Munich to his imperial friend saying that he wished he could have left at once for Potsdam and the Neues Palais, for 'I am quite overcome with the desire to kiss my beloved Kaiser's hand after all the trouble we have had with this child of sorrows, the Army Bill! It is as though a heavy burden has been lifted from my soul after all the difficulty and anxieties which the child of sorrows caused even for me here in Bavaria! I see the adoption of the bill as a great political success. With this the first firm stone has been laid in the work of reconstruction after the unfortunate School Bill.'[143]

## THE KAISER AND THE CONSERVATIVES

As has already been shown in an earlier chapter Kaiser Wilhelm, for all his inconsistency, tended towards the liberal rather than the conservative end of the party spectrum in domestic politics during the Caprivi years,[144] and the same can be said of the period after the School Bill crisis. Indeed it was most strikingly demonstrated in relation to the troublesome question of mass anti-Semitism, which came to a head once more around 1892. Although full of anti-Semitic prejudices to which he occasionally gave crude expression, the Kaiser was very far from approving the loutish anti-Semitism displayed by the likes of Hermann Ahlwardt, who was elected to the Reichstag in the winter of 1892 but was at the same time condemned to a harsh prison sentence for publishing the inflammatory pamphlet *Judenflinten*.[145] The trial of Ahlwardt coincided with the conference of the German Conservative Party at Berlin-Tivoli, at which the members adopted by a large majority an anti-Semitic clause in the official party manifesto. Waldersee, although himself a vehement anti-Semite, had for some time warned of the threat posed by the radical anti-Semitic movement, which he saw as a new form of socialism. Nonetheless he greeted this controversial decision by the Conservatives as the best tactic for taking the wind out of the sails of rabble-rousers such as Ahlwardt, Liebermann von Sonnenberg and Böckel. In his diary for 18 December 1892 the General reflected on this worrying development: 'A new element, which has long existed but has been disregarded by our national leaders, has suddenly appeared in the political affairs of this country and has rapidly acquired importance; it is anti-Semitism! I have been observing its development for years and in my opinion its leaders, at least in so far as they have appeared in public, are very dubious creatures, like Liebermann, Ahlwardt and their cronies. But I also have the impression that the movement is deeply anchored in the population, and I am convinced that it has much justification. Its aims are not clear, but if it is allowed to grow unchecked and unmodified it must inevitably lead to socialism and become like the social democratic movement. I have often warned Conservatives against throwing in their lot with anti-Semitism, because with such disreputable leaders alliances of that kind are far too easy to exploit for attacks. The Conservatives have recently held a conference in Berlin at which expressions of anti-Semitic beliefs received overwhelming support. People said that this is now the mood in broad sections of the population of this country; we must take account of it if we want to keep our hold over them.' Doing so, Waldersee considered, was 'fully justified'.[146]

The attitude adopted by the Reich Chancellor and the Foreign Office towards this thorny question was diametrically opposed to Waldersee's – Caprivi made a speech in the Reichstag against anti-Semitism for which he received much praise – and they strove, not without success, to persuade the Kaiser to publicly condemn the new development in the Conservative Party. Holstein warned that Waldersee's position had been greatly strengthened by the adoption of the anti-Semitic clause in the party manifesto. Until recently the General had had 'a negligibly small hold' on the Conservatives because they considered him an 'unprincipled self-seeker'; in fact he had had the backing of 'none but the anti-Semites'. But now, since the Tivoli conference, the Conservative Party was 'overrun by anti-Semites: Waldersee's position has thus been strengthened at a stroke; he sees the moment coming when he will be able to dictate laws and conditions to the Kaiser'.[147] The Kaiser must therefore be induced to make a public declaration against anti-Semitism, Holstein argued. He welcomed the fact that the Chancellor had 'asked His Majesty to express his disapproval to the Conservatives of the demagogic attitude of the party conference'. But instead of doing so in unmistakable terms, Holstein complained, the Kaiser had 'called out laughingly to Manteuffel when they next met: "You and your friends ought all to be hanged!" Naturally Manteuffel does not see that as a criticism', he reported to Eulenburg.[148] The latter therefore stressed, in a very persuasive letter he wrote to the Kaiser on 17 December 1892, his conviction that 'in the interests of Your Majesty it is *essential* to adopt a clear-cut attitude towards anti-Semitism – *in whatever form*, to demonstrate very seriously that You stand by the Reich Chancellor's attitude'. 'I am no lover of the Jews, nor is Your Majesty – we have exchanged views on that from time to time', Eulenburg recalled. But as a result of the Conservative Party joining forces with the demagogues of the anti-Semitic movement, the political situation in Germany had been given a 'crooked face' which needed a timely box on the ears to straighten it out. 'The ugly face I mean is the latest move of the Conservative ultras towards anti-Semitism', wrote the Count in his inimitable style. 'It sticks out its tongue at all of us – at Your Majesty too!' The Reich Chancellor had already ensured that anti-Semitism had been 'knocked over the head'; 'but everything depends on there being *not the slightest doubt* that Your Majesty is behind him – otherwise Your Majesty's sympathy for the anti-Semites will be used to drive a wedge between Your Majesty and the Reich Chancellor . . . There are serious reservations about anti-Semitism itself, in the form in which it appears. When Your Majesty has successfully weathered the political transition brought about by the departure of Prince Bismarck and his faction, *then* it may perhaps be possible to establish a means of attending to the justified complaints of anti-Semitism.' But on grounds of self-preservation alone the state must make a strong stand against mass anti-Semitism in its present form, 'for the slightest suspicion of silent complicity on Your Majesty's part would shake the monarchical principle *to its foundations*. Your Majesty would become a *"roi des gueux"* – and with that Hohenzollern is lost . . . If the word is spread everywhere . . . that everything has its price – military and civilian – if respect for authority is taken away from country people, clergy, minor officials – by the anti-Semites in competition with the Social Democrats – the seed will soon bear fruit which sees all *property-owners* as corrupt . . .'[149]

The determined and impressive action taken by Caprivi, Holstein and Eulenburg did not fail to have the desired effect on the Kaiser's attitude to the German Conservatives, as Waldersee was to be the first to discover. The General complained bitterly that the Chancellor had 'had the bad manners, or indeed the baseness, to speak about it in the Reichstag and he has of course worked on the Kaiser in the same sense. The latter is naturally furious with the Conservatives again and has willingly harnessed himself to Caprivi's carriage which is deep in the mud. A few days ago . . . he was very unfriendly to Manteuffel, the leader of the Conservatives on this question, and on the 16th he had a long, heated conversation with Count Schulenburg Beetzendorf on the subject. There is no question that he will personally try to work on other Conservatives as well.'[150] In the Kaiser's hostile attitude to the Conservatives Waldersee saw the confirmation of his earlier suspicion that Wilhelm in fact wanted to throw in his lot with the liberals.[151] 'What I tried to foretell six months ago now seems to me to be becoming more probable: the Kaiser is heading in the liberal direction, and if he does not get as far as Eugen Richter [on the radical left] immediately, he will at least catch up with [the more moderate leader Heinrich] Rickert. I think that would in fact be the best possible thing', he added bitterly. 'He must first find out what these people are like, and I shall not be surprised if he soon becomes a friend of the Jews and in the end even allows those Jewish scoundrels to become officers.'[152]

After some initial hesitation, Wilhelm took similar action on another question that aroused party political passions at this time: the commercial treaties with Austria-Hungary, Italy and Russia. Since the autumn of 1891 Caprivi, who had no experience of economic matters, had had to concern himself with the renewal of these trade agreements which Bismarck had made ten years earlier. He soon became convinced that in view of Germany's rapid industrialisation and urbanisation the high corn duties which his predecessor had conceded to the great landowners east of the Elbe could no longer be justified. In taking this view the Chancellor had the backing of his closest adviser, the Chief of the Reich Chancellery Karl Goering, who was credited with Left Liberal leanings.

Naturally he came into increasing conflict with the protectionist interests of the East Elbian landed aristocracy, who formed a powerful nucleus within the German Conservative Party, and likewise with Miquel and other Prussian ministers.[153] When the commercial treaties with the Danube monarchy, Italy and Belgium were ratified on 18 December 1891 the Kaiser expressed his warm thanks to Caprivi in a speech at Teltow, to the fury of the Conservatives, and raised 'this simple Prussian General', as he described him, to the rank of count.[154]

At the beginning of 1893, when it became known that Caprivi's government intended to conclude a commercial treaty with Russia as well, the Prussian landowners formed the Agrarian League to try to protect their interests. Waldersee noted with bitterness the Kaiser's hostile attitude to this 'powerful' popular movement and the landed classes it represented, which had hitherto been the mainstay of the Prussian monarchy. 'That *this* Kaiser would lend his hand to the ruin of the agricultural community, in which his most reliable people are still to be found, from which the state gets its strongest support, I would have thought impossible a few years ago. When I think of the promises he has made, how he has sworn never to allow any harm to come to agriculture! What will become of his reputation; no one can rely on him and on his word again.' The General gloomily predicted a speeding-up of the process by which the families of the old nobility were abandoning their estates and being replaced by people who had made their money in trade and industry. 'The army will take this hard too', he feared.[155]

It was perhaps characteristic of Kaiser Wilhelm II that he chose to see the protests of the Agrarian League against Caprivi's free trade policy as directed against himself.[156] Before long a wide gulf had opened up between him and the Conservative landed aristocracy of Prussia, a development that temporarily improved relations between him and Caprivi. As the Postmaster-General, Heinrich von Stephan, told Waldersee in October 1893, the Agrarians' attacks were less of a threat for Caprivi, 'because the Kaiser is in complete agreement with him on the agricultural question'.[157] Press reports of these attacks were immediately shown to the Kaiser who, as Miquel confirmed, was 'infuriated' by them.[158] Waldersee commented with dismay that it would be 'very sad' if the Kaiser, who had often declared that he would protect agriculture, 'let down the people who trusted his word on this question too'.[159] When in late November 1893 the Kaiser received the news that the vote for the return to Germany of the Jesuits had been carried in the Reichstag with the help of a few Conservatives, he remarked to Waldersee that the names of these deputies should be taken down, and 'none of them will ever be invited to the Schloss again. Then he expressed his displeasure with the Conservatives in general.' He went on to say that 'they did not know what they wanted and were really no longer a coherent party at all'.[160] During the parliamentary debates on the commercial treaties there were fierce clashes between the Conservatives and the Chancellor, in which the Kaiser did not hesitate to intervene. 'It would be right and proper for him not to interfere', Waldersee wrote on 15 December 1893. 'But he cannot resist doing so, and this is one of the causes of the confused state of affairs we are in.'[161]

Ultimately the ferocity of Wilhelm's antagonism towards the East Elbian landed nobility in the winter of 1893–4 can be explained only in terms of the foreign policy hopes he pinned on the trade treaty with Russia. 'The Kaiser himself was quite deliberately courting the Tsar now', Thomas Nipperdey writes, rightly pointing out that the trade treaty represented an attempt to renew the rapprochement with Russia, and was intended 'in effect to replace the Reinsurance Treaty' which had lapsed in 1890.[162] When the ratification of the Russian trade treaty by the Reichstag seemed in jeopardy, Wilhelm personally took up the cudgels for the treaty and informed the Conservative deputy and Speaker of the Reichstag, Albert von Levetzow, 'that anyone who wore military uniform and frequented the court must vote for the government, or at least abstain'.[163] At a dinner for members of parliament given by the Chancellor the Kaiser again expressed his support for the trade treaty, remarking that he had no desire 'to wage war with Russia for the sake of 100 stupid Junkers', whereupon Levetzow, otherwise a quiet, venerable figure, countered by declaring to the Kaiser's face 'with raised voice and great determination' that the loyalty of the Conservatives to the monarchy was beyond all doubt, even if after careful examination they should consider it their duty to vote against the treaty. He added 'with deep emotion' that this day was the saddest of his life. 'And truly the Kaiser has no more loyal subject!', Waldersee lamented, adding that the other Conservatives present also left the dinner 'deeply dismayed'.[164] The Kaiser had even 'uttered threats' against Count Kanitz, the Master of Ceremonies at court, Waldersee recorded.[165] A few weeks later Wilhelm said, again addressing Kanitz: 'The trade treaty must go through: I have given Tsar Alexander my word!!!!'[166] He informed Duke Johann Albrecht of Mecklenburg that he was having all known Agrarians who came to Berlin watched by the police in order to form an impression of their alleged state of distress. Waldersee doubted that the monarch would go quite so far, although he admitted 'that the Kaiser encourages informers to report to him on this subject, as he always enjoys doing, and that there are certainly plenty of scoundrels around who add fuel to the flames by such gossip'.[167] In spite of threats of this kind, when the trade treaty with Russia came to the vote on 16 March 1894, the Conservatives rejected it, with only a few exceptions – Count Dönhoff and Prince Karl zu Hohenlohe-Schillingsfürst, the son of the Statthalter of Alsace-Lorraine, voted in favour, according to Waldersee, purely 'out of fear of the Kaiser'.[168] When the treaty was nevertheless ratified with the support of the Centre, the Polish deputies, the two Progressive parties and the Social Democrats, Wilhelm again hastened to send the glad news by telegraph to his grandmother.[169] Philipp Eulenburg was not entirely wide of the mark when he wrote to the Kaiser on 11 March saying that the ratification of the Russian trade treaty, which was 'of epoch-making importance both politically and economically', was his *great, personal* achievement'.[170]

After this success the Kaiser, while vacationing at Abbazia on the Adriatic, was so taken up with the pleasures of 'water sports, tennis, vulture-shooting and the fleet' that for the time being he took no further interest in matters of domestic legislation, as his companion Eulenburg, whom he had just promoted to the post of ambassador in Vienna, reported.[171] On his return, however, a fresh source of conflict between him and the East Elbian landowners arose in the form of the canal question. As Eulenburg recalled: 'When . . . the Kaiser came back from Abbazia to Berlin in mid-April his mood . . . was dominated particularly by the fact that the Conservatives, as a result of the undeniably serious plight of agriculture, had adopted a position diametrically opposed to the government, which at the instigation of the Kaiser had . . . put forward draft legislation for the construction of canals.' Eulenburg rightly stressed that this canal policy had been 'inspired by the Kaiser himself and pursued with his impulsive zeal'. The German Conservative Party, which had only reluctantly agreed to the construction of the Elbe–Trave canal, now refused to approve a further 55 million marks for the building of the Dortmund–Ems canal. But the Kaiser, as Eulenburg recorded, 'took this refusal as an insult aimed at him *personally* (!), ordered the names of all members of the Conservative Party who had voted against the canal to be struck off the court list (!) and wanted to "remove from office" the court chamberlains among them, which was only prevented thanks to the intervention of my cousin, the Oberhofmarschall Count August Eulenburg. What increased the Kaiser's rage (I cannot use any other word) even more was that with his impulsive instinct he sensed behind the attitude of the agrarian Conservatives – probably not without reason – machinations by Prince Bismarck. The blows which certain notorious hotheads aimed at the government during the negotiations in an extremely blunt (not to say *brutal Junkerish*) tone were really the last straw. For the Kaiser, who had unfortunately made an all too *personal* commitment to the construction of the canals, took this tone as a personal rebuff *to him* by the Conservatives and would not be placated. The cruel way in which the Great Elector had crushed the aristocracy and Frederick the Great's treatment of refractory nobles were frequently cited as the only proper way of teaching the insolent aristocracy a lesson.'[172] An eloquent example of this method of dealing with the aristocracy occurred in February 1894 when the Kaiser was informed that the Catholic Count Hompesch had said the Centre Party would not approve more than 2 million marks for the monument to Kaiser Wilhelm I. In the hearing of a large number of people Wilhelm II declared: 'I shall have the fellow thrown down the stairs if he comes into the Schloss.'[173] The domineering tone which Wilhelm II used towards the aristocracy was no different, as we shall see, from that which he used in his dealings with the Reich Chancellor.

A survey of the crisis-ridden relationship between the Kaiser and his Chancellor in the middle years of Caprivi's period of office thus continues to reveal a contradictory picture in which neither the monarch nor the leading statesman of the Reich appears unequivocally dominant. Certainly, Wilhelm II succeeded in halting Count Zedlitz's highly controversial Prussian School Bill in March 1892. But this was only after a long period of indecision and by unwittingly provoking a serious ministerial crisis which caused considerable damage to the reputation of the monarchy and to the cohesion of the Prussian and Reich government. The great army increase of the summer of 1893 was unquestionably the product of the Kaiser's personal initiative, but its passage through the Reichstag was only achieved by the abandonment of the three-year service which the Kaiser, remembering his 'grandpapa's' heroic stand in the Prussian constitutional conflict of the 1860s, had sworn never to give up. With the aid of contemporary correspondence and diaries we have been able to follow month after month of upheavals caused in both these instances by the dualistic division of power between Kaiser and Chancellor. As the sources also show, in a third extremely controversial instance, the trade treaty with Russia, Wilhelm II stood shoulder to shoulder with Caprivi against the East Elbian landed aristocracy which should have formed the natural mainstay of the Hohenzollern monarchy and had become the sworn enemy of the Chancellor they called 'the man without an inch of land or a blade of grass'.

It was a matter of universal speculation how long this crisis-ridden system of divided power could go on. No one seriously doubted, however, that it would be the Kaiser and not the Chancellor who emerged victorious, for while the position of the unpretentious Chancellor-General was becoming visibly weaker, that of the young Kaiser was growing stronger. Caprivi's surprising commitment to Zedlitz and his reactionary School Bill had shaken the confidence of the anticlerical Liberal bourgeoisie of all shades of opinion in his judgement, without winning him the support of the orthodox Protestants or of the Catholic population. Through his obstinate insistence on giving up the minister-presidency of Prussia to Botho Eulenburg he lost control over the Prussian Ministry of State, a fatal development which was aggravated by Wilhelm II's wilful manner of making appointments. In the endless battle over two-year military service

Caprivi proceeded to make bitter enemies of the influential military at court and at the 'front', who had the backing of some of the federal princes and members of the imperial family. Finally the new elections in the summer of 1893 brought Agrarians and anti-Semites into the Reichstag, who literally persecuted the increasingly isolated Chancellor with fanatical hatred. The future, on the other hand, belonged to the young monarch. Since he could not afford a second change of chancellor in the first few years following Bismarck's dismissal he had been obliged, for the time being, to hold on to the stubborn Caprivi and support the measures he demanded, even sometimes against his will. But at the latest by the spring of 1894, four years after Bismarck's departure, when the Kaiser was widely considered to have given sufficient proof of steadiness, a change of chancellor might again be contemplated. Even in the dualist phase which we examined in chapter 15 and in this chapter the enormous potential power which the crown possessed through the 'kingship mechanism' had already become apparent. Senior officers refused to speak of the Army Bill except in laudatory terms because they knew that the Kaiser saw 'every contradiction almost as an act of malice';[174] the officials of the Wilhelmstrasse became increasingly reserved even in their 'intimate private utterances' because they were aware 'that H.M. . . . is very sensitive to the slightest criticism';[175] and even experienced parliamentarians expressed surprise at 'the fear of the Kaiser that reigns in the Reichstag'.[176] If Wilhelm II thus had enormous potential to exercise both direct and indirect influence on the formulation of domestic policy in the Reich and in Prussia even under Caprivi, his freedom of action in the sphere of foreign policy, where he was not obliged to compromise with the Chancellor and was not subject to any sort of parliamentary control, was infinitely greater.

# CHAPTER EIGHTEEN

# Dynastic diplomacy

## WILHELM II BETWEEN RUSSIA AND GREAT BRITAIN

IN chapter 14 we were able to trace the way in which the non-renewal of the secret treaty with Russia, the attempted rapprochement between Germany and Britain and the renegotiation of the Triple Alliance with Austria-Hungary and Italy in May 1891 helped bring about a strengthening of ties between the Tsarist empire and the French Republic, a menacing development to which Wilhelm II reacted with apprehension and anger. In the period following this Franco-Russian fraternisation, which found its most dramatic expression in the enthusiastic reception of the French fleet at Kronstadt in July–August 1891, the Kaiser tried desperately to restore the former friendly relationship between the two empires through his dynastic ties with the Russian imperial family – the sister of his grandfather Wilhelm I was the grandmother of Tsar Alexander III. His advances were repeatedly met with a contemptuous and wounding rebuff. He was particularly offended by the fact that in the autumn of 1891 the Tsar bypassed Berlin on his way from Copenhagen to St Petersburg without taking the slightest notice of him. He complained angrily to his grandmother Queen Victoria that the Tsar had thought fit 'to snub us in the most untoward manner, without any cause whatever, thereby putting aside the simplest rules of international courtesy en vogue between European courts'.[1] Following conversations with Wilhelm in Hanover and Springe, Waldersee noted: 'The Kaiser is very bitter against Tsar Alexander and quite rightly so, but also through his own fault. He had in fact hoped for a visit in Berlin and unfortunately went so far as to propose travelling to Danzig, but once again the Tsar evaded it under the pretext of being in deep mourning. This will naturally increase Russian arrogance still more, while we feel increasingly humiliated.'[2] There were alarming signs that internationally, and above all in Russia, Germany and its Kaiser were 'no longer as highly regarded as they were a few years ago'. Prince Ernst zu Hohenlohe, who had meanwhile been appointed to the German embassy in St Petersburg, reported in January 1892 that on Wilhelm II's birthday 'not a single grand duke [had] appeared at the embassy to offer congratulations, and very few other people called, whereas previously the house had been overrun on such days'. The ambassador, General von Schweinitz, had walked up and down his room in his uniform, 'smiling grimly', while the servants in full ceremonial dress stood expectantly around. Schweinitz commented: 'I feel like a lady who is receiving, and who is put to shame in front of her own servants because no one comes.'[3] In the autumn of 1892 Wilhelm himself was forced to admit that 'my relations with St Petersburg really no longer exist'.[4] The military representative in Russia, Lieutenant-Colonel Karl von Villaume, remarked in a conversation with Waldersee that it was only abroad that one could judge how much Germany's standing had fallen since Bismarck's dismissal. 'The only good thing was that people credited the Kaiser with great energy, and thought that he might suddenly let fly or bring off some unexpected coup', to which Waldersee retorted: 'One can only wonder what will happen when the world realises that he is basically a weak man from whom one can indeed expect strong words, but no deeds.'[5] Looking back on developments in foreign affairs since Bismarck's fall, Waldersee commented dejectedly at the end of 1893 that 'things can seldom have changed as rapidly and completely between 1890 and now as in this sphere'.[6]

If Wilhelm's Russian relations saw his attempts at rapprochement and his protestations of peaceful intentions[7] as dishonest and manipulative, it was not least because of the great military expansion which he had pursued since July 1891, as well as his own frequent belligerent utterances, which found their way to Russia through countless different channels. As Waldersee was dismayed to hear during a visit to Berlin in April 1892, Tsar Alexander himself was convinced that Germany was devising 'plans of attack' on Russia. 'Unfortunately careful investigations have shown that our Kaiser is probably to blame for the Russian attitude', he wrote, for Wilhelm had 'repeatedly and most imprudently made remarks against Russia and about how he intended to beat the Russians. I know of 3 or 4 such instances, and the last one I heard of was in Remplin, at the wedding of the Prince [Albert] of [Saxe-]Altenburg and the Princess [Helene] of [Mecklenburg-]Strelitz, at which numerous Russians were present. I do not doubt that such remarks are made even more frequently in the circle of his family, and they are of course passed around at once. The Empress Frederick and her daughters alone would ensure they were spread about . . . It is small wonder if such a dull-witted and timorous man as Tsar Alexander actually becomes obsessed with the idea that we wanted to launch a war. But it is terrible that Kaiser Wilhelm can cause such damage by making rash speeches.'[8] Months later Prince Albert of Saxe-Altenburg confirmed to Waldersee that Alexander III had told him 'that Kaiser Wilhelm II had given grounds for suspicion [in Russia] by his remarks, to most of which he had probably given no thought whatsoever'. The General commented that the Tsar was absolutely right.[9]

The threat to Germany represented by the Franco-Russian alliance seemed all the more dangerous to Wilhelm II because the Vatican, and equally the Catholic Centre Party and the South German particularists, drew new hope from it for their own aspirations. The Kaiser saw in the increasingly self-assured attitude of the Vatican 'yet another proof that the ultramontanes are totally crazy and intoxicated with confidence and victorious frenzy. This has been brought about by their friendship with the French, and by the hope, nourished by this friendship, that the Triple Alliance will soon be destroyed by France *and Russia*. Exactly the same mood as was shown in the shameless and quite indescribable speeches and conduct [of the Catholic conference] in Mainz . . . We must take vigorous steps against the ultras and teach them a sharp lesson, firmly and coolly, with Protestant-German confidence, and this must also be aired *in the press*, clearly and unmistakably, the sooner the better.'[10] Waldersee likewise pointed to the significance of reports in circulation that 'the Holy Father [had] allied himself to our enemies'. 'If the Pope openly sides with our enemies in the event of war, our Catholics will be put in an extremely difficult position and one cannot expect a surge of patriotic feeling from the majority of them.' He wondered, moreover, 'how we are to incite the Poles to rebel if we do not have the Catholic clergy firmly on our side!' 'Our situation is really getting worse and worse!', he commented in despair.[11]

In the early summer of 1892 wounded dynastic pride threatened to take a heavy toll on relations between Germany and Russia when Tsar Alexander declared that during his forthcoming visit to Kiel he did not wish to come to Berlin or Potsdam, which so deeply offended Wilhelm II that he refused to countenance visiting the Tsar in Kiel. For days the Reich Chancellor and the Foreign Office strove in vain to convince the Kaiser that to refuse the Tsar's suggestion outright, as he proposed to do, would be '*too* rude'; a postponement of his visit to Kiel for a few days would be quite 'rude enough'. 'Can you imagine the effect of our Kaiser putting off the Tsar for 4 days because He has told a Silesian Count [Hans von Oppersdorff] that he is coming to stay with him!', Holstein asked Philipp Eulenburg, who was staying with the Kaiser in Prökelwitz in East Prussia. 'Do you think that such a thing has ever happened to the Tsar?'[12] Unmoved by the barrage of telegrams from Berlin, Wilhelm refused to alter his decision not to go to Kiel 'under any circumstances' and demanded that the

22. Three Emperors in a boat – Wilhelm II, Alexander III and the future
Tsar Nicholas II in Kiel on 7 June 1892

Foreign Office draft his negative response to the Tsar. The Foreign Secretary
telegraphed to Eulenburg to say that this was quite impossible, 'as the European
situation and the position of Germany are at stake'. Finally the Kaiser agreed that
Marschall could come and see him at Prökelwitz. The latter described his difficult
negotiations with Wilhelm in his diary. 'I make my report to him, explain the
historical relationship between Russia and Prussia and warn him against *cutting
off the link completely*, for that would be playing into France's hands.' By way of
a counter-proposal Marschall suggested a visit by the Kaiser to Kiel from 5 to
8 June, as the French were planning to hold a chauvinistic gymnastic festival
in Nancy at that time. 'That strikes home. H.M. accepts. Immediate telegram
to R[eich] C[hancellor]. Thank God!' It was 'a memorable day', Marshall later
recorded.[13]

　　On 7 June 1892 Alexander III and Wilhelm II finally met on their yachts
amidst a thunder of gun salutes and cheers in the flag-bedecked harbour at Kiel,
accompanied by Prince Heinrich and the heir to the Russian throne, Tsarevich
Nicholas. Wilhelm described the meeting to his mother: 'The Czar's visit went off
very well. He was in the best of spirits & extreemly [sic] amiable. His son Niky has

greatly developed & is a charming well bred boy with agreeable manners. The
weather was glorious & the old place looked its best. The Yacht is an enormous
vessel, rather like a mailsteamer from the outside, but beautiful inside, all done
up in Maple wood.'[14] After a conversation with Marschall the British ambassador
reported that the meeting of the Emperors had passed off extremely satisfactorily
for both sides and had made a considerable contribution to the safeguarding
of peace in Europe.[15] The German Foreign Office informed the embassy in
St Petersburg that the interview had 'gone off very well'. 'Both Emperors were
in a very good mood and behaved much more warmly towards each other than
previously.' The young Prince Hohenlohe reflected: 'Even if the meeting does not
produce any fundamental change, the good impression that it made on the Tsar
is of some value, as the tension which existed before was largely due to personal
causes.'[16] Queen Victoria expressed her satisfaction to her grandson that the
harmony between the two monarchs had made peace secure and dispelled the
anxieties 'which an estrangement between you & him seemed to have caused'.[17]

In reality, as Waldersee heard, both monarchs were play-acting. The General
doubted whether they had been alone even for five minutes; at any rate no political discussions had taken place. Not only had Tsar Alexander been determined to
avoid them, but the Tsarevich Nicholas, who had not left his father's side for an
instant, had also ensured that his father could not be inveigled into any serious
conversation by Wilhelm II. Waldersee found it regrettable that Wilhelm had
insisted on taking the *Hohenzollern* out to meet the Tsar, although the latter
had expressly tried to prevent this by telegraphing that he wanted to visit Kiel
and would not leave his ship until he arrived there. 'In spite of this our Kaiser
could not resist sailing a little way out towards the Tsar and then leading him in',
the General complained.[18] In the autumn of 1894, when Alexander lay dying,
Waldersee was still bemoaning the fact that Wilhelm had 'often bored [the Tsar]
dreadfully by his . . . importunity', adding that the heir to the Russian throne,
Nicholas, had also 'remained completely indifferent to the many kindnesses and
attentions and advances' towards him 'because I am sure he did not think they
were sincere'.[19]

Whatever the meeting of the Emperors in Kiel achieved, it was overshadowed
by the fact that at precisely the same time the Russian Grand Duke Constantine
had attended the mass gathering of French chauvinists in Nancy to which
Marschall had drawn the Kaiser's attention. The apparently pro-German attitude
of the Tsar in Kiel took on a different aspect when it transpired that Alexander
III had not only been informed of Constantine's intention of visiting Nancy,
but had written to him to give his approval. Ernst Hohenlohe reported that it
was 'widely assumed that the idea originated with the Russian ambassador in
Paris, Mohrenheim (a Jew), and that he had intended it to reduce the impact of

the Kiel meeting, a cleverly thought out and successful chess move.'[20] Herbert Bismarck, disheartened by the turn German policy was taking, predicted in July 1893 that 'H.M. will find himself at war with Russia and the result will certainly be disastrous.'[21]

### THE RUSSIAN FAMINE

With the Franco-Russian encirclement of Germany growing ever more constrictive, an unhoped-for way out seemed suddenly to be provided in the shape of a natural disaster on an enormous scale. The catastrophic food crisis in Russia caused by a succession of bad harvests had, since the summer of 1891, led to much conjecture in the courts, chancelleries and general staffs of Europe as to whether Russia was still in a position to wage war at all, or indeed whether the country was not heading inexorably towards its ruin. The Empress Frederick hoped that the Russian famine would bring a few years of peace during which the French would also be compelled to keep quiet, and that more trusting relationships in Europe would develop as a result of these conditions. 'If a *few years* of quiet development are passed, I always trust war will become more & more unlikely – only *alas* one must be prepared for it, & these preparations when on a scale as they are here are an *immense* evil & danger', she wrote to her mother at the end of 1891.[22] Friedrich von Holstein too thought the threat posed by Russia much reduced, as it 'will be destroyed in the foreseeable future by the internal damage it has suffered'. 'The only danger for us', he told Prince Hohenlohe, 'is French chauvinism', but with no hope of Russian support the French would have no desire for a war of revenge.[23] For his part Hohenlohe confirmed from the St Petersburg embassy that in view of the famine neither the Tsar nor Foreign Minister Giers had any wish to start a war. But he stressed that in the Russian capital 'there was widespread apprehension that, with our Kaiser's unpredictable nature, Russia's plight might be exploited for an aggressive move on the part of the Triple Alliance'. For that very reason the pacific comments made by Caprivi in his speech in Osnabrück, which had attracted much attention, had been received with relief.[24] Privately, however, even Caprivi expressed the opinion that if it should come to a revolution in Russia Germany should not stand idly by, but must strive 'to destroy the mighty empire, and therefore not to shrink from taking a risk'. The 'final goal' of his policy, the Chancellor indicated in early 1892, was the creation of the 'United States of Europe', in order to make Europe economically independent of America.[25]

From the outset the news of the famine in Russia had a peculiar fascination for Wilhelm II, for he too saw in the catastrophe the possibility of the total collapse of the mighty Russian Empire, the danger of a diversionary Russian attack outwards and finally also a chance to eliminate the weakened Russian rival permanently by military means. During a hunting trip to Rominten in East Prussia in October 1891 he criticised the Chancellor's pacific speech in Osnabrück. 'Now, what is this speech aiming at? First, the Chancellor could have mentioned it to me beforehand, second in such grave circumstances he exposes himself to the danger that next time he will be driven *ad absurdum* by public opinion, and third we *need* a mood of unrest in Germany so as to push through the unavoidably necessary military increases. Such a mood suits me perfectly, for if the German lights his pipe and puts on his dressing gown he simply cannot be governed . . . The key to the whole situation is the urgent necessity for strengthening the army. That is the goal which *must* be reached. I have sought the opinions of the King of Saxony, the Regent of Bavaria, etc., and have received, particularly from the former, wholehearted agreement. The Prince Regent also agreed with me – but he is like an old peasant who finds everything too expensive. The situation in Russia is incalculable. No one can tell the outcome of this famine. According to a secret report the Warsaw hotels are already being used as winter quarters for the troops! That is not merely military activity, it is mobilisation! . . Austria's inaction throws everything on to *our shoulders*. They do not stand by us, they simply leave us in the lurch in military matters! *We* are now more than ever obliged to go ahead – and as his contribution the Chancellor makes a peace speech in Osnabrück!'[26] The following month Waldersee lamented that 'in his present mood' the Kaiser was 'naturally' reacting to the 'very alarming' reports on the famine in Russia 'with delight'. 'He interprets them to suit himself, and exaggerates a great deal too; news of the effects of the failed [Russian] attempt to raise a loan in France also interested him greatly, but here too he interpreted everything in his own favour.'[27]

It is striking how often and at what length Wilhelm discussed the implications of the Russian crisis in his letters to his grandmother. In December 1891 he wrote saying: 'I think this fearful calamity will – with Gods help – for some time to come keep the Russians from making war upon their unsuspecting neighbours.'[28] In a long letter of 12 April 1892 he commented: 'The news that reached me from Russia are manifold; but all end with the same terrible gloomy outlook . . . Notwithstanding all what the Czar may say & fancy, the quite hopeless condition in which 17 of the Governments of the best "Black Earth" are, is perfectly appalling. A gentleman well versed in matters of national economy & finance, & who lived in Petersburg for over 20 years, told me that Russia was marching with giant strides towards its ruin *if* the Czar did not at last wake up. If the country is to be saved from a catastrophe, the only way for it is the immediate reducing of the army and navy on a large scale. This is the only manner to save money, neither Germany or France will give Russia a rouble more. Should the present Minister of Finance die or be disabled, his successor will have to place this fact plainly before the Czar. It is more than probable, the Ruler of all the Russians will not accept the proposal of reducing his forces, as it would create a terrible uproar in the war party & the Slavophil camp, inwardly; & outwardly give the world at large the spectacle of the "Colossus on feet of Clay". Then says my informant the country is utterly lost; & in a shorter or longer lapse of time the whole Realm will come to grief with a fearful crash. As for making war on other people, he went on, that was quite out of the question, as the whole of the transport system on the lines have been utterly muddled [sic], so that a lot of engines & waggons have up [to] the number of 500 & 14000 respectively been broken down or spoiled by snowdrifts [sic], so that they are beyond hope of repair. – Government has done much – as much as money can do – to help the people; they have payed [sic] 190 millions of roubles to the districts 20 mill: to General Annekoff for labour schemes; & in private a like sum has been raised. But how about next winter nobody knows; as the conditions will be the same & the money will probably fail! Nearly the same report has been made to our Foreign Office by H. v. Bleichröder here, who seems to be backing out of Russia with his money.'[29]

Lord Salisbury, to whom the Queen showed the Kaiser's letter, agreed with his opinion of the situation in Russia but pointed out that the illness of the two strongest men in the Russian government, Vishnegradski and Giers, made the outcome difficult to foresee. 'It is impossible to say now who it is that is guiding that vast machine', he wrote, '& under such conditions, a reckless policy is quite a possibility.' If the Queen had an opportunity, on her forthcoming visit of condolence to Darmstadt, to speak to the Kaiser, she should urge greater 'calmness' on him, both in his actions and in his all too frequent speeches.[30]

Not much calmness was in evidence for the time being, however. In his birthday letter to his grandmother, written on 22 May 1892 while he was hunting at Schlobitten in East Prussia, the Kaiser again brought up the subject of the Russian threat. 'The way in which the Russians prepare for their future inroad into Germany is illustrated by the fact not withstanding the terrible calamity at home they are pushing up 5 new Infantry Divisions against the frontier of Eastern Prussia & Galizia, including the formation of the new 18th Army Corps at Dunaburg. The Divisions come from Finland, Saratow, Caucasus respectively. General Gowrko proudly remarked to a french [sic] officer, who passed Warsaw a few weeks ago: "Je suis le poing de la Russie sur la poitrine de l'Allemagne, un mot de Czar et je l'enfonce!!! Puisse't-il se passer que ce mot d'ordre soit bientôt donné"!! An agreeable neighbour! – Besides I am informed by a Russian friend of mine – a gentleman of the good old school & traditions – that in March, when they thought Caprivi would leave & Bismarck come in, he heared [sic] two Generals in the Emperor's Palace say: "Si cela arrive on a ordonné en haut, d'immédiatement publier le texte du traité secret entre la France et nous"! My faith in the Peace is however *not* shaken but I trust in Prussia, my good conscience & my army.'[31]

## HOPES OF AN ALLIANCE WITH BRITAIN

The strategic purpose that lay behind this correspondence with Queen Victoria is not difficult to discern. No one recognised more clearly than Wilhelm II that with the Franco-Russian pact it had become more desirable than ever to win the support – at least tacit – of Great Britain. After the Kaiser's visit to Britain in the summer of 1893 Waldersee quite rightly observed that 'he still wishes to persuade England to join the Triple Alliance',[32] and six months later Wilhelm himself declared: 'We cannot manage on the continent without England . . . England must play its part in European politics.'[33] Undaunted by the change of government in London, where Gladstone's Liberal ministry (with Lord Rosebery as foreign secretary) had replaced the supposedly more pro-German Conservative government led by Lord Salisbury,[34] the Kaiser continued his efforts to use his close dynastic ties with the British royal family to gain political advantages for his country. But it was precisely on the dynastic level that countless points of friction and rivalry stood in the way of achieving the goal of an Anglo-German alliance.[35] In the rejection of the Kaiser's attempts at rapprochement, which were seen as importunate in Windsor too, we may detect one possible germ of the Anglo-German naval rivalry through which, a mere ten years later, the British Empire would be driven into the arms of France and Russia.

Wilhelm II's tendency to impose himself where he was not welcome became all too apparent in the spring of 1891 when Queen Victoria asked him to delay his visit to England until after the wedding of Prince Aribert of Anhalt and Princess Louise of Schleswig-Holstein, the younger daughter of Prince and Princess Christian (Lenchen), on 6 July, as the presence of the Kaiser would put the bridegroom's father, Duke Friedrich of Anhalt, too much in the shade.[36] The Kaiser, however, was determined to attend the wedding, which he had been instrumental in bringing about, and wrote to his uncle, Arthur Duke of Connaught: 'Now this I must say is very extraordinary, & very surprising! With Aunt Lenchens wish & permission *I alone* brought the whole match together, I had the whole of the writing & arguing etc. to do, I coaxed the Duke into an answer affirmative & lastly I pay out of my own pocket just as much as Grandmama though the two do not belong to my house or family! I have allready

[sic] promised Aribert to assist at his wedding & also the Anhalts so that they would be very much mortified if we were not there for the ceremony. Now for the "etiquette" question. The fear of the Queen that she could not honour the Duke enough in my presence is ungrounded. 1). At my court – & so in all the courts of the continent – the parents of the bridal pair are placed on the same rank as ours for the festivities. 2). So it was for the old Anhalts at Uncle Frederic Charles wedding, at which the late king of Hanover was present they ranked with him under the form of "unbeschadet des Ranges" taken from the old French court regulations "sauf le rang". 3). The same was done for my mother in law at Yayas wedding, when the Kings of Saxony & Greece were present; also the Prince & Princess of Lippe at Vickys wedding wer[e] treated in the same manner. It is "ganz selbstverständlich" [quite taken for granted] with us that the "Schwiegereltern haben den pas vor allen anderen Herrschaften die eingeladen sind 'unbeschadet des Ranges'" [parents-in-law take precedence over all other ladies and gentlemen who are invited, "rank notwithstanding"]. So that I should think that there is not the slightest difficulty.' Wilhelm assured his uncle that the Senior Master of Ceremonies, Count August zu Eulenburg, who knew everything about such matters, had confirmed his opinion and could provide any further information required. 'By these lines', he concluded, 'you will see that after all I have gone through for Louise & Aribert for whose happiness I worked from sheer [sic] friendship & love to Aunt Helena & the dear girl, that I feel rather hurt at beeing [sic] "abgewinkt" [put off] only out of an etiquette question which in reality is none.'[37] Queen Victoria was compelled to give way and invite her grandson both to the wedding of the young couple and to the silver wedding celebrations, held at the same time, of the bride's parents.[38] Nevertheless, as we have already seen, the Kaiser's visit to Britain that summer was universally considered a great success.[39]

Building on this success, Wilhelm hoped to consolidate the improved relations between the two countries through regular visits to his grandmother. But in June 1892, when he announced his intention of visiting her again on the Isle of Wight, Queen Victoria made it unmistakably plain that such visits were not at all to her liking. She sent word to the British ambassador in Berlin that 'the Queen *never invited the Emperor*. On the contrary she merely said if he came in his yacht she would be glad to see him at luncheon or dinner but could not lodge him at Osborne this year. But she wd. be very thankful if he did *not* come.'[40] Nor had she any desire, so soon after the death of her grandson the Duke of Clarence, to hear the brass band which Wilhelm wished to bring to perform for her during his visit.[41] To Wilhelm himself she wrote on 29 June: 'You understand, dear Willy, that I *cannot* lodge you this year, *at Osborne*, – but shall be delighted to see you to luncheon or dinner. It is most kind of you to offer to bring over the fine Band, but I have not had any Military Band whatever this year on account of our deep mourning & wd. therefore advise their not coming this year.'[42]

Wilhelm did nevertheless visit his grandmother at Osborne for a week at the beginning of August 1892. He slept on board the *Kaiseradler*, as the old *Hohenzollern* was now called, but joined the Queen and the rest of the royal family for several dinner parties at Osborne, dressed in his British admiral's uniform. He took part in the Cowes regatta in his new yacht *Meteor*, which he proudly boasted was the finest in all England (and which was almost entirely manned by British sailors), and at first won almost every prize available.[43] He wrote delightedly to his mother: 'I am so glad to see dear Grandmama again & to be able to breathe Osborne's balmy air, together with having the pleasure of sailing a good yacht of my own in the Royal Yacht Squadron Fleet. Meteor has made a brave show of herself this summer & has won 7 first prizes & 3 second ones; . . . the yacht has been pronounced as the swiftest of the whole of England.'[44] He was bitterly disappointed when over the next few days his yacht was beaten by *Iverna*, *Queen Mab* and the smaller *Corsair*, which belonged to Admiral Victor Montagu. 'Fortune has not smiled upon the German Emperor during the week of yacht racing', commented *The Times* on 6 August 1892.[45] As a result of these experiences at Cowes in the summer of 1892 the Kaiser put forward a proposal to his uncle the Prince of Wales, as commodore of the Royal Yacht Squadron, for a new race exclusively for larger yachts of over 100 tons – *Meteor* was 116 tons – for which he would give a Challenge Shield to the value of £90.[46] The offer was gratefully accepted.[47] The sailing rivalry between Wilhelm and his uncle which began in this way was, however, to have a fateful effect on their political relationship.

The marriage of the Duke of York (now heir presumptive and later King George V) and Princess Victoria Mary (May) of Teck, who had been engaged to his late brother Eddy, was to take place on 6 July 1893. As the day approached, Wilhelm was confident that he would be invited to the festivities at Windsor. But Queen Victoria again instructed her ambassador in Berlin to make it clear to the German government 'that it will be quite impossible . . . to invite the Emperor to the wedding of the Duke of York'; she would not be able to show the numerous guests sufficient honour if the German Emperor were present.[48] The decided tone of this instruction wounded Wilhelm all the more deeply because shortly afterwards his brother Heinrich received a letter from the Queen herself warmly inviting him and his wife Irène – another of the Queen's grandchildren – to the wedding. Both wished 'very much' to attend but they could not accept the invitation without the permission of the Kaiser. And Wilhelm refused, on the grounds that Heinrich's duties in the navy 'excluded the undertaking of any external official or family engagement'.[49] Not without justification Prince

Heinrich's Marshal of the Court, Albert Freiherr von Seckendorff, suspected that 'palace intrigues and difficulties on both sides of the Channel' were at the bottom of this extraordinary ruling.[50] He blamed the British side for 'uncle–nephew trouble', but also assumed, quite correctly, that the Kaiser was annoyed that not he but Heinrich had been invited to the wedding. The sudden emphasis on the Prince's naval duties was strange, he thought, considering the protracted Mediterranean cruise and 'many other pleasurable episodes' which Heinrich had been allowed to enjoy. During the past two summers Heinrich had made 'lengthy pleasure-trips to England' with the Kaiser's approval. As the Kaiser's brother Prince Heinrich was expected to go to Berlin for every court ball. Seckendorff could not think that a five-day trip to London for a family wedding could have serious military consequences.[51] Senden-Bibran, the Chief of the Naval Cabinet, confirmed Seckendorff's assumption that the reason for Wilhelm II's attitude lay in wounded vanity. 'The Kaiser is angry', he wrote, 'perhaps because He would prefer to go himself, and is not wanted.'[52] Seckendorff stressed that Heinrich and Irène had behaved quite correctly and had an absolutely clear conscience. To his direct question to Princess Irène, 'whether anything had been done by her or by the Prince [Heinrich] to bring about the invitation from England', she had responded with an unqualified 'No'.[53] This time the Kaiser gave in. On 14 June the Queen sent him a telegram from Balmoral thanking him for giving his brother and Irène permission to attend the wedding.[54] Wilhelm himself stayed away until the Cowes regatta at the end of July 1893.

Outwardly the Kaiser's eight-day visit, a sumptuous affair, passed off very satisfactorily. The new *Hohenzollern* – 'an enormous ship, painted white', as Queen Victoria observed after sailing around her – was universally admired; the German ship's band, this time consisting exclusively of string instruments, played 'beautifully' during the meal and the newly appointed Flügeladjutant Count Kuno von Moltke delighted his distinguished audience by playing an improvised piece on the piano, weaving together his own compositions, tunes from Wagner and 'God Save the Queen' (or 'Heil Dir im Siegerkranz').[55] Even on the water Anglo-German understanding seemed to be in the ascendant when the Prince of Wales's racing yacht *Britannia* won the Kaiser's Challenge Cup. Prince Hohenlohe-Langenburg, who as a relative and now secretary at the German embassy had ample opportunity to observe Wilhelm at close quarters,[56] wrote admiringly of him: 'The English were quite delighted with the Kaiser. He was in the best of moods the whole time and charming to everyone. He really has something uncommonly fascinating about him, and I was especially struck by his sharp, lively and intelligent expression.' During a visit to the Portsmouth docks the Kaiser's knowledgeable questions and comments astonished the British naval officers.[57]

And yet behind the glittering scenes personal animosity, threat of war and —
for a brief moment — imperial panic prevailed. Count Philipp zu Eulenburg,
visiting England for the first (and last) time on this occasion, had a conversation
with the Prince of Wales on the latter's yacht, while the Kaiser was absorbed
in captaining the vessel.[58] The heir to the British throne spoke sarcastically of
his nephew's 'colonial sport', which he claimed to find as puzzling as Wilhelm's
love for the navy. The Prince of Wales, Eulenburg reported, commented with a
malicious glance that 'it was certainly very nice that his nephew was interested
in ships'. 'But when one saw him rushing about so much with his paralysed arm,
like up on deck, one could not help fearing that he would do himself harm.'[59]

The situation suddenly took a serious turn when Britain and France found
themselves on the brink of war in Siam (Thailand) and the prospect of Great
Britain joining the Triple Alliance, as Wilhelm had hoped, seemed to be within
reach.[60] On the night of 30 July 1893 the Queen sent her grandson a telegram
from the Foreign Secretary, Lord Rosebery, reporting that the French government had sent an ultimatum demanding the withdrawal of the British gunboats
lying off Bangkok; Rosebery had rejected the French demand and asked for an
immediate interview with the German ambassador, Hatzfeldt.[61] The attitude of
the German embassy was reflected in a letter written by Ernst Hohenlohe to his
father immediately after the crisis: 'France and England were a hair's breadth
away from war with each other. As I learnt from official correspondence Italy
too would probably not have remained inactive in the event of war. We should
not have stood idly by either, and there would have been a European war.'[62]

Philipp Eulenburg's diary contains a striking description of the almost panic-
stricken reaction of the Kaiser to the threat of war which had so suddenly flared
up. 'Immediately on our return to the *Hohenzollern* the Kaiser took me into
his saloon and he had completely lost his nerve. In fact I have never seen him
so agitated and had to summon all my wits to calm him down with reasoned
arguments. After the French fleet's visit to Kronstadt in 1891 this was the second
great shock to befall him following the non-renewal of the secret treaty with
Russia . . . The Kaiser declared "that England's navy was weaker than the
combined Russian and French navies. Even with the help of our small navy
England would still be weaker. The French were now trying to drive Russia into
action, and given Tsar Alexander's hostile attitude towards Him [Wilhelm II]
this could well succeed. Our army was not yet strong enough to fight against
France and Russia at the same time. The French had chosen their moment
skilfully. To do nothing, and wait until the waves closed over one's head, was
impossible. All Germany's prestige would be lost if we did not take a leading
role, and if we were not a world power we would cut a sorry figure."' Eulenburg
tried to console the Kaiser with the (accurate) observation that Britain would

not fight France but would try to reach a settlement. If it nevertheless came to war, the Germans could for the present be amused spectators. 'If we succeeded in playing such a role in a war between the other powers, we should not do badly out of it. Above all the Kaiser should not let himself be trapped into making any kind of binding declaration, but should listen with a benevolent smile to what the English say, and keep as quiet as possible.' The diplomats Kiderlen Wächter and Wolff Metternich, summoned to join in the discussion, supported Eulenburg's arguments. 'When they left', the Kaiser's friend recalled, 'the Kaiser seemed calmer, but looked miserable – pale and biting his lip nervously. I felt terribly sorry for him. Having arrived over here with all his great song and dance about ships he suddenly felt driven into a modest little corner, and politically shut out.'[63] Rosebery's 'hesitant conduct' in the crisis certainly restored peace, but the 'diplomatic defeat' which Great Britain had suffered, in the Kaiser's eyes, shook his confidence in the Liberal Foreign Secretary who was soon to become Prime Minister. 'The unpleasant result', Prince Hohenlohe commented, 'is that in India the English now have France nearby, as well as Russia as a neighbour.'[64] Throughout the world as well as at home the British Empire was in crisis, the young diplomat wrote. 'One cannot resist taking a certain malicious pleasure in this. But it would of course be fatal if this became the source of a world conflagration.'[65]

Partly because Hatzfeldt fell ill, and partly because of Rosebery's cool nature, the Siam crisis did not lead to the close Anglo-German co-operation for which the Kaiser had hoped, and he left the British Foreign Secretary in no doubt of his dissatisfaction over this. When Hatzfeldt reported a conversation with Rosebery in November 1893, in which the latter stated that he had urged on the Cabinet the importance of increasing the navy and that with the prospect of serious complications arising, he would seek the support of Germany and its allies, Wilhelm took the entire credit for this apparent change in British foreign policy, writing on the report from London: 'The sudden new about-turn by Rosebery, which astonishes Hatzfeldt, reverting to complete openness and confidential consultation with us, stems from my initiative. I found a safe opportunity of sending a message to Rosebery telling him bluntly that I would not tolerate this game of hide-and-seek with me any longer and that if he still valued My friendship and affection at all and hoped for support from us, he must return to the old relationship of complete honesty. Otherwise I would not be prepared to talk to him again. It seems to have worked.'[66]

The extent to which the Kaiser regarded himself as a silent ally of Great Britain against the Franco-Russian alliance becomes clear from his critical remarks about the weakness of the Royal Navy in the Mediterranean. When the newly appointed German ambassador in St Petersburg, General von Werder, reported that the

Russians had sent five warships to Toulon which would remain in the area for a year, the Kaiser saw this as a threat to British supremacy in the Mediterranean and not, as in fact was the intention of Russia and France, as an action directed against Germany.[67] Wilhelm expressed his concern in a comment on Werder's report: 'This reinforcement will be welcome to France and brings the number of anti-English battleships up to 19. A raid on the Dardanelles is only a matter of time now.'[68] Four months later he passed on to the British ambassador secret information that a Russian general, who had recently been with Tsar Alexander at Fredensborg, had indicated that the Russian ships now in the Mediterranean were heading for Alexandretta (the present Turkish port of Iskenderun). As Russia's access to Constantinople through the Balkans was blocked, it had to create a route southwards through Asia Minor for itself, the Kaiser declared. When Malet observed that Cyprus might therefore prove itself useful at last, the Kaiser responded: 'Yes . . . if you have got the ships. I am convinced France is working for a triple alliance in the Mediterranean and trying to induce Spain to join it by promise of help towards the recovery of Gibraltar. You must be very wary as to what is passing in Morocco.'[69] In communicating information of this kind Wilhelm cherished hopes of deepening the opposition between Britain and France and driving a wedge between France and Russia. Similarly, Waldersee calculated at this juncture that 'the stronger France feels in the Mediterranean, the more she will strive for sole supremacy there, which will bring her into conflict with England at first – which can only be to our advantage – and later also with Russia, as soon as she rules over Constantinople'.[70]

## THE KAISER'S 'THIRST FOR UNIFORMS'

Kaiser Wilhelm II's inner attachment to Britain and his British relations often showed itself in ceremonial forms, as for instance when he wrote to his grandmother on 12 January 1894 asking permission to appoint his uncle Albert Edward, Prince of Wales, à la suite of the German Dragoon Regiment of which he had made the Queen colonel-in-chief. 'My passion since my early days for H.M. Redcoats & their history', he wrote, 'has always been a very warm one; the more so as they so often fought side by side with our soldiers! This puts into my mind wether [sic] You, as 'Chef' of our Dragoon Guards, would allow me to place Uncle Bertie à la suite of Your Regiment on my birthday. This day beeing [sic] the 25th anniversary of my entry into the I Regiment of the Guards & as such, a list of military honours is to be issued on the 27th, & it would give me great pleasure as well as be a great honour to the Regiment. Father & son would then both be in Your "Queens Own Regiment".'[71] The intention behind this imperial initiative was no secret to the British military attaché Colonel

and even pointed out that the first five or six years which Wilhelm had spent in the army in his teens could hardly count as 'service'.[83] At the same time Ponsonby wrote on the Queen's behalf to Knollys, the Duke of Cambridge and Lord Rosebery, explaining 'that it would be impossible at the present time when there is no special reason to confer the highest military rank upon the Emperor'.[84] The Prince of Wales was furious and ordered his luckless Private Secretary to telegraph to the Queen that he very deeply regretted her decision and only wished that he had not been drawn into this unfortunate affair.[85] In a letter he added that the ministers who had advised against granting the distinction were less competent in such questions than himself, the Prince of Wales. The opinion of the Commander-in-Chief ought to have been taken into account as well. In his view neither Rosebery nor Campbell-Bannerman was 'infallible'; both were talking 'rank nonsense when they say that because the Queen makes Her grandson, who is likewise half an Englishman, a Field Marshal She must give other Sovereigns who are no relations the same rank'. The decision was even more painful to him because Wilhelm had just sent him his new Prussian uniform by a special envoy.[86]

Victoria was shaken by the strength of her son's obstinate reaction to her decision. In stark contrast to Wilhelm's attitude to his constitutional advisers the Queen pointed out that she was obliged to accept the advice of her responsible ministers.[87] The Duke of Cambridge likewise expressed his regret at the Queen's decision. Swaine, he said, would not have made his suggestion if he had not received a hint from the highest quarters that the Kaiser wished to wear British uniform on his visits to Britain. As Wilhelm was already an admiral there would be no difficulty about making him a field marshal too. By conferring regiments and uniforms on members of the British royal family the Kaiser had demonstrated his attachment to his grandmother and his uncles; he, the Duke, could not understand why his courtesies had not been answered by the simple gesture of conferring the uniform upon him, when it obviously meant so much to him.[88] Even the former Prime Minister Lord Salisbury spoke out in favour of conferring the distinction on Wilhelm. 'If present Foreign Policy is to keep well with Germany the grant would be wise for personal considerations weigh heavily', he commented.[89]

Although Queen Victoria had got her way, her ill-feeling towards Wilhelm was still unmistakable weeks later. After a visit to court in March 1894 Prince Hohenlohe reported to his father: 'The Queen's expression seemed rather stern when I conveyed the Kaiser's greetings to her, and she did not say a word in reply. Has something happened there again?'[90] In fact neither the Prince of Wales nor the Duke of Cambridge had given up the campaign on the Kaiser's behalf and Rosebery, who had meanwhile succeeded Gladstone as prime minister, felt compelled to strengthen his case against the grant of the distinction. This time he pointed out that, if in addition to his admiral's rank the Kaiser were also made a field marshal, there would be nothing left to give him in the future. Rosebery feared 'that it will simply leave the German Emperor unsatiated while yet young', which could have an undesirable effect, for 'so marked an additional honour should only be given at a time when it is necessary to display either signal gratitude or signal friendship. Now there is at the present moment no necessity for the display of any extraordinary friendship, still less for the demonstration of any extraordinary gratitude.'[91]

In spite of all this, however, Queen Victoria eventually felt obliged to fulfil her grandson's original and dearest wish: on the occasion of the marriage of her grandson Ernst Ludwig, Grand Duke of Hesse Darmstadt, at Coburg on 21 April 1894 she appointed Kaiser Wilhelm II colonel-in-chief of the 1st Royal Dragoons, a cavalry regiment.[92] He sent ecstatic thanks for this exceptional distinction – it was the first time in British military history that a foreign sovereign had appeared in the Army List – writing to her from the Wartburg: 'The kindness & love with which You have treated me have quite overwhelmed me! I am afraid that under the impression of the so unexpected & joyful surprize You prepared for me, I did not find the right words to express my feelings. Deeply & sincerely do I thank You for the great honour which You conferred upon me by making me hon. Colonel of the Royals. I am moved, deeply moved at the idea that I now too can wear beside the naval uniform the traditional British "Red Coat". How many brave & brillant [sic] soldiers have worn it & before all my beloved Grandpapa! The congratulations I receive from all parts show me, how much this token of Your kindness is valued here, & how glad they are here that the bonds of friendship between our countries & armies have received a new addition. I shall be very happy to wear the uniform of a so distinguished & brave Regiment, & am impatiently looking forward to the moment when I can meet my brother officers.'[93]

When a deputation from the regiment arrived in Berlin in June 1894 to present itself to the Kaiser he telegraphed enthusiastically to his grandmother that he had found the detachment quite exemplary. 'We are very glad to see the Officers of the Royals as our Brothers in Arms in our midst.'[94] In a speech which was reported with satisfaction in the British press Wilhelm declared how proud he was to be Colonel-in-Chief of the regiment. 'I have thus become a member of the body of British officers, and a tie, which has for a long series of years united the British and Prussian Armies is thus bound anew.'[95] At a musical evening in the Neues Palais on 10 June attended by the British deputation the Kaiser wore the new red Dragoons uniform and his composition, 'Song to Ägir', was given its first performance.[96] Swaine was delighted with the warmth of the reception given

23. Kaiser Wilhelm II in the uniform of the First Royal Dragoons, Aldershot 1894

the British officers.[97] Kiel Week then provided a further opportunity for demonstrations of Anglo-German friendship. The new relationship was overshadowed only a little by an initiative taken by Rosebery on the Congo question, which was condemned in Berlin as shameless; the Kaiser, it was reported, was 'particularly resentful' because he suspected 'that Lord Rosebery assumed that as the Queen's grandson He would not put up a fight'.[98]

When the great white and gold yacht *Hohenzollern*, bedecked with the German national flag, the Kaiser's personal standard and the white flag of the Royal Yacht Squadron, once again moored at Cowes in August of that year for the annual regatta, the Kaiser was wearing the uniform of the 1st Royal Dragoons.[99] He was at first disappointed that no detachment of the regiment had appeared to welcome him, but no one had thought to remind the Royals that the Kaiser was now their Colonel-in-Chief.[100] Nonetheless before returning to Germany Wilhelm, accompanied by his retinue – Adjutant-General von Plessen and the Flügeladjutanten Count Kuno von Moltke, Count Arnim and Major von Scholl – inspected his regiment at Aldershot and led it in a march-past before his uncle Prince Arthur, Duke of Connaught. 'The sight of these fine troops under his command is never to be forgotten', he telegraphed enthusiastically to the Queen.[101]

One cannot doubt the genuineness of his gratitude to his grandmother nor the honesty of his sense of belonging to the British royal family and the British army, expressed in his letter to the Queen of 24 August 1894. 'Most beloved Grandmama', he wrote from the Neues Palais, 'Your great kindness to me & all my gentlemen has left us all full of the most agreeable & indelible souvenirs. The stay at Cowes was enhanced by the dinners at dear old Osborne which I so adore, & which my entourage has come to love as much as I do; fascinated by the kind & benevolent "acceuil" [sic] of the much revered Queen. The [Cowes] "Week" is my real holiday & I must with all my heart thank You for the kind & warm reception which I met at Your hands. I hope & trust that next year – should it please Providence that we all be well – I will be able to bear home that only trophy I really covet, & I work for through the whole of the year "Her Majesty's Cup". Aldershot was a great success & all the arrangements for our stay at the pavilion were perfect. What a delightful place that is, how splendid the view & the air so bracing! Uncle Arthur was attention itself & managed the Military affairs in a first rate manner. The review was a lovely sight & my officers who never had seen a British parade before were deeply impressed by it. I am glad to say the Squadron of the Royals which You so kindly ordered over for me looked splendid & won an all round applause. The field day was very attractive & showed the brilliant marching qualities as also of endurance of the troops who were well handled. It gave me a great pleasure to be able to associate with so many nice comrades in arms & to think that I was looked upon as one of their own, belonging to "the thin Red Line" of England too!'[102]

## THE POLISH QUESTION AND THE RUSSIAN TRADE TREATY

Farcical as the Kaiser's search for colourful uniforms may seem to us, Wilhelm II's personal initiatives in foreign policy undoubtedly had their serious side even in these early years. His hopes for Britain's support in a possible military conflict with Russia and France were fanned by his private correspondence with the American friend of his youth, Poultney Bigelow, whom Hinzpeter angrily accused in early 1893 of having talked the Kaiser into believing he was a second Alexander the Great, destined to conquer the East.[103] Bigelow was a strict Protestant, an anti-Semite and an enemy of Russia, who referred to the present as the 'ante bellum' – the pre-war time – and who used his widely read books and articles (he had just published his book *The German Emperor and His Eastern Neighbours*) to pursue the goal of inciting the Americans and the British to make common cause with Germany in a war against Russia, by appealing to their shared Protestantism.[104] On 18 August 1892 he wrote to the Kaiser: 'Your English visit I see added much to your popularity there, particularly the manly way in which you measured yourself with them [at sailing] . . . No Prime Minister can unmake alliances that are founded in mutual personal admiration; & whether Gladstone rules or Salisbury I fancy that no Government there can do much to stem the popular tide that runs against Russia . . . It is only necessary to make the British Public understand that Russia's movements are, not merely hostile to Austria & Germany, but to her own mercantile interests.'[105] Bigelow passed on alarming news to the Kaiser to the effect that Russia was keeping only one army division east of Moscow, while all the others were stationed between that city and Russia's border with Germany and Austria.[106] He also stated that he was in close contact with the Russian exiles Volkovsky and Stepniak, who published the periodical *Free Russia* in London and whose only fault in his eyes was that they considered the German Emperor as a new Bonaparte who was intent only on increasing his own power. He suggested to the Kaiser – and this was 1892, not 1917 – that Germany should secretly infiltrate this anarchist movement and place skilful agents in Königsberg, Thorn, Cracow and Brodnica with the aim of working for the liberation of Poland and the reannexation of Russia's Baltic provinces to the Reich.[107] It was possible that Bigelow himself would soon be travelling to the Baltic, but first he was awaiting the visit of a Polish friend who would bring him important information from Warsaw.[108]

The alarming effect which the American millionaire's exhortations had on Wilhelm II became apparent not only in the latter's correspondence with Queen Victoria, as we saw earlier,[109] but also in a conversation with his friend Philipp Eulenburg during the Scandinavian cruise of July 1892. At Tromsø the Kaiser, who prided himself on having acted in this delicate question without the knowledge of his Foreign Office, confided to Eulenburg his hopes of a forthcoming union of Russian Poland with Germany. He boasted that he had good reason to be pro-Polish. 'Having already secretly learnt that the mood in Posen and Russian Poland has swung round entirely in my favour, remarkable revelations reached

me through the American Bigelow, my old friend from my youth and student
days, from Warsaw where he was carrying out studies for a book commissioned
by his government. When he was admitted to some of the Polish clubs which
have sprung up under the agonizing pressure of Russian domination and which
he was able to enter through confidential contacts, he discovered to his astonishment that all the interest, all the hopes of the Poles are directed towards me,
that every sitting begins with a toast to me. They are full of hope for liberation
from the Russian yoke, and in a war with Russia all Poland would range itself on
my side with the express intention of being annexed by *me*.' The Kaiser denied
that the motive behind the Polish freedom movement was the establishment of
an independent Polish empire. The educated elements had given up this hope
in view of their political weakness, he claimed. 'They want to come under *Prussia*. Bigelow writes confirming this in a way that leaves *no room for doubt*. If
necessary Poland could of course be made into a province of the Reich. Alsace
and Lorraine have been kept in good order as such. I have *not* passed Bigelow's
interesting communications to the Foreign Office. The Polish question would be
taken under their political wing, so to speak – and I am considering the matter
for the time being from a purely *military* standpoint. For the General Staff and
the deployment of the army it is a very great gain to have Poland on our side.' A
General Staff officer had recently travelled to Poland, the Kaiser confided, and
had found Bigelow's information confirmed to the letter. Even if a few Poles
were still working for national independence that was 'cura posterior' (a concern
for the future), Wilhelm opined. '*For the time being I* am their goal, and we must
remember that.'[110]

   The hopes that Wilhelm cherished of a Polish uprising on the outbreak of war
between Russia and Germany had a direct effect on both domestic and foreign
policy. In 1893 he conferred an order on the leader of the Polish party in the
Reichstag, Joseph von Koscielski and held up the Poles as models of Prussian
loyalty.[111] Waldersee watched with consternation as this policy, disastrous in his
eyes, took its course. When he was told in confidence by the pro-government
editor of the *Hamburger Korrespondent* 'that everything has been arranged by
us in such a way that in the event of a war with Russia an insurrection would
break out throughout Poland!!', the former Chief of the General Staff could not
believe his ears and wrote scornfully: 'With such simpletons as we now have in
charge of our diplomacy I am afraid it is not impossible that such nonsense is
believed.'[112] He foresaw with deep concern that 'there is scarcely any sphere in
which the Kaiser will have to face worse disappointments than in this'. It would
be impossible to satisfy the Poles, who naturally aspired towards an independent
state. Only if there were a firm intention of waging war against Russia could

the former Chief of the General Staff see any benefit in the Kaiser's Polish
policy. 'If it were the case that we definitely intended to wage war at a given
time, and to make use of the Poles, I should certainly be in favour of making
careful preparations for our strike', he wrote in October 1893, 'but not in such
a misguided way as now.'[113] The present German policy towards Poland 'would
make sense only if we wanted to launch an attack in the spring, which of course
we have no intention of doing'.[114]

The secret contacts which the German General Staff made with the anti-
Russian nationalists in Russian Poland on the orders of the Kaiser did not remain
secret for long and proved very inconvenient when the Kaiser and the Wilhelmstrasse were forced to concede, in the autumn of 1893, that the hopes they
had cherished since 1890 of an alliance with Great Britain had foundered on
the island kingdom's 'Splendid Isolation', and that a new rapprochement with
Russia would therefore be desirable. Waldersee, who as we have seen was well
informed about the subversive activities of the General Staff in Russian Poland,
was in no doubt about the damaging effect of this on German–Russian relations.
'Insurrection in the kingdom [sic] has been discussed in the most irresponsible
way with influential Poles, and all kinds of promises have been made to them.
All this has been closely watched in Russia and of course as a result their mistrust
of us has increased and their garrisons have been strengthened.'[115] 'The final
result can only be that we shall make a lasting enemy of Russia without satisfying the Poles', he predicted.[116] In the quest for improved relations with Russia
Wilhelm II himself seemed to grasp that through his secret contacts with the
Polish independence movement he had succeeded only in arousing suspicion in
St Petersburg. At all events, in Thorn on 22 September 1894 he made a speech
which struck a completely different note. He now declared unequivocally that
the Polish fellow citizens of this West Prussian town 'may count on my favour and
support . . . but only if they truly feel themselves to be Prussian subjects . . . For
only if we stand together shoulder to shoulder like a phalanx is it possible to
bring the struggle with subversion to a triumphant end.' In words not designed
to encourage the Poles on the other side of the Russian border to throw in their
lot with Prussia he threatened: 'I can also be very unpleasant, and if it is required,
that is what I shall be.'[117] It was not until the First World War that plans for
fomenting revolution in Russian Poland (and elsewhere) were revived.

Wilhelm II pinned his hopes for better relations with Russia chiefly on his
personal relationship with the heir to the throne, Tsarevich Nicholas, who despite
the coolness and reserve he had shown hitherto, accepted an invitation to the
wedding of the Kaiser's youngest sister Margarethe (Mossy) and Prince Friedrich
Karl of Hesse-Kassel (Fischy) in Berlin in January 1893.[118] On 26 January the

Kaiser visited the barracks of the Tsar Alexander Regiment of Grenadier Guards with the Tsarevich, and proposed a cordial toast in the officers' mess to the latter's father, which was intended both as a gesture of personal friendship and as 'a serious appeal for the union of monarchies against revolution'.[119] Raising his glass, he declared 'All of us see in Your Imperial Father not only the exalted Chief of the Regiment, not only our most distinguished comrade, but above all the upholder of long-lasting monarchical tradition, of tried and tested friendship and of the inner bonds forged by close links with my illustrious predecessors, sealed in former times with the blood of both Russian and Prussian regiments on the battlefield before the enemy.'[120] As the Kaiser reported to his grandmother, he had the opportunity to talk at length to the Tsarevich, who only a few months later was to assume absolute sovereignty over the gigantic Russian Empire. 'Niki' had shown 'sound judgement & a quiet clear mind', and had proved that he 'understands European questions much better than most of his countrymen & family; I hope that on the whole his visit will have a good effect on our relations in general.'[121] In a letter to Kaiser Franz Joseph, Wilhelm summed up the main points of his discussions with the future Tsar, whom he expected to bring about a shift in Russian policy away from France and towards the Triple Alliance. 'Far from having aggressive tendencies, the Triple Alliance had purely defensive aims in view', Wilhelm assured the Tsarevich. 'When the treaty was concluded the powers had in mind the grave dangers which threatened the monarchies from France, through the dissemination of republican propaganda. It was after all chiefly from Paris that all revolutionary doctrines were being spread, the aim of which was to undermine monarchical traditions in all countries in all manner of [missing word]. These common dangers were therefore to be seen primarily as the basis of the Alliance, and any power that wished to defend the interests of peace and of monarchy in the same way could join this Alliance at any time. The common interests of the three Allied powers were, however, by no means limited to the political sphere. The Triple Alliance sought to bring the European powers closer to each other in the economic sphere as well, through trade treaties. In so doing it aimed both to reduce the causes of friction between European states and also, above all, to counteract the danger which threatened the entire trade of Europe, in that the republic of North America was proving increasingly inclined to snatch for itself the entire trade of South America as well.' Nicholas had listened to these observations with interest, Wilhelm reported to Vienna, and had shown 'a pronounced aversion towards France'. At his request he had given him 'the above-mentioned "aphorisms" on politics in writing as an aide-mémoire, as he wanted to report the contents to his father in minute detail', the Kaiser wrote. 'If I should have succeeded, by what I said, in removing

some of the Tsar's suspicion of the Triple Alliance, and in proving its usefulness
for the monarchical principle, I should be very glad. I may add that both the
King of Saxony and the Grand Duke of Baden have had long conversations of
similar import with the Tsarevich, which will certainly not have failed to make
an impression on him. Much will depend on whether he manages to use the
information he has gathered in an appropriate way vis-à-vis his father. May he
succeed, for the good of all concerned.'[122] These declarations once again show
the hegemonial aims which lay at the heart of the foreign policy pursued by
Kaiser Wilhelm, however inconsistent the individual initiatives might appear to
be.[123]

The visit to Berlin by the heir to the Russian throne was in fact to have
momentous consequences, for during the marriage festivities Nicholas fell in
love with the Kaiser's Hessian cousin Alix, whose sister Ella had been the great
love of Wilhelm's youth, and whose other sister Irène was married to his brother
Heinrich. In April the following year, when the young Grand Duke Ernst Ludwig
of Hesse and by Rhine, brother of the Darmstadt princesses, married Princess
Viktoria Melitta of Saxe-Coburg and Gotha, it was Kaiser Wilhelm himself who
succeeded in overcoming the religious scruples of his Hessian cousin, which she
had hitherto seen as an obstacle to marriage with the Tsarevich. At Coburg she
agreed to marry Nicholas. As the Kaiser's eldest sister Charlotte recorded in a
letter, this success put her two brothers Wilhelm and Heinrich 'in bounding
spirits: the Emperor specially, after he had brought the Russian engagement on
of my cousin Alix: they look nice & happy & may her future remain so: certainly
outwardly it is a grand partie & match, but upon close & nearby reflexion, not
an enviable position'.[124] Queen Victoria too had mixed feelings at the thought
that her favourite granddaughter would soon be living so far away from her. 'I
grieve to see her also carried off so far away', she wrote to the Kaiser.[125] Wilhelm,
however, pinned great political hopes on his new connection with Nicholas, who
had 'Germany on his mind!' and with whom he had 'priority' because 'I made
the match for him!'[126]

In his public speeches likewise Wilhelm II adopted a tone towards Russia that
had rarely been heard from him since the fall of Bismarck. In February 1894 he
declared in an address to the officers of the First Regiment of Guards that 'he saw
himself as guardian of the peace of Europe and had from his youth learned to
see this as his role'. Waldersee was surprised, recalling the 'completely different
tone' of earlier utterances in which Wilhelm had announced that he wanted 'to
smash the French and the Russians and parade into Berlin etc. . . . What kind of
feelings must the Kaiser have if he ever allows himself an hour of calm reflection
and remembers everything he has wanted and said! We must be prepared for
many more sudden shifts and about-turns.'[127]

The corner-stone of the policy of rapprochement with Russia which the German leadership was pursuing, in ignorance of the fact that after lengthy negotiations in December 1893 Russia and France had undertaken to give each other military support in the event of a German attack, was the trade treaty, which held considerable advantages for Germany's eastern neighbour and which was eventually accepted after bitter political argument by the Reichstag in March 1894.[128] Wilhelm II had great expectations of the Russian trade treaty, which he described as 'one of the greatest achievements ever attained for Prussia and Germany'. He hoped it would both improve German–Russian relations and turn Russia against the French Republic. Echoing the 'fundamental idea' he had expressed in July 1892 and again in January 1893 of Germany's 'Napoleonic' domination in Europe, he announced at a Crown Council held in the Berlin Schloss on 18 February 1894: 'Our supremacy is to be demonstrated to Europe not only by our army but also through our trade policy, and a customs union of European nations is to be considered the goal of our future development, in order to be able to take up the economic struggle with North America.' The latter country was seeking 'to push us out of our principal market, South America, by establishing itself there through pacts with democratic movements. The rebellion in Chile was led by North American envoys, and now they are playing the same game in Brazil.' While the USA was playing the democratic card in this way, the conclusion of the trade treaty with Russia, so important for Germany and Europe, had been 'of decisive significance for the relationship between the two dynasties', the Kaiser declared. It was his belief that the moment at which Russia showed Germany its willingness to co-operate on trade policy had been 'the moment when His Majesty the Tsar of Russia, returning from Denmark, had realised the sad state of Russian agriculture and had given the order for the conclusion of the treaty to be proceeded with in earnest'. Wilhelm welcomed the conclusion of the treaty 'with all my heart' and emphasised that 'a good political relationship between nations whose economic relations are bad cannot last long'. He expressed his hope to the ministers of state that the trade treaty would bring about a 'strengthening of relations between Russia and Germany and [a] loosening of those between Russia and France'.[129] These ambitious international expectations explain the Kaiser's determination to push through the trade treaty despite the virulent opposition of the East Elbian agrarians and his angry outburst of February 1894, quoted earlier, that he had no desire 'to wage war with Russia for the sake of 100 stupid Junkers'.[130]

For an anti-Russian hothead like Waldersee, Wilhelm's swing towards Russia was incomprehensible. He reacted with scorn to the Kaiser's assertion that the rejection of the trade treaty by the Reichstag would lead to war with Russia 'in 3 months at the latest', and that in the course of it he would have to surrender the right bank of the Vistula. 'So the Kaiser has reached the point not only of being afraid of the Russians – I have long known that – but also of admitting it openly', he wrote mockingly in his diary. 'He thinks he can maintain peace by giving in, and he will achieve the opposite. How cocksure the Russians must feel when they hear that we are afraid of them, that we are prepared to give up provinces without a fight; I am convinced that it brings us closer to war. What are our people to think when they hear such ideas from the Kaiser, when they were assured only six months ago that once the Army Bill was passed we would be equal to any enemy.' According to what the Kaiser had said, which had been telegraphed all over the country, it must be clear to everyone 'that Russia has us entirely in her power', the General feared. 'As soon as the Tsar makes a threat, we give in! That must lead to a setback, such a state of affairs is demeaning. What jubilation there will be in France.'[131] 'This is the Kaiser who smashes everything!', Waldersee exclaimed in disgust some days later. 'The German Reich was so great and so much feared only a few years ago, and abroad too, especially in Russia, people felt that Kaiser Wilhelm II was an extraordinarily energetic man and that one must be prepared for him to be very quick to draw his sword; people were really afraid of him and that was a great guarantee of peace. That is all over now.'[132]

The news that Alexander III was seriously ill with Bright's disease, which reached the Kaiser on his return from England in mid-August 1894, revived his fear that the weakness of the Tsar might be exploited by the Slavophile military leadership of Russia to begin major redeployments of troops against Germany. As the support of Britain seemed more essential than ever in this situation, it was certainly not by chance that Wilhelm passed on details of the threatening development on his eastern frontier to his grandmother. In spite of the serious cholera epidemic in Western Russia and Poland the Russians were in the process of setting up three new army corps on the German–Russian border and were moving one or even two divisions from the Caucasus to Poland, he wrote to her on 24 August 1894. 'The rest of the Army is beeing [sic] moved up into closer formations & quarters, so that by next summer I shall have 10 Corps & 8 Cavalry divisions on my frontier. An outlook we think rather serious as we only have 5 Corps & 1 Cavalry Division to dispose of. We fancy that they want to strike an unexpected blow in the East, & to keep us from helping anybody they are going to attack, they have marschalled [sic] the enormous forces on our frontier. This state of affairs with an ill if not half dying Emperor unable to control the Slavophile party is rather ticklish & we must with great care & attention observe what is going on at Petersburg.'[133] It was not until his friend Nicky succeeded to the throne in October and immediately afterwards married Wilhelm's cousin Alix, who bore the name Alexandra following her reception into the Russian Orthodox church, that there seemed to be any prospect of a new era in Russo-German relations.

## WILHELM II AND FRANCE

The relatively peace-loving phase which the Kaiser can be seen to have gone through in 1893–4 had its effect even on his attitude towards France. As the co-operation between Russia and France became increasingly visible and was publicly and enthusiastically celebrated in both countries (in Kronstadt, Nancy and Toulon), the danger of a French war of revenge with Russian support loomed distinctly larger. Wilhelm reacted to this threat by alternating between conciliatory signals on the one hand and aggressively menacing gestures on the other. Thus when the former President of the Third Republic, the Comte de MacMahon, died on 17 October 1893, he ordered a wreath to be laid on the coffin, which Waldersee predictably saw as another sign of weakness. The 'hatred of the French for us' was as strong as ever, he considered, and their 'intention of seeking revenge in the end' was 'unalterably fixed'. The Kaiser, on the other hand, was 'only too ready to believe what he hopes'; by having the wreath laid on MacMahon's coffin he thought he would be able to accomplish 'moral victory', but this was 'a complete misunderstanding of the French character'. In the opinion of the former Chief of the General Staff, 'with Russians as with the French one must show one's strength and let them see that one is not afraid of them'.[134] Only a few weeks later in a telegram to Philipp Eulenburg Wilhelm gave vent to his feelings about a failed French assassination attempt against him and the Reich Chancellor. The 'Gallic blackguards', he declared, had 'sent Caprivi and me a time bomb each. Toulon-Paris has made them cocky. Likewise the incredible utterances of kleindeutsch particularism which is showing its ugly face everywhere. This is the result! But God has prevented it and I thank Him for the preservation of our good Caprivi! But these days it is doubly necessary for all Germans to rally round the banner of the Kaiser and the Reich! He who fails to do so is an enemy, and woe to him who wishes to be my enemy! Wilhelm I. R.'[135]

When the French President Sadi Carnot was stabbed to death by the Italian anarchist Caserio in Lyon on 24 June 1894 Wilhelm sent a telegram of condolence to the widow of the murdered politician which caused universal astonishment, especially in France, where the Kaiser had long been seen as the arch-enemy. In a sycophantic letter which Wilhelm proudly forwarded to Caprivi, Hinzpeter congratulated him on this apparently wondrous change in German policy towards France. The former tutor wrote: 'How far Your Majesty's telegram to Mme Carnot was combined with a political purpose I cannot of course know. But my

French correspondence shows so clearly that it has achieved such a purpose that I am taking the liberty of drawing attention to it. This correspondence fairly well represents the average ideas and attitudes of the French and comes from the same people who told me as their firm opinion, not very long ago, that Kaiser Wilhelm II had only one purpose in life, which was to destroy France and that he spent his days searching for an opportunity to achieve this. This conviction may have been shaken by other things, but by nothing so much as this telegram. This has transformed the picture they have of the Kaiser.'[136]

The impression initially created that the Kaiser wished to bring about a shift towards France in German policy was, however, an illusion. Wilhelm did indeed pardon two French officers who had been condemned to long prison sentences for espionage, and personally ensured that the pardon was announced on the same day as Carnot's funeral. Nonetheless he did so only in response to a request from the French ambassador, Jules Herbette, who had gone to Kiel to thank the Kaiser for the message of condolence to Carnot's widow; he had no thought of changing the direction of German foreign policy.[137] This is borne out by a conversation between Waldersee and Verdy at the Swiss resort of Engelberg in the summer of 1894, in the course of which the former Minister of War, who had continued to maintain close contacts with Schlieffen, told the latter's predecessor of the new requirements that the Kaiser had laid down for waging war in the West and in the East. 'The Kaiser wants to take the offensive against France at once and has therefore weakened the Eastern army by 2–3 corps!', Waldersee indignantly recorded after hearing Verdy's information. 'He is doing exactly what the French hope and what they have prepared for. We shall be throwing ourselves at the positions they have reinforced with permanent fortifications and we all have every prospect of being sent back with bloody heads.' During his time as Chief of the General Staff Waldersee had planned to entice the French forward and then to counterattack them; by using such tactics, he believed, there was a good prospect of breaking through the French line of fortifications, but not by the Kaiser's offensive strategy. 'In my opinion Schlieffen ought to be prepared to sacrifice his post to prevent the Kaiser from carrying out his immature ideas', he wrote.[138] When Waldersee met the Grand Duke of Baden on the island of Mainau not long afterwards, the latter was also surprised to hear of the Kaiser's intention 'to go on the offensive from Lorraine at an early stage'. Grand Duke Friedrich had thought that 'my proposals, which also had Schlieffen's approval, still held good', the General noted. 'I could only tell him that Schlieffen's views had certainly remained the same, but that he has given way to the will of the Kaiser. The great danger that we incur in this way was perfectly plain to the Grand Duke.'[139]

Waldersee, Verdy and the Grand Duke of Baden were by no means the only ones who felt profoundly unsettled by the manner — mercurial, ill-considered and emotionally charged but always imperious and intolerant of any opposition — in which Wilhelm II intervened in every aspect of domestic, foreign and military policy. Shortly after his accession, and particularly after Bismarck's dismissal, the conviction was spreading that this irresponsible manner of ruling the country could easily lead to the collapse of the Prusso-German monarchy and the end of the German Reich.

# CHAPTER NINETEEN

# The rude awakening

A T the time of the young Kaiser's accession in 1888, the prevailing mood almost everywhere was favourable, sometimes even enthusiastic. To compare this with the growing sense of foreboding which was perceptible only a few years later in leading political circles, at all levels of society and in every region of the Reich as well as abroad, is to gain some idea of the damage which Wilhelm II, over a very short period, had succeeded in inflicting on the standing of the Hohenzollern monarchy. The hectic round of state visits on which he had embarked immediately after the death of his father, the fall of the Bismarcks followed by the dismissal of several ministers of the old school, the removal from the imperial entourage of Oberhofmarschall von Liebenau and the older generals – Versen, Waldersee, Wittich and Wedel – all this had helped open the eyes of the world to the dangerously vulnerable position into which this inexperienced and unpredictable young monarch had manoeuvred himself. Even for those who knew nothing of the aggressive, often obscene tone which characterised the imperial entourage and who had not read the (hurriedly locked away) autocratic and insulting marginal comments written by the Kaiser on diplomatic reports, there could be no doubt that these changes in the leadership of both Prussia and the Reich, at the imperial court and in the army, were motivated by his desire to exercise a kind of personal autocracy. Indeed, Wilhelm himself gave notice of his wholly anachronistic ideas of divine right, personal rule and dynastic ancestor-worship in countless maxims, speeches and edicts which alarmed and horrified all who heard them. There was the motto, 'sic volo sic jubeo', which he inscribed on his portrait for the Minister of Ecclesiastical Affairs, Gustav von Gossler, the Golden Book of the city of Munich in which he wrote 'suprema lex regis voluntas', the speech of 20 February 1891 to the provincial diet of Brandenburg in which he railed against 'the spirit of disobedience' and called on the people to follow him blindly in the task 'which Heaven has laid upon me', the Düsseldorf speech of May 1891 in which he declared that there was only one ruler in the Reich, and that was himself, the imperial rescript of October 1891 on prostitution which none of the ministers had countersigned, the Brandenburg speech of February 1892 in which he challenged the 'dissatisfied grumblers' to shake 'the dust of Germany from their feet' and invited the people to follow him on the path traced out for them by God – who had 'taken endless trouble with . . . Our House' – to a great and glorious future, the address to the commanding generals in which he threatened to drive out the 'half-crazy Reichstag' if it continued to oppose him. All in all, there was certainly no lack of public indications of Wilhelm II's extraordinary quasi-absolutist conception of his role as kaiser and king. A hundred years after the French Revolution, in defiance of the democratic trends of his day and in an empire which was rapidly developing into the foremost industrial power in the world, he set out to exercise the kind of 'personal rule' to which Charles I, Louis XIV, Napoleon, the Russian tsars and the kings of Prussia in the pre-parliamentary era had aspired.

### THE LAMENTATIONS OF THE EMPRESS FREDERICK

No one who has read the first volume of this biography will be surprised to learn that in the eyes of the Kaiser's mother his words and deeds only confirmed the fears she had long harboured. As early as 15 March 1890, anticipating the disaster which was taking place that very morning in the Wilhelmstrasse, the Dowager Empress bewailed the lack of a firmly anchored constitutional structure in the Reich, as a result of which the entire decision-making authority in this powerful nation now rested in the hands of her impulsive son, 'How one does bless a constitution like the British one, when one sees a young man totally without knowledge & experience – playing the Despot, without anything to prevent him fr. running into danger or mischief', she wrote in distress to Queen Victoria. '*Not one* older man or older relation is there to give a little timely advice, to warn & to give a gentle hint – both in political & important matters, – or in *family* & *court* matters.'[1] A week later, after Bismarck's departure, she reflected: 'The *System* Bismark [sic] was intensely *corrupt* and *bad*, – *this* is however not the reason that W. wanted the change, & this he does not even see through. The genius & prestige of Pce B. might *still* have been useful & valuable for Germany & for the cause of *peace*, – *especially* with so inexperienced & imprudent a sovereign, – & I fear that he will be missed in that respect, as I *also* fear that the combination wh. is to replace him will *not* be strong enough! – W. fancies he can do every thing himself – *you know* he *cannot*. A little modesty and "Selbst Erkenntnis" [self-knowledge] wd. show him that he is *not* the genius

24. The Empress Frederick in 1900

or the "Frederick the Great" he imagines.' 'I fear he will get into trouble', she
added, especially because his 'love of playing the Despot & of showing off is
very great'.[2] On 25 March, after Prince and Princess Bismarck had called on
her to take their leave, the Empress wrote to her mother: 'I am afraid W. is a
most thorough despot & has some very queer ideas on this subject in his head.'[3]
Without Bismarck Wilhelm would behave like a tsar and cause a sensation by
ruling Germany by ukase, his mother predicted apprehensively. 'Everything
must be done in a hurry & be *startling*!! – & emanate or seem to emanate from
one source!'[4] Wilhelm was 'so unpredictable that one must always be prepared
for some completely unexpected coup!'[5] Like many other people she found
Wilhelm's fondness for pompous ceremonies both ridiculous and alarming. In
December 1890 she described the grand memorial parade with military bands
and cannon-fire which her son had organised in honour of the Great Elector,

and commented that she thought it very far-fetched, but 'W. does do the very oddest things, the element of show off, noise and "sensation", dramatic effects etc. is very preponderant, and in these serious times seems to me *very* youthful.'[6] The ministry that would suit Wilhelm best, she remarked sarcastically, would be composed of fantasists and eccentrics like Jules Verne, Richard Wagner, Lord Randolph Churchill, Lord Charles Beresford and a few bold African explorers. She had no doubt that her son would be reckless in whatever course he pursued, and the future filled her with anxiety.[7]

By the spring of 1891, a year after Bismarck's dismissal, the Kaiser had taken to proclaiming his ideas of absolute rule even more loudly than before. His mother predicted terrible catastrophe for the monarchy, Germany and the whole of Europe, writing to Freifrau von Stockmar: 'My son . . . enjoys his "power" to the full – the exercise of "personal rule", the satisfaction of every one of his caprices. – Everyone yields, everyone flatters and honours him and he is almost a megalomaniac. *Nowhere* can I see any *deeper, more serious* aspirations, nor any more spontaneous, nobler impulses – modesty, goodwill and piety.'[8] 'How frightful the speech in Düsseldorf was!', she exclaimed in another letter of May 1891.[9] And on the third anniversary of Wilhelm's accession she commented in a letter to Queen Victoria: 'It is indeed misfortune for us *all* that W. was called to the position he occupies so unprepared – (worse than unprepared) – imbued with prejudices, false notions & mistaken ideas; – that so *unripe* of character & judgement power was put into his hands, which alas he so often abuses! To me the grief is that he *might* have developed into something so much better if his dear Father could have been at the head of affairs for 20 or even 15 years.'[10] In December 1891 she reflected sadly: 'Oh *how* different all might be if that vile party who brought on 1848 & drove F[riedrich] W[ilhelm] IV off his head; – terrorized my Father in Law, & formed the body guard of Bismarkism [sic], broke Fritz's heart, and *destroyed* all the work of *our* Lives, took *entire* possession of our Son, *hunted* me & all *our* friends down, – did *not* exist!'[11]

In November 1891, after Wilhelm had promulgated his rescript on prostitution in the official *Reichsanzeiger* without ministerial countersignature, in Russian style, the Empress Frederick wrote perceptively to Queen Victoria: 'It is *so* unconstitutional and I do fear that if he thinks Germany can be governed by "Ukases" he will find out his mistake! – It is imprudent to *strain* the law and overstep the bounds of monarchical power & authority, in *our* days – in *Europe* – it will *not do*, – what it is doing in Russia where personal government is *daily* showing its worst side every one sees! – There cannot fail to be a Crash *there* some day.'[12] At the same time she lamented to Baroness Stockmar: 'I am quite beside myself over this "Declaration"! We *are* after all a constitutional country – if only very little, unfortunately – but *sadly* this seems not to have been taken

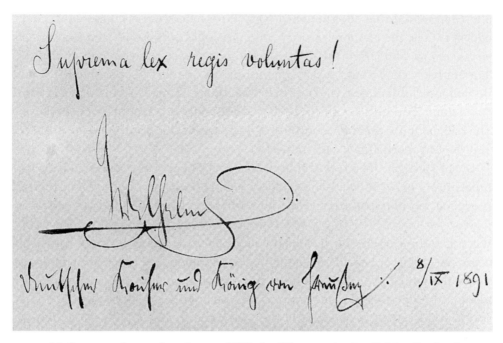

25. Suprema lex regis voluntas: Wilhelm II's entry in the Golden Book of
the City of Munich, 1891

into account at all on high, and the idea seems to be that one can and must
rule by "Ukases" – it is always the same deplorable trait that shows itself everywhere! "L'état c'est moi" – and it is – the *last* attempt at personal government
in Europe! I am only afraid that this "last attempt" will be a miserable failure –
for the time for such things is past, and I should be sorry if what could be useful
in certain circumstances in having authority and power, – were brought to an
end – because people refuse to accept the overstepping of that power.'[13] The
Empress's worst fears were realised only days later when it became known that
Wilhelm had written the absolutist dictum 'suprema lex regis voluntas' in the
Golden Book of the city of Munich. As she wrote to the Queen, 'I think he *can*
hardly understand *what* a bévue he is making when *he* writes such a thing!!! –
A Czar, an infallible Pope, the Bourbons and our poor Charles I might have
written such a sentence, – but a constitutional monarch in the 19th Century!! So
young a man, – the son of *his* father – & *your grandson* – not to speak of a child of
mine – should neither have nor express such a maxim!! It is like what he wrote
under his Picture to Min: Gossler in Spring, wh. caused so much comment!'[14]
When Wilhelm once again seized the opportunity to make a strong speech at
the swearing-in of recruits at the end of the year, his mother lamented: 'W. has
alas made a terrible new speech to the Recruits wh. is very freely criticised.'[15] A

week later she wrote again to the Queen: 'If I *had* a *shadow* of influence I should implore W. to make no speeches in public for they are too terrible & not to write into books & under photographs – it makes ones hair stand on end! Here at Berlin people are becoming accustomed to the *very* strange utterances etc . . . & think it a peculiar style to wh. it is well not to attach too great importance, it is put down to ignorance & childish impetuosity.'[16]

After the *'most imprudent'* second Brandenburg speech of February 1892 in which he promised to lead his people towards 'a glorious destiny', the Empress Frederick, aghast, commented that Wilhelm was playing 'a most dangerous game' in exercising his rule in so irresponsible a manner. 'Here am I condemned to sit here and look on, in silence, without being able to say *one word* in warning, and knowing that the hideous mistakes made may lead to terrible consequences . . . I now watch as from *a grave* . . . the reckless course pursued by my own son . . . *no one* sensible has *any* influence – *no* one about him *warns* or *gives* advice. The worst of it is that *we* shall perhaps all have to pay for *his* ignorance & imprudence.'[17] Again referring to this speech, she wrote to her second daughter Moretta in Bonn: 'Willy has made a great speech again, wh. rather distresses me! . . . In our days a nation like Germany will *not* be led by the *will* of one person, especially that of a young & inexperienced man. – That perhaps did in *Prussia* in the days of Fred. Will. I & of Fred. the Great, but those days are *past*. *Modern* Life is too complicated for a sovereign to be like the Chieftain of a Clan in the olden time – personal govt. is no more possible or desirable! I sadly fear your Brothers do not quite see or understand this, and I am often *so* troubled and anxious! It is what I feared & foresaw when beloved Papa was taken who understood his times. Caprivi, whom I honour & respect & trust in every way, is too much of a *soldier* to be a *statesman* such as is needed in such ticklish times!'[18] In a letter to her mother she reverted to her earlier simile of a hen that has hatched a duck's egg. 'I wish I could put a padlock on his mouth for all occasions where speeches are made in public', she lamented. 'The Bismark [sic] education & the School of the Emp: William's entourage have made him what he is – & *their* teaching brings us these results.' She disclaimed all responsibility for the way her son had developed. 'His dear Father & *I* are in no ways responsible for his extraordinary ideas! We were for *constitutional* Liberty, for *quiet steady* progress, for *unobtrusive but unobstructed* evolution, – for *individualism* & the development of *culture*. *Not* for Imperialism, Caesarism, State Socialism etc . . .!!'[19] Two days later, in another lamentation addressed to the Queen, she described Wilhelm as 'a source of constant anxiety to me!', adding that 'the pernicious influence of the Bismarks [sic], of *certain* military circles & Junkers have so filled his head with ideas wh. I consider most false and dangerous, and which he takes up with the conviction & naiveté, of ignorance and inexperience. – There is *no* one there to advise or counteract the baneful turn given to his opinions! What *will* it come to!! – He was *snatched* out of our hands, all our wise friends were put to silence! . . . I assure you I tremble for him with all his rashness and obstinacy etc . . . He is a big Baby. Henry & Bernhard understand politics *no better* than he does! Some of his Aide de Camps [sic] were beside themselves with *enthusiasm* about this speech, wh. quite brought the perspiration to my forehead when I read it!! The speech was – alas – *not* an ebullition of the moment, he had written it all *down before* & took it with him & made Oberpräsident v. Achenbach prompt him! I should have *refused* & told him that such a speech was *impossible*. Afterwards the Ministers tried to weed out all the expressions wh. were a *great* deal stronger still – and therefore the "Staatsanzeiger" in which it was printed in its present form appeared 3 hours later than usual! . . . It is too despairing to see people rushing headlong into mistakes & on *quite* the wrong tack – & not to be able to stop them. *All* those who are blind enough to hate constitutional liberty admire and applaud him, and all the orthodox set! Why is it they do not see that they are playing the game of socialism (as Pce Bismark was!!).'[20]

At the end of March 1892, after the funeral of her equally liberal-minded brother-in-law, Grand Duke Ludwig IV of Hesse and by Rhine, the fourth anniversary of her husband's accession as Kaiser and the second anniversary of Bismarck's dismissal, the Empress Frederick looked back forlornly over political developments in Berlin. Of Wilhelm and his latest Brandenburg speech she wrote to her mother: 'He will *not* admit that the speech was a mistake in any way – & thinks the criticisms all pure spite and wickedness, but *some* that were shown him have annoyed him – wh. everybody is *thankful* for, as heretofore they have made *no* impression whatsoever – and it is hope[d] this may stagger him a little and make him a little more prudent & careful! I myself do *not* think so, – he is *so* imbued with false ideas that it would want a *constant* & *daily* & *powerful* influence to open his eyes, *explain* things in their true light. He does not understand *what* a Constitution *is*! He does not know a single member of the Liberal Party, he never reads *one* of the really good sensible newspapers!! If he only had the same political instinct that dear Louis [Ludwig IV of Hesse] had!!'[21]

In May 1892 Wilhelm II aroused widespread criticism when he commended a grenadier who had opened fire on some loutish passers-by, killing one and wounding another, in a speech to the regiment and rewarded him with a signed photograph of himself. The Empress Frederick was horrified by this fresh display of tactlessness on the part of her son. '*What* must people think when the sovereign *praises* the soldier openly for firing on another man, just as much his subject & entitled to as much protection. It is one more of the many bévues that startle &

alarm me! – He makes himself terribly unpopular.'[22] When Queen Victoria also expressed horror at the favour shown by Wilhelm to the soldier, Vicky commented that the incident had reminded her of some of her son's earlier actions: the award of the Order of the Black Eagle to Puttkamer, whom his dying father had dismissed; the telegram to Treitschke, who had so vilely attacked his, Wilhelm's, parents; the public praise for Gustav Freytag's inflammatory book. All these actions led in the same dangerous direction. 'Will there *ever* be an awakening from these mistaken ideas?', she asked. 'All the flattery etc . . . have made them take a firm root in W.'s mind!'[23]

With the crisis over the School Bill and the ensuing political turmoil, the worst fears which the widowed Empress, as a powerless critic of the Bismarck system, had harboured for decades, seemed to be realised. In a heartbreaking Cassandra-like lament addressed to Bogumilla von Stockmar at the end of April 1892 she wrote, virtually anticipating the entire catastrophe of German history yet to come: 'What an utterly *abominable* and *despicable* piece of anti-Semitism that miserable Norddeutsche Zeitung and the Conservative Party have achieved again. It is really shaming! – In Prussia generally things which a sensible, cultivated people can scarcely tolerate in modern times are gaining the upper hand! *Personal government* is exercised "ad absurdum" and the Conservative Party is behaving in such a grotesque and impossible way that no one can take them *au sérieux* any more! – But the *consolation is to be found in this* too – and my hopes are rooted in it. Perhaps the present government will have the effect that people will at last see and learn *what* must be done in order to guard against all possible extravagances – and how our constitution *must* develop and be extended – to protect freedom – and to protect the monarchy too! – Perhaps the Bismark [sic] system will be followed by a rebirth of the constitution of the German Reich on *solid* foundations – on firm principles of constitutional freedom . . . The government *will* gradually *be obliged*, if it does not wish to be still further endangered, to help in building up a strong, healthy structure on a *broad* base, if Germany is not to slide further and further down into evil ways and into a republic or even a socialist state. The latter state could never last; there would be chaos – and then reaction – dictatorship and God knows what other ravages!' Switching into English she expressed her feelings about Wilhelm's conduct: 'For *me* it is *most bitter hard* and disappointing to see all the aspirations and aims of our Lives *defeated & brought to nought* – and *that* by the very one who, it *might* have been *hoped*, would have carried them on, if he had been allowed to come under the influence of his Parents & their friends – instead of having his mind wharped & his opinions poisoned by others.' She begged her friend to burn her letter, 'for *even now* one cannot tell one's best friends in writing what one thinks, however good and loyal one's intentions are'.[24]

When the Army Bill was rejected by the Reichstag in May 1893 and Wilhelm gave vent to his anger in his speech at Tempelhof, his mother was incensed by this renewed demonstration of his anti-constitutional attitude: 'I was grieved and horrified to hear the frightful speech!', she wrote to Baroness Stockmar. 'I can *never* understand how a child of mine – a grandson of my father's – can understand nothing at all of the *meaning*, the sense and the value of a constitution,    and that *all* his views are so diametrically opposed to mine! . . . So much egoism, so much selfishness pains me deeply, – even if I am often disarmed by his truly childish naivety and ignorance! It is *not my* fault, and I am not responsible for this, it is the seed planted by Bismark [sic] which is coming up – and overgrowing everything! – The entire younger generation is in thrall to Bismark!'[25] She complained to her daughter Moretta on 18 May: 'I am miserable about things at Berlin. He [Wilhelm] is making one blunder after another! The speeches are quite dreadful, & the incessant whirl of amusement in wh. he lives in such serious times make a very bad impression, he neglects his duties and shows himself to be very selfish! For *me* his Mother it is very humiliating and distressing.'[26]

### CRITICISM IN THE IMPERIAL FAMILY AND AT COURT

It would be a grave mistake to dismiss the Empress Frederick's harsh criticism of her son as little more than the expression of the bitter personal disappointment or of the 'un-Prussian' attitude of this liberal-minded 'Engländerin', for it is a demonstrable fact that other members of the imperial family, as well as many ruling princes at German and foreign courts, shared the same fears and voiced the same complaints, often with damaging effects on the reputation of the Hohenzollern monarchy. Thus for instance Wilhelm's sister Sophie, the Crown Princess of Greece, was reported by Waldersee to have 'spoken out in the most contemptuous and hostile way against her brother Wilhelm at St Petersburg, and said, among other things, that the whole family thought he was mad'.[27] During a visit to Berlin in the spring of 1892 the diplomat Bernhard von Bülow was shocked by the hypercritical mood which he found not only among foreign diplomats there, but also in the Kaiser's own family, among whom he named the Crown Princess of Greece and the Grand Duchess Ella of Russia in particular. He reported anxiously to his friend Philipp Eulenburg that the Empress Frederick was 'less unpopular than before in many circles. Prince Heinrich is also said to have joined in the general chorus of criticism against our most gracious sovereign in Darmstadt and in England. Et tu quique! His own relations – especially all the Russian, Danish, English and Greek elements and the whole Rumpenheim clique – are very hostile towards our most gracious sovereign.'[28]

Even Bernhard of Saxe-Meiningen, who was married to the Kaiser's elder sister Charlotte and who in fact shared Wilhelm's reactionary and militaristic views, was increasingly inclined to make openly critical remarks about his brother-in-law.[29] After Wilhelm's second speech to the provincial diet of Brandenburg the Kaiserin's brother, Duke Ernst Günther of Schleswig-Holstein, went so far as to criticise the 'not always very felicitous' speeches of the Kaiser.[30] Prince Ernst zu Hohenlohe-Langenburg, related both to the Kaiserin and to the British royal family, wrote to his father not long afterwards saying that things were 'getting more and more lively here [in Germany]'; Wilhelm's speech in Brandenburg resembled 'a declaration of infallibility and has been greeted everywhere with malicious pleasure, scorn or anger depending on which party people support'.[31] Prince Heinrich VII Reuss, who had been German ambassador in Vienna for many years and was married to a Princess of Saxe-Weimar-Eisenach, recognised Wilhelm II's good qualities even after he himself had been rudely dismissed from his post, but deeply deplored the fact that these qualities were 'so often cancelled out by inconsistency and excessive haste but above all by arrogance!' He had heard, he informed Carl Wedel, that 'Philli [Eulenburg] and his allies had succeeded in teaching their patron the Nietzschean theory of the Übermensch, and this had got somewhat out of control. This could explain many things. I try my best to see any sign of improvement, and if I find one, for instance that he talks less, something else immediately comes along to destroy my hopes.'[32] Duke Georg II of Saxe-Meiningen was unusually perceptive in commenting to a friend after the Kaiser's belligerent speech at Erfurt that it was 'very much in doubt whether things will remain as quiet as they have been since the [1870–1] war with France, or whether we are not in fact heading for colossal storms, perhaps even before my reign is over. It seems to me that there is a more and more chauvinist attitude in the highest place in this country – perhaps because of the realisation that armed peace is gradually ruining us, but perhaps also because the frequent sight of large numbers of German soldiers bolsters confidence in one's own strength. But what will we achieve, even at best, if we go on the offensive? The maintenance of the status quo. We already have that! But if it goes wrong, what then?'[33] The old Duke died a few weeks before war broke out in 1914.

It is particularly telling that the two German federal princes who had stood by the Kaiser in his bitter contest with the Bismarcks, Grand Duke Friedrich I of Baden and King Albert I of Saxony, also strongly criticised Wilhelm very soon after the dismissal of the founder of the Reich. In the summer of 1890, for instance, the Grand Duke and Grand Duchess expressed themselves in 'decidedly . . . anxious' terms about the Kaiser and bemoaned the fact that he very frequently took 'overhasty action' and was losing ground with the public. Although at that time they clung to the view that 'with all [Wilhelm's] good qualities one could nevertheless still hope for the best',[34] such hopes were all too quickly dashed. When the Grand Duke met Waldersee in October 1890 the latter recorded that the conversation immediately came round to the Kaiser, 'and the Grand Duke told me, after I had given him my impressions, that he regretted to have to say that he shared my views entirely'. Friedrich added that he had lately discussed the same subject with Caprivi in Baden and had expressed his fear 'that pushy people might easily acquire influence these days', whereupon the Reich Chancellor had answered that this was unfortunately already the case.[35] After spending an evening with the Grand Duke and his wife on the island of Mainau in the summer of 1894 Waldersee commented that as both of them had always set 'an outstanding example of devotion to duty and of regal dignity' it was 'really no wonder if they were deeply disturbed about the Kaiser and considered the present time a very serious one'.[36] The Grand Duchess Luise, Wilhelm's aunt, declared that what she felt most strongly with the Kaiser was 'the lack of imperial dignity which one cannot fail to notice if one has but seen the daily life of the Kaiser and his relations with his entourage'. She said that she fully recognised, as she had always done, 'the Kaiser's rare qualities, his quick understanding and his knowledge on all kinds of subjects . . . but she is shocked by his volatility and hastiness. His many ill-considered decisions are of course an inevitable result of this', General von Waldersee concluded. For his part the Grand Duke singled out for particular criticism the Kaiser's craving for pleasure and lack of seriousness. Wilhelm had been to visit the Grand Duke for three days (as Waldersee recounted) but had gone shooting every morning and had spent in all only half an hour in private conversation with his uncle. The Grand Duke described as particularly characteristic the manner in which Wilhelm had made up his mind on the important question of the return of the Redemptorist Order to Germany. His decision had been taken 'at Kiel, without interrupting the pleasures of the regatta week, during a 15-minute audience'.[37]

The King of Saxony was scarcely less critical in his comments on the new style of government. Six months after Bismarck's fall he told Caprivi that he was 'a little hurt' that 'I am almost never asked for my advice now, as I used to be in the days of the old Kaiser and under the present Kaiser too, in former days.'[38] While hunting at Königswusterhausen in December 1890 Waldersee had several conversations with the King, who fully shared the Chief of the General Staff's growing anxiety about the Kaiser.[39] The following autumn when King Albert met Waldersee at Wilhelmshöhe he remarked that although he thought highly of the Kaiser he knew 'many of his weaknesses and hoped he would gradually calm down'.[40] Towards the end of 1894 the King tried to persuade the Kaiser 'not to ask strangers for advice, but only the responsible ministers'. He had no success.[41]

It should perhaps be no surprise to find members of the Kaiser's closest entourage among his sternest critics, since they were the most likely to suffer from his changeable moods. After the Scandinavian cruise of 1890 a member of Wilhelm's accompanying suite commented to Waldersee: 'You should be glad that you were not with us; it was dreadful. Bad weather most of the time, and being crammed together in a small space soon became an ordeal. Moreover the Kaiser did not even have *one* serious conversation; apart for playing games with the navy, of which the latter is heartily sick, there was nothing but the most infantile fooling around. It is alarming to see how the Kaiser is deteriorating, and becoming increasingly nervy and irritable as well. Where will it lead?'[42] During the hunt at Grunewald in January 1891, to Waldersee's 'utter astonishment' the Chief of the Civil Cabinet, Hermann von Lucanus, engaged him in lengthy conversation 'about the Kaiser and above all about the general mood of dissatisfaction; this I could only confirm, unfortunately', the Chief of the General Staff recorded. 'Only I could not tell him that he himself was probably partly to blame because he gave the Kaiser such bad advice.'[43] The following year the General noted that he had again had a long conversation with Lucanus, who had 'complained bitterly about the Kaiser's dislike of work, which was growing stronger rather than decreasing'.[44] At the beginning of 1891 Waldersee recorded in his diary that the former tutor, Hinzpeter, 'in terms that one could scarcely credit', had strongly condemned the Kaiser's 'lack of respect for the truth'.[45] A senior official of the Kaiserin's household, the Oberhofmeister Freiherr von Mirbach, deeply deplored the Kaiser's 'erratic behaviour and lack of devotion to duty'.[46] At a service in Potsdam in December 1890 Wilhelm found the sermon tedious and demanded the sacking of the clergyman in question. The latter's superior conceded that he was not a gifted preacher, but he was still young and, moreover, had outstanding talent for pastoral care. 'And now he is to be got rid of without further ado, on the whim of our All-Highest Sovereign!', Waldersee commented angrily. 'Things are going from bad to worse!'[47]

For those in the know at the Hohenzollern court the appointment of Prince Chlodwig zu Hohenlohe-Schillingsfürst as Reich chancellor and Prussian minister-president in October 1894 represented a last chance to call a halt to the young Kaiser's autocratic behaviour, which was increasingly seen as disastrous. Thus for instance no less a person than Kaiserin Auguste Viktoria's chamberlain, Bodo von dem Knesebeck, courageously wrote to Prince Hohenlohe's son Alexander in the very early days of the new chancellorship, with the warning that 'the Kaiser does not see the consequences of the present situation because he does not yet understand how much he himself is to blame for it'. No one but Prince Hohenlohe was in a position to place conditions on the Kaiser which would protect the Chancellor from unpleasant surprises, the chamberlain argued.

He went on: 'The period during which the Prince is in control of affairs must become a period of training for the K[aiser], otherwise the situation will remain untenable. For although all other factors change the K[aiser] remains, and this constant factor must have its unpredictable element removed. I should like to think that there is still time to do this, and that it is not impossible, given the presence of such great gifts. But herein lies the kernel of all evil and part of the reason why this change is taking place under circumstances which have an element of tragedy. I cannot give any other name to the fact that to take on this office, which has no equal in Europe, is to make a sacrifice that is beyond measure!' Knesebeck added that he regarded the future 'with insurmountable anxiety'.[48]

In high-ranking army circles and above all among the military officers at court who were in constant attendance on the Kaiser, a particularly pessimistic mood prevailed. Adjutant-General von Wittich was among the most emphatic and outspoken critics of Wilhelm II. As early as the summer of 1890 Waldersee recorded that Wittich spoke 'in the most disparaging way' about the Kaiser, and indeed 'quite openly'.[49] Not long afterwards, following a long conversation with the Adjutant-General about the alarming development of the Kaiser's personality, the Chief of the General Staff noted that Wittich had 'expressed himself exactly in accordance with my own views on the Kaiser, his character and his deterioration and blamed it all on the Coburg blood. I believe he has hit the nail on the head.'[50] Waldersee also described in his diary how Wittich had criticised the Kaiser 'with a vengeance' after the New Year reception for the commanding generals in January 1892 and had complained that 'he was becoming more and more great and infallible'.[51] The views of Max von Versen, who as adjutant-general had been 'very close' to the Kaiser, were no less critical. When Waldersee met him on 19 December 1890 he found Versen 'very disappointed', and recorded that the General thought 'exactly as I do about the Kaiser's development'. Above all, Versen complained 'that the Kaiser had become far less dependable' – that no one ever knew 'how he stood with him'. 'Those immediately about him have reached the stage . . . where no one dares to say anything, neither the Cabinet chiefs nor Wittich, nor any of the Flügeladjutanten nor even a Hofmarschall. Everyone fears for his post.' Versen also agreed with Waldersee that Bismarck had 'suppressed people's personalities', but under Kaiser Wilhelm II 'we see the same thing happening, only in a stronger and more dangerous form'.[52] When the two Generals met again in the summer of 1891 Waldersee recorded that Versen was still 'very critical' of Wilhelm and entirely shared Waldersee's opinion 'that his development had taken quite a different course from what one might have expected'.[53] The new Adjutant-General, Hans von Plessen, whom many had expected to have a good influence on the Kaiser, was a disappointment, for he had 'as good as no influence at all' and was 'cowardly as well', Waldersee wrote in the summer of 1894. 'In short, wherever one looks there is dissatisfaction, ill-humour and discouragement, and not only in the higher ranks of the army, but among all independent, well-meaning people. Unfortunately I am not the only one who is convinced that we are going downhill all the time and that a catastrophe is inevitable.'[54] Even the once fiercely loyal Chief of the Military Cabinet, Wilhelm von Hahnke, eventually had no scruples in joining in the adverse criticism of the Kaiser expressed by his fellow generals.[55] Four years after Bismarck's dismissal Hahnke's enemy and rival Waldersee recorded that he was 'discontented' and 'anxious to get out'.[56] A year later Waldersee summed up the mood of the Chief of the Military Cabinet in a contemptuous note in his diary. 'Hahnke is very discontented but has not the energy to leave; he says quite openly that no one can tell today whether he will still be in favour tomorrow and that one has to be constantly prepared to hear that what is coal-black today is declared snow-white tomorrow.'[57] The former Minister of War General von Verdy was another who observed 'with great concern how everything is gradually deteriorating, and that it is the Kaiser himself who is responsible. In his view one of the worst things is that the Kaiser lacks nobility of mind. Unfortunately this is only too true, and the effects of this are truly disastrous', the former Chief of the General Staff commented.[58] Indeed, no less a man than the old Field Marshal Count Helmuth von Moltke 'expressed very great anxiety about the Kaiser' when Waldersee visited him in Kreisau in October 1890.[59] When Moltke died in April 1891 there were many who were deeply affected by his death, not only because they felt the loss of 'one of the last great men of the most glorious period of our history'. Prince Ernst zu Hohenlohe spoke for many when he expressed the view that 'under the present system of rushing ahead with everything' Moltke, 'as the guardian of the old traditions whom everyone respected, still seemed capable of preventing much of what the people of the new era come up with in their excess of enthusiasm'.[60]

## COUNT VON WALDERSEE'S AWAKENING

The process of disenchantment was of course more painful for Waldersee himself than for anyone else. Once Wilhelm's closest confidant and the man who had done more than anyone to spur him on, first against his parents and then against the Bismarcks, it is a harrowing experience to read the unexpurgated version of his diaries and to watch the transformation which took place in his judgement of the young Kaiser. Like someone waking from a dream, Moltke's successor as chief of the General Staff was suddenly brought face to face with what he had failed to see before, and was able to recognise the disastrous mistake he had made.

In increasingly harsh terms he condemned the Kaiser's autocratic behaviour, his vanity and courting of popularity, his love of pomp, his extravagance, self-indulgence and superficiality, his constant interference in army business and in matters of civil administration, his inconsistency and thoughtlessness, his incessant and unfortunate speeches, his inconsiderate treatment of colleagues and subjects, the coarse and undignified tone of his entourage, his receptiveness to flattery and gossip relayed by irresponsible outsiders and not least his inability to tolerate well-meaning criticism.

The more negative his attitude to Wilhelm became and the more fatalistic a view he took of the future of Prussia–Germany, the more desperately he wondered whether he was not judging Wilhelm too harshly. In February 1894, for instance, he commented: 'I wish to God that I were able to write something good about the Kaiser. I sometimes wonder whether I am unjust and prejudiced in my judgement, but I cannot escape the conviction that our sovereign has no clear idea of his aims and is utterly unpredictable.'[61] On several occasions Waldersee asked himself whether he had any right to commit such critical comments on the Kaiser to paper at all, but again he concluded that, although he must hope that his remarks would 'remain undiscovered for a long time', it was nevertheless fitting 'that truth should be honoured and records such as this are necessary for the history which will have to be written one day of this very strange Kaiser and character'.[62] Demonstrably, there were certain experiences which the General shrank from recording in writing, although some of these were precisely the events which confirmed his general opinion of the Kaiser.[63] It goes without saying that Waldersee had no inkling that the editor of his diaries would later delete innumerable critical passages on Wilhelm in order to transmit to posterity an embellished picture of this sovereign and so distort the historical truth for decades to come.

It would certainly be a mistake for us to take every negative utterance of the fallen and increasingly bitter Chief of the General Staff at its face value. Not only because of the obvious frustration of his personal ambitions, but also because of very fundamental differences in attitude towards both domestic and foreign policy, we shall do well to ask ourselves from time to time whether we share the precepts on which Waldersee founded his criticisms of Wilhelm. On trade policy, for instance, the General took a view favouring the great landed proprietors and agriculture in general which, in the light of actual economic development, seems even more abstruse to us today than it did to his contemporaries. His only response to the steady growth of social democracy, as we shall see, was to advocate a highly dangerous policy of preventive war against the workers by which military force would be used to achieve the abolition of universal suffrage. The paranoid comments throughout his diary about the 'enormous power of the Jews' and his longing for 'a powerful personality . . . to make a clean sweep' occasionally make the General seem like a herald of a later nationalistic movement with which few would wish to be associated.[64] Nor should we forget, in assessing Waldersee's harsh criticism of the restrained foreign policy of the 'New Course', his own preferred solution to the strategic dilemma of the German Reich. The remedy which he repeatedly advocated was the formation of a Greater German Reich to which not only the German provinces of Austria but also a germanised Bohemia would be annexed. And that was not all: after the 'next' war against France he advocated that Germany should not claim any financial reparations but instead 'again take land'; in so doing 'we must remove the population from there to France and settle the land thus depopulated with people from Germany'.[65] Even taking his extreme views into account, however, we are left with such a formidable body of criticism of Wilhelm II's personality and style of rule that Waldersee's unexpurgated diaries must rank among the most revealing sources on the true events behind the scenes of the Wilhelmine Reich.

Waldersee's rude awakening can be dated to the summer of 1890, six months before his dismissal as chief of the General Staff, when he returned to Berlin after a long holiday and became aware of the criticism of the Kaiser which was being increasingly widely expressed. 'It is alarming what I have heard said about the Kaiser in 3 days in Berlin', he wrote in dismay on 12 August. 'There really is a universal sense of disappointment.'[66] Only one thought ran through all the Kaiser's actions, the Chief of the General Staff complained even at this early stage, and that was 'concern for his personal position. He wants to be popular!' The 'rapidly developed vanity' of the Kaiser was the basic weakness of his personality, Waldersee observed, adding: 'I thought his father a very vain man who enjoyed dressing up in fine clothes and posing; he set great store by outward ornament like orders and was delighted to be cheered by a few street boys. – But he [Wilhelm] outdoes all that by far. He fishes for ovations and – as of course follows from that – is very open to flattery. All this has developed so quickly that I am constantly surprised by what he does. As Prince Wilhelm he seemed to have many of the excellent qualities of his grandfather, he was modest and simple in his way of life, avoided attracting attention, did not like being escorted by adjutants and was very considerate towards old people. Now he loves splendour to an alarming degree and is beginning to behave like Louis XIV; he likes acting the patron, throws money away uselessly and does not worry himself at all about finances; he conducts himself with as much pomp as possible and likes nothing better than noisily cheering crowds; he is ruthless and odious towards the army; he has reached the point where he has a very high estimation of his abilities and thinks himself superior to everyone, but unfortunately this is a gross illusion and adds to the impression that there is very little behind it.

His great strength is a decided skill in dealing with people: he has a beguiling charm that few can resist. He often uses it with officers and thus wins hearts wherever he goes and does not stay long. But 2 years have been long enough to reveal the truth and the initial enthusiasm has cooled down now.'[67]

Not surprisingly, the clash with Wilhelm during the imperial manoeuvres in September 1890 sharpened the General's awareness of his weaknesses. After the manoeuvres Waldersee retreated to Russian Poland to stay with Count Guido Henckel von Donnersmark, and there reflected at length on what had become of the great hopes he had once harboured. Though it was scarcely six months since Bismarck's dismissal, for which he himself bore considerable responsibility, Waldersee too now recognised that Wilhelm II had 'come to the throne very much too early!' The realisation which was gradually dawning on him that Wilhelm 'was not, after all, the right man to lead the Fatherland out of the many dangers which threaten it' had now become a certainty. The Kaiser was certainly 'full of good intentions and idealistic ideas', but 'he did not have the clarity of vision to see that the approval of the masses, which he won surprisingly quickly, and the picture which those at home and abroad who did not know him formed of him and which the newspapers reflected back to him was not based on deeds, nor on the truth. His vanity having grown considerably, he very soon began to believe that he really was something quite special and clear signs of delusions of grandeur now began to appear.'[68] In his musings Waldersee constantly reverted to the 'extraordinarily highly developed . . . vanity' of the Kaiser, which he considered to be the 'mainspring of most of his behaviour'.[69]

For all his criticism General Waldersee at this time still emphasised that Wilhelm also had good qualities – a quick understanding, a good memory and a certain confidence in speaking – which enabled him to give an impression of being well informed in almost any domain. 'Furthermore, although he is outwardly hard, often very ruthless and indeed inclined to use ruthlessness to impress, he has a certain good nature and shows kindness towards those who have served him well.' The young Kaiser also had unusual aptitude for handling people, Waldersee acknowledged. 'He can win anyone over with beguiling charm and impress them with skilful, agreeable and often very amusing conversation. Anyone who does not know him very well falls under the spell of his personality, which of course is immensely enhanced by his position as Kaiser. Whether the Kaiser has real courage I do not yet know', the Chief of the General Staff commented in this character sketch of September 1890. 'He is a fearless rider and this is of course not to be dismissed, but whether he can show steadfastness in difficult times, take on great responsibilities and remain calm under enemy fire only experience will show. Hearing him speak one would be inclined to answer this question in the affirmative; but I have sufficient experience of life to have my doubts as yet. His concern for his personal safety is said to be great; his lack of consideration towards officers, civil servants and well-meaning people is matched by great consideration for the workers. He has already often threatened to smash the Centre, the Progressives, the feudal aristocracy and I do not know who else, but so far only people who are too weak or too monarchically inclined to resist have been given a taste of his power.'[70]

In time, however, the opinions which Waldersee expressed about his once so greatly admired Kaiser, King and Supreme War Lord became more and more pessimistic and scathing. Wilhelm was 'utterly unpredictable', he complained in an entry of 4 October 1890. 'Today he sings the praises of one party, tomorrow of another; he criticises the Jews and yet gets involved with people of Jewish origin; today he promises to support agriculture but tomorrow he does something likely to ruin it; he shows interest in industry and big business but is actually hostile and disparaging towards it; he dismisses Bismarck partly because he was supposed to have got involved with Windthorst and then stands calmly by while Caprivi enters into active dealings with him; he declares the aristocrats the noblest of his subjects and then threatens to shatter the factious aristocracy (which no one has heard of); today he is full of hatred and contempt for Russia and yet he pays court to the Russians in such a way that they themselves laugh at it; the Austrians are pitiful people on one occasion and his loyal and excellent allies on another. Is he a really pious man and a convinced Christian, or does he only pretend to be so; is he a trustworthy man or not − we do not know. These are all comments which one often hears now', the Chief of the General Staff concluded. He himself believed that the Kaiser 'actually has no firmly held convictions on any subject; he stumbles from one risky idea to another and there is no set plan behind his actions. There is *no subject* on which his opinions are clearly formed as yet.'[71] Another serious problem, as Waldersee observed, was that Wilhelm 'no longer [had] the slightest desire to do any work'. 'His amusements, whether playing about with the army or more especially the navy, travelling, shooting etc. come before everything else; and because these things come first he actually has scarcely any time for work. He reads very little, extracts from the newspaper being perhaps his most regular reading matter; he hardly writes any more himself, except for annotations on reports, and thinks the best audiences are those which are over soonest. Such a way of conducting business can last for quite a time before it becomes apparent to the outside world, but it cannot be kept up in the long run without causing very serious harm, and I believe it has reached that point already. It is truly scandalous how the court circular deceives the general public about the activities of the Kaiser. According to it he is at work from morning till night!'[72] Waldersee also had good grounds for observing that Wilhelm had 'an unusually lively imagination' and was thus 'very prone to exaggeration'; consequently his own duty as chief of the General Staff was 'to be doubly careful and to weigh things up calmly'.[73]

The Kaiser's weakness for flattery and for gossip peddled by irresponsible advisers made it infinitely more difficult for those who held political responsibility under the constitution to carry out their duties, Waldersee complained in November 1890. The old Kaiser Wilhelm had never allowed anyone to speak to him about third parties, 'unless it was within their competence. His entourage, with the exception of the Cabinet Chiefs, therefore had no influence. There was no one who could boast that he had the Kaiser's ear, or whose influence others feared.' Things were very different under Wilhelm II. The young Kaiser loved gossip 'and gives it free rein, allowing all those in his entourage to express opinions on others, and indeed encouraging them to do so. He thinks that by listening to people outside the official orbit he will be well informed about everything and know more than his ministers. He fails to see that 9/10 of his people simply tell him what he wants to hear! He does not notice how many people he offends, how many whose trust and therefore support he loses, how much he stirs people up against each other and all in all causes great damage.'[74] Waldersee accused not only the Kaiser's entourage but also outsiders of telling the Kaiser what he wanted to hear, which in turn he blamed on Wilhelm's vanity. 'I hear complaints from many sides of how much people flatter the Kaiser', he wrote in December 1890. But such eulogies were often 'provoked' by Wilhelm himself 'by his asking "What did you think of my speech?" or "Did I not do that well?", after which few people have the courage to tell him what they really think. But the good people often go straight up to him and come out with the most tedious flattery, sometimes about something he has done, sometimes in a more roundabout way by running down people against whom they know the Kaiser is prejudiced. All decent-thinking people are very concerned about this, if they know anything about what is going on, and many are deeply disheartened.'[75] On 10 January 1891, shortly before his dismissal as Chief of the General Staff, Waldersee reflected that 'these days . . . no one is sure of his life; that is what is so strange and disturbing about the state we are in; everyone feels unsafe because he does not know how far the Kaiser can be trusted; he who is in good odour today may be destroyed by gossip in a month! Gossip from the most insignificant people can be enough to bring discredit on respected people in high places, and the changes get faster and faster. It clearly shows a degree of nervous strain.'[76] 'Seldom has anyone disappointed expectations as much as he. Until he changes, until he realises that he is only a dilettante in all the countless areas into which he ventures with such confidence and makes up his mind to call on experienced people, until he decides not to tolerate gossip and to get rid of unqualified advisers, nothing can change and everything will get worse and worse.'[77] There was in fact no improvement and in later years the General again strongly condemned Wilhelm II's willingness to listen to slander, which in his eyes had become a cancer on the Prusso-German monarchy. 'This is the principal cause of our malady', he wrote in 1893. 'This is what produces the insecurity that weighs everything down; this is what breeds a false, bungling, contemptible, unprincipled spirit, and we may be destroyed by it.'[78] The mood in Berlin in general was worse than ever, Waldersee commented in January 1893, but above all at court. 'The closer one comes to the atmosphere of the court, the more one is repelled; there is an incredible stirring up of enmity and mistrust etc. Not a day goes by without someone being torn down and slandered.'[79]

For a short time in 1893 Waldersee allowed himself to hope that there had been a slight improvement in the 'mostly obscene' tone habitually used at the Hohenzollern court. In March that year he recorded that 'people who see the Kaiser often are reported to have remarked that he adopts a better tone in his conversations now. He had got into very bad habits through his contact with Herbert Bismarck and enjoyed hearing and telling dirty jokes, unfortunately also in the presence of servants. Among the people in his entourage Colonel Kessel also had a particularly bad effect on him. If there should really be a change for the better it would be an excellent thing', the General commented, clearly not quite convinced.[80] And indeed visitors to the imperial court continued to be struck by 'the bad tone among the members of the Kaiser's entourage'. During the visit paid by the Kaiser and Kaiserin to Rome in May 1893 the 'bad manners' and 'very arrogant, demanding and disagreeable' attitude of their suite were said to have made a particularly unpleasant impression. One could be sure, Waldersee warned on hearing various reports of the Kaiser's behaviour in Rome, that stories about it would do the rounds of all the courts of Europe, where they would be received with much malicious pleasure.[81]

Waldersee singled out the anniversaries of Kaiser Wilhelm I's death, Wilhelm II's accession and Bismarck's dismissal, as well as the young Kaiser's birthday, as opportunities to launch into brooding recollections or dark forebodings of the future of the Reich, repeatedly asking himself how he could have been so utterly deceived. In January 1891 he looked back with distress on the development of the political and religious views of the Kaiser, now aged thirty-two. In the spring of 1888, as crown prince, Wilhelm had maintained 'a firm, devout Lutheran attitude' and had had the courage to express this openly, Waldersee recollected. 'He had very decidedly conservative convictions of the kind that a sovereign who wishes to keep his throne today must have and cultivate, untroubled by the clamour of the unprincipled and unthinking masses. And what do we see barely 3 years later? A Kaiser who is led by fear of the Social Democrats, who believes he can create a position for himself by concessions to those who clamour for them, by courting popularity, by abandoning his firm Lutheran standpoint. He has been told that a king should not represent any strict confessional standpoint; there is some sense in that if one puts the emphasis on *represent*; he certainly should not persecute people with different beliefs, whether Catholics, Protestants, sectarians or Jews or anything else. But he should *have* a firm standpoint and not shrink from expressing it . . . He must show that he is the defender of the Lutheran Church and must hold unreservedly to the creed which is read out every Sunday in our Lutheran churches . . . Unfortunately Kaiser Wilhelm is now going the way of holding to no one, so he will eventually fall out with everyone.'[82] In Waldersee's eyes the Kaiser had quite the wrong conception of his role as supreme bishop of the Lutheran Church. 'How different I had imagined things would be when the Kaiser came to the throne', he sighed at the end of 1891. 'I dreamt of a Lutheran king in whom all fellow believers in Europe would see their powerful defender'; instead the Protestant camp was in conflict and the Catholics were being courted.[83] Waldersee was bewildered when he again received reports of the Kaiser's spiritualist leanings. Philipp Eulenburg, he wrote, had already been strongly urged, even before the first Scandinavian cruise, 'not to encourage the Kaiser in his spiritualist views, but to calm him and try to bring him round to a more level-headed way of thinking'. To begin with, Eulenburg had kept his word, but during the Kaiser's most recent visit to Munich Eulenburg had introduced the Kaiser to a spiritualist medium. When in a trance this woman had been asked by Wilhelm what attitude he should take to a friend in Russia, by which he of course meant Alexander III. 'Is it . . . not appalling that such a farce should be allowed?', Waldersee exclaimed. 'If our sovereign can be influenced in such a way, the welfare of the Fatherland is in the hands of swindlers and beyond hope. We may be facing a new edition of Friedrich Wilhelm II and Bischoffwerder!'[84]

Reminiscing at the beginning of 1891 on the past three years, the Chief of the General Staff commented bitterly on the disappointment of the hopes he had placed in the young Wilhelm. 'When I look back to the spring of 88, when the Kaiser was Crown Prince . . . and remember how he trusted me and how I hoped that he would become an excellent kaiser who would lead the country and show himself indifferent to the clamour of the masses and firm in his religious convictions, who would be devoted to the army and cherish all that is noble and good; when I think how it would have been the greatest possible satisfaction to me to help him in my field, and how well justified I was in having these hopes, I am bound to say that there has been a very great change indeed.' Looking back still further, Waldersee recalled: 'Prince Wilhelm was simple in his way of life, his speech; he did not like to be surrounded by a large suite, he was modest and considerate towards older people, had a certain respect for those who had served

well in our wars; he was hard-working, liked writing and wrote a great deal —
indeed sometimes too much — he had firmly held Lutheran beliefs and the
courage to express them openly; he rejected excessive luxury and was very critical
of gambling and the excesses of the racecourse.' 'And how do things look barely
3 years later?', Waldersee asked himself, gloomily answering his own question:
'He has become volatile, reluctant to work and unwilling to concentrate on one
subject for long. He treats the army badly and is inconsiderate towards older
people; his conviviality and bonhomie, which always made him popular at first,
do not last, so that the good impression soon fades, especially among those who
see him often. Quite unexpectedly, he has developed a very marked weakness
for showy display, grand ceremonies and luxury.' The Kaiser undoubtedly had
good sides — a quick understanding and 'a desire to attain what is good' — and
Waldersee had not quite abandoned all hope that these aspects of his character
would win through and overcome his undesirable tendencies.[85] Only a few days
after this diary entry Waldersee was sacked as chief of the General Staff.

Even after his transfer to the command of the IX Army Corps in Altona,
General Count Alfred von Waldersee remained on excellent terms with the
military officers and senior officials at the Berlin court, with Prince Heinrich
at Kiel, with his fellow generals and with the landed aristocracy. He continued
to see and correspond with both current and former ministers as well as party
leaders and journalists of various shades of opinion. He went to Berlin frequently
and travelled the country on official tours of inspection or hunting trips. He must
therefore continue to rank as one of the best-informed sources on the innermost
workings of the court and of the world of high politics. It should therefore be
no surprise that his open breach with Wilhelm II and his removal from the
court in January 1891 did not result in any qualitative change in his attitude
to his former hero. On the contrary, his judgement remained as sound — and as
harsh — as ever.

Soon after his dismissal Waldersee commented with growing concern on
Wilhelm II's despotic form of rule and frivolous lifestyle. 'Intelligent and very
well-disposed people complain that he has less and less inclination to work or
to listen to the opinion of others', he remarked. 'He does not give anyone the
chance to speak, but expresses his own opinion with the greatest confidence and
apparently will not allow any contradiction. With the life he leads there is indeed
scarcely any time for work, especially as any free time is often lamentably wasted;
for instance lately on the journey to Göhrde he played a very silly card game
with Lucanus and Hahnke for almost 3 hours in the train. He could have got so
much useful work done with those two . . . during that time.' For the first time
Waldersee felt compelled to give serious consideration to the possibility that the
Kaiser, of whom he had for years had such high hopes, might be mentally ill.[86]

'What is always the saddest thing for me', he wrote on Wilhelm II's thirty-third birthday, 'is to look into the Kaiser's heart and character.'[87]

Like everyone else the General was appalled when he read the newspaper report of the Kaiser's second speech to the Brandenburg provincial diet in February 1892. His remarks would 'quite justifiably [cause] bad blood' everywhere, Waldersee wrote in dismay, for they bore witness yet again 'to such boundless arrogance! He wants to lead Germany to glory and happiness and has done nothing so far but to drag her down. How great was the old Kaiser Wilhelm in his modesty, compared to this.'[88] It was 'deeply sad' to see 'how rapidly the standing of the Kaiser has diminished'. The foreign press was writing 'quite dreadful things' about him. 'In foreign newspapers one finds more and more comments about the Kaiser's mental state; many say quite openly that he has already gone mad!' As the speech coincided with the radical protest by all the liberal parties against the School Bill and with widespread street demonstrations by workers, it had given many people 'goose-flesh'. There was many an echo of the period leading up to the revolutionary events of 1848: 'The indecisiveness of those in charge, the confusion at the very top, where all kinds of unauthorised people have their say – all this is a repeat of the situation which brought about the events of '48', Waldersee remarked (just as the Empress Frederick had done) in his diary.[89]

On 1 March 1893 Wilhelm II gave his annual address at the gala dinner of the Brandenburg provincial diet. This time, in spite of the usual emphasis on his divine right, the speech had a rueful note. The Kaiser expressed his gratitude to his former mentor, Oberpräsident Heinrich von Achenbach, who had made a flattering introductory speech, for the 'firm confidence' placed in him as 'father of the people'. This was 'the finest reward which I and My trusted counsellors [can receive] in our work'. He acknowledged that the present time could not be compared with the 'glorious days gone by' of his grandfather. 'The noble form of our great departed Kaiser Wilhelm is ever present to our eyes with his mighty triumphs', he proclaimed; but those successes had been possible only because 'my grandfather had the most firm belief in his divinely appointed office combined with the most unwearied devotion to duty . . . Well, gentlemen, I grew up and was reared by him in these traditions', Wilhelm II declared. 'I too cherish the same belief. My highest reward is, therefore, to labour night and day for my people and their welfare. But I do not disguise from myself the fact that I can never make all the members of our nation equally happy and contented.'[90] 'Does he really believe that people trust him and his advisers?', Waldersee wondered when he read the speech in the newspaper. 'It is precisely because there is no trust, but general mistrust instead, that we are in such a bad way. The reference to his divine mission will hardly please the liberal gentlemen.

He claims to work day and night for the welfare of his people! Unfortunately all too many people know that he really does no work at all. In general there is rather a melancholy flavour to the speech', the General commented. 'Not very long ago he wanted to make the whole world happy; now the numbers are shrinking considerably.'[91] Waldersee found it 'comical' how every sentence of the Kaiser's speech was highlighted and analysed in the press, and wrote: 'If the people suspected how little thought is given to the Kaiser's individual words on such occasions! Often he actually does not know what he has said, and yet as is well known he has often said things that were highly questionable, but none were taken any further. He has often made threats, but he has never carried out a threat.' The elegiac tone which characterised this speech, the General claimed, was symptomatic. 'I have been aware of this mood for some time now', he commented. And he predicted, 'It only needs some great disappointment to come along, and with his character there is no question that despondency will follow, although at first he will not have the slightest hesitation in throwing the blame on others.'[92]

Looking back critically on the first five years of the young Kaiser's rule in June 1893 Waldersee wrote: 'He has often gone as far as to depict his grandfather as a tired old man who scarcely knew what was going on around him in his latter years. In fact the old gentleman was of incalculable value to us all, particularly as far as the socialist question was concerned. His venerable personality, known throughout the world for the conscientiousness and devotion to duty he showed until his dying day, with all his past, and the fact that he never gave any reason for malicious tongues to wag, was for us a bulwark against the tide of revolution. The present Kaiser, on the other hand, positively cultivates Social Democrats. Many people, particularly abroad, credit him with great energy, but the great majority in this country no longer do. People have realised that he is inclined to vacillate and therefore cannot to be relied on to stick to any course on which he has started; countless thoughtless remarks . . . have greatly encouraged the suspicion that he is a ruthless autocrat at heart; in the eyes of many, his versatility is merely a sign of superficiality; his private life is watched closely, and people conclude that he devotes most of his time to pleasure. His love of splendour is compared with the simplicity of his grandfather. No ruler in our times can be accused of such things and escape unscathed. They create a harmful atmosphere and this expresses itself by people becoming inflamed and voting for social democracy. It would not be fair to say that the Kaiser is chiefly to blame, but he is unquestionably very much to blame, as are all those who advise him. There was no need for us to have been brought so low as we have been!'[93] The wish, evident on all sides, for independent-minded men to come to the fore was quite clearly directed against the Kaiser, as it was believed that no member of the present regime would dare to tell him the truth, for fear of losing his position. 'I am sorry to say that there is undoubtedly much truth in this', Waldersee commented in the summer of 1894. 'The Kaiser thinks his opinion is the only right one, even if he often changes it. Apart from Bismarck and Minister Zedlitz I cannot think of anyone who faced up to him firmly and persisted in his own opinion.'[94] Waldersee reacted with disbelief to the passage in the Kaiser's speech at Königsberg on 6 September 1894, in which he claimed that his door was open to all. Such a remark might impress the unthinking masses, he said, but 'anyone in the know is all too well aware that for all his outward openness, the Kaiser is practically inaccessible. How many people have already tried to give him their views! They almost never manage it because the Kaiser will not listen to anyone who he thinks wants to instruct him or give him good advice. Even people in his closest entourage often do not succeed in saying a single word to him in private. And yet he boldly asserts that his door is open to everyone.'[95]

Among those closer to the Kaiser, Waldersee recorded in January 1895, the conviction was growing that it was 'impossible for any chancellor to work with the Kaiser so long as he conducts business as he has done so far'. Caprivi had swallowed far too much, and his successor Prince Chlodwig zu Hohenlohe-Schillingsfürst had already 'had many difficult moments because of the Kaiser's high-handed interference. The view is gradually gaining ground that the constitution must be developed further in order to keep greater control of the Kaiser's powers! This is how far we have come, 7 years after Wilhelm I's death!'[96] Similar despondent remarks occur in the General's diary on the fifth anniversary of Bismarck's dismissal. 'What twists and turns the Kaiser has already brought about!', he sighed in the spring of 1895. 'Neither Caprivi nor Hohenlohe is chiefly to blame for the lack of stability, but only the Kaiser. And it will go on until he realises that he must stop intervening personally in every matter of importance. It is quite remarkable how this can have gone on for 5 years already, and that both Caprivi and Hohenlohe, as well as the other ministers involved, have accepted it. They are none of them men of character; Zedlitz was the only one. How harshly history will judge this time in years to come! And at this grave moment when only strength of character can help us the Kaiser's chief occupation is breaking characters. One day he will come to suffer greatly for what he has done.'[97] When Waldersee was approached several times by conservative and even liberal politicians in Berlin who remarked, with a view to his becoming a candidate for the Reich chancellorship, that what was needed was 'above all an energetic man who will also be able to cope with the Kaiser', the General turned down this improbable request with the characteristic argument that 'the Kaiser has not yet reached the point of realising that he cannot continue to do business like this for much longer, and he has no intention of giving way to a chancellor or, to put it a better way, to let him work for him and stay in the background. That would require more experience.'[98]

Although his personal relationship to the Kaiser and Kaiserin slowly improved after Wilhelm conferred the Order of the Black Eagle on him in January 1895, to the point that even outsiders began to fear his influence again,[99] Waldersee did not alter his pessimistic view of Wilhelm's personality and style of rule. 'The most alarming thing, in my view, is that I still think that the Kaiser does not know what to do', he wrote at the beginning of 1896, after listing the major problems that confronted the Reich in both domestic and foreign policy. 'He has certain aims, but they are not clearly thought out, nor does he know how and by what means he wants to attain them. And as he still does not fully recognise the seriousness of the domestic situation, nor, in my opinion, properly understand the significance of the parties, and wants to reign Himself, intervening first in one place and then in another, often very rashly, and as there is no strong chancellor nor a united Ministry, it really is no wonder if we are regarded as being on a very uncertain course.'[100]

In the summer of 1896 Waldersee recorded that the Kaiser's mood was gradually becoming 'very embittered, he considers that most people are bad and complains of disloyalty and lack of gratitude . . . and refuses to see that the truth is the other way about. He himself is to blame: he has offended, deceived and let down so many loyal, able people that it is no wonder that many of them are disappointed and deeply hurt and leave him. Unlike his grandfather he does not have the gift of winning hearts and binding them to him; to begin with he captivates and enchants them with his charm and kindness, but it gradually fades and eventually he repels them. Years ago I put forward the theory', he wrote, 'that the Kaiser was ageing prematurely and would become an embittered man at odds with the world, and today I am convinced that he is well on the way to this.' Reflecting the views of someone 'very close to the Kaiser' Waldersee continued: 'in addition, he is as convinced as ever of his infallibility and superiority; he never makes a mistake; if anything goes wrong others are always to blame. Unfortunately he is not getting any more conscientious or hard-working; on the contrary, his desire to work is constantly dwindling; there is no sign of thoroughness and conscientiousness. With his exceptional gifts he can understand anything he wants to understand, but he never goes below the surface.'[101] In June 1896 Waldersee used the occasion of the eighth anniversary of Wilhelm's accession to take stock of the external and internal position of the Reich and of the Kaiser's achievements. The result was anything but encouraging. The world was like a great army camp living in a state of unnatural tension that would soon erupt, he observed. The danger of an international conflict was all the greater because the old European powers had now been joined by Japan, China and the

United States. Within Germany too the state of affairs was becoming increasingly untenable everywhere. 'Where the first clash will be God only knows', he wrote, adding prophetically that 'the next decades have every prospect of seeing great catastrophes'. Commenting on Kaiser Wilhelm himself, who ought to have taken control of this difficult situation, he wrote: 'Tomorrow is the anniversary of Kaiser Friedrich's death! The present Kaiser has been on the throne for 8 years now. He took up his duties with such fine and inspired ideas, and what has he achieved? Have we gone forwards or backwards? I have absolutely no hesitation in saying backwards. If the Kaiser were really the man he thought himself, if he had the gift of being able to use his exceptional abilities in the right way, if he were less vain, if he were more conscientious, if he had more knowledge of people and of the world and less inclination to surround himself with flatterers and yes-men, and if above all he had more courage, he could well have steered the world in a different direction, given the colossal power of the position he has inherited.' Instead, Waldersee had found it 'almost inconceivable how much he is impressed by outward splendour, great spectacles etc., and he commits the fatal error of believing others are equally impressed. A great parade, a ceremonial entry with a colour escort, 1000 bellowing louts and 10,000 foolish people waving handkerchiefs and shouting hurrah give him a feeling of well-being and confidence.' The magnificent reception which Wilhelm had put on for the Chinese Viceroy Li Hung Tschang had given him huge pleasure. The Kaiser was convinced 'that he had achieved something great, made an enormous impression, served the Fatherland well', Waldersee scoffed.[102]

After closely observing the Kaiser and his entourage 'in the broader sense' at Kiel and Travemünde that summer Waldersee wrote a scathing account of his impressions in his diary. In the imperial entourage no one trusted anyone else, he observed, and all were 'afraid of the Kaiser. He is quite well aware of this and encourages it, because in this way he hears a great deal of gossip and keeps control; only in one sphere does he fail to see how he is deceived and is up against a king rat, and that is foreign affairs, where the old sinners [by which he meant Friedrich von Holstein above all] continue to rule the roost and know how to influence him as they want . . . In Kiel, where Lucanus was also present, I was again much struck by the strange circumstances in which we find ourselves, and by the foolishness of the great mass of mankind . . . The Kaiser has always been of an autocratic nature, and although he has often let slip autocratic remarks he is regarded nevertheless as a sovereign who respects the constitutional procedures and on the whole is guided by them. But that is unfortunately untrue. He despises these procedures and actually practises absolute rule in any domain in which he cares to involve himself, which means that he does this regularly in foreign affairs, the army and the navy, and in other areas according to the circumstances, whenever he feels like seizing upon them. Uncle Chlodwig [the Reich Chancellor, Prince Hohenlohe] only puts up a mild resistance from time to time, but is in general absolutely compliant; the chiefs of Cabinet work on the other areas. Now this would be quite all right if the Kaiser were as industrious and clear-thinking a sovereign as Frederick the Great, whose Cabinet chiefs were only the obedient agents of his will . . . He could rule like that because he knew very few pleasures and was always at work. But now pleasure has become the most important thing, time for work is reduced to the minimum and at the same time the influence of the Cabinet chiefs is far-reaching and too great. We saw the same thing with Fried[rich] Wilhelm II and III and evil consequences inevitably followed.'[103] In mid-August 1896 Waldersee noted in his diary: 'The Kaiser intends to direct foreign policy and command the army as an autocrat In the long run that is not feasible and it must lead to constant friction.'[104]

In October 1896 the General commented scathingly that it was now becoming clear 'what the Kaiser has achieved in his short reign by way of destroying characters, creating confusion in the country, stirring up the parties against each other and cultivating despicable people. The sycophancy and lack of character of the members of his entourage and all those with whom he surrounds himself is said to be on the increase. To complete this attractive picture of the court, no one trusts anyone else. If two people converse quietly together, the others immediately become suspicious and feel uncomfortable. No one feels really at ease! Philipp Eulenburg is still considered his best and most true friend. Once when someone urged him to fulfil his duty as a friend and speak frankly to the Kaiser, he burst into tears and said: Oh no, I cannot say unpleasant things to him! And this is the stuff of which our men of influence are made!'[105] In March 1897, during celebrations in Berlin for the centenary of the birth of Kaiser Wilhelm I, Waldersee spoke to Counts August and Botho Eulenburg, the Oberstkämmerer (Principal Chamberlain) Christian Kraft, Hereditary Prince of Hohenlohe-Oehringen (a nephew of the Reich Chancellor), the House Minister von Wedell-Piesdorf, Chief of the Naval Cabinet Admiral Freiherr von Senden-Bibran, Commanding General of the VIII Army Corps in Koblenz Vogel von Falckenstein, former Minister of War von Verdy du Vernois and several members of the Reichstag and other old acquaintances. He recorded that all of them felt 'great anxiety' and 'deep discontent' with regard to the Kaiser. Their chief grounds for complaint were Wilhelm's interference in foreign policy, the accelerated expansion of the fleet and his latest speech to the Brandenburg provincial diet, which had 'caused offence to all parties'. Summing up his impressions, the General commented: 'The feeling against the Kaiser is said to be very bad among broad sections of the people.' 'In fact the parties are all either hostile or deeply discontented and disturbed. It has now reached the point where everything that our sovereign does and says or might have said is bitterly criticised. His autocratic tendencies have gradually been recognised for what they are, and people know that he no longer pays heed to anyone else's opinion, knows *everything* better and is a wiser judge of *every* subject than anyone else. I should be less concerned if his nerves were in a perfectly healthy state; one could then be certain that he would learn from experience. But I am convinced that he is not capable of facing serious reversals; his nerves would give way and he would collapse, which would be the worst thing for us.'[106]

A review of the many highly critical comments about the Kaiser which General von Waldersee made in his diary over the years from 1890 to 1897 reveals that they constantly revolve around the same points. Only in one regard is there a distinct linear development, which in fact reflects the actual course of events. In the later years the diary accurately records the dominant role which the monarch was now in a position to play, above all in the formulation of foreign policy and in military and naval affairs. Otherwise Waldersee's constant criticism, despite all the allowances he makes for the Kaiser's positive qualities (his quick understanding, his good memory, his engaging friendliness in personal contacts, his amusing conversation and confidence in speaking), can be generally summed up as follows:

- The autocratic tendency verging on megalomania which Wilhelm II displayed in his speeches and sayings as the foremost champion of the principle of 'personal monarchy' led to a dangerous overestimation of his abilities. Deluding himself that he was infallible, he refused to tolerate any opposition.
- In spite of his exaggerated opinion of himself Wilhelm in Waldersee's eyes had no firm goals. The driving force behind his actions was vanity and desire for popularity, combined with an overactive, perhaps even diseased imagination. This gave rise to the Kaiser's notorious unpredictability.
- The Kaiser's autocratic pretensions were not based on the conscientious exercise of his role as monarch; on the contrary, they were accompanied by reluctance to work and a love of distraction and amusement. The result was superficiality and dilettantism.
- His autocratic attitude expressed itself in ruthlessness and severity towards his responsible advisers in the Reich and Prussian governments as well as in the army. Strong characters were broken; weaker ones became despondent and submissive. Wilhelm preferred to rule with mediocrities rather than with the ablest men in the land.
- In order to win personal prestige and to be able to assert himself over his ministers the Kaiser relied on information brought him by irresponsible outsiders and unauthorised members of his entourage, who of course generally told

him what he wanted to hear. The result of this gossip-mongering was general discord and a poisoned atmosphere, above all at court, and a pronounced feeling of insecurity among all those who held high office. Waldersee castigated Wilhelm II's inability to arouse a sense of loyalty in his advisers.

- As far as Wilhelm's character was concerned, the General deeply deplored his susceptibility to flattery, his love of pomp and luxury and his tendency towards obscenity.

- Like many of his contemporaries in Germany and abroad, Waldersee was increasingly inclined to wonder whether the Kaiser ought still to be regarded as mentally normal at all. I shall return to this point below.

For all his insight into the problematical nature of 'personal monarchy' under a ruler like Wilhelm II, Waldersee had no real solution of the dilemma to suggest, unlike Holstein and Marschall von Bieberstein, who (as we shall see) tried to force the Kaiser to abandon his disastrous style of rule by confronting him with repeated collective resignations by the Reich Chancellor and the entire Ministry of State. His only, paradoxical-sounding response was that Wilhelm should suffer a few serious setbacks, since only through such calamities could one hope for an improvement in his character. It had long been his hope, he stated in May 1890, 'that the year 1890 would bring sombre experiences, and with them, regeneration'; but it was already 'almost June, without anything of the kind having happened'.[107] Like Hinzpeter at the Gymnasium in Kassel more than fifteen years earlier, Waldersee now saw a salutary taste of humiliation as the only remedy for imperial arrogance. He even sent up a prayer: 'If God in His goodness would but . . . send him disappointments and anxieties! He would render great service to our Fatherland and spare us much evil.'[108] A year later, when the international situation was becoming acute and the sense of crisis was taking hold within the country too, Waldersee again drew hope from the thought that 'the Kaiser will for once be confronted by the seriousness of life; hitherto almost everything he has done has succeeded, which has spoilt him and given him an immense opinion of his own ability. He can only be helped by serious experiences and setbacks. May God grant that they come, without damaging our interests too much meanwhile.'[109] But the time never came for the 'self-examination and self-recognition' on which the General pinned his hopes. 'Unfortunately we are still a very long way from that', he admitted helplessly in December 1892.[110] It is perhaps not altogether fanciful, however, for us to imagine the ageing General sitting up in bed at dead of night to wonder whether the anachronistic 'Personal Monarchy' which Bismarck had bequeathed to the Germans was really the most appropriate system of government for a vibrant and rapidly industrialising nation of 60 million people at the threshold to the twentieth century.

## CONSTERNATION IN THE WILHELMSTRASSE

After March 1890 Friedrich von Holstein, the Grey Eminence of the Foreign Office, who together with Waldersee and others had secretly advised the young monarch against Bismarck in the dismissal crisis, had rapidly become the most embittered enemy of the Chief of the General Staff. Yet he found himself learning the same painful lessons of disappointment as Waldersee. Holstein was particularly shocked by the Kaiser's undignified public appearances and his high-handed absolutist speeches, which led him to fear that Wilhelm might squander his inheritance of monarchical capital within a very short time. In early 1891 he warned that an unhappy and dangerous mood was beginning to spread throughout the Reich, and that, although it could be blamed partly on slander, the Kaiser himself bore much of the responsibility. As he wrote to Eulenburg, everyone was afraid that the Kaiser would go 'mad' like Ludwig II of Bavaria. It was said that he was suffering from 'delusions of grandeur, but had no moral courage'.[111] Unfortunately, Holstein stated, he could not but confirm 'that the position of His Majesty in the country is not improving; on the contrary. The serious-minded North German simply cannot understand why the Kaiser would order the troops in Potsdam and Berlin to the lake shore to watch him sailing in a torpedo boat in his admiral's uniform. There have been the most despicable jokes about it this last week — and that is the worst thing: people laugh.'[112] The Kaiser's speech to the Brandenburg provincial diet on 20 February 1891 completely shattered Holstein's confidence. He wrote in despair: 'It shows a misunderstanding of the times we live in. In 1891, when nothing is believed and everything is doubted, blind trust "through thick and thin" is not so easy to achieve.' Like many other observers Holstein thought the Kaiser's speech more suited to a historical melodrama than to the present political scene. 'This last speech is the most inopportune thing he has yet managed to do. The "Progressives" pretend to admire it in their newspapers. But when they talk, I mean the Left Liberals, it sounds quite different. Today one of them said: "If one listens to the speech with one's eyes shut, one thinks one is hearing [the melodramatic playwright Ernst von] Wildenbruch." . . . After the speech the talk about Ludwig II has started up again.' Holstein asked Eulenburg, as the Kaiser's friend, whether there was anyone in the imperial entourage, which 'criticises him so bravely behind his back', who 'does it to his face? Surely they cannot all approve of the speech.'[113] 'The worst thing . . . is that the Kaiser is increasingly regarded in parliamentary circles as mentally unwell', he warned.[114] At the end of 1891 Holstein again expressed his concern. 'It is sad that His Majesty still treats everything like a game. He will pay dearly for it before long, for things happen very quickly these days.'[115]

As head of the Political Department of the Foreign Office, Holstein was particularly alarmed by the Kaiser's increasing tendency to intervene personally in foreign affairs without consulting the appropriate authorities. A few days after the first Brandenburg speech he wrote to Eulenburg complaining that Wilhelm's action in sending the Empress Frederick to Paris had 'greatly increased mistrust of the Kaiser and of the way he rules'. The 'repeated conduct of His Majesty in foreign affairs' whereby he took political decisions 'as if he were dealing with court matters' was causing great disquiet. As examples of such intervention Holstein named not only the Paris incident but also Wilhelm's letter of condolence to the widow of the French painter Meissonier and the Flügeladjutant Wedel's mission to Copenhagen. 'All that is decreed without paying much attention to the Foreign [Office]', he objected. 'The public is beginning to realise that His Majesty is his own foreign minister, and this causes great uneasiness . . . In Germany this has greatly increased mistrust of the Kaiser and of the way he rules', he warned, and predicted that if Caprivi and Marschall did not stand up more firmly to the Kaiser 'we shall see all kinds of strange things happening'.[116] Within the diplomatic corps discontent arose from the fact that since Bismarck's dismissal almost every post as envoy had been given to someone from the army or the consular body.[117] Wilhelm's propensity to treat 'diplomats as a corps of irregulars which is to get its troops and its training through elements from God knows where' offended Holstein so much that in September 1892 he threatened to resign. The pleasure he took in his work was disappearing fast, he said.[118]

Like Waldersee, the Geheimrat saw Wilhelm's restlessness and lack of seriousness as diminishing the prestige of the monarchy, even as a threat to the survival of the Hohenzollern throne. He expressed his concern to Eulenburg in February 1891: 'On the 28th His Majesty is going to the Kaiserhof to attend the celebrations of the Bonn student fraternity Borussia. I have not met a single person . . . who does not think this a very regrettable idea. By going everywhere, eating everywhere, speaking everywhere His Majesty lowers himself too much. If he then suddenly decides to exert his authority, like the Great Elector or Frederick the Great, he is not taken seriously . . . You know that it goes against my innermost nature to criticise the Kaiser. But I am afraid I cannot do otherwise. Much of what is happening is the Kaiser's own fault.'[119] Holstein's comment can be compared with Waldersee's reaction to Wilhelm's behaviour a few weeks later in Bonn, 'where he goes out drinking with the student corps with a student's cap on his head and directs the whole nonsense himself'. 'It is simply unworthy of a kaiser!', the General raged. Such 'childish nonsense' would 'deeply offend pro-monarchical feeling and the Kaiser will inevitably lose all respect', he feared. 'Today in ermine robes, tomorrow dressed for the beer garden – it will not do, we cannot put up with it in the long run. It deeply offends monarchical feeling and gradually destroys it. Crown princes have been able to get away with such behaviour; they were forgiven for it as soon as they showed their seriousness on the throne. Sovereigns cannot do so with impunity.' What appalled Waldersee most was the fact that Wilhelm accompanied Grand Duke Adolf of Luxemburg to the station in Bonn wearing student fraternity costume. In his eyes, the Kaiser's 'undignified behaviour' had reached its peak. It was 'a blow in the face for all sovereigns. The German ruling princes, among whom there is already so much bad feeling, will be deeply offended and will tell themselves that such a thing could happen to them too.'[120] The anger aroused by Wilhelm's unseemly behaviour in Bonn had wide repercussions, as Holstein and Waldersee feared. Arthur von Brauer, the envoy from Baden, criticised the Kaiser's speech there, commenting that the public did not understand 'how H.M. could publicly praise institutions like student duelling which are now offences under the law of the land and which the Catholic Church punishes with lesser excommunication . . . The idleness and extravagance in the corps also give little cause for this institution, which the overwhelming majority of students detest, to be glorified in the highest quarters.'[121]

Just as the Empress Frederick had done, Holstein described the saying 'suprema lex regis voluntas' inscribed by the Kaiser in the Golden Book of Munich as a 'disaster for the nation'. 'He makes himself not so much hated as ridiculous', he wrote to Eulenburg. 'He is held in increasing contempt.'[122] Eulenburg was distressed to find himself compelled to write warning letters to his 'hotly beloved Kaiser' and to advise him to use the motto 'Ich Dien' at the first possible opportunity – forgetting that this was the motto of the Prince of Wales and that Wilhelm had recently used precisely this phrase to mock his uncle.[123]

At the Foreign Office no one doubted that socialists, democrats, Catholics and particularists were doing all they could to stir up ill-will towards the Kaiser, and that the Bismarck faction was doing the same, often to even greater effect. For that very reason, however, Wilhelm's frivolous and restless style of rule was strongly condemned as providing an easy target for his enemies. As Foreign Secretary Adolf Marschall von Bieberstein warned immediately after the Düsseldorf speech of 4 May 1891: 'The tendency to damage and discredit the present government, and more particularly His Majesty, by systematically spreading confusion and *anxiety* among the people, is becoming so evident everywhere, and is so clearly the weapon used by our enemies, that only *one* tactic is open to the government, and that is to act always and everywhere as a *calming* influence. Every word that is likely to create anxiety furthers our enemies' plans, and most of all when it comes from the highest quarters . . . In this connection I would mention as an example the fact that one of our foremost stockbrokers, when asked by an acquaintance of mine what effect the speech had had on the stock market, replied with a smile "None at all; we have long been accustomed to such things." What can we expect to happen at times when matters are serious and every word should be seen as an appeal to defend the most sacred possessions of the Fatherland?'[124] Not only at the Foreign Office but also among the Prussian ministers the uncomfortable feeling prevailed that the country was sailing helplessly towards a catastrophe. Thus, after a long conversation with Finance Minister Miquel Waldersee recorded that the latter was also 'very pessimistic and also has no illusions about the Kaiser'.[125]

Wilhelm's second Brandenburg speech of 24 February 1892 could not but have a disastrous effect on the mood among responsible statesmen. 'Oh these wretched speeches!', sighed the leader of the Conservative Party, Otto von Helldorff-Bedra, whose loyalties were normally with the Kaiser. 'When will he learn the caution that is so vital?'[126] The Reich Chancellor saw in the reception given to the speech the 'proof of how suspicious of autocratic tendencies people in all circles have become. They are drawing conclusions from all the Kaiser's speeches, taken together, which they find unacceptable. All parties agree on that.' The general critical mood had been in evidence again over Wilhelm's plans for the Berlin cathedral, Caprivi continued. 'It becomes very difficult to carry out business objectively when one constantly comes up against the suspicion that we are dealing with whims and caprices of the monarch, and when there is less and less inclination to co-operate with the monarch. I do not take a pessimistic view and I believe that this will be overcome, but we must not stretch our credit too much to begin with.'[127]

A few months later Wilhelm's plans to hold a lottery to raise funds to embellish the surroundings of the Berlin Schloss provoked such violent criticism that the idea had to be abandoned. Holstein warned despairingly that building plans of this kind inevitably revived the memory of the fairy-tale castles of the deranged King Ludwig II of Bavaria. He declared: 'The Kaiser is not in a position to be able to do such things at present.' If the Ministry of State gave way to the Kaiser on this question it would be 'the object of public contempt'.[128] Philipp Eulenburg likewise thought the planned lottery 'highly dangerous' and warned that with the present angry mood in Bavaria the Kaiser's building plans 'almost forcibly' reminded people of the castles built by the late King. Reporting in his official capacity to Marschall, he stated his opinion that 'in the interest of our All-gracious sovereign it is very much to be hoped . . . that the fantastic projects . . . will prove to be only fantasies, or that they will at least be reduced to a modest scale'. Wilhelm wrote bitterly in the margin of Eulenburg's report: 'Really, Philipp! et tu Brute!'[129]

If such anxieties were shared even by the Kaiser's closest friend, who according to Waldersee had a 'completely idealised picture of the Kaiser',[130] it is scarcely surprising that his enemies were delighted. In the Bismarck camp malicious jokes circulated about the latest symptoms of illness said to have been noticed in the Kaiser.[131] From the Wilhelmstrasse came a stream of increasingly urgent warnings that Wilhelm must be on his guard against poisonous attacks by the pro-Bismarck faction if he did not want to risk his throne. As Holstein wrote to Eulenburg in April 1892: 'His Majesty knows that his enemies are watching him. The April issue of the Contemporary Review contains an article, "William". Translated from German. The cleverest and bitterest thing which has yet been written attacking the Kaiser. His Majesty has read the article . . . You will see from it that the Kaiser must weigh his words and deeds more carefully than hitherto if he does not want − metaphorically speaking − to be thrown to the dogs.'[132] The following month Alfred von Kiderlen-Wächter sent the same article, with the Kaiser's annotations, to Eulenburg, commenting that the latter would see from it 'what insidious attacks are still being made against His Majesty'. Certain turns of phrase such as 'burden of vanity', 'sword of the Prussian officer' and the like were, he said, unmistakably expressions used by the Bismarcks − 'they *could not* be invented by an *Englishman*'.[133] Eventually Eulenburg felt compelled to warn the Kaiser of the acute risk he was running by his autocratic behaviour. 'Our good German people will never favour a single large national party', he wrote to Wilhelm in August 1892. 'But Bismarck as the standard-bearer of parliament against the Kaiser with "absolutist tendencies" (which the people will see in every word that Your Majesty utters and in all Your many visits and journeys at home and abroad, because our philistine countrymen will never get it into their heads that Your Majesty can work during these changes of scenery!) − *that* is a watchword that has caught on.'[134]

Eulenburg's letter made little impression and changed nothing in the Kaiser's way of life or style of rule. Waldersee noted at the end of 1892 that he frequently heard the expression 'le roi s'amuse' in connection with the shooting expeditions on which Wilhelm had been engaged for weeks on end. Socialists and Progressives had long been running a book on how much time he would have left for audiences.[135] In the summer of 1894 calculations appeared in the press showing that in the course of the past twelve months Wilhelm had spent no less than 199 days on his travels, as a result of which the joke on the streets of Berlin was that the Kaiser had said 'I have no time to rule.'[136]

In the Wilhelmstrasse the premonition was gaining ground that Wilhelm II's reign might turn out to be the prelude to a republic and could even end with his execution. As early as September 1892 Holstein commented in dismay that 'our Master' had 'no instinct for the masses' and exclaimed: 'What humiliations await

him!'[137] 'Would we have thought it possible 5 years ago for . . . the court to descend
to the depths it has reached today?', he asked in a letter to Eulenburg, adding that
the Kaiser 'even treats ruling as a sport. Is he likely to die on the throne?? He is
not the man, nor is this the time, to play around with the people like a giant toy.
I am much more inclined to believe in the coming of the German Republic –
which Bismarck has already prepared the way for – than [as Eulenburg feared]
in the disintegration of the Reich. The Liberals who are loyal to the Reich and
who are being antagonised are much more likely to turn to the republic than to
particularism.'[138]

A year later Holstein wrote to Eulenburg: 'You cannot imagine how much the
feeling against H.M. in the country has intensified in the last 4 weeks. "Travel
mania, avoidance of work, frivolity" stand out above all the other accusations
against him. The R[eich] C[hancellor] is accused of not being firm enough with
the Kaiser. The future belongs to a R[eich] c[hancellor] who knows how to "keep
the whims of the Kaiser in check" . . . I am very depressed. We have worked all
these years to create or maintain a position for H.M. in the eyes of the outside
world. But it is all wasted effort if he ruins his own position within the country.
Nor should we overlook the fact   and Marschall made the same observation
in very bad humour yesterday – that the respect and recognition which H.H.
[Bismarck] receives from the public is on the increase once more, because people
are saying to themselves: "The man is right, one cannot do business with the
Kaiser."'[139] In a further letter to Eulenburg at this time Holstein commented
dejectedly: 'I am afraid that his constantly rising unpopularity means a more
dismal future for H.M. than he suspects.'[140]

After Caprivi's dismissal in October 1894 the sense of crisis in the country
reached a new peak. In the *Zukunft* Maximilian Harden published an article
entitled 'The Giant Toy', in which he compared the Kaiser with King Charles I,
who was beheaded in 1649. Holstein bewailed the fact that 'the feeling against
the Kaiser among the public is quite appalling. People talk more and more
of Ludwig II. *It cannot go on much longer like this* . . . The Kaiser suspects
nothing of all this; he behaves with such carelessness that even I am sometimes
worried about his mental equilibrium.' The latest chancellor crisis had done him
great harm, Holstein concluded.[141] It was Wilhelm II's misfortune, he declared
in another letter to Eulenburg at the beginning of 1895, 'that his glow-worm
character reminds people of Friedrich Wilhelm IV and Ludwig II. Neither of
us has any influence over the conclusions which the German people will draw
from this similarity.'[142] Only those who 'long for a Bismarckian dictatorship or
a republic' could draw any comfort from the present situation in Germany, he
wrote to Eulenburg during the first weeks of Hohenlohe's chancellorship. 'That
the regime of His Majesty Wilhelm the Second is the prelude to one of these

two forms of government is a possibility which I am afraid I cannot exclude. His Majesty retained a certain respect for our stubborn Caprivi. He claps "Uncle" Hohenlohe on the back and says: "Well, you certainly have brought a long wish list with you" and leaves after two minutes, whereupon Hohenlohe returns from Wildpark [station in Potsdam] to Berlin with his fat portfolio full of things that have not been dealt with. That, dear friend, is an operetta regime, but not one that a European nation at the end of the 19th century will put up with.'[143] The young Kaiser was unconscious of any danger. Convinced of his own infallibility he continued, unperturbed, to build up his personal power. But how *did* German society at the end of the nineteenth century react to this anachronistic 'operetta regime'?

# CHAPTER TWENTY

# The predictable disaster: Wilhelm II
# and the 'public soul' of Germany

## 'THERE MAY BE EVIL TIMES TO COME'

No more than a few months after Bismarck's dismissal, well-placed observers like the Empress Frederick, Chief of the General Staff Count von Waldersee and Geheimrat Friedrich von Holstein – as should be more than evident from the preceding chapter – were already haunted by the fear that the superficial, impulsive and wholly anachronistic style of Wilhelm II's rule might lead to the downfall of the Hohenzollern monarchy, the proclamation of a republic or the imposition of a dictatorship. His grandiose aspirations to the role of autocratic sovereign by divine right in an increasingly critical, industrialised mass age made the danger of failure all too plain. When in January 1891 a portrait of Wilhelm II by Max Koner, which the Kaiser had commissioned for the German embassy in Paris, was exhibited in honour of the Kaiser's birthday, it made a deeply disquieting impression on many people. The Baden envoy Arthur von Brauer reported in surprise to Karlsruhe that the life-size oil painting was causing a stir in Berlin. 'The pose chosen by the artist is thought too theatrical, the stance is almost provocative and the field marshal's baton is unusually large and prominent. [The ambassador to France] Count Münster, who saw the picture here, gave a very disparaging opinion of it; in conception and manner it was very inappropriate for Paris. He even expressed his doubts in the highest quarters, but without success. The picture went off to Paris. Meanwhile Countess Asseburg had taken the opportunity to tell H.M. with the kind of ruthless frankness that only a lady can get away with that the picture was "very unattractive and absolutely impossible for Paris" because it would invite mockery from the Parisians. Her words made an impression; H.M. sent a telegram to Paris ordering the picture not to be unpacked and to be returned.'[1] On Waldersee the portrait made a

26. Max Koner's portrait of Kaiser Wilhelm II, January 1891 – a declaration of war?

'sad impression' because it showed the monarch 'as he really thinks and feels – immensely vain and self-confident!' The Kaiser was shown standing 'in an incredibly challenging attitude, in Garde du Corps uniform with a black cuirass and a purple mantle, leaning on a long field marshal's baton. It gives everyone the feeling that he is trying to impress the French and is saying to them: "beware of picking a fight with me".' One would not be able to give a true verdict on the portrait for another ten or twenty years, the Chief of the General Staff opined. 'If he has achieved great deeds by then, it will be an excellent picture; if things go differently, it will be simply ridiculous.'[2] Only three years later, when Wilhelm II's unpopularity at all levels of society throughout the Reich had reached critical proportions, Waldersee could no longer doubt that the throne of the Hohenzollerns, in which he had once had so much faith as a bastion against democratisation, had become very shaky. 'The Kaiser is now reaping what he sowed', he declared. 'In the first few years everything seemed to go very well and he was obviously very lucky too; regrettably this soon gave him arrogant and conceited feelings which made him blind to the real circumstances; he thought he could do everything himself, that he understood everything and could control the politics of the whole world, and what was the result? May the good Lord not turn aside from us completely, but protect us. There may be evil times to come.'[3] When the fifth volume of Treitschke's *German History* was published later that year many readers were struck by the resemblance between the first years of the reign of the Prussian King Friedrich Wilhelm IV and the present. Distraught, Waldersee asked himself: 'Are we to find ourselves in the same terrible plight as in 1848? God forbid, but it is very probable that we are heading in that direction.'[4]

Observers abroad often saw most clearly the immense risks inherent in the all-or-nothing game in which the Kaiser was engaged. As early as May 1890 the French historian Ernest Lavisse drew attention to the ambitious aims of the young Kaiser in an influential article in the *Figaro*, in which he emphasised the dangers that lay not only in the Kaiser's exceptionally powerful position but also in his character. 'In the person of Wilhelm II power and youth form a fascinating contrast', he wrote. 'Wilhelm II is not content with reigning; he wants to govern, like his forefathers who put Prussia together piece by piece with their own royal hands.' For this reason alone the dismissal of Bismarck had been a simple, quite natural necessity in Wilhelm's eyes: 'His property was in the hands of another: he took his property for himself.' The Germany whose government he had now personally taken over had 'immense reserves of loyalty, fidelity and patience' towards Wilhelm II. 'It is no longer at odds with itself, as it once was, for ruling princes both great and small, kings, grand dukes and dukes, are gradually disappearing in the majesty of empire . . . The parties are fragments which will not unite, but Germany wishes to be united and indivisible and to remain so. The only form which this unity can take at the present time is monarchy; the only monarch is the King of Prussia. Germany is personified in Kaiser Wilhelm II, and Germany gives him such power that he is able to take great risks.' And so Wilhelm, 'he alone and always he', would 'bear the burden of the day. In political battles he will always be personally engaged, exposed and visible to all. It is for him to find the solution to all questions . . . But not all questions are soluble . . . Should expectations remain unfulfilled, who will bear the responsibility? The Kaiser. This responsibility is not without danger', Lavisse warned. A further difficulty, in the historian's eyes, lay in the fact that, although Wilhelm had a modern air, he was 'a contemporary of the past'; he was indeed 'an anachronism' in his innermost convictions. 'Kaiser by the grace of God! I can assure you that this title is no empty formula for Wilhelm II', Lavisse stressed. 'His belief is entirely sincere.' Other characteristics of the monarch would have an equally marked impact on the style and content of German policy. 'Rapidity in action, a predilection for oratory, a lively mind and a thirst for greatness. The Kaiser seems even to have a taste for the impossible.' As to foreign policy, Wilhelm spoke of the Triple Alliance politely but without enthusiasm, as if he thought the alliance with Austria-Hungary and Italy a little *passé*. 'But to pursue colonial policy on a par with England and to come to agreements with her, to pay visits to the Queen of England and the Emperor of Russia, to repeat these visits, to review the English Navy in the uniform of an English admiral and to take the salute of the Russian Army in the uniform of the Russian Army . . . – that is fine, that is grand, that is impossible!' The future of Wilhelm II and of Germany was therefore still unclear and uncertain. 'The young Kaiser . . . attracts universal attention to a high degree; he is in favour with public opinion and deserves this distinction above all because of the grandeur of his vision and . . . also most especially because of the presentiment of certain dangers which he has expressed. Let the danger come: the Kaiser will not flinch. He is courageous to the point of audacity, he looks ahead with confidence, he strides onwards, the figure of an ideological soldier, into the unknown.'[5]

The uneasy feeling of witnessing a highly risky game of chance which Lavisse conveys here in somewhat romanticised and veiled terms was given much sharper expression by the Portuguese writer and diplomat José Maria Eça de Queirós shortly afterwards. In a most perceptive comment on the recklessly uncompromising attitude which flowed from the Wilhelmine concept of the role of the kaiser he wrote in 1891: 'Wilhelm II literally gambles with those terrible iron dice of which Bismarck once spoke.' He too predicted that Wilhelm would one day *either* 'calmly and majestically direct the destiny of Europe from his palace in Berlin', *or else* find himself sitting in a London hotel room rummaging 'for the battered double crown of Germany and Prussia in his little exile's travelling

27. 'The Kaiser's Dream'. Cartoon in the British journal *Truth*, December 1890, showing Wilhelm II's progress from birth (bottom right) to exile (top left) and the partition of Germany after a lost war

bag'.[6] As early as the end of 1890 the British republican journal *Truth* had published a caricature entitled 'The Kaiser's Dream' which predicted the future course of Wilhelm II's reign with breathtaking perspicacity (fig. 27). A series of images shows the political crisis after Bismarck's fall, the dangerously growing discontent of the German population, the attempt to avert internal crisis by an external war and the subsequent defeat and disintegration of the Reich into several republics. The Kaiser and the other deposed monarchs seek asylum in London with their exiles' travelling bags. In fact it was only in this last detail – the place of exile – that the caricaturist's uncannily accurate prediction failed to come true.

After Bismarck's departure – the celebrated 'Dropping the Pilot' caricature by Sir John Tenniel in *Punch* had already hinted at Wilhelm's foolhardy role in the dismissal crisis – it was the Kaiser's Brandenburg speech of February 1892 which did the most to set alarm bells ringing abroad. The Baden envoy in Berlin reported in disgust, but not without anxiety, that 'the imperial speech and the riots have of course provided the foreign press with a very welcome opportunity to paint our situation in the blackest colours and dish up the most incredible lies about both events for foreign readers . . . The most shameless of them is, as always, the Paris Figaro, which claims to have had telegraphic reports that as a result of the speech people in Berlin are saying que l'Empereur "ne dispose pas entièrement de ses facultés"! Unfortunately such idiocies are widely believed in foreign countries which are less well disposed towards us, and so they help make the general political situation worse, however filthy and nonsensical such products of the press are in themselves.'[7] In London, in an article entitled 'The Holy German Empire' published on 26 February 1892, the *St James's Gazette* drew attention to the alarming anachronism of the Kaiser's autocratic perorations, although at the same time putting forward the view that strong leadership would be welcomed by the German people as long as it brought unity and order. 'There is something very strange, and at first sight very much out of date, in this young man's enunciation, in words stronger than any English King has used since the days of Henry VIII, of the principle, *Quod principi placet, legis habet vigorem*; and no wonder that in Germany and elsewhere men are asking what the end of it will be. Is the Emperor a hot-headed young man inflated with an inordinate conception of his own power and capacity, and destined out of sheer obstinacy and vanity to jeopardize his throne and endanger his country? . . . The majority of the German people care little for Constitutional Government. They want a strong man at the head of affairs, an efficient administration, and a settled policy . . . If it is believed that the Emperor's policy can keep Germany strong and united, and prevent the forces of discord and disorder gaining ground, it will have the support of the people. But no one will deny that the oratorical recklessness which is one of the Kaiser's most marked characteristics is in itself a source of danger. As long as he confines his frankness to questions of internal policy no great harm is done; but let him make a speech in the same strain . . . on a subject of international difficulty, and the whole of Europe would be in a blaze. His glorification of Rossbach and Dennewitz was not very wise; and a large section of Frenchmen have not forgotten or forgiven the allusion in a recent speech to "the Corsican *parvenu*". It is true that the Emperor frequently insists on his desire for peace, but unless he can keep a watch on his lips it is quite possible that he may himself be the cause of war . . . A highly interesting figure is this young ruler, with his unbounded belief in himself and his firm conviction that Providence is his ally and will never desert him, or Prussia. He is all the more picturesque because he is an anachronism. He talks the language of the old Hohenzollern tradition − with modern variations. But the experiment of governing a great civilized country under a patriarchate is a curious one to be attempting in the year 1892.'[8]

## THE GERMAN 'PUBLIC SOUL' AND THE KAISER

But how did the German people react to the imperial announcement of divine right and autocracy? Was the German 'public soul' (Heinrich Mann) really so unpolitical, as Lavisse and the author of the article in the *St James's Gazette* claimed, as to care little for constitutional forms and to accept Wilhelm II's autocracy as the price which had to be paid for national unity and internal order? Did the German nation even see its own image in Kaiser Wilhelm II, as Walther Rathenau maintained after the fall of the monarchy, and as is still willingly believed by (crypto-)monarchists today? In Rathenau's famous and often-quoted comment on Wilhelm in 1919, 'This people, at this time, consciously and unconsciously, wanted him thus and not otherwise. They wanted themselves and him to be thus and not otherwise.' 'Never before has a symbolic human being been so perfectly reflected in an epoch, nor an epoch in a human being. Not for a single day could Germany have been governed as it was governed, without the consent of the people.'[9] In the light of the contemporary sources, which bear ample witness to the growing unrest and anger among all social classes throughout the county, Rathenau's retrospective judgement must be firmly rejected, not from personal prejudice or ideological bias but out of respect for the truth and for the real feelings of that generation of the German people.

Waldersee's 'rude awakening' in the summer of 1890 was causally linked to his perception of the growing unpopularity of the Kaiser among the citizenry. There was 'absolutely no question but that the feeling against the Kaiser [was] growing fast', he commented in his diary only a few weeks after Bismarck's fall.[10] In May 1890 Waldersee noted that in the army, the political parties and the population as a whole 'a feeling of dissatisfaction with him [Wilhelm II] has become more widespread; I thought that he would have very fanatical admirers among the young, but they of all people . . . are said to complain bitterly about him and criticise his vanity and love of playing soldiers'. This mood was all the more dangerous, Waldersee observed, because the Bismarcks were clearly doing their best to spread the message from Friedrichsruh 'that the Kaiser is mad'.[11] Three months later the Chief of the General Staff's anxiety was increasing. To judge from German newspapers, he said, one would think that there was 'no more popular man and ruler . . . than Kaiser Wilhelm'; yet this impression was deceptive. He had found that 'the number of dissatisfied people is immense; and yet this is not even hinted at in the press. It worries me greatly, but mostly because the army is strongly affected by this mood.'[12] He was shocked by the 'growing discontent with the Kaiser among wide sections of the population' and attributed this alarming development to the fact that Wilhelm had no sense of purpose and acted only out of egoism and vanity.[13] After the 'absurd' speech at Düsseldorf in which Wilhelm had declared that he alone was master in the Reich and that he would tolerate no other, the General commented: 'Unfortunately we have already reached the point that the Kaiser is no longer taken seriously;

people have already heard so many wonderful speeches from him that they are only amused by them.'[14] The Catholic General Walther Freiherr von Loë, who had come to Berlin in October 1890 on the occasion of the visit of King Leopold II of the Belgians, was astonished to find that the mood in the capital had changed so much in a year.[15] Three years later Loë had become more deeply pessimistic still about the state of Germany, describing it as 'almost beyond hope'.[16]

Waldersee's forebodings about the disastrous future facing the monarchy under Wilhelm II were reinforced by what he himself observed while travelling around the country on tours of inspection or on leave. In September 1890 he commented that during recent months he had journeyed widely, whether in South Germany, East Prussia, Schleswig or Silesia or on the Rhine, had spoken to a great variety of people – the Grand Duke of Baden, King Albert and Prince Georg of Saxony, Prince Albrecht of Prussia, countless generals, big landowners and industrialists, ministers, provincial administrators and other senior officials – and had found the same feeling of insecurity and apprehension in all of them. 'Everywhere anxiety about the future and doubts about the Kaiser being the man to take us forward; most people even thought that he is having a destructive effect.' Waldersee added that he would be prepared to swear 'that lately I have found *not a single person* who had any confidence'.[17]

In October 1890 Waldersee recorded with concern that he was 'constantly receiving reports of the growing feeling against the Kaiser; it has now reached the best middle-class circles. In South Germany it is growing, and recently in Saxony too; in Bavaria I hear people are saying quite openly that he is mentally ill.'[18] In November, when members of parliament returned to Berlin for the new legislative term, Waldersee heard 'more opinions from the provinces, of course; unfortunately they bear witness to widespread discontent, especially with the Kaiser; he has in fact disappointed everyone – with the exception of the Social Democrats'.[19] Not long afterwards Waldersee recorded that he had spoken to Franz Fischer, the Berlin correspondent of the National Liberal *Kölnische Zeitung*, as well as to a banker (whom he did not further identify) and a general. 'With all 3 the conversation soon came round to the Kaiser and they were of one mind in thinking that the mood is getting persistently worse. They represent completely different milieux', the General commented.[20] When he met Theobald von Bethmann Hollweg early the next year while hunting in Buckow, the future Reich Chancellor assured him that 'in all sections of the population the mood is unfavourable'.[21]

In January 1891 Waldersee was horrified to observe that even among the ordinary people of Berlin the enthusiasm for the Kaiser which had been apparent until recently had completely vanished. At the consecration of the Friedenskirche he was struck by 'how coolly the people in the streets behaved towards the Kaiser; only 6 months ago all the streets leading to the church would have been decorated; this time there were only a few flags on the houses closest to the church and at most a few 100 people'. When the Chief of the General Staff commented on this to the Berlin Chief of Police the latter shrugged and said that this was simply 'an expression of the general mood'.[22] A year later Waldersee noticed that on the Kaiser's birthday the usual illuminations were limited to Unter den Linden and a very few other streets, 'as all Berliners are aware of a gradual waning of enthusiasm for the Kaiser'.[23] After talking the situation over in detail with civil servants and politicians in Berlin Waldersee was distressed to have to acknowledge that 'the increasing ill-feeling is unquestionably the main topic of all conversation'.[24]

Holstein, forced to watch helplessly while Wilhelm alienated his own people with one autocratic pronouncement after another and put the future of the monarchy at risk, took a no less critical view. He wrote despondently to Philipp Eulenburg in November 1891 reporting that in response to Wilhelm's disastrous inscription in the Golden Book of the City of Munich, 'suprema lex regis voluntas',[25] the anthem 'Heil Dir im Siegerkranz' had been shouted down in public. 'That is a sign of the times. Bismarck's position is much stronger than six months ago. People were also heard shouting "salus publica suprema lex" at the station', Holstein registered in dismay. 'More and more people are deserting the Kaiser. He has not yet noticed it, but come the moment when he needs to call on the devotion of the people and their trust in him – then he will notice what he has brought upon himself. Our sovereign seems predestined to suffer terrible defeats, for the ruler's success depends on the trust and love of those who do his bidding. No intelligent person can want an absolute state in Germany today. All the suspicions about the Kaiser's mental health are emerging again like a poisonous miasma . . . Things are not going badly in general – only His Majesty!'[26] Scarcely had Holstein uttered this lament when the Kaiser made a speech which again sparked rumours about his 'state of mental health', and this time – as Holstein pointed out – in all the parties.[27] When an anonymous satirical article appeared in the Berlin *Lokalanzeiger* at about this time Holstein saw it as a sad symptom of the general mood of the population that this edition of the newspaper, which normally had a circulation of 12,000, was so quickly sold out that it was changing hands for five marks. He sent a copy to Eulenburg with the remark that the malicious article owed its success to the fact that it 'corresponds to the picture that people have of H. Majesty'. It was significant that the paper had been sold principally to officers, for that showed 'how the Kaiser's position has been undermined, especially in the army', he wrote. 'His Majesty has seen the lampoon and is very angry about it', Holstein continued. 'To counteract this

kind of thing His Majesty must show *seriousness of character* . . . I am beginning
to get tired of these incidents.'[28]

The journalist Dr Franz Fischer, who as Berlin correspondent of the quasi-
official *Kölnische Zeitung* had good contacts both at the Foreign Office and among
the Rhenish-Westphalian industrialists, was elegiac in his comments. In a broad
survey of public opinion a year after Bismarck's dismissal he declared: 'When our
Kaiser came to the throne everyone breathed freely again, all hearts were drawn
to him, a new confidence and a lively spirit of enterprise took hold everywhere;
the upsurge in our industry, which had lain fallow for so long, was unmistakable.
Today the exact opposite is true . . . And what is worst is that the reason for the
general mistrust and uneasiness is precisely the picture which numerous people
in all types of profession, the army, the civil service, the academic world, but
above all the world of commerce, have formed of His Majesty the Kaiser, with or
without good reason. Our government, especially the Reich Chancellor himself,
may do their utmost to counteract the present dissatisfaction by proposing good
laws and taking excellent administrative measures, but it will not achieve its goal.
For the conviction is steadily growing that the entire body of ministers are not
independent men who act in good faith, but more or less puppets, who blindly
follow the whims and caprices of their imperial master. But such incredible
legends are circulated about the Kaiser – and what is still more insane – they
are so completely believed, even in royalist circles, that people think the most
impossible things and the most extraordinary administrative measures are not
only quite possible but very probable. At the very least the Kaiser is universally
portrayed as a gentleman who is extremely erratic in his thinking, irresolute in
his decisions, rash in his speeches, inconsistent in his preferences and unable to
tolerate opposition. Private attempts to refute these false ideas are fruitless. On
the contrary, the smallest trifles, such as the frequency with which the garrisons
visited by the Kaiser are called out, or the recent transfer of the torpedo boat
to Berlin, only provide fresh reasons for making a mountain out of a molehill.
One is constantly hearing: the old Kaiser would never have done such-and-
such!!'[29]

The well-informed Baden envoy described the mood of the people in equally
sombre terms in December 1891, looking back over developments since Bismarck's departure. 'The theme of "suprema lex regis voluntas" was very far
from played out', Brauer commented sarcastically, 'when news of the Kaiser's
speech at the swearing-in of the recruits in Potsdam reached the wider public.
At first people thought it was a hoax or a malicious invention. But soon it was
confirmed by people who had heard it with their own ears that H.M. really
did say the words attributed to him. The Commanding General of the Corps
of Guards, General von Meerscheidt-Hüllessem, immediately realised what

dangerous consequences the Kaiser's words could have and after H.M. had left he made a short speech to the assembled troops in which he said it was the duty of everyone present not to allow any of the all-highest remarks to become public knowledge. Of course this well-meaning command, addressed to such a large number of soldiers among whom there were probably Social Democrats, was doomed to failure. The all-highest words caused utter panic among the most timid spirits, and I have the impression that they were expressly exploited by the Kaiser's enemies to stir up fear and indignation – among the propertied classes, as if the Kaiser could make rash decisions dangerous to trade and commerce – and among the workers, as if the Kaiser might feel the inclination or the need to have them "shot down".' Commenting on the abrupt change in Wilhelm II's attitude to the workers Brauer wrote: 'At the beginning of his reign, imbued with ardent, optimistic dedication to his exalted calling, the Kaiser was full of joyous confidence that he had a mission to resolve the social question. The great popularity which he undoubtedly enjoyed at first deluded him into believing that it would be easy for him to outshine the Bebels, the Liebknechts etc. with the mass of workers, and to win their confidence. Hence the great energy which he put into organising the international social welfare conference, showing a personal interest in social welfare legislation, attending the Council of State and getting rid of the Anti-Socialist Bill. There have been more than enough utterances by H.M. to show that he expected his efforts to succeed very quickly and to bring about a sudden and complete transformation in the attitude of the misguided masses. He may therefore have felt bitter that in this respect he had nothing but disappointments: social democracy is becoming a more and more significant factor, and the early signs of the formation of an imperial workers' party, which the Kaiser hoped for, have had no lasting result. Given H.M.'s character it is very understandable, psychologically, if these disappointments have brought about a complete reversal of his attitude. I am afraid the Kaiser has now become convinced that nothing can be achieved amicably and that the worker question can be resolved only by force and on the principle of "the sooner the better". Thus for some time now he has repeatedly referred to "dangers from within", culminating in his recent remark about "shooting down brothers and friends".'[30]

Even before the Brandenburg speech of February 1892 a dangerously hostile mood, which came close to erupting in street protests, had built up towards the Kaiser. The Empress Frederick's inclination was to withdraw to the Taunus mountains or even to England, but when she reluctantly returned to Berlin in December 1891 for the season she observed with distress that her son was 'not at all popular!' and that his 'public utterances' were 'much criticized'.[31] 'I am miserable about affairs here – & W's growing great unpopularity, wh. *cannot astonish* me; he does not feel it or observe it & is as self confident as ever alas', she wrote.[32] The widowed Empress's assessment of the situation was amply borne out by the foreign diplomats stationed in the various capital cities within Germany. The British minister in Dresden, for instance, reported to London in December 1891 that 'uneasiness exists in Germany among patriotic & loyal people because their faith in the discretion & wisdom of the Crown has been so rudely & often shaken'.[33] A mocking character sketch of Kaiser Wilhelm in the London journal *Truth*, which was widely sold and discussed in Germany, attracted the comment from Waldersee (who had been given it by the Adjutant-General von Wittich, of all people) that it contained 'incredible things about the Kaiser and could only have been written by people with very close knowledge of him and the Prince of Wales, who comes out of it worst, and of the life and atmosphere in the English [royal] family'. The General had to admit that after reading it he was distressed 'that so much ridicule can be heaped on the Kaiser; of course it is immensely exaggerated, but unfortunately it identifies weaknesses in him with absolute accuracy'.[34]

Following this, Wilhelm II's speech to the Brandenburg provincial diet on 24 February 1892 provoked a disastrous public reaction both in Germany and abroad. Because the speech coincided, as already mentioned, with widespread agitation over the School Bill and major street protests by the unemployed in Berlin, the Kaiser's autocratic utterances seemed almost deliberately framed with class conflict in mind. The Reich Chancellor remarked philosophically that the street riots were 'of no importance', and that it had been an excellent thing that the Kaiser 'rode out once . . . in order to show courage. A repetition of the insolence shown on that occasion would be undesirable, however, since it would not be preventable without a police escort. So I was glad that the Kaiser gave up the idea of riding out again yesterday.'[35] According to Arthur von Brauer, a 'grumbling, pessimistic mood' had now 'taken hold of almost the entire nation . . . and poisoned our public life'.[36] The Kaiser's mother welcomed the news that Wilhelm had withdrawn to Hubertusstock, for otherwise there would probably have been more street demonstrations on the second anniversary of Bismarck's dismissal.[37] The British ambassador, reporting on the Kaiser's speech, commented that it had been strongly condemned everywhere, and deservedly so. Its critics maintained that Wilhelm had thrown down the gauntlet of imperial will to his people and had made it impossible for them to look up to him as an impartial sovereign. Even Wilhelm's supporters deplored the superficiality of his remarks; but, according to Sir Edward Malet, they warned against reading too much into them. The offensive phrase about the grumblers who were to shake the dust of Germany from their feet, for instance, was merely an allusion to an allegorical play by Ernst von Wildenbruch which the Kaiser had admired recently. Similarly the passage (particularly badly received in Britain) in which the Kaiser had spoken of the Almighty as 'our old ally' of Rossbach and Dennewitz had scarcely attracted any attention in Germany, as it was simply a well-known quotation from Field Marshal Blücher. In spite of all these explanations and excuses, however, the speech had been very strongly criticised, Malet reported, 'and His Majesty's Ministers, to whom it came as a complete surprise, will no doubt endeavour to guard against such an occurrence in the future. All the comments in the papers have been laid before His Majesty and it is hoped that the general condemnation of the Speech in the English papers of all shades will have a salutary effect.'[38] And indeed General von Verdy was able to report to Waldersee, from conversations with members of the inner circle of the imperial entourage, that 'His Majesty has lately read *everything* which has been published about his recent speech and the School Bill . . . and is said to be very depressed about it – at least for the moment.'[39] A few months later, when the British military attaché Leopold Swaine returned to Berlin after an absence of three years, he was shocked by the extent to which public opinion had changed. 'What strikes me more than anything, comparing the present time with that which I left behind me 3 years ago, is the way in which the Emperor is abused – openly abused – by all classes of society, even by the Army. The Country feels and knows that the Emperor lacks good advisers. The People are unsettled and no one knows what the next move is likely to bring.' It was very much to be feared, he warned, that 'matters will drift from bad to worse, and all confidence in the existing régime is fast leaking out'.[40]

The Kaiser was also attacked in parliament for the first time when the Left Liberal leader Eugen Richter made a critical speech, which won support from all the parties, in the Prussian House of Representatives in May 1892. 'The speech will certainly have a very profound effect on the Kaiser', Waldersee commented, for 'it is a harsh lesson which the country is teaching the Kaiser, and yet it is very sad that we have already reached this point'.[41] The following year it was the critical speeches of the Social Democrat August Bebel which created the most alarm in royalist circles. Waldersee found it 'positively outrageous . . . how people attack the Kaiser himself nowadays. Bebel was clever enough not to name him directly, but no one could possibly have misunderstood him.'[42] A shocked Brauer reported from Berlin at the end of 1892: 'There has probably never been such widespread and deep-rooted dissatisfaction with the existing state of affairs since the Reich was founded, and – what is worse – such despondency. Only the generations to come will be able to appreciate fully the extent of the monarchical feeling, national pride, calm and objective judgement and love

of Kaiser and Reich which has been destroyed in the past two years. We who
are living through it can gauge the extent of what we have lost from outward
manifestations only; the inward transformation of the feelings and attitudes of
the German people remains concealed from us as yet.'[43]

Not long after Bismarck's dismissal it became plain to observers in Berlin
that despite their initial enthusiasm foreign diplomats and journalists were also
taking an increasingly negative view.[44] After the second Brandenburg speech
and the School Bill crisis of the spring of 1892 this foreign criticism reached new
and disquieting heights. The future Foreign Secretary and Reich Chancellor
Bernhard von Bülow, on a visit to Berlin, was horrified by the 'shameless' way
in which foreign diplomats in the German capital found fault with the Kaiser
and the Hohenzollern court. 'They criticise everything and spread the most
incredible news about us', he wrote indignantly.[45] The reports, which reached
Paris and St Petersburg from Berlin at this time, did indeed draw an alarming
picture, not only of the political situation in Germany but also of the Kaiser
himself. In March 1892 Holstein read a secret agent's report from Paris according
to which the French Prime and Foreign Minister Alexandre Ribot considered
the Kaiser 'mentally unsound, on the basis of ambassadorial and other reports'
from Berlin. The agent concluded that 'the relevant ambassadorial report must
have indicated that the "retraite" of the Kaiser to Hubertusstock was necessary
on account of the mental state of the monarch; in addition the Quai d'Orsay is
receiving reports from Berlin . . . that the view that the Kaiser is temporarily of
unsound mind is gaining increasing acceptance in "exalted" circles in Berlin,
especially in international diplomatic circles there. Some of the articles in the
Parisian press, which for months has been maintaining at regular intervals
that the German Kaiser is mad, are . . . inspired by the Foreign Ministry here
[in Paris].'[46] Holstein commented tersely to Philipp Eulenburg that he knew
'not from Schweinitz but from private letters from St Petersburg' that Tsar
Alexander III thought exactly the same.[47]

There was of course no need for secret reports from abroad to document
the decline of confidence in the Prusso-German monarchy. The Reichstag
elections, held by universal secret ballot for men, sent all too clear a message.
The growth of the Marxist–republican Social Democratic Party seen in the
Reichstag elections of February 1890, disastrous enough in itself as far as the
monarchy was concerned, proved in the elections of the summer of 1893 to be
only the beginning of an inexorable upward trend which continued until after
the First World War. Since the Catholic Centre maintained its share of the vote
(19 per cent) undiminished until 1912, the result was that the reservoir of parties
loyal to the Kaiser continued to shrink – like the 'Peau de Chagrin' in Balzac's
portrait of the Bourbon monarchy in post-revolutionary France – in spite of

the losses suffered by the internally divided Left Liberals. In 1893 there were 4.35 million votes for the opposition parties which Bismarck had condemned as 'enemies of the Reich', as against 2.48 million for the former Kartell parties which had been regarded as 'staatserhaltend' or state-supporting. Five years later, in the Reichstag elections of 1898, this trend persisted: 4.43 million voted for the SPD, the Centre and the Left Liberal Parties while the former Kartell managed to attract no more than 2.17 million votes.[48]

Wilhelm's monarchist critics were of course aware that this decline could not be attributed solely to the Kaiser; they acknowledged that the growing criticism of the monarchy in public opinion was part of a general move towards democratisation which could be seen to be happening in other countries too. In their analyses, nevertheless, they laid much of the blame at his door. Contemplating the confused state of domestic politics in Germany, it did not take Waldersee long to realise that the hopes which he had once pinned on the Hohenzollern monarchy as a bulwark against the democratic tendencies of the day would not be fulfilled under Wilhelm II. When the Kaiser came to power, Waldersee observed, he had still hoped that the German Reich would become a 'stronghold' against the socialist movement, from which all the other European states could derive support. But already by September 1890 he had to admit that 'this hope has been bitterly disappointed'.[49] Two years later he wrote reflectively: 'I no longer have any doubt that we are facing great catastrophes which will shake the whole of Europe and may bring about a completely new era. I am far from throwing all the blame on the Kaiser now; but he did much to set in train the movement towards the abyss. While his grandfather was alive the whole world looked up to us, sensing that Germany was a pillar of firm, healthy strength, a rock on which the waves of revolution would break, a house beneath whose roof shelter might be found in troubled times. All this the grandson has destroyed in an astonishingly short time. He is continuing his work of destruction and still believes, in his immensely exaggerated estimation of his own capabilities, that he is the right man at the helm. On all sides one hears people expressing the wish for a real man, and nothing speaks more eloquently for the fact that no one believes in him any more.'[50] In the summer of 1894 the General again took stock of the international situation, observing no less despondently that things looked 'pretty bad in the world'. Many countries – Hungary, Italy, France, Britain, Serbia and Bulgaria – were in the grip of government crises. 'One would think that conditions here were ideal; but unfortunately this is not the case. Thank God we do not have parliamentary rule yet; the comings and goings of ministers still depend largely on the sovereign, or at least not on the Chambers. But it is true to say that the world is simmering and seething and I am inclined to think that great turmoil lies ahead. In the lifetime of Kaiser

Wilhelm I people had much confidence in Germany and saw her as a firmly grounded, robust power on which one could depend for support in bad times. Sadly that has now changed. In only a few days' time the present Kaiser's reign will have lasted for six years. What must he think of his achievements, if he takes the time to reflect calmly on the past? Many illusions of the early days have probably vanished. He wanted to make Germany greater and more feared and to make the country happy internally. Have we become greater? No, our reputation has declined and our enemies have become arrogant; Russia now believes she rules the world. And how do things stand within the country? No one is really content; countless people are embittered and offended; the Social Democrats scornfully proclaim that their cause is flourishing . . . It may be that the old ways in our country and throughout Europe have become outworn and must pass away. Nevertheless I think that men of action could still turn events in a different direction.'[51] Waldersee was repeatedly confronted with evidence that the growing ill-feeling was directed against the Kaiser himself. 'Within the country things look no better; indeed they look decidedly worse than a year ago, when it was clear that there had already been a deterioration', he noted in his diary at the end of 1894. 'The mood of dissatisfaction, ill-feeling and pessimism has undoubtedly spread and is more vociferously expressed, especially in South Germany; it is also directed much more pointedly against the Kaiser . . . Absolutely no one has any real confidence in him any more; this is inexpressibly sad, but unfortunately true.'[52] The ill-feeling was very widespread and the perception that the Kaiser was to blame was gaining ground everywhere. 'Seldom has anyone disappointed expectations as much as he.'[53]

The growing discontent of the population with Wilhelm II's autocratic conduct in the years following the fall of Bismarck was exemplified by the huge success of the satirical pamphlet *Caligula. A Study of Roman Caesaromania*, in which the liberal historian Ludwig Quidde drew an unmistakable and extremely critical portrait of Wilhelm II under the pretext of a scholarly analysis of classical sources. His aim, as he said himself, was to point out 'the dangers of the unrestrained exercise of a morbidly affected . . . autocratic mind'.[54] With thirty-four editions and hundreds of thousands of copies sold, Quidde's *Caligula* was by far the most successful political publication in the history of the Reich. It led to an intense debate – albeit conducted in coded terms – in newspapers of every party political slant on the personality and style of rule of the young Kaiser.[55] Quidde had insisted on his name appearing as the author. His calculation that no public prosecutor would be able to admit publicly to having spontaneously thought of Kaiser Wilhelm II in reading this analysis of a deranged Roman emperor did not quite work out as he hoped. Although he did not receive a jail sentence of four to five years, as his lawyer had feared, he was compelled to serve three months in Stadelheim prison and his career as a historian was ruined.[56]

Quidde's detention happened at a moment when convictions for contraventions of the laws of *lèse-majesté* (paragraphs 94–101 of the penal code) reached their peak. According to the lists of cases compiled annually by the Imperial Office of Statistics, in the thirty years of the last German Emperor's reign there were 12,196 prosecutions and no less than 9,212 convictions for *lèse-majesté* in all the German federal states, but the cases were by no means evenly distributed across the three decades (see table 1).[57] Although in the last years of Bismarck's rule and the first years of the New Course prosecutions remained below 800 annually and convictions as a rule below 600, both figures shot upwards from 1892 onwards. there were 922 prosecutions with 670 convictions in 1893, 952 prosecutions with 720 convictions in 1894, 858 prosecutions with 644 convictions in 1895 and 844 prosecutions with 623 convictions in 1896. Thereafter the number of trials for *lèse-majesté* declined rapidly, however: the number of guilty verdicts sank to below 300 around the turn of the century, and by the time of the outbreak of war only about twenty people a year were being convicted of this crime. This striking decline can be partly attributed to changed methods of collecting statistics.[58] Another reason for it, however, lay in the growing realisation of the Kaiser and the government authorities that these sensational trials could prove very harmful for the reputation of the monarchy, particularly as it was almost impossible to secure convictions in South Germany, while even in Prussia the judges were less and less inclined to impose the full sentence. In April 1893 Maximilian Harden was tried for *lèse-majesté* but acquitted by the presiding judge on the grounds that respect for a prince could also be shown by upholding the truth before him.[59] In the end the Kaiser announced through an All-Highest proclamation of 27 January 1907, his birthday, that instances of *lèse-majesté* committed through ignorance, thoughtlessness or otherwise without malice would not in future be punished.[60] That the decline in the numbers punished for infringements of the *lèse-majesté* laws cannot be seen as indicating a resurgence of Wilhelm II's popularity is, again, demonstrated by the sources. In 1897 Waldersee was still recording that 'the feeling against the Kaiser . . . is unfortunately widespread'; 'how much worse it has gradually become!'[61]

Waldersee and other commentators were repeatedly struck by the lenience shown towards the Kaiser by the Liberal and Social Democratic press; it was no wonder, they thought, that he had false ideas of his popularity. The explanation for this strange phenomenon, according to the General, was that the press and 'all the parties flirt with him' in the hope of winning his support. 'But if one speaks to party members of any persuasion' one only ever heard expressions of 'doubt and despair'. Waldersee added apprehensively: 'Where it will all lead is

Table 1 *Prosecutions and convictions for infringements of the laws relating to* lèse-majesté, *1882–1918*

| Year | Prosecutions | Convictions |
| --- | --- | --- |
| 1882 | 587 | 487 |
| 1883 | 564 | 443 |
| 1884 | 538 | 438 |
| 1885 | 537 | 412 |
| 1886 | 558 | 456 |
| 1887 | 763 | 615 |
| 1888 | 820 | 654 |
| 1889 | 750 | 557 |
| 1890 | 794 | 581 |
| 1891 | 783 | 593 |
| 1892 | 788 | 581 |
| 1893 | 922 | 670 |
| 1894 | 952 | 720 |
| 1895 | 858 | 644 |
| 1896 | 844 | 623 |
| 1897 | 602 | 429 |
| 1898 | 632 | 486 |
| 1899 | 545 | 402 |
| 1900 | 385 | 300 |
| 1901 | 394 | 299 |
| 1902 | 348 | 284 |
| 1903 | 370 | 287 |
| 1904 | 338 | 258 |
| 1905 | 216 | 179 |
| 1906 | 235 | 193 |
| 1907 | 132 | 107 |
| 1908 | 50 | 34 |
| 1909 | 21 | 14 |
| 1910 | 21 | 17 |
| 1911 | 24 | 14 |
| 1912 | 30 | 23 |
| 1913 | 21 | 19 |
| 1914 | 81 | 64 |
| 1915 | 96 | 75 |
| 1916 | 71 | 55 |
| 1917 | 42 | 29 |
| 1918 | 31 | 21 |
| Total | 15743 | 12063 |

28. The Kaiser and his sons – an unconventional portrait

not yet quite clear to me, but that things are going badly I do not doubt for an instant. We are gradually going down in the estimation of other countries; all our enemies are beginning to feel pleased with themselves while at home pessimism is taking over.'[62] Four years later he commented: 'From the Liberals down to the Social Democrats, all are convinced that he [Wilhelm II] is working in their interest and they cover him with compliments, or at least do not attack him.

They are well aware of what he really is at heart, his arrogance, *voluntas regis* etc.'[63]

When the Reichstag elections of 1893 brought an increase of almost 25 per cent in Social Democrat votes Waldersee commented that the Kaiser ought really to see now 'that all his plans for reform and all his fine intentions have failed and that his advisers à la Douglas, Hinzpeter, Helldorf [sic] and his gang have advised him badly. He is hardly likely to acknowledge that he has contributed a great deal to the development of social democracy himself, but it is . . . undoubtedly true.'[64] After the speech of November 1893 in which the Kaiser had proclaimed to the newly sworn-in recruits of the Berlin garrison: 'You have *no will* of your own from now on, there is only *one will* for you and that is *my will*!', Waldersee predicted that the Social Democrats would be delighted with it, for 'no one brings them more recruits than the Kaiser'.[65]

### THE 'STATE-SUPPORTING' PARTIES LOSE CONFIDENCE

Almost more alarming than the steady growth of the so-called anti-Reich parties during the first years of Wilhelm II's reign was the mounting discontent among those sections of the population on which the monarchy depended for its support. Only a matter of months after Bismarck's dismissal the pro-Bismarck Fronde had already begun to take root, especially in the southern and western regions of the Reich and among the students (the elite of the future), and to create enmity between influential bourgeois circles and the Kaiser. During these same years, as we have seen, the anti-Semitic campaign made great advances among the rural population and caused the venerable Conservative Party, the party of the landowning Prussian aristocracy, to embrace anti-Semitism in its official Tivoli programme in 1892. Meanwhile the Pan-German League, founded in 1890, was putting the cautious foreign and colonial policies of the New Course under increasing nationalistic pressure. And finally the Agrarian League, founded at much the same time, became the focus of all discontented elements in rural areas, uniting them in a dangerous mass agitation against the moderate policies of the government.

These menacing developments were of course regarded with the greatest anxiety by all observers with a political axe to grind. After a conversation with the right-wing editor of the *Deutsches Wochenblatt*, Arendt, Waldersee recorded in the winter of 1891 that the latter was 'very pessimistic', especially about 'the decline of the prestige of the monarchy, in particular in the circles hitherto considered well-disposed . . . even including civil servants and officers'.[66] Watching the growing dissatisfaction among the very parties which were formerly regarded as being loyally supportive of the state – the Conservatives, Free Conservatives and National Liberals – the General repeatedly commented that 'the Kaiser alone' was to blame for this development, for 'without realising what he was doing', he was working for 'the disintegration of the well-disposed parties'.[67] At the beginning of 1892 Waldersee was dismayed to observe that the mood throughout the country was 'very gloomy and uneasy among all who consider themselves the supporters of the state, in other words among the mass of the rural population, whether from the peasant or the great landowning classes, among all civil servants, in the army, among most industrialists, in academic circles, but also among countless ordinary people who are good patriots at heart. The fundamental cause is as regrettable as it is clear to me: it lies *entirely in the Kaiser himself*.'[68] Two years later this aristocratic, arch-conservative General noted in his diary: 'In all the circles in which I move, whose thinking I share and to which, through my personal circumstances, I belong, the prevalent mood is one of the most pronounced dissatisfaction and ill-will.' This 'great ill-will towards the Kaiser . . . however, has spread to much wider circles; I would even say that it is general, although this is not apparent outwardly; but that is not surprising, because the press is highly circumspect, which is also the reason why the Kaiser no doubt suspects very little of all this.'[69]

In South Germany, where Catholic particularism was continuing to gather momentum and veneration for Bismarck among the nationalist-minded bourgeoisie was growing to an alarming degree, the mood of antagonism towards the Kaiser was universal. As early as March 1891 a Bavarian Count, writing to Eulenburg, warned of the serious decline of belief in the idea of the Reich, which was being further accelerated by 'skilfully circulated mistrust of the Kaiser'. 'Last year the talk over beer, wine and tea was of the Kaiser's foolishness; this year only of his excitability, overhastiness etc.'[70] At a banquet in honour of Bismarck in Stuttgart in 1891, Eulenburg reported to Berlin, many people remained seated when the Kaiser's health was drunk.[71] The Baden envoy often found himself compelled to point out that pro-Bismarck rallies turned out to be 'not so much to honour Bismarck as to demonstrate against Wilhelm II'.[72] 'H.M. is unfortunately blamed more and more by the nation for everything that is wrong, and thus also for the Bismarck scandals!', he reported in July 1892, after Bismarck's triumphal progress to Vienna on the occasion of his son Herbert's wedding had led to a series of mass ovations for the former Chancellor. 'There is a desire to put the Kaiser in the wrong, and the criticism of the former Chancellor for his present conduct is nearly always accompanied by the corollary that "none of this would have happened if H.M. had kept the Prince in office!" . . . But in private conversation both among the upper classes and among lesser folk a deep grudge against H.M. comes to the fore everywhere, and it is our duty not to conceal the fact that H.M.'s popularity among the people has again suffered a heavy loss on account of recent events.'[73] Prince Bernhard of Saxe-Meiningen, who was married to Wilhelm II's sister, complained in 1894 that in South Germany even army officers made a show of supporting particularism. In the learned circles to which the Kaiser's brother-in-law also had access the feeling against the Kaiser was 'dreadful'. The general verdict was that this state of affairs could not go on much longer. 'He was sure that even now the Kaiser had not the slightest idea of how people really felt', Waldersee noted after a conversation with the Prince.[74]

The middle classes in the great cities of the west and north of Germany were no less angry and alienated. In 1892 Waldersee recorded that employers, especially industrialists, were 'in great anxiety'; there was insecurity throughout the commercial classes and even the teaching profession, writers and some lawyers felt 'deeply offended'.[75] In 1894, as commanding general in Altona, he had a confidential conversation with a 'well-intentioned and intelligent' citizen of Hamburg who told him 'how unpopular the Kaiser has become and how openly this is discussed at the higher levels of society; although I am well aware of this', Waldersee observed, 'I thought it expedient to show surprise'.[76] Shortly before this he had recorded in his diary, after a meeting with the military author Major Johannes Scheibert, that this 'absolutely reliable, unselfish, loyal man' was 'deeply shocked at the situation in Berlin' and had 'nothing but scorn and contempt . . . for the Kaiser'. 'He says that it is absolutely extraordinary how people talk about the Kaiser in the most disrespectful way in restaurants, even of the better class, in bars, in trams etc.'[77]

The bitter feud between Wilhelm II and Bismarck not only had disastrous consequences for the Kaiser in its effect on the National Liberal bourgeoisie; it also contributed to the growing alienation between Wilhelm and the traditional supporters of the Hohenzollern monarchy, the Conservative landed aristocracy of Prussia. Early in 1891 Holstein was dismayed to observe that the Conservatives under Limburg-Stirum were beginning to form a faction not only against the Chancellor but also against the Kaiser. In this 'open defiance' of their King, he said, 'the rumours of mental illness in the Kaiser play a part. It is scarcely ever mentioned, but many people, in all parties, think that the "carnival" cannot last much longer . . .'[78] In November 1891 Holstein reported to Eulenburg with horror that while conferring an order on Wilhelm von Rauchhaupt, the leader of the Conservatives, the Kaiser had said: 'But as you know, dear Rauchhaupt, regis voluntas suprema lex.' It was indicative of the mood among the Conservatives, the diplomat commented, that Rauchhaupt had expressed his intention of resigning his seat.[79] The Kaiser was 'very angry with the Conservatives', and there would be no lack of ill-considered speeches in the future, Waldersee predicted bitterly in 1892.[80] In 1894, as already mentioned, the normally placid Conservative

President of the Reichstag Albert von Levetzow was moved to raise his voice against the Kaiser and afterwards observed that this day was the saddest of his life; the other Conservatives present had also left the meeting with their King 'deeply upset' by it.[81] 'What great damage the Kaiser has done to himself and to the whole situation with his unfortunate passion for acting as spokesman on all matters of importance!', Waldersee exclaimed.[82] He reacted with bitter irony on hearing the following month that the Kaiser had sent the 'wretched' Count Dönhoff, who had voted for the Russian trade treaty 'purely out of fear of the Kaiser', a congratulatory telegram which read: 'Bravo! Done like a true nobleman.' 'That is the kind of person that H.M. likes', was Waldersee's scathing comment. 'Kaiser Friedrich and Kaiser Wilhelm I, who had a true sense of what is fitting in a nobleman, must be turning in their graves . . . If one could still take the Kaiser at all seriously in what he says, now would be the right moment to renounce noble rank.'[83] It was very much to be feared, Waldersee believed, 'that Germany has already passed its highest point', although, as he acknowledged, 'when Kaiser Wilhelm II came to the throne I certainly had a very different idea of how the country would develop'.[84]

The General became increasingly concerned about the steadily worsening mood in country areas, a mood which he compared with that of the years between 1808 and 1812, when Prussian history had reached what was then its lowest ebb. In the autumn of 1892 he recorded that he was receiving more and more comments from Silesia, Brandenburg and Saxony which testified to deep unhappiness, sometimes even despair, in rural circles. Even in monarchist families there the opinion had taken hold 'that the blame for the confused state of affairs in the country, for the general sense of insecurity, lay entirely with the Kaiser. Even in the circles that I have in mind royalist feeling is declining', he noted. 'People feel forgotten, and they see how the Kaiser is playing into the hands of the revolutionary parties.'[85] After a hunting trip to Silesia that winter he recorded that 'critical comments on the Kaiser are increasingly frequent and at the same time it is very apparent that people are remembering his grandfather more and more'.[86]

The crisis in the relationship between Wilhelm II and Prussia's Conservative rural population deepened dramatically in the winter of 1893–4 when the Kaiser gave his support to Caprivi's tariff policy favouring industry, commerce and labour. Waldersee watched in consternation as Wilhelm put himself at odds with the natural allies of the crown. Running down the Junkers had always been a favourite pastime on the Liberal side, the General commented scathingly, 'but now they are really flushed with victory, as the Kaiser has also spoken out against the Junkers . . . No one likes to mention the fact that the whole peasant class stands behind the Junkers.'[87] The longstanding mainstays of the government, namely the peasants and the small landed proprietors of the old Prussian provinces, were gradually being driven into the most extreme opposition. The Kaiser was now convinced that he was 'fighting a battle with the rebellious Junkers, like his forefathers. Catchwords like that always impress him', Waldersee mocked in early 1894.[88] When the Kaiser surprisingly proclaimed himself the protector of the aristocracy and of agriculture in his speech at Königsberg in September 1894 Waldersee could hardly believe his ears. 'What kind of nonsense is our gracious master babbling now', he exclaimed. 'His Liberal so-called admirers will pull very sour faces when they hear that he identifies himself with the aristocracy . . . But what are people to think, when he proudly claims to have kept his word that he would protect agriculture, whereas in fact he has dealt it the hardest of blows with the trade treaties.'[89] The fact was, Waldersee commented, that not only the landed nobility was disgruntled, 'but the entire section of the population, amounting to millions more, who live from agriculture'. Until a few years ago, in his view, the peasant class, or at least the Lutheran part of it, constituted 'the most dependable Conservative element that could be found'. In the old Prussian provinces this group were 'good Hohenzollernites', and in Mecklenburg, Holstein and Hanover they were still at least 'thoroughly conservative'. If its leaders were now intimidated by the government, he warned, the whole peasant class would switch over to the anti-government camp and would in future vote for the Progressive Democrats, the Anti-Semites or the Socialists.[90] Waldersee was repeatedly confronted with evidence that the ill-feeling in the country was directed against the Kaiser. This was 'really very sad, but no wonder . . . with his tendency to put himself forward everywhere'.[91]

The Berlin correspondent of the *Kölnische Zeitung* painted an alarming picture of the mood in the Reich in 1895, above all among the increasingly radical small farmers, writing: 'From ever more widespread circles we are receiving reliable information about a growing ill-feeling towards the person of His Majesty our Kaiser; in South Germany, where the upsurge of national feeling had been strongest in the last twenty years, radical elements are growing in the most alarming way; the numbers in Württemberg bear eloquent witness to this. In North Germany the Agrarian League has sown a seed which will produce the most dangerous of all fruit. For the time being the present Conservative leaders still believe they are in control of the movement, but plenty of indications that they are mistaken are already beginning to appear: in Bavaria with the peasant leaguers, on the Rhine in agricultural circles linked to the Centre Party. The Conservatives have thought it necessary to harness the small farmers to their cause . . . It cannot end well . . . The present movement can be held back for another year; the great landowners may also be able to rein in the Agrarian League for another year. But then our small farmers will notice that their leaders have been leading them around by the nose, and then they will become as bad and as dangerous as our present revolutionary parties. The game that the present Conservative Party is playing is equally dangerous for the state and the monarchy.'[92]

## DISCONTENT IN THE ARMY

In its original text Waldersee's diary also provides us with an excellent source on the mood of the army, about which the Chief of the General Staff was particularly concerned, since he saw the armed forces as the natural and essential mainstay of the Hohenzollern throne. We have already seen the extent to which the other military officers closest to the Kaiser shared Waldersee's critical attitude.[93] The generals at court were not alone, however. Like them, the commanding generals of the seventeen army corps, the officers of the General Staff and of the Prussian Ministry of War and even younger officers who were to succeed to positions of leadership in the coming years were even now, in the aftermath of Bismarck's dismissal, expressing harsh views about their Supreme War Lord. Waldersee's diary records that at the 1892 New Year reception the Kaiser made a deplorable impression on the commanding generals by simply rejecting as 'nonsense' the changes to army uniform which many of them had requested. Afterwards, he noted, Adjutant-General von Wittich 'roundly' criticised the Kaiser and said 'he was getting more and more grand and infallible'.[94] After the Kaiser's New Year address to the commanding generals two years later Waldersee recounted that the generals had 'mostly looked embarrassed' and had 'smiled strangely'; nor had any of them had the slightest scruples afterwards about making derogatory remarks about the monarch. 'I was very distressed', the former Chief of the General Staff admitted, 'for never has the Kaiser expressed such feeble, I might even say childish, views in these speeches; he really lacks knowledge and experience and the worst thing is that he does not feel the least need to broaden them, for he thinks he knows everything very well and better than anyone else.'[95] On the same occasion in January 1895 the critical comments of the commanding generals were 'quite openly expressed in the most appalling way'. The Commanding General of the Guards made a 'particularly audacious' contribution, Waldersee commented.[96] Five years after Bismarck's fall he described the mood among senior officers as 'despondent', adding that 'Hahnke is highly discontented . . . General Winterfeld, the great Comm[anding] General of the Corps of Guards, is also very depressed about the Kaiser, and even people like Bissing are beginning to lose heart.'[97]

Even at this early stage Waldersee made repeated complaints about the sycophantic behaviour of the army officers attached to the court and the other favourites whom the Kaiser had collected around him. The behaviour of Freiherr Gustav von Meerscheidt-Hüllessem since his appointment as commanding general of the Corps of Guards was in his view thoroughly symptomatic of the corrupt atmosphere at the Hohenzollern court which Wilhelm had encouraged. Hüllessem accepted 'completely and unquestioningly everything the Kaiser did with the corps, which is often absolutely incredible', and he even encouraged the Kaiser in this habit. 'He is very often in the Kaiser's company, especially at the countless meals for the officers, and he tries to amuse the Kaiser with jokes which are always coarse and mostly obscene. Even young officers think it is unbecoming for him to lower himself to act as a jester', Waldersee noted disapprovingly. The award of the Order of the Black Eagle to Hüllessem on the occasion of the military review of 18 August had caused universal head-shaking, he wrote. 'We have not been accustomed to such things at reviews, and it will be seen more as a reward for unconditional obedience.' As Hüllessem's private life was 'very questionable' – he lived with a woman to whom he was not married – such an exalted order 'really did not look well' upon him.[98] Commenting on Winterfeld, Meerscheidt-Hüllessem's successor as commanding general of the Guards, Waldersee recorded that there was much indignation in well-informed circles, for 'as soon as the Kaiser [can] be seen on the horizon he [becomes] coarse, obviously in the hope of impressing our gracious master thereby . . . But he is just the sort of man to like an appointment close to the Kaiser', Waldersee added caustically.[99] In later years too Waldersee strongly criticised the attitude of the Kaiser, which led senior officers to curry favour with him by rudeness towards subordinates.[100]

A further reason for the growing unrest among the generals was Wilhelm II's personal interference in appointments and promotions in the officer corps. There was universal dismay, for instance, when Prince Friedrich of Hohenzollern-Sigmaringen, whom Wilhelm, under the influence of Countess Elisabeth Wedel, had formerly abhorred as a dangerous intriguer,[101] was promoted to commanding general of the III Army Corps in the autumn of 1893. Waldersee strongly condemned the preferential treatment shown to this 'indolent' Prince, for he was 'a very insignificant man, without a trace of passion for his career, without ambition – not even of smart appearance, and very poorly trained as a soldier'. For the proud former Chief of the General Staff it was 'truly not an uplifting feeling to hold the same post as such a lamentable General'.[102] When shortly after this the Kaiser gave Prince Hohenzollern yet another appointment, as a member of the National Defence Committee, Waldersee commented scathingly: 'If the Kaiser intended to diminish the significance and prestige of the Committee in the eyes of the army he could not have made a better choice than to nominate this General, who is as uneducated as he is insignificant and uninteresting, to the Committee. The sole reason is to have another more compliant man on it.'[103] Waldersee condemned out of hand the Kaiser's inclination to give preferential treatment in the army to 'minor princes'. 'I have nothing against the Hereditary Prince of Meiningen, although I am afraid that he loses his head easily', he wrote; 'but Pce Hohenzollern, Hereditary G[rand] D[uke Friedrich] of Baden and [Hereditary Duke Peter of] Oldenburg, Prince Leopold [of Bavaria] etc. are quite useless as senior troop commanders.' The Kaiser was altogether 'a very incompetent judge of men' and deluded himself greatly in selecting officers for the most senior positions. 'What mistakes he has already made!'[104]

Waldersee was particularly shocked to see how much his successor as chief of the General Staff, Count Alfred von Schlieffen, was dominated by the Kaiser and even allowed the latter to dictate the strategic guidelines for a future war to him.[105] In March 1892 the Kaiser made such 'derogatory' remarks about Schlieffen in front of numerous General Staff officers in the Tiergarten that in his predecessor's view Schlieffen ought to have resigned.[106] In 1892, in the hope of curing him of the offensive habit of personally evaluating military exercises in the General Staff offices, Wilhelm was 'very cunningly' informed that there was an outbreak of measles there![107] With a view to avoiding such difficulties in the future the officers developed a system by which a Flügeladjutant asked the General Staff confidentially for Schlieffen's solution and then, on the basis of this information, worked out with the Kaiser what opinion he should express. At the evaluation session the Kaiser could then demonstrate that he had found exactly the right solution![108] The 'lamentable' part of the Kaiser's evaluations, according to Waldersee, was that he was 'either guided by preconceived ideas or by momentary and always hastily formed impressions'; that was also the reason why most army commanders became 'uncertain and agitated' whenever the Kaiser was in the vicinity.[109] 'He obviously has not the least idea of the damage he does to himself and to everything', the General commented anxiously.[110] In later years Wilhelm II continued to do as he pleased in military matters, and the most senior officers followed his bidding. When in the spring of 1895, after weeks of preparation, Schlieffen made his report to the Kaiser on the forthcoming manoeuvres in the Uckermark and happened to mention Prenzlau, where the Prussian army had surrendered to the French in 1806, the Supreme War Lord declared 'that in view of the sad associations of this name he did not wish to have any manoeuvre there! Now poor Schlieffen has to abandon the very laborious preparations he has made and start all over again. The Kaiser also added', Waldersee recorded in his diary, 'that according to the map the terrain in the Uckermark did not seem suitable for cavalry, but he intended to take command himself, with large masses of cavalry, and anyway he would like to have the manoeuvres in Pomerania.' The former Chief of the General Staff commented bitterly: 'I hope he does not suspect what toil and trouble he causes with such caprices.'[111]

The growing discontent of the officer corps and the increasingly critical attitude of the younger officers in particular made Waldersee especially fatalistic. In the summer of 1890, when he was still Chief of the General Staff, he recorded that it was sad but 'unfortunately . . . already to a great extent the case', that the army was deeply dissatisfied with the Kaiser. 'Great mistrust has grown up, and there is no affection at all; there is a feeling of coldness and of great ill-will . . . Above all, the Kaiser should have bound the army to himself; such a thing cannot be bequeathed; it must be won. Kaiser Wilhelm I did this and what a fine relationship there was between him and the army, how profound was the feeling of solidarity and mutual security!'[112] Not long after Bismarck's dismissal Waldersee drew up a list in his diary of the manifold reasons for Wilhelm II's unpopularity in the army. His 'great preference' for the navy and the Guards and his consequent neglect of the line regiments, and especially of the infantry, were resented. There were complaints that the Kaiser showed 'considerably less courtesy' towards senior officers 'than they had been accustomed to with his grandfather', and that he passed harsh judgements 'most of which are probably expressed quite thoughtlessly and which verge on brutality'. In general the Kaiser's excessively strong expression of his will 'about things which the sovereign does not thoroughly understand', coupled with his arrogant attitude towards the judgement of experienced people, was responsible for frequent transfers and even reprimands for senior officers, which 'are regarded as being based entirely on his personal feelings'. Not least, Wilhelm's 'habit of speaking openly to junior officers about their superiors' caused deep dissatisfaction. Finally, the Chief of the General Staff recorded, the Kaiser had squandered the confidence which the officer corps had initially shown towards him by indulging his 'passion for playing soldiers', which expressed itself principally in frequent and utterly senseless orders for troops to be called out. A feeling of insecurity and discontent was apparent everywhere among senior officers, who spoke openly of the 'tactlessness' of the Kaiser and of the 'ruthlessness' of his Military Cabinet.[113]

A year after Bismarck's fall and shortly after his own transfer to Altona, Waldersee inveighed against the Kaiser's constant and harmful interference in army matters. Wilhelm had already ordered 'countless innovations', he complained, 'mostly little more than tomfoolery', among other things the 'unfortunate' arming of the cavalry regiments with lances. He had been 'very premature in trusting his own judgement', 'which only caused offence and did not impress anyone, because it was based on dilettantism'. His 'currying favour with the masses even at the expense of the army' had deeply offended the officer corps. 'Now, after 3 years, the inevitable result is that the army feels that its relationship to its War Lord has fundamentally changed and has of course become much cooler and more distant than before, and that confidence in the Kaiser's military talents has not grown at all; on the contrary, lack of confidence in his ability has spread', the General wrote.[114] He also strongly criticised the Kaiser's demand that new recruits should be paraded before him. If they had not practised this the parades went badly and the Kaiser was dissatisfied; if on the other hand the soldiers practised the parade drill so as to please the Kaiser, valuable weeks of basic training were wasted, which 'turned all the principles of our military training upside down. What utter confusion everyone is thrown into, and how it ruins people's characters', Waldersee commented despairingly.[115] He went on to condemn, as a well-meaning but 'very unfortunate . . . idea of the Kaiser', the encouragement of competition in the army through the award of medals for shooting and imperial prizes for riding, which had caused much 'envy, quarrelling, cheating, deception and discord'. The General emphasised that these 'evils, which are already very evident', were giving rise to widespread anxiety.[116] However much a militarist at heart, even Waldersee could not condone Wilhelm's praise for the grenadier who had shot and fatally wounded civilians. The Kaiser's action would 'cause great and very lasting harm', he predicted; this was 'yet another sign of utter immaturity of judgement'.[117] Wilhelm's behaviour in 1893, when numerous officers were caught gambling and he took a strongly censorious attitude, was considered 'incredible and injudicious' by all the army commanders, especially as he had recently not only allowed gambling during court hunting expeditions but had himself watched it.[118] In the summer of 1895 Waldersee again recorded with deep concern that 'the Kaiser could not be less popular in the army; he lacks his grandfather's great talent for winning hearts. He captivates people at first, but then repels them.'[119] Numerous observers, including the journalist Franz Fischer, the diplomat Philipp Eulenburg and the Empress Frederick, expressed similar views about the growing discontent within the army.[120]

Senior officers were particularly disgusted by Wilhelm II's liking for surrounding himself with cheering crowds when he went on manoeuvre. Thus for instance when the imperial manoeuvres of 1893 were held in the French-speaking part of Alsace-Lorraine the women, schoolchildren and servants at the German garrison had to be taken to the troop reviews to cheer, and this had to be done in such a way as to enable the Kaiser to see them several times on the same day.[121] This had been 'a complete and utter sham', wrote Waldersee,[122] who was very far from being the only one who regarded the Kaiser's taking personal command at manoeuvres as a dangerous farce. The saying 'the Kaiser always wins' was mockingly peddled around the entire army, and the arbiters at manoeuvres were indeed given direct instructions to ensure that he did.[123] The Kaiser's brother-in-law Prince Bernhard, who took part in the disastrous autumn manoeuvres in Silesia in 1890 in command of the Second Guards Infantry Division, deplored not only the harm which this undesirable practice did to the army, but also the effect on the Kaiser himself. It was spoiling the 'gracious sovereign' and doing him no favour, he declared, and 'nobody who truly wished him well should do such a thing'.[124] After the above-mentioned cavalry manoeuvre in Lorraine in the autumn of 1893 the Kaiser's personal direction of the attack was 'unanimously unfavourably criticised' by the officers – although not in such a way that Wilhelm heard about it.[125] In a conversation with Waldersee the Grand Duke of Baden remarked that his nephew had assembled the troops in too much of a hurry, ordered them to move before they had finished assembling and then moved them forwards without sufficient reconnaissance. The result had been that the mounted troops on one flank had ridden into marshy ground in which numerous horses had got stuck. To cap it all Wilhelm had attacked his own troops! At first the generals had hoped, according to the Grand Duke, that Wilhelm would conclude from this experience that to command cavalry in great numbers was no easy task. But Waldersee had to break the news to Wilhelm's uncle that although at first the Kaiser had been 'fully under the impression of having failed, as soon as he began the ride home he was told by some despicable flatterers that he had in fact led his troops very well, and his good mood returned immediately'.[126] General Viktor von Podbielski, who was taking a cure at Karlsbad at the same time as Reich Chancellor von Caprivi, informed Waldersee afterwards that during those imperial manoeuvres the Kaiser had 'concerned himself almost exclusively with the cavalry and put it to the most unbelievable use'. Podbielski had also heard complaints from several senior cavalry officers 'about constant orders and counter-orders' from the Kaiser; there had never been such great confusion. The attack which the Kaiser led with twelve regiments was, moreover, 'nothing but a copy of an identical attack which General Krosigk had performed before the Kaiser shortly beforehand near Salzwedel, the only difference being that the one in Lorraine had missed the enemy', the two Generals told each other in consternation.[127] How little Wilhelm had learned from this experience became evident a year later, when at the manoeuvres in East Prussia he again insisted on commanding a cavalry corps, with equally unfortunate results.[128] Again, before the imperial manoeuvres in the early autumn of 1895 in Western Pomerania – Wilhelm had personally chosen this region in the belief that it was particularly suitable for cavalry attacks – Waldersee wrote of the participating officers' fear of the Kaiser's 'passion' for commanding 'enormous contingents of cavalry', although he had always come to grief in doing so hitherto. 'For a cavalry

commander he is far too reckless and inexperienced.'[129] 'Commanding large
units of cavalry is an unfortunate obsession of the Kaiser's; he hopes to create an
impressive effect by doing so, but he achieves the opposite.'[130] In addition the
General made the very valid point that with the 'enormously increased firepower'
of modern weapons it was 'absolute folly' to set so much store by the cavalry.[131]

If the generals were unanimous in considering the Kaiser's personal command
at manoeuvres in peacetime highly damaging, the idea of his taking command
himself in a war filled them with utter consternation. Waldersee, it is true, had
his doubts as to whether at the decisive moment, when required 'to draw the
sword and cut the knot', Wilhelm would really have the courage to start a war,
in spite of all his bloodthirsty utterances.[132] Nevertheless for him, as for all the
other army commanders, it was beyond doubt that Wilhelm II, as supreme war
lord, would personally assume overall command over the nation's armed forces
in the event of war breaking out. 'The possibility that the Kaiser will wish to
direct operations himself in a war is a thought that fills one with grave concern',
Waldersee confided to his diary in the spring of 1891.[133] A few months later
the King of Saxony confirmed that it was of course true that Kaiser Wilhelm II
'must take overall command in war wherever he goes', 'but he must do it like
his grandfather, that is, he must take advice'. The King agreed with Waldersee
'that in spite of all his passion for military matters and all his abilities the Kaiser
does not have what it takes to command an army'.[134] Waldersee, of course,
knew Wilhelm's excessive self-confidence too well to be able to believe that he
would in fact listen to the generals whose advice he should follow. His constantly
recurring nightmare was therefore that 'in his immense overestimation of his
own competence' Wilhelm might take over command himself if a major war
broke out.[135] 'I believe many people are now terrified at the thought that the
Kaiser will want to take command himself in war!', Waldersee wrote after the
imperial manoeuvres in Lorraine in the autumn of 1893.[136] The unanimous
opinion among the generals was that 'the Kaiser himself is not the man for this
task', he wrote. As the Austrian generals likewise had 'not the slightest confidence
in the ability of the Kaiser to direct major operations', the Austrian army had
already distanced itself to a regrettable degree from its German counterpart,
and the realisation that Schlieffen had no influence on the monarch had also
considerably increased the danger of a 'lukewarm war effort' on the part of
Germany's ally.[137] The most that Waldersee dared hope for himself was that
in the event of war he would be appointed to a command in the east against
the Russians, where he would be able to use his own initiative in discharging
his responsibilities. 'In the west my army is tied to other armies and all are
under the direct control of the Kaiser, in whose leadership I, like many others,
unfortunately have no confidence at all', he wrote in July 1894. 'With his rashness,

his certainty of knowing better than anyone else and his vanity he is capable of creating the most appalling confusion and Schlieffen is not the man to guide him. If the Chancellor, the Minister of War and Hahnke too – as Verdy heard from Hahnke – were also to join the high command I foresee things getting very bad indeed.'[138] Waldersee's desire to have the eastern command was given short shrift by the Kaiser, however, with the remark: 'I do not like the idea of having the King of Saxony in the west. Just give him command in the east.' As Waldersee commented in despair, 'trivial personal interests thus become the deciding factor in a matter on which the good of the Fatherland might well depend'.[139]

It was not Count Schlieffen but Kaiser Wilhelm II who determined the deployment and strategy of the Prusso-German army. A year after his dismissal as chief of the General Staff Waldersee recorded in his diary: 'The Kaiser wants to send more troops to the west in case of war – which I told Schlieffen he would – and it seems the latter is willing to give in and even thinks in general that nothing needs to be done in the east.' Waldersee bitterly predicted that these plans would lead to the loss of the right bank of the Vistula and the province of Silesia.[140] Even the belligerent Waldersee was shocked by the Kaiser's aggressive predilection for an attacking strategy. Wilhelm's belief that one ought 'always to attack and then to follow up rapidly' could lead 'in a very short time to the destruction of whole divisions', the General warned.[141] In his address to the commanding generals in January 1895 Wilhelm demanded that the policy 'of attacking the enemy wherever we see him, regardless of whether he has even 4 times the strength!' must be maintained. The generals assembled in the Berlin Schloss found it particularly offensive that on this occasion the Kaiser held up as a model to them the victorious Japanese, 'who went on the attack everywhere with tremendous daring, and knocked the Chinese down, although they were superior in number'. The monarch had completely overlooked the fact, they objected, 'that there is nothing approaching an organised Chinese army, but only a mass of troops who are lamentably badly armed and even more badly led'. Indignantly Waldersee asked: 'Has any army ever understood offensive tactics better than us in the last 3 wars? Have troops ever gone on the attack more bravely than ours? Truly not! And now the miserable Japanese are held up as an example to us! That is indeed hard and we do not deserve it!'[142]

## OF 'UNBOUNDED LOVE' FOR 'THE BEST OF ALL KINGS'

It was not of course Holstein, Marschall or Grand Duke Friedrich of Baden, nor the Empress Frederick or Waldersee, and certainly not the inexorably growing mass of 'grumblers' in the general population, who were to be the decisive influence on the course of the government crisis in the next few years. This role was to be played by two men of quite a different stamp who idolised the Kaiser. The ambassador Count Philipp zu Eulenburg and his close friend Bernhard von Bülow were very well aware of the extent to which they differed from most statesmen, officials, diplomats and officers in their estimation of their young ruler, but they revelled in their 'ideal' alternative view. After a secret meeting between the two men in the South Tyrol in January 1896 Eulenburg wrote revealingly to Wilhelm II: 'Our discussions and exchange of feelings had one sure foundation: unbounded love for our King . . . If the great mass of politicians had heard our conversations during these days they would not have believed their ears, it would have seemed *impossible* to them – for personal, human love for the best of all kings and natural warm friendship between ourselves – how is that to be rightly understood in our complicated world?'[143]

Neither man held back in expressing his love for Wilhelm, and at least as far as Eulenburg is concerned there can be no doubt that his assurances of love and gratitude were deeply felt and sincerely meant. It did not embarrass him to tell the Kaiser to his face that he was the 'kindest, best sovereign that Prussia has ever had'.[144] For him, Wilhelm II was 'the kindest, most gracious of Kaisers and the most sympathetic of friends!',[145] for whom he constantly 'yearned'. 'Who understands me better than Yr Majesty? – and how many things only come to fruition as a result of talking them over with so understanding and kind a Kaiser!'[146] Even after many years of their friendship the sight of the Kaiser's 'beloved' handwriting continued to throw Eulenburg into a state of ecstasy. 'Oh what joy!', he wrote in the summer of 1897 in answer to a letter from Wilhelm. 'Your Imperial and Royal Majesty cannot conceive how happy Your long, gracious, *immensely interesting* letter has made me! Yesterday evening after receiving it I was quite unable to sleep. Happiness, gratitude, the contents – my head and heart were spinning with it all!'[147] At Christmas 1895 after receiving a letter from the Kaiser he had written: 'I read the words of the first pages, which contained so much kindness and friendship, over and over again and thought how wonderfully God has ordered my life. But since He has directed it thus, I hope that He will also give me the mental and physical strength I need in order to serve Your Majesty in the way that I most fervently wish.'[148] When the Flügeladjutant and military attaché Georg von Hülsen brought another letter from Wilhelm to him to Vienna, the ambassador expressed his delight 'at Your Majesty's dear presence near me! . . . It was as if Your Majesty were sitting beside me and speaking to me – I heard Your voice – and especially the emphases, accompanied by lively gestures of the hand. In friendship, what pleasure one has in the *particular characteristics* of the person one loves.'[149] Philipp Eulenburg and his closest friends, the Flügeladjutant Count Kuno von Moltke and Axel Freiherr von Varnbüler, Württemberg's envoy and representative in the Bundesrat in Berlin, did indeed call Kaiser Wilhelm II 'das Liebchen' – the darling one – to each other, as their arch-enemies were later to claim.[150]

Eulenburg also took the greatest delight in the annual Scandinavian cruises and the other frequent excursions and hunting expeditions on which he accompanied the Kaiser, in spite of the considerable strain they entailed and the often tricky political problems which had to be solved in the course of them. 'I am still revelling in the memory of the *wonderful* trip and of all Your Majesty's kindness to me, and I never cease to think of my beloved Kaiser with the deepest gratitude', he wrote after the Scandinavian trip of the summer of 1893.[151] Only a few months later, after a journey to the Adriatic with Wilhelm, he wrote ecstatically: 'I must . . . once again tell Your Majesty how *indescribably grateful* I am for all the kindness which Your Majesty again showed me, and how the shining memory of our splendid Venetian journey will rank among the most wonderful experiences of my life!'[152] After the Scandinavian cruise of the summer of 1895 the ambassador and imperial favourite expressed his gratitude with the words: 'The sun of Your Majesty's *golden friendship* shines more and more brightly upon me. The best and highest ornament of a human being, the touchstone of his *true* worth. God bless my most beloved Kaiser for it.'[153]

Gratitude for his rapid promotion, first as envoy (Oldenburg, Stuttgart and Munich) and then to the post of ambassador at Vienna, naturally played an important part in Eulenburg's relationship with Wilhelm, but he repeatedly affirmed (and with some credibility) that the personal friendship of the Kaiser meant far more to him than the outward glamour or material advantages of his position. In his first letter after taking up his appointment as ambassador he wrote with evident pleasure: 'These are the first lines Your Majesty will receive from me from Vienna! . . . dictated by a sense of immeasurable gratitude towards my beloved Kaiser, who showers me with honours and distinctions and gives me even more than all this splendour: true friendship, the highest and most glorious blessing!'[154] Eulenburg considered himself and the Kaiser – as also Bülow – kindred souls, whose nature was different from that of their ordinary fellow humans. He wrote to Wilhelm bewailing the 'artificiality of city life' after a stay in a forest region with the Kaiser. 'Very few people understand these feelings as intensively as Yr Majesty feels them. For that one needs the *truly* dual nature of one who can both dream and be awake at the same time – like Yr Majesty, and perhaps myself too. We have a long way to go before it is common to find two souls in one breast!'[155]

Moved by what he felt sure was the Kaiser's reciprocal affection for him, in the winter of 1898 Eulenburg gave expression to this certainty in a letter to his imperial friend. In thanking him for a telegram from Damascus he declared: 'I know Yr Majesty's loyalty which, although it is becoming increasingly strange in these times characterised by egoism, gives such a noble stamp to Yr Majesty's personality. That is why I understand this sign of friendship and feel happy and grateful for it! But in this case I am almost inclined to believe in "transmitted effect", telepathy, for my thoughts have been so *constantly*, so *intensively* directed towards Yr Majesty at this time – with both anxiety and sympathy – that I believe Yr Majesty must have felt it!' Alluding to the fact that Wilhelm had said some comforting words to him about his brother Friedrich (Fredi), who had been forced to leave the army because he had been accused of homosexuality, the Kaiser's best friend continued: 'I should like to say something else to Yr Majesty – something quite personal which I did not dare say in Rominten because I was too deeply moved (which Yr Majesty does not like!). But my heart is so full of ardent gratitude that I cannot stay silent any longer. I know very well what Yr Majesty wished to convey to me by putting my picture – that old face – on your writing table (which I feel is almost too much!). I understood very well the *love* that out of deep human sympathy you wished to show to an old friend who was suffering inwardly from a mortal wound. The silent eloquence of this act touched me beyond words – did me an *infinite amount of good*! God bless Yr Majesty a thousand times for it!'[156]

The diplomat Alfred von Bülow had belonged to the 'Liebenberg Round Table' centred around Eulenburg since they had studied together in Leipzig and Strassburg; his brother Adolf, as we saw in the first volume of this biography, decisively influenced Prince Wilhelm's political education in an autocratic and militaristic sense as his personal adjutant.[157] Another brother of Alfred, the ambassador in Rome Bernhard von Bülow, was of course to play a more significant role still in the life of Wilhelm II as secretary of state at the Foreign Office from 1897 to 1900 and then from 1900 to 1909 as Reich chancellor and Prussian minister-president. It was chiefly thanks to his intimate friendship with Philipp Eulenburg, as we shall show, that Bülow rose to these heights.

The language which Bernhard von Bülow used in his correspondence with Eulenburg about the Kaiser was scarcely less effusive than that of the Kaiser's favourite, and yet one cannot escape the impression that the only purpose of Bülow's idolisation of the monarch was to manipulate Eulenburg to his own advantage. In his letters to 'dearest Philipp' Bülow constantly and cynically emphasised exactly what this 'sisterly soul' (Bülow's description of their relationship) wanted to hear, namely that Wilhelm II was a man 'of genius' and would accomplish great deeds in the future, always providing, of course, that he received the right advice. As early as 1892 he assured Eulenburg that he had 'confidence in the Kaiser's destiny. He will work his way through, not only to be a great ruler, but also to win recognition from many who misjudge him now.'[158] After a visit to Berlin he wrote enthusiastically: 'I found His Majesty kind, natural, looking well, fresh, full of life, intellect, ideas, and thoughtful and intelligent in everything he said. With the right people about him, serving and interpreting him, he will stand his ground, will be able to stand his ground.'[159] After another visit to court the following year Bülow wrote to his friend: 'Dearest Philipp, I have just come from the Neues Palais. His Majesty immensely kind – as brilliant, lively, interesting as possible. I was deeply moved when I was able to kiss his hand and thank him for so much graciousness. His face had such a kind expression, almost soft, in spite of all his energy. It pleases me to give him pleasure.'[160] In later years too the tone of Bülow's letters to Eulenburg remains precisely attuned to the latter's sensibilities. 'In my mind I have the dear Kaiser's fine, bright eyes constantly before me, with such a moving expression (because they are so trustful and fixed on the noblest of goals).'[161] 'It only makes me love our dear, beloved Kaiser all the more when I see him being attacked so much. I always think of his wide eyes, the eyes of both a child and a genius . . .'[162] Just like Eulenburg, Bülow wrote ecstatically of a letter from Wilhelm: 'Our beloved sovereign's letter to me has moved me profoundly. Even if he were not the Kaiser one could not but wish him well with all one's heart. What would I not do for such a sovereign! But for the very reason that I love him so much I do not want him *to do himself any harm*.'[163] 'I already belonged to our Kaiser body and soul', he wrote from Rome in 1896 after Wilhelm's visit to Italy; 'but this time he has utterly *and completely* conquered me.' 'It is impossible to be near him without being swept away by so much life, intellect, strength and goodness. The miasma of false perceptions and exaggerations, the fog of slander and malice fall away and his true image emerges in all its vigour and versatility. One cannot help being terribly fond of him *once one really knows him*.'[164]

Whether such declarations of love were sincerely meant or were merely a cynical pretence calculated to win, or at any rate to maintain, Eulenburg's confidence and support for Bülow himself, they led to a flight from reality into an idealised dream world from which neither man would awake until the damage they had done, in their blindness, was beyond repair. In February 1892, that is to say at a moment when the leading elite in Germany were throwing up their hands in horror at Wilhelm II's autocratic utterances and foreign newspapers were beginning to talk openly of his mental illness, Bülow was affirming his mystical belief in the Kaiser's spirit of genius and in Prussia's destiny to an infatuated Eulenburg. 'The doubts and complaints about our All-gracious sovereign are a sad – and alarming – phenomenon, and also politically harmful, both at home and abroad, but it has not made me lose my confidence in the future', he attested. The Kaiser, he maintained, possessed 'the qualities – such as steadfastness, courage, a quick understanding – which can neither be acquired nor instilled from outside;

His faults, which are mostly no more than the reverse side of these qualities, can be gradually reduced or completely cured by experience'.[165] Bülow dismissed Geheimrat von Holstein's 'prophecies of doom' as to the consequences of Wilhelm's absolutist speeches and style of government, merely remarking that the diplomat was too pessimistic. 'In people of great mind and temperament one must not take every word in such deadly earnest.'[166] 'I shall not allow all these long-drawn-out prophecies of doom to rob me of the complete confidence I have in our beloved sovereign. My overall impression is, as it has always been, that in general His Majesty not only has the right thing in mind, but also achieves it with clarity, freshness and brilliance of vision. It is only the form in which it is expressed which still occasionally lacks subtlety, and is sometimes a little careless too. Where strength and initiative abound, this usually happens. But it is people of precisely this nature who learn through their own experience.'[167] 'Do not let us be robbed either of our belief in the country's destiny, or of our confidence in the personality of the Kaiser', urged the future Reich Chancellor in a letter to Eulenburg in early 1895. 'Even if our dear Kaiser has occasionally slipped up over this or that on a matter of form, He has always reined in His strong will and lively temperament when reasons of state have been paramount, and he will continue to do so, which is the lodestone that has guided his house to greatness.'[168] In October 1895 Bülow gave further encouragement to Eulenburg's dangerous illusions with an effusive assurance of his fellow feeling: 'I understand so well that you are becoming increasingly attached to our All-Highest sovereign. I too, who do not know him nearly as well as you and am far less close to him, feel more and more at one with him inwardly. Not only because I am a royalist – not of the head but of the heart, the Prussian monarchy is in the end the most important thing for me – but also because of his individuality. His letter to the Tsar is a work of genius! How much he has to give! May God protect him!' Alluding to Holstein, Bülow added: 'malicious dwarves always abound where heroes hold sway'.[169] Even after taking up office as foreign secretary, apparently blind to reality, Bülow wrote his friend a letter of surpassing sycophancy which he no doubt hoped would be laid before the Kaiser. 'I grow fonder and fonder of the Kaiser. He is so important!! Together with the Great King and the Great Elector he is by far the most important Hohenzollern ever to have lived. In a way I have never seen before he combines genius – the most authentic and original genius – with the clearest *bon sens*. His vivid imagination lifts me like an eagle high above petty detail, yet he can judge soberly what is or is not possible and attainable. And what vitality! What a memory! How quick and sure his understanding! In the Crown Council this morning I was completely overwhelmed! He gave an exposé on the water questions, which are so complicated, and mentioned all the material and administrative aspects involved in as precise and detailed a way as any expert minister could have done, but with a vigour, vividness, broadness of overall vision, in short with a genius that no minister could even begin to achieve. May God preserve our great monarch and the noblest of men!'[170]

To counter the forcible return of Wilhelm II to the principle of reasons of state contemplated by Holstein, Marschall von Bieberstein, Bronsart von Schellendorf and Alexander Hohenlohe, Philipp Eulenburg and Bernhard Bülow together developed a strange, wholly irrational political philosophy centred on their romantic love for the Kaiser. Neither the state nor the welfare of the nation but their 'completely and utterly monarchist way of thinking' and above all their 'personal love and gratitude for our All-Gracious sovereign' formed the guiding principle of all political thought and action.[171] Eulenburg formulated the central tenet of this philosophy quite openly in a letter which he wrote to Kuno Moltke on 15 June 1895, the seventh anniversary of Wilhelm II's accession, declaring that as a good Prussian and a monarchist one could 'come to only one conclusion, to give unqualified support *to the Kaiser*. If we do not work towards considering *Him* as the personification of Germany — even if his qualities make it hard work for us! — we shall lose *everything*.' For him personally this 'idealistic' standpoint was the product not only of cerebral cogitation but also of his inmost feelings, Eulenburg confessed, since 'my heart and my emotions lead me to the very place where my logic as a supporter of the monarchical principle and of my King also leads me'.[172] The consequences of this attitude — as Eulenburg also recognised — were not particularly beneficial either to the idea of the state or to the welfare of the German people; indeed the contrary was true. He wrote to Bülow in the summer of 1896: 'The Kaiser has the kind of nature which wishes to experience things *for itself* and not to be guided by information about the experiences of others . . . Of course I shall never make this comment anywhere except here, as everyone would rebel at the idea that the Kaiser wants to find things out *for Himself*; i.e. in some cases even at the expense of the people. But I think that as long as we wish to be and are a monarchy the King's character must be taken into consideration. The republican trend of our times demands that the king conform to a pre-set pattern . . . The Kaiser combines in Himself, more than I have ever been able to observe in any other person, two completely different natures: the chivalrous — in the sense of the finest period of the Middle Ages, with its piety and mysticism — and the modern . . . The *chivalrous* side of the Kaiser is very dominant — perhaps more than H.M. Himself realises . . . If I now transpose the effect of this imperial personality into politics, I am obliged to conclude that H.M. must look for His *natural support* from the Conservatives, from the Conservatives in the good sense — and that is confirmed by looking at Prussian history. In the long run the king of Prussia cannot do without the Conservatives . . . I think therefore that the Kaiser's individuality will find its *equilibrium* in political life on a sensible Conservative basis. Everything about the Kaiser's strong, powerful nature stands in such a remarkable conflict with the domination of Liberal–Progressive or Liberal–Catholic (Centre) thinking that this in itself gives rise to the impression of indecision which all Germany is complaining about.'[173] Guided by these tenets, Eulenburg and Bülow piloted the Kaiser through the stormy waters of the endless government crises of the years 1894–7, thereby bringing him into still greater conflict with his own people. Not until many years later did they realise what a fatal mistake they had made.[174]

# CHAPTER TWENTY-ONE

# Caprivi's dismissal

## THE KAISER AND HIS REICH CHANCELLOR

IF Leo von Caprivi had hoped that his withdrawal from the top post in Prussia would at least leave him freedom of action in the affairs of the Reich, this proved all too soon to be an illusion. In September 1893 the Chancellor made the painful discovery that the Kaiser would not even allow him to choose his closest colleagues in the Reich government. Having heard 'much good' of Count Arthur von Posadowsky-Wehner during a hunting expedition in Posen, Wilhelm insisted on appointing him successor to Freiherr von Maltzahn-Gültz as secretary of state at the Reich Treasury.[1] In political circles the choice of this outsider caused 'general astonishment';[2] it was presumed that one of the reasons why the Kaiser had hit upon Posadowsky was that he mistakenly believed that the Count was of Polish extraction. Wilhelm was still paying court to the Poles, Waldersee wrote, and thought that in choosing Posadowsky he had 'pulled off a skilful coup in this direction'; but the Poles were laughing heartily at this idea, for 'Posadowski [sic] comes from an old Silesian Lutheran family and had nothing Polish about him except the i.'[3] Whatever the truth of the matter, the Reich Chancellor found himself compelled to obey the Kaiser's command. The three candidates whom he had himself put forward for the Treasury after consulting Miquel were simply passed over. As he had never met Posadowsky, Caprivi made enquiries about him from the Oberpräsident of the province of Posen, Wilamowitz-Möllendorff. He could not of course have known that Lucanus, on the instructions of the Kaiser, had taken care that the Oberpräsident's response would be favourable.[4] After a personal meeting with Posadowsky in Berlin the Chancellor declared himself ready on 3 August to entrust him with the Treasury, but following a meeting with Miquel (who had wanted the appointment to go to Aschenborn) Posadowsky himself had second thoughts and asked Caprivi to choose someone else. Caprivi therefore telegraphed the Kaiser, who was taking part in the Cowes regatta with his yacht *Meteor*, asking 'May I tell the Count that Yr Majesty wishes to entrust the office to him and appeal to his patriotism?' 'Yes, most certainly', the Kaiser wired back, whereupon Posadowsky accepted the appointment.[5] But when the Chancellor sent the Kaiser a telegram two days later asking permission to announce Posadowsky's appointment, if necessary, he received the curt reply from England: 'Commission to be sent to me in Heligoland. Announcement without my signature is inadmissible.'[6]

With that the affair was by no means settled, for Posadowsky had not been able to familiarise himself with his tasks and declared that he was not in a position to chair the conference of all German finance ministers which was about to take place at Frankfurt am Main. The Reich Chancellor and Miquel therefore proposed that the handover be delayed until 1 September so that the outgoing Secretary of State, Maltzahn, could still preside at the Frankfurt session. This, however, again met with an insulting rejection from the Kaiser, who sent a telegram from Heligoland, dictated to Kiderlen, insisting that either Posadowsky or Miquel, but on no account Maltzahn, should take the chair at the ministerial conference in Frankfurt.[7] The Chancellor's patience finally snapped. In unusually resolute terms Caprivi pointed out that the conference in Frankfurt had already begun under Maltzahn's chairmanship. Posadowsky could not have presided at the conference, in the first place because he had not yet mastered the complicated business in hand, but in the second place also because he was not yet in the service of the Reich, since the Kaiser had not yet signed his commission of appointment. In Berlin all those concerned had decided on 1 September as the date on which Posadowsky would assume office, so that he had time to wind up his provincial duties and transfer to the service of the Reich. In the meantime Maltzahn would produce a written report on the deliberations in Frankfurt.[8]

On All-Highest orders Kiderlen informed the Reich Chancellor in a letter from Kiel on 12 August that His Majesty had been 'put under duress by the fact that the commission had been laid before him on 8th August, the day of the opening of the ministers' conference in Frankfurt am Main, and He had no longer been in a position, . . . confronted by a fait accompli, to come to a decision as to the chairmanship of the conference. H.M. expressed the view that a *proposal* submitted to Him was pointless if the proposed measure had already been taken . . . H.M. went on to express the hope that in future proposals to be submitted to Him by the Reich offices would be sent in sufficient time to make it unnecessary to start carrying out the measure submitted to the All-Highest decision until *after* the decision of His Majesty.'[9] The Chancellor refused to accept this carefully worded reprimand, responding with a telegram which pointed out firmly that the start of the finance ministers' conference had been fixed 'weeks ago'. He, the Reich Chancellor, had 'considered himself justified in appointing the chairman of this purely preparatory meeting on his own initiative'. He had 'by no means mentioned the matter in order to seek [an] All-Highest decision, but only in answer to a question from His Majesty'.[10]

The Kaiser had nevertheless succeeded in getting his candidate appointed to the Reich Treasury and had thereby, for the first time, personally selected the head of one of the internal offices of the Reich. As a result Posadowsky enjoyed a degree of independence within the Reich leadership which further weakened the Chancellor's authority. This became apparent only a few months later when Caprivi reprimanded his new colleague for having 'obeyed a telegraphic order from His Majesty The Kaiser' without informing him, as his superior, in advance. Posadowsky emphatically rejected the charge of 'incorrect conduct in the exercise of his official duties' and asked the Reich Chancellor, 'in view of the . . . manner of the reproof issued to me . . . to have the goodness to recommend to His Majesty The Kaiser my immediate discharge from my office'. As Caprivi was unwilling to enter into any further argument with the Kaiser at this juncture, he had no alternative but to make his peace with Posadowsky,[11] who remained in government office until 1907 – at first at the Treasury and from 1897 at the Reich Office of the Interior – and became a significant driving force in domestic politics in Wilhelmine Germany. But Caprivi's days were numbered.

Posadowsky's appointment coincided with a violent conflict between Wilhelm and his Chancellor-General over a decision made by Caprivi to restrict the scope of the imperial manoeuvres in Baden and Württemberg, which were badly affected by drought. The monarch saw this as an inadmissible infringement by the civilian authorities of the Reich of his prerogative as supreme war lord. Waldersee, having discussed the matter with members of the imperial entourage – he expressly named Hahnke, August Eulenburg, Lucanus and Plessen as his informants – recorded in August 1893 that 'a break-up between the Kaiser and the Chancellor is imminent', as Caprivi's 'slackness' in restricting the manoeuvres in South-West Germany without obtaining the Kaiser's prior approval had gone down 'very badly' with the latter and had 'greatly embittered' him. From his own experience Waldersee knew 'very well that once the Kaiser is in the grip of a bad mood like this, it very easily spreads, especially when it is encouraged'.[12]

How bad relations between the Kaiser and his Chancellor had become after their arguments over Posadowsky's appointment and the Württemberg manoeuvres of the summer of 1893 is apparent from the long letter which Philipp Eulenburg wrote to Caprivi from the *Hohenzollern* after his visit to England with Wilhelm, in order to warn the Chancellor of the 'ill-feeling' towards him which the Kaiser had begun to display. Caprivi's proposal to appoint the moderate Centre leader Freiherr von Huene as secretary of state at the Reich Treasury had already greatly annoyed the Kaiser, Eulenburg reported. He went on: 'Although this matter was settled in accordance with His Majesty's wishes by the appointment of Count Posadowsky, it still irritates him now. The attitude adopted by the Centre in the Reichstag has put His Majesty in such a thoroughly bad mood that the Catholics will be "excommunicated" for a long time to come. His Majesty's dissatisfaction is related to this attitude.' But Wilhelm's annoyance at the abandonment of the Württemberg manoeuvres was more serious still, Eulenburg warned. This affair 'has made His Majesty . . . very angry indeed and he strongly resisted all attempts on my part to persuade him to take an objective view. His Majesty shares General von Hahnke's opinion in this matter and also has the support of the Grand Duke of Baden. The fact that the imperial authority in Württemberg was undermined by the changes made independently [by the civilian Reich authorities] to the arrangements for the manoeuvres, and the Foreign Office's handling of this matter, which His Majesty and his military suite consider as the inviolable domain of the army – these are two constantly recurring themes which arouse His Majesty's anger towards Your Excellency and which particularly affect Herr von Marschall too. I had hoped that the week at Cowes would mitigate these impressions. But this was an illusion. His Majesty returned to them with undiminished anger . . . His Majesty's anger . . . reached such a degree and his language was so forceful that I felt compelled to remind His Majesty very seriously of the dangers which could arise from such anger and from the possibility of a violent argument with Your Excellency.' Eulenburg strongly urged Caprivi not to think of resigning in his forthcoming meeting with the Kaiser. He had pointed out to the Kaiser, he wrote, 'that a sudden chancellor crisis just as he returned from a pleasure-trip would certainly cause an astonished Germany to put all the blame on him. I likewise drew His Majesty's attention to the fact that Your Excellency might say, by way of clearing up the ill-feeling prevailing between you, that government business had to go on when His Majesty was on pleasure-trips. Your Excellency does not need to be told that this unleashed a storm of indignation, but on this occasion too His Majesty kindly treated me with his habitual consideration. Now that I have given you this account of the state of affairs, which is strictly accurate, Your Excellency will be in a position to prepare yourself for "what is to come" and – I venture to express this fervent plea with the greatest respect! – I hope that Your Excellency, having all the facts at your disposal, will be able to steer clear of the rocks which threaten the Kaiser and us all if a storm should suddenly provoke the chancellor crisis which we dread . . . A conversation I have had with His Majesty today has left me the impression that my arguments have softened the intensity of

His Majesty's feelings. May God grant that it is so. I cannot bear to think what dangerous consequences for Germany and the Kaiser there would be if an acute crisis were suddenly to arise!'[13] Eulenburg was relieved to hear from his cousin the Oberhofmarschall on 17 August 1893 that the meeting between the Kaiser and Caprivi had passed off without a chancellor crisis. 'The interview with the Reich Chancellor went off well, fortunately, so that both parties are satisfied, although for very different reasons', August Eulenburg reported. 'H.M. says that the Chancellor said his "pater peccavi" [Father, I have sinned], while the latter maintains that H.M. did not have the courage even to mention "these trifles, which were really not worth a crisis", so that he, the Chancellor, had had to take the initiative himself.'[14]

The Kaiser's extreme anger over the affair of the manoeuvres had by no means subsided, however. On 16 September 1893, when the Chancellor was on the point of departing on leave, he was held back by a telegram from the Kaiser 'reproaching him in the most violent and impolite way for this alleged misdeed of his'.[15] After an encounter in October 1893 with the Finance Minister von Miquel and the Oberhofmarschall August Eulenburg at the unveiling ceremony of the memorial to Kaiser Wilhelm I in Bremen, Waldersee noted that the Kaiser had in fact 'inwardly' broken with Caprivi.[16] The ill-feeling was by no means one-sided, for the Chancellor was now also beginning to complain loudly about the difficulties he had to face because 'one could almost never be sure of the Kaiser; if he approved something, one could never be sure that a Flügeladjutant or a Cabinet chief would not arrive a few hours later with a different expression of his will'.[17] In the summer of 1892 Caprivi had still been able to say: 'Even if I am angry, when he (H.M.) looks at me kindly with his fine eyes, my anger disappears.' But this mood had long since been replaced by quite a different one.[18] From what he heard from Berlin, Waldersee accurately concluded that the Chancellor too was now 'in a highly irritable state'.[19]

It is difficult to imagine the cold arrogance with which the Kaiser had treated his Reich Chancellor since the School Bill crisis, and even more since the clash over the Württemberg manoeuvres. His hostile marginal comments on a report by Caprivi of 30 November 1893 give us an unusual insight into the relationship between the two men. Caprivi, who was after all constitutionally responsible for directing foreign policy, commented on a report by the military attaché in Rome, Colonel von Engelbrecht, on the Italian financial crisis. The monarch's scornful marginalia reached their peak in his response to Caprivi's offer to explain his own views in audience. 'No thank you!', Wilhelm wrote; he was 'perfectly well aware' of the Reich Chancellor's views.[20]

Waldersee saw a further sign of the growing estrangement between Wilhelm and Caprivi in the appointment of General Walter Bronsart von Schellendorf as Kaltenborn's successor as Prussian minister of war, for according to August Eulenburg the choice of this fiery General was not only made without the Chancellor's agreement, but 'was in fact even directed against him'. Waldersee found it incomprehensible that the Chief of the Military Cabinet should have recommended this choice, for Hahnke surely could not have wanted a strong minister of war. 'But the Kaiser will also realise that he will have to treat the Minister of War differently from now on', Waldersee predicted.[21] He was astonished to hear from Bronsart himself how much pressure the Kaiser had put on him to accept the War Ministry. Bronsart, 'after repeated attempts to resist, had had no alternative but to accept, after the way the Kaiser had appealed to him'.[22] The former Chief of the General Staff foresaw serious conflicts, since he could not imagine that Bronsart would accept 'the present state of affairs'.[23] And indeed it was not long before serious friction arose between Wilhelm and this General, who, unlike his two predecessors, was not prepared to suffer ill-treatment by the Kaiser in silence.

The Kaiser's arrogant lack of regard for the Reich Chancellor was conspicuous in other actions, as for instance in January 1894, when after discussing the situation in Cameroon in the officers' mess at Kiel he appointed a certain Captain von Natzmer of the Guards Rifles as governor of the colony on the recommendation of one of the officers. Out of the blue, on 2 January, the Chancellor received an All-Highest cipher telegram which left him and the Foreign Secretary speechless. It read: 'The recent events in Cameroon have once again proved the old, well-tried theory that civilian governors are not suitable for African conditions. The complete transformation that has taken place in East Africa since Herr [Colonel] von Schele arrived confirms this evidence. It is high time things changed in Cameroon too. Neither Governor Zimmerer, who is hated in all commercial circles as a loudmouth, nor a born subaltern like Herr Leist is capable of being of lasting use in Cameroon, with the breadth of vision required, as the population has virtually no respect at all for them. We also have to rely too much on force to be able to dispense with a military governor in Cameroon as well as elsewhere for the time being. In addition, I have heard that Leist has been guilty of a serious crime against morality by allowing gross immorality with Dahomeian women, which has completely destroyed his authority among the whites (above all the commandant of the garrison and his people) and the blacks. The new military governor must therefore go out immediately with the company of Marine Infantry which I am sending there. The most suitable candidate is Captain von Natzmer of the Guards Rifle Battalion, who has already been listed as a possible governor of East Africa because of his outstanding qualities. I have directed him to report to the Foreign Office immediately. Leist must be recalled at once. Wilhelm I. R.'[24] On investigation, Caprivi and Marschall discovered that the

Kaiser had heard both through the Chief of the Naval Cabinet and through his brother Prince Heinrich that the colonial troops from Dahomey, former slaves whose freedom had been purchased by Germany, were not paid any wages until they had 'served out' the equivalent of the purchase price, and were therefore compelled to make their wives earn money through prostitution.[25] On 2 January the Foreign Secretary noted in his diary 'The R[eich] C[hancellor] and I decided to go and see H.M. this afternoon and if necessary threaten to resign.'[26] In the end the two statesmen managed to convince the Kaiser that a detailed investigation into the accusations against Leist must be instituted first, and that to this end the Foreign Office should send a commission of inquiry out to Cameroon. They also persuaded him not to appoint Natzmer governor 'for the time being'.[27] Wilhelm was 'very gracious' on this occasion and cancelled Natzmer's appointment, Marschall recorded, but the confrontation had been 'necessary'.[28] The dispatch of a ship with a detachment of marine infantry, which the Kaiser had ordered at the same time, was not countermanded. 'The Kaiser has had his way after all', Waldersee noted tersely.[29] When Marschall remonstrated with Admiral von Senden for having 'gossiped to H.M. about affairs in Cameroon', he was rebuffed. 'He denies saying anything.'[30]

On the pretext that the Foreign Office was incompetent, Wilhelm II continued to intervene peremptorily in foreign policy and in diplomatic appointments. Philipp Eulenburg reported to his friend Bernhard von Bülow in the spring of 1894 that the Kaiser had 'thrown overboard *any* consideration' for the Foreign Office 'and only speaks of it with disdain'. He would not make any changes in its administration, however, because he 'derives increasing pleasure from deciding on policy matters *himself*, and sees justification for this in the "incompetence of the house"'.[31] Holstein too complained of the Kaiser's growing 'high-handedness' and observed that 'from his [Wilhelm's] point of view the best argument for keeping Caprivi must be that *no* successor to Caprivi would allow His Majesty so much freedom'.[32] The deep anxiety caused in the Foreign Office by an unsupervised exchange of telegrams between Wilhelm and the Tsar in late 1893 was exemplified by one diplomat's observation that it would be highly desirable 'if our All-Gracious sovereign were accompanied by a diplomatic adviser even on short journeys, or if he made it a strict rule never to send off politically important telegrams of that kind without previous checking by the Foreign Office'.[33] But as the disastrous 'Willy–Nicky' correspondence, which began only a few months later, was to prove, the Kaiser would not have dreamt of subjecting his correspondence with a foreign monarch to any form of official inspection.

The increasingly autocratic behaviour of the Kaiser in matters of foreign affairs was also repeatedly demonstrated in the appointments and dismissals of ambassadors and envoys, which as a rule went against the wishes of the Reich Chancellor. What Caprivi did not begin to suspect for some time (and even then only dimly) was the humiliating truth that in making these dispensations from above the Kaiser was often merely carrying out suggestions for appointments which had been secretly urged on him by Philipp Eulenburg, and which as often as not originated in the Political Department of the Foreign Office; the choices, in other words, of the Chancellor's direct subordinates. This strange mechanism can be seen operating in a whole succession of diplomatic appointments following the School Bill crisis. In one instance Marschall, Kiderlen-Wächter and Holstein wanted General Bernhard von Werder, who was on good terms with Tsar Alexander, appointed ambassador in St Petersburg in succession to Lothar von Schweinitz. Caprivi, however, was against the appointment of this elderly, unmarried General who had no particular diplomatic talent. In order to circumvent the Reich Chancellor's opposition the three top Foreign Office officials decided to persuade the Kaiser, through Eulenburg, to declare himself in favour of Werder. Eulenburg was to hint to Wilhelm that the Tsar had expressed a wish for Werder to be appointed.[34] The plot hit a snag, for the Kaiser was so determined to send Count Alvensleben to St Petersburg as ambassador that Eulenburg's question as to 'what the attitude of His Majesty might be if a particular wish of the Tsar had been received – concerning General von Werder, perhaps – provoked a very sharp rebuff'.[35] Only a few days later, however, the Kaiser telegraphed the Chancellor saying that the Russian ambassador Count Shuvalov had read him a telegram from the Tsar asking for Werder as ambassador. 'Our Kaiser replied that the most important thing for him was that his ambassador had the confidence of the Tsar', Holstein wrote triumphantly to Eulenburg. Werder was appointed.[36] The intrigue successfully over, a relieved Eulenburg was able to report to Bülow: 'After some anxious moments I heard that His Majesty had at once yielded to the wishes expressed and had now fully realised (almost *too* much – for we love superlatives!) the advantage we have gained from the present situation.'[37]

If the Reich Chancellor was duped and the Kaiser manipulated by the Holstein–Eulenburg team in this case, the type of intrigue they practised can be seen even more clearly in the dismissal of the ambassador in Rome, Count Solms, at the end of 1893, and his replacement by Bernhard von Bülow, who had manoeuvred himself into the good graces of the Kaiser's favourite. After Bülow had drawn attention to his own suitability for the post (he was married to an aristocratic Italian lady whose mother, he claimed, was King Umberto's best friend),[38] Eulenburg wrote to Wilhelm II suggesting that Solms be dismissed and Bülow appointed in his place. 'The critical remarks which Your

Majesty made to me in Berlin about Ambassador Solms', he wrote, 'have made me wonder whether Your Majesty is perhaps intending to prepare for a change in this post on the occasion of Your visit to Rome. All kinds of thoughts have occurred to me which I should like to lay before Your Majesty with my most humble duty for Your consideration: a kind of box of tools to be used in any way You wish. The question is, who is to be the successor. In my most humble opinion there is only one person, although Your Majesty has chosen him for Paris: Bernhard Bülow. For the time being old Münster with his long legs, long strides and booming voice can still play the part of the aurochs [extinct wild ox] in the monkey park so well that Bernhard could go to Rome *en attendant*.'[39] When, during the Kaiser's visit to Rome, Count Solms omitted to inform him of a garden party to be held by an English peer living there, the stage was set for a change of scene. Eulenburg wrote to the Kaiser again giving him advice for the audience which the Reich Chancellor was about to attend. 'May I most respectfully suggest to Your Majesty that You might defuse what would be a highly unpleasant crisis at this moment by *Yourself* bringing up the subject of Italy *first* and saying: "Solms will not do any longer – once he has gone matters will certainly improve." I have no scruples in giving Your Majesty this advice, because Solms has already sent his wine-cellar away – so he is beginning to settle his affairs in Rome. This turn of events puts the whole matter in quite a different light. Your Majesty knows whom *I* would recommend for Rome.'[40] The Kaiser answered at once, exactly as Eulenburg had hoped: 'All right! I have duly put paid to Solms, with the Chancellor's approval, and *Bülow's* appointment to Rome is to be announced!'[41] To take Bülow's place in Bucharest, at Holstein's urgent request Caprivi had given the Kaiser the choice of Count Casimir von Leyden or Count Anton Monts, which drew from Wilhelm II the response: 'I prefer Leyden; Monts is such a pessimist.'[42] Naturally Leyden was appointed. Malet reported perspicaciously to London that the ruthless dismissal of Count Solms and the surprising appointment of Bülow as ambassador in Rome had not come about through a decision by the Reich Chancellor or the Foreign Secretary, whose constitutional responsibility it was, but had been 'entirely due to the Emperor'.[43]

The Chancellor was understandably offended, not only by the manner of the ambassadors' appointments but also by the private correspondence which Wilhelm II conducted with some of them. But his protests had little effect.[44] Early in 1894 the Kaiser expressed his regret for having betrayed to the Chancellor a letter he had received from Bülow, a mistake he would never normally make. He resolved to be more careful in future, sending a message to Bülow through Philipp Eulenburg: 'But he *commands* you to write to Him whenever you consider it necessary. His Majesty has a similar arrangement with Hatzfeldt and He said that if He did not maintain direct contact with certain of His most distinguished diplomats in this way, He would soon be landed in trouble by the Reich Chancellor and the Secretary of State.' 'So you see', the Kaiser's best friend commented to the future Secretary of State and Reich Chancellor, 'I was right when I told you that your letter-*intermezzo* has had the desired effect.'[45]

Not only did the Kaiser continue to correspond with Bülow, but he gave him advance notice of his plan, which was to be kept 'absolutely secret from the Foreign Office', to meet King Umberto in Venice to discuss the question of a reconciliation between the Italian state and the Vatican, in which he wished to play the 'honest broker'. By taking this initiative, 'which could become a new milestone in the peace-making policy of the German Kaiser', Wilhelm hoped to strengthen monarchical feeling in Italy, reduce the French, American and Jesuit influence in the curia and – not least – improve his relationship with his own Catholic subjects. As he wrote to Bülow on 28 March 1894, shortly before his departure for Abbazia, 'It must not be forgotten that the idea of reconciliation could easily be seized upon by other people and either exploited for their own benefit or, as in the case of Gaul [i.e. France], undermined. Hence the wish that the German Kaiser might perhaps bring it about. He would also put himself in a very strong and impressive position vis-à-vis his Centre and fanatical priests in Germany if he were successful in this work of reconciliation. I must ask you to treat the Venice matter as *completely secret*, and also to make sure that the same is done on il Re's [the King's] side. I shall visit Pola and can dash over to Venice from there. I would inform il Re about the little trip in advance, and then he could also make a chance visit there without indicating any reason, and so we would meet! W.'[46] As Eulenburg, who accompanied the Kaiser to Abbazia, reported to his intimate friend Bülow, the Kaiser had become so excited in thinking about the idea of reconciliation 'with his characteristic enthusiasm' that the political advantage to be gained from it had become 'a shining vision' to him. 'In fact H.M. is like a child looking forward to the trip to Venice and to politicking with King Umberto and the two of us!' But Eulenburg was at a loss as to how the affair could be managed 'without creating an enormous uproar in the Foreign Office'. And besides: 'Is it even possible for H.M. to interfere in Italy's internal affairs in this way?'[47]

A more striking example still of the Kaiser's use of his personal power to make and unmake appointments was the replacement of Heinrich VII Prince Reuss, ambassador for many years in Vienna, by Philipp Eulenburg himself, whose appointment as Prussian envoy in Munich in 1891 had already been widely seen as an act of favouritism by Wilhelm II. With fine irony, but also hitting the nail on the head, Reuss wrote to Holstein on 3 January 1894: 'When one no longer has the confidence of one's sovereign, one can no longer render such good service as before. I wish my successor, who is armed with this invaluable possession, success in gaining the trust of the people here [in Vienna] so that the *cause* does not suffer.'[48] Eulenburg's influence on the Kaiser can be clearly seen in the fact that to all intents and purposes he picked his own successor as envoy in Munich, Max Freiherr von Thielmann. When he had second thoughts about his choice and wrote to the Kaiser, 'Your Majesty is quite right in describing Thielmann as unsuitable for Munich. His Jewish extraction and abrupt manners make him best fitted for a post where the nobility does not play such an important part as here [in Munich]', it was too late to rescind the appointment. The Kaiser telegraphed his friend to say that his letter had arrived half an hour too late. 'Everything has already been settled in accordance with your earlier suggestion! Alea jacta sunt!'[49]

The high degree of dependence of the leading German statesmen on the wishes and moods of the young Kaiser is further exemplified by the state of insecurity into which they were thrown when it was rumoured in January 1894 that Wilhelm II had had a conversation lasting an hour and a half with General Paul von Leszczynski. The rumour alone was enough to cause speculation that the General might be appointed Reich chancellor. In Waldersee's opinion, if the rumour of a meeting were confirmed 'it would certainly be significant and the Kaiser must have some plan for the General'. Leszczynski was undoubtedly a very competent and experienced general but as far as politics were concerned he was 'highly questionable'. Waldersee had 'often heard him talking complete nonsense; his Polish blood is all too obvious, he is very lively but always unsteady'. But he could talk 'like a book – and that is enough to impress the Kaiser'. 'I cannot think of him as a candidate for the chancellorship; in my view that should be an impossibility', but 'unfortunately these days one must always be prepared for such things'.[50] If a mere conversation between Wilhelm and a rather insignificant General could give rise to rumours of an imminent change of chancellor, anything that could be taken for a sign of a rapprochement between the Kaiser and the Bismarcks came close to provoking complete hysteria in the Wilhelmstrasse.

### THE 'RECONCILIATION' WITH BISMARCK

The attacks made by the Bismarcks not only on the men of the New Course but also on himself were so insulting to the Kaiser that in the summer of 1891 he was still uttering furious threats that he would set 'his colleagues, the field marshals and commanding generals' on to the old 'Iron Chancellor' and have him stripped of his uniform. He was reported to have declared to the generals that 'if Prince Bismarck continued to behave as hitherto his patience would soon be at an end and he would not hesitate to send him straight to Spandau [prison] if necessary'.[51] At this time a reconciliation with the former Reich Chancellor still seemed absolutely unthinkable. But only six months later Friedrich von Holstein felt compelled to warn strongly against the Kaiser visiting Friedrichsruh. He suspected the Flügeladjutanten Gustav von Kessel and Count Carl von Wedel, the Adjutant-General von Wittich and the Kaiserin's Hofmeister Hugo Freiherr von Reischach of having persuaded the Kaiser that he was so strong and powerful that he could take the first step towards reconciliation with the Bismarcks without loss of face. But such a step, Holstein argued, would be seen by the nation as submission rather than reconciliation, and Wilhelm would thereby be subjecting himself to Prince Bismarck's authority. 'Can you see the Princess, Herbert, the Rantzaus and the Bills moving into 77 [Wilhelmstrasse] again?', Holstein asked Eulenburg. Kessel would then become 'senior medical attendant with a grand title' and Reischach would be made an ambassador.[52]

Another six months later the Wilhelmstrasse officials were panic-stricken when it became known that Prince Bismarck was planning to travel to Vienna for his son Herbert's marriage to Countess Marguerite Hoyos, taking advantage of this occasion to make a 'Greater Germany' tour by visiting Kaiser Franz Joseph, King Albert of Saxony and Prince Regent Luitpold of Bavaria. Under pressure from Caprivi and Marschall, who in turn had been urged to take a firm line by Holstein and Kiderlen Wächter, Wilhelm wrote to Franz Joseph in mid-June 1892 asking his 'dear friend' not to receive the disgraced former Chancellor. At the same time Prince Reuss, the ambassador in Vienna, was instructed not to take any notice of the Bismarck wedding. Kiderlen described the Kaiser's letter to Franz Joseph as '*excellent*' and commented triumphantly that it was 'His Majesty's own work, for the pusillanimous Reich Chancellor would never have advised such a thing'.[53] In this letter Wilhelm reminded the Austrian Emperor that a 'major coup' achieved by Bismarck 'was the secret treaty – à double fond – with Russia, which was concluded behind Your back and which I dissolved'. 'Since his retirement', Wilhelm continued, 'the Prince has waged war on me, Caprivi, my ministers &c in the most perfidious manner . . . Incomprehensible though it is, he launches his fiercest attacks against the *Triple Alliance* (his own creation, of which he is so proud) and above all against our resolute solidarity with You and Your excellent people. His outrageous attitude towards Your country in the matter of the trade treaties is still too well known to waste words over it.' Bismarck's apparent 'desire for reconciliation' with Kaiser Franz Joseph, Wilhelm declared, was nothing but another 'humbug' on his part 'which is aimed only at arousing the love of sensation and the curiosity of the stupid masses'. Bismarck, the monarch complained, was 'as artful and cunning as can be in trying to turn things round so that it seems to the world that I am the one who is making the first approach'. With this purpose in mind Bismarck had devised the idea of an audience with Kaiser Franz Joseph as the 'climax of his programme', Wilhelm wrote. 'Ignoring my court and the Kaiserin in the rudest way he takes himself off to Dresden and Vienna to present himself there at once and play the part of the loyal old man.' Wilhelm therefore asked the Austrian Emperor, 'as a loyal friend', not to put him in a difficult position by receiving 'my disobedient subject' 'before he has made an approach to me and said his peccavi'. Wilhelm had made it clear to the people who had always been ready to mediate between them that he expected 'an unambiguous letter' from Bismarck, 'in which he asks to be received back into favour. I would not commit myself to anything before that.' As the Prince was still very far from taking this first step Wilhelm asked Franz Joseph not to receive him.[54] On 16 June 1892 the Austro-Hungarian Foreign Minister Count Kálnoky informed the German ambassador in Vienna that Kaiser Franz Joseph had refused to grant an audience to Bismarck and Herbert.[55]

The Bismarcks' campaign seemed to the statesmen in the Wilhelmstrasse all the more dangerous because even their former arch-enemy Waldersee, after a visit to Friedrichsruh, took up the cause of reconciliation between Wilhelm and Bismarck and, declaring that his 'sole endeavour' was to serve his All-Highest sovereign, proposed himself as Reich chancellor at this critical moment.[56] Caprivi hurried to Potsdam to persuade the Kaiser not to yield to this pressure for reconciliation. In his presence Wilhelm immediately wrote out a reply to Waldersee's initiative: 'Dear Count, The rumours which are sprouting like mushrooms in the press everywhere, alluding in various ways to "reconciliation" or "rapprochement" etc. between the Prince and Myself, make it seem advisable to come back to what you suggested to me in Kiel. You expressed the opinion that the Prince was tired of his campaign and yearned to be on pleasant terms with me again. But to "jump the ditch" – as the cavalry say – was very difficult for him. You said, however, that you were quite convinced that when the right time came for him you would be able to make it easier for him by offering to mediate. I should like to repeat, absolutely precisely, my answer at that time: that it was all very well, but the first step must be taken by the Prince, whatever happens. He must formulate his request or wish to be permitted to renew relations with me quite *unambiguously, in writing, directly to Me*. I shall not agree to anything else. You must keep this in mind as an unalterable principle. With many good wishes to your wife, Your sincerely devoted King Wilhelm R.'[57]

The Kaiser's displeasure at this escalation of the Bismarckian Fronde lingered on for some time yet. During the Scandinavian cruise that summer he complained to Eulenburg that it was shameful 'that the Kaiser is obliged to fight so hard against my former Chancellor and my Ambassador, who has been playing an infamous role'; Prince Reuss's days were therefore also numbered, he said.[58] In the Bismarck camp too hatred for the Kaiser and the men of the New Course reached new heights. In 1893 Philipp Eulenburg described the 'terrible fury of Herbert, Bill and Rantzau' as having given them a new family motto: 'May the blood of the Old Man be avenged on the Kaiser and his children.'[59] Faced with a growing pro-Bismarck cult, Wilhelm and his advisers were obliged to put on a semblance of goodwill in order to prevent the Bismarcks from getting the better of them. Thus there were earnest discussions behind the scenes as to how the Kaiser and the government should react to the death of the 'Iron Chancellor' in order to minimise the danger of the Bismarck family exploiting what would be an event of national importance to attack the crown. The idea of offering the dying Prince Bismarck an apartment in one of the Berlin palaces was rejected since it was clear, as Caprivi said, that 'the Prince will then become a political focus against which no power in the world can prevail'. Instead, on Caprivi's advice, the Kaiser sent a telegram from Hungary on 19 September 1893 offering Bismarck the imperial palace in Wiesbaden for the winter. The latter expressed his thanks but declined the offer.[60] The following month there was a further exchange of letters between Wilhelm II and Bismarck, which was seen as an attempt at rapprochement on the part of the Kaiser.[61]

The question of whether the Bismarcks possessed letters from Wilhelm 'which could be dangerous for His Majesty in the hands of [the journalist] Maximilian Harden' was particularly highly charged.[62] 'The most awkward and difficult question, which we must discuss, is the possible – perhaps even probable – *misuse of imperial correspondence* by the Bismarck family', Eulenburg wrote to Holstein on 7 October 1893. 'I spoke to His Majesty about it yesterday and asked him to tell me absolutely precisely what may have remained in the family's hands. The Kaiser spent a long time going over all the phases of his dealings with the Prince with me. There is apparently *nothing* for the time of Kaiser Friedrich (the most suspect to me!), as His Majesty firmly maintains. There were, however, dubious points concerning private letters from Prince Wilhelm from St Petersburg. These communications are of a *very* intimate nature – among other things they deal with the subject of the Prince *offering* Constantinople to the Russians. I doubt that the Prince has deposited the correspondence in the official files. But I do not doubt that the well-known, vigorous tone of the Kaiser's style will cause a quite extraordinary sensation in the world and will drive Austria, which at present is on better terms with Russia than we are, *even more* into Russia's arms out of retrospective shock.' The Kaiser's friend went on to consider how the letters could be recovered from the Bismarcks.[63]

In view of the vehemence with which the Kaiser rejected these attempts at rapprochement and mediation in the summer of 1892 and of the difficult discussions the following autumn about the dangers which the death of the founder of the Reich might bring for the monarch, the volte-face which Wilhelm performed in January 1894 when he ceremoniously received Prince Bismarck in the Berlin Schloss on the occasion of his thirty-fifth birthday was quite extraordinary. His action shows not only how successfully the Bismarckians in his entourage – his brother Prince Heinrich, his uncle the Prince Regent Albrecht of Brunswick, the Flügeladjutant Gustav von Kessel, the Oberhofmarschall August Count zu Eulenburg and his brother Botho, as well as the Finance Minister Johannes von Miquel – had worked to bring about the reconciliation, but also, and above all, how little the Kaiser cared by this time about keeping Caprivi's government in office. In April 1893, with the appointment as Flügeladjutant of Count Kuno (Tütü) von Moltke – who was an intimate friend of both 'Phili' Eulenburg and the new Württemberg envoy in Berlin, Axel Varnbüler, and the uncle of the painter Franz von Lenbach and thus on the best of terms with the Bismarckian clique in Munich[64] – yet another admirer of Bismarck entered the imperial entourage. He was to play a key role in the dramatic reconciliation of 26 January 1894.

As an unmistakable sign of his dissatisfaction with Caprivi and his advisers in the Wilhelmstrasse,[65] the Kaiser sent Kuno Moltke to Friedrichsruh on 22 January with a bottle of vintage Rhenish wine to invite the former Reich Chancellor to visit him in Berlin on his birthday. No sooner had Prince Bismarck accepted the invitation than Wilhelm II sent a telegram announcing the fact to his grandmother but completely distorting the truth of the matter: 'The congratulatory message I sent to Friedrichsruh through my Aide de Camp so touched the old Prince Bismarck that he immediately sent me an answer begging to be allowed to pay his respects to me tomorrow and to congratulate me on my jubilee. Am so thankful that this at last is possible.'[66] When the Foreign Secretary called on the Kaiser and Kaiserin on the morning of 23 January the Kaiser triumphantly showed him a letter and asked 'Whose handwriting is this?', whereupon Marschall replied 'Prince Bismarck'. The Secretary of State noted with dismay that 'H.M. has arranged this himself without any consultation.' At Marschall's request Wilhelm at first agreed that the news should be announced by the official government, but then sent Kuno Moltke to the Foreign Office 'with the Kaiser's orders that it should all be kept secret.' 'That will not do', the statesman commented, adding 'I go and see H.M. with Moltke and express my opinion strongly and frankly that the government itself must make the announcement so as not to appear to be put out and give the Bismarcks the chance to exploit the situation. Moltke contradicts. Rather a violent scene. H.M. gives way. 1 o'clock to the Reichstag. I tell everyone about it. Great joy.' Two days later, however, August Eulenburg came to the Foreign Office 'in rather an agitated state' with an article from the *Berliner Tageblatt* which alluded to collaboration between the Oberhofmarschall and the Foreign Secretary in the reconciliation with Bismarck. 'H.M. was furious about it', Eulenburg explained, 'and said it was to be denied in the *Reichsanzeiger*.' 'Done', Marschall noted tersely.[67] On the same day an announcement appeared in the official gazette indicating that Flügeladjutant von Moltke had been sent to Prince Bismarck on the Kaiser's own personal initiative and that even in government circles no one had been aware of the All-Highest 'magnanimous decision'. With that the disavowal of the Reich government was complete. In such circumstances, Prince Chlodwig zu Hohenlohe-Schillingsfürst commented in his journal, he would not wish to be the Reich chancellor. Barely ten months later, nevertheless, he was.[68]

It was characteristic of the lack of a sense of political responsibility in the Wilhelmstrasse that none of the government officials who had been exposed by the monarch in this way thought of resigning. Marschall was even relieved to be able to record, after conversations with Wilhelm and Philipp Eulenburg in the next few days, that 'H.M. is not thinking of making any changes in appointments.'[69] The Kaiser's favourite knew better, however, and recognised this clash between the Flügeladjutanten and the leading statesmen as the defining moment in which Marschall had irrevocably lost the monarch's confidence. The Kaiser told Eulenburg bluntly on 26 January 1894 that the Foreign Secretary had behaved so badly 'that my gentlemen thought he could not be kept on for much longer'.[70] Kuno Moltke wrote to Eulenburg describing Marschall as 'crazy and *insolent*'; he was no Prussian and therefore could not see German matters from a Prussian point of view. The Kaiser's standing among the people had changed overnight as a result of the reconciliation, Moltke enthused, going on to claim that 'the cheering of the people was tremendous yesterday [Wilhelm's birthday] again when the Kaiser went to give the password, and he realised that the crowds were not just a yelling *canaille*'. 'When I think of him tears still come to my eyes; in unselfish love for him let us rejoice as old friends and as loyal children of our Fatherland.'[71] Against such blind adulation the grey bureaucrats at their green baize desks in the Wilhelmstrasse stood little chance.

Waldersee was overwhelmed by this 'great event' and found it difficult to form a clear picture of what it meant. A reconciliation between the Kaiser and Bismarck must include Herbert Bismarck; but that was only possible, in his view, in conjunction with a 'complete change of system'. 'Might Caprivi really step down?', he wondered in some agitation. 'It may still be simply that the Kaiser hopes to win the Prince round by showing him great courtesy, and to persuade him to keep quiet.' Even then the ovations in the streets of Berlin would make a great impression on the Kaiser, the General wrote, for 'the old man is now

29. Prince Bismarck, supported by Prince Heinrich, in Berlin, January 1894

the popular one, while Caprivi is the dull philistine who does not know how to win people's hearts. How nervous they must be in the Wilhelmstrasse!' Abroad, where people had never understood why the Kaiser had got rid of such an asset as Bismarck, the reconciliation would be regarded as a perfectly natural step, Waldersee observed, while in Germany there were forced smiles to be seen among the Liberals, who were most anxious that Caprivi's position should not be undermined. Waldersee himself believed, however, that the Kaiser had 'finished' with Caprivi; all that remained was to arrange for the succession. Caprivi must get the Russian trade treaty through the Reichstag, but thereafter the Kaiser would certainly let him go. 'The Kaiser cannot be good friends with him and with

Bismarck and family at the same time', Waldersee commented, for 'the one excludes the other'. The time had clearly arrived for momentous decisions.[72] From a 'very subterranean source' Waldersee heard of a 'violent scene' which the Kaiser was said to have had with his mother in the Berlin Schloss. She had reproached her son 'for having sent a message to Bismarck without saying a word to her about it, and it was in any case much too soon for a reconciliation. The Kaiser is said to have replied that he needed Bismarck to get the Russian trade treaty through, and moreover circumstances were such that Caprivi would soon leave. The servants claim to have heard all this, in the Schloss itself; if it were really true, it would be a nice sign of the reliability and loyalty of these people', the General commented sarcastically.[73]

Several times in the course of these crucial days Wilhelm showed by deliberately slighting Herbert Bismarck that the reconciliation did not in fact include him, but only his father. At the investiture held at the Schloss on 21 January the Kaiser completely ignored his former Foreign Secretary, confidential adviser and drinking companion, which was all the more noticeable since numerous other royal personages, court officials and ministers treated Herbert with conspicuous friendliness. Observers were particularly struck by the repeated attempts which Prince Heinrich, Prince Regent Albrecht and the otherwise reserved August Eulenburg made to bring the younger Bismarck up to the Kaiser during the *cercle*. Although the Kaiser 'very obviously' avoided him, however, these attempts at a rapprochement at court were generally interpreted as the beginning of the end of the Caprivi era.[74] 'My appearance at the Order celebrations caused much excitement', Herbert reported to his father immediately afterwards. 'The Kaiserin spoke kindly to me, I had very long and friendly conversations with Prince Heinrich and Albrecht, both asked me to send you their greetings. During the *cercle* I stood in the last window embrasure, and was fetched from there on the instructions of S. Kanitz and A. Eulenburg; "I was to stay in the front row as H.M. wanted to see me." I followed and was asked twice more by both of them to stay at the front, "the Flügeladjutant knew about it" – but in the end H.M. was too embarrassed, he spoke to 4 or 5 indifferent people, 7 or 8 steps from me, talking to each for a conspicuously long time, and then turned to the opposite side from me on his way out of the hall. Botho Eulenburg greeted me with very noticeable warmth, but it was Miquel who compromised himself most with me. He talked very loudly, sent you greetings and wished you would come back, and showed contempt for the present leadership. With everyone so close together a great many people must have heard him.'[75]

If Herbert interpreted the Kaiser's conduct as embarrassment on this occasion, Wilhelm's insulting behaviour on his birthday – the day after he had received the ex-Chancellor at the Schloss – left no room for doubt that his disregard for the younger Bismarck was deliberate. On 28 January Herbert sent another report to Friedrichsruh: 'Yesterday after I had taken part in the *défilé* at court I waited for more than 20 minutes in the White Hall in case H.M. wanted to hear about your journey home. Everyone else left the Schloss immediately after their march-past. As the place was thinning out very much by now, I asked 2 friendly gentlemen of the court, of whom I sent one to A. Eulenburg, whether I should wait any longer. The answer came: "no, you are already attracting attention by staying, and if H.M. passes you later, when there are only royalties in the hall apart from you, you will be in trouble". A. Eulenburg undertook to tell H.M. that you arrived home safely, and that I would be at the gala opera performance. – During the very long interval at the opera I at first stayed behind, and various royalties spoke to me in a very friendly manner (the Albrechts, the Hermann Weimars, Hereditary Prince Meiningen etc.); the one who asked the most and was the most gracious was the King of Saxony; all sent you warm greetings. Afterwards I stood 3 or 4 steps away from the Kaiser, who spoke to Aug. Dönhoff for at least $\frac{1}{4}$ hour . . . then shook the hand of some nonentity standing in front of me and turned away. In the same way H.M. walked straight past me when he returned to his box . . . The impression it gave was that I was to be cut dead. Presumably H.M. thinks that *you* can be of use to him in his present difficulties, but that it makes no difference if I am badly treated.'[76]

### THE *KLADDERADATSCH* ATTACKS

The hysterical reaction in the Wilhelmstrasse to the reconciliation between the Kaiser and Bismarck becomes more understandable still in the light of the fact that, not long beforehand, the satirical journal *Der Kladderadatsch* had published vicious attacks on three conspirators named Count Troubadour, Austernfreund (Oysterfriend) and Spätzle (Noodles), whom everyone immediately recognised as Philipp Eulenburg, Holstein and Kiderlen-Wächter.[77] As the articles were clearly based on inside information, a sense of almost panic-stricken insecurity and paranoia filled the corridors of the Foreign Office. 'Why are we *three* always named together?', Kiderlen asked Eulenburg. 'Who is it who knows so much about our business? Who is it who hates only us, and associates with the people Kladderadatsch praises, Schlözer, Reuss etc.? Who knows about such private matters as that Reuss proposed you as his successor? It seems to me that there is one natural suspicion, which I do not wish to express yet, but which I shall look into carefully.'[78] Holstein was firmly convinced that the attacks had been ordered by Herbert Bismarck and/or Waldersee, that the Silesian magnate Count Guido von Henckel-Donnersmarck was the paymaster and that sinister police agents were involved in the campaign. In mid-April the Grey

Eminence of the Wilhelmstrasse, who was blind in one eye, seconded by the former Flügeladjutant General Moritz von Bissing, challenged Count Henckel to a duel. He asked General Waldersee to be his second, but refused to take part in the duel with Holstein.[79] Although duelling was illegal, at the instigation of his military suite the Kaiser demanded that Kiderlen shoot it out with Henckel and the editor of *Kladderadatsch*, Wilhelm Polstorff, before there could be any question of his accompanying the Kaiser on his travels again. Henckel rejected Kiderlen's challenge, declaring that he had no connection with the newspaper attacks, but Polstorff demanded a postponement of the duel for four weeks. As a result Kiderlen was unable to accompany the Kaiser on his trip to the Adriatic. On 18 April 1894 the Swabian diplomat fought a duel with the editor in the Grunewald and seriously wounded him with the third bullet. Both men were condemned to four months' imprisonment, but were released after a few weeks.[80]

In the politically and socially exposed position in which he found himself, it was the lack of a single word of appreciation from the Kaiser which affected Friedrich von Holstein most deeply. Despondently he wrote to Eulenburg at the end of 1893: 'If, in my joyless existence, I now have to endure His Majesty standing by and smiling coldly while I am pelted with dirt, if he can tolerate the fact that the Berlin police are, and remain, notoriously hostile towards the New Course, he cannot be surprised if I hand over my cards to someone else . . . before long . . . It is not those wretched attacks against me which make me angry. It is His Majesty's attitude which offends me: he does not lift a finger, but seems to find it enjoyable when a lot of filth is let loose.'[81] In January 1894 Holstein lamented that he and his colleagues were 'quite helpless to deal with the present attacks, for one has no idea against whom one should take action'. 'And the longer the people behind the Kladderadatsch are convinced they cannot be found, the more insolent they will become in their libels . . . I am utterly outraged by the way the Kaiser lets his supporters down. Why does he not appoint a decent chief of police? We have been betrayed and sold.'[82] Two months later the Privy Councillor renewed his complaints: 'What is so discouraging about the situation is the Kaiser's coquetry and unreliability. There is no pleasure in serving a master who lets one down . . . His Majesty ruins everything . . . with his lust for political adultery.'[83] Holstein's grievances about lack of support from the Kaiser bear eloquent witness to the effectiveness of the 'kingship mechanism', by which the monarch could, with a mere word or a simple gesture, discriminate for or against the rival politico-social cliques.

Eulenburg tried to lure Wilhelm into action by arguing that the *Kladderadatsch* attacks were also directed against him, the Kaiser.[84] He pointed out that Holstein was suffering from sleeplessness and extreme nervous strain and urged Wilhelm to cheer him up by conferring an order on him, and likewise to bestow some mark of his favour on the Reich Chancellor, whose position had been undermined by the systematically circulated rumours of a crisis.[85] He also informed the Kaiser that the National Liberal Reichstag deputy, Heinrich Prince zu Schönaich-Carolath, was spreading the story among journalists that 'H.M. the Kaiser's penchant for spiritualism' had played a decisive role in the choice of Axel Varnbüler as envoy from Württemberg, and that Eulenburg too was supposedly a spiritualist and was 'in the highest favour with H.M. precisely because he shared this mentality'. Prince Carolath had named Count von Henckel-Donnersmarck as his source.[86] Replying to this letter on 11 January 1894 the Kaiser joked that Eulenburg's information had 'helped considerably to further my studies of so-called polite or court society'. He had acted rapidly upon it, putting Adjutant-General von Plessen in the picture without even hinting at Eulenburg's name. 'He wrote a very nice but firm letter, as if on his own accord, to Butter-Heinrich [Prince Carolath]. The enclosed reply from the Butterfürst [Anton, ruling Prince of Schönaich-Carolath] will show you the effect. Either – as the letter must have been written with the guidance of Isidor Lachmannski [this is an allusion to Henckel-Donnersmarck, who was married to the Jewish Frenchwoman Marquise Blanche de Païva, née Lachmann] – Butteranton is telling a pack of lies, or your informant has grossly deceived you. It would be interesting to find out which.'[87]

Since the Kaiser eventually sided with Holstein, Kiderlen and Eulenburg in this unpleasant affair, albeit without great enthusiasm,[88] Henckel and Waldersee found themselves in an increasingly difficult position. In May 1894 Henckel approached Eulenburg through the Bismarckian journalist Hugo Jacobi, asking him to intervene with the Kaiser on his behalf, which the newly appointed ambassador in Vienna declined to do, remarking that a man like Henckel, with his untold millions, must surely be in a position to prove himself innocent of the *Kladderadatsch* attacks by finding out the true identity of the perpetrator. The very next day Jacobi was authorised by Henckel to send Eulenburg a pneumatic dispatch informing him that the 'sources' were still in official employment and had even sat at the Reich Chancellor's table with Holstein and Kiderlen at the Kaiser's last birthday celebrations.[89] Armed with this information, Marschall was at once able to demand an explanation from two of the disaffected officials in the Foreign Office, Ernst Freiherr von Bothmer and Ludwig Raschdau, whereupon the attacks immediately ceased. But the fact that Marschall decided to take action as discreetly as possible against the culprits led Eulenburg to conclude, not without reason, that the attacks against his powerful subordinates, Holstein and Kiderlen, had not been entirely unwelcome to the Foreign Secretary.[90] As we have seen, it was not least as a result of the machinations of Holstein and

Kiderlen with Eulenburg and the Kaiser against Caprivi and Marschall that the internal cohesion between the men of the New Course had broken down.

An unbridgeable gulf now began to open not only between Marschall and Caprivi on the one hand and the top officials in the Political Department of the Foreign Office on the other, but also between Philipp Eulenburg and Holstein. 'In the past few days I have had an instinctive and very painful feeling that something has come between you and me', Holstein wrote to his erstwhile ally in April 1894.[91] The future course of the reign of Kaiser Wilhelm II was to be decisively influenced by the parting of the ways between Eulenburg – who in his blindness continued to support the Kaiser uncritically, with the backing of Bülow in Rome and of Kuno Moltke, Axel Varnbüler and August and Botho Eulenburg in Berlin – and Holstein, who was to make one last attempt to spur on the statesmen in the Wilhelmstrasse to resist the growing personal power of the young Kaiser.

Philipp Eulenburg's decision to abandon the alliance he had formed with Holstein back in 1886, electing instead to go his own way, can be dated almost precisely to 20 March 1894, the fourth anniversary of Bismarck's dismissal. It was on this day that he drew up a memorandum for Wilhelm II in which he argued that the Kaiser could now dispense with the services of Caprivi and the other men of the New Course if he wanted. 'To make the present situation clear', he stated, 'I must go back to the time when His Majesty parted company with Prince Bismarck in 1890. The *necessity* of dismissing Prince Bismarck with which His Majesty found himself confronted led to the appointment of civil servants who were *not congenial* to the Prince . . . As it was very widely believed that after the death of Prince Bismarck Germany would collapse, and as the complication now arose that the Prince not only left the political stage, but also threw his great weight behind an attack on the Kaiser's government, which his departure had put in a very difficult position, it was natural that his successors in the Foreign Office would be considered "inadequate".' He, Eulenburg, had at that time made it his mission in life to help 'guard the Kaiser and the Fatherland against the grave danger of his having to lay down his arms in the battle for public support waged by the Prince. His Majesty would *never* have been able to recover personally from the blow of a defeat; Prussia could not have made up for the setback to the monarchy except with difficulty, perhaps only after a successful war. It was therefore important not only to keep the "New Men" in the posts entrusted to them by His Majesty *much* longer than the entire opposition thought possible, but also to make their work as *successful* as possible. Both can be considered "accomplished" after an interval of 4 years. The "reconciliation" with Prince Bismarck in *Berlin* and the fact that he has actually left the ranks of those maliciously opposing His Majesty forms, as it were, the keystone of a building which reached its culmination in the Russian trade treaty . . . This success for the Prussian monarchy, this victory for His Majesty the Kaiser, in spite of the fact that it exhausted all the strength that was invested in it, is *no Pyrrhic victory*. The "King of Prussia" is now no longer "checkmated" if He sees fit to bring about a gradual change in the personalities who have been systematically fought against . . . The immense difficulty of keeping the "New Men" in place lay not only in the characters themselves, but also in their ignorance of public affairs. It also lay in the fact that His Majesty, with his profound sense of duty, was endeavouring to learn how to govern, and adequate experience can often be acquired only at one's own and other people's expense. It was natural that there should be friction, and there were countless things behind the scenes which had to be settled, prevented, got rid of or found – without coming to His Majesty's attention – in order to achieve our goal, which took quite a toll on my nerves . . . Only a year ago I should have been filled with the greatest anxiety by the realisation that His Majesty completely ignores the Reich Chancellor, that is, he regards the latter's ability to direct internal and external policy as non-existent, and by his complete loss of confidence in the Secretary of State. *Today* – after His Majesty's new government has stayed the course for four years – I do not see this fact as fatally damaging, because I no longer need fear for the Kaiser and the monarchy if it should come to a break. It is my opinion, however, that within a certain period either His Majesty must recover his confidence entirely or there *must indeed* be a change, because the *first requirement for fruitful co-operation* must be that the Kaiser has confidence in *the particular people* in government office who have to deal with the questions on which the weal and woe of Germany and Prussia depend.' Eulenburg fully recognised Holstein's merits: it was his experience and his unparalleled hard work alone which had saved Caprivi and Marschall in the first years of the New Course. But since 1892 the Chancellor and the Foreign Secretary had begun to act increasingly independently, 'like fledglings which have hopped out of the nest'. 'It was a period of many mistakes and blunders', the Kaiser's friend lamented. 'After this period mistakes were even made with a certain self-confidence.' The Kaiser's trust in the leadership of the Reich had been shaken on the one hand by these 'mistakes', but on the other hand also by the feeling that Holstein, 'who shows marked peculiarities in his private life (which have earned him the reputation of being "half-mad", and much hatred besides), actually held the reins in the sphere *most important* to His Majesty, rather than his Chief [Marschall]'. It was nevertheless absolutely essential that the Kaiser recover confidence in the Wilhelmstrasse. 'The Foreign Office must be the *natural, self-evident* tool, mouthpiece, machine with which the Kaiser works. From the moment the Kaiser has the feeling that the machine is not running smoothly, it *must* be oiled, for the Kaiser cannot find better machinery for His Own use. The impression which His Majesty has at present can be changed only if His Majesty has absolute trust in the Secretary of State, and – that is something which Marschall can no longer achieve. For the time being a change is no doubt impossible . . . But after a certain interval I would advise His Majesty to make a change for the reasons I have stated. In making a new appointment to this post His Majesty will no doubt, for reasons of gratitude as well, wish to treat Holstein considerately . . . To show gratitude to him it would be desirable to choose a secretary of state with whom he would be happy to work. But this secretary of state must nevertheless be regarded *publicly as an independent man.* The choice is narrow. I can suggest only Bülow . . . Bülow is held in the highest regard abroad, he is acceptable to nearly all parties and in any case he will suit the Reich Chancellor, *whoever he might be.* There is a certain feeling in the country that he would be the right man and, as I know him very well, I can also confirm that he would be the right man for His Majesty . . . Provided that the latter makes his complete peace with the House of Bismarck and finds an ambassadorial post for Herbert (perhaps in London). The Reich Chancellor is in a similar situation to Marschall. He has been considerably strengthened by the Russian trade treaty, and the gratitude of his Kaiser will secure his position for the time being. But whether the Chancellor will keep his nerve and stand fast in the face of a campaign waged more fiercely than ever before in the press and behind the scenes is another question. Even at the time of the worst conflict, when Prince Bismarck was in office, the press did not create such an uproar, and only the feeling that His Majesty the Kaiser will maintain his solidarity with his principal advisers can give him the courage to "stay the course".' The question was therefore becoming urgent, Eulenburg went on, as to 'whom His Majesty would chose as successor? A general would be faced with *very great difficulties*, since the best general had not proved satisfactory to His Majesty. Furthermore, if the idea should take hold in the army that the Reich chancellor *had* to be a general, politics would invade the highest ranks of the army and every officer would think less of carrying "the field marshal's baton" than "the inkwell of Wilhelmstrasse 77" in his kit bag.' The only solution which he could see, Eulenburg reasoned, was 'to put the political confusion within the country under the control of a man of *very great* experience both in parliamentary matters and in internal affairs, that is to say Minister-President Botho Eulenburg. On the one hand, he has a good relationship with Miquel as a colleague, and on the other he would have in B. Bülow, to whom he has been close for many years, a secretary of state at his side on whom he could rely in foreign policy matters. In making these observations I am guided by the fact that this combination would be accepted without misgivings by a surprisingly broad spectrum of opinion – and that this change would be the only one which could be carried out without great convulsions.'[92] Situating himself firmly in the power vacuum left since Bismarck's fall between the crown and the state, Philipp Eulenburg assumed the role of the omniscient arbitrator whose place it was to pronounce on the capacities and future of the constitutional 'responsible government'. In this document of March 1894 he sketched out for the first time the combination – Botho Eulenburg as Reich chancellor with Bernhard Bülow as foreign secretary – which he was to continue to advocate throughout the countless crises of the next three years. Rarely in modern history does one see as clearly as in this instance the destructive role which a favourite can play within a system of Personal Monarchy.

## THE REVIVAL OF THE *COUP D'ETAT* PLANS

Immediately before the Scandinavian cruise of the summer of 1894 'considerable ill-feeling' prevailed between the Kaiser and Caprivi, which encouraged renewed speculation about a change of chancellor, particularly as there was growing concern over the general atmosphere of confusion and lack of leadership.[93] In accordance with the principle of the 'kingship mechanism', the monarch's loss of confidence in his principal advisers led to a further shrinking of Caprivi's power and at the same time to struggles and conflicts within the leadership of the Reich and the Prussian state. Arthur von Brauer, who had meanwhile returned to Karlsruhe as prime minister of Baden, gave a cogent analysis of the chaos behind the gleaming façade of Berlin in a letter to his Grand Duke in the autumn of 1894. 'To continue to speak of dualism in the government today would be to make oneself guilty of euphemism. It is not dualism, but at least "quadrilateralism": . . . Caprivi, Eulenburg, Miquel, Posadowsky, each with his supporters, face each other like four great enemy parties who agree only on one thing, that "it cannot go on like this and that H.M. must decide". "His Majesty's Government", in the sense of a unit, simply no longer exists . . . All those involved . . . cling so doggedly to their point of view that I believe that H.M. will *at last* have to come to a decision on the question of appointments. But it is characteristic that no party is certain of victory or even pretends to be so. No one knows which way H.M. will lean, and many people think a *tertius gaudens* [a third party] might well succeed both.'[94] After a visit to the capital Waldersee summed up the confusion behind the scenes in similar terms: 'The most profound mistrust and hatred between Caprivi and Miquel, Caprivi distrusts [Botho] Eulenburg and of course also the Kaiser, Bronsart on strained terms with Caprivi, but in serious conflict with the Kaiser, meanwhile all are the best of friends outwardly.'[95] In the Wilhelmstrasse Caprivi's position was regarded as in such danger that Philipp Eulenburg, at Holstein's instigation, was obliged to warn the Kaiser that if he conferred the Order of the Black Eagle on Miquel, as he apparently intended, the Chancellor would immediately resign. The Kaiser denied having any such intention and sent a telegram in answer to his friend's letter saying 'Had a good laugh over it! Who could think up such rubbish. And to think that you were taken in! Wilhelm I. R.'[96] Be that as it may, the sense of insecurity in the highest government circles was palpable.

Speculation about possible successors to Caprivi now grew increasingly lively. In March 1894 Minister of War Bronsart remarked during a visit to Waldersee in Altona that 'the separation of the posts of chancellor and minister-president causes continual problems; in fact the situation is untenable, but it nevertheless goes on'. Both Generals were of the opinion that Botho Eulenburg would be the best successor to Caprivi; if he were appointed Reich chancellor not only would the separation of the two offices be removed, but the lamentably bad relationship between the Conservatives and the Kaiser would also rapidly improve under him.[97] The Prussian Minister-President and Minister of the Interior, who like Caprivi complained that it was 'truly difficult to govern with this sovereign!', seemed, however, to lack the 'will to power'.[98] When in the following weeks it became increasingly obvious that Botho Eulenburg was a 'complete nonentity', other candidates for the chancellorship began to be discussed.[99] In the summer of 1894 rumours circulated that it was not Botho, but his cousin the Kaiser's favourite Philipp Eulenburg who was to be appointed to succeed Caprivi. The former Chief of the Admiralty, General von Stosch, told Rudolf von Bennigsen that the Kaiser had said to a close friend: 'I can get on with Caprivi, but I do not warm to him. The man lacks imagination, he does not understand when I tell him about further thoughts I have. I shall have a younger man as his successor, who is closer to me personally and to whom I owe no sort of debt as a result of his past. *He shall be my man only*.' Stosch presumed that the Kaiser had his friend Eulenburg in mind for the highest office, although he doubted that Eulenburg 'could be so reckless as to accept the chancellorship'.[100] Waldersee was among the many who regarded the favourite as the most unsuitable candidate imaginable for this responsible position. 'I will not presume to pass judgement on Eulenburg's diplomatic capabilities, but I am quite prepared to believe that he might be a passable foreign minister', he wrote. 'He is unsuitable to be chancellor because he has much too feminine a nature, without any vigour; and then there are his spiritualist leanings. I think he would lead us to rack and ruin. But he would suit the Kaiser very well, of course.'[101] The former Minister of Ecclesiastical Affairs, Count Robert von Zedlitz-Trützschler, who visited Waldersee at Altona in August that year, also saw an obstacle in Philipp Eulenburg's effete personality and in the spiritualist interests which he apparently shared with the Kaiser.[102]

'If Zedlitz were to become chancellor I would be happy and begin to hope that many things in this country might improve. The Kaiser could not choose anyone more appropriate', the arch-conservative Waldersee commented.[103]

At the end of June 1894 two events coincided that were to push the chancellor crisis, long since brewing, into an acute phase. At a by-election in the Hamburg constituency of Pinneberg a Social Democrat was elected, and in Lyon the French President, Sadi Carnot, was assassinated by an Italian anarchist. Waldersee commented on the first of these events that the Kaiser 'would not mind if quite a few more [Social Democrats] got into the Reichstag; for then the sensible people would pull themselves together', while he himself believed 'that we ought to make up our minds now to take vigorous action', as otherwise one might 'easily miss the right moment'.[104] Although the Kaiser was again talking about defeating the socialists and the anarchists the General was afraid that the monarch would lack the resolve to take such a step. 'The good Kaiser did indeed plan, under the influence of his immature youthful impulses, to make all mankind happy, and was even convinced that he could do it; what did he achieve? He made the masses greedier and class hatred has merely increased. Now he dreams of shooting down the Social Democrats, who have not the slightest intention of giving him the opportunity to do so.'[105]

The murder of Carnot led to deliberations in all European countries on how to combat anarchism most effectively. Waldersee had grave doubts as to whether the right means would be used. 'I do not believe that important decisions will be made, least of all here', he wrote on 6 July 1894. 'It is no use executing or locking up 100 scoundrels or so and keeping 1000 or so in fear of their lives; we must pursue the causes of the movement and put a stop to the way in which these people can openly and freely incite the lower classes against the upper classes, the unpropertied class against the property-owners, and bring religion into disrepute. But unfortunately through neglect we have already slipped a long way down, and if action is not taken soon we shall go rapidly downhill. The Kaiser, who surely wants what is best, does not begin to see the full picture; he likes to say that he will shoot down all ringleaders, but does not realise that it will never come to an uprising; the leaders of the movement see that they are making steady progress and they will be careful not to give any reason for shooting at them.' In Germany no one had had the courage to take action even against those Social Democrats who openly advocated the destruction of the existing order and left the room when toasts were drunk to the Kaiser. 'From my knowledge of the persons involved, fear of assassination attempts is already playing a part [in Wilhelm II's mind]', Waldersee complained. He would offer his services, he declared, if action was to be taken against the revolutionary parties, but 'the men of today in our government would of course have to disappear', and in general 'pretty well everything would have to be tackled differently from before'.[106]

The inevitable result of Wilhelm II's determination to use the general fear and anger aroused by the assassination in Lyon as an opportunity to take action against 'revolutionary tendencies' – by which he meant both anarchism and socialism – was to bring to a head the conflict between the Prussian Ministry of State under the leadership of Botho Eulenburg and Miquel on the one hand, and the Reich administration under Caprivi and Marschall on the other. The former advocated a large-scale operation in the Reich, which did not exclude the possibility of repeated dissolution of the Reichstag and, as a last resort, a *coup d'état*. The latter, however, considered it sufficient to introduce in the Prussian Landtag (not in the Reichstag) a law of association which would be acceptable to parliament. In mid-July 1894 Holstein and Caprivi explained to the Württemberg envoy, Varnbüler, the catastrophic consequences which would follow the introduction of a harsh anti-socialist bill into the democratically elected Reichstag. The Privy Councillor declared that 'His Majesty was in favour of making use of the present favourable moment and the fear of daggers and bombs in the middle classes; and since the Prussian Ministry of State, especially Botho Eulenburg, had spoken out against taking action through legislation in the [Prussian] Landtag, if their influence prevailed there was a danger that the Reich Chancellor would be forced to introduce into the Reichstag a bill which, in both his and Holstein's opinion, would certainly be rejected both by the present Reichstag and, after it had been dissolved, by a newly elected Reichstag.' The Reich Chancellor likewise stressed to Varnbüler that the Reichstag would not in any circumstances vote for a new anti-socialist bill; to take action in the Reich would therefore inevitably lead to the dissolution of parliament, to a *coup d'état* and to the imposition by force of a new electoral system. The consequences, it was feared in the Wilhelmstrasse, might be civil war and even the disintegration of the German Reich.[107]

The Kaiser thus found himself once again facing a choice between two rival groups representing opposing points of view. After lengthy discussions with Philipp Eulenburg and Kiderlen on the Scandinavian cruise he at first opted for the moderate course recommended by Caprivi and sent a telegram on 24 July to the Minister-President, ordering Prussian law to be tightened up. The chances of a bill against 'revolutionary tendencies' being accepted by the Reichstag were slight, he explained, echoing the views of the Reich government exactly. 'On the other hand it seems to me possible, for the time being, to achieve what Saxony already has by taking the path of legislation in *Prussia*. I wish appropriate proposals to be submitted to me through the Ministry of State. Absolute secrecy is essential. Audience on my return.'[108] On receiving this message Botho Eulenburg told his cousin Philipp that he would have a suitable bill drafted as instructed, but that he had asked the Kaiser to postpone 'the All-Highest decision as to whether to choose this or the more advisable, more comprehensive course of legislation for the Reich' until he was at Königsberg at the beginning of September, as until then almost all the ministers would be away on leave.[109]

After taking soundings in Berlin and discussing the subject at length with Botho in Munich on 29 August 1894, on his return to Vienna Philipp Eulenburg wrote the Kaiser a letter which gives us another clear glimpse of the 'kingship mechanism' and which was to be of decisive significance for the course of the crisis and the fate of Caprivi. As a result of his enquiries the Kaiser's close friend reported that 'a conflict has arisen between my cousin and the Reich Chancellor . . . over the question which Your Majesty commanded me to discuss with him. I must freely admit that after my conversation with him [Botho] I could not avoid the impression that his nerve is as strong as could possibly be desired, and even stronger than in another quarter . . . He told me that the danger from the anarchists and the socialists was much too serious to be counteracted otherwise than through the *Reichstag*. Only a rigorous anti-socialist law could provide the means of control which was so urgently needed. Of course this bill would *have* to be passed. It was not entirely out of the question that the present Reichstag, given the generally prevailing mood and the use of the whip, might accept the bill. But it was doubtful. At any rate a new Reichstag (in the event of resistance) would *also* have to be dissolved and if there were *another* rejection the government would have to bring in a *new electoral law*. It would be a matter of bending or breaking. The monarchy *needed* to act with rigour in such an important question . . . The idea of changing the law of association through the [Prussian] Landtag was wrong because it was a weak measure . . . A change in the law of association in Prussia would be nothing but a fiasco. This argument is *directly opposed* to that of the Reich Chancellor and is hard to refute. The Reich Chancellor will not contemplate another dissolution of the Reichstag *in any circumstances*, because he foresees difficulties with the federal states. So he would turn *this question* into *another* resigning issue. I do not doubt that the federal states would indeed make difficulties. Württemberg because it is democratic, Bavaria out of particularist aspirations. But on the other hand the question is too much of a *national* one for the federal governments not to co-operate if the Reich government shows it is in earnest and threatens reprisals. The Reich Chancellor would not "co-operate" in any case because he neither would nor could put the case for the bill in the Reichstag. Botho Eulenburg spoke *brilliantly* in favour of the anti-socialist laws in 1878. He would be able to do it. He would of course have to become an authorised member of the Bundesrat first. If we assume that Your Majesty wished to bring the question before the Reichstag, then a change of chancellor would come first. That would be a dramatic introduction to the proposed action. But the new Chancellor would reorganise the Ministry. (I doubt that Marschall would stay on as secretary of state in that case, – and I am not sure whether Botho Eulenburg would remain as minister-president. But only *he* could put the case for the bill.) – But now let us assume that the Reich Chancellor stays and Botho Eulenburg goes. In that case I can only repeat the *unanimous* opinion of statesmen and officials of all party groups, which is that dual government would then cease. It is only the remarkably conciliatory and at the same time loyal personality of my cousin that has enabled this form of government to survive . . . That is more or less what my enquiries have revealed. A conundrum, a vicious circle. I cannot give Your Majesty any advice – except perhaps to discuss the situation frankly with Botho Eulenburg. He is after all the most eminent *statesman* whom Your Majesty has, and he is also honourable and considerate. Marschall and Miquel are interested parties; the Reich Chancellor is obstinate. Lucanus (with whom I am on very close terms and whose diligence I admire) is not senior enough to be consulted on questions of *great* moment. Your Majesty will of course make the best of this complicated situation for yourself, but a discussion with an experienced statesman might reveal new points of view to Your Majesty which would be useful – and might perhaps help clarify the important choice to be made between the Reichstag and the Landtag in the anti-socialist question . . . It seems to me that the situation will not become acute until after the Chancellor's return from Karlsbad – that is, probably when Your Majesty is in Rominten [on 23 September].'[110]

On receiving this letter the Kaiser arranged to call on Botho Eulenburg on the afternoon of 2 September. They spent an hour discussing the situation. Afterwards the Minister-President reported to his cousin that the Kaiser had explained to him at great length 'that at first he had been in favour of taking the aforementioned action in Prussia, but that he had since become convinced – it was easy for me to see how – that this would not be adequate, but that the matter must be tackled in the Reich and that it was essential that it be carried through. He was well aware that it was a momentous matter, but he was determined to carry it through and he believed he could count on the co-operation of the federal allies, as he already knew he could on that of the Kings of Saxony and Württemberg . . . When I suggested that it would surely be necessary first to come to an understanding on the matter with the leading statesman, His Majesty agreed, but commented that if the latter would not see to it someone else would, and also expressed the opinion that only a general could be considered for that role. This gave me the chance to press the point that if this happened the opportunity should be taken of reversing the separation of the highest offices in the Reich and in Prussia, and that I myself would not stand in the way. His

Majesty protested very emphatically against the latter suggestion, however. The discussion came to an end on the point that all preparations should be made as agreed and that the decision should be taken after the return of the Chancellor and the Kaiser, that is in the second half of October.'[111] Botho Eulenburg's brother, the Oberhofmarschall August Eulenburg, confirmed in a letter to their cousin Philipp that the conversation which the latter had engineered between the Kaiser and the Minister-President had 'worked wonders'. After 'a very long and thorough discussion' the Kaiser had 'changed tack completely' and '*such* complete agreement . . . had been achieved that they even talked about the most far-reaching consequences of possible changes of appointments'.[112]

### THE FALL OF CAPRIVI AND BOTHO EULENBURG

The day after his conversation with the Minister-President the Kaiser left Potsdam for East Prussia, where he was to direct the army manoeuvres. When Botho Eulenburg arrived in Königsberg, the East Prussian capital, the Kaiser invited him to luncheon with the King of Saxony, who was likewise in favour of large-scale action against 'revolutionary tendencies' in the Reich.[113] On 6 September 1894 Wilhelm made a speech at Königsberg which signalled the beginning of the end for Caprivi. 'With deep sadness in his heart', he said, he had been compelled to recognise 'that in the circles of the nobility close to me my best intentions have been misunderstood and sometimes challenged, and even the word opposition has reached my ears. Gentlemen! It is a nonsense for Prussian nobles to form an opposition against their king; it is only justified if the king is at their head, as the history of Our House teaches us. How often have my forefathers been obliged to confront misguided members of one class for the good of the whole! The successor of the man who became sovereign duke in Prussia in his own right will walk in the footsteps of his great ancestor; just as the first King [Friedrich I] said ex me mea nata corona [from me my crown is born] and his great son [Friedrich Wilhelm I] established his authority as firmly as a rocher de bronce [sic], I too, like my Imperial Grandfather, represent the Divine Right of Kings. Gentlemen! Whatever oppresses you, I feel too, for I am the greatest landowner in our nation and I know very well that we are going through difficult times. My thoughts are daily directed towards helping you; but you must support me in this, not by causing an uproar, not by using the methods of the professional parties of opposition that you have so often rightly fought against; no, but by addressing yourselves trustfully to your sovereign. My door is always open to each one of my subjects, to whom I gladly lend my ear. Follow that path from now on, and I shall consider everything that has happened as expunged!' Alluding to the memorial to his grandfather which he had unveiled that morning the Kaiser continued: 'Before us stands the statue of Kaiser Wilhelm I holding the sword of the Reich aloft in his right hand, a symbol of justice and order. It reminds us all of other duties, of the hard struggle against the efforts of those who attack the very foundations of our national and social life. Now, gentlemen, it is to you that My call is addressed. Go and fight for religion, for morality and order, against the parties seeking to overthrow them! Like the ivy which winds itself around the gnarled trunk of the oak tree, adorns it with its foliage and protects it when storms rage through its crown, the Prussian nobility encircles My House. May it, together with the entire nobility of the German nation, become a shining example to those of our people who are still hesitating. Come, then, let us go into this battle together! Onwards with God, and shame on him who lets his King down. In the hope that East Prussia will be the first province to join the front line of this war, I raise my glass!'[114] Two days later Wilhelm told Botho Eulenburg, when the latter took his leave in Marienburg, 'that He would inform the Chancellor of what He had decided by cipher telegram and that I myself might write to Karlsbad [to Caprivi] with further details, which I have already done'. 'I am very anxious to know what the answer will be', Botho wrote to his cousin, whom he asked to burn his letter at once.[115]

After the speech at Königsberg Waldersee had a sense that 'we are about to witness a change in the internal political scene and I think the Eulenburg family has plucked up courage to act against Caprivi'.[116] While the Kaiser was at Rominten for several days' shooting during the last week of September Philipp Eulenburg had a further opportunity to work on the monarch along the same lines as his cousin Botho.[117] Always inclined to regard the wishes and impulses of the Kaiser as a legitimate starting-point for any policy to be followed, the ambassador at Vienna, who had not been at his post for months, found himself increasingly at odds with his erstwhile ally Holstein.[118] He confided to his new confidant and prompter, Bülow, whom he looked upon as future Foreign Secretary and Reich Chancellor,[119] on 30 September 1894: 'I am . . . basically of the opinion that the Königsberg speech has had such a significant effect that it is impossible to take *half*-measures now. The Kaiser's appeal has electrified the people and if His government brings *weak* proposals before them or fails to bring any at all, the Kaiser's standing, which has just risen, will be *completely* and hopelessly ruined. Beside this consideration all Holstein's oversubtle, Bismarck-fearing calculations wither away to nothing.'[120]

At Rominten the Kaiser's friend drew up a detailed *aide-mémoire* in which he summed up the advantages and disadvantages of forcible action in the Reich, and read it out to the monarch on 27 September on the latter's return from a shooting expedition. In this highly revealing document he stated that 'the *advantages* of introducing a bill into the Reichstag with the object . . . of giving the Reich government a firm basis on which to combat socialism and the revolutionary parties are 1. that the external situation is eminently peaceful at the moment. The Tsar's serious illness guarantees peace for some time and at the same time puts a curb on the French, whose inclination is always to exploit any possibility of serious trouble in the German Reich to strike out at us . . . 2. The present combination of federal princes makes it advantageous to take action now: King Albert of Saxony can be counted on, King Wilhelm of Württemberg likewise, and the old Prince Regent of Bavaria is weighed down by great fear of the socialists. In a few years' time the picture may be quite different. The 3 Kingdoms will, in the foreseeable future, find themselves governed by princes who are less firm in their convictions, which may rule out fruitful action. 3. The moment is opportune in view of the confusion among the parties and the general discontent. It may not be possible to eliminate this discontent, but the slogan "War against revolution" has sufficient appeal to bring about a change for the better, rally those who have strayed and show them the path towards unity. The government is also in a position to show the firm hand and firm will which the misled masses have become accustomed to calling for. 4. The moment is opportune because the universal need for protection against revolution provides a useful electioneering slogan in the event of dissolution of the Reichstag.' Eulenburg set out equally clearly the disadvantages of a draconian measure in the Reichstag. 'The *dangers* of bringing in a strong bill in the Reichstag are undoubtedly serious, as one cannot count on its being accepted except in a more moderate form. As soon as it overstepped the mark, the majority of the Reichstag would oppose it and the Reich government would have to proceed to dissolution in order to maintain its own reputation. It is *possible*, but not certain, that the bill could be forced through the new Reichstag. It is much more likely that there would be conflict between the Reichstag and the Reich government, which could be brought to an end only by radical means (a change in the electoral system and perhaps force of arms). The difficulties which a deliberate alteration of the electoral system would entail in the Reich would be as follows: 1. As the constitution of the Reich, by its incorporation into the constitutions of the separate federal states, has become part of their constitutions, but there are *responsible ministers* in the federal states (as in Bavaria and Württemberg), these Ministries would be open to impeachment by their Landtage if they took sides with a Reich government that violated the constitution of the Reich. For this reason these federal governments will not give their support, and the Kings of Bavaria and Württemberg will have to take up the battle within their own domains if they dismiss their Ministries. Nor will they find any other Ministries to take on this battle; they will have to lead the fight *in person, against* the tide. Neither Prince Regent Luitpold nor King Wilhelm [of Württemberg] is the man to do this. Neither has the courage to fight his way through rebellions (these would be likely in Stuttgart). 2. The only way of coming to an agreement with the Reich government and *participating* in the conflict would be on the basis of a *revision* of the Reich constitution of 1871, whereby for instance the Bavarian government, in return for the alteration of the electoral system . . . might demand *advantages* which would inevitably change Bavaria's current position in the Reich to the detriment of Prussia's hegemony. That is the area in which the Bavarian Landtag, the Württemberg Landtag etc. would agree to negotiate. Prussia could not tolerate such a weakening of its position, and although the federal princes may honestly intend to stand by Prussia, out of this a conflict may arise which 3. requires force of arms. This would in fact lead to the spectacle of the Reich *in the process of disintegration.* The damage to our national and international standing would be immense. The danger of a French invasion would come to the fore at the same time. And there is another respect in which the conflict in the Reich would be dangerous. The concurrence of Prince Bismarck in the announcements of His Majesty in Königsberg, Thorn etc. may be sincere. In the event of a conflict in the Reich, with all its consequences, i.e. if the situation should become chaotic, the Kaiser would, *par la force des choses*, be *compelled* to call for Bismarck. That would be his Canossa, the effect of which would be to cause damage to the Prussian throne and to leave the Kaiser personally and politically played out.'[121]

As the Kaiser's stay at Rominten drew to a close, Eulenburg had the impression that Wilhelm had already decided on large-scale action in the Reich and hence on a change of chancellor. As he reported to Bülow, the dangers of a *coup d'état* in the Reich which he had listed in his *aide-mémoire* did not worry the Kaiser 'because he *seems* to want a *decision*. He does not say so openly − on the contrary, he would deny it.' The Cabinet Chiefs Lucanus and Hahnke, who had both come to Rominten, also seemed to Eulenburg to be trying to influence the Kaiser towards dismissing Caprivi. 'The ring around the Chancellor is tightening. Lucanus, the angry little terrier, has already got the big dog *firmly* by the hind leg. He was here yesterday. Hahnke is helping him. He was here today.'[122] On 28 September Eulenburg told his cousin the Minister-President that he could expect to take over as Reich chancellor in the near future. 'I have the feeling that His Majesty wants to "sort things out". Lucanus has been here, and he too seemed to me to be in a hurry. I have thought a great deal about the best moment for the change and am still not sure. It might be more effective for you to make your entrance after the dissolution of the Reichstag. On the other hand I should like to have avoided a chancellor departing as a result of a vote in the Reichstag. We have not yet reached that point.'[123] A conversation with the Kaiser on 29 September, in which the favourite attempted to mediate, nearly precipitated a crisis when it became apparent that important documents had been withheld from the monarch by the Chancellor and the Foreign Office, just as in the Bismarck crisis of 1890. Eulenburg recorded the conversation in dialogue form in a letter to Bülow:

*Myself*: In order to put Your Majesty fully in the picture about the situation I have brought with me the relevant reports received from the three kingdoms in the course of the summer. Although Y.M. is familiar with them, it would perhaps be a good thing to look through them again.

*H.M.*: What reports? I do not know of any.

*Myself*: (very shocked!): They will perhaps have been submitted to Y.M. in extenso . . .

*H.M.*: No, *most certainly* not. Well, let us see why these far from unimportant documents have been withheld from me!

*Myself*: (I read the reports, which are extremely important.)

*H.M.*: So it was because the federal states *agree* with taking action through the Reich! *That* was the reason! . . . I have been *systematically* kept in the dark in an irresponsible way, by Marschall *and* Caprivi. I am used to their doing that, of course; but this is the limit.

'So as you see, my old Bernhard', Eulenburg's letter continued, 'these people are digging their *own* graves! It used to make the Kaiser furious when Bismarck withheld important reports from him. Caprivi knows that as well as Marschall. With the sincere intention of enlightening H.M. on the unpredictable consequences of taking excessively strong action if there were conflict in the Reich I used the material officially at my disposal in order to impress the point on him!! Could anyone have imagined that reports from the three kingdoms would not be laid before the Kaiser when they concerned a question which has occupied H.M. almost exclusively for 4 months? Really, there is nothing one can do.'[124]

The Kaiser's irritation with Caprivi in these final days of the latter's chancellorship is evident from the audience he gave the Reich Chancellor on 5 October 1894 at his hunting lodge at Hubertusstock. Marschall recorded that 'His Majesty's antagonism towards the Reichstag . . . was immediately apparent when the ceremony to mark the completion of the new Reichstag building was mentioned. It was only with great difficulty that His Majesty could be persuaded to abide by his earlier decision to attend the ceremony. The discussion of the bill to be brought before the Reichstag after it had convened brought matters to a head. The Reich Chancellor declared himself ready in principle to introduce an anti-revolution bill, but considered it necessary that it should be announced in the speech from the throne. His Majesty categorically opposed this: the Reichstag must be taken completely *by surprise*, he said, as soon as the fiscal reform bill had been accepted, and the dissolution of the Reichstag must follow at once. The Reich Chancellor pointed out that this was not a practicable way of proceeding, as the revolution question had already been discussed in the press for weeks and questions would immediately be asked on the subject in the first days of the session . . . It would be impossible to hold back. At the same time C[aprivi] stated the view that the bill must be in a form that did not *a priori* exclude any possibility of acceptance by the Reichstag, for otherwise there would inevitably be convulsions and crises which would have the opposite effect to the political aim of the measure – the suppression of revolution. His Majesty now brought up the subject of a *coup d'état*, whereupon the Chancellor set out in detail the dangers of a *coup d'état* in the Reich, pointing out that it was impossible to destroy part of the constitution of the Reich without damaging the whole creation etc. His Majesty dismissed these arguments and launched into a long and enthusiastic exposition of the entire *coup d'état* programme which he had agreed with the King of Saxony. The Reich Chancellor tried to stress the merits of his point of view and finally remarked – as His Majesty remained obdurate – that His Majesty would have to choose another Reich Chancellor to carry out this policy, since his conscience and his convictions made it impossible for him to put forward a policy which he feared would "ruin the Kaiser and the Reich". His Majesty declared that he would not accept the Chancellor's resignation; it was for Him to decide what standpoint every official should adopt at a time of conflict – and the Kaiser, not the official, knew the soul of the German people and bore the responsibility before God; he appealed to the soldier who had once told Him that he would allow himself to be shot dead for His sake. Caprivi responded that he was still ready to do so, but that he could not act against his conscience and put forward a policy which he regarded as harmful to the Kaiser. There followed a long discussion. His Majesty expressed the view that Caprivi's resignation would allow his enemies to crow over him and would expose him – the Kaiser – to the suspicion that he had been "forced to get rid of a chancellor". Finally His Majesty alluded to the possibility of a deteriorating situation with regard to foreign relations – the death of the Tsar was imminent, complications were beginning to arise, C[aprivi] could not desert him at this time. C[aprivi] answered that the present state of affairs in the world of high politics in fact constituted a grave warning against following a domestic policy which would inevitably lead to crises and convulsions and might end in catastrophe. As C[aprivi] would not give way, His Majesty took a milder tone and asked for details of the draft anti-revolution bill. C[aprivi] said that it was still in preparation and that he would communicate with the Prussian Ministry of State about the details of it. His Majesty agreed, and with that the audience came to an end. The Reich Chancellor stayed for dinner. His Majesty led the conversation at table in a cheerful and relaxed way and took leave of C[aprivi] as kindly and graciously as always . . . The Reich Chancellor emphasised that the discussion was occasionally very heated, but there had been no hurtful words on either side. He is also convinced that His Majesty will not drop him now, although of course he is also *absolutely adamant* that he will refuse to co-operate in a *coup d'état*. The key to the situation now lies with the Prussian Ministry of State.'[125] On 12 October, at a session of the Crown Council, Caprivi spoke out against a harsh law and therefore against a *coup d'état* policy, while Botho Eulenburg advocated both. Astonishingly, Miquel took Caprivi's side, along with Bosse, the Minister of Ecclesiastical Affairs, and Berlepsch, the Trade Minister. The Kaiser, however, 'persisted in his advocacy of a rigorous measure'.[126]

The Chancellor was in a strange position, Waldersee noted at this time, for while he had publicly refused to take measures against 'revolutionary tendencies', the Kaiser had demanded just such measures. Conservatives, Free Conservatives and National Liberals were willing to co-operate but the parties which supported Caprivi – the Catholic Centre, the Left Liberals, Democrats and Social Democrats – could not support such a policy. 'The situation could not be more confused, and one would think that light must eventually dawn on the Kaiser', the former Chief of the General Staff commented. 'Leaving aside the Centre – although I think these people the most dangerous of all – if Eugen Richter, [Leopold] Sonnemann and [August] Bebel warmly support Caprivi in their newspapers and say that he is their man, it ought surely to open his eyes!'[127] The Kaiser had left Rominten for Hubertusstock, where both Caprivi and Botho Eulenburg had visited him, Waldersee noted, adding that negotiations were underway there, during which it was 'the specific aim' of the Minister-President to 'hoist the Chancellor out of the saddle so as to take his place'. 'The Eulenburg family' evidently thought the time had come to bring Caprivi down and replace him with Botho. 'They worked hard, and apparently successfully, during the manoeuvres in [East] Prussia and at Rominten.' The Chancellor's enemies had found an unexpected ally in the King of Saxony, who had previously supported Caprivi but who had now become afraid of the social democratic movement in his own country and who had convinced the Kaiser at Königsberg that things 'could not go on like this any longer'. 'Hence the constant emphasis on the fight against revolutionary tendencies in the imperial speeches.'[128] This last remark related to another speech of Wilhelm's calling for decisive action and undermining Caprivi's moderate policies. On 18 October 1894 he declared: 'Just as in 1861, when my grandfather undertook the reorganisation of His armed forces – misunderstood by many, contested by still more, the future proved him gloriously right – just as in those days, discord and mistrust prevails among the people today. The only pillar on which our Reich stood was the army. It is the same today!'[129] Even the militaristic Waldersee criticised Wilhelm for having emphasised 'too sharply' that 'the army also stands against internal enemies', by which he had 'again stirred up unrest quite unnecessarily'. The Kaiser's remark that the army was 'the only reliable support for the throne against revolution' had caused universal offence. 'It would be a sorry state of affairs for us if that were true', Waldersee commented, adding, 'unfortunately, however, he has a particular aptitude for offending and embittering the people who are his true and staunch supporters'.[130]

On 26 October 1894 both Caprivi and Botho Eulenburg were dismissed. It was no accident that this happened at Liebenberg, Philipp Eulenburg's country house. The direct cause was an article in the *Kölnische Zeitung*, obviously Wilhelmstrasse-inspired, in which the Chancellor made known the Kaiser's decision to support his moderate policy and not the provocative class-warfare policy of the Minister-President. The real reason, however, is to be found in Caprivi's long since untenable relationship with the Kaiser on the one hand, and with the Eulenburg clique on the other. 'The solution to the puzzle', Waldersee reflected when news of the double dismissal reached him, 'lies simply in the fact that the Kaiser had already had enough of his Chancellor a long time ago and was glad to be able to get rid of him now.'[131] The General rightly pointed out that 'relations between Caprivi and the Kaiser have been strained for almost a year and there has been much friction which has helped bring about the final clash'. The Chancellor had felt obliged 'to make representations to the Kaiser about the fact that he was negotiating with others behind his back', and this 'very much displeased' the Kaiser. After the dismissal, Waldersee recorded, Wilhelm declared that he had been compelled to part with Caprivi 'because he became increasingly uncongenial to me and wanted to have me under his tutelage'.[132] Later the Kaiser complained that Caprivi 'never did me a single favour'.[133] The dismissal showed, Waldersee commented, 'that it is difficult to work with the Kaiser, and for people who have some self-respect it is impossible in the long run. He is secretive; one soon has the impression that he is not being open, which naturally breeds mistrust. Caprivi allowed this to go on for far too long, chiefly out of vanity, because he felt powerful and great as chancellor, and now he has to bear the great disappointment of having the Kaiser declare his firm support for him, and then calmly dismiss him 5 days later, while saying very unkind things about him. Caprivi has also complained bitterly to various people and has said that it is really impossible to govern with our sovereign. He is very put out. And the fact that Caprivi's departure was clumsily handled, like almost everything that the Kaiser does – or thinks he does – on his own account, will damage the Kaiser's reputation even more. The whole world will say: what a way to behave, and what vacillation!'[134]

The simultaneous dismissal of Botho Eulenburg Waldersee attributed partly to the latter's mistaken tactics and partly to the Kaiser's fear of falling entirely into the hands of the Eulenburg family. In his opinion Botho, who had fully recognised 'the unhealthy aspect of the separation of offices', ought to have brought about the break with Caprivi far sooner. Instead he had held back cautiously 'until he went on the offensive a few months ago'. It had also been of decisive importance that the Minister-President had powerful opponents in his struggle with Caprivi. Above all, 'the entire entourage of the Kaiserin [was] on Caprivi's side . . . Might someone or other perhaps have told the Kaiser that he was completely in the hands of the Eulenburgs?', Waldersee wondered, answering his own question with the comment that 'it is possible that the Kaiserin might have done so'.[135] He himself could scarcely conceal his glee at Caprivi's fall. This 'great, and yet so small, man' had 'passed into oblivion full of bitterness' and had 'richly deserved this end', he wrote to Verdy, adding, 'May his ashes rest in peace! I hope never to hear or see anything of him again.' He reported that the Kaiser had exclaimed, in a similar mood: 'Thank God that I am rid of that tiresome fellow; I could not have borne him any longer.'[136] For his part, Caprivi showed his resentment at his treatment by failing to send his good wishes to the Kaiser either for the New Year or for his birthday.[137]

The Austro-Hungarian Foreign Minister Count Kálnoky had not the slightest doubt that Caprivi was the victim of an ingenious plot by the Eulenburgs which neither the Chancellor nor the Kaiser had seen through. When Philipp Eulenburg returned to his ambassadorial post in Vienna in mid-November 1894 after an absence of several months he gave a 'very extended' account, first to Kaiser Franz Joseph and then to him, Kálnoky, of the events leading up to the 'fall of Count Caprivi, staged at Liebenberg', which the Foreign Minister regarded as a 'catastrophe'. Kálnoky summarised the essential details of Eulenburg's account in a derisively mocking confidential letter to the Austrian ambassador in Berlin. Eulenburg, he said, had embroidered on the story of the dismissal 'at great length' and 'in a rather muddled way' with 'innumerable trivial details' and had dressed it up in 'particularly Eulenburgish wrappings'. The Kaiser had arrived at Liebenberg in the belief that his last attempt at reconciliation had succeeded and that Caprivi would therefore remain in office. 'So it was only at Liebenberg, where the Kaiser was surrounded exclusively by the influence of the Eulenburg clique, that the plot which had evidently been in preparation for a long time was carried out.' At Liebenberg Caprivi's comments in the press had been 'interpreted as unseemly crowing over Botho Eulenburg', and the Chancellor was depicted as the ally of the left-wing fractions and of the Centre Party. 'Whether the gentlemen intended Minister-President Count Eulenburg to fall likewise, I would doubt, and I am inclined to think that the speed with which Kaiser Wilhelm cut the knot and dismissed *both* rivals came as a surprise to the originators of the intrigue. In his impatience at being constantly burdened with these personal incompatibilities . . . Kaiser Wilhelm brought the whole situation to an end through what was perhaps too sudden a decision, but one whose logical justification cannot be denied. But various circumstances give me reason to believe that the clique was taken aback . . . The Kaiser is unwittingly caught in the web which has been spun around him – I hope the moment will nevertheless come when he will see through their activities and strike out at them. General Caprivi was no match for these people, he was too honest and too ponderous to be able to understand these cunning intrigues, nor, unfortunately, did he know how to behave with the young Kaiser. This business may cause much more mischief and I cannot see any improvement unless the Kaiser's good sense and good impulses find a way out.'[138] The faltering hopes for Wilhelm II's common sense which the Austrian Foreign Minister still clung to here were to vanish in the following years, under the weak chancellorship of Prince Chlodwig zu Hohenlohe-Schillingsfürst. But before we turn to the relationship between Kaiser and Chancellor under the so-called Newest Course, we shall investigate the largely unknown role of Wilhelm II as head of the House of Hohenzollern, a family beset with scandals.

# CHAPTER TWENTY-TWO

# Head of the family

WILHELM II was not only German Emperor and King of Prussia, Supreme War Lord and Principal Bishop of the Lutheran Church but also head of the Prussian royal family and all its branches. His power over the personal life of the numerous members of the House of Hohenzollern was great, whether exercised by direct command or indirectly through arranged marriages, promotions, allowances from his Privy Purse or the allocation of living quarters in royal palaces. Nor did he fail to take full advantage of it, unwelcome though this was to many of those affected. 'Of course W. *is* the head of the family both "de jure" and "de facto"', the Empress Frederick remarked in a letter to Queen Victoria. '*Alas* it is so, & I know it to my *cost*, & try to bear the fact as best I can! But it does not give him the *moral* right & authority to interfere, and therefore when he does so in family affairs it can only embitter.'[1] And indeed from the first years of his reign his attempts to maintain strict control over the private life of his close relatives led to bitter clashes and sensational scandals which not only damaged the reputation of the monarchy at home in Germany but were instantly relayed to his more distant relatives in England, Russia, Denmark, Greece and the other German states, arousing further hostility towards the young Kaiser and his wife.

Those most affected (apart from the reigning Kaiserin Auguste Viktoria and the imperial couple's seven children) after the death of Kaiserin Augusta in January 1890 were the Kaiser's widowed mother, who went to live as far as possible from Berlin, in the Taunus (at first at Bad Homburg and later, when Schloss Friedrichshof was completed, at Kronberg), his brother Prince Heinrich, who as a naval officer lived in Kiel with his young family, his eldest sister Charlotte, married to Hereditary Prince Bernhard of Saxe-Meiningen, his sister Sophie (Fozzie) who had married the Crown Prince of the Hellenes (Greece), Constantine (Tino),

## The imperial family

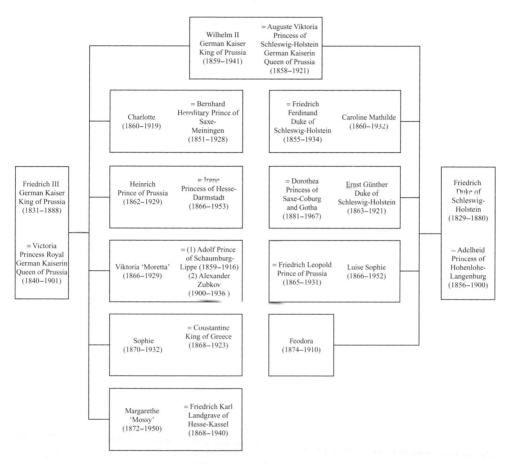

30. The imperial family tree

in October 1889 and lived in Athens, and his sisters Viktoria (Moretta) and Margarethe (Mossy), both still unmarried at the beginning of 1890 and living with their mother in Bad Homburg. The Kaiser's close family circle also included the Kaiserin's mentally disturbed mother, her brother and sisters and their spouses: Duchess Adelheid of Schleswig-Holstein, Duke Ernst Günther of Schleswig-Holstein-Sonderburg-Augustenburg, who was still single at this time; Princess Caroline Mathilde (Calma), who had married Friedrich Ferdinand, Duke of Schleswig-Holstein-Sonderburg-Glücksburg in 1885; Princess Luise Sophie (Yaya), who had married Prince Friedrich Leopold of Prussia in the summer of 1889; and the youngest sister Feodora (Baby), who lived only until 1910.

THE REIGNING KAISERIN

In the first years of the New Course the relationship between Wilhelm and Auguste Viktoria (Dona) was still close and affectionate.[2] On 22 October 1891, the Kaiserin's thirty-third birthday, Waldersee wrote: 'May God bestow rich blessings upon her and bring the Kaiser ever closer to her.' His wish seemed to be fulfilled.[3] The letters the Kaiser wrote to his wife have not survived, but her replies (although only a limited number remain) continually express great love and happiness, as well as sorrow at his frequent absences. 'Oh it is sometimes really like a dream!', she wrote in the summer of 1892. 'How many blessings, how much love I have from my darling. God has certainly been wonderfully gracious to us! And he will continue to help us, he will give me courage to stand by you in your difficult position! However much people attack you and try to make your life difficult, they will not come between us. − Love can do so much.'[4] 'Yes, my darling, my longing is as strong as ever', she wrote to her husband during his Scandinavian cruise in 1892. 'Poor darling', we read in a letter of 15 July 1892, 'I wish I could come and sooth[e] my darling now and then for love does sooth[e] the worries sometimes [original English]. Isn't that so, my darling?'[5] She heaped banal advice upon him, such as 'I hope you are taking good care of yourself, going to bed *early* and eating properly . . . I am glad my little husband goes swimming and doesn't read all the newspapers.'[6]

The few surviving letters from Auguste Viktoria to her husband give us unusual insights into the emotional life and the private domestic world of the imperial couple. They confirm Philipp Eulenburg's surprised observation around the turn of the century that the 'imperial marriage-bed' had been elevated into a true 'cult' by the Kaiserin.[7] When Wilhelm decided to spend a few days at Wilhelmshaven at the end of his 1890 Scandinavian cruise and before his journey to England, instead of hurrying back to his wife, she wrote to him reproachfully saying that it made her cry 'every time I think that I could have been with you for almost 3 days, oh my darling, it is fearfully hard when one loves one's little husband so much . . . God grant that our days together in Berlin will be all the nicer, as the children are all away and we can pretend that it is our first married year. What do you think, darling? . . . Your little wife, who loves you so passionately and longs for you very much, kisses you and strokes you quite softly as you like it.'[8] Alluding to his approaching visit to England she warned him: 'I hope you will not pay court to the beautiful daughters of Albion too much, or else I shall appear to you in your dreams again but not as nicely as before.'[9] A few weeks later, when the Kaiser was on his way to Vienna, she wrote to her 'dear, sweet darling': 'I kiss you all over & always pray for you, that you keep well and that nothing happens to you.'[10] Two years later she promised him, as in the first years of their marriage, 'loving kisses all over & on my place'.[11]

Even without the Kaiser's letters to her, it is possible to conclude from some of Dona's replies that the couple's erotic feelings were mutual. In the summer of 1892, for instance, they communicated their dreams to each other in the form of drawings. 'Your drawings make me feel quite excited', the Kaiserin wrote in one letter.[12] She willingly agreed to his particular wishes, which were evidently (as shown in his letters to his mother from Kassel and his correspondence with Miss Love)[13] inspired by a fetishist fascination with her hands and gloves. 'I shall let you have all your little pleasures', she promised him in expectation of his return. 'I always have gloves on at night now to take care of my hands! − How dear and nice of you to send me more drawings and I am looking forward to them so much ... You naughty little husband for thinking that I might perhaps not give my little husband such a nice welcome as he imagines. You know how awfully much I love you, and if I am well, *how* willing I am to do everything. Come back as soon as you can my own darling and you will not be disappointed', she wrote in mid-July 1892, eight weeks before the birth of her daughter.[14]

In describing her dreams to Wilhelm, Dona was patently using feminine wiles to strengthen her hold on him. 'My dear, sweet darling', one of her letters of the summer of 1892 reads. 'Last night I dreamt of you so vividly, darling. At first you were quite out of my reach, then you came to me and I clung to you so tightly so as not to let you go again. You were wearing something very strange on your head, but in my dream I told you how well it suited you, and then of course you had to go away again.'[15] Some of the Kaiserin's dreams, however, reveal her deepest fears. Thus in September 1890 she told her husband: 'Last night I dreamt of the French Revolution, with hordes of women milling about, it was terribly upsetting. May God protect us from such things.'[16]

The influence which she exerted on Wilhelm II is rarely easily detected, but it is probably safe to assume that it was particularly active where social life and political appointments were concerned but also, principally, in questions of the children's upbringing and family matters in general.[17] It was demonstrated, for example, when in 1895 the Kaiser was urged both by the Chancellor and by Eulenburg to receive the second wife of Count Hatzfeldt, the German ambassador in London. In reply, Wilhelm told Eulenburg that he greatly regretted 'that nothing could be done in this matter. The Kaiserin had *refused in such decided terms* to receive the Countess that it was useless to make any further attempt. "We men take a less serious view", H.M. said, "and I sincerely wish that it could be done. But in these questions I cannot give orders to the Kaiserin. It is her domain. I cannot command her to receive someone who has made herself

unacceptable to society." When H.M. appealed to me [Eulenburg wrote] and
to my knowledge of the Kaiserin's character and conduct, I certainly could not
deny that it was a difficult state of affairs.' It was a fact that the Kaiserin had
a *'great* aversion to divorced women' and even the Kaiser could do nothing to
change that.[18] As we shall see, Auguste Viktoria was equally intractable when
Princess Sophie of Prussia and Princesses Ella and Alix of Hesse adopted the
Greek and the Russian Orthodox faiths respectively.[19]

There are nevertheless indications that at this time, as in earlier years,
Wilhelm found it tedious and constricting to be in constant proximity to his wife,
heavily influenced as she was by her Oberhofmarschall von Mirbach and by the
three pious '*Kreuzzeitung* ladies-in-waiting', Countess Therese von Brockdorff,
Countess Mathilde von Keller and Claire von Gersdorff.[20] It is true that soon
after his accession he had broken off the extramarital relationships in which
he had indulged in the 1880s; but the fact that he still felt the need to get
away from home is attested not only by Dona's constant complaints. Philipp
Eulenburg, whose friendship with the Kaiser was now 'firmer than ever' and
was observed jealously by the Kaiserin,[21] commented tellingly after the summer
cruise of 1890: 'These Scandinavian voyages are a sort of fiord carnival. It is in
fact H.M.'s "season" – minus feminine conversation, which is as he likes it.'[22]
Early in 1891 the Kaiser brought together all the men who had accompanied
him on the two previous Nordic cruises. A 'Nordland' Society was established,
with the Kaiser as master and his travelling companions as members. On this
occasion Waldersee met Count Emil Görtz, who 'entertained the company with
humorous recitations'.[23] Such attempts to escape from the wife whom he sometimes found cloyingly sweet and clinging should not, however, mislead us into
assuming – as many of his contemporaries and a few later commentators thought
they could detect – that Wilhelm despised women in general and felt at ease
only in the company of men.[24]

For Auguste Viktoria, more than for her husband, the building of churches
was a major preoccupation. When the Church of the Ascension in Berlin was
consecrated in June 1890 Waldersee noted approvingly that thanks to the 'energetic action of the Kaiser and Kaiserin . . . the appalling shortage of churches
in Berlin [was] at last in the process of being remedied to some extent'. Since
Wilhelm's accession, work had started, or was planned, on the construction of
ten new churches, and the Kaiserin had single-handedly raised the money for
the Church of the Ascension, Waldersee recorded.[25] Seven years later there were
no less than twenty-two new churches in Berlin, which had been built with
private funds collected by Mirbach – 'chiefly from Jews', it was said – in the
name of the Kaiserin.[26] In the Foreign Office too it was well known that in
such matters the Kaiserin was the driving force. Kiderlen complained in 1893

that 'all kinds of "Protestant" causes will approach Her Majesty the Kaiserin, and I am afraid of Her Majesty's inclinations and Mirbach's influence, which is very narrow-minded in these things'.[27] Auguste Viktoria's 'Protestant' attitude almost led to an international incident when she 'obstinately and for a considerable length of time' refused to call on the Pope during her visit to Rome in 1893. 'The gracious lady had religious scruples and thought that as the leading Protestant reigning lady she ought to ignore the Roman bishop. It took all H[is] M[ajesty]'s powers of persuasion and several reports from the Foreign Office to overcome H[er] M[ajesty]'s objections', Arthur von Brauer wrote confidentially to his Grand Duke.[28]

Contradictory as it may seem, the pietism which many derided (or simply regretted) in the Kaiserin did not by any means prevent her from displaying a lamentable arrogance and − with the passage of time − an excessive love of luxury. The Empress Frederick and her daughters, above all, were affronted by the Kaiserin's haughty behaviour.[29] 'Dona enjoys her position intensely & her whole face expresses the most intense satisfaction', Wilhelm's mother complained shortly before Bismarck's dismissal. 'Her pride is so great and she thinks she knows better than everyone because she is the Empress.' 'She meddles in *every* thing the family does, *every little* trifle is reported to her & she orders & directs in a way very galling for the others.'[30] It was simply 'offensive' for her daughters and her daughter-in-law Irène to be ordered about by Dona.[31] The young Kaiserin had 'something condescending & patronizing wh[ich] irritates me & rubs one up the wrong way; − & she orders her sisters in Law about as if she were the Empress Augusta, wh[ich] makes me *frantic* sometimes'.[32] In January 1891 the Empress Frederick had a further reproach for her daughter-in-law: 'Poor thing she seems to think that she has to exercise a sort of police supervision of the whole family in *all* things! This is not called for either by her position or her age or her experience. The Empress Augusta whose ideas were of another century also thought this, & Dona fancies she has stepped into *her* shoes (over my head) and must continue this! To me it is most galling!'[33] The blame for this presumptuous behaviour lay with the constant flattery heaped upon her by her entourage, against which no sensible influence could make itself felt at the Hohenzollern court. 'The flattery that is lavished on *both* of them is enough to turn anybody's head, & it is no wonder that theirs *is* turned!', Vicky wrote to Queen Victoria. 'Poor Dona' was therefore quite convinced 'that all William & she do & think & say is perfect'.[34] Dona's highly intelligent mother-in-law did not entertain the possibility that she herself gave the young Kaiserin a sense of inferiority which caused her to put on airs. But less enlightened members of the family − particularly the Kaiser's eldest sister Charlotte − also showed little understanding for Dona's arrogant behaviour.[35]

Soon after the fall of Bismarck complaints began to be heard, especially from Protestant critics like Waldersee, about the excessive love of luxury and pleasure which characterised the court of the young imperial couple. Family festivities became more and more grandiose and expensive and even the pious Kaiserin wore an extravagant quantity of jewellery.[36] It was often Wilhelm himself who encouraged his wife in her growing taste for splendour. In the winter 'season' of 1893–4 Philipp Eulenburg wrote to his mother describing a concert in the Marble Hall of the Neues Palais at which the Kaiserin had appeared 'in a gown of blue velvet combined with yellow muslin, large diamond and sapphire jewellery – not very well dressed'. By way of explanation he added: 'The Kaiser sometimes thinks up these things himself.'[37] Meanwhile the young sisters of the Kaiser and the Kaiserin went from one ball to another and caused much gossip by their behaviour.[38] Waldersee deplored the moral decline which he detected at the Berlin court and in the Kaiser's personal conduct too. 'There is no better illustration of how times have changed than the contrast between the Kaiser's prohibition of racing on Sunday in 1888 and his invitation, 2 years later, to a sleigh-ride and a ball on Sunday! Things are going backwards step by step', he wrote in early 1891.[39]

From 1894 onwards there are increasing indications that not only Wilhelm but also his wife, now thirty-five years old, suffered some kind of nervous crisis. She went on a starvation diet to lose weight, but although this was successful[40] she became increasingly irritable, particularly over her husband's 'incessant' and 'restless' activity.[41] 'Ostensibly because of her throat' but in fact 'on account of the state of her nerves', in 1894 she insisted on taking an Easter holiday with her children at Abbazia on the Adriatic. She was horrified, however, when the Kaiser, who had gladly agreed to her plan, wanted to give her a yacht, 'because Her Majesty thinks that this would increase the danger of this expedition becoming an annual event'.[42] The following year when Wilhelm announced that he intended to go on a Mediterranean cruise in an English yacht with the Kaiserin, she was '*in despair* and begged me to do what I could to prevent the journey', as Eulenburg recorded.[43] At the end of 1897 the Kaiserin's nervous exhaustion led to a complete breakdown. As August Eulenburg informed his cousin Philipp, she suffered 'such severe nervous shock that one cannot get any sense out of her. His Majesty, with his usual impetuosity, declared that a stay in the South (Riviera) was absolutely necessary, an idea which did not please the All-Highest patient at all, and now we are engaged in the cross-fire which we have seen so often, as you know.'[44] The marital crisis to which the Oberhofmarschall was alluding now became a persistent problem. During his Scandinavian cruise of 1898 the Kaiser discussed his relationship with the Kaiserin at length with his best friend, who immediately passed on what he had heard to the Foreign Secretary and future

Chancellor, Bernhard von Bülow. 'The poor woman's nerves have been so ruined by child-care and royal duties that H[is] M[ajesty] does not believe her present calm state can last . . . There was such a fight in Homburg that the Kaiserin almost lost all control of herself. Then there have been angry scenes between Therese Brockdorff and the Kaiser, which ended with the Kaiser dismissing the good Countess. H[is] M[ajesty] complained in the strongest possible terms about the intolerable disturbances which the Kaiserin inflicts on Him while he is working or resting by constantly bursting in and pestering him with nursery matters. I have the impression that peace prevails for the time being — and might also continue at Wilhelmshöhe, as they lead a country life when they stay there; but knowing the Kaiserin as I do, I fear the problems may increase in spite of all cures and precautionary measures.'[45]

The relationship between Wilhelm and Dona in the following years was shaken by so many crises that their doctors and members of their immediate entourage feared both might suffer a serious nervous breakdown.[46] In a letter to the Kaiserin's personal physician, the Kaiser complained that she had 'fired off unbelievable telegrams' to him because he had inspected a pigsty at Urville on his own, without her. 'The Kaiserin's nerves are in a condition which worries me very much', he wrote.[47] In the autumn of 1900 at Rominten there were such 'appalling scenes' between husband and wife over the education of their sons Auwi and Oskar that the Kaiser spoke to Eulenburg 'in great distress and anxiety' of the possibility that his wife might need to be sent to a clinic for nervous disorders. 'The poor dear Kaiserin really seems to be in a bad nervous condition', Eulenburg reported to Bülow after he had seen her rush after the Kaiser 'like a madwoman', when she had 'screamed and raved so much' that Wilhelm did not know what to do. On the train to Tilsit, where he was to unveil a memorial to Queen Louise of Prussia, the Kaiser launched into 'a very sad, painful outpouring of his feelings' which lasted for hours, and during which he told his friend that the Kaiserin had 'made scenes the *whole night*, crying and screaming'; it had been 'an absolute paroxysm'. He had 'begged her *on bended knee*' to be reasonable, but in vain. 'I am completely at loss', the Kaiser confessed. 'What am I to do? These crises and scenes are killing me. I cannot stand it. The Kaiserin is ill — ill because of a daily routine which is absolutely *impossible* for a Kaiserin. She cannot be a "bourgeois" mother, a loving wife and a ruling Kaiserin at the same time. She has reached the end of her tether and is becoming an "impossibility" to herself and to me. Advice must be sought . . . The thought of seeing the poor Kaiserin consigned to a cold-water treatment hospital is so frightful that I cannot take it in!' This reference to a mental hospital was evidence enough for Eulenburg of what the Kaiser really feared: that the Kaiserin might 'lapse into eccentricity in the same way as her mother'. But it was not only Auguste Viktoria's nerves which needed to be cured, the Kaiser said; in her outward appearance too it was already possible 'to see the effect of the shattered nerves in her lined, prematurely aged face and her grey hair'. Eulenburg tried to console his imperial friend with the thought that the Kaiserin was indeed suffering from a '*temporary* impairment of the nervous system', but that the doctors would undoubtedly find a way to cure it. Writing to Foreign Secretary von Bülow, however, he confessed his fear that these developments would 'unfortunately have a very distinct and severe effect on the private life of the Kaiser for the time being and may perhaps become significant in *political* matters by *affecting his nerves*'. Moreover, he warned, the imperial marriage itself was in danger if 'the Kaiserin *eventually* makes herself *unbearable* to the Kaiser by continuing to make intolerable scenes'. The 'comment about premature ageing' was 'a symptom which should not be overlooked'.[48] Eulenburg finally advised the Kaiser, who was 'so oppressed by fear of the dreadful scenes' made by the Kaiserin, to leave the 'imperial marriage-bed' as soon as a nocturnal scene began and to lock the doors to his own room.[49] Wilhelm accepted his friend's advice with 'childlike naivety', but nevertheless showed 'a certain masculine pride' when, surprisingly, the 43-year-old Kaiserin proved to be expecting a child a year later. The fact that she hid her condition from the Kaiser and defied her doctors' orders by accompanying her husband to the manoeuvres and afterwards to Cadinen and Rominten, where she suffered a miscarriage, earned the disparaging comment from the Kaiser's favourite that 'her love for H.M. is like the passion of a cook for her sweetheart who shows signs of cooling off. This method of forcing oneself upon him is certainly not the way to keep the beloved's affection.'[50]

## PRINCE AND PRINCESS HEINRICH

Although he was stationed at Kiel and frequently stayed with his wife's family in Darmstadt, Wilhelm's 'devoted and obedient little brother' Heinrich, as he called himself,[51] was duty-bound to come to Berlin for all major court functions, all important state ceremonies, national festivals and ceremonies such as the opening and closing of the Reichstag and of the Landtag; he was also expected to attend major military reviews and the autumn manoeuvres. At important dinners and festivities his wife Irène was also obliged to be present. She was the sister of Princess Victoria of Battenberg, who lived in England, and also of the future Tsarina Alexandra and of Grand Duchess Sergei (Ella) of Russia. The frequent journeys to Berlin were troublesome enough, but Prince and Princess Heinrich had the additional problem of where to stay while they were there, since for many years they had no satisfactory accommodation in the capital. At first they stayed at the Empress Frederick's palace or in the Schloss itself, but this was only a temporary solution. After the death of Kaiserin Augusta, Wilhelm decided that his brother should take over the royal palace of Unter den Linden, where their grandfather had lived, as his permanent residence in Berlin. But the old Kaiser's daughter, Grand Duchess Luise of Baden, refused to remove her parents' furniture from the palace and to give up her own right of residence, with the result that Heinrich and his family never felt at home there. In 1893 the Kaiser decided to have the Niederländisches Palais fitted up for his brother, but the question of the old palace of Unter den Linden remained unresolved.[52] It was not until they acquired Schloss Hemmelmark in Schleswig in the summer of 1896 that Heinrich and Irène gained a greater degree of independence from the Berlin court, a source of much pride and pleasure to them.[53]

When the reigning Kaiserin asserted to Philipp Eulenburg in the autumn of 1895 that 'Prince Heinrich, who formerly loved his brother tenderly', had been 'turned against him by sister Charlotte',[54] the evidence suggests that this was at best only partly true, for signs of an estrangement between Wilhelm and Heinrich can be detected long before this.[55] We have already seen in an earlier chapter the ill feeling which arose between the brothers when Heinrich and Irène, but not the Kaiser, were invited to England for the wedding of the Duke of York in 1893.[56] With characteristic modesty Heinrich strongly resisted Wilhelm's plan to promote him to the ranks of general and of admiral. As his Adjutant Freiherr von Seckendorff reported to the Chief of the Naval Cabinet, the Prince would be 'extremely upset' if this premature promotion were to take place. Since his appointment as naval captain and colonel in the army the Prince had been afraid that 'the pressure to go further would become increasingly strong and impossible to resist', Seckendorff wrote. Prince Heinrich, however, very much wished to make his own way in the navy, 'to which he is deeply attached by inclination and by his whole nature'. In the Prince's name his Adjutant pleaded 'that His Majesty might be prepared to postpone the promotion of His Royal Highness until the time when His Royal Highness is due, by *seniority*, to become a general', for it was not in fact possible 'to be a general in the army and a captain in the navy'. If the promotion should be imperative at the beginning of 1893, the Prince would have to 'accept with resignation'.[57]

Within only a few years of Wilhelm II's accession, Heinrich and his Hessian–English wife were regarded by insiders as belonging to the rebellious faction of the imperial family which had formed around the Empress Frederick. Although the widowed Empress had at first complained of Heinrich's habit of following Wilhelm everywhere and of visiting him almost every month while he never had time to visit his mother, by the summer of 1891 she was defending him against the Kaiser's attempts to control his life, protesting that 'nothing irritates me more than when Henry is pulled up, found fault with & interfered with

31. The Empress Frederick with her family at Friedrichshof. Standing, from left to right: Princess Irène of Prussia, Crown Princess Sophie of Greece, Princess Charlotte of Saxe-Meiningen, Kaiserin Auguste Viktoria, the Empress Frederick, Princess Viktoria of Schaumburg-Lippe, Princess Margarethe of Hesse. Sitting: Prince Adolf of Schaumburg-Lippe, Prince Friedrich Karl of Hesse, Prince Heinrich of Prussia, Kaiser Wilhelm II, Crown Prince Constantine of Greece, Prince Albert of Schleswig-Holstein, Grand Duke Ernst Ludwig of Hesse

by W. & his people, it makes me quite savage!'[58] The following spring Grand Duke Sergei returned from the funeral of Grand Duke Ludwig IV of Hesse at Darmstadt bringing 'very gloomy' accounts of what was happening in Germany: Kaiser Wilhelm was 'mentally ill' and had 'fallen out' with Princess Irène.[59] Bernhard Bülow was shocked to discover during a visit to Berlin that 'Prince Heinrich . . . [had] joined in the general chorus of criticism of our all-gracious sovereign in Darmstadt and in England'. 'His own relations – especially all the Russian, Danish, English and Greek ones, the whole Rumpenheim clique is very hostile towards our all-gracious sovereign.'[60]

At the beginning of 1893 open conflict finally broke out between the two brothers. Under the influence of his wife, and increasingly that of his mother too, Heinrich rebelled against the obligations which the Kaiser tried to impose on him. His request for an increase in his appanage was brusquely rejected by Wilhelm as 'quite out of the question'.[61] They also quarrelled violently 'about the royal family's religious affairs' – presumably in connection with the change of religion of Crown Princess Sophie of Greece (a sister of Wilhelm and Heinrich) and of Grand Duchess Ella (Princess Irène's sister).[62] The crisis finally reached its peak in early 1893 when instead of announcing his arrival in Berlin to the Kaiser, Heinrich committed the impropriety of sending him word through a servant that he would be lunching in the Querallee. The Kaiser insisted 'that the Prince should inform him of his arrival by telegram and seek his orders *or* have himself personally announced on arrival by the Flügeladjutant on duty; he had always followed this procedure with his grandfather'.[63]

The estrangement between the brothers prompted the Kaiser to ask the Chief of the Naval Cabinet in February 1893 to investigate the 'difficulties in the relationship' between him and Prince and Princess Heinrich and to suggest to him how 'these difficulties could be permanently put to rights'. After taking extensive soundings Admiral von Senden summarised his conclusions. 'In the first years of Y[our] M[ajesty]'s reign Prince H[einrich] was completely absorbed in his naval service. The Prince had only one ambition: to devote himself fully and completely to Y.M. through the All-H[ighest] service.' But this wish of Heinrich's had been seriously undermined by the influence of Princess Irène, who had grown up in completely un-Prussian surroundings in Darmstadt and England, the Admiral claimed. The Princess insisted on 'isolation' and 'completely free self-determination' and took 'a firm stand' against any influence from Berlin. 'Y.M. knows from experience', Senden wrote, 'that H[er] R[oyal] H[ighness] was brought up in circumstances in which the inner circle [of her family] had ideas which were quite at variance with all the traditions and time-honoured conventions of the [Prussian] court and of the [Hohenzollern] family . . . These ideas later gained the upper hand when H.R.H. married and sought to distance herself and her husband from Prussian ways, which she did with increasing success.' 'The former home of the Princess, where the simple, free habits of a happy childhood could be kept up, became the Prince's home too. Their rare visits to Berlin became merely an oppressive burden to them as they became increasingly estranged from the court there.' To solve the problem, Senden suggested that a three-man committee, consisting of the chiefs of the Military and Naval Cabinets and a third trustworthy person, should be entrusted with the task of conveying the commands and wishes of the Kaiser as head of the imperial family to the Prince and his wife, in order to achieve harmony at least in outward things.[64]

One important reason for Heinrich's reserve and Irène's wish to be allowed to lead as private a family life as possible was not mentioned in Senden's report:

even as a small child their son Waldemar, born in March 1889, was exhibiting the unmistakable signs of haemophilia. The Empress Frederick tried to console herself and her own mother with the thought that apart from this *one* defect in his constitution the child was strong and healthy. Furthermore, unlike her youngest brother Leopold, who had bled to death in Cannes in 1884, the little Prince Waldemar was of a quiet disposition, she claimed. 'I think it a very favorable sign that he has had no outward bleeding – & that he is of a quiet placid temperament, wh. poor dear Leo of course was not! This dear little man will not fret and worry about everything like our poor Leo, who was so sensitive & put himself so often needlessly into such a state.'[65]

In view of the strained relationship with his brother it is not surprising that the Kaiser very rarely entrusted him with important political tasks. Wilhelm II's proposal that Russia should join the Triple Alliance and seize the Straits, which Heinrich conveyed to his brother-in-law Nicholas II in November 1894, remained (at least until the first Russian revolution of 1905) an exception.[66] But the Kaiser also lacked confidence in Heinrich's capabilities, probably not without reason. Although Prince Heinrich would have become regent on behalf of the young Crown Prince in the event of the death or abdication (frequently contemplated in 1895–7) of Wilhelm II,[67] he was regarded as 'superficial, obstinate and insignificant' within the family and in political circles in general.[68] In the summer of 1896, after one of many clashes between the Prussian Prince and the heir to the Bavarian throne, Prince Ludwig, Philipp Eulenburg complained: 'Prince Heinrich's behaviour is terribly *immature*. Until all the courts in Europe have assessed him at his true, stupid worth and *properly* judged what he says and does, he can still do much harm. What kind of a regent would he make if – God forbid – something happened to our sovereign.'[69] Eulenburg was astounded, however, when shortly after this he heard from Plessen and Lyncker that Prince Heinrich had told them that Prince Ludwig was quite within his rights; the German ruling princes 'did not have to put up with anything from the Kaiser and had a perfect right to their own independence. The whole "German rubbish-heap" would not hold together for much longer anyway.' Wilhelm's best friend wondered whether he should tell the Kaiser about this remark, for it was 'certainly almost rebellion in his own house!'[70]

Only a year later the Prince proved to the world that such derogatory views of his intellectual capabilities were no exaggeration, when at the embarkation of German troops for China he proclaimed in the presence of his imperial brother: 'For me, fame and laurels have no allure; I am drawn by one thing alone: to bring the gospel of Your Majesty's sacred person to foreign lands, to preach it to everyone who wants to hear and also to those who do not want to hear.'[71] In July 1899 in conversation with Eulenburg Wilhelm expressed what the former considered 'an accurate opinion of Prince Heinrich', saying that he was 'a completely feminine, dependent character, and afflicted with anglomania' – a remark which perhaps says as much about the Kaiser's preoccupations as about the personality of his brother.[72]

## THE KAISER'S SISTERS

In the early years of his reign Wilhelm II's relationship with his four sisters, Charlotte (Hereditary Princess of Saxe-Meiningen), Viktoria (Moretta), Sophie and Margarethe (Mossy), was characterised by violent upheavals which were caused partly by the continuing bitter conflict between the Kaiser and his mother, partly by the arrogant, status-conscious and at the same time petty-minded Protestant attitude of his wife, but also partly by the behaviour of some of his sisters, which did not always seem suitably royal. Soon after Wilhelm's accession Princess Sophie was married to Crown Prince Constantine (Tino) of Greece, Princess Viktoria to Prince Adolf of Schaumburg-Lippe and Princess Margarethe to Prince Friedrich Karl (Fischy) of Hesse-Kassel. Given the close relationship of the Hohenzollerns to the British, Russian, Danish and Greek royal families it was inevitable that family quarrels would also have serious consequences for international relationships between the powers.

While the three younger sisters, at first still unmarried, sided with their suffering mother, the eldest sister Charlotte and her husband Bernhard, Hereditary Prince of Saxe-Meiningen, took a decisive stand in favour of the young Kaiser. The Empress Frederick complained bitterly in a letter to Stockmar's widow in February 1891 that the hostility shown towards her by Wilhelm and Dona was shared by Charlotte and Bernhard (and at this time also by Prince Heinrich). 'My 3 eldest children *still* take the San Remo attitude – it makes such a *gulf* between me and them, and that hurts so much.'[73] 'There is *no* one to help me!', she wrote, in her isolation, to Queen Victoria on 5 December 1890. 'Henry *cannot* and also does *not* understand. Bernhard & Charlotte have worked against me for 3 years ... W. & Dona have the power & I am nothing but a defenceless *widow*!'[74] She had received no sign of life 'from those whose mother I have the misfortune to be!', she wrote bitterly, on her return to the Rhine after a visit to England.[75] Although Prince Heinrich gradually came round to her side, the widowed Empress continued to find her eldest daughter's behaviour 'most odd'; she 'fights shy of me, hardly comes near me'.[76] Her son-in-law Bernhard was also 'impertinent' and 'ill-bred' towards her and took every opportunity of making 'a rude & sneering remark'.[77] Not long afterwards she again complained that 'the behaviour of W. & Dona – of Bernhard and Charlotte is a *constant* worry & trouble to me – but I have quite given *them* up, and trouble my head no more about them'.[78]

32. The Kaiser's four sisters. From top to bottom: Margarethe, Sophie, Viktoria
and Charlotte

The close political and social contact which Bernhard and Charlotte maintained with the young Kaiser and Kaiserin, and which brought them certain career advantages (as we shall see), did not exclude conflict with Wilhelm and Auguste Viktoria, however. In 1896 Charlotte complained of the 'arrogant condescensions!!!!' of the Kaiserin, whom she ungraciously described as 'disgusting, old and ugly as if she were 50'.[79] The constant disputes over precedence between the Kaiser's eldest sister and his wife, the Hereditary Princess's erratic, pleasure-seeking lifestyle, together with her husband's often offensive manner, gave rise to gossip and criticism in the family (and well beyond it). The Empress Frederick often expressed sorrow at her daughter's superficial, restless life and was deeply concerned by her numerous extramarital relationships and her tendency towards malicious intrigues, through which Charlotte caused great mischief. 'Charlotte *must* go everywhere, and put herself "en evidence" – she *never* can keep quiet, and is always gadding about', she complained in a letter to her daughter Moretta.[80] When she heard that her eldest daughter had decided to learn Spanish, the Empress predicted that no more would come of it than of her earlier attempts to learn Italian and Russian, for Charlotte simply had no talent for languages. She welcomed her daughter's plan nevertheless, for it was better 'when she has a sensible occupation to keep her at home instead of constantly having visitors & paying visits and flying about from morning to night, and leading such a foolish, aimless life, wh[ich] ends in mischief-making'.[81] What she meant by this remark is evident from a letter in which she begged the newly married Moretta to be 'a tender loving good & unselfish little wife!' and 'never to be to him what Charlotte is to Bernhard!'[82] In a letter of 28 November 1890, which she asked Moretta to burn, she indicated which married princesses behaved dutifully despite marital problems and which could certainly not be regarded as good examples. 'I am so anxious for you to be a good wife as Dona, Calma, Yaya, Louisa Hohenzollern, Irene, Viktoria Battenberg, Ella & so many others are – and *not* like our poor Charlotte, or my poor sister Louise [Marchioness of Lorne] or Anastasia [Grand Duchess of Mecklenburg] etc . . . that give one such anxiety & do not make their Homes comfortable & happy – & are so much talked about in the world – & their names not mentioned with the respect one would wish. Aunt Minny [the Tsarina Marie Feodorovna], Aunt Olga [Queen of Greece], Elisabeth of Roumania, Pcss Wied are also such examples of good Hausfrauen – Aunt Beatrice [Battenberg], poor Aunt Helen [Duchess of Albany], the Queens of Holland & Spain. God knows *all* the Husbands of these Ladies were *not* patterns of perfection & excellence, therefore it must often have been a struggle to keep up to the mark & do their *duty*!'[83]

The Empress Frederick thought her eldest daughter's malicious tongue very dangerous, and not without reason. A compulsive gossip, she told the

Flügeladjutant Carl Wedel in early 1891 that while on a visit to Moretta in
Bonn her mother had 'done all she could to stir up feelings against the Kaiser
and told her son-in-law, Prince Adolf Schaumburg, dreadful stories about him'.[84]
The Empress Frederick felt particularly threatened by the close relationship
between Charlotte and the degenerate court of Duke Ernst II of Saxe-Coburg
and Gotha, her late father's brother, whom the widowed Empress considered
one of her worst enemies[85] and who was universally regarded as a 'morally very
inferior man', 'thoroughly unprincipled, false, lying, a braggart and an intriguer'.
In Waldersee's eyes, for instance, there was scarcely anyone 'who did less credit
to his throne than this Coburger'.[86] Every time the Empress Frederick heard
that her daughter was at Coburg she foresaw trouble. 'Charlotte is at Coburg
again; I am always rather alarmed at all the nonsense, mischief & gossip she carries about, wh[ich] one believes, not knowing what confusion she always makes.
There is a great deal of harm done in that way perhaps even unintentionally.'[87]
That her anxiety was not unfounded we shall soon see from the events connected
with her daughter Moretta's marriage plans and with the change of religion of
Crown Princess Sophie of Greece.

In 1893, as a result of a violent quarrel between Bernhard of Saxe-Meiningen
and his brother-in-law Wilhelm, the Hereditary Prince angrily resigned from
the army and withdrew to Meiningen with his wife.[88] Not long afterwards,
surprisingly, Bernhard accepted the Kaiser's offer of the command of the 22nd
Division, hitherto held by Prince Friedrich of Hohenzollern, and moved to Kassel
with Charlotte.[89] But the couple remained on bad terms with the Kaiser and
Kaiserin. When Charlotte paid a visit to Prince Ernst zu Hohenlohe-Langenburg
in London in January 1894 the latter reported to his father that the Kaiser's sister
had 'poured out endless complaints. She and Bernhard seem to be very annoyed,
and he wants to resign soon.'[90] The feud between Wilhelm and Bernhard was so
serious that the Prince of Wales could not receive his niece Charlotte at Sandring-
ham because of this 'unpleasantness'.[91] The couple were all the more delighted
at the surprising appointment, on the occasion of the old Kaiser's birthday, of
the Hereditary Prince as general in the infantry and commanding general of
the VI Army Corps in Breslau. Charlotte wrote happily to a friend on 25 March
1895 in a mixture of English and German: 'These lines . . . come from a beaming Commandirende Generalin [commanding general's wife]. I wish you could
have witnessed on the morning of 22nd the rushing screaming of Bernh. & his 2
aide de camps [sic], to my quiet writing table I was working at! Telephone from
William Glückwunsch [congratulations] zum 6. Corps u. General d. Infanterie.
I was stunned & tears rushed to my eyes, as the telegramm came: so fine in
commemorating our beloved g[ran]d father etc.! I *never* before saw my husband
*so* perfectly delighted & wild! A dream fulfilled & what a delightful future in

every way! From all sides the gratulations pour in, really touching. And I!! well I feel proud of my husband, & only longed for *my* Father to witness our joy & his beloved cherished Silesia.'[92] In officer circles, not surprisingly, there was much annoyance at this preferential treatment of a brother-in-law, which gave the impression that the Kaiser could hand out senior army commands to members of his family like Easter presents. The promotion of the Hereditary Prince 'in one big leap' had 'caused much bad blood in the army, and quite rightly', Waldersee commented. 'We are quite happy to accept that Prussian princes should be advanced more rapidly, but if the minor princelings are given these advantages too it is a blow in the face for the army; . . . and what is more, these princes are almost without exception wretched creatures. The Meiningen fellow is perhaps the best of them, but he has considerable weaknesses; and I also think that as commanding general, and in Breslau of all places, he will soon cause much offence. Wherever he has served he has made himself universally disliked through his extreme rudeness; he has no manners and does not know how to behave in distinguished company. His tendency to make overhasty judgments and express them without due caution will cause many problems, particularly in Silesia; for instance he is very fond of indulging in brutal tirades against the Catholics, and that alone may soon create a rumpus.'[93]

Prince Bernhard repeatedly vented his feelings with great passion and violence not only against Catholics but also against Social Democrats, the liberal press and the parliamentary system in general. In his eyes, the Reichstag was a 'disgrace to German political life', 'the vilest representative body a great people has ever had in its history' and a 'collection of oxen and villains who take pleasure in keeping their nation small and powerless'.[94] The newly appointed Commanding General was to come into conflict above all with the 'swamp', the 'All-Highest, All-Gracious' Prussian Ministry of War.[95] When the Ministry refused him permission to build additional stabling behind the general headquarters at Breslau – a decision which put the Commanding General in a 'fuming rage' in which he wanted to 'throw everything over' – the Hereditary Princess defiantly approached a Jewish horse-dealer who had offered to build better stables for half the price. 'So the whole Province will see the Emperor's sister *helped by a kind Jew*', Charlotte wrote angrily to Baroness Heldburg.[96] Prince Bernhard took the view, which had more than a little bearing on Wilhelm II's future position of power, that the commanding generals should close ranks against 'interferences' by the War Ministry. Above all in questions of military training the commanding generals should take their orders 'only from His Majesty', he insisted.[97]

During their time at Breslau there was a noticeable cooling of relations between the Meiningens and the imperial court, above all where the Kaiserin, that 'conceited goose' as her sister-in-law called her, was concerned.[98] 'For various reasons' she did not 'fit in *there* any longer', Charlotte told her doctor.[99] In October 1896 Prince Bernhard and his wife received 'such an insulting and impudent' letter from the Kaiserin that they were tempted to withdraw from public life and retire to Meiningen. On the grounds that the (apparently distraught) wife of their Hofmarschall, Karl-August Freiherr Roeder von Diersburg, had left him, Auguste Viktoria had concluded that Charlotte was having an affair with Roeder. She issued an ultimatum that the Hofmarschall must resign from his position. According to Dona's letter 'the Kaiser did not yet know about it', 'but if there was no change she would have to tell him, and he would not stand for any nonsense'. Bernhard and Charlotte were determined, as the latter told her father-in-law, to show the world that they were 'above such *filth*' and 'would not drop a faithful servant on the basis of tittle-tattle'. 'This new impertinent interference by Her [the Kaiserin] is too bad and you can imagine how indignant B[ernhard] and I are. If she sends a rude answer and stirs up my brother against us, we shall come to Meiningen immediately, for She knows how to make W. flare up in no time at all! We have proofs enough!!! God knows who repeated this gossip to her, and it proves to us once again that one can *not* get on with her . . . Slander and gossip, envy and jealousy are now common currency in the "highest circle!"'[100] Prince Bernhard, equally enraged by the 'dreadfully rude, arrogant tone of the so-called gracious lady', protested that the Kaiserin had no right 'to watch over what Charlotte does and does not do as if she were "head of the family" and . . . to issue reprimands and orders to her'. That was the reason, he explained to his father, why he did not wish to remain in Prussia. 'In Berlin they maintain the fiction that every Prussian princess, even after her marriage, is still under the control of the king and queen as heads of the House [of Hohenzollern]. This fiction, which shows contempt for the honour and independence of the other German reigning houses, is what I have to stand up to.' Leaving the army and retiring to Meiningen was perhaps the only lasting protection against the demeaning attitude of the Kaiser and Kaiserin, the Hereditary Prince considered. 'It is after all not the first time that the Kaiserin has interfered in my domestic affairs in the most outrageous way', he complained. 'She does it to show that she has the upper hand even over princesses who have married out of the royal house.'[101] The incident threatened to have wide repercussions, especially as the King of Saxony offered to go and see the Kaiserin immediately and make it clear to her that Charlotte no longer belonged to the House of Hohenzollern. In the end matters were settled when Roeder brought his wife back to Breslau and made a point of appearing in society with her, but the anger aroused by Dona's presumptuous behaviour continued to rankle and was by no means confined to the

House of Meiningen.[102] When Charlotte learnt to ride a bicycle in the summer of 1898 she remarked that she was determined to resist any interference from the Kaiserin, who had already forbidden her sister Calma and her daughters to indulge in this 'indecent' sport.[103]

The life of Wilhelm II's eldest sister was increasingly overshadowed by porphyria, the rare metabolic disease which she had inherited from her mother, as has since been conclusively proved. The severe symptoms of this hereditary condition, which had been apparent since her twenty-fifth birthday – unbearable stomach pain, colic, paralysis in the arms and legs, sleeplessness, feverish sweats, constipation, palpitations, blistering skin rashes, dark red urine and periodic mental confusion – have been described in the first volume of this biography and more fully elsewhere.[104] The Empress Frederick was alarmed to hear of the signs of the illness which she had long predicted: Charlotte was suffering from 'fits of violent excitement'; she suddenly became 'so very thin' in 1893; her legs swelled up and were very painful; she had 'rheumatism' and daily headaches, was nervy and sleepless and had 'so little blood'. In August 1894 the Hereditary Princess sought the help of the celebrated doctor, Professor Ernst Schweninger, who was also Bismarck's personal physician. He diagnosed 'anaemia and nervous breakdown'. It was only many decades later that medical science identified porphyria as a distinguishable form of illness.[105] Until her death on 1 October 1919 Wilhelm II's eldest sister remained a patient of Schweninger and his colleague from Baden, the doctor and psychiatrist Georg Groddeck.

It cannot be ruled out that the second eldest sister Viktoria (called Moretta or Vicksey by her mother) also suffered from porphyria. At any rate she too made herself conspicuous by her behaviour throughout her life – she was widely regarded as a nymphomaniac – and had to be treated at a clinic in Bad Schwalbach in 1893 for 'persistent anaemia', disruption of haemoglobin production, stomach cramps, backache and loss of weight.[106] Soon after Wilhelm II's accession and after he had placed a definitive ban on Moretta's marriage to Prince Alexander of Battenberg,[107] the Kaiser began to look around for a suitable husband for his sister. He hit upon the youngest son of the ruling Prince of Schaumburg-Lippe, Prince Adolf, born in the same year as himself, good-looking and not without means, whom he had met in Bückeburg and who was at this time in military service as first lieutenant in the Bonn Hussars. As we have seen, at the beginning of 1889 Wilhelm commissioned Philipp Eulenburg to make secret investigations into the financial circumstances and private life of Prince Adolf. Eulenburg gave a positive report in February, although the question of the Lippe succession was still completely unresolved.[108] At the end of 1889 Eulenburg was sent on another secret mission to Bückeburg, where after protracted negotiations with Prince Adolf's father he succeeded in arranging for the young Prince to pay a discreet call on the Empress Frederick and her two unmarried daughters in Italy.[109]

At first the widowed Empress seemed to accept her son's decision as irrevocable. After a visit to Bad Homburg by Prince Adolf in June 1889 she wrote resignedly to Queen Victoria that he was certainly 'good looking & agreeable but of course not much of a parti!' The only other possible candidate for Moretta's hand was Prince Philipp of Württemberg, but as a Catholic he was less suitable, she commented at this time.[110] In reality, however, she continued working actively in secret to find what she considered a more suitable husband for her favourite daughter. As late as the summer of 1890, only a few months before the wedding which took place in November, she introduced Moretta to Hereditary Prince Ernst zu Hohenlohe-Langenburg, but this attempt was again frustrated by Wilhelm's determination to stick to his decision. 'My son has chosen *this* alliance', the widowed Empress wrote bitterly to Hermann Hohenlohe,[111] while in her letters to her own mother she complained furiously that Wilhelm was 'much pleased at having had *his* way! He has crushed & ruined without scruple *so much*, much – that he triumphs now of course.'[112] All three Victorias – the Queen, the Empress Frederick and her daughter Moretta – had the greatest hopes, however, for an English naval officer of noble birth named Captain Maurice Archibald Bourke.[113]

In a long letter of 12 June 1890 which the old Queen copied out, with numerous omissions, before destroying the middle pages of the original, the Empress Frederick had again seemed prepared to put a brave face on the Schaumburg-Lippe marriage. According to the Queen's copy she complained that she had 'cried so much I feel quite ill', but since 'William wishes this marriage particularly' she had accepted it as inevitable. She was also prepared to believe that Prince Adolf was 'thoroughly trustworthy & good & I am sure he will try to make her happy' and that Moretta too 'will try her utmost to do her duty'.[114] But what had she said in the many pages which the Queen did not copy out, but burnt? Strangely enough we know about their contents from a copy of another letter, which made the already disastrous relations between Kaiser Wilhelm II and his mother and sister even worse and could also have put his attachment to his grandmother the Queen under severe strain.

On 21 July 1890 Kaiserin Auguste Viktoria wrote a letter to Wilhelm II in which we find not only her own comments about the affair, but also those of the Duchess of Edinburgh and the Kaiser's sister Charlotte. From this remarkable and undoubtedly authentic document it becomes clear that Moretta was still in love with Captain Bourke after her engagement to Prince Adolf, that her mother favoured a match with this latest object of her daughter's affections, that the Empress Frederick had almost persuaded Queen Victoria to give her blessing to this step, and finally that Wilhelm and Dona had been fully informed about Moretta's new infatuation and the machinations of her mother and Queen Victoria since March 1890. In the letter the Kaiserin passed on to her husband an unwelcome piece of news which she had just heard from Charlotte. The latter, Dona explained to Wilhelm, had received a letter from her Aunt Marie of Edinburgh (a Russian Grand Duchess by birth, married to the heir to the Duchy of Coburg, Alfred, Duke of Edinburgh, the Empress Frederick's second brother). Charlotte gave the letter to Dona to copy – a striking example of the 'mischief-making' for which the Hereditary Princess had made herself feared. Duchess Marie's letter to Charlotte said: 'I must tell you that very disagreeable things are going on now, for poor Granny [Queen Victoria] has got once more completely bamboozled by your Mama [Empress Frederick], & the whole of the Bourke story was discussed with most disastrous results. First Granny talked [sic] it to Moretta, who took it quite lightly, said that she never took the episode au serieux ect. [sic] So Granny gave her a scolding and for once was quite sensible. But then she talked it over with your Mama, who told her a very different story: that Moretta was still madly in love with the gallant Captain, would have waited for him five or six years if necessary, followed him to the end of the world, and more of that sort of bosh and nonsense adding, that when Bourke broke it off, it nearly broke Moretta's heart. Whereupon dear . . . Granny shed romantic tears of real sorrow over the sad episode telling your Mama that if she had known it before this new engagement with Adolph . . . *she* (Granny) *would have certainly helped Moretta to accomplish this match!!!* Good heavens! The only thing that would rather have frightened her, she added, was *that dreadful tyrant William* who always takes things so badly & makes rows about anything. On his account also, Moretta was obliged to accept this new partie but would never forget her love for Bourke, the most charming individual in the world! Poor Granny wrote to me pages & pages about it, her mind is in a terrible state . . . She pretends now, that *you* poor Carolus [Charlotte] have created this mischief etc. She was evidently put up again by your Mama and begins again to hate William, but that will all disappear when he comes here [England] and again turns her round. I am going to write to him and prepare a little the ground for a careful & impressive talk with foolish Granny. – But what is downright wicked of your Mother, is so utterly to destroy Granny's present joy at the idea of Moretta's marrying at last und einen ächten Prinzen [and a real Prince], for she *was* very pleased, the old lady, & now her old mind is again tormented by romantic ideas of another thwarted attachment & eternal pinings for another man! But now only I *fully* see how right we were to stop the whole thing last March by telling William & how right our suppositions were that they both meant to settle the Bourke affair with

Granny when they came to England in June. Thank God a thousand times that we did it then, & prevented a most infernal row between your Mama Granny & William . . . *But* I should not be the least astonished if your Mama would try to bring it about again. God preserve us from further scandals, but somehow, I do not feel reassurance yet, that Moretta will really marry that very nice Adolph, so good looking, I think, & with such charming honest fine eyes. We are all quite taken with him & think her a lucky girl.' It was also a very bad thing, the Duchess wrote to Charlotte, that on their way to Princess Sophie's wedding in Athens the Empress Frederick and her daughters Moretta and Mossy had travelled in the *Surprise*, the very ship in which Captain Bourke was serving. 'What do you say to this story, darling?', Dona asked her husband indignantly after copying out the letter. 'But I told you recently that I did not think we could be sure of Vicky [Moretta] until the wedding had taken place. – I thought it my duty to write all this to you, darling, before you go to England, so that you can give Grandmama a good talking-to, for this is really going *too far*, when a girl, particularly a princess, *is engaged*, that her own mother is probably trying to break it off! You must also make it clear to Grandmama that Vicky [Moretta] must not travel back in the Surprise, for the constant contact with the man, when someone is like Vicky [Moretta] if she gets very worked up, she might well do something quite frightful and then tell you that there were reasons which compelled her to marry the fellow. With Victoria [Moretta] anything is possible, in my opinion! – Poor darling, I am so sorry, also because you had so much trouble with the whole Adolph business.'[115]

In the end all three Victorias yielded to the Kaiser's will. After Prince Adolf had travelled to Venice to meet the Empress Frederick and Moretta, the Empress reported to her mother fairly optimistically that 'Moretta seems to take great interest now in the preparation for the wedding & future Home, though she is very low sometimes and there is not much enthusiasm.'[116] And when Wilhelm arrived at Osborne on 4 August 1890 he was in fact successful, as the Duchess of Edinburgh had predicted, in convincing 'Granny' of the advantages of the match. Not least because he had brought about the marriage, he was in a particularly good mood and talked to the Queen at length about the reasons for Bismarck's dismissal, telling her 'how badly he had behaved, trying to intrigue against him with Russia'.[117]

In September 1890 the Empress Frederick reported that Moretta was again deeply depressed. 'The nearer the wedding approaches the more cast down she is', she wrote in one of her letters.[118] Once the wedding had taken place in the Berlin Schloss on 19 November 1890, however, the Empress Frederick urged her daughter to do her 'duty' and to be a faithful, 'good housewife', as we have seen.[119] She was relieved to be able to tell her mother at the end of 1890 that Moretta was now 'satisfied with her fate'.[120] Other members of court society who knew how much pressure Wilhelm had brought to bear in order to achieve this match were not optimistic about its future. 'I am quite sure that the couple do not suit each other and that the marriage can never be a happy one', Waldersee wrote on the day of the wedding.[121] Only a few years later Moretta's bizarre behaviour (and appearance) were causing indignation in the family. Her eccentricity reached its height in 1927 when as a widow aged sixty-one − Adolf had died in 1916 − she married a 27 year-old Russian gigolo, Alexander Zubkov, who moved into the Schaumburg Palace in Bonn with her and ruined her financially. It is not without irony that her second marriage ceremony was conducted according to the Russian Orthodox rite.[122]

Shortly after Moretta's first marriage there occurred one of the most unpleasant scandals in the history of the Hohenzollern family. It was triggered by the announcement made by the Crown Princess of Greece, Wilhelm's sister Sophie − during the wedding celebrations in Berlin in November 1890 − that she was to enter the Greek Orthodox Church.[123] The Kaiser's consternation at this is revealed by the savage marginal comments he wrote on the diplomatic dispatches from Athens, culminating in the exclamation: 'What a disgrace, what a humiliation for my whole house. What a sin against my father in his grave.'[124] Dona's outrage − which was further fuelled by the old rivalry between the Augustenburg and the Glücksburg lines, of which the latter had succeeded in winning the Greek throne[125] − at the Crown Princess's proposed change of religion was so great that the Kaiser told Waldersee that he blamed the premature birth of his son Joachim, born three weeks early, on the affair. He went on to complain that his mother had shown herself to be 'completely without religion', had 'nothing but scorn and contempt' for Christian belief and had even claimed that his sister's change of religion was no business of his, the Kaiser's, and that 'she could become a Jew if she felt like it'. Wilhelm had thereupon declared that he would forbid his sister to set foot on Prussian soil if she changed her religion, 'which naturally produced a further storm of indignation against the Kaiser' − his mother angrily declaring that in future she would neither visit nor receive him, if he carried out his threat to ban Sophie from Prussia. Wilhelm went on to speak 'very bitterly and despondently' about his mother and commented that she was 'only in Berlin to make mischief and to harm him'.[126] He told Hugo Freiherr von Reischach, his Hofmarschall, that his mother had treated him so badly that he had been reduced to tears.[127] The next day, when the Empress Frederick tried to visit the Kaiserin at the Schloss after her confinement, the Kaiser would not allow her to enter but promptly took her back to her carriage.[128] The gulf between Wilhelm's mother and his wife became even wider when Dona rejected the Empress Frederick's offer to hold the child during the baptism with

33. Princess Viktoria (Moretta), the Kaiser's sister, with her second husband
Alexander Zubkov

the curt remark that 'William does not want it as you are not the Godmother.'[129]
After this clash the Empress wrote to her daughter Moretta, who was on her
honeymoon voyage to Malta and Egypt: 'I have been told *not* to go & see Dona
at the Schloss so I leave for Kiel tomorrow with my Mossy! The parting from
Sophie was terrible! *She* feels & I feel that she will never come back to Berlin, &
it has nearly broken our hearts! There was *not* a *soul* of W's *or* Dona's court or

a single official at the Railway Station, & W. was exceedingly rude to me again yesterday!' Only the thought that her youngest daughter was still unmarried and therefore needed her protection against the Kaiser as head of the family had prevented her from making a complete break with Wilhelm, she told Moretta.[130]

When Wilhelm nevertheless came to the station next day to say goodbye to his mother and Mossy, the Empress Frederick interpreted this gesture as a sign of remorse – 'perhaps that is his way of admitting that he has gone too far', she wrote.[131] When she arrived at Kiel she was relieved to find that her son Heinrich and his wife took her side in this family conflict.[132] 'I try & not think of the Schloss & of Berlin so much – that gives me such pain', she wrote to Moretta on Christmas Eve.[133] 'I was certain you would be as vexed & disgusted at the tiresome row & the utterly unnecessary quarrel Will: & Dona picked with poor dear Sophie & me! . . . I was *so* grieved & hurt for Tino, as it was so dreadfully rude to him.'[134] In order to counteract Wilhelm's 'contortion of *facts*', the widowed Empress commented to Queen Victoria that 'if he says that his sister is to be received *without Royal honours* in Prussia, because she has changed her religion, he simply shows he does not know the A.B.C. of his "métier" wh[ich] is to be civil to other royal families. It is rude & illbred & ridiculous, & makes me feel utterly ashamed of him; – & must disgust all sensible people.'[135] In her letters from Kiel she continued to complain of Wilhelm's hurtful behaviour towards the Greek Crown Prince and Princess, which had culminated in his failure to come to the station either to meet or to take leave of Sophie and Tino, or even to send a prince or a court official to represent him. At St Petersburg, on the other hand, the Tsar, the Tsarina, the whole imperial family and the entire court had gone to see the heir to the Greek throne and his wife on to their train; and the old Kaiser Wilhelm had always met his sisters, his daughter Luioo, his aunts and his female cousins personally at the station.[136] When King George of Greece heard how the Kaiser had treated his heir and his wife, he would find it incredible 'that a man can be so foolish and childish when he is 32 years of age, and holds so high a position', she predicted.[137] She expressed the hope that Wilhelm would realise, with time, 'that he cannot carry out threats of the kind – if they are ever so solemnly made (as these were) – without consequences wh[ich] *must* destroy the peace of the family forever, – and show him in the light of a tyrant & bully – wh[ich] I think in spite of his love of showing his power & authority he would not like. That such heartlessness & "Rücksichtslosigkeit" [lack of consideration] has left a *deep* impression on me, you cannot wonder . . . But I feel his *rudeness* & undutiful conduct to *me* far less than I do his rudeness to his *sister* – who has gone away most deeply *disgusted* & hurt. – He has no heart, & she [Dona] has no tact – & they are both so convinced of their own perfection that they *will* run with their heads against the wall some day in all "naiveté".'[138] She passed on copies of the correspondence between Wilhelm and King George, which the latter had sent to her from Athens, to London, and did not mince her words over the Kaiser's 'preposterous' telegram to the King. 'He seems to be copying Peter the Great, Frederick William I, Napoleon or some such conspicuous tyrant', she wrote to Sophie. 'To a free-born Briton, as I thank God I am, such ideas, so little in harmony with the XIX Century and personal liberty and independence, are simply abhorrent; and this my own son!'[139] On the basis of this information Queen Victoria and the Prince of Wales naturally took sides strongly against Wilhelm and Dona.[140] The Queen asked her daughter to make known to the King of Greece 'that I deeply deplore what I think most *inconceivable* conduct on W's part', while the heir to the British throne condemned Wilhelm's attitude as 'pompous, ridiculous and unkind'.[141]

Wilhelm's and Dona's offensive behaviour only strengthened Crown Princess Sophie in her resolve to be received into the Greek Orthodox Church at Easter in 1891.[142] As her mother wrote to Bogumilla von Stockmar in March 1891, 'the scenes to which her brother and his wife subjected her have confirmed her in her decision and it will be carried out all the more quickly as a result!' Wilhelm, she commented, was so unpredictable that they must be prepared for another 'demonstration of fury and power', but on the other hand it was not impossible that he would at last realise 'how misguided it was to treat his poor sister so – and that by doing so he has achieved exactly what he wished to prevent'.[143] On 19 April 1891 Wilhelm read out to his Flügeladjutant Carl von Wedel a letter from the Crown Princess in which she confirmed her announced conversion to the Greek Orthodox Church. In his reply Wilhelm spoke of the 'disgrace' which his sister had brought upon the House of Hohenzollern and the country, of her 'violation of the oath she had taken at her confirmation' and of the 'insult to the memory of her father and grandfather'. He forbade her to cross the Prussian frontier for the next three years. Wedel's attempts to calm the Kaiser were rejected out of hand.[144]

While the Kaiser's eldest sister also expressed herself as 'very much enraged' by Sophie's conversion,[145] his younger sisters Moretta and Mossy were entirely on the Crown Princess's side and declared themselves 'absolutely *infuriated*' by Wilhelm's behaviour.[146] Moretta did her best, at first, to bridge the gulf between mother and son by pointing out that Wilhelm had 'a curious sort of character' and did not like to admit it 'when he has done a foolish act'.[147] But her attempts at mediation were frustrated by the hostile correspondence between her brother and Sophie. 'Dear me!', she sighed when her mother sent her copies of their letters. 'It's very sad – I hardly know what to say or think & am in a very difficult position wanting to help everybody . . . I *perfectly* understand her [Sophie's] feelings – & *he* [Wilhelm] may seem a tyrant etc. etc. but perhaps *his* answer was misunderstood & he may regret his hastyness & rough ways towards his

34. Crown Prince Constantine of Greece with his wife Sophie, the Kaiser's sister

little sister!' 'Really what "Zustände" [goings-on] there are in our family – will
it never get any better?'[148]

The Kaiser's mother, above all, could not understand her son's intolerance. 'He
has absolutely *no heart*', she commented in a letter to Sophie. 'It is perhaps *not*
his fault . . . but it is a fact. There is no sentiment in his nature . . . He is, besides,
not *learned* enough to understand that our Christian Religion has centuries ago
divided into branches.' He was therefore convinced that 'the Prussian Church
[is] the only right one'. But basically it was not the religious differences between
the faiths but 'his silly vanity and pride of being "head of the family"' that was at
the root of Wilhelm's conduct, she thought.[149] The 'foolish prohibition' banning
his sister from crossing the Prussian frontier for the next three years infuriated
her and robbed her of all sleep. 'It is really *too* unheard of', she wrote to Sophie.
'It is a piece of *tyranny* and *injustice* which fills me with *contempt*, indignation
and disgust . . . It is a piece of despotism from which *every* right-minded person
*must* turn away with pity and derision . . . It is really dreadful to think that
he fancies he can do *all* and *everything* he likes!'[150] She complained bitterly in
a letter to Baroness Stockmar: 'I have few joys to brighten my life, but that of
having my Sophie with me ought not to be snatched from me by *him* who *should*
be looking after me, and who has already brought so much suffering on me.'[151]

In spite of the prohibition Crown Prince Constantine visited his mother-in-
law in the Taunus while the Crown Princess and their infant son at first stayed
behind in Heidelberg, on the other side of the Prussian frontier. Only after
Reich Chancellor von Caprivi interceded on her behalf did Wilhelm II allow his
sister to visit her mother.[152] On 30 May 1891 the Empress Frederick was at last
reunited with her daughter Sophie, her husband and their newborn son George
at Bad Homburg.[153] They were visited there by the elderly King Christian IX of
Denmark, father of the King of Greece. The widowed Empress reported proudly
to Moretta in Bonn that she had written to Wilhelm to thank him, not for giving
permission for her to see Sophie, since he had no right either to give or to refuse
it, but because in the end he had not put any obstacles in the way of the visit.[154]

It was indicative of the power which Wilhelm could exercise as head of the
family and also as supreme war lord that his brother-in-law Prince Adolf of
Schaumburg-Lippe was fearful of being drawn into the family quarrel. When
Moretta travelled to Bad Homburg to be with her mother and her two younger
sisters for the third anniversary of her father's death, Prince Adolf excused
himself on the pretext that he could not leave his squadron.[155] 'That is the price
I have to pay for her [Moretta] having married a German prince who is only a
Rittmeister [captain in the cavalry]. He has to do *all* W. wishes . . . & he *only*
looks to the "Emperor", therefore he did *not* come here to see Sophie & Tino,
though I invited him 3 times!!!', the Empress wrote bitterly to Queen Victoria.[156]

The following summer, when Sophie and Tino were staying in Copenhagen, Wilhelm sent his sister word that he hoped her forthcoming visit to Bad Homburg would do her good. Relieved, the Empress Frederick wrote to Moretta: 'Do not fear there will be disagreeables this time. W. has expressed his pleasure at hearing that Sophie is coming to Germany! If one only takes the matter simply & naturally *now*, it will be all right; & last year's mess quite forgotten.'[157] The Empress neverthless expressed complete agreement with the decision of the Greek Crown Prince and Princess not to attend her youngest daughter Mossy's wedding, which was to take place in Berlin in November 1892. 'Tino & Sophie are not thinking of coming to Mossy's wedding!', she told Moretta. 'I am sure *no* objection would be offered at Berlin; but . . . after the *insults* William has offered them and the affront his behaviour was to the King, [the] whole Greek family and to me; I should not think it becoming or dignified to go to the Court at Berlin.'[158] Not until the summer of 1894 was it possible for the Greek Crown Prince and Princess to visit the Kaiser in Berlin in circumstances that were at least outwardly normal.[159] Nonetheless a certain acrimony persisted in their relationship with the Kaiser and Kaiserin for years, which had a corrosive effect not only in Athens but also in St Petersburg, Copenhagen and London.[160]

Wilhelm's attitude to his sister's conversion naturally had wide repercussions and contributed to his already considerable unpopularity and isolation among the principal royal families of Europe. Queen Olga of Greece – a Russian Grand Duchess by birth – sent copies of Wilhelm's letter to Sophie to the Tsar and to Queen Victoria.[161] As we have seen, the Empress Frederick also sent her mother copies of the letters and telegrams which Wilhelm and King George had exchanged, together with a letter which she herself had received from the latter.[162] The incident had brought Prince Heinrich back on to his mother's side again, and Princess Charlotte expressed justifiable anxiety that 'the conduct of the Kaiser towards his sister' might be 'used in Homburg to create a rift between the two brothers'.[163]

The alienation of the German Kaiser and Kaiserin from their British, Russian, Danish, Greek and Hessian relations was intensified by the conversion of Grand Duchess Ella, Wilhelm II's Hessian cousin who was married to Grand Duke Sergei of Russia, to the Orthodox faith, which took place at the same time and aroused equally strong feelings in Berlin. Ella's father, the Kaiser claimed, had wept uncontrollably at the news of her conversion. For his part, Wilhelm said, he entirely shared the opinion of Grand Duchess Maria Pavlovna, the Mecklenburg-born wife of Grand Duke Vladimir of Russia, that it was 'a disgrace for a German Protestant princess to go over to the Orthodox faith in Russia at a time when both the Lutheran Church and her compatriots there were being persecuted and oppressed in the most ruthless and unjust manner'. He wholeheartedly agreed with her comment that 'the great, powerful German Reich and its Kaiser' were now 'the stronghold and the refuge' of the Lutheran Church, so that Ella, by her conversion, would become 'an apostate and a traitor to her faith and her Fatherland'. Like the Grand Duchess, Wilhelm also believed that Ella's motives were 'an inordinate pursuit of popularity, a desire to improve her position at court, a great lack of intelligence and also a want of true religiousness and patriotic feeling'. She had never felt herself to be a German, he maintained, for as a child she had thought of herself as Hessian first and English second; and then after her marriage she had become Russian. The aim which Ella and her husband were pursuing through this dramatic step was to make themselves popular at the Russian court again, after they had 'completely lost their former favoured position through the thoroughly clumsy and tactless way in which they had set in train the project of marrying her sister [Alix] to the Grand Duke, the heir to the throne'. In spite of the Tsarina's refusal to allow Princess Alix ever to come to St Petersburg again, Grand Duke Sergei and his wife Ella had not given up hope of engineering the marriage between Alix and Nicholas, but they had realised that 'it would first be necessary to recover their former influential position of trust with Their All-Highest Majesties', and to accomplish this the Grand Duchess did not even shrink from changing her religion.[164] When Princess Alix likewise converted to the Russian Orthodox faith on her marriage to Tsar Nicholas II − Wilhelm prided himself on having brought about this match − the Kaiser and Kaiserin were shocked: the latter would '*never*' forgive this conversion, Eulenburg noted.[165]

By contrast, the search for a husband for the Kaiser's youngest sister Margarethe (Mossy) went reasonably smoothly. Princess Margarethe lived with her mother in Bad Homburg, but found the town 'like a tomb' and longed for the 'paradise' of social life in Berlin.[166] In German diplomatic circles it was rumoured for a time that the Empress Frederick was pursuing an alliance between her youngest daughter and the heir to the Russian throne, Nicholas, but it seems unlikely that this was true, given the Empress's strong anti-Russian feelings. Nevertheless when the ambassador Bernhard von Bülow got wind of this alleged plot he warned that if it happened Princess Margarethe would 'presumably soon turn into a full-blooded Russian and enemy of Germany, cf. Crown Princess Sophie of Greece and Grand Duchess Sergei [Ella]', and that she would 'stir up trouble for her Imperial brother from the very start'.[167] Be that as it may, for a long time Princess Mossy cherished ardent hopes of marrying Prince Max of Baden, the future Reich Chancellor, in which she was encouraged by both her mother and her sisters Moretta and Sophie, although they suspected that the attraction was not mutual and that the Prince 'would not dream' of marrying her.[168] After various other candidates had been considered, including Prince

Wilhelm Ernst of Saxe-Weimar-Eisenach and Prince Ernst Ludwig of Hesse-Darmstadt, the Princess's choice fell, surprisingly, on Max of Baden's best friend, Prince Friedrich Karl (Fischy) of Hesse, who proposed to her and was accepted on 19 June 1892 in the garden of Schloss Philippsruhe. There was now an anxious moment while the family awaited the reaction of the Kaiser, whose consent to the marriage had to be obtained. Prince Friedrich Karl set out at once for Berlin in some agitation; meanwhile the Empress Frederick wrote to her son explaining how the engagement had come about so suddenly and asking him to give it his blessing. Accompanied by Charlotte and Bernhard Meiningen, Louise and Aribert Anhalt and Albert Saxe-Altenburg, Friedrich Karl travelled from Berlin to Potsdam, where Wilhelm signified his approval of the engagement and announced it to the remainder of the family with evident pleasure. The Kaiserin's reaction on hearing the news, however, was 'cold as usual', which the Empress Frederick suspected was because 'it is not her brother Ernst Günther'.[169]

Wilhelm's agreement did not, however, signify the slightest willingness to consent to anything else his mother might wish. Shortly after her daughter's engagement the Empress asked Philipp Eulenburg to visit her secretly at Schloss Friedrichshof. She asked him to persuade her son during his Scandinavian cruise to allow her new son-in-law to leave the army. Wilhelm refused, arguing that with Prince Friedrich Karl's 'philosophising, melancholy' character, he needed 'contact with soldiers and military service' to provide 'the necessary counterbalance'.[170] The Kaiser's mother did nevertheless win one concession. When Wilhelm expressed his intention of inviting Duke Ernst II of Saxe-Coburg to his youngest sister's wedding, the bride's mother declared that in that case she would not attend the ceremony. No invitation was sent.[171]

### THE 'RUTTING DUKE' ERNST GÜNTHER OF SCHLESWIG-HOLSTEIN

The relationship between the young imperial couple and Duke Ernst Günther, Kaiserin Auguste Viktoria's only brother, proved especially problematic. The Duke's secondment to the General Staff in the summer of 1890 had already attracted criticism;[172] but when a year later the Kaiser promoted him captain on the General Staff the officer corps was outraged. Waldersee, who had just been dismissed as chief of the General Staff, commented furiously: 'The Duke got himself seconded to the General Staff because he found winter service at Potsdam tedious and uncongenial.' It was no great misfortune, certainly, 'if someone of his type is nominally employed on the General Staff', for 'no one takes it seriously, and especially not in the present case, where the person in question is utterly lacking in both training and competence'. But that the Kaiser should make his brother-in-law a fully fledged General Staff officer was 'a slap in the face for the

General Staff, a humiliation of a corps which is highly respected throughout the world'.[173]

In spite of such privileged treatment the Duke always felt slighted, not only by Wilhelm II but also by the other members of the Hohenzollern family and by other royals of his own rank. In the spring of 1891 he complained that he had not been invited to the celebration of the engagement of his cousin Louise, Princess of Schleswig-Holstein, to Prince Aribert of Anhalt – 'and that the Kaiser responded by saying that I had not had any idea [about the forthcoming marriage]'. His irritation with Wilhelm's attitude towards him was also apparent from his remark that his uncle, Prince Christian of Schleswig-Holstein, who lived in England, was the only person of whom he could be sure that he was 'not constantly influenced by having to consider the wishes of the All-Highest personages'.[174] Ernst Günther was generally considered unusually immature and conceited. The Empress Frederick thought him 'a most foolish young man', although 'his sisters naturally think him perfection'.[175] His sister-in-law Moretta described him baldly as 'that idiot'.[176] Kiderlen-Wächter complained of the Duke's irresponsible gossiping, while Karl Samwer criticised his capriciousness and vanity. 'The only constant in him is egoism.'[177] Count von der Gröben, who was able to observe the young Duke closely during the imperial couple's visit to England in July 1891, gave a 'hair-raising' description of his behaviour there and deplored the fact that he had aroused 'universal indignation by his arrogance, rudeness and insensitivity'.[178] Prince Christian also complained bitterly about his nephew's outrageous behaviour. As Prince Hohenlohe reported in a letter to Langenburg, Ernst Günther had 'expressed himself in such a rude and stupid way in his correspondence with Uncle Christian' that 'the only possible explanation was that he was not quite in his right mind'. Christian had read out to him several passages from Ernst Günther's letters, 'which certainly defied description', Hohenlohe commented.[179]

On the marriage of his sister to the future Kaiser and King, Duke Ernst Günther had received a donation of a million marks, in addition to which he benefited from an annual appanage of 300,000 marks from the state as well as a private income of around 200,000 marks. In spite of this he was perpetually in trouble financially, partly as a result of ill-advised building projects. Even after his promotion to the rank of major in the summer of 1895, from which he had hoped he would achieve a certain 'liberation', it was said that he was still 'up to his ears in debt'.[180] He nevertheless aspired to a brilliant role at the centre of court society in Berlin, and to demonstrate this he organised a 'Corso-Fest' consisting of 'races, carnival of flowers etc.' on the Berlin trotting racecourse in the summer of 1891, which was attended by the Kaiser and Kaiserin.[181] As the only son of the late Duke Friedrich of Schleswig-Holstein-Sonderburg-Augustenburg he took it upon himself to try to settle his family's unresolved 'Hoheit question' (the title and precedence of 'Hoheit', 'Highness') but found it 'very difficult to get anywhere with the German ruling princes'. He complained that he had had to endure 'several very unkind remarks', especially from Duke Ernst II of Saxe-Coburg and Gotha. Like the Duke of Coburg, Duke Georg II of Saxe-Meiningen had opposed him on this question, whereas the Dukes of Anhalt and Saxe-Altenburg had expressed their agreement.[182] When the Kaiserin's brother took up the cudgels on the Schleswig-Holstein question in 1895 in a newspaper article appearing under a pseudonym, his initiative led to 'very strong attacks against Ernst Günther', whom Bismarck accused of 'aggressive insolence' in the *Hamburger Nachrichten*. Bismarck's criticisms in turn provoked 'great indignation in H.M.', as the Reich Chancellor Prince Hohenlohe noted.[183]

But what caused the greatest embarrassment of all to the Kaiser and Kaiserin was Ernst Günther's obsessive and tempestuous hunt for a bride. In the summer of 1890 he decided to go to England for the 'Season', 'not with the express intention of marrying *à tout prix*', he assured his uncle Christian, 'but to have an opportunity of looking around'. For obvious reasons he was not thinking of the daughters of the Prince of Wales, but he would 'very gladly . . . marry one of the daughters of the country, provided she were well brought up, pleasing etc. for with the lack of choice among Princesses this *still* seems to me to be the most favourable solution'. The upper echelons of the German aristocracy had nothing to offer a man in his position, he felt, since most girls from these circles had been very little out in the world, and moreover one would have 'a constant following of dependant [sic] relatives in the country'. Catholicism was the hindrance as far as Austrian young ladies were concerned. Ernst Günther therefore asked his uncle to give him 'certain hints' as to suitable marriageable Englishwomen.[184] His intention of marrying an Englishwoman was, however, thwarted by the Kaiser himself, for as the young Duke complained in October 1890, he 'would not hear of a *parti* with the English aristocracy'.[185]

When Princess Victoria Mary (May) of Teck, a princess of morganatic Württemberg descent on her father's side, whose mother was Queen Victoria's cousin Princess Mary Adelaide of Cambridge, was suggested as a possible wife for Ernst Günther, the Empress Frederick reported to Windsor that 'Dona was much offended & said to me that her Brother would not dream of making such a mésalliance!!!'[186] May Teck was destined for far greater things, however: she was betrothed in December 1891 to the (albeit rather strange) eldest son of the Prince of Wales, Albert Victor Duke of Clarence, known to his family as Eddy and next in line after his father to the throne of the United Kingdom of Great Britain and Ireland. When Wilhelm heard of the engagement he wrote hypocritically to his 'dearest Grandmother': 'What happy & interesting news! Eddy is engaged! I

congratulate You with all my heart & am glad that the choice has met with your
approval. He is indeed a lucky creature & may look forward to a happy life! For
a handsomer & more accomplished young Princess is rarely to be found. I saw
much of her last year, & I must say "Sie gefiel mir ausnehmend gut" ["I thought
her exceptionally nice"]. I am sure the country at large will ring with joy &
merry will this Xmas be for You & the whole of the United Kingdom. I am very
glad for Uncle Bertie.'[187] After the Duke of Clarence's sudden death in January
1892 shortly before the wedding, in June 1893 Princess May of Teck married his
brother the Duke of York, who succeeded to the British throne in 1910 as King
George V and reigned until 1936 with Queen Mary at his side. Like the Battenberg marriage of Queen Victoria's youngest daughter Beatrice,[188] this marriage
aroused disapproval in Germany, and not only in the imperial house. Cardinal
Prince Gustav zu Hohenlohe-Schillingsfürst, the brother of the future Reich
Chancellor, was astounded and wrote from the Vatican: 'I think the marriage of
the Princess of Teck quite extraordinary . . . I cannot understand why the Queen
has approved this marriage too.' He ironically advised his cousin Hermann to see
that the Crown Prince of Italy was married off to the Kaiserin's youngest sister as
soon as possible, 'otherwise yet another Principessa May will get in the way'.[189]

   In the summer of 1893 Ernst Günther horrified Wilhelm II and the Kaiserin
by proposing to the widowed Duchess of Aosta, Laetitia, a Princess Bonaparte by
birth, in Paris, and it was only at the last moment that the German ambassador,
Count Münster, succeeded in frustrating this plan.[190] A year later the Duke tried
his luck with the beautiful and clever Princess Hélène of Orléans, whom he
had met in Cairo. The late heir to the British throne, the Duke of Clarence,
had been 'very much in love with her', it was said, and she would have had
the prospect of becoming Queen of England had the Pope given his consent
to this marriage.[191] Philipp Eulenburg, to whom the Kaiser and Kaiserin had
entrusted the task of thwarting this latest venture by Ernst Günther, reported to
his mother in April 1894 that 'the Kaiserin is in floods of tears. The Kaiser refuses
to approve the match under any circumstances and sees it as an intrigue by the
Orléans family, who "want to make themselves a good name through the House
of Hohenzollern".'[192] Eulenburg commented despairingly to Bernhard Bülow
that Ernst Günther was 'like a rutting stag in spring. Perhaps even stupider. The
poor Kaiserin *wept* in front of me in her divine Silver Rococo Saloon! H.M. was
only angry for political and personal reasons and has taken steps through the
Empress Frederick to warn the Orléans off. I am afraid there will be a family
row anyway, for the rutting Duke is giving himself airs as the head of the House
of Holstein and showing off.'[193]

   Like the Kaiser and Eulenburg, Bülow also saw 'enormous danger' for
Germany in a marriage between the ambitious and 'perfidious' French princess

35. Duke Ernst Günther of Schleswig-Holstein, the Kaiserin's brother

and Duke Ernst Günther, who would be 'like wax in her hands'. It would lead to 'unpredictable consequences – and unpredictable trouble'. In the first place the Orléans family were zealous Catholics and would create a focus of anti-national ultramontane elements in Berlin; second they were 'passionately French' and would devote all their efforts towards furthering France's greatness, power and revenge. 'There is so much that she [Hélène] could find out, betray, prevent, stir up! What an opening she would give to our worst enemies! With her the Trojan horse would come within our walls', he warned. In the third place the family's position in France would be improved by the marriage, and for Germany there was no more dangerous form of rule in France than that of the Orléans. And finally, the scheming Princess Marie of Orléans, who had been married to Prince Waldemar of Denmark since 1885, would exploit her cousin Hélène's marriage 'to lay mines' in North-West Germany which could 'cause great destruction by exploding at critical moments'. For all these reasons it was essential that the marriage be prevented, Bülow considered, and this could best be done through Queen Victoria and Prince Christian of Schleswig-Holstein. Kaiser Wilhelm should declare, he advised, that he would never give his consent to the marriage and would never receive Ernst Günther and his wife; furthermore he would never allow the couple to live in Prussia, in particular in Schleswig-Holstein.

But although the prohibition of the marriage must be very firm, Bülow warned, it should be very carefully expressed so that it could not be exploited by the Danish royal family in order to turn Tsar Alexander III against Wilhelm II.[194]

Eulenburg set out the case to the German ambassador in Paris as follows: 'The Kaiser would see in such an alliance the desire of the Orléans to improve their position – he would also fear intrigues in Berlin . . . I should add that it would be difficult to persuade the Duke, whose heart is easily inflamed, to give up or desist from giving in to a *coup de tête*. It would therefore be a question of taking precautions on the other side and frightening off the Orléans from entering into an alliance with the Kaiser's brother-in-law . . . In my view much depends on the personality of the Princess. If she is of the same type as her sister [sic] Waldemar of Denmark one might have to be prepared for trouble, for the Duke is *not a very clever* man and is easily led. I imagine that you would probably know ways and means of conveying a placatory message to the Orléans. If they want the match, however, it will be impossible to do anything about it. In the end people always think that a *brouille* cannot last for ever and that it is only a question of time before the Duchess of Holstein-Orléans will be seen at the Berlin Schloss.'[195] From his experience of the womanising Duke in Paris the previous summer, in his reply to Eulenburg Münster could only confirm the worst fears of the Kaiser's friend. Unlike the Duchess of Aosta, Princess Hélène of Orléans would not be receptive to his arguments against the marriage, although Münster agreed that such an alliance would be 'extremely *harmful*'.[196] Eulenburg forwarded the ambassador's letter to the Kaiser with the comment that 'the business of Duke E[rnst] G[ünther]'s engagement is really *highly* dangerous . . . I think Prince Christian might after all be better as an intermediary with the Orléans than the Empress Frederick.'[197] For several more weeks the Kaiserin was tormented by the Duke's 'foolish rush to find a bride'.[198] Then on 25 June 1895 Princess Hélène married Emmanuel, Duke of Aosta, at Kingston-upon-Thames, leaving Ernst Günther to begin his search all over again.

The Duke's next project drove the Kaiser and his wife to distraction. In the spring of 1896 he announced his intention of marrying the eighteen-year-old Johanna von Spitzemberg, who was not of royal birth. She was the daughter of Baroness Hildegard von Spitzemberg and a niece of the Württemberg envoy Axel Freiherr von Varnbüler. In March 1896 Eulenburg found himself compelled, as he wrote, 'to torment [the Kaiser] yet again, alas, with a marriage project of Duke Ernst Günther's!' He sent Wilhelm a copy of a letter from Varnbüler but urged him not to react to Ernst Günther's plan until 'the news reaches Your Majesties *through* the Duke', for Varnbüler and Eulenburg would be put 'in an *impossible* position if the Duke found out that the matter had been brought to Your Majesty's attention directly'. Eulenburg also advised the Kaiser not to say anything to the Kaiserin about her brother's intention for the time being, for it would 'only fill Her Majesty with anxiety again and detract from the beneficial effect of the journey [to Italy]. It would also be very difficult to dissuade Her Majesty from writing – and then . . . Axel and I would be in a very unpleasant position!'[199] The Kaiser telegraphed in fury from Palermo: 'Am quite outraged at your news; all the more as the selfsame young man recently asked me to negotiate with another lady for him, which is already in progress. Find his behaviour indescribable. Please warn Axel at once. His niece is too good for such a wretch.'[200] Not until May did Ernst Günther admit to the Spitzemberg family, as Axel Varnbüler informed Eulenburg, that the Kaiser had 'suggested another girl [to him] – namely the daughter of our beloved lion, hippopotamus and dervish-howl-mimic' Count Emil Görtz. When it turned out that the eldest Görtz daughter was already spoken for, Countess Anna Görtz declared that she would invite the Duke to Schlitz soon, 'to give him the opportunity of meeting the second daughter'.[201] On 19 May Eulenburg wrote to Varnbüler from Prökelwitz on behalf of a grateful Kaiser to tell him that during a shooting trip to Schloss Primkenau, the Holstein family seat in Silesia, there had been 'serious arguments' with Ernst Günther. 'When the Duke tried to put off the match with the Görtz daughter for three more weeks "because his heart was engaged", the Kaiser answered that the Duke no doubt had the right to marry whom he wished, but that He and the Kaiserin were determined, if he entered into a marriage with a lady who was not of the appropriate rank, *never to receive her*. He must make his arrangements accordingly. Furthermore he [Ernst Günther] would prevent the Kaiserin from coming to Primkenau, because she would never set foot in the house if the marriage were not of appropriate rank. The Duke was quite flabbergasted.' According to the second sister of the Kaiserin and the Duke, Princess Calma of Schleswig-Holstein-Sonderburg-Glücksburg, Eulenburg continued, Ernst Günther had already lost interest in Johanna Spitzemberg; he had spoken definitely of marrying one of the Görtz daughters.[202] Varnbüler was not convinced, however, that 'the danger' was over, for Ernst Günther had renewed his wish to continue to pay court to his niece, and even if Johanna Spitzemberg had commented that she did not like Ernst Günther at all and could not imagine ever being able to love and marry him, Baroness Spitzemberg was nonetheless rather more taken with the ducal title than was desirable.[203] Eulenburg warned his friend that a marriage between Ernst Günther and Johanna would cost him his position as Württemberg's envoy and delegate to the Bundesrat. 'The Kaiserin, who is full of gratitude for your support for her views, would be overcome with thirst for revenge if she found herself in the position of perhaps having to call you and your wife Uncle and Aunt', he explained; and the Kaiser would also treat him with hostility if the marriage took place. 'I therefore beg you earnestly to go on lovingly fostering your niece's *anti*pathy. And that is not a difficult task given *this* personality. I have *never* met such a wayward fellow!'[204]

On 28 May 1896 Kaiser Wilhelm II finally contacted Varnbüler directly to put an end to the matter. 'My dear Axel', he wrote, 'I take up my pen with a heart full of distress and anxiety, to appeal to you in the matter of my brother-in-law, about which you informed me through Phili. First of all, my dear Axel, accept my own and the poor, greatly suffering Kaiserin's warmest thanks for your loyal, honest attitude in this affair, which the Duke unfortunately kept carefully hidden from us. I expected nothing else from you, of course, but the Kaiserin's praise for your conduct must give you consolation and encouragement in a situation so painful for you too. You have behaved as an upright and honourable friend to me, which I shall not forget. But now to the matter itself. Phili has of course explained to you exactly what has passed between the Kaiserin and her brother as well as what I discussed with him in Primkenau . . . Now, my dear Axel, I have had enough of these constant charades and manoeuvres. The poor Kaiserin already has enough to worry and upset her, but this affair is breaking her heart. You know that the Kaiserin has told the Duke expressly that if he takes your niece she will have no more to do with him and she will be cut off once and for all from coming home to Primkenau. The thought of never returning to the home of her forefathers, never being able to pray beside the coffin of her dear, idolised father again, so overwhelmed the Kaiserin that she burst into floods of bitter tears. I cannot bear to see such despair and wretchedness any longer; it must be stopped. Only yesterday I again made clear to the Duke what a miserable situation would be created for him, for the family and above all for his intended bride. She would not be recognised, could never appear at court with him and never be seen in the family circle . . . I then told the Duke that as head of one of the oldest and most distinguished German princely houses, heaven had laid obligations upon him which compelled him to remain within certain limits, which I had already relaxed by allowing him to choose among the families of the old mediatised and ruling counts and princes, but to go further was quite out of the question. I ended the conversation by saying that I expected to hear from him at the beginning of next month that everything was settled. But you, dear Axel, must help with this. Advise your sister to go away at once and take your niece with her . . . So I ask you, dear Axel, to put a stop to the affair once and for all by a *fait accompli*. Your true friend and King, Wilhelm I. R.'[205]

At the same time Wilhelm revived his efforts to arrange a marriage between his brother-in-law and Countess Anna Görtz, the nineteen-year-old daughter of his friend the mediatised Reichsgraf (Imperial Count) 'Em' Görtz, her previous marriage plans having meanwhile come to nothing. On his return from

Prökelwitz the Kaiser held discussions with Countess Sophia Görtz, first at the Neues Palais and then at the Hotel Continental. His old friend was understandably agitated when news of this reached him at Schlitz, and on 23 May he wrote to the Kaiser: 'Your Majesty can well imagine how affected I was by the subject of your conversation, of which my wife informed me immediately – affected on the one hand by the joyful hope of seeing a fine and happy future ahead for my dear Anna, with God's help, but also by anxiety as to how the complication which *previously* arose, for reasons which my wife did not conceal from Your Majesty, would be settled. If I now take up my pen to write about this matter, it is in the conviction that no further impediment to Your Majesty's gracious intentions need be anticipated from another quarter. The conduct of the other party, at least, is such that we can scarcely believe that any further step will be taken from there. We are afraid that obstacles on grounds of health may be the reason. I can assure Your Majesty that we shall be happy, in these circumstances, to see the accomplishment of that other alliance indicated by Your Majesty. Naturally we are saying nothing to our daughter about it, nor shall we say anything until the gentleman himself wishes it. It seems to me that the first requirement is that it should happen as naturally as possible. In order to ensure this – that is to say, to ensure it for *both* sides – I am also particularly disinclined to try to bring about the rapprochement which we too now wish, by an invitation to Schlitz. As there has been so little contact hitherto, such an invitation would be difficult to explain in a non-committal manner, and it would certainly attract a great deal of attention! We have thought of another way of bringing about a closer acquaintance between them, as desired. There is no reason why my wife and I should not come to Berlin with Anna for a few days "to visit the two exhibitions there". That will give the gentleman the opportunity to call on us at our hotel, which in turn will lead naturally and quite inconspicuously to further contact in a way which is not at all binding on either party. If, as I may perhaps hope, this plan recommends itself to Your Majesty, it would only be a question of deciding on an appropriate moment and of letting the other side know.' Görtz asked the Kaiser to inform Ernst Günther of this plan, 'all the more because Your Majesty is the only person through whom this matter *can* be arranged!' In 'the interests of all sides!' he urged, Wilhelm should act, and 'the sooner the better'.[206]

The satyric saga of the 'Rutting Duke' did not come to an end, and that only temporarily, until he married Princess Dorothea (Dora) of Saxe-Coburg and Gotha in August 1898, the daughter of the Vienna-based Prince Philipp of Saxe-Coburg and Gotha. If a match between the German Kaiserin's brother and a sixteen-year-old Catholic Princess was problematic enough in itself – Prince Heinrich wrote from Vladivostok that he was glad his mother had not been present at the wedding of 'that d——d fool to a child!'[207] – the outrage was all the

greater because the engagement coincided with a scandal of epic proportions in
the bride's family.[208] Not only had Dora's mother, Princess Louise, a member of
the Belgian branch of the Coburg family, forged the name of her sister Crown
Princess Stephanie on countless bills of exchange, but in February 1898 the father
of the young bride had fought a duel with his wife's Croatian lover, Lieutenant
Mattachich-Keglevich. Shortly before her daughter's marriage to Duke Ernst
Günther, Mattachich was arrested for fraud and Princess Louise of Saxe-Coburg
and Gotha was shut away in a lunatic asylum and deprived of her rights. 'These
are all most unpleasant matters!', Eulenburg exclaimed in despair and not without reason in a letter to the Kaiser.[209]

### SCANDAL AT SCHLOSS GLIENICKE

Almost as scandalous as Ernst Günther's life was that of the Kaiserin's younger
sister, Luise Sophie, known as Yaya, and her husband Prince Friedrich Leopold
of Prussia, a cousin of the Kaiser and brother of Princess Louise Margaret, the
wife of Queen Victoria's third son Prince Arthur, Duke of Connaught. Yaya
and Fritz Leopold lived at Schloss Glienicke and had four children, although
there was little sign of domestic bliss in the marriage. 'I fear there is much
unhappiness', the Empress Frederick wrote regretfully about the relationship
between Yaya and Fritz Leopold.[210] The Princess was distinctly plain – the
widowed Empress commented with dismay in December 1891 that 'the poor
thing is too distressingly ugly – really quite startling' – and although she dressed
very well and had beautiful hair, she had 'such a temper that it never goes smooth
there'.[211] Waldersee described Prince Fritz Leopold as a 'foolish, incompetent
man' who treated his wife 'with appalling lack of consideration'.[212] Charlotte of
Saxe-Meiningen spread the rumour that the Prince was 'not quite right in his
high mind & intellect, or else he is a brute'.[213] Perhaps as a defiant reaction to her
husband's maltreatment of her, the Kaiserin's younger sister became 'so fearfully
arrogant . . . that even [Prince] Heinrich, who is certainly a good-natured fellow,
doesn't speak to her any more'.[214]

The numerous critical remarks made by the couple about the Kaiser, which
were deliberately reported to him, combined with Yaya's often improper
behaviour, led in the winter of 1895–6 to one of the most sensational scandals in the history of the Prusso-German court. The indolent, difficult Fritz
Leopold[215] committed the error of failing to send word immediately to the
Kaiser, as head of the family, of a skating accident suffered by his wife, for which
Wilhelm rewarded both his cousin and his sister-in-law Yaya with fourteen
days of house arrest. Schloss Glienicke was surrounded by sentries from the 1st
Guards Regiment, which led to wild speculation in the press that the Princess

had attempted to commit suicide or that Fritz Leopold had been unmasked as a political conspirator. '*Who could* imagine the simple truth!', exclaimed the Empress Frederick, who saw Wilhelm's action as yet another expression of a reactionary spirit of the deepest dye. 'Despotic spirit and autocratic ways − & ideas of 200 years ago were not taught by Fritz & me − & not learnt from *us* − as *we* often suffered under a thralldom wh[ich] was very irksome, of wh[ich] [Wilhelm] *never knew anything*.'[216] Throughout the ruling houses of Germany the news that the Kaiserin's sister had been placed under house arrest was greeted with incredulity.[217]

The Senior Marshal of the Court and Palace, Count August zu Eulenburg, who shared the general view that the Kaiser's reaction had been excessive, gave his cousin Philipp an account of the affair. 'The outward cause of the conflict, which had been flickering in the embers for a long time because of constant disobedience and opposition from Glienicke, particularly on the female side, was the Princess's falling through the ice when she was yet again skating without an escort. This accident was then kept completely secret from the Neues Palais for the whole day, and when the Kaiserin happened to call at Glienicke that afternoon she was turned away on the pretext that the Princess had a bad cold and had gone to bed. A violent argument between His Majesty and the Prince then led to the imposition of house arrest . . . It was high time for them to be taught a proper lesson, even if it took an excessive form − as unfortunately frequently happens here.'[218] In a revealing comment on the background to the incident Philipp Eulenburg wrote: 'There is an open feud between Prince Friedrich − who is, to put it mildly, *quite* crazy − and his wife, the Kaiserin's sister, on the one hand, and the Kaiser and Kaiserin on the other. The Prince absolutely refuses to comply with the wishes and "commands" of his cousin, and his wife is equally unwilling to do what the Kaiserin wishes. A kind of minor rebellion in domestic affairs. The Friedrich Leopolds spent most of their time squabbling, threw every adjutant and Hofmarschall out of the house after a very short time, and behaved in an unsuitable manner. The Prince's open defiance finally led to the arrest − and the whole of Potsdam, or rather Berlin, is in a state of high excitement. Indeed this must surely be the first time since Frederick the Great that a member of the Prussian royal family has been placed under arrest with a military guard on his castle, and in this case one is as surprised at Prince Friedrich Leopold and his wife as at His Majesty himself.'[219] Eulenburg wrote to the Kaiser on 20 January 1896: 'The incredible affair of Prince Friedrich Leopold is upsetting people. I hope Their Royal Highnesses will go away for a long holiday, for *it is necessary for the peace of mind of Your Majesty and the Kaiserin* that you should be spared these tiresome rebellions at Glienicke, which are so trying on the nerves, for a while . . .'[220]

Through their close dynastic ties with the royal house of Prussia the British royal family was also drawn into the quarrel, which was not without danger in view of the fact that precisely at this time Anglo-German relations were under great strain because of the Transvaal crisis and the Kruger telegram.[221] Queen Victoria was kept up to date with events by almost daily letters from her daughter Vicky. On 1 January 1896 she wrote to her mother about this 'sad affair': 'I am much upset at William's having put Fritz Leopold & "Yaya" under arrest . . . This is a highhanded measure wh[ich] I am afraid will only exasperate Fritz L. and Louise-Sophie – & make relations very strained ever after.' Wilhelm's behaviour reminded her of painful times in the past – of his conduct in 1888 and 1889 and of his attitude to his sister Sophie's conversion. 'What a strange way of treating one's family!', she exclaimed in bewilderment. 'I cannot say *how* I regret this unseemly proceeding!!!' When she expressed her disapproval to the Kaiserin, Dona replied: 'Discipline must be enforced & kept up in the family.' But even leaving aside the inappropriateness of the punishment, the Empress Frederick pointed out, the airing of this family quarrel in the press was certainly very harmful for Wilhelm's reputation.[222]

Queen Victoria, who at first intended to stay out of the quarrel, nevertheless felt compelled to comment cautiously on it in response to a letter from Wilhelm justifying his conduct. 'It was very careless of her [Yaya] to attempt to walk on the ice, with no servant at hand, & it was very wrong of Fritz Leopold to speak disrespectfully of you both, but when people get into a passion they are often not aware of what they say, & I think those who repeat such expressions to you deserve great blame. It would surely have been better not to arouse any bitterness of feeling by such an arbitrary act as putting a Relation & a General Officer under arrest. Why not have sent for him or written to him to reprimand him? I fear the effect of the measures you have taken will not tend to the peace & harmony of the family & will cause a scandal.'[223] On 8 January 1896 Wilhelm was able to report to his grandmother that the measures against Fritz Leopold and Yaya had had a very beneficial effect. The Prince had shown remorse, so that the arrest could be rescinded.[224] But despite the ostensible reconciliation, inwardly Fritz Leopold continued to seethe with anger at his treatment. 'Unfortunately the storm continues to rage unpleasantly here, even if the waves have subsided outwardly', Captain von Heuduck wrote to August von Mackensen on 2 February 1896.[225] After a meeting with Fritz Leopold in October 1896 Waldersee too had the feeling that he would 'very soon have another clash with the Kaiser'. 'I could see again what an unhappy character the Prince has . . . He . . . allowed himself to make some very questionable remarks.'[226] Wilhelm himself expressed the view in 1899 that Friedrich Leopold was among those princes who 'might adopt a dangerous and hostile attitude under certain circumstances'. But his cousin would 'certainly be locked up in a madhouse soon', he commented.[227] Some years later he scribbled angrily on the margin of a petition from Friedrich Leopold: 'Unbelievable! I give the orders here! And that is that!'[228]

## ARIBERT AND LOUISE OF ANHALT

Wilhelm II had played the matchmaker in another Berlin marriage in which the family relationships between the Houses of Hohenzollern, Schleswig-Holstein and Saxe-Coburg and Gotha were almost impossible to unravel. In December 1890 he personally announced the betrothal of Prince Aribert of Anhalt and Princess Louise Augusta of Schleswig-Holstein, born in 1872, daughter of Prince Christian and Princess Helena ('Lenchen').[229]

Wilhelm's role in bringing about this union, which was ill-starred from the beginning, had been far from merely ceremonial, however. A few days before the betrothal his Aunt Lenchen had begged him for financial support, as the marriage would be impossible without it. She had told him that 'Grandmama [Queen Victoria] is so keen about this *partie* [sic] coming off' that she had declared herself ready to give the bride 10,000 marks a year  As they, the bride's parents, could also give her 10,000 marks a year and Duke Friedrich of Anhalt had promised the Prince 30,000 marks, only 10,000 marks more were needed in order to reach the sum of 60,000 marks a year which would be required for the young couple to live on. Lenchen therefore asked Wilhelm for the remaining 10,000 marks and pointed out that the dowry of 20,000 marks that Louise would bring to the marriage from her grandmother and parents was 'far more than any P[rince]ss of Schleswig-Holstein has *ever* brought as a marriage portion, & I cannot help thinking, *more* than *very many German* princesses ever bring their husbands!'[230] Wilhelm agreed.[231] In spite of his generosity, as we have already seen, Queen Victoria asked the Kaiser not to come to England until after the wedding at the beginning of July 1891, ostensibly because his presence would put the bridegroom's father too much in the shade. Wilhelm, however, insisted on being present at the marriage which he had been chiefly responsible for bringing about. The Queen was obliged to give in and invite her grandson to the young couple's wedding.[232]

For a while Princess Louise of Anhalt became the 'direct channel from the Kaiser to the Queen [Victoria]'; it was, for example, through 'the Ariberts' that Wilhelm's enquiry about a possible visit to England in 1898, as well as the Queen's negative reply, were directed.[233] But all too soon this marriage ended in divorce. The Princess became dangerously anorexic[234] and separated from her husband around the turn of the century, when her husband's homosexuality could no longer be doubted. The separation became the subject of angry correspondence between the Kaiser and Kaiserin on the one hand and the British royal family on the other, in the course of which Christian of Schleswig-Holstein even threatened to appear before the Bundesrat to explain the grounds for the divorce, which the Kaiser would not permit 'under any circumstances'.[235] After the divorce in 1900 the Princess ostentatiously resumed her maiden name.

### THE KOTZE AFFAIR

One Sunday in January 1891 Charlotte, Hereditary Princess of Saxe-Meiningen, and her brother-in-law Duke Ernst Günther organised a lively skating party and dance at a hunting lodge at Grunewald which was to have serious – and finally even fatal – consequences.[236] Among the fifteen participants, apart from the Kaiser's sister and her brother-in-law, were Prince Friedrich Karl (Fischy) of Hesse, Count Friedrich of Hohenau with his wife Charlotte (Lottka), Louis Ritter von Berger and his wife Sophie with her sister Eva, the officers Max and Paul Freiherren Schuler von Senden, Ludwig Freiherr von Knorring and the Masters of Ceremonies, Leberecht von Kotze and Karl Freiherr von Schrader with their respective wives, Elisabeth née von Treskow, and Alide née de Villier. The following morning some of the nocturnal revellers received disgusting anonymous letters, which not only contained obscene accusations of the worst kind but were also characterised by disdainful snobbery towards the guests who were not from the highest ranks of the aristocracy. But what was astounding about the letters, which were written in a disguised hand in block capitals and posted in Berlin, was that they described intimate events of which only eyewitnesses could have been aware. The assumption was that the writer had been at the skating party. But who could it have been?

In the course of the next four years several hundred such letters were sent. The recipients included Hereditary Princess Charlotte, Duke Ernst Günther, the Empress Frederick, Princess Margarethe (Mossy) of Prussia, Prince Friedrich Karl of Hesse, Prince and Princess Aribert of Anhalt, Prince Max of Baden, Prince Karl Egon zu Fürstenberg, Prince Hermann zu Stolberg-Wernigerode, Prince Friedrich Karl zu Hohenlohe-Oehringen, Count and Countess Eberhard von Dohna, Baron and Baroness Hugo von Reischach, the Chamberlain Edgard von Wedel, the Masters of Ceremonies von Kotze and von Schrader, and the brothers Friedrich and Wilhelm Hohenau, who were the sons of Prince Albrecht of Prussia (1809–72) by his morganatic marriage to Rosalie von Rauch. But the actual target of these truly repellent letters was Lottka, the strikingly beautiful, tall young wife of the homosexual Count Fritz Hohenau. She was Charlotte von der Decken by birth, and was contemptuously mocked as 'the stinking one', 'stinking Lotte' or 'Lottchen of Prussia' in the letters. She was accused of having pushed her way into the highest ranks of court society and of behaving in an unseemly way at court, but above all of leading a wild sexual life with high-born men and women: Prince 'Fichi' or 'Vischi' [sic] of Hesse, Prince Aribert of Anhalt, Prince Max of Baden, Prince Friedrich Karl zu Hohenlohe, Prince Hermann zu Stolberg, Prince Heinrich XIX Reuss of the junior branch, Prince Franz-Joseph of Battenberg, Eberhard Count von Dohna, the Freiherren Max and Paul Schuler von Senden, Hugo von Reischach and Ludwig von Knorring, as well as the English-born Princess Louise of Anhalt, were repeatedly named as her lovers and participants in her 'orgies' in the brothel of a certain Frau Hagenauer. Even the name of Herbert Bismarck crops up a few times in this connection. One typical letter of April 1892 to Princess Louise of Anhalt reads: 'The Countess's peculiar mania consists in a real lust to have the closest possible, that is to say sexual, relationship with all princes, and it gives her a special, irresistible thrill to steal a newly married husband from his young wife. As most men lack the energy to resist the captivating beauty of this woman, she has already caused untold mischief, especially as she suffers from a dreadfully infectious abdominal disease . . . which is almost invariably transmitted to the man through sexual relations, and on account of which Count Hohenau has long since been forbidden all sexual relations by his doctors.'[237] As the motive for these attacks the letters indicate expressly that what the writer (or writers) wanted was 'to destroy the reputation of Countess Hohenau, who has completely ruined people very close to us, in Berlin'.[238] If other people such as Hugo von Reischach and Louise von Anhalt were attacked, this was as a rule only in order to keep them away from Countess Hohenau. While Princess Louise was accused of having a lesbian relationship with the Countess, Reischach, the Empress Frederick's Hofmarschall, received a letter in February 1892 claiming that he was 'a Würt[t]emberger of the most suspect ancestry . . . whose father is said to have killed himself and whose mother, sister and brother have a highly dubious reputation'; he should therefore take care 'not to tread on the toes of Prussian people in high places' if he did not want to lose the 'brilliant position [he had] usurped here'.[239] One can imagine only too well the fury and frustration of the recipients of these letters that it proved impossible to find the source of the poison.

In the approximately thirty defamatory letters placed at the disposal of the military tribunal which later investigated the case – most had been destroyed at once by the recipients – the Kaiser himself was scarcely mentioned. There was only one letter, addressed to Ernst Günther on 23 January 1893 – just before the marriage of the Kaiser's youngest sister Mossy to Prince Friedrich Karl (Fischy) of Hesse – in which the libellous comments centred around the monarch. The letter claimed that Countess Hohenau, who was otherwise 'very extravagant', was holding back in the case of Ernst Günther, 'because she wishes Y[our]

H[ighness], as Her Majesty's brother, to continue to believe in her virtue. For the lovely Lottchen has . . . no less a goal than to be embraced by the strong arms of H.M. himself one day. She has been planning it for a long time, and whenever there is an opportunity she puts herself in H.M.'s way and pursues him with lascivious glances or shows her naked bosom as at the last court . . . But her masterstroke is to be launched tomorrow. Tomorrow afternoon at four o'clock L. will show herself off in the greatest splendour in front of H.M., appearing as a circus rider at a party which is to be staged with colossal pomp, and everyone agrees that she looks absolutely superb and plays her part to perfection. One cannot deny that she sets to work with wonderful energy and that her plan is excellently conceived, aiming first of all to captivate H.M. and to allow herself to be admired in front of all the princes of Europe, but also to awaken in the mind of the poor bridegroom old memories of earlier lovers' trysts, and to estrange his heart permanently from his wife.'[240] That the 'poor bridegroom' meant Prince Friedrich Karl of Hesse is clear from a postcard, sent a few days earlier to a Countess who is not further identified, which read: 'We hear that in order to keep her hold over Vischi [sic] and if possible to catch another prince as well, stinking Lotte has arranged a great party at which she will appear as a circus rider and only royalties will be invited. We shall not fail to elucidate those in high places further on the purpose of the exercise and the public danger involved in the enterprise, for which the impoverished Lieutenant is forced to sacrifice 1000 marks, so that Vischi will always have pleasant memories of those lovers' trysts in the Yorkstrasse [where the Hohenaus lived] and his heart will be permanently estranged from poor Mossi.'[241]

Who could have been the author of such letters? Whoever it was, he or she was familiar with the nicknames of princes and princesses and knew a great deal about the most private affairs of people of the highest social rank. Sometimes the letters were signed 'Bertha M.', and the writer is also identified elsewhere as a woman: it is indicated that the person in question was once connected with Princess Helena of Schleswig-Holstein, the mother of Princess Louise of Anhalt, in England.[242] Other letters suggest that several people are involved: they are signed 'The Committee' or 'One for many'. In March 1894 Countess Lottka Hohenau received a letter in which it was claimed that the writer of the anonymous letters was 'quite definitely the Duke of Holstein', the Kaiserin's brother, and Ernst Günther was also named as 'the anonymous letter writer' to House Minister Wilhelm von Wedell-Piesdorf. But as these denunciations were, paradoxically, also written in sinister block capitals, they were given little credence at first.[243]

On 16 June 1894 Master of Ceremonies Leberecht von Kotze was suddenly arrested on the orders of the Kaiser and personally conducted to the military prison in the Lindenstrasse by Chief of the Military Cabinet General Wilhelm von Hahnke, after Commandant Flügeladjutant von Scholl, who had been ordered to carry out the arrest, had failed to find the suspected culprit at his lodgings. The immediate reason for the arrest was the discovery of twelve pieces of blotting paper. They had been found by the group around Schrader and the Hohenaus on the desk of the Master of Ceremonies and in the Casino club and they showed several separate words, including the name 'Lottchen von Preussen', in capital letters. Kotze hotly protested his innocence, showed the Chief of the Military Cabinet two letters 'in the well-known hand' which he himself had received, and declared that he considered 'only women capable of the kind of thing being blamed on him'.[244]

The arrest of Kotze, which Hahnke had advised but which the Principal Chamberlain responsible for disciplinary matters at court, Prince Otto zu Stolberg-Wernigerode, had expressly warned against, caused a sensation and was, as Philipp Eulenburg recorded, 'deeply regretted in the interests of the monarchy' by all true royalists who had any understanding of the situation.[245] Only too soon it proved to be a grave mistake, not only politically and socially but also in legal terms, for since it was a case of libel, and thus of an offence requiring an offical complaint from the injured party, the arrest ordered by the Kaiser had been unlawful because no legal proceedings had been instituted. It was only several days later that Aribert Anhalt, Fritz Hohenau and Ernst Günther could be persuaded to bring an action for libel.[246] Since Kotze was a seconded captain of cavalry and was therefore subject to military jurisdiction, the military authorities were commissioned to investigate the case. This too turned out to have unforeseen political consequences, however, for the fact that the scandal now had to be dealt with in secret, in order to protect the Kaiser against accusations of perversion of justice, had more than a little to do with his and Hahnke's subsequent insistence on military prosecutions being held in camera, which in turn was to poison Wilhelm's relationship with the Reich Chancellor (as we shall see) for years to come.[247] The Bavarian envoy, Count Lerchenfeld, at once recognised the dangers for the monarchy which could arise from the overhasty and unlawful order by the Kaiser for the arrest. The press, he predicted, would use the case 'against the person of His Majesty the Kaiser . . . and find further material in it for attacks against the constitution of Prussian military courts'. He went on to bemoan the fact that the action taken by Wilhelm showed once again 'how ill-equipped His Majesty the Kaiser's closest entourage is for the task of drawing our sovereign's attention to the consequences of his decisions'.[248] Waldersee also regarded Kotze's arrest as a precipitate and ill-considered step. 'The whole affair is so entangled and some of it is of such a delicate nature that the best thing would be just to get rid of it.'[249] 'It is very regrettable', he wrote, 'that the affair is not being settled quietly; the arrest was certainly overhasty and probably quite illegal. But what is ever done with due consideration these days!'[250] Baroness Spitzemberg was no less outraged, and commented, with hindsight, that 'the whole horrible business, which did untold harm in our circles, could have been dealt with quietly if the Kaiser, instead of rushing in, had waited for Stolberg's memorandum and acted accordingly – frightful!'[251]

Kotze's arrest by order of the Kaiser was particularly surprising because his Master of Ceremonies had hitherto stood high in his favour. Described as good-looking, ridiculously dressed, hypercorrect and zealous in his duties and yet humorous and full of *joie de vivre*, he had been adept at entertaining the Kaiser, whom he 'idolised' – he is said once to have worn a startling green cravat for the sole reason that Wilhelm was going hunting – with piquant tittle-tattle from Berlin court society.[252] Although he had made many enemies at court through his affected behaviour it seemed doubtful from the outset that this naïve and 'funda-mentally decent man' was at all capable of thinking up 'such sophisticated anony-mous libels' as the letters contained.[253] At an officers' meeting at Breslau at the end of June 1894 opinion among army commanders was divided, but even those who thought Kotze guilty had to admit that he must have had 'other helpers'.[254]

The evidence of Kotze's guilt was always meagre and it soon collapsed alto-gether. The suspect sheets of blotting-paper with the disguised handwriting could have been used by someone else – by his adversary Baron Schrader, for instance, who used the same office. A graphologist was consulted and gave it as his expert opinion that the author of the libellous letters was not Kotze but must have been a woman – more precisely, 'a person of pathologically effeminate tendencies and of a vain and affected appearance'.[255] When the Chief of the Military Cabinet received another anonymous letter three days after the arrest – the Master of Ceremonies had no access to writing materials in prison! – even he realised that at worst Kotze could only have been guilty of aiding and abetting. 'We have not yet found the perpetrator', he admitted.[256] On 5 July 1894 the Governor of Berlin, General von Pape, as the responsible judicial authority, temporarily released the unfortunate courtier from captivity and reported to the Kaiser that the enquiries made indicated that there were 'insufficient grounds' for the sus-picion that Kotze had written the anonymous letters.[257] Unwilling to accept that his own conduct should thus become subject to exposure, the Kaiser ordered that the investigation should continue under the supervision of the Commander of the III Army Corps, General Prince Friedrich von Hohenzollern-Sigmaringen. Both the Governor of Berlin and Principal Chamberlain Prince zu Stolberg-Wernigerode, who by reporting the blotting-paper evidence to the Kaiser had unintentionally provided the motive for Kotze's arrest, had no alternative but to resign.[258] After taking evidence in detail – the transcripts filled approximately a thousand pages – the court martial, which was composed of officers of the Railway Regiment, finally began proceedings against Kotze in March 1895. He was accused of having committed libel, 'or aided and abetted therein', 'in common with other persons'. After only a few days, however, the tribunal recommended that Kotze be acquitted on grounds of lack of evidence. After some hesitation the Kaiser, as supreme war lord, gave his consent.[259]

In striking contrast to his precipitate order for Kotze's arrest, the Kaiser now forced his brother-in-law Ernst Günther, Count Fritz Hohenau and Prince Aribert of Anhalt, who had been the principal plaintiffs, to make written apologies and then to call and leave their cards on Kotze. 'So the flow has been checked from above, a blessing', his sister Charlotte commented.[260] Wilhelm was supported in this conciliatory attitude by the Kaiserin, who now took a decided stand for Kotze. A private letter to a member of the British royal household from the military attaché, Colonel Swaine, indicates that Prince Christian of Schleswig-Holstein, Ernst Günther's uncle and father-in-law of Prince Aribert, also played a decisive role in putting an end to this sordid affair.[261] Waldersee noted that Count Schlieffen, as Duke Ernst Günther's superior officer, had also helped bring about the reconciliation – 'a sad mission indeed' for the Chief of the General Staff. He suspected, however, that there was no prospect of a satisfactory end to the whole unpleasant business yet, since it was still not known 'who the culprit is; many people still believe that it was Kotze . . . The affair has by no means been laid to rest.'[262] The Reich Chancellor, Prince Hohenlohe, also considered that the situation was still explosive, commenting to his son that battle continued to rage at court between 'the Wedell, Lucanus and Hahnke clique and the Schrader, Reischach, Christian Krafft [Hereditary Prince zu Hohenlohe-Oehringen] clique. Hohenau, Aribert and Ernst Günther have made their peace, while the Schrader side is still unreconciled and bears a grudge against the aforementioned for having backed down. I am keeping to my resolve to do no more than observe.'[263]

With the Kaiser's confirmation of the acquittal the scandal entered its blood-stained final phase. As courts martial in Prussia took no oral evidence and conducted their proceedings in camera, Leberecht von Kotze now felt compelled to defend his honour publicly by challenging those of his accusers who had not apologised to fight it out with pistols.[264] It would be another case, Waldersee remarked bitterly, 'of an innocent man being put in the position of allowing himself to be shot dead in accordance with our so-called ideas of social standing; for if Kotze is to shoot it out with all those who maintained that he was the culprit, he will have so many duels on his hands that he will undoubtedly come to harm'. 'There would be far too many people who had sinned against Kotze . . . , including the Kaiser himself, since he ordered the arrest, which was utterly wrong.'[265] The

Chancellor urged the Kaiser to prevent the duels, as the middle classes would hold the Kaiser responsible for the original arrest and thus for the 'bad turn events had taken'. 'Since everything which affects the mood of the population towards Your Majesty is of great importance to me, and since I am always at pains to eliminate anything which could occasion ill-feeling towards Your M., the prospect of a duel with an unfortunate outcome for Herr von Kotze fills me with an anxiety which is all the greater because I am afraid that such an outcome could be exploited in a manner unfavourable to Y. M.', the elderly Prince wrote.[266] Even if the Kaiser had agreed to the Chancellor's request, the latter's well-meaning intervention came too late: on 13 April 1895, in a duel fought under very harsh conditions with Freiherr von Reischach, Kotze was shot in the thigh on the eighth exchange of bullets.[267] By way of a conciliatory gesture the Kaiser sent Kotze flowers and an Easter egg.

Full of sympathy for the wounded man and his wife Elisabeth, the Kaiser's sister Charlotte wrote: 'Kotze at last pronounced free, but since yesterday badly wounded, consequences of the first duel. I shudder when I think of the others that must come still: his wife is *so* courageous & behaves admirably; her letters all these days to me are "bewunderungswürdig" [admirable] from strength of mind & will: but the long 10 months strain must soon tell on her nerves: dear thing how I long to help & comfort her now!!'[268] Waldersee too was incensed at this new trial by fire which the unfortunate Kotze had to endure. 'The wretched Kotze affair has reached a temporary conclusion through the acquittal of this actually very foolish and harmless man, who was accused and arrested with such inordinately excessive haste', he wrote the day after the duel. 'What a quantity of dust and dirt has been stirred up to absolutely no purpose! There has already been a duel and Kotze has been shot in the leg by his chief accuser, Reischach. It makes me very angry that Kotze was obliged to fight a duel because of our completely misguided ideas . . . Are all the countless slanderers to go unpunished? That would be truly outrageous. In the decree introducing the disciplinary courts the Kaiser said: "I will not tolerate anyone in my army who impugns the honour of a comrade in a criminal manner." Why is no use made of this admirable sentiment?' Not without reason many newspapers expressed the opinion that, if laws were now to be passed to protect religion and morality, they would have to be applied first 'against the highest ranks of society'.[269]

As the next step towards his rehabilitation, on the advice of his Jewish defence lawyer, Fritz Friedmann, who was regarded as a brilliant man, Kotze lodged a formal complaint against Schrader for slander, but after his complaint had been repeatedly rejected by the public prosecutor's office, a duel between the two former colleagues seemed inevitable.[270] Waldersee had already predicted this outcome, which he strongly condemned, in August 1894 after a conversation with

Zedlitz-Trützschler. The former Minister of Ecclesiastical Affairs had expressed the opinion, the General noted, that 'nothing could be proved against Kotze, but suspicion continued to rest on him', so that it would probably be a matter of duels between him and his accusers in the end. The scandal was certainly 'deeply shaming and it throws a dark shadow over court society in Berlin', the former Chief of the General Staff wrote. But to settle it through a duel would be quite wrong, in his view. 'If Kotze is innocent his accusers must be treated as slanderers and hounded out; if he is guilty he must be got rid of. But what use is shooting?'[271]

In December 1895 Wilhelm II again intervened disastrously in the scandal when he angrily overturned the verdict of a disciplinary tribunal conducted by the Rathenow Hussars, which had found for Schrader and against Kotze, describing it as 'very partisan', and ordered a new investigation by a tribunal from the Hanoverian King's Uhlans. The officers whose verdict had been repudiated felt compelled to submit their resignations, and the Rathenow Hussar Regiment was further punished by receiving no All-Highest congratulatory telegram at its jubilee celebrations. General Prince Friedrich von Hohenzollern, whom the Kaiser blamed for the leaking of the verdict to the press, was dismissed in an insulting manner from his post as commander of the III Army Corps.[272]

Philipp Eulenburg congratulated the Kaiser on his rejection of the tribunal's verdict.[273] Other observers, however, were disturbed by the continuing escalation of the scandal and by the Kaiser's increasingly irritable mood. 'This affair really must be settled soon', Waldersee commented in March 1896.[274] The Austrian ambassador reported from Berlin on the widespread and growing nervousness caused by 'the lack of proper stability', while the Bavarian envoy, Lerchenfeld, pointed out that the precipitate dismissal of Prince Hohenzollern in direct connection with the Kotze affair involved a considerable risk for the crown. The Commander could have been unobtrusively retired three or four months later without any damage to the monarchy, but 'this affair, which has been dealt with in an unfortunate manner from the very start, has already caused a great deal of mischief. A number of people have lost their position in society. The court is divided and its reputation has suffered and the crown itself has not escaped unharmed, in consequence of the sudden change in the All-Highest attitude and the overhasty intervention of His Majesty the Kaiser.'[275] Count Monts reported to the German ambassador in Rome on the 'bad mood' of the Kaiser, commenting that it was directed principally against the Conservatives; but in addition to this 'the Jewish bankers and financiers are very offended about the cancelled procession at the subscription ball: there are no court balls, because H.M. is going to pay back Berlin society for the Kotze affair. In short, as in the days of Frederick William IV, the outlook's pretty gloomy.'[276]

Meanwhile the new disciplinary tribunal in Hanover reached the same conclusion as its predecessor at Rathenow. Schrader had not been guilty of defama-
tion; Kotze, on the other hand, had dishonoured his profession and must resign
his officer's commission. But in April 1896 the Kaiser rejected this verdict too,
thereby confirming Kotze's right to demand satisfaction and clearing the way
(albeit unintentionally) for a duel between his two Masters of Ceremonies. On
Good Friday, 10 April 1896, Schrader was fatally wounded in an exchange of fire
on the Ravensberg at Potsdam. He died the next day.[277] Eulenburg was with the
Kaiser and Kaiserin on the *Hohenzollern* at Venice when Wilhelm read out the
telegram announcing that Kotze had shot Schrader. The Kaiserin's face turned
'dark red and she immediately and vehemently exclaimed: "That is right!"'[278]
The Empress Frederick reacted quite differently to the news of Schrader's death.
'We are horrified here at the Duel wh[ich] has taken place at Potsdam and that
unfortunate H. v. Schrader has been killed by that horrid Kotze', she wrote to
her mother.[279] Waldersee likewise deplored this fatal outcome, and particularly
the lamentable fact 'that the Kaiser [had] actually encouraged duels'. 'Public
opinion is considerably aroused and I think it very probable that the matter will
be discussed in the Reichstag', he wrote.[280]

As a result of the sensational duels which Kotze fought with Reischach and
Schrader the origin of the whole affair – the authorship of the obscene letters –
had almost been forgotten. Indeed, among those in the know the suspicion was
not infrequently voiced that this outcome was exactly what had been wished
and intended from the outset – that Kotze had been induced to sacrifice himself
to protect someone else, and had been 'rescued' by the Kaiser for this very
reason.[281] In September 1894 Arthur von Brauer had written to the Grand Duke
of Baden stating that the true culprit was 'a very highly placed person'; so much
so, indeed, that he *ought* not to be found out. Brauer did not dare commit the
name to paper.[282]

Although conclusive evidence is lacking and will probably never be found, in
the light of research there are increasingly strong indications that the author
of the anonymous letters was none other than Ernst Günther, the Kaiserin's
brother. Philipp Eulenburg was in a particularly good position to discover the
truth behind the scandal, not only because he was the Kaiser's closest confidant
in this thorny affair, as in many others, and because he was also kept up to date
with developments by his cousin August Eulenburg,[283] but also because he was
a close friend of the brothers Dietrich and Georg von Hülsen, whose mother
was the sister of Kotze's mother-in-law.[284] Furthermore he was repeatedly asked
for advice in the affair by his old friend Christian Krafft, Hereditary Prince
zu Hohenlohe-Oehringen, Stolberg's successor as principal chamberlain.[285] For
Eulenburg, as for the Hülsens and also the Marshal of the Palace, Maximilian
Freiherr von Lyncker, it was always clear that there was '*no question* of Kotze

being guilty'. For a time the Kaiser's friend suspected the other Master of Ceremonies, Karl von Schrader, who had had numerous 'relationships' in exalted circles, of having written the obscene letters with the help of his '*very* pretty, *very* elegant' Dutch wife. During the Scandinavian cruise of 1894, however, Eulenburg heard that there was 'a trail leading to *Duke Ernst Günther*', who had connections with 'ladies of the *demi-monde*' with whom Schrader also consorted. Following this discovery Eulenburg discussed 'the unfortunate affair' with the Kaiser, whom he described as 'almost more agitated than I have ever seen him. The police at Berlin had told Him that they *had called a halt* to their investigation of the affair, because the trail led to the Duke.' The '*weak and extremely* confused' Ernst Günther had even written letters to the Kaiser, Eulenburg recorded, 'which *almost* described himself as guilty!!' Wilhelm had banned his brother-in-law from entering his house, but had used another scandalous story as the pretext, namely that the Duke had lost his badge of the Order of the Black Eagle, which was later found under the bed of a Berlin woman with whom he was infatuated. Eulenburg summed up the situation in a memorandum of April 1895 in which he recorded that the secret police officer Eugen von Tausch believed that Ernst Günther was guilty, while Kotze and his friends accused both the Duke and Schrader of being the perpetrators, claiming that 'actresses of *the most disreputable kind*' had been supplied 'by both of them (as has been established)' with information 'about all kinds of private matters at Fritz Hohenau's house' and also about 'all kinds of incidents in court society'.[286] In January 1895 Philipp Eulenburg reported to Friedrich von Holstein 'that the Kotze affair is said to have taken an unfavourable turn for Schrader lately. Police Lieutenant von Tausch has some incriminating evidence for which no one has yet asked him. I am afraid that out of consideration for *brother-in-law Duke E[rnst] G[ünther]* things will be kept quiet, and that consequently this evil affair will become completely obscured in the end, but it has dealt Berlin society a blow from which it will not recover.'[287]

Lieutenant von Tausch was also in close touch with General Waldersee, who by his own account had already heard the rumours of Ernst Günther's complicity many months before Kotze's arrest. He noted in mid-July 1894 that he had heard the suspicion voiced 'more than a year ago' that – as 'the whole world' was now whispering – the culprit was 'Duke Ernst Günther in collaboration with his mistress'. This being so, it was 'scarcely possible . . . to pursue the matter any further . . . No doubt there will be great efforts to kill off the affair.'[288] A month later he saw his prediction confirmed, noting that 'strenuous attempts are now being made' to prevent the Kotze affair from being solved, 'because the scandal affects the most exalted circles' and 'truly appalling facts' would come to light. 'Once again this seems to indicate that a great deal is rotten in the state.'[289]

Other thoroughly credible sources confirm the conclusions reached by Eulen-burg and Waldersee. Soon after taking over the Reich chancellorship in the autumn of 1894 Prince Hohenlohe recorded that 'the Ernst Günther affair' was 'so complicated that I think it advisable to keep out of it'. The Kaiser had sent Hahnke to Ernst Günther to ask him whether he was the author of the anony-mous letters. 'E.G. replied that if he had not been Chief of the Military Cabinet he would have answered him with a horsewhip, but in the circumstances he would merely show him the door.' According to the Chancellor the Kaiserin's brother was suspected not only by Hahnke but also by the Chief of Police in Berlin, Bernhard Freiherr von Richthofen, Adjutant-General von Plessen and the Kaiserin's Oberhofmeister von Mirbach. As if this coalition were not power-ful enough, allegations against Ernst Günther were also made by Prince Aribert of Anhalt and his wife Louise, who accused the Kaiserin's brother of having taken part in the 'disgraceful deed'. Everything now depended on the Kaiser's attitude. But he hesitated. Hohenlohe noted in his journal: 'E.G. wanted to justify himself to the Kaiser, but the latter refuses to listen to what he has to say until Kotze's trial is over.'[290] It was perhaps after this confrontation that the 'confused' Duke began the correspondence with Wilhelm in which he 'almost' admitted his guilt. Nor do the self-pitying letters which Ernst Günther wrote to his uncle Christian de-monstrate a convincing indignation at the widespread allegations against him.[291]

Further compromising details about the not exactly exemplary private life of the Kaiserin's brother – the lost Order of the Black Eagle, stories of fraudulent cheques, his demands for the return of presents given to his mistress and for her expulsion by the police, together with many other 'unpleasant matters' – threatened to come to light in the course of the trial of Eugen von Tausch in 1897. The newspapers took this opportunity of reporting openly that Tausch had named Ernst Günther to the Kaiser 'as the author of the anonymous letters, for which alleged evidence was produced', and had thereby caused 'great anger on the part of the Kaiser' against his brother-in-law.[292] The supposition widely expressed at this time that the obscene letters had been written by Duke Ernst Günther (and perhaps also by Karl Schrader) in collusion with 'actresses of *the most disreputable kind*' seems convincing. It explains much (although by no means everything) which has remained problematic about the affair: the uncanny inside knowledge, the snobbish attitude towards 'invaders' like Lottka Hohenau and Hugo Reischach, the allegedly 'feminine' handwriting and the 'pathologically effeminate' mentality of the letters, the horrified reaction of those in the know to the precipitate arrest ordered by the Kaiser and the conciliatory attitude suddenly adopted by Wilhelm towards Kotze on hearing of the strong suspicions of his own brother-in-law's guilt, and finally the way in which the explosive affair was 'obscured' in order to prevent the actual perpetrator being discovered.

Apart from Ernst Günther there was only one other 'very exalted person-age' in the immediate proximity of the Kaiser who was suspected of having been involved in the sordid anonymous letter campaign: Wilhelm's eldest sister Charlotte, Hereditary Princess of Saxe-Meiningen, who was so fond of 'mischief-making'. In his memorandum on the Kotze case Philipp Eulenburg affirms that 'an important figure in Berlin society' is prepared to 'swear' that this 'fairly – depraved' Princess was the author of the letters, because she hated Lottka Hohenau for reasons unknown to him.[293] A recent study has revived this contem-porary rumour with the suggestion – albeit without documentary evidence – that Charlotte might have collaborated with her brother's brother-in-law Ernst Günther.[294] This hypothesis is contradicted by the fact that on 26 June 1894 the Hereditary Princess wrote a revealing letter full of indignation about Kotze's arrest, in which she convincingly demonstrates not only his, but her own, inno-cence. As this private letter was certainly not destined for public consumption it can hardly be interpreted as an elaborate attempt to exculpate herself; we therefore have little alternative but to accept the Princess's protestations at face value. The letter, addressed to her father-in-law's third wife, Freifrau Ellen von Heldburg, reads: 'The Kotze scandal and his shocking arrest has affected me *very much*, especially because *she* [Elisabeth von Kotze] is my oldest and best friend. We know only what is in the newspapers and are until now firmly convinced of his innocence: we have known him for 16 years and until the court convicts him I consider [him] *not* guilty: he is such a loyal, slightly stupid man that *I* do not believe him capable of such nastiness, nor does Bernhard: the wretched pieces of blotting-paper do not prove anything; he would not commit such carefully worked out stuff to paper either in the Ceremonial Office or in the officers' mess. Nor could he have carried on with this *nastiness* systematically for 4 years, when we have travelled so much together and spent time together and often read the anonymous letters together. I have just received a pitiful letter from her [Elisabeth] K[otze]; she has seen her husband in prison and says he was admirably calm and firmly convinced that God would help him and show that he was innocent, and also that the truth would certainly come to light. Neither of them can yet grasp what is happening, or what will happen. There will be more than enough nastiness and filth, suspicions, slander etc. to come. I cannot under-stand my brother's *rash*!!! action in causing such a public scandal when he has always favoured him, and he an officer and holding an important post at court. Qui vivra verra! is all I can say. *I* had the first anonymous letter 4 years ago & up to last year they continued, some very vile, but never for one moment dreamed of accusing *him* poor man . . . But enough, the whole thing disgusts me too much.'[295]

Although many details of the Kotze affair remained concealed from the public at large, it created an appalling impression of moral decline at the court and even in the imperial family itself. With the fatal outcome of the affair, if not before, the Kaiser and his entourage were subjected to a barrage of criticism; there was 'deep indignation against the irresponsible advisers' who had counselled the Kaiser to interfere actively in the affair.[296] The conservative *Reichsbote* bewailed the fact that the Kotze case had 'destroyed more royalist feeling in the country than years of ideological work by true supporters of the monarchy could build up again'. The democratic *Berliner Tageblatt* pointed out that healthy popular sentiment could not but be harmed 'when men in the immediate entourage of the Kaiser flout all the laws of the land, all the prohibitions of the Church', and the liberal *Vossische Zeitung* was no less indignant that such things could take place at a time when 'the people are to be forced to pay more respect to the law by an anti-revolutionary measure; when scarcely a week goes by without the foundation stone of a new church being laid; and when social democracy is reproached for having a philosophy which offends against all morality and good sense'.[297] Maximilian Harden sharpened his pen to castigate the court as an obsolete establishment imposing itself 'like a mythological fossil . . . on to modern times'. The court scandal had shown up the 'whole danger' of an institution which 'keeps a modern ruler in the daintily tied bonds of a defunct rococo constraint', he wrote in *Die Zukunft*.[298] 'Berlin society', Philipp Eulenburg commented from Vienna in 1895, 'has probably never been as vulnerable to public criticism as now. Torn apart into factions which accuse each other of perpetrating the filthy anonymous attacks, it bears the very imprint of decay.'[299] It is not impossible that this scandal, which was discussed throughout the press and in countless sensational pamphlets,[300] even had an influence on the development of psychoanalysis. At any rate at the very time when Sigmund Freud recognised the power of the human sexual drive, numerous observers of the affair expressed very similar ideas. Thus Waldersee commented that the scandal had afforded 'sad insights into the highest circles in Berlin'. He was as convinced as ever, he wrote, 'that most of the numerous persons involved have a guilty conscience; each knows sordid stories about the other; they have made enemies of each other and now they are all as frightened as each other'.[301] And Charlotte Meiningen, Wilhelm II's sister, who had of course herself been suspected of involvement in the anonymous letters, expressed her sense of foreboding when she wrote: 'You cannot imagine the lies, the dirt, the nastiness of which there is now documentary evidence. And they came from the grandest people at court, and the leading figures of the *haute volée*! A sign of our times! Certainly sad and wretched enough. I shudder to think what harm humanity can do.'[302]

# CHAPTER TWENTY-THREE

# The Kaiser and the 'Newest Course'

## THE APPOINTMENT OF 'UNCLE CHLODWIG' AS REICH CHANCELLOR AND MINISTER-PRESIDENT

On 26 October 1894 Kaiser Wilhelm II sent a telegram from Potsdam to Prince Chlodwig zu Hohenlohe-Schillingsfürst, Statthalter of Alsace-Lorraine, reading: 'Request Your Highness to come here at once by the next express train and to bring Herr von Köller. Matters of importance to the Reich are concerned. Wilhelm I. R.'[1] Three days earlier, when he went to Liebenberg to shoot, Wilhelm had announced to his host Philipp Eulenburg the 'happy ending of the *ninth* crisis!', thus indicating that he still counted on both the Reich Chancellor, Count von Caprivi, and the Prussian Minister-President and Minister of the Interior, Count Botho Eulenburg, remaining in office. Not until the latter appeared at Liebenberg on 24 October to ask to be relieved of his duties did the Kaiser gradually realise that he would have to think of a successor for both posts. 'I have seldom seen him so helpless', commented Philipp Eulenburg in his diary.[2] How did Wilhelm II's choice come to fall on the 75-year-old Hohenlohe-Schillingsfürst, of all people? The Prince had been Bavarian Minister-President and Foreign Minister at the time of the foundation of the Reich (1866–70); but now, afflicted with infirmities of age and speech, a shrunken figure 'with his head bent to one side', he made a pitiful impression on all who saw him.[3] It is chiefly to Philipp Eulenburg's correspondence that we must look for further enlightenment.

The separation of the two highest offices, introduced in 1892 as an emergency solution, had been widely regarded from the outset as an arrangement that could not last. By the time open conflict broke out between Caprivi and Botho Eulenburg in the autumn of 1894 this view had been well and truly confirmed.

On 27 September the Baden envoy in Berlin, Eugen von Jagemann, reported that it was now clear that the divergence between the governmental hierarchies of the Reich and Prussia could not continue any longer; the press, he added, was talking of the forthcoming reunification of the two supreme offices and pointing to Philipp Eulenburg 'as the coming man, the only man to have any real influence on H.M. the Kaiser'.[4] At the same time the Grand Duke of Baden wrote from Lorraine to Philipp Eulenburg, who was with the Kaiser at Rominten at the time, urging that the 'functions of the Reich chancellor and the Prussian minister-president' should be reunited in one person; but that a new man would be required, for neither Caprivi nor Botho Eulenburg was fitted for both posts. In the whole of Germany there was only one statesman who stood above party and had 'a broad, clear vision, wise foresight and great firmness as a leader', and that was the Statthalter at Strassburg, Prince Chlodwig zu Hohenlohe-Schillingsfürst. He should become Reich Chancellor and Minister-President of Prussia. But since it was no longer possible for one person to manage the affairs of the Prussian state and those of the Reich on his own, Hohenlohe, who was old and must be spared, would have to have a 'vice-chancellor' and 'vice-minister-president' under him, who would later rise to become Reich chancellor and minister-president. For this post of vice-chancellor and vice-minister-president *cum jure succedendi* Philipp Eulenburg himself was the only possible candidate, the Grand Duke maintained.[5]

When news of this suggestion reached Bernhard von Bülow in Rome via a letter from Eulenburg, he immediately objected that Hohenlohe was too old to bear so great a responsibility; furthermore, as a Bavarian and former Minister-President of Bavaria he was not a suitable person to take over the Prussian minister-presidency. Bülow therefore adapted the Grand Duke of Baden's plan, suggesting that the supreme leadership of the country should be entrusted to *three* men: Prince Hohenlohe (either the Statthalter or his cousin Prince Hermann zu Hohenlohe-Langenburg) as Reich chancellor, Philipp Eulenburg as vice-chancellor and Botho Eulenburg as Prussian minister-president.[6] It was clear, however, that such a triumvirate would only increase the impression of the weakness of the Reich Chancellor.[7] With the fall of Botho and the (only too understandable) refusal of Philipp Eulenburg to take on high office in the harsh political limelight of Berlin, this proposed combination in any case came to nothing.

During the Kaiser's visit to Liebenberg Philipp Eulenburg was forced to recognise, after his cousin had announced his intention of resigning, that there was now no longer any prospect of the reconciliation for which the Kaiser still hoped between Botho and Caprivi. He therefore warned the Kaiser that it would be necessary to find a new man for both posts, which would not be easy, for this person must be 'neither Conservative nor Liberal . . . neither Ultramontane nor Radical . . . neither a churchman nor an atheist' – an 'impossible mythical creature', as the Kaiser remarked. Eulenburg went on to tell him that the Grand Duke of Baden had recently recommended Prince Chlodwig zu Hohenlohe-Schillingsfürst 'as a transition to someone else, who would have to be found'. The Kaiser seized on the idea at once and decided to write to Hohenlohe, as there could be no question of Caprivi staying on without Botho Eulenburg.[8] The very next day Philipp Eulenburg received from his cousin August a telegram which confirmed his supposition: 'Both going. The watchword is Chlodwig.'[9]

In telegraphing to Hohenlohe on 26 October Wilhelm not only asked the Statthalter to take the next express train to Berlin and to bring his Under-Secretary of State, Ernst Matthias von Köller, but also invited both men to stay at the Neues Palais. When Alexander, the Prince's younger son, who had also hurried to Potsdam, saw the magnificent apartments in the palace his first impression was of a beautiful cage in which his father was to be imprisoned.[10] At the same time Prince Hohenlohe received a letter from his close friend in the Foreign Office, Friedrich von Holstein, who strongly urged him not to accept the post of Reich chancellor definitely '*unless all your conditions are fulfilled with regard to government appointments*'.[11] In order to ensure that his advice was heard the Geheimrat had travelled out to Magdeburg to meet the Prince.[12] The actions of Wilhelm II and Holstein on 26 October 1894 mark the beginning of a conflict between the Kaiser and the Wilhelmstrasse which was to overshadow the next two and a half years, ending in the spring of 1897 with the victory of the Kaiser over the Reich Chancellor, the secretaries of state and the Prussian ministers. And it was indeed the control of public appointments, as will become evident, that proved the decisive weapon in the hands of the crown.

On his arrival at the Neues Palais Hohenlohe began by pointing out to the Kaiser the considerations which weighed against his taking over the Reich chancellorship and the Prussian minister-presidency respectively: '1. Age, poor memory, illness. 2. Poor public speaker. 3. Unfamiliarity with Prussian laws and politics. 4. Not a soldier. 5. Insufficient means. I could probably manage without the Statthalter's salary, but not in Berlin. I shall be ruined. My Russian connections [Princess Hohenlohe]. I have been in public life for almost thirty years, am seventy-five years old and do not wish to start something which I know will be too much for me.'[13] The Prince's wife Marie, who had inherited large estates in Western Russia, made a fruitless attempt to frustrate the appointment of her husband as Reich chancellor by sending a telegram to the Kaiserin, a niece of Chlodwig Hohenlohe. Auguste Viktoria merely wired back with a phrase that perhaps said more than she intended: 'The Prince is sacrificing himself for the Kaiser and the Reich . . .'[14] The Kaiser must nevertheless have promised the

Prince on this first occasion, in return for his acceptance of the chancellorship, to arrange for the 'removal of the financial difficulties' at the expense of the crown, by which means he was later able to secure Hohenlohe's dependence on him.[15] Soon after this he informed the new Reich Chancellor that he intended to address him as 'Du' and to treat him as his uncle, which 'of course' would be a one-sided arrangement only.[16]

In the confusion of the crisis Wilhelm seems at first to have intended to maintain the division between the supreme offices in the Reich and in Prussia and to appoint Heinrich von Boetticher minister-president of Prussia, for in his first interview with Hohenlohe he stipulated that Köller, who was designated for the post of Prussian interior minister, should become 'minister-president later . . . instead of Boetticher'. Boetticher's promotion, however, was opposed by Holstein, who wanted him 'out of the way' completely. After further negotiations with Holstein on the one hand and Wilhelm and Lucanus, the Chief of the Civil Cabinet, on the other, Hohenlohe recorded laconically: 'We'll leave Boetticher where he is, since Köller refuses and there is no one else.'[17] Wilhelm was able to telegraph to his grandmother in England in the late afternoon of 28 October the glad news that 'Uncle Chlodwig Hohenlohe has accepted the reunited post of Chancellor and President of Ministry. The outward policy remains exactly the same as it was before.'[18] There was no further reference to the idea of a vice-chancellor and a vice-minister-president.

Prince Hohenlohe also succeeded in appointing some of his younger relatives to provide necessary reinforcement for his team. Since Karl Goering, the former head of the Reich Chancellery, had resigned with Caprivi, Holstein suggested to Hohenlohe that the Vortragender Rat Heinrich von Günther be promoted to head of the Reich Chancellery and Hohenlohe's son Alexander, who had been a Free Conservative deputy in the Reichstag since 1893, appointed second-in-command of this small department.[19] Instead of Günther, Hohenlohe decided to appoint Freiherr Kurt von Wilmowski, who had hitherto worked in the Prussian Ministry of Agriculture, as head of the Reich Chancellery, while Alexander Hohenlohe was brought into the Foreign Office with the pro forma rank of counsellor; his task was to support his father in all his duties, 'like a kind of crown prince'.[20] Count Clemens von Schönborn-Wiesentheid, a cavalry captain whose brother had been married to Prince Hohenlohe's deceased daughter Stephanie, was also formally appointed to the Foreign Office, although he actually served as a personal adjutant to the new Reich Chancellor. Cardinal Gustav zu Hohenlohe, the Chancellor's brother – another brother was a member of the Prussian Upper House, a third was Senior Master of the Court at the Habsburg court – wrote to one of the federal princes giving equal weight to the prospects of success and failure facing the new regime: 'God grant Clodwig [sic] patience and good

36. Prince Chlodwig zu Hohenlohe-Schillingsfürst, Reich Chancellor 1894–1900

health. The honour is great but so is the burden, and I am worried about him, although I am also very glad that he has such an exalted post, and that he will be able to do much good and avert many an evil.'[21] For Waldersee it was more than doubtful that Hohenlohe was 'at all the right man' to overcome the difficult situation in which the Reich found itself. He was certainly 'wise, experienced, very cautious and perfectly suited to conduct a skilful defensive action. But that is not what is needed now', for it had become noticeable lately 'that from all sides dissatisfaction is focused on H.M.'.[22]

In spite of the assurances that he had received from Wilhelm the elderly Prince soon suspected that it had been 'perhaps a mistake, after all', to have yielded to the pressure put on him by the Kaiser. Alexander Hohenlohe, who knew the 'world of politics and the court at Berlin' well, openly admitted that his father lacked the necessary 'ruthless energy . . . without which a Reich chancellor cannot ward off his numerous political opponents and jealous enemies'. Chlodwig Hohenlohe did not have 'the initiative and the strength which the statesman there must possess in order to carry through his policy in parliament'. But the 75-year-old especially lacked the physical stamina 'to survive the gruelling life at the court of such a restless and self-willed monarch as the young Kaiser, who had ruled for only a few years'. Prince Alexander feared for his elderly father, who would now be 'exposed to the dangers and acts of malice' which were unavoidably bound up with the post of Reich chancellor. 'I sometimes felt as if I were sitting on the box next to an old coachman who could no longer get a proper grip on the reins in his hands, and yet I was not permitted to intervene and take the reins and whip out of his hands', he later recalled. It was abundantly clear to the Chancellor's son that those who had worked on the Kaiser behind the scenes to obtain his appointment wanted the post of chancellor to be held only by a man who would be a tool in their hands. 'I soon saw that his official life would from now on be a gruelling, day-to-day struggle against open attacks and intrigues, and even more from hidden sources; that in this milieu the vilest means and the most poisonous weapons were put to use and that a man like him, who . . . was not belligerent by nature . . . , must soon be defeated by the poisonous newts and toads among whom he found himself.'[23] That Hohenlohe saw himself as a 'transition to someone else' is clear from the mere fact that he extracted a promise from the Kaiser to guarantee his pension even if he were obliged to resign within two years.[24]

## THE NEW MINISTERS

Just as they had done at the time of Bismarck's resignation in March 1890, after the fall of Caprivi and Botho Eulenburg, the Prussian ministers met on 27 October 1894 at Boetticher's house, and as before they discussed the crucial question of whether they could exert a collective influence on the formation of the new government, or would simply have to accept the will of the monarch. The Minister of Ecclesiastical Affairs, Dr Robert Bosse, expressed the opinion 'that we should all place our portfolios at His Majesty's disposal in the most loyal manner', while Boetticher (exactly as four and a half years earlier) pointed out that such a step 'was not the Prussian way and that we could not cause the Kaiser trouble at such a difficult time'. He informed his seven ministerial colleagues that the Kaiser had already summoned Hohenlohe and Köller to Potsdam and had decided to put an end to the division of offices – 'the root of all evil'. Bosse insisted that the ministers at least had the right to record their approval of the monarch's decisions regarding appointments, which Boetticher could not deny; but he insisted that the fact that the ministers had this right should not hinder the monarch from 'selecting and appointing His ministers personally'. The ministers were dismayed, however, to hear from the Minister of Agriculture, Wilhelm von Heyden-Cadow, that 'the not-yet-appointed future Minister of the Interior von Köller, on the instructions of the likewise not-yet-appointed future Minister-President Prince Hohenlohe', had put it to him that he should hand in his resignation. Bosse complained bitterly in early November of his colleagues' refusal to resign *en bloc* as he had suggested. 'Now the Ministry of State is acquiring an entirely different character from before, over our heads. But now it is too late . . .'[25]

In telegraphing his orders to Hohenlohe on 26 October to bring with him to Berlin the Under-Secretary of State responsible for the interior administration of the Reich province of Alsace-Lorraine, Ernst Matthias von Köller, the Kaiser had pre-empted the choice of the new Prussian minister of the interior. His intention from the outset was evidently to create a counterweight to the Catholic, liberal, South German Reich Chancellor in the person of the arch-conservative Köller. On 26 October Wilhelm told the Bavarian, Baden and Württemberg envoys that Köller was 'one of my staunchest Prussian Conservatives'.[26] With the appointment of this 'typical' Prussian Junker, as Alexander Hohenlohe rightly perceived, his father's government had acquired from the very outset 'an unpleasant appearance which did not accord with his political views nor with his entire political record'. 'My fears were later proved right to an even greater extent than I had anticipated', he wrote in his memoirs.[27] Even Waldersee, who in principle shared the Interior Minister's conservative standpoint, commented only a few weeks after his appointment that he thought Köller 'completely unsuited to his position'.[28] Köller's assumption of the role of the Kaiser's special representative in the Ministry of State was to lead to the first major government crisis of the 'Newest Course' before long.[29]

Although Prince Hohenlohe was unable to prevent the appointment of an arch-conservative Minister of the Interior, he was successful in resisting the equally right-wing candidates proposed by the Kaiser for the Ministries of Agriculture and Justice. Wilhelm was intent on appointing the Regierungspräsident of Breslau, Dr Georg von Heydebrand und der Lasa, 'personally known' to the Kaiser and brother of the future leader of the German Conservative Party, as the new minister of agriculture. 'He was active in Königsberg for a long time', the Kaiser wrote; he 'knows the agrarian campaign and its antics through and through, is himself a very great landowner and always behaved very correctly and calmly during the great agrarian agitation. He is fresh and vigorous, and a very suitable person.'[30] The previous day Hohenlohe had proposed the moderate Oberpräsident of Posen, Freiherr Hugo von Wilamowitz-Möllendorf, for the post and was most unwilling to accept the extreme right-wing Heydebrand as a member of his administration, particularly as the latter's superior, Oberpräsident Prince Hermann von Hatzfeldt-Trachenberg, described him as 'domineering, brusque and . . . very conceited' and commented ironically that he would be ideal as minister of the interior if one were aiming to stir up a constitutional conflict and as minister of agriculture if one wished to introduce a state monopoly on grain.[31] Hohenlohe therefore rejected Wilhelm's proposal with unusual firmness, on the grounds that Heydebrand was 'too much of a

Conservative Party man' who, combined with Köller, would create too strong a reactionary bias in the Ministry of State, thereby alienating all the other parties. 'If Heydebrand is taken on, I shall have to go', he resolutely declared. 'All my life I have been regarded, and have acted, as a moderate Liberal. I cannot become a Conservative Agrarian at the end of my life.'[32] On 6 November, when Hohenlohe came to see him at the Neues Palais, the Kaiser gave up his advocacy of Heydebrand after the Prince had argued 'with resounding success' that his appointment would be tantamount to a 'pater peccavi' on the part of the Kaiser vis-à-vis the agrarian movement.[33] Kaiser and Chancellor finally agreed on the Landesdirektor at Hanover, Ernst Freiherr von Hammerstein-Loxten, who had been suggested by the Oberpräsident of the province, the National Liberal Rudolf von Bennigsen. Hammerstein was also regarded, however, as 'such a determined agrarian' that even Germany's ally Austria-Hungary expected him to introduce an unacceptably protectionist tariff policy.[34]

Like Heyden, Prussian Minister of Justice Ludwig Hermann von Schelling was called on to hand in his resignation at this time of crisis. But while Hohenlohe had been responsible for the departure of the Minister of Agriculture, the dismissal of Schelling was entirely the work of the Kaiser, who sent the Chief of the Civil Cabinet to the Minister armed with the notorious blue letter. Hohenlohe begged the Kaiser to leave Schelling in office at least until the completion of his fifty years of service in December, but his request was curtly refused.[35] Wilhelm demanded the appointment of Hermann von Tessendorf, who had acted with extreme severity against the Centre Party and the Social Democrats during the Bismarck era. The Secretary of State of the Reich Justice Office, Arnold Nieberding, warned that the appointment of Tessendorf as Prussian minister of justice would be interpreted as 'signifying the introduction of harsh repression of the press, political associations and the right of public assembly, using all possible means'.[36] The newly appointed Reich Chancellor strongly urged the Kaiser to give up the idea of Tessendorf and instead to consider appointing the Director of the Reichsbank, Richard Koch, as minister of justice. Wilhelm abruptly turned down this request too. In his usual imperious style he wrote on Hohenlohe's submission: 'Koch is not the right man to reform the totally deplorable condition of the Prussian judiciary with the necessary ruthlessness and determination. His character is not suited for a ministerial post. Tessendorf must regain control over the law courts of Prussia and cleanse the Augean stables . . . I decided to appoint him justice minister fifteen months ago. The most reliable investigators have described him as the right man . . . Furthermore it is completely against my principles to appoint someone who is unknown to me to a Ministry, as I must always know exactly what I am letting myself in for.'[37] Hohenlohe therefore found himself compelled to offer the Ministry of Justice to Tessendorf. The latter was realistic enough, however, to see that as probably the most hated man in Germany he would face opposition from all parties. He refused the post. Hohenlohe now hesitantly suggested the President of the High Court at Celle, Karl Heinrich von Schönstedt, although he thought at first that Schönstedt 'might not satisfy His Majesty's requirements'. But Wilhelm declared himself willing to accept Schönstedt as minister of justice and worked harmoniously with him until 1905.[38]

Of crucial significance for the political conflicts between the Kaiser and the Reich administration over the next two and a half years was the decision in October 1894 to keep on Adolf Marschall von Bieberstein as secretary of state at the Foreign Office. Since the clash between Marschall and the Flügeladjutant Kuno von Moltke over Bismarck's visit to the Berlin Schloss in January 1894 vigorous attempts had been made to turn the Kaiser against the Foreign Secretary, as Holstein informed Prince Hohenlohe on 26 October. Holstein considered Marschall indispensable, however, and declared that he himself would resign if Marschall were forced to leave. Moreover in several letters to Philipp Eulenburg, as well as in his letter to Hohenlohe at this time, the Privy Councillor advocated the appointment of Marschall as Prussian minister without portfolio, arguing that it was 'a matter of political survival' for Hohenlohe himself to have him in the Ministry of State as a counterweight to Miquel.[39] Hohenlohe finally succeeded not only in keeping the Badenese statesman at the Foreign Office – 'Marschall is to stay, because otherwise the Foreign Office will fall apart', he noted after a conversation with the Kaiser on 28 October[40] – but also in making him a member of the Prussian Ministry of State. Because of the elderly Prince's lack of skill at public speaking, Marschall's talent as an orator in both the Reichstag and the Prussian Landtag, as well as his good relations with the Centre Party, also helped ensure that he remained in office.[41] Many people even assumed that he would soon be appointed Reich secretary for the interior instead of Boetticher.[42] But only days later the Kaiser's hostile behaviour towards the Foreign Secretary made it plain that Wilhelm 'obviously wants to pick a quarrel with Marschall'.[43] On 17 November 1894 Holstein had to advise the new Chancellor to take over the responsibility for reporting to the Kaiser on foreign policy 'until Marschall's standing with H.M. improves'.[44] It soon became apparent that Wilhelm was no longer willing to work with either Marschall or Boetticher.

Finally, a new appointment also had to be made to Chlodwig Hohenlohe's erstwhile post as Statthalter of Alsace-Lorraine. Originally the Kaiser had intended to nominate the departing Prussian Minister-President, Botho Eulenburg, to this position, which was much sought after because of the high salary and generous funds for official expenses attached to it, but Hohenlohe was determined not to accept the chancellorship if Eulenburg became Statthalter.[45] A letter from

Philipp Eulenburg convinced the Kaiser that it would be wiser to send a South German prince like Carl Egon zu Fürstenberg (although he was married to a French Princess) or Hermann zu Hohenlohe-Langenburg, the Kaiserin's uncle, to Strassburg as Statthalter. With a characteristic telegram from the Kaiser — 'Have appointed you my Statthalter in Alsace-Lorraine. Refusal not possible. Wilhelm I. R.' — Hohenlohe-Langenburg ('Uncle Hermann' as the Kaiser called him) was given the posting and Botho Eulenburg was left empty-handed.[46]

In contrast, another idea of the new Reich Chancellor which he hoped — perhaps erroneously — would strengthen his position, above all at the imperial court, failed to come to fruition. This was the appointment of the Kaiser's friend Philipp zu Eulenburg as minister of the royal house in place of Wedell-Piesdorf. It is probably correct to assume that this thought had its origin in the Grand Duke of Baden's suggestion that the elderly Chancellor should be given the support of a vice-chancellor who would be expected to succeed him. A first attempt by the new Chancellor to suggest Philipp Eulenburg to the Kaiser as house minister was frustrated when Wilhelm expressed doubts 'as to whether Eulenburg had sufficient experience in financial management' — a remark from which Holstein concluded that the Kaiser 'does not think Phil. Eul. suitable to be house minister. That is just going too far for H.M., as far as money matters are concerned.'[47] What was more, Wilhelm had 'a decidedly guilty conscience' with regard to Botho Eulenburg and was playing with the idea of appointing him, rather than Philipp Eulenburg, in place of Wedell-Piesdorf, 'whom His Majesty has in fact long wished . . . to be rid of'.[48] After further negotiations Hohenlohe was able to remind the ambassador in Vienna in January 1895 that he had shared his views 'on the importance of this post for H.M.' and had assured him of his readiness to 'make the patriotic sacrifice and take over the House Ministry'.[49] Eulenburg laid down both financial and institutional conditions, acting initially as if he intended to accept the post; but in the end he had to recognise that his special friendship with the Kaiser would not survive daily dealings with him on an official footing, and he saw to it that the negotiations came to nothing.[50]

In looking back over these momentous decisions on political appointments made in the late autumn of 1894, one is struck above all by the element of chance and the lack of forethought which governed the choice of the new men for the highest offices. The new Reich Chancellor and Minister-President Hohenlohe-Schillingsfürst did not come under consideration at all until a few days before his appointment, when the Kaiser suddenly saw himself compelled by Botho Eulenburg's unexpected resignation to think of a successor for both him and Caprivi. Hohenlohe, who from the beginning was regarded only as a 'transition to someone else who will have to be found', had been suggested by the Grand Duke of Baden, but even he only considered Hohenlohe's appointment feasible in

conjunction with that of a younger statesman who would take over the two
highest offices after a few months or years. When this solution proved impossible because of Philipp Eulenburg's refusal to take on such a responsible office
Wilhelm II had recourse to the idea — we do not know who suggested it —
of appointing the ultra-conservative Köller as minister of the interior in order
to provide a Prussian counterbalance for the South German Reich Chancellor
and Minister-President. Apart from Hohenlohe himself Köller remained the
only minister whose selection in the autumn of 1894 can be attributed solely
to the Kaiser. As we have seen, Wilhelm's attempt to appoint another two
arch-conservatives, Heydebrand and Tessendorf, as ministers of agriculture
and justice respectively, was unsuccessful, although it was indicative of the
monarch's imperious and almost class-struggle-obsessed mood, with which the
new Reich Chancellor most certainly had to reckon in making his counter-
proposals (Hammerstein-Loxten and Schönstedt). In his negotiations, as a condition of his acceptance of the two supreme offices, Hohenlohe was not only able
to extract several material promises from the Kaiser but also to secure the appointment of his son Alexander as his permanent adviser and of Count Schönborn as
his personal adjutant. The choice of Prince Hermann zu Hohenlohe-Langenburg
as Statthalter must also be seen as an impulsive choice by the Kaiser after his wish
to reward Botho Eulenburg with this post had been frustrated by the new Chancellor's opposition. Lastly, Chlodwig Hohenlohe also succeeded, much against
the will of Wilhelm II, in keeping on Heinrich von Boetticher as secretary of
state of the interior and Adolf Freiherr Marschall von Bieberstein as secretary
of state at the Foreign Office. Both were to play a central role in the forthcoming
battle of the Wilhelmstrasse against the growing might of the Kaiser and his
entourage.

## THE KAISER AND THE HOHENLOHE GOVERNMENT

In what way had the relationship between the Kaiser and the executive shifted
as a result of the change of chancellor and ministers in October 1894? How much
power did Wilhelm II possess under the chancellorship of his wife's uncle; what
influence did he exercise on the formulation of German domestic and foreign
policy under the 'Newest Course'? How did the venerable Prince Hohenlohe
regard his responsibilities as Reich chancellor and minister-president — did he
see himself, in relation to the monarch, as supreme leader of the 'responsible
government' or rather as the executive agent of the imperial will? And what
role did the Prussian ministers and the secretaries of state of the Reich offices
play in these decisive years? Were they — either singly or collectively — willing
and able to take independent political decisions and to carry them through? The

answers that one is compelled to give to these questions on the basis of the very explicit contemporary sources are shocking and depressing even today.

As soon as the new Reich Chancellor took office Friedrich von Holstein had urged upon him the importance of firmness with the Kaiser, in order to bring about, at least in foreign policy, 'a change for the better *from the start*', for 'the way in which H.M. has gradually become accustomed to discuss policy with every Tom, Dick or Harry cannot be compatible in the long run with the orderly pursuit of business'.[51] Despite isolated acts of protest, however, Hohenlohe hesitated to offer any resistance to the Kaiser's craving for power. At the close of 1894 he reflected that his relationship with the Kaiser was still too new 'for me to climb up on my high horse and reproach him about his conduct'.[52] After six months in office his hopes of an improvement in his relations with the Kaiser had become very modest. 'Monarchs are human like others and have an inclination towards a comfortable life, in which one should disturb them only in emergencies', he observed.[53] Not without irony he wrote on 7 January 1895, in a letter to Eulenburg: 'In my relationship with His Majesty all is well. I do not take it amiss if His Majesty gets one of his valets to telegraph to the cipher office and orders a dispatch-rider to be sent to Petersburg in the evening. What is bad is that the little, silent, cautious Tsar will soon be several lengths ahead of our Kaiser in public opinion. But nothing can be done about it.'[54] In January 1896 he is said to have remarked: 'I have taken a firm decision not to get angry about anything and I let everything take its course. If I wanted to do anything else I would have to resign at least once a week.'[55] When he came under increasing pressure from Holstein in the next few months to put a stop to the interferences of the Kaiser, his Cabinet chiefs and Flügeladjutanten, the Reich Chancellor rejected the diplomat's demand with the telling argument that in the end he would rather resign 'than govern with the Kaiser in an unfriendly relationship. The purpose of my existence in the Reich chancellor's palace is after all none other than to prevent overhasty decisions. An independent regime, in which the Kaiser walks alongside as a defeated man, so to speak, is unthinkable with this sovereign. It is also against my nature.'[56] Nor had he any desire, Hohenlohe added, 'to take on the role of victor over the defeated Kaiser, as it were. That is not for me.'[57]

From the outset there were rumours of a change of chancellor,[58] and as early as 24 November 1894 the Austrian ambassador reported from Berlin: 'As far as the stability of the new regime is concerned, there is much pessimism here in general; . . . many people say [Hohenlohe] is only a stand-in and they think that Kaiser Wilhelm intends Count Philipp Eulenburg to take over this post in the foreseeable future.'[59] In the spring of 1895 Waldersee expressed the opinion 'that Hohenlohe has long since had enough and has often regretted taking on the position'.[60] Although he 'very often' avowed that he was 'of a different opinion from the Kaiser on many questions', he had 'given in completely and renounced any idea of independence'.[61] In fact all observers already agreed at this time that the new Chancellor was 'not much more than a nullity'.[62] 'Hohenlohe scarcely even attracts mockery any more. To be precise, he does not come into the reckoning at all. The Kaiser could not have chosen a more pitiful Chancellor', Waldersee commented damningly in May 1895.[63] A week later he noted in his diary: 'If the question were asked in the Reichstag: what is your opinion of Hohenlohe's chancellorship or of the Newest Course? the *unanimous* verdict would be one of incompetence. Such a state of affairs has never existed before, and yet I can see no sign of a change.'[64]

Through his informants at court and in the officer corps Waldersee also became aware of the elderly Chancellor's increasing financial dependence on the Kaiser: Hohenlohe had abused his position in order to win far-reaching concessions for his wife's Russian property. 'Furthermore he has also managed to take very good care of the numerous branches of the Hohenlohe family', the General recorded.[65] Indeed it is one of the most scandalous events of the third Reich Chancellor's term of office that the Kaiser, at Hohenlohe's instigation, secretly used crown funds to triple his official annual salary of 54,000 marks. On 15 December 1894 an anonymous letter appeared in the press according to which Hohenlohe was to receive 100,000 marks from the Kaiser to top up his salary. Although a denial had to be issued, Hohenlohe and Philipp Eulenburg continued to negotiate over the secret subsidy. 'I have to make it clear to the Kaiser that the poor Reich Chancellor must not be allowed to suffer from yet another burden as well as that of his work', Eulenburg emphasised in January 1895.[66] At the beginning of February he sent a letter to the Kaiser pointing out that the Reich chancellor's salary was 'really *disgracefully* small'. The Prince's financial difficulties were made still more acute by the unpredictability of his 'miserly' wife Princess Marie, although she was obliged to support their sons Moritz and Alexander and their wives. 'So this puts the old Prince under pressure', Eulenburg wrote. 'Unfortunately since the news of Your Majesty's gracious intentions mysteriously leaked out . . . it has become impossible to help the Prince as planned. But Your Majesty will no doubt graciously keep this situation in mind. When he agreed to make the sacrifice of coming to Berlin the Prince was reassured by the certainty that he would be *provided for* in material terms. This turn of events has greatly affected him. It is *impossible* for Your Majesty to help from Your own pocket because the family is so large. But unforeseen advantages might *occasionally* arise which could be directed towards the Prince.'[67] It is safe to assume that the much-criticised political weakness of the Reich Chancellor was bound up with his secret financial dependence on the Kaiser. It was not long before Holstein was complaining that 'Hohenlohe [is being] worked upon by his wife and son to do nothing that might threaten the Kaiser's goodwill towards the Hohenlohe family.'[68]

Waldersee wrung his hands in despair over the way in which the German Reich was being governed. He commented acidly that Wilhelm II had realised after only a few weeks that with Hohenlohe's appointment he had 'dug up a semi-corpse', and that his behaviour had become correspondingly imperious.[69] In February 1895 he noted gloomily that Hohenlohe had now been Reich Chancellor for more than three months and that it should have become clear where he was heading. In reality, however, 'no firm programme [had been] settled with the Kaiser', who was continuing 'to make policy decisions on his own initiative'.[70] In a letter to Verdy in April 1895 Waldersee again complained of the confusion and indecision of the government, produced on the one hand by the constant interference of the Kaiser and on the other by the completely passive attitude of Hohenlohe. 'The wavering back and forth will go on until a mighty row breaks out', he prophesied. 'I had thought that Hohenlohe would quietly assess the situation first, but then come forward with some programme or some recognisable aim. But that was an illusion. Now I am convinced that he is glad just to get through without a row, and accepts everything.'[71] With every month of Hohenlohe's chancellorship, Waldersee wrote, the general conviction was growing stronger 'that the Kaiser's personal intervention is chiefly to blame for the sad state of affairs in which we find ourselves'. 'Previously it was only hinted at, but now people say it more clearly: that he takes no notice of the opinions of the ministers, but that they completely submit to his wishes and opinions; if these took a *consistent* course it would be all right; but as they change, and often very rapidly, one would think that the ministers must be in an impossible position. But this is not the case, for these gentlemen always knuckle under. They certainly complain that the Kaiser is impossible to get along with . . . but they do not leave. If there were a Ministry which was united under the leadership of the Chancellor, and in which they supported each other, the Kaiser would also be different; but he is clever enough to see that he would draw the short straw in that case, and he positively enjoys playing off one minister against another.'[72] Again in February 1896 Waldersee recalled Marschall's remark during the opening ceremony of the Kaiser Wilhelm Canal at Kiel the previous summer: 'This is too much for anyone to bear: one thing today and another tomorrow, and again a few days later.' Waldersee himself considered that under the present circumstances the Reich Chancellor and the Foreign Secretary were in a 'degrading' position which they ought not to accept, 'all the more because the whole world knows how things are. The Kaiser is his own chancellor and has only compliant ministers.' As a result it was not surprising that there was 'widespread mistrust', he said.

'No mortal being can tell us what the future will bring; but one thing I know for sure: we have no purposeful, clear and consistent leadership, either at home or in foreign affairs.'[73] During the laying of the foundation stone of the memorial for Kaiser Wilhelm I in Berlin on 18 August 1895 Waldersee had the opportunity of speaking to many acquaintances about the confused state of both domestic and foreign politics. All were agreed about the dire state of affairs and declared that it could not go on. 'Everyone is disgruntled and chasing in different directions; the ministers criticise each other and work only for themselves. Whether in domestic or foreign policy, there are orders today and counter-orders tomorrow and something else again the day after.' The General went on to express the opinion that there was absolutely no prospect of a change for the better in the near future. 'We shall go on wavering about in the same way for a long time and we shall gradually sink even lower in the process.'[74]

There is no doubt that under Prince Hohenlohe's chancellorship neither he nor the Prussian Ministry of State but Kaiser Wilhelm II — together with his advisers at court — was the decisive political factor.[75] Even if his personal power did not reach its peak until after the great reshuffle of secretaries of state and ministers in the summer of 1897, the sources show clearly the extent to which, during the first three years of the 'Newest Course', he was already not only setting the general political course of the country, but also intervening, sometimes down to the smallest detail, at least in the particular areas which interested him, which included both domestic and foreign policy, military and naval matters, art, science and, not least, the economy. At Prökelwitz in 1895 he gave Philipp Eulenburg a clear exposition of his conception of the proper relationship between himself, the Reich chancellor and the Prussian Ministry of State. The Kaiser had declared quite distinctly, Eulenburg reported to the astonished Reich Chancellor on 24 May, 'that he *quite categorically* refused to tolerate any quarrelling, discord and divergence within the Ministry. It was for Your Highness to ensure this homogeneity; decisions upon the principles of government were his own and Your Highness's business alone — he would "throw out" those who presumed to have *personal* views. Only Your Highness had the right to take a view and express it to His Majesty; the individual ministers must limit themselves to following the principles laid down . . . His Majesty stated further that he relied upon Your Highness always to inform him immediately of anything that happened in the government in any sphere.'[76] It was around this time that the Kaiser commented 'in very forceful tones that He would not tolerate individual political action by ministers'. 'It was for *Him* alone to govern with his minister-president . . .'[77]

This method of government did not of course produce the kind of objective decision-making which the Reich and its population deserved, but a regime that was characterised by personal passion and impulse, by court intrigue, backstairs influences and interdepartmental rivalries. Already in February 1895 the Foreign Secretary was complaining bitterly that it was 'a nice state of affairs that one constantly has to contend not only with foreign states but also with H.M. and his irresponsible advisers'.[78] At the same time Friedrich von Holstein recorded with consternation that 'the Kaiser is governing *with* the Cabinets *against* the constitutional organs of government. There is no one to act as intermediary between the latter and the Kaiser, as Wilmowski and Lehndorff did under Kaiser Wilhelm I. Without anyone to mediate there is bound to be a clash. I do not deny that I should like to be gone before the clash comes. *After* the clash, i.e. Hohenlohe's resignation, the Kaiser will go for a trial of strength. The more important federal princes, led by Bavaria, will oppose him and he will fail. That will destroy the Kaiser's prestige and he will be faced with a period of humiliation. *I* can do nothing to prevent it. For His Majesty now follows the advice of Hahnke against Bronsart (Minister of War), of Senden against [Admiral] Hollmann and of Lucanus against the whole Ministry of State.'[79]

Holstein could not believe his eyes or ears when he learned that on the occasion of his birthday in January 1895 the Kaiser intended to confer 'the rank of ministers of state' on his Oberhofmarschall, Count August zu Eulenburg, and the Chief of the Civil Cabinet, Hermann von Lucanus. The Ministry of State, without meeting for consultation, immediately and unanimously took the view that this was not permissible, as 'minister of state' was an *office* and not a rank or title, and Hohenlohe only just managed to put a stop to the Kaiser's plan. The Privy Councillor's verdict on the affair was that 'if the idea had been carried out the Hohenlohe regime would probably have succumbed from the sheer weight of ridicule. To have a fawning courtier as a minister — that has never happened in Prussian history, not even in the absolutist period.' He commented with deep concern that this affair was 'typical'. 'The Kaiser, who has no idea of constitutional law, can be persuaded to take the most utterly incredible decisions through the combined efforts of A[ugust] E[ulenburg], Hahnke and the apothecary [Lucanus].' He added sarcastically: 'Instead of minister of state August E. is being made lieutenant-general and Lucanus is getting the rank of "behind the ministers of state".'[80] A few weeks later Philipp Eulenburg surprised Holstein with a report on the relative power of the court officials, drawing particular attention to the rivalry between the increasingly influential Lucanus on the one hand and the Kaiser's military suite on the other. A strong movement against Lucanus had developed in the Kaiser's entourage, he claimed. '*He alone* is held responsible for *everything* the Kaiser says and all his political utterances . . . There is nothing that is not blamed on Lucanus. The bad mood among the maison militaire and other people in the imperial entourage has not sprung from any wish to put a particular successor in his place. There was *never* any question of that. I attribute it principally to the ever more powerful position of Lucanus.' Any attempt to get rid of the Chief of the Civil Cabinet would only have the opposite effect. 'His Majesty has grown *too* accustomed to him not to treat *any action* against him as a "nasty intrigue" and to strengthen his position still more.'[81]

By the early summer of 1896 the numerous ministerial crises and scandals were causing highly critical comments in the press and parliament about Kaiser Wilhelm II's style of government. People spoke 'quite openly about illegal influences on the Kaiser, in particular Hahnke and Lukanus [sic] and Flügel Adjutanten in general', noted Waldersee, who was forced to admit that there was 'much truth' in this criticism. 'The Kaiser wants to rule autocratically', he wrote on 3 May 1896, 'and in fact does so fully in military matters and foreign affairs; he only rarely intervenes in other areas, but there too his will is supposed to be paramount. Of course a great deal of hostility is building up against the Cabinet chiefs . . . The fact that other third persons also often join in the discussions with the Kaiser is beyond question. If Hohenlohe were an energetic man he would have gone long ago or else he would have insisted on a change.'[82] All such attacks on the irresponsible advisers were 'in fact directed against the Kaiser', Waldersee rightly observed.[83] Berlin was in a state of 'hopeless confusion', he commented not long afterwards. 'Hohenlohe is exhausted in every sense; he would like to get out as soon as possible and he lets everything take its own course. The ministers are each going their own ways, and are no doubt using the press in their own particular interests too. None of this seems to upset the Kaiser and he is only anxious to enable good old Uncle Chlodwig to stay on.'[84] A year later the mayor of Altona, Giese, reported after a visit to Berlin: 'No minister knows anything about the others; each claims that he does not know what the Kaiser actually wants; the Kaiser no longer communicates; Hohenlohe is completely indolent etc.'[85] This, then, is what the government of the Kaiserreich looked like from within, five years after Bismarck's dismissal. Only rarely were outsiders able to catch a glimpse of Wilhelm's autocratic style and the disturbing compliance of his ministers.

### THE OPENING OF THE KAISER WILHELM CANAL IN JUNE 1895

The international celebrations to mark the opening of the Kiel Canal in June 1895, that is to say exactly seven years after his accession, provided a particularly clear illustration of the personal power of Wilhelm II in action, working in conjunction with the rapidly increasing commercial and industrial power of Germany. Not only at the ceremony itself, when he was the natural focus of attention during the laying of the foundation stone of the memorial at the eastern end of the canal, but also in the preparations for the gigantic and costly celebrations in Hamburg and Kiel, he played a dominant and decisive role. Even the technical problems which arose during the construction of the Kaiser Wilhelm Canal were overcome rather more rapidly than the experts thought advisable as a result of an imperial command. Waldersee, who as commanding general at Altona was responsible for security measures — the fear of assassination attempts being unusually great because so many prominent public figures would be present — commented in April 1895, 'the Kaiser has overcome the opposition of the technicians by giving definite orders that the canal absolutely must be ready at the beginning of June ... But there is now great anxiety as to whether the procession through the canal on 20 June will be a success.' Countless pessimists claimed that the procession would not work, and after the event considerable damage was indeed discovered, caused by the premature opening procession through the canal.[86]

In March 1895 the Kaiser summoned a conference to discuss the opening ceremony without first approaching the long-serving Secretary of the Reich Office of the Interior, Heinrich von Boetticher. His action led to a letter of protest from Hohenlohe, who had to ask Wilhelm to receive Boetticher alone, before the conference, in recognition of his services in the construction of the canal. Boetticher complained bitterly of the influence of Plessen and the two Moltkes in the Kaiser's entourage, who drove the sovereign 'to more and more extreme ideas' and demanded enormous sums of money — there was talk of two million.[87] The Kaiser replied on 30 March to the Reich Chancellor's letter with the sarcastic mockery that characterised his manner with 'Uncle Chlodwig': 'Dear Uncle, I received your letter last night when my night-shirt was already flapping round me and I thought it meant we were about to mobilise! The contents were reassuring, however. It shall be as you wish. Instead of taking umbrage, by my reckoning the gentle Heinrich ought to be grateful that we want to help him carry the burden and share it out! Your letter quite rightly emphasises his great services for the canal, the project he lives for!, and far be it from me to belittle them. On the contrary! But in order that he can *devote himself entirely to his canal*, which he must, it is best that he should not concern himself with other things, otherwise the Privy Councillorish mind will be troubled with distractions which will have a harmful effect. The mere fact that in answer to almost all the questions of principle which were put to him from the naval side concerning the canal he could supply only inadequate information or none at all shows that he still needs to acquire a thorough knowledge of his "pet project". This is all the more evident because since we were both in Kiel in November 94 I have asked Boetticher to tell me in broad outline how the programme should be arranged, as he gave the end of June as the deadline! From November until now he has had 4 months! All the questions concerning the *canal* could have been committed to paper and submitted to me long since! From what you tell me about the two representatives of Lloyd's – the gentle Heinrich's doubts about their being called in on financial grounds – I gather that you support my summoning of a committee under you! This *doubtfulness* is precisely what is wrong with him and threatens to expose us to ridicule! He has so many doubts he never gets anywhere! This Lloyd's question could have been settled months ago by a short discussion with the gentlemen, so why was it not done? Now is the time to act, so I implore you to harden your heart against all objections! *It must be done!* If you can make the gentle Heinrich see it in the light of co-operation he will be content not to have to bear the enormous responsibility on his own! Let him worry about his canal and his ships and guests; we shall take care of the rest! Your devoted nephew Wilhelm I. R.'[88]

It was in the same autocratic spirit that Wilhelm conducted the meeting which he convened on 1 April 1895 to plan the opening ceremony. It was attended by civilian statesmen (Reich Chancellor Prince Hohenlohe, Secretary of State for the Interior von Boetticher, Prussian Minister of Public Works Karl von Thielen, Reich Postmaster-General Heinrich von Stephan and the Oberpräsident of Schleswig-Holstein, Georg Steinmann), admirals (Navy Secretary Friedrich von Hollmann, Commanding Admiral Wilhelm von Knorr, Chief of the Naval Cabinet Gustav Freiherr von Senden-Bibran), generals (Chief of the Military Cabinet Wilhelm von Hahnke, and Commanding General in Altona Alfred Count von Waldersee), Senior Marshal of the Court Count August zu Eulenburg, Albert Ballin, the owner of the Hamburg Packet line, a representative of the Bremen shipping company Lloyd and a landowner as a representative of agriculture. The Kaiser began by drawing attention to the difficulties which would be created in Kiel by the arrival of large crowds of people for the opening of the canal, and recommended the establishment of a committee with three subcommittees to take responsibility for accommodation, food and entertainment for the visiting masses. With the sole exception of the military precautions suggested by Waldersee, the Kaiser raised objections to the suggestions made by all the other participants, and his views were accepted. When Boetticher pointed out that two million marks would be required for the celebrations but that the Reichstag would not approve such a sum, the Kaiser ordered that it should be requested nonetheless. To Boetticher's suggestion that seventy-five members of the Reichstag should be invited the Kaiser responded that this was far too few, whereupon the figure was raised to 150. The elderly Reich Chancellor made 'a very pitiable impression' on Waldersee during the negotiations. As the General recorded, only Albert Ballin had the courage to stand up to the Kaiser in defence of his own point of view, although even he did not succeed in getting his way. In a particularly 'painful scene' Wilhelm II declared that the German princes must be accommodated on board the Lloyd's of Bremen ship during the celebrations, whereupon Ballin, as representative of the Hamburg Packet, objected that this would be a 'very painful' and 'very severe' blow to Hamburg and its company, which was providing two ships. The Kaiser 'flatly' refused Ballin's strong plea for a change of plan, remarking that he had given his word to Lloyd's of Bremen some time ago. 'The Kaiser then explained to Herr Ballin that he was quite wrong. Hamburg was extraordinarily favoured in having the honour of putting up the Kaiser himself (which is costing Hamburg over a million marks), in addition to which the *ambassadors* would be in a packet ship, and since they represented the sovereigns the Hamburg Packet was in fact receiving preferential treatment!!! When Ballin asked for the princes to be divided up, the Kaiser objected, very kindly for all those present, that such gentlemen could not be mixed with other people; they had to keep to their own society!' In describing the scene Waldersee commented that he thought 'everyone felt how unfair the Kaiser was being towards Hamburg, from which he was asking such large sacrifices; but unfortunately he has a talent for offending people in a quite extraordinary way'. Summing up his impressions of the day, the General wrote: 'the Kaiser's speech [was] very clear and his arguments, as usual, quite skilful, but the whole thing was characterised by a certain cursoriness which was probably very noticeable to all those present; there had no doubt been preliminary discussions with younger people who lack judgement . . . Some very extraordinary ideas were expressed.'[89]

Wilhelm presided over a further meeting to discuss the opening of the canal, this time in Kiel, which confirmed Waldersee's worst fears about the attitude of Ministers Boetticher, Köller and Hammerstein-Loxten to the Kaiser. He had expected nothing else, he said, than that Boetticher would say exactly what the Kaiser wanted to hear; but he had thought otherwise of Köller. And yet he too 'echoed the Kaiser's every word, nor did he have any scruples in talking of the agitation stirred up by the Conservatives. Hammerstein was perhaps the best of the three, but his desire to please the Kaiser was also obvious; none of the three let slip a single word, a single hint of an opinion differing from the Kaiser's; oh what a sorry trio!' It had been very depressing for him to observe yet again 'how people agree with everything the Kaiser says and no one makes even the most diffident attempt to put forward a different view'. Köller had particularly annoyed him with his way of 'persistently pushing himself forward' and submitting proposals to the Kaiser instead of taking decisions himself. After the meeting Waldersee recorded that the naval officers present complained that the Kaiser 'wants to decide everything himself and never alters his own opinions'.[90] In May 1895 he noted in his diary that he was 'genuinely sorry for the gentlemen from the navy, but especially the canal authorities. The problems mostly arise from the fact that the Kaiser wants to decide everything himself and gives hasty orders which soon turn out to be impracticable, and that too many authorities want to have a voice in the matter. Minister Boetticher, the Comm[anding] Admiral, the Chief of the Naval Cabinet, the Ob[er]Hofmarschall's office, Minister Thielen, the Minister of the Interior etc.: each wants to have his say and is partly under an obligation to do so anyway; sometimes agreement is reached with great difficulty, only to be overturned by the Kaiser.'[91]

Shortly before the opening celebrations Waldersee succeeded in preventing the Kaiser from committing a serious *faux pas*. The monarch had expressed the wish to be received on arrival in Hamburg by a guard of honour at the station and another at the town hall, and to be escorted by a squadron of Hussars. Waldersee had to point out to the Military Cabinet that Hamburg was not part of Prussia but a sovereign state which had invited the Kaiser and the other German ruling princes, and therefore had the right to decide for itself how it would receive them. Waldersee assumed, probably not without reason, that both Wilhelm and Hahnke would be annoyed by his intervention, but they conceded the point nonetheless and informed the city of Hamburg through its envoy in Berlin that the sovereign would agree to the arrangements made by the Senate. Even the official reception of the German ruling princes, 'which the Kaiser had been very much against', had now been approved by him, Waldersee recorded. The city fathers were relieved, for their part, having feared that a conflict with the Kaiser might develop out of this question. The German princes were also worried that 'the Kaiser might act inconsiderately towards the federal state of Hamburg'.[92] In constantly making unfriendly remarks about Hamburg and its mayors, Waldersee observed disapprovingly, Wilhelm was completely failing to recognise that the city was taking the greatest possible trouble to give him a magnificent and very expensive reception.[93] Oberpräsident of Schleswig-Holstein Georg Steinmann later felt compelled to resign because the Kaiser persisted in treating him badly.[94]

The opening celebrations, staged at a cost of several million marks, were among the most magnificent ceremonies of the entire Wilhelmine era. 'It will be a more splendid gathering than has perhaps ever been seen and it should put the opening of the Suez Canal in the shade', Waldersee predicted in the spring.[95] The innumerable sovereigns, royalties and diplomats – including the future King George V of England, an Austrian Archduke and an Italian Prince – were invited to a luncheon in the Hamburg Zoological Gardens on 19 June, for the Kaiser had decided from the outset that the ceremony would begin in Hamburg; the city was reluctantly obliged to accept 'the inevitable'.[96] That evening, with a storm brewing, a great gala dinner took place in the unfinished town hall, presided over by the Kaiser who replied 'in suitable words' to a speech by the Mayor of Hamburg, Lehmann. After dinner, in pouring rain, the 'somewhat tipsy' guests were offered coffee on an island constructed for the occasion in the Alster lake at a cost of 700,000 marks, before being taken by train to Brunsbüttel and delivered to the ships – the Kaiser to the new white-and-gold *Hohenzollern* – in which they were to stay. The same night the ships, accompanied by cheering and brass band music, sailed down the Elbe to the canal. But as the convoy ran aground several times it did not arrive at Holtenau or Kiel until the later afternoon of 20 June. The weather was still very wet, so that the Navy Ball was 'dreadfully spoilt by rain'. On the morning of 21 June the ceremony of the laying of the foundation stone of the memorial at the Baltic Sea end of the canal took place. The Reich Chancellor escorted the Kaiser and Kaiserin to the podium, near which stood the sovereigns, ruling princes and other high office-holders. Hohenlohe read out the document that was to be placed in the foundation stone; the Bavarian Foreign Minister Freiherr von Crailsheim gave an address and handed the Kaiser the trowel; 'then all the designated people struck the stone with a hammer, after which I gave three cheers for the Kaiser', Hohenlohe wrote.[97] That evening a banquet for 1,050 people took place at Kiel, during which the Kaiser read out a lengthy speech written by Hohenlohe, Boetticher and Lucanus. It was warmly applauded. After dinner the Kaiser conversed 'very enthusiastically' with the French naval officers present, who were 'very surprised by the Kaiser's technical knowledge'; one of them said 'Votre Majesté parle comme un mécanicien.' Next day a great naval exercise was held, during which the German battleships sailed out in single line ahead towards Denmark to meet four other ships coming in the other direction. 'There was a lot of firing. After that had gone on for some time everyone returned to their previous anchorage for lunch', the Reich Chancellor noted drily, plainly relieved that there had been no assassination attempts during the celebrations.[98] The French and Russian fleets which had met in the Baltic and sailed in line ahead into the harbour at Kiel, keeping up a constant flow of reciprocal greetings, made themselves disagreeably conspicuous.[99] The 'shameless' spying activities of two Russian officers, who went around photographing all forts and batteries, also made a bad impression in Kiel and Wilhelm complained personally about them in a letter to the Tsar.[100] Holstein deplored the fact that as a result of the lavish celebrations French chauvinism, which had 'nodded off for lack of stimulus', was once again 'wide awake'. If the joint arrival of the two fleets proved to be symptomatic of a Franco-Russian alliance, he warned, 'they will also be keen to go on the attack soon'.[101] Waldersee, moreover, was full of contempt for Hinzpeter, who had said of the Kaiser during the celebrations that he was 'very good at making public appearances, but he can do nothing else', from which the

General concluded that Hinzpeter 'does not seem to be very much in favour with the Kaiser at the moment, or else he was trying to provoke others into making comments'.[102]

The lavish provisions made for the international press by order of Prussian Interior Minister von Köller, who had 'previously taken care to obtain the Kaiser's blessing' for them, were an indication of things to come. 'No one has ever paid such court to these people as we are seeing here', Waldersee commented acidly. 'A ship was specially designated for them, an officer was allocated to the ship to provide them with information, they were given special places everywhere and paid compliments on all sides . . . We have totally capitulated to this great power! Eyewitnesses have told me that a good half of the group consisted of Jews', Waldersee complained, unpleasantly surprised by the success of this press policy – and of the free drinks. The 'wretched rascals from the press' had 'gone into ecstasies' and had had no qualms about 'rating Wilhelm II's success above those of Wilhelm I', he commented in disgust.[103]

Philipp Eulenburg was enraptured by the great success of the canal celebrations which the Kaiser had personally organised and wrote to Holstein commenting that Wilhelm was with good reason 'in very high spirits' about it. 'Everything was absolutely splendid and a great success. The vast array of ships a magnificent sight. The passage through the canal and the laying of the foundation stone extraordinarily impressive.'[104] Even the usually sceptical Waldersee had to admit that the celebrations had been a triumph and that the Kaiser had played his part admirably. That the canal voyage had been accomplished at all, the General observed, was 'a personal success for the Kaiser', since he had simply overridden the technicians' reservations. The Kaiser's speech, the review and the naval exercise had created a 'powerful' impression. 'There is not the slightest doubt that the Kaiser himself did very well, which is not to be underestimated, seeing that the whole world sent representatives . . . In summing up my impressions . . . I have to say that the opening of the canal signifies a great success for the Kaiser; most of those who attended were very impressed both by the festivities and by his personality. Even an ill-disposed person could not deny that he played his part very well. How sad it is that his outstanding gifts are so much reduced by his many failings – almost exclusively weaknesses of character – and that no one, in fact, is really willing to serve him and happy in his service.'[105]

# CHAPTER TWENTY-FOUR

# An enemy of the people

## KAISER WILHELM II VERSUS PARLIAMENT AND NATION

THE brilliant success of the Kiel Canal opening celebrations should not blind us to the fact that parliamentary and public opinion continued to be anything but favourable to the Kaiser.[1] In the Wilhelmstrasse, and above all in the Political Department of the Foreign Office which, with the Reich Chancellor, effectively controlled the state apparatus, there was deep concern over the future of the monarchy under Wilhelm II. On 11 November 1894 Holstein warned the newly appointed Chancellor that the manner in which Caprivi had been ousted had dealt a further severe blow to the Kaiser's standing with the people. Moreover 'H.M.'s extremely brusque treatment of the architect [Paul] Wallot', who was responsible for the new Reichstag building, had created a very bad impression. The 'outrageous tone' lately adopted towards the Kaiser by the press undoubtedly found an echo in public opinion, he warned. 'I consider the position of the Kaiser to be increasingly *endangered*, unless he decides to act with more circumspection than hitherto. By *endangered* I mean that no parliamentary majority can be obtained for anything any more. The moment may come, if the Kaiser continues to treat parliament and people as *quantités négligeables*.'[2] A few months later Holstein told the German ambassador in Rome, Bülow, that the Kaiser had 'no notion what kind of future he is preparing for himself. He does not suspect that the most popular man in Germany would be a chancellor who was known to press his thumb in the Kaiser's eye and who obviously did so.'[3] The Privy Councillor went on to quote a remark confided to him by an unnamed man who saw the Kaiser frequently: 'If one hears what is being said, if one sees how His Majesty is steering *blindly* towards his doom – it makes one weep.'[4] Alexander Hohenlohe likewise warned against the 'policy of force, hitting out blindly', which Wilhelm

II and his irresponsible advisers evidently favoured, and drew attention to the Kaiser's unpopularity, which was being exploited by the pro-Bismarck faction to stir up discontent at every possible opportunity. 'The fact that a conflict in the Reich would entail inestimable risks for the survival of the Reich itself, seeing how unpopular, indeed one could almost say discredited, H.M. has undeniably become, needs no further demonstration', the Reich Chancellor's son declared in February 1895. The Kaiser had been discredited, in Prince Alexander's view, chiefly because of 'the inconsistency of H.M.'s decisions and ideas, which is obvious to the general public, and the fear, caused by one surprise after another, of what the next day might bring'.[5]

Wilhelm seems to have been fully aware of the hostile mood among the people, for during a visit to the Reich chancellor's palace on 14 December 1894 he remarked to Hohenlohe that 'he knew very well that he was unpopular and had often heard that people called out insults or shook their fists at him when he was out in his carriage'.[6] But it never occurred to him to tone down his reactionary anti-parliamentary views. On the contrary, the dismissal of the reform-minded Caprivi had a liberating effect on him, as if he no longer needed to go against his own convictions and take account of the state of the parties in the Reichstag or the mood of the people. The contempt which the Kaiser felt for the Reichstag emerges clearly from a malicious letter he wrote to Philipp Eulenburg on 9 December 1894 after the ceremony to mark the completion of the new Reichstag building. 'The dedication of the Reich monkey-house went ahead with all due ceremony and splendour and never a false note. Wallot was in raptures and stuck close by me when he noticed that I neither knocked his top hat in nor made any rude remarks. Especially as he has become a privy councillor. His rapture was so great that when I commanded him to escort the Kaiserin, as she was in front of us and stopped at every door because she didn't know which way to go, he rushed up to her with the words "By special command of His Majesty" and publicly offered her *his arm*! How about that!'[7]

The Kaiser's ill-tempered attitude towards the Reichstag was reciprocated in full measure, for neither the Social Democrats nor the Centre Party, nor indeed the Left-Liberal parties, had any intention of meekly accepting Wilhelm II's increasingly autocratic tendencies, together with the ever more apparent influence on him of the three Cabinet Chiefs and the Flügeladjutanten and the policy of conflict and incitement of class antagonism which had been pursued by him and the court since mid-1894. At the first session of the new Reichstag on 6 December 1894 the Social Democrat fraction, who had hitherto been in the habit of leaving the chamber during the ceremonial opening of parliament, demonstrated their displeasure at the harsher new course by remaining ostentatiously seated when the Kaiser was cheered. Wilhelm reacted to this protest by the workers' party with aggressive indignation. 'The first session of parliament proved to my great delight to be an emphatic demonstration in favour of the [anti-revolutionary] bill. The Reichstag was in *uproar* at the outrageous rudeness of those left-wing scoundrels and 10 minutes later accepted the latter's first motion on the bill with the help of the Centre! In a *good* Berlin *bar* the Socialists would have been given a thorough thrashing and thrown out of the door. The Reichstag is *far* too cowardly. Soon it will reach the point where some-one will propose abandoning the cheers for the Kaiser so as to spare the feelings of the Left.'[8]

After the turbulent session of 6 December the Prussian Ministry of State, led by Interior Minister von Köller, decided to institute proceedings against the deputy Wilhelm Liebknecht for *lèse-majesté*, for which the consent of the Reichs-tag was required. The Reich Chancellor pointed out that it would probably be impossible to obtain such consent, since it would be voted down principally by the Centre Party and the deputies from the Rhineland, Bavaria and Württemberg. In the event of rejection, however, 'a dissolution in the name of H.M.' could not be risked. In any case, Hohenlohe emphasised, he refused to begin his chancel-lorship with a defeat. He wrote to the Kaiser stating his case with great firmness. 'Action against the Social Democrats is necessary, but only when they give cause. Laws against them do not help. They lead to conflict with the Reichstag, disso-lution and partial *coup d'état* and increase the power and influence of the Social Democrats. If Y.M. wishes to pursue such a policy it is not for me to say anything against it. But *I shall not participate in it*, and in that case Y.M. would do better to appoint a general as Reich chancellor. I shall be glad to return to private life.'[9] On 14 December the Kaiser acknowledged that neither the prosecution of Liebknecht nor the anti-revolutionary bill could be used as the pretext for a dissolution. Instead he devised another plan which could lead to a change in the electoral system: this was 'to draw up an economic, but not merely agrarian, programme and to dissolve on the basis of that'. He also played with the idea of having a single election for both Reichstag and Landtag.[10] In the cautious style of the courtier – 'Y.M.'s idea . . . is certainly a very happy one, . . . but . . .' – the Reich Chancellor had to convince the Kaiser of the impracticability of his plan for a dissolution on such grounds.[11]

Waldersee regarded this development as highly dangerous, seeing the demon-stration of 6 December as 'a rejection of the Kaiser by the Social Democrats'. Unlike Hohenlohe, however, he welcomed Köller's resolute action in deciding to prosecute the Social Democrat deputy, for if the Reichstag rejected the motion to penalise the Social Democrats it would have to be dissolved, with all the consequences that would arise from dissolution. For the reactionary General this episode proved that the state must now counterattack against the socialist movement before it was too late. 'What will happen if many more Social Democrats get into the Reichstag?', he asked. 'In the end that will mean that the Reichstag rules the Kaiser. I hope we are fast approaching the decisive moment; but is our good Hohenlohe the man to play for high stakes? I say no.'[12] When he learned from the newspapers that the Reichstag committee, as Hohenlohe had predicted, had voted against the prosecution of the Social Democrats by a large majority, Waldersee was disappointed, commenting that 'it really is not a good beginning for a new course'.[13] He was therefore heartened, on meeting Wilhelm in Hanover in mid-December, to hear how preoccupied the Kaiser was with the whole question of the Social Democrats. But Wilhelm had not 'made it clear what is to be done about it, and in the end he always takes comfort in imagining street battles during which we quickly manage to shoot down the rebels. The idea of taking a firm decision to face all the consequences, even the most extreme, whether on this occasion or with the anti-revolutionary bill, is never mentioned, and so we shall probably go on in the same aimless way as before.'[14] However much the Kaiser's anger may have been aroused, however often he may have been sorely tempted to abolish universal suffrage through a violent *coup d'état*, to Waldersee's regret he never came to a firm decision to order such a breach of the constitution on his own initiative.

The Kaiser saw a second opportunity to vent his displeasure with the Reichstag when in the spring of 1895 the Centre, the Left Liberals, the Poles, Guelphs, Alsatians and Social Democrats voted against sending a telegram congratulating Prince Bismarck on his eightieth birthday. 'With his usual haste' the Kaiser – who could barely be prevented from dissolving parliament over the affair – telegraphed to Friedrichsruh on 23 March to give forcible expression to his indignation.[15] The 'outrage telegram', as Marschall dubbed it, ran: 'I wish to express to Your Highness my deep sense of outrage at the resolution just passed by the Reichstag. It is utterly contrary to the feelings of all German princes and their peoples.' It led many to wonder – not without reason, Marschall noted – 'why H.M. dismissed the Prince in 1890'.[16] Once again Waldersee criticised the Kaiser's unthinking and overhasty action, which had aggravated the situation unnecessarily and lost him the advantage, for had it not been for his telegram the greater part of the nation and 'in particular, by far the majority of people abroad' would have condemned the Reichstag's resolution. Instead, Waldersee predicted, there would be howls of indignation against the Kaiser in Catholic and democratic circles and counter-demonstrations could certainly be expected.[17] After speaking to numerous gentlemen from Berlin at the birthday celebrations at Friedrichsruh, Waldersee recorded that a state of 'great agitation' prevailed among them. It had been established that 'the Kaiser sent off the telegram without speaking to Hohenlohe or any of the ministers, who were naturally extremely surprised. With the public in such a highly excitable state of mind anything is possible . . . If matters become even more acute, however, momentous events might follow and might even lead to a *coup d'état* and to the dissolution of the German Reich. This is not a new idea: for years people have been saying "things cannot go on like this; the Reich was founded on the voluntary union of the princes and therefore they can equally well dissolve the contract". One's next thought is naturally that the Reich will be re-established, but that universal suffrage will be abolished at the same time. In fact a great rift *has* occurred in the unity of Germany since the memorable 23 March [1895]. The Kaiser has shown the greatest possible severity towards a majority in the Reichstag which in all probability cannot be got rid of by dissolving the Reichstag and holding new elections. What is to be done? Either he must yield or he must take the consequences of a complete break; perhaps this is the greatest decision with which he has ever been confronted. Many people are already saying that Hohenlohe must go, because life is beginning in earnest now.'[18] The Kaiser had even intended to make 'a speech attacking the Reichstag' during the banquet in honour of Prince Bismarck on 1 April 1895, which Hohenlohe only just managed to prevent.[19]

Waldersee watched in bewilderment as political affairs nevertheless continued to follow their usual course, and the Kaiser even invited the new President of the Reichstag, Rudolf Freiherr von Buol-Berenberg, a member of the Centre Party, to a dinner in honour of Bismarck at the Schloss. 'How can the Kaiser get on with a Reichstag whose attitude has deeply offended him and which he has insulted in front of the whole world?' The inevitable consequence of such inconsistency, he commented, would be that 'what the Kaiser says is no longer taken seriously'.[20] Later Waldersee discovered the real story of how the telegram to Bismarck had come about. The Kaiser had sent one of his Flügeladjutanten to the Reichstag to find out the result of the vote straight away. When he was told of the rejection of the congratulatory telegram he immediately drew up his telegram and took it with him to see the Reich Chancellor, from whom he demanded the dissolution of the Reichstag. When Hohenlohe realised (as he put it) 'that I could not talk him out of both, I confined myself to deterring him from dissolving the Reichstag'. 'This demonstrates with absolute clarity how little influence Hohenlohe has on him', Waldersee aptly remarked, 'and also that he would not dream of risking his position. I have no doubt at all that if Hohenlohe had stood firm the Kaiser would have given way and the telegram would not have been sent.'[21]

In addition to the dinner which he gave at the Berlin Schloss for Bismarck's birthday, Wilhelm II made the journey to Friedrichsruh on 26 March, accompanied by the Crown Prince and numerous dignitaries, to offer his congratulations to the old man.[22] Both for the benefit of outside observers and within his own family Wilhelm sought to present a highly romanticised picture of the visit and to exploit its propaganda possibilities. As he wrote to his mother on 5 April 1895 from the *Hohenzollern*, 'the day at Friedrichsruh went off very well, the old Prince looked very well but his nerves were much shattered. He was extremely affected & nearly always crying, very often kissing my hand, & lamented the death of his wife, whom he sorely misses, & whose decease made him as he said "a broken down man". He was very happy to see our boy & as often as he could stroked his head & hair.'[23] In spite of the fine speeches made on the occasion, however,[24] in Waldersee's view it was evident that the relationship between the Kaiser and Bismarck continued to be cool on both sides. 'They are both play-acting', he noted afterwards. 'The Kaiser is outdoing himself in attentiveness . . . but it is all mere pretence. The Kaiser does not speak to him at all about affairs of state and still harbours the old grudge instilled into him by Caprivi; Bismarck still has the feeling that no real amends have been made to him. And that will not change!'[25] Even the appointment of Count Wilhelm von Bismarck as Oberpräsident of the province of East Prussia, which was 'the Kaiser's own idea' − 'yet another interference in other people's business', as Waldersee grumbled − and which was taken as a sign of improved relations between the Kaiser and the Bismarck family, turned out to be a *faute de mieux* solution, for Wilhelm II had offered the post successively to Botho Eulenburg, Count August von Dönhoff and the ex-Minister Gustav von Gossler, and had resorted to Bill Bismarck only when all the others had turned it down.[26] Bismarckians like Count Carl von Wedel and Prince 'Septi' Reuss were quick to detect the self-interested aim behind Wilhelm's ostentatious attentions to Bismarck, namely to demonstrate publicly that the veneration of the founder of the Reich was the particular preserve of the Kaiser and the monarchy. After the visit to Friedrichsruh, which Wedel described in detail in a letter to Reuss, the latter replied: 'I think your comments about it are absolutely right, and also as regards the [Kaiser's] almost childish anger with the old man . . . The fact that he refuses to understand what B[ismarck] is and always will be to the German people is quite enough to make me doubt that he has normal powers of comprehension. You were quite right to try to combat this delusion he has, as if he were trying to put the "one and only" in the shade; and what you say is so true, that B. deserves to be measured by a different scale from other men. The fact that he cannot grasp this shows his small-mindedness.'[27] Similar views could be heard at this time even within inner government circles. Minister of War Bronsart told Philipp Eulenburg − 'naively', as the latter thought − that it was important 'that His Majesty ask old Prince Bismarck for advice from time to time';[28] Bronsart was 'very worked up' and had spoken to him 'very *foolishly* about the relationship

H.M. wishes, but in an inconspicuous manner'.[40] He subsequently made it plain that although he was prepared, 'at the special request of His Majesty', to take whatever action was within the bounds of possibility, he himself was convinced that it would be best not to introduce any bill at all.[41]

On 2 September, the twenty-fifth anniversary of the battle of Sedan, as Marschall recorded in his diary, Wilhelm made 'a strong speech against the Social Democrats and then raised his glass to me in a toast. After dinner I toned the speech down a little with Lucanus and discovered from him that an anti-socialist law is planned, and is to be laid before the Reichstag.'[42] Even in the modified version of his speech the Kaiser described the Social Democrats as 'a traitorous gang' and as 'a band of men unworthy to bear the name of Germans'.[43] The ensuing protests from the Social Democrats gave the Kaiser what he saw as an opportunity to take advantage of the alleged national 'storm of indignation' against the workers' movement in order to get an additional short and sharp legislative measure, under which anyone who caused a public nuisance by reviling the memory of any deceased German prince would be punished with imprisonment, passed quickly by the Reichstag. He told Minister of Justice Schönstedt, as Marschall recorded, that 'he wanted only a single clause, so as to protect the reputation of the old Kaiser, for he was not so stupid as to give the Socialists the pleasure of an exceptional law'.[44]

The leading role which both Hermann von Lucanus, the Chief of the Civil Cabinet, and the Kaiser's friend Philipp Eulenburg played in engineering these reactionary measures demonstrates the extent to which the political initiative in such questions had passed from the Wilhelmstrasse to the irresponsible advisers at court. Together they became convinced that because of the tense external situation the Kaiser could not risk a resignation by Hohenlohe. Eulenburg therefore set himself the task of placating the old Chancellor with the argument that the measure in question was only a limited one, both in Prussia and in the Reich, and that it had good prospects of success. 'As His Majesty's measure is limited to single §§ [clauses], and the Kaiser is *absolutely* determined to do *something* – (His latest observations about the socialists culminated in the view that we must proceed *step by step*, using every opportunity that arises) – I think it is a good thing if the Kaiser is not opposed when He *limits* Himself, as He evidently has done . . . I can confirm, moreover, that *Lucanus* really does not want a major measure, but is doing his best to keep the All-Highest wishes in check.' Lucanus and Eulenburg took the view that the Kaiser must be talked out of his plan to spend the winter on an English yacht, which he had rented at great expense, in the Mediterranean, since the presence of the monarch in Berlin would be absolutely indispensable during the negotiations over the two bills.[45]

While shooting at Rominten in East Prussia in September 1895 the Kaiser had a long conversation with Eulenburg during which he spoke of the behaviour of the Social Democratic Party at the Sedan anniversary celebrations. The ambassador sent the Chancellor a detailed account of the Kaiser's remarks. 'He began with a passionate attack on Kaiser Wilhelm I's former companions and adjutants, who in his opinion should have intervened personally to defend the honour of the old Kaiser against insult. If they had beaten Herr Bebel and his gang over the head at the editorial offices of the *Vorwärts* the mood of the whole of Berlin would have been on their side and the people, fired with patriotism, would have destroyed the printing house and given the Social Democrats a fright for the first time. The Kaiser demands that this insult to His grandfather, which has gone unpunished, should be redressed by the clauses to be laid before the Reichstag. The Kaiser's intention is only to call for atonement for the offence to the late German Kaiser and he seemed to have little inclination to demand the same for deceased German princes in general . . . He wished it to be left to each individual Landtag of the German Reich to safeguard the memory of its own prince.' Wilhelm had rejected each of the numerous arguments which Eulenburg put forward against the measures he had demanded. He claimed that Köller had 'the whole [Prussian] Landtag in his pocket' and would get the laws through with very little trouble. In general, Eulenburg reported, the Kaiser harboured 'great illusions' about Köller. The Kaiser's friend could tell from many of his remarks 'that the main impulse behind the Kaiser's wish to put the heaviest possible shackles on the social democratic movement is the fear that some misfortune might befall the Kaiserin or the children. He wants to protect His family, as we would wish to protect ourselves from a mad dog, for as a monarch faced by this mob He finds himself in a position in which we personally do not find ourselves, or only in exceptional cases. With reference to the appeal to the people that He had made in his speeches, He said that, having given it full consideration, He had suggested that He should be accorded the legal means to protect the peaceful elements in the state (NB His children) from assassination attempts; if that did not work, the time would have to come when He would demand, and also achieve, these means. If there were then an outcry he would be in a position to say that he had no other alternative, after his appeal to the people had gone unheard.' As the Kaiser was well aware that in acting this way he would be falling into Bismarck's trap, Eulenburg believed that 'these things will not be seriously considered until after the death of Prince Bismarck – unless some atrocity by the anarchists gave the Kaiser an earlier opportunity to carry out what he wishes'.[46]

While Wilhelm was hunting at Rominten Eulenburg received a twelve-page letter from Marschall arguing strongly against the Kaiser's plans to strengthen the Prussian anti-association law. In modern society, he maintained, the formation of associations had become an absolutely indispensable weapon for those with less economic power against the superior strength of capital.[47] Eulenburg's description of the Kaiser's reaction to this speaks volumes. In a secret letter of 1 October he wrote to the Chancellor: 'As I had touched upon the bill in a conversation shortly beforehand and had found His Majesty not exactly inclined to give up his plans, I asked for an audience today and tried to read out Herr von Marschall's letter to him. The Kaiser is no lover of lengthy analyses, and the only way I could make sure that he paid at least a certain amount of attention to the carefully worked out conclusions was by telling him that the only reason for the Secretary of State's detailed letter was the following: Herr von Marschall was firmly convinced that the personal safety of His Majesty and of the imperial family would be threatened from the moment that the Kaiser took severe measures against the socialists and aroused their resentment against him . . . Even this explanation did not prevent His Majesty from making critical comments about it. He even let fall the remark that Herr von Marschall should not interfere in this question, which was entirely an internal matter; his South German views were inappropriate to Prussian affairs, which cried out for a revision of the law of association. His – the Kaiser's – personal safety was in danger with or without a law, and if the punishment or restriction of the Social Democrats' organisational activities could be achieved, that would answer a need for which the remedy had to be found.'[48] When a few days later the Kaiser learned from the newspapers that a factory-owner in Mülhausen had been murdered, he telegraphed angrily to the Statthalter in Strassburg: 'Yet another victim of the revolutionary movement stirred up by the socialists. If only our people would pull themselves together!'[49] In his speech to the Cuirassier Guards Regiment at Breslau on 2 December the Kaiser again expressed his fury at what he saw as the unpatriotic behaviour of the Social Democrats at the twenty-fifth anniversary celebrations in the autumn. He reaffirmed his solidarity with his 'comrades' in the army and, as Waldersee commented, was 'carried away in intemperate expressions about the Social Democrats', to the extent that 'everyone was in a state of high anxiety because the Ob[er]b[ür]germeister and also reporters were present; the speech was later pruned for the benefit of the latter'.[50]

The Kaiser's attitude to his Catholic subjects – a third of the population of the Reich – and to their parliamentary representatives was scarcely less aggressive than to the rapidly growing Social Democratic workers' movement.[51] When Dr Clemens Freiherr von Heeremann, a Centre Party member, attacked Minister of Ecclesiastical Affairs, Education and Medicine Robert Bosse during the debate on the Teachers' Income Bill in the Prussian House of Representatives on 30 January 1896, and shortly afterwards Viktor Rintelen, a Centre Party representative in the Reichstag, announced his party's demands for changes to family and marriage law during the Reichstag's discussions of the Civil Code, the Kaiser wrote furiously to Hohenlohe: 'Greatly distressed as I was by Heeremann's disgraceful, Jameson-like attack on Bosse, I am absolutely outraged by Rintelen's speech on the Civil Code, which I have just read . . . A piece of legislation which has been completed with the approval of the entire German people, and which was praised as the crowning glory of the edifice when you introduced it at **my** *command* [sic], is threatened with destruction by the Centre; of course they do it in the hope of *bargaining*! Any minister of mine who dares to hint at the slightest accommodation or even concession to such an unpatriotic rabble ceases that very instant to be a minister. And although it is after the event, since unfortunately *the government side said nothing*, I wish you to condemn Rintelen's declaration very strongly at the next session and to emphasise the broad national point of view. Wilhelm I. R.'[52] Summoning all his patience, Prince Hohenlohe had to point out to the Kaiser that Rintelen was 'a foolish old chatterbox' whose remarks could not be regarded as expressions of his party's opinion. There was no question of concessions to the Centre Party, which would accept the Civil Code anyway, and if the Kaiser regretted the lack of response to Rintelen from the government benches, the Prince 'most humbly' begged him to read 'the masterly, patriotic speech' which Professor Gottlieb Planck had made as chairman of the committee on the Civil Code.[53]

Wilhelm's outbursts of rage against the Social Democratic Party and the Centre, however, should not mislead us into assuming that he was now in sympathy with the extreme-right agrarian Conservatives. On the contrary, considerable personal and political differences continued to divide him from them. Although the speech he made on 18 February 1895 at a reception for the leaders of the Agrarian League gave the impression that he was now 'seriously intending to go over to the agrarian camp',[54] even in this speech the Kaiser deplored the agitation stirred up by the agrarian movement, which 'could not but deeply wound my heart as Father of My People'.[55] Referring to the speech in a letter to Philipp Eulenburg Wilhelm commented that 'the Conservatives and Agrarian League are completely mad . . . I received the delegation from the League, although very much *contre coeur*, because *Hohenlohe personally and repeatedly asked me to do so*. In my speech you will have read between the lines the rude remarks I gave them to swallow.'[56]

A week later, in his annual speech to the provincial diet of Brandenburg, Wilhelm spoke of the 'thorny task' he faced as 'Margrave', and emphatically rejected the demands of the agrarians. Although he promised to support the agricultural classes as strongly as he could, he warned them not to 'harbour exaggerated hopes, let alone to demand that Utopia be brought about'. No class could expect to be given preference at the expense of the others, he declared. 'It is the duty of the sovereign to weigh the interests of all classes against each other . . . so that the general interests of the great Fatherland are safeguarded.'[57]

Waldersee expressed his dismay in his diary. 'The good mood and confidence that were gradually beginning to take hold among the Conservatives will be badly shaken by a speech made by the Kaiser at the dinner of the Brandenburg provincial diet. I am convinced that he expressed himself in a way that he did not intend, for he surely cannot contradict what he said to the leaders of the Agrarian League scarcely 8 days ago. It is a most unfortunate idea to make speeches all the time; he has already done himself so much harm in this way. The Liberals, who were deeply depressed 8 days ago, are of course jubilant ... He loves to call himself 'Father of the People', but unfortunately this is greeted only with smiles and mockery, and when he says that people should follow him with confidence, they naturally say: very gladly, but we should like to have some idea of where he is leading us.'[58] There was 'great despondency and even indignation' about the 'complete about-turn in the Kaiser's mood' among the Conservatives, Waldersee observed. People rightly suspected that the influence of Hinzpeter and Helldorff was behind it, but the result was that 'confidence in the Kaiser is dwindling'. 'He rallies the aristocracy to the struggle against revolution, but now, by withdrawing his interest from the country people, he is driving them towards the revolutionary parties in droves.'[59]

Serious disappointment was in store for Waldersee and the right-wing Conservatives on another score. In May 1896 the Kaiser sent Hinzpeter a strangely worded telegram which was intended to be passed on to the Saarland heavy industrialist, Carl Freiherr von Stumm-Halberg, and in which he attacked former Court Preacher Adolf Stoecker. 'Stoecker has met the end which I predicted years ago', Wilhelm wrote, alluding to Stoecker's departure from the Conservative Party. 'Political pastors are an absurdity', he declared, concluding with words which, as the Liberal newspapers commented critically, sounded like a marginal note by Frederick the Great or even his father the Soldier King. 'The reverend gentlemen should look after the souls of their flocks and leave politics out of it, since that is none of their business.'[60] Waldersee thought it showed 'unforgivable tactlessness on the part of Messrs Hinzpeter and Stumm to publish such a telegram; they both know the Kaiser very well and are aware that ... he frequently expresses himself crudely in conversation, although afterwards he often scarcely knows what he said, and in the same way he is prone to dash off a telegram and does not weigh his words; if he had thought calmly about it the Kaiser would never have written such muddled stuff, and Stumm and Hinzpeter have done him a very bad service. Of course the whole of the Liberal press is exulting in it.'[61] Two days later Waldersee was more critical in his comments. 'The Kaiser's telegram has quite rightly caused a great scandal, and I think it will have bad after-effects. There will soon come a time when our gracious sovereign will badly need the help of the clergy. I am truly sorry for the Lutheran clergymen; they will not know what to do, but many will go in the very dangerous direction taken by [Friedrich] Naumann.'[62]

## MINISTERIAL AND CHANCELLOR CRISES

Clearly, Wilhelm's increasingly autocratic behaviour, his insistence on personally determining every measure of internal and external policy and his flaunting of repressive, anti-parliamentary and anti-Catholic attitudes put the statesmen of the Reich and Prussia under great strain. As Hohenlohe was timid, elderly and frail and, with very rare exceptions, never crossed swords with the monarch, the ministers had little alternative but to enter the lists against the Kaiser. For a while, under Hohenlohe, the Prussian Ministry of State acquired an importance that it had not possessed since the appointment of Bismarck more than thirty years earlier. Foreign and naval policy, which were matters for the Reich, remained outside the competence of the Ministry; nor did it have any say at all in 'purely military' affairs, being a civil authority. But as far as domestic policy was concerned, not only in Prussia but in the Reich as a whole, in the first two-and-a-half years of the new chancellorship the ministers of state, now a committee of eleven, formed a kind of government cabinet which met to discuss and to try to reach decisions on every question that arose. That it was unable, particularly in these crisis-ridden years, to assert itself successfully against the iron will of Wilhelm II, was one of the most fateful developments of the Kaiser's reign and is hence one of the most important themes of this book.

The underlying weakness of the Prussian Ministry of State as an organ of government was its heterogeneity, which itself was the natural consequence of the impulsive and inconsistent manner in which the Kaiser made ministerial appointments. The ministry which Hohenlohe took over in November 1894 as Prussian minister-president and minister of foreign affairs consisted of men whose political opinions were as varied as their characters. Vice-President von Boetticher was a survival (although somewhat weakened since the embarrassing revelations of financial impropriety in 1891) from the Bismarck era. Minister of Trade Hans Hermann Freiherr von Berlepsch had been appointed to the Ministry of State by Wilhelm II in early 1890 with the express task of carrying through the Kaiser's social reform programme against Bismarck. Johannes von Miquel, appointed finance minister a few months later, the former leader of the National Liberal Party and Oberbürgermeister of Frankfurt, had moved decidedly towards the right since taking office; now, as a confidant of Herbert Bismarck, Waldersee and Count Henckel von Donnersmarck, he constituted a link to the agrarian movement and the Bismarckian Fronde. Dominated by Miquel, Thielen, who had been appointed minister of railways in 1891, scarcely played a political role at all. Bosse, promoted minister of ecclesiastical affairs, education and medicine after the School Bill crisis of 1892, was even less inclined to venture on to the slippery political ice. Minister of War Walter Bronsart von Schellendorf, however, whose older brother had held the same post in the latter days of the Bismarck era, was a fiery General possessed of great self-confidence and extensive connections. Karl Heinrich von Schönstedt, the Minister of Justice appointed with Hohenlohe in November 1894, and Freiherr von Hammerstein-Loxten, appointed minister of agriculture at the same time, lacked experience at first and played no distinctive role outside their particular domains. Ernst Matthias von Köller, on the other hand, who had been appointed minister of the interior in November 1894 by telegraphic order from the Kaiser, saw himself from the outset as the Kaiser's right-hand man in the Ministry of State. Finally there was Adolf Freiherr Marschall von Bieberstein, the Reich Foreign Secretary from South Baden, who in the course of his parliamentary activity in the previous seven years had developed a relationship of trust with the leaders of the Centre group in particular, and who had been appointed to the Prussian Ministry of State as minister without portfolio in the autumn of 1894, on the insistence of Holstein and as a condition for Hohenlohe's acceptance of the chancellorship. This 'fellow from Baden', as Wilhelm called him, almost inevitably incurred the anger of the increasingly 'Prussian' monarch.

After only a few weeks there was a violent dispute between the Kaiser and the Foreign Secretary which almost cost the latter his position. Irritated beyond measure because the Reichstag, and first and foremost the Centre Party, was threatening to reject his demands for the navy, and spurred on by the former Jesuit Count Paul Hoensbroech, who had converted to Protestantism and whom the Kaiser had received against the Reich Chancellor's advice,[63] Wilhelm gave orders to his Oberhofmarschall, August Eulenburg, never to invite '*any* member of the Centre to a court function ever again'. He accused Marschall, who had arranged for the leader of the Centre Party, Dr Ernst Lieber, to be invited to the last court ball on 6 February, of having repeatedly tried to make him talk to Lieber on that occasion, against his will. After the ball the Kaiser let loose a torrent of 'very strong language' against Marschall and said that he was 'sick of this fellow from Baden, who had no Prussian feeling in him'. On 14 February 1895 Alexander Hohenlohe warned his father that he could expect an 'onslaught against Marschall' when the Kaiser came to see him that day.[64] When the monarch arrived at the Foreign Office in the morning he behaved 'very ungraciously' towards the Secretary of State, refused to shake hands with him, complained 'in the strongest possible terms' about the Reichstag, which evidently wished 'to destroy the navy', and went over to speak to the Reich Chancellor.[65] Holstein also reported that the Kaiser was 'in a rotten mood' and had been whipped up against Marschall principally by Hoensbroech and Lucanus.[66]

The letter that Wilhelm II wrote on 12 February 1895 from his hunting lodge at Hubertusstock to his friend 'Phili' Eulenburg left the ambassador at Vienna in no doubt 'that a separation from Herr von Marschall is to be expected in the near future'.[67] 'You will be surprised that I am writing from here', the Kaiser began. 'But when such grave times are approaching, and everyone in Berlin gets more and more insane, angry and impossible, one has to get out for a moment to keep a cool head and sound judgement. For I want to be able to judge everything that happens absolutely fairly. The incident which compels me to write to you is unfortunately another one of a personal nature. Our friend Marschall's behaviour towards me at the recent court ball surpassed everything that had happened before. After he had made himself unpleasantly conspicuous to me and to other onlookers for a long time by standing in my way and blocking doorways, he forced me to talk to him. He then told me that Herr Lieber was standing just there at the back, near me. An excellent man who was very well disposed towards the navy and was the right person to help the bill through, if I would speak to him! I replied that it was highly improper for him to confront me with such situations in my own house. Herr Lieber was a downright scoundrel who had been invited without my knowledge or permission. When he attacked the Army Bill last year he called the Hohenzollerns and the Protestants a band of murderous fire-raisers and the Germans in the South as "willy-nilly Prussians" from which he acquired the nickname of the willy-nilly Prussian throughout Bavaria. If he was prepared to agree to the ships, he should do it out of conviction, for the Fatherland, not as a present to me in return for talking to him. After that I left him standing there looking very crestfallen. He then went off and – without saying a word about what had happened – tried to get [Prince] Heinrich involved with Lieber. He [Heinrich] answered by telling him to give the swine a kick in the a . . . My Marshal of the Court [Egloffstein] told me later that Lieber had been invited just before the ball by Marschall's personal arrangement, without my permission, and was not even on the list!! That is going too far, and there will be consequences!'[68] The day after the court ball, during a visit to the Wilhelmstrasse, Wilhelm expressed his anger that Hoensbroech had not been accepted into the diplomatic service; 'he had given up his religion so that he could remain loyal to his King', and he, Wilhelm, would make sure that he was given an appointment in Prussia. In the course of a conversation with Marschall the Kaiser became 'very abusive towards Catholics in general' and said that it was quite useless showing any consideration towards the Centre. 'He would perhaps – since we had been trying in vain to do business with the Centre for six years – rally the Protestants around Him and start the Thirty Years War again.'[69]

The incident at the court ball when the Kaiser had flown into 'a furious temper' and turned his back on Lieber, and Marschall had received 'an even stronger snub' from Prince Heinrich, was confirmed by the accounts given by two of the Flügeladjutanten who were with Wilhelm at Hubertusstock, Gustav von Kessel and Hans von Arnim, whom Wilhelm ordered to write to Eulenburg as well. 'His Majesty dislikes being waylaid by anyone at balls, but most of all by his officials who are trying to bring people forward for him to speak to, without telling him anything about it beforehand, in order to advance parliamentary or other causes. As German kaiser he will not lend himself to this kind of thing. And absolutely not in the case of this Dr L.' As a result of this incident the Kaiser's attitude towards Marschall was highly critical, Kessel gleefully remarked, 'and in my opinion a change is in the offing, sooner or later . . . I consider M. to be easily replaceable, a man of narrow vision who goes around flattering everybody.' The Kaiser was right to be angry at Marschall's tactics, the Flügeladjutant added. 'He has given orders that L. is never to be invited again.' Arnim likewise declared that he could only agree with the Kaiser's view of Marschall's conduct and had come to the conclusion that the Foreign Secretary's demeanour was 'typical of the whole character of this man, from whom it was impossible to expect a policy in the grand style'.[70] Philipp Eulenburg rightly observed, on receiving these letters, that they spoke volumes about the blatant influence of the Flügeladjutanten on the Kaiser. '*At last* the Flügeladjutanten and the Supreme Headquarters have shot Marschall down! They are completely at their ease in writing to me. On the *orders* of the Kaiser!! My good Arnim's views on the *duties of a secretary of state*, or the qualities that such a person should *not* have – say more than an entire book about what I call "adjutant politics" . . . What would Hohenlohe, Holstein and Marschall say if I showed them *these* letters!!'[71]

But even Eulenburg, ever loyal to the Kaiser, considered Marschall doomed because of the purely personal dislike which the Kaiser and his entourage felt towards him.[72] As he commented to Holstein, Marschall had 'just as little ability as Caprivi to win friends among the entourage of H.M.'. The Kaiser's entourage had not turned against Hohenlohe, he assured Holstein, 'because he has the kindly manner of the grand seigneur and is polite by nature. Although the narrow-minded court ladies may talk against the *Catholic* Chancellor, this issue is taken up by the military and civilian entourage of H.M. only in order to bring up Marschall's "undignified" flirtation with the Centre Party. You know that H.M. has felt a pronounced antipathy to Marschall for almost two years.' Eulenburg went on to declare that it was only in order not to lose Holstein himself that he had worked to have Marschall kept on in the Hohenlohe government the previous autumn. 'The weakness of the Hohenlohe Cabinet lay and lies in Marschall, because he has no friends in Prussia and because the Kaiser hasn't liked him for two years.' After the incident at the court ball Eulenburg no longer had the slightest doubt that the Kaiser would get rid of Marschall. 'I tell you frankly', he wrote to Holstein, 'that in my opinion Hohenlohe would be stronger if Marschall went, because in the long run the antipathy of H.M. will become unbearable and because the King after all has the right to select his own ministers.'[73] Eulenburg also wrote to the Reich Chancellor with a view to distancing him from Marschall, so as to avoid the danger of a chancellor crisis arising from Marschall's impending dismissal. Meanwhile he wrote to the Kaiser strongly advising him to appoint Bernhard von Bülow as Marschall's successor.[74]

The Kaiser's reaction to his friend's letter was, to put it mildly, unexpected. He sent a telegram dismissing the whole 'stupid story' of Marschall, Lieber and the court ball as a carnival joke and telling Eulenburg to stop trying to oust the 'wounded M.' from his post.[75] This was followed up with a letter in characteristic style commenting on the letters from Marschall and Alexander Hohenlohe giving their version of the incident, which Eulenburg had sent him: 'My dear Philippus, The contents of this letter have left me dumbfounded with astonishment! Such a farrago of nonsense as Crown Prince Alexander [i.e. the Reich Chancellor's son] has dreamt up has seldom been written down in black and white. He is doing far more harm than 100 newspaper articles in [Maximilian Harden's] Die Zukunft. How can any sensible person who knows me and sees me every day, knows exactly whom I see and who is seen with me, which can be verified at any moment, imagine such rubbish! . . . I am so happy with old Hohenlohe, for everything is working so well and comfortably; whenever either of us wants something, we immediately exchange notes and discuss it, so that nothing can happen behind the scenes! Which is a paradise for me. But now I suddenly find that I have been quite mistaken! And that the nonsense is worse than before! And that it comes precisely from the place where it ought to be found least! Why didn't Alexander give the tale-bearers a direct slap in the face instead of just believing this outrageous rubbish! . . . I had settled the entire ball affair *with the Prince* [Hohenlohe] long ago, and had forgotten all about it. And then you come along with your grand plans for reshuffles! Wretched creature, leave me in peace with such stuff! Write and tell these people that they should be ashamed to believe such rubbish, and leave all those whom you want to make dance around like puppets sitting quietly at their posts! Thank God it is carnival time, otherwise I should have been really rude to you. I can *assure* you that I have spoken to *no one* at all about government business, or about Hohenlohe, out of sheer concern for nonsense of this kind, if for no other reason. Please make the widest possible use of this letter! As far as the Centre are concerned, you will have seen that I have dined with Arenberg and Kopp. With the former I had a detailed political conversation about the Anti-Revolution Bill, which, according

to a later report he made to me, had a very good effect on his party!! Well then!?
Where does that leave the bad treatment of the Centre, 3 gentlemen from which
were promoted to major on 27th!? It is only natural that I should not tolerate
tactlessness at parties where I am host, and if the Catholic side wanted to try
to link that with something, it would be even more unjust! . . . I couldn't care
less about Marschall: for all I care he can stay till his fat coagulates, and I am
letting Schele go for Hohenlohe's sake, although he is being sacrificed to the
villainous tricks of Kayser, who wants to be minister for the colonies! So tell me
please, dearest Philippus, what reason is there for all these insinuations? Please
make sure that the truth of the matter is made *quite clear*, straight away, and
be very rude! to all and sundry! If Hohenlohe goes, I'll go too! Your loyal friend
Wilhelm I. R.'[76]

But if the Kaiser had decided to keep on Marschall – who denied having asked
the Kaiser more than once to talk to Lieber and claimed not to have spoken to
Prince Heinrich at all[77] – for the time being, the crisis soon came to affect the
entire government. In Holstein's view 'the whole affair is a sneak attack, taking
advantage of the nervous irritability of the Kaiser'.[78] Only a few days after the
court ball incident Minister of War Bronsart had 'a scene with the Kaiser because
the latter doubted the loyalty of the Catholic officers'. 'The Minister of War was
so angry about it', Holstein telegraphed to Bülow in Rome, 'that he told Herr
von Lucanus yesterday that in his opinion the entire Ministry should resign, or
impose conditions.'[79] The idea of collective resignation by the entire Ministry
of State, in order to force the Kaiser to give up his methods of personal rule, was
gaining ground all the time.

In the early summer of 1895 Prince Hohenlohe found himself face to face
with a second, well-nigh intractable ministerial crisis which arose from what
had become irreconcilable differences between the Kaiser and Minister of Trade
Hans Hermann von Berlepsch, a convinced advocate of social reform. After a
joint audience with the reactionary Minister of the Interior, Köller, on 12 May
1895, Hohenlohe noted that 'the Kaiser has reservations about setting a standard
working day'.[80] Three days later Berlepsch informed the Reich Chancellor that
he intended 'to ask the Kaiser and King to relieve me of my office' because he
had reached the conclusion 'that it has become impossible to make any further
progress in the foreseeable future with the social reforms which I think absolutely
indispensable'.[81] Not for the first time the Chancellor found himself compelled
to call on the services of Philipp Eulenburg as mediator.[82] When Eulenburg,
who was at Prökelwitz in East Prussia with the Kaiser, brought up the subject
of the opposition between the pro-reform Berlepsch and the ultra-conservative
Köller, 'His Majesty took sides against Herr von Berlepsch with some vigour' –
as Eulenburg reported to Hohenlohe – 'and referred to the fact that He and Your

Excellency, in the presence of Herr von Köller, had established the basis on which "the process of governing" was to be conducted.' Eulenburg strongly advised Hohenlohe to postpone dealing with matters of contention within the Ministry of State until the parliamentary recess, or if this were impossible, to inform the Kaiser of them without delay, to avoid the impression of 'secretiveness'.[83] But Berlepsch was unwilling to remain in office against his own convictions and handed in his resignation. On 8 June 1895 the Chancellor described in his journal the humiliating treatment he received from the monarch. 'At 6 o'clock I received an invitation to dine at the Marmorpalais. After supper the Kaiser, who was waiting for me with Lucanus, summoned me and showed me Berlepsch's letter. He refuses to let Berlepsch go. He said he had appointed him to carry out social legislation in accordance with the resolutions of 1890. He still wished this to be done; but as the originator of these measures he could also order a slowing-down. Berlepsch's resignation would signify a wish to change direction, and that was not his intention. But German industry must not be too heavily burdened and must not be made incapable of competing with foreign countries. H.M. had written comments on Berlepsch's letter which he read out to me . . . I am to be sent a written communication as well.'[84]

The Kaiser ultimately succeeded in delaying the Trade Minister's resignation for the duration of the summer. On 28 June Berlepsch went to see Hohenlohe with the news that the Chief of the Civil Cabinet had written to him to say that 'it would be some time yet' before the Kaiser would take a decision on his resignation. Berlepsch declared, however, that he could not remain in the Ministry any longer. 'If the Kaiser thought a reduction of the pace of social legislation were necessary, he respected this point of view but could not share it, in view of all his endeavours hitherto, without discrediting himself in the eyes of the Reichstag and of the world in general', as Hohenlohe recorded. Since the Kaiser was away, however, Berlepsch admitted that he had no alternative but to wait. The Reich Chancellor, equally resigned, commented: 'For the moment I can do nothing, as the Kaiser cannot be reached.'[85] It was not until he returned from his Scandinavian cruise and just before his departure for England that Wilhelm found an opportunity to explain to Berlepsch why he refused to accept his resignation. In a letter from the Neues Palais on 31 July 1895, evidently drafted by Lucanus, he wrote: 'I am unable to grant your request to be allowed to resign from the office of minister of trade and industry. You rightly emphasise that to abandon the social policy set out by Me in my order of 4 February 1890 and repeatedly referred to in speeches from the throne would result in severe damage to the interests of the Fatherland. Nothing is further from my mind, however, than to give up this course, and least of all would I approve a policy which sought to introduce repression by force, instead of humane legislation and administration, in relation to questions of social welfare. But this mistaken notion would inevitably be aroused by your resignation, because people would be inclined to see the change of minister as the expression of a systemic change. If therefore there is no difference of principle between Me and you with regard to the aims of our social policy, the only matter in question is the way in which we should continue on the path we are treading, as best befits our political and economic circumstances as a whole. It is true that in this regard I consider the maintenance of a slow tempo to be required at present . . . Nevertheless I do not wish all activity in the sphere of social welfare to cease, even at present; but I wish to prevent the great excitement which has unfortunately been caused by the agrarian agitation being further increased by parliamentary discussion of great social policy questions, such as the regulation of maximum working hours and the establishment of representation for the workers. There is, however, another sphere of social policy which still needs to be settled and which can be tackled without danger, together with further work to develop present arrangements for the amelioration of the position of the workers. This is the question of the organisation of craftsmen. I do not doubt that for the sake of accomplishing this task, with which all the state-supporting parties have a certain sympathy, you will be willing to continue to place your well-tried skill at My disposal and that you will add new services to those you have already rendered in such great measure. You will have My full confidence and My gratitude as your King in this endeavour. I therefore look forward to your suggestions for the improvement and protection of the craftsman's profession as soon as possible. Wilhelm R.'[86]

In the midst of this ministerial crisis Miquel launched an attempt to exploit the Kaiser's current mood, which had again become markedly 'Prussian', to increase his own influence, as Prussian finance minister, on the financial affairs of the Reich. But this was met with determined opposition on Wilhelm II's part. In a secret letter dated 24 May 1895 Philipp Eulenburg told the Chancellor that, although the Kaiser had expressed himself 'very strongly' to the effect that he 'no longer felt disposed to sacrifice Prussian financial interests to the Reich', on the other hand he had '*categorically*' rejected an extension of the powers of the Prussian finance minister at the expense of the Reich chancellor and the Reich Treasury. 'I have the impression', Eulenburg wrote, 'that H. Majesty considers this All-Highest decision as definitive, and that He particularly hopes that it will provide the *very keenly* desired settlement, and that no further reference to the matter will be forthcoming.'[87]

The double ministerial crisis of May 1895 led to a general discussion in Prökelwitz on the fundamental question of how the Kaiser, the Reich Chancellor and the Ministry of State should determine the guidelines of Prusso-German domestic policy. Philipp Eulenburg drew the Kaiser's attention to the various

shades of opinion within the Ministry of State, which could lead to more serious
conflicts and thereby endanger 'the homogeneity of His Majesty's government'.
As Eulenburg reported to Hohenlohe, the Kaiser had *quite categorically* forbidden any controversial disputes within the Ministry and called upon the Chancellor to ensure the 'homogeneity' of the leadership of both the Reich and Prussia.
Only the chancellor had the right 'to take a view and express it to His Majesty;
the individual ministers must limit themselves to following the principles laid
down'.[88]

There was one minister, however, who was not prepared to allow the guidelines
for his sphere of responsibility to be determined by the Kaiser, and who had
indeed expressed grave doubts from the outset about whether the monarch could
still be regarded as mentally normal at all. This was the self-confident Minister
of War, General Walter Bronsart von Schellendorf. Bronsart had already aroused
Wilhelm's anger in the autumn of 1894, as Waldersee recorded in his diary, by
paying a visit to the Conservative member of the Reichstag, Count Julius von
Mirbach-Sorquitten, whom the Kaiser detested. 'The Kaiser . . . reprimanded the
Minister of War to his face for it and received a rather sharp answer from Bronsart,
who also wrote at once to Hahnke saying that he had been very unwilling to
become a minister, thought himself very ill-suited to it and would be glad to
resign.' Waldersee thought it 'sad that the Kaiser is already on such a bad footing
with the really very effective Minister of War, after barely a year'.[89] Another
violent clash between the monarch and the Prussian Minister of War is vividly
depicted in a letter from Marschall. On 17 February 1895 he wrote to Philipp
Eulenburg: 'After a dinner at Hahnke's house, which I attended with my wife, I
went into the smoking room where a lively conversation was going on between
Bronsart and Lucanus, into which the former drew me. Bronsart was recounting
a scene which he had on Thursday morning – the day on which His Majesty
treated me so ungraciously – with the Kaiser: "he had never thought he would
have to speak to his King in that way". During his report to the monarch he
had described the progress of the budget committee's discussions of the military
budget and had expressed himself very satisfied with and appreciative of the
Centre, which had approved all the items which he had considered particularly
important. At this His Majesty had become very ungracious and had expressed
the greatest offence not only at the Centre but in particular at Catholic officers,
who he said would throw off their uniforms and desert their King at the decisive
moment. His Majesty's words had been so insulting that he, Bronsart, had risen
to his feet and protested loudly against these insults; he thought he had turned
deathly pale with emotion and had found it very difficult to control himself.
His Majesty had not replied and the audience came to an end. He would never,
and would never wish to, experience such a scene again. The blame for it lay

with *the unscrupulous people who spur the Kaiser on – who they were, he did not know.* Lucanus kept very quiet and did not contradict Bronsart when he bitterly criticised the fact that Count Hoensbroech had been led up to speak to the Kaiser, when it was probably he who had stirred him up so much. These things make the position of the ministers utterly impossible; one wears oneself out in parliament trying to achieve something, and then anonymous advisers come along and ruin everything. Things cannot go on like this.'[90] The Foreign Secretary noted in his diary at this time that Bronsart had said to the Chief of the Civil Cabinet: 'The irresponsible advisers should all be sent to the scaffold.'[91] During the canal-opening ceremony at Kiel, Bronsart spoke 'in a highly conspicuous way' and 'with great irritation' about the Kaiser, and also suddenly burst out with the remark that Lucanus was 'the greatest criminal of the century'.[92]

General von Bronsart's renewed threat to resign was all the more dangerous for the Kaiser because the Minister of War, since taking office, had been working on a highly popular reform of military courts – in harmony with the wishes of the majority of the Reichstag and of the people he wished to introduce public trials, conducted *viva voce* rather than solely in writing – to which the Kaiser vehemently objected. It was not just that Bronsart would have gone out in a blaze of glory over of this issue, however. Neither the Reich Chancellor, who as Bavarian minister-president had introduced a similar measure and felt he could not now be 'more Prussian than a Prussian general', nor the majority of the Prussian ministers were prepared to remain in office if the Minister of War resigned. Hence the Bronsart crisis threatened to become a general government crisis which might have catastrophic consequences for the Kaiser's standing.[93] This question more than any other overshadowed German domestic politics during the first two years of Hohenlohe's chancellorship.

A week after the discussion between Wilhelm and Eulenburg at Prökelwitz in May 1895 about the principles governing the relationship between the Kaiser, the Chancellor and the Ministry of State, Hohenlohe tried in vain to bring up the subject of the fundamental differences between the monarch and the Minister of War on the increasingly highly charged issue of court martial reform. 'I was unable to carry out my intention of speaking to H.M. about Bronsart except in a limited way', he recorded with weary resignation on 31 May 1895. 'The Kaiser was not available to speak to throughout the boat trip, nor on the Pfaueninsel.' When the Chancellor approached the Kaiser just before dinner and began to speak of Bronsart, the court martial question and the danger of the Minister's resignation, 'he did not allow me to finish, but said that in these difficult times a minister ought not to abandon his king. He claimed that the Minister of War had declared himself in agreement with him; they were of one mind, and during a journey from Magdeburg to Berlin they had come to an understanding . . . After these remarks he went in to dinner and the conversation was over. I then had to ask the Minister of War about it, and he told me that it was all untrue.'[94] Later the Kaiser remarked to Philipp Eulenburg 'that he had half ruined his army with the two years' service and *under no circumstances* could he now be induced to ruin it *completely*'. Eulenburg was in no doubt that the Kaiser would be prepared to lose Hohenlohe over this issue.[95]

In the following weeks the crisis intensified dramatically when Bronsart wished to put before the Reichstag the proposed new regulations for courts martial, introducing public hearings on all questions not of purely military content, while the Kaiser, backed by Plessen and Hahnke, persisted in refusing to allow the bill to go forward in this form. When Bronsart again threatened to resign in mid-August 1895 the Kaiser's response, as Waldersee recorded, was to say to him: 'You cannot desert me now. And, after all, I gave you the Black Eagle very early.' Later Wilhelm made the War Minister a present of a French cannon, which led Waldersee to comment that 'the Kaiser is extraordinarily skilful in managing these things and has often been successful before. After such acts of kindness, which, it must also be said, he performs with irresistible charm, the reaction is always to say: the Kaiser has been so infinitely gracious, I really cannot go now.'[96] Wilhelm was now convinced that the whole question had been definitely laid aside and that Bronsart had given his assurance that he would 'let [the matter] rest completely'. Eulenburg was therefore horrified to hear in the autumn of 1895 that Bronsart had not given up his plans for reform and was threatening to take the Chancellor and the Ministry of State with him.[97] In an 'alarming' debate carried out in the press by both camps, Hahnke and Plessen – rightly, in Waldersee's view – were identified as the people responsible for 'hindering Bronsart's efforts with the Kaiser'. 'It is deplorable that the only real problems faced by such a man should be with the Kaiser', Waldersee commented, 'when the sovereign ought after all to do everything he can to retain such a powerful asset. But unfortunately it has got to the point where the only people in favour are those who accept the All-Highest whims without question, as the Cabinet chiefs do. For the moment H.M. does not have the sense to see that this destroys characters and causes untold harm, because in the end only pitiful wretches are left in power, but he will suffer badly from it when it is too late.'[98]

While the Kaiser was shooting at Liebenberg in October 1895 news arrived that the Minister of War, in spite of the Kaiser's veto, but with the support of the entire Ministry of State except Köller,[99] had introduced the issue of the regulation of courts martial into the Reichstag. 'It was extremely painful and distressing for me', Eulenburg recalled, 'to have to explain to my beloved Kaiser, while he was doing me the honour of being my guest, the position in which he now found himself.' The War Minister's conduct had acted on him 'like a bomb'. The Kaiser's friend eventually succeeded in persuading Wilhelm that to sack Bronsart was out of the question, since Hohenlohe and the Ministry of State had to be kept in office. Together they decided that the government should be ordered to consult the commanding generals, which would delay a decision for at least nine months.[100] Eulenburg wrote at once to the Chancellor reporting that the Kaiser was '*very angry indeed* at Bronsart's behaviour'. He had been absolutely confident that the question had been postponed and regarded it as an act of '*perfidy*' engineered from Friedrichsruh that it had been brought up again. On the other hand he did not intend 'to allow Bronsart to go *under any circumstances* at present, so as not to give him the opportunity of making a grand exit'. The Kaiser had also shown very little understanding for Hohenlohe's view that he could not remain in office if Bronsart should fall over this issue, Eulenburg stated. The only solution therefore lay in the postponement of the matter. 'The poor Kaiser has been very affected by this business – I hope that it will be possible to arrange for the postponement.'[101]

On his return to Berlin the Kaiser immediately went to see the Chancellor to vent his feelings on the matter. Hohenlohe heard him out before cautiously explaining his own point of view. As he had introduced public hearings for military courts as minister-president of Bavaria he could not now, as Reich chancellor, bring in a bill which excluded public hearings without appearing ridiculous and earning the contempt of the Reichstag. If Bronsart resigned over this bill he too must take his leave. The Kaiser recognised the force of this argument, 'but let out a stream of accusations against the Minister of War, complaining that the latter had sought the support of foreign sovereigns for his views and had persuaded the King of Saxony to use his influence with him, the Kaiser, in favour of public trials. That was high treason and he would have liked to take the Black Eagle away from the Minister of War and throw him out of the army.' In this 'fit of bad temper' Wilhelm repeated his accusation that Bismarck was behind the crisis; he was 'very angry' about it and his patience was at an end. When Hohenlohe pointed out that respected generals such as Loë and Albedyll were also in favour of the reform of military courts, the Kaiser disputed this, insisting that 'all the commanding generals were against it'. 'He summoned the help of Plessen, who was waiting in the ante-room. Plessen defended the Kaiser's point of view, but weakly. Finally the Kaiser decided to send Plessen to the Minister of War again, to induce him not to resign now and to agree that the matter be postponed until another session.'[102] That same evening the Kaiser was able to telegraph to Hohenlohe that he had had a long and friendly conversation with Bronsart, who had agreed to the postponement of the tiresome affair until after the commanding generals had been consulted.[103] Eulenburg was even able to report to the Grand Duke of Baden that during this discussion Bronsart had 'assured His Majesty of his loyalty with tears in his eyes and declared that he was willing to stay in office and to agree to the consultation'.[104]

But the truce proved short-lived. On 15 November Captain Count Bogdan von Hutten-Czapski, an influential member of the Prussian Upper House, reporting to Holstein on the Kaiser's mood, commented that the 'defenceless ancestors' were 'still alive and the poor soldiers will continue in future to be sentenced behind closed doors'. The Minister of War was complaining 'bitterly about the daily interference of H.M. in official matters, especially in armament questions which involved the senseless expenditure of large sums; irresponsible advisers always had some new invention on tap that caught the fancy of the Kaiser and brought disorder into the administration; Hahnke's influence in military and Lucanus's influence in political affairs made the routine transaction of official business impossible, etc.'. Bronsart took particular offence at the way in which the Kaiser had reacted to an article of 4 November 1895 in the *Münchener Neueste Nachrichten*, which had reported on the secret decision of the Ministry of State to introduce public military trials even against the Kaiser's will if necessary. General von Hahnke had been sent by Wilhelm to put the Minister of War 'on the carpet', and had given him a 'fairly severe' dressing-down about the article. 'In the past two years I have witnessed many fights between the Kaiser and Bronsart', Hutten-Czapski remarked, 'but have never seen the latter so wrought up. As I heard from the Chancellor, the Kaiser too is very irritated. This mood, or rather this bad mood, the importance of the problems at issue, and the volatile character of the participants arouses fears about a catastrophe; this would be all the more unfortunate because Bronsart is very well liked in the Reichstag, and above all he would fall as the protagonist of a reform that is popular in the whole Reich, which in turn would significantly increase the difficulties of the government.' Bronsart was also angry with Köller, who had been the only member of the Ministry of State to vote against public trials, so as to put himself across to the Kaiser as the champion of the traditions of the army, Hutten-Czapski reported. Bronsart suspected, probably rightly, that Köller was behind the Munich newspaper article, the purpose of which had been to 'damage' him and the Chancellor in the eyes of the Kaiser. Köller was an 'enfant terrible' who had frequently been very tactless in the Reichstag and who was now trying to 'win recognition from the Kaiser at the expense of his colleagues', the Count commented.[105]

On 18 November 1895, at a meeting of the Ministry of State, Bronsart accused the Minister of the Interior to his face not only of being responsible for the Munich newspaper article but also of having told the Kaiser and Generals Hahnke and Plessen, while the court was hunting at Letzlingen on 15 and

16 November, of his vote against court martial reform.[106] It was now unthinkable for Bronsart and Köller to continue to work together. Moreover even the least politically minded ministers were indignant at the Interior Minister's disloyal behaviour. Thielen and Schönstedt spoke out 'very firmly', and Hammerstein-Loxten reproached Köller for having given all the ministers 'the unpleasant impression . . . that he wanted to "curry favour" with H.M. by mentioning his dissenting vote and by subsequently talking to Hahnke and Plessen'. By 27 November 1895 it was clear to Hohenlohe that he would have to tell the Kaiser that the entire Ministry of State was united against Köller and demanded his resignation.[107] When he went to Potsdam the next day at the request of the Ministry to explain to the Kaiser why Köller and the other ministers could no longer work satisfactorily together, he found Wilhelm disinclined to take any notice of the matter. The Kaiser declared 'quite definitely, and in not very obliging terms, that he would not dismiss Köller. He was the only man on whose energy he could count if force ever needed to be used.' 'I then withdrew', the Reich Chancellor recorded, 'but stayed to luncheon in the Neues Palais, where the Kaiser resumed his usual manner. But the refusal affected my standing with the ministers and officials. Even Wilmowski took the view that I could not accept this. I now drew up my resignation letter.' But deeply angered as he was, Prince Hohenlohe did not send the letter, for he was unwilling to inflict such an embarrassment on the Kaiser just before the opening of the Reichstag.[108]

Instead he summoned the ministers to a meeting to report on the insulting treatment he had received in the Neues Palais and at the same time to tell them that he nevertheless had doubts as to whether it would be loyal to confront the Kaiser with a ministerial crisis three days before the opening of the Reichstag. Some of the ministers (Marschall, Boetticher, Berlepsch and Thielen) spoke out in favour of decisive action, others took a softer line; but as neither Miquel nor Bronsart was present the ministers postponed their decision until the following day.[109] On 1 December 1895 the Chancellor had to write to the Kaiser informing him that in the unanimous opinion of his ministerial colleagues no further profitable co-operation with Köller could be ensured, and that in the prevailing circumstances the latter had declared himself ready to submit his resignation to the Kaiser. He, Hohenlohe, must 'humbly submit' to the Kaiser 'that He should graciously accept the resignation of Minister von Köller'.[110]

The news of the crisis reached Philipp Eulenburg on 29 November at Merano. He wrote to the Kaiser expressing his sympathy, but warning strongly against a change of chancellor. 'I cannot bear Your Majesty to be tormented by continual crises', he wrote. 'I can still clearly remember the expression on Your Majesty's face when I took my leave in the Neues Palais and You said: "I cannot go through a third chancellor crisis." Now it has reached that point again.' As a result of this crisis, Eulenburg warned, Wilhelm faced the alternative of dismissing either Hohenlohe and the entire Ministry, or Köller alone. He must let Köller go, for otherwise he would 'bring about a crisis which, given the extremely complex European situation, would alarm Europe and brand Your Majesty as an inconstant and arbitrary ruler'. 'No chancellor crisis – *no change of chancellor* – at this moment', Eulenburg urged. 'That would create the impression for which Friedrichsruh has been lying in wait with eager anticipation: now the Kaiser has gone far enough! Now is the time for the Chancellor whom I, Bismarck, have in my hand, whether he is called Waldersee, Schweinitz or whatever!' The Kaiser must not dismiss Hohenlohe; 'the next change of chancellor must be left to a greater power than Your Majesty – death, to which the old Prince will unfortunately fall victim in the foreseeable future'.[111] The letter had the desired effect. On the morning of 2 December, on the train from Wildpark to Berlin, Köller had his last audience with the Kaiser, at the end of which he handed in his letter of resignation. It was accepted at once.[112] On the same day the Kaiser sent a telegram summoning Eulenburg to Breslau. Matters were not at all as Eulenburg believed, Wilhelm claimed.[113]

The 'mental state' of the Kaiser during their meeting at Breslau made a lasting impression on Eulenburg. 'I was so deeply affected, indeed shaken, . . . to see my beloved Kaiser suffering so much at Breslau', he afterwards wrote to Wilhelm himself.[114] 'I have never seen our beloved sovereign so agitated and so depressed at the same time', he wrote to Lucanus, echoing these words almost exactly in a letter to the Chancellor: 'I have never seen the Kaiser more agitated – but in particular, never *more depressed* than in Breslau.'[115] He telegraphed to Holstein expressing concern because 'His Majesty is deeply hurt.'[116] 'I happen to love H.M. personally very much', he wrote later, 'and to see a person suffer deeply whom one has taken to one's heart – that is not my strong point.' The Kaiser had really 'suffered *deeply*', and Eulenburg's meeting with him in Breslau had taken on 'the character of the heartfelt outpourings of a tormented spirit'. Eulenburg had therefore begged 'the dear old gentleman', the Reich Chancellor, to 'take into account this feeling of our suffering King'.[117]

At the Breslau meeting the Kaiser declared to his friend that the thought of another chancellor crisis had 'thrown Him into utter despair'. 'In fact he had never been reduced to such a dreadful state, because he had felt so deeply and painfully hurt by the *insult* to him which the action of the Ministry of State represented; he had never suffered a personal affront like this before, and he could not understand how his Uncle Hohenlohe had been able to lend himself to it: no doubt it was because of his age . . . He had completely lost his confidence in the entire Ministry.' Eulenburg believed that the Kaiser's antipathy towards the Ministry had been 'worked up to the maximum' under the influence of his military suite – Wilhelm had been accompanied to Breslau by both Moltkes, Kuno and Helmuth. If he, the Kaiser, stated that he continued to have confidence in Köller, the Ministry could not simply respond that Köller no longer had the confidence of the Ministry, Wilhelm declared. He was firmly convinced that such a 'rebellion' could not have originated 'in the mind of a *Prussian* minister'; 'Marschall was behind it, for he was constantly putting the constitution forward. The Kaiser also left it open to conjecture that the old democrat Miquel might have taken some pleasure in outvoting the King of Prussia.'[118] Eulenburg was also of the opinion that in this case the Prussian Ministry of State had 'in fact behaved like a Cabinet in a parliamentary state'. Behind it all he detected Marschall's Badenese attitudes, Hohenlohe's South German feelings, Bronsart's 'thirst for revenge' and the inner convictions of 'the old democrat' Miquel.[119]

In any event Kaiser Wilhelm II demanded satisfaction for the 'gross insubordination' of the Ministry of State. His idea was, he said, that the entire Ministry should hand in its resignation by way of atonement, which he would then refuse to accept.[120] On hearing of this suggestion by the Kaiser, Marschall at once commented, 'That is what we aimed above all to avoid by acting in the way we did, since H.M. would then in fact have been in a position of constraint.'[121] Eulenburg also pointed out to the Kaiser that the collective resignation of the Ministry of State would have to remain a secret, for 'if it became known that the entire Ministry had tendered its resignation, and the Ministry then stayed on while Köller left, public opinion would *inevitably* draw the conclusion that handing in their resignations was their method of getting rid of Köller – and that this method *succeeded*'. In addition, if a collective resignation were publicly announced, a chancellor crisis might well follow, which must be avoided at all costs because it would seriously threaten the stability of the country. The formal resignation of the Ministry was necessary as an example for the future, but for the present it must be kept strictly confidential, Eulenburg argued. He was, he added, 'quite miserable' because 'I cannot bear to see Your Majesty in torment any longer!'[122]

On 5 December 1895 the Chief of the Civil Cabinet was able to report to Eulenburg that his arguments against the public announcement of the collective resignation of all the ministers had persuaded the Kaiser to abandon his idea altogether. Instead he had agreed with the Reich Chancellor that Köller would not be dismissed for the time being, but would merely be sent away on holiday, and that the Ministry of State would receive a 'firm order' in which its 'improper conduct' would be 'censured, and the rights of the crown emphatically upheld'. 'I thank God', Lucanus wrote, 'that there is some progress and that our Imperial Master will be given satisfaction without any more grave crises arising from it. His Majesty's mood has also improved as a result.'[123] Waldersee, however, recorded after the Kaiser had been shooting at Springe on 7 December, that Wilhelm was still 'in a decidedly serious mood' because of Köller's enforced resignation.[124] His anger with the Reich Chancellor and the ministers expressed itself in an 'unguarded remark' he made at this time and which was repeated by one of his Flügeladjutanten. At a function attended, among others, by Hohenlohe, Boetticher, Marschall and Berlepsch, the Kaiser pointed at them and called out mockingly: 'Aha, look at the Convention sitting over there!'[125]

The 'firm order', probably drafted by Lucanus, that Wilhelm II addressed to the Prussian Ministry of State on 9 December 1895 very clearly reflects the Prussian conception of 'personal monarchy', as opposed to parliamentary monarchy. In his capacity as king of Prussia Wilhelm rebuked the Ministry of State for its behaviour in the Köller crisis, which was 'inappropriate to the position in which the Ministry of State in Prussia stands in relation to the king. In the Prussian monarchy the appointment and dismissal of ministers is the constitutional right of the king, and the king's confidence alone is decisive in that regard. If therefore the Ministry of State, although aware that My confidence in Minister von Köller remained undiminished, induced the latter to hand in his resignation, the Ministry of State has thereby created a situation which may well be not unusual in states ruled by a parliamentary system, but which has no precedent in Prussia. It is my intention, however, to maintain in full the historical and constitutional rights and prerogatives of My crown and in due course to transmit them undiminished to my successors. I am compelled by the present case to announce this to the Ministry of State, so that its significance as a precedent for all time may be recognised.'[126]

Wilhelm II continued to urge his uncle the Reich Chancellor to stick to the 'old Prussian point of view' in dealing with the ministers, namely 'that a Prussian minister is in the agreeable position of not having to worry about the success or failure of any bill put forward by him in case he might have to resign on account of it. For he has *not* achieved office at the wish or under the mandate of one or other party in the Chamber. On the contrary, my ministers are appointed quite freely by me as a mark of All-Highest confidence; and as long as they possess this confidence they need not concern themselves with anything else. They are in a better position than in other constitutional states. I should be very grateful to you if you would occasionally remind the ministers very specifically about this principle, since as a result of their morally corrupting dealings with parliaments they are occasionally affected by attacks of constitutionalism, or, as with Miquel, infected by an old parliamentarian . . . Your faithful Nephew and King Wilhelm I. R.'[127]

More than ever, the Kaiser was determined to give an unmistakable demonstration of his right to decide on appointments in choosing a new minister of the interior. His first thought, characteristically, was to nominate the Chief of his Civil Cabinet, Hermann von Lucanus, as successor to Köller, which – since all the ministers declared this choice 'impossible'[128] – reawakened the danger of collective resignation by the Ministry of State. Philipp Eulenburg warned urgently of the consequences of another conflict. If the Kaiser gained the impression that '*the Ministry to which he has had to give way over Köller is exploiting its victory*, either there will be a storm which will change everything and alarm the world, or it will put him into a mental state which I fear *even more*: loss of the self-confidence that we *need*, that is *essential*. That would mean that the Kaiser is *completely* in the power of Lucanus – or of some other person.'[129] But although Wilhelm gave up the idea of appointing Lucanus, he also rejected the unanimous suggestions of the ministers, who recommended the Oberpräsident of Westphalia, Konrad Studt, the Regierungspräsident in Cologne, Oswald Freiherr von Richthofen, and the Secretary of State at the Reich Treasury, Count Posadowsky.[130] On 8 December the Kaiser sent Hohenlohe a telegram informing him that after detailed discussions he had appointed the Regierungspräsident of Düsseldorf, Eberhard Freiherr von der Recke von dem Horst, as minister of the interior.[131] As the Reich Chancellor rightly observed, the Kaiser had chosen the new minister entirely by himself.[132]

After the Köller crisis Eulenburg fell back on his old formula, according to which the Kaiser should take the most important political decisions in agreement with the Reich Chancellor, after which the ministers simply had to carry them out. He put it to Holstein on 7 December that Wilhelm was convinced that in the Köller crisis he had overstepped the mark of 'what a self-confident Prussian king may do'. Care must therefore be taken in future 'that H.M. should never feel he is being overridden by the entire Ministry of State, but only that he is facing *the definite firm will of the Chancellor, man to man*'.[133] 'The main focus must be placed on the understanding between H.M. and the Chancellor. At the expense of the *whole* Ministry, as far as I am concerned', he declared in a letter to Bülow.[134] 'He [Hohenlohe] will always have Y.M.'s confidence if he takes decisions alone with Y.M.', Eulenburg wrote to the Kaiser. 'If he obeys Y.M.'s will, Y.M. will also take account of the wishes which *he* may perhaps express at some time with regard to appointments. In my Prussian heart the only conceivable alliance is "the king with his minister-president and chancellor" against the ministers, not "the minister-president with all the ministers" against the king – if it is inevitable that controversial questions arise.'[135] According to the Kaiser's favourite, whose influence, with both the Kaiser and the Chancellor, was now at its height, everything depended, as he told the latter, on ensuring that 'what happens from now on should be decided *in dialogue between H. Maj. and Yr. Highness*. If the ministers do not accept what Yr. Highness has discussed and agreed with H. Maj., another resignation by this or that minister would *strengthen Yr. Highness's position vis-à-vis His Majesty immensely*, because H. Majesty would have to recognise it as the result of firm support for *His* wishes.' This form of decision-making had always been what the Kaiser wanted, Eulenburg emphasised.[136] '*Je ne demande pas mieux*', the 'dear old gentleman' replied, but added awkwardly that he was often afraid that, even when he wanted to speak to the Kaiser urgently, he was a nuisance to him. 'If I am wrong in thinking so, I shall be all the more pleased.'[137] The treatment that he was to receive over the next few months both in foreign affairs and at home could only confirm his worst fears.

# CHAPTER TWENTY-FIVE

# Wilhelm and world politics

## THE KAISER AND THE FOREIGN POLICY OF THE NEWEST COURSE

**D**URING the chancellorship of his 'Uncle Chlodwig', Wilhelm II controlled the foreign policy of the German Reich to an even greater extent than he had been able to do in Caprivi's time.[1] His activity in this sphere was no longer limited to an occasional intervention in the Wilhelmstrasse's otherwise carefully calculated diplomatic games of finesse; he now determined the guidelines of foreign policy himself in characteristically impetuous and emotional fashion, often after discussing them with this or that favourite, Flügeladjutant, naval officer, ambassador or other visitor to the court, and expected his orders to be carried out by the Reich Chancellor and the Foreign Office. In the chancelleries of the European powers – including those of Germany's allies – there was concern at the harsher, more aggressive note to be detected in German foreign policy, which was generally attributed to Wilhelm II's personal influence. Thus for instance in November 1894 the usually circumspect Austrian Foreign Minister, Count Kálnoky, complained to the British ambassador, Sir Edmund Monson, in an unmistakable reference to the Kaiser, that German policy was now characterised by 'sudden impulse'.[2] A year later Martin Gosselin, then British chargé d'affaires in Berlin, went a step further and reported that the rumour was rife in Berlin that the Kaiser was suffering from hallucinations. He added, not without reason, 'It becomes, indeed, a serious matter if a Sovereign who possesses a dominant voice in the foreign policy of the Empire is subject to hallucinations & influences which must in the long run warp his judgement, & render Him liable at any moment to sudden changes of opinion which no one can anticipate or provide against.'[3] Waldersee thought much the same, commenting in his diary in 1896: 'If only our Kaiser would keep his hands off foreign policy; it is a field which he thinks he has mastered, but in fact he does everything wrong. It must be a sad task to be chancellor or secretary of state for foreign affairs! But these good people are willing to accept any kind of mistreatment; in my opinion they sin against both the Kaiser and the Fatherland by doing so.'[4]

Some of the new Reich Chancellor's closest colleagues, however, would not have disagreed with these criticisms. In December 1895 Friedrich von Holstein spoke of the 'unprecedented direct interference of the Kaiser in Foreign Office business', which was not only a vote of no confidence in Hohenlohe, Marschall and Holstein himself, but constituted 'an immense danger, because of the Kaiser's naïvety and lack of experience'. 'The Kaiser his own Reich chancellor' was a perilous formula whatever the circumstances, the Privy Councillor continued, 'but most definitely now, with this impulsive and unfortunately very superficial sovereign, who knows nothing of constitutional law, of political events, of diplomatic history and − of how to handle people'.[5] Marschall too voiced his discontent at this time. 'Things are going badly with H.M. He constantly interferes in foreign policy. A monarch must have the last word, H.M. always wants to have the first word, and this is a cardinal error.'[6]

At the end of 1894 or early in 1895 Prince Alexander Hohenlohe, at the request of his father, drafted a revealing letter of protest to the Kaiser. The first version of the letter contained a passage reading: 'There are two ways in which foreign policy can be conducted in monarchical states: either as in Russia, where the Tsar is his own minister of foreign affairs and the minister merely carries out the orders, or as here, where the minister of foreign affairs is responsible not only to H.M the Kaiser, but also to the country.' As this emphasis on the constitution would certainly have aroused the anger of the Kaiser, this passage was crossed out and replaced by a milder version: 'I have always held fast to the principle that foreign policy must be conducted in accordance with Your M's commands. The fulfilment of these commands is the duty of the Reich chancellor and the Foreign Office respectively. The Reich chancellor must take care that the instructions sent by him or the Foreign Office to the ambassadors do not conflict with any commands which might be sent directly from Y.M. to the ambassadors, or with communications which Y.M. thinks fit to send to foreign sovereigns. The interests of Y.M. require that measures be taken to avoid any possibility of contradiction or misunderstanding. This can only be the case, however, if Y.M. is graciously pleased to inform me of any direct communications to foreign sovereigns, in so far as they concern the progress of diplomatic negotiations.' The fact that even this watered-down plea was never sent speaks volumes.[7] Instead, where foreign affairs were concerned Prince Hohenlohe adopted the attitude disparaged by his son as the 'Russian' way: that of the minister simply following the orders of the Kaiser. An example of this is provided by his 'reverent' phraseology in the summer of 1895 when he sought the instructions of his All-Highest Sovereign on a question affecting an alliance, which was after all a matter of vital importance to the Reich. 'Y.M. would place me under a debt of reverent thanks', he wrote, 'if Y.M. would be pleased to inform me by telegraph of Y.M.'s All-[Highest] will, so that, according to the circumstances, I would be in a position to adopt the attitude corresponding to Y.M.'s will.'[8]

As we have already had occasion to see, the influence which Kaiser Wilhelm II exercised on the formulation of foreign policy manifested itself in the highly personal way in which he took decisions on appointments. He alone decided – often after discussions with his friend Philipp Eulenburg, perhaps during his Scandinavian cruises or on hunting expeditions – who should go where as ambassador or envoy,[9] but he was just as likely to make such decisions of his own accord. He regarded the filling of senior diplomatic posts as the crown's prerogative; as a rule he had not the slightest qualms in ignoring the advice of Hohenlohe, despite the decades of diplomatic experience the Reich Chancellor had to offer as former Bavarian Minister-President, German ambassador in Paris and Statthalter in Strassburg. When for example in 1895 Hohenlohe recommended the then Prussian envoy in Stuttgart, Theodor von Holleben, for the difficult post of Beijing, Wilhelm turned down the Reich Chancellor's suggestion on the grounds that Holleben's recall from Stuttgart would be 'unwelcome' to the King of Württemberg.[10] The Kaiser was also chiefly responsible for the sudden replacement of the German ambassador at St Petersburg, General von Werder, by the former Marshal of the Court Hugo Prince von Radolin in the spring of 1895. The advice which Holstein gave his friend Radolin on his appointment is evidence of the pernicious influence which the gossip-loving, indiscreet Kaiser exercised on the diplomatic profession: 'take pains to write interesting reports on the Kaiser's account. But then be careful in your criticisms about things which, if repeated in St Petersburg, might cause trouble for you. One never knows.'[11]

There were a few instances when the Kaiser allowed himself to be persuaded by the Reich Chancellor's representations to give way over an appointment. But such concessions were exceptions which merely confirmed the rule: foreign policy during Prince Hohenlohe's chancellorship, as Wolfgang J. Mommsen has rightly commented, was dominated by the 'uncontrolled personal rule' of Wilhelm II.[12] As he had done before, the Kaiser invited German ambassadors abroad to correspond directly with him, bypassing the Reich Chancellor and the Foreign Office, and took it amiss if they did not respond to their sovereign's invitation. Count Paul von Hatzfeldt, who had been the German Reich's representative in London for many years, attributed the Kaiser's noticeably unfriendly attitude towards him to the fact that he had 'never made use of his repeated permission to write to him directly'. The ambassador justified his refusal to do so on the grounds that 'in the first place it does not accord with my way of doing business to make policy behind the chancellor's back', and 'furthermore, although I can keep quiet and blindly carry out what I am told to do, I cannot express specific agreement when it would not correspond with my convictions to do so', which had frequently been the case recently.[13]

What was more, the Kaiser repeatedly and without the knowledge of the Reich Chancellor or the Foreign Office called on the ambassadors and military attachés of foreign powers in Berlin to discuss vitally important and secret foreign relations matters with them, or to make revelations of breathtaking significance. Hohenlohe had hardly moved into the Reich chancellor's palace when he found that the Kaiser, in direct negotiations with the Japanese envoy Aoki, had proposed a trade treaty between Japan and Germany.[14] In January 1895 he asked the Russian ambassador, Count Shuvalov, the real reasons for the Franco-Russian rapprochement – receiving the answer that it was the result of the non-renewal of the secret Reinsurance Treaty in the spring of 1890 – and told the astonished ambassador that the Triple Alliance could become a Quadruple Alliance if Russia joined. The Reich Chancellor and the Foreign Secretary did not hear of these ventures into high politics until the next morning.[15] Waldersee was shocked by the manner in which Wilhelm spoke of the heir to the Bavarian throne in the presence of the Russian ambassador. Although Shuvalov was seated at the same small table as the Kaiser, Wilhelm gave vent to 'extremely critical remarks about Prince Ludwig of Bavaria, in the presence of a foreign ambassador! It sent cold shivers down the spines of those listening, and some of them tried to divert the conversation on to something else, but in vain. The Kaiser does not seem to realise that it is Shuvalov's duty, even if the Kaiser regards him as a personal friend, to send home a report of the conversation.'[16]

Early in the morning of 18 January 1895 the Kaiser paid a surprise visit – 'without the slightest word to the Chancellor'[17] – to the French embassy and complained vehemently to the ambassador, Jules Herbette, about the fall of President Casimir-Périer. It was events of this kind, he explained to the bewildered representative of the neighbouring republic, that had made him an enemy of parliamentarism.[18] At the same time, in marginal notes on diplomatic reports, the Kaiser urged that strictly confidential negotiations be held between the monarchies of Europe in order to agree 'a common line' against revolution which could become the basis of operations if indeed, as he expected, 'something surprising' should happen in Paris.[19] Both Hohenlohe and Holstein were furious at this wilful interference by the Kaiser in diplomatic affairs,[20] and Waldersee was no less indignant at Wilhelm's initiative, which showed that the Kaiser had no real idea of the effect which his interference had on foreign policy. 'He fails to understand that this is an important political act possibly entailing considerable consequences', the General complained, adding 'Hohenlohe was very unhappy about it himself, but seems to have said nothing.'[21] On 25 January the Kaiser appeared at the Reich Chancellor's palace; as Hohenlohe told Holstein, he was seeking to justify his marginal comments. 'He said he would hear nothing about an action by the powers against France. Therein he agreed with me. What H.M. is considering is the following: he fears that in the event of the formation of a revolutionary socialistic government, one or another of the *monarchical* governments might betray the solidarity of the monarchical governments . . . and establish relations with the revolutionary government in France. H.M. would like to prevent this and make certain that the solidarity of the monarchical governments did not "crumble". "How this is to be arranged", so says H.M., "is a problem for cleverer people than I."'[22] The following year Herbette, who had been French ambassador for ten years, had to be recalled from Berlin after an incident during a ball at the Opera House, when the Kaiser asked him whether the recall of the French military attaché, the Comte de Foucauld, could be cancelled. When Herbette answered in the negative, the Kaiser abruptly and ostentatiously turned on his heel, after which the ambassador's position, in spite of attempts at reconciliation on all sides, was fatally undermined.[23] Wilhelm even went so far as to discuss high politics with the French ambassador in London, Baron de Courcel, during a visit to the Isle of Wight.[24]

In the spring of 1896 the Secretary of State at the Foreign Office joined forces with Holstein in urging the Reich Chancellor to threaten resignation in order to stop the Kaiser's direct discussions with foreign ambassadors. 'They say I should make the Kaiser refrain from all conversation with the ambassadors. If the Kaiser did not agree I should have no alternative but to go', the elderly Prince noted in his journal. But he went on to comment resignedly: 'The Kaiser's conversations with the ambassadors cannot be prevented. If I had regarded that as a reason for resigning I should have had occasion enough to go. To leave him in the lurch now, when the situation is becoming serious, would be simple dereliction of duty.'[25]

Wilhelm of course continued to annotate diplomatic reports with insulting remarks, as for instance in September 1895 when the German envoy in Lisbon reported that the Marquis de Soveral, hitherto Portuguese ambassador in London, had been appointed foreign minister. 'The blue monkey!', Wilhelm II scribbled on the report. 'It is amazing what heights a mandrill can reach.' In 1897 he wrote in the margin of further reports from Lisbon: 'The blue monkey is either a villain in the pay of England, or a great fathead! . . . I think he is a fathead.'[26] Similarly, the Kaiser made no secret of his annoyance at the appointment of Lobanov as Russian foreign minister in February 1895.[27] Not surprisingly, his telegrams and aggressive speeches constantly created a stir, especially when they concerned sensitive international questions. In the spring of 1895 Waldersee observed that the mood in France was becoming 'more hostile towards us as a result of the Kaiser's latest speeches'.[28] In September, while shooting at Rominten, he sent telegrams to the Reich Chancellor and the Chief of the Military Cabinet ordering them to submit proposals to him as to how Germany should respond to recent French armament plans.[29] Three weeks later the General welcomed the 'very strong' speech which the Kaiser had made at the dedication of the memorial to his father on the battlefield at Wörth, and in which he had emphasised that Germany would never surrender the Reich territory of Alsace-Lorraine; the speech had been just what was needed, in response not only to the vociferous demands for revenge coming from the French, but also to the 'many feeble spirits' in Germany itself, who saw the surrender of Lorraine as a way out of the international dilemma.[30]

But Wilhelm II's most dangerous activity, in terms of foreign policy, was the personal correspondence which he conducted with other monarchs and which the Reich Chancellor often did not see at all, or did not see until weeks after it had been written.[31] The notorious 'Willy–Nicky' correspondence, which began with the accession of the young Tsar Nicholas II in November 1894 and which aroused universal anger when it was published by the Bolsheviks in 1918, will be examined later in this chapter. Somewhat less explosive was the correspondence between Wilhelm II and King Umberto of Italy, and yet in the spring of 1896, when the Italian army had suffered a catastrophic defeat near Adua in the Tigre province of Ethiopia, this correspondence led to a fundamental disagreement between Hohenlohe and the Kaiser over the latter's personal diplomacy.

On 8 March 1896 Hohenlohe felt compelled to object to the dispatch of the former military attaché in Rome, now Flügeladjutant Colonel von Engelbrecht, to King Umberto with a letter written by Wilhelm himself.[32] Once again it was Holstein who had impressed upon the Chancellor the dangers of surrender. 'If Your Highness gives way, this kind of thing will be repeated *de plus fort en plus fort* . . . If it should come to the point — which I doubt — of Your Highness having to threaten resignation, please consider my own also at your disposal.'[33] Not least because he felt obliged to protect the ambassador at Rome, Bülow, from Engelbrecht's intrigues, the Prince nerved himself to write to the monarch stating that the Flügeladjutant's mission could not be permitted to go ahead. Such a step, he said, would inaugurate a policy for which he could not accept responsibility.[34] The Kaiser's reply is characteristic of his attitude to the conduct of foreign policy in general. 'Dear Uncle', he wrote, 'Your letter, which I have just received, and which prevents me from carrying out my intention of relieving poor King Umberto's situation, came as a most painful surprise. In it you say that he would be hurt by such a step! I see from this that you are not familiar with what happened concerning the question of army formations. In Bismarck's time, that is to say 7 years ago, the question arose and *enquiries were made in Berlin* by Italy as to what the reaction here would be if there were a reduction of cadres. The Prince [Bismarck] was very worried about it and moved heaven and earth *to prevent it*, as a result of which, through heavy pressure and Engelbrecht's single-minded skill this question was eventually postponed and the *Italians retained*, with a heavy heart but *by Germany's express official desire*, the very expensive organisation they had. Indeed even the King gave me *his word* during my visit to Rome, jamais je ne laisserai toucher à l'Armée. Now he is in a position of constraint: he cannot take a decision to do something until I release him from his word and he is given a free hand from here, which he does *not* have now. As he is very gentle and warm-hearted and has such close links with me, my letter would console him, give him courage and calm him. Furthermore, it in fact contains the same phrase that Bülow used in speaking to [Foreign Minister] Sermoneta yesterday on my behalf in accordance with your instructions, that whatever they did, Italy's value as our ally would not be affected. But as we *forbade* Italy 7 years ago to reduce its corps, we now bear *full responsibility* if the King consequently has to face difficult inner conflicts or other problems. I therefore urgently beg you to allow the letter to be sent so as to release the King from his word and give him back his freedom of action. He has already been advised by telegram that my letter is coming. Your devoted nephew Wilhelm I. R.'[35]

This time, surprisingly, Hohenlohe stood firm. He pointed out to the Kaiser that a word to the Italian ambassador in Berlin would suffice to allay the scruples of the King of Italy, whereas to send Engelbrecht to Rome would undermine Bülow's position. He therefore considered the Colonel's mission 'inadmissible for political reasons'.[36] And as Holstein had predicted, the Kaiser did in fact climb down, although with such bad grace that Hohenlohe's worst fears were realised. In reply to the Chancellor's objections he wrote: 'Dear Uncle, I believe I detect in your second letter of last night a certain sharpness which I cannot entirely reconcile with the subject it concerns. The very strong opposition which you express, in a way I do not fully understand, against Engelbrecht's so-called "mission", and which at the end of the letter culminates in a kind of threatening rejection, of course obliges me to give up the idea of carrying out my wish. So he will not go. Although I had sent a telegram to the King [Umberto] announcing that he would be coming with a letter. Now I shall have to find some excuse. I acted with the best intentions and hoped to give my ally some comfort and reassurance, which he urgently needed. I had loyally kept you informed of everything and shown you everything in advance, and now it has all come to nothing. You must of course bear the responsibility for it and for whatever consequences it may have.

But one expression in your letter pained me deeply and that is the sentence: "Engelbrecht's mission would weaken Bülow's position!" I can only conclude from this that you think me capable of personally going behind the backs of my own officials, whom I have myself appointed. I need hardly say that Engelbrecht had orders to call on Bülow at once and talk to him. It is equally clear that my Flügeladjutant is a welcome visitor to the ambassador, especially when – as in this case – he has spent nearly 10 years in the embassy in question, and that as the bearer of a letter from his sovereign it redounds to the credit of the ambassador to help him gain an audience. Particularly as the matter in question was of a purely military-technical nature and one with which the adjutant had been familiar for many years, while the ambassador, in spite of all his experience, is only a civilian and therefore cannot judge or understand purely military matters in the same way as a professional soldier who, furthermore – in this case – has himself conducted all the negotiations over these matters. It was also quite clear that Bülow is my personal, intimate friend, upon whom I have just conferred a Grand Cross for his outstanding services, and whom I would have to be mad, or a wicked intriguer, to want to harm or weaken in his position. Having examined both my own motives and the step I contemplated, it seems to me that it would in fact have been a help to you. But I have received a harsh rejection from you and it has hurt me all the more because I have given you so many proofs of my complete dependence on you and confidence in you in the course of this last winter. I have not entertained a single political idea or taken a single step without anxiously discussing it in detail with you, at the risk of pestering you with my frequent visits, or of looking almost incapable of independent action in the eyes of the world. So it weighs all the more heavily on me for being so unexpected, that you should accuse me of taking a step that would prevent you from carrying out your policy and weaken the ambassador's position; in other words, first you think I am capable of hatching intrigues behind your back, and second you think a Royal Prussian Colonel and Flügeladjutant capable of lending his hand to such an activity. I am sure that if you consider this affair calmly you will give up your completely groundless suspicions and will realise that my plan to send Engelbrecht would no more have harmed Bülow than the "mission" of Colonel and Flügeladjutant von Moltke to the Tsar harmed Radolin's position. On the contrary, it was of the greatest value to him. I hope your confidence in me will return, for one can often hold very different opinions about things and also argue about them sometimes, but that is no reason to suspect each other of evil motives, especially not in your truly devoted nephew Wilhelm I. R.'[37] This time it was the Chancellor's turn to apologise 'most humbly' for the expressions used in his 'hurriedly written' letter. He had 'hitherto always tried', he wrote to the Kaiser during a meeting of the Ministry of State, 'to express myself to

Y.M. only in a manner which expressed the deep reverence and loyal devotion which I have in my heart for Y.M.'.[38] He had 'absolute confidence in Y.M.'s wisdom and prudence' and hoped that he would be able to give proof of this in the future. Although his behaviour had displeased the Kaiser, he particularly begged him not to be deterred by this from 'honouring me with All-Highest visits. The discussions I have with Y.M. in person are the highlights of my arduous existence, and to receive Y.M.'s commands orally certainly contributes more to the satisfactory conduct of affairs than lengthy written reports.'[39]

Two days later the Kaiser sent his letter to King Umberto to Rome after all, but through Bülow, with orders to give the letter to the King unopened. The ambassador was obliged to guess from the King's remarks what the letter contained. Bülow felt compelled to urge the Chancellor 'not to mention *to anyone* the fact that this letter had been sent', although he was prepared to accept that it was 'doubtless a sign of conciliatory feeling' that he, and not the special messenger Engelbrecht, had been entrusted with the transmittal of the letter in the end.[40] Just as Holstein had done, Bülow warned of the 'incommensurable dangers of "rule by adjutant"'.[41] In similar vein Count Münster, the longstanding ambassador in Paris, asked despairingly: 'What is the point of the Wilhelmstrasse, when its business is divided among the Flügeladjutanten? One of old Kaiser Wilhelm's greatest qualities was that he never interfered in the business of the various departments and officials of the state!'[42]

During his Mediterranean cruise the following month Wilhelm II had an opportunity to comfort 'His Majesty's friend and ally' Umberto in person over the defeat in Tigre. When the King lamented the fact that 200 officers whom he knew personally had died in vain in Africa, the Kaiser responded that it was the lot of the soldier and an honour to die a soldier's death. 'The Italian officers who had fallen in Africa had died loyal to their King and for the glory of their flag. The honour of the Italian army had been upheld.' The example of Frederick the Great showed that defeats could be overcome; it was only a matter of knowing how to 'make up for them at the opportune moment and in the right place'. 'Revenge was a dish which had to be served cold. Instead of battling *contre vent et marée* in Eritrea, Italy ought to collect and strengthen itself militarily, financially and in its internal political situation.' Since the French had helped the Abyssinians by sending them money, arms and even a large number of officers, Italy must take revenge on *them*. 'The right moment to pay back the French', the Kaiser commented, 'must . . . be awaited with a cool head; the reckoning would come in the end not in the mountains and ravines of Tigre but on Middle European terrain.' As far as the Russian flirtation with Abyssinia was concerned, in Wilhelm's view it was 'a product of the increasingly evident hostility between Russia and England. This historic antagonism, which dominated the overall situation in Europe, was becoming noticeable outside our continent. It was not in the interest of Italy to put itself between the bear and the whale.' Umberto was particularly impressed by the Kaiser's remarks about developments in the Muslim world, in which an 'explosion of Islamic fanaticism' might be in the offing, which would be of great significance for Anglo-Russian rivalry.[43] These utterances in themselves give a clear indication of the militaristic and belligerent direction in which Wilhelm was now making his growing influence felt. They were far from the only pronouncements by the Kaiser which seemed to anticipate the future course of German foreign policy in a sometimes alarming manner.

## WILHELM II AND THE SCANDINAVIAN CRISIS

The crisis-ridden developments in many parts of the world – in the Far East, where Japan and China were at war, in the collapsing Turkish empire, in the Horn of Africa, where Italy's colonial aspirations were causing dissension among the great powers, and in Madagascar, where the French were establishing a hold – presented Wilhelm with ample opportunities to bring his own, or rather Germany's, ambitions to the fore. But the issue which particularly concerned him at this time, because of his personal acquaintance with the Swedish royal family, into which his cousin Viktoria of Baden had married, was that of the threat posed by the Norwegian independence movement to the unity of the King- dom of Sweden and Norway. As always, he saw a popular rebellion of this kind as a menace to the monarchical principle. In addition to this he feared that the independence of Norway might lead to that country being divided between Russia and Britain, which he was not prepared to countenance without German involvement in the south of the country. During the Scandinavian crisis of July 1893 he had already gone so far as to give orders, in a telegram to Caprivi, for the occupation of southern Norway in the event of a national uprising against the rule of the King of Sweden. His message ran: 'In case it should come to an open rebellion in Norway and the King were not able to suppress it, and if he should appeal to us and other friendly monarchies for aid, Count von Wedel [the German envoy] should be instructed that I am naturally ready to help and My navy is at his disposal. It is our duty, wherever monarchies are under threat, to spring to their aid and support them. Just as we did so morally in Portugal, we must be ready in case we have to do so physically in Norway.'[44] Three years later, when the situation in Scandinavia had become even more acute, the Kaiser subjected Prince Hohenlohe to a long lecture on the Norwegian question, which he believed could lead to the break-up of the union with Sweden at any moment. King Oscar was indecisive and could not cope with the increasingly radical Nor- wegian population, Wilhelm maintained. 'Generous supplies of Russian money were circulating in the country and, if the union were abandoned, it was to be feared that Russia would carry out its long-cherished plan and occupy part of Norway in the region of Tromsoe. The English would not be happy with that, and so they would also occupy part of the country, and in that case we should have to make haste to take the southern part of Norway, before the Danes did so. For we could not tolerate Denmark establishing a hold there . . . We would have to maintain a close watch and instruct the consul to keep us abreast of the situation by daily telegrams, for it might be necessary to send out a fleet, if Russia and England went ahead.'[45] During the Scandinavian cruise that year Kaiser Wilhelm had a serious discussion with the King of Sweden and Norway, which Philipp Eulenburg summed up in a memorandum as follows: 'Germany is the natural friend of Scandinavia, because it cannot be in favour of Russian expansion in the Baltic. If Scandinavia falls apart, however, and Russia takes over the north of Norway, while England perhaps takes Bergen, Germany may be compelled to occupy the southern areas of Norway. In order to avoid this eventuality, which would be extremely troublesome for Germany, Scandinavia must restore order *itself*, and in a forceful manner.' The possibility could not be ruled out, however, that 'even if Sweden intends to restore order in Norway by force, Russia will use the unrest as an excuse to take action for her own part, and perhaps occupy Tromsö and Bodö . . . It can be assumed that England will then occupy Bergen. A peaceful settlement between England and Russia could no doubt still be achieved by holding a conference, but *an agreement between these two powers* over Norway would be *at our expense*. For the existence of Sweden would be endangered by an agreement which was reached on the basis of occupation of Norwegian ports. The country would soon fall into Russia's lap like a ripe fruit. Germany could not tolerate such a shift in the balance of power in the Baltic. But then we should find ourselves faced with an unpopular war. Accordingly, German interests would be best served if the *integrity* of the present Scandinavia were maintained. It cannot be safely assumed that an Anglo-Russian war will develop from the Norwegian question. If England acquires a Norwegian port, she will probably be content with that. In the event that Russia occupies a Norwegian port, we should probably have to remain as spectators and wait to see how the conflict of interests between Russia and England developed. If it reaches the point that England occupies a Norwegian port, we should have to occupy Stavanger, and probably Christiania [now Oslo] too, to protect our own interests. That will put us on a better footing as the situation develops. We could later attach conditions to the surrender of what we had taken by way of security, or indeed we could protect Sweden better from the Russian threat by maintaining our occupation. His Majesty *is inclined to favour* such an occupation in the event that England and Russia proceed to occupy ports.'[46]

That summer, on board the *Hohenzollern*, Wilhelm II dictated to Philipp Eulenburg a letter with racist overtones addressed to Crown Prince Gustaf of Sweden. He did not send a copy to the Reich Chancellor until two months later. The developments in Norway, the Kaiser's letter explained, filled him 'with genuine anxiety'. Norway wanted at all costs to break away from the union with Sweden, and was thereby threatening 'the survival of both kingdoms and the stability of European peace. Given the gentle disposition and sensitive conscience of the King [of Sweden], it is a popular trick to draw his attention to the apparently sacred nature of the Norwegian constitution and to his oath upon it, so as to set him at war with his own conscience . . . But in the end it must come to conflict. And that is because the Norwegian constitution has proved to be completely inadequate, and has put the survival of the union under threat by placing the King in a powerless position. In other words: the King of Norway must now give way to the King of the union. The latter has also taken an oath: to maintain the union whatever happens.' 'I beseech you', Wilhelm exhorted the Crown Prince, 'to keep the King in constant remembrance of this point . . . If the King does not succeed *soon and once for all* in bringing about calm and lasting stability in Norway, it is inevitable that foreign states will intervene. Russia, as your neighbour, will be the first to put its finger into the pie. Under the appearance of friendly help on the grounds that the persistently disorderly state of affairs in the country was a danger to her own frontier population, she would march into Norway in a charmingly friendly way and help restore calm there as she did before in Hungary [in 1849]. Perhaps there would then be a telegram to the Tsar from the General entrusted with the task, sounding just like the one sent on that occasion: "All Norway is at Your Majesty's feet!" Russian money and Russian intrigues have prepared the ground well enough in Norway, especially among the radicals, for a party to be established at an opportune moment, which will call for Russian help. Russia would make sure that her friendly services were paid for with the Norwegian port she has long desired to have, together with the obligatory hinterland. This would be a *casus belli* for England. But if the latter should decide, in accordance with the Falstaffian rule, that discretion is the better part of valour, she would also take possession of a Norwegian port as a security, by arrangement with Russia. Under no circumstances could I accept that Slavs and Britons should share sovereignty over the Germanic North Sea without asking me or without my permission. I should therefore be likewise compelled to occupy the southern part of Norway in order to safeguard my trade and my coast. The union would thus be destroyed, and what would become of Sweden? Locked in by Russia on all sides as far as the North Sea, she would gradually succumb to the embrace of this colossus and be absorbed by it. Now that I have seen the magnificent Angermanälv, I do not doubt for a moments that it will be the first thing that Russia takes from Sweden. So the fate of your House would be sealed, along with that of your country. It might perhaps be possible to save Sweden from being absorbed directly into Russia if she were to join the German Reich's customs union. This could guarantee the King the survival of his kingdom and of his dynasty – after the loss of Norway. But what would this be in comparison to the glorious position which your father now holds and which, God willing, will be held by many more descendants of his House? There is another side of this affair which I should like you to consider: all my aims and endeavours, all my ideas in the political sphere, are directed towards bringing the Germanic races in the world, especially in Europe, closer together and forging strong links between them, in order to protect ourselves more surely against the Slav–Czech invasion which threatens us all to a most dangerous degree. Sweden–Norway is one of the principal factors in this alliance of Germanic peoples. What will happen if this great Nordic union of states suddenly falls apart and is perhaps absorbed by the Slavs (Russians)? In this context, the whole European Germanic North constitutes Germany's left flank, or indeed that of Europe itself, and is therefore of great importance for our security. Its disappearance would expose our flank and would represent a serious threat for us all. The monarchical principle as such would also be very severely affected. The Kings of Portugal, Serbia and Greece have already brought it into disrepute. May your father be preserved from being counted among such a crew. His duty as monarch and king is to set aside his personal feelings and obey the dictates of his duty, which demands that he establish respect and obedience towards kingly authority in his domains. At this moment the peace of Europe, and its survival, lie in the hands of your father. May this peace not be threatened or even destroyed by his giving in at the wrong moment! I thought it my duty to explain the circumstances to you once more, quite frankly and honestly, because so much depends on the decisions of your father. My warning is that of a true friend, whose intentions towards your country and your House are honourable. My plea is that of one colleague to another, to help him in his work. May it not go unheeded! You may use this letter as you think best. Wilhelm.'[47] One wonders how the Crown Prince of Sweden and Norway reacted to this 'warning' from his powerful neighbour.

Two months later, at Rominten, Wilhelm again sat down with Eulenburg to compose words of advice for Crown Prince Gustaf. The King of Sweden should work only with the really loyal, pro-union elements in Norway and should on no account make deals with 'revolution', Wilhelm warned. 'No more than water [deals] with fire.' For the King it was vital that he choose as his advisers only such men as 'watch over the crown like knights with the Holy Grail'. As for King Oscar's desire for a defensive alliance with Germany, the Kaiser felt compelled to decline. 'Russia knows that she would find us in her way if she wanted to lay her hand on Norway. What difference would it make to this relationship if . . . I *bound* myself by *treaty* to use force of arms in response to a Russian invasion of Norway? It would mean only that Russia would get the impression that Germany *wanted* to set itself up against Russia, whereas I am glad to be able to state that there are *no direct* points of conflict between Russia and Germany at present. If Russia *creates* such points – fair enough, then Germany will fight a just war if she is attacked. But I would be taking a heavy responsibility on myself if *I* tried to create points of conflict which were aimed at injuring Russia, and which would moreover be highly unpopular in Germany.' Unlike in the July letter, Wilhelm this time stressed the 'natural alliance between Germany and England', both of whom wished to maintain the status quo in Scandinavia. Sweden, he assured the Crown Prince, could always count on the support of both powers against a Russian attack even without contractual agreements. 'But if Sweden feels the *need* to make public connections with powerful states, nothing would prevent her identifying herself with the peaceful aims which the Triple Alliance set itself. That would issue a warning to Russia *without any hostile intent* being shown, for Europe at last believes in the peaceful aims of the Triple Alliance, and the opinion of chauvinistic Frenchmen and pan-Slavic Russians is of no consequence in this regard.' As with the earlier letter, the Reich Chancellor – and only he – was informed of this missive, with its highly risky assurances, only after it had been sent.[48] How the letter was received in the Swedish–Norwegian royal house is once again not known.

## THE KAISER AND THE WAR IN EAST ASIA

Ever since the outbreak of the Sino-Japanese war in the summer of 1894 Wilhelm II had followed the progress of the campaign by land and by sea with unusually intense interest. At the beginning of 1895 he gave two lengthy lectures on the sea battles of the war which were to be of great significance for the development of the German warship building programme, as we shall see in a later chapter.[49] From the beginning he took the Japanese side and expressed his views so strongly at every possible opportunity that everyone in his entourage felt obliged to take a similar line. The Chancellor and the Foreign Office tried in vain to warn of the dangers of such partisanship not only for future relations with China but also for relations with the other great powers, who had their own interests in East Asia to defend. Waldersee too, who saw 'something almost childish' in Wilhelm's partisan attitude, warned anxiously that such bias was highly unwise in political terms. 'In Berlin everyone from the Kaiser down, and in his case particularly ostentatiously, was on the side of Japan and they celebrated Japanese victories almost as if they were German. Anyone who was not for Japan was considered stupid or malicious', he wrote retrospectively when the war ended in the spring of 1895 with total defeat for China.[50] In the Foreign Office the Kaiser's open bias in favour of Japan had been 'very unwelcome', Waldersee noted, 'because people in China are aware of it, take it very much amiss and draw the natural conclusion that Germany's policy is hostile towards China. This is in fact not the case and it is in our interest to remain neutral for the time being. But our good master cannot resist not only giving free rein to his personal feelings on every question, but also expressing them publicly.' 'Japan is rapidly making itself independent of Europe; it is active in all spheres; and if it gets to the point of no longer using imports from us and closing itself to them, then we derive no benefit from our friendship. On the other hand, if China opens itself up to more contact with Europe, it can be assumed that our industry will be able to make massive sales there', commented the General who, five years later, after the suppression of the Boxer Rebellion, was to make a triumphal entry into Beijing as 'Weltmarschall'.[51]

Wilhelm II hoped that a victory by Japan over China would lead to the establishment of a German empire in East Asia. At an audience on 2 November 1894 the Kaiser had already instructed the newly appointed Chancellor to make sure that when peace was concluded Germany was given 'compensation through the cession of Formosa' (now Taiwan). 'Since we protected Japan from intervention by England', he argued, 'we had a right to compensation, and Formosa was a good coaling station. We must likewise try to get Mozambique. We were dependent on England for our coaling stations, and this must stop.' The Kaiser had yielded only on one point, Prince Hohenlohe recorded. He had given up the idea of selling two old ships to Japan, which he had suggested in a letter on 30 October, in view of the reservations expressed by the Chancellor.[52] While still in Strassburg Hohenlohe had had to point out to the Kaiser in a cipher telegram that, of all the powers, Britain had the strongest interest in keeping China in its entirety as a buffer state; but a German demand for Formosa might give the signal for the Chinese empire to be carved up. Furthermore, it was possible that Japan itself had its eye on the island of Formosa as a reward for victory. 'Any intervention by Germany' in East Asia, he warned, would inevitably 'awaken the suspicion of *all* the powers at this moment'.[53]

The following spring, when the war ended in an overwhelming victory for Japan, Wilhelm reverted to his demand for Formosa. In a pencilled note to the Chancellor dated 19 March 1895 he wrote: 'I have made a marginal comment about Formosa because I recently spoke about it to Admiral Knorr, who knows the island. The Pescadores Islands, which are very close by, provide excellently protected anchorage and also a harbour defended by forts. The island of Formosa is largely still in its original state, inhabited by somewhat belligerent natives. Has great treasures to offer, however, especially coal, primarily in the north-east, and undoubtedly valuable. If Japan has no *special* interest in it, it would surely be important to secure this stock of coal and a coaling station by treaty, as a reward for good behaviour as a neutral.' He doubted that France, which was completely absorbed in the annexation of Madagascar, would want to 'embroil itself' in 'a second Madagascar' with Formosa.[54]

When Japan, in the peace of Shimonoseki, succeeded in obtaining not only the independence of Korea and a full indemnity but also the cession of Formosa, the Pescadores and the peninsula of Liaotung to itself, the German Kaiser's enthusiasm for the Empire of the Rising Sun suddenly disappeared. Instead he now ordered the Chancellor to take action with Russia and France against Japan and Great Britain in the hope that by this means it might still be possible to acquire a coaling station – perhaps Wei-hai-wei on the Shantung peninsula. On 11 April 1895 Hohenlohe recorded in his journal: 'At today's audience H.M. observed that he still stood by his plan of co-operating with Russia. H.M. assumes that England has come to an understanding with Japan through secret agreements. Japan will have made commercial concessions to England, and in return England has undertaken not to oppose the peace conditions. If it comes to peace, England will see to it that the Chinese receive a few advantages and will then obtain concessions from China. This can be counteracted by concerted action by Russia, Germany and France. H.M. believes that we could obtain territory in Shantung, in particular Wei-hai-wei. For that it would be necessary to have the iron-clad *Kaiser* brought into service, so that by dispatching it to join the Russian fleet we could ensure that England did not take Wei-hai-wei away from us. Upon my remarking that one must first be sure that Russia would not abandon its war plans again, H.M. expressed the opinion that it could not do so. For us, the Kaiser commented, co-operation with Russia was a great advantage, and if France and Italy joined in, this would constitute an impressive force opposing England, against which country H.M. seems to be very embittered at the moment.'[55] A week later the Kaiser gave the Chief of his Naval Cabinet instructions to discuss with the Foreign Secretary and the former German envoy in Beijing, Maximilian von Brandt, the question of whether it would be useful to inform the Russian government of Wilhelm's intention of acquiring Wei-hai-wei as a base. The reason for the Kaiser's instructions was that Germany, as Senden-Bibran recorded, 'as a result of the very limited naval forces available on the spot' would probably not be strong enough to enforce its claims without Russian support.[56] Thus the momentous decision to collaborate with Russia and France in forcing the Japanese to withdraw from Liaotung and then to seek to establish a coaling station on the Chinese coast can be attributed beyond all doubt to Wilhelm II himself.[57] On this question, in which Anglo-German antagonism and even the future isolation of Germany began to emerge, the Reich Chancellor simply accepted the 'All-Highest will' of the Kaiser.[58]

The monarch had no scruples in coming forward with detailed instructions for the further handling of the East Asian question and in particular the evacuation of the Liaotung peninsula. In the process he showed that he not only grasped the diplomatic and military implications but also fully understood the political advantages that could be gained on the home front from a conclusive success in the Far East. He ordered that it should first be established in Paris 'with absolute certainty and authenticity' what attitude the French Foreign Minister, Hanotaux, took towards the Russian demands on Japan. 'From a conversation which I had with Baron de Courcel [the French ambassador in London] at Cowes I gathered that France has hitherto disagreed with Russia on the question of evacuation . . . Until the reply comes from Paris', the Kaiser continued, 'I would suggest that the matter should be treated in a dilatory manner as far as Russia is concerned. If France abandons its reservations, then we can join in too, and we must try to influence Japan in a conciliatory and reassuring way. If Russia should decide to occupy Korean territory or a seaport, that would be the moment for us to occupy Wei-hai-wei without delay, to prevent the English or the French forestalling us as in Africa. A *fait accompli* always wins more respect from other states than recriminations. Our people would be happy and enthusiastic: it would make an excellent impression on them and boost the nation's self-confidence very much. You know of course that during the spring I secured the Tsar's written agreement in advance to the occupation of an area in China. It would therefore also be necessary for our cruiser division to be instructed to cruise in the vicinity of Wei-hai-wei or in the Gulf of Petshili at the appropriate moment, in an innocent way but with the necessary telegraph connections, so that on receipt of telegraphic instructions they could at once raise the flag there. For this to be carried out smoothly as far as China is concerned, I recommend the Brand[t]–Li-Hung-Tshang connection. Naturally all this must remain absolutely secret.'[59] While staying at Rominten with Eulenburg in September 1895 the Kaiser had a message sent to the Reich Chancellor asking what progress had been made with the occupation of Wei-hai-wei. The elderly Prince's reply was curt: 'As long as the Japanese are there we cannot land. War with China and Japan at the same time is too much.'[60] In Waldersee's eyes, the Kaiser's startling volte-face in turning against Japan after the peace settlement when he had taken the Japanese side so strongly during the war was characteristic of Wilhelm's attitude to politics in general. The 'sudden change' proved once again, he wrote, 'that we must be prepared for surprising moves at any time; hitherto they happened more often in domestic policy; but this is a pretty powerful one in foreign policy'.[61]

## THE UNSUCCESSFUL COURTSHIP OF RUSSIA

The co-operation which Wilhelm II had ordered with Russia and France after the peace of Shimonoseki was not aimed solely at the pursuit of his ambitions in East Asia. It was part of a highly personal and at times even secret initiative, the purpose of which was to bring Russia into the Triple Alliance, thereby restoring the Three Emperors' League of the Bismarck era. This enterprise arose from the Kaiser's conviction that thanks to his personal friendship with Nicholas II, who had succeeded to the throne on the death of his father on 1 November 1894, and thanks to the numerous family ties which linked him to the Russian imperial house, he would be able to effect a complete transformation of Russia's international political orientation. He could not only pride himself on having brought about the marriage between his Darmstadt cousin Alix of Hesse and the Tsarevich; Wilhelm's brother Heinrich was married to the young Tsarina's sister, while another sister, Ella, had been the love of Wilhelm's youth and now lived at the Russian imperial court as the wife of Grand Duke Sergei. As we shall see, in his private correspondence with 'Nicky' and in numerous oral communications Wilhelm repeatedly used two arguments which were intended to make alliance with Germany seem an enticing prospect to the young Tsar. These were that Nicholas must protect 'Christian' Europe from the 'Yellow Peril' in the East while Wilhelm made sure that peace was preserved in Europe; and that Russia could take Constantinople and the Straits whenever it wanted, and need fear no opposition from Germany or Austria-Hungary. Even under the most favourable conditions a secret dynastic policy of such breathtaking arrogance would have had little chance of succeeding in the last years of the nineteenth century; but as Russia had long since concluded not only a military convention but also a formal alliance with the French Republic Wilhelm II's grandiose initiative was completely hopeless.

When the news of Tsar Alexander III's serious illness reached Rominten in September 1894, Wilhelm had expressed his confident expectation that 'a total change in political circumstances' would now come about 'through the accession of the heir to the throne', over whom he had 'influence'; he was therefore determined to travel to Russia for the funeral, he had declared.[62] When Philipp Eulenburg sent a diplomatic dispatch from Vienna commenting on the ill-humour of Count Kálnoky, the Austro-Hungarian Foreign Minister, Wilhelm's hopes of Russian friendship were highlighted by his marginal comments:

37. Wilhelm II with his British relations and the newly engaged couple, Nicholas of
Russia and Alix of Hesse, Coburg 1894

Nicholas II was 'German-minded! That is why Kalnocky [sic] is annoyed.' 'Yes,
because the heir to the throne is on good terms with us and I arranged his marriage for him, I have "priority" with him! And that annoys Kalnocky.'[63] On 18
October 1894 he told the sceptical Waldersee that 'the heir to the throne is very
well disposed towards Germany, I know him very well and the Grand Duke of
Hesse has confirmed it to me'.[64]

    Like Hohenlohe and the Foreign Office, Waldersee recognised both the illu-
sory basis and the colossal dangers of Wilhelm's courtship of Russian favour. A
few weeks before the accession of Nicholas II the General had already summed

up the situation. 'The way he forces his friendship upon them has been seen there as dishonest; as it has also been seen – unfortunately rightly so – as an indication of fear, it has done us a great deal of harm. The present Tsar [Nicholas] has been clever enough for years to behave in a very reserved, watchful way towards our Kaiser, nor has he responded in the slightest to the almost importunate advances made to him. Certain events during his visit to Springe in '89, which I would rather not commit to paper, made a lasting impression on the then heir to the throne.'[65] Waldersee wrote mockingly of Wilhelm II in November 1894: 'As he considers himself a powerful politician, now that a new Tsar has ascended the Russian throne he has plenty of opportunity to develop his talent. England is courting Russian friendship with all her might, and is trying to compete with the French . . . The best course would be for us not to behave as yet another suitor but to remain elegantly aloof, confident of our strength; that is the only way in which we can impress the Russians. The young Tsar is in the agreeable position of allowing himself to be courted by all the world and waiting calmly, without taking a single step to be accommodating. His advisers will certainly encourage him in that direction.'[66]

The disappointment of the hopes which the Kaiser had pinned on the young Russian sovereign was not long in coming. When Wilhelm visited Hohenlohe in the Reich chancellor's palace for the first time on 14 December 1894 – he remarked that the place was still as dark as it had been in his predecessors' time – it was plain that considerable disillusionment had set in. He agreed with the Chancellor that it was important to maintain a very reserved attitude towards the new Tsar; matters would become clearer and German–Russian relations would improve with time.[67] The coolness shown by the Russians towards Prince Heinrich and the Prussian officers (Plessen, Helmuth von Moltke, Villaume and Saussin) who accompanied him to St Petersburg at the time of the Tsar's accession, together with the rejection of Wilhelm's suggestion that their respective military aides-de-camp should be appointed, as they had been in the past, members of each other's *maison militaire*, showed all too clearly that there was no sign of an improved relationship as yet; on the contrary, some observers expressed the opinion that Germany's position in Russia was 'lost for ever'. 'The Kaiser is the poorer by one illusion', Waldersee commented in December 1894.[68] A few weeks later he registered his delight at hearing that 'the Kaiser has completely abandoned his illusions about Russia and Tsar Nicholas, who loves us so tenderly; that is great progress, even if it must also have been a grave disappointment'.[69] By April 1895 at the latest Wilhelm was forced to recognise 'that the mood in Russia is the worst it could possibly be for us', Waldersee noted. He commented contemptuously of Wilhelm that 'six months ago he still wanted to put the young Tsar in his pocket and control him!'[70]

News from Russia confirmed the fear harboured from the outset that the young Tsar would turn out to be a weak man who allowed himself to be governed by his mother, not only politically but even in the details of daily life. Wilhelm was indignant at a report from Prince Albert of Saxe-Altenburg that the Dowager Tsarina Maria Feodorovna, born a Danish princess, had said on returning to St Petersburg 'that much had not gone as it should have during her absence'. Nicholas had been unable 'to summon up a single word in response!!', the Kaiser complained.[71] Waldersee too recorded that the Dowager Tsarina had 'no greater wish than to humiliate us and the game of intrigue against us will be taken up with new vigour in Copenhagen'. The young Tsarina Alexandra, of whom the Kaiser had had such high expectations, was obviously a completely insignificant woman.[72]

The fact that Wilhelm was already on bad terms with the Darmstadt family, which had been very much under the influence of Queen Victoria since the premature deaths first of Grand Duchess Alice and then of Grand Duke Ludwig IV, also contributed to the Tsar's coolness and reserve towards him. Nor was the domineering and characteristically prudish way in which Wilhelm tried to impose his will during the preparations for the Russian wedding calculated to prejudice Nicholas and Alexandra, as Princess Alix was now called, or her brother Ernst Ludwig, in the Kaiser's favour. On 2 November 1894 in a conversation with Hohenlohe Wilhelm spoke 'rather heatedly' about the forthcoming marriage between Nicholas and Alix, and 'criticised the Grand Duke [Ernst Ludwig], who was a baby, very severely for not having travelled to Livadia with his sister in order to make arrangements for the marriage to be concluded there, as it is being delayed at the instigation of the Queen of Denmark'. The Kaiser had already made 'serious representations' to the Russian ambassador about it, Hohenlohe noted, and had asserted that 'the Princess could not come back to Germany unmarried, that was simply impossible and would be taken very much amiss throughout Germany. But to stay there with her fiancé, unmarried, would go against moral traditions here. He would give Prince Heinrich, who was to go to the funeral at St Petersburg, instructions in this sense.'[73]

In spite of the rejection of his attempts to curry favour, Wilhelm continued his efforts, through private letters and other communications to Nicholas II, to divert Russian foreign policy away from Europe and towards the east and south. Within a few days of the Tsar's accession he had already sent Nicholas the first of a total of seventy-five private letters. In the next twelve months six more letters were to follow, which he showed to his 'responsible' advisers only after having sent them, if at all. In vain Holstein urged the Reich Chancellor to make it plain to the Kaiser 'that there is a limit beyond which Your Highness would not allow even His Majesty to make a habit of going'.[74] Eulenburg's assurance that

Wilhelm's letters concerned trifles, and that on any serious question he would ask the Chancellor's advice first, was very far from the truth, as he himself was soon to realise with horror.[75]

At the end of April 1895 Wilhelm wrote a letter to the young Tsar in which he encouraged Russia to expand further to the east and at the same time announced that Germany wished for a base in East Asia. 'I shall certainly do all in my power to keep Europe quiet and also guard the rear of Russia so that nobody shall hamper your action towards the Far East', he assured Nicholas. 'For that is clearly the great task of the future for Russia to cultivate the Asian Continent and to defend Europe from the inroads of the Great Yellow race. In this you will always find me on your side ready to help you as best I can. You have well understood that call of Providence and have quickly grasped the moment; it is of immense political and historical value and much good will come of it. I shall with interest await the further development of our action and hope that, just as I will gladly help you settle the question of eventual annexations of portions of territory for Russia, you will kindly see that Germany may also be able to acquire a Port somewhere where it does not "gêne" you.'[76] The Tsar's reply, in which he stated that he had no objection if Germany wanted to acquire 'something' in the Far East, was shown to the Reich Chancellor by Wilhelm II under the seal of secrecy.[77]

The celebrations for the opening of the Kaiser Wilhelm Canal at Kiel in the summer of 1895 provided the monarch with a further opportunity to pursue his attempts at manipulation. Philipp Eulenburg recorded with dismay during the Scandinavian cruise that Wilhelm had told him that during the Kiel festivities he had held discussions with Grand Duke Alexis Alexandrovich, the Tsar's Francophile uncle, and the Russian Admiral Schillings on the mission of Russian policy in the Far East. The Kaiser had put it to the Grand Duke, Eulenburg, wrote, 'that He would protect Russia's back as long as she fulfilled her Christian duties towards Mongols and Buddhists in East Asia. His Majesty had an even more wide-ranging conversation with Admiral Schillings, to whom he described the dangers which threaten Europe from the continuing development of the yellow race. *Only Russia* could fulfil the great East Asian cultural mission, and *Germany* would regard it as her duty to protect Russia's borders in the west unless Germany were attacked by other states with Russia's knowledge. He told Schillings he should say this in St Peterburg, also to the Tsar. Schillings was extremely surprised and delighted. His Majesty hopes his words will have a good effect on the attitude of Russian society.' The Kaiser went on to tell his astonished friend that he had written to the Tsar not long ago, 'after I had received your letter about your conversation with [the Russian ambassador] Osten-Sacken in Vienna. The Tsar had told you through Osten-Sacken that Russia understood

38. The Kaiser's original sketch of 30 April 1895, warning of the Yellow
Peril in the East

that Germany had to use all her power to overcome radical tendencies. Russia
would *guarantee* Germany peace on her eastern frontier if he (Kaiser Wilhelm)
would undertake to maintain peace in Europe. I (Kaiser Wilhelm) replied to the
Tsar as follows: "As you have informed me of your decisions through Philipp
Eulenburg, I *pledge* myself for my part to cover your back while you are engaged
in East Asia. My ships in East Asia are also at your disposal." The Tsar answered
me in very affectionate and grateful terms. I (Kaiser Wilhelm) therefore think
that the situation is clear. If the Tsar breaks his word, well, he must answer before
God for it. For my part I consider myself bound by my word and I shall keep it.'[78]
Only a few days later, on board the *Hohenzollern*, to Eulenburg's consternation
Wilhelm II read him another letter which he had sent to the Tsar 'through the
*Naval Attaché* (!) at St Petersburg, Kalau vom Hofe', and which was 'written in
English and about 7 octavo pages long'.[79] In this letter the Kaiser commented on
his conversations with Alexis and Schillings, with whom he said he had had 'a
serious word about East Asian affairs'. In the course of these talks, he wrote, he
had emphasised 'how our interests were entwined in the Far East, that my ships
had been ordered to second yours in case of need when things looked doubtful,
that Europe had to be thankful to you that you so quickly had perceived the

39. The sketch as completed by Hermann Knackfuss: 'Nations of Europe, protect your holiest possessions! Wilhelm I. R.'

great future for Russia in the cultivation of Asia and in the Defence of the Cross and the old Christian European culture against the inroads of the Mongols and Buddhism, that it was natural that if Russia was engaged in this tremendous work you wished to have Europe quiet and your back free; and that it was natural and without doubt that this would be my task and that I would let nobody try to interfere with you and attack from behind in Europe during the time you were fulfilling the great mission which Heaven has shaped for you. That was as sure as Amen in Church!'[80]

Eulenburg, who had hitherto regarded the private correspondence of the two Emperors as harmless, was thus suddenly forced to recognise its highly dangerous nature. Shocked by this revelation, he noted on 5 July that 'this correspondence has been kept absolutely secret *until now*. I am unfortunately not yet in a position to be able to inform the Reich Chancellor about it because I am under an obligation to the Kaiser to keep quiet. His Majesty *must and shall* release me from this obligation.'[81] A week later, after hearing about the latest letter to 'Nicky', he wrote in alarm: 'His Majesty has thus *committed himself – without Hohenlohe*. This gives me yet more problems to solve, which fill me with *dread*! Nicky will of course *not* keep quiet and *Alexei the Frenchman* even less. If Hohenlohe hears of the letter from someone *other than me*, he will go at once. And yet he *must* know about it!'[82] But worse was to come.

On 30 April 1895, while staying with his old friend Count Emil von Görtz at Schlitz in the Vogelsberg, Wilhelm II sketched the picture entitled 'Against the Yellow Peril', on which he wrote the caption: 'Nations of Europe, protect your holiest possessions!'[83] Philipp Eulenburg was delighted when he saw Hermann Knackfuss's finished version of it at Rominten. He wrote to Kaiserin Auguste Viktoria on 29 September: 'I am quite under the spell of this truly magnificent work. The idea is uplifting and the execution masterly. When I immerse myself in the contemplation of the picture I am filled with the feeling that all Europe must indeed answer the call of the beloved Kaiser to unite in peaceful harmony for the sake of the cross and the holiest goods, but then the uneasy feeling steals over me that the evil in those men who oppose as an enemy power the good which manifests itself in the Kaiser's being will now cause them to tear down and attack with their ingenious criticism that which has sprung from the high-mindedness and noble heart of the Kaiser.'[84] To his mother Eulenburg wrote enthusiastically: 'The Kaiser has given me a magnificent engraving of the *wonderful* allegorical picture executed by Prof. Knackfuss from His Majesty's sketch: the peoples of Europe, represented as female figures, are called upon by St Michael to defend *the cross* against unbelief, heathenism etc. You will like it . . . It is a beautiful idea in a beautiful form.'[85] The Kaiser sent this drawing to the Tsar from Rominten at the end of September 1895. In his accompanying letter he explained that he had had the idea for the picture during the joint German–Russian action in the Far East in the spring, when he had realised the 'danger to Europe and our Christian Faith' emanating from that part of the world. It showed 'the powers of Europe represented by their respective Genii called together by the Arch-Angel Michael, – sent from Heaven, – to *unite* in resisting the inroad of Buddhism, heathenism and barbarism for the Defence of the Cross. Stress is especially laid on the *united* resistance of *all* European powers, which is just as necessary also against our common internal foes, anarchism, republicanism, nihilism.'[86]

While the Kaiser was hunting at Rominten news arrived of a plan to reinforce the French army with Algerian troops, who were to be stationed on the eastern border of France. This roused Wilhelm II to declare that such a measure 'was in fact nothing less than a threat of war'. He considered it his duty to take counter-measures, for one could not 'watch motionlessly as hostile neighbours tighten the noose more and more'.[87] His letter to Nicholas II also referred to this question. The decision of the French parliament to recall an army corps from Algeria and Tunisia and 'to form a *new* continental Corps on *my Western Frontier*' had 'fallen like a thunderbolt on Germany and has created a deep feeling of alarm', he claimed. Together with the existing French forces, which were already overwhelmingly strong, the new corps represented 'a serious danger to my country'. The honours heaped on the Russian Foreign Minister Lobanov and

General Dragomirov by France at the same time had, furthermore, awakened the 'ugly' impression in the German people that 'Russia would like France to be offensive against Germany' with the hope of Russian help. 'Such a serious danger will cause me to strongly increase my army, to be able to cope with such fearful odds', Wilhelm II wrote to the Tsar. 'I perfectly know that you personally do not dream of attacking us, but still you cannot be astonished that the European Powers get alarmed how the presence of your officers and high officials in *official way* [sic] in France fans the inflammable Frenchman into a white heated passion and strengthens the cause of Chauvinism and Revanche! God knows that I have done all in my power to preserve the European Peace, but if France goes on openly or secretly encouraged like this to violate all rules of international courtesy and Peace in peace times, one fine day, my dearest Nicky, you will find yourself nolens volens suddenly embroiled in the most horrible of wars Europe ever saw! Which will by the masses and by history perhaps be fixed on you as the cause of it.' The Tsar, Wilhelm continued, was young and inexperienced; moreover, because he was in mourning he was living in seclusion and therefore did not know what was going on behind the scenes. 'I have some experience of Politics, and see certain unmistakable symptoms, so I hasten to you, my friend, to plead in the name of the Peace of Europe; if you are allied for better, for worse with the French, well then, keep those damned rascals in order and make them sit still, if not, then don't let your Men who go to France make the French believe that you are allied and get reckless and turn their heads till they lose them, and we have to fight in Europe instead [of] for it against the East! Think of the awful responsibility for the shocking bloodshed!'[88] Philipp Eulenburg, who was at Rominten with the Kaiser, had great difficulty in copying this explosive letter for the Reich Chancellor. 'I am a poor Englishman; I had to copy the letter in a great hurry and could not read all of the Kaiser's difficult handwriting', he admitted; Hohenlohe would therefore have to 'work it out' if something were not clear. The copy was intended for Hohenlohe alone and should not be made known to the Foreign Office. 'The fact of the letter being sent . . . will of course displease Holstein very much', Eulenburg predicted, anxious to have time to consider the best way of explaining the Kaiser's action to the Privy Councillor. Not that the 'vigorous language' of the letter gave the Kaiser's friend and ambassador cause for concern. 'His Majesty was angered by the news of the reinforcement of the French army, and as the famous picture was about to be sent to the Tsar anyway, the Kaiser enclosed the political admonition with it.' Furthermore the reinforcement would probably not take place, and 'as a result the Kaiser's present anger will probably also disappear'.[89]

It is not without irony that the man whom the Kaiser chose for the task of delivering this letter and the drawing to St Petersburg was his Flügeladjutant

Helmuth von Moltke, who was later to play a decisive role, as Chief of the General Staff, in the preparation and provocation of the First World War.[90] In the first audience he granted Moltke, the Tsar showed surprise at the news of a forthcoming enlargement of the French army, but he expressed himself fully in agreement with the Flügeladjutant when the latter, on the instructions of 'the most distinguished representative of the monarchical principle' (as Moltke described Kaiser Wilhelm II), drew attention to the danger 'that a possibly victorious France would engender a flood of republican spirit which could be disastrous for the already socially churned-up ground in which the old monarchies were rooted'. Moltke also discussed with other members of the Tsar's family the danger of a Franco-German war and the possibility of collaboration between 'the two Emperors'.[91] Nicholas II received the Colonel again on 3 October at Tsarskoe Selo, where they had a wide-ranging conversation in French on the domestic and foreign political situation. He repeatedly emphasised his peaceful intentions, above all towards Germany. The two countries had not waged war against each other for 150 years, nor did they have any 'conflicting interests' now. Russia was principally an agricultural country and would have to concentrate on internal development for a long time to come; it was dependent on trade with industrialised Germany. He would do everything in his power to keep the French quiet. 'For the time being the French have Madagascar on their plate', the Tsar remarked; and they would be absorbed with that for at least a year. Even after that he would never allow a war. Kaiser Wilhelm had evidently allowed himself to be too provoked by newspaper extracts in the seclusion of his hunting lodge at Rominten, Nicholas observed. He himself read one German (the *Kölnische Zeitung*), one French (*Le Temps*), one English and one Russian newspaper every day, but he did not set much store by newspapers, for he knew 'how they are made. Some Jew or other sits there making it his business to stir up the passions of different peoples against each other and the people, who mostly have no political opinion of their own, are guided by what they read. That is why I shall never set the Russian press free as long as I live. The Russian press shall write only what I want . . . and my will alone shall prevail throughout the country', he said.[92]

When Moltke's telegram arrived at Rominten with the news that Nicholas knew nothing of the French military plans, 'His Majesty was transfixed with astonishment.' The Tsar obviously had '*no idea* of what is going on!', he exclaimed.[93] The Kaiser dismissed Eulenburg's suspicion that the Russian sovereign had been 'play-acting' with Moltke. 'No, . . . that is quite out of the question', he declared. 'The Tsar is absolutely *genuine* by nature. It can only be assumed that people are playing a terribly dangerous game with him.'[94] It was not until a six-page 'schoolboyish' letter from Nicholas arrived at Hubertusstock

that the Kaiser discovered, with some relief, that the Tsar had not taken his letter amiss and was willing to continue the confidential correspondence with his
fellow monarch.[95] All in all, however, the Tsar's reply amounted to a disappointing rejection of the 'well-meaning suggestions of our All-gracious sovereign', as
Holstein sarcastically commented.[96] The Privy Councillor confirmed that 'the
impression that H.M. had of Franco-Russian intentions, after Colonel Moltke's
return, is a very disturbing one'. 'H.M. made remarks', he reported to the German
ambassador at St Petersburg, Prince Radolin, 'to the effect that the Tsar did not
seem to be informed, that Lobanov might be up to all sorts of tricks'.[97]

On 25 October 1895, again without consulting the Reich Chancellor and the
Foreign Office, Wilhelm wrote another – the seventh – highly political letter to
Nicholas II. The Tsar's autocratic views on the press were 'exactly the same as
mine', he declared; but its influence, although always harmful, mendacious and
nonsensical, varied from country to country according to the 'spirit in which the
People of the different races are brought up'. 'Your subjects and mine are slower
at thought, sober and quieter in their conclusions they draw as [sic] for instance
Southerners or the French. The Roman and Gallic races are more easily roused,
incensed and more ready to jump to conclusions, and once having flared up are
more dangerous to peace than the Teutonic or Russian Race.' It was true that
'every Sovereign is sole master of his countrie's [sic] interests and he shapes his
policy accordingly', yet the danger to 'our Principle of Monarchism' represented
by the constant visits by Russian princes, grand dukes, statesmen and generals
to the French Republic should not be underestimated. In Russia and Germany
'Republicans [were] Revolutionists de natura' and were consequently 'treated –
rightly too – as people who must be shot or hung'. The much-fêted visits by
the Russian royalties to France thus only caused confusion, the Kaiser argued.
'The R[épublique] F[rançaise] is from the source of the great Revolution and
propagates and is bound to do so, the ideas of it. Don't forget that [President]
Faure . . . sits on the throne of the King and Queen of France "by the Grace of
God" whose heads Frenchmen Republicans cut off! The Blood of their Majesties
is still on that country! Look at it, has it since then ever been happy or quiet again?
Has it not staggered from bloodshed to bloodshed? And in its great moments did
it not go from war to war? till it soused all Europe in streams of blood? Till at
last it had the Commune over again? Nicky take my word on it the curse of God
has stricken that People forever! We Christian Kings and Emperors have only
one holy duty imposed on us by Heaven, that is to uphold the Principle "von
Gottes Gnaden" ["by the grace of God"], we can have good relations with the
R.F. but never be intime with her!' Once again the German Kaiser undertook to
protect Russia's back 'from anybody in Europe', in the event of its being 'seriously
engaged' in the Far East, and promised, if that were the case, to ensure 'that all

be kept quiet, and that nothing would happen from me also to France, provided I was not attacked'.[98]

### THE BALKANS AND A BLANK CHEQUE FOR AUSTRIA

At the same time as making these repeated attempts to divert Russia's attention to the east, Kaiser Wilhelm II – again on his own initiative and in direct imitation of the mission to Brest-Litovsk which he had carried out in September 1886 on Bismarck's instructions[99] – embarked on the risky undertaking of encouraging the Russians to annex Constantinople and capture the Dardanelles. In his first conversation with Hohenlohe on foreign policy, on 2 November 1894, he made it clear that in the event of a Russian advance he intended to remain strictly neutral on this tricky question and to make his position known both in St Petersburg and in Vienna. He told the newly appointed Reich Chancellor that in Austria the possibility had been mentioned to him that Russia intended to force a passage through the Dardanelles, and that a wish had been expressed that Germany should take a stand on this. 'H.M. refused to do so, as it was his opinion . . . that we had no interest in risking the life a single grenadier for that', the Chancellor recorded. 'Russia needed the key to the door for her navy and this need not matter to us.'[100] Without the prior knowledge of the Reich Chancellor or the Foreign Office the Kaiser solemnly assured the Russian leadership, both through the Grand Duke of Mecklenburg-Schwerin and through his own brother Prince Heinrich, who went to St Petersburg for the funeral of Alexander III, that he was ready *'to come to an understanding with Russia and attached no importance to the Straits from the German point of view'*. To Geheimrat von Holstein it was quite clear that the official German policy would now have to follow the same lines as this imperial initiative. 'The question of whether His Majesty would have done better to wait until he was approached on the matter is no longer relevant', he wrote in December, when he heard of the Kaiser's action. 'It has happened and is presumably being discussed at all the All-Highest tea tables in St Petersburg, Copenhagen, London etc. In order that Germany should not appear frivolous or deceitful we must adapt all our official comments so as not to contradict what the Kaiser said.' Even Philipp Eulenburg, who liked to console himself with the thought that his 'beloved Kaiser' might perhaps sometimes be 'too precipitate in political action, but never does anything really foolish – indeed usually does something of genius', thought it 'bad' that Russia 'received by word of mouth a secret assurance from His Majesty that he had no objection to the capture of C[onstantinople]'.[101]

Wilhelm took a similarly pro-Russian and anti-Austrian line towards another potential source of conflict in the Balkans which threatened to explode at any moment: Bulgaria. In defiance of the official policy pursued by the Wilhelm-strasse, in the autumn of 1894 he instructed the military attaché at Vienna, Colonel von Deines, to make it clear to the Austrian Chief of the General Staff, Feldzeugmeister Beck, 'that in the event of complications concerning Bulgaria we should not feel obliged to intervene actively on Austria's behalf'. According to Waldersee, Deines carried out this order, but when Foreign Minister Kálnoky checked up on the matter with the Foreign Office in Berlin he was told that the military attaché was interfering in politics in an unauthorised manner. 'I cannot wait to hear how the Kaiser will react to this', the General exclaimed. 'What is strange is that last year in Güns he assured Feldzeugm. Beck of exactly the opposite.'[102] When Wilhelm outlined his ideas on foreign policy to the new Chancellor three weeks later he commented, with regard to the growing tension between Bulgaria and Russia, that it was 'still very questionable whether Bulgaria will accept Russian sovereignty. Austria could take what she wanted for herself. He spoke disparagingly of Kálnoky.'[103] During the Scandinavian cruise in July 1895 Wilhelm cherished hopes of 'a completely passive attitude on the part of Austria' in the Bulgarian question; the assassination of the former Prime Minister Stefan Stambulov, in his opinion, was to be blamed on the behaviour of the government of Prince Ferdinand of Saxe-Coburg and Gotha and ought not to lead to Austrian intervention.[104]

In the autumn of 1895, however, Wilhelm II's attitude towards Russia and Austria-Hungary with regard to Balkan policy suddenly underwent a momentous change. In October the Kaiser was still urging a policy of expansion both in East Asia and in the Near East on the Russian leadership and assuring them of the benevolent neutrality of Germany.[105] And when Eulenburg reported from Vienna in early November 1895 that Kálnoky's successor Count Goluchowski had said that the Straits question concerned Germany 'just as much' as Austria, Wilhelm wrote dismissively on the report: 'ahem! in simple terms: we should help prevent the Russians getting into Stamboul. I shall not risk the life of a Pomeranian grenadier any more for Stamboul than for London.'[106] In a three-sided conversation with Philipp Eulenburg and the Austrian ambassador Count Ladislaus von Szögyény on 6 November 1895 the Kaiser discussed the handling of the crisis which would be caused by the apparently imminent break-up of Turkey. With a map of the Balkan peninsula spread out in front of him he strongly urged Szögyény to persuade Austria to make its claims for compensation plain. As the first step towards dividing up the Ottoman Empire would probably come from England, he said, it would 'perhaps be opportune for Austria, Germany and Russia – the three Emperors – to come to an understanding on what was to be done'. The Austrian ambassador expressed reservations about an expansion of Austria too far south because of the proximity of Greece, of which the Kaiser spoke 'contemptuously'. Szögyény reacted most touchily when Wilhelm floated the idea that in the division Italy could be given Albania. Eulenburg summed up the impressions that the Austrian ambassador must have gained from this meeting in these terms: 'Kaiser W. is still very irritated with England and thinks her capable of every possible political enormity, but he will not go against the Berlin Treaty. The Kaiser will give us (Austrians) strong and emphatic support if it should come to a division of Turkey. If we attack or allow ourselves to be *driven* into a hostile action by England we cannot count on his help. The Kaiser thinks the situation in the Balkans is very serious, almost hopeless, and he shows a tendency to support Russia – although only if Austria comes away with the equivalent of what Russia gains.'[107]

Friedrich von Holstein was horrified when he saw Eulenburg's report on the conversation, for the Kaiser's remarks to Szögyény showed that Wilhelm was no longer prepared to defend Austria-Hungary's status as a great power, and moreover that he assumed that the Franco-Russian alliance was a dead letter and had been, or could be, replaced by a Russian–German combination. 'If the Austrians take H.M.'s utterances *au pied de la lettre* it will mean the end of the Triple Alliance, because it will be *meaningless* for Austria', he warned. 'But I doubt that H.M.'s utterances will be taken literally. Their credibility is belied by the obstinacy with which H.M. treats the Franco-Russian alliance, which is very much in existence, as a *quantité négligeable* – a view probably shared by no one else today.'[108] The fact that the imperial endorsement 'Agreed' then appeared on a memorandum by Marschall, in which he had put forward exactly the opposite point of view on the Balkan question, added to the consternation in the Foreign Office. 'This is another surprise. If the Kaiser approves the views of the Foreign Office – *who* is then responsible for the confusion? Phil. Eulenburg himself?? Or both?' In despair, Holstein urged the elderly Chancellor to ask the Kaiser at his next audience for permission to write to Eulenburg saying that he, the Kaiser, considered it premature to discuss 'future eventualities in the Balkans' at the present time. In spite of the sleepless nights the Kaiser's interferences had already caused him, the Privy Councillor vowed to do his utmost to prevent 'poets [meaning Eulenburg] and dilettantes [Wilhelm II] from destroying the Triple Alliance while the Franco-Russian liaison remains in force'.[109]

When the Kaiser appeared at the Reich Chancellor's palace on 13 November 1895 for the customary audience, Hohenlohe and Marschall felt obliged to ask him the fundamental question of whether the government's conduct of German foreign policy was 'in harmony with the intentions of H.M.' or not. Using Holstein's exact words, the Reich Chancellor asserted that the preservation of Austria-Hungary's status as a great power had been 'one of the foremost, if not the foremost, aim of our foreign policy for decades'. If Germany were now to declare that it would not under any circumstances take part in a war over the Straits, it might be taken to mean that the policy it had hitherto pursued towards Austria was being abandoned. Such a shift would be all the more risky because in Austria too there were political and ethnic groups who wished for co-operation with Russia rather than with Germany and Italy and who saw 'an alliance between Russia, Austria and France as an opportunity to destroy Hungary and recover the position Austria had lost in Germany (the restoration of the status quo before 1866)'. These parties were not in the majority in Austria, but they would gain increased support if it were widely believed that the Triple Alliance were unwilling 'to take steps at the critical moment to support Austria's position as a great power'. The danger of such a shift in German policy was also great because Germany's relations with Russia still left much to be desired, as had been evinced not only by the 'rather cold' reserve of the Tsar but also by 'the inconsiderate behaviour of the Russian Master of Ceremonies with regard to the rank to be accorded to Prince Heinrich at the coronation'. From this it could be deduced that Russia 'values her French entente more highly than intimacy with us'. Germany would therefore be wrong 'to risk our other friendly relationships for the sake of an uncertain Russian friendship'. At the end of the audience the Kaiser declared himself in agreement with the arguments put forward by Hohenlohe and Marschall.[110]

Wilhelm now swung violently against Russia, not only for the objective reasons presented by his responsible advisers but also because his advances to St Petersburg received a snub. He was especially deeply wounded by the rejection of the suggestion he had made by telegram on 8 November that Russia and Germany should make common cause in the Turkish question.[111] 'H.M. is beginning to be quite angry with the Tsar because of the repeated cool rebuffs', Holstein reported to the German ambassador in Russia. 'H.M. would like to restore the Holy Alliance, but Lobanov, who runs the Tsar, won't desert France . . . Our Kaiser was very irritated for instance when in reply to his telegraphic proposal for an agreement *à deux* about the present Turkish difficulties, the Tsar referred him very briefly and coolly to the ambassadors of the powers in Constantinople.' Radolin should say nothing in St Petersburg about Wilhelm's annoyance, Holstein advised. 'H.M. will do enough of that himself. He treated Grand Duke Vladimir miserably, always answered in German to his French, etc.'[112]

Anger with Russia was not the only reason behind the belligerent mood of Wilhelm II and his closest advisers at this time. Another was the hope that complications abroad could help solve the deepening political crisis at home. Philipp Eulenburg expressed the view to Bülow that the serious international situation in the east had 'a refreshing, distracting character' which made him hope, 'for the sake of the dear Fatherland', 'that the situation there would not be cleared up too quickly'.[113] He admitted to Holstein that 'in general my wish is that things will not calm down in the Orient yet. Not that it should go as far as war, into which we should be drawn by Austria, but that there should be a certain unrest to distract people at home. Occupying minds with a little gentle excitement is better than the most splendid government bills and the finest leading articles in the *Nord[deutsche] Z[eitun]g*.'[114] Waldersee was ready with similar advice for the monarch: 'in my opinion it [is] in our interest to let others quarrel'.[115] After talking to members of the imperial entourage the General was hopeful at the close of the year of 1895 that plans were afoot 'to complicate the situation still further'. He reaffirmed his opinion that 'foreign policy can have a good influence on the situation at home'; it was unfortunately 'an unhealthy sign that we cannot help ourselves from within'.[116] After a conversation with Wilhelm II he recorded with satisfaction in his diary that the Kaiser had declared 'there were many indications that things would get serious in the spring'.[117]

It was in this warlike, anti-Russian frame of mind that Kaiser Wilhelm II summoned the Austrian ambassador to see him late in the evening of 13 November 1895 at the station, in order to explain 'the ultimate goals of German policy . . . on matters affecting the East' to him. According to Szögyény the Kaiser emphasised that he was in complete agreement with the Reich Chancellor and Baron Marschall in making the following 'highly important remarks': 'The survival of Turkish rule in Europe seems to me very doubtful, as you know; nevertheless, in the present circumstances I consider the preservation of the status quo in the European Orient as the most urgent task facing all the powers at this time.' Britain, Austria-Hungary and Italy were those primarily involved; Germany's role was only secondary, 'but she is very firmly involved. I am perfectly convinced that Austria-Hungary will not allow herself to be driven to any acts of provocation; but if complications should nevertheless arise, as a consequence of which Austria-Hungary saw her position as threatened – then it would be for Austria-Hungary, not for us, to decide whether this were actually the case – and in this case I declare quite plainly that I shall stand at Austria-Hungary's side with all the forces at my disposal, without any further enquiry as to whether the *casus foederis* existed in accordance with our treaty of alliance . . . Your All-Highest sovereign may be quite sure that if at any moment the position of the Austro-Hungarian monarchy is at issue, as to which the decisive judgement rests solely and entirely with Him and His All-Highest advisers, my entire fighting forces will be immediately and unconditionally at his disposal.'[118]

Would it be going too far to see this 'quite open' definition of the official German attitude on the Balkan question as anticipating the fatal 'blank cheque' which Kaiser Wilhelm offered the same ambassador, Szögyény, on 5 July 1914 in reply to a letter from Kaiser Franz Joseph, and which demonstrably strengthened the will of the government in Vienna to go to war? Did the Kaiser remember his declaration of 13 November 1895 in later years, and did the government of Austria-Hungary regard the Kaiser's promise as a considered expression of official German government policy or only as an eccentric initiative on the part of the monarch? Thirteen years after the late-night meeting at the station, at the height of the crisis over the annexation of Bosnia, Wilhelm II still remembered perfectly clearly the fateful, solemn assurance which he had given Szögyény to transmit to his emperor in November 1895. At the reception held at the Berlin opera house on 21 October 1908 the Kaiser reminded the Austrian ambassador that in 1895 he had declared 'in the most categorical way' 'that he did not regard loyalty to the alliance simply as a matter of keeping to the letter of our treaty, but that he would stand loyally at our [Austria-Hungary's] side on every issue, whether great or small'. He had even said, Wilhelm II went on, that 'Kaiser Franz Joseph was a Prussian field marshal, and consequently he had only to command and the whole Prussian army would obey his orders.'[119]

Count Szögyény did not have to take the Kaiser's word that he was speaking also in the name of the Reich Chancellor and of the Foreign Secretary. On 14 November 1895 Hohenlohe informed him that he was 'in complete agreement' with the Kaiser Wilhelm's declaration.[120] It was no wonder that Goluchowski regarded the declaration as the 'most important enunciation' on the part of Germany 'since the conclusion of the Austro-German alliance', and commented that 'its warmth and resolve put all previous statements in the shade'.[121] Unlike his later successor as Foreign Minister, Count Berchtold, Goluchowski will have had no doubts as to who ruled in Berlin.

# CHAPTER TWENTY-SIX

# Great Britain and the spectre of encirclement

## THE KAISER AND THE BRITISH

THE harder line which German foreign policy was now following and which was generally attributed to the growing influence of Wilhelm II naturally caused disquiet in London, where the weak Liberal ministry under Lord Rosebery lost the general election and Lord Salisbury returned to Downing Street in July 1895 as prime minister and foreign secretary. The dangerous interplay between the authorities in Berlin and the increasingly nationalistic German press was viewed with particular apprehension by British observers. Martin Gosselin, the perceptive chargé d'affaires at the embassy in Berlin, commented in a dispatch of 5 November 1894 that the semi-official press, the Kaiser and the Reich government were now all noticeably more hostile in their attitude towards Britain. He reported that the *Kölnische Zeitung*, which was close to the Foreign Office, had threatened that Germany would create difficulties for England if the empire continued to impede German colonial expansion, while Marschall, the Foreign Secretary, had recently remarked 'that so long as England disputes every scrap of territory with Germany he does not see how the relations of the two countries can improve. The Emperor is keenly in favour of German Colonial development and the new Govt. is believed to be [in favour] of a more forward policy than the last.'[1]

It was not only Germany's new colonial appetite but also Wilhelm II's attempted courtship of Russia, German collaboration in the Far East with Russia and France against Japan, the sudden incursions of German foreign policy into the highly sensitive Dardanelles question and, not least, the talk in Berlin of a continental league against Britain, which for the first time brought the government in London face to face with the urgent problem of whether the security of the island realm and of its global interests could continue to be safeguarded by a policy of 'splendid isolation'. And, if not, the question arose of whether, in abandoning its non-aligned position, the country might not achieve better protection by joining with France and Russia than with the Triple Alliance. By 1895 – several years before the alliance between the United Kingdom and Japan (1902) and the ententes with France (1904) and Russia (1907) – the international isolation of the German Reich was already beginning to emerge with alarming clarity. Towards the end of 1894 the long-serving German ambassador in London, Paul Hatzfeldt, warned that a shift in British public feeling towards the Triple Alliance would have consequences which no ministry could prevent. Britain was already 'casting about elsewhere', blaming this 'on our alienation of herself', and the result might be 'the formation of a group that would be extraordinarily dangerous' both for Germany and for Austria-Hungary.[2] At the same time the French ambassador in Berlin, Jules Herbette, who could scarcely conceal his delight at the antagonism between Germany and Britain, commented in conversations with Marschall on the likelihood that a triple alliance between France, Russia and Great Britain would be stronger than that between Germany, Austria and Italy.[3] Early in 1895 Waldersee, filled with dark forebodings of disaster, voiced the fear that the German collaboration with France and Russia in East Asia which the Kaiser had ordered might anger Britain and might even result in the encirclement of the Reich by all three great powers. 'If we make a determined enemy of England', he predicted, 'the danger is that Russia and France will then disown us.'[4] Presciently, he expressed anxiety that Britain had 'taken our action very much amiss', for although this was scarcely perceptible 'under Rosebery's slack and apparently moribund Ministry', 'we should soon feel it if Salisbury took the helm'.[5]

The conflict of interest between Germany and Britain in the eastern Mediterranean, repeatedly exacerbated by Kaiser Wilhelm's personal diplomacy, had also put the previously harmonious relationship between the two countries under visible strain since the end of 1894. In a 'highly confidential' conversation with the military attaché Colonel Swaine in November the Kaiser brought up the subject of the Straits and tried to find out, by dropping what he thought was a 'harmless' question into the conversation, whether the understanding reached between the British government and Russia 'concerned the Dardanelles as well as India'. Swaine's reply clearly indicated, according to Wilhelm, 'that essentially that was the case, and that the question of opening up [the Straits] is already being seriously considered'. 'At the end of the conversation I remarked *en passant*', Wilhelm continued, 'that if England was really absolutely serious about wanting to ensure peace and be good neighbours with Russia in Asia by opening up the Dardanelles, I hoped she would inform the other powers of it in good time and not spring a surprise à la Congo Treaty on Europe; that would ill befit John Bull. The Colonel entirely shared this view and promised to take the hint, if he should hear any more about the question.' To this the Kaiser appended the instruction: 'Hatzfeldt to be informed of this at once. Petersburg, Rome, Stamboul, Vienna to be informed.'[6]

Rosebery's replacement by the Marquess of Salisbury in July 1895, which the Kaiser at first enthusiastically welcomed,[7] most certainly did not lead to a more trusting relationship between Wilhelm and the British government. After a dinner on 5 August 1895 'with Queenie', as Kiderlen disrespectfully called her, the Kaiser held a long conversation at Cowes with Salisbury about the partition of the Ottoman Empire as the most effective solution of the Near Eastern question.[8] Hatzfeldt was relieved to be able to assure Holstein that this time Wilhelm had not allowed himself to be 'carried away into anything dangerous'. 'The most important part seems to have been that H.M. defended the idea that Turkey wasn't going to collapse as quickly as Salisbury thought.'[9] Wilhelm told the Reich Chancellor, however, that when the Ottoman Empire came to be divided Salisbury evidently wanted to give the Italians Tripoli, Morocco 'and all kinds of things', and to let the Austrians have Salonika and the Russians Constantinople.[10] After the interview the Kaiser 'quite unexpectedly' gave Hatzfeldt what amounted to an order 'to write to him directly and personally, if anything important happened here [in England] with regard to the Near East and a possible partition'.[11]

The Kaiser remained deeply suspicious of Salisbury's Near Eastern policy over the next few months. When news of more Armenian massacres came through in October 1895 — Wilhelm indignantly complained that the role played by the European great powers vis-à-vis the Sultan was 'more than pathetic' and that they would do better to fire 'a cannon-ball into Yildiz'[12] — he suspected that Britain might use the shedding of 'Christian blood' in Turkey as a pretext to allow Russian ships to sail through the Dardanelles without consulting Germany and the other signatories to the Berlin Treaty.[13] When the Empress Frederick also urged her son to act against the 'Turkish business',[14] Wilhelm sent the Chancellor a telegram demanding vigorous German intervention in the Near Eastern question, contrary to the course being followed by the Foreign Office. 'If Russia and England come to an understanding over Egypt and the Dardanelles so that one gets the former and the other the latter, where does that leave us?', he demanded impatiently, urging that measures be taken to prevent an Anglo-Russian agreement.[15] Holstein, schooled in Bismarckian ways, pointed out how advantageous such an accord between Great Britain and Russia would be for Germany, for it would create a deep gulf between Russia and France. 'So why should *we* get involved in trying to prevent it?', he asked. 'Whether it becomes a reality or not, this plan holds no dangers for us. But there is *serious* danger for Germany in H.M.'s intended anti-English attitude and mistrustful opposition of England, which, in view of the apparent *Russian-French-German* agreement on Mediterranean questions, might so soften up England and Italy that the former would give up Egypt and the Mediterranean, and the latter give up the Triple Alliance.'[16] The Privy Councillor's arguments went unheeded. A few days later the Kaiser again called on Colonel Swaine and complained that Salisbury's strange attitude since his return to power was creating the suspicion everywhere that Britain intended to change its Mediterranean policy. The universal view, he now claimed, was that Britain wanted 'to give Constantinople to Russia, to win France round by concessions in Egypt and to take the Dardanelles herself'. 'I looked the Colonel straight in the eye as I said this', the Kaiser recorded; 'he was visibly startled.' Neither Germany nor the other signatory powers would tolerate such a breach of the Berlin Treaty, Wilhelm warned the dismayed military attaché.[17]

Wilhelm seems not to have shared the fears of Holstein, Waldersee and others of an imminent encirclement of Germany brought about by collaboration between Britain, France and Russia. One of the ideas which dominated his thinking at this time was that Britain was facing an international crisis and could be forced by German pressure to associate itself formally with the Triple Alliance. It was in this expectation that in the spring of 1895, when news arrived that the Russian Mediterranean squadron had suddenly departed for the Far East, he commented jubilantly: 'I hear England is alarmed at this. Which is quite good for us. Rosebery's famous entente cordiale with Russia does not seem very sound. And in the end England will return penitently into the arms of the Triple Alliance.'[18] A long private letter which he received in September 1895 from Sir Edward Sullivan, a rich Englishman with whom he had spoken on various occasions at Cowes, made a strong impression on Wilhelm. Following up on their discussions, Sullivan's letter contained observations on the state of the British army and navy and on British policy which the Kaiser found extremely interesting. Philipp Eulenburg, who was staying with him at Rominten when the letter arrived, recorded that the information supplied by the Englishman amounted to 'a damning criticism of the present situation and leads to the conclusion that England's total isolation will force her to seek support in the form of an alliance, for the days when England made others do her work for her are over. England's natural allies are the members of the Triple Alliance, especially Germany. Sullivan's portrayal of how England would react to a French invasion is also of great interest. He comes to the sad conclusion, for England, that it would be an easy matter for France to catch England off her guard. The French have a better fleet than the English, and with combined action by the Russians

the English fleet could be defeated in the Mediterranean, or cornered so effectively that practically nothing would stand in the way of a French landing at the
unfortified ports. Very shortly afterwards France could dictate peace terms to
London.' Eulenburg went on to record that 'after reading this letter the Kaiser
embarked on a long discussion of English policy and the state of affairs there.
He told me that He had always made it very plain, not to the Queen and her
ministers but to persons who He knew would pass on His remarks, that England
can only expect support from the Triple Alliance, should she decide to ally herself
formally with it. Without written, binding agreements she had no hope . . . The
gloomy picture that Sullivan sketched of England's powerlessness brought the
thought of England's downfall vividly before His Majesty's mind's eye, and in
view of the common factors of race and religion, and of many and various other
important links, His Majesty came to the conclusion that in every respect the
consequences of such an eventuality could be incalculably great for us, and that
it required the most serious consideration.'[19] To put the future Foreign Secretary
and Reich Chancellor Bülow into the picture, Philipp Eulenburg gave him the
comforting news that 'His Majesty would be quite happy for England to be "shot
and wounded" – but he does *not* want England's downfall. That is absolutely
certain.'[20]

   The threatening tone of German policy – above all the German expectation
that Great Britain would bind itself by treaty to the Triple Alliance against France
and Russia, together with the Reich's excessive expansionist claims all over the
world – was attributed by the British government principally to Wilhelm II himself, whom Lord Salisbury, on the basis of recent reports from Berlin according to
which the Kaiser suffered from hallucinations, regarded as mentally unsound.[21]
Indeed, recalling John Erichsen's strong warnings in the spring of 1888,[22] he
even feared that Queen Victoria's grandson might go completely out of his mind.
According to a memorandum by the new British ambassador in Berlin, Sir Frank
Lascelles, the Prime Minister commented despondently to him on 4 December
1895 that 'The conduct of the German Emperor is very mysterious and difficult to explain. There is a danger of his going completely off his head . . . In
commercial and colonial matters Germany was most disagreeable. Her demand
for the left bank of the Volta was outrageous, so much so that Lord Salisbury
thought it must have been the idea of the Emperor himself as no responsible
statesman could have put it forward. The rudeness of German communications,
much increased since Bismarck's time, was perhaps due to the wish of smaller
men to keep up the traditions of the great Chancellor . . . In the Far East, the
Germans are up to every sort of intrigue, asking for concessions & privileges
of all sorts, with a view to cutting us out. The only way of meeting them is by

countermining, & we are in a position to do so.'[23] The spectre of encirclement was slowly but surely taking shape.

## BRITISH INSULTS

Wilhelm II's *Schadenfreude* at the possible 'downfall of England' was in part a reaction to various insulting rebuffs which he had received at the hands of his royal relations, the British government and the London press and which contributed in no small measure to a completely unnecessary exacerbation of the conflict of interests which did in fact exist between the two countries.[24] A typical example of the kind of wounding snub delivered to him by the British royal family occurred in connection with the inauguration of the Kiel Canal in June 1895. Wilhelm was almost childish in his enthusiasm to show off the great maritime achievement represented by the North Sea–Baltic canal for the benefit of his English relations. In a telegram to his grandmother he expressed confidence that the canal would further 'the union of nations' and contribute to the 'peaceful development of their wealth'. He thanked her for sending Prince George and the entire Channel Squadron to take part in the celebrations and informed her that on 20 June, the anniversary of her accession, the German fleet had joined with the British fleet in firing a salute.[25] Again on 12 July Wilhelm wrote enthusiastically to the Queen from Stockholm about the successful co-operation between the German and British fleets at Kiel. 'Let me thank You sincerely once more for Your having kindly sent Georgy to represent You at Kiel; & for the appearing of the fine Channel Squadron under the Flag of Lord W. Kerr. The sight of the whole assembled ships was really worth seeing & as the neucleus [sic] of the gathering the sight of the Channel Squadron in its uniformity of Type was most imposing . . . The relations between our officers were cordial & intimate & proved the ties of esteem & friendship excisting [sic] between our Navies.'[26] In reality such assurances of friendship bordered on hypocrisy, for the participation of the Duke of York, the future King George V, in the inauguration ceremony had been preceded by almost unbelievably insulting behaviour on the part of the Prince of Wales and his son. When Swaine suggested that in view of the fact that the Kaiser was an honorary admiral of the Royal Navy and that Austria and Italy were to be represented at Kiel by members of their royal families, a British prince should be sent to the ceremony,[27] the Prince of Wales asked in all seriousness for enquiries to be made as to whether the date of the inauguration of the canal could be postponed, as otherwise the ceremony would clash with Ascot Week.[28] Prince George's attitude to his German cousin's invitation was scarcely less insulting. Before his departure for Hamburg the young duke had informed the British ambassador in Berlin that he would be embarrassed if the Kaiser conferred an honorary rank in the Imperial Navy on him; he would be glad to accept any other German distinction but it was not possible for him to wear German naval uniform. When the Kaiser instructed the ambassador to be asked the reason for this astonishing statement the answer conveyed to Wilhelm by Hohenlohe was that 'the responsibility for this attitude undoubtedly lay with the Duke's mother, who as Your Majesty knows is very anti-German and obstinate, and to whom the Duke probably gave his promise on the matter'.[29] Even during Wilhelm's visit to Cowes in August 1895, to which he had looked forward like a child,[30] the Prince of Wales distinguished himself by his gross discourtesy, according to the imperial entourage. Kiderlen-Wächter reported to Berlin: 'Fat old Wales has again been inconceivably rude to H.M. On our arrival he let H.M. wait three-quarters of an hour before he came on board. When H.M. was talking with Salisb[ury] the day before yesterday, Wales came up twice to interrupt the conversation. The first time he completely failed, but the second time he succeeded in separating them.'[31] Waldersee, who was astonishingly accurately informed about events in Britain, heard not only that the Prince of Wales had made fun of the Kaiser 'in the most brazen way', but also that the Queen's third son Arthur, Duke of Connaught, had refused an invitation from the Kaiser to attend manoeuvres on the grounds that he had something else to do. 'They evidently think over there that they can cope with the Kaiser better if they treat him badly; they are well aware that he is impressed by English life, English wealth and luxury and can easily be fobbed off with the multitude of pleasures offered to him. I have been able to watch for years how he, who had nothing but mockery for England as Prince Wilhelm, has gradually become an anglomane', Waldersee noted regretfully. His own anglophobia, unlike that of the Kaiser, was not inclined to swing repeatedly over into anglomania.[32]

There were other reasons why Wilhelm's extended stay on the Isle of Wight in unremittingly rainy weather was not an unalloyed pleasure either for him or for his hosts.[33] As a result of new competition rules the Kaiser lost the races both for the Queen's Cup, which he coveted, and for the Meteor Challenge Shield, to his rival, his Uncle Bertie. The monarch had brought a thirty-strong military band with him, which played at every banquet, whether on the terrace in front of Osborne House or at the Royal Yacht Squadron in Cowes. Kiderlen, the Swabian diplomat known for his biting mockery, reported sardonically from Cowes that the Kaiser had given the British 'a special treat by bringing along a fleet of four battleships and a dispatch boat. They block the course of the racing vessels, every few moments they get an attack of *salutirium*, the sailors are flooding Cowes, the Queen has to invite the commanders, etc.!'[34]

The relationship between Kaiser Wilhelm and his grandmother, on the other hand, took a decidedly favourable turn when they agreed together that General Viscount Wolseley should be appointed to succeed the outgoing British ambassador in Berlin, Sir Edward Malet, who had asked to be relieved of his post after eleven stressful years.[35] It is astonishing to see the extent to which the Kaiser felt entitled to choose the new ambassador himself, in agreement with his grandmother. As we shall see, his restless activity on behalf of Wolseley cast a cloud over his relationship with Salisbury's government. The Kaiser turned down the Queen's first suggestion that Lord Cromer should go to Berlin, but he was positively enthusiastic when she brought up Wolseley's name. He said that he wanted a soldier and would welcome Wolseley's appointment with the greatest pleasure.[36] When Philip Eulenburg heard of the Kaiser's efforts to obtain Wolseley's appointment he groaned: 'A hero! A general! An Englishman! – who can withstand that!' The Russian ambassador in Berlin would not have a chance against such a rival.[37] The Kaiser's hidden motive, however, was probably quite different. Wolseley was also regarded at this time as the most likely candidate to take over the supreme command of the British army. His appointment as ambassador in Berlin would therefore leave the way open for the Kaiser's uncle, Arthur Duke of Connaught, to be appointed commander-in-chief, and this, or so Wilhelm believed, would bring potential advantages for Germany, since Connaught was married to a Prussian princess.

The trouble began when the Queen, who had meanwhile discovered that the new Conservative government did not after all want Wolseley as commander-in-chief,[38] sent word to Wilhelm that she would be grateful if he would grant Salisbury a second audience, whereupon at 3.30 p.m. the Kaiser summoned the Prime Minister by telephone to see him at 4 o'clock. Salisbury excused himself, saying that he had to see the Queen at Osborne House at that time. He did not say that he would come to see the Kaiser after his audience with the Queen. The Kaiser then sent him a message saying that he would wait for him on board the *Hohenzollern* until 6.30. This message, however, did not reach the Prime Minister, as he did not return to his rooms after seeing the Queen (or so he maintained later), but went into the park, where he was caught by a downpour until shortly before 8 p.m. The same evening Hatzfeldt wrote to Salisbury to say that he could come and see the Kaiser the next morning, 7 August, but the Prime Minister evaded this invitation too on the grounds that he unfortunately had to return to London very early in the morning.[39] 'William is a little sore at your not coming to see him', the Queen warned her Prime Minister in a cipher telegram of 8 August.[40]

Although Hatzfeldt was convinced that everything had happened as Salisbury claimed,[41] and Kiderlen was relieved that there had been no second conversation

with the Kaiser – 'I am quite happy that the talk did not take place', he wrote
to Holstein; 'I have more confidence in Hatzf[eldt]'s talks with Sal[isbury] than
in those of H.M.!' – they nevertheless racked their brains over the reasons for
Salisbury's behaviour. Kiderlen guessed that Queen Victoria's wish to appoint
her son Arthur rather than Wolseley as commander-in-chief might well be the
root cause. Writing to Holstein, this was his interpretation of the comedy of
manners on the Isle of Wight: 'As you know, the Queen spoke with H.M. about
Wolseley as the successor of Malet. The main purpose in sending Wolseley is
to get rid of him here and to make Connaught commander-in-chief. H.M. of
course knows that too and that is why he is so much for Wolseley for he thinks it
is "most important" (!) that Connaught be made commander-in-chief . . . Now
it is possible that the Queen worked out this little plan with her nephew without
first asking Salisb[ury], in the certain belief that he would make no difficulties
for her on this point as Rosebery would have done. Now perhaps Salisb. bucked
after all – because it is certainly strange that he said nothing about it either to
H.M. or to Hatzf[eldt]. In that case it is quite possible that it was for this reason
that he did not want to see H.M. again, to avoid having to talk with him about
Wols[eley].'[42]

The Queen's correspondence, published in 1931, shows that Kiderlen had hit
the nail on the head. On 8 August 1895 she sent a message to Minister of War
Lord Lansdowne, asking him to tell Wolseley 'that the Emperor is very anxious
to have him at Berlin. H.M. fears Emperor will be greatly disappointed if he
does not go.'[43] Wolseley, however, made no attempt to conceal the fact that he
would prefer to be commander-in-chief.[44] The Queen was furious to hear that
Lansdowne, without her permission, had offered the General both posts and had
left the choice to him. 'The Emperor will be grievously disappointed.'[45] Salisbury
and Lansdowne had to explain patiently to the Queen that the appointment of
her son Arthur as commander-in-chief in succession to her cousin, the Duke of
Cambridge, would have had serious political drawbacks.[46]

Such restriction of the sovereign's freedom of choice was exactly what
Wilhelm II detested about the British constitutional system. He was mortified at the failure of his plans, telegraphing to Queen Victoria on 12 August:
'Very surprised and deeply grieved at the unexpected turn the matter we wished
has taken.'[47] He informed Lord Salisbury through Hatzfeldt that he still wished
to have 'a soldier or Grand Seigneur' as British ambassador at Berlin, causing the
Prime Minister to protest that such interference from an outside source would
rightly anger the diplomatic corps, added to which there were only two great
landed proprietors who could even be considered, and in both cases the talent
for diplomacy was 'more largely developed in the wife than in the husband'.
He proposed at first to transfer the career diplomat Sir Edmund Monson from

Vienna to Berlin and to send Sir Nicholas O'Conor to Vienna as ambassador.[48] Queen Victoria countered by suggesting Lord Londonderry, Lord Jersey or Sir Francis Grenfell for the Berlin post.[49] Finally it was agreed that the ambassador at St Petersburg, Sir Frank Lascelles, should be transferred to Berlin. He seemed to satisfy the social demands of the Kaiser, even though his wife was not of exalted birth.[50] In a letter of 28 August to her grandson, after apologising at length for the confusion that had occurred, the Queen made great play of the excellent qualities possessed by Lascelles. 'Long & anxiously did I go over with Lord Salisbury various names we discussed', she assured Wilhelm; 'and at length we agreed that Sir F. Lascelles, now at St. Petersburg, wd. be the fittest. He is one of our best Diplomatists, a very able man of Lord Harewood's family; his Mother was a Sister of the D[uche]ss of Sutherland, whose Husband was a great friend of your Grandfather and Gt Uncle of Papa's, and my 1st Mistress of the Robes & great friend. He is also 1st Cousin to the Duke of Devonshire. – His wife is a clever agreeable person but she is not good looking, nor a *Grande Dame*. There might have been several *Grandes Dames*, but the husbands wd. not have done. – In this choice I have been most anxious to find someone who wd. be agreeable to you & wd. do all he cd. to maintain the best relations between the 2 Countries.'[51] The Kaiser accepted Lascelles but was nevertheless disappointed. 'H.M. had been looking forward to having a field-marshal with a suitable wife, and is peeved that this is not going to happen', Hatzfeldt reported to Berlin.[52]

The Kaiser suffered yet another painful setback during his visit to England in the summer of 1895, this time from the scathing personal attacks made on him by the press. Their effect on him was deeply and enduringly wounding, especially as the newspapers concerned, most of which had reported favourably on his earlier visits, were those that he regarded as close to the government. He did not understand the extent to which the British press had become a powerful and troublesome entity independent of the government. As Waldersee had predicted, neither Germany's collaboration with Russia and France against Japan nor the Wilhelmstrasse's newly declared interest in Southern Africa did Wilhelm II any favours in political and journalistic circles in London.[53] Most notably, an article in the *Standard* criticised German policy in the Far East and advised Wilhelm to take lessons in political wisdom from his grandmother during his visit to the Isle of Wight. 'The Kaiser has probably never been told the truth in such strong terms', Waldersee declared. He found it incomprehensible that Wilhelm continued to enjoy himself in England instead of leaving at once, for – as the General commented – he must have been very offended by the article, particularly by its insulting schoolmasterish tone, and could not have found it easy 'not to allow himself to be irritated by all these lectures and admonitions'.[54]

And indeed the barb implanted by the *Standard*'s malicious article left a deep wound, as we shall see.

On 10 August the Kaiser and his suite left Cowes amid cheering crowds and set out for Lowther Castle in Westmorland, the seat of Lord Lonsdale, a close friend since 1892, whom he had seen in September 1894 at the manoeuvres in East Prussia and more recently during the Kiel Week regatta, as well as at Cowes.[55] From Lowther, in spite of the bad weather, he went on expeditions to Ullswater and Windermere (clad, unusually for him, in a light-coloured civilian suit, a brown overcoat and a black bowler) with the other guests, who included Karl von Eisendecher and several members of the Churchill family, who were related to Lonsdale. He shot red grouse on Wemmersgill Moor and went out cycling.[56] Documents sent to Lord Lonsdale a year later and forwarded by him to the Chief Constable in Carlisle claimed that when the Kaiser arrived at Lowther a bomb attack on him planned from Switzerland had been foiled only just in time, but further police and diplomatic investigations revealed that it was more likely to have been an unsuccessful blackmail attempt.[57] More than a hundred years later no explanation can be found for this puzzling episode, of which the Kaiser was told nothing. For him, his stay in the rain-swept green hills of the Lake District remained an unforgettable experience. 'With a heavy heart I left Lowther and am unable to find words to thank you and Lonsdale for the kind hospitality shown to myself and my suite', he wrote to his hostess from the *Hohenzollern* on his way home. 'The memory of my stay will ever be most delightful . . . Compliments to all who made Lowther a second Paradise. William I. R.'[58] Staying with the Lonsdales was the only happy experience for Wilhelm during his visit to England in August 1895, from which he had hoped for so much.

This visit undoubtedly marked a turning-point in Anglo-German relations and hence in the international situation as a whole. In London, not only at court and in government circles but also in public opinion, impatience with Germany's conspicuously volatile and unreliable foreign policy, aggravated to no small degree by Kaiser Wilhelm's importunate behaviour, had given rise to a new, threatening tone which conveyed the unmistakable message: 'If you do not go along with us as we wish, we shall go against you.'[59] From this Waldersee concluded that it was more important than ever for Germany to maintain 'a reserved but confident stance and an independent policy'.[60] He strongly criticised the Kaiser's importunate efforts to win friends. 'The greatest failing of Kaiser Wilhelm's policy', he commented, 'is that he wants to be on good terms with the Russians, the French, the English and even the Sultan, and pays court to them in a dangerous way; he inevitably falls between two stools. I do not even wish to mention his attentions to Austria and Italy; but they too are quite excessive and no less unwise. If we stand proudly aloof, run after no one but give the clear impression that we are confident of our power, others will come and ask for our support. If we continue as we are, we cannot but lose public respect.'[61] The only pleasing aspect of the insulting attitude adopted in Great Britain, in the General's eyes, was the anger expressed about it 'more or less unanimously' throughout the German press. 'The whole nation' was positively 'outraged . . . by the impudence of the English', he commented in his diary of 13 August 1895, adding with satisfaction that at last 'some sort of national feeling' was beginning to stir in Germany.[62] From now on, indeed, reciprocal prejudices and feelings of hatred began to stir on both sides of the North Sea. Fanned by the press, they could no longer be held in check by the respective governments, especially as in the young German Reich the temptation to enter into a pact with the devil, in the shape of the dangerous new power of the media, not infrequently proved irresistible.

## THE AIMS OF GERMAN COLONIAL POLICY

The German Empire had become a 'global empire', Kaiser Wilhelm II announced at the impressive state banquet held in the White Hall of the Berlin Schloss on 18 January 1896 to celebrate the twenty-fifth anniversary of the founding of the Reich.[63] Waldersee took a sceptical view of this claim, for it really could not be justified by 'our colonies, which are after all still very pitiful, . . . and although we keep up an extensive trade with all parts of the world, this surely does not qualify us as a global empire either. If the Kaiser aspired to such a thing, we should have to seize it; but where? and from whom? The millions of Germans who have emigrated are no longer German nationals and do not concern us, nor do most of them want anything from us.'[64] Still less of a colonial enthusiast in the accepted sense than Waldersee was the new Reich Chancellor Chlodwig Hohenlohe, for rather than seeking to acquire territories in the tropics, he called for the emigration of the surplus population of Germany to be encouraged, principally to Argentina and southern Brazil. In early 1895 he wrote to his cousin Hermann zu Hohenlohe-Langenburg condemning Bismarck's colonial policy: 'The Bismarckian conception was one of the great man's mistakes. When great men have stupid ideas, their stupidity is in proportion to their greatness. In heaven's name, what are we supposed to do with the 500,000–700,000 people added to the population of Germany every year? In the end the Germans will have no alternative but to eat each other up. I consider it one of the most urgent tasks of the Reich government to encourage emigration and to organise it as well as possible.'[65]

In October 1895 the Kaiser likewise declared the 'strengthening of the German presence' in southern Brazil to be an urgent objective of Germany's foreign policy.[66] His interest in expanding German colonial possessions in Africa had recently suffered a setback as a result of his discovery that neither he nor the government of the Reich but the German-African Company was the rightful owner of the colonies there. As Philipp Eulenburg told the Colonial Director in the Foreign Office, Paul Kayser, '*in complete confidence*' in September 1895, the Kaiser was very angry that 'according to the treaties concluded, the entire area of the colonies – and even any additional territory that is acquired – remains in the hands of the German-African Company and not in those of His Majesty's government. From the moment he learned this His Majesty's interest in the colonies was as good as extinguished. The Kaiser can neither direct the flood of German emigrants there and make plans for the colonies, nor take any pleasure in troops who fight only for a company of German capitalists.'[67]

Rather than the acquisition of territory overseas, Wilhelm II's attention was now directed principally towards finding suitable coaling stations and naval bases, which in turn was attributed to the influence exercised on him (and deplored by the civilian leadership of the Reich) by naval and army officers. During a visit to the Wilhelmstrasse in January 1895 he demanded the creation of an integrated organisation for colonial troops. The current system by which each colony organised its own troops must be replaced by a single colonial army of which the Marine Infantry would form the core.[68] The Secretary of State of the Reich Navy Office, Admiral Friedrich von Hollmann, found this demand unacceptable. He threatened to resign and was supported in his stance by the Reich Chancellor, who saw the Kaiser's demand as an infringement of his responsibility for the conduct of foreign policy.[69] Again in September 1895 Hohenlohe complained of the strong influence of the navy on the Kaiser in colonial matters when the latter blocked the creation of a separate Colonial Office. 'The navy should really not have anything to do with the administration of the colonies', he wrote to his cousin Hermann. 'But H.M. is still too much under the influence of the navy to accept a proposal aiming to bring that about.' Hohenlohe deplored the 'the military culture' in the colonies which led to a situation in which 'our colonies are being used to accommodate useless officers, when a governor with a few officials and a number of Sudanese would be quite adequate'. Against the Kaiser's will nothing could be done, however, and Hohenlohe also feared that Paul Kayser's 'personality' was 'not calculated to help change H.M.'s mind'.[70]

The influence of the navy and the army on the Kaiser's colonial policy showed itself principally in his repeated attempts to pressurise the Reich government into acquiring ports, coastal strips and islands which he considered would be useful to Germany's naval forces. At Hohenlohe's first audience on 2 November 1894 Wilhelm demanded, as we have seen, not only the annexation of the island of Formosa (Taiwan) but also the acquisition of Mozambique, as Germany was dependent on Britain for coaling stations and this must stop.[71] In July 1895 Waldersee noted in his diary that Germany now intended to take 'serious steps as regards Morocco'.[72] In the spring of 1896 Morocco again emerged as an objective of German colonial policy. After a conversation with Count Christian von Tattenbach, the German envoy in Tangier, the Kaiser called at the Reich chancellor's palace in a 'highly agitated' state, with the news that France wanted to buy the Canary Islands from Spain; Germany must therefore have something in Morocco by way of compensation. As the Chancellor recorded, Wilhelm began by discussing the advantages of a colony but in the end contented himself with the idea of acquiring a coaling station – 'and then we shall see what is to be done next'. At the Kaiser's suggestion Tattenbach was ordered 'to pursue the matter there'.[73] On All Highest orders the warship *Moltke* was instructed to remain at Gibraltar 'in order to be ready if any action were to be undertaken on the Moroccan coast'.[74] A week later Hohenlohe had to urge the Kaiser to allow the *Moltke* to proceed on its way, as the rumour about the purchase of the Canary Islands by France had proved groundless. He went on to point out that the survival of the Triple Alliance might be threatened if Germany were to take action in Morocco immediately after the catastrophic defeat which the Italian army had suffered at Adua on 1 March.[75] The Kaiser, whom Hohenlohe found 'in a cheerful mood' this time, recognised the dangers to be feared from an action in Morocco and authorised the warship's departure from Gibraltar.[76] In July 1896 Wilhelm, anticipating not only a possible Anglo-French agreement on respective spheres of interest in North Africa, but also a Moroccan crisis unleashed by this, wrote on a report from Rome: 'The English squadron is *à portée* off Tangier! Might a little agreement with France at the expense of Italy and Spain be in the offing, with Morocco for England, Tunis and Tripoli for France? Please keep a lookout in Morocco! Because we shall have our say too!'[77] Only nine years later the German demand for compensation in Morocco for a very similar Anglo-French agreement in North Africa would unleash the first of the great pre-war crises.

In eastern and southern Africa, meanwhile, an increasingly critical situation was developing and the detached stance hitherto taken by Germany was fast becoming a thing of the past. In the summer of 1894 Sir Edward Malet drew attention to the fact that in the interest of Anglo-German understanding Wilhelm II's attitude over the demarcation of the two countries' possessions and spheres of influence in central Africa had been very moderate.[78] Only a few months later, however, it was only too plain to the statesmen of both countries that the Kaiser's attitude had changed. Remarks that he made to Swaine on 21 November 1894 led to a lively exchange between the British Foreign Secretary, Lord Kimberley, and the German ambassador in London, in the course of which Hatzfeldt deplored the growing antagonism between Germany and Britain in East Africa. 'Count Hatzfeldt said he had for 8 years tried to make a closer alliance between England and the triple alliance but that England refused and he was sorry to perceive there were signs of irritation in Germany against England's Colonial Policy.'[79] In his diary for 7 August 1895 Waldersee predicted that 'our Colonial people' would be 'very unhappy' at the new turn British policy was taking, for they would 'very soon realise in Africa . . . that England has no intention of giving up anything at all there; if *we* do not give up, there will be plenty of points of conflict there. Only if things go badly for England will she co-operate with us.'[80]

## THE MALET INCIDENT

Far more dangerous than Anglo-German rivalry in East Africa, of course, was the tense relationship between the British Cape Colony under Cecil Rhodes and the Boer republics of Transvaal and the Orange Free State, in which not only the Kaiser but also the Reich government, backed by inflamed public opinion in Germany, interfered forcefully and with fatal results, as we shall soon see. Ever since the discovery of enormous gold and diamond deposits in the two Boer states in the 1860s the rural idyll was over for these descendants of Dutch immigrants. Thousands of 'Uitlanders', mainly British, had poured in to prospect for gold and precious stones. Among the most successful of them was Cecil Rhodes, who had come to South Africa at the age of seventeen and had since become one of the richest men in the world. In addition to his diamond business, which controlled 90 per cent of world production, Rhodes had risen to become Prime Minister of Cape Colony in 1890. As the first step on the way to bringing the whole of southern and eastern Africa under British rule Rhodes planned to gain control of the two Boer states with the help of an armed uprising by the Uitlanders. Four thousand rifles and three machine guns were smuggled into Johannesburg and plans were made to capture the arsenal in Pretoria. In October 1895 Leander Starr Jameson, a friend of Rhodes, led a private army of 500 men (including three serving British officers), with six machine guns and three field guns, to the western border of the Transvaal to await the moment for invasion. The rebellion which they were to support was planned for 28 December.[81]

The rapidly developing situation was watched with growing surprise and displeasure by both the Kaiser and the Foreign Office in Berlin. There were about 5,000 citizens of the German Reich living in the Transvaal at this time; German investments there amounted to nearly 500 million marks. In Germany public opinion identified itself to a large extent with the Boers, that small nation of 'Protestant farmers of Germanic origin' who were being threatened, as it seemed, by the 'plutocratic Anglo-Saxons'. The German Consul-General in Pretoria, Franz von Herff, had taken the opportunity of a banquet at the German Club in the town in honour of the Kaiser's birthday in January 1895, at which President of the Transvaal 'Ohm' Krüger was present, to assure the latter that the German Reich was not indifferent to fate of the Transvaal. The President had replied that, although his small country was like a child among the great powers, if the great power Britain tried to trample on his country, the great power Germany would be able to prevent this. These remarks had been enough to cause a serious diplomatic confrontation between London and Berlin: the British ambassador pointedly reminded the German Foreign Secretary of the status of the Transvaal under international law from the British point of view: Great Britain had annexed the country in 1877; four years later and again in 1884 it had recognised the sovereignty of the republic, but with the proviso that the Transvaal must not form any alliance with another state without British consent. Marschall contested this interpretation, made angry allusions to Cecil Rhodes's intentions and his anti-German utterances, and protested against the Cape Colony's plan to force the Transvaal into an economic union with it.[82] The repeated warnings of the government in London that as far as South Africa was concerned the most vital interests of the British Empire were at stake seemed not to have been understood in Berlin, probably because there was no desire to understand them.[83]

The following months brought further Anglo-German conflicts in this highly sensitive region. On the occasion of a visit by the German cruiser *Condor* Wilhelm II sent the President of the Transvaal the telegram which came to be known as 'the first Krüger telegram' and which, as Waldersee recorded, was 'particularly badly received' in London.[84] In October 1895 there was a second clash between Marschall and Malet when the latter, on the point of retiring as ambassador in Berlin, declared during his farewell visit to the Wilhelmstrasse that there was only one 'black spot' in the otherwise friendly relations between Germany and Britain, and that was the support which the Germans were giving the Boers in their hostile attitude towards Great Britain in the Transvaal. This was an intolerable state of affairs for Britain and if Germany persisted in its attitude serious complications could follow.[85] Marschall rejected Malet's critical remarks with such robustness that the Kaiser, for once, had nothing but praise for him for sending the ambassador away with a flea in his ear. Like the Foreign Secretary, Wilhelm poured scorn on the British threat, 'when they need us so much in Europe!' He too thought it outrageous that Malet should 'make us take the blame for Rhodes's arrogance!',[86] and considered the ambassador's warning an 'impertinence' which must be repudiated 'with the requisite energy'.[87] Writing to the Tsar, he commented that Malet had used 'very blustering words, about

Germany behaving badly to England in Africa', and had threatened 'that it [England] would not stand it any longer and that after buying off the French by concessions in Egypt they were at liberty to look after us. He was even so undiplomatic to utter the word "war"! saying that even England would not shrink from making war upon me if we did not knock down in Africa.'[88]

Infuriated beyond measure by the 'utterly incomprehensible' attitude of Lord Salisbury, who was unwilling to join the Triple Alliance, the Kaiser fiercely attacked British policy in a conversation with Leopold Swaine on 25 October 1895 that had a far-reaching effect on Anglo-German relations. He began by castigating Britain's Mediterranean policy and threatening to set up a continental league against it.[89] Then, according to his own account of the conversation, he told Swaine that Malet had made 'the most astonishing accusations of malicious conduct by us towards England' on his departure. 'Indeed, he had even gone so far as to utter the unbelievable word "war"; thus for the sake of a few square miles full of negroes and palm trees England had threatened her only real friend, the German Kaiser, grandson of Her Majesty the Queen of Great Britain and Ireland, with war.' Wilhelm rejected out of hand Swaine's attempt to explain away the words of the outgoing ambassador as a misunderstanding that ought to be cleared up as soon as possible. He retorted that 'this tone, even though it was surprising to hear it from so mild a man as Malet, matched the tone of the English press towards Germany', and went on to tell Swaine that 'the government press in particular behaved in the most unwarrantable way towards me. Germany and the Triple Alliance had been continually insulted and taunted, and a good part of my seven years of hard work to bring my Reich and England closer together on the basis of common interests and mutual respect in order to solve great cultural issues, had been destroyed . . . It was not compatible with the interests of my country to go along with all the whims of English policy and to react to vague hints and enigmatic utterances by English statesmen. Such conduct by England positively forced me to make common cause with France and Russia, both of which could have about a million men on my borders ready to invade, while England did not even have a kind word for me.' 'I ended the conversation', the Kaiser continued, 'with a strong warning that the only way England could escape from her present complete *isolement*, in which she found herself because of her "policy of selfishness and bullying", was to take an open and unqualified stand either on the side of the Triple Alliance or against it. The former course would have to be in the form customary among continental powers, i.e. under signed and sealed guarantee. The Colonel seemed profoundly shaken and affected.'[90] The Reich Chancellor, informing the German ambassadors in London and Rome of this conversation, softened the Kaiser's anti-British tone considerably by affirming that as soon as British policy adopted a more definite course 'His Majesty's remarks directed against England, in which He was expressing His thoughts about the current situation rather than voicing a fixed principle, will no longer have any practical application.'[91] By contrast, the impression made on the British government by Swaine's account of the Kaiser's comments was powerful in the extreme. The document was printed and circulated to all Cabinet ministers, one of whom wrote to the military attaché saying that it was 'the most important document you have ever sent to us from Berlin'.[92]

Although Hatzfeldt reported several times to Berlin that Malet had acted without instructions,[93] Philipp Eulenburg observed during the Kaiser's stay at Liebenberg at the end of October that Wilhelm was 'still very indignant' about Malet's behaviour,[94] The Kaiser expressed the opinion 'that he would not regard the Malet incident about the Transvaal as settled until he had been informed officially by some suitable person (unfortunately the new ambassador won't be here for another six weeks) that Lord Salisbury does *not* share Malet's views'.[95] The Kaiser's 'irritation' with Britain continued to manifest itself in the aggressive marginal comments which he wrote on diplomatic papers.[96] The Foreign Secretary had difficulty in preventing him from sending a telegram to Bülow in Rome with instructions to warn the Italians against Britain and 'cut them off' from Britain if possible. Holstein's comment was that in Marschall's place he would rather have walked out.[97] In mid-November 1895 Eulenburg reported to Bülow that although the Malet incident had been settled the Kaiser 'is very annoyed with England and will remain so'.[98] The Kaiser's irritation at 'England's brazenness' had wide repercussions and even led to a plea from Kaiser Franz Joseph that 'Kaiser Wilhelm should not be too hostile towards England, as that would put Austria into an extremely difficult position.'[99] It was not until 17 November that the Kaiser accepted that 'the British Premier . . . has formally said his *peccavi*', commenting with satisfaction that 'the rude answer . . . has fulfilled its purpose perfectly'.[100] In December 1895, however, Waldersee confided to his diary after long conversations with Wilhelm in Hanover and Springe that the Kaiser had 'criticised English policy . . . very sharply'.[101] Only two weeks later the most serious crisis of confidence in Anglo-German relations in the pre-war period broke out as a result of an act of 'unbelievable stupidity'.[102] How did it happen, and what role did the Kaiser play in it?

## THE KRÜGER TELEGRAM

At the end of December 1895 the rapidly worsening situation in southern Africa had been causing 'great agitation' in the Wilhelmstrasse for days.[103] On 31 December at 1.30 p.m. the Foreign Office received news of the incursion into the Transvaal by Jameson and his irregular army. Consul-General von Herff tele-graphed to say that President Krüger considered Jameson's action to be a breach of the London Convention of 1884 and was counting on the support of Germany and France. Herff asked for the protection of a landing party from the cruiser *Seeadler* to defend the Germans whose life and property seemed under serious threat. He described the Jameson Raid as 'unscrupulous land-grabbing'. On receiving this news the Foreign Secretary immediately sent a telegram to the Kaiser and then travelled to Potsdam with the Director of the Colonial Department, Paul Kayser, for consultations with the monarch. Wilhelm approved the decision to order the landing party of fifty marines on board the *Seeadler* to go to Pretoria to protect the Germans there. A second cruiser was dispatched to Delagoa Bay.[104] When a second telegram arrived from Herff on 1 January together with an open telegram from the Germans in Pretoria begging Wilhelm II 'to intervene at once to prevent untold misery and bloodshed', Marschall again went to the Schloss to inform the Kaiser.[105]

We know from the Reich Chancellor's journal that Wilhelm II was in a highly excitable state at this time, not least as a result of the Köller crisis, and that his behaviour towards the Minister of War was so violent that Bronsart had diffi-culty in restraining himself from 'drawing swords'; the General doubted that the Kaiser was 'entirely normal' mentally, and had 'grave concerns about the future'.[106] When the news from South Africa arrived, the Kaiser condemned Cecil Rhodes as a 'monstrous villain' and scrawled on a report from Cape Town: 'This is a gross stock exchange swindle cooked up by *German Jews*.'[107] Waldersee, who sat next to the Kaiser at the New Year dinner for the commanding generals, looked on as Wilhelm received 'a long telegram about the Transvaal, which caused him some agitation; he said that it had been established that uniformed English officers had taken part in Mr Jameson's expedition, and he foresaw serious complications'.[108] In a conversation with Lascelles on 1 January 1896 he expressed the hope that Jameson and all his followers would be captured and shot.[109] The *Times* correspondent Valentine Chirol informed the ambas-sador that 'the Emperor was so rabid when the news first reached him that he thought of sending back his English uniforms with the remark that they were only fit to be worn by South African bandits'. Wilhelm was also reported to have claimed that 'there was at all events one part of Africa over which England could not claim Suzerainty and that was Egypt'. Conveying these remarks in a private letter to Salisbury, Lascelles sighed: 'It will be a serious matter if the Emperor becomes actively hostile towards us, and he is so impulsive and impetuous that this is a contingency which must be considered.' The situa-tion, Sir Frank added, was 'far more unsatisfactory than I could have believed possible'.[110]

On 2 January the Kaiser wrote to the Tsar taking up the idea of a continental league against Great Britain. 'The political horizon is peculiar just now. Armenia and Venezuela are open questions England brought up, and now suddenly the Transvaal Republic has been attacked in a most foul way as it seems not without England's knowledge. I have used very severe language in London and have opened communications with Paris for common defence of our endangered interests, as French and German colonists have immediately joined hands of their own accord to help the outraged boers. I hope you will also kindly consider the question, as it is one of principle of upholding treaties once concluded. I hope that all will come right, but come what may, I never shall allow the British to stamp out the Transvaal!'[111] In fact the British government had immediately distanced itself from the attack. On 30 December Colonial Secretary Joseph Chamberlain formally condemned Jameson's action and ordered the recall of his troops and the punishment of the British officers involved. On 1 January 1896 Hatzfeldt reported, after a conversation with Salisbury, that he was convinced that the government in London had not been behind the Jameson Raid and that it was being honest in distancing itself publicly from him [112]

At 10 a.m. on 3 January 1896 the Kaiser, accompanied by Naval Secretary Admiral Friedrich von Hollmann, Commanding Admiral Eduard von Knorr and Chief of the Naval Cabinet Admiral Gustav Freiherr von Senden-Bibran, arrived at the Reich chancellor's palace, where Hohenlohe, Marschall and Paul Kayser were waiting for him. Geheimrat von Holstein was in a neighbouring room. 'The South African question was discussed', the Reich Chancellor noted in a brief account of the proceedings. 'Marschall proposed a telegram to Krüger, which was accepted. Then possible support for the Boers was discussed. Colonel Schele was summoned and ordered to travel to South Africa to investigate what kind of help might be given to the Boers. Holstein, Kayser and Marschall are against it.'[113] Marschall's diary throws rather more light on the strange process by which the decision was eventually reached to send the notorious Krüger telegram and above all indicates the pressure under which the 'responsible' statesmen, Hohenlohe, Marschall, Holstein and Kayser, were put by the monarch and the three Admirals. The Foreign Secretary writes: 'At 10 o'clock attended conference with H.M., together with Reich Chancellor, Hollmann, Knorr and Senden. H.M. put forward some weird and wonderful plans. Protectorate over the Transvaal, which I at once talked him out of. Mobilisation of the marines. Dispatch of troops to the Transvaal. When the Reich Chancellor objected: "That would mean war with England", H.M. replied: "Yes, but only on land." Then it was decided to send Schele on a reconnaissance mission to the Transvaal. Also an unfortunate idea. Finally, at my suggestion, H.M. sent a congratulatory telegram to President Krüger.'[114] The telegram, as is well known, was expressed in terms that were particularly offensive to Great Britain in that the Kaiser congratulated Krüger for having succeeded, 'without appealing for the help of friendly powers, in guarding the independence of your country against attacks from outside'.[115]

The impression given by these entries in the diaries of the statesmen involved is that the telegram, which was in fact suggested by Marschall and not by the Kaiser, was a hastily concocted compromise solution to prevent Wilhelm's more far-reaching and far more dangerous 'weird and wonderful' plans – the declaration of a German protectorate and the dispatch of troops, even at the risk of war with Britain – from being realised. Since the telegram was written in the first person and personally signed by Wilhelm II, in the eyes of the world he was seen from the outset as the person who actually initiated it. Historians too have frequently portrayed him, with his 'pathological urge to act', as solely responsible for it.[116] Perceptive contemporaries like the Empress Frederick, Sir Frank Lascelles, Valentine Chirol, Baroness Spitzemberg, Princess Daisy of Pless, the Bavarian envoy Count Hugo von Lerchenfeld and Hermann Freiherr von Eckardtstein, however, rightly emphasised the shared responsibility of the leaders of the Wilhelmstrasse for the telegram,[117] and more recent research has also demonstrated convincingly that well before 3 January Marschall and Holstein had turned strongly against Britain, that they expressed quite as much indignation as the Kaiser at the Jameson Raid and that initially they too were thoroughly satisfied with the effect of the congratulatory telegram to Krüger.[118]

It is indisputable that in the context of the Transvaal crisis the German Foreign Office, as much as the Kaiser himself, envisaged a kind of continental league between the Triple Alliance and the Franco-Russian alliance, with the aim of teaching Britain a lesson and demonstrating the value of German friendship. On 30 December 1895 Marschall had noted: 'Holstein has plans for a new anti-English policy.'[119] The very next day – but before news of the Jameson Raid arrived – the Foreign Secretary, adopting Holstein's line of thought, warned the new British ambassador, Lascelles, 'that if England overestimated the antagonism between the alliances of European states and thought she could get away with anything, this could prove to be a mistaken calculation, and in the end the idea that the continental powers could come to an agreement and enrich themselves at England's expense might find fertile ground in which to grow'.[120] On 1 January 1896 Marschall explained his 'train of thought' to the French ambassador, Herbette, as follows: 'England is counting on the antagonism between the continental powers and believes she can do anything she pleases. Could not the great continental groups agree together on specific purposes, and set aside all issues which might lead to a European war?'[121]

When the Jameson Raid brought the Transvaal crisis to a head, Holstein and Marschall, quite independently of the Kaiser, made it plain that they too considered the challenge to the independence of the Boer state as *casus foederis*, and therefore as activating treaty obligations. On 2 January the Foreign Secretary commented in his diary: 'It is a very frightening situation. If the Boers are beaten, we shall have to take action.'[122] He had already instructed Hatzfeldt, on receiving Herff's first telegram, to make official enquiries in London as to whether the Salisbury government approved of Jameson's action and warned that if the occasion arose he might have to break off diplomatic relations with Britain.[123] In spite of the ambassador's assurances that the British government had sincerely and publicly distanced itself from Jameson, Marschall raised the stakes with a note which Hatzfeldt was to hand over in London, and which culminated in the declaration 'that we protest against the invasion and cannot accept infringement of the independence of the Transvaal'. Not until the telegram announcing the defeat of Jameson arrived in Berlin that evening did the Foreign Secretary step back from the edge of the abyss, hastily instructing Hatzfeldt not to hand over the note with its ultimatum.[124] Fortunately, because Lord Salisbury happened to be out of London, the document was lying unread at the Foreign Office and the ambassador succeeded in recovering it before it was opened.[125]

Both Marschall and Holstein also agreed that the Krüger telegram should be published immediately – a logical step, since one of the main aims of official German policy was (and remained for the next few years) to teach Britain the 'lesson' that 'they need us'.[126] Indeed Marschall was more than satisfied with the initial public reaction to the telegram, as his diary entry for 3 January reveals. 'Our press is magnificent. All the parties are of one mind; even Auntie Voss [the liberal *Vossische Zeitung*] wants to fight.' He was also struck by the 'remarkably favourable' reaction of the French press.[127] But it was a different matter when the 'outrageous', 'insolent', 'foolish' and 'utterly insane' articles in the British press, even threatening 'a switch to the Franco-Russian side by England', reached Berlin. Marschall was obliged to write replies to the attacks for the *Kölnische Zeitung* and the *Norddeutsche Allgemeine*, and tried to prove first to the Kaiser and then to the British ambassador, on the basis of official documents, that the telegram had been factually correct: Britain's sovereignty over the Transvaal had indeed been stipulated in 1881, but in his view it had been revoked by the 1884 convention.[128]

Looking back over the workings of the decision-making process in Berlin in these first few days of 1896, it does in fact seem highly probable that the Krüger telegram came to be written only because the civilian statesmen in the Wilhelmstrasse wanted to prevent Wilhelm II from making infinitely worse demands and were put under enormous pressure by him in terms both of time and of his expectations. It is even possible that following Jameson's surrender and Hatzfeldt's retrieval of the German note from Downing Street the Anglo-German

crisis might have been reasonably peacefully settled on 2 January, had not
the Kaiser appeared at the Reich chancellor's palace the next morning with
his 'extraordinary plans'. At the same time the evidence now available clearly
shows that the responsible Reich authorities, above all Marschall and Holstein,
must bear a much greater share of responsibility for the telegram than public
opinion at the time, and subsequent historical writing, attributed to them. Their
'new anti-English policy', which aimed to force Britain to attach itself to the
Triple Alliance against its will, would have driven it into the arms of France
and Russia even without the Krüger telegram – just as was to happen when the
German blackmail policy was pursued further through the intensified battleship
building programme.[129] But of course the fact that Wilhelm II was nevertheless
seen as the sole, or the main, culprit responsible for writing the fateful telegram
had its roots in the whole egocentric style of personal rule which he exercised.
The young Anglo-German Eyre Crowe, who was making a name as an expert
on Germany in the British Foreign Office at the time, commented quite rightly
at the height of the Transvaal crisis: 'When the Emperor complains, as he does
to us, of being *personally* attacked in the press here, surely that is the natural
and legitimate consequence of his very *personal* way of governing and mixing
himself up so prominently in every act of govt. Why, for instance, that *personal*
telegram? . . . If you want to govern with a big "I", you may have all the glory,
but you must also take the defeat.'[130]

### REACTIONS TO THE KAISER'S TELEGRAM

The Kaiser's congratulatory telegram to Krüger, and above all the reference to
'the independence of your country towards the outside world' and the insinuation
that 'friendly powers' like Germany would have come to the Transvaal's aid if
necessary, had the effect of 'a flash of lightning in a powder-keg' on public
opinion in Britain.[131] The newspapers were full of vicious attacks on the Kaiser
for days; he received numerous insulting anonymous letters and the officers of
his own regiment, the 1st Royal Dragoons, turned his portrait to the wall. Only
a few days after the telegram a new Royal Navy fighting unit of two battleships
and four cruisers set sail for the Mediterranean.

   The violence of the public reaction in Britain to the telegram came as an
unpleasant surprise not only for the German Foreign Office but also for many
other members of the German administration. The Reich Navy Secretary,
Admiral von Hollmann, asked the British military attaché Swaine in consternation why people in Britain were so angry with Germany. The Kaiser's telegram
had been 'perfectly harmless', he claimed, whereupon Swaine replied that the
British reaction was not directed against the German nation but only against

the Kaiser; against him, however, there was such strong feeling that his former popularity had completely disappeared, so much so 'that it would be impossible for His Majesty to visit Cowes this year'. The German Admiral was left to console himself with the thought that 'any idea of war between the two countries was out of the question, as "the Elephant could not fight the Whale"'. Hollmann had admitted that the Kaiser was still very prejudiced against Britain because of the article in the *Standard* the previous August, the military attaché added in his report on the conversation.[132]

As a result of the 'paroxysm of fury' which the telegram had unleashed in British public opinion, the mood in German diplomatic circles, where dreams of a continental league against Great Britain had so recently flourished, switched to an almost panic-stricken fear of a combination between Britain and France against Germany. From London, Hatzfeldt urged extreme caution, 'since if there were any further reason, however slight, England might come to an agreement with France and give up Egypt'. A visit to Cowes by Wilhelm would be extremely dangerous, he warned, for 'at the very least the Kaiser would be booed'.[133] Friedrich von Holstein heard that Courcel, the French ambassador in London, had thought there might be war between Britain and Germany and had assured Lord Salisbury that in that event Britain could be sure of the support of France, 'for France had only one enemy and that was Germany'.[134] Count Münster, the German ambassador in Paris, who had earlier been *en poste* in London for several years, condemned the telegram and warned that Britain might now turn away from Germany and towards France. The 'most tragic result' of the crisis was 'the mistrust and hatred that has grown up between the two great civilised states of Europe', he wrote to Holstein 'I know and felt for a long time that this existed latently . . . Our Kaiser saw only the surface of things, sand is always thrown in his eyes when he comes on a visit; this is how I explain how H.M. sent the telegram, without realising in advance that it was a match to set fire to an accumulation of inflammatory material; I do not believe that it will really come to war. I hope not. God preserve us from that. The Queen and the men in control are too level-headed for that.' But even without war the political and economic damage was very great. The British Admiralty had made use of the crisis to strengthen the Royal Navy enormously, and signs of an Anglo-French rapprochement could be seen everywhere.[135] When a report by Münster containing these warnings was submitted to the Kaiser he commented bitterly in the margin that the new British squadron would have created a sensation if it had appeared in the Mediterranean before. 'Now, under the pretext of "Transvaal—made in Germany" it is put into commission quite harmlessly and naturally and can reinforce the Mediterranean quite undisturbed. The English should be very grateful to me instead of criticising me.'[136]

Like the peace-loving Münster, the anglophobe General Count von Waldersee saw the outcry in Britain as the expression of a longstanding rivalry. It would certainly have been better, in his opinion, if Wilhelm had not sent the telegram, and yet it had not been 'a crime' and England could not have taken the Kaiser's action so badly unless 'she had a very guilty conscience'. The General took the view that the violent British reaction also reflected 'a long-held grudge' against Germany. He conceded that 'our colonial policy has made England uneasy and she persistently intrigues against us . . . The Kaiser has unquestionably acted overhastily in certain cases.' 'Why send ships to Delagoa Bay? They cannot be of any use, but they give England an excuse to be suspicious of us.'[137] Like Marschall, the General had at first believed that the opportunity of creating a continental league against Britain was within reach. 'So far Europe is still siding against England', he wrote on 7 January. The confused picture would soon clear, he predicted, since 'England in her madness' was driving Germany into getting closer to Russia and France. 'Will they respond?', he wondered anxiously. 'We may be facing very serious events and everything depends on skilful hands on our side. God grant that we have them.'[138] As the grave consequences of the imperial telegram began to emerge, however, Waldersee's thoughts became darker. He wondered how the German princes would react to the Kaiser's initiative. 'I think it not impossible that Bavaria might try to express reservations over the unilateral action of the Kaiser.'[139] The more the storm raged in the press the more Waldersee's anxiety grew, and he too began to see a war against Britain, France and Russia at the same time as within the realm of possibility. 'In England people seem to have gone quite mad', he wrote on 10 January. 'People rage against us in public, even in polite society, and speak and write about our Kaiser with outrageous insolence. The newspapers seem to have instructions to stir up and confuse public opinion and there are calls for naval armament as if a war were imminent. I hope we shall keep calm, and especially the Kaiser himself. But it is nevertheless possible that England, having brought so much disgrace on herself, is now planning a great coup. If we had skilful diplomats that would not be serious, but I am afraid that we do not. Hostile feelings towards us in France and Russia may gain the upper hand when people see that we are in an uncomfortable position. We cannot wage war against England; our strength rests entirely on the fact that we can either be a very valuable ally for England, or, if we can come to an understanding with her enemies, cause her great difficulties. But all this requires very careful work and a cool head.'[140]

Although he did not think the danger of war acute, the former Chief of the General Staff was compelled to acknowledge that Germany's international position had become significantly worse as a result of British hostility. In January 1896 he wrote: 'I had hoped that we would use the turmoil in the Far East to create divisions between the other powers, while we stood quietly by for the time being; but now in no time at all exactly the opposite has happened, and we are in the foreground! I am sure England is not seriously thinking of war, but the gravity of the situation is recognised there, and they are preparing themselves to face whatever arises.' Waldersee considered that a weakening of the Triple Alliance would be one of the direct results of British antagonism, for Italy would always have to co-operate with the United Kingdom, while Austria-Hungary would also want to remain on good terms with it. He personally would not be sorry if this happened, so long as it led to improved relations with Russia; but that was unlikely, for Russia was 'not at all inclined to come closer to us, quite apart from the fact that influential circles there would take the greatest possible pleasure in seeing us isolated'. So, following the Krüger telegram, the picture of an isolated Germany in an increasingly dangerous global situation was beginning to emerge. All countries were 'exerting their energies to the utmost' to arm themselves, and 'those on the continent have now been joined by England, Japan and China', Waldersee observed. Even the United States of America was making 'great efforts on the maritime front'. 'So there is a truly massive accumulation of explosive material and an apparently insignificant matter can easily set it ablaze.'[141]

When the storm in the British press began to die down on 12 January 1896 Waldersee likewise grew calmer in his assessment of the situation, although his comments showed the ambiguity of his attitude towards Britain. In his heart of hearts he welcomed the Anglo-German confrontation because it had at last proved to 'the many anglomanes . . . that English policy [is] two-faced, utterly false and exclusively egotistical'. It was unquestionably best for Germany 'to be permanently on a good footing with England, and if possible allied with her, but that is absolutely ruled out as long as England merely wants to exploit us and at the same time has the unbelievable temerity to make difficulties for us in our colonial policy *everywhere*. I hope that the outrageous spite and impertinence towards the Kaiser of which the English press has been guilty will never be forgotten.'[142] Waldersee, like Tirpitz and other enemies of Great Britain, often sought comfort in the thought that the vituperation from London would at least ensure 'that the Kaiser will be somewhat cured of his anglomania'.[143]

The Krüger telegram naturally led to bitter arguments not only in public but also within the royal family, putting Anglo-German relations under lasting strain. With the help of her daughter Beatrice, Queen Victoria gave her grandson a dressing-down, expressing her distress and surprise at his 'outrageous' and 'dreadful' telegram. 'Our great wish', she declared, 'has always been to keep on the best of terms with Germany, trying to act together, but I fear Your Agents in the Colonies do the very reverse which deeply grieves us.'[144] The Prince of

Wales spoke furiously of the hostile and completely unnecessary interference of the Kaiser in matters that did not concern him, which was all the more offensive because he was the Queen's grandson, constantly affirmed his love for England and held high rank in both the British army and the Royal Navy. It was out of the question for him to visit Cowes this year.[145] In February, in conversation with a high-ranking German delegation, the heir to the throne and his son George again expressed resentment at the Krüger telegram, which they saw as an insult, and furthermore one that had been delivered 'by a relation, an English admiral etc.'.[146] The Empress Frederick, who was in Berlin at this time, likewise criticised her son's telegram as 'a deplorable mistake'. She too emphasised how important it was 'for England & Germany to get on well together & be good friends!' and expressed the astonishingly progressive view, which would not be out of place in a historical conference today, that 'the whole foolish German Colonial Enterprize in Africa was encouraged by Pce Bismarck – as he quietly admitted – to be a thorn in England's side & an apple of discord – a question wh. he could put forward at any moment when he wanted to raise popular feeling here against England, to keep the nations asunder!' The German colonies were expensive and uneconomical, but they flattered the 'inordinate national vanity & chauvinism'.[147]

Wilhelm answered his grandmother's rebuke with a hypocritical assurance that his anger had been directed not against Britain but against the international 'mob of golddiggers' who had rebelled against the Queen. This letter, of which the Kaiser had discussed his own draft line for line with the Reich Chancellor,[148] is one of the strangest documents he ever penned in English and is given here in full. 'Most beloved Grandmama', he wrote from the Neues Palais on 8 January, 'Your kind letter just reached me in presence of Uncle Hohenlohe who had come for his "Vortrag" [audience], so I was able to immediatly [sic] speak to him about the affair. As you kindly express it so it is. Never was the telegram intended as a step against England or your government. By Sir Frank [Lascelles] as well as by the Embassy in London we knew that Government had done everything in its power to stop the freebooters, but that the latter had flatly refused to obey, & in a most unprecedented manner went & surprised a neighbouring country in deep peace! As Sir Frank himself told me when I asked him about the fact, on New Years day, these men were flibustiers [filibusters] or rebels, I hinted that we ought to join & cooperate in keeping them from doing mischief. But I never heard anything about the matter anymore. The reasons for the telegram were 3 fold. First in the name of "Peace" as such which had been suddenly violated, & which I always, following Your glorious example, try to maintain everywhere. This course of action has till now so often earned Your so valuable approval. Secondly for our Germans in Transvaal & our Bondholders at home with an invested capital of 250–300 millions & local commerce of the coast of 10–12 millions which were in danger in case fighting broke out in the towns. Thirdly. As Your Government & Ambassador had both made clear that the men were acting in open disobedience to Your orders they were rebels, I of cours[e] thought that they were a mixed mob of golddiggers quickly summoned together, who are generally known to be strongly mixed with the scum of all nations, never suspecting that there were real Englishmen or officers among them. Now to me rebels against the will of H. Most Gracious Majesty the Queen are to me the most execrable beeings [sic] in the world & I was so incensed at the idea of your orders having been disobeyed & thereby, Peace & the security also of my fellow countrymen endangered, that I thought it necessary to show that publicly! It has I am sorry to say been totally misunderstood by the British Press. I was standing up for law, order & obedience to a Sovereign whom I rever[e] & adore & whom to obey I thought paramount for her subjects. Those were my motives, & I challenge anybody who is a gentle man to point out where there is anything hostile to England in this!? The Secretary of Transvaal was even at his audience the day before yesterday cautioned by me to warn his Government on no account to do anything that could be interpreted as beeing [sic] hostile to England. The gunboat in Delagoa was only to land in case street fight & incendiarism broke out to protect the German consulate as they do in China or elsewhere but was forbidden to take any active part in the row; nothing more. As to the silly idea in the press that I was or wanted to behave hostilely to England I with a clear conscience refer to L. Salisbury, who has material enough in his hands from the last years to know my thoughts & what I do for England. But the English press has been rather rash in its conjectures & having since some months freely lavished its displeasure on our devoted heads, the home press still sore about certain Standard articles which appeared when I was at Cowes, & which were unkind to me personally – which wounded German amour propre more deeply than the authors may have thought – this made people rather hot & rash. But I hope & trust that this will soon pass away, as it is simply nonsense that two great nations nearly related in kinsmanship & religion, should stand aside & view each other askance, with the rest of Europe as lookers on, what would the Duke of Wellington & old Blücher say if they saw this? As to the wishes You expressed regarding the relations in Afrika [sic] in general & the question of the Agents I have immediatly [sic] communicated to Prince Hohenlohe who will give the matter his serious attention. So I hope that soon all will come right.'[149] The Queen found her grandson's attempts to exculpate himself 'lame and illogical', but after discussing it with Salisbury thought it advisable not to pursue the matter, as the 'real rebuke' he deserved would only annoy him still more.[150]

## THE KAISER AND BRITAIN AFTER THE KRÜGER TELEGRAM

Wilhelm II's ingratiating response to his grandmother's reproaches suggests that he was trying to make good the massive damage caused to Germany's relations with Great Britain by his telegram to Krüger. There was further evidence of this in numerous other gestures he made, which seemed to destroy the hopes of anti-British statesmen in Germany that the Kaiser's 'anglomania' was at last over. When for instance the long-serving British military attaché, Leopold Swaine, took his leave at the end of February 1896 Wilhelm spoke effusively of his regret at the departure of this 'personal friend', and caused general astonishment by conferring the star of the Order of the Red Eagle Second Class on Swaine.[151] For the funeral of Prince Henry ('Liko') Battenberg, who had died while serving in the Ashanti war on the Gold Coast, Wilhelm sent such a large deputation to London that even the Empress Frederick was embarrassed.[152] Waldersee was deeply disappointed, and saw this action as a sign that 'our gracious sovereign [has] no idea how to exercise restraint'. The British would only see the gesture as 'a kind of apology', he feared, adding: 'the people in Berlin who thought the Kaiser had been cured of his love of England for a long time do not know him well. I truly do not want us to be on bad terms with England, but I do not want us to run after her.'[153] Count Anton Monts, Philipp Eulenburg's successor as Prussian envoy in Munich, who like many others at this time questioned the Kaiser's sanity, commented mockingly: 'H.M. is very upset about . . . the estrangement of the English, as he can hardly now go to Cowes!! That is why he is running after these people again, alas, which is exactly the opposite of what he should be doing! He sends an entirely superfluous deputation of the Gardes-du-Corps, a private letter to his tippling grandmother, and a message as unknown to the Foreign Ministry as the letter is, to be delivered personally to the old hucksteress by his Flügeladjutant Arnim . . . In short, the outlook's pretty gloomy, just as in the days of Friedrich Wilhelm IV.'[154] Even the elderly Reich Chancellor thought it risible that Flügeladjutant von Arnim, whom the Kaiser had sent to London for the Battenberg funeral, would come back with favourable but completely untrue reports on the mood there, 'because he has to do so in order to give H.M. courage and revive his hopes of Cowes'.[155]

Although the prospect of a visit to Cowes was ruled out for the time being, the Kaiser stuck to his plan to go on a Mediterranean cruise – albeit not as originally intended in an English yacht rented through Lord Lonsdale but in the *Hohenzollern*[156] – in the spring.[157] The Empress Frederick was astonished at the idea, but nevertheless suggested to Wilhelm that while in Genoa he might pay an hour's visit to Queen Victoria and his widowed aunt Beatrice in Cimiez.[158] The Kaiser replied that he had already discussed this idea with 'Uncle

Chancellor', who had advised against a visit to France. 'He quite understood the feelings prompting me, but positively . . . declared that such an interview was *impossible* if intended on *French territory*. The Southerner is most excitable, incognito quite out of the question & an orange peel or apple enough to create international difficulties. So that if it is impossible to meet *on the water* (Bay of Villefranche?) I am unable to see dear Grandmama as long as she is in *France* on terra firma.'[159] After further negotiations with 'Uncle Hohenlohe' Wilhelm expressed the hope that the Queen would agree to meet him on the Italian side of the border.[160] As the Kaiser did not wish to put the Queen under any obligation to come, he asked his mother to sound out the Queen, and although in the end the meeting between the two sovereigns did not take place, the Empress Frederick's mediation nevertheless helped improve relations between Wilhelm and his mother.[161] She was able to report to the Queen in the spring of 1896 that the personal relationship with her son was no longer strained. 'He is quite nice to me and I have forgiven him with all my heart the cruel wrong he did me; but of course we meet seldom and I am a complete outsider, powerless to prevent the countless blunders & mistakes that grieve me so much – unable to do any good, – in constant anxiety about him & the course of events and the future. I even perceive that William tries to give me pleasure here and there and I am always very grateful for it – and pleased when things go well with him and when he does the right thing no matter whether it be great or small.'[162]

It seems, therefore, that after the Krüger telegram the Kaiser was advocating a conciliatory policy towards Britain with which leading spirits in the German army and diplomatic service did not agree. But does this picture of a Kaiser who in his heart of hearts was in fact an 'anglomane' accord with reality? Were not his feelings for his mother's country altogether more complicated, contradictory and impulsive? In fact, comments made by Wilhelm II during these very weeks, while tension was running high, clearly indicate that his friendly gestures were purely manipulative and designed to deceive British policy-makers as to his real purpose: to force Britain into a formal association with the Triple Alliance, including obligations in the event of war.

When Waldersee saw the Kaiser again on 18 January 1896 at the annual celebration of the founding of the Reich he noted that Wilhelm was 'deeply disgruntled' with Great Britain, a feeling which his entourage thought likely to last. Although he had been reconciled with his 'quite sensible' grandmother to a certain extent, Waldersee commented, he had 'had to swallow really outrageous rudeness from England', which he would not forget. He had become convinced 'on the basis of good information', the General continued, 'that we shall never be able to count on England with any certainty, but that the English have the immense effrontery not only to demand that we help them, but also to do nothing at all in return. He has probably given up his favourite idea of making England join the Triple Alliance, in which intelligent people have probably never been able to believe. But what is to happen now is quite uncertain. Russia and France have been more on our side in general, but that by no means presupposes that they would also be prepared to act with us. In both countries there is very widespread antagonism towards us and it will depend which of us proceeds more skilfully, we or the English. If it is the latter, we may find ourselves very isolated.' Waldersee welcomed not only Wilhelm's critical view of Britain, but also the 'pleasing' fact that the Krüger telegram had made the Kaiser 'popular . . . throughout Germany'.[163]

On the evening of 3 March 1896 – the day on which news arrived of the devastating defeat of the Italian army at Adua in Abyssinia – Wilhelm II received Sir Frank Lascelles for a two-hour, wide-ranging conversation which the diplomat, as Hohenlohe noted, saw as 'initiating good relations with England'.[164] As the Kaiser told the Chancellor the next day, he had pointed out to the ambassador that it was impossible 'that England could come to an understanding with France, as France's links with Russia were far too strong', and Russia 'considered it her principal task to destroy England'. The great mistake of British policy, the Kaiser had said, was that instead of supporting Italy in Africa Britain made difficulties for it there. 'Franco-Russian policy was working against Italy's action in Abyssinia with a view to gaining a firm foothold or power there with which to block the way to India for the English.' After the Italian defeat at Adua Britain must give Italy either military assistance from Egypt or financial help. Hohenlohe's summary of the conversation continues: 'After His Majesty had drawn attention to the danger threatening England that her route to India might be cut off, he stressed that England would have only the route round the Cape. But here too dangers loomed, for the French intended to buy the Canary Islands from the Spaniards and to make difficulties for England on that route too.'[165] The statesmen officially in control of German foreign policy received further information about Wilhelm's conversation with Lascelles from the ambassador himself, who sent Marschall a copy of his telegram to Salisbury reporting on the interview. According to this, the Kaiser had told the ambassador that Russia's aim was 'to destroy' both Austria-Hungary and Great Britain and, although peaceful means were to be used initially, Russia was also fully prepared 'to wage war, even if it lasted ten years'. Russia had declared to France that the recovery of Alsace-Lorraine was out of the question. Instead the Russian plan was 'to annex Bulgaria and the Balkan states as well as Austria's Slavic territories, and to detach Germany from Austria by offering her [i.e. Germany] the German provinces'. Russia would also drive the Italians out of the Horn of Africa and establish itself there, in order to 'get control of the sea route to India'. At the same time it would raise the Egyptian question again and also compensate the French with the Canary Islands. 'This plan', the Kaiser had claimed, 'was not only approved by Russian statesmen but had been sanctioned by Tsar Nicholas. Although His Majesty had been badly treated by the English press and by certain English statesmen, he considered it his duty to draw England's attention to this danger; he was delighted that the English fleet had been expanded and expected that England would join the Triple Alliance or at any rate come to Italy's aid in her desperate situation.'[166]

The Kaiser's conversation with Lascelles once again threw the Wilhelmstrasse into a state of bad-tempered confusion. In his journal the Reich Chancellor noted that both Marschall and Holstein were 'full of resentment against H.M.', because he had advised the British ambassador that Britain should (perhaps by sending an expedition to Dongola in the Sudan) go to the help of the Italians after their defeat. Giving this advice after the Transvaal crisis was, in their view, 'an action contrary to the dignity of Germany', which might even lead to war between Germany and both France and Russia. The elderly Prince Hohenlohe saw the situation differently, although he too described it as 'serious'. 'The ill-humour of the English towards us is not the result of the conversation between H.M. and Sir Frank and of the call to England to help the Italians, but it is the consequence of our colonial policy and of the prosperity of our industry and the competition it has created in world trade. The activities we have pursued for years in South Africa, and which culminated in the Kaiser's telegram, have finally aroused English resentment. But to blame H.M. for it, when the Foreign Office is responsible . . . , would be unjust.'[167] Hohenlohe may have judged correctly to some extent, but one cannot help wondering whether he fully recognised the momentous nature of the Kaiser's initiative. Not only was it an attempt to help Italy and restore better relations with Britain, but it also had the dual aim of preventing an Anglo-French rapprochement, which would amount to a *de facto* entente between the three world powers, Britain, France and Russia, against Germany, and forcing Britain into a binding union with the Triple Alliance. The expedition to Dongola which Britain did in fact mount in March 1896 was regarded by Wilhelm II as entirely due to him – Salisbury had simply followed the advice he had given to Lascelles, he claimed; he had never thought 'that the English would fall into the trap so easily'.[168] The Kaiser himself put his machiavellian motives for suggesting the Dongola expedition into these words: 'The goal has been achieved. England has gone into action, she is compromised and the flirtation with Gallo-Russia has been interrupted. It is all I wanted. I am satisfied. W.'[169] He remarked gleefully to the Reich Chancellor that he thought the British would 'get a hiding in their Dongola campaign', and told Prince Alexander Hohenlohe that although Britain had undertaken the expedition to

Dongola 'for purely selfish reasons', they would soon 'come crawling to us on their knees, if we just let them wriggle'.[170] The goal (which was also to give rise to the future battleship building race) of making life difficult for the 'arrogant Britons'[171] in the expectation that they would join the Triple Alliance was a constant but extremely costly miscalculation at the heart of the new German foreign policy.[172]

After the conversation with Lascelles the Kaiser boasted that 'he had never made such rude remarks about an ambassador's country to his face as he had to Lascelles'.[173] Only later did Holstein hear privately from Hatzfeldt, who as he said would sooner have had his hand cut off than report officially on it, about the British Prime Minister's distressed reaction to Wilhelm II's conversation with the ambassador. Salisbury, 'who had just begun once again to become more candid and more confidential', was 'literally horrified . . . because he saw herein proof that he would again be confronted with all sorts of demands and that he could not hope for a calmer conduct of policy on our part'. Salisbury had ended by saying: '*Je vous avoue que cette agitation croissante m'inquiète vivement* [I confess that this growing agitation worries me greatly].' Since then Hatzfeldt had sensed a renewed reserve in Salisbury in discussing political questions, which made him very anxious with regard to Anglo-German relations.[174] Even in the restrained official language of diplomacy there was no mistaking the Prime Minister's despair when, in response to the Kaiser's remarks to Lascelles, he once again tried to make the principles of British policy in Europe clear to the Wilhelm-strasse. Great Britain wished to be on a friendly footing with Germany as in ear-lier days, and was indeed willing to come closer to the Triple Alliance, Salisbury explained. But it would 'never make a promise which entailed the obligation to go to war in any future eventuality'. Such a commitment, which in any case was unnecessary thanks to the country's position as an island, would never be accepted by public opinion. 'Whether this policy was sensible or not it was the only one possible in England; during his previous ministry from 1886 to 1892 . . . His Majesty the Emperor had been content with it; why was he not so now?'[175] One answer to this question must be that since that time the power of Kaiser Wilhelm II had grown enormously. In the first half of 1896, as the next chapter will show, he succeeded in making the breakthrough to Personal Monarchy in the final battle against the 'responsible government'.

# CHAPTER TWENTY-SEVEN

# Endgame: the breakthrough to decisive personal power

## A HIGHLY CHARGED EMOTIONAL STATE

O BSERVERS both in Germany and abroad were at one in the opinion that Wilhelm II was particularly on edge and excitable in the first few months of 1896. His close family circle, court society (with the house arrest at Schloss Glienicke and the Kotze scandal) and even the cabinets of Europe (with the Dardanelles question, the Transvaal crisis, relations with Britain and naval expansion) witnessed outbursts of rage and impetuous actions which could not but be regarded as extremely worrying, indeed pathological, in their nature. But the event which angered him most was the ultimatum he was given by the Reich Chancellor and the entire Ministry of State in the Köller crisis of December 1895, which he regarded as an inadmissible infringement of his most sacred prerogatives as king of Prussia. In the months that followed Wilhelm II not only showed through his aggressive, autocratic attitude and vindictive comments how deeply offended he was by the collective action of the constitutional authorities; he also made it absolutely plain that he would not hesitate to seize supreme decision-making power in Prussia and in the Reich once and for all. On the advice of his best friend Philipp Eulenburg, his three Cabinet Chiefs Hahnke, Lucanus and Senden and the ubiquitous Flügeladjutanten, he sacked the supposed ringleaders of the 'ministerial revolt' – Bronsart von Schellendorf, Marschall von Bieberstein and Boetticher – and replaced them with men like Bülow who had promised to be nothing but 'executive tools of His Majesty'. With the dismissal of General Bronsart as minister of war in August 1896 the 'responsible government' finally lost all scope for independent action and the way was clear for Kaiser Wilhelm II to exercise 'real personal rule'.

When Hinzpeter visited Berlin in January 1896 he at once noticed that a fundamental shift of power had taken place since the Köller crisis. He told Boetticher that 'the position of the Reich Chancellor was no longer what it had been'; on the other hand that of the Chief of the Civil Cabinet, Lucanus, had 'grown much bigger'.[1] The Chancellor complained to Eulenburg that he had received no answer to a written request for an audience and had been so hurt by this that he felt he might have to distance himself more from the Kaiser and avoid private audiences with him altogether.[2] During a visit to Berlin in March 1896 Eulenburg noted that the Kaiser's antipathy towards Marschall was now '*insurmountable*'. When Eulenburg drew attention to the Foreign Secretary's parliamentary successes Wilhelm replied: 'That is just the trouble: his position gets better and better and I dislike him more and more. What can one do?'[3] The monarch's rancour towards the Chancellor and the ministers made itself powerfully felt at a dinner on 30 April 1896 when he rounded on all the ministers except Thielen and Hammerstein. He asked the new Minister of the Interior, von der Recke, for news of 'good, honest Köller', and commented: 'He was brought down by the same sort of disgraceful intrigues that are going on now.' Addressing the Foreign Secretary, he said: 'I tell you, Marschall, I shall not tolerate these press campaigns much longer. I demand that you put a stop to this business. If it goes on I shall move my headquarters to Berlin and arm my Flügeladjutanten with pistols to go and kill the villain who is behind it. The attacks are not against Hahnke but against me.' Marschall's reply was blunt: 'Yes, they are indeed against Your Majesty.' The Kaiser had a similar exchange with Bronsart. When Wilhelm concluded his remarks by saying that things could not go on as they were, the Minister of War answered frankly: 'I quite agree with Your Majesty, things cannot go on like this.' The Kaiser turned away in a fury, retorting: 'Yes, but I do not mean it in the same way as you.'[4] Wilhelm displayed petulant contempt for the responsible statesmen at every possible opportunity. In May, instead of enquiring after the health of the elderly Reich Chancellor, who was ill, he summoned him to Potsdam in bad weather, although he himself was in Berlin every day. His reaction to a perfectly reasonable suggestion from the Ministry of State that three noblemen and three wealthy commoners be appointed to the Prussian Upper House was to decide, after a report from Lucanus, to approve the appointment of the nobles and reject that of the three middle-class candidates. Holstein concluded disconsolately that 'Reich Chancellor and Ministry of State *ne comptent pour rien* these days. Nothing is done except by His Majesty and the Cabinets.'[5]

If Wilhelm yielded to representations from the statesmen of the Wilhelmstrasse it was only rarely and under enormous pressure. A typical example occurred in the early summer of 1896 when the situation in the German colony of South West Africa became so serious that the colonial officials there made an urgent request for a few hundred mounted infantrymen to be sent out. They also demanded the introduction of compulsory military service for citizens of the Reich living in the colony. Hohenlohe, Marschall, Bronsart, Admiral Hollmann and the Commanding Admiral of the Navy, Eduard von Knorr, were firmly in favour of sending the requested number of Volunteers to the colony. The Chief of the Naval Cabinet alone recommended instead that a naval battalion – 'notwithstanding the fact that no troops have had less training in riding', as Holstein acidly remarked – be sent out to this desert terrain instead, 'and – His Majesty supported Senden'. Furthermore, the Military Cabinet under Hahnke held out against the introduction of compulsory military service in South West Africa. Only after a joint audience with the Kaiser attended by the Reich Chancellor, the Foreign Secretary, the Director of the Colonial Department Dr Kayser and the Minister of War, together with Senden and Hahnke, was the 'responsible government' able to assert its authority in both questions.[6]

The vexed question of the succession to the minor princedom of Lippe gave rise to a dispute which provides a perfect example of Wilhelm's attitude towards his most senior officials and towards the federal constitution of the Reich in general. Since the death of the childless Prince Woldemar of Lippe-Detmold on 20 March 1895, Wilhelm II's brother-in-law, Prince Adolf of Schaumburg-Lippe, had assumed the regency on behalf of the mentally ill Prince Alexander, on the basis of a decree of 1890. This settlement, however, was stated by Count zu Lippe-Biesterfeld to be invalid, and the Landtag of Lippe also doubted its legality. The Landtag's decision to have the dispute over the succession settled by the Reich court in Leipzig was challenged by several of the German federal princes, who saw it as a curtailment in principle of their sovereignty. They demanded instead that the dispute be settled through a compromise reached between all parties involved. Hohenlohe informed the Kaiser in a submission of 20 April 1896, drafted by Marschall, that as Reich chancellor he had been charged by the Bundesrat with the task of bringing about such a compromise. He had ascertained that all the parties to the dispute were prepared to accept the decision of an arbitration tribunal presided over by the King of Saxony, who would have the right to select a number of judges from the Reich court for this purpose. Hohenlohe had taken the necessary steps to establish whether and under what conditions the King of Saxony would be prepared to preside over the tribunal.[7]

The Kaiser's furious reaction to this independent action by the Reich Chancellor shows how strongly he felt that he had been bypassed, especially in a matter of this kind. 'Do I still rule at all!?', he wrote in the margin of the submission. The King of Saxony certainly could not choose the judges 'without even asking or informing me!' The tribunal must be held 'under a chairman to be selected by *me* from 2 Princes to be chosen by each of the parties'. 'I am astonished that such a highly important question has been settled in this very surprising manner, without consulting me and obtaining my agreement. Only *one* man in the Reich can be the arbitrator in this question and that is *the German Kaiser*! Any other alternative is *unthinkable*.' All the other princes to whom he had spoken took 'absolutely the same view!', he claimed. Only Duke Georg II of Saxe-Meiningen, whose youngest son Friedrich was married to a Countess zu Lippe-Biesterfeld, had expressed support for the claims of the Biesterfeld line, the Kaiser declared, adding, 'The indignation here at the Duke of Meiningen is very great. Wilhelm I. R.'[8] The Kaiser's sisters added fuel to the fire by persuading him that a decision in favour of the Biesterfeld line would be 'a victory for democracy'. Both Charlotte and Moretta had no scruples in spreading the rumour that the mother of the reigning Countess zu Lippe-Biesterfeld had formerly worked as a shop assistant, while her father had been an American small-holder. The 'Biests' were '*disgusting, common*' people who had taken on princely airs. 'Can the German princes tolerate *such* a pack of worthless wretches?? . . . By this criterion any Herr Müller or Fräulein Schulz could become regent . . . What would Grandpapa or Papa have said?'[9] Wilhelm II undoubtedly thought of the succession dispute in similar terms.[10]

On 22 April 1896 Lucanus came to the Chancellor with the news that the Kaiser was 'very annoyed' and had declared in no uncertain terms that there was only one arbitrator in the Reich, and that was himself. The Chief of the Civil Cabinet suggested that the approach to the King of Saxony be withdrawn 'until the Kaiser had calmed down', which the Chancellor declined to do on the grounds that the Bundesrat, inclusive of the Prussian vote, had entrusted him with the task of bringing about an agreement between the parties involved by means of an arbitration tribunal, and that he had carried out this task. 'It is not clear to me what occasion there would have been for *the Kaiser's* intervention.'[11] In a further submission to the Kaiser he warned that it would be unwise to call into question the solution which had been reached. It would inevitably wreck the chances of any compromise and would thus perpetuate the present state of affairs and seriously damage the monarchical principle.[12] This missive was likewise returned to Hohenlohe with an angry comment scrawled on it in pencil. 'The request which I sanctioned related only to the discussion in the Bundesrat. The further steps which the Reich Chancellor wanted to take or took were not possible without my opinion being ascertained and needed to be discussed with me first. That was not done. I have once again been confronted with an extremely painful *fait accompli*. It is unacceptable that in a question with such serious consequences the Reich Chancellor should negotiate independently over the Kaiser's head with German princes, and even offer them the position of arbitrator, without my knowledge and permission. I stand by my opinion that in this matter the only right course is a princely court with judicial advisers under a chairman appointed by me. Moreover an opportunity could perfectly well have been found in Vienna [in mid-April 1896] during the audience at the German embassy to discuss this matter with me; why did this not happen? Quarrels between Reich princes cannot be settled by any court; it can only be done by the princes presided over by the Kaiser or by a representative, e.g. the Reich chancellor, designated chairman by All-Highest order. Wilhelm I. R.'[13]

The Chancellor reacted unusually firmly to this 'most ungracious marginal comment', declaring: 'With the best will in the world I cannot do the man *this* favour.'[14] He sent a cipher telegram to the Kaiser explaining the complicated legal situation again and persisting in the opinion he had previously expressed. There was no prospect of the parties in dispute accepting a princely court in the form demanded by the Kaiser. He 'reverently and urgently' begged the monarch not to do anything to disavow the negotiations which he, as Reich chancellor, had conducted on the instructions of the federal governments. Hohenlohe, who was himself a mediatised prince, noted privately at the time that this was not a quarrel between Reich princes but a dispute over a succession within one and the same princely house, whose members could come to whatever agreement they wished. But even in a quarrel between princes of the Reich the Kaiser did not hold the position of arbitrator. 'In the old days the Kaiser was the supreme feudal lord and the princes were his vassals. That has changed now. The Kaiser is *primus inter pares* and the princes are his allies.'[15] On 4 May 1896 Lucanus finally informed the Chancellor that the Kaiser realised that he would have to accept a tribunal, but to save face he insisted that some way should be found of 'acknowledging the Kaiser's authority'.[16]

Holstein and Marschall were brought to the brink of despair by this latest manifestation of the Kaiser's anachronistic views. What would have happened, they wondered, if the government had yielded to Wilhelm's desire to have the same power of disposal over Lippe and other federal lands of the German Reich 'as Charlemagne had over vacant fiefs?' Holstein doubted 'whether the Kaiser knows that the present German princes are his allies, while the German princes at the time of Charlemagne were his vassals'. Bismarck had designed the constitution of the Reich in such a way that the federal princes would rely on the support of the Reich government against the particularist elements in their states. 'But if the instincts of our present Kaiser were translated into action, the feeling of security within the Reich on the part of the individual federal princes would be wholly lost.'[17] Equally worrying for the Wilhelmstrasse was the

Kaiser's impulsive behaviour, of which this latest incident was yet another crass example. The Kaiser had the 'unfortunate habit', Holstein commented bitterly, 'of talking all the more rapidly and incautiously the more a matter interests him'. He went on to reflect that 'the chief danger in the life of Kaiser Wilhelm II is that he is and remains absolutely unconscious of the effect which his speech and actions have upon princes, public men, and the masses'. Consequently, Holstein observed, the most vital task for any government under Wilhelm's rule would be to counteract this danger and neutralise the effects of the Kaiser's character as far as possible.[18]

There was an unpleasant epilogue to this conflict during the Scandinavian cruise of July 1896. 'With deep sorrow and grief', Wilhelm wrote to his 'dear Lucanus' of the 'unbelievable stage' which the 'wretched Lippe affair' had reached. 'Yesterday I received by messenger the draft agreement for the arbitration tribunal in the Lippe affair, together with the final record of proceedings, which were sent for me to see and put into execution if I thought fit.' He had not signed the document, as he wanted it amended. 'In the passage referring to the possibility of the king not acting as arbitrator for any reason it is stated that the parties should be free to choose another prince of the Reich as they see fit! I crossed that out and with Ct. Eulenburg's agreement I wrote "the parties are to apply to the Kaiser, who will select another arbitrator". I had just finished reading it through when a telegram arrived from the Foreign Office to the effect that "through an indiscretion the agreement had already been published in the †Zeitung and I should therefore hurry up and sign it as soon as possible"! I am outraged at this unbelievable incident! The leaking *in politicis* at the higher levels is quite unprecedented. I ciphered the Reich Chancellor at once to say that I could not yet sign in such circumstances, because of an indiscretion, and that I was contemplating further amendments. He should at once order an investigation and establish who the culprit was and punish him as appropriate. Or if people in high places should be compromised, he should disgrace them publicly. I would not sign until the investigation, which should be announced, was over. Please see to anything further which might be necessary . . . Your affectionate Wilhelm I. R.'[19]

Although he was eventually forced to give way over the Lippe succession dispute,[20] the autocratic attitude which Wilhelm II displayed towards the federal princes in this affair as in many others − for instance his decree to the German princes of November 1887, which Bismarck ordered 'to be burnt without delay'[21] − manifested itself alarmingly in yet another case in the summer of 1896. During the festivities in Moscow for the coronation of Tsar Nicholas II, which Prince Ludwig of Bavaria was attending as representative of Prince Luitpold, the Prince Regent, Prince Ludwig protested vociferously against a speech in which he and the other German princes present had been described as the 'suite' of Prince Heinrich, the Kaiser's brother. 'We are not vassals but allies of the German Kaiser', he objected. Thinking to take the sting out of this embarrassing incident,[22] the Bavarian Count Konrad von Preysing-Lichtenegg-Moos suggested that Prince Ludwig should 'take the road to Canossa', as it were, by going straight from Moscow to see the Kaiser, accompanied by Preysing himself. Preysing's suggestion was strongly supported by the Foreign Office, Philipp Eulenburg and Monts, the Prussian envoy in Munich, since it was feared that otherwise Prince Ludwig would become 'the focus of inflammatory particularist demonstrations' on his return to Bavaria.[23] But in spite of the Reich Chancellor's carefully argued support for this course, Wilhelm II refused to receive Count Preysing, who had previously been a Centre Party delegate in the Reichstag.[24] When Eulenburg asked him about it, the Kaiser declared roundly: 'I do not receive a man who has openly lied to me' – an allusion to Preysing's vote against the Army Bill in the Reichstag in the summer of 1893.[25]

The Kaiser's meeting with the heir to the Bavarian throne, the future Ludwig III, on 29 June at Kiel, was not exactly a harmonious occasion, not least because, as the Bavarian envoy Count Lerchenfeld knew from experience, it was 'impossible to get anywhere' with Wilhelm when he was 'with his fleet among the sailors'.[26] Just before he left for his Scandinavian cruise the Kaiser telegraphed to the Chancellor from Wilhelmshaven: 'Prince Ludwig of Bavaria made his journey to Canossa yesterday. The course which the conversation took showed that far from regretting his unpatriotic and un-German conduct the Prince laboured under the impression that he had done a great deed for the German princes in general. He used the expression that it had made his blood boil to hear the word "suite", and he had therefore given vent to his oppressed feelings. He maintained that they were not vassals but were unfortunately often treated, or had been treated, as such. I at once dismissed this assertion very sharply and challenged him to name one instance which proved what he had said, but he could not do so and corrected himself, but claimed to know that there was a certain party whose aim was to have the princes of the Reich treated in that way (i.e. as vassals). My comment that I knew nothing of a princes' party put an end to all further comment. He then went on to refer to the fact that they had all been sent to Moscow as representatives of their independently ruling dynasties. But that did not seem to have been quite clear to the Russians, as they had been treated summarily, in spite of the fact that they had their own envoys, while my representative had been accorded the most honourable status. This prompted me to give the noble gentleman a lecture on the fact that the individual South German states were not – thank God – required to represent the Reich abroad nor to take responsibility for war and peace. Bavaria, Württemberg and

Saxony did not conduct great international policy; the fact that they had been allowed to keep their envoys was an act of courtesy and their main purpose was to maintain good family relations between the courts. The whole responsibility for the welfare of the Reich, its relations with foreign countries, were a matter for the Kaiser alone and I was therefore not prepared to allow any meddling, and for that reason I deplored the fact that through his remark, even if made *bona fide*, the impression had been created abroad that things were not going as well as they should in the German Reich. Wrong conclusions would be drawn, and wrong conclusions could easily lead to fatal decisions which might possibly lead to serious consequences.' After an interruption, the Kaiser continued this remarkable account of his conversation with Prince Ludwig. 'The Prince then mentioned that he had been pleased to see, from the great enthusiasm for his courageous support for the threatened right [of the princes] expressed in telegrams and letters sent to him from Bavaria and also from elsewhere in the Reich, that he had in fact done the right thing. There would also be great celebrations and ovations in Bavaria on his return, and he had therefore come here first, so that these ovations should not be misunderstood. The Centre had unfortunately treated the affair rashly and used it to its own advantage, which greatly displeased him. I responded that the ovations in Bavaria were a matter of complete indifference to me; as far as the Centre was concerned, it had at last shown how inimical it really was to the Reich in its thinking, and had opened the eyes of even the most stupid among the German people to its ultimate goals. In doing so it had forfeited all confidence and respect and had thoroughly confirmed its anti-Reich tendencies . . . I asked the Prince, in case he intended to make any speeches on the occasion of the expected ovations for his courageous support for the German princes whose freedom had been threatened, to give his audience the correct explanation of the expression "allies" or "allied governments". People seemed to have a completely wrong idea of it in his Fatherland. Bavaria was not an ally of Prussia or of another state in the sense of e.g. Austria or Italy with Germany, it did not have the power or freedom to loosen or dissolve its ties with the German Reich and to act as a free agent. It ought not to be forgotten that apart from the bonds created by the blood which the German tribes shed together 25 years ago to recover their unity, we were bound by the iron bond of a common Reich constitution, just as we shared a common system of justice and common finances. But above all we had a common Reich army under a war lord, and that was the Kaiser. Anyone who sought to detach himself from such ties, for whatever reason, was committing a breach of the constitution and would bring the full consequences of this on his own head. The Prince was silent, apparently very dismayed, and looked extremely embarrassed. Moreover, I went on to say, his colleagues were not at all edified by his behaviour, as far as I had heard. He maintained that he knew the opposite to be true, and even believed that they were very grateful to him. To cut off further long-winded repetitive arguments which threatened to go round in circles, I observed that I had just spoken to the German princes at Kyffhäuser and had received quite a different picture of the situation from their comments about him, but asked him to excuse me from passing them on to him. I was grateful to him, however, for coming and for discussing the matter with Me. The question did not concern My Person, but the German Reich, which I had the honour to represent and personify, and to which he had offered the requisite satisfaction by his visit. He took his leave, thanking me for receiving him and remarking that he considered that he had done his duty and regretted that it had been wrongly interpreted. Wilhelm I. R.'[27] Prince Ludwig, who had expected a friendlier reception after having done penance, understandably took lasting offence at this arrogant lecture and complained that the Kaiser had 'bawled him out'.[28] When the Kaiser repeated the 'very clear' words of his telegram to Eulenburg during the Scandinavian cruise, the latter concluded that this dressing-down would serve only to deepen the gulf which already existed between Wilhelm and the 'very touchy and resentful Wittelsbacher'.[29]

## THE BRONSART CRISIS AND THE HOLSTEIN PLOT

The decisive battle for power which took place in the first half of 1896 was not, however, between Wilhelm and the federal princes but between him and the 'responsible government', that is to say the Reich Chancellor and the ministers of state. Among the key figures in the dispute was the argumentative War Minister General Bronsart von Schellendorf, whose reform plans had been at the heart of the Köller crisis and still threatened to trigger an explosion even after the forced dismissal of the Interior Minister.[30] At the beginning of the year, after a conversation with Wilhelm, Waldersee accurately summed up the situation in his diary, noting that 'the Kaiser was decidedly put out . . . by the fact that the entire Ministry forced him to choose between dismissing Köller or the Ministry. He gave in, but as Bronsart played the most important part in the affair, he is *particularly* put out with him.'[31] Bronsart was also 'very disgruntled', he added, and ready to resign if the Kaiser continued to oppose his policy for the reform of courts martial.[32] The conflict erupted stormily after the Kaiser's speech at the New Year reception of the commanding generals. 'Perhaps without fully realising the consequences of what he was saying', Waldersee commented, Wilhelm had spoken out about 'several serious issues', thereby provoking the Minister of War into submitting his resignation. Referring to the kernel of Bronsart's reform programme, the new regulations for courts martial under

which public (instead of secret) and oral (instead of written) prosecutions would
be introduced for the army, the Kaiser said 'he firmly maintained the stand
adopted by his grandfather in rejecting public hearings, and was confirmed in
this by many expert opinions'. He then declared that the fourth half-battalions
introduced by Caprivi as a concession to the Reichstag in 1893 must be abolished
'in the very near future'; in 1899 increases in the army estimates would in any
case have to come, and 'then we should be faced with the burning question of
whether it would not be as well to *reintroduce 3-year military service*'. Finally
the Supreme War Lord expressed his 'clear and well thought-out' (according to
Waldersee) views on the question of armaments. At present, he said, the Italian
army had a rifle that could be regarded as the best in the world; 'whether we
can proceed to adopt it is a question that still needs to be investigated; it depends
also on changing to a new gunpowder and the question of cost would be very
momentous'. A new rapid-firing gun had been built for the artillery and had
proved effective; he had ordered 200 to be made initially, which were destined
for the frontier corps and would 'ensure great superiority for us'.[33]

The reception was scarcely over before the Minister of War told Waldersee
angrily that the Kaiser's remarks about the courts martial, which showed that he
had taken an 'absolutely definite' stand on the question, were unacceptable to him
and 'he would be handing in his resignation today'.[34] The violent thunderstorm
which broke that New Year's afternoon in 1896, and which brings to mind the
inkstand scene of 15 March 1890, was so alarming that even the loyal Chief of
the Military Cabinet had to admit that 'the Kaiser had gone too far and had lost
all sense of moderation'. The Chancellor, who received various reports of the
incident, commented: 'The scene . . . was such that the War Minister had difficulty
in restraining himself.' Bronsart himself told Hohenlohe that 'he would have
reached for his sword if it had been anyone else'. It caused consternation in the
General, who expressed the opinion 'that H.M. did not seem quite normal and he
was extremely worried for the future'.[35] During the dinner to which Walter von
Loë had invited his fellow generals on the evening of 1 January Bronsart was still
burning with anger.[36] It was not until the next day that the Kaiser saw the error
of his ways and invited Bronsart to dinner, during which he told him in front
of Hahnke and Plessen that he had been 'too hasty' and asked his forgiveness,
whereupon the Minister of War withdrew his resignation.[37] In Waldersee's
eyes the Kaiser had acted wisely in making a tactical surrender, for if Bronsart
had resigned at that time over the issue of public courts martial it would have
'aroused widespread feeling against the Kaiser outside the army'. Nevertheless
Waldersee had no doubt that the 'rift' between Wilhelm II and Bronsart was now
irreparable, for 'mutual trust' had been 'considerably undermined by a whole
series of differences of opinion'. The Kaiser would never forget 'a thing like that'

40. General Walter Bronsart von Schellendorf, Prussian War Minister 1893–1896

and would 'wait for a more favourable moment to rid himself of Bronsart', he predicted.[38]

The long-drawn-out conflict of the next few months was thus preordained, for while Wilhelm continued to refuse steadfastly to concede public courts martial, the Minister of War remained 'very much annoyed' by this All-Highest attitude, and determined to hand in his resignation 'certainly before the end of this year'.[39] But as Bronsart could count on the ardent support of the overwhelming majority of the German people and of the parties represented in the Reichstag for his modernising measures, neither the Reich Chancellor nor the other Prussian ministers felt able to take a less reformist line on this question than the fiery Prussian General himself. If he resigned because the Kaiser refused his assent to the reforms, Hohenlohe and all the ministers of state would have to resign too. The fatal deadlock which had forced the Kaiser to dismiss his favourite minister in the Köller crisis had arisen again. But this time it was to have a different outcome.

At first the Kaiser tried to avoid a decision on the explosive question of court martial reform on the pretext that he wanted to seek expert opinions on the subject from the commanding generals, but that these would not be ready until the end of the year. When the Reich Chancellor submitted a laboriously worked-out compromise solution to him in March 1896, Wilhelm was at first 'stunned and *extremely incensed* with Hohenlohe',[40] but under Philipp Eulenburg's soothing influence he turned down the suggestion on the grounds of the consultation with the generals. 'In accordance with what you had agreed I settled with the War Minister that in a question of such fundamental importance the army, i.e. the comm. generals, should be consulted first', he wrote to his 'dear Uncle' on 14 March. 'After he had thanked me, touched by my willingness to co-operate, and declared that whichever way the army voted he would accept it unconditionally, I sent for the documents from the War Min[istry] with a view to preparing a memorandum for the commanding generals. The documents were handed over hesitantly and late and were very voluminous, so that the work will require months. The date for the replies was then set at the winter of 96, for which your agreement was also obtained, so as to give those who were being consulted sufficient time and latitude to answer. Consequently nothing can be done in the matter until this year is out, I shall not comment until the army has spoken, until then I am not in a position to speak.'[41] In an audience on 16 March 1896 Wilhelm warned the elderly Chancellor against Bronsart and Marschall. The former was aiming to create a rift between Hohenlohe and the Kaiser while the latter wanted to become Reich chancellor.[42]

Friedrich von Holstein and Foreign Secretary Freiherr von Marschall were so enraged by the autocratic and militaristic behaviour of the Kaiser on the one hand and the spineless manoeuvrings of the Reich Chancellor on the other – Holstein complained that Wilhelm and his advisers at court had 'softened the old gentleman . . . so much' that 'he has lost all trace of resistance' – that they became the *de facto* allies of the War Minister against Wilhelm and his favourite Eulenburg.[43] Since 1895 Holstein had been conducting a fascinating debate with Eulenburg on constitutional developments since Bismarck's fall and in particular on the dangers of Wilhelm II's personal style of government, which as we shall shortly see was to have serious practical consequences in the spring and summer of 1896. Not long after Hohenlohe had taken office Holstein had written to Eulenburg setting out the fundamental difference between their ideas of the role of the monarchy in modern society. 'You support the principle . . . that the people must submit to the Kaiser. I consider this principle impracticable, as far as the *German* people and the *German* Kaiser are concerned . . . But the Kaiser, unfortunately, shares *your* views . . . in that at every possible opportunity he flies in the face of public opinion and behaves – much more than Nicholas II does – like an autocrat.'[44] Since then the disagreement between these former allies had intensified almost to the point of an open breach. At the end of 1895 Holstein commented in a letter to Eulenburg, looking back, that 'for the first time in the new year both of us, you and I, were *not* pulling in the same direction. I certainly consider myself a royalist, but I do not favour absolute submission to His Majesty's

41. The Grey Eminence of the German Foreign Office:
Geheimrat Friedrich von Holstein

every line of thought in the same degree as you. As I know how honest you are I do not reproach you at all, and I honestly hope that you will not come to reproach yourself one day, when you see where all this leads.'[45] When the Bronsart crisis entered its most acute phase at the beginning of 1896, Holstein delivered a lecture to the Kaiser's favourite on his attitude. 'You instinctively incline to an autocratic regime no matter whether it be Russian patriarchal or *despotisme éclairé* on the French model. I am in favour of a moderate use of a practicable system of constitutional co-operative government which, with the exception of St Petersburg and Constantinople, is in operation in the rest of the European and civilised world. My opinion is, I know, unfashionable at the court here. "A strong government which can manage without the Reichstag" is Admiral von Senden's ideal, and not his alone. You also belong, perhaps without knowing it, to those who believe that every political, military and legal question is best decided directly by the Kaiser. The old English Cavaliers held similar beliefs . . . To be sure they first ruined the Stuarts, and then they died or ruined themselves in misery and want; but from an ethical standpoint they remain disinterested types of superb chivalry. I am not so chivalrous, I am for the possible, and since it seems to me that "governing without a Reichstag" is at present impossible in Germany, I would prefer that this Chancellor's political existence between this Kaiser and this Reichstag were not made impossible.'[46]

In his blinkered monarchism and personal devotion to the Kaiser Eulenburg failed to recognise the dangers to which his erstwhile ally was alluding in this letter. In his reply he strenuously denied having joined the 'autocratic tendency'; it was not he but Holstein, who did not know the Kaiser personally, whose political views had undergone a change since Wilhelm's accession, the Kaiser's friend claimed. 'The Holstein of 1888 with his Old Prussian loyalty to the King has certainly not become an anti-monarchist, but he has become a parliamentarian.' He and Holstein nevertheless continued to share the same political ground. 'We both serve . . . the Kaiser', Eulenburg maintained. 'One with love, the other without love.' Holstein should never forget the intimate personal bond which united them, he insisted. 'For that to be possible it is necessary to have a certain – I would almost say feminine – sensitiveness that is peculiar to us both.'[47] But in his letters to Bernhard von Bülow, whom he had recommended to the Kaiser as a future Reich chancellor, he adopted a harsher tone. He dismissed Holstein's growing disquiet with the all too simple psychological explanation that the Privy Councillor had become enraged by 'the progressively developing political sense of the Kaiser' because he was 'no longer in sole control'.[48]

This fundamental conflict led to an enthralling final battle for the future of the monarchy in the German Reich, fought out in the spring and summer of 1896. With the help of Marschall and later also of Alexander Hohenlohe, Holstein worked on a plan which he hoped would break the autonomy of the Prussian crown to the advantage of the 'responsible government' and by extension to that of parliament. In the event that the Kaiser refused to approve Bronsart's popular reform programme, Hohenlohe should threaten to resign along with the entire government, as in the Köller crisis. Philipp Eulenburg, on the other hand, saw it as his principal task to undermine this disgraceful plot, in which he was sure that Bronsart was also complicit, in order to rescue the unlimited decision-making power of his beloved Kaiser from the constitutional control exerted by the Wilhelmstrasse and the Reichstag.

As early as 1 February 1896 Holstein went to see the Reich Chancellor and urged the necessity of 'forcing the Kaiser to approve the court martial bill on the lines proposed by Bronsart'. He had no success at all. 'I shall take care not to provoke another conflict now', Prince Hohenlohe noted in his journal at the time.[49] A few weeks later the Chancellor commented that 'H[olstein]'s proposal amounts to using the present situation in order to put H.M. in a position of constraint by means of a demand by the entire Ministry of State that only a Court Martial Reform Bill conceding public trials be brought into the Reichstag. In Holstein's opinion, H.M. will not now be able to withstand the Ministry's pressure and will therefore give way, and my position will thereby become so strong that no one would dare simply to show me the door, as they now intend.'[50] Only days later the Reich Chancellor returned to the subject, noting that 'the proposal to exploit the present situation to push through the court martial question with public trials which the Ministry of State has determined upon is to be carried out by first raising the matter in the press and the Reichstag and then sending a categorical demand from the Ministry of State to H.M. that he allow the draft bill . . . to be laid before the Bundesrat. Now, it is said, the Kaiser would be forced to give way. If the present opportunity is missed, the fear is that H.M. will dismiss the Ministry in the autumn without further ado, and will try to push through the court martial bill without public trials, as well as his fleet plans, with the help of a different Reich chancellor and a different Ministry. H.M. ought therefore to be put in a position of constraint, as in the Köller case.'[51] In June Holstein again implored the Chancellor to take advantage of this propitious moment to curb the personal power of the Kaiser. On 15 June 1896 – the eighth anniversary of Wilhelm II's accession – he came into Hohenlohe's office, as the Chancellor recorded, and insisted 'that things could not go on like this, that I must take a firmer stand with the Kaiser . . . The Kaiser – in his opinion – thinks he can do anything he likes and does not have the necessary respect for me.'[52]

Eulenburg got wind of this conspiracy on a visit to Berlin in March. He was outraged: Holstein, Marschall and Bronsart had a '*very evil attitude*' towards the Kaiser – the word 'very' was underlined three times. All three were working towards a decisive crisis 'which will destroy His Maj[esty]'s authority and deliver him bound hand and foot'. As in the Köller crisis 'the three conspirators' wanted to bring about a situation in which the Reich Chancellor would have to declare his '*solidarity* with the Ministry against H. Maj[esty]'. Hohenlohe, who wished to remain in office for the time being and depart on peaceful terms with the Kaiser later on, recognised the danger which lay in the court martial question above all. Like Eulenburg, he was afraid that Holstein, Marschall and Bronsart would use the press and the Reichstag to try to force him to take a stand against the Kaiser. In their present opposition to the Kaiser the conspirators were 'quite unrestrained, and shrinking from nothing, like certain people (including Holstein) before the dismissal of Prince Bismarck. I can only tell you that I am *horrified*!', Eulenburg wrote to Bülow.[53] Three days later he reported exhaustedly: 'These have been very difficult days, dearest Bernhard! . . . Only His Maj[esty]'s love and his gratitude for the patching up I have done can compensate for the real damage to my nerves . . . There is *no doubt whatsoever* about the existence of the Holstein-Marschall-Bronsart *League* . . . The exploitation of positions of constraint in order to pull the rope tight around the Kaiser's neck has become *systematic* and premeditated. Holstein goes so far as to use every petty detail for this practice, which *revolts* me *deeply* . . . It is *beyond all doubt* that this group is provoking rows *of all kinds* in order to bring Hohenlohe into conflict with the Kaiser in such a way as to demonstrate Hohenlohe's solidarity with the others and so *force* His Majesty to give way.' Eulenburg had nevertheless succeeded, he reported, in separating Hohenlohe from the conspirators and bringing him together with the Kaiser. He added that he had also achieved a partial reconciliation with Holstein on the basis of 'mutual *personal* inclination' and of foreign policy, although their differences on domestic policy were greater than ever. Holstein had even advised him 'to give up all mediation in the interest of H. Maj. now and altogether!!', the Count commented indignantly. 'So the system feels threatened by Hohenlohe's willingness to give in and my friendly influence!'[54]

While the Kaiser was visiting Abbazia, Eulenburg and Bülow met secretly in Venice to discuss their strategy against the 'conspirators' of the Wilhelmstrasse.[55] Meanwhile, Holstein, Marschall and Bronsart were using their contacts with the press to suggest that Eulenburg would succeed Hohenlohe on the basis of his opposition to court martial reform, while maintaining that Hohenlohe and the entire Ministry of State were totally united behind modernisation. Eulenburg had no doubt that the Kaiser would connect this press campaign with the Foreign Office. 'The "positions of constraint" which we have discussed and feared are coming to the fore, and this game can really only end with a violent solution', he wrote to Bülow on 29 April. At the very moment that he made this prediction he received 'very angry' and '*extremely* excited' telegrams from the Kaiser which took the words out of his mouth. 'Prince Hohenlohe very wretched and overwrought. M. and B. are playing their crazy game worse than ever in the most impudent way. All hell is let loose and there will have to be a thunderbolt. Wilhelm I. R.' For the first time Eulenburg wondered whether in these circumstances it would not be better for Bülow to come to Berlin as secretary of state at the Foreign Office initially, instead of becoming Reich chancellor straight away. If the Kaiser appointed Botho Eulenburg as Hohenlohe's immediate successor, the whole Foreign Office – including Holstein – would be 'blown sky high' and Bülow would therefore have an easier start on his ascent to the supreme position in the Reich, becoming chancellor in a few years' time. 'Farewell, my dearest Bernhard. How hard it is not to have you with me at such times as this!', lamented Eulenburg, who was about to leave for Budapest.[56] He begged the Kaiser to avoid a crisis at all costs until he returned. 'I do not want Your Majesty to face this infamous intrigue . . . without my help. After all I know the terrain in all its nuances better than anyone else close to Your Majesty.'[57]

Holstein, Marschall and others in Berlin tried in vain to bring the Kaiser's favourite back down to earth by emphasising the dangers for the survival of the monarchy which a ministerial and chancellor crisis would entail. If the Kaiser were to dismiss Bronsart or even allow him to resign without having first conceded public courts martial, 'a crisis such as the Kaiser had never even come near to experiencing' would arise, they warned. A partial ministerial crisis was out of the question because the departure of the Minister of War would make the departure of the whole Ministry of State inevitable and 'the situation of the whole Reich and of the Kaiser in particular' would then 'with great speed . . . become very serious'.[58] Throughout Germany 'the worst possible impression' had been created by the fact that the promised consultation of the commanding generals on the question of court martial reform had still not started after six months, while leading advocates of the reform among the generals had been compulsorily pensioned off, and the Kotze affair had not only drawn universal attention to the 'disastrous activities' of the imperial entourage but also given a practical demonstration of the iniquity of secret hearings. Yet in spite of the public indignation, Marschall pointed out to Eulenburg, the Kaiser's entourage was pushing him into 'such a highly charged emotional state that he is blaming his ministers for the press and demanding *the impossible* from them, namely to silence the press'. If this attitude on the Kaiser's part caused a ministerial crisis he would be in '*appalling danger*', for no politician who had a modicum of reputation to lose would be willing to enter a government that would inevitably be considered by public opinion as advocating '*the predominance of the Cabinets and the abandonment of court martial reform*'. 'And amid all the pandemonium that this would inevitably let loose in Germany the wearer of the crown would undoubtedly be the injured party.'[59] The Secretary for the Interior, Boetticher, sounded a similar warning. 'The German Kaiser has never experienced a crisis such as the one that is now on the way. He has no idea what it will be like!'[60] Holstein looked back philosophically at the Kaiser's development since the conflict with Bismarck over the Stoecker meeting in the winter of 1887, when Wilhelm, as he put it, had completely lost his 'stomach for politics' thanks to the '*toujours* Chancellor'. 'As a result of that he has taken to Cabinet pudding, but he will find that even more indigestible in the long run. He cannot govern the German Reich for long with third- and fourth-rate irresponsible advisers.'[61]

The Holstein–Marschall plot – there is no proof for the suspicion harboured by Eulenburg and the Kaiser that Bronsart was part of it – was thwarted by Chlodwig Hohenlohe's refusal to take action against the monarch. The 77-year-old Prince, who prided himself on being particularly well placed to deflect the Kaiser's worst decisions thanks to his relationship with the imperial family, his illustrious position in society and his long and distinguished political career,[62] was not the man to make a show of strength against the Kaiser. He admitted that Holstein's plan might possibly succeed, but he had 'serious reservations', above all in view of the consequences for himself, for 'the result of such a forcible action would . . . be to make my position with the Kaiser intolerable. H.M. saw our action in the Köller affair as an infringement of his rights as king and still bears a grudge against the Ministry for it. A second *coup* of the same kind would aggravate this impression and create mistrust in H.M. which would make my task more difficult. It cannot be supposed that the Kaiser would accept the suppression of his role in the long term. The clash would not be prevented but only postponed.'[63] In the end he would rather go 'than govern with the Kaiser in an unfriendly relationship', the Reich Chancellor reflected. The previous eighteen months had surely shown that one could also govern peaceably with the Kaiser, he observed with short-sighted self-satisfaction. At any rate he had 'no desire to take on the role of the conqueror, as it were, ruling over the conquered Kaiser. That is not my style.' In a passage which betrays the wholly passive attitude which he took to his obligations as Reich chancellor and to his responsibilities towards the German nation, Prince Hohenlohe wrote in his diary: 'The purpose of my existence in the Reich chancellor's palace is in fact none other than to hold back precipitate decisions. An independent regime with the Kaiser at its side in the role of a conquered man, as it were, is unthinkable with this sovereign. It also goes against my nature.'[64] In June the elderly Prince was still refusing to 'stage a clash' on his own initiative. 'If the Kaiser wants to get rid of Bronsart I cannot change that', he wrote resignedly. 'The Kaiser will stay the way he is . . . So why make a great fuss now?'[65] The constitutional crisis over Bronsart and the new court martial regulations was nevertheless moving ineluctably towards its finale, with or without the 'conspiracy' in the Wilhelmstrasse.

### CONFRONTATION IN PRÖKELWITZ

The situation became acute when the War Minister announced at the meeting of the Ministry of State on 3 May 1896 that he would hand in his resignation at the end of the parliamentary session. The whole Ministry thereupon decided 'to advise H.M. to approve the introduction of the court martial regulations' as otherwise the situation for 'those remaining' would be *untenable*.[66] During a 'satisfactory' audience the following morning, Marschall gained the impression that the Kaiser would yield, but this very soon proved to be an illusion.[67] On that same day Wilhelm telegraphed to Eulenburg at Budapest saying 'Shall never seek popularity with the street rabble at the expense of my army, stand by my often repeated view: it is the same as that of my late lamented grandfather.'[68] An audience of an hour and a half which the Reich Chancellor had on 8 May brought no agreement either. Instead of embarking on the 'burning' question of the reform of military courts the Kaiser made derogatory remarks about the War Minister, on whom he laid all the blame for the crisis, but who could not be dismissed now as it would make him more dangerous still. Alexander Hohenlohe deeply regretted that his father, in his 'gentle and considerate way', had not succeeded in having the main issue out with the Kaiser. The Prince would have to make the government statement in the Reichstag himself, and in it he must make a firm announcement of the introduction of public courts martial, the Chancellor's son argued, for any weak or dilatory declaration would be received with scornful laughter in parliament, while public opinion would continue its assault on the 'irresponsible advisers' of the Kaiser. And that was not all. If the Reich Chancellor made a statement that did not satisfy the Reichstag he would inevitably expose himself to the danger that the War Minister, who by nature was certainly not likely to show the same consideration for the Kaiser, would unilaterally make such a positive declaration – 'with clattering spurs and rattling sabre . . . but to the delight of the Reichstag' – that Hohenlohe and the whole Ministry would be made fools of for all time. As for the Kaiser, 'however much H.M. rejects parliamentarism in general', Prince Alexander maintained, 'and however much he is inclined to belittle the power of public opinion, he still has too much English blood in his veins not to have an acute sense of such nuances'. But Prince Chlodwig zu Hohenlohe, who had 'sacrificed even the last years of his life in unparalleled patriotic devotion to his Kaiser – would be condemned to sit on the ruins of his well-earned reputation, which he was forced to allow to be destroyed out of consideration for the Kaiser's mood over a question which was not even important', and would have to console himself 'with some diamond-hung chain or other'. In Alexander's view his father did not deserve such a fate. The Kaiser would have to give in, if he wanted to avoid a crisis 'which could shake the whole state edifice as never before'.[69] Waldersee, who would have considered Bronsart's resignation an 'absolutely inconceivable' loss for the government, also took the view that the Kaiser would give in. 'He will do it as he did with the School Bill and the 2 year military service', he predicted.[70] He was mightily mistaken.

Philipp Eulenburg now employed truly machiavellian cunning to develop plans to distance the Reich Chancellor and the other ministers from Bronsart. He began by suggesting to the Kaiser that he should have the courts martial bill submitted to the Bundesrat not, as the normal procedure would be, as a Prussian proposal but as a presidial bill – that is to say, a measure put forward by the Reich government. The bill would of course have to accord with the decisions taken by the Ministry of State, as otherwise Bronsart would resign, and Hohenlohe and all the ministers would do likewise. But the moment that the reform bill was laid before the Bundesrat, the Kaiser could dismiss Bronsart without risking a collective resignation by the other ministers. The presidial bill could then be amended later by the Prussian government with reference to the expert opinions of the commanding generals. 'The authorisation for the introduction of this bill, which is granted by the *Kaiser*, does not bind the *King of Prussia*', Eulenburg argued.[71]

A few days later he thought up another even more sophisticated feint. The Reichstag was shortly to debate the fourth battalions, in the course of which an interpellation was to be expected on the military courts issue. The Reich Chancellor should therefore announce to the Reichstag that this military matter was being examined by all army and corps commanders, who would submit their findings to the Kaiser in the autumn. After this announcement, Eulenburg observed, Bronsart would be able to remain in office to begin with – 'especially if Yr. Majesty strokes him occasionally'. In the autumn, however, the Kaiser should suddenly convene an 'Areopagus of the most senior Prussian military', in which the royal princes, the Reich Chancellor and possibly a few federal princes would also take part. In order to be effective, however, this 'second act' must take the form of a 'surprise attack' on Bronsart. The 'Areopagus' could then declare itself against the introduction of public courts martial, for, as Eulenburg believed, 'there is still sufficient military feeling in Germany to vindicate the right of *such* an assembly, *presided over by the Kaiser*, to decide on the question of public trials'.[72]

Eulenburg's ploy was in danger of being thwarted by the firm conviction of the statesmen in the Wilhelmstrasse that, if the responsible government were not to be totally discredited, the Reich Chancellor would have to make a definite promise in his statement to the Reichstag that the bill to be introduced in the autumn would ensure public courts martial. If the statement did not say this, Marschall warned, it would amount to an admission that 'the views of the *responsible* government had not yet been accepted at the highest level, but rather that the irresponsible advisers had gained the upper hand'. This would become the signal for the Reichstag to debate the position of the Cabinets in the German system of government. If the Kaiser did not give his consent, therefore, 'a fatal position of constraint' would arise as a matter of course in a few days' time.[73]

For Eulenburg, who was passing through Berlin 'with a heavy heart' on his way to visit the Kaiser on the Dohna family's estate of Prökelwitz in East Prussia, as he did every year at this time,[74] the responsible government's proposed course was nothing but a South German liberal conspiracy against the Prussian militarist monarchy. The 'well-known' group (in which he now included Prince Alexander Hohenlohe) had driven the Reich Chancellor 'into a corner' and was presenting the Kaiser with 'what amounts to an ultimatum', he wrote to Bülow in alarm. 'There is something Bavarian-Badenese-Radical in the air which plans to do violence to the King of Prussia . . . The way out which I took so much trouble to find will not work, because Hohenlohe refuses.'[75] Secret consultations with his cousin Botho in Berlin only confirmed Eulenburg's impression that the proposed – '*completely unnecessary*' – statement by the Chancellor was both a 'measure of force against the Kaiser' and a symptom of the 'South

German–liberal desire to represent the Ministry as the stronghold of liberal opinion'. After further discussions with Holstein, Marschall and Prince Alexander he reported to Rome: 'In spite of all their fury with the War Minister the entire band is hypnotised by him and I see absolutely no way out now – unless the Kaiser gives way (which I hardly consider possible) or else manages by means of a very urgent expression of his will to change the Chancellor's decision concerning the declaration . . . That too seems improbable and I am expecting a showdown.'[76] On his arrival in East Prussia, on the Kaiser's instructions Eulenburg appealed for the help of the Chief of the Civil Cabinet. Lucanus was asked to get in touch with Hohenlohe in order to 'prevent the statement by the Reich Chancellor which the Ministry is demanding, or more precisely to strengthen Prince Hohenlohe's resistance to what is quite obviously an intrigue by the Ministry, which cannot but lead irretrievably to a break, for His Majesty has no intention of changing his views in the face of a *position of constraint* . . . I am afraid, however, that it will not succeed.'[77] Meanwhile, the prophecies of doom arriving from Holstein in Berlin provided a reminder that the future of Germany and of the Hohenzollern monarchy was at stake in this dangerous game of poker. In a cipher telegram of 16 May he warned that 'an acute constitutional conflict in the most unfavourable conditions imaginable is imminent at any moment'.[78]

The same day the Kaiser wrote to the Reich Chancellor from Prökelwitz warning him expressly of the possibility 'that one or other of my ministers who is frightened of parliament might press for a joint statement by the Ministry of State' on court martial reform. This, he insisted, was impossible for three reasons: first, the matter could be dealt with only by him and Hohenlohe as minister-president; in the second place it was not a political but a 'purely technical, military' question which could be decided 'only by the supreme war lord'; and finally the consultation of the generals was in process and must not be prejudiced by a statement in parliament. 'I cannot rid myself of the fear', the Kaiser continued, 'that the restless spirits in the Ministry are preparing some *coup* behind our backs and want to take you by surprise with a joint statement which you will be expected to make to parliament and which will probably go against our agreements of the 8th [of May]. But that would be a serious offence against the crown and its wearer. The Ministry cannot and may not make any statement on questions of principle without previously submitting the wording to me and obtaining my agreement after I have examined it. If individual ministers tried to do this nevertheless, they would be liable to prosecution.' Wilhelm went on to say that he considered 'the interpellation which has already been announced as a ploy ordered by one of the troublemakers in the Ministry so as to plunge you and all of us into conflicts which are quite unnecessary and in the course of which the person in question is aiming to take your place . . . So watch out for ambushes

whether by individuals or by the entire Ministry and do not allow yourself to be
led astray or forced into declarations which put me in a difficult position.' The
previous autumn, the Kaiser added, the War Minister had given him his word of
honour that he would on no account allow the question of court martial reform
to be combined with that of the fourth battalions in the Reichstag. 'I shall hold
him to that and you must play that card too if he gets up to any tricks', the Kaiser
ordered, with a final exhortation to the Chancellor 'not to worry too much about
all the rubbish other people and a few ill-mannered louts in the Ministry like
to indulge in; good hunting for Monday, make sure you shoot the interpellation
down like a good stag'.[79] The Kaiser's appeal was seconded by Eulenburg, who
sent the Reich Chancellor a cipher telegram making it clear that Wilhelm would
regard a statement to the Reichstag in the name of the whole Ministry, without
his authorisation, 'as a constraint, as in the Köller crisis'. It was essential that
Hohenlohe's statement be couched in evasive terms and it must not contain the
'extreme wishes' of the Minister of War.[80] Even the Kaiserin was mobilised to
put pressure on her elderly uncle. In a note of 17 May she urged the Chancellor
to stand up for the Kaiser when he spoke to the Reichstag, and to take control of
the ministers who were trying to make trouble again. 'The Kaiser has often given
way for your sake, even when it was difficult for him, but in military matters
I know he takes a firm stand and will continue to do so', she assured him. 'For
the good of all', and because it was clear 'how difficult the ministers often make
things for the Kaiser', he, the Chancellor, should give way this time.[81]

    Before the letters from East Prussia had arrived in Berlin, Hohenlohe had
written to the Kaiser saying that he intended to reply to any interpellation in the
Reichstag on the subject by stating that the new court martial bill, which would
be 'based on the principles of modern legal opinion', was now in preparation and
would be ready to be laid before parliament at its next session in the autumn.[82]
The Kaiser peremptorily wired back via Eulenburg ordering that the phrase
'draft bill based on modern legal opinion' should be 'omitted, as it is superfluous
and will lead to misunderstandings; above all it is an insult to the army as it
exposes the previous procedure as not in accordance with modern legal opinion and would cause great anger'. Hohenlohe could state that the reform bill
would represent a considerable step forward and would take account of modern legal opinion in so far as it was compatible with 'military organisation and
the particular requirements of the army' and did not have any damaging effect
on discipline but maintained it 'absolutely intact'. Furthermore the Chancellor
should not commit himself to any date for the completion of the bill but at the
very most say that it would 'probably' be laid before the Reichstag in its next
session. Finally, the Kaiser 'ordered' the Reich Chancellor to inform the Chief
of the Military Cabinet, General von Hahnke, 'at once' of the contents of his

telegram.[83] Eulenburg sent Holstein an unequivocal warning that the Kaiser was 'absolutely intractable' on this question; it was entirely in Hohenlohe's hands what course the crisis would now take. 'According to the way he decides it the future will take shape.'[84]

It is not difficult to imagine the reaction of the leading statesmen in the Wilhelmstrasse to these All-Highest orders from the hunting lodge at Prökelwitz. Marschall described the Kaiser's letter of 17 May as 'incredible'. In it the Kaiser warned Prince Hohenlohe 'against resolutions by the Ministry as a whole which might impose declarations on him' and maintained 'that the court martial regulations are a purely military question which only he can decide upon, etc.'.[85] When the Kaiser's telegram arrived on 18 May Marschall noted furiously that the Kaiser was dictating 'word for word' what the Reich Chancellor should say in the Reichstag, including 'a phrase which, not in so many words but in its sense, is directed against public hearings. H[is] H[ighness] is determined not to have anything to do with it.'[86] Holstein telegraphed to Eulenburg that he had 'never seen the Prince so furious in the 22 years I have known him. Reason for anger: continuing bad treatment and unfair mistrust on the part of His Majesty.'[87] On 18 May, with the help of his 'General Staff', as Holstein called the small group of advisers around the Reich Chancellor, Hohenlohe drew up the statement which he would make that afternoon in answer to the interpellation in the Reichstag. The moment of truth had arrived.

In response to a question from the leader of the Centre Party, Dr Ernst Lieber, about the slow progress of the work on court martial reform, the Reich Chancellor, adopting some of the Kaiser's wording but nevertheless remaining faithful to his own views and those of the Ministry of State on the subject, stated that he 'definitely expected' to be able to lay the new regulations before the Reichstag in the coming autumn, and that the bill would be 'based on the principles of modern legal opinion, subject to the particular requirements of military organisation'.[88] That same evening, in response to Hohenlohe's telegram informing the Kaiser of the terms of his statement, a second cipher telegram arrived from Eulenburg conveying the monarch's bitterly disappointed reaction. The wording used by the Reich Chancellor had gone much further than the text which Wilhelm, 'after careful consideration, had Himself composed'. It would arouse expectations, 'particularly with regard to public hearings', 'which in the interests of the army His Majesty could not fulfil'. It had also been the Kaiser's deliberate intention to avoid specifying the deadline to which Hohenlohe had now committed himself.[89] Eulenburg followed this up with a letter to the Chancellor revealing that the Kaiser had been 'very upset' and 'quite beside himself' on receiving his telegram. As Eulenburg had feared 'an outburst of passion' if the Kaiser were to wire a response himself, he had persuaded Wilhelm to go out stalking and leave the telegram to him. It was to be hoped, he said, that 'the storm will have died down on his return from the forest'. But the Chancellor should be aware that the monarch was still 'absolutely opposed' to making any concession on the question of public hearings. 'As far as *public access* is concerned there is . . . *nothing* to be done', the Kaiser's friend warned. 'On that the Kaiser is absolutely *committed*.'[90] The elderly Prince's answer to Eulenburg's reproaches, which he had formulated himself before Marschall arrived to see him at 10 o'clock in the morning, was unusually acrimonious. It read: 'I am the Reich Chancellor and not a Chancellery official, and ought to know what to say.'[91]

Proud words indeed from the holder of the highest offices in Prussia and the Reich, and a refreshing contrast to the constant spectacle of a 'responsible government' giving way. If Prince Hohenlohe had acted in the spirit of this principle – if he had followed the advice of Holstein, Marschall, Bronsart and his own son and asserted himself against the Kaiser or resigned his office – would the Wilhelmstrasse have become the decision-making centre of German policy again, as it had been in Bismarck's day? The answer that probably has to be given to this question is doubly depressing. In the previous seven years Wilhelm II had acquired so much power that it would no longer have been possible to put the clock back. For the Reich Chancellor to have insisted on his primacy in decision-making, at a time when he had no reliable backing in the Reichstag or from public opinion, would only have led to his dismissal and that of the other ministers, and hence to a national crisis with unforeseeable consequences. But in any case Hohenlohe simply did not act in accordance with the admirable principle he had so proudly expressed. Once again, step by step, he capitulated. Within weeks the promising clarion call of 19 May 1896 was being drowned out by the roll of drums beating the retreat.

## THE RECONSTITUTION OF THE GOVERNMENT BY THE CROWN

Eulenburg's first concern was to avert an immediate government crisis. The same day, 19 May 1896, he sent the Chancellor a placatory message from the imperial hunting lodge. 'The Kaiser was at first perplexed by your answer today. Then he was upset for a moment, but afterwards his attitude became calmer, and remains so . . . The anger has abated. He is in a good, cheerful mood again.'[92] He urged Prince Alexander to persuade his father to remain in office. 'The Kaiser's excitable state' must not give the Reich Chancellor reason to conclude that he should resign, although this would be only too understandable given the 'volatile nature' of the monarch. 'I am glad that it turned out in the way it did!', Eulenburg asserted. 'But I *really do not* think the time has come for far-reaching decisions by the Prince.'[93] In a secret note intended only for Chlodwig Hohenlohe, however,

Eulenburg informed him that, although the Kaiser wished to keep him, the Chancellor, in office, he did intend to dismiss Bronsart and Marschall. 'The resentment towards the Minister of War – but also towards Marschall – is *very* great and will probably lead to a clash in the not too distant future.'[94]

Although it suited Wilhelm to keep Hohenlohe in office – indeed he was to remain Reich chancellor and Prussian minister-president until October 1900 – the statement made by the Chancellor on his own initiative in the Reichstag on 18 May had nonetheless 'left a wound in the Kaiser's heart'[95] which had perceptibly diminished Wilhelm's willingness to co-operate even with him. To Philipp Eulenburg, the monarch's loss of trust seemed reason enough for a major government reshuffle. The aim which he and the Kaiser's other advisers at court now pursued was therefore to re-structure the Reich government from above, so that in future the will of the monarch, rather than that of the Reich chancellor, the secretaries of state and the ministers of state, would determine Germany's destiny. The role which Eulenburg played as Wilhelm II's confidant in this national crisis was so dominant that Holstein remarked that he sometimes could not tell 'what was H.M. and what was Phil. Eul.'.[96] Another diplomat, casting doubt on rumours that Eulenburg himself would shortly be appointed Reich chancellor, commented that he had always regarded the favourite as 'a charming dilettante' who would not be so 'foolish' as to 'step out of the shadows of the irresponsible adviser's role'. He could not imagine, either, that it would suit the Kaiser to let him out of 'the behind-the-scenes business . . . which he seems to manage to the All-Highest satisfaction'. Whomever the Kaiser appointed as Reich chancellor, however, the sad truth was that he would not follow the principle of 'who is the most effective, but who is the most obedient'.[97]

The chief difficulty which Wilhelm and Eulenburg faced in the summer of 1896 was that of Bronsart's proposed reform of the military judicial system, supported as it was both by the Chancellor and the Ministry of State and by public opinion, while the Kaiser had absolutely no intention of conceding it. On the Scandinavian cruise Wilhelm, 'with obvious irritation but also with very marked energy', declared that he would never be persuaded to change his mind. Although the danger of a change of chancellor filled him 'with extreme concern', he would take even this upon himself, since 'I would despise myself if I were to sacrifice my convictions on this question.'[98] Wilhelm remained obdurate in his antipathy for the Minister of War and the resignation of this key figure could not be far off. Hohenlohe complained that the Kaiser spoke 'in such derogatory terms' about Bronsart that the General felt he 'could not honourably continue to serve'. A few friendly words from the Kaiser would be enough to pacify him, the Chancellor commented; but he knew that 'H.M. will . . . not want to do that.'[99] On a visit to the court at the end of May Waldersee too observed that the Kaiser had 'completely broken' with the War Minister and 'often says so in the harshest possible terms'. Wilhelm accused Bronsart of 'inciting the other ministers against him and attacking the Military Cabinet and the influence of the Flügeladjutanten in the press, and he says he is absolutely certain of this . . . It is the same old story: the Kaiser listens to gossip and believes everything!'[100] As he had previously announced, Bronsart handed in his resignation on 17 June after the closure of the Reichstag session, but hinted that he was prepared to go on leave for the time being, in case the Kaiser should refuse to allow him to resign immediately.[101] A few days later Waldersee heard that Bronsart was to take three months' leave, but – like Verdy five years earlier[102] – would not return to his post thereafter. 'He has completely fallen out with the Kaiser', he commented. 'We shall soon see the Kaiser's 5th minister of war: a good turnover in 8 years!'[103] Wilhelm and Eulenburg had thus gained three months in which to drive a wedge between the Reich Chancellor and the outgoing War Minister.

Nothing shows more clearly the extent to which the most important decisions in the German Reich were now being taken by the Kaiser and his confidential advisers than the discussions which Eulenburg held in May 1896 with the Kaiser and Lucanus on the future composition of the Reich government and the course which domestic policy should follow in consequence. In two letters to Bülow of 24 May and 8 June 1896 the Kaiser's favourite reported, with astonishing condescension, on the progress of these discussions, which were to seal the fate of the Hohenlohe regime. After his conversations with Wilhelm in Prökelwitz Eulenburg was convinced that the relationship of trust between Kaiser and Chancellor could never be restored. 'But what can one do if the Kaiser no longer wants to ride this horse?', he asked. 'It is tired and will not take any more ditches. There is no point in my singing its praises. I know how gladly it carries its master, how well the old animal has ridden in the past, how exactly it understands every signal during exercises, how well known it is and how soft and good its name sounds! If H.M. has lost the desire to ride it, it will not be given the right aids and will not jump as it should.' Eulenburg expressed horror at the prospect of the crises which a third change of chancellor would bring, shaking Germany and its neighbours 'to the core', but he maintained that the sole decisive factor for him was the welfare of the 'beloved' Kaiser. 'I look at what it means for the intellectual development of our beloved Kaiser, and I try to decide on the basis of events and of His character how one should carry on life for the best, how can *the Kaiser* carry on his life for the best?' Eulenburg was convinced that 'the King's character must be taken into consideration as long as we are a monarchy and wish to remain one'. But Kaiser Wilhelm II, his friend declared, represented to an astonishing degree a combination of 'two totally different natures': 'the knightly – reminiscent of the finest days of the Middle Ages, with all their piety and mysticism – and the modern', although the knightly side was 'very predominant'. 'If I now transfer the effect of the Kaiser's personality on to politics', Eulenburg continued revealingly, 'I come to the inevitable conclusion that H.M. must find His *natural point of support* in the Conservatives, the Conservatives in the good sense – and that is confirmed by looking at Prussian history. The king of Prussia cannot long remain without the Conservatives . . . I think, therefore, that the Kaiser's individuality will find its equilibrium in politics on a sensible Conservative basis. The whole of the Kaiser's vital, dynamic being stands in such remarkable contradiction to the predominance of Liberal-Progressive or Liberal-Catholic (Centre) ideas that this has been one of the main reasons for the feeling of unsteadiness about which the whole of Germany is complaining.' The Conservative Party, for its part, would have no choice but to find its way back to the monarchy, Eulenburg predicted, for 'a king of Prussia who, like our dear King, is *la fine fleur* of kingship, and a Conservative Party that adopts democratic and demagogical airs, are mutually incompatible – but must also be brought together again *par la force des choses*'. The conclusion to be drawn from these reflections was obvious to Eulenburg. In the new government, above all, '*Prussians* must now dominate', and 'the single will of the Kaiser in His Ministry' must be made perfectly clear. Of course for the sake of the German Reich the wheel must not be turned too far to the right, he pointed out; on the contrary, extremely skilful men must be appointed who could master the art of ruling 'conservatively in Prussia and liberally in the Reich'. If this talented, predominantly Prussian, moderate Conservative, unified government were but in place, Eulenburg maintained, the 'myth of adjutant-politics', so damaging for the monarchy, could be scotched, for on the one hand the new government would be at peace with the adjutants, 'because there would be the greatest possible harmony of political views between it and H.M.'s entourage', and on the other the Kaiser would 'treat the Ministry with the same confidence as His adjutants'.[104]

On the practical question of choosing successors to the present government, Eulenburg and Wilhelm II at first had different ideas. Eulenburg's suggestion that his cousin Botho should be appointed Reich chancellor with Bernhard von Bülow as foreign secretary was initially turned down by Wilhelm because Lucanus had told him that as minister of the interior Botho Eulenburg had shown so little vigour in dealing with the Conservatives 'that it was inconceivable that he should hold the foremost position in the Reich in such difficult circumstances'. For this reason, Wilhelm declared, he had decided to appoint Bülow Reich chancellor immediately. 'He was tired of crises, He needed a chancellor who would stay for 20 years and more.' He dismissed Philipp Eulenburg's argument that he should not make use of Bülow in the present crisis especially if he wanted to retain him as chancellor for a long time; 'it seemed to be a firm decision',

Eulenburg recorded, and 'I did not insist.' But as he was still convinced of the advantages of a 'strongly Prussian' chancellorship under Botho Eulenburg, with Bülow as foreign secretary and Posadowsky as secretary of the interior, the Kaiser's friend decided to call on the Chief of the Civil Cabinet at Potsdam on his way back from East Prussia to Vienna on 24 May, in order to talk him out of his fear of the 'excessive power of the Eulenburgs'.[105]

Like Eulenburg, Bülow believed that in the final analysis the conflict between the crown and the Wilhelmstrasse turned on the question of who should have the final power of decision in the land. 'What is really at issue?', he asked. 'It is this: that His Majesty's prestige and plenitude of power, which was usurped [by Bismarck] in 1890 and which as a result of various events in the last year seems threatened, if not shaken, should be restored in the eyes of the army and the country.' The Kaiser should not, however, be forced into choosing between subordinating himself to the Ministry of State led by Bronsart and Marschall on the one hand, and provoking a '*casse-cou* policy' with 'dissolutions of the Reichstag, *coup d'état*, break-up of the Reich federation and general chaos' on the other. It was also open to him to dismiss the rebellious ministers and, having shown the army and the people that he would not allow his will to be broken, he could then come to a compromise solution with the new ministers on the question of court martial reform. The Kaiser's candidate for the chancellorship was well aware under what ordinance he would have to succeed Marschall or Hohenlohe. 'My standpoint will always be the same', he assured Eulenburg, who by now was cruising in the North Sea with the Kaiser. 'I am always at our dear sovereign's disposal – wherever, whenever and however he wishes . . . All I want is to be a card in the Kaiser's hand with which he wins as many tricks as possible.'[106] A week later, knowing full well that Eulenburg would read his letter out to the Kaiser, Bülow enlarged on his theme in terms that could not fail to be understood. 'I am filled solely and purely with burning love for our revered Kaiser and sovereign, profound devotion to Prussia and Germany . . . I would be a different kind of chancellor from my predecessors. Bismarck was a power in his own right, a Pepin, a Richelieu. Caprivi and Hohenlohe regarded or regard themselves as the representatives of the "government" and to a certain extent of the parliament in relation to His Majesty. I would regard myself as the executive tool of His Majesty, so to speak his political Chief of Staff. With me personal rule – in the good sense – would really begin.' But for precisely that reason he should be brought in as Reich chancellor at the right moment and not too early, he warned, for 'if this attempt at real personal rule were to fail, things would look black for our beloved Kaiser!'[107]

In the course of endless conversations during the Scandinavian cruise in July 1896 Wilhelm and Eulenburg devised a series of carefully thought-out plans addressing every eventuality – Hohenlohe's resignation *with* a subsequent *coup d'état*, Hohenlohe's resignation *without* a *coup d'état*, Hohenlohe's continuation in office with the proviso of sacrificing Bronsart, Marschall and Boetticher. There was only one possibility which they did not consider: a surrender by the Kaiser on the court martial reform question. To him this signified the preservation of 'the dignity of the crown' and the maintenance of his personal power as kaiser, king and supreme war lord. In numerous letters from the *Hohenzollern* the Kaiser's best friend set out to convince the two key figures in the 'responsible government', Hohenlohe and Holstein, of Wilhelm's absolute determination, and therefore of the futility of their resistance, on this question. And since Eulenburg's threats of the catastrophic consequences of a ministerial and chancellor crisis were far from being empty attempts at intimidation, the statesmen of the Wilhelmstrasse, conscious of their responsibility, eventually fell victim to their own prophecies of doom.

In their machinations Wilhelm and his friend began by recognising, on the one hand, that the 'clash' must not take place during the Scandinavian cruise, as this would put Eulenburg and the adjutants accompanying the Kaiser into a 'disagreeable position' and would awaken the impression that the Kaiser was allowing himself 'to be influenced in an outrageous manner'. On the other hand they realised that they must get their way by the end of August or the beginning of September at the latest, that is to say before the Reichstag reassembled and Bronsart finally departed.[108] At the very start of the cruise it became obvious to Eulenburg that Wilhelm had 'no clear sense' of the full implications of his attitude – he wanted to make immediate changes, replacing Hohenlohe by Bülow, Marschall by Brinken and Bronsart by Hähnisch.[109] It was therefore 'with some hesitation' that the Kaiser's friend wrote to the Chancellor on the Kaiser's instructions on 5 July informing him that Wilhelm would '*on no account*' give way on the court martial question. A catastrophe was therefore inevitable in the autumn unless Hohenlohe himself was prepared to give way and sanction the dismissal of Bronsart and Marschall. 'The King has the right to be influenced by personal feelings in forming an opinion of his ministers', the favourite again insisted. Marschall would be given an embassy (Constantinople) and Bernhard Bülow would be appointed secretary of state at the Foreign Office. Once a new minister of war had been appointed, Hohenlohe could modify his position on public courts martial for the Kaiser's sake. If he did so he would be able to look forward to a 'peaceful, dignified' retirement in the future. Otherwise there would be a serious constitutional conflict for which Hohenlohe would have to bear the responsibility. A passage dictated by Wilhelm, which Eulenburg later toned down to spare the elderly Chancellor's feelings, contained the threat that 'in the event of very serious attack' the Kaiser 'might even be *compelled* to vindicate his crown . . . and use forcible means'. 'Although it would make his heart bleed, he could announce to the world that the declaration of principle made by his Uncle the Chancellor in parliament accorded neither with his wishes nor with the orders which he had conveyed to Your Highness in the form of words which he himself had drawn up after he was consulted.'[110] Eulenburg also wrote to Holstein stating that after his conversation with Wilhelm in Norway it was clear to him that the Hohenlohe system in the form it had taken hitherto was 'done for', and that Marschall must be dismissed and Bülow brought into the government as future chancellor. 'The unremitting agitation against Marschall has aroused what appears to me to be such insurmountable dislike against him on the part of H.M.', he wrote. On the other hand Bülow must not be branded as an anti-public courts martial candidate for the chancellorship. If Bülow should be tarred with this brush and therefore refuse even an *urgent request* from the Kaiser to come to Berlin, there was a chance that 'H.M. out of ill-humour would suddenly appoint Wald[ersee] or would turn to Botho E[ulenburg].'[111] Eulenburg repeatedly warned the leading spirits in the Wilhelmstrasse that the Kaiser would not yield on the question of court martial reform.[112] Although he fully recognised the benefits to be gained from Bülow's appointment as foreign secretary under Hohenlohe – 'It would be a blessing for you to work with Hohenlohe for a little while longer', he wrote to his friend in Rome – Eulenburg was convinced that the Prince's response would be negative and that Bülow would therefore be appointed Reich chancellor immediately.[113]

Writing to his son, the Chancellor commented bitterly that the air of the North Sea had evidently stimulated 'the All-Highest vitality'. Eulenburg had informed him in a letter from Norway 'that H.M. has not changed his opinion with regard to public access [to courts martial], that he wants to get rid of Marschall and Bronsart and that he expects me to submit to all of this'.[114] In reply to Eulenburg's letter Hohenlohe stated that to give up the principle of open courts martial would be political suicide for him, for he would be heaped with 'scorn and ridicule' and 'a ridiculed Reich chancellor' would no longer be able to render any worthwhile service to the Kaiser. He would therefore continue to try to find a formula that would allow the Kaiser to give his consent to the public military trials which had been promised to the Reichstag. If such a compromise could be found, however, Bronsart would be 'the only man' who could make this formula palatable to the Reichstag. He therefore had serious reservations about the immediate departure of Bronsart and equally about the removal of Marschall at this juncture.[115] The 77-year-old Reich Chancellor also hinted indirectly to the Kaiser's friend that he cherished certain hopes which might induce him to leave office in a manner that would avoid conflict. 'If it could be arranged for me to be transferred back to Strassburg [as Statthalter] that would of course be the most pleasing solution and it would prevent any suggestion of a rift. I should be able to celebrate my golden wedding there next winter.'[116]

The only person who firmly resisted the far-reaching plans contemplated by Wilhelm and Eulenburg was Geheimrat Friedrich von Holstein. He continued to warn of the disastrous consequences of the national crisis, akin to civil war, which would ensue if the Kaiser did not give way on the court martial question and Bronsart, Hohenlohe, Marschall and the entire Ministry of State were to resign as a result.[117] The Kaiser must on no account bring about a constitutional conflict of this order with the Reichstag unless he had secured a written commitment from the principal German federal princes that they would support him 'through thick and thin'. If a number of ruling princes, headed by Bavaria, should suddenly refuse to co-operate with him in taking further action against parliament once the conflict had begun, 'the Kaiser will find himself in a serious position because the power of the princes would be augmented by that of all the opposition parties . . . This, my dear E[ulenburg], is the heart and soul of the whole matter, because it is here a question of the preservation or weakening of the imperial authority. All the other questions – for example ministerial appointments – are of secondary importance.'[118] If the Kaiser provoked the conflict without making quite sure of the support of the rulers of Bavaria, Saxony and Württemberg, he would be heading for 'a political defeat the consequences of which will be felt during his entire reign', Holstein warned.[119] The Kaiser himself was 'too eminent a person' to expose himself to the risk of a rejection from Munich, Dresden or Stuttgart, but Eulenburg could take soundings with the three rulers on his behalf.[120]

The persistent warnings and threats in Holstein's letters did not go unheeded in the imperial camp. Even Adjutant-General von Plessen spoke of the urgent need to avoid a chancellor crisis now; the 'growing possibility of a clash filled him with anxiety'.[121] In a memorandum of 21 July Eulenburg acknowledged that the resignation of Hohenlohe, Marschall and Bronsart would 'cause the greatest astonishment and agitation throughout Germany'. '*It will not be understood and it will show His Majesty in the wrong light.*' After such a sensational clash the new chancellor would be plunged into a situation of conflict in which he would inevitably be defeated. He would have no party in the Reichstag on his side, for the Centre and the Liberals would be fiercely opposed to him, while the Conservatives, who were still very much in conflict with the crown, would likewise withhold their support from Hohenlohe's successor. The Reichstag would therefore refuse to approve any more expenditure; dissolution would be inevitable, but new elections would only make the situation worse. With Holstein's warnings in mind, Eulenburg concluded: 'The conflict with the Reichstag can be carried through only with the full agreement of the federal princes, above all that of the [three] kings. They must make binding, written declarations, so that they do not try to extract advantages for themselves — (revision of the Treaty of Versailles, for instance) — out of Prussia's difficulties at the crucial moment. That would spread the conflict to the federal states and would entail the risk that foreign countries might exploit the strife to attack Germany.'[122] When Eulenburg put these concerns to the Kaiser he was unperturbed. The King of Saxony and the Grand Duke of Baden, he asserted, were indeed on Bronsart's side on the question of open courts martial, but they would not pose any danger in the event of a conflict, and even Bavaria, where the Wittelsbach princes might be tempted to make common cause with the Liberals, nationalists and particularists to 'trip up Prussia', did not greatly worry him. 'I have seventeen army corps and am therefore the master of the situation', he declared coolly.[123]

Although this train of thought by no means persuaded Wilhelm and Eulenburg to abandon their plans, they were nevertheless forced to consider whether it would not be preferable to postpone Bülow's candidacy for the chancellorship and appoint a transitional chancellor who would be prepared to see the constitutional conflict through to the end, if Hohenlohe remained intransigent.[124] In a decisive conversation in the *Hohenzollern* on 23 July 1896 Eulenburg told the Kaiser of the Reich Chancellor's negative response to his letter of 5 July and discussed the dangerous state of affairs which would arise if Hohenlohe and the entire government of the Reich and Prussia resigned in protest at the pressure on them. Wilhelm continued to maintain that surrender on public courts martial was 'completely out of the question' for him. 'I have scarcely ever seen the Kaiser so strongly affected', Eulenburg reported to Bülow. 'His eyes were brimming with tears when he said "I should think myself a miserable creature if I gave in on a question which my forefathers recognised as necessary and right! How could I show my face before them in Heaven? — although I am certainly not worthy to go there! And how would I stand *with the army*, which would see it as the destruction of all its protective walls, the army in whose eyes I already bear the heavy responsibility of having accepted the two-year service!"' For a whole hour the Kaiser listened 'with an attention that was really touching' while his friend set out the 'serious dangers' which would arise from Hohenlohe's resignation and the resultant conflict with the Reichstag. 'It made a very profound impression on His Majesty. The beloved Kaiser had not fully realised the possible consequences', Eulenburg commented.[125]

At a later stage in this memorable conversation, Eulenburg argued that in view of the foreseeable political complications Wilhelm II must find another successor for Hohenlohe, instead of putting Bülow, who was to be 'a Reich chancellor who would *last*', in an almost hopeless position. When Eulenburg went on to name his cousin Botho or, of all people, General von Bronsart to take on the role of transitional chancellor, the Kaiser exclaimed in astonishment: 'That reminds me of a suggestion by old Hahnke, who told me I should make the Minister of War my adjutant-general in waiting, to shut his mouth. I indignantly refused at that time – but today, the way you have described it makes me wonder whether this suggestion might perhaps be the solution in the present state of affairs? Bronsart is not dismissed, but *promoted* and receives an *exceptional mark* of favour from me. Then Hohenlohe has no reason to go. Bronsart is removed from office and replaced – but because I appoint him to *my* service, not because of the wretched court martial reform.' The 'German Reich Chancellor Hohenlohe' could then 'make a concession to the Prussian Prime Minister Hohenlohe' without burdening his conscience, the Kaiser observed happily. Eulenburg declared himself ready to pass on these suggestions at once to Hohenlohe and was further authorised by the Kaiser to offer him the postponement of Marschall's dismissal as well.[126]

In a letter to the Chancellor on 23 July, couched in terms as 'warm' as possible, Eulenburg emphasised that on the question of public hearings the monarch was still unable to give way on any account, for he must remain true to his 'most sacred conviction', to which he was bound by the well-tried tradition upheld by his forebears. Wilhelm had said, 'with tears in his eyes', 'I *cannot* sacrifice my conviction – I would think myself wicked! My uncle will sacrifice his Bavarian traditions when he sees my sincere goodwill to be as accommodating as possible with him!' But the Kaiser was prepared to make 'a great sacrifice' to the Chancellor on two other points. First, the replacement of Marschall by Bülow could be postponed and, second, on quitting the Ministry of War Bronsart could be promoted to adjutant-general in waiting to the Kaiser. Any idea that the Military Cabinet and the Kaiser's military suite had won a victory over Bronsart would be counteracted by his promotion, and the Reich Chancellor would thus be free to accept the opinion of the new minister of war and of the commanding generals of all seventeen Prussian army corps on the question of the court martial bill.[127]

The ensnaring of Prince Hohenlohe was, however, only one of the options that the Kaiser and his good friend 'Phili' were keeping open. At the same time they prepared themselves for conflict with the Reichstag and even for a possible *coup d'état* with all its consequences – civil war and military intervention by foreign powers. In his conversation of 23 July 1896 with Wilhelm, Eulenburg particularly emphasised that he had '*not the slightest scruples*' about entering into conflict with the parliament 'because Prussia is strong enough to fight it out'. If Hohenlohe refused to accept the Kaiser's offer a crisis would follow, Eulenburg noted calmly that evening. 'In that case Botho Eulenburg with Bernhard B. as secretary of state seems to me to have the best chance. But it is not inconceivable

that Bronsart could emerge as "war chancellor" – and that might not be a bad
thing, in a really hopeless situation.'[128]


## THE BREAKTHROUGH

At the end of July 1896 two non-political developments compelled Wilhelm to
break off his Scandinavian cruise early and return to Germany. First, he received
news – prematurely, as it turned out – that Bismarck was dying, and he was
determined to exploit the propaganda value of this historic event by making a
dramatic appearance at his deathbed. The other reason was that his right ear was
giving trouble and there were fears of inflammation of the brain. Accompanied
by Eulenburg, Wilhelm hurried to Schloss Wilhelmshöhe overlooking Kassel,
where Dr Moritz Trautmann was secretly waiting and was to carry out a major
operation on his right middle ear.[129] With the Kaiser's return the decisive battle
was imminent.

During the train journey from Kiel to Kassel, Eulenburg worked out the
programme for the future drawing together the threads of the discussions
of the past four weeks. On 1 August 1896, during a sunny walk in the park at
Wilhelmshöhe, he read it out to the Kaiser, subsequently handing it to him as
an *aide-mémoire*. This breathtaking exposé, which demonstrates with startling
clarity the extent to which the imperial camp held the upper hand in its final
battle with the 'responsible' government of the Reich, is undoubtedly one of
the most impressive documents of the Wilhelmine era, showing as it does how
carefully the Kaiser and his secret advisers had prepared themselves for every
eventuality. If Hohenlohe were to give way and remain in office, Eulenburg's
memorandum stated, Bronsart would be replaced by General von Hähnisch,
Boetticher by Posadowsky and – after a few months – Marschall by Radolin
or Brinken. But if Hohenlohe insisted on resigning, Bronsart, Marschall and
Boetticher must be dismissed together by the beginning of September at the latest. Thereafter there were two possibilities for the Kaiser. In the event that 'His
Majesty *does not want a policy of force*' he should appoint Botho Eulenburg as
Reich chancellor and Bernhard Bülow as foreign secretary and vice-president of
the Prussian Ministry of State. This combination would mean 'a Prussian, moderate course with an anti-revolutionary tendency – [but] not anti-constitutional
or anti-Reichstag'. Botho would outlive his usefulness 'after a few years' and
Bülow could then 'ease himself in' to the post of Reich chancellor. But the Kaiser
and his friend also calmly faced the possibility of a breach of the constitution. 'In
the event that His Majesty is not afraid of a policy of *forcible settlement* or cannot
avoid it', the memorandum provided for Bülow to be kept in reserve until after
the 'fierce battles' were over. In this case the Kaiser could take either Bronsart or

Waldersee as Reich chancellor instead of Botho Eulenburg. The appointment of a '*belligerent*' general of this kind as chancellor would in itself signify 'the government throwing down the gauntlet, a marked shift towards so-called reaction, which would arouse the *strongest* opposition throughout the Reich and might even lead to the dissolution of the Reichstag; it would at any rate exacerbate the difficulties with the Bavarians, Württembergers and Saxons enormously', as Eulenburg observed. He himself preferred the 'great combination (Eulenburg–Bülow)' as 'the more favourable solution', but acknowledged that the 'sudden cessation of the Hohenlohe era' would hold great dangers. The '*greatest possible efforts*' should therefore be made to keep the old Prince in office, as far as this was compatible with 'His Majesty's principles and dignity'[130] After his walk with the Kaiser Eulenburg noted enthusiastically: 'For me this walk will always remain most memorable; it will be decisive in many ways. How kind, clever, simple and clear the Kaiser was. I had the feeling that we were closer to each other than before.' He had explained the content of his memorandum 'very thoroughly' to Wilhelm, 'entering into every detail. He agreed *unreservedly*, so that the exposé . . . must be considered as his programme.'[131]

The soothing telegrams and letters which he had received from the *Hohenzollern* led Holstein to conclude, rightly, that Wilhelm and Eulenburg intended to delay the decisive moment until they had spoken to the Reich Chancellor himself. With the modest means at his disposal – for apart from his cynical intellect and the power of his pen he had no way to exert influence – the Privy Councillor led the intellectual resistance of the 'responsible government' to the monarch's plans to seize power. He informed the Vortragender Rat, Karl von Lindenau, who was with Hohenlohe at Alt-Aussee in Austria, that he no longer believed there would be 'a row overnight, but deduce[d] from the various Imperial pronouncements the intention of saving up some crucial questions – business or personal – for the next *verbal* discussion with the Chancellor in the hope of being able to bowl him over with his innate *Suada* aided by some dramatic gestures. I imagine that any such discussion with the Kaiser must be very embarrassing for *anyone who wants to be polite* for the simple reason that H.M. can come closer to the limits of parliamentary freedom of speech than another mortal.' Holstein therefore advised that all outstanding questions should be settled in writing by the Reich Chancellor, as in that way the risky 'effects of the moment' would not play such an important role as in a discussion face to face. In order to avoid a meeting with the Kaiser Hohenlohe should therefore stay somewhere in South Germany while the crucial decisions were taken.[132]

On 26 July 1896 the Kaiser telegraphed to the Reich Chancellor to say that he had decided to return from his Scandinavian cruise a few days earlier than planned, and to go to Wilhelmshöhe. 'Philipp Eulenburg will accompany me and travel by way of Kassel directly to Aussee in order to discuss the situation with you.'[133] When the true reason for the sudden curtailment of the cruise – the resurgence of the Kaiser's ear trouble – became known in the Foreign Office, Holstein saw it as confirmation of a suspicion that he had harboured for weeks and had mentioned to those closest to him, namely that 'the events of the last few days were not free from pathological features'. How else could one describe the Kaiser's 'temperamental remarks' on 'the Lippe case, Bronsart, Marschall and the fleet programme' which had reached Berlin from the *Hohenzollern* over the past four weeks, he asked. But if the Kaiser were in any way not of sound mind there was an even more urgent need than before 'to uphold the personality and the *prestige* of the Chancellor as the *fixed point* around which the whole conception of the Reich and its supporters can come together'. The 'political personality' of Prince Hohenlohe was 'today even more than a month ago an indispensable, almost irreplaceable, political working capital for the German Reich'. Court martial reform and the 'enormous budget for the limitless fleet programme' – like the resistance against two-year military service under Caprivi – had been 'blown up artificially' by the Kaiser's entourage in order to reduce the Reich Chancellor's power, which they found uncomfortable, Holstein argued. In his forthcoming negotiations with Eulenburg the Reich Chancellor must therefore take care, for his own sake and that of the German people, that his position was not diminished, for the moment that he abandoned the standpoint he had taken in his statement to the Reichstag and capitulated to the imperial entourage, Hohenlohe would cease to 'represent anything firm and definite, and from that day onwards the Kaiser can get rid of him without fearing public indignation'. On the other hand, the more resolute the Chancellor was in what he said, the more careful the Kaiser would be. 'All unbalanced persons are like that!'[134] Holstein even advised the Reich Chancellor to allude to the danger of the Kaiser being declared incapable in his discussion with Eulenburg. Hohenlohe should tell him that 'a sick Kaiser must be more circumspect than a healthy one, since otherwise *the idea of placing him under guardianship* would be mooted in some corner of the Reich at the first opportunity, and the thought would never die out'. In mentioning Wilhelm's illness the Chancellor could 'point out frankly and unequivocally that the rule of the Kaiser, both with regard to the German princes and the German people, would be made much more difficult if the existence of this illness became known, and that this should be a warning to the Kaiser to be careful'.[135] The news that 'the illness has reappeared after lying quiescent for several years' would make a profound impression, the Privy Councillor urged in a last letter before Eulenburg's arrival at Alt-Aussee. 'Throughout the Reich there will be a general feeling of uncertainty, which may lead to disintegration and revolution if it is allowed to develop.' It was therefore Hohenlohe's duty to declare to the Kaiser 'with absolute firmness' that he must stay in office, 'but under conditions that correspond to the interests of the monarchy, namely that I [the Chancellor] remain at the head of a Cabinet capable of dealing with the problems brought before it in the interests of the crown and the country'.[136]

For his part, Hohenlohe assured Holstein that he would tell Eulenburg 'categorically' that the abandonment of public courts martial was an 'impossibility', and that he would consider the departure of Bronsart and Marschall 'disastrous'.[137] Privately, however, he noted that he wished to find 'a way out', 'out of consideration for the personality and position of the Kaiser'. He would gladly resign, but he could see that the Kaiser would be in a difficult position if he resigned over court martial reform.[138] When the Kaiser telegraphed from Wilhelmshöhe to tell him of his ear operation the Chancellor wired back with his 'humble' thanks for the 'gracious' telegram and asked 'most respectfully for news of Your Majesty's health soon'.[139] So even before Eulenburg's arrival the elderly Prince seems to have inwardly abandoned the idea of resistance on grounds of principle. In any case he had nothing with which to counter the programme so firmly decided upon by the Kaiser and his friend at Wilhelmshöhe.

In the meantime Eulenburg had travelled from Wilhelmshöhe via Hallstadt, where he met Bülow, and joined Prince Hohenlohe at Alt-Aussee, with the task of bringing about an ultimate solution to the long-running government crisis.[140] During their encounter of 3–5 August 1896, in which, as Hohenlohe himself acknowledged, it was a question of 'to be or not to be', Eulenburg behaved as if he were certain of victory and was not in the least embarrassed to be regarded 'as a torpedo in the imminent crisis'. As he had agreed in his conversations with the Kaiser on the *Hohenzollern* he explained to the Chancellor that the monarch could not concede open courts martial in any circumstances; he considered that his 'bounden duty'. But he was sincerely ready to consider a reform of the old court martial regulations taking in a few other features of 'modern' thinking and, if the reform bill were rejected by the Bundesrat or the Reichstag because it did not include public hearings, it could be introduced in Prussia. This reform was 'in accordance not only with the convictions of the Supreme War Lord but also of the Prussian army' and therefore could be supported by the civil government with a good conscience. As far as Bronsart was concerned, the Kaiser would relieve him of his functions as war minister and appoint him his adjutant-general in waiting, which would prevent the General's resignation from appearing to reflect sharp differences of opinion between the Kaiser and the government. 'I replied to Eulenburg', Hohenlohe recorded after the meeting, 'that the appointment of Bronsart as adjutant-general would not change the fact that he was no longer minister of war. Furthermore that these complicated suggestions would not cancel the fact that I had given up open courts martial. Bronsart's position would be enhanced, and I would be disgraced. I drew attention to the looming conflict with the Reichstag; for since 1871 no question had preoccupied public opinion as much as this one. If I gave up my standpoint, in political terms I would be a lost man.' At the same time the Prince recognised that this was 'a matter of complete indifference both to H.M. and Count Philipp Eulenburg'. 'What happens to me does not interest them, so long as the Kaiser's caprice and the Military Cabinet's will is carried out.' Hohenlohe even had the impression that Eulenburg wanted to remove him from his post, 'whether for his own motives or to please the Kaiser'. At any rate Eulenburg had made it clear to him that he could remain in office only provided that he 'submitted to the All-Highest will. That I shall not do.'[141]

For his part, Eulenburg gained the impression that Hohenlohe had taken many of his arguments on board. The Prince had become 'very pensive' and needed a few days to reflect, he reported to the Kaiser. If pressure were put on him to make up his mind immediately he would take it as 'a rude ultimatum from Your Majesty' and would throw all arguments overboard again. 'I beg Your Majesty's gracious forgiveness for this decision – but I could not thoughtlessly provoke a rejection.' But a 'very friendly letter from Yr. Majesty' could have a good effect on the Chancellor, Eulenburg advised. The news of the imminent death of Bismarck had already affected him deeply.[142] When he had taken his leave Hohenlohe had thanked Eulenburg 'with feeling' and had again expressed the hope that he would still be able to find 'some way out'.[143]

Eulenburg had barely left Alt-Aussee when a telegram arrived from Wilhelmshöhe with a pressing invitation from the Kaiser to the Reich Chancellor to go there. The invitation – 'obviously something arranged by E[ulenburg] with H.M.' – was expressed in such a way that Hohenlohe could not refuse, nor even return to Berlin first.[144] On 8 August the elderly Chancellor and his son Alexander therefore made the journey to Wilhelmshöhe via Munich. He found the Kaiser, who was clearly afraid that Hohenlohe would refuse to accept Bronsart's appointment as adjutant-general, 'very much on edge'. But on this point the Prince yielded at once without dissension. The Kaiser then set out 'the whole plan as drawn up by Eulenburg'. In the end the Chancellor agreed to wait for the expert opinion of the generals on the contentious question of public courts martial, although he knew very well that 'the commanding generals will say only what the Kaiser orders'. Meanwhile, the Kaiser said, Hohenlohe need have no scruples about going away to Werki, his wife's Russian estate, since a final answer on the court martial question could not be expected until the beginning of October.[145] In thus agreeing to postpone the critical moment until the autumn the Prince's desire to seek his own material advantage again played a discreditable role. In order to 'look after his Russian interests' he asked permission to be present at the Kaiser's forthcoming meeting with the Tsar and Tsarina at Breslau; he also expressed the wish that his son Alexander be appointed Bezirkspräsident (district president) of Colmar in Alsace.[146]

Wilhelm II himself left a typically heartless account of these decisive negotiations with the Reich Chancellor and his son. In a letter of 14 August to Eulenburg he reported that 'old Uncle' had been 'hale and hearty and very sensible'. 'Especially after his long conferences with Lucanus and Hahnke. In order to get him out of the state which you rightly describe as stagnation in his support for public hearings, it was made very clear to him that the main issue was not public access but the Central Military Court presided over by a general directly under the Kaiser. The South Germans were opposed to this. But as long as it was not conceded the entire reform bill would collapse and would not come before the Reichstag. This point was an absolutely indispensable condition for the Kaiser and he must get it accepted first. This was something quite new for the old man and he was grateful when he saw that the rejection which could be expected from the Bundesrat would give him a bridge over which he could retreat. Alexander was no use at all here. He talked all kinds of rubbish, stirred his father up the whole time and in the end had to be very roughly silenced by Lucanus that evening, in a violent dispute in which he got very worked up arguing for public access. This grass-green young clown, who has never served in the army and couldn't tell a Pioneer from a Garde du Corps, does a great deal of damage and compromises the old man by spreading a lot of irresponsible gossip which he invents. I therefore spoke very strongly and seriously to my uncle about his offspring, which shocked the old man very much, but he was very grateful. He went away with the impression that I was as steady as a rock and that public hearings were a nonsense, and with my permission to think about finding a way out in the above-mentioned manner. To bolster him up against his "colleagues" I gave him a written assurance that Bronsart's dismissal would not affect the declarations in the Reichstag. For the rest I insisted very strongly and warmly on his importance and on the need for him to stay for the sake of political affairs, and asked him to stick to what we had both agreed and not let himself be browbeaten by every unauthorised "adviser" who came along. He promised to do all this and as he left he said, "I shall let the matter rest entirely, speak to no one about it and keep very quiet in Berlin." He went on his way and we were very pleased.'[147]

When his three months of leave were over the normally so defiant General Bronsart von Schellendorf endured the undignified farce of 'promotion' to adjutant-general to the Kaiser, which no one could take seriously.[148] To succeed him as minister of war the Kaiser chose not General von Hähnisch but the Commander of the 25th Division, General Heinrich von Gossler, of whom he telegraphed delightedly to Eulenburg that he was 'in agreement with me on all questions' and wanted 'only to be his Kaiser's general'.[149] Gossler, he commented in a later message, was 'an old friend of mine, and we have already fought many a battle in the Ministry of War together'.[150] The public reaction to Bronsart's dismissal and Gossler's appointment was disastrous.[151] The Reich Chancellor noted in his journal that both decisions had caused 'an enormous uproar' and the Kaiser had done himself 'terrible harm' by his action. It was 'very sad', he commented, adding that the future looked 'black' to him. But instead of learning from this experience Wilhelm condemned the attacks in the press 'against government by the Cabinets, which of course is basically no more than personal rule', as 'expressions of high treason'.[152] Waldersee also expressed indignation at the decisions. 'There is universal regret at Bronsart's resignation', he commented, 'and dismay over the successor is almost as widespread. Indeed I believe the Kaiser could not have made an unluckier choice.'[153] Germany could never have a more effective war minister than Bronsart, in his view, and Gossler was 'a very dubious successor', who was perhaps hard-working and competent but was 'an extremely unprincipled and ambitious person'. 'He can be turned in any direction and certainly suits the Kaiser down to the ground', he wrote. 'I am very worried by this choice.'[154] The rift between Bronsart and the Kaiser could not of course be disguised by his appointment to the court. Only a few months later, in his next New Year address to the commanding generals, the Supreme War Lord declared with uncontrolled fury that he had 'felt compelled to dismiss the General from the army, relieve him of his post as adjutant-general and request him to absent himself from the celebrations of the Order of the Black Eagle. Thereupon he abruptly turned on his heel, said goodbye and vanished.' It was only with difficulty that the 'very agitated' Chief of the Military Cabinet succeeded in persuading the Kaiser that the order to Bronsart should be toned down.[155] Months afterwards it was still being said in political circles that the former War Minister had been forbidden by imperial order to go within a two-mile radius of Berlin.[156]

The violent public reaction to Bronsart's fall might still have enabled Hohenlohe, even at this late stage, to preserve the power of the chancellorship by taking a firm stand. Not only Holstein and other Foreign Office officials but also his own family and members of the South German professorate were urging him to stand by his principles, and their efforts were not entirely unsuccessful.[157] As Eulenburg had to explain with some anxiety to the Kaiser, their earlier hope that the Prince could retire without reference to court martial reform was now ruled out. Extreme caution was necessary in dealing with the Chancellor, for he had very strong feelings about the 'historical figure' he cut, and if he should gain the impression that he might be dismissed in the autumn he would 'much rather go *now* in a blaze of glory'. It was also most important, the Kaiser's friend advised, to delay the appointment of Alexander Hohenlohe as Bezirkspräsident until after the chancellor crisis was finally over. 'The prospect of relieving the burden on the Princess [Hohenlohe]'s purse is a strong reason to stay on for this rather cynical part mediatised, part Sarmatian princely family – a kind of patent axle on the Chancellor's carriage.'[158] But when the Reich Chancellor sent a telegram from Berlin seeking to make clear that he still stood by the 'principle of public access' Eulenburg did not hesitate to tell him plainly that this declaration, which had 'awakened memories of the Köller crisis', had 'annoyed' the Kaiser. The monarch was 'very certain, very *firm*' on this question and might easily be provoked to 'sudden, very extreme steps' by continued resistance from the Chancellor.[159] Hohenlohe again gave way, and Wilhelm and his best friend observed with relief that 'the Hohenlohe crisis . . . is over'.[160] And with the 'disappearance of the crisis' they were again confident that 'Hohenlohe will be able to spend the rest of his life in office. Then other arrangements will also be more peaceful and simple to make.'[161] And indeed, in the course of the next few months Wilhelm II and Philipp Eulenburg, together with the other advisers at court – August Eulenburg, the three Cabinet Chiefs and the adjutant-generals and Flügeladjutanten – were able to make almost all the changes in personnel which they had worked out together during the Scandinavian cruise and subsequently at Wilhelmshöhe.

### THE REICH CHANCELLOR AS THE KAISER'S 'STRAW DOLL'

When he looked back a year later over the events of the summer of 1896 Prince Hohenlohe was only too painfully aware that in those crucial weeks he had lost the last vestiges of the Reich chancellor's independent power to the Kaiser. He wrote ruefully to his son Prince Alexander: 'If I had offered my resignation at that time, I would either have departed a popular man, or forced the Kaiser to give way . . . Now there is little to be done.'[162] He noted privately on 22 May 1897 that 'the government cannot go on as it is now. If H.M. wants to rule by himself, I cannot act as his straw man. If H.M. had approved the court martial bill years ago . . . the whole storm would not have arisen. If H.M. chooses all the ministers himself, the government will lose more and more consistency and respect . . . Without authority, government is impossible. If I cannot get the Kaiser's consent to measures I regard as necessary, then I have no authority . . . I cannot stay if H.M. removes Marschall against my will and if Holstein goes. Likewise I cannot stay if the Kaiser appoints ministers without consulting me . . . I cannot govern against public opinion as well as against the Kaiser. To govern against the Kaiser and the public is to hang in mid-air. That is impossible.'[163]

During his summer holiday on his estate in Bohemia he recorded that 'The entire attitude of H.M. in recent months . . . proves that the Kaiser is determined to choose another Reich chancellor, or at least to inaugurate a new system. He wants to support himself more on the right, to use Miquel to this end, and to tolerate me for the time being as a straw man until he has found the right chancellor. If I accept this plan I shall . . . be utterly discredited.'[164] 'The fact is', he recognised, 'that I have lost my authority over the Kaiser, and as a result I have no *raison d'être*.'[165] To remain in office as a 'half-dead Reich chancellor' was impossible for him, he declared with apparent resolve in mid-June 1897.[166] 'The role of the Reich chancellor who merely carries out the orders of H.M. does not appeal to me at all', he wrote to his son,[167] echoing this sentiment in a clear-sighted letter to a South German friend: 'If the Kaiser wants to be his own Reich chancellor he will have to appoint a straw doll. I have no desire to be one.'[168]

Seldom has the desolate situation of the Reich chancellor under Wilhelm II been as unsparingly laid bare as in these self-critical comments by Hohenlohe. But the elderly Prince did not act in accordance with the insight he showed. Admittedly, from time to time he noted down proud declarations which he intended to make to the Kaiser – in one such, written in March 1897, he expressed regret that Wilhelm was not the Tsar of Russia; the constitution was not of his making but he must uphold it – but it is more than doubtful that he ever made use of them.[169] He threatened to resign when Wilhelm II appointed Tirpitz in place of Admiral Friedrich Hollmann, the Secretary of State at the Reich Navy Office and as such responsible to the Reich Chancellor, but he did not succeed in reversing the Kaiser's decision.[170] And he went so far as to hand in his resignation on 31 May 1897 when the Kaiser peremptorily demanded the immediate resignation of Heinrich von Boetticher as Reich secretary for the interior and vice-president of the Prussian Ministry of State, but backed down at once after receiving a few flattering lines from the Kaiser brought to him by Lucanus.[171] The Reich Chancellor, now aged seventy-eight, constantly found reasons why it seemed 'easier' or more effective to postpone his retirement.[172]

Until his departure in October 1900 'Chlodwig, the old mummy', as his opponents unkindly nicknamed him,[173] endured the most outrageous rudeness from the Kaiser without reacting as he owed it to himself and to the German people to do. In the summer of 1897, as the so-called responsible Reich chancellor, he accepted a series of appointments and dismissals of momentous significance, which transformed the Reich and Prussian government into an administrative machine with the sole purpose of carrying out the Kaiser's will. Marschall von Bieberstein was replaced as foreign secretary by Bernhard von Bülow and shipped off to Constantinople as ambassador. Count Arthur von Posadowsky

was appointed secretary at the Reich Office of the Interior in place of Boetticher; the former ambassador in Washington, Max Freiherr von Thielmann,
was nominated to the Reich Treasury Office and General Viktor von Podbielski, a Conservative member of the Reichstag, to the Reich Post Office. Finance
Minister Johannes von Miquel was promoted to vice-president of the Prussian
Ministry of State, with instructions to steer a 'more Prussian' course in internal
affairs; Admiral Alfred Tirpitz, with his plan to build a 'giant fleet', enthusiastically supported by Wilhelm II, took Hollmann's place as navy secretary. Bülow,
meanwhile, prepared himself – at first still as secretary of state at the Foreign
Office – to take over the Reich chancellorship, a post in which he himself had
said that he would act as the 'executive tool' of the Kaiser and 'so to speak his
political Chief of Staff'. With that, 'personal rule – in the good sense – would
really begin'.[174] If, as was said of Hohenlohe, the 'historical figure' he cut in
German history was his main motivation, it is certainly clear that in the summer of 1896, in his narrow-minded obsession with his personal reputation and
his constant search for a 'good' way of quitting his post, he shamefully gambled
away what little remained of the autonomy of the 'responsible government',
which he had taken over from the upright General von Caprivi barely two years
earlier. In the last four years of Prince Hohenlohe's period in office the German
Reich chancellor was downgraded to the 'straw doll of the crown'.

Hohenlohe's pathetic spinelessness towards the Kaiser is all the more shocking
because he was repeatedly reminded by old friends of the principles at stake in
the conflict with the monarch. The Bavarian public servant, Hohenlohe's former
colleague Otto Freiherr von Völderndorff-Waradein, writing to the Prince in
June 1897, fully acknowledged that the position of Reich chancellor as defined
by Bismarck's Reich constitution had been far beyond the powers of any man
and that it needed to be reduced, perhaps by delegating Prussian internal affairs
to a reliable deputy. But he pointed out that 'it is quite a different matter when
the Kaiser wants to be his own Reich chancellor. That is of course even more
beyond the powers of any man and would be sheer self-deception. For in practice
decisions would be taken only by irresponsible secondary figures, who usually
have only a one-sided knowledge and opinion of the real state of affairs, and
who would make their views seem plausible to the monarch.' Völderndorff
went on to say that he would deeply regret it if Prince Hohenlohe ended his
'glorious' life as a 'delivery boy', and advised him to resign from all his offices.
'The elections to the next Reichstag will most certainly turn out very badly', he
added as a further reason for resignation.[175] Another old friend, Léon Dacheux,
the Superior of the great seminary at Strassburg, wrote to Hohenlohe saying that
in his eyes what was going on in Berlin was a constitutional conflict between the
system of absolutism and a nineteenth-, almost twentieth-century system. 'But

the system of Louis XIV, which has continued under the successors of Frederick the Great, no longer accords with the ideas of our own times.' A *coup d'état* such as that carried out by Louis Napoleon on 2 December 1851 could of course be attempted, but it would not provide a lasting solution; on the contrary, a violent measure of that kind would be the death-blow for the Hohenzollern monarchy. 'I like to believe that the German people will not put up barricades, but an abyss will open between the people and the throne, at least in the western provinces, and the bourgeoisie and the lower classes, especially in the Rhineland towns, will become increasingly republican, and the love which the nation has for the monarchy will be struck dead.'[176] A few weeks later Abbé Dacheux expressed regret that Hohenlohe had not resigned with Marschall and Boetticher. The honourable name of the Prince was too good to serve as camouflage for the introduction of 'more compliant' people 'who lend themselves to anything that the monarch demands, according to his own impulses or the influence of others'. With unerring accuracy the wise old priest warned that the Chancellor would achieve nothing by giving in. 'You are being demolished bit by bit.'[177]

# CHAPTER TWENTY-EIGHT

# Personal Monarchy: Wilhelm II at the summit of his power

## THE FACE OF PERSONAL MONARCHY

HAVING got off relatively lightly with the dismissal of War Minister Bronsart von Schellendorf – the much-feared major government crisis had not after all materialised – Kaiser Wilhelm II had reached the zenith of his personal power, objectively speaking. And yet he was clearly far from satisfied. He showed less restraint than ever in giving vent to his autocratic, indeed aggressive claims to power in defiance of the Reich and Prussian government, the Reichstag and the overwhelming majority of the German people, whose attitude towards him was becoming increasingly critical. Every restriction placed on his power irritated him: he wanted to be in command and expected unconditional obedience. 'I know no constitution, I know only what I want', he exclaimed.[1] 'All of you know nothing', he asserted peremptorily to his admirals. 'I alone know something, I alone decide!'[2] Count August Eulenburg, the Oberhofmarschall, commented at the beginning of 1897 that the links between the court and the Wilhelmstrasse were 'in effect completely severed', and 'if any attempt is made to resume contact sparks fly every time, if there is not an actual explosion'.[3] It was becoming clear to those in high places who had dealings with him that 'the Kaiser could not get accustomed to the idea that his power was restricted by the Reichstag. The idea of ruling without the Reichstag never left his mind, and was encouraged by one sector of his entourage.'[4] The Reich Chancellor tried in vain to persuade the Kaiser that his power was limited by the constitution. The longstanding rights which he had inherited as king of Prussia still held good, Prince Hohenlohe acknowledged, 'in so far as the Prussian constitution had not placed limits on them. [But] in the Reich the Kaiser had only the rights which the Reich constitution accorded to him.' To this Wilhelm retorted that 'he did not care about public opinion. He knew that he was not loved and that people criticised him; but that did not deter him . . . The South German democratic states did not trouble him. He had 18 army corps and was quite able to deal with the South Germans.'[5] In May 1897 the British ambassador reported to London with growing anxiety on the unrest that was taking hold in Germany. He commented that the parliamentary debates on the laws on *lèse-majesté* and the reactionary law of association, the backstage intrigues at court seeking to influence the government's policies, and not least the manner in which the Kaiser repeatedly dealt out public insults to the Reichstag, the Social Democrats, the pro-Bismarck movement and even the Conservatives, had caused a gulf of mistrust to open up between Wilhelm II and the German people.[6]

Wilhelm's aggressiveness can be partly explained by the fact that he had been forced to put off until mid-1897 the dismissal of the 'loathed' and 'detested' Marschall, the Foreign Secretary, and likewise that of the Secretary for the Interior, Boetticher, of whom he had grown tired. Marschall's decision to 'go public' − in the winter of 1896–7 he appeared as chief prosecution witness in the case against Police Commissioner Eugen von Tausch, the police agent Lützow and the journalist Leckert, in the course of which highly compromising information about Ernst Günther and the Kotze affair, the Miss Love scandal, Mirbach's dishonest activities over church subscriptions and underhand machinations by Waldersee came to light − was the last straw.[7] In October 1896 Wilhelm exclaimed bitterly: 'I cannot stand Marschall any longer!'; his patience was at an end, regardless of what further parliamentary successes the Foreign Secretary might achieve.[8] While the court was hunting at Springe in December he telegraphed to the Reich Chancellor stating that he must get rid of Marschall and added, tellingly, that 'his entire entourage was of the same opinion'. At the beginning of 1897 Waldersee commented that 'everyone in the Kaiser's personal entourage including Hahnke, who has returned from leave', was against keeping Marschall and that they had 'repeatedly said so'. When an unsolicited report of some kind arrived from South Germany, sharply criticising 'Marschall's tactlessness and arrogance', Wilhelm declared: 'I see it is quite impossible for me to work with these South German ministers, they do not understand me, I shall find myself some North Germans or Old Prussians again; I shall get rid of the other lot by spring at the latest.'[9] He wrote angrily to his 'dearest Phili' complaining that in Berlin 'as usual people constantly invent things, slander, criticise etc. but above all refuse to obey orders. In the Ministry, as Boetticher recently put it, showing how well he knows his own faults, everyone "muddles along" calmly, except that rage and fury against Marschall has quite taken hold among his colleagues and has united them firmly against him. They will thank me if they live to see the day when that d . . . d South German vanishes from the scene.'[10]

The Kaiser reacted angrily to every flicker of independent spirit from the Reich Chancellor. It was only half in jest that he remarked reproachfully in October 1897, as Hohenlohe reported to his son in some surprise, that the old Chancellor 'had tyrannised him!'[11] Several times Wilhelm complained of the Chancellor's habit of accepting the 'orders' of his Kaiser only to question them again subsequently. 'My old uncle is dear and kind as always, but more and more reluctant to keep any promise he has made to me. In the last few months there have been several more flagrant instances when I had arranged what was to happen verbally and sometimes even in writing, only to be most kindly informed in those well-known little *billets doux* that to his very great regret what we had *agreed* was quite out of the question. The worthy gentleman calls the *orders* of his King and Master *agreements*! Well, I shall let things go on as they are until the spring, but then, dear Phili, even if you fling yourself on your knees before me, too bad! Then there must be a clean sweep, or we shall be ruined! Morally and physically! I shall not be able to bear it any longer by then!'[12]

The sharp orders which Wilhelm fired off at the Chancellor in tones of military command are probably without equal in the history of European monarchy. The flavour of these dispatches, letters, marginal notes and speeches is exemplified by an open telegram to Hohenlohe of 4 January 1897, in which the Kaiser rejected his advice not to respond to an item in an insignificant local newspaper concerning his attitude to duelling. It reads: 'What the *public* think or do not think of me is quite immaterial. The report ... will *confuse the army* and other *decent people*. The *démenti* is therefore to be issued immediately. As we know from famous examples, publicity is of course most salutary, and I have as much right to it as my subjects. My answer. W.'[13] The Kaiser's attitude to duels had already given rise to a brusque telegram from the Neues Palais a few weeks earlier. 'I have seen in the press that the Reichstag intends to use an interpellation to criticise and challenge My right to grant pardon in cases of duels', Wilhelm telegraphed to the Chancellor. That was, he said, 'a piece of shamelessness which represents a direct attack on My personal rights and privileges. On no account will I allow this. In the event that they do have such an intention, therefore, there must be immediate talks with the members of the Reichstag to make it clear to them that this interpellation must be stopped. If the Reichstag should nevertheless insist on bringing in the interpellation, I would regard this as a direct attack on My Person and the crown, whose constitutional rights I have to defend, and I would respond to this attack immediately by dissolving the Reichstag. Wilhelm I. R.'[14] In similar tones Wilhelm denounced the *Kölnische Zeitung*, of which the Foreign Office often made use for its own diplomatic purposes and which, according to the Kaiser, 'in spite of all warnings, admonitions etc.', had not only 'had the effrontery' to publish articles 'insulting to my adjutant-generals and a

Commanding General of my army [i.e. Waldersee], but had furthermore instituted direct personal attacks on Adjutant-General von Hahnke again. I therefore command that the offices of this newspaper should immediately be barred by the Foreign Office until further orders from me, and that all authorities in the country should be instructed not to give the paper any further news or to receive any of its representatives. Anyone disobeying this command can regard himself as dismissed from my service.'[15] In August 1897 the Kaiser was still raging against the 'nonsense in the press', which was the work of 'the remnant of the men who used to cause mayhem in the Foreign Office' – in this case he meant Holstein – and demanded that this 'stop immediately and the press must be given orders to that effect!'[16] When President of the Reichstag Count Ballestrem presumed to reprimand Prussian Minister of Trade Ludwig Brefeld the Kaiser sent a thunderous telegram to the Chancellor declaring peremptorily that 'he has no right to reprimand one of My ministers and I will not have it, once and for all. He should be told this. Brefeld is to be praised for speaking so well in favour of the bill.'[17]

In the summer of 1898 Wilhelm caused much bad blood by sending an offensive telegram *en clair* in response to a petition from the Count Regent Ernst of Lippe-Biesterfeld that the commanding officer of the troops stationed in Detmold should accord him and his family the honours customarily paid to a ruling prince. 'Your letter received', the Kaiser wired back. 'Commanding General's orders are as approved by me after consultation. The regent gets what is due to a regent, nothing more. Furthermore I wish it to be understood once and for all that I will not tolerate the tone in which you thought fit to write to me. W. R.'[18] Hohenlohe complained that the Kaiser was still obsessed with the idea of a tribunal of princes to settle these succession disputes, consisting of three sovereigns on each side with him, the Kaiser, holding the casting vote as chairman. 'Naturally no German sovereign would agree to that', he commented.[19] The stir which this episode caused among the public, who did not always fully understand the esoteric subtleties of these princely squabbles, was great and did nothing to improve the standing of the monarchy.[20] The 'state-supporting' newspapers warned that the German Reich, united by blood, iron and tears, would fall apart if the dignity and rights of the federal princes were not upheld; the opposition press, on the other hand, made little attempt to hide its glee at the imperial gift to particularists, republicans and socialists.[21] Public opinion was scarcely less surprised and affronted by the Kaiser's telegram to Hinzpeter of 1899, in which he compared himself with the Great Elector and declared that 'just as with my ancestor, there is in me an indomitable will to follow the path which I have recognised as right, regardless of all opposition, without wavering. Wilhelm I. R.'[22]

In view of the increasing criticism directed at him from all sides it is under-standable that Wilhelm II took refuge in the support of the Liebenberg circle around Philipp Eulenburg, in which he was idolised, as well as of the trusted members of his (predominantly military) entourage and of the army, suppos-edly still loyal to him. In a revealing speech to the regiments of the imperial bodyguard – the First Guards Regiment of Foot, the Gardes-du-Corps and the Hussar Body Guards – on the tenth anniversary of his accession in June 1898, he said in tones of self-pity: 'Seldom, indeed, has a time of such trouble passed over the head of a successor to a throne, who had to see his grandfather and his father die within so short a time. The crown was burdened with heavy anxieties. On all sides men doubted me; on all sides I encountered misconceptions. Only in *one* quarter was there confidence and belief in me, and that was in the army. And supported by it, and relying upon our God as of old, I undertook my heavy office, knowing well that the army was the main support of my country, the main pillar of the Prussian throne, to which God's decree had called me.'[23]

Like a feudal lord 'bound by common bonds of loyalty' to his army and navy, albeit on the threshold of the twentieth century, Kaiser Wilhelm tried to shield them from all political criticism. When the Chancellor warned him in November 1897 that the speech he was about to make at the swearing-in of naval recruits at Kiel would be read with close attention in St Petersburg and in Paris, where people would be on the look-out for grounds for suspicion of his foreign policy, the Supreme War Lord snarled back at him insultingly that 'speeches at swearings-in of recruits are *never* political in content, for politics have no place in either army or navy, and therefore do not concern Paris or Petersburg in the least. As I cannot but suppose that Y[our] H[ighness] was prompted by someone else to write the final passage, I would ask Y.H. to deliver the appropriate reprimand from Your sovereign and Kaiser in the clearest possible terms to the gentleman in question. Such promptings are highly improper and I refuse once and for all to tolerate them.'[24] Prince Hohenlohe courageously replied that as principal adviser to the Kaiser he had felt it his duty to draw his sovereign's attention to the fact that his speeches would attract malevolent attention abroad; he had required no prompting to recognise this danger.[25]

If the Kaiser's offensively peremptory tone in dealing with the constitutional organs of government was bad enough, his aggressive tendencies were even more noticeable in his comments on the elected representatives of the people. At the beginning of 1897 he learned that the seventy-year-old Social Democrat Wilhelm Liebknecht had made a 'fiery speech' in Holland, and saw it as a 'glaring confirmation' of the necessity of suppressing the workers' movement by military means. He ordered the Reich Chancellor to submit proposals as to 'what can be done against active members of the Reichstag who preach revolution abroad during the parliamentary session'.[26] A few weeks later, in a speech to the Brandenburg provincial diet which aroused indignation throughout the country, he again called for a '*fight against revolution*, with every means at our command'. The Social Democratic Party, which dared to 'attack the foundations of the state, which rebels against religion, and which does not even spare the person of the All-Highest sovereign, must be crushed. I shall rejoice to know that every man's hand is in mine, be he workman, prince or sovereign, if only I have his help in this conflict! . . . Then we shall work in the right spirit, and will not desist in the struggle to free our country from this malady [in fact he described the workers' movement as a "plague"[27]], which is invading not only our people but also our family life, and, above all, is striving to shake the position of woman, the most sacred thing that we Germans know. I hope, therefore, to see my Brandenburgers rally round me if the fiery signal should be raised.'[28]

In April 1897, after the Reichstag had rejected the greater part of the naval estimates, Kaiser Wilhelm sent an ill-advised letter to his brother Heinrich, which the latter read out to the crew of his cruiser. 'I deeply regret', the Kaiser wrote, 'that I cannot place a better ship at your disposal for the celebrations [of the Diamond Jubilee of Queen Victoria in London] than the *König Wilhelm*, while other nations will put on a splendid show with their proud battleships. This is the sad consequence of the behaviour of those unpatriotic people who succeeded in preventing the provision of the most badly needed ships. But I shall not rest until I have brought My navy up to the same level as the army.'[29] According to other accounts the Kaiser described the Reichstag deputies as 'scoundrels without a fatherland' or 'rogues'. At a crisis meeting of the Ministry of State Prince Hohenlohe was asked to send the Kaiser newspaper extracts showing the effect of his letter and to request permission to issue a *démenti*, since otherwise an interpellation in the Reichstag on the Kaiser's personal rule was to be feared. 'It is a very unpleasant business', the Chancellor commented. He was relieved to hear that the leader of the Centre Party was prepared to postpone the interpellation in view of the mood abroad.[30]

The Kaiser, who was staying with his friend Emil Görtz at Schlitz in the Vogelsberg, was of course adamant that there should be no *démenti*. Kiderlen-Wächter, who had gone with the Kaiser as representative of the Foreign Office, reported to the Reich Chancellor that at the first mention of a possible interpellation 'His Majesty flared up: what He and his brother wrote to each other was no one else's business, least of all the Reichstag's; that was the only answer the government should give. After the initial storm had died down I told His Majesty that I was sure Your Highness would give the Reichstag the answer His Majesty wished, but that a negative answer from the government would not prevent the Reichstag from indulging in remarks that would inevitably have a bad effect both at home and abroad.' The Kaiser had certainly welcomed the news given him by Kiderlen that Hohenlohe was negotiating with the Centre with a view to preventing the interpellation. But when Kiderlen 'went on to say that all kinds of different versions [of the Kaiser's letter] were circulating and that certain expressions in particular (I cited "scoundrels without a fatherland") had caused bad blood, and that it was therefore thought desirable at least to be able to deny that these expressions had been used, His Majesty reverted to the claim that the letter was a private matter between Him and his brother. When I interjected that the letter had acquired a different character because of the publicity given it by Prince Heinrich, His Majesty refused to accept this but simply went on repeating that He could write what He wished to his brother.' Summing up his discussion with the Kaiser Kiderlen concluded 'that His Majesty realises how inopportune the letter was, but will not admit it. Nor have I any doubt that the strong expressions are authentic; for when I cited them His Majesty was visibly very embarrassed.'[31]

Even before Kiderlen's report arrived in Berlin the Reich Chancellor received an open telegram from the Kaiser which provided clear confirmation of Kiderlen's account. 'Yr Highness's letter and enclosures received. I was already familiar with the latter. Making private expressions of opinion subjects for discussion in the press is somewhat reminiscent of the beginning of the Convention; possible interpellations and debates are even more so; it betrays a determination on the part of parliament to interfere in personal affairs, which has never arisen except in revolutionary times . . . I do not care in the slightest what the press writes or does not write about me. But I will not allow any interference in my personal affairs. It is a good thing that the proposed demand was turned down: if it had come to an interpellation I would have responded with dissolution. There must be no *démenti*. Wilhelm I. R.'[32] The unbridgeable gulf which had opened up between the monarch on the one side, and the constitution as understood by the Reich government and the parliament on the other, is vividly illustrated by the note which Hohenlohe made after receiving the Kaiser's telegram: 'This is not a question of private expressions of opinion but of an insult to the Reichstag. The private expression of opinion loses this character when it is read out *officially* to the crew of an imperial warship by an admiral. The dissolution of the Reichstag would not protect Prince Heinrich from a libel suit. If I were a member of the Reichstag I would start legal proceedings against H.R.H. [Prince Heinrich]. § 24 of the Reich constitution. For the dissolution of the Reichstag during the parliamentary term a resolution of the Bundesrat with the consent of the Kaiser is required.'[33]

The loudest outcry, however, was reserved for Wilhelm II's remark in his Brandenburg speech of 26 February 1897 that in comparison with his grandfather,

42. Wilhelm Imperator Rex: the Kaiser at the height of his personal power

who would have been canonised in the Middle Ages, Bismarck and Moltke had been nothing but 'lackeys and pygmies', who had the honour of carrying out the ideas of 'Kaiser Wilhelm the Great'.[34] As soon as the speech was over, worried Flügeladjutanten hurried from chair to chair, asking the guests not to mention the 'salient parts' of the speech.[35] Although this initially prevented the worst expressions from becoming public knowledge, supporters of the monarchy were deeply alarmed by them. Holstein quoted the remark of a prominent

Conservative to the effect that the Kaiser could have given Bismarck whatever names he liked, 'but to call him a pygmy – No! he *must* be wrong in the head.'[36] The Prussian envoy in Munich, Count Monts, reported with consternation on the mood in Bavaria: 'Our enemies here find it scarcely necessary . . . to hide their delight any longer over the exalted orator, who really is no longer responsible for his actions. The nationalist-minded people here are like a flock of frightened chickens. The average cultured South German politician, even the clerical, is indignant at the falsification of history so beloved by His Majesty, and at his description of Moltke and Bismarck as minions of the illustrious sovereign.' The monarchy itself was undermining 'all monarchical convictions . . . from above', the envoy warned, and 'the only patch of dry ground which the representative of the Reich still has to stand on in Bavaria . . . is shrinking fast. Another flood like the torrent of words from Brandenburg will wash it away completely.'[37] Utterly discouraged, Monts wrote to Philipp Eulenburg commenting that 'the mood in the west and south of Germany is deplorable. Our numerous enemies are jubilant, and are quietly preparing for the disintegration of the Reich. Our friends are disgusted with the Kaiser. The bitterness goes deeper than ever before . . . Many are saying secretly that H.M. is insane; already there are hints to this effect in the press . . . What I think of H.M. I dare not even say, but I fear that he is completely finished now, here in the south. Perhaps the masses will still shout hurrah during the manoeuvres, but the hearts of the patriotic middle classes are now surely lost to him for ever . . . Does His Majesty know all this, and that his vague romantic ideas are completely at variance with the mood of the nation? The great capital which he inherited from Wilhelm I is dwindling away all the time, even the most loyal, most monarchically minded men are losing faith in everything that was most sacred to them, and terrifying prospects are opening up.'[38]

In the Reichstag, as was to be expected, criticism of the Kaiser in the spring of 1897 was the strongest yet heard. In mid-March Julius Bachem, the editor of the Catholic *Kölnische Volkszeitung*, suggested to the leaders of the Centre Party that they should use the parliamentary debate on the naval estimates as an opportunity to protest against Wilhelm II's personal rule. 'Everyone now realises that the Kaiser's personality and intervention lie at the root of our present crisis', he wrote. 'Someone in the Reichstag should say very plainly indeed how perturbed the people are at this excess of imperial initiative; how urgently they desire that the monarch take more notice of the realities of political life . . . In a word: a most loyal but earnest declaration should be directed at the Kaiser . . . The speech would be greeted by the people as an act of deliverance . . . When similar situations arose in England and Holland, men raised their voices in determined and glorious protest. Why should not that happen here?'[39] As the Centre Party rejected this suggestion on the grounds that such an action would only strengthen the Kaiser's prejudice against the Catholics, it was left to the leader of the Left Liberal Party, Eugen Richter, to make an impressive speech pillorying the system of Personal Monarchy. On 18 May 1897 in the Reichstag this democrat of the old school put into words exactly what millions of people in the country, right up to the highest echelons of the civil and military administration, were feeling. 'Where today can we find a unified, purposeful will, which is not affected by sudden impulses, but is able to pursue its goal steadily, with prudence and good sense? Where are the ministers? Wherever you look there are only compliant courtiers who agree with every opinion from above, promoted bureaucrats, dashing Hussars turned politician, lackeys, but in the conventional sense of the word. The [Free Conservative] Deputy von Kardorff has spoken of the decline of monarchical feeling since the death of Kaiser Friedrich. In Germany the monarchical system can expect to last for a long time, because the monarchy is bound up with the evolution of the nation itself. It is all the more regrettable that the stock of monarchical feeling is being used up in a way which I should not have thought possible ten years ago, and not as a result of Social Democratic agitation, no – but as a result of events which are beyond the reach of parliamentary discussion, events which provoke criticism, not only among ordinary citizens but also deep within the civil service and the officer corps. Germany is a monarchical, constitutional country, but although it may still be possible to rule Russia according to the principles of *sic volo sic jubeo* or *regis voluntas suprema lex*, the German people will not allow themselves to be ruled like that for long.' Richter's remarks were greeted with a storm of applause both from the deputies and from the public galleries.[40] 'The speech created a huge sensation and unfortunately received widespread enthusiastic applause', Waldersee noted. Richter had 'torn the whole government apart in a way that had never been done before . . . Of course the main target of the attacks was the Kaiser.'[41] As the 'wretched' Boetticher had not been able to summon up the words to repudiate Richter's 'insults', the 'highly incensed' and 'embittered' Kaiser demanded his immediate resignation.[42]

## THE KAISER AND WALDERSEE'S *COUP D'ETAT* PLANS

It is not surprising that, faced with this situation and this atmosphere, Wilhelm should again have toyed with the idea of freeing himself from the democratically elected Reichstag by means of forcible constitutional change. Already in November 1896 the newly appointed War Minister, General von Gossler, had gone to the Reichstag with the Kaiser's instructions, as he told Boetticher, 'to provoke a conflict'.[43] The Saarland industrialist and Free Conservative Reichstag deputy

Karl Ferdinand Freiherr von Stumm-Halberg was likewise given 'orders' 'in a very heated manner' by Wilhelm while walking with him in the Tiergarten, to go to the Reichstag and say that 'if the Navy Bill were not accepted, the Kaiser would cause a great rumpus [and] kick the ministers out'.[44] He had other representatives such as the Prince zu Wied, the Conservative Party leader Otto Freiherr von Manteuffel and the National Liberal deputy Friedrich Hammacher sounded out in the spring of 1897 as to what conditions the former Kartell parties would set in exchange for their support for a *coup d'état* policy and a naval expansion programme.[45] 'Never before have we been threatened so openly with a *coup d'état*', observed a member of the Centre Party.[46] At the end of March 1897 the Reich Chancellor recorded his impressions after a visit to the Schloss, noting that it was 'evident that the Kaiser is under the influence of men who tell him that he can inaugurate a great era of conflict, change the Reich constitution, get rid of universal suffrage and build countless cruisers'.[47] But who were these people who were pressing for a *coup d'état*, and how seriously should we take Wilhelm's threats to use force against the Reichstag?

In his immediate entourage influential people like Admiral von Senden and Adjutant-General von Plessen spoke out in favour of repression of the workers' movement and abolition of the Reichstag.[48] Wilhelm's brother-in-law Hereditary Prince Bernhard of Saxe-Meiningen, the Commanding General at Breslau, described the creation of 'a protective barrier against the socialist threat' as the most urgent task of domestic policy. The ordinary German was 'a narrow-minded brute totally lacking in political instinct' who in his 'pettifoggery and dullness' had committed the enormous mistake of putting 'parliamentary decisions into the horny hands of the stupidest, worst and vilest elements', that is to say 'those who are nothing, have nothing, know nothing and can do nothing.' 'Socialism is nothing more than the instinctive hatred of the poor and stupid for the rich and clever', he declared. 'Such crack-brained, grotesque ideas could only appear and gain influence among people as politically stupid as the Germans!' The chief failing of those in power, in the eyes of this royal Prince and General, was 'that they did not get on with it a long time ago, without worrying about existing laws on paper, and do what the public good requires, i.e. send the socialists about their business'. 'Why does intelligence and efficiency allow itself to be ruled by stupidity and madness?', he angrily demanded.[49]

Apart from these influences at court it was demonstrably Waldersee, above all, who advised the Kaiser to adopt a *coup d'état* policy – albeit in the belief that Wilhelm would never dare resort to a breach of the constitution. As early as 1895, as commanding general in what was then the Prussian port and industrial city of Altona, Waldersee had had occasion to discuss the 'totally disorganised state of affairs' with Conservative members of the Reichstag as well as with the former War Minister Verdy, who had contacts in liberal financial and academic circles. All were agreed that 'momentous decisions' would soon have to be faced and that Waldersee, and not Hohenlohe, was the right chancellor for this task. 'The gentlemen who talk of a *coup d'état* and say that things cannot go on as they are do not realise that the Kaiser is still very far from believing that momentous decisions need to be taken, and especially far from recognising that he himself is principally to blame for the situation in which we find ourselves.' Since the Kaiser 'would never stop dabbling in politics himself and becoming actively involved', Waldersee observed, he himself had no desire to become Reich chancellor; nor was the Kaiser intending to offer him the post.[50] One of Waldersee's sources who spent much time at court confirmed the General's view that Wilhelm II was not planning to carry out a *coup d'état*. 'Believe me, however resolutely he speaks about it, if things really become serious with the Social Democrats he will never allow shooting!'[51]

In the course of 1895 Waldersee's views on the Kaiser began to lose some of their earlier severity. The distinctions and attentions he received – promotion to colonel-general with the rank of field marshal, the Order of the Black Eagle and two ostentatious visits to him at Altona by the Kaiser – helped soften his criticism. He now laid much more blame on bad advisers around the monarch and recorded, after Wilhelm's visit on 16 December 1895, that he had the impression 'that the Kaiser has at last realised that he has been greatly deceived by swindlers and malicious busybodies'. Waldersee was now ready to put past grievances behind him and believed for a time that he was 'back on the old footing with the Kaiser again'.[52] The reasons for the change in the tone of the General's comments, however, are to be found in his own situation in life rather than in any change in the Kaiser's political views. Illness, together with social and financial problems, induced a certain melancholy in Waldersee. He was increasingly preoccupied with his imminent retirement from the army, with his withdrawal from politics and society and with thoughts of his death, which he supposed was now near. In the winter of 1896–7 he faced a serious crisis when Marschall revealed the contacts he had had with Police Commissioner von Tausch and other dubious individuals. In this painful situation the General was only too well aware of how dependent he was on the protection of the Kaiser. On the occasion of 27 January 1897, Wilhelm's thirty-eighth birthday, he wrote in his diary: 'When I look back over the past year in the Kaiser's life, I have reason only to be grateful; he has been kind and affectionate towards me every time we have met. God grant that he remain consistent now and protect me from the intrigues of Marschall and his people.'[53] Three weeks later he heard that 'darker and darker clouds' were gathering over his 'affair', and noted that 'in the end everything will depend on whether the Kaiser remains firm'.[54] Through his improved relationship with

Wilhelm, however, Waldersee regained his influence over him and thereby over the course of political events. And this, as we shall shortly see, very nearly led to violent consequences. Shooting down workmen, violation of the constitution, civil war, dissolution of the German Reich and foreign war − all came under discussion.

Waldersee thought he detected hopeful signs of a change in the Kaiser's attitude at the time of the unveiling of the memorial to Wilhelm I at Kiel on 24 November 1896. He found Wilhelm 'in good spirits', but 'very irritated with Bismarck', who had recently betrayed the secret of the Reinsurance Treaty with Russia in the *Hamburger Nachrichten*. In his annoyance, in the presence of hundreds of young officers the Kaiser declared that 'very highly placed people' had committed 'high treason against him and the nation'.[55] On this occasion Waldersee noted that the Kaiser considered universal suffrage a misfortune, and was 'preoccupied with the question of what should take its place. I made no bones about saying "Your Majesty is strong enough to undertake anything; only it must be tackled with vigour."'[56] The impressively well-organised strike of 18,000 dock workers in the Hamburg area, which had begun in the autumn of 1896 and was to last for several months, did not fail to have an effect on Wilhelm. During his second visit to Waldersee at Altona the Kaiser demanded 'energetic action' against the strikers, and his parting words to the General at the station were 'Just deal firmly with it, and there is no need to ask permission.' The Commanding General had to explain to the Kaiser that he could not lawfully intervene as long as the workers did not disturb the peace. 'We need laws against agitation etc.', which the present Reichstag would never approve, he complained.[57] Privately he noted that 'using armed force against hungry workers is really no pleasure. There is no question of really rebellious movements such as the Kaiser seems to think we are facing . . . If they should happen I would suppress them with the utmost severity.'[58]

Not only the Hamburg strike but also what seemed to be an increasingly hopeless parliamentary situation, which the Reichstag elections, due in the summer of 1898, would only make worse, strengthened Waldersee in his conviction that 'it is now high time for us to take big decisions'. He calculated that after the new elections the composition of the Reichstag would render the country virtually ungovernable. The Conservatives would lose a considerable number of votes to the Agrarian League and the Anti-Semites, the National Liberals would lose most of their seats to the progressive parties, the Centre, which was becoming increasingly democratic, would get rid of 'its few good elements', and the Social Democrats, who would win votes from all parties, could easily double their vote. 'How can anyone govern with that?', the General wondered despondently. 'Why shut one's eyes to it! If energetic action is not taken soon, the German Reich may be in a very parlous state in a few years. If anything needs to be done, then the sooner it is done, the better; any delay is harmful.'[59]

On 22 January 1897, bypassing the Reich and Prussian governments, Waldersee sent the Kaiser a memorandum which demanded a preventive war against the workers' movement as soon as possible.[60] He drew attention to the fact that the 'party of revolution' was steadily gaining ground and 'while carefully avoiding any disturbance or rebellion, eventually it will choose the moment to pit its strength against that of the state'.[61] 'But if the battle is inevitable', he went on to infer, with military logic, 'the state has nothing to gain by waiting', for 'the longer the revolutionary party is allowed to develop its organisation, the stronger it will get; the further it spreads, the more difficult the battle will be and the more harmful its consequences for the people'.[62] As always, it was for the Kaiser to decide on the future of the Reich. 'I cannot wait to hear what the Kaiser will say about it', Waldersee wrote after delivering the memorandum. 'I think he will do nothing, for if he wants to do anything he will have to appoint new ministers and embark on the great struggle with a clear vision.'[63]

When Waldersee went to Kiel on 30 January 1897 for the baptism of Prince Sigismund of Prussia (Prince Heinrich's son), Hahnke told him that the Kaiser had been 'very pleased' with the memorandum. 'As soon as the Kaiser saw me', Waldersee's diary continues, 'he shook my hand and said: I thank you very much for the memorandum; I am very glad that someone is at last telling the truth openly. I read it out at the recent meeting of the Ministry of State. You should have seen the gentlemen's faces: they looked as if they wished the earth would swallow them up.' This remark, loudly voiced over the lunch table, was heard by many of the guests and 'caused quite a sensation'. Even more significant was the 45-minute conversation between the two men which took place the same evening. In the course of it the Kaiser indicated to Waldersee that he did not want to take any action on the socialist question for the time being but that he was thinking of using it as an election slogan and was 'quite convinced that it would be necessary to tackle the matter firmly'. Wilhelm concluded by saying to Waldersee: 'I think the immediate future is very serious; if it becomes too hot for me, you must take your turn.' This, the General recorded, was the first time that the Kaiser had offered him (if only as a hint) the post of chancellor. Wilhelm then added: 'I know that you will do the job well if shooting becomes necessary.' On taking his leave Waldersee assured the Kaiser 'that if he wanted to make use of me for firm action, he would not be disappointed; but it must not be postponed for too long, or I would be too old', to which Wilhelm answered: 'Well, we shall see.' On the basis of this conversation and other impressions he received at Kiel, Waldersee became convinced 'that the Kaiser really intends to make me chancellor if certain circumstances arise. He is thoroughly dissatisfied with the attitude of Hohenlohe and the Ministry at the moment, and he lets them feel it too.'[64] The ministers would certainly complain that he was interfering in things which did not concern him; 'but they cannot very well do so knowing that the Kaiser was very pleased with my memorandum'.[65] A few days after the meeting at Kiel Waldersee stated with some confidence in a letter to Verdy that he thought 'the conviction has taken hold in the highest quarters that we cannot go on like this any longer; but I also know that from there to the point of resolving to take a decisive step a great deal of time may pass'.[66]

The Kaiser's Brandenburg speech on 26 February, in which he called for a 'fight against revolution, with all the means at our command', aroused universal fears that emergency laws against social democracy were about to be introduced. 'People in all the parties that make up the majority in the Reichstag, that is to say the anti-Reich parties, are terrified of the Kaiser taking energetic measures; there is a gloomy feeling that something bad is in the air', Waldersee recorded.[67] This was the moment when, as we have seen, the party leaders Stumm, Wied, Manteuffel and Hammacher were sent to the Reichstag by Wilhelm with threats of a *coup d'état*.[68] Nevertheless Waldersee was again doubtful of whether the Kaiser would find 'the courage to take a great decision'.[69] 'I am convinced', he wrote on 1 April 1897, 'that the Kaiser will do nothing.'[70] 'My general impression is that the Kaiser has not yet come to any firm decision, and as far as I am concerned, he is not thinking of appointing me [as Reich chancellor] at the moment. As he has become decidedly irresolute, I also think that if he closes the Reichstag soon and nothing very out of the ordinary happens, he will soon be distracted in his ideas by other impressions, journeys etc. and will simply leave everything as it is.'[71]

Only two weeks later Waldersee heard about the Kaiser's letter to Prince Heinrich describing the majority in the Reichstag as 'rogues' or 'scoundrels without a fatherland'. Although on the one hand the General was indignant at this latest gaffe − 'It really is a misfortune that the Kaiser lets himself be so carried away with fury', he wrote − on the other hand he could not help hoping that this 'powerful' aggravation of the situation might bring about the desired constitutional conflict. 'What will the Reichstag do?', he was eager to know. 'Possibly it will come to conflict very soon. Will not Hohenlohe go at once now? . . . But what an inheritance for his successor to take on!'[72] In the next few days 'powerful antagonism' towards the Kaiser made itself felt in the press, which in Waldersee's eyes indicated 'that the pace is quickening towards a crisis'.[73] The General was surprised, however, when the Centre Party decided to put up with the 'kick' from the Kaiser and take no action. 'The Kaiser must think . . . that he can trample on them at the moment', Waldersee commented.[74] Once again this gave him hope that Wilhelm would steel himself for the great coup against the Reichstag. He wondered 'whether the Kaiser will act soon or not until the autumn; at most he has until the autumn, but it would be better if he sent the Reichstag home soon . . . then appointed a new chancellor and gave him the time until November to prepare the really serious campaign'.[75]

How would Waldersee have acted if he had been appointed chancellor in the spring of 1897, which for a time seemed entirely possible? In his reply to the War Minister's request to the commanding generals to put forward their views on the handling of an internal crisis in case of need – a request which was 'obviously prompted by the memorandum I presented to the Kaiser', Waldersee believed – he demanded the abolition of universal suffrage for Reichstag elections, on the grounds that it had 'demonstrably' failed to prove its value. If the federal states did not *all* agree with this measure, Prussia would have to withdraw from the German Reich and re-create the Reich on a new basis.[76] (Bismarck had considered a similar *coup d'état* plan just before his dismissal, as we saw earlier.)[77] In conjunction with this internal policy of force, Waldersee was in favour of engineering a European war, in which Germany would not of course be involved at first. 'Such a war, which skilful diplomacy ought to be able to bring about, would be the best thing that could happen for us at this truly difficult time', he told Verdy, adding: 'I believe it would lead to better economic circumstances, a better internal situation and also better external affiliations . . . If matters should eventually reach a point where we had to intervene actively, we would bring such a powerful weight into the balance that it would be resolved in our favour.' 'The idea is morally questionable', the General admitted, 'but I think it is worth considering nevertheless. If we go on living as we have done hitherto, carelessly and without purpose, we shall slide, gradually at first, but soon much faster, down the slippery slope on which we find ourselves.'[78] Verdy agreed with his friend and expressed similar views. 'The ideal goal is still to strengthen the internal structure of our country on a healthy basis . . . and to reinforce the power of our position in external relations.' Domestic policy must be aimed at bringing about 'the collapse of the constitutional parliamentary institutions', 'which undermine all authority and reduce the state to the plaything of the parties; in the process both roots and branches must be cut away; both universal suffrage and freedom of the press etc. etc.' As far as foreign policy was concerned, the aim was 'to recover the prestige which we enjoyed after 1870'; this could be achieved only by the 'reunion' with Germany of the German provinces of the Habsburg empire, for which of course the support of Russia would be required. This would have to be purchased with the offer of Constantinople and of further Russian expansion in Asia.[79]

It was decisive for the future of Germany that the willingness to contemplate a *coup d'état* which Kaiser Wilhelm II had so clearly demonstrated in the first months of 1897 had meanwhile receded. Evidence of this is provided by the imperial marginalia on a letter from Eulenburg of 8 April, in which the Kaiser's friend referred to the soundings which Wilhelm had taken with Wied, Stumm and Manteuffel, news of which had reached his ears. 'Absolute lies!', the monarch scrawled in the margin in angry denial. 'I have never spoken to these men about it! Just as I have never mentioned the word *coup d'état* to the Prince [Hohenlohe]. The whole story is pure *fabrication*! I gave no such instructions and have received no answers.'[80] He telegraphed to Eulenburg *en clair* saying that 'not a syllable' of this information was true; but he was not surprised at it, 'since it is now considered good form, in order to cover up their own weakness and debility, for people to invent the most fabulous lies about me and spread them around. Wilhelm I. R.'[81] When he met Eulenburg in Vienna on 21 April the Kaiser gave his friend his word 'that He had *never* said a word either to Stumm or to Manteuffel or to Wied in the sense alleged, and had scarcely spoken to these gentlemen at all . . . If old Hohenlohe imagines that I am planning a *coup d'état*, he is playing a dishonest game too. He *knows* that I have no such intention . . . I perhaps spoke to him once in confidence about the possibility or impossibility of changing the electoral law − but I am sure you have done that too, we have *all* done that! To deduce a policy of force from that − that is bad faith! . . . I have only once spoken lately to the Grand Duke of Baden about the electoral law *in an academic sense*, without any ulterior motive, purely by chance.' The whole story of his *coup d'etat* plans had been invented by the men in the Wilhelmstrasse, who were operating 'a thoroughly *malicious* system' to further their own purposes 'at the *expense of their Kaiser*', Wilhelm claimed. Eulenburg's 'blood boiled' when his beloved Kaiser told him of this tissue of lies.[82]

It is by no means easy to unravel the tangle of conflicting sources on this critical episode. One is disinclined to take even Eulenburg's indignant protestations to Bülow and Holstein at face value, given the insouciance with which he had discussed the option of a *coup d'état* and all its consequences with the Kaiser in 1896, and had planned the appointment of either Waldersee or Bronsart as Reich chancellor in the event of just such a coup.[83] It seems probable, however, that the instructions given to Wied, Manteuffel and Stumm, of which Holstein had been told by Count Monts, who in turn had heard of them from the Conservative Party leader Heydebrand,[84] did not spring from any actual *coup d'état* plan but were intended chiefly as attempts to intimidate the Reichstag. Furthermore, in his purely 'academic' discussion of the question with the Reich Chancellor and the Grand Duke of Baden, the Kaiser's lively temper and the aggressive tone in which he customarily spoke of parliament and the opposition parties might easily have given rise to the false impression that he had serious intentions of embarking on a policy of force in violation of the constitution. Waldersee's often repeated view, shared by other members of the military, that the Kaiser would never give orders to shoot on his own initiative, rings all the more true because the General deeply deplored this attitude. It is at any rate clear that, although Wilhelm may from time to time have toyed with the idea of a *coup d'état*, under the influence of Waldersee, Senden and other officers, he had dropped the idea by mid-April 1897 at the latest. Instead he now pinned his hopes on the newly appointed statesmen Bülow and Tirpitz, with whose assistance he intended to pursue an exciting new foreign and naval policy. But at the same time, as far as domestic policy was concerned, he put his trust in the efficacy of a backward-looking monarchical ideology at the centre of which stood the grandfather whom he revered above everything, the heroic figure of the 'Heldenkaiser'.

## THE CULT OF 'KAISER WILHELM THE GREAT'

What was going on in Wilhelm II's mind when he insulted his principal advisers, spoke disparagingly in public about Bismarck and Moltke, criticised the Reichstag and the nation in the most violent terms and praised his ancestors, and above all his grandfather, to the skies? In response to the steadily rising democratic tide and the increasingly vociferous criticism both of the Kaiser himself and of his quasi-absolutist rule, he propagated an amalgam of dynastic ancestor-worship, falsification of history along militaristic and chauvinistic Prusso-German lines and Christian manichaeism – a monarchical ideology which can only be described as utterly inappropriate for a modern, multi-cultural industrial society with strong federalist features. What were Bavarians, Saxons, Württembergers, Badeners, Hessians, Guelphs, Hanseatic citizens, Alsatians, Poles and Danes to make of the Kaiser's speech of 26 February 1897, in which he said of his 'Royal Grandfather of most blessed memory' that there must be a special significance in the fact that God had 'selected' a Brandenburger as his 'instrument' in the creation of the German Reich? What will their feelings have been on reading the passages in the speech in which he declared that 'Wilhelm the Great' had prepared himself for his calling for years, 'with the great thoughts already fully formed in his mind, which were to enable him to bring the Reich into being once more. We see how he first of all raised an army of the hired peasant sons of his provinces, and constituted them into a powerful, splendidly equipped force. We see how, by means of his army, he succeeded gradually in acquiring predominant power in Germany and in raising Brandenburg–Prussia to the leading position. This having been done, the moment arrived for him to call upon the entire Fatherland to rally round him, and on the field of battle he united those who had been adversaries.' What were Prussian Protestants, let alone Catholics, Jews and atheists, to make of the declaration by their sovereign and principal bishop that Kaiser Wilhelm I, 'if [he] had lived in the Middle Ages . . . would have been canonised, and bands of pilgrims would have travelled from all lands to offer up prayers at his tomb'? Fortunately this was still the case, the hero's grandson asserted, adding that 'the door of his sepulchre stands open' and his loyal subjects could daily delight in 'seeing this splendid old man and his statues'.[85]

That such utterances were not a momentary aberration but articles of faith in a monarchical ideology dressed up as a religion is demonstrated by numerous other speeches which the young Kaiser made at the dedication of memorial churches or monuments to commemorate the hundredth birthday of 'Wilhelm the Great' – for instance on Mount Kyffhäuser in the Harz or at the Deutsches Eck in Koblenz. Even the birthday of his father, whom he scarcely ever mentioned otherwise, provided him with the opportunity to preach his dynastic-Christian cult to the army in 1896 and 1897.[86] The Protestant element of the ideology was also much in evidence in the speech which the Kaiser made at the swearing-in of recruits in Berlin on 18 November 1897, giving great offence both in Germany and abroad. 'He who is not a good Christian is neither a good man nor a Prussian soldier, and can under no circumstances perform what is required of a soldier in the Prussian army', he proclaimed. 'Your duty is not light; it demands of you self-discipline and self-denial, the two highest qualities of the Christian; also absolute obedience and submission to the will of your superiors . . . On you my glorious ancestors look down from heaven; on you the statues of the kings and above all the monument to the great Kaiser look down . . . Your duty now is to show your loyalty to Me and to defend our highest goods, whether against an enemy abroad or at home, to obey when I command, and to stand by Me.'[87] We have had too many opportunities to observe the real depth of Wilhelm II's veneration for his grandfather to doubt that such declamations reflected genuine feeling on his part. But one does not need to be a Machiavelli to recognise that these speeches were also motivated by a desire to manipulate his subjects' Christian beliefs and their patriotic vision of their history for his own benefit and that of the Hohenzollern monarchy. Lavish and expensive publications glorifying the 'Heldenkaiser' also appeared, aimed at bolstering the unsteady throne.[88] The memory of the old Kaiser, Wilhelm II believed, was 'the best way of collecting the parties which support the state together in a patriotic decision'.[89]

This aim came to the fore particularly strongly when in the autumn of 1896 Wilhelm demanded that a commemorative medal should be issued, 'as a Reich matter', on the occasion of the unveiling of the memorial on 22 March 1897, the hundredth birthday of his grandfather, to all members of the army and the navy and to every Prussian and Reich government official, and not only to those who were currently in active service but also to all those who had served under the old Kaiser. To no avail, Prince Hohenlohe drew the Kaiser's attention to the constitutional and financial objections to this idea.[90] In the German Reich orders and decorations were regarded, 'in accordance with the constitutional structure of the Reich, as flowing from the territorial sovereignty of the rulers of the individual states', he pointed out. This was the reason why there had been no orders or decorations emanating from the Reich itself. The Chancellor went on to point out what an enormous quantity of medals the Kaiser was proposing to distribute. 'Even if only the total number of *active* members of the German army and the Imperial Navy (607,105 persons) and the total number of *active* Prussian officials and Reich officials living in Prussia (460,648 persons) were taken into account, the number of recipients would amount to more than a million. The cost of a copper medal with an eyelet, loop and ribbon is approximately 3 marks 10 pfennigs; the total cost of production for a million recipients would thus exceed three million marks.' If in addition to this it were wished to confer the medal on the civil servants and members of the armed forces who had served under Wilhelm I, as the Kaiser demanded, the number of recipients would rise to between three and four million. The requisite sums could be made available from Reich resources only by legislation, the Chancellor emphasised, which would require a bill to be submitted to the Bundesrat and then to the Reichstag. Even if no problems arose in the Bundesrat − although both Bavaria and Württemberg had already voiced reservations − it was out of the question that the Reichstag would approve several million marks for the purpose. On the contrary, 'the discussion would be highly unpleasant and would in all probability end in a defeat for the government, which would be all the more painful because the opposition would be directed at a personal wish of Your Majesty'. Finally the Chancellor referred to the 'regrettable, but indubitable fact' that 'numerous members of the army become members of the Social Democratic Party again after their discharge', and that in the lower ranks of the civil service there were also elements hostile to the state, so that the danger could not be ruled out that 'these people might get up to mischief with the medals conferred upon them, throw them away or sell them'. For all these reasons, as principal adviser to the crown, Hohenlohe argued that the commemorative medal should be instituted as a Prussian decoration, and that it should be issued only to the actual participants in the ceremony of the unveiling of the memorial on 22 March. If the number of recipients could be limited to about 50,000, the requisite sum of 155,000 marks could be taken out of the 'Kaiserlicher Dispositionsfonds' − a solution already suggested by Posadowsky in October − 'thereby avoiding parliamentary involvement altogether'.[91]

The Kaiser's response to this well-reasoned report by the Reich Chancellor was to write a curt note on it saying 'No. My order stands. W.'[92] A telegraph message from Bückeburg followed: 'The celebration of the hundredth anniversary of the birthday of the first *German* Kaiser of a Reich of the *German* nation, from the *German* House of Hohenzollern, has quite a different significance for Germany and the whole world from that of the coronation of the King of Prussia in 1861. This is a unique phenomenon such as has never occurred in history before, and very strong emphasis must therefore be placed on it, particularly for the benefit of the subversive elements. For the ordinary soldier who has lived through this year and who wears the portrait of the great Kaiser on his breast, it will be a talisman against unpatriotic temptations when he leaves the army.'[93] The Kaiser returned to the charge in a further letter, in which he declared himself 'most painfully surprised' by the contents of the Chancellor's memorandum. 'Having announced my will on this matter at the meeting of the Ministry of State at Hubertusstock [in October], I had a conversation 4 weeks later with Herr von Bötticher in which I discussed all eventualities and procedures and gave him all the necessary instructions. As a result of this a model of the medal was submitted to Me, which I accepted after making minor alterations, and which is therefore already in preparation. The question of obtaining funds was also considered at that time, and I had occasion then to point out to Herr von Bötticher the impropriety of using the Allerhöchster Dispositionsfond, which is chiefly intended for the support of the poor, widows and orphans and for artistic purposes, to this end. That is quite out of the question for me! The Reichstag must therefore be approached and asked for the money. In order to keep the amount down as much as possible, however, I am willing to allow a limitation. As I have already personally informed the army and the navy that they are to receive such a medal, none of the armed forces can be excluded. All the more so because it is a question of commemorating the Supreme War Lord, the Supreme Campaign Commander and the creator of the Reich, the victor of three wars! For the civil service, on the other hand, it is not necessary, as they did not have such direct contact with the great Kaiser as My Army. I will therefore strike the 460,648 civil servants off the list; this is the equivalent of a sum of 1,428,009 marks. Subtract this from 3,000,000 marks, which leaves 1,571,991. This sum is surely not too high for the commemoration of My grandfather, in view of the enormous surpluses this year and the increase of the national wealth by 3 billion marks! Asking for this small sum in the Reichstag should be a real pleasure! If the Reichstag should be so miserable and unpatriotic as to refuse it, they can be sure of a getting a beating in the streets and they will lose the last remnant of the people's respect. It would be an honourable defeat for the government, which would do us credit in the eyes of all. Besides, the memory of the Kaiser is the best way of collecting the parties which support the state together in a patriotic decision. The Centre will take care not to be left sitting alone on a bench with Bebel and company again, opposing their *Old Sovereign*. The matter only needs arranging with a bit of tact and care.' Wilhelm indignantly rejected Hohenlohe's argument that Social Democrats among the soldiers would not treat the commemorative medal with respect. 'As for the implied accusation against the army and the attitude of its members that it produces Social Democrats *en masse*', he angrily declared, 'as supreme war lord I categorically repudiate it as a serious insult!' 'It is certainly an undeniable fact that many are Social Democrats when they are taken on. But the percentage of those converted by its grand ideals, its educational influence and the moral and religious invigoration which it provides, is – praise God! – great. – And even if there are bad apples here and there, the great majority of those discharged join veterans' associations and continue to behave in a patriotic spirit. If it came to a comparison between the army and the 460,000 civil servants as to which was the more utterly reliable in their views and in their loyalty to Kaiser and Reich, the army would certainly not come off worst.' As supreme war lord he had the indisputable right to confer medals on the army and the navy. 'If the sum should be refused I shall take care of the rest. Wilhelm I. R.'[94] At the beginning of the New Year the Kaiser was able to report to his best friend in Vienna that 'the question of the medals for 22 March is settled, as Miquel has most kindly placed unexpected revenue surpluses at my disposal, so that this affair can be dealt with on a *Prussian* footing.'[95]

The cult of Kaiser Wilhelm I was of course not only an expression of his genuine veneration for his beloved grandfather, nor was it only calculated political propaganda for the benefit of the increasingly threatened Hohenzollern monarchy. It was also in good measure a projection of the vision he cherished of his own role as ruler, and of his supposed historical mission, on to the revered, transcendental figures of his Hohenzollern ancestors. This manifested itself almost literally in the grand historical costumed festivities which he held in the Berlin Schloss and at which he himself, as was avidly reported in all the newspapers, appeared as the Great Elector or as Frederick the Great. For the hundredth birthday of his venerated grandfather in March 1897 it was inevitable that there would be a court ball in the costumes of a hundred years earlier. To the roll of drums, Wilhelm II processed from the Picture Gallery to the White Hall at the head of the Company of Life Guards and the Bodyguard of Gendarmerie and seated himself on the throne. The adjutant-generals and Flügeladjutanten then marched in, halting at the throne on the imperial command and presenting arms. Very much against her will, at the Kaiser's command 'the poor Kaiserin, . . . red-faced and with quivering lips', had to inspect the line-up of adjutants. Minuets, gavottes, waltzes and Ländler were danced to music of the period taken from the Royal Library. The result was a glittering picture of the

43. The Kaiser and his entourage dressed in the style of 1797, the year of his
grandfather's birth. The diminutive figure in a frock coat to the left of the
monarch is the painter Adolf von Menzel

last years of the eighteenth century re-created at the threshold of the twentieth,
a spectacle of magnificent uniforms, lavish costumes and rich colours exceeding
anything the participants had ever seen. One of them, the Flügeladjutant Count
Kuno von Moltke, commented to his friend Eulenburg that 'the darling [i.e.
Kaiser Wilhelm II] had too low a forehead, but otherwise he looked very good,
and happy', whereas Chief of the Naval Cabinet Freiherr von Senden-Bibran,
who had dressed up as an English pirate admiral in a narrow-shouldered coat
with his epaulettes askew and a piece of loose white cotton-wool on his head as
a wig, merely looked ridiculous.[96]

If this historical masquerade was greeted with astonishment by public opinion, the response to Ernst von Wildenbruch's allegorical drama 'Willehalm',
which received its first performance at a gala evening likewise in honour of
the hundredth birthday of Kaiser Wilhelm I, was one of sheer embarrassment,
especially since it was rumoured that whole sections of this piece of Germanic
hagiography, in which the 'enslaved German soul' was set free by the 'young
King's son Willehalm', had been partly written by Wilhelm II himself.[97] What
is undoubtedly true is that the final scene planned by Wildenbruch, in which
the heroic old Kaiser entered Valhalla, was cut out at the behest of Wilhelm
II and his artistically inclined Flügeladjutanten, Kuno Moltke and Georg von

Hülsen. Instead, on their orders, the play ended with the death of the old hero, while the 'soul of Germany' bent over the dead man and placed the consecrating kiss of all Germany on his forehead, to the sound of a funeral march. Although Moltke found the play 'profoundly serious and affecting' and praised Wildenbruch for producing a work worthy of the 'grief, not yet dulled, for the noble, beloved departed one',[98] Prince Hohenlohe was certainly expressing the general opinion when he described the piece as 'deplorable'.[99] At any rate the ruling German princes, who had come to Berlin for the centenary, considered the performance 'the greatest humiliation inflicted on them since 1866'.[100] Abroad, parallels were drawn between Wilhelm II, Friedrich Nietzsche, who was now mentally deranged, and the destructive urge, with all its overtones of narcissistic resentment, which had emerged in the early compositions of Richard Strauss; heads were shaken, and it was said that in Germany there was 'a scent of Nero in the air'.[101]

## THE 'GREAT FARCE' OVER BISMARCK'S DEATH

On 30 July 1898, ten years after the death of 'his' Kaiser, Prince Otto von Bismarck died at Friedrichsruh, aged eighty-three. Until the last moment it was Wilhelm II's 'dearest wish', as Bülow called it, to exploit the internationally historic importance of this event as propaganda for himself and his dynasty, by hurrying to the bedside of the national idol. The danger had long been recognised within the imperial entourage that otherwise 'the mighty man' could 'take millions of hearts with him to the grave', which 'would no longer beat for our Kaiser'.[102] Since 1892 at the latest Wilhelm had realised, as one historian has rightly observed, that he would have to give Bismarck 'a magnificent burial if he wanted to inherit from him'.[103] And to the end Bismarck and those around him denied the hated monarch − the 'stupid boy', as the founder of the Reich still called him on his deathbed − this satisfaction.[104]

Since Bismarck's dismissal, Wilhelm's attitude to his dangerously powerful, fractious subject had fluctuated wildly, as we have seen. The initial show of concern had soon given way to helpless rage, culminating in his publicly expressed threat in the summer of 1891 that he would lock Bismarck up in Spandau.[105] Again, during the 'grand tour of Greater Germany' made by the founder of the Reich in 1892 on the occasion of his son Herbert's marriage in Vienna, the Kaiser's anger against him knew no bounds.[106] Yet only a year later, while Bismarck lay ill at Kissingen, Wilhelm sent him a telegram from Hungary making a point of offering one of the royal residences for his convalescence.[107] This phase of ostentatious reconciliation − encompassing, as we have seen, Bismarck's visit to Berlin for the Kaiser's birthday in 1894, the Kaiser's indignant telegram and his emotional visit to Friedrichsruh in March 1895 after the Reichstag had refused to congratulate the former Reich Chancellor on his eightieth birthday[108] – came to an abrupt end in October 1896 when Bismarck revealed to the press the state secret of the Russian Reinsurance Treaty and its non-renewal. Wilhelm II telegraphed to Kaiser Franz Joseph saying that the newspaper articles contained 'what I told you of at our first meeting after his dismissal, and you and the world will now understand even better why I dismissed the Prince'.[109] Beside himself with anger – he regarded the disclosure of the secret as a betrayal of his grandfather[110] – he again spoke of imprisonment and confinement in a fortress.[111] He declared to his friend Eulenburg that 'in order to preserve his crown and his personal dignity' he would have to resort to *'forcible measures'* against the Prince if he betrayed any more secrets. The Kaiser was above all afraid of his letter of 1886 concerning the offer of Constantinople to Russia becoming known, and considered that its publication would 'ruin him in the eyes of Europe and also of Germany'. In any case the bond between him and Prince Bismarck was now severed and there could never be 'any sign of a connection ever again'.[112] Hohenlohe tried to calm the enraged Kaiser down by pointing out that, if he were incarcerated, the eighty-year-old founder of the Reich might die in prison. 'Then the question of the funeral would arise. The Kaiser would naturally want to make it a ceremonial occasion and would of course be present at it. Would it be worthy of so great a monarch to allow the funeral of his first and most famous chancellor to take place in a second-class fortress?' At this Wilhelm gradually regained his composure.[113] His fury nevertheless broke out again in the notorious speech of 26 February 1897 in which he called Bismarck the 'pygmy' and 'lackey' of Kaiser Wilhelm the Great. His refusal to send Bismarck a telegram of good wishes on his eighty-second birthday on 1 April 1897 was a further sign of his ill-will and was widely deplored, even in the Centre Party.[114]

Thus in the spring of 1897 Wilhelm's relations with the Bismarck family had sunk to a new low. When the diplomat Rear Admiral Karl von Eisendecher discussed 'the Friedrichsruh question' with the Kaiser, he found that the subject produced 'a very bad mood in our Royal master'. He warned Wilhelm that he would never succeed in 'estranging the old Chancellor from the heart of the people'. The Kaiser, Eisendecher recalled, 'violently resisted every attempt at a rapprochement and explained with some passion the reasons why an initiative on his part was completely out of the question now'. Eisendecher had therefore been delighted to hear that a new effort was to be made after all to bring about reconciliation. Although a 'really good, friendly relationship' would never be possible, given the lack of 'forbearance . . . in both gentlemen', who could not 'forgive and forget', it was nevertheless imperative that an 'outward bridge' should be built, for 'the old Prince will close his eyes for the last time in the foreseeable future, [and] the situation would be disastrous for H.M. if matters were still as they have been since the Russian treaty bombshell'.[115]

On 19 July 1897 Wilhelm II instructed the Chief of his Naval Cabinet to inform Prince Bismarck that the ship *Ersatz Leipzig* was to be named after him on 25 September, and to ask whether Bismarck's daughter Marie, Countess Rantzau, would perform the ceremony and the Prince himself attend the launch of the ship as the Kaiser's guest.[116] Bismarck turned down the imperial invitation with the harsh comment that he had no wish to serve as a table ornament.[117] The Kaiser, understandably, was deeply hurt by his 'curt refusal' on the grounds that his daughter was not well enough to take part in the launch, which was a full two months away. On board the *Hohenzollern* the chief fear was that Bismarck would make it known through the press that he had turned down the invitation, which would put 'our All-Highest sovereign in a painful situation'.[118] This did not happen, however, and Bülow advised that another attempt should be made to persuade the Bismarck family to attend the launch. At the beginning of August, therefore, Tirpitz, who was originally to have gone to Friedrichsruh in September to canvass Bismarck's support for his fleet building programme, was asked instead to visit the Prince as soon as possible, in the hope that he would be able to prevail upon him to allow one of his daughters-in-law to perform the naming ceremony.[119] 'This setting to rights', as Tirpitz put it, was 'a difficult and *thankless* task, but it had to be done for the sake of His Majesty and of the launch itself. I succeeded as far as it was at all possible to succeed given the circumstances and personalities involved, especially with people as obsessed as they are at Friedrichsruh.'[120] In his private record of the visit on 22 August, the newly appointed Navy Secretary noted that Bismarck had drunk one and a half bottles of champagne while he was there. He had remarked spitefully of Caprivi, whom he described as 'wooden', that as Reich chancellor it was only to be expected that he would carry out a campaign of revenge against landowners; after all he had 'spent 22 years as a lieutenant in Berlin without a penny by way of an allowance, and had always seen the wealthy cavalry officers whose fathers had landed property'. He spoke 'affectionately' of Kaiser Friedrich III, who had 'stuck up for him in spite of Vicky, even during his illness', but he refused to countenance any rapprochement with Wilhelm II. Speaking English because of the coachman's presence he said to Tirpitz: 'Tell your master I only want to be let alone ("let alone" was constantly repeated). I have no wish for myself any more. My task is done. I want to die in peace. There is no future left for me, no hope.'[121]

In spite of the Prince's request to be left in peace the Kaiser did not give up his ambition to turn Bismarck's funeral into a great state occasion for the benefit of the monarchy. By giving the first large iron-clad the name of *Bismarck* – in the end a few members of the family did in fact attend the ceremony at Kiel on 25 September 1897 — and by subsequently sending a flattering telegram to the Prince, he restored the link with Friedrichsruh.[122] In December 1897 he found an excuse to send his brother there to enquire after Bismarck's state of health and to extract a promise from the Prince's personal physician, Ernst Schweninger, that he would warn the Kaiser at once by telegraph of any deterioration in his elderly patient's condition.[123] Contrary to the doctors' optimistic assurances, Prince Heinrich gained the impression that 'the end was near', and advised the Kaiser to come to Friedrichsruh himself, whereupon Wilhelm sent a telegram from Rendsburg announcing his intention of coming to dinner on 16 December with fourteen people, among whom were Bülow, Tirpitz, Miquel, Lucanus, Helmuth von Moltke and the imperial physician Rudolf Leuthold.[124] When the conversation at table degenerated into the usual exchange of petty anecdotes, and the Kaiser even dragged up 'a few old barrack-room jokes', Moltke whispered in dismay to Tirpitz that it was 'frightful' to behave in such a superficial and undignified way in the presence of the great man. Suddenly, and quite out of context, Bismarck made a remark which imprinted itself on the memory of all those present. 'Your Majesty', he said, 'as long as You have this corps of officers You can of course do whatever You like; if that were no longer the case, it would be quite a different matter.'[125] By an enormous effort of will the dying Prince had succeeded in duping the Kaiser and his retinue one last time about his state of health. Reassured, August Eulenburg reported to his cousin Philipp that Bismarck was after all not in such a bad way; he had shown great 'mental alertness' at the dinner.[126]

On 28 July 1898, two days before the death of the founder of the Reich, Schweninger caused great surprise by leaving Friedrichsruh, thereby successfully creating the impression intended by the Bismarck family that his patient's condition was 'not quite as bad' as the newspapers had reported.[127] When he arrived in Berlin the doctor confided to his friend Maximilian Harden that Bismarck's death would mark the start of 'a great farce'; it was 'appalling to think of it'. The Kaiser was already sending constant telegrams from Norway.[128] Early in the morning of 31 July — Bismarck had died that night — Wilhelm telegraphed to Waldersee from Bergen. 'Prince Bismarck is said to be gravely ill', the message ran. 'As Schweninger told me two days ago that he was well I can only suppose that he lied to me and is deceiving me about [his patient's] condition. Go at once on *my orders* to Friedrichsruh and find out how His Highness is, and telegraph to me at Reval where I shall arrive on 2nd, or here if possible by this evening, or if it is urgent to the Consul at Elsinore.'[129] Only minutes later the news of Bismarck's death was received on the *Hohenzollern*. 'Deeply distressed', the Kaiser telegraphed to the Reich Chancellor: 'I had intended, when unfavourable news suddenly reached Us on 27th from newspaper dispatches, to sail directly to Kiel. Unfortunately on the same day I received a telegram from Schweninger telling me that the news was pure invention, that the Prince's condition had not changed! . . . Unfortunately that turns out to have been a lie!'[130] The Bismarck clique had succeeded in making the Kaiser appear indifferent to what was a deeply affecting event for the whole of Germany. Wilhelm nevertheless gave orders for an immediate return home. He intended to be at Kiel on 1 August and to stand by the Prince's coffin at Friedrichsruh a day later.[131]

With the obvious aim of placing himself at the head of the Bismarck movement, which had been so damaging for him hitherto, Wilhelm now set in train plans for a spectacular national act of mourning. In an effusive telegram to Herbert Bismarck he bewailed the loss 'of Germany's great son, whose loyal service in the work of reuniting the Fatherland won him the lifelong friendship of My grandfather, His Majesty the great Kaiser who rests in the Lord, and the undying gratitude of the entire German people for all time. I shall prepare the last resting place for his earthly remains in the cathedral in Berlin beside My ancestors. Wilhelm I. R.'[132] In an official proclamation to the Reich Chancellor he declared that he felt compelled to 'give expression before the world to the unanimous grief and the grateful admiration with which the entire nation is filled today, and to make a vow in the name of the nation to uphold and to build upon what he, the great Chancellor, had created under Kaiser Wilhelm the Great, and if need be to sacrifice life and property to defend it'.[133] While still in Norwegian waters he ordered the half-masting of flags and court and army mourning, sent a sixty-strong guard of honour to Friedrichsruh and ordered Senior Master of Ceremonies August Eulenburg to prepare the programme for a great funeral ceremony in Berlin.[134] He sent a telegram to the sculptor Reinhold Begas asking him to design a sarcophagus for the cathedral in Berlin. He personally gave directions to Begas, Ernst Ihne and Anton von Werner as to the artistic arrangements for the grandiose funeral service, to which all the federal princes and countless prominent personages were to be invited. His idea was that the catafalque should be erected on the terrace in front of the Reichstag, and that after a military ceremony in the Königsplatz the funeral procession, with Wilhelm at its head, should then proceed through the Brandenburg Gate along Unter den Linden to the cathedral. 'At least some of the mythical power of the dead man was to be transferred on to the person of the young Kaiser through this symbolic act', Lothar Machtan writes. The burial of the national hero in the Hohenzollern vault was to help raise the monarchy 'to a higher form of legitimacy'.[135]

But the entire plan in all its pomp and ceremony was thwarted by Bismarck's testamentary stipulation, dating from 1896, that he should be buried very simply at Friedrichsruh, beneath a gravestone with the inscription: *Bismarck, born 1.IV.1815, a loyal German servant of Kaiser Wilhelm*, a wish which his family was determined to respect.[136] 'Am I expected to hand over my father's body to be dragged off to Berlin so that the Kaiser can use it to fish for popularity?', Herbert Bismarck asked a former colleague of the Prince.[137] Nonetheless the Kaiser, arriving 'in a tense mood' at Kiel, decided to travel to Friedrichsruh the next day so that he could at least attend the funeral there. He forced the Kaiserin, who had just arrived from Wilhelmshöhe and was intending to travel to Coburg for her brother Ernst Günther's wedding,[138] to dress in mourning for Bismarck immediately, treating her to 'a long lecture' in front of Bülow, Philipp Eulenburg and others to the effect that the German people would never forgive her if she showed the slightest lack of admiration for the late Chancellor.[139]

At this juncture Wilhelm had not yet given up hope of being able to bury Bismarck in the cathedral in Berlin, in a sarcophagus donated by him and designed by Begas, and the preliminary works for a grand commemorative ceremony in front of the Reichstag building at first went ahead as planned. In the end, however, he had to be content with a modest memorial service in the Kaiser Wilhelm Gedächtniskirche.[140] His disappointment was even greater at Friedrichsruh itself. When he arrived there on the evening of 2 August with the Kaiserin, Bismarck's coffin had already been sealed, and everyone guessed the family's motives. Baroness Spitzemberg, who had revered the Prince, noted in her diary: 'The fact that the coffin was closed before the Kaiser arrived was undoubtedly prompted by the wish not to allow the man who had inflicted such a burning injury on the dead man to see him – and perhaps they did not believe they had the self-control to keep calm when they saw the living Kaiser looking upon their dead father!! . . . Blood is blood, and the Bismarcks are defiant, violent people, untamed by education or culture, and not of a noble disposition. If the Princess [Johanna von Bismarck] had been alive she would never have allowed him to look, but would have stood by the body of her Siegfried and cursed Hagen, who fatally insulted and harmed him!!'[141] Even from the grave Bismarck continued his fight for revenge against the Hohenzollerns with the publication of the first two volumes of his *Gedanken und Erinnerungen*, which were to be followed in 1918 by the third volume, directed particularly against Wilhelm II.

Nonetheless the 'Great Stealer of our People's hearts' was dead, and the young Kaiser felt as if he had awoken from a nightmare. After the memorial service at the Gedächtniskirche on 4 August he summoned the Reich Chancellor and all the ministers to the sacristy and declared: 'Today the curtain has come down on a long act in our history. Now a new act begins, in which the leading role falls to me.'[142] But no document from the Kaiser's pen testifies more eloquently to the relief he felt at his supposedly final victory in the long and bitter struggle against his overpowering rival in the Sachsenwald than the triumphant letter which he wrote, in English, to his mother from Rominten on 25 September 1898. In it he claimed that Bismarck's lifelong aim had been 'to be glorified and admired and worshipped by the People at the expense of our Dynasty and House, which he made the good People of Germany believe *he* was ever ready to die for, & which *he* had raised to the German Imperial Throne! . . . His ultimate ends are correctly stated by you, and the ways and means he adopted. But against one complaint you utter in your letter I must strongly protest! He is sayed [sic] to have turned away the hearts from their Parents of your 3 eldest children!! What the 2 others have to say for themselves, I do not know, but for my part I simply but firmly & with a clear consience [sic] am able to answer: "No!" He never dared, & I never should have allowed him, to talk about either you or dear Papa in my presence! But if you mean to allude to the possibility of my lending a hand to the overthrowal [sic] of the then allmighty [sic] Chancellor in the days of dear Papa's Reign, I quite openly confess that I was dead against it, & for a very good reason. The death of Grandpapa had so totally upset & even unnerved the country, that it was quite out of its mind; and in a state of hysterics. In this state it looked at B[ismarck] & *not* at *us* as the sole transmitter and *keeper* of the old tradition – it was wholly wrong, & was his own crafty doing – but it was *a fact*! Had Papa – & I with him – sent B. home, then such a storm would have broken lose [sic] against him & *you*, that we would have simply been powerless to stay it & you would have embitterd [sic] poor Papa's last days, spoilt the splendid, ineffaceable figure he had in his People's eye & fancy & endangered your *stay* with us, yes perhaps made it *impossible*. For the moment B. was the Master of the situation & the Empire! And the House of Hohenzollern was nowhere! Had we only even tried to touch him, the whole of the German Princes – I was secretly informed of this – would have arisen like one man & would have made us take back the Chancellor, to whom we – & especially later I – would have been delivered over bound hand & foot! The situation was simply impossible. I from that moment perfectly understood the terrible task, you then did not foresee, which Heaven had shaped for me; the task of rescuing the Crown from the overwhelming shadow of its Minister, to set the person of the Monarch in the first row at "his" place, to save the honour & the future of our House from the corrupting influence of the Great Stealer of our People's hearts & to make "him" atone for what he harmed Papa, you & even Grandpapa. Appaling [sic] enough for a young man of 30! to have to begin a reign with, after such a glorious one, having just passed! I however felt what was my duty & thank God He helped me! Without Him I was lost. When the strife waxed hot & B. began his most daring tricks against me, not recoiling before even High Treason, I sent a message to him saying: It seems to me as if he was riding into the lists *against* the House of

Hohenzollern *for* his *own family*; if it were so I warned him, that this was useless as in that he *must* be the loser. The reply was what I had expected; & I felled him, stretching him in the sand, for the sake of my Crown, & our House! Now since that terrible year, I had to bear up with the storm of Germany's feelings, & the vilest tricks of the enraged & passionate B! The same poor Papa & you would have had to bear! I bore it quietly, without flinching, the Royal standard firmly in my hand, the shield with the Black & White quarterings on my arm & God above, alone I bore it for 8 long years! Where is he now? The storm has calmed, the Standard waves high in the breeze, comforting every anxious look cast upwards; the Crown sends its rays "by the Grace of God" into Palace & hut, & – pardon me if I say so – Europe & the World listen to hear "what does the German Emperor say or think", & not what is the will of his Chancellor! To my notion in one point Papa's theory of the continuation of the Old Empire in the new one is right; he allways [sic] maintained & so do I! for ever & for ever, there is only *one real Emperor* in the world, & that is the *German*, regardless of his Person & qualities, but by *right* of a *thousand years tradition*. And his Chancellor has to *obey*!'[143] As Bülow very pertinently remarked, this letter, veering back and forth between self-pity and romantic monarchical arrogance, is perhaps more indicative of Wilhelm II's mentality than anything else he wrote.[144]

## THE KAISER AS 'HIS OWN REICH CHANCELLOR'

Since Bronsart's dismissal, and even more since the forced resignations of Marschall and Boetticher, Wilhelm II had maintained such direct personal control over German domestic, foreign and arms policy that he was widely regarded as 'his own Reich chancellor'. As we have seen, as soon as the Reichstag had adjourned in the summer of 1897 he brought about the long-planned restructuring of the Reich and Prussian government entirely on his own initiative. Not only was he directly responsible for the appointment of Heinrich von Gossler as minister of war and of Alfred Tirpitz as secretary of state at the Reich Navy Office, but the most important posts in the civil administration also changed hands entirely in accordance with his wishes.[145] Waldersee, in Potsdam for the funeral of General von Albedyll on 16 June 1897, learned of the details of the great reshuffle. 'The strangest change of recent days' and of Wilhelm's personal style of government, he commented, was the appointment of General Viktor von Podbielski as successor to the late Heinrich von Stephan as secretary of state at the Reich Post Office. Podbielski, as Waldersee remarked, had long been 'decidedly out of favour and it is only as a result of his conduct as a [Conservative] member of the Reichstag that he has risen a little; but the Kaiser has nevertheless always treated him with marked coldness, until he called him over during the races at Hoppegarten on 14th [June 1897] and told him he wanted to make

44. Bernhard von Bülow, German Foreign Secretary 1897–1900
and Reich Chancellor 1900–1909

him a secretary of state.'[146] This became the pattern for Wilhelm II's selection
of most ministers and secretaries of state from now onwards, and in 1909 and
1917 even for that of the Reich chancellor. On the whole, the arch-conservative
Waldersee welcomed the changes among the leading figures of the government
in the summer of 1897 as a sign 'that the Kaiser now intends to choose different,
much better people than before; he has turned against the South Germans and
wants Old Prussians; God grant that he continue in this direction: he will find
plenty of able people.'[147] The South German Reich Chancellor was soon complaining that he could not hold his own against the Prussian excellencies and
Junkers; they were 'too numerous, too powerful and have the kingdom and the
army on their side'.[148]

The new system, in which the monarch and his entourage were at least
outwardly in harmony with the ministers, seemed to be working smoothly at first.
Bülow reported enthusiastically to his patron Philipp Eulenburg in February
1898 that everything was going 'wonderfully well' in terms of politics. 'The mood

in the country has completely changed', which was not in any way due to his own talent, but to the Kaiser's genius. 'My only real merit is that I understand the aims and intentions of our dear master', the Foreign Secretary and future Reich Chancellor asserted hypocritically. 'Where are the eternal chancellor crises now?', he asked. 'How the once stubborn, refractory and conspiratorial ministers have changed into the meekest little lambs! What has happened to all the agitation against the "Cabinets", the alleged camarilla, the army, the fleet plans and the "limitless" aims! . . . And have not the other much more dangerous threats been averted with God's help? I cannot remember them without shuddering, for those threats were real.'[149] Only with time did Bülow and Eulenburg come to realise what a price they had paid for the apparent harmony between the crown and the government. Only with time did they recognise that the 'much more dangerous threats' of which Holstein, Marschall and Bronsart had warned had not disappeared.

In countless details of German policy the 'will' of the Kaiser, ten years after his accession, could now be seen to be the decisive factor, with the Reich and Prussian governments as mere administrative organs carrying out the imperial 'commands'.[150] Although the Ministry of State held discussions as to whether it might not be tactically advisable, in view of the forthcoming Reichstag elections, to make a concession to the Centre by allowing the return of a few religious orders, the question was decided by the Kaiser, who took the line of 'absolute rejection'.[151] Equally, despite the fact that the ministers and secretaries of state conducted lengthy negotiations with the party leaders in the Landtag or Reichstag committees on the Accountancy Bill, the 'Lex Heinze' against prostitution, the peacetime army establishment or the Meat Inspection Bill, many of their decisions were overturned 'in a mood of extreme indignation' by Wilhelm II 'on the All-Highest initiative and with great animation'.[152] Even with regard to the choice of the next archbishop of Cologne, which the Ministry of State discussed in July 1899, the Kaiser stipulated which two bishops were the only ones who could be considered for the post.[153] No question was too trivial for an expression of the imperial will. In a five-page letter Wilhelm personally explained to his aunt Luise why the Augusta Foundation for young girls would have to be moved to another site because of the rapid industrial expansion in Berlin. The safety, and above all 'the undisturbed blossoming of the tender young plants', was 'quite inconceivable' in the midst of 'thousands of factory workers and lightermen', he wrote.[154] Often, however, the decisions taken by the Kaiser concerned matters of the utmost gravity for German policy.

Wilhelm summoned Crown Councils or appeared unannounced at meetings of the Ministry of State far more frequently than before, in order to inform the ministers of his wishes.[155] Occasionally he overwhelmed the Ministry with detailed instructions. 'A strange sort of Crown Council', one experienced minister noted after one such meeting at the Neues Palais. 'Yesterday none of us was asked for our counsel on anything.'[156] The way in which the monarch now controlled the machinery of government is strikingly demonstrated by the Crown Council held on 15 February 1898 in the Schloss. The meeting was almost entirely taken up by an imperial speech. Wilhelm spoke first of the measures which were necessary to prevent flood damage, and which he ordered the government to put before the Prussian Landtag in the autumn as a draft bill. Then he ordered a redistribution of responsibilities between various Prussian ministries: the Waterways and Buildings Department was to be separated from the Ministry of Public Works and divided up between the other ministries, while the Ministry of Ecclesiastical Affairs, Education and Medicine should hand over its responsibility for medicine to the Interior Ministry. The only duty remaining for the Ministry of State was to 'work out the details' of these imperial ideas. Urgent matters such as the courts martial bill, which the Reich Chancellor wished to discuss, were postponed by Wilhelm until 'later'.[157]

Even if the elderly Prince Hohenlohe was surprised by this new style of government, his preordained successor, Bülow, who prefaced his letters to the Kaiser in bombastic style: 'Most Serene, most Mighty Kaiser and King! All-gracious Kaiser, King and Sovereign!',[158] appeared to be carried away by the 'genius' which Wilhelm II, this 'most noble and most important of all princes', had shown at the Crown Council. 'I grow fonder and fonder of the Kaiser', he wrote to Eulenburg after the meeting on 15 February. 'He is so important!! Together with the Great King and the Great Elector he is by far the most important Hohenzollern ever to have lived. In a way I have never seen before he combines genius – the most authentic and original genius – with the clearest *bon sens*. His vivid imagination lifts me like an eagle high above every petty detail, yet he can soberly judge what is or is not possible and attainable. And what vitality! What a memory! How quick and sure his understanding! In the Crown Council this morning I was completely overwhelmed! He gave an *exposé* of the terribly complicated waterways question – with all that that entailed in the way of material and departmental problems – which no departmental minister could have equalled for precision and accuracy. Yet it was done with a freshness, an attractiveness, a breadth of vision, in short with a brilliance far beyond the reach of any minister. God preserve this great monarch and noblest of men for us!'[159]

The Kaiser sought to control the Ministry of State, that is to say the only collective decision-making body in the Prusso-German government, in various ways. In the Crown Council of 7 October 1898 he impressed upon the ministers that they 'ought not to offer to resign over every difference of opinion', as one of them recorded in his diary. They had 'the honour to be his ministers; he had chosen us because we were the best he could find. We were not parliamentary ministers but ministers of the King of Prussia, and so long as he was satisfied with us, our task was simply to do our duty.'[160] Wilhelm naturally insisted more than ever on his right to dismiss ministers who no longer enjoyed the 'All-Highest confidence', and to replace them with men of his choice; in the ministerial reshuffle of September 1899 the 'responsible government' only just succeeded in persuading the monarch to concede that 'even in cases in which the Ministry of State [had not been] formally instructed to make suggestions for appointments to vacant ministerial posts', they would at least be informed *pro forma* of the names of their new colleagues.[161] In addition, Wilhelm brought in measures intended to strengthen his hold over the government machine. In September 1898 Miquel, in his capacity as vice-president, informed the other ministers of state that 'His Majesty the Kaiser and King has been pleased to stipulate . . . that from now on all decisions of the Royal Ministry of State concerning Reich affairs, and especially those relating to the instruction of the Prussian vote in the Bundesrat, must receive All-Highest approval before being put into effect.'[162] Although some of the ministers doubted whether it would always be possible to carry out this command, given the Kaiser's frequent absences from Berlin, the Ministry nevertheless decided 'to take cognizance of His Majesty's order and to act accordingly'.[163] Hohenlohe succeeded in thwarting a further controlling measure which Wilhelm thought up, but it was nevertheless indicative of Wilhelm's perception of what was within his power as king and kaiser (and also of the great confidence enjoyed by the 'rising sun', Bülow).[164] This was the wish expressed by the Kaiser in the autumn of 1898 to appoint an official of his Civil Cabinet to keep the minutes of the Ministry of State, 'in order to remain *au courant* about what is said' there. As the Reich Chancellor realised, he would have been 'compromised in the eyes of the entire senior bureaucracy' if he had given in to this ploy. He therefore 'urged Bülow . . . to dissuade the Kaiser from the idea. If he does not succeed, I shall go . . . If Bülow really wants me to stay, he must use his influence with the Kaiser, so that the latter does not make it impossible for me to stay.'[165] Hohenlohe's counter-proposal that Head of the Reich Chancellery Karl Freiherr von Wilmowski should be allotted the task of keeping the Ministry's minutes was rejected by the Kaiser for the reason — also typical of Wilhelm — that Wilmowski had encouraged the Chancellor to write 'rude letters to H.M.'.[166]

It was almost inevitable that Wilhelm II's authoritarian rule would undermine both the unity of the Reich and Prussian leadership and the authority of the Reich Chancellor. The Kaiser's habit of dealing directly with individual ministers or secretaries of state, who then carried out his wishes on his instructions and without further discussion, had a particularly detrimental effect. When, for instance, the Minister of War bypassed the Reich Chancellor to deliver 'what was unmistakably a reprimand from the Kaiser' to the Statthalter of Alsace-Lorraine, Prince Hermann zu Hohenlohe-Langenburg saw this insulting action as representing a danger that he, as Statthalter, might be reduced to the status of a mere Oberpräsident and the Reich territory of Alsace-Lorraine to that of a Prussian province.[167] In 1899 even the loyal General von Hahnke felt compelled to protest against the War Minister's habit of putting 'All-Highest decisions' into practice unilaterally and without previous consultation with the government.[168]

Despite the firm opposition of the ministers – who for the first time since Bronsart's dismissal discussed the possibility of a 'formal protest of the Ministry of State *in corpore*' – in March 1898 the Kaiser succeeded in appointing Reich Navy Secretary Admiral Alfred Tirpitz as a member of the Prussian Ministry of State with full voting rights. In vain Miquel, Posadowsky and most of the other ministers pointed out that the navy was a *Reich* organisation and nothing to do with Prussian affairs, and that the Kaiser's wish therefore amounted to 'an organisational change in the supreme departments of state which was contradictory both to the constitution and to the realities of political life', and that public opinion both in Prussia and in the other federal states would react with indignation to such a step. Both Hohenlohe and Bülow emphasised that the Kaiser would not back down and that any attempt to change his mind was 'hopeless'.[169]

Another piece of bureaucratic reorganisation, peremptorily demanded by Tirpitz and ordered by Wilhelm II after violent clashes over departmental responsibilities, proved positively disastrous. The tripartite administration of the navy introduced in 1889 was abolished in 1899 when the High Command was dissolved, to make it easier for the Kaiser to intervene directly in naval affairs.[170] But the break-up of the Naval High Command into several posts with direct access to the Kaiser, as we shall see, was only one aspect of a massive increase in the power of the Reich Navy Office, which was to give Tirpitz – for as long as he had the Kaiser's support – a tremendous amount of influence in shaping German foreign policy. The Foreign Office perceptively drew attention to the dangers inherent in Tirpitz's proposed reorganisation of the naval administration in a memorandum of 25 June 1898. 'If the Secretary of State at the Reich Navy Office extends his sphere of action, as he wishes, to all German overseas interests, and furthermore receives a power of command which is free of all parliamentary and other constitutional responsibility, he will acquire an authority superior to that of all other Reich Offices. Foreign policy, at least as far as it is overseas, will henceforth become a condominium between the Reich Navy Office and the Foreign Office.'[171] Wilhelm II nevertheless decided in favour of the reorganisation demanded by Tirpitz.

As far as the authority of the Reich Chancellor was concerned, Hohenlohe initially consoled himself with the thought that even if he could no longer take the initiative, he could still prevent decisions which he considered wrong or harmful. With time he lost even this justification for his existence. He complained increasingly loudly that the post of Reich chancellor had become 'nothing but a façade'; 'if H.M. wants to play Reich chancellor himself, there is nothing for me to do'.[172] As Hohenlohe's son Alexander clearly recognised, the chancellor's status had been reduced to that of an imperial 'scapegoat'. 'And if H.M. needs another scapegoat he will easily find one. The future Reich chancellor will not and cannot be anything else, unless circumstances change completely. And there is little prospect of that.'[173] He wrote to his father expressing his irritation that the newspapers never reported 'that the Kaiser has been to see you or that you have been to see the Kaiser, whereas I am constantly reading that Bülow has been to see him and he has been to see Bülow'.[174] 'A Reich chancellor whom the Kaiser avoids is in a ridiculous position', the old Prince himself admitted, complaining that he was obliged to spend more and more time simply to avoid 'putting H.M. into a bad mood with me'.[175] Hohenlohe's requests for audiences were often ignored – 'he finds Bülow more comfortable', the Chancellor commented. Often he had to make his report to the Kaiser during dinner at the Schloss or on a train journey to some hunting lodge or other, and to use this time to seek the Kaiser's 'commands' on the most important questions of domestic and foreign policy, such as when the Reichstag or Landtag should be convened, whether they should be dissolved or merely closed, and who should be given which appointment as Oberpräsident. Before the Kaiser departed on his journey to Constantinople, Palestine and Damascus in 1898 the Reich Chancellor was obliged to ask for an All-Highest decision on what was to be done in the event of war breaking out during the Kaiser's absence.[176] In domestic affairs too, the decisions of the Kaiser held a central place in the political life of the nation.

## TWO DIFFERENT CHALLENGES: THE HARD LABOUR BILL AND THE CANAL REBELLION

On 6 September 1898, while he was on manoeuvres, without so much as a word to the Reich Chancellor in advance, Wilhelm made a speech at Oeynhausen in Westphalia in which he announced harsh legislation 'for the protection of those willing to work'. Under its provisions, he declared, 'anyone – whoever he is and whatever he is called – who seeks to prevent a German workman who is willing to carry out his work from doing so, or even to incite him to strike, will be punished with imprisonment'.[177] In his posthumously published memoirs Bülow explained the 'exaggerated harshness of the Kaiser's language' as a defiant reaction on Wilhelm's part to the support for the workers expressed by Hinzpeter, who had been sitting opposite him at table.[178] However that may be, this unexpected initiative on the part of the monarch plunged the 'responsible government', the Reichstag and German public opinion in general into a crisis that was to last for over a year.

The reaction of the government authorities to the Kaiser's intervention in the delicate question of workers' disputes in a modern industrial society speaks volumes. The luckless Chancellor commented sarcastically that it was certainly true that it would be useful for anti-strike legislation to be tightened up, 'but for that one needs the federal governments and the Reichstag, not an imperial speech at a manoeuvre. I have less and less desire to serve under this sovereign.' He could not take responsibility 'if the Kaiser insists that incitement to strike be punished by *hard labour*', he declared.[179] Posadowsky, who was responsible for social policy, was beside himself with anger at the Kaiser's interference. The head of the Reich Chancellery, Wilmowski, found the Secretary for the Interior 'in a deeply depressed and agitated state' because the Oeynhausen speech had 'ruined all his plans'. Posadowsky, like the Chancellor, was considering resignation, Wilmowski reported.[180] Nevertheless, after detailed discussions in the Ministry of State, he set about drafting a bill for the 'protection of free working conditions'. The Chancellor forwarded the draft to Bülow, who was accompanying the Kaiser on his Near Eastern voyage, on 10 November 1898, quite rightly doubting that it would 'completely satisfy H.M.'.[181] That his pessimism was thoroughly justified is evinced by the All-Highest marginal comments on the draft bill. Where it provided for a penalty of 'imprisonment for at least one month', the Kaiser demanded 'at least one year'; where 'imprisonment for at least six months' was proposed, he increased the punishment to 'hard labour for not less than two years', and he changed clause 8, which stipulated 'imprisonment for at least three months' for an offence to 'hard labour for up to three years'.[182] After Wilhelm's return from Palestine Hohenlohe commented ironically that 'the All-Highest proposals' still went 'far beyond the comprehension of serious legal experts'.[183] 'H.M. is still convinced that the workers must be protected by a harsh law'; it would therefore be necessary to 'proceed very gently and cautiously . . . to bring about a law which is halfway reasonable'.[184]

All the details of the handling of the controversial bill in the Reichstag were decided by the Kaiser himself. Even the Chief of the Civil Cabinet was reluctant to mention the so-called Hard Labour Bill while making his report to the Kaiser on 1 May 1899, but when the Kaiser asked a direct question about it he had no alternative but to explain the serious reservations about the bill. Wilhelm dismissed these out of hand and said that the government should continue to try to get the bill through the Reichstag, showing how completely he misjudged the mood in the country. In the Kaiser's opinion, if the bill came to grief in parliament, 'the blame would fall on the Reichstag', the Chancellor recorded. 'This would damage the Reichstag in the eyes of the many people, particularly in industrial circles, who supported measures against Social Democratic terrorism . . . H.M. is not afraid of any criticism of the bill which may arise during the summer; "people will of course criticise it". He does not care how much or how little. So he intends to let matters take their course, and then if the bill fails because there is no quorum, he will decide whether to adjourn or to close. If H.M. stands by his decision, we shall try to get the bill through the Bundesrat and then submit it to the Reichstag.'[185] This was done on 2 June. When the Reichstag adjourned four weeks later without having reached a decision on this hotly debated measure, the Kaiser telegraphed from Kiel expressing his warm appreciation to the Chancellor for the vigorous manner in which he had supported the Hard Labour Bill. 'The bourgeoisie has apparently capitulated for the moment, against its better judgement, to socialism, which *attacked* it *en rase campagne*. The government must fight all the harder, therefore the bill *must* be reintroduced in the autumn, and the House must accept it or else disappear.'[186] Obediently Hohenlohe promised to carry out the 'All-Highest commands'.[187] Neither the unanimous view of the 'responsible government' that there was no prospect of getting the bill through the Reichstag, nor a memorandum by the Grand Duke of Baden pointing out that the 'horse-trading' associated with it would divide the parties which supported the state and strengthen social democracy, had any effect in persuading the Kaiser to abandon the bill.[188]

Even Bülow was shocked to be told in July 1899 by Philipp Eulenburg, who was with the Kaiser on his Scandinavian cruise, of the open telegram that Wilhelm had sent to the Civil Cabinet. Accepting a request by the mayor of Dortmund that the Kaiser postpone his visit for the opening of the Dortmund–Ems Canal, Wilhelm telegraphed: 'Agree with proposal and very touched by feelings of citizens of Dortmund. Will visit, if at all this year, only after the bill for the protection of those willing to work has been accepted. I have promised the willing workers in Westphalia this and will not go there until I can bring them this gift.' Bülow tried desperately to suppress at least the second half of this telegram.[189] Although Wilhelm eventually allowed himself to be persuaded to take part in the festivities in Dortmund, no one could induce him to give up the Hard Labour Bill. At the end of October, after discussing the matter at length with the monarch, Bülow told the Chancellor that he regarded 'the withdrawal of the bill by His Majesty as completely out of the question'.[190] The result was another heavy defeat for the government and above all for the Kaiser. On 20 November 1899 the bill which he had personally announced fourteen months earlier in Oeynhausen was comprehensively – and even unanimously, as far as the hard labour clause was concerned – rejected by the Reichstag.

Not content with uniting the democratically elected German parliament against him over a bill which he had personally announced without the prior knowledge or approval of anyone in the government, the Kaiser managed simultaneously to provoke the 'Old Prussian' landed nobility, the officials of the Prussian provincial administration and even some of great peers of the realm into open rebellion against him. His passionate support for the plan to build a central canal linking the Rhine, the Ems, the Weser and the Elbe for the benefit of trade and industry brought him into conflict with the Conservative majority in the Prussian Lower House which had been elected under the three-class franchise and which under normal circumstances could be regarded as a pillar of loyal support for crown.[191] In November 1898, just a few weeks after announcing the Hard Labour Bill in Oeynhausen, the Kaiser left Hohenlohe in no doubt that he had 'set his mind' on getting the canal through in spite of the firm opposition of the East Elbian agrarians.[192] In April 1899 the Chancellor noted with alarm that Wilhelm was 'still enthusiastically in favour' of the Canal Bill and was determined to dissolve the Prussian Landtag if it rejected the measure.[193] The monarch even threatened those officials of the provincial adminsitration – the Regierungspräsidenten and Landräte – who had seats in the House with dishonourable discharge from their posts if they voted against the project,[194] thereby turning the Canal Bill into a deep crisis of confidence between the crown and the Conservatives, many of whom, it was claimed, opposed it chiefly 'out of hatred for H.M.'.[195]

The question of what should be done if the Landtag rejected the bill, so openly supported by the monarch, split the Prussian Ministry into two camps, as Hohenlohe and the Foreign Office considered the dissolution of the parliament essential, while Miquel and his followers were anxious at all costs to avoid an election campaign in which the state would be pitted against the Conservatives. Wilhelm was at first fully persuaded of the necessity of a dissolution in order to uphold the dignity of the crown. In May 1899, in marginal comments on a report from Munich, he expressly threatened the ministers Miquel, Recke, Hammerstein and Thielen with summary dismissal. Blind to his own lamentable lack of backbone, the Chancellor commented: 'If such a thing were said to me, my resignation letter would be in the All-Highest hands the next day. But these gentlemen think differently.'[196] The following month Bülow informed Hohenlohe that in the Kaiser's view dangerous consequences 'for the monarchical principle' would follow if the government accepted the defeat of a bill 'which had received the endorsement of the All-Highest person' without insisting on the dissolution of parliament. 'If the House of Deputies does not accept the Canal Bill, he must and will dissolve the House in order to uphold his personal dignity and in fulfilment of his duties as sovereign.' Bülow even had the impression, from the 'All-Highest ill-humour', that 'further opposition to the Canal Bill on the part of the Conservatives [would] influence the whole attitude of His Majesty towards the Conservatives for a long time to come'. This consideration would have to be borne in mind, the Foreign Secretary and future Reich Chancellor warned, in regard to 'all further legislative action in the next few years (in particular the Trade Treaties)'.[197]

In an audience at Wilhelmshöhe Miquel succeeded in persuading the Kaiser, in spite of his earlier telegram refusing to go Westphalia until the Hard Labour Bill had been accepted, to attend the festivities for the opening of the Dortmund–Ems Canal after all. On 10 August 1899 Wilhelm therefore set out for the Ruhr where, accompanied by the Reich Chancellor and the ministers, he spent the night at the Krupps' magnificent house, the Villa Hügel.[198] The next day he made a speech at the opening ceremony in Dortmund in which he committed himself 'with all possible vigour' personally to the construction of the central canal as part of an 'absolutely necessary . . . great work' which the Great Elector and Frederick the Great had begun and which, following 'the achievements of My grandfather' in re-establishing 'a strong, united Reich obeying a single will', must now be extended across the whole of Germany.[199]

Only five days after the Dortmund speech the Chancellor had to inform the Kaiser that the Canal Bill would almost certainly be defeated in the Landtag. Voting against it would be 128 Conservatives, 47 Free Conservatives and 26 Centre Party members, so that its passage would depend on the 13 Polish deputies whose attitude was not yet clear.[200] Wilhelm rapidly grasped the significance of these figures: many of the deputies who held posts in the Prussian provincial administration were prepared to vote against the government's bill. In a telegram from Wilhelmshöhe he stated that it was clear from Hohenlohe's figures 'that a number of My officials are among the opponents. This gives me occasion to point out once again that I am determined not to tolerate opposition on principle from political officials in a matter of such great and general importance and that the deputies in question must therefore understand that they will have to bear the consequences of their conduct . . . Furthermore I am sure that My Ministry of State, both as a whole and in all its constituent parts, will continue to devote all its strength to defending the bill.'[201] That very day the construction of the central canal, which Wilhelm had so strongly and publicly advocated, was rejected on the second reading, in a roll-call vote, by a majority of 228 to 126 with 65 abstentions.[202] The Kaiser immediately telegraphed from Metz ordering Interior Minister von der Recke to summon the Regierungspräsidenten and Landräte who had voted against the bill and to tell them in his name that at the third reading they must at least abstain from voting, or else they would lose their posts. He considered it incompatible with the duties of a royal official, he wrote, to vote against a government bill 'as long as they are in My service'.[203]

The opposition to the Canal Bill, which was led by the leader of the Conservatives, Count Limburg-Stirum, and the Centre Party deputy Count Ballestrem, was regarded by the Kaiser as an insult directed at himself. In his anger he fired off open dispatches viciously attacking Limburg-Stirum, who had a Jewish mother, to Bülow, although as foreign secretary he had no responsibility at all in the matter. 'The Conservative parties in their boundless narrowness and Junker arrogance have thrown down a gauntlet in challenge to me; I shall take it up', he threatened. 'This is rank stupidity, mixed with ill-will, and exploited by a Jew-boy. I am determined to make the party feel my anger through social punishments, and so to compel it to do its work after all.' The punishment, he declared, would be the 'exclusion of Limburg and his associates from society'.[204] In a further telegram to Bülow he gave orders that in all the newspapers to which the government had access 'the attention of the Conservative Party should be very emphatically drawn to the consequences which the rejection of the Canal Bill at the third reading would have for our internal political situation and especially for relations between the Conservatives and the crown'.[205] This was followed in September by yet another telegram: 'The traditional pillars of throne and altar, which have always been spoilt by the Royal House, have turned against their Lord, and that under the lead of that fellow Limburg of Jewish descent. Let loose all your press dogs and rain down cudgel blows on the party.'[206] The Kaiserin was so anxious about her husband's agitated state of mind that in her 'fear' she appealed to Bülow to write a calming letter to Wilhelm. 'It is really needed! . . . Ah, it has been a bad summer! May God continue to help us.'[207]

Suddenly, to the consternation of Hohenlohe and Holstein, the Kaiser gave up all talk of dissolving the Landtag because he believed he would need the votes of the Conservatives in the Reichstag for the Hard Labour Bill, despite the fact that it had no hope of success.[208] Both statesmen were firmly convinced that if the Canal Bill were definitively rejected the Landtag would have to be dissolved 'to strengthen the authority of the government and save the reputation of the crown'.[209] They were supported in this view by most of the ministers, who again discussed whether they should all resign, or at least place their portfolios at the Kaiser's disposal if he refused to grant a dissolution.[210] But such decisions had long since ceased to lie with the government; they depended entirely on the will of the monarch. Hohenlohe's diary note after the meeting of the Ministry of State – 'We shall see what Lucanus brings from the Kaiser and then meet again tomorrow' – was symptomatic of the balance of power which now prevailed.[211] When the Chief of the Civil Cabinet brought him the imperial decision, which was against dissolution of the Landtag, the old Prince nerved himself to send

Wilhelm a telegram warning urgently of the danger of 'serious damage to monarchical authority in Prussia and in the Reich' if 'a pronouncement like Count [Limburg-]Stirum's answer to Your Majesty's Dortmund speech' were allowed to go unpunished.[212] In all political circles the predominant opinion was that, after the Kaiser had spoken out so decidedly in favour of the bill, failure to dissolve parliament would be taken as a sure sign that imperial utterances need no longer be taken seriously.[213] Wilhelm II nevertheless decided against dissolution.

On 25 August 1899 the Kaiser summoned a Crown Council at which Hohenlohe and all the ministers with the exception of Miquel 'urgently' recommended dissolution.[214] Wilhelm responded with a long speech in which, as Bülow recalled, he treated the whole question from a military point of view 'When a regiment mutinies ... it is not disbanded on that account, for that would be an injury to the army . . . But the ringleaders are brought to the front and shot. On the analogy of this all officials, especially the Regierungspräsidenten and the Landräte, who had voted against the Canal Bill must now be dismissed.'[215] Instead of arranging for new elections, at which the Conservatives, as Hohenlohe hoped, would have suffered 'a healthy defeat', the Kaiser ordered the suspension of the so-called canal rebels from their posts, a ban on participation in the Agrarian League for all officials and the sacking of the ministers von der Recke and Bosse.[216] The two replacement ministers – Freiherr von Rheinbaben as minister of the interior and Dr Studt as minister of ecclesiastical affairs – were of course 'selected by the Kaiser'.[217] Once again the Reich Chancellor wondered whether the Kaiser had any intention of keeping him in office, if this was how he was to be treated. 'The difficulty is that I do not know what H.M. has in mind', he complained in October 1899, a year before he finally retired.[218]

The disciplinary action taken against the provincial officials caused much bad blood, and even within the imperial family it was condemned as 'simply outrageous and *fin de siècle!*'[219] When Philipp Eulenburg joined the Kaiser at Rominten in October 1899 he gained the impression that Wilhelm himself suspected that he had 'aggravated the situation most unfortunately by his personal intervention'. 'Not everyone learns the lessons of time', the Kaiser's confidant commented philosophically; but he had not yet given up hope 'that our Master and Kaiser will *not* be one of those who do not learn!'[220] The serious consequences of the disciplinary measures against the recalcitrant officials manifested themselves when two of the highest officers of the Prusso-German court, the Oberstjägermeister and Chancellor of the High Order of the Black Eagle, Duke Heinrich XI of Pless, and the Oberstkämmerer Prince Christian Krafft zu Hohenlohe-Oehringen (Ujest) resigned on the grounds that they too were opponents of the Canal Bill and did not wish to be treated any better than the officials who had been banned from court because of the way they had voted.[221] The deep impression that this affair made on the East Elbian aristocrats is clearly demonstrated by a bitter petition addressed to the Kaiser by Count Finck von Finckenstein auf Simnau, complaining 'that the blow which Your Majesty has dealt us and which found its expression in the banishment of the court officials has pierced us all to the heart. I can assure Your Majesty that I still feel the effects of that blow today, because there is something profoundly humiliating, almost degrading, in it.'[222] Wilhelm summoned Bülow to the Neues Palais, 'in visible agitation', and greeted him with the words: 'The great ones of my court are abandoning me.'[223] In his replies to Pless and Ujest, Wilhelm stressed that he did not wish to forbid his court officials on principle to vote against government bills; in the 'very special' case of the Canal Bill, however, what had been at stake was legislation of very great economic significance for the whole of Germany, for which he had pledged his personal support. 'In My speech at Dortmund I publicly stated in clear and unambiguous terms that I considered the Canal Bill as a subject in which I took the greatest possible personal interest and to which I gave my personal support; and I see its implementation as an essential requisite for the healthy, prosperous development of the entire economic life of our nation. In questions of such outstanding, crucial importance for our whole country, to which I think it my duty to give my personal support, I can and must expect that the officers of My court will not place themselves in direct and hostile opposition to Myself.' He went on to express the hope that Pless and Ujest would reconsider their decision.[224] In the end the Kaiser won over Pless by offering his son-in-law Prince Solms the post of principal chamberlain vacated by Ujest.[225]

Wilhelm II's constant demands on the two Berlin parliaments, unmatched by any corresponding willingness to entertain the wishes of the parties whose votes he needed, drove the elderly Chancellor to the brink of despair. The notes which he made for himself in November 1899 for an audience with the Kaiser sum up the government's dilemma: 'We demand the increase of the fleet, the central canal and the capitulation of the Reichstag, which is to agree to the Bill for the Protection of the Workers. But the demands which parliament makes are rejected. How then can a majority be obtained for what the government wishes.'[226] Although he constantly pondered whether he would not do better to retire, given these difficult and humiliating circumstances, Prince Hohenlohe remained in office until October 1900.

Ever since the appointment of Bülow as foreign secretary and Posadowsky as interior secretary in the summer of 1897, Hohenlohe had had the feeling that his position as Reich chancellor was under threat. Just before his resignation, looking back over his period of office, he recorded that 'when Bülow took Marschall's place, I had a rival beside me. Likewise with Posadowsky, although he was unable to usurp my position with the Kaiser. Bülow worked slowly and cautiously, but unremittingly, to achieve his goal of taking my place with the Kaiser. There was nothing I could do to prevent it. I could not unseat him from his position with the Kaiser, who preferred him. So fate had to take its course, until catastrophe came.'[227] What the old Prince could not have known was that Bülow's appointment as Reich chancellor and Prussian minister-president had been a foregone conclusion since the Scandinavian cruise of July 1896 at the latest, long before his arrival in the Wilhelmstrasse. Indeed Hohenlohe's role in the last four years of his term of office as chancellor, after he had given in to the forced dismissal of War Minister von Bronsart, had little but the name in common with Bismarck's tenure of that post. The most important questions of both domestic and foreign policy were no longer decided at the green baize tables of the Wilhelmstrasse but by the Kaiser in person; and he listened to Philipp Eulenburg and Bülow, August Eulenburg and Lucanus, Senden-Bibran, Plessen and the Flügeladjutanten, but only seldom, and usually reluctantly, accepted the advice of the chief 'responsible' statesman. One last time, in a memorandum of October 1900 giving the reasons for his resignation, Hohenlohe described the omnipotence of the Kaiser and the powerlessness of the Reich chancellor. The decision to send troops to China to suppress the Boxer Rebellion had been taken without his participation, he declared. He had not even been informed in advance of Waldersee's appointment as commander-in-chief of the international expedition against the rebels. 'Everything relating to foreign policy is discussed and decided by H.M. and Bülow. The departmental heads work out questions of domestic policy without my participation because they know H.M. does not listen to my advice . . . All personnel questions are decided without my advice and even without my knowledge.' In the press and in the Reichstag he was held responsible for policies about which he knew nothing.[228] On 17 October 1900 at an audience in Bad Homburg, Kaiser Wilhelm II gratefully accepted Hohenlohe's resignation from all his offices.[229] 'Uncle Chlodwig' had served his purpose, and Bülow was able to slip smoothly into his shoes, just as he and Eulenburg and the Kaiser had always planned.

# CHAPTER TWENTY-NINE

# The Kaiser, art and architecture

## WILHELM II AND THE 'NATIONAL ROLE' OF THE ARTS

WILHELM II's rise to the summit of his personal power at the turn of the twentieth century cannot be adequately explained in terms of the structure of the Reich constitution established by Bismarck, in which the hereditary prerogatives of the Prussian crown, with its extra-constitutional power of military command, had remained intact, although this factor was undeniably central to the campaign waged by the Kaiser and his entourage against the organs of 'responsible' government. Nor is it enough to put the psychological and material venality, the weakness of character and the submissiveness of the civilian government officials under the microscope, highly significant as these considerations also were in the decisive power struggles of the 1890s, as the preceding chapters have shown. In order to comprehend Wilhelm's remarkable success against his adversaries in the Wilhelmstrasse it is also essential to take account of the almost superhuman energy and versatility of this extraordinarily forceful monarch, which, combined with his impressive memory and his articulacy, made it easy for him to get the better of almost everyone he spoke to — especially since most of those concerned were still dazzled by the lustre of the crown.

It was not only in politics in the narrower sense, however, that this ability to assert himself proved a sharp sword with which the Kaiser could cut through the Gordian knot of government bureaucracy. There was scarcely an aspect of public life on which he did not think himself entitled to pronounce, indeed to decide. Untroubled by self-doubt, he intervened powerfully in matters of science and technology, ship-building and canal construction, architecture, memorial design, sculpture and painting, costume and stage design, music, crafts and horticulture. He composed songs, drew pictures, designed new uniforms for the navy, for hunting, for overseas colonial troops. Archaeological digs, for instance at the Saalburg in the Taunus, at the Citadel in Metz,[1] at Troy and Baalbek or later on Corfu, particularly attracted his attention. Paul Seidel could not get over his astonishment at the variety of Wilhelm II's artistic activity. 'Whether it be the show-pieces of military spectacle, such as flags, banners and drums, whether it be costly gold or silver prizes for races, sailing or rowing regattas, or magnificent chains of office conferred by Him on rectors of Universities, mayors and conductors of victorious male-voice choirs in singing competitions, abbesses' staves for the heads of charitable institutions which have grown out of former convents, or whether it be merely simple photograph frames for His personal use to preserve memories of people and travels – even to the smallest such task the Kaiser devotes a keen interest, prefers to explain His wishes personally to the artists who are to carry them out, and indeed often produces a design in His own hand as a basis for the work.'[2] A British caricature published in February 1898 shows a day in the life of the restless German sovereign (see illustration 45). He rises at 4 a.m., holds a military review before breakfast, writes a play and composes an opera. After breakfast he paints a picture – the theme being 'The Subjugation of the World' – gives his children military drill, changes the map of Africa and China and sends a telegram to Krüger. Then he makes a fiery speech to the Reichstag, teaches a boot-maker his trade, meets 'a few Emperors', gives an interview to the editor of a satirical journal, dines with Lord Lonsdale and spends the rest of the evening smoking, drinking, singing and duelling until 2 a.m.[3] Critics accused most monarchs of this era of ignorance of the world, preoccupation with their own pleasure and indifference to the sufferings of their subjects. But not Wilhelm II. In his case more calm, reserve, modesty and dignified thoughtfulness would have been more appropriate and at any rate less dangerous for the survival of the monarchy.

It goes without saying that Wilhelm's interventions in the artistic world were hardly less controversial than his role in politics. Here too, by emphasising the themes of Christian chivalry, Germanic nationalism and Brandenburg–Prussian dynastic history, he strove to strengthen the Hohenzollern monarchy and to demonise the forces in the nation which he considered his enemies – Catholics, Jews, South Germans, democrats, socialists and other 'grumblers' and 'scoundrels without a fatherland'. His drawing of 1896, 'Niemand zu Liebe, Niemand zu Leide!' ('beholden to none, harming none') (illustration 46) shows a young knight in shining armour with the black-and-white cross of the Teutonic Order on his breast and his tunic adorned with the black eagle of Prussia, sword and shield in hand to protect the women and children who are playing violins and flutes in the idyllic setting of a Romanesque church behind him. In the foreground,

45. 'A Day with the German Emperor'. Alfred Bryan's cartoon in *Moonshine*,
26 February 1898

46. 'Beholden to none, harming none'. The Kaiser's manichaean sketch of 1896,
as completed by Hermann Knackfuss

at the feet of the Knight of the Grail, dark devilish figures with horns and vampire
wings writhe helplessly in hellfire. In November 1896 the German Kaiser and
King of Prussia had this highly symbolic drawing published by the official Reich
printers in a version completed by Hermann Knackfuss.[4] Any lingering doubts
that the youthful knight was intended to represent the Kaiser himself should be
dispelled by Wilhelm's Christmas present to Reich Chancellor Prince Hohenlohe

in 1898: a bronze statuette of himself in the guise of a Teutonic knight leaning on his sword, with the inscription 'Credo'.[5] There was indisputable evidence of 'political trains of thought', running 'like red threads . . . through all the Kaiser's patronage of art', as the contemporary art historian Gerhard Malkowsky commented in his book *Art in the Service of the State*.[6]

Wilhelm's political aims emerge clearly in the restoration of the old German knights' castles – such as Marienburg in the east and Hohkönigsburg[7] in the west – for which he showed great enthusiasm. At the 'dedication ceremony in characteristic knightly style' in the restored West Prussian castle of Marienburg on 5 June 1902 Wilhelm II called on the German people 'to defend their national goods' against 'Polish presumption'.[8] But it was above all the restoration of the Saalburg, the Roman frontier fort near Bad Homburg, which gave him the opportunity, at the beginning of the new century, to voice the ambitious expectations which underpinned his patronage of this archaeological activity. On 11 October 1900 Kaiser and Kaiserin, 'greeted by fanfares of Roman tubas, entered the flower-bedecked gateway and made their way along the *Via triumphalis* to the square in front of the shrine'. At the laying of the foundation stone of what was to be the restored fort, Wilhelm addressed the thousands of guests and spectators. 'My first thought today is one of sorrowful gratitude to my unforgettable father, Kaiser Friedrich III. The Saalburg owes its resurrection to His energy, His enthusiastic purpose. Just as far away in the east of the Kingdom the mighty castle [the Marienburg] which once brought the seed of German culture to the East rose up anew at his bidding and is now close to its completion, so too, on the heights of the soaring Taunus, the old Roman fort has risen again like the phoenix from its ashes, bearing witness to Roman power, a link in the powerful iron chain which Rome's legions laid around the mighty empire, and which, at the bidding of the Roman Emperor, Caesar Augustus, imposed his will on the world and opened the whole world to Roman culture, which found fertile ground above all in Germania. So I dedicate this stone with a first stroke in memory of Kaiser Friedrich III; a second for German youth, the younger generation who I trust will learn here, in the museum that is coming into being, what a world empire means; and a third for the future of our German Fatherland, to which I trust it may be granted in future times, through the united efforts of princes and peoples, their sovereigns and their citizens, to become as powerful, as firmly united and as influential as the Roman world empire once was, so that in the future the saying which in the old days was: *civis Romanus sum*, may henceforward be: I am a German citizen.'[9]

Since in the artistic world he had no Bismarck, Caprivi, Holstein or Bronsart to contend with, nor any collective forum like the Prussian Ministry of State, and since the imperial initiatives in architecture, memorial design or painting needed no approval from the elected representatives of the people, Wilhelm II was comparatively free to bring his personal influence to bear on these matters in Prussia, and above all in Berlin itself. Outside Prussia too he could exert a direct influence as 'supreme head' of the Reich railways and postal service, monitoring and directing the architecture of stations and post offices as he thought fit.[10] Many of the artists, moreover, fought for the monarch's favour, and were even less inclined than the government officials to oppose the wishes of their Kaiser. They were hopelessly divided among themselves, which also made it easier for Wilhelm to intervene. He was able to look down on them all with lofty condescension when he reported to his mother in February 1893 on the progress of the numerous building projects under way in Berlin. 'At the wish of [Lord Mayor] Zelle in the name of Berlin we went & had a look at the models of Grandmama's statue. [The sculptor] Prof. [Friedrich] Schaper has made the best model so his was chosen, it was the same the town council had hit upon. Its place will be between Opera & Gr$^{d}$papa's Palace . . . The art circles are all more or less ablaze with rival strifes. [Reinhold] Begas is having a shindy with [Ernst] Ihne about Grandpapa's Monument. [The sculptor Alexander] Calandrelli is beeing [sic] pulled down because his model for Frederic the first Elector has been accepted. [The painter August] v Heydon has fallen out with [Anton von] Werner. Zelle & the Council of Berlin are beeing [sic] pitched into by other wise ones, because they want to enlargen [sic] the Königstein Bridge & Schlossplatz, & because they chose Schaper & not the other ones. Alltogether [sic] a happy family!'[11]

A vivid example of the powerful influence exerted by the Kaiser on the artistic world is provided by the visit which he paid to the dress rehearsal of Ernst Wichert's play *Aus eignem Recht* (*In his own right*), accompanied by Lucanus and the Flügeladjutanten Dietrich von Hülsen and Count Kuno von Moltke, in late 1893. Wichert and the director, Ludwig Barnay, were delighted when the Kaiser not only praised the play but also suggested a few improvements in the script, which were eagerly accepted. Wichert noted enthusiastically afterwards: 'It was the most impressive theatrical performance I have ever seen. The hushed silence in the festively lit room, the ardent efforts of all the actors to give of their best, the concentration of attention on one single spectator whose verdict would be decisive, the natural inner agitation of being constantly aware of *this* spectator in *this* play, and finally the growing certainty of success in the expression of such a magnanimous judge – all combined to make an unforgettable impression, beside which the question of what fate lay in store for my play became quite secondary for the moment. That I did not allow my pleasure to be spoilt by foreseeing that now I could be really sure of the most violent attacks will, I think, be understood.'[12]

## THE KAISER AND ARCHITECTURE

However unbridgeable the gulf between Wilhelm and his mother in their political views, in the artistic sphere they saw eye to eye, and above all in the Empress Frederick's last years, when she was suffering from cancer and in great pain, the Kaiser's correspondence with her about the renovation of the royal palaces and the progress of the many building projects in the centre of Berlin gave the Kaiser the opportunity to behave in a conciliatory and even solicitous way towards her. The letters which he wrote to her at the end of 1899 show the close cooperation between mother and son and the leading personal role which the Kaiser played in architectural questions. On 4 November he wrote from the Neues Palais: 'Most beloved Mama. The valuable hints which You kindly have given me in your letter about the library and the Monbijou Museum, were most interesting for me. They were all the more à propos as the matter is now under serious consideration of the Government, & as the Hausminister has now formally concluded an agreement with Minister Miquel as to the sum which is to be paid by the state to the Crown for the "Akademieviertel". After having studied the matter I have sent for the Cultusminister, who reported to me today. It seems according to his tale that Your proposals coincide with the views of the Ministers . . . I then told the Minister that Ihne would be the best man for the new library buildings & that it was my wish that he should be given the order to draw up the plans. With reference to the Alte Museum, the plaster casts can not yet be removed till the new house has been built, which has not yet been begun. The Ateliers & the School for Musik are in course of construction now first; so that for the present there will be no room for the removal of the Hohenzollern Museum to the Old Museum. But the Minister has promised to keep his eye on the question & to report to me as soon as the revirement will be possible. I am charmed at the opportunity of beeing [sic] able to turn Monbijou into a habitable residence & think that it will turn out to be an excellent Villino . . . As soon as the new "Dom" is finished – which by the bye [sic] has turned out a most magnificent building – the "Interimskirche" & a house next to it will vanish & allow of the enlarging of the grounds. The "Kaiser Friedrich Museum" is progressing most favourably & is all ready showing what a fine ornament it will be to that part of the town.'[13]

Only two weeks later he wrote to her full of gratitude for her suggestions for the renovation of the Neues Palais. 'All the interesting remarks You made & plans You developed in Your last letters have been put before the "High Court" of Ihnes eversmiling person & are beeing [sic] pondered upon by him. The Apollo-Saal plan is the first & most important. He . . . is in the act of preparing a sketch of the whole thing. The work of cleansing the gobelins has been most carefully done & everyone who has seen those finished is astonished at the brillancy [sic] of the colours & the fine drawing of the figures! The sums which will I am afraid cost something about a quarter of a million must be "floated" by the sale of the old mews & Academy to the State, & I hope to realise a good sum by it. Perhaps it will even be possible to polish up the stairs leading to our rooms & to simplify the too multifarious colours with which the taste of former Schloss- & Bau-Räthe have bedombed [sic] the ceilings & walls under the name of "Abtönung" [colour gradation] i.e. for instance certain light blue skies with "little stars" in gold twinkling down upon the astonished guests who must "wonder what they are", & how they came there! We have begun to hang some large pictures on the walls & find that they do very well!'[14]

Not only the interiors of the royal castles and palaces, but also the appearance of the city of Berlin, which was changing at lightning speed – between 1880 and 1900 the population of the capital doubled to two million – and of other German cities was personally influenced by Wilhelm II to a degree scarcely even suspected today. Although the Berlin Schloss itself was blown up in 1950 on the orders of the Politbüro, numerous other landmarks of the capital which survived the Allied bombing and the Red Army onslaught in some form or other, or were restored after 1945 – the Dom, the Kaiser Wilhelm Gedächtniskirche, several other churches and a number of government buildings – have features which can be traced directly to the last Kaiser.[15] To be precise, up until the end of 1904, through his personal involvement the Kaiser played a fundamental role in the appearance of a total of 163 new buildings for the government of the Reich or the Prussian state.[16] In and around Berlin alone, 58 new churches were built in this period, all of them owing their foundation and design to the Kaiser and Kaiserin. As the total cost of this church-building campaign ran to more than 34 million marks, not a few Berliners will occasionally have breathed the prayer: 'Oh Lord, hold back Thy blessings!' In the Prussian provinces the number of churches built in the first half of Wilhelm II's reign is estimated at several hundred.[17] Well over sixty Reich Post Office buildings (for instance in Strasburg, Ülzen, Cologne, Hanover-Linden, Berlin Tempelhofer Ufer, Karlsruhe, Memel and Königsberg) and numerous stations (including Hamburg Central Station, designed in 1903) owed their final form to instructions given by the Kaiser in his own hand.[18]

On the basis of the very full comments which he wrote in the margins of the designs and which were always meticulously carried out by the commissioning authorities, we can see how radically and in what detail Wilhelm intervened in the architects' plans, and also what guidelines he was following. For the Brandenburg provincial government building in Potsdam, for instance, he ordered that 'the gables over the windows of the 1st floor (1 flight up) should be made rounded at the top, not broken but full, as marked, with uninterrupted mouldings (see Neues Palais), leaving out the intermediary cartouches. The balusters at the windows on the same floor should not be rectangular but round. The small mouldings above the windows of the 1st floor should be uninterrupted, the gables over the windows should be kept flat, not projecting. Consoles should be omitted. On the upper floor the ornament between the windows should be removed. The mouldings should be uninterrupted. On the cupola the torches should be removed. The upper section should be a round lantern like on the wings of the Neues Palais (Frederick the Great's apartments and Ladies' Wing). Light arrangement of columns in the same material as shown in the drawing. The cartouches planned for the alcoves on the central building should be omitted. Over the entrance a projecting, broad balcony should be added, leaving out the heavy cartouches and figures, like in the central building of the Neues Palais (garden front). The Imperial monogram should be placed in the cartouches on the gables of both projecting wings. The projecting bay window in the right wing should be roofed with copper and kept simple without cartouches. The railing round the lantern on the cupola should be kept light and transparent. It is too heavy. Possibly wrought iron. Examples: balustrade at Wilhelmsthal near Kassel – Neues Palais, window railings. At the top beneath the two groups on the central building the projections should be omitted keeping an uninterrupted line. The sloping roofs over the windows in the projecting wings should be omitted. The cupola over the stairwell in the left lateral wing should be round, and the form of the upper section correspondingly round. It is noticeable that the upper part of the roof structure is too high in relation to the cupola. If possible, lower it in order to give more emphasis to the cupola. A coloured tracing containing the alterations should be prepared and glued on to the design for consideration, after which the design should be re-submitted.'[19] Otherwise, one hopes, the Kaiser was quite pleased with the architect's work! Wilhelm added similar instructions to countless designs by experienced architects.[20] One may argue with the Kaiser's taste, but there is no denying his direct, personal involvement in the architecture of numerous major buildings. Even in cases where the buildings no longer exist today, the architects' second plans for each show that the Kaiser's orders were always faithfully carried out.[21]

As a rule Wilhelm II's concern was above all to preserve the historical character of a city and to ensure, as he wrote, that all building projects took account of 'the character and peculiarities of the towns for which the buildings were proposed', and that at the same time 'all stereotyping . . . should be avoided'.[22] For major government buildings the Kaiser preferred the neo-Gothic style, as for instance for the Post Office building in Strassburg, and made sure that all the elements of a building were stylistically correct.[23] On one occasion he criticised the round

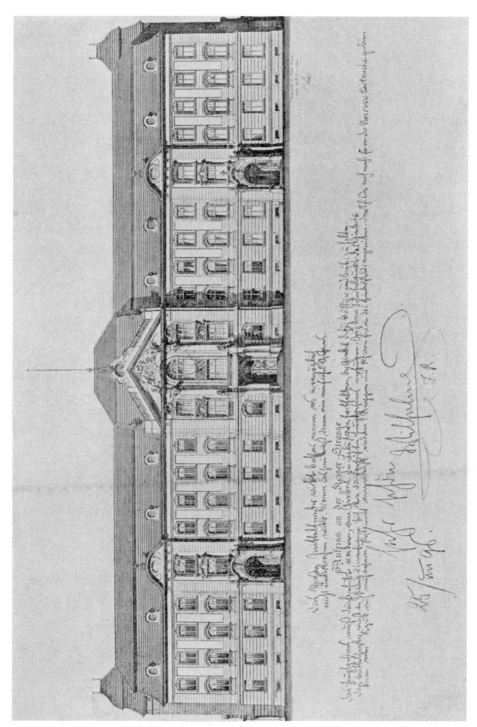

47. The architect's design for the main office of the postal service in Karlsruhe, with the Kaiser's commanded alterations

windows which the architects had included in buildings which were otherwise Gothic in style. 'Straight window heads are more correct in the Gothic, if pointed arches are not used', he noted reprovingly on one plan. 'Straight windows or arched windows are used in the Gothic style, but not rounded arches', he wrote on another, and 'round arches have no place in the Gothic' on a third.[24] For the new Post Office in Ülzen he specified that 'the rosettes would perhaps be best set right into the window frame as in Gothic models. The slanting window-sills would look good in glazed bricks, if not too expensive.'[25] The Kaiser rejected the first design for the Post Office in Hanover-Linden with the remark: 'The front of the house does not look Gothic enough and does not correspond with the fine, strictly Gothic gable.'[26]

Where the hundreds of churches that he had built in Berlin and the Prussian provinces were concerned, Wilhelm II exercised his personal influence 'to a far-reaching extent', as the loyal Seidel wrote admiringly in 1907. Here he drew 'almost without exception on the glorious works of the Middle Ages', taking as his principal model the 'Brandenburg–Gothic brick church of the Cistercians, which the Kaiser loved'.[27] Thus with the 'church-building movement inspired by the throne', according to Seidel, began 'the aspiration, both on the part of the authorities and among many private architects, with regard to the question of style and architectural design, no longer to try to create something modern and new with their plans, but to rely once more on medieval Gothic models'. Seidel goes on to inform us that at the turn of the year in 1889/90 Wilhelm took an intense interest in the Romanesque buildings on the Rhine. 'He had a large number of photographs of the famous Romanesque churches of the Rhineland sent to him, including reproductions of numerous details, especially the many different types of ornament.' He was particularly struck by the parish church and the imperial palace in Gelnhausen, the Dom at Limburg, the monastery of Maria-Laach in the Eifel, the Bonn Münster and the celebrated Romanesque churches at Andernach, Sinzig and of course Cologne. Later he brought back photographs from his journeys to Norway and Italy and put these too at the disposal of the architects Max Spitta and Franz Schwechten. In this way Wilhelm arrived at what seems to us the somewhat paradoxical conviction that the Romanesque style of architecture was 'particularly . . . suitable for Lutheran churches'.[28]

The influence of the medieval churches on the Rhine was already apparent in Spitta's design for the Gnadenkirche, the church that Wilhelm decided to build in 1890 in memory of the late Kaiserin Augusta, as also in Schwechten's Romanesque design for the Kaiser Wilhelm Gedächtniskirche. Every detail – 'both of the exterior of the building and of the internal decoration' – of these two churches, which Seidel described as 'favourite works of the Kaiser', was planned by Wilhelm II himself. Both architects, Spitta and Schwechten, were expected to report to him at least once a month, 'when He discussed everything with them. He preferred the stricter early Romanesque character of Spitta's Gnadenkirche and consequently had changes made more often to the Kaiser Wilhelm Gedächtniskirche. The choir at Gelnhausen was used as the basis for the choirs of both churches. The Kaiser himself chose the site of the Gnadenkirche in the Invalidenpark, and likewise the much-disputed site of the Kaiser Wilhelm Gedächtniskirche, which the building authorities wished to place on an axis to the Hauptstrasse which passed by it. The Kaiser, on the other hand, decided on the . . . diagonal position, on the model of the Bonn Münster. While the churches were under construction He frequently visited the sites and the studios erected there for the sculptors, and held consultations with the architects, making use of the constantly increasing knowledge he had gained from his travels and his studies.'[29] In the next few years numerous other churches were built, again 'under the special personal care and concern of the Kaiser', in Berlin and the surrounding area, as also in Danzig (the Lutherkirche), Bad Homburg (the Church of the Redeemer), Hanover (the Garrison Church) and elsewhere.[30] To mention one last instance of the Kaiser's church-building activity, from 1892 he worked 'energetically' and 'with particular care and love', as Seidel states, to promote the construction of the Romanesque Church of the Redeemer in Jerusalem. Here too the Kaiser directed the project 'in every detail' in consultation with the architect, in this case Adler. He even drew the massive Romanesque tower himself, based on photographs he had taken in Tivoli during his visit to Rome in 1893.[31]

Wilhelm II devoted his remarkable energy not only to the building of new churches, but also to the restoration of old ones. Seidel lists the cathedrals at Havelberg, Wesel, Magdeburg, Brandenburg, Metz, Maria-Laach and Trier and states that the Kaiser always studied the restoration plans closely and took a strict line on 'stylistically correct works appropriate to each epoch'. He also intervened actively in the renovation of the garrison churches in Berlin and Potsdam, insisting on the removal of 'inartistic and tasteless elements' and the restoration of the 'perfectly formed art of their time'. The high altar at Maria-Laach was a gift from Wilhelm II, designed by Spitta on the basis of his instructions.[32] He was also personally responsible for the decoration of St Elizabeth's apartments in the Wartburg.[33]

Thanks to his interest in the decorative elements of church interiors, including stained glass, mural painting, mosaics and sculpture, these arts enjoyed a great revival during his reign, as the faithful Seidel records. New stained-glass works were founded in Freiburg, Frankfurt and Munich.[34] According to Seidel, 'the art of glass mosaics for church decoration owes its introduction and flourishing development in Germany to the epoch-making church-building movement instigated by the Kaiser and Kaiserin'.[35] The small glass mosaic company of Puhl and Wagner was expanded with the Kaiser's support, thanks to which, according to Seidel, within ten years it had overtaken all its European rivals. The Kaiser scrutinised its designs for the Berlin churches, frequently visited its workshops and promoted its work by giving it major commissions.[36]

He was in fact tireless in his interest in all the details of church building. 'Always one of the first donors', he was responsible for the installation of church bells and organs in many churches, which gave 'an extraordinary stimulus' to organ-building and to church music in general. 'In the larger churches, above all in the Kaiser Wilhelm Gedächtniskirche and the [Berlin] Dom, the Kaiser ordered the erection of large organ galleries, so that the glorious old church music, much of which had been forgotten, could be revived for the Church and for church services.'[37] Indeed the Dom above all, the ground plans of which he had taken over from his parents and which, after long years of controversy over its construction, was finally completed in February 1905, must be regarded as largely Wilhelm II's own architectural creation.

## THE 'DEAREST WISH OF THE ALL-HIGHEST': THE BUILDING OF THE DOM AT BERLIN

The construction of 'a cathedral worthy of the Protestant Church and of the Reich' was from the outset rightly regarded as 'a long-cherished and favourite wish of His Majesty the Kaiser'.[38] Wilhelm's parents had devoted much time to working out the details of the projected Dom in consultation with the architect Julius Raschdorff, but in the end it was left to their energetic son to bring their plans to fruition. As early as 26 June 1888, immediately after his accession, Wilhelm II asked for a report on the progress of the project. Although no decision had yet been taken on the shape of the Dom and its link with the Schloss, he issued a Cabinet Order of 9 July 1888 stating that 'It is My will that the project for the erection of a Dom in My capital city and residence of Berlin . . . should be vigorously pursued. The execution of this plan in accordance with the intentions of the late lamented Kaiser and King Friedrich is for me a sacred legacy. I wish the building to mark the climax of the work on the Dom project in which His Majesty the departed Kaiser and King was engaged for many years.'[39] Wilhelm began by rejecting out of hand the unanimous recommendation of the imperial commission on the project that Raschdorff's planned link between the Schloss and the Dom should not be accepted. It was no business of the commission, he commented, 'how I go to church!' He likewise rejected the idea of announcing a new architectural competition (the earlier one, in 1867, had not produced a satisfactory winning design), declaring that it was his wish 'that the design

produced by Geheim Rat Professor Raschdorff in accordance with the intentions
of Their Majesties my father, Kaiser and King Friedrich, who rests in God,
and my mother, Kaiserin and Queen Friedrich, should be the basis of future
proceedings, without prejudice to modifications which may prove to be necessary
on closer inspection.'[40] Seidel relates triumphantly that 'the opposition which
Kaiser Wilhelm the Great was unable to overcome was thrust aside by our Kaiser's
youthful energy. He no longer allowed the project to be buried in commissions
and competition juries, but placed Himself . . . at the head of the authorities
supervising the building, by reserving for Himself the right to determine and
personally decide on every question of any significance.'[41]

Although Raschdorff was retained as architect, in spite of serious reservations
on the part of the Conservatives,[42] his design was considerably revised. The
original estimate for the cost of the project was 22 million marks in all, but it
soon became apparent that the Landtag would never provide such a sum and
would approve 10 million at the most. In an order to Raschdorff of 12 December
1890 the Kaiser therefore stipulated 'that the project for the Dom to be built here
will be limited to the construction of a worthy House of God corresponding to the
needs of the congregation, and a Royal Vault, and the total costs, including the
cost of the interim church and of the demolition of the present Dom, must not
exceed 10 million marks'.[43] Raschdorff stated that the Dom could be built to his
design for this sum, provided that it was reduced in size. A building committee
was set up to ensure that expenditure did not exceed 10 million marks. With
Raschdorff as superintendent of works and Wilhelm II as commissioning client,
contracts were signed allowing the monarch considerable freedom of action.
'The right is reserved to Your Majesty to order alterations to the plan, to suspend
building works or to dismiss the architect of the Dom at any time.'[44]

At every stage of the project Kaiser Wilhelm, who often presided in person
over the meetings of the building committee, put forward his ideas, and he also
contributed directly to the decorative details by personally drawing revisions
from time to time. 'You need only let Me know, and I will always be ready to
come', he told the superintendents of works and artists.[45] After one visit to the
studio of the sculptor Schott, who was making models for the angel figures which
were to encircle the cupola, the Kaiser gave instructions 'that instead of the rococo
form, the more severe Renaissance form should be chosen'.[46] A press report of
this visit stated that 'the Kaiser examined every detail and with powerful strokes
drew the cupola, and an angel figure in the Renaissance style, in the sculptor's
sketchbook'.[47] For the painting of the cupola Wilhelm suggested landscapes
with biblical features rather than figurative scenes. Even minor details like the
weather vane did not escape the imperial attention.[48] Seidel, who was able to
consult the minutes of the building committee and artists' diaries, comments
admiringly on the 'burden of work' which 'His Majesty took upon himself and

saw through to the end'. 'Step by step he took the final decision as to the execution of the details of the . . . project.'[49] The Kaiser took a particular interest in the vault, which he ordained should be as accessible as possible to the public and should 'help the visitor, by means of monuments . . . and inscriptions, to understand the development of the Prussian royal house, and with it that of the Brandenburg–Prussian state, in its historical sequence'.[50] His enthusiasm for building was only rarely disturbed by the idea that with every such intervention he would inevitably arouse controversy and criticism and thereby lay the monarchy open to attack.[51]

In April 1893 Wilhelm reported to his mother on the demolition of the old building. 'The old Dome is now attacked by Raschdorff & his Myrmidons & is coming down with a vengeance. The whole of the roof is gone, the two small towers too; the cupola has disappeared & they ar[e] taking off the cross now. In a month nothing more will have been left of it.'[52] But he had to turn down the Empress Frederick's attempts to make a few more alterations to the new Dom at the last minute. 'I am very sorry if it does not correspond to Your ideas!', he wrote in the summer of 1894; 'but all the wishes You expressed in former years were immediately transmitted to the Committee which superintends the construction, for the benefit of Raschdorff. And as far as was possible without fundamentally altering the plans he has acted on these suggestions. But on the other hand it was impossible to wait any longer for the beginning [of the building work] as Parliament would not have voted the money; & besides the plans had had time enough to be matured with regard to the "Grundriss" [ground plan] & the general dimensions. Considering that Papa himself told me that Raschdorff had been working on the plans by his commands since the last 10 or 15 years & that the plans were what he liked best. The size was given by the very large numbers of the "Domgemeinde" [congregation of the Dom] which has grown so very large. As for the details nothing has been settled at all & I would be thankful for any advice which You would give me, or to the Committee, or Raschdorff himself.'[53] On 17 July 1894 the laying of the foundation stone at last took place, in the presence of the Kaiser and Kaiserin; a document written by the Kaiser was sealed into the wall at the same time.[54]

It was originally hoped that the Dom would be completed by the turn of the century, but there were already delays in the summer of 1896, caused by strikes. Another factor was the increasing influence on the project exerted by Anton von Werner, thanks to the confidence placed in him by Wilhelm. His interventions led to alterations in the design which caused further delays.[55] In the end, the building took eleven years instead of six, as had been planned. While the final work was still in progress, preparations began for the consecration: as always, it was the Kaiser's chief concern that this should be a magnificent affair.

Since the Berlin Dom was intended to be seen as 'the central church for German Protestantism as a whole', all the Protestant federal princes and representatives of all Protestant churches in Germany and abroad were invited to the consecration. On 27 February 1905 the court, led by the 'Most Illustrious couple in Protestant Christendom' (whose twenty-fourth wedding anniversary it happened to be), entered the Dom for the consecration ceremony.[56]

Although the Kaiser was thoroughly satisfied with the building he had created, and received praise from many quarters for it, some naturally took a critical view. Hofmarschall Count Robert von Zedlitz-Trützschler noted in his diary: 'First, the site is badly chosen, for it is a large building standing in far too small a space. The cupola is too big for the lower section, and particularly inside the absence of the double nave which one is accustomed to seeing in a Dom of this kind is a great disadvantage. In general the whole thing is pretentious and invites comparison with other great cathedrals.' Of the 'outwardly splendid' consecration ceremony this court official, always of a critical turn of mind, wrote: 'Just as if the whole thing were a reflection of our time, I did not feel in an especially uplifted or spiritual mood during the service. Both clergymen gave magnificent addresses, but there was much sycophancy in their words which troubled me. I wonder if they themselves believed a quarter of the things they made such a fuss about? They particularly enjoyed praising the glorious work and its creator, by which of course they meant the Kaiser.'[57] Baroness Spitzemberg's mood on this 'divinely beautiful day' was not dissimilar. 'Princes and "notabilities" had been drummed up from all sides, as the usually so cautious [diplomat, Eduard von] Derenthall said, "as if it were for the consecration of a St Peter's, not a hideous Berlin church!" For a purely Prussian, at the most German Protestant occasion, why this exaggerated pomp, this cosmopolitan, pretentious behaviour which no one believes is genuine and which therefore makes one inwardly protest at it? I can only wonder that the population of a great city can have such leisure, curiosity and patience, which manifests itself afresh at every such spectacle; today they were there in their tens of thousands from the Schloss to the Stern, just to see a few court carriages rattling past, *voilà tout*.'[58]

## 'YOUR MAJESTY, THAT WILL NOT DO!': PAUL WALLOT AND THE REICHSTAG BUILDING

There were of course limits to the power of the Kaiser, and in architectural policy just as in domestic policy in general these limits were set in the first instance by the Reichstag, whose building, opened in December 1894, remains one of the most notable and historically significant buildings in Berlin today. Unlike the Dom and numerous churches and government buildings of the Wilhelmine era, however, the Reichstag building bears no signs of imperial interference, not least because of the timing of its construction, for the architect Paul Wallot had started work on the building on the eastern side of the Königsplatz back in 1884. When Wilhelm II succeeded to the throne the basic structure was already complete up to roof height, and the facing was already in a relatively advanced state, despite repeated strikes. Wallot was nevertheless well aware of the significance of the Kaiser's attitude and wrote to his friend and colleague Friedrich Bluntschli in January 1889: 'The Kaiser . . . took an evident and really knowledgeable interest in my poor efforts, and was moreover very gracious. It is of the greatest importance for the progress of the work that the Kaiser took this attitude.'[59]

Shortly thereafter, however, when Wallot was received in audience by the Kaiser at the Neues Palais to report on the building, the first disagreements arose. According to the record of this incident written by the architect Eugen Bracht, this project and that of the Dom were fundamentally different as far as the legal position was concerned, for the Reichstag itself, or rather the building committee elected by it, was the 'commissioning client', and neither the Kaiser nor the Reich government had any right to 'meddle' in it. 'For the Kaiser, however, "participation" always played a major role; he saw it as his mission to exert his influence on this most important building of his reign, and was obviously accustomed to official architects such as Schwechten etc. accepting the interference of the imperial blue pencil . . . After Wallot had shown the plans to H.M. and touched on the existing problems, the latter was at once ready with his opinion, and clapping Wallot on the shoulder he said, confident of victory: "My son – we shall do it like this", and was about to start drawing, or had already started, when Wallot, in his determined way, drawing himself up to his full height, replied: "Your Majesty, that will not do!" There must have been something, not only in the words, but also in the tone, that H.M. was not used to hearing – he saw himself being rejected as fellow builder and, with that, Wallot had acquired as implacable an enemy as can possibly be imagined.'[60] So much for Bracht's recollection. Probably more authentic is the description which Wallot himself gave of the successfully resisted attempt by the Kaiser to influence the Reichstag building, in a letter of 28 January 1889 to his colleague August Reichensperger. 'Then . . . the subject of the cupola came up. Here I was the victor . . . Quite seriously, in the whole affair and especially with the cupola a huge responsibility has been placed on me and I must fulfil it if I do not want to become a bedfellow of the late Herostratus . . . It took place at the Neues Palais in Potsdam; it was quite interesting to see the "Juvenis imperator" living in the rooms used by his great ancestors. H.M. was also quite gracious and he even called me "My son", but then he wrote an ordinance in which he declared that he was not satisfied. When this was read out to the Reichstag building committee some of these pillars immediately collapsed; although it was not in fact difficult to stand them up again afterwards, once the "experts" had spoken up for me.'[61]

This memorable clash at Potsdam in January 1889 soured the relationship between Wilhelm II and Wallot. While work on the building rapidly progressed – the cupola was completed at the end of 1891 and the glazing began the following spring – the Kaiser, characteristically, did not mince his words in criticising it. He wrote to his mother in February 1893: 'The Houses of Parliament outside the Brandenburg gate are growing more & more hideous, the scaffolding having mostly disappeared, the Reichstags-Bau-Commission, whose lack of taste vyes [sic] with its moneysquandering propensity, is fighting pitched battles among the members, because they cannot make up their minds whose statues are to be placed inside – what the Berliners call – the Reichs-Treibhaus [the Reich hothouse]. The Centre wont have Luther there & want a Pope, Conser: & Liberals declare they would see the Centre d—d first, before the statue of a Pope entered the precincts of the mansion. And all this at last comes before the patient ears of your poor firstborn offspring!'[62]

Although these private remarks by the Kaiser did not become public knowledge, when he condemned the Reichstag building as 'the height of bad taste' during his visit to Rome a few weeks later he aroused indignation throughout Europe. As Michael Cullen has shown, all artists and architects at once took Wallot's side, and not only in Germany, where the Kaiser's unpopularity was greater than ever before.[63] Understandably annoyed, Wallot wrote to Bluntschli on 6 May 1893: 'Only a few words today, so that you can see that I am still alive and that the blast from the imperial whipper-snapper hasn't knocked me down. What can one do when one is attacked like that, and from such a quarter? Although I am glad to say that the imperial loudmouth – who is always trying to be astonishing and witty, without really being so at all – is pretty well alone in his view, it is not a trifling matter to be pilloried in front of all the world like that. The shabbiest thing about it is that the imperial prattler came out with his criticism in front of people of whom only the smallest proportion is in a position to check up on his judgement, i.e. to see the building in Berlin for themselves. What is more, people who are far away do not know how things really are here. Begas is the slanderer who has his ear and whose genius and judgement the Kaiser and his dear Mama . . . absolutely swear by . . . And all the charming things that Reinhold [Begas] has poured into Wilhelm's ears over the years, he now bawls out in his barrack-room style in Rome and at any rate thought – . . . enough said – he is a common, despicable brute, for whom Germany will have to pay the price in other ways. For one can probably assume that the Kaiser behaves in exactly the same way in other fields, for instance the military, as he does in the artistic sphere. It is merely easier for us to see what he gets up to in the latter sphere.'[64]

While Wallot was showered with honours by both German and foreign institutions and committees – not least as a defiant reaction to the Kaiser's hostile attitude – Wilhelm showed him his displeasure through petty acts of spite which often created a huge furore. In 1894, instead of awarding the great Gold Medal of the Berlin Exhibition to the architect, as the jury had unanimously decided and Minister of Ecclesiastical Affairs Bosse had recommended, the Kaiser gave it to the society painter Vilma Parlaghy. Instead of the Order of the Red Eagle, for which Wallot's name had been put forward by the responsible authorities, the Kaiser merely conferred the title of Geheimer Baurat on him when the massive Reichstag building was at last completed.[65] A contemporary art critic commented with cynical irony: 'I remember . . . that in 1894 the Kaiser struck off the great Gold Medal, for which Wallot's name had been unanimously put forward, from the list submitted to him, and conferred this same great Gold Medal of 1894, for which Wallot did not seem to him to be sufficiently well qualified, on Vilma Parlaghy . . . The Kaiser showed the Reichstag architect how benevolent and gracious a judge of art he was by awarding him . . . the small Gold Medal, and as appreciation must be given a scale, he awarded the great Gold Medal to Vilma Parlaghy, for which not a single one of the jurors had put her name forward. In so saying I mean only that in matters of art the Kaiser has always been absolutely constant in following his sacred conviction.'[66]

By virtue of the 'kingship mechanism', the monarch's displeasure proved a stumbling block for the architect in many ways. Thus in November 1892 Wallot complained in a letter to Reichensperger that 'the ultimate cause of all this bother is H. Majesty, who has withdrawn his favour both from this building and from myself. How have I deserved this? I don't know. But let's forget it.'[67] At the end of 1893 the architect commented perceptively on the difficulties with which he had found himself struggling since the quarrel with the Kaiser. 'I say that the man up there is to blame and that is true. This pressurising is quite pointless; it is only because he is full of his own importance; he does not wish the building well and he wants to make his power felt over it. So he attacks the Minister and the latter bears down on me . . . What is more, I am not alone in my anger. In a mere 3 to 4 years the Kaiser has managed to squander all the great wealth of devotion and monarchical feeling in the nation which he inherited.'[68] Six months later the irritated Wallot again wondered why 'His Majesty heaps all his kindness on men like Schwechten and Raschdorff. And why does he pour the whole torrent of his crass ignorance over my poor head? I don't know. But probably he was very hurt when I rejected an apotheosis of his grandfather and father painted by Keller-Karlsruhe as inappropriate for the Reichstag building. As I discovered afterwards, the Grand Duke of Baden had used his influence very strongly on behalf of this picture and the National Gallery had to swallow it in the end . . . Bötticher will have said to His Majesty: "Well, Your Majesty, as far as I am concerned – I would of course have thought the picture very appropriate for the new Reichstag building – but one cannot do anything with this stubborn architect Wallot – the fellow is really obstinate." And soon afterwards His Majesty was making remarks – I was a wilful, pigheaded person.'[69]

We are already familiar with the aggressive, anti-parliamentary account, mockingly directed against the commoner Wallot, of the 'dedication of the Reich monkey-house' on 5 December 1894, which Wilhelm II sent to his friend 'Phili' Eulenburg.[70] Wallot gives us a rather different picture of the grandiose ceremony on the completion of the building. He writes: 'The dedication took place on the 5th – the building was ready for use. A "throne" was constructed in great haste in the rotunda in the lobby, opposite the entrance, and stands erected up above . . . At 12 o'clock H.M. appeared. He tried to shorten the time from the carriage into the lobby and make it amusing, by talking about all the money we had been rolling in. At the time, I could see, he was not quite sure how I would behave towards his exalted person after all that had gone before. When he did the rounds after the ceremony – which lasted over an hour – he tried to be kind. He avoided any direct praise – even of things which everyone likes. He got out of it by saying something like: "Yes of course, my mother told me about it." His mother, my old anti-patroness, being a clever woman, had taken care to visit the House at the eleventh hour, i.e. a few days before the dedication. When we were leaving the refreshment rooms and the Kaiserin [Auguste Viktoria], who was in front, hesitated for a moment, unsure which way she should go, H.M. said: "Wallot, give my wife your arm, otherwise we shan't get anywhere." Naturally I had to walk on ahead, and I told H[er] M[ajesty] of H.M.'s command, and equally naturally and fortunately H[er] M[ajesty] did not react to my kind offer. I begged H[er] M[ajesty] to be kind enough to excuse me – I had been obliged to take the Kaiser's wish as a command – if I had done something stupid, I hoped She would put it down to my inexperience in such matters. The situation was utterly ridiculous – what do you think of this "Majesty" – this revoker of medals? And when it was all over and the soldiers down below were marching past in goose-step, and the great Lord took his leave, he said to H[err] v. Bötticher: "Well, shall I give him the great Gold medal after all?" So as not to need to have heard this magnificent generosity on the part of the sovereign, I quickly slipped behind a curtain at the side. You ask whether H.M.'s attitude to the building would be more favourable from now on – it would of course be very nice for the building . . . and for me too. But this will certainly not be the case. Of course – if I were a power to be reckoned with – but such a little mite of an architect, there is no reason for one to modify one's imperial opinion for him.'[71]


## THE KAISER AND PAINTING

No one who is aware of the great interest which Wilhelm II's parents took in art, and above all of the Empress Frederick's undoubted talent for painting,[72] will be surprised that their son followed developments in painting with close attention. Here too he repeatedly, and in the end to the detriment of the monarchy, interfered in the factional struggles of artists. During his time at the gymnasium in Kassel he had attended drawing lessons at the academy of art, and only a few years later – modesty was never a hindrance with him – to his father's regret he publicly exhibited an oil painting depicting a German ship engaged in firing practice off the coast of Japan.[73] With his usual uncritical admiration for his Kaiser, Seidel tells us of the Monarch's 'favourite art'. 'Already early in his life a burning interest in marine painting was awakened in the soul of the young Prince Wilhelm.' Two teachers, the marine painters Carl Salzmann and Hans Bohrdt, fostered this early passion. Seidel goes so far as to claim that 'with the Kaiser's great gift . . . only the fulfilment of higher duties have prevented Him from acquiring the technical mastery necessary for an exclusively artistic activity in this field'.[74] Both Salzmann and Bohrdt have left striking descriptions of the Kaiser's activity as a painter. The former recalled how 'one autumn evening in 1893 I received a telegram summoning me to Berlin. I took the first and fastest train, but did not arrive at the Royal Schloss until a quarter past ten. I was at once taken to the Kaiser, who called out humorously: "So here he is at last! Where have you been hiding, I have had the whole of Berlin searched for you." The royal party had probably just returned from a theatre or a concert, for Her Majesty the Kaiserin and her ladies were in full evening dress, and likewise the gentlemen in attendance. The Kaiser, wearing the Litewka [an officer's off-duty jacket], was standing in front of an easel and was trying to draw a marine picture in charcoal and chalk on a large board. With the explanatory words "We are building a new iron-clad soon, 'Ersatz Preussen', and I would like to publish a pictorial representation of it, showing how the ship will look in the water; help me with it" and with short, energetic strokes the Kaiser drew a small profile view at the edge of the board, showing what he knew of the ship from the plan. In the middle of the beautiful, brightly lit room stood one of the adjutants, who was reading aloud from a large open newspaper a speech made by an opposition leader in the Reichstag, on which the Kaiser frequently made brief comments, half turning away from the easel.'[75] Hans Bohrdt describes a Scandinavian cruise on which he accompanied the Kaiser, and during which Wilhelm was occupied with designing a commemorative certificate for the navy. 'He showed the same keen enthusiasm as when he painted at the Schloss, except that his work was frequently interrupted to look at the beauties of nature which the "Hohenzollern" was passing. Then work would stop for quite a long time, and after the joys of nature the Kaiser found it hard to get back to the design; sometimes he put the drawing aside for the whole day.'[76]

Wilhelm II's passion for marine painting was of course an expression of his obsession with the navy as a whole, but it also had direct consequences for painting and crafts. As supreme war lord, according to Salzmann he personally gave permission for 'artists who wish to perfect their skills specifically in naval painting to be taken on voyages of some length in training ships, and also to be taken to sea exercises in the large iron clads. The big merchant navy companies also frequently and most obligingly grant artists absolutely free passage in their great steamers sailing both to the North and to southern countries. It is likewise due to the great interest which the Kaiser takes in this branch of art that in 1894 on the Kaiser's own initiative a course of instruction in sea- and ship-painting was established at the Royal Academic College for graphic arts in Berlin.'[77] And just as he scrutinised every detail and made corrections to architectural plans for government buildings and churches, Wilhelm decided on the interior arrangement of the new warships which were built at his instigation. According to Seidel, he strove to 'combine the stern necessities of military purposes with a simple but tasteful appearance. His Majesty personally decides upon and determines every detail of these living quarters, whether it is the composition of the walls, the materials for the furniture or the porcelain table service which is under consideration.'[78]

Wilhelm II's best-known and most reproduced drawing, however, was not a depiction of some sea-battle but the sketch which has already been mentioned and illustrated, 'Nations of Europe, protect your holiest possessions', which was completed by the painter Hermann Knackfuss and was intended to convince Tsar Nicholas II of his mission as protector of Christendom against the 'Yellow Peril' in the East.[79] In a letter to the Tsar which the future Chief of the General Staff Helmuth von Moltke delivered to St Petersburg, the Kaiser explained the deeper meaning of the drawing. 'Dearest Nicky', he wrote, in English as always, 'I worked it [the sketch] out with an artist – a first class draughtsman – and after it was finished had it engraved for public use. It shows the powers of Europe represented by their respective Genii called together by the Arch-Angel Michael, – sent from Heaven, – to *unite* in resisting the inroad of Buddhism, heathenism and barbarism for the Defence of the Cross. Stress is especially laid on the *united* resistance of *all* European powers, which is just as necessary also against our

common internal foes, anarchism, republicanism, nihilism. I venture to send
you an engraving begging you to accept it as a token of my warm and sincere
friendship to you and Russia.'[80] The next day the Tsar telegraphed his thanks
for 'the charming picture' which Moltke had brought him. Recent research in
the Moscow Archives has revealed the Tsar's laconic diary entry on his receipt of
the drawing. It reads: 'Received the Kaiser's aide-de-camp, Moltke, with a letter
and an engraving for me from the boring Mr Wilhelm.'[81] The Kaiser had copies
of the lithograph sent to other crowned heads of Europe, and gave it to his wife
for Christmas in 1896.[82] Knackfuss also 'completed' numerous other sketches by
the Kaiser, as for instance the provocative 'Beholden to none, harming none',
mentioned earlier in this chapter.[83] As Ferdinand Avenarius bitingly remarked
in 1901, Knackfuss's drawings were so 'weak . . . that we could not understand
why the opinion that they came from the Kaiser himself was not contradicted
in the Kaiser's interest'.[84]

   The instructions that the Kaiser gave between 1893 and 1899 for the painting
of the throne room in the Palazzo Caffarelli, the German Embassy on the Capitol
in Rome, showed little consideration for the feelings of Italians. The painter
Hermann Prell was ordered to paint a cycle of seasons of the year simultaneously
relating the Edda saga with the express intention of impressing the Italians.[85]
The project not only testifies anew to Wilhelm II's dynastic and nationalistic
understanding of art and his love of the world of the ancient Germanic sagas; it
also demonstrates his ambivalent attitude towards Italian art, which fluctuated
between admiration and arrogance.[86] The new masterpiece on the Capitol was
also intended to outshine the French. As Prell told his wife, the Kaiser was
obsessed with the wish that 'if the French allow their Pal[azzo] Farnese to fall
into decay', 'an all the more beautiful, truly German palace' should be created
on the Capitol, 'for if the Romans see a stylish palace up there, they will conclude
that we are a stylish people'.[87]

   Wilhelm of course followed the planning and execution of the project with
great interest, and here too he intervened in the artistic formulation of the work.[88]
He spoke with enthusiasm of the advantages of mural painting. The 'genre
rubbish' depicting scenes from common life displayed in exhibitions nowadays
was 'all stupid stuff', he commented. 'Only wall painting, even if it isn't fresco,
can produce great art today.' After Prell had submitted preliminary sketches to
him in June 1894 and had expressed doubts as to whether the Germanic sagas
were really suitable for the throne room in Rome, Wilhelm admitted that he had
himself been anxious 'about whether a Renaissance palace, where no one would
understand them, was the right place for Odin [i.e. Wotan] and Thor; but the
myths of the seasons, which all nations used allegorically and in which the names
of the gods did not arise, would be easily understood by Italian viewers too'.[89]

When he visited Prell's Dresden studio in September 1896 to inspect the work in its early stages, the Kaiser expressed his satisfaction with it, only suggesting a few alterations to *Winter*, as Prell reported to his wife. 'What he said was so good and right, the concluding sequence was not pleasing, he would like to have the calm of the first one repeated, no more brown fellows, a blue-green mood – in short, all my own opinions.'[90] The opinions of the Kaiser and the artist were less harmonious, however, when it came to a nude of the Valkyrie seen from the back, which Wilhelm, no doubt under 'feminine influence', ordered to be removed in December 1898.[91] When Prell objected that very similar nudes could be found even in the Vatican, Wilhelm's answer was that, unlike the depictions in the Vatican, the naked Valkyrie was seated, 'on a fiery steed'. 'In this position the buttocks are spread apart and broadened, and therefore in her movement the naked rider, being so large and with the all too voluptuous lower part of her broad back, makes an unaesthetic, offensive impression on the viewer', and must therefore be removed.[92]

It was not until 1903, four years after the dedication of the *Gesamtkunstwerk* initiated by him on the Capitol, that Wilhelm was able to see the painted throne room for himself. Count Monts, by then the German ambassador in Rome, described his visit. 'H.M. was burning with curiosity to see the Throne Room which had been restored, if by no means beautified, under his aegis. He appeared at the Embassy unannounced and quite alone on the first morning of his stay in Rome. First he had all the windows in the room darkened, so as to be able to judge the effect of the frescoes by [artificial] light. Knowing how fond he was of expressing his feelings, I expect Wilhelm II would have declared himself satisfied if he had liked it . . . We were alone in the room; we calmly discussed the restoration work and, indirectly, its failure.'[93]

Although such attempts to exert political influence at home and abroad in the 1890s by means of pictures that were little better than caricatures tended to prove counterproductive, Wilhelm was nevertheless able, through the 'kingship mechanism', to control artistic policy very effectively, and to stem the tide of Impressionism and other modern movements in favour of historicism, which had been the only officially sanctioned style in Germany hitherto, at least for a few more years – although it may be wondered at what price. Another monarch might have thought it wise to remain aloof from the battle of the artists. Wilhelm intervened personally.

Hugo von Tschudi, one of the principal promoters of modern art in Germany, had become director of the National Gallery in Berlin in 1896. He was convinced that knowledge of recent French art was absolutely essential to the understanding of developments in contemporary German art. As director, in spite of the strictly nationalist and conservative policy of the National Art Committee,

which controlled the art collections and purchase funds, he managed, by means
of donations, to build up a considerable collection of modern European art,
which included among other things French Impressionists and modern German painters.[94] As the gallery lacked space, by 1898 a rearrangement of the
paintings had become indispensable. But Tschudi's decision to give preferential treatment to the French works and to hang the older German pictures on
the upper floors provoked strong opposition from official artistic circles. The
traditionalists, drawing attention to the inscription 'To German Art' on the
National Gallery, insisted that it should be dedicated exclusively to the art of the
Fatherland.[95] The matter was also hotly and repeatedly debated in the Landtag.
On 11 April 1899 the Kaiser paid a visit to the National Gallery to investigate
the rumours circulating about the modern paintings. He was accompanied by
the Minister of Ecclesiastical Affairs, Dr Bosse, the Chief of the Civil Cabinet,
Lucanus, and two Flügeladjutanten, General Friedrich von Scholl and Captain Count Oskar von Platen zu Hallermund. Anton von Werner had also been
ordered to attend, and as Wilhelm entered the building he said to the painter, 'It
is time I inspected this place.' Werner, the Kaiser's favourite artist and chairman
of the National Art Committee, has left us a striking account of the conversation
between Wilhelm and Tschudi as they toured the Gallery. 'Herr von Tschudi
explained the pictures. On seeing Böcklin's portrait with the skeleton . . . H.M.
said he would rather see a genius or something of the kind instead of the skeleton. H.M. did not conceal his dislike of Böcklin. Nature did not look like that,
He did not like the fantastic, the untrue . . . Coming to Ad[olf von] Menzel's
"Iron Rolling Mill" H.M. to Tschudi: "You see, that is genuine and truthful, a
celebration of work, and not all that filthy, degenerate, repulsive side which the
modern painters always emphasise in their depictions of workers now" . . . H.M.
wanted nothing to do with [Max] Liebermann and F[ritz] v. Uhde . . . With
Millet, in response to H.M.'s challenge: "Now just tell me what you see in that",
v. Tsch[udi] tried to make Millet out as a kind of Rembrandt. H.M.: "No no, in
that case we would rather have the real Rembrandt." The others too, such as
Fragiacomo and Segantini, were met with head-shaking and opposition from
H.M.'[96] The departmental head in the Prussian Ministry of Ecclesiastical Affairs
and Education, Ludwig Pallat, blamed Wilhelm's hostile reaction on Anton von
Werner and Tschudi's other enemies, commenting: 'He did not conceal his disapproval of the modern art, especially the French, but seems not to have expressed
himself particularly strongly about it. On the other hand, the artists hostile to
Tschudi, led by Anton von Werner, spread stories of disapproving remarks by
the Kaiser – the Frenchification must stop, the French must be removed from
the gallery and suchlike. Even if the Kaiser did not say such things, he seems to
have been influenced by those circles towards their views.'[97]

Whatever the truth of that, four months after his visit to the National Gallery, Wilhelm issued an order in which he took a decided stand against Tschudi and the Impressionists. 'In the course of my visit to the National Gallery in the spring of this year I observed that paintings which, by virtue of the subjects they depict, seem particularly likely to have an educational influence on the visitors, and which through their artistic merit represent the art of the nation in an outstanding fashion, have been removed from their advantageous positions and replaced by examples of the modern tendency in painting. I do not approve of these changes, and I wish the works in question to be put back in their old places and the more recent pictures to be moved to a less prominent place. At the same time I require that in future all acquisitions for the National Gallery, whether by purchase or donation, should first be submitted for my approval. Please make the necessary arrangements accordingly. Signed. Wilhelm R. Neues Palais, 29 August 1899.'[98] Tschudi had no choice but to obey, and before the end of the year Bosse's successor as minister for ecclesiastical affairs, Konrad Studt, was able to announce to the Kaiser that the re-hang of the Impressionists on the second floor had been completed. Wilhelm's ban on Tschudi's previous freedom to make purchases, however, proved much more draconian in its effect. In 1902 Alfred Lichtwark described the paradoxical situation in which the Director of the National Gallery now found himself. 'He has at his disposal the richest private means that a museum in Europe can attract, and he could bring together a first-rate collection in no time at all, except that his superior authorities don't dare accept it as a gift or recommend its acceptance to the Kaiser.'[99] By means of the 'kingship mechanism', Wilhelm had accorded the powerful protection of the state to the old salon art of the historical and battle painters, but at what cost! The glorious splendour of German Expressionism, which is still universally marvelled at as a brightly gleaming 'gash of fire' (Christos Joachimides) in the darkness, was shut out; it flourished, not in the capital of the Reich, but in Munich and Dresden, Darmstadt and Dachau, Worpswede, Weimar and Wuppertal, Düsseldorf and Hagen.[100]

Just as in politics Wilhelm had to rely on the advice of unofficial favourites such as Philipp Eulenburg in order to get his way against the constitutional authorities, in the world of artistic politics he had his 'artists' camarilla', which enabled him to exercise his personal rule. Apart from Ihne, Raschdorff and Schwechten, Salzmann and Bohrdt, Begas and Knackfuss, he listened above all to the advice of Anton von Werner, who had already played an important role as court painter to Wilhelm's grandfather and his parents, but who now, under Wilhelm II, rose to be unquestionably the most important influence on official artistic policy. The young Kaiser not only heaped honours upon him; he gave him the most important posts in the artistic world in Berlin. He became Director of the Academy, member

of the Prussian National Art Committee, Chairman of the Union of Berlin
Artists, Chairman of the Members' Association of the Academy, Chairman of
the Berlin Local Association and Principal Chairman of the United German Art
Association.[101] Werner's enemies accused him of being more imperial than the
Kaiser.[102] As in the political sphere, the relationship between Wilhelm and his
favourite in the artistic world was founded on mutual idolisation, as Werner's
diaries testify. '[It is] amazing what expert knowledge, objectivity and total
lack of preconceived ideas the Kaiser brings to the examination of such artistic
questions, always with sound common sense', we read in one entry. And in
another: 'I am always happy to be able to see and speak to the Kaiser on such
occasions, and to take pleasure in his clear gaze and his fresh, lively nature. In his
whole nature he is always so unaffected and natural, and even surprises like this
one [Wilhelm had unexpectedly conferred an order on a young painter] spring
from a right feeling or have a carefully considered purpose.'[103]

The Kaiser showed a keen interest not only in painting, but also in graphic art,
photography and the new medium of film, and here too he was ready to intervene
with imperial advice and instructions. Seidel writes admiringly of his detailed
discussions of the various methods of graphic reproduction with the director of
the chalcographic department of the Reich printing works, in which he showed a
remarkable breadth of knowledge and gave expert instructions on the execution
of commissions. In the sphere of photography the Kaiser took a lively interest
in the problem of producing coloured photographs directly from nature. 'By
hearing reports from the experts, particularly . . . from the Technical College in
Charlottenburg, and by having the relevant experiments demonstrated to him,
the Kaiser is fully informed about the various more or less successful work in
this field, and if any progress is reported the Kaiser always demands a report on
it', Seidel tells us, going on to describe approvingly how for one of the exterior
shots the monarch wore 'his green hunting coat with black breeches, the orange
sash of the Order of the Black Eagle over his white waistcoat and a red nosegay
in his buttonhole'.[104]

Although Wilhelm often gave offence by the unusual intensity and ubiqui-
tousness of his personal interventions in the sphere of art, he also earned himself
great credit in the more traditional princely role of collector and patron.[105] It
was thanks to him that the collections of the Gemäldegalerie, the Skulpturen-
abteilung and the Kupferstichkabinett in Berlin achieved international status
during his reign. As early as April 1889 Wilhelm gave the Gemäldegalerie a
special grant from the Allerhöchster Dispositionsfonds which enabled it to buy
a large collection of the early works of Adolf von Menzel.[106] Collections of
non-European art, above all the Islamic and East Asian Department, were also
established at this time, and several very fruitful archaeological expeditions to

the Aegean, the Near East and Egypt took place entirely as a result of his personal support.[107]

The fact that egotistical Realpolitik could be at work even in such apparently selfless patronage is shown by the case of the Schack Gallery, which the Kaiser magnanimously allowed the city of Munich to keep in 1894. He sent a telegram to the Mayor saying: 'I see from the telegrams that Count Schack has bequeathed his picture gallery to Me. This art treasure, which has become so dear to the artists and citizens of Munich as well as to all Germans, shall be preserved for Munich. May the people of Munich see in this a new proof of My Imperial favour and of My interest in their well-being, just as I take pleasure in owning a house in your beautiful city, as an Imperial symbol, in whose halls every devotee of art will be My welcome guest.'[108] It was Philipp Eulenburg who had drawn the attention of his imperial friend to the political advantages of leaving Count Schack's art collection in the Bavarian capital – albeit as imperial property and in a specially erected building, so that it was plain for all to see that it belonged to the Kaiser – instead of removing it to Berlin, as he was under strong pressure to do. Such an action, Eulenburg pointed out, would make Wilhelm popular in Bavaria and throughout South Germany. 'There would be a storm of gratitude and appreciation', he promised, and 'an imperial *property* in Munich, recognisable by emblems etc., would help to promote the idea of the Reich'. In addition to this, Eulenburg stressed, 'the withdrawal of the favour would always be a sword of Damocles hanging over the city', which would allow to Kaiser to exert a certain pressure on Bavaria. These political advantages, in his opinion, outweighed the purely artistic benefits of transferring the collection to Berlin.[109] Soon afterwards Eulenburg was able to report to his protégé Bülow in Rome that 'the affair of the Schack picture gallery went off splendidly. H.M. was really magnificent and bought the house for 400,000 without blinking. Nothing could have made him more popular in the South than this coup! The particularist–ultramontane party is beside itself over this *Kaiser's House* in Munich.'[110]

### THE SIEGESALLEE AND 'GUTTER ART'

Not only because he saw himself as a sculptor *manqué* – according to Seidel he once said that 'if he had not been Kaiser, he would most like to have been a sculptor' – but also because he believed that the most immediate way of reaching ordinary people was through memorial art, Wilhelm II had always taken an intense interest in sculpture. He produced numerous designs of his own (for instance for the First Regiment of Foot Guards memorial on the battlefield at St Privat, and for the national memorial in Memel) and personally chose the sites for memorials (such as the equestrian statue of Kaiser Wilhelm I on the

Deutsches Eck at Koblenz).[111] As with all other forms of art, he intervened even in the smallest details of whatever project had taken his interest, especially where the supposed didactic effect of the work on his subjects was concerned.[112]

It was no coincidence that in memorial sculpture as in architecture, opposition to the Kaiser's ideas for putting dynastic history to pedagogical use should again come from the Reichstag. The parliamentary committee responsible for the memorial to Kaiser Wilhelm I that was to be erected in front of the Berlin Schloss had originally allowed Wilhelm II to choose both the site and the style of the equestrian statue of his grandfather. But in January 1894 the design which Wilhelm had approved came under harsh criticism from the committee, which, not surprisingly, he bitterly resented. 'The time when everything went well and people did everything to please him has gone', Waldersee commented on hearing of this, although he was confident that the Kaiser would get his way in the end.[113] His prediction was to be more than fulfilled with the row of statues of all thirty-two Hohenzollerns in front of the new Reichstag building.

Of all the artistic projects with which Kaiser Wilhelm II was associated, the Siegesallee, begun in 1895 and completed in 1901, was the most peculiarly his own. His idea of stimulating national pride and admiration for the Hohenzollern dynasty through a form of sculpture park had manifested itself early on. In Kiel 'a series of monuments commemorating the naval heroes who founded our navy in the most difficult of circumstances, or who won the first laurels in the wreath of its fame', commissioned by Wilhelm, was erected in front of the Naval Academy. The Kaiser himself produced most of the designs for these monuments.[114] He placed statues of his ancestors from the House of Orange, for which he likewise prepared the designs, on the terrace of the Berlin Schloss.[115] On 27 January 1895, his thirty-sixth birthday, he had an announcement published in a special edition of the *Reichsanzeiger* and *Königlich Preussischer Staatsanzeiger* which read: 'Almost a quarter of a century has passed since the German people, following the call of their princes, rose in unison to repel the foreign attacker, and through glorious victories, albeit fought with heavy sacrifices, achieved the unification of the Fatherland and the re-establishment of the Reich. My capital city and residence of Berlin played a full part in the development of German cities which ensued . . . As a mark of my appreciation of the city and in commemoration of the glorious past of our Fatherland I therefore wish to create a lasting adornment for My capital city and residence of Berlin, which will portray the development of the history of the Fatherland from the foundation of the Mark of Brandenburg to the restoration of the Reich. The object of my plan is to erect in the Sieges-allee marble statues of the princes of Brandenburg and Prussia, beginning with Albrecht the Bear and ending with Kaiser and King Wilhelm I, and beside each of them the image of a man specially characteristic of his time, whether he be

48. The Siegesallee in Berlin

soldier, statesman or citizen, in a continuous series. I shall meet the costs of the entire work from My Privy Purse. Reserving for Myself the further decisions to be made, it is My pleasure to acquaint the Magistrate and the City Councillors with this plan on My birthday today.'[116] Wilhelm succeeded in taking the city fathers completely by surprise with this imperial 'gift'. As Seidel points out, his aim was to create a pictorial history lesson, which, like the Hohenzollern vault in Berlin Dom, would bring the history of Brandenburg–Prussia vividly to life for the people through its ruling princes. The Hohenzollern monarchy would gain stability, and the young Prusso-German empire historical legitimacy, through the depiction of a gradual evolution passing from generation to generation of rulers and culminating in the German Reich. The whole concept, as Uta Lehnert has convincingly argued, was a grandiloquent 'Réclame Royale'.[117]

The Kaiser was more directly involved with this building project than with any other. He entrusted the historical and artistic supervision of the scheme to the court historian Reinhold Koser and his old favourite Reinhold Begas respectively. He also had the last word in the choice of the twenty-five other sculptors employed, and commissioned 'Em' Görtz, the friend of his youth, to execute the statue of Margrave Ludwig II. Equally, it was entirely his decision to position the statues in two lines, which were to extend from the Königsplatz to the Kemperplatz and back.[118] He even issued detailed instructions for the execution of each monument. In consultation with Begas he prescribed that the statues, thirty-two in all, should be erected at equal intervals, in chronological order. Each statue should be framed by a semi-circular bench surmounted with busts of two characteristic contemporary figures. After inspecting an early model, the Kaiser ordered the statues in their surrounds to be moved further back into the Tiergarten and the steps to be raised.[119] He also decided on the dimensions of the figures and chose the material to be used, which was Carrara marble. He gave instructions that the statues of the rulers were to show them as young men; they were not to be open to mockery, and they must be historically accurate: every uniform button, it was said, must be correct.[120] Under Koser's supervision historians were commissioned to supply precise information on the appearance, dress, character and historical background of each figure.[121]

As soon as the preliminary works were completed a small model had to be produced first, followed by a large one; the final version was then carved in stone, usually not by the sculptors themselves but by Italian or German stonemasonry firms. Each of the models had to be approved by the Kaiser and even the fees required imperial authorisation for each instalment. This in itself was reason enough for the artists to be afraid to oppose the Kaiser's decisions.[122] He was always accompanied by a large entourage on his visits to their studios; his wife often came, and Begas almost always.[123] Here again Seidel emphasises the Kaiser's technical interest. 'At every stage of the work His Majesty took care to see for himself the progress made and never tired of encouraging and helping with word and deed. Many an afternoon the Kaiser would spend visiting one studio after another, and this work with the artists gave him some of his pleasantest hours of relaxation.'[124] Not all the artists regarded the imperial visits as an honour. When, for example, Rudolf Siemering announced to the Kaiser in the spring of 1899 that he had completed his clay model of Friedrich Wilhelm I, he asked to be given timely warning of Wilhelm's visit so as to be able to prepare himself; furthermore, he said, he did not wish to see Herr Begas in his studio ever again![125] Fritz Schaper, to whom the Kaiser had given the commission for the statue of the Great Elector, suffered a nervous breakdown in 1899 and had to spend several months in a sanatorium.[126]

The first three monuments were unveiled on 22 March 1898, the birthday of the old Kaiser Wilhelm. At the All-Highest request this ceremony was a simple affair without music or speeches. The expense of the unveiling ceremonies depended on the historical significance which Wilhelm II accorded to each ruler, but he was always at pains to create a period ambience. He selected the guests, instructing the College of Heralds to search for living descendants of the figures represented in the monuments to be invited to the ceremonies. He dressed in the clothes of each period, as if he were about to meet the prince immortalised in marble in person. At particularly special ceremonies he even gave a military salute to his stone ancestors; he is said to have stood for a full minute saluting Frederick the Great.[127] On 30 March 1901 the unveiling of the monuments to the Great Elector, King Friedrich Wilhelm III and Kaiser Wilhelm I took place. Lehnert aptly describes this spectacle as a 'showpiece for the imperial troops', through which the 'pre-eminent importance of the military as the mainstay of the monarchy' was to be demonstrated. 'The artistic message, by contrast, was completely drowned out.'[128] This spectacular event had been planned originally for 22 March, Wilhelm I's birthday, but it had to be postponed for eight days because Wilhelm II had been wounded in an assassination attempt at Bremen.

With the unveiling of the last of the thirty-two statues in December 1901 the realisation of Wilhelm's ambitious idea had been completed, and the didactic effect which he hoped it would have on the population did not entirely fail to materialise. According to some accounts it became a highly popular pastime to go for walks along the Siegesallee and play 'cheerful guessing games' as to who the figures were. But among the many million inhabitants of Berlin, not a few found the retrospective self-glorification of the Hohenzollern dynasty tasteless and ridiculous, especially as the ancestors represented included figures such as Heinrich the Child or Otto the Lazy, who positively invited mockery. It was not long before the lines of statues had acquired the nicknames of Corpse Avenue or Puppets' Parade among the people, and as a result of damage to the sculptures measures to protect the monuments at night were considered. In any case workers in Berlin, the great majority of whom voted Social Democrat, and the rural population in the surrounding provinces, never went into the Tiergarten, or only very rarely. Among educated people, and above all among artists and art critics, the predominant reaction was one of anger or mockery. Count Ernst zu Reventlow spoke of 'artistic sycophancy', Ferdinand Avenarius of 'pseudo-art with a political purpose, for the glorification of the dynasty', Karl Scheffler of trivial and meaningless 'court art'.[129] The poet Wilhelm Holzamer described the Siegesallee bitterly as the greatest obstacle that could have been placed in the way of art. 'It was an *imperial* commission', he wrote, but 'My God, what can it be, this avenue of white benches with little busts on them . . . A broad street, marked out on each side into 16 equal parts . . . and each of the 32 marked-out places filled with the same arrangement: bench, busts, pedestal, figure of a ruler . . . That was the directive — and the directive was that this history of Brandenburg should not be the people's history, nor intellectual or cultural history, nor a history of deeds, but the history of a dynasty . . . , an avenue to show off a family in marble, in which a portrait of a prince was itself the meaning — and meaning enough.'[130] 'What depths German art has reached', Fritz Schaper lamented after one of the unveiling ceremonies in the Siegesallee.[131] Max Liebermann went further still and called the Siegesallee a crime against good taste which he could not bear to look at except through dark glasses.[132] And after the First World War Heinrich Vogeler posed the question: 'Can we use the word culture at all, in describing the period in the life of our people before 1914, when the Siegesallee was created?'[133] Far from reconciling the German people with the late-absolutist Hohenzollern monarchy as represented by Wilhelm II, the Siegesallee has come to be regarded as a 'preposterous' and 'outlandish' symbol of the contrasts and illusions which were to be the downfall of Wilhelmine Germany.[134]

On 18 December 1901 the Kaiser invited all the artists who had rendered meritorious service by their work in the Siegesallee or in the Pergamon Museum to a gala dinner in the Schloss, at which Begas and Schaper were accorded the particular distinction of being seated next to the Kaiser. This was the occasion on which Wilhelm II made the half-hour speech which has gone down in history as the 'gutter speech', in which he explained the thinking behind the Siegesallee and expressed his abhorrence for modern art. He said:

> I joyfully take this opportunity to express to you in the first place my congratula-
> tions, and in the second place my thanks for the admirable way in which you have
> helped me to realise my original idea. The drawing up of the programme for the
> Siegesallee occupied a number of years, and it was Prof. Dr Koser, the esteemed
> historiographer of my House, who enabled me to set you gentlemen your task in
> a comprehensible form. When once the historical basis had been found, it was
> possible to take a further step, and directly the personalities of the princes had
> been settled, it was possible also, resting on historical research, to settle on the
> more important men who helped them in their work. In this manner originated
> the groups, and, to a certain extent influenced by history, the form which the
> group should take was arranged. When once this portion of the programme had
> been completed, naturally came the most difficult part of all, the question: will it
> be possible, as I hoped, to find so many artists in Berlin who will be able to work
> on a uniform scheme to carry out this programme? In approaching the solution of
> this problem, I had in my mind, in the event of its successful accomplishment, to
> show the world that the most favourable condition for the solution of an artistic
> problem was not to be found in the calling of committees, or in the appointment
> of all kinds of prize courts and competitions, but that the old way practised in
> ancient classical times, and also subsequently in the Middle Ages, that is to say,
> the direct intercourse of the person who gives the commission with the artist,
> affords the best guarantee for an artistic result and successful performance of
> the task. I am therefore specially obliged to Professor Reinhold Begas, because
> when I approached him with this thought in my mind, he declared to me without
> hesitation that there was absolutely no doubt that enough artists could always be
> found in Berlin to carry out such an idea without difficulty, and with his assistance,
> and thanks to the acquaintances which I had made among the sculptors of this

city by means of my visits to exhibitions and studios, I have indeed succeeded in gathering together a staff, the greater part of which I see assembled round me today, with the help of which I could undertake this task. I feel sure that you cannot refuse to bear me witness that with regard to the programme I have worked out I have made the treatment of it as easy as possible for you, that I have set and laid down the limits of your commission in general terms; but in every other respect I have given you the most absolute freedom, not only freedom in combination and composition, but even freedom to throw into the work so much of your own individuality, as every artist must do in order to impart to a work of art his own individual character; for every true work of art should contain in itself a grain of the artist's individual character. I believe, if I may use the term, that on the completion of the Siegesallee, we may record this experiment as successful. It only needed personal intercourse between him who gave the commission and the artist who executed it to banish every doubt, to answer every question, and no difficulties of a more serious kind presented themselves. I think, therefore, that from this point of view we may altogether look back on our Siegesallee with satisfaction. You have each in your own way performed the task to the best of your ability, and I am conscious that I have helped you by allowing the fullest measure of freedom and leisure, as indeed I consider necessary for the artist. I have never entered into details, but have contented myself with merely giving the initiative, the original impulse. With pride and joy the thought fills me today that Berlin can boast to the whole world of a body of artists who have been able to accomplish this magnificent work. It shows that the Berlin School of Sculpture stands upon a level which can scarcely have been surpassed, even in the time of the Renaissance, and I think that every one of you will admit without a touch of envy that the active example of Reinhold Begas, and his conception of the whole subject, based upon his knowledge of the antique, has been the guide of many of you in the execution of this great task. In this respect, too, we might draw a parallel with the great artistic performances of the Middle Ages and the Italians, inasmuch as the sovereign and art-loving Prince, who gave the commission to the artists, also found the masters, to whom a number of young men attached themselves, so that a definite school thereby grew up and enabled them to perform excellent work. Well, gentlemen, today, at the same hour, the Pergamon Museum has been opened at Berlin. I consider this, too, to be a very important episode in the history of our art, and a good omen and a fortunate coincidence. What will be presented in this building to the admiring visitor is a wealth of beauty, the most splendid that can be conceived collected in one place.

How is it with art in general throughout the world? It takes its models and draws from the springs of great mother Nature, and she, Nature, in spite of her great, apparently unrestricted, boundless freedom yet moves according to everlasting laws, which the Creator has set for Himself, and which can never be transgressed or broken without endangering the development of the world. Just so it is with art, and when we look at the splendid remains of classical antiquity there comes across us again the selfsame feeling: Here, too, prevails an eternal permanent law — the law of beauty, the law of harmony, the law of aesthetic. This law is expressed by ancients in such a marvellous, overpowering way and such perfect form, that we, with all our modern delicacy of feeling and all our practical skill, are proud if we are told, with regard to some specially excellent performance, 'this is almost as good as was done nineteen hundred years ago' — almost! With this thought in mind I should like to urgently impress upon you the idea that sculpture has still for the most part remained untouched by the so-called modern tendencies and movements. It still stands there noble and sublime; maintain it so, and do not allow yourselves to be induced by any judgement of men or any far-fetched doctrine to forsake those principles on which it is based. Art which exceeds the laws and limits which I have indicated is no longer art, but mere mechanical skill, mere craftsmen's work, and that art must never become. Under the much-used word freedom, and under its banner, artists often degenerate into monstrosity and exaggeration and conceit. The man who breaks away from the law of beauty, the feeling for aesthetic and harmony of which every human heart is sensible, even when it is unable to give it expression, and finds his main principle in the thought of some special tendency, some definite solution of what are rather technical problems, sins against the prime spring and origin of art. Yet again, art must be helpful, must influence our people in an educative way; it must also make it possible for the lower classes of society, when hard toil and labour are over, to rise again to ideals. The great ideals have become for us Germans a permanent possession, while other nations have more or less lost them. The German nation is now the only people left which is called upon in the first place to protect and cultivate and promote these great ideals, and one of these great ideals is that we should render it possible for our working and toiling classes to take pleasure in the beautiful, and to work up and out of their everyday range of thought. If art, as is frequently the case now, does nothing more than represent misery as still more hideous than it actually is, it thereby sins against the German people. The cultivation of ideals is at the same time the greatest work of civilisation; and if in this respect we wish to be and remain a model to other nations, the whole German people must assist in the work; and if civilisation is to fully perform its task, it must permeate to the lowest ranks of the people. That result can only be brought about if Art lends her hand to the task, if she elevates instead of sinking into the gutter. As the sovereign of this country I often feel with some vexation that art in the person of its masters does not combat such tendencies with sufficient energy. I do not for one moment fail to see that many a strenuous character is to be found among the adherents of these tendencies, whose intentions are perhaps of the best, but nonetheless, he is on a false track. The true artist needs no mountebank tricks, no puffs in the press, no connection. I do not believe that the great masters of art whom you regard as your models, either in ancient Greece or in Italy, or in the time of the Renaissance, ever resorted to advertising, as it is today frequently practised in the press, to give special prominence to their ideas. They worked according to the abilities that God gave them, and for the rest they let people talk. The honest and true artist must also act on like principles. Art which descends to advertising is no longer art, even if it be lauded a hundred or a thousand times over. Every man, however simple-minded he may be, has a feeling for what is beautiful or ugly, and to cultivate this feeling still further among our people, I need the help of all of you, and for producing in this Siegesallee a piece of such work I give you my special thanks. Gentlemen, even now I can inform you that the impression which the Siegesallee makes upon strangers is quite overpowering. All over the world an extreme respect for German art is observable. May it ever remain at this high level, and may my grand and great-grandchildren, if I should have any, ever see such masters standing at their side. Then, I am convinced, will our people be able to love what is beautiful and ever to prize their ideals.[135]

Had the Kaiser limited himself to the battle against modern tendencies in art, his backward-looking influence would certainly have been great, and regrettable from an aesthetic point of view. His activity in this sphere, however, would have been an internal matter with which his own people would have had to contend. But he was not content merely to throw down the gauntlet to French Impressionism, the Jugendstil, Expressionism and modern architecture, nor just to challenge the alleged 'enemies of the Reich' among the German political parties with a succession of provocative speeches and open telegrams. With his new *Weltpolitik* and the fleet building programme begun in 1897 he drove the oceanic world power of Great Britain into the arms of France and Russia and thereby set in train the fatal encirclement of the German Reich. Along with the dismissal of Bismarck in 1890 and the triggering of war in July 1914, this development must undoubtedly count among the most critical errors of judgement in the thirty years of Wilhelm's reign. We shall now look more closely into how it came about.

# CHAPTER THIRTY

# The challenge: from continental policy
# to *Weltpolitik*

KAISER Wilhelm II's success in securing supreme decision-making power
for himself in the summer of 1896 coincided with Germany's transition
to an ambitious foreign policy which left the careful, self-imposed limitations
of the Bismarck and Caprivi eras far behind. Its goal was the elevation of the
German Reich to the status of a world power on a level with the three established
imperial powers, Great Britain, France and Russia, and the two new arrivals on
the scene, the United States of America and Japan. The driving forces behind
Germany's shift from a European-based policy to one which looked out to the
world beyond have been the subject of close scholarly analysis in recent decades
and have often given rise to controversy. But although there will continue to be
differences in the evaluation of the individual causes of this development, historians are unanimous in agreeing that economic, ideological and domestic factors
were at work that together made a change of direction towards an expansive foreign policy well-nigh inevitable.[1] When Wilhelm II proudly announced, at the
spectacular state banquet in the White Hall of the Berlin Schloss in celebration
of the twenty-fifth anniversary of the foundation of the Reich on 18 January
1896, that the German Empire had become a world empire,[2] he was alluding
not only to Germany's enormous economic upsurge and the impressive increase
in its population, through which the country had become the leading European
industrial power. The Kaiser's words were also calculated to win approval among
those who were untroubled by the Bismarckian nightmare of encirclement and
impatient to throw off the cautious continental security policy pursued under
the New Course, act with strength and determination throughout the world and
ensure that at long last Germany too had a fitting 'place in the sun'. As we have
already seen on frequent occasions in previous chapters, the expectation that

spectacular foreign policy successes would restore the damaged image of the monarchy also played its part in this transition to *Weltpolitik*.[3]

For anyone who examines the rich documentary sources on this development, however, it will quickly become apparent that, although the urge for expansion was enthusiastically supported by part of the German population, the idiosyncratic character of the foreign policy that was actually pursued was not the result of irresistible pressure from below, but arose instead from government decisions in which the Kaiser and his entourage played a dominant role.[4] In other words, had Germany been a country governed by a parliamentary system, the impulse towards expansionism would not have been strong enough to overcome what was in fact considerable resistance among the population to a reckless *Weltpolitik*, as exemplified by the Cassandra call of Prince Hohenlohe's former Bavarian colleague, Otto Freiherr von Völderndorff, writing in November 1897. He warned that 'unless the colonial and world power policy [was] abandoned, the ruin of Germany and the most grave political complications must inevitably follow'.[5] But even if the constitutionally responsible authorities in the Wilhelmstrasse had merely retained their previous power, the result would certainly have been a more cautious German foreign policy than that which in fact came about under the pressure of Wilhelm II's constant restlessness and his irresistible urge to stir up trouble. As Paul Kennedy has very rightly observed, 'Even if one suspects that Germany without Wilhelm would have pursued an expansionist course in any case, the fact surely remains that he gave a "push" and a sense of urgency to the whole programme of *Weltpolitik*, especially in its distant aim of becoming the "successor to England" in the colonial field.'[6] Thomas Nipperdey also points out cogently the extent to which German *Weltpolitik*, characterised as it was by 'aimlessness and hectic restlessness, constantly changing plans and ideas', by 'hyperactivity' and 'the desire to be everywhere', was also imbued with 'a tendency imposed upon it by the Kaiser to show off and to seek prestige'.[7] In this chapter I shall attempt to show, on the basis of the documentary sources, the appalling degree to which Wilhelm II was responsible for the fact that in the eyes of the other great powers the German Reich rapidly became a malevolent rogue state, which was not prepared to abide by the recognised rules of the international community but which, on the contrary, was lying in wait for any opportunity to overturn the existing world order to its own advantage.

## WILHELM AND WELTPOLITIK

It is scarcely surprising that the establishment of the system of 'personal monarchy' had an effect on foreign policy that was even more serious than its impact on domestic affairs. In the field of international relations Wilhelm had a free hand to do as he wished, without bureaucratic − let alone parliamentary − let or hindrance. In institutional terms alone, the right he claimed to decide everything personally prevented the formation of a collective forum in which the various foreign policy options open to the Reich could be objectively discussed. But in psychological terms too the effects of the Kaiser's domination over the 'responsible' authorities of the Wilhelmstrasse were immeasurable. The British military attaché, Lieutenant-Colonel Sir James Grierson, quite rightly observed in 1899 that 'His Majesty, what with the doctrine of divine right and the state of abject discipline to which he has reduced all around him, is getting into a state of "Grössenwahnsinn" [megalomania], and expects the policy of every other state to be changed to meet his views or something very like it, under penalty of his displeasure.'[8]

If Philipp Eulenburg's reaction to the dizzying speed with which the Kaiser's foreign policy developed was to retreat more and more into his shell, there was as always no lack of voices encouraging the Kaiser to believe that he was an extraordinary genius or even a saint, whose historic mission was to lead Germany to world domination. When the Kaiser went to Kiel in December 1897 for the embarkation of the German troops who were being sent to capture Kiaochow on the north-eastern coast of China, his brother Prince Heinrich, who was in command of the squadron conveying the troops, declared: 'Neither fame nor laurels hold any allure for me; I am drawn by only one thing: to announce the gospel of Your Majesty abroad, to preach it to everyone who wants to hear it, and also to those who do not want to hear it.'[9] 'It was as if we were embarking on a Crusade!', groaned Eulenburg,[10] while Baroness Spitzemberg commented that it was 'a dreadful thing, this passionate way of speaking and this bragging'.[11] Poultney Bigelow, the American writer and friend of Wilhelm's youth, congratulated him on the seizure of Kiaochow and spurred him to even greater deeds: he should reform and modernise the whole of China, and 'when you have cleaned up the Chinese Augean stable you will be a bigger man than Napoleon ever was − then come to America & be proclaimed Emperor of Yankeeland . . . − we shall soon have civil war again and every man with money in the bank will welcome a dictator − a strong reforming man', he added jokingly.[12]

Among those most deeply implicated in cultivating the Kaiser's dreams of world power was Dr Hinzpeter, former tutor to the two Hohenzollern brothers, now living in retirement in Bielefeld. Expressing his regret that ill-health had prevented him from attending Prince Heinrich's embarkation at Kiel, he wrote enthusiastically to Wilhelm II in December 1897: 'It would have been a sublime sight for me, to watch the Kaiser sending his fleet on a bold voyage and his brother on a magnificent adventure, Germany's first step on the path of truly global policy, now under the leadership of the Hohenzollerns in a double sense.'[13] A year later, when the Reich acquired the Caroline Islands in the Pacific, Hinzpeter felt compelled to inform his Kaiser that 'to calculate the value of the object by the number of square kilometres and inhabitants is really a very feeble attempt to denigrate it. Of course Germany is unfortunately in the first stage of its colonial policy, where it is only a matter of getting a firm footing in those places where the future of the world will be decided. And that, after all, is what the occupation of these groups of islands has achieved in such an outstanding way that it must be obvious even to the lay person. It truly warms my heart to see the figure of the Kaiser growing gradually but steadily in stature and brilliance.'[14] And for his imperial pupil's fortieth birthday Hinzpeter sent his congratulations with a remark pitched with unerring accuracy to match Wilhelm II's inner motivation: 'May it be granted to Your Majesty to create a place in the world for the German Reich like that which Your Majesty's grandfather created for it in Europe.'[15]

With his grandiose desire to make his mark, Wilhelm not only drove the new *Weltpolitik* forwards at a far greater speed that the experienced officials in the Reich Chancellor's palace and the Foreign Office considered wise. His sudden and unpredictable initiatives on the world stage also had the effect of greatly irritating and alarming the governments of the other powers. Repeatedly driven to the edge of desperation, the statesmen in London, Paris and St Petersburg saw themselves confronted not only with a dangerous international rival but also with an excessively powerful and hyperactive ruler who seemed to be not quite responsible for his actions. No less disturbed were the German diplomats, who had occasion enough to throw up their hands in horror at the Kaiser's inconsistencies. In November 1896 Friedrich von Holstein listed Wilhelm II's contradictory interventions in international politics over the previous few months and wondered despairingly what the outcome would be. 'On 30 August the Kaiser warns . . . the English against the Russians. On 25 October the Kaiser telegraphs the Chancellor saying it is necessary to ally ourselves with Russia and France, as a security for our colonies against the threat of English attack. On 12 November the Kaiser telegraphs the Reich Chancellor to say that he has warned Grand Duke Vladimir [of Russia] against England. On 21 November he tells the English ambassador that he will always stand by England and is also prepared, in order to bring about a better understanding, to exchange the greater part of the German colonies for a coaling station. Where will it all end?'[16] It was obvious 'that a great state cannot be ruled in this way, and that a great people will not be ruled in this way', Holstein observed.[17] When the German ambassador at St Petersburg, Hugo Prince Radolin, who had been Wilhelm's Oberhofmarschall ten years before as Count von Radolinski, complained at the beginning of 1897 of 'how dangerous this personal intervention' of the Kaiser in foreign policy was,[18] Holstein could only reply 'That H.M.'s interference makes our work infinitely more difficult is something to make one cry out to heaven. Though I am tough, I am gradually losing my nerve. The international situation in itself is not at all unfavourable for us . . . But to turn it to advantage one must know how to wait. This is something H.M. doesn't know how to do at all.'[19] In the spring of 1897 Holstein complained to Philipp Eulenburg that there was 'much that is sad in the Imperial marginalia to the report from London no. 38 which is being sent to you . . . Here H.M. emphasises that "it is our duty to establish closer relations with Gaul" and "to aid [Gaul] in its task as a main bulwark of European culture against the barbaric preponderance of the East". So here we have the third foreign policy programme within six months: first, closer relations with Russia and France to protect our colonies against England; then, the cession of our colonies to that same England with the sole exception of East Africa; now, after the Darmstadt fiasco and the refusal regarding the Jubilee, both Russia and England are over and done with and we are to seek our salvation with Gaul. We are simply dealing with a sensitive character who gives vent to *personal* displeasure in *practical* affairs. What material these three programmes in six months would have afforded a Bismarck for handing in his resignation!'[20] Chancellor Prince Hohenlohe urged Eulenburg to take a tolerant view of Holstein's 'disgruntled mood', for he was after all 'from the old Bismarckian school, where everything was weighed up and decided in the gloomy ground-floor room of the Reich chancellor's palace, and where the monarch took care not to disturb Bismarck's *circulos*. Then along comes a sovereign who is eager for action, who wants to have his say and who creates confusion by his contacts with ambassadors, for he creates contradictions between what he says and what the Foreign Office says, and sometimes even contradicts his own remarks to the various ambassadors. The diplomat of the old school is not used to that. Moreover H[olstein] does not know H.M. and does not feel the softening influence of that personal sympathy which our gracious sovereign's kindness calls forth.'[21] For Holstein it was not of course a matter of injured vanity, but of war and peace and the future of the German Reich. He complained again and again of the Kaiser's interventions, which were likely to cause trouble in European political affairs and to 'focus the mistrust of the other great powers on to Germany'. In his draft for a letter of protest from the Reich Chancellor to the Kaiser, which Hohenlohe did not in the end send, Holstein wrote: 'Apart from the fact that it is strictly incompatible with my position as responsible adviser for Y[our] M[ajesty] to decide on war and peace without my knowledge, Your Majesty . . . will recognise what harm and even danger is entailed in giving direct advice to foreign ambassadors.'[22]

## THE WILHELMINE CONTINENTAL POLICY

Wilhelm II's oscillation between Russia, France and Great Britain, as reflected in Holstein's alarmed comments, shows with depressing clarity the dangers of war which the ill-considered European policy of the Reich already threatened to bring about, even before it ventured out on to the high seas and into the great wide world. What was the Kaiser aiming to achieve with his constantly changing attempts to curry favour with the other European powers? Were they motivated by any concept, any recognisable unifying idea? Let us begin by looking at the relationship with Russia and the hope for a union of continental powers under German leadership.

The idea of a continental league against Britain and/or the United States had, as we have seen, held a certain fascination for Wilhelm from the outset. As early as 1892 he had spoken of 'Napoleonic supremacy' as his actual goal in Europe,[23] and in 1899 he was still comparing himself unashamedly with Napoleon and Lord Nelson too, writing to his mother: 'Nelson is for me as far as Naval Policy & strategy are concerned "the Master" & I shape my naval ideas & plans from his! The same as I have learnt most of my military principles I adopt & follow from Napoleon the first. These two great rivals, yet masters in their own way are my task masters!'[24] At the Crown Council of 18 February 1894 he had expressed the idea, in regard to the Russo-German trade treaty, that German 'supremacy' in Europe should be demonstrated not only through military strength but also through a fiscal union of all European states against America.[25] In the summer of 1896 he reverted to this idea, not least as a result of the deterioration of Anglo-German relations following the Krüger telegram – he was looking forward to having his English uncles 'crawling around in front of me again soon', he wrote[26] – and also of the election of the Republican protectionist William McKinley as president of the United States. Tsar Nicholas II told the astonished Reich Chancellor Hohenlohe in early September 1896, after his meeting with Wilhelm II at Breslau, that Wilhelm had spoken to him 'of a customs union against the United States . . . and had appealed to him to canvass opinion in Paris in favour of it'.[27] In the confident belief that he could be 'sure' of the Tsar, Wilhelm triumphantly announced to his friend Eulenburg that on his visit to Paris Nicholas would declare himself ready 'to go hand in hand with France to the defence of the continent of Europe'. 'Our programme is: . . . to bring Europe together in the struggle against MacKinley [sic] and America in a common defensive customs union, with or without England, depending on the circumstances.'[28] And in a bombastic speech at Görlitz on 7 September he said of Nicholas II: 'We are all still under the spell of the fresh young figure of the knightly Emperor . . . He, the War Lord commanding the most powerful army, wishes only to see his troops used in the service of civilisation and for the protection of peace. In perfect accord with Me, his efforts are directed towards bringing together all the peoples of the European continent in order to unite them on the basis of common interests, for the protection of our holiest possessions.'[29] As this effusive toast had supposedly been approved in advance by the Tsar, Wilhelm and Eulenburg saw it as 'the point of departure [for] the unification of Europe' and 'the programme, as it were, for the immediate future of the European world'. The 'old friendship' between Wilhelm and Nicholas had 'come to life again', Eulenburg recorded after his arrival at the imperial hunting lodge of Hubertusstock on 4 October 1896. The Tsar was 'full of sincerity', the Kaiser had 'great trust in him and thinks the days at Breslau and Görlitz will bear good fruit'.[30] According to Eulenburg, who was in a position to know, the 'continental union against America, possibly also against England', was a favourite goal of Wilhelm II's foreign policy. 'How grateful the German people must be to such a Kaiser', he wrote enthusiastically, alluding to the friendship between Wilhelm and the Tsar.[31]

In reality, the meeting of the two Emperors aroused the impression in almost all commentators that Germany was running after the Tsar out of fear of Russian power. And that was not all: Wilhelm's attempts to play off the world empires, Russia and Britain, against each other only strengthened the determination of the Tsar, Queen Victoria and Lord Salisbury to bank on reaching mutual understanding in future crises.[32] During his meeting with the British Prime Minister at Balmoral on 27 September 1896 the Tsar, as Salisbury recorded in a 'very secret' memorandum for the Cabinet, was very critical of the German Emperor. 'He said that the Emperor was a very nervous man; he (the Emperor of Russia) was a quiet man, and he could not stand nervous men. He could not endure a long conversation with the Emperor William, as he never knew what he would do or say. I understood him to say that the Emperor William's manners were bad; that he would poke him in the ribs, and slap him on the back like a schoolboy.'[33] These remarks by the Tsar will have done little to dispel Salisbury's long-held concerns about the mental state of Queen Victoria's grandson. In Paris too Nicholas complained about Wilhelm II's nervous restlessness. 'The Emperor William . . . is a great talker', he told the Foreign Minister Gabriel Hanotaux. 'All one needs do is listen to him, which is what I did. He talked to me of everything, with a great desire to make himself agreeable to me and captivate me.' In complete contrast to the Kaiser's expectations, the Tsar declared his intention of standing by the alliance with France and not allowing himself to be put off by Wilhelm. He even spoke publicly of a 'deep feeling of being brothers in arms' between the two armies.[34] Although it was now scarcely possible to doubt the existence of a real Franco-Russian alliance, the Kaiser assured the Austrian ambassador Szögyény that there was 'at the most' a military convention, and certainly not a treaty of alliance, between the two countries.[35] The full significance of the Franco-Russian alliance as the basis of a Triple Entente to secure peace, directed against Germany and in particular against the Kaiser, is shown by Salisbury's satisfied comment that the Dual Alliance was 'a decided check to the Emperor William, who, if he had elbow-room, would certainly be nasty for us. Family quarrels have made him really bitter against this country, and I am always glad to see him "hobbled".'[36]

The widespread impression that Wilhelm was running after the young Tsar was made a great deal worse by Wilhelm himself when in October 1896 he decided to go to Wiesbaden for a few days while the Tsar and Tsarina were staying at Darmstadt, on the assumption that it would be easy to arrange another encounter with Nicholas there. Both Wilhelm and Hohenlohe were therefore deeply shocked when the Tsar sent a telegram turning down the suggestion of a meeting at Wiesbaden. Nicholas and Alexandra, who were in Bad Homburg on 17 October for the dedication of the Russian Chapel and visited the Empress Frederick in neighbouring Kronberg, were not even prepared to wait two or three hours the following day until Wilhelm arrived at Wiesbaden.[37] On the advice of the Chancellor, who was concerned about the negative impression that it would make abroad if the two Emperors did not meet at all, Wilhelm announced his intention of paying a short visit to Darmstadt on 19 October, which the Tsar and Tsarina returned the following day by calling on Wilhelm briefly at Wiesbaden.[38] But both meetings turned out to be diplomatic disasters. In Darmstadt, where in addition to Nicholas and Alexandra the latter's sister Ella, her brother Ernst Ludwig and Grand Duke Sergei (Ella's husband and Nicholas's uncle) were staying, the German Emperor, who still looked pale and depressed after the operation on his ear, was made to feel the cold contempt of his Russian and Hessian relatives. Eulenburg was indignant at the deliberate humiliation to which Wilhelm was subjected, and reported to Bülow: 'Those individuals the Grand Duke of Hesse and Grand Duke Sergei are *the absolute worst* in Darmstadt, and undoubtedly influence the Emperor Nicholas's view of things . . . Sergei hates our master, and the young Grand Duke would take the greatest of pleasure in accepting a Kingdom of Hesse, enlarged by Baden, from the Tsar and his allied Republic [France]. One should not forget that a German prince who is not a nationalist, like this one, always signifies a certain danger.'[39] The return visit to Wiesbaden the next day by the Tsar and his wife, accompanied by Ernst Ludwig, was conspicuously short and did nothing to improve relations. The memorandum which Wilhelm handed to the Tsar at Wiesbaden, 'On the need to form a politico-mercantile coalition of the European states against the USA', lay neglected by Nicholas for months before he decided to shelve it, on the advice of his ministers.[40]

As Eulenburg was able to observe, this experience with Nicholas had 'deeply affected' his imperial friend Wilhelm. 'I could see very clearly in the features of the beloved Kaiser the *degree* of the moral impression it made on him. H.M. looked *shocking* when I saw him on 22 October after his visit to Wiesbaden. The Tsar's refusal of the invitation to Wiesbaden was very brusque. The subsequent visit he paid to the Empress [Alexandra] in Darmstadt hurt H.M. because of the way in which he was received. The Tsar, the Empress [Alexandra], the Grand Duke [of Hesse] and Grand Duke Sergei and their wives were choosing precious stones which they had had sent from France. Our Kaiser stood by − a seventh person on the sideline. After that the Tsar's visit to Wiesbaden brought no warmth. It was timed to the minute. H.M. told me very little about it. I could feel how it tormented Him.'[41] Waldersee found Wilhelm's behaviour towards the Tsar undignified and incomprehensible, and expressed deep anxiety over it in his diary after a meeting with Wilhelm at Schwerin. 'The Kaiser insists on running after his cousin, one could even say throwing himself at him, and puts up with it when the latter coldly sends him packing. Even at the court at Darmstadt it was plain to see that people have nothing but scorn for our Kaiser's behaviour; they are under partly English, partly Russian influence there and have not the slightest trace of feeling for us [Prussia], not even for Germany. The Russians have nothing but scorn and derision; it really is profoundly sad and the attitude of our Kaiser is almost incomprehensible; in fact it can only be explained as fear of a war. But in this respect the worthy gentleman has followed the worst possible path: a firm, confident attitude will give us much more security than this miserable grovelling!'[42]

As if all that were not enough, the Tsar sent a message, delivered to the Kaiser by Grand Duke Vladimir at a family wedding, asking him not to write any more letters in future; Nicholas would not answer them. His father − Tsar Alexander III − would never have permitted such a correspondence, he declared, especially since Wilhelm's letters, as he had now discovered, had been written without the previous knowledge of the Reich Chancellor.[43] As is well known, Wilhelm took no notice of the Tsar's request and carried on regardless with the highly political 'Willy–Nicky' correspondence. He attributed Nicholas's hostile behaviour to the influence of his Danish mother. As he commented maliciously in a letter to Emperor Franz Joseph in early 1898, Russian foreign policy was obviously based on the principle *'fiat voluntas − Imperatricis Matris − pereat mundus*! [The Empress Mother's will be done − let the world perish!] The poor Emperor [Nicholas] is to be pitied and has no easy task, but I trust him more than his Minister!'[44] Others, like Baroness Spitzemberg, were more inclined to attribute the Tsar's unfriendliness to Wilhelm II's importunate behaviour, which discomfited those at whom it was directed, compelled them to respond with reserve or a direct rebuff, and put them into 'a complicated, false position, out of which a grudge develops against the person who caused it – very sad, because it has very serious consequences', she observed.[45] Unquestionably, the exclusion of Wilhelm from the Russian-Hessian-English family circle foreshadowed the later diplomatic encirclement of the Wilhelmine Reich.

Not for nothing was mistrust of Wilhelm II and his seemingly unfathomable foreign policy growing in St Petersburg, Paris and London, for at the same time as he was proposing a continental coalition against the Atlantic powers, America and Britain, Wilhelm was putting out feelers towards France, and not long after the Wiesbaden fiasco he went so far as to launch a 'new programme', 'that is to say, co-operation between Germany and France against Russia'.[46] In August 1896, in a marginal note on a report by Eulenburg, he directed that Germany must persuade the French Foreign Minister of the virtues of mutual co-operation, and 'give a warm welcome to any attempt at rapprochement with us which Hanotaux shows signs of making'.[47] These hopes of a Franco-German rapprochement were fostered by Eulenburg, who was on the best of terms with his 'old friend' Raymond Lecomte at the French embassy in Berlin, and introduced him to the Kaiser.[48] Eulenburg was evidently endeavouring to avert the threat of a world war through such contacts. Although he tried to soothe the anxieties of Franz Joseph over the Franco-Russian alliance by assuring him that 'in Europe *Germany and Austria* are the rulers, and our alliance paralyses the madness of the Franco-Russian extravagance', he was warned by Count Anton von Wolkenstein, who had been Austrian ambassador at St Petersburg for many years, that France would now have Russia behind it if it 'struck out'. Passing on the warning to Wilhelm, Eulenburg wrote: 'An untenable state of affairs in Paris could seek an outlet through war and rapidly set the world on fire; for it is no longer a question of a duel between Germany and France [alone].'[49]

Shortly after the meeting between the two Emperors at Breslau, in a conversation with the British military attaché Sir James Grierson, Kaiser Wilhelm expressed anxiety about the possibility of a French attack on Germany, in connection with the anticipated effect of the Tsar's visit to Paris on the monarchist and Bonapartist movements there. Supporters of these movements would greet the Tsar with shouts of 'Vive l'Empereur', which would make them nostalgic for the old 'idées napoléoniennes', Wilhelm remarked, 'and the reestablishment of an Empire or Monarchy in France would, he fears, mean war with Germany, as, to solidify the dynasty, probably the first thing would be an attempt to recover Alsace and Lorraine'.[50] Early in 1897, when Wilhelm again urged the Reich

Chancellor, in a series of letters and marginal comments, to attempt a rapprochement with France, Hohenlohe had to point out to him that there would be little
prospect of success unless Germany were prepared to return Alsace-Lorraine to
France.[51] Holstein commented sarcastically on this latest idea of the Kaiser's in a
letter to Eulenburg: 'The moment H.M. already sees approaching when France
will seek our alliance as a *substitute* for the alliance with Russia – that moment
is still a long way off so far as human reckoning can judge. Before that time
comes – if it ever does – we will have to get around a good many sharp corners.
H.M. is only harming himself by speaking about this possibility with politicians
at this early date.'[52] Eulenburg, to whom Hohenlohe appealed for support in this
situation, assured him that he need not take the Kaiser's marginal notes seriously.
'An *entente* with France is something which His Majesty and I have frequently
discussed', he admitted, but 'always as something for the future, very far off,
and perhaps *never* to be a useful eventuality. But of course the *conversation itself*
always had the character of the *activity*, as is characteristic of His Majesty. The
marginal notes are also of *this character*. His Majesty will be easily persuaded.
And what harm has His Majesty's restlessness done, in the end? We are stronger
than ever at the moment as far as international affairs are concerned!'[53] In the
next few years Wilhelm's thoughts repeatedly returned to the idea of a Franco-
German agreement against Russia, especially on occasions when the young Tsar
and Tsarina tried to avoid a meeting with him or Russian military activity on
the frontier made him anxious.[54] In September 1899 he spoke to the Alsatian
politician Hugo Freiherr Zorn von Bulach 'of co-operation with France'; that
was 'the only salvation for France', he said. On this occasion he referred to the
Russians as 'riff-raff'.[55]

## A POLICY FOR THE FUTURE

How then did these continental aims – and it should be remembered that they
were never abandoned – relate to the new overseas policy that was now coming
increasingly to the fore? In this context the memorandum entitled 'Future policy', written in 1896 by Prince Heinrich's personal adjutant Georg Alexander
Müller, who was later to become Chief of the Kaiser's Naval Cabinet, is a most
revealing document. In it Müller boldly stated that world history was now dominated by the economic struggle. This struggle was at its most intense in Europe,
where 'above all as a result of the world domination of England' the peoples living there had no room for free expansion. 'The war which could – and many say
must – result from this situation of conflict would according to the generally
accepted opinion in our country have the aim of breaking England's world
domination in order to open up the necessary colonial possessions for the central

European states which need to expand', that is to say Germany, Austria-Hungary and Italy, and perhaps also the Scandinavian countries and Switzerland. 'But Germany stands far ahead in the need and indeed the right to expand', Müller claimed. And yet even in combination with the other Triple Alliance powers Germany would not have anything like the strength required 'in this great battle for economic survival . . . to break England's world domination'. It would therefore be necessary to join with France and Russia to form a continental league. 'In France we would gain a considerable increase in naval power; and in Russia an ally who would be able to attack the British Empire on land.' But in Müller's eyes the disadvantages of such a course were obvious. The 'destruction of the British world empire' would benefit not Germany, but the United States, France and above all Russia, which 'would naturally take India and therewith the lion's share of the spoils'. The Germans, at the very latest the next generation of them, would have to suffer 'because we permitted Russia's power to grow to the skies'. 'No', Prince Heinrich's Adjutant exclaimed, 'at that price we would rather not become a colonial power at all.' In an astonishing about-turn of the kind that was to become characteristic of the general ambiguity of Wilhelmine foreign policy until about 1912, Müller considered the possibility that instead of acting *against* Britain, Germany might act *with* it, in order to become a great colonial and world power. As Britain had the same interest in keeping down Russia as Germany itself, the latter could perhaps count on British support 'in the acquisition of territory outside Europe', he reasoned. By a happy chance Britain was after all 'our natural ally because we are both of the same race', which would add an idealistic element to the shared economic struggle, that is to say 'the preservation of the Germanic race against the Slav and Romance peoples'. Granted, if both Germanic races were to have a share in world domination Britain would probably expand more rapidly than Germany thanks to its much more powerful armaments, 'but even if Great Britain became stronger still, it could never become as dangerous for us as a stronger Russia would be', Müller declared. Reich Chancellor von Caprivi, he stated, had believed that 'Germany had no chance at all of becoming a world power, and consequently his policy was designed only to maintain [Germany's] position on the European continent.' This policy, 'now so widely ridiculed', would have been brilliantly vindicated 'if the German people were not coming to accept an entirely different opinion of their ability and duty to expand', the naval officer argued. In view of this development, however, the swing towards expansion either *with* Britain against the Franco-Russian alliance or as the leading power in a continental league *against* Britain was indispensable. Here too it was a case of 'all or nothing', Müller maintained. Either Germany must 'harness the total strength of the nation, ruthlessly, even if it means accepting the risk of a great war, or we limit ourselves to continental power alone. The middle way of contenting ourselves with a few leftover pieces of East Africa and the South Sea Islands without . . . suitability for settlement by Germans; of maintaining a fleet too strong for the mere defence of our coastline yet too weak for the pursuance of *Weltpolitik* – all this implies a dispersal of our strength . . . which Caprivi's policy logically wished to see diverted to the army.' Müller went on to ask whether Caprivi's policy would turn out to have been right. He hoped not. 'It would admittedly bring the present nation comfortable days without serious conflicts and excitements, but as soon as our exports began noticeably to decline the artificial economic edifice would start to crumble and existence therein would become very unpleasant indeed. Now, the Caprivi policy has been officially abandoned, and the new Reich government will hesitantly put to the nation the question – in the form of the new Navy Bill [planned by Wilhelm II and Tirpitz] – of whether the other policy, *Weltpolitik*, really can be adopted. Let us hope that this question receives an enthusiastic "Yes" for an answer, but also that then a change comes over our external relations in favour of an understanding with England, beside whom there is still a lot of room on this earth which is available or could be made available.'[56]

The memorandum by Georg Müller, who, though destined soon to become one of the most powerful men in German politics, was at this time a mere corvette-captain, was certainly not an officially binding document, but the ideas that are considered in it with such breathtaking insouciance are absolutely characteristic of the 'bid for world power' for which Wilhelmine Germany was preparing itself even before the turn of the century, and are therefore worth closer analysis here. The first combination discussed by Müller, that of a continental league of the Triple Alliance and the Dual Alliance against Great Britain, immediately raises the question: why should France and Russia accept German leadership? Had they not created the Dual Alliance only a few years earlier precisely in order to protect their security and sovereignty against the mightiest military power in the world? Both France and Russia had already become gigantic empires and their potential for expansion – in Asia, in the Near East and in Africa – was by no means exhausted. Why should they be tempted to participate in a break-up of the British world empire, the purpose of which was to raise the German Reich to the status of a hegemonial world power? After the 'great battle' both would be helplessly vulnerable to the superior power of Germany. The Kaiser's siren song of a European economic union against the United States of America could not prevail against the well-justified reservations of the French and the Russians. And if France and Russia were not willing to enter into the idea of a continental league under German leadership, would it not become necessary to use force to compel them to join the Triple Alliance? And where would that leave 'the problem of England'?

Even if Müller's first scenario of a continental league were not expressly designed to destroy British world domination, Britain would have been compelled to make use of all the power and influence at its disposal to prevent the European powers combining. The maintenance of the 'balance of power' on the continent had after all been the indispensable guiding principle of British foreign policy for centuries. Great Britain's interests in this respect undoubtedly coincided with the French and Russian desire for security, however great the differences between these three world powers might have been overseas. Thus even to get the continental league off the ground Germany would have had to overcome British supremacy, which was indeed the actual intention behind the battleship building programme, the early stages of which we shall examine shortly. And it was precisely this massive fleet building plan which – quite logically – was to lead to the increasingly close ties between Britain, France and Russia to protect the security of all three against Germany. None other than Wilhelm's uncle King Edward VII summed up the compelling logic of the British policy of *entente* when he remarked that if Britain dropped France and Russia out of fear of the German navy, it would give Germany the opportunity 'of demolishing her enemies, one by one, with us sitting by with folded arms, & she would then probably proceed to attack us'.[57] Müller's first suggestion thus led to an impasse, and not only for the reason he himself adduced, that Russia might become too strong by taking over India.

The prospects of success were no better, however, for the second possibility reviewed and preferred by him, that of an Anglo-German alliance to 'keep down' Russia and its western ally. Would not the establishment of a shared world domination by the two 'Germanic' world empires necessarily have entailed a war against the Dual Alliance which would naturally have given the German Reich supremacy on the continent of Europe? But even if Anglo-German collaboration had been limited to overseas acquisitions, as Müller suggested, the expansion of German power could not be expected to stop at that, for Berlin would have been exposed to the irresistible temptation, once it had acquired an enormous colonial empire, to broaden its narrow power base in Europe at the expense of France and Russia. And what form would the relationship between the two 'Germanic world empires' take? At one point in his memorandum Müller muses that it was perhaps not impossible 'that two so-to-speak satiated colonial powers . . . could coexist peaceably and use any surplus political power to further the struggle for the supremacy of the Germanic race', but this was not his considered view. Rather, he felt sure that an enlarged Britain and Germany would 'sooner or later but with absolute inevitability have to go to war to decide which of the two should dominate'. Moreover, he fantasised, it was by no means certain 'that the British world empire would be the stronger of the two Germanic states, for the lead which Great Britain now has over us means that she will be faced correspondingly sooner with the natural tendency for colonies to break away to form independent states'. One can all too readily understand, therefore, why the British government was unwilling to allow Germany 'the areas she needs for expansion whenever foreign empires collapse'.[58]

But if each of the routes to world power and 'world domination' indicated by Müller was as presumptuous and impracticable as the other, what is clear beyond any doubt is that the intensification of Germany's efforts in *both* directions – towards the creation of a continental league together with Russia and France against Great Britain and the forced imposition of an Anglo-German alliance against France and Russia – *simultaneously* was bound to lead to disaster. Even before the turn of the century, through the fatal zigzag course of expansionism it was pursuing all over the globe, the German Reich was coming into conflict with the world empires of Great Britain, France, Russia, Japan and the United States, all of which were to be among its enemies in the First World War.

## ARMENIAN ATROCITIES AND THE CRETAN CRISIS

The kind of wilful, unpredictable, emotionally charged policy which both the Wilhelmstrasse and the governments of the established powers now had to face manifested itself as early as 1896 and 1897 in Wilhelm II's furious interventions in the critical situation in the eastern Mediterranean, where the German Reich had previously remained strictly aloof. The atrocities carried out in and around Constantinople in the summer of 1896, when up to 8,000 Christian Armenians were murdered, caused horror throughout Europe.[59] The regard in which the Kaiser had held Sultan Abdul Hamid II since his visit to Yildiz in the autumn of 1889 had completely vanished as a result of the massacres, at least for the time being.[60] He repeatedly demanded that the Turkish ruler, whom he now described as a 'wretched scoundrel', be deposed.[61] Wilhelm believed he could see through the Sultan's motives for the mass murder of the Armenians, and that they were part of a cynical diversionary strategy. In September 1896 he wrote on a report by the German ambassador, Baron Saurma, from Constantinople, that even more serious than the Armenian question in itself was 'the growing discontent of the Mohammedans in all circles, especially the army. Effendimis [the Sultan] knows it very well, and at first resorted to arrests and drownings. But as that did not help, he lets the Mohammedans loose on the Armenians as Christians, so as to curry favour with them.'[62] In December 1896 in a letter to Queen Victoria he wrote of the Sultan: 'May Allah soon take him to were [sic] it is very hot – [he] seems to be bent upon amusing himself aux depens of the Powers, "les 6 *im*=Puissances", as he calls them.'[63]

From the outset the Kaiser poured scorn on the inactivity of the great powers. At the end of July 1896, when the position of the Armenians in Turkey was becoming dangerous, Wilhelm had expressed the fear that 'all the Christians' there might be 'slaughtered', and criticised the lack of international intervention. 'And the Christian powers are to look calmly on, and if possible support it by a blockade!! Shame on us all!'[64] But when the crisis became acute he categorically rejected Marschall's urgent recommendation that German warships be sent to the eastern Mediterranean. 'No. They would in any case be too late and could not go through the Dardanelles', he wrote on the Foreign Secretary's cipher telegram. 'Anyway, England and France are there!' 'If the whole of the English and French, as well as the Russian, Italian etc., Mediterranean squadrons have been no use, a German ship will not be any use either.'[65] Only months later Wilhelm's attitude to the Sultan and the Ottoman Empire was to change completely again.

In early 1897 the rebellion against Turkish rule in Crete flared up anew. The leaders proclaimed union with Greece, and war between Greece and Turkey seemed inevitable. Under pressure from public opinion the Greek government sent a warship and a cargo ship to Crete on 6 February; a few days later the Greek fleet was mobilised, and Prince George of Greece, the second son of the King, crossed over to Crete with four torpedo boats.[66] During this crisis the Kaiser allowed himself to be led by strong anti-British and anti-Greek feelings. He distrusted London's intentions and was convinced that Britain was aiming to take advantage of the collapse of the Ottoman Empire.[67] When Hatzfeldt reported in January 1897 that Salisbury doubted that the ambassadors' conference meeting in Constantinople to solve the crisis could succeed, and that he thought it probable that in the end Austria would have to step in to prevent action by Russia, the Kaiser commented on this news with an explosive marginal note: 'I see, just as I thought, for want of an army Austria must act as slave labour in England's interests, and once that is under way, the Triple Alliance will have to follow, after which Salisbury will set Gaul on our heels! Then *vogue la galère* and *adieu* Africa for us?!'[68] On another report from Hatzfeldt, in which he described the proposal of the international conference to set up a supreme council of state in Turkey, the Kaiser expressed his suspicion that Britain was merely trying 'to compel Russia to intervene, so as to be able to play off Austria against her'.[69] Obsessed with his mistrust of Salisbury, he constantly tried to 'unmask' the real intentions of the British in the crisis.[70] He suspected, for instance, that Salisbury had made promises to Italy as to how it could profit from the collapse of Turkey at the expense of Austria.[71] Lascelles, no doubt recalling Lord Salisbury's warning of December 1895, reported that Wilhelm's behaviour appeared 'to verge on insanity'. He was 'violently excited against England' and 'in a wild state of excitement' over Crete, the ambassador informed the British Prime Minister, bemoaning the fact that 'His Majesty should have elected to be his own Minister for Foreign Affairs during this crisis.'[72]

Wilhelm favoured severe measures against Greece, which he likewise deeply distrusted. On 14 February 1897 he wrote to his mother: 'Everybody is very preoccupied here by the sudden & unexpected turn affairs have taken in Crete by the most untoward immixtion [sic] of the Greeks, who are in the act of setting fire to the whole of Europe if they persist in their rashness! For I just got the news that the King has given the order to mobilize his Army! If Heaven does not avert the catastrophy [sic], we are on the eve of very grave events & may before the year is many months older be plunged in the most terrific broils!'[73] Against the wishes of the Chancellor and the Foreign Office, who were in favour of an intervention by the powers on the spot, Wilhelm suggested a joint blockade of Piraeus, in direct conversations with the British, Austrian and Russian ambassadors.[74] He wanted to prove to the world, he wrote, that things could be managed 'even without England', for 'the continent must show the British for once that they are not the best at running it'.[75] Colonel Grierson described the Kaiser's hectic attempts to make the running in this affair in a letter to Sir Arthur Bigge of 20 February 1897. 'The Emperor is constantly visiting the ambassadors . . . and trying to win the Powers round to his proposal of a blockade of the Greek coast. The other day he went to the Austrian Embassy at 9 a.m. and found the Ambassador in bed. After rousing him, he came on to the British Embassy where the same thing was repeated. Apart from public opinion in England it seems to me all the same that the Emperor is right in his idea of nipping the danger to the peace of Europe in the bud, but I cannot see why Germany, whose interests in the Mediterranean are infinitesimal compared to those of other Powers, and who at this moment has not a single ship in Cretan or Greek waters (though one is *en route*), should take the lead . . . I very much fear that there will now be a new flood of vituperations against British policy in the German papers.'[76] When the German warship mentioned in Grierson's letter, the *Kaiserin Augusta*, arrived in the Eastern Mediterranean, the Kaiser demanded that its commander be instructed 'to act above all in unison with the *Russian* and *Austrian* admirals, and not to hesitate to take the severest measures − including shooting with live ammunition − if Greece pays no heed to warnings'.[77] Action at sea would make sense only if 'instead of a few cannon shots, a sharp naval engagement puts an abrupt end to the Greek fleet. For it has powerful torpedoes, and in return for "a few cannon shots" it could sink the ships with a few torpedoes during the night.'[78]

Just as after the Krüger telegram a year earlier, the Kaiser bewailed the fact that Germany's navy was not strong enough for international crises. 'This shows one once again how much Germany suffers from the *lack* of a *strong fleet*, as it cannot make itself felt effectively in the Concert [of Europe]. If, instead of one ship, we had had a strong cruiser division with armoured cruisers in Crete, Germany could immediately have blockaded Athens on her own initiative in February, *alone*, and thereby swept along the other powers with us and forced them willy-nilly to join in. As it is, in the end nothing happened, and the one who thwarts all plans, paralyses all energy and to whom after all that consideration is shown is England! And why? *Because she has the strongest fleet!* Our 1,000,000 Grenadiers are *no* help to us there!'[79]

In this crisis Kaiser Wilhelm found himself in conflict not only with his own Foreign Office and the agreed policy of the great powers, but also with the passionate feelings of his sister Crown Princess Sophie and his mother and grandmother. His contempt for the Greek royal family, with its close ties with Copenhagen, London and St Petersburg, played a decisive role in his hostile attitude towards Greek aspirations. He described the sons of King George I as 'louts without any education', and commenting on the influence of the Dowager Empress Marie of Russia, the Princess of Wales and the ladies of the Danish court on the Greek question he said: 'These petticoats should keep their fingers out of things.'[80] He scornfully rejected the humanitarian arguments of his sister, mother and grandmother, who were shocked by the atrocities committed by the Turks against the Cretan population.[81] Once again the Empress Frederick could only consider her son's heartlessness as an incomprehensible barrier to a better relationship between them. 'Of course I do not mention the subject to William, whose violence is unabated', she wrote to Queen Victoria.[82] 'What it is to me – as a Mother – to see my own son embarked on a course which threatens ruin & destruction to his own sister & brother in law & their family, I cannot tell you!!!'[83] After a visit which the Kaiser had paid to her at Kronberg she reported to Windsor: 'William . . . did not disguise that all his sympathies were with the Turks. – He believes everything that is in *disfavour* of the Greeks.'[84]

In spite of the blockade instigated by Wilhelm II, Greek troops crossed the Thessalian frontier on 10–11 April 1897, setting in motion the war with Turkey.[85] Fears were now beginning to be expressed in all the capitals of Europe about the escalation of the crisis, especially when the Greek army suffered a series of defeats. On 25 April Queen Victoria appealed to the Tsar – a further sign of British co-operation with the Franco-Russian alliance – 'to use all your powerful influence to bring about an armistice and terminate this disastrous war which, I am sure, must distress you as much as it does me. I earnestly trust that you will be able to agree to Lord Salisbury's proposal for joint action with you and France.'[86] At the beginning of May the representatives of the Russian, British, French and Italian governments in Constantinople suggested an armistice between Greece and Turkey, although without making it a condition that Athens should recognise the autonomy of Crete and the Greek troops should be withdrawn from the island, both points on which Wilhelm II had insisted as prerequisites. Instead, as Hohenlohe informed the Kaiser, the ambassadors 'merely expressed the hope that the Greek government, out of gratitude for the successful mediation, would agree to those demands later'. In view of this fact, the Chancellor advised the Kaiser 'that His Majesty should maintain the attitude He has held hitherto in the interest of European peace, and also impress this point of view upon the Austro-Hungarian ambassador. For it is beyond question that the Greek government will not agree to the demands of the powers except under the pressure of a direct threat of war.' The Kaiser unreservedly accepted Hohenlohe's suggestion. 'Have spoken to the ambassador in the sense indicated below and quite unambiguously, leaving him in no doubt that I shall not participate unless Greece has knuckled under and promised unconditional withdrawal of troops from and autonomy for Crete, and has submitted unconditionally to the verdict of the great powers.'[87]

In consequence, Queen Victoria's efforts to persuade Wilhelm that it was necessary for all the powers to negotiate an armistice as soon as possible[88] received short shrift from the Kaiser. In reply to a telegram from the Queen he wrote: 'The Powers have arranged that the Proposal of an Armistice must be begged for by Greece, with the promise to be added by the same Power that she is ready unconditionally to submit to the verdict of the Powers and immediately to recall her Troops from Creta, the Autonomy of which she has to accept. This is conditio sine qua non. Before Greece has not expressed her will in the above named way, intervention is out of the question. It is the Russian government who, I think, is most fit to take the lead in this matter. William I. R.'[89] Taken aback, the Queen wrote in her diary: 'Received a rude answer from William, sent en clair, whilst my telegram was in cypher.'[90] Even when he received a cry for help from his sister Sophie, begging him to prevent 'further bloodshed' and 'to hasten the mediation which has been proposed by the powers, for my sake',[91] the Kaiser answered that he could do nothing so long as Greece refused to submit to the powers, recognise the autonomy of Crete and 'restore the rights she has infringed, by withdrawing her troops from there'. Not until Greece showed itself willing to accept these conditions did the German ambassadors in Athens and Constantinople have the Kaiser's instructions 'to enter into discussions with the representatives of the other powers regarding mediation', as he replied to his sister on 12 May.[92]

A few days later Wilhelm was in a position to report triumphantly to his grandmother that Greece had agreed to the conditions he had specified. 'I am happy to be able to communicate to you that after the King and the Government had begged for my intervention through Sophy and after having officially notified to my minister and again through Sophy to me personally that they unconditionally accepted the conditions I had proposed I have ordered Baron v. Plessen to take the necessary steps to restore Peace in conjunction with the representatives of the other powers. William I. R.'[93] Once again the Queen noted with astonishment in her journal, 'Received another grandiloquent telegram, also en clair, from William saying that Willy of Greece [King George I of Greece] had begged through Sophy for his intervention.'[94] Wilhelm's self-satisfaction was even more evident in the telegram that he sent to his mother the same day: 'After Sophie had begged for mediation and had been acquainted with my conditions which she transmitted to the King – the Gov[t] have unconditionally accepted them and I have unconditionally instructed my Minister at Athens to join the Powers in the work of restoring peace. – War is at an end now!' The Empress Frederick sent a copy of this 'curious telegram from him, in the usual strangely bombastic style', to her mother, and added anxiously: 'What a strange way of doing things – why all *himself* instead of his foreign office!!'[95]

When the peace negotiations came to an end in September 1897 the Chancellor congratulated the monarch on the success of his policy. In reply, the Kaiser wrote: 'If, in Your Highness's opinion, my firm stand helped to further the cause of peace, its success is essentially due to the prudence of Your Highness and of the agencies which succeeded in putting my ideas, as agreed with Your Highness, into practical effect.'[96] In his own estimation, of course, his role during the crisis had been so crucial that he was the only person who could, or should, make any statement to the Reichstag about it. In a telegram from Hubertusstock he complained about Marschall, who had promised the Reichstag to provide more information about Germany's Cretan policy in due course. 'There should be no question of this without my orders and without previous consultation with me.' The Kaiser was 'the only person whose place it is to inform the Reichstag about it', and he had already ordered Hohenlohe to convene a meeting of the Reichstag at the Schloss for this purpose. 'Your Highness thought this idea a good one in every respect and approved it, but thought that it was too soon to make a statement to the Reichstag. That has nevertheless happened, without my prior knowledge and consent, and I must express my astonishment at it.' From now on, Wilhelm insisted, he would himself keep parliament informed on the crisis. 'All interpellations or discussions concerning Crete in which the Reichstag requests further information must be notified to me, with an indication of the proposed reply . . . I have very consciously taken a step which is intended to preserve peace in Europe once more, and I am firmly resolved to continue to take charge of the matter myself . . . I have no doubt that I shall succeed with God's help in once again preventing a world conflagration, if it is possible.'[97]

The following year, when Wilhelm visited the Sultan in Yildiz during his spectacular Near Eastern tour, both the bitter rancour and the cunning political calculation which had motivated him in the Cretan crisis found expression in an emotionally charged letter to the Tsar. Full of hatred for Britain, the 'meddlesome Power' which he held responsible for the rebellion on the island, he told Nicholas II that he had involved his fleet in the crisis 'because I felt and saw that a certain Power was using us all others as catspaws to get us to help her to take Crete or Suda bay, and I would not be of the party who are expected to appear with bread and salt and on the top the keys of Crete praying the said Power to kindly look after the welfare of these poor darling "Cretans who may one and all roast in hell"!' If the Christians in Crete succeeded in driving the Muslims off the island the effect would be disastrous, the Kaiser declared. 'What a terrible blow to the prestige of the Christian in general in the eyes of the Mussulman and renewal of hatred you can hardly imagine! The Powers concerned in Crete have played a foolish and a most dangerous game.' The Tsar should never forget 'that the Mahometans [are] a tremendous card in our game in case you or I were suddenly confronted by a war with the certain meddlesome Power! You as the master of millions of Mahometans must be the best judge of this.' 'If you quietly go on following the lead of the other Power in Crete as has been done till now', Wilhelm warned the Tsar, 'the effect will be deplorable upon your own Mahometan subjects and on Turkey . . . Therefore I implore you to give this matter once more your most serious attention and if possible find means by which you can save the Sultan from a dangerous and compromising situation envers ses sujets and solve the Cretan question in a manner acceptable to him. Don't forget that his Army fought valiantly and victoriously *for Crete* . . . and reconquered the Province. It would never forget or forgive another Power the expulsion of their brothers in arms and their Master from a reconquered Province! What a splendid opportunity for you to step in and save the Sultan from disgrace, the world from bloody war and gain the gratitude of all Mahometans! Otherwise revolution may come, and the Sultan's blood may one day be at your door! . . . All hoping eyes are turned to the great Emperor of the East; will he bring the hoped for solution?'[98]

## WILHELM'S PLANS FOR A GERMAN-JEWISH HOMELAND IN PALESTINE

The Kaiser's journey to Constantinople, Haifa, Jerusalem, Bethlehem, Beirut and Damascus in the autumn of 1898 is certainly one of the strangest episodes in his not exactly uneventful life, especially as he not only met the 'wretched scoundrel' Abdul Hamid, whom had recently wished to see deposed, and set himself up as protector of all the Muslims in the world, but also contemplated, for a short time but in all seriousness, proclaiming a Jewish homeland in Palestine under his patronage. How, and through whom, did this astonishing idea come to the German Kaiser, who in spite of his friendship with a few prominent German Jews was anything but pro-Jewish by inclination? What was his aim, and what prevented the plan from taking off? As this failed project affects one of the sorest points of German–Jewish relations in the past hundred years, it is not surprising that it has been the subject of much detailed research.[99]

With their enormous suite – the Kaiserin's three ladies in waiting, her Ober-hofmeister Mirbach, the Oberhofmarschall August Eulenburg and the Ober-stallmeister Ernst von Wedel, two personal physicians, Leuthold and Ilberg, the Adjutant-Generals and Flügeladjutanten Plessen, Kessel, Scholl, Mackensen and Pritzelwitz, the three Cabinet Chiefs Hahnke, Lucanus and Senden, the Foreign Secretary Bernhard Bülow and many others, including eighty maids, servants and bodyguards – the German Kaiser and Kaiserin left Berlin on 11 October 1898 in the imperial train. The ostensible reason for the journey to the Orient was the dedication of the Church of the Redeemer in Jerusalem on 31 October. More far-reaching hopes and plans, however, lay behind it. In memory of the journey through the Holy Land which his father had made in 1869 on the way to the opening of the Suez Canal, Wilhelm now wished to visit the holy places in his turn, in a kind of pilgrimage with the Kaiserin, while at the same time using the opportunity to make contact with the various German settlers in Palestine.[100] As always, the desire to promote the image of the monarchy played its part: through the dissemination in Germany of pictures and descriptions of the journey, useful propaganda was to be derived from the iconography of the imperial visit to the sacred sites of Christianity. On the orders of the Kaiser a tropical uniform was designed expressly for the tour, and the horses, specially broken in for him, which he would need for his theatrical entry into Jerusalem, were sent out in advance by sea. Poets (Frank Wedekind), caricaturists (Thomas Theodor Heine) and publishers (Albert Langen) who made fun of the imperial crusader in the satirical journal *Simplicissimus* were punished with long prison sentences or had to flee abroad.[101]

In view of the smouldering national and religious conflicts in the Near East the greatest caution was of course necessary if Wilhelm II's tour was not to prove the spark that set the powder keg alight.[102] The Kaiser's original plan to include a visit to Cairo had to be abandoned because of the serious danger of an assassination attempt – the Empress Elisabeth of Austria, whom Wilhelm had worshipped in his youth, was murdered by an Italian anarchist on 10 September 1898 on Lake Geneva – and because of the Anglo-French conflict in the upper Nile.[103] Nonetheless, after his help in the Cretan crisis Wilhelm expected his visit to Sultan Abdul Hamid II at Constantinople to bring about a decided improvement in relations between Germany and the Ottoman Empire, which, as everyone was well aware, might easily lead to complications with Russia, France and Britain. It is therefore all the more surprising that Wilhelm was willing, shortly before his journey, to consider the proclamation of a German protectorate over a Jewish homeland in Palestine, and to suggest this idea to the Sultan.

Documentary sources show that the initiative for this came not from Wilhelm but from Theodor Herzl, the founder of modern Zionism. In June 1895, shortly before he began drafting his influential book *Der Judenstaat*, he declared: 'I shall go to the German Kaiser, and he will understand me, as he has been brought up to appreciate great things. I shall say to the German Kaiser: Let our people go.'[104] Although he was well aware that a Jewish state called into being with Germany's help would have to pay 'the most usurious interest',[105] the German route to the realisation of his far-reaching plans was Herzl's preferred option. The German Reich would provide not only protection, but the model for the internal structure of the aristocratic Jewish republic which he wished to found. 'To live under the protection of this strong, great, moral, splendidly governed, tightly organised Germany can only have the most salutary effect on the Jewish national character', he wrote in his diary. 'At one stroke we would obtain a completely ordered internal and external legal status.' And the Germans would also profit from this alliance, for 'through Zionism it will again become possible for Jews to love this Germany, to which our hearts have been attached despite everything!'[106]

It was of course one thing to appeal to the Kaiser, but quite another to persuade the monarch to grant him an audience. In fact it was William H. Hechler, the eccentric Anglo-German chaplain at the British embassy in Vienna, who paved the way for Herzl's approach to the imperial court. He sent the Grand Duke of Baden three copies of *Der Judenstaat* and persuaded the Kaiser's uncle to receive Herzl at Karlsruhe on 22 April 1896.[107] In time Grand Duke Friedrich proved to be a benevolent, if hesitant, patron of the Zionists. For his part Wilhelm II had hitherto shown little interest in Zionism, although he was aware of the central aim of the movement and occasionally – albeit mockingly – expressed himself in favour of it. In May 1891, when he heard of the negotiations between America and Russia over the acquisition of land in Argentina for the persecuted Jews of Russia, he remarked 'Oh, if only we could send ours there too.'[108] In April 1896 the Kaiser visited Karlsruhe, and when the Grand Duke and Hechler tried to draw his attention to Herzl's ideas he called out jokingly to his uncle's guest: 'Hechler, I hear you want to become a minister of the Jewish State.'[109] A year later, on reading a report on the First Zionist Congress, Wilhelm wrote in the margin: 'I am very much in favour of the Mauschels going to Palestine, the sooner they clear off there the better. I shall put no obstacles in their way.'[110] The All-Highest sovereign's anti-Semitic scrawl does at least show that common ground existed between Herzl and the Kaiser. As the Zionist leader had noted in 1895, 'the anti-Semites are becoming our most reliable friends'.[111] When Herzl wrote to the Kaiser on the Grand Duke's advice, asking for an audience, he received the reply that the monarch could not receive him, but asked him to submit a written report on the Zionist Congress. On 1 December 1897 Herzl sent the Kaiser his pamphlet *The Basel Congress*.[112] The first contact had been made.

The fact that for a short while during the autumn of 1898 Wilhelm showed rather more sympathy for the Zionist dream was largely thanks to the efforts of Hechler, the Grand Duke of Baden and Philipp Eulenburg. Hechler was convinced that the Ark of the Covenant, containing the Ten Commandments inscribed by the hand of God and the original manuscript of the first part of the Old Testament written by Moses, was awaiting discovery on Mount Nebo to the east of the River Jordan. Kaiser Wilhelm, the Anglican chaplain urged, should persuade the Sultan to cede the Holy Land with Transjordania to him, so as to be able to prove to the world at last that God and Moses had personally written these Judaeo-Christian texts.[113] On 28 July 1898 Grand Duke Friedrich, after repeated requests from Hechler and Herzl, finally wrote to his imperial nephew. Although he enclosed material about the Zionist movement, his letter was mainly concerned with Hechler's 'discovery' of the whereabouts of the Ark of the Covenant. The Grand Duke urged the Kaiser to make use of his forthcoming tour of the Near East to persuade the Sultan to cede the territory in question to him, naturally without revealing the real reason for his request, the Ark.[114]

The Kaiser's reply was guarded. He would send the enclosed Zionist material to Eulenburg, who would make him an oral report on it.[115] Despite this initial caution, events now began to move rapidly. On 2 September the Grand Duke received Hechler and Herzl for a two-hour audience on the Isle of Mainau in Lake Constance. The Zionist leader was amazed by the Grand Duke's 'grandiose' willingness to discuss with him 'the most secret German political matters and . . . the intentions of the Kaiser'. The Grand Duke had learned from Adolf Marschall von Bieberstein, who had meanwhile been accredited as German ambassador in Constantinople, that the Sultan was favourably disposed towards the Zionist cause. As a result of Germany's support for Turkey in the crisis over Crete, Abdul Hamid had complete confidence in the Kaiser, Grand Duke Friedrich continued, and so German influence in Constantinople was now unlimited. 'If our Kaiser drops a word to the Sultan, it will certainly be heeded', he asserted. He went on to disclose that the Kaiser had shown a very marked interest in the

Ark of the Covenant, the discovery of which would be a world sensation. The
Grand Duke asked Herzl whether he had the intention of founding a state in
Palestine and advised him to recognise the Sultan's overlordship for the time
being; a generation later one would be able to see what could be done. But he
warned Herzl to be patient. The other powers had suddenly become suspicious
of German intentions in Palestine, and Herzl would only add fuel to the fire if
he pressed for an audience with the Kaiser.[116]

On 8 September Herzl appealed to the German ambassador in Vienna, Philipp
Eulenburg. He offered to provide the Kaiser's friend with further information
about the Zionist movement, and stressed that he needed to speak to the Kaiser
before his visit to the Near East.[117] Since Wilhelm was to be in Vienna for
the funeral of the murdered Empress Elisabeth on 17 September, Herzl hoped
he might be granted an audience on that day.[118] As he described his plans to
Eulenburg on 16 September, the ambassador became 'visibly fascinated'. What
made the strongest impression was Herzl's hint that the Zionists would have
to turn to Britain if German support were not forthcoming. He strongly urged
that Herzl should meet his friend Bernhard von Bülow, who would be coming
to Vienna with the Kaiser.[119]

Following an unproductive meeting with the new Foreign Secretary, Herzl left
for Paris, Amsterdam and London without having met the Kaiser. From Paris he
wrote to Eulenburg setting out his principal arguments again. He emphasised
that with the establishment of a Jewish homeland in Palestine 'an element of
German culture' would be brought to the eastern shore of the Mediterranean;
that an 'ordered exodus' of the Jewish proletariat would take the wind out of the
sails of the socialist movement in Europe; and that, with the decrease of anti-
Semitic agitation that would follow, wealthy Jews would be happy to remain
in their present countries. Moreover 'the influx of an intelligent, economically
energetic people' would bring new strength to the Ottoman Empire. France was
in turmoil over the Dreyfus affair and was in no position to oppose a German
initiative. With even greater urgency Herzl renewed his plea for an audience
with the Kaiser before his journey to Constantinople. 'One word from the Kaiser
can have the greatest consequences for the shaping of things in the Orient. His
journey to the Holy Land can attain the significance of a historic turning-point
in the Orient, if the return of the Jews is initiated', he urged.[120]

Eulenburg, who was staying with the Kaiser at Rominten, evidently used
Herzl's letter as an *aide-mémoire* in his conversations with Wilhelm. At any rate
it is clear that the monarch adopted Herzl's arguments in the letter he wrote
to the Grand Duke of Baden on 29 September 1898. He began by thanking his
uncle for sending the material on Zionism, which he had worked through with
Eulenburg. 'The result of my researches is now as follows: . . . The basic idea

[of the movement] has always interested me and even aroused my sympathy. After studying the material you kindly sent me I have now come to the conclusion that we are dealing here with a question of the most far-reaching significance. I have therefore had careful approaches made to the promoters of this idea and have thus been able to find out that the transfer to the land of Palestine of those Israelites who are ready to go has been most excellently prepared for and is even perfectly financially sound in every respect. I have therefore said in response to a question from the Zionists whether I would be prepared to receive a delegation of them in audience, that I would be happy to receive a deputation in Jerusalem on the occasion of our visit there.' He was convinced, the Kaiser continued, 'that the settlement of the Holy Land by the wealthy and hard-working nation of Israel would soon bring to the former unsuspected prosperity' — and thus also lead to a significant economic revival for Turkey. 'The Turk would then get well again, i.e. he would receive money in the natural way, *without needing to borrow*, then he will no longer be sick, will be able to build his own roads and railways without having to rely on foreign companies and then it won't be so easy for him to be partitioned. Q.E.D! In addition, the energy, creativity and efficiency of the tribe of Sem would be diverted to worthier goals than the sucking dry of the Christians, and many an oppositional Semite now supporting the Social Democrats would clear off to the East, where there is more rewarding work to be done . . . Now I realise that nine-tenths of all Germans would recoil in horror if they were to discover that I sympathised with the Zionists or would even, as I intend to do if asked, place them under my protection!' But Wilhelm had his retort ready: 'Our dear God knows even better than we do that the Jews killed Our Saviour, and he has punished them accordingly. But neither the anti-Semites nor others, myself included, have been asked or empowered by Him to bully these people after our own fashion *in majorem Dei Gloriam*!' One must love one's enemies, the Kaiser piously reminded his uncle. And besides, 'from an earthly, realistic political standpoint it should not be forgotten that, considering the immense and extremely dangerous power which International Jewish capital represents, it would after all be of huge advantage to Germany if the world of the Hebrews looked up to it in gratitude?! Everywhere the hydra of the coarsest, ghastliest anti-Semitism is raising its dreadful head, and the terrified Jews — ready to leave those countries where danger threatens — are looking around for a protector. Well then, those who have returned to the Holy Land shall enjoy protection and security, and I shall intercede on their behalf with the Sultan.'[121]

As one can readily understand, Herzl was utterly overwhelmed when he learned from a letter from Eulenburg that the Kaiser was ready to take on the protectorate of the Jewish state. Wilhelm had shown a 'complete and profound understanding' of the movement and was ready to take up its cause *'urgently'*

with the Sultan. The monarch did not wish to meet Herzl before his departure
for Constantinople, as such a meeting could not be kept secret, but he was looking
forward to receiving a Zionist deputation in Palestine. In a 'top secret' postscript
Eulenburg suggested that Herzl should nevertheless come to Constantinople on
17 October in case the Kaiser needed a final briefing before he spoke to the
Sultan. In addition, he offered to receive Herzl at Liebenberg, his estate in the
Mark Brandenburg, before his departure for the Orient.[122]

At Liebenberg, Eulenburg repeated his view that Wilhelm had now become
quite accustomed to the idea of a protectorate, and did not doubt that the Sultan
would welcome his proposal. 'Wonderful, wonderful!', Herzl wrote delightedly.
When Eulenburg warned that Germany would not go to war on behalf of the
Zionists, a discussion followed on the probable reaction of the great powers to
German sponsorship of a Jewish homeland in the Near East. Eulenburg's view
was that 'since a protectorate was involved, the matter could not remain concealed
for long. Therefore he thought it best to come right out with it, immediately
and demonstratively.' As far as Russia was concerned, the ambassador was more
sanguine than the Zionist. 'If the worst comes to the worst, our Kaiser could
write [the Tsar] a letter and win him over to Zionism', Eulenburg assured Herzl.
'Since Russia has no objections to the departure of the Jews, no obstacles will be
placed in the way of the cause.'[123]

Herzl spent the next day on tenterhooks at the Neues Palais, where Eulenburg and the Grand Duke were conferring with the Kaiser. The Grand Duke
subsequently confirmed Eulenburg's impression that the Kaiser was 'full of
enthusiasm' for the Zionist cause. On the grounds of a positive report received
from Marschall, he was sure that the Sultan would react favourably. 'The Kaiser
has now undertaken to mediate and he intends to go through with it', the Grand
Duke assured Herzl. Wilhelm intended to receive Herzl both at Constantinople
and at Jerusalem. Later, when Herzl met Bülow and Hohenlohe, the chill wind
of political realism made itself felt for the first time. The elderly Chancellor
wanted to know how much territory Herzl was claiming: whether as far north
as Beirut or even beyond. He asked whether Herzl wanted to found a state, and
how he thought Turkey would respond to such an initiative. The Foreign Secretary denied all knowledge of a favourable report from Marschall. Herzl had to
console himself with the thought that in the end what really counted was the
Kaiser himself.[124]

On 13 October 1898 Herzl and four other Zionist leaders left Vienna on the
Orient Express. On the way they agreed to ask for the territory between Gaza
and the Euphrates, for which they would seek autonomous status within the
Ottoman Empire. On their arrival at Constantinople, however, things did not go
well at first. Marschall brusquely declared that he did not know Herzl and had

no time to receive him. Herzl then appealed to August Eulenburg, and sent him a letter for the Kaiser in which he begged for an audience.[125] The long-awaited meeting, at which Bülow was also present, finally took place on the evening of 18 October 1898.

Herzl was at first irritated by the anti-Semitic undertone of the hour-long conversation which ensued. The Kaiser declared that he would very much welcome the settlement of some German-Jewish 'elements' in Palestine. 'I am thinking of Hesse, for example, where there are usurers at work among the rural population. If these people took their possessions and went to settle in the colonies, they could be more useful.' Bülow added to the anti-Semitic tone by complaining that 'the Jews' had shown themselves ungrateful to the House of Hohenzollern and were now to be found among the oppositional parties. If the Kaiser proclaimed a protectorate in Palestine, he would expect the Jews to show their gratitude. Nevertheless, Herzl succeeded in getting his 'entire plan' across. 'Everything, everything', he later noted with relief. The Kaiser 'listened to me magnificently' and agreed that the plan for a Jewish homeland was 'completely natural'. And when Bülow expressed doubts about the Turkish reaction, Wilhelm exclaimed: 'But surely it will make an impression if the German Kaiser concerns himself with it and shows an interest in it . . . After all, I am the only one who still sticks by the Sultan. He puts stock in me.' He asked Herzl what he should demand of the Sultan, to which Herzl replied: 'A Chartered Company – under German protection'.[126] Sensing that he was 'approaching the climax of my tragic [sic!] enterprise', Herzl and his team left for Palestine.

We do not know in which of his conversations with the Sultan the Kaiser raised the subject of a German protectorate in Palestine. All that is known is that Abdul Hamid rejected the idea so brusquely that his imperial guest did not feel able to pursue the matter further.[127] But the Zionist plan was of course nothing new to the Turkish government, which had long since agreed upon its own policy on the matter. In spite of Marschall's (alleged) report to the contrary, the Sultan had never wavered in his opposition to the project. According to his daughter he declared, 'I cannot sell even a foot of land for it does not belong to me but my people . . . The Jews may spare their millions. When my empire is divided, perhaps they will get Palestine for nothing. But only our corpse can be divided. I will never consent to vivisection.'[128] As the records in the Yildiz Archives show, the Sultan's position was unanimously supported by his advisers. All were opposed to the idea of burdening the empire with yet another national and religious problem which the European powers would only exploit to their own advantage. The Ottoman ambassadors abroad warned that the real aim of the Zionists was the formation of an independent Jewish state which would not be limited to Palestine; such a state would become the focus of worldwide

Jewish activity. They also realised that the establishment of a Jewish state in the Holy Land would fuel the 'Arab Awakening' which would destroy the Ottoman Empire. On the orders of Abdul Hamid, the Council of Ministers had developed a programme to counter the Zionist danger at home and abroad.[129] Against this background, the Sultan's determined attitude should have come as no surprise to Wilhelm II.[130]

Although Herzl was not yet aware of it, Wilhelm's attitude to Zionism had in any case abruptly gone into reverse. Suddenly overwhelmed with admiration for the quasi-absolutist Sultan and the monotheistic rigour of Islam – a sentiment which found expression in the letter of 20 October to the Tsar quoted earlier in this chapter[131]– and out of reach of the influence of Eulenburg and the Grand Duke of Baden, but open to the dictates of *raison d'état* as presented to him by Tewfik Pasha, the Turkish ambassador in Berlin who was travelling with him, and Bülow, both of whom pointed out to him that Britain, France and Russia would never tolerate a German satellite state in the Near East, Wilhelm reverted to the indifferent, almost scoffing opposition to the Zionist idea which had characterised his attitude until his conversion by Eulenburg at Rominten three weeks earlier. His interest in Zionism proved fleeting and superficial. Motivated from the beginning by anti-Semitic prejudice and egoistical calculation, his intention of proclaiming a German protectorate over a Jewish homeland in Palestine rapidly faded away after Abdul Hamid's rebuff.

The Kaiser and his suite sailed into Haifa on 25 October 1898. When Wilhelm landed that afternoon, it was, as the official account of the voyage announced, the first time since the visit of Friedrich II of Hohenstaufen in 1228 that a German emperor had set foot on the soil of the Holy Land. By the time the imperial party set out on the dusty ride to Jaffa, they had been joined by numerous clergymen and over 500 others who had arrived in four steamers. The cortege needed no less than 230 tents, 120 carriages, 1,300 horses and mules, 100 coachmen and 600 drivers, 12 cooks and 60 waiters. This colossal caravan was guarded by a regiment of the Turkish army, and the German warships which had accompanied the travellers fired off thunderous salvoes every time the imperial standard appeared on the horizon.[132] On the way Wilhelm had a brief meeting by the roadside with Herzl before travelling on to Jerusalem for the principal event of the journey – the dedication of the Church of the Redeemer on 31 October.[133]

When he received Herzl and his four companions, who had all received a blessing from the Reverend William Hechler beforehand, in his encampment outside Jerusalem, Wilhelm addressed them only in non-committal platitudes. 'The land needs . . . water and shade', he told the Zionists. 'The settlements which I have seen, both the German ones and those of your countrymen, may serve as a model of what can be done with the land. There is room for all . . . The idea behind your movement . . . is a healthy one.' When Herzl remarked that the water supply could be secured by damming the river Jordan, although it would be very expensive, the Kaiser replied in his familiar tone: 'Well, you have plenty of money . . . More money than all of us.' 'He said neither Yes nor No', Herzl commented disconsolately after the meeting. He nevertheless took comfort in the thought that his efforts had not been in vain. 'This short audience will be preserved for time immemorial in the history of the Jewish people, and it is not impossible that it will also have historic consequences.'[134]

Although Wilhelm had lost interest in the Zionist cause, Herzl's idea of proclaiming a German protectorate in the Orient was too alluring to be abandoned altogether. From Jerusalem the Kaiser travelled via Beirut to Damascus, where on 8 November he astounded the world by announcing that he considered himself the protector of all the Muslims in the world. Intoxicated by his reception in the Syrian city, Wilhelm declared himself 'moved at the thought of standing in the place where one of the most chivalrous rulers of all time, the great Sultan Saladin, once stayed'. Today, he added, Sultan Abdul Hamid and 'the 300 million Mahomedans who live scattered throughout the world and who revere him as their Caliph, [may] rest assured that the German Kaiser will be their friend for all time!'[135] He telegraphed to the Grand Duke of Baden telling him that Damascus was 'a pearl among the cities of the world'; his entry into the city had been 'the most overwhelmingly enthusiastic which I have ever experienced, with the exception of [Buda]Pest'. He interpreted the enthusiasm as 'an expression of the gratitude of the Muslim world . . . to the German Reich for its loyalty and friendship towards the Sultan, a handsome reward for our often scorned policy'.[136] The All-Highest crusader made no secret of his disappointment with what he had seen in Palestine, however. The land was 'a dismal arid heap of stones', he wrote to his mother on his way home. 'The want of shade & water is appalling . . . Jerusalem is very much spoilt by the large quite modern suburbs, which are mostly formed by the numerous Jewish colonies . . . 60,000 of these people were there, greasy & squalid, cringing & abject, doing nothing but making themselves obnoxious equally to Christian & Mussulman by trying to fleece these neighbours from every farthing they manage to earn. Shylocks by the score!'[137]

If the project of an imperial protectorate over a Jewish homeland in Palestine was an illusion from the outset, for Wilhelm his Near Eastern tour was an unforgettable landmark in his life, which he was also determined to exploit publicly. His sister Charlotte could not believe her ears when she heard of his intention of making a ceremonial entry into Berlin, as if he had won a war.[138]

A sumptuously illustrated volume, together with cheaper popular publications and colourful children's books, made sure that the myth of the imperial pilgrimage was disseminated throughout the country.[139] And in his next speech to the Brandenburg provincial diet Wilhelm took care to make capital out of his supposed triumph in Palestine to attack the enemies of the Reich within its borders, by declaring: 'Of all the impressions I received, the most sublime and moving was . . . that of standing on the Mount of Olives and seeing the place, at its foot, where the mightiest battle which has even been fought on earth, the battle for the salvation of humanity, was fought by the One. This fact moved Me on that day to swear My oath of allegiance to heaven as it were anew, that I would leave nothing untried in order to unite My People and to remove whatever might divide them. But during my stay in that distant land and in all those different places, where the woods and the water which are so dear and so lovely to us Germans are absent, my thoughts turned to the Brandenburg lakes with their clear dark waters and the Brandenburg forest of oak and pine, and I thought to Myself that although we are sometimes looked down upon in Europe, we are much better off in the Mark than abroad . . . Yes, gentlemen, the tree which we see growing, and which we have to foster, is the German Imperial oak . . . My journey to the Holy Land and its sacred places will also be valuable to me in my task of protecting, tending and cultivating this tree, and, like a good gardener, of pruning the superfluous branches and attacking the vermin which gnaw at its roots in order to exterminate them. I hope, therefore, it will be vouchsafed to me to see this picture: the oak grown into a magnificent tree, and the German Michael standing before it, his hand on his sword-hilt, gazing across the frontier, ready to protect it. Secure is that peace which stands behind the shield and under the sword of the German Michael . . . Let it, therefore, be the aim of us Germans at least to stand together firm as a solid rock! Against this *rocher de bronze* of the German nation, both far beyond the seas and here at home in Europe, may every wave that threatens peace dash itself in vain!'[140]

## THE ANNEXATION OF KIAOCHOW

In the interval between the conclusion of peace negotiations over Crete in September 1897 and Wilhelm II's voyage to the Orient in the autumn of 1898, another opportunity had arisen for him to indulge his compulsive urge for action, this time drawing him far out into the Pacific and the South Seas – and also into potential conflict with Russia, China, Japan, the United States and Britain. Since 1894 he had talked of the need for a German naval base on Formosa or on the Chinese coast, and since November 1896 he and the naval authorities had identified the bay of Kiaochow, on the Shantung peninsula in north-eastern

China, as the most suitable starting-point for a German empire in East Asia. Since then Berlin had in effect been waiting for China to provide Germany with a pretext – through some violation of German rights – for seizing Kiaochow with the little port of Tsingtau.[141] During his visit to Peterhof in August 1897 Wilhelm had expressed keen interest in acquiring this port as a coaling station, and had gained the impression that Russia would agree in principle to 'shared use' of Kiaochow with Germany for this purpose.[142] When on 6 November 1897 the news reached Berlin that two German missionaries had been murdered in Shantung, Wilhelm saw this as the long-awaited pretext to gain a foothold in China by the occupation of Kiaochow. He wrote excitedly to the Foreign Office: 'I have just read in the press the news of the attack on the German Catholic Mission in Shantung, which is under my protection. Full atonement for this must be exacted through vigorous intervention by the fleet . . . I am now quite determined to give up our excessively cautious policy, which is already regarded as weak throughout East Asia, and to use all severity and if necessary the most brutal ruthlessness towards the Chinese, to show at long last that the German Kaiser is not to be trifled with, and that it is a bad thing to have him as an enemy . . . Energetic action is all the more called for because it will enable me to prove once again to my Catholic subjects, including the ultramontanes, that their well being is as close to my heart as that of, and that they can count on my protection as much as, my other subjects.'[143] He gave instructions for an order to be sent to Admiral Otto von Diederichs as follows: 'Proceed at once ⌊to⌋ Kiaochow with your whole squadron, occupy appropriate positions and places there and then exact full atonement in the way which seems the most appropriate to you. The greatest possible vigour is ordered. The goal of your voyage is to be kept secret.'[144]

The Kaiser's aggressive zeal and 'driving energy', now piling the pressure on the Wilhelmstrasse once again,[145] also manifested itself in the telegram which he sent to Bernhard von Bülow, who was still in Rome, on 7 November. 'Our conversation about Kiaochow, . . . at the end of which you emphasised that it was high time to give our wavering, lukewarm policy in East Asia more vigour, has had rapid results, more rapid than we expected . . . The Chinese have at last given us the reason and "incident" for which your predecessor Marschall waited so long. I decided to take action at once . . . The eyes of all, both Asians and Europeans living there, are upon us, and everyone is wondering whether we will put up with it or not.'[146] As Bülow's biographer Gerd Fesser points out, the newly appointed Foreign Secretary was not overjoyed at the prospect of beginning his term of office with a Russo-German conflict. 'At a safe distance in Rome . . . he went to ground, in effect, and remained stubbornly silent.'[147] It was therefore left to Hohenlohe to calm the excited Kaiser down and prevent him from taking any disastrous steps. In accordance with Wilhelm's orders the Chancellor instructed the German envoy in China to demand full satisfaction from the Chinese government; but he warned the Kaiser of the dangerous consequences of a quarrel with Russia over Kiaochow. 'If Your Majesty . . . wishes to give the Squadron Commander orders to take action at once, it might be necessary to choose somewhere other than Kiaochow, as in order to occupy Kiaochow in accordance with the agreement reached between Your Majesty and the Emperor of Russia at Peterhof, Russian consent would have to be sought.'[148]

As a result of Hohenlohe's warning, the Kaiser did at least take the precaution of personally consulting the Tsar again on his attitude to this delicate question. The ambiguous reply which he received to his enquiry – Nicholas telegraphed: 'Can neither give nor withhold consent to your sending a German squadron to Kiaochow as I have just heard that this port was only temporarily ours in 1895–6' – Wilhelm happily interpreted as indicating approval of a German occupation, and he again demanded swift and energetic action. 'We must use this excellent opportunity without delay, before another great power provokes China or comes to her aid! Now or never', he wrote to the Reich Chancellor.[149] For Bülow's benefit he set out in hypocritical terms the justification for his willingness to clarify Russia's position by means of a telegram to Nicholas. 'Deeply humiliating as it is that the German Reich should practically have to ask permission from St Petersburg to protect and avenge its Christian dependants in China, and to use for that purpose a place which out of excessive modesty it did not occupy three years ago, although this could easily have been done, I have not hesitated for a moment to take this step, for the good of my country.' Wilhelm went on to declare that he did not share the Tsar's concern 'that severe punishments in the east of China will perhaps cause agitation and insecurity and widen the gulf between the Chinese and the Christians'. On the contrary: 'thousands of German Christians will breathe a sigh of relief when they hear that the German Kaiser's ships are near by, hundreds of German traders will exult in the knowledge that the German Reich has at last won a firm foothold in Asia, hundreds of thousands of Chinese will tremble when they feel the iron fist of the German Reich bearing down on their necks, and the whole German Reich will rejoice that its government has done a manly deed . . . But let the world learn the lesson once and for all from this incident, that where I am concerned: "Nemo me impune lacessit." Wilhelm I. R.'[150] Like many of his utterances from this period, these words read like a draft of the notorious 'Hun speech' of 1900.

The concern felt by the Chancellor and the Foreign Office that with his precipitate order to Diederichs the Kaiser had disregarded Russian reservations to a dangerous degree soon proved justified when on 9 November news reached Berlin that Russia insisted at the very least on maintaining its prior right of anchorage ('priorité de mouiller') in Kiaochow.[151] As the deputy Secretary of State at the Foreign Office, Rotenhan, explained to the Kaiser on 10 November, this declaration by Russian Foreign Minister Muraviev meant 'that if a foreign power were allowed to take the port, Russia's priority must in all circumstances be secured. In order to safeguard this right the commander of the Russian squadron in the Far East had been given orders that as soon as German ships entered the port, Russian ships should be sent there likewise.'[152] Hohenlohe was dismayed, and remonstrated with the Russian ambassador. 'It has been our intention from the first to come to an agreement with you, and to do nothing that was unwelcome to you. If your Emperor had indicated to us from the first that our action was unwelcome to him, I [would have] very firmly opposed the navy's plans. The contents of the Emperor [Nicholas]'s telegram persuaded me otherwise. Now that our Kaiser is committed, I am bound to make the dignity of the Kaiser and of the Reich my first consideration.'[153] The danger of a Russo-German conflict was particularly acute because Diederichs, who had set sail on the Kaiser's orders, could no longer be reached by telegraph. 'Things really look very bad', Hohenlohe lamented on 10 November 1897. He tried to console himself with the thought that 'the Russians are [only] trying to frighten us. I cannot believe that the Emperor of Russia will declare war on us because of Kiaochow Bay. There is a danger that H.M. will send a telegram to the Tsar at once. And what will it say?'[154] Holstein cautioned Hohenlohe that 'the Russian declaration is so brutally explicit that it scarcely seems necessary to give the Kaiser any advice. He alone will know whether he wants war with Russia or not. We shall now have to be very careful with our action in China.'[155] Even Tirpitz believed that war with Russia was a possibility, and advised calling a halt to the 'dangerous' action.[156] Nevertheless the Chancellor avoided a confrontation with Wilhelm. 'I shall not write or telegraph to the Kaiser, but wait until he brings up the subject himself', he told Rotenhan.[157] He was to regret his passivity later.[158] But the Kaiser did not allow the Russian objections to trouble him greatly. He wrote to the Foreign Office: 'Count Muraviev's note corresponds perfectly to the character of this mendacious gentleman . . . We should attempt to come to an arrangement with Russia to acquire the rights to Kiaochow, if necessary by purchase. Even Russia will yield to a *fait accompli*, and will certainly not start a war on account of Kiaochow, as she needs us in the East.'[159]

The cruiser division under the command of Diederichs arrived in the Bay of Kiaochow on 14 November 1897 and landed a force of 30 officers, 77 petty officers and 610 sailors, although this was to have been done only 'if the Chinese reply is unsatisfactory.'[160] The Chancellor succeeded in persuading the Kaiser 'that the Squadron Commander should desist from making a proclamation or occupying Chinese territory until the Chinese reply arrives and is unsatisfactory'.[161]

Nevertheless, at a hastily convened meeting at the Reich chancellor's palace on 15 November, presided over by Wilhelm, it was decided that an unsatisfactory reply should be engineered by deliberately setting unacceptable conditions. The minutes of the meeting stated quite openly: 'Our demands to China are to be set at such a level that they cannot be fulfilled and therefore justify further seizure.'[162] During the discussion the Kaiser made his aims in Kiaochow clear: 'Permanent occupation of the bay is to be envisaged. His Majesty remarked that he stood by the fact that the Emperor Nicholas had given telegraphic approval. Two years ago the Tsar had already expressed his agreement to Germany taking a port in China, while thanking him for our support for Russian policy in the Far East . . . His Majesty therefore does not believe there will be war with Russia, and is convinced that the seizure will be welcomed with jubilation by public opinion in Germany, and that in the Reichstag too the Centre will appreciate and support this imperial intervention for the protection of the Catholic missions.'[163]

In spite of the Kaiser's confidence the threat of conflict with Russia continued to loom. On 18 November Hohenlohe had to inform Wilhelm that both the Russian government and the Tsar himself had spoken out against the German claims to a port in China. 'The tone and content of the Russian document leave no room for doubt that the Emperor Nicholas has been persuaded to take the view that Your Majesty intended to make improper use of his telegram, to the detriment of Russian rights, which it had never been the Emperor's intention to relinquish. The *amour propre* of the Emperor will not easily get over this impression', Hohenlohe warned. He therefore suggested that delaying tactics be used for the time being; the Tsar should be told 'that the Russian fleet can of course remain in Kiaochow Bay too, and that we would undoubtedly come to an agreement over future plans'.[164] The Kaiser annotated this document: 'Completely agree with Yr. H[ighness]'s suggestion. Their famous right of *premier mouillage* will in no way be infringed by our occupation and later seizure. Russians can stay anchored there until they are blue in the face. But that cannot prevent us building a coaling station and docks there.'[165]

It was still uncertain not only how Russia would react, but also what the response of the Chinese government would be to the annexation of a sizeable piece of territory and the dispatch of several warships under the command of the Kaiser's brother Prince Heinrich. But Wilhelm ignored the reservations of both the Wilhelmstrasse and the Minister of War. On 24 November 1897 he wrote to the Foreign Office: 'That the Chinese know exactly what we want is certain; that they will wage war is highly unlikely, as they have neither ships nor money and the number of troops in Shantung is not great. The fact that Heinrich is being sent and the second division formed must of course be mentioned [in a telegram to China], as everyone knows it and it shows that the Imperial House does not for a moment hesitate to risk the lives of its members for the honour of Germany. Wilhelm I. R.'[166] Two days later he wrote to Hohenlohe: 'In about three weeks the *Kaiserin Augusta* will arrive [in China]; Prince Heinrich and the rest of the ships not until February [1898]. So that the crews do not remain away from their ships any longer than absolutely necessary, the moment has now come to form the colonial force, charter the steamer and embark them as soon as possible. I expect an answer tomorrow morning so that I can give my orders. No one is in any more doubt about our intentions. A longer delay is impossible. That it is not for Russia to say anything in Kiaochow is as clear as daylight. The battle at Nikki [in West Africa] between France and England will bring about an interesting situation; at any rate it is favourable for us.'[167] On 29 November 1897 the Reich Chancellor noted with concern that War Minister General Heinrich von Gossler had told him 'that he had received an order to make available two heavy batteries for dispatch to China, together with about 1,000 men. The War Minister is very worried about it and says that this gives the Kiaochow affair a very serious character, and that H.M. cannot have fully realised its consequences. For if these troops were thrown out by the Chinese we should be at war with China. He has no doubt that the Chinese are strong enough to sweep our troops away, as there are troops trained by our officers in Tientsin. But the Prussian army could not tolerate a defeat. War with China would therefore be inevitable, and this would cost hundreds of millions. Even sending the batteries and troops will cost 10 million. The other ministers present shared the concerns of the War Minister.' 'I know nothing about the dispatch of the batteries', the Reich Chancellor admitted helplessly. 'It looks as if the whole War Ministry is in uproar. The ministers take the view that the Kiaochow question will have a very unfavourable effect on the Navy Bill. To judge from the War Minister's remarks, the mood in the army does not seem favourable to the Chinese venture. What will the "federal governments" say to it? If things continue at this pace, we shall have a war with China. The powers will see to that.'[168] Not until the occupation of Port Arthur (now Lushun) by Russia in December 1897 did Bülow succeed in defusing the Russo-German crisis.[169]

The 'driving' role which Kaiser Wilhelm II personally – and sometimes in uncanny anticipation of his fatal orders at the beginning of the crisis of July 1914 – played in November 1897 over the seizure of Kiaochow is unmistakable. Putting his trust in his friendly relationship with Nicholas II, he repeatedly disregarded the reservations expressed by those who foresaw disaster – not only the Reich Chancellor and the Foreign Office but also the army and the navy – and confronted his experienced advisers with one *fait accompli* after another through his inflammatory orders.[170] During the Boxer Rebellion of 1900 Hohenlohe

admitted, in retrospect, that, although he had not supported the Kaiser's occupation policy in the Kiaochow episode, he had not opposed it resolutely enough
either. 'You are quite right', he told his son, 'when you say that we would have
done better to leave the Chinese alone. The seizure of Kiaochow at any rate
added to the exasperation of the yellow beasts. That occupation, which the navy
inspired the Kaiser to undertake, is of no use to us. But once Tirpitz and Bülow
had excited H.M.'s interest (in 1897), there was nothing I could do, and I did
not want to incur the usual accusation of "being in a blue funk". But I was
wrong and should have protested against it with the Ministry.'[171] Wilhelm, on
the other hand, notched up the capture of Kiaochow as a triumph for his personal diplomacy, and his friend Eulenburg congratulated him 'from the bottom
of [his] heart' on his success, 'for which we have to thank Your Majesty's energetic initiative, *and nothing else*'.[172] On 8 January 1898, writing to the Austrian
Emperor, Wilhelm commented: 'Our Chinese affair has gone off well, thanks
to the previous agreement with the Emperor [Nicholas II] *in person* and has
shown the pigtailed gentlemen of the East that the good missionaries are not to
be regarded as mere wild game to be hunted down',[173] to which Franz Joseph
replied by sending his congratulations 'on the new, promising world position in
which Your Reich finds itself'.[174] Meanwhile Wilhelm congratulated Nicholas II
on the occupation of Port Arthur, expressing his hope for 'Christian' co-operation
with the words: 'Russia and Germany at the entrance of the Yellow Sea may be
taken as represented by St George and St Michael shielding the Holy Cross in
the Far East and guarding the Gates to the Continent of Asia. May you be able
fully to realise the plans you often unrolled to me; my sympathy and help shall
not fail in case of need.'[175]

In Kiel on 15 December 1897 to bid farewell to the troops departing for the
occupation of Kiaochow under the command of Prince Heinrich, the Kaiser
addressed his brother with the words: 'If anyone . . . should ever venture to wish
to hurt or harm us in the due exercise of our rights, smash him with an iron
fist! and, if it be God's will, weave a laurel wreath around your young brow
which no one in the whole German Reich will begrudge you!'[176] Heinrich had
to forgo his laurel wreath, for on 4 January 1898 China signed a lease by which
the German Reich received the Bay of Kiaochow and the surrounding area,
together with railway and mining concessions in the province of Shantung and
tariff privileges, for ninety-nine years. A territory of 150,000 square kilometres
with more than 33 million inhabitants had become a German zone of influence
under the administration of the Reich Navy Office (not the Foreign Office).[177]
With this step, however, Germany had entered into latent conflict not only with
the other European great powers, as before, but also with the aspiring world
powers in the Pacific: Japan and the United States.

49. The Kaiser and his three eldest sons at Kiel with Prince Heinrich on the latter's embarkation for China in December 1897

## PRINCE HEINRICH OF PRUSSIA IN THE PACIFIC OCEAN

The letters of 'Henry the Navigator' (as the Kaiser's brother was jokingly called at the Foreign Office) from the Far East to Wilhelm and his mother in Kronberg give us a good picture of the geopolitical struggle in the Pacific Ocean, in which the German Reich was now keen to play a part. 'Once in the Far East', Prince Heinrich wrote from the *Deutschland*, which had arrived in Hong Kong, in April 1898, 'the world looks very much different from what it does in Berlin, London or Friedrichshof!'[178] As commandant of the East Asian squadron Heinrich had great hopes for Germany's future in the Far East and the South Seas. In a letter to his mother of February 1899 he observed: 'I doubt it not that Germany's future lies in the East.'[179] And at the same time he wrote to his brother from Amoy (now Xiamen): 'In itself China has few pleasures and only momentary satisfaction to offer the European, but our future no doubt lies here all the same.' The Manchu dynasty was obviously coming to an end, he commented, and it was not impossible that there would be a rebellion sooner or later in this 'gigantic empire', and that 'people would try to proclaim a Chinaman as ruler. – What then? How will the great powers react to this! I do not believe there will be a peaceful partition of China; jealousy between the individual European nations is too great for that! England would certainly claim the Yangtze region and thus acquire the lion's share right into the heart of China. Russia will certainly move towards Peking under some pretext or other. – I can see only one way out of this dilemma, consisting in an alliance between England, Germany and Russia. All the other nations, including Japan and America, are absolutely unreliable!' The prospects of acquiring the island of Formosa, which had been occupied by Japan since the Sino-Japanese war, seemed particularly promising to Prince Heinrich. He suggested entering into negotiations with Japan for the purchase of this 'enormously rich' island; the German government could raise the money for it by selling German firms concessions for the export of the island's produce. 'Formosa would not need to become a colony at first', the Prince explained to his brother, who in this case was sceptical. 'It could however be placed under German protection as a means of getting our hands on it for the time being.' Later, admittedly, the 'wild tribe . . . (of Malayan origin)', which would not allow any foreigner into the interior of the island, would have to be 'tamed' by Chinese troops trained by German officers. The chief object for the moment, however, was simply that 'the protection of our Reich would be made possible', Heinrich urged. 'The Japanese are said to have realised already how weak they are, and are bleeding to death financially. If you were willing to authorise me, I should gladly negotiate with the Emperor of Japan in due course, or put out a feeler.' Although Wilhelm II rejected this request in a typically biting marginal comment − 'Heaven preserve me from that! Heinrich's political ideas are still very Utopian!' − only a few years earlier, as we have seen, he had himself peremptorily demanded the annexation of Formosa.[180]

Not only was there no desire in the Wilhelmstrasse to negotiate with Japan for the acquisition of Formosa; it was even feared, at first, that the seizure of Kiaochow might lead to war with the Empire of the Rising Sun, a war which Germany could hardly win. Soon after taking office Bülow had to warn the Kaiser of the hopelessness of such a war and to suggest that it might be advisable to take over a less controversial port than Kiaochow. 'The probable consequences of a German−Japanese war are . . . so unfavourable that German policy must set itself the task of preventing, as far as possible, the disruption of German− Japanese relations, which for our enemies would be an unexpected stroke of luck', he cautioned. Germany could avoid this danger, however, if it made it plain to the Japanese 'that we are no longer opposed *in principle* to their establishing themselves *anywhere* on the East Asian *mainland, as we were* in 1895, but rather that we are inclined to recognise the legitimacy of "live and let live" for Japan too'.[181] The Kaiser went even further in a note he wrote on Bülow's letter: 'We can also give moral support to Japan's protest over [the American appropriation of] Hawaii and thereby draw it away from America.' But he rejected Bülow's suggestion that another East Asian port should be taken over as a base, pointing out that 'Amoy and Samsah . . . , like Korea, are closer to Tokyo or Formosa than Kiaochow.' Nor did he share the Foreign Secretary's anxiety about war with Japan, for the reason that − as he wrote − 'Our fleet is most definitely superior to the Japanese.'[182] On 12 December 1897, in consultation with the Naval High Command, he set the course 'for a war which is to be expected shortly with Japan'.[183]

Although this particular war was in fact avoided until 1914, armed conflict did break out in the Far East only a few weeks later, from which Germany expected to profit. On the eve of the Spanish−American war in April 1898 Prince Heinrich reported to his mother: 'Everything looks most warlike out here, & the American Commodore is constantly waiting for the declaration of war between Spain & the U.S. Japan is supposed to prepare for war to side with England against Russia, so they say here. God knows what the end will be.'[184] Germany's relations with the United States, in addition to those with Japan, were beginning to play a more important role in the thinking of Prince Heinrich and his fellow officers. He was gratified to hear of the first signs of a reawakening of patriotic feeling among the millions of ethnic Germans who had emigrated to America. The new German *Weltpolitik*, he commented to his mother in June 1898, had roused the Germans in the United States to their senses at last, 'hereby proving that the population of the U.S. does not *only* consist of english people, as has been lately professed by the two "english speaking races."' He had nothing but contempt, of course, for Germany's transatlantic rivals on the world stage. 'Have the Yanks . . . in any way shown their superiority in the way of colonisation to the Spaniards', he asked after the American capture of the Philippines. The 40,000-strong US army in Manila was nothing but 'a set of illdisciplined cowboys & bushrangers & a perfect set of ruffians . . . Their officers and generals have been described to me as unfit & untrained for their work!'[185] When Germany acquired the Caroline, Palau and Mariana Islands in the Pacific after the defeat of Spain in the war against the United States, Heinrich expressed his satisfaction 'that we have taken over a new colony in this part of the world', even if the direct economic advantages should prove minimal. 'We are badly in need of a coaling station & as such, they will be of great value', he declared. 'Furthermore this new possession, I hope, will help to increase our navy in general, as well as our squadron out here.'[186]

In his geopolitical aspirations, the brother whom Wilhelm II considered to be an anglophile was torn between his admiration for the British Empire and his goal of helping Germany to attain the status of a world power. 'I wish I could give many of our narrowminded countrymen at home an idea of Great Britain's position on this globe of ours! For it is a marvel to see how that British nation has settled all over the world', he wrote to his mother in February 1898. At the same time, he admitted, 'involuntarily one wishes the same for ones own country, the position of which alas is so very much different & so very much more difficult'.[187] But his admiration for the British Empire could rapidly swing over into rivalry and hostility, as his threatening comment only a few weeks later shows. 'Until now I have tried to make friends with the English, but should I find, that they intend harming us in any way out here, I shall stop that policy of mine . . . That England is to a degree jealous of "beastly Germany" having taken possession of the very best harbour in China is known to all of us! . . . I am trying to serve my country out here & I mean to do it thoroughly! I shall "consider every man my enemy who speaks ill of my sovereign", to use Nelson's words!'[188] Later that year Anglo-American co-operation in Samoa gave him further cause for complaint. 'The way certain other nations try to cut Germany out in every way does not seem over friendly . . . I am fully aware of the one fact though, that politics have got nothing to do with sympathies or antipathies, but that every nation has to seek its own interest where or when it is to be found!'[189]

In anticipation of a great struggle between Britain and Russia in the Far East Prince Heinrich instinctively sided with the former, but only as long as he saw advantages for his own country in so doing. He welcomed the news that Russia had seized Port Arthur and that Britain had taken Wei-hai-wei in retaliation as a symptom of increasing antagonism between the two countries. 'I am right glad that England has undertaken this task, thereby also ridding us of the presence of the Japanese in China, who have no business to be among us Europeans here', he wrote in April 1898. 'I surmise that Russia will take the whole of Korea & comfortably settle down there, thereby increasing her empire still more in size. Anyhow I hope our people at home will have the good sense to see things in this light & let both nations fight it out, if necessary! It would be such fun! The British fleet out here is strong enough to hold its own against the Russian fleet & they would be quite a match for each other.'[190] A few months later his hopes for a war in which Britain and Germany would combine against Russia seemed about to be realised. Writing to his mother in October 1898 from Kiaochow, he commented: 'I have seen them of late, those beloved Russians, & know pretty well, what they are aiming at! Peking on one side, Korea on the other, that's their "little plan". They are the greatest danger to us & Great Britain in the Far East & longing for a brush with the latter! So they openly told us! . . . I have a great mistrust in the Russians & am convinced they mean mischief! . . . If Russia moves towards Peking her influence over the Chinese Empire will be very great & Great Britain's and Germany's commerce endangered.'[191] And two weeks later he remarked: 'The only nation who is able to stop Russia by force is England! I wish to God, I was allowed to fight on the British side against those Russian barbarians!'[192] It was precisely the British Empire, however, that was to prove the greatest impediment to the realisation of Wilhelmine Germany's dreams of world power

# CHAPTER THIRTY-ONE

# The Kaiser and England

## THE 'WORLD-SAVING IDEA' OF AN ANGLO-GERMAN ALLIANCE

IN spite of the dozens of intimate letters to his mother, grandmother and other English relations, Wilhelm's real feelings about Britain, and the inner motivation for his policy towards the country, sometimes seem well-nigh impossible to work out. His comments contradict each other so often and so completely that one is tempted – as has already been remarked – to regard any positive comment or gesture as mere camouflage to disguise his real intentions.[1] But is such an explanation, even if it contained a core of truth, sufficient to clarify the confusion, or were the Kaiser's true feelings towards his mother's homeland characterised by a muddled, profoundly ambivalent love–hatred, as is often claimed? Did his bombastic self-glorification really conceal a deeply felt longing to earn the respect of the British, and in particular of his revered grandmother? Was his aggressive behaviour only the result of his hurt feelings because the much-admired world empire allegedly treated him as a *quantité négligeable*? Could not the British royal family and the government in London have shown more consideration for Wilhelm II's peculiar sensitivity, in order to ease Anglo-German tensions? Was there, as Bernhard von Bülow claimed, a 'fundamentally fanatical' conspiracy against the Kaiser, characterised by 'very unfair misjudgement and latent hatred', throughout the courts of Europe, embracing almost the entire 'English-Battenberg-Hessian-Danish . . . *cousinage*', which sought to undermine Wilhelm's efforts to improve relations?[2] We shall continue to be confronted with these problems, both in connection with the battlefleet building programme and the complications which dogged Anglo-German relations right up until the outbreak of war in 1914. For Wilhelm's biographer it is small comfort that even those who were closest to the Kaiser were often unable to solve the riddle.

It is undoubtedly true that certain comments and actions on the British side hurt the Kaiser unnecessarily and rarely failed to evoke a defiant response from him. Queen Victoria, the Prince of Wales and, increasingly, Lord Salisbury too, who had previously been prepared to make concessions to Wilhelm's apparently insatiable conceit and love of pomp by conferring titles and other honours upon him, gave up such attempts at placating him after the Krüger telegram, and instead expressed their displeasure through insulting rebuffs. The Kaiser showed little understanding of his grandmother's decision not to invite him to Cowes in the summer of 1896 because of the anger aroused by the notorious telegram. His sense of injury was increased when he heard that the elderly King of Saxony had been invited to England, although he was not related to the royal family. He expressed his feelings in a note in the margin of the report from Dresden containing the news: 'I am not to go to Cowes but the King is even going to London etc.! It seems he is the First throughout the Reich now!'[3]

But what hurt Wilhelm particularly was the negative reply he received from Queen Victoria to his request in January 1897 to be allowed to bring some of his children to her Diamond Jubilee celebrations in June of that year.[4] He should not come over for her Jubilee at all, the old Queen wrote, but wait until the usual time for his visit in the late summer, and come not to London but to Osborne House on the Isle of Wight. And that was not all: since Wilhelm had not nominated his brother to be his official representative at the celebrations in London, she would invite Heinrich and Irène to the Jubilee 'as my grand children', for on this important occasion she wanted to have as many of her grandchildren around her as possible. Wilhelm noted bitterly on this letter: 'and I am the eldest grandchild'.[5] His distress at his grandmother's unjust behaviour made itself felt in many of his comments, and not least in his maltreatment of his brother.[6] Deeply disappointed, he wrote to the Queen on 10 June 1897: 'As . . . I shall not have the pleasure of offering my congratulations for Your Jubilee as I did 10 Years ago, I must with a heavy heart resort to pen & ink. To be the first & eldest of Your grandchildren & yet to be precluded from taking part in this unique fête, while cousins & far relations will have the privilege of surrounding You & cheering You during the coming happy days, whilst I may not be with them, nay the first of all is deeply mortifying; & I feel like a charger chained in the stables who hears the bugle sounding, & stamps & champs his bit, because he cannot follow his Regiment! I had hoped to lead the Royals as their Colonel past their Sovereign, if not as her Escort & to join their cheers when they salute their Queen in the exuberance of their loyal pride, & that only a few days after "our Waterloo" day, & in the great final charge I would have borne my sword proudly before the saluting point at the head of that magnificent Regiment side by side with Uncle George[,] Uncle Arthur, Uncle Bertie & so many others,

3 generations in arms! But it was all idle dreams! But such dreams are hard to give up for a passionate soldier!'[7]

No less significant for the relations between the two countries was the growing irritation of the Prime Minister, Lord Salisbury, with the Kaiser, whom he not only considered vain, impulsive and unreliable, but now also saw as a malevolent warmonger.[8] The Krüger telegram and the conflicts with the German Reich over Zanzibar in the late summer of 1896, then over the Cretan crisis and the Pacific, did little to improve Anglo-German relations, especially as the press on both sides did its best to inflame public opinion. Shortly after the seizure of Kiaochow Hatzfeldt reported from London that Germany could not at present count on much goodwill on the part of the British cabinet, and added: 'Certain remarks by Lord Salisbury . . . give me reason to believe that our opponents here have lately been trying to turn him against us again. That is the only explanation I can find for the fact that yesterday he reverted to what are supposedly old grievances, namely the Krüger telegram and our action against the pretender in Zanzibar, with a certain bitterness, although he admitted that the press here has done us a great deal of wrong.'[9]

It is worth noting that Wilhelm made visible efforts, at least from time to time, to influence both German and British public opinion in a more favourable direction. During the conflict over the controversial succession in Zanzibar, for instance, there was malicious anti-British comment in the German press which led the Empress Frederick to remark despairingly: 'The German newspapers are not pleasant reading – this is a fresh opportunity for the most bitter unjust & violent attacks on England. It makes me so savage that sometimes I cannot finish reading the articles – they are so unfair & sneering & nasty.'[10] On this occasion the Kaiser not only shared his mother's anger but even took demonstrative action against the anglophobic press campaign. Clad in the red uniform of the Royal Dragoons, he received the British ambassador, his family and all the members of the embassy at the Schloss for a theatrical performance and a dinner and declared that the invitation was intended to be seen as a 'pro-English demonstration', in view of the anti-British attitude of the Foreign Office under Marschall and of the regrettable mood in the country, which was still being fuelled by Bismarck in the press. At this time the strange rumour was also doing the rounds that the Kaiser intended to give up all the colonies except German East Africa, because the cost of administering them was more than the value of all the trade with them, and because no more than about 3,000 Europeans in all, including the colonial officials and the security forces, had settled in the German colonies.[11] On 22 November 1896 Sir Frank Lascelles secretly informed Lord Salisbury that the Kaiser had proposed that, as Germany could not develop all the colonies it possessed, it might be wiser for it 'to concentrate her energies on a single one

30. Kaiser Wilhelm II in England after the death of his grandmother
Queen Victoria in January 1901

and give up the rest'; he hoped that Britain might then compensate it with a coaling station.[12]

The message was unmistakable; and yet only a few weeks earlier Wilhelm had expressed quite different sentiments with regard to Britain. In a letter of 24 October 1896 to her mother, which she asked the Queen to burn immediately, the Empress Frederick gave a moving but fatalistic *tour d'horizon* of Anglo-German relations, which she had recently discussed with Wilhelm during a visit he had paid her from Wiesbaden. As daughter of the Prince Consort and widow of Kaiser Friedrich III she felt only love for Germany, but she was '*miserable*' over the latest development in Germany, and as she was now nothing but 'my poor

William's mother', she could only watch helplessly while he acted in a way which was 'so often deluded & mistaken!!' 'I can do *nothing, nothing*', she lamented. As ever, in her eyes the root of the evil lay in the warping of the German spirit caused by Bismarck's foundation of the Reich and his long years of authoritarian rule. 'The vanity of the Chauvinists etc. has been *so flattered* & *cultivated* by P$^{ce}$ Bismarck that it has now overrun the country like a noxious weed.' As to the foreign policy of the Newest Course, she found it extremely distressing to see Germany 'pursue a policy of systematic unfriendliness to England, but so it *is* . . . I perceive a systematic *enmity* in Germany to the "Welt Stellung" [world status] of the British Empire, and an endeavour to take advantage of this commercial rivalry by making all sorts of *political waves* in order to hinder and checkmate England (vide Zanzibar) . . . Instead of the bands of *closest* friendship such as *our − now* fast disappearing − generation had *fondly dreamt of* & worked & lived for with untiring devotion and enthusiasm I see a system of *enmity* with *an aim* & a *purpose*.' The widowed Empress did not dispute that her son was playing the leading role in this system, but she persuaded herself that his anti-British policy was a kind of misunderstanding. 'William admires England very much and is very fond of you − & especially enjoys himself *in* England, − but he is not steady & coolheaded and farsighted enough to see that to strain every nerve for Germany to succeed in outdoing England, & *wrest* fr[om] her the position of supremacy she has in the world, is simply *nonsense*! It is a ridiculous, fantastic and wild idea; − but appeals to his imagination & love of the *marvellous*, the *sensational* & exaggerated!' She went on to warn the Queen of the unlimited fleet building plans which her son cherished and which were aimed against Britain. 'I hear that "Krupp" − the *greatest* manufacturer we have, who has a colossal fortune − has been ordered to buy some Docks near Wilhelmshafen, "Germania Docks", in order (it is supposed) to be able to have english shipbuilders & employ engineers etc. to design & build ships for the German Navy that shall beat the English.' She herself naturally wished Germany to be trusted and respected in the world, and hoped 'to see her people *free*, happy & prosperous, her liberty & culture progressing in every way, − but *not* embarking *now*, when there is still *so* much to be done at home on adventurous enterprizes, quarrel with her best friends & make herself universally disliked'.[13]

A year later the former British military attaché in Berlin, Colonel Sir Leopold Swaine, who had once been very close to the Kaiser, found himself in Berlin again and was struck by the anti-British feeling that had now become widespread in Germany, a development which he blamed in the first instance on Wilhelm. 'The feeling between the two countries has not been of the best for some time', he commented. 'Colonial antagonism as well as commercial rivalries have been partly to blame for this; but the principal culprit is the Emperor who cannot recover from his annoyance that the "famous Kruger" telegram had exactly the opposite result to what he anticipated.' What was more, in recent times the Kaiser had gone further than German public opinion and the Foreign Office wanted in his policy, which was directed principally against Britain, the Colonel observed. In view of German sensitivities and of the general reverence for Bismarck, who was probably dying, it would be advisable, he believed, for Queen Victoria to appoint someone soon to represent her at the funeral of the founder of the Reich. 'The veneration for Bismarck in Germany is as great as ever it was and has, if anything, been enhanced by the mess things have got into since he left office for which the Emperor, whether rightly or wrongly, is solely blamed. Any show, in spite of the angry abuse showered upon us by the German press, which we can make of honouring their great Statesman is certain of having a salutary effect on all the right-minded people in Germany and on those whose opinions we value. We are an old nation and can afford to be magnanimous vis-à-vis to an upstart one.'[14]

It is not without irony that at precisely the time when anglophobic sentiment was flaring up in Germany, influential circles in Britain were putting out feelers towards an alliance with Germany. The negotiations for an Anglo-German alliance which were conducted behind the scenes in the spring of 1898 and again in 1901 are the subject of a still unresolved controversy between historians, in which one side interprets the talks as the great 'missed opportunity' of pre-war diplomacy, while the other sees them as no more than a series of illusions and misunderstandings.[15] How did Kaiser Wilhelm behave in this potentially crucial moment in world history? How, and through what channels, did he learn of the British soundings, and what attitude did he take to the possibility of an alliance with his mother's homeland, before this opportunity proved to be an illusion? The correspondence of the royal family, which is generally neglected by diplomatic historians, can throw new light on this well-researched and yet still controversial question.

In mid-January 1898, while shooting at Buckow, the Kaiser took the British military attaché Grierson aside and discussed the threats of Anglo-French conflict on the upper Nile with him, as well as the German occupation of Kiaochow. He then switched to the subject of Anglo-German relations and said with obvious annoyance, as Grierson reported to London, 'that for eight years he had tried to be friends and allies with us but had failed and now had to go on alone and forward German interests. We would never again have such a chance of an ally on the continent, for never again would a grandson of the Queen of Great Britain be on the German throne, and more to the same effect. Then he said to me "Is there a British policy at all? What is your idea of the policy?" So I said that I was no politician, but that my idea was that our government would join neither the Triple nor the Dual alliance, as to join one would embroil us with the other and we did not want to embroil ourselves with anybody. We were strong enough to hold our own against either group, and it seemed unlikely that they would combine. Then he said: "There you are mistaken. They can combine and they *shall* combine. Socialism will compel the monarchs of Europe to combine for mutual assistance, and the great danger to be guarded against is the yellow race of the Far East. My allegorical picture ["Nations of Europe"] will yet be realized." Then he asked if I had seen his picture in "Punch" as Emperor of China, and said that the Empress was furious about it, but he thought it rather a good joke. "But", he said, "your people do not realize how monarchs are looked on on the continent, and so long as those journal attacks are made on me you cannot expect the German press to remain silent.'"[16]

Before Wilhelm expressed this complaint, Queen Victoria had attempted on her own initiative to persuade the London press to take a more positive line. Early in 1898 she asked Sir Theodore Martin to contact the leading editors and urge them to be less hostile and more objective in their coverage of Germany and the Kaiser. On 13 January Martin told the Queen that all the editors to whom he had spoken, and above all the editor of *The Times*, had deplored the 'very bitter feeling against the Germans' which prevailed all over Britain and which could be attributed only in a small degree to trade rivalry. Even the humorous journal *Punch* would moderate its mockery and its caricatures, Martin assured the Queen.[17] The restraint of the British press soon had a noticeable effect on the German newspapers, and in Berlin court society the English Princess Aribert of Anhalt, who was credited with having great influence on Wilhelm II, contributed considerably to the improvement in Anglo-German relations. In addition, the unusually warm reception which Prince Heinrich was given in Gibraltar, Aden, India and Hong Kong during his voyage to the Far East was appreciated at the Berlin court as a welcome gesture of friendship.[18] Finally, the old Duke of Cambridge, Queen Victoria's cousin, expressed support for an Anglo-German rapprochement. At Cannes, where he had met the German ambassador in Paris, Count Münster, the Duke had pointed out that, although the Prince of Wales had for a time succeeded in prejudicing the Queen against Germany, which had prevented relations between the countries improving, 'that had not lasted, and at heart the old Queen loves and in some respects admires her grandson very much'. It was well known that the heir to the British throne did not harbour either anger or love for long, Münster told the Reich Chancellor in a secret letter, and therefore it was not impossible that even Albert Edward would now seek a better relationship with Germany.[19] Thus on a monarchical level friendly feelers had been put out on both sides of the North Sea before the statesmen and diplomats began their tentative political talks in March 1898.

In the imperial entourage, however, forces were at work to try to sabotage the improvement in Anglo-German relations which was gathering impetus. Grierson complained that there were those about the Kaiser who 'who stick at nothing to damage England and everything English in the Emperor's eyes'.[20] These irresponsible mischief-makers did great damage by spreading false and malicious rumours which the Kaiser only too willingly believed.[21] One of the chief culprits in this respect was the Chief of the Naval Cabinet, Gustav Freiherr von Senden-Bibran,[22] who told the Kaiser after a visit to England that, although he had been very kindly received by the Queen, the Prince of Wales had been deliberately discourteous to him. He had received him in the equerries' room, had been unfriendly and had not once enquired after the Kaiser and Kaiserin. As a result of this assertion by Senden, the Kaiser called on the British ambassador in February 1898 'in a most excited state', in order to express his fury at the poor treatment of the Admiral 'His Majesty told Sir Frank Lascelles that this continued hostility evinced towards him by the Prince of Wales would prevent his coming to Cowes & would even possibly have serious results upon the relations between the two countries.'[23] The ambassador immediately reported the incident to Salisbury, who relayed the telegram to the Prince of Wales. The latter wrote to Lascelles rejecting Senden's assertions and instructing the luckless ambassador to tell the Kaiser that he, the heir to the British throne, refused to have anything further to do with Senden.[24] As had happened over the Vienna incident almost ten years earlier,[25] Prince Christian of Schleswig-Holstein, who was about to visit his daughter Princess Aribert in Berlin, was asked by the Queen to have a serious word with Wilhelm about his relationship with the Prince of Wales.[26]

When Lascelles carried out the Prince of Wales's instructions on 16 March 1898, the Kaiser expressed his regret, but said that he 'that he had great hopes that an improvement in the relations of the two Courts would soon take place, as important Personages were attempting to bring about an arrangement'. He named his mother as the driving force behind the initiative. Two days later, when the members of the British embassy were received by the Empress Frederick, Lascelles raised the subject of the Kaiser's remarks with her, whereupon the Empress expressed surprise that her name had been mentioned in this connection. She indicated, however, that she had had the idea 'that The Emperor should run over to Scotland during his annual cruise in the North Sea, and pay a visit to The Queen at Balmoral'.[27]

The Empress Frederick and other advocates of a rapprochement between Germany and Great Britain regretted that Wilhelm would not be going to Cowes in the summer of 1898 as usual, because of the Senden incident. But they had great hopes for the Kaiser's visit to Egypt, Malta and Gibraltar, which he had planned to make immediately following his journey to Constantinople,

Palestine and Damascus in the autumn of 1898.[28] Staff at the British embassy were astonished to discover that the Kaiser had not only heard that the improved tone of the London newspapers had been brought about by the personal orders of Queen Victoria, but even knew the name of her intermediary. 'He must have some very well informed correspondents at home', remarked Grierson, who was constantly surprised by the Kaiser's marked friendliness towards him.[29] There were reports of admiring comments made by Wilhelm II in May on the deeds of the British army on the upper Nile, and of his wish for a closer connection between the two countries. He spoke to Grierson of the successes of the 'Yankees' in the war against Spain, and commented 'that Europe will have to combine against them'. But in order for that to happen, England and Germany would have to co-operate, for 'we can do nothing against America unless England is with us'. As the military attaché noted with surprise, 'he never seems to be free from this dream of an European coalition'.[30]

It was only now that the politicians stepped in to the Anglo-German talks which had been going on, if only intermittently, at the monarchical level since the beginning of the year. The German seizure of Kiaochow and the Russian occupation of Port Arthur had roused fears in London that a general partition of China was in the offing, and this, together with the French advances into the Niger region and on the upper Nile, led the British government to question the wisdom of maintaining its policy of isolation. On 25 March 1898 an initial exploratory conversation took place between Arthur Balfour, who had taken charge at the Foreign Office during Salisbury's illness, and Hatzfeldt, the German ambassador.[31] Four days later the influential Colonial Secretary, Joseph Chamberlain, met the ambassador at Alfred de Rothschild's house, and to Hatzfeldt's astonishment proposed a full alliance between Great Britain and the Triple Alliance against France and Russia. When Salisbury was informed by his nephew Balfour of Chamberlain's unauthorised diplomatic initiative, the Prime Minister's response was scathing, not only on the disloyal conduct of his Cabinet colleague, but also, and principally, on the subject of Wilhelm II, whom he described as the greatest impediment to improved relations with Germany. 'The one object of the German Emperor since he has been on the throne has been to get us into a war with France', he declared bluntly. He regarded an alliance with Germany 'with some dismay, for Germany will blackmail us heavily'.[32] But in spite of his mistrust of Germany, and in particular of the Kaiser, after his return to Downing Street Salisbury nevertheless indicated in a conversation with the Austro-Hungarian ambassador in London, Count Deym, that the time might be ripe for Britain to enter into alliances to protect its interests. The British government, Hatzfeldt reported to Berlin, was however afraid that Germany would place unacceptable conditions on its friendship, 'particularly as regards colonies'. The Kaiser, as usual, covered Hatzfeldt's dispatch with marginal comments, which clearly reveal his own attitude to the idea of an Anglo-German agreement. Where reference was made to the fact that Salisbury was considering possible alliances, Wilhelm wrote: 'Here he is directly contradicting all the statements he made to us at the end of the eighties and beginning of the nineties, when we were trying to persuade him to join the Triple Alliance, or rather to draw closer to Italy! England must therefore be finding the situation sticky now.' Beside a reference to the likelihood that the German price for alliance with Britain would be too high, he commented: 'But we haven't been properly asked yet, or received a request.' Apart from the concession of British possessions in Borneo, Germany must also, 'if possible', get 'Samoa, [the] Carolines and one of the Philippine Islands'. He did not understand, Wilhelm commented finally, why Salisbury had dropped these hints to Deym, 'and not to Hatzfeldt or to me by Lascelles'.[33]

A few days later Wilhelm received a nineteen-page letter from his mother – now ill with cancer at Kronberg – which she asked him to burn at once, and in which she argued that an alliance between Germany and Britain might well be the last chance for world peace, and begged her son to accept the offer of alliance which she was sure London would make very soon. 'I *know* for a fact that in England part of the Govt. are *seriously inclined* to enter into a *real alliance* with Germany, a thing wh[ich] has never happened before, – and to my idea, and that of 100.000[s] of Germans – the *most blessed* that could happen *not only* for the 2 Countries but for the *world* and civilization!! – The moment *never* may come again – how grand it would be, & how *wise* – if you grasped the outstretched hand wh[ich] if I understand rightly Mr. Chamberlain is seriously & honestly offering!! – For *yourself*, your *own* position, your *own* future, for Germany, I could conceive no more magnificent opportunity. Misunderstandings would be swept away – and *peace* secured! We need not fear the Russians or the French, – nor both of them together and can *afford* to be on the *best* of terms with them. All the *great standing questions* of the day could be solved quietly & amicably & *without* war! – The *security* & prosperity of Europe increased *immensely*. – That Italy & Austria would only be too pleased to join is without doubt, and this combination would be so strong, that there would be no need to feel uncomfortable about Russia & France, who might be left to enjoy their alliance unharassed & undisturbed, & who then would *not* be likely to wish to attack *any* one, for with the German Army & english Fleet combined, *who* would take up the gauntlet?' Although she otherwise stayed out of politics, the Empress Frederick said, she had decided to take this step because neither Hohenlohe nor Bülow knew Great Britain, 'and therefore perhaps are not so keenly alive to the *immense* importance of an alliance between the 2 great Germanic & Protestant nations, wh[ich] for 50 years has been the dream of so many true patriots but prevented by the vicissitudes of political phases of a momentary kind! *All* quarrels all misunderstandings *disappear* & *melt* like snow – wh[ich] seems *so entirely natural* & right. It seems to me as if you can have this ripe fruit, of inestimable value, in the hollow of your hand if you will & can but seize it! Time presses and I am so afraid that if english statesmen see Germany does not care to respond to the idea they must look *else where* – that would be disastrous, *now* is the time & *now* the hour!' Obviously suspecting that Wilhelm would steer a narrow nationalistic course whatever happened, his mother repeatedly stressed the advantages which an alliance with the United Kingdom, which Japan and the United States could also join, would have not only for humanity in general but also for the German Reich. 'The moment has *come*!', she urged. It was a historic, deeply significant, richly promising opportunity which should be seized with both hands. The Anglo-German alliance embodied 'a world-saving idea', which Wilhelm must take hold of, not only for the benefit of mankind, Christianity and civilisation but also in the interests of Germany, for through it German influence in the world would become greater than ever before. The new century would have a more promising start than had ever been seen. '*My* father's dream & *your* father's dream, and what they worked & slaved for, would come true, though *they* are no more! For *you* it would be the most immense satisfaction & for dear Grandmama too! *No one* would exult more than Uncle Bertie – & as for me, I could sing "nunc dimittis"' and die at peace', Wilhelm's mother concluded.[34] No one in Britain knew that she was aware of these plans, which had originated with Chamberlain and which Salisbury might not support at all, the Empress Frederick confided to her son. He must therefore keep the matter absolutely secret.[35]

Wilhelm II's reaction to this 'world-saving' opportunity was both triumphant and fearful. Without consulting the Reich Chancellor or the Foreign Office, on 30 May 1898 he wrote a letter to Tsar Nicholas II in which he spoke of the 'enormous offers' which the British were ready to make to him, and then suggested that the Tsar might like to outbid the British offer! 'Dearest Nicky', he wrote, 'With a suddenness wholely [sic] unexpected to me I am placed before a grave decision which is of vital importance to my country, and which is so far reaching that I cannot foresee the ultimate consequences. The traditions in which I was reared by my beloved Grandfather of blessed memory as regards our two houses and countries, have as you will own, always been kept up by me as a holy bequest from him, and my loyalty to you and your family is, I flatter myself, above any suspicion. I therefore come to you as my friend and "confident" [sic] to lay the affairs before you as one who expects a frank and loyal answer to a frank and loyal question . . . About Easter a Celebrated Politician [Chamberlain] proprio motu suddenly sent for my Ambassador and à brûle pourpoint offered him a *treaty of* Alliance with England! Count Hatzfeldt, utterly astonished, said he could not quite make out how that could be after all that had passed between us since 1895. The answer was that the offer was made in real earnest and was sincerely meant. My Ambassador said he would report, but that he doubted very much whether Parliament would ever ratify such a treaty England till now always having made clear to anybody who wished to hear it, that it never by any means would make an Alliance with any Continental Power whoever it may be! Because it wished to keep its liberty of action . . . The answer was that the prospect had completely changed and that this offer was the consequence. After Easter the request was *urgently* renewed but by my commands cooly [sic] and dilatorily answered in a colourless manner. I thought the affair had ended. Now however the request has been renewed for the third time in such an unmistakable manner, putting a *certain short term* to my definite answer and accompanied by such enormous offers showing a wide and great future opening for my country, that I think it my duty to Germany duly to reflect before I answer. Now before I do it, I frankly and openly come to you, my esteemed friend and cousin, to inform you, as I feel that it is a question so to say of life and death. We two have the same opinions, we want peace, and we have sustained and upheld it till now! What the tendence [sic] of the Alliance is, you will well understand, as I am informed that the Alliance is to be with the Triple Alliance and with the addition of Japan and America, with whom pourparlers have already been opened! What the chances are for us in refusing or accepting you may calculate yourself! Now as my old and trusted friend I beg you to tell me what you can offer me and will do if I refuse. Before I take my final decision and send my answer in this difficult position, I must be able to see clearly, and clear and open without any backthoughts must your proposal be, so that I can judge and weigh in my mind before God, as I should, what is for the good of the Peace of my Fatherland and of the world. You need not fear for your Ally, in any proposal you make should he be placed in a combination wished by you. With this letter dearest Nicky I place my whole faith in your silence and discretion to *everybody* and write as in old times my Grandfather would have written to your Grandfather Nicholas I! May God help you to find the right solution and decision! It is for the next generation! But time is pressing so, please answer soon! Your devoted friend Willy. P. S. Should you like to meet me anywhere to arrange by mouth I am ready every moment at sea, or on land to meet!'[36] The Tsar, supremely indifferent to the Kaiser's dramatic letter, replied that the British had recently made similar approaches to him too.[37]

Although they were well aware that the contents of the Kaiser's letter, which they themselves had seen only after the event and in an inaccurate version, would be reported to London, the experienced and supposedly 'responsible' diplomats in the Wilhelmstrasse merely shrugged their shoulders over Wilhelm II's intervention. On Bülow's instructions the compromising document was quietly filed away in the confidential records of the Foreign Office. Friedrich von Holstein, who eighteen months earlier had seemed ready to go the barricades in protest against personal rule, now scoffed at the 'excited' Kaiser's exaggerated expectations, and at his evident fear of attack by the Royal Navy if Britain's offers were rejected. His dread of incurring British enmity, Holstein believed, had been apparent in a memorandum written by the Kaiser on 31 May, which had read: 'At the beginning of the next century we would have a battlefleet which, with *others* which will also have grown, could represent a real danger to England's fleet. Hence the intention either to force us into an alliance or to destroy us before we have become strong, like Holland in times past.'[38] Hatzfeldt too shook his head over the Kaiser's expectations and anxieties. He saw no sign of the 'enormous offers' of which the Kaiser dreamt. 'The feared naval attack is even more improbable. As far as can be humanly foreseen it could take place only if we ourselves first took up a hostile attitude', the ambassador commented — a remark which, no doubt unwittingly, expressed Wilhelm's guilt complex over his anti-British fleet building plans. From a conversation with Salisbury, Hatzfeldt gained the impression that, although the British government wished to be on good terms with Germany, it had no intention of suggesting a formal agreement.[39]

The reply, bristling with anti-British resentment, which Wilhelm wrote to his mother's letter on 1 June 1898, and of which he subsequently sent a copy to the Wilhelmstrasse, represents what is probably the most revealing assessment of Anglo-German relations, as he saw them, since his accession. In it he acknowledged that he had been fascinated by what his mother had said. 'The idea of an Alliance of the Anglo-Saxon race is not new, the accession of Germany to it however is so, as far at least as the English Government is concerned. Let me make a short sketch of our relations. In the first 6 years of my reign I tried to the very utmost of my powers . . . to elicit from L[ord] S[alisbury] a word implying approval of the idea of a[n] Anglo German cooperation & Convention. But it was utterly without any result, as he invariably allways [sic] ended in the same refrain: "An English Government cannot & never will form an Alliance with *any continental power* for the simple reason, that Parliament would hardly ever ratify such an instrument & because England prefers to keep its *liberty of action*, therefore I am unable to fullfill [sic] your wishes."!! So I let the matter drop & with a heavy heart gave up the task, which was a difficult one, though dear to me seeing that I worked on the same lines dear Papa, & Grandpapa (Consort) had shaped. In numerous phases of Foreign Affairs, notably in the Siamese Imbroglio (under the Liberal Government of L[ord] Rosebery) I staunchly stood by England & volunteered my help L[ord] R[osebery] so warmly begged for with Grandmama's consent at Osborne in 1894 [sic]! But instead of thanks or of help in our colonising enterprises, I got nothing whatever. I for the last 3 years have been abused, ill-treated & a butt to any bad joke any musikhall [sic] singer or fishmonger or pressman thought fit to let fly at me! – Notwithstanding all this two years ago I tried hard to have L[ord] S[alisbury] help to give us a coaling station in China, he flatly refused in a language that only Hatzfeld knew how to interpret so that no serious action came out of it! So pushed back, illtreated & riled by Grt Britain & her Prime Minister instead from her I got from Russia in a few conversations with the Emperor all I wanted & even more than I ever hoped for! This as "eine kleine Orientirung" [to set the record straight a little]. Now with respect to what you wrote about the Alliance of England-Amerika & Germany, this has very much interested me. The idea has been ventilated in the papers since 2 months & also sundry allusions & suggestions from Mr. Ch[amberlain] have been wafted over here by the same breezes. But as they were not officially transmitted as coming from the government or Prime Minister nobody very much heeded them as they seemed to be merely a repetition of the articles in the Press. By your letter I see for the first time that the thing is ment [sic] in earnest, & purports to be an overture, at least so it was ment [sic] by Mr. Ch[amberlain]. If that is the case & if as I gather there is a certain speed wished in the treatment of this question, then why in the name of all that is diplomatic use & sense, does not the *Prime Minister* make a *real* proposal? Why does Cabinet not make real propositions to serve as base for pourparlers? Why does the Cabinet not empower L[ord] S[alisbury] or L[ord] S[alisbury] Mr. Ch[amberlain] under his authority to expound the terms of a treaty to me? Private conversations & even statements before others are all very well, but do not represent the right way to a Treaty of Alliance! Besides if even Mr. Ch[amberlain] & as it seems *part* of the Cabinet are in earnest & begin to treat with me in the above informal manner, who will ever guard me against a sudden desaveu in the House of Lords by the Premier, or in Parliament by Balfour if they found popular feeling not in the lines they expected, as long as L[ord] S[alisbury] is in such a bad way with Mr. Ch[amberlain] & has not implicitly bound himself to this affair by officially authorising his Ministers to enter into negotiations?! England would not feel anything, but a *miscarried* try at an Alliance with her brings Russia & France down on my head & over my frontier on the same day!? – These are some of the difficulties which have cropped up in my mind since I have given your letters serious attention, & are the consequences of the treatment I have gone through at the hands of the British Government & notably L[ord] S[alisbury], & the result of the experience I had in the 10 years of my reign of

British Foreign Politics! Should Government wish to get out of the "splendid isolation", promote the idea of a "rapprochement" to me and the formation of an Alliance, then let the British Premier speak out openly & manly & officially as it is "d'usage" among Great Powers, & I will with pleasure listen & consider! But he can never expect me to "slip in by the back door" like a thief at night whom one does not like to own before ones richer friends. I will be most grateful if I can have any information how the things are going on.'[40]

In her reply of 3 June 1898 the Empress Frederick tried to reassure her son. No one would expect him to go in 'by the back door' in a matter of such importance. She could sympathise with his complaints about many of the things said against him by public opinion in Britain, but in Britain too certain comments by the German press had caused offence and it might in fact take some time for people there to recover their trust in German intentions. 'But these are, I hope, *passing* shadows, and I wish with all my heart that the idea floating in people's minds of an alliance may take *shape & form* and be brought forward in an official & decided way.' One could only wait and hope that nothing would happen in Berlin or London to ruin this opportunity.[41] When weeks again went by without further progress, however, the widowed Empress was forced to acknowledge that, while Wilhelm hoped, as she did, for an understanding in the near future, leading statesmen in both capitals were at best prepared to handle the matter only in a dilatory fashion. She was certain, she wrote to her mother, 'that William *is most* anxious for a rapprochement with England and *hopes* with all his heart that England *will come* forward in some sort of way & meet him halfway'. Prince Hohenlohe was not exactly anti-British, but if only on account of his Russian property, which he wished to keep, he was pro-Russian. Bülow was in favour of an agreement between Germany and Britain, but not for many years to come. In Britain, she believed, Chamberlain supported the idea of an understanding with Germany, while Salisbury was against it. If the Prime Minister would only come forward with a concrete proposal, she was sure Wilhelm would be ready to agree to it; Lascelles knew this too. 'Wm. thinks the moment propitious – & would be anxious for the idea to take shape & form! . . . I am sure W. wd. make every endeavour to "enfiler" a "rapprochement" with England, – but fears it wd. not be reciprocated by Ld. S[alisbury].'[42]

When Queen Victoria showed this letter to Salisbury, he strongly disputed the Empress Frederick's interpretation of events. 'It appears that she, and the German Emperor are of the opinion that in the communications which are going on about colonial territory between England and Germany, Mr. Chamberlain is anxious to meet the wishes of Germany while Lord Salisbury is opposing them. Lord Salisbury never wishes to discuss the actions of a colleague. But he feels bound to inform Your Majesty that this view of the comparative action of Lord Salisbury and Mr. Chamberlain is not correct – it is the very reverse of the truth.'[43] This distinctly unclear pronouncement by Salisbury touched on the Anglo-German negotiations over the future of the Portuguese colonies but left the central question of a full alliance between Germany and Great Britain, which was what mattered to the Empress Frederick, unanswered.

Wilhelm's hopes for 'enormous offers' from Britain, encouraged principally by his mother's well-meaning letters, were reflected in a memorandum written in the Wilhelmstrasse and approved by him on 15 June 1898. In it Germany's desiderata in its negotiations with Britain on the Portuguese colonies were listed.[44] These were, in West Africa, a naval base in the Canaries or the Cape Verde Islands; the island of Fernando Po in the Gulf of Guinea; the re-drawing of the frontier between Togo and the British colony of the Gold Coast; Angola, or at least the southern regions of Mossamedes and Benguela; and the British enclave of Walvis Bay on the Namibian coast. In East Africa Germany hoped to acquire Zanzibar and Pemba, together with the extension of the southern limits of German East Africa down to the Zambezi, which would have meant the assim-ilation of the Malawi of today, with its capital of Blantyre. In Asia the Kaiser and the Wilhelmstrasse expected to gain Portuguese Timor, the Sulu archipelago (with Jolo) in the South Philippines and at least one of the larger islands in the Philippines, preferably Mindanao. And, finally, they counted on acquiring exclusive possession of the Caroline Islands and the Samoan Islands in the South Pacific.[45] These far-reaching expectations – which in fact represented no more than a rough outline of the geopolitical goals of the new German leadership and did not begin to take into account Germany's possible ambitions in other parts of the world such as the Near East, the Caribbean and South America – were likewise thwarted by Salisbury's determined opposition. At the end of July 1898 he informed the Queen that in view of public opinion in Britain and the colonies he had rejected Hatzfeldt's demands for Blantyre and Walvis Bay, Samoa and Tonga in compensation for the British seizure of Delagoa Bay. First, he stated, Britain had already secured the right to Delagoa Bay in the event of Portugal giving it up, and second it could at most give up Walvis Bay in exchange for Togo. 'C[oun]t Hatzfeldt expressed great regret at Lord Salisbury's decision & hinted that if Germany could find no resource in friendship with England she must turn to Russia.'[46]

Wilhelm II's disappointment and fury with Salisbury knew no bounds. He scrawled marginal notes on Hatzfeldt's report calling the British Prime Minis-ter a 'shameless scoundrel!' and describing his behaviour as 'positively Jesuitical, monstrous and insolent!' 'If he has to take the feeling in his colonies into consid-eration', the Kaiser raged, 'I have to take the feeling of the German people into consideration, and that is what counts for *me*. It shows once again that the noble

Lord is trifling with us and shifting around simply because he is not afraid of us, because *we have no fleet*, which those stupid donkeys in the Reichstag have constantly denied me throughout the 10 years of my reign. Well, I stay here on my bond and shall make *no more concessions*.'[47] During the Scandinavian cruise that summer Eulenburg recorded that 'His Majesty is furious with the English and to my regret particularly enjoys expressing himself very frankly in front of foolish naval officers.'[48] Wilhelm remarked bitterly that he expected that 'England (allied to America?) will take our colonies away one day, because she is bound to come to the conclusion that we cannot take on a war.'[49] He also gave vent to his feelings in an angry telegram to his mother which she forwarded to Windsor. The Empress Frederick was at first convinced that there must have been a misunderstanding and wrote to her son: 'I think I may say without indiscretion – *trusting* that you will keep it *to yourself*, – that in England there *has* been an impression that you had been particularly kind and friendly in your expressions to different people you had met, naval & others, while at the same time the ambassador maintained gt. stiffness & coldness. I dare say this puzzled very much . . . and most likely made people not quite know wh. way the wind blew.' She acknowledged that Great Britain had to remain on good terms with Russia, 'but on the other hand I cannot bring myself to believe that Russia's intentions *can* be very friendly to England though the Emperor (*Nicky*) is so devoted to Grandmama & likes England so much'.[50] She must have reported to her mother on Wilhelm's disappointment in similar terms, for in returning the Kaiser's telegram and the Empress Frederick's letters to the Queen Salisbury remarked incredulously: 'The Emperor William is wonderful.'[51] Hatzfeldt's conduct at the negotiations 'did not at all correspond with the Emperor's strange telegram', he commented; on the contrary, he had remained friendly regardless of the difference in the positions taken by the two countries.[52] But Salisbury was anxious that the Empress Frederick should not pass on his own comments to the Kaiser. The latter would certainly tell others about them and thereby create the impression that Salisbury was intriguing with the Kaiser against Chamberlain. 'The German Emperor takes offence very easily', he commented in exasperation, adding that he did not understand 'what it is he refers to when he speaks of his overtures having been received with "something between a joke and a snub" . . . The truth is that on questions of territorial cession the German Emperor and public opinion here take very opposite views. It would be impossible to do what the German Emperor desires without incurring the reproach of deserting British interests and making undue concessions . . . When the public is excited on the subject as they are now, it is too strong to be resisted.'[53] When Salisbury again fell ill, it was left to Balfour to bring the negotiations on the Portuguese colonies to a tolerably satisfactory conclusion on the basis that in return for British recognition of the German claim to Timor, Germany would abandon all claims to the Boer republics in South Africa and to the island of Zanzibar.[54]

In an attempt to re-launch the stalled talks on the idea of an alliance, the Empress Frederick invited the British ambassador to Schloss Friedrichshof at Kronberg while the Kaiser was visiting her there. Again on this occasion Wilhelm made no secret of his disappointment and anger 'at the manner in which He considered that He had been treated by Your Majesty's Government', as Lascelles reported to the Queen after his meeting with the Kaiser on 21 August 1898. 'He complained at the scant consideration shown in England for German interests, and the curt refusal which His demands usually met with.' The ambassador seized the opportunity to explain to the Kaiser that his demands for colonial expansion in Africa were generally considered 'exorbitant' in Britain. But he also indicated that there was a genuine desire in Britain for better relations with Germany, and that some influential circles were even prepared to envisage a formal, if strictly defensive, alliance under which treaty obligations would come into force only if one of the two countries were attacked by two powers simultaneously. In the following days and months the ambassador was more than once surprised by the exaggerated importance which the Kaiser attributed to this somewhat hypothetical statement which had not even been formally committed to paper. The day after the meeting, the Empress Frederick showed Lascelles a telegram she had just received from Wilhelm, in which he expressed gratitude for the ambassador's 'energetic intercession'. It had decidedly altered the position, he said, and ensured that there would be a favourable conclusion for both sides. This was followed next day by a telegram direct to Lascelles from the Kaiser, in which Wilhelm described their discussion at Kronberg as highly satisfactory and stated that he had telegraphed appropriate instructions to Berlin and London. The attempts Lascelles made to correct the false impression the Kaiser had evidently gained from the conversation at Kronberg had no effect, as events were to show.[55]

Meanwhile the Kaiser's advisers in the Wilhelmstrasse, confident in the expectation that Britain would in time offer far more favourable conditions for an alliance with Germany, set out to persuade their master that Germany should maintain its neutrality between Britain and Russia, so that at the right moment — and with its new battlefleet — it could intervene for its own benefit in the war that would inevitably break out between these two rival world empires. German policy, as Bülow explained to the Kaiser, must maintain 'independence from both sides'; war between Russia and Britain would come 'all the sooner, the less both sides believe that we wished for any such thing!'[56] On 19 August 1898 Bülow described the aim of his foreign policy to Wilhelm as a 'firm and independent position between England and Russia, independent of both sides, but with the possibility of co-operating with one or the other, as soon as it suits Y.M.'.[57] By the end of the year Holstein was able to assure his confidant Hatzfeldt in London that they had steered the Kaiser back to the official line: the 'free hand' policy. 'H.M. realises the advantages there are for us in playing the part of spectators for as long as possible.'[58] Postponing the day of reckoning did not imply that Germany's designs had been abandoned, however, and by August 1900 Bülow was assuring his Kaiser of the victorious role he was destined to play. 'How true it is that in Your Majesty's reign the British are playing the same role as the French did under the Great Elector, and the Austrians under Frederick the Great. Dealing with the British is immensely laborious, immensely difficult and requires immense patience and skill. But just as the Hohenzollern eagle drove the two-headed Austrian eagle from the battlefield and clipped the wings of the Gallic cockerel, so will it vanquish the English leopard with God's help and Your Majesty's strength and wisdom.'[59]

## THE IMPERIAL WARMONGER

Patience, wisdom and skill were not exactly the Kaiser's strong points. After Salisbury had put paid to his colonial aspirations, Wilhelm turned back to the continent, and in particular to Russia. On 18 August 1898 he wrote to Tsar Nicholas castigating the perfidious English, who had conducted negotiations with him but had 'never quite uncovered [their] hand; they are trying hard, as far as I can make out, to find a continental army to fight for their interests! But I fancy they won't easily find one, at least not *mine*! Their newest move is the wish to gain France over from you, and they in consequence have suddenly decided to send the Duke of Connaught to the French Army Manoeuvres.'[60] During his tour of the Orient the Kaiser at first tried to incite the Tsar against Britain, and then set his sights on the goal he had accused the British of pursuing, by attempting to drive a wedge between Russia and its ally France. On 28 September 1898 the French had given way to the British at Fashoda, as France was unwilling to risk taking on Britain's overwhelming naval power.[61] Wilhelm wrote maliciously to his 'dearest Nicky' from Damascus: 'The hatred of the English is strong and growing more and more intense − no wonder − whilst in the same time apace with it grows the open contempt of France, which has lost all the respect it once possessed of old! That is the unavoidable consequence of the terrible quagmire the French are now floundering about in their interior affairs, splashing the dirt right and left till the whole of Europe reeks with the stench! . . . Here [in the Near East] people look upon them as on a dying nation, especially since the last and most ignominious retreat of the French from Faschoda! What on earth has possessed them?! After such a first rate well arranged and plucky expedition of poor and brave [Major] Marchand? They were in a first rate position and able to help us others all in Africa who are so[r]ely in need of strong help! The news here have [sic] come as a thunderbolt on the Eastern people, nobody would believe them! At all events if it is true, what the papers say, that Count Mouravieff [the Russian Foreign Minister] councelled [sic] France to take this foolish step he was singularly and exceptionally ill advised, as it has given your *"friends and allies"* a mortal blow here and brought down their ancient prestige here never to rise again! The Moslems call it France's second Sedan.'[62]

At the same time Wilhelm pursued his efforts to incite Britain to go to war with France. On his way home from the Orient he wrote to his mother, who was visiting her native land (for the last time), from Messina on 20 November 1898, saying that the British fleet, which he had admired at Malta, was 'ready for imminent use should Britain want its ships for a quick blow. The speeches of the British ministers seem to show pretty clearly that Great Britain means business [sic] this time & that the moment has come for her to settle the accounts with France on the whole globe. This *may* lead to war. But the moment – militarily spoken – is well chosen as nobody will dream of helping France – who has understood to make itself disagreeable to every body in the world –, by its perpetual intrigues & the self asserting vanity with which it upholds its pretentions. Should it come to war, I of course in private as Grandmama's grandson will pray for the success of her arms with all my heart – which is to me of no doubt whatever – as France is no equal to England on the Sea. Officially as head of the German Empire I would uphold a strict & benevolent neutrality. Should a second Power think fit to attack England from the rear, whilst it is fighting, I would act according to our arrangements made with Sir Frank Lascelles.'[63] When Queen Victoria had this letter sent to him, Lord Salisbury was understandably surprised to read of agreements of whose existence he knew nothing but which had apparently been made between the German sovereign and the British ambassador in Berlin.[64]

Lascelles again found himself compelled to make it plain to the Kaiser that the spontaneous remarks he had made during their meeting at Kronberg, from which Wilhelm had evidently drawn false conclusions, had been purely informative and in no way binding.[65] On 19 December he dined with the Kaiser at Potsdam and brought up the subject of the letter that Wilhelm had written to his mother from Messina. Once again Wilhelm persuaded himself that he had come to 'most satisfactory agreement' with Lascelles, writing to the Empress Frederick afterwards: 'I was able to tell him, that I had a conversation with the Russian Ambassador [Count Osten-Sacken], who seemed much alarmed at the situation in Europe & elsewhere, & that in the end I was able to make him understand, that in the case England was in the necessity of "settling accounts" with France, no general conflagration in Europe would be the result for the simple reason that the fight would be *purely on the water*. But we two beeing [sic] eminently land powers with fleets not to speak of, the very best thing would be to sit as quiet as possible & to look on; the French army not beeing [sic] engaged it would do no great harm to France if she lost a few ships & colonies & it would do none to Russia or us! "Ruhe ist die erste Bürgerpflicht." ["The main thing is to keep calm."] This greatly relieved the old gentleman who left me saying "Ah il me tombe une pierre du Coeur."'[66]

When a report arrived at Potsdam from Hatzfeldt two days later describing Salisbury's attitude to France as conciliatory and peaceable, Wilhelm dismissed the Prime Minister's words as pure sophistry in view of the British naval preparations which he knew to be under way, and wrote an angry marginal comment rejecting Salisbury's assertion that these measures had been planned the previous spring, long before the Fashoda crisis, and therefore had nothing to do with the present situation. The measures were 'being carried out only now! Furthermore Fashoda could have been foreseen a year ago! I told Grierson [in January 1898] during the hare shoot at Buckow that we had received news that Marchand had reached the upper Nile and was preparing to sail down it. Which gave him a colossal fright; then he pulled himself together quickly, laughed and said it was nonsense!' Against Salisbury's joking remark, reported by Hatzfeldt, that if the Admiralty were still making war preparations it must be doing so privately in its own room, as he, the Prime Minister, knew nothing about it, Wilhelm II noted: 'That I can quite believe! Since H. Excellency has not even the faintest glimmer of an idea about the navy and ships, as I discovered for myself, the last part is absolutely right!' As supreme war lord the German Kaiser knew much more about such things than the civilian Prime Minister of a parliamentary nation. 'Mobilisation is generally planned and prepared in a room and not on the street, nor in Tsung-li-Yamen!!' – by which he meant the parliament at Westminster. When Salisbury referred to Russia's peaceful intentions and expounded his favourite theory that a war between Britain and Russia was scarcely conceivable if only because there was no battlefield on which the two powers could fight each other, Wilhelm remarked spitefully: 'Well! When the Caucasian grenadiers come knocking on the door at Herat he will change his tune.' The Prime Minister's conviction that Britain need not fear a Russian attack on India received nothing but scorn from the Kaiser, who annotated this passage: 'Well! That is at the very least colossally irresponsible and shows he is badly informed about Russian troop movements in the East!' The only matter which gave the British leader cause for anxiety was the unpredictable situation in Macedonia, on which the Kaiser commented furiously: 'Quite right. And perhaps the English war preparations are also intended to encourage the Macedonians, and then, when there is a rebellion there they are hoping for a general mess so that they can get Crete, Suda [Bay], Dardanelles, French fleet etc. in one fell swoop; St Petersburg must therefore be urged to keep things *quiet* in the Balkans; and above all to hobble that scoundrel [Prince] Ferdinand [of Bulgaria] by his mutton legs. For he *is planning something*, and the House of Coburg reaches far up into the North! If Russia becomes embroiled in the Balkans – which Salisbury certainly hopes – she will be out of the way in Asia and he is rid of the problem, while the Austrians and Germans have it on their plate! – So *Effendimis* [Sultan Abdul Hamid II] must be encouraged at all costs to keep his European troops ready to fight on the Bulgarian frontier and to strengthen them so as to teach Ferdinand a lesson at once. To make Sir Fr. Lascelles aware of the real seriousness of the situation, since he treats the Macedonians more like a bad joke and refused to take the Bulgarian seriously, I told him that Ferdinand would undoubtedly try to create havoc down there; if he did so and provoked a European conflagration in the process, *I* would *have him murdered without further ado*, for *"fire raisers"* of that kind must be got rid of at once, and I did not go to the Orient for nothing!! The ambassador's face was a picture! But I think the "Coburger" may well be *warned*! – In his usual masterly way Salisbury has said nothing that he might have to *take back* later or that was *absolutely untrue*, but between the lines he says a great deal, and glosses over everything! – In the passage about India he is perhaps being dishonest in hiding his anxiety.'[67]

Bülow had scarcely had time to order these imperial outbursts to be locked away with the Foreign Office's secret records when he found himself compelled to consign another batch of correspondence, bedecked with revealing marginal notes in the All-Highest hand, to the Wilhelmstrasse's iron safe. In February 1899 Cecil Rhodes, who was to pass through Berlin on his return from Egypt, sent the Kaiser two books with a flattering accompanying letter in which he said that Wilhelm must feel very alone, since the Germans did not understand their Kaiser's 'big ideas'.[68] Although Rhodes was extremely unpopular in Germany, on Bülow's advice Wilhelm agreed to receive him, scrawling a characteristic note on the Foreign Secretary's submission: 'Well! It will create a splendid scandal among my dim-witted subjects, but I don't care. If I could I would hang Cecil Rh:, but as that isn't possible I shall make use of him. But it will cause a great sensation!'[69] In fact, as Rhodes had predicted, the two men got on extremely well at their meeting on 11 March. On the Kaiser's orders, less than three days later a treaty had been drawn up and signed, granting Rhodes the right to lay his Cape-to-Cairo telegraph and railway line through German East Africa. Rhodes asked the Kaiser 'why he did not go for Mesopotamia as a colonizing ground to which H.M. replied that this was a project he had had for years'. At dinner later at the British embassy the conversation came round to the Krüger telegram.

Lascelles's blood froze in his veins with terror, but Rhodes apologised for his role in the Jameson Raid and said to the Kaiser: 'I was a naughty boy, I did behave badly; you were quite right, but my people . . . thought that if I was to be punished, it was they who should do it and that no one else should interfere.' Finally the Kaiser gave him a large signed portrait of himself.[70] Writing to his mother about the meeting, Wilhelm described Rhodes as 'a most energetic man & marvellous organiser. I have of course promised to help him as far as is in my power so that he may be able to see the wish of his life fullfilled.'[71] To Lascelles he expressed the view that, 'with a man like Rhodes for a minister, he would do anything'.[72] Rhodes, for his part, also did his best to bring about warmer relations between Britain and Germany, and in particular between Wilhelm and his uncle, who it was safe to assume would succeed to the British throne before very long. In a letter to the Prince of Wales he expressed his confidence in the Kaiser's goodwill. 'I feel sure he is most anxious to work with England, and I think he is fond of the English; he must be so, for after all he is half an Englishman. I think he is very sensitive, for he spoke about the way the English papers had abused him. I heard in Berlin, on good authority, and I am sure, Sir, you will not mind my repeating it, that he thinks you do not like him, and that he is very anxious to gain your good opinion . . . I think . . . we ought to try and work with Germany, and the Emperor is really Germany, at least, it appeared to me to be so when I was in Berlin, Ministers doing just as he desires and the Reichstag most docile . . . It seems to me that in view of the complications in the world we must work with some nation, and Germany seems the best . . . I am sure of this that, if you showed him good feeling when he came to England, it would immensely influence his mind.'[73]

Although the Kaiser had been forced to give up his hopes for a war between Britain and France for the time being, he continued to make no secret of his view that the former had missed a historic opportunity. 'How funny it is to read about you all in the South of France when I remember our correspondence in October & November about the forthcoming probable war with France!', he wrote to his mother on 26 March 1899. 'In ways of course this state of things is to be preferred & I fully understand Grandmama not wanting to finish her Reign with fighting. But simply taken from a cool political point of view: England has missed a grand opportunity which will never come again. France unprepared, the Continent uncertain; Russia not ready, Germany a Friendly neutral, & England herself ready & stronger than ever! What a great pity! With every year the odds will be heavier! For France has awakened & is quietly but thoroughly preparing herself for the great struggle.'[74] The Empress Frederick, who had meanwhile arrived in Bordighera, replied that England would indeed have had a good chance of success if war had broken out with France the previous November or December, 'but the aim of politics is to avoid such struggles *if possible* and it *was* possible'. One must always hope for a friendly solution of outstanding questions, she commented, 'without plunging nations into the misery of war; no one can tell when and how they will end, and the responsability [sic] is too great to risk bringing on a struggle because one's chances are good, and those of one's adversary are not'.[75] The Empress's humane arguments made no impression whatever. Lieutenant-Colonel Grierson was astonished to hear from the Kaiser during a dinner in late March 1899 what a mistake Britain had made 'in not going to war with France over Fashoda. He said that we should never have such a chance again, and that the situation was just like that before Frederick the Great at the beginning of the 1st Silesian War. *He* had arranged everything to keep Russia out of the war', and now the Russians were cocking a snook at him. 'Every nation in Europe was building battleships and though we [British] might build we could not find men to put into our ships, and we should end by losing our supremacy. He said that England was no longer Nelson's England, and all this "because Grandmama wants to go to Cimiez"!' Commenting on Salisbury's agreements with France and Russia, the Kaiser asserted that England had made great concessions to the former and should not expect Russia to keep its promises.[76]

## THE COBURG SUCCESSION

As if there were not already enough contentious issues between Britain and Germany in the sphere of *Weltpolitik* and between the two ruling houses, the sudden death of the young Prince Alfred of Saxe-Coburg and Gotha, only son of the reigning Duke Alfred (Affie), who was himself gravely ill, precipitated a conflict over the succession to the two Thuringian duchies of Coburg and Gotha which caused further strain between Wilhelm and his English relations. Duke Alfred's next successor would have been his younger brother Prince Arthur, Duke of Connaught, who had the advantage of being married to a Prussian princess, but who was unwilling to give up his career in the British army. Connaught's son Arthur, born in 1883, could have taken over the succession; after him, the next in line was Charles Edward (Charlie), Duke of Albany, the still underage son of Prince Leopold, Queen Victoria's youngest son, who had died of haemophilia in 1884.[77] From the outset the question of the succession threatened to become an affair of state, for while Queen Victoria was adamant that according to Coburg laws of succession it was absolutely nothing to do with the Kaiser, Wilhelm himself saw it from a German national perspective and insisted that the young successor – whether Arthur or Charles Edward – must at least be educated in Germany.[78] Wilhelm felt thoroughly snubbed when he heard in March 1899 that several members of the English Coburg family had had a meeting in the

South of France, where the Queen was on holiday, to discuss the succession. He pointed out to Grierson that he too was 'a member of the Royal Family and happened also to be German Emperor'; he had therefore expected to be asked for his opinion on a question of the succession to a German throne. He had not even been directly informed of the family's decision, he complained, but believed that the choice had fallen upon young Arthur of Connaught. He had no objection to this decision, but must insist, as German kaiser, that the Prince move to Germany if only to learn the language, which in spite of his Prussian mother he did not speak perfectly, and as a German prince he must join the German army. As Lascelles reported to Lord Salisbury, Grierson had received the impression from this conversation 'that the Emperor felt he had been slighted about the question of the Coburg Gotha succession and was sore in consequence'. The ambassador had also taken soundings at the German Foreign Office, which left no room for doubt that this was an affair 'upon which the Emperor felt very strongly'. He drew the Prime Minister's attention to the difficult position in which the young Prince Arthur would find himself if he moved to Germany as heir to the Duchy without the Kaiser's blessing.[79] The Queen, the Empress Frederick and the Prince of Wales were not at all surprised by Wilhelm's annoyance, but thought it would be wrong to make any apology. 'He seems greatly annoyed at not having been consulted about the Coburg-succession which "unter uns" [between ourselves] is no real concern of his, but as you know only *too* well [he] *must* meddle with everything', the heir to the British throne complained to his sister.[80]

During a meeting arranged at the suggestion of the Empress Frederick between the Duke of Coburg, his brother the Duke of Connaught and Wilhelm II at the Wartburg on 21 April 1899, the latter reiterated his conditions on the succession question and added threateningly that, if the family did not accept them, he would have a bill introduced into the Reichstag excluding foreign princes from succeeding to any German throne. Later he dropped this threat, presumably, as Grierson commented, because he realised that the bill would not receive sufficient support in the Reichstag.[81] But the Duke of Connaught was unwilling to give up his life in Britain and his position in the British army 'to begin life anew as a German and a German officer', as the Kaiser insisted. He was also uncomfortably aware that Wilhelm had the support of the German press and public opinion, which was hostile to a 'foreigner' succeeding in Coburg, and therefore declared himself ready to renounce the Coburg throne both for himself and for his son.[82] The other English members of the family feared the effect of Wilhelm II's emotional outbursts on the international political scene and agreed that it would be advisable for the Connaughts to renounce their rights in favour of the young Duke of Albany, especially in view of the danger that the family might lose its right to the Coburg succession altogether.[83] After a further meeting between Wilhelm and his uncle Arthur, this time in Kassel on 27 May, at least an outward semblance of harmony was achieved with the agreement that both Connaughts, father and son, would renounce the succession and that it would fall to 'little Albany'.[84] It was only a little over a year later, on the death of his uncle Alfred on 30 July 1900, that Charles Edward was to succeed to the Duchy of Saxe-Coburg and Gotha, although under the guardianship of Hereditary Prince Ernst zu Hohenlohe-Langenburg until 1905. Other problems which arose at the same time as the succession crisis in Coburg were not so easily overcome.

### THE KAISER, LORD SALISBURY AND QUEEN VICTORIA

For some time now Wilhelm's contempt for the British Prime Minister and Foreign Secretary, which was entirely mutual, had assumed dangerous dimensions and put a strain on relations between the two countries. In November 1896 the Kaiser had accused the British government of giving financial support to the Hamburg dockers' strike for its own economic benefit. Salisbury had responded with a sharply worded dispatch to Lascelles which the Kaiser took very much amiss. As the Reich Chancellor noted with concern on 2 December 1896, the Kaiser was determined to go and see the British ambassador and make it plain to him 'that, given the feeling against England prevalent in Germany now, it would have the worst possible effect in Germany if it were discovered that England was encouraging a strike that deeply affected Germany's economic situation. Lascelles would then be exposed to the danger, according to Wilhelm, that the Berliners might break his windows.' The Kaiser had rejected the ambassador's claim that it was not London financiers, but perhaps British socialists, who were supporting the strike, on the grounds that the latter 'did not have . . . enough money and must have received funds from the English financial barons'. One can imagine the effect that these accusations had on Salisbury and Queen Victoria.[85] A few years later, not least because of the disappointment of Germany's hopes in the Samoan question, open conflict was to break out between Wilhelm II and the Prime Minister.[86]

Queen Victoria marked the fortieth birthday of her firstborn grandson on 27 January 1899 with an anxious comment in her journal: 'I wish he were more prudent and less impulsive at such an age!'[87] Wilhelm himself had a surprisingly accurate grasp of his grandmother's opinion of him and wrote to her on the occasion of his birthday saying: 'I fully understand how extraordinary the fact must seem to you that the tiny, weeny little brat you often had in your arms and dear Grandpapa swung about in a napkin has reached the forties! Just half of your prosperous and successful life! [My life] is full of heavy unceasing work, and animated with my untiring trials to emulate such grand example as you set us all. It is often full of moments when I fancy the strain is too strong and the burden too heavy to bear . . . I venture to believe that, where the Sovereign will sometimes shake her wise head often over the tricks of her queer and impetuous colleague, the good and genial heart of my Grandmother will step in and show that, if he sometimes fails, it is never from want of goodwill, honesty, or truthfulness, and thus mitigate the shake of the head by a genial smile of warm sympathy and interest!' He went on to say how delighted he was by her invitation to him to visit her at Cowes or Balmoral.[88]

Like Salisbury, the old Queen did not take Wilhelm's expressions of friendship entirely at their face value. In a conversation with the Prime Minister on 17 February 1899 she agreed with him that, 'while William appeared to wish to be on good terms with us, he did not wish that we should be so with other countries and in particular Russia, whom he was always trying to set against us. Lord Salisbury does not at all believe the stories he tells.'[89] On 1 March 1899, shortly before her departure for the South of France, Queen Victoria wrote to the Tsar warning him, in words that presaged future developments, against the Kaiser's double-dealing. Wilhelm, she said, 'takes every opportunity of impressing upon Sir F. Lascelles that Russia is doing all in her power to work against us; that she offers alliances to other Powers and has made one with the Ameer of Afghanistan against us. I need not say that I do not believe a word of this, neither do Lord Salisbury nor Sir F. Lascelles. But I am afraid William may go and tell things against us to you, just as he does about you to us. If so, pray tell me openly and confidentially. It is so important that we should understand each other, and that such mischievous and unstraightforward proceedings should be put a stop to. You are so true yourself, that I am sure you will be shocked at this.'[90]

A few weeks later, in conversation with the British military attaché Grierson, the Kaiser delivered himself of an extraordinary tirade on the subject of Salisbury and the 'disgraceful' foreign policy of Great Britain. He was evidently feeling deeply hurt again, this time at not being invited to Queen Victoria's eightieth birthday on 24 May 1899 – for a time he even threatened to turn up uninvited[91] – but wounded feelings aside, the attack was of such virulence that at the British embassy, the Wilhelmstrasse, Downing Street and Windsor Castle there were serious concerns about his sanity. As Grierson reported to his ambassador, Lascelles, the Kaiser began by venting his feelings on the Coburg succession question, and then suddenly declared bluntly that he found British policy 'quite incomprehensible'. 'He said that for years he had been the one true friend to Great Britain on the continent of Europe, and had done everything to help her policy and assist her, and that he had received nothing in return but ingratitude, culminating in our behaviour in the Samoan affair, which, he said, had undone all the good he had effected in the way of cultivating friendly relations between the two countries. Some day, when it was too late, we should regret it. He had particularly desired to be in England on her Majesty's [80th] Birthday, and present all his children to the Queen, but that was now impossible. His consistent enemy throughout had been Lord Salisbury, and, while the latter remained Prime Minister, it would be impossible for him to come to England. Formerly it was the people of Great Britain who kept back the Government from war, now it was the Government which was holding back the people. The City and Mr. Chamberlain were all for war. They had failed to get war with France, and now they wanted war with Germany, which would be an easier thing for them as she had fewer ships than France.' The military attaché went on to suggest to his superior, with careful circumspection, that 'from the above Your Excellency will not fail to see that his Majesty was talking somewhat at random, for, by his own statement, his "enemy" Lord Salisbury was keeping back the people from making war on Germany!' Grierson felt compelled to add that, nevertheless, 'His Majesty's tone throughout this conversation was calm and dispassionate.'[92] During the conversation, which was in English, Wilhelm II had put on 'his gravest face and most impressive manner', but had otherwise been extremely friendly. But the military attaché seriously wondered whether the All-Highest sovereign might not be unhinged. He told the Queen's Private Secretary that he could not help fearing, given the doctrine of divine right and the state of subservient discipline to which the Kaiser had reduced all those around him, that he might be in a state of 'Grössenwahnsinn' (megalomania), in which he expected every other nation to change its policy in accordance with his views. Grierson did not think it wise to commit all his impressions to paper and asked Sir Arthur Bigge for a personal meeting during his forthcoming visit to London.[93] When Sir Frank Lascelles discussed the Kaiser's outburst with Bülow, the Foreign Secretary was visibly embarrassed. As the ambassador reported to Salisbury, Bülow declared 'that it was not for him to criticize in any way the language of his sovereign, but I, who knew the Emperor so well, must know that His Majesty's impetuosity sometimes led to exaggeration of expression . . . His Majesty was in fact more than half an Englishman, and was extraordinarily sensitive to anything which He could regard as a slight either from the Royal Family or from Her Majesty's Government.'[94] Salisbury himself was stunned by the Kaiser's completely unfounded accusations, which he regarded as the expression of a guilty conscience. 'So groundless is the charge', he wrote to Lascelles, 'that I cannot help fearing that it indicates a consciousness on the part of His Majesty that he cherishes some design which is bound to make me his enemy — and that he looks forward to the satisfaction of saying I told you so. It is a great nuisance that one of the main factors in the European calculation should be so ultra human. He is as jealous as a woman because he does not think the Queen pays him enough attention.'[95]

The Kaiser's angry assertion that he would not be able to come to Britain as long as Salisbury was still in occupation at Downing Street as prime minister provoked his grandmother to write a stern letter to her grandson on 18 May 1899, which served only to deepen the gulf between the two monarchs. She was hearing 'such very strange reports', she wrote, according to which he would not be welcome at Cowes this year. He should remember, however, that she had personally written to invite him and had also told his Flügeladjutant, Löwenfeld, when he was at Osborne, how much she was looking forward to Wilhelm's visit in August. 'I feel I must write to tell you how grieved I am at these false reports which have all emanated from Germany. As I am convinced that you cannot possibly be aware of this, I feel I must write this to you in order that you can make enquiries as to how such unfounded statements have got about, & put a stop to them. I am quite sure that you will be as much pained as I am, for I am convinced that you will be the first to assist me in clearing up a matter which may so easily make bad blood.'[96]

Queen Victoria's unusual tone was not without effect on Wilhelm. He telegraphed to Bülow on 20 May in dismay, stating that he had just 'received a rather angry letter' from the Queen, in which she complained of the false rumour that he had not been invited to Cowes this year and asked for the matter to be set straight, so that there should be no bad blood between the two countries. 'The letter gives me the impression', the Kaiser commented, 'that it was written in some agitation. Her Majesty's assertion, as far as I can remember, is completely invalid. Since My return from the Orient I have never seen any remark in any newspaper which even hinted at the absence of an invitation to Me from the Queen. I think it is more likely that some unpleasant intrigue is at work here. The absence of an invitation to her eightieth birthday (which even My Mother tried to obtain for Me in Cimiez) has been skilfully confused with the visit to Cowes. That may have been combined recently with the announcement conveyed by Lascelles on my instructions that I could not come to Cowes in view of the agitated state of public opinion in Germany because of Samoa, and that I therefore deeply regretted that in consequence of Her Majesty's refusal to allow Me and My family to visit her for her eightieth birthday, I had to forgo the pleasure of paying my respects to My grandmother in this important year. As Her Majesty can no longer read herself, I am afraid that the royal lady who acts as her secretary will have artfully confused these facts in reporting them to her, which has given rise to this strange accusation by the Queen. It is very striking that Her Majesty, who speaks to Me *for the first time in her life* of public opinion in

Germany, and apparently sets much store by it, makes not the slightest mention of the Samoa affair, although it has been so enormously upsetting and hurtful for our public.'[97] In view of Wilhelm's claim that the Queen's accusation must have been due to a misunderstanding, it may be worth pointing out that he too had misunderstood his grandmother's letter, for nowhere in it does she refer to newspaper reports or to German public opinion.

Wilhelm's pique over his family's exclusion from his grandmother's eightieth birthday celebrations manifested itself again at the banquet which he held in Berlin in honour of the occasion. He expressed his fury to the British ambassador over the bombardment of Samoa by British and American ships, which had caused considerable damage to German possessions, 'thereby causing the greatest indignation among all classes in Germany against England. Tho[ugh] England evidently treated Germany as a nonentity and ignored her Fleet, yet the time might come when England would have to respect it, and he only hoped that then it would not be too late, and that Germany might have formed combinations not agreeable to England. The feeling of irritation in Germany was so bitter, that he could not visit Cowes this year. All the good relations which existed between the two countries at the beginning of the year were now completely destroyed by British action in Samoa. His Majesty alluded to the large sums of money sent from England to bribe the American press to attack Germany & said Her Majesty's Government ought to have known of it, and they had taken no steps to counteract this evil influence. He praised Mr. Rhodes, and regretted more influential Englishmen did not visit Berlin. The Emperor's farewell words to the Ambassador were, "Tell your people to behave themselves properly", after which he quoted the speech of Dean Liddell to an undergraduate "You have not only imperilled your immortal soul, but you have incurred my serious displeasure" – the impression conveyed on the Ambassador being that the apologue conveyed a fairly accurate description of His Majesty's mind.'[98] Queen Victoria described Lascelles's report as 'an extraordinary account of William's impertinent & outrageous language'.[99]

On 27 May 1899 the Kaiser wrote a nine-page letter to his grandmother from Wilhelmshöhe which she described as 'a most violent attack on Ld. Salisbury & our supposed treatment of Germany' and which is indeed a document probably without parallel in modern European history.[100] 'I think it my duty to point out that public feeling over here has been very much agitated & stirred to its depths by the most unhappy way in which Lord Salisbury has treated Germany in the Samoan buisiness [sic]. After we had formed the South African agreement – which I settled very much against the will of our Colonial circles – the People in Germany thought that a new base had been laid for mutual understanding & goodwill in foreign & colonial questions. Then came our military demonstrations

on the Waterloo Place in Hannover for the Victors of Omdurman, which was
a sign of the warm interest taken by our Army in the deeds of their British
Brothers in Arms. My visit to Malta – as alas I could not extend my journey to
Egypt – was a sign of affectionate interest in your Fleet & your Flag, of which
I am so proud to be an Admiral. And last not least, with an utter disregard for
public opinion – which was very sore about this – & in the teeth of a most
violent opposition from all ranks of society in Germany I received Sir [sic] Cecil
Rhodes. Only showing thereby that I thought it my duty to do all in my power
to help your Government in the work of peace & goodwill, for the benefit of
my country. As a "rendu" for all this Lord Salisbury has treated Germany in
the Samoan Question in a way which was utterly at variance with the manners,
which regulate the relations between great Powers according to European rules
of civility. He not only left my Government for months without an answer to its
proposals, dating from Autumn last year, but he even refrained from expressing
his or the Governments regrets after the first acts of violence by Commander
Sturdee & the other ships had occurred at Samoa. A fact the more unintelligible
as the President of the U.S.A. immediately sent word to say how sorry he was
such acts had happened on the part of American officers & men. On the contrary
the British ships went on for days & weeks bombarding socalled "positions"
of socalled "rebels" – though noone knows against whom they "rebelled" – &
thereby burning & destroying plantations & houses belonging to my subjects
with a loss of hundreds of thousands of marks without even so much as an
excuse having been made, & that on an Island which by three fourths is in
German hands. This way of treating Germany's feelings & interests has come
upon the People like an electric shock & has evoked the impression that Lord
Salisbury cares for us no more than for Portugal, Chili [sic], or the Patagonians,
& out of this impression the feeling has arisen that Germany was beeing [sic]
despised by his government, & this has stung my subjects to the quick. This fact
is looked upon as a taint to the National honour & to their feelings of self respect.
Therefore I am most sorry to have to state that popular feeling in Germany is
just now very bitter on England, & as I found out during my spring visit to the
South of Germany that feeling is the same with the simple labourer as with their
Princes, it is unanimous. Most disheartening for my honest labours to bring the
two countries to understand eachother [sic] better. If this sort of highhanded
treatment of German affairs by Lord Salisbury is suffered to continue, I am afraid
that there will be a permanent source of misunderstandings & recriminations
between the two Nations, which may in the end lead to bad blood. I of course
have been silent as to what I have *personally* gone through these last six months,
the shame & pain I have suffered, & how my heart has bled when to my despair
I had to watch how the arduous work of years was destroyed – to make the two

Nations understand eachother & respect their aspirations & wishes — by one blow by the highhanded & disdainful treatment of Ministers who have never come over to stay here & to study our institutions, & People, & hardly ever have given themselves the trouble to understand them. Lord Salisbury's Government must learn to respect & treat us as equals, as long as he cannot be brought to do that, People over here will remain distrustful & a sort of coolness will be the unavoidable result. It is very probable that the news of the dissatisfaction over here with regard to the Samoan affairs may have reached your informant in a roundabout way & led him to believe it had to do with the visit to Cowes, but that is not the case. What a great pity it is that you could not pass by Strassburg or any other station where I could have met you & had a quiet talk with you in your carriage, about all this grievous mess. Now you will understand dear Grandmama why I so ardently hoped to be able to go over for your birthday. That visit would have been perfectly understood over here, as the duty of the grandson to his grandmother, putting "Emperor" etc. apart, & as according to the family ties, & nobody would have said a word against it. The more so as the children were to be shown greatgrandmama. But a pleasure trip to Cowes after all that has happened, & with respect to the temperature of our public opinion here is utterly impossible now. I had not the heart to write about all these disagreeable matters to you, as I did not want to worry you, & because I hoped that Lord Salisbury would change his mind again, & therefore gulped everything down & held my tongue. But as you have yourself kindly inquired about the state of public opinion in Germany, I thought it my duty to state the facts as they are. I can assure you there is no man more deeply grieved & unhappy than me! and all that on account of a stupid Island which is a hairpin to England compared to the thousands of square miles she is annexing right & left unopposed every year . . . Goodbye most beloved Grandmama. With much love & respect believe me ever your most dutiful & devoted grandson William I. R.'[101]

It is not particularly surprising that the Prime Minister categorically and comprehensively rejected the Kaiser's outrageous accusations. He assured the Queen that he had sent for the relevant records and had found not a single ground for Wilhelm's complaints. 'Either the German Emperor has been misled by certain correspondents he has in England — mostly intriguing men; or he is simply angry that England should have made agreements with Russia and France. His outspoken desire that there should be a war between England and France this spring probably indicates that his indignation has been created by recent agreements. He [Salisbury] entirely concurs with Your Majesty in thinking that it is quite new for a Sovereign to attack in a private letter the Minister of another Sovereign; especially one to whom he is so closely related. It is not a desirable innovation and might produce some confusion.'[102] The eighty-year-old Queen delivered an indignant reprimand to her grandson. She had been extremely surprised by his letter, she wrote on 12 June. 'The tone in which you write about Lord Salisbury I can only attribute to a temporary irritation on your part, as I do not think you would otherwise have written in such a manner, & I doubt whether any Sovereign ever wrote in such terms to another Sovereign, — & that Sovereign his own Grandmother, about their Prime Minister. I never should do such a thing, & I never personally attacked, or complained of Prince Bismarck, though I knew well what a bitter enemy he was to England & all the harm he did.' Salisbury had completely refuted the accusations that Wilhelm had made against him, in a memorandum which she was enclosing with her letter, she added.[103] 'Old Victoria's rude letter has hurt Him unutterably deeply!', Philipp Eulenburg reported to his friend Bülow.[104] In July 1899 the Kaiser was still speaking of his 'deeply wounded feelings over the way he has been treated by his grandmother and her family'.[105]

Anyone tempted to think that with this brusque reprimand of Kaiser Wilhelm II by Queen Victoria Anglo-German relations must have reached their lowest possible level should remember that the secret aims of the German battlefleet building programme, initiated in 1897 by the Kaiser and Admiral Alfred Tirpitz and directed against Great Britain, were still hidden from London. Once it dawned on the British what kind of menacing superweapon was being created on the other side of the North Sea for use against them, it would only be a matter of time before Britain joined the Franco-Russian Dual Alliance, thus completing the 'encirclement' of Germany.

# CHAPTER THIRTY-TWO

# Wilhelm and the birth of the German battlefleet

## THE KAISER'S 'LIMITLESS FLEET PLANS'

THE resolve gradually formed by Kaiser Wilhelm II in the 1890s to build a 'giant fleet' of battleships with which to confront Great Britain was one of the most momentous and catastrophic decisions of his long reign, along with his dismissal of Bismarck in early 1890 and his role in the outbreak of the First World War in 1914. 'From the beginning to the end of the *Flottenpolitik*, the Kaiser played a critical and fatal role', writes Paul Kennedy, whose masterly analysis of the Anglo-German antagonism before 1914 is second to none.[1] Relations between Germany and Britain, already corroded by the mutual distrust which had characterised them since 1896, were irreparably damaged by this decision and, having made the painful discovery of its vulnerability on the world political stage during the Boer War,[2] Britain was rapidly driven into the arms of Japan, France and Russia. But how did Wilhelm's personal passion for the sea come to provide the impetus for a fatal armaments race between the two neighbours on the North Sea? What was the Kaiser's purpose in pursuing this 'limitless' naval policy, which he personally instigated and carried through against the will of parliament, the statesmen of the Wilhelmstrasse and even some leading members of the officer corps?

The young Kaiser's 'passion for the navy', which as we have seen can be traced back to his childhood, had cast its shadow over the policy of his government from the start.[3] Even his brother Heinrich, whose whole life revolved around his career as a naval officer, complained in a letter to Tirpitz in 1893 that it was 'impossible to avoid conversations about the navy . . . in one's day-to-day dealings with His Majesty!'[4] Wilhelm's frequent and vociferous demands for the expansion of the fleet, however, had proved fruitless — with the exception of four battleships accepted in the estimates for 1889 – for it was not long before the impression had arisen in the Reichstag that naval construction was more a question of the Kaiser's predilections than of political and strategic necessity. The Left Liberal Reichstag deputy Eugen Richter coined the expressive phrase 'limitless fleet plans' for these demands, arguing that they must be blocked on political and financial grounds. The Reichstag consistently rejected all Wilhelm II's expansion plans from 1890 onwards, especially after the naval authorities had provided the Kaiser's critics with additional ammunition by demanding a large sum of money for the refurbishment of the imperial yacht *Hohenzollern*.[5]

It was not only the Kaiser's personal enthusiasm which proved an impediment to the expansion of the German navy at first. His plans also lacked any systematic basis, and he annoyed the Reichstag by unnecessary confrontations. A further obstacle was the ineptitude of Secretary of State at the Reich Navy Office Admiral Friedrich Hollmann, who enjoyed the Kaiser's favour, indeed even his friendship, but completely failed to persuade the Reichstag of the necessity of expanding the fleet, possibly because he himself was not convinced of it.[6] Admittedly, naval planning was rendered particularly complicated at this period by the fact that tactical conceptions varied widely, against a background of extraordinarily rapid technological development in warship building. But that Hollmann could stand up in front of the Reichstag in early 1894 and declare that the funds requested for the building of new ships had been included in the estimates by the naval authorities 'without any plan' is rightly described by the military historian Wilhelm Deist as 'disarmingly naïve and helpless'.[7] In several respects Hollmann's attitude resembles that of the Kaiser: both wanted to enlarge the navy, both favoured a cruiser fleet and neither was able to put forward a convincing strategic scenario in which this fleet would serve a purpose commensurate with the expenditure involved in creating it. Consequently the German fleet stagnated in the first years of Wilhelm II's reign. It was old-fashioned and consisted of a motley collection of ships of different types. Its relative strength even decreased during this period, and it fell to fifth or sixth place in the world.

Wilhelm found this development extremely painful, especially since he saw it as the purpose of his reign and his historic task to raise Germany to the status of a naval power. In his memoirs Bülow relates a conversation in which he compared the Kaiser with the Soldier King. Just as the latter created the army which had been indispensable to the rise of Prussia, Wilhelm aimed to create an equivalent naval power to ensure the continued advancement of Prussia–Germany. 'You have often said yourself that your ideal would be, like that of Friedrich Wilhelm I, to forge the weapon which your son or, still better, your grandson will one day use', he told Wilhelm.[8] The comparison with the 'Heldenkaiser', Wilhelm I, was even more compelling, however. The young monarch constantly compared himself with his grandfather, who at the time of the constitutional conflict had strengthened the army in the face of what had at first seemed a hopeless struggle against the parliament. In fact it was precisely this vision of his own role that was largely to blame for Wilhelm II's problems, since he could only picture the expansion of the fleet as a victory wrung out of the 'stupid' Reichstag after a fierce battle, if necessary through dissolution or even a *coup d'état*. It occurred to him either not at all or only sporadically that he could have got his way by a systematic effort to win over the opposition, by co-operation rather than confrontation, and there was no one in his entourage who would have given him the necessary encouragement. On the contrary, Senden, Plessen and others constantly stoked up his prejudices against parliamentarism.

From the outset Wilhelm repeatedly gave notice that he would not rest until he had achieved his aim of enlarging the fleet. Soon after his accession he declared to a group of naval officers that, just as his grandfather had once said that his last thoughts would be with the army, he promised them that his last thoughts would be with the navy.[9] In 1897 he assured his brother Heinrich that he would not be content 'until I have brought My navy up to the same level as the army'.[10] The army officers in the Kaiser's entourage were very soon afraid that Wilhelm's passion for the navy would be to the detriment of the land forces. Chief of the Military Cabinet General von Hahnke remarked anxiously in 1892 'that the Kaiser would abandon the strengthening of the army for the sake of a few warships without a second thought'.[11] Waldersee too, as we have seen, was alarmed by the 'fanatical love for the navy', with which the Kaiser was obsessed.[12] Wilhelm 'no longer [has] the passion he should for the army . . . ; he has had the chance to look over the fleet and is full of it'.[13] Writing to his friend the former War Minister von Verdy, in April 1895, Waldersee asked sarcastically: 'Are you not sorry that you did not send your son into the navy? Anyone who is now not of the opinion that the main focus of all warfare is on the sea is an ignoramus and has not moved with the times.'[14] In all political circles the word was that 'the Kaiser's only real interest is in the navy'; everything else was 'pretty well indifferent' to him.[15]

If Wilhelm II was unable to make any progress with the plans he pursued with such ardour for the expansion of the fleet, it was not through any lack of ideas; his fault was rather that he had too many ideas and failed to bring them together into any systematic order. As early as the first year of his reign he had been prompt to suggest what the navy needed. He devoted a disproportionate amount of time to the theatrical aspect of the fleet, and to questions of prestige.[16] While receiving reports from the navy secretary or the chief of the Naval Cabinet Wilhelm liked to be shown plans and photographs of German or foreign warships, as the later chief of the Naval Cabinet, Georg Alexander von Müller, reported. Müller considered this a waste of time: 'The major part of the valuable time for reports [was] usually taken up with such things, which had little significance except to entertain the Kaiser. There were rarely decisions to be taken on them, and if there were, they related to quite unimportant trifles like the position of the smokestacks of a cruiser, from an aesthetic point of view, the form of a ship's bow or the decoration of the bow and stern of new ships that were to be built.'[17] His plans for the fleet were equally dilettantish and amounted to little more than demanding more money for ships from the Reichstag. 'Naves esse aedificandas', he said simply, and this was symptomatic of his attitude to the fleet in the Hollmann era.[18] In February 1895 he remarked that a general had advised him to take out a loan of a billion for the navy 'and then start building ships with it'. It did not occur to Wilhelm to work out an organic plan for the increases, develop a tactical and strategic concept to aim at, as happened with the later battlefleet programme, and then put forward systematic demands for the supply of the types of ship needed.[19]

By the autumn of 1893 there were increasing signs that the Kaiser at last meant business with the fleet plans he had so long cherished. 'I see . . . to my regret from His Majesty's marginal comments', Holstein wrote, 'that He is considering the idea [of an expansion of the fleet] – I hope only theoretically for the moment.'[20] Kiderlen had the same impression and wrote on 1 October 1893: 'From the All-Highest margin[alia] it almost seems that he is intending to make increased demands for the navy *this* year. That could cause new conflicts with the Reichstag.' But having recently approved the great Army Bill, he pointed out, the Reichstag ought 'to be allowed a little time for a breather'.[21] Political observers agreed that the Reichstag would reject these plans, but Waldersee already suspected that the Kaiser would get his way in the end. The imperial wishes, he wrote, had been 'indignantly' turned down by all and sundry, but 'to judge from experience, many of those who are now beating their breasts and declaring "not a single mark more for the navy" will be a lot tamer later, after they have been subjected to all kinds of influence in Berlin, and these are naturally mostly Conservatives who do not like denying the Kaiser anything'.[22] For the time being, however, the fleet plans came to nothing. After Miquel had submitted a memorandum on the financial position of Prussia and the Reich to him, Wilhelm declared himself ready 'to give up all increased demands for the navy for this year'. Waldersee welcomed this decision, commenting that the money would 'not have been granted in any circumstances', and that the battles it would have caused would have been 'extremely unpleasant'.[23]

## FROM CRUISERS TO THE BATTLEFLEET

Wilhelm's enthusiasm for the navy was nourished by both political and literary events. In his eyes, his belief that the navy was indispensable to the future of Germany and to its continued rise in the world was confirmed by Alfred Thayer Mahan's work, *The Influence of Sea Power upon History*. Its thesis of the decisive significance of sea power was exactly to his taste. He wrote to an American friend: 'I am just now not reading but devouring Captain Mahan's book and am trying to learn it by heart. It is a first-class book and classical on all points.'[24] The Sino-Japanese war of 1894–5 seemed to him to provide compelling proof of the accuracy of Mahan's theories, and he followed its course with fascination.[25] The naval engagements were his principal interest, and in particular the battle of the Yalu estuary on 17 September 1894. The state of feverish excitement into which Wilhelm was projected caused a certain alarm. Marschall, the Foreign Secretary, recorded in his diary on 2 February 1895: 'H.M. is again very much preoccupied with the navy. I asked him to keep quiet and trust me, as I had hopes.' Three days later he noted: 'In the morning H.M. He has nothing but the navy in his head.'[26]

Having been provided with such a striking example of the significance of sea power by events in the Far East, Wilhelm was anxious to make positive progress with his naval construction plans at long last. The conclusions he was prepared to draw for German armaments policy from the superiority of the Japanese in their planning and conduct of the war can be seen in the two-hour extempore lecture which he gave to about 500 officers at the Royal War Academy in Berlin on 8 February 1895, using numerous drawings and tables. He began by expressing his admiration for the prudence with which the Japanese had prepared for the campaign over a ten-year period, 'in a completely modern way'. Of decisive importance, in his view, was the close co-operation between the warships, the merchant navy and the army over the landing in Korea, which had made the Japanese victories on the mainland possible. Using merchant ships, 12,000–13,000 men had been landed in $1\frac{1}{2}$ days. The Kaiser had high praise for the Japanese landing operation: 'Here, for the first time, very large numbers of troops were transported overseas; no nation has ever carried out a practice exercise for this before. It is astonishing how well Japan worked out and provided for everything in this respect.' But Wilhelm placed most weight on the decisive sea battle of the two fleets at the mouth of the Yalu. The Japanese fleet, he emphasised, had been numerically smaller but of better quality than the Chinese. It had 'consisted only of modern armoured cruisers', which had been built in Britain, France and, using these as models, partly also in Japan itself. The Chinese fleet, on the other hand, had consisted of two large and

three smaller armoured warships, five cruisers and a few small ships, which
were all obsolete and inferior to the Japanese ships, especially in their speed.
A whole series of other shortcomings counted against the Chinese fleet: there
were not enough exploding shells for the Chinese artillery, the experience and
tactical training of the commanders left much to be desired, the communications
system was inadequate, there was no integrated command of the fleet at all. It
was quite a different matter with the Japanese, whose admiral, in Wilhelm II's
opinion, 'acted in general in accordance with the same tactical principles which
we have recognised as correct as a result of our exercises'. But, above all, the
ships themselves were the decisive factor. The victory of the Japanese could
be attributed to the fact that 'they were equipped with a series of cruisers in
good order, which were capable of reaching a speed of 20 knots, while the
Chinese could not achieve more than 10 knots'. Moreover 'the warlike spirit
inherent in the Japanese, in contrast to their enemies . . . which makes their
whole conduct in this war so appealing to us', had likewise contributed to their
victory. 'Towards 5 o'clock the battle had reached its conclusion and the rays
of the setting sun lit up the flag of the Rising Sun of the Mikado, fluttering
victoriously in the wind . . . Through this sea-battle the Japanese succeeded in
securing an immensely important victory for their country, i.e. through their
supremacy at sea they paved the way for the further operations of the army,
which now strides ahead from victory to victory. The Japanese capture of the
enemy capital of Peking should be certain.'

   From this analysis of the course of the war in the Far East Wilhelm drew two
significant conclusions: first, that a good fleet 'can be of very critical importance
in a campaign', and second 'that even if the fleet is smaller, it must above all consist
of excellent *matériel* which fulfils all modern requirements'.[27] Both conclusions
were calculated to lend weight to the Kaiser's wish to strengthen the German
fleet. From various contemporary sources we know that on numerous occasions
in the winter of 1894–5 Wilhelm brought out his shipping tables, drew attention
to the shortfall in the German fleet by making comparisons with the numbers
of ships possessed by different nations, and presented his analysis of the great
sea-battle at the mouth of the Yalu. It is equally clear from his remarks that
at this juncture he was seeking to build a fleet of modern armoured cruisers,
which would destroy the enemy fleets in a war fought principally on land against
Russia, France and possibly Denmark, and which would be in a position to keep
the trade routes across the Atlantic open. It is important to note, however, that
the idea of throwing down the gauntlet to the British Empire by building a
large fleet of battleships was still very far from his mind.[28] True, he pressed for
a rapid expansion of the navy, but the demand for four new cruisers which he
put forward through the Navy Secretary in 1895 was comparatively modest.[29]

Another incident demonstrates how much the Kaiser's naval plans were dominated by the desire for impressive German warships to be seen in all four corners of the earth – a policy of prestige, in other words. On 31 January 1895 he appeared at the Reich chancellor's palace and demanded the withdrawal of the lone German warship stationed off Samoa on the grounds that the British ship that was also there was three times as big. 'If we wanted to increase the diminished German influence in Samoa we should have to make our presence felt with several German ships; this was not possible in the present state of the navy. H.M. does not want to give up Samoa', Hohenlohe remarked, 'but he thinks the presence of the ship there now is inadequate and therefore superfluous.'[30]

Wilhelm was now also making efforts to persuade the Reichstag to share his enthusiasm for the fleet. On 8 January 1895 he invited several of its members, mainly from the Conservative Party, together with the delegate of the Hanseatic cities in the Bundesrat, Krüger, to Potsdam. The Badenese envoy, Eugen von Jagemann, reported to Karlsruhe that the Kaiser had again given a 'two-hour extempore lecture' to this audience, in which he had shown 'great expertise and prudence'. He had 'described the German armed forces in relation to the Russian and French', and had then discussed 'the state of the navy, pointing out the more important German and foreign types of ship, often using his own drawings'. The obvious purpose of the lecture, Jagemann commented, was to influence opinion in the Reichstag in favour of approving the requested cruiser corvettes, for in the Kaiser's view the number of cruisers was insufficient for service abroad and for the protection of the merchant navy. In the last half hour of the lecture, however, the Kaiser had set out, 'as a future prospect, the need to acquire more iron-clads, which are decisive in sea-battles'.[31] In contrast to his previous tactics, therefore, the Kaiser was trying to win over the Reichstag by argument; but he made the mistake, according to Jagemann, of inviting only deputies who needed no persuading.

The Kaiser wanted more ships; but what exactly did he want? Was the reference to iron-clads in his lecture an early hint of what was to come? We know from Tirpitz's memoirs that this reference can be traced to a report that he himself had made to the Kaiser the previous day and which had left such a strong impression on the latter that he adopted elements of it for his lecture.[32] Nonetheless, at this time Wilhelm thought above all in terms of a cruiser fleet. This is abundantly clear from both of the lectures he gave, on 8 January and 8 February 1895, in which he had dealt not only with the sea-battle off the Yalu estuary but also with the types of ship in the German navy. He began by deploring the fact that, although Germany had the second-largest merchant fleet in the world, the country had no adequate cruiser fleet capable of protecting German interests worldwide. As he regarded his audience as landlubbers, he explained the differences between the various types of warship, first from a historical perspective and then progressing to current ship-building policy. Using drawings and tables he carefully explained the difference between battleships of the first class or ships of the line on the one hand, and armoured cruisers or armoured deck cruisers on the other. To give the officers of the War Academy 'at least some idea' of what a modern ship of the line looked like, the Kaiser showed them a picture which he had drawn with Salzmann's help showing the *Ersatz Preussen*, which was in the process of being built.[33] Such ships of the line fought in large tactical groups on the battle line, according to Wilhelm II, and could not be used separately. By way of contrast he showed them the armoured cruiser *Ersatz Leipzig*, which was also equipped with heavy guns and had belt armour, but unlike the ship of the line it was designed 'to engage with several opponents on its own, to chase them, and to do as much damage to them as it could with its big, long-range guns, and to keep the area allocated to it clear'. Of this type of ship the French had thirteen, the Russians ten, Italy five, the United States three and 'Germany none'. 'It is very difficult, strangely enough', the Kaiser remarked, 'to make any progress in this country on the question of armoured cruisers, as a secret terror fills the people in the Reichstag at the very mention of this name [*Panzerkreuzer*]. They are afraid that the wool is being pulled over their eyes, and that an absolutely monstrous weapon is to be built.' He went on to point out that the position was no better with more lightly protected cruisers. Here too the Franco-Russian Dual Alliance enjoyed a crushing superiority over the Triple Alliance. Taking everything into account, the Triple Alliance powers had five armoured cruisers, thirty-two armoured deck cruisers and thirty-one unprotected cruisers (which of course could play only a secondary role in war), while France, Russia and Denmark together possessed twenty-three armoured cruisers, forty-six armoured deck cruisers and forty-one unprotected cruisers. 'That means that there are 68 battle units of the Triple Alliance against 110 on the other side.' If one added the big armoured battleships or ships of the line, there would be a total of 133 'ships of all types usable in battle . . . on the side of the Triple Alliance against 201 of the other trio'. From these figures one could see 'how enormously the French and Russian fleets [had] developed'.[34]

These remarks again left no room for doubt that in the Kaiser's eyes the antagonist, as far as the German fleet was concerned, was the Franco-Russian Dual Alliance, and that he set most store by the cruiser fleet, ships of the line being mentioned only incidentally. He was particularly preoccupied with armoured cruisers. Deploring the hopeless state of the German fleet, he went on to comment that the German ships, with the exception of the *Irene*, were 'absolutely unfitted' to engage in 'any serious battle . . . and if any major conflicts should arise in the course of the Sino-Japanese war, or attempts at partition between the European states, the German Reich would be absolutely incapable of enforcing a single claim'. The three ships which were representing the German Reich abroad at the moment, he said, were still equipped with masts and rigging like the old frigates of the time of Nelson and had no rapid-fire guns or armoured deck, so that they would be defenceless against a modern cruiser. 'A single Japanese armoured cruiser would be enough to shoot our entire German cruiser squadron to pieces', Wilhelm declared. The situation was so bad that it could be assumed that 'in 1896 the German Reich would not have a single ship sailing out there in the world'.[35]

What conclusions did the Kaiser draw from this? He demanded that cruisers be built, namely the replacement of nine first-class armoured cruisers, fifteen second-class cruisers and twelve fourth-class cruisers 'so as to be able at least to provide moderately decent protection for our overseas trade and to get the necessary respect for our flag'. Together with the smaller ships this would mean 36 new ships with 756 guns, including 3 flagships. 'The German Reich could quite easily have had this number, if in the last 10 years 1 armoured cruiser and perhaps 2 second-class cruisers had been requested and gradually built each year. Instead, the Reichstag has . . . consistently struck out every single replacement ship, and so we have arrived at this deplorable state of affairs.' At present there was '*no more than one* ship being built' in Germany, the Kaiser complained. 'If things go on as they are at the moment, i.e. absolute refusal on the part of our parliament', the Chief of Staff of the Naval High Command had explained to him 'that by 1899 the German battlefleet will no longer be capable of leaving harbour at all. The German fleet will then be confronted with 10 brand new Russian first-class battleships and about 21 new French first-class battleships in the Channel, while Germany at the moment has only 5 armoured battleships. All the rest are second-class and according to modern principles no longer fit for a battle at sea.'[36]

Once again the question is: what did the Kaiser want? He spoke about decisive sea-battles and battleships, in other words a battlefleet. But he also spoke of armoured cruisers, lighter armed cruisers and small cruisers which were to enable German interests to be enforced worldwide. He demanded several types of ship for various uses on the high sea. So at this point it cannot yet be said that his ideas were fixed on a fleet of battleships; the armoured cruiser still had priority for him. How, and against whom, did he see these ships being used in a war?

Wilhelm's audience in the War Academy consisted of army officers who on the whole did not share the imperial enthusiasm for the navy. He tried to arouse their interest by making observations on 'the use of the fleet in relation to the army'. Following the logic of his remarks on the Sino-Japanese war, he made the axiomatic pronouncement that 'only he who controls the sea is in a position well and truly to get the better of his opponent and thus to maintain untrammelled freedom of action in military operations, which otherwise he could not afford'. If the French fleet, vastly superior to the German, should drive back or destroy the few German ships confronting it in a future war, it could blockade the German coast, stop all trade and even enable troops to be landed on the German coast. 'If we imagine the situation in reverse, if we were confronting France with our fleet in the same way as it confronts us, it would be the most natural thing for us to use our fleet to defeat the French fleet wherever it appeared, to blockade French ports, to transport a large part of the army and to land them rapidly so that they could quickly advance on Paris and be within the walls of the capital within a few days, while the enemy awaited attack from the east behind the triple reinforcements of their defensive forts. In spite of its inferior strength, in spite of its inadequate *matériel*, the German fleet has decided to pursue this idea nonetheless, in so far as it is at all feasible', the Kaiser affirmed, in an access of wishful thinking that was entirely typical of him and some of the leading naval officers. 'The intention is to bring all the ships together, hurl them against the enemy and if possible force him to fight, and, if God gives us victory, to gain victory too.' The Kaiser emphasised not only this strategically important use of the fleet in the event of a war on the continent, but also its value for 'providing food for our great armed forces'. 'The German army needs to eat', he pointed out. In 1870, on its advance into France, the German army had had no threat from the rear and could therefore obtain food supplies from Hungary, Russia and southern Austria. 'That will not be the case now. Not a single grain will come over the Russian border; Austria needs her own supplies herself. So we have no alternative but to bring in supplies by sea. But our supply route lies directly off the great French ports of Cherbourg, Brest, Rochefort, where the French have their armoured cruisers etc. etc. lying in wait to intercept any foreign ship. It therefore naturally follows that our fleet, instead of staying where it is for so-called coastal protection, as the Reichstag always envisaged, should aim to gain control of the Channel so as to repulse any interception by the French energetically from the outset. For that we need a whole series of fast armoured cruisers.' Its value in a war against France, Russia and probably Denmark was thus the principal reason for a strong German fleet. But the Kaiser also had visions of another possible use of the navy: war at sea against the United States. America, with its thirty-seven cruisers, was a country 'with which we could find ourselves in collision at any moment, partly because of what we might wish for abroad, e.g. because of Samoa or the like, partly because of wishes we might have at home, if for example our agriculture had a particular wish to export something, or to prevent some import which was unwelcome to it'. Without an effective battlefleet 'the German Reich would be absolutely incapable of getting its way at all against America, if America did not wish it'.[37]

One has the impression from this document that Wilhelm, presumably with the assistance of the Chief of his Naval Cabinet Senden, marshalled every conceivable argument to justify the naval expansion which he so ardently desired. But what is significant, and of particular importance for us here, is that in conjuring up this wide-ranging and often unrealistic strategic panorama in February 1895 the Kaiser made no mention at all of war with Great Britain. True, he commented that with its 205 warships Britain was only a little stronger than Russia, France and Denmark put together, and that 'former claims of English supremacy at sea' no longer had any validity. But the difference between the strength of the German and British navies was so great that Wilhelm simply left it out of account in his comparative tables. Indeed he expressly ruled out any parallels, saying that Britain 'cannot serve as a point of comparison for us, for as a marine nation it has completely abnormal criteria and is based entirely on the fleet'. Although he nevertheless mentioned the numbers of British ships being built it was only in order to underline the enormous disparity between the two countries.[38] But it was precisely in this context, as we shall see, that a disastrous transformation was to take place in his attitude over the next eighteen months.

The personal initiative which the Kaiser had taken in this question was in itself enough to arouse criticism from many of his compatriots, especially in the army. Waldersee noted sceptically in his diary for 10 February 1895: 'It is certainly a new idea for a Kaiser to speak on such a matter to such a large audience . . . That the Kaiser can speak well, that he has a great love for the navy and knows a great deal about its affairs, and that he considers a considerable increase necessary – all that is well known. That any member of the Reichstag, or at least an appreciable number of them, will become more amenable as a result of his lecture, is completely out of the question. But it may well provoke a great deal of criticism, and then I can see it having a bad effect in that people will become suspicious and say the Kaiser is gradually demanding more and more, and such a colossal increase that it will be beyond our financial means I also believe that it is impossible for us to achieve the aim of creating a first-class fleet which would also be capable of protecting German commerce all over the world. For that we should first have to win great victories on land, which would enable us to maintain a smaller army. But is there any prospect of that?'[39] Waldersee considered the Kaiser's naval armament plans excessive, and did not think himself alone in taking this view. Two days later he noted: 'The Kaiser, who is always particularly obsessed by some question or other, is now completely absorbed with the expansion of the navy and as usual is inclined to go too far. In fact no one agrees with what he wants or thinks it is even possible, except a few young naval officers. The people in the Reichstag who go along with it probably do it only to keep on good terms with the Kaiser.'[40] The pro-government Berlin

correspondent of the National Liberal *Kölnische Zeitung*, Franz Fischer, shared
this view, and reported to Eulenburg on 17 February 1895 that the 'apparently
enormous demands for funds for the navy on which His Majesty's two lectures
are said to have been based', and which were estimated at a billion marks –
to be raised by 1899 – were being discussed with alarm in the Reichstag.[41] It
was perhaps precisely against this background of huge sums for the navy that
the comparatively modest demand for the four new cruisers was approved, by
the Reichstag with very little fuss.[42] Wilhelm had evidently doubted that even
this demand would succeed, and had therefore sent his Flügeladjutant Kuno
Moltke to Friedrichsruh again on 11 January 1895 to take Bismarck drawings
he himself had made of American warships. He had 'only one thought', as
Eulenburg assured Holstein, which was 'the approval of the cruisers. That was
the actual motive for Moltke's journey and for all his friendly gestures.'[43] When
they were approved, Wilhelm was delighted and telegraphed to Hohenlohe on
1 March 1895: 'Am overjoyed at the good news. What a splendid result in the
vote. The Reichstag has the pleasant feeling of having done a good deed for the
preservation of the greatness of the Fatherland and for our industry. It has given
me great pleasure.'[44] He was, as Holstein recorded, 'as happy as a lark about his
four cruisers'.[45]

And yet, not long ago, the Kaiser had declared that thirty-six cruisers were
absolutely essential. He showed no more consistency in the key question of
the battlefleet (which Senden demanded) as against the cruiser fleet (which
Hollmann advocated).[46] But he remained obdurate on one point: the creation of
a strong fleet in the longer term. And at the same time a highly significant change
came about as to the purpose for which the fleet was to be built up. Hitherto the
Kaiser's fleet plans had been formulated with an eye to co-operation between
the Triple Alliance powers and Great Britain. The German fleet, as the Kaiser
had often stressed, should work with the Royal Navy and Britain should remain
'Mistress of the Seas',[47] and his previous plans for the expansion of the fleet
had not deviated from this basic idea. But now his thoughts began to turn in a
new and fatal direction, for at the beginning of 1896 it occurred to the Kaiser
that he could exploit events in South Africa, the Jameson Raid, the Krüger
telegram and the strong British reaction to it, to pursue his naval construction
plans.[48] The mechanism was exactly the same as he had used during the Sino-
Japanese war: he tried to take advantage of actual crises to make it clear to public
opinion how urgently Germany needed a strong fleet. But this time, unlike on
the earlier occasion, his conduct had a strongly anti-British note. Twice during
the Chancellor's audiences in early January 1896, when the battle between the
British and the German press over the Krüger telegram was at its height, Kaiser
Wilhelm – anxious to make the most of the 'heightened political mood of the

moment' – peremptorily demanded that a loan of 'several hundred million' be taken out to build a battle fleet. At the same time he called for a committee to be established, consisting of the secretaries of state at the Foreign Office, the Reich Treasury and the Reich Navy Office, together with the Prussian Finance Minister, to discuss 'the enlargement of the fleet'.[49] He rejected Hohenlohe's objections to both demands in a revealing document of 8 January 1896, in which he commented that 'a distinction should be made between the firm plan for the expansion of the navy adopted as a result of the report of the High Command of 1 December, and my aims, which have arisen because of the Transvaal and about which I spoke to you. The two plans complement each other. But while the expansion plan must be worked out well in advance, in order to take the general position of the Reich in the world into account, the idea which the Transvaal has engendered, and which is based on urgent short-term needs, is intended to fill a momentary, but serious, gap. In many parts of the world, where the situation is getting increasingly critical, the Reich has inadequate or non-existent means of upholding its considerable interests. In the Mediterranean there is neither a squadron . . . nor even *one ship* fit to uphold our interests. We have had to resort to a training ship. In the whole of America, whether east, central or west, there is not a single gunboat to protect hundreds of thousands of Germans and millions of marks of our capital; and in Venezuela the situation could at any moment turn into one in which the fleet [would need] to show the flag to protect German property. In East Asia our only fighting division has been tied down for almost a year pursuing special local interests, with no prospect of being released. And now we have the Transvaal question too, which has shown very clearly indeed that the ever-shrinking navy does not have a sufficient number of ships to do justice to the world position of the Reich at all. We shall never again have such a favourable opportunity of proving to the country that the navy cannot continue in its present state. The movement which is sweeping through our people is a deep one, and the Reichstag, even if it hesitates, will be forced to take this mood into account! But with every day, every week that passes without any action, once the Reichstag has assembled, the optimistic mood will fade, the Reichstag will sink into the mud courtesy of Kanitz, Stoecker, Hammerstein etc., the parties which are uplifted and united now as a result of the 18th Jan. [an allusion to Wilhelm's speech on the 25th anniversary of the foundation of the Reich] will disintegrate, and if the poor navy's estimates are discussed and chewed over then, there will be such discord and lack of enthusiasm that even the better elements in the Reichstag will not be able to be persuaded of the necessity of enlarging the navy. For present needs it is not necessary to have a great plan; all that is needed is immediate replacement, not by building new ships at home but by *purchasing* armoured cruisers and cruisers as rapidly as possible wherever we can get them. Meanwhile cruisers would have to be laid down at home, the number of which depends on the efficiency of our shipyards. All the cruisers would then have to be taken into account in the programme which is still being worked out and which has to be submitted next year, to which reference would have to be made. These thoughts which I have briefly sketched out for you should give you the basis on which I wish the question to be considered and handled. Whether the Reichstag will have any inclination or enthusiasm for it is beside the point; our *duty* is to [make] the situation perfectly plain to them even at the risk of rejection. Wilhelm I. R.'[50]

One thing is more than clear from this document. The Kaiser's almost hysterical eagerness to do something for the navy outweighed any consideration of the political wisdom of what he was advocating. Without stopping to think, he leapt at the chance of exploiting the anglophobic current of German public opinion for the indiscriminate, unsystematic purchase of ships, his only concern being that this apparently favourable moment might slip through his fingers. Marschall von Bieberstein complained on 8 January 1896 that 'H.M. wants to get "a few hundred millions" from the Reichstag for ship-building. Hohenlohe is to make a big speech in the Reichstag to take advantage of the present mood.'[51] Again, when the Foreign Secretary had a long conversation with the Kaiser on 11 January about his correspondence with Queen Victoria on the Transvaal crisis, he noted afterwards that the constant 'refrain' had been 'enlargement of the fleet'.[52] Holstein's explanation for the Kaiser's 'pathological excitement' was that 'the illusion that he will get a few hundred millions – he ranges between 100 and 300 in what he says – at a stroke, has made him incapable of judging anything calmly . . . All this makes for an uncanny impression of excessive haste. The Kaiser's nerves have never been stimulated by anything so much as by the temptations of "the great fleet programme".'[53] Eulenburg did his best to calm the Geheimrat by arguing that 'despite all H.M.'s nervousness' the Kaiser was pushing ahead so far with his demands for the fleet merely 'because only by means of shock tactics applied to all branches of the administration is he able to achieve any results at all'. 'H.M. wants a lot, but not the impossible', he assured Holstein.[54] In the Wilhelmstrasse the imperial entourage was suspected of adding fuel to these demands for the fleet. Holstein also blamed 'the little Kayser', who wanted an independent Reich Colonial Office and was using his influence on the monarch through Hinzpeter, and Admiral Senden for fanning the flames of Wilhelm's enthusiasm for the navy. The Kaiser was 'in a state of pathological excitement' and was demanding 'at least 100 million immediately for the acquisition of ships', he wrote. As well as Kuno Moltke, Senden had now been sent to Friedrichsruh with naval plans, and Bismarck had promised his support.[55] The Kaiser's aversion, which was already considerable, to the idea of having to wring his fleet programme out of the Reichstag, was further inflamed by the anti-British and anti-parliamentarian promptings of his entourage.[56]

Given the situation in 1896, Wilhelm of course had no alternative at first but to trust to his Chancellor. The elderly Prince Hohenlohe was likewise obliged, against his own convictions, to undertake the task of sounding out opinion in the Reichstag on the Kaiser's idea of a loan for the fleet. The result, as was to be expected, was devastating. The leaders of the Centre, the National Liberals and the Conservatives in the Reichstag categorically rejected the Kaiser's wish for a loan. Hohenlohe wrote to him on 14 January 1896 to report on his findings. Fritzen, the leader of the Centre Party, had said that if his group agreed to the loan they would vanish from the scene at the next elections, for the population was already weighed down by the burden of taxation and it was impossible to impose further burdens on the country. The leader of the Conservatives, Levetzow, had replied that agriculture was in such a parlous state that an exceptional appropriation for the navy would not receive a single vote from his party. Both Fritzen and Levetzow had also pointed out that such a demand at the present moment would be seen by the people as a prelude to war with the British Empire, and it would have to be turned down for that reason alone. Only Oberpräsident von Bennigsen, the leader of the National Liberals, had been prepared to consult the members of his group, although he was not hopeful of a positive result. From these soundings Hohenlohe concluded 'that there [was] no trace of enthusiasm in the Reichstag for an enlargement of the fleet itself at this moment'. The introduction of a Loan Bill would inevitably lead to a massive defeat for the government, which would be greeted with *Schadenfreude* in other European countries and especially in Great Britain, 'as a personal defeat for Y[our] M[ajesty]'.[57] Together with Hollmann and Marschall, Hohenlohe urged on the Kaiser the view that it was necessary to work out a long-term 'plan for the setting up of the fleet', which could be carried out only 'over the years'.[58] He was anxious to put the naval construction plans on to a systematic basis, which they had hitherto lacked, and thereby to counter the general impression that naval expansion was only an imperial hobby. 'I am eager to know how he will react', Marschall noted, having concluded from the Kaiser's good mood on 14 January that he evidently did not yet know anything 'about the result of the enquiries about the navy'.[59]

The perceptive Friedrich von Holstein, meanwhile, foresaw complications indicative of the political mood in Germany, where there was no shortage of advocates of naval expansion in nationalist circles. He viewed with alarm a scenario in which the Kaiser's initiative might be supported principally by chauvinist groups. Colonialist and pan-German elements led by Duke Johann Albrecht of Mecklenburg and the Colonial Director Paul Kayser had already convened a mass meeting at the Kroll opera house in Berlin, at which 'rousing speeches and resolutions in favour of [a] grand fleet expansion programme' were planned, Holstein wrote to Philipp Eulenburg on 14 January 1896.[60] Once again the ambassador tried to protect Wilhelm and pointed out that with his 'exaggerated, pushing demands' he was only trying to obtain 'the largest possible naval appropriation'. By strongly supporting the Kaiser's wishes Marschall would also be able to strengthen his own position, which was very necessary, Eulenburg added.[61]

When the Kaiser heard the next day how the parties in the Reichstag stood on the naval expansion question he reacted with fury and defiance. Ober-hofmarschall Count August zu Eulenburg recorded that on the morning of 15 January Wilhelm had been 'very depressed about his disappointed hopes for the navy and of course he had little good to say about the Reichstag'.[62] If the members of parliament would not agree to his fleet plans, then he would show them what it was like to be without a fleet, he said. The following day, 16 January 1896, he gave orders for all German warships to be withdrawn from China and Delagoa Bay. The Kaiser's order, which the Chief of the Naval Cabinet conveyed to the Naval High Command, read: 'Have informed Freiherr von Marschall today that, as the Reichstag has so little sense of what the honour of our Fatherland means in relation to England abroad, and no one has any feeling for or interest in the navy, I can no longer allow My Home Fleet to remain in a weakened state in view of the uncertain prospects this spring. *Kaiser* should therefore return immediately, after repairs, and likewise the cruiser squadron, which should follow next month, with the exception of *Arcona*. The cruisers from Lourenço Marques should be sent to Zanzibar, as I do not wish them to stay there because of the concentration of English ships. The High Command is to give orders accordingly. Wilhelm I. R.'[63] It was only with difficulty that Hohenlohe and Marschall succeeded in having the imperial order countermanded.[64]

Wilhelm's anger at the rejection of his plans for naval construction rebounded on those who, in his opinion, had not given sufficient support to his ideas. Chief among them was the Reich Chancellor; and in the second place the Secretary of State at the Reich Navy Office, Hollmann. After a visit to the capital Waldersee noted that the Kaiser was 'enraged' with the Chancellor, adding: 'the reason for his anger with Hohenlohe is that the Kaiser wanted a big loan for naval purposes – 300 million – and had already begun negotiations with the "Vulkan" [shipyard] on that basis, and Hohenlohe explained to him that it would not work; he had consulted Fritzen, Bennigsen and Levetzow, that is, the leaders of the Centre, the National Liberals and the Conservatives, and they told him that there was no chance of getting such a bill through'. Waldersee, who was on the best of terms with the Conservatives, was however of the opinion that

Hohenlohe had not made a serious attempt to negotiate with the party leaders, as he 'personally had no desire, naturally enough, to tackle such a big question'. But now, Waldersee continued, there might be dangerous political consequences. The Kaiser had been 'beside himself', he wrote; his language suggested that 'the decision to change chancellors is definite'. In his displeasure the Kaiser had threatened 'to bring back all the cruisers, then there will soon be great uproar in the seaports, and all the Colonial people will join in'. In Waldersee's view Admiral Hollmann would also have to to resign as Reich navy secretary, as he had said 'that we did not have enough manpower to man a much larger fleet'.[65] Holstein shared the view that the Kaiser would try to get rid of all those who had let him down over the fleet plan, and thought that Wilhelm would use the question of the large demand for additional funds for the navy as a lever to bring about Hohenlohe's fall in the same way as he had used the Anti-Revolutionary Bill to engineer Caprivi's dismissal.[66]

The signs of the Kaiser's deep displeasure were not long in manifesting themselves. When the elderly Prince Hohenlohe asked for a joint audience for himself, Hollmann, Marschall and Admiral Knorr to discuss naval affairs, he received no answer for days. He then asked Hollmann 'if he knew anything'. As Hohenlohe recorded in his diary, the Admiral replied that he had spoken to the Kaiser at a beer party given by Senden, and that Wilhelm had said that Hohenlohe and Hollmann 'had let the Kaiser down and did not want to do anything He would therefore have to wait . . . At the same time, the Kaiser expressed himself in such a way that Hollmann is convinced that the Kaiser hopes to find a Reich chancellor who will put forward large naval demands, dissolve the Reichstag if necessary and execute a *coup d'état*.' Hohenlohe took this news calmly. 'That is all right with me', he noted. 'In fact, though, I cannot see whom the Kaiser can find to carry out this experiment.'[67] Once again Holstein sent off an alarmed message to Eulenburg in Vienna. 'The Kaiser is extremely worked up. He wants to demand enormous funds for the Navy, *at least* 100 million, and thinks that by dissolving the Reichstag he will be able to get a more compliant parliament.' The Privy Councillor considered the Kaiser's plan quite impracticable and warned that 'the next Reichstag will be dreadful, it will not approve anything, and the German princes will *not* join in a Reich *coup d'état* campaign. Then the Kaiser will have his political Jena and will not recover from it any better than Friedrich Wilhelm IV from his ride [through the streets of Berlin] with the [revolutionary] flag on 20 March 1848.'[68]

Not until early February was a kind of armistice achieved between Kaiser and Chancellor on the fleet question, when Wilhelm visited the old Prince, who instead of being 'rude', as the 'embittered elements in the Ministry' demanded, only touched 'in passing and in courteous terms on the discourtesy of the Kaiser' in ignoring his request for an audience. In the course of their tête-à-tête the Kaiser expressed his willingness to leave the ship *Kaiser* in China. He also gave his consent for the Reichstag to be told that no further demands for funds for the navy would be made during the current session. Instead, as Wilhelm now agreed, a systematic procedure should be followed and new ships built on the basis of a carefully worked-out programme.[69] Waldersee suspected that the Kaiser had only seemingly abandoned his far-reaching ambitions for the fleet, noting in his diary on 9 February 1896 that Wilhelm had indeed temporarily postponed his naval expansion plans until the autumn, 'but that he should give up his plans I think is out of the question, nor will he forgive Hohenlohe, Marschall and Hollmann for having caused him problems in this'. The entire liberal camp, according to Waldersee, was terrified that the Kaiser might appoint a 'bold general' as chancellor, with the aim of bringing about a reactionary shift in internal policy and of carrying out his fleet programme. 'To judge from what they say the Kaiser must be surrounded with dangerous intriguers who constantly encourage him in his ideas, whereas the wretched hypocrites know perfectly well that the Kaiser himself is the instigator and leader of the movement.'[70]

Naturally these setbacks in no way dimmed the ardour of Wilhelm II's enthusiasm for the navy. On a train journey to Genoa on 23–4 May 1896 the Kaiser, who was in a good mood, talked 'chiefly about the navy'. Kiderlen-Wächter, who was accompanying the Kaiser on his Mediterranean journey as representative of the Foreign Office, reported to Berlin that Wilhelm had 'just received a plan from a certain Captain Diederichs for building an armoured vessel in a new style – obviously commissioned work! Entirely in accordance with H.M.'s ideas, with particularly powerful armament which is H.M.'s hobby-horse. How the Reichstag will rejoice, and Hollmann, who already had so much trouble in talking H.M. out of his last idea, will be happier still. That last idea of the Kaiser's was very lovely, only it could not float.'[71] The Kaiser as ship-builder might have been a butt for the diplomat's secret mockery, but no one laughed at his visions of naval power. His 'limitless' fleet plans were still creating a 'somewhat eerie feeling' in Berlin in March 1896, especially as there were still fears that the Reichstag might be dissolved on account of them. 'That the Kaiser will pursue his goal resolutely I do not doubt for a moment', Waldersee wrote on 3 March 1896. Even among naval officers there were 'divided opinions', as numerous 'well-respected officers [thought] such a great enlargement scarcely feasible'.[72]

### TIRPITZ ANTE PORTAS

Thus in the spring of 1896 the battle lines were drawn. The Kaiser wanted to enlarge the fleet, but was confronted by the direct opposition of the Reichstag and the rather more passive resistance of his Chancellor, the Foreign Office and even the Secretary of State of the Reich Navy Office, who, as Holstein reported to Vienna, was openly saying 'the way the country has been governed hitherto cannot go on'.[73] In early July 1896, during an audience at Wilhelmshöhe lasting several hours and also attended by Senden and Plessen, Hollmann set out 'all his reservations about the submission to the Reichstag of a fleet plan spread out over years'. The parliament would never agree to such a plan, the Secretary of State stressed. It would lead to repeated dissolutions of the Reichstag, but a *coup d'état* was an impossibility in a federal Reich. Hollmann therefore proposed that 'the fleet plan should be completely abandoned and [we] should limit [ourselves] to demanding from the Reichstag only what was necessary each year to maintain and renew the fleet'. Asked by the Kaiser for their opinion, Plessen said that he agreed with Hollmann, while Senden vigorously opposed his suggestions. Surprisingly, the Kaiser eventually declared that he could see that Hollmann was right. 'It was too late now. Last year's enthusiasm and the impression made by his speech on 18 January [1896] should have been used . . . Now the great plan would have to be abandoned, considered as a study and laid aside, and there should be no more talk of it.'[74] During the Scandinavian cruise of 1896 too it was clear that the opposition from all sides had momentarily destroyed his faith in his plan. As he told Philipp Eulenburg, his demands now consisted only 'in the idea of "replacement" of the existing old ships with new, whereby the old ships [could] still [be] used in the second line in an auxiliary role'. If the Reichstag granted these 'itemised demands' each year the target would gradually be reached. Germans demanded 'strong action in overseas countries, with the appropriate ships', Wilhelm claimed. It would be illogical for them 'to demand an energetic German policy all over the world and then refuse to grant the navy what it needs'. 'England's uncouth behaviour in the Transvaal question, on which the whole of Germany was united, would not have happened if Germany had been in a position, with a reasonably good fleet, to have had the slightest say in the matter.' The Kaiser's ideas of expanding the fleet through 'acceptable' annual demands were in express contrast to the 'absolutely inordinate and very unclear' demands for the navy put forward by Senden, whom Wilhelm criticised 'very harshly', and whose 'boundless obstinacy' and complete 'obsession' he strongly condemned on this occasion.[75]

These remarks by Wilhelm were, however, prompted by the circumstances of the moment and by no means reflected his longer-term intentions. With his declaration Hollmann had after all gone back on the agreements reached in February and had pronounced any enlargement of the navy practically impossible. The Kaiser was now forming the resolve, as Waldersee had already guessed, to put the realisation of his fleet plans into other hands. The replacement of the responsible authorities, above all Hollmann, did not take place at once, but the search for suitable successors was in full swing, and Senden, as chief of the Naval Cabinet, played a major role in it. This fanatical navalist constantly encouraged Wilhelm in his fleet plans and tried to win him over to a change of personnel. In a submission to the Kaiser in the spring of 1896 he argued that Hollmann should be replaced as secretary at the Reich Navy Office by Rear-Admiral Alfred Tirpitz. Hollmann had shown no initiative in regard to either the Reichstag or the Reich Chancellor and had thereby proved that he was not equal to the far reaching tasks which would fall to the holder of his office in the future. 'He lacks the qualities required to promote such an important question on his own, to take the lead in it, to weigh up the means to achieve the goal and to blaze the trail, supported by the commands of His Majesty', the Chief of the Naval Cabinet wrote. 'Given the opposition that a great naval programme will come up against in the Reichstag, the navy needs determined action on the part of the Reich Chancellor (R[eich N[avy O[ffice]), a man who will constantly stimulate interest, who will set the resources of the country in motion and who will be inventive in finding ways to promote such a goal.' Admittedly, Senden acknowledged, it would be sensible to wait until the navy estimates for 1896–7 had been accepted before replacing Hollmann. But his successor should be found and prepared in advance.[76]

Senden had already picked out Tirpitz for the post of navy secretary some time before; indeed he had systematically built him up for the role. In the above-mentioned memorandum he drew attention to Tirpitz's professional qualifications for the post, which were undeniably outstanding, but at the same time he warned that his preferred candidate had a difficult character. 'If the choice should fall on Adm[iral] Tirpitz the unusual personality of this officer would have to be taken into account', he cautioned. Tirpitz had 'a very energetic, one might say ruthless nature, which needs curbing rather than driving forwards. He is ambitious, not particular about the means he uses, of a sanguine disposition: elated at one moment, depressed the next, but never letting up in his energetic activity, however despondent he might seem . . . He could not be treated like Adm[iral] H[ollmann], he is too self-confident and convinced of his own quality for that. He is not a compliant character who accepts an opinion at once at face value. On the contrary, he considers everything very carefully and then expresses his reservations very clearly and objectively. If his objections are not accepted then he accepts the decision and carries it out unflinchingly in accordance with his superior's wishes . . . He has been very spoilt in his naval career and has probably never had a superior officer who was his equal among the chiefs of the Admiralty . . . His Majesty will have to do full justice to his competence, follow his suggestions, give him room to manoeuvre, if they are to work profitably

51. Admiral Alfred von Tirpitz, State Secretary of the Reich Navy Office 1897–1916

together.' In spite of these difficulties the Chief of the Naval Cabinet considered Tirpitz 'the most suitable man . . . to bring the navy forward in this difficult situation'.[77]

Apart from Senden's support, the influence of Prince Heinrich on the appointment of Tirpitz should not be underestimated. He described the admiral as his 'master' and himself as his 'pupil' and 'truest and most gratefully devoted friend and comrade'. With the backing of his personal adjutant, Captain Georg Alexander Müller, who was to succeed Senden as chief of the Naval Cabinet, from 1896 the Kaiser's brother warmly advocated not only Tirpitz's appointment but also the creation of the battlefleet which Tirpitz demanded.[78] Like Tirpitz, Prince Heinrich strongly condemned Wilhelm II's Krüger telegram. He even dismissed the Kaiser's hopes of being able to exploit the excited state of public opinion in the aftermath of the telegram to expand the navy, since 'our failure . . . was not great enough to prove to the public at large how stupid and incredibly

short-sighted it was'. 'If anyone at all shows any enthusiasm for the fleet question', the Prince wrote to Tirpitz in February 1896, 'he speaks of "cruisers" and
his conscience is clear!' But it was obvious, he went on, 'that cruisers are a nonsense without a strong core provided by the battlefleet at home'. He expressed
his hope that Tirpitz would soon take Hollmann's place and that the 'cruiser
danger' would thereby be avoided. 'The Monarch's love for His Navy is unfortunately not always helpful to its sound development!', Wilhelm's brother wrote.
But, as he recognised, certain *naval officers* are *also* to blame for this state of
affairs'.[79]

Senden had already asked Tirpitz, in December 1895, to set out his ideas
on the future development of the battlefleet for submission to the Kaiser, as a
counterpart to a memorandum produced by the Naval High Command. Tirpitz's
views are well known. He was convinced that Germany's position in the world
could be secured only by a large battlefleet, but not by cruisers; that a battlefleet
would enhance the Reich's value as an ally, also in Britain's estimation; that
a skilful propaganda campaign should be conducted to win over the German
people, who were still sceptical, to a fleet programme of this magnitude; and
that the Reich Navy Office must become the central authority in control of the
navy in order to carry out this bold long-term project, which at this time Tirpitz
saw as taking twelve years to complete. 'If we had an absolute monarchy the
Kaiser would have the liberty to decide, on the basis of his advisers' proposals,
exactly how strong the navy should be', he argued in February 1896 in a letter
to Senden. In those circumstances the present division of responsibilities among
the senior naval authorities might still make sense. But the fact was 'that the
Kaiser cannot simply act according to his will in creating his navy, but has to
reckon with a series of other factors and with the will . . . of the nation', and
therefore all naval interests should be brought together under one authority, the
Reich Navy Office, which must create a stronger position for itself in relation to
the other government authorities, the Bundesrat, the Reichstag and the population in general.[80] This was all the more necessary, Tirpitz wrote to his mentor
Admiral von Stosch, for *'our policy hitherto has been completely lacking in a sense
of the political significance of sea power* . . . Our policy does not recognise that
Germany's value as an ally even for European states often lies not in our army
but in the navy . . . In my opinion Germany will rapidly fall from her position as a
great power in the next century unless these general naval interests are energetically, promptly and systematically pursued now. Not least also because there is a
strong palliative against educated and uneducated Social Democrats in the great
new national task and the economic profit associated with it.'[81] In his memorandum for the Kaiser, Tirpitz put forward the convincing argument that with
a fleet of seventeen battleships even the biggest naval power – Britain – would

adopt an accommodating attitude towards Germany, which could never be achieved with ocean-going cruisers. But without a battlefleet the German people would be perpetually 'subject to the whims of the Anglo-Saxons'.[82] As Jonathan Steinberg rightly pointed out in 1965 and as Volker Berghahn, Wilhelm Deist, Paul Kennedy and Michael Epkenhans have subsequently proved beyond all doubt: 'This was the programme which Tirpitz pursued without rest from that day until the outbreak of war in 1914.'[83]

Alfred Tirpitz was no stranger to the Kaiser. Wilhelm had already pronounced him 'the future mainstay of the navy' in 1891.[84] As Prince Heinrich's remarks suggest, however, Wilhelm and Tirpitz were by no means of one mind on everything. The Kaiser wanted a fleet, but for a long time, as we have seen, he had no intention of directing it against Great Britain. Tirpitz, on the other hand, wanted to build his fleet expressly to confront Britain. Wilhelm wanted armoured ships for home defence, principally against the Franco-Russian Dual Alliance, and a cruiser fleet to show the flag and protect German interests overseas – in other words, different types of ships for different purposes. Tirpitz, however, was vehemently opposed to the cruiser fleet. It seemed to him unusable on principle, because it would always be dependent on British goodwill. On one thing, however, the Kaiser and the Admiral were agreed: Germany needed a large fleet if it did not wish to lose its status as a great power in the coming decades. Tirpitz had no choice but to work with the Kaiser, although he did not disguise his contempt for the monarch. And in 1896, after his numerous failed attempts to launch, in grand style, the fleet building programme he so passionately desired, Wilhelm could see no alternative but to dismiss the inept and recalcitrant Hollmann and entrust the task to the most energetic personality in the navy. And the best candidate by a long chalk, according to the Naval Cabinet and the Kaiser's own brother, was Tirpitz. At the end of January 1896 Senden arranged an audience for Tirpitz, in the course of which the Kaiser informed the Admiral that in the near future he would able to take over the Reich Navy Office as Hollmann's successor. At this meeting Tirpitz, showing great self-confidence, presented his plans and demands to the Kaiser.[85]

His appointment hung fire, however, because in March 1896 Marschall and Hollmann succeeded in obtaining the Reichstag's approval for a few cruisers, while for parliamentary reasons Hohenlohe was opposed to any change at the Reich Navy Office. Tirpitz saw this as a threat to the battlefleet plan which had already been approved in principle by the Kaiser, and wrote despondently to Senden on 20 March 1896: 'The way our interests are being represented in the Reichstag, indeed the whole situation, could hardly be less favourable. The Secretary of State at the F[oreign] O[ffice] supports the Navy Bill, blows a fanfare for cruisers and shoots at sparrows with a cannon. What kind of gunpowder is going to make any impression later when really serious demands are put forward? The Secretary of State at the Reich Navy Office beats his breast and says: as long as I stand here no limitless plan will be brought in, i.e. no iron-clads. Then the wicked uncle will turn up in April. The Reichstag sees what is happening and . . . at the very least undermines future demands by approving a few ships this time . . . According to people who know what goes on in the Reichstag, this manner of proceeding will have made it almost impossible for any iron-clads to be approved for years . . . That is the situation and you will of course know best whether the best solution might not be to leave the present secretary of state where he is for a few more years. The worst thing is that the whole nation has been poisoned with this nonsense about cruisers.' He went on to ask, in obvious irritation, whether 'His Majesty would adhere to his earlier decision nevertheless'.[86] The Kaiser set about rebuilding Tirpitz's morale. On 31 March Senden, writing from the *Hohenzollern*, informed the Admiral that 'His Majesty shares the view expressed in your letter of 20 March that a new secretary of state would arouse mistrust in the present situation in parliament . . . His Majesty will therefore defer making any change for the moment, but asks me to tell you expressly that postponement does not mean cancellation, and that His Majesty will make a point of using his influence in line with the ideas which you expressed both in your report of 3/1 96 and in the discussion at the end of January.'[87] When the Kaiser returned to Berlin on 29 April after his Mediterranean cruise, Tirpitz was on the point of leaving for China to take over command of the East Asian cruiser squadron.

    Whether at this time Tirpitz really believed that he would still have a chance to realise his plans is doubtful. But in fact his appointment and his great fleet building programme had only been postponed, as the Kaiser had said, especially as naval officers and the imperial entourage, above all Senden, constantly kept up the pressure for expansion. Holstein wrote that Wilhelm was being encouraged by 'Senden and Co.' to believe that 'it is only due to the ineptitude, ill-will and lack of interest on the part of his government that the money for the gigantic fleet hasn't yet been granted, or that the first steps have not yet been taken to secure the appropriations − for instance, a *coup d'état*, change of constitution, etc. Hence the imperial bad mood against the government that is aired in nasty marginal comments.'[88] After meeting the Kaiser at Kiel and Travemünde in late June 1896 Waldersee recorded that Wilhelm 'evidently felt happiest at sea and among navy people . . . I now have no doubt that the Kaiser is sticking to his great navy plans, which he hinted at in January, and that he will come up with very big demands in the autumn. Of course he is constantly spurred on by the naval officers who flatter him appallingly and to whom he continues to show great friendliness. What concerns me about the whole thing is that the Chief of the Naval Cabinet, Senden, is a singularly insignificant man.'[89] The Empress Frederick was deeply shocked to realise, after a visit from Wilhelm in October 1896, that her son's intentions were now to seize for himself the hegemonial position hitherto held by Great Britain by building 'ships for the German Navy that shall beat the english', as she reported to Queen Victoria. 'William admires England very much and is very fond of you', she wrote; 'but he is not steady & cool headed and far sighted enough to see that to strain every nerve for Germany to succeed in outdoing England & *wresting* fr[om] her the position of supremacy she has in the world – is simply *nonsense!*'[90]

In the imperial entourage, meanwhile, efforts were being made not only to get rid of Hollmann, but also to undermine the position of the Chancellor, and here again the prime mover was the Chief of the Naval Cabinet. In the summer of 1896, during a visit to England, Senden declared that 'the great fleet programme must be pushed through and that the Kaiser intended to push it through. Hohenlohe, however, was too old for this sort of thing, and therefore the Kaiser was often talking about bringing in new blood.' Those who heard him assumed he meant Bernhard von Bülow.[91] The Kaiser expressed similar sentiments to Waldersee at Kiel in late January 1897 in the conversation described in chapter 28.[92] After his remarks about the possible need for a violent *coup d'état*, Wilhelm drew a graph in coloured pencils 'showing the growth of the French and German navies, and began talking about the need for the expansion of our fleet. Finally he gave me the drawing and recommended me to study it', Waldersee recorded.[93] He suspected that Wilhelm would have to appoint a new chancellor, as much to implement a domestic policy of force as to carry out the expansion of the fleet, and wrote: 'The fact that the Kaiser gave me the drawing and emphasised strongly that a great deal would have to be done for the navy soon, combined with Hohenlohe's opposition to the naval plans, suggests to me that a change of chancellor might arise out of this question.' Even if, 'with this very lively gentleman' one could never know 'what else might crop up to change things', one should never forget 'that with the Kaiser developments sometimes happen very quickly, and I know that in recent weeks he has often spoken of his intention of making a major change in the spring'.[94] These documents show clearly how determined the Kaiser already was, even *before* Tirpitz's appointment, which it was generally thought would happen in the autumn,[95] to implement a 'gigantic fleet plan' at all costs.

Meanwhile it was becoming increasingly clear that the Reichstag, not least out of opposition to Wilhelm II, would reject the comparatively moderate addition to the fleet which the government was seeking.[96] Hollmann had a last chance in March 1897, and presented the Reichstag with a new plan. He asked for 40 million marks for cruisers, torpedo boats and an iron-clad. The political omens were bad and there was little hope that the Secretary would win approval for the estimates. As early as 4 February Hohenlohe informed Eulenburg: 'The Kaiser is thinking of letting Hollmann go at the end of the year because he is not the right man to put the gigantic fleet plan into effect. I can already tell you today that that gigantic fleet plan is a practical impossibility. The present Reichstag will not accept it, at least not so soon before the elections; and if the voters even suspect that something like that is afoot, the next Reichstag will be even worse than the present one.'[97] Holstein too was again beset by anxiety that the Kaiser was heading towards a 'Reich coup', which the federal princes would never support. He regarded the 'gigantic fleet' as the 'real goal . . . to achieve which the Kaiser is prepared to gamble the peace, one might even say the existence, of the Reich'.[98] These were no imaginary fears, for Wilhelm did not hesitate to issue threats and attempt to intimidate his opponents. He clashed with the Reich Chancellor and Hollmann when he set up imperial committees on the naval question without their consent.[99] He threatened military intervention if the South Germans opposed his plans.[100] And on 5 March he told Hohenlohe that it was his duty, just as it had been his grandfather's with the army, to ensure that the navy was strong enough to fulfil its tasks.[101] If the Reichstag refused him the funds required, 'he would go ahead with construction and send the bill to the Reichstag later'.[102]

As we have already seen, Wilhelm also tried to intimidate the members of parliament, above all the Centre Party, whose support was crucial if the fleet plans were to receive parliamentary approval, by threatening dissolution and a coup d'état.[103] But this proved counterproductive and failed to achieve anything. Hollmann did not succeed in getting the estimates accepted by the Reichstag;[104] instead, they were cut by some 12 million marks. On the grounds of this drastic reduction Wilhelm demanded that the luckless Secretary of State tender his resignation – which, as Hohenlohe pointed out to the monarch, was inadmissible, since under the Reich constitution the secretary of state at the Reich Navy Office was answerable to the Reich chancellor, and therefore it was he, the Chancellor, and not Hollmann, who would have to resign.[105]

Wilhelm II was beside himself with rage. When Waldersee came to Berlin in mid-March 1897 for the confirmation of the youngest son of the Prince Regent of Brunswick he found a state of 'growing confusion'. The Kaiser came up to him at once and held an animated discussion about the naval estimates, which had just been rejected, and about foreign affairs in general. 'What do you say to the rejection of the ships in the Reichstag committee?', he asked angrily. As Waldersee recorded in his diary, 'a conversation now developed from which it was plain that the Kaiser is extremely embittered. He told me that both Hollmann and the Chancellor had tendered their resignations, that he would accept Hollmann's but that in Hohenlohe's case he wanted to think it over; he would close the Reichstag as soon as the budget debate was over. He expressed himself particularly strongly about the Centre and said "The whole thing is a fight by the Catholic Church against the Protestant Kaiserdom." Unfortunately this revelation has come to him a little late', wrote Waldersee. 'I then asked him how he stood with the German princes, in case relations with the Reichstag deteriorated still further, and he replied that the Prince Regent of Bavaria could not be trusted at all. I told him that the Centre was undoubtedly motivated by malice; it had taken offence against him for various reasons and was taking this opportunity to pick a quarrel, to show him its power, and moreover it knew very well that the rejection of 2 cruisers and a few torpedo boats was not sufficiently important to enable Him to use it as grounds for dissolution . . . From this conversation and from other information I received it was clear to me that the Kaiser does not know what to do; he is deeply hurt and also very dissatisfied with both Hohenlohe and Marschall, but does not yet know what further action to take. Evidently he has not yet decided on a great step, but is still considering that he might *perhaps* have a change of chancellor after the closure of the Reichstag.'[106]

No one was in any doubt that the Kaiser alone was the driving force behind the expansion of the fleet. Waldersee recorded on 19 March 1897 that Wilhelm had 'not accepted' the rejection of the two cruisers by the Reichstag committee and had sent Hohenlohe, Marschall and Hollmann 'into the fray', but again without success. 'What will the Kaiser do?', the General wondered, when the increased naval estimates were rejected in committee for the third time. 'After everything that has happened he ought to do something energetic and Hohenlohe really should not stay on. But I think nothing will happen, nor will Hohenlohe go, so that the dangerous situation will continue. It is very sad how freely the Kaiser is drawn into the Reichstag debates; people say quite calmly that he alone is pushing for the expansion of the navy, and unfortunately that is quite true.'[107] The Kaiser's defiant attitude towards the Reichstag was also apparent in the 'strange' proposal, which had been 'quite seriously discussed', that the naval estimates should be submitted to the Prussian Landtag. 'I have got used to thinking that anything is possible', Waldersee sighed. 'So why shouldn't such an idea find its supporters too?'[108]

### THE FIRST NAVY BILL

Wilhelm did indeed seem to be ready to consider anything to prevent his fleet programme from foundering altogether. He contemplated dismissing Hohenlohe and talked of his grandfather and the situation in 1861; on the other hand, he was heartily tired of haggling with the Reichstag over every detail of the naval estimates.[109] The only way out seemed to be to draw up a new plan providing for a fleet of a fixed strength, and this was the course he now followed, even before Tirpitz took over the Reich Navy Office.[110] He gave instructions for a Navy Bill to be drafted, stipulating that the German fleet must be half as large as the combined Russian and French fleets.[111] On 7 April 1897 he consulted Commander-in-Chief of the Navy Admiral Eduard von Knorr and the interim head of the Reich Navy Office, Admiral Büchsel, as to how large such a fleet would need to be. Knorr, who had at his disposal the calculations made by his former Chief of Staff, Tirpitz, submitted a plan which specified two squadrons of ships of the line and twelve additional ships, that is to say a total of twenty-eight ships of the line, seven large and twenty-one small cruisers, as the necessary strength. In addition to this there were the twelve existing armoured coastal ships.[112] The Reich Navy Office, meanwhile, worked out the substantial sums that would be required for this construction plan.[113] At a conference held on 19 May 1897 Wilhelm had the plan significantly modified, in particular ordering a considerable increase in the cruiser component. In his view the composition of the fleet should be statutorily fixed at twenty-five ships of the line, eight first-class cruisers, thirty second-class cruisers, sixteen fourth-class cruisers, five gunboats, fourteen torpedo division boats and ninety-six torpedo boats. The whole programme was to be completed by 1 April 1910. At the same time a replacement programme for ships that were to be put out of service was to be implemented. The costs would amount to 54 million marks a year, reaching a total of 833 million by 1910. The crucial question, of course, was how the Reichstag could be induced to pass such a law.[114]

In fact the Kaiser himself was still the greatest obstacle to the acceptance of what were regarded as his limitless demands for the navy. In August 1897 Philipp Eulenburg felt compelled to inform his beloved friend that opinion throughout Germany was unfavourable and that the Reichstag was arming itself 'for a kind of policy of resistance' against his naval plans. 'The resistance is unfortunately directed very much against Your Majesty personally, because the German philistines see the approaching Navy Bill more as pandering to a hobby of Your Majesty's than fulfilling Germany's need. The opposition of all political shades is taking this line – a *lamentable* picture of German narrow-mindedness! In view of this undeniable fact it seems to me *tactically necessary* that the *professional* standpoint and that *alone* should be brought to the fore. And Tirpitz is the man for that. I think that it is important for *tactical* reasons that *Your Majesty* should now do as little as possible in the matter, so as to leave the emphasis on the *professionals* in public.' To spare his friend's feelings, Eulenburg added: 'Your Majesty knows very well that I – and all who have some insight into naval affairs – cannot but consider that it is precisely Your Majesty whose *professional* opinion carries the most weight, but the great masses *do not believe it.*'[115] On the very day that this letter was written Alfred Tirpitz, who had meanwhile returned from East Asia, came to see the Kaiser at Wilhelmshöhe for his first audience as secretary of state at the Reich Navy Office. A difficult and disastrous partnership had begun.

At first the Kaiser had hardly been able to wait for the Admiral to take office. Tirpitz, he wrote on 2 April 1897, was 'one of the most talented and notable personalities he had ever come across. He could become anything, even Reich chancellor.' He was a 'tough customer' and would not allow himself to be 'fobbed off' by either the Reich Treasury Office, the Reich Chancellor, the Reichstag or the federal governments as Hollmann had done.[116] The object of all this praise was less enthusiastic about his All-Highest master. After their crucial first meeting at Wilhelmshöhe on 18–19 August 1897 Tirpitz noted that the Kaiser 'made many remarks that showed that he does not live in the real world The Germans only needed to be properly shaken up and to feel the reins. He would throw a firm anti-socialist law and an army cadre law at them for the next elections, and that would soon make them vote for the navy. He let fly with outrageous attacks on Bronsart, saying he had turned the whole country against him, and that was his thanks for the Order of the Black Eagle.' Wilhelm did not agree to the new Navy Secretary's request that he should give up his opposition to the new court martial regulations so as to encourage the Reichstag to be more accommodating on the fleet question, but he approved all the Admiral's proposals relating to the Navy Bill itself.[117] According to its provisions, the fleet was at first to comprise twenty-one ships of the line, eight (existing) armoured coastal ships, sixteen large and thirty small cruisers – considerably fewer than the Kaiser had stipulated only a few weeks earlier.[118] Prince Heinrich was surprised by the modesty of the naval estimates. They were 'cut down to the minimum', he wrote to Tirpitz after studying the bill, but were also 'based on an absolutely realistic and objective approach . . . Common sense tells one that any child must be able to see the necessity of it.' But Tirpitz's task would be no easy one, he warned, promising that 'you may be sure of my help whenever it is needed'.[119] In a memorandum which he drew up for the Kaiser after his audience Tirpitz made it plain that the fleet he built would be directed not only against Russia and France but at the same time against Great Britain.[120]

The support given by Wilhelm II and his brother to Tirpitz's plans, which in fact amounted to a fundamental shift in German foreign policy, was all the more critical because the new Navy Secretary, who in constitutional terms was under the direct control of the Reich chancellor, was being pressed by Prince Hohenlohe and other members of the Reich government to give up his dramatic fleet plans. Tirpitz told the Chief of the Naval Cabinet in confidence on 11 August 1897 'that attempts have been made to induce me to abandon the larger, longer-term demands for the navy and to limit my demands to replacing a few ships. I turned down this request very firmly and threatened to resign.'[121] Support for the gigantic fleet plan could certainly not be expected from Bismarck, whom Tirpitz visited on 22 August at Friedrichsruh, as we have seen. After his conversation with the 82-year-old former Chancellor the Admiral noted despondently that Bismarck had not grasped the fact that it was in Great Britain's power to 'wrestle Germany down' by imposing a strict blockade. 'He was thinking of the political situation of England in 1869 and does not understand how powerful her position is in 1897.'[122] The diplomat Rear-Admiral Karl von Eisendecher made a similar observation. 'From what I know of the Prince [Bismarck], I am not surprised by his somewhat cool attitude, prejudiced by ideas adopted from Roon, towards our efforts for the navy. He always treated the fleet in a rather offhand manner, and above all without any knowledge of the subject, and he was never enthusiastic about developing the fleet.'[123] Only the Grand Duke of Baden, whom Tirpitz met while taking a cure at Bad Ems, declared himself ready to give the Navy Bill his warm support.[124]

Wilhelm II was soon proved right in thinking that Tirpitz would be very different from Hollmann when it came to dealing with the political authorities. First, he succeeded in systematically building up enthusiasm for the navy, thereby putting the Reichstag under pressure 'from below', as it were. In June 1897 he unleashed a propaganda campaign, about which there had been previous deliberations, but which was nevertheless genuinely his own work.[125] The Kaiser reported enthusiastically to Eulenburg: 'Tirpitz has just organized a huge office which . . . will look after *maritima* in some 1,000–1,500 newspapers and magazines. In the great university towns all over the country the professor class has met us willingly and is going to co-operate by speaking, writing, and teaching about Germany's need to possess a strong fleet.'[126] Next, Tirpitz took the members of the Reichstag by surprise with the clarity of his language and the logic of his demands for two battle squadrons. The deputies expressed satisfaction with the new style in which they were being treated. As Volker Berghahn writes, Tirpitz succeeded in winning them over with tactics that combined concealment of his true plans, pressure, the element of surprise produced by his sensible and systematic approach, clarity of presentation and moderate initial demands. They were no longer confronted with demands for a hotchpotch of different types of ship, the purpose of which was never explained, as in the Hollmann era. Instead, they were presented with a clear concept, the aim of which was home defence with moderately sized battle squadrons, and the deputies had no desire to deny their consent to this well-integrated plan.[127] Wilhelm did what he could to smooth Tirpitz's path. He helped him both against the opposition within the navy and against Miquel.[128]

After the Navy Bill had been passed by the Reichstag by 272 votes to 139 on 28 March 1898, giving the navy a budget of 408 million marks, Tirpitz was fêted by the Kaiser, who invited him to dinner and, as we have seen, appointed him a Prussian minister of state with a seat and a vote in the Ministry of State, in spite of the strong resistance of the other ministers. This appointment was to help him strengthen his position at the expense of the civil government of the Reich.[129] Wilhelm swept aside the constitutional objections to his action, declaring in a letter to Hohenlohe: 'Certainly the navy is not under the control of the Prussian authorities, but it is under that of the King of Prussia, who is German Emperor. And like the army it is a component part of our national defences, with absolutely equal rights and equal value, and may therefore also be so bold as to crave a hearing at the illustrious gatherings of the Ministry of State. The magnificent development of our trade, its repercussions on Prussian affairs, the opening up of great areas in the market, in the national economy etc., will give Prussia an increasingly predominant position. Moreover the Admiral, who had only just come home from China, cheerfully took on the enormous task *alone*, in spite of being in poor health, of educating an *entire* population of 50 million unruly, uninformed, bad-tempered Germans and of converting them to a completely opposite point of view, and in eight months he achieved what seemed incredible to everyone. A powerful man indeed! Anyone who can carry out such a gigantic undertaking so splendidly, even contrary to the opinion of most of the ministers, must be in my Ministry, and with full rights! Nor can it be anything but an honour for this most learned body to be able to count such a man among its number and, I hope, to be inspired to energetic work by the fresh impetus and the broad outlook that he will bring to it.'[130]

Kaiser Wilhelm continued to give Tirpitz his support, as for instance over the elimination of the navy's other decision-making authority. In 1899, as we have seen, he dismantled the Naval High Command, replacing it with several separate posts answerable directly to him, on the grounds that this would make it easier for him to intervene in naval affairs. Wilhelm told his brother Heinrich that the 'principal motive' for the reform was 'so that the navy can feel that the monarch is actually its chief, as with the army'. Prince Heinrich replied from Shanghai expressing his bewilderment at this arrangement, commenting at the same time in a letter to the Chief of the Naval Cabinet that he had 'never yet seen anyone who had any doubts about the direct relationship between the monarch and the navy, but that now he might easily be held responsible for much that was not his fault at all! Somebody must tell the Kaiser the plain truth!' The new organisation was 'incomprehensible' to him; he and his officers had been 'speechless' when they heard the news, especially since before his departure from Germany he had written advocating the retention of the High Command. He did not understand, he wrote, how anyone could take on the responsibility of recommending a reorganisation of this kind.[131]

## THE 'GIGANTIC FLEET PLAN' AND ITS AIMS

Tirpitz seems from the outset to have regarded the Navy Bill of 1898, which many considered astonishingly moderate, as only the first step in an ambitious plan that was intended to secure for Germany the status of a world power alongside Great Britain, the United States and Russia.[132] Before his meeting with Wilhelm II at Wilhelmshöhe in August 1897 he had explained to the Chief of the Naval Cabinet his reason for holding back initially: there was no need, he said, 'to argue now for funds which need not be requested until later'.[133] Soon after the Navy Bill was passed, therefore, he was planning the next stage. In April 1898, when he demanded the break-up of the Naval High Command and the transfer of the entire responsibility for the navy into his own hands, he argued that 'in the economic struggle in which the nations will inevitably be engaged in the next century . . . it will become increasingly necessary to defend Germany's maritime interests with military power'; this being the case, the Navy Bill certainly provided a 'secure basis for the Reich's naval power', but it must be brought up to 'the required strength'.[134] The ominous nature of the 'Tirpitz plan' is much more evident in these reflections on future developments than in the apparently modest Navy Bill of 1898. Nor was it long before the British recognised that the types of ship being built by Tirpitz represented a direct threat to their worldwide maritime power at its most sensitive point, that is to say in the North Sea, and began to take far-reaching strategic and diplomatic measures to counteract it. The fatal 'road into the abyss', as Prince Lichnowsky called it, lay open.

As Senden had warned, the new Secretary of State at the Reich Navy Office proved to be an extremely difficult character. Almost the complete antithesis of Bernhard von Bülow, 'slippery as an eel' by nature, who was appointed foreign secretary at the same time, Tirpitz was determined to get what he wanted or resign. Even in these early years he repeatedly held a pistol at the Kaiser's head with threats or actual requests to resign, in order to force Wilhelm to give in. When the Reich Chancellor told Wilhelm in October 1898 that Tirpitz was thinking of resigning, Wilhelm commented that the Admiral was a 'neurasthenic' who was unable to 'obey'.[135] He also repeatedly used these same Bismarckian methods to force his supporters to implore him to stay. 'You are *indispensable* and *irreplaceable*!', Prince Heinrich assured him after one such threat to resign. 'Try to speak privately to the Kaiser, I beg you. He is human as we all are, and will listen to calm, objective arguments from you! Objectively speaking you are right; but I beg you to make allowances for humans and their failings . . . I myself fully and completely support you, your work in the past and I hope in the future for the benefit of the navy, as I have hitherto.'[136]

On the other hand it is undeniable that in spite of his prickly character Tirpitz tried to make allowances for the Kaiser's vanity, the better to achieve his own ends. Before every audience he made detailed notes for himself, not only on the subject to be discussed but also on the form of words in which he could most effectively convey his wishes to the monarch. He made frequent use of the courtier's device of implying that the Kaiser himself was the initiator of a proposed measure. A typical note, in this instance for an audience on 28 November 1898, reads: 'If I have understood Y[our] M[ajesty] correctly, in our conduct over the next few years we should aim to create a situation which will facilitate the introduction of an amendment to the Navy Law.'[137] In the course of this audience Tirpitz persuaded Wilhelm to put the decisions which he took on the basis of their joint discussions into the form of All-Highest Cabinet Orders, 'so that they cannot be departed from without careful examination and a new decision by Your Majesty'.[138] In other words, Tirpitz institutionalised the Personal Monarchy in his own interest by establishing a system of imperial commands. The reason which he gave for this move was that the future expansion of the fleet must proceed along planned lines in order to ensure its success. The previous years had shown 'how much the progress of our fleet has suffered from the fact that no specific target for each stage and no corresponding systematic procedure' had existed.[139]

The frequent audiences and memoranda in which Tirpitz set out his far-reaching ideas to the Kaiser leave no room for doubt that Wilhelm II was well aware of the anti-British aims of the 'Tirpitz plan' and also that he was fully in sympathy with them. At the above-mentioned audience of 28 November 1898 he agreed to the Admiral's suggestion that the next stage should be to request a third squadron 'complete with cruiser groups and torpedo boat divisions, as a squadron to be at Your Majesty's disposal for use abroad'. In order to push ahead as fast as possible with the expansion of the fleet the Kaiser approved the postponement of coastal defence works, as Tirpitz had persuaded him that these could not be carried out at the same time as 'the rapid creation of a fleet'. 'For the sake of Germany's political position and to make it easier to preserve peace while avoiding the risk of serious political humiliation' as well as 'in case of war' it was 'incomparably more important to create a fleet quickly than to

52. Wilhelm II as admiral of the fleet in 1899

strengthen coastal defences', he urged.[140] In another report Tirpitz pointed out to the Kaiser how little the importance of the navy in warfare had been appreciated since 1870. No one had understood that 'supremacy at sea' must be 'the primary goal', therefore no one had accepted the obvious consequences of this in terms of the types of ship and the structure of the fleet; 'no one has grasped that coasts, colonies and commercial interests can only be protected by [a] battlefleet with a unified structure under a unified command'; no one had seen what history proved, that is to say 'that everything is decided by (concentration of forces) [and] battle'. As long as these old-fashioned ideas prevailed Britain would continue to enjoy supremacy at sea, he argued, referring to Mahan's theories. Germany must therefore concentrate its efforts entirely on the rapid creation of a battlefleet. The cruiser warfare which had hitherto been expected to happen would indeed play 'a certain role in the future too, but it will be at the great bases Suez, Gibraltar, Singapore, the Channel, that is to say at strategic points, that concentration of forces and therefore battle will take place'.[141]

Tirpitz's audience at the East Prussian hunting lodge of Rominten on 28 September 1899 marked another crucial stage. This time the Admiral proposed that the next phase of the battlefleet building programme be brought forward. He emphasised that it was his intention, as far as possible, to include 'all unpopular demands' in the next Navy Bill, and 'to state the purpose of the development from the outset'. For the home fleet he proposed to ask for statutory funding for forty ships of the line, eight large cruisers, twenty-four small cruisers and ninety-six large torpedo boats. For the overseas fleet he planned to demand five ships of the line, one large cruiser, three small cruisers, four to six gunboats and a flotilla of torpedo boats for Asia, and two to three large cruisers, three small cruisers and one to two gunboats for America. This target was to be reached in two phases. In the first phase the focus would be on the Third Squadron, the overseas ships and the modernisation of older ships, while in the second phase the ships of the Siegfried class would be replaced by ships of the line. The Secretary of State dangled an enticing, glorious and completely illusory future before his sovereign, whose obsession with the fleet and craving for recognition he knew well how to exploit. 'As soon as [the] goal has been achieved', he promised, 'Your Majesty will have an effective strength of 45 fully equipped ships of the line. A strength so considerable that it is inferior to none but England. But even in relation to England we undoubtedly have a good chance of success in terms of our geographical situation, defence system, mobilisation, torpedo boats, tactical training, planned organisational development, integrated command through the monarch. Apart from the fact that in a conflict our prospects would by no means be hopeless, England will have lost, both on general political grounds and simply from the sober point of view of the businessman, any inclination to attack us, and will consequently have conceded to Your Majesty such a degree of sea power that Your Majesty will be able to pursue a grandiose overseas policy.' According to his own notes, Tirpitz went on to say: 'If Your Majesty agrees and commands that I should proceed with this aim in mind, I promise Your Majesty to devote all my efforts to accomplishing it. [There will, however, be] no possibility of success unless all naval measures are in accordance with and subservient to this great aim . . . The creation of an effective fleet [is] such an indispensable necessity for Germany that without it the country would face ruin. 4 World Powers. Russia, England, America and Germany. Because 2 of these World Powers can be reached only by sea, national power at sea is of prime importance.' 'Salisbury's dictum – the great states are becoming greater and stronger, the small ones smaller and weaker – is my view too', Tirpitz affirmed, adding, 'As Germany has lagged behind particularly in relation to sea power, [it is] a question of life and death for Germany as a world power and a great civilised state to make up for what has been missed. Both so as to create and maintain sea power in the narrower sense (fleet) and because it signifies power in itself, Germany must keep her population German and develop further into an industrial and commercial nation on a worldwide scale . . . With commercial and industrial development on this scale the points of contact and conflict with other nations will grow, and therefore power, sea power, is indispensable if Germany is not to go rapidly downwards.' The Kaiser, the Secretary noted with satisfaction, expressed his agreement with this point of view and authorised him to proceed along these lines. He had already discussed the question with Senden, who was of the same mind but feared that it would not be easy to get the plan through parliament. 'His Majesty commented that these difficulties were not important', Tirpitz noted; 'if need be, the iron pot will then smash the earthenware pot.'[142]

## THE NAVY BILL OF 1900

During his audience at Rominten Tirpitz had spoken of bringing forward the second phase of his great plan, but by this he had meant that the second Navy Bill should be introduced in 1901 or 1902. He had even asked the Kaiser not to speak publicly about it too soon, but had underestimated both Wilhelm's passion for the navy and his machiavellian tendency. As in 1896 after the Transvaal crisis, he saw Salisbury's intransigent stand on the question of the Portuguese colonies, which he described as a 'violation of German colonial interests', as an opportunity to exploit the disappointment of German expectations to drum up support for fleet building and to spike the guns of the 'stupid Reichstag'.[143] And as feelings were again running high against Britain after the outbreak of the Boer War on 11 October 1899, Wilhelm was sure, as before, that the ideal moment to strengthen the fleet had arrived. At the launch of the ship of the line *Karl der Grosse* in Hamburg on 18 October 1899, without the prior knowledge of the Navy Secretary he made a speech which included the celebrated remark: 'A strong German fleet is sorely needed.'[144] At his next audience on 23 October Tirpitz was obliged to express his gratitude for this mark of imperial support, but in reality he was indignant at the Kaiser's impulsive action. He needed more time for the careful preparation of the bill and also to build up popular support for it. He sought the Kaiser's permission to declare publicly 'that no new bill was being planned for 1900' and to hint at 1901 instead.[145] But the ball had been set rolling and could not be stopped, especially as questions were bound to be asked in the Reichstag about the Kaiser's remark. In the end Tirpitz decided not to apply the brakes but to go ahead, if public opinion were indeed thought to be favourable as a result of the events in South Africa.[146] He assured Hohenlohe that he had not known about the Kaiser's speech in advance, but that it must now be followed up. In his view a second Navy Bill would now have to be introduced in the autumn of 1900, and also it would be necessary to offer the Centre Party the repeal of the anti-Jesuit law in exchange for their support.[147] Hohenlohe, on the other hand, was sceptical and considered the moment inopportune, for numerous parliamentary reasons. In addition, he did not believe that German public opinion really shared the Kaiser's conviction that a strong fleet was necessary. 'I do not think the enthusiasm produced by His Majesty's speech in Hamburg was so great that public opinion and the Reichstag will happily agree to the idea behind the new bill', he wrote.[148] In the end Hohenlohe's desire to postpone the matter was overtaken by the publication in the *Norddeutsche Allgemeine Zeitung* of a remark by Tirpitz which gave the impression that 'the plan to increase the navy [had] already been *decided* by H.M.'.[149] In this way, as Berghahn comments, Tirpitz had thrust aside the Reich Chancellor's objections 'in a manner . . . that was characteristic of the constitutional practice [he] adopted of direct interaction with the monarch'.[150] Wilhelm was more convinced than anyone that the favourable moment must be seized. On 2 November he sent telegrams to the German federal princes stressing the 'necessity' of the enlargement of the fleet and making clear 'that He intended to have a new bill introduced in the Reichstag this winter'.[151] The Reich Chancellor had no alternative but to write to the governments of all the German states himself, as also to the Statthalter of Alsace-Lorraine, to explain the necessity of strengthening the fleet and inform them that the new bill would be introduced soon.[152]

But unlike Hohenlohe and Tirpitz, who intended to bring about a parliamentary majority for the bill by careful and conciliatory methods, the Kaiser continued on his usual collision course with the Reichstag. He had grave reservations about the Admiral's suggestion that the repeal of the anti-Jesuit law should be offered to the Centre as 'compensation', he declared.[153] It was at least his spoken intention to dissolve the Reichstag if necessary. Wilhelm's complete refusal to think in terms of parliamentary feasibility and to make concessions to the parties whose support was crucial drove the old Reich Chancellor to the verge of distraction.[154] Even Eulenburg, Bülow and Lucanus were now complaining about the Kaiser's habit of 'frequently [making] pronouncements without contacting the government at all, so that no one in official circles is prepared for them, and they then have to be modified or changed to restore harmony'.[155] But Wilhelm was untroubled by any scruples. On his return from his visit to England in November 1899 he telegraphed to the Chancellor from Flushing: 'I see from German press commentaries shown to me at Port Victoria that there are doubts as to whether the Navy Bill will be accepted by the Reichstag. Your Highness knows from My expressions of My will in the Crown Council and from what I recently told Your Highness at your house after dinner, that I am determined to dissolve the Reichstag if it should refuse to agree to the strengthening of our naval armed forces, which is absolutely essential for our security and our future. All other thoughts and considerations must take second place to this question, which is one of life or death for the Reich. In this question there is no going back for Me, just as for My revered late grandfather there was none in the question of army reorganisation. If we did not use the present moment to complete and expand the Navy Bill of 1898 we should be guilty of a political mistake which could never be rectified. From the standpoint of foreign policy too, the present moment is favourable and right. Not only did the Emperor of Russia recently congratulate Me on my speech at Hamburg and on the planned strengthening of the fleet, but during My visit to England, which has gone off in the most satisfactory manner in every respect, I have received assurances both from the court and the English ministers and from the officers of the Royal Navy with whom I have been in contact that the proposed strengthening of our sea power would be welcomed in England. I therefore fully expect that My government will be fully united and show absolute determination in putting forward the Navy Bill, so as to ensure that it is accepted for the good of the Fatherland. Wilhelm I. R.'[156]

At the turn of the century two German mail steamers were seized by the British on suspicion of carrying contraband for the Boers, a suspicion which turned out to be false.[157] A 'furious' wave of anti-British emotion swept through Germany and the Kaiser's first thought was once again to turn this opportunity to advantage.[158] Years later, in exile, he still took malicious pleasure in recalling the moment when Bülow received the telegram containing this very welcome piece of news, in his own and Tirpitz's presence. He had quoted the English proverb, 'It's an ill wind that blows nobody good', he wrote, and Tirpitz had exclaimed: 'Now we have the wind we need to bring our ship into harbour; the Navy Bill will go through. Your Majesty ought to confer an Order on the English commander as a reward for getting the Navy Bill through.' He then noted that the Reich Chancellor (sic!) ordered champagne, 'and so we three drank to the bill, its passage and the future German fleet, in gratitude to the English navy which had been so helpful'.[159]

The extent to which this triumphant retrospective description was coloured by wishful thinking is shown by the impatient telegram which Wilhelm actually sent on 10 January 1900 to Prince Hohenlohe, who was of course still Reich Chancellor at the time, and in which he showed how little comprehension he had of Tirpitz's careful parliamentary preparations. 'I have today personally given the Secretary of State at the Reich Navy Office, Admiral Tirpitz, the clearest instructions to introduce the Navy Bill within 8 days at the latest. The Admiral made some difficulties on the grounds that it had not yet been "polished" in every detail, and said that he wished to wait a little longer. I consider this wrong. Opinion throughout the population has become so aroused by the capture of the German Reich post steamers by England, and the anger over this insult is growing so much that sooner or later it will try to make itself felt with elemental violence. The first thing will be popular meetings, protest meetings and even more vicious attacks against England and the Queen herself than have already been made. That would considerably disrupt our negotiations with regard to the steamers and might drive the English to extremes against us if there are further setbacks. So the strong build-up of "explosive pressure" here must find an outlet in a way that puts patriotism to the best use for our country. And that is the immediate introduction of the Navy Bill. The Reichstag is in a position of constraint between the crown, the Bundesrat and the people, who are demanding the Navy Bill with increasing vehemence. The Admiral is rather conceited, and wants to "cut a good figure", as one says. So he is still tinkering with and working over his speeches and his bill, to prepare himself for all possible questions and objections. But all that is quite superfluous now. He has had plenty of time from 18 October (Hamburg) until the middle of January to get the bill ready in general outline. It is well known that under Prince Bismarck bills were sometimes drafted and settled in one night. With this [bill] it will not be a question of elaborate arguments or elegant verbal duels, but the bill will simply be introduced and the Reichstag will refer it to its committees, where it will in any case be favourably settled, with the help of pressure from the entire nation. The Admiral can show off all his flowery turns of phrase and all his skill in defence of the bill in the committees. The shorter and drier the speeches are kept at its introduction the better it will be. At such major political moments as the present one, the great stream of the German national idea, which is at last flowing strongly, must be used quickly. Count von Bülow and Herr von Lucanus are fully informed and share my view in every respect. I therefore beg Your Highness to pursue this matter in the way which I have indicated . . . Wilhelm I. R.'[160]

The bill was completed on 25 January 1900. The Kaiser again applied pressure for it to make faster progress, and arranged for it to go straight to the Bundesrat, 'bypassing the Prussian Ministry of State'.[161] In public too he continued to stir up support for the navy, declaring for instance, at the reception on 13 February 1900 for his brother on his return from East Asia, that the 'joyful and enthusiastic' welcome given to Prince Heinrich by 'all classes of people in My residence of Berlin' was an 'unambiguous sign of how great the support for the strengthening of our sea power [had] become'. 'The German people are at one with their princes and their Kaiser', he went on, 'in their wish to set up a new milestone in their mighty development by creating a great fleet to fulfil their needs. Just as Wilhelm the Great created the weapon with the help of which we have become Black, White and Red again [sic!], so the German people are setting out to forge the weapon through which, if God wills, they will remain Black, White and Red throughout all eternity, both at home and abroad.' Thanks to Tirpitz's skilful tactics in making the additional demands for funds look plausible to the Reichstag with reference to unforeseeable developments in arms technology, and above all in winning over the Centre, the government succeeded in getting the second Navy Bill through.[162] Carried along on a wave of anti-British emotion, the Reichstag voted in favour of the measure on 12 June 1900.[163] With this, the Anglo-German antagonism that had already begun to manifest itself to some extent in recent years became an inexorable, indeed merciless conflict which, as we know, was in the end to be fought out not on the high seas but in the trenches of the First World War.

The unequal and uncomfortable partnership between Wilhelm II and his 'evil spirit', Tirpitz, which began in 1895 and was to continue until it came to a stormy end in 1916, proved catastrophic for Germany and the world.[164] The forced battleship building programme robbed German foreign policy of its freedom of manoeuvre. Only a few years after the Navy Bill the diplomats of the Wilhelmstrasse were forced to accept the 'encirclement' of the German Reich by Great Britain, France and Russia, as helplessly as if they had been in chains. Yet the 'limitless' battlefleet programme, driven forward incessantly by Tirpitz with the support of Wilhelm II, continued unabated, and neither the increasingly vociferous warnings of the German ambassadors in London nor the efforts of the Reich chancellors, Bülow and Bethmann Hollweg, nor even the opponents of the Tirpitz plan within the navy and the army, were able to persuade the Kaiser to give way. Wilhelm's passion for the navy, fed by his urge to gain recognition and by dark feelings of hatred for his mother's homeland, had led him, like an addict, into the hands of another naval fanatic who alone seemed able to carry through the 'gigantic fleet plan' which he so fervently desired, in defiance of the Reich government and the Prussian Ministry of State, the Reichstag and the majority of the German people.[165] By withdrawing the trust he had placed in Tirpitz Wilhelm II had it in his power at any time to put a stop to the disastrous battleship building programme, directed as it was towards the overthrow of Great Britain's position as a world power and the supplanting of the balance of power in Europe by German domination. But he did so only after the Iron Dice of War had begun to roll.

# CHAPTER THIRTY-THREE

# 'Young Germany, Your Kaiser!',
## or
## what was wrong with Wilhelm II?

### THE NEW CENTURY

THE beginning of a new century, then as now, was an occasion for recollection of the past and conjecture about the future, and at the turn of the twentieth century Kaiser Wilhelm II, who now stood at the zenith of his power and yet seemed, so far, not to have himself under control, naturally played an important part in these reflections both in Germany and further afield. What did people think of him, and how did this affect their hopes and fears for the future? Contemporary comments vary widely in their assessment of him, and we shall examine just a few of them. In the admiring eyes of the Archduke Franz Ferdinand of Austria-Hungary, Wilhelm II was 'the grandest fellow in Europe',[1] while Tolstoy reviled him as 'one of the most abhorrent, not to say the most ridiculous representatives of imperial power'.[2] Among his most ardent admirers was an Englishman living in Vienna, who enthusiastically embraced the German language and German culture and was later to marry Wagner's daughter, but who in 1900 had not yet met the Kaiser: it was not until the winter of 1901 that Philipp Eulenburg was to introduce the racial theorist Houston Stewart Chamberlain to Wilhelm II at Liebenberg.[3] Writing in the weekly periodical *Jugend* in the summer of 1900, Chamberlain, the author of *The Foundations of the Nineteenth Century*, predicted a glorious future for the German Reich under its energetic, youthful Kaiser. 'The reign of Wilhelm II has the character of the dawning of a new day', was the jubilant comment of this 'evangelist of race', who twenty-three years later was to praise Adolf Hitler at Bayreuth as the saviour of Germany in its hour of greatest need.[4] Wilhelm II, according to Chamberlain, was 'in fact the first German Kaiser'. He had understood that it was his historic mission to 'ennoble' the world through 'German knowledge, German philosophy, German art and – if

God wills – German religion'. 'Only a Kaiser who undertakes this task is a true Kaiser of the German people', he declared. Wilhelm had recognised that the spread of the 'higher' German language and culture could be achieved only by power, and that power meant sea power above all. The son of an English admiral, Chamberlain asserted confidently that 'without a fleet nothing can be done'. But 'equipped with a great fleet, Germany is embarking on the course to which Cromwell showed England the way, and she can and must steer resolutely towards the goal of becoming the first power in the world. She has the moral justification for it and therefore also the duty.'[5] The picture of Wilhelm II which the militaristic Young Germany League drew in its propaganda piece, *Jung Deutschland, Dein Kaiser!* ('Young Germany, Your Kaiser!'), on the eve of the First World War was to be very similar.[6]

A considerably more sober, indeed more anxious, evaluation of the future prospects of the German Reich comes from the pen of the long-standing Austro-Hungarian ambassador in Berlin, Count Ladislaus von Szögyény. In a report of 5 February 1900 he too drew attention to the battlefleet plans and visions of world domination which now set the tone of imperial Germany's policy, but he did not fail to recognise the enormous dangers of such a challenge to the established world powers. 'The leading German statesmen, and above all Kaiser Wilhelm, have their eyes fixed on the distant future; their efforts are directed towards making Germany's position as a world power, which has taken great strides forward in recent times, a dominant one and in due course they are counting on becoming England's heirs in this respect. But in Berlin people are well aware that Germany is not in a position to come into this inheritance today, nor for a long time to come, and for this reason the collapse of English world power in the near future would not be at all welcome, as no one is in the slightest doubt that Germany's ambitious plans can at the moment only be a dream for the future. – Nevertheless Germany is already eagerly working with all her might to prepare herself for her self-appointed future mission.' In this connection Szögyény drew particular attention to the 'incessant preoccupation with the increase of German naval forces, and to the constantly repeated remarks referring to this aim which are made by H.M. the German Kaiser and his leading statesmen'. But this policy, he pointed out, was planned on a long-term basis. That both Wilhelm and Bülow were reluctant to give in to the present 'wave of popular feeling' against Britain on account of the Boer War and adopt a position that was 'too antagonistic towards England' could be attributed to their pragmatic recognition that they could not expect to enter into the 'possible inheritance which they so ardently desired', that of 'Great Britain's colonial power', except in 'the very distant future'. 'As to the period of time which will elapse before then, Kaiser Wilhelm has the least illusions of all, as he repeatedly indicated that he would certainly not live to see the realisation of these ambitious plans Himself, but He considered it His duty to prepare His country as well as possible for what could be expected to happen.' The ambassador went on to emphasise that German aspirations for world power had caused anxiety not only in Britain but also in Russia, and were indeed seen there as a mortal danger. He could well understand, he commented, why Russia 'would very much like to put a stop to the all too rapid realisation of Germany's aspirations before it is too late', for 'there can be no doubt of how dangerous it would be for Russia if Germany achieved an overwhelming position not only as the strongest land power in central Europe but also in the whole world'. Rightly predicting what was to happen, Szögyény pointed to the possibility that Britain and Russia would come to an agreement on the many unresolved questions that divided the two world empires. 'The spectre of a general coalition against Germany which always haunted Prince Bismarck still has a hold over people's minds here today', he reported. 'There is probably no need to spell out what role England would play in such an eventuality, and for this reason alone it seems quite natural that on the German side strenuous efforts will be made to avoid any serious damage to the relations between the cabinets of Berlin and London.'[7]

The Bismarckian Maximilian Harden was certainly among the most embittered critics of the Wilhelmine *Weltpolitik*. For him it was absolutely axiomatic that the full responsibility for that policy lay with Wilhelm II, together with the Liebenberg circle around Philipp Eulenburg, whom the Kaiser raised to the rank of prince on 1 January 1900. 'The Kaiser is his own Reich chancellor', he wrote in the periodical *Die Zukunft*, of which he was the editor, in 1902. 'All the important political decisions of the past twelve years have been made by him.'[8] For Harden too, the turn of the century and in particular the speech which 'the imperial War Lord' made on 27 July 1900 at Bremerhaven on the embarkation of the German troops who were to suppress the Boxer Rebellion under Waldersee's command, provided him with the occasion to express his views on the Kaiser. He launched his fiercest attack to date upon Wilhelm in his article 'The Fight with the Dragon', which was immediately confiscated, while Harden was sentenced to six months' imprisonment.[9] In his so-called Hun speech the Kaiser, alluding to his 'great immortal grandfather' and the Great Elector, had again used the sort of bloodthirsty militaristic turn of phrase which is familiar to us from his marginal comments and his earlier speeches, and which this time, in spite of the attempts of Bülow and the Flügeladjutanten to suppress the actual words, leaked out and shocked the world. The use of the word 'Huns' throughout the English-speaking world as a term of abuse for the Germans, particularly in both world wars and sometimes even today, can be traced back directly to the Kaiser's command to his troops in 1900 to conduct themselves in China 'like the Huns under their King Attila a thousand years ago', so that 'the name of Germany [shall] become known in China to such effect that no Chinaman will ever again

53. The Kaiser making his 'Hun Speech' in Bremerhaven on 27 July 1900

dare so much as to look askance at a German'. 'Pardon will not be given, prisoners will not be taken', he proclaimed. 'Whoever falls into your hands will fall to your sword.' The soldiers should 'set an example of manly self-control and discipline', and of 'traditional German excellence' as they had learned 'from our military history'; 'God's blessing' would ensure 'that Christianity becomes established in that country. That is what you stand for with your oath of allegiance!'[10]

54. A French comment on Wilhelm II's 'Hun Speech'

This speech, which aroused 'anxious unease' everywhere, convinced Harden that Germany had reached a 'monarchical crisis' as a result of Wilhelm II's Personal Monarchy. In this system there was no one who could force 'the widely roaming fantasy' of the Kaiser 'into the narrow bounds of common reality'. 'No one chases away sweet illusions and warns against setting too much store by the skilfully created but also artificial magnificence of the Reich. Everyone tries to gild the lily. Germany is immeasurably rich; Germany has a mission to become the first among all industrial and commercial nations, and in order to come closer to this goal she must carry her victorious standards overseas; and the Kaiser of the Germans, like the crowned heroes in the days of the crusades, must endeavour to conquer the world for the Gospel. The dreamers and the sly speculators whisper these things into the sovereign's ear ... In times of peace and calm it is a harmless fallacy, or at least it causes no serious mischief; in times of chaos and confusion it may become a catastrophe.' With unerring accuracy Harden recognised the dynastic cult of the Hohenzollerns practised by Wilhelm, who had always been taught to see his ancestors 'only in legendary, transfigured form', as a major cause of his isolation from the real world and of his growing alienation from the German people, which – he expressly warned – could lead to assassination attempts. 'He who was raised to the throne so early, who takes pride in being the son of his forefathers, looks back and compares. What small means his ancestors had, and what mighty things they achieved nonetheless! Shall he alone, the richly endowed heir of their accumulated strength, be allotted none of the tasks without which the life of the monarch is not worth living and which transform the *roi fainéant* into the benefactor of the Reich?' 'It is perhaps this kind of mood', Harden suggested, 'that has given rise to the general tone of the speeches calling for revenge.' The Kaiser would probably be very surprised to discover how differently most Germans saw the world and their history, how little they had in common with the 'exuberance' of his 'romantic dreams of crusades'. To them 'the splendour of the Reich is in some danger. They see it in a difficult territorial position, surrounded by lurking suspicion and envy, unprepared at home, dependent on unreliable or weak allies abroad, with rapidly increasing prosperity, but lacking the riches which could allow the Reich to risk the gigantic battle with Great Britain, North America and Russia for world power and worldwide commercial supremacy.' The danger of assassination attempts by anarchists was rooted in the alienation between a monarch with autocratic inclinations and his people, for 'where the belief is allowed to grow that all political action springs from the mind of the monarch, the delusion will always take root in some sick or overheated brain that the violent elimination of a ruler who is hated by the impoverished masses is a heroic act from which good will come for the people.' And Harden quite rightly concluded from this observation that the monarchical form of government could be tolerated in the twentieth century only if the crown limited itself to its representational functions under the constitution. 'Kings and emperors can escape the flatterer's poison and the murderer's dagger only if they content themselves with the role that has been allotted to them since the constitutional struggles of our century: the role of the ceremonial representative of nationhood, removed from the squabbles of everyday life, safeguarded by special laws behind golden bars, whose carefully considered words are his deeds, who can do good and can never be held responsible for evil.'[11]

### THE BROKEN SPELL: PHILIPP EULENBURG AND HIS 'LIEBCHEN'

The system of Personal Monarchy practised by Wilhelm II and seen by him as especially 'Prussian' represented the exact opposite of the constitutional form of monarchical government. By the turn of the century there was scarcely a single matter of personnel, domestic, foreign or military policy which was not decided by the Kaiser, scarcely ever a public occasion which he allowed to pass without making a speech, scarcely a field in which he did not feel called to make his strongly held opinions known, scarcely a 'colleague' among the monarchs of Europe whom he did not pester with correspondence and visits and offend with jocular digs in the ribs, scarcely a single diplomatic document which he did not bedeck with crude marginal comments. It is therefore hardly surprising that he himself, and still more those who had to live and work with him, began to complain of the great burden of work thus accumulated. His life was 'full of heavy and unceasing work', he wrote to his grandmother in 1899, and there were often 'moments when I fancy the strain is too strong and the burden too heavy to bear'.[12] That winter, he told his friend Philipp Eulenburg, he had had 'a difficult time politically', during which without Bülow he would have found himself 'in a terrible position'. 'What you are for him and for *everyone*, *he* knows best', Eulenburg told Bülow, reporting a remark of Wilhelm's.[13] On 22 June 1899 the Kaiser raised Bülow to the rank of count.

With Bülow's appointment as secretary of state at the Foreign Office in the summer of 1897 (and then as Hohenlohe's successor as Reich chancellor and Prussian minister-president in October 1900) Eulenburg had attained the goal for which he had worked tirelessly behind the scenes, against all the prophecies of doom emanating from the Wilhelmstrasse and throughout countless government crises: the establishment of the Personal Monarchy of Wilhelm II. Nor did the Kaiser fail to give generous recognition to his closest friend's loyal efforts. On the tenth anniversary of his accession he sent Eulenburg an affectionate telegram thanking him warmly for his friendship and support over the past years.[14] Eulenburg expressed his delight in a letter to Hermann von Lucanus, the Chief of the Civil Cabinet. 'The Kaiser has sent me such a moving telegram of thanks, in such – I can only say exuberant – terms, that I am deeply touched and quite overcome. It is quite true that I have *thoroughly* worn myself out and tormented myself for him for 10 years. But . . . he is a *unique, wonderful* Master – we both know that *very* well!'[15]

And indeed the new system, under Bülow's auspices, seemed at first to function very well. August Eulenburg reported from Berlin that since Bülow had taken office 'everything looks rosy', and following the successful passage of the first Navy Bill his cousin Philipp jubilantly exclaimed: 'Could anyone imagine a more magnificent demonstration of consistency, initiative and vision than the way the "limitless plans" of our poor dear Master have turned out, when he was called impulsive, inconsistent and foolish?'[16] Yet the triumphant feelings of the Kaiser's secret advisers were short-lived. For Eulenburg this was the beginning of a time of cruel suffering which was to lead to his enforced resignation from his post as ambassador in 1902 and to culminate four years later in the sensational trials for perjury and homosexual offences which were sparked by Harden's attacks (supported by Holstein) on him and Count Kuno von Moltke in *Die Zukunft*.[17] Blackmail by a Viennese bath attendant in the spring of 1896[18] was followed by the scandal-ridden divorces of his brother Friedrich and his intimate friend Kuno Moltke, whom the Kaiser had appointed military attaché at the Viennese embassy shortly beforehand. In both cases 'Phili' Eulenburg had himself been in danger of being unmasked, but in both cases Kaiser Wilhelm – unlike later, in the terrible days of the trials – showed his loyalty. The imperial favourite was relieved to observe that in spite of Friedrich Eulenburg's enforced dismissal from the army Wilhelm spoke to Philipp 'quite in the old way' while they were together on board the *Hohenzollern* in July 1898. 'In his manner and conduct His Majesty has kept up the old friendly ways with me and even when the full entourage is present he speaks mainly to me', Eulenburg wrote in relief to Bülow.[19] And even when Kuno Moltke's disastrous marriage failed because of the all too intimate relationship between the newly appointed military attaché and the ambassador, Eulenburg himself, the warm relations between the Kaiser and his best friend remained intact. Hearing from Eulenburg of Moltke's marriage problems, another friend, the Württemberg envoy Axel Freiherr von Varnbüler, assured Moltke that the Kaiser would understand everything and protect him. 'The Liebchen', Varnbüler wrote, 'is man enough to put a stop to nasty gossip – and he knows and loves you too well in your peculiarity to allow even the shadow of blame to fall upon you.'[20] Varnbüler's prediction was to prove correct.[21] In fact it was not the Kaiser who lost faith in Eulenburg but Eulenburg who lost faith in the Kaiser.

In the summer of 1897 the tone of Eulenburg's references to his 'dearly beloved' Kaiser in his letters to Bülow was still that of earlier days: 'I felt that my love for him . . . was bursting into flame.'[22] He was 'deeply moved' to hear Wilhelm's self-critical lament that he did not feel anything when he dismissed officers or officials, and that he reproached himself bitterly for this. 'Something is missing in me that others have. All poetic feeling in me is dead – has been killed', the Kaiser had confessed. 'Experiences and experiments in his youth have artificially dammed the balancing qualities in his nature', Eulenburg observed sympathetically. But he still believed that the Kaiser's nature would prove stronger than these constraints.[23] Soon, however, Eulenburg saw his 'Liebchen' in quite another light, as if scales had fallen from his eyes. From the spring of 1898 he began to show concern over the effect of the Kaiser's personality abroad. Over the next months and years this concern was to grow into a panic-stricken terror. He warned of the increasing dislike of Wilhelm felt not only by the Tsar and Tsarina but also at the German courts, like Coburg and Darmstadt, which had close family ties with Britain, and of the threat which this represented.[24] 'We must be very careful', he wrote to Bülow. 'And especially our beloved sovereign. His manner annoys insignificant and weak characters even more than it irritates those who are naturally opposed to him. Even his strong handshake makes people uncomfortable, and that Darmstadt alliance which he himself brought about [Nicholas and Alexandra] is turning into a dangerous breeding ground for hysterical modern bacilli which find nourishment wherever Siegfried's fist is feared or is considered "vulgar".'[25] The new Foreign Secretary agreed that the greatest care was needed, for 'there is much jealousy and antipathy towards the German people abroad, among the nations from Paris to Moscow and Prague and from London to New York, and at the courts there is much very unfair misjudgement and lurking hatred againt His Majesty. Not only Princess Beatrice but almost the entire English-Battenbergian-Hessian-Danish etc. *cousinage* is quietly plotting against His Majesty . . . We shall gain the day only if we work fearlessly but also wisely, with clear vision but also with a skilful hand. Now is not the time for rash experiments; too violent swings of the pendulum could have disastrous results; we need steadiness, calm and shrewdness.'[26] Although Bülow had recently compared Wilhelm II with Frederick the Great he now had premonitions of trouble. 'It is a misfortune', he lamented, 'that our beloved, highly talented Kaiser so easily goes too far and gives too much rein to his temperament and sometimes to his imagination';[27] and Eulenburg, no less anxious, complained of 'that energetic mood' which his imperial friend so often displayed and which made it so hard to maintain a calm, confidence-building foreign policy.[28] In the following months Eulenburg and Bülow exchanged increasingly worried comments about the trouble Wilhelm was causing – his 'frequent visits to ambassadors', his demand for 'a "German" Asia Minor', the 'most extraordinary comments' he had made on the Russian succession on hearing of the sudden death of the Tsar's brother in 1899 – all of which put Bülow's efforts at risk. 'I follow it all with deep feelings of friendship with you; I *feel* what you are suffering', Eulenburg wrote to the Foreign Secretary in February 1899.[29]

The two former admirers of the Kaiser also discussed his 'irritation . . . with Austria and the Austrian court' with concern as early as 1898.[30] In particular, there was deep animosity between Wilhelm and the heir to the Austrian throne, Franz Ferdinand, as a result of the Kaiser's jokes, which had wounded the Archduke '*terribly* deeply', the ambassador reported. At the station in Berlin the Kaiser had greeted the haughty Habsburger with the words: 'Don't imagine that I have come to receive *you*. I am expecting the Crown Prince of Italy.' Worse, in Budapest after a conversation with the Archduke, Wilhelm had remarked that he had not thought that he would be so clever, whereupon Franz Ferdinand,

'white with rage', had exclaimed: 'Did he take me for a cretin?' But in Eulenburg's opinion the chief reason for their mutual antipathy lay in the Archduke's
jealousy of Germany's growing power. 'A strong Germany with a ruler of genius
is too favourable a soil for the evil character bacilli that dominate the heir to the
Habsburg throne', he wrote to Bülow in May 1899.[31] A more serious issue than
the relationship with the Danube monarchy, however, was that of Germany's
relations with Russia and Britain. During the Scandinavian cruise of 1899 Eulenburg set out to persuade the Kaiser, who was enraged with both world empires,
'that in the end it is preferable to *run after* Russia *and* England than to *anger*
them both'.[32]

   This voyage was also one of painful disillusionment for the Kaiser's friend.
While going for a walk along the seashore on 14 July 1899 Wilhelm and
Eulenburg had a memorable conversation about the danger of an enforced abdication by the Kaiser, which not unnaturally made a deep impression on the
latter. Wilhelm's friend strongly urged him to show more caution 'at home and
abroad'. 'In a dangerous situation of the kind which could perhaps be caused or
aggravated by an incautious act on His Majesty's part, the government [could
be] *forced out.* That could be followed by a campaign in the Reich to make the
Kaiser abdicate or to deprive him of his rights. A structure like the German state
was a delicate, subtle creation – a work of art in a glass case . . . If the work of art
were not treated with sufficient care the anger of the people would be aroused.
The Kaiser grew very grave at this remark and asked again *who* could have such
ideas?' Eulenburg refused to name names but quoted a comment by the late
Cardinal Prince Gustav zu Hohenlohe-Schillingsfürst, the Reich Chancellor's
brother, who had warned that 'the Kaiser should be *very much* on his guard, *very*
careful. I know for a fact that the idea of declaring him of unsound mind is in
many minds, and that very many people, including highly placed personalities,
would be glad to help institute proceedings to do so.' Eulenburg should warn
the Kaiser, the Cardinal had said. 'Very much against his usual practice', the
ambassador recorded, 'the Kaiser did not end this conversation with a joke or an
energetic verbal jab of the broadsword à la 1st Guards Regiment but remained
lost in thought.' Later Wilhelm reverted to this conversation and admitted that
'even close to him there were elements who might possibly adopt a dangerous
and hostile attitude, e.g. the bigoted, Hanoverian-minded Prince Albrecht [of
Prussia, the Regent of Brunswick], also Prince Friedrich Leopold [of Prussia] –
who incidentally was bound to be locked up in a madhouse soon'.[33]

   But Eulenburg's exhortations to calm and caution were of no avail. 'The life
of a kaiser like our master functions like a natural element. It is a cloud that
is sometimes white, sometimes grey, sometimes black, and contains rain, hail,
storms – and in particular a great deal of electricity', he sighed.[34] A few days

after the conversation on the seashore the Kaiser's favourite heard of Wilhelm's telegrams to Hinzpeter at Bielefeld and to the city of Dortmund, which horrified him.[35] He wrote despairingly to Bülow that it was 'really a mystery to me why the Kaiser has to adopt that loud, resounding, energetic tone just because of a memorial to the Great Elector, and why Hinzpeter publishes the telegram!'[36] Shortly afterwards he reported that 'the bomb of the Bielefeld telegram' had evidently not been enough; the Kaiser had now brought the telegram to the city of Dortmund to show him in his cabin, 'with the satisfied smile of a wise statesman', Eulenburg wrote to the Foreign Secretary. 'I must admit that it filled me with consternation . . . The consequences are obvious – and the Kaiser does not see them! . . . An action like that makes the prospects for the future look so hopeless that it makes me very sad indeed!'[37] Not only he but the entire suite on board the *Hohenzollern* were perplexed and appalled by the telegrams, he added. 'I see a kind of bitterness emerging everywhere. In the past I used to argue with two or at most three grumblers; now everyone is grumbling, without exception, in an exhausted, hopeless way that gives the whole suite an oriental character of fatalism – and of bad-tempered fear of the Sultan.' 'Seeing this makes me very melancholy', Eulenburg confessed. 'There is so much I should like to say to him – then his Caliphate chokes me.'[38]

It was only now that Eulenburg recognised the brutal aggressiveness and also the shameful political ignorance of the Kaiser he had idolised for so long. When news arrived on 21 July 1899 of unrest among workmen at Augsburg, Wilhelm reacted with 'great satisfaction' and loudly declared at table: 'Good! . . . Carry on! The moment is coming where we must *act*. And I shall let *nothing* hold me back – not even the Ministry, which will simply be "out on its ear" if it does not co-operate. Be so good as to read my speeches which have been printed and published since my accession. You will clearly see that I have warned the German people, at first in a friendly way and then in earnest, of the dangers which threaten them within the country. The German middle class has completely *failed*! The government must *act*, otherwise all will be lost. If a serious conflict has arisen abroad and there is a possibility that half of the army is tied down within the country by a general strike, we are *lost*. And at the last Hamburg strike England already had its finger in the pie, and did quite well out of it. So the time has come to take action. I have already made enquiries as to how far my military powers go in relation to the constitution. *The Minster of War has told me* that I can declare a state of emergency throughout *the entire Reich at any time.* (!!!) Matters will not improve until the troops drag the Social Democratic leaders out of the Reichstag and gun them down. We need a law under which to be a Social Democrat is enough to get oneself exiled to the *Carolines*.' The Kaiser '*hoped*' there would be 'looting' during the unrest among workers in Berlin and other major cities, he said, because then 'but only after a few hundred middle-class shops have been destroyed' it would be possible to carry out 'a *very* severe blood-letting'.[39]

On some evenings the conversation at dinner in the *Hohenzollern* switched to foreign affairs. The Kaiser spoke at length about his meeting with Cecil Rhodes, who he said had advised him to consider the 'acquisition and opening up of *Mesopotamia*' as his allotted 'task'. The Englishman had told him he should 'build the railway through Asia Minor to the Euphrates – the land route to India', and had remarked that the Kaiser had surely not gone to Jerusalem because of the holy places but had pursued 'other aims' there. The Kaiser had been delighted at this, he said, and had answered: 'You have guessed right! I shall build this railway and reopen these lands of ancient civilisation to the world!'[40]

Hearing these effusions from the monarch whom he had blindly supported through endless struggles and crises since his accession made Philipp Eulenburg feel 'thoroughly unwell', he admitted. The realisation was at last beginning to dawn on him that the Bismarcks, Holstein, Caprivi, Marschall, Waldersee, Wittich, Bronsart and all the other warning voices with their predictions of disaster had not been entirely wrong in trying to put an end to the personal rule of *this* Kaiser. He wrote to his political ally Bülow, whom he had worked for years to raise to the highest offices in the Reich, on 21 July 1899, feeling 'out of sorts and sad': 'In the 11 years of his reign the Kaiser has become very much quieter as far as his outer being is concerned', he commented. 'Spiritually, however, there has not been the slightest development. He is unchanged in his explosive manner. Indeed even harsher and more sudden, as his self-esteem has grown with experience – which is no experience. For his "individuality" is stronger than the effect of experience. That could be a way of describing something else – but it is *not* anything else. He does not belong in our era.' 'Such strong natures cannot help but cause convulsions when they are at the head of a nation', the Kaiser's friend continued. 'We are approaching a moment when a decision will be reached as to whether the epoch or the Kaiser will be the stronger. I am afraid that he will be the loser.'[41]

Shortly before the end of the cruise Eulenburg found another opportunity to warn the Kaiser of the dangers that lay in his autocratic tendencies. The widespread and growing dissatisfaction was beginning to give him 'an uncanny feeling', he told Wilhelm, 'because the parties which are usually so divided are coming together in their common resentment towards Your Majesty'. The old battle with the Bismarcks was still playing a part in the present situation, he went on. 'It culminates in a dangerous conflict between Your Majesty's *personality* and the people as a whole. The undoubtedly *modern* side of Your Majesty ... is almost progressive in character, but it is paralysed by an energy which makes itself felt too *harshly* in public. By your speeches and telegrams Your Majesty gives the impression of wanting to resurrect the *absolute* monarchy. But that is no longer understood by *any* party throughout the Reich . . . Parliamentarism is deeply rooted in all Germans.' The Kaiser retorted 'rather sharply' that he claimed for himself 'the same freedom of speech as every German man! I must *say* what I want, so that the sensible elements know what to do and whom to *obey*. If I were *silent*, the completely "finished" middle classes would have no idea what to do! . . . You are only afraid that I might use force against parliament.' But 'somehow or other it must come to a clash one day. Everything is going that way, and so one has to *accept* that there will be a fight.' Eulenburg warned strongly against this attitude, which would only rouse the people even more against the Kaiser. 'The anger will be directed against the absolute Kaiser', and he must do everything to avoid 'arousing disastrous and dangerous conflicts!'[42]

The next few months brought no improvement in the sombre mood of the Kaiser's friend, now Prince zu Eulenburg-Hertefeld. He wrote anxiously to the Chief of the Civil Cabinet: 'As long as you, Your Excellency, work closely with Bernhard Bülow and watch over the interests of our beloved sovereign, I sleep soundly. But I tell you frankly that my blood sometimes runs cold when I think of the possibility of a change in this regard!'[43] Shortly afterwards he sent Lucanus another 'heartfelt sigh over the internal situation in Germany'. He was 'not without concern for our beloved sovereign. His position is becoming more and more precarious at home − and more and more splendid abroad. But the latter can balance out the former only *for a time*.'[44] 'I feel how much our *genuine* love for our beloved sovereign binds us together − our *caring* love for Him! . . . I *tremble* at the thought that the Kaiser might lose you! . . . I sometimes wonder whether he realises what we have to bear for Him? I am almost inclined to say no.'[45]

At the end of 1899 Eulenburg called on the Grand Duke of Baden and told him of his serious concern 'about the increasing irritation of public opinion against the Kaiser'. 'He had had frequent opportunities to discuss this state of affairs with the Kaiser and to draw his attention to the dangers for the future', the Grand Duke afterwards reported to the Reich Chancellor. 'Eulenburg went on to tell me that he had had a long talk with Lucanus about this whole business and had urged him to make it increasingly clear to the Kaiser how difficult his position was in relation to public opinion. Lucanus then said that he had done so . . . Count Bülow has also spoken to Eulenburg in the same sense, and has complained very much about the difficulties he faces.'[46] How must these men have felt when they looked back at the endless ministerial and chancellor crises of the past ten years, in which they had consistently taken sides with the crown against the responsible statesmen!

The new century brought no relief, but rather the reverse. Wilhelm took the Boxer Rebellion and the murder of the German envoy in China, as Eulenburg remarked, 'as a *personal* insult', for which he was determined to seek '*revenge*'.[47] He telegraphed to a horrified Bernhard Bülow saying: 'The German envoy must be avenged by my troops. Peking must be razed to the ground.'[48] When he realised that the troops under Waldersee's command would arrive too late to capture Beijing, according to Bülow he was 'so beside himself . . . that he completely lost control' and instructed Eulenburg at Kiel to convey his orders to the Foreign Office to conclude a defensive and offensive alliance with Japan, which Eulenburg only managed with great difficulty – he called it his 'great battle' – to prevent.[49] The Scandinavian cruise of July 1900 which followed this episode was, if possible, even more worrying than that of the previous year. In an attempt to avoid rousing the Kaiser's feelings, Eulenburg begged all his companions on board ship to 'regale H.M. with the most harmless possible stories and to avoid politics', and he himself, 'with the greatest impudence', changed the subject from foreign politics to 'the most banal and trivial matters'. In vain! Already on 15 July Eulenburg had to report to Bülow that there had been 'a violent outbreak' that morning, which 'worries me very much'. He had gone for a walk on deck with the Kaiser and Georg Hülsen and had been telling harmless theatre stories, when the Kaiser suddenly started talking furiously about Berlin society and especially about the Conservatives. 'His violence in conversation was terrifying', Eulenburg commented. 'I must admit that I saw an *abyss of hate and bitterness* within him, which nothing can change . . . H.M. *cannot control himself any more* when he is filled with anger. Yesterday he did not even notice that there were sailors near by, he simply raved on, so that they could hear every word he said. Hülsen was so terrified that he was taken ill . . . I consider our present situation a very dangerous one; I see no way out . . . I feel as though I were sitting on a barrel of gunpowder.' Eulenburg could think of no other alternative 'but to await events and to pray to God that His Majesty will not be obliged to confront any complicated problems, for repeated scenes, like the one I witnessed in Kiel, would surely lead to a nervous crisis, the character of which cannot be foretold . . . These things affect me very much. I had such faith in the Kaiser's ability – and in the good that time would do, but now I am losing faith in both and I see a human being whom I love deeply suffering so much without being able to help.'[50] 'I am sometimes very frightened, and I am seriously worried. I am worried about you too, my dearest Bernhard', he wrote to Bülow. 'How are you going to be able to steer the ship with a Captain who is not well??'[51] 'I am very, very anxious about the future.' It was clear to him, Eulenburg added, that 'His Majesty must not remain a single day without reliable diplomatic advice.'[52] Just one week later Wilhelm made his rabid 'Hun speech' at Bremerhaven.

55. Philipp Eulenburg's last Scandinavian cruise with the Kaiser, July 1903. Eulenburg is on the extreme left of the main group, holding a champagne glass; Wilhelm is in the centre, wearing a white cap and white shoes.

During the last Scandinavian cruise in which he was to take part, that of the summer of 1903,[53] Eulenburg's experiences were so shattering that he had the nightmarish feeling of having put the fate of his countrymen into the hands of a madman. The Kaiser's 'nervousness', he told Bülow, now Reich chancellor, had changed considerably in the past two or three years. 'Although in the past (I am thinking of the war in China) he gave me much cause for concern with his fearful passion, his speeches etc., at least his behaviour was caused by his being "completely obsessed" with *one* idea . . . Today things are different: he is no longer painfully obsessed with any *one* thing which weighs down on him and will not let him rest; he is difficult to handle and complicated in *all* things no matter how trivial. *No one* can make even the most harmless remark about the weather, travelling plans or other completely indifferent things without provoking a violent objection, an insulting response or even an outburst of rage.' 'The Kaiser's *earnestness*' had become 'a *real torment*' to him, Eulenburg wrote, 'when he builds up his houses of cards and violently abuses people and things, constantly contradicting himself. How long can it be before his outbursts of hatred against "the dirty, obstinate, stupid, poor, badly dressed Germans, who should follow the example of Englishmen and Americans", will leak out into the world through naval officers, paymasters, engineers, sailors and messenger boys?' He had talked 'at great length' with the imperial physician, Rudolf Leuthold, about 'our poor dear Master', 'who wanders around as if in a dream world and boosts his ego into an ever greater phantom. I asked him [Leuthold] whether I had been *right* in observing that his nervousness is expressing itself increasingly strongly while his self-control is becoming weaker and weaker? Leuthold shares this view, and his anxiety has increased.' Bülow should therefore be prepared for 'a slow transformation of the mental and emotional condition of our dear Master'. 'Ask God for *strength*', he advised the Reich Chancellor, 'for without His help you will be almost in despair.' He himself, the Kaiser's friend wrote, often felt 'the tears welling up in me, when I hear our dear, kind Master (whom I still thank for *so much*, especially his *loyalty*, in spite of all the suffering he has caused me) – making wild attacks against all kinds of windmills, and see his face quite distorted with anger. Almost every day there are conversations like that, remarks like that . . . There is no question of self-control any more. Sometimes he seems to have *completely* lost all self-discipline.'[54] Frequently, as Eulenburg continued in his report to Bülow in the next few days, the Kaiser would be roused to 'explosions of high spirits' by jokes and funny stories told by his travelling companions on board the *Hohenzollern*, but lighter moments like these could not disguise the fact that the Kaiser was seriously unwell and was not in control of himself. With a 'completely distorted . . . pale, nervous face' and 'gesticulating excitedly', he would speak of war and revenge. 'The poor, poor Kaiser', sighed his closest friend. 'How he destroys everything around him that should be his mainstay and his pride!' All those on board were 'shocked by the fact, which becomes more apparent all the time, that H.M. sees and judges *all* things and *all* men purely from his personal standpoint. Objectivity is lost completely; subjectivity rides on a biting and stamping stallion – contradiction celebrates daily triumphs in his own utterances.' 'Pale, ranting wildly, looking restlessly about him and piling lie on lie', Wilhelm made 'such a terrible impression' on Eulenburg and all those on the Scandinavian cruise that, as Eulenburg exclaimed, 'I still cannot get over it! I could hardly sleep a wink at night. "Not in good health" is perhaps the gentlest way one can put it.' 'I am filled with deep sadness', Eulenburg confessed. 'I can hardly wait for the hour of my release from this royal cage . . . Leuthold is at his wits' end. But he considers all his medical plans more or less impracticable. So *nothing* happens. It is an appalling wait for *some* kind of crisis. And everyone here on board waits with him.'[55]

## NEURASTHENIA, MENTAL ILLNESS, BAD BLOOD – WHAT WAS WRONG WITH WILHELM II?

Philipp Eulenburg's increasingly anguished expressions of alarm from 1899 onwards are striking, but in fact only reflect, if rather more dramatically than usual, what other well-informed observers had been lamenting for some time. Blinded by his love for the Kaiser, it took him much longer to recognise the central problem of the Personal Monarchy, which lay in the character of Wilhelm II. It will not have escaped the reader's notice how regularly the suspicion had arisen since the beginning of his reign that Wilhelm II could not be entirely sound in body and mind, and that such suspicions were expressed in all circles around the Kaiser, whether by his own family, his more distant royal relations, his entourage of courtiers, court society in Berlin, the officer corps, higher civil servants, political parties of all shades of opinion or foreign diplomats and journalists. Anxious comments had been made by relatives and other observers about his outward appearance even in the very early days following his accession. Queen Victoria's cousin Princess Augusta Caroline of Cambridge, the Hereditary Grand Duchess of Mecklenburg-Strelitz, wrote in 1888 after a visit from the young Kaiser: 'I don't think he looks well, very brown-yellow, pulled out yet in some way, puffed.'[56] Similarly when he travelled through Munich a few weeks later it was remarked that he did not look well.[57] A year later Dr Leuthold was expressing anxiety about the detrimental effect on Wilhelm's health of his hectic lifestyle. Although conceding that the Kaiser had got over a bout of influenza without the accompanying nervous symptoms from which he usually suffered, Leuthold ascribed his illness to exhaustion caused by his ceaseless round of shooting

expeditions. There was no denying, he declared, that 'the travelling, the official functions, the shooting [have] gradually become too much for the Kaiser'.
Already in these early days Leuthold urged Eulenburg to persuade Wilhelm
to lead a quieter life.[58] After Bismarck's dismissal concerns of this kind began
to be much more frequently expressed in the imperial entourage. 'The Kaiser
looked very seedy', a senior naval officer recorded after seeing him on a visit to
Wilhelmshaven in the spring of 1890.[59] After the Scandinavian cruise in July
that year Eulenburg reported that the sea voyage had not done the Kaiser any
good. 'His restlessness has increased rather than diminished and he takes too
little sleep.' Leuthold had stated bluntly that 'things could not go on like that',
and Eulenburg too had the feeling that 'H.M. is doing himself harm and simply
must have eight hours' sleep if he wants to keep going any longer.'[60] During
the following year's cruise the Kaiser slipped on a wet deck and fell on his back,
dislocating his right kneecap. After the kneecap had been put back in place a
plaster cast had to be applied, although the knee was swollen and bleeding.[61] For
his mother, of course, this accident was nothing new. 'William has put out his
knee pan several times!', she wrote to the Queen. 'He is very knock kneed and as
a child he had not strong "Knie Bänder" . . . He has *not* his balance as one side is
lighter than the other in consequence of the arm – wh[ich] makes him awkward
on his legs . . . He sprained one leg fencing at Bonn (when I went to look after
him) – *once* dancing & once swimming.'[62] In the winter of 1896–7, when the
Kaiser's nervous irritability gave particular cause for concern, diplomats reported
that he was suffering badly from a carbuncle on the knee and looked 'very care-
worn and thin'.[63] Philipp Eulenburg was shocked by Wilhelm's appearance in
October 1896, after his ear operation and the humiliating encounter with the
Russian imperial family at Darmstadt.[64]

It was not only the Kaiser's physical health that gave rise to anxiety from
early on, but also, and principally, his mental condition. Very much in the spirit
of the times, those about him often explained the monarch's alarming state of
mind in terms such as 'nervous tension' or 'neurasthenia'.[65] When Waldersee
saw Wilhelm at Kiel in 1891 and thought him 'rather worn out', he commented
that it seemed to him 'as others had already claimed – that a certain nervous
depression had set in'.[66] A little later, after meeting the Kaiser and Kaiserin
again he wrote: 'This time I noticed that the Kaiser was not as fresh as usual; he
complained of being overtired, and the Kaiserin said to me twice: "Wilhelm must
have more sleep, he is completely exhausted." But there is in fact no real reason
for the Kaiser to be overtired; I am afraid it is his nerves which are beginning to
give way.'[67] In November 1892 Waldersee again noted in his diary: 'The Kaiser
has a cold and has cried off two shoots; it is said that he is also suffering from a
certain moral depression, as happened last year.'[68]

Gradually the opinion took hold that the Kaiser's restless and peculiar behaviour might be not the cause but the symptom of a serious emotional disorder. Hinzpeter, who had earlier seen the 'salutary humiliation' of his arrogant pupil as the only way of improving his character, had adopted a completely different approach since Wilhelm's accession. It was not repression but constant encouragement that was now required, in order to ward off the danger of a nervous breakdown. In a conversation with Schottmüller in January 1891, in which the latter complained that the Kaiser began many things but finished none, Hinzpeter is reported to have said: '*That does not matter at all; the main thing is that I keep him busy all the time*; if he does not have something new all the time he falls into apathy.' Waldersee, who recorded this remark, continued: 'He [Hinzpeter] then spoke utterly cynically about the Kaiser's ear complaint, saying that it could easily lead to death or mental disorder, so Prince Heinrich ought really to live in Berlin to prepare himself for a possible regency.'[69]

In March 1892 – this was the time of the School Bill crisis, during which Caprivi resigned as Prussian minister-president[70] – when Waldersee heard that the Kaiser had been unwell for several days, he saw this as the beginning of the nervous breakdown which he had for a long time expected to happen. Wilhelm was not actually ill, he said, 'but only very pulled down, fatigued, disgruntled'; he complained of too much work. 'If his nerves were better, I would hope that he would begin to improve now, but as they are notoriously bad I am afraid it will soon get to the point where he loses heart completely.' Wilhelm had come to the throne with the ambitious aim of being recognised as an 'acclaimed ruler, esteemed and feared by the whole world'. 'He himself, who became quite giddy with the apparent successes of the early days, who believes he knows everything better than anyone else, who thinks his opinion on every subject is the right one, now sees that many things are going badly in Germany, that the mood is turning against him. Now he finds himself involved in serious internal conflicts; at the moment it is true that he is still inclined to blame everything on others, and is still as self-confident and arrogant as before in what he says, but I think that this is nothing but bragging; his inner mood is beginning to change.' It was to be feared, Waldersee commented, that the Kaiser's 'so easily overtaxed nerves' might fail him completely. 'What will happen if he begins to waver even more, if he becomes really discouraged, I do not know', he wrote. 'I only know that we shall go down even more.'[71] 'To my very great regret I have to say that he is an unreliable, weak character.'[72] In the summer of 1892 Waldersee went so far as to express the apparently paradoxical hope that a nervous breakdown on the part of the monarch might save the Reich from the ruin that otherwise lay in store for it. Deeply anxious, he wrote of Wilhelm II that 'he may well destroy all his grandfather's work; if he goes on for a few more years as he has done up to now, it will be inevitable. Perhaps our salvation lies in his nerves breaking down so that he will let others take over.'[73] After the chancellor crisis of October 1894, during which the bad state of the Kaiser's nerves was 'often' mentioned, Waldersee commented: 'I said long ago that there was absolutely no doubt he would soon come to the end of his tether.'[74]

When Waldersee went to Berlin in January 1896 for the twenty-fifth anniversary of the founding of the Reich and for the chapter meeting of the Order of the Black Eagle, he recorded after several conversations with the Kaiser that Wilhelm was 'deeply out of sorts in himself and his nerves are again beginning to make themselves felt'. The reason for his irritability, according to the General, was 'the affair of Prince [Friedrich] Leopold, in which he has again been much too hasty', and which had 'very much upset' both the Kaiser and the Kaiserin. In addition to this there were his 'anger at the Köller affair, which he has not yet quite got over, [and] his quarrel with Bronsart at the New Year'; finally, the Transvaal crisis and 'the behaviour of the English' had left him 'deeply disgruntled'.[75] At this time, as we have seen, the signs of an 'unhealthy excitability' in the Kaiser were increasing, and were becoming apparent in an extremely aggressive attitude towards both his own people and foreign powers. Holstein commented that it filled him with alarm to hear how the Kaiser had been speaking recently. 'Everything makes an uncanny, rushed impression', the Privy Councillor wrote. 'The Kaiser's nerves' seemed more tense than ever before.[76] A few weeks later Wilhelm felt compelled to withdraw to his hunting lodge at Hubertusstock because of a nervous attack. Waldersee recorded in his diary on 16 February 1896: 'The Kaiser is very annoyed and his nerves are in a bad way, as I was already aware from what people close to him had told me in January. He has gone to Hubertusstock to recover; it is no doubt quite a good thing that it has become necessary, but sad. How will our sovereign be able to go on, if he already has nervous disorders at the age of 36. He should simply hold back more, and not try to control everything. That is just what he cannot manage and it has already done us much harm. But I scarcely think that he has reached the point of realising that *he alone* is to blame if the cart has got stuck in the mud.'[77]

On 23 October 1896 the wedding of the Hereditary Grand Duke of Oldenburg to Duchess Elisabeth of Mecklenburg took place at Schwerin, an occasion on which Waldersee saw the Kaiser and many old acquaintances from the imperial entourage. 'I found the Kaiser not looking well', he wrote afterwards. 'Years ago I predicted that his nerves would soon let him down; I think that moment has almost come. First of all the condition of his ear has deteriorated again since the Scandinavian cruise, and the reappearance of this complaint has depressed him very much. In addition to that all kinds of annoyances, partly political,

partly domestic, have arisen, and his nervous state has *often* been apparent in a
melancholy mood, lack of energy, emotional outbursts etc. To combat this there
is a constant search for distraction and restlessness, but it is clear that this is not
a good idea and that it is more likely to have the opposite effect. If anything
serious should arise now, e.g. major political disappointments, which can very
easily happen, there will be a breakdown! And then what? We could be in a
really serious situation with this worn-out old Chancellor, these ministers, most
of whom are pathetic, the lamentable Cabinet chiefs and finally the effeminate
and distinctly second-rate Prince Heinrich, who is the only stand-in available!'[78]
Similar sentiments were expressed a few days later by Finance Minister Johannes
von Miquel, of whom Waldersee wrote: 'For the first time I found him in an
anxious mood about the Kaiser, both as to his influence on the machinery of
state and as to his health.'[79] 'I should be less worried if his nerves were quite
healthy', the General wrote. 'Then one could say that experience would have a
purging effect on him. But I am convinced that he is not capable of enduring
serious setbacks; his nerves would give way and he would collapse, which would
be the most terrible thing for us.'[80]

Naturally it seemed no more satisfactory to his contemporaries than it does to
us to explain Wilhelm II's unstable state of health merely in terms of his 'nerves'.
Many went further and expressed the suspicion that he was 'mentally ill' or would
become so in time. The uncomfortable feeling that Wilhelm II was in some way
not normal, a feeling which every speech, telegram, marginal note or other conspicuously odd action helped to nurture, spread throughout Europe with alarming speed after his accession. Already in 1890 highly placed people who had been
in his grandfather's entourage were speaking of the young Wilhelm's 'hereditary taint'.[81] Immediately following Bismarck's dismissal Holstein warned that
the Kaiser was considered to be 'frankly speaking not quite right in the head',
and predicted that 'this spectre of mental illness will haunt the sovereign all his
life'.[82] Hinzpeter and others soon began to speak of 'Caesaromania', a diagnosis
that was on everyone's lips after the publication of Ludwig Quidde's *Caligula*
pamphlet.[83] Wilhelm's own sister Sophie, the Crown Princess of Greece, as we
have seen, expressed herself 'in the most contemptuous and hostile way' about
him at St Petersburg and added that 'the whole family thought he was mad'. In
Berlin the Empress Frederick and her daughters were suspected of spreading
such rumours.[84] Grand Duke Sergei of Russia, who was married to Princess Ella
of Hesse-Darmstadt, stated bluntly that he thought the Kaiser was 'mentally
ill',[85] while at the same time the French Foreign Ministry came to the conclusion that Wilhelm was 'emotionally disturbed' and 'temporarily of unsound
mind'.[86]

Early in 1891 Waldersee felt compelled to register the 'extremely sad but very
significant fact' that 'serious, patriotically minded men are really considering

the idea that the Kaiser is very gradually succumbing to a mental disorder. This would certainly be the greatest misfortune that could befall the Fatherland, especially if the development were slow. May we be spared this by God's grace!'[87] In December that year the General wrote again in his diary: 'It is said that the question is being openly and widely discussed, especially among doctors, of whether a mental illness is slowly developing, perhaps in connection with the ear complaint. This would be the most terrible thing that could happen, first for the Kaiser himself . . . but then for the Fatherland. What misfortunes may occur until then and what else may arise from it is completely unforeseeable.'[88]

After the dismissal of Caprivi and Botho Eulenburg, which was decided upon at the Eulenburg estate of Liebenberg, such fears intensified. The chargé d'affaires at the British embassy, Martin Gosselin, reported in November 1895, shortly before the Köller crisis came to a head, that there were 'curious rumours going about Berlin as to the Emperor's health. Count Phi[lip]p Eulenburg . . . is known to have a wonderful influence over His Majesty; & not infrequently this is attributed . . . to the mesmeric power which it is asserted His Excellency is able to exert over his Sovereign.' Gosselin had also heard that the Kaiser was suffering from hallucinations, which found their expression in such things as the famous 'yellow peril' picture. The diplomat continued: 'If there should be any truth in these rumours, it would account for much that is otherwise inexplicable: it becomes, indeed, a serious matter if a Sovereign who possesses a dominant voice in the foreign policy of the Empire is subject to hallucinations & influences which must in the long run warp his judgement, & render Him liable at any moment to sudden changes of opinion which no one can anticipate or provide against.'[89]

In Germany comparisons were frequently made between Wilhelm II's 'glow-worm character' and the mentally deranged Kings Friedrich Wilhelm IV of Prussia and Ludwig II of Bavaria.[90] Prussian War Minister General Bronsart von Schellendorf commented after his alarming clash with the Kaiser in January 1896, as we have seen, 'that H.M. did not seem quite normal' and that it was very worrying for the future.[91] After the Brandenburg speech of February 1897, in which he had described Bismarck and Moltke as pygmies and lackeys of his sainted grandfather, and the historical fancy-dress party for the hundredth birthday of Wilhelm I on 22 March, the rumours that Wilhelm II was mentally deranged became common currency. The East Elbian leaders of the German Conservative Party declared that they considered the Kaiser 'not quite normal'; the King of Saxony commented that he was obviously 'unstable', and his uncle, Grand Duke Friedrich of Baden, spoke 'in a very worrying way about the psychological side of the matter, about the loss of touch with reality'.[92] Count Monts reported with horror from Munich that in South Germany the Kaiser was considered 'clearly no longer a responsible person'.[93] The resentment against him among patriotic people was deeper than ever before, and people were saying secretly that 'H.M. is insane', he wrote.[94] 'What is the point of all this work and effort. Nobody believes one when one describes the Kaiser as he was, for example on his visit here, so simple, understanding, clear, moderate and quiet. – It is as if from time to time our master were seized by an evil spirit, benighting his mind and compelling him to make speeches which deeply insult the nation.'[95] It was out of the question, Monts continued, 'that the disorder could be anything but psychological'; he could see Wilhelm II 'going the same way . . . as King Friedrich Wilhelm IV, who like H.M. had become excited and intoxicated by his own words, after which a state of despondency usually followed, which made it necessary for him to shut himself away . . . for days on end'.[96] Bismarck told a Bavarian writer that he had recognised 'the Kaiser's abnormal mental condition' as early as 1888, and had resisted his dismissal as chancellor only because he had been afraid of a national catastrophe.[97] After meeting Philipp Eulenburg in April 1897 Bülow noted that Eulenburg had spoken of the 'inclination' which existed even in the Kaiser's family 'to put H.M. into care', and had mentioned the Empress Frederick and Prince Heinrich. The view 'that H.M. is mentally ill' was being spread both from the Bismarckian side and from the Foreign Office. Eulenburg had discussed this danger with Leuthold, who (according to hasty notes made by Bülow) had expressed the opinion 'that H.M. did not have any maniacal characteristics; on the contrary, it was more that he was too fragmented in his ideas' and 'changeable'; in the view of the Kaiser's physician the 'only danger was that H.M. would put too much strain on his nerves [and] then break down'.[98] During the Scandinavian cruise in the summer of 1900 Leuthold still believed that the Kaiser's alarming outbursts of fury could be attributed to 'a certain weakness of the nervous system', but 'he emphatically denies any possibility of mental disorder'.[99] On the basis of such assurances Bülow felt able to calm the Reich Chancellor's fears when, upon Bülow's taking office as foreign secretary in October 1897, Prince Hohenlohe asked him if he considered Wilhelm II to be 'mentally quite normal'.[100] When he took Hohenlohe's place three years later, however, Bülow had to warn the Kaiser through Eulenburg that there was a danger that the next incautious move on the part of the Kaiser might lead to a coalition between the German federal princes and the Reichstag with the object of forcing him to abdicate.[101]

Members of Wilhelm's own family felt that the 'lackey' and 'Hun' speeches, along with numerous other instances of aggressive and peculiar behaviour, confirmed their earlier forebodings about him.[102] His eldest sister Charlotte spoke in March 1897 of her '*serious* fears', and later repeatedly expressed the opinion that her brother really ought to be in Professor Schweninger's clinic, where she herself was receiving treatment for her painful hereditary illness.[103] In 1908 she decided that 'as a true Prussian' she should set about having Wilhelm placed under a kind of collective regency of all the federal princes. She wrote to her doctor: 'I want to persuade the German princes to go to the Kaiser in a body . . . and to offer him their help, in the interest of the Reich and in the name of their peoples, under clearly stated conditions. I think it is imperative that they should work together and keep together, and it is the only thing which could still make an impression. [Prince] Ludwig [of Bavaria] would have to be the spokesman, in the name of his father and of the grand dukes, [and of] Saxony and Württemberg.'[104] The lamentations of Wilhelm's mother, his other sisters and his own wife quoted in the chapter on the imperial family show that they were no less anxious and despondent.[105] In later years even Wilhelm II's eldest son admitted to doubts about his father's mental state. 'I know my father very well . . . It is claimed that genius and madness are very close to each other. There have been moments when, seeing the strange expression in his eyes, I have doubted his sanity.'[106]

Naturally enough the question of the mental condition of the eccentric German Kaiser was the subject of lively and often wildly speculative discussion in the foreign press. After the Brandenburg speech of February 1897 Waldersee commented that the British and American newspapers were spreading the story 'with the greatest impudence' that the Kaiser was 'of unsound mind'.[107] When Wilhelm hurt his eye during the Scandinavian cruise that summer, and at the same time the 26-year-old son of General von Hahnke, who was travelling with the Kaiser's party, was killed in an accident during a bicycling expedition on shore, an article appeared in the Canadian press – and was widely reprinted elsewhere – linking these two accidents, with appalling insinuations against the Kaiser. The young Gustav von Hahnke, the writer of the article deduced, had hit the Kaiser in the face after being insulted by him, and had been made to pay for it with his life.[108] The *New York Times* expressed the opinion at about this time that the German monarch, already a 'surprising' man, would 'sooner or later "go queer" altogether'.[109] Newspaper articles and pamphlets with titles such as 'Is Kaiser Wilhelm of Normal Mind?'[110] frequently appeared. After the outbreak of war in 1914 such publications became a veritable flood.

Conjectures of this kind by irresponsible journalists were by no means insignificant in an age of unrestricted media attention, but naturally the opinions of the crowned heads and the leading statesmen of Europe had a more direct effect on relations between the great powers in the period leading up to the First World War. And these opinions, as this biography has shown, were scarcely more favourable to Wilhelm II. Russian General A. A. Mossolov, who was for many years the head of the Court Chancellery under Nicholas II, tellingly records in his memoirs that both the imperial couple and their entourage considered the Kaiser, whom they found importunate and very often quite insufferable, 'raving mad'.[111] As we have seen in many instances above, Wilhelm's personality, which was regarded as disturbed, had a direct effect on British foreign policy.[112] As early as the autumn of 1888 Lord Salisbury had remarked, à propos of the Vienna incident, that he thought 'the Emperor William must be a little off his head'.[113] The British Prime Minister and Foreign Secretary not only developed a strong personal antipathy towards the Kaiser but also became convinced that Wilhelm could be neither trusted nor believed.[114] He frequently wondered whether the Kaiser was perhaps 'not "all there"'; he considered him a danger to peace and 'the most dangerous enemy we had in Europe', because he was 'mad enough for anything'.[115] In December 1895, after reading Martin Gosselin's report on the Kaiser's apparent hallucinations and the hypnotic influence of Philipp Eulenburg over him, Salisbury warned the new British ambassador in Berlin, Sir Frank Lascelles, of the danger that Wilhelm might in time go 'completely off his head'.[116] It did not take long for the new ambassador to report that the German Emperor's behaviour appeared to 'verge on insanity'.[117] Upon what were these forebodings based?

Apart from the 'neurasthenia' and 'mental disorder' to which Kaiser Wilhelm II's strangeness was attributed, contemporary observers also ascribed it to a hereditary or organic condition. Besides his ear complaint, which at a very early stage had given rise to fears of an infection penetrating the wall of the skull, with resultant brain damage,[118] a second theory as to the possible cause of his odd behaviour was in circulation at the Hohenzollern court, namely that it was due to his Coburg or Guelphic 'blood'. In October 1890 Waldersee recorded that Adjutant-General Adolf von Wittich had expressed 'exactly the same opinion as I have about the Kaiser, his character and his decline, and blamed everything on the Coburg blood. I think he has hit the nail on the head.'[119] Again in early 1892 he wrote: 'Oh, this infamous Coburg blood, mixed with the Guelphic, which makes itself so sadly felt in reckless behaviour!'[120] Two years later Waldersee was even more convinced that the 'Coburg blood' was responsible for the bizarre personality of the Kaiser, whom he compared with his great-uncle, Duke Ernst II of Saxe-Coburg and Gotha. He commented: 'For me, having had the advantage of knowing Duke Ernst of Coburg and having lived through both his rise and his decline, the similarity of the two characters becomes increasingly apparent; but at the same time I cannot but recognise that at heart the Kaiser is much nobler, and that is the Hohenzollern in him. At the moment, however, the Coburg blood is causing very dangerous impulses to emerge.'[121] When Quidde's *Caligula* pamphlet with its unmistakable portrayal of Wilhelm II's megalomaniac, power-loving personality appeared shortly afterwards, Waldersee recalled similar comments which members of the imperial entourage had made in the past. 'On looking through it I was reminded', he wrote, 'that 4 years ago General

Wittich referred to tendencies of Caesaromania, and that he also put forward the assertion that the Kaiser visibly derives an agreeable nervous stimulus from the mention of massive losses when he makes speeches about military history. Nevertheless, in spite of the numerous really striking analogies, I should like to think that the way in which our Kaiser is developing need not lead to a sad end. It is true that I very rarely see him now, but when I do I observe him very closely, and I cannot say that I can detect any real disorder. If he did have any really alarming tendencies they would have developed much more in the past 6 years. What has worried me for a long time is the evident predominance of the Guelphic–Coburg blood, which is certainly disturbing enough in itself.'[122]

The news that the Kaiser had to have an operation to remove a small cyst on his cheek on 1 June 1894 led to further pessimistic forecasts. Waldersee noted anxiously in his diary: 'A rumour had been going round for 3 months that he had a swelling under one ear, and all sorts of other rumours were immediately linked with this. According to what I recently heard from people who had seen the Kaiser it is true that a clearly visible swelling had appeared. It is perhaps not surprising that this gives rise to serious thoughts. What has God in store for us?'[123] At the height of the power struggle between the Kaiser and the Chancellor in the summer of 1896, when Trautmann had to carry out a radical operation on the Kaiser's right ear at Wilhelmshöhe,[124] Friedrich von Holstein recalled the comments of Sir Felix Semon, the German-born throat specialist who practised at the British court and was also close to Bismarck. Four or five years earlier Semon had claimed, according to Holstein, that 'the restlessness of the present Kaiser [was] the precisely definable first stage of a psychiatric condition, but one which in the beginning should be considered and treated from the physiological rather than from the psychological standpoint'.[125] What half-physiological, half-psychiatric illness can Semon have meant by this?

A document quoted in the first volume of this biography is of particular relevance in this connection. It refers to a conversation which Sir Schomberg McDonnell, private secretary to the Prime Minister Lord Salisbury at the time, had with Surgeon-General John Erichsen in March 1888, just after the death of Kaiser Wilhelm I and the accession of the fatally ill Kaiser Friedrich III. McDonnell immediately reported the conversation verbally to Salisbury. As he later recalled, Erichsen came to see him to bring some extremely important and alarming news for the Prime Minister. He told McDonnell that 'when Prince William of Prussia was 14 or 16 . . . his condition gave rise to some anxiety', and that German doctors had sent him detailed notes on the case at the time. These had convinced him that Wilhelm 'was not, and never would be, a normal man'; that 'he would always be subject to sudden accesses of anger; and that when angry he would be quite incapable of forming a reasonable or temperate judgement on the subject under consideration'; that 'while it was not probable that he would actually become insane, some of his actions would probably be those of a man not wholly sane'. From this diagnosis Erichsen drew the worrying conclusion that the future Kaiser Wilhelm II could 'possibly be a danger for Europe' if he came to the throne. When McDonnell passed on Erichsen's comments to Salisbury, the Prime Minister 'was of course immensely interested', the former private secretary recounted, adding that on several occasions in later years 'when the Emperor committed some indiscretion he used to say privately the single word "Erichsen"'.[126]

The information brought by Erichsen explains the importance which Lord Salisbury accorded to Gosselin's report on the 'hallucinations' of the Kaiser and the apparently hypnotic effect of Eulenburg upon him, and also his warning to Lascelles in December 1895 that Wilhelm might eventually become 'completely mad'. But what was the illness which Erichsen believed he had diagnosed in the young Wilhelm on the basis of the medical notes sent him by his German colleagues? In the first volume of this biography attention was drawn to the fact that the British royal family suffered from two hereditary diseases: haemophilia, which manifested itself for the first time in some of Queen Victoria's children and was passed by them to the ruling families of Hesse-Darmstadt, Prussia (Prince Heinrich's sons), Russia (Tsarevich Alexei) and Spain,[127] and porphyria, a hereditary metabolic disorder which causes attacks of mental confusion and painful physical symptoms. The best-known case of porphyria is that of King George III, Queen Victoria's grandfather and great-great-grandfather of Wilhelm II. Unlike haemophilia, which is sex-specifically transmitted, porphyria is passed on by a dominant gene: about half the children of an affected parent will inherit the mutation, whether they are male or female. Recent DNA research has shown beyond doubt, as has already been mentioned, that Kaiser Wilhelm II's eldest sister Charlotte, the Hereditary Princess of Saxe-Meiningen, and her daughter Feodora, Princess Reuss of the younger line, suffered from porphyria variegata.[128] Could it be that Charlotte's 'big brother' also inherited this mutation from his mother?

Unlike in his sister's case, there seems to be virtually no evidence that Wilhelm II suffered from the physical symptoms of the illness – unbearable abdominal pain and headaches, sleeplessness, vomiting, colic, feverish sweating, constipation, rapid heart beat, paralysis in the arms and legs, blister-like skin rashes and dark red urine. On the other hand the attacks of mental and emotional disorder so frequently complained of would accord with such a hypothesis. Perhaps one day DNA research will bring the certainty, one way or the other, which presently eludes the historian. But the possibility that a documentary-based scholarly approach might shed light even on this complex medical question should not be underestimated. On 31 May 1918, when all Europe lay in ruins and the worst fears of the Empress Frederick, the Bismarcks, Holstein, Bronsart and in the end even Eulenburg were beginning to come true, Wilhelm II's youngest son was examined by the distinguished psychiatrist Professor Robert Gaupp. Prince Joachim, Gaupp concluded, was incurably ill, both mentally and physically. Two years later, in a state of frenzy, he was to take his own life. The Kaiser's son, the psychiatrist wrote, spoke too fast; he had sudden facial tics; he was extremely easily emotionally and sexually aroused; he was inclined to 'violent, uncontrollably exploding outbursts of anger in which all self-control [was] lost'; his thinking, in spite of a quick understanding, was superficial; his behaviour was 'determined by momentary impulses'; his 'highly developed ego' meant that he felt 'unjustly injured' by any resistance he met to the pursuit of his passionate wishes, and reacted 'with outbursts of rage'. Also symptomatic of Joachim's disorder was his inability to keep to decisions he had taken, and 'a certain weakness in giving way to the temptations of the outside world and to impulsive urges and moods'. In addition, he had 'vaso-motor disorders' and 'a rapid fluctuation in the blood supply to the face'. The overall condition of 'physical and psychological irregularity', Gaupp concluded in his report, 'points to an *innate abnormal tendency*'.[129] Had both father and son, even if not to the same degree, and of course over and above all their other psychological and physical problems, inherited the royal hereditary malady of porphyria from their Guelph ancestors? In the present state of knowledge this possibility, which would explain much, cannot be excluded. At the British court, at any rate, there was support for this opinion. In November 1908 Lord Esher, a confidant of King Edward VII, wrote in his diary of Kaiser Wilhelm II: 'I am sure that the taint of George III is in his blood.'[130]

# Notes

PREFACE TO THE ENGLISH EDITION

1 See the contributions in Annika Mombauer and Wilhelm Deist, eds., *The Kaiser. New Research on Wilhelm II's Role in Imperial Germany*, Cambridge 2003.

2 Christian Baechler, *Guillaume II le Kaiser*, Paris 2003. Other recent studies include Jost Rebentisch, *Die vielen Gesichter des Kaisers. Wilhelm II. in der deutschen und britischen Karikatur (1888–1918)*, Berlin 2000; Lothar Reinermann, *Der Kaiser in England. Wilhelm II. und sein Bild in der britischen Öffentlichkeit*, Paderborn, Munich, Vienna, Zürich 2001; Stefan Samerski, ed., *Wilhelm II. und die Religion. Facetten einer Persönlichkeit und ihres Umfelds*, Berlin 2001; Thomas Hartmut Benner, *Die Strahlen der Krone. Die religiöse Dimension des Kaisertums unter Wilhelm II. vor dem Hintergrund der Orientreise 1898*, Marburg 2001; Douglas Mark Klahr, 'The Kaiser Builds in Berlin. Expressing National and Dynastic Identity in the Early Building Projects of Wilhelm II', dissertation, Providence, RI 2002; Holger Afflerbach, ed., *Wilhelm II. als Oberster Kriegsherr im Ersten Weltkrieg. Quellen aus der militärischen Umgebung des Kaisers 1914–1918*, Munich 2004.

3 Quoted in John C. G. Röhl, 'The Kaiser's Germany as Seen from Beachy Head on a Clear Day. Autobiographical Reminiscences of an Anglo-German Historian', in Stefan Berger, Peter Lambert and Peter Schumann, eds., *Historikerdialoge. Geschichte, Mythos und Gedächtnis im deutsch-britischen kulturellen Austausch 1750–2000*, Göttingen 2003, p. 128.

4 Max Weber to Friedrich Naumann, 14 December 1906, quoted in Wolfgang J. Mommsen, *War der Kaiser an allem schuld? Wilhelm II. und die preußisch-deutschen Machteliten*, Munich 2002, p. 7.


PREFACE TO THE GERMAN EDITION

1 John C. G. Röhl, *Young Wilhelm. The Kaiser's Early Life 1859–1888*, translated from the German by Jeremy Gaines and Rebecca Wallach, Cambridge 1998.

2 John C. G. Röhl, *Germany without Bismarck. The Crisis of Government in the Second Reich, 1890–1900*, London 1967.

3 John C. G. Röhl, ed., *Philipp Eulenburgs politische Korrespondenz*, 3 vols., Boppard-am-Rhein 1976–83.

4 See Hans-Ulrich Wehler, *Deutsche Gesellschaftsgeschichte*, vol. III, *Von der 'Deutschen Doppelrevolution' bis zum Beginn des Ersten Weltkrieges, 1849–1914*, Munich 1995, pp. 1016–20.

5  See for example Nicolaus Sombart, *Wilhelm II. Sündenbock und Herr der Mitte*, Berlin 1996, and Giles MacDonogh, *The Last Kaiser. William the Impetuous*, London 2000.

6  Geoff Eley, 'The View from the Throne: The Personal Rule of Kaiser Wilhelm II', *Historical Journal*, 28, 2 (1985), pp. 469–85.

7  See e.g. Norman Rich, *Friedrich von Holstein. Politics and Diplomacy in the Era of Bismarck and Wilhelm II*, 2 vols., Cambridge 1965; Isabel V. Hull, *The Entourage of Kaiser Wilhelm II, 1888–1918*, Cambridge 1982; Hull, 'Persönliches Regiment', in John C. G. Röhl, ed., *Der Ort Kaiser Wilhelms II. in der deutschen Geschichte*, Munich 1991; Paul Kennedy, 'The Kaiser and German Weltpolitik. Reflexions on Wilhelm II's Place in the Making of German Foreign Policy', in John C. G. Röhl and Nicolaus Sombart, eds., *Kaiser Wilhelm II – New Interpretations*, Cambridge 1982; Katharine A. Lerman, *The Chancellor as Courtier. Bernhard von Bülow and the Governance of Germany 1900–1909*, Cambridge 1990; Thomas A. Kohut, *Wilhelm II and the Germans. A Study in Leadership*, Oxford, New York 1991; Lamar Cecil, *Wilhelm II*, 2 vols., Chapel Hill, London 1989–96; Christopher Clark, *Kaiser Wilhelm II*, London 2000; Roderick R. McLean, *Royalty and Diplomacy in Europe, 1890–1914*, Cambridge 2001; Holger Afflerbach, 'Wilhelm II as Supreme Warlord in the First World War', *War in History*, 5 (1998), pp. 427–49.

8  But see Thomas Nipperdey, *Deutsche Geschichte 1866–1918*, 2 vols., Munich 1990–2, vol. II, *Machtstaat vor der Demokratie*, pp. 475–85.

9  Heinrich Otto Meisner, *Denkwürdigkeiten des General-Feldmarschalls Alfred Grafen von Waldersee*, 3 vols., Stuttgart, Berlin 1922–3.

1   THE ACCESSION

1  Kaiser Wilhelm II, Armee-Befehl, 15 June 1888, Geheimes Staatsarchiv (GStA) Berlin, Rep. 92 Scholz Papers, No. 11.

2  Kaiser Wilhelm II, An die Marine!, proclamation of 15 June 1888, ibid.

3  Admiral Gustav Freiherr von Senden-Bibran, Aufzeichnungen über das Jahr 1888, Bundesarchiv-Militärarchiv (BA-MA) Freiburg, Senden-Bibran Papers N160/11, p. 21.

4  Kaiser Wilhelm II, An Mein Volk!, proclamation of 18 June 1888, GStA Berlin, Rep. 92, Scholz Papers, No. 11.

5  Széchényi to Kálnoky, 19 June 1888, Haus-, Hof- und Staatsarchiv (HHStA) Vienna, PA III 134. Cf. *Truth*, 23, 599, 21 June 1888, p. 1065. Reactions to Wilhelm's proclamations are collected together in Politisches Archiv des Auswärtigen Amtes (PA AA), R 3446.

6  Helmuth von Moltke to Eliza von Moltke, 17 and 19 June 1888, Eliza von Moltke, ed., *Generaloberst Helmuth von Moltke. Erinnerungen, Briefe, Dokumente 1877–1916. Ein Bild vom Kriegsausbruch, erster Kriegsführung und Persönlichkeit des ersten militärischen Führers des Krieges*, Stuttgart 1922, pp. 141–2.

7  See Crown Prince Wilhelm to Waldersee, 14 June 1888, GStA Berlin, Waldersee Papers, B I No. 42.

8  Count Alfred von Waldersee, diary entry for 19 June 1888, ibid.; printed in Heinrich Otto Meisner, ed., *Denkwürdigkeiten des General-Feldmarschalls Alfred Grafen von Waldersee*, 3 vols., Stuttgart, Berlin 1922–3, I, p. 405 (cited below as Meisner).

9  Rudolf Vierhaus, ed., *Das Tagebuch der Baronin Spitzemberg. Aufzeichnungen aus der Hofge-sellschaft des Hohenzollernreiches*, Göttingen 1960, diary entry for 28 June 1888, p. 253.

10  Spitzemberg, diary entry for 28 June 1888, ibid., p. 252.

11  Széchényi to Kálnoky, 24 June 1888, HHStA Vienna, PA III 134.

12  Ibid.; Spitzemberg, diary entry for 28 June 1888, *Tagebuch*, p. 252; Prince Wilhelm of Württemberg to Prince Adolphus von Teck, 2 July 1888, Royal Archives (RA) Geo V. CC50/176. On the situation at the Stuttgart court, see Philipp Eulenburg to Kaiser Wilhelm II,

5 July 1888, printed in John C. G. Röhl, ed., *Philipp Eulenburgs politische Korrespondenz*, 3 vols., Boppard am Rhein 1976–83, I, No. 185.

13  Széchényi to Kálnoky, 24 June 1888, HHStA Vienna, PA III 134.

14  Helmuth von Moltke to Eliza von Moltke, 25–7 June 1888, Moltke, *Erinnerungen, Briefe, Dokumente*, pp. 142–7.

15  See e.g. *The Standard*, 26 June 1888.

16  Kaiser Wilhelm II to Kögel, 22 June 1888, GStA Berlin, Kögel Papers No. 5.

17  Helmuth von Moltke to Eliza von Moltke, 26 June 1888, Moltke, *Erinnerungen, Briefe, Dokumente*, pp 143ff.

18  Ibid.

19  Széchényi to Kálnoky, 24 June 1888, HHStA Vienna, PA III 134; Kaiser Wilhelm II, Thronrede bei der Eröffnung des Deutschen Reichstages, 25 June 1888, *Centralblatt Deutschlands*, 25 June 1888.

20  Helmuth von Moltke to Eliza von Moltke, 26 June 1888, Moltke, *Erinnerungen, Briefe, Dokumente*, pp. 143ff.

21  Die Thronrede Kaiser Wilhelms II., *Centralblatt Deutschlands*, 25 June 1888. The speech from the throne is printed in Johannes Penzler, ed., *Die Reden Kaiser Wilhelms II. in den Jahren 1888–1895*, Leipzig (n.d.), pp. 11ff.

22  *The Standard*, 26 June 1888.

23  Ibid., 26 and 27 June 1888.

24  Kaiser Wilhelm II to Kaiserin Augusta, 11 July 1888, GStA Berlin, BPHA Rep. 53J Lit. P No. 14a.

25  Spitzemberg, diary entry for 28 June 1888, *Tagebuch*, pp. 252–3.

26  Empress Frederick to Queen Victoria, 29 June 1888, RA Z42/5, printed in Sir Frederick Ponsonby, ed., *Letters of the Empress Frederick*, London 1928, pp. 322–3.

27  Empress Frederick, diary entry for 27 June 1888, GStA Berlin BPH Rep. 52 No. 3.

28  Kaiser Wilhelm II, Thronrede bei Eröffnung des Landtages, 27 June 1888, Penzler, *Reden Kaiser Wilhelms II. in den Jahren 1888–1895*, pp. 15ff.

29  Spitzemberg, diary entry for 28 June 1888, *Tagebuch*, pp. 252–3.

30  Herbert Bismarck's notes, 5 October 1888, in J. Lepsius, A. Mendelssohn-Bartholdy and F. Thimme, eds., *Die Große Politik der europäischen Kabinette 1871–1914*, 40 vols., Berlin 1922–7, VI, No. 1352; Prince Bismarck to Herbert Bismarck, 5 October 1888, cited ibid., p. 346, footnote.

31  Philipp Eulenburg to Kaiser Wilhelm II, 15 October 1888, *Eulenburgs Korrespondenz*, I, No. 199. See Eulenburg to his mother, 4 October 1888, ibid., No. 197.

32  Empress Frederick, diary entry for 25 December 1888, GStA Berlin, BPH Rep. 52 No. 3.

33  Waldersee, diary entry for 14 October 1888, GStA Berlin, Waldersee Papers; cf. Meisner, II, p. 7.

34  Douglas, speech of 4 October 1888, printed in *Norddeutsche Allgemeine Zeitung*, No. 474, 7 October 1888.

35  See the fully documented account of Wilhelm's education in Kassel and Bonn in John C. G. Röhl, *Young Wilhelm. The Kaiser's Early Life, 1859–1888*, Cambridge 1998, pp. 201–28 and 274–305.

36  Douglas, speech of 4 October 1888, *Norddeutsche Allgemeine Zeitung*, No. 474, 7 October 1888.

37  Cited in F. Hellwig, *Carl Freiherr von Stumm-Halberg*, Heidelberg, Saarbrücken 1936, p. 516.

38  Cf. Nicolaus Sombart, '"Ich sage, untergehen." Zum zweiten Band von Philipp Eulenburgs politischer Korrespondenz', *Merkur*, 385 (June 1980), pp. 542–54.

39  Eulenburg to Count Kuno von Moltke, 15 June 1895, *Eulenburgs Korrespondenz*, III, No. 1112.

40 Eissenstein to Kálnoky, 29 October 1888, HHStA Vienna, PA III 134.

41 Empress Frederick to Queen Victoria, 9 April 1889, RA Z44/26.

42 Waldersee, diary entry for 13 November 1889, GStA Berlin, Waldersee Papers; cf. Meisner, II, pp. 76–7.

43 Wedell to Kaiser Wilhelm II, 19 November 1890, cited in John C. G. Röhl, *The Kaiser and His Court. Wilhelm II and the Government of Germany*, Cambridge 3rd edn 1996, pp. 86 and 237.

44 Waldersee, diary entry for 2 December 1888, GStA Berlin, Waldersee Papers; omitted from Meisner, II, pp. 24–5.

45 Waldersee, diary entry for 2 December 1888, GStA Berlin, Waldersee Papers; cf. Meisner, II, pp. 24–5.

46 Waldersee, diary entry for 12 December 1888, GStA Berlin, Waldersee Papers; omitted from Meisner, II, pp. 25–6.

47 *Stenographische Berichte des Preußischen Abgeordnetenhauses*, 13th session, 9 and 12 February 1889, pp. 319ff., 351–2.

48 Waldersee, diary entry for 2 December 1888, GStA Berlin, Waldersee Papers; Meisner, II, pp. 24–5.

49 See Peter Domann, *Sozialdemokratie und Kaisertum unter Wilhelm II. Die Auseinandersetzung der Partei mit dem monarchischen System, seinen gesellschafts- und verfassungspolitischen Voraussetzungen*, Wiesbaden 1974; Marina Cataruzza, 'Das Kaiserbild in der Arbeiterschaft am Beispiel der Werftarbeiter in Hamburg und Stettin', in John C. G. Röhl, ed., *Der Ort Kaiser Wilhelms II. in der deutschen Geschichte*, Munich 1991, pp. 131–44.

50 See the article in favour of an imperial civil list in *Der Schwäbische Merkur*, 7 February 1889, PA AA, Preußen 1 No. 1d, Bd 1 secr., together with Bismarck's sceptical marginal comment.

51 Note of 26 January 1889, GStA Berlin, 2.2.1. No. 3085. See Waldersee, diary entry for 13 November 1889, GStA Berlin, Waldersee Papers; cf. Meisner, II, pp. 76–7.

52 Lerchenfeld to Berchem, 16 August 1888, PA AA, R 3474.

53 Rantzau to Berchem, 18 August 1888, PA AA, R 3474.

54 Eissenstein to Kálnoky, 3 November 1888, HHStA Vienna, PA III 134.

55 See Röhl, *Kaiser and His Court*, pp. 73–4.

56 The loyal address of the Catholic archbishops and bishops of Prussia of 29 August 1888 together with Kaiser Wilhelm II's reply is to be found in PA AA, R 3448.

57 It is a measure of the worldwide significance attached to the accession of Wilhelm II that the imperial house of Japan requested an account of the educational principles which Hinzpeter had used in preparing him for the throne: Count Robert von Zedlitz-Trützschler to Kaiser Wilhelm II, 17 October 1891, Lucanus to Zedlitz, 19 October 1891, Bosse to Kaiser Wilhelm II, 13 September 1892, Prince T. Arisugawa of Japan to Kaiser Wilhelm II, 11 October 1892, GStA Berlin, 2.2.1. No. 3085.

58 See the article 'Kaiser Wilhelm II. und die Süddeutschen', *Der Schwäbische Merkur*, 5 September 1888, PA AA, R 3447.

59 Ibid.

60 Dr Paul Kayser, memorandum of 7 September 1889, PA AA, R 3448.

61 *Badische Presse*, 4 October 1889, PA AA, R 3448.

62 Edouard Simon, *L'Empereur Guillaume II et la première année de son règne*, Paris 1889. See Edouard Simon to Kaiser Wilhelm II, 27 July 1889, Lucanus to Bismarck, 27 August 1889, Berchem to Bismarck, 31 August 1889, PA AA, R 3448.

63 Ernest Lavisse, 'L'Empereur d'Allemagne', *Figaro*, 21 May 1890, PA AA, R 3448.

64 *Perseveranza*, 27 May 1890, PA AA, R 3448.

65 Poultney Bigelow, translation of an article in *Kurjer Codzienny*, 11 May 1890, PA AA, Nordamerika 6 No. 4.

66 Harold Frederic, *The Young Kaiser. William II of Germany. A Study in Character Development on a Throne*, London 1891. See Empress Frederick to Queen Victoria, 10 July 1891, RA Z50/57.

67 Sir Edward Malet to Lord Salisbury, 14 June 1888, RA I56/86.

68 Empress Frederick to Queen Victoria, 15 April 1889, RA Z44/30. See also Lord Salisbury to Queen Victoria, 9 March 1889, RA A67/51. See below, p. 91.

69 Empress Frederick to Queen Victoria, 27 April 1889, RA Z44/33.

70 Empress Frederick to Queen Victoria, 30 October 1889, RA Z46/31.

71 Széchényi to Kálnoky, 4 July 1888, HHStA Vienna, PA III 134.

72 Spitzemberg, diary entry for 19 August 1888, *Tagebuch*, pp. 253–4.

73 Waldersee, diary entry for 7 July 1888, GStA Berlin, Waldersee Papers; Meisner, I, pp. 411–12.

74 Waldersee, diary entry for 26 August 1888, GStA Berlin, Waldersee Papers; cf. Meisner, II, p. 1.

75 Széchényi to Kálnoky, 26 January 1889, HHStA Vienna, PA III 136.

76 Kaiser Wilhelm II, order to the Reich Chancellor of 28 January 1889, Széchényi to Kálnoky, 30 January 1889, HHStA Vienna, PA III 136.

77 Széchényi to Kálnoky, 9 February 1889, ibid. See below, p. 181.

78 Széchényi to Kálnoky, 26 March 1889, HHStA Vienna, PA III 136.

79 Count August zu Eulenburg to Philipp Eulenburg, 27 March 1889, *Eulenburgs Korrespondenz*, I, No. 216.

80 Malet, report of 27 March 1889, RA I57/19.

81 Széchényi to Kálnoky, 28 March 1889, HHStA Vienna, PA III 136.

82 Széchényi to Kálnoky, 9 January 1889, ibid. Ordered by Kálnoky, the report was sent to the embassies in St Petersburg, London, Paris, Rome and Constantinople.

## 2    THE FIRST STATE VISITS

1 Kaiser Wilhelm II, marginal comment on Bülow's report of 26 December 1904, PA AA, R 18858.

2 Széchényi to Kálnoky, 24 June 1888, HHStA Vienna, PA III 134.

3 Kaiser Franz Joseph to Kaiser Wilhelm II, draft telegram, June 1888, HHStA Vienna, Kabinettsarchiv, Geheimakten 2.

4 Kaiser Franz Joseph to Kaiser Wilhelm II, 17 June 1888, ibid. The exchange of letters between Franz Joseph and Wilhelm was published in *Neue Freie Presse* on 31 July and 7 August 1921.

5 Kaiser Wilhelm II to Kaiser Franz Joseph, 23 June 1888, HHStA Vienna, Kabinettsarchiv, Geheimakten 2. See *Große Politik*, VI, No. 1342. A draft of Franz Joseph's reply of 10 July 1888 is located in HHStA Vienna, Kabinettsarchiv, Geheimakten 2.

6 Waldersee, diary entry for 23 June 1888, Meisner, I, pp. 406ff. See Széchényi to Kálnoky, 21 June 1888, HHStA Vienna, PA III 134.

7 Kaiser Wilhelm II to Kaiserin Augusta, 11 July 1888, GStA Berlin, BPHA Rep. 53J Lit. P No. 14a.

8 Kaiser Wilhelm II to Crown Prince Rudolf, 12 July 1888, newspaper clipping from *L'écho de Paris*, 3 September 1895, PA AA, Österreich 86 No. 1. See Brigitte Hamann, 'Das Leben des Kronprinzen Rudolf von Österreich-Ungarn nach neuen Quellen', diss., Vienna 1977. A copy of Wilhelm's letter was sent by Rudolf to the Quai d'Orsay in July 1888. In the autumn of 1895 a French translation was then published in a Paris newspaper: Brigitte Hamann, *Rudolf, Kronprinz und Rebell*, Vienna, Munich 1978, pp. 361–2.

9 Queen Victoria, diary entry for 27 June 1888, RA QVJ, in George Earle Buckle, ed., *The Letters of Queen Victoria*, Third Series, 3 vols., London 1930, I, p. 421. See Empress Frederick to Queen Victoria, 8 July 1888, RA Z42/9. Cf. Albert Edward Prince of Wales to Empress Frederick, 11 July 1888, RA Add A5.

10 Queen Victoria to Kaiser Wilhelm II, 3 July 1888, RA I56/82, in Buckle, *Letters of Queen Victoria*, I, pp. 423–4.

11 Kaiser Wilhelm II to Queen Victoria, 6 July 1888, RA I56/84, in Buckle, *Letters of Queen Victoria*, I, pp. 424–5.

12 See *Young Wilhelm*, pp. 805–8.

13 Count Herbert Bismarck, Aufzeichnungen aus dem Herbst 1891, BA Koblenz, Bismarck Papers FC 3018 N; Tsar Alexander III to Kaiser Wilhelm II, 24 June 1888, PA AA, R 3613.

14 Kaiser Wilhelm II to Crown Prince Rudolf, 12 July 1888, newspaper clipping from *L'écho de Paris*, 3 September 1895, PA AA, Österreich 86 No. 1. Cf. Hamann, *Rudolf, Kronprinz und Rebell*, p. 361.

15 Senden-Bibran, Aufzeichnungen über das Jahr 1888, BA-MA Freiburg, Senden-Bibran Papers N160/11, p. 21.

16 Empress Frederick, diary entry for 13 July 1888, GStA Berlin, BPH Rep. 52 No. 3.

17 Széchényi to Kálnoky, 4 July 1888, HHStA Vienna, PA III 134.

18 Senden-Bibran, Aufzeichnungen über das Jahr 1888, BA-MA Freiburg, Senden-Bibran Papers N160/11, p. 22.

19 Alfred von Kiderlen-Wächter to Holstein, 16 July 1888, in Norman Rich and M. H. Fisher, eds., *The Holstein Papers. The Memoirs, Diaries and Correspondence of Friedrich von Holstein 1837–1909*, 4 vols., Cambridge 1956–63, III, No. 271.

20 Waldersee, diary entry for 1 July 1888, Meisner, I, p. 410.

21 Herbert Bismarck to his father, 14 July 1888, BA Koblenz, Bismarck Papers FC 3005 N.

22 Herbert Bismarck to his father, 16 July 1888, ibid.; Kiderlen-Wächter to Holstein, 16 July 1888, *Holstein Papers*, III, No. 271.

23 Count Herbert Bismarck, Aufzeichnungen aus dem Herbst 1891, BA Koblenz, Bismarck Papers FC 3018 N.

24 Kiderlen-Wächter to Holstein, 19 July 1888, *Holstein Papers*, III, No. 272; Senden-Bibran, Aufzeichnungen über das Jahr 1888, BA-MA Freiburg, Senden-Bibran Papers N160/11, p. 24. See also Kiderlen-Wächter to Holstein, 25 July 1888, *Holstein Papers*, III, No. 273.

25 Senden-Bibran, Aufzeichnungen über das Jahr 1888, BA-MA Freiburg, Senden-Bibran Papers N160/11, p. 24.

26 Herbert Bismarck, memorandum, 25 July 1888, *Große Politik*, VI, No. 1346; Herbert Bismarck, Aufzeichnungen aus dem Herbst 1891, BA Koblenz, Bismarck Papers FC 3018 N. See also Kiderlen-Wächter to Holstein, 25 July 1888, *Holstein Papers*, III, No. 273.

27 Senden-Bibran, Aufzeichnungen über das Jahr 1888, BA-MA Freiburg, Senden-Bibran Papers N160/11, p. 25.

28 Herbert Bismarck to Rantzau, 22 July 1888, BA Koblenz, Bismarck Papers FC 3014 N.

29 Kiderlen-Wächter to Holstein, 25 July 1888, *Holstein Papers*, III, No. 273. Cf. the description in Senden-Bibran, Aufzeichnungen über das Jahr 1888, BA-MA Freiburg, Senden-Bibran Papers N160/11, pp. 25–6.

30 Kiderlen-Wächter to Holstein, 19 and 25 July 1888, *Holstein Papers*, III, No. 272 and 273.

31 Kiderlen-Wächter to Holstein, 25 July 1888, ibid., No. 273.

32 Senden-Bibran, Aufzeichnungen über das Jahr 1888, BA-MA Freiburg, Senden-Bibran Papers N160/11, p. 26. For the relationship between Wilhelm and Ella, see *Young Wilhelm*, pp. 325–37.

33 Kiderlen-Wächter to Holstein, 25 July 1888, *Holstein Papers*, III, No. 273; Herbert Bismarck to Rantzau, 26 July 1888, BA Koblenz, Bismarck Papers FC 3014 N.

34 Herbert Bismarck to Rantzau, 26 July 1888, BA Koblenz, Bismarck Papers FC 3014 N.

35 Kiderlen-Wächter to Holstein, 25 July 1888, *Holstein Papers*, III, No. 273.

36 Waldersee, diary entry for 10 July 1888, Meisner, I, p. 412; Waldersee to Holstein, 26 July 1888, *Holstein Papers*, III, No. 275.

37 Pourtalès to Holstein, 25 July 1888, *Holstein Papers*, III, No. 274.

38 Schweinitz to Bismarck, 25 July 1888, *Große Politik*, VI, No. 1347.

39 Count W. N. Lamsdorff, diary entries for 30 January/11 February 1889, cited in George F. Kennan, *The Decline of Bismarck's European Order. Franco-Russian Relations, 1879–1890*, Princeton 1979, p. 398.

40 Sir Robert Morier to Sir Henry Ponsonby, 22 January 1889, RA I57/11; Ponsonby to Queen Victoria, 31 January 1889, RA I57/12.

41 Széchényi to Kálnoky, 2 August 1888, HHStA Vienna, PA III 134.

42 Senden-Bibran, Aufzeichnungen über das Jahr 1888, BA-MA Freiburg, Senden-Bibran Papers N160/11, pp. 24–5.

43 Waldersee to Verdy, 13 July 1888, GStA Berlin, Waldersee Papers B1 No. 53.

44 Waldersee to Holstein, 26 July 1888, *Holstein Papers*, III, No. 275.

45 Empress Frederick to Queen Victoria, 16 August 1888, RA Z42/31; Senden-Bibran, Aufzeichnungen über das Jahr 1888, BA-MA Freiburg, Senden-Bibran Papers N160/11, p. 28.

46 Empress Frederick to Queen Victoria, 16 August 1888, RA Z42/31.

47 Senden-Bibran, Aufzeichnungen über das Jahr 1888, BA-MA Freiburg, Senden-Bibran Papers N160/11, p. 27.

48 Herbert Bismarck to Rantzau, 29 July 1888, BA Koblenz, Bismarck Papers FC 3014 N.

49 Kaiser Wilhelm II to Eulenburg, 28 August–4 September 1888, *Eulenburgs Korrespondenz*, I, No. 194.

50 See Birgit Marschall, *Reisen and Regieren. Die Nordlandfahrten Kaiser Wilhelms II.*, Heidelberg 1991, pp. 80–101; also Klaus von See, *Barbar Germane Arier. Die Suche nach der Identität der Deutschen*, Heidelberg 1994, p. 16.

51 Kiderlen-Wächter to Holstein, 25 July 1888, *Holstein Papers*, III, No. 273.

52 Senden-Bibran, Aufzeichnungen über das Jahr 1888, BA-MA Freiburg, Senden-Bibran Papers N160/11, p. 28.

53 Kiderlen-Wächter to Holstein, 25 July 1888, *Holstein Papers*, III, No. 273.

54 See Waldersee to Holstein, 26 July 1888, ibid., No. 275.

55 Senden-Bibran, Aufzeichnungen über das Jahr 1888, BA-MA Freiburg, Senden-Bibran Papers N160/11, p. 29.

56 Széchényi to Kálnoky, 2 August 1888, HHStA Vienna, PA III 134.

57 See below, pp. 67–72.

58 Kaiser Wilhelm II to Kaiserin Augusta, 9 August 1888, GStA Berlin, Brand.-Preuß. Hausarchiv, Rep. 53J Lit. P. No. 14a.

59 Herbert Bismarck to Rantzau, 29 July 1888, BA Koblenz, Bismarck Papers FC 3014 N.

60 Kaiser Wilhelm II to Kaiserin Augusta, 9 August 1888, GStA Berlin, Brand.-Preuß. Hausarchiv, Rep. 53J Lit. P. No. 14a.

61 Rantzau to Berchem, 16 August 1994, PA AA, R 3474.

62 Eissenstein to Kálnoky, 26 September 1888, HHStA Vienna, PA III 134.

63 Kaiser Wilhelm II to Kaiserin Augusta, 10 October 1888, GStA Berlin, Brand.-Preuß. Hausarchiv Rep. 53J Lit. P. No. 14a.

64 Raschdau to Holstein, 13 October 1888, *Holstein Papers*, III, No. 279.

65 Prince Ernst zu Hohenlohe-Langenburg to his father, 6 January 1889, Hohenlohe-Zentralarchiv Neuenstein, Hermann Hohenlohe-Langenburg Papers, Bü. 56.

66 Waldersee, diary entry for 21 October 1888, GStA Berlin, Waldersee Papers; Meisner, II, p. 10.

67 Kaiserin Auguste Viktoria to Kaiser Wilhelm II, 13 October 1888, GStA Berlin, BPHA Rep. 53T Preußen: An Kaiser Wilhelm II., Bd III; Herbert Bismarck to Wilhelm Bismarck, 19 October 1888, in Walter Bußmann, ed., *Staatssekretär Graf Herbert von Bismarck. Aus seiner politischen Privatkorrespondenz*, Göttingen 1964, No. 369.

68 Christopher Duggan, *Creare la nazione. Vita di Francesco Crispi*, Rome, Bari 2000, pp. 664–7.

69 Cardinal Gustav von Hohenlohe-Schillingsfürst to Duke Georg II of Saxe-Meiningen, 27 December 1888, Thüringisches Staatsarchiv Meiningen, HA 361.

70 Raschdau to Holstein, 13 October 1888, *Holstein Papers*, III, No. 279.

71 Herbert Bismarck to Wilhelm Bismarck, 19 October 1888, in Bußmann, *Staatssekretär*, No. 369.

72 Herbert Bismarck to Holstein, 15 and 17 October 1888, *Holstein Papers*, III, Nos. 280–1.

73 Empress Frederick to Queen Victoria, 27 April 1889, RA Z44/33.

74 Holstein, diary entry for 24 October 1888, *Holstein Papers*, II, pp. 379–80.

75 Salisbury to Queen Victoria, 23 October 1888, RA A67/14.

76 Holstein, diary entry for 24 October 1888, *Holstein Papers*, II, pp. 379–80.

77 Cited in Duggan, *Creare la nazione*, p. 667.

78 Cf. Heinz-Joachim Fischer, 'Kaiserliche Eskapaden in der Ewigen Stadt. Was das Vatikanische Geheimarchiv über den Besuch Wilhelms II. in Rom enthüllt', *Frankfurter Allgemeine Zeitung*, 7 August 1996, p. 6.

79 Holstein, diary entry for 22 October 1888, *Holstein Papers*, II, pp. 378–9.

80 Cited in Christoph Weber, *Quellen und Studien zur Kurie und zur vatikanischen Politik unter Leo XIII.*, Tübingen 1973, pp. 40–1. See also Waldersee, diary entries for 16 and 21 October and 1, 2, 4, 7 and 26 November 1888, GStA Berlin, Waldersee Papers; also Raschdau to Holstein, 13 October 1888, *Holstein Papers*, III, No. 279. See Herbert Bismarck to Kaiser Wilhelm II, 21 October 1888, BA Koblenz, Bismarck Papers FC 2986 N; partially printed in Bußmann, *Staatssekretär*, No. 370. Cf. Count zu Solms to Holstein, 2 November 1888, *Holstein Papers*, III, No. 282. See also Kurd von Schlözer, *Letzte römische Briefe 1882–1894*, Stuttgart, Berlin, Leipzig 1924, pp. 119–37; Friedrich Noack, *Das Deutschtum in Rom seit dem Ausgang des Mittelalters*, 2 vols., Berlin, Leipzig 1927, I, pp. 665–6, 689–90, II, p. 646; James E. Ward, 'Leo XIII and Bismarck. The Kaiser's Vatican Visit of 1888', *Review of Politics*, 24 (1962), pp. 392–414.

81 Herbert Bismarck to Holstein, 15 October 1888, *Holstein Papers*, III, No. 280.

82 Waldersee, diary entry for 21 October 1888, GStA Berlin, Waldersee Papers; cf. the abridged and distorted version in Meisner, II, p. 10.

83 Waldersee, diary entries for 1 4, and 7 November 1888, GStA Berlin, Waldersee Papers; omitted from Meisner, II, pp. 13, 15–16.

84 Cardinal Gustav von Hohenlohe-Schillingsfürst to Duke Georg II of Saxe-Meiningen, 27 December 1888, Thüringisches Staatsarchiv Meiningen, HA 361.

85 Holstein, diary entry for 24 October 1888, *Holstein Papers*, II, pp. 379–80.

86 Queen Victoria to Sir Theodore Martin, 4 November 1888, RA Y172/82.

87 Queen Victoria to Empress Frederick, 6 November 1888, RA Add U32/612.

88 Grand Duke Ludwig IV of Hesse-Darmstadt to Empress Frederick, 13 October 1888, GStA Berlin, BPH Rep. 52 No. 3, pp. 338–44.

89 Herbert Bismarck to his father, 9 October 1888, in Bußmann, *Staatssekretär*, No. 368.

90 Ibid.

91 Eissenstein to Kálnoky, 20 October 1888, HHStA Vienna, PA III 134.

3   THE KAISER AND HIS MOTHER

1 Empress Frederick to Queen Victoria, 18, 20, 23 and 24 June, 5 and 21 July 1888, RA Z41/65–6, Z42/2–3, 7, 19; Ponsonby, *Letters of the Empress Frederick*, pp. 319–27.

2 Empress Frederick to Queen Victoria, 27 and 30 July, 13, 29 and 30 August 1888, RA Z42/23–4, 29, 40–1. See Rainer von Hessen, ed., *Victoria Kaiserin Friedrich. Mission und Schicksal einer englischen Prinzessin in Deutschland*, Frankfurt, New York 2002.

3 Empress Frederick to Queen Victoria, 18 June 1888, in Ponsonby, *Letters of the Empress Frederick*, pp. 319–21; see also 30 August and 1 September 1888, RA Z42/41–2.

4 Empress Frederick to Queen Victoria, 29 September 1888, RA Z43/11.

5 Empress Frederick, diary entry for 4 July 1888, GStA Berlin BPH Rep. 52 No. 3; Empress Frederick to Queen Victoria, 5 July 1888, in Ponsonby, *Letters of the Empress Frederick*, pp. 325–6.

6 Empress Frederick to Queen Victoria, 28 September 1888, RA Z43/10.

7 Empress Frederick to Queen Victoria, 22 August 1888, RA Z42/36, in Ponsonby, *Letters of the Empress Frederick*, pp. 329–31.

8 Empress Frederick to Queen Victoria, 21 August 1888, RA Z42/34.

9 Empress Frederick to Queen Victoria, 30 August 1888, RA Z42/41.

10 Empress Frederick to Queen Victoria, 27 July 1888, RA Z42/23.

11 Empress Frederick to Queen Victoria, 16 August 1888, RA Z42/31. See above, ch. 2.

12 Empress Frederick to her daughter Princess Viktoria of Schaumburg-Lippe, 28 January 1891, Archiv der Hessischen Hausstiftung (AdHH) Schloss Fasanerie. The Empress commented along similar lines to her daughter Sophie. See Arthur Gould Lee, *The Empress Frederick Writes to Sophie, Her Daughter, Crown Princess and Later Queen of the Hellenes*, London 1955, p. 77. See also Queen Victoria to Kaiser Wilhelm II, 24 January and 4 March 1891, GStA Berlin, BPHA Rep. 52 W3 No. 11.

13 See Empress Frederick to Queen Victoria, 13 December 1890, RA Z49/43.

14 Empress Frederick to Queen Victoria, 22 August 1888, RA Z42/36, in Ponsonby, *Letters of the Empress Frederick*, pp. 329–30.

15 Empress Frederick to Queen Victoria, 7 July 1888, RA Z42/8; Empress Frederick to Queen Victoria, 13 July 1888, AdHH Schloss Fasanerie; Empress Frederick, diary entry for 30 July 1888, GStA Berlin BPH Rep. 52 No. 3.

16 Empress Frederick to Queen Victoria, 23 August 1888, RA Z42/37.

17 Waldersee, diary entry for 18 December 1890, GStA Berlin, Waldersee Papers; cf. Meisner, II, p. 167.

18 Empress Frederick to Queen Victoria, 16 August 1888, RA Z42/31.

19 Empress Frederick to Queen Victoria, 28 September 1888, RA Z43/10.

20 Empress Frederick to Queen Victoria, 12 September 1888, RA Z42/46.

21 Empress Frederick to Queen Victoria, 10 December 1890, RA Z49/39. See below, pp. 505–12.

22 Empress Frederick to Queen Victoria, 2 November 1888, RA Z43/32.

23 Empress Frederick to Queen Victoria, 5 July 1888, in Ponsonby, *Letters of the Empress Frederick*, pp. 325–6.

24 Empress Frederick, diary entry for 20 June 1888, GStA Berlin BPH Rep. 52 No. 3; cited in Egon Caesar Conte Corti, *The English Empress. A Study in the Relations between Queen Victoria and Her Eldest Daughter, Empress Frederick of Germany*, London 1957, p. 306. See also Empress Frederick to Queen Victoria, 5 July 1888, RA Z42/7.

25 Empress Frederick to Queen Victoria, 30 July 1888, RA Z42/24.

26 See Empress Frederick to Queen Victoria, 5 July 1888, RA Z42/7.

27 Empress Frederick, diary entry for 17 June 1888, GStA Berlin BPH Rep. 52 No. 3, quoted in part in Corti, *English Empress*, p. 304.

28 Empress Frederick, diary entry for 25 June 1888, GStA Berlin BPH Rep. 52 No. 3, quoted in Corti, *English Empress*, p. 306; Empress Frederick to Queen Victoria, 5, 7, 12 and 16 July 1888, RA Z42/7–8, 11 and 13. See also Empress Frederick to Queen Victoria, 23, 25 and 29 August and 14 September 1888, RA Z42/37–8, 40, 43.

29 Empress Frederick to Queen Victoria, 29 August 1888, RA Z42/40.

30 Kaiser Wilhelm II to Minister of Justice von Friedberg and House Minister von Wedell, 3 December 1888, GStA Berlin, 2.2.1. No. 3115; Prince Ernst zu Hohenlohe-Langenburg

to his father, 6 January 1889, Hohenlohe-Zentralarchiv Neuenstein, Hermann Hohenlohe-Langenburg Papers, Bü. 56; Empress Frederick to Queen Victoria, 21 January 1889, AdHH Schloss Fasanerie (copy in RA Z60A/10); Széchényi to Kálnoky, 30 January 1889, HHStA Vienna, PA III 136. See Ponsonby, *Letters of the Empress Frederick*, pp. 339-65.

31 Empress Frederick to Queen Victoria, 25 October 1888, AdHH Schloss Fasanerie; Empress Frederick to Queen Victoria, 27 April 1889, RA Z44/33.

32 Holstein, diary entry for 24 October 1888, *Holstein Papers*, II, pp. 379-80.

33 Friedberg to Lucanus, 21 October 1888, Kaiser Wilhelm II to Friedberg, 27 October 1888, Lucanus to Friedberg, 27 October 1888, GStA Berlin, 2.2.1. No. 3115; Empress Frederick to Queen Victoria, 25 October 1888, AdHH Schloss Fasanerie; Eissenstein to Kálnoky, 29 October 1888, HHStA Vienna, PA III 134; Empress Frederick, diary entries for 17 and 28 October and 2 November 1888, GStA Berlin, BPH Rep. 52 No. 3; Bogumilla Freifrau von Stockmar to Empress Frederick, 2 November 1888, ibid., pp. 392-4; Lucanus to Tessendorff, 8 November 1888, GStA Berlin, 2.2.1. No. 3115. Many documents on the 'Morier affair' are to be found at Windsor Castle in RA I/57.

34 Empress Frederick to Queen Victoria, 20 and 22 March 1889, RA Z44/15 and 17.

35 Empress Frederick to Queen Victoria, 30 October 1888, RA Z43/31.

36 Empress Frederick to Queen Victoria, 29 March 1889, RA Z44/20, cited in Ponsonby, *Letters of the Empress Frederick*, pp. 369-70.

37 Empress Frederick, diary entries for 17 and 28 October 1888, GStA Berlin, BPH Rep. 52 No. 3; Empress Frederick to Queen Victoria, 16, 17 and 20 October 1888, RA Z43/24, 25 and 27; Grand Duke Ludwig IV of Hesse-Darmstadt to Empress Frederick, 17 October and 3 November 1888, GStA Berlin, BPH Rep. 52 No. 3, pp. 349-52 and 396-9. Empress Frederick to Queen Victoria, 27 April 1889, RA Z44/33.

38 Empress Frederick to Queen Victoria, 30 October 1888, RA Z43/31.

39 Empress Frederick to Queen Victoria, 2 November 1888, RA Z43/32, in Ponsonby, *Letters of the Empress Frederick*, pp. 357-61.

40 Empress Frederick, diary entries for 5-7 and 12-13 November and 8 December 1888, GStA Berlin BPH Rep. 52. No. 3; Empress Frederick to Kaiser Wilhelm II, 7 November 1888, GStA Berlin, BPHA Rep. 52T No. 13.

41 Empress Frederick to Queen Victoria, 2 November 1888, RA Z43/32, in Ponsonby, *Letters of the Empress Frederick*, pp. 357-61.

42 Ibid.

43 Empress Frederick to Queen Victoria, 10 November 1888, RA Z43/36, in Ponsonby, *Letters of the Empress Frederick*, pp. 361-4.

44 Empress Frederick to Queen Victoria, 23 June 1888, RA Z42/2.

45 Empress Frederick to Queen Victoria, 13 August 1888, RA Z42/29.

46 Empress Frederick to Queen Victoria, 2 November 1888, RA Z43/32, in Ponsonby, *Letters of the Empress Frederick*, pp. 357-61.

47 Empress Frederick to Queen Victoria, 26 September 1888, RA Z43/8.

48 Empress Frederick to Queen Victoria, 29 June 1888, RA Z42/5, in Ponsonby, *Letters of the Empress Frederick*, pp. 322-3.

49 Empress Frederick to Queen Victoria, 16 August 1888, RA Z42/31.

50 Empress Frederick, diary entries for 23 and 29 December 1888, GStA Berlin, BPH Rep. 52 No. 3.

51 Empress Frederick to Queen Victoria, 2 November 1888, RA Z43/32, in Ponsonby, *Letters of the Empress Frederick*, pp. 357-61.

52 Ibid.

53 Queen Victoria to Kaiser Wilhelm II, 3 July 1888, RA I56/82; Empress Frederick to Queen Victoria, 7 July 1888, RA Z42/8.

54  Empress Frederick to Queen Victoria, 13 August 1888, RA Z42/29.

55  Empress Frederick to Queen Victoria, 5 July 1888, RA Z42/7, in Ponsonby, *Letters of the Empress Frederick*, pp. 325–6. See also Empress Frederick to Queen Victoria, 27 July 1888, RA Z42/23.

56  Empress Frederick to Queen Victoria, 26 September 1888, RA Z43/8.

57  Empress Frederick to Queen Victoria, 3 September 1888, RA Z42/43.

58  Empress Frederick to Queen Victoria, 23 June 1888, RA Z42/2.

59  Albert Edward Prince of Wales to Empress Frederick, 29 June 1888, RA Add A5/479/20.

60  Albert Edward Prince of Wales to Empress Frederick, 4 July 1888, RA Add A5/479/21.

61  Albert Edward Prince of Wales to Empress Frederick, 29 June 1888, RA Add A5/479/20.

62  Albert Edward Prince of Wales to Empress Frederick, 4 July 1888, RA Add A5/479/21.

63  Albert Edward Prince of Wales to Empress Frederick, 27 June 1888, RA Add A5.

64  Empress Frederick, diary entry for 22 June 1888, GStA Berlin BPH Rep. 52 No. 3.

65  Ibid.

66  Empress Frederick, diary entry for 28 June 1888, ibid.

67  Empress Frederick to Queen Victoria, 7 July 1888, RA Z42/8; Empress Frederick to Queen Victoria, 12 October 1888, RA Z43/21.

68  Empress Frederick, diary entry for 28 June 1888, GStA Berlin BPH Rep. 52 No. 3, quoted in Corti, *English Empress*, p. 309.

69  Empress Frederick, diary entry for 2 July 1888, GStA Berlin BPH Rep. 52 No. 3.

70  Empress Frederick to Queen Victoria, 27 August 1890, RA Z49/10.

71  See *Young Wilhelm*, pp. 666–8.

72  Empress Frederick, diary entry for 2 July 1888, GStA Berlin BPH Rep. 52 No. 3; Empress Frederick to Queen Victoria, 29 June and 5 July 1888, in Ponsonby, *Letters of the Empress Frederick*, pp. 322–3, 325.

73  Empress Frederick to Queen Victoria, 13 and 16 August, 1 and 24 September 1888, RA Z42/29, 31, 42 and Z43/7; Empress Frederick, diary entry for 1 September 1888, GStA Berlin BPH Rep. 52 No. 3; Empress Frederick to Prince Hermann zu Hohenlohe-Langenburg, 22 September 1888, Hohenlohe-Zentralarchiv Schloss Neuenstein, Hermann Hohenlohe-Langenburg Papers, Bü. 105.

74  Empress Frederick to Queen Victoria, 7 July and 29 September 1888, RA Z42/8 and Z43/11.

75  Empress Frederick to Queen Victoria, 15, 20 and 27 April 1889, RA Z44/30, 31 and 33.

76  Empress Frederick, diary entries for 30 September and 1 October 1888, GStA Berlin BPH Rep. 52 No. 3; Empress Frederick to Queen Victoria, 28 September 1888, RA Z43/10.

77  *Young Wilhelm*, p. 679.

78  Empress Frederick, diary entry for 20 June 1888, GStA Berlin, BPH Rep. 52 No. 3; Empress Frederick to Queen Victoria, 20 June 1888, RA Z41/66; Empress Frederick to Queen Victoria, 12 July and 24 October 1888, AdHH Schloss Fasanerie.

79  Empress Frederick to Queen Victoria, 20 and 24 June 1888, RA Z41/66, Z42/3.

80  Empress Frederick, diary entry for 10 July 1888, GStA Berlin, BPH Rep. 52 No. 3; Empress Frederick to Queen Victoria, 16 July 1888, RA Z42/13.

81  Empress Frederick to Queen Victoria, 18 July 1888, RA Z42/14; Empress Frederick, diary entry for 18 July 1888, GStA Berlin, BPH Rep. 52 No. 3.

82  Empress Frederick to Queen Victoria, 12 July 1888, AdHH Schloss Fasanerie; Empress Frederick to Queen Victoria, 16 and 18 July 1888, RA Z42/13, 15.

83  Empress Frederick, diary entry for 19 July 1888, GStA Berlin, BPH Rep. 52 No. 3.

84  Empress Frederick to Queen Victoria, 20 July 1888, RA Z42/18.

85  Empress Frederick, diary entry for 21 July 1888, GStA Berlin, BPH Rep. 52 No. 3; Empress Frederick to Queen Victoria, 21 July 1888, RA Z42/19. See also the Empress Frederick's notes of 14 August 1888, GStA Berlin, BPHA Rep. 52J, general, No. 5; Wedell to Kaiser Wilhelm II, 30 August 1888, GStA Berlin, 2.2.1. No. 3085.

86 Herbert Bismarck to his father, 4 August 1888, BA Koblenz, Bismarck Papers FC 3005 N, printed in part in Bußmann, *Staatssekretär*, No. 363.

87 Empress Frederick to Queen Victoria, 20 July 1888, RA Z42/18.

88 Empress Frederick to Queen Victoria, 18 July 1888, RA Z42/15.

89 The Empress handed over another collection of her letters to Windsor in the spring of 1891: Empress Frederick to Bogumilla Freifrau von Stockmar, 17 February 1891, AdHH Schloss Fasanerie.

90 Empress Frederick, diary entries for 22, 23 and 26 July 1888, GStA Berlin, BPH Rep. 52 No. 3. Cf. Queen Victoria to Empress Frederick, 25 July 1888, RA Add U32/570.

91 Empress Frederick to Queen Victoria, 13 September [?] 1888, RA Z43/2. In January 1891 the Empress Frederick received back the letters which she had written to the Kaiserin Augusta: Empress Frederick to Queen Victoria, 13 January 1891, RA Z50/5.

92 'Secret. Memo'd concerning the collecting of material for a Life of Fritz', Empress Frederick to Queen Victoria, 13 September [?] 1888, RA Z43/2; Empress Frederick to Queen Victoria, 14 September 1888, RA Z43/3, in Ponsonby, *Letters of the Empress Frederick*, pp. 341–3. See Empress Frederick to Queen Victoria, 17 and 22 September 1888, RA Z43/4 and Z43/6.

93 Empress Frederick, diary entry for 20 September 1888, GStA Berlin, BPH Rep. 52 No. 3.

94 Empress Frederick, diary entry for 23 September 1888, GStA Berlin, BPH Rep. 52 No. 3.

95 Empress Frederick to Queen Victoria, 24 September 1888, RA Z43/7, in Ponsonby, *Letters of the Empress Frederick*, pp. 344–5. See also Empress Frederick, diary entry for 25 September 1888, GStA Berlin, BPH Rep. 52 No. 3.

96 See Ponsonby, *Letters of the Empress Frederick*, pp. 359–60.

97 Empress Frederick, diary entry for 26 September 1888, GStA Berlin, BPH Rep. 52 No. 3; Wedell to Kaiser Wilhelm II, 25 September 1888, GStA Berlin, 2.2.1. No. 3115; Empress Frederick to Queen Victoria, 27 September 1888, RA Z43/9.

98 Eissenstein to Kálnoky, 23 September 1888, HHStA Vienna, PA III 134.

99 Empress Frederick to Queen Victoria, 24 September 1888, RA Z43/7, in Ponsonby, *Letters of the Empress Frederick*, pp. 364–5; also Empress Frederick, diary entry for 25 September 1888, GStA Berlin, BPH Rep. 52 No. 3.

100 Empress Frederick to Queen Victoria, 26 September 1888, RA Z43/8, in Ponsonby, *Letters of the Empress Frederick*, pp. 345–6.

101 Empress Frederick to Queen Victoria, 29 September 1888, RA Z43/11, in Ponsonby, *Letters of the Empress Frederick*, pp. 348–50.

102 Herbert Bismarck to Holstein, 30 September 1888, *Holstein Papers*, III, No. 276.

103 Empress Frederick, diary entry for 1 October 1888, GStA Berlin, BPH Rep. 52 No. 3.

104 Empress Frederick to Queen Victoria, 2 October 1888, RA Z43/13, in Ponsonby, *Letters of the Empress Frederick*, pp. 350–1.

105 Empress Frederick to Queen Victoria, 11 October 1888, RA Z43/20, in Ponsonby, *Letters of the Empress Frederick*, pp. 351–2.

106 Empress Frederick to Queen Victoria, 12 October 1888, RA Z43/21, in Ponsonby, *Letters of the Empress Frederick*, p. 352.

107 Empress Frederick to Queen Victoria, 20 October 1888, RA Z43/27, in Ponsonby, *Letters of the Empress Frederick*, pp. 353–4.

108 Empress Frederick to Queen Victoria, 30 October 1888, RA Z43/31, in Ponsonby, *Letters of the Empress Frederick*, pp. 355–6.

109 Empress Frederick to Kaiser Wilhelm II, 29 October 1888, sent on 8 November, GStA Berlin, BPHA Rep. 52T No. 13; copy ibid., BPH Rep. 52 No. 3, pp. 384–7.

110 Empress Frederick, diary entries for 5, 6 and 12 November 1888, GStA Berlin, BPH Rep. 52 No. 3.

111 Empress Frederick to Kaiser Wilhelm II, 7 November 1888, GStA Berlin, BPHA Rep. 52T No. 13. See also Empress Frederick, diary entry for 13 November 1888, GStA Berlin, BPH

Rep. 52 No. 3. Cf. Holstein, diary entry for 11 November 1888, *Holstein Papers*, II, pp. 382–3. See also Kaiserin Auguste Viktoria to Kaiserin Augusta, 16 November 1888, GStA Berlin, BPHA Rep. 52 W3 No. 4 Victoria, Dok. No. 45.

112 Empress Frederick to Queen Victoria, 2 November 1888, RA Z43/32, in Ponsonby, *Letters of the Empress Frederick*, pp. 357–61.

113 See e.g. Princess Victoria of Battenberg to Queen Victoria, 16 and 29 June 1888, RA Add U166/50–1; Princess Viktoria (Moretta) of Prussia to Queen Victoria, 27 June 1888, RA Z83/27; Princess Margarethe of Prussia to Queen Victoria, 28 June 1888, RA Z83/28. Cf. also Grand Duchess Augusta Caroline of Mecklenburg Strelitz to Eulenburg, 7 August 1888, in *Eulenburgs Korrespondenz*, I, No. 189.

114 Queen Victoria's Journal (QVJ), 27 June 1888, printed in Buckle, *Letters of Queen Victoria*, I, p. 421. See also Queen Victoria to Lord Salisbury, 28 June 1888, RA I56/79.

115 Queen Victoria to Princess Victoria of Battenberg, RA Add U173/143.

116 Queen Victoria to Princess Maria Anna of Prussia, 30 July 1888, RA Vic Addl Mss A7/259.

117 The exchange of letters is printed in Buckle, *Letters of Queen Victoria*, I, pp. 423–5. See above, ch. 2.

118 Queen Victoria to Albert Edward Prince of Wales, 17 July 1888, RA I56/86a.

119 Queen Victoria to Albert Edward Prince of Wales, 24 July 1888, RA I56/86b.

120 Queen Victoria to Empress Frederick, 25 July 1888, RA Add U32/570.

121 Queen Victoria to Kaiser Wilhelm II, 3 July 1888, RA I56/82. See Albert Edward Prince of Wales to Empress Frederick, 4 July 1888, RA Add A5/479/21.

122 Kaiser Wilhelm II to Queen Victoria, 6 July 1888, RA I56/84.

123 See above, pp. 33–4.

124 See above, p. 29; Kaiser Wilhelm II, marginal comments, 4 July 1888, PA AA, Asservat No. 4.

125 Empress Frederick to Queen Victoria, 20 June 1888, RA Z41/67, quoted in Corti, *English Empress*, p. 308. See also Empress Frederick, diary entry for 20 June 1888, GStA Berlin BPH Rep. 52 No. 3.

126 See *Truth*, 16 August 1888, p. 277.

127 Winterfeldt to Herbert Bismarck, 30 June 1888, PA AA, R 5668.

128 Kaiser Wilhelm II, marginal comment, 5 July 1888, PA AA, Asservat No. 4.1.

129 Leopold Swaine to Sir Henry Ponsonby, 4 July 1888, in Ponsonby, *Letters of the Empress Frederick*, p. 324.

130 Queen Victoria to Sir Henry Ponsonby, [7 July 1888], RA I56/77. Cf. Ponsonby, *Letters of the Empress Frederick*, p. 324.

131 Sir Edward Malet to Lord Salisbury, 14 July 1888, RA I56/86; also Count Herbert Bismarck, diary, 3 and 7 July 1888, BA Koblenz, Bismarck Papers FC 3018 N.

### 4 AN OMINOUS FAMILY QUARREL

1 Kaiser Wilhelm II, speech of 16 August 1888, Penzler, *Reden Kaiser Wilhelms II. in den Jahren 1888–1895*, pp. 19–21. Cf. Count Georg von Werthern to Eulenburg, 9 September 1888, *Eulenburgs Korrespondenz*, I, No. 195.

2 Empress Frederick to Queen Victoria, 25 August 1888, RA Z42/38, in Ponsonby, *Letters of the Empress Frederick*, pp. 333–4.

3 Empress Frederick to Queen Victoria, 25 August 1888, RA Z42/38. See Ponsonby, *Letters of the Empress Frederick*, pp. 333–4.

4 Empress Frederick to Queen Victoria, 26 August 1888, RA Z42/39, in Ponsonby, *Letters of the Empress Frederick*, pp. 336–7.

5 Albert Edward Prince of Wales to Prince Christian of Schleswig-Holstein, 3 April 1889, in Buckle, *Letters of Queen Victoria*, I, p. 489. See Ponsonby, *Letters of the Empress Frederick*, p. 338; Corti, *English Empress*, p. 305.

6 Rantzau to Berchem, 28 August 1888, PA AA, R 3447.

7 Count Herbert Bismarck, Aufzeichnungen aus dem Jahre 1891, BA Koblenz, Bismarck Papers FC 3018 N.

8 Herbert Bismarck, memorandum, 25 July 1888, *Große Politik*, VI, No. 1346.

9 Pourtalès to Herbert Bismarck, 21 September 1888, PA AA, R 3447.

10 Swaine to Albert Edward Prince of Wales, 3 September 1888, RA Z281/1.

11 Empress Frederick, diary entries for 3 and 5 September 1888, GStA Berlin BPH Rep. 52 No. 3; Albert Edward Prince of Wales to Empress Frederick, 6 September 1888, RA Add A5. See above, p. 41.

12 Swaine to Albert Edward Prince of Wales, 3 September 1888, RA Z281/1.

13 Ellis to Swaine, 12 September 1888, RA Z281/2.

14 Swaine to Albert Edward Prince of Wales, 20 September 1888, RA Z281/3.

15 Swaine to Albert Edward Prince of Wales, 5 October 1888, RA Z281/12; Count Herbert Bismarck, diary entry for 19 February 1889, BA Koblenz, Bismarck Papers FC 3018 N.

16 Ellis to Swaine, 25 September 1888, RA Z281/4.

17 Queen Victoria to Arthur Duke of Connaught, 27 September 1888, RA Vic Addl Mss A15/5166. See also Queen Victoria to Princess Victoria of Battenberg, 2 October 1888, RA Add U173/145.

18 See *Truth*, 27 September 1888, p. 529.

19 Crown Prince Rudolf to Crown Princess Stephanie, 12 September 1888, cited in Hamann, *Rudolf, Kronprinz and Rebell*, p. 363.

20 Paget to Albert Edward Prince of Wales, 25 September 1888, RA Z281/5.

21 Salisbury to Paget, cipher telegram, 30 September 1888, RA Z281/7.

22 Paget to Salisbury, cipher telegram, 1 October 1888, RA Z281/8.

23 Paget to Albert Edward Prince of Wales, 1 and 5 October 1888, RA Z281/9, 11.

24 Paget to Sir Frank Lascelles, cipher telegram, 4 October 1888, RA Z281/10; Albert Edward Prince of Wales to Queen Victoria, 5 October 1888, RA Z280/65; Paget to Albert Edward Prince of Wales, 5 October 1888, RA Z281/11.

25 Queen Victoria to Salisbury, 15 October 1888, RA T9/111; Albert Edward Prince of Wales to Empress Frederick, 31 October 1888, RA Add A5/479/34.

26 Swaine to Ellis, 27 September 1888, RA Z281/6.

27 Salisbury, memorandum, 13 October 1888, RA T9/110, in Buckle, *Letters of Queen Victoria*, I, pp. 438–40.

28 Salisbury to Queen Victoria, 15 October 1888, RA T9/112, in Buckle, *Letters of Queen Victoria*, I, pp. 441–2.

29 Queen Victoria to Salisbury, 15 October 1888, RA T9/111, in Buckle, *Letters of Queen Victoria*, I, pp. 440–1. See also Queen Victoria to Salisbury, 13 November 1888, RA Z280/67.

30 Paget to Ponsonby, 13 November 1888, RA Z280/68; Salisbury to Queen Victoria, 18 November 1888, RA Z280/69.

31 Queen Victoria to Kaiserin Augusta, 14 November 1888, GStA BPHA Rep. 52 W3 No. 4 Victoria, Dok. No. 47.

32 Kaiserin Augusta to Queen Victoria, 17 November 1888, ibid., Dok. No. 48. On Wilhelm's treatment during his stay in London in the summer of 1887, see *Young Wilhelm*, pp. 682–9.

33 Albert Edward Prince of Wales to Queen Victoria, 1 November 1888, RA Z280/66.

34 Albert Edward Prince of Wales to Empress Frederick, 31 October 1888, RA Add A5/479/34.

35 Alexandra Princess of Wales to Prince George, 17 October 1888, RA Geo V, AA31/1.

36  Albert Edward Prince of Wales to Empress Frederick, 31 October 1888, RA Add A5/479/34. See also Albert Edward Prince of Wales to Empress Frederick, 23 November 1888, ibid.

37  Arthur Duke of Connaught to Queen Victoria, 25 October 1888, RA Z185/25.

38  Count Herbert Bismarck, Aufzeichnungen aus dem Jahre 1891, BA Koblenz, Bismarck Papers FC 3018 N.

39  Count Herbert Bismarck, diary entries for 31 August–16 September 1888, ibid.

40  Count Herbert Bismarck, diary entries for August–October 1888, ibid.

41  Adolf von Deines, report of August 1888, PA AA, R 8593.

42  Kaiser Wilhelm II, marginal notes on Deines's report of 30 August 1888, PA AA, Asservat No. 4.

43  Rantzau to Auswärtiges Amt, 4 September 1888, PA AA, R 5900, Geheime Acten betreffend den Prinzen von Wales.

44  Berchem, draft of 6 September 1888, ibid. See above, pp. 73–7.

45  Reuss, report of 13 September 1888, PA AA, R 5900.

46  See also Bismarck to Kaiser Wilhelm II, 20 September 1888, *Große Politik*, VI, No. 1351.

47  Herbert Bismarck to his father, 16 September 1888, BA Koblenz, Bismarck Papers FC 3005 N.

48  Count Herbert Bismarck, diary, August–October 1888, BA Koblenz, Bismarck Papers FC 3018 N. See also the retrospective note in Herbert Bismarck, Aufzeichnung, pp. 56–7, ibid.

49  Empress Frederick to Queen Victoria, 20 April 1889, RA Z44/31, in Ponsonby, *Letters of the Empress Frederick*, pp. 370–3. See Prince Christian of Schleswig-Holstein to Sir Henry Ponsonby, 13 May 1889, RA Z281/46; also Prince Ernst zu Hohenlohe-Langenburg to his father, 9 June 1889, Hohenlohe Zentralarchiv Neuenstein, Hermann Hohenlohe-Langenburg Papers, Bü. 56.

50  Queen Victoria to Albert Edward Prince of Wales, 7 February 1889, RA I57/17, in Buckle, *Letters of Queen Victoria*, I, pp. 467–8. See also Ponsonby to Knollys, 12 and 15 February 1889, RA Z281/13 and 14.

51  Albert Edward Prince of Wales to Queen Victoria, 8 February 1889, RA Z498/49.

52  Queen Victoria to Salisbury, 27 February 1889, RA A67/46, in Buckle, *Letters of Queen Victoria*, I, p. 473.

53  Salisbury to Queen Victoria, 9 March 1889, RA A67/51. See Prince Ernst zu Hohenlohe-Langenburg to his father, 4 March 1889, Hohenlohe Zentralarchiv Neuenstein, Hermann Hohenlohe-Langenburg Papers, Bü. 56.

54  Count Herbert Bismarck, Aufzeichnung, pp. 64ff., BA Koblenz, Bismarck Papers FC 3018 N; diary entry for 6 March 1889, ibid.

55  Herbert Bismarck to Rantzau, 30 July 1889, ibid., FC 3014 N, in Bußmann, *Staatssekretär*, No. 386. See also Count Herbert Bismarck, Aufzeichnung, pp. 66ff., BA Koblenz, Bismarck Papers, FC 3018 N.

56  Queen Victoria to Empress Frederick, 12 March 1889, RA Vic Add Mss U32/619.

57  Prince Ernst zu Hohenlohe-Langenburg to his father, 19 May 1889, Hohenlohe Zentralarchiv Neuenstein, Hermann Hohenlohe-Langenburg Papers, Bü. 56.

58  Knollys to Ponsonby, 13 March 1889, RA Addl Mss A12/1641. See also George Duke of Cambridge to Ponsonby, 16 March 1889, RA W11/36.

59  Herbert Bismarck to Kaiser Wilhelm II with marginal comments by the Kaiser, 17 March 1889, BA Koblenz, Bismarck Papers FC 2986 N; Salisbury to Queen Victoria, 20 March 1889, RA A67/59; Waldersee, diary entry for 25 March 1889, GStA Berlin, Waldersee Papers; omitted from Meisner, II, p. 47.

60  Count Herbert Bismarck, Aufzeichnung, pp. 55ff., BA Koblenz, Bismarck Papers FC 3018 N.

61  Salisbury to Queen Victoria, 29 March 1889, RA A67/48, in Buckle, *Letters of Queen Victoria*, I, pp. 483–5; Prince Ernst zu Hohenlohe-Langenburg to his father, 19 May 1889, Hohenlohe

Zentralarchiv Neuenstein, Hermann Hohenlohe-Langenburg Papers, Bü. 56; Count Herbert Bismarck, diary entries for 21–31 March 1889, BA Koblenz, Bismarck Papers FC 3018 N.

62  Albert Edward Prince of Wales to Prince Christian of Schleswig-Holstein, 3 April 1889, RA T9/119, in Buckle, *Letters of Queen Victoria*, I, pp. 487–9.

63  Count Herbert Bismarck, diary entry for 8 April 1889, BA Koblenz, Bismarck Papers FC 3018 N.

64  Prince Christian of Schleswig-Holstein, Report on my conversations with the Emperor, 16 April 1889, RA Z281/34. See Buckle, *Letters of Queen Victoria*, I, pp. 491–3.

65  Count Herbert Bismarck, diary entry for 9 April 1889, BA Koblenz, Bismarck Papers FC 3018 N.

66  Malet to Albert Edward Prince of Wales, cipher telegram, 9 April 1889, RA Z281/17.

67  Albert Edward Prince of Wales to Prince Christian of Schleswig-Holstein, 10 April 1889, RA Z281/18 and 19, in Buckle, *Letters of Queen Victoria*, I, pp. 492–3.

68  Salisbury to Knollys, 10 April 1889, RA Z281/20.

69  Salisbury to Albert Edward Prince of Wales, 11 April 1889, RA Z281/22.

70  Prince Christian of Schleswig-Holstein, Report on my conversation with the Emperor, 16 April 1889, RA Z281/34; Malet to Albert Edward Prince of Wales, cipher telegram, 11 April 1889, RA Z281/21.

71  Malet to Albert Edward Prince of Wales, cipher telegram, 12 April 1889, RA Z281/26.

72  Albert Edward Prince of Wales to Malet, cipher telegram, 13 April 1889, RA Z281/27.

73  Albert Edward Prince of Wales to Prince Christian of Schleswig-Holstein, 16 April 1889, RA Z281/33.

74  Prince Christian of Schleswig-Holstein, Report on my conversations with the Emperor, 16 April 1889, RA Z281/34.

75  Ibid.

76  Malet to Salisbury, 13 April 1889, RA Z281/28.

77  Ponsonby to Queen Victoria, 20 April 1889, RA I57/24, in Buckle, *Letters of Queen Victoria*, I, p. 494.

78  Albert Edward Prince of Wales to Salisbury, 16 April 1889, RA Z281/32.

79  Albert Edward Prince of Wales to Prince Christian of Schleswig-Holstein, 19 April 1889, RA Z281/37.

80  Albert Edward Prince of Wales to Prince Christian of Schleswig-Holstein, 19 April 1889, RA Z281/36.

81  Queen Victoria to Albert Edward Prince of Wales, 21 April 1889, RA Z281/38.

82  Empress Frederick to Queen Victoria, 20 and 27 April 1889, RA Z44/31 and 33. See Ponsonby, *Letters of the Empress Frederick*, p. 370.

83  Prince Ernst zu Hohenlohe-Langenburg to his father, 28 April 1889, Hohenlohe Zentralarchiv Neuenstein, Hermann Hohenlohe-Langenburg Papers, Bü. 56.

84  Queen Victoria to Albert Edward Prince of Wales, 21 April 1889, RA Z281/38.

85  Prince Christian of Schleswig-Holstein to Albert Edward Prince of Wales, 28 April 1889, RA Z281/39.

86  Prince Ernst zu Hohenlohe-Langenburg to his father, 19 May 1889, Hohenlohe Zentralarchiv Neuenstein, Hermann Hohenlohe-Langenburg Papers, Bü. 56.

87  Summary of 'Incident at Vienna', May 1889, RA Z281/40.

88  Prince Ernst zu Hohenlohe-Langenburg to his father, 11 and 19 May 1889, Hohenlohe Zentralarchiv Neuenstein, Hermann Hohenlohe-Langenburg Papers, Bü. 56. Cf. Knollys to Ponsonby, 23 May 1889, RA Z281/66.

89  Lord Salisbury to Queen Victoria, 11 May 1889, RA Z280/71. Cf. Count Herbert Bismarck, Aufzeichnung, p. 59, BA Koblenz, Bismarck Papers FC 3018 N.

90  Ponsonby to Queen Victoria, 13 May 1889, RA Z280/72.

 91 Knollys to Ponsonby, 12 May 1889, RA Z281/45.

 92 Ponsonby to Queen Victoria, 13 May 1889, RA Z280/72; Prince Christian of Schleswig-Holstein to Ponsonby, 13 May 1889, RA Z281/46.

 93 Drafts by Salisbury and Ponsonby, amended by Queen Victoria, May 1889, RA Z281/55; Ponsonby to Knollys, 22 May 1889, RA Z281/60; Knollys to Ponsonby, 22 May 1889, RA Z281/61; Ponsonby to Queen Victoria, Queen Victoria to Ponsonby, 23 May 1889, RA Z281/67.

 94 Knollys to Ponsonby, 23 May 1889, RA Z281/66; Ponsonby to Albert Edward Prince of Wales, 23 May 1889, RA E63/42.

 95 Ponsonby to Knollys, 23 May 1889, RA Z281/64. Cf. Ponsonby to Prince Christian of Schleswig-Holstein, 25 May 1889, in Buckle, *Letters of Queen Victoria*, I, p. 500.

 96 Queen Victoria to Kaiser Wilhelm II, telegram, 24 May 1889, GStA Berlin, BPHA Rep. 52 W3 No. 11.

 97 Queen Victoria to Kaiser Wilhelm II, 25 May 1889, GStA Berlin, BPH Rep. 53 No. 156; copy by the Prince of Wales in RA Addl Mss A/4/11.

 98 Albert Edward Prince of Wales to Empress Frederick, 29 May 1889, RA Addl Mss A/4/12.

 99 Herbert Bismarck to Kaiser Wilhelm II, 28 May 1889, GStA Berlin, BPH Rep. 53 No. 156; diary entry for 28 May 1889, BA Koblenz, Bismarck Papers FC 3018 N.

100 Ponsonby to Prince Christian of Schleswig-Holstein, 1 June 1889, in Buckle, *Letters of Queen Victoria*, I, p. 501.

101 Kaiser Wilhelm II to Queen Victoria, 28 May 1889, copy, RA T9/161.

102 Queen Victoria to Albert Edward Prince of Wales, copy, 1 June 1889, RA Z280/74; Arthur Duke of Connaught to Queen Victoria, 3 June 1889, RA Z186/32.

103 Knollys to Ponsonby, 2 and 4 June 1889, RA Z281/86 and 89; Ponsonby to Queen Victoria, 5 June 1889, RA Z280/75.

104 Empress Frederick to Queen Victoria, 3 June 1889, RA Z45/10.

105 Prince Ernst zu Hohenlohe-Langenburg to his father, 9 June 1889, Hohenlohe Zentralarchiv Neuenstein, Hermann Hohenlohe-Langenburg Papers, Bü. 56.

106 Salisbury's draft of a letter from Queen Victoria to Kaiser Wilhelm II, 4 June 1889, copy in Ponsonby's hand with amendments by the Queen, RA Z281/88.

107 Ibid.

108 Marlborough House draft, 7 June 1889, RA Z281/99; Ponsonby to Salisbury, 7 June 1889, RA Z281/95.

109 Salisbury to Ponsonby, 7 June 1889, RA Z281/98.

110 Ponsonby to Prince Christian of Schleswig-Holstein, 8 June 1889, in Buckle, *Letters of Queen Victoria*, I, p. 501.

111 Knollys to Prince Christian of Schleswig-Holstein, 8 June 1889, in Buckle, *Letters of Queen Victoria*, I, pp. 501–2; Prince Christian of Schleswig-Holstein to Ponsonby and to Knollys, 11 June 1889, RA Z281/103 and 104.

112 Ponsonby to Prince Christian of Schleswig-Holstein, 8 June 1889, in Buckle, *Letters of Queen Victoria*, I, p. 501.

113 Count Herbert Bismarck, Aufzeichnung, pp. 60–1, BA Koblenz, Bismarck Papers FC 3018 N.

114 Malet to Queen Victoria, 15 June 1889, in Buckle, *Letters of Queen Victoria*, I, pp. 503–4; RA QVJ, 23 July 1889; Ponsonby to Queen Victoria, 23 July 1889, RA A67/82; Queen Victoria to Princess Victoria of Hesse, 7 August 1889, RA Add U173/154.

115 Salisbury to Queen Victoria, 27 July 1889, RA I57/44, in Buckle, *Letters of Queen Victoria*, I, p. 518. Bismarck's letter of 12 October 1889 expressing his gratitude to Queen Victoria is in RA I57/64.

116 Kaiser Wilhelm II to Malet, 14 June 1889, RA I57/33, in Buckle, *Letters of Queen Victoria*, I, p. 504.

117 Count Herbert Bismarck, Aufzeichnung, pp. 67–8, BA Koblenz, Bismarck Papers FC 3018 N.

118 Eulenburg to Herbert Bismarck, 17 July 1889, *Eulenburgs Korrespondenz*, I, No. 228.

119 Arthur Duke of Connaught to Sir Howard Elphinstone, 5 August 1889, RA Vic Addl Mss A25/795.

120 Count Herbert Bismarck, Aufzeichnung, pp. 70ff., BA Koblenz, Bismarck Papers FC 3018 N.

121 Casimir Count von Leyden to Ponsonby, 15 June 1889, RA Z281/107.

122 Kaiser Wilhelm II to Queen Victoria, 23 June 1889, RA I57/36, in Buckle, *Letters of Queen Victoria*, I, p. 505.

123 Queen Victoria to Princess Victoria of Battenberg, 7 August 1889, RA Add U173/154.

124 Count Herbert Bismarck, Aufzeichnung, p. 70, BA Koblenz, Bismarck Papers FC 3018 N.

125 RA QVJ, 2–8 August 1889, in Buckle, *Letters of Queen Victoria*, I, pp. 520–2.

126 RA QVJ, 2 August 1889.

127 Queen Victoria to Princess Victoria of Battenberg, 7 August 1889, RA Add U173/154.

128 E. Phipps, report from Vienna, 20 August 1889, RA I57/55.

129 RA QVJ, 5 and 6 August 1889.

130 RA QVJ, 7 August 1889.

131 Count Herbert Bismarck, Aufzeichnung, pp. 72–3, BA Koblenz, Bismarck Papers FC 3018 N.

132 RA QVJ, 2–8 August 1889, in Buckle, *Letters of Queen Victoria*, I, pp. 520–2; Queen Victoria to Arthur Duke of Connaught, 9 August 1889, RA Vic Addl Mss A15/5343.

133 Count Herbert Bismarck, Aufzeichnung, pp. 75–6, BA Koblenz, Bismarck Papers FC 3018 N.

134 See Lothar Reinermann, *Der Kaiser in England. Wilhelm II. und sein Bild in der britischen Öffentlichkeit*, Paderborn, Munich, Vienna, Zürich 2001, pp. 89ff.

135 RA QVJ, 2–8 August 1889, in Buckle, *Letters of Queen Victoria*, I, pp. 520–2; Queen Victoria to Arthur Duke of Connaught, 9 August 1889, RA Vic Addl Mss A15/5343.

136 Salisbury to Queen Victoria, 8 August 1889, in Buckle, *Letters of Queen Victoria*, I, p. 523.

137 Kaiser Wilhelm II to Queen Victoria, 10 August 1889, RA I57/49, in Buckle, *Letters of Queen Victoria*, I, pp. 523–4; Queen Victoria's reply, ibid., p. 524.

138 W. Beauclerk to Lord Salisbury, 17 August 1889, RA I57/54.

139 Kaiser Wilhelm II to Queen Victoria, 17 August 1889, RA I57/53, in Buckle, *Letters of Queen Victoria*, I, pp. 526–7. See below, pp. 156–8.

140 Herbert Bismarck to his father, 5 October 1889, in Bußmann, *Staatssekretär*, No. 390; Kaiser Wilhelm II to Queen Victoria, telegram, 9 October 1889; Queen Victoria to Kaiser Wilhelm II, 9 October 1889, RA I57/60–1.

141 Vice Admiral Paul Hoffmann, diary entries for 26–8 October 1889, Hoffmann Papers, in the possession of Dr Margot Leo-Hoffmann, Freiburg.

142 Kaiser Wilhelm II to Queen Victoria, telegram, 30 October 1889; Queen Victoria to Kaiser Wilhelm II, 31 October 1889, RA I57/67–8.

143 Salisbury to Queen Victoria, 31 October 1889; Sir Edmund Monson to Salisbury, 31 October 1889, RA I57/69–70.

144 On Erichsen's report to Salisbury on Wilhelm's mental health, see *Young Wilhelm*, pp. 322–3 and below, pp. 1065–6.

145 Salisbury to Queen Victoria, 24 October 1889, RA I57/66.

146 Salisbury to Queen Victoria, 2 November 1889, RA I57/71.

147 Prince Ernst zu Hohenlohe-Langenburg to his father, 16 October 1889, Hohenlohe-Zentralarchiv Neuenstein, Hermann Hohenlohe-Langenburg Papers, Bü. 56.

148 Phipps, report from Vienna, 20 August 1889, RA I57/55.

149 Sir Arthur Nicolson, report from Budapest, 27 August 1889, RA I57/55.

150 Herbert Bismarck to Rantzau, 30 July 1889, BA Koblenz, Bismarck Papers, FC 3014 N, in Bußmann, *Staatssekretär*, No. 386.

151 Ponsonby to Queen Victoria, 8 August 1889, in Buckle, *Letters of Queen Victoria*, I, p. 523.

152 Count Herbert Bismarck, Aufzeichnung, pp. 76ff., BA Koblenz, Bismarck Papers FC 3018 N.

153 Empress Frederick to Queen Victoria, 17 August 1889, RA Z45/41.

### 5 THE YOUNG KAISER: A SKETCH DRAWN FROM LIFE

1 See above, pp. 12–16.

2 Dr G. Hinzpeter, *Kaiser Wilhelm II. Eine Skizze nach der Natur gezeichnet*, Bielefeld 1888, p. 3. Hinzpeter's role and influence on the future Kaiser are dealt with in detail in *Young Wilhelm*.

3 Hinzpeter, *Kaiser Wilhelm II.*, pp. 3–15.

4 Kaiser Wilhelm II to Kaiserin Augusta, 11 July 1888, GStA Berlin, BPHA Rep. 53J Lit. P No. 14a.

5 Kaiser Wilhelm II to Queen Victoria, 6 July 1888, RA I56/84.

6 Kiderlen-Wächter to Holstein, 16 July 1888, *Holstein Papers*, III, No. 271.

7 Kiderlen-Wächter to Holstein, 19 July 1888, ibid., No. 272. Bismarck's promemoria for Wilhelm II is printed in *Große Politik*, VI, No. 1343, pp. 311–14.

8 Count Herbert Bismarck, Aufzeichnungen aus dem Herbst 1891, BA Koblenz, Bismarck Papers FC 3018 N. The memorandum on German–Russian relations the Chancellor had drafted for Wilhelm is located in PA AA, Deutschland 131 secr.

9 Kiderlen-Wächter to Holstein, 25 July 1888, *Holstein Papers*, III, No. 273.

10 Ibid.

11 Ibid.

12 Kiderlen-Wächter to Holstein, 16 July 1888, ibid., No. 271.

13 Széchényi to Kálnoky, 2 August 1888, HHStA Vienna, PA III 134.

14 Waldersee to Holstein, 26 July 1888, *Holstein Papers*, III, No. 275.

15 Waldersee, diary entry for 26 August 1888, GStA Berlin, Waldersee Papers; omitted from Meisner, II, p. 1.

16 Waldersee, diary entry for 11 October 1888, GStA Berlin, Waldersee Papers; cf. Meisner, II, pp. 6–7.

17 Waldersee, diary entry for 13 October 1888, GStA Berlin, Waldersee Papers; cf. Meisner, II, p. 7.

18 Széchényi to Kálnoky, 26 January 1889, HHStA Vienna, PA III 136.

19 Empress Frederick to Queen Victoria, 2 November 1888, RA Z43/32.

20 Herbert Bismarck to his father, 5 October 1888, BA Koblenz, Bismarck Papers FC 3005 N, in Bußmann, *Staatssekretär*, No. 366.

21 Herbert Bismarck to Rantzau, 4 July 1889, BA Koblenz, Bismarck Papers FC 3014 N, in Bußmann, *Staatssekretär*, No. 382.

22 Holstein to Radolin, 28 November 1889, *Holstein Papers*, III, No. 300.

23 Holstein, diary entry for 24 October 1888, ibid., II, pp. 427–8.

24 Prince Ernst zu Hohenlohe-Langenburg to his father, 1 November 1888, Hohenlohe-Zentralarchiv Neuenstein, Hermann Hohenlohe-Langenburg Papers, Bü. 55.

25 Eulenburg to Holstein, 6 August 1889, *Eulenburgs Korrespondenz*, I, No. 230.

26  Vice-Admiral Paul Hoffmann, diary entry for 23 October 1889, Hoffmann Papers, Freiburg.
27  Ibid.
28  Hoffmann, diary entries for 24–5 October and 9 and 11 November 1889, ibid.
29  Hoffmann, diary entry for 25 October 1889, ibid.
30  Hoffmann, diary entry for 7 November 1889, ibid.
31  Waldersee, diary entry for 13 November 1889, GStA Berlin, Waldersee Papers; cf. Meisner, II, pp. 76–7.
32  Waldersee, diary entry for 13 November 1889, GStA Berlin, Waldersee Papers; cf. Meisner, II, pp. 76–7. See also Waldersee, diary entry for 3 January 1890, GStA Berlin, Waldersee Papers; omitted from Meisner, II, p. 87.
33  Waldersee, diary entry for 5 January 1890, GStA Berlin, Waldersee Papers; cf. Meisner, II, p. 87.
34  Kaiser Wilhelm II to Bismarck, telegram, 17 January 1890, cited in *Eulenburgs Korrespondenz*, I, p. 420.
35  Kaiser Wilhelm II to Empress Frederick, 25 September 1898, AdHH Schloss Fasanerie. A copy is printed in *The Memoirs of Prince von Bülow*, 4 vols., London and New York 1931–2, I, pp. 230–2. See below, pp. 871–3.
36  Kaiser Wilhelm II, dictated notes on a conversation with Pope Leo XIII, 23 April 1893, in Chlodwig Fürst zu Hohenlohe-Schillingsfürst, Karl Alexander von Müller, ed., *Denkwürdigkeiten der Reichskanzlerzeit*, Stuttgart, Berlin 1931, pp. 608–11.
37  Charles Seymour, ed., *The Intimate Papers of Colonel House*, 4 vols., Boston, New York 1926–8, II, p. 139.
38  Kaiser Wilhelm II to Crown Prince Gustaf of Sweden and Norway, 25 July 1895, printed in Hohenlohe, *Denkwürdigkeiten der Reichskanzlerzeit*, pp. 102–5.
39  Bismarck noted on Prince Reuss's report of 28 April 1888: 'To be locked away on account of the marginalia of H[is] I[mperial] H[ighness]' (*Große Politik*, VI, pp. 301–2).
40  See PA AA, Asservat No. 4.1, 2–5.
41  On Bülow's report of 1 March 1889, Bismarck noted: 'This document is to be locked away, a copy is to be kept with the non-secret files under A 3728 without the margin[alia]' (PA AA, Asservat No. 4).
42  Kaiser Wilhelm II, marginal note on a report of 9 January 1892 from Petropolis, ibid.
43  Kaiser Wilhelm II, marginal note on a report of 24 June 1893 from Luxemburg, ibid.
44  Kaiser Wilhelm II, marginal notes on Schlözer's report of 4 October 1890 and Bülow's report of 22 October 1890, ibid.
45  Kaiser Wilhelm II, marginal notes on Bülow's reports of 14, 16, 21, 24 February, 7 March, 13 April, 15 May, 6 and 12 November 1889, 22 November 1891, as well as on Herbert Bismarck's report of 6 April 1889, ibid.
46  Kaiser Wilhelm II, marginal note on Alvensleben's report from Brussels of 8 March 1889, ibid.
47  Kaiser Wilhelm II, marginal note on Bülow's report of 1 June 1889, ibid.
48  Kaiser Wilhelm II, marginal note on Lichnowsky's report of 15 July 1891, ibid.
49  Kaiser Wilhelm II, marginal note on Bülow's report of 17 March 1889, ibid. See also Kaiser Wilhelm II, marginal note on Reuss's report of 23 May 1891, and his marginal note on Eulenburg's report of 7 May 1896, ibid.
50  Kaiser Wilhelm II, marginal note on Bülow's report of 14 April 1889, PA AA, R 9845.
51  Kaiser Wilhelm II, marginal note on Bülow's report of 11 March 1889, PA AA, Asservat No. 4.1.
52  Kaiser Wilhelm II, marginal note on Bülow's report of 20 December 1888, ibid. See Waldersee, diary entry for 20 April 1889, GStA Berlin, Waldersee Papers; cf. Meisner, II, p. 49.
53  Wilhelm II, marginal note on report A8118, BA Koblenz, Bismarck Papers FC 2986 N.

54 Kaiser Wilhelm II, marginal note on Reuss's report of 6 November 1888, PA AA, Asservat No. 4.1.

55 Kaiser Wilhelm II, marginal note on Reuss's report of 22 December 1888 with a comment by Bismarck, ibid.

56 Kaiser Wilhelm II, marginal note on a report from Belgrade of 2 January 1889, ibid.

57 Kaiser Wilhelm II, marginal note on Reuss's and Bray's reports of 23 January, 8 and 23 February and 3 March 1889, PA AA, R 11618.

58 Kaiser Wilhelm II, marginal note on Consul Schroeder's report from Beirut of 28 May 1889, PA AA, Asservat No. 4. See also Kaiser Wilhelm II, marginal note on Reuss's report from Vienna of 22 March 1889, ibid.

59 Kaiser Wilhelm II, marginal note on Radowitz's report from Therapia of 23 October 1891, ibid.

60 Kaiser Wilhelm II, marginal note on Alvensleben's report from Brussels of 8 March 1889, ibid. On Ferdinand's marital plans, see Wilhelm's marginal note on Bülow's report of 5 May 1889, ibid.

61 Kaiser Wilhelm II, marginal note on Lichnowsky's report of 15 July 1891, ibid.

62 Kaiser Wilhelm II, marginal note on articles in the *Berliner Tageblatt* of 28 February and 20 March 1889, ibid.

63 Kaiser Wilhelm II, marginal note on Schweinitz's report of 3 July 1889, ibid.

64 Kaiser Wilhelm II, marginal note on Schweinitz's report of 24 May 1891, ibid.

65 Kaiser Wilhelm II, marginal note on Leyden's report of 8 December 1890, ibid.

66 Kaiser Wilhelm II, marginal note on Schweinitz's report of 30 December 1891, ibid.

67 Kaiser Wilhelm II, marginal note on Alfred von Bülow's report from St Petersburg of 20 July 1891, ibid.

68 Kaiser Wilhelm II, marginal note on Count Rex's report from St Petersburg of 14 September 1892, ibid.

69 Kaiser Wilhelm II, marginal note on de Maistre's report from Athens of 25 September 1889, ibid.

70 Kaiser Wilhelm II, marginal note on an article in the *Standard* of 25 December 1889, ibid.

71 Kaiser Wilhelm II, marginal note on Brincken's report of 23 October 1888, PA AA, Asservat No. 4.1.

72 Empress Frederick to Queen Victoria, 1 August 1890, RA Z48/44.

73 For a more detailed assessment, see below, pp. 643–50.

74 Kaiser Wilhelm II, marginal note on Wesdehlen's report of 10 November 1890, PA AA, Asservat No. 4.

75 Kaiser Wilhelm II, marginal note on Kiderlen-Wächter's report from Copenhagen of 9 March 1897, ibid.

76 Kaiser Wilhelm II, marginal note on Wesdehlen's report of 3 February 1894, ibid.

77 Kaiser Wilhelm II, marginal note on Wesdehlen's report of 9 November 1892, ibid.

78 Kaiser Wilhelm II, marginal note on Kiderlen-Wächter's from Copenhagen of 9 March 1897, ibid.

79 Kaiser Wilhelm II, marginal note on Wesdehlen's report of 17 February and 2 March 1892, ibid.

80 Kaiser Wilhelm II, marginal note on Wesdehlen's report of 28 January 1891, ibid.

81 Kaiser Wilhelm II, marginal note on Waecker-Gotter's report of 31 January 1891, ibid.

82 Hoffmann, diary entry for 26 October 1889, Hoffmann Papers, Freiburg. See also Kaiser Wilhelm II, marginal note on Wesdehlen's report of 28 January 1891, PA AA, Asservat No. 4.1.

83 Kaiser Wilhelm II, marginal note on Wesdehlen's report of 10 November 1890, ibid.

84 Hoffmann, diary entries for 28–30 October 1889, Hoffmann Papers, Freiburg.

85  Hoffmann, diary entry for 31 October–3 November 1889, ibid.

86  Hoffmann, diary entry for 3 November 1889, ibid.

87  Hoffmann, diary entry for 5 November 1889, ibid.

88  Hoffmann, diary entry for 4 November 1889, ibid.

89  See Margarete Jarchow, *Hofgeschenke. Wilhelm II. zwischen Diplomatie und Dynastie 1888–1914*, Hamburg 1998, pp. 35 and 183.

90  Hoffmann, diary entry for 6 November 1889, Hoffmann Papers, Freiburg.

91  Hoffmann, diary entry for 4 November 1889, ibid.

92  Hoffmann, diary entry for 6 November 1889, ibid.

93  Ibid.

94  Empress Frederick to Queen Victoria, 4 November 1889, RA Z46/32.

95  Hoffmann, diary entry for 1 November 1889, Hoffmann Papers, Freiburg.

96  Kaiser Wilhelm II to Prince Otto von Bismarck, 12 June 1889, BA Koblenz, Bismarck Papers FC 2986 N.

97  Malet to Salisbury, 11 June 1889, RA I57/29.

98  Kaiser Wilhelm II, marginal notes on newspaper clippings of 24 May 1890, PA AA, Asservat No. 4.1.

99  Waldersee, diary entry for 15 January 1892, GStA Berlin, Waldersee Papers; omitted from Meisner, II, p. 229.

100  Swaine to Ponsonby, 1 July 1892, RA I59/89.

101  Kaiser Wilhelm II, marginal note on Eulenburg's report from Munich of 18 January 1894, PA AA, Asservat No. 4.

102  Kaiser Wilhelm II, marginal note on Schweinitz's report of 3 March 1889, PA AA, Asservat No. 4.1.

103  Waldersee, diary entry for 12 October 1893, GStA Berlin, Waldersee Papers; cf. Meisner, II, p. 295.

104  Kaiser Wilhelm II, marginal note on Wesdehlen's report of 25 August 1888, PA AA, Asservat No. 4.1.

105  Waldersee, diary entry for 10 October 1891, GStA Berlin Waldersee Papers; omitted from Meisner II, p. 218.

106  Herbert Bismarck to Rantzau, 4 January 1889, BA Koblenz, Bismarck Papers FC 3014 N.

107  Eulenburg to Herbert Bismarck, 3 January 1889, *Eulenburgs Korrespondenz*, I, No. 209. See also Herbert Bismarck to his father, 30 December 1888, BA Koblenz, Bismarck Papers FC 3005 N.

108  Kaiser Wilhelm II to Eulenburg, 27 February 1889, *Eulenburgs Korrespondenz*, I, No. 213. See Eulenburg's reply of 1 March 1889, ibid., No. 214.

109  Herbert Bismarck to Rantzau, 3 February 1889, BA Koblenz, Bismarck Papers FC 3014 N.

110  Széchényi to Kálnoky, 31 January and mid-February 1889, HHStA Vienna, PA III 136.

111  Kaiser Wilhelm II to Queen Victoria, 14 February 1889, RA Z500/3.

112  Kaiserin Auguste Viktoria to Kaiser Wilhelm II, 23 September 1890, GStA Berlin, BPHA Rep. 53T Preußen: An Kaiser Wilhelm II., Bd IV.

113  Hoffmann, diary entry for 8 November 1889, Hoffmann Papers, Freiburg.

114  Morley, quoted in Jonathan Steinberg, 'Kaiser Wilhelm and the British', in Röhl and Sombart, *Kaiser Wilhelm II – New Interpretations*, p. 127.

115  Max Freiherr von Holzing-Berstett to his wife, 21 May 1910, Generallandesarchiv Karlsruhe, Holzing Papers, No. 116/21.

116  Kaiser Wilhelm II, speech of 23 August 1888, Penzler, *Reden Kaiser Wilhelms II. in den Jahren 1888–1895*, pp. 21–3.

117  Werthern to Eulenburg, 9 September 1888, *Eulenburgs Korrespondenz*, I, No. 195.

118  Holstein, diary entry for 11 November 1888, *Holstein Papers*, II, pp. 382–3.

119 Kaiser Wilhelm II, marginal note on Hohenlohe's report of 16 April 1898, PA AA, Asservat No. 4.

120 Kaiser Wilhelm II, marginal note on von der Goltz's report of 12 April 1891, ibid.

121 Kaiser Wilhelm II, marginal note on Hohenlohe's report of 13 March 1897, ibid.

122 Holstein, diary entry for 11 November 1888, *Holstein Papers*, II, pp. 382–3.

123 Kaiser Wilhelm II, marginal note on Radowitz's report from Madrid of 14 May 1893, PA AA, Asservat No. 4.

124 Kaiser Wilhelm II, marginal note on Count Rex's report of 14 September 1892, ibid.

125 Kaiser Wilhelm II, marginal note on an article in *Le Temps* of 29 March 1889, ibid.

126 Kaiser Wilhelm II, marginal note on an article in *Hamburger Korrespondent* of 25 August 1889, ibid.

127 Bismarck's comment on the article 'Zum 18. October' in *Berliner Zeitung*, PA AA, R 3447. See Empress Frederick to Queen Victoria, 21 October 1888, RA Z43/28. See also Grand Duke Ludwig IV of Hesse-Darmstadt to Empress Frederick, 17 October 1888, GStA Berlin, BPH Rep. 52 No. 3, pp. 349–52.

128 Kaiser Wilhelm II, speech of 27 October 1888, Penzler, *Reden Kaiser Wilhelms II. in den Jahren 1888–1895*, pp. 27–9.

129 Press reactions to the Kaiser's speech are collected in PA AA, R 3447.

130 Eissenstein to Kálnoky, 29 October 1888, HHStA Vienna, PA III 134.

131 Beauclerk to Salisbury, 28 October 1888, RA I56/97.

132 Holstein, diary entry for 29 October 1888, *Holstein Papers*, II, pp. 380–1.

133 Herbert Bismarck to his father, 31 October 1888, PA AA, R 3447.

134 Rottenburg to Herbert Bismarck, 1 November 1888, ibid.

135 Kaiser Wilhelm II, marginal note on Dönhoff's report of 2 January 1889, PA AA, Asservat No. 4.

136 Kaiser Wilhelm II, marginal note on Rantzau's report from Munich of 24 September 1889, ibid.

137 Kaiser Wilhelm II, marginal note on Rantzau's report from Munich of 3 June 1889, ibid.

138 Kaiser Wilhelm II, marginal note on Eisendecher's report from Karlsruhe of 13 July 1889 as well as on Münster's report from Paris of 21 October 1892, ibid.

139 Kaiser Wilhelm II, marginal note on Otto Bülow's and Below's reports of 24 November and 20 December 1898 from Rome, ibid.

140 Kaiser Wilhelm II, marginal note on Reuss's report from Vienna of 10 June 1889, ibid.

141 Waldersee, diary entry for 13 November 1888, GStA Berlin, Waldersee Papers; omitted from Meisner, II, pp. 18–19.

142 Waldersee, diary entry for 7 September 1888, GStA Berlin, Waldersee Papers. This passage was heavily crossed out by Meisner in the original diary and omitted from the published version. See Meisner, II, p. 3.

143 Waldersee, diary entry for 11 October 1888, GStA Berlin, Waldersee Papers. The original diary has at this point been so badly mutilated by Meisner that the text cannot be deciphered with any certainty. Cf. Meisner, II, p. 6.

144 Waldersee, diary entry for 29 October 1891, GStA Berlin, Waldersee Papers; omitted from Meisner, II, pp. 219–20.

145 Kaiser Wilhelm II, marginal note on a report in the *Daily News* of 29 March 1889, PA AA, Asservat No. 4.

146 Kaiser Wilhelm II, marginal note on a Vienna newspaper article of 12 May 1889, ibid.

147 Kaiser Wilhelm II, marginal note on Schlözer's report from Rome of 23 November 1889, ibid.

148 Prince Ernst zu Hohenlohe-Langenburg to his father, 24 May 1889, Hohenlohe-Zentralarchiv Neuenstein, Hermann Hohenlohe-Langenburg Papers, Bü. 56.
149 Kaiser Wilhelm II, marginal note on an article in the *Daily News* of 15 June 1889, PA AA, Asservat No. 4.
150 Kaiser Wilhelm II, marginal note on Schlözer's report of 4 October 1890, ibid.
151 Kaiser Wilhelm II, marginal note on Schweinitz's report of 24 May 1891, ibid.
152 Waldersee, diary entry for 29 October 1888, GStA Berlin, Waldersee Papers; Meisner, II, pp. 12–13.
153 Cosima Wagner to Kaiser Wilhelm II, 23 August 1888, PA AA, R 3474.
154 Lucanus to Prince Otto von Bismarck, 18 September 1888, PA AA, R 3474.
155 See *Eulenburgs Korrespondenz*, I, pp. 191–4.
156 *Hamburger Nachrichten*, quoted in *Münchener Neueste Nachrichten*, 12 October 1888, PA AA, Preußen 1 No. 1d, Bd I.
157 Prince Otto von Bismarck to Kaiser Wilhelm II, 20 September 1888, PA AA, R 3474.
158 Note by Holstein, 15 and 21 October 1888, ibid.
159 Herbert Bismarck to Lucanus, 31 October 1888, ibid.
160 Herbert Bismarck to Rantzau, 5 August 1888, BA Koblenz, Bismarck Papers FC 3014 N.
161 Rantzau to Herbert Bismarck, 6 August 1888, BA Koblenz, Bismarck Papers FC 3028 N; Herbert Bismarck to Rantzau, 12 August 1888, ibid., FC 3014 N. Cf. Hans Rall, *Wilhelm II. Eine Biographie*, Graz, Vienna, Cologne 1995, pp. 84ff.
162 Waldersee, diary entry for 27 February 1894, GStA Berlin, Waldersee Papers; omitted from Meisner, II, p. 309.

### 6   FIRST STEPS IN FOREIGN AFFAIRS

1 PA AA, Asservat No. 4.1.
2 Prince Wilhelm of Prussia, marginal notes on Deines's report from Vienna of 5 February 1888, PA AA, Asservat No. 4.1.
3 Herbert Bismarck to Kaiser Wilhelm II, 11 November 1888, BA Koblenz, Bismarck Papers FC 2986 N.
4 Waldersee, diary entries for 19–22 November 1888, GStA Berlin, Waldersee Papers; omitted from Meisner, II, p. 21.
5 Waldersee, diary entry for 27 January 1889, GStA Berlin, Waldersee Papers; cf. Meisner, II, p. 34.
6 Waldersee, diary entry for 25 March 1889, GStA Berlin, Waldersee Papers; cf. Meisner, II, p. 47.
7 Prince Wilhelm of Prussia, marginal note on Deines's report from Vienna of 5 February 1888, PA AA, Asservat No. 4.1.
8 Kaiser Wilhelm II, marginal note on Yorck's report of 31 July 1888, ibid.; cited in *Große Politik*, VI, p. 341.
9 Kaiser Wilhelm II, marginal note on Yorck's report of 14 October 1888, PA AA, Asservat No. 4.1.
10 Kaiser Wilhelm II, marginal note on the military attaché's report from Paris of 14 November 1888, ibid.
11 Kaiser Wilhelm II, marginal note on a report from St Petersburg of 5 November 1888, ibid.
12 Kaiser Wilhelm II, marginal note on Rechenberg's report from Warsaw of 10 November 1888, ibid.; Waldersee, diary entry for 15 November 1888, GStA Berlin, Waldersee Papers; Meisner, II, p. 19. Cf. the Kaiser's marginal notes on a report from St Petersburg of 27 June 1888, PA AA, Asservat No. 4.1.

13 Prince Otto von Bismarck to Kaiser Wilhelm II, 19 August 1888, *Große Politik*, VI, No. 1350.

14 Waldersee, diary entry for 1 January 1889, GStA Berlin, Waldersee Papers; omitted from Meisner, II, p. 27. See below, pp. 210–16 and 218–25.

15 Kaiser Wilhelm II, speech of 16 August 1888, Penzler, *Reden Kaiser Wilhelms II. in den Jahren 1888–1895*, pp. 19–21. See above, p. 73.

16 See Kaiser Wilhelm II, marginal note on a report from Monts of 28 August 1888, PA AA, Asservat No. 4.1.

17 Kaiser Wilhelm II, note of 3 November 1888, BA Koblenz, Bismarck Papers FC 2986 N.

18 Kaiser Wilhelm II, marginal note dated 21 December 1889 on Schweinitz's report of 11 December 1889, PA AA, Asservat No. 4.

19 Waldersee, diary entry for 8 September 1888, GStA Berlin, Waldersee Papers; omitted from Meisner, II, p. 4.

20 Waldersee, diary entry for 2 March 1889, GStA Berlin, Waldersee Papers; largely omitted from Meisner, II, p. 42.

21 Waldersee, diary entry for 15 April 1889, GStA Berlin, Waldersee Papers; omitted from Meisner, II, p. 48.

22 Waldersee, diary entry for 20 April 1889, GStA Berlin, Waldersee Papers; omitted from Meisner, II, p. 49.

23 Waldersee, diary entry for 28 October 1888, GStA Berlin, Waldersee Papers; cf. Meisner, II, p. 12.

24 Waldersee, diary entry for 27 October 1888, GStA Berlin, Waldersee Papers; Meisner, II, p. 12.

25 Waldersee, diary entry for 28 October 1888, GStA Berlin, Waldersee Papers; cf. Meisner, II, p. 12.

26 Waldersee, diary entry for 1 November 1888, GStA Berlin, Waldersee Papers; cf. Meisner, II, p. 13, where key passages have been omitted.

27 Waldersee, diary entry for 3 November 1888, GStA Berlin, Waldersee Papers; numerous passages omitted from Meisner, II, p. 14.

28 Waldersee, diary entry for 6 November 1888, GStA Berlin, Waldersee Papers; abridged in Meisner, II, p. 15.

29 Waldersee, diary entry for 11 November 1888, GStA Berlin, Waldersee Papers; abridged and distorted in Meisner, II, pp. 17–18.

30 Waldersee, diary entry for 13 November 1888, GStA Berlin, Waldersee Papers; Meisner, II, pp. 18–19; Waldersee to Verdy du Vernois, 26 November 1888, GStA Berlin, Waldersee Papers, B I No. 53. See also Holstein, diary entry for 11 November 1888, *Holstein Papers*, II, pp. 382–3; Herbert Bismarck to his father, 30 December 1888, BA Koblenz, Bismarck Papers FC 3005 N.

31 Prince Otto von Bismarck to Waldersee, 24 November 1888 and Waldersee's coded reply of the same day, PA AA, R 1009.

32 Waldersee, diary entry for 27 November 1888, GStA Berlin, Waldersee Papers; omitted from Meisner, II, p. 23.

33 Waldersee, diary entry for 12 December 1888, GStA Berlin, Waldersee Papers; omitted from Meisner, II, pp. 25–6.

34 Waldersee, diary entry for 1 January 1889, GStA Berlin, Waldersee Papers; omitted from Meisner, II, p. 27.

35 Waldersee, diary entries for 21 and 26 January 1889, GStA Berlin, Waldersee Papers; cf. Meisner, II, pp. 32–3.

36 Eulenburg's note of 17 February 1889, *Eulenburgs Korrespondenz*, I, pp. 328–9.

37 Holstein to Eulenburg, 6 February 1889, ibid., No. 211.

38 Eulenburg's note of 17 February 1889, ibid., pp. 328–9. See Herbert Bismarck to Bülow, 28 October 1888, in Bußmann, *Staatssekretär*, No. 371. For Herbert Bismarck's view, see Salisbury to Queen Victoria, 29 March 1889, RA A67/48.

39 See Waldersee, diary entries for 21 October, 9 and 25 November and 2 December 1888, GStA Berlin, Waldersee Papers; Meisner, II, pp. 10, 16–17 and 22ff.

40 Waldersee, diary entry for 21 January 1889, GStA Berlin, Waldersee Papers; omitted from Meisner, II, p. 32.

41 Waldersee, diary entries for 1 and 3 November 1888, GStA Berlin, Waldersee Papers; cf. Meisner, II, pp. 13–14.

42 Waldersee, diary entry for 9 November 1888, GStA Berlin, Waldersee Papers; printed only in part in Meisner, II, pp. 16–17.

43 Waldersee, diary entry for 12 November 1888, GStA Berlin, Waldersee Papers; cf. Meisner, II, p. 18.

44 Kaiser Wilhelm II, marginal note on Deines's report of 20 December 1888, PA AA, R 8594.

45 Kaiser Wilhelm II, marginal note on Deines's report of 20 December 1888, PA AA, Asservat No. 4.1.

46 Kaiser Wilhelm II, marginal note on a report from Vienna of 19 October 1888, ibid.

47 Kaiser Wilhelm II, marginal note on Count Monts's report of 18 January 1889, ibid.

48 Kaiser Wilhelm II, marginal note on Reuss's report of 22 December 1888, ibid. See above, pp. 121–2.

49 Paul Hoffmann, diary entry for 10 November 1889, Hoffmann Papers, Freiburg.

50 Waldersee, diary entry for 22 April 1889, GStA Berlin, Waldersee Papers; cf. Meisner, II, p. 49.

51 Waldersee, diary entries for 1 and 21 January 1889, GStA Berlin, Waldersee Papers; cf. Meisner, II, pp. 27, 32.

52 Waldersee, diary entry for 25 January 1889, GStA Berlin, Waldersee Papers; omitted from Meisner, II, p. 33.

53 Waldersee, diary entry for 1 January 1889, GStA Berlin, Waldersee Papers; omitted from Meisner, II, p. 27.

54 Waldersee, diary entry for 21 January 1889, GStA Berlin, Waldersee Papers; cf. Meisner, II, p. 32.

55 Ibid.

56 Waldersee, diary entry for 25 March 1889, GStA Berlin, Waldersee Papers; omitted from Meisner, II, p. 47.

57 Waldersee, diary entry for 5 April 1889, GStA Berlin, Waldersee Papers; largely omitted from Meisner, II, p. 48.

58 Colonel Euan Smith to Salisbury, 20 November 1888, RA I56/99–100.

59 Prince Ernst zu Hohenlohe-Langenburg to his father, 10 September 1889, Hohenlohe-Zentralarchiv, Schloss Neuenstein, Hermann Hohenlohe-Langenburg Papers, Bü. 56. See also the exchange between the Sultan of Zanzibar and Kaiser Wilhelm II of 2 June and 15 August 1889, in PA AA, R 3579.

60 Herbert Bismarck to his father, 16 September 1888, BA Koblenz, Bismarck Papers FC 3005 N. Cf. Herbert Bismarck to Holstein, 30 September 1888, *Holstein Papers*, III, No. 276.

61 Herbert Bismarck to Rantzau, 30 July 1889, BA Koblenz, Bismarck Papers FC 3014 N, in Bußmann, *Staatssekretär*, No. 386.

62 Kaiser Wilhelm II, marginal note on his conversation with Admiral von Knorr of 11 September 1888, PA AA, Asservat No. 4.1.

63 Kaiser Wilhelm II, marginal note on Hatzfeldt's report of 30 November 1888, ibid.

64 Kaiser Wilhelm II, marginal note on Hatzfeldt's report of 12 December 1888, ibid.

65 Kaiser Wilhelm II, Gedankensplitter über den Krieg in Transvaal, 21 December 1899, RA W60/28, and Weitere Gedankensplitter über den Transvaalkrieg, 4 February 1900, RA W60/67.

66 Count Herbert Bismarck, Aufzeichnungen, pp. 62–70, BA Koblenz, Bismarck Papers FC 3018 N.

67 Kaiser Wilhelm II, marginal note on report No. A 17256/89 from East Africa, PA AA, Asservat No. 4.1.

68 Herbert Bismarck, diary entries for 15 and 17 February 1890, BA Koblenz, Bismarck Papers FC 3018 N.

69 Empress Frederick to Queen Victoria, 20 April 1889, RA Z44/31, in Ponsonby, *Letters of the Empress Frederick*, pp. 370–3.

70 Herbert Bismarck to Rantzau, 30 July 1889, BA Koblenz, Bismarck Papers FC 3014 N, in Bußmann, *Staatssekretär*, No. 386. See Kaiserin Auguste Viktoria to Kaiser Wilhelm II, 1 July 1889, GStA BPHA Rep. 53T Preußen: An Kaiser Wilhelm II., Bd III.

71 Kiderlen-Wächter to Holstein, 19 July 1888, *Holstein Papers*, III, No. 272.

72 Senden-Bibran, Aufzeichnungen über das Jahr 1888, BA-MA Freiburg, Senden-Bibran Papers N160/11, p. 27.

73 Hoffmann, diary entries for 21 October and 11 November 1889, Hoffmann Papers, Freiburg.

74 Hoffmann, diary entry for 9 November 1889, ibid.

75 Hoffmann, diary entries for 22 October and 11 November 1889, ibid.

76 Hoffmann, diary entry for 8 November 1889, also 25 October 1889, ibid.

77 Kaiser Wilhelm II, Jugenderinnerungen, dictated on 2 April 1926, Mewes Papers, in the possession of Oberst Joachim von Natzmer, Munich. Cf. Kaiser Wilhelm II, *Aus meinem Leben 1859–1888*, Berlin, Leipzig 1927, pp. 274–5.

78 Kaiser Wilhelm II, Jugenderinnerungen, dictated on 2 April 1926, Mewes Papers, in the possession of Oberst Joachim von Natzmer, Munich.

79 See Hoffmann, diary entry for 22 October 1889, Hoffmann Papers, Freiburg. For the relationship between Wilhelm and his brother Heinrich, see below, pp. 628–33.

80 Prince Heinrich of Prussia to Kaiser Wilhelm II, telegram, 31 March 1889, GStA Berlin, BPHA Rep. 52 V1 No. 13.

81 Waldersee to Holstein, 26 July 1888, *Holstein Papers*, III, No. 275.

82 Waldersee, diary entry for 9 October 1888, GStA Berlin, Waldersee Papers; cf. Meisner, II, p. 4.

83 Waldersee, diary entry for 6 November 1888, GStA Berlin, Waldersee Papers; omitted from Meisner, II, p. 15.

84 Kaiser Wilhelm II, Jugenderinnerungen, dictated on 2 April 1926, Mewes Papers, Munich. Cf. Kaiser Wilhelm II, *Aus meinem Leben*, p. 263. 'Not one word' of the ex-Kaiser's dictated memoirs were used by the ghost writers of the book. See Kurt Jagow to Friedrich Mewes, 9 April 1926, Mewes Papers, Munich.

85 Bülow, *Memoirs*, II, p. 30.

86 Waldersee, diary entry for 11 November 1888, GStA Berlin, Waldersee Papers; abridged and distorted in Meisner, II, pp. 17–18.

87 Prince Christian of Schleswig-Holstein, Report on my conversations with the Emperor, 16 April 1889, RA Z281/34; Malet to Salisbury, 3 February 1889, RA I57/14; Herbert Bismarck to Kaiser Wilhelm II, 17 March 1889, with marginal notes of the Kaiser, BA Koblenz, Bismarck Papers FC 2986 N.

88 Kaiser Wilhelm II to Queen Victoria, 17 August 1889, RA I57/53, in Buckle, *Letters of Queen Victoria*, I, pp. 526–7.

89 Kaiser Wilhelm II, marginal note on an article in the *Manchester Guardian*, 3 August 1889, PA AA, Asservat No. 4.

90 Kaiser Wilhelm II to Queen Victoria, 22 December 1889, RA I57/75.

91 Grand Duchess Augusta Caroline of Mecklenburg-Strelitz to Count Adolphus von Teck, 7 September 1888, RA Geo V CC50/184.

7   THE PILLARS OF IMPERIAL POWER

1 Holstein to Eulenburg, 5 May 1896, *Eulenburgs Korrespondenz*, III, No. 546.

2 See Röhl, *Kaiser and His Court*, pp. 70–106.

3 See Konrad Breitenborn, *Im Dienste Bismarcks. Die politische Karriere des Grafen Otto zu Stolberg-Wernigerode*, Leipzig 3rd edn 1986, pp. 331–2; Breitenborn, ed., *Die Lebenserinnerungen des Fürsten Otto zu Stolberg-Wernigerode*, Wernigerode 1996, pp. xvi–xviii.

4 See Bismarck to Crown Prince Wilhelm, 3 May 1888, Albedyll to Kaiser Wilhelm II, 23 June 1888, PA AA, R 3433. See also Breitenborn, *Im Dienste Bismarcks*, pp. 341–2; Eissenstein to Kálnoky, 3 November 1888, HHStA Vienna, PA III 134; Holstein, diary entry for 22 October 1888, *Holstein Papers*, II, pp. 380–1.

5 Széchényi to Kálnoky, 30 June and 4 July 1888, HHStA Vienna, PA III 134. Cf. Holstein, diary entry for 22 October 1888, *Holstein Papers*, II, pp. 380–1.

6 Waldersee, diary entry for 7 July 1888, GStA Berlin, Waldersee Papers; Meisner, I, p. 411.

7 Kaiser Wilhelm II to Kaiserin Augusta, 11 July 1888, GStA Berlin, BPHA Rep. 53J Lit. P No. 14a.

8 Waldersee, diary entry for 20 November 1896, GStA Berlin, Waldersee Papers; omitted from Meisner, II, p. 377.

9 Széchényi to Kálnoky, 2 August 1888, HHStA Vienna, PA III 134.

10 Empress Frederick to Queen Victoria, 10 July 1891, RA Z50/57.

11 Széchényi to Kálnoky, 30 June 1888, HHStA Vienna, PA III 134.

12 See Holstein, diary entry for 22 October 1888, *Holstein Papers*, II, pp. 380–1.

13 Széchényi to Kálnoky, 4 July 1888, HHStA Vienna, PA III 134.

14 For the career of Versen, who died in early 1893, see Alfred Freiherr von Werthern, *General von Versen. Ein militärisches Zeit- und Lebensbild. Aus hinterlassenen Briefen und Aufzeichnungen*, Berlin 1898.

15 Waldersee, diary entries for 20 July 1891 and 8 October 1893, GStA Berlin, Waldersee Papers; cf. Meisner, II, pp. 212–13 and 294–5.

16 Empress Frederick to Queen Victoria, 9 January 1892, RA Z52/14.

17 Swaine to Ponsonby, 1 July 1892, RA I59/89.

18 Waldersee, diary entry for 29 March 1889, GStA Berlin, Waldersee Papers; omitted from Meisner, II, p. 48. See also ibid., pp. 294–5.

19 For details of Wittich's dismissal and his role at the court, see below, ch. 16.

20 Széchényi to Kálnoky, 21 June 1888, HHStA Vienna, PA III 134.

21 Swaine to Ponsonby, 1 July 1892, RA 59/89.

22 Holstein to Eulenburg, 7/8 April 1895, *Eulenburgs Korrespondenz*, III, No. 1101; Eulenburg to Holstein, 16 April 1895, ibid., No. 1104.

23 Empress Frederick to Queen Victoria, 13 August 1890, RA Z49/5. On Zitzewitz's sudden death, see Empress Frederick to her daughter Princess Viktoria of Schaumburg-Lippe, 27 February 1892, AdHH Schloss Fasanerie.

24 Empress Frederick to Queen Victoria, 4 July 1891, RA Z50/55.

25 Empress Frederick to Queen Victoria, 9 November 1891, RA Z51/43. See Holstein to Eulenburg, 7/8 April 1895, *Eulenburgs Korrespondenz*, III, No. 1101; Eulenburg to Holstein, 16 April 1895, ibid., No. 1104.

26 Waldersee, diary entry for 8 December 1888, GStA Berlin, Waldersee Papers; Meisner, II, p. 25.

27 Rudolf Schmidt-Bückeburg, *Das Militärkabinett der preußischen Könige und deutschen Kaiser. Seine geschichtliche Entwicklung und staatsrechtliche Stellung 1787–1918*, Berlin 1933, pp. 177ff.; Waldersee, diary entry for 23 June 1888, GStA Berlin, Waldersee Papers; Meisner, I, p. 406.

28 Rudolf Graf von Stillfried-Alcántara, *Ceremonial-Buch für den Königlich-Preußischen Hof*, Berlin 1871–8, p. iv.

29 Graf Carl von Wedel, *Zwischen Kaiser und Kanzler*, Leipzig 1943, p. 187; also Wedel, promemoria of 13 June 1894, in the possession of Graf Gustav von Wedel, Frankfurt a.M.

30 Waldersee, diary entry for 22 October 1894, GStA Berlin, Waldersee Papers; omitted from Meisner, II, p. 327.

31 Senden-Bibran, Aufzeichnungen über das Jahr 1888, BA-MA Freiburg, Senden-Bibran Papers N160/11, pp. 38–40.

32 Waldersee, diary entry for 26 August 1888, GStA Berlin, Waldersee Papers; cf. Meisner, II, p. 1.

33 Princess Viktoria of Schaumburg-Lippe to Empress Frederick, 9 May 1891, AdHH Schloss Fasanerie.

34 Waldersee, diary entry for 17 September 1891, GStA Berlin, Waldersee Papers; omitted from Meisner, II, pp. 216–17.

35 Bodman to Brauer, 7 March 1897, in Walther Peter Fuchs, ed., *Großherzog Friedrich I. von Baden und die Reichspolitik 1871–1907*, 4 vols., Stuttgart 1968–80, III, No. 1657.

36 Eulenburg to Kaiser Wilhelm II, 15 April 1893, *Eulenburgs Korrespondenz*, II, No. 791.

37 Holzing-Berstett to his mother, 12 August 1905, Generallandesarchiv Karlsruhe, Holzing Papers, No. 116/11.

38 Holzing-Berstett to his mother, 3 September 1905, ibid.

39 Heinrich Prinz von Schönburg-Waldenburg, *Erinnerungen aus kaiserlicher Zeit*, Leipzig 1929, pp. 132–3.

40 Walter Görlitz, ed., *Der Kaiser . . . Aufzeichnungen des Chefs des Marinekabinetts Admiral Georg Alexander v. Müller über die Ära Wilhelms II.*, Göttingen 1965, pp. 188–9.

41 Waldersee, diary entry for 22 October 1888, GStA Berlin, Waldersee Papers; cf. Meisner, II, p. 10.

42 Hoffmann, diary entries for 4 and 12 November 1889, Hoffmann Papers, Freiburg.

43 Waldersee, diary entry for 22 October 1888, GStA Berlin, Waldersee Papers; cf. Meisner, II, p. 10.

44 Waldersee, diary entry for 19 November 1888, GStA Berlin, Waldersee Papers; cf. Meisner, II, p. 21.

45 Waldersee, diary entry for 29 August 1888, GStA Berlin, Waldersee Papers; cf. Meisner, II, p. 2.

46 Waldersee, diary entry for 5 November 1888, GStA Berlin, Waldersee Papers; cf. Meisner, II, p. 15.

47 Waldersee, diary entry for 26 August 1888, GStA Berlin, Waldersee Papers; cf. Meisner, II, p. 1; Széchényi to Kálnoky, 26 January 1889, HHStA Vienna, PA III 136.

48 Waldersee, diary entry for 26 November 1888, GStA Berlin, Waldersee Papers; cf. Meisner, II, pp. 22–3.

49 Waldersee, diary entry for 29 August 1888, GStA Berlin, Waldersee Papers; cf. Meisner, II, p. 2.

50 See Mathilde Gräfin von Keller, *Vierzig Jahre im Dienst der Kaiserin. Ein Kulturbild aus den Jahren 1881–1921*, Leipzig 1935, pp. 131–2; also *Young Wilhelm*, pp. 257ff.

51 Waldersee, diary entry for 26 November 1888, GStA Berlin, Waldersee Papers; cf. Meisner, II, pp. 22–3. See also the entries for 22 October and 19 November 1888, GStA Berlin, Waldersee Papers; cf. Meisner, II, pp. 10 and 21.

52  August Eulenburg to Philipp Eulenburg, 27 March 1889, *Eulenburgs Korrespondenz*, I, No. 216; Waldersee, diary entry for 29 March 1889, GStA Berlin, Waldersee Papers; omitted from Meisner, II, p. 48.

53  Waldersee, diary entry for 14 April 1889, GStA Berlin, Waldersee Papers; omitted from Meisner, II, p. 48.

54  Széchényi to Kálnoky, 16 June 1888, HHStA Vienna, PA III 134.

55  Kaiser Wilhelm II to Kaiserin Augusta, 11 July 1888, GStA Berlin, BPHA Rep. 53J Lit. P No. 14a.

56  Waldersee, diary entry for 11 October 1888, GStA Berlin, Waldersee Papers; Meisner, II, p. 6.

57  Holstein to Eulenburg, 23 September 1895, cited in *Eulenburgs Korrespondenz*, III, p. 1579.

58  Waldersee, diary entry for 26 October 1894, GStA Berlin, Waldersee Papers; omitted from Meisner, II, pp. 327–8.

59  See the brief character sketch in Röhl, *Kaiser and His Court*, pp. 142–3.

60  Kaiser Wilhelm II to Miessner, 13 December 1888, GStA Berlin, BPH Rep. 53 No. 400.

61  See *Young Wilhelm*, pp. 456 and 503–4.

62  See Holstein, diary entry for 22 October 1888, *Holstein Papers*, II, pp. 380–1. For Wilhelm's campaign against the Union Club, see *Young Wilhelm*, pp. 507–15.

63  Waldersee, diary entry for 16 June 1888, GStA Berlin, Waldersee Papers; cf. Meisner, I, p. 405.

64  Waldersee, diary entry for 20 June 1888, GStA Berlin, Waldersee Papers. The text printed in Meisner, I, p. 405, is incomplete. Kaiser Wilhelm II, *Ereignisse und Gestalten aus den Jahren 1878–1918*, Berlin, Leipzig 1922, p. 20. Wilhelm von Hahnke was married to Josefine von Bülow (1842–1911).

65  RA QVJ, 5 August 1889.

66  Waldersee, diary entry for 2 February 1891, GStA Berlin, Waldersee Papers; omitted from Meisner, II, p. 184.

67  Waldersee, diary entry for 10 October 1890, GStA Berlin, Waldersee Papers; cf. Meisner, II, p. 153.

68  Waldersee, diary entry for 19 January 1891, GStA Berlin, Waldersee Papers; omitted from Meisner, II, p. 176.

69  Waldersee, diary entry for 17 May 1891, GStA Berlin, Waldersee Papers; omitted from Meisner, II, p. 207.

70  See Walther Hubatsch, *Der Admiralstab und die obersten Marinebehörden in Deutschland 1884–1945*, Frankfurt a.M. 1958; Jonathan Steinberg, *Yesterday's Deterrent. Tirpitz and the Birth of the German Battle Fleet*, London 1966; Volker R. Berghahn, *Der Tirpitz-Plan. Genesis und Verfall einer innenpolitischen Krisenstrategie unter Wilhelm II.*, Düsseldorf 1971.

71  Jörg-Uwe Fischer, *Admiral des Kaisers. Georg Alexander von Müller als Chef des Marine- kabinetts Wilhelms II.*, Frankfurt a.M. 1992, pp. 29–30.

72  See Alfred von Tirpitz, *Erinnerungen*, Leipzig 1919, p. 36.

73  Müller to Tirpitz, 8 December 1889, cited in Fischer, *Admiral des Kaisers*, p. 34.

74  Széchényi to Kálnoky, 4 July 1888, HHStA Vienna, PA III 134.

75  Senden-Bibran, Aufzeichnungen über das Jahr 1888, BA-MA Freiburg, Senden-Bibran Papers N160/11, pp. 13ff.

76  Kaiser Wilhelm II, *Aus meinem Leben*, p. 273.

77  Senden-Bibran, Aufzeichnungen über das Jahr 1888, BA-MA Freiburg, Senden-Bibran Papers N160/11, pp. 33ff.

78  Ibid., p. 36.

79  Ibid.

80  Ibid., p. 38.

81  Bülow, *Memoirs*, II, p. 65.

82  Eulenburg to Holstein, 16 July 1896, cited in Röhl, *Kaiser and His Court*, p. 236.

83 Berghahn, *Tirpitz-Plan*, p. 189 n. 79.

84 Holstein to Bülow, 6 June 1896, cited in Isabel V. Hull, *The Entourage of Kaiser Wilhelm II, 1888–1918*, Cambridge 1982, p. 179.

85 See *Truth*, 22 November 1888, p. 898.

86 Waldersee, diary entry for 5 July 1888, GStA Berlin, Waldersee Papers; cf. Meisner, I, pp. 410–11.

87 Waldersee, diary entry for early August 1888, GStA Berlin, Waldersee Papers; cf. Meisner, I, p. 414.

88 See above, pp. 154–5.

89 Herbert Bismarck to his father, BA Koblenz, Bismarck Papers FC 3005 N.

90 Waldersee to Verdy, 26 November 1888, GStA Berlin, Waldersee Papers, B I No. 53.

91 See Schmidt-Bückeburg, *Militärkabinett*, pp. 175–6.

92 Waldersee to Verdy, 2 December 1888, GStA Berlin, Waldersee Papers, B I No. 53. See also Herbert Bismarck to his father, 30 December 1888, BA Koblenz, Bismarck Papers FC 3005 N.

93 Waldersee, diary entries for 8 and 26 April 1889, GStA Berlin, Waldersee Papers; cf. Meisner, II, pp. 48ff.

94 Bismarck's marginal comments on Herbert Bismarck's notes of April 1890, BA Koblenz, Bismarck Papers.

95 Hereditary Prince Bernhard of Saxe-Meiningen to Colmar Freiherr von der Goltz, 20 October 1898 and 9 April 1899, BA-MA Freiburg, v. d. Goltz Papers N737, Zug. 161/95.

96 Holzing-Berstett to his father, 4 January 1904, Generallandesarchiv Karlsruhe, Holzing Papers, No. 116/11.

97 Hereditary Prince Bernhard of Saxe-Meiningen to von der Goltz, 20 October 1898, BA-MA Freiburg, v. d. Goltz Papers N737, Zug. 161/95.

98 See below, p. 301.

99 Waldersee, diary entry for 23 June 1888, GStA Berlin, Waldersee Papers; cf. Meisner, I, p. 406.

100 Waldersee, diary entry for 9 October 1888, GStA Berlin, Waldersee Papers; omitted from Meisner, II, pp. 4–5.

101 Wedel, *Zwischen Kaiser und Kanzler*, p. 137.

102 Swaine to Ponsonby, 1 July 1892, RA I59/89.

103 Széchényi to Kálnoky, 29 December 1888, HHStA Vienna, PA III 134.

104 Széchényi to Kálnoky, 9 January 1889, ibid., PA III 136.

## 8 THE DOMINATION OF THE BISMARCKS

1 Herbert Bismarck to his father, 9 October 1888, BA Koblenz, Bismarck Papers FC 3005 N; in Bußmann, *Staatssekretär*, No. 368.

2 See *Young Wilhelm*, pp. 720–37.

3 Count Herbert Bismarck, 'Notizen V', BA Koblenz, Bismarck Papers FC 3018 N.

4 Herbert Bismarck to Rantzau, 17 June 1888, ibid., FC 3014 N.

5 Herbert Bismarck to his brother, 23 June 1888, in Bußmann, *Staatssekretär*, No. 362.

6 Herbert Bismarck to Holstein, 15 October 1888, *Holstein Papers*, III, No. 280.

7 Herbert Bismarck to Holstein, 17 October 1888, ibid., No. 281.

8 Rantzau to Herbert Bismarck, 29 August 1888, BA Koblenz, Bismarck Papers FC 3028 N.

9 Herbert Bismarck to Rantzau, 30 August 1888, ibid., FC 3014 N.

10 Prince Otto von Bismarck to Herbert Bismarck, 7 December 1888, PA AA, R 1009.

11 Herbert Bismarck to his father, 30 December 1888, BA Koblenz, Bismarck Papers FC 3005 N.

12 Bismarck left for Varzin on 8 June 1889 and did not return to Berlin until 24 January 1890: Count Herbert Bismarck, diary 1888–90, BA Koblenz, Bismarck Papers FC 3018 N.

13 Herbert Bismarck to his father, 9 June 1889, ibid., FC 3005 N; in Bußmann, *Staatssekretär*, No. 376.

14 Salisbury to Queen Victoria, 15 October 1888, RA T9/112, in Buckle, *Letters of Queen Victoria*, I, pp. 441–2.

15 Széchényi to Kálnoky, 9 February 1889, HHStA Vienna, PA III 136. See above, p. 24.

16 Széchényi to Kálnoky, 23 February 1889, HHStA Vienna, PA III 136.

17 Empress Frederick to Queen Victoria, 20 April 1889, RA Z44/31.

18 In the entire period from 12 July 1888 to 24 January 1890 the Chancellor was in Berlin only for the first six months of 1889. See Waldersee, diary entry for 27 March 1889, GStA Berlin, Waldersee Papers; cf. Meisner, II, p. 47.

19 Heinrich von Eckardt, Aufzeichnung vom 8. November 1889, GStA Berlin, BPH Rep. 53 No. 29.

20 Count Herbert Bismarck, diary 1888–90, BA Koblenz, Bismarck Papers FC 3018 N.

21 Széchényi to Kálnoky, 26 January 1889, HHStA Vienna, PA III 136.

22 Empress Frederick to Queen Victoria, 20 April 1889, RA Z44/31.

23 See e.g. Herbert Bismarck to Kaiser Wilhelm II, 11 November 1888, BA Koblenz, Bismarck Papers FC 2986 N. For earlier examples, see *Young Wilhelm*, pp. 417–18.

24 Herbert Bismarck to Rantzau, 17 June 1888, BA Koblenz, Bismarck Papers FC 3014 N.

25 Waldersee, diary entry for 13 November 1889, GStA Berlin, Waldersee Papers; cf. Meisner, II, pp. 76–7. See also Waldersee, diary entry for 3 January 1890, GStA Berlin, Waldersee Papers; omitted from Meisner, II, p. 87.

26 Széchényi to Kálnoky, 26 January 1889, HHStA Vienna, PA III 136. For the Geffcken case, see above, pp. 62–6.

27 Széchényi to Kálnoky, 26 January 1889, HHStA Vienna, PA III 136.

28 See Philipp Graf zu Eulenburg-Hertefeld, *Aus 50 Jahren. Erinnerungen, Tagebücher und Briefe aus dem Nachlaß des Fürsten*, Berlin 2nd edn 1925, pp. 81–107; Louis L. Snyder, 'Political Implications of Herbert von Bismarck's Marital Affairs, 1881, 1892', *Journal of Modern History*, 36 (1964), pp. 155–69; Otto Pflanze, *Bismarck and the Development of Germany*, 3 vols., Princeton 1963–90, III, pp. 55–6.

29 Count Herbert Bismarck, diary 1888–90, BA Koblenz, Bismarck Papers FC 3018 N.

30 Waldersee, diary entry for 28 February 1889, GStA Berlin, Waldersee Papers; largely omitted from Meisner, II, p. 41. On 27 February 1889 Herbert Bismarck wrote in his diary: 'In the evening ball at my place. 67 people. To bed at 6 a.m.': Count Herbert Bismarck, diary 1888–90, BA Koblenz, Bismarck Papers FC 3018 N.

31 Waldersee, diary entry for 28 February 1889, GStA Berlin, Waldersee Papers; largely omitted from Meisner, II, p. 41.

32 Waldersee, diary entry for 9 June 1889, GStA Berlin, Waldersee Papers; cf. Meisner, II, p. 53.

33 Waldersee, diary entry for 12 October 1889, GStA Berlin, Waldersee Papers; omitted from Meisner, II, p. 70.

34 See Herbert Bismarck to Rantzau, 24 July 1889, BA Koblenz, Bismarck Papers FC 3014 N.

35 Waldersee, diary entry for 12 October 1889, GStA Berlin, Waldersee Papers; omitted from Meisner, II, p. 70.

36 Waldersee, diary entry for 28 February 1889, GStA Berlin, Waldersee Papers; abridged and distorted in Meisner, II, pp. 41–2.

37 Waldersee, retrospective diary entry, GStA Berlin, Waldersee Papers; cf. Meisner, II, pp. 63–4.

38 Waldersee, diary entry for 12 October 1889, GStA Berlin, Waldersee Papers; omitted from Meisner, II, p. 70.

39  Waldersee, diary entry for 13 November 1889, GStA Berlin, Waldersee Papers; Meisner, II, p. 77.

40  Waldersee, diary entry for 15 April 1889, GStA Berlin, Waldersee Papers; cf. Meisner, II, p. 48.

41  Waldersee, diary entry for 16 October 1889, GStA Berlin, Waldersee Papers; omitted from Meisner, II, p. 73. See Waldersee, diary entry for 10 November 1889, GStA Berlin, Waldersee Papers; printed under an incorrect date in Meisner, II, p. 76.

42  Count Herbert Bismarck, diary entry for 7 June 1889, BA Koblenz, Bismarck Papers FC 3018 N.

43  Waldersee, diary entry for 2 January 1890, GStA Berlin, Waldersee Papers; largely omitted from Meisner, II, p. 86.

44  Waldersee, diary entry for 18 January 1890, GStA Berlin, Waldersee Papers; cf. Meisner, II, p. 95.

45  See *Young Wilhelm*, pp. 713–15.

46  Herbert Bismarck to his father, 5 October 1888, BA Koblenz, Bismarck Papers FC 3005 N; in Bußmann, *Staatssekretär*, No. 366.

47  Eulenburg to Kaiser Wilhelm II, 5 July 1888, *Eulenburgs Korrespondenz*, I, No. 185.

48  Kaiser Wilhelm II to Eulenburg, 28 July 1888, Eulenburg to Kaiser Wilhelm II, 1 August 1888, ibid., I, No. 187. A facsimile of this Skaldengesang, published in 1892, is printed in See, *Barbar Germane Arier*, pp. 18–19.

49  Kaiser Wilhelm II to Eulenburg, 28 August–4 September 1888, *Eulenburgs Korrespondenz*, I, No. 194.

50  Eulenburg to Kaiser Wilhelm II, 11 September 1888, ibid., No. 196.

51  Eulenburg to his mother, 4 October 1888, ibid., No. 197.

52  Herbert Bismarck to his father, 5 October 1888, in Bußmann, *Staatssekretär*, No. 366.

53  Eulenburg to his mother, 4 October 1888, *Eulenburgs Korrespondenz*, I, No. 197.

54  Eulenburg to Kaiser Wilhelm II, 15 October 1888, ibid., No. 199.

55  Eulenburg to his mother, 8 July 1888, ibid., No. 186. See also Herbert Bismarck to Rantzau, 12 September 1888, BA Koblenz, Bismarck Papers FC 3014 N.

56  Herbert Bismarck to his father, 5 October 1888, in Bußmann, *Staatssekretär*, No. 366.

57  Eulenburg to his mother, 4 October 1888, *Eulenburgs Korrespondenz*, I, No. 197; Herbert Bismarck to his father, 5 October 1888, in Bußmann, *Staatssekretär*, No. 366.

58  Herbert Bismarck to his father, 5 October 1888, in Bußmann, *Staatssekretär*, No. 366.

59  Prince Otto von Bismarck to Herbert Bismarck, 7 October 1888, ibid., No. 367. See also the Chancellor's marginal notes on his son's letter, ibid., pp. 524–5.

60  Prince Otto von Bismarck to Herbert Bismarck, 7 October 1888, ibid., No. 367; the Chancellor's marginal notes, ibid., pp. 524–5. Herbert Bismarck's reply of 8 October 1888 is located in BA Koblenz, Bismarck Papers FC 3005 N. Cf. Herbert Bismarck to Holstein, 15 October 1888, *Holstein Papers*, III, No. 280.

61  Eulenburg to Herbert Bismarck, 15 October 1888, *Eulenburgs Korrespondenz*, I, No. 198.

62  Eulenburg to Kaiser Wilhelm II, 15 October 1888, ibid., I, No. 199.

63  Kaiser Wilhelm II to Eulenburg, 31 October 1888, in Eulenburg, *Aus 50 Jahren*, p. 197.

64  Eulenburg to Kaiser Wilhelm II, 1 November 1888, *Eulenburgs Korrespondenz*, I, No. 201.

65  Eulenburg to Herbert Bismarck, 1 November 1888, ibid., No. 202.

66  Rantzau to Herbert Bismarck, 5 [?] November 1888, cited ibid., p. 320.

67  Eulenburg to his mother, 17 December 1888, ibid., No. 207.

68  Ibid.

69  Eulenburg to Grand Duchess Augusta Caroline of Mecklenburg-Strelitz, 8 April 1889, ibid., No. 217.

70  Eulenburg to Kaiser Wilhelm II, 22 December 1888, ibid., No. 208.

71 Eulenburg to Kaiser Wilhelm II, 15 October 1888, ibid., No. 199. See *Young Wilhelm*, pp. 713–15.

72 Eulenburg to Holstein, 4 February 1889, *Holstein Papers*, III, No. 287.

73 Eulenburg to Kaiser Wilhelm II, 15 October 1888, *Eulenburgs Korrespondenz*, I, No. 199.

74 Eulenburg to Kaiser Wilhelm II, 19 November 1888, ibid., No. 205.

75 Eulenburg to his father, 21 November 1888, ibid., No. 206.

76 Széchényi to Kálnoky, 9 January 1889, HHStA Vienna, PA III 136.

77 Eulenburg, diary entry for 17 January 1889, *Eulenburgs Korrespondenz*, I, p. 327.

78 Empress Frederick to Queen Victoria, 1 and 6 April 1889, RA Z44/21, 24 and 25. See below, pp. 639–43.

79 Kaiser Wilhelm II to Eulenburg, 27 February 1889, *Eulenburgs Korrespondenz*, I, No. 213.

80 Eulenburg to Kaiser Wilhelm II, 1 March 1889, ibid., No. 214.

81 See *Young Wilhelm*, pp. 485–8.

82 Ibid., pp. 502–7.

83 See ibid., pp. 499–05.

84 Count Herbert Bismarck, diary entry for 9 May 1889, BA Koblenz, Bismarck Papers FC 3018 N.

85 Eulenburg to Holstein, 18 February 1894, *Eulenburgs Korrespondenz*, II, No. 911. See also Waldersee, diary entry for 26 November 1888, GStA Berlin, Waldersee Papers; cf. Meisner, II, pp. 22–3.

86 In the six months from December 1888 to May 1889, the Kaiser received Herbert Bismarck in audience fifty-seven times; the corresponding figure for the six months from June to November 1889 is twenty-two: Count Herbert Bismarck, diary 1888–90, BA Koblenz, Bismarck Papers FC 3018 N; also Herbert Bismarck, 'Notizen V', ibid.

## 9  THE BISMARCK CRISIS BEGINS

1 Waldersee, diary entry for 3 June 1889, GStA Berlin, Waldersee Papers; cf. Meisner, II, p. 53.

2 See Kaiser Wilhelm II to Kaiserin Augusta, 28 September 1889, GStA Berlin, Rep. 5J Lit. P No. 14a.

3 *Badische Presse*, Karlsruhe, 4 October 1889. See above, ch. 1.

4 Waldersee, diary entry for 4 May 1889, GStA Berlin, Waldersee Papers; omitted from Meisner, II, p. 50.

5 See Waldersee, diary entries for 24 April and 4 May 1889, GStA Berlin, Waldersee Papers; omitted from Meisner, II, pp. 49–50.

6 Széchényi to Kálnoky, 26 January 1889, HHStA Vienna, PA III 136.

7 Waldersee, diary entry for 13 November 1889, GStA Berlin, Waldersee Papers; cf. Meisner, II, pp. 76–7.

8 See above, ch. 7.

9 Wilhelm's decision against the widening of the remit of the Reich Railway Office serves as an example. See below, pp. 225–6.

10 Waldersee, diary entry for 25 February 1889, GStA Berlin, Waldersee Papers; cf. Meisner, II, p. 40.

11 For example on 21 and 26 February and 13 and 23 March 1889: Waldersee, diary entries for those dates, GStA Berlin, Waldersee Papers.

12 Waldersee, diary entry for 18 March 1889, ibid.; Meisner, II, pp. 45–6.

13 For example on 4, 6 and 21 February and 13 March 1889: Count Herbert Bismarck, diary, BA Koblenz, Bismarck Papers FC 3018 N.

14 Waldersee, diary entry for 1 April 1889, GStA Berlin, Waldersee Papers; Meisner, II, p. 48.

15  Waldersee, diary entry for 2 March 1889, GStA Berlin, Waldersee Papers; cf. Meisner, II, p. 42. See also the diary entry for 12 March 1889, ibid., pp. 44–5. See Wilhelm's marginal notes on Deines's (5 February and 20 December 1888), Yorck's (14 October 1888) and Huene's reports (14 November 1888), PA AA, Asservat 4.1.

16  Count Herbert Bismarck, 'Notizen V', BA Koblenz, Bismarck Papers FC 3018 N.

17  Waldersee, diary entry for 3 February 1890, GStA Berlin, Waldersee Papers; omitted from Meisner, II, p. 99.

18  Waldersee, diary entry for 1 May 1889, GStA Berlin, Waldersee Papers; omitted from Meisner, II, p. 50.

19  Waldersee, diary entry for 15 April 1889, GStA Berlin, Waldersee Papers; cf. Meisner, II, p. 48.

20  See Herbert Bismarck to Rantzau, 27 June 1889, BA Koblenz, Bismarck Papers FC 3014 N; in Bußmann, *Staatssekretär*, No. 380.

21  Waldersee, diary entry for 26 March 1889, GStA Berlin, Waldersee Papers; cf. Meisner, II, p. 47.

22  Waldersee, diary entry for 19 March 1889, GStA Berlin, Waldersee Papers; omitted from Meisner, II, p. 46.

23  See above, pp. 191–7.

24  See above, pp. 173–6.

25  Count Herbert Bismarck, diary, 29 January and 19 February 1889, BA Koblenz, Bismarck Papers FC 3018 N.

26  Waldersee, diary entry for 19 and 25 February and 18 March 1889, GStA Berlin, Waldersee Papers; cf. Meisner, II, pp. 39–40, p. 46.

27  Waldersee, diary entry for 25 April and 1 May 1889, GStA Berlin, Waldersee Papers; omitted from Meisner, II, pp. 49–50.

28  Waldersee, diary entry for 6 April 1889, GStA Berlin, Waldersee Papers; largely omitted from Meisner, II, p. 48.

29  Wilhelm II, marginal note of April 1889, PA AA, Asservat 4.1.

30  Wilhelm II, marginal note on Brandt's report from Beijing of 15 July 1890, ibid.

31  Waldersee, diary entry for 6 April 1889, GStA Berlin, Waldersee Papers; omitted from Meisner, II, p. 48.

32  Waldersee, diary entry for 12 May 1889, GStA Berlin, Waldersee Papers; omitted from Meisner, II, p. 50.

33  Count Herbert Bismarck, diary, 22 July 1889, BA Koblenz, Bismarck Papers FC 3018 N.

34  Count Herbert Bismarck, diary, 20 May and 15 August 1889, ibid.

35  Count Herbert Bismarck, diary, 14 and 16 May 1889, ibid.

36  Waldersee, diary entry for 19 May 1889, GStA Berlin, Waldersee Papers; cf. Meisner, II, pp. 50–1.

37  Waldersee, diary entry for 20 May 1889, GStA Berlin, Waldersee Papers; cf. Meisner, II, pp. 51–2.

38  Waldersee, diary entry for 2 June 1889, GStA Berlin, Waldersee Papers; omitted from Meisner, II, p. 53.

39  Holstein to Eulenburg, 28 September 1889, *Eulenburgs Korrespondenz*, I, No. 235.

40  Waldersee, diary entry for 4 May 1889, GStA Berlin, Waldersee Papers; Meisner, II, p. 50.

41  See below, pp. 225–7.

42  Count Herbert Bismarck, 'Notizen V', BA Koblenz, Bismarck Papers FC 3018 N; diary, 12 and 15 May 1889, ibid.

43  See the Kaiser's speeches of 14 and 16 May 1889, Penzler, *Reden Kaiser Wilhelms II. in den Jahren 1888–1895*, pp. 53–7. See Christopher Clark, *Kaiser Wilhelm II*, London 2000, pp. 37ff., who rightly points out the unprecedented nature of the young monarch's intervention.

44 Waldersee, diary entry for 19 May 1889, GStA Berlin, Waldersee Papers; cf. Meisner, II, p. 50.

45 Bismarck to Kaiser Wilhelm II, 25 May 1889, in Meisner, II, p. 451.

46 Robert Freiherr Lucius von Ballhausen, *Bismarck-Erinnerungen*, Stuttgart, Berlin 1920, p. 497. For the machiavellian motives behind Bismarck's tactics during the miners' strike, see Lothar Gall, *Bismarck. Der weisse Revolutionär*, Frankfurt a.M., Berlin, Vienna 1980, pp. 690–1.

47 Eulenburg to Herbert Bismarck, 19 May 1889, *Eulenburgs Korrespondenz*, I, No. 221; Count Herbert Bismarck, diary, 20 May 1889, BA Koblenz, Bismarck Papers FC 3018 N.

48 Holstein to Eulenburg, 23 May 1889, *Eulenburgs Korrespondenz*, I, No. 222.

49 Count Herbert Bismarck, 'Notizen V', BA Koblenz, Bismarck Papers FC 3018 N.

50 Ibid.

51 Waldersee, diary entry for 19 May 1889, GStA Berlin, Waldersee Papers; cf. Meisner, II, p. 51.

52 Waldersee, diary entry for 2 and 3 June 1889, GStA Berlin, Waldersee Papers; cf. Meisner, II, p. 53; Herbert Bismarck to Rantzau, 4 July 1889, BA Koblenz, Bismarck Papers FC 3014 N, in Bußmann, *Staatssekretär*, No. 382; Count Herbert Bismarck, diary, 5 June 1889, BA Koblenz, Bismarck Papers FC 3018. See also Waldersee, diary entry for 9 June 1889, GStA Berlin, Waldersee Papers; omitted from Meisner, II, p. 53, but cf. Meisner, II, pp. 63–4.

53 Count Herbert Bismarck, diary, 8 May and 4 June 1889, BA Koblenz, Bismarck Papers FC 3018.

54 Waldersee, retrospective diary entry written in later years, GStA Berlin, Waldersee Papers; cf. Meisner, II, pp. 63–4. Cf. Herbert Bismarck to Rantzau, 4 July 1889, BA Koblenz, Bismarck Papers FC 3014 N; in Bußmann, *Staatssekretär*, No. 382.

55 Holstein to Eisendecher, 5 July 1889, *Holstein Papers*, III, No. 292.

56 Prince Otto von Bismarck to Eisendecher, 4 July 1889, cited ibid., p. 313, n. 1.

57 Holstein to Eisendecher, 11 July 1889, ibid., No. 293.

58 Waldersee, retrospective diary entry written in later years, GStA Berlin, Waldersee Papers; cf. Meisner, II, pp. 63–4. Cf. Herbert Bismarck to Rantzau, 4 July 1889, BA Koblenz, Bismarck Papers FC 3014 N; in Bußmann, *Staatssekretär*, No. 382.

59 Count Herbert Bismarck, 'Notizen V', BA Koblenz, Bismarck Papers FC 3018 N.

60 Waldersee, retrospective diary entry written in 1892, GStA Berlin, Waldersee Papers; cf. Meisner, II, pp. 55–6.

61 Cited above, p. 204.

62 Waldersee, diary entry for 25 March 1889, GStA Berlin, Waldersee Papers; omitted from Meisner, II, p. 47.

63 Waldersee, diary entry for 15 April 1889, GStA Berlin, Waldersee Papers; omitted from Meisner, II, p. 48.

64 Waldersee, diary entry for 7 July 1889, GStA Berlin, Waldersee Papers; cf. Meisner, II, pp. 54–9.

65 Count Herbert Bismarck, 'Notizen V', BA Koblenz, Bismarck Papers FC 3018 N; Count Herbert Bismarck, diary, 11 June 1889, ibid.

66 Kaiser Wilhelm II to Prince Otto von Bismarck, 12 June 1889, ibid., FC 2986 N.

67 Waldersee, diary entry for 7 July 1889, GStA Berlin, Waldersee Papers; cf. Meisner, II, pp. 54–9.

68 Waldersee, retrospective diary entry written in 1892, GStA Berlin, Waldersee Papers; cf. Meisner, II, pp. 55–6. See also Herbert Bismarck to his father, 14 June 1889, BA Koblenz, Bismarck Papers FC 3005 N; in Bußmann, *Staatssekretär*, No. 377.

69 Rantzau to Herbert Bismarck, 1 July 1889, cited in Bußmann, *Staatssekretär*, pp. 541–2, n. 5.

70 Herbert Bismarck to Rantzau, 4 July 1889, BA Koblenz, Bismarck Papers FC 3014 N; in Bußmann, *Staatssekretär*, No. 382.

71 Herbert Bismarck to his father, 14 June 1889, BA Koblenz, Bismarck Papers FC 3005 N; in Bußmann, *Staatssekretär*, No. 377.

72 Herbert Bismarck to Rantzau, 4 July 1889, BA Koblenz, Bismarck Papers FC 3014 N; in Bußmann, *Staatssekretär*, No. 382.

73 Eulenburg to Holstein, 6 August 1889, *Eulenburgs Korrespondenz*, I, No. 230.

74 Count Herbert Bismarck, 'Notizen V', BA Koblenz, Bismarck Papers FC 3018 N.

75 Waldersee, diary entry for 7 July 1889, GStA Berlin, Waldersee Papers; cf. Meisner, II, pp. 54–9.

76 Holstein to Eulenburg, 3 July 1889, *Eulenburgs Korrespondenz*, I, No. 225.

77 Holstein to Herbert Bismarck, late June 1889, in Bußmann, *Staatssekretär*, No. 379.

78 Herbert Bismarck to Rantzau, 27 June 1889, BA Koblenz, Bismarck Papers FC 3014 N; in Bußmann, *Staatssekretär*, No. 380. See also Herbert Bismarck to Eulenburg, 24 June 1889, *Eulenburgs Korrespondenz*, I, No. 224.

79 Herbert Bismarck to Rantzau, 4 July 1889, BA Koblenz, Bismarck Papers FC 3014 N; in Bußmann, *Staatssekretär*, No. 382.

80 Ibid.

81 Ibid.

82 Prince Otto von Bismarck to Eisendecher, 1 July 1889, cited from the Foreign Office files in *Holstein Papers*, III, p. 313, n. 3.

83 Rantzau's marginal notes on Herbert Bismarck to Rantzau, 6 July 1889, BA Koblenz, Bismarck Papers FC 3014 N; in Bußmann, *Staatssekretär*, No. 383.

84 Herbert Bismarck to Rantzau, 8 July 1889, BA Koblenz, Bismarck Papers FC 3014 N; in Bußmann, *Staatssekretär*, No. 385.

85 Holstein to Eisendecher, 5 July 1889, *Holstein Papers*, III, No. 292.

86 Herbert Bismarck to Rantzau, 6 July 1889, BA Koblenz, Bismarck Papers FC 3014 N; in Bußmann, *Staatssekretär*, No. 383.

87 Eulenburg to Herbert Bismarck, 17 July 1889, Holstein to Eulenburg, 2 August 1889, Eulenburg to Holstein, 6 August 1889, *Eulenburgs Korrespondenz*, I, Nos. 228–30; Kaiserin Auguste Viktoria to Kaiser Wilhelm II, 12, 13, 15, 16, 17 and 18 July 1889, GStA Berlin, BPHA Rep. 53T Preußen: An Kaiser Wilhelm II., Bd III.

88 Waldersee, retrospective addendum to 9 July 1889, GStA Berlin, Waldersee Papers; cf. Meisner, II, pp. 58–9.

89 Waldersee, restrospective note written in 1892, GStA Berlin, Waldersee Papers; cf. Meisner, II, pp. 55–6.

90 *Hamburger Nachrichten*, 19 June 1889. See *Berliner Tageblatt* of 20 June 1889.

91 Waldersee, diary entry for 7 July 1889, GStA Berlin, Waldersee Papers; omitted from Meisner, II, p. 54.

92 Ibid.; cf. Meisner, II, pp. 54–9.

93 Wilhelm II, marginal note, 20 June 1889, PA AA, R 1009.

94 See Meisner, II, pp. 60ff.

95 Eulenburg to Holstein, 6 August 1889, *Eulenburgs Korrespondenz*, I, No. 230.

96 Waldersee, diary entry for 7 July 1889, GStA Berlin, Waldersee Papers; cf. Meisner, II, pp. 54–9.

97 Waldersee, diary entry for 26 December 1889, GStA Berlin, Waldersee Papers; largely omitted from Meisner, II, p. 85.

98 Waldersee, diary entry for 7 December 1889, GStA Berlin, Waldersee Papers; omitted from Meisner, II, p. 81.

99 Waldersee, diary entry for 25 March 1889, GStA Berlin, Waldersee Papers; cf. Meisner, II, p. 47.

100 Herbert Bismarck to his father, 14 June 1889, BA Koblenz, Bismarck Papers FC 3005 N.

101 Waldersee, diary entries for 2 and 3 June 1889, GStA Berlin, Waldersee Papers; cf. Meisner, II, p. 53.

102 Waldersee, diary entry for 6 October 1889, GStA Berlin, Waldersee Papers; cf. Meisner, II, p. 69.

103 Count Herbert Bismarck, Aufzeichnung, pp. 76ff., BA Koblenz, Bismarck Papers FC 3018. See above, pp. 107–8.

104 Prince Ernst zu Hohenlohe-Langenburg to his father, 13 November 1889, Hohenlohe-Zentralarchiv Neuenstein, Hermann Hohenlohe-Langenburg Papers, Bü. 56.

105 Count Herbert Bismarck, Aufzeichnung, pp. 84–5, BA Koblenz, Bismarck Papers FC 3018. Cf. Salisbury to Queen Victoria, 24 October 1889, RA I57/66.

106 Waldersee, diary entry for 16 October 1889, GStA Berlin, Waldersee Papers; omitted from Meisner, II, p. 73.

107 Waldersee, diary entry for 21 October 1889, GStA Berlin, Waldersee Papers; omitted from Meisner, II, p. 73.

108 Waldersee, diary entry for 10 October 1889, GStA Berlin, Waldersee Papers; cf. Meisner, II, p. 69.

109 Count Herbert Bismarck, Aufzeichnung, pp. 84ff., BA Koblenz, Bismarck Papers FC 3018 N. See Herbert Bismarck to his father, 5 October 1889, in Bußmann, *Staatssekretär*, No. 390.

110 Herbert Bismarck's note on the imperial hunt at Hubertusstock, October 1889, BA Koblenz, Bismarck Papers FC 3005.

111 Holstein to Radolin, 15 October 1889, *Holstein Papers*, VI, No. 294.

112 Waldersee, diary entry for 12 and 16 October 1889, GStA Berlin, Waldersee Papers; Meisner, II, pp. 70 and 73.

113 Waldersee, diary entry for 12 October 1889, GStA Berlin, Waldersee Papers; Meisner, II, p. 70. Holstein to Radolin, 15 October 1889, *Holstein Papers*, III, No. 294.

114 Count Herbert Bismarck, Aufzeichnung, p. 86, BA Koblenz, Bismarck Papers FC 3018.

115 Waldersee, diary entry for 13 October 1889, GStA Berlin, Waldersee Papers; omitted from Meisner, II, p. 71.

116 Waldersee, retrospective note written in later years, GStA Berlin, Waldersee Papers; cf. Meisner, II, p. 70. Cf. Holstein to Radolin, 15 October 1889, Reuss to Holstein, 5 November 1889, *Holstein Papers*, III, Nos. 294 and 299.

117 Grand Duchess Olga, the daughter of Alexander III, cited in Ian Vorres, *The Last Grand Duchess*, London 1964, p. 66. The episode is recounted almost verbatim in Alexander Grand Duke of Russia, *Once a Grand Duke*, New York 1932, p. 174. For the growing concern of the Tsar over the mental health of Wilhelm II, see below, pp. 297–301.

118 Count Herbert Bismarck, Aufzeichnung, pp. 88–9, BA Koblenz, Bismarck Papers FC 3018 N.

119 Waldersee, diary entry for 15 October 1889, GStA Berlin, Waldersee Papers; Meisner, II, p. 70.

120 Waldersee, retrospective note written in later years, GStA Berlin, Waldersee Papers; Meisner, II, p. 72.

121 Count Herbert Bismarck, Aufzeichnung, p. 89, BA Koblenz, Bismarck Papers FC 3018 N.

122 Count Herbert Bismarck, Aufzeichnung, pp. 89–90, ibid. See Tsar Alexander III to Kaiser Wilhelm II, 18 November 1889, Kaiser Wilhelm II to Tsar Alexander III, 5 December 1889, PA AA, R 3571.

123 Waldersee, diary entry for 14 December 1894, GStA Berlin, Waldersee Papers; cf. Meisner, II, pp. 332–3.

124 Count Herbert Bismarck, Aufzeichnung, pp. 90–1, BA Koblenz, Bismarck Papers FC 3018 N.

125 Waldersee, diary entries for 3 and 5 November 1889, GStA Berlin, Waldersee Papers; cf. Meisner, II, p. 75.

126 See Kaiser Wilhelm II to Queen Victoria, telegram, 17 October 1889, RA I57/65.

127 Kaiser Wilhelm II to Kaiser Franz Joseph, 20 October 1889, HHStA Vienna, Kabinettsarchiv, Geheimakten 2.

128 Waldersee, diary entry for 23 October 1889, GStA Berlin, Waldersee Papers; Meisner, II, p. 74.

129 Kaiser Franz Joseph to Kaiser Wilhelm II, 24 October 1889, HHStA Vienna, Kabinettsarchiv, Geheimakten 2.

130 Waldersee, diary entry for 5 November 1889, GStA Berlin, Waldersee Papers; omitted from Meisner, II, p. 75.

131 Waldersee, diary entry for 17 November 1889, GStA Berlin, Waldersee Papers; Meisner, II, pp. 77-8.

132 Herbert Bismarck to Holstein, 21 October 1889, Solms to Holstein, 26 October 1889, *Holstein Papers*, III, Nos. 295-6.

133 Waldersee, diary entry for 17 November 1889, GStA Berlin, Waldersee Papers; omitted from Meisner, II, p. 78. See above, pp. 125-6.

134 Waldersee, diary entry for 3 November 1889, GStA Berlin, Waldersee Papers; omitted from Meisner, II, p. 75.

135 Waldersee, diary entry for 8 December 1889, GStA Berlin, Waldersee Papers; Meisner, II, pp. 81ff.

136 Waldersee, diary entry for 27 October 1889, GStA Berlin, Waldersee Papers; largely omitted from Meisner, II, p. 75.

137 Waldersee, diary entry for 5 November 1889, GStA Berlin, Waldersee Papers; cf. Meisner, II, pp. 75-6.

138 Waldersee, diary entry for 31 October 1889, GStA Berlin, Waldersee Papers; omitted from Meisner, II, p. 75.

139 Waldersee, diary entry for 7 December 1889, GStA Berlin, Waldersee Papers; printed in Meisner, II, p. 81, under an incorrect date.

140 Waldersee, diary entry for 2 January 1890, GStA Berlin, Waldersee Papers; cf. Meisner, II, pp. 85-6.

141 Ibid.

142 Waldersee, diary entry for 23 December 1889, GStA Berlin, Waldersee Papers; omitted from Meisner, II, pp. 83ff.

143 Waldersee, diary entry for 8 December 1889, GStA Berlin, Waldersee Papers; Meisner, II, p. 81.

144 Holstein to Radolin, 5 December 1889, *Holstein Papers*, III, No. 301.

145 Herbert Bismarck to his father, 9 December 1889, BA Koblenz, Bismarck Papers FC 3005 N. See also Bußmann, *Staatssekretär*, Nos. 551-3.

146 Count Herbert Bismarck, 'Notizen V', BA Koblenz, Bismarck Papers FC 3018 N; also Prince Otto von Bismarck to Herbert Bismarck, 10 December 1889, telegram, PA AA, R 1009; Herbert Bismarck to his father, 9 and 10 December 1889, with the Chancellor's marginal notes, BA Koblenz, Bismarck Papers FC 3005 N.

147 Herbert Bismarck to his father, 10 December 1889, BA Koblenz, Bismarck Papers FC 3005 N.

148 Herbert Bismarck to his father, 9 December 1889, ibid.

149 Verdy to Waldersee, 10 December 1889, GStA Berlin, Waldersee Papers, No. 53; also Waldersee, diary entry for 10 December 1889, GStA Berlin, Waldersee Papers; omitted from Meisner, II, p. 82.

150 Herbert Bismarck to his father, 9 and 10 December 1889, with marginal comments by the Chancellor, BA Koblenz, Bismarck Papers FC 3005 N.

151 Waldersee, diary entry for 10 December 1889, GStA Berlin, Waldersee Papers; omitted from Meisner, II, p. 82.

152 Count Herbert Bismarck, 'Notizen V', BA Koblenz, Bismarck Papers FC 3018 N.

153 Waldersee, diary entry for 11 December 1889, GStA Berlin, Waldersee Papers; omitted from Meisner, II, p. 83.

154 Count Herbert Bismarck, 'Notizen V', BA Koblenz, Bismarck Papers FC 3018 N; diary, 13 December 1889, ibid.

155 Herbert Bismarck to his father, 13 December 1889, ibid., FC 3005 N; in Bußmann, *Staatssekretär*, No. 394.

156 Herbert Bismarck to his father, 31 December 1889, BA Koblenz, Bismarck Papers FC 3018 N; in Bußmann, *Staatssekretär*, No. 395.

157 Herbert Bismarck to his father, 7 January 1890, BA Koblenz, Bismarck Papers FC 3018 N.

158 Holstein to Eulenburg, 26 December 1889, *Eulenburgs Korrespondenz*, I, No. 270.

159 Eulenburg to Kaiserin Auguste Viktoria, 30 December 1889, ibid., No. 274.

160 Eulenburg to Holstein, 28 December 1889, ibid., No. 272.

## 10   THE KAISER, THE CHANCELLOR AND THE KARTELL

1 Bunsen to Morier, 14 September 1889, Balliol College Oxford, Morier Papers, Box 42.

2 Herbert Bismarck to his father, 4 August 1888, BA Koblenz, Bismarck Papers FC 3005 N; in Bußmann, *Staatssekretär*, No. 363. See Hermann Oncken, *Rudolf von Bennigsen. Ein deutscher liberaler Politiker. Nach seinen Briefen und hinterlassenen Papieren*, 2 vols., Stuttgart, Leipzig 1910, II, pp. 543–7.

3 Herbert Bismarck to Rantzau, 5 August 1888, BA Koblenz, Bismarck Papers FC 3014 N.

4 Herbert Bismarck to Rantzau, 12 August 1888, ibid.; Rantzau to Herbert Bismarck, 29 August 1888, ibid., FC 3028 N; Werthern to Eulenburg, 9 September 1888, *Eulenburgs Korrespondenz*, I, No. 195; Lucius von Ballhausen, *Bismarck-Erinnerungen*, pp. 583–4.

5 See above, p. 12.

6 Douglas, Speech of 4 October 1888, *Norddeutsche Allgemeine Zeitung*, No. 474, 7 October 1888.

7 See Eissenstein to Kálnoky, 13 October 1888, HHStA Vienna, PA III 134.

8 Douglas, speech of 4 October 1888, *Norddeutsche Allgemeine Zeitung*, No. 474, 7 October 1888.

9 Herbert Bismarck to Wilhelm Bismarck, 19 October 1888, in Bußmann, *Staatssekretär*, No. 369.

10 Stoecker to Waldersee, 22 March 1889, GStA Berlin, Waldersee Papers. See above, p. 204.

11 Eissenstein to Kálnoky, 13 October 1888, HHStA Vienna, PA III 134.

12 Kaiserin Auguste Viktoria to Kaiser Wilhelm II, 11 October 1888, GStA Berlin, BPHA Rep. 53T Preußen: An Kaiser Wilhelm II., Bd III.

13 Waldersee, diary entry for 7 September 1888, GStA Berlin, Waldersee Papers; cf. Meisner, II, p. 3.

14 Waldersee, diary entry for 7 November 1888, GStA Berlin, Waldersee Papers; Meisner, II, p. 16.

15 Waldersee, diary entry for 23 October 1888, GStA Berlin, Waldersee Papers; cf. Meisner, II, p. 11.

16 Waldersee, diary entries for 11, 14, 17, and 23 October 1888, GStA Berlin, Waldersee Papers; cf. Meisner, II, pp. 5–11.

17 Freiherr von Hammerstein, 'Das monarchische Gefühl', *Kreuzzeitung*, late January 1889.

18 Széchényi to Kálnoky, 30 January 1889, HHStA Vienna, PA III 136.

19 Waldersee, diary entry for 19 March 1889, GStA Berlin, Waldersee Papers; omitted from Meisner, II, p. 46.

20 Waldersee, diary entry for 9 October 1889, GStA Berlin, Waldersee Papers; omitted from Meisner, II, p. 69.

21 Waldersee, diary entry for 9 July 1889, GStA Berlin, Waldersee Papers; Meisner, II, p. 60.

22 Herbert Bismarck to Rantzau, 27 June 1889, BA Koblenz, Bismarck Papers FC 3014; in Bußmann, *Staatssekretär*, No. 380.

23 Prince Otto von Bismarck to Lutz, 6 August 1889, Bismarck, *Die gesammelten Werke*, 15 vols., Berlin 1923–35, VIc, p. 416.

24 Waldersee, diary entry for 9 July 1889, GStA Berlin, Waldersee Papers; cf. Meisner, II, p. 60.

25 Holstein to Eulenburg, 28 September 1889, *Eulenburgs Korrespondenz*, I, No. 235.

26 Holstein to Eulenburg, 28 and 30 September 1889, ibid., Nos. 235–6.

27 Holstein to Eulenburg, 30 September 1889, ibid., No. 236.

28 See Otto Gradenwitz, *Bismarcks letzter Kampf, 1888–1898*, Berlin 1924, p. 76; Lucius von Ballhausen, *Bismarck-Erinnerungen*, pp. 503–4; Waldersee, diary entry for 6 October 1889, GStA Berlin, Waldersee Papers; cf. Meisner, II, p. 69.

29 Herbert Bismarck to Prince Otto von Bismarck, 5 October 1889, BA Koblenz, Bismarck Papers FC 3005 N; in Bußmann, *Staatssekretär*, No. 390.

30 Holstein to Eulenburg, 8 October 1889, *Eulenburgs Korrespondenz*, I, No. 237.

31 Waldersee, diary entry for 27 October and 1 and 25 November 1889, GStA Berlin, Waldersee Papers; cf. Meisner, II, pp. 75, 80.

32 Waldersee, diary entry for 4 November 1889, GStA Berlin, Waldersee Papers; omitted from Meisner, II, p. 75.

33 Waldersee, diary entry for 21 October 1889, GStA Berlin, Waldersee Papers; Meisner, II, pp. 73–4.

34 See Meisner, II, p. 73, n. 2.

35 See for example Holstein to Eulenburg, 6 and 12 November 1889, *Eulenburgs Korrespondenz*, I, Nos. 246 and 250.

36 Eulenburg to Kaiser Wilhelm II, 25 October 1889, ibid, No. 241.

37 Eulenburg to Kaiser Wilhelm II, 29 October 1889, ibid., No. 242.

38 Eulenburg to Grand Duke Friedrich I of Baden, 30 October 1889, ibid., No. 243.

39 Holstein to Eulenburg, 4 November 1889, ibid., No. 244.

40 Holstein to Eulenburg, 5 November 1889, ibid., No. 245.

41 Eulenburg to Holstein, 10 November 1889, ibid., No. 248.

42 Kaiser Wilhelm II to Prince Otto von Bismarck, telegram, 6 November 1889, cited in Holstein to Eulenburg, 9 November 1889, ibid., No. 247.

43 Lucanus to Boetticher, telegram, 6 November 1889, cited in Holstein to Eulenburg, 6 November 1889, ibid., No. 246.

44 Holstein to Eulenburg, 9 November 1889, ibid., No. 247. See also Eulenburg to Kaiser Wilhelm II, 10 November 1889, ibid., No. 249.

45 Eulenburg to Holstein, 19 November 1889, ibid., No. 254.

46 Holstein to Radolin, 5 December 1889, *Holstein Papers*, III, No. 301.

47 Holstein to Eulenburg, 12 December 1889, *Eulenburgs Korrespondenz*, I, No. 265. The Frankfurt speech is printed in Penzler, *Reden Kaiser Wilhelms II. in den Jahren 1888–1895*, pp. 82–4.

48 Waldersee, diary entry for 17 November 1889, GStA Berlin, Waldersee Papers; cf. Meisner, II, p. 78.

49 Prince Otto von Bismarck to Kaiser Wilhelm II, 9 November 1889, BA Berlin, Reichskanzlei, No. 863, cited in *Eulenburgs Korrespondenz*, I, No. 247, n. 1.

50 Ibid.; also Brauer to Lerchenfeld, 27 October 1889, BA Berlin, Reichskanzlei, No. 863, cited in *Eulenburgs Korrespondenz*, I, No. 243, n. 3.

51 Holstein to Eulenburg, 12 November 1889, *Eulenburgs Korrespondenz*, I, No. 250. See also Holstein to Ida von Stülpnagel, 13 November 1889, Helmuth Rogge, *Friedrich von Holstein. Lebensbekenntnis in Briefen an eine Frau*, Berlin 1932, p. 152.

52 Pflanze, *Bismarck and the Development of Germany*, III, pp. 368–9. See also below, pp. 436–50.

53 Waldersee, diary entry for 13 November 1889, GStA Berlin, Waldersee Papers; cf. Meisner, II, pp. 76–7.

54 Count Herbert Bismarck, 'Notizen II', April 1890, pp. 48–9, BA Koblenz, Bismarck Papers FC 3018 N.

55 Eulenburg to Herbert Bismarck, 25 January 1889, *Eulenburgs Korrespondenz*, I, No. 210.

56 Holstein to Eulenburg, 4 November 1889, ibid., No. 244.

57 Eulenburg to Holstein, 10 November 1889, ibid., No. 248.

58 Eulenburg to Holstein, 19 November 1889, Holstein to Eulenburg, 12 December 1889, ibid., Nos. 254 and 265.

59 Hinzpeter to Kaiser Wilhelm II, 4 January 1890, BA Berlin, Reichskanzlei, No. 1816, cited in *Eulenburgs Korrespondenz*, I, p. 403. See also Hinzpeter to Bismarck, 7 January 1890, BA Berlin, Reichskanzlei, No. 1816.

60 Hinzpeter to Eulenburg, 8 January 1890, *Eulenburgs Korrespondenz*, I, No. 277.

61 Kaiser Wilhelm II, marginal notes on Hinzpeter's letter of 4 January 1890, BA Berlin, Reichskanzlei, No. 1816, cited in *Eulenburgs Korrespondenz*, I, p. 403.

62 Herbert Bismarck to his father, 6 January 1890, BA Koblenz, Bismarck Papers FC 3005 N; in Bußmann, *Staatssekretär*, No. 396.

63 Bismarck to Hinzpeter, 5 January 1890, Bismarck to Kaiser Wilhelm II, 7 January 1890, BA Berlin, Reichskanzlei, No. 1816, cited in *Eulenburgs Korrespondenz*, I, p. 403.

64 Herbert Bismarck to his father, 8 January 1890, BA Berlin, Reichskanzlei, No. 1816, cited in *Eulenburgs Korrespondenz*, I, p. 403.

65 Herbert Bismarck to his father, 9 January 1890, BA Berlin, Reichskanzlei, No. 1816, cited in *Eulenburgs Korrespondenz*, I, p. 403.

66 Schwartzkoppen to Herbert Bismarck, 9 January 1890, BA Berlin, Reichskanzlei, No. 1816, cited in *Eulenburgs Korrespondenz*, I, p. 403.

67 Marschall, diary entry for 10 January 1890, cited in *Eulenburgs Korrespondenz*, I, p. 403.

68 Hinzpeter to Kaiser Wilhelm II, 15 January 1890, BA Berlin, Reichskanzlei, No. 1860.

69 Kaiser Wilhelm II to Bismarck, telegram, 17 January 1890, cited in *Eulenburgs Korrespondenz*, I, p. 420.

70 Eulenburg to Hinzpeter, 9 January 1890, ibid., No. 278.

71 Lerchenfeld, report of 2 April 1890, in Karl Alexander von Müller, 'Die Entlassung. Nach den bayerischen Gesandtschaftsberichten', *Süddeutsche Monatshefte*, 19/1 (December 1921), p. 140. See below, p. 321.

72 Waldersee, diary entries for 11 and 12 January 1890, GStA Berlin, Waldersee Papers; cf. Meisner, II, pp. 88–9.

73 Waldersee, diary entries for 20 and 21 January 1890, GStA Berlin, Waldersee Papers; omitted from Meisner, II, p. 95.

74 See Holstein to Eulenburg, 26 December 1889, Eulenburg to Holstein, 28 December 1889, *Eulenburgs Korrespondenz*, I, Nos. 270 and 272.

75 Waldersee, diary entry for 11 January 1890, GStA Berlin, Waldersee Papers; cf. Meisner, II, pp. 88–9.

76 Waldersee, diary entry for 15 February 1890, GStA Berlin, Waldersee Papers; omitted from Meisner, II, p. 102.

77 Waldersee, diary entry for 11 January 1890, GStA Berlin, Waldersee Papers; cf. Meisner, II, pp. 88–9.

78  Waldersee, diary entry for 20 and 21 January 1890, GStA Berlin, Waldersee Papers; omitted from Meisner, II, p. 95.

79  Waldersee, diary entry for 3 January 1890, GStA Berlin, Waldersee Papers; cf. Meisner, II, p. 86.

80  Waldersee, diary entry for 8 January 1890, GStA Berlin, Waldersee Papers; cf. Meisner, II, p. 87.

81  Waldersee, diary entry for 12 January 1890, GStA Berlin, Waldersee Papers; cf. Meisner, II, p. 89.

82  *Norddeutsche Allgemeine Zeitung*, 12 January 1890, cited in Meisner, II, p. 89, n. 3. See alsoWaldersee, diary entry for 13 January 1890, GStA Berlin, Waldersee Papers; Meisner, II, p. 90.

83  Waldersee, diary entry for 12 January 1890, GStA Berlin, Waldersee Papers; cf. Meisner, II, p. 89.

84  Waldersee, diary entry for 18 January 1890, GStA Berlin, Waldersee Papers; Meisner, II, p. 94.

85  Herbert Bismarck, notes of April 1890, pp. 48–50, with the Reich Chancellor's marginal comment 'cherchez la femme', BA Koblenz, Bismarck Papers.

86  Waldersee, diary entry for 12 January 1890, GStA Berlin, Waldersee Papers; cf. Meisner, II, p. 90.

87  Eulenburg to Waldersee, 17 January 1890, in Meisner, II, p. 92.

88  Eulenburg to Holstein, 17 January 1890, *Eulenburgs Korrespondenz*, I, No. 284. See Röhl, *Germany without Bismarck. The Crisis of Government in the Second Reich, 1890–1900*, London, Berkeley and Los Angeles 1967, p. 35.

89  Eulenburg to Holstein, 29 January 1890, Eulenburg to Hinzpeter, 3 February 1890, *Eulenburgs Korrespondenz*, I, Nos. 294 and 304.

90  The correspondence between Herbert Bismarck and his father reveals the close co-operation of both with Liebenau at the court. See Bußmann, *Staatssekretär*, Nos. 366, 368 and 390.

91  Waldersee, diary entry for 29 August and 22 October 1888, GStA Berlin, Waldersee Papers; cf. Meisner, II, pp. 2 and 10.

92  Waldersee, diary entry for 5 November 1888, GStA Berlin, Waldersee Papers; cf. Meisner, II, p. 15.

93  Waldersee, diary entry for 22 October 1888, GStA Berlin, Waldersee Papers; cf. Meisner, II, p. 10.

94  August Eulenburg to Philipp Eulenburg, 1 February 1890, *Eulenburgs Korrespondenz*, I, No. 298.

95  Waldersee, diary entry for 17 November 1889, GStA Berlin, Waldersee Papers; omitted from Meisner, II, p. 77.

96  Ibid. Cf. Meisner II, p. 77.

97  Waldersee, diary entry for 25 November 1889, GStA Berlin, Waldersee Papers; cf. Meisner, II, p. 80.

98  Waldersee, diary entry for 27 November 1889, GStA Berlin, Waldersee Papers; largely omitted from Meisner, II, p. 80.

99  Eulenburg to Kaiser Wilhelm II, 3 December 1889, *Eulenburgs Korrespondenz*, I, No. 262; Waldersee, diary entries for 2 and 7 December 1889, GStA Berlin, Waldersee Papers; omitted from Meisner, II, p. 81; Waldersee to Eulenburg, 8 December 1889, *Eulenburgs Korrespondenz*, I, No. 263; August Eulenburg to Philipp Eulenburg, 12 December 1889, ibid., No. 264.

100 Waldersee, diary entries for 11 and 23 December 1889, GStA Berlin, Waldersee Papers; omitted from Meisner, II, pp. 82–3. See Waldersee to Eulenburg, 8 December 1889, *Eulenburgs Korrespondenz*, I, No. 263. See also August Eulenburg to Philipp Eulenburg, 12 December 1889, ibid., No. 264.

101 August Eulenburg to Philipp Eulenburg, 23 December 1889, cited in *Eulenburgs Korrespondenz*, I, p. 393.
102 Eulenburg to Grand Duke of Baden, 25 December 1889, ibid., No. 269.
103 Waldersee, diary entry for 9 January 1890, GStA Berlin, Waldersee Papers; cf. Meisner, II, p. 87.
104 August Eulenburg to Philipp Eulenburg, 21 January 1890, *Eulenburgs Korrespondenz*, I, No. 289.
105 August Eulenburg to Philipp Eulenburg, 15 February 1890, ibid., No. 323.
106 See Stolberg-Wernigerode to Reuss, 5 June 1890, cited ibid., p. 543.
107 On Liebenau's dismissal, see below, pp. 331–3.
108 Herbert Bismarck to his father, 9 and 10 December 1889, BA Koblenz, Bismarck Papers, FC 3005 N,
109 Herbert Bismarck to his father, 24 September 1889, ibid.
110 Waldersee, diary entry for 11 December 1889, GStA Berlin, Waldersee Papers; cf. Meisner, II, p. 82.
111 Waldersee, diary entry for 31 January 1890, GStA Berlin, Waldersee Papers; omitted from Meisner, II, p. 99.
112 Waldersee, diary entry for 18 January 1890, GStA Berlin, Waldersee Papers; Meisner, II, p. 94.
113 Waldersee to Eulenburg, 13 January 1890, printed with omissions in Meisner, II, pp. 90–2. See *Eulenburgs Korrespondenz*, I, p. 453; also Waldersee to Eulenburg, 12 February 1890, ibid., No. 321.
114 Eulenburg to Waldersee, 17 January 1890, printed with omissions in Meisner, II, p. 92.
115 Holstein to Eulenburg, 12 December 1889, *Eulenburgs Korrespondenz*, I, No. 265.
116 Eulenburg to Kaiser Wilhelm II, 1 January 1890, ibid., No. 276.
117 Marschall, diary entries for 5 and 13 January 1890, cited ibid., p. 402; Eulenburg to Kaiser Wilhelm II, 15 January 1890, ibid., No. 280; but cf. Lindau to Eulenburg, 17 January 1890, ibid., No. 285.
118 Waldersee, diary entry for 14 January 1890, GStA Berlin, Waldersee Papers; largely omitted from Meisner, II, p. 93.
119 Waldersee, diary entry for 18 January 1890, GStA Berlin, Waldersee Papers; cf. Meisner, II, p. 94.
120 Waldersee, diary entry for 30 January 1890, GStA Berlin, Waldersee Papers, Meisner, II, p. 98.
121 Waldersee, diary entries for 26 and 28 December 1889, GStA Berlin, Waldersee Papers; cf. Meisner, II, pp. 83–4.

## 11 CONSTITUTIONAL CONFLICTS

1 Eulenburg, note of January 1914, cited in *Eulenburgs Korrespondenz*, I, p. 406.
2 Waldersee, diary entries for 27 November and 7 December 1889, GStA Berlin, Waldersee Papers; omitted from Meisner, II, pp. 80–1.
3 Waldersee, diary entry for 24 November 1889, GStA Berlin, Waldersee Papers; Meisner, II, pp. 79–80.
4 Waldersee, diary entry for 25 November 1889, GStA Berlin, Waldersee Papers; omitted from Meisner, II, p. 80.
5 For details of Bismarck's *coup d'état* plans in the dismissal crisis, see Hans Delbrück, 'Staatsstreichpläne als Ursachen von Bismarcks Rücktritt. Sensationelle Enthüllungen', *Neues Wiener Journal*, 11 December 1913; Egmont Zechlin, *Staatsstreichpläne Bismarcks und Wilhelms II., 1890–1894*, Stuttgart, Berlin 1929; Werner Pöls, *Sozialistenfrage und Revolutionsfurcht in ihrem Zusammenhang mit den angeblichen Staatsstreichplänen*

*Bismarcks*, Lübeck, Hamburg 1960; John C. G. Röhl, 'Staatsstreichplan oder Staatsstreich-bereitschaft? Bismarcks Politik in der Entlassungskrise', *Historische Zeitschrift*, 203 (1966), pp. 610–24; also Clark, *Kaiser Wilhelm II*, pp. 39ff.

6 Waldersee, diary entry for 11 December 1889, GStA Berlin, Waldersee Papers; cf. Meisner, II, p. 83.

7 Waldersee, diary entry for 26 December 1889, GStA Berlin, Waldersee Papers; largely omitted from Meisner, II, p. 85.

8 Waldersee, diary entry for 2 January 1890, GStA Berlin, Waldersee Papers; cf. Meisner, II, p. 86.

9 Waldersee, diary entry for 17 November 1889, GStA Berlin, Waldersee Papers; Meisner, II, p. 78.

10 Waldersee, diary entry for 27 November 1889, GStA Berlin, Waldersee Papers; omitted from Meisner, II, p. 80.

11 See Waldersee, diary entries for 4 and 8 December 1889, GStA Berlin, Waldersee Papers; omitted from Meisner, II, p. 81.

12 Eulenburg, note of January 1914, cited in *Eulenburgs Korrespondenz*, I, pp. 406–7. See Eulenburg to Kaiser Wilhelm II, 15 January 1890, ibid., No. 280; Eulenburg to Holstein, 17 January 1890, ibid., No. 284.

13 Kaiser Wilhelm II, marginal notes on *Münchener Neuesten Nachrichten*, 5 March 1891, PA AA, Asservat No. 4.

14 For the historiography of Wilhelm II's social welfare initiative, see Lamar Cecil, *Wilhelm II, vol. I, Prince and Emperor, 1859–1900*, Chapel Hill, London 1989, p. 133, and Clark, *Kaiser Wilhelm II*, pp. 38–9, who portrays Wilhelm's motives in a rather idealistic light.

15 Holstein to Eulenburg, 1 and 4 February 1890, *Eulenburgs Korrespondenz*, I, Nos. 299 and 306.

16 Empress Frederick to Queen Victoria, 15 February 1890, RA Z47/32.

17 Empress Frederick to Queen Victoria, 19 February 1890, RA Z47/34.

18 Salisbury to Queen Victoria, 24 February 1890, RA L16/36.

19 Waldersee, diary entries for 20 and 21 January 1890, GStA Berlin, Waldersee Papers; omitted from Meisner, II, p. 95. See Holstein to Eulenburg, 26 December 1889, *Eulenburgs Korrespondenz*, I, No. 270.

20 Waldersee, diary entries for 3 and 8 February 1890, GStA Berlin, Waldersee Papers; largely omitted from Meisner, II, p. 100.

21 Waldersee, diary entry for 22 December 1894, GStA Berlin, Waldersee Papers; omitted from Meisner, II, p. 334.

22 Marschall, diary entry for 29 January 1890, cited in *Eulenburgs Korrespondenz*, I, p. 428. See Holstein to Eulenburg, 4 February 1890, ibid., No. 306; Lucius von Ballhausen, *Bismarck-Erinnerungen*, p. 514.

23 Hinzpeter to Eulenburg, 23 January 1890, *Eulenburgs Korrespondenz*, I, No. 291.

24 Eulenburg to Holstein, 3 February 1890, ibid., No. 303.

25 Eulenburg to Hinzpeter, 3 February 1890, ibid., No. 304.

26 Hinzpeter to Eulenburg, 8 January 1890, ibid., No. 277.

27 Hinzpeter to Eulenburg, 2 February 1890, ibid., No. 302.

28 Hinzpeter to Eulenburg, 23 January and 6 February 1890, ibid., Nos. 291 and 307.

29 Hinzpeter to Eulenburg, 6 February 1890, ibid., No. 307.

30 Marschall, diary entry for 12 January 1890, cited ibid., p. 411; Marschall's report of 15 January 1890, in Gradenwitz, *Bismarcks letzter Kampf*, pp. 120–1.

31 Holstein to Eulenburg, 15 January 1890, *Eulenburgs Korrespondenz*, I, No. 283.

32 In Hugo Graf Lerchenfeld-Koefering, *Erinnerungen and Denkwürdigkeiten, 1843–1925*, Berlin 1934, pp. 355ff.

33 Eulenburg to Holstein, 17 January 1890, *Eulenburgs Korrespondenz*, I, No. 284. See above, pp. 248-9.

34 Eulenburg to Freyschlag, 14 January 1890, *Eulenburgs Korrespondenz*, I, No. 279; Eulenburg to Lutz, 18 January 1890, ibid., No. 286.

35 Eulenburg to Kaiser Wilhelm II, 20 January 1890, ibid., No. 288.

36 Holstein to Eulenburg, 15 January 1890, ibid., No. 283.

37 Marschall, diary entries for 19-23 January 1890, cited ibid., p. 412.

38 Waldersee, diary entry for 22 January 1890, GStA Berlin, Waldersee Papers; cf. Meisner, II, pp. 95-6.

39 Herbert Bismarck to his father, 23 January 1890, BA Koblenz, Bismarck Papers FC 3005 N.

40 Boetticher to Prince Otto von Bismarck, cipher telegram, 23 January 1890, ibid. See Georg Freiherr von Eppstein, ed., *Fürst Bismarcks Entlassung. Nach den hinterlassenen, bisher unveröffentlichten Aufzeichnungen des Staatssekrotärs des Innern, Staatsministers Dr. Karl Heinrich von Boetticher und des Chefs der Reichskanzlei unter dem Fürsten Bismarck Dr. Franz Johannes von Rottenburg*, Berlin 1920, pp. 143-5.

41 Herbert Bismarck to his father, cipher telegram, 23 January 1890, BA Koblenz, Bismarck Papers FC 3005 N.

42 Herbert Bismarck to his father, letter and telegrams, 23 January 1890, ibid.

43 Holstein to Eulenburg, 27 January 1890, *Eulenburgs Korrespondenz*, I, No. 293; Holstein to Herbert Bismarck, 24 January 1890, *Holstein Papers*, III, No. 302.

44 Eulenburg to Holstein, 25 January 1890, *Eulenburgs Korrespondenz*, I, No. 292.

45 Waldersee, diary entry for 25 January 1890, GStA Berlin, Waldersee Papers; Meisner, II, p. 96.

46 Herbert Bismarck to his father, 19 and 20 January 1890, BA Koblenz, Bismarck Papers FC 3005 N.

47 Minutes of the Crown Council meeting of 24 January 1890, in Eppstein, *Bismarcks Entlassung*, pp. 157-65.

48 Empress Frederick to Queen Victoria, 15 February 1890, RA Z47/32; also Ponsonby to Queen Victoria, 15 February 1890, RA I58/18, and Salisbury to Queen Victoria, 15 February 1890, RA L16/33.

49 Malet to Queen Victoria, 22 March 1890, RA I58/33-4.

50 Minutes of the Crown Council meeting of 24 January 1890, in Eppstein, *Bismarcks Entlassung*, p. 157; Bismarck, *Die gesammelten Werke*, XV, pp. 491ff. See Ernst Engelberg, *Bismarck. Das Reich in der Mitte Europas*, Berlin 1990, p. 561; Rall, *Wilhelm II*, pp. 90-1.; Clark, *Kaiser Wilhelm II*, pp. 41-2.

51 On Kayser's relationship to the German-Jewish community on the one hand, and the Bismarcks on the other, see Spitzemberg, diary entry for 14 February 1898, *Tagebuch*, p. 365.

52 Kayser to Eulenburg, 15 January 1890, *Eulenburgs Korrespondenz*, I, No. 281.

53 Franz Fischer, note of 15 January 1890, ibid., No. 282; Holstein to Eulenburg, 15 January 1890, ibid., No. 283.

54 Kayser to Eulenburg, 15 January 1890, ibid., No. 281. The original memorandum was located in the files of the Hausarchiv, now in GStA Berlin, BPHA Rep. 53 EIII No. 3. In Merseburg it was subsequently incorporated into the files of the Civil Cabinet as 2.2.1. No. 29960/1.

55 The text of Kayser's exposé is printed in Eppstein, *Bismarcks Entlassung*, pp. 146-51. See Bismarck, *Die gesammelten Werke*, XV, pp. 491ff. See also Eulenburg to Holstein, 9 March 1890, *Eulenburgs Korrespondenz*, I, No. 341.

56 Holstein to Eulenburg, 27 January 1890, *Eulenburgs Korrespondenz*, I, No. 293; Boetticher, Zur Geschichte der Entlassung des Fürsten Bismarck am 20. March 1890, in Eppstein,

*Bismarcks Entlassung*, pp. 33–78. In the official transcipt there is no mention of Bismarck's threat to resign: ibid., pp. 162–5.

57  Eppstein, *Bismarcks Entlassung*, p. 47.

58  Kaiser Wilhelms II, speech of 25 January 1890, Penzler, *Reden Kaiser Wilhelms II. in den Jahren 1888–1895*, pp. 87–9. The speech had been written by Boetticher and Bosse. See Eppstein, *Bismarcks Entlassung*, pp. 47–8; Waldersee, diary entry for 25 January 1890, GStA Berlin, Waldersee Papers; cf. Meisner, II, p 96.

59  Waldersee, diary entry for 25 January 1890, GStA Berlin, Waldersee Papers; Meisner, II, p. 97; Malet, report of 8 February 1890, RA I58/15.

60  Marschall, diary entry for 25 January 1890, cited in *Eulenburgs Korrespondenz*, I, p. 423.

61  Waldersee, diary entry for 25 January 1890, GStA Berlin, Waldersee Papers; cf. Meisner, II, p. 96.

62  Waldersee, diary entry for 25 January 1890, GStA Berlin, Waldersee Papers; cf. Meisner, II, p. 97.

63  Holstein to Eulenburg, 1 February 1890, *Eulenburgs Korrespondenz*, I, No. 299.

64  Holstein to Eulenburg, 27 January 1890, ibid., No. 293; Eulenburg to Holstein, 29 January 1890, ibid., No. 294; Eulenburg to Kaiser Wilhelm II, 30 January 1890, ibid., No. 296.

65  Holstein to Eulenburg, 1 and 4 February 1890, ibid., Nos. 299 and 306.

66  Holstein to Eulenburg, 4 February 1890, ibid., No. 306.

67  Marschall, diary entry for 30 January 1890, cited ibid., p. 426.

68  Holstein to Eulenburg, 1 and 4 February 1890, ibid., Nos. 299 and 306.

69  Hinzpeter to Eulenburg, 6 February 1890, ibid., No. 307.

70  Eulenburg to Holstein, 3 February 1890, ibid., No. 303; Eulenburg to Hinzpeter, 3 February 1890, ibid., No. 304.

71  Kayser to Eulenburg, 1 February 1890, ibid., No. 300.

72  Waldersee, diary entry for 12 January 1890, GStA Berlin, Waldersee Papers; cf. Meisner, II, p. 90.

73  Waldersee to Eulenburg, 13 January 1890, printed with omissions in Meisner, II, pp. 90–2.

74  Waldersee, diary entry for 25 January 1890, GStA Berlin, Waldersee Papers; cf. Meisner, II, p. 97.

75  On 27 January 1890 Marschall noted in his diary: 'The Kaiser wants him [Bismarck] to confine himself to the Foreign Office and give up domestic affairs:' cited in *Eulenburgs Korrespondenz*, I, p. 427. See below, pp. 273–5.

76  Eulenburg to Holstein, 3 February 1890; Eulenburg to Hinzpeter, 3 February 1890, *Eulenburgs Korrespondenz*, I, Nos. 303 and 304.

77  Minutes of the Crown Council meeting of 26 January 1890, in Eppstein, *Bismarcks Entlassung*, pp. 166–7.

78  Holstein to Eulenburg, 31 January 1890, August Eulenburg to Philipp Eulenburg, 1 February 1890, Franz Fischer to Eulenburg, 2 February 1890, *Eulenburgs Korrespondenz*, I, Nos. 297, 298 and 301; cf. *Holstein Papers*, III, pp. 324–5; Waldersee, diary entry for 27 January 1890, GStA Berlin, Waldersee Papers; partly omitted from Meisner, II, p. 98.

79  Holstein to Eulenburg, 27 January and 12 February 1890, *Eulenburgs Korrespondenz*, I, Nos. 293 and 320; Rudolf Lindau to Eulenburg, 6 February 1890, ibid., No. 308.

80  Eulenburg to Holstein, 29 January 1890, ibid., No. 294.

81  Boetticher, Geschichte der Entlassung, in Eppstein, *Bismarcks Entlassung*, pp. 51–2.

82  Kayser to Eulenburg, 1 February 1890, *Eulenburgs Korrespondenz*, I, No. 300.

83  Fischer to Eulenburg, 2 February 1890, ibid., No. 301.

84  Kayser to Eulenburg, 6 and 7 February 1890, ibid., Nos. 310 and 314. Cf. Holstein to Eulenburg, 6 and 7 February 1890, ibid., Nos. 309 and 313.

85  Eulenburg to Kayser, 7 February 1890, ibid., I, No. 312.

86 Eulenburg to Kaiser Wilhelm II, 7 February 1890, Eulenburg to Kayser, 7 February 1890, Eulenburg to Holstein, 9 February 1890, ibid., Nos. 311, 312 and 316.

87 Minutes of the Ministry of State, 7 and 9 February 1890, quoted ibid., p. 443. A list of the members of the Prussian Council of State can be found in Eppstein, *Bismarcks Entlassung*, pp. 211–17.

12  BISMARCK'S FALL FROM POWER

1 Boetticher, Geschichte der Entlassung, in Eppstein, *Bismarcks Entlassung*, p. 49.

2 Ibid.; Holstein to Eulenburg, 4 February 1890, *Eulenburgs Korrespondenz*, I, No. 306.

3 August Eulenburg to Philipp Eulenburg, 1 February 1890, ibid., No. 298.

4 See Röhl, *Germany without Bismarck*, pp. 37–8.

5 Marschall, diary entry for 27 January 1890, cited in *Eulenburgs Korrespondenz*, I, p. 427.

6 Ernst Gagliardi, *Bismarcks Entlassung*, 2 vols., Tübingen 1927–41, pp. 69–70.

7 Lerchenfeld, report of 30 January 1890, Lerchenfeld, *Erinnerungen*, pp. 357–8.

8 Lucius von Ballhausen, *Bismarck-Erinnerungen*, p. 516; Bismarck, *Die gesammelten Werke*, XV, pp. 505–6; Holstein to Eulenburg, 9 and 10 February 1890, *Eulenburgs Korrespondenz*, I, Nos. 317–18.

9 Waldersee, diary entry for 9 February 1890, GStA Berlin, Waldersee Papers; largely omitted from Meisner, II, pp. 101–2.

10 Lucius von Ballhausen, *Bismarck-Erinnerungen*, p. 515; Boetticher, Geschichte der Entlassung, in Eppstein, *Bismarcks Entlassung*, pp. 60ff.

11 Waldersee, diary entry for 9 February 1890, GStA Berlin, Waldersee Papers; largely omitted from Meisner, II, pp. 101–2.

12 Lerchenfeld, report of 8 February 1890, in Müller, 'Die Entlassung', pp. 146ff.

13 Boetticher, Geschichte der Entlassung, in Eppstein, *Bismarcks Entlassung*, pp. 54 and 62.

14 Malet to Salisbury, 12 February 1890, RA I58/16.

15 Lerchenfeld, report of 10 February 1890, Lerchenfeld, *Erinnerungen*, pp. 359ff.; Boetticher, Geschichte der Entlassung, in Eppstein, *Bismarcks Entlassung*, pp. 62–3.

16 Marschall, report of 11 February 1890 in Gradenwitz, *Bismarcks letzter Kampf*, pp. 127ff.; Holstein to Eulenburg, 12 February 1890, *Eulenburgs Korrespondenz*, I, No. 320.

17 August Eulenburg to Philipp Eulenburg, 9 March 1890, *Eulenburgs Korrespondenz*, I, No. 342.

18 Boetticher, Geschichte der Entlassung, in Eppstein, *Bismarcks Entlassung*, p. 50.

19 Holstein to Eulenburg, 4 February 1890, *Eulenburgs Korrespondenz*, I, No. 306; Herbert Bismarck to Eulenburg, 3 February 1890, Eulenburg, *Aus 50 Jahren*, p. 291.

20 Malet, report of 8 February 1890, RA I58/15.

21 Malet to Salisbury, 12 February 1890, RA I58/16. The Kaiser and his advisers were incensed by Bismarck's habit of discussing his differences with Wilhelm with foreign ambassadors. See Holstein to Reuss, 5 March 1890, *Berliner Monatshefte*, No. 15, 1937, pp. 327–8.

22 Herbert Bismarck to his brother, 16 February 1890, in Bußmann, *Staatssekretär*, No. 402.

23 Empress Frederick to Queen Victoria, 19–21 February 1890, RA Z47/34.

24 See Miquel's assumption in Waldersee, diary entry for 8 February 1890, GStA Berlin, Waldersee Papers; Meisner, II, p. 100.

25 See Pflanze, *Bismarck and the Development of Germany*, III, pp. 368–9; cf. Gall, *Bismarck*, pp. 689ff.

26 See above, pp. 233–4.

27 Holstein to Eulenburg, 27 January 1890, *Eulenburgs Korrespondenz*, I, No. 293.

28 Holstein to Eulenburg, 7 February 1890, ibid., No. 313; Eulenburg to Kaiser Wilhelm II, 8 February 1890, ibid., No. 315.

29  Holstein to Eulenburg, 10 and 26 February 1890, ibid., Nos. 318 and 325.

30  Marschall, diary entry for 12 February 1890, ibid., p. 450; Waldersee, diary entries for 3 and
    5 February 1890, GStA Berlin, Waldersee Papers; cf. Meisner, II, pp. 99–100.

31  Marschall, report of 12 February 1890, in Gradenwitz, *Bismarcks letzter Kampf*, pp. 131–2;
    Salisbury to Queen Victoria, 15 February 1890, RA L16/33.

32  Holstein to Eulenburg, 7 and 10 February 1890, *Eulenburgs Korrespondenz*, I, Nos. 313 and
    318. See Kayser to Eulenburg, 7 February 1890, Eulenburg to Kaiser Wilhelm II, 8 February
    1890, ibid., Nos. 314–15. After a meeting with Holstein and Paul Kayser on 7 February,
    Marschall noted: 'I am convinced the Reich Chancellor is aiming for a fiasco' (cited ibid.,
    p. 444).

33  Waldersee, diary entry for 30 January 1890, GStA Berlin, Waldersee Papers; partly omitted
    from Meisner, II, p. 99.

34  Waldersee, diary entry for 9 February 1890, GStA Berlin, Waldersee Papers; cf. Meisner, II,
    p. 101.

35  Waldersee, diary entries for 3, 8, 9 and 10 February 1890, GStA Berlin, Waldersee Papers;
    largely omitted from Meisner, II, p. 100.

36  Waldersee, diary entries for 3, 8, 9 and 19 February 1890, GStA Berlin, Waldersee Papers;
    largely omitted from Meisner, II, pp. 100, and 104.

37  Waldersee, diary entry for 8 February 1890, GStA Berlin, Waldersee Papers; omitted from
    Meisner, II, p. 100.

38  Waldersee, diary entry for 10 February 1890, GStA Berlin, Waldersee Papers; several impor-
    tant passages omitted from Meisner, II, p. 101.

39  Waldersee to Eulenburg, 12 February 1890, *Eulenburgs Korrespondenz*, I, No. 321. See
    Waldersee, diary entry for 15 February 1890, GStA Berlin, Waldersee Papers; omitted from
    Meisner, II, p. 102.

40  Waldersee, diary entry for 15 February 1890, GStA Berlin, Waldersee Papers; cf. Meisner, II,
    p. 102.

41  Waldersee, diary entry for 16 February 1890, GStA Berlin, Waldersee Papers; distorted in
    Meisner, II, p. 102.

42  Waldersee, diary entry for 18 February 1890, GStA Berlin, Waldersee Papers; largely omitted
    from Meisner, II, p. 103.

43  Waldersee, diary entry for 20 February 1890, GStA Berlin, Waldersee Papers; Meisner, II,
    pp. 104–5.

44  Waldersee, diary entry for 20 February 1890, GStA Berlin, Waldersee Papers; omitted from
    Meisner, II, p. 105.

45  Waldersee, diary entry for 20 February 1890, GStA Berlin, Waldersee Papers; omitted almost
    entirely from Meisner, II, p. 104.

46  Waldersee, diary entry for 23 February 1890, GStA Berlin, Waldersee Papers; cf. Meisner, II,
    pp. 105–6.

47  Ibid.

48  For Eulenburg's activities in Berlin in the period 14–23 February 1890, see *Eulenburgs
    Korrespondenz*, I, pp. 454–6.

49  Eulenburg, diary entries for 14–22 February 1890, ibid.

50  Eulenburg to Kaiser Wilhelm II, 22 February 1890, ibid., No. 324.

51  See Gradenwitz, *Bismarcks letzter Kampf*, p. 110; Röhl, *Germany without Bismarck*, pp. 42–3.

52  Kaiser Wilhelm II to Queen Victoria, 24 February 1890, RA I58/21.

53  Eulenburg to Kaiser Wilhelm II, 22 February 1890, *Eulenburgs Korrespondenz*, I, No. 324.

54  Bismarck's report to Kaiser Wilhelm II of 26 February 1890, in Bismarck, *Die gesammelten
    Werke*, VIc, pp. 432–3.

55  Kayser to Holstein, 28 February 1890, *Holstein Papers*, III, No. 306.

56 Waldersee, diary entry for 1 March 1890, GStA Berlin, Waldersee Papers; cf. Meisner, II, p. 108.

57 Eulenburg to Kaiser Wilhelm II, 22 February 1890, *Eulenburgs Korrespondenz*, I, No. 324.

58 Waldersee, diary entry for 16 February 1890, GStA Berlin, Waldersee Papers; omitted from Meisner, II, p. 103.

59 Marschall, diary entry for 20 February 1890, cited in *Eulenburgs Korrespondenz*, I, p. 455.

60 Stolberg-Wernigerode to Reuss, 22 February 1890, cited ibid.

61 See below, pp. 286–7.

62 Waldersee, diary entry for 26 February 1890, GStA Berlin, Waldersee Papers; cf. Meisner, II, pp. 106–7.

63 Marschall, report of 27 February 1890, Gradenwitz, *Bismarcks letzter Kampf*, p. 140; also Boetticher, Geschichte der Entlassung, in Eppstein, *Bismarcks Entlassung*, pp. 55–8.

64 Waldersee, diary entry for 1 March 1890, GStA Berlin, Waldersee Papers; cf. Meisner, II, p. 107. The Kaiser's speech is printed in Eppstein, *Bismarcks Entlassung*, pp. 173–6. See Boetticher's account of the debates of the Council of State, Geschichte der Entlassung, ibid., pp. 58ff.

65 Waldersee, diary entry for 1 March 1890, GStA Berlin, Waldersee Papers; cf. Meisner, II, p. 107.

66 Kayser to Eulenburg, 1 March 1890, *Eulenburgs Korrespondenz*, I, No. 328. Eulenburg sent this letter to the Kaiser on 3 March. See ibid., No. 332; GStA Berlin, BPHA Rep. 53 E III No. 3.

67 Holstein to Eulenburg, 2 March 1890, *Eulenburgs Korrespondenz*, I, No. 329. See Kayser to Eulenburg, 2 March 1890, ibid., No. 330.

68 Eulenburg to Holstein, 28 February 1890, ibid., No. 326.

69 Waldersee, diary entry for 1 March 1890, GStA Berlin, Waldersee Papers; omitted from Meisner, II, p. 108.

70 Kayser to Eulenburg, 1 March 1890, *Eulenburgs Korrespondenz*, I, No. 328.

71 Holstein to Eulenburg, 2 March 1890, ibid., No. 329.

72 Waldersee, diary entry for 1 March 1890, GStA Berlin, Waldersee Papers; cf. Meisner, II, p. 108.

73 Bernhard Vogel, Dieter Nohlen and Rainer-Olaf Schultze, *Wahlen in Deutschland. Theorie-Geschichte-Dokumente, 1848–1970*, Berlin 1971, pp. 290–1.

74 See Rauchhaupt to Hammerstein, 20 February 1890, Hans Leuß, *Wilhelm Freiherr von Hammerstein*, Berlin 1905, pp. 83–4.

75 Waldersee, diary entry for 23 February 1890, GStA Berlin, Waldersee Papers; cf. Meisner, II, p. 106.

76 Waldersee, diary entry for 5 March 1890, GStA Berlin, Waldersee Papers; omitted from Meisner, II, pp. 111–12.

77 Waldersee, diary entry for 2 March 1890, GStA Berlin, Waldersee Papers; cf. Meisner, II, p. 109.

78 Waldersee, diary entry for 5 March 1890, GStA Berlin, Waldersee Papers; omitted from Meisner, II, pp. 111–12.

79 Waldersee, diary entry for 23 February 1890, GStA Berlin, Waldersee Papers; cf. Meisner, II, p. 106.

80 Waldersee, diary entry for 1 March 1890, GStA Berlin, Waldersee Papers; important passages omitted from Meisner, II, pp. 108–9.

81 Waldersee, diary entry for 4 March 1890, GStA Berlin, Waldersee Papers; cf. Meisner, II, p. 110.

82 Waldersee, diary entry for 1 March 1890, GStA Berlin, Waldersee Papers; cf. Meisner, II, pp. 107–8.

83  Eulenburg to Holstein, 28 February 1890, *Eulenburgs Korrespondenz*, I, No. 326.

84  Minutes of the meeting of the Prussian Ministry of State of 2 March 1890, printed in Zechlin, *Staatsstreichpläne Bismarcks und Wilhelms II.*, pp. 178ff. The last sentence was crossed out by Bismarck, evidently because it revealed too much of his intentions.

85  Marschall, diary entry for 2 March 1890, cited in *Eulenburgs Korrespondenz*, I, p. 463.

86  Holstein to Eulenburg, 2 March 1890, ibid., No. 329.

87  Kayser to Eulenburg, 2 and 4 March 1890, ibid., Nos. 330 and 333.

88  Eulenburg to Kaiser Wilhelm II, 3 March 1890, ibid., No. 332.

89  Marschall, diary entry for 3 March 1890, cited ibid., p. 476.

90  Marschall, diary entries for 3–4 March 1890, cited in Röhl, *Germany without Bismarck*, p. 52.

91  Marschall, diary entry for 4 March 1890, cited ibid., p. 53.

92  Kaiser Wilhelm II to Eulenburg, 5 March 1890, *Eulenburgs Korrespondenz*, I, p. 477.

93  Eulenburg to Holstein, 5 March 1890, ibid., No. 334.

94  Eulenburg to Kaiser Wilhelm II, 10 March 1890, ibid., No. 344.

95  The Kaiser's note and Boetticher's reply are printed in Eppstein, *Bismarcks Entlassung*, pp. 177–8. See also August Eulenburg to Philipp Eulenburg, 9 March 1890, *Eulenburgs Korrespondenz*, I, No. 342. For Bismarck's furious reaction to the decoration of Boetticher, see Bismarck, *Die gesammelten Werke*, XV, pp. 509–10.

96  Eulenburg to Herbert Bismarck, 8 March 1890, *Eulenburgs Korrespondenz*, I, No. 340.

97  Bleichröder to Lord Rothschild, 10 March 1890, Rothschild Archives London, RAL XI/64/1. See also the similar letter of 7 March 1890, ibid.

98  Eulenburg to Kaiser Wilhelm II, 7 March 1890, Eulenburg to Herbert Bismarck, 8 March 1890, *Eulenburgs Korrespondenz*, I, Nos. 336 and 340. For Eulenburg's appointment, see above, pp. 191–7.

99  Kayser to Eulenburg, 5 and 7 March 1890, Eulenburg to Kaiser Wilhelm II, 7 March 1890, Marschall to Eulenburg, 12 March 1890, ibid., Nos. 335–7 and 349.

100  Kayser to Eulenburg, 12 March 1890, ibid., No. 347.

101  See Bleichröder to Lord Rothschild, 7 and 10 March 1890, Rothschild Archives London, RAL XI/64/1.

102  Holstein to Eulenburg, 7 March 1890, *Eulenburgs Korrespondenz*, I, No. 338. See Stig Förster, *Der doppelte Militarismus. Die deutsche Heeresrüstungspolitik zwischen Status-quo-Sicherung und Aggression 1890–1913*, Stuttgart 1985, p. 31.

103  Holstein to Eulenburg, 7 March 1890, *Eulenburgs Korrespondenz*, I, No. 338.

104  Eulenburg to Kaiser Wilhelm II, 8 March 1890, ibid., No. 339; Marschall, diary entry for 8 March 1890, cited ibid., p. 482.

105  Waldersee, diary entries for 8 and 10 March 1890, GStA Berlin, Waldersee Papers; cf. Meisner, II, p. 113.

106  Marschall, diary entry for 11 March 1890, cited in *Eulenburgs Korrespondenz*, I, p. 489.

107  Holstein to Eulenburg, 11 March 1890, ibid., No. 345.

108  Eulenburg to Holstein, 12 March 1890, Eulenburg to Grand Duke of Baden, 13 March 1890, ibid., Nos. 334 and 350. Cf. Eulenburg's note of 12 March, ibid., p. 489.

109  Karl Bachem, *Vorgeschichte, Geschichte und Politik der Deutschen Zentrumspartei*, 9 vols., Cologne 1927–32, V, pp. 116ff.; IX, pp. 93ff.; Marschall, diary entry for 13 March 1890, cited in *Eulenburgs Korrespondenz*, I, p. 492.

110  Kayser to Eulenburg, 12 March 1890, *Eulenburgs Korrespondenz*, I, No. 348.

111  Marschall to Eulenburg, 12 March 1890, ibid., No. 349.

112  Marschall, report of 15 March 1890, in Gradenwitz, *Bismarcks letzter Kampf*, pp. 147–8.

113  Waldersee, diary entry for 12 March 1890, GStA Berlin, Waldersee Papers; Meisner, II, p. 114.

114 Waldersee, diary entry for 9 March 1890, GStA Berlin, Waldersee Papers; Meisner, II, p. 113.

115 Waldersee, diary entry for 13 March 1890, GStA Berlin, Waldersee Papers; partly omitted from Meisner, II, p. 114.

116 Waldersee, diary entry for 25 January 1890, GStA Berlin, Waldersee Papers; largely omitted from Meisner, II, pp. 96–7.

117 Waldersee, diary entry for 15 February 1890, GStA Berlin, Waldersee Papers; omitted from Meisner, II, p. 102.

118 Waldersee, diary entry for 15 March 1890, GStA Berlin, Waldersee Papers; cf. Meisner, II, pp. 114–16.

119 Waldersee, diary entry for 2 March 1890, GStA Berlin, Waldersee Papers; cf. Meisner, II, p. 109.

120 Waldersee, diary entry for 5 March 1890, GStA Berlin, Waldersee Papers; largely omitted from Meisner, II, pp. 111–12.

121 Waldersee, diary entry for 8 March 1890, GStA Berlin, Waldersee Papers; omitted from Meisner, II, p. 112.

122 Waldersee, diary entry for 5 March 1890, GStA Berlin, Waldersee Papers; omitted from Meisner, II, pp. 111–12.

123 Waldersee, diary entry for 8 March 1890, GStA Berlin, Waldersee Papers; omitted from Meisner, II, p. 113. Cf. Bleichröder to Rothschild, 19 and 20 March 1890, Rothschild Archives London, RAL XI/64/1.

124 Kayser to Eulenburg, 5 and 7 March 1890, Eulenburg to Kaiser Wilhelm II, 7 March 1890, *Eulenburgs Korrespondenz*, I, Nos. 335–7.

125 Bismarck to August Eulenburg, 14 March 1890, cited ibid., p. 499.

126 Waldersee, diary entry for 4 March 1890, GStA Berlin, Waldersee Papers; cf. Meisner, II, p. 110.

127 Waldersee, diary entry for 15 March 1890, GStA Berlin, Waldersee Papers; Meisner, II, p. 114.

128 Bismarck, *Gedanken und Erinnerungen*, III, pp. 81–7. For the following, see Bernard Miall, transl., *New Chapters of Bismarck's Autobiography*, London, 1921, pp. 166–76.

129 Malet to Queen Victoria, 22 March 1890, RA I58/33–4.

130 Kaiser Wilhelm II, marginal notes on articles in *Vossische Zeitung* of 30 November 1903 and in *Berliner Tageblatt* of 2 December 1903, PA AA, R 1009.

131 Waldersee, diary entry for 15 March 1890, GStA Berlin, Waldersee Papers; cf. Meisner, II, pp. 114–16.

132 Waldersee, diary entry for 17 March 1890, GStA Berlin, Waldersee Papers; cf. Meisner, II, pp. 117–18.

133 Bismarck, *Gedanken und Erinnerungen*, III, pp. 87–8.

134 Waldersee, diary entry for 17 March 1890, GStA Berlin, Waldersee Papers; cf. Meisner, II, pp. 117–18.

135 Bismarck, *Gedanken und Erinnerungen*, III, p. 94; Bleichröder to Rothschild, 17, 18 and 20 March 1890, Rothschild Archives London, RAL XI/64/1.

136 Waldersee, diary entry for 17 March 1890, GStA Berlin, Waldersee Papers; cf. Meisner, II, pp. 117–18.

137 Bismarck, *Gedanken und Erinnerungen*, III, pp. 89–90. The decision not to renew the Reinsurance Treaty with Russia is discussed below, pp. 334–43.

138 The minutes are printed in Bismarck, *Gedanken und Erinnerungen*, III, pp. 163–70.

139 Printed in Bismarck, *Gedanken und Erinnerungen*, III, pp. 95–100.

140 Waldersee, diary entry for 19 March 1890, GStA Berlin, Waldersee Papers; cf. Meisner, II, pp. 118–19. On the choice of Caprivi as Bismarck's successor, see below, pp. 320–4.

141  Bismarck, *Gedanken und Erinnerungen*, III, p. 100. See also the comments of General Paul Bronsart von Schellendorf in Arnold Oskar Meyer, *Bismarck. Der Mensch und der Staatsmann*, Stuttgart 2nd edn 1949, p. 654.

142  Engelberg, *Bismarck. Das Reich in der Mitte Europas*, pp. 557ff.

143  Waldersee, diary entry for 25 January 1890, GStA Berlin, Waldersee Papers; largely omitted from Meisner, II, pp. 96–7.

144  Hoffmann, diary, 22 March 1890, Hoffmann Papers, Freiburg.

145  Hoffmann, diary, 23 April 1890, ibid.

146  Hinzpeter to Kaiser Wilhelm II, 22 May 1899, GStA Berlin, BPHA Rep. 53J Lit. H No. 1.

147  Hinzpeter to Studt, 9 March 1895, Stadt- und Landesbibliothek Dortmund, Studt Papers 7824.

148  Kayser to Eulenburg, 2 March 1890, *Eulenburgs Korrespondenz*, I, No. 330.

149  Waldersee, diary entry for 8 February 1890, GStA Berlin, Waldersee Papers; largely omitted from Meisner, II, p. 100.

150  See below, pp. 388–96.

151  Marschall, report of 15 March 1890, in Gradenwitz, *Bismarcks letzter Kampf*, pp. 147–8.

152  Bismarck, *Gedanken und Erinnerungen*, III, p. 80.

153  Leonhard von Muralt, *Bismarcks Verantwortlichkeit*, Göttingen 1955.

154  Hinzpeter to Studt, 9 March 1895, Stadt- und Landesbibliothek Dortmund, Studt Papers 7824.

13  THE HAPHAZARD TRANSITION: FROM THE BISMARCKS TO
THE NEW COURSE

1  Waldersee claimed that Bismarck's behaviour had 'clearly displayed the hallmark of the most disgusting *Jewish tricks of the trade* [den Stempel widerwärtigster *jüdischer Mache*]': Waldersee, diary 1890, fol. 48, GStA Berlin, Waldersee Papers; cf. Meisner, II, p. 123.

2  Wedel, *Zwischen Kaiser und Kanzler*, pp. 72ff.

3  Waldersee, diary 1890, fol. 48, GStA Berlin, Waldersee Papers; omitted from Meisner, II, p. 122; Wedel, *Zwischen Kaiser und Kanzler*, pp. 72ff.

4  Malet to Queen Victoria, 29 March 1890, RA I58/36.

5  Wedel, *Zwischen Kaiser und Kanzler*, p. 71.

6  Ibid., p. 68.

7  Malet to Queen Victoria, 29 March 1890, RA I58/36.

8  Printed in Bismarck, *Gedanken und Erinnerungen*, III, pp. 101–5.

9  Kaiser Wilhelm II to Hinzpeter, 22 March 1890, printed in Wedel, *Zwischen Kaiser und Kanzler*, pp. 62–3. On Hinzpeter's advice the telegram was published as if it had been addressed to Emil Görtz; see ibid., pp. 99–100 and 115–16.

10  Ibid., pp. 91ff. See below, pp. 335–8.

11  Pourtalès to Holstein, 20 or 21 March 1890, *Holstein Papers*, III, No. 308.

12  Count Anton Monts to Wedel, 24 March 1890, Wedel Papers, Frankfurt a.M. The letter is printed in Wedel, *Zwischen Kaiser und Kanzler*, pp. 56–9.

13  Reuss to Wedel, 2 April 1890, Wedel Papers, Frankfurt a.M.; also Eulenburg's letters to Holstein and to Kaiser Wilhelm II of 8 April 1890, *Holstein Papers*, III, No. 313 with enclosure.

14  Kaiser Franz Joseph to Prince Otto von Bismarck, 22 March 1890, HHStA Vienna, Kabinettsarchiv Geheimakten 2.

15  Prince Otto von Bismarck to Kaiser Franz Joseph, 26 March 1890, ibid.

16  For the following, see Wilhelm von Schweinitz, ed., *Denkwürdigkeiten des Botschafters General Hans Lothar von Schweinitz*, 2 vols., Berlin 1927, II, p. 265.

17  Eulenburg to Holstein, 25 April 1890, *Holstein Papers*, III, No. 317.

18  Bülow, *Memoirs*, I, p. 234.

19  Kaiser Wilhelm II to Kaiser Franz Joseph, 3–5 April 1890, HHStA Vienna, Kabinettsarchiv Geheimakten 2. The letter is printed in Hanns Schlitter, 'Briefe Kaiser Franz Josephs I. und Kaiser Wilhelms II. über Bismarcks Rücktritt' *Österreichische Rundschau*, 58 (1919), pp. 100ff.

20  Kaiser Franz Joseph to Kaiser Wilhelm II, 12 April 1890, Entwurf, HHStA Vienna, Kabinettsarchiv Geheimakten 2; printed in Schlitter, 'Briefe', pp. 100ff.

21  Kaiser Wilhelm II to Kaiser Franz Joseph, 14 April 1890, HHStA Vienna, Kabinettsarchiv Geheimakten 2.

22  Kaiser Wilhelm II to Queen Victoria, telegram, 19 March 1890, RA I58/27. See Salisbury to Queen Victoria, cipher telegram, 20 March 1890, RA I58/30.

23  Malet to Queen Victoria, memorandum, 22 March 1890, RA I58/34.

24  Malet to Queen Victoria, 22 March 1890, RA I58/33. See the Queen's diary entry for 29 March 1890, RA QVJ.

25  Kaiser Wilhelm II to Queen Victoria, 27 March 1890, RA 158/32. See the Queen's reply of 31 March 1890, GStA Berlin, BPHA Rep. 52 W3 No. 11.

26  Salisbury to Queen Victoria, 7 April 1890, RA I58/39.

27  Eulenburg, notes of 12 July 1896, *Eulenburgs Korrespondenz*, III, No. 1239.

28  Spitzemberg, entry of 10 September 1908, *Tagebuch*, p. 487.

29  Hoffmann, diary entries for 22 and 24 March and 23 April 1890, Hoffmann Papers, Freiburg. Hoffmann was present on 22 April 1890 when Prince Heinrich told the Kaiser at Wilhelmshaven: 'At the time I said that Caprivi was the last person you would take.'

30  See above, pp. 225–7.

31  Marschall, diary entry for 29 January 1890, cited in Röhl, *Germany without Bismarck*, p. 59.

32  See Bismarck's later comments on these events, *Norddeutsche Allgemeine Zeitung*, 28 June 1892.

33  Waldersee, diary entry for 18 February 1890, GStA Berlin, Waldersee Papers; in Meisner this passage is omitted, II, p. 103.

34  Eulenburg to Kaiser Wilhelm II, 7 and 8 March 1890, *Eulenburgs Korrespondenz*, I, Nos. 336 and 339; Eulenburg to Holstein, 9 March 1890, ibid., No. 341.

35  See ibid., p. 503.

36  Ibid.

37  Waldersee, diary entry for 3 October 1894, GStA Berlin, Waldersee Papers; cf. Meisner, II, p. 330.

38  Empress Frederick to Queen Victoria, 22 March 1890, RA Z48/5.

39  Empress Frederick to Queen Victoria, 25 March 1890, RA Z48/6; also Empress Frederick to Queen Victoria, 29 March 1890, RA Z48/8.

40  See e.g. Wedel, *Zwischen Kaiser und Kanzler*, pp. 66, 78ff., 111–12, 125.

41  See Engelberg, *Bismarck. Das Reich in der Mitte Europas*, pp. 587–8.

42  Hereditary Prince Bernhard of Saxe-Meiningen to Waldersee, 29 November 1891, GStA Berlin, Waldersee Papers No. 36.

43  Schlözer, *Letzte römische Briefe, 1882–1894*, p. 158.

44  Cited in Waldersee, diary entry for 31 August 1890, GStA Berlin, Waldersee Papers; omitted from Meisner, II, p. 142.

45  Waldersee, diary entry for 20 March 1890, GStA Berlin, Waldersee Papers; cf. Meisner, II, p. 119.

46  Waldersee, diary entry for 18 February 1890, GStA Berlin, Waldersee Papers; largely omitted from Meisner, II, p. 103; also the diary entries for 19 and 20 March 1890, GStA Berlin, Waldersee Papers; omitted from Meisner, II, pp. 118ff.

47 See Röhl, *Germany without Bismarck*, p. 44.

48 *Eulenburgs Korrepondenz*, I, p. 506; also Waldersee, diary entry for 20 March 1890, GStA Berlin, Waldersee Papers; omitted from Meisner, II, p. 119.

49 Holstein to Eisendecher, 26 March 1890, *Holstein Papers*, III, No. 309. Herbert Bismarck's letter of resignation is printed in Bußmann, *Staatssekretär*, No. 405.

50 Waldersee, diary entry for 23 March 1890, GStA Berlin, Waldersee Papers; omitted from Meisner, II, p. 122.

51 Wedel, *Zwischen Kaiser und Kanzler*, pp. 68–71.

52 Malet to Queen Victoria, 29 March 1890, RA I58/36.

53 Waldersee, diary entry for 17 March 1890, GStA Berlin, Waldersee Papers; omitted from Meisner, II, p. 118.

54 Eulenburg to Kaiser Wilhelm II, 26 March 1890, *Eulenburgs Korrepondenz*, I, No. 369. See Waldersee, diary entry for 17 March 1890, GStA Berlin, Waldersee Papers; omitted from Meisner, II, p. 118.

55 Waldersee, diary entry for 17 March 1890, GStA Berlin, Waldersee Papers; omitted from Meisner, II, p. 118; Holstein to Eulenburg, 26 March 1890, *Eulenburgs Korrespondenz*, I, No. 368.

56 Holstein to Eulenburg, 26 March 1890, *Eulenburgs Korrespondenz*, I, No. 368.

57 August Eulenburg to Philipp Eulenburg, 22 March 1890, ibid., No. 363; see *Holstein Papers*, I, p. 148; Holstein to Eulenburg, 26 March 1890, *Eulenburgs Korrespondenz*, I, No. 368; Marschall, report of 27 March 1890, ibid., p. 512.

58 Stolberg-Wernigerode to Reuss, 28 March 1890, ibid., pp. 512–13.

59 Wedel, *Zwischen Kaiser und Kanzler*, p. 65.

60 Monts to Wedel, 24 March 1890, Wedel Papers, Frankfurt a.M.

61 Holstein to Eulenburg, 26 March 1890, *Eulenburgs Korrespondenz*, I, No. 368. In 1885 Bernhard von Bülow had married the divorced Countess Marie Dönhoff, an Italian friend of the then Crown Princess Victoria. See *Young Wilhelm*, p. 549.

62 Marschall, report of 27 March 1890, *Eulenburgs Korrespondenz*, I, p. 512.

63 Holstein to Eulenburg, 26 March 1890, ibid., No. 368; Eulenburg to Kaiser Wilhelm II, 26 March 1890, ibid., No. 369. According to Wedel, *Zwischen Kaiser und Kanzler*, p. 66, Limburg-Stirum was also recommended to the Kaiser by Alvensleben.

64 Eulenburg's memorandum for Kaiser Wilhelm II of 20 March 1894, *Eulenburgs Korrespondenz*, II, No. 933.

65 Monts to Wedel, 24 March 1890, Wedel Papers, Frankfurt a.M., printed in Wedel, *Zwischen Kaiser und Kanzler*, pp. 56–9.

66 Wedel, *Zwischen Kaiser und Kanzler*, pp. 64–7.

67 Marschall, report of 27 March 1890, *Eulenburgs Korrespondenz*, I, p. 512.

68 Waldersee, diary entry for 22 March 1890, GStA Berlin, Waldersee Papers; omitted from Meisner, II, p. 121.

69 Holstein to Eulenburg, 26 March 1890, *Eulenburgs Korrespondenz*, I, No. 368.

70 Eulenburg to Kaiser Wilhelm II, 26 March 1890, ibid., No. 369.

71 Marschall, report of 27 March 1890, ibid., p. 512; Waldersee, diary 1890, fol. 44, GStA Berlin, Waldersee Papers; cf. Meisner, II, p. 122.

72 Wedel, *Zwischen Kaiser und Kanzler*, pp. 62ff.; Waldersee, diary 1890, fol. 44, GStA Berlin, Waldersee Papers; cf. Meisner, II, p. 122.

73 Wedel, *Zwischen Kaiser und Kanzler*, pp. 64–5.

74 Stolberg-Wernigerode to Reuss, 28 March 1890, *Eulenburgs Korrespondenz*, I, pp. 512–13.

75 Waldersee, diary entries for 27 and 30 May 1890, GStA Berlin, Waldersee Papers; Meisner, II, p. 129.

76 For details, see Wedel, *Zwischen Kaiser und Kanzler*, pp. 102–8.

77 Prince Ernst zu Hohenlohe-Langenburg to his father, 2 April 1890, Hohenlohe-Zentralarchiv Neuenstein, Hermann Hohenlohe-Langenburg Papers, Bü. 57.

78 Holstein to Eulenburg, 10 February 1890, *Eulenburgs Korrespondenz*, I, No. 318.

79 Wedel, *Zwischen Kaiser und Kanzler*, p. 74; also above, p. 248.

80 Minutes of the meeting of the Prussian Ministry of State of 17 March 1890, printed in Bismarck, *Die gesammelten Werke*, XV, pp. 570ff. and Eppstein, *Bismarcks Entlassung*, pp. 179ff.

81 Eppstein, *Bismarcks Entlassung*, pp. 68–9.

82 Empress Frederick to Queen Victoria, 22 March 1890, RA Z48/5.

83 Waldersee, diary entry for 20 April 1890, GStA Berlin, Waldersee Papers; omitted from Meisner, II, p. 124; August Eulenburg to Philipp Eulenburg, 27 March 1890, *Eulenburgs Korrespondenz*, I, No. 371.

84 Kiderlen-Wächter to Holstein, 1 July 1890, *Holstein Papers*, III, No. 324.

85 A copy of the All-Highest Order of 23 May 1890 is to be found in the files of the Civil Cabinet, GStA Berlin, 2.2.1 No. 3007/1. See Waldersee, diary entries for 23–4 May 1890, GStA Berlin, Waldersee Papers; cf. Meisner, II, pp. 128–9; also Stolberg-Wernigerode to Reuss, 5 June 1890, cited in *Eulenburgs Korrespondenz*, I, p. 543.

86 Wedel, *Zwischen Kaiser und Kanzler*, pp. 108–9.

87 Waldersee, diary entries for 23 and 24 May 1890, GStA Berlin, Waldersee Papers; cf. Meisner, II, pp. 128–9.

88 Liebenau to House Minister Wilhelm von Wedell, 4 June 1890, Liebenau to Flügeladjutant Count Carl von Wedel, 4 June 1890, Wedel Papers, Frankfurt a.M.

89 Wedel, *Zwischen Kaiser und Kanzler*, p. 109.

90 Empress Frederick to Queen Victoria, 27 May and 4 June 1890, RA Z48/24 and 27.

91 Empress Frederick to Queen Victoria, 27 May, 4 and 19 June 1890, RA Z48/24, 27 and 34–5.

92 Waldersee, diary entry for 22 January 1894, GStA Berlin, Waldersee Papers; cf. Meisner, II, p. 304.

14   IN BISMARCK'S FOOTSTEPS: THE CONDUCT OF FOREIGN POLICY
UNDER THE NEW COURSE

1 See Hans Hallmann, ed., *Zur Geschichte und Problematik des Deutsch-Russischen Rückversicherungsvertrages von 1887*, Darmstadt 1968; Norman Rich, *Friedrich von Holstein. Politics and Diplomacy in the Era of Bismarck and Wilhelm II*, 2 vols., Cambridge 1965; George F. Kennan, *The Decline of Bismarck's European Order. Franco-Russian Relations, 1879–1890*, Princeton 1979; Klaus Hildebrand, *Das vergangene Reich. Deutsche Außenpolitik von Bismarck bis Hitler, 1871–1945*, Stuttgart 1995, pp. 118ff. and 155ff.; Konrad Canis, *Von Bismarck zur Weltpolitik. Deutsche Außenpolitik 1890 bis 1902*, Berlin 1997; Volker Ullrich, *Die nervöse Großmacht 1871–1918. Aufstieg und Untergang des deutschen Kaiserreichs*, Frankfurt a.M. 1997.

2 See Hildebrand, *Das vergangene Reich*, pp. 118–22.

3 Canis, *Von Bismarck zur Weltpolitik*, p. 26.

4 Diary of the Russian diplomat Count Lamsdorff, 19 December 1889, *Berliner Monatshefte* 9, 1931, pp. 158–77; Hallmann, *Rückversicherungsvertrag*, p. 167.

5 See *Große Politik*, VII, No. 1924.

6 See Bismarck's memorandum for Kaiser Wilhelm II of 19 August 1888, *Große Politik*, VI, No. 1350. See above, pp. 141–2. Kaiser Friedrich III on the other hand was not informed of the existence of the secret treaty with Russia. See Lamsdorff, diary entry for 4 March 1889, in Hallmann, *Rückversicherungsvertrag*, p. 165.

7 *Große Politik*, VII, No. 1367.

8 Ibid., No. 1366.

9 Wedel, *Zwischen Kaiser und Kanzler*, pp. 36–7.

10 *Große Politik*, VII, No. 1367.

11 Schweinitz, *Denkwürdigkeiten des Botschafters*, II, pp. 396–406.

12 Lamsdorff, diary entries for 9/21 March 1890, in Hallmann, *Rückversicherungsvertrag*, pp. 167–9.

13 Ibid., p. xxxv.

14 Rich, *Friedrich von Holstein*, I, p. 310; Hallmann, *Rückversicherungsvertrag*, p. xxxv.

15 Holstein to Eisendecher, 16 April 1890, *Holstein Papers*, III, No. 315.

16 Holstein to Eulenburg, 22 March 1890, *Eulenburgs Korrespondenz*, I, No. 364.

17 Hallmann, *Rückversicherungsvertrag*, p. xxxviii.

18 *Große Politik*, VII, No. 1368.

19 See Holstein to Eisendecher, 26 March 1890, Holstein to Herbert Bismarck, 5 April 1890, and Herbert Bismarck to Holstein, 5 April 1890, in *Holstein Papers*, III, Nos. 309, 311–12.

20 Lamsdorff, 14/26 March 1890, in Hallmann, *Rückversicherungsvertrag*, p. 172.

21 Schweinitz, *Denkwürdigkeiten*, ibid., p. 197.

22 Ibid., p. xlii.

23 Ibid., pp. 197–8.

24 Ibid., pp. 198–9; also Schweinitz, *Briefwechsel*, pp. 264–6.

25 *Große Politik*, VII, No. 1392.

26 Lamsdorff, diary for 7 January 1895, in Hallmann, *Rückversicherungsvertrag*, p. 186.

27 Wedel, *Zwischen Kaiser und Kanzler*, pp. 68–9.

28 See *Große Politik*, VII, Nos. 1372–3.

29 Ibid., Nos. 1374–7.

30 Ibid., No. 1378.

31 Ibid.

32 See e.g. Rich, *Friedrich von Holstein*, I, pp. 322ff.

33 Thomas Nipperdey, *Deutsche Geschichte 1866–1918*, Vol. II, *Machtstaat vor der Demokratie*, Munich 1992, p. 622.

34 Waldersee, diary entry for 2 February 1891, GStA Berlin, Waldersee Papers; cf. Meisner, II, p. 184.

35 Waldersee, diary entry for 25 September 1890, GStA Berlin, Waldersee Papers; cf. Meisner, II, pp. 149–50.

36 Waldersee, diary entry for 24 April 1890, GStA Berlin, Waldersee Papers; cf. Meisner, II, p. 124.

37 Waldersee, diary entry for 11 August 1890, GStA Berlin, Waldersee Papers; cf. Meisner, II, pp. 137–8.

38 Waldersee, diary entry for 13 September 1891, GStA Berlin, Waldersee Papers; omitted from Meisner, II, p. 216.

39 Waldersee, diary entry for 5 November 1891, GStA Berlin, Waldersee Papers; cf. Meisner, II, p. 221.

40 Wedel, *Zwischen Kaiser und Kanzler*, pp. 95–6.

41 Ibid., pp. 155 and 185.

42 Waldersee, diary entry for 24 April 1890, GStA Berlin, Waldersee Papers; cf. Meisner, II, p. 124. See Eulenburg to Holstein, 25 April 1890, *Holstein Papers*, III, No. 317.

43 Wedel, *Zwischen Kaiser und Kanzler*, p. 109. Cf. Solms to Holstein, 13 June 1890, *Holstein Papers*, III, No. 320.

44 Waldersee, diary entry for 11 August 1890, GStA Berlin, Waldersee Papers; cf. Meisner, II, pp. 137–8.

45 Waldersee, diary entry for 6 March 1891, GStA Berlin, Waldersee Papers; cf. Meisner, II, p. 198.

46  Waldersee, diary entry for 27 November 1891, GStA Berlin, Waldersee Papers; omitted from Meisner, II, p. 223.

47  Waldersee, diary entry for 4 January 1892, GStA Berlin, Waldersee Papers; omitted from Meisner, II, pp. 228–9.

48  Waldersee, diary entry for 30 January 1892, GStA Berlin, Waldersee Papers; cf. Meisner, II, p. 232.

49  Waldersee, diary entry for 30 November 1891, GStA Berlin, Waldersee Papers; omitted from Meisner, II, p. 224.

50  Waldersee, diary entry for 19 January 1891, GStA Berlin, Waldersee Papers; omitted from Meisner, II, p. 176. See Canis, *Von Bismarck zur Weltpolitik*, p. 68.

51  Waldersee, diary entry for 23 March 1890, GStA Berlin, Waldersee Papers; cf. Meisner, II, p. 122.

52  Wedel, *Zwischen Kaiser und Kanzler*, p. 101.

53  Kaiser Wilhelm II, speeches of 14 and 15 May 1890, Penzler, *Reden Kaiser Wilhelms II. in den Jahren 1888–1895*, pp. 112–16.

54  Waldersee, diary entry for 21 May 1890, GStA Berlin, Waldersee Papers; omitted from Meisner, II, p. 128.

55  Kaiser Wilhelm II, marginal notes on Pourtalès's report of 8 July 1890, PA AA, Asservat No. 4.

56  Prince Ernst zu Hohenlohe-Langenburg to his father, 29 August 1890, Hohenlohe-Zentralarchiv Neuenstein, Prince Hermann zu Hohenlohe-Langenburg Papers, Bü. 57.

57  See Kaiser Wilhelm II, marginal note on consular telegram of 31 October 1891 on Alexander III's travel plans: 'Couldn't care less' (PA AA, Asservat No. 4).

58  Wedel, *Zwischen Kaiser und Kanzler*, pp. 121–2; Waldersee, diary entry for 22 December 1890, GStA Berlin, Waldersee Papers; Meisner, II, p. 170.

59  Waldersee, diary entry for 1 September 1890, GStA Berlin, Waldersee Papers; Meisner, II, p. 142.

60  Wedel, *Zwischen Kaiser und Kanzler*, pp. 121–2.

61  Waldersee, diary entry for 1 September 1890, GStA Berlin, Waldersee Papers; cf. Meisner, II, p. 142.

62  See Waldersee's diary entry for 6 March 1891, in Meisner, II, pp. 197–8.

63  Empress Frederick to Queen Victoria, 3 February 1891, RA Z50/12. For the background to these attempts to reach an understanding with France, see Canis, *Von Bismarck zur Weltpolitik*, p. 90. But cf. Brauer to Turban, 21 February 1891, Fuchs, *Großherzog von Baden*, III, No. 1104.

64  Waldersee, diary entry for 26 February 1891, GStA Berlin, Waldersee Papers; omitted from Meisner, II, pp. 196–7. But see Waldersee's diary entry for 6 March 1891, Meisner, II, pp. 197–8.

65  Empress Frederick to Kaiser Wilhelm II, 21 February 1891, GStA Berlin, Brand.-Preuß. Hausarchiv, Rep. 52T No. 13.

66  Münster to Holstein, 5 March 1891, *Holstein Papers*, III, No. 335; also Empress Frederick to Queen Victoria, 8 April 1891, RA Z50/37.

67  Empress Frederick to her daughter Princess Viktoria of Schaumburg-Lippe, 28 February 1891, AdHH Schloss Fasanerie.

68  Empress Frederick to Queen Victoria, 29/30 March and 2 April 1891, RA Z50/29 and 32.

69  Verdy to Waldersee, 24 May 1891, GStA Berlin, Waldersee Papers, No. 53.

70  Empress Frederick to Bogumilla Freifrau von Stockmar, 18 March 1891, AdHH Schloss Fasanerie; also Brauer to Turban, 1 March 1891, Fuchs, *Großherzog von Baden*, III, No. 1107; Empress Frederick to Queen Victoria, 24 March 1891, RA Z50/24.

71 Kaiser Wilhelm II, marginal notes on the report from Vienna of 23 May 1891, PA AA, Asservat No. 4.

72 Ibid.

73 Wedel, *Zwischen Kaiser und Kanzler*, pp. 156ff.

74 Waldersee, diary entry for 16 November 1890, GStA Berlin, Waldersee Papers; cf. Meisner, II, p. 160.

75 In Penzler, *Reden Kaiser Wilhelms II. in den Jahren 1888–1895*, pp. 174–5.

76 Wedel, *Zwischen Kaiser und Kanzler*, pp. 174–9; also Brauer to Turban, 23 April 1891, Fuchs, *Großherzog von Baden*, III, No. 1110.

77 Waldersee, diary entry for 21 April 1891, GStA Berlin, Waldersee Papers; Meisner, II, p. 204.

78 Waldersee, diary entry for 21 April 1891, GStA Berlin, Waldersee Papers; cf. Meisner, II, pp. 204–5.

79 Waldersee, diary entry for 17 May 1891, GStA Berlin, Waldersee Papers; omitted from Meisner, II, p. 207.

80 On the foreign policy of the New Course, see Rainer Lahme, *Deutsche Außenpolitik 1890–1894. Von der Gleichgewichtspolitik Bismarcks zur Allianzstrategie Caprivis*, Göttingen 1990; also Rich, *Friedrich von Holstein*, I, pp. 287ff.; Ralf Forsbach, *Alfred von Kiderlen-Wächter (1852–1912). Ein Diplomatenleben im Kaiserreich*, 2 vols., Göttingen 1997; Canis, *Von Bismarck zur Weltpolitik*, pp. 17–137; Ullrich, *Nervöse Großmacht*, pp. 182–8.

81 On 31 May 1890 Waldersee and War Minister von Verdy had a joint audience with the Kaiser at which the monarch approved the 'completely altered' and 'very bold' operations plans for the eastern front presented to him by the General Staff: Waldersee, diary entry for 31 May 1890, GStA Berlin, Waldersee Papers; cf. Meisner, II, p. 129.

82 Waldersee, diary entry for 1 May 1890, GStA Berlin, Waldersee Papers; omitted from Meisner, II, p. 126.

83 Wedel, *Zwischen Kaiser und Kanzler*, p. 83.

84 Ibid., p. 80.

85 Waldersee, diary entry for 25 July 1890, GStA Berlin, Waldersee Papers; omitted from Meisner, II, p. 132. Cf. Waldersee's similar comments of January 1889, above, p. 149.

86 Waldersee, diary entry for 8 June 1890, GStA Berlin, Waldersee Papers; omitted from Meisner, II, p. 131.

87 Wedel, *Zwischen Kaiser und Kanzler*, pp. 85 and 88. See Kaiser Franz Joseph's similar concerns, cited above, p. 308.

88 Wedel, *Zwischen Kaiser und Kanzler*, p. 80.

89 Waldersee, diary entry for 25 July 1890, GStA Berlin, Waldersee Papers; Meisner, II, p. 131.

90 Waldersee, diary entry for 4 May 1890, GStA Berlin, Waldersee Papers; cf. Meisner, II, p. 126.

91 Eulenburg to Holstein, 25 April 1890, *Holstein Papers*, III, No. 317.

92 Waldersee, diary entry for 4 May 1890, GStA Berlin, Waldersee Papers; cf. Meisner, II, p. 126.

93 Waldersee, diary entry for 28 October 1890, GStA Berlin, Waldersee Papers; omitted from Meisner, II, p. 156.

94 See Canis, *Von Bismarck zur Weltpolitik*, pp. 58–60.

95 Waldersee, diary entry for 4 May 1890, GStA Berlin, Waldersee Papers; cf. Meisner, II, p. 126.

96 Waldersee, diary entry for 24 May 1890, GStA Berlin, Waldersee Papers; omitted from Meisner, II, p. 129.

97 Waldersee, diary entry for 8 May 1890, GStA Berlin, Waldersee Papers; omitted from Meisner, II, p. 127.

98 Salisbury to Queen Victoria, 23 May 1890, RA I58/49. See Buckle, *Letters of Queen Victoria*, I, p. 606.

99 RA QVJ, 7 August 1890.

100  Emin Pasha's original orders were to extend the border between the German and the British spheres of influence in East Africa as far as possible in Germany's favour. See Wissmann's order to Emin of 30 March 1890 in Georg Schweitzer, *Emin Pasha. His Life and Work*, 2 vols., London 1898, II, pp. 41–2. The Anglo-German colonial treaty of 1 July 1890 committed the Reich government to accepting an agreed boundary. See Schmidt to Emin, 30 August and 7 September 1890, Schweitzer, *Emin Pasha*, II, pp. 97ff. For Emin Pasha's adventurous life and his death, see Gaetano Casati, *Ten Years in Equatoria*, London 1891; Carl Peters, *New Light on Dark Africa; Being the Narrative of the German Emin Pasha Expedition*, London, New York, Melbourne 1891; Vita Hassan, *Die Wahrheit über Emin Pascha*, 1893; F. Stuhlmann, *Mit Emin Pascha ins Herz von Afrika*, 1894; A. J. A. Symons, *Emin, Governor of Equatoria*, London 1928.

101  Prince Hermann zu Hohenlohe-Langenburg to Kaiser Wilhelm II, 25 December 1890, Hohenlohe-Zentralarchiv Neuenstein, Hermann Hohenlohe-Langenburg Papers, Bü. 109.

102  Kaiser Wilhelm II to Prince Hermann zu Hohenlohe-Langenburg, 27 December 1890, ibid.

103  Prince Hermann zu Hohenlohe-Langenburg to Kaiser Wilhelm II, December 1890, ibid.

104  Schweitzer, *Emin Pasha*, II, pp. 294–5.

105  See Canis, *Von Bismarck zur Weltpolitik*, pp. 57–63.

106  Waldersee, diary entry for 25 July 1890, GStA Berlin, Waldersee Papers; Meisner, II, pp. 131–2.

107  Wedel, *Zwischen Kaiser und Kanzler*, pp. 116–17. Cf. Queen Victoria to Salisbury, 11 and 12 June 1890, RA I58/50–1.

108  Prince Ernst zu Hohenlohe-Langenburg to his father, 13 August 1890, Hohenlohe-Zentralarchiv Neuenstein, Hermann Hohenlohe-Langenburg Papers, Bü. 57.

109  Kaiser Wilhelm II, speech of 10 August 1890, Penzler, *Reden Kaiser Wilhelms II. in den Jahren 1888–1895*, pp. 121–4.

110  Ibid., pp. 123–4.

111  Kaiser Wilhelm II to Queen Victoria, 16 February 1891, RA E56/40 and 41; Queen Victoria to Kaiser Wilhelm II, 4 March 1891, GStA Berlin, BPHA Rep. 52 W3 No. 11.

112  Kaiser Wilhelm II to Queen Victoria, telegram, 26 February 1891, RA I59/4.

113  Salisbury to Queen Victoria, March 1891, RA I59/9 and 14.

114  Hoffmann, diaries for 22–3 April 1890, Hoffmann Papers, Freiburg.

115  Empress Frederick to her daughter Princess Viktoria of Schaumburg-Lippe, 19 January 1891, AdHH Schloss Fasanerie. For Wilhelm's relationship with his brother, see below, pp. 628–33.

116  Kiderlen-Wächter to Holstein, 7 July 1890, *Holstein Papers*, III, No. 321.

117  Kiderlen-Wächter to Holstein, 19 July 1890, ibid., No. 324.

118  Kiderlen-Wächter to Holstein, 21 September 1890, ibid., No. 328.

119  Wedel, *Zwischen Kaiser und Kanzler*, p. 157.

120  Ibid., p. 173.

121  Waldersee, diary entry for 6 September 1890, GStA Berlin, Waldersee Papers; omitted from Meisner, II, p. 142.

122  Waldersee, diary entry for 18 February 1890, GStA Berlin, Waldersee Papers; in Meisner this last passage is omitted, II, p. 103.

123  Waldersee, diary entry for 11 October 1890, GStA Berlin, Waldersee Papers; omitted from Meisner, II, p. 154.

124  Waldersee, diary entries for 20 December 1890 and 17 January 1891, GStA Berlin, Waldersee Papers; cf. Meisner, II, pp. 168 and 176.

125  See Canis, *Von Bismarck zur Weltpolitik*, pp. 71–87.

126  Waldersee, diary entry for 3 July 1891, GStA Berlin, Waldersee Papers; cf. Meisner, II, pp. 211–12.

127 Waldersee, diary entry for14 July 1891, GStA Berlin, Waldersee Papers; omitted from Meisner, II, p. 212.

128 Rumbold to Ponsonby, 24 June 1891, RA I59/29.

129 See Roderick R. McLean, *Royalty and Diplomacy in Europe, 1890–1914*, Cambridge 2001, p. 87.

130 *Daily Telegraph*, 6 July 1891, *Times*, 10 July 1891, RA I59/31–3.

131 *Daily Telegraph*, 11 July 1891, RA I59/34–5.

132 *Morning Post*, 13 July 1891, RA I59/37.

133 See e.g. *Standard*, 4 July 1891, RA I59/30.

134 Kaiser Wilhelm II, speech of 10 July 1891, cited from *Daily Telegraph*, 11 July 1891, RA I59/34.

135 *Morning Post*, 13 July 1891, *Standard*, 14 July 1891, RA I59/37–8.

136 This portrait now hangs in Osborne House. See Jarchow, *Hofgeschenke*, pp. 52–3.

137 Prince Ernst zu Hohenlohe-Langenburg to his father, 16 October 1891, Hohenlohe-Zentralarchiv Schloss Neuenstein, Hermann Hohenlohe-Langenburg Papers, Bü. 58.

138 Kaiser Wilhelm II to Queen Victoria, 14 July 1891, RA I59/39.

139 Kaiser Wilhelm II to Queen Victoria, 20 July 1891, RA I59/42.

140 Kaiser Wilhelm II to Queen Victoria, 12 August 1891, RA I59/45.

141 Kaiser Wilhelm II to Queen Victoria, 22 May 1892, RA I59/80.

142 Empress Frederick to Queen Victoria, 26 August 1891, RA Z51/15.

143 Prince Heinrich of Prussia to Kaiser Wilhelm II, 16 August 1891, BA-MA Freiburg, Senden-Bibran Papers, N160/10.

144 Prince Heinrich of Prussia to Kaiser Wilhelm II, 21 August 1891, ibid.

145 Waldersee, diary entry for 15 July 1891, GStA Berlin, Waldersee Papers; omitted from Meisner, II, p. 212.

146 Canis, *Von Bismarck zur Weltpolitik*, pp. 67–71.

147 Waldersee, diary entry for 15 July 1891, GStA Berlin, Waldersee Papers; omitted from Meisner, II, p. 212.

148 Canis, *Von Bismarck zur Weltpolitik*, p. 63.

149 Empress Frederick to Queen Victoria, 8 September 1891, RA Z51/21.

150 Kaiserin Auguste Viktoria to Kaiser Wilhelm II, 26/28 July 1891, GStA Berlin, BPHA Rep. 53T Preußen: An Kaiser Wilhelm II., Bd IV.

151 Waldersee, diary entry for 27 August 1891, GStA Berlin, Waldersee Papers; omitted from Meisner, II, p. 215.

152 Ibid.

153 Waldersee, diary entry for 13 and 25 September 1891, GStA Berlin, Waldersee Papers; omitted from Meisner, II, pp. 216 and 218.

154 Waldersee, diary entry for 13 August 1891, GStA Berlin, Waldersee Papers; omitted from Meisner, II, pp. 214–15.

155 Waldersee, diary entry for 17 September 1891, GStA Berlin, Waldersee Papers; cf. Meisner, II, p. 217.

156 Kaiser Wilhelm II, marginal notes on Bülow's report of 11 August 1891 and on the report from Egypt of 6 April 1892, PA AA, Asservat No. 4.

157 Kaiser Wilhelm II, marginal notes on Bülow's report of 22 November 1891, ibid.

158 Kaiser Wilhelm II, speech at Erfurt, 14 September 1891, Penzler, *Reden Kaiser Wilhelms II. in den Jahren 1888–1895*, pp. 192–3.

159 Caprivi to Kaiser Wilhelm II, cipher telegram, 17 September 1891, Kaiser Wilhelm II to Caprivi, telegram *en clair*, 18 September 1891, PA AA, Asservat No. 4.

160 Empress Frederick to Queen Victoria, 19 September 1891, RA Z51/26.

161 Waldersee, diary entry for 25 September 1890, GStA Berlin, Waldersee Papers; cf. Meisner, II, pp. 149–50.

162 Waldersee, diary entries for 24 April and 11 August 1890, GStA Berlin, Waldersee Papers; cf. Meisner, II, pp. 124 and 137–8.

163 Eulenburg's notes of 11 July 1892, *Eulenburgs Korrespondenz*, II, No. 688.

164 Kaiser Wilhelm II to Kaiser Franz Joseph, 31 January 1893, HHStA Vienna, Kabinettsarchiv Geheimakten 2.

165 Kaiser Franz Joseph to Kaiser Wilhelm II, 5 February 1893, ibid.

166 Eulenburg to Kaiser Wilhelm II, 16 April 1893, *Eulenburgs Korrespondenz*, II, No. 793.

167 Kaiser Wilhelms II, dictated notes on a conversation with Pope Leo XIII, 23 April 1893, in Hohenlohe, *Denkwürdigkeiten der Reichskanzlerzeit*, pp. 608–11. See above, p. 118.

168 Minutes of the Crown Council of 18 February 1894, GStA Berlin; cited more fully below, p. 499. See Canis, *Von Bismarck zur Weltpolitik*, pp. 121–2.

169 Kaiser Wilhelm II to Crown Prince Gustaf of Sweden and Norway, 25 July 1895, printed in Hohenlohe, *Denkwürdigkeiten der Reichskanzlerzeit*, pp. 102–5.

## 15 THE DUALISM OF POWER

1 Waldersee, diary entry for 4 May 1890, GStA Berlin, Waldersee Papers; omitted from Meisner, II, p. 126.

2 Cabinet order of 14 April 1890, in Gradenwitz, *Bismarcks letzter Kampf*, p. 114.

3 Kiderlen-Wächter to Holstein, 7 and 15 July 1890, *Holstein Papers*, III, Nos. 321–2. See Forsbach, *Kiderlen-Wächter*, I, p. 98.

4 Kaiser Wilhelm II to Queen Victoria, 25 December 1890, RA I58/63.

5 Holstein to Brandt, 26 December 1890, *Holstein Papers*, III, No. 332.

6 Waldersee, diary entry for 26 December 1890, GStA Berlin, Waldersee Papers; omitted from Meisner, II, p. 171.

7 Waldersee, diary entry for 20 April 1890, GStA Berlin, Waldersee Papers; omitted from Meisner, II, p. 124.

8 Ibid.

9 Waldersee, diary entries for 20–2 March and 20 April 1890, GStA Berlin, Waldersee Papers; cf. Meisner, II, pp. 119ff. and 124.

10 Wedel, *Zwischen Kaiser und Kanzler*, p. 109. Cf. Solms to Holstein, 13 June 1890, *Holstein Papers*, III, No. 320.

11 Brauer to Turban, 17 December 1890, Fuchs, *Großherzog von Baden*, III, No. 1089.

12 For the genesis of Verdy's Army Bill, see above, pp. 291–2.

13 Waldersee, diary entry for 8 June 1890, GStA Berlin, Waldersee Papers; cf. Meisner, II, pp. 130–1.

14 Waldersee, diary entry for 20 April 1890, GStA Berlin, Waldersee Papers; omitted from Meisner, II, p. 124. Cf. Meisner, II, pp. 132ff.

15 Wedel, *Zwischen Kaiser und Kanzler*, p. 115. Cf. Waldersee, diary entry for 7 June 1890, GStA Berlin, Waldersee Papers; Meisner, II, p. 130. See Förster, *Der doppelte Militarismus*, pp. 31ff.

16 Kiderlen-Wächter to Holstein, 21 September 1890, *Holstein Papers*, III. No. 328; also Brauer to Turban, 11 October 1890, Fuchs, *Großherzog von Baden*, III, No. 1076.

17 Waldersee, diary entry for 25 July 1890, GStA Berlin, Waldersee Papers; Meisner, II, p. 133.

18 Waldersee, diary entry for 7 October 1890, GStA Berlin, Waldersee Papers; omitted from Meisner, II, p. 153.

19 But cf. Waldersee, diary entry for 2 October 1890, GStA Berlin, Waldersee Papers; omitted for the most part from Meisner, II, pp. 151–2. See below, p. 412.

20 Waldersee, diary entry for 3 September 1890, GStA Berlin, Waldersee Papers; omitted from Meisner, II, p. 142.

21 Waldersee, diary entry for 25 July 1890, GStA Berlin, Waldersee Papers; Meisner, II, p. 134.

22 Waldersee, diary entry for 2 October 1890, GStA Berlin, Waldersee Papers; omitted from Meisner, II, pp. 151–2.

23 See below, pp. 433–4.

24 Wedel, *Zwischen Kaiser und Kanzler*, p. 133.

25 Ibid., pp. 117–18.

26 Waldersee, diary entry for 2 October 1890, GStA Berlin, Waldersee Papers; omitted from Meisner, II, pp. 151–2.

27 Waldersee, diary entry for 19 August 1890, GStA Berlin, Waldersee Papers; cf. Meisner, II, p. 140.

28 Waldersee, diary entry for 2 October 1890, GStA Berlin, Waldersee Papers; cf. Meisner, II, pp. 151–2.

29 Waldersee, diary entry for 21 October 1890, GStA Berlin, Waldersee Papers; Meisner, II, p. 155.

30 Minutes of the Prussian Ministry of State, 16 June 1890, in Röhl, *Germany without Bismarck*, pp. 60–1.

31 Waldersee, diary entry for 25 July 1890, GStA Berlin, Waldersee Papers; Meisner, II, p. 134; Wedel, *Zwischen Kaiser und Kanzler*, p. 116.

32 Wedel, *Zwischen Kaiser und Kanzler*, pp. 109–10.

33 See Hans Herzfeld, *Johannes von Miquel. Sein Anteil am Ausbau des Deutschen Reiches bis zur Jahrhundertwende*, 2 vols., Detmold 1938; Röhl, *Germany without Bismarck*, pp. 61–2; Wedel, *Zwischen Kaiser und Kanzler*, pp. 130–1.

34 Waldersee, diary entry for 10 December 1890, GStA Berlin, Waldersee Papers; cf. Meisner, II, p. 165.

35 Waldersee, diary entry for 5 August 1893, GStA Berlin, Waldersee Papers; omitted from Meisner, II, pp. 291–2.

36 Empress Frederick to Bogumilla Freifrau von Stockmar, 11 and 18 April 1891, AdHH Schloss Fasanerie.

37 Minutes of the Prussian Ministry of State, 30 September 1890, in Röhl, *Germany without Bismarck*, p. 62; Wedel, *Zwischen Kaiser und Kanzler*, p. 130.

38 Minutes of the Prussian Ministry of State, 30 September 1890, in Röhl, *Germany without Bismarck*, p. 62; Wedel, *Zwischen Kaiser und Kanzler*, p. 130; also Waldersee, diary entry for 16 November 1890, GStA Berlin, Waldersee Papers; omitted from Meisner, II, p. 161.

39 Waldersee, diary entry for 19 January 1891, GStA Berlin, Waldersee Papers; omitted from Meisner, II, p. 176.

40 Wedel, *Zwischen Kaiser und Kanzler*, p. 125.

41 Röhl, *Germany without Bismarck*, p. 63.

42 Ibid., p. 77.

43 Kiderlen-Wächter to Holstein, 21 September 1890, *Holstein Papers*, III, No. 328.

44 Wedel, *Zwischen Kaiser und Kanzler*, p. 128.

45 Kiderlen-Wächter to Holstein, 21 September 1890, *Holstein Papers*, III, No. 328.

46 Waldersee, diary entry for 3 October 1890, GStA Berlin, Waldersee Papers; omitted from Meisner, II, p. 152.

47 Kiderlen-Wächter to Holstein, 21 September 1890, *Holstein Papers*, III, No. 328.

48 Waldersee, diary entry for 10 October 1890, GStA Berlin, Waldersee Papers; omitted from Meisner, II, p. 154.

49 Waldersee, diary entry for 11 October 1890, GStA Berlin, Waldersee Papers; omitted from Meisner, II, p. 154.

50 Boetticher and Marschall to Flügeladjutant on duty, 14 October 1891, with the Kaiser's marginal notes, PA AA, Preußen 1 No. 1d, Bd I; Kaiser Wilhelm II to Boetticher, 14 October 1891, PA AA, Asservat No. 4.

51 Waldersee, diary entry for 2 November 1891, GStA Berlin, Waldersee Papers; cf. Meisner, II, pp. 220–1.

52 Wedel, *Zwischen Kaiser und Kanzler*, pp. 110–15.

53 Waldersee, diary entry for 18 November 1890, GStA Berlin, Waldersee Papers; Meisner, II, p. 162.

54 Waldersee, diary entry for 1 February 1891, GStA Berlin, Waldersee Papers; Meisner, II, p. 184; also Wedel, *Zwischen Kaiser und Kanzler*, p. 152.

55 Waldersee, diary entry for 1 February 1891, GStA Berlin, Waldersee Papers; omitted from Meisner, II, p. 184.

56 Empress Frederick to Bogumilla Freifrau von Stockmar, 18 March 1891, AdHH Schloss Fasanerie.

57 Wedel, *Zwischen Kaiser und Kanzler*, p. 115.

58 Waldersee, diary entry for 17 August 1890, GStA Berlin, Waldersee Papers; cf. Meisner, II, p. 130.

59 Brauer, report of 7 December 1890, in Fuchs, *Großherzog von Baden*, III, No. 1088.

60 See below, pp. 405–9.

61 See e.g. Clark, *Kaiser Wilhelm* II, pp. 60–1. Cf. Nipperdey, *Deutsche Geschichte 1866–1918*, Vol. I, *Arbeitswelt und Bürgergeist*, Munich 1990, p. 535. For the effect of the Kaiser's speech on Prussian secondary schools, See, *Barbar Germane Arier*, p. 148.

62 Kaiser Wilhelm II, speech of 4 December 1890, Penzler, *Reden Kaiser Wilhelms II. in den Jahren 1888–1895*, pp. 152–62. Cf. Louis Elkind, transl., *The German Emperor's Speeches: Being a Selection from the Speeches, Edicts, Letters and Telegrams of the Emperor William II*, New York, London, Bombay 1904, pp. 160–1. See Waldersee, diary entry for 5 December 1890, GStA Berlin, Waldersee Papers; Meisner, II, p. 164.

63 Brauer to Turban, 7 December 1890, Fuchs, *Großherzog von Baden*, III, No. 1088.

64 Waldersee, diary entry for 6 December 1890, GStA Berlin, Waldersee Papers; omitted from Meisner, II, p. 164.

65 Waldersee, diary entry for 10 December 1890, GStA Berlin, Waldersee Papers; cf. Meisner, II, p. 165.

66 Waldersee, diary entry for 14 December 1890, GStA Berlin, Waldersee Papers; cf. Meisner, II, p. 166.

67 Kaiser Wilhelm II, speech of 17 December 1890, Penzler, *Reden Kaiser Wilhelms II. in den Jahren 1888–1895*, pp. 163–7; Elkind, *German Emperor's Speeches*, pp. 166–7.

68 Waldersee, diary entry for 14 January 1891, GStA Berlin, Waldersee Papers; Meisner, II, p. 175.

69 Waldersee, diary entry for 25 January 1891, GStA Berlin, Waldersee Papers; omitted from Meisner, II, p. 177.

70 Empress Frederick to Queen Victoria, 24 March 1891, RA Z50/24.

71 Wedel, *Zwischen Kaiser und Kanzler*, p. 187.

72 Röhl, *Germany without Bismarck*, p. 78, n. 2.

73 Waldersee, diary entry for 27 October 1890, GStA Berlin, Waldersee Papers; omitted from Meisner, II, p. 156.

74 Wedel, *Zwischen Kaiser und Kanzler*, p. 172.

75 Count Udo Stolberg, ibid., p. 115.

76 Kaiser Wilhelm II, speech at the Brandenburg provincial diet, 20 February 1891, Penzler, *Reden Kaiser Wilhelms II. in den Jahren 1888–1895*, pp. 168–71.

77 Kaiser Wilhelm II, speech at the Rhenish provincial diet, 4 May 1891, ibid., pp. 176–8; Wedel, *Zwischen Kaiser und Kanzler*, p. 179.

78 Kaiser Wilhelm II, speech of 24 February 1892, Penzler, *Reden Kaiser Wilhelms II. in den Jahren 1888–1895*, pp. 207–10; Elkind, *German Emperor's Speeches*, pp. 292–4. See Marschall, diary entry for 24 February 1892, cited in *Eulenburgs Korrespondenz*, II, p. 780.

79  Brauer to Grand Duke Friedrich I of Baden, 26 February 1892, Fuchs, *Großherzog von Baden*, III, No. 1159; also Brauer to Turban, 1 March 1892, ibid., No. 1162.

80  Holstein to Eulenburg, 16 March 1891, *Eulenburgs Korrespondenz*, I, No. 485.

81  Eulenburg to Kaiser Wilhelm II, 23 March 1891, ibid., No. 493.

82  Holstein to Eulenburg, 16 March 1891, ibid., No. 485.

83  On Kiderlen's role, see Forsbach, *Kiderlen-Wächter*, I, pp. 120ff.

84  Kiderlen-Wächter to Holstein, 3 August 1891, *Holstein Papers*, III, No. 345.

85  Kaiser Wilhelm II, marginal note on an article in the *Hamburger Nachrichten* of 21 September 1891, PA AA, Asservat No. 4.

86  Kaiser Wilhelm II to King Albert of Saxony, 1 February 1892, GStA Berlin, BPH Rep. 53 No. 377.

87  Waldersee, diary entry for 31 October 1891, GStA Berlin, Waldersee Papers; omitted from Meisner, II, p. 220; Brauer, report of 29 October 1891, Fuchs, *Großherzog von Baden*, III, No. 1137; also below, pp. 507–8.

88  Waldersee, diary entry for 20 July 1891, GStA Berlin, Waldersee Papers; Meisner, II, pp. 212–13.

89  Waldersee, diary entry for 31 October 1891, GStA Berlin, Waldersee Papers; cf. Meisner, II, p. 220.

90  Waldersee, diary entry for 17 November 1891, GStA Berlin, Waldersee Papers; cf. Meisner, II, p. 222.

91  Waldersee, diary entry for 18 November 1891, GStA Berlin, Waldersee Papers; printed in part in Meisner, II, p. 222.

92  Verdy to Waldersee, 24 May 1891, GStA Berlin, Waldersee Papers No. 53.

93  See Förster, *Der doppelte Militarismus*, pp. 36ff.

94  See Holstein to Eulenburg, 17 June 1891, *Eulenburgs Korrespondenz*, I, No. 525.

95  Kaiser Wilhelm II to Kaltenborn, 15 June 1891, BA-MA Freiburg, KGFA W10/50266.

96  Kaiser Wilhelm II to Caprivi, 15 June 1891, printed from the original in the files of the Reichskanzlei (Militärsachen 2b vol. I 1255 Mappe 13) in Heinrich Otto Meisner, 'Der Reichskanzler Caprivi', *Zeitschrift für die gesamte Staatswissenschaft*, 3 (1955), pp. 742–3.

97  Waldersee, diary entry for 6 December 1891, GStA Berlin, Waldersee Papers; omitted from Meisner, II, pp. 224–5.

98  Holstein to Eulenburg, 16 and 17 June 1891, *Eulenburgs Korrespondenz*, I, Nos. 523 and 525.

99  Caprivi to Kaiser Wilhelm II, 16 June 1891, in Meisner, 'Reichskanzler Caprivi', p. 744.

100  Holstein to Eulenburg, 16 June 1891, Eulenburg to Holstein, 17 June 1891, *Eulenburgs Korrespondenz*, I, Nos. 523 and 524.

101  Kaiser Wilhelm II to Caprivi, 16 June 1891, in Meisner, 'Reichskanzler Caprivi', pp. 744–5.

102  Holstein to Eulenburg, 17 June 1891, *Eulenburgs Korrespondenz*, I, No. 525.

103  Kiderlen-Wächter to Holstein, 10 August 1891, *Holstein Papers*, III, No. 346; also Eulenburg to Caprivi, 31 July 1891, *Eulenburgs Korrespondenz*, I, No. 530.

104  Waldersee, diary entry for 13 August 1891, GStA Berlin, Waldersee Papers; cf. Meisner, II, pp. 214–15.

105  Caprivi, Denkschrift betreffend die weitere Entwicklung der deutschen Wehrkraft, Caprivi to Kaltenborn, 27 August 1891, BA-MA Freiburg, W10/50266.

106  See below, pp. 456–65; also Förster, *Der doppelte Militarismus*, pp. 40–1.

107  Holstein to Eulenburg, 17 June 1891, *Eulenburgs Korrespondenz*, I, No. 525.

108  See Empress Frederick to Queen Victoria, 19 December 1891, RA Z52/7.

109  Kaiser Wilhelm II to Queen Victoria, 19 December 1891, RA I59/55. See Waldersee, diary entry for 19 December 1891, GStA Berlin, Waldersee Papers; omitted from Meisner, II, p. 227.

110 Caprivi to Holstein, 27 January 1892, *Holstein Papers*, III, No. 355. See Holstein to Kaiser Wilhelm II, 30 January 1892, ibid., No. 358.

111 Eulenburg to Holstein, 4 February 1892, ibid., No. 359.

112 Prince Ernst zu Hohenlohe-Langenburg to his father, 28 January 1892, Hohenlohe-Zentralarchiv Neuenstein, Hermann Hohenlohe-Langenburg Papers, Bü. 59.

113 Waldersee, diary entry for 21 November 1891, GStA Berlin, Waldersee Papers; Meisner, II, p. 223.

114 Waldersee, diary entry for 24 April 1890, GStA Berlin, Waldersee Papers; cf. Meisner, II, p. 124.

115 Kaiser Wilhelm II, marginal notes on the article 'Warnungszeichen' in *Hamburger Nachrichten*, 26 March 1890, Wedel Papers, Frankfurt a.M.; cited in Wedel, *Zwischen Kaiser und Kanzler*, pp. 67–8.

116 Wedel, *Zwischen Kaiser und Kanzler*, pp. 67–8.

117 Ibid., pp. 95–6.

118 Waldersee, diary entry for 24 April 1890, GStA Berlin, Waldersee Papers; cf. Meisner, II, p. 124.

119 Waldersee, diary entry for 1 May 1890, GStA Berlin, Waldersee Papers; omitted from Meisner, II, p. 126.

120 Waldersee, diary entry for 4 May 1890, GStA Berlin, Waldersee Papers; omitted from Meisner, II, p. 126.

121 Waldersee, diary entry for 24 April 1890, GStA Berlin, Waldersee Papers; omitted for the most part from Meisner, II, p. 124.

122 Waldersee, diary entry for 4 May 1890, GStA Berlin, Waldersee Papers; cf. Meisner, II, p. 126.

123 Waldersee, diary entry for 3 September 1890, GStA Berlin, Waldersee Papers; omitted from Meisner, II, p. 142.

124 Wedel, *Zwischen Kaiser und Kanzler*, pp. 110–15. Cf. ibid., p. 152.

125 Waldersee, diary entry for 25 September 1890, GStA Berlin, Waldersee Papers; cf. Meisner, II, p. 149.

126 Waldersee, diary entry for 1 September 1890, GStA Berlin, Waldersee Papers; cf. Meisner, II, p. 142.

127 Waldersee, diary entries for 30 August and 3 September 1890, GStA Berlin, Waldersee Papers; cf. Meisner, II, pp. 141–2.

128 Wedel, *Zwischen Kaiser und Kanzler*, p. 131.

129 Waldersee, diary entry for 22 November 1890, GStA Berlin, Waldersee Papers; omitted from Meisner, II, p. 163.

130 Eulenburg to Holstein, 30 January 1892, *Holstein Papers*, III, No. 357.

131 Waldersee, diary entry for 28 November 1891, GStA Berlin, Waldersee Papers; cf. Meisner, II, pp. 223–4.

132 Waldersee, diary entry for 24 April 1890, GStA Berlin, Waldersee Papers; cf. Meisner, II, p. 124.

133 Waldersee, diary entry for 16 March 1892, GStA Berlin, Waldersee Papers; Meisner, II, pp. 234–5.

134 Brauer, reports of 11 and 17 February and 19 December 1891, cited in Röhl, *Germany without Bismarck*, pp. 75–6.

135 Waldersee, diary entry for 16 November 1890, GStA Berlin, Waldersee Papers; omitted from Meisner, II, p. 161.

136 Wedel, *Zwischen Kaiser und Kanzler*, p. 132.

137 Waldersee, diary entry for 29 October 1890, GStA Berlin, Waldersee Papers; Meisner, II, p. 156.

138 Waldersee, diary entry for 4 November 1890, GStA Berlin, Waldersee Papers; omitted from Meisner, II, p. 157.

139 Waldersee, diary entry for 1 November 1890, GStA Berlin, Waldersee Papers; omitted from Meisner, II, p. 157.

140 Waldersee, diary entry for 4 November 1890, GStA Berlin, Waldersee Papers; omitted from Meisner, II, p. 157; Empress Frederick to Queen Victoria, 11 November 1890, RA Z49/33.

141 Wedel, *Zwischen Kaiser und Kanzler,* pp. 129–30 and 151.

142 Ibid.; also Brauer to Grand Duke Friedrich, 9 November 1890, Fuchs, *Großherzog von Baden*, III, No. 1081.

143 Empress Frederick to Queen Victoria, 11 November 1890, RA Z49/33.

144 Wedel, *Zwischen Kaiser und Kanzler*, p. 130.

145 Waldersee, diary entries for 16 and 18 November 1890, GStA Berlin, Waldersee Papers; cf. Meisner, II, pp. 161–2.

146 Waldersee, diary entry for 4 November 1890, GStA Berlin, Waldersee Papers; omitted from Meisner, II, p. 157.

147 Waldersee, diary entry for 7 November 1890, GStA Berlin, Waldersee Papers; omitted from Meisner, II, p. 158.

148 Waldersee, diary entry for 23 November 1890, GStA Berlin, Waldersee Papers; omitted from Meisner, II, p. 163. Cf. Waldersee's retrospective note of 21 November 1894 in Meisner, II, p. 332.

149 Waldersee, diary entry for 3 January 1891, GStA Berlin, Waldersee Papers; cf. Meisner, II, p. 174.

150 Waldersee, diary entry for 2 January 1891, GStA Berlin, Waldersee Papers; omitted from Meisner, II, p. 172.

151 Wedel, *Zwischen Kaiser und Kanzler*, p. 172.

152 Count Karl von Kalnein to Eulenburg, 8 March 1892, *Eulenburgs Korrespondenz*, II, No. 602. See below, ch. 29.

153 Waldersee, diary entry for 9 January 1891, GStA Berlin, Waldersee Papers; omitted from Meisner, II, p. 174.

154 Waldersee, diary entry for 10 January 1891, GStA Berlin, Waldersee Papers; cf. Meisner, II, p. 175.

155 Waldersee, diary entry for 18 January 1891, GStA Berlin, Waldersee Papers; omitted from Meisner, II, p. 176.

156 Wedel, *Zwischen Kaiser und Kanzler*, p. 192.

157 Waldersee, diary entry for 22 June 1891, GStA Berlin, Waldersee Papers; cf. Meisner, II, pp. 209–10.

158 Waldersee, diary entry for 2 November 1891, GStA Berlin, Waldersee Papers; cf. Meisner, II, pp. 220–1.

159 Wedel, *Zwischen Kaiser und Kanzler*, p. 108.

160 Ibid., p. 116.

161 Waldersee, diary entry for 27 October 1890, GStA Berlin, Waldersee Papers; omitted from Meisner, II, p. 156.

162 Above, pp. 401–3.

163 Waldersee, diary entry for 21 November 1890, GStA Berlin, Waldersee Papers; abridged in Meisner, II, p. 163.

164 Waldersee, diary entry for 4 January 1891, GStA Berlin, Waldersee Papers; cf. Meisner, II, p. 174.

165 Waldersee, diary entries for 19 and 24 November 1890, GStA Berlin, Waldersee Papers; cf. Meisner, II, pp. 162ff.

166　Waldersee, diary entry for 27 October 1890, GStA Berlin, Waldersee Papers; omitted from Meisner, II, p. 156.

167　Waldersee, diary entry for 14 January 1891, GStA Berlin, Waldersee Papers; cf. Meisner, II, p. 175.

168　Holstein to Eulenburg, 17 March 1891, Eulenburg to Holstein, 19 March 1891, *Eulenburgs Korrespondenz*, I, Nos. 489-90.

169　See Thomas A. Kohut, *Wilhelm II and the Germans. A Study in Leadership*, New York, Oxford 1991, p. 286.

170　Waldersee, diary entry for 7 December 1890, GStA Berlin, Waldersee Papers; cf. Meisner, II, p. 164.

171　Waldersee, diary entry for 10 December 1890, GStA Berlin, Waldersee Papers; cf. Meisner, II, pp. 164-5.

172　Waldersee, diary entry for 9 January 1891, GStA Berlin, Waldersee Papers; cf. Meisner, II, p. 171.

173　Waldersee, diary entry for 19 January 1891, GStA Berlin, Waldersee Papers; cf. Meisner, II, p. 176.

174　Bigelow to Kaiser Wilhelm II, 26 January 1893, GStA Berlin, Brand.-Preuß. Hausarchiv Rep. 53J Lit. B. No. 10 Bigelow 1.

175　Waldersee, diary entry for 14 January 1891, GStA Berlin, Waldersee Papers; cf. Meisner, II, p. 175.

176　Waldersee, diary entries for 11 and 27 April 1890, GStA Berlin, Waldersee Papers; omitted from Meisner, II, pp. 124 and 138; also above, pp. 168-9.

177　Wedel, *Zwischen Kaiser und Kanzler*, pp. 108, 116 and 125; Waldersee, diary entry for 1 June 1890, GStA Berlin, Waldersee Papers; Meisner, II, p. 129.

178　Waldersee, diary entry for 11 August 1890, GStA Berlin, Waldersee Papers; omitted from Meisner, II, p. 138.

179　Waldersee, diary entry for 4 October 1890, GStA Berlin, Waldersee Papers; cf. Meisner, II, pp. 151-2.

180　Waldersee, diary entry for 20 December 1890, GStA Berlin, Waldersee Papers; omitted from Meisner, II, p. 169.

181　Waldersee, diary entry for 21 October 1894, GStA Berlin, Waldersee Papers; cf. Meisner, II, p. 327. See *Eulenburgs Korrespondenz*, III, pp. 1535, 1639-40, 1848-9 and 1951-2.

182　Wedel, *Zwischen Kaiser und Kanzler*, p. 142.

### 16　THE FALL OF THE COURT GENERALS

1　See *Young Wilhelm*, pp. 424-30, 490-515, 599-629 *et passim*.

2　Ibid., pp. 455-62, as well as above, pp. 197-9.

3　Hoffmann, diary entries for 22 and 24 March and 23 April 1890, Hoffmann Papers, Freiburg. See above, p. 320.

4　Wedel, *Zwischen Kaiser und Kanzler*, p. 128.

5　See above, pp. 225-7; also Cecil, *Wilhelm II*, I, pp. 182-4.

6　Waldersee, diary entry for 29 January 1891, GStA Berlin, Waldersee Papers; Meisner, II, p. 180.

7　Kiderlen-Wächter to Holstein, 19 July and 21 September 1890, *Holstein Papers*, III, Nos. 324 and 328.

8　Wedel, *Zwischen Kaiser und Kanzler*, p. 129.

9　Eulenburg to Holstein, 1 August 1890, *Holstein Papers*, III, No. 327.

10　Wedel, *Zwischen Kaiser und Kanzler*, p. 129. See above, pp. 373-5.

11　Waldersee to Verdy, 30 October 1891, GStA Berlin, Waldersee Papers No. 53.

12 Waldersee, diary entry for 7 June 1890, GStA Berlin, Waldersee Papers; omitted from Meisner, II, p. 130.

13 Waldersee, diary entry for 30 August 1890, GStA Berlin, Waldersee Papers; cf. Meisner, II, pp. 141–2.

14 Waldersee, diary entry for 13 September 1890, GStA Berlin, Waldersee Papers; cf. Meisner, II, p. 144.

15 Waldersee, diary entry for 10 October 1890, GStA Berlin, Waldersee Papers; cf. Meisner, II, p. 153.

16 Eulenburg to Holstein, 1 August 1890, *Holstein Papers*, III, No. 327.

17 See Heinrich Otto Meisner, *Militärattachés und Militärbevollmächtigte in Preußen und im Deutschen Reich. Ein Beitrag zur Geschichte der Militärdiplomatie*, Berlin 1957, pp. 56–7 and 73ff.; Gerhard Ritter, *Die deutschen Militär-Attachés und das Auswärtige Amt. Aus den verbrannten Akten des Großen Generalstabes*, Heidelberg 1959, pp. 21ff. and 33ff. The letters from Holstein to Eulenburg of 6 and 27 November 1890 and 10 January 1891 are informative on this issue: *Eulenburgs Korrespondenz*, I, Nos. 433, 444 and 464; also Forsbach, *Kiderlen-Wächter*, I, pp. 104–5.

18 Waldersee, diary entry for 10 August 1890, GStA Berlin, Waldersee Papers; cf. Meisner, II, pp. 135–6.

19 Waldersee, diary entry for 10 August 1890, GStA Berlin, Waldersee Papers; omitted from Meisner, II, p. 137.

20 Waldersee, diary entry for 11 September 1890, GStA Berlin, Waldersee Papers; cf. Meisner, II, p. 144.

21 Kiderlen-Wächter to Holstein, 21 September 1890, *Holstein Papers*, III, No. 328.

22 Waldersee, diary entry for 11 September 1890, GStA Berlin, Waldersee Papers; cf. Meisner, II, p. 144.

23 Kiderlen-Wächter to Holstein, 21 September 1890, *Holstein Papers*, III, No. 328.

24 Waldersee, diary entries for 21 and 24 September 1890, GStA Berlin, Waldersee Papers; cf. Meisner, II, pp. 145–9; also Wedel, *Zwischen Kaiser und Kanzler*, pp. 126ff.

25 Kiderlen-Wächter to Holstein, 21 September 1890, *Holstein Papers*, III, No. 328.

26 Waldersee, diary entries for 21 and 24 September 1890, GStA Berlin, Waldersee Papers; cf. Meisner, II, pp. 145–9; also Wedel, *Zwischen Kaiser und Kanzler*, pp. 126ff.

27 Kiderlen-Wächter to Holstein, 21 September 1890, *Holstein Papers*, III, No. 328.

28 Waldersee, diary entry for 24 September 1890, GStA Berlin, Waldersee Papers; cf. Meisner, II, p. 148.

29 Waldersee, diary entry for 21 September 1890, GStA Berlin, Waldersee Papers; cf. Meisner, II, pp. 145ff.

30 Waldersee, diary entry for 25 September 1890, GStA Berlin, Waldersee Papers; omitted from Meisner, II, p. 151.

31 Waldersee, diary entry for 21 September 1890, GStA Berlin, Waldersee Papers; cf. Meisner, II, pp. 145ff. See Wedel, *Zwischen Kaiser und Kanzler*, pp. 125–6.

32 Kiderlen-Wächter to Holstein, 21 September 1890, *Holstein Papers*, III, No. 328.

33 Waldersee, diary entry for 11 September 1890, GStA Berlin, Waldersee Papers; omitted from Meisner, II, p. 145.

34 Waldersee, diary entry for 3 October 1890, GStA Berlin, Waldersee Papers; Meisner, II, p. 152.

35 Waldersee, diary entry for 21 September 1890, GStA Berlin, Waldersee Papers; cf. Meisner, II, pp. 145–6; also the diary entry of 9 October 1890, GStA Berlin, Waldersee Papers; omitted from Meisner II, p. 154.

36 Kiderlen-Wächter to Holstein, 21 September 1890, *Holstein Papers*, III, No. 328.

37 Wedel, *Zwischen Kaiser und Kanzler*, p. 126.

38 Waldersee, diary entry for 9 October 1890, GStA Berlin, Waldersee Papers; omitted from Meisner, II, p. 153.

39 Waldersee, diary entry for 16 October 1890, GStA Berlin, Waldersee Papers; omitted from Meisner, II, p. 155.

40 Wedel, *Zwischen Kaiser und Kanzler*, p. 128.

41 Caprivi's instruction of 11 December 1890 is printed in Meisner, *Militärattachés*, pp. 73ff.; see Waldersee's marginal notes in Ritter, *Militär-Attachés*, pp. 33ff.

42 Waldersee, diary entry for 13 December 1890, GStA Berlin, Waldersee Papers; Meisner, II, p. 165.

43 Waldersee, diary entry for 17 December 1890, GStA Berlin, Waldersee Papers; cf. Meisner, II, pp. 166–7.

44 Holstein to Brandt, 26 December 1890, *Holstein Papers*, III, No. 332.

45 Waldersee, diary entry for 2 January 1891, GStA Berlin, Waldersee Papers; omitted from Meisner, II, p. 173.

46 Wedel, *Zwischen Kaiser und Kanzler*, pp. 134 and 148. See above, p. 403.

47 Waldersee, diary entries for 15 and 16 January 1891, GStA Berlin, Waldersee Papers; cf. Meisner, II, pp. 175–6.

48 Wedel, *Zwischen Kaiser und Kanzler*, pp. 147–8.

49 Waldersee, diary entry for 25 January 1891, GStA Berlin, Waldersee Papers; omitted from Meisner, II, p. 177.

50 Waldersee, diary note of late January 1891, GStA Berlin, Waldersee Papers; omitted from Meisner, II, p. 177.

51 Waldersee, diary entry for 28 January 1891, GStA Berlin, Waldersee Papers; cf. Meisner, II, pp. 177–8.

52 Wedel, *Zwischen Kaiser und Kanzler*, p. 137.

53 Waldersee, diary entry for 28 January 1891, GStA Berlin, Waldersee Papers; cf. Meisner, II, p. 179; also Waldersee to Grand Duke of Baden, 28 January 1891, Fuchs, *Großherzog von Baden*, III, No. 1094.

54 Wedel, *Zwischen Kaiser und Kanzler*, pp. 139–40.

55 Ibid., p. 142.

56 Waldersee, diary entry for 31 January 1891, GStA Berlin, Waldersee Papers; cf. Meisner, II, pp. 180ff. On Holstein's and Philipp Eulenburg's role, and that played by the other Foreign Office officials mentioned in connection with Waldersee's downfall, see Holstein to Eulenburg, 10 January, 3 February and 27 March 1891, *Eulenburgs Korrespondenz*, I, Nos. 464, 470 and 495; August Eulenburg to Philipp Eulenburg, 1 February 1891, ibid., No. 469; Philipp Eulenburg to August Eulenburg, 14 February 1891, ibid., No. 472; and Waldersee to Eulenburg, 18 February 1891, ibid., No. 474. See also Waldersee to Verdy, 18 February 1891, GStA Berlin, Waldersee Papers.

57 Waldersee, diary entry for 1 February 1891, GStA Berlin, Waldersee Papers; cf. Meisner, II, p. 182.

58 Waldersee, diary entry for 2 February 1891, GStA Berlin, Waldersee Papers; omitted from Meisner, II, p. 184.

59 Waldersee, diary entry for 6 February 1891, GStA Berlin, Waldersee Papers; omitted from Meisner, II, pp. 185–6.

60 Wedel, *Zwischen Kaiser und Kanzler*, pp. 142–8.

61 Ibid., p. 150.

62 See Röhl, *Kaiser and His Court*, p. 128.

63 Eulenburg to Holstein, 6 August 1889, *Eulenburgs Korrespondenz*, I, No. 230.

64 Waldersee, diary entry for 17 November 1889, GStA Berlin, Waldersee Papers; omitted from Meisner, II, p. 78.

65  Waldersee, diary entry for 23 March 1890, GStA Berlin, Waldersee Papers; omitted from Meisner, II, p. 122.

66  See Wedel, *Zwischen Kaiser und Kanzler*, pp. 71–8, 81–93, 119–25, 157–62 *et passim*.

67  Ibid., p. 149. On the transfer of Count Ernst von Wedel from the service of Grand Duke Carl Alexander of Saxe-Weimar-Eisenach to the Kaiser's court as Oberstallmeister, see the unpublished memoirs of Wedel's daughter Countess Alice zu Lynar, in the possession of Count Peter von Wedel, Bad Driburg.

68  Kaiser Wilhelm II to Caprivi, 9 May 1891, *Große Politik*, VII, pp. 295–6. See Helmuth Rogge, *Holstein und Hohenlohe. Neue Beiträge zu Friedrich von Holsteins Tätigkeit als Mitarbeiter Bismarcks und als Ratgeber Hohenlohes*, Stuttgart 1957, pp. 358ff.; also Holstein to Eulenburg, 10 May 1891, *Eulenburgs Korrespondenz*, I, No. 514.

69  Holstein to Eulenburg, 10 May 1891, *Eulenburgs Korrespondenz*, I, No. 514.

70  Count Carl von Wedel, promemoria, 13 June 1894, Wedel Papers, Frankfurt a.M.

71  Ibid.

72  See Eulenburg to Holstein, 6 November 1891 and 27 April 1892, *Eulenburgs Korrespondenz*, I, No. 552, and II, No. 647.

73  Prince Ernst zu Hohenlohe-Langenburg to his father, 13 June 1892, Hohenlohe-Zentralarchiv Neuenstein, Hermann Hohenlohe-Langenburg Papers, Bü. 59.

74  Eulenburg to Holstein, 20 July 1892, *Holstein Papers*, III, No. 374.

75  Wedel, promemoria, 13 June 1894, Wedel Papers, Frankfurt a.M.

76  Ibid.

77  Ibid.

78  Ibid.

79  Eulenburg to Holstein, 2 September 1892, *Eulenburgs Korrespondenz*, II, No. 696.

80  Kiderlen-Wächter to Eulenburg, 3 March 1893, ibid., No. 778.

81  On this intrigue, see Holstein to Eulenburg, 7, 18 and 21 November 1892, *Eulenburgs Korrespondenz*, II, Nos. 727, 732 and 736; Eulenburg to Caprivi, 14 November 1892, ibid., No. 730; Eulenburg to Holstein, 19 November 1892, ibid., No. 733.

82  Malet to Lord Rosebery, 20 December 1893, RA I59/115.

83  Wedel, promemoria, 13 June 1894, Wedel Papers, Frankfurt a.M.

84  Ibid.

85  Wedel, *Zwischen Kaiser und Kanzler*, pp. 181–93.

86  See above, pp. 162–3.

87  Széchényi to Kálnoky, 23 February 1889, HHStA Vienna, PA III 136.

88  Waldersee, diary entry for 26 August 1888, GStA Berlin, Waldersee Papers; cf. Meisner, II, p. 1.

89  Waldersee, diary entry for 9 October 1888, GStA Berlin, Waldersee Papers; omitted from Meisner, II, pp. 4–5.

90  Waldersee, diary entry for 26 November 1888, GStA Berlin, Waldersee Papers; cf. Meisner, II, pp. 22–3.

91  Waldersee, diary entry for 30 August 1890, GStA Berlin, Waldersee Papers; cf. Meisner, II, pp. 141–2.

92  Waldersee, diary entry for 19 August 1890, GStA Berlin, Waldersee Papers; omitted from Meisner, II, p. 140; similarly, Waldersee to Verdy, 28 May 1891, GStA Berlin, Waldersee Papers, No. 53.

93  Waldersee, diary entry for 19 August 1890, GStA Berlin, Waldersee Papers; omitted from Meisner, II, p. 140.

94  Waldersee, diary entry for 19 August 1890, GStA Berlin, Waldersee Papers; omitted from Meisner, II, p. 140.

95  Waldersee to Verdy, 28 May 1891, GStA Berlin, Waldersee Papers, No. 53.

96 Verdy to Waldersee, 24 May 1892, ibid.

97 Waldersee, diary entry for 13 October 1892, ibid.; omitted from Meisner, II, pp. 265–6.

98 Empress Frederick to Queen Victoria, 13 August 1892, RA Z53/24. See Waldersee's diary entry for 29 August 1892, Meisner, II, p. 264.

99 Kaiser Wilhelm II to Hans von Plessen, telegram, 29 December 1892, BA-MA Freiburg, Plessen Papers, Msg 1/3117.

100 Waldersee, diary entry for 22 October 1894, GStA Berlin, Waldersee Papers; omitted from Meisner, II, p. 327.

101 Waldersee, diary entry for 14 December 1894, GStA Berlin, Waldersee Papers; omitted from Meisner, II, p. 333.

102 Colonel Russell, report of 13 February 1891, RA I59/2.

103 Waldersee, diary entry for 17 December 1894, GStA Berlin, Waldersee Papers; cf. Meisner, II, p. 334.

17 THE SCHOOL BILL CRISIS AND THE FRAGMENTATION OF POWER

1 Waldersee, diary entry for 2 May 1891, GStA Berlin, Waldersee Papers; omitted from Meisner, II, pp. 207–8.

2 Waldersee to Verdy, 28 May 1891, GStA Berlin, Waldersee Papers, No. 53.

3 See Nipperdey, *Deutsche Geschichte 1866–1918*, I, pp. 535–6.

4 Empress Frederick to her daughter Princess Viktoria of Schaumburg-Lippe, 1 March 1892 *et passim*, AdHH Schloss Fasanerie.

5 Oncken, *Bennigsen*, II, pp. 557–63.

6 Eulenburg to Holstein, 22 January 1892, *Eulenburgs Korrespondenz*, II, No. 574.

7 Prince Ernst zu Hohenlohe-Langenburg to his father, 7 March 1892, Hohenlohe-Zentralarchiv Neuenstein, Hermann Hohenlohe-Langenburg Papers, Bü. 59.

8 Waldersee, diary entry for 20 February 1892, GStA Berlin, Waldersee Papers; omitted from Meisner, II, p. 232.

9 Hereditary Prince Bernhard of Saxe-Meiningen to Waldersee, 30 January 1892, GStA Berlin, Waldersee Papers No. 36.

10 See above, pp. 233–4.

11 Eulenburg to Kaiser Wilhelm II, 21 [sic] January 1892, Johannes Haller, *Aus dem Leben des Fürsten Philipp zu Eulenburg-Hertefeld*, Berlin, 1924, p. 66.

12 Holstein to Eulenburg, 24 January 1892, *Eulenburgs Korrespondenz*, II, No. 575.

13 Holstein to Eulenburg, 27 January 1892, ibid., No. 578. See Oncken, *Bennigsen*, II, pp. 557–63.

14 Waldersee, diary entries for 30 January and 6 February 1892, GStA Berlin, Waldersee Papers; these passages are omitted from Meisner, II, p. 232; also Brauer to Turban, 1 February 1892, Fuchs, *Großherzog von Baden*, III, No. 1150.

15 Waldersee, diary entry for 21 February 1892, GStA Berlin, Waldersee Papers; cf. Meisner, II, pp. 232–3.

16 Waldersee, diary entry for 12 March 1892, GStA Berlin, Waldersee Papers; cf. Meisner, II, p. 234; also Brauer to Turban, 6 February 1892, Fuchs, *Großherzog von Baden*, III, No. 1151.

17 Kaiser Wilhelm II, speech of 17 December 1890, Penzler, *Reden Kaiser Wilhelms II. in den Jahren 1888–1895*, pp. 163–7; Elkind, *German Emperor's Speeches*, p. 167.

18 Eulenburg to Holstein, 22 January 1892, *Eulenburgs Korrespondenz*, II, No. 574.

19 Helldorff to Eulenburg, 7 March 1892, ibid., No. 600; also Brauer to Turban, 16 February 1892, Fuchs, *Großherzog von Baden*, III, No. 1154.

20 On Kaiser Wilhelm II's speech of 24 February 1892, see above, pp. 384–5.

21 Above, pp. 233–4.

22 Holstein to Eulenburg, 27 January 1892, *Eulenburgs Korrespondenz*, II, No. 578.

23 Eulenburg to Holstein, 28 and 29 January and 14 February 1892, *Holstein Papers*, III, Nos. 356, 357 and 361.

24 Eulenburg to Holstein, 28 and 29 January 1892, ibid., Nos. 356 and 357; also August Eulenburg to Philipp Eulenburg, 14 February 1892, *Eulenburgs Korrespondenz*, II, No. 587; Holstein to Eulenburg, 17, 18 and 27 February 1892, ibid., Nos. 588, 590 and 593.

25 Eulenburg to Holstein, 22 February 1892, *Holstein Papers*, III, No. 362.

26 Holstein to Eulenburg, 1 March 1892, *Eulenburgs Korrespondenz*, II, No. 596; Eulenburg to Holstein, 5 March 1892, *Holstein Papers*, III, No. 364.

27 Eulenburg to Kaiser Wilhelm II, 10 March 1892, *Eulenburgs Korrespondenz*, II, No. 604.

28 Helldorff to Eulenburg, 24 October 1892, ibid., No. 723.

29 Helldorff to Eulenburg, 7 March 1892, ibid., No. 600.

30 See above, pp. 384–5.

31 Empress Frederick to Queen Victoria, 20 March 1892, RA Z52/34. Wilhelm's inner-ear illness is described at some length in ch. 13 of *Young Wilhelm*, pp. 306–24.

32 Cf. Brauer to Turban, 18 March 1892, Fuchs, *Großherzog von Baden*, III, No. 1166.

33 August Eulenburg to Philipp Eulenburg, 19 March 1892, *Eulenburgs Korrespondenz*, II, No. 617.

34 Leuthold to Eulenburg, 15 March 1892, ibid., No. 607.

35 Malet to Ponsonby, 22 and 25 March 1892, RA I59/63 and 66; Malet to Salisbury, 2 April 1892, RA I59/68.

36 Kaiser Wilhelm II to Queen Victoria, 15 March 1892, RA S25/53.

37 Helldorff to Eulenburg, 24 March 1892, *Eulenburgs Korrespondenz*, II, No. 628.

38 August Eulenburg to Philipp Eulenburg, 19 March 1892, ibid., No. 617.

39 Helldorff to Eulenburg, 24 March 1892, ibid., No. 628.

40 Brauer to Turban, 19 March 1892, Fuchs, *Großherzog von Baden*, III, No. 1167.

41 August Eulenburg to Philipp Eulenburg, 19 March 1892, *Eulenburgs Korrespondenz*, II, No. 617; Verdy to Waldersee, Sunday, ? March 1892, GStA Berlin, Waldersee Papers No. 53.

42 Kaiser Wilhelm II, marginal note on Caprivi's letter of resignation of 19 March 1892 cited in Herzfeld, *Johannes von Miquel*, II, p. 306. See *Eulenburgs Korrespondenz*, II, p. 808.

43 Holstein to Eulenburg, 18 March 1892, *Eulenburgs Korrespondenz*, II, No. 613.

44 Eulenburg to Kaiser Wilhelm II, 19 March 1892, ibid., No. 615. On the Guelph Fund and the bribing of King Ludwig II of Bavaria in 1870, see ibid., p. 801; R. Nöll von der Nahmer, *Bismarcks Reptilienfonds*, Mainz 1968, pp. 142–61; H. Maatz, *Bismarck und Hannover 1866–1898*, Hildesheim 1971; S. A. Stehlin, *Bismarck and the Guelph Problem 1866–1890*, The Hague 1973; Hans Rall, *König Ludwig II. und Bismarcks Ringen um Bayern*, Munich 1973.

45 Eulenburg to Caprivi, 19 March 1892, *Eulenburgs Korrespondenz*, II, No. 616.

46 Verdy to Waldersee, March 1892, GStA Berlin, Waldersee Papers No. 53; Marschall's diary entry for 20 March 1892, *Eulenburgs Korrespondenz*, II, p. 813.

47 Holstein to Eulenburg, 31 March 1892, *Eulenburgs Korrespondenz*, II, No. 634.

48 Verdy to Waldersee, March 1892, GStA Berlin, Waldersee Papers No. 53.

49 Holstein to Eulenburg, 18 and 19 March 1892, *Eulenburgs Korrespondenz*, II, Nos. 613 and 618.

50 Holstein to Eulenburg, 19 March 1892, ibid., No. 618; Helldorff to Eulenburg, 24 March 1892, ibid., No. 628.

51 August Eulenburg to Philipp Eulenburg, 19 March 1892, ibid., No. 617.

52 August Eulenburg to Philipp Eulenburg, 20 March 1892, cited ibid., No. 619; Marschall's diary entry for 20 March 1892, ibid., p. 814.

53 Holstein to Eulenburg, 20 March 1892, ibid., No. 620; August Eulenburg to Philipp Eulenburg, 20 March 1892, ibid., No. 621.

54 August Eulenburg to Philipp Eulenburg, 20 March 1892, ibid., No. 621; Holstein to Eulenburg, 21 and 23 March 1892, ibid., Nos. 623 and 625; Marschall's diary entry for 21 March 1892, cited ibid., p. 819; Brauer to Turban, 20–2 March 1892, Fuchs, *Großherzog von Baden*, III, Nos. 1168–71.

55 August Eulenburg to Philipp Eulenburg, 23 March 1892, *Eulenburgs Korrespondenz*, II, No. 626.

56 On Bosse's appointment as minister for ecclesiastical affairs, see the extracts from his diary cited ibid., pp. 822–3. See also Helldorff to Eulenburg, 24 March 1892, ibid., No. 628.

57 Brauer to Grand Duke of Baden, 25 March 1892, Fuchs, *Großherzog von Baden*, III, No. 1174.

58 Malet to Salisbury, 2 April 1892, RA I59/68.

59 Eulenburg to Holstein, 26 March 1892, *Holstein Papers*, III, No. 366.

60 Kaiser Wilhelm II to Queen Victoria, 12 April 1892, RA I59/72.

61 See Eulenburg to Holstein, 26 March 1892, *Holstein Papers*, III, No. 366.

62 Empress Frederick to Queen Victoria, 24 March 1892, RA Z52/35.

63 Kaiser Wilhelm II to Lucanus, 18 April 1892, cited in *Eulenburgs Korrespondenz*, II, p. 855; Marschall, diary entries, 12–21 April, cited ibid.

64 Empress Frederick to Queen Victoria, 13 August 1892, RA Z53/24. See also Spitzemberg, *Tagebuch*, p. 301.

65 Marschall, diary entry for 12 April 1892, cited in *Eulenburgs Korrespondenz*, II, p. 844.

66 Verdy to Waldersee, 11 May 1892, GStA Berlin, Waldersee Papers No. 53.

67 Waldersee, diary entry for 28 March 1892, ibid.; Meisner, II, pp. 236–7.

68 Waldersee, diary entry for 14 April 1892, GStA Berlin, Waldersee Papers; cf. Meisner, II, pp. 238–9.

69 Waldersee, diary entry for 16 April 1892, GStA Berlin, Waldersee Papers; omitted from Meisner, II, pp. 239–40.

70 Waldersee, diary entry for 28 April 1892, GStA Berlin, Waldersee Papers; omitted from Meisner, II, p. 240.

71 Waldersee, diary entry for 12 June 1892, GStA Berlin, Waldersee Papers; cf. Meisner, II, pp. 244–5.

72 Waldersee, diary entry for 28 April 1892, GStA Berlin, Waldersee Papers; omitted from Meisner, II, p. 240.

73 Waldersee, diary entry for 29 April 1892, GStA Berlin, Waldersee Papers; omitted from Meisner, II, p. 240.

74 Waldersee, diary entry for 8 May 1892, GStA Berlin, Waldersee Papers; Meisner, II, pp. 240–1.

75 See e.g. Waldersee, diary entries for 7 October, 13 November and 1 December 1892, GStA Berlin, Waldersee Papers; Meisner, II, pp. 265 and 269.

76 Waldersee, diary entry for 7 October 1892, GStA Berlin, Waldersee Papers; omitted from Meisner, II, p. 265.

77 Eulenburg to Holstein, 20 July 1892, *Holstein Papers*, III, No. 374.

78 Waldersee, diary entry for 28 April 1892, GStA Berlin, Waldersee Papers; omitted from Meisner, II, p. 240.

79 Waldersee, diary entry for 29 April 1892, GStA Berlin, Waldersee Papers; omitted from Meisner, II, p. 240.

80 Kaiserin Auguste Viktoria to Kaiser Wilhelm II, 3–4 July 1892, GStA Berlin, BPHA Rep. 53T Preußen: An Kaiser Wilhelm II., Bd IV.

81 Kiderlen-Wächter to Holstein, 13 July 1892, *Holstein Papers*, III, No. 372.

82 Kaiserin Auguste Viktoria to Kaiser Wilhelm II, 14–15 July 1892, GStA Berlin, BPHA Rep. 53T Preußen: An Kaiser Wilhelm II., Bd IV.

83 Kaiser Wilhelm II to Caprivi, 20 July 1892, printed in *Holstein Papers*, III, No. 373, enclosure.

84 Kiderlen-Wächter to Holstein, 20 July 1892, ibid., No. 373; Eulenburg to Holstein, 20 July 1892, ibid., No. 374.

85 Kaiser Wilhelm II to Zelle, 7 October 1892, printed in *Eulenburgs Korrespondenz*, II, p. 945.

86 Holstein to Eulenburg, 27 September 1892, ibid., No. 707.

87 Waldersee, diary entries for 7, 9 and 13 October 1892, GStA Berlin, Waldersee Papers; omitted from Meisner, II, p. 265.

88 Waldersee, diary entry for 28 October 1892, GStA Berlin, Waldersee Papers; omitted from Meisner, II, p. 267. See also Empress Frederick to Queen Victoria, 24 October 1891, RA Z51/40.

89 Waldersee, diary entries for 7, 9 and 13 October 1892, GStA Berlin, Waldersee Papers; omitted from Meisner, II, p. 265.

90 See above, pp. 388–96; also Förster, *Der doppelte Militarismus*, pp. 36ff.

91 See e.g. Caprivi to Eulenburg, 28 February 1892, Eulenburg to Kaiser Wilhelm II, 14 August 1892, *Eulenburgs Korrespondenz*, II, Nos. 595 and 693; Caprivi to Bennigsen, 29 September 1892, Oncken, *Bennigsen*, II, pp. 577–9.

92 Waldersee, diary entry for 28 September 1892, GStA Berlin, Waldersee Papers; omitted from Meisner, II, p. 265; Kiderlen-Wächter to Colmar von der Goltz, 21 December 1892, BA-MA Freiburg, von der Goltz Papers, N737/21.

93 Both letters are cited above, pp. 389–91.

94 See Empress Frederick to her daughter Princess Viktoria of Schaumburg-Lippe, 28 October 1892, AdHH Schloss Fasanerie.

95 Waldersee, diary entry for 29 October 1891, GStA Berlin, Waldersee Papers; cf. the totally distorted version in Meisner, II, pp. 219–20. See also Waldersee, diary entries for 1 and 5 November 1892, GStA Berlin, Waldersee Papers; omitted from Meisner, II, pp. 267–8.

96 Waldersee, diary entry for 2 May 1891, GStA Berlin, Waldersee Papers; omitted from Meisner, II, p. 206.

97 Waldersee, diary entry for 20 January 1892, GStA Berlin, Waldersee Papers; Meisner, II, p. 231.

98 Waldersee, diary entries for 16 and 25 October 1891, GStA Berlin, Waldersee Papers; omitted from Meisner, II, pp. 218–19.

99 Waldersee, diary entry for 29 October 1891, GStA Berlin, Waldersee Papers; omitted from Meisner, II, pp. 218–19.

100 See Brauer to Turban, 29 June 1892, Fuchs, *Großherzog von Baden*, III, No. 1191.

101 Hereditary Prince Bernhard of Saxe-Meiningen to Waldersee, 9 October 1891, GStA Berlin, Waldersee Papers No. 36.

102 Hereditary Prince Bernhard of Saxe-Meiningen to Waldersee, 30 January 1892, ibid.

103 Hereditary Prince Bernhard of Saxe-Meiningen to Waldersee, 12 October 1892, ibid.

104 Waldersee, diary entry for 30 January 1892, GStA Berlin, Waldersee Papers; omitted from Meisner, II, p. 232.

105 Waldersee, diary entry for 10 August 1892, in Meisner, II, p. 259. See Fuchs, *Großherzog von Baden*, III, pp. 166–78, especially Kaiser Wilhelm II to Grand Duke of Baden, 6 November 1892, ibid., No. 1206, and Grand Duke of Baden to Kaiser Wilhelm II, 14 November 1892, ibid., No. 1209.

106 Waldersee, diary entry for 30 January 1892, GStA Berlin, Waldersee Papers; omitted from Meisner, II, p. 232.

107 Marschall, diary entry for 29 August 1892, cited in *Eulenburgs Korrespondenz*, II, p. 925.

108 Marschall, diary entry for 16 September 1892, cited ibid., p. 940.

109 See Eulenburg's notes of 24 September 1892, in Haller, *Eulenburg*, pp. 89–91; *Holstein Papers*, III, No. 376.

110 Waldersee and Verdy, 3 February 1893, GStA Berlin, Waldersee Papers No. 53.

111 Eulenburg's notes of 24 September 1892, in Haller, *Eulenburg*, p. 90.

112 Waldersee, diary entry for 31 August 1892, GStA Berlin, Waldersee Papers; omitted from Meisner, II, p. 264.

113 Brauer to Grand Duke of Baden, 22 October 1892, Fuchs, *Großherzog von Baden*, III, No. 1201.

114 Hereditary Prince Bernhard of Saxe-Meiningen to Waldersee, 12 October 1892, GStA Berlin, Waldersee Papers No. 36.

115 Eulenburg to Holstein, 30 September 1892, *Holstein Papers*, III, No. 376; also Eulenburg to Kaiser Wilhelm II, 10 September 1892, *Eulenburgs Korrespondenz*, II, No. 702.

116 Waldersee, diary entry for 19 October 1892, GStA Berlin, Waldersee Papers; cf. Meisner, II, p. 266.

117 Brauer, reports of 6, 17 and 20 November 1892, Fuchs, *Großherzog von Baden*, III, Nos. 1207, 1210–11.

118 Waldersee, diary entry for 1 November 1892, GStA Berlin, Waldersee Papers; omitted from Meisner, II, p. 267.

119 Ibid.

120 Waldersee, diary entry for 1 December 1892, GStA Berlin, Waldersee Papers; omitted from Meisner, II, p. 270.

121 Waldersee, diary entries for 20 November, 3 and 15 December 1892, GStA Berlin, Waldersee Papers; omitted from Meisner, II, p. 270; cf. p. 272.

122 Kaiser Wilhelm II to Kaiser Franz Joseph, 31 January 1893, HHStA Vienna, Kabinettsarchiv Geheimakten 2.

123 Waldersee, diary entry for 20 November 1892, GStA Berlin, Waldersee Papers; omitted from Meisner, II, p. 270; also Waldersee's entry of 3 December 1892, GStA Berlin, Waldersee Papers.

124 Kiderlen-Wächter to Eulenburg, 18 December 1892, Holstein to Eulenburg, 23 December 1892, Eulenburg to Kaiser Wilhelm II, 29 December 1892, *Eulenburgs Korrespondenz*, II, Nos. 752–4.

125 Holstein to Eulenburg, 1 January 1893, ibid., No. 755.

126 Waldersee, diary entry for 3 January 1893, GStA Berlin, Waldersee Papers; abridged in Meisner, II, p. 274.

127 Waldersee, diary entry for 6 January 1893, GStA Berlin, Waldersee Papers; omitted from Meisner, II, p. 275. See also Waldersee, diary entry for 19 March 1893, GStA Berlin, Waldersee Papers; cf. Meisner, II, pp. 287–8.

128 Prince Ernst zu Hohenlohe-Langenburg to his father, 26 January 1893, Hohenlohe-Zentralarchiv Neuenstein, Hermann Hohenlohe-Langenburg Papers, Bü. 60. Cf. Caprivi to Eulenburg, 17 January 1893, *Eulenburgs Korrespondenz*, II, No. 762; Brauer to Turban, 5 January 1893, Fuchs, *Großherzog von Baden*, III, No. 1218.

129 Caprivi to Eulenburg, 30 April 1893, *Eulenburgs Korrespondenz*, II, No. 799. See Brauer to Grand Duke of Baden, 1 May 1893, Fuchs, *Großherzog von Baden*, III, No. 1256.

130 Eulenburg to Kaiser Wilhelm II, 16 April 1893, *Eulenburgs Korrespondenz*, II, No. 793; Kiderlen-Wächter to Eulenburg, 15 April 1893, ibid., p. 1065.

131 See Förster, *Der doppelte Militarismus*, pp. 63ff.

132 Waldersee, diary entry for 11 May 1893, GStA Berlin, Waldersee Papers; omitted from Meisner, II, p. 289.

133 Eulenburg, diary entry for 6 May 1893, *Eulenburgs Korrespondenz*, II, p. 1074.

134 Brauer to Grand Duke of Baden, 7 May 1893, Fuchs, *Großherzog von Baden*, III, No. 1267.

135 Kaiser Wilhelm II, 9 May 1893, Penzler, *Reden Kaiser Wilhelms II. in den Jahren 1888–1895*, p. 230; Elkind, *German Emperor's Speeches*, pp. 216–17.

16 Prince Ernst zu Hohenlohe-Langenburg to his father, 13 June 1892, Hohenlohe-Zentralarchiv Neuenstein, Hermann Hohelohe-Langenburg, Bü. 59. Cf. Canis, *Von Bismarck zur Weltpolitik*, p. 105.

17 Queen Victoria to Kaiser Wilhelm II, 14 and 29 June 1892, GStA Berlin, BPHA Rep. 52 W3 No. 11.

18 Waldersee, diary entry for 11 June 1892, GStA Berlin, Waldersee Papers; cf. Meisner, II, pp. 241–2.

19 Waldersee, diary entry for 9 October 1894, GStA Berlin, Waldersee Papers; cf. Meisner, II, pp. 323–4.

20 Prince Ernst zu Hohenlohe-Langenburg to his father, 13 June 1892, Hohenlohe-Zentralarchiv Neuenstein, Hermann Hohelohe-Langenburg, Bü. 59.

21 Herbert Bismarck to his father, 11 July 1893, BA Koblenz, Bismarck Papers FC 3005 N.

22 Empress Frederick to Queen Victoria, 19 December 1891, RA Z52/7.

23 Prince Ernst zu Hohenlohe-Langenburg to his father, 13 June 1892, Hohenlohe-Zentralarchiv Neuenstein, Hermann Hohelohe-Langenburg, Bü. 59.

24 Prince Ernst zu Hohenlohe-Langenburg to his father, 13 December 1891, ibid., Bü. 58.

25 Waldersee, diary entry for 19 January 1892, GStA Berlin, Waldersee Papers; cf. Meisner, II, pp. 229–30.

26 As reported in Eulenburg to Holstein, 8 October 1891, *Holstein Papers*, III, No. 349.

27 Waldersee, diary entry for 21 November 1891, GStA Berlin, Waldersee Papers; printed only in part in Meisner, II, p. 223.

28 Kaiser Wilhelm II to Queen Victoria, 8 December 1891, RA I59/53.

29 Kaiser Wilhelm II to Queen Victoria, 12 April 1892, RA I59/72.

30 Salisbury to Queen Victoria, 22 April 1892, RA I59/78.

31 Kaiser Wilhelm II to Queen Victoria, 22 May 1892, RA I59/80.

32 Waldersee, diary entry for 7 August 1893, GStA Berlin, Waldersee Papers; omitted from Meisner, II, p. 292.

33 Cited in *Holstein Papers*, III, p. 411.

34 See Paul Kennedy, *The Rise of the Anglo-German Antagonism 1860–1914*, London 1980, pp. 212ff.

35 See McLean, *Royalty and Diplomacy*, pp. 78ff.

36 The marriage of Aribert Anhalt and Louise Holstein is described below, pp. 663–4. See also Marie Louise Princess of Schleswig-Holstein, *My Memories of Six Reigns*, London 1956, pp. 66ff.

37 Kaiser Wilhelm II to Arthur Duke of Connaught, 11 March 1891, RA Addl Mss A15/5680.

38 Malet to Ponsonby, 19 March 1891, RA I59/10; Malet to August Eulenburg, 24 March 1891, RA I59/11.

39 See above, pp. 360–4.

40 Queen Victoria to Ponsonby, 15 June 1892, RA I59/86.

41 Ponsonby to Malet, 16 June 1892, RA I59/87.

42 Queen Victoria to Kaiser Wilhelm II, 29 June 1892, GStA Berlin, BPHA Rep. 52 W3 No. 11.

43 See Kristin Lammerting, *Meteor. Die kaiserlichen Segelyachten*, Cologne 1999, pp. 30–47.

44 Kaiser Wilhelm II to his mother, 28 July 1892, AdHH Schloss Fasanerie.

45 *Times*, 2–6 August 1892; *Standard*, 3–8 August 1892; *Daily Telegraph*, 4 August 1892, RA I59/91.

46 Kaiser Wilhelm II to Albert Edward Prince of Wales, 23 October 1892, RA L21/70.

47 Albert Edward Prince of Wales to Kaiser Wilhelm II, 31 October 1892, RA L21/73.

48 Malet to Queen Victoria, [late] May 1893, RA I59/100.

49 Seckendorff to Senden-Bibran, 14 June 1893, BA-MA Freiburg, Senden-Bibran Papers N160/2.

50  Ibid.

51  Seckendorff to Senden-Bibran, 16 June 1893, ibid.

52  Cited ibid.

53  Seckendorff to Senden-Bibran, 15 and 16 June 1893, ibid.

54  Queen Victoria to Kaiser Wilhelm II, telegram, 14 June 1893, GStA Berlin, BPHA Rep 52 W3 No. 11. See Heinrich's report to the Kaiser of 9 July 1893 on his experiences in London, BA-MA Freiburg, Senden-Bibran Papers N160/2.

55  RA QVJ, 29 July–6 August 1893.

56  See Prince Ernst zu Hohenlohe-Langenburg to his father, 16 July 1893, Hohenlohe-Zentralarchiv Neuenstein, Hermann Hohenlohe-Langenburg Papers, Bü. 60.

57  Prince Ernst zu Hohenlohe-Langenburg to his father, 10 August 1893, ibid.

58  See Eulenburg's notes, Am Hofe von England, in Philipp Fürst zu Eulenburg-Hertefeld, *Das Ende König Ludwigs II. und andere Erlebnisse*, Leipzig 1934, pp. 212–45.

59  See *Große Politik*, VIII, No. 1752.

60  On the Siam crisis, see Rich, *Friedrich von Holstein*, I, pp. 350ff.; Lahme, *Deutsche Außen-politik*, pp. 395ff.; Canis, *Von Bismarck zur Weltmacht*, pp. 116–18.

61  See *Große Politik*, VIII, No. 1752.

62  Prince Ernst zu Hohenlohe-Langenburg to his father, 10 August 1893, Hohenlohe-Zentralarchiv Neuenstein, Hermann Hohenlohe-Langenburg Papers, Bü. 60. See also Prince Ernst's letter of 16 July 1893, ibid.

63  Cited in Haller, *Eulenburg*, pp. 84–5.

64  Prince Ernst zu Hohenlohe-Langenburg to his father, 10 August 1893, Hohenlohe-Zentralarchiv Neuenstein, Hermann Hohenlohe-Langenburg Papers, Bü. 60.

65  Prince Ernst zu Hohenlohe-Langenburg to his father, 28 August 1893, ibid.

66  Kaiser Wilhelm II, marginal notes on Hatzfeldt's report of 18 November 1893, cited in *Holstein Papers*, III, p. 446.

67  See Canis, *Von Bismarck zur Weltpolitik*, pp. 119–20.

68  Kaiser Wilhelm II, marginal notes on Werder's report from St Petersburg of 8 July 1893, PA AA, Asservat No. 4.

69  Malet to Rosebery, 7 November 1893, RA I59/113.

70  Waldersee, diary entry for 29 November 1893, GStA Berlin, Waldersee Papers; omitted from Meisner, II, p. 299.

71  Kaiser Wilhelm II to Queen Victoria, 12 January 1894, RA I60/1.

72  Swaine to Ponsonby, 12 January 1894, RA I60/2.

73  Swaine to Ponsonby, 13 January 1894, RA I60/3.

74  Albert Edward Prince of Wales to Queen Victoria, 16 and 19 January 1894, RA I60/5 and 14; Knollys to Ponsonby, 20 January RA I60/17.

75  Ponsonby to Queen Victoria, 16 January 1894, RA I60/6.

76  Queen Victoria, marginal notes on Ponsonby's letters of 15, 17 and 18 January 1894, RA I60/4, 8 and 10; Queen Victoria to Malet and to Prince of Wales, secret telegrams, 19 January 1894, RA I60/11; Malet's reply of 20 January 1894, RA I60/18.

77  Henry Campbell-Bannerman to Ponsonby, 18, 19 and 24 January 1894, RA I60/9, 12 and 37; Queen Victoria, marginal note of 27 January 1894, RA I60/46.

78  Rosebery to Ponsonby, 27 January 1894, RA I60/55.

79  George Duke of Cambridge to Ponsonby with Queen Victoria's marginal notes, 20 January 1894, RA I60/24.

80  Ponsonby, notes, 23 January 1894, RA I60/36; QVJ, 23 January 1894.

81  Knollys to Ponsonby, 22 and 24 January RA I60/31 and 39.

82  Ponsonby to Swaine, 24 January 1894, RA I60/41; Swaine's reply of 27 January 1894, RA I60/56.

83 Queen Victoria to Kaiser Wilhelm II, 25 January 1894, GStA Berlin, BPHA Rep. 52 W3 No. 11.

84 Ponsonby to Queen Victoria, 24 January 1894, RA I60/42.

85 Knollys to Ponsonby, 26 January 1894, RA I60/46.

86 Knollys to Ponsonby, 27 January 1894, RA I60/57.

87 Knollys to Ponsonby, 26 January 1894, RA I60/51; Ponsonby to Queen Victoria, 26 January 1894, RA I60/52 and 53.

88 George Duke of Cambridge to Ponsonby, 26 January 1894, RA I60/48.

89 Salisbury to Ponsonby, 26 January 1894, RA I60/47.

90 Prince Ernst zu Hohenlohe-Langenburg to his father, 8 March 1894, Hohenlohe-Zentralarchiv Neuenstein, Hermann Hohenlohe-Langenburg Papers, Bü. 61.

91 Rosebery to Queen Victoria, 11 April 1894, RA I60/62.

92 Queen Victoria to Kaiser Wilhelm II, 28 April 1894, GStA Berlin, BPHA Rep. 52 W3 No. 11.

93 Kaiser Wilhelm II to Queen Victoria, 24 April 1894, RA I60/64.

94 Kaiser Wilhelm II to Queen Victoria, telegram, 8 June 1894, RA I60/72.

95 Kaiser Wilhelm II, toast to Royal Dragoons, 7 June 1894, Penzler, *Reden Kaiser Wilhelms II. in den Jahren 1888–1895*, pp. 269–70; Engish version from *Standard*, 11 June 1894, RA I60/73.

96 See the article 'The Emperor William and the Dragoons', ibid.

97 Swaine to Queen Victoria, 15 June 1894, RA I60/75; Malet to Queen Victoria, 16 June 1894, RA I60/77.

98 Holstein to Eulenburg, 12 and 16 June 1894, Eulenburg to Holstein, 16 June 1894, Kálnoky to Eulenburg, 17 June 1894, Eulenburg to Kaiser Wilhelm II, 18 June 1894, *Eulenburgs Korrespondenz*, II, Nos. 975–80; also Kaiser Wilhelm II to his mother, 21 June 1894, AdHH Schloss Fasanerie.

99 RA QVJ, 6–13 August 1894; *Daily Telegraph*, 7 August 1894; *Times*, 7 August 1894, RA I60/81.

100 Major-General Sir Leopold Swaine, *Camp and Chancery in a Soldier's Life*, London 1926, pp. 215–16; McLean, *Royalty and Diplomacy*, pp. 78–9.

101 Kaiser Wilhelm II to Queen Victoria, 13 and 15 August 1894, RA I60/84 and 88; Kaiser Wilhelm II to Arthur Duke of Connaught, 15 August 1894, RA L4/26a; Kaiser Wilhelm II to Prince Albert Edward of Wales, 24 August 1894, RA L4/26b.

102 Kaiser Wilhelm II to Queen Victoria, 24 August 1894, RA I60/91.

103 Bigelow to Kaiser Wilhelm II, 26 January 1893, GStA Berlin, BPHA Rep. 53J Lit. B No. 10 Bigelow 1. See above, pp. 407–8. See Poultney Bigelow, *Prussian Memories 1864–1914*, New York 1916.

104 Bigelow to Kaiser Wilhelm II, 20 July 1892, GStA Berlin, BPHA Rep. 53J Lit. B No. 10 Bigelow 1. Bigelow enclosed his article 'The Czar's Western Frontier', which had just been published in *Harper's Magazine*.

105 Bigelow to Kaiser Wilhelm II, 18 August 1892, GStA Berlin, BPHA Rep. 53J Lit. B No. 10 Bigelow 1.

106 Bigelow to Kaiser Wilhelm II, 26 January 1893, ibid.

107 Bigelow to Kaiser Wilhelm II, 20 July 1892, ibid. Stepniak (in reality Sergei Kravchinski) had stabbed to death the chief of the Russian secret police in 1878.

108 Bigelow to Kaiser Wilhelm II, 18 August 1892, ibid.

109 See above, pp. 479–80.

110 Eulenburg's note of 11 July 1892, in *Eulenburgs Korrespondenz*, II, No. 688.

111 Waldersee, diary entry for 6 August 1893, GStA Berlin, Waldersee Papers; omitted from Meisner, II, p. 292.

112 Waldersee, diary entry for 3 November 1893, GStA Berlin, Waldersee Papers; omitted from Meisner, II, p. 299; but cf. ibid., p. 298.

113 Waldersee, diary entry for 16 October 1893, GStA Berlin, Waldersee Papers; omitted from Meisner, II, p. 296.

114 Waldersee, diary entry for 15 November 1893, GStA Berlin, Waldersee Papers; omitted from Meisner, II, p. 299.

115 Waldersee, diary entry for 30 September 1894, GStA Berlin, Waldersee Papers; cf. Meisner, II, p. 323.

116 Waldersee, diary entry for 16 October 1893, GStA Berlin, Waldersee Papers; omitted from Meisner, II, p. 296.

117 Kaiser Wilhelm II, speech of 22 September 1894, Penzler, *Reden Kaiser Wilhelms II. in den Jahren 1888–1895*, pp. 278–9.

118 On this marriage, see below, pp. 650–1.

119 Eulenburg to Kaiser Wilhelm II, 5 February 1893, *Eulenburgs Korrespondenz*, II, No. 767.

120 Kaiser Wilhelm II, toast of 26 January 1893, Penzler, *Reden Kaiser Wilhelms II. in den Jahren 1888–1895*, pp. 222–3.

121 Kaiser Wilhelm II to Queen Victoria, 28 January 1893, RA I59/98. See Waldersee, diary entry for 20 October 1894, GStA Berlin, Waldersee Papers; Meisner, II, p. 326.

122 Kaiser Wilhelm II to Kaiser Franz Joseph, 31 January 1893, HHStA Vienna, Kabinettsarchiv Geheimakten 2.

123 See above, pp. 366–70.

124 Hereditary Princess Charlotte of Saxe-Meiningen to Helene Freifrau von Heldburg, 26 April 1894, Thüringisches Staatsarchiv Meiningen, HA 342.

125 Queen Victoria to Kaiser Wilhelm II, 28 April 1894, GStA Berlin, BPHA Rep. 52 W3 No. 11.

126 Kaiser Wilhelm II, marginal notes on Eulenburg's report from Vienna, PA AA, Asservat No. 4.

127 Waldersee, diary entry for 24 February 1894, GStA Berlin, Waldersee Papers; printed only in part in Meisner, II, p. 309.

128 See Canis, *Von Bismarck zur Weltpolitik*, pp. 120–7.

129 Minutes of the Crown Council of 18 February 1894, GStA Berlin, cited in part in Canis, *Von Bismarck zur Weltpolitik*, pp. 121–2. Canis points out that the most telling sections of the minutes were omitted by the editors of *Große Politik*.

130 Waldersee, diary entry for 9 February 1894, GStA Berlin, Waldersee Papers; printed only in part in Meisner, II, pp. 306–7. See above, p. 469. See also Philipp Eulenburg to Botho Eulenburg, 9 February 1894, *Eulenburgs Korrespondenz*, II, No. 900.

131 Waldersee, diary entry for 9 February 1894, GStA Berlin, Waldersee Papers; printed only in part in Meisner, II, pp. 306–7.

132 Waldersee, diary entry for 15 February 1894, GStA Berlin, Waldersee Papers; heavily abridged and distorted in Meisner, II, p. 308.

133 Kaiser Wilhelm II to Queen Victoria, 24 August 1894, RA I60/91.

134 Waldersee, diary entry for 29 October 1893, GStA Berlin, Waldersee Papers; omitted from Meisner, II, p. 298.

135 Kaiser Wilhelm II to Eulenburg, 29 November 1893, telegram, *Eulenburgs Korrespondenz*, II, No. 852.

136 Hinzpeter to Kaiser Wilhelm II, 30 June 1894, PA AA, Asservat No. 4.

137 Malet to Queen Victoria, 14 July 1894, RA I60/80.

138 Waldersee, diary entry for 1 August 1894, GStA Berlin, Waldersee Papers; Meisner, II, pp. 318–19.

139 Waldersee, diary entry for 6 August 1894, GStA Berlin, Waldersee Papers; omitted from Meisner, II, p. 320.

19   THE RUDE AWAKENING

1  Empress Frederick to Queen Victoria, 15 March 1890, RA Z48/2.

2  Empress Frederick to Queen Victoria, 22 March 1890, RA Z48/5.

3  Empress Frederick to Queen Victoria, 25 March 1890, RA Z48/6.

4  Empress Frederick to Queen Victoria, 8 April 1890, RA Z48/11.

5  Empress Frederick to Bogumilla Freifrau von Stockmar, 29 March 1891, AdHH Schloss Fasanerie.

6  Empress Frederick to Queen Victoria, 1 December 1890, RA Z49/39; also Empress Frederick to her daughter Princess Viktoria of Schaumburg-Lippe, 1 March 1892, AdHH Schloss Fasanerie.

7  Empress Frederick to Queen Victoria, 8 April 1890, RA Z48/11.

8  Empress Frederick to Bogumilla Freifrau von Stockmar, 7 April 1891, AdHH Schloss Fasanerie.

9  Empress Frederick to Bogumilla Freifrau von Stockmar, 9 May 1891, ibid.

10  Empress Frederick to Queen Victoria, 12 June 1891, RA Z50/45.

11  Empress Frederick to Queen Victoria, 12 December 1891, RA Z52/5.

12  Empress Frederick to Queen Victoria, 4 November 1891, AdHH Schloss Fasanerie.

13  Empress Frederick to Bogumilla Freifrau von Stockmar, 4 November 1891, ibid.

14  Empress Frederick to Queen Victoria, 16 November 1891, RA Z51/46.

15  Empress Frederick to Queen Victoria, 5 December 1891, RA 52/2.

16  Empress Frederick to Queen Victoria, 12 December 1891, RA 52/5.

17  Empress Frederick to Queen Victoria, 16 February 1892, RA 52/20. See also Empress Frederick to Queen Victoria, 20 May 1892, RA Z52/51.

18  Empress Frederick to her daughter Princess Viktoria of Schaumburg-Lippe, 25 February 1892, AdHH Schloss Fasanerie.

19  Empress Frederick to Queen Victoria, 27 February 1892, RA 52/25.

20  Empress Frederick to Queen Victoria, 29 February 1892, RA 52/29; also Empress Frederick to her daughter Princess Viktoria of Schaumburg-Lippe, 8 March 1892, AdHH Schloss Fasanerie.

21  Empress Frederick to Queen Victoria, 20 March 1892, RA Z52/34.

22  Empress Frederick to Queen Victoria, 14 May 1892, RA Z52/48.

23  Empress Frederick to Queen Victoria, 20 May 1892, RA Z52/51. See also Empress Frederick to Queen Victoria, 24 October 1891, RA Z51/40.

24  Empress Frederick to Bogumilla Freifrau von Stockmar, 26 April 1892, AdHH Schloss Fasanerie.

25  Empress Frederick to Bogumilla Freifrau von Stockmar, 17 May 1893, ibid.

26  Empress Frederick to her daughter Princess Viktoria of Schaumburg-Lippe, 18 May 1893, AdHH Schloss Fasanerie.

27  Waldersee, diary entry for 16 April 1892, GStA Berlin, Waldersee Papers; cf. Meisner, II, pp. 239–40.

28  Bülow to Eulenburg, 6 April 1892, *Eulenburgs Korrespondenz*, II, No. 641.

29  Waldersee, diary entry for 30 December 1894, GStA Berlin, Waldersee Papers; omitted from Meisner, II, p. 334.

30  Duke Ernst Günther of Schleswig-Holstein to Prince Christian of Schleswig-Holstein, 16 December 1891, RA Add A18/G1.

31  Prince Ernst zu Hohenlohe-Langenburg to his father, 7 March 1892, Hohenlohe-Zentralarchiv Neuenstein, Hermann Hohenlohe-Langenburg Papers, Bü. 59.

32  Reuss to Wedel, 2 September 1895, Wedel Papers, Frankfurt a.M.

33  Georg II Duke of Saxe-Meiningen to Carl Werder, 21 September 1891, Thüringisches Staatsarchiv Meiningen, HA 395/II.

34 Waldersee, diary entry for 7 August 1890, GStA Berlin, Waldersee Papers; cf. Meisner, II, p. 135.

35 Waldersee, diary entry for 21 October 1890, GStA Berlin, Waldersee Papers; cf. Meisner, II, pp. 155–6.

36 Waldersee, diary entry for 3 August 1894, GStA Berlin, Waldersee Papers; omitted from Meisner, II, p. 319.

37 Waldersee, diary entry for 6 August 1894, GStA Berlin, Waldersee Papers; printed only in part in Meisner, II, pp. 319–20.

38 Wedel, *Zwischen Kaiser und Kanzler*, p. 127.

39 Waldersee, diary entry for 17 December 1890, GStA Berlin, Waldersee Papers; omitted from Meisner, II, p. 167.

40 Waldersee, diary entry for 13 September 1891, GStA Berlin, Waldersee Papers; omitted from Meisner, II, p. 216.

41 Hohenlohe, undated note, printed in Hohenlohe, *Denkwürdigkeiten der Reichskanzlerzeit*, p. 32.

42 Waldersee, diary entry for 12 August 1890, GStA Berlin, Waldersee Papers; omitted from Meisner, II, p. 138.

43 Waldersee, diary entry for 10 January 1891, GStA Berlin, Waldersee Papers; printed only in part in Meisner, II, pp. 174–5.

44 Waldersee, diary entry for 1 November 1892, GStA Berlin, Waldersee Papers; cf. Meisner, II, p. 267.

45 Waldersee, diary entry for 9 January 1891, GStA Berlin, Waldersee Papers; cf. Meisner, II, p. 174.

46 Waldersee, diary entry for 26 October 1894, GStA Berlin, Waldersee Papers; cf. Meisner, II, pp. 327–8.

47 Waldersee, diary entry for 7 December 1890, GStA Berlin, Waldersee Papers; omitted from Meisner, II, p. 164.

48 Bodo von dem Knesebeck to Alexander Hohenlohe, 29 October 1894, Hohenlohe, *Denkwürdigkeiten der Reichskanzlerzeit*, p. 4.

49 Waldersee, diary entry for 19 August 1890, GStA Berlin, Waldersee Papers; omitted from Meisner, II, p. 140.

50 Waldersee, diary entry for 11 October 1890, GStA Berlin, Waldersee Papers; omitted from Meisner, II, p. 154.

51 Waldersee, diary entry for 4 January 1892, GStA Berlin, Waldersee Papers; omitted from Meisner, II, pp. 228–9.

52 Waldersee, diary entry for 19 December 1890, GStA Berlin, Waldersee Papers; cf. Meisner, II, p. 168.

53 Waldersee, diary entry for 20 July 1891, GStA Berlin, Waldersee Papers; omitted from Meisner, II, pp. 212–13.

54 Waldersee, diary entry for 27 June 1894, GStA Berlin, Waldersee Papers; omitted from Meisner, II, p. 315.

55 Waldersee, diary entry for 5 January 1894, GStA Berlin, Waldersee Papers; Meisner, II, pp. 301ff.

56 Waldersee, diary entry for 27 June 1894, GStA Berlin, Waldersee Papers; omitted from Meisner, II, p. 315.

57 Waldersee, diary entry for 21 August 1895, GStA Berlin, Waldersee Papers; cf. Meisner, II, pp. 356–7.

58 Waldersee, diary entry for 18 July 1894, GStA Berlin, Waldersee Papers; omitted from Meisner, II, p. 317.

59 Waldersee, diary entry for 20 October 1890, GStA Berlin, Waldersee Papers; cf. Meisner, II, p. 155.

60　Prince Ernst zu Hohenlohe-Langenburg to his father, 1 May 1891, Hohenlohe-Zentralarchiv Neuenstein, Hermann Hohenlohe-Langenburg Papers, Bü. 58.

61　Waldersee, diary entry for 27 February 1894, GStA Berlin, Waldersee Papers; printed only in part in Meisner, II, p. 309.

62　Waldersee, diary entry for 5 January 1894, GStA Berlin, Waldersee Papers; Meisner, II, pp. 301ff.

63　See e.g. Waldersee, diary entry for 14 December 1894, GStA Berlin, Waldersee Papers; Meisner, II, pp. 332ff.

64　Waldersee, diary entry for 12 October 1895, GStA Berlin, Waldersee Papers; omitted from Meisner, II, p. 361.

65　Waldersee, diary entry for 10 August 1895, GStA Berlin, Waldersee Papers; omitted entirely from Meisner, II, p. 356.

66　Waldersee, diary entry for 12 August 1890, GStA Berlin, Waldersee Papers; omitted from Meisner, II, p. 138.

67　Waldersee, diary entry for 11 August 1890, GStA Berlin, Waldersee Papers; cf. Meisner, II, pp. 137–8.

68　Waldersee, diary entry for 25 September 1890, GStA Berlin, Waldersee Papers; cf. Meisner, II, p. 149.

69　Waldersee, diary entry for 25 September 1890, GStA Berlin, Waldersee Papers; omitted from Meisner, II, p. 149.

70　Waldersee, diary entry for 25 September 1890, GStA Berlin, Waldersee Papers; cf. Meisner, II, pp. 149–51.

71　Waldersee, diary entry for 4 October 1890, GStA Berlin, Waldersee Papers; printed only in part in Meisner, II, pp. 152–3.

72　Waldersee, diary entry for 4 October 1890, GStA Berlin, Waldersee Papers; cf. Meisner, II, p. 153.

73　Waldersee, diary entry for 16 November 1890, GStA Berlin, Waldersee Papers; cf. Meisner, II, p. 161.

74　Waldersee, diary entry for 24 November 1890, GStA Berlin, Waldersee Papers; cf. Meisner, II, pp. 163–4.

75　Waldersee, diary entry for 20 December 1890, GStA Berlin, Waldersee Papers; cf. Meisner, II, p. 169.

76　Waldersee, diary entry for 10 January 1891, GStA Berlin, Waldersee Papers; omitted from Meisner, II, p. 175.

77　Waldersee, diary entry for 3 January 1892, GStA Berlin, Waldersee Papers; omitted from Meisner, II, p. 228.

78　Waldersee, diary entry for 3 January 1893, GStA Berlin, Waldersee Papers; cf. Meisner, II, p. 274.

79　Waldersee, diary entry for 6 January 1893, GStA Berlin, Waldersee Papers; omitted from Meisner, II, p. 275.

80　Waldersee, diary entry for 17 March 1893, GStA Berlin, Waldersee Papers; omitted from Meisner, II, p. 286.

81　Waldersee, diary entries for 11, 12 and 16 June 1893, GStA Berlin, Waldersee Papers; cf. Meisner, II, p. 290.

82　Waldersee, diary entry for 18 January 1891, GStA Berlin, Waldersee Papers; omitted from Meisner, II, p. 176.

83　Waldersee, diary entry for 1 November 1891, GStA Berlin, Waldersee Papers; omitted from Meisner, II, p. 220.

84　Waldersee, diary entry for 18 November 1891, GStA Berlin, Waldersee Papers; cf. Meisner, II, p. 222.

85  Waldersee, diary entry for 18 January 1891, GStA Berlin, Waldersee Papers; omitted from Meisner, II, p. 176. See also the very negative judgement of 6 February 1891, omitted from Meisner, II, pp. 185–6.

86  Waldersee, diary entry for 22 December 1891, GStA Berlin, Waldersee Papers; cf. Meisner, II, p. 228.

87  Waldersee, diary entry for 27 January 1892, GStA Berlin, Waldersee Papers; omitted from Meisner, II, pp. 231–2.

88  Waldersee, diary entry for 26 February 1892, GStA Berlin, Waldersee Papers; Meisner, II, pp. 233–4.

89  Waldersee, diary entries for 3 and 7 March 1892, GStA Berlin, Waldersee Papers; both entries are omitted from Meisner, II, p. 234.

90  Kaiser Wilhelm II, speech of 1 March 1893, Penzler, *Reden Kaiser Wilhelms II. in den Jahren 1888–1895*, pp. 226–7; Elkind, *German Emperor's Speeches*, pp. 294–5.

91  Waldersee, diary entry for 3 March 1893, GStA Berlin, Waldersee Papers; omitted from Meisner, II, p. 286.

92  Waldersee, diary entry for 5 March 1893, GStA Berlin, Waldersee Papers; omitted from Meisner, II, p. 286.

93  Waldersee, diary entry for 23 June 1893, GStA Berlin, Waldersee Papers; cf. Meisner, II, pp. 290–1.

94  Waldersee, diary entry for 7 June 1894, GStA Berlin, Waldersee Papers; cf. Meisner, II, p. 314.

95  Waldersee, diary entry for 12 September 1894, GStA Berlin, Waldersee Papers; cf. Meisner, II, p. 322.

96  Waldersee, diary entry for 15 January 1895, GStA Berlin, Waldersee Papers; cf. Meisner, II, pp. 334–6.

97  Waldersee, diary entries for 14 and 17 March 1895, GStA Berlin, Waldersee Papers; cf. Meisner, II, pp. 339–40.

98  Waldersee, diary entry for 25 January 1895, GStA Berlin, Waldersee Papers; cf. Meisner, II, pp. 336–7.

99  Eulenburg to Holstein, 21 January 1895, *Eulenburgs Korrespondenz*, II, No. 1075; Holstein to Eulenburg, 7 April 1895, ibid., No. 1101; Waldersee, diary entry for 28 January 1895, GStA Berlin, Waldersee Papers; cf. Meisner, II, pp. 336–7.

100  Waldersee, diary entry for 21 January 1896, GStA Berlin, Waldersee Papers; omitted from Meisner, II, pp. 365–6.

101  Waldersee, diary entry for 8 June 1896, GStA Berlin, Waldersee Papers; cf. Meisner, II, pp. 370–1.

102  Waldersee, diary entry for 14 June 1896, GStA Berlin, Waldersee Papers; omitted from Meisner, II, p. 371.

103  Waldersee, diary entry for 28 June 1896, GStA Berlin, Waldersee Papers; cf. Meisner, II, pp. 371–2.

104  Waldersee, diary entry for 15 August 1896, GStA Berlin, Waldersee Papers; omitted from Meisner, II, p. 372.

105  Waldersee, diary entry for 25 October 1896, GStA Berlin, Waldersee Papers; cf. the abridged version in Meisner, II, pp. 374–5.

106  Waldersee, diary entry for 16 March 1897, GStA Berlin, Waldersee Papers; cf. Meisner, II, pp. 393ff.

107  Waldersee, diary entry for 20 May 1890, GStA Berlin, Waldersee Papers; omitted from Meisner, II, p. 128.

108  Waldersee, diary entry for 25 September 1890, GStA Berlin, Waldersee Papers; omitted from Meisner, II, pp. 149ff.

109  Waldersee, diary entry for 20 August 1891, GStA Berlin, Waldersee Papers; omitted from Meisner, II, p. 215.

110  Waldersee, diary entry for 19 December 1892, GStA Berlin, Waldersee Papers; omitted from Meisner, II, p. 272.

111  Holstein to Eulenburg, 10 January 1891, *Eulenburgs Korrespondenz*, I, No. 464.

112  Holstein's note of March 1891, BA Koblenz, Eulenburg Papers, 1891, p. 81.

113  Holstein to Eulenburg, 22 February 1891, *Eulenburgs Korrespondenz*, I, No. 477; cf. ibid., No. 479. But see Bülow to Eulenburg, 13 March 1893, ibid., II, No. 785, where Bülow describes the Kaiser's Brandenburg speech as 'excellent'.

114  Holstein to Eulenburg, 16 March 1891, ibid., I, No. 485.

115  Holstein to Eulenburg, 1 December 1891, ibid., No. 559.

116  Holstein to Eulenburg, 28 February 1891, ibid., No. 481.

117  See Kiderlen-Wächter to Eulenburg, 3 March 1893, ibid., II, No. 778.

118  Holstein to Eulenburg, 4 September 1892, ibid., No. 697.

119  Holstein to Eulenburg, 22 February 1891, ibid., I, No. 477; cf. ibid., No. 479.

120  Waldersee, diary entries for 11 and 17 May 1891, GStA Berlin, Waldersee Papers; heavily abridged in Meisner, II, p. 207.

121  Brauer to Turban, 9 May 1891, Fuchs, *Großherzog von Baden*, III, No. 1116.

122  Holstein to Eulenburg, 16 November 1891, *Eulenburgs Korrespondenz*, I, No. 555.

123  Eulenburg to Kaiser Wilhelm II, 28 November and 19 December 1891, ibid., Nos. 556 and 566.

124  Marschall to Eulenburg, 6 May 1891, ibid., No. 513.

125  Waldersee, diary entry for 4 January 1892, GStA Berlin, Waldersee Papers; omitted from Meisner, II, pp. 228–9.

126  Helldorff to Eulenburg, 7 March 1892, *Eulenburgs Korrespondenz*, II, No. 600.

127  Caprivi to Eulenburg, 28 February 1892, ibid., No. 595. See Count Karl von Kalnein to Eulenburg, 8 March 1892, ibid., No. 602.

128  Holstein to Eulenburg, 27 April and 7 May 1892, ibid., Nos. 646 and 650.

129  Eulenburg to Holstein, 27 April 1892, ibid., No. 647; Eulenburg to Marschall, 2 and 5 May 1892, PA AA, Preußen 1 No. 1d, Bd I; Holstein to Eulenburg, 3 and 7 May 1892, *Eulenburgs Korrespondenz*, II, Nos. 648 and 650.

130  Waldersee, diary entry for 13 January 1891, GStA Berlin, Waldersee Papers; cf. Meisner, II, p. 175.

131  Herbert Bismarck to his father, 23 August 1892, BA Koblenz, Bismarck Papers FC 3005N.

132  Holstein to Eulenburg, 27 April 1892, *Eulenburgs Korrespondenz*, II, No. 646.

133  Kiderlen-Wächter to Eulenburg, 10 May 1892, ibid., No. 651.

134  Eulenburg to Kaiser Wilhelm II, 12 August 1892, ibid., No. 691.

135  Waldersee, diary entry for 13 November 1892, GStA Berlin, Waldersee Papers; Meisner, II, p. 269.

136  Waldersee, diary entry for 18 August 1894, GStA Berlin, Waldersee Papers; Meisner, II, p. 320. See Richard J. Evans, ed., *Kneipengespräche im Kaiserreich. Stimmungsberichte der Hamburger Politischen Polizei 1892–1914*, Reinbek bei Hamburg 1989, pp. 328ff.

137  Holstein to Eulenburg, 4 September 1892, *Eulenburgs Korrespondenz*, II, No. 697.

138  Holstein to Eulenburg, 4 September 1892, ibid., No. 698.

139  Holstein to Eulenburg, 7 August 1893, ibid., No. 814.

140  Holstein to Eulenburg, 11 August 1893, ibid., No. 815.

141  Holstein to Eulenburg, 9 and 11 November 1894, ibid., Nos. 1045 and 1047.

142  Holstein to Eulenburg, 17 February 1895, ibid., III, No. 1089.

143  Holstein to Eulenburg, 27 November 1894, ibid., II, No. 1052.

### 20 THE PREDICTABLE DISASTER: WILHELM II AND
### THE 'PUBLIC SOUL' OF GERMANY

1 Brauer to Turban, 28 January 1891, Fuchs, *Großherzog von Baden*, III, No. 1096.

2 Waldersee, diary entry for 18 January 1891, GStA Berlin, Waldersee Papers; omitted from Meisner, II, p. 176.

3 Waldersee, diary entry for 20 October 1894, GStA Berlin, Waldersee Papers; omitted from Meisner, II, pp. 324ff.

4 Waldersee, diary entry for 17 December 1894, GStA Berlin, Waldersee Papers; cf. Meisner, II, pp. 333-4.

5 Ernest Lavisse, *Figaro*, May 1890; German translation in *Börsen-Courier*, 23 May 1890.

6 José Maria Eça de Queirós, 'O imperador Guilherme' (1891), in *Echos de Pariz*, Porto 4th edn 1920, translated by Professor Dr Erwin Koller.

7 Brauer to Turban, 1 March 1892, Fuchs, *Großherzog von Baden*, III, No. 1162.

8 'The Holy German Empire', *St James's Gazette*, 26 February 1892, RA 59/59.

9 Walther Rathenau, *Der Kaiser*, Berlin 1919, pp. 24-5. See Nicolaus Sombart, *Wilhelm II. Sündenbock und Herr der Mitte*, Berlin 1996, p. 11 *et passim*. Cf. Thomas Kohut, *Wilhelm II and the Germans*, pp. 125ff.

10 Waldersee, diary entry for 18 August 1890, GStA Berlin, Waldersee Papers; omitted from Meisner, II, p. 140.

11 Waldersee, diary entry for 18 May 1890, GStA Berlin, Waldersee Papers; omitted from Meisner, II, p. 128.

12 Waldersee, diary entry for 10 August 1890, GStA Berlin, Waldersee Papers; omitted from Meisner, II, pp. 136-7.

13 Waldersee, diary entry for 11 August 1890, GStA Berlin, Waldersee Papers; cf. Meisner, II, pp. 137-8.

14 Waldersee, diary entry for 11 May 1891, GStA Berlin, Waldersee Papers; omitted in large part from Meisner, II, pp. 206-7.

15 Waldersee, diary entry for 31 October 1890, GStA Berlin, Waldersee Papers; omitted from Meisner, II, p. 157.

16 Loë to Waldersee, 16 November 1893, extracts printed in Meisner, II, pp. 454-6. See Waldersee, diary entry for 18 November 1893, GStA Berlin, Waldersee Papers; the key passages are omitted from Meisner, II, p. 299.

17 Waldersee, diary entry for 24 September 1890, GStA Berlin, Waldersee Papers; cf. Meisner, II, p. 149.

18 Waldersee, diary entry for 3 October 1890, GStA Berlin, Waldersee Papers; omitted from Meisner, II, p. 152.

19 Waldersee, diary entry for 24 November 1890, GStA Berlin, Waldersee Papers; omitted from Meisner, II, p. 163.

20 Waldersee, diary entry for 12 December 1890, GStA Berlin, Waldersee Papers; omitted from Meisner, II, p. 165.

21 Waldersee, diary entry for 3 January 1891, GStA Berlin, Waldersee Papers; omitted from Meisner, II, p. 174.

22 Waldersee, diary entry for 19 January 1891, GStA Berlin, Waldersee Papers; omitted from Meisner, II, p. 176.

23 Waldersee, diary entry for 31 January 1892, GStA Berlin, Waldersee Papers; omitted from Meisner, II, p. 232.

24 Waldersee, diary entry for 26 February 1891, GStA Berlin, Waldersee Papers; omitted from Meisner, II, pp. 196-7.

25 See illus. 25, p. 508.

26  Holstein to Eulenburg, 16 November 1891, *Eulenburgs Korrespondenz*, I, No. 555.

27  Holstein to Eulenburg, 17 March and 19 April 1891, ibid., Nos. 489 and 503.

28  Holstein to Eulenburg, 27 March 1891, ibid., No. 495.

29  Franz Fischer to Eulenburg, 19 April 1891, ibid., No. 503.

30  Brauer to Turban, 6 December 1891, Fuchs, *Großherzog von Baden*, III, No. 1142.

31  Empress Frederick to Queen Victoria, 5 December 1891, RA Z52/2.

32  Empress Frederick to Queen Victoria, 8 March 1892, RA Z52/30.

33  Strachey, report from Dresden, 4 December 1891, RA I59/52.

34  Waldersee, diary entry for 22 January 1892, GStA Berlin, Waldersee Papers; omitted from Meisner, II, p. 231.

35  Caprivi to Eulenburg, 28 February 1892, *Eulenburgs Korrespondenz*, II, No. 595. See Kalnein to Eulenburg, 8 March 1892, ibid., No. 602.

36  Brauer to Turban, 6 March 1892, Fuchs, *Großherzog von Baden*, III, No. 1163.

37  Empress Frederick to Queen Victoria, 20 March 1892, RA Z52/34.

38  Malet to Salisbury, 5 March 1892, RA Z59/61.

39  Verdy to Waldersee, March 1892, GStA Berlin, Waldersee Papers No. 53.

40  Swaine to Ponsonby, 1 July 1892, RA I59/89.

41  Waldersee, diary entry for 11 May 1892, GStA Berlin, Waldersee Papers; omitted from Meisner, II, p. 241.

42  Waldersee, diary entry for 29 November 1893, GStA Berlin, Waldersee Papers; omitted from Meisner, II, p. 299.

43  Brauer to Grand Duke of Baden, 31 December 1892, Fuchs, *Großherzog von Baden*, III, No. 1217.

44  Waldersee, diary entry for 8 March 1891, GStA Berlin, Waldersee Papers; omitted from Meisner, II, p. 198.

45  Bülow to Eulenburg, 6 April 1892, *Eulenburgs Korrespondenz*, II, No. 641.

46  Holstein to Eulenburg, 1 April 1892, ibid., No. 638.

47  Holstein to Eulenburg, 31 March 1892, ibid., No. 634.

48  See Ritter and Niehuss, *Wahlgeschichtliches Arbeitsbuch*, pp. 38–42.

49  Waldersee, diary entry for 24 September 1890, GStA Berlin, Waldersee Papers; cf. Meisner, II, p. 149.

50  Waldersee, diary entry for 18 December 1892, GStA Berlin, Waldersee Papers; omitted from Meisner, II, p. 272.

51  Waldersee, diary entry for 7 June 1894, GStA Berlin, Waldersee Papers; cf. Meisner, II, p. 314.

52  Waldersee, diary entry for 30 December 1894, GStA Berlin, Waldersee Papers; omitted from Meisner, II, p. 334.

53  Waldersee, diary entry for 3 January 1892, GStA Berlin, Waldersee Papers; omitted from Meisner, II, p. 228.

54  Ludwig Quidde, *Caligula. Eine Studie über römischen Cäsarenwahnsinn*, Leipzig 12th edn 1894; Quidde, *Erinnerungen*, cited in Hans-Ulrich Wehler, ed., *Caligula. Schriften über Militarismus und Pazifismus*, Frankfurt a.M. 1977, p. 24.

55  The reaction to Quidde's pamphlet is analysed extensively in Martin Kohlrausch, 'Monarchie und Massenöffentlichkeit. Veränderungen in der Rezeption des wilhelminischen Kaisertums, 1890–1925', diss., Florence 2002. See Joachim Radkau, *Das Zeitalter der Nervosität. Deutschland zwischen Bismarck und Hitler*, Munich, Vienna 1998, pp. 275–6; Gisela Brude-Firnau, *Die literarische Deutung Kaiser Wilhelms II. zwischen 1889 und 1989*, Heidelberg 1997, pp. 32–9.

56  See Hans Wehberg, *Ludwig Quidde. Ein deutscher Demokrat und Vorkämpfer der Völkerverständigung*, Offenbach 1948; Utz-Friedbert Taube, *Ludwig Quidde. Ein Beitrag zur Geschichte des demokratischen Gedankens in Deutschland*, Munich 1963; Wehler, *Caligula*; John C. G. Röhl, *Kaiser Wilhelm II. Eine Studie über Cäsarenwahnsinn*, Munich 1989.

57  I am grateful to Dr Jost Rebentisch of Cologne for drawing my attention to these interesting official statistics. See Jost Rebentisch, *Die vielen Gesichter des Kaisers. Wilhelm II. in der deutschen und britischen Karikatur (1888–1918)*, Berlin 2000, pp. 58 and 60.

58  From 1897 onwards the official figures include only cases involving insults to the Kaiser or other ruling princes in Germany, not to lesser members of the royal families.

59  On Harden's article 'Monarchen-Erziehung' in the *Zukunft* of 31 December 1892 and the subsequent trial, see Bernd-Uwe Weller, *Maximilian Harden und die 'Zukunft'*, Bremen 1970, p. 109. Harden was sentenced to six months in prison for *lèse-majesté* on the basis of his articles 'Pudel Majestät', 'An den Kaiser' and 'Großvaters Uhr', published in the *Zukunft* in 1898: Hans Dieter Hellige and Ernst Schulin, eds., *Walther Rathenau Gesamtausgabe*, vol. VI, *Briefwechsel Walther Rathenau–Maximilian Harden*, Munich, Heidelberg 1983, pp. 314–21.

60  Kaiser Wilhelm II, All-Highest Proclamation of 27 January 1907. See 'Der Kaiser und die Majestätsbeleidigung' in *Vossische Zeitung* of 28 January 1907; also the minutes of the Prussian Ministry of State meeting of 25 March 1907, GStA Berlin.

61  Waldersee, diary entry for 19 March 1897, GStA Berlin, Waldersee Papers; omitted from Meisner, II, p. 395.

62  Waldersee, diary entry for 24 September 1890, GStA Berlin, Waldersee Papers; cf. Meisner, II, p. 149.

63  Waldersee, diary entry for 27 February 1894, GStA Berlin, Waldersee Papers; printed only in part in Meisner, II, p. 309; also the diary entry for 18 August 1894, GStA Berlin, Waldersee Papers; omitted from Meisner, II, pp. 320–1.

64  Waldersee, diary entry for 23 June 1893, GStA Berlin, Waldersee Papers; cf. Meisner II, pp. 290–1.

65  Waldersee, diary entries for 18 and 21 November 1893, GStA Berlin, Waldersee Papers; cf. Meisner, II, p. 299. See the watered-down version of the speech in Penzler, *Reden Kaiser Wilhelms II. in den Jahren 1888–1895*, p. 255.

66  Waldersee, diary entry for 22 December 1891, GStA Berlin, Waldersee Papers; cf. Meisner, II, p. 228.

67  Waldersee, diary entry for 29 October 1891, GStA Berlin, Waldersee Papers; omitted from Meisner, II, pp. 219–20.

68  Waldersee, diary entry for 3 January 1892, GStA Berlin, Waldersee Papers; omitted from Meisner, II, p. 228. See Brauer to Turban, 20 December 1891 and 22 May 1892, Fuchs, *Großherzog von Baden*, III, Nos. 1143 and 1184.

69  Waldersee, diary entry for 17 December 1893, GStA Berlin, Waldersee Papers; completely omitted from Meisner, II, p. 300.

70  Count Friedrich Yrsch to Eulenburg, March and 7 April 1891, *Eulenburgs Korrespondenz*, I, Nos. 487 and 497.

71  Eulenburg to Holstein, 12 April 1891, ibid., No. 498.

72  Brauer to Turban, 19 June 1892, Fuchs, *Großherzog von Baden*, III, No. 1190.

73  Brauer to Turban, 12 July 1892, ibid., No. 1193.

74  Waldersee, diary entry for 30 December 1894, GStA Berlin, Waldersee Papers; omitted from Meisner, II, p. 334. See Brauer to Turban, 8 January 1892, Fuchs, *Großherzog von Baden*, III, No. 1145.

75  Waldersee, diary entry for 9 March 1891, GStA Berlin, Waldersee Papers; omitted from Meisner, II, p. 198.

76  Waldersee, diary entry for 17 December 1894, GStA Berlin, Waldersee Papers; omitted from Meisner, II, pp. 333–4. On the popular mood in Hamburg, see Evans, *Kneipengespräche*, pp. 322ff. *et passim.*

77  Waldersee, diary entry for 23 August 1894, GStA Berlin, Waldersee Papers; omitted from Meisner, II, p. 322.

78  Holstein to Eulenburg, 17 March 1891, *Eulenburgs Korrespondenz*, I, No. 489.

79  Holstein to Eulenburg, 16 November 1891, ibid., No. 555.

80  Waldersee, diary entry for 3 January 1892, GStA Berlin, Waldersee Papers; omitted from Meisner, II, p. 228.

81  Waldersee, diary entry for 20 February 1894, GStA Berlin, Waldersee Papers; omitted from Meisner, II, p. 308. See above, p. 469.

82  Waldersee, diary entry for 14 February 1894, GStA Berlin, Waldersee Papers; omitted from Meisner, II, p. 308.

83  Waldersee, diary entry for 11 March 1894, GStA Berlin, Waldersee Papers; cf. Meisner, II, p. 310.

84  Waldersee, diary entry for 20 February 1894, GStA Berlin, Waldersee Papers; omitted from Meisner, II, p. 308.

85  Waldersee, diary entry for 13 November 1892, GStA Berlin, Waldersee Papers; omitted from Meisner, II, p. 269.

86  Waldersee, diary entry for 1 December 1892, GStA Berlin, Waldersee Papers; omitted from Meisner, II, p. 270.

87  Waldersee, diary entry for 14 February 1894, GStA Berlin, Waldersee Papers; omitted from Meisner, II, p. 308.

88  Waldersee, diary entry for 5 January 1894, GStA Berlin, Waldersee Papers; omitted from Meisner, II, p. 303.

89  Waldersee, diary entry for 9 September 1894, GStA Berlin, Waldersee Papers; omitted from Meisner, II, p. 322.

90  Waldersee, diary entry for 5 January 1894, GStA Berlin, Waldersee Papers; omitted from Meisner, II, p. 303.

91  Waldersee, diary entry for 18 December 1894, GStA Berlin, Waldersee Papers; omitted from Meisner, II, p. 334.

92  Fischer to Eulenburg, 17 February 1895, *Eulenburgs Korrespondenz*, III, No. 1090.

93  See above, chs. 16 and 19.

94  Waldersee, diary entry for 4 January 1892, GStA Berlin, Waldersee Papers; omitted from Meisner, II, pp. 228–9.

95  Waldersee, diary entry for 5 January 1894, GStA Berlin, Waldersee Papers; Meisner, II, pp. 301ff.

96  Waldersee, diary entry for 15 January 1895, GStA Berlin, Waldersee Papers; omitted from Meisner, II, pp. 334ff.

97  Waldersee, diary entry for 21 August 1895, GStA Berlin, Waldersee Papers; cf. Meisner, II, pp. 356–7.

98  Waldersee, diary entry for 6 September 1891, GStA Berlin, Waldersee Papers; cf. Meisner, II, pp. 215–16.

99  Waldersee, diary entry for 27 June 1894, GStA Berlin, Waldersee Papers; omitted from Meisner, II, p. 315.

100  Waldersee, diary entry for 21 July 1895, GStA Berlin, Waldersee Papers; cf. Meisner, II, pp. 353ff.

101  See *Young Wilhelm*, pp. 490ff.

102  Waldersee, diary entry for 15 October 1893, GStA Berlin, Waldersee Papers; cf. Meisner, II, pp. 295–6.

103  Waldersee, diary entry for 10 November 1893, GStA Berlin, Waldersee Papers; omitted from Meisner, II, p. 299.

104  Waldersee, diary entry for 21 July 1895, GStA Berlin, Waldersee Papers; omitted from Meisner, II, pp. 353–5.

105  Waldersee, diary entry for 4 January 1892, GStA Berlin, Waldersee Papers; omitted from Meisner, II, pp. 228–9. See below, p. 572.

106 Waldersee, diary entry for 13 March 1892, GStA Berlin, Waldersee Papers; cf. Meisner, II, p. 234.

107 Waldersee, diary entry for 13 March 1892, GStA Berlin, Waldersee Papers; cf. Meisner, II, p. 234.

108 Waldersee, diary entry for 6 March 1893, Meisner, II, p. 286.

109 Waldersee, diary entry for 21 August 1895, GStA Berlin, Waldersee Papers; omitted from Meisner, II, pp. 356–7.

110 Waldersee, diary entry for 13 March 1892, GStA Berlin, Waldersee Papers; cf. Meisner, II, p. 234.

111 Waldersee, diary entries for 6 April and 4 May 1895, GStA Berlin, Waldersee Papers; cf. Meisner, II, pp. 344–5 and 347.

112 Waldersee, diary entry for 10 August 1890, GStA Berlin, Waldersee Papers; omitted from Meisner, II, pp. 136–7.

113 Waldersee, diary entries for 6 May and 11 September 1890, GStA Berlin, Waldersee Papers; cf. Meisner, II, pp. 126–7 and 144.

114 Waldersee, diary entry for 9 March 1891, GStA Berlin, Waldersee Papers; omitted from Meisner, II, p. 198.

115 Waldersee, diary entry for 14 December 1894, GStA Berlin, Waldersee Papers; cf. Meisner, II, p. 333.

116 Waldersee, diary entries for 21 July and 8 August 1895, GStA Berlin, Waldersee Papers; cf. Meisner, II, pp. 353–5.

117 Waldersee, diary entry for 14 May 1892, GStA Berlin, Waldersee Papers; omitted from Meisner, II, p. 241.

118 Waldersee, diary entry for 3 December 1893, GStA Berlin, Waldersee Papers; omitted from Meisner, II, p. 299.

119 Waldersee, diary entry for 21 July 1895, GStA Berlin, Waldersee Papers; omitted from Meisner, II, pp. 353–5.

120 Waldersee, diary entries for 10 and 13 January 1891, GStA Berlin, Waldersee Papers; cf. Meisner, II, pp. 174–5; Empress Frederick to Queen Victoria, 29 August 1891, RA Z51/16.

121 Waldersee, diary entry for 10 November 1893, GStA Berlin, Waldersee Papers; distorted and printed under an incorrect date in Meisner, II, p. 298.

122 Waldersee, diary entry for 16 October 1893, GStA Berlin, Waldersee Papers; omitted from Meisner, II, p. 296. See also Loë to Waldersee, 16 November 1893, partially printed in Meisner, II, pp. 454–6.

123 Waldersee, diary entry for 9 October 1895, GStA Berlin, Waldersee Papers; omitted from Meisner, II, p. 360.

124 Hereditary Prince Bernhard of Saxe-Meiningen to Waldersee, 9 October 1891, GStA Berlin, Waldersee Papers No. 36.

125 Waldersee, diary entry for 4 October 1893, GStA Berlin, Waldersee Papers; omitted from Meisner, II, p. 294.

126 Waldersee, diary entry for 6 August 1894, GStA Berlin, Waldersee Papers; omitted from Meisner, II, p. 320.

127 Waldersee, diary entry for 15 October 1893, GStA Berlin, Waldersee Papers; cf. Meisner, II, pp. 295–6.

128 Waldersee, diary entry for 22 October 1894, GStA Berlin, Waldersee Papers; omitted from Meisner, II, p. 327.

129 Waldersee, diary entry for 12 July 1895, GStA Berlin, Waldersee Papers; Meisner, II, p. 352.

130 Waldersee, diary entries for 6 April and 4 May 1895, GStA Berlin, Waldersee Papers; cf. Meisner, II, pp. 344–5 and 347.

131 Waldersee, diary entry for 29 October 1895, GStA Berlin, Waldersee Papers; omitted from Meisner, II, p. 361.

23 Waldersee, diary entry for 19 October 1893, GStA Berlin, Waldersee Papers; Meisner, II, p. 297.

24 Kaiser Wilhelm II to Caprivi, cipher telegram, 2 January 1894, PA AA, Preußen 1 No. 1d, Bd I. See also Jagemann to Brauer, 14 January 1894, Fuchs, *Großherzog von Baden*, III, No. 1309.

25 Marschall to Caprivi, 4 January 189[4], PA AA, Preußen 1 Nr 1d, Bd I.

26 Marschall, diary entry for 2 January 1894, cited in *Eulenburgs Korrespondenz*, II. p. 1180. See also Spitzemberg, diary, p. 318.

27 Caprivi, draft telegram of 4 January 1894, PA AA, Preußen 1 No. 1d, Bd I.

28 Marschall, diary entry for 2 January 1894, cited in *Eulenburgs Korrespondenz*, II. p. 1180. See also Spitzemberg, diary, p. 318.

29 Waldersee, diary entry for 9 January 1894, GStA Berlin, Waldersee Papers; Meisner, II, p. 303.

30 Marschall, diary entry for 4 January 1894, cited in *Eulenburgs Korrespondenz*, II. p. 1180.

31 Eulenburg to Bülow, 2 April 1894, ibid., No. 948.

32 Holstein to Eulenburg, 7 December 1893, ibid., No. 859.

33 Pourtalès to Eulenburg, 2 December 1893, ibid., p. 1156.

34 Holstein to Eulenburg, 7 November 1892, ibid., No. 727.

35 Eulenburg to Caprivi, 14 November 1892, ibid., No. 730.

36 Holstein to Eulenburg, 18 November 1892, Eulenburg to Holstein, 19 November 1892, ibid., Nos. 732 and 733.

37 Eulenburg to Bülow, 28 February 1893, ibid., No. 776.

38 Bülow to Eulenburg, 27 March 1893, ibid., No. 789.

39 Eulenburg to Kaiser Wilhelm II, 15 April 1893, ibid., No. 790.

40 Eulenburg to Kaiser Wilhelm II, 4 December 1893, ibid., No. 857.

41 Kaiser Wilhelm II to Eulenburg, 6 December 1893, ibid., No. 858.

42 Holstein to Eulenburg, December 1893, ibid., No. 859.

43 Malet to Rosebery, abstract, 20 December 1893, RA I59/115; Reuss to Wedel, 9 January 1894, Wedel Papers, Frankfurt a.M.

44 See Caprivi's letter of protest to Bülow of 8 March 1894, *Eulenburgs Korrespondenz*, II, p. 1239.

45 Eulenburg to Bülow, 27 March 1894, ibid., No. 941. See also ibid., p. 1239, as well as Nos. 924, 929 and 930.

46 Kaiser Wilhelm II to Bülow, 28 March 1894, ibid., No. 944.

47 Eulenburg to Bülow, 28 March 1894, ibid., No. 943.

48 Reuss to Holstein, 3 January 1894, *Holstein Papers*, III, No. 397.

49 Eulenburg to Kaiser Wilhelm II, 7 March 1894, Kaiser Wilhelm II to Eulenburg, 8 March 1894, *Eulenburgs Korrespondenz*, II, Nos. 922–3.

50 Waldersee, diary entry for 21 January 1894, GStA Berlin, Waldersee Papers; omitted from Meisner, II, p. 304.

51 Brauer to Turban, 6 and 8 June 1891, Fuchs, *Großherzog von Baden*, III, Nos. 1121–2.

52 Holstein to Eulenburg, 7 and 10 December 1891, *Eulenburgs Korrespondenz*, I, Nos. 561–2; Empress Frederick to Queen Victoria, 5 and 12 December 1891, in Ponsonby, *Letters of the Empress Frederick*, pp. 430–2.

53 Kiderlen-Wächter to Eulenburg, 15 June 1892, *Eulenburgs Korrespondenz*, II, No. 680. See the correspondence on this crisis ibid., pp. 879–902.

54 Kaiser Wilhelm II to Kaiser Franz Joseph, 13 June 1892, in Gradenwitz, *Bismarcks letzter Kampf*, pp. 240–2.

55 Kálnoky to Reuss, 16 June 1892, in Otto Gradenwitz, ed., *Akten über Bismarcks großdeutsche Rundfahrt vom Jahre 1892*, Heidelberg 1922, No. 12.

56 Waldersee to Kaiser Wilhelm II, 13 June 1892, in Meisner, II, pp. 245–6; Gradenwitz, *Akten*, pp. 3–4. See Kiderlen-Wächter to Eulenburg, 15 June 1892, *Eulenburgs Korrespondenz*, II,

No. 680; also Eulenburg's notes on a conversation with Waldersee on 29 June 1892, ibid., p. 918.

57 Kaiser Wilhelm II to Waldersee, 10 June 1892, GStA Berlin, Waldersee Papers No. 42. See Holstein to Eulenburg, 9 June 1892, *Eulenburgs Korrespondenz*, II, No. 671.

58 Eulenburg's notes of 26 June 1892, *Eulenburgs Korrespondenz*, II, No. 685.

59 Eulenburg to Holstein, 2 October 1893, ibid., No. 828.

60 Caprivi to Eulenburg, 18 September 1893, ibid., No. 825.

61 Prince Otto von Bismarck to Kaiser Wilhelm II, 21 October 1893, ibid., p. 1118; Eulenburg to Kaiser Wilhelm II, 24 October 1893, ibid., No. 831.

62 Caprivi to Eulenburg, 18 September 1893, ibid., No. 825.

63 Eulenburg to Holstein, 7 October 1893, ibid., No. 830.

64 Eulenburg to Varnbüler, 19 April 1893, ibid., No. 796. See also Eulenburg to Kaiser Wilhelm II, 12 August 1892, ibid., No. 691.

65 See Eulenburg, *Aus 50 Jahren*, pp. 257–68. See also Hohenlohe, *Denkwürdigkeiten*, II, pp. 508ff.; Spitzemberg, *Tagebuch*, pp. 319ff.

66 Kaiser Wilhelm II to Queen Victoria, telegram, 25 January 1894, RA I60/45. See also Brauer to Jagemann, 26 January 1894, Fuchs, *Großherzog von Baden*, III, p. 288, footnote.

67 Marschall, diary entries for 22–5 January 1894, cited in *Eulenburgs Korrespondenz*, II, pp. 1197–8.

68 Hohenlohe, *Denkwürdigkeiten*, II, p. 510; Bülow, *Memoirs*, IV, pp. 656–6.

69 Marschall, diary entry for 26 January 1894, cited in *Eulenburgs Korrespondenz*, II, p. 1198.

70 Eulenburg, *Aus 50 Jahren*, p. 267.

71 Kuno Moltke to Eulenburg, 25 and 28 January 1894, *Eulenburgs Korrespondenz*, II, Nos. 889 and 890. Cf. Eulenburg's reply of 1 February 1894, ibid., No. 891. See Fuchs, *Großherzog von Baden*, III, No. 1322.

72 Waldersee, diary entry for 25, 26 and 28 January 1894, GStA Berlin, Waldersee Papers; printed only in part in Meisner, II, p. 305.

73 Waldersee, diary entry for 29 January 1894, GStA Berlin, Waldersee Papers; cf. Meisner, II, p. 305.

74 Waldersee, diary entries for 22 and 26 January 1894, GStA Berlin, Waldersee Papers; cf. Meisner, II, p. 304.

75 Count Herbert von Bismarck to his father, 21 January 1894, BA Koblenz, Bismarck Papers FC 3005 N. See also Jagemann to Brauer, 25 January 1894, Fuchs, *Großherzog von Baden*, III, No. 1316.

76 Herbert Bismarck to his father, 28 January 1894, BA Koblenz, Bismarck Papers FC 3005 N.

77 The first article, entitled 'Der vierte Mann im Skat', appeared on 24 December 1893. On this scandal, see above all Helmuth Rogge, 'Die Kladderadatsch-Affäre. Ein Beitrag zur inneren Geschichte des Wilhelminischen Reichs', *Historische Zeitschrift*, vol. 195/1 (August 1962), pp. 90–130.

78 Kiderlen-Wächter to Eulenburg, 14 January 1894, *Eulenburgs Korrespondenz*, II, No. 885.

79 Pourtalès to Eulenburg, 18 April 1894, ibid., No. 957.

80 See ibid., p. 1255; also Forsbach, *Kiderlen-Wächter*, I, pp. 129, 131, 137ff. On the question of duelling in imperial Germany, see Ute Frevert, *Ehrenmänner. Das Duell in der bürgerlichen Gesellschaft*, Munich 1991; Tobias C. Bringmann, *Reichstag und Zweikampf. Die Duellfrage als innenpolitischer Konflikt des deutschen Kaiserreichs 1871–1918*, Freiburg 1997.

81 Holstein to Eulenburg, 28 December 1893, *Eulenburgs Korrespondenz*, II, No. 872.

82 Holstein to Eulenburg, 10 January 1894, ibid., No. 881.

83 Holstein to Eulenburg, 22 March 1894, ibid., No. 936.

84 Eulenburg to Kaiser Wilhelm II, 9 January 1894, ibid., No. 880.

85 Eulenburg to Kaiser Wilhelm II, 23 January 1894, ibid., No. 887.

86  See Eulenburg to Varnbüler, 18 December 1893, ibid., No. 865; Eulenburg to Kaiser Wilhelm II, 13 January 1894, ibid., No. 884.

87  Kaiser Wilhelm II to Eulenburg, 11 January 1894, ibid., No. 882.

88  See the extensive correspondence on this issue ibid., particularly Nos. 949, 950, 960, 964, 972 and 974.

89  Eulenburg to Kaiser Wilhelm II, 7 May 1894, ibid., No. 962. See Eulenburg's account of these murky dealings in Eulenburg to Kuno Moltke, 15 June 1895, ibid., No. 1112.

90  See Marschall's diary entries for May 1894, cited ibid., p. 1300.

91  Holstein to Eulenburg, 18 April 1894, ibid., No. 956.

92  Eulenburg's note for Kaiser Wilhelm II of 20 March 1894, ibid., No. 933.

93  Waldersee, diary entry for 20 August 1894, GStA Berlin, Waldersee Papers; cf. Meisner, II, p. 321. See Prince Ernst zu Hohenlohe-Langenburg to his father, 2 April and 11 June 1893, Hohenlohe-Zentralarchiv Neuenstein, Hermann Hohenlohe-Langenburg Papers, Bü. 60.

94  Brauer to Grand Duke Friedrich I of Baden, 12 and 14 September 1894, Fuchs, *Großherzog von Baden*, III, No. 1341 and 1343.

95  Waldersee, diary entry for 20 October 1894, GStA Berlin, Waldersee Papers; cf. Meisner, II, p. 326.

96  Kaiser Wilhelm II to Eulenburg, telegram, 13 March 1894, *Eulenburgs Korrespondenz*, II, p. 1249.

97  Waldersee, diary entry for 30 March 1894, GStA Berlin, Waldersee Papers; omitted from Meisner, II, p. 312.

98  Waldersee, diary entry for 21 October 1894, GStA Berlin, Waldersee Papers; omitted from Meisner, II, p. 327.

99  Waldersee, diary entries for 8 and 29 August 1894, GStA Berlin, Waldersee Papers; Meisner, II, p. 322.

100  Stosch to Bennigsen, 3 July 1894, printed in Oncken, *Bennigsen*, II, p. 591.

101  Waldersee, diary entry for 16 July 1894, GStA Berlin, Waldersee Papers; omitted from Meisner, II, p. 317.

102  Waldersee, diary entry for 20 August 1894, GStA Berlin, Waldersee Papers; largely omitted from Meisner, II, p. 321.

103  Waldersee, diary entry for 20 August 1894, GStA Berlin, Waldersee Papers; cf. Meisner, II, p. 321.

104  Waldersee, diary entry for 25 June 1894, GStA Berlin, Waldersee Papers; omitted from Meisner, II, p. 315.

105  Waldersee, diary entry for 28 June 1894, GStA Berlin, Waldersee Papers; omitted from Meisner, II, p. 315.

106  Waldersee, diary entry for 6 July 1894, GStA Berlin, Waldersee Papers; cf. Meisner, II, pp. 315–16.

107  Varnbüler to Eulenburg, 16 July 1894, *Eulenburgs Korrespondenz*, II, No. 984; Fischer to Eulenburg, 16 July 1894, ibid., No. 985.

108  Kaiser Wilhelm II to Botho Eulenburg, 24 July 1894, ibid., p. 1333.

109  Botho Eulenburg to Philipp Eulenburg, 26 July 1894, ibid., No. 987.

110  Eulenburg to Kaiser Wilhelm II, 30 August 1894, ibid., No. 989. See also Eulenburg to Grand Duke of Baden, 5 September 1894, ibid., No. 990.

111  Botho Eulenburg to Philipp Eulenburg, 9 September 1894, ibid., No. 991.

112  August Eulenburg to Philipp Eulenburg, 9 September 1894, ibid., No. 992.

113  Botho Eulenburg to Philipp Eulenburg, 9 September 1894, ibid., No. 991.

114  Kaiser Wilhelm II, speech of 6 September 1894, Penzler, *Reden Kaiser Wilhelms II. in den Jahren 1888–1895*, pp. 274–7.

115  Botho Eulenburg to Philipp Eulenburg, 9 September 1894, *Eulenburgs Korrespondenz*, II, No. 991.

116 Waldersee, diary entry for 20 September 1894, GStA Berlin, Waldersee Papers; cf. Meisner, II, p. 323. See Major Ebmeyer, 'Caprivis Entlassung', *Deutsche Revue*, 47/4 (1922), pp. 193ff.; also Jagemann to Brauer, 20 and 28 September and 4 October 1894, Fuchs, *Großherzog von Baden*, III, Nos. 1347, 1351 and 1354.

117 See Eulenburg to Holstein, 25 September 1894, *Eulenburgs Korrespondenz*, II, No. 997.

118 For the growing conflict between Eulenburg and Holstein, especially in regard to their opinion of the Kaiser, see Eulenburg to Bülow, 12 October and 25 December 1894, *Eulenburgs Korrespondenz*, II, Nos. 1023–4 and 1069.

119 Eulenburg had been praising the extraordinary political talents of Bülow in his letters to the Kaiser since early 1892. See Eulenburg to Kaiser Wilhelm II, 12 March 1892, ibid., No. 605. See also above, pp. 575–9.

120 Eulenburg to Bülow, 30 September 1894, *Eulenburgs Korrespondenz*, II, No. 1006.

121 Eulenburg's note of 27 September 1894, ibid., No. 1002.

122 Eulenburg to Bülow, 30 September 1894, ibid., No. 1006.

123 Philipp Eulenburg to Botho Eulenburg, 28 September 1894, ibid., No. 1003.

124 Eulenburg to Bülow, 30 September 1894, ibid., No. 1006.

125 Marschall to Eulenburg, 6 October 1894, ibid., No. 1013. See also Eulenburg to Bülow, 6 October 1894, ibid., No. 1015.

126 Eulenburg's note of 13 October 1894, Haller, *Eulenburg*, p. 150.

127 Waldersee, diary entry for 10 October 1894, GStA Berlin, Waldersee Papers; omitted from Meisner, II, p. 324.

128 Waldersee, diary entry for 20 October 1894, GStA Berlin, Waldersee Papers; cf. Meisner, II, pp. 324ff.

129 Kaiser Wilhelm II, speech of 18 October 1894, cited from E. Schröder, *Zwanzig Jahre Regierungszeit. Ein Tagebuch Kaiser Wilhelms II. Vom Antritt der Regierung, 15. Juni 1888 bis zum 15. Juni 1908 nach Hof- und anderen Berichten*, Berlin 1909, pp. 183ff.

130 Waldersee, diary entries for 21 and 22 October 1894, GStA Berlin, Waldersee Papers; cf. Meisner, II, p. 327.

131 Waldersee, diary entry for 30 October 1894, GStA Berlin, Waldersee Papers; Meisner, II, pp. 329–30.

132 Waldersee, diary entry for 29 October 1894, GStA Berlin, Waldersee Papers; largely omitted from Meisner, II, pp. 328–9.

133 Cited in Hatzfeldt to Holstein, 6 March 1895, *Holstein Papers*, III, No. 453.

134 Waldersee, diary entry for 29 October 1894, GStA Berlin, Waldersee Papers; mostly omitted from Meisner, II, pp. 328–9.

135 Waldersee, diary entry for 31 October 1894, GStA Berlin, Waldersee Papers; cf. Meisner, II, p. 330.

136 Waldersee to Verdy, 9 January 1895, GStA Berlin, Waldersee Papers No. 53.

137 Waldersee, diary entry for 9 April 1895, ibid.; cf. Meisner, II, p. 345.

138 Kálnoky to Szögyény, 14 November 1894, copy, BA Berlin, Nowak Papers No. 47.

## 22 HEAD OF THE FAMILY

1 Empress Frederick to Queen Victoria, 27 August 1890, RA Z49/10.

2 The early years of Wilhelm's and Dona's marriage are recounted in the first volume of this biography. See *Young Wilhelm*, pp. 325–66 and 452ff.

3 Waldersee, diary entry for 22 October 1891, GStA Berlin, Waldersee Papers; omitted from Meisner, II, p. 218. See Princess Viktoria of Schaumburg-Lippe to Empress Frederick, 26 and 30 October 1891, AdHH Schloss Fasanerie.

4 Kaiserin Auguste Viktoria to Kaiser Wilhelm II, 31 July 1892, GStA Berlin, BPHA Rep. 53T Preußen: An Kaiser Wilhelm II., Bd IV.

5 Kaiserin Auguste Viktoria to Kaiser Wilhelm II, 14–15 July 1892, ibid.

6 Kaiserin Auguste Viktoria to Kaiser Wilhelm II, 3–5 July 1892, ibid.

7 Eulenburg to Bülow, 1 October 1900, *Eulenburgs Korrespondenz*, III, No. 1434.

8 Kaiserin Auguste Viktoria to Kaiser Wilhelm II, 21 June 1890, GStA Berlin, BPHA Rep. 53T Preußen: An Kaiser Wilhelm II., Bd IV.

9 Kaiserin Auguste Viktoria to Kaiser Wilhelm II, 24 July 1890, ibid.

10 Kaiserin Auguste Viktoria to Kaiser Wilhelm II, 23 September 1890, ibid.

11 Kaiserin Auguste Viktoria to Kaiser Wilhelm II, 3–5 July 1892, ibid.

12 Kaiserin Auguste Viktoria to Kaiser Wilhelm II, 14 July 1892, ibid.

13 See *Young Wilhelm*, pp. 235–42 and 460; also above, pp. 197–9.

14 Kaiserin Auguste Viktoria to Kaiser Wilhelm II, 19/20 July 1892, GStA Berlin, BPHA Rep. 53T Preußen: An Kaiser Wilhelm II., Bd IV.

15 Kaiserin Auguste Viktoria to Kaiser Wilhelm II, 5 July 1892, ibid.

16 Kaiserin Auguste Viktoria to Kaiser Wilhelm II, 21 September 1890, ibid.

17 See Eulenburg to Bülow, 23–5 September 1900 and 26 September 1901, *Eulenburgs Korrespondenz*, III, Nos. 1427–9 and 1454.

18 Eulenburg to Holstein, 22 June and 21 July 1895, ibid., Nos. 1114 and 1118.

19 See below, pp. 643–50.

20 See e.g. Eulenburg to Bülow, 29 September 1899, *Eulenburgs Korrespondenz*, III, No. 1403.

21 Kiderlen-Wächter to Holstein, 19 July 1890, *Holstein Papers*, III, No. 324; Eulenburg to Bülow, 1 October 1900, *Eulenburgs Korrespondenz*, III, No. 1434.

22 Eulenburg to Holstein, 1 August 1890, *Holstein Papers*, III, No. 327.

23 Waldersee, diary entry for 12 January 1891, GStA Berlin, Waldersee Papers; omitted from Meisner, II, p. 175. On Emil Görtz's efforts to amuse the Kaiser, see Röhl, *Kaiser and his Court*, p. 16.

24 Empress Frederick to Queen Victoria, 27 December 1890, RA Z49/48; Kaiser Wilhelm II to his mother, 14 September 1892, AdHH Schloss Fasanerie; Queen Victoria to Kaiser Wilhelm II, 24 January and 4 March 1891, GStA Berlin, BPHA Rep. 52 W3 No. 11; Empress Frederick to her daughter Princess Viktoria of Schaumburg-Lippe, 28 January 1891, AdHH Schloss Fasanerie; also Lee, *Empress Frederick Writes to Sophie*, p. 77; Nicolaus Sombart, 'The Kaiser in His Epoch. Some Reflexions on Wilhelmine Society, Sexuality and Culture', in Röhl and Sombart, *Kaiser Wilhelm II. New Interpretations*, pp. 287–311; Sombart, *Wilhelm II.*, pp. 66ff., 159ff. *et passim*.

25 Waldersee, diary entry for 2 June 1890, GStA Berlin, Waldersee Papers; omitted from Meisner, II, p. 130.

26 Empress Frederick to Queen Victoria, 7 January 1897, AdHH Schloss Fasanerie. The important part played by the Kaiser and Kaiserin in the building of new churches in Berlin and the provinces is discussed more fully in chapter 29 below.

27 Kiderlen-Wächter to Eulenburg, 16 April 1893, *Eulenburgs Korrespondenz*, II, No. 795.

28 Brauer to Grand Duke of Baden, 9 April 1893, Fuchs, *Großherzog von Baden*, III, No. 1238.

29 Empress Frederick to Queen Victoria, 20 August 1890, RA Z49/7.

30 Empress Frederick to Queen Victoria, 15 March 1890, RA Z48/2.

31 Empress Frederick to Queen Victoria, 27 August 1890, RA Z49/10.

32 Empress Frederick to Queen Victoria, 16 December 1890, RA Z49/44.

33 Empress Frederick to Queen Victoria, 20 January 1891, RA Z50/6.

34 Empress Frederick to Queen Victoria, 15 March 1890, RA Z48/2; also Empress Frederick to her daughter Princess Viktoria of Schaumburg-Lippe, 13 December 1890, AdHH Schloss Fasanerie.

35 Prince Ernst zu Hohenlohe-Langenburg to his father, 24 October 1890, Hohenlohe-Zentralarchiv Neuenstein, Hermann Hohenlohe-Langenburg Papers, Bü. 57. See below, pp. 633–9.

36  Empress Frederick to her daughter Princess Viktoria of Schaumburg-Lippe, 28 January 1891, AdHH Schloss Fasanerie.

37  Eulenburg to his mother, 13 December 1893, *Eulenburgs Korrespondenz*, II, No. 863.

38  See e.g. Prince Ernst zu Hohenlohe-Langenburg to his father, 8 February 1891, Hohenlohe-Zentralarchiv Neuenstein, Hermann Hohenlohe-Langenburg Papers, Bü. 58.

39  Waldersee, diary entries for 10 and 12 January 1891, GStA Berlin, Waldersee Papers; omitted from Meisner, II, p. 175; also the entry for 23 November 1890, Meisner, II, p. 162.

40  See Eulenburg's notes, 12/13 October 1895, *Eulenburgs Korrespondenz*, III, No. 1145.

41  Kaiserin Auguste Viktoria to Eulenburg, 22 December 1893, ibid., II, No. 868.

42  Eulenburg to Bülow, 9 March 1894, ibid., No. 924; also Holstein to Eulenburg, 16 February 1894, ibid., No. 910; Eulenburg to his mother, 6 March 1894, ibid., p. 1245.

43  Eulenburg's notes, 12/13 October 1895, ibid., III, No. 1145.

44  August Eulenburg to Philipp Eulenburg, 27 December 1897, ibid., No. 1352.

45  Eulenburg to Bülow, 20 July 1898, ibid., No. 1380.

46  Eulenburg to Bülow, 14 July 1900, ibid., No. 1419.

47  Kaiser Wilhelm II to Dr Zunker, 23 September 1900, cited in Eulenburg to Bülow, 25 September 1900, ibid., No. 1429.

48  Eulenburg to Bülow, 23, 24 and 25 September 1900, ibid., Nos. 1427–9.

49  Eulenburg to Bülow, 1 October 1900, ibid., No. 1434.

50  Eulenburg to Bülow, 29 September and 1 October 1901, ibid., Nos. 1455–6; Bülow, *Memoirs*, I, p. 607.

51  Prince Heinrich of Prussia to Kaiser Wilhelm II, 23 January 1893, BA-MA Freiburg, Senden-Bibran Papers N160/10.

52  Seckendorff to Senden-Bibran, 24 November 1890, 8 and 10 January 1891, ibid., N160/2; Empress Frederick to her daughter Princess Viktoria of Schaumburg-Lippe, 3 and 13 February 1891, AdHH Schloss Fasanerie; Empress Frederick to Bogumilla Freifrau von Stockmar, 29 March 1891, ibid.; Senden-Bibran to Seckendorff, 21 February 1893, Seckendorff to Senden-Bibran, 24 February and 25 March 1893, BA-MA Freiburg, Senden Papers N160/2.

53  Empress Frederick to Queen Victoria, 22 July 1896, AdHH Schloss Fasanerie.

54  Eulenburg's notes, 12/13 October 1895, *Eulenburgs Korrespondenz*, III, No. 1145.

55  See for example Seckendorff to Senden-Bibran, 26 April 1891, BA-MA Freiburg, Senden Papers N160/2.

56  Above, pp. 483–4. See Empress Frederick to Queen Victoria, 25 March 1897, AdHH Schloss Fasanerie, and below, pp. 967–8.

57  Seckendorff to Senden-Bibran, 12 January 1891, BA-MA Freiburg, Senden Papers N160/2; also Seckendorff's letter of 5 June 1893, ibid.

58  Empress Frederick to Queen Victoria, 22 August 1891, postscript, RA Z51/14; 26 August 1891, RA Z51/15.

59  Holstein to Eulenburg, 1 April 1892, *Eulenburgs Korrespondenz*, II, No. 638.

60  Bülow to Eulenburg, 6 April 1892, ibid., No. 641.

61  Senden-Bibran to Seckendorff, 21 February 1893, BA-MA Freiburg, Senden-Bibran Papers N160/2.

62  Senden-Bibran to Kaiser Wilhelm II, 11 February 1893, ibid., N160/1.

63  Senden-Bibran to Seckendorff, 21 February 1893, ibid., N160/2.

64  Senden-Bibran to Kaiser Wilhelm II, 11 February 1893, ibid., N160/1.

65  Empress Frederick to Queen Victoria, 17 and 22 August 1891, RA Z51/12 and 14. See Charlotte Zeepvat, *Prince Leopold. The Untold Story of Queen Victoria's Youngest Son*, London 1998.

66  For Wilhelm's offer to the Tsar, see below, p. 760.

67  See e.g. Holstein to Eulenburg, 27 September 1895, *Eulenburgs Korrespondenz*, III, No. 1135.

68  Eulenburg's memorandum, 12/13 October 1895, ibid., No. 1145.

69 Eulenburg to Holstein, 12 June 1896, ibid., p. 1698. See also Eulenburg to Kuno Moltke, 1 February 1894, ibid., II, No. 891.

70 Eulenburg to Holstein, 5 July 1896, appendix I, *Holstein Papers*, III, No. 554.

71 See Eulenburg to Bülow, 18 December 1897, *Eulenburgs Korrespondenz*, III, No. 1354, and August Eulenburg to Philipp Eulenburg, 27 December 1897, ibid., No. 1352.

72 Eulenburg to Bülow, 12 July 1899, ibid., No. 1397.

73 Empress Frederick to Bogumilla Freifrau von Stockmar, 8 February 1891, AdHH Schloss Fasanerie; also Empress Frederick to her daughter Princess Viktoria of Schaumburg-Lippe, 9 February 1891, AdHH Schloss Fasanerie.

74 Empress Frederick to Queen Victoria, 5 December 1890, RA Z49/40.

75 Empress Frederick to Bogumilla Freifrau von Stockmar, 11 April 1891, AdHH Schloss Fasanerie.

76 Empress Frederick to her daughter Princess Viktoria of Schaumburg-Lippe, 5 December 1890, ibid.

77 Empress Frederick to Queen Victoria, 5 April 1891, RA Z50/34; Empress Frederick to Bogumilla Freifrau von Stockmar, 7 April 1891, AdHH Schloss Fasanerie.

78 Empress Frederick to her daughter Princess Viktoria of Schaumburg-Lippe, 5 and 19 June 1891, ibid. Cf. Princess Viktoria of Schaumburg-Lippe to Empress Frederick, 4 June 1891, ibid.; also Lee, *Empress Frederick Writes to Sophie*, p. 89.

79 Hereditary Princess Charlotte of Saxe-Meiningen to Professor Ernst Schweninger, 7 September 1896, Schweninger Papers, BA Berlin; Hereditary Princess Charlotte of Saxe-Meiningen to Ellen Freifrau von Heldburg, 9 July 1896, Thüringisches Staatsarchiv Meiningen, HA 342.

80 Empress Frederick to her daughter Princess Viktoria of Schaumburg-Lippe, 31 October 1892 and 8 January 1893, AdHH Schloss Fasanerie.

81 Empress Frederick to her daughter Princess Viktoria of Schaumburg-Lippe, 15 November 1891, cited from the extract in the catalogue of the auctioneers Butterfield & Butterfield, Los Angeles, 17 June 1998, No. 2396.

82 Empress Frederick to her daughter Princess Viktoria of Schaumburg-Lippe, 24 February 1891, AdHH Schloss Fasanerie.

83 Empress Frederick to her daughter Princess Viktoria of Schaumburg-Lippe, 28 November 1890, ibid.

84 Wedel, *Zwischen Kaiser und Kanzler*, pp. 180–1.

85 See Lee, *Empress Frederick Writes to Sophie*, pp. 56–7.

86 Waldersee, diary entry for 12 October 1893, GStA Berlin, Waldersee Papers; cf. Meisner, II, p. 295.

87 Empress Frederick to Queen Victoria, 20 August 1890, RA Z49/8; also Empress Frederick to Queen Victoria, 31 March 1891, RA Z50/30.

88 Empress Frederick to her daughter Princess Viktoria of Schaumburg-Lippe, 9–12 July 1893, AdHH Schloss Fasanerie. See also Kiderlen to Eulenburg, 28 September 1892, *Eulenburgs Korrespondenz*, II, No. 709.

89 Empress Frederick to her daughter Princess Viktoria of Schaumburg-Lippe, 27 October 1893, AdHH Schloss Fasanerie.

90 Prince Ernst zu Hohenlohe-Langenburg to his father, 15 January 1894, Hohenlohe-Zentralarchiv Neuenstein, Hermann Hohenlohe-Langenburg Papers, Bü. 61.

91 Albert Edward Prince of Wales to Queen Victoria, 16 January 1894, RA I60/5.

92 Hereditary Princess Charlotte of Saxe-Meiningen to Ellen Freifrau von Heldburg, 25 March 1895, Thüringisches Staatsarchiv Meiningen, HA 342.

93 Waldersee, diary entry for 24 March 1895, GStA Berlin, Waldersee Papers; cf. Meisner, II, pp. 340–1.

94 Hereditary Prince Bernhard of Saxe-Meiningen to Colmar Freiherr von der Goltz, 28 September, 3 November and 23 December 1899, BA-MA Freiburg, von der Goltz Papers, N737 Zug. 161/95.

95 Hereditary Prince Bernhard of Saxe-Meiningen to Colmar Freiherr von der Goltz, 20 October 1898 and 9 April 1899, ibid.

96 Hereditary Princess Charlotte of Saxe-Meiningen to Ellen Freifrau von Heldburg, 14 June 1895, Thüringisches Staatsarchiv Meiningen, HA 342.

97 Hereditary Prince Bernhard of Saxe-Meiningen to Waldersee, 30 March 1895, GStA Berlin, Waldersee Papers.

98 Hereditary Princess Charlotte of Saxe-Meiningen to Ellen Freifrau von Heldburg, 7 October 1897, Thüringisches Staatsarchiv Meiningen HA 342.

99 Hereditary Princess Charlotte of Saxe-Meiningen to Schweninger, BA Berlin, Schweninger Papers No. 130.

100 Hereditary Princess Charlotte of Saxe-Meiningen to Duke Georg II of Saxe-Meiningen, 1 November 1896, Thüringisches Staatsarchiv Meiningen, HA 342; Hereditary Princess Charlotte of Saxe-Meiningen to Ellen Freifrau von Heldburg, 5, 7 and 11 November 1896, ibid.; also Ellen Freifrau von Heldburg to Hereditary Princess Charlotte of Saxe-Meiningen, 4 November 1896, ibid.

101 Hereditary Prince Bernhard of Saxe-Meiningen to his father, 6 November 1896, ibid., HA 341; Kaiserin Auguste Viktoria to Hereditary Prince Bernhard of Saxe-Meiningen, 5 November 1896, copy, ibid.

102 Hereditary Princess Charlotte of Saxe-Meiningen to Ellen Freifrau von Heldburg, 7 and 27 December 1896, 11, 15 and 27 January and 7 October 1897, ibid., HA 342.

103 Hereditary Princess Charlotte of Saxe-Meiningen to her mother, 1 and 5 June 1898, AdHH Schloss Fasanerie.

104 See *Young Wilhelm*, pp. 105ff., and John C. G. Röhl, Martin Warren and David Hunt, *Purple Secret. Genes, 'Madness' and the Royal Houses of Europe*, London 1998, especially ch. 7.

105 Röhl, Warren and Hunt, *Purple Secret*, pp. 139–40.

106 Empress Frederick to her daughter Princess Viktoria of Schaumburg-Lippe, 8 March, 3 April, 1 and 19 June 1892 and 19 October 1893, AdHH Schloss Fasanerie.

107 See *Young Wilhelm*, pp. 516–46 and 800–5.

108 Kaiser Wilhelm II to Eulenburg, 27 February 1889, *Eulenburgs Korrespondenz*, I, No. 213. See above, p. 197.

109 Eulenburg to Kaiser Wilhelm II, 17 December 1889, *Eulenburgs Korrespondenz*, I, No. 266.

110 Empress Frederick to Queen Victoria, 19 June 1889, RA Z45/17; also Lee, *Empress Frederick Writes to Sophie*, pp. 66–7.

111 Empress Frederick to Prince Hermann zu Hohenlohe-Langenburg, 12 June 1890, Hohenlohe-Zentralarchiv Neuenstein, Hermann Hohenlohe-Langenburg Papers, Bü. 105.

112 Empress Frederick to Queen Victoria, 19 June 1890, RA Z48/34–5; also Lee, *Empress Frederick Writes to Sophie*, pp. 66–7.

113 Captain Bourke (1853–1900), second son of the 6th Earl of Mayo, was much liked in the British royal family and was on good terms not only with the Empress Frederick but also with the Prince of Wales and the Duke of York, later King George V, whom he accompanied to the opening ceremony of the Kiel Canal in 1895. See Empress Frederick to Queen Victoria, 3 February 1892, RA Z52/17; Albert Edward Prince of Wales to Empress Frederick, 18 September 1900, RA Add A 4/178. For the anxieties of the Empress Frederick, see Hannah Pakula, *An Uncommon Woman. The Empress Frederick, Daughter of Queen Victoria, Wife of the Crown Prince of Prussia, Mother of Kaiser Wilhelm*, New York 1995, p. 537.

114 Empress Frederick to Queen Victoria, 12 June 1890, RA Z48/30.

115 Kaiserin Auguste Viktoria to Kaiser Wilhelm II, 21 July 1890, GStA Berlin, BPHA Rep. 53T Preußen: An Kaiser Wilhelm II., Bd IV.

116 Empress Frederick to Queen Victoria, 7 August 1890, RA Z49/3.

117 RA QVJ, 4–6 August 1890.

118 Empress Frederick to Queen Victoria, 10 September 1890, RA Z49/14.

119 Empress Frederick to her daughter Princess Viktoria of Schaumburg-Lippe, 24 February 1891, AdHH Schloss Fasanerie.

120 Empress Frederick to Queen Victoria, 5 December 1890, RA Z49/40.

121 Waldersee, diary entry for 18 November 1890, GStA Berlin, Waldersee Papers; Meisner, II, p. 162.

122 For this embarrassing episode, see J. J. Lynx, *The Great Hohenzollern Scandal*, London 1965.

123 The Baden political documents edited by Walther Peter Fuchs contain numerous references to this issue. See in particular Brauer to Turban, 23 April and 2 May 1891, Fuchs, *Großherzog von Baden*, III, Nos. 1110–11; Empress Frederick to Grand Duke of Baden, 6 and 15 May 1891, ibid., Nos. 1113 and 1117; Grand Duke of Baden to Empress Frederick, 16 May 1891, ibid., No. 1118.

124 Brauer to Hardeck, 27 June 1891, ibid., No. 1125.

125 Empress Frederick to Queen Victoria, 5 September 1891, RA Z51/20.

126 Waldersee, diary entry for 18 December 1890, GStA Berlin, Waldersee Papers; cf. Meisner, II, p. 167; also Lee, *Empress Frederick Writes to Sophie*, p. 73.

127 Lee, *Empress Frederick Writes to Sophie*, p. 73.

128 Waldersee, diary entries for 19 and 20 December 1890, GStA Berlin, Waldersee Papers; Meisner, II, pp. 167–8.

129 Empress Frederick to Queen Victoria, 25 and 28 January 1891, RA 50/8 and 10; also Lee, *Empress Frederick Writes to Sophie*, p. 77.

130 Empress Frederick to her daughter Princess Viktoria of Schaumburg-Lippe, 19 December 1890, AdHH Schloss Fasanerie.

131 Empress Frederick to her daughter Princess Viktoria of Schaumburg-Lippe, 21 December 1890, ibid.

132 Empress Frederick to her daughter Princess Viktoria of Schaumburg-Lippe, 22 December 1890, ibid., also Lee, *Empress Frederick Writes to Sophie*, p. 73.

133 Empress Frederick to her daughter Princess Viktoria of Schaumburg-Lippe, 24 December 1890, AdHH Schloss Fasanerie.

134 Empress Frederick to her daughter Princess Viktoria of Schaumburg-Lippe, 1 January 1891, ibid.

135 Empress Frederick to Queen Victoria, 12 June 1891, RA Z50/45; also Lee, *Empress Frederick Writes to Sophie*, p. 73.

136 Empress Frederick to Queen Victoria, 22 December 1890, RA Z49/45.

137 Lee, *Empress Frederick Writes to Sophie*, p. 74.

138 Empress Frederick to Queen Victoria, 27 December 1890, RA Z49/48; also Empress Frederick to Queen Victoria, 9 and 20 January 1891, RA Z50/3 and Z50/6; Empress Frederick to her daughter Princess Viktoria of Schaumburg-Lippe, 24 February 1891, AdHH Schloss Fasanerie.

139 Empress Frederick to Crown Princess Sophie, January 1891, cited in Lee, *Empress Frederick Writes to Sophie*, p. 76.

140 Ibid., p. 74.

141 Queen Victoria to Empress Frederick, January 1891, cited in Lee, *Empress Frederick Writes to Sophie*, p. 77; also ibid., pp. 88–9.

142 Empress Frederick to Queen Victoria, 29 March 1891, RA Z50/29.

143 Empress Frederick to Bogumilla Freifrau von Stockmar, 29 March 1891, AdHH Schloss Fasanerie.

144 Wedel, *Zwischen Kaiser und Kanzler*, pp. 175–6.

145 Ibid., p. 180.

146 Empress Frederick to Bogumilla Freifrau von Stockmar, 18 and 19 May 1891, AdHH Schloss Fasanerie.

147 Princess Viktoria of Schaumburg-Lippe to Empress Frederick, 2 June 1891, ibid.

148 Princess Viktoria of Schaumburg-Lippe to Empress Frederick, 6, 8, 9 and 18–22 May 1891, ibid.

149 Cited in Lee, *Empress Frederick Writes to Sophie*, pp. 85–6.

150 Cited ibid., pp. 86ff.

151 Empress Frederick to Bogumilla Freifrau von Stockmar, 18 and 19 May 1891, AdHH Schloss Fasanerie.

152 Wedel, *Zwischen Kaiser und Kanzler*, p. 190. See Princess Viktoria of Schaumburg-Lippe to Empress Frederick, 29 May 1891, AdHH Schloss Fasanerie.

153 Empress Frederick to Bogumilla Freifrau von Stockmar, 1 June 1891, Empress Frederick to Princess Viktoria of Schaumburg-Lippe, 1 June 1891, Princess Viktoria of Schaumburg-Lippe to Empress Frederick, 31 May 1891, ibid.; also Lee, *Empress Frederick Writes to Sophie*, p. 89.

154 Empress Frederick to her daughter Princess Viktoria of Schaumburg-Lippe, 2 June 1891, AdHH Schloss Fasanerie.

155 Empress Frederick to Queen Victoria, 15 June 1891, RA Z50/46.

156 Empress Frederick to Queen Victoria, 26 August 1891, RA Z51/15.

157 Empress Frederick to her daughter Princess Viktoria of Schaumburg-Lippe, 1 June 1892, AdHH Schloss Fasanerie.

158 Empress Frederick to her daughter Princess Viktoria of Schaumburg-Lippe, 28 June 1892, ibid.

159 Kaiser Wilhelm II to his mother, 21 June 1894, ibid.

160 See Empress Frederick to Queen Victoria, 6 August 1896, ibid.; Kaiser Wilhelm II to his mother, 13 September 1896, ibid.

161 Wedel, *Zwischen Kaiser und Kanzler*, p. 190. See Princess Viktoria of Schaumburg-Lippe to Empress Frederick, 29 May 1891, ibid.

162 Empress Frederick to Queen Victoria, 16 January 1891, RA Z50/4.

163 Wedel, *Zwischen Kaiser und Kanzler*, p. 190. See Princess Viktoria of Schaumburg-Lippe to Empress Frederick, 29 May 1891, AdHH Schloss Fasanerie.

164 Military attaché in St Petersburg to Kaiser Wilhelm II, 1 March 1891, with numerous marginal comments by the Kaiser, PA AA, Rußland 82 No. 1 secr; also Empress Frederick to her daughter Princess Viktoria of Schaumburg-Lippe, 9 March 1892, AdHH Schloss Fasanerie.

165 Eulenburg's notes, 12/13 October 1895, *Eulenburgs Korrespondenz*, III, No. 1145.

166 Empress Frederick to her daughter Princess Viktoria of Schaumburg-Lippe, 6 April 1892, AdHH Schloss Fasanerie; also Lee, *Empress Frederick Writes to Sophie*, p. 71.

167 Bülow to Eulenburg, 6 April 1892, *Eulenburgs Korrespondenz*, II, No. 641.

168 See Lee, *Empress Frederick Writes to Sophie*, p. 71.

169 Empress Frederick to Kaiser Wilhelm II, 20 June 1892, GStA Berlin, BPHA Rep. 52T No. 13; Empress Frederick to her daughter Princess Viktoria of Schaumburg-Lippe, 3, 20 and 22 June 1892, AdHH Schloss Fasanerie; Empress Frederick to Queen Victoria, 20 and 23 June 1892, RA Z53/7 and 8.

170 See *Eulenburgs Korrespondenz*, II, p. 903.

171 Waldersee, diary entry for 13 December 1890, GStA Berlin, Waldersee Papers; Meisner, II, p. 166.

172 Duke Ernst Günther of Schleswig-Holstein to Prince Christian of Schleswig-Holstein, 2 August 1890, RA Add A18/G1.

173 Waldersee, diary entry for 7 June 1891, GStA Berlin, Waldersee Papers; Meisner, II, p. 209.

174 Duke Ernst Günther of Schleswig-Holstein to Prince Christian of Schleswig-Holstein, 10 March 1891, RA Add A18/G1.

175 Empress Frederick to Queen Victoria, 16 December 1890, RA Z49/44.

176 Princess Viktoria of Schaumburg-Lippe to Empress Frederick, 18 May 1891, AdHH Schloss Fasanerie.

177 Kiderlen-Wächter to Eulenburg, 12 December 1892, *Eulenburgs Korrespondenz*, II, No. 748; Karl Samwer to Prince Christian of Schleswig-Holstein, 7 October 1891, RA Add A18/L2.

178 Prince Ernst zu Hohenlohe-Langenburg to his father, 16 October 1891, Hohenlohe-Zentralarchiv Schloss Neuenstein, Hermann Hohenlohe-Langenburg Papers, Bü. 58.

179 Prince Ernst zu Hohenlohe-Langenburg to his father, 27 July 1893, Hohenlohe-Zentralarchiv Neuenstein, Hermann Hohenlohe-Langenburg Papers, Bü. 60. See also Duke Ernst Günther of Schleswig-Holstein to Prince Christian of Schleswig-Holstein, 12 October 1893, RA Add A18/G1. See *Holstein Papers*, III, No. 385.

180 Eulenburg to Varnbüler, 10 and 19 May 1896, *Eulenburgs Korrespondenz*, III, No. 1227; Duke Ernst Günther of Schleswig-Holstein to Prince Christian of Schleswig-Holstein, 29 June 1895, RA Add A18/G1.

181 Prince Ernst zu Hohenlohe-Langenburg to his father, 9 May 1891, Hohenlohe-Zentralarchiv Schloss Neuenstein, Hermann Hohenlohe-Langenburg Papers, Bü. 58.

182 Duke Ernst Günther of Schleswig-Holstein to Prince Christian of Schleswig-Holstein, 10 March 1891, RA Add A18/G1.

183 Prince Chlodwig zu Hohenlohe to Prince Alexander Hohenlohe, 27 May 1895, Hohenlohe, *Denkwürdigkeiten der Reichskanzlerzeit*, pp. 72-3. See Bismarck's article 'Zur schleswig-holsteinschen Frage', *Hamburger Nachrichten*, 23 May 1895, reprinted in Hermann Hofmann, *Fürst Bismarck 1890-1898*, 2 vols., Stuttgart, Berlin, Leipzig 1913, II, pp. 300-2.

184 Duke Ernst Günther of Schleswig-Holstein to Prince Christian of Schleswig-Holstein, 2 August 1890, RA Add A18/G1.

185 Duke Ernst Günther of Schleswig-Holstein to Prince Christian of Schleswig-Holstein, 15 October 1890, RA Add A18/G1.

186 Empress Frederick to Queen Victoria, 26 November 1891, RA Z51/49.

187 Kaiser Wilhelm II to Queen Victoria, 8 December 1891, RA I59/53.

188 For the marriage of Princess Beatrice to Prince Heinrich (Liko) of Battenberg, see *Young Wilhelm*, pp. 520-3.

189 Cardinal Prince Gustav zu Hohenlohe-Schillingsfürst to Prince Hermann zu Hohenlohe-Langenburg, 25 July 1893, Hohenlohe-Zentralarchiv Schloss Neuenstein, Hermann Hohenlohe-Langenburg Papers, Bü. 85.

190 Münster to Eulenburg, 22 April 1894, *Eulenburgs Korrespondenz*, II, No. 959.

191 Ibid.

192 Eulenburg's note of 16 April 1894, ibid., p. 1287.

193 Eulenburg to Bülow, 7 May 1894, ibid., No. 963.

194 Bülow to Eulenburg, 21 April 1894, ibid., No. 958.

195 Eulenburg to Münster, 16 April 1894, ibid., No. 954.

196 Münster to Eulenburg, 22 April 1894, ibid., No. 959.

197 Eulenburg to Kaiser Wilhelm II, 26 April 1894, ibid., No. 960.

198 Eulenburg to Bülow, 7 May 1894, ibid., No. 963.

199 Eulenburg to Kaiser Wilhelm II, 29 March 1896, ibid., III, No. 1204; also Eulenburg to Varnbüler, 5 April 1896, ibid., No. 1207.

200 Kaiser Wilhelm II to Eulenburg, 4 April 1896, ibid., No. 1206.

201 Varnbüler to Eulenburg, 1 and 6 May 1896, cited ibid., p. 1661.

202 Eulenburg to Varnbüler, 19 May 1896, ibid., No. 1227.

203 Varnbüler to Eulenburg, [May 1896], ibid., No. 1229.

204 Eulenburg to Varnbüler, 25 May 1896, ibid., No. 1230.

205 Kaiser Wilhelm II to Varnbüler, 28 May 1896, ibid., No. 1231.

206 Görtz to Kaiser Wilhelm II, 23 May 1896, GStA Berlin, BPHA Rep. 53J Lit. G. No. 5.

207 Prince Heinrich of Prussia to his mother, 11 September 1898, AdHH Schloss Fasanerie. See Empress Frederick to Queen Victoria, 17 April 1897, ibid.

208 Duke Ernst Günther of Schleswig-Holstein to Prince Christian of Schleswig-Holstein, 27 April 1897 and 15 June 1898, RA Add A18/G1.

209 Eulenburg to Kaiser Wilhelm II, 4 April and 18 May 1898, *Eulenburgs Korrespondenz*, III, Nos. 1365 and 1371.

210 Empress Frederick to her daughter Princess Viktoria of Schaumburg-Lippe, 2 December 1891, AdHH Schloss Fasanerie; also her letter of 9 December 1892, ibid.

211 Empress Frederick to her daughter Princess Viktoria of Schaumburg-Lippe, 7 December 1891, ibid.; Empress Frederick to Queen Victoria, 12 December 1891, RA Z52/5.

212 Waldersee, diary entry for 23 November 1890, GStA Berlin, Waldersee Papers; cf. Meisner, II, p. 162.

213 Cited in Prince Ernst zu Hohenlohe-Langenburg to his father, 10 January 189[2], Hohenlohe-Zentralarchiv Neuenstein, Hermann Hohenlohe-Langenburg Papers, Bü. 59.

214 Prince Ernst zu Hohenlohe-Langenburg to his father, 14 June 1890, ibid., Bü. 57.

215 See the correspondence of Major von Krosigk with August von Mackensen, BA-MA Freiburg N39/45; also Heuduck to Mackensen, 9 June 1896, ibid.

216 Empress Frederick to Queen Victoria, 4 and 6 January 1896, AdHH Schloss Fasanerie.

217 Hereditary Princess Charlotte of Saxe-Meiningen to Ellen Freifrau von Heldburg, 11 November 1896, Thüringisches Staatsarchiv Meiningen, HA 342.

218 August Eulenburg to Philipp Eulenburg, 6 January 1896, *Eulenburgs Korrespondenz*, III, No. 1186.

219 See ibid., p. 1634.

220 Eulenburg to Kaiser Wilhelm II, 20 January 1896, ibid., No. 1190.

221 See below, ch. 26.

222 Empress Frederick to Queen Victoria, 1 January 1896, AdHH Schloss Fasanerie.

223 Queen Victoria to Kaiser Wilhelm II, 5 January 1896, RA O45/169.

224 Kaiser Wilhelm II to Queen Victoria, 8 January 1896, RA Z500/5; draft in the files of the Auswärtiges Amt, PA AA; printed in Hohenlohe, *Denkwürdigkeiten der Reichskanzlerzeit*, pp. 154–6.

225 Heuduck to Mackensen, 4 February 1896, Mackensen Papers, BA-MA N39/45.

226 Waldersee, diary entry for 31 October 1896, GStA Berlin, Waldersee Papers; cf. Meisner, II, pp. 375–6.

227 Eulenburg to Bülow, 12 July 1899, *Eulenburgs Korrespondenz*, III, No. 1397.

228 Kaiser Wilhelm II, marginal notes on Prince Friedrich Leopold of Prussia to Kaiser Wilhelm II, 5 July 1904, Burg Hohenzollern.

229 Duke Ernst Günther of Schleswig-Holstein to Prince Christian of Schleswig-Holstein, 10 March 1891, RA Add A18/G1; Empress Frederick to her daughter Princess Viktoria of Schaumburg-Lippe, December 1890, AdHH Schloss Fasanerie; also Empress Frederick to Queen Victoria, 5 December 1890, RA Z49/40. See Princess Marie Louise, *My Memories of Six Reigns*, pp. 66–109.

230 Princess Helena of Schleswig-Holstein to Kaiser Wilhelm II, 29 November 1890, GStA Berlin, BPHA Rep. 53J Lit. S No. 25; also Empress Frederick to her daughter Princess Viktoria of Schaumburg-Lippe, 10 December 1890, AdHH Schloss Fasanerie.

231 See Eulenburg to Bülow, 1 October 1900, *Eulenburgs Korrespondenz*, III, No. 1434.

232 See Kaiser Wilhelm II to Duke Arthur of Connaught, 11 March 1891, RA Addl Mss A15/5680, cited above, pp. 481–2; also Malet to Ponsonby, 19 March 1891, RA I59/10; Malet to August Eulenburg, 24 March 1891, RA I59/11.

233 Eulenburg to Bülow, 11 July 1898, *Eulenburgs Korrespondenz*, III, No. 1378; also Grierson to Bigge, 5 February 1898, RA I61/34.

234 Empress Frederick to her daughter Princess Viktoria of Schaumburg-Lippe, 19 April, 19 and 27 October 1893, AdHH Schloss Fasanerie.

235 Prince Christian of Schleswig-Holstein to Eulenburg, 1 October 1900, Eulenburg to Bülow, 1 October 1900, *Eulenburgs Korrespondenz*, III, Nos. 1433–4.

236 Waldersee, diary entries for 10 and 12 January 1891, GStA Berlin, Waldersee Papers; omitted from Meisner, II, p. 175. On the Kotze scandal, see Bringmann, *Reichstag und Zweikampf*, pp. 152–224. See the earlier accounts of the affair published by Caesar Schmidt in Zürich: Anon., *Das Geheimnis des Ceremoniemeisters. Hofroman aus der jüngsten Vergangenheit. Von Carl Fürst von . . . (in Preußen verboten)*; Dr Fritz Friedmann, *Der deutsche Kaiser und die Hofkamarilla. I. Der Fall Kotze. II. Wilhelm II. und die Revolution von oben*, Zürich 1896; Anon. [H. von Langen-Allenstein], *Herr von Tausch und die Verfasser der anonymen Briefe der Hofgesellschaft*, Zürich 1897.

237 Anonymous to Princess Louise of Anhalt, 7 April 1892, GStA Berlin, PK 1, HA Rep. 89, No. 3307/10, fol. 40ff.; also the letter dated 15 June 1892 to Count Wilhelm Hohenau, cited in Bringmann, *Reichstag und Zweikampf*, p. 157.

238 Anonymous to Prince Aribert of Anhalt, 10 March 1893, GStA Berlin, PK 1, HA Rep. 89, No. 3307/10, fol. 83ff.

239 Ibid.; to Hugo Freiherr von Reischach, 5 February 1892, ibid., pp. 26–7. In another of the letters addressed to Reischach his mother was described as a 'Jewess and a professional'. See Bringmann, *Reichstag und Zweikampf*, p. 157.

240 Anonymous to Duke Ernst Günther of Schleswig-Holstein, 23 January 1893, GStA Berlin, PK 1, HA Rep. 89, No. 3307/10, fol. 78ff.

241 Anonymous to 'Frau Gräfin', 10 January 1893, ibid., fol. 76.

242 Anonymous to Princess Louise of Anhalt, 7 April 1892, ibid., fol. 40ff.; to Prince Aribert of Anhalt, 10 March 1893, ibid., fol. 83ff.

243 Anonymous to Countess Hohenau, 1 March 1894, ibid., letter No. 40; Anonymus to Wedell-Piesdorff, 17 May 1894, ibid., fol. 120.

244 Hahnke to Kaiser Wilhelm II, 16 June 1894, GStA Berlin, PK 1, HA Rep. 89, No. 3307/2.

245 Philipp Eulenburg, memorandum Der Fall Kotze, BA Koblenz, Eulenburg Papers, typescript for April 1895, pp. 332–354b.

246 See Brauer to Grand Duke of Baden, 13 September 1894, Fuchs, *Großherzog von Baden*, III, No. 1342.

247 See Marschall to Eulenburg, 30 April 1896, *Eulenburgs Korrespondenz*, III, No. 1211; Monts to Eulenburg, 7 August 1896, ibid., No. 1254.

248 Lerchenfeld's report 28 June 1894, cited in Bringmann, *Reichstag und Zweikampf*, p. 172.

249 Waldersee, diary entry for 24 June 1894, GStA Berlin, Waldersee Papers; omitted from Meisner, II, p. 315.

250 Waldersee, diary entry for 27 June 1894, GStA Berlin, Waldersee Papers; omitted from Meisner, II, p. 315.

251 Spitzemberg, diary, 12 April 1896, *Tagebuch*, p. 343.

252 For Kotze's character, see Bringmann, *Reichstag und Zweikampf*, pp. 166–7; Bülow, *Memoirs*, IV, p. 213; Philipp Eulenburg, Der Fall Kotze, in BA Koblenz, Eulenburg Papers, typescript for April 1895, pp. 332–354b.

253 See the documentation in Bringmann, *Reichstag und Zweikampf*, p. 173.

254 Waldersee, diary entry for 27 June 1894, GStA Berlin, Waldersee Papers; omitted from Meisner, II, p. 315.

255 Cited in Bringmann, *Reichstag und Zweikampf*, p. 173.

256 Hahnke to O. Meding, 4 August 1894, GStA Berlin, PK 1, HA Rep. 89, No. 3307/2.

257 Pape to Kaiser Wilhelm II, 5 July 1894, Bringmann, *Reichstag und Zweikampf*, p. 174. See Waldersee, diary entry for 5 July 1894, GStA Berlin, Waldersee Papers; omitted from Meisner, II, p. 315.

258 Bringmann, *Reichstag und Zweikampf*, pp. 174–5.

259 See ibid., pp. 180–3.

260 Hereditary Princess Charlotte of Saxe-Meiningen to Ellen Freifrau von Heldburg, 20 May 1895, Thüringisches Staatsarchiv Meiningen, HA 342.

261 Swaine to Sir Arthur Bigge, 9 June 1895, RA I60/109.

262 Waldersee, diary entry for 23 May 1895, GStA Berlin, Waldersee Papers; cf. Meisner, II, p. 349.

263 Chlodwig Hohenlohe to Alexander Hohenlohe, 27 May 1895, Hohenlohe, *Denkwürdigkeiten der Reichskanzlerzeit*, p. 72.

264 See Marschall to Eulenburg, 30 April 1896, *Eulenburgs Korrespondenz*, III, No. 1211.

265 Waldersee, diary entry for 20 August 1894, GStA Berlin, Waldersee Papers, cf. Meisner, II, p. 321.

266 Hohenlohe to Kaiser Wilhelm II, 12 April 1895, Hohenlohe, *Denkwürdigkeiten der Reichskanzlerzeit*, p. 59; also Holstein to Eulenburg, 26 January 1895, *Eulenburgs Korrespondenz*, II, No. 1078.

267 Chlodwig Hohenlohe to Prince Hermann zu Hohenlohe-Langenburg, 13 April [erroneously dated October] 1895, Hohenlohe-Zentralarchiv Neuenstein, Hermann Hohenlohe-Langenburg Papers, Bü. 86.

268 Hereditary Princess Charlotte of Saxe-Meiningen to Ellen Freifrau von Heldburg, 14 April 1895, Thüringisches Staatsarchiv Meiningen, HA 342.

269 Waldersee, diary entries for 14 and 18 April 1895, GStA Berlin, Waldersee Papers; cf. Meisner, II, pp. 345–6.

270 See August Eulenburg to Philipp Eulenburg, 17 December 1894, *Eulenburgs Korrespondenz*, II, No. 1066. See Bringmann, *Reichstag und Zweikampf*, pp. 178 and 189ff.

271 Waldersee, diary entry for 20 August 1894, GStA Berlin, Waldersee Papers; cf. Meisner, II, p. 321.

272 Kaiser Wilhelm II to Eulenburg, 25 December 1895, *Eulenburgs Korrespondenz*, III, No. 1178; Bringmann, *Reichstag und Zweikampf*, pp. 195ff. See Prince Friedrich of Hohenzollern to Colmar Freiherr von der Goltz, 24 February 1896, von der Goltz Papers, BA MA N737/25.

273 Eulenburg to Kaiser Wilhelm II, 2 January 1896, *Eulenburgs Korrespondenz*, III, No. 1184.

274 Waldersee, diary entry for 3 March 1896, GStA Berlin, Waldersee Papers; omitted from Meisner, II, pp. 368–9.

275 Szögyeny's report of 6 February 1896, Lerchenfeld's report of 6 February 1896, cited in Bringmann, *Reichstag und Zweikampf*, pp. 196 and 198.

276 Monts to Bülow, 24 February 189[6], cited in Bülow, *Memoirs*, I, pp. 32ff.

277 Details in Bringmann, *Reichstag und Zweikampf*, pp. 197–202.

278 Philipp Eulenburg, Der Fall Kotze, in BA Koblenz, Eulenburg Papers, typescript for April 1895, pp. 351–2. On the occasion of the Kaiser's birthday in January 1902, Leberecht von Kotze was awarded the Order of the Red Eagle third class.

279 Empress Frederick to Queen Victoria, 12 April 1896, AdHH Schloss Fasanerie.

280 Waldersee, diary entry for 15 April 1896, GStA Berlin, Waldersee Papers; omitted from Meisner, II, p. 369.

281 Count Bogdan von Hutten-Czapski, *Sechzig Jahre Politik und Gesellschaft*, 2 vols., Berlin 1936, I, p. 263; Lerchenfeld's report of 6 February 1896, cited in Bringmann, *Reichstag und Zweikampf*, p. 208.

282 Brauer to Grand Duke of Baden, 13 September 1894, Fuchs, *Großherzog von Baden*, III, p. 311.

283 August Eulenburg to Philipp Eulenburg, 17 December 1894, *Eulenburgs Korrespondenz*, II, No. 1066.

284 See Eulenburg to Holstein, 16 April 1895, ibid., III, No. 1104.

285 See Eulenburg to Kaiser Wilhelm II, 16 April 1896, BA Koblenz, Eulenburg Papers, typescript for April 1895, pp. 347–51.

286 Philipp Eulenburg, Der Fall Kotze, BA Koblenz, Eulenburg Papers, typescript for April 1895, pp. 345–6.

287 Eulenburg to Holstein, 21 January 1895, *Eulenburgs Korrespondenz*, II, No. 1075.

288 Waldersee, diary entry for 16 July 1894, GStA Berlin, Waldersee Papers; cf. Meisner, II, p. 317.

289 Waldersee, diary entries for 12, 18 and 20 August 1894, GStA Berlin, Waldersee Papers; not in Meisner, II, pp. 320–1.

290 Hohenlohe, undated note, Hohenlohe, *Denkwürdigkeiten der Reichskanzlerzeit*, pp. 35–6.

291 Duke Ernst Günther of Schleswig-Holstein to Prince Christian of Schleswig-Holstein, 29 June 1895 and 26 April 1896, RA Add A18/G1.

292 Karl Samwer to Prince Christian of Schleswig-Holstein, 10 February 1897, RA Add A18/L2.

293 Philipp Eulenburg, Der Fall Kotze, in BA Koblenz, Eulenburg Papers, typescript for April 1895, p. 353.

294 Bringmann, *Reichstag und Zweikampf*, pp. 208ff.

295 Hereditary Princess Charlotte of Saxe-Meiningen to Ellen Freifrau von Heldburg, 26 June 1894, Thüringisches Staatsarchiv Meiningen, HA 342; also Hereditary Princess Charlotte of Saxe-Meiningen to Ellen Freifrau von Heldburg, 14 April 1895, cited above, p. 670, and 1 November 1896, Thüringisches Staatsarchiv Meiningen, HA 342.

296 Marschall to Eulenburg, 30 April 1896, *Eulenburgs Korrespondenz*, III, No. 1211.

297 *Berliner Tageblatt*, 14 April 1895, *Vossische Zeitung*, 14 April 1895 and 11 April 1896, cited in Bringmann, *Reichstag und Zweikampf*, pp. 185 and 214.

298 Harden, *Die Zukunft*, 7 July 1894, cited in Bringmann, *Reichstag und Zweikampf*, p. 215.

299 Philipp Eulenburg, Der Fall Kotze, BA Koblenz, Eulenburg Papers, typescript for April 1895, p. 334.

300 See Bringmann, *Reichstag und Zweikampf*, pp. 210ff.

301 Waldersee, diary entry for 23 May 1895, GStA Berlin, Waldersee Papers; cf. Meisner, II, p. 349.

302 Hereditary Princess Charlotte of Saxe-Meiningen to Ellen Freifrau von Heldburg, 20 May 1895, Thüringisches Staatsarchiv Meiningen, HA 342.

23 THE KAISER AND THE 'NEWEST COURSE'

1 Kaiser Wilhelm II to Hohenlohe, telegram, 26 October 1894, in Hohenlohe, *Denkwürdigkeiten der Reichskanzlerzeit*, p. 1.

2 Haller, *Eulenburg*, pp. 153ff.

3 Otto Hammann, *Der neue Kurs*, Berlin 1918, p. 137.

4 Jagemann, report, 27 September 1894, cited in Röhl, *Germany without Bismarck*, p. 119.

5 Grand Duke of Baden to Eulenburg, 25 September 1894, *Eulenburgs Korrespondenz*, II, No. 998. See Eulenburg to Bülow, 30 September 1894, ibid., No. 1006.

6 Bülow to Eulenburg, 6 October 1894, ibid., No. 1016.

7 Eulenburg to Bülow, 27 October 1894, ibid., No. 1038.

8 Haller, *Eulenburg*, pp. 154, 157–8.

9 Ibid., p. 155. See also Nipperdey, *Deutsche Geschichte*, II, pp. 709–10; Ullrich, *Nervöse Groß-macht*, pp. 155ff.

10 Alexander von Hohenlohe, *Aus meinem Leben*, Frankfurt a.M. 1925, p. 226.

11 Holstein to Hohenlohe, 26 October 1894, Hohenlohe, *Denkwürdigkeiten der Reichskanz-lerzeit*, pp. 1–2; Grand Duke of Baden to Hohenlohe, 26 October 1894, Fuchs, *Großherzog von Baden*, III, No. 1371.

12 Alexander Hohenlohe, *Aus meinem Leben*, p. 226.

13 Hohenlohe, note of October 1894, Hohenlohe, *Denkwürdigkeiten der Reichskanzlerzeit*, p. 4.

14 Alexander Hohenlohe, *Aus meinem Leben*, p. 225.

15 Hohenlohe's notes of 27 October 1894, Hohenlohe, *Denkwürdigkeiten der Reichskanzlerzeit*, p. 3.

16 Hohenlohe's notes of 2 November 1894, ibid., p. 7.

17 Hohenlohe's notes of 27–8 October 1894, ibid., p. 3.

18 Kaiser Wilhelm II to Queen Victoria, telegram, 28 October 1894, RA I60/97.

19 Holstein to Hohenlohe, 26 October 1894, Hohenlohe, *Denkwürdigkeiten der Reichskanz-lerzeit*, pp. 1–2.

20 Eulenburg to Kaiser Wilhelm II, 3 November 1894, *Eulenburgs Korrespondenz*, II, No. 1042.

21 Cardinal Prince Gustav zu Hohenlohe to Duke Georg II of Saxe-Meiningen, 7 November 1894, Thüringisches Staatsarchiv Meiningen, HA 361.

22 Waldersee to Verdy, 9 January 1895, GStA Berlin, Waldersee Papers No. 53.

23 Alexander Hohenlohe, *Aus meinem Leben*, pp. 235–40.

24 John C. G. Röhl, *Deutschland ohne Bismarck. Die Regierungskrise im Zweiten Kaiserreich 1890–1900*, Tübingen 1969, p. 270, n. 16.

25 Röhl, *Germany without Bismarck*, p. 123.

26 Jagemann, report of 26 October 1894, cited ibid.

27 Alexander Hohenlohe, *Aus meinem Leben*, pp. 224–5.

28 Waldersee to Verdy, 9 January 1895, GStA Berlin, Waldersee Papers No. 53.

29 See below, pp. 721–31.

30 Kaiser Wilhelm II to Hohenlohe, 5 November 1894, cited in Röhl, *Germany without Bismarck*, p. 124.

31 Hohenlohe, *Denkwürdigkeiten der Reichskanzlerzeit*, p. 134.

32 Hohenlohe, undated note, ibid., p. 10.

33 Hohenlohe's notes, 6 November 1894, ibid., pp. 10–11.

34 Kálnoky to Szögyény, 14 November 1894, copy, BA Berlin, Nowak Papers No. 47.

35 Schelling, letter of resignation, 2 November 1894. See Röhl, *Germany without Bismarck*, pp. 124–5.

36 Nieberding to Hohenlohe, 4 November 1894, Hohenlohe to Kaiser Wilhelm II, 4 November 1894, cited ibid., p. 125.

37 Kaiser Wilhelm II, marginal notes on Hohenlohe's report of 4 November 1894, Kaiser Wilhelm II to Hohenlohe, 5 November 1894, cited ibid.

38 On these negotiations, see ibid., pp. 125–6.

39 Holstein to Hohenlohe, 26 October 1894, Hohenlohe, *Denkwürdigkeiten der Reichskanz-lerzeit*, pp. 1–2. See Eulenburg to Bülow, 6 and 12 October 1894, *Eulenburgs Korrespondenz*, II, Nos. 1015 and 1024.

40 Hohenlohe's note of 28 October 1894, Hohenlohe, *Denkwürdigkeiten der Reichskanzlerzeit*, p. 3.

41 See Count Anton Monts's remarks in Bülow, *Memoirs*, I, pp. 28ff.; also Gosselin's report of 3 November 1894, RA I60/98.

42 Kálnoky to Szögyény, 14 November 1894, copy, BA Berlin, Nowak Papers No. 47.

43 Holstein to Hohenlohe, 11 November 1894, Hohenlohe, *Denkwürdigkeiten der Reichskanzlerzeit*, p. 11.

44 Holstein to Hohenlohe, 17 November 1894, ibid., p. 15.

45 Alexander Hohenlohe, *Aus meinem Leben*, pp. 226–7.

46 Ibid., pp. 228; Hohenlohe's notes of 27 October 1894, Hohenlohe, *Denkwürdigkeiten der Reichskanzlerzeit*, p. 3.

47 Hohenlohe's notes of 6 November 1894, ibid., pp. 10–11.

48 August Eulenburg to Philipp Eulenburg, 17 December 1894, *Eulenburgs Korrespondenz*, II, No. 1066.

49 Hohenlohe to Eulenburg, 20 January 1895, Hohenlohe, *Denkwürdigkeiten der Reichskanzlerzeit*, p. 30.

50 Eulenburg to Bülow, 7 November 1894, *Eulenburgs Korrespondenz*, II, No. 1043; Eulenburg to Holstein, 7 November 1894, ibid., No. 1044; Bülow to Eulenburg, 10 November 1894, ibid., No. 1046; Eulenburg to Kaiser Wilhelm II, 14 November 1894 and 23 January 1895, ibid., Nos. 1049 and 1076; Eulenburg to Hohenlohe, 22 January 1895, Hohenlohe, *Denkwürdigkeiten der Reichskanzlerzeit*, p. 30; Eulenburg to Holstein, 22 January 1895, *Holstein Papers*, III, No. 436.

51 Holstein to Hohenlohe, 17 November 1894, Hohenlohe, *Denkwürdigkeiten der Reichskanzlerzeit*, p. 15.

52 Hohenlohe, diary entry for 31 December 1894, ibid., p. 27.

53 Chlodwig Hohenlohe to Prince Hermann zu Hohenlohe-Langenburg, 21 April 1895, Hohenlohe-Zentralarchiv Neuenstein, Hermann Hohenlohe-Langenburg Papers, Bü. 86.

54 Hohenlohe to Eulenburg, 7 January 1895, *Eulenburgs Korrespondenz*, II, p. 1441.

55 Waldersee, diary entry for 21 January 1896, GStA Berlin, Waldersee Papers; cf. Meisner, II, pp. 365–6.

56 Hohenlohe, note of 28 February 1896, Hohenlohe, *Denkwürdigkeiten der Reichskanzlerzeit*, pp. 181–2.

57 Hohenlohe, diary entry for 2 March 1896, ibid., p. 186.

58 See Bülow to Eulenburg, 5 January 1895, *Eulenburgs Korrespondenz*, II, No. 1073.

59 Szögyény to Kálnoky, 24 November 1894, cited ibid., p. 1401.

60 Waldersee, diary entry for 28 April 1895, GStA Berlin, Waldersee Papers; omitted from Meisner, II, p. 346.

61 Waldersee, diary entry for 8 May 1895, GStA Berlin, Waldersee Papers; omitted from Meisner, II, p. 348.

62 Waldersee, diary entry for 9 April 1895, GStA Berlin, Waldersee Papers; cf. Meisner, II, p. 345.

63 Waldersee, diary entry for 12 May 1895, GStA Berlin, Waldersee Papers; omitted from Meisner, II, p. 349.

64 Waldersee, diary entry for 19 May 1895, GStA Berlin, Waldersee Papers; omitted from Meisner, II, p. 349.

65 Waldersee, diary entry for 10 October 1895, GStA Berlin, Waldersee Papers; omitted from Meisner, II, p. 360.

66 Eulenburg to Holstein, 11 and 21 January 1895, *Eulenburgs Korrespondenz*, II, No. 1075; Alexander Hohenlohe to Eulenburg, 14 January 1895, ibid., p. 1447; also Jagemann to Brauer, 19 December 1894 and 5 January 1895, Fuchs, *Großherzog von Baden*, III, Nos. 1400 and 1405.

67 Eulenburg to Kaiser Wilhelm II, 5 February 1895, *Eulenburgs Korrespondenz*, II, No. 1079.

68 Holstein to Eulenburg, 22 December 1895, ibid., III, No. 1175.

69 Waldersee, diary entry for 11 June 1895, GStA Berlin, Waldersee Papers; omitted from Meisner, II, p. 350.

70 Waldersee, diary entry for 17 February 1895, GStA Berlin, Waldersee Papers; omitted from Meisner, II, p. 339.

71 Waldersee to Verdy, 12 April 1895, GStA Berlin, Waldersee Papers No. 53.

72 Waldersee, diary entry for 22 April 1895, GStA Berlin, Waldersee Papers; omitted from Meisner, II, p. 346.

73 Waldersee, diary entry for 4 February 1896, GStA Berlin, Waldersee Papers; printed only in part in Meisner, II, p. 367.

74 Waldersee, diary entry for 21 August 1895, GStA Berlin, Waldersee Papers; cf. Meisner, II, p. 356.

75 See Harden's article 'Hohenzollern oder Hohenlohe', *Die Zukunft*, February 1895.

76 Eulenburg to Hohenlohe, 24 May 1895, Hohenlohe, *Denkwürdigkeiten der Reichskanzlerzeit*, pp. 71–2.

77 Eulenburg to Holstein, 22 June 1895, *Eulenburgs Korrespondenz*, III, No. 1114.

78 Marschall, diary entry for 17 February 1895, cited ibid., p. 1469.

79 Holstein to Bülow, 7 February 1895, ibid., No. 1082.

80 Holstein to Eulenburg, 26 January 1895, ibid., No. 1078.

81 Eulenburg to Holstein, 16 April 1895, ibid., No. 1104.

82 Waldersee, diary entry for 3 May 1896, GStA Berlin, Waldersee Papers; omitted from Meisner, II, p. 369.

83 Waldersee, diary entry for 10 May 1896, GStA Berlin, Waldersee Papers; omitted from Meisner, II, p. 369.

84 Waldersee, diary entry for 14 May 1896, GStA Berlin, Waldersee Papers; printed only in part in Meisner, II, pp. 369–70.

85 Waldersee, diary entry for 31 May 1897, GStA Berlin, Waldersee Papers, omitted from Meisner, II, pp. 397–8.

86 Waldersee, diary entries for 28 April, 18 May, 28 June and 10 July 1895, GStA Berlin, Waldersee Papers; omitted from Meisner, II, pp. 346, 349 and 351–2.

87 Holstein to Eulenburg, 7 April 1895, *Eulenburgs Korrespondenz*, III, No. 1101. See Jagemann to Brauer, 8 April 1895, Fuchs, *Großherzog von Baden*, III, p. 422 note.

88 Kaiser Wilhelm II to Hohenlohe, 30 March 1895, Hohenlohe, *Denkwürdigkeiten der Reichskanzlerzeit*, pp. 57–8.

89 Waldersee, diary entry for 2 April 1895, GStA Berlin, Waldersee Papers; cf. Meisner, II, pp. 343–4.

90 Waldersee, diary entry for 6 April 1895, GStA Berlin, Waldersee Papers; cf. Meisner, II, pp. 344–5.

91 Waldersee, diary entry for 18 May 1895, GStA Berlin, Waldersee Papers; omitted from Meisner, II, p. 349.

92 Waldersee, diary entry for 12 June 1895, GStA Berlin, Waldersee Papers; cf. Meisner, II, p. 350.

93 Waldersee, diary entry for 6 April 1895, GStA Berlin, Waldersee Papers; cf. Meisner, II, pp. 344–5.

94 Waldersee, diary entry for 15 October 1896, GStA Berlin, Waldersee Papers; cf. Meisner, II, pp. 372–3.

95 Waldersee, diary entry for 23 February 1895, GStA Berlin, Waldersee Papers; omitted from Meisner, II, p. 339.

96 Waldersee, diary entry for 23 February 1895, GStA Berlin, Waldersee Papers; omitted from Meisner, II, p. 339. See Evans, *Kneipengespräche*, p. 138.

97 Hohenlohe, diary entry for 19 June 1895, Hohenlohe, *Denkwürdigkeiten der Reichskanzlerzeit*, pp. 79–80.

98 Hohenlohe, diary entry for 23 June 1895, ibid., p. 80.

99 Waldersee, diary entry for 23 June 1895, GStA Berlin, Waldersee Papers; Meisner, II, pp. 350–1.

100 Eulenburg, notes of 13 and 28 July 1895, *Eulenburgs Korrespondenz*, III, Nos. 1117 and 1119; Kaiser Wilhelm II to Tsar Nicholas II, 10 July 1895, Walter Goetz, ed., *Briefe Wilhelms II. an den Zaren 1894–1914*, Berlin 1920, pp. 292ff.

101 Holstein to Eulenburg, 17 June 1895, *Eulenburgs Korrespondenz*, III, No. 1113.

102 Waldersee, diary entry for 23 June 1895, GStA Berlin, Waldersee Papers; Meisner, II, pp. 350–1.

103 Waldersee, diary entries for 27 and 28 June 1895, GStA Berlin, Waldersee Papers; cf. Meisner, II, pp. 351–2.

104 Eulenburg to Holstein, 22 June 1895, *Eulenburgs Korrespondenz*, III, No. 1114.

105 Waldersee, diary entries for 23 and 28 June 1895, GStA Berlin, Waldersee Papers; cf. Meisner, II, pp. 350ff.

24   AN ENEMY OF THE PEOPLE

1 See Harden's attacks on Hohenlohe and the Kaiser in *Die Zukunft* of 14 December 1894. See *Eulenburgs Korrespondenz*, II, p. 1436.

2 Holstein to Hohenlohe, 11 November 1894, Hohenlohe, *Denkwürdigkeiten der Reichskanzlerzeit*, p. 11.

3 Holstein to Bülow, 15 February 1895, *Holstein Papers*, III, No. 443.

4 Holstein to Bülow, 21 February 1895, ibid., No. 447.

5 Alexander Hohenlohe to Eulenburg, 17 February 1895, Hohenlohe, *Denkwürdigkeiten der Reichskanzlerzeit*, pp. 42–4.

6 Hohenlohe, diary entry for 14 December 1894, ibid., p. 23.

7 Kaiser Wilhelm II to Eulenburg, 9 December 1894, *Eulenburgs Korrespondenz*, II, No. 1060. See Eulenburg's telling reply of 14 December 1894, ibid., No. 1063; also Jagemann to Brauer, 2 October 1894, Fuchs, *Großherzog von Baden*, III, No. 1353.

8 Kaiser Wilhelm II to Eulenburg, 9 December 1894, *Eulenburgs Korrespondenz*, II, No. 1060.

9 Hohenlohe, undated notes, Hohenlohe, *Denkwürdigkeiten der Reichskanzlerzeit*, pp. 20–1.

10 Hohenlohe, diary entry for 14 December 1894, ibid., p. 23.

11 Hohenlohe, undated notes, ibid., pp. 31–2.

12 Waldersee, diary entries for 7 and 9 December 1894, GStA Berlin, Waldersee Papers; omitted from Meisner, II, p. 332.

13 Waldersee, diary entry for 14 December 1894, GStA Berlin, Waldersee Papers; cf. Meisner, II, pp. 332–3.

14 Waldersee, diary entry for 14 December 1894, GStA Berlin, Waldersee Papers; omitted for the most part from Meisner, II, pp. 332–3.

15 Waldersee, diary entry for 24 March 1895, Meisner, II, p. 340. See Marschall's diary entry for 23 March 1895, Fuchs, *Großherzog von Baden*, III, p. 410, note.

16 Kaiser Wilhelm II to Bismarck, telegram, 23 March 1895, in Hohenlohe, *Denkwürdigkeiten der Reichskanzlerzeit*, p. 53. Bismarck's reply is to be found in GStA Berlin, BPH Rep. 53 No. 140; see also Marschall to Hohenlohe, 31 March 1895, Hohenlohe, *Denkwürdigkeiten der Reichskanzlerzeit*, p. 58.

17 Waldersee, diary entry for 24 March 1895, GStA Berlin, Waldersee Papers; cf. Meisner, II, pp. 340–1. See Jagemann to Brauer, 24 and 25 March 1895, Fuchs, *Großherzog von Baden*, III, Nos. 1429 and 1431.

18 Waldersee, diary entry for 25 March 1895, GStA Berlin, Waldersee Papers; omitted from Meisner, II, p. 341.

19 Holstein to Eulenburg, 7 April 1895, *Eulenburgs Korrespondenz*, III, No. 1101.

20 Waldersee, diary entry for 28 March 1895, GStA Berlin, Waldersee Papers; cf. Meisner, II, pp. 341–2.

21 Waldersee, diary entry for 2 April 1895, GStA Berlin, Waldersee Papers; cf. Meisner, II, p. 342. See Hohenlohe's notes on his conversation with the Kaiser of 24 March 1895, Hohenlohe, *Denkwürdigkeiten der Reichskanzlerzeit*, pp. 53–4.

22 Waldersee, diary entry for 28 March 1895, Meisner, II, pp. 341–2.

23 Kaiser Wilhelm II to his mother, 5 April 1895, AdHH Schloss Fasanerie.

24 Kaiser Wilhelm II's two speeches of 26 March 1895 are printed in Penzler, *Reden Kaiser Wilhelms II. in den Jahren 1888–1895*, pp. 301–3.

25 Waldersee, diary entry for 28 March 1895, GStA Berlin, Waldersee Papers; cf. Meisner, II, pp. 341–2.

26 Waldersee, diary entries for 17 March and 2 April 1895, GStA Berlin, Waldersee Papers; cf. Meisner, II, pp. 339–40 and 342.

27 Reuss to Wedel, 2 September 1895, Wedel Papers, Frankfurt a.M.

28 Eulenburg to Holstein, 22 June 1895, *Eulenburgs Korrespondenz*, III, No. 1114.

29 Eulenburg to Hohenlohe, 12 September 1895, Hohenlohe, *Denkwürdigkeiten der Reichskanzlerzeit*, pp. 97–8.

30 Eulenburg to Kuno Moltke, 15 June 1895, *Eulenburgs Korrespondenz*, III, No. 1112.

31 Eulenburg to Holstein, 22 June 1895, ibid., No. 1114. Bismarck's speech is printed in Bismarck, *Die gesammelten Werke*, XIII, pp. 605–8.

32 Eulenburg to Holstein, 1 October 1895, *Eulenburgs Korrespondenz*, III, No. 1141.

33 Empress Frederick to Bogumilla Freifrau von Stockmar, 14 April 1895, AdHH Schloss Fasanerie.

34 Kaiser Wilhelm II to Hohenlohe, 11 May 1895, Hohenlohe, *Denkwürdigkeiten der Reichskanzlerzeit*, p. 63. A facsimile of the telegram is printed ibid., pp. 64–5.

35 Kaiser Wilhelm II to Hohenlohe, 23 August 1895, ibid., pp. 92–3.

36 Marschall, diary entry for 25 August 1895, cited in *Eulenburgs Korrespondenz*, III, p. 1526.

37 Holstein to Eulenburg, 28 August 1895, ibid., No. 1124.

38 Hohenlohe to Kaiser Wilhelm II, undated, Hohenlohe, *Denkwürdigkeiten der Reichskanzlerzeit*, p. 93.

39 Kaiser Wilhelm II to Hohenlohe, 31 August 1895, ibid., p. 94.

40 Hohenlohe to Köller, 31 August 1895, ibid., p. 94.

41 Eulenburg to Hohenlohe, 21 September 1895, ibid., pp. 99–100; Waldersee, diary entry for 12 October 1895, GStA Berlin, Waldersee Papers, omitted from Meisner, II, pp. 361–2.

42 Marschall, diary entry for 2 September 1895, cited in *Eulenburgs Korrespondenz*, III, p. 1526.

43 Kaiser Wilhelm II, speech of 2 September 1895, in Schröder, *Tagebuch Kaiser Wilhelms II.*, pp. 216–17.

44 Marschall, diary entry for 6 September 1895, cited in *Eulenburgs Korrespondenz*, III, p. 1527.

45 Eulenburg to Hohenlohe, 12 September 1895, Hohenlohe, *Denkwürdigkeiten der Reichskanzlerzeit*, pp. 97–8.

46 Eulenburg to Hohenlohe, 21 September 1895, ibid., pp. 99–100.

47 Marschall to Eulenburg, 29 September 1895, *Eulenburgs Korrespondenz*, III, No. 1140.

48 Eulenburg to Hohenlohe, 1 October 1895, Hohenlohe, *Denkwürdigkeiten der Reichskanzlerzeit*, pp. 111–12. See also Eulenburg to Marschall, 2 October 1895, *Eulenburgs Korrespondenz*, III, No. 1142.

49 Kaiser Wilhelm II to Hohenlohe-Langenburg, 8 October 1895, Hohenlohe-Zentralarchiv Neuenstein, Hermann Hohenlohe-Langenburg Papers, Bü. 308.

50 Waldersee, diary entry for 9 December 1895, GStA Berlin, Waldersee Papers; omitted from Meisner, II, p. 362. Cf. the watered-down version of the speech in Penzler, *Reden Kaiser Wilhelms II. in den Jahren 1888–1895*, pp. 321–3.

51  See Holstein to Eulenburg, 21 February 1895, *Eulenburgs Korrespondenz*, III, No. 1093.

52  Kaiser Wilhelm II to Hohenlohe, 4 February 1896, Hohenlohe, *Denkwürdigkeiten der Reichs-kanzlerzeit*, pp. 164–5.

53  Hohenlohe to Kaiser Wilhelm II, 5 February 1896, ibid., p. 165.

54  Waldersee, diary entry for 12 February 1895, GStA Berlin, Waldersee Papers; omitted from Meisner, II, p. 338.

55  Kaiser Wilhelm II, speech to the leaders of the Agrarian League, 18 February 1895, Penzler, *Reden Kaiser Wilhelms II. in den Jahren 1888–1895*, pp. 294–5.

56  Kaiser Wilhelm II to Eulenburg, 21 February 1895, *Eulenburgs Korrespondenz*, III, No. 1094.

57  Kaiser Wilhelm II, speech of 24 February 1895 to the Brandenburg provincial diet, Penzler, *Reden Kaiser Wilhelms II. in den Jahren 1888–1895*, pp. 295–6.

58  Waldersee, diary entry for 25 January 1895, GStA Berlin, Waldersee Papers; cf. Meisner, II, pp. 336–7.

59  Waldersee, diary entry for 10 March 1895, GStA Berlin, Waldersee Papers; cf. Meisner, II, p. 339.

60  Erich Eyck, *Das Persönliche Regiment Wilhelms II. Politische Geschichte des Deutschen Kaiserreiches von 1890 bis 1914*, Zürich 1948, p. 157.

61  Waldersee, diary entry for 12 May 1896, GStA Berlin, Waldersee Papers; omitted from Meisner, II, p. 369.

62  Waldersee, diary entry for 14 May 1896, GStA Berlin, Waldersee Papers; omitted from Meisner, II, p. 369; Waldersee, diary entry for 17 May 1896, GStA Berlin, Waldersee Papers; omitted from Meisner, II, p. 370.

63  Cf. Chlodwig Hohenlohe to Prince Hermann zu Hohenlohe-Langenburg, 8 March 1895, Hohenlohe-Zentralarchiv Neuenstein, Hermann Hohenlohe-Langenburg Papers, Bü. 86.

64  Alexander Hohenlohe to his father, 14 February 1895, Hohenlohe, *Denkwürdigkeiten der Reichskanzlerzeit*, p. 39. See Hohenlohe's draft of a letter to the Kaiser, not sent, 12 February 1895, ibid., pp. 38–9.

65  Marschall to Eulenburg, 17 February 1895, *Eulenburgs Korrespondenz*, III, No. 1088.

66  Holstein to Bülow, 15 February 1895, *Holstein Papers*, III, No. 443.

67  Eulenburg to Hohenlohe, 16 February 1895, Hohenlohe, *Denkwürdigkeiten der Reichskanz-lerzeit*, pp. 39–40.

68  Kaiser Wilhelm II to Eulenburg, 12 February 1895, *Eulenburgs Korrespondenz*, II, No. 1083.

69  Holstein to Bülow, 7 February 1895, ibid., No. 1082; Marschall to Eulenburg, 17 February 1895, ibid., No. 1088.

70  Gustav von Kessel to Eulenburg, 13 February 1895, Hans von Arnim to Eulenburg, 14 February 1895, ibid., Nos. 1084 and 1085.

71  Eulenburg, diary entry, cited ibid., II, p. 1462. See Eulenburg's reply to the Kaiser of 14 February 1895, ibid., No. 1086; Eulenburg to Hohenlohe, 16 February 1895, Hohenlohe, *Denkwürdigkeiten der Reichskanzlerzeit*, pp. 39–42.

72  Eulenburg to Kaiser Wilhelm II, 22 February 1895, *Eulenburgs Korrespondenz*, III, No. 1095.

73  Eulenburg to Holstein, 19 February 1895, *Holstein Papers*, III, No. 446.

74  Eulenburg to Hohenlohe, 16 February 1895, Hohenlohe, *Denkwürdigkeiten der Reichskanz-lerzeit*, pp. 39–42; Eulenburg to Kaiser Wilhelm II, 18 February 1895, *Eulenburgs Korre-spondenz*, III, No. 1091. See Hohenlohe's reply to Eulenburg of 21 February 1895, ibid., No. 1092.

75  Kaiser Wilhelm II to Eulenburg, telegram, 21 February 1895, ibid., III, p. 1481.

76  Kaiser Wilhelm II to Eulenburg, 21 February 1895, ibid., No. 1094.

77  Marschall to Eulenburg, 17 February 1895, ibid., No. 1088.

78  Holstein to Bülow, 21 February 1895, *Holstein Papers*, III, No. 447; Similar: Holstein to Eulenburg, 21 February 1895, *Eulenburgs Korrespondenz*, III, No. 1093.

79 Holstein to Bülow, 17 February 1895, *Holstein Papers*, III, No. 444; Holstein to Eulenburg, 17 February 1895, *Eulenburgs Korrespondenz*, III, No. 1089.

80 Hohenlohe's notes of 12 May 1895, Hohenlohe, *Denkwürdigkeiten der Reichskanzlerzeit*, pp. 63–4.

81 Berlepsch to Hohenlohe, 15 May 1895, ibid., p. 65.

82 Hohenlohe to Eulenburg, 22 May 1895, ibid., pp. 68–70.

83 Eulenburg to Hohenlohe, 24 May 1895, ibid., pp. 71–2.

84 Hohenlohe, diary entry for 8 June 1895, ibid., p. 75.

85 Hohenlohe, diary entry for 28 June 1895, ibid., pp. 82–3.

86 Kaiser Wilhelm II to Berlepsch, 31 July 1895, ibid., p. 86.

87 Eulenburg to Hohenlohe, 24 May 1895, ibid., pp. 70–1.

88 Eulenburg to Hohenlohe, 24 May 1895, ibid., pp. 71–2. See above, p. 691.

89 Waldersee, diary entry for 20 October 1894, GStA Berlin, Waldersee Papers; cf. Meisner, II, p. 326.

90 Marschall to Eulenburg, 17 February 1895, *Eulenburgs Korrespondenz*, III, No. 1088.

91 Marschall, diary entry for 10 February 1895, cited ibid., p. 1409; also *Holstein Papers*, III, No. 444.

92 Eulenburg to Holstein, 22 June 1895, *Eulenburgs Korrespondenz*, III, No. 1114.

93 Eulenburg to Kaiser Wilhelm II, 4 August 1895, ibid., No. 1121.

94 Hohenlohe, notes of 31 May 1895, Hohenlohe, *Denkwürdigkeiten der Reichskanzlerzeit*, p. 74. See the discrepant account in Eulenburg to Grand Duke of Baden, 6 November 1895, *Eulenburgs Korrespondenz*, III, No. 1153.

95 Eulenburg to Holstein, 29 February 1896, *Holstein Papers*, III, No. 530.

96 Waldersee, diary entry for 10 October 1895, GStA Berlin, Waldersee Papers, cf. Meisner, II, p. 360.

97 Grand Duke of Baden to Eulenburg, 26 October 1895, Eulenburg to Grand Duke of Baden, 6 November 1895, *Eulenburgs Korrespondenz*, III, Nos. 1149 and 1153.

98 Waldersee, diary entry for 25 November 1895, GStA Berlin, Waldersee Papers; omitted from Meisner, II, p. 361. See Marschall's diary entry for 17 November 1895, cited in *Eulenburgs Korrespondenz*, III, p. 1593.

99 See Grand Duke of Baden to Eulenburg, 26 October 1895, *Eulenburgs Korrespondenz*, III, No. 1149.

100 Eulenburg to Grand Duke of Baden, 6 November 1895, ibid., No. 1153.

101 Eulenburg to Hohenlohe, 29 October 1895, Hohenlohe, *Denkwürdigkeiten der Reichskanzlerzeit*, p. 114.

102 Hohenlohe, diary entry for 31 October 1895, ibid., pp. 114ff.

103 Kaiser Wilhelm II to Hohenlohe, 31 October 1895, ibid., p. 116.

104 Eulenburg to Grand Duke of Baden, 6 November 1895, *Eulenburgs Korrespondenz*, III, No. 1153.

105 Hutten-Czapski to Holstein, 15 November 1895, *Holstein Papers*, III, No. 500.

106 See Hohenlohe, *Denkwürdigkeiten der Reichskanzlerzeit*, pp. 124–5.

107 Hohenlohe, diary entry for 27 November 1895, ibid., p. 125; Marschall, diary entries for 26 and 29 November 1895, cited in *Eulenburgs Korrespondenz*, III, p. 1593; Holstein to Eulenburg, 29 November 1895, ibid., Nos. 1159–60. On the Köller crisis, see also Nipperdey, *Deutsche Geschichte*, II, pp. 710–11; Clark, *Kaiser Wilhelm II*, pp. 78–9.

108 Hohenlohe to Kaiser Wilhelm II, 29 November 1895, Hohenlohe, *Denkwürdigkeiten der Reichskanzlerzeit*, pp. 126–7. See Marschall to Eulenburg, 20 December 1895, *Eulenburgs Korrespondenz*, III, No. 1174.

109 Hohenlohe, diary entry for 29 November 1895, Hohenlohe, *Denkwürdigkeiten der Reichskanzlerzeit*, p. 127.

110 Hohenlohe to Kaiser Wilhelm II, 1 December 1895, ibid., pp. 129–30.

111 Eulenburg to Kaiser Wilhelm II, 29 November 1895, *Eulenburgs Korrespondenz*, III, No. 1161; Eulenburg to Hohenlohe, 29 November 1895, Hohenlohe, *Denkwürdigkeiten der Reichskanzlerzeit*, pp. 127–8. See Holstein to Bülow, 29 November 1895, *Holstein Papers*, III, No. 505; Eulenburg to Holstein, 29 November 1895, ibid., No. 506.

112 Holstein to Eulenburg, 2 December 1895, *Eulenburgs Korrespondenz*, III, No. 1163.

113 See Haller, *Eulenburg*, p. 160.

114 Eulenburg to Kaiser Wilhelm II, 6 December 1895, *Eulenburgs Korrespondenz*, III, No. 1168.

115 Eulenburg to Lucanus, 7 December 1895, ibid., No. 1170; Eulenburg to Hohenlohe, 6 December 1895, Hohenlohe, *Denkwürdigkeiten der Reichskanzlerzeit*, pp. 137–8.

116 Eulenburg to Holstein, 4 December 1895, *Eulenburgs Korrespondenz*, III, p. 1603.

117 Eulenburg to Holstein, 7 December 1895, *Holstein Papers*, III, No. 508.

118 Eulenburg's notes of 3 December 1895, Haller, *Eulenburg*, pp. 160–1.

119 Eulenburg to Bülow, 6 December 1895, *Eulenburgs Korrespondenz*, III, No. 1169.

120 Eulenburg's notes of 3 December 1895, Haller, *Eulenburg*, pp. 160–1.

121 Marschall, diary entry for 4 December 1895, cited in *Eulenburgs Korrespondenz*, III, p. 1602.

122 Eulenburg to Kaiser Wilhelm II, 3 December 1895, ibid., No. 1164. See Eulenburg to Holstein, 7 December 1895, *Holstein Papers*, III, No. 508.

123 Lucanus to Eulenburg, 5 December 1895, *Eulenburgs Korrespondenz*, III, No. 1166.

124 Waldersee, diary entry for 9 December 1895, GStA Berlin, Waldersee Papers; omitted from Meisner, II, p. 362.

125 Holstein to Eulenburg, 22 December 1895, *Eulenburgs Korrespondenz*, III, No. 1175.

126 Kaiser Wilhelm II, order to the Prussian Ministry of State, 9 December 1895, Hohenlohe, *Denkwürdigkeiten der Reichskanzlerzeit*, p. 139.

127 Kaiser Wilhelm II to Hohenlohe, 6 May 1896, ibid., p. 218.

128 Holstein to Eulenburg, 5 December 1895, *Eulenburgs Korrespondenz*, III, No. 1165. Cf. Hohenlohe to Eulenburg, 9 December 1895, Hohenlohe, *Denkwürdigkeiten der Reichskanzlerzeit*, pp. 138–9; also Eulenburg to Holstein, 7 December 1895, *Holstein Papers*, III, No. 508.

129 Eulenburg to Hohenlohe, 6 December 1895, Hohenlohe, *Denkwürdigkeiten der Reichskanzlerzeit*, pp. 137–8.

130 See ibid., p. 138. Cf. Eulenburg to Holstein, 7 December 1895, *Holstein Papers*, III, No. 508; Lucanus to Hohenlohe, 7 December 1895, Hohenlohe, *Denkwürdigkeiten der Reichskanzlerzeit*, p. 138.

131 Kaiser Wilhelm II to Hohenlohe, 8 December 1895, *Denkwürdigkeiten der Reichskanzlerzeit*, p. 138. See Hohenlohe to Eulenburg, 9 December 1895, ibid., pp. 138–9; also Marschall, diary entries for 5 and 8 December 1895, cited in *Eulenburgs Korrespondenz*, III, p. 1606.

132 Hohenlohe to Eulenburg, 9 December 1895, Hohenlohe, *Denkwürdigkeiten der Reichskanzlerzeit*, pp. 138–9.

133 Eulenburg to Holstein, 7 December 1895, *Holstein Papers*, III, No. 508.

134 Eulenburg to Bülow, 6 December 1895, *Eulenburgs Korrespondenz*, III, No. 1169.

135 Eulenburg to Kaiser Wilhelm II, 6 December 1895, ibid., No. 1168.

136 Eulenburg to Hohenlohe, 6 December 1895, Hohenlohe, *Denkwürdigkeiten der Reichskanzlerzeit*, pp. 137–8.

137 Hohenlohe to Eulenburg, 9 December 1895, ibid., pp. 138–9; also Chlodwig Hohenlohe to Prince Hermann zu Hohenlohe-Langenburg, 27 December 1895, Hohenlohe-Zentralarchiv Neuenstein, Hermann Hohenlohe-Langenburg Papers, Bü. 86.

## 25  WILHELM AND WORLD POLITICS

1  See Canis, *Von Bismarck zur Weltpolitik*.

2  Sir Edmund Monson, report of 8 November 1894, RA I60/101.

3  Gosselin to Salisbury, 29 November 1895, cited in *Eulenburgs Korrespondenz*, III, pp. 1484–5.

4  Waldersee, diary entry for 22 October 1896, GStA Berlin, Waldersee Papers; printed only in part in Meisner, II, pp. 373–4.

5  Holstein to Eulenburg, 26 December 1895, *Eulenburgs Korrespondenz*, III, No. 1180.

6  Marschall, diary entry for 25 December 1895, Marschall Papers, Schloss Neuershausen.

7  Alexander Hohenlohe, draft letter from his father to the Kaiser, 1894/5, Hohenlohe, *Denkwürdigkeiten der Reichskanzlerzeit*, p. 27.

8  Hohenlohe to Kaiser Wilhelm II, undated [August 1895], ibid., pp. 93–4.

9  See e.g. Eulenburg to Marschall, 2 October 1895, *Eulenburgs Korrespondenz*, III, No. 1142; also Eulenburg's notes of 11 July 1892, ibid., II, No. 688; Eulenburg to Holstein, 2 October 1892, *Holstein Papers*, III, No. 377.

10  Chlodwig Hohenlohe to Prince Hermann zu Hohenlohe-Langenburg, 29 September 1895, Hohenlohe-Zentralarchiv Neuenstein, Hermann Hohenlohe-Langenburg Papers, Bü. 86.

11  Holstein to Radolin, 4 June 1895, *Holstein Papers*, III, No. 464.

12  Wolfgang J. Mommsen, *Großmachtstellung und Weltpolitik, 1870–1914. Die Außenpolitik des Deutschen Reiches*, Frankfurt a.M. 1993, p. 123. See Canis, *Von Bismarck zur Weltpolitik*, p. 14.

13  Hatzfeldt to Holstein, 15 March 1896, *Holstein Papers*, III, No. 532.

14  Hohenlohe's notes of 2 November 1894, Hohenlohe, *Denkwürdigkeiten der Reichskanzlerzeit*, p. 8, n. 3.

15  Hohenlohe's notes of 12 January 1895, ibid., p. 29. See Kaiser Wilhelm II to Hohenlohe, 16 January 1895, Hohenlohe's undated notes, ibid., pp. 29–31.

16  Waldersee, diary entry for 25 January 1895, GStA Berlin, Waldersee Papers; cf. Meisner, II, p. 336.

17  Ibid.

18  Herbette's report of 18 January 1895, *Documents Diplomatiques Français 1871–1914*, Ministère des Affaires Etrangères, ed., 41 vols., Paris 1929–36, XI, pp. 541ff.

19  Kaiser Wilhelm II, marginal notes on Eulenburg's report from Vienna of 17 January 1895, cited in *Holstein Papers*, III, p. 491.

20  See Holstein to Bülow, 23 January 1895, ibid., III, No. 437.

21  Waldersee, diary entry for 25 January 1895, GStA Berlin, Waldersee Papers; cf. Meisner, II, p. 336.

22  Hohenlohe to Holstein, 25 January 1895, *Holstein Papers*, III, No. 438.

23  Waldersee, diary entry for 3 March 1896, GStA Berlin, Waldersee Papers; cf. Meisner, II, p. 368; Hohenlohe, diary entry for 5 March 1896, Hohenlohe, *Denkwürdigkeiten der Reichskanzlerzeit*, p. 187.

24  Kaiser Wilhelm II to Hohenlohe, 31 August 1895, *Denkwürdigkeiten der Reichskanzlerzeit*, pp. 94–5. See below, p. 748.

25  Hohenlohe's report of 7 March 1896, Hohenlohe, *Denkwürdigkeiten der Reichskanzlerzeit*, pp. 191–2.

26  Kaiser Wilhelm II, marginal notes on the reports of 21 September 1895 and 18 and 19 April 1897, PA AA, Asservat No. 4.

27  Monson, telegram from Vienna, 28 February 1895, RA I60/105. See Eulenburg to Hohenlohe, 5 March 1895, Hohenlohe, *Denkwürdigkeiten der Reichskanzlerzeit*, p. 50.

28  Waldersee, diary entry for 2 April 1895, GStA Berlin, Waldersee Papers; omitted from Meisner, II, pp. 342ff.

29 Eulenburg's notes, 27 September 1895, *Eulenburgs Korrespondenz*, III, No. 1136.

30 Waldersee, diary entry for 20 October 1895, GStA Berlin, Waldersee Papers; omitted from Meisner, II, p. 361.

31 See Hohenlohe, *Denkwürdigkeiten der Reichskanzlerzeit*, p. 26. See Goetz, *Briefe Wilhems II. an den Zaren*, p. 288.

32 Hohenlohe's notes of 8 March 1896, Hohenlohe, *Denkwürdigkeiten der Reichskanzlerzeit*, p. 193.

33 Holstein to Hohenlohe, 8 March 1896, ibid., pp. 193–4.

34 See Marschall to Eulenburg, two telegrams, 8 March 1896, *Eulenburgs Korrespondenz*, III, Nos. 1193 and 1194; Eulenburg to Kaiser Wilhelm II, 9 March 1896, ibid., No. 1196.

35 Kaiser Wilhelm II to Hohenlohe, 8 March 1896, Hohenlohe, *Denkwürdigkeiten der Reichskanzlerzeit*, p. 194.

36 Hohenlohe to Kaiser Wilhelm II, 8 March 1896, ibid., pp. 194–5.

37 Kaiser Wilhelm II to Hohenlohe, 9 March 1896, ibid., pp. 195–6. Cf. Eulenburg to Bülow, 13 March 1896, *Eulenburgs Korrespondenz*, III, No. 1198.

38 Hohenlohe to Kaiser Wilhelm II, 9 March 1896, Hohenlohe, *Denkwürdigkeiten der Reichskanzlerzeit*, p. 196.

39 Hohenlohe to Kaiser Wilhelm II, 10 March 1896, ibid., pp. 197–8.

40 Bülow to Hohenlohe, 19 March 1896, ibid., p. 201.

41 Bülow to Holstein, 19 March 1896, *Holstein Papers*, III, No. 533.

42 Münster to Holstein, 19 March 1896, ibid., No. 534.

43 Bülow to Hohenlohe, 13 April 1896, Hohenlohe, *Denkwürdigkeiten der Reichskanzlerzeit*, pp. 208–11.

44 Kaiser Wilhelm II to Caprivi, telegram, 12 July 1893, cited in Folke Lindberg, *Kunglig utrikespolitik. Studier i svensk utrikespolitik under Oscar II och fram till borggårdskrisen*, Stockholm 1966, p. 110. See Eulenburg's notes of 11 July 1892, in *Eulenburgs Korrespondenz*, II, No. 688.

45 Hohenlohe, diary entry for 22 February 1895, Hohenlohe, *Denkwürdigkeiten der Reichskanzlerzeit*, p. 45.

46 Eulenburg's notes of 22 July 1895, *Eulenburgs Korrespondenz*, III, pp. 1516–17. See also ibid., No. 1119.

47 Kaiser Wilhelm II to Crown Prince Gustav of Sweden and Norway, 25 July 1895, printed in Hohenlohe, *Denkwürdigkeiten der Reichskanzlerzeit*, pp. 102–5.

48 Kaiser Wilhelm II to Crown Prince Gustav of Sweden and Norway, 27 September 1895, printed ibid., pp. 108–10.

49 Below, ch. 32.

50 Waldersee, diary entries for 4 and 23 May 1895, GStA Berlin, Waldersee Papers; cf. Meisner, II, pp. 347 and 349.

51 Waldersee, diary entry for 15 February 1895, GStA Berlin, Waldersee Papers; largely omitted from Meisner, II, pp. 338–9.

52 Hohenlohe's notes of 2 November 1894, Hohenlohe, *Denkwürdigkeiten der Reichskanzlerzeit*, pp. 7–8. See Marschall's diary entry for 31 October 1894, cited in *Eulenburgs Korrespondenz*, II, p. 1406.

53 Hohenlohe to Kaiser Wilhelm II, 18 November 1894, Hohenlohe, *Denkwürdigkeiten der Reichskanzlerzeit*, pp. 15–16.

54 Kaiser Wilhelm II, undated notes, printed ibid., pp. 52–3. See Holstein's notes of 27 March 1895, ibid., pp. 55–6.

55 Hohenlohe, diary entry for 11 April 1895, ibid., p. 58.

56 Senden-Bibran to Kaiser Wilhelm II, 22 April 1895, BA-MA Freiburg, Senden-Bibran Papers.

57  Holstein to Radolin, 18 June 1895, *Holstein Papers*, III, No. 470. See Radolin to Holstein, 10 August 1895, ibid., No. 483. See also Hohenlohe to Holstein, 6 August 1895, ibid., No. 481; also *Große Politik*, IX, Nos. 2285–90. Cf. Hohenlohe, diary entry for 10 September 1895, Hohenlohe, *Denkwürdigkeiten der Reichskanzlerzeit*, p. 96.

58  Hohenlohe to Kaiser Wilhelm II, undated [August 1895], Hohenlohe, *Denkwürdigkeiten der Reichskanzlerzeit*, pp. 93–4. See above, pp. 733–4.

59  Kaiser Wilhelm II to Hohenlohe, 31 August 1895, Hohenlohe, *Denkwürdigkeiten der Reichskanzlerzeit*, pp. 94–5. Cf. Holstein to Eulenburg, 2 and 7/8 April 1895, *Eulenburgs Korrespondenz*, III, No. 1101.

60  Hohenlohe to Eulenburg, 24 September 1895, *Eulenburgs Korrespondenz*, III, No. 1131.

61  Waldersee, diary entries for 4 and 23 May 1895, GStA Berlin, Waldersee Papers; cf. Meisner, II, pp. 347 and 349.

62  Eulenburg to Marschall, 30 September 1894, *Eulenburgs Korrespondenz*, III, No. 1008.

63  Kaiser Wilhelm II, marginal notes on Eulenburg's report from Vienna, PA AA, Asservat No. 4.

64  Waldersee, diary entry for 20 October 1894, GStA Berlin, Waldersee Papers; cf. Meisner, II, p. 326.

65  Waldersee, diary entries for 6 and 14 December 1894, GStA Berlin, Waldersee Papers; cf. Meisner, II, pp. 332–3. See above, p. 221. Cf. Kaiser Wilhelm II to Tsar Nicholas II, 8 November 1894, in Goetz, *Briefe Wilhelms II. an den Zaren*, pp. 287–8; Tsar Nicholas II to Kaiser Wilhelm II, 8 November 1894, Hohenlohe, *Denkwürdigkeiten der Reichskanzlerzeit*, p. 8.

66  Waldersee, diary entry for 21 November 1894, GStA Berlin, Waldersee Papers; omitted from Meisner, II, p. 332.

67  Hohenlohe, diary entry for 14 December 1894, Hohenlohe, *Denkwürdigkeiten der Reichskanzlerzeit*, p. 23.

68  Waldersee, diary entries for 6 and 14 December 1894, GStA Berlin, Waldersee Papers; cf. Meisner, II, pp. 332–3. Cf. Kaiser Wilhelm II to Tsar Nicholas II, 8 November 1894, Goetz, *Briefe Wilhelms II. an den Zaren*, pp. 287–8; Tsar Nicholas II to Kaiser Wilhelm II, 8 November 1894, Hohenlohe, *Denkwürdigkeiten der Reichskanzlerzeit*, p. 8.

69  Waldersee, diary entry for 25 January 1895, GStA Berlin, Waldersee Papers; this passage is omitted from Meisner, II, pp. 336–7.

70  Waldersee, diary entry for 2 April 1895, GStA Berlin, Waldersee Papers; omitted from Meisner, II, pp. 342ff.

71  Eulenburg's notes of 28 July 1895, *Eulenburgs Korrespondenz*, III, No. 1119.

72  Waldersee, diary entry for 21 August 1895, GStA Berlin, Waldersee Papers; this passage is omitted from Meisner, II, pp. 356–7.

73  Hohenlohe's notes of 2 November 1894, Hohenlohe, *Denkwürdigkeiten der Reichskanzlerzeit*, p. 7.

74  Holstein to Hohenlohe, 25 December 1894, ibid., p. 26.

75  Hohenlohe, diary entry for 26 December 1894, ibid.

76  Kaiser Wilhelm II to Tsar Nicholas II, 26 April 1895, Goetz, *Briefe Wilhelms II. an den Zaren*, pp. 290–2.

77  Friedrich Curtius, ed., *Denkwürdigkeiten des Fürsten Chlodwig zu Hohenlohe-Schillingsfürst*, 2 vols., Stuttgart 1906, II, p. 521.

78  Eulenburg's notes, 5 July 1895, *Eulenburgs Korrespondenz*, III, No. 1116.

79  Eulenburg's notes, 13 July 1895, ibid., No. 1117.

80  Kaiser Wilhelm II to Tsar Nicholas II, 10 July 1895, Goetz, *Briefe Wilhelms II. an den Zaren*, pp. 292–4.

81  Eulenburg's notes, 5 July 1895, *Eulenburgs Korrespondenz*, III, No. 1116.

82 Eulenburg's notes, 13 July 1895, ibid., No. 1117; also Eulenburg's notes of 28 July 1895, ibid., No. 1119.

83 The original sketch of Wilhelm II's world-famous drawing sports the signature 'Em u W 30/IV 95 Schlitz'. It is reproduced in Hans Wilderotter and Klaus-D. Pohl, eds., *Der letzte Kaiser. Wilhelm II. im Exil*, Gütersloh, Munich 1991, p. 321.

84 Eulenburg to Kaiserin Auguste Viktoria, 29 September 1895, *Eulenburgs Korrespondenz*, III, p. 1549.

85 Eulenburg to his mother, late September 1895, ibid., p. 1549.

86 Kaiser Wilhelm II to Tsar Nicholas II, 26 September 1895, Goetz, *Briefe Wilhelms II. an den Zaren*, pp. 294–6.

87 Eulenburg's notes, 27 September 1895, *Eulenburgs Korrespondenz*, III, No. 1136.

88 Kaiser Wilhelm II to Tsar Nicholas II, 26 September 1895, Goetz, *Briefe Wilhelms II. an den Zaren*, pp. 294–6.

89 Eulenburg to Hohenlohe, 28 and 30 September 1895, Hohenlohe, *Denkwürdigkeiten der Reichskanzlerzeit*, p. 102; also Radolin to Holstein, 28 September 1895, *Holstein Papers*, III, No. 487.

90 For Moltke the Younger, see Annika Mombauer, *Helmuth von Moltke and the Origins of the First World War*, Cambridge 2001.

91 Helmuth Moltke to Kaiser Wilhelm II, telegram of 30 September 1895, printed in Hohenlohe, *Denkwürdigkeiten der Reichskanzlerzeit*, p. 110. See Moltke's report to the Kaiser in *Große Politik*, IX, pp. 365–6.

92 Helmuth Moltke to Kaiser Wilhelm II, report on his farewell audience with Nicholas II, 3 October 1895, GStA Berlin, BPH Rep. 53 No. 116.

93 Eulenburg to Holstein, 1 October 1895, *Eulenburgs Korrespondenz*, III, No. 1141. See Radolin to Eulenburg, 2 October 1895, ibid., No. 1143.

94 Eulenburg to Hohenlohe, 1 October 1895, Hohenlohe, *Denkwürdigkeiten der Reichskanzlerzeit*, pp. 111–12.

95 Eulenburg's notes, 12/13 October 1895, *Eulenburgs Korrespondenz*, III, No. 1145.

96 Holstein to Eulenburg, 19 November 1895, ibid., No. 1156.

97 Holstein to Radolin, 30 October 1895, *Holstein Papers*, III, No. 496.

98 Kaiser Wilhelm II to Tsar Nicholas II, 25 October 1895, Goetz, *Briefe Wilhelms II. an den Zaren*, pp. 297–300. The Reich Chancellor was not shown this letter until 30 October. See Hohenlohe, *Denkwürdigkeiten der Reichskanzlerzeit*, p. 116.

99 Eulenburg's notes of 28 July 1895, *Eulenburgs Korrespondenz*, III, No. 1119. On the meeting of the then Prince Wilhelm with Tsar Alexander III at Brest-Litovsk, see *Young Wilhelm*, pp. 570–84.

100 Hohenlohe's notes of 2 November 1894, Hohenlohe, *Denkwürdigkeiten der Reichskanzlerzeit*, pp. 7–8. See Marschall's diary entry for 31 October 1894, cited in *Eulenburgs Korrespondenz*, II, p. 1406.

101 Eulenburg to Bülow, 12 November 1895, *Eulenburgs Korrespondenz*, III, No. 1154.

102 Waldersee, diary entry for 9 October 1894, GStA Berlin, Waldersee Papers; omitted from Meisner, II, p. 324.

103 Hohenlohe's notes of 2 November 1894, Hohenlohe, *Denkwürdigkeiten der Reichskanzlerzeit*, pp. 7–8. See Marschall's diary entry for 31 October 1894, cited in *Eulenburgs Korrespondenz*, II, p. 1406.

104 Eulenburg's notes, 28 July 1895, *Eulenburgs Korrespondenz*, III, No. 1119.

105 See Lobanov's report to the French Foreign Minister Hanotaux in *Documents Diplomatiques Français*, XII, p. 264.

106 Kaiser Wilhelm II, marginal notes, *Große Politik*, X, p. 147.

107 Eulenburg to Marschall, 6 November 1895, Hohenlohe, *Denkwürdigkeiten der Reichskanzlerzeit*, pp. 117–18.

108 Holstein to Bülow, 8 November 1895, ibid., p. 119. Cf. Hatzfeldt to Holstein, 10 November 1895, *Holstein Papers*, III, No. 497.

109 Holstein to Hohenlohe, 12 November 1895, Hohenlohe, *Denkwürdigkeiten der Reichskanzlerzeit*, p. 120. See Eulenburg to Kaiser Wilhelm II, 31 December 1895, *Eulenburgs Korrespondenz*, III, No. 1183.

110 Hohenlohe's notes of 13 November 1895, Hohenlohe, *Denkwürdigkeiten der Reichskanzlerzeit*, pp. 120–1. See Hutten-Czapski to Holstein, 15 November 1895, *Holstein Papers*, III, No. 500.

111 See the exchange of telegrams of 8 and 9 November 1895, *Große Politik*, X, Nos. 2452–3.

112 Holstein to Radolin, 16 November 1895, *Holstein Papers*, III, No. 501.

113 Eulenburg to Bülow, 12 November 1895, *Eulenburgs Korrespondenz*, III, No. 1154.

114 Eulenburg to Holstein, 16 November 1895, ibid., No. 1155.

115 Waldersee, diary entry for 9 December 1895, GStA Berlin, Waldersee Papers; omitted from Meisner, II, p. 362.

116 Waldersee, diary entry for 31 December 1895, GStA Berlin, Waldersee Papers; these passages are omitted from Meisner, II, p. 363.

117 Waldersee, diary entry for 9 December 1895, GStA Berlin, Waldersee Papers; omitted from Meisner, II, p. 362.

118 Szögyény, telegram, 14 November 1895, cited in Helmut Krausnick, 'Holstein, Österreich-Ungarn und die Meerengenfrage im Herbst 1895. Persönliches Regiment oder Regierungspolitik?', in *Forschungen zu Staat und Verfassung. Festgabe für Fritz Hartung*, Berlin 1958, pp. 519–20. See *Große Politik*, X, pp. 203–7.

119 Szögyény, report of 21 October 1908, in *Österreich-Ungarns Außenpolitik von der Bosnischen Krise 1908 bis zum Kriegsausbruch 1914*, Vienna, Leipzig 1930, p. 278. See Krausnick, 'Holstein, Österreich-Ungarn und die Meerengenfrage', pp. 485ff.

120 Szögyény, telegram, 14 November 1895, Krausnick, 'Holstein, Österreich-Ungarn und die Meerengenfrage', p. 520.

121 *Große Politik*, X, pp. 205ff.

## 26  GREAT BRITAIN AND THE SPECTRE OF ENCIRCLEMENT

1 Gosselin, report of 5 November 1894, RA I60/100.

2 Hatzfeldt to Holstein, 19 December 1894, *Holstein Papers*, III, No. 430.

3 Malet, report of December 1894, RA I60/104.

4 Waldersee, diary entry for 25 April 1895, GStA Berlin, Waldersee Papers; omitted from Meisner, II, p. 346.

5 Waldersee, diary entry for 23 May 1895, GStA Berlin, Waldersee Papers; omitted from Meisner, II, p. 349.

6 Kaiser Wilhelm II, marginal comment on Hatzfeldt's report of 11 November 1894, *Große Politik*, IX, No. 2161.

7 See Kaiser Wilhelm II to Queen Victoria, 12 July 1895, RA I60/119, in Buckle, *Letters of Queen Victoria*, II, pp. 535–6.

8 *Große Politik*, X, No. 2385.

9 Kiderlen-Wächter to Holstein, 7 August 1895, Hatzfeldt to Holstein, 14 August 1895, *Holstein Papers*, III, Nos. 482 and 486.

10 Hohenlohe's notes of 18 August 1895, Hohenlohe, *Denkwürdigkeiten der Reichskanzlerzeit*, p. 88.

11 Hatzfeldt to Holstein, 14 August 1895, *Holstein Papers*, III, No. 486.

12 Kaiser Wilhelm II, marginal notes, *Große Politik*, X, pp. 85, 102, 119, 134 *et passim*.

13 Kaiser Wilhelm II to Hohenlohe, 9 October 1895, Hohenlohe, *Denkwürdigkeiten der Reichskanzlerzeit*, pp. 112–13.

14 See the Kaiser's notes on the conversation with his mother, ibid., p. 123; also Empress Frederick to Queen Victoria, 1 January 1896, AdHH Schloss Fasanerie.

15 Kaiser Wilhelm II to Hohenlohe, 20 October 1895, *Große Politik*, X, No. 2437.

16 Holstein to Bülow, 23 October 1895, *Holstein Papers*, III, No. 490.

17 Kaiser Wilhelm II to Marschall, 25 October 1895, *Große Politik*, XI, No. 2579.

18 Kaiser Wilhelm II, undated notes, printed in Hohenlohe, *Denkwürdigkeiten der Reichskanzlerzeit*, pp. 52–3.

19 Eulenburg's notes, 24 September 1895, *Eulenburgs Korrespondenz*, III, No. 1129. See Eulenburg's notes of 12/13 October 1895, ibid., No. 1145.

20 Eulenburg to Bülow, 12 November 1895, ibid., No. 1154.

21 See Gosselin to Salisbury, 29 November 1895, ibid., II, pp. 1484–5.

22 See *Young Wilhelm*, pp. 318–19, and below, pp. 1065–6.

23 Lascelles, notes on a conversation with Salisbury of 4 December 1895, cited in Kennedy, *Anglo-German Antagonism*, pp. 219–20.

24 For the hostility of the British press at this time, see Reinermann, *Der Kaiser in England*, pp. 145ff.

25 Kaiser Wilhelm II to Queen Victoria, telegram, 20 June 1895, RA I60/117.

26 Kaiser Wilhelm II to Queen Victoria, 12 July 1895, RA I60/119, in Buckle, *Letters of Queen Victoria*, II, pp. 535–6.

27 Swaine to Bigge, 24 March 1895, RA I60/106.

28 Knollys to Bigge, 18 April 1895, RA I/108.

29 Hohenlohe to Kaiser Wilhelm II, 10 June 1895, Hohenlohe, *Denkwürdigkeiten der Reichskanzlerzeit*, p. 76.

30 See Kaiser Wilhelm II to Queen Victoria, 12 July 1895, RA I60/119, in Buckle, *Letters of Queen Victoria*, II, pp. 535–6.

31 Kiderlen-Wächter to Holstein, 7 August 1895, *Holstein Papers*, III, No. 482.

32 Waldersee, diary entry for 21 August 1895, GStA Berlin, Waldersee Papers; cf. Meisner, II, pp. 356–7.

33 See Hatzfeldt to Holstein, 14 August 1895, *Holstein Papers*, III, No. 486.

34 Kiderlen-Wächter to Holstein, 7 August 1895, ibid., No. 482.

35 Malet to Bigge, 1 August 1895, in Buckle, *Letters of Queen Victoria*, II, pp. 542–3; also Swaine to Bigge, 16 August 1895, RA I60/129.

36 RA QVJ, 6 August 1895, in Buckle, *Letters of Queen Victoria*, II, pp. 544–5; Queen Victoria to Salisbury, 8 August 1895, RA I60/121, printed ibid., p. 547; Salisbury to Bigge, 9 August 1895, RA I60/125, ibid., p. 548.

37 Eulenburg to Holstein, 11 August 1895, *Holstein Papers*, III, No. 484.

38 Lansdowne to Queen Victoria, 7 August 1895, in Buckle, *Letters of Queen Victoria*, II, pp. 545–6.

39 Kiderlen-Wächter to Holstein, 7 August 1895, *Holstein Papers*, III, No. 482.

40 Queen Victoria to Salisbury, 8 August 1895, RA I60/121, Salisbury to Queen Victoria, 8 August 1895, RA I60/123, both in Buckle, *Letters of Queen Victoria*, II, pp. 547–8.

41 Hatzfeldt to Holstein, 14 August 1895, *Holstein Papers*, III, No. 486; Waldersee, diary entry for 21 August 1895, GStA Berlin, Waldersee Papers; cf. Meisner, II, p. 356.

42 Kiderlen-Wächter to Holstein, 7 August 1895, *Holstein Papers*, III, No. 482.

43 Bigge to Lansdowne, 8 August 1895, in Buckle, *Letters of Queen Victoria*, II, p. 547.

44 Lansdowne to Bigge, 10 August 1895, ibid., p. 548.

45 Queen Victoria to Salisbury, 11 and 12 August 1895, ibid., pp. 549–50.

46 Salisbury to Queen Victoria, 11 August 1895, Lansdowne to Queen Victoria, 14 August 1895, Salisbury to Bigge, 16 August 1895, ibid., pp. 549–54.

47 Kaiser Wilhelm II to Queen Victoria, 12 August 1895, RA I60/126.

48 Salisbury to Bigge, 16 and 19 August 1895, in Buckle, *Letters of Queen Victoria*, II, pp. 553–5.

49 Bigge to Queen Victoria, 20 August 1895, RA I60/130.

50 For Wilhelm II and the appointment of Lascelles as ambassador, see Willem-Alexander van't Padje, 'At the Heart of the Growing Anglo-German Imperialist Rivalry: Two British Ambassadors in Berlin, 1884–1908', DPhil. diss., Oxford 2001, pp. 29ff.

51 Queen Victoria to Kaiser Wilhelm II, 28 August 1895, GStA Berlin, Brand.-Preuß. Hausarchiv, Rep. 52 W3 No. 11; copy in RA I60/132. Cf. Buckle, *Letters of Queen Victoria*, II, pp. 560–1.

52 Hatzfeldt to Holstein, 14 August 1895, *Holstein Papers*, III, No. 486. Malet's farewell address was printed in *The Times*, 14 October 1895, RA I60/134.

53 See below, pp. 779–83.

54 Waldersee, diary entry for 7 August 1895, GStA Berlin, Waldersee Papers; omitted from Meisner, II, p. 356.

55 Kaiser Wilhelm II to Queen Victoria, 12 August 1895, RA I60/126.

56 Lonsdale Papers, Lowther.

57 J. Meyer to Lord Lonsdale, 10 June and 29 July 1896, Chief Constable P. Clarke to Lord Lonsdale, 15 August 1896, Clarke to Meyer, 15 August 1896, Frederick Adams to Clarke, 26 August 1896, Lonsdale Papers, Cumbria Record Office, Carlisle.

58 Kaiser Wilhelm II to Countess of Lonsdale, 15 August 1895, Lonsdale Papers, Cumbria Record Office, Carlisle. Cf. Waldersee, diary entry for 21 August 1895, GStA Berlin, Waldersee Papers; omitted from Meisner, II, pp. 356–7.

59 Waldersee, diary entry for 7 August 1895, GStA Berlin, Waldersee Papers; omitted from Meisner, II, p. 356.

60 Ibid.

61 Waldersee, diary entry for 8 August 1895, GStA Berlin, Waldersee Papers; cf. Meisner, II, p. 356.

62 Waldersee, diary entries for 10 and 13 August 1895, GStA Berlin, Waldersee Papers; omitted from Meisner, II, p. 356.

63 Kaiser Wilhelm II, speech of 18 January 1896, Penzler, *Reden Kaiser Wilhelms II. in den Jahren 1896–1900*, Leipzig 1904, pp. 9–10.

64 Waldersee, diary entry for 31 January 1896, GStA Berlin, Waldersee Papers; omitted from Meisner, II, pp. 366–7.

65 Chlodwig Hohenlohe to Prince Hermann zu Hohenlohe-Langenburg, 8 March 1895, Hohenlohe-Zentralarchiv Neuenstein, Hermann Hohenlohe-Langenburg Papers, Bü. 86.

66 Kaiser Wilhelm II, marginal notes of 6 October 1895, cited in Nancy Mitchell, *The Danger of Dreams. German and American Imperialism in Latin America*, Chapel Hill, London 1999, pp. 114–15.

67 Eulenburg to Kayser, 24 September 1895, *Eulenburgs Korrespondenz*, III, No. 1130.

68 Hohenlohe, note of 31 January 1895, Hohenlohe, *Denkwürdigkeiten der Reichskanzlerzeit*, p. 32.

69 Alexander Hohenlohe to Eulenburg, 17 February 1895, ibid., pp. 42–44.

70 Chlodwig Hohenlohe to Prince Hermann zu Hohenlohe-Langenburg, 29 September 1895, Hohenlohe-Zentralarchiv Neuenstein, Hermann Hohenlohe-Langenburg Papers, Bü. 86.

71 Hohenlohe, diary entry for 2 November 1894, Hohenlohe, *Denkwürdigkeiten der Reichskanzlerzeit*, pp. 7–8. See above, pp. 745–6.

72 Waldersee, diary entry for 10 July 1895, GStA Berlin, Waldersee Papers; omitted from Meisner, II, p. 352.

73 Hohenlohe, diary entry for 1 March 1896, Hohenlohe, *Denkwürdigkeiten der Reichskanzlerzeit*, p. 185.

74 Hohenlohe to Kaiser Wilhelm II, 7 March 1896, ibid., p. 188.

75 Ibid.

76 Ibid., pp. 190–1.

77 Kaiser Wilhelm II, marginal notes on Bülow's report from Rome of 21 July 1896, *Große Politik*, XI, p. 295.

78 Malet to Queen Victoria, 16 June 1894, RA I60/77.

79 Lord Kimberley, report of 21 November 1894, RA I60/102.

80 Waldersee, diary entry for 7 August 1895, GStA Berlin, Waldersee Papers; omitted from Meisner, II, p. 356.

81 Elizabeth Longford, *Jameson's Raid: The Prelude to the Boer War*, London 1984.

82 See Matthew S. Seligmann, *Rivalry in Southern Africa, 1893–1899. The Transformation of German Colonial Policy*, London 1998, pp. 70–4.

83 See Kennedy, *Anglo-German Antagonism*, p. 220.

84 Waldersee, diary entry for 21 August 1895, GStA Berlin, Waldersee Papers; omitted from Meisner, II, pp. 356–7. See G. W. F. Hallgarten, *Imperialismus vor 1914. Die soziologischen Grundlagen der Außenpolitik europäischer Großmächte vor dem Ersten Weltkrieg*, 2 vols., Munich 1963, I, pp. 372–3; Seligmann, *Rivalry*, pp. 74–5; Canis, *Von Bismarck zur Weltpolitik*, pp. 166–7.

85 Marschall's notes of 15 October 1895, *Große Politik*, XI, No. 2578. For the ensuing crisis, see van't Padje, 'Anglo-German Imperialist Rivalry', pp. 185–93.

86 Kaiser Wilhelm II, marginal notes, *Große Politik*, XI, No. 2578, p. 7.

87 Holstein to Eulenburg, 28 October 1895, *Holstein Papers*, III, No. 492.

88 Kaiser Wilhelm II to Tsar Nicholas II, 25 October 1895, Goetz, *Briefe Wilhelms II. an den Zaren*, pp. 297–300.

89 See above, pp. 759–60.

90 Kaiser Wilhelm II to Marschall, 25 October 1895, *Große Politik*, XI, No. 2579.

91 Proclamation of 27 October 1895, *Große Politik*, XI, No. 2579, pp. 10–11, note.

92 See *Große Politik*, XI, No. 2579, p. 11, note.

93 See the exchange of telegrams between 29 October and 17 November 1895 with the Kaiser's marginal notes, *Große Politik*, XI, Nos. 2581–4.

94 Eulenburg to Holstein, 28 October 1895, *Holstein Papers*, III, No. 492; also Eulenburg to Bülow, 12 November 1895, *Eulenburgs Korrespondenz*, III, No. 1154.

95 Eulenburg to Holstein, 29 October 1895, *Holstein Papers*, III. No. 493.

96 Holstein to Eulenburg, 2 November 1895, *Eulenburgs Korrespondenz*, III, No. 1152.

97 Ibid.

98 Eulenburg to Bülow, 12 November 1895, ibid., No. 1154.

99 Eulenburg to Marschall, 6 November 1895, in Hohenlohe, *Denkwürdigkeiten der Reichskanzlerzeit*, pp. 117ff. See Eulenburg to Holstein, 31 January 1896, *Holstein Papers*, III. No. 525.

100 Kaiser Wilhelm II, marginal notes on Marschall's report of 17 November 1895, *Große Politik*, XI, No. 2584.

101 Waldersee, diary entry for 9 December 1895, GStA Berlin, Waldersee Papers; omitted from Meisner, II, p. 362.

102 Gerd Fesser, 'Ohrfeige für England. Die brisante Depesche Wilhelms II. an Burenpräsidenten "Ohm" Krüger', *Die Zeit*, 5 January 1996, p. 28. See Rich, *Friedrich von Holstein*, II, p. 469; Kennedy, *Anglo-German Antagonism*, pp. 220ff.

103 Marschall, diary entries for 28 and 31 December 1895, Marschall Papers, Schloss Neuershausen. See below, pp. 786–8.

104 Marschall, diary entry for 31 December 1895, Marschall Papers, Schloss Neuershausen.

105 Marschall, diary entry for 1 January 1896, ibid.

106 Hohenlohe, diary entry for 3 January 1896, Hohenlohe, *Denkwürdigkeiten der Reichskanzlerzeit*, p. 151; also above, p. 727, and below, pp. 799–807.

107 Kaiser Wilhelm II, marginal notes on reports from Cape Town, cited in Jochen Laufer, 'Die deutsche Südafrikapolitik 1890–1898 im Spannungsfeld zwischen deutsch–englischen Beziehungen, Wirtschaftsinteressen und Expansionsforderungen in der bürgerlichen Öffentlichkeit', diss., Humboldt-Universität Berlin 1986, p. 213.

108 Waldersee, diary entry for 5 January 1896, GStA Berlin, Waldersee Papers; cf. Meisner, II, p. 363.

109 Eyre Crowe to his mother, 9 January 1896, Crowe Papers, Bodleian Library, Oxford.

110 Lascelles to Salisbury, 4 January 1896, quoted in van't Padje, 'Anglo-German Imperialist Rivalry', pp. 89–90.

111 Kaiser Wilhelm II to Tsar Nicholas II, 2 January 1896, Goetz, *Briefe Wilhelm II. an den Zaren*, pp. 300–1.

112 Canis, *Von Bismarck zur Weltpolitik*, p. 179.

113 Hohenlohe, diary entry for 3 January 1896, Hohenlohe, *Denkwürdigkeiten der Reichskanzlerzeit*, p. 151.

114 Marschall, diary entry for 3 January 1896, Marschall Papers, Schloss Neuershausen. Cf. Alexander Hohenlohe's retrospective account of February 1914 in Hohenlohe, *Denkwürdigkeiten der Reichskanzlerzeit*, pp. 612–13.

115 Kaiser Wilhelm II to President Krüger, telegram, 3 January 1896, *Große Politik*, XI, pp. 31–2.

116 See above all *Große Politik*, I, pp. 287–9; Eyck, *Das Persönliche Regiment*, pp. 131ff.; Michael Balfour, *The Kaiser and His Times*, London 1975, pp. 193–4; Robert K. Massie, *Dreadnought. Britain, Germany and the Coming of the Great War*, New York 1991, pp. 222–5; Cecil, *Wilhelm II*, I, pp. 285–8.

117 Empress Frederick to Queen Victoria, 4 January 1896, cited in Sir Sidney Lee, *King Edward VII: A Biography*, 2 vols., London 1925–7, I, p. 727; Lascelles to Salisbury, 7 January 1896, van't Padje, 'Anglo-German Imperialist Rivalry', pp. 94ff.; Spitzemberg, diary entry for 5 January 1896, *Tagebuch*, pp. 340–1; D. Chapman-Huston, ed., *The Private Diaries of Princess Daisy of Pless, 1873–1914*, London 1950, p. 50; Lerchenfeld to Crailsheim, 7 January 1896, cited in Ekkehard-Teja P. W. Wilke, *Political Decadence in Imperial Germany. Personnel–Political Aspects of the German Government Crisis 1894–1897*, Urbana, Chicago, London 1976, p. 168; Hugo Graf Lerchenfeld-Koefering, *Erinnerungen und Denkwürdigkeiten*, Berlin 1935, pp. 373 and 385; Baron von Eckardstein, *Ten Years at the Court of St James, 1895–1905*, London 1921, pp. 84–6.

118 See Laufer, 'Deutsche Südafrikapolitik', pp. 98ff.; Seligmann, *Rivalry*, pp. 92ff.; Canis, *Von Bismarck zur Weltpolitik*, pp. 178ff.; Clark, *Kaiser Wilhelm II*, p. 133.

119 Marschall, diary entry for 30 December 1895, Marschall Papers, Schloss Neuershausen. See Holstein to Hatzfeldt, 1 January 1896, in G. Ebel, *Botschafter Paul Graf von Hatzfeldt. Nachgelassene Papiere 1838–1901*, 2 vols., Boppard am Rhein 1976, pp. 1065–6.

120 Marschall, diary entry for 31 December 1895, Marschall Papers, Schloss Neuershausen.

121 Marschall, diary entry for 1 January 1896, ibid.

122 Marschall, diary entry for 2 January 1896, ibid.

123 Fesser, 'Ohrfeige für England', p. 28.

124 Marschall, diary entry for 2 January 1896, Marschall Papers, Schloss Neuershausen.

125 Ibid.

126 Canis, *Von Bismarck zur Weltpolitik*, p. 181.

127 Marschall, diary entries for 3 and 4 January 1896, Marschall Papers, Schloss Neuershausen. See Dönhoff's report of 6 January 1896 on the unanimous praise for the Krüger telegram in the Saxon press, PA AA. See Evans, *Kneipengespräche*, pp. 346–7.

128 Marschall, diary entries for 4–11 January 1896, Marschall Papers, Schloss Neuershausen.

129 See below, ch. 28.

130  Eyre Crowe to his mother, 9 January 1896, Crowe Papers, Bodleian Library, Oxford.

131  Fesser, 'Ohrfeige für England', p. 28.

132  Swaine, report of January 1896, RA I60/149.

133  Hohenlohe, diary entry for 9 February 1896, Hohenlohe, *Denkwürdigkeiten der Reichskanz-lerzeit*, p. 169. See Monts to Bülow, 24 February 189[6], in Bülow, *Memoirs*, I, pp. 32ff.; Hatzfeldt to Holstein, 28 April 1896, *Holstein Papers*, III, No. 543.

134  Holstein to Bülow, 22 April 1896, *Holstein Papers*, III, No. 541. See Seligmann, *Rivalry*, pp. 128–9.

135  Münster to Holstein, 13 January 1896, *Holstein Papers*, III, No. 521.

136  Kaiser Wilhelm II, marginal comments on Münster's report from Paris of 16 January 1896, PA AA, Asservat No. 4, printed in *Große Politik*, XI, p. 82. See the Kaiser's angry comment 'all bosh' on Hatzfeldt's report from London of 17 January 1896, cited in *Holstein Papers*, III, p. 586.

137  Waldersee, diary entry for 7 January 1896, GStA Berlin, Waldersee Papers; omitted from Meisner, II, p. 364.

138  Ibid.

139  Waldersee, diary entry for 10 January 1896, GStA Berlin, Waldersee Papers; cf. Meisner, II, p. 364.

140  Ibid.

141  Waldersee, diary entry for 11 January 1896, GStA Berlin, Waldersee Papers; omitted for the most part from Meisner, II, p. 364.

142  Waldersee, diary entry for 12 January 1896, GStA Berlin, Waldersee Papers; cf. Meisner, II, pp. 364–5.

143  Waldersee, diary entry for 10 January 1896, GStA Berlin, Waldersee Papers; cf. Meisner, II, p. 364. Cf. Tirpitz to Stosch, 13 February 1896, printed in Tirpitz, *Erinnerungen*, pp. 54–6.

144  RA QVJ, 3 and 5 January 1896; Queen Victoria to Kaiser Wilhelm II, 5 January 1896, RA O45/169, in Buckle, *Letters of Queen Victoria*, III, pp. 7ff. Cf. the slightly different version in RA O45/55.

145  Knollys to Bigge, 4 January 1896, in Buckle, *Letters of Queen Victoria*, III, pp. 7–8.

146  Hohenlohe, diary entry for 9 February 1896, Hohenlohe, *Denkwürdigkeiten der Reichskanz-lerzeit*, p. 169.

147  Empress Frederick to Queen Victoria, 4 and 11 January 1896, AdHH Schloss Fasanerie. See also Münster to Holstein, 13 January 1896, *Holstein Papers*, III, No. 521.

148  According to Anton Monts, the Kaiser's 'private' letter was not shown to the officials in the Wilhelmstrasse. See Bülow, *Memoirs*, I, p. 32, and below, p. 794. In actual fact the files of the Auswärtiges Amt contain Wilhelm II's original draft with numerous alterations in his own hand. The version printed in Hohenlohe's *Denkwürdigkeiten der Reichskanzlerzeit* (pp. 154–6) is based on a copy made by the Chancellor of this improved text. The letter eventually sent to Windsor differs again in some of its wording from that version. Cf. Cecil, *Wilhelm II*, I, p. 288.

149  Kaiser Wilhelm II to Queen Victoria, 8 January 1896, RA Z500/5. The Queen sent copies of Wilhelm's letter and of her reply to her eldest daughter: Empress Frederick to Queen Victoria, 18 January 1896, AdHH Schloss Fasanerie.

150  See Cecil, *Wilhelm II*, I, p. 288.

151  Kaiser Wilhelm II to Queen Victoria, Queen Victoria to Kaiser Wilhelm II, 23 February 1896, RA I60/146–7; Swaine to Bigge, 2 March 1896, RA I60/151.

152  Empress Frederick to Queen Victoria, 4 February 1896, AdHH Schloss Fasanerie.

153  Waldersee, diary entry for 4 February 1896, GStA Berlin, Waldersee Papers; cf. Meisner, II, p. 367. Cf. Holstein to Hohenlohe, 8 March 1896, Hohenlohe, *Denkwürdigkeiten der Reichskanzlerzeit*, p. 192.

154 Monts to Bülow, 24 February 189[6], in Bülow, *Denkwürdigkeiten*, I, pp. 34. Cf. Bülow, *Memoirs*, I, p. 32.

155 Hohenlohe, diary for 9 February 1896, Hohenlohe, *Denkwürdigkeiten der Reichskanzlerzeit*, p. 169. See Monts to Bülow, 24 February 189[6], in Bülow, *Memoirs*, I, pp. 32ff.; Hatzfeldt to Holstein, 28 April 1896, *Holstein Papers*, III, No. 543.

156 Eulenburg's notes of 12/13 October 1895, *Eulenburgs Korrespondenz*, III, No. 1145. Both the Kaiserin and Senden-Bibran were outraged at the Kaiser's decision to rent a yacht in England.

157 Waldersee, diary entry for 3 March 1896, GStA Berlin, Waldersee Papers; omitted from Meisner, II, pp. 368–9. In January 1896, Waldersee recorded that the Kaiser had now decided neither to visit Cowes in the summer nor to rent an English yacht for his Mediterranean cruise in the spring, saying: 'With that I am giving up the one thing that I really enjoy' (Waldersee, diary entry for 21 January 1896, GStA Berlin, Waldersee Papers; cf. Meisner, II, pp. 365–6). The Kaiser and Kaiserin began their Mediterranean cruise – in a German yacht – on 28 March 1896.

158 Empress Frederick to Queen Victoria, 29 February 1896, AdHH Schloss Fasanerie, Empress Frederick to Kaiser Wilhelm II, 13 March 1896, GStA Berlin, BPHA Rep. 52T No. 13.

159 Kaiser Wilhelm II to Empress Frederick, 14 March 1896, AdHH Schloss Fasanerie.

160 Kaiser Wilhelm II to his mother, undated [March 1896] and 18 March 1896, ibid.; Hohenlohe, diary entry for 16 March 1896, Hohenlohe, *Denkwürdigkeiten der Reichskanzlerzeit*, p. 199.

161 Empress Frederick to Queen Victoria, 19, 24, 26 and 28 March 1896, AdHH Schloss Fasanerie.

162 Empress Frederick to Queen Victoria, 12 April 1896, ibid.

163 Waldersee, diary entry for 21 January 1896, GStA Berlin, Waldersee Papers; cf. Meisner, II, pp. 365–6.

164 Hohenlohe, diary entry for 5 March 1896, Hohenlohe, *Denkwürdigkeiten der Reichskanzlerzeit*, p. 187.

165 Hohenlohe to Hatzfeldt, 4 March 1896, *Große Politik*, XI, No. 2770.

166 Marschall, note of 4 March 1896, ibid., No. 2771.

167 Hohenlohe, diary entry for 7 March 1896, Hohenlohe, *Denkwürdigkeiten der Reichskanzlerzeit*, pp. 191–2; also Hohenlohe to Holstein, 8 March 1896, ibid., pp. 192–3.

168 Kaiser Wilhelm II, marginal notes on Hatzfeldt's report from London of 12 March 1896, *Große Politik*, XI, p. 241; Kiderlen-Wächter to Holstein, 25 March 1896, *Holstein Papers*, III, No. 537. The editors of the *Große Politik der Europäischen Kabinette* were also convinced that the British Dongola expedition could be 'traced back directly to Wilhelm II': *Große Politik*, XI, p. 235.

169 Kaiser Wilhelm II, marginal notes on Radolin's report from St Petersburg of 21 March 1896, *Große Politik*, XI, p. 168.

170 Hohenlohe, diary entry for 16 March 1896 with note, Hohenlohe, *Denkwürdigkeiten der Reichskanzlerzeit*, p. 199. For Salisbury's motives, see *Große Politik*, XI, No. 2698ff., and Holstein to Radolin, 22 March 1896, *Holstein Papers*, III, No. 536.

171 Kaiser Wilhelm II, marginal notes on Bülow's report from Rome of 13 May 1896, *Große Politik*, XI, p. 253.

172 The part played by the Kaiser in Germany's decision to build a fleet of battleships is fully explored in chapter 32.

173 Kiderlen-Wächter to Holstein, 25 March 1896, *Holstein Papers*, III, No. 537.

174 Hatzfeldt to Holstein, 15 March 1896, ibid., No. 532.

175 Marschall's notes of 13 March 1896, *Große Politik*, XI, No. 2779.

27   ENDGAME: THE BREAKTHROUGH TO DECISIVE PERSONAL POWER

1 Marschall, diary entry for 25 January 1896, cited in *Eulenburgs Korrespondenz*, III, pp. 1639–40.

2 Eulenburg to Kaiser Wilhelm II, 27 February 1896, ibid., No. 1192.

3 Eulenburg to Bülow, 13 March 1896, ibid., No. 1198. See Bülow's reply of 20 March 1896, ibid., No. 1201.

4 Holstein to Eulenburg, 1 May 1896, ibid., No. 1213.

5 Holstein to Eulenburg, 6 May 1896, ibid., No. 1219.

6 Holstein to Eulenburg, 5 May 1896, *Holstein Papers*, III, No. 546.

7 Hohenlohe to Kaiser Wilhelm II, 20 April 1896, Hohenlohe, *Denkwürdigkeiten der Reichskanzlerzeit*, pp. 213–14.

8 Kaiser Wilhelm II, marginal notes of 21 April 1896, GStA Berlin, Zivilkabinett 2.2.1. No. 13162/1.

9 Princess Viktoria of Schaumburg-Lippe to Kaiser Wilhelm II, 21 July 1897, GStA Berlin, 2.2.1. No. 13162/1; Hereditary Princess Charlotte of Saxe-Meiningen to Ellen Freifrau von Heldburg, 14 April 1895, Thüringisches Staatsarchiv Meiningen, HA 342. For Charlotte's intrigues in the Lippe succession dispute, see Röhl, *Kaiser and His Court*, p. 90.

10 Kaiser Wilhelm II to his mother, 5 April 1895, AdHH Schloss Fasanerie.

11 Hohenlohe, diary entry for 22 April 1896, Hohenlohe, *Denkwürdigkeiten der Reichskanzlerzeit*, p. 214; Hohenlohe to Lucanus, 22 April 1896, GStA Berlin, Zivilkabinett 2.2.1. No. 13162/1.

12 Hohenlohe to Kaiser Wilhelm II, 22 April 1896, Hohenlohe, *Denkwürdigkeiten der Reichskanzlerzeit*, p. 214.

13 Kaiser Wilhelm II to Hohenlohe, 23 April 1896, ibid., p. 215.

14 Holstein to Eulenburg, 5 May 1896, *Holstein Papers*, III, No. 546.

15 Hohenlohe to Kaiser Wilhelm II, 23 April 1896, GStA Berlin, Zivilkabinett 2.2.1. No. 13162/1; printed in part in Hohenlohe, *Denkwürdigkeiten der Reichskanzlerzeit*, pp. 215–16.

16 Hohenlohe, diary entry for 4 May 1896, Hohenlohe, *Denkwürdigkeiten der Reichskanzlerzeit*, pp. 215–16.

17 Holstein to Eulenburg, 5 May 1896, *Holstein Papers*, III, No. 546.

18 Ibid.

19 Kaiser Wilhelm II to Lucanus, 16 July 1896, GStA Berlin, Rep. 89, No. 13162/1.

20 The Lippe succession crisis would preoccupy the Kaiser for many months to come and would lead to further disputes with the Chancellor and the King of Saxony. See the documents and letters in GStA Berlin, 2.2.10. No. 2796; GStA Berlin, 2.2.1. No. 13162/1; Hohenlohe, *Denkwürdigkeiten der Reichskanzlerzeit*, pp. 390 and 407–8.

21 See *Young Wilhelm*, pp. 737–40.

22 See Karl Möckl, *Die Prinzregentenzeit. Gesellschaft und Politik während der Ära des Prinzregenten Luitpold in Bayern*, Munich 1972, pp. 393ff. See Prince Ernst zu Hohenlohe-Langenburg to his father, 13 June 1896, Hohenlohe-Zentralarchiv Neuenstein, Hermann Hohenlohe-Langenburg Papers, Bü. 62.

23 Marschall to Hohenlohe, 18 June 1896, Hohenlohe, *Denkwürdigkeiten der Reichskanzlerzeit*, pp. 236–7.

24 Hohenlohe to Kaiser Wilhelm II, 23 June 1896, ibid., pp. 237–8.

25 Eulenburg to Holstein, 5 July 1896, Enclosure I, *Holstein Papers*, III, No. 554.

26 Dieter Albrecht, ed., Hugo Graf Lerchenfeld-Kœfering, *Kaiser Wilhelm II. als Persönlichkeit und Herrscher*, Regensburger Historische Forschungen, Vol. 11, Kallmünz 1985, pp. 29ff. For the Kaiser's mood in Kiel in June 1896 see below, p. 828.

27 Kaiser Wilhelm II to Hohenlohe, telegram, 30 June 1896, Hohenlohe, *Denkwürdigkeiten der Reichskanzlerzeit*, pp. 238–40.

28 Lerchenfeld-Koefering, *Kaiser Wilhelm II. als Persönlichkeit und Herrscher*, p. 31.

29 Eulenburg to Holstein, 5 July 1896, Enclosure I, *Holstein Papers*, III, No. 554.

30 See Hull, *Entourage*, pp. 216ff.

31 Waldersee, diary entry for 5 January 1896, GStA Berlin, Waldersee Papers; cf. Meisner, II, p. 363.

32 Waldersee, diary entry for 9 December 1895, GStA Berlin, Waldersee Papers; omitted from Meisner, II, p. 362.

33 Waldersee, diary entry for 5 January 1896, GStA Berlin, Waldersee Papers; cf. Meisner, II, p. 363.

34 Ibid.

35 Hohenlohe, diary entry for 3 January 1896, Hohenlohe, *Denkwürdigkeiten der Reichskanzlerzeit*, p. 151; also Holstein to Eulenburg, 2 January 1896, *Holstein Papers*, III, No. 1185.

36 Waldersee, diary entry for 5 January 1896, GStA Berlin, Waldersee Papers; cf. Meisner, II, p. 363.

37 Hohenlohe, diary entry for 3 January 1896, Hohenlohe, *Denkwürdigkeiten der Reichskanzlerzeit*, p. 151; also Holstein to Eulenburg, 2 January 1896, *Eulenburgs Korrespondenz*, III, No. 1185.

38 Waldersee, diary entry for 5 January 1896, GStA Berlin, Waldersee Papers; cf. Meisner, II, p. 363.

39 Waldersee, diary entry for 3 March 1896, GStA Berlin, Waldersee Papers; omitted from Meisner, II, pp. 368–9.

40 Eulenburg to Bülow, 13 March 1896, *Eulenburgs Korrespondenz*, III, No. 1198.

41 Kaiser Wilhelm II to Hohenlohe, 14 March 1896, Hohenlohe, *Denkwürdigkeiten der Reichskanzlerzeit*, pp. 198–9.

42 Hohenlohe, diary entry for 16 March 1896, ibid., p. 199.

43 Holstein to Eulenburg, 19 June 1896, *Eulenburgs Korrespondenz*, III, No. 1234.

44 Holstein to Eulenburg, 17 February 1895, ibid., No. 1089.

45 Holstein to Eulenburg, 17 December 1895, ibid., No. 1171. Several passages of this letter are printed in Haller, *Eulenburg*, pp. 181–2; also Holstein to Bülow, 18 December 1895, *Holstein Papers*, III, No. 511. See Eulenburg to Holstein, 19 December 1895, ibid., No. 513; Eulenburg to Hohenlohe, 19 December 1895, Hohenlohe, *Denkwürdigkeiten der Reichskanzlerzeit*, pp. 143–4.

46 Holstein to Eulenburg, 9 February 1896, *Holstein Papers*, III, No. 528.

47 Eulenburg to Holstein, 14 February 1896, Haller, *Eulenburg*, pp. 194–5; Eulenburg to Holstein, 19 February 1896, *Holstein Papers*, III, No. 529. See Otto Hammann, *Bilder aus der letzten Kaiserzeit*, Berlin 1922, pp. 14–15.

48 Eulenburg to Bülow, 12 November 1895, *Eulenburgs Korrespondenz*, III, No. 1154.

49 Hohenlohe, diary entry for 1 February 1896, Hohenlohe, *Denkwürdigkeiten der Reichskanzlerzeit*, p. 164.

50 Hohenlohe, note of 28 February 1896, ibid., pp. 181–2; also Hohenlohe's comments of 3 May 1896, ibid., pp. 216–17.

51 Hohenlohe, diary entry for 2 March 1896, ibid., p. 186.

52 Hohenlohe, diary entry for 15 June 1896, ibid., p. 235.

53 Eulenburg to Bülow, 13 March 1896, *Eulenburgs Korrespondenz*, III, No. 1198. See Bülow's reply of 20 March 1896, ibid., No. 1201.

54 Eulenburg to Bülow, 16 March 1896, ibid., No. 1199.

55 Eulenburg to Bülow, 29 March 1896, ibid., No. 1203; Bülow to Eulenburg, 1 April 1896, ibid., No. 1205.

56 Eulenburg to Bülow, 29 April 1896, ibid., No. 1208. A facsimile of Wilhelm's telegram to Eulenburg of 29 April 1896 is to be found in the Conrad Haussmann Papers, Stuttgart.

See also Eulenburg to Holstein, 30 April 1896, *Holstein Papers*, III, No. 544; Eulenburg to Hohenlohe, 1 May 1896, Hohenlohe, *Denkwürdigkeiten der Reichskanzlerzeit*, p. 216.

57 Eulenburg to Kaiser Wilhelm II, 29 April 1896, *Eulenburgs Korrespondenz*, III, No. 1209.

58 Holstein to Eulenburg, 1 May 1896, ibid., No. 1213 (Eulenburg sent this letter to the Kaiser from Pest); Eulenburg to Kaiser Wilhelm II, 3 May 1896, ibid., No. 1215.

59 Marschall to Eulenburg, 30 April 1896, ibid., No. 1211.

60 Cited in Holstein to Eulenburg, 1 May 1896, ibid., No. 1212.

61 Ibid.

62 See Alexander Hohenlohe to Völderndorff, 20 February 1896, Hohenlohe, *Denkwürdigkeiten der Reichskanzlerzeit*, pp. 175–6.

63 Hohenlohe, diary entry for 2 March 1896, ibid., p. 186.

64 Hohenlohe, note of 28 February 1896, ibid., pp. 181–2; Hohenlohe, diary entry for 2 March 1896, ibid., p. 186.

65 Hohenlohe, diary entry for 15 June 1896, ibid., p. 235.

66 Marschall, diary entry for 3 May 1896, cited in *Eulenburgs Korrespondenz*, III, p. 1673; Holstein to Eulenburg, telegram, 3 May 1896, cited ibid., p. 1677.

67 Marschall, diary entry for 4 May 1896, cited ibid., p. 1674.

68 Kaiser Wilhelm II to Eulenburg, telegram, 4 May 1896, ibid., No. 1217.

69 Alexander Hohenlohe to Eulenburg, 11 May 1896, Hohenlohe, *Denkwürdigkeiten der Reichskanzlerzeit*, pp. 220–3.

70 Waldersee, diary entry for 3 May 1896, GStA Berlin, Waldersee Papers; omitted from Meisner, II, p. 369.

71 Eulenburg to Kaiser Wilhelm II, 5 May 1896, *Eulenburgs Korrespondenz*, III, No. 1218.

72 Eulenburg to Kaiser Wilhelm II, 7 May 1896, ibid., No. 1220.

73 Marschall to Eulenburg, telegram, 9 May 1896, ibid., No. 1221; also Alexander Hohenlohe to Eulenburg, 11 May 1896, Hohenlohe, *Denkwürdigkeiten der Reichskanzlerzeit*, pp. 220–3.

74 For the Kaiser's shooting trips to Prökelwitz and Rominten, see Andreas Gautschi, *Wilhelm II. und das Waidwerk. Jagen und Jagden des letzten Deutschen Kaisers. Eine Bilanz*, Hanstedt 2000, pp. 30ff. and 44ff.

75 Eulenburg to Bülow, 13 May 1896, *Eulenburgs Korrespondenz*, III, No. 1222.

76 Eulenburg to Bülow, 16 May 1896, ibid., No. 1223.

77 Eulenburg to Lucanus, 16 May 1896, ibid., No. 1224.

78 Holstein to Eulenburg, telegram, 16 May 1896, ibid., No. 1225.

79 Kaiser Wilhelm II to Hohenlohe, 16 May 1896, Hohenlohe, *Denkwürdigkeiten der Reichskanzlerzeit*, pp. 225–6.

80 Eulenburg to Hohenlohe, 17 May 1896, ibid., p. 227.

81 Kaiserin Auguste Viktoria to Hohenlohe, 17 May 1896, ibid., pp. 226–7.

82 Hohenlohe to Kaiser Wilhelm II, 16 May 1896, ibid., pp. 224–5. See also the telegram of 17 May 1896 drafted for the Chancellor by Marschall, Holstein, Wilmowski and Alexander Hohenlohe, ibid., p. 227. See Marschall, diary entry for 16 May 1896, *Eulenburgs Korrespondenz*, III, p. 1684.

83 Eulenburg and Kaiser Wilhelm II to Hohenlohe, telegram, 17 May 1896, Hohenlohe, *Denkwürdigkeiten der Reichskanzlerzeit*, p. 228.

84 Eulenburg to Holstein, 17 May 1896, *Holstein Papers*, III, No. 548.

85 Marschall, diary entry for 17 May 1896, cited in *Eulenburgs Korrespondenz*, III, p. 1684.

86 Marschall, diary entry for 18 May 1896, cited ibid.

87 Holstein to Eulenburg, 19 May 1896, cited ibid.

88 Hohenlohe to Kaiser Wilhelm II, telegram, 18 May 1896, Hohenlohe, *Denkwürdigkeiten der Reichskanzlerzeit*, pp. 228–9.

89 Eulenburg to Hohenlohe, telegram, 17 May 1896, ibid., p. 229.

90 Eulenburg to Hohenlohe, 18 May 1896, ibid., pp. 229–31.

91 Hohenlohe to Eulenburg, telegram, 19 May 1896, ibid., p. 231; Marschall, diary entry for 19 May 1896, cited in *Eulenburgs Korrespondenz*, III, p. 1684.

92 Eulenburg to Hohenlohe, 19 May 1896, Hohenlohe, *Denkwürdigkeiten der Reichskanzlerzeit*, pp. 231–2.

93 Eulenburg to Alexander Hohenlohe, 19 May 1896, ibid., p. 232; also Eulenburg to Holstein, 19 May 1896, *Holstein Papers*, III, No. 549.

94 Eulenburg to Hohenlohe, 18 May 1896, Hohenlohe, *Denkwürdigkeiten der Reichskanzlerzeit*, pp. 229–31.

95 Eulenburg to Hohenlohe, 5 July 1896, *Eulenburgs Korrespondenz*, III, No. 1235.

96 Lindenau to Holstein, 5 August 1896, *Holstein Papers*, III, No. 580.

97 Heinrich VII Prince Reuss to Count Carl von Wedel, 18 July 1896, Wedel Papers, Frankfurt a.M.

98 Eulenburg to Holstein, 5 July 1896, Enclosure II, *Holstein Papers*, III, No. 554.

99 Hohenlohe to Eulenburg, 20 May 1896, Hohenlohe, *Denkwürdigkeiten der Reichskanzlerzeit*, p. 233.

100 Waldersee, diary entry for 8 June 1896, GStA Berlin, Waldersee Papers; cf. Meisner, II, pp. 370–1.

101 Alexander Hohenlohe to his father, 17 June 1896, Hohenlohe, *Denkwürdigkeiten der Reichskanzlerzeit*, pp. 235–6.

102 Above, p. 374.

103 Waldersee, diary entry for 21 June 1896, GStA Berlin, Waldersee Papers; omitted from Meisner, II, p. 371.

104 Eulenburg to Bülow, 8 June 1896, *Eulenburgs Korrespondenz*, III, No. 1233. Cf. Eulenburg to Kaiser Wilhelm II, 20 January 1896, ibid., No. 1190.

105 Eulenburg to Bülow, 24 May 1896, ibid., No. 1228.

106 Bülow to Eulenburg, 16 July 1896, ibid., No. 1242.

107 Bülow to Eulenburg, 23 July 1896, ibid., No. 1245. Eulenburg read Bülow's letter to the Kaiser on 1 August: ibid., p. 1713.

108 Eulenburg to Bülow, 7 and 23 July 1896, ibid., Nos. 1237 and 1246.

109 Eulenburg to Bülow, 23 July 1896, ibid., No. 1246.

110 Eulenburg to Hohenlohe, 5 and 6 July 1896, ibid., Nos. 1235–6.

111 Eulenburg to Holstein, 12 July 1896, *Holstein Papers*, III, No. 558; also Eulenburg to Holstein, 3 August 1896, *Eulenburgs Korrespondenz*, III, No. 1248, Eulenburg to Holstein, telegram, 4 August 1896, *Holstein Papers*, III, No. 576. See Hohenlohe to Holstein, 5 August 1896, ibid., No. 579; printed in part in Hohenlohe, *Denkwürdigkeiten der Reichskanzlerzeit*, pp. 250–1.

112 Eulenburg to Holstein, 26 July 1896, *Holstein Papers*, III, No. 570.

113 Eulenburg to Bülow, 7 July 1896, *Eulenburgs Korrespondenz*, III, No. 1237.

114 Hohenlohe to Alexander Hohenlohe, 18 July 1896, Hohenlohe, *Denkwürdigkeiten der Reichskanzlerzeit*, p. 242. See Hohenlohe, diary entry for 1 July 1896, ibid., p. 240.

115 Hohenlohe to Eulenburg, 16 July 1896, *Eulenburgs Korrespondenz*, III, No. 1240.

116 Hohenlohe to Eulenburg, 16 July 1896, ibid., No. 1241.

117 See Holstein to Eulenburg, 22 December 1895, ibid., No. 1175; Holstein to Eulenburg, 9 February 1896, *Holstein Papers*, III, No. 528.

118 Holstein to Eulenburg, 10 July 1896, *Holstein Papers*, III, p. 622.

119 Holstein to Eulenburg, 18 July 1896, ibid., No. 564 Enclosure.

120 Holstein to Eulenburg, 14 July 1896, ibid., No. 559; also Holstein to Kiderlen-Wächter, 10 July 1896, ibid., No. 557.

121 Quoted in Bülow to Eulenburg, 23 July 1896, *Eulenburgs Korrespondenz*, III, No. 1245.

122 Eulenburg, note of 21 July 1896, ibid., No. 1243; also Bülow to Eulenburg, 23 July 1896, ibid., No. 1245.

123 Eulenburg, note of 15 July 1896, *Holstein Papers*, III, No. 561.

124 Eulenburg, note of 21 July 1896, *Eulenburgs Korrespondenz*, III, No. 1243; also Bülow to Eulenburg, 23 July 1896, ibid., No. 1245.

125 Eulenburg to Bülow, 23 July 1896, ibid., No. 1246.

126 Ibid.

127 Eulenburg to Hohenlohe, 23 July 1896, ibid., No. 1244.

128 Eulenburg to Bülow, 23 July 1896, ibid., No. 1246.

129 For further details, see *Young Wilhelm*, pp. 319–20.

130 Eulenburg, note of 1 August 1896, *Eulenburgs Korrespondenz*, III, No. 1247.

131 Eulenburg, diary entry for 1 August 1896, ibid., III, p. 1720.

132 Holstein to Lindenau, 24 July 1896, *Holstein Papers*, III, No. 567.

133 Kaiser Wilhelm II to Hohenlohe, telegram, 26 July 1896, cited ibid., p. 633.

134 Holstein to Lindenau, 24 and 27 July 1896, ibid., Nos. 567 and 572; also Holstein to Eulenburg, telegram, 4 August 1896, ibid., No. 577; Monts to Eulenburg, 7 August 1896, *Eulenburgs Korrespondenz*, III, No. 1254.

135 Holstein to Lindenau, 29 July 1896, *Holstein Papers*, III, No. 573.

136 Holstein to Lindenau, 1 August 1896, ibid., No. 575.

137 Hohenlohe to Holstein, 27 July 1896, ibid., No. 571.

138 Hohenlohe, undated note, Hohenlohe, *Denkwürdigkeiten der Reichskanzlerzeit*, p. 248.

139 Hohenlohe to Kaiser Wilhelm II, cipher telegram, 4 August 1896, PA AA, Preußen 1 No. 1d, Bd I.

140 Eulenburg, diary entries for 1–3 August 1896, *Eulenburgs Korrespondenz*, III, pp. 1720–1.

141 Eulenburg, note of 4 August 1896, ibid., No. 1249; Hohenlohe, diary entry for 4 August 1896, Hohenlohe, *Denkwürdigkeiten der Reichskanzlerzeit*, pp. 249–50; also Hohenlohe to Holstein, 5 August 1896, *Holstein Papers*, III, No. 579. Cf. Hohenlohe, *Denkwürdigkeiten der Reichskanzlerzeit*, pp. 253–4.

142 Eulenburg to Kaiser Wilhelm II, telegram and letter of 4 August 1896, *Eulenburgs Korrespondenz*, III, Nos. 1251–2.

143 Eulenburg to Kaiser Wilhelm II, 5–6 August 1896, ibid., No. 1253.

144 Lindenau to Holstein, 5 August 1896, *Holstein Papers*, III, No. 580.

145 Hohenlohe, diary entry for 8 August 1896, Hohenlohe, *Denkwürdigkeiten der Reichskanzlerzeit*, pp. 251–2; also the undated note, ibid., p. 253. See Kiderlen-Wächter to Eulenburg, 10 August 1896, *Holstein Papers*, III, No. 581.

146 August Eulenburg to Philipp Eulenburg, 11 August 1896, *Eulenburgs Korrespondenz*, III, No. 1255.

147 Kaiser Wilhelm II to Eulenburg, 14 August 1896, ibid., No. 1259.

148 Eulenburg to Kaiser Wilhelm II, 12 and 18 August 1896, ibid., Nos. 1256 and 1261.

149 Kaiser Wilhelm II to Eulenburg, telegram, 13 August 1896, ibid., No. 1257.

150 Kaiser Wilhelm II to Eulenburg, 14 August 1896, ibid., No. 1259.

151 Empress Frederick to Queen Victoria, 17 August and 12 September 1896, AdHH Schloss Fasanerie. Marschall described Gossler as 'wholly incapable, especially in parliament': diary entry for 14 August 1896, *Eulenburgs Korrespondenz*, III, p. 1732.

152 Hohenlohe's diary for 24 August 1896, Hohenlohe, *Denkwürdigkeiten der Reichskanzlerzeit*, pp. 256–7.

153 Waldersee, diary entry for 20 August 1896, GStA Berlin, Waldersee Papers; cf. Meisner, II, p. 372.

154 Waldersee, diary entry for 16 August 1896, GStA Berlin, Waldersee Papers; omitted from Meisner, II, p. 372.

155 Waldersee, diary entries for 6 and 20 January 1897, GStA Berlin, Waldersee Papers; cf. Meisner, II, pp. 382ff.

156 Jagemann to Brauer, 8 April 1897, Fuchs, *Großherzog von Baden*, III, No. 1679.

157 Eulenburg to Kaiser Wilhelm II, 12 August 1896, *Eulenburgs Korrespondenz*, III, No. 1256. See the bitterly angry letter that Hohenlohe now wrote to Eulenburg but did not send: Hohenlohe, *Denkwürdigkeiten der Reichskanzlerzeit*, pp. 253–4; also Holstein to Eulenburg, 13 August 1896, *Holstein Papers*, III, No. 583. Marschall wrote in his diary on 14 August: 'Holstein is furious with Philipp Eulenburg' (*Eulenburgs Korrespondenz*, III, p. 1732.).

158 Eulenburg to Kaiser Wilhelm II, 12 and 24 August 1896, *Eulenburgs Korrespondenz*, III, Nos. 1256 and 1262.

159 Eulenburg to Hohenlohe, 24 August 1896, Hohenlohe, *Denkwürdigkeiten der Reichskanzlerzeit*, pp. 254–5.

160 Eulenburg, note of 4 October 1896, *Eulenburgs Korrespondenz*, III, No. 1265.

161 Eulenburg to Kaiser Wilhelm II, 14 and 24 August 1896, ibid., Nos. 1258 and 1262.

162 Hohenlohe to his son Alexander, 7 June 1897, Hohenlohe, *Denkwürdigkeiten der Reichskanzlerzeit*, p. 352.

163 Hohenlohe's diary for 22 May 1897, ibid., pp. 342–3.

164 Hohenlohe's diary for 5 June 1897, ibid., pp. 351–2.

165 Hohenlohe's diary for 3 June 1897, ibid., p. 350.

166 Hohenlohe's diary for 19 June 1897, ibid., pp. 358–9.

167 Hohenlohe to his son Alexander, 29 August 1897, ibid., pp. 379–80.

168 Hohenlohe to Otto Freiherr von Völderndorff-Waradein, undated [summer 1897], ibid., p. 344.

169 Hohenlohe, undated note [March 1897], ibid., p. 311.

170 Hohenlohe, diary entry for 8 March 1897, ibid., p. 312; Hohenlohe to Kaiser Wilhelm II, 9 March 1897, ibid., pp. 312–13.

171 Hohenlohe to Kaiser Wilhelm II, 31 May 1897, Lucanus to Hohenlohe, 1 June 1897, Kaiser Wilhelm II to Hohenlohe, 1 June 1897, ibid., pp. 346–7.

172 See for example Hohenlohe, diary entries for 1 and 22 June and 17 October 1897, ibid., pp. 347, 359 and 392–3.

173 Herbert Bismarck to Bülow, 18 October 1900, printed in facsimile in Bülow, *Memoirs*, I, p. 389.

174 See above, p. 826.

175 Völderndorff to Hohenlohe, 22 June 1897, Hohenlohe, *Denkwürdigkeiten der Reichskanzlerzeit*, pp. 359–60.

176 Dacheux to Hohenlohe, 19 May 1897, ibid., pp. 340–1.

177 Dacheux to Hohenlohe, 4 August 1897, ibid., pp. 374–5.

28 PERSONAL MONARCHY: WILHELM II AT THE SUMMIT OF HIS POWER

1 Holstein to Bülow, 5 March 1897, cited in Röhl, *Germany without Bismarck*, p. 212.

2 Holstein to Eulenburg, 3 March 1897, *Eulenburgs Korrespondenz*, III, No. 1300.

3 August Eulenburg to Philipp Eulenburg, 9 February 1897, ibid., p. 1773.

4 Holstein to Eulenburg, 30 November 1896, *Holstein Papers*, III, No. 587.

5 Hohenlohe, notes of 7 March 1897, Hohenlohe, *Denkwürdigeiten der Reichskanzlerzeit*, pp. 311–12.

6 Lascelles, report of 14 May 1897, RA I61/19.

7 See Dieter Fricke, 'Die Affäre Leckert-Lützow-Tausch und die Regierungskrise von 1897 in Deutschland', *Zeitschrift für Geschichtswissenschaft*, 7 (1960).

8 Eulenburg to Bülow, 26 October 1896, *Eulenburgs Korrespondenz*, III, No. 1268; also Eulenburg, notes of 4 October 1896, ibid., No. 1265; Hohenlohe, diary entries for 25 November
   1896 and 22 May 1897, Hohenlohe, *Denkwürdigkeiten der Reichskanzlerzeit*, pp. 279 and
   343; Eulenburg to Kaiser Wilhelm II, 8 December 1896, *Eulenburgs Korrespondenz*, III,
   No. 1283.

9 Waldersee, diary entry for 6 January 1897, GStA Berlin, Waldersee Papers; cf. Meisner, II,
   pp. 382-3.

10 Kaiser Wilhelm II to Eulenburg, 5 January 1897, *Eulenburgs Korrespondenz*, III, No. 1287.

11 Hohenlohe to his son Alexander, 31 October 1897, Hohenlohe, *Denkwürdigkeiten der Reichskanzlerzeit*, p. 398.

12 Kaiser Wilhelm II to Eulenburg, 5 January 1897, *Eulenburgs Korrespondenz*, III, No. 1287.
   See Hohenlohe, diary entries for 6 September and 17 October 1897, Hohenlohe,
   *Denkwürdigkeiten der Reichskanzlerzeit*, pp. 381-2 and 392.

13 Kaiser Wilhelm II to Hohenlohe, 4 January 1897, *Denkwürdigkeiten der Reichskanzlerzeit*,
   pp. 288-91.

14 Kaiser Wilhelm II to Hohenlohe, 15 November 1896, ibid., pp. 278-9.

15 Kaiser Wilhelm II to Hohenlohe, 7 January 1897, ibid., p. 291. See the Chancellor's reply,
   ibid., pp. 291-2.

16 Kaiser Wilhelm II, marginal comment on Eulenburg's report from Vienna of 16 August 1897,
   PA AA, Asservat No. 4.

17 Kaiser Wilhelm II to Hohenlohe, 26 June 1899, Hohenlohe, *Denkwürdigkeiten der Reichskanzlerzeit*, pp. 508-9.

18 Kaiser Wilhelm II to Count Ernst zu Lippe-Biesterfeld, 17 June 1898, ibid., pp. 454-5. See
   Hohenlohe to Völderndorff, 24 June 1898, as well as his diary entry for 2 August 1898, ibid.,
   pp. 455-6.

19 Hohenlohe to Völderndorff, 26 November 1898, ibid., pp. 471-2.

20 Empress Frederick to Kaiser Wilhelm II, 25 November 1898 and 24 January 1899, GStA
   Berlin, BPHA Rep. 52T No. 13.

21 See Bülow, *Memoirs*, I, pp. 217-18.

22 Kaiser Wilhelm II to Hinzpeter, July 1899, cited in Schröder, *Tagebuch Kaiser Wilhelms II.*,
   pp. 328-9; also Prince Heinrich of Prussia to Empress Frederick, 29 August 1899, AdHH
   Schloss Fasanerie.

23 Kaiser Wilhelm II, speech of 16 June 1898, Penzler, *Die Reden Kaiser Wilhelms II. in den
   Jahren 1896-1900*, pp. 96-8; Elkind, *German Emperor's Speeches*, p. 226.

24 Kaiser Wilhelm II to Hohenlohe, 21 November 1897, Hohenlohe, *Denkwürdigkeiten der
   Reichskanzlerzeit*, p. 417. Cf. Kaiser Wilhelm II's marginal notes on Hohenlohe's report of
   21 November 1897 in PA AA, Preußen 1 No. 1d, Bd I.

25 Hohenlohe to Kaiser Wilhelm II, 22 November 1897, Hohenlohe, *Denkwürdigkeiten der
   Reichskanzlerzeit*, p. 417.

26 Kaiser Wilhelm II to Hohenlohe, undated [January 1897], ibid., p. 296; printed in facsimile
   ibid., pp. 304-5.

27 See below, pp. 849-51. For the real text of the Kaiser's speech, see Kuno Moltke to Eulenburg,
   1 March 1897, *Eulenburgs Korrespondenz*, III, No. 1299.

28 Kaiser Wilhelm II, speech of 26 February 1897, Penzler, *Reden Kaiser Wilhelms II. in den
   Jahren 1896-1900*, pp. 38-41; Elkind, *German Emperor's Speeches*, p. 301.

29 Kaiser Wilhelm II to Prince Heinrich of Prussia, April 1897, from the version in *Berliner
   Lokal-Anzeiger*, 25 April 1897, PA AA, Preußen 1 No. 1d, Bd I.

30 Hohenlohe, diary entry for 29 April 1897, Hohenlohe, *Denkwürdigkeiten der Reichskanzlerzeit*, pp. 332-3. See Hohenlohe to Marschall, 27 April 1897, PA AA, Preußen 1 No. 1d,
   Bd I.

31 Kiderlen-Wächter to Hohenlohe, 30 April 1897, Hohenlohe, *Denkwürdigkeiten der Reichskanzlerzeit*, p. 334.

32 Kaiser Wilhelm II to Hohenlohe, 30 April 1897, ibid., p. 333.

33 Hohenlohe, notes, undated [30 April 1897], ibid., p. 335.

34 Kaiser Wilhelm II, speech of 26 February 1897, Penzler, *Reden Kaiser Wilhelms II in den Jahren 1896–1900*, pp. 38–41. See Kuno Moltke to Eulenburg, 1 March 1897, *Eulenburgs Korrespondenz*, III, No. 1299.

35 Bülow, *Memoirs*, I, pp. 38–9. Cf. Bülow to Eulenburg, 17 March 1897, *Eulenburgs Korrespondenz*, III, No. 1307; also Kuno Moltke to Eulenburg, 1 March 1897, ibid., No. 1299.

36 Holstein to Bülow, 5 April 1897, cited in Röhl, *Germany without Bismarck*, p. 212; Spitzemberg, *Tagebuch*, pp. 352–3; Theodor Fontane, *Briefe an Georg Friedländer*, Heidelberg 1954, p. 311.

37 Monts to Holstein, 2 March 1897, *Eulenburgs Korrespondenz*, III, No. 1301.

38 Monts to Eulenburg, 20/21 March 1897, ibid., No. 1309.

39 Julius Bachem to Karl Bachem, 15 March 1897, cited in Röhl, *Germany without Bismarck*, p. 216.

40 Eugen Richter, speech of 18 May 1897, in Eyck, *Das Persönliche Regiment*, pp. 171–2.

41 Waldersee, diary entry for 24 May 1897, GStA Berlin, Waldersee Papers; omitted from Meisner, II, pp. 396–7.

42 Hohenlohe, diary entry for 31 May 1897, Hohenlohe, *Denkwürdigkeiten der Reichskanzlerzeit*, pp. 345–6.

43 Holstein to Bülow, 23 November 1896, cited in Röhl, *Germany without Bismarck*, p. 207. See also Holstein to Eulenburg, 24 November 1896, *Holstein Papers*, III, No. 586; Haller, *Eulenburg*, p. 204.

44 Hohenlohe to Eulenburg, 25 March 1897, Hohenlohe, *Denkwürdigkeiten der Reichskanzlerzeit*, pp. 322–3.

45 Eulenburg to Kaiser Wilhelm II, 8 April 1897, *Eulenburgs Korrespondenz*, III, No. 1313, Enclosure I.

46 Karl Bachem, cited in Röhl, *Germany without Bismarck*, p. 215.

47 Hohenlohe, diary entry for 30 March 1897, Hohenlohe, *Denkwürdigkeiten der Reichskanzlerzeit*, pp. 326–7.

48 See Holstein to Eulenburg, 9 February 1896, *Holstein Papers*, III, No. 528; Holstein to Bülow, 17 February 1897, ibid., IV, No. 605.

49 Hereditary Prince Bernhard of Saxe-Meiningen to Colmar Freiherr von der Goltz, 10 October 1899, BA-MA Freiburg, von der Goltz Papers N737 Zug. 161/95. See also Prince Bernhard's letter to his father, 16 August 1900, Thüringisches Staaatsarchiv Meiningen, HA 341.

50 Waldersee, diary entry for 7 February 1895, GStA Berlin, Waldersee Papers; cf. Meisner, II, p. 338.

51 Waldersee, diary entry for 31 January 1895, GStA Berlin, Waldersee Papers; cf. Meisner, II, p. 338, where the date given is incorrect.

52 Waldersee, diary entry for 17 December 1895, GStA Berlin, Waldersee Papers; cf. Meisner, II, p. 362.

53 Waldersee, diary entry for 28 January 1897, GStA Berlin, Waldersee Papers; omitted from Meisner, II, pp. 385ff.

54 Waldersee, diary entry for 16 February 1897, GStA Berlin, Waldersee Papers; cf. Meisner, II, p. 392.

55 Waldersee, diary entry for 25 November 1896, GStA Berlin, Waldersee Papers; cf. Meisner, II, p. 377.

56 Ibid.

57 Waldersee, diary entry for 29 November 1896, GStA Berlin, Waldersee Papers; printed only in part in Meisner, II, p. 377.

58 Waldersee, diary entry for 2 December 1896, GStA Berlin, Waldersee Papers; printed only in part in Meisner, II, p. 377.

59 Waldersee, diary entry for 28 January 1897, GStA Berlin, Waldersee Papers; omitted from Meisner, II, pp. 385ff.

60 Waldersee's memorandum of 22 January 1897 is printed in Meisner, II, pp. 386–9.

61 Waldersee, diary entry for 28 January 1897, GStA Berlin, Waldersee Papers; omitted from Meisner, II, p. 385.

62 Waldersee's memorandum of 22 January 1897, Meisner, II, pp. 386–9.

63 Waldersee, diary entry for 28 January 1897, GStA Berlin, Waldersee Papers; omitted from Meisner, II, pp. 385ff.

64 Waldersee, diary entry for 31 January 1897, GStA Berlin, Waldersee Papers; cf. Meisner, II, pp. 389ff.

65 Waldersee, diary entry for 19 February 1897, GStA Berlin, Waldersee Papers; omitted from Meisner, II, p. 392. See Waldersee to Verdy, 5 February 1897, GStA Berlin, Waldersee Papers No. 53.

66 Ibid. General Adolf von Deines also approved of Waldersee's memorandum: Waldersee, diary entry for 4 March 1897, GStA Berlin, Waldersee Papers; omitted from Meisner, II, p. 393.

67 Waldersee, diary entry for 1 April 1897, GStA Berlin, Waldersee Papers; omitted from Meisner, II, p. 396.

68 Above, pp. 852–60.

69 Waldersee, diary entry for 26 March 1897, GStA Berlin, Waldersee Papers; Meisner, II, p. 395.

70 Waldersee, diary entry for 1 April 1897, GStA Berlin, Waldersee Papers; omitted from Meisner, II, p. 396.

71 Waldersee, diary entry for 16 March 1897, GStA Berlin, Waldersee Papers; cf. Meisner, II, pp. 393ff.

72 Waldersee, diary entry for 26 April 1897, GStA Berlin, Waldersee Papers; omitted from Meisner, II, p. 396.

73 Waldersee, diary entry for 2 May 1897, GStA Berlin, Waldersee Papers; omitted from Meisner, II, p. 396.

74 Waldersee, diary entry for 16 May 1897, GStA Berlin, Waldersee Papers; omitted from Meisner, II, p. 396.

75 Waldersee, diary entry for 26 April 1897, GStA Berlin, Waldersee Papers; omitted from Meisner, II, p. 396.

76 Waldersee to Gossler, 20 February 1897, Meisner, II, pp. 388–9, note. See Waldersee, diary entry for 19 February 1897, GStA Berlin, Waldersee Papers; omitted from Meisner, II, p. 392.

77 See above, p. 288.

78 Waldersee to Verdy, 5 February 1897, GStA Berlin, Waldersee Papers No. 53.

79 Verdy to Waldersee, 25 February 1897, ibid.

80 Kaiser Wilhelm II, marginal comments on Eulenburg to Kaiser Wilhelm II, 8 April 1897, *Eulenburgs Korrespondenz*, III, No. 1313, Enclosure I.

81 Kaiser Wilhelm II to Eulenburg, 20 April 1897, quoted in Eulenburg to Bülow, 24 April 1897, ibid., No. 1317.

82 Eulenburg to Bülow, 24 April 1897, ibid.; also Eulenburg to Holstein, 11 May 1897, ibid., No. 1318.

83 See above, pp. 832–3.

84 See Marschall's diary entry for 2 April 1897, quoted in *Eulenburgs Korrespondenz*, III, p. 1813.

85 Kaiser Wilhelm II, speech of 26 February 1897, Penzler, *Reden Kaiser Wilhelms II. in den Jahren 1896–1900*, pp. 38–41; Elkind, *German Emperor's Speeches*, p. 300.

86 Kaiser Wilhelm II, speeches in Berlin on 12 November and in Kiel on 24 November 1896, speech in Berlin, 18 October 1897, Penzler, *Reden Kaiser Wilhelms II. in den Jahren 1896–1900*, pp. 35–6. and 67–8.

87 Kaiser Wilhelm II, speech in Berlin, 18 November 1897, ibid., pp. 70–2; Elkind, *German Emperor's Speeches*, p. 226.

88 See e.g. Wilhelm Oncken, ed., *Unser Heldenkaiser. Festschrift zum hundertjährigen Geburtstage Kaiser Wilhelms des Großen*, Berlin 1897; Bernhard von Kugler, *Deutschlands größter Held. Jubel-Ausgabe zur hundertjährigen Gedächtnisfeier des Geburtstags weiland Sr. Majestät Kaiser Wilhelm I.*, Dresden 1893.

89 Kaiser Wilhelm II to Hohenlohe, 6 December 1896, copy in Bundesarchiv Koblenz, Boetticher Papers, 23. See below, pp. 863–4.

90 Eulenburg, notes of 27 October 1896, *Eulenburgs Korrespondenz*, III, No. 1269.

91 Hohenlohe to Kaiser Wilhelm II, 5 December 1896, GStA Berlin, BPHA Rep. 53 Lit. H. No. 2. Cf. Hohenlohe, undated note [early December 1896], Hohenlohe, *Denkwürdigkeiten der Reichskanzlerzeit*, pp. 285–6; also Posadowsky to Boetticher, 20 October 1896, BA Koblenz, Boetticher Papers, 23.

92 Kaiser Wilhelm II, marginal notes on Hohenlohe's report of 5 December 1896, GStA Berlin, BPHA Rep. 53 Lit. H. No. 2.

93 Kaiser Wilhelm II to Hohenlohe, 6 December 1896, telegram, Hohenlohe, *Denkwürdigkeiten der Reichskanzlerzeit*, pp. 285–6.

94 Kaiser Wilhelm II to Hohenlohe, 6 December 1896, letter from Springe, copy in BA Koblenz, Boetticher Papers, 23. See Röhl, *Germany without Bismarck*, pp. 206–7.

95 Kaiser Wilhelm II to Eulenburg, 5 January 1897, *Eulenburgs Korrespondenz*, III, No. 1287.

96 Kuno Moltke to Eulenburg, 1 March 1897, ibid., No. 1299.

97 Hohenlohe, diary entry for 24 March 1897, Hohenlohe, *Denkwürdigkeiten der Reichskanzlerzeit*, pp. 321–2; Jagemann to Brauer, 8 April 1897, Fuchs, *Großherzog von Baden*, III, No. 1679.

98 Kuno Moltke to Eulenburg, 1 March 1897, *Eulenburgs Korrespondenz*, III, No. 1299.

99 Hohenlohe, diary entry for 24 March 1897, Hohenlohe, *Denkwürdigkeiten der Reichskanzlerzeit*, pp. 321–2.

100 Hohenlohe, diary entry for 27 March 1897, ibid., pp. 323–4.

101 Romain Rolland, 'Journal Intime, 22. Januar 1898', in *Cahiers Romain Rolland*, III, *Richard Strauß et Romain Rolland*, Paris 1951, p. 118.

102 Bodo von dem Knesebeck to Eulenburg, 9 December 1893, cited in Lothar Machtan, *Bismarcks Tod und Deutschlands Tränen. Reportage einer Tragödie*, Munich 1998, p. 89. See also ibid., p. 100.

103 Ibid., p. 99.

104 See ibid., pp. 75ff.

105 Wedel, *Zwischen Kaiser und Kanzler*, p. 192. See above, pp. 590–1.

106 See above, pp. 591–2.

107 Kaiser Wilhelm II to Bismarck, 19 September 1893, in Schröder, *Tagebuch Kaiser Wilhelms II.*, pp. 151–2.

108 Above, pp. 594–7 and 703–6.

109 Kaiser Wilhelm II to Kaiser Franz Joseph, 29 October 1896, HHStA Vienna, Kabinettsarchiv Geheimakten 2.

110 Eulenburg, note of 8 November 1896, Bülow, note of 7 April 1897, *Eulenburgs Korrespondenz*, III, Nos. 1272 and 1312.

111 Kaiser Wilhelm II to Hohenlohe, 28 October 1896, Hohenlohe to Kaiser Wilhelm II, 29 October 1896, Hohenlohe, *Denkwürdigkeiten der Reichskanzlerzeit*, pp. 270–1.

112  Eulenburg, notes of November 1896, *Eulenburgs Korrespondenz*, III, No. 1272. Wilhelm's letter to Bismarck of 11 September 1886 on his negotiations with Alexander III is printed in *Young Wilhelm*, pp. 580–3.

113  Bülow, *Memoirs*, IV, pp. 677–8. See also Eulenburg to Kaiser Wilhelm II, 26 November 1896, *Eulenburgs Korrespondenz*, III, No. 1280.

114  Hohenlohe, diary entry for 27 March 1897, Hohenlohe, *Denkwürdigkeiten der Reichskanzlerzeit*, pp. 323–4.; Jagemann to Brauer, 8 April 1897, Fuchs, *Großherzog von Baden*, III, No. 1679.

115  Eisendecher to Tirpitz, 1 September 1897, BA-MA Freiburg, Tirpitz Papers N253/4.

116  Senden to Tirpitz, 19 July 1897, ibid.

117  Tirpitz to Senden, 11 August 1897, ibid.

118  Tirpitz to Prince Heinrich of Prussia, 29 October 1897, ibid.

119  Senden to Tirpitz, 4 August 1897, ibid. See Wilmowski to Hohenlohe, 24 August 1897, Hohenlohe, *Denkwürdigkeiten der Reichskanzlerzeit*, p. 379.

120  Tirpitz to Prince Heinrich of Prussia, 29 October 1897, BA-MA Freiburg, Tirpitz Papers N253/4.

121  Tirpitz, notes on a visit to Friedrichsruh, 22 August 1897, ibid.

122  Senden to Tirpitz, 3 September 1897, ibid.; Hans Blum, *Fürst Bismarck und seine Zeit. Eine Biographie für das deutsche Volk*, Munich 1899, p. 61.

123  Machtan, *Bismarcks Tod*, p. 35.

124  August Eulenburg to Philipp Eulenburg, 27 December 1897, *Eulenburgs Korrespondenz*, III, No. 1352.

125  Tirpitz, *Erinnerungen*, pp. 93–4; Bülow, *Memoirs*, I, p. 204.

126  August Eulenburg to Philipp Eulenburg, 27 December 1897, *Eulenburgs Korrespondenz*, III, No. 1352; also Jagemann's report of 20 December 1897, Fuchs, *Großherzog von Baden*, III, No. 1793.

127  See Philipp Eulenburg's essay 'Bismarck stirbt', in Eulenburg, *Aus 50 Jahren*, pp. 270–80.

128  Maximilian Harden to K. Harden, 29 July 1898, cited in Machtan, *Bismarcks Tod*, p. 62.

129  Kaiser Wilhelm II to Waldersee, 31 July 1898, GStA Berlin, Waldersee Papers, BI No. 42. See Meisner, II, p. 417.

130  Kaiser Wilhelm II to Hohenlohe, 31 July 1898, quoted in Machtan, *Bismarcks Tod*, p. 70.

131  Ibid., p. 132.

132  Blum, *Fürst Bismarck und seine Zeit*, p. 139; Eulenburg, *Aus 50 Jahren*, p. 273.

133  Johannes Penzler, *Fürst Bismarck nach seiner Entlassung. Leben und Politik des Fürsten seit seinem Scheiden aus dem Amte auf Grund aller authentischen Kundgebungen*, 7 vols., Leipzig 1897–8, VII, p. 492.

134  Machtan, *Bismarcks Tod*, p. 133.

135  Ibid., pp. 133–4.

136  Posadowsky to Hohenlohe, 31 July 1898, cited ibid., pp. 134–5; Eulenburg, *Aus 50 Jahren*, p. 273.

137  Arthur von Brauer, *Im Dienste Bismarcks. Persönliche Erinnerungen*, Berlin 1936, pp. 403 and 407.

138  See Duke Ernst Günther of Schleswig-Holstein to Prince Christian of Schleswig-Holstein, 14 August 1898, RA Add A18/G1.

139  Bülow, *Memoirs*, I, pp. 224–5.

140  Hohenlohe, diary entry for 2 August 1898, Hohenlohe, *Denkwürdigkeiten der Reichskanzlerzeit*, pp. 456–8; Machtan, *Bismarcks Tod*, pp. 135–6.

141  Spitzemberg, diary entry for 2 August 1898, cited in Machtan, *Bismarcks Tod*, p. 138; Cf. Spitzemberg, *Tagebuch*, p. 373. See Bülow, *Memoirs*, I, pp. 224ff.

142 Kaiser Wilhelm II, speech of 4 August 1898, cited in Bülow, *Memoirs*, I, pp. 228–9.

143 Kaiser Wilhelm II to his mother, 25 September 1898, AdHH Schloss Fasanerie. Cf. Bülow, *Memoirs*, I, pp. 230–2. See Empress Frederick to Kaiser Wilhelm II, 22 and 27 September, 24 October and 25 November 1898, GStA Berlin, BPHA Rep. 52T No. 13 and 13a.

144 Bülow, *Memoirs*, I, p. 229.

145 See above, pp. 840–1.

146 Waldersee, diary entries for 16 and 17 June 1897, GStA Berlin, Waldersee Papers; cf. Meisner, II, p. 399.

147 Waldersee, diary entries for 16 and 17 June 1897, GStA Berlin, Waldersee Papers; cf. Meisner, II, p. 399.

148 Hohenlohe, diary entry for 15 December 1898, Hohenlohe, *Denkwürdigkeiten der Reichskanzlerzeit*, p. 473. But cf. Alexander Hohenlohe's comment, ibid., p. 474.

149 Bülow to Eulenburg, 15 February 1898, *Eulenburgs Korrespondenz*, III, No. 1362.

150 Hohenlohe to his son Alexander, 29 August 1897, Hohenlohe, *Denkwürdigkeiten der Reichskanzlerzeit*, pp. 379–80.

151 Hohenlohe, diary entry for 8 May 1898, ibid., p. 444.

152 Bülow to Hohenlohe, 12 October 1898, BA Berlin, Reichskanzlei No. 237; Hohenlohe, diary entry for 20 November 1898, Hohenlohe, *Denkwürdigkeiten der Reichskanzlerzeit*, pp. 469–70; Hohenlohe, diary entry for 27 February 1899, ibid., p. 486; Hohenlohe to Völderndorff, 11 March 1899, ibid., p. 489; also Grierson to Bigge, 18 March 1899, RA I62/6; Bülow to Hohenlohe, 15 March 1900, Hohenlohe, *Denkwürdigkeiten der Reichskanzlerzeit*, p. 568; Hohenlohe, diary entry for 15 March 1900, ibid.

153 See Hohenlohe, *Denkwürdigkeiten der Reichskanzlerzeit*, pp. 511–12.

154 Kaiser Wilhelm II to Grand Duchess Luise of Baden, 30 August 1899, GStA Berlin, BPH Rep. 53 No. 55.

155 Such meetings took place on 16 March, 7 October and 30 December 1896, 26 January, 13 February and 14 October 1897, 1 January, 15 February and 7 October 1898 and 13 June and 23 August 1899.

156 Bosse, diary entry for 14 October 1897, cited in Röhl, *Germany without Bismarck*, p. 259.

157 Hohenlohe, diary entry for 15 February 1898, Hohenlohe, *Denkwürdigkeiten der Reichskanzlerzeit*, p. 428. See BA Koblenz, files of the Prussian Ministry of Justice, P135/2050.

158 Bülow to Kaiser Wilhelm II, 10 March 1897, GStA Berlin, BPHA Rep. 53J Lit. B. No. 16a.

159 Bülow to Eulenburg, 15 February 1898, *Eulenburgs Korrespondenz*, III, No. 1362.

160 Bosse, diary entry for 7 October 1898, cited in Röhl, *Germany without Bismarck*, p. 259.

161 Miquel to all Prussian ministers, 2 September 1899, BA Berlin, Reichskanzlei No. 1461. See Thielen to Boetticher, 7 September 1899, BA Koblenz, Boetticher Papers.

162 Miquel to all Prussian ministers, 22 September 1898, BA Koblenz, files of the Prussian Ministry of Justice, P135/4385.

163 Minutes of the Prussian Ministry of State, 24 September 1898, ibid.

164 Alexander Hohenlohe to his father, 13 July 1897, Hohenlohe, *Denkwürdigkeiten der Reichskanzlerzeit*, p. 370.

165 Hohenlohe to Völderndorff, 25 October 1898, ibid., pp. 464–5.

166 Hohenlohe, diary entry for 20 November 1898, ibid., pp. 469–70.

167 Prince Hermann zu Hohenlohe-Langenburg to Prince Chlodwig zu Hohenlohe-Schillingsfürst, 7 March 1898, ibid., p. 433.

168 Hahnke, memorandum of 2 October 1899, BA Berlin, Reichskanzlei, Geschäftsgang 1 Vol. 6 No. 360.

169 Minutes of the Prussian Ministry of State, 22 and 28 March 1898, GStA Berlin.

170 See Tirpitz to Kaiser Wilhelm II, 24 April 1898, Knorr, memorandum of 21 May 1898 with Tirpitz's marginal notes, Tirpitz to Kaiser Wilhelm II, 28 May 1898, Tirpitz to Hohenlohe,

28 May 1898, Kaiser Wilhelm II to Tirpitz, 1 and 14 June 1898, Tirpitz to Hohenlohe, 14 June 1898, Tirpitz to Wilmowski, 16 June 1898, BA Berlin, Reichskanzlei No. 1612.

171  Memorandum entitled 'Bemerkungen zu der Differenz zwischen Oberkommando der Marine und Reichsmarineamt', 25 June 1898, BA Berlin, Reichskanzlei No. 1612.

172  Hohenlohe to Völderndorff, 5 October and 28 December 1898, Hohenlohe, *Denkwürdigkeiten der Reichskanzlerzeit*, pp. 462 and 475. See Völderndorff to Hohenlohe, 22 June 1897, ibid., pp. 359–60.

173  Alexander Hohenlohe to his father, 20 September 1900, ibid., p. 583.

174  Alexander Hohenlohe to his father, 10 January 1899, ibid., pp. 478–9.

175  Hohenlohe to his son Alexander, 7 January 1900, ibid., p. 554; Hohenlohe to Völderndorff, 18 March 1899, ibid., p. 490.

176  Hohenlohe to Völderndorff, 5 October 1898, ibid., p. 462; Hohenlohe, diary entries for 30 April, 6 October and 15 December 1898 and 27 February 1899, ibid., pp. 443–4, 462–3, 473–4 and 486; also Alexander Hohenlohe to Prince Hermann zu Hohenlohe-Langenburg, 19 June 1899, Hohenlohe-Zentralarchiv Schloss Neuenstein, Hermann Hohenlohe-Langenburg Papers, Bü. 294.

177  Kaiser Wilhelm II, speech of 6 September 1898 in Oeynhausen, Penzler, *Reden Kaiser Wilhelms II. in den Jahren 1896–1900*, pp. 111–13.

178  Bülow, *Memoirs*, I, p. 234.

179  Hohenlohe to Völderndorff, 25 October 1898, Hohenlohe, *Denkwürdigkeiten der Reichskanzlerzeit*, pp. 464–5; Hohenlohe to his son Alexander, 9 September 1898, ibid., p. 458; Hohenlohe to Grand Duke of Baden, [October 1899], ibid., p. 532.

180  Wilmowski to Hohenlohe, 12 September 1898, ibid., p. 459.

181  Hohenlohe to Bülow, 10 November 1898, ibid., pp. 468–9.

182  Röhl, *Germany without Bismarck*, p. 262.

183  Hohenlohe to his son Alexander, 26 November 1898, Hohenlohe, *Denkwürdigkeiten der Reichskanzlerzeit*, p. 471.

184  Hohenlohe to Völderndorff, 26 November 1898, ibid., pp. 471–2.

185  Hohenlohe to [Posadowsky?], 1 May 1899, ibid., p. 498. See Hohenlohe, diary entry for 11 May 1899 and Hohenlohe to his son Alexander, 17 May 1899, ibid., pp. 501–2.

186  Kaiser Wilhelm II to Hohenlohe, telegram, 26 June 1899, ibid., pp. 508–9.

187  Hohenlohe to Kaiser Wilhelm II, 26 June 1899, ibid., p. 509.

188  Hohenlohe to Grand Duke of Baden, undated, ibid., p. 532.

189  Kaiser Wilhelm II to Lucanus, telegram, quoted in Bülow to Auswärtiges Amt, 22 July 1899, ibid., pp. 512–13.

190  Wilmowski to Hohenlohe, 23 October 1899, ibid., pp. 532–3.

191  See Hannelore Horn, *Der Kampf um den Bau des Mittellandkanals. Staat und Politik*, Cologne, Opladen 1964.

192  Hohenlohe, diary entry for 20 November 1898, Hohenlohe, *Denkwürdigkeiten der Reichskanzlerzeit*, pp. 469–70.

193  Hohenlohe to his son Alexander, 13 April 1899, ibid., p. 495.

194  Bülow, *Memoirs*, I, p. 293.

195  Hohenlohe, diary entry, undated [May 1899], Hohenlohe, *Denkwürdigkeiten der Reichskanzlerzeit*, p. 501.

196  Hohenlohe to his son Alexander, 17 May 1899, ibid., pp. 501–2.

197  Bülow to Hohenlohe, 26 June 1899, ibid., p. 508.

198  Miquel to Hohenlohe, 8 August 1899, ibid., p. 515; Hohenlohe to his son Alexander, 11 August 1899, ibid., pp. 515–16.

199  Kaiser Wilhelm II, speech at Dortmund, 11 August 1899, Penzler, *Reden Kaiser Wilhelms II. in den Jahren 1896–1900*, pp. 159ff.; Elkind, *German Emperor's Speeches*, pp. 309–10.

200 Hohenlohe to Kaiser Wilhelm II, 16 August 1899, Hohenlohe, *Denkwürdigkeiten der Reichs-kanzlerzeit*, pp. 516–17.

201 Kaiser Wilhelm II to Hohenlohe, 17 August 1899, ibid., p. 517; Hohenlohe's reply, ibid.

202 Hohenlohe to Kaiser Wilhelm II, 17 August 1899, ibid., p. 518.

203 Kaiser Wilhelm II to von der Recke, 18 August 1899, ibid., p. 518.

204 Kaiser Wilhelm II to Bülow, August 1899, cited in Bülow, *Denkwürdigkeiten*, I, p. 295. Cf. the translation in Bülow, *Memoirs*, I, p. 293.

205 Bülow to Auswärtiges Amt, 18 August 1899, Hohenlohe, *Denkwürdigkeiten der Reichskanz-lerzeit*, p. 518.

206 Kaiser Wilhelm II to Bülow, September 1899, cited in Bülow, *Denkwürdigkeiten*, I, p. 296; cf. *Memoirs*, I, p. 294.

207 Kaiserin Auguste Viktoria to Bülow, 18 August 1899, cited in Bülow, *Memoirs*, I, p. 293.

208 Hohenlohe, diary entry for 11 August 1899, Hohenlohe, *Denkwürdigkeiten der Reichskanz-lerzeit*, p. 516; Holstein to Hohenlohe, 19 August 1899, ibid., p. 519.

209 Hohenlohe, diary entry for 20 August 1899, ibid., pp. 519–20.

210 Hohenlohe, diary entry for 22 August 1899, ibid., p. 522.

211 Hohenlohe, diary entry for 20 August 1899, ibid., pp. 519–20.

212 Hohenlohe to Kaiser Wilhelm II, 21 August 1899, ibid., pp. 521–2. See Alexander Hohenlohe to his father, 22 August 1899, ibid., p. 522.

213 Hutten-Czapski to Hohenlohe, 23 August 1899, ibid., pp. 469–70; Hohenlohe, diary entry for 27 August 1899, ibid., pp. 523–4.

214 Hohenlohe to his son Alexander, 25 August 1899, ibid., p. 523.

215 Bülow, *Memoirs*, I, p. 295.

216 Hohenlohe to his son Alexander, 25 August and 13 September 1899, Hohenlohe, *Denkwürdigkeiten der Reichskanzlerzeit*, pp. 523 and 526; Hohenlohe, diary entry for 7 March 1900, ibid., p. 567; Bülow, *Memoirs*, I, pp. 295–6; Lucanus to Kaiser Wilhelm II, 27 August 1899, GStA Berlin, BrPrHA Rep. 53J Lit. L No. 12.

217 Miquel to Hohenlohe, 4 September 1899, Hohenlohe, *Denkwürdigkeiten der Reichskanz-lerzeit*, pp. 525–6.

218 Hohenlohe to his son Alexander, 6 October 1899, ibid., p. 531.

219 Hereditary Princess Charlotte of Saxe-Meiningen to Schweninger, BA Berlin, Schweninger Papers 90 Schw. 4 No. 130; Hereditary Prince Bernhard of Saxe-Meiningen to Colmar Freiherr von der Goltz, 10 October 1899, BA-MA Freiburg, von der Goltz Papers N737 Zug. 161/95.

220 Eulenburg to Hohenlohe, 2 October 1899, Hohenlohe, *Denkwürdigkeiten der Reichskanz-lerzeit*, p. 531.

221 Duke Heinrich XI von Pless to Kaiser Wilhelm II, 21 October 1899, GStA Berlin, BPHA Rep. 53J Lit. P No. 1; Prince Christian Krafft zu Hohenlohe-Oehringen to August Eulenburg, 21 October 1899, GStA Berlin, BPHA Rep. 53 E. III No. 4.

222 Count Hans Finck von Finckenstein-Simnau to Kaiser Wilhelm II, 23 May 1900, Finck to August Eulenburg, 22 May 1900, August Eulenburg to Finck, 28 May 1900, GStA Berlin, BPHA Rep. 53 E. III No. 4.

223 Bülow, *Memoirs*, I, p. 295.

224 Kaiser Wilhelm II to Duke Heinrich XI von Pless, 24 October 1899, GStA Berlin, BPHA Rep. 53J Lit. P No. 3; Kaiser Wilhelm II to Prince Christian Krafft zu Hohenlohe-Oehringen, 25 October 1899, GStA Berlin, BPHA Rep. 53 E. III No. 4.

225 Bülow, *Memoirs*, I, p. 296.

226 Hohenlohe, notes of 6 November 1899, Hohenlohe, *Denkwürdigkeiten der Reichskanzlerzeit*, p. 538.

227 Hohenlohe, diary entry for 17 October 1900, ibid., p. 592.

228 Hohenlohe's undated notes, [October 1900], ibid., p. 582. Cf. the draft resignation letter ibid., pp. 581–2; also Hohenlohe to his son Alexander, 8 and 10 October 1900, ibid., p. 589.

229 Kaiser Wilhelm II to Hohenlohe, 17 October 1900, ibid., pp. 592–3; Hohenlohe, diary entry for 16 October 1900, ibid., pp. 591–2.

### 29 THE KAISER, ART AND ARCHITECTURE

1 Hammerstein to Kaiser Wilhelm II, 10 April 1899, Hohenlohe-Zentralarchiv Schloss Neuenstein, Hermann Hohenlohe-Langenburg Papers, Bü. 312.

2 Paul Seidel, *Der Kaiser und die Kunst*, Berlin 1907, p. 255.

3 Cartoon by Alfred Bryan in *Moonshine*, 26 February 1898, reprinted in Jost Rebentisch, *Die vielen Gesichter des Kaisers. Wilhelm II. in der deutschen und britischen Karikatur (1888–1918)*, Berlin 2000, p. 381.

4 Kaiser Wilhelm II, 'Niemand zu Liebe, Niemand zu Leibe!', signed 'Berlin, 28.XI.96, W.', GStA Berlin, BPHA Rep. 53 No. 270.

5 See Hohenlohe, *Denkwürdigkeiten der Reichskanzlerzeit*, p. 474.

6 Gerhard Malkowsky, *Die Kunst im Dienste der Staatsidee. Hohenzollernsche Kunstpolitik vom Großen Kurfürsten bis auf Wilhelm II*, Berlin 1912, p. 237.

7 See Alexander Hohenlohe to his father, 5 May 1899, Hohenlohe, *Denkwürdigkeiten der Reichskanzlerzeit*, p. 499.

8 See Hartmut Boockmann, *Die Marienburg im 19. Jahrhundert*, Frankfurt, Berlin, Vienna 1982, pp. 38–9 and 167ff. Cf. Seidel, *Kaiser und die Kunst*, pp. 60ff. and 66–70.

9 Kaiser Wilhelm II, speech at the Saalburg, 11 October 1900, Seidel, *Kaiser und die Kunst*, pp. 53–4.

10 Jarchow, *Hofgeschenke*, p. 86. See *Der Kunstwart*, 11th year, vol. 13 (April 1898), p. 36.

11 Kaiser Wilhelm II to his mother, 20 February 1893, AdHH Schloss Fasanerie. The Empress Frederick's reply of 25 February 1893 is located in GStA Berlin, BPHA Rep. 52T No. 13.

12 Ernst Wichert, 'Eine Generalprobe vor dem Kaiser', December 1893, GStA Berlin, BPHA Rep. 53 No. 179; also Poultney Bigelow to Kaiser Wilhelm II, December 1893, ibid., BPHA Rep. 53J Lit. B No. 10 Bigelow 1.

13 Kaiser Wilhelm II to Empress Frederick, 4 November 1899, AdHH Schloss Fasanerie.

14 Kaiser Wilhelm II to Empress Frederick, 18 November 1899, ibid.

15 See Wolf Jobst Siedler, *Abschied von Preußen*, Berlin 1991.

16 Seidel, *Kaiser und die Kunst*, p. 38.

17 Ibid., pp. 74–6.

18 Ibid., pp. 40ff.; Jürgen Julier, ed., *Kaiserlicher Kunstbesitz. Aus dem holländischen Exil Haus Doorn*, Berlin 1991, p. 259.

19 Seidel, *Kaiser und die Kunst*, p. 35.

20 See the illustrations ibid., pp. 32–3, 36–7, 40, 42–3 and 48.

21 Ibid., p. 38.

22 Seidel, *Kaiser und die Kunst*, p. 40. For further examples see ibid., pp. 31, 41 and 43.

23 Kaiser Wilhelm II, marginal notes on the design for the Post Office in Strassburg, 18 June 1895, ibid., pp. 40–1.

24 Kaiser Wilhelm II, marginal notes on the designs for the Post Offices in Güsten (Anhalt), Geestemünde and Königsberg, ibid., pp. 40–1 and 43.

25 Kaiser Wilhelm II, marginal notes on the design for the Post Office in Ülzen, ibid., p. 43.

26 Kaiser Wilhelm II, marginal notes on the design for the Post Office in Hanover-Linden, ibid., p. 43.

27 Ibid., p. 76.

28 Ibid., pp. 77–8.

29 Ibid., p. 80. Wilhelm also chose Schwechten as the architect for the Residenzschloss in Posen: ibid., p. 38.

30 See the list ibid., p. 82.

31 Ibid., p. 83.

32 Ibid., p. 98.

33 See ibid., pp. 102–4.

34 Ibid., pp. 98–9.

35 Ibid., p. 100.

36 Ibid., pp. 102–4.

37 Ibid., pp. 108–10.

38 Kalnein to Eulenburg, 8 March 1892, *Eulenburgs Korrespondenz*, II, No. 602.

39 Kaiser Wilhelm II, All-Highest Cabinet Order of 9 July 1888, Seidel, *Kaiser und die Kunst*, p. 92.

10 Carl Wolfgang Schümann, *Der Berliner Dom im 19. Jahrhundert*, Berlin 1980, pp. 245–6.

41 Seidel, *Kaiser und die Kunst*, p. 92.

42 See Kalnein to Eulenburg, 8 March 1892, *Eulenburgs Korrespondenz*, II, No. 602.

43 Schümann, *Berliner Dom*, p. 248; also Julius Schneider, *Die Geschichte des Berliner Doms*, Berlin 1993, p. 67.

44 Schümann, *Berliner Dom*, p. 251.

45 Seidel, *Kaiser und die Kunst*, p. 93.

46 Schümann, *Berliner Dom*, p. 252.

47 Ibid., p. 252.

48 Ibid., p. 253.

49 Seidel, *Kaiser und die Kunst*, p. 93.

50 Schümann, *Berliner Dom*, p. 247.

51 Ibid., p. 252.

52 Kaiser Wilhelm II to his mother, 20 February 1893, AdHH Schloss Fasanerie. The Empress Frederick's reply of 25 February 1893 is located in GStA Berlin, BPHA Rep. 52T No. 13.

53 Kaiser Wilhelm II to his mother, 21 June 1894, AdHH Schloss Fasanerie.

54 The document is printed in Seidel, *Kaiser und die Kunst*, pp. 92–3.

55 Schümann, *Berliner Dom*, p. 253; also Schneider, *Geschichte des Berliner Doms*, pp. 68–9.

56 The sermon of Oberhof- and Domprediger Dryander is printed in Seidel, *Kaiser und die Kunst*, pp. 94–7.

57 Robert Graf von Zedlitz-Trützschler, *Zwölf Jahre am deutschen Kaiserhof*, Berlin, Leipzig 1923, pp. 114–15.

58 Spitzemberg, diary entry for 27 February 1905, *Tagebuch*, pp. 445–6.

59 Wallot to Bluntschli, 3 January 1889, quoted in Michael S. Cullen, *Der Reichstag. Die Geschichte eines Monumentes*, Berlin 1983, p. 201.

60 Cited ibid., pp. 202–3.

61 Wallot to Reichensperger, 28 January 1889, ibid., pp. 204–5.

62 Kaiser Wilhelm II to his mother, 20 February 1893, AdHH Schloss Fasanerie. The Empress Frederick's reply of 25 February 1893 is located in GStA Berlin, BPHA Rep. 52T No. 13.

63 See Hohenlohe, diary entry for 14 December 1894, Hohenlohe, *Denkwürdigkeiten der Reichskanzlerzeit*, p. 23.

64 Wallot to Bluntschli, 6 April 1893, cited in Cullen, *Reichstag*, pp. 219–20.

65 See ibid., pp. 226ff. and 232–3.

66 Maximilian Rapsilber, 'Der Kaiser als Kunstrichter', in L. Leipziger, ed., *Der Roland von Berlin. Eine Wochenschrift für das Berliner Leben*, vol. 2, part 25, 23 June 1904, p. 59; copy in GStA Berlin, 2.2.12., Oberhofmarschallamt, fasc. 135.

67 Wallot to Reichensperger, 27 November 1892, cited in Cullen, *Reichstag*, p. 215; Friedrich von Thiersch to Bluntschli, 6 November 1892, ibid., p. 216.

68 Wallot to Bluntschli, 28 December 1893, ibid., p. 220.

69 Wallot to Bluntschli, 27 June 1894, ibid., pp. 220–1.

70 Above, p. 701.

71 Wallot to Bluntschli, 16 January 1895, cited in Cullen, *Reichstag*, pp. 242–6.

72 See Inge Eichler, 'Victoria als Malerin, Sammlerin und Mäzenin', in Rainer von Hessen, ed., *Victoria Kaiserin Friedrich (1840–1901). Mission und Schicksal einer englischen Prinzessin in Deutschland*, Frankfurt a M. 2002, pp. 134–50; Karoline Müller and Friedrich Rothe, eds., *Victoria von Preußen 1840–1901*, Berlin 2001, *passim*.

73 See *Young Wilhelm*, pp. 212–13 and 559–62. The oil painting exhibited in 1886 is reproduced in Seidel, *Kaiser und die Kunst*, p. 237. See also Wilhelm's work of 1876, ibid., p. 221.

74 Ibid., pp. 219–22.

75 Cited ibid., pp. 240–2.

76 Ibid., p. 250.

77 Ibid., pp. 242–3.

78 Ibid., p. 225.

79 See above, pp. 754–6.

80 Goetz, *Briefe Wilhelms II. an den Zaren*, pp. 294–6.

81 Cited in Elisabeth Heresch, *Nikolaus II. 'Feigheit, Lüge und Verrat'. Leben und Ende des letzten russischen Zaren*, Munich 1992, p. 101.

82 Jarchow, *Hofgeschenke*, pp. 69–70 and 141.

83 The finished work is reproduced above, p. 891.

84 Ferdinand Avenarius, 'Hofkunst und andere Kunst', *Der Kunstwart*, vol. 15, part 3 (November 1901), p. 87.

85 See Hartwig Fischer, *Ein Wilhelminisches Gesamtkunstwerk auf dem Kapitol. Hermann Prell und die Einrichtung des Thronsaals in der Deutschen Botschaft zu Rom 1894–1899*, Basel 1998.

86 See ibid., pp. 67–8 and 127.

87 Prell to his wife, 9 June 1896, ibid., pp. 52–3.

88 See Eulenburg to Bülow, 4 July 1898, *Eulenburgs Korrespondenz*, III, No. 1377.

89 Fischer, *Wilhelminisches Gesamtkunstwerk*, pp. 52–3.

90 Prell to his wife, 3 September 1896, cited ibid., pp. 91–2.

91 Ibid., p. 130.

92 The Kaiser's Privy Purse to Prell, 4 January 1899, cited ibid., p. 130.

93 Karl-Friedrich Nowak and Friedrich Thimme, eds., *Erinnerungen und Gedanken des Botschafters Anton Graf Monts*, Berlin 1932, p. 99. But cf. Wilhelm's positive comments in Fischer, *Wilhelminisches Gesamtkunstwerk*, p. 135.

94 Nicolaas Teeuwisse, *Vom Salon zur Sezession. Berliner Kunstleben zwischen Tradition und Aufbruch zur Moderne 1871–1900*, Berlin 1986, pp. 197–207.

95 Ibid., p. 207.

96 Excerpts from Anton von Werner's lost diaries, in Dominik Bartmann, *Anton von Werner. Zur Kunst und Kunstpolitik im Deutschen Kaiserreich*, Berlin 1985, p. 217.

97 Ludwig Pallat, *Richard Schöne, Generaldirektor der Königlichen Museen zu Berlin. Ein Beitrag zur Geschichte der preußischen Kunstverwaltung 1872–1905*, 1959, p. 327, cited in Bartmann, *Anton von Werner*, pp. 217–18.

98 Cited in Teeuwisse, *Vom Salon zur Sezession*, pp. 213–14.

99 Alfred Lichtwark, *Briefe an die Kommission für die Verwaltung der Kunsthalle*, vol. XI, 1903, p. 193, cited ibid., p. 214.

100 See Peter Paret, *Die Berliner Secession. Moderne Kunst und ihre Feinde im Kaiserlichen Deutschland*, Frankfurt a.M., Berlin, Vienna, 1983.

101 Bartmann, *Anton von Werner*, pp. 32–3.

102 Ibid., pp. 178 and 267.

103 Seidel, *Kaiser und die Kunst*, p. 198.

104 Ibid., pp. 212–14.

105 See Bartmann, *Anton von Werner*, p. 177.

106 Teeuwisse, *Vom Salon zur Sezession*, p. 95; Seidel, *Kaiser und die Kunst*, p. 194.

107 Teeuwisse, *Vom Salon zur Sezession*, p. 161.

108 Seidel, *Kaiser und die Kunst*, p. 144.

109 Eulenburg to Kaiser Wilhelm II, 16 April 1894, *Eulenburgs Korrespondenz*, II, No. 953.

110 Eulenburg to Bülow, 7 May 1894, ibid., No. 963. See also No. 966.

111 Seidel, *Kaiser und die Kunst*, pp. 161 and 176–7; Lutz Tittel, 'Monumentaldenkmäler von 1871 bis 1918', in Ekkehard Mai and Stephan Waetzoldt, eds., *Kunstverwaltung, Bau- und Denkmalkunst im Kaiserreich*, Berlin, 1981.

112 See for example Seidel, *Kaiser und die Kunst*, p. 181.

113 Waldersee, diary entry for 19 January 1891, CStA Berlin, Waldersee Papers; omitted from Meisner, II, p. 304.

114 Seidel, *Kaiser und die Kunst*, p. 228.

115 Ibid., p. 174.

116 *Reichs-Anzeiger*, special edition, Sunday, 27 January 1895, in Uta Lehnert, *Der Kaiser und die Siegesallee. Réclame Royale*, Berlin 1998, p. 22.

117 See ibid., pp. 15–22.

118 Ibid., p. 39.

119 Ibid., p. 67.

120 Ibid., p. 70.

121 Ibid., pp. 52 and 78.

122 Ibid., p. 79.

123 *Berliner Lokal-Anzeiger*, No. 571, 6 December 1899, cited ibid., p. 80.

124 Seidel, *Kaiser und die Kunst*, p. 168.

125 Lehnert, *Siegesallee*, p. 79.

126 Ibid., pp. 262 and 292–3.

127 Ibid., p. 245.

128 See the detailed account of the ceremony ibid., pp. 244–52.

129 Ibid., pp. 288–9.

130 Wilhelm Holzamer, *Die Siegesallee. Kunstbriefe an den deutschen Michel*, Leipzig 1902, cited ibid., p. 288.

131 Schaper to his wife, 3 May 1900, ibid., p. 292.

132 Barbara Tuchman, *Proud Tower*, New York 1966, p. 303.

133 Cited in Lehnert, *Siegesallee*, p. 293.

134 Gerhard Masur, *Imperial Berlin*, London 1971, p. 212; Ronald Taylor, *Berlin and Its Culture. A Historical Portrait*, New Haven, London 1997, p. 169; Alexandra Richie, *Faust's Metropolis. A History of Berlin*, London 1998, p. 231.

135 Kaiser Wilhelm II, speech of 18 December 1901, Johannes Penzler, ed., *Die Reden Kaiser Wilhelms II. in den Jahren 1901–Ende 1905*, Leipzig n.d., pp. 57–63; Elkind, *German Emperor's Speeches*, pp. 185–9.

### 30   THE CHALLENGE: FROM CONTINENTAL POLICY TO *WELTPOLITIK*

1 See Hildebrand, *Deutsche Außenpolitik 1871–1918*, pp. 32ff.; Hildebrand, *Das vergangene Reich*, pp. 190ff.; Canis, *Von Bismarck zur Weltpolitik*, pp. 138ff.

2 Kaiser Wilhelm II, speech of 18 January 1896, Penzler, *Reden Kaiser Wilhelms II. in den Jahren 1896–1900*, pp. 9–10. See also Elkind, *German Emperor's Speeches*, pp. 141–2.

3 See above, pp. 763–4 and 858 also Canis, *Von Bismarck zu Weltpolitik*, pp. 223ff.

4 Szögyény to Goluchowski, 5 February 1900, cited in Paul Kennedy, 'The Kaiser and German Weltpolitik. Reflexions on Wilhelm II's Place in the Making of German Foreign Policy', in Röhl and Sombart, *Kaiser Wilhelm II. New Interpretations*, p. 158.

5 Völderndorff to Hohenlohe, 9 November 1897, Hohenlohe, *Denkwürdigkeiten der Reichskanzlerzeit*, pp. 401–2.

6 Kennedy, 'Kaiser and German Weltpolitik', pp. 158–9.

7 Nipperdey, *Deutsche Geschichte*, II, p. 632.

8 Grierson to Bigge, 4 May 1899, RA I62/10a.

9 Prince Heinrich of Prussia, speech of 15 December 1897, Penzler, *Reden Kaiser Wilhelms II. in den Jahren 1896–1900*, pp. 80–1.

10 Eulenburg to Bülow, 18 December 1897, *Eulenburgs Korrespondenz*, III, No. 1354.

11 Spitzemberg, diary entry for 19 December 1897, *Tagebuch*, p. 362.

12 Bigelow to Kaiser Wilhelm II, January 1898, GStA Berlin, BPHA Rep. 53J Lit. B No. 10.

13 Hinzpeter to Kaiser Wilhelm II, 9 December 1897, ibid., BPHA Rep. 53J Lit. H. No. 1.

14 Hinzpeter to Kaiser Wilhelm II, 12 June 1899, ibid.

15 Hinzpeter to Kaiser Wilhelm II, 4 February 1899, ibid.

16 Holstein to Eulenburg, 24 November 1896, *Eulenburgs Korrespondenz*, III, No. 1279.

17 Holstein to Eulenburg, 24 November 1896, *Holstein Papers*, III, No. 586.

18 Radolin to Holstein, 18 January 1897, ibid., IV, No. 596.

19 Holstein to Radolin, 19 January 1897, ibid., No. 597.

20 Holstein to Eulenburg, 3 February 1897, ibid., No. 599. See *Große Politik*, XII, No. 3104. For Wilhelm's inclination towards France at this time, see also Holstein to Hatzfeldt, 14 April 1897, *Holstein Papers*, IV, No. 609.

21 Hohenlohe to Eulenburg, 3 March 1897, Hohenlohe, *Denkwürdigkeiten der Reichskanzlerzeit*, p. 309; Eulenburg to Hohenlohe, 1 March 1897, ibid., p. 308.

22 Holstein's undated draft, ibid., p. 309, n. 1.

23 See above, p. 367.

24 Kaiser Wilhelm II to Empress Frederick, 20 February 1899, AdHH Schloss Fasanerie.

25 See above, p. 499.

26 Kaiser Wilhelm II, marginal notes on Münster's report from Paris of 26 May 1896, *Große Politik*, XI, No. 2853.

27 Hohenlohe, diary entry for 6 September 1896, Hohenlohe, *Denkwürdigkeiten der Reichskanzlerzeit*, pp. 260–1. For the meeting of the two emperors in Breslau, see Canis, *Von Bismarck zur Weltpolitik*, pp. 205–6; McLean, *Royalty and Diplomacy*, pp. 31–2.

28 Kaiser Wilhelm II to Eulenburg, 9 September 1896, *Große Politik*, XI, No. 2861.

29 Kaiser Wilhelm II, speech in Görlitz, 7 September 1896, Penzler, *Reden Kaiser Wilhelms II. in den Jahren 1896–1900*, pp. 32–3.

30 Eulenburg, note of 4 October 1896, *Eulenburgs Korrespondenz*, III, No. 1265.

31 Eulenburg to Kaiser Wilhelm II, 22 August 1897, ibid., No. 1340.

32 Margaret M. Jefferson, 'Lord Salisbury's Conversations with the Tsar in Balmoral, 27 and 29 September 1896', *Slavonic and East European Review*, 39 (1960–1), pp. 216–22; Canis, *Von Bismarck zur Weltpolitik*, p. 207.

33 Jefferson, 'Salisbury's Conversations with the Tsar', p. 220; Andrew Roberts, *Salisbury. Victorian Titan*, London 2000, pp. 643–4.

34 Hanotaux, note of 12 October 1896, *Documents Diplomatiques Français*, XII, p. 781; McLean, *Royalty and Diplomacy*, p. 32; *Große Politik*, XI, p. 369. See also Nicholas II to his mother, 2 October 1896, in E. J. Bing, ed., *The Letters of the Tsar Nicholas and the Empress Marie*, London 1937, pp. 119–25.

35 Canis, *Von Bismarck zur Weltpolitik*, pp. 207–8.

36 Salisbury to Goschen, 6 September 1897, cited in Kennedy, *Anglo-German Antagonism*, p. 233.

37 Empress Frederick to Queen Victoria, 17 October 1896, AdHH Schloss Fasanerie; Alexander Hohenlohe to his father, 8 October 1896, Hohenlohe, *Denkwürdigkeiten der Reichskanzlerzeit*, pp. 388–9.

38 Hohenlohe to Kaiser Wilhelm II, 16 October 1896, Hohenlohe to his son Alexander, 17 October 1896, ibid., pp. 268–9; Kaiser Wilhelm II to Hohenlohe, 20 October 1896, *Große Politik*, XI, No. 2868.

39 Eulenburg to Bülow, 26 October 1896, *Eulenburgs Korrespondenz*, III, No. 1268.

40 Kaiser Wilhelm II, memorandum 'On the need to form a politico-mercantile coalition of the European states against the USA', printed in Russian translation in A. A. Fursenko, *Bor'ba za razdel Kitaya i amerikanskaya doktrina otkritich dverei 1895–1900*, Moscow, Leningrad 1956, pp. 209–12.

41 Eulenburg, note of 8 November 1896, *Eulenburgs Korrespondenz*, III, No. 1272.

42 Waldersee, diary entry for 25 October 1896, GStA Berlin, Waldersee Papers; badly distorted in Meisner, II, pp. 374–5.

43 Holstein to Hatzfeldt, 27/28 November 1896, Hatzfeldt, *Nachgelassene Papiere*, II, No. 692.

44 Kaiser Wilhelm II to Kaiser Franz Joseph, 8 January 1898, HHStA Vienna, Kabinettsarchiv Geheimakten 2. See Holstein to Hatzfeldt, 27/28 November 1896, Hatzfeldt, *Nachgelassene Papiere*, II, No. 692; McLean, *Royalty and Diplomacy*, p. 32.

45 Spitzemberg, diary entry for 18 November 1896, *Tagebuch*, p. 348.

46 Hohenlohe to Eulenburg, 4 February 1897, Hohenlohe, *Denkwürdigkeiten der Reichskanzlerzeit*, p. 297. See also Hohenlohe to Kaiser Wilhelm II, draft of January 1897, ibid., p. 296.

47 Kaiser Wilhelm II, marginal notes on Eulenburg's report of 19 August 1896, *Große Politik*, XI, p. 328.

48 Eulenburg to Kaiser Wilhelm II, 7 June 1896, *Eulenburgs Korrespondenz*, III, p. 1741; Eulenburg to Kaiserin Auguste Viktoria, 15 October 1896, ibid., No. 1266.

49 Eulenburg to Kaiser Wilhelm II, 14 November 1896, ibid., No. 1275.

50 Grierson to Bigge, 14 September 1896, RA I60/156a. But cf. above, pp. 347–8.

51 Hohenlohe to Kaiser Wilhelm II, January 1897, Hohenlohe, *Denkwürdigkeiten der Reichskanzlerzeit*, pp. 296–7.

52 Holstein to Eulenburg, 3 February 1897, *Holstein Papers*, IV, No. 599.

53 Hohenlohe to Eulenburg, 4 February 1897, Eulenburg to Hohenlohe, 8 February 1897, Hohenlohe, *Denkwürdigkeiten der Reichskanzlerzeit*, pp. 297–8.

54 Hohenlohe, diary entry for 27 February 1899, Hohenlohe to his son Alexander, 24 September 1899, ibid., pp. 486 and 527.

55 Alexander Hohenlohe to his father, 18 September 1899, ibid., pp. 526–7.

56 Georg Alexander (from 1900 von) Müller, memorandum of 1896 entitled 'Zukunftspolitik', in Görlitz, *Der Kaiser* pp. 36–41. See John C. G. Röhl, ed., *From Bismarck to Hitler. The Problem of Continuity in German History*, London 6th edn 1984, pp. 56–60.

57 Knollys to Hardinge, 13 November 1909, Cambridge University Library, Hardinge Papers, 18; cited in John C. G. Röhl, 'Der Kaiser und England', in Wilfrid Rogasch, ed., *Victoria & Albert, Vicky & The Kaiser. Ein Kapitel deutsch-englischer Familiengeschichte*, Berlin 1997, p. 175. See McLean, *Royalty and Diplomacy*, p. 155.

58 Müller, 'Zukunftspolitik', pp. 39–40.

59 Empress Frederick to Queen Victoria, 25 September 1896, AdHH Schloss Fasanerie. On the Armenian question, see Jost Dülffer, 'Die Kreta-Krise und der griechisch-türkische Krieg 1890–1898', in Jost Dülffer, Hans-Otto Mühleisen and Vera Torunsky, eds., *Inseln als Brennpunkte internationaler Politik*, Cologne 1986, pp. 30 and 36–39; William L. Langer, *The Diplomacy of Imperialism 1890–1902*, New York 2nd edn 1965, pp. 321–50.

60 Gerd Fesser, *Der Traum vom Platz an der Sonne. Deutsche 'Weltpolitik' 1897–1914*, Bremen 1996, p. 19; Lascelles to Salisbury, 28 August 1896, RA I60/154.

61 Kaiser Wilhelm II, marginal notes on Saurma's report from Constantinople, 22 August 1896, PA AA, Asservat No. 4; marginal notes on Marschall's telegrams of 28 and 29 August 1898, *Große Politik*, XII, 1, No. 2898 and 2901. See Dülffer, 'Kreta', p. 36; Langer, *Diplomacy*, p. 326.

62 Kaiser Wilhelm II, marginal notes on Saurma's report from Constantinople, 19 September 1896, *Große Politik*, XII, 1, No. 2904.

63 Kaiser Wilhelm II to Queen Victoria, 18 December 1896, RA I60/161. This passage has been omitted from Buckle, *Letters of Queen Victoria*, III, p. 109.

64 Kaiser Wilhelm II, marginal notes on Saurma's report from Constantinople, 29 July 1896, *Große Politik*, XII, 1, No. 2893.

65 Kaiser Wilhelm II, marginal notes on Marschall's telegrams of 29 August 1896, ibid., Nos. 2899 and 2900.

66 See *Große Politik*, XII, 2, especially Nos. 3137, 3150 and 3151. For the Crete crisis and its background, see Langer, *Diplomacy*, pp. 315ff.; Rich, *Friedrich von Holstein*, II, pp. 477ff., Dülffer, 'Kreta', pp. 13–59.

67 Kaiser Wilhelm II, marginal notes on the Empress Frederick's letter, 17 February 1897, printed in Hohenlohe, *Denkwürdigkeiten der Reichskanzlerzeit*, p. 301.

68 Hatzfeldt to Hohenlohe, 7 January 1897, *Große Politik*, XII, 1, No. 3100.

69 Hatzfeldt and Hohenlohe, 15 January 1897, ibid., No. 3102. See also Kaiser Wilhelm II to Hohenlohe, 15 January 1897, ibid., No. 2932.

70 See Marschall's notes of 21 February 1897 with Kaiser Wilhelm II's marginal notes, ibid., 2, No. 3166.

71 Ibid. See also Kaiser Wilhelm II, marginal notes on Hatzfeldt's report from London, 14 April 1897, ibid., No. 3222.

72 Lascelles to Salisbury, 20 February 1897, quoted in van't Padje, 'Anglo-German Imperialist Rivalry', p. 109.

73 Kaiser Wilhelm II to Empress Frederick, 14 February 1897, AdHH Schloss Fasanerie.

74 See *Große Politik*, XII, 2, No. 3152, especially the notes on p. 327. Cf. Kaiser Wilhelm II's marginal notes on Marschall's report of 21 February 1897, ibid., No. 3166; marginal notes on the report from the envoy in Athens, Freiherr von Scheel-Plessen to Hohenlohe, 28 March 1897, ibid., No. 3215.

75 Hohenlohe to Kaiser Wilhelm II, 22 February 1897, ibid., No. 3168, with marginal notes, p. 347.

76 Grierson to Bigge, 20 February 1897, RA I61/2a.

77 Kaiser Wilhelm II, marginal comments on Marschall's notes of 21 February 1897, *Große Politik*, XII, 2, No. 3166.

78 Hohenlohe to Kaiser Wilhelm II, 15 February 1897, ibid., No. 3152, with the Kaiser's marginal notes, p. 328.

79 Kaiser Wilhelm II, marginal notes on Scheel-Plessen's report from Athens, 28 March 1897, ibid., No. 3215.

80 Kaiser Wilhelm II, marginal notes on Kiderlen-Wächter's report from Copenhagen of 9 March 1897, PA AA, Asservat No. 4.

81 Crown Princess Sophie of Greece to Empress Frederick, 12 February 1897, enclosure to Empress Frederick to Kaiser Wilhelm II, 17 February 1897, printed in Hohenlohe, *Denkwürdigkeiten der Reichskanzlerzeit*, p. 303. See also Crown Princess Sophie of Greece to Empress Frederick, 23 April 1897, copy in Empress Frederick to Queen Victoria, 27 April 1897, AdHH Schloss Fasanerie; Queen Victoria to Wilhelm II, 17 February 1897, Hohenlohe, *Denkwürdigkeiten der Reichskanzlerzeit*, p. 303. See Buckle, *Letters of Queen Victoria*, III, pp. 135–6.

82 Empress Frederick to Queen Victoria, 23 March 1897, AdHH Schloss Fasanerie.

83 Empress Frederick to Queen Victoria, 4 April 1897, ibid.

84 Empress Frederick to Queen Victoria, 28 April 1897, ibid.

85 See *Große Politik*, XII, 2, Nos. 3219 and 3220.

86 Queen Victoria to Tsar Nicholas II, 25 April 1897, in Buckle, *Letters of Queen Victoria*, III, p. 154.

87 Hohenlohe to Kaiser Wilhelm II, 10 May 1897, *Große Politik*, XII, 2, No. 3231, with marginal notes, pp. 417–18.

88 Queen Victoria to Kaiser Wilhelm II, 7 May 1897, transmitted by Gough to August Eulenburg, GStA Berlin, BPHA Rep. 53 J. Lit. G. No. 13.

89 Kaiser Wilhelm II to Queen Victoria, draft, ibid.; text of the telegram in RA H40/22.

90 RA QVJ, 7/8 May 1897.

91 Crown Princess Sophie of Greece to Kaiser Wilhelm II, 9 May 1897, *Große Politik*, XII, 2, No. 3232; Wilhelm's reply, ibid., No. 3233.

92 Kaiser Wilhelm II to his sister Sophie, 12 May 1897, ibid., No. 3238.

93 Kaiser Wilhelm II to Queen Victoria, 13 May 1897, RA H40/56.

94 RA QVJ, 13 May 1897.

95 Empress Frederick to Queen Victoria, 14 May 1897, AdHH Schloss Fasanerie. For the peace negotations, see *Große Politik*, XII, 2, Nos. 3248, 3249 and 3250.

96 Kaiser Wilhelm II to Hohenlohe, 24 September 1897, Hohenlohe, *Denkwürdigkeiten der Reichskanzlerzeit*, p. 386.

97 Kaiser Wilhelm II to Hohenlohe, 23 February 1897, *Große Politik*, XII, 2, No. 3169. See also Hohenlohe, *Denkwürdigkeiten der Reichskanzlerzeit*, p. 305.

98 Kaiser Wilhelm II to Tsar Nicholas II, 20 October 1898, Goetz, *Briefe Wilhelms II an den Zaren*, pp. 313–15. A somewhat inaccurate copy is to be found in PA AA, Preußen 1 No. 1d, Bd I.

99 On the following see Ernst Freiherr von Mirbach, ed., *Das deutsche Kaiserpaar im Heiligen Lande im Herbst 1898. Mit Allerhöchster Ermächtigung Seiner Majestät des Kaisers und Königs bearbeitet nach authentischen Berichten und Akten*, Berlin 1899; Theodor Herzl, *Gesammelte zionistische Werke*, 5 vols., Tel Aviv 1934; Hermann Ellern and Bessi Ellern, *Herzl, Hechler, the Grand Duke of Baden and the German Emperor 1896–1904*, Tel Aviv 1961; Alexander Bein, *Erinnerungen und Dokumente über Herzls Begegnung mit Wilhelm II, Zeitschrift für die Geschichte der Juden*, 1964; Julius H. Schoeps, *Theodor Herzl 1860–1904. Wenn ihr wollt, ist es kein Märchen. Eine Text-Bild-Monographie*, Vienna 1995; Jan Stefan Richter, *Die Orientreise Kaiser Wilhelms II. 1898*, Hamburg 1997; John C. G. Röhl, 'Herzl and Kaiser Wilhelm II. A German Protectorate in Palestine?', in Ritchie Robinson and Edward Timms, eds., *Theodor Herzl and the Origins of Zionism*, Edinburgh 1997, pp. 27–38; Alex Carmel and Ejal Jakob Eisler, *Der Kaiser reist ins Heilige Land. Die Palästinareise Wilhelms II. 1898. Eine illustrierte Dokumentation*, Stuttgart 1999.

100 See Kaiser Wilhelm II to Tsar Nicholas II, 18 August 1898, Goetz, *Briefe Wilhelms II. an den Zaren*, pp. 311–12. Cf. Grand Duke Carl Alexander of Saxe-Weimar-Eisenach to Kaiser Wilhelm II, 11 October 1898, GStA Berlin, BPHA Rep. 53J Lit. S No. 2.

101 See Wedekind's satirical poem 'Im heiligen Land' and Heine's cartoon 'Palästina' in *Simplicissimus*, 3, No. 31, September 1898. See Ernestine Koch, *Albert Langen. Ein Verleger in München*, Munich, Berlin 1969, pp. 8 and 92.

102 See Bismarck's warning, cited in Hellige and Schulin, *Rathenau und Harden*, pp. 322–3.

103 See Posadowsky to Hohenlohe, 25 September 1898, Hohenlohe to Posadowsky, 28 September 1898, Hohenlohe, *Denkwürdigkeiten der Reichskanzlerzeit*, pp. 460–1; see Hellige and Schulin, *Rathenau und Harden*, Nos. 14 and 15.

104 Cited in Schoeps, *Herzl*, p. 87.

105 Herzl, diary entry for 15 November 1898. Translations are taken from Raphael Patal, ed., *The Complete Diaries of Theodor Herzl*, translated by Harry Zohn, 5 vols., New York, London 1960.

106 Herzl, diary entry for 8 October 1898.

107 William H. Hechler to Grand Duke Friedrich I of Baden, 26 March and 18 April 1898, Ellern and Ellern, *Herzl*, Nos. 1 and 2; Fuchs, *Großherzog von Baden*, III, Nos. 1532–3; Herzl to Grand Duke of Baden, 26 April 1898, Ellern and Ellern, *Herzl*, No. 3; Fuchs, *Großherzog von Baden*, III, No. 1537.

108 Kaiser Wilhelm II, marginal notes on Schweinitz's report from St Petersburg, 24 May 1891, PA AA, Asservat No. 4.

109 Herzl, diary entry for 23 April 1896; Isaiah Friedman, *Germany, Turkey and Zionism 1897–1918*, Oxford 1977, p. 57.

110 Kaiser Wilhelm II, marginal notes of 1 October 1897, PA AA, No. R 529.

111 Herzl, diary entry for 12 June 1895.

112 Herzl to Kaiser Wilhelm II, 22 October and 1 December 1897, Ellern and Ellern, *Herzl*, Nos. 10 and 11; Herzl to Grand Duke of Baden, 22 October 1897, Fuchs, *Großherzog von Baden*, III, No. 1759.

113 Desmond Stewart, *Theodor Herzl, Artist and Politician*, London 1974, p. 260.

114 Grand Duke of Baden to Kaiser Wilhelm II, 28 July 1898, Ellern and Ellern, *Herzl*, No. 12; Fuchs, *Großherzog von Baden*, IV, No. 1879.

115 Kaiser Wilhelm II to Grand Duke of Baden, 29 August 1898, Fuchs, *Großherzog von Baden*, IV, No. 1884.

116 Herzl, diary entry for 3 September 1898. See Herzl to Grand Duke of Baden, 8 September 1898, Ellern and Ellern, *Herzl*, No. 14; Fuchs, *Großherzog von Baden*, IV, No. 1888.

117 Herzl, diary entry for 9 September 1898.

118 Herzl, diary entry for 15 September 1898.

119 Herzl, diary entry for 16 September 1898.

120 Herzl to Eulenburg, 24 September 1898, *Eulenburgs Korrespondenz*, III, No. 1386.

121 Kaiser Wilhelm II to Grand Duke of Baden, 29 September 1898, Ellern and Ellern, *Herzl*, No. 16; Bein, *Herzls Begegnung mit Wilhelm II.*, pp. 44ff.; Fuchs, *Großherzog von Baden*, IV, No. 1892. See *Eulenburgs Korrespondenz*, III, pp. 1920ff.

122 Eulenburg to Herzl, 27 September 1898, Bein, *Herzls Begegnung mit Wilhelm II.*, pp. 44ff.; Fuchs, *Großherzog von Baden*, IV, No. 1891. See *Eulenburgs Korrespondenz*, III, No. 1387. See Herzl, diary entry for 2 October 1898.

123 Herzl, diary entry for 6 October 1898.

124 Herzl, diary entry for 9 October 1898.

125 Herzl, diary entries for 15–17 October 1898; Herzl to Kaiser Wilhelm II, 18 October 1898, draft, ibid.

126 Herzl, diary entries for 19–21 October 1898.

127 Herzl, diary entry for 3 January 1901.

128 Ayse Osmanoglu, *Avec mon Père le Sultan Abdulhamid de son palais à sa prison*, Paris 1991, p. 54. See Philip Mansel, *Constantinople, City of the World's Desire, 1453–1924*, London 1995, pp. 321–2.

129 Bulent Mim Kemal Öke, 'Ottoman Policies towards Zionism', MPhil. diss., Cambridge 1979, pp. 61–92.

130 Bülow, *Memoirs*, I, p. 250. Cf. Friedman, *Germany, Turkey and Zionism*, p. 79; Öke, 'Ottoman Policies towards Zionism', p. 91.

131 See above, p. 944; also Bülow, *Memoirs*, I, pp. 253–4.

132 Mirbach, *Das deutsche Kaiserpaar im Heiligen Lande*, pp. 86 and 99–100.

133 Herzl, diary entry for 29 October 1898.

134 Herzl, diary entry for 2 November 1898.

135 Kaiser Wilhelm II, speech of 8 November 1898 in Damascus, Penzler, *Reden Kaiser Wilhelms II. in den Jahren 1896–1900*, pp. 126–7.

136 Kaiser Wilhelm II to Grand Duke of Baden, 7 November 1898, PA AA, Preußen 1 No. 1d, Bd I. Cf. Hereditary Princess Charlotte of Saxe-Meiningen to Empress Frederick, 13 November 1898, AdHH Schloss Fasanerie.

137 Kaiser Wilhelm II to Empress Frederick, 20 November 1898, AdHH Schloss Fasanerie, printed in facsimile in Carmel and Eisler, *Heilige Land*, pp. 173–4.

138 Hereditary Princess Charlotte of Saxe-Meiningen to Empress Frederick, 1 December 1898, AdHH Schloss Fasanerie. See also Hohenlohe, diary entry for 20 November 1898, Hohenlohe, *Denkwürdigkeiten der Reichskanzlerzeit*, pp. 469–70; Kaiser Wilhelm II, speech of 1 December 1898 on his return to Berlin, Penzler, *Reden Kaiser Wilhelms II. in den Jahren 1896–1900*, pp. 127–8.

139 See Mirbach, *Das deutsche Kaiserpaar im Heiligen Lande*; Hans Forsten, *Unser Kaiser in Palästina. Reise Kaiser Wilhelms II. und der Kaiserin Auguste Victoria nach dem gelobten Lande*, Berlin 1898, Adolf Meyer, *Ins Heilige Land. Reisebilder von der großen Festfahrt nach Jerusalem im Oktober und November 1898*, Berlin 1899; Pastor Ludwig Schneller, *Die Kaiserfahrt durch's heilige Land*, Leipzig 1899; Richard Schott, *Eine Fahrt nach dem Orient. Zur Erinnerung an den Einzug des deutschen Kaisers und der Kaiserin in Jerusalem, Herbst 1898*, Berlin, Eisenach, Leipzig 1898; Friedrich Zange, *Die Jerusalemfahrt Kaiser Wilhelms II. im Lichte der Geschichte*, Berlin 1899; Marie von Bodelschwingh, *Aus Heiligem Land. Den Kindern erzählt*, Bielefeld 1899; Paul von Frankenberg, *Kaiser Wilhelms II. Reise nach Jerusalem*, Berlin 1899. See further Thomas Hartmut Benner, *Die Strahlen der Krone. Die religiöse Dimension des Kaiserstums unter Wilhelm II. vor dem Hintergrund der Orientreise 1898*, Marburg 2001.

140 Kaiser Wilhelm II, speech of 3 February 1899, Penzler, *Reden Kaiser Wilhelms II. in den Jahren 1896–1900*, pp. 144–8; cf. Elkind, *German Emperor's Speeches*, p. 303. See *Young Wilhelm*, pp. 304–5.

141 Fesser, *Platz an der Sonne*, pp. 11–12; Jost Dülffer, Martin Kröger and Rolf-Harald Wippich, *Vermiedene Kriege. Deeskalation von Konflikten der Großmächte zwischen Krimkrieg und Erstem Weltkrieg 1865–1914*, Munich 1997, pp. 475–6. See also *Große Politik*, XIV, No. 3669, note.

142 *Große Politik*, XIV, Nos. 3679 and 3680. See Dülffer et al., *Vermiedene Kriege*, p. 477.

143 Kaiser Wilhelm II to Auswärtiges Amt, 6 November 1897, *Große Politik*, XIV, No. 3686.

144 Ibid., No. 3687.

145 See Dülffer et al., *Vermiedene Kriege*, p. 477.

146 Kaiser Wilhelm II to Bülow, 7 November 1897, *Große Politik*, XIV, No. 3690.

147 Fesser, *Platz an der Sonne*, p. 13.

148 Hohenlohe to Kaiser Wilhelm II, 6 November 1897, *Große Politik*, XIV, No. 3688; Holstein to Eulenburg, 23 November 1897, *Eulenburgs Korrespondenz*, III, No. 1353.

149 Kaiser Wilhelm II to Hohenlohe, 7 November 1897, *Große Politik*, XIV, No. 3689.

150 Kaiser Wilhelm II to Bülow, 7 November 1897, ibid., No. 3690.

151 Dülffer et al., *Vermiedene Kriege*, p. 478.

152 Rotenhan to Kaiser Wilhelm II, 10 November 1897, *Große Politik*, XIV, No. 3693.

153 Hohenlohe, *Denkwürdigkeiten der Reichskanzlerzeit*, p. 413.

154 Hohenlohe to Rotenhan, 10 November 1897, ibid., p. 412.

155 Holstein to Hohenlohe, 9 November 1897, ibid., p. 411. See Fesser, *Platz an der Sonne*, p. 13.

156 Tirpitz to Hohenlohe, 10 November 1897, Hohenlohe, *Denkwürdigkeiten der Reichskanzlerzeit*, p. 412.

157 Hohenlohe to Rotenhan, 10 November 1897, ibid.

158 See below, p. 960.

159 Cited in Rotenhan to Bülow, 11 November 1897, *Große Politik*, XIV, No. 3695; Dülffer et al., *Vermiedene Kriege*, p. 478.

160 Fesser, *Platz an der Sonne*, p. 13.

161 Hohenlohe to Kaiser Wilhelm II, 11 November 1897, *Große Politik*, XIV, No. 3696.

162 Memorandum of 15 November 1897, ibid., No. 3701. See Dülffer et al., *Vermiedene Kriege*, pp. 479–80.

163 Memorandum of 15 November 1897, *Große Politik*, XIV, No. 3701.

164 Hohenlohe to Kaiser Wilhelm II, 18 November 1897, ibid., No. 3707.

165 Kaiser Wilhelm II, marginal notes, Hohenlohe to Kaiser Wilhelm II, 18 November 1897, ibid. See Dülffer et al., *Vermiedene Kriege*, p. 481.

166 Kaiser Wilhelm II to Auswärtiges Amt, 24 November 1897, Hohenlohe, *Denkwürdigkeiten der Reichskanzlerzeit*, p. 418.

167 Kaiser Wilhelm II to Hohenlohe, 26 November 1897, ibid., p. 419.

168 Hohenlohe, diary entry for 29 November 1897, ibid.

169 Dülffer et al., *Vermiedene Kriege*, p. 481; Fesser, *Platz an der Sonne*, p. 14.

170 See e.g. Bülow to Hatzfeldt, 2 December 1897, *Holstein Papers*, IV, No. 636; also Hohenlohe to Holstein, 31 December 1897, ibid., No. 640.

171 Hohenlohe to his son Alexander, 8 July 1900, Hohenlohe, *Denkwürdigkeiten der Reichskanzlerzeit*, p. 578. Cf., however, ibid., p. 424.

172 Eulenburg to Kaiser Wilhelm II, 23 December 1897, *Eulenburgs Korrespondenz*, III, No. 1355.

173 Kaiser Wilhelm II to Kaiser Franz Joseph, 8 January 1898, HHStA Vienna, Kab. Archiv, Geheimakten 1.

174 Kaiser Franz Joseph to Kaiser Wilhelm II, 11 January 1898, ibid.

175 Kaiser Wilhelm II to Tsar Nicholas II, 19 December 1897, *Große Politik*, XIV, No. 3739.

176 Kaiser Wilhelm II, speech of 15 December 1897 in Kiel, Penzler, *Reden Kaiser Wilhelms II. in den Jahren 1896–1900*, pp. 78–80.

177 Fesser, *Platz an der Sonne*, pp. 14–15.

178 Prince Heinrich of Prussia to Empress Frederick, 10 April 1898, AdHH Schloss Fasanerie.

179 Prince Heinrich of Prussia to Empress Frederick, 20 February 1899, ibid.

180 Prince Heinrich of Prussia to Kaiser Wilhelm II, 4 February 1899, GStA Berlin, BPHA Rep. 52 V1 No. 13a. See above, pp. 745–9.

181 Bülow to Kaiser Wilhelm II, 13 December 1897, *Große Politik*, XIV, No. 3732.

182 Kaiser Wilhelm II, marginal notes on Bülow's report of 13 December 1897, ibid.

183 Cited in Dülffer et al., *Vermiedene Kriege*, p. 485.

184 Prince Heinrich of Prussia to Empress Frederick, 10 April 1898, AdHH Schloss Fasanerie.

185 Prince Heinrich of Prussia to Empress Frederick, 1 June 1898, ibid.

186 Prince Heinrich of Prussia to Empress Frederick, 6 May and 9 August 1899, ibid.

187 Prince Heinrich of Prussia to Empress Frederick, 8 February 1898, ibid.

188 Prince Heinrich of Prussia to Empress Frederick, 10 April 1898, ibid.

189 Prince Heinrich of Prussia to Empress Frederick, 1 June 1898, ibid.

190 Prince Heinrich of Prussia to Empress Frederick, 8 April 1898, ibid.

191 Prince Heinrich of Prussia to Empress Frederick, 24 October 1898, ibid.

192 Prince Heinrich of Prussia to Empress Frederick, 6 November 1898, ibid. See also Heinrich's letter of 27 December 1898, ibid.

### 31 THE KAISER AND ENGLAND

1 See above, ch. 26.

2 Bülow to Eulenburg, 20 July 1898, *Eulenburgs Korrespondenz*, III, No. 1381.

3 Kaiser Wilhelm II, marginal notes on Dönhoff's report of 5 May 1896, PA AA, Asservat No. 4.

4 Kaiser Wilhelm II to Queen Victoria, 2 January 1897, RA I61/1.

5 Queen Victoria to Kaiser Wilhelm II, 17 February 1897, in Hohenlohe, *Denkwürdigkeiten der Reichskanzlerzeit*, p. 303.

6 Grierson to Bigge, 20 February 1897, RA I61/2a. See above, pp. 628–33.

7 Kaiser Wilhelm II to Queen Victoria, 10 June 1897, RA Z500/7.

8 See above, p. 798, and below, pp. 991–8.

9 Hatzfeldt to Hohenlohe, 11 December 1897, *Große Politik*, XIV, No. 3730.

10 Empress Frederick to Queen Victoria, 29 August 1896, AdHH Schloss Fasanerie.

11 Grierson to Bigge, 24 November 1896, RA I60/160.

12 Lascelles to Salisbury, 22 November 1896, quoted in van't Padje, 'Anglo-German Imperialist Rivalry', pp. 102–3.

13 Empress Frederick to Queen Victoria, 24 October 1896, AdHH Schloss Fasanerie.

14 Swaine to Bigge, 16 November 1898, RA I61/27.

15 See Kennedy, *Anglo-German Antagonism*, pp. 231ff.; J. A. S. Grenville, *Lord Salisbury and Foreign Policy*, London 1964, pp. 148–76; J. L. Garvin and J. Amery, *Life of Joseph Chamberlain*, 6 vols., London 1932–69, III, pp. 251ff.; Friedrich Meinecke, *Geschichte des deutsch-englischen Bündnisproblems*, Munich, Berlin 1927, pp. 85–114; Gerhard Ritter, *Die Legende von der verschmähten englischen Freundschaft 1898/1901*, Leipzig 1929; Roberts, *Salisbury*, pp. 689ff.; Peter Winzen, *Bülows Weltmachtkonzept. Untersuchungen zur Frühphase seiner Außenpolitik 1897–1901*, Boppard am Rhein 1977, pp. 156ff.; Gregor Schöllgen, *Imperialismus und Gleichgewicht. Deutschland, England und die orientalische Frage 1871–1914*, Munich 1992, pp. 86ff.; Hildebrand, *Das vergangene Reich*, pp. 213ff.

16 Grierson to Bigge, 21 January 1898, RA I61/32a. The cartoon of Wilhelm II as Emperor of China appeared in *Punch* on 15 January 1898. See Röhl, 'Der Kaiser und England', p. 178.

17 Sir Theodore Martin to Queen Victoria, 13, 14 and 16 January 1898, RA I61/30–32; Bigge to Queen Victoria, 26 January 1898, RA I61/33.

18 Grierson to Bigge, 5 February 1898, RA I61/34.

19 Münster to Hohenlohe, 23 February 1898, Hohenlohe, *Denkwürdigleiten der Reichskanzlerzeit*, p. 431.

20 Grierson to Bigge, 26 February 1898, RA I61/35a.

21 See George Duke of York to Bigge, 9 March 1898, RA I61/36.

22 See Holstein to Eulenburg, 10 November 1897, *Eulenburgs Korrespondenz*, III, No. 1352.

23 Bigge to Queen Victoria, 14 March 1898, RA I61/37.

24 Grierson to Bigge, 26 February and 6 March 1898, RA I61/35a–b; Bigge to Queen Victoria, 14 March 1898, RA I61/37 and Add A18/Y10; Eulenburg to Bülow, 11 July 1898, *Eulenburgs Korrespondenz*, III, No. 1378.

25 See above, ch. 4.

26 Prince Christian of Schleswig-Holstein to Albert Edward Prince of Wales, undated [March 1898] RA Add A18/Y10.

27 Lascelles to Albert Edward Prince of Wales, 25 March 1898, RA I61/39.

28 Ibid.; Grierson to Bigge, 7 May 1898, RA I61/46a.

29 Grierson to Bigge, 28 May 1898, RA I61/48a. See Kaiser Wilhelm II to Tsar Nicholas II, 30 May 1898, in Goetz, *Briefe Wilhelms II. an den Zaren*, pp. 309–11. The Kaiser was in close touch in England with, among others, the Earl of Lonsdale und Sir Edward Sullivan. See Lonsdale to Kaiser Wilhelm II, 4 August and 28 September 1898, GStA Berlin, BPHA Rep. 53J Lit. L. No. 9 and Lit. V. No. 1-W No. 1; Sullivan to Kaiser Wilhelm II, 7 January 1899, ibid., Lit. S. Nos. 15–21.

30 Grierson to Bigge, 7 May 1898, RA I61/46a.

31 *Große Politik*, XIV, 1, No. 3781.

32 Cited in Roberts, *Salisbury*, p. 690. See Paul Kennedy, *The Samoan Tangle. A Study in Anglo-German-American Relations 1878–1900*, Dublin 1974, p. 157.

33 Hatzfeldt to Auswärtiges Amt, 22 May 1898, with Kaiser Wilhelm II's marginal notes, *Holstein Papers*, IV, No. 654; also Lonsdale to Kaiser Wilhelm II, 4 August 1898, GStA Berlin, BPHA Rep. 53J Lit. L. No. 9; Kennedy, *Samoan Tangle*, pp. 138–9 and 155ff.

34 Empress Frederick to Kaiser Wilhelm II, 29 May 1898, GStA Berlin, BPHA Rep. 52T No. 13. Cf. Empress Frederick to Hatzfeldt, 30 May 1898, Hatzfeldt, *Nachgelassene Papiere*, II, No. 725; Holstein to Hatzfeldt, 8 June 1898, ibid., No. 727.

35 Empress Frederick to Kaiser Wilhelm II, 31 May 1898, GStA Berlin, BPHA Rep. 52T No. 13.

36 Kaiser Wilhelm II to Tsar Nicholas II, 30 May 1898, Goetz, *Briefe Wilhelms II. an den Zaren*, pp. 309–11. A copy of a draft of this letter is to be found in the files of the Auswärtiges Amt, PA AA, Preußen 1 No. 1d Bd 1.

37 See *Große Politik*, XIV, 1, Nos. 3803–4; Rich, *Friedrich von Holstein*, II, pp. 582–5; Canis, *Von Bismarck zur Weltpolitik*, pp. 282 and 286.

38 Cited in Holstein to Hatzfeldt, 31 May 1898, *Holstein Papers*, IV, No. 656. See Kaiser Wilhelm II's note, *Große Politik*, XIV, 1, No. 3799.

39 Hatzfeldt to Holstein, 2 June 1898, *Holstein Papers*, IV, No. 658. See Hatzfeldt to Auswärtiges Amt, 2 June 1898, *Große Politik*, XIV, 1 No. 3800; Roberts, *Salisbury*, p. 691.

40 Kaiser Wilhelm II to Empress Frederick, 1 June 1898, draft, PA AA, Preußen 1 No. 1d, Bd I, printed in *Holstein Papers*, IV, No. 657. This document was placed in the secret files of the Auswärtiges Amt on Bülow's instructions.

41 Empress Frederick to Kaiser Wilhelm II, 3 June 1898, PA AA, Preußen 1 No. 1d, Bd I.

42 Empress Frederick to Queen Victoria, 15 July [June?] 1898, RA I61/52, in Buckle, *Letters of Queen Victoria*, III, pp. 258–9.

43 Salisbury to Queen Victoria, 21 June [July?] 1898, RA I61/50, in Buckle, *Letters of Queen Victoria*, III, pp. 259–60.

44 On the negotiations, see Rich, *Friedrich von Holstein*, II, pp. 586–7; Grenville, *Salisbury and Foreign Policy*, pp. 177–98; Kennedy, *Samoan Tangle*, pp. 130ff.

45 Bülow to Hatzfeldt, 8 June 1898, *Große Politik*, XIV, 1, Nos. 3804–6; also ibid., Nos. 3835–6. See Eugen Fischer, *Holsteins großes Nein. Die deutsch-englischen Bündnisverhandlungen von 1898–1901*, Berlin 1925, p. 65; A. S. Jerussalimski, *Die Außenpolitik und die Diplomatie des deutschen Imperialismus Ende des 19. Jahrhunderts*, Berlin 1954, pp. 614–15; Kennedy, *Samoan Tangle*, pp. 138–9 and 155ff.

46 Salisbury to Queen Victoria, 27 July 1898, RA I61/53.

47 Kaiser Wilhelm II, marginal notes on Richthofen to Eulenburg, 20 July 1898, PA AA, IA England 78 No. 1 secr., Bd. IV, R 5802; cited in Kennedy, *Samoan Tangle*, p. 130. The Kaiser's marginal comments were omitted by the editors of *Große Politik*.

48 Eulenburg to Bülow, 11 July 1898, *Eulenburgs Korrespondenz*, III, No. 1378.

49 Eulenburg to Bülow, 23 July 1898, ibid., No. 1383.

50 Empress Frederick to Kaiser Wilhelm II, 29 June 1898, GStA Berlin, BPHA Rep. 52T No. 13. See Lonsdale to Kaiser Wilhelm II, 4 August 1898, ibid., Rep. 53J Lit. L. No. 9.

51 Salisbury to Queen Victoria, 2 August 1898, RA I61/62.

52 Salisbury to Queen Victoria, 10 August 1898, RA I61/63, in Buckle, *Letters of Queen Victoria*, III, pp. 263–4.

53 Salisbury to Queen Victoria, 4 August 1898, in Buckle, *Letters of Queen Victoria*, III, pp. 262–3. Cf. the version of this letter, dated 1 August 1898, in RA I61/57.

54 Balfour to Queen Victoria, 26 August 1898, RA I61/65, 65a and b.

55 Lascelles to Queen Victoria, 9 December 1898, RA I61/78. See below, pp. 985–7.

56 Bülow to Kaiser Wilhelm II, 24 August 1898, *Große Politik*, XIV, 1, No. 3867.

57 Bülow to Kaiser Wilhelm II, 19 August 1898, GStA Berlin, BPHA Rep. 53J Lit. B. No. 16a, cited in Canis, *Von Bismarck zur Weltpolitik*, p. 288.

58 Holstein to Hatzfeldt, 22 December 1898, Canis, *Von Bismarck zur Weltpolitik*, p. 293.

59 Bülow to Kaiser Wilhelm II, 6 August 1900, GStA Berlin, BPHA Rep. 53J Lit. B. No. 16a, cited in Röhl, 'Kaiser und England', p. 174.

60 Kaiser Wilhelm II to Tsar Nicholas II, 18 August 1898, copy in PA AA, Preußen 1 No. 1d, Bd I, in Goetz, *Briefe Wilhelms II. an den Zaren*, pp. 311–12.

61 Kaiser Wilhelm II to Tsar Nicholas II, 20 October 1898, copy in PA AA, Preußen 1 No. 1d, Bd I, in Goetz, *Briefe Wilhelms II. an den Zaren*, pp. 313–15. See Ludwig Bittner, 'Neue Beiträge zur Haltung Kaiser Wilhelms II. in der Faschoda-Frage', *Historische Zeitschrift*, 162 (1940); Langer, *Diplomacy*, pp. 566–70; Kennedy, *Samoan Tangle*, p. 157.

62 Kaiser Wilhelm II to Tsar Nicholas II, 9 November 1898, in Goetz, *Briefe Wilhelms II. an den Zaren*, pp. 315–18. The copy of a draft of this letter, dated 8 November 1898, differs in several respects from the version actually sent. See PA AA, Preußen 1 No. 1d, Bd I.

63 Kaiser Wilhelm II to Empress Frederick, 20 November 1898, AdHH Schloss Fasanerie, printed in facsimile in Carmel and Eisler, *Der Kaiser reist ins Heilige Land*, pp. 173–4. See also Kaiser Wilhelm II to Queen Victoria, 16 November 1898, in Buckle, *Letters of Queen Victoria*, III, p. 311.

64 Salisbury to Queen Victoria, 26 November 1898, RA I61/77.

65 Lascelles to Queen Victoria, 9 December 1898, RA I61/78. See above, p. 983.

66 Kaiser Wilhelm II to Empress Frederick, 20 December 1898, AdHH Schloss Fasanerie. Cf. the copy in RA I61/80. See also Lascelles to Queen Victoria, 24 December 1898, RA I61/81, in Buckle, *Letters of Queen Victoria*, III, pp. 321–2; Empress Frederick to Kaiser Wilhelm II, 25 December 1898, GStA Berlin, BPHA Rep. 52T No. 13.

67 Kaiser Wilhelm II, marginal notes on Hatzfeldt's report from London of 22 December 1898, PA AA, Asservat No. 4. Hatzfeldt's report is printed without the Kaiser's marginal notes in *Große Politik*, XIV, 2, pp. 405ff. Cf. Bigge to Queen Victoria, 25 December 1898, RA I61/82, in Buckle, *Letters of Queen Victoria*, III, pp. 322–3; also Kaiser Wilhelm II to Queen Victoria, 29 December 1898, RA I61/83, ibid., pp. 323–4.

68 Rhodes to Kaiser Wilhelm II, 26 February 1899, GStA Berlin, BPHA Rep. 53J Lit R. No. 12.

69 Kaiser Wilhelm II, marginal notes on Bülow's report of 23 February 1899, PA AA, Asservat No. 4.

70 Grierson to Bigge, 18 March 1899, RA I62/6. On Wilhelm's wish for a 'German Asia Minor', see Eulenburg to Bülow, 10–11 July 1899, *Eulenburgs Korrespondenz*, III, No. 1396.

71 Kaiser Wilhelm II to Empress Frederick, 26 March 1899, AdHH Schloss Fasanerie.

72 Grierson to Bigge, 18 March 1899, RA I62/6; Kennedy, *Samoan Tangle*, p. 162.

73 Rhodes to Albert Edward Prince of Wales, undated [March 1899], in Buckle, *Letters of Queen Victoria*, III, pp. 349–51.

74 Kaiser Wilhelm II to Empress Frederick, 26 March 1899, AdHH Schloss Fasanerie.

75 Empress Frederick to Kaiser Wilhelm II, 30 March 1899, PA AA, Preußen 1 No. 1d, Bd I.

76 Grierson to Bigge, 1 April 1899, RA I62/9a.

77 See RA QVJ, 6 February 1899, in Buckle, *Letters of Queen Victoria*, III, p. 337. See Hartmut Pogge von Strandmann, 'Nationalisierungsdruck und königliche Namensänderung in England. Das Ende der Großfamilie europäischer Dynastien', in Gerhard A. Ritter and Peter Wende, eds., *Rivalität und Partnerschaft. Studien zu den deutsch-britischen Beziehugen im 19. und 20. Jahrhundert. Festschrift für Anthony J. Nicholls*, Paderborn 1999, pp. 69–91; also Kennedy, *Samoan Tangle*, pp. 180–1.

78 RA QVJ, 15 March and 9 April 1899, in Buckle, *Letters of Queen Victoria*, III, pp. 347–8 and 356; Pogge von Strandmann, 'Nationalisierungsdruck', pp. 74–5 and 77.

79 Lascelles to Salisbury, 31 March 1899, RA I62/9; Grierson to Bigge, 1 April 1899, RA I62/9a; Grierson to Lascelles, 3 May 1899, in Buckle, *Letters of Queen Victoria*, III, pp. 357ff. See Pogge von Strandmann, 'Nationalisierungsdruck', pp. 75–6.

80 Albert Edward Prince of Wales to Empress Frederick, 25 April 1899, cited in Pogge von Strandmann, 'Nationalisierungsdruck', p. 77; also Buckle, *Letters of Queen Victoria*, III, p. 356.

81 Grierson to Bigge, 4 May 1899, RA I62/10a.

82 Arthur Duke of Connaught to Queen Victoria, 22 April 1899, RA Vic/Add A 35/484, cited in Pogge von Strandmann, 'Nationalisierungsdruck', p. 77.

83 Queen Victoria to Empress Frederick, 3 May 1899, Albert Edward Prince of Wales to Empress Frederick, 2 May 1899, Alfred Duke of Coburg to Queen Victoria, 8 May 1899, cited in Pogge von Strandmann, 'Nationalisierungsdruck', pp. 78–9.

84 Kaiser Wilhelm II to Queen Victoria, 27 May 1899, cited in Pogge von Strandmann, 'Nationalisierungsdruck', p. 80. See Agatha Ramm, ed., *Beloved and Darling Child. Last Letters between Queen Victoria and Her Eldest Daughter 1886–1901*, Stroud 1990, pp. 231–2.

85 Hohenlohe, note of 2 December 1896, Hohenlohe, *Denkwürdigkeiten der Reichskanzlerzeit*, pp. 284–5. Wilhelm's accusations were discussed by Salisbury and the Queen on 2 December 1896: RA QVJ.

86 See above all Kennedy, *Samoan Tangle*, pp. 178ff.; Canis, *Von Bismarck zur Weltpolitik*, pp. 313ff.

87 RA QVJ, 27 January 1899, in Buckle, *Letters of Queen Victoria*, III, p. 336.

88 Kaiser Wilhelm II to Queen Victoria, 2 February 1899, in Buckle, *Letters of Queen Victoria*, III, pp. 336–7.

89 RA QVJ, 17 February 1899, in Buckle, *Letters of Queen Victoria*, III, pp. 340–1.

90 Queen Victoria to Tsar Nicholas II, [March?] 1899, RA I62/22, in Sir Sidney Lee, *King Edward VII. A Biography*, 2 vols., London 1925–7, I, p. 741, and in Buckle, *Letters of Queen Victoria*, III, pp. 343–4.

91 Lascelles to Salisbury, 11 March 1899, in Kennedy, *Samoan Tangle*, p. 180.

92 Grierson to Lascelles, 3 May 1899, RA I62/10, in Buckle, *Letters of Queen Victoria*, III, pp. 357–9.

93 Grierson to Bigge, 4 May 1899, RA I62/10a.

94 Lascelles to Salisbury, 5 May 1899, RA I62/11, printed in part in Buckle, *Letters of Queen Victoria*, III, pp. 359–60.

95 Salisbury to Lascelles, 10 May 1899, cited in Kennedy, *Samoan Tangle*, p. 182.

96 Queen Victoria to Kaiser Wilhelm II, 18 May 1899, GStA Berlin, BPHA Rep. 52 W3 No. 11.

97 Kaiser Wilhelm II to Bülow, 20 May 1899, quoted in Bülow to Hohenlohe, 21 May 1899, Hohenlohe, *Denkwürdigkeiten der Reichskanzlerzeit*, pp. 503–4.

98 Lascelles, report from Berlin, 26 May 1899, RA I62/12. The Kaiser was particularly hurt when he heard that his cousin Grand Duke Ernst Ludwig of Hesse-Darmstadt had been invited to attend the Queen's birthday celebrations: Holstein to Hatzfeldt, 13 May 1899, Hatzfeldt, *Nachgelassene Papiere*, II, No. 757; McLean, *Royalty and Diplomacy*, p. 92.

99 RA QVJ, 5 June 1899, in Buckle, *Letters of Queen Victoria*, III, p. 381.

100 RA QVJ, 1 June 1899.

101 Kaiser Wilhelm II to Queen Victoria, 27 May 1899, RA I62/14, in Buckle, *Letters of Queen Victoria*, III, pp. 375–9. See Eyck, *Das Persönliche Regiment*, p. 234.

102 Salisbury to Queen Victoria, 3 June 1899, RA I62/15, in Buckle, *Letters of Queen Victoria*, III, p. 379. See Salisbury's memorandum of the same day, ibid., pp. 379–81.

103 Queen Victoria to Kaiser Wilhelm II, 12 June 1899, RA I62/19, ibid., pp. 381–2. See Salisbury to Queen Victoria, 14 June 1899, RA I62/21.

104  Eulenburg to Bülow, 10–11 July 1899, *Eulenburgs Korrespondenz*, III, No. 1396.

105  Eulenburg to Bülow, 4 July 1899, ibid., No. 1395.

### 32  WILHELM AND THE BIRTH OF THE GERMAN BATTLEFLEET

1  Kennedy, 'The Kaiser and German Weltpolitik', p. 162.

2  On the eve of the Boer War, one German general wrote to another: 'If only our fleet were at the stage [. . .] where we could use the war in South Africa [. . .] for a surprise attack [on England]': Mudra to Colmar Freiherr von der Goltz, 2 October 1899, BA-MA Freiburg, von der Goltz Papers, N737 Zug. 228/95.

3  See above, pp. 153–8 and 355–60.

4  Prince Heinrich of Prussia to Tirpitz, 24 October 1893, BA-MA Freiburg, Tirpitz Papers N253/183.

5  Wilhelm Deist, *Flottenpolitik und Flottenpropaganda. Das Nachrichtenbureau des Reichsmarineamtes 1897–1914*, Stuttgart 1976, pp. 20–1.

6  See Waldersee, diary entry for 9 March 1897, GStA Berlin, Waldersee Papers, omitted from Meisner, II, p. 393.

7  Deist, *Flottenpolitik und Flottenpropaganda*, p. 23; Cecil, *Wilhelm II*, I, p. 303.

8  Bülow, *Memoirs*, II, p. 62.

9  Cecil, *Wilhelm II*, I, p. 298.

10  Kaiser Wilhelm II to Prince Heinrich of Prussia, April 1897, *Berliner Lokal-Anzeiger*, 25 April 1897, PA AA, Preußen 1 No. 1d, Bd I. See above, p. 848.

11  Waldersee, diary entry for 28 April 1892, GStA Berlin, Waldersee Papers; omitted from Meisner, II, p. 240.

12  Waldersee, diary entry for 29 April 1892, GStA Berlin, Waldersee Papers; omitted from Meisner, II, p. 240. See above, pp. 155 and 359.

13  Waldersee, diary entry for 10 September 1892, GStA Berlin, Waldersee Papers; omitted from Meisner, II, p. 264.

14  Waldersee to Verdy, 12 April 1895, GStA Berlin, Waldersee Papers.

15  Waldersee, diary entry for 10 March 1895, Meisner, II, p. 339.

16  Cecil, *Wilhelm II*, I, p. 313. See Massie, *Dreadnought*, pp. 150ff; Thomas Kohut, *Wilhelm II and the Germans*, pp. 177ff.; also above, pp. 33ff.

17  Görlitz, *Der Kaiser*, p. 29. Cf. Paul Simsa, *Marine intern. Entwicklung und Fehlentwicklung der deutschen Marine 1888–1939*, Stuttgart 1972, p. 23.

18  Hildebrand, *Das vergangene Reich*, p. 202.

19  Holstein to Bülow, 7 February 1895, *Eulenburgs Korrespondenz*, II, No. 1082.

20  See Holstein to Eulenburg, 5 October 1893, ibid., p. 1114.

21  Kiderlen-Wächter to Eulenburg, 1 October 1893, ibid., No. 827.

22  Waldersee, diary entry for 16 October 1893, GStA Berlin, Waldersee Papers; omitted from Meisner, II, p. 296.

23  Waldersee, diary entry for 19 October 1893, GStA Berlin, Waldersee Papers; cf. Meisner, II, p. 297.

24  Cecil, *Wilhelm II*, I, p. 299.

25  Waldersee, diary entry for 14 December 1894, GStA Berlin, Waldersee Papers; omitted from Meisner, II, pp. 332–3. See also the diary entry for 15 February 1895, Meisner, II, pp. 338–9.

26  Marschall, diary entries for 2–9 February 1895, cited in *Eulenburgs Korrespondenz*, II, p. 1459.

27  Kaiser Wilhelm II, lecture of 8 February 1895 in the Königliche Kriegs-Akademie, BA-MA Freiburg, N160/13.

28 See Cecil, *Wilhelm II*, I, p. 300.

29 Ibid., p. 303.

30 Hohenlohe, diary entry for 31 January 1895, Hohenlohe, *Denkwürdigkeiten der Reichskanzlerzeit*, p. 32.

31 Jagemann, report of 9 January 1895, Fuchs, *Großherzog von Baden*, III, No. 1407.

32 Tirpitz, *Erinnerungen*, p. 49; Steinberg, *Yesterday's Deterrent*, p. 72; Franz Uhle-Wettler, *Alfred von Tirpitz in seiner Zeit*, Hamburg, Berlin, Bonn 1998, p. 68.

33 See above, p. 908.

34 Kaiser Wilhelm II, lecture of 8 February 1895, BA-MA Freiburg, N160/13.

35 Ibid.

36 Ibid.

37 Ibid.

38 Ibid.

39 Waldersee, diary entry for 10 February 1895, GStA Berlin, Waldersee Papers; omitted from Meisner, II, p. 338.

40 Waldersee, diary entry for 12 February 1895, GStA Berlin, Waldersee Papers; omitted from Meisner, II, p. 338.

41 Fischer to Eulenburg, 17 February 1895, *Eulenburgs Korrespondenz*, III, No. 1090.

42 Cecil, *Wilhelm II*, I, p. 303.

43 Eulenburg to Holstein, 21 January 1895, *Eulenburgs Korrespondenz*, II, No. 1075.

44 Kaiser Wilhelm II to Hohenlohe, 1 March 1895, Hohenlohe, *Denkwürdigkeiten der Reichskanzlerzeit*, p. 49. See Waldersee, diary entry for 24 February 1895, GStA Berlin, Waldersee Papers; omitted from Meisner, II, p. 339.

45 Holstein to Radolin, 2 March 1895, *Holstein Papers*, III, No. 452.

46 Uhle-Wettler, *Tirpitz*, p. 87.

47 Cecil, *Wilhelm II*, I, p. 294.

48 See above, pp. 783ff.

49 Hohenlohe to Kaiser Wilhelm II, 7 January 1896, in Hohenlohe, *Denkwürdigkeiten der Reichskanzlerzeit*, pp. 152–3.

50 Kaiser Wilhelm II to Hohenlohe, 8 January 1896, ibid., pp. 153–4.

51 Marschall, diary entry for 8 January 1896, Marschall Papers, Schloss Neuershausen.

52 Marschall, diary entries for 8, 11 and 13 January 1896, ibid.

53 Holstein to Eulenburg, 25 January 1896, *Eulenburgs Korrespondenz*, III, No. 1191; *Holstein Papers*, III, p. 589, n. 2.

54 Eulenburg to Holstein, 31 January 1896, *Holstein Papers*, III, No. 525.

55 Holstein to Eulenburg, 13 and 25 January 1896, *Eulenburgs Korrespondenz*, III, Nos. 1188 and 1191.

56 Cf. Steinberg, *Yesterday's Deterrent*, pp. 90–1.

57 Hohenlohe to Kaiser Wilhelm II, 14 January 1896, Hohenlohe, *Denkwürdigkeiten der Reichskanzlerzeit*, pp. 156ff. .

58 Hohenlohe, undated note, Hohenlohe to Kaiser Wilhelm II, 7 January 1896 and diary entry for 22 January 1896, ibid., pp. 151–61. See Holstein to Eulenburg, 14 January 1896, *Eulenburgs Korrespondenz*, III, No. 1189.

59 Marschall, diary entries for 12–16 January 1896, Marschall Papers, Schloss Neuershausen. See *Eulenburgs Korrespondenz*, III, p. 1637.

60 Holstein to Eulenburg, 14 January 1896, *Eulenburgs Korrespondenz*, III, No. 1189.

61 Eulenburg to Holstein, 14 January 1896, cited ibid., p. 1637.

62 August Eulenburg to Hohenlohe, 15 January 1896, Hohenlohe, *Denkwürdigkeiten der Reichskanzlerzeit*, pp. 158–9.

63 Kaiser Wilhelm II to Senden, 16 January 1896, ibid., p. 159.

64 Marschall, diary entries for 13–16 January 1896, Marschall Papers, Schloss Neuershausen; Hohenlohe to Kaiser Wilhelm II, 17 January 1896, Kaiser Wilhelm II to Hohenlohe, 17 January 1896, Holstein to Hohenlohe, undated, and Hohenlohe, note for his son Alexander of 18 January 1896, Hohenlohe, *Denkwürdigkeiten der Reichskanzlerzeit*, pp. 160–1.

65 Waldersee, diary entry for 21 January 1896, GStA Berlin, Waldersee Papers; cf. Meisner, II, pp. 365–6.

66 Holstein to Hatzfeldt, 16 January 1896, *Holstein Papers*, III, No. 522.

67 Hohenlohe, diary for 25 January 1896, Hohenlohe, *Denkwürdigkeiten der Reichskanzlerzeit*, p. 162.

68 Holstein to Eulenburg, 25 January 1896, *Eulenburgs Korrespondenz*, III, No. 1191.

69 Hohenlohe, diary entry for 1 February 1896, Hohenlohe, *Denkwürdigkeiten der Reichskanzlerzeit*, p. 164.

70 Waldersee, diary entry for 9 February 1896, GStA Berlin, Waldersee Papers; printed only in part in Meisner, II, p. 367.

71 Kiderlen-Wächter to Holstein, 29 March 1896, *Holstein Papers*, III, No. 537.

72 Waldersee, diary entry for 3 March 1896, GStA Berlin, Waldersee Papers; printed only in part in Meisner, II, pp. 368–9.

73 Holstein to Eulenburg, 13 and 25 January 1896, *Eulenburgs Korrespondenz*, III, Nos. 1188 and 1191.

74 Hohenlohe, diary entry for 2 July 1896, Hohenlohe, *Denkwürdigkeiten der Reichskanzlerzeit*, pp. 240–1.

75 Eulenburg, note of 9 July 1896, *Eulenburgs Korrespondenz*, III, No. 1238.

76 Senden, undated memorandum [spring 1896], BA-MA Freiburg Senden Papers N160/11 fol. 45ff. See Steinberg, *Yesterday's Deterrent*, p. 94.

77 Senden, undated memorandum [spring 1896], BA-MA Freiburg, Senden Papers N160/11 fol. 45ff.

78 Cf. Müller's memorandum of 1896, above, pp. 934–8.

79 Prince Heinrich of Prussia to Tirpitz, 21 February 1896, BA-MA Freiburg, Tirpitz Papers N253/183.

80 Tirpitz to Senden, 15 February 1896, ibid., Senden Papers N160/5.

81 Tirpitz to Stosch, 21 December 1895 and 13 February 1896, Tirpitz, *Erinnerungen*, pp. 52–6.

82 Deist, *Flottenpolitik und Flottenpropaganda*, pp. 52–61.

83 Steinberg, *Yesterday's Deterrent*, p. 84. For Tirpitz's intentions, see above all Berghahn, *Der Tirpitz-Plan*; Paul M. Kennedy, 'Tirpitz, England and the Second Navy Law of 1900. A Strategical Critique', *Militärgeschichtliche Mitteilungen*, 2 (1970); Michael Epkenhans, *Die wilhelminische Flottenrüstung 1908–1914. Weltmachtstreben, industrieller Fortschritt, soziale Integration*, Munich 1991; Massie, *Dreadnought*, pp. 160ff.

84 Uhle-Wettler, *Tirpitz*, p. 53.

85 Steinberg, *Yesterday's Deterrent*, pp. 81ff.; Uhle-Wettler, *Tirpitz*, pp. 90–3.

86 Tirpitz to Senden, 20 March 1896, BA-MA Freiburg, Senden Papers N160/5. See Steinberg, *Yesterday's Deterrent*, p. 95.

87 Senden to Tirpitz, 31 March 1896, BA-MA Freiburg, Senden Papers N160/5. See Steinberg, *Yesterday's Deterrent*, p. 96.

88 Holstein to Bülow, 17 February 1897, *Holstein Papers*, IV, No. 605.

89 Waldersee, diary entry for 28 June 1896, GStA Berlin, Waldersee Papers; cf. Meisner, II, pp. 371–2.

90 Empress Frederick to Queen Victoria, 24 October 1896, AdHH Schloss Fasanerie; cited in Röhl, 'Der Kaiser und England', p. 169.

91 Holstein to Kiderlen-Wächter, 13 August 1896, *Holstein Papers*, III, No. 582.

92  See above, pp. 856–7.

93  Waldersee, diary entry for 31 January 1897, GStA Berlin, Waldersee Papers; Meisner, II, p. 390.

94  Waldersee, diary entry for 31 January 1897, GStA Berlin, Waldersee Papers; cf. Meisner, II, p. 391.

95  Berghahn, *Tirpitz-Plan*, p. 97.

96  Ibid., p. 95.

97  Ibid., pp. 97–8.

98  Ibid., p. 98.

99  Röhl, *Germany without Bismarck*, pp. 212ff.

100 Berghahn, *Tirpitz-Plan*, p. 100.

101 Ibid., p. 99.

102 Ibid.

103 See above, pp. 852–3.

104 Berghahn, *Tirpitz-Plan*, p. 100.

105 Hohenlohe, note of 8 March 1897, Hohenlohe to Kaiser Wilhelm II, 9 and 15 March 1897, Kaiser Wilhelm II to Hohenlohe, 15 and 16 March 1897, Hohenlohe, *Denkwürdigkeiten der Reichskanzlerzeit*, pp. 312–20.

106 Waldersee, diary entry for 16 March 1897, GStA Berlin, Waldersee Papers; cf. Meisner, II, pp. 393ff.

107 Waldersee, diary entry for 20 March 1897, GStA Berlin, Waldersee Papers; printed only in part in Meisner, II, p. 395.

108 Waldersee, diary entry for 30 May 1897, GStA Berlin, Waldersee Papers; cf. Meisner, II, p. 397.

109 Berghahn, *Tirpitz-Plan*, pp. 101–2.

110 Ibid., p. 102.

111 Ibid., p. 103.

112 Ibid., p. 105.

113 Ibid.

114 Ibid., p. 106.

115 Eulenburg to Kaiser Wilhelm II, 18 August 1897, *Eulenburgs Korrespondenz*, III, No. 1339.

116 Berghahn, *Tirpitz-Plan*, p. 106.

117 Tirpitz, notes on his visit to the Kaiser, 18–20 August 1897, BA-MA Freiburg, Tirpitz Papers N253/4.

118 Berghahn, *Tirpitz-Plan*, pp. 108–9.

119 Prince Heinrich of Prussia to Tirpitz, 17 October 1897, Tirpitz to Prince Heinrich of Prussia, 29 October 1897, BA-MA Freiburg, Tirpitz Papers N253/4.

120 Berghahn, *Tirpitz-Plan*, pp. 108–9.

121 Tirpitz to Senden, 11 August 1897, BA-MA Freiburg, Tirpitz Papers N253/4.

122 Tirpitz, notes on his visit to Bismarck, 22 August 1897, ibid.

123 Eisendecher to Tirpitz, 1 September 1897, ibid.

124 Tirpitz to Senden, 11 August 1897, ibid. See Kaiser Wilhelm II to Hohenlohe, 23 August 1897, Hohenlohe, *Denkwürdigkeiten der Reichskanzlerzeit*, pp. 377–8.

125 Berghahn, *Tirpitz-Plan*, p. 119.

126 Bülow, *Memoirs*, I, p. 133. See W. Marienfeld, *Wissenschaft und Schlachtflottenbau in Deutschland 1897–1906*, Frankfurt a.M. 1957; Deist, *Flottenpolitik und Flottenpropaganda*, pp. 71–145 *et passim*.

127 Bülow, *Memoirs*, I, pp. 111–12; Berghahn, *Tirpitz-Plan*, p. 123.

128 Berghahn, *Tirpitz-Plan*, p. 125.

129 Kaiser Wilhelm II to Tirpitz, 24 March 1898, BA-MA Freiburg, Tirpitz Papers N253/4; Cecil, *Wilhelm II*, I, p. 317. See above, p. 878.

130  Kaiser Wilhelm II to Hohenlohe, 27 March 1898, Hohenlohe, *Denkwürdigkeiten der Reichs-kanzlerzeit*, p. 436.

131  Prince Heinrich of Prussia to Senden, 19 April 1899, BA-MA Freiburg, Senden-Bibran Papers N160/4.

132  See Volker R. Berghahn, 'Zu den Zielen des deutschen Flottenbaus unter Wilhelm II.', *Historische Zeitschrift*, 210/1 (February 1970), pp. 46, 53 *et passim*.

133  Tirpitz to Senden, 11 August 1897, BA-MA Freiburg, Tirpitz Papers N253/4.

134  Tirpitz to Kaiser Wilhelm II, 24 April 1898, Hohenlohe, *Denkwürdigkeiten der Reichskanz-lerzeit*, pp. 441–2. See above, p. 878.

135  Hohenlohe, diary entry for 6 October 1898, *Denkwürdigkeiten der Reichskanzlerzeit*, pp. 462–3.

136  Prince Heinrich of Prussia to Tirpitz, 8 June 1901, BA-MA Freiburg, Tirpitz Papers N253/183.

137  Tirpitz, notes for an audience with the Kaiser on 28 November 1898, ibid. N253/4.

138  Tirpitz, secret notes, presented to the Kaiser on 28 November 1898, ibid.

139  Ibid.

140  Ibid.

141  Tirpitz, notes for an audience with the Kaiser, undated, BA-MA Freiburg, Tirpitz Papers N253/4, fol. 227.

142  Tirpitz, notes of 29 September 1899 on an audience with the Kaiser in Rominten on 28 September 1899, ibid. N253/5.

143  Kaiser Wilhelm II, marginal notes on Richthofen to Eulenburg, 20 July 1898, Eulenburg to Richthofen, 22 July 1898, PA AA, IA England 78 No. 1 secr., Bd. IV, R 5802.

144  Wilmowski to Hohenlohe, 24 October 1899, Hohenlohe, *Denkwürdigkeiten der Reichskanz-lerzeit*, p. 533; Hohenlohe, note of 26 October 1899, ibid., pp. 534–5; Hohenlohe, diary entry for 5 November 1899, ibid., pp. 537–8. See Tirpitz, *Erinnerungen*, pp. 104–5; also Kaiser Wilhelm II to Hohenlohe, 10 January 1900, Hohenlohe, *Denkwürdigkeiten der Reichskanz-lerzeit*, pp. 555–6; Berghahn, *Tirpitz-Plan*, p. 211.

145  Tirpitz, notes on the events between 28 September and 17 November 1899, BA-MA Freiburg, Tirpitz Papers N253/5.

146  Berghahn, *Tirpitz-Plan*, p. 213.

147  Wilmowski to Hohenlohe, 25 October 1899, Hohenlohe, note of 26 October 1899, Hohen-lohe, *Denkwürdigkeiten der Reichskanzlerzeit*, pp. 533–4.

148  Hohenlohe to Tirpitz, 26 October 1899, BA-MA Freiburg, Tirpitz Papers N253/6, printed in Hohenlohe, *Denkwürdigkeiten der Reichskanzlerzeit*, pp. 533–4.

149  Hohenlohe to Tirpitz, 29 October 1899, BA-MA Freiburg, Tirpitz Papers N253/6.

150  Berghahn, *Tirpitz-Plan*, p. 214.

151  Tirpitz, notes on the events between 28 September and 17 November 1899, BA-MA Freiburg, Tirpitz Papers N253/5.

152  Hohenlohe to the prime ministers of the individual German states, 6 November 1899, ibid. N253/6.

153  Bülow to Hohenlohe, 25 October 1899, Hohenlohe, *Denkwürdigkeiten der Reichskanzlerzeit*, p. 533.

154  Hohenlohe, note of 6 November 1899, ibid., p. 538. See above, p. 886.

155  Grand Duke of Baden to Hohenlohe, 10 and 15 November 1899, Hohenlohe, *Denkwürdigkeiten der Reichskanzlerzeit*, pp. 539 and 545.

156  Kaiser Wilhelm II to Hohenlohe, 29 November 1899, BA-MA Freiburg, Tirpitz Papers N253/5, in Hohenlohe, *Denkwürdigkeiten der Reichskanzlerzeit*, p. 547.

157  See *Große Politik*, XV, pp. 441ff.; Cecil, *Wilhelm II*, I, p. 334.

158  Grierson to Bigge, 6 January 1900, RA I62/76b. See Kennedy, *Anglo-German Antagonism*, pp. 239–40.

159 Kaiser Wilhelm II, *Ereignisse und Gestalten*, pp. 196–7.

160 Kaiser Wilhelm II to Hohenlohe, 10 January 1900, Hohenlohe, *Denkwürdigkeiten der Reichskanzlerzeit*, p. 547. See Tirpitz to Hohenlohe, 16 January 1900, BA-MA Freiburg, Tirpitz Papers N253/5.

161 Kaiser Wilhelm II to Hohenlohe, undated, Hohenlohe, *Denkwürdigkeiten der Reichskanzlerzeit*, p. 557.

162 Tirpitz to Hohenlohe, 27 April 1900, ibid., p. 571.

163 Cecil, *Wilhelm II*, I, p. 335.

164 See Spitzemberg, diary entry for 29 September 1912, *Tagebuch*, pp. 548–9.

165 See Holger Afflerbach, *Der Dreibund. Europäische Großmacht- und Allianzpolitik vor dem Ersten Weltkrieg*, Vienna, Cologne, Weimar 2002, pp. 363ff.

## 33   'YOUNG GERMANY, YOUR KAISER!', OR WHAT WAS WRONG WITH WILHELM II?

1 Archduke Franz Ferdinand of Austria-Hungary to Baron Beck, 28 August 1900, cited in Robert A. Kann, 'Kaiser Wilhelm II. und Thronfolger Franz Ferdinand in ihrer Korrespondenz', in Kann, *Erzherzog Franz Ferdinand Studien*, Vienna 1976, p. 50. But cf. Eulenburg to Bülow, 26 May 1899, *Eulenburgs Korrespondenz*, III, No. 1394 and below, p. 1049.

2 Tolstoy to Prince Grigory Wolkonsky, 4/16 December 1899, quoted in R. F. Christian, ed., *Tolstoy's Letters*, 2 vols., London 1978, II, No. 458.

3 See Eulenburg, *Erlebnisse an deutschen und fremden Höfen*, pp. 321–58; Houston Stewart Chamberlain, *Briefe 1882–1924 und Briefwechsel mit Kaiser Wilhelm II.*, 2 vols., Munich 1926, II, pp. 131–275; Geoffrey G. Field, *Evangelist of Race. The Germanic Vision of Houston Stewart Chamberlain*, New York 1981.

4 Houston Stewart Chamberlain, 'Kaiser Wilhelm II', *Jugend*, I, No. 22 (1900), pp. 370ff.; Chamberlain to Adolf Hitler, 7 October 1923, Chamberlain, *Briefe*, II, pp. 124–6.

5 Chamberlain, 'Kaiser Wilhelm II.', pp. 370ff.

6 Ernst Heinrich Bethge, *Jung Deutschland, Dein Kaiser!*, Langensalza 1913.

7 Szögyény, report of 5 February 1900, HHStA Vienna, PA III/153, cited in part in Kennedy, *Anglo-German Antagonism*, p. 241.

8 Maximilian Harden, *Die Zukunft*, No. 40, 1902, p. 340.

9 Weller, *Maximilian Harden*, pp. 113–14; Hellige, *Rathenau und Harden*, pp. 160ff. and 332.

10 See Bernd Sösemann, 'Die sog. Hunnenrede Wilhelms II. Textkritische und interpretatorische Bemerkungen zur Ansprache des Kaisers vom 27. Juli 1900 in Bremerhaven', *Historische Zeitschrift*, vol. 222 (1976), pp. 349–50; Sösemann, 'Wir sollen sein ein einig Volk von Schlächtern', *Frankfurter Allgemeine Zeitung*, 27 July 2000.

11 Maximilian Harden, 'Der Kampf mit dem Drachen', *Die Zukunft*, No. 32, 11 August 1900, pp. 225–36. For the generational shift more generally, see Martin Doerry, *Übergangsmenschen. Die Mentalität der Wilhelminer und die Krise des Kaiserreichs*, Weinheim, Munich 1986; Thomas Kohut, *Wilhelm II and the Germans*; Ullrich, *Nervöse Grossmacht*; Radkau, *Das Zeitalter der Nervosität*.

12 Kaiser Wilhelm II to Queen Victoria, 2 February 1899, in Buckle, *Letters of Queen Victoria*, III, pp. 336–7. See above, pp. 991–2.

13 Eulenburg to Bülow, 4–7 July 1899, *Eulenburgs Korrespondenz*, III, No. 1395. See Kaiser Wilhelm II to Eulenburg, 15 June 1899, ibid., p. 1941.

14 Kaiser Wilhelm II to Eulenburg, 15 June 1898, cited in Bülow, *Memoirs*, I, p. 218; cf. Eulenburg to Bülow, 15 June 1898, *Eulenburgs Korrespondenz*, III, No. 1375; also Eulenburg to Bülow, 12–19 July 1899, ibid., No. 1397.

15 Eulenburg to Lucanus, 16 June 1898, *Eulenburgs Korrespondenz*, III, No. 1376.

16 August Eulenburg to Philipp Eulenburg, 23 March 1898, ibid., p. 1887; Eulenburg to Bülow, 22 March 1898, ibid., No. 1364.

17 See Hull, *Entourage*, pp. 109–45, and Hull, 'Kaiser Wilhelm II and the "Liebenberg Circle"', in Röhl and Sombart, *Kaiser Wilhelm II. New Interpretations*, pp. 193–220; also Cecil, *Wilhelm II*, pp. 98–122. For the trials of Eulenburg and Kuno Moltke, see Karsten Hecht, 'Die Harden-Prozesse. Strafverfahren, Öffentlichkeit und Politik im Kaiserreich', diss., Munich 1997.

18 See *Eulenburgs Korrespondenz*, III, Nos. 1294 and 1422 and p. 1977.

19 Eulenburg to Bülow, 4 and 20 July 1898, ibid., Nos. 1377 and 1380. See Bülow to Eulenburg, 27 May 1898, ibid., No. 1372.

20 Varnbüler to Kuno Moltke, 15 April 1898, ibid., No. 1366.

21 See Varnbüler to Kuno Moltke, 4 June 1898, ibid., No. 1373; Eulenburg to Kaiser Wilhelm II, 16 August and 15 November 1898 and 9 May 1899, ibid., Nos. 1385, 1389 and 1393.

22 See e.g. Eulenburg to Bülow, 26 July 1897, ibid., No. 1335.

23 Eulenburg's note of 26 July 1897, *Eulenburgs Korrespondenz*, III, No. 1335.

24 See Roderick R. McLean, 'Kaiser Wilhelm II and His Hessian Cousins. Intra-state Relations in the German Empire and International Dynastic Politics, 1890–1918', *German History*, 19/1 (2001), pp. 28–53.

25 Eulenburg to Bülow, 22 March 1898, *Eulenburgs Korrespondenz*, III, No. 1364.

26 Bülow to Eulenburg, 20 July 1898, ibid., No. 1381.

27 Ibid.

28 Eulenburg to Bülow, 10–11 July 1899, ibid., No. 1396.

29 Eulenburg to Bülow, 11 February and 10–11 July 1899, ibid., Nos. 1390 and 1396.

30 Eulenburg to Bülow, 20 July 1898, ibid., No. 1380.

31 Eulenburg to Bülow, 26 May 1899, ibid., No. 1394. Cf. Bülow, *Memoirs*, I, pp. 398–9.

32 Eulenburg to Bülow, 10–11 July 1899, *Eulenburgs Korrespondenz*, III, No. 1396.

33 Eulenburg to Bülow, 12–19 July 1899, ibid., No. 1397.

34 Eulenburg to Bülow, 20–22 July 1899, ibid., No. 1399.

35 See above, p. 663.

36 Eulenburg to Bülow, 12–19 July 1899, *Eulenburgs Korrespondenz*, III, No. 1397.

37 Eulenburg to Bülow, 20–2 July 1899, ibid., No. 1399.

38 Eulenburg to Bülow, 26–7 July 1899, ibid., No. 1400.

39 Eulenburg to Bülow, 20–2 July 1899, ibid., No. 1399.

40 Ibid.

41 Ibid.

42 Eulenburg to Bülow, 26–27 July 1899, ibid., No. 1400.

43 Eulenburg to Lucanus, 5 December 1899, ibid., No. 1405.

44 Eulenburg to Lucanus, 10 December 1899, ibid., No. 1408.

45 Eulenburg to Lucanus, 2 January 1900, ibid., No. 1412.

46 Grand Duke of Baden to Hohenlohe, 10 November 1899, Hohenlohe, *Denkwürdigkeiten der Reichskanzlerzeit*, pp. 539–40.

47 Eulenburg, note of 27 July 1900, cited in Haller, *Eulenburg*, p. 257.

48 Kaiser Wilhelm II to Bülow, 19 June 1900, *Große Politik*, XVI, No. 4527.

49 See Bülow, *Memoirs*, I, p. 452; Eulenburg to Bülow, 14 July 1900, *Eulenburgs Korrespondenz*, III, No. 1419.

50 Eulenburg to Bülow, 14–15 July 1900, *Eulenburgs Korrespondenz*, III, No. 1419. Cf. Bülow, *Memoirs*, I, pp. 452–3.

51 Eulenburg to Bülow, 18 July 1900, *Eulenburgs Korrespondenz*, III, No. 1420.

52 Eulenburg to Bülow, 21 July 1900, ibid., No. 1421.

53 See Eulenburg, *Mit dem Kaiser als Staatsmann und Freund auf Nordlandreisen*, 2 vols., Dresden 1931, II, pp. 315–71.

54 Eulenburg to Bülow, 21 July 1903, *Eulenburgs Korrespondenz*, III, No. 1497.

55 Eulenburg to Bülow, 26–8 July and 9 August 1903, ibid., Nos. 1498 and 1499.

56 Grand Duchess Augusta Caroline of Mecklenburg-Strelitz to George Duke of Cambridge, 30 August 1888, RA Vic Addl Mss A8/2689.

57 Count Georg von Werthern to Eulenburg, 22 October 1888, *Eulenburgs Korrespondenz*, I, No. 200.

58 Dr Rudolf Leuthold to Eulenburg, 25 December 1889, ibid., No. 268.

59 Vice Admiral Paul Hoffmann, diary for 22–3 April 1890, Hoffmann Papers, Freiburg

60 Eulenburg to Holstein, 1 August 1890, *Holstein Papers*, III, No. 327.

61 Kaiser Wilhelm II to Queen Victoria, telegram, 29 July 1891, RA I59/43.

62 Empress Frederick to Queen Victoria, 6 August 1891, RA Z51/7.

63 Grierson to Bigge, 2 April 1897, RA I61/4a.

64 See above, p. 932.

65 See Radkau, *Zeitalter der Nervosität*, particularly pp. 275ff.; also Ullrich, *Nervöse Grossmacht*.

66 Waldersee, diary entry for 20 August 1891, GStA Berlin, Waldersee Papers; omitted from Meisner, II, p. 215.

67 Waldersee, diary entry for 17 September 1891, GStA Berlin, Waldersee Papers; cf. Meisner, II, p. 217.

68 Waldersee, diary entry for 25 November 1892, GStA Berlin, Waldersee Papers; omitted from Meisner, II, p. 270.

69 Waldersee, diary entry for 9 January 1891, GStA Berlin, Waldersee Papers; cf. Meisner, II, p. 174.

70 See above, ch. 17.

71 Waldersee, diary entry for 16 March 1892, GStA Berlin, Waldersee Papers; printed in part in Meisner, II, pp. 234–5.

72 Waldersee, diary entry for 25 September 1892, GStA Berlin, Waldersee Papers; omitted from Meisner, II, p. 265.

73 Waldersee, diary entry for 31 August 1892, GStA Berlin, Waldersee Papers; omitted from Meisner, II, p. 264.

74 Waldersee, diary entry for 21 November 1894, GStA Berlin, Waldersee Papers; omitted from Meisner, II, p. 332.

75 Waldersee, diary entry for 21 January 1896, GStA Berlin, Waldersee Papers; cf. Meisner, II, pp. 365–6.

76 Holstein to Eulenburg, 25 January 1896, *Eulenburgs Korrespondenz*, III, No. 1191; Eulenburg to Holstein, 31 January 1896, *Holstein Papers*, III, No. 525.

77 Waldersee, diary entry for 16 February 1896, GStA Berlin, Waldersee Papers; omitted from Meisner, II, p. 367.

78 Waldersee, diary entry for 25 October 1896, GStA Berlin, Waldersee Papers; cf. the distorted version in Meisner, II, pp. 374–5.

79 Waldersee, diary entry for 31 October 1896, GStA Berlin, Waldersee Papers; cf. Meisner, II, pp. 375–6.

80 Waldersee, diary entry for 16 March 1897, GStA Berlin, Waldersee Papers; cf. Meisner, II, pp. 393ff.

81 Bodman, report of 7 March 1897, Fuchs, *Großherzog von Baden*, No. 1657.

82 See Holstein to Eulenburg, 4 and 11 April 1890, *Eulenburgs Korrespondenz*, I, Nos. 379 and 384. Cf. above, p. 534.

83 Holstein to Eulenburg, 6 December 1890, *Eulenburgs Korrespondenz*, I, No. 452. See above, pp. 556–7.

84 Waldersee, diary entry for 16 April 1892, GStA Berlin, Waldersee Papers; cf. Meisner, II, pp. 239–40. See above, p. 512.

85 Holstein to Eulenburg, 1 April 1892, *Eulenburgs Korrespondenz*, II, No. 638.

86 Report from Paris, 22 March 1892, ibid., pp. 839–40; also Hull, *Entourage*, p. 16.

87 Waldersee, diary entry for 23 February 1891, GStA Berlin, Waldersee Papers; omitted from Meisner, II, pp. 189ff.

88 Waldersee, diary entry for 22 December 1891, GStA Berlin, Waldersee Papers; cf. Meisner, II, p. 228.

89 Gosselin to Salisbury, 29 November 1895, cited in *Eulenburgs Korrespondenz*, III, pp. 1484–5.

90 Holstein to Eulenburg, 17 February 1895, ibid., No. 1089. See Bülow, *Memoirs*, I, pp. 135–6 and 174–5.

91 Hohenlohe, *Denkwürdigkeiten der Reichskanzlerzeit*, p. 151. See above, p. 808.

92 Holstein to Bülow, 24 March and 2 April 1897, cited in Röhl, *Kaiser and His Court*, p. 22.

93 Monts to Holstein, 2 March 1897, in *Eulenburgs Korrespondenz*, III, No. 1301; cf. Bülow, *Memoirs*, I, p. 39.

94 Monts to Eulenburg, 20/21 March 1897, *Eulenburgs Korrespondenz*, III, No. 1309.

95 Ibid.

96 Bodman, report of 4 March 1897, Fuchs, *Großherzog von Baden*, III, No. 1654.

97 Bodman, report of 7 March 1897, ibid., No. 1657.

98 Bülow, note of 7 April 1897, *Eulenburgs Korrespondenz*, III, No. 1312.

99 Eulenburg to Bülow, 14–15 July 1900, ibid., No. 1419. Cf. Bülow, *Memoirs*, I, p. 453.

100 Bülow, *Memoirs*, I, pp. 135 and 175.

101 Bülow to Eulenburg, 22 November 1900, Eulenburg to Kaiser Wilhelm II, 22 November 1900, *Eulenburgs Korrespondenz*, III, Nos. 1439 and 1440.

102 Hereditary Princess Charlotte of Saxe-Meiningen to Ellen Freifrau von Heldburg, 15 March 1897, Thüringisches Staatsarchiv Meiningen, HA 342.

103 Hereditary Princess Charlotte of Saxe-Meiningen to Schweninger, 26 March 1897, 4 April 1901 and 4 June 1903, cited in Röhl, *Cäsarenwahnsinn*, p. 28.

104 Hereditary Princess Charlotte of Saxe-Meiningen to Schweninger, 5 December 1908, cited ibid., pp. 28–9.

105 See above, ch. 22.

106 Hopman, report of 3 February 1915, cited in Holger Afflerbach, ed., *Wilhelm II. als Oberster Kriegsherr im Ersten Weltkrieg. Quellen aus der militärischen Umgebung des Kaisers 1914–1918*, Munich 2004.

107 Waldersee, diary entry for 6 April 1897, GStA Berlin, Waldersee Papers; cf. Meisner, II, p. 396.

108 Alvensleben, report from Brussels of 24 October 1897, PA AA, IA Preußen 1 No. 1d, Bd VIII. This version of events on board the *Hohenzollern* in July 1897 also gained currency in Germany. See Friedrich Percyval Reck-Malleczewen, *Tagebuch eines Verzweifelten*, Berlin, Bonn 1981, pp. 109–10. See Marschall, *Reisen und Regieren*, pp. 198ff.

109 *New York Times*, 28 November 1897, cited in Mitchell, *Danger of Dreams*, p. 22.

110 Wolf von Schierbrand, 'Is Kaiser Wilhelm II of Normal Mind?', *Lippincott's*, 78 (November 1906), pp. 619–25.

111 A. A. Mossolov, *At the Court of the Last Tsar*, London 1935, pp. 202–10.

112 T. G. Otte, '"The Winston of Germany": The British Foreign Policy Élite and the Last German Emperor', *Canadian Journal of History*, December 2001, pp. 471–504.

113 Salisbury to Paget, 16 October 1888, cited in Otte, '"Winston"', p. 478.

114 Lord George Hamilton, *Parliamentary Reminiscences and Reflections, 1886–1906*, London 1922, p. 137.

115 Cited in Roberts, *Salisbury*, p. 555. See Otte, '"Winston"', pp. 479–80.

116 Lascelles, note of 4 December 1895, cited above, p. 770.

117 Lascelles to Salisbury, 16 February 1897, quoted in van't Padje, 'Anglo-German Imperialist Rivalry', p. 109. See above, pp. 992–4.

118 For the medical condition of Prince Wilhelm's ear, see ch. 13 of *Young Wilhelm*.

119 Waldersee, diary entry for 11 October 1890, GStA Berlin, Waldersee Papers; omitted from Meisner, II, p. 154.

120 Waldersee, diary entry for 21 March 1892, GStA Berlin, Waldersee Papers; omitted from Meisner, II, p. 236.

121 Waldersee, diary entry for 15 February 1894, GStA Berlin, Waldersee Papers; omitted from Meisner, II, p. 308.

122 Waldersee, diary entry for 29 April 1894, GStA Berlin, Waldersee Papers; cf. Meisner, II, p. 313.

123 Waldersee, diary entry for 2 June 1894, GStA Berlin, Waldersee Papers; omitted from Meisner, II, p. 314.

124 See above, p. 832.

125 Holstein to Lindenau, 29 July 1896, *Holstein Papers*, III, No. 573.

126 Sir Schomberg McDonnell to King George V, 26 October 1914, cited in *Young Wilhelm*, pp. 318–19.

127 See D. M. Potts and W. T. W. Potts, *Queen Victoria's Gene. Haemophilia and the Royal Family*, Stroud 1995, and Zeepvat, *Prince Leopold*.

128 See Röhl, Warren and Hunt, *Purple Secret*, and above, p. 639.

129 Professor Robert Gaupp, medical report of 31 May 1918, Archiv des vormals regierenden preußischen Königshauses, Burg Hohenzollern; my italics.

130 Lord Esher, diary entry for 21 November 1908, Esher Papers, Churchill Archives Centre, Cambridge, cited in Röhl, Warren and Hunt, *Purple Secret*, p. 311.

# Archival sources

1. Geheimes Staatsarchiv (GStA) Berlin and Merseburg:
   Brandenburg-Preußisches Hausarchiv
   Files of the Civil Cabinet
   Minutes of the Prussian Crown Council
   Minutes of the Prussian Ministry of State
   Files of the Kotze Case
   Papers of Rudolf Kögel
   Papers of Karl Friedrich Nowak
   Papers of Adolf von Scholz
   Papers of Count Alfred von Waldersee
2. Bundesarchiv (BA) Berlin (formerly Zentrales Staatsarchiv Potsdam):
   Files of the Reichskanzlei
   Papers of Ernst Schweninger
3. Politisches Archiv des Auswärtigen Amtes (PA AA) Berlin (formerly in Bonn):
   Asservat No. 4
   Files of the German Foreign Office
4. Cambridge University Library:
   Papers of Sir Charles Hardinge
5. Churchill Archives Centre, Cambridge:
   Papers of Viscount Esher
6. Cumbria Record Office, Carlisle:
   Papers of Lord Lonsdale
7. Stadt- und Landesbibliothek Dortmund:
   Papers of Konrad Studt
8. Archiv der Hessischen Hausstiftung (AdHH) Schloss Fasanerie:
   Papers of Kaiserin Victoria (the Empress Frederick) and Kaiser Friedrich III
9. Bundesarchiv-Militärarchiv (BA-MA) Freiburg:
   Papers of Colmar Freiherr von der Goltz
   Papers of Hans von Plessen
   Papers of Gustav Freiherr von Senden-Bibran
   Papers of Alfred von Tirpitz

10. Bismarck-Archiv Schloss Friedrichsruh:
    Papers of Prince Otto von Bismarck
    Papers of Count Herbert von Bismarck
11. Archiv des vormals regierenden preußischen Königshauses, Burg Hohenzollern:
    Papers of Kaiser Wilhelm II
12. Generallandesarchiv (GLA) Karlsruhe:
    Papers of Max Freiherr von Holzing-Berstett
13. Bundesarchiv (BA) Koblenz:
    Files of the Prussian Ministry of Justice
    Papers of Prince Otto von Bismarck
    Papers of Count Herbert von Bismarck
    Papers of Heinrich von Boetticher
    Papers of Robert Bosse
    Papers of Bernhard von Bülow
    Papers of Count Philipp zu Eulenburg-Hertefeld
14. Rothschild Archives London (RAL):
    Letters of Gerson Bleichröder
15. Thüringisches Staatsarchiv Meiningen (ThStaMgn):
    House Archive of the ducal family of Saxe-Meiningen
16. Hohenlohe-Zentralarchiv Schloss Neuenstein:
    Papers of Prince Hermann zu Hohenlohe-Langenburg
    Papers of Prince Ernst zu Hohenlohe-Langenburg
17. Bodleian Library, Oxford:
    Papers of Sir Eyre Crowe
18. Haus-, Hof- und Staatsarchiv (HHStA) Vienna:
    Kabinettsarchiv Geheimakten
    Ambassadors' Reports from Berlin
19. Royal Archives (RA) Windsor:
    Papers of Queen Victoria
    Papers of Albert Edward Prince of Wales
    Papers of King George V
    Papers of Prince Christian of Schleswig-Holstein
20. Privately held papers:
    Papers of Vice-Admiral Paul Hoffmann, Freiburg im Breisgau
    Papers of Lord Lonsdale, Lowther, Cumbria
    Papers of Countess Alice zu Lynar, Bad Driburg
    Papers of Adolf Freiherr Marschall von Bieberstein, Neuershausen
    Papers of Friedrich Mewes, Munich
    Papers of Count Carl von Wedel, Frankfurt a.M.
    Papers of Count Ernst von Wedel, Bad Driburg

# Select bibliography

Abret, Helga, *Die Majestätsbeleidigungsäffare des 'Simplicissimus'-Verlegers Albert Langen. Briefe und Dokumente zu Exil und Begnadigung 1898–1903*, Frankfurt, New York 1985

Adam, Juliette, *Guillaume II 1890–1899*, Paris 1917

*The Schemes of the Kaiser*, London 1917

Afflerbach, Holger, *Der Dreibund. Europäische Großmacht- und Allianzpolitik vor dem Ersten Weltkrieg*, Vienna 2002

'Wilhelm II as Supreme Warlord in the First World War', in Mombauer and Deist, *The Kaiser* ed., *Wilhelm II. als Oberster Kriegsherr im Ersten Weltkrieg. Quellen aus der militärischen Umgebung des Kaisers 1914–1918*, Munich 2004

Albrecht, Dieter, ed., Hugo Graf Lerchenfeld-Köfering, *Kaiser Wilhelm II. als Persönlichkeit und Herrscher*, Regensburger Historische Forschungen, Vol. 11, 1985

Alexander Grand Duke of Russia, *Once a Grand Duke*, New York 1932

Anon. [H. von Langen-Allenstein], *Herr von Tausch und die Verfasser der anonymen Briefe der Hofgesellschaft*, Zürich 1897

Anon., *Das Geheimnis des Ceremoniemeisters. Hofroman aus der jüngsten Vergangenheit. Von Carl Fürst von ... (in Preußen verboten)*

*Kaiserreden. Reden und Erlasse, Briefe und Telegramme Kaiser Wilhelms des Zweiten, ein Charakterbild des deutschen Kaisers*, Leipzig 1902

*The Private Life of Two Emperors. William II of Germany and Francis Joseph of Austria*, 2 vols., London 1905

*Unser Kaiser und sein Volk! Deutsche Sorgen. Von einem Schwarzseher*, Freiburg, Leipzig 7th edn 1906

*Unser Kaiser, 25 Jahre der Regierung Kaiser Wilhelms II., 1888–1913*, Berlin, Leipzig 1913

*The Real Kaiser. An Illuminating Study*, New York 1914

*The Last of the War Lords. New Lights on the Life and Personality of Kaiser Wilhelm II, His Relations with Britons and Americans, with Artists and Writers, and Some Account of His Love-Affairs*, London 1918

*Semi-Imperator, 1888–1919*, Munich 1919

*Wilhelms II. Abschiedsbrief an das deutsche Volk. Den Deutschen ein Spiegel*, Berlin 2nd edn 1922

*Drei deutsche Kaiser. Wilhelm I., Friedrich III., Wilhelm II. Ihr Leben und ihre Zeit, 1858–1918*, Freiburg, Würzburg 1987

Arren, Jules, *Wilhelm II. Was er sagt, was er denkt*, Leipzig 1911

Avenarius, Ferdinand, 'Hofkunst und andere Kunst', *Der Kunstwart*, vol. 15, part 3, November 1901

Bachem, Karl, *Vorgeschichte, Geschichte und Politik der Deutschen Zentrumspartei*, 9 vols., Cologne 1927–32

Baechler, Christian, *Guillaume II le Kaiser*, Paris 2003

Balfour, Michael, *The Kaiser and His Times*, London 1975

Bartmann, Dominik, *Anton von Werner. Zur Kunst und Kunstpolitik im Deutschen Kaiserreich*, Berlin 1985

Bein, Alexander, *Erinnerungen und Dokumente über Herzls Begegnung mit Wilhelm II.*, *Zeitschrift für die Geschichte der Juden*, 1964

Benner, Thomas Hartmut, *Die Strahlen der Krone. Die religiöse Dimension des Kaisertums unter Wilhelm II. Vor dem Hintergrunde der Orientreise 1898*, Marburg 2001

Benson, E. F., *The Kaiser and His English Relations*, London, New York 1936

Bérard, Victor, *La France et Guillaume II*, Paris 1907

Berghahn, Volker R., 'Zu den Zielen des deutschen Flottenbaus unter Wilhelm II.', *Historische Zeitschrift*, 210/1, February 1970, pp. 34–100

    *Der Tirpitz-Plan. Genesis und Verfall einer innenpolitischen Krisenstrategie unter Wilhelm II.*, Düsseldorf 1971

    'Des Kaisers Flotte und die Revolutionierung des Mächtesystems vor 1914', in Röhl, *Der Ort Kaiser Wilhelms II.*

Bernstein, Hermann, *The Willy–Nicky Correspondence, Being the Secret and Intimate Telegrams Exchanged between the Kaiser and the Tsar*, New York 1918

Beseler, Dora von, *Der Kaiser im englischen Urteil*, Stuttgart 1932

    *Der Kaiser in Vergangenheit und Gegenwart. Gedanken zum 75. Geburtstag Kaiser Wilhelm II.*, Leipzig 1934

Bethge, Ernst Heinrich, *Jung Deutschland, Dein Kaiser!*, Langensalza 1913

Beumelburg, Werner, *Wilhelm II. und Bülow*, Oldenburg 1932

Beynes, N., *L'Empereur Guillaume*, Paris 1915

Bigelow, Poultney, *The German Emperor and His Eastern Neighbours*, New York 1892

    *Prussian Memories 1864–1914*, New York 1916

    *Prussianism and Pacifism. The Two Wilhelms between 1848 and 1918*, New York, London, 1919

Bing, E. J., ed., *The Letters of the Tsar Nicholas and the Empress Marie*, London 1937

Bismarck, Otto Fürst von, *Die gesammelten Werke*, 15 vols., Berlin 1923–35

Bittner, Ludwig, 'Neue Beiträge zur Haltung Kaiser Wilhelms II. in der Faschoda-Frage', *Historische Zeitschrift*, 162 (1940), pp. 540–50

Blum, Hans, *Fürst Bismarck und seine Zeit. Eine Biographie für das deutsche Volk*, Munich 1899

    *Bismarck. Ein Buch für Deutschlands Jugend und Volk*, Heidelberg 1903

Bodelschwingh, Marie von, *Aus Heiligem Land. Den Kindern erzählt*, Bielefeld 1899

Bodenheimer, M., *Die Zionisten im kaiserlichen Deutschland*, Bensberg 1972

Boelcke, Willi A., *Krupp und die Hohenzollern in Dokumenten. Krupp-Korrespondenz mit Kaisern, Kabinettschefs und Ministern 1850–1918*, Frankfurt a.M. 1970

Boockmann, Hartmut, *Die Marienburg im 19. Jahrhundert*, Frankfurt, Berlin, Vienna 1982

Borkenhagen, Hermann, 'Kaiser Wilhelms II. Schuld', *Flugschrift der DNVP*, Berlin 1920

Bornhak, Conrad, *Deutsche Geschichte unter Kaiser Wilhelm II.*, Leipzig, Erlangen 2nd edn 1921

Brauer, Arthur von, *Im Dienste Bismarcks. Persönliche Erinnerungen*, Berlin 1936

Breitenborn, Konrad, *Im Dienste Bismarcks. Die politische Karriere des Grafen Otto zu Stolberg-Wernigerode*, Leipzig 3rd edn 1986 ed., *Die Lebenserinnerungen des Fürsten Otto zu Stolberg-Wernigerode*, Wernigerode 1996

Bringmann, Tobias C., *Reichstag und Zweikampf. Die Duellfrage als innenpolitischer Konflikt des deutschen Kaiserreichs 1871–1918*, Freiburg 1997

Brude-Firnau, Gisela, *Die literarische Deutung Kaiser Wilhelms II. zwischen 1889 und 1989*, Heidelberg 1997

Buchner, Max, *Kaiser Wilhelm II., seine Weltanschauung und die Deutschen Katholiken*, Leipzig 1929

Buckle, George Earle, ed., *The Letters of Queen Victoria*, Third Series, 3 vols., London 1930

Bülow, Bernhard Fürst von, *Denkwürdigkeiten*, 4 vols., Berlin 1930–1

    *The Memoirs of Prince von Bülow*, 4 vols., London and New York 1931–2

Burmeister, Hans W., *Prince Philipp zu Eulenburg-Hertefeld, 1847–1921. His Influence on Kaiser Wilhelm II and His Role in the German Government, 1888–1902*, Wiesbaden 1981

Bußmann, Walter, ed., *Staatssekretär Graf Herbert von Bismarck. Aus seiner politischen Privatkorrespondenz*, Göttingen 1964

Canis, Konrad, *Bismarck und Waldersee*, Berlin 1980

    *Von Bismarck zur Weltpolitik. Deutsche Außenpolitik 1890 bis 1902*, Berlin 1997

Carmel, Alex and Eisler, Ejal Jakob, *Der Kaiser reist ins Heilige Land. Die Palästinareise Wilhelms II. 1898. Eine illustrierte Dokumentation*, Stuttgart 1999

Carnegie, Andrew, *William II, German Emperor & King of Prussia*, Dunfermline 1913

Casati, Gaetano, *Ten Years in Equatoria*, 2 vols., London 1891

Cataruzza, Marina, 'Das Kaiserbild in der Arbeiterschaft am Beispiel der Werftarbeiter in Hamburg und Stettin', in Röhl, *Der Ort Kaiser Wilhelms II.*

Catling, A. H., *The Kaiser under the Searchlight*, London 1914

Cecil, Lamar, *The German Diplomatic Service, 1871–1914*, Princeton 1976

    *Wilhelm II.* volume I. *Prince and Emperor, 1859–1900*, Chapel Hill, London 1989

    *Wilhelm II.* volume II. *Emperor and Exile, 1900–1941*, Chapel Hill, London 1996

Chamberlain, Houston Stewart, 'Kaiser Wilhelm II.' *Jugend*, 1900

    *Briefe 1882–1924 und Briefwechsel mit Kaiser Wilhelm II.*, 2 vols., Munich 1926

Chamier, Jacques D., *Ein Fabeltier unserer Zeit*, Zürich 1938

Chickering, Roger, *We Men Who Feel Most German. A Cultural Study of the Pan-German League, 1886–1914*, Boston, London, Sydney 1984

Christian, R. F., ed., *Tolstoy's Letters*, 2 vols., London 1978

Clark, Christopher, *Kaiser Wilhelm II*, London 2000

Conradi, Hermann, *Wilhelm II. und die junge Generation. Eine zeitpsychologische Betrachtung*, Leipzig 1889

Corti, Egon Caesar Conte, *Wenn... Sendung und Schicksal einer Kaiserin*, Graz, Vienna, Cologne 1954

    *The English Empress. A Study in the Relations between Queen Victoria and Her Eldest Daughter, Empress Frederick of Germany*, London 1957

Cowles, Virginia, *The Kaiser*, New York 1963

Craig, Gordon A., *The Politics of the Prussian Army, 1640–1945*, New York 1955

Cullen, Michael S., *Der Reichstag. Die Geschichte eines Monumentes*, Berlin 1983

Cunliffe-Owen, Marguerite, *Imperator et Rex, William II of Germany*, New York 1904

Curtius, Friedrich, ed., *Denkwürdigkeiten des Fürsten Chlodwig zu Hohenlohe-Schillingsfürst*, 2 vols., Stuttgart 1906

Daudet, Ernest, *Guillaume II et François Joseph*, Paris 1916

Davis, Arthur N., *The Kaiser I Knew. My Fourteen Years with the Kaiser*, London 1918

Deist, Wilhelm, *Flottenpolitik und Flottenpropaganda. Das Nachrichtenbureau des Reichsmarineamtes 1897–1914*, Stuttgart 1976

    'Kaiser Wilhelm II. als Oberster Kriegsherr', in Röhl, *Der Ort Kaiser Wilhelms II.*

*Militär, Staat und Gesellschaft. Studien zur preußisch-deutschen Militärgeschichte*, Munich 1991

Delbrück, Hans, 'Staatsstreichpläne als Ursachen von Bismarcks Rücktritt. Sensationelle Enthüllungen', *Neues Wiener Journal*, 11 December 1913

Dickenson, Asa Don, *The Kaiser. A Book about the Most Interesting Man in Europe*, New York 1914

*Documents Diplomatiques Français 1871–1914*, Ministère des Affaires Etrangères, ed., 41 vols., Paris 1929–36

Dod, Karl C., *The Friendship of Wilhelm II and Nicholas II and Its International Implications, 1894–1905*, Urbana, IL, 1934

Doerry, Martin, *Übergangsmenschen. Die Mentalität der Wilhelminer und die Krise des Kaiserreichs*, Weinheim, Munich 1986

Domann, Peter, *Sozialdemokratie und Kaisertum unter Wilhelm II. Die Auseinandersetzung der Partei mit dem monarchischen System, seinen gesellschafts- und verfassungspolitischen Voraussetzungen*, Wiesbaden 1974

Dryander, Ernst von, *Wollte der Kaiser Krieg?*, Berlin 1919
   *Erinnerungen aus meinem Leben*, Bielefeld, Leipzig 1922

Dubber, Ursula, *Wilhelm II und England, 1898–1914*, Heidelberg 1944

Duchhardt, Heinz, 'Der 18. Januar 1701 und die europäische Monarchie', *Majestas*, 10, 2002, pp. 151–66

Duggan, Christopher, *Creare la nazione. Vita di Francesco Crispi*, Rome, Bari 2000

Dülffer, Jost, 'Die Kreta-Krise und der griechisch-türkische Krieg 1890–1898', in Dülffer, Jost, Mühleisen, Hans-Otto and Torunsky, Vera, eds., *Inseln als Brennpunkte internationaler Politik*, Cologne 1986

Dülffer, Jost, Kröger, Martin and Wippich, Rolf-Harald, *Vermiedene Kriege. Deeskalation von Konflikten der Großmächte zwischen Krimkrieg und Erstem Weltkrieg 1865–1914*, Munich 1997

Ebel, G., *Botschafter Paul Graf von Hatzfeldt. Nachgelassene Papiere 1838–1901*, 2 vols., Boppard am Rhein 1976

Ebmeyer, Major, 'Caprivis Entlassung', *Deutsche Revue*, 47/4, 1922

Eça de Queirós, José Maria, 'O imperador Guilherme' (1891), in *Echos de Pariz*, Porto 4th edn 1920

Eckardstein, Baron von, *Ten Years at the Court of St James, 1895–1905*, London 1921

Eckardt, Julius von, *Aus den Tagen von Bismarcks Kampf gegen Caprivi*, Leipzig 1920

Elkind, Louis, ed., *The German Emperor's Speeches: Being a Selection from the Speeches, Edicts, Letters and Telegrams of the Emperor William II*, New York, London, Bombay 1904

Ellern, Hermann and Ellern, Bessi, *Herzl, Hechler, the Grand Duke of Baden and the German Emperor 1896–1904*, Tel Aviv 1961

Endres, Franz Carl, *Die Tragödie Deutschlands. Im Banne des Machtgedankens bis zum Zusammenbruch des Reiches. Von einem Deutschen*, Stuttgart 3rd edn 1924

Engelberg, Ernst, *Bismarck. Das Reich in der Mitte Europas*, Berlin 1990

Epkenhans, Michael, *Die wilhelminische Flottenrüstung 1908–1914. Weltmachtstreben, industrieller Fortschritt, soziale Integration*, Munich 1991
   'Wilhelm II and "His" Navy, 1888–1918', in Mombauer and Deist, *The Kaiser*

Eppstein, Georg Freiherr von, ed., *Fürst Bismarcks Entlassung. Nach den hinterlassenen, bisher unveröffentlichten Aufzeichnungen des Staatssekretärs des Innern, Staatsministers Dr. Karl Heinrich von Boetticher und des Chefs der Reichskanzlei unter dem Fürsten Bismarck Dr. Franz Johannes von Rottenburg*, Berlin 1920

Erck, Alfred and Schneider, Hannelore, *Georg II. von Sachsen-Meiningen. Ein Leben zwischen ererbter Macht und künstlerischer Freiheit*, Zella-Mehlis, Meiningen 1997

Erfurt, Erich, *Bismarcks Sturz und die Änderung der deutschen Politik*, Berlin 1940

Eulenburg-Hertefeld, Philipp Fürst zu, *Aus 50 Jahren. Erinnerungen, Tagebücher und Briefe aus dem Nachlaß des Fürsten*, Berlin 2nd edn 1925

  *Mit dem Kaiser als Staatsman und Freund auf Nordlandreisen*, 2 vols., Dresden 1931

  *Das Ende König Ludwigs II. und andere Erlebnisse*, Leipzig 1934

  *Erlebnisse an deutschen und fremden Höfen*, Leipzig 1934

Evans, Richard J., ed., *Kneipengespräche im Kaiserreich. Stimmungsberichte der Hamburger Politischen Polizei 1892–1914*, Reinbek bei Hamburg 1989

Everling, Friedrich, *Der Kaiser. Wie er war – wie er ist*, Berlin 1934

Eyck, Erich, *Die Monarchie Wilhelms II nach seinen Briefen, seinen Randbemerkungen und Zeugnissen seiner Freunde*, Berlin 1924

  *Das persönliche Regiment Wilhelms II. Politische Geschichte des Deutschen Kaiserreiches von 1890 bis 1914*, Zürich 1948

Farrar, Lancelot L., *Divide and Conquer*, New York 1978

Fellner, Fritz, 'Wilhelm II. und das wilhelminische Deutschland im Urteil österreichischer Zeitgenossen', in Röhl, *Der Ort Kaiser Wilhelms II*

Fesser, Gerd, *Reichskanzler Bernhard Fürst von Bülow. Eine Biographie*, Berlin 1991

  'Ohrfeige für England. Die brisante Depesche Wilhelms II. an Burenpräsidenten "Ohm" Krüger', *Die Zeit*, 5 January 1996

  *Der Traum vom Platz an der Sonne. Deutsche 'Weltpolitik' 1897–1914*, Bremen 1996

  *Die Kaiserzeit. Deutschland 1871–1918*, Erfurt 2000

Fiebig-von Hase, Ragnhild, *Lateinamerika als Konfliktherd der deutsch-amerikanischen Beziehungen 1890–1903*, 2 vols., Göttingen 1986

  'Die Rolle Kaiser Wilhelms II. in den deutsch-amerikanischen Beziehungen, 1890–1914', in Röhl, *Der Ort Kaiser Wilhelms II.*

  'The Uses of "Friendship". The "Personal Regime" of Wilhelm II and Theodore Roosevelt, 1901–1909', in Mombauer and Deist, *The Kaiser*

Field, Geoffrey G., *Evangelist of Race. The Germanic Vision of Houston Stewart Chamberlain*, New York 1981

Fink, Carole, Hull, Isabel V. and Knox, MacGregor, eds., *German Nationalism and the European Response, 1890–1945*, Norman, OK, 1985

Fischer, Eugen, *Holsteins großes Nein. Die deutsch-englischen Bündnisverhandlungen von 1898–1901*, Berlin 1925

Fischer, Franz, 'Zur Entlassung Bismarcks. Unveröffentlichte Briefe aus dem Archiv der Kölnischen Zeitung', *Kölnische Zeitung*, 14/15 January 1921

Fischer, H. W. H., *Private Lives of William II and His Consort and the Secret History of the Court of Berlin 1888–1898 from the Papers and Diaries Extending over a Period Beginning June 1888 to the Spring of 1898, of Ursula, Countess of Eppinghoven*, New York 1898–9

  *Secret Life of the Kaiser from Birth to Exile, from the Private Papers and Diaries of Baroness von Larisch-Reddern*, New York 1919

  *Behind the Scenes with the Kaiser 1888–1922. The True Story of the Kaiser as He Lived, Loved, Played and Warred, by the Baroness von Larisch*, New York 1922

Fischer, Hartwig, *Ein Wilhelminisches Gesamtkunstwerk auf dem Kapitol. Hermann Prell und die Einrichtung des Thronsaals in der Deutschen Botschaft zu Rom 1894–1899*, Basel 1998

Fischer, Heinz-Joachim, 'Kaiserliche Eskapaden in der Ewigen Stadt. Was das Vatikanische Geheimarchiv über den Besuch Wilhelms II. in Rom enthüllt', *Frankfurter Allgemeine Zeitung*, 7 August 1996

Fischer, Jörg-Uwe, *Admiral des Kaisers. Georg Alexander von Müller als Chef des Marinekabinetts Wilhelms II.*, Frankfurt a.M. 1992

Fischer-Sallstein, Conrad, *Prinz Heinrich in Kiautschau. Reisen zu Wasser und zu Lande des Prinz-Admirals in Indien, China, Japan (1898–1900)*, Berlin 1900

Fontane, Theodor, *Briefe an Georg Friedländer*, Heidelberg 1954

Fontenoy, Marquise de, *William II, Germany: Francis Joseph, Austria-Hungary*, Philadelphia 1900

Forsbach, Ralf, *Alfred von Kiderlen-Wächter (1852–1912). Ein Diplomatenleben im Kaiserreich*, 2 vols., Göttingen 1997

Forsten, Hans, *Unser Kaiser in Palästina. Reise Kaiser Wilhelms II. und der Kaiserin Auguste Victoria nach dem gelobten Lande*, Berlin 1898

Förster, Stig, *Der doppelte Militarismus. Die deutsche Heeresrüstungspolitik zwischen Status-quo-Sicherung und Aggression 1890–1913*, Stuttgart 1985

Fox, Edward Lyell, *Wilhelm Hohenzollern & Co.*, New York 1917

Franke, Lydia, 'Die Randbemerkungen Wilhelms II. in den Akten der auswärtigen Politik als historische und psychologische Quelle', diss., Berlin 1933

Frankenberg, Paul von, *Kaiser Wilhelms II. Reise nach Jerusalem*, Berlin 1899

Franz, Eckhardt G., ed., *Erinnertes. Aufzeichnungen des letzten Großherzogs Ernst Ludwig von Hessen und bei Rhein*, Darmstadt 1983

Frederic, Harold, *The Young Emperor. William II of Germany. A Study in Character Development on a Throne*, London 1891

Freksa, Friedrich, *Menschliche Rechtfertigung Wilhelms II. Nach seinen Randbemerkungen in den Akten des Auswärtigen Amtes*, Munich 1920

Frevert, Ute, *Ehrenmänner. Das Duell in der bürgerlichen Gesellschaft*, Munich 1991

Fricke, Dieter, 'Die Affäre Leckert-Lützow-Tausch und die Regierungskrise von 1897 in Deutschland', *Zeitschrift für Geschichtswissenschaft*, 7, 1960

Fried, Alfred H., *The German Emperor and the Peace of the World*, London, New York 1912

Friedländer, Prof. Dr Adolf Albrecht, *Wilhelm II. Versuch einer psychologischen Analyse*, Halle 1919

Friedman, Isaiah, *Germany, Turkey and Zionism 1897–1918*, Oxford 1977

Friedmann, Fritz, *Der deutsche Kaiser und die Hofkamarilla. I. Der Fall Kotze, II. Wilhelm II. und die Revolution von oben*, Zürich 1896

Frobenius, Herman, *Die Hohenzollern. Geschichte Brandenburg-Preußens und des Deutschen Reiches unter den Hohenzollern*, Berlin n.d.

Fuchs, Georg, *Der Kaiser, die Kultur und die Kunst. Betrachtungen über die Zukunft des deutschen Volkes aus den Papieren eines Unverantwortlichen*, Munich, Leipzig 1904

Fuchs, Walther Peter, ed., *Großherzog Friedrich I. von Baden und die Reichspolitik 1871–1907*, 4 vols., Stuttgart 1968–80

Fursenko, A. A., *Bor'ba za razdel Kitaya i amerikanskaya doktrina otkritich dverei 1895–1900*, Moscow, Leningrad 1956

Gagliardi, Ernst, *Bismarcks Entlassung*, 2 vols., Tübingen 1927–41

Gall, Lothar, *Bismarck. Der weisse Revolutionär*, Frankfurt a.M., Berlin, Vienna 1980

Garvin, J. L. and Amery, J., *Life of Joseph Chamberlain*, 6 vols., London 1932–69

Gauss, Christian, *The German Emperor as Shown in His Public Utterances*, New York 1922

Gautschi, Andreas, *Wilhelm II. und das Waidwerk. Jagen und Jagden des letzten Deutschen Kaisers. Eine Bilanz*, Hanstedt 2000

Gerard, James W., *My Four Years in Germany*, London, New York, Toronto 1917
    *Face to Face with Kaiserism*, London, New York, Toronto 1918

Gisevius, Hans B., *Der Anfang vom Ende. Wie es mit Wilhelm II. begann*, Zürich 1971

Goetz, Walter, ed., *Briefe Wilhelms II. an den Zaren 1894–1914*, Berlin 1920

Gollwitzer, Heinz, *Die Gelbe Gefahr. Geschichte eines Schlagworts. Studien zum imperialistischen Denken*, Göttingen 1962

*Geschichte des weltpolitischen Denkens*, 2 vols., Göttingen 1972–82

Görlitz, Walter, ed., *Regierte der Kaiser? Kriegstagebücher, Aufzeichnungen und Briefe des Chefs des Marine-Kabinetts Admiral G. A. von Müller, 1914–1918*, Göttingen 1959

ed., *Der Kaiser . . . Aufzeichnungen des Chefs des Marinekabinetts Admiral Georg Alexander v. Müller über die Ära Wilhelms II.*, Göttingen 1965

Gradenwitz, Otto, ed., *Akten über Bismarcks großdeutsche Rundfahrt vom Jahre 1892*, Heidelberg 1922

*Bismarcks letzter Kampf, 1888–1898*, Berlin 1924

Grand-Carteret, John, *Les célébrités vues par l'image 'Lui' devant l'objectif caricatural*, Paris 1906

Grenville, J. A. S., *Lord Salisbury and Foreign Policy*, London 1964

Grunder, Horst, *Christliche Mission und deutscher Imperialismus*, Paderborn 1982

Grunow, Alfred, *Der Kaiser und die Kaiserstadt*, Berlin 1970

Gutsche, Willibald, *Wilhelm II. Der letzte Kaiser des Deutschen Reiches. Eine Biographie*, Berlin 1991

Guttmann, Bernhard, *Schattenriß einer Generation 1888–1919*, Stuttgart 1950

Haller, Johannes, *Aus dem Leben des Fürsten Philipp zu Eulenburg-Hertefeld*, Berlin 1924

Hallgarten, G. W. F., *Imperialismus vor 1914. Die soziologischen Grundlagen der Außenpolitik europäischer Großmächte vor dem Ersten Weltkrieg*, 2 vols., Munich 1963

Hallmann, Hans, ed., *Zur Geschichte und Problematik des deutsch-russischen Rückversicherungsvertrages von 1887*, Darmstadt 1968

Hamann, Brigitte, 'Das Leben des Kronprinzen Rudolf von Österreich-Ungarn nach neuen Quellen', diss., Vienna 1977

*Rudolf, Kronprinz und Rebell*, Vienna, Munich 1978

Hammann, Otto, *Der neue Kurs*, Berlin 1918

*Um den Kaiser, Erinnerungen aus den Jahren 1906–1909*, Berlin 1919

*Bilder aus der letzten Kaiserzeit*, Berlin 1922

Hammer, S. C., *Wilhelm II, et blad au Tysklands nyeste historie*, Kristiania 1915

Hank, Manfred, *Kanzler ohne Amt. Fürst Bismarck nach seiner Entlassung 1890–1898*, Munich 1977

Hansen, Heinrich E., 'Die "Hunnenrede" Kaiser Wilhelms II. in Bremerhaven', *Jahrbuch der Männer vom Morgenstern*, 50, 1969, pp. 207–31

Harden, Maximilian, "Der Kampf mit dem Drachen", *Die Zukunft*, No. 32, 11 August 1900

Hartau, Friedrich, *Wilhelm II in Selbstzeugnissen und Bilddokumenten*, Reinbek bei Hamburg 1978

Hartung, Fritz, *Das persönliche Regiment Kaiser Wilhelms II.*, Berlin 1952

Hassan, Vita, *Die Wahrheit über Emin Pascha*, 1893

Hecht, Karsten, 'Die Harden-Prozesse. Strafverfahren, Öffentlichkeit und Politik im Kaiserreich', diss., Munich 1997

Heinsick, Paul, *Wilhelm II., Friedenskaiser oder nicht?*, Leipzig 1915

Helfritz, Hans, *Wilhelm II. als Kaiser und König. Eine historische Studie*, Zürich 1954

Hellige, Hans Dieter and Schulin, Ernst, eds., *Walther Rathenau Gesamtausgabe*, vol. VI, *Briefwechsel Walther Rathenau–Maximilian Harden*, Munich, Heidelberg 1983

Hellwig, F., *Carl Freiherr von Stumm-Halberg*, Heidelberg, Saarbrücken 1936

Hemmi, Beate, *Wilhelm II. und die Reichsregierung im Urteil schweizerischer diplomatischer Berichte*, Zürich 1964

Heresch, Elisabeth, *Nikolaus II. 'Feigheit, Lüge und Verrat'. Leben und Ende des letzten russischen Zaren*, Munich 1992

Herre, Franz, *Wilhelm II. Monarch zwischen den Zeiten*, Cologne 1993

Hervier, Paul-Louis, *The Two Williams. Studies of the Kaiser and the Crown Prince*, London 1916

Herwig, Holger H., *The German Naval Officer Corps. A Social and Political History, 1890–1918*, Oxford 1973

'*Luxury' Fleet. The Imperial German Navy 1888–1918*, London 1987

Herzfeld, Hans, *Johannes von Miquel. Sein Anteil am Ausbau des Deutschen Reiches bis zur Jahrhundertwende*, 2 vols., Detmold 1938

Herzl, Theodor, *Gesammelte zionistische Werke*, 5 vols., Tel Aviv 1934

Heyking, Elisabeth von, *Tagebücher aus vier Weltteilen, 1886–1904*, Leipzig 1926

Hilarus, *Jung Wilhelm. Heitere Bilder aus der Jugendzeit Kaiser Wilhelms II.*, Berlin 1910

Hildebrand, Klaus, *Deutsche Außenpolitik 1871–1918*, Munich 1989

*Das vergangene Reich. Deutsche Außenpolitik von Bismarck bis Hitler, 1871–1945*, Stuttgart 1995

Hill, David J., *Impressions of the Kaiser*, New York, London 1918

Hintze, Otto, *Die Hohenzollern und ihr Werk. Fünfhundert Jahre vaterländischer Geschichte*, Berlin 2nd edn 1915

Hinzpeter, Georg Ernst, *Kaiser Wilhelm II. Eine Skizze nach der Natur gezeichnet*, Bielefeld 1888

Hoche, Jules, *L'Empereur Guillaume II intim*, Paris 1913

Hofmann, Hermann, *Fürst Bismarck 1890–1898*, 2 vols., Stuttgart, Berlin, Leipzig 1913

Hohenlohe, Alexander von, *Aus meinem Leben*, Frankfurt a.M. 1925

Hohenlohe-Schillingsfürst, Chlodwig Fürst zu, *Denkwürdigkeiten*, 2 vols., Stuttgart, Leipzig 1907

Müller, Karl Alexander von, ed., *Denkwürdigkeiten der Reichskanzlerzeit*, Stuttgart, Berlin 1931

Horn, Hannelore, *Der Kampf um den Bau des Mittellandkanals. Staat und Politik*, Cologne, Opladen 1964

Hubatsch, Walther, *Der Admiralstab und die obersten Marinebehörden in Deutschland 1884–1945*, Frankfurt a.M. 1958

Hull, Isabel V., *The Entourage of Kaiser Wilhelm II, 1888–1918*, Cambridge 1982

'Kaiser Wilhelm II and the "Liebenberg Circle"', in Röhl and Sombart, *Kaiser Wilhelm II. New Interpretations*

'"Persönliches Regiment"', in Röhl, *Der Ort Kaiser Wilhelms II.*

'Military Culture, Wilhelm II and the End of the Monarchy in the First World War', in Mombauer and Deist, *The Kaiser*

Hutten-Czapski, Bogdan Graf von, *Sechzig Jahre Politik und Gesellschaft*, 2 vols., Berlin 1936

Jacks, William, *The Life of His Majesty William the Second, German Emperor, with a Sketch of His Hohenzollern Ancestors*, Glasgow 1904

Jarchow, Margarete, *Hofgeschenke. Wilhelm II. zwischen Diplomatie und Dynastie 1888–1914*, Hamburg 1998

Jefferson, Margaret M., 'Lord Salisbury's Conversations with the Tsar in Balmoral, 27 and 29 September 1896', *Slavonic and East European Review*, 39, 1960–1

Jerussalimski, A. S., *Die Außenpolitik und die Diplomatie des deutschen Imperialismus Ende des 19. Jahrhunderts*, Berlin 1954

Jonge, J. A., *Wilhelm II.*, Amsterdam 1986

Julier, Jürgen, ed., *Kaiserlicher Kunstbesitz. Aus dem holländischen Exil Haus Doorn*, Berlin 1991

Kanghi-Tschu, *Deutschland, der Kaiser und Simplizissimus. Aus den Berichten eines chinesischen Diplomaten*, Munich 1911

Kann, Robert A., 'Kaiser Wilhelm II. und Thronfolger Franz Ferdinand in ihrer Korrespondenz', in Kann, Robert A., *Erzherzog Franz Ferdinand Studien*, Vienna 1976, pp. 46–85

Kautsky, Karl, *The Guilt of Wilhelm Hohenzollern*, London 1920

Kautzsch, W., *Intimes des Berliner Hoflebens unter Wilhelm II.*, Berlin 1922

Keller, Mathilde Gräfin von, *Vierzig Jahre im Dienst der Kaiserin. Ein Kulturbild aus den Jahren 1881–1921*, Leipzig 1935

Kennan, George F., *The Decline of Bismarck's European Order. Franco-Russian Relations, 1879–1890*, Princeton 1979

*The Fateful Alliance. France, Russia and the Coming of the First World War*, New York 1984

Kennedy, J. M., *The War Lord: A Character Study of Kaiser Wilhelm II by Means of His Speeches, Letters and Telegrams*, London 1914

Kennedy, Paul, 'Tirpitz, England and the Second Navy Law of 1900. A Strategical Critique', *Militärgeschichtliche Mitteilungen*, 1970, 2

*The Samoan Tangle. A Study in Anglo-German-American Relations 1878–1900*, Dublin 1974

*The Rise of the Anglo-German Antagonism 1860–1914*, London 1980

'The Kaiser and German Weltpolitik. Reflexions on Wilhelm II's Place in the Making of German Foreign Policy', in Röhl and Sombart, *Kaiser Wilhelm II. New Interpretations*

Klahr, Douglas Mark, 'The Kaiser Builds in Berlin. Expressing National and Dynastic Identity in the Early Building Projects of Wilhelm II', diss., Providence, RI, 2002

Klaussmann, A. O., ed., *The Kaiser's Speeches, Forming a Character Portrait of Wilhelm II*, New York, London 1903

Koch, Ernestine, *Albert Langen. Ein Verleger in München*, Munich, Berlin 1969

Koffler, Dosio, *Wilhelm II.*, Berlin 1931

Kohlrausch, Martin, 'Monarchie und Massenöffentlichkeit. Veränderungen in der Rezeption des wilhelminischen Kaisertums, 1890–1925', diss., Florence 2002

Kohut, A., *Kaiser Wilhelm II als Denker. Goldene Worte und Aussprüche aus seinen Reden, Erlässen, Gesprächen, Briefen und Telegrammen*, Lüneburg 1913

Kohut, Thomas A., *Wilhelm II and the Germans. A Study in Leadership*, Oxford, New York, 1991

Kosposth, K. A., *Wie ich zu meinem Kaiser stand. Persönliche Erinnerungen an Kaiser Wilhelm II.*, Breslau 1924

Kracke, Friedrich, *Prinz und Kaiser. Wilhelm II. im Urteil seiner Zeit*, Munich 1960

Krausnick, Helmut, *Neue Bismarck-Gespräche. Vier unveröffentlichte politische Gespräche des Kanzlers mit österreich-ungarischen Staatsmännern sowie ein Gespräch Kaiser Wilhelms II.*, Hamburg 1940

*Holsteins Geheimpolitik in der Ära Bismarck, 1886–1890*, Hamburg 1942

'Holstein, Österreich-Ungarn und die Meerengenfrage im Herbst 1895. Persönliches Regiment oder Regierungspolitik?', in *Forschungen zu Staat und Verfassung. Festgabe für Fritz Hartung*, Berlin 1958

Krockow, Christian Graf von, *'Unser Kaiser'. Glanz und Sturz der Monarchie*, Munich 1996

*Kaiser Wilhelm II. und seine Zeit. Biographie einer Epoche*, Berlin 1999

Kroll, Frank-Lothar, ed., *Preussens Herrscher. Von den ersten Hohenzollern bis Wilhelm II.*, Munich 2000

Kugler, Bernhard von, *Deutschlands größter Held. Jubel-Ausgabe zur hundertjährigen Gedächtnisfeier des Geburtstags weiland Sr. Majestät Kaiser Wilhelm I.*, Dresden 1893

Kürenberg, Joachim von, *War alles falsch? Das Leben Kaiser Wilhelms II.*, Bonn 1951

Kurtz, Harold, *The Second Reich. Kaiser Wilhelm II and His Germany*, London, New York 1970

Lahme, Rainer, *Deutsche Außenpolitik 1890–1894. Von der Gleichgewichtspolitik Bismarcks zur Allianzstrategie Caprivis*, Göttingen 1990

Lamber, Juliette, *Guillaume II (1890–1899)*, Paris 1917

Lambi, Ivo Nikolai, *The Navy and German Power Politics, 1862–1914*, Boston, London, Sydney 1984

Lammerting, Kristin, *Meteor. Die kaiserlichen Segelyachten*, Cologne 1999

Lamprecht, Karl, *Der Kaiser. Versuch einer Charakteristik*, Berlin 1916

Lamsdorff, Wladimir N., *Dnevnik 1886–1892*, 2 vols., Moscow 1926–34

'Die Nichterneuerung des Rückversicherungsvertrages. Auszüge aus dem Tagebuch des russischen Außenministers Grafen Wladimir Nikolajewitsch Lamsdorff', *Berliner Monatshefte*, 9, 1931, pp. 158–77

Lanessan, J., *L'Empire germanique sous la direction de Bismarck et de Guillaume II*, Paris 1915

Langer, William L., *The Franco-Russian Alliance, 1890–1894*, Cambridge 1929
  *European Alliances and Alignments, 1871–1890*, New York 2nd edn 1956
  *The Diplomacy of Imperialism 1890–1902*, New York 2nd edn 1965

Laufer, Jochen, 'Die deutsche Südafrikapolitik 1890–1898 im Spannungsfeld zwischen deutsch-englischen Beziehungen, Wirtschaftsinteressen und Expansionsforderungen in der bürgerlichen Öffentlichkeit', diss., Humboldt-Universität Berlin 1986

Le Mang, Erich, *Die persönliche Schuld Wilhelms II. Ein zeitgemäßer Rückblick*, Dresden 1919

Lee, Arthur Gould, *The Empress Frederick Writes to Sophie, Her Daughter, Crown Princess and Later Queen of the Hellenes*, London 1955

Lee, Sir Sidney, *King Edward VII. A Biography*, 2 vols., London 1925–7

Legge, Edward, *The Public and Private Life of Kaiser Wilhelm II*, London 1915
  *King Edward, the Kaiser and the War*, London 1917

Lehnert, Uta, *Der Kaiser und die Siegesallee. Réclame Royale*, Berlin 1998

Lepsius, J., Mendelssohn-Bartholdy, A. and Thimme, F., eds., *Die Große Politik der europäischen Kabinette, 1871–1914*, 40 vols., Berlin 1922–7

Lerchenfeld-Koefering, Hugo Graf, *Erinnerungen und Denkwürdigkeiten, 1843–1925*, Berlin 1934
  *Kaiser Wilhelm II. als Persönlichkeit und Herrscher*, Kallmünz 1985

Lerman, Katharine Anne, *The Chancellor as Courtier. Bernhard von Bülow and the Governance of Germany 1900–1909*, Cambridge 1990
  'The Chancellor as Courtier. The Position of the Responsible Government under Kaiser Wilhelm II, 1900–1909', in Röhl, *Der Ort Kaiser Wilhelms II.*
  'The Kaiser's Elite? Wilhelm II and the Berlin Administration 1890–1914', in Mombauer and Deist, *The Kaiser*

Leudet, Maurice, *Guillaume II intim*, Paris 1897

Leuß, Hans, *Wilhelm Freiherr von Hammerstein*, Berlin 1905

Liman, Paul, *Der Kaiser 1888–1909. Ein Charakterbild Kaiser Wilhelms II.*, Leipzig 1909

Lindberg, Folke, *Kunglig utrikespolitik. Studier i svensk utrikespolitik under Oscar II och fram till borggårdskrisen*, Stockholm 1966

Longford, Elizabeth, *Jameson's Raid. The Prelude to the Boer War*, London 1984

Lowe, Charles, *The German Emperor, William II*, London 1895

Lucius von Ballhausen, Robert Freiherr, *Bismarck-Erinnerungen*, Stuttgart, Berlin 1920

Ludwig, Emil, *Wilhelm der Zweite*, Berlin 1926

Lugaro, Ernesto, *An Emperor's Madness or National Aberration?*, London, New York 1916

Lynx, J. J., *The Great Hohenzollern Scandal*, London 1965

Maatz, H., *Bismarck und Hannover 1866–1898*, Hildesheim 1971

Maccotta, Giuseppe, *Guillermo II, la Germania e l'Europa 1888–1914*, Rome 1934

MacDonogh, Giles, *The Last Kaiser. William the Impetuous*, London 2000

Machtan, Lothar, *Bismarcks Tod und Deutschlands Tränen. Reportage einer Tragödie*, Munich 1998

Malkowsky, Gerhard, *Die Kunst im Dienste der Staatsidee. Hohenzollernsche Kunstpolitik vom Großen Kurfürsten bis auf Wilhelm II.*, Berlin 1912

Mann, Golo, *Wilhelm II.*, Munich 1964

Mansel, Philip, *Constantinople, City of the World's Desire, 1453–1924*, London 1995

Marie Louise Princess of Schleswig-Holstein, *My Memories of Six Reigns*, London 1956

Marienfeld, W., *Wissenschaft und Schlachtflottenbau in Deutschland 1897–1906*, Frankfurt a.M. 1957

Marschall, Birgit, *Reisen und Regieren. Die Nordlandfahrten Kaiser Wilhelms II.*, Heidelberg 1991

Martin, Rudolf, *Deutsche Machthaber*, Berlin, Leipzig 1910

Massie, Robert K., *Dreadnought. Britain, Germany and the Coming of the Great War*, New York 1991

Masur, Gerhard, *Imperial Berlin*, London 1971

Maute, Hans-Ernst, *Die Februarerlasse Kaiser Wilhelms II. und ihre gesetzliche Ausführung. Unter besonderer Berücksichtigung der Berliner Internationalen Arbeiterschutzkonferenz von 1890*, Bielefeld 1984

Mazel, Henri, *La Psychologie du Kaiser*, Paris 1919

McCabe, Joseph, *The Kaiser. His Personality and Career*, London 1915

McLean, Roderick R., 'Kaiser Wilhelm II and His Hessian Cousins. Intra-state Relations in the German Empire and International Dynastic Politics, 1890–1918', *German History*, 19/1, 2001

   *Royalty and Diplomacy in Europe, 1890–1914*, Cambridge 2001

   'Dreams of a German Europe. Wilhelm II and the Treaty of Björkö of 1905', in Mombauer and Deist, *The Kaiser*

Mehnert, Ute, *Deutschland, Amerika und die 'Gelbe Gefahr'. Zur Karriere eines Schlagworts in der Großen Politik 1905–1917*, Stuttgart 1995

Meinecke, Friedrich, *Geschichte des deutsch-englischen Bündnisproblems*, Munich, Berlin 1927

Meinhold, Paul, *Wilhelm II., 25 Jahre Kaiser und König*, Berlin 1912

Meisner, Heinrich Otto, ed., *Denkwürdigkeiten des General-Feldmarschalls Alfred Grafen von Waldersee*, 3 vols., Stuttgart, Berlin 1922–3

   *Militärattachés und Militärbevollmächtigte in Preußen und im Deutschen Reich. Ein Beitrag zur Geschichte der Militärdiplomatie*, Berlin 1957

Meyer, Adolf, *Ins Heilige Land. Reisebilder von der großen Festfahrt nach Jerusalem im Oktober und November 1898*, Berlin 1899

Meyer, Arnold Oskar, *Bismarck. Der Mensch und der Staatsmann*, Stuttgart 2nd edn 1949

Mirbach, Ernst Freiherr von, ed., *Das deutsche Kaiserpaar im Heiligen Lande im Herbst 1898. Mit Allerhöchster Ermächtigung Seiner Majestät des Kaisers und Königs bearbeitet nach authentischen Berichten und Akten*, Berlin 1899

Mitchell, Nancy, *The Danger of Dreams. German and American Imperialism in Latin America*, Chapel Hill, London 1999

Möckl, Karl, *Die Prinzregentenzeit. Gesellschaft und Politik während der Ära des Prinzregenten Luitpold in Bayern*, Munich 1972

Moltke, Eliza von, ed., *Generaloberst Helmuth von Moltke. Erinnerungen, Briefe, Dokumente 1877–1916. Ein Bild vom Kriegsausbruch, erster Kriegsführung und Persönlichkeit des ersten militärischen Führers des Krieges*, Stuttgart 1922

Mombauer, Annika, *Helmuth von Moltke and the Origins of the First World War*, Cambridge 2001

   'Wilhelm, Waldersee and the Boxer Rebellion', in Mombauer, and Deist, *The Kaiser*

Mombauer, Annika and Deist, Wilhelm, eds., *The Kaiser. New Research on Wilhelm II's Role in Imperial Germany*, Cambridge 2003

Mommsen, Wilhelm, *Bismarcks Sturz und die Parteien*, Stuttgart 1924

Mommsen, Wolfgang J., *Der Autoritäre Nationalstaat. Verfassung, Gesellschaft und Kultur des deutschen Kaiserreiches*, Frankfurt a.M. 1990

   'Kaiser Wilhelm II and German Politics', *Journal of Contemporary History*, 25/2–3, May–June 1990, pp. 289–316

*Großmachtstellung und Weltpolitik, 1870–1914. Die Außenpolitik des Deutschen Reiches*, Frankfurt a.M. 1993

*War der Kaiser an allem schuld? Wilhelm II. und die preußisch-deutschen Machteliten*, Munich 2002

Morré, Harold, *20 Jahre S. M. Heitere Bilder zu ernsten Ereignissen*, Berlin 1909

Mosse, Werner E., ed., *Juden im Wilhelminischen Deutschland 1890–1914*, Tübingen 1976

Mossolov, A. A., *At the Court of the Last Tsar*, London 1935

Müller, Karl Alexander von, 'Die Entlassung. Nach den bayerischen Gesandtschaftsberichten', *Süddeutsche Monatshefte*, 19/1, December 1921

Muralt, Leonhard von, *Bismarcks Verantwortlichkeit*, Göttingen 1955

Muret, Maurice, *Guillaume II*, Paris 1940

Naumann, Friedrich, *Demokratie und Kaisertum*, Berlin 3rd edn 1904

Neyen, Emil, *Wilhelm II. Sein Werk. 450 Millarden neuer Schulden und 21 fliehende Könige*, Berlin 1919

Nichols, J. Alden, *Germany after Bismarck. The Caprivi Era, 1890–1894*, Cambridge 1958

Niemann, Alfred, *Kaiser und Heer. Das Wesen der Kommandogewalt und ihre Ausübung durch Kaiser Wilhelm II.*, Berlin 1921

*Wanderungen mit Kaiser Wilhelm II.*, Leipzig 1924

Nipperdey, Thomas, *Deutsche Geschichte 1866–1918*, Vol. I, *Arbeitswelt und Bürgergeist*, Munich 1990

*Deutsche Geschichte 1866–1918*, Vol. II, *Machtstaat vor der Demokratie*, Munich 1992

Noack, Friedrich, *Das Deutschtum in Rom seit dem Ausgang des Mittelalters*, 2 vols., Berlin, Leipzig 1927

Nöll von der Nahmer, R., *Bismarcks Reptilienfonds*, Mainz 1968

Nostiz, Herbert von, *Bismarcks unbotmäßiger Botschafter, Fürst Münster von Derneburg (1820–1902)*, Göttingen 1968

Noussanne, Henri de, *The Kaiser as He Is: or, the Real William II (Le Veritable Guillaume II)*, New York, London 1905

Nowak, Karl-Friedrich and Thimme, Friedrich, eds., *Erinnerungen und Gedanken des Botschafters Anton Graf Monts*, Berlin 1932

Öke, Bulent Mim Kemal, 'Ottoman Policies towards Zionism', MPhil. diss., Cambridge 1979

Oncken, Hermann, *Rudolf von Bennigsen. Ein deutscher liberaler Politiker. Nach seinen Briefen und hinterlassenen Papieren*, 2 vols., Stuttgart, Leipzig 1910

Oncken, Wilhelm, ed., *Unser Heldenkaiser. Festschrift zum hundertjährigen Geburtstage Kaiser Wilhelms des Großen*, Berlin 1897

Osmanoglu, Ayse, *Avec mon Père le Sultan Abdulhamid de son palais à sa prison*, Paris 1991

*Österreich-Ungarns Außenpolitik von der Bosnischen Krise 1908 bis zum Kriegsausbruch 1914. Diplomatische Aktenstücke des österreichisch-ungarischen Ministerium des Äußern*, selected by Ludwig Bittner, Alfred F. Pribram, Heinrich Srbik and Hans Uebersberger, edited by Ludwig Bittner and Hans Uebersberger, 9 vols., Vienna, Leipzig 1930

Otte, Thomas, '"The Winston of Germany." The British Foreign Policy Élite and the Last German Emperor', *Canadian Journal of History*, December 2001, pp. 471–504

Otto, Berthold, *Wilhelm II. und wir! Die Kaiserartikel des 'Deutschen Volksgeistes' aus den Jahren 1919–1925*, Berlin 1925

Padje, Willem-Alexander van't, 'At the Heart of the Growing Anglo-German Imperialist Rivalry. Two British Ambassadors in Berlin, 1884–1908', DPhil. diss., Oxford 2001

Pakula, Hannah, *An Uncommon Woman. The Empress Frederick, Daughter of Queen Victoria, Wife of the Crown Prince of Prussia, Mother of Kaiser Wilhelm*, New York 1995

Paléologue, Maurice, *Guillaume II et Nicolas II*, Paris 1934

Palmer, Alan, *The Kaiser. Warlord of the Second Reich*, New York 1916

Paulmann, Johannes, *Pomp und Politik. Monarchenbegegnungen in Europa zwischen Ancien Régime und Erstem Weltkrieg*, Paderborn, Munich, Vienna, Zürich 2000

Penzler, Johannes, ed., *Fürst Bismarck nach seiner Entlassung. Leben und Politik des Fürsten seit seinem Scheiden aus dem Amte auf Grund aller authentischen Kundgebungen*, 7 vols., Leipzig 1897–8

*Die Reden Kaiser Wilhelms II. in den Jahren 1888–1895*, Leipzig, n.d.

ed., *Die Reden Kaiser Wilhelms II. in den Jahren 1896–1900*, Leipzig 1904

*Die Reden Kaiser Wilhelms II. in den Jahren 1901–Ende 1905*, Leipzig n.d.

Perris, George, *Germany and the German Emperor*, London 1912

Peters, Carl, *New Light on Dark Africa; Being the Narrative of the German Emin Pasha Expedition*, London, New York, Melbourne 1891

Peters, Evelene, *Roosevelt und der Kaiser, ein Beitrag zur Geschichte der deutsch-amerikanischen Beziehungen, 1895–1906*, Leipzig 1936

Pezold, Dirk von, *Cäsaromanie und Byzantinismus bei Wilhelm II.*, Cologne 1971

Pfeil und Klein-Ellguth, Hans Graf von, *Mein Kaiser! Der Fall Zedlitz-Trützschler und Wilhelms II. wahres Gesicht*, Leipzig 1924

Pflanze, Otto, *Bismarck and the Development of Germany*, 3 vols., Princeton 1963–90

Philipp, Ferdinand, *Bismarcks vertrauliche Gespräche u. a. über Wilhelm II.*, Dresden 1927

Pless, Daisy Fürstin von, *Tanz auf dem Vulkan. Erinnerungen an Deutschlands und Englands Schicksalswende*, 2 vols., Dresden 2nd edn 1930

Pogge von Strandmann, Hartmut, 'Der Kaiser und die Industriellen', in Röhl, *Der Ort Kaiser Wilhelms II.*

'Nationalisierungsdruck und königliche Namensänderung in England. Das Ende der Groß-familie europäischer Dynastien', in Ritter, Gerhard A. and Wende, Peter, eds., *Rivalität und Partnerschaft. Studien zu den deutsch-britischen Beziehungen im 19. und 20. Jahrhundert. Festschrift für Anthony J. Nicholls*, Paderborn 1999

'Rathenau, Wilhelm II and the Perception of Wilhelminismus', in Mombauer and Deist, *The Kaiser*

Pöls, Werner, *Sozialistenfrage und Revolutionsfurcht in ihrem Zusammenhang mit den angeblichen Staatsstreichplänen Bismarcks*, Lübeck, Hamburg 1960

Pommerin, Reiner, *Der Kaiser und Amerika. Die USA in der Politik der Reichsleitung, 1890–1917*, Cologne 1986

Ponsonby, Sir Frederick, ed., *Letters of the Empress Frederick*, London 1928

*Briefe der Kaiserin Friedrich*, Berlin 1929

Posadowsky, Arthur Graf, *Weltwende. Gesammelte politische Aufsätze*, Stuttgart 2nd edn 1920

Potts, D. M. and Potts, W. T. W., *Queen Victoria's Gene. Haemophilia and the Royal Family*, Stroud 1995

Prince, Morton, *The Psychology of the Kaiser. A Study of His Sentiments and Obsessions*, London 1915

Pudor, Heinrich, *Kaiser Wilhelm II. und Rembrandt als Erzieher*, Dresden 2nd edn 1891

Quidde, Ludwig, *Caligula. Eine Studie über römischen Cäsarenwahnsinn*, Leipzig 12th edn 1894

*Der deutsche Pazifismus während des Weltkrieges, 1914–1918*, Boppard am Rhein 1979

Rachfahl, Felix, *Kaiser und Reich 1888–1913. 25 Jahre preußisch-deutsche Geschichte. Festschrift zum 25-jährigen Regierungsjubiläum Wilhelms II., deutschen Kaisers, Königs von Preussen*, Berlin 1913

Radkau, Joachim, *Das Zeitalter der Nervosität. Deutschland zwischen Bismarck und Hitler*, Munich, Vienna 1998

Radziwill, Princess Catherine, *Sovereigns and Statesmen of Europe*, London, New York, Toronto, Melbourne 1915

Radziwill, Princess Marie, *This Was Germany. An Observer at the Court of Berlin*, London 1937

Rall, Hans, *König Ludwig II. und Bismarcks Ringen um Bayern*, Munich 1973
  *Wilhelm II. Eine Biographie*, Graz, Vienna, Cologne 1995
Ramm, Agatha, ed., *Beloved and Darling Child. Last Letters Between Queen Victoria and Her Eldest Daughter 1886–1901*, Stroud 1990
Rapsilber, Maximilian, 'Der Kaiser als Kunstrichter', in Leipziger, L., ed., *Der Roland von Berlin. Eine Wochenschrift für das Berliner Leben*, vol. 2, part 25, 3 June 1904
Raschdau, Ludwig, *Unter Bismarck und Caprivi. Erinnerungen eines deutschen Diplomaten aus den Jahren 1885–1894*, Berlin 1939
  *In Weimar als preußischer Gesandter. Ein Buch der Erinnerung an deutsche Fürstenhöfe, 1894–1897*, Berlin 1939
Rathenau, Walther, *Der Kaiser*, Berlin 1919
Rebentisch, Jost, *Die vielen Gesichter des Kaisers. Wilhelm II. in der deutschen und britischen Karikatur (1888–1918)*, Berlin 2000
Reck-Malleczewen, Friedrich Percyval, *Tagebuch eines Verzweifelten*, Berlin, Bonn 1981
Reif, Heinz, *Adel im 19. und 20. Jahrhundert*, Munich 1999
  ed., *Adel und Bürgertum in Deutschland*, 2 vols., Berlin 2000
Reifland, Ursula, 'Das persönliche Regiment Wilhelms II. in der Zeit der Kanzlerschaft Bülows', unpublished manuscript, Berlin 1951
Reinermann, Lothar, *Der Kaiser in England. Wilhelm II. und sein Bild in der britischen Öffentlichkeit*, Paderborn, Munich, Vienna, Zürich 2001
Reischach, Hugo Freiherr von, *Unter drei Kaisern*, Berlin 2nd edn 1925
Reventlow, Ernst Graf von, *Kaiser Wilhelm II. und die Byzantiner*, Munich 1906
  *Der Kaiser und die Monarchisten*, Berlin 1913
  *Glanz und Tragödie Wilhelms II.*, Stuttgart 1938
  *Von Potsdam nach Doorn*, Berlin 1940
Rich, Norman, *Friedrich von Holstein, Politics and Diplomacy in the Era of Bismarck and Wilhelm II*, 2 vols., Cambridge 1965
Rich, Norman and Fisher, M. H., eds., *Die Geheimen Papiere Friedrich von Holsteins*, 4 vols., Göttingen 1956–63
  *The Holstein Papers. The Memoirs, Diaries and Correspondence of Friedrich von Holstein 1837–1909*, 4 vols., Cambridge 1956–63
Richie, Alexandra, *Faust's Metropolis. A History of Berlin*, London 1998
Richter, Jan Stefan, *Die Orientreise Kaiser Wilhelms II. 1898*, Hamburg 1997
Ritter, Gerhard, *Die Legende von der verschmähten englischen Freundschaft 1898/1901*, Leipzig 1929
  *Die deutschen Militär-Attachés und das Auswärtige Amt. Aus den verbrannten Akten des Großen Generalstabes*, Heidelberg 1959
Ritter, Gerhard A., *Die Arbeiterbewegung im Wilhelminischen Reich*, Berlin 1959
Ritter, Gerhard A. and Niehuss, M., *Wahlgeschichtliches Arbeitsbuch. Materialien zur Statistik des Kaiserreichs, 1871–1918*, Munich 1980
Roberts, Andrew, *Salisbury. Victorian Titan*, London 2000
Robolsky, Hermann, *Kaiser Wilhelm II. und seine Leute*, Berlin 1891
Rogge, Helmuth, *Friedrich von Holstein. Lebensbekenntnis in Briefen an eine Frau*, Berlin 1932
  *Holstein und Hohenlohe. Neue Beiträge zu Friedrich von Holsteins Tätigkeit als Mitarbeiter Bismarcks und als Ratgeber Hohenlohes*, Stuttgart 1957
  'Die Kladderadatsch-Affäre. Ein Beitrag zur inneren Geschichte des Wilhelminischen Reichs', *Historische Zeitschrift*, 195/1, August 1962, pp. 90–130
Roggenbach, Franz von, *Im Ring der Gegner Bismarcks. Denkschriften und politischer Briefwechsel Franz von Roggenbachs mit Kaiserin Augusta und Albrecht von Stosch*, Stuttgart 1943

Röhl, John C. G., 'Staatsstreichplan oder Staatsstreichbereitschaft? Bismarcks Politik in der Entlassungskrise', *Historische Zeitschrift*, 203, 1966, pp. 610–24

*Germany without Bismarct. The Crisis of Government in the Second Reich, 1890–1900*, London, Berkeley, Los Angeles 1967

ed., *Philipp Eulenburgs politische Korrespondenz*, 3 vols., Boppard am Rhein 1976–83

*Kaiser Wilhelms II. Eine Studie über Cäsarenwahnsinn*, Munich 1989

ed., *Der Ort Kaiser Wilhelms II. in der deutschen Geschichte*, Munich 1991

*The Kaiser and his Court. Wilhelm II and the Government of Germany*, 3rd edn, Cambridge 1996

*Young Wilhelm. The Kaiser's is Early Life, 1859–1888*, Cambridge 1998

'Der Kaiser und England', in Rogasch, Wilfrid, ed., *Victoria & Albert, Vicky & The Kaiser. Ein Kapitel deutsch-englischer Familiengeschichte*, Berlin 1997

'Herzl and Kaiser Wilhelm II. A German Protectorate in Palestine?', in Robinson, Ritchie and Timms, Edward, eds., *Theodor Herzl and the Origins of Zionism*, Edinburgh 1997

'The Kaiser's Germany as Seen from Beachy Head on a Clear Day. Autobiographical Reminiscences of an Anglo-German Historian', in Berger, Stefan, Lambert, Peter and Schumann, Peter, eds., *Historikerdialoge. Geschichte, Mythos und Gedächtnis im deutsch-britischen kulturellen Austausch 1750–2000*, Göttingen 2003

Röhl, John C. G. and Sombart, Nicolaus, eds., *Kaiser Wilhelm II – New Interpretations*, Cambridge 1982

Röhl, John C. G., Warren, Martin and Hunt, David, *Purple Secret. Genes, 'Madness' and the Royal Houses of Europe*, London 1998

Rolland, Romain, 'Journal Intime, 22. Januar 1898', in *Cahiers Romain Rolland*, III, *Richard Strauß et Romain Rolland*, Paris 1951

Roth, Erwin, *Preußens Gloria in Heiligen Land. Die Deutschen und Jerusalem*, Munich 1973

Routier, Gaston, *Guillaume II à Londres et l'union franco-russe*, Paris 1894

Samerski, Stefan, ed., *Wilhelm II. und die Religion. Facetten einer Persönlichkeit und ihres Umfelds*, Berlin 2001

Saunders, George, *Builder and Blunderer. A Study of Emperor William's Character and Foreign Policy*, New York 1914

*The Last of the Huns*, London, New York 1914

Scheuner, Ulrich, 'Die Kunst als Staatsaufgabe im 19. Jahrhundert', in Mai, Ekkehard and Waetzoldt, Stephan, eds., *Kunstverwaltung, Bau- und Denkmalkunst im Kaiserreich*, Berlin 1981

Schierbrand, Wolf von, *The Kaiser's Speeches*, New York 1903

'Is Kaiser Wilhelm II of Normal Mind?', *Lippincott's*, 78, November 1906

Schlitter, Hanns, 'Briefe Kaiser Franz Josephs I. und Kaiser Wilhelms II. über Bismarcks Rücktritt', *Österreichische Rundschau*, 58, 1919

Schlözer, Kurd von, *Letzte römische Briefe 1882–1894*, Stuttgart, Berlin, Leipzig 1924

Schmidt-Bückeburg, Rudolf, *Das Militärkabinett der preußischen Könige und deutschen Kaiser. Seine geschichtliche Entwicklung und staatsrechtliche Stellung 1787–1918*, Berlin 1933

Schmidt-Pauli, Edgar von, *Der Kaiser. Das wahre Gesicht Wilhelms II.*, Berlin 1928

Schneider, Julius, *Die Geschichte des Berliner Doms*, Berlin 1993

Schneller, Pastor Ludwig, *Die Kaiserfahrt durch's heilige Land*, Leipzig 1899

Schoeps, Julius H., *Theodor Herzl 1860–1904. Wenn ihr wollt, ist es kein Märchen. Eine Text-Bild-Monographie*, Vienna 1995

Schöllgen, Gregor, *Imperialismus und Gleichgewicht. Deutschland, England und die orientalische Frage 1871–1914*, Munich 1992

Schönburg-Waldenburg, Heinrich Prinz von, *Erinnerungen aus kaiserlicher Zeit*, Leipzig 1929

Schott, Richard, *Eine Fahrt nach dem Orient. Zur Erinnerung an den Einzug des deutschen Kaisers und der Kaiserin in Jerusalem, Herbst 1898*, Berlin, Eisenach, Leipzig 1898

Schottelius, Herbert and Deist, Wilhelm, eds., *Marine und Marinepolitik im kaiserlichen Deutschland 1871–1914*, Düsseldorf 1972

Schröder, E., *Zwanzig Jahre Regierungszeit. Ein Tagebuch Kaiser Wilhelms II. Vom Antritt der Regierung, 15. Juni 1888 bis zum 15. Juni 1908 nach Hof- und anderen Berichten*, Berlin 1909

Schröder, Wilhelm, *Das persönliche Regiment, Reden und sonstige öffentliche Äusserungen Wilhelms II.*, Munich 1907

Schümann, Carl-Wolfgang, *Der Berliner Dom im 19. Jahrhundert*, Berlin 1980

Schüssler, Wilhelm, *Bismarcks Sturz*, Leipzig 3rd edn 1922

    *Deutschland zwischen Rußland und England. Studien zur Außenpolitik des Bismarckischen Reiches, 1879–1914*, Leipzig 1940

    *Kaiser Wilhem II., Schicksal und Schuld*, Göttingen 1962

Schwabe, Klaus, ed., *Das diplomatische Korps, 1871–1945*, Boppard am Rhein 1985

Schweinitz, Wilhelm von, ed., *Denkwürdigkeiten des Botschafters General Hans Lothar von Schweinitz*, 2 vols., Berlin 1927

    ed., *Briefwechsel des Botschafters General v. Schweinitz*, Berlin 1928

Schweitzer, Georg, *Emin Pasha. His Life and Work*, 2 vols., London 1898

Schwering, Axel von, *The Berlin Court under Wilhelm II*, London, New York 1915

See, Klaus von, *Barbar Germane Arier. Die Suche nach der Identität der Deutschen*, Heidelberg 1994

Seidel, Paul, *Der Kaiser und die Kunst*, Berlin 1907

Seligmann, Matthew S., *Rivalry in Southern Africa, 1893–1899. The Transformation of German Colonial Policy*, London 1998

    'Military Diplomacy in a Military Monarchy? Kaiser Wilhelm II and His Relations with British Service Attachés', in Mombauer and Deist, *The Kaiser*

Sexau, Richard, *Kaiser oder Kanzler. Der Kampf um das Schicksal des Bismarck-Reiches*, Berlin 1936

Seymour, Charles, ed., *The Intimate Papers of Colonel House*, 4 vols., Boston, New York 1926–8

Shaw, Stanley, *William of Germany*, New York, London 1913

    *The Kaiser 1859–1914*, London 1914

Shel'king, Eugeni, *The Game of Diplomacy*, London 1900

Siedler, Wolf Jobst, *Abschied von Preußen*, Berlin 1991

Simon, Christian, 'Kaiser Wilhelm II. und die deutsche Wissenschaft', in Röhl, *Der Ort Kaiser Wilhelms II.*

Simon, Edouard, *L'Empereur Guillaume II et la première année de son règne*, Paris 1889

Simsa, Paul, *Marine intern. Entwicklung und Fehlentwicklung der deutschen Marine 1888–1939*, Stuttgart 1972

Smith, Alson J., *In Preußen keine Pompadour. Wilhelm II. und die Gräfin Waldersee*, Stuttgart 1965

Snyder, Louis L., 'Political Implications of Herbert von Bismarck's Marital Affairs, 1881, 1892', *Journal of Modern History*, 36, 1964, pp. 155–69

    *Diplomacy in Iron. The Life of Herbert von Bismarck*, Malabar, FL, 1985

Sombart, Nicolaus, '"Ich sage, untergehen." Zum zweiten Band von Philipp Eulenburgs politischer Korrespondenz', *Merkur*, 385, June 1980

    'The Kaiser in His Epoch. Some Reflexions on Wilhelmine Society, Sexuality and Culture', in Röhl and Sombart, *Kaiser Wilhelm II – New Interpretations*

    'Der Kaiser und seine Kritiker. Gedanken zur Problematik der Beurteilung Wilhelms II.', *Wissenschaftskolleg Jahrbuch*, 1982/3, pp. 310–34

    *Wilhelm II. Sündenbock und Herr der Mitte*, Berlin 1996

Sonntag, Josef, *Schuld und Schicksal. Die Tragödie Wilhelms II.*, Leipzig 1927

Sösemann, Bernd, 'Die sog. Hunnenrede Wilhelms II. Textkritische und interpretatorische Bemerkungen zur Ansprache des Kaisers vom 27. Juli 1900 in Bremerhaven', *Historische Zeitschrift*, 222, 1976, pp. 342–58

ed., *Theodor Wolff. Die Wilhelminische Epoche. Fürst Bülow am Fenster und andere Begegnungen*, Frankfurt a.M. 1989

*Theodor Wolff. Ein Leben mit der Zeitung*, Munich 2000

'Hollow-Sounding Jubilees. Forms and Effects of Public Self-Display in Wilhelmine Germany', in Mombauer and Deist, *The Kaiser*

Stehlin, S. A., *Bismarck and the Guelph Problem 1866–1890*, The Hague 1973

Stein, Adolf, *Wilhelm II.*, Leipzig 1909

*Bülow und der Kaiser*, Berlin 1931

Steinberg, Jonathan, *Yesterday's Deterrent. Tirpitz and the Birth of the German Battle Fleet*, London 1966

'Kaiser Wilhelm and the British', in Röhl and Sombart, *Kaiser Wilhelm II – New Interpretations*

Stern, Fritz, *Gold and Iron. Bismarck, Bleichröder and the Building of the German Empire*, New York 1977

Stewart, Desmond, *Theodor Herzl, Artist and Politician*, London 1974

Stibbe, Matthew, 'Kaiser Wilhelm II. The Hohenzollerns at War', in Hughes, Matthew and Seligmann, Matthew, eds., *Leadership in Conflict 1914–1918*, Barnsley 2000, pp. 265–83

'Germany's "Last Card". Wilhelm II and the Decision in Favour of Unrestricted Submarine Warfare in January 1917', in Mombauer and Deist, *The Kaiser*

Stillfried-Alcántara, Rudolf Graf von, *Ceremonial-Buch für den Königlich-Preußischen Hof*, Berlin 1871–8

Stöber, Gunda, *Pressepolitik als Notwendigkeit. Zum Verhältnis von Staat und Öffentlichkeit im Wilhelminischen Deutschland 1890–1914*, Stuttgart 2000

Stolberg-Wernigerode, Otto Graf von, *Wilhelm II.*, Lübeck 1933

Stöwer, Willy, *Zur See mit Pinsel und Palette, Erinnerungen von Prof. Willy Stöwer*, Braunschweig 1929

Straub, Eberhard, *Albert Ballin. Der Reeder des Kaisers*, Berlin 2001

Stribrny, Wolfgang, *Bismarck und die deutsche Politik nach seiner Entlassung (1890–1898)*, Paderborn 1977

Stuhlmann, F., *Mit Emin Pascha ins Herz von Afrika*, 1894

Svanström, Ragnar, *Kejsaren. En bok om Wilhelm II*, Stockholm 1978

Swaine, Sir Leopold, *Camp and Chancery in a Soldier's Life*, London 1926

Syberkrop, Louis, *From the Cradle to the Madhouse, a Biography of Wilhelm II and a Prophecy of His Demise*, Creston 1917

Symons, A. J. A., *Emin, Governor of Equatoria*, London 1928

Taube, Utz-Friedbert, *Ludwig Quidde. Ein Beitrag zur Geschichte des demokratischen Gedankens in Deutschland*, Munich 1963

Taylor, Ronald, *Berlin and Its Culture. A Historical Portrait*, New Haven, London 1997

Teeuwisse, Nicolaas, *Vom Salon zur Sezession. Berliner Kunstleben zwischen Tradition und Aufbruch zur Moderne 1871–1900*, Berlin 1986

Tesdorpf, Paul, *Die Krankheit Wilhelms II.*, Munich 1919

Tirpitz, Alfred von, *Erinnerungen*, Leipzig 1919

*Der Aufbau der deutschen Weltmacht*, Stuttgart 1924

Tittel, Lutz, 'Monumentaldenkmäler von 1871 bis 1918', in Mai, Ekkehard and Waetzoldt, Stephan, eds., *Kunstverwaltung, Bau- und Denkmalkunst im Kaiserreich*, Berlin 1981

Topham, Anne, *Memories of the Kaiser's Court*, New York 1914

Tuchman, Barbara, *Proud Tower*, New York 1966

Uhle-Wettler, Franz, *Alfred von Tirpitz in seiner Zeit*, Hamburg, Berlin, Bonn 1998

Ullrich, Volker, *Die nervöse Großmacht 1871–1918. Aufstieg und Untergang des deutschen Kaiser-reichs*, Frankfurt a.M. 1997

Viereck, George Sylvester, *The Kaiser on Trial*, Richmond, VA, 1937

Vierhaus, Rudolf, ed., *Das Tagebuch der Baronin Spitzemberg. Aufzeichnungen aus der Hofge-sellschaft des Hohenzollernreiches*, Göttingen 1960

Viktoria Luise, Herzogin von Braunschweig, *Deutschlands letzte Kaiserin*, Göttingen 1971

Vogel, Bernhard, Nohlen Dieter, and Schultze, Rainer-Olaf, *Wahlen in Deutschland. Theorie-Geschichte-Dokumente, 1848–1970*, Berlin 1971

Vollmar, Georg, *Socialism and the German Kaiser*, London 1903

Vorres, Ian, *The Last Grand Duchess*, London 1964

Ward, James E., 'Leo XIII and Bismarck. The Kaiser's Vatican Visit of 1888', *Review of Politics*, 24, 1962

Weber, Christoph, *Quellen und Studien zur Kurie und zur vatikanischen Politik unter Leo XIII.*, Tübingen 1973

Wedel, Graf Carl von, *Zwischen Kaiser und Kanzler*, Leipzig 1943

Wehberg, Hans, *Ludwig Quidde. Ein deutscher Demokrat und Vorkämpfer der Völkerver-ständigung*, Offenbach 1948

Wehler, Hans-Ulrich, ed., *Caligula. Schriften über Militarismus und Pazifismus*, Frankfurt a.M. 1977

   *Das Deutsche Kaiserreich 1871–1918*, Göttingen 5th edn 1983

   *Deutsche Gesellschaftsgeschichte*, vol. III, *Von der 'Deutschen Doppelrevolution' bis zum Beginn des Ersten Weltkrieges, 1849–1914*, Munich 1995

Weitowitz, Rolf, *Deutsche Politik und Handelspolitik unter Reichskanzler Leo von Caprivi, 1890–1894*, Düsseldorf 1978

Weller, Bernd-Uwe, *Maximilian Harden und die 'Zukunft'*, Bremen 1970

Wendel, Friedrich, *Wilhelm II. in der Karikatur*, Dresden 1926

Werthern, Alfred Freiherr von, *General von Versen. Ein militärisches Zeit- und Lebensbild. Aus hinterlassenen Briefen und Aufzeichnungen*, Berlin 1898

White, Arnold, *Is the Kaiser Insane? A Study of the Great Outlaw*, London 1915

Whittle, Tyler, *The Last Kaiser. A Biography of William II, German Emperor and King of Prussia*, London 1977

Wilderotter, Hans and Pohl, Klaus-D., eds., *Der letzte Kaiser. Wilhelm II. im Exil*, Gütersloh, Munich 1991

Wile, Frederic, *Men around the Kaiser. The Makers of Modern Germany*, Indianapolis 1914

Wilhelm II, *Vergleichende Geschichtstabellen von 1878 bis zum Kriegsausbruch, 1914*, Leipzig 1921

   *Ereignisse und Gestalten aus den Jahren 1878–1918*, Berlin, Leipzig 1922

   *Aus meinem Leben 1859–1888*, Berlin, Leipzig 1927

Wilke, Ekkehard-Teja P. W., *Political Decadence in Imperial Germany. Personnel–Political Aspects of the German Government Crisis 1894–1897*, Urbana, IL, London 1976

Wilson, Lawrence, *The Incredible Kaiser. A Portrait of William II*, New York 1965

Windelband, Wolfgang, *Herbert Bismarck als Mitarbeiter seines Vaters*, Stuttgart 1921

Winzen, Peter, *Bülows Weltmachtkonzept. Untersuchungen zur Frühphase seiner Außenpolitik 1897–1901*, Boppard am Rhein 1977

   'Zur Genesis von Weltmachtkonzept und Weltpolitik', in Röhl, *Der Ort Kaiser Wilhelms II.*

   *Bernhard Fürst von Bülow. Weltmachtstratege ohne Fortune – Wegbereiter der großen Katas-trophe*, Göttingen, Zürich 2003

Ydewalle, Charles d', *Guillaume II*, Brussels 1972

Zange, Friedrich, *Die Jerusalemfahrt Kaiser Wilhelms II. im Lichte der Geschichte*, Berlin 1899

Zechlin, Egmont, *Staatsstreichpläne Bismarcks und Wilhelms II., 1890–1894*, Stuttgart, Berlin 1929

Zedlitz-Trützschler, Robert Graf von, *Zwölf Jahre am deutschen Kaiserhof*, Berlin, Leipzig 1923

Zeepvat, Charlotte, *Prince Leopold. The Untold Story of Queen Victoria's Youngest Son*, London 1998

Zelinsky, Hartmut, *Richard Wagner. Ein deutsches Thema. Eine Dokumentation zur Wirkungsgeschichte Richard Wagners 1876–1976*, Berlin, Vienna 1983

    'Kaiser Wilhelm II., die Werk-Idee Richard Wagners und der "Weltkampf"', in Röhl, *Der Ort Kaiser Wilhelms II.*

Zentner, Kurt, *Kaiserliche Zeiten. Wilhelm II. und seine Ära in Bildern und Dokumenten*, Munich 1964

# Index

WITHDRAWN